BUSINESS LAW

TWELFTH EDITION

The Ethical, Global, and E-Commerce Environment

Jane P. Mallor

A. James Barnes

Thomas Bowers

Arlen W. Langvardt

all of Indiana University

Boston   Burr Ridge, IL   Dubuque, IA   Madison, WI   New York   San Francisco   St. Louis
Bangkok   Bogotá   Caracas   Kuala Lumpur   Lisbon   London   Madrid   Mexico City
Milan   Montreal   New Delhi   Santiago   Seoul   Singapore   Sydney   Taipei   Toronto

The McGraw·Hill Companies

BUSINESS LAW: THE ETHICAL, GLOBAL, AND E-COMMERCE ENVIRONMENT
Published by McGraw-Hill/Irwin, a business unit of The McGraw-Hill Companies, Inc., 1221
Avenue of the Americas, New York, NY, 10020. Copyright © 2004, 2001, 1998, 1995, 1992,
1989, 1986, 1982, 1978, 1974, 1970, 1966, 1961, 1959, 1955, 1951, 1946 by The McGraw-
Hill Companies, Inc. All rights reserved. No part of this publication may be reproduced or
distributed in any form or by any means, or stored in a database or retrieval system, without
the prior written consent of The McGraw-Hill Companies, Inc., including, but not limited to,
in any network or other electronic storage or transmission, or broadcast for distance learning.
Some ancillaries, including electronic and print components, may not be available to
customers outside the United States.

This book is printed on acid-free paper.

3 4 5 6 7 8 9 0 DOW/DOW 0 9 8 7 6 5 4

ISBN 0-07-256200-5

Publisher: *John E. Biernat*
Executive editor: *Andy Winston*
Developmental editor: *Sarah Reed*
Marketing manager: *Lisa Nicks*
Media producer: *Tony Sherman*
Project manager: *Jim Labeots*
Production supervisor: *Debra R. Sylvester*
Design team leader: *Mary L. Christianson*
Senior supplement producer: *Susan Lombardi*
Senior digital content specialist: *Brian Nacik*
Cover design: *Ryan Brown*
Cover images: *©PhotoDisc*
Typeface: *10/12 Times Roman*
Compositor: *Carlisle Communications, Ltd.*
Printer: *R. R. Donnelley*

Library of Congress Cataloging-in-Publication Data

Business law: the ethical, global, and e-commerce environment / Jane P. Mallor ...[et al].
  12th ed.
    p. cm.
  Rev. ed. of: Business law and the regulatory environment / Jane P. Mallor ... [et al.]
  11th ed. 2001.
  Includes index.
  ISBN 0-07-256200-5 (alk. paper)
    1. Commercial law—United States—Cases. 2. Business law—United States—Cases. 3.
  Commercial law—United States. 4. Business law—United States. I. Mallor, Jane P. II.
  Business law and the regulatory environment.
  KF888.B8 2004
  346.7307—dc21   2003044178

www.mhhe.com

THE AUTHORS

Jane P. Mallor has been a member of the Business Law faculty at Kelley School of Business, Indiana University, since 1976. She has a B.A. from Indiana University and a J.D. from Indiana University School of Law. She has been admitted to the Indiana Bar, the Bar of the Southern District of Indiana, and the Bar of the U.S. Supreme Court. She is a member of the Academy of Legal Studies in Business.

Professor Mallor has taught a range of courses, including an introductory legal environment course and a graduate-level legal concepts course, real estate law, university pedagogy courses for business doctoral students, and most recently, graduate and undergraduate courses on Internet law and e-commerce. She is a member of Indiana University's Faculty Colloquium for Excellence in Teaching and was a Lilly Postdoctoral Teaching Fellow. She has won a number of teaching awards, including the Amoco Foundation Award for Distinguished Teaching, the Dow Technology Teaching Award, and the Innovative Teaching Award. Her research has focused primarily on punitive damages, product liability, and employment rights. Her work has been published in law reviews such as *Hastings Law Journal, North Carolina Law Review, American Business Law Journal,* and *Notre Dame Lawyer.*

A. James Barnes, J.D., is Professor of Public and Environmental Affairs and Adjunct Professor of Law at Indiana University in Bloomington. He previously served as Dean of the School of Public and Environmental Affairs (SPEA). His teaching interests include environmental law, alternative dispute resolution, law and public policy, and ethics and the public official. He has written, testified, and spoken extensively on environmental issues and has considerable international experience dealing with environmental officials in other countries. He currently consults on a variety of environmental matters.

From 1985 to 1988, Professor Barnes served as the deputy administrator of the U.S. Environmental Protection Agency. As the agency's number two official, he gained extensive experience in environmental policy making and administration. From 1983 to 1985, he was the EPA General Counsel, and in the early 1970s participated in the formation of EPA and served as the chief of staff to its first administrator, William D. Ruckelshaus.

Professor Barnes also served as a trial attorney for the U.S. Department of Justice and as general counsel for the U.S. Department of Agriculture from 1981 to 1983, where he dealt with a wide variety of public policy issues, including environmental issues involving the Forest Service, Soil and Conservation Service, and federal agriculture programs. For six years, from 1975 to 1981, he had a commercial and environmental law practice with the firm of Beveridge and Diamond in Washington, D.C.

Thomas Bowers is Argosy Gaming Faculty Fellow in the Kelley School of Business at Indiana University, Bloomington. He is co-director of the Kelley MBA Sports and Entertainment Academy. Focusing primarily on the law of business organizations, securities regulation, professional responsibility, and business ethics, Dr. Bowers teachers two courses in the Kelley School's Systems and Accounting Graduate Program. His students have honored him with 15 outstanding teaching awards. He joined the faculty at Indiana University after obtaining a B.S. in finance from The Ohio State University and a J.D. from New York University.

Arlen W. Langvardt, Professor of Business Law, joined the faculty of Indiana University's Kelley School of Business in 1985. Professor Langvardt earned a Bachelor of Arts degree (summa cum laude) from Hastings College in 1976 and a Juris Doctor degree (with distinction) from the University of Nebraska in 1981.

From 1981–85, Professor Langvardt was a trial attorney with firms in Nebraska. He tried cases in a variety of legal areas, including tort, contract, constitutional, and miscellaneous commercial cases, as well as criminal and domestic relations cases.

Professor Langvardt has received several teaching awards and honors at the undergraduate and MBA levels. His graduate-level teaching assignments have included Legal Concepts and Trends Affecting Business, Managing Legal and Ethical Risk, Legal Issues in Marketing Management, and Legal Issues in the Arts. At the undergraduate level, he has taught Legal Environment of Business, Legal Aspects of Marketing, Commercial Law, Personal Law, and Law and the Arts.

Most of Professor Langvardt's research focuses on the First Amendment's application in contexts such as advertising regulation, trademark protection, and corporate defamation. He has published numerous articles in law journals and business journals, including the *Minnesota Law Review,* the *American Business Law Journal,* the *Journal of Marketing,* the *Trademark Reporter, the Villanova Law Review,* and the *Kansas Law Review.* Professor Langvardt has won several research awards from professional associations, including the Holmes/Cardozo Award from the American Business Law Association (now the Academy of Legal Studies in Business). The Brand Names Education Foundation selected him as winner of the 1992 Ladas Memorial Award for writing the best trademark law article published in 1991. By invitation of the Brand Names Education Foundation, Professor Langvardt delivered the 1992 Boal Memorial Lecture (part of a lecture series on trademark and unfair competition law) at the Georgetown University Law Center. In 2000, he was named the Kelley School's Murray Robinson Faculty Fellow, in recognition of his teaching, research, and service efforts. Professor Langvardt also serves as chair of the Kelley School's Department of Business Law.

Professor Langvardt and his wife, Mary, are the parents of Kyle and Tara.

PREFACE

This is the Twelfth UCC Edition (and the nineteenth overall edition) of a business law text that first appeared in 1935. Throughout its nearly 70 years of existence, this book has been a leader and an innovator in the fields of business law and the legal environment of business. One reason for the book's success is its clear and comprehensive treatment of the standard topics that form the traditional business law curriculum. Another reason is its responsiveness to changes in these traditional subjects and to new views about that curriculum. In 1976, this textbook was the first to inject regulatory materials into a business law textbook, defining the "legal environment" approach to business law. Over the years, this textbook has also pioneered by introducing materials on business ethics, corporate social responsibility, global legal issues, and e-commerce law. The Twelfth edition continues to emphasize change by integrating these four areas into its pedagogy.

Continuing Strengths

The Twelfth UCC Edition continues the basic features that have made its predecessors successful. They include:

- *Comprehensive Coverage.* We believe that the text continues to excel both in the number of topics it addresses and the depth of coverage within each topic. This is true both of the basic business law subjects that form the core of the book and also of the regulatory and other subjects that are said to constitute the "legal environment" curriculum.
- *Style and Presentation.* This text is written in a style that is direct, lucid, and organized, yet also relatively relaxed and conversational. For this reason, we often have been able to cover certain topics by assigning them as reading without lecturing on them. As always, key points and terms are emphasized; examples, charts, figures, and concept summaries are used liberally; and elements of a claim and lists of defenses are stated in numbered paragraphs.
- *Case Selection.* We try very hard to find cases that clearly illustrate important points made in the text, that should interest students, and that are fun to teach. Except when older decisions are landmarks or continue to best illustrate particular concepts, we also try to select recent cases. Our collective in-class teaching experience with recent editions has helped us determine which of those cases best meet these criteria.

- *AACSB Curricular Standards.* The AACSB's curriculum standards say that both undergraduate and MBA curricula should include ethical and global issues; should address the influence of political, social, legal and regulatory, environmental, and technological issues on business; and should also address the impact of demographic diversity on organizations. In addition to its obvious stress on legal and regulatory issues, the book contains chapters on business ethics, the legal environment for international business, and environmental law, as well as Ethics in Action boxes. By putting legal changes in their social, political, and economic context, several text chapters enhance students' understanding of how political and social changes influence business and the law. Chapter 51's discussion of employment discrimination law certainly speaks to the subject of workplace diversity. Finally, the Twelfth UCC Edition examines many specific legal issues involving e-commerce and the Internet.

Features

The Twelfth Edition introduces six new features:

Opening Vignettes precede the chapter discussion in order to give students a context for the law they are about to study. Many opening vignettes raise issues that come from the corporate social responsibility crisis that students have read about the last few years.

Ethics in Action boxes are interspersed where ethical issues arise, asking students to consider the ethics of actions and laws. The Sarbanes–Oxley Act of 2002 is often featured in the ethics boxes.

Cyberlaw in Action boxes discuss e-commerce and Internet law at the relevant points of the text.

The Global Business Environment boxes address the legal and business risks that arise in international business transactions, including being subject to the laws of other countries. By integrating the global business environment boxes in each chapter, students are taught that global issues are an integral part of business decision making.

Log On boxes direct students to Internet sites where they can find additional legal and business materials that will aid their understanding of the law.

Online Research Problems close each chapter by challenging students to use their Internet research skills to expand their understanding of the chapter.

v

This edition also retains four features of previous editions:

Concept Reviews appear throughout the chapters. These Concept Reviews visually represent important concepts presented in the text to help summarize key ideas at a glance and simplify students' conceptualization of complicated issues.

Cases include the judicial opinions accompanying court decisions. These help to provide concrete examples of the rules stated in the text, and to provide a real-life application of the legal rule.

Problem Cases are included at the end of each chapter to provide review questions for students.

Key Terms are bolded throughout the text and defined in the Glossary at the end of the text for better comprehension of important terminology.

Important Changes in This Edition

The chapters in the Twelfth UCC Edition have been reorganized slightly. For instance, the chapter on the legal environment for international business was deleted and the content was reworked into the relevant chapters including the new Global Business Environment boxes. Also, Chapter 46 now includes coverage of auditors, consultants, and securities professionals.

As usual, there are many new cases, the text has been thoroughly updated, and a good number of problem cases have been replaced with new ones. The cases continue to include both hypothetical cases as well as real-life cases so that we can target particular issues that deserve emphasis. The Twelfth UCC Edition's most substantive changes are as follows:

- The **Sarbanes–Oxley Act of 2002** is covered throughout the Twelfth UCC Edition. This important legislation that intends to rein in corporate fraud is featured prominently in Chapters 4, 43, 45, and 46. See especially the Ethics in Action boxes on pages 945, 951, 1009, 1027, 1032, and 1047.
- Chapter 4 is a wholly-revised ethics chapter titled "Business Ethics, Corporate Social Responsibility, Corporate Governance, and Critical Thinking." This highly readable and practical chapter contains a logical exposition of ethical thinking and includes new sections with guidelines for making ethical decisions and resisting requests to act unethically.

- Chapter 4 now includes a critical discussion of three familiar enemies of business ethics: moral relativism, psychological egoism, and ethical egoism.
- In addition to acquiring five new text cases, Chapter 8, which now bears the title "Intellectual Property and Unfair Competition," includes discussions of copyright infringement issues in Internet-related contexts, the Copyright Term Extension Act of 1998, and the Anti-cybersquatting Consumer Protection Act of 1999.
- The contracts chapters integrate e-commerce issues at various points. Examples include treatments of the proposed Uniform Computer Information Transactions Act in Chapter 9, shrinkwrap and clickwrap contracts in Chapter 10, and digital or electronic signatures in Chapter 16.
- Chapter 20's discussion of product liability now discusses the new *Restatement (Third) of Torts: Product Liability.*
- Chapters 37 to 44 add business planning materials that help persons creating partnerships, LLPs, corporations, and other business forms. New materials give practical solutions that help business planners determine the compensation of partners in an LLP, ensure a return on investment for shareholders, anticipate management problems in partnerships and corporations, and provide for the repurchase of owners' interests in partnerships and corporations.
- Chapter 40 is restructured to give greater emphasis to the law affecting limited liability companies and covers the Uniform Limited Liability Company Act.
- New materials on complying with management duties give practical advice to boards of directors as well as consultants and investment bankers assisting corporate management. The new materials help managers make prudent business decisions. For example, a practical framework on how to comply with business judgement rule is on pages 938 and 939.
- Chapter 46, newly titled "Legal and Professional Responsibilities of Auditors, Consultants, and Securities Professionals," covers the liability of professionals in general, with new emphasis on investment bankers, securities brokers, and securities analysts. The revised chapter is relevant not only to students studying accounting and auditing, but also to finance majors and MBA students who will work in the consulting and securities industries.
- Chapters 36–38 have been updated to reflect the fact that a majority of the states have adopted the Revised Uniform Partnership Act.
- Chapter 40, which now bears the title "Limited Liability Companies, Limited Partnerships, and Limited Li-

ability Limited Partnerships" has been revised to reflect the creation of a new business form, the limited liability limited partnership.

- Chapters 40 and 44 incorporate Internet issues by discussing the recent efforts of Internet companies to avoid state sales taxes through subsidiary corporations, and by including recent S.E.C. changes that permit Internet marketing of initial public offerings.
- In addition to including a new case that moves vertical maximum price-fixing from the per se category to rule-of-reason category, Chapter 49 includes the Justice Department's case against Microsoft.

Acknowledgments

We would like to thank the many reviewers who have contributed their ideas and time to the development of the Twelfth Edition. Our sincere appreciation to the following:

Kenneth Ackman, *Miami-Dade Community College, Kendall*

Miriam Albert, *Fordham University*

Joseph Allegretti, *Siena College*

Laura Barelman, *Wayne State University*

Lia Barone, *Norwalk Community College*

Karen Barr, *Pennsylvania State University*

Perry Binder, *Georgia State University*

Robert Bing, *William Paterson University*

William Bockanic, *John Carroll University*

Glenn Boggs, *Florida State University*

Joyce Boland-DeVito, *St. John's University*

Harvey Boller, *Loyola University*

Myra Bruegger, *Southeastern Community College*

Jeff Bruns, *Bacone College*

William Burke, *Trinity University*

Jeanne Calderon, *New York University*

Leandro Castillo, *Monterey Peninsula College*

Tom Cavenagh, *North Central College*

Mark Conrad, *Fordham University*

Kathryn Coulter, *Mt. Mercy College*

Richard Custin, *Carthage College*

Barbara Danos, *Louisiana State University*

Diana Dawson, *Florida Atlantic University, Boca Raton*

Patrick Deane, *South Suburban College*

Alexander Devience, *DePaul University*

John Dowdy, *University of Texas, Arlington*

Paul Dwyer, *Siena College*

Craig Ehrlich, *Babson College*

Tony Enerva, *Lakeland Community College*

Richard Finkley, *Governors State University*

Mahmoud Gaballa, *Mansfield University*

Sam Garber, *DePaul University*

Robert Garrett, *American River College*

Donna Gitter, *Fordham University*

Cheryl Gracie, *Washtennaw Community College*

Dale Grossman, *Cornell University, Ithaca*

Patricia Hermann, *Coastal Bend College, Beeville*

Scott Hoover, *Lipscomb University*

Phillip Howard, *Ball State University*

Walt Janoski, *Luzerne County Community College*

Catherine Jones-Rokkers, *Grand Valley State University*

Warren Keck, *Thiel College*

Kevin Kern, *Rhodes College*

Nancy Kubasek, *Bowling Green State University*

Elvin Lashbrooke, *Michigan State University, East Lansing*

Andrew Laviano, *University of Rhode Island, Kingston*

Daniel Levin, *Minnesota State University, Mankato*

Anne Levy, *Michigan State University, East Lansing*

Avi Liveson, *Hunter College*

Victor Lopez, *SUNY, Delhi*

James MacDonald, *Weber State University*

Linda Marquis, *Northern Kentucky University*

Jim Marshall, *Michigan State University, East Lansing*

Brent McClintock, *Carthage College*

Brad McDonald, *Northern Illinois University*

Jane McNiven, *Ivy Tech State College*

Russell Meade, *Gardner-Webb University*

Ronald Meisberg, *University of Maryland, College Park*

Georthia Moses, *Morris College*

Stephen Mumford, *Gwynedd Mercy College*

Marlene Murphy, *Governors State University*

Tonia Murphy, *University of Notre Dame*

Jim Owens, *California State University, Chico*

Sandra Perry, *Bradley University*

Ellen Pierce, *University of North Carolina*

Greg Rabb, *Jamestown Community College*

Roger Reinsch, *University of Wisconsin, La Crosse*

Daniel Reynolds, *Middle Tennessee State University*

Bob Richards, *Oklahoma State University*

Marvin Robertson, *Harding University*

Susan Samuelson, *Boston University*

Kurt Saunders, *California State University, Northridge*

David Scalise, *University of San Francisco*

Anne Schacherl, *Madison Area Technical College*

Robert Schupp, *University of North Florida*

Sean Scott, *St. Petersburg College*

Keith Shishido, *Santa Monica College*

Harold Silverman, *Bridgewater State College*

Jay Sklar, *Temple University*

Bradley Sleeper, *St. Cloud State University*

Michael Sommerville, *St. Mary's University*

John Sparks, *Grove City College*

John Thomas, *Northampton Community College*

David Trostel, *University of the Ozarks*

Donna Utley, *Okaloosa-Walton Community College*

Janet Velasquez, *Kansas City Community College*

Douglas Woods, *Wayne College*

We also acknowledge the assistance of Professor Sarah Jane Hughes of the Indiana University Law School, graduate assistant Paul Mitchell, and research assistant Kyle Langvardt.

Jane P. Mallor
A. James Barnes
Thomas Bowers
Arlen W. Langvardt

A GUIDED TOUR

A New Kind of Business Law Experience

The Twelfth Edition of **Business Law** has been reorganized to focus on global, ethical, and e-commerce issues affecting legal aspects of business. The new edition contains a number of new features as well as an exciting new supplements package. Please take a few moments to page through some of the highlights of this new edition.

OPENING VIGNETTES

Each chapter begins with an opening vignette that presents students with a mix of real-life and hypothetical situations and discussion questions. These stories provide a motivational way to open the chapter and get students interested in the chapter content.

2

THE RESOLUTION OF PRIVATE DISPUTES

Victoria Wilson, a resident of Illinois, wishes to bring an invasion of privacy lawsuit against XYZ Co. because XYZ used a photograph of her, without her consent, in an advertisement for one of the company's products. Wilson will seek money damages of $150,000 from XYZ, whose principal offices are located in New Jersey. A New Jersey newspaper was the only print media outlet in which the advertisement was published. However, XYZ also placed the advertisement on the firm's website. This website may be viewed by anyone with Internet access, regardless of the viewer's geographic location.

Consider the following questions regarding Wilson's case as you read Chapter 2:

- Where, in a geographic sense, may Wilson properly file and pursue her lawsuit against XYZ?
- Must Wilson pursue her case in a state court, or does she have the option of litigating in federal court?
- Assuming that Wilson files her case in a state court, what strategic option may XYZ exercise if it acts promptly?
- Regardless of the court in which the case is litigated, what procedural steps will occur as the lawsuit proceeds from beginning to end?

BUSINESS LAW COURSES normally examine many substantive legal rules—laws that tell us how to behave in business and in society. Examples include the rules of contract, tort, and agency law, as well as those of many other legal areas addressed later in this text. Most of these rules are applied by courts as they decide civil cases involving private parties. This chapter lays a foundation for the text's discussion of substantive legal rules by examining the court systems of the United States and by outlining how civil cases proceed from beginning to end. The chapter also explores related subjects, including *alternative dispute resolution*, a collection of processes for resolving private disputes outside the court systems.

State Courts and Their Jurisdiction

The United States has 52 court systems—a federal system plus a system for each state and the District of Columbia. This section describes the various types of state courts. It also considers the important subject of *jurisdiction*, something a court must have if its decision in a case is to be binding on the parties.

Courts of Limited Jurisdiction

Minor criminal cases and civil disputes involving small amounts of money or specialized matters frequently are decided in *courts of limited jurisdiction*. Examples include traffic courts, probate courts, and small claims courts. Such courts often handle a large number of cases. In some of these courts, procedures may be informal and parties unrepresented by attorneys often argue their own cases. Courts of limited jurisdiction often are not courts of record—meaning that they may not keep a transcript of the proceedings conducted. Appeals from their decisions therefore require a new trial (a trial *de novo*) in a trial court.

Trial Courts

Courts of limited jurisdiction find the relevant facts, identify the appropriate rule(s) of law, and combine the

4

BUSINESS ETHICS, CORPORATE SOCIAL RESPONSIBILITY, CORPORATE GOVERNANCE, AND CRITICAL THINKING

You work for N-Rot Company, a large energy trading company. N-Rot's chief financial officer (CFO) asks you to create a $50,000,000-asset energy services partnership with Martin Lowell Company, an investment banking firm. The CFO tells you, "Make sure the partnership has some positive cash flow over the next two years, but don't worry about whether the partnership will make money long term. Just make sure you convince Martin Lowell to partner with us, and that our ownership is only around 8 percent so that we don't have to record any liabilities from the venture on our balance sheet."

The purpose of the partnership, the CFO explains, is to generate income for N-Rot for the current year without materially affecting N-Rot's assets or liabilities. The CFO also tells you, "Convince our auditors, Armen Andrusian LLP, to book in the current year all the partnership's projected earnings for the next two years. If Andrusian resists, tell them that we can always find someone else to take over the $100,000,000 in consulting business we give them every year."

The CFO continues, "We'll make you a manager of the partnership, which will pay you about $900,000 a year. Also, I'll ask Martin Lowell to allocate some IPO [initial public offering] shares to you. The IPO shares I've been getting from Martin Lowell have been going up three to five times the first day of trading. This will be a good deal for you. You can make $300,000 every time, almost risk free."

Finally, the CFO says, "Remember where the paper shredder is. If things get a little hot around here, be sure to use it."

- Do you see any potential ethical problems with what the CFO has asked you to do?
- What principles and guidelines help you decide what to do?
- How do you resist the CFO's request for you to create the partnership without jeopardizing your career and without harming N-Rot?

Why Study Business Ethics?

Enron. Arthur Andersen. WorldCom. Tyco. Adelphia. Global Crossing. ImClone. These business names from the front pages of 2002 and 2003 conjure images of unethical and socially irresponsible behavior by corporations and their executives. The United States Congress, employees, investors, and other critics of the power held and abused by some corporations and their management have demanded that corporate wrongdoers be punished and that future wrongdoers be deterred. Consequently shareholders, creditors, and state and federal attorneys general have brought several civil and criminal actions against wrongdoing corporations and their executives. Congress has also got in the action, passing the Sarbanes–Oxley Act of 2002, which increased penalties for corporate wrongdoers and established rules

REVISED CHAPTER 4 ON ETHICS

With ethics in the forefront now, the authors have greatly expanded this chapter and incorporated recent events. The chapter defines several ethical theories and discusses their strengths and weaknesses, as well as providing a guideline for ethical decision making.

CYBERLAW IN ACTION BOXES

In keeping with today's technological world, these boxes describe and discuss actual instances of how e-commerce and the Internet are affecting business law today.

ETHICS IN ACTION BOXES

These boxes appear throughout the chapters and offer critical thinking questions and situations that relate to ethical/public policy concerns.

THE GLOBAL BUSINESS ENVIRONMENT BOXES

Since global issues affect people in many different aspects of business, this material now appears throughout the text instead of in a separate chapter on international issues. This feature brings to life global issues that are affecting business law.

LOG ON BOXES

These appear throughout the chapters and direct students, where appropriate, to relevant websites that will give them more information about each featured topic. Many of these are key legal sites that may be used repeatedly by business law students and business professionals alike.

CONCEPT REVIEW

What Terminates Offers?

- Their own terms
- Lapse of time
- Revocation

- Rejection
- Death or insanity of offeror or offeree
- Destruction of subject matter

- Intervening illegality

CONCEPT REVIEWS

These boxes visually represent important concepts presented in the text to help summarize key ideas at a glance and simplify students' conceptualization of complicated issues.

ONLINE RESEARCH PROBLEMS

These end-of-chapter research problems drive students to the Internet and include discussion questions so they can be used in class or as homework.

10. Soldau was fired by Organon, Inc. He received a letter from Organon offering to pay him double the normal severance pay if he would sign a release giving up all claims against the company. The letter incorporated the proposed release, which Soldau signed, dated, and deposited in a mailbox outside a post office. When he returned home, Soldau found that he had received a check from Organon in the amount of the increased severance pay. He returned to the post office and persuaded a postal employee to open the mailbox and retrieve the release. Soldau cashed Organon's check and subsequently filed an age discrimination suit against Organon. Was Soldau bound by the release?

Online Research: Finding Contracts on the Internet

1. *Finding Contracts on the Internet* Surf the web and find an example of a click-wrap and an example of what the court in *Specht* calls a "browse-wrap."

2. Find a User Agreement (also called Terms of Use Agreement) on any website. How does the User Agreement that you find indicate that a user's acceptance to the terms of the agreement will be shown?

Lewis v. Abbott Laboratories   189 F. Supp. 2d 590 (S. D. Miss. 2001)

Abbott Laboratories manufactured and sold the Life Care PCA, a pump that delivers medication into a person intravenously at specific time intervals. Beverly Lewis sued Abbott in a Mississippi State Court, alleging that a defective Life Care PCA had injured her by delivering an excessive quantity of morphine. Abbott served Lewis with a request for admission calling for her to admit that her damages did not exceed $75,000.00. Lewis did not answer the request for admission. Abbott then removed the case to the U.S. District Court for the Southern District of Mississippi, predicating the court's subject matter jurisdiction on diversity of citizenship and an amount in controversy exceeding $75,000. Lewis moved to have the case remanded to the state court on the ground that her silence had amounted to an admission that her damages were less than $75,000.00.

Wingate, District Judge Generally, in diversity cases, the courts determine the amount in controversy from the complaint itself, unless it appears, in some way shown, that the amount stated in the complaint is not claimed in good faith. The United States Supreme Court in *Horton v. Liberty Mutual Insurance Company*, 367 U.S. 348 (1961) stated that "in deciding this question of good faith we have said that it must appear to a legal certainty that the claim is really for less than the jurisdictional amount to justify dismissal." This "legal certainty" test is applied to jurisdictional amount questions in removed cases, as well as cases originally brought in federal court. So, this court lacks jurisdiction if it is apparent, to a legal certainty, that Lewis cannot, or is not entitled to, recover the jurisdictional minimum.

Of course, when a plaintiff does not desire to try his case in the federal court, he may resort to the expedient of suing for less than the jurisdictional amount, and though he would be justly entitled to more, the defendant cannot remove the

case. Thus, if a plaintiff pleads damages less than the jurisdictional amount, he can bar a defendant from removing the case to federal court.

This court finds that while Lewis failed to respond to a request for admissions relative to this court's jurisdictional amount, Abbott still has not established that Lewis' current claim for damages . . . is above this court's minimum jurisdictional amount of $75,000.00. By failing to answer the request for admissions, Lewis, under state law, . . . admitted that her damages do not exceed $75,000.00. Upon this occurrence, Lewis's complaint is in no different posture from one where plaintiff explicitly pleaded an amount below this court's jurisdictional limit. Under either or both of these scenarios, defendant, to justify removal, must present this court more than a hunch or suspicion that the amount in controversy exceeds $75,000.00. Abbott has not met that burden.

Case remanded to Mississippi state court.

CASES

The cases in each chapter help to provide concrete examples of the rules stated in the text.

PROBLEMS AND PROBLEM CASES

Problem cases appear at the end of each chapter for student review.

Problems and Problem Cases

1. Mr. and Mrs. Abelman engaged the Capitol Termite and Pest Control Company to treat their home for a termite infestation. The chemical used by Capitol was Gold Crest Termite manufactured by Velsicol Chemical Corporation. Velsicol sold the Gold Crest Termite to a distributor, which in turn sold it to Capitol in bulk—in 55-gallon drums. Capitol did not specifically buy materials for each termite job. One 55-gallon drum would service many homes. Employees of Capitol pumped the chemical from the 55-gallon drums into a 5-gallon pail at Capitol's premises. The solution was then poured from the 5-gallon pail into a 1-gallon pail, which they filled half full. Next, the half-gallon of Gold Crest Termite was poured into a fixed 50-gallon tank on the back of Capitol's trucks and then the tank was filled to capacity with water. This solution was then applied to the Abelman's residence by employees of Capitol. The Abelmans abandoned their home the day after Capitol completed treatment. Three years later they brought suit against Capitol and Velsicol contending that the termiticide had caused personal injuries and property damages. Among other things, they claimed there was a breach of express and implied warranties provided by the Uniform Commercial Code (discussed in Chapter 20). Velsicol and Capitol sought to dismiss these claims on the ground that there had not been a sale of goods and thus no warranties had arisen. Was the contract to obtain treatment for termites a sale of goods under the Uniform Commercial Code?

2. Keith Russell, a boat dealer, contracted to sell a 19-foot Kinvater boat to Robert Clouser for $8,500. The agreement stipulated that Clouser was to make a down payment of $1,700, with the balance due when he took possession of the boat. According to the contract, Russell was to retain possession of the boat in order to install a new engine and drive train. While the boat was still in Russell's possession, it was completely destroyed when it struck a seawall. Transamerica, Russell's insurance company, refused to honor Russell's claim for the damages to the boat. The insurance policy between Transamerica and Russell covered only watercraft under 26 feet in length that were not owned by Russell. Transamerica argued that the boat was not covered by the policy since Russell still owned it at the time of the accident. Did Russell have title to the boat at the time of the accident?

3. Club Pro Golf Products was a distributor of golf products. It employed salesmen who called on customers to take orders for merchandise. The merchandise was

sent by Club Pro directly to the purchaser and payment was made by the purchaser directly to Club Pro. A salesman for Club Pro, Carl Gude, transmitted orders for certain merchandise to Club Pro for delivery to several fictitious purchasers. Club Pro sent the merchandise to the fictitious purchasers at the fictitious addresses where it was picked up by Gude. Gude then sold the merchandise, worth approximately $19,000, directly to Simpson, a golf pro at a golf club. Gude then retained the proceeds of sale for himself. Club Pro discovered the fraud and brought suit against Simpson to recover the merchandise. Did Simpson get good title to the merchandise he purchased from Gude even though Gude had obtained it by fraud?

4. Shaker Valley Auto & Tire purchased a pickup truck at an auction and brought the vehicle for service to Fred Madore Chevrolet-Pontiac-Oldsmobile, an automobile dealership that sells and services vehicles. A few weeks later, Madore sold the truck to Winston Titus. Titus was unaware of Shaker Valley's ownership of the vehicle. In a subsequent court proceeding, both Titus and Shaker Valley claimed valid title to the truck. Shaker Valley argued that it never authorized the sale of the vehicle and that Madore had no title to transfer to Titus because Shaker Valley never transferred title to Madore. Does Titus have good title to the truck under the Code?

5. Legendary Homes, a home builder, purchased various appliances from Ron Mead T.V. & Appliance, a retail merchant selling home appliances. They were intended to be installed in one of Legendary Homes's houses and were to be delivered on February 1. At 5 o'clock on that day, the appliances had not been delivered. Legendary Homes's employees closed the home and left. Sometime between 5 and 6:30, Ron Mead delivered the appliances. No one was at the home so the deliveryman put the appliances in the garage. During the night, someone stole the appliances. Legendary Homes denied it was responsible for the loss and refused to pay Ron Mead for the appliances. Ron Mead then brought suit for the purchase price. Did Legendary Homes have the risk of loss of the appliances?

6. The Cedar Rapids YMCA bought a large number of cases of candy from Seaway Candy under an agreement by which any unused portion could be returned. The YMCA was to sell the candy to raise money to send boys to camp. The campaign was less than successful, and 668 cases remained unsold. They were returned to Seaway Candy by truck. When delivered to the common carrier, the candy was in good condition; when it arrived at Seaway four days later, it had melted and was completely

INSTRUCTOR AND STUDENT SUPPLEMENTS

INSTRUCTOR'S MANUAL

The Instructor's Manual consists of objectives, suggestions for lecture preparation, recommended references, answers to problems and problem cases, and suggested answers to the Online Research Problems and Opening Vignettes. It also includes answers to the Student Study Guide questions.

YOU BE THE JUDGE DVD-ROM

This **new** DVD (included with each new copy of the text) features ten interactive case videos that showcase courtroom arguments of business law cases. This interactive DVD gives students the opportunity to watch profile interviews of the plaintiff and defendant, read background information, hear each case, review the evidence, make their decision, and then access an actual, unscripted judge's decision and reasoning. There are also instructor's notes available with each video to help prepare you for classroom discussion. Cases include topics such as sexual harassment, fraud, liability, and oral contracts.

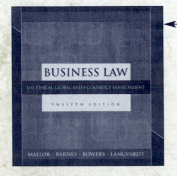

POWERPOINT® PRESENTATION

The PowerPoint presentation includes nearly 500 slides that provide lecture outline material, as well as slides that expand on important concepts and figures in the text.

SUPPLEMENTS

TEST BANK

The Test Bank consists of true-false, multiple choice, and short essay questions in each chapter. Approximately 35 questions are included per chapter. The Test Bank is also available in computerized format so you can create your own tests.

INSTRUCTOR'S RESOURCE CD

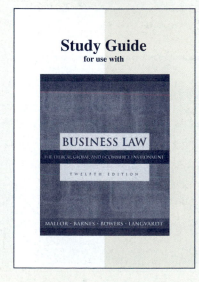

The Instructor's Resource CD includes the Instructor's Manual, the computerized test bank, and the PowerPoint presentation all on one CD so you can format your lectures.

STUDENT STUDY GUIDE

The Student Study Guide contains additional test questions for students so they can review and study the main concepts for each chapter. It also contains the Uniform Commercial Code articles.

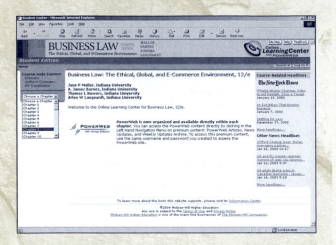

ONLINE LEARNING CENTER

www.mhhe.com/mallor12e

The Online Learning Center (OLC) is a website that follows the text chapter-by-chapter. The Twelfth Edition OLC contains case updates, Business Law in the News updates, quizzes and review terms for students to study from, downloadable supplements for the instructors, and links to professional resources for students and professors.

VIDEOS

Two video packages are available. One includes 120 minutes of business law cases taken from the business law telecourse videos. The other includes the video material from the DVD (profile interviews, courtroom arguments, and the judge's verdict) reformatted for VHS for those who may not have access to a DVD-Rom in the classroom.

POWERWEB

PowerWeb is an online tool that provides high quality, peer-reviewed content including up-to-date articles from leading periodicals and journals, current news, weekly updates with assessments, interactive exercises, Web research guide, study tips, and much more! Access PowerWeb through the Online Learning Center or at www.dushkin.com/powerweb. Access to PowerWeb is provided with each new copy of the book.

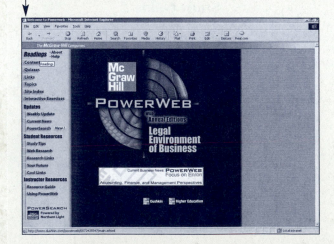

BRIEF CONTENTS

CONTENTS

Part Four   *Sales*

Part Seven   *Commercial Paper*

Contents xxvii

45 Securities Regulation 984
Purposes of Securities Regulation 985
Securities and Exchange Commission 985
SEC Actions 985
What Is a Security? 986
Securities Act of 1933 989
Registration of Securities under the 1933 Act 990
Mechanics of a Registered Offering 990
Registration Statement and Prospectus 990
Section 5: Timing, Manner, and Content of Offers and Sales 991
Exemptions from the Registration Requirements of the 1933 Act 993
Securities Exemptions 993
Transaction Exemptions 993
Intrastate Offering Exemption 993
Private Offering Exemption 994
Small Offering Exemptions 995
Securities Offerings on the Internet 996
Transaction Exemptions for Nonissuers 996
Sale of Restricted Securities 996
Consequence of Obtaining a Securities or Transaction Exemption 997
Liability Provisions of the 1933 Act 1000
Liability for Defective Registration Statements 1000
Other Liability Provisions 1004
Criminal Liability 1005
Securities Exchange Act of 1934 1005
Registration of Securities under the 1934 Act 1006
Holdings and Trading by Insiders 1007
Proxy Solicitation Registration 1008
Liability Provisions of the 1934 Act 1010
Liability for False Statements in Filed Documents 1010
Section 10(b) and Rule 10b-5 1010
Elements of a Rule 10b-5 Violation 1010
Criminal Liability 1018
Tender Offer Regulation 1018
Private Acquisitions of Shares 1019
State Regulation of Tender Offers 1019
The Foreign Corrupt Practices Act 1020
The Payments Prohibition 1020
Record-Keeping and Internal Controls Requirements 1020
State Securities Law 1020
Registration of Securities 1021

46 Legal and Professional Responsibilities of Auditors, Consultants, and Securities Professionals 1025
General Standard of Performance 1026
Professionals' Liability to Clients 1028
Contractual Liability 1028
Tort Liability 1028
Breach of Trust 1032
Securities Law 1033
Professionals' Liability to Third Persons: Common Law 1033
Negligence and Negligent Misrepresentation 1033
Fraud 1038

Professionals' Liability to Third Parties: Securities Law 1039
Securities Act of 1933 1039
Securities Exchange Act of 1934 1041
State Securities Law 1047
Limiting Professionals' Liability: Professional Corporations and Limited Liability Partnerships 1047
Qualified Opinions, Disclaimers of Opinion, Adverse Opinions, and Unaudited Statements 1048
Criminal, Injunctive, and Administrative Proceedings 1048
Criminal Liability under the Securities Laws 1048
Other Criminal Law Violations 1051
Injunctions 1051
Administrative Proceedings 1051
Securities Exchange Act Audit Requirements 1052
Ownership of Working Papers 1052
Professional–Client Privilege 1053

Part Eleven   *Regulation of Business*

47 Administrative Agencies 1058
Origins of Administrative Agencies 1059
Agency Creation 1059
Enabling Legislation 1059
Administrative Agencies and the Constitution 1060
Agency Types and Organization 1064
Agency Types 1064
Agency Organization 1065
Agency Powers and Procedures 1065
Nature, Types, and Source of Powers 1065
Investigative Power 1066
Rulemaking Power 1068
Adjudicatory Power 1070
Controlling Administrative Agencies 1071
Presidential Controls 1071
Congressional Controls 1071
Judicial Review 1072
Information Controls 1076
Freedom of Information Act 1077
Privacy Act of 1974 1079
Government in the Sunshine Act 1079
Issues in Regulation 1080
"Old" Regulation versus "New" Regulation 1080
"Captive" Agencies and Agencies' "Shadows" 1080
Deregulation versus Reregulation 1080

48 The Federal Trade Commission Act and Consumer Protection Laws 1085
The Federal Trade Commission 1086
The FTC's Powers 1086
FTC Enforcement Procedures 1086
Anticompetitive Behavior 1087
Deception and Unfairness 1087
Deception 1088
Unfairness 1091
Remedies 1091

APPENDIX A   *The Constitution of the United States of America 1223*

LIST OF CASES

FOUNDATIONS OF AMERICAN LAW

1

THE NATURE OF LAW

Assume that you have taken on a management position at MKT Corp. If MKT is to make sound business decisions, you and your management colleagues must be aware of a broad array of legal considerations. These may range, to use a nonexhaustive list, from issues in contract, agency, and employment law to considerations suggested by tort, intellectual property, securities, and constitutional law. Sometimes legal principles may constrain MKT's business decisions; at other times, the law may prove a valuable ally of MKT in the successful operation of the firm's business.

Of course, you and other members of the MKT management group will rely on the advice of in-house counsel (an attorney who is an MKT employee) or of outside attorneys who are in private practice. The approach of simply "leaving the law to the lawyers," however, is likely to be counterproductive. It often will be up to nonlawyers such as you to identify a potential legal issue or pitfall about which MKT needs professional guidance. If you fail to spot the issue in a timely manner and legal problems are allowed to develop and fester, even the most skilled attorneys may have difficulty rescuing you and the firm from the resulting predicament. If, on the other hand, your failure to identify a legal consideration means that you do not seek advice in time to obtain an advantage that applicable law would have provided MKT, the corporation may lose out on a beneficial opportunity. Either way—i.e., whether the relevant legal issue operates as a constraint or offers a potential advantage—you and the firm cannot afford to be unfamiliar with the legal environment in which MKT operates.

This may sound intimidating, but it need not be that way. The process of acquiring a working understanding of the legal environment of business begins simply enough with these basic questions:

• What major types of law apply to the business activities and help shape the business decisions of firms such as MKT?
• What ways of examining and evaluating law may serve as useful perspectives from which to view the legal environment in which MKT and other businesses operate?
• What role do courts play in making or interpreting law that applies to businesses such as MKT and to employees of those firms, and what methods of legal reasoning do courts utilize?

Types and Classifications of Law

The Types of Law

Constitutions Constitutions, which exist at the state and federal levels, have two general functions.[1] First, they set up the structure of government for the political unit they control (a state or the federal government). This involves creating the branches and subdivisions of the government and stating the powers given and denied to each. Through its **separation of powers,** the U.S. Constitution establishes a Congress and gives it power to legislate or *make* law in certain areas, provides for a chief executive (the president) whose function is to execute or *enforce* the laws, and helps create a federal judiciary to *interpret* the laws. The U.S. Constitution also structures the relationship between the federal government and the states. In the process, it respects the principle of **federalism** by recognizing the states' power to make law in certain areas.

The second function of constitutions is to prevent other units of government from taking certain actions or passing certain laws. Constitutions do so mainly by prohibiting government action that restricts certain individual rights. The Bill of Rights to the U.S. Constitution is an example.

Statutes Statutes are laws created by elected representatives in Congress or a state legislature. They are stated in an authoritative form in statute books or codes. As you will see, however, their interpretation and application are often difficult.

Throughout this text, you will encounter state statutes that were originally drafted as **uniform acts.** Uniform acts are model statutes drafted by private bodies of lawyers and/or scholars. They do not become law until they are enacted by a legislature. Their aim is to produce state-by-state uniformity on the subjects they address. Examples include the Uniform Commercial Code (which deals with a wide range of commercial law subjects), the Revised Uniform Partnership Act, and the Revised Model Business Corporation Act.

Common Law The **common law** (also called judge-made law or case law) is law made and applied by judges

[1] Chapter 3 discusses constitutional law as it applies to government regulation of business

as they decide cases not governed by statutes or other types of law. Although common law exists only at the state level, both state courts and federal courts become involved in applying it. The common law originated in medieval England and developed from the decisions of judges in settling disputes. Over time, judges began to follow the decisions of other judges in similar cases, called **precedents.** This practice became formalized in the doctrine of *stare decisis* (let the decision stand). As you will see later in the chapter, *stare decisis* is not completely rigid in its requirement of adherence to precedent. It is flexible enough to allow the common law to evolve to meet changing social conditions. The common law rules in force today, therefore, often differ considerably from the common law rules of earlier times.

The common law came to America with the first English settlers, was applied by courts during the colonial period, and continued to be applied after the Revolution and the adoption of the Constitution. It still governs many cases today. For example, the rules of tort, contract, and agency discussed in this text are mainly common law rules. In some instances, states have codified (enacted into statute) some parts of the common law. States and the federal government also have passed statutes superseding the common law in certain situations. As discussed in Chapter 9, for example, the states have established special rules for contract cases involving the sale of goods by enacting Article 2 of the Uniform Commercial Code.

This text's torts, contracts, and agency chapters often refer to the *Restatement*—or *Restatement* (*Second*) or (*Third*)—rule on a particular subject. The *Restatements* are collections of common law (and occasionally statutory) rules covering various areas of the law. Because they are promulgated by the American Law Institute rather than by courts, the *Restatements* are not law and do not bind courts. However, state courts often find *Restatement* rules persuasive and adopt them as common law rules within their states. The *Restatement* rules usually are the rules followed by a majority of the states. Occasionally, however, the *Restatements* stimulate changes in the common law by suggesting new rules that the courts later decide to follow.

Equity The body of law called **equity** historically concerned itself with accomplishing "rough justice" when common law rules would produce unfair results. In medieval England, common law rules were technical and rigid and the remedies available in common law courts were too few. This meant that some deserving parties could not obtain adequate relief. As a result, separate equity courts began hearing cases that the common law

CYBERLAW IN ACTION

When an applicable statute conflicts with a common law rule, the statute controls. This principle played a key role in *Blumenthal v. Drudge,* 992 F. Supp. 44 (D.D.C. 1998). There, a federal statute dealing with Internet service providers was held to protect America Online (AOL) from defamation liability that AOL might have faced if the statute had not displaced one of defamation's common law rules.

In 1997, the Drudge Report, a free Internet gossip page hosted by AOL, reported that Sidney Blumenthal, a newly appointed aide in the Clinton Administration, had "a spousal abuse past that [had] been effectively covered up." Blumenthal and his wife brought a defamation action against AOL and Matt Drudge, the operator of the page. AOL moved for summary judgment, arguing that a provision in the federal Communications Decency Act of 1996 (CDA) protected AOL from liability for any content appearing in Drudge's column. The court agreed and granted summary judgment in AOL's favor.

The effect of the CDA provision relied upon by AOL cannot be understood without some background concerning a particular aspect of defamation law. As you will see when the tort of defamation is addressed in Chapter 6, the common law of defamation typically provides that a *publisher* of a writer's defamatory statement is liable to the same extent that the writer is liable. For instance, a newspaper would be considered the publisher of a defamatory statement in an article it prints, because the newspaper, having considerable editorial control over the content of the article, would have had the ability to remove the defamatory statement. If this common law rule had controlled in *Blumenthal* and if AOL could credibly have been characterized as a publisher, AOL would have been at risk, along with Drudge, of liability for defamation.

Enter the CDA, however. Its § 230(c) states that "[n]o provider or user of an interactive computer service shall be treated as the publisher or speaker of any information provided by another information content provider." Drudge was "another information content provider," defined in the statute as "any person or entity that is responsible, in whole or in part, for the creation or development of information provided through the Internet or any other interactive computer service." Reasoning that AOL was a "provider . . . of an interactive computer service" for purposes of § 230(c), the court held that AOL could not be treated as the "publisher" of statements made by Drudge in the Drudge Report. Although § 230(c) did not expressly mention defamation and the CDA was generally designed to deal with matters other than defamation, legislative history indicated that § 230(c) was enacted to counteract earlier court decisions in which information content providers in positions similar to AOL's were held liable, as publishers, for defamation. With the court concluding that the CDA provision prevented application of the common law rule regarding publishers, AOL could not be held liable to the Blumenthals.

The CDA made one of the Blumenthals' arguments—that the *Washington Post* would be held liable if it had published Drudge's story without doing anything to edit or verify it—irrelevant by granting special status to interactive computer service providers. Had it been "writing on a clean slate," the court observed, it would have taken the Blumenthals' position. The court noted that "AOL [had] certain editorial rights with respect to the content provided by Drudge and disseminated by AOL, including the right to require changes in content and to remove it; and it [had] affirmatively promoted Drudge as a new source of unverified instant gossip on AOL." Moreover, AOL was "not a passive conduit like the telephone company, a common carrier with no control and therefore no responsibility for what is said over the telephone wires." The court commented that in view of AOL's "right to exercise editorial control over those with whom it contracts and whose words it disseminates, it would seem only fair to hold AOL to the liability standards applied to a publisher." Recognizing, however, that the "slate" on which it wrote was not "clean," the court held that it was bound by the "different policy choice" made by Congress: to protect Internet service providers from defamation liability without regard for whether they play an active role in deciding what content is provided and what content is not.

---

courts could not resolve fairly. In these equity courts, procedures were flexible, and rigid rules of law were deemphasized in favor of general moral maxims.

Equity courts also provided several remedies not available in the common law courts (which generally awarded only money damages or the recovery of property). The most important of these *equitable remedies* was—and continues to be—the **injunction,** a court order forbidding a party to do some act or commanding him to perform some act. Others include the contract remedies of **specific performance** (whereby a party is ordered to perform according to the terms of her contract), **reformation** (in which the court rewrites the contract's terms to reflect the parties' real intentions), and **rescission** (a cancellation of a contract in which the parties are returned to their precontractual position).

As was the common law, equity principles were brought to the American colonies and continued to be used after the Revolution and the adoption of the Constitution. Over time, however, the once-sharp line between law and equity has become blurred. Nearly all states have abolished separate equity courts and have enabled courts to grant whatever relief is appropriate, whether it be the legal remedy of money damages or one of the equitable remedies discussed above. Equitable principles have been blended together with common law rules, and some traditional equity doctrines have been restated as common law or statutory rules. An example is the doctrine of unconscionability discussed in Chapter 15.

Administrative Regulations and Decisions As Chapter 47 reveals, the administrative agencies established by Congress and the state legislatures have acquired considerable power, importance, and influence over business. A major reason for the rise of administrative agencies was the collection of social and economic problems created by the industrialization of the United States that began late in the 19th century. Because legislatures generally lacked the time and expertise to deal with these problems on a continuing basis, the creation of specialized, expert agencies was almost inevitable.

Administrative agencies obtain the ability to make law through a *delegation* (or grant) of power from the legislature. Agencies normally are created by a statute that specifies the areas in which the agency can make law and the scope of its power in each area. Often, these statutory delegations are worded so broadly that the legislature has, in effect, merely pointed to a problem and given the agency wide-ranging powers to deal with it.

The two types of law made by administrative agencies are **administrative regulations** and **agency decisions.** As do statutes, administrative regulations appear in a precise form in one authoritative source. They differ from statutes, however, because the body enacting regulations is not an elected body. Many agencies have an internal courtlike structure that enables them to hear cases arising under the statutes and regulations they enforce. The resulting agency decisions are legally binding, though appeals to the judicial system are sometimes allowed.

Treaties According to the U.S. Constitution, **treaties** made by the president with foreign governments and approved by two-thirds of the U.S. Senate are "the supreme Law of the Land." As will be seen, treaties invalidate inconsistent state (and sometimes federal) laws.

Ordinances State governments have subordinate units that exercise certain functions. Some of these units, such as school districts, have limited powers. Others, such as counties, municipalities, and townships, exercise various governmental functions. The enactments of counties and municipalities are called **ordinances;** zoning ordinances are an example.

Executive Orders In theory, the president or a state's governor is a chief executive who enforces the laws but has no law-making powers. However, these officials sometimes have limited power to issue laws called **executive orders.** This power normally results from a legislative delegation.

Priority Rules

Because the different types of law conflict, rules for determining which type takes priority are necessary. Here, we briefly describe the most important such rules.

1. According to the principle of **federal supremacy,** the U.S. Constitution, federal laws enacted pursuant to it, and treaties are the supreme law of the land. This means that federal law defeats conflicting state law.

2. Constitutions defeat other types of law within their domain. Thus, a state constitution defeats all other state laws inconsistent with it. The U.S. Constitution, however, defeats inconsistent laws of whatever type.

3. When a treaty conflicts with a federal statute over a purely domestic matter, the measure that is later in time usually prevails.

4. Within either the state or the federal domain, statutes defeat conflicting laws that depend on a legislative delegation for their validity. For example, a state statute defeats an inconsistent state administrative regulation.

5. Statutes and any laws derived from them by delegation defeat inconsistent common law rules. For example, either a statute or an administrative regulation defeats a conflicting common law rule.

Classifications of Law

Three common classifications of law cut across the different types of law. These classifications involve distinctions between: (1) criminal law and civil law; (2) substantive law and procedural law; and (3) public law and private law. One type of law might be classified in each of these ways. For example, a burglary statute would be criminal, substantive, and public; a rule of contract law would be civil, substantive, and private.

Criminal and Civil Law **Criminal law** is the law under which the government prosecutes someone for committing a crime. It creates duties that are owed to the public as a whole. **Civil law** mainly concerns obligations that private parties owe to each other. It is the law applied when one private party sues another. The government, however, may also be a party to a civil case. For example, a city may sue, or be sued by, a construction contractor. Criminal penalties (e.g., imprisonment or fines) differ from civil remedies (e.g., money damages or equitable relief). Although most of the legal rules in this text are civil law rules, Chapter 5 deals specifically with the criminal law.

Even though the civil law and the criminal law are distinct bodies of law, the same behavior will sometimes violate both. For instance, if A commits an act of physical violence on B, A may face both a criminal prosecution by the state and B's civil suit for damages.

Substantive Law and Procedural Law **Substantive law** sets the rights and duties of people as they act in society. **Procedural law** controls the behavior of government bodies (mainly courts) as they establish and enforce rules of substantive law. A statute making murder a crime, for example, is a rule of substantive law. The rules describing the proper conduct of a trial, however, are procedural. This text focuses on substantive law. Chapters 2 and 5, however, examine some of the procedural rules governing civil and criminal cases.

Public and Private Law **Public law** concerns the powers of government and the relations between government and private parties. Examples include constitutional law, administrative law, and criminal law. **Private law** establishes a framework of legal rules that enables parties to set the rights and duties they owe each other. Examples include the rules of contract, property, and agency.

Jurisprudence

The various types of law sometimes are called *positive law*. Positive law comprises the rules that have been laid down (or posited) by a recognized political authority. Knowing the types of positive law is essential to an understanding of the American legal system and the topics discussed in this text. Yet defining *law* by listing these different kinds of positive law is no more complete or accurate than defining "automobile" by describing all the vehicles going by that name. To define law properly, some say, we need a general description that captures its essence.

The field known as **jurisprudence** seeks to provide such a description. Over time, different schools of jurisprudence have emerged, each with its own distinctive view of law.

Legal Positivism

One feature common to all types of law is their enactment by a governmental authority such as a legislature or an administrative agency. This feature underlies the definition of law adopted by the school of jurisprudence known as **legal positivism.** Legal positivists define law as the *command of a recognized political authority*. As the British political philosopher Thomas Hobbes observed, "Law properly, is the word of him, that by right hath command over others."

The commands of recognized political authorities may be good, bad, or indifferent in moral terms. To legal positivists, such commands are valid law regardless of their "good" or "bad" content. In other words, positivists see legal validity and moral validity as entirely separate questions. Some (but not all) positivists say that every properly enacted positive law should be enforced and obeyed, whether just or unjust. Similarly, positivist judges usually try to enforce the law as written, excluding their own moral views from the process.

Natural Law

At first glance, legal positivism's "law is law, just or not" approach may seem to be perfect common sense. It presents a problem, however, for it could mean that *any* positive law—no matter how unjust—is valid law and should be enforced and obeyed so long as some recognized political authority—no matter how wicked—enacted it. The school of jurisprudence known as **natural law** takes issue with legal positivism by rejecting the positivist separation of law and morality.

Natural law adherents usually contend that some higher law or set of universal moral rules binds all human beings in all times and places. The Roman statesman Marcus Cicero described natural law as "the highest reason, implanted in nature, which commands what ought to be done and forbids the opposite." Because this higher law determines what is ultimately good and ultimately bad, it serves as a criterion for evaluating positive law. To Saint Thomas Aquinas, for example, "every human law has just so much of the nature of law, as it is derived from the law of nature." To be genuine law, in other words, positive law must resemble the law of nature by being "good"—or at least by not being "bad."

Unjust positive laws, then, are not valid law under the natural law view. As Cicero put it: "What of the many deadly, the many pestilential statutes which are imposed on peoples? These no more deserve to be called laws than the rules a band of robbers might pass in their assembly." An "unjust" law's supposed invalidity does not translate into a natural law defense that is recognized in court, however. The *Lynch* case, which follows shortly, makes this point quite clear.

Although a formal natural law defense is not recognized in court, judges may sometimes take natural law-oriented views into account when interpreting the law. As compared with positivist judges, judges influenced by natural law ideas may be more likely to read constitutional provisions broadly in order to strike down positive laws they regard as unjust. They also may be more likely to let morality influence their interpretation of the law. Of course, neither judges nor natural law thinkers always agree about what is moral and immoral—a major difficulty for the natural law position. This difficulty allows legal positivists to claim that only by keeping legal and moral questions separate can we obtain stability and predictability in the law.

United States *v.* Lynch   *1996 U.S. App. Lexis 32729 (2 d Cir. 1996)*

The Freedom of Access to Clinic Entrances Act (FACE), a federal statute, provides for penalties against anyone who "by force or threat of force or by physical obstruction . . . intentionally injures, intimidates or interferes . . . with any person . . . in order to intimidate such person . . . from obtaining or providing reproductive health services." Lynch and Moscinski blocked access to the Women's Medical Pavilion (WMP), a clinic offering such services. The government sought an injunction prohibiting Lynch and Moscinski from impeding access to or coming within fifteen feet of the clinic. A federal district court issued the injunction after finding that Lynch and Moscinski had violated the statute by making entrance to the clinic unreasonably difficult. Lynch and Moscinski moved to amend the order on the ground that the court's opinion had not addressed their natural law argument. The district court denied the motion, and Lynch and Moscinski appealed.

Per Curiam Defendants concede that they willfully intended to impede and did impede access to the WMP. At the hearing, defendants essentially offered no challenge to the Government's evidence, nor did they present any evidence of their own. Their only defense was their contention, which they argued at length, that the FACE statute protects the taking of innocent human life, and is therefore contrary to natural law and accordingly null and void.

Defendants' sole contention on appeal is that the district court declined to address their only defense based on natural law. We find it abundantly clear from the record that the district court considered and rejected this defense. Judge Sprizzo stated, "I don't recognize my authority to refuse to issue an injunction under natural law," and "I don't have the right to act my own private conscience." He pointedly explained to defense counsel:

That seal above my head says . . . this is Caesar's court. This is not a church, this is not a temple, this is not a mosque. And we don't live in a theocracy. This is a court of law. I will look at all the legal issues.

Thus did the district court fully and forcefully address and deny defendants' natural law defense.

We agree with the district court's conclusion that natural law cannot furnish a valid basis upon which to nullify the FACE statute, or the injunction issued pursuant to it. Defendants cite, among others, Pope John Paul II's encyclical, *Evangelium Vitae,* Thomas Aquinas' *Summa Theologia,* and Ronald Dworkin's *Taking Rights Seriously.* For better or worse, as the case may be, these texts do not control our decision in this case. "[T]he Constitution and the laws passed pursuant to it are the supreme laws of the land, binding alike upon states, courts, and the people." *Testa v. Katt,* U.S. Supreme Court (1946). Defendants do not argue that FACE is unconstitutional. They argue instead that FACE (and abortion) are anathema, and thus violate principles superior to the Constitution. Under Supreme Court precedent, well-settled constitutional principles, and the rule of stare decisis, we decline to invalidate a federal statute (on its face or as applied) on the basis of natural law principles.

Judgment in favor of government affirmed.

American Legal Realism

To some, the debate between natural law and legal positivism may seem unreal. Not only is natural law unworkable, such people might say, but sometimes positive law does not mean much either. For example, juries sometimes pay little attention to the legal rules that are supposed to guide their decisions, and prosecutors have discretion concerning whether to enforce criminal statutes. In some legal proceedings, moreover, the background, biases, and values of the judge—and not the positive law—determine the result. An old joke reminds us that justice sometimes is what the judge ate for breakfast.

Remarks such as these typify the school of jurisprudence known as **American legal realism.** Legal realists regard the law-in-the-books as less important than the *law in action*—the conduct of those who enforce and interpret the positive law. American legal realism defines law as the *behavior of public officials (mainly judges) as they deal with matters before the legal system.* Because the actions of such decisionmakers—and not the rules in the books—really affect people's lives, the realists say, this behavior is what deserves to be called law.

It is doubtful whether the legal realists have ever developed a common position on the relation between law and morality or on the duty to obey positive law. They have been quick, however, to tell judges how to behave. Many realists feel that the modern judge should be a social engineer who weighs all relevant values and considers social science findings when deciding a case. Such a judge would make the positive law only one factor in her decision. Because judges inevitably base their decisions on personal considerations, the realists assert, they should at least do this honestly and intelligently. To promote this kind of decisionmaking, the realists have sometimes favored fuzzy, discretionary rules that allow judges to decide each case according to its unique facts.

Sociological Jurisprudence

Sociological jurisprudence is a general label uniting several different approaches that examine law within its social context. The following quotation from Justice Oliver Wendell Holmes is consistent with such approaches:

> The life of the law has not been logic: it has been experience. The felt necessities of the time, the prevalent moral and political theories, intuitions of public policy, avowed or unconscious, even the prejudices which judges share with their fellow-men, have had a good deal more to do than the syllogism in determining the rules by which men should be governed. The law embodies the story of a nation's development through many centuries, and it cannot be dealt with

as if it contained only the axioms and corollaries of a book of mathematics.[2]

Despite these approaches' common outlook, there is no distinctive sociological definition of law. If one were attempted, it might go as follows: *Law is a process of social ordering reflecting society's dominant interests and values.*

Different Sociological Approaches By examining examples of sociological legal thinking, we can add substance to the definition just offered. The "dominant interests" portion of the definition is exemplified by the writings of Roscoe Pound, an influential 20th-century American legal philosopher. Pound developed a detailed and changing catalog of the social interests that press on government and the legal system and thus shape positive law. An example of the definition's "dominant values" component is the *historical school* of jurisprudence identified with the 19th-century German legal philosopher Friedrich Karl von Savigny. Savigny saw law as an unplanned, almost unconscious, reflection of the collective spirit of a particular society. In his view, legal change could only be explained historically, as a slow response to social change.

By emphasizing the influence of dominant social interests and values, Pound and Savigny undermine the legal positivist view that law is nothing more than the command of some political authority. The early 20th-century Austrian legal philosopher Eugen Ehrlich went even further in rejecting positivism. He did so by identifying two different "processes of social ordering" contained within our definition of sociological jurisprudence. The first of these is positive law. The second is the "living law," informal social controls such as customs, family ties, and business practices. By regarding both as law, Ehrlich sought to demonstrate that positive law is only one element within a spectrum of social controls.

The Implications of Sociological Jurisprudence

Because its definition of law includes social values, sociological jurisprudence seems to resemble natural law. Most sociological thinkers, however, are concerned only with the *fact* that moral values influence the law, and not with the goodness or badness of those values. Thus, it might seem that sociological jurisprudence gives no practical advice to those who must enforce and obey positive law.

Sociological jurisprudence has at least one practical implication, however: a tendency to urge that the law must change to meet changing social conditions and values. In

---

[2]Holmes. *The Common Law* (1881).

ETHICS IN ACTION

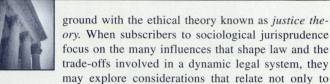

Some schools of jurisprudence discussed in this chapter—most notably *natural law* and the various approaches lumped under the *sociological jurisprudence* heading—concern themselves with the relationship between law and notions of morality. These schools of jurisprudence involve considerations related to key aspects of ethical theories that will be explored in Chapter 4, which addresses ethical issues arising in business contexts.

Natural law's focus on rights thought to be independent of positive law has parallels in ethical theories that are classified under the *theory of rights* (or *rights theory*) heading. In its concern over unjust laws, natural law finds common ground with the ethical theory known as *justice theory*. When subscribers to sociological jurisprudence focus on the many influences that shape law and the trade-offs involved in a dynamic legal system, they may explore considerations that relate not only to rights theory or justice theory but also to two other ethical theories, *utilitarianism* and *profit maximization*. As you study Chapter 4 and then later chapters, keep the schools of jurisprudence in mind. Think of them as you consider the extent to which a behavior's probable legal treatment and the possible ethical assessments of it may correspond or, instead, diverge.

---

other words, the law should keep up with the times. Some might stick to this view even when society's values are changing for the worse. To Holmes, for example, "[t]he first requirement of a sound body of law is, that it should correspond with the actual feelings and demands of the community, *whether right or wrong.*"[3]

Other Schools of Jurisprudence

During approximately the past 30 years, legal scholars have fashioned additional ways of viewing law, explaining why legal rules are as they are, and exploring supposed needs for changes in legal doctrines. For example, the *law and economics* movement examines legal rules through the lens provided by economic theory and analysis. This movement's influence has extended beyond academic literature, with law and economics-oriented considerations, factors, and tests occasionally appearing in judicial opinions dealing with such matters as contract, tort, or antitrust law.

The *critical legal studies* (CLS) movement tends to regard law as inevitably the product of political calculation (mostly of the right-wing variety) and longstanding class biases on the part of lawmakers, including judges. Articles published by CLS adherents provide controversial assessments and critiques of legal rules. Given the thrust of CLS and the view it takes of lawmakers, however, one would be hard-pressed to find CLS adherents in the legislature or the judiciary.

Other schools of jurisprudence that have acquired notoriety in recent years examine law and the legal system from the vantage points of particular groups of persons or sets of ideas. Examples include the feminist legal studies perspective and the gay legal studies movement.

The Functions of Law

In societies of the past, people often viewed law as unchanging rules that deserved obedience because they were part of the natural order of things. Most lawmakers today, however, treat law as a flexible tool or instrument for the accomplishment of chosen purposes. For example, the law of negotiable instruments discussed later in this text is designed to stimulate commercial activity by promoting the free movement of money substitutes such as promissory notes, checks, and drafts. Throughout the text, moreover, you see courts manipulating existing legal rules to achieve desired results. One strength of this *instrumentalist* attitude is its willingness to adapt the law to further the social good. A weakness, however, is the legal instability and uncertainty those adaptations often produce.

Just as individual legal rules advance specific purposes, law as a whole serves many general social functions. Among the most important of those functions are:

1. *Peacekeeping.* The criminal law rules discussed in Chapter 5 further this basic function of any legal system. Also, as Chapter 2 suggests, the resolution of private disputes serves as a major function of the civil law.

2. *Checking government* power *and* promoting personal freedom. Obvious examples are the constitutional restrictions examined in Chapter 3.

---

[3]The italics have been added for emphasis.

3. *Facilitating planning and the realization of reasonable expectations.* The rules of contract law discussed in Chapters 9–18 help fulfill this function of law.

4. *Promoting economic growth through free competition.* The antitrust laws discussed in Chapters 48–50 are among the many legal rules that help perform this function.

5. *Promoting social justice.* Throughout this century, government has intervened in private social and economic affairs to correct perceived injustices and give all citizens equal access to life's basic goods. Examples include the employer–employee regulations treated in Chapter 51.

6. *Protecting the environment.* The most important federal environmental statutes are discussed in Chapter 52.

Obviously, the law's various functions can conflict. The familiar clash between economic growth and environmental protection is an example. Chapter 5's cases dealing with the constitutional aspects of criminal cases illustrate the equally familiar conflict between effective law enforcement and the preservation of personal rights. Only rarely does the law achieve one end without sacrificing others. In law, as in life, there generally is no such thing as a free lunch. Where the law's objectives conflict, lawmakers may try to strike the best possible balance among those goals. This suggests limits on the law's usefulness as a device for promoting particular social goals.

Legal Reasoning

This text seeks to describe important legal rules affecting business. As texts generally do, it states those rules in what lawyers call "black letter" form, using sentences saying that certain legal consequences will occur if certain events happen. Although it provides a clear statement of the law's commands, this black letter approach can be misleading. It suggests definiteness, certainty, permanence, and predictability—attributes the law frequently lacks. To illustrate, and to give you some idea how lawyers and judges think, we now discuss the two most important kinds of legal reasoning: **case law reasoning** and **statutory interpretation.**[4] However, we first must examine legal reasoning in general.

Legal reasoning is basically deductive, or syllogistic. The legal rule is the major premise, the facts are the minor premise, and the result is the product of combining the two. Suppose a state statute says that a driver operating an automobile between 55 and 70 miles per hour must pay a $50 fine (the rule or major premise) and that Jim Smith drives his car at 65 miles per hour (the facts or minor premise). If Jim is arrested, and if the necessary facts can be proved, he will be required to pay the $50 fine. As you will now see, however, legal reasoning often is more difficult than this example would suggest.

Case Law Reasoning

In cases governed by the common law, courts find the appropriate legal rules in prior cases called *precedents.* The standard for choosing and applying prior cases to decide present cases is the doctrine of *stare decisis,* which states that like cases should be decided alike. That is, the present case should be decided in the same way as past cases presenting the same facts and the same legal issues. If a court decides that an alleged precedent is not sufficiently like the present case and should not control the present decision, it *distinguishes* the prior case.[5]

Because every present case differs from the precedents in some respect, it is always possible to spot a factual distinction. For example, one could attempt to distinguish a prior case because both parties in that case had black hair, whereas one party in the present case has brown hair. Of course, such a distinction would be ridiculous, because the difference it identifies is insignificant in moral or social policy terms. A valid distinction involves a widely accepted ethical or policy reason for treating the present case differently from its predecessor. Because people disagree about moral ideas, public policies, and the degree to which they are accepted, and because all these factors change over time, judges may differ on the wisdom of distinguishing a prior case. Although this is a source of uncertainty in the common law, it also gives the common law the flexibility to adapt to changing social conditions.

When a precedent has been properly distinguished, the common law rule it stated does not control the present case. The court deciding the present case may then fashion a new common law rule to govern the case. Consider, for instance, an example involving the employment-at-will rule, the pre-

---

[4]The reasoning courts employ in constitutional cases resembles that used in common law cases, but often is somewhat looser. On the way courts decide constitutional cases, see Chapter 3.

[5]Also, though they exercise the power infrequently, courts sometimes completely *overrule* their own prior decisions.

vailing common law rule regarding employees in the United States. Under this rule, an employee may be fired at any time—and without any reason, let alone a good one—unless a contract between the employer and the employee guaranteed a certain duration of employment or established that the employee could be fired only for certain recognized legal causes. Most employees are not parties to a contract containing such provisions. Therefore, they are employees-at-will. Assume that in a precedent case, an employee who had been doing good work challenged his firing, and that the court hearing the case ruled against him on the basis of the employment-at-will rule. Also assume that in a later case, a fired employee has challenged her dismissal. Although the fired employee would appear to be subject to the employment-at-will rule applied in the seemingly similar precedent case, the court deciding the later case nevertheless identifies an important difference: that in the later case, the employee was fired in retaliation for having reported to law enforcement authorities that her employer was engaging in seriously unlawful business-related conduct. A firing under such circumstances appears to offend public policy, notwithstanding the general acceptance of the employment-

at-will rule. Having properly distinguished the precedent, the court deciding the later case would not be bound by the employment-at-will rule set forth in the precedent and would be free to develop a public policy-based exception under which the retaliatory firing would be deemed wrongful. (Chapter 51 will reveal that courts in a number of states have adopted such an exception to the employment-at-will rule.)

The *Hagan* case, which follows, provides a further illustration of the process of case law reasoning. In *Hagan*, the Florida Supreme Court scrutinizes various precedents as it attempts to determine whether Florida's courts should retain, modify, or abolish a common law rule under which a plaintiff in a negligence case could not recover damages for emotional harm unless she also sustained some sort of impact that produced physical injuries—i.e., injuries to her body. (Negligence law is discussed in depth in Chapter 7.) Ultimately, the court determines that under circumstances of the sort presented in the case, damages for emotional distress should be recoverable even in the absence of a physical injury-producing impact.

Hagan v. Coca-Cola Bottling Co.   *776 So. 2d 275 (Fla. Sup. Ct. 2000)*

Linda Hagan and her sister Barbara Parker drank from a bottle of Coke which they both agreed tasted flat. Hagan then held the bottle up to a light and observed what she and Parker thought was a used condom with "oozy stringy stuff coming out of the top." Both women were distressed that they had consumed some foreign material and Hagan immediately became nauseated. The bottle was later delivered to Coca-Cola for testing. Concerned about what they had drunk, the women went to a health care facility the next day and were given shots. The medical personnel at the facility told them they should be tested for HIV-AIDS. Hagan and Parker were then tested and informed that the results were negative. Six months later, both women were again tested for HIV, and the results were again negative.

Hagan and Parker brought a negligence action against Coca-Cola. Coca-Cola's beverage analyst testified at trial that he had initially thought, as Hagan and Parker had, that the object in the bottle was a condom. However, upon closer examination, he concluded that the object was a mold, and that, to a "scientific certainty," the item floating in the Coke bottle was not a condom.

At the conclusion of the trial, the jury returned a verdict in favor of the plaintiffs, awarding $75,000 each to Hagan and Parker. The trial court reduced the jury award to $25,000 each to Hagan and Parker. Both sides appealed to the Fifth District Court of Appeal.

The appellate court reversed the jury awards and concluded that under case law concerning the impact rule, Hagan and Parker had not established a claim because neither had suffered a physical injury. Under a special procedure allowed by Florida law, certain dissenting and concurring appellate court judges sent a certified question to the state Supreme Court asking whether the impact rule should be abolished or amended in Florida.

Anstead, Judge   We have for review a decision from the Fifth District Court of Appeal in which the court certified a question to be of great public importance: Should the impact

rule be abolished or amended in Florida? Because we conclude that there was an impact here and the impact rule does not bar the claim, we rephrase the certified question [to ask whether] the impact rule preclude[s] a claim for damages for emotional distress caused by the consumption of a foreign substance in a beverage product where the plaintiff suffers no accompanying physical injuries[.]

Hagan and Parker (hereinafter "appellants") assert that a person should not be barred from recovering damages for emotional distress caused by the consumption of a beverage containing a foreign substance simply because she suffered distress but did not suffer any additional physical injury at the time of consumption. Therefore, appellants contend that the "impact rule" should not operate to preclude relief under the circumstances of this case. We agree with appellants and hold that the impact rule does not apply to cases where a plaintiff suffers emotional distress as a direct result of the consumption of a contaminated beverage.

We begin by acknowledging that although many states have abolished the "impact rule," several states, including Florida, still adhere to the rule. This court, while acknowledging exceptions, has accepted the impact rule as a limitation on certain claims as a means for "assuring the validity of claims for emotional or psychic damages." *R. J. v. Humana of Florida, Inc.* (1995). Generally stated, the impact rule requires that before a plaintiff may recover damages for emotional distress, she must demonstrate that the emotional stress suffered flowed from injuries sustained in an impact. Notwithstanding our adherence to the rule, this Court has noted several instances where the impact rule should not preclude an otherwise viable claim.

For example, this Court modified the impact rule in bystander cases by excusing the lack of a physical impact. In such cases, recovery for emotional distress would be permitted where one person suffers "death or significant discernible physical injury when caused by psychological trauma resulting from a negligent injury imposed on a close family member within the sensory perception of the physically injured person." *Champion v. Gray* (1985). We also have held that the impact rule does not apply to claims for intentional infliction of emotional distress, wrongful birth, negligence claims involving stillbirth, and bad faith claims against an insurance carrier.

We believe that public policy dictates that a cause of action for emotional distress caused by the ingestion of a contaminated food or beverage should be recognized despite the lack of an accompanying physical injury. In *Doyle v. Pillsbury Co.* (1985), for example, this Court observed that the impact rule would not bar a cause of action for damages caused by the ingestion of a contaminated food or beverage. There, the plaintiffs, Mr. and Mrs. Doyle, opened a can of peas and observed an insect floating on top of the contents.

Mrs. Doyle jumped back in alarm, fell over a chair and suffered physical injuries. The plaintiffs sued the Pillsbury Company, Green Giant Company, and Publix Supermarkets, alleging negligence, strict liability, and breach of warranty. The trial court granted summary judgment in favor of the defendants, finding that the impact rule barred the plaintiffs' cause of action, and the intermediate appellate court affirmed.

On review, this Court approved of the outcome but disapproved of the application of the impact rule. We initially recognized that ingestion of a food or drink product is a necessary prerequisite to a cause of action against restaurants, manufacturers, distributors and retailers of food. In doing so, we impliedly found that ingestion of a foreign food or substance constitutes an impact. [We wrote:]

> "This ingestion requirement is grounded upon foreseeability rather than the impact rule. The public has become accustomed to believing in and relying on the fact that packaged foods are fit for consumption. A producer or retailer of food should foresee that a person may well become physically or mentally ill after consuming part of a food product and then discovering a deleterious foreign object, such as an insect or rodent, in presumably wholesome food or drink. The manufacturer or retailer must expect to bear the costs of the resulting injuries. The same foreseeability is lacking where a person simply observes the foreign object and suffers injury after the observation. The mere observance of unwholesome food cannot be equated to consuming a portion of the same. We should not impose virtually unlimited liability in such cases. When a claim is based on an inert foreign object in a food product, we continue to require ingestion of a portion of the food before liability arises. Because Mrs. Doyle never ingested any portion of the canned peas, the trial court properly granted summary judgment against the Doyles. *Doyle v. Pillsbury Co.* (1985).

Other jurisdictions have reached a similar conclusion, one, in fact, involving virtually the same facts presented here. In *Wallace v. Coca-Cola Bottling Plants, Inc.*, [Me. (1970)], the plaintiff drank from a Coke bottle which contained an unwrapped condom. The plaintiff became ill after he returned home and thought about his experience. The Maine Supreme Court held that where the plaintiff demonstrates a causal relationship between the negligent act and the reasonably foreseeable mental and emotional suffering by a reasonably foreseeable plaintiff, damages for emotional suffering are recoverable despite the lack of a "discernable trauma from external causes." The court found that such requirements had been met: "The foreign object was of such a loathsome nature it was reasonably foreseeable its presence would cause nausea and mental distress upon being discovered . . . The mental distress was manifested by the vomiting."

Several years later [in *Culbert v. Sampson Supermarkets Inc.,* 444 A.2d 433 [Me. (1982)], the Maine Supreme Court overruled *Wallace* to the extent that it had required a plaintiff to demonstrate actual physical manifestations of the mental injury. In overruling any physical injury requirement, the court noted that it could have permitted recovery in *Wallace* even under the impact rule because the condom had come in contact with the plaintiff. We find the reasoning of the Maine Supreme Court to be instructive, and consistent with our analysis in Doyle, to the extent it concludes that a plaintiff may recover for emotional injuries caused by the consumption of a contaminated food or beverage despite the lack of an additional physical injury.

As this Court [has] recognized [before], the impact rule does not apply where emotional damages are a "consequence of conduct that itself is a freestanding tort apart from any emotional injury." *Tanner v. Hartog,* (1997). [W]e hold that a plaintiff need not prove the existence of a physical injury in order to recover damages for emotional injuries caused by the consumption of a contaminated food or beverage. [T]hose who market foodstuffs should foresee and expect to bear responsibility for the emotional and physical harm caused by someone consuming a food product that is contaminated by a foreign substance. Further, since we have concluded that there was an impact in the case at hand by the ingestion of a contaminated substance, and the impact rule does not bar the action, we decline to rule on the broader question posed by the district court's certified question.

Intermediate appellate court decision reversed, and case remanded.

Statutory Interpretation

Because statutes are written in one authoritative form, their interpretation might seem easier than case law reasoning. However, this is not so. The natural ambiguity of language serves as one reason courts face difficulties when interpreting statutes. The problems become especially difficult when statutory words are applied to situations the legislature did not foresee. In some instances, legislators may deliberately use ambiguous language when they are unwilling or unable to deal specifically with each situation the statute was enacted to regulate. When this happens, the legislature expects courts and/or administrative agencies to fill in the details on a case-by-case basis. Other reasons for deliberate ambiguity include the need for legislative compromise and legislators' desire to avoid taking controversial positions.

To deal with the problems just described, courts use various techniques of statutory interpretation. As you will see shortly, different techniques may dictate different results in a particular case. Sometimes judges employ the techniques in an instrumentalist or result-oriented fashion, emphasizing the technique that will produce the result they want and downplaying the others. It is therefore unclear which technique should control when different techniques yield different results. Judges have considerable latitude in this regard.

Plain Meaning Courts begin their interpretation of a statute with its actual language. If the statute's words have a clear, common, accepted meaning, courts often employ the *plain meaning rule*. This approach calls for the court to apply the statute according to the usual meaning of its words, without concerning itself with anything else. In the *Rucker* case, which follows, the Supreme Court takes a plain meaning approach to interpretation of a federal statute.

Department of Housing and Urban Development v. Rucker
122 S. Ct. 1230 (U.S. Sup. Ct. 2002)

The Anti-Drug Abuse Act of 1988 provides that each "public housing agency shall utilize leases which . . . provide that any criminal activity that threatens the health, safety, or right to peaceful enjoyment of the premises by other tenants or any drug-related criminal activity on or off such premises, engaged in by a public housing tenant, any member of the tenant's household, or any guest or other person under the tenant's control, shall be cause for termination of tenancy." 42 U.S.C. §

1437d (1)(6). Department of Housing and Urban Development (HUD) regulations implementing the Act authorize local public housing authorities to evict for drug-related activity of persons listed in the statute even if the tenant did not know of the activity.

The Oakland Housing Authority (OHA) instituted eviction proceedings in state court against William Lee, Barbara Hill, and Pearlie Rucker, alleging that they had violated a lease provision obligating tenants to "assure that . . . any member of the household, a guest, or another person under the tenant's control, shall not engage in . . . any drug-related criminal activity on or near the premises." Allegedly, the respective grandsons of Lee and Hill were caught smoking marijuana in the apartment complex parking lot, Rucker's daughter was found with cocaine and a crack cocaine pipe three blocks from Rucker's apartment, and, on three instances within a two-month period, seventy-five year old Herman Walker's caregiver and two others were found with cocaine in Walker's apartment. Lee, Hill, and Rucker claimed to have been unaware of their grandsons' and daughter's illegal drug abuse, and Walker fired his caregiver upon receiving the eviction notice.

In response to OHA's actions, Lee, Hill, Rucker, and Walker (hereinafter referred to as "the tenants") filed an action in federal district court, arguing that the Anti-Drug Abuse Act does not authorize the eviction of innocent tenants, and that if it did, it would be unconstitutional. They sought and won a preliminary injunction enjoining the enforcement of HUD's regulations and the corresponding provision in the OHA lease against innocent tenants. The Ninth Circuit Court of Appeals upheld the preliminary injunction. HUD appealed, and the Supreme Court granted certiorari.

Rehnquist, Chief Justice HUD and OHA say that § 1437d(*l*)(6) requires lease terms that allow a local public housing authority to evict a tenant when a member of the tenant's household or a guest engages in drug-related criminal activity, regardless of whether the tenant knew, or had reason to know, of that activity. The tenants say it does not. We agree with HUD and OHA.

That this is so seems evident from the plain language of the statute. It provides that "each public housing authority shall utilize leases which . . . provide that . . . any drug-related criminal activity on or off such premises, engaged in by a public housing tenant, any member of the tenant's household, or any guest or other person under the tenant's control, shall be cause for termination of tenancy." The Court of Appeals thought the statute did not address "the level of personal knowledge or fault that is required for eviction." Yet Congress' decision not to impose any qualification in the statute, combined with its use of the term "any" to modify "drug-related criminal activity," precludes any knowledge requirement. As we have explained, "the word 'any' has an expansive meaning, that is, 'one or some indiscriminately of whatever kind.' " *United States v. Gonzales,* (1997). Thus, *any* drug-related activity engaged in by the specified persons is grounds for termination, not just drug-related activity that the tenant knew, or should have known, about.

The Court of Appeals also thought it possible that "under the tenant's control" modifies not just "other person," but also "member of the tenant's household" and "guest." The court ultimately adopted this reading, concluding that the statute prohibits eviction where the tenant "for a lack of knowledge or other reason, could not realistically exercise control over the conduct of a household member or guest." But this interpreta-

tion runs counter to basic rules of grammar. The disjunctive "or" means that the qualification applies only to "other person." Indeed, the view that "under the tenant's control" modifies everything coming before it in the sentence would result in the nonsensical reading that the statute applies to "a public housing tenant . . . under the tenant's control." HUD offers a convincing explanation for the grammatical imperative that "under the tenant's control" modifies only "other person": "by 'control,' the statute means control in the sense that the tenant has permitted access to the premises." 66 Fed. Reg. 28781 (2001). Implicit in the terms "household member" or "guest" is that access to the premises has been granted by the tenant. Thus, the plain language of § 1437d(*l*)(6) requires leases that grant public housing authorities the discretion to terminate tenancy without regard to the tenant's knowledge of the drug-related criminal activity.

Nor was the Court of Appeals correct in concluding that this plain reading of the statute leads to absurd results. The statute does not *require* the eviction of any tenant who violated the lease provision. Instead, it entrusts that decision to the local public housing authorities, who are in the best position to take account of, among other things, the degree to which the housing project suffers from "rampant drug-related or violent crime," 42 U.S.C. § 11901(2), "the seriousness of the offending action," 66 Fed. Reg., at 28803, and "the extent to which the leaseholder has . . . taken all reasonable steps to prevent or mitigate the offending action," *ibid.* It is not "absurd" that a local housing authority may sometimes evict a tenant who had no knowledge of the drug-related activity. Such "no-fault" eviction is a common "incident of tenant responsibility under normal landlord–tenant law and practice." 56 Fed. Reg., at 51567.

And, of course, there is an obvious reason why Congress would have permitted local public housing authorities to conduct no-fault evictions: Regardless of knowledge, a tenant who "cannot control drug crime, or other criminal activities by a household member which threaten health or safety of other residents, is a threat to other residents and the project." 56 Fed. Reg., at 51567. With drugs leading to "murders, muggings, and other forms of violence against tenants," and to the "deterioration of the physical environment that requires substantial governmental expenditures," 42 U.S.C. § 11901(4), it was reasonable for Congress to permit no-fault evictions in order to "provide public and other federally assisted low-income housing that is decent, safe, and free from illegal drugs," § 11901(1).

The Court of Appeals held that HUD's interpretation "raises serious questions under the Due Process Clause of the Fourteenth Amendment," because it permits "tenants to be deprived of their property interest without any relationship to individual wrongdoing." The government is not attempting to criminally punish or civilly regulate respondents as members of the general populace [, however]. It is instead acting as a landlord of property that it owns, invoking a clause in a lease to which respondents have agreed and which Congress has expressly required. [The cases relied on by the tenants] cast no constitutional doubt on such actions.

The Court of Appeals sought to bolster its discussion of constitutional doubt by pointing to the fact that respondents have a property interest in their leasehold interest, citing *Greene v. Lindsey,* (1982). This is undoubtedly true, and *Greene* held that an effort to deprive a tenant of such a right without proper notice violated the Due Process Clause. But, in the present cases, such deprivation will occur in the state court where OHA brought the unlawful detainer action against respondents. There is no indication that notice has not been given by OHA in the past, or that it will not be given in the future. Any individual factual disputes about whether the lease provision was actually violated can, of course, be resolved in these proceedings.

We hold that Congress has directly spoken to the precise question at issue. Section 1437d(*l*)(6) requires lease terms that give local public housing authorities the discretion to terminate the lease of a tenant when a member of the household or a guest engages in drug-related activity, regardless of whether the tenant knew, or should have known, of the drug-related activity.

Judgment of Court of Appeals reversed, and case remanded for further proceedings.

Legislative History and Legislative Purpose

Some courts, such as the Supreme Court in a case that appears later in this section, refuse to follow a statute's plain meaning when its legislative history suggests a different result. Almost all courts resort to legislative history when the statute's language is ambiguous. A statute's legislative history includes the following sources: reports of investigative committees or law revision commissions that led to the legislation; transcripts or summaries of hearings of legislative committees that originally considered the legislation; reports issued by such committees; records of legislative debates; reports of conference committees reconciling two houses' conflicting versions of the law; amendments or defeated amendments to the legislation; other bills not passed by the legislature but proposing similar legislation; and discrepancies between a bill passed by one house and the final version of the statute.

Sometimes a statute's legislative history provides no information or conflicting information about its meaning, scope, or purposes. Some sources prove to be more authoritative than others. The worth of debates, for instance, may depend on which legislator (e.g., the sponsor of the bill or an uninformed blowhard) is quoted. Some sources are useful only in particular situations; prior unpassed bills and amendments or defeated amendments are examples. Consider, for instance, whether mopeds are covered by an air pollution statute applying to "automobiles, trucks, buses, and other motorized passenger or cargo vehicles." If the statute's original version included mopeds but this reference was removed by amendment, it is unlikely that the legislature wanted mopeds to be covered. The same might be true if six similar unpassed bills had included mopeds but the bill that was eventually passed did not, or if one house had passed a bill including mopeds but mopeds did not appear in the final version of the legislation.

Courts use legislative history in two overlapping but distinguishable ways. They may use it to determine what the legislature thought about the specific meaning of statutory language. They may also use it to determine the overall aim, end, or goal of the legislation. In this second case, they then ask whether a particular interpretation of the statute is consistent with this legislative purpose. To illustrate the difference between these two uses of legislative history, suppose that a court is considering whether our pollution statute's "other motorized passenger or cargo vehicles" language includes battery-powered vehicles. The court might scan the legislative history for specific references to battery-powered vehicles or other indications of what the legislature thought about their inclusion. However, the court might also use the same history to determine the overall aims of the statute, and then ask whether including battery-

powered vehicles is consistent with those aims. Because the history probably would reveal that the statute's purpose was to reduce air pollution from internal combustion engines, the court might well conclude that battery-powered vehicles should not be covered.

In the following case, *United Steelworkers v. Weber*, the Supreme Court rejects the plain meaning technique when it interprets a major employment discrimination statute. Instead, the Court interprets the statute in light of its legislative history and purpose and thereby reaches a result contrary to the result that the plain meaning technique would have produced.

United Steelworkers v. Weber   *443 U.S. 193 (U.S. Sup. Ct. 1979)*

As part of its collective bargaining agreement with the United Steelworkers of America, the Kaiser Aluminum and Chemical Company established a new on-the-job craft training program at its Gramercy, Louisiana plant. The selection of trainees for the program was based on seniority, but at least 50 percent of the new trainees had to be black until the percentage of black skilled craft workers in the plant approximated the percentage of blacks in the local labor force.

Brian Weber was a rejected white applicant who would have qualified for the program had the racial preference not existed. He sued Kaiser and the union in federal district court, arguing that the racial preference violated Title VII of the 1964 Civil Rights Act. Section 703(a) of the act stated: "It shall be an unlawful employment practice for an employer . . . to discriminate against any individual with respect to his compensation, terms, conditions, or privileges of employment, because of such individual's race, color, religion, sex, or national origin." Section 703(d) had a similar provision specifically forbidding racial discrimination in admission to apprenticeship or other training programs. Weber's suit was successful, and the federal court of appeals affirmed. Kaiser and the union appealed to the U.S. Supreme Court.

Brennan, Justice   The only question before us is whether Title VII forbids private employers and unions from voluntarily agreeing upon bona fide affirmative action plans that accord racial preferences in the manner and for the purpose provided in the Kaiser-USWA plan. That question was expressly left open in *McDonald v. Santa Fe Trail Transp. Co.* (1976), which held, in a case not involving affirmative action, that Title VII protects whites as well as blacks from racial discrimination.

Weber argues that Congress intended in Title VII to prohibit all race-conscious affirmative action plans. His argument rests upon a literal interpretation of sections 703(a) and (d) of the act. Those sections make it unlawful to discriminate because of race in the selection of apprentices for training programs. Since, the argument runs, *McDonald* settled that Title VII forbids discrimination against whites as well as blacks, and since the Kaiser-USWA plan discriminated against white employees solely because they are white, it follows that the plan violates Title VII.

Weber's argument is not without force. But it overlooks the fact that the Kaiser-USWA plan is an affirmative action

plan voluntarily adopted by private parties to eliminate traditional patterns of racial segregation. It is a familiar rule, that a thing may be within the letter of the statute and yet not within the statute, because not within its spirit. Sections 703(a) and (d) must therefore be read against the background of the legislative history of Title VII and the historical context from which the act arose. Examination of these sources makes clear that an interpretation that forbade all race-conscious affirmative action would bring about an end completely at variance with the purpose of the statute and must be rejected.

Congress's primary concern in enacting the prohibition against racial discrimination in Title VII was the plight of the Negro in our economy. Before 1964, blacks were largely relegated to unskilled and semi-skilled jobs. Because of automation the number of such jobs was rapidly decreasing. As a consequence the relative position of the Negro worker was steadily worsening. Congress feared that the goal of the Civil Rights Act—the integration of blacks into the mainstream of American society—could not be achieved unless this trend were reversed. Accordingly, it was clear to Congress that the crux of the problem was to open employment opportunities for Negroes in occupations which have traditionally been closed to them, and it was to this problem that Title VII's prohibition against racial discrimination in employment was primarily addressed.

Given this legislative history, we cannot agree with Weber that Congress intended to prohibit the private sector from taking effective steps to accomplish the goal that Congress designed Title VII to achieve. It would be ironic indeed if a law triggered by a nation's concern over centuries of racial injustice and intended to improve the lot of those who had been excluded from the American dream for so long, constituted the first legislative prohibition of all voluntary, private, race-conscious efforts to abolish traditional patterns of racial segregation and hierarchy.

We need not define the line between permissible and impermissible affirmative action plans. It suffices to hold that the challenged plan falls on the permissible side of the line.

The purposes of the plan mirror those of the statute. Both were designed to break down old patterns of racial segregation and hierarchy, and to open employment opportunities for Negroes in occupations which have been traditionally closed to them. At the same time the plan does not unnecessarily trammel the interests of the white employees. Nor does the plan create an absolute bar to the advancement of white employees; half of those trained in the program will be white. Moreover, the plan is a temporary measure. Preferential selection of craft trainees will end as soon as the percentage of black skilled craft workers approximates the percentage of blacks in the local labor force. We conclude therefore that the plan falls within the area of discretion left by Title VII to the private sector voluntarily to adopt affirmative action plans designed to eliminate conspicuous racial imbalance in traditionally segregated job categories.

Judgment reversed in favor of Kaiser and the union.

General Public Purpose   Occasionally, courts construe statutory language in the light of various *general public purposes*. These purposes are not the purposes underlying the statute in question; rather, they are widely accepted general notions of public policy. In a 1983 case, for example, the Supreme Court used the general public policy against racial discrimination in education as one argument for denying tax-exempt status to a private university that discriminated on the basis of race.

Prior Interpretations   Courts sometimes follow prior cases and administrative decisions interpreting a statute, regardless of the statute's plain meaning or legislative history. The main argument for following these prior interpretations is to promote stability and certainty by preventing each successive court that considers a statute from adopting its own interpretation. The courts' willingness to follow a prior interpretation depends on such factors as the number of past courts adopting the interpretation, the authoritativeness of those courts, and the number of years that the interpretation has been followed.

Maxims   Maxims are general rules of thumb employed in statutory interpretation. There are many maxims, which courts tend to use or ignore at their discretion. One example of a maxim is the *ejusdem generis* rule, which says that when general words follow words of a specific,

limited meaning, the general language should be limited to things of the same class as those specifically stated. Suppose that the pollution statute quoted earlier listed 12 types of gas-powered vehicles and ended with the words "and other motorized passenger or cargo vehicles." In that instance, *ejusdem generis* probably would dictate that battery-powered vehicles not be included.

Limits on the Power of Courts

By now, you may think that anything goes when courts decide common law cases or interpret statutes. Many factors, however, discourage courts from adopting a freewheeling approach. Their legal training and mental makeup cause judges to be likely to respect established precedents and the will of the legislature. Many courts issue written opinions, which expose judges to academic and professional criticism if the opinions are poorly reasoned. Lower court judges may be discouraged from innovation by the fear of being overruled by a higher court. Finally, political factors inhibit judges. For example, some judges are elected, and even judges with lifetime tenure can sometimes be removed.

An even more fundamental limit on the power of courts is that they cannot make or interpret law until parties present them with a case to decide. In addition, any such case must be a real dispute. That is, courts generally limit themselves to genuine, existing "cases or

THE GLOBAL BUSINESS ENVIRONMENT

Just as statutes may require judicial interpretation when a dispute arises, so may treaties. The techniques that courts use in interpreting treaties correspond closely to the statutory interpretation techniques discussed in the text. In *McKesson HBOC, Inc. v. Islamic Republic of Iran,* 271 F.3d 1101 (D.C. Cir. 2001), for instance, the court concluded that a provision in a treaty between the United States and Iran must be interpreted in light of the treaty's purpose.

McKesson, an American company, owned a minority interest in an Iranian dairy. Following Iran's 1979 Islamic Revolution, the dairy stopped paying McKesson's dividends, cut off the flow of capital to McKesson, and froze out McKesson's board members. After years of litigation, the U.S. District Court for the District of Columbia granted summary judgment in favor of McKesson, holding that the Iranian government had expropriated McKesson's equity in the dairy and ordering that Iran pay more than $20 million in compensation. Iran appealed, arguing that the district court erred in interpreting the 1955 Treaty of Amity as permitting McKesson's pursuit of an expropriation claim in a

U.S. court. Iran cited a treaty provision stating that "property of nationals and companies of either High Contracting Party, including interests in property, shall receive the most constant protection and security within the territories of the other High Contracting Party." According to Iran, this provision would allow Iranian citizens and firms to bring property-related claims in U.S. courts and American citizens and firms to pursue such claims in Iranian courts, but should not be read to allow what McKesson, a U.S. firm, did: bring an expropriation claim in a U.S. court.

The U.S. Court of Appeals for the District of Columbia Circuit rejected Iran's argument, pointing out that even though the treaty's language suggests that a party from one country will have legal protections in the other country, it does not say that the protections can only be enforced in the other country. The interpretation urged by Iran should not be adopted, the court said, because it "flatly conflicts with the treaty's purpose—protecting property of U.S. nationals—particularly because Iran's post-revolutionary courts cannot provide adequate remedies for U.S. claims."

---

controversies" between real parties with tangible opposing interests in the lawsuit. Courts generally do not issue *advisory opinions* on abstract legal questions unrelated to a genuine dispute, and do not decide *feigned controversies* that parties concoct to seek answers to such questions. Courts may also refuse to decide cases that are insufficiently *ripe* to have matured into a genuine controversy, or that are *moot* because there no longer is a real dispute between the parties. Expressing similar ideas is the doctrine of **standing to sue,** which normally requires that the plaintiff have some direct, tangible, and substantial stake in the outcome of the litigation.

State and federal **declaratory judgment** statutes, however, allow parties to determine their rights and duties even though their controversy has not advanced to the point where harm has occurred and legal relief may be necessary. This enables them to determine their legal position without taking action that could expose them to liability. For example, if Darlene believes that something she plans to do would not violate Earl's copyright on a work of authorship but she recognizes that he may take a contrary view, she may seek a declaratory judgment on the question rather than risk Earl's lawsuit by proceeding to do what she had planned. Usually, a declaratory judgment is awarded only when the parties' dispute is sufficiently advanced to constitute a real case or controversy.

APPENDIX

Reading and Briefing Cases

Throughout this text, you will encounter cases—the judicial opinions accompanying court decisions. These cases are highly edited versions of their much longer originals. What follows are explanations and pointers to assist you in studying cases.

1. Each case has a *case name* that includes at least some of the parties to the case. Because the order of the parties may change when a case is appealed, do not assume that the first party listed is the plaintiff (the party suing) and the second the defendant (the party being sued). Also, because some cases have many plaintiffs and/or many defendants, the parties discussed in the court's opinion sometimes differ from those found in the case name.

2. Each case also has a *citation,* which includes the volume and page number of the legal reporter in which the full case appears, plus the year the case was decided. *United Steelworkers v. Weber,* for instance, begins on page 193 of volume 443 of the United States Reports (the official reporter for U.S. Supreme Court decisions), and was decided in 1979. (Each of the many different legal reporters

has its own abbreviation. The list is too long to include here.) In the parenthesis accompanying the date, we also give you some information about the court that decided the case. For example, "U.S. Sup. Ct." is the United States Supreme Court, "3d Cir." is the U.S. Court of Appeals for the Third Circuit, "S.D.N.Y." is the U.S. District Court for the Southern District of New York, "Minn. Sup. Ct." is the Minnesota Supreme Court, and "Mich. Ct. App." is the Michigan Court of Appeals (a Michigan intermediate appellate court). Chapter 2 describes the various kinds of courts.

3. At the beginning of each case, there is a *statement of facts* containing the most important facts that gave rise to the case.

4. Immediately after the statement of facts, we give you the case's *procedural history*. This history tells you what courts previously handled the case you are reading, and how they dealt with it.

5. Next comes your major concern: the *body of the court's opinion*. Here, the court determines the applicable law and applies it to the facts to reach a conclusion. The court's discussion of the relevant law may be elaborate; it may include prior cases, legislative history, applicable public policies, and more. The court's application of the law to the facts usually occurs after it has arrived at the applicable legal rule(s), but also may be intertwined with its legal discussion.

6. At the very end of the case, we complete the procedural history by stating the court's *decision*. For example, "Judgment reversed in favor of Smith" says that a lower court judgment against Smith was reversed on appeal. This means that Smith's appeal was successful and Smith wins.

7. The cases' main function is to provide concrete examples of rules stated in the text. (Frequently, the text tells you what point the case illustrates.) In studying law, it is easy to conclude that your task is finished once you have memorized a black letter rule. Real-life legal problems, however, seldom present themselves as abstract questions of law; instead, they are hidden in particular situations one encounters or particular actions one takes. Without some sense of a legal rule's real-life application, your knowledge of that rule is incomplete. The cases help provide this sense.

8. You may find it helpful to *brief* the cases. There is no one correct way to brief a case, but most good briefs contain the following elements: (1) a short statement of the relevant facts; (2) the case's prior history; (3) the question(s) or issue(s) the court had to decide; (4) the answer(s) to those question(s); (5) the reasoning the court used to justify its decision; and (6) the final result. Using "P" and "D" for the plaintiff and defendant, a brief of the *Weber* case might look this way:

United Steelworkers v. Weber

Facts The Ds were a private employer and a union that had voluntarily established a craft training program through a collective bargaining agreement. The procedures for selecting the program's trainees favored black workers over white workers by establishing an affirmative action feature for the former. P, a white worker who was denied access to the program, would have qualified had the racial preference not existed.

History P sued the Ds under Title VII of the 1964 Civil Rights Act, which forbids employment discrimination on the basis of race. He won in federal district court and the court of appeals affirmed. The Ds appealed to the U.S. Supreme Court.

Issue Does this voluntary racial preference favoring black workers violate Title VII's ban on racial discrimination in employment?

Answer No.

Reasoning Even though Title VII's plain meaning appears to favor P and a prior interpretation holds that Title VII forbids racial discrimination against both whites and blacks, neither point is decisive. The reason is that holding for P would frustrate Title VII's purpose. Title VII's legislative history and its historical context make clear that its aim was to integrate blacks into the American mainstream. This was especially true in the area of employment, an area in which blacks were falling behind. The Ds' preference helped further this purpose because it helped blacks get better jobs, and declaring the preference illegal would have frustrated the purpose. Moreover, the prior interpretation of the relevant Title VII did not occur in a case presenting affirmative action issues.

Result Court of appeals decision reversed; Ds win.

Problems and Problem Cases

1. Susan Donahue allowed her two Irish Setters to run off-leash at Clippenger Field, an area clearly marked "restricted to equestrian use only." When Ann Gibson went horse riding there, Donahue's dogs went after the horse, causing it to throw Gibson against a

tree. Gibson sued Donahue for damages. Donahue claimed immunity from Gibson's action under an Ohio statute that, in recognition of the "inherent risk of equine activity," protects "an equine activity sponsor, equine activity participant, equine professional, veterinarian, farrier, or other person" from liability. Does Donahue's argument have merit?

2. Suppose that Congress passes a federal statute that conflicts with a state constitutional provision. The state argues that the constitutional provision should prevail over the statute because constitutions are a higher, more authoritative kind of law than statutes. Is this argument correct? Why or why not?

3. In 1949, three Los Angeles deputy sheriffs heard that Antonio Rochin was selling narcotics. They entered Rochin's home one morning in search of evidence and forced open the door to his bedroom. They spotted two capsules on the nightstand beside the bed where Rochin was sitting. The deputies asked, "Whose stuff is this?" and Rochin put the capsules into his mouth. The officers jumped Rochin, trying to force the capsules from his mouth, but were unsuccessful. They handcuffed him and took him to a hospital, where they had a doctor forcibly insert a tube into Rochin's stomach and chemically induce vomiting. Within the vomit disgorged from Rochin's stomach were two morphine capsules. Did the deputies' method of obtaining information violate the Due Process Clause of the Fourteenth Amendment?

4. State A passes a statute declaring that those who sell heroin are to receive a mandatory 30-year prison sentence. Describe this statute in terms of the three classifications of law stated in the text—criminal/civil, substantive/procedural, and public/private.

5. Nation X is a dictatorship in which one ruler has the ultimate lawmaking power. The ruler issues a statute declaring that certain religious minorities are to be exterminated. An international convocation of jurisprudential scholars meets to discuss the question, "Is Nation X's extermination statute truly law?" What would be the typical natural law answer to this question? What would be the typical legal positivist response? Assume that all of those present at the convocation think that Nation X's statute is morally wrong.

6. Nation Y has enacted positive laws forbidding consensual sexual relations between unmarried adults. However, the police of Nation Y rarely enforce these laws, and even when they do, prosecutors never bring charges against violators. What observation would legal realists make about this situation? In order to determine what a believer in natural law would think about these laws, what else would you have to know?

7. Many states and localities used to have so-called Sunday Closing laws—statutes or ordinances forbidding certain business from being conducted on Sunday. A few may still have such laws. Often, these laws have not been obeyed or enforced. What would an extreme legal positivist tend to think about the duty to enforce and obey such laws? What would a natural law exponent who strongly believes in economic freedom tend to think about this question? What about a natural law adherent who is a Christian religious traditionalist? What observation would almost any legal realist make about Sunday Closing laws? Looking at these laws from a sociological perspective, finally, what social factors help explain their original passage, their relative lack of enforcement today, and their continued presence on the books despite their lack of enforcement?

8. The Supreme Court of State X is about to decide on the constitutionality of a statute restricting some controversial activity. Three of the court's justices—Justices A, B, and C—are taking the coming decision very seriously. In an effort to determine the true rule of law that governs the case, Justice A is reading and rereading all the relevant precedents and legislative history. In order to determine what result is morally right, Justice B is reading books on moral philosophy. To determine what the public thinks, finally, Justice C is reading every available public opinion poll on the behavior at issue in the case. Which schools of jurisprudence do Justices A, B, and C exemplify?

9. One wheel of a pre-1916 automobile manufactured by the Buick Motor Company was made of defective wood. Buick could have discovered the defect had it made a reasonable inspection after it purchased the wheel from another manufacturer. Buick sold the car to a retail dealer, who then sold it to MacPherson. While MacPherson was driving his new Buick, the defective wheel collapsed and he was thrown from the vehicle. Was Buick, which did not deal directly with MacPherson, liable for his injuries?

10. Mary Holmes, postmaster at the U.S. Post Office in Poncha Springs, Colorado, responded to an inquiry

by employees of Consumer Insurance Group (CIG) about a bulk mailing. The CIG employees informed Holmes that CIG was receiving the per-pound bulk postal rate at the post office in Howard, Colorado. After confirming this information with the postmaster in Howard, Holmes granted CIG the per-pound rate. Upon further investigation, however, Holmes discovered that CIG's pieces did not satisfy certain weight requirements and were thus ineligible for the per-pound rate. She contacted the postmaster in Howard and let him know that CIG was not entitled to the per-pound rate. Two years later, Holmes learned from a different postmaster in Howard that CIG was receiving the per-pound rate. She notified her superior that CIG was defrauding the Postal Service by providing false information in order to get a lower rate. The Postal Inspection Service began an investigation that exposed the fraud. Holmes received a $500 award and a letter of appreciation from the Postal Service. Holmes later filed suit against CIG under the False Claims Act, which authorizes a "person" to bring a civil action against a party that defrauds the government. The action, according to the False Claims Act, is "for the person and for the United States Government." The "person" who brought the case becomes entitled to a portion of the proceeds recovered in the action or in a settlement of it. Such a case is called a *qui tam* action. Is Holmes a "person" who may properly maintain a qui tam action under the False Claims Act?

Online Research: The American Law Institute

Earlier in this chapter, mention was made of the *Restatements* drafted by the American Law Institute (ALI) with regard to a large number of areas of the law. Visit ALI's website at http://www.ali.org. After reviewing material at that site, answer these questions:

1. How long has ALI been preparing and issuing the *Restatements*?

2. In what ways does ALI collaborate with the National Conference of Commissioners on Uniform State Laws?

THE RESOLUTION OF PRIVATE DISPUTES

Victoria Wilson, a resident of Illinois, wishes to bring an invasion of privacy lawsuit against XYZ Co. because XYZ used a photograph of her, without her consent, in an advertisement for one of the company's products. Wilson will seek money damages of $150,000 from XYZ, whose principal offices are located in New Jersey. A New Jersey newspaper was the only print media outlet in which the advertisement was published. However, XYZ also placed the advertisement on the firm's website. This website may be viewed by anyone with Internet access, regardless of the viewer's geographic location.

Consider the following questions regarding Wilson's case as you read Chapter 2:

- Where, in a geographic sense, may Wilson properly file and pursue her lawsuit against XYZ?
- Must Wilson pursue her case in a state court, or does she have the option of litigating in federal court?
- Assuming that Wilson files her case in a state court, what strategic option may XYZ exercise if it acts promptly?
- Regardless of the court in which the case is litigated, what procedural steps will occur as the lawsuit proceeds from beginning to end?

BUSINESS LAW COURSES normally examine many substantive legal rules—laws that tell us how to behave in business and in society. Examples include the rules of contract, tort, and agency law, as well as those of many other legal areas addressed later in this text. Most of these rules are applied by courts as they decide civil cases involving private parties. This chapter lays a foundation for the text's discussion of substantive legal rules by examining the court systems of the United States and by outlining how civil cases proceed from beginning to end. The chapter also explores related subjects, including *alternative dispute resolution,* a collection of processes for resolving private disputes outside the court systems.

courts. It also considers the important subject of *jurisdiction,* something a court must have if its decision in a case is to be binding on the parties.

Courts of Limited Jurisdiction

Minor criminal cases and civil disputes involving small amounts of money or specialized matters frequently are decided in *courts of limited jurisdiction.* Examples include traffic courts, probate courts, and small claims courts. Such courts often handle a large number of cases. In some of these courts, procedures may be informal and parties unrepresented by attorneys often argue their own cases. Courts of limited jurisdiction often are not courts of record—meaning that they may not keep a transcript of the proceedings conducted. Appeals from their decisions therefore require a new trial (a trial *de novo*) in a trial court.

Trial Courts

Courts of limited jurisdiction find the relevant facts, identify the appropriate rule(s) of law, and combine the

State Courts and Their Jurisdiction

The United States has 52 court systems—a federal system plus a system for each state and the District of Columbia. This section describes the various types of state facts and the law to reach a decision. State trial courts do the same, but differ from inferior courts in two key ways. First, they are not governed by the subject-matter restrictions or the limits on civil damages or criminal penalties that govern courts of limited jurisdiction. Cases involving significant dollar amounts or major criminal penalties usually begin, therefore, at the trial court level. Second, trial courts are courts of record that keep detailed records of hearings, trials, and other proceedings. These records become important if a trial court decision is appealed. The trial court's fact-finding function may be handled by the judge or by a jury. Determination of the applicable law, however, is always the judge's responsibility. In cases pending in trial courts, the parties nearly always are represented by attorneys.

States usually have at least one trial court for each county. It may be called a circuit, superior, district, county, or common pleas court. Most state trial courts can hear a wide range of civil and criminal cases, with little or no subject matter restriction. They may, however, have civil and criminal divisions. If no court of limited jurisdiction deals with these matters, state trial courts may also contain other divisions such as domestic relations courts or probate courts.

Appellate Courts

State appeals (or appellate) courts generally decide only legal questions. Instead of receiving new evidence or otherwise retrying the case, appellate courts review the record of the trial court proceedings. Although appellate courts correct legal errors made by the trial judge, they usually accept the trial court's findings of fact. Appellate courts also may hear appeals from state administrative agency decisions. Some states have only one appeals court (usually called the supreme court), but most also have an intermediate appellate court. The U.S. Supreme Court sometimes hears appeals from decisions of the state's highest court.

Jurisdiction and Venue

The party who sues in a civil case (the plaintiff) cannot sue the defendant (the party being sued) in whatever court the plaintiff happens to prefer. Instead, the chosen court—whether a state court or a federal court—must have jurisdiction over the case. Jurisdiction is a court's power to hear a case and to issue a decision binding on the parties. In order to render a binding decision in a civil case, a court must have not only subject-matter jurisdiction but also in personam jurisdiction or in rem jurisdiction. Even if a

court has jurisdiction, applicable **venue** requirements must also be satisfied in order for the case to proceed in that court.

Subject-Matter Jurisdiction   Subject-matter jurisdiction is a court's power to decide the *type* of dispute involved in the case. Criminal courts, for example, cannot hear civil matters. Similarly, a $500,000 claim for breach of contract cannot be pursued in a small claims court.

In Personam Jurisdiction   Even a court with subject-matter jurisdiction cannot decide a civil case unless it also has either **in personam jurisdiction** or **in rem jurisdiction.** In personam jurisdiction is based on the residence, location, or activities of the defendant. A state court has in personam jurisdiction over defendants who are citizens or residents of the state (even if situated out-of-state), who are within the state's borders when process is served on them (even if nonresidents),[1] or who consent to the court's authority (for instance, by entering the state to defend against the plaintiff's claim).[2] The same principle governs federal courts' in personam jurisdiction over defendants.

In addition, most states have enacted "long-arm" statutes that give their courts in personam jurisdiction over certain out-of-state defendants. Under these statutes, nonresident individuals and businesses become subject to the jurisdiction of the state's courts by, for example, doing business within the state, contracting to supply goods or services within the state, or committing a tort (a civil wrong) within the state. Some long-arm statutes are phrased with even broader application in mind. Federal law, moreover, permits federal courts to rely on state long-arm statutes as a basis for obtaining in personam jurisdiction over nonresident defendants.

Even if a long-arm statute applies, however, a state or federal court's assertion of in personam jurisdiction over an out-of-state defendant is subject to federal due process standards. The *Butler* case, which follows, addresses long-arm statute and due process issues arising in an Internet sales context. Although the court in *Butler* is a federal district court in Alabama, the same analysis of the key issues would have been appropriate if the case had been filed in an Alabama state court.

---

[1]Service of process is discussed later in the chapter.
[2]In many states, however, out-of-state defendants may make a *special appearance* to challenge the court's jurisdiction without consenting to the court's authority.

Butler v. Beer Across America   83 F.Supp.2d 1261 (N.D. Ala. 2000)

Lynda Butler's son, a minor, was at home unsupervised while his parents were on vacation. He ordered 12 bottles of beer from the website of a microbrewery club, Beer Across America. The beer was shipped from Illinois, where the sale was made, to the Butlers' Alabama residence. Ms. Butler learned of the sale when she found several bottles of beer from the shipment in the family refrigerator. Under Alabama's Civil Damages Act, which provides for a civil action by the parent of a minor against anyone who knowingly and illegally sells liquor to the minor, Butler sued Beer Across America and two related Illinois corporations in an Alabama state court. Based on a claim of diversity of citizenship, Beer Across America removed the action to the U.S. District Court for the Northern District of Alabama.

Hancock, District Judge   [This case presents] the following question: whether personal jurisdiction properly may be asserted by a federal court sitting in diversity in Alabama over . . . Illinois defendants in an action arising from a sale made in Illinois, solely in response to an order placed by an Alabama resident via the Internet.

[A] multipart analysis [applies]. The first part requires a consideration of state law because the reach of a federal diversity court's jurisdictional power over a nonresident defendant may not exceed the limits allowed under state law. If a basis for personal jurisdiction is found under the state's long-arm statute, the court then conducts a two-part due process analysis.

As one arm of the due process analysis, the court initially must determine whether at least minimum contacts exist between the defendant and the jurisdiction. The significant question is whether "the defendant's conduct and connection with the forum State are such that he should reasonably anticipate being haled into court there." *World-Wide Volkswagen Corp.* v. *Woodson,* 444 U.S. 286, 297 (1980). The level and nature of such conduct and connections may support either general or specific jurisdiction. General jurisdiction may be exercised when a defendant's contacts with the forum are sufficiently numerous, purposeful, and continuous, as to render fair an assertion of power over the defendant by that state's courts no matter the nature or extent of the relationship to the forum entailed in the particular litigation; if general jurisdiction is established, absolutely no connection need be shown between the state and the claim for the defendant to be summoned constitutionally before that forum's courts. In contrast, specific jurisdiction may be based upon less extensive contacts, but jurisdiction will lie only in those matters which are related to or which arise from those contacts. Regardless of the specific or general nature of the contacts in question, for purposes of satisfying due process, . . . "it is essential in each case that there be some act by which the defendant purposefully avails itself of the privilege of conducting activities within the forum State, thus invoking the benefits and protection of its laws." *Hanson* v. *Denckla,* 357 U.S. 235, 253 (1958). Jurisdiction will not be supported be-

cause of random, fortuitous, or attenuated contacts. However, even if minimum contacts are found, the court must still address the second prong of the due process analysis.

[D]ue process mandates a consideration of the fairness in forcing the defendant to litigate in a foreign forum. This fairness inquiry is rooted in *International Shoe Co.* v. *Washington,* 326 U.S. 310 (Sup. Ct. 1945), and its pronouncement that a nonresident defendant must "have certain minimum contacts with [the forum] such that maintenance of the suit does not offend 'traditional notions of fair play and substantial justice.'" To answer this inquiry into "fair play and substantial justice," the court will examine the nature of the defendant's contacts with the forum in light of additional factors, including the burdens on the defendant of litigating in the foreign forum; the interests of the forum state in overseeing the litigation; the interests of the plaintiff in efficient, substantial relief; the interests of the interstate judicial system in economical dispute resolution; and the joint interests of the states in promoting basic social policies. The Court now applies this extended analysis to the facts of the present case. [Our] initial inquiry concerns the reach of Alabama's long-arm statute. The Alabama long-arm statute provides:

A person has sufficient contacts with the state when that person . . . otherwise ha[s] some minimum contact with this state and, under the circumstances, it is fair and reasonable to require the person to come to this state to defend an action . . . so long as the prosecution of the action against a person in this state is not inconsistent with the constitution of this state or the Constitution of the United States.

Consequently, the reach of Alabama's long-arm jurisdiction extends to the full limits of federal due process. [T]he state law and due process analyses [therefore] collapse into a single inquiry.

To support general jurisdiction, Butler cites not only the sale to her son but also the defendants' sales (in Illinois) to other Alabama residents [and companies]. However, Butler has not offered any competent evidence to seriously controvert the defendants' averments that they are not registered to do business in Alabama; that they own no property in the state; that they maintain no offices in the state; that they have no agents in Alabama; that their key personnel have never even visited the state; and that they do not place advertisements with Alabama media outlets . . . or engage in any other significant promotions targeting the state. What Butler has offered is simply not sufficient to conclude that Beer Across America can be brought before an Alabama tribunal [under general jurisdiction principles].

Although specific jurisdiction presents a different question, the ultimate answer is the same. Alabama courts have found sufficient minimum contacts to support in personam jurisdiction over nonresident defendants in other actions related to out-of-state sales of goods to Alabama residents for use in this state, but the contacts in those cases differed both in kind and extent from the de minimis connections in the instant case. First, the Alabama state court cases involved the sale of automobiles . . . worth thousands of dollars, as opposed to the less than $ 25.00 purchase here. More important than the size of the purchases, however, the sellers in [these cases] had actively courted the Alabama market through advertisements on regional and local radio stations, in regional newspapers, and through the mails. Evidence was also offered in one case that the defendant's agent had even solicited sales within Alabama. Here, Beer Across America does not advertise with local or regional media specifically targeting the Alabama market, and plaintiff's son was never directly solicited by defendants by any means prior to placing his order. Also, [in two of the automobile sale cases], the sale in question was not an isolated transaction but one in a series of car sales made by the same defendant to the same Alabama plaintiff. The defendant in [another case] regularly sold [cars] to Alabama residents. In contrast, Beer Across America did not enter into any continuing relationship with plaintiff's son, but rather made a single sale amounting to $24.95. The defendants' total sales . . . to Alabama residents . . . represent, on average, only a few hundred orders per year, with Internet orders . . . accounting for a mere 3 to 4 percent of that total. That plaintiff's son's order was placed over Beer Across America's Internet site . . . is another important distinction between the instant case and prior Alabama decisions, which all involved some degree of personal interaction between the plaintiffs and the nonresident defendants or their agents.

The fact that many companies have established virtual beachheads on the Internet and the fact that the Internet is now accessible from almost any point on the globe have created complex, new considerations in counting minimum contacts for purposes of determining personal jurisdiction. [According to a leading decision, *Zippo Mfg. Co.* v. *Zippo Dot Com, Inc.,* 952 F. Supp. 1119 (1997)] jurisdiction is proper when the defendant does business over the Internet by entering into contracts with residents of other states which involve the knowing and repeated transmission of computer files over the Internet. In personam jurisdiction is improper, however, when the nonresident defendant has established a passive Internet site, which acts as little more than an electronic billboard for the posting of information. Between those two extremes lies a gray area "where a defendant has a website that allows a user to exchange information with a host computer." *Mink* v. *AAAA Development LLC,* 190 F.3d 333, 336 (5th Cir. 1999). [T]here, the determination turns on the nature of the information transmitted and on the degree of interaction. Applying these principles to the present case, clearly Beer Across America's site does not even anticipate the regular exchange of information across the Internet, much less provide for such interaction. Rather, it is closer to an electronic version of a postal reply card; the limited degree of interactivity available on the defendants' website is certainly insufficient to satisfy the minimum contacts requirement.

Furthermore, considerations of "fair play and substantial justice" do not support personal jurisdiction over the nonresident defendants in this action. The court recognizes that "modern transportation and communication have made it much less burdensome for a party sued to defend himself in a [distant] State," but the difficulties of geography still impose a not insubstantial burden on a defendant seeking to mount an effective defense against a potentially substantial claim in a remote jurisdiction to which that party has no real ties. *McGee* v. *International Life Ins. Co.,* 355 U.S. 220 (1957). Although Alabama has a legitimate interest in protecting its residents, it has no interest in effectively regulating out-of-state sales of alcohol. Similarly, plaintiff claims no actual injuries but merely seeks to punish and deter defendants, yet the state of Illinois has criminal and administrative procedures in place to accomplish the same task.

Butler has failed to make a prima facie case of personal jurisdiction over the defendants. However, simply because this court lacks jurisdiction does not mean that the defendants are completely immune from plaintiff's suit. The evidence . . . leads the court to find that personal jurisdiction would be proper in the Northern District of Illinois. Therefore, the defendants' motion to dismiss is denied but this action is hereby transferred to [that court].

Action transferred to federal court in Illinois district because federal court in Alabama district lacks in personam jurisdiction.

In Rem Jurisdiction In rem jurisdiction is based on the presence of *property* within the state. It empowers state courts to determine rights in that property even if the persons whose rights are affected are outside the state's in personam jurisdiction. For example, a state court's decision regarding title to land within the state is said to bind the world.[3]

Venue Even if a court has jurisdiction, it may be unable to decide the case because **venue** requirements have not been met. Venue questions arise only after jurisdiction is established or assumed. In general, a court has venue if it is a territorially fair and convenient forum in which to hear the case. Venue requirements applicable to state courts typically are set by state statutes, which normally determine the county in which a case must be brought. For instance, the statute might say that a case concerning land must be filed in the county where the land is located, and that other suits must be brought in the county where the defendant resides or is doing business. If justice so requires, the defendant may be able to obtain a *change of venue*. This can occur when, for example, a fair trial would be impossible within a particular county.

Role of Forum Selection Clauses Contracts sometimes contain a clause reciting that disputes between the parties regarding matters connected with the contract must be litigated in the courts of a particular state. Such a provision is known as a **forum selection clause.** Depending on its wording, a forum selection clause may have the effect of addressing both jurisdiction and venue issues. Although forum selection clauses may appear in agreements whose terms have been hammered out by the parties after extensive negotiation, they fairly often are found in form agreements whose terms were not the product of actual discussion or give-and-take. For example, America Online, Inc. (AOL)

may include a forum selection clause in a so-called "clickwrap" document that sets forth the terms of its Internet-related services—terms to which AOL subscribers are deemed to have agreed by virtue of utilizing AOL's services. Forum selection clauses, whether expressly bargained for or included in a clickwrap agreement, are generally enforced by courts unless they are shown to be unreasonable in a given set of circumstances. Assume, for instance, that AOL's terms of services document calls for the courts of Virginia to have "exclusive jurisdiction" over its subscribers' disputes with the company, but that a subscriber sues AOL in a Pennsylvania court. Unless the subscriber performs the difficult task of demonstrating that application of the clickwrap agreement's forum selection clause would be unreasonable, the Pennsylvania court will be likely to dismiss the case and to hold that if the subscriber wishes to litigate the claim, he or she must sue in an appropriate Virginia court.

Federal Courts and Their Jurisdiction

Federal District Courts

In the federal system, lawsuits usually begin in the federal district courts. As do state trial courts, the federal district courts determine both the facts and the law. The fact-finding function may be entrusted to either the judge or a jury, but determining the applicable law is the judge's responsibility. Each state is designated as a separate district for purposes of the federal court system. Each district has at least one district court, and each district court has at least one judge.

District Court Jurisdiction There are various bases of federal district court civil jurisdiction. The two most important are **diversity jurisdiction** and **federal question jurisdiction.** One traditional justification for diversity jurisdiction is that it may help protect out-of-state defendants from potentially biased state courts. *Diversity jurisdiction* exists when: (1) the case is between citizens of different states, and (2) the amount in controversy exceeds $75,000. In the *Lewis* case, which appears shortly, the court concludes that the requirements of diversity jurisdiction were not met. Diversity jurisdiction also exists in certain cases between citizens of a state and citizens or governments of foreign nations, if the amount in controversy

---

[3]Another form of jurisdiction, *quasi in rem jurisdiction* or *attachment jurisdiction,* also is based on the presence of property within the state. Unlike cases based on in rem jurisdiction, cases based on quasi in rem jurisdiction do not necessarily determine rights in the property itself. Instead, the property is regarded as an extension of the out-of-state defendant—an extension that sometimes enables the court to decide claims unrelated to the property. For example, a plaintiff might attach the defendant's bank account in the state where the bank is located, sue the defendant on a tort or contract claim unrelated to the bank account, and recover the amount of the judgment from the account if the suit is successful.

THE GLOBAL BUSINESS ENVIRONMENT

Chapter 1 contained a discussion of Iran's unsuccessful attempt to rely on the Treaty of Amity as a basis for avoiding liability in *McKesson HBOC, Inc.* v. *Islamic Republic of Iran,* 271 F.3d 1101 (D. C. Cir. 2001). As the earlier discussion revealed, a federal district court ruled in favor of McKesson on its claim that after the 1979 Islamic Revolution, Iran expropriated McKesson's equity in an Iranian dairy and wrongfully withheld dividends to which McKesson would have been entitled by virtue of its minority ownership interest.

In its appeal to the U.S. Court of Appeals for the District of Columbia Court, Iran raised an alternative argument: that the Foreign Sovereign Immunities Act of 1976 (FSIA) deprived U.S. courts of subject matter jurisdiction over the case. Subject to exceptions listed in the statute, the FSIA grants immunity from federal court jurisdiction to all foreign sovereigns, as well as their agents and instrumentalities. McKesson contended that Iran in this case fell under an exception for "any case . . . in which the action is based upon a commercial activity . . . of the foreign state . . . that . . . causes a direct effect in the United States." The Court of Appeals agreed with McKesson. The facts revealed that the domestic effect of freezing out the American company was sufficiently "direct" to give jurisdiction under the FSIA exception.

Iran countered by arguing that even if some elements of its expropriation had direct effects in the United States, federal courts did not have jurisdiction over the claim regarding the dairy's withholding of dividends. Iran relied on *Kingdom of Saudi Arabia* v. *Nelson,* 507 U.S. 349 (1993), in which the Supreme Court held that a fact which could not independently have served as grounds for jurisdiction could not serve as a basis for a foreign state's liability. The court rejected Iran's argument, observing that *Nelson* held only that "commercial-activity jurisdiction cannot exist unless the commercial activity forming the basis for jurisdiction also serves as the predicate for the plaintiff's substantive cause of action." In this case, McKesson had demonstrated direct and substantial domestic effects stemming from, and established federal jurisdiction with respect to, its cause of action: the freezing of commercial activity. Regardless of whether the withholding of dividends could alone have been grounds for jurisdiction, said the court, it had contributed to a "net effect"—the freezing of commercial activity—that furnished the basis for both jurisdiction and potential liability. Although the Court of Appeals ultimately remanded the case to the district court on an unrelated ground that is not relevant here, it affirmed the lower court's holding that jurisdiction existed under the "commercial activity" exception to the FSIA.

---

exceeds $75,000. Under diversity jurisdiction, a corporation normally is a citizen of both the state where it has been incorporated and the state where it has its principal place of business.

Federal question jurisdiction exists when the case arises under the Constitution, laws, or treaties of the United States. The "arises under" requirement normally is met when a right created by federal law is a basic part of the plaintiff's case. There is no amount-in-controversy requirement for federal question jurisdiction.

Diversity jurisdiction and federal question jurisdiction are forms of subject matter jurisdiction. Even if one of the two forms exists, a federal district court must also have in personam jurisdiction in order to render a decision that is binding on the parties. As noted earlier in the chapter, the analysis of in personam jurisdiction issues in the federal court system is essentially the same as in the state court systems. Further limiting the plaintiff's choice of federal district courts are the federal system's complex venue requirements, which are beyond the scope of this text.

Concurrent Jurisdiction and Removal The federal district courts have *exclusive jurisdiction* over some matters. Patent cases, for example, must be litigated in the federal system. Often, however, federal district courts have *concurrent jurisdiction* with state courts—meaning that both state and federal courts have jurisdiction over the case. For example, a plaintiff might assert state court in personam jurisdiction over an out-of-state defendant or might sue in a federal district court under that court's diversity jurisdiction. A state court, moreover, may sometimes decide cases involving federal questions. Where concurrent jurisdiction exists and the plaintiff opts for a state court, the defendant has the option to *remove* the case to an appropriate federal district court, assuming the defendant acts promptly.

In the *Lewis* case, which follows, a federal district court concludes that concurrent jurisdiction did not exist and that the defendant's attempt to remove the case to federal court was improper.

Lewis v. Abbott Laboratories   189 F. Supp. 2d 590 (S. D. Miss. 2001)

Abbott Laboratories manufactured and sold the Life Care PCA, a pump that delivers medication into a person intravenously at specific time intervals. Beverly Lewis sued Abbott in a Mississippi State Court, alleging that a defective Life Care PCA had injured her by delivering an excessive quantity of morphine. Abbott served Lewis with a request for admission calling for her to admit that her damages did not exceed $75,000.00. Lewis did not answer the request for admission. Abbott then removed the case to the U.S. District Court for the Southern District of Mississippi, predicating the court's subject matter jurisdiction on diversity of citizenship *and an amount in controversy exceeding $75,000.00. Lewis moved to have the case remanded to the state court on the ground that her silence had amounted to an admission that her damages were less than $75,000.00.*

Wingate, District Judge   Generally, in diversity cases, the courts determine the amount in controversy from the complaint itself, unless it appears, or is in some way shown, that the amount stated in the complaint is not claimed in good faith. The United States Supreme Court in *Horton* v. *Liberty Mutual Insurance Company,* 367 U.S. 348 (1961) stated that "in deciding this question of good faith we have said that it must appear to a legal certainty that the claim is really for less than the jurisdictional amount to justify dismissal." This "legal certainty" test is applied to jurisdictional amount questions in removed cases, as well as cases originally brought in federal court. So, this court lacks jurisdiction if it is apparent, to a legal certainty, that Lewis cannot, or is not entitled to, recover the jurisdictional minimum.

Of course, when a plaintiff does not desire to try his case in the federal court, he may resort to the expedient of suing for less than the jurisdictional amount, and though he would be justly entitled to more, the defendant cannot remove the case. Thus, if a plaintiff pleads damages less than the jurisdictional amount, he can bar a defendant from removing the case to federal court.

This court finds that while Lewis failed to respond to a request for admissions relative to this court's jurisdictional amount, Abbott still has not established that Lewis' current claim for damages . . . is above this court's minimum jurisdictional amount of $75,000.00. By failing to answer the request for admissions, Lewis, under state law, . . . admitted that her damages do not exceed $75,000.00. Upon this occurrence, Lewis's complaint was in no different posture from one where plaintiff explicitly pleaded an amount below this court's jurisdictional limit. Under either or both of these scenarios, defendant, to justify removal, must present this court more than a hunch or suspicion that the amount in controversy exceeds $75,000.00. Abbott has not met that burden.

Case remanded to Mississippi state court.

Specialized Federal Courts

The federal court system also includes certain specialized federal courts, including the Court of Federal Claims (which hears claims against the United States), the Court of International Trade (which is concerned with tariff, customs, import and other trade matters), the Bankruptcy Courts (which operate as adjuncts of the district courts), and the Tax Court (which reviews certain IRS determinations). Usually, the decisions of these courts can be appealed to a federal court of appeals.

Federal Courts of Appeals

The U.S. courts of appeals do not engage in fact-finding. Instead, they review only the legal conclusions reached by lower federal courts. As Figure 1 shows, there are 13 circuit courts of appeals: 11 numbered circuits covering several states each; a District of Columbia circuit; and a separate federal circuit.

Except for the Court of Appeals for the Federal Circuit, the most important function of the U.S. courts of appeals is to hear appeals from decisions of the federal district courts. Appeals from a district court ordinarily proceed to the court of appeals for that district court's region. Appeals from the District Court for the Southern District of New York, for example, go to the Second Circuit Court of Appeals. The courts of appeals also hear appeals from the Tax Court, from many administrative agency decisions, and from some Bankruptcy Court decisions. The Court of Appeals for the Federal Circuit hears a wide variety of specialized appeals, including some patent and trademark matters, Court of Federal Claims decisions, and decisions by the Court of International Trade.

CYBER LAW IN ACTION

Chapter 1 discussed issues raised in *Blumenthal* v. *Drudge* concerning the liability of Internet service providers in defamation suits. Now we turn to the jurisdictional issue raised in the case, reported at 992 F. Supp. 44 (D.D.C. 1998). The Blumenthals sued Drudge in the District Court for the District of Columbia. Important events, however, had taken place in California, where Drudge published and transmitted his column and the allegedly defamatory document had been placed on an Internet website. Drudge, who resided in California, asserted that the D.C. court did not have in personam jurisdiction over him. He therefore sought dismissal or transfer of the case to a federal court in California.

"In order for this court to maintain in personam jurisdiction over a nonresident defendant," wrote the court, "jurisdiction must be proper under the District of Columbia long-arm statute and consistent with the demands of the process." The long-arm statute reads:

A District of Columbia court may exercise in personam jurisdiction over a person, who acts directly or by an agent, as to a claim for relief arising from the person's . . . causing tortious injury in the District of Columbia by an act or omission outside the District of Columbia if he regularly does or solicits business, engages in any other persistent course of conduct, or derives substantial revenue from goods used or consumed or services rendered, in the District of Columbia.

It was undisputed that Drudge's "act" had taken place outside the District of Columbia and that the "tortious injury" to the Blumenthals had occurred inside it. Therefore, the Court only had to find that Drudge "regularly [did] or solicit [ed] business, engage[d] in . . . [a] persistent course of conduct, or derive[d] substantial revenue from goods used or consumed or services rendered in the District of Columbia" in order to conclude that the D.C. long-arm statute had been satisfied.

The Blumenthals pointed out that Drudge's website was available 24 hours a day to D.C. residents and that D.C. residents' e-mail addresses were included on Drudge's mailing list. Additionally, they argued that he solicited contributions and collected money from District of Columbia residents and that he had visited the District of Columbia twice, including once for a promotional interview on C-SPAN. Drudge countered that even though D.C. residents received transmissions from him, he had not targeted D.C. residents specifically.

For example, Drudge had known only the e-mail addresses, and not the geographic addresses, of the subscribers to his mailing list. Moreover, fewer than 15 D.C. residents had made contributions totaling $250. Drudge's visits to D.C., he said, were so sporadic and infrequent that they could not possibly constitute a "persistent" course of action.

The court noted that a website's interactivity and the sufficiency of non-Internet-related contacts are the key criteria in jurisdiction disputes of this nature. In the words of the court, interactivity means that a website "involv[es] more than just the maintenance of a home page; it must allow browsers to interact directly with the website on some level." The court concluded that the exchange of e-mails—requests for subscriptions from browsers to the website, transmissions from the website to users on the mailing list, and other communications—between Drudge and his readers added up to "the epitome of website interactivity."

Rejecting Drudge's argument that he had not specifically targeted D.C. residents, the court noted that even though the Drudge Report had not advertised in physical locations or local newspapers in D.C., its effects were meant to be felt most strongly in D.C. The Drudge Report was "directly related to the political world of the Nation's capital and [featured] 'inside the beltway' gossip and rumor;" it targeted D.C. residents "by virtue of the subjects [Drudge] cover[ed]," reasoned the court. The small size of the monetary contributions from D.C. residents, was unimportant, the court said, because Drudge's solicitations were consistently made to D.C. residents.

The court also concluded that Drudge's interview with C-SPAN and his constant telephone and mail contact with D.C. gossip sources were sufficient non-Internet-related contacts with the District of Columbia. Drudge's Internet-related and non-Internet related contacts satisfied the D.C. long-arm statute and constituted the minimum contacts required for in personam jurisdiction to be consistent with due process. The court therefore denied Drudge's motion to dismiss or transfer the case.

The U.S. Supreme Court

The United States Supreme Court, the highest court in the land, is mainly an appellate court. It therefore considers only questions of law when it decides appeals from the federal courts of appeals and the highest state courts.[4]

Today, most appealable decisions from these courts fall within the Supreme Court's *certiorari* jurisdiction, under

[4]In special situations that do not often arise, the Supreme Court will hear appeals directly from the federal district courts.

Figure 1   *The Thirteen Federal Judicial Circuits*

First Circuit (*Boston, Mass.*) Maine, Massachusetts, New Hampshire, Puerto Rico, Rhode Island

Second Circuit (*New York, N.Y.*) Connecticut, New York, Vermont

Third Circuit (*Philadelphia, Pa.*) Delaware, New Jersey, Pennsylvania, Virgin Islands

Fourth Circuit (*Richmond, Va.*) Maryland, North Carolina, South Carolina, Virginia, West Virginia

Fifth Circuit (*New Orleans, La.*) Louisiana, Mississippi, Texas

Sixth Circuit (*Cincinnati, Ohio*) Kentucky, Michigan, Ohio, Tennessee

Seventh Circuit (*Chicago, Ill.*) Illinois, Indiana, Wisconsin

Eighth Circuit (*St. Louis, Mo.*) Arkansas, Iowa, Minnesota, Missouri, Nebraska, North Dakota, South Dakota

Ninth Circuit (*San Francisco, Calif.*) Alaska, Arizona, California, Guam, Hawaii, Idaho, Montana, Nevada, Northern Mariana Islands, Oregon, Washington

Tenth Circuit (*Denver, Colo.*) Colorado, Kansas, New Mexico, Oklahoma, Utah, Wyoming

Eleventh Circuit (*Atlanta, Ga.*) Alabama, Florida, Georgia

District of Columbia Circuit (*Washington, D.C.*)

Federal Circuit (*Washington, D.C.*)

which the Court has discretion whether to hear the appeal. The Court hears only a small percentage of the many appeals it is asked to decide under its certiorari jurisdiction.

Nearly all appeals from the federal courts of appeals are within the Court's certiorari jurisdiction. Appeals from the highest state courts are within the certiorari jurisdiction when: (1) the validity of any treaty or federal statute has been questioned; (2) any state statute is challenged as repugnant to federal law; or (3) any title, right, privilege, or immunity is claimed under federal law. The Supreme Court usually defers to the states' highest courts on questions of state law and does not hear appeals from those courts if the case involves only such questions.

In certain rare situations, the U.S. Supreme Court has **original jurisdiction,** which means that it acts as a trial court. The Supreme Court has *original and exclusive* jurisdiction over all controversies between two or more states. It has *original,* but not exclusive, jurisdiction over cases involving foreign ambassadors, ministers, and like parties; controversies between the United States and a state, and cases in which a state proceeds against citizens of another state or against aliens.

Civil Procedure

Civil procedure is the set of legal rules establishing how a civil lawsuit proceeds from beginning to end.[5] Because civil procedure sometimes varies with the jurisdiction in question,[6] the following presentation summarizes the most widely accepted rules governing civil cases in state and federal courts. Knowledge of these basic procedural matters will be useful if you become involved in a civil lawsuit. Such knowledge will also help you understand the cases in this text.

In any civil case, the *adversary system* is at work. Through their attorneys, the litigants take contrary positions before a judge and possibly a jury. To win a civil case, the plaintiff must prove each element of his, her, or its claim by a *preponderance of the evidence.*[7] This stan-

---

[5]Criminal procedure is discussed in Chapter 5.

[6]In the following discussion, the term *jurisdiction* refers to one of the 50 states, the District of Columbia, or the federal government.

[7]In a criminal case, however, the government must prove the elements of the alleged crime beyond a reasonable doubt. This standard of proof is discussed in Chapter 5.

dard of proof requires the plaintiff to show that the greater weight of the evidence—by credibility, not quantity—supports the existence of each element. In other words, the plaintiff must convince the fact-finder that the existence of each factual element is more probable than its nonexistence. The attorney for each party presents his or her client's version of the facts, tries to convince the judge or jury that this version is true, and attempts to rebut conflicting factual allegations by the other party. Each attorney also seeks to persuade the court that his or her reading of the law is correct.

Service of the Summons

A **summons** notifies the defendant that he, she, or it is being sued. The summons typically names the plaintiff and states the time within which the defendant must enter an *appearance* in court (usually through an attorney). In most jurisdictions, it is accompanied by a copy of the plaintiff's complaint (which is described below).

The summons is usually served on the defendant by an appropriate public official after the plaintiff has filed her case. To ensure that the defendant is properly notified, statutes, court rules, and constitutional due process guarantees set standards for proper service of the summons. For example, personal delivery to the defendant almost always meets these standards. Many jurisdictions also permit the summons to be left at the defendant's home or place of business. Service to corporations often may be accomplished by delivery of the summons to the firm's managing agent. Many state long-arm statutes permit out-of-state defendants to be served by registered mail. Although inadequate service of process may sometimes defeat the plaintiff's claim, the defendant who participates in the case without making a prompt objection to the manner of service will be deemed to have waived the objection.

The Pleadings

The **pleadings** are the documents the parties file with the court when they first state their respective claims and defenses. They include the **complaint,** the **answer,** and, in some jurisdictions, **the reply.** Traditionally, the pleadings' main function was to define and limit the issues to be decided by the court. Only those issues raised in the pleadings were considered part of the case, amendments to the pleadings were seldom permitted, and litigants were firmly bound by allegations or admissions contained in the pleadings. Although many jurisdictions retain some of these rules, most have relaxed them significantly. The main reason is the modern view of the

purpose of pleading rules: that their aim is less to define the issues for trial than to give the parties general notice of each others' claims and defenses.

The Complaint   The complaint states the plaintiff's claim in separate, numbered paragraphs. It must allege sufficient facts to show that the plaintiff would be entitled to legal relief and to give the defendant reasonable notice of the nature of the plaintiff's claim. The complaint also must state the remedy requested.

The Answer   Unless the defendant makes a successful motion to dismiss (described below), he must file an answer to the plaintiff's complaint within a designated time after service of the complaint. The amount of time is set by applicable law, with 30 to 45 days being typical. The answer responds to the complaint paragraph by paragraph, with an admission or denial of each of the plaintiff's allegations.

An answer may also include an **affirmative defense** to the claim asserted in the complaint. A successful affirmative defense enables the defendant to win the case even if all the allegations in the complaint are true and, by themselves, would have entitled the plaintiff to recover. For example, suppose that the plaintiff bases her lawsuit on a contract that she alleges the defendant has breached. The defendant's answer may admit or deny the existence of the contract or the assertion that the defendant breached it. In addition, the answer may make assertions that, if proven, would provide the defendant an affirmative defense on the basis of fraud committed by the plaintiff during the contract negotiation phase.

Furthermore, the answer may contain a **counterclaim.**[8] A counterclaim is a *new* claim by the defendant arising from the matters stated in the complaint. Unlike an affirmative defense, it is not merely an attack on the plaintiff's claim, but is the defendant's attempt to obtain legal relief. In addition to using fraud as an affirmative defense to a plaintiff's contract claim, for example, a defendant might counterclaim for damages caused by that fraud.

The Reply   In some jurisdictions, the plaintiff is allowed or required to respond to an affirmative defense or a counterclaim by making a reply. The reply is the plaintiff's point-by-point response to the allegations in

---

[8]In appropriate instances, a defendant also may file a *cross claim* against another defendant in the plaintiff's suit, or a *third-party complaint* against a party who was not named as a defendant in the plaintiff's complaint.

the answer or counterclaim. In jurisdictions that do not allow a reply to an answer, the defendant's new allegations are automatically denied. Usually, however, a plaintiff who wishes to contest a counterclaim must file a reply to it.

Motion to Dismiss

Sometimes it is evident from the complaint or the pleadings that the plaintiff does not have a valid claim. In such a situation, it would be wasteful for the litigation to proceed further. The procedural device for ending the case at this early stage is commonly called the **motion to dismiss.** This motion often is made after the plaintiff has filed her complaint. A similar motion allowed by some jurisdictions, the **motion for judgment on the pleadings,** normally occurs after the pleadings have been completed. A successful motion to dismiss means that the defendant wins the case. If the motion fails, the case proceeds.

The motion to dismiss may be made on various grounds—for example, inadequate service of process or lack of jurisdiction. The most important type of motion to dismiss, however, is the motion to dismiss for failure to state a claim upon which relief can be granted, sometimes called the **demurrer.** This motion basically says "So what?" to the factual allegations in the complaint. It asserts that the plaintiff cannot recover even if all of his allegations are true because no rule of law entitles him to win on those facts. Suppose that Potter sues Davis on the theory that Davis's bad breath is a form of "olfactory pollution" entitling Potter to recover damages. Potter's complaint describes Davis's breath and the distress it causes Potter in great detail. Even if all of Potter's factual allegations are true, Davis's motion to dismiss almost certainly will succeed. There is no rule of law allowing the "victim" of another person's bad breath to recover damages from that person.

Discovery

When a civil case begins, litigants do not always possess all of the facts they need to prove their claims or establish their defenses. To help litigants obtain the facts and to narrow and clarify the issues for trial, the state and federal court systems permit each party to a civil case to exercise **discovery** rights. The discovery phase of a lawsuit normally begins when the pleadings have been completed. Each party is entitled to request information from the other party by utilizing the forms of discovery described in this section. Moreover, for civil cases pending in federal court, the Federal Rules of Civil Procedure require each party to provide the other party certain basic information at an early point in the case, even though the other party may not have made a formal discovery request.

Discovery is available for information that is not subject to a recognized legal privilege and is relevant to the case or likely to lead to other information that may be relevant. Information may be subject to discovery even if it would not ultimately be admissible at trial under the legal rules of evidence. The scope of permissible discovery is thus extremely broad. Yet it is not without limits, as the court in the *Blumenthal* case (which follows shortly) reminds the parties. The broad scope of discovery stems from a policy decision to minimize the surprise element in litigation and to give each party the opportunity to become fully informed regarding facts known by the opposing party. Each party may then formulate trial strategies on the basis of that knowledge.

The *deposition* is one of the most frequently employed forms of discovery. In a deposition, one party's attorney conducts an oral examination of the other party or of a likely witness (usually one identified with the other party). The questions asked by the examining attorney and the answers given by the deponent—the person being examined—are taken down by a court reporter. The deponent is under oath, just as he or she would be if testifying at trial, even though the deposition occurs on a pretrial basis and is likely to take place at an attorney's office or at some location other than a courtroom. Some depositions are videotaped.

Interrogatories and *requests for admissions* are among the other commonly utilized forms of discovery. Interrogatories are written questions directed by the plaintiff to the defendant, or vice-versa. The litigant on whom interrogatories are served must provide written answers, under oath, within a time period prescribed by applicable law (30 days being typical). Requests for admissions are one party's written demand that the other party admit or deny, in writing, certain statements of supposed fact or of the application of law to fact, within a time period prescribed by law (30 days again being typical). The other party's failure to respond with an admission or denial during the legal time period is deemed an admission of the statements' truth or accuracy. The *Lewis* case, which appears earlier in the chapter, illustrates this effect of a failure to respond.

Requests for production of documents or other physical items (e.g., videotapes, photographs, and the like) are a discovery form employed by the parties in many civil cases. When the issues in a case make the opposing litigant's physical or mental condition relevant, a party may seek discovery in yet another way by filing a *motion for a court order requiring* that the opponent undergo *a physical or mental examination.* With the exception of the discovery form mentioned in the previous sentence, discovery generally takes place without a need for court orders or other judicial supervision. Courts become involved, however, if a party objects to a discovery request on the basis of privilege or other recognized legal ground, desires an order compelling a noncomplying litigant to respond to a discovery request, or seeks sanctions on a party who refused to comply with a legitimate discovery request or abusively invoked the discovery process. In the *Blumenthal* case, the court rejects the privilege objections raised by each party to the other's discovery requests.

Blumenthal v. Drudge   *1999 U.S. Dist. LEXIS 7045 (D.D.C. 1999)*

Chapter 1 and an earlier section in this chapter discussed certain issues in Blumenthal v. Drudge, *in which a Clinton administration aide and his wife alleged that they were defamed by AmericaOnline (AOL) and Matt Drudge, operator of an Internet gossip column (the Drudge Report). The U.S. District Court for the District of Columbia dismissed the claim against AOL on the ground that under the Communications Decency Act of 1997, AOL could not be held liable for defamation. Because the court rejected Drudge's jurisdiction-based objection, the case against Drudge proceeded.*

One year later both Drudge and the Blumenthals had filed motions in the district court to compel discovery from the opposing party. Drudge demanded that the Blumenthals answer: 1) a number of interrogatories and requests for production of documents to which the Blumenthals filed late objections; 2) a request for Sidney Blumenthal's notes of conversations with several journalists; and 3) questions that Blumenthal had refused to answer at his deposition on grounds of executive privilege. Drudge also asked the court to impose monetary sanctions, pursuant to the Federal Rules of Civil Procedure (FRCP), on the Blumenthals and their attorneys. In this request, Drudge alleged that improper conduct on the part of the plaintiffs and their counsel had necessitated the court's involvement in the parties' discovery dispute.

The Blumenthals moved to compel Drudge to respond to: 1) interrogatories and requests for documents over which Drudge asserted the attorney–client privilege but which appeared to have been shared with third parties who were not lawyers; 2) interrogatories and document requests regarding Drudge's sources of information regarding plaintiff; and 3) interrogatories and document requests regarding the membership of Drudge's legal defense fund.

Friedman, District Judge   There is such mistrust and suspicion [between the opposing parties and their respective attorneys that they have not made an adequate attempt] to resolve discovery disputes. [Although the court] declines the defendant's request for the imposition of sanctions, it reminds counsel of a few rudimentary principles.

First, if Mr. Blumenthal, [as described in the plaintiffs' written opposition to Drudge's motion,] is "a very busy man, involved in many high stakes matters that require constant attention" and Mrs. Blumenthal also is "busy in her job," perhaps they are too busy to be plaintiffs in this lawsuit. Plaintiffs brought this lawsuit and thereby voluntarily subjected themselves to the discovery process, which by its nature is not always pleasant and not always compatible with one's personal or business travel schedules or professional obligations. If plaintiffs are too busy for discovery, they are free to drop their lawsuit.

Second, defendant is reminded that not all subjects are relevant to the claims brought against him or the legitimate defenses he might raise. Nor is the exploration of such wide-ranging subjects likely to lead to the discovery of admissible evidence. This court cannot fathom, . . . why defendant and his counsel believe it is appropriate to ask plaintiffs questions about Geraldo Rivera, Henry Hyde, Robert Dole, the emotional state or alleged extramarital relationships of various public figures, grand jury subpoenas, the "vast right wing conspiracy," or the address of the parents of the girlfriend of a particular reporter. There are limits under the FRCP, as well as limits set by both common sense and common decency. Litigation is not just another arrow in the quiver of those with a political agenda or who are practitioners of the "gotcha" mentality of some journalists and purveyors of infotainment.

I. Drudge's Motion to Compel

A. Drudge's Written Discovery Requests

Drudge first argues that the Blumenthals waived all objections to his written discovery requests by serving their responses after they were due. While [the FRCP provide that] "any ground not stated in a timely objection [to an interrogatory] is waived unless the party's failure to object is excused by the court for good cause shown," the rule by its terms gives the court discretion to excuse the failure. The same principle applies to written document requests.

Discovery deadlines are intended to ensure the efficient progress of a lawsuit. If the Blumenthals' counsel were not able to meet a discovery deadline, they should have sought an agreement with Drudge's lawyer to submit their responses at a later date. If such consent was not provided . . . , the Blumenthals' counsel should then have sought an extension of time from the court by motion. Nonetheless, in the exercise of its broad discretion, the court finds that the Blumenthals have not waived their right to raise their objections even at this late date.

B. Mr. Blumenthal's Notes

Drudge asks the court to compel the Blumenthals to produce notes made by Mr. Blumenthal containing the substance of his conversations with various journalists, including David Brock. Mr. Blumenthal asserted in his deposition that he was seeking information for use in this litigation through his conversations with [the] journalists and that he prepared the notes at the request of his attorneys. He therefore argues that the notes are protected by the attorney–client privilege.

"The attorney–client privilege protects confidential communications made between clients and their attorneys when the communications are for the purpose of securing legal advice or services." *In re Lindsey,* 158 F.3d 1263, 1267 (D.C. Cir. 1998). As described, Mr. Blumenthal's notes do not appear to contain protected information since they contain only the substance of conversations between a nonlawyer, Mr. Blumenthal, and . . . other third parties who also are not lawyers. [The notes therefore] cannot be information communicated "for the purposes of securing legal advice or services." *In re Lindsey,* 158 F.3d at 1267. The argument that the notes of Mr. Blumenthal's conversations with Mr. Brock and other journalists are attorney–client protected communications is far-fetched, if not frivolous.

C. Executive Privilege

Drudge has moved to compel Mr. Blumenthal's answers to a number of deposition questions relating to his work as an advisor to the President of the United States. Mr. Blumenthal refused to answer each of these questions, raising the executive, or presidential communications, privilege.

The presidential communications privilege "is a governmental privilege intended to promote candid conversations between the President and his advisors concerning the exer-

cise of his Article II duties." *In re Grand Jury Proceedings,* 5 F. Supp. 2d 21, 25 (D.D.C. 1998). The privilege is "limited to communications 'in performance of [a President's] responsibilities,' 'of his office,' and made 'in the process of shaping policies and making decisions.'" *In re Sealed Case,* 121 F.3d 729, 744 (D.C. Cir. 1997) (quoting *Nixon* v. *Adm'r of General Services,* 433 U.S. 425 (1977)).

Mr. Blumenthal acknowledges that neither he nor his counsel can invoke executive privilege. The President alone possesses this authority. Still, Mr. Blumenthal does have an obligation to preserve the presidential communications privilege long enough for the President to invoke it if he so desires. If Drudge wishes to pursue the lines of questioning to which Mr. Blumenthal asserted executive privilege, he may reopen the deposition of Mr. Blumenthal and provide the Blumenthals either with sufficient notice so that they may secure the presence of a White House lawyer or with a list of the subjects for the deposition that might touch on privileged areas so the Blumenthals can request White House review in advance. If the President chooses to invoke executive privilege and Drudge seeks court review, the court will consider the merits of the claim at that time.

II. The Blumenthals' Motion to Compel
A. Attorney–Client Privilege

The Blumenthals argue that Drudge improperly invoked the attorney–client privilege in response to a number of their [discovery] requests. First, the Blumenthals requested that Drudge identify all communications to which Drudge was a party that addressed the allegedly defamatory information at issue in this case. Drudge claimed that many of these communications were protected by the attorney–client privilege. Even if Drudge is correct that the *substance* of the communications is privileged in some cases, he has no right to decline to *identify* the privileged communications.

[According to the FRCP], a party invoking a privilege must "describe the nature of the documents, communications, or things not produced or disclosed in a manner that, without revealing information itself privileged or protected, will enable other parties to assess the applicability of the privilege or protection." [Therefore,] Drudge at least must describe the parties to the communications, the dates on which the communications occurred, and their general subject matter.

The Blumenthals also request that the court compel Drudge to answer interrogatories regarding communications with third parties and the production of documents that were shared with third parties. The majority of the communications and the documents at issue apparently involved or were shared with David Horowitz, president of the Individual Rights Foundation. Normally, the attorney–client privilege is destroyed once information is shared with any person other than the attorney and the client because the presence of a third party is inconsistent with the client's intent that the communication remain confidential.

Drudge contends, however, that the attorney–client privilege extends to Mr. Horowitz because Drudge has retained him as a "litigation consultant" who is using his media, journalistic and political consulting experience to assist Drudge's attorneys. The court is more than a little skeptical of this claim. Here, it appears that Mr. Horowitz was retained for the value of his own advice, not to assist Drudge's attorneys in providing their legal advice. The communications with Mr. Horowitz were not made for the purpose of obtaining advice from a lawyer and therefore are not protected by the attorney–client privilege. They must be disclosed.

The Blumenthals also point out that several documents on Drudge's privilege log were electronic mail messages that were forwarded by Drudge's counsel to Drudge or his co-counsel. If any of these messages originally were sent by third parties, then the message is not privileged. Drudge may redact any privileged communications between himself and counsel that were added to the original electronic mail message from a third party, but he must produce the original electronic mail message.

B. Information Regarding Drudge's Sources

The Blumenthals also objected to Drudge's withholding of information about his sources for the allegedly defamatory information that is the subject of this litigation. Drudge maintains that such information is protected under the First Amendment.

While the First Amendment provides some protection for the identity of a reporter's confidential sources, there is no absolute bar to disclosure of confidential. The reporter's privilege is only a qualified privilege that can be overcome by a sufficient showing of need by the party seeking the information. The protections of the First Amendment may be overcome when (1) the information cannot be discovered through alternative sources, (2) the party seeking the information has exhausted all reasonable alternative means of identifying the source, and (3) the information sought goes to the heart of the plaintiff's claim. The Blumenthals have proffered nothing to satisfy their burden, and the court cannot find that the First Amendment's protections have been outweighed absent such a showing.

C. The Membership of Drudge's Legal Defense Fund

Finally, the Blumenthals request the court to compel the disclosure of the membership of Drudge's legal defense fund. While the Blumenthals assert that the information could lead to the discovery of information relating to Drudge's sources of information, they provide no grounds for this conclusion. Certainly, without a more substantial basis to the request it must be denied because the disclosure of the list might implicate the First Amendment right to association of the fund members. Because the Blumenthals have not satisfied their burden of showing that the membership list is within the scope of permissible discovery, and because such discovery might implicate the First Amendment rights of the fund members, Drudge will not be forced to disclose it.

Plaintiffs' and defendant's motions to compel each granted in part and denied in part; defendant's motion for sanctions denied.

Documents and similar items obtained through the discovery process may be used at trial if they fall within the legal rules governing admissible evidence. The same is true of discovery material such as answers to interrogatories and responses to requests for admissions. If a party or other witness who testifies at trial offers testimony that differs from her statements during a deposition, the deposition may be used to impeach her—i.e., to cast doubt on her trial testimony. A litigant may offer as evidence, at trial, the deposition of

a witness who died prior to trial or meets the legal standard of unavailability to testify in person. In addition, selected parts or all of the deposition of the opposing party or of certain persons affiliated with the opposing party may be used as evidence at trial, regardless of whether such a deponent is available to testify "live."

Participation in the discovery process may require significant expenditures of time and effort, not only by the attorneys but also by the parties and their employees. As the court indicates in *Blumenthal,* parties who see themselves

ETHICS IN ACTION

The broad scope of discovery rights in a civil case will often entitle a party to seek and obtain copies of records, memos, and other documents from the opposing party's files. In many cases, some of the most favorable evidence for the plaintiff will have come from the defendant's files, and vice-versa. If your firm is, or is likely to be, a party to civil litigation and you know that the firm's files contain records or documents that may be damaging to the firm in the litigation, you may be faced with the temptation to alter or destroy the potentially damaging items. This temptation poses serious ethical dilemmas. Is it morally defensible to change the content of records or documents on an after-the-fact basis, in order to lessen the adverse effect on your firm in pending or probable litigation? Is document destruction ethically justifiable when you seek to protect your firm's interests in a lawsuit?

If the ethical concerns are not sufficient by themselves to make you leery of involvement in document alteration or destruction, consider the potential legal consequences for yourself and your firm. The much-publicized collapse of the Enron Corporation in 2001 led to considerable scrutiny of the actions of the Arthur Andersen firm, which had provided auditing and consulting services to Enron. An Andersen partner, David Duncan, pleaded guilty in 2002 to a criminal obstruction of justice charge that accused him of having destroyed, or having instructed Andersen employees to destroy, certain Enron-related records in order to thwart a Securities and Exchange Commission (SEC) investigation of Andersen. As this book went to press in 2002, a jury found the Andersen firm guilty of obstruction of justice. In that case, the U.S. Justice Department alleged that Andersen altered or destroyed records pertaining to Enron in order to impede the SEC investigation of Andersen. This criminal conviction, even if it were to be overturned in an appeal that Andersen vowed to lodge, appeared highly likely to have a devastating effect on the firm.

Of course, not all instances of document alteration or destruction will lead to criminal prosecution for obstruction of justice. Other consequences of a noncriminal but clearly severe nature may result, however, from document destruction that interferes with legitimate discovery requests in a civil case. In such instances, courts have broad discretionary authority to impose appropriate sanctions on the document-destroying party. These sanctions may include such remedies as court orders prohibiting the document-destroyer from raising certain claims or defenses in the lawsuit, instructions to the jury regarding the wrongful destruction of the documents, and court orders that the document-destroyer pay certain attorney's fees to the opposing party.

Stevenson v. *Union Pacific Railroad Co.,* 2001 U.S. Dist. LEXIS 21787 (E. D. Ark. 2001), furnishes a useful example. In the discovery phase of this civil case concerning a deadly car–train collision at a railroad crossing, the surviving spouse and the estate of the deceased requested access to the audio record of communications between the train crew and dispatchers at the general time of the collision. Such audio records may be helpful to a determination of what caused an accident of this nature. Union Pacific (UP) policy called for the company to keep audio records of train crew–dispatcher communications for a 90-day period, after which time UP would reuse the tapes by taping new communications over what had been recorded. With more than 90 days having passed since the accident at issue in *Stevenson,* UP had already taped over the audio communication concerning the accident. The plaintiffs moved for sanctions against UP for destruction of the audio record.

As the *Stevenson* court noted, sanctions may be imposed on a litigant for destruction of documents or other records if two elements existed: (1) the litigant knew or should have known that the documents or other records were, or would become, relevant to pending or probable litigation; and (2) the destruction prejudiced the opposing party. The district judge in *Stevenson* determined from listening to other accident tapes of the same type that they usually reveal significant information and that the audio record sought by the plaintiffs would have been discoverable had it been preserved. He also concluded that the destruction of the audio record had prejudiced the plaintiffs because, with the passage of time, the train crew would have forgotten certain details and sensory impressions that the tape would likely have revealed.

The district judge did not regard UP's 90-day tape-retention policy as inherently unreasonable or as the product of bad faith in general. Nevertheless, he imposed sanctions against UP on the ground that UP, having been regularly involved in crossing collisions and litigation, should reasonably have expected a lawsuit over the collision. UP therefore should have preserved the tape. "Considering the materiality of the tape, and UP's knowledge of that materiality," wrote the court, there was "no reason to adhere to a 90-day retention policy when there has been a serious injury or death, other than to keep the voice tape out of the hands of [the plaintiffs]. The 90-day period may well be reasonable in other cases, but under these circumstances, it is manifestly unreasonable, and adherence to the retention policy [in this instance] amounts to bad faith."

Similar issues arose in *Stevenson* regarding UP's adherence to the company's retention policy for track inspection records. In accordance with time guidelines set forth in the firm's retention policy, UP destroyed certain track inspection records for which the plaintiffs had made a discovery request. The destroyed records would have been likely to contain information relevant to allegations being made by the plaintiffs regarding conditions at the crossing where the accident occurred. Therefore, the court concluded that the destruction of the records had prejudiced the plaintiffs.

After observing that UP's destruction of the audio record and the track inspection records neither "square[d] with the discovery rules, nor with 'traditional notions of fair play and justice,'" the district judge stated that UP "has either made an effort to keep evidence out of the hands of [the plaintiffs] or it has remained willfully blind and uninformed, intending to rely on its document retention policies to avoid discovery. Either way, sanctions are appropriate." The court chose two severe sanctions. First, it announced an intention to instruct the jury that (a) UP had destroyed the audio record and the track in-spection records when those items should have been pre-served, and (b) the jury was entitled to presume that the de-stroyed items' content would have been adverse to UP's inter-ests. Second, the court ordered UP to compensate the plaintiffs for a broad range of "costs incurred and time spent by [the plaintiffs] showing that [UP]'s left hand did not know what its right hand knew." These expenses would include attorney's fees associated with the preparation of the motion for sanctions and related briefs and with appearances at sanctions-related hearings, as well as the travel, telephone, and deposition ex-penses that the plaintiffs would not have had to incur if UP had complied with their legitimate discovery requests.

as too busy to comply with discovery requests may need to think seriously about whether they should remain a party to pending litigation. The discovery process may also trig-ger significant ethical issues, such as those associated with uses of discovery requests simply to harass or cause ex-pense to the other party, or the issues faced by one who does not wish to hand over legitimately sought material that may prove to be damaging to him or to his employer.

Summary Judgment

Summary judgment is a device for disposing of relatively clear cases without a trial. It differs from a demurrer be-cause it involves factual determinations. To prevail, the party moving for a summary judgment must show that: (1) there is no genuine issue of material (legally significant) fact, and (2) she is entitled to judgment as a matter of law. A moving party satisfies the first element of the test by us-ing the pleadings, relevant discovery information, and affi-davits (signed and sworn statements regarding matters of fact) to show that there is no real question about any signif-icant fact. She satisfies the second element by showing that, given the established facts, the applicable law clearly man-dates that she win.

Either or both parties may move for a summary judg-ment. If the court rules in favor of either party, that party wins the case. (The losing party may appeal, however.) If the parties' summary judgment motions are denied, the case proceeds to trial. The judge may also grant a partial summary judgment, which settles some issues in the case but leaves others to be decided at trial.

The Pretrial Conference

Depending on the jurisdiction, a **pretrial conference** is either mandatory or held at the discretion of the trial judge. At this conference, the judge meets informally with the attorneys for both litigants. He or she may try to get the attorneys to stipulate, or agree to, the resolution of certain issues in order to simplify the trial. The judge may also urge them to convince their clients to settle the case by coming to an agreement that eliminates the need for a trial. If the case is not settled, the judge enters a pretrial order that includes the attorneys' stipulations and any other agreements. Ordinarily, this order binds the parties for the remainder of the case.

The Trial

Once the case has been through discovery and has sur-vived any pretrial motions, it is set for trial. The trial may be before a judge alone (i.e., a bench trial), in which case the judge makes findings of fact and reaches conclusions of law before issuing the court's judgment. If the right to a jury trial exists and either party demands one, the jury finds the facts. The judge, however, continues to deter-mine legal questions.[9] During a pretrial jury screening process known as *voir dire,* biased potential jurors may be removed for cause. In addition, the attorney for each party is allowed a limited number of *peremptory chal-lenges,* which allow him to remove potential jurors with-out having to show bias or other cause.

---

[9]The rules governing availability of a jury trial are largely beyond the scope of this text. The U.S. Constitution guarantees a jury trial in federal court cases "at common law" whose amount exceeds $20. Most states have similar constitutional provisions, often with a higher dollar amount. Also, Congress and the state legislatures have chosen to allow jury trials in various other cases.

Trial Procedure At either a bench trial or a jury trial, the attorneys for each party make opening statements that outline what they expect to prove. The plaintiff's attorney then presents her client's case-in-chief by calling witnesses and introducing documentary evidence (relevant documents and written records, videotapes, and other evidence having a physical form). The plaintiff's attorney asks questions of her client's witnesses in a process known as direct examination. If the plaintiff is an individual person rather than a corporation, he is very likely to testify. The plaintiff's attorney may choose to call the defendant to testify. In this respect, civil cases differ from criminal cases, in which the Fifth Amendment's privilege against self-incrimination bars the government from compelling the defendant to testify. After the plaintiff's attorney completes direct examination of a witness, the defendant's lawyer cross-examines the witness. This may be followed by re-direct examination by the plaintiff's attorney and re-cross examination by the defendant's lawyer.

Once the plaintiff's attorney has completed the presentation of her client's case, defense counsel presents his client's case-in-chief by offering documentary evidence and the testimony of witnesses. The same process of direct, cross-, re-direct, and re-cross-examination is followed, except that the examination roles of the respective lawyers are reversed. After the plaintiff and defendant have presented their cases-in-chief, each party is allowed to present evidence rebutting the showing made by the other party. Throughout each side's presentations of evidence, the opposing attorney may object, on specified legal grounds, to certain questions asked of witnesses or to certain evidence that has been offered for admission. The trial judge utilizes the legal rules of evidence to determine whether to sustain the objection (meaning that the objected-to question cannot be answered by the witness or that the offered evidence will be disallowed) or, instead, overrule it (meaning that the question may be answered or that the offered evidence will be allowed).

After all of the evidence has been presented by the parties, each party's attorney makes a closing argument summarizing his or her client's position. In bench trials, the judge then usually takes the case under advisement rather than issuing a decision immediately. The judge later makes findings of fact and reaches conclusions of law, renders judgment, and, if the plaintiff is the winning party, states the relief to which the plaintiff is entitled.

Jury Trials At the close of a jury trial, the judge ordinarily submits the case to the jury after issuing **instruc-** tions that set forth the legal rules applicable to the case. The jury then deliberates, makes the necessary determinations of the facts, applies the applicable legal rules to the facts, and arrives at a **verdict** on which the court's judgment will be based.

The verdict form used the vast majority of the time is the *general verdict,* which requires only that the jury declare which party wins and, if the plaintiff wins, the money damages awarded. The jury neither states its findings of fact nor explains its application of the law to the facts. Although the nature of the general verdict may permit a jury, if it is so inclined, to render a decision that is based on bias, sympathy, or some basis other than the probable facts and the law, one's belief regarding the extent to which juries engage in so-called "jury nullification" of the facts and law is likely to be heavily influenced by one's attitude toward the jury system. Most proponents of the jury system may be inclined to believe that "renegade" juries, though regrettable, are an aberration, and that the vast majority of juries make a good-faith effort to decide cases on the basis of the facts and controlling legal principles. Some jury system proponents, however, take a different view, asserting that juries *should* engage in jury nullification when they believe it is necessary to accomplish "rough justice." Those who take a dim view of the jury system perceive it as fundamentally flawed and as offering juries too much opportunity to make decisions that stray from a reasonable view of the evidence and the law. Critics of the jury system have little hope of abolishing it, however. Doing so would require amendments to the U.S. Constitution and many state constitutions, as well as the repeal of numerous federal and state statutes.

Another verdict form known as the *special verdict* may serve to minimize concerns that some observers have about jury decisions. When a special verdict is employed, the jury makes specific, written findings of fact in response to questions posed by the trial judge. The judge then applies the law to those findings. Whether a special verdict is utilized is a matter largely within the discretion of the trial judge. The special verdict is not frequently employed, however.

Directed Verdict Although the general verdict gives the jury considerable power, the American legal system also has devices for limiting that power. One device, the **directed verdict,** takes the case away from the jury and provides a judgment to one party before the jury gets a chance to decide the case. The motion for a directed verdict may be made by either party; it usually occurs after the other (nonmoving) party has presented her evidence. The moving party asserts that the evidence, even when viewed favorably to the other party, leads to only one result and need not be considered by the jury. Courts differ on the test governing a motion for a directed verdict. Some deny the motion if there is *any* evidence favoring the nonmoving party, whereas others deny the motion only if there is *substantial* evidence favoring the nonmoving party. More often than not, trial judges deny motions for a directed verdict.

Judgment Notwithstanding the Verdict On occasion, one party wins a judgment even after the jury has reached a verdict against that party. The device for doing so is the **judgment notwithstanding the verdict** (also known as the judgment *non obstante veredicto* or judgment n.o.v.). Some jurisdictions provide that a motion for judgment n.o.v, cannot be made unless the moving party previously moved for a directed verdict. In any event, the standard used to decide the motion for judgment n.o.v. usually is the same standard used to decide the motion for a directed verdict.

Motion for a New Trial In a wide range of situations that vary among jurisdictions, the losing party can successfully move for a new trial. Acceptable reasons for granting a new trial include legal errors by the judge during the trial, jury or attorney misconduct, the discovery of new evidence, or an award of excessive damages to the plaintiff. Most motions for a new trial are unsuccessful, however.

Appeal

A final judgment generally prevents the parties from relitigating the same claim. One or more parties still may appeal the trial court's decision, however. Normally, appellate courts consider only alleged errors of law made by the trial court. The matters ordinarily considered "legal" and thus appealable include the trial judge's decisions on motions to dismiss, for summary judgment, for directed verdict or judgment notwithstanding the verdict, and for a new trial. Other matters typically considered appealable include trial court rulings on service of process and admission of evidence at trial, as well as the court's legal conclusions in a nonjury trial, instructions to the jury in a jury case, and decision regarding damages or other relief. Appellate courts may *affirm* the trial court's decision, *reverse* it, or affirm one part of the decision and reverse another part. One of three things ordinarily results from an appellate court's disposition of an appeal: (1) the plaintiff wins the case; (2) the defendant wins the case; or (3) the case is *remanded* (returned) to the trial court for further proceed-

ings if the trial court's decision is reversed in whole or in part. For example, if the plaintiff appeals a trial court decision granting the defendant's motion to dismiss and the appellate courts affirm that decision, the plaintiff loses. On the other hand, if an appellate court reverses a trial court judgment in the plaintiff's favor, the defendant could win outright, or the case might be returned to the trial court for further proceedings consistent with the appellate decision.

Enforcing a Judgment

In this text, you may occasionally see cases in which someone was not sued even though he probably would have been liable to the plaintiff, who sued another party instead. One explanation is that the first party was "judgment-proof"—so lacking in assets as to make a civil lawsuit for damages a waste of time and money. The defendant's financial condition also affects a winning plaintiff's ability to collect whatever damages she has been awarded.

When the defendant fails to pay as required after losing a civil case, the winning plaintiff must enforce the judgment. Ordinarily, the plaintiff will obtain a *writ of execution* enabling the sheriff to seize designated property of the defendant and sell it at a judicial sale to help satisfy the judgment. A judgment winner may also use a procedure known as *garnishment* to seize property, money, and wages that belong to the defendant but are in the hands of a third party such as a bank or employer. Legal limits exist, however, concerning the portion of wages that may be garnished. If the property needed to satisfy the judgment is located in another state, the plaintiff must use that state's execution or garnishment procedures. Under the U.S. Constitution, the second state must give "full faith and credit" to the judgment of the state in which the plaintiff originally sued. Finally, when the court has awarded an equitable remedy such as an injunction, the defendant may be found in contempt of court and subjected to a fine or a jail term if he fails to obey the court's order.

Class Actions

So far, our civil procedure discussion has proceeded as if the plaintiff and the defendant were single parties. Various plaintiffs and defendants, however, may be parties to one lawsuit. In addition, each jurisdiction has procedural rules stating when other parties can be *joined* to a suit that begins without them.

One special type of multiparty case, the **class action,** allows one or more persons to sue on behalf of themselves and all others who have suffered similar harm from substantially the same wrong. Class action suits by consumers, environmentalists, and other groups now are common events. The usual justifications for the class action are that: (1) it allows legal wrongs causing losses to a large number of widely dispersed parties to be fully compensated, and (2) it promotes economy of judicial effort by combining many similar claims into one suit.

The requirements for a class action vary among jurisdictions. The issues addressed by class action statutes include the following: whether there are questions of law and fact common to all members of the alleged class; whether the class is small enough to allow all of its members to join the case as parties rather than use a class action; and whether the plaintiff(s) and their attorney(s) can adequately represent the class without conflicts of interest or other forms of unfairness. To protect the individual class members' right to be heard, some jurisdictions have required that unnamed or absent class members be given notice of the case if this is reasonably possible. The damages awarded in a successful class action usually are apportioned among the entire class. Establishing the total recovery and distributing it to the class, however, pose problems when the class is large, the class members' injuries are indefinite, or some members cannot be identified.

Alternative Dispute Resolution

Lawsuits are not the only devices for resolving civil disputes. Nor are they always the best means of doing so. Settling private disputes through the courts can be a cumbersome, lengthy, and expensive process for litigants. With the advent of a litigious society and the increasing caseloads it has produced, handling disputes in this fashion also imposes ever-greater social costs. For these reasons and others, various forms of **alternative dispute resolution (ADR)** have assumed increasing importance in recent years. Proponents of ADR cite many considerations in its favor. These include ADR's: (1) quicker resolution of disputes; (2) lower costs in time, money, and aggravation for the parties; (3) lessening of the strain on an overloaded court system; (4) use of decisionmakers with specialized expertise; and (5) potential for compromise decisions that promote and reflect consensus between the parties. Those who are skeptical of ADR worry about its potential for sloppy, biased, or lawless decisions. They also worry that it may sometimes mean second-class jus-

tice for ordinary people who deal with powerful economic interests. Sometimes, for example, agreements to submit disputes to alternative dispute resolution are buried in complex standard-form contracts drafted by a party with superior size, knowledge, and business sophistication and are unknowingly agreed to by less knowledgeable parties. Such clauses, critics charge, may compel ADR proceedings before decisionmakers who are biased in favor of the stronger party.

Common Forms of ADR

Settlement The settlement of a civil lawsuit is not everyone's idea of an alternative dispute resolution mechanism. It is an important means, however, of avoiding protracted litigation—one that often is a sensible compromise for the parties. Most cases settle at some stage in the proceedings described previously. The usual settlement agreement is a contract whereby the defendant agrees to pay the plaintiff a sum of money, in exchange for the plaintiff's promise to release the defendant from liability for the plaintiff's claims. Such agreements must satisfy the requirements of contract law discussed later in this text. In some cases, moreover, the court must approve the settlement in order for it to be enforceable. Examples include class actions and litigation involving minors.

Arbitration Arbitration is the submission of a dispute to a neutral, nonjudicial third party (the *arbitrator*) who issues a binding decision resolving the dispute. Arbitration usually results from the parties' agreement. That agreement normally is made before the dispute arises (most often through an *arbitration clause* in a contract). As noted in the *Circuit City* case, which follows shortly, the Federal Arbitration Act requires judicial enforcement of a wide range of agreements to arbitrate claims. This means that if a contract contains a clause requiring arbitration of certain claims but one of the parties attempts to litigate such a claim in court, the court is very likely to dismiss the case and compel arbitration of the dispute.

Arbitration may also be compelled by other statutes. One example is the *compulsory arbitration* many states require as part of the collective bargaining process for certain public employees. Finally, parties who have not agreed in advance to submit future disputes to arbitration may agree upon arbitration after the dispute arises.

Arbitration usually is less formal than regular court proceedings. The arbitrator may or may not be an attorney. Often, she is a professional with expertise in the subject matter of the dispute. Although arbitration hearings often resemble civil trials, the applicable procedures, the rules for admission of evidence, and the record-keeping requirements typically are not as rigorous as those governing courts. Arbitrators sometimes have freedom to ignore rules of substantive law that would bind a court.

The arbitrator's decision, called an *award,* is filed with a court, which will enforce it if necessary. The losing party may object to the arbitrator's award, but judicial review of arbitration proceedings is limited. Possible grounds for overturning an arbitration award include: (1) a party's use of fraud, (2) the arbitrator's partiality or corruption, and (3) other misconduct by the arbitrator.

In *Circuit City,* which follows, the Supreme Court considers whether the Federal Arbitration Act requires enforcement of an agreement to resolve employment disputes through arbitration.

Circuit City Stores, Inc. v. Adams   532 U.S. 105 (U.S. Sup. Ct. 2001)

Adams, a worker hired at a Circuit City electronics retail store in California, signed an application that included an agreement to resolve all future employment disputes exclusively by binding arbitration. Later, Adams filed a state-law-based employment discrimination suit against Circuit City in a California state court. Circuit City then filed suit in a federal district court, asking the court to enjoin the state-court action and compel arbitration under the Federal Arbitration Act (FAA). The district court granted the order, and Adams appealed. The Court of Appeals for the Ninth Circuit reversed and remanded, reasoning that the FAA did not cover employment contracts. Circuit City sought review by the United States Supreme Court, which granted certiorari.

Kennedy, Justice   Congress enacted the FAA in 1925 [as] a response to hostility of American courts to the enforcement of arbitration agreements. [T]he FAA compels judicial enforcement of a wide range of written arbitration agreements. The FAA's coverage provision, § 2, provides that

> [a] written provision in any maritime transaction or a contract evidencing a transaction involving commerce to settle by arbitration a controversy thereafter arising out of such contract or transaction, or the refusal to perform the whole or any part thereof, . . . shall be valid, irrevocable, and enforceable, save upon such grounds as exist at law or in equity for the revocation of any contract.

Section 1 of the FAA excludes from the FAA's coverage "contracts of employment of seamen, railroad employees, or any other class of workers engaged in foreign or interstate commerce." Adams contends that we need not address the meaning of the § 1 exclusion provision to decide the case in his favor. In his view, an employment contract is not a "contract evidencing a transaction involving interstate commerce" at all, since the word "transaction" in § 2 extends only to commercial contracts. This line of reasoning proves too much, for it would make the § 1 exclusion provision superfluous. If all contracts of employment are beyond the scope of the Act under the § 2 coverage provision, the separate exemption for "contracts of employment of seamen, railroad employees, or any other class of workers engaged in . . . interstate commerce" would be pointless. If, then, there is an argument to be made that arbitration agreements in employment contracts are not covered by the Act, it must be premised on the language of the § 1 exclusion provision itself.

Adams, endorsing the reasoning of the Court of Appeals . . . that the provision excludes all employment contracts, relies on the asserted breadth of the words "contracts of employment of . . . any other class of workers engaged in . . . commerce." Referring to our construction of § 2's coverage provision in *Allied-Bruce Terminix Cos* v. *Dobson* (1995)—concluding that the words "involving commerce" evidence the congressional intent to regulate to the full extent of its commerce power—Adams contends § 1's interpretation should have a like reach, thus exempting all employment contracts.

This reading of § 1, however, runs into an immediate and . . . insurmountable textual obstacle. Unlike the "involving commerce" language in § 2, the words "any other class of workers engaged in . . . commerce" constitute a residual phrase, following, in the same sentence, explicit reference to "seamen" and "railroad employees." Construing the residual phrase to exclude all employment contracts fails to give independent effect to the statute's enumeration of the specific categories of workers which precedes it; there would be no need for Congress to use the phrases "seamen" and "railroad employees" if those same classes of workers were subsumed within the meaning of the "engaged in . . . commerce" residual clause. The wording of § 1 calls for the application of the maxim *ejusdem generis,* the statutory canon that "where general words follow specific words in a statutory enumeration, the general words are construed to embrace only objects similar in nature to those objects enumerated by the preceding specific words." 2A N. Singer, *Sutherland on Statutes and Statutory Construction* §47.17 (1991) Under this rule of construction the residual clause should be read to give effect to the terms "seamen" and "railroad employees," and should itself be controlled and defined by reference to the enumerated categories of workers which are recited just before it.

The application of the rule *ejusdem generis* in this case . . . is in full accord with other sound considerations bearing upon the proper interpretation of the clause. For even if the term "engaged in commerce" stood alone in § 1, we would not construe the provision to exclude all contracts of employment from the FAA. Congress uses different modifiers to the word "commerce" in the design and enactment of its statutes. [The Court has held that the] phrase "affecting commerce" indicates Congress's intent to regulate to the outer limits of its authority under the Commerce Clause. [In **Allied Bruce,** the Court reached the same conclusion regarding the] "involving commerce" phrase, the operative words for the reach of the basic coverage provision in § 2, [of the FAA]. Unlike those phrases, however, the general words "in commerce" and the specific phrase "engaged in commerce" are understood to have a more limited reach. In *Allied-Bruce* itself the Court said [that] the words "in commerce" [have not been] read as expressing congressional intent to regulate to the outer limits of authority under the Commerce Clause.

In sum, the text of the FAA forecloses the construction of § 1 followed by the Court of Appeals . . . a construction which would exclude all employment contracts from the FAA. Section 1 exempts from the FAA only contracts of employment of transportation workers.

As the conclusion we reach today is directed by the text of § 1, we need not assess the legislative history of the exclusion provision. We do note, however, that [Adams] places greatest reliance upon testimony before a Senate subcommittee hearing suggesting that the exception may have been added in response to the objections of the president of the International Seamen's Union of America. Legislative history is problematic even when the attempt is to draw inferences from the intent of duly appointed committees of the Congress. It becomes far more so when we consult sources still more steps removed from the full Congress and speculate upon the significance of the fact that a certain interest group sponsored or opposed particular legislation. We ought not attribute to Congress an official purpose based on the motives of a particular group that lobbied for or against a certain proposal.

[F]or parties to employment contracts not involving the specific exempted categories set forth in § 1, . . . there are real benefits to the enforcement of arbitration provisions. [T]he advantages of the arbitration process [do not] disappear when transferred to the employment context. Arbitration agreements allow parties to avoid the costs of litigation, a benefit that may be of particular importance in employment litigation, which often involves smaller sums of money than disputes concerning commercial contracts. The considerable complexity and uncertainty that the construction of § 1 urged by Adams would introduce into the enforceability of arbitration agreements in employment contracts would call into doubt the efficacy of alternative dispute resolution procedures adopted by many of the Nation's employers, in the process undermining the FAA's proarbitration purposes. [A]rbitration agreements can be enforced under the FAA without contravening the policies of congressional enactments giving employees specific protection against discrimination prohibited by federal law.

Judgment of the Court of Appeals reversed, and case remanded.

Stevens, Justice, dissenting [T]he original [draft of the FAA] was opposed by representatives of organized labor, most notably the president of the International Seamen's Union of America, because of their concern that the legislation might authorize federal judicial enforcement of arbitration clauses in employment contracts and collective-bargaining agreements. In response to those objections, the chairman of the American Bar Association committee that drafted the legislation emphasized at a Senate Judiciary Subcommittee hearing that "it is not intended that this shall be an act referring to labor disputes at all."[A]nother supporter of the bill, then Secretary of Commerce Herbert Hoover, suggested that "if objection appears to the inclusion of workers' contracts in the law's scheme, it might be well amended by stating 'but nothing herein contained shall apply to contracts of employment of seamen, railroad employees, or any other class of workers engaged in interstate or foreign commerce.' " The legislation was reintroduced in the next session of Congress with Secretary Hoover's exclusionary language added to § 1, and the amendment eliminated organized labor's opposition to the proposed law.

That amendment is what the Court construes today. History amply supports the proposition that it was an uncontroversial provision that merely confirmed the fact that no one interested in the enactment of the FAA ever intended or expected that § 2 would apply to employment contracts.

A method of statutory interpretation that is deliberately uninformed . . . may produce a result that is consistent with a court's own views of how things should be, but it may also defeat the very purpose for which a provision was enacted. That is the sad result in this case.

Court-Annexed Arbitration   In this form of ADR, certain civil lawsuits are diverted into arbitration. One example might be cases in which less than a specified dollar amount is at issue. Most often, court-annexed arbitration is mandatory and is ordered by the judge, but some jurisdictions merely offer litigants the option of arbitration. The losing party in a court-annexed arbitration still has the right to a regular trial.

Mediation   In mediation, a neutral third party called a *mediator* helps the parties reach a cooperative resolution of their dispute by facilitating communication between them, clarifying their areas of agreement and disagreement, helping them to see each other's viewpoints, and suggesting settlement options. Mediators, unlike arbitrators, cannot make decisions that bind the parties. Instead, a successful mediation process results in a *mediation agreement*. Such agreements normally are enforced under regular contract law principles.

Mediation is used in a wide range of situations, including labor, commercial, family, and environmental disputes. It may occur by agreement of the parties after a dispute has arisen. It also may result from a previous contractual agreement by the parties. Increasingly, court-annexed mediation is either compelled or made available by courts in certain cases.

Summary Jury Trial   Sometimes settlement of civil litigation is impeded because the litigants have vastly different perceptions about the merits of their cases. In such cases, the summary jury trial may give the parties a needed dose of reality. The summary jury trial is an abbreviated, nonpublic mock jury trial that does not bind the parties. If the parties do not settle after completion of the summary jury trial, they still are entitled to a regular court trial. There is some disagreement over whether courts can compel the parties to take part in a summary jury trial.

Minitrial   A minitrial is an informal, abbreviated private "trial" whose aim is to promote settlement of disputes. Normally, it arises out of a private agreement that also describes the procedures to be followed. In the typical minitrial, counsel for the parties present their cases to a panel composed of senior management from each side. Sometimes a neutral advisor such as an attorney or a retired judge presides. This advisor may also offer an opinion about the case's likely outcome in court. After the presentations, the managers attempt to negotiate a settlement.

Other ADR Devices

Other ADR devices include: (1) *med/arb* (a hybrid of mediation and arbitration in which a third party first acts as a mediator, and then as an arbitrator); (2) the use of *magistrates* and *special masters* to perform various tasks during complex litigation in the federal courts; (3) *early neutral evaluation* (ENE) (a court-annexed procedure involving early, objective evaluation of the case by a neutral private attorney with experience in its subject matter); (4) *private judging* (in which litigants hire a private referee to issue a decision that may be binding but that usually does not preclude recourse to the courts); and (5) *private panels* instituted by an industry or an organization to handle claims of certain kinds (e.g., the Better Business Bureau). In addition, some formal legal processes are sometimes called ADR devices. Examples include small claims courts and the administrative procedures used to handle claims for veterans' benefits or Social Security benefits.

Problems and Problem Cases

1. Peters sues Davis. At trial, Peters's lawyer attempts to introduce certain evidence to help make his case. Davis's attorney objects, and the trial judge refuses to allow the evidence. Peters eventually loses the case at the trial court level. On appeal, his attorney argues that the trial judge's decision not to admit the evidence was erroneous. Davis's attorney argues that the appellate court cannot consider this question, because appellate courts review only errors of *law* (not fact) at the trial court level. Is Davis's attorney correct? Why or why not?

2. Eric Baker, who had agreed in his employment application to resolve any employment-related dispute through arbitration, was fired after suffering a seizure on the job. Baker did not initiate arbitration proceedings. Instead, he filed a charge of discrimination with the Equal Employment Opportunity Commission (EEOC). Alleging that Baker's employer violated the Americans with Disabilities Act (ADA), the EEOC filed an enforcement action against the employer in federal court. The EEOC sought an injunction and punitive damages against the employer, and backpay, reinstatement, and compensatory damages for Baker. The Federal Arbitration Act (FAA) does not allow Baker to step outside the bounds of his agreement by bringing a judicial action against Waffle House. Does it prohibit the EEOC from bringing such an action, demanding victim-specific relief for Baker?

3. Albert Knowles, an Alabama truck driver, died of natural causes in California while hauling produce from Alabama to California. After Knowles's body was discovered inside his truck, it was taken to Hems Brothers Mortuaries, where Damon Reference Laboratories performed an autopsy at the request of the local coroner. Both Hems and Damon did business in California. In response to a request from an Alabama funeral home, Hems prepared Knowles's body for shipment and arranged for it to be flown to his hometown. Hems billed the Alabama funeral home for these services and for the price of a casket. It also mailed a statement to Knowles's wife.

Mrs. Knowles did not view her husband's body after its return to Alabama and before its burial. No one positively identified the body as that of Mr. Knowles during this period. After the burial, Mrs. Knowles received an autopsy report from Damon describing a body different from her husband's. She had the buried body exhumed so that she could verify that it was her husband's. It was. The body had been buried nude, had been packed in cotton in a "disaster pouch," was terribly discolored, and was lying in an awkward position. Mrs. Knowles described it as looking like "a monster." Mrs. Knowles then sued Hems and Damon in an Alabama court for the wrongful mishandling of her husband's body. Neither Damon nor Hems had contacts with Alabama other than those described earlier, and each moved to dismiss the claim because the court lacked in personam jurisdiction.

Due process requires that a defendant have certain minimum contacts with a state in order to be subject to its jurisdiction. Alabama's long-arm statute reaches to the limits of due process. Were Damon and Hems correct in arguing that the Alabama court lacked in personam jurisdiction?

4. Paul sues Dicken in a state trial court in Smith County. Both Paul and Dicken have spent their entire lives inside the state in question. Both parties live in Jones County, and the land at issue also is located there. Smith County is 200 miles from Jones County. Dicken's attorney argues that the Smith County trial court lacks *jurisdiction* over the case because the land in question is not located in Smith County. Is Dicken's attorney correct?

5. State two differences between a motion to dismiss for failure to state a claim upon which relief can be granted (or demurrer) and a motion for summary judgment.

6. Jerrie Gray worked at a Tyson Foods plant where she was exposed to comments, gestures, and physical contact that, she alleged, constituted sexual harassment. Tyson disputed the allegation, arguing that the behavior was not unwelcome, that the complained-about conduct was not based on sex, that the conduct did not affect a term, condition, or privilege of employment, and that proper remedial action was taken in response to any complaint by Gray of sexual harassment. During the trial in federal court, a witness for Gray repeatedly volunteered inadmissible testimony that the judge had to tell the jury to disregard. At one point, upon an objection from the defendant's counsel, the witness asked, "May I say something here?" The judge told her she could not. Finally, after the jury left the courtroom, the witness had an angry outburst that continued into the hallway, in view of some of the jurors.

The jury awarded Gray $185,000 in compensatory and $800,000 in punitive damages. Tyson believed that it should not have been liable, that the awards of damages were excessive and unsupported by evidence, and that the inadmissible evidence and improper conduct had tainted the proceedings. What courses of action may Tyson pursue?

7. Preston is the plaintiff in a civil lawsuit against Dalton. During the discovery phase of the case, Dalton's attorney took Preston's deposition. The trial of the case is in process. Dalton's attorney has offered Preston's deposition as evidence. Preston's attorney has objected, arguing that Preston is neither dead nor unavailable to testify in person, and that the deposition therefore should not be allowed admitted into evidence. Is Preston's attorney correct?

8. What is the main difference between a motion for a directed verdict and a motion for judgment notwithstanding the verdict?

9. The state of New Jersey says it is sovereign over certain landfilled portions of Ellis Island. The state of New York disagrees, asserting that it is sovereign over the whole of the island. New Jersey brings an action in the U.S. District Court for the Southern District of New York. Should the court hear the case?

10. Jackson was born in Texas but has had no contact with that state for 20 years. Jackson's father dies. A Texas court interprets the father's will so that Jackson receives none of the father's property, which is located in Texas. Assume that the court had jurisdiction to make this decision. What *kinds* of jurisdiction did it have?

Online Research: The American Arbitration Association

The American Arbitration Association (AAA) furnishes dispute resolution services in cases that fall within a wide variety of legal categories identified on the AAA's official website. Locate and review the organization's website. Then prepare a list of the legal categories of cases concerning which the AAA provides dispute resolution services.

3

BUSINESS AND THE CONSTITUTION

A federal statute and related regulations prohibited producers of beer from listing, on a product label, the alcohol content of the beer in the container on which the label appeared. The regulation existed because the U.S. government believed that if alcohol content could be disclosed on labels, certain producers of beer might begin marketing their brand as having a higher alcohol content than competing beers. The government was concerned that "strength wars" among producers could then develop, that consumers would seek out beers with higher alcohol content, and that adverse public health consequences would follow. Because it wished to include alcohol content information on container labels for its beers, Coors Brewing Co. filed suit against the United States government and asked the court to rule that the statute and regulations violated Coors's constitutional right to freedom of speech.

Consider the following questions as you read Chapter 3:

• On which provision in the U.S. Constitution was Coors relying in its challenge of the statute and regulations?

• Does a corporation such as Coors possess the same constitutional right to freedom of speech possessed by an individual human being, or does the government have greater latitude to restrict the content of a corporation's speech?

• The alcohol content disclosures that Coors wished to make with regard to its product would be classified as *commercial speech*. Does commercial speech receive the same degree of constitutional protection that political or other noncommercial speech receives?

• Which party—Coors or the federal government—won the case, and why?

CONSTITUTIONS SERVE TWO general functions. First, they set up the structure of government, allocating power among its various branches and subdivisions. Second, they prevent government from taking certain actions—especially actions that restrict individual or, as suggested by the Coors scenario with which this chapter opened, corporate rights. This chapter examines the U.S. Constitution's performance of these functions and considers how that performance affects government regulation of business.

An Overview of the U.S. Constitution

The U.S. Constitution exhibits the principle of **separation of powers** by giving distinct powers to Congress,

the president, and the federal courts. Article I of the Constitution establishes a Congress composed of a Senate and a House of Representatives, gives it sole power to legislate at the federal level, and sets out rules for the enactment of legislation. Article I, section 8 also defines when Congress can make law by stating its *legislative powers*. Three of those powers—the commerce, tax, and spending powers—are discussed later in the chapter.

Article II gives the president the *executive power*—the power to execute or enforce the laws passed by Congress. Section 2 of that article lists other presidential powers, including the powers to command the nation's armed forces and to make treaties. Article III gives the *judicial power* of the United States to the Supreme Court and the other federal courts later established by Congress. Article III also determines the types of cases the federal courts may decide.

Besides creating a separation of powers, Articles I, II, and III set up a system of **checks and balances** among Congress, the president, and the courts. For example, Article I, section 7 gives the president the power to veto legislation passed by Congress, but allows Congress to override such a veto by a two-thirds vote of each House. Article I, sections 2 and 3 and Article II, section 4 provide that the president, the vice president, and other federal officials may be impeached and removed from office by a two-thirds vote of the Senate. Article II, section 2 states that treaties made by the president must be approved by a two-thirds vote of the Senate. Article III, section 2 gives Congress some control over the Supreme Court's appellate jurisdiction.

The Constitution recognizes the principle of **federalism** in the way it structures power relations between the federal government and the states. After Article I, section 8 lists the powers Congress holds, Article I, section 9 lists certain powers that Congress cannot exercise. The Tenth Amendment provides that those powers the Constitution neither gives to the federal government nor denies to the states are reserved to the states or the people.

Article VI, however, makes the Constitution, laws, and treaties of the United States supreme over state law. As will be seen, this principle of **federal supremacy** may cause federal statutes to *preempt* inconsistent state laws. The Constitution also puts limits on the states' lawmaking powers. One example is Article I, section 10's command that states shall not pass laws impairing the obligation of contracts.

Article V sets forth the procedures for amending the Constitution. The Constitution has been amended 27 times. The first 10 of these amendments comprise the Bill of Rights. Although the rights guaranteed in the first 10 amendments once restricted only federal government action, most of them now limit state government action as well. As you will learn, this results from their *incorporation* within the Due Process Clause of the Fourteenth Amendment.

The Evolution of the Constitution and the Role of the Supreme Court

According to the legal realists discussed in Chapter 1, written "book law" is less important than what public de-

cision makers *actually do.* Using this approach, we discover a Constitution that differs from the written Constitution just described. The actual powers of today's presidency, for instance, exceed anything one would expect from reading Article II. As you will see, moreover, some constitutional provisions have acquired a meaning different from their meaning when first enacted. American constitutional law is much more evolving than static.

Many of these changes result from the way one public decisionmaker—the U.S. Supreme Court—has interpreted the Constitution over time. Formal constitutional change can be accomplished only through the amendment process. Because this process is difficult to employ, however, amendments to the Constitution have been relatively infrequent. As a practical matter, the Supreme Court has become the Constitution's main "amender" through its many interpretations of constitutional provisions. Various factors help explain the Supreme Court's ability and willingness to play this role. Because of their vagueness, some key constitutional provisions invite diverse interpretations; "due process of law" and "equal protection of the laws" are examples. In addition, the history surrounding the enactment of constitutional provisions sometimes is sketchy, confused, or contradictory. Probably more important, however, is the perceived need to adapt the Constitution to changing social conditions. As the old saying goes, Supreme Court decisions tend to "follow the election returns." (Regardless of where one finds himself or herself on the political spectrum, the old saying has taken on a new twist after *Bush* v. *Gore,* the historic 2000 decision summarized later in this chapter.)

Under the power of **judicial review,** courts can declare the actions of other government bodies unconstitutional. How courts exercise this power depends on how they choose to read the Constitution. This means that courts—especially the Supreme Court—have political power. Indeed, the Supreme Court's nine justices are, to a considerable extent, public policymakers. Their beliefs are important in the determination of how America is governed. This is why the justices' nomination and confirmation often involve so much political controversy.

Yet even though the Constitution frequently is what the courts say it is, judicial power to shape the Constitution has limits. Certain limits spring from the Constitution's language, which sometimes is quite clear. Others result from the judges' adherence to the *stare decisis* doctrine discussed in Chapter 1. Perhaps the most significant limits on judges' power, however, stem from the tension between modern judicial review and democracy. Legislators are chosen by the people, whereas judges—especially appellate level judges—often are appointed, not elected. Today, judges exercise political power by declaring the actions of legislatures unconstitutional under standards largely of the judiciary's own devising. This sometimes leads to charges that courts are undemocratic, elitist institutions. Such charges put political constraints on judges because courts depend on the other branches of government—and ultimately on public belief in judges' fidelity to the rule of law—to make their decisions effective. Judges, therefore, may be reluctant to declare statutes unconstitutional because they are wary of power struggles with a more representative body such as Congress.

The Coverage and Structure of This Chapter

This chapter examines certain constitutional provisions that are important to business; it does not discuss constitutional law in its entirety. These provisions help define federal and state power to regulate the economy. The U.S. Constitution limits government regulatory power in two general ways. First, it restricts *federal* legislative authority by listing the powers Congress can exercise. These are known as the **enumerated powers.** Federal legislation cannot be constitutional if it is not based on a power specifically stated in the Constitution. Second, the U.S. Constitution limits both *state and federal* power by placing certain **independent checks** in the path of each. In effect, the independent checks establish that even if Congress has an enumerated power to legislate on a particular matter or a state constitution authorizes a state to take certain actions, there still are certain protected spheres into which neither the federal government nor the state government may reach.

Accordingly, a federal law must meet two general tests in order to be constitutional: (1) it must be based on an enumerated power of Congress, and (2) it must not collide with any of the independent checks. For example, Congress has the power to regulate commerce among the states. This power might seem to allow Congress to pass legislation forbidding women from crossing state lines to buy or sell goods. Yet such a law, though arguably based on an enumerated power, surely would be unconstitutional because it conflicts with an independent check— the equal protection guarantee discussed later in the chapter. Today, the independent checks are the main limitations on congressional power. The most important reason for the 20th-century decline of the enumerated powers limitation is the perceived need for active federal regulation of economic and social life. Recently, however, the enumerated powers limitation has begun to assume somewhat more importance, as will be seen.

After discussion of the most important state and federal powers to regulate economic matters, the chapter explores certain independent checks that apply to the federal government and the states. The chapter then examines some independent checks that affect the states alone. It concludes by discussing a provision—the Takings Clause of the Fifth Amendment—that both recognizes a governmental power and limits its exercise.

State and Federal Power to Regulate

State Regulatory Power

Although state constitutions may do so, the U.S. Constitution does not list the powers state legislatures can exercise. The U.S. Constitution does place certain independent checks in the path of state law-making, however. It also declares that certain powers (e.g., creating currency and taxing imports) can be exercised only by Congress. In many other areas, though, Congress and the state legislatures have *concurrent powers*. Both can make law within those areas unless Congress preempts state regulation under the supremacy clause. A very important state legislative power that operates concurrently with many congressional powers is the **police power,** a broad state power to regulate for the public health, safety, morals, and welfare.

Federal Regulatory Power

Article I, section 8 of the U.S. Constitution specifies a number of ways in which Congress may legislate concerning business and commercial matters. For example, it empowers Congress to coin and borrow money, regulate commerce with foreign nations, establish uniform laws regarding bankruptcies, create post offices, and regulate copyrights and patents. The most important congressional powers contained in Article I, section 8, however, are the powers to regulate commerce among the states, to lay and collect taxes, and to spend for the general welfare. Because they now are read so broadly, these three powers are the main constitutional bases for the extensive federal social and economic regulation that exists today.

The Commerce Power   Article I, section 8 states that "The Congress shall have Power . . . To regulate Commerce . . . among the several States." The original reason for giving Congress this power to regulate *inter-state commerce* was to nationalize economic matters by blocking the protectionist state restrictions on interstate trade that were common after the Revolution. As discussed later in the chapter, the *commerce clause* serves as an independent check on state regulation that unduly restricts interstate commerce. Our present concern, however, is the commerce clause's role as a source of congressional regulatory power.

The literal language of the commerce clause simply gives Congress power to regulate commerce that occurs among the states. Today, however, the clause is regarded as an all-purpose federal police power enabling Congress to regulate most activities within a state's borders (*intra*state matters). How has this transformation occurred?

The most important step in the transformation was the Supreme Court's conclusion that the power to regulate *interstate* commerce includes the power to regulate *intrastate* activities that affect interstate commerce. For example, in the *Shreveport Rate Cases* (1914), the Supreme Court upheld the Interstate Commerce Commission's regulation of railroad rates within Texas (an intrastate matter outside the language of the commerce clause) because those rates affected rail traffic between Texas and Louisiana (an interstate matter within the clause's language). This "affecting commerce" doctrine eventually was used to justify federal police power measures with significant intrastate reach. For instance, the Supreme Court upheld the application of the 1964 Civil Rights Act's "public accommodations" section to a family-owned restaurant in Birmingham, Alabama. It did so because the restaurant's racial discrimination affected interstate commerce by reducing the restaurant's business and limiting its purchases of out-of-state meat, and by restricting the ability of blacks to travel among the states.

As the above example suggests, Congress may now regulate many predominantly intrastate activities. In our highly interdependent society, almost all intrastate activities have some effect on interstate commerce. This has led some observers to believe that the intrastate reach of the commerce clause is unlimited. In the following *Morrison* case, however, the Supreme Court made it clear that the commerce power still has some limits.

United States v. Morrison   *529 U.S. 598 (U.S. Sup. Ct. 2002)*

In 42 U.S.C. § 13981, which was part of the Violence Against Women Act, Congress provided a federal civil remedy for victims of gender-motivated violence. Christy Brzonkala, a former student at a Virginia university, brought a claim under § 13981 against two male students who allegedly had raped her and caused her to experience severe emotional distress. When the defendants attacked § 13981 on constitutional grounds, the United States intervened in the case to defend the statute's constitutionality. A federal district court, holding that Congress did not have constitutional authority to enact § 13981, dismissed Brzonkala's claim. A panel of the U.S. Court of Appeals for the Fourth Circuit reversed, but upon rehearing, the full Fourth Circuit upheld the district court's decision. The U.S. Supreme Court granted certiorari.

Rehnquist, Chief Justice Every law enacted by Congress must be based on one or more of its powers enumerated in the Constitution. Congress explicitly identified the source of federal authority on which it relied in enacting § 13981. It said that a "federal civil rights cause of action" is established "pursuant to the affirmative power of Congress . . . under . . . section 8 of Article I of the Constitution."

Due respect for the decisions of a coordinate branch of Government demands that we invalidate a congressional enactment only upon a plain showing that Congress has exceeded its constitutional bounds. With this presumption of constitutionality in mind, we [consider] whether § 13981 falls within Congress' power under Article I, § 8. Brzonkala and the United States rely upon the third clause of the Article, which gives Congress power "to regulate Commerce with foreign Nations, and among the several States, and with the Indian Tribes."

[O]ur interpretation of the Commerce Clause has changed as our Nation has developed. [S]ince *NLRB* v. *Jones & Laughlin Steel Corp.*(1937), Congress has had considerably greater latitude in regulating conduct and transactions under the Commerce Clause than our previous case law permitted. *United States* v. *Lopez,* (1995), emphasized, however, that even under our modern, expansive interpretation of the Commerce Clause, Congress' regulatory authority is not without effective bounds:

"Even [our] modern-era precedents which have expanded congressional power under the Commerce Clause confirm that this power is subject to outer limits.

In *Jones & Laughlin Steel,* the Court warned that the scope of the interstate commerce power 'must be considered in the light of our dual system of government and may not be extended so as to embrace effects upon interstate commerce so indirect and remote that to embrace them, in view of our complex society, would effectually obliterate the distinction between what is national and what is local and create a completely centralized government' " (quoting *Jones & Laughlin Steel*).

As we observed in *Lopez,* modern Commerce Clause jurisprudence has "identified three broad categories of activity that Congress may regulate under its commerce power." First, "Congress may regulate the use of the channels of interstate commerce." Second, "Congress is empowered to regulate and protect the instrumentalities of interstate commerce, or persons or things in interstate commerce, even though the threat may come only from intrastate activities." [Third,] "Congress' commerce authority includes the power to regulate those activities having a substantial relation to interstate commerce, . . . i.e., those activities that substantially affect interstate commerce."

Brzonkala and the United States . . . seek to sustain § 13981 as a regulation of activity that substantially affects interstate commerce.

Since *Lopez* most recently canvassed and clarified our case law governing this third category of Commerce Clause regulation, it provides the proper framework for [analyzing] § 13981. In *Lopez,* we held that the Gun-Free School Zones Act of 1990, which made it a federal crime to knowingly possess a firearm in a school zone, exceeded Congress' authority under the Commerce Clause. Several significant considerations contributed to our decision.

First, we observed that [the enactment] was "a criminal statute that by its terms has nothing to do with 'commerce' or any sort of economic enterprise, however broadly one might define those terms." [Brzonkala, the United States, and the dissenting Justices] downplay the role that the economic nature of the regulated activity plays in our Commerce Clause analysis. But a fair reading of *Lopez* shows that the noneconomic, criminal nature of the conduct at issue was central to our decision. *Lopez's* review of Commerce Clause case law demonstrates that where we have sustained federal regulation of intrastate activity based upon the activity's substantial effects on interstate commerce, the activity has been some sort of economic endeavor.

The second consideration that we found important in [*Lopez*] was that the statute contained "no express jurisdictional element which might limit its reach to a discrete set of firearm possessions that additionally have an explicit connection with or effect on interstate commerce." Third, we noted [in *Lopez*] that neither [the statute] "nor its legislative history contains express congressional findings regarding the effects upon interstate commerce of gun possession in a school zone."

Finally, our decision in *Lopez* rested in part on the fact that the link between gun possession and a substantial effect on interstate commerce was attenuated. The United States argued that the possession of guns may lead to violent crime, and that violent crime "can be expected to affect the functioning of the national economy in two ways. First, the costs of violent crime are substantial, and, through the mechanism of insurance, those costs are spread throughout the population. Second, violent crime reduces the willingness of individuals to travel to areas within the country that are perceived to be unsafe." We rejected [the] "costs of crime" . . . argument because [it] would permit Congress to "regulate not only all violent crime, but all activities that might lead to violent crime, regardless of how tenuously they relate to interstate commerce."

With these principles . . . as reference points, the proper resolution of the present case is clear. Gender-motivated crimes of violence are not, in any sense of the phrase, economic activity. While we need not adopt a categorical rule against aggregating the effects of any noneconomic activity in order to decide these cases, thus far in our Nation's history our cases have upheld Commerce Clause regulation of intrastate activity only where that activity is economic in nature.

Like the Gun-Free School Zones Act at issue in *Lopez,* § 13981 contains no jurisdictional element establishing that the federal cause of action is in pursuance of Congress' power to regulate interstate commerce. [Congress did not, for instance, provide that the statute would be violated by one who *crossed state lines* to commit an act of gender-motivated violence.] Although *Lopez* makes clear that such a jurisdictional element would lend support to the argument that § 13981 is sufficiently tied to interstate commerce, Congress elected to cast § 13981's remedy over a wider, and more purely intrastate, body of violent crime.

In contrast with the lack of congressional findings that we faced in *Lopez,* § 13981 *is* supported by numerous findings regarding the serious impact that gender-motivated violence has on victims and their families. But the existence of congressional findings is not sufficient, by itself, to sustain the constitutionality of Commerce Clause legislation.

In these cases, Congress' findings are substantially weakened by the fact that they rely so heavily on a method of reasoning that we have already rejected as unworkable if we are to maintain the Constitution's enumeration of powers. Congress found that gender-motivated violence affects interstate commerce

> "by deterring potential victims from traveling interstate, from engaging in employment in interstate business, and from transacting with business, and in places involved in interstate commerce; . . . by diminishing national productivity, increasing medical and other costs, and decreasing the supply of and the demand for interstate products."

Given these findings and [the] arguments [made by the petitioners, Brzonkala and the United States], the concern we expressed in *Lopez*—that Congress might use the Commerce Clause to completely obliterate the Constitution's distinction between national and local authority—seems well founded. The reasoning that petitioners advance seeks to follow the but-for causal chain from the initial occurrence of violent crime (the suppression of which has always been the prime object of the States' police power) to every attenuated effect upon interstate commerce. If accepted, petitioners' reasoning would allow Congress to regulate any crime as long as the nationwide, aggregated impact of that crime has substantial effects on employment, production, transit, or consumption. Indeed, if Congress may regulate gender-motivated violence, it would be able to regulate murder or any other type of violence since gender-motivated violence, as a subset of all violent crime, is certain to have lesser economic impacts than the larger class of which it is a part.

We accordingly reject the argument that Congress may regulate noneconomic, violent criminal conduct based solely on that conduct's aggregate effect on interstate commerce. The Constitution requires a distinction between what is truly national and what is truly local. In recognizing this fact we preserve one of the few principles that has been consistent since the Clause was adopted. The regulation and punishment of intrastate violence that is not directed at the instrumentalities, channels, or goods involved in interstate commerce has always been the province of the States. Indeed, we can think of no better example of the police power, which the Founders . . . reposed in the States, than the suppression of violent crime and vindication of its victims.

Brzonkala's complaint alleges that she was the victim of a brutal assault. But Congress' effort in § 13981 to provide a federal civil remedy [cannot] be sustained under the Commerce Clause. If the allegations here are true, no civilized system of justice could fail to provide her a remedy for the conduct of [the wrongdoers]. But under our federal system that remedy must be provided by the Commonwealth of Virginia, and not by the United States.

Judgment of Court of Appeals affirmed.

The Taxing Power Article I, section 8 of the Constitution states that "The Congress shall have Power To lay and collect Taxes, Duties, Imposts and Excises." The main purpose of this *taxing power* is to provide a means of raising revenue for the federal government. The taxing power, however, may also serve as a regulatory device. Because the power to tax is the power to destroy, Congress may choose, for instance, to regulate a disfavored activity by imposing a heavy tax on it. Although some past regulatory taxes were struck down, today the reach of the taxing power is seen as very broad. Sometimes it is said that a regulatory tax is constitutional if its purpose could be furthered by another power belonging to Congress. The broad scope of the commerce power may therefore mean that the taxing power has few limits.

The Spending Power If taxing power regulation uses a federal club, congressional *spending power* reg-ulation employs a federal carrot. Article I, section 8 also gives Congress a broad ability to spend for the general welfare. By basing the receipt of federal money on the performance of certain conditions, Congress can use the spending power to advance specific regulatory ends. Conditional federal grants to the states for instance, are common today.

Over the past 60 years, congressional spending power regulation routinely has been upheld. There are limits, however, on its use. First, an exercise of the spending power must serve *general* public purposes rather than particular interests. Second, when Congress conditions the receipt of federal money on certain conditions, it must do so clearly. Third, the condition must be reasonably related to the purpose underlying the federal expenditure. This means, for instance, Congress probably could not condition a state's receipt of federal highway money on the state's adoption of a one-house legislature.

Independent Checks on the Federal Government and the States

Even if a regulation is within Congress's enumerated powers or a state's police power, it still is unconstitutional if it collides with one of the Constitution's *independent checks*. This section discusses three checks that limit both federal and state regulation of the economy: freedom of speech; due process; and equal protection. Before discussing these guarantees, however, we must consider three foundational matters.

Incorporation

The Fifth Amendment prevents the federal government from depriving "any person of life, liberty, or property, without due process of law." The Fourteenth Amendment creates the same prohibition with regard to the states. The literal language of the First Amendment, however, restricts only federal government action. Moreover, the Fourteenth Amendment says that no *state* shall "deny to any person . . . the equal protection of the laws."

Thus, although due process clearly applies to both the federal government and the states, the First Amendment seems to apply only to the federal government and the Equal Protection Clause only to the states. The First Amendment's free speech guarantee, however, has been included within the "liberty" protected by Fourteenth Amendment due process as a result of Supreme Court decisions. The free speech guarantee, therefore, restricts state governments as well as the federal government. This is an example of the process of *incorporation* by which almost all Bill of Rights provisions now apply to the states. The Fourteenth Amendment's equal protection guarantee, on the other hand, has been made applicable to federal government action through incorporation of it within the Fifth Amendment's Due Process Clause.

Government Action

People often talk as if the Constitution protects them against anyone who might threaten their rights. However, most of the Constitution's individual rights provisions block only the actions of *government* bodies, state and federal.[1] Private

---

[1] However, the Thirteenth Amendment, which bans slavery and involuntary servitude throughout the United States, does not have a state action requirement. Some state constitutions, moreover, have individual rights provisions that lack a state action requirement.

behavior that denies individual rights, while perhaps forbidden by statute, is very seldom a constitutional matter. This **government action** or **state action** requirement forces courts to distinguish between governmental behavior and private behavior. Judicial approaches to this problem have varied over time.

Before World War II, only formal arms of government such as legislatures, administrative agencies, municipalities, courts, prosecutors, and state universities were deemed state actors. After the war, however, the scope of government action increased considerably, with various sorts of traditionally private behavior being subjected to individual rights limitations. The Supreme Court, in *Marsh* v. *Alabama* (1946), treated a privately owned company town's restriction of free expression as government action under the *public function* theory because the town was nearly identical to a regular municipality in most respects. In *Shelley* v. *Kraemer* (1948), the Court held that when state courts enforced certain white homeowners' private agreements not to sell their homes to blacks, there was state action that violated the Equal Protection Clause. Later, in *Burton* v. *Wilmington Parking Authority* (1961), the Court concluded that racial discrimination by a privately owned restaurant located in a state-owned and state-operated parking garage was unconstitutional state action, in part because the garage and the restaurant were intertwined in a mutually beneficial "symbiotic" relationship. Among the other factors leading courts to find state action during the 1960s and 1970s were extensive government regulation of private activity and government financial aid to a private actor.

The Court, however, severely restricted the reach of state action during the 1970s and 1980s. Since then, private behavior generally has not been held to constitute state action unless a regular unit of government is directly *responsible* for the challenged private behavior because it has coerced or encouraged such behavior. The public function doctrine, moreover, has been limited to situations in which a private entity exercises powers that have *traditionally* been *exclusively* reserved to the state; private police protection is a possible example. In addition, government regulation and government funding have become somewhat less important factors in state action determinations. Despite all these changes, however, state action doctrine has not returned to its narrow pre–World War II definition. Some uncertainty remains in this area, as brief discussion of two cases will demonstrate.

Consider, first, the Supreme Court's decision in *Rendell-Baker* v. *Cohn,* (1982). There, the Court rejected various constitutional challenges to the firing of teachers and counselors at a private school for maladjusted high school students because no state action was present. Although the school was extensively regulated by the state, that did not matter because no state regulation compelled or even influenced the challenged firings. The school depended heavily on state funding, but that fact was not sufficient for state action either. The Court also rejected a "symbiosis" argument with little discussion. Finally, it found the public function doctrine inapplicable because the education of maladjusted high school students, though public in nature, is not *exclusively* a state function.

In a 2001 decision, however, a six-justice majority of the Supreme Court concluded that the Tennessee Secondary School Athletic Association (TSSAA) was a state actor for purposes of the Constitution's Fourteenth Amendment when it enforced an association rule against a member school. The TSSAA, a privately organized, not-for-profit entity, regulated interscholastic sports competition among public and private high schools in Tennessee. Although no school was required to join the TSSAA, nearly all public schools and many private schools had done so. All members of the association's governing bodies were school officials, most of whom were from public schools. Public school systems provided considerable financial support for the TSSAA, which worked closely with the state board of education, a governmental body. For many years, the TSSAA was designated in a state board of education rule as the regulator of athletics in the state's public schools. Stressing the "pervasive entwinement of public institutions and public officials in [the TSSAA's] composition and workings" and the lack of any "substantial reason to claim unfairness in applying constitutional standards to it," the Supreme Court held in *Brentwood Academy* v. *Tennessee Secondary School Athletic Association* that the TSSAA was a government actor.

Brentwood Academy's "entwinement" rationale appears to provide an additional way in which state action can be found, though the Court emphasized that each decision on the state action issue is highly fact-specific. It is too early to tell whether *Brentwood Academy* will spearhead a movement toward more expansive applications of government action principles.

Means-Ends Tests

Throughout this chapter, you will see tests of constitutionality that may seem strange at first glance. One example is the test for determining whether laws that discriminate on the basis of sex violate equal protection. This test says that to be constitutional, such laws must be substantially related to the achievement of an important government purpose. The Equal Protection Clause does not contain such language. It simply says that "No State shall . . . deny to any person . . . the equal protection of the laws." What is going on here?

The sex discrimination test just stated is a **means-ends test** developed by the Supreme Court. Such tests are judicially created because no constitutional right is absolute, and because judges therefore must weigh individual rights against the social purposes served by laws that restrict those rights. In other words, means-ends tests determine how courts strike the balance between individual rights and the social needs that may justify their suppression. The "ends" component of a means-ends test specifies how *significant* a social purpose must be in order to justify the restriction of a right. The "means" component states how *effectively* the challenged law must promote that purpose in order to be constitutional. In the sex discrimination test, for example, the challenged law must serve an "important" government purpose (the significance of the end) and must be "substantially" related to the achievement of that purpose (the effectiveness of the means).

Some constitutional rights are deemed more important than others. Accordingly, courts use tougher tests of constitutionality in certain cases and more lenient tests in other situations. Sometimes these tests are lengthy and complicated. Throughout the chapter, therefore, we will simplify by referring to three general kinds of means-ends tests:

1. *The rational basis test.* This is a very relaxed test of constitutionality that challenged laws usually pass with ease. A typical formulation of the rational basis test might say that government action need only have a *reasonable* relation to the achievement of a *legitimate* government purpose to be constitutional.

2. *Intermediate scrutiny.* This comes in many forms; the sex discrimination test discussed above is an example.

3. *Full strict scrutiny.* Here, the court might say that the challenged law must be *necessary* to the fulfillment of a *compelling* government purpose. Government action that is subjected to this rigorous test of constitutionality is almost always struck down.

Business and the First Amendment

The First Amendment provides that "Congress shall make no law . . . abridging the freedom of speech." Despite its absolute language ("*no* law"), the First Amendment does not prohibit every law that restricts speech. As

Justice Oliver Wendell Holmes famously remarked, the First Amendment does not protect someone who falsely shouts "Fire!" in a crowded theater. Although the First Amendment's free speech guarantee is not absolute, government action restricting the content of speech usually receives very strict judicial scrutiny. One justification for this high level of protection is the "marketplace" rationale, under which the free competition of ideas is seen as the surest means of attaining truth. The marketplace of ideas operates most effectively, according to this rationale, when restrictions on speech are kept to a minimum and all viewpoints can be considered.

During recent decades, the First Amendment has been applied to a wide variety of government restrictions on the expression of individuals and organizations, including corporations. This chapter does not attempt a comprehensive discussion of the many applications of the freedom of speech guarantee. Instead, it explores basic First Amendment concepts before turning to an examination of the free speech rights of corporations.

Political and Other Noncommercial Speech

Political speech—expression that deals in some fashion with government, government issues or policies, public officials, or political candidates—is often described as being at the "core" of the First Amendment. Various Supreme Court decisions have held, however, that the freedom of speech guarantee applies not only to political speech but also to noncommercial expression that does not have a political content or flavor. According to these decisions, the First Amendment protects speech of a literary or artistic nature, speech dealing with scientific, economic, educational, and ethical issues, and expression on many other matters of public interest or concern. Government attempts to restrict the content of politi-

CYBERLAW IN ACTION

The Children's Internet Protection Act (CIPA) denied federal funding to public libraries that failed or refused to use Internet filtering software to block material harmful to minors. Although filtering software blocks much of the material it targets, it does not block all of it. It also blocks some materials similar to items many libraries carry in hard copy. A group of libraries, library associations, and Web publishers brought suit against the United States in a federal district court, attacking CIPA on First Amendment grounds. In accordance with a CIPA provision, a special three-judge court was convened to hear the case. The plaintiffs argued that the statute's conditional requirement to use Internet filtering software would lead to content-based restrictions on patrons' access to constitutionally protected materials and thus violated the First Amendment.

The court agreed with the plaintiffs that the content restrictions contemplated by CIPA implicated First Amendment interests sufficiently to trigger the form of analysis known as "strict scrutiny." Speech restrictions under strict scrutiny are permissible only if they are narrowly tailored to fulfill a compelling state interest and no alternatives restricting less speech can fulfill that interest. The court recognized that in enacting CIPA, Congress sought to further the compelling state interests of preventing the dissemination of obscenity and child pornography and protecting minors from material harmful to them.

Nevertheless, the court concluded that in view of the inherent nature of Internet filtering systems, it was impossible for a library to comply with CIPA without restricting large amounts of non-obscene, non-pornographic material to which library patrons should have access under the First Amendment. The speech restrictions associated with CIPA's filtering requirement swept too broadly—meaning that the statute was not narrowly tailored.

Continuing its analysis, the court noted existence of effective alternatives that would restrict less speech. Libraries, the court observed, could have patrons agree to Internet use policies so that they know they should not use library terminals to access illegal content (e.g., obscene material). Library staff could later scan Internet use logs and revoke policy violators' terminal access. Minors could be protected from materials harmful to them if they were allowed to use only those terminals in constant view of library staff. Alternatively, minors' Internet access could be filtered at the request of parents. To protect patrons—especially minors—from viewing offensive materials on other patrons' screens, libraries could install "privacy screens" that make viewing at an angle impossible. The court found all these alternatives to be less restrictive of speech, viable, and, in all likelihood, effective.

Because the court held that CIPA's filtering requirement violated the First Amendment, its May 2002 opinion enjoined the government from withholding the relevant federal funding from libraries that did not utilize the filtering contemplated by CIPA.

cal or other noncommercial speech normally receive full strict scrutiny when challenged in court. Unless the government is able to meet the exceedingly difficult burden of proving that the speech restriction is *necessary* to the fulfillment of a *compelling government purpose,* a First Amendment violation will be found. Because government restrictions on political or other noncommercial speech trigger the full strict scrutiny test, such speech is referred to as carrying "full" First Amendment protection.

Do *corporations,* however, have the same First Amendment rights that individual human beings possess? The Supreme Court has consistently provided a "yes" answer to this question. Therefore, if a corporation engages in political or other noncommercial expression, it is entitled to full First Amendment protection, just as an individual would be if he or she engaged in such speech. This does not mean, however, that all speech of a corporation is fully protected. Some corporate speech is classified as **commercial speech,** a category of expression to be examined shortly. As will be seen, commercial speech receives First Amendment protection but not the full variety extended to political or noncommercial speech. The mere fact, however, that a profit motive underlies speech does not make the speech commercial in nature. Books, movies, television programs, musical works, works of visual art, and newspaper, magazine, and journal articles are normally classified as noncommercial speech—and are thus fully protected—despite the typical existence of an underlying profit motive. Their informational, educational, artistic, or entertainment components are thought to outweigh, for First Amendment purposes, the profit motive.

Commercial Speech   The exact boundaries of the commercial speech category are not certain, though the Supreme Court has usually defined commercial speech as speech that proposes a commercial transaction. As a result, most cases on the subject involve advertisements for the sale of products or services or for the promotion of a business. In 1942, the Supreme Court held that commercial speech fell outside the First Amendment's protective umbrella. The Court reversed its position, however, during the 1970s. It reasoned that informed consumer choice would be furthered by the removal of barriers to the flow of commercial information in which consumers would find an interest. Since the mid-1970s, commercial speech has received an intermediate level of First Amendment protection if it deals with a lawful activity and is nonmisleading. Commercial speech receives no protection, however, if it misleads or seeks

to promote an illegal activity. As a result, there is no First Amendment obstacle to federal or state regulation of deceptive commercial advertising. (Political or other noncommercial speech, on the other hand, generally receives—with very few exceptions—full First Amendment protection even if it misleads or deals with unlawful matters.)

Because nonmisleading commercial speech about a lawful activity receives intermediate protection, the government has greater ability to regulate such speech without violating the First Amendment than when the government seeks to regulate fully protected political or other noncommercial speech. The Supreme Court developed, more than 20 years ago, a still-controlling test that amounts to intermediate scrutiny. Under this test, a government restriction on protected commercial speech does not violate the First Amendment if the government proves each of these elements: that a *substantial government interest* underlies the restriction; that the restriction *directly advances* the underlying interest; and that the restriction is *no more extensive than necessary* to further the interest. It usually is not difficult for the government to prove that a substantial interest supports the commercial speech restriction. Almost any asserted interest connected with the promotion of public health, safety, or welfare will suffice. The government is likely to encounter more difficulty, however, in proving that the restriction at issue directly advances the underlying interest without being more extensive than necessary—the elements that address the "fit" between the restriction and the underlying interest. If the government fails to prove any element of the test, the restriction violates the First Amendment.

Although the same test has been used in evaluating commercial speech restrictions for more than two decades, the Supreme Court has varied the intensity with which it has applied the test. From the mid-1980s until 1995, the Court sometimes applied the test loosely and in a manner favorable to the government. The Court has applied the test—especially the "fit" elements—more strictly since 1995, however. Two key effects have occurred: (1) the government has found it more difficult to justify restrictions on commercial speech; and (2) the gap between the intermediate protection for commercial speech and the full protection for political and other noncommercial speech has effectively become smaller than it was 10 to 15 years ago. Although the Court has hinted in recent cases that it might consider formal changes in commercial speech doctrine (so as to enhance First Amendment protection for commercial speech), it had not made formal doctrinal changes as of the time this book went to press in 2002.

The following two cases, both of which were decided in 2002, illustrate the First Amendment concepts and issues discussed above. In *Thompson* v. *Western States Medical Center,* a commercial speech decision, the Supreme Court applies the intermediate scrutiny test to a federal statute that restricted pharmacists from advertising compounded drugs. The case illustrates the significant rigor with which the Court has applied the test during the past several years. In *Kasky* v. *Nike, Inc.,* the Supreme Court of California addresses a classification question: whether Nike engaged in fully protected noncommercial speech or, instead, commercial speech, when it made allegedly misleading statements in the course of a public relations campaign designed to refute claims about its overseas labor practices.

Thompson v. Western States Medical Center   *122 S. Ct. 1497 (U.S. Sup. Ct. 2002)*

The Food and Drug Administration Modernization Act of 1997 (FDAMA) exempts "compounded drugs" from the rigorous Food and Drug Administration approval process that new drugs must ordinarily undergo. Compounded drugs are "cocktails" whose ingredients are combined, mixed, or altered by pharmacists or doctors to accommodate patients with individualized needs. Providers of compounded drugs, however, are exempted from the approval process only if they adhere to certain approval conditions set by the FDAMA. These conditions require, among other things, that the drugs be "unsolicited" and that the providers "not advertise or promote the compounding of any particular drug, class of drug, or type of drug." A group of pharmacies specializing in compounded drugs filed a complaint in a federal district court against the U.S. Secretary of Health and Human Services and the commissioner of the FDA, alleging that the FDAMA's advertising restrictions violated the First Amendment. The district court granted the pharmacies' motion for summary judgment, and, upon the government's appeal, the U.S. Court of Appeals for the Ninth Circuit affirmed. The government appealed to the U.S. Supreme Court, which granted certiorari.

O'Connor, Justice In *Virginia Board of Pharmacy* v. *Virginia Citizens Consumer Council, Inc.*(1976), the first case in which we explicitly held that commercial speech receives First Amendment protection, we explained the reasons for this protection: "It is a matter of public interest that [economic] decisions, in the aggregate, be intelligent and well-informed. To this end, the free flow of commercial information is indispensable." Indeed, we recognized that a "particular consumer's interest in the free flow of commercial information . . . may be as keen, if not keener by far, than his interest in the day's most urgent political debate."

Although commercial speech is protected by the First Amendment, not all regulation of such speech is unconstitutional. In *Central Hudson Gas & Electric Corp.* v. *Public Service Commission* (1980), we articulated a test for determining whether a particular commercial speech regulation is constitutionally permissible. Under that test we ask as a threshold matter whether the commercial speech concerns unlawful activity or is misleading. If so, then the speech is not protected by the First Amendment. If the speech concerns lawful activity and is not misleading, however, we next ask "whether the asserted governmental interest is substantial." If it is, then we "determine whether the regulation directly advances the governmental interest asserted," and,

finally, "whether it is not more extensive than is necessary to serve that interest." Each of these latter three inquiries must be answered in the affirmative for the regulation to be found constitutional.

The Government . . . does not argue that the prohibited advertisements would be about unlawful activity or would be misleading. Instead, the Government argues that the FDAMA satisfies the remaining three prongs of the *Central Hudson* test.

The Government asserts [in its brief] that [two] substantial interests underlie the FDAMA. The first is an interest in "preserving the effectiveness and integrity of the [FDA's] new drug approval process and the protection of the public health that it provides." The second is an interest in "preserving the availability of compounded drugs for those individual patients who, for particularized medical reasons, cannot use commercially available products that have been approved by the FDA."

Preserving the effectiveness and integrity of the [FDA's] new drug approval process is clearly an important governmental interest, and the Government has every reason to want as many drugs as possible to be subject to that approval process. The Government also has an important interest, however, in permitting the continuation of the practice of compounding so that patients with particular needs may obtain medications suited to those needs. And it would not make sense to require compounded drugs created to meet the unique needs of individual patients to undergo the testing required for the new drug approval process. Pharmacists do not make enough money from small-scale compounding to make safety and efficacy testing of their compounded drugs economically feasible, so requiring such testing would force pharmacists to stop providing compounded drugs. Given this, the Government needs to be able to draw a line [that distinguishes] compounded drugs produced on such a small scale that they could not undergo safety and efficacy testing from drugs produced and sold on a large enough scale that they could undergo such testing.

The Government argues that the FDAMA's speech-related provisions provide just such a line, i.e., that, in the terms of *Central Hudson,* they "directly advance the governmental interests asserted." Those provisions use advertising as the trigger for requiring FDA approval—essentially, as long as pharmacists do not advertise particular compounded drugs, they may sell compounded drugs without first undergoing safety and efficacy testing and obtaining FDA approval. If they advertise their compounded drugs, however, FDA approval is required. The Government explains that traditional (or, in its view, desirable) compounding responds to a physician's prescription and an individual patient's particular medical situation, and that . . . advertising is [neither necessary to nor] typically associated with compounding for particular individuals. In contrast it is typically associated, the Government claims, with large-scale production of a drug for a substantial market.

The Government seems to believe that without advertising it would not be possible to market a drug on a large enough scale to make safety and efficacy testing economically feasible. Assuming it is true that drugs cannot be marketed on a large scale without advertising, the FDAMA's prohibition on advertising compounded drugs might indeed "directly advance" the Government's interests. Even assuming that it does, however, the Government has failed to demonstrate that the speech restrictions are "not more extensive than is necessary to serve [those] interests." In previous cases addressing this final prong of the *Central Hudson* test, we have made clear that if the Government could achieve its interests in a manner that does not restrict speech, or that restricts less speech, the Government must do so.

Several non-speech-related means of drawing a line between compounding and large-scale manufacturing might be possible here. First, it seems that the Government could use the very factors the FDA relied on to distinguish compounding from manufacturing in its Compliance Policy Guide [, which preceded enactment of the FDAMA]. For example, the Government could ban the use of "commercial scale manufacturing or testing equipment for compounding drug products." It could prohibit pharmacists from compounding more drugs in anticipation of receiving prescriptions than in response to prescriptions already received. It could prohibit pharmacists from "offering compounded drugs at wholesale to other state licensed persons or commercial entities for resale." Alternately, it could limit the amount of compounded drugs . . . that a given pharmacist or pharmacy sells out of state. Another possibility . . . would be capping the amount of any particular compounded drug . . . that a pharmacist or pharmacy may make or sell in a given period of time. It might even be sufficient to rely solely on the non-speech-related provisions of the FDAMA, such as the requirement that compounding only be conducted in response to a prescription or a history of receiving a prescription.

The Government has not offered any reason why these possibilities, alone or in combination, would be insufficient to prevent compounding from occurring on such a scale as to undermine the new drug approval process. Indeed, there is no hint that the Government even considered these or any other alternatives. Nowhere in the legislative history of the FDAMA or petitioners' briefs is there any explanation of why the Government believed forbidding advertising was a necessary, as opposed to merely convenient, means of achieving its interests. If the First Amendment means anything, it means that regulating speech must be a last—not first—resort. Yet here it seems to have been the first strategy the Government thought to try.

Even if the Government had argued that the FDAMA's speech-related restrictions were motivated by a fear that advertising compounded drugs would put people who do not need such drugs at risk by causing them to convince their doctors to prescribe the drugs anyway, that fear would fail to justify the restrictions. [T]his concern amounts to a fear that people would make bad decisions if given truthful information about compounded drugs. We have previously rejected the notion that the Government has an interest in preventing the dissemination of truthful commercial information in order to prevent members of the public from making bad decisions with the information.

Judgment of the Court of Appeals affirmed.

Kasky v. Nike, Inc.   45 P.3d 243 (Cal. Sup. Ct. 2002)

Nike, Inc. mounted a public relations campaign in order to refute news media allegations that its labor practices overseas were unfair and unlawful. This campaign involved the use of press releases, letters to newspapers, a letter to university presidents and athletic directors, and full-page advertisements in leading newspapers. Relying on California statutes designed to curb false and misleading advertising and other forms of unfair competition, California resident Mark Kasky filed suit in a California court on behalf of the general public of the state. Kasky contended that Nike had made false statements in its campaign and that the court should therefore grant the legal relief contemplated by the California statutes. Nike demurred on the ground, among others, that the First Amendment barred Kasky's action. The court, holding Nike's campaign to be fully protected under the First Amendment as noncommercial speech, sustained Nike's demurrer and dismissed Kasky's complaint. Kasky appealed, and the California Court of Appeal affirmed. The Supreme Court of California granted Kasky's petition for review.

Kennard, Justice   The U.S. Supreme Court has not adopted an all-purpose test to distinguish commercial from noncommercial speech under the First Amendment, nor do we propose to do so here. A close reading of the high court's commercial speech decisions suggests, however, that it is possible to formulate a limited-purpose test. We conclude, therefore, that *when a court must decide whether particular speech may be subjected to laws aimed at preventing false advertising or other forms of commercial deception,* categorizing a particular statement as commercial or noncommercial speech requires consideration of three elements: the speaker, the intended audience, and the content of the message.

In typical commercial speech cases, the *speaker* is likely to be someone engaged in commerce—that is, generally, the production, distribution, or sale of goods or services—or someone acting on behalf of a person so engaged. [T]he *intended audience* is likely to be actual or potential buyers or customers of the speaker's goods or services, or persons acting for actual or potential buyers or customers, or persons (such as reporters or reviewers) likely to repeat the message to or otherwise influence actual or potential buyers or customers. Considering the identity of both the speaker and the target audience is consistent with, and implicit in, the U.S. Supreme Court's commercial speech decisions. The Court has frequently spoken of commercial speech as speech proposing a commercial transaction, thus implying that commercial speech typically is communication between persons who engage in such transactions.

In addition, the factual content of the message should be commercial in character. In the context of regulation of false or misleading advertising, this typically means that the speech consists of representations of fact about the business operations, products, or services of the speaker (or the individual or company that the speaker represents), made for the purpose of promoting sales of, or other commercial transactions in, the speaker's products or services. This is consistent with . . . the Supreme Court's commercial speech decisions

[, including *Bolger* v. *Youngs Drug Products Corp.,* 463 U.S. 60 (1983), in which the Court identified "product references" as a usual characteristic of commercial speech]. By "product references," we do not understand the Court to mean only statements about the price, qualities, or availability of individual items offered for sale. Rather, we understand "product references" to include also, for example, statements about the manner in which the products are manufactured, distributed, or sold, about repair or warranty services that the seller provides to purchasers of the product, or about the identity or qualifications of persons who manufacture, distribute, sell, service, or endorse the product. Similarly, references to services would include not only statements about the price, availability, and quality of the services themselves, but also, for example, statements about the education, experience, and qualifications of the persons providing or endorsing the services. This broad definition of "product references" is necessary, we think, to adequately categorize statements made in the context of a modern, sophisticated public relations campaign intended to increase sales and profits by enhancing the image of a product or of its manufacturer or seller.

Our understanding of the content element of commercial speech is also consistent with the reasons that the Court has given for denying First Amendment protection to false or misleading commercial speech. The Court stated [, in *Virginia State Board of Pharmacy* v. *Virginia Citizens Consumer Council, Inc.,* 425 U.S. 748 (1976),] that false or misleading commercial speech may be prohibited because the truth of commercial speech is "more easily verifiable by its disseminator" and because commercial speech, being motivated by the desire for economic profit, is less likely than noncommercial speech to be chilled by proper regulation.

Apart from this consideration of the identities of the speaker and the audience, and the contents of the speech, we find nothing in the U. S. Supreme Court's commercial speech decisions that is essential to a determination that particular speech is commercial in character. Although in *Bolger* the Court noted that the [commercial] speech at issue there was in a traditional advertising format, the court cautioned that it was not holding that this factor would always be necessary to the characterization of speech as commercial. Advertising format is by no means essential to characterization as commercial speech.

Here, the first element—a commercial speaker—is satisfied because the speakers—Nike and its officers and directors—are engaged in commerce. The second element—an intended commercial audience—is also satisfied. Nike's letters to university presidents and directors of athletic departments were addressed directly to actual and potential purchasers of Nike's products, because college and university athletic departments are major purchasers of athletic shoes and apparel. [Kasky] has alleged that Nike's press releases and letters to newspaper editors, although addressed to the public generally, were also intended to reach and influence actual and potential purchasers of Nike's products. Specifically, plaintiff has alleged that Nike made these statements about its labor policies and practices "to maintain and/or increase its sales and profits." To support this allegation, [he] has included as an exhibit a letter to a newspaper editor, written by Nike's director of communications, referring to Nike's labor policies practices and stating that "consumers are savvy and want to know they support companies with good products and practices" and that "during the shopping season, we encourage shoppers to remember that Nike is the industry's leader in improving factory conditions."

The third element—representations of fact of a commercial nature—is also present. In describing its own labor policies, and the practices and working conditions in factories where its products are made, Nike was making factual representations about its own business operations. In speaking to consumers about working conditions and labor practices in the factories where its products are made, Nike addressed matters within its own knowledge. The wages paid to the factories' employees, the hours they work, the way they are treated, and whether the environmental conditions under which they work violate local health and safety laws, are all matters likely to be within the personal knowledge of Nike executives, employees, or subcontractors. Thus, Nike was in a position to readily verify the truth of any factual assertions it made on these topics.

In speaking to consumers about working conditions in the factories where its products are made, Nike engaged in speech that is particularly hardy or durable. Because Nike's purpose in making these statements, at least as alleged in [Kasky's] complaint, was to maintain its sales and profits, regulation aimed at preventing false and actually or inher-

ently misleading speech is unlikely to deter Nike from speaking truthfully or at all about the conditions in its factories. To the extent that application of these laws may make Nike more cautious, and cause it to make greater efforts to verify the truth of its statements, these laws will serve the purpose of commercial speech protection by [, as noted in *Virginia Board of Pharmacy,*] "insuring that the stream of commercial information flows cleanly as well as freely."

Because Nike was acting as a commercial speaker, because its intended audience was primarily the buyers of its products, and because the statements consisted of factual representations about its own business operations, we conclude that the statements were commercial speech for purposes of applying state laws designed to prevent false advertising and other forms of commercial deception. Nike argues [, however,] that its allegedly false and misleading statements were not commercial speech because they were part of "an international media debate on issues of intense public interest." This argument falsely assumes that speech cannot properly be categorized as commercial speech if it relates to a matter of significant public interest or controversy. As the U.S. Supreme Court has [made clear], commercial speech commonly concerns matters of intense public and private interest. The individual consumer's interest in the price, availability, and characteristics of products and services "may be as keen, if not keener by far, than his interest in the day's most urgent political debate" (quoting *Virginia Board of Pharmacy*).

Nike's speech is not removed from the category of commercial speech because it is intermingled with noncommercial speech. To the extent Nike's press releases and letters discuss policy questions such as the degree to which domestic companies should be responsible for working conditions in factories located in other countries, or what standards domestic companies ought to observe in such factories, or the merits and effects of economic "globalization" generally, Nike's statements are noncommercial speech. Any content-based regulation of these noncommercial messages would be subject to the strict scrutiny test for fully protected speech. But Nike may not "immunize false or misleading product information from government regulation simply by including references to public issues" (quoting *Bolger*). Here, the alleged false and misleading statements all relate to the commercial portions of the speech in question—the description of actual conditions and practices in factories that produce Nike's products—and thus the proposed regulations reach only that commercial portion.

We also reject Nike's argument that regulating its speech to suppress false and misleading statements is impermissible because it would restrict or disfavor expression of one point of view (Nike's) and not the other point of view (that of the critics of Nike's labor practices). The argument is misdirected because the regulations in question do not suppress points of view but instead suppress false and misleading statements of fact. Moreover, differential treatment of speech about products and services based on the identity of the speaker is inherent in the commercial speech doctrine as articulated by the U.S. Supreme Court. A noncommercial speaker's statements criticizing a product are generally noncommercial speech, for which damages may be awarded only upon proof of both falsehood and actual malice. A commercial speaker's statements in praise or support of the same product, by comparison, are commercial speech that may be prohibited entirely to the extent the statements are either false or actually or inherently misleading.

We conclude, accordingly, that the trial court and the Court of Appeal erred in characterizing as noncommercial speech Nike's allegedly false and misleading statements about labor practices and working conditions in factories where Nike products are made. In concluding . . . that Nike's speech at issue here is commercial speech, we do not decide whether that speech was, as plaintiff has alleged, false or misleading. [That issue, as well as others, should be addressed on remand.]

Court of Appeal decision reversed and case remanded.

Due Process

The Fifth and Fourteenth Amendments require that the federal government and the states observe **due process** when they deprive a person of life, liberty, or property. Due process has both *procedural* and *substantive* meanings.

Procedural Due Process The traditional conception of due process, called **procedural due process,** establishes the *procedures* that government must follow when it takes life, liberty, or property. Although the requirements of procedural due process vary from situation to situation, their core idea is that one is entitled to adequate *notice* of the government action to be taken against him and to some sort of *fair trial or hearing* before that action can occur.

For purposes of procedural due process claims, *liberty* includes a very broad and poorly defined range of freedoms. It even includes certain interests in personal reputation. For example, the firing of a government employee may require some kind of due process hearing if it is publicized, the fired employee's reputation is sufficiently damaged, and her future employment opportunities are restricted. The Supreme Court has said that procedural due process *property* is not created by the Constitution but by existing rules and understandings that stem from an independent source such as state law. These rules and understandings must give a person a *legitimate claim of entitlement* to a benefit, not merely some need, desire, or expectation for it. This definition includes almost all of the usual forms of property, as well as utility service, disability benefits, welfare benefits, and a driver's license. It also includes the job rights of tenured public employees who can be discharged only for cause, but not the rights of untenured or probationary employees.

Substantive Due Process Procedural due process does not challenge rules of *substantive law*—the rules that set standards of behavior for organized social life. For example, imagine that State X makes adultery a crime and allows people to be convicted of adultery without a trial. Arguments that adultery should not be a crime go to the substance of the statute, whereas objections to the lack of a trial are procedural in nature.

Sometimes, the due process clauses have been used to attack the substance of government action. For our purposes, the most important example of this **substantive due process** occurred early in the 20th century, when courts struck down various kinds of social legislation as denying due process. They did so mainly by reading freedom of contract and other economic rights into the liberty and property protected by the Fifth and Fourteenth Amendments, and then interpreting "due process of law" to require that laws denying such rights be subjected to means-ends scrutiny. The best-known example is the Supreme Court's 1905 decision in *Lochner* v. *New York,* in which it struck down a state law setting maximum hours of work for bakery employees because the statute limited freedom of contract and did not directly advance the legitimate state goal of promoting worker health.

Since 1937, however, this "economic" form of substantive due process has been largely abandoned by the Supreme Court and has not amounted to a significant check on government regulation of economic matters. Substantive due process attacks on such regulations now trigger only a lenient type of rational basis review and thus have had little chance of success. During the 1970s and 1980s, however, substantive due process became increasingly important as a device for protecting *noneconomic* rights. The most important example is the constitutional right of privacy, which consists of several rights that the Supreme Court regards as fundamental and as entitled to significant constitutional protection. The Court has declared that these include the rights to marry, have children and direct their education and upbringing, enjoy marital privacy, use contraception, and elect to have an abortion. Laws restricting these rights must be narrowly tailored to meet a compelling government purpose in order to avoid being declared unconstitutional.

Equal Protection

The Fourteenth Amendment's equal protection clause says that "[n]o State shall . . . deny to any person . . . the equal protection of the laws." Because the equal protection guarantee has been incorporated within Fifth Amendment due process, it also restricts the federal government. As currently interpreted, the equal protection guarantee potentially applies to all situations in which government *classifies* or *distinguishes* people. The law inevitably makes distinctions among people, benefiting or burdening some groups but not others. Equal protection doctrine, as developed by the Supreme Court, sets the standards such distinctions must meet in order to be constitutional.

The Basic Test   The basic equal protection standard is the *rational basis* test described earlier. This is the standard usually applied to social and economic regulations that are challenged as denying equal protection. As the following case indicates, this lenient test usually does not impede state and federal regulation of social and economic matters.

City of Dallas v. Stanglin	*490 U.S. 19 (U.S. Sup. Ct. 1989)*

The city of Dallas, Texas adopted an ordinance restricting admission to so-called "Class E" dance halls to persons between the ages of 14 and 18. However, it did not impose similar age limitations on most other establishments where teenagers might congregate—for example, skating rinks. Charles Stanglin, who in one building operated both a Class E dance hall and a roller-skating rink, sought an injunction against enforcement of the ordinance in a Texas trial court. One of his arguments was that the ordinance denied equal protection because its distinction between Class E dance halls and other establishments for teenagers was irrational. The Texas trial court upheld the ordinance, but a higher Texas court struck down its age restriction. The city appealed to the U.S. Supreme Court.

Rehnquist, Chief Justice   The Dallas ordinance implicates no suspect class. The question remaining is whether the classification survives rational basis scrutiny under the equal protection clause. The city has chosen to impose a rule that separates 14- to 18-year-olds from what may be the corrupting influences of older teenagers and young adults. An urban planner for the city testified: "Older kids can access drugs and alcohol, and they have more mature sexual attitudes, more liberal sexual attitudes in general. . . . And we're concerned about mixing up these individuals with youngsters [who] have not fully matured."

Stanglin claims that this restriction has no real connection with the city's stated objectives. Except for saloons and teenage dance halls, he argues, teenagers and adults in Dallas may associate with each other, including at the skating area of his rink. We think Stanglin's arguments misapprehend the nature of rational basis scrutiny, which is the most relaxed and tolerant form of judicial scrutiny under the equal protection clause. If the classification has some reasonable basis, it does not offend the Constitution simply because the classification is not made with mathematical nicety or because in practice it results in some inequality.

The rational basis standard is true to the principle that the Fourteenth Amendment gives the federal courts no power to impose upon the states their views of what constitutes wise economic or social policy.

In the local economic sphere, it is only the invidious discrimination, the wholly arbitrary act, which cannot stand consistently with the Fourteenth Amendment. The city could reasonably conclude that teenagers might be susceptible to corrupting influences if permitted to frequent a dance hall with older persons [and that] limiting dance hall contacts between juveniles and adults would make less likely illicit or undesirable juvenile involvement with alcohol, illegal drugs, and promiscuous sex. It is true that the city allows teenagers and adults to roller-skate together, but skating involves less physical contact than dancing. The differences between the two activities may not be striking, but differentiations need not be striking in order to survive rational basis scrutiny.

Texas court decision striking down the age limitation reversed.

Stricter Scrutiny The rational basis test is the basic equal protection standard. Some classifications, however, receive tougher means-ends scrutiny. According to Supreme Court precedent, laws that discriminate regarding **fundamental rights** or **suspect classes** must undergo more rigorous review.

Although the list of rights regarded as "fundamental" for equal protection purposes is not completely clear, it includes certain criminal procedure protections as well as the rights to vote and engage in interstate travel. Laws creating unequal enjoyment of these rights receive full strict scrutiny. In 1969, for instance, the Supreme Court struck down the District of Columbia's one-year residency requirement for receiving welfare benefits because that requirement unequally and impermissibly restricted the right of interstate travel.

An equal protection claim involving the fundamental right to vote was addressed recently and in high-profile fashion, by the Supreme Court in *Bush* v. *Gore* (2000). The historic decision is summarized below.

Equal Protection and Related Issues in Bush v. Gore

An equal protection claim concerning the fundamental right to vote served as a key basis on which a five-justice majority of the U.S. Supreme Court ruled in favor of then-Governor George W. Bush in *Bush* v. *Gore,* 531 U.S. 98 (2000). This controversial decision halted presidential election recounts that had been ordered by the Florida Supreme Court and ended then-Vice President Albert Gore's judicial challenges of Florida's 2000 presidential election results. With those results showing Governor Bush as an extremely narrow winner of Florida's popular vote and with that state's crucial electoral votes therefore going his way, candidate Bush achieved the Electoral College margin he needed to become President Bush. For the first time in more than 100 years, the President-elect was a candidate who had lost the national popular vote but had won the controlling Electoral College tally.

The Majority Opinion

The justices in the *Bush* v. *Gore* majority (Chief Justice Rehnquist and Justices O'Connor, Scalia, Kennedy, and Thomas) concluded that the manual recount ordered by Florida's highest court was constitutionally infirm because it did not contain standards sufficiently specific to address the danger that different reviewers of ballots would apply different standards to determine whether a valid vote had been cast. Relying on a state statute, the Florida Supreme Court had adopted the "intent of the voter" as the standard to govern the recount. Nevertheless, the U.S. Supreme Court majority noted that without more specific content to guide recount workers' determinations of voter intent, there was too great a likelihood that the "intent of the voter" standard would be applied inconsistently.

For instance, in reviewing punch-card ballots concerning which a counting machine did not detect a vote because they had not been "punched in a clean complete way by the voter," one group of manual counters might treat a mere indentation on a ballot (i.e., a "dimpled chad") as a valid vote. Another group of counters, however, might find a valid vote only if there was at least a partial tearing of the indented area (i.e., a "hanging chad"). Other counters might apply varying standards regarding the amount of chad left hanging and the relationship to a probable intent to cast a vote. There was, accordingly, a significant risk that the recount process would "value one person's vote over that of another." This risk was unacceptable under equal protection principles, the majority reasoned, given the fundamental nature of the right to vote and the strict scrutiny applied to government actions that discriminate with regard to exercise of the right. The majority concluded that the recount ordered by Florida's highest court failed to provide adequate "assurance that the rudimentary requirements of equal treatment [of voters] and fundamental fairness [to voters] are satisfied."

Rather than remand the case to the Florida courts for development of appropriately specific standards to govern the recount, the majority observed that there was no time for the formulation of such standards and the completion of a recount in accordance with them. Time was an insurmountable problem, the majority observed, because it was already December 12, 2000. The December 12 date of the Court's decision was also the date contemplated by a federal election law, 3 U.S.C. § 5. Section 5 provided that if selection of a state's presidential electors—a matter dependent on the outcome of the state's popular vote—was completed by December 12, the validity of the chosen electors would be conclusive and could not be challenged in January, when the electoral votes to be cast on December 18 would be opened and tallied. The December 12 "safe-harbor" date was one that Florida's legislature would have wanted to meet when it enacted the state's election laws and established that the state's electors would be persons pledged to the state's popular vote winner. The five justices in the majority therefore reasoned that any further recount-related activity could not—and should not—occur.

In closing their opinion, the five justices in the majority acknowledged the obvious significance of the decision and made comments seemingly designed to blunt criticism of the decision and of the Court:

None are more conscious of the vital limits on judicial authority than are the members of this Court, and none stand more in admiration of the Constitution's design to leave the selection of the President to the people . . . and to the political sphere. When contending parties invoke the process of the courts, however, it becomes our unsought responsibility to resolve the federal and constitutional issues the judicial system has been forced to confront.

The Dissenting Opinions

The four dissenters (Justices Stevens, Souter, Ginsburg, and Breyer) wrote separate opinions that spared little in their criticism of the Court's decision. Although Justices Souter and Breyer agreed with the majority's conclusion that the lack of specific standards to govern the determination of valid votes during the recount posed an equal protection problem, they strongly disagreed with the majority's termination of the recount. They would have remanded the case to the Florida courts for the determination of specific, uniform standards and would have allowed the recount to proceed under those standards. Justices Stevens and Ginsburg took the position that no substantial equal protection problem existed. Any possible danger that a given voter's vote would not be counted consistently with someones else's vote during the recount was no greater, they contended, than a statistically provable danger: that votes cast on punch-card ballots used in certain counties were at higher risk of not being detected by counting machines than votes cast on different sorts of ballots used in other counties. Assuming that the latter would not pose a serious equal protection concern, why, they reasoned, should the former?

All four dissenters agreed that the termination of the recount meant that thousands of punch-card ballots concerning which a counting machine did not detect a vote (because the chad had not been completely perforated and/or detached) would not be evaluated at all during a recount process, even though the voter would have intended to cast a vote. The dissenters contended that the "disenfranchisement" of those voters surely should have raised concerns at least as great as those on which the majority focused and should have counseled against termination of the recount if, indeed, the majority was concerned about safeguarding the fundamental right to vote.

Justices Stevens, Souter, Ginsburg, and Breyer also faulted the majority for giving distorted significance to the December 12 "deadline" contemplated by 3 U.S.C. § 5. As the dissenters pointed out, a state's failure to have its electors selected by December 12 (because the state's popular vote winner had not yet been determined) did not mean that the state would forfeit the ability to participate in the Electoral College process. Missing the December 12 "safe-harbor" date would only have meant that the state's later-identified electors would not have to be regarded as conclusively valid if a dispute arose concerning the counting of electoral votes in January 2001. If any such dispute arose, federal law called for it to be resolved by Congress, which would still be free to accept a state's supposed slate of electors even though the "safe-harbor" date of December 12 had been missed. The dissenters also noted that if a state failed to select its electors by December 12 but selected them by December 18, the electors could participate in the December 18 casting of electoral votes. Moreover, Justice Ginsburg observed, a federal statute provided that if a state did not participate in the December 18 casting of electoral votes and had not otherwise communicated its electoral votes by December 27, Congress was to request an immediate certified response from the state's secretary of state.

The dissenters' point was that December 12 was not a critical deadline, and that there was more time than the majority represented for Florida to complete the recount, determine a popular vote winner, select its electors, and register its electoral votes. The dissenters saw no reason for the Court's decision not to let that process run its course and produce whatever outcome it would yield.

Justice Stevens observed that "[a]lthough we may never know with complete certainty the identity of the winner of this year's Presidential election, the identity of the loser is perfectly clear. It is the Nation's confidence in the judge as an impartial guardian of the rule of law."

Justice Breyer issued a similar lament:

[I]n this highly politicized matter, the appearance of a split decision runs the risk of undermining the public's confidence in the Court itself. That confidence . . . has been built slowly over many years, some of which were marked by a Civil War and the tragedy of segregation. It is a vitally necessary ingredient of any successful effort to protect basic liberty and, indeed, the rule of law itself. [The Court's decision] risk[s] a self-inflicted wound—a wound that may harm not just the Court, but the Nation.

Certain "suspect" bases of classification also trigger more rigorous equal protection review. As of 2002, the **suspect classes** and the level of scrutiny they attract are as follows:

1. *Race and national origin.* Classifications disadvantaging racial or national minorities receive the most rigorous kind of strict scrutiny and are almost never constitutional. Still, the Supreme Court has sometimes upheld

ETHICS IN ACTION

As discussion in this chapter reveals, Supreme Court precedent establishes that when government action discriminates on the basis of race or sex, the action will receive heightened scrutiny from the court in an equal protection case. Sexual orientation, however, has not been treated by the Supreme Court as a classification basis that justifies heightened scrutiny. This means that the lenient rational basis review will be employed by a court deciding an equal protection case in which the government is alleged to have discriminated on the basis of sexual orientation. In a *legal* sense, then, the government has more latitude to regulate in ways that draw lines on the basis of persons' sexual preference than in ways that classify on the basis of persons' race or gender. Now view this set of issues from an *ethical* perspective. Should the government be any more free to take actions that discriminate against homosexuals—or, for that matter, against heterosexuals—than it is to take actions that discriminate on the basis of race or sex? As you consider this question, you may wish to examine Chapter 4's discussion of ethical theories and ethical decision making.

government-required affirmative action plans and what critics have called reverse racial discrimination—government action that benefits racial minorities and allegedly disadvantages whites. In 1989, however, a majority of the Court concluded that state action of this kind should receive the same full strict scrutiny as discrimination *against* racial or national minorities. Reversing a 1990 ruling, a 1995 Supreme Court decision held that this is true of federal government action as well as state action. These developments have curtailed certain government-created affirmative action programs but have not eliminated them.

2. *Alienage.* Classifications based on one's status as an alien also receive strict scrutiny of some kind, but this standard almost certainly is not as tough as the full strict scrutiny normally used in race discrimination cases. Under the "political function" exception, moreover, laws restricting aliens from employment in positions that are intimately related to democratic self-government only receive *rational basis* review. This exception has been read broadly to allow the upholding of laws that exclude aliens from being state troopers, public school teachers, and probation officers.

3. *Sex.* Although the Supreme Court has been hesitant to make a formal declaration that sex is a suspect class,

for nearly 30 years laws discriminating on the basis of gender have been subjected to a fairly rigorous form of *intermediate scrutiny.* As the Court said in 1996, such laws require an "exceedingly persuasive" justification. The usual test is that government action discriminating on the basis of sex must be *substantially* related to the furtherance of an *important* government purpose. Under this test, measures discriminating against women have almost always been struck down. The Supreme Court has said that laws disadvantaging men receive the same scrutiny as those disadvantaging women, but this has not prevented the Court from upholding men-only draft registration and a law making statutory rape a crime for men alone. In the *Nguyen* case, which follows shortly, the Supreme Court rejects an equal protection claim involving alleged sex discrimination.

4. *Illegitimacy.* Classifications based on one's illegitimate birth receive a form of *intermediate scrutiny* that probably is less strict than the scrutiny given gender-based classifications. Under this vague standard, the Court has struck down state laws discriminating against illegitimates in areas such as recovery for wrongful death, workers' compensation benefits, social security payments, inheritance, and child support.

Nguyen v. Immigration and Naturalization Service
533 U.S. 53 (U.S. Sup. Ct. 2001)

A federal statute, 8 U.S.C. § 1409, sets requirements for acquisition of U.S. citizenship by a child born outside the United States to unwed parents, only one of whom is a U.S. citizen. If the mother is the U.S. citizen, the child acquires citizenship at birth. Section 1409(a) states that if the father is the citizen parent, the child requires citizenship only if, before the child reaches the age of 18, (1) the child is legitimized under the law of the child's residence or domicile, (2) the father acknowledges paternity in writing under oath, or (3) paternity is established by a competent court.

Tuan Anh Nguyen was born in Vietnam to a Vietnamese mother and a U.S. citizen father, Joseph Boulais. At the age of 6, Nguyen came to the United States, where he became a lawful permanent resident and was raised by his father. When Nguyen was 22, he pleaded guilty in a Texas court to two counts of sexual assault. The United States Immigration and Naturalization Service (INS) initiated deportation proceedings against Nguyen, and an immigration judge found him deportable. While Nguyen's appeal to the United States Board of Immigration Appeals was pending, Boulais obtained from a state court an order of parentage that was based on DNA testing. The board dismissed Nguyen's appeal, denying his citizenship claim on the ground that he had not established compliance with 1409(a). Nguyen and Boulais appealed to the United States Court of Appeals for the Fifth Circuit, which rejected their contention that § 1409 was gender-discriminatory in violation of the Constitution's equal protection guarantee. The U.S. Supreme Court granted certiorari in order to resolve a conflict between the Fifth Circuit's decision and those of two other circuit courts of appeal that had held § 1409 unconstitutional.

Kennedy, Justice   [Section 1409] governs the acquisition of United States citizenship by persons born to one United States citizen parent and one noncitizen parent when the parents are unmarried and the child is born outside of the United States or its possessions. The statute imposes different requirements for the child's acquisition of citizenship depending upon whether the citizen parent is the mother or the father. The question before us is whether the statutory distinction is consistent with the equal protection guarantee embedded in the Due Process Clause of the Fifth Amendment.

For a gender-based classification to withstand equal protection scrutiny, it must be established "'at least that the [challenged] classification serves "important governmental objectives and that the discriminatory means employed" are "substantially related to the achievement of those objectives."'" *United States* v. *Virginia* (1996) (quoting [two earlier decisions]). For reasons to follow, we conclude § 1409 satisfies this standard. Given that determination, we need not decide whether some lesser degree of scrutiny [applies] because the statute implicates Congress' immigration and naturalization power.

Before considering the important governmental interests advanced by the statute, two observations are in order. First, a citizen mother expecting a child and living abroad has the right to re-enter the United States so the child can be born here and be a 14th Amendment citizen. [T]he statute simply ensures equivalence between two expectant mothers who are citizens abroad if one chooses to reenter for the child's birth and the other chooses not to return, or does not have the means to do so. This equivalence is not a factor if the single citizen parent living abroad is the father. [U]nlike the unmarried mother, the unmarried father as a general rule cannot control where the child will be born.

Second, although § 1409(a)(4) requires certain conduct to occur before the child of a citizen father, born out of wedlock and abroad, reaches 18 years of age, it imposes no limitations on when an individual who qualifies under the statute can claim citizenship. The statutory treatment of citizenship is identical in this respect whether the citizen parent is the mother or the father. A person born to a citizen parent of either gender may assert citizenship, assuming compliance with statutory preconditions, regardless of his or her age. And while the conditions necessary for a citizen mother to transmit citizenship under § 1409 exist at birth, citizen fathers and/or their children have 18 years to satisfy the requirements of § 1409(a)(4).

The statutory distinction relevant in this case, then, is that § 1409(a)(4) requires one of three affirmative steps to be taken if the citizen parent is the father, but not if the citizen parent is the mother: legitimation; a declaration of paternity under oath by the father; or a court order of paternity. Congress' decision to impose requirements on unmarried fathers that differ from those on unmarried mothers is based on the significant difference between their respective relationships to the potential citizen at the time of birth. [T]he imposition of the requirement for a paternal relationship, but not a maternal one, is justified by two important governmental objectives.

The first governmental interest to be served is the importance of assuring that a biological parent–child relationship exists. In the case of the mother, the relation is verifiable from the birth itself. The mother's status is documented in most instances by the birth certificate or hospital records and the witnesses who attest to her having given birth.

In the case of the father, the uncontestable fact is that he need not be present at the birth. Fathers and mothers are not similarly situated with regard to the proof of biological parenthood. The imposition of a different set of rules for making that legal determination with respect to fathers and mothers is neither surprising nor troublesome from a constitutional perspective. Section 1409(a)(4)'s provision of three options for a father seeking to establish paternity—legitimation, paternity oath, and court order of paternity—is designed to ensure an acceptable documentation of paternity.

The requirement of § 1409(a)(4) represents a reasonable conclusion by the legislature that the satisfaction of one of several alternatives will suffice to establish the blood link between father and child required as a predicate to the child's acquisition of citizenship. Given the proof of motherhood that is inherent in birth itself, it is unremarkable that Congress did not require the same affirmative steps of mothers.

The second important governmental interest furthered in a substantial manner by § 1409(a)(4) is the determination to ensure that the child and the citizen parent have some demonstrated opportunity or potential to develop not just a relationship that is recognized . . . by the law, but one that consists of the real, everyday ties that provide a connection between child and citizen parent and, in turn, the United States. In the case of a citizen mother and a child born overseas, the opportunity for a meaningful relationship between citizen parent and child inheres in the very event of birth.

The same opportunity does not result from the event of birth, as a matter of biological inevitability, in the case of the unwed father. Given the 9-month interval between conception and birth, it is not always certain that a father will know that a child was conceived, nor is it always clear that even the mother will be sure of the father's identity. This fact takes on particular significance in the case of a child born overseas and out of wedlock.

Principles of equal protection do not require Congress to ignore [] reality. [The high frequency with which Americans travel abroad] demonstrate[s] the critical importance of the Government's interest in ensuring some opportunity for a tie between citizen father and foreign born child which is a reasonable substitute for the opportunity manifest between mother and child at the time of birth. Indeed, especially in light of the number of Americans who take short sojourns abroad, the prospect that a father might not even know of the conception is a realistic possibility. Even if a father knows of the fact of conception, moreover, it does not follow that he will be present at the birth of the child. Thus, there is no assurance that the father and his biological child will ever meet. Without an initial point of contact with the child by a father who knows the child is his own, there is no opportunity for father and child to begin a relationship. Section 1409 takes the unremarkable step of ensuring that such an opportunity, inherent in the event of birth as to the mother–child relationship, exists between father and child before citizenship is conferred upon the latter.

Nguyen and Boulais argue in addition that, rather than fulfilling an important governmental interest, § 1409 merely embodies a gender-based stereotype. There is nothing irrational or improper in the recognition that at the moment of birth—a critical event in the statutory scheme and in the whole tradition of citizenship law—the mother's knowledge of the child and the fact of parenthood have been established in a way not guaranteed in the case of the unwed father. This is not a stereotype.

[With] facilitation of a relationship between parent and child [having been shown to be] an important governmental interest, the question remains whether the means Congress chose to further its objective—the imposition of certain additional requirements upon an unwed father—substantially relate to that end. [I]t should be unsurprising that Congress decided to require that an opportunity for a parent–child relationship occur during the formative years of the child's minority. In furtherance of the desire to ensure some tie between this country and one who seeks citizenship, various other statutory provisions concerning citizenship and naturalization require some act linking the child to the United States to occur before the child reaches 18 years of age.

In this difficult context of conferring citizenship on vast numbers of persons, the means adopted by Congress are in substantial furtherance of important governmental objectives. The fit between the means and the important end is exceedingly persuasive.

In analyzing § 1409(a)(4), we are mindful that the obligation it imposes with respect to the acquisition of citizenship by the child of a citizen father is minimal. This circumstance shows that Congress has not erected inordinate and unnecessary hurdles to the conferral of citizenship on the children of citizen fathers in furthering its important objectives. Only the least onerous of the three options provided for in § 1409(a)(4) must be satisfied. The statute can be satisfied on the day of birth, or the next day, or for the next 18 years. In this case, the unfortunate, even tragic, circumstance is that Boulais did not pursue, or perhaps did not know of, these simple steps and alternatives. Any omission, however, does not nullify the statutory scheme.

To fail to acknowledge even our most basic biological differences—such as the fact that a mother must be present at birth but the father need not be—risks making the guarantee of equal protection superficial, and so disserving it. Mechanistic classification of all our differences as stereotypes would operate to obscure those misconceptions and prejudices that are real. The distinction embodied in the statutory scheme here at issue is not marked by misconception and prejudice, nor does it show disrespect for either class. The difference between men and women in relation to the birth process is a real one, and the principle of equal protection does not forbid Congress to address the problem at hand in a manner specific to each gender.

Fifth Circuit's decision affirmed.

O'Connor, Justice, dissenting   No one should mistake the majority's analysis for a careful application of this Court's equal protection jurisprudence concerning sex-based classifications. Today's decision instead represents a deviation from a line of cases in which we have vigilantly applied heightened scrutiny to such classifications to determine whether a constitutional violation has occurred. I trust that the depth and vitality of these precedents will ensure that today's error remains an aberration.

Independent Checks Applying Only to the States

The Contract Clause

Article I, section 10 of the Constitution States: "No State shall . . . pass any . . . Law impairing the Obligation of Contracts." Known as the *contract clause,* this provision deals with state laws that change the parties' performance obligations under an *existing* contract *after* that contract has been made.[2] The original purpose of the contract clause was to strike down the many debtor relief statutes passed by the states after the Revolution. These statutes impaired the obligations of existing private contracts by relieving debtors of what they owed to creditors. In two early 19th-century cases, however, the contract clause also was held to protect the obligations of *governmental* contracts, charters, and grants.

The contract clause probably was the most important constitutional check on state regulation of the economy for much of the 19th century. Beginning in the latter part of that century, the clause gradually became subordinate to legislation based on the states' police powers. By the mid-20th century, most observers treated the clause as being of historical interest only. In 1977, however, the Supreme Court gave the contract clause new life by announcing a fairly strict constitutional test governing situations in which a state impairs *its own* contracts, charters, and grants. Such impairments, the Court said, must be "reasonable and necessary to serve an important public purpose."

During recent decades, the Court has continued its deference toward state regulations that impair the obligations of *private* contracts. Consider, for instance, *Exxon Corp.* v. *Eagerton* (1983). For years, Exxon had paid a severance tax under Alabama on oil and gas it drilled within the state. As the tax increased, appropriate provisions in Exxon's contracts with the purchasers of its oil and gas allowed Exxon to pass on the amounts of the increases to the purchasers. Alabama, however, enacted a law that not only increased the severance tax but also forbade producers of oil and gas from passing on the increase to purchasers. Exxon filed suit, seeking a declaration that the law's pass-on prohibition was unconstitutional under the Contract Clause. Affirming Alabama's highest court, the U.S. Supreme Court observed that the Contract Clause allows the states to adopt broad regulatory measures without having to be concerned that private contracts will be affected. The pass-on prohibition was designed to advance a broad public interest in protecting consumers against excessive prices and was applicable to all oil and gas producers regardless of whether they were then parties to contracts containing pass-on provisions. Therefore, the Court reasoned, the Alabama statute did not violate the Commerce Clause.

Burden on Interstate Commerce

In addition to empowering Congress to regulate interstate commerce, the commerce clause limits the states' ability to *burden* such commerce. This limitation is not expressly stated in the Constitution. Instead, it arises by implication from the commerce clause and reflects that clause's original purpose of blocking state protectionism and ensuring free interstate trade. The burden-on-commerce limitation operates independently of congressional legislation under the commerce power or other federal powers. If appropriate federal regulation is present, the preemption questions discussed in the next section may also arise.

Many different state laws can raise burden-on-commerce problems. For example, state regulation of transportation (e.g., limits on train or truck lengths) has been a prolific source of litigation. The same is true of state restrictions on the importation of goods or resources, such as laws forbidding the sale of out-of-state food products unless they meet certain standards. Such restrictions

---

[2]Under the Fifth Amendment's due process clause, standards similar to those described in this section apply to the federal government.

sometimes benefit local economic interests and reflect their political influence. Burden-on-commerce issues also arise if states try to aid their own residents by blocking the export of scarce or valuable products, thus denying out-of-state buyers access to those products.

In part because of the variety of state regulations it has had to consider, the Supreme Court has not adhered to one consistent test for determining when such regulations impermissibly burden interstate commerce. In a 1994 case, the Court said that if a state law *discriminates* against interstate commerce, the strictest scrutiny will be applied in the determination of the law's constitutionality. Discrimination is *express* when state laws treat local and interstate commerce unequally on their face. In a 1992 case, for example, the Supreme Court considered an Oklahoma statute that required Oklahoma coal-fired electric generating plants producing power for sale in the state to burn at least 10 percent Oklahoma-mined coal. The Court stated that because this measure treated Oklahoma coal differently from out-of-state coal, it expressly discriminated against interstate commerce and deserved very strict scrutiny. Because the Court suspected that the Oklahoma statute had protectionist motivations and because the alleged justifications for it were weak, the Court found the law unconstitutional.

State laws might also discriminate even though on their face, they seem neutral regarding interstate commerce. This occurs when their *effect* is to burden or hinder such commerce. In one case, for example, the Supreme Court considered a North Carolina statute that required all closed containers of apples sold within the state to bear only the applicable U.S. grade or standard. The State of Washington, the nation's largest apple producer, had its own inspection and grading system for Washington apples. This system generally was regarded as superior to the federal system. The Court struck down the North Carolina statute because it benefited local apple producers by forcing Washington sellers to regrade apples sold in North Carolina (thus raising their costs of doing business) and by undermining the competitive advantage provided by Washington's superior grading system.

On the other hand, state laws that regulate even-handedly and have only incidental effects on interstate commerce are constitutional if they serve legitimate state interests and their local benefits exceed the burden they place on interstate commerce. There is no sharp line between such regulations and those that are almost always unconstitutional under the tests discussed above. In a 1981 Supreme Court case, a state truck-length limitation that differed from the limitations im-

posed by neighboring states failed to satisfy the tests for constitutionality. The Court concluded that the measure did not further the state's legitimate interest in highway safety because the trucks banned by the state generally were as safe as those it allowed. In addition, whatever marginal safety advantage the law provided was outweighed by the numerous problems it posed for interstate trucking companies.

Finally, laws may unconstitutionally burden interstate commerce when they *directly regulate* that commerce. This can occur, for example, when state price regulations require firms to post the prices at which they will sell within the state and to promise that they will not sell below those prices in other states. Because they affect prices in other states, such regulations directly regulate interstate commerce and usually are unconstitutional.

Federal Preemption

The constitutional principle of **federal supremacy** dictates that when state law conflicts with valid federal law, the federal law is supreme. In such a situation, the state law is said to be *preempted* by the federal regulation. The central question in most federal preemption cases is the intent of Congress. Thus, such cases often present complex questions of statutory interpretation.

Federal preemption of state law generally occurs for one or more of four reasons:

1. *There is a literal conflict between the state and federal measures, so that it is impossible to follow both simultaneously.*

2. *The federal law specifically states that it will preempt state regulation in certain areas.* Similar statements may also appear in the federal statute's legislative history. Courts sometimes find such statements persuasive even when they appear only in the legislative history and not in the statute itself.

3. *The federal regulation is pervasive.* If Congress has "occupied the field" by regulating a subject in great breadth and/or in considerable detail, such action by Congress may suggest an intent to displace state regulation of the subject. This may be especially likely where Congress has given an administrative agency broad regulatory power in a particular area.

4. *The state regulation is an obstacle to fulfilling the purposes of the federal law.* Here, the party challenging the state law's constitutionality typically claims that the state law interferes with the purposes she attributes to the federal measure (purposes usually found in its legislative history).

The *Rush Prudential* case, which follows, primarily addresses the second, of the above reasons for federal preemption. In this 2002 decision, the Supreme Court dismayed health maintenance organizations (HMOs) by holding that a federal statute dealing with employee benefit plans did not preempt an Illinois statute that entitled recipients of health coverage from an HMO to an independent medical review of the HMO's denials of certain medical claims.

Rush Prudential HMO, Inc. v. Moran   *122 S. Ct. 2151 (U.S. Sup. Ct. 2002)*

Section 4–10 of the Illinois Health Maintenance Organization (HMO) Act entitles recipients of health coverage from such organizations to an independent medical review of denials of certain benefits. Rush Prudential, an HMO, provided medical services for employee welfare benefit plans covered by the federal Employee Retirement Income Security Act of 1974 (ERISA). Debra Moran, a beneficiary of one of these plans, began having medical problems. Her doctor administered certain "conservative" treatments, but when Moran's condition had not improved, the doctor suggested to Moran that she go to a specialist who had developed an unconventional treatment for her condition. Rush denied Moran the treatment on the ground that under the terms of Rush's Certificate of Group Coverage, the treatment was not "medically necessary."

Moran demanded an independent medical review of Rush's denial under the Illinois HMO Act. Rush did not provide the review, so Moran sued in an Illinois state court to compel Rush's compliance with the state law. In the meantime, she underwent the unconventional treatment her doctor had suggested. After a year of litigation, the state court found in Moran's favor, enforcing the Illinois HMO Act and compelling independent medical review.

The resulting review revealed that Moran's treatment was necessary. Rush's medical director disagreed, however, and again denied Moran's claim. In response, Moran amended her claim in state court to seek reimbursement for the treatment. Rush removed the case to federal court, arguing that ERISA governed Moran's complaint and that ERISA's civil enforcement provisions preempted the Illinois HMO Act. The district court agreed with Rush, and denied Moran's claim on the ground that the state law was preempted by ERISA. On Moran's appeal, the Seventh Circuit reversed, holding that ERISA did not preempt the substantive portions of the Illinois HMO Act. The decision conflicted with the Fifth Circuit's treatment of a similar provision of Texas law, so the U.S. Supreme Court granted certiorari.

Souter, Justice   The issue in this case is whether the statute, as applied to health benefits provided by a health maintenance organization under contract with an employee welfare benefit plan, is preempted by ERISA. We hold it is not.

To "safeguard . . . the establishment, operation, and administration" of employee benefit plans, ERISA sets "minimum standards . . . assuring the equitable character of such plans and their financial soundness," and contains an express preemption provision that ERISA "shall supersede any and all State laws insofar as they may now or hereafter relate to any employee benefit plan. . . ." A saving clause then reclaims a substantial amount of ground with its provision that "nothing in this subchapter shall be construed to exempt or relieve any person from any law of any State which regulates insurance, banking, or securities." The "unhelpful" drafting of these antiphonal clauses occupies a substantial share of this Court's time. In trying to extrapolate congressional intent in a case like this, when congressional language seems simultaneously to preempt everything and hardly anything, we have no choice but to temper the assumption that the ordinary meaning . . . accurately expresses the legislative purpose, with the qualification that "the historic police powers of the States were not [meant] to be superseded by the Federal Act unless that was the clear and manifest purpose of Congress." *Rice v. Santa Fe Elevator Corp.* (1947).

It is beyond serious dispute that under existing precedent § 4–10 of the Illinois HMO Act "relates to" employee benefit plans within [ERISA's meaning]. The state law bears "indirectly but substantially on all insured benefit plans," *Metropolitan Life Insurance Co.* v. *Massachussetts* (1985), by requiring them to submit to an extra layer of review for certain benefit denials if they purchase medical coverage from any of the common types of health care organizations covered by the state law's definition of HMO. As a law that "relates to" ERISA plans, § 4–10 is saved from preemption only if it also "regulates insurance" under [ERISA's saving clause].

In *Metropolitan Life,* we said that in deciding whether a law "regulates insurance" under ERISA's saving clause, we [employ] a "common-sense view of the matter," under which "a law must not just have an impact on the insurance industry, but must be specifically directed toward that industry." *Pilot Life Ins. Co.* v. *Dedeaux* (1987). Although this is not the place to plot the exact perimeter of the saving clause, it is generally fair to think of the . . . "common-sense" [approach] as parsing the "who" and the "what": when insurers are regulated with respect to their insurance practices, the state law survives ERISA. The common-sense enquiry focuses on primary elements of an insurance contract, which are the spreading and underwriting of a policyholder's risk. The Illinois statute addresses these elements by defining "health maintenance organization" by reference to the risk that it bears.

Rush contends that seeing an HMO as an insurer distorts the nature of an HMO, which is, after all, a health care provider, too. This, Rush argues, should determine its characterization, with the consequence that regulation of an HMO is not insurance regulation within the meaning of ERISA. The answer to Rush is, of course, that an HMO is both: it provides health care, and it does so as an insurer. Nothing in the saving clause requires an either-or choice between health care and insurance in deciding a preemption question, and as long as providing insurance fairly accounts for the application of state law, the saving clause may apply. There is no serious question about that here, for it would ignore the whole purpose of the HMO-style of organization to conceive of HMOs without their insurance element.

Congress has understood [this point] from the start, when the phrase "Health Maintenance Organization" was established and defined in the [federal] HMO Act of 1973. [That statute] was intended to encourage the development of HMOs

as a new form of health care delivery system, and when Congress set the standards that the new health delivery organizations would have to meet to get certain federal benefits, the terms included requirements that the organizations bear and manage risk. The Senate Committee Report explained that federally qualified HMOs would be required to provide "a basic package of benefits, consistent with existing health insurance patterns," and the very text of the Act assumed that state insurance laws would apply to HMOs. In other words, one year before it passed ERISA, Congress itself defined HMOs in part by reference to risk, set minimum standards for managing the risk, showed awareness that States regulated HMOs as insurers, and compared HMOs to "indemnity or service benefits insurance plans." Rush cannot checkmate common sense by trying to submerge HMOs' insurance features beneath an exclusive characterization of HMOs as providers of health care.

Given that § 4–10 regulates insurance, ERISA's mandate that "nothing in this subchapter shall be construed to exempt or relieve any person from any law of any State which regulates insurance" . . . forecloses preemption.

Seventh Circuit's decision affirmed; Illinois HMO Act held not to be preempted by ERISA.

The Takings Clause

The Fifth Amendment states that "private property [shall not] be taken for public use, without just compensation." Because this **takings clause** has been incorporated within Fourteenth Amendment due process, it applies to the states. Traditionally, it has come into play when the government formally condemns land through its power of **eminent domain,**[3] but it has many other applications as well.

The takings clause both recognizes government's power to take private property and limits the exercise of that power. It does so by requiring that when *property* is subjected to a governmental *taking,* the taking must be for a *public purpose* and the property owner must receive *just compensation.* We now consider these four aspects of the takings clause in turn.

1. *Property.* The takings clause protects other property interests besides land and interests in land. Although its full scope is unclear, the clause has been held to cover takings of personal property, liens, trade secrets, and contract rights.

2. *Taking.* Because of the range of property interests it may cover, the takings clause potentially has a broad scope. Another reason for the clause's wide possible application is the range of government activities that may be considered takings. Of course, the government's use of formal condemnation procedures to acquire private property is a taking. There also may be a taking when the government physically invades private property or allows someone else to do so.

It has long been recognized, moreover, that extensive overly land use regulation may so diminish the value of property or the owner's enjoyment of it as to constitute a taking. Among the factors courts consider in such "regulatory taking" cases are: the degree to which government deprives the owner of free possession, use, and disposition of his property; the overall economic impact of the regulation on the

---

[3]Eminent domain and the takings clause's application to land use problems are discussed in Chapter 24.

owner; and how much the regulation interferes with the owner's reasonable investment-backed expectations regarding the future use of the property. In *Lucas* v. *South Carolina Coastal Council* (1992), the Supreme Court held that, there is an automatic taking when the government denies the owner *all* economically beneficial uses of the land. When this is not the case, courts tend to apply some form of means-ends scrutiny in determining whether land use regulation has gone too far and thus amounts to a regulatory taking.

3. *Public use.* Once a taking of property has occurred, it is unconstitutional unless it is for a public use. Because courts now apply a relaxed version of the rational basis test to resolve "public use" questions, the test is normally easy to meet.

4. *Just compensation.* Even if a taking of property is for a public use, it still is unconstitutional if the property owner does not receive just compensation. Although the standards for determining just compensation vary with the circumstances, the basic test is the fair market value of the property (or of the lost property right) at the time of the taking.

Problems and Problem Cases

1. While Larry Dean Dusenbery was in prison because of a conviction on federal drug charges, the Federal Bureau of Investigation (FBI) began a process seeking forfeiture, pursuant to the Controlled Substances Act (CSA), of cash and items that had been seized in a search of the residence where Dusenbery was arrested. The FBI was required under the CSA to publish notice of its intention to seek forfeiture and to mail notice to all those who appeared to have an interest in the property. If, 20 days after the notice was published, no person had claimed an interest, the cash and the items would become the property of the government. As required by law, the FBI sent to Dusenbery, by certified mail, letters declaring the FBI's intention to forfeit the property. The letters were addressed to the residence where Dusenbery was arrested, to an address in the town in which Dusenbery's mother lived, and to Dusenbery, in care of the Federal Correctional Institution (FCI) where he was housed. When the FBI received no claim by anyone to any interest in the property within the 20-day period referred to above, it began the forfeiture process.

Nearly five years later, Dusenbery filed a motion in federal court seeking return of his property, alleging that his due process rights had been violated because the FBI's notice of its intention to forfeit the property had never actually reached Dusenbery's cell. Were Dusenbery's due process rights violated?

2. 44 Liquormart, a licensed Rhode Island liquor store, ran a newspaper advertisement containing an implied reference to its bargain prices. For this reason, the state's Liquor Control Administrator levied a fine of $400 on 44 Liquormart under Rhode Island statutes forbidding public price advertising for alcoholic beverages. 44 Liquormart argued that the statutes under which it was fined violated the First Amendment. Was 44 Liquormart correct?

3. The Master Settlement Agreement (MSA) settled litigation between major tobacco manufacturers and numerous states seeking reimbursement for money spent on their citizens tobacco-related health problems. Under the MSA, the tobacco manufacturers agreed to make a number of concessions, including paying for the participating states' tobacco-related health care costs. Virginia, a party to the MSA, passed a qualifying statute providing that any manufacturer selling tobacco in Virginia must either sign the MSA as a subsequent participating manufacturer or place a monetary amount determined by the number of cigarettes sold in Virginia into an escrow fund. This escrow fund would serve as a pool from which Virginia could draw damages in the event that it wished to sue a non-MSA participant tobacco manufacturer. The manufacturer could either recover the money annually, insofar as it exceeded what the manufacturer would have paid under the MSA, or completely after 25 years.

Star Scientific (Star) is a relatively small technology-based tobacco company that attempts to reduce carcinogens in its product. It was not a party to the litigation leading up to the MSA, and because it could not afford the financial burden, it did not sign on as a subsequent participating member. Therefore, in compliance with Virginia's qualifying statute, it deposited $11.6 million into the escrow fund. Star then filed an action in the United States District Court for the Eastern District of Virginia alleging that the qualifying statute violated its rights under the Due Process Clause, first, by attempting to compel it to sign an agreement settling a case to which it was never a party, and second, by forcing it to put money in an escrow fund for 25 years, thereby depriving it of its property. Pointing out that subsequent participating manufacturers were not obligated to pay any damages so long as their market shares stayed within certain bounds, Star also alleged that the statute had violated its rights under the Equal Protection Clause by treating manufacturers not participating in the MSA more harshly than others.

Finally, Star alleged that the qualifying statute violated its rights under the Commerce Clause by assessing an escrow payment on cigarettes sold in Virginia through distributors. Star asserted that the statute regulated transactions and weighed down commerce beyond Virginia's borders by forcing Star to police sales of and make payments on cigarettes it sold to out-of-state distributors, which then sold the cigarettes in Virginia. Should Star succeed with these arguments?

4. The United States Olympic Committee (USOC) is a federally chartered private corporation. Under the Amateur Sports Act, it has broad powers to handle U.S. participation in international athletic competition and to promote amateur athletics within this country. In addition to granting the USOC its charter, Congress imposed certain regulatory requirements upon it and also gave it some funding. Congress also gave the USOC near-exclusive rights in the commercial and promotional use of the term *Olympic*. When the USOC sued to protect those rights, the defendant argued that its discriminatory enforcement of them violated the equal protection clause.

Suppose that you are an attorney for the defendant in this case. Based on the discussion in the text, what arguments would you make for the proposition that the USOC's enforcement of its rights was state action? Do you think that those arguments will succeed today? Why or why not?

5. A Stratton, Ohio ordinance prohibited "canvassers" from "going in and upon" private residential property to promote a "cause" without first obtaining a permit from the office of the mayor. The ordinance sought to prevent fraud and crime and to protect residents' privacy. Permits were free of charge, and were routinely issued after an applicant had filled out a "Solicitor's Registration Form." After receiving a permit, a solicitor was authorized to go upon the premises she had listed on the registration form. At a resident's or a policeman's request, the solicitor was required to display the permit. If a resident had filled out a "No Solicitation Registration Form" from the mayor's office and posted a "no solicitation" sign on his property, not even solicitors with permits were allowed to enter the premises unless the resident had listed them as exceptions on the "No Solicitation Registration Form."

The Watchtower Bible and Tract Society of New York, a society and congregation of Jehovah's Witnesses that distributed and published religious materials, did not apply for a permit. Watchtower claimed that God orders Jehovah's Witnesses to preach the gospel, and that applying for a permit would insult God by subordinating the scripture to local code. Watchtower therefore brought an action

in federal court seeking to have the village of Stratton enjoined from enforcing the solicitation ordinance. Watchtower contended that the ordinance violated First Amendment rights to free speech, free press, and the free exercise of religion. Was Watchtower's allegation correct?

6. On August 26, while employed as a policeman at a state university, Richard Homar was arrested by the state police and charged with a drug felony. University officials then suspended Homar without pay. Although the criminal charges were dismissed on September 1, Homar's suspension remained in effect. On September 18, he finally was provided the opportunity to tell his side of the story to university officials. Subsequently, he was demoted to groundskeeper. He then filed suit under a federal civil rights statue, claiming that university officials' failure to provide him with notice and a hearing before suspension without pay had violated due process. Had it?

7. A small town adopts an ordinance that, among other regulatory measures, requires a permit for certain applications of pesticides. A property owner applies for a permit to spray a portion of his land from the air. The town grants him a permit, but refuses to let him spray by air and restricts the areas in which he can spray. The property owner sues the town, seeking a declaratory judgment that the pesticide ordinance is preempted by the Federal Insecticide, Fungicide, and Rodenticide Act (FIFRA), a federal statute addressing many aspects of pesticide control. In particular, FIFRA addresses pesticide registration and classification, applicator certification, inspection of pesticide production facilities, and the possible ban and seizure of pesticides that fail to meet federal requirements. If the property owner is to succeed, how must he demonstrate preemption? What are his chances of winning?

8. The Minnesota legislature passed a statute banning the sale of milk in plastic nonrefillable, nonreusable containers. However, it allowed sales of milk in other nonrefillable, nonreusable containers such as paperboard cartons. One of the justifications for this ban on plastic jugs was that it would ease the state's solid waste disposal problems because plastic jugs occupy more space in landfills than other nonreturnable milk containers. A group of dairy businesses challenged the statute, arguing that its distinction between plastic containers and other containers was unconstitutional under the equal protection clause. What means-ends test or level of scrutiny applies in this case? Under that test, is easing the state's solid waste disposal problems a sufficiently important *end?* Under that test, is there a sufficiently close "fit" between the classification and that end to make the statutory *means* constitutional? In answering the last question, assume for the sake of argument that there were better ways of alleviating the solid waste disposal problem than banning plastic jugs while allowing paperboard cartons.

9. Oklahoma statutes set the age for drinking 3.2 beer at 21 for men and 18 for women. The asserted purpose behind the statutes (and the sex-based classification that they established) was traffic safety. The statutes were challenged as a denial of equal protection by male residents of Oklahoma. What level of scrutiny would this measure receive if *women* had been denied the right to drink 3.2 beer until they were 21 but men had been allowed to consume it at age 18? Should this standard change because the measure discriminates against *men?* Is the male challenge to the statute likely to be successful?

10. While it was preparing a comprehensive land-use plan in the area, the Tahoe Regional Planning Agency (TRPA) imposed two moratoria on development of property in the Lake Tahoe Basin. The moratoria together lasted 32 months. A group of property developers affected by the moratoria filed suit in federal court alleging that the moratoria constituted an unconstitutional taking without just compensation. Were the developers correct?

11. Persons who wish to practice midwifery in New Jersey first must obtain a midwifery license from the state board of medical examiners. Candidates for a license must pass an examination of midwifery, possess good moral character, and receive a diploma from a school of midwifery or maternity hospital. They also must get a New Jersey-licensed physician to endorse their application. A practicing midwife who was not licensed in New Jersey, several couples who wanted a midwife's assistance for future births, and several women who wanted to be midwives sued the state, claiming that its licensing scheme violated due process. Was this claim correct?

12. After nine years and eight months of service, Perry McClendon was fired from his sales job with the Ingersoll-Rand Company. Believing that Ingersoll-Rand fired him to avoid pension obligations that would have arisen after 10 years of service, McClendon sued the firm for wrongful discharge. During the litigation, Ingersoll-Rand argued that McClendon's common law claim was preempted by the Employee Retirement Income Security Act (ERISA). ERISA has a provision stating that: "[T]he provisions of this subchapter and subchapter III of this chapter shall supersede any and all State laws insofar as they may now or hereafter relate to any employee benefit plan [covered by relevant ERISA provisions]." Does this language preempt McClendon's claim?

Online Research: The U.S. Constitution

Locate the U.S. Constitution by using an online source. Review the Constitution and then answer the following questions:

- Which articles and sections deal with the qualifications that persons must have in order to serve as a member of the House of Representatives, as a Senator, and as President of the United States? How do those respective qualifications differ?
- What article and section addresses the subject of a presidential veto of a bill passed by the House and the Senate? What is necessary in order for the House and Senate to override a presidential veto?
- Of the 18th, 19th, and 20th centuries, which one accounts for the smallest number of properly ratified amendments to the Constitution?
- Which amendment gave Congress the power to levy an income tax?

BUSINESS ETHICS, CORPORATE SOCIAL RESPONSIBILITY, CORPORATE GOVERNANCE, AND CRITICAL THINKING

You work for N-Rot Company, a large energy trading company. N-Rot's chief financial officer (CFO) asks you to create a $50,000,000-asset energy services partnership with Martin Lowell Company, an investment banking firm. The CFO tells you, "Make sure the partnership has some positive cash flow over the next two years, but don't worry about whether the partnership will make money long term. Just make sure you convince Martin Lowell to partner with us, and that our ownership is only around 8 percent so that we don't have to record any liabilities from the venture on our balance sheet."

The purpose of the partnership, the CFO explains, is to generate income for N-Rot for the current year without materially affecting N-Rot's assets or liabilities. The CFO also tells you, "Convince our auditors, Armen Andrusian LLP, to book in the current year all the partnership's projected earnings for the next two years. If Andrusian resists, tell them that we can always find someone else to take over the $100,000,000 in consulting business we give them every year."

The CFO continues, "We'll make you a manager of the partnership, which will pay you about $900,000 a year. Also, I'll ask Martin Lowell to allocate some IPO [initial public offering] shares to you. The IPO shares I've been getting from Martin Lowell have been going up three to five times the first day of trading. This will be a good deal for you. You can make $300,000 every time, almost risk free."

Finally, the CFO says, "Remember where the paper shredder is. If things get a little hot around here, be sure to use it."

- Do you see any potential ethical problems with what the CFO has asked you to do?
- What principles and guidelines help you decide what to do?
- How do you resist the CFO's request for you to create the partnership without jeopardizing your career and without harming N-Rot?

Why Study Business Ethics?

Enron. Arthur Andersen. WorldCom. Tyco. Adelphia. Global Crossing. ImClone. These business names from the front pages of 2002 and 2003 conjure images of unethical and socially irresponsible behavior by corporations and their executives. The United States Congress, employees, investors, and other critics of the power held and abused by some corporations and their management have demanded that corporate wrongdoers be punished and that future wrongdoers be deterred. Consequently shareholders, creditors, and state and federal attorneys general have brought several civil and criminal actions against wrongdoing corporations and their executives. Congress has also got in the action, passing the Sarbanes–Oxley Act of 2002, which increased penalties for corporate wrongdoers and established rules designed to deter and prevent future wrongdoing. The purpose of the statute is to encourage and enable corporate executives to be ethical and socially responsible.

But statutes and civil and criminal actions can go only so far in directing business managers down an ethical path. And while avoiding liability by complying with the law is one reason to be ethical and socially responsible, there are noble and economic reasons that encourage current and future business executives to study business ethics.

Although it is tempting to paint all businesses and all managers with the same brush that colors unethical and irresponsible corporations and executives, in reality corporate executives are little different from you, your friends, and your acquaintances. All of us from time to time fail to do the right thing, and we know that people have varying levels of commitment to acting ethically. The difference between most of us and corporate executives is that they are in positions of power that allow them to do greater damage to others when they act unethically or socially irresponsibly. They also act under the microscope of public scrutiny.

It is also tempting to say that current business managers are less ethical than managers historically. But as Federal Reserve Chairman Alan Greenspan said, "It is not that humans have become any more greedy than in generations past. It is that the avenues to express greed have grown enormously."

This brings us to the first and most important reason why we need to study business ethics: to make better decisions for ourselves, the businesses we work for, and the society we live in. As you read this chapter, you will study not only the different theories that attempt to define ethical conduct, but more importantly you will learn to use a framework or strategy for making decisions. This framework will increase the likelihood you have considered all the facts affecting your decision. By learning a methodology for ethical decision making and studying common thinking errors, you will improve your ability to make ethical decisions.

Another reason we study ethics is to understand ourselves and others better. While studying the various ethical theories, you will see concepts that reflect your own thinking and the thinking of others. This chapter, by exploring ethical theories systematically and pointing out the strengths and weaknesses of each ethical theory, should help you understand better why you think the way you do and why others think the way they do. By studying ethical theories, learning a process for ethical decision making, and understanding common reasoning fallacies, you should also be better able to decide how you should think and whether you should be persuaded by the arguments of others. Along the way, by better understanding where others are coming from and avoiding fallacious reasoning, you should become a more persuasive speaker and writer.

There are also cynical reasons for executives to study business ethics. By learning how to act ethically and in fact doing so, businesses forestall public criticism, reduce lawsuits against them, prevent Congress from passing onerous legislation, and make higher profits. For many corporate actors, however, these are not reasons to act ethically, but instead the natural consequences of so acting.

While we are studying business ethics, we will also examine the role of the law in defining ethical conduct. Some argue that it is sufficient for corporations and executives to comply with the requirements of the law; commonly, critics of the corporation point out that since laws cannot and do not encompass all expressions of ethical behavior, compliance with the law is necessary but not sufficient to ensure ethical conduct. This introduces us to one of the major issues in the corporate social responsibility debate.

THE GLOBAL BUSINESS ENVIRONMENT

Unethical Business Practices in China

American executives are not alone in being charged with unethical and illegal business practices. In China in 2002, for example, prosecutors charged executives of Zhengzhou Baiwen Company with accounting fraud. A partly state-owned company, Baiwen executives were charged with manipulating the company's books to hide losses. As a result, Baiwen was able to obtain Chinese government approval to sell new shares to investors in 1997.

The crackdown on Baiwen executives suggests that Chinese regulators are treating accounting fraud more seriously than in the past. Unlike the American public who, thanks to a free press, read daily newspaper stories of scandals at American corporations, Chinese investors are largely unaware of the extent of accounting problems at Chinese companies whose stock is listed on the Chinese stock exchange. Chinese market regulators estimate that almost half the 1,500 listed Chinese companies have committed some form of accounting irregularity.

The Corporate Social Responsibility Debate

Although interest in business ethics education has increased greatly in the last 30 years, that interest is only the latest stage in a long struggle to control corporate misbehavior. Ever since large corporations emerged in the late 19th century, such firms have been heroes to some and villains to others. Large corporations perform essential national and global economic functions, including raw material extraction, energy production, transportation, and communication, as well as providing consumer goods and entertainment to millions of people.

Critics, however, claim that corporations in their pursuit of profits ruin the environment, mistreat employees, sell shoddy and dangerous products, produce immoral television shows and motion pictures, and corrupt the political process. Critics claim that even when corporations provide vital and important services, business is not nearly as accountable to the public as are organs of government. For example, the public has little to say about the election of corporate directors or the appointment of corporate officers. This lack of accountability is aggravated by the large amount of power that big corporations wield in America and much of the rest of the world.

These criticisms and perceptions have led to calls for changes in how corporations and their executives make decisions. The main device for checking corporate misdeeds has been the law. The perceived need to check abuses of business power was a force behind the New Deal laws of the 1930s and extensive federal regulations enacted in the 1960s and 1970s. Some critics, however, believe that legal regulation, while an important element of any corporate control scheme, is insufficient by itself. They argue that businesses should adhere to a standard of ethical or socially responsible behavior that is higher than the law.

One such standard is the stakeholder theory of corporate social responsibility. It holds that rather than merely striving to maximize profits for its shareholders, a corporation should balance the interests of shareholders against the interests of other corporate stakeholders, such as employees, suppliers, customers, and the community. To promote such behavior, some corporate critics have proposed changes that increase the influence of the various stakeholders in the internal governance of a corporation. We will study many of these proposals later in the chapter. You will also learn later that an ethical decision-making process requires a business executive to anticipate the effects of a corporate decision on the various corporate stakeholders.

Despite concerns about abuses of power, big business has contributed greatly to the unprecedented abundance in America and elsewhere. Partly for this reason and partly because many businesses attempt to be ethical actors, critics have not totally dominated the debate about control of the modern corporation. Defenders of businesses argue that in a society founded on capitalism, profit maximization should be the main goal of businesses: the only ethical norms firms must follow are those embodied in the law or those impacting profits. In short, they argue that businesses that maximize profits within the limits of the law are acting ethically. Otherwise, the marketplace would discipline them for acting unethically by reducing their profits.

Fed Chairman Alan Greenspan wrote in 1963 that moral values are the power behind capitalism. He wrote, "Capitalism is based on self-interest and self-esteem; it holds integrity and trustworthiness as cardinal virtues and makes them pay off in the marketplace, thus demanding that men survive by means of virtue, not of vices." Note that companies that are successful decade after decade, like Proctor & Gamble and Johnson & Johnson, adhere to society's core values.

We will cover other arguments supporting and criticizing profit maximization later in the chapter, where we will consider fully proposals to improve corporate governance and accountability. For now, however, having set the stage for the debate about business ethics and corporate social responsibility, we want to study the definitions of ethical behavior.

Ethical Theories

For centuries, religious and secular scholars have explored the meaning of human existence and attempted to define a "good life." In this section, we will define and examine some of the most important theories of ethical conduct.

As we cover these theories, much of what you read will be familiar to you. The names may be new, but almost certainly you have previously heard speeches and read writings of politicians, religious leaders, and commentators that incorporate the values in these theories. You will discover that your own thinking is consistent with one or more of the theories. You can also recognize the thinking of friends and antagonists in these theories.

None of these theories are necessarily invalid, and many people believe strongly in any one of them. Whether you believe your theory to be right and the others to be wrong, it is unlikely that others will accept what you see as the error of their ways and agree with all your values. Instead, it is important for you to recognize that people's ethical values can be as diverse as human culture. Therefore, no amount of argumentation appealing to theories you accept is likely to influence someone who subscribes to a different ethical viewpoint.

This means that if you want to be understood by and to influence someone who has a different ethical underpinning than you do, you must first determine his ethical viewpoint and then speak in an ethical language that will be understood and accepted by him. Otherwise, you and your opponent are like the talking heads on nighttime cable TV news shows, whose debates often are reduced to shouting matches void of any attempt to understand the other side.

The four ethical theories we will study are rights theory, justice theory, utilitarianism, and profit maximization. Some of these theories focus on results of our decisions or actions: do our decisions or actions produce the right results? Theories that focus on the consequences of a decision are **teleological** ethical theories. For example, a teleological theory may justify a manufacturing company laying off 5,000 employees, because the effect is to keep the price of manufactured goods low and to increase profits for the company's shareholders.

Other theories focus on the decision or action itself, irrespective of what results it produces. Theories that focus on decisions or actions alone are **deontological** ethical theories. For example, a deontological theory may find unacceptable that any competent employee loses his job, even if the layoff's effect is to reduce prices to consumers and increase profits.

LOG ON

Go to
www.utm.edu/research/iep/
The Internet Encyclopedia of Philosophy gives you background on all the world's great philosophers from Aenesidemus to Zeno. You can also study the development of philosophy from ancient times to the present. Many of the world's great philosophers addressed the question of ethical or moral conduct.

First, we will cover rights theory, which is a deontological theory. Next will be justice theory, which has concepts common to rights theory, but a focus primarily on

outcomes. Our study of ethical theories will conclude with two additional teleological theories, utilitarianism and profit maximization.

Rights Theory

Rights theory encompasses a variety of ethical philosophies holding that certain human rights are fundamental and must be respected by other humans. The focus is on each individual member of society and her rights. As an actor, each of us faces a moral compulsion not to harm the fundamental rights of others.

Kantianism Few rights theorists are strict deontologists, and one of the few is 18th century philosopher Immanuel Kant. Kant viewed humans as moral actors that are free to make choices. He believed humans are able to judge the morality of any action by applying his famous **categorical imperative.** One formulation of the categorical imperative is, "Act only on that maxim whereby at the same time you can will that it shall become a universal law." This means that we judge an action by applying it universally.

Suppose you want to borrow money even though you know that you will never repay it. To justify this action using the categorical imperative, you state the following maxim or rule: "When I want money, I will borrow money and promise to repay it, even though I know I won't repay." According to Kant, you would not want this maxim to become a universal law, because no one would believe in promises to repay debts and you would not be able to borrow money when you want. Thus, your maxim or rule fails to satisfy the categorical imperative. You are compelled, therefore, not to promise falsely that you will repay a loan.

Kant had a second formulation of the categorical imperative: "Always act to treat humanity, whether in yourself or in others, as an end in itself, never merely as a means." That is, we may not use or manipulate others to achieve our own happiness. In Kant's eyes, if you falsely promise a lender to repay a loan, you are using that person because she would not agree to the loan if she knew all the facts.

Modern Rights Theories Strict deontological ethical theories like Kant's face an obvious problem: the duties are absolute. We can never lie and never kill, even though most of us find lying and killing acceptable in some contexts, such as in self defense. Responding to these difficulties, some modern philosophers have proposed mixed deontological theories.

THE GLOBAL BUSINESS ENVIRONMENT

The Golden Rule in the World's Religions and Cultures

Immanuel Kant's Categorical Imperative, which is one formulation of Rights Theory, has its foundations in the Golden Rule. Note that the Golden Rule exists in all cultures and in all countries of the world. Here is a sampling.

BUDDHISM: Hurt not others in ways that you would find hurtful.

CHRISTIANITY: Do to others as you would have others do to you.

CONFUCIANISM: Do not to others what you would not like yourself.

GRECIAN: Do not that to a neighbor which you shall take ill from him.

HINDUISM: This is the sum of duty: do nothing to others which if done to you would cause you pain.

HUMANISM: Individual and social problems can only be resolved by means of human reason, intelligent effort, and critical thinking joined with compassion and a spirit of empathy for all living beings.

ISLAM: No one of you is a believer until he desires for his brother that which he desires for himself.

JAINISM: In happiness and suffering, in joy and grief, we should regard all creatures as we regard our own self.

JUDAISM: Whatever is hateful to you, do not to another.

NATIVE AMERICAN SPIRITUALITY: Respect for all life is the foundation.

PERSIAN: Do as you would be done by.

ROMAN: Treat your inferiors as you would be treated by your superiors.

SHINTOISM: The heart of the person before you is a mirror. See there your own form.

SIKHISM: As you deem yourself, so deem others.

TAOISM: Regard your neighbor's gain as your own gain, and your neighbor's loss as your own loss.

YORUBAN: One going to take a pointed stick to pinch a baby bird should first try it on himself to feel how it hurts.

ZOROASTRIANISM: That nature alone is good which refrains from doing to another whatsoever is not good for itself.

There are many theories here, but one popular theory requires us to abide by a moral rule unless a more important rule conflicts with it. In other words, our moral compulsion is not to compromise a person's right unless a greater right takes priority over it.

For example, members of society have the right not to be lied to. Therefore, in most contexts you are morally compelled not to tell a falsehood. That is an important right, because it is critical to a society that we be able to rely on someone's word. If, however, you could save someone's life by telling a falsehood, such as telling a lie to a criminal about where a witness who will testify against him can be found, you probably will be required to save that person's life by lying about his whereabouts. In this context, the witness's right to live is a more important right than the criminal's right to hear the truth. In effect, one right "trumps" the other right.

What are these fundamental rights? How do we rank them in importance? Seventeenth century philosopher John Locke argued for fundamental rights that we see embodied in the constitutions of modern democratic states: the protection of life, liberty, and property. Libertarians and others include the important rights of free-

dom of contract and freedom of expression. Modern liberals, like Berthold Brecht, argued that all humans have basic rights to employment, food, housing, and education. In the 1990s, the right to health care became part of the liberal rights agenda.

Strengths of Rights Theory The major strength of rights theory is that it protects fundamental rights, unless some greater right takes precedence. This means that members of modern democratic societies have extensive liberties and rights that they need not fear will be taken away by their government or other members of society.

Criticisms of Rights Theory Most of the criticisms of rights theory deal with the near absolute yet relative value of the rights protected, making it difficult to articulate and administer a comprehensive rights theory. First, it is difficult to achieve agreement about which rights are protected. Rights fundamental to modern countries like the United States (such as many women's rights) are unknown or severely restricted in countries like Pakistan or Saudi Arabia. Even within one country, citizens disagree on the existence and ranking of rights. For example, some Americans argue that the right to health care is an important need that should be met by government or a person's employer. Other Americans believe funding universal health care would interfere with the libertarian right to limited government intervention in our lives.

In addition, rights theory does not concern itself with the costs or benefits of requiring respect for another's right. For example, rights theory probably justifies the protection of a neo-Nazi's right to spout hateful speech, even though the costs of such speech, including damage to relations between ethnic groups, may far outweigh any benefits the speaker, listeners, and society receives from the speech.

Moreover, rights theory promotes moral fanaticism and creates a sense of entitlement reducing innovation, entrepreneurship, and production. If, for example, I am entitled to a job, a place to live, food, and health care regardless of how hard I work, how motivated am I to work to earn those things?

Justice Theory

In 1971, John Rawls published his book *A Theory of Justice,* the philosophical underpinning for the bureaucratic welfare state. Rawls reasoned that it was right for governments to redistribute wealth in order to help the poor and disadvantaged. He argued for a just distribution of society's resources by which a society's benefits and burdens are allocated fairly among its members.

Rawls expressed this philosophy in his **Greatest Equal Liberty Principle**: each person has an equal right to basic rights and liberties. He qualified or limited this principle with the **Difference Principle**: social inequalities are acceptable only if they cannot be eliminated without making the worst-off class even worse off. The basic structure is perfectly just, he wrote, when the prospects of the least fortunate are as great as they can be.

Rawls's justice theory has application in the business context. Justice theory requires decision makers to be guided by fairness and impartiality. It holds that businesses should focus on outcomes: are people getting what they deserve? It would mean, for example, that a business deciding in which of two communities to build a new manufacturing plant should consider which community has the greater need for economic development.

Chief among Rawls's critics was his Harvard colleague Robert Nozick. Nozick argued that the rights of the individual are primary and that nothing more was justified than a minimal government that protected against violence and theft and ensured the enforcement of contracts. Nozick espoused a libertarian view that unequal distribution of wealth is moral if there is equal opportunity. Applied to the business context, Nozick's formulation of justice would permit a business to choose between two manufacturing plant sites after giving each community the opportunity to make its best bid for the plant. Instead of picking the community most in need, the business may pick the one offering the best deal.

Strengths of Justice Theory The strength of Rawls's justice theory lies in its basic premise, the protection of those who are least advantaged in society. Its motives are consistent with the religious and secular philosophies that urge humans to help those in need. Many religions and cultures hold basic to their faith the assistance of those who are less fortunate.

Criticisms of Justice Theory Rawls's justice theory shares some of the criticisms of rights theory. It treats equality as an absolute, without examining the costs of producing equality, including reduced incentives for innovation, entrepreneurship, and production. Moreover, any attempt to rearrange social benefits requires an accurate measurement of current wealth. For example, if a business is unable to measure accurately which employees are in greater need of benefits due to their wealth level, application of justice theory may make the business a Robin Hood in reverse: taking from the poor to give to the rich.

Utilitarianism

Utilitarianism requires a decision maker to maximize utility for society as a whole. Maximizing utility means achieving the highest level of satisfactions over dissatisfactions. This means that a person must consider the benefits and costs of her actions to everyone in society.

A utilitarian will act only if the benefits of the action to society outweigh the societal costs of the action. Note that the focus is on society as a whole. This means a decision maker may be required to do something that harms her if society as a whole is benefited by her action.

A teleological theory, utilitarianism judges our actions as good or bad depending on their consequences. This is sometimes expressed as "the ends justify the means."

Utilitarianism is most identified with 19th century philosophers Jeremy Bentham and John Stuart Mill. Bentham argued that maximizing utility meant achieving the greatest overall balance of pleasure over pain. A critic of utilitarianism, Thomas Carlyle, called utilitarianism "pig philosophy," because it appeared to base the goal of ethics on the swinish pleasures of the multitude.

Mill thought Bentham's approach too narrow and broadened the definition of utility to include satisfactions such as health, knowledge, friendship, and aesthetic delights. Responding to Carlyle's criticisms, Mill also wrote that some satisfactions count more than others. For example, the pleasure of seeing wild animals free in the world may be a greater satisfaction morally than shooting them and seeing them stuffed in one's den.

How does utilitarianism work in practice? It requires that you consider not just the impact of decisions on yourself, your family, and your friends, but also the impact on everyone in society. Before deciding whether to ride a bicycle to school or work rather than to drive a car, a utilitarian would consider the wear and tear on her clothes, the time saved or lost by riding a bike, the displeasure of riding in bad weather, her improved physical condition, her feeling of satisfaction for not using fossil fuels, the cost of buying more food to fuel her body for the bike trips, the dangers of riding near automobile traffic, and a host of other factors that affect her satisfaction and dissatisfaction.

But her utilitarian analysis doesn't stop there. She has to consider her decision's effect on the rest of society. Will she interfere with automobile traffic flow and decrease the driving pleasure of automobile drivers? Will commuters be encouraged to ride as she does and benefit from doing so? Will her lower use of gasoline for her car reduce demand and consumption of fossil fuels, saving money for car drivers and reducing pollution? Will her and other bike riders' increased food consumption drive up food prices and make it less affordable for poor families? This only scratches the surface of her utilitarian analysis.

The process we used above, so-called **act utilitarianism,** judges each act separately, assessing a single act's benefits and costs to society's members. Obviously, a person cannot make an act utilitarian analysis for every decision. It would take too much time.

Utilitarianism recognizes that human limitation. **Rule utilitarianism** judges actions by a rule that over the long run maximizes benefits over costs. For example, you many find that taking a shower every morning before school or work maximizes society's satisfactions, as a rule. Most days, people around you will be benefited by not having to smell noisome odors, and your personal and professional prospects will improve by practicing good hygiene. Therefore, you are likely to be a rule utilitarian and shower each morning, even though some days you may not contact other people.

Many of the habits we have are the result of rule utilitarian analysis. Likewise, many business practices, such

as a retailer's regular starting and closing times, also are based in rule utilitarianism.

Strengths of Utilitarianism What are the strengths of utilitarianism as a guide for ethical conduct? It is easy to articulate the standard of conduct: you merely need to do what is best for society as a whole. Is also coincides with values of most modern countries like the United States: it is capitalist in nature by focusing on total social satisfactions, benefits, welfare, and wealth, not on the allocations of pleasures and pains, satisfactions and dissatisfactions, and wealth.

Criticisms of Utilitarianism Those strengths also expose some of the criticisms of utilitarianism as an ethical construct. It is difficult to measure one's own pleasures and pains and satisfactions and dissatisfactions, let alone those of all of society's members. In addition, those benefits and costs almost certainly are unequally distributed across society's members. It can foster a tyranny of the majority that may result in morally monstrous behavior, such as a decision by a 100,000-person community to use a lake as a dump for human waste because only one person otherwise uses or draws drinking water from the lake.

That example exhibits how utilitarianism differs from rights theory. While rights theory may protect a person's right to clean drinking water regardless of its cost, utilitarianism considers the benefits and costs of that right as only one factor in the total mix of society's benefits and costs. In some cases, the cost of interfering with someone's right may outweigh the benefits to society, resulting in the same decision that rights theory produces. But where rights theory is essentially a one-factor analysis, utilitarianism requires a consideration of that factor and a host of others as well.

A final criticism of utilitarianism is that it is not constrained by law. Certainly, the law is a factor in utilitarian analysis. Utilitarian analysis must consider, for example, the dissatisfactions fostered by not complying with the law and by creating an environment of lawlessness in a society. Yet the law is only one factor in utilitarian analysis. The pains caused by violating the law may be offset by benefits the violation produces. Most people, however, are rule utilitarian when it comes to law, deciding that obeying the law in the long run maximizes social utility.

Profit Maximization

Profit maximization as an ethical theory requires a decision maker to maximize a business's long-run profits within the limits of the law. It is based in the *laissez faire* theory of capitalism first expressed by Adam Smith in the 18th century and more recently promoted by liberal economists such as Milton Friedman and Thomas Sowell. Liberal economists argue total social welfare is optimized if humans are permitted to work toward their own selfish goals. The role of governments and law is solely to ensure the workings of a free market by not interfering with economic liberty, eliminating collusion among competitors, and promoting accurate information in the marketplace.

By focusing on results—maximizing total social welfare—profit maximization is a teleological ethical theory. It is closely related to utilitarianism, but it differs fundamentally in how ethical decisions are made. While utilitarianism maximizes social utility by focusing the actor on everyone's satisfactions and dissatisfactions, profit maximization optimizes total social utility by narrowing the actor's focus, requiring the decision maker to make a decision that merely maximizes profits for himself or his organization.

Strengths of Profit Maximization How can we define ethical behavior as acting in one's selfish interest? As you probably already learned in a microeconomics course, this apparent contradiction is explained by the consequences of all of us being profit maximizers. By working in our own interests, we compete for society's scarce resources (iron ore, labor, and land, to name a few), which are allocated to those people and businesses that can use them most productively. By allocating society's resources to their most efficient uses, as determined by a free market, we maximize total social utility or benefits. Society as a whole is bettered if all of us compete freely for its resources by trying to increase our personal or business profits. If we fail to maximize profits, some of society's resources will be allocated to less productive uses that reduce society's total welfare.

In addition, profit maximization results in ethical conduct because it requires society's members to act within the constraints of the law. A profit maximizer, therefore, acts ethically by complying with society's mores as expressed in its laws.

Moreover, each decision maker and business is disciplined by the marketplace. Consequently, profit maximization analysis probably requires a decision maker to consider the rights protected by rights theory and justice theory. Ignoring important rights of employees, customers, suppliers, communities, and other stakeholders may negatively impact a corporation's profits. A business

that engages in behavior that is judged unethical by consumers and other members of society is subject to boycotts, adverse publicity, demands for more restrictive laws, and other reactions that damage its image, decrease its revenue, and increase its costs.

Consider for example, the reduced sales of Martha Stewart branded goods at K-Mart after Ms. Stewart was accused of trading ImClone stock while possessing inside information. Consider also the fewer number of upcoming college graduates willing to work for Enron in the wake of adverse publicity and indictments against Enron's executives for misstating its financial results. Finally, note the higher cost of capital for firms like WorldCom as investors bid down the stock price of companies accused of accounting irregularities and other wrongdoing.

All these reactions to perceived unethical conduct impact the business's profitability in the short and long run, motivating that business to make decisions that comply with ethical views that transcend legal requirements.

Criticisms of Profit Maximization The strengths of profit maximization as a model for ethical behavior also suggest criticisms and weaknesses of the theory. Striking at the heart of the theory is the criticism that corporate managers are subject to human failings that make it impossible for them to maximize corporate profits. The failure to discover and process all relevant information and varying levels of aversion to risk can result in one manager making a different decision than another manager. Group decision making in the business context introduces other dynamics that interfere with rational decision making. Social psychologists have found that groups often accept a higher level of risk than they would as individuals. There is also the tendency of a group to internalize the group's values and suppress critical thought.

Furthermore, even if profit maximization results in an efficient allocation of society's resources and maximization of total social welfare, it does not concern itself with how wealth is allocated within society. In America, more than 50 percent of all wealth is held by 10 percent of the population. To some people, that wealth disparity is unacceptable. To liberal economists, wealth disparity is a necessary component of a free market that rewards hard work, acquired skills, innovation, and risk taking. Yet critics of profit maximization respond that market imperfections and a person's position in life at birth interfere with his ability to compete.

Critics charge that the ability of laws and market forces to control corporate behavior is limited, because it requires lawmakers, consumers, employees, and other constituents to detect unethical corporate acts and take appropriate steps. Even if consumers notice irresponsible behavior and inform a corporation, a bureaucratic corporate structure may interfere with the information being received by the proper person inside the corporation. If instead consumers are silent and refuse to buy corporate products because of perceived unethical acts, corporate management may notice a decrease in sales, yet attribute it to something other than the corporation's unethical behavior.

Critics also argue that equating ethical behavior with legal compliance is a tautology in countries like the United States where businesses distort the lawmaking process by lobbying legislators and making political contributions. It cannot be ethical, they argue, for businesses to comply with laws reflecting the interests of businesses.

Profit maximization proponents respond that many laws restraining businesses are passed despite businesses lobbying against those laws. The recently enacted Sarbanes–Oxley Act of 2002, which increases penalties for wrongdoing executives, requires CEOs to certify financial statements, and imposes internal governance rules on public companies, is such an example. So are laws restricting drug companies from selling a drug unless it is approved by the Food & Drug Administration and requiring environmental impact studies before a business may construct a new manufacturing plant. Moreover, businesses are nothing other than a collection of individual stakeholders, which includes employees, shareholders, and their communities. When they lobby, they lobby in the best interests of all these stakeholders.

Critics respond that ethics transcends law, requiring in some situations that businesses adhere to a higher standard than required by law. We understand this in our personal lives. For example, despite the absence of law dictating for the most part how we treat friends, we know that ethical behavior requires us to be loyal to friends and to spend time with them when they need our help. In the business context, a firm may be permitted to release employees for nearly any reason, except the few legally banned bases of discrimination (such as race, age, and gender), yet some critics will argue businesses should not terminate an employee for other reasons currently not banned by most laws (such as sexual orientation or appearance). Moreover, these critics further argue that businesses—due to their influential role in a modern society—should be leaders in setting a standard for ethical conduct.

Profit maximizers respond that such an ethical standard is difficult to define and hampers efficient decision making. Moreover, they argue that experience shows the

law has been a particularly relevant definition of ethical conduct. Consider that all the recent corporate scandals would have been prevented had the executives merely complied with the law. For example, Enron executives illegally kept some liabilities off the firm's financial statements. An Arthur Andersen partner illegally destroyed evidence. Tyco and Adelphia executives illegally looted corporate assets. Had these executives simply complied with the law and maximized their firms' long-run profits, none of the recent ethical debacles would have occurred.

Critics of profit maximization respond that the recent corporate crises at companies like Enron and WorldCom prove that flaws in corporate governance encourage executives to act unethically. These examples, critics say, show that many executives do not maximize profits for their firms. Instead, they maximize their own profits at the expense of the firm and its shareholders. They claim that stock options and other incentives intended to align the interests of executives with those of shareholders promote decisions that raise short-term profits to the long-run detriment of the firms. They point out that many CEOs and other top executives negotiate compensation plans that do not require them to stay with the firm long term and which allow them to benefit enormously from short-term profits. Executive greed, encouraged by these perverse executive compensation plans, also encourage CEOs and other executives to violate the law.

Defenders of business, profit maximization, and capitalist economics point out that it is nearly impossible to stop someone who is bent on fraud. A dishonest executive will lie to shareholders, creditors, board members, and the public and also treat the law as optional. Yet enlightened proponents of the modern corporation accept that there are problems with corporate management culture that require changes. They know that an unconstrained CEO, ethically uneducated executives, perverse compensation incentives, and inadequate supervision of executives by the firm's CEOs, board of directors, and shareholders present golden opportunities to the unscrupulous person and make unwitting accomplices of the ignorant and the powerless.

Improving Corporate Governance and Corporate Social Responsibility Even if we cannot stop all fraudulent executives, we can modify the corporate governance model to educate, motivate, and supervise executives and thereby improve corporate social responsibility. Corporate critics have proposed a wide variety of cures, all of which have been implemented to some degree and with varying degrees of success.

ETHICS IN ACTION

Halliburton Company's Statement of Ethical Business Practices

Oil services giant Halliburton Company is one of many American corporations to adopt an ethics code. Here is Halliburton's statement of "Ethical Business Practices." Particularly relevant is the last paragraph.

Ethical Business Practices

Company policy requires employees to observe high standards of business and personal ethics in the conduct of their duties and responsibilities. Employees must practice honesty and integrity in every aspect of dealing with other Company employees, the public, the business community, stockholders, customers, suppliers, and government authorities.

Company policy prohibits unlawful discrimination against employees, stockholders, directors, officers, customers, or suppliers on account of race, color, age, sex, religion, or national origin. All persons shall be treated with dignity and respect and they shall not be unreasonably interfered with in the conduct of their duties and responsibilities.

No employee should be misguided by any sense of loyalty to the Company or a desire for profitability that might cause him or her to disobey any applicable law or Company policy. Violation of Company policy will constitute grounds for disciplinary action, including, when appropriate, termination of employment.

Ethics codes Many large corporations and several industries have adopted codes of ethics or codes of conduct to guide executives and other employees. The Sarbanes–Oxley Act of 2002 requires a public company to disclose whether it has adopted a code of ethics for senior financial officers, and to disclose any change in the code or waiver of the code's application.

There are two popular views of such codes. One sees the codes as genuine efforts to foster ethical behavior within a firm or an industry. The other view regards them as thinly disguised attempts to make the firm function better, to mislead the public into believing the firm behaves ethically, to prevent the passage of legislation that would impose stricter constraints on business, or to limit competition under the veil of ethical standards. Even where the first view is correct, ethical codes fail to address concretely all possible forms of corporate misbehavior. Instead, they often emphasize either the behavior required for the firm's effective internal function, such as not accepting gifts from customers, or the relations between competitors within a particular industry, such as prohibitions on some types of advertising.

Better corporate ethics codes make clear that the corporation expects employees not to violate the law in a mistaken belief that loyalty to the corporation or corporate profitability requires it. An example is the Halliburton statement of "Ethical Business Practices," which appears in an Ethics in Action box. Such codes work best, however, when a corporation also gives its employees an outlet for dealing with a superior's request to do an unethical act. That outlet may be the corporate legal department or corporate ethics office.

Ethical Instruction Some corporations require their employees to enroll in classes that teach ethical decision making. The idea is that a manager trained in ethical conduct will recognize unethical actions before they are taken and deter herself and the corporation from the unethical acts.

While promising in theory, in practice many managers are resistant to ethical training that requires them to examine their principles. They are reluctant to set aside a set of long-held principles with which they are comfortable. Therefore, there are some doubts whether managers are receptive to ethical instruction. Even if the training is accepted, will managers retain the ethical lessons of their training and use it, or will time and other job-related pressures force a manager to think only of completing the job at hand?

Moreover, what ethical values should be taught? Is it enough to teach only one, a few, or all the theories of ethical conduct? Corporations mostly support profit maximization, because it maximizes shareholder value. But should a corporation also teach rights theory and expect its employees to follow it? Or should rights theory be treated as only a component of profit maximization?

Most major corporations today express their dedication to ethical decision making by having an ethics officer who is not only responsible for ethical instruction, but also in charge of ethical supervision. The ethics officer may attempt to instill ethical decision making as a component of daily corporate life by sensitizing employees to the perils of ignoring ethical issues. The ethics officer may also be a mentor or sounding board for all employees who face ethical issues.

Whether an ethics officer is effective, however, is determined by the level of commitment top executives make to ethical behavior and the position and power granted to the ethics officer. For example, will top executives and the board of directors allow an ethics officer to nix an important deal on ethical grounds or will they replace the ethics officer with another executive whose ethical views permit the deal? Therefore, probably more important than an ethics officer is a CEO with the character to do the right thing.

Greater Shareholder Role in Corporations Since shareholders are the ultimate stakeholders in a corporation in a capitalist economy, some corporate critics argue that businesses should be more attuned to shareholders' ethical values and that shareholder control of the board of directors and executives should be increased. This decentralization of ethical decision making, the theory goes, should result in corporate decisions that better reflect shareholders' ethical values.

Yet this decentralization of power flies in the face of the rationale for the modern corporation, which in part is designed to centralize management in the board of directors and top officers and to free shareholders from the burden of managing their investments in the corporation. Significant efficiencies are lost if corporate executives are required to divine and apply shareholders' ethical values before making a decision.

In addition, divining the shareholders' ethical viewpoint may be difficult. While nearly all shareholders are mostly profit driven, a small minority of shareholders have other agendas, such as protecting the environment or workers' rights, regardless of the cost to the corporation. It is often not possible to please all shareholders.

Nonetheless, increasing shareholder democracy by enhancing the shareholders' role in the nomination and election of board members is essential to uniting the interests of shareholders and management. So is facilitating the ability of shareholders to bring proposals for ethical policy to a vote of shareholders. In the last several years, for public companies at least, the Securities and Exchange Commission has taken several steps to increase shareholder democracy. These steps, which are covered fully in Chapter 45, are having their intended effect. In 2002 shareholders of EMC Corporation approved a proposal recommending that the company's board comprise a majority of independent directors. That same year, Mentor Graphics Corporation shareholders voted in a resolution

that any significant stock option plan be shareholder-approved. Moreover, in 2002 the New York Stock Exchange and NASDAQ required companies listed on those exchanges to submit for shareholder approval certain actions, such as approval of stock option plans.

Consider All Stakeholders' Interests Utilitarianism analysis clearly requires an executive to consider a decision's impact on all stakeholders. How else can one determine all the benefits and costs of the decision? Likewise, modern rights theory also dictates considering all stakeholders' rights, including not compromising an important right unless trumped by another. Kant's categorical imperative also mandates a concern for others by requiring one to act as one would require others to act.

Critics of corporations and modern proponents of profit maximization argue that more responsible and ethical decisions are made when corporate managers consider the interests of all stakeholders, including not only shareholders, but also employees, customers, suppliers, the community, and others impacted by a decision. For profit maximizers, the wisdom of considering all stakeholders is apparent, because ignoring the interests of any stakeholder may negatively affect profits. For example, a decision may impact a firm's ability to attract high quality employees, antagonize consumers, alienate suppliers, and motivate the public to lobby lawmakers to pass laws that increase a firm's cost of doing business. This wisdom is reflected in the Guidelines for Ethical Decision Making, which you will learn in the next section.

Nonetheless, there are challenges when a corporate manager considers the interests of all stakeholders. Beyond the enormity of identifying all stakeholders, stakeholders' interests may conflict, requiring a compromise that harms some stakeholders and benefits others. In addition, the impact on each stakeholder group may be difficult to assess accurately.

For example, if a manager is considering whether to terminate the 500 least productive employees during an economic downturn, the manager will note that shareholders will benefit from lower labor costs and consumers may find lower prices for goods, but the manager also knows that the terminated employees, their families, and their communities will likely suffer from the loss of income. Yet if the employees terminated are near retirement and have sizable retirement savings or if the termination motivates employees to return to college and seek better jobs, the impact on them, their families, and their communities may be minimal or even positive. On the other hand, if the manager makes the decision to retain the employees, shareholder wealth may decrease and economic inefficiency may result, which harms all society.

Independent Boards of Directors In some of the instances in which corporate executives have acted unethically and violated the law, the board of directors was little more than a rubber stamp or a sounding board for the CEO and other top executives. The CEO hand picked a board that largely allowed the CEO to run the corporation with little board supervision.

CEO domination of the board is a reality in most large corporations, because the market for CEO talent has skewed the system in favor of CEOs. Few CEOs are willing to accept positions in which the board exercises real control. Often, therefore, a CEO determines which board members serve on the independent board nominating committee and selects who is nominated by the committee. Owing their positions to the CEO and earning handsome fees sometimes exceeding $100,000, many directors are indisposed to oppose the CEO's plans.

For more than three decades, corporate critics have demanded that corporate boards be made more nearly independent of the CEO. The corporate ethical crisis of 2002 has increased those calls for independence. The New York Stock Exchange and NASDAQ require companies with securities listed on the exchanges to have a majority of directors independent of the company and top management. Their rules also require independent management compensation, board nomination, and audit committees. The Sarbanes–Oxley Act of 2002 requires public companies to have board audit committees comprising only independent directors.

One criticism of director independence rules is the belief that no director can remain independent after joining the board, because every director receives compensation from the corporation. There is a concern that an independent director, whose compensation is high, will side with management to ensure his continuing nomination, election, and receipt of high fees.

More extreme proposals of corporate critics include recommendations that all corporate stakeholders, such as labor, government, environmentalists, and communities, have representation on the board or that special directors or committees be given responsibility over special areas, such as consumer protection and workers' rights. Other critics argue for contested elections for each board vacancy. Few corporations have adopted these recommendations.

While honestly motivated, these laws and recommendations often fail to produce greater corporate social responsibility because they ignore the main reason for management's domination of the board: the limited time, information, and resources that directors have. One solution is to give outside directors a full-time staff with power to acquire information within the corporation. This solution, while providing a check on management, also may produce inefficiency by creating another layer of management in the firm.

In addition, some of the recommendations complicate management by making the board less cohesive. Conflicts between stakeholder representatives or between inside and outside directors may be difficult to resolve. For example, the board could be divided by disputes between shareholders who want more dividends, consumers who want lower prices, and employees who want higher wages.

Changing the Internal Management Structure Some corporate critics argue that the historic shift of corporate powers away from a public corporation's board and shareholders to its managers is irreversible. They recommend, therefore, that the best way to produce responsible corporate behavior is to change the corporation's management structure.

The main proponent of this view, Christopher Stone, recommended the creation of offices dedicated to areas such as environmental affairs and workers' rights, higher educational requirements for officers in positions like occupational safety, and procedures to ensure that important information inside and outside the corporation is directed to the proper person within the corporation. He also recommended that corporations study certain important issues and create reports of the study before making decisions.

These requirements aim to change the process by which corporations make decisions. The objective is to improve decision making by raising the competency of decision makers, increasing the amount of relevant information they hold, and enhancing the methodology by which decisions are made.

More information held by more competent managers using better tools should produce better decisions. Two of the later sections in this chapter in part reflect these recommendations. The Guidelines for Ethical Decision Making require a decision maker to study a decision carefully before making a decision. This includes acquiring all relevant facts, assessing a decision's impact on each stakeholder, and considering the ethics of one's decision from each ethical perspective. In addition, the Critical Thinking section below will help you understand when fallacious thinking interferes with a manager's ability to make good decisions.

Eliminating Perverse Incentives and Supervising Management Even if a corporation modifies its internal management structure by improving the decision-making process, there are no guarantees more responsible decisions will result. To the extent unethical corporate behavior results from faulty perception and inadequate facts, a better decision-making process helps. But if a decision maker is motivated solely to increase short-term profits, irresponsible decisions may follow. When one examines closely the corporate debacles of 2002, three things are clear: the corporate wrongdoers acted in their selfish interests, the corporate reward system encouraged them to act selfishly, illegally, and unethically, and the wrongdoers acted without effective supervision. These facts suggest other changes that should be made in the internal management structure.

During the high flying stock market of the 1990s, stock options were the compensation package preferred by high level corporate executives. Shareholders and boards of directors were more than willing to accommodate them. On one level, stock options seem to align the interests of executives with those of the corporation and it shareholders. Issued at an exercise price usually far below the current market price of the stock, stock options have no value until the corporation's stock price exceeds the exercise price of the stock options. Thus, executives are motivated to increase the corporation's profits, which should result in an increase in the stock's market price. In the 1990s stock market, in which some stock prices were doubling yearly, the exercise price of executives' stock options was quickly dwarfed by the market price. Executives exercised the stock options, buying and then selling stock, and in the process generating profits for a single executive in the tens and hundreds of millions of dollars. Shareholders also benefited from the dramatic increase in the value of their stock.

So what is the problem with stock options? As executives accepted more of their compensation in the form of stock options and became addicted to the lifestyle financed by them, some executives felt pressure to keep profits soaring to ever higher levels. In companies like Enron and WorldCom, which had flawed business models and suspect accounting practices, some executives were encouraged to create business deals that had little if any economic justification and could be accounted for in ways that kept profits growing. In what were essentially pyramid schemes, once the faulty economics of the deals were understood by prospective partners, no new deals were possible and the schemes crashed like houses of cards. But until the schemes were discovered, many executives, including some who were part of the fraudulent schemes, pocketed ten and hundreds of millions of dollars in stock option profits.

The Sarbanes–Oxley Act of 2002 attempts to recover fraudulently obtained stock option profits by requiring the CEO and CFO to reimburse the company when the corporation is required to restate its financial statements filed with the SEC. The CEO and CFO must disgorge any bonus or stock compensation that was received within 12 months after a false financial report was filed with the SEC.

It is easy to see how fraudulent actions subvert the objective of stock options to motivate executives to act in the best interests of shareholders. Adolph Berle, however, has argued for more than 30 years that stock options are flawed compensation devices that allow executives to profit when stock market prices rise in general, even when executives have no positive effect on profitability. He proposed that the best way to compensate executives is to allow them to trade on inside information they possess about a corporation's prospects, information they possess because they helped produce those prospects. His proposal, however, is not likely ever to be legal compensation because insider trading creates the appearance that the securities markets are rigged.

Even with incentives in place to encourage executives to inflate profits artificially, it is unlikely that the recent fraudulent schemes at Enron, WorldCom, and other companies would have occurred had there been better scrutiny of upper management and its actions by the CEO and the board of directors. At Enron, executives were given great freedom to create partnerships that allowed Enron to keep liabilities off the balance sheet yet generate income that arguably could be recognized in the current period. It is not surprising that this freedom from scrutiny when combined with financial incentives to create the partnerships resulted in executives creating partnerships that had little economic value to Enron.

Better supervision of management is mostly the responsibility of the CEO, but the board of directors bears this duty also. We addressed earlier proposals to create boards of directors that are more nearly independent of the CEO and, therefore, better able to supervise the CEO and other top managers. Primarily, however, better supervision is a matter of attitude, or a willingness to devote time and effort to discover the actions of those under your charge and to challenge them to justify their actions. It is not unlike the responsibility a parent owes to a teenage child to scrutinize her actions and her friends to make sure that she is acting consistent with the values of the family. So too, boards must make the effort to scrutinize their CEOs and hire CEOs who are able and willing to scrutinize the work of the managers below them.

Yet directors must also be educated and experienced. Poor supervision of management has also been shown to be partly due to some directors' ignorance of business disciplines like finance and accounting. Unless board members are able to understand accounting numbers and other information that suggests management wrongdoing, board scrutiny of management is a process with no substance.

The Law   The law has been a main means of controlling corporate misdeeds. Lawmakers usually assume that corporations and executives are rational actors that can be deterred from unethical and socially irresponsible behavior by the threats law presents. Those threats are fines and civil damages, such as those imposed and increased by the Sarbanes–Oxley Act of 2002. For deterrence to work, however, corporate decision makers must know when the law's penalties will be imposed, fear those penalties, and act rationally to avoid them.

To some extent, the law's ability to control executive misbehavior is limited. As we discussed earlier in this chapter, corporate lobbying may result in laws reflecting the views of corporations, not society as a whole. Some corporate executives may not know the law exists. Others may view the penalties merely as a cost of doing business. Some may think the risk of detection is so low that the corporation can avoid detection. Other executives believe they are above the law, that it does not apply to them out of arrogance or a belief that they know better than lawmakers. Some rationalize their violation of the law on the grounds that "everybody does it."

Nonetheless, for all its flaws, the law is an important means by which society controls business misconduct. Of all the devices for corporate control we have considered, only market forces and the law impose direct penalties for corporate misbehavior. Although legal rules have no special claim to moral correctness, at least they are knowable. Laws also are the result of an open political process in which competing arguments are made and evaluated. This cannot be said about the intuitions of a corporate ethics officer, edicts from public

THE GLOBAL BUSINESS ENVIRONMENT

Foreign Businesses Face Tougher Laws in U.S. than at Home

Although American executives accused of defrauding shareholders are prosecuted or hauled before congressional hearings, wrongdoing managers in the rest of the world often escape the grasp of their countries' regulators. In most of Asia, Europe, and Latin America, regulations and enforcement are weak. Some legal systems are poorly equipped to handle executive misconduct. The Japanese Securities and Exchange Surveillance Commission has only 360 employees and no power to file civil suits or bring administrative actions against corporate wrongdoers. It brings about seven cases a year, compared to the 50 usually brought by the United States Securities and Exchange Commission.

Taiwan's Securities and Futures Commission has no power to conduct its own investigations, and local prosecutors who do have that power have little expertise in market and accounting fraud. Germany has been labeled the Wild West, with numerous scandals in newly public companies, yet few actions against the perpetrators. The German Association for Shareholder Protections, a shareholder rights group, regularly brings abuse allegations to state prosecutors, yet the cases are often too complicated for untrained prosecutors to handle. Fewer than 5 percent are investigated. In Italy, false accounting was decriminalized in 2001, making it merely a misdemeanor.

Yet if those executives manage foreign businesses that register their securities on a stock exchange in the United States, such as the New York Stock Exchange, the Sarbanes–Oxley Act of 2002 requires them to comply with some of the act's toughest provisions. More than 1,300 foreign corporations, such as Sony, Nokia, and Daimler Chrysler, and their executives could be affected by the act's provisions that ban loans to officers, require independent audit committees, and impose personal liability on officers for errors in the corporate books.

Foreign governments and businesses have already started lobbying to be granted exemptions from the Sarbanes–Oxley Act. The European Union wrote to U.S. legislators that the act gives the SEC unjustified authority over foreign auditing firms that could chill trans-Atlantic trade. The EU warned that it may consider regulating American auditing firms. The president of the Japanese Institute of Certified Public Accountants argued that the act places U.S. law above Japanese securities and CPA law, violates international treaties, and infringes Japanese sovereignty.

As it does with many of its financial rules, the United States is expected to exempt foreign businesses from some of the requirements of the Sarbanes–Oxley Act, especially those that conflict with their home countries' laws, such as the ban on loans to officers. Foreign businesses are not expected to receive exemptions from other provisions, such as the requirement that CEOs certify the accuracy of financial statements. That part of the law may affect the decision whether foreign businesses continue to list their securities on U.S. stock exchanges.

interest groups, or the theories of economists or philosophers, except to the extent they are reflected in law. Moreover, in mature political systems like the United States, respect for and adherence to law is a well-entrenched value.

Where markets fail to promote socially responsible conduct, the law can do the job. For example, the antitrust laws discussed in Chapters 48–50, while still controversial, have eliminated the worst anticompetitive business practices. The federal securities laws examined in Chapters 45 and 46 arguably restored investor confidence in the securities markets after the stock market crash of 1929. Although environmentalists often demand more regulation, the environmental laws treated in Chapter 52 have improved the quality of water and reduced our exposure to toxic substances. Employment regulations discussed in Chapter 51—especially those banning employment discrimination—have forced significant changes in the American workplace. Thus, the law has an accomplished record as a corporate control device.

Indeed, sometimes the law does the job too well, often imposing a maze of regulations that deter socially valuable profit seeking without producing comparable benefits. The Fed's Greenspan once wrote, "Government regulation is not an alternative means of protecting the consumer. It does not build quality into goods, or accuracy into information. Its sole 'contribution' is to substitute force and fear for incentive as the 'protector' of the consumer."

The hope is that the Sarbanes–Oxley Act of 2002 will restore investor confidence in audited financial statements and corporate governance. It will be interesting to observe the legacy of that act to see if it improves corporate governance by imposing higher standards or reduces corporate efficiency by deterring high quality corporate executives from accepting positions in corporations.

Guidelines for Ethical Decision Making

Now that you understand the basics of ethical theories and the issues in the corporate governance debate, how do you use this information to make decisions for your business that are ethical and socially responsible? That is, what process will ensure that you have considered all the ethical ramifications and arrived at a decision that is good for your business, good for your community, good for society as a whole, and good for you.

Figure 1 lists nine factors in the Guidelines for Ethical Decision Making. Let's consider each Guideline and explain how each helps you make better decisions.

What Facts Impact My Decision?

This is such an obvious component of any good decision that it hardly seems necessary to mention. Yet it is common that people make only a feeble attempt to acquire *all* the facts necessary to a good decision.

Many people enter a decision-making process biased in favor of a particular option. As a result, they look only for facts that support that option. You have seen this done many times by your friends and opponents, and since you are an honest person, you have seen yourself do this as

---

Figure 1   *Guidelines for Ethical Decision Making*
1. What **FACTS** impact my decision?
2. What are the **ALTERNATIVES**?
3. Who are the **STAKEHOLDERS**?
4. How do the alternatives impact **SOCIETY AS A WHOLE**?
5. How do the alternatives impact **MY BUSINESS FIRM**?
6. How do the alternatives impact **ME, THE DECISION MAKER**?
7. What are the **ETHICS** of each alternative?
8. What are the **PRACTICAL CONSTRAINTS** of each alternative?
9. What **COURSE OF ACTION** should be taken and how do we **IMPLEMENT** it?

well from time to time. In addition, demands on our time, fatigue, laziness, ignorance of where to look for facts, and aversion to inconvenience someone who has information contribute to a reluctance or inability to dig deep for relevant facts.

Since good decisions cannot be made in a partial vacuum of information, it is important to recognize when you need to acquire more facts. That is primarily the function of your other classes, which may teach you how to make stock market investment decisions, how to audit a company's financial records, and how to do marketing research.

For our purposes, let's consider this example. Suppose we work for a television manufacturing company that has a factory in Sacramento, California. Our company has placed you in charge of investigating the firm's decision whether to move the factory to Juarez, Mexico. What facts are needed to make this decision, and where do you find those facts?

Among the facts you need are: What are the firm's labor costs in Sacramento and what will those costs be in Juarez? How much will labor costs increase in subsequent years? What is the likelihood of labor strife in each location? What is and will be the productivity level of employees in each city? What are and will be the transportation costs of moving the firm's inventory to market? What impact will the move have on employees, their families, the communities, the schools, and other stakeholders in each community? Will Sacramento employees find other jobs in Sacramento or elsewhere? How much will we have to pay in severance pay?

How will our customers and suppliers be impacted by our decision? If we move to Juarez, will our customers boycott our products even if our televisions are better and cheaper than before? If we move, will our suppliers' costs increase or decrease? How will our profitability be affected? How will shareholders view the decision? Who are our shareholders? Do we have a lot of Mexican shareholders, or do Americans dominate our shareholder list? What tax concessions and other benefits will the City of Sacramento give our firm if we promise to stay in Sacramento? What will Ciudad Juarez and the government of Mexico give us if we move to Juarez? How will our decision impact U.S.–Mexican economic and political relations?

This looks like a lot of facts, but we have only scratched the surface. You can probably come up with another 100 facts that should be researched. To give you another example of how thorough managers must be to make prudent decisions, consider that the organizers for the 2000 Summer Olympics in Sydney, Australia, created 800 different terrorist scenarios before developing an anti-terrorism plan.

You can see that to some extent we are discussing other factors in the Guidelines as we garner facts. The factors do overlap to some degree. Note also that some of the facts you want to find are not facts at all, but estimates, such as cost and sales projections. We'll discuss in the Eighth Guideline the practical problems with the facts we find.

What Are the Alternatives?

A decision maker must be thorough in listing the alternative courses of actions. For many of us, the temptation is to conclude that there are only two options: to do something or not to do something. Let's take our decision whether to move our factory to Juarez, Mexico. You might think that the only choices are to stay in Sacramento or to move to Juarez. Yet there are several combinations that fall in between those extremes.

For example, we could consider maintaining the factory in Sacramento temporarily, opening a smaller factory in Juarez, and gradually moving production to Mexico as employees in Sacramento retire. Another alternative is to offer jobs in the Juarez factory to all Sacramento employees who want to move. If per-unit labor costs in Sacramento are our concern, we could ask employees in Sacramento to accept lower wages and fringe benefits or to increase their productivity.

There are many other alternatives that you can imagine. It is important to consider all reasonable alternatives. If you do not, you increase the risk that the best course of action was not chosen only because it was not considered.

Who Are the Stakeholders?

In modern societies, where diversity is valued as an independent virtue, considering the impacts of your decision on the full range of society's stakeholders has taken on great significance in prudent and ethical decision making. While a public corporation with thousands of shareholders obviously owes a duty to its shareholders to maximize shareholder wealth, corporate managers must also consider the interests of other important stakeholders, including employees, suppliers, customers, and the communities in which they live. Stakeholders also include society as a whole, which can be defined as narrowly as your country or more expansively as an economic union of countries, such as the European Union of 15 countries, or even the world as a whole.

Not to be omitted from stakeholders is you, the decision maker, who is also impacted by your decisions for your firm. The legitimacy of considering your own selfish interests will be considered fully in the Sixth Guideline.

Listing all the stakeholders is not a goal by itself, but helps the decision maker apply more completely other factors in the Ethical Guidelines. Knowing whom your decision affects will help you find the facts you need. It also helps you evaluate the alternatives using the next three Guidelines: how the alternatives we have proposed impact society as whole, your firm, and the decision maker.

How Do the Alternatives Impact Society as a Whole?

We covered some aspects of this Guideline above when we made an effort to discover all the facts that impact our decision. We can do a better job discovering the facts if we try to determine how our decision impacts society as a whole.

For example, if the alternative we evaluate is keeping the factory in Sacramento after getting property tax and road building concessions from the City of Sacramento, how is society as a whole impacted? What effect will tax concessions have on the quality of Sacramento schools (most schools are funded with property taxes)? Will lower taxes cause the Sacramento infrastructure (roads and governmental services) to decline to the detriment of the ordinary citizen? Will the economic benefits to workers in Sacramento offset the harm to the economy and workers in Juarez?

Will our firm's receiving preferential concessions from the Sacramento government undermine the ordinary citizen's faith in our political and economic institutions? Will we contribute to the feelings of some citizens that government grants privileges only to the powerful? Will our staying in Sacramento foster further economic growth in Sacramento? Will staying in Sacramento allow our suppliers to stay in business and continue to hire employees who will buy goods from groceries and malls in Sacramento?

What impact will our decision have on efforts to create a global economy in which labor and goods can freely travel between countries? Will our decision increase international tension between the United States and Mexico?

Note that the impact of our decision on society as a whole fits neatly with one of the ethical theories we discussed earlier: utilitarianism. Yet profit maximization, rights theory, and justice theory also require a consideration of societal impacts.

How Do the Alternatives Impact My Firm?

The most obvious impact any alternative has on your firm is its effect on the firm's bottom line: what are the firm's profits. Yet that answer requires explaining, because what you really want to know is what smaller things leading to profitability are impacted by an alternative.

For example, if our decision is to keep the factory in Sacramento open temporarily and gradually move the plant to Juarez as retirements occur, what will happen to employee moral and productivity in Sacramento? Will our suppliers in Sacramento abandon us to serve more permanent clients instead? Will consumers in Sacramento and the rest of California boycott our televisions? Will they be able to convince other American laborers to boycott our TVs? Will a boycott generate adverse publicity and media coverage that will damage our brand name? Will investors view our firm as a riskier business, raising our cost of capital?

Again, you can see some redundancy here as we work through the guidelines, but that redundancy is alright, for it ensures that we are examining all factors important to our decision.

How Do the Alternatives Impact Me, the Decision Maker?

At first look, considering how a decision you make for your firm impacts *you* hardly seems to be a component of ethical and responsible decision making. The term "selfish" probably comes to mind.

Many of the corporate ethical debacles of the last few years comprised unethical and imprudent decisions that probably were motivated by the decision makers' selfish interests. Several of Enron's off-balance sheet partnerships, while apparently helping Enron's financial position, lined the pockets of conflicted Enron executives holding stocks options and receiving management fees from the partnerships. WorldCom's decision to seek more and larger acquisition targets was in part motivated by some executives' selfish goal to maintain a high stock price that made their stock options valuable.

Despite these examples, merely because a decision benefits you, the decision maker, does not always mean it is imprudent or unethical. Even decisions by some Enron executives in the late 1990s, while motivated in part by the desire to increase the value of the executives' stock options, could have been prudent and ethical if the off-balance sheet partnerships had real economic value to Enron (as they did when Enron first created off-balance sheet partnerships in the 1980s) and accounting for them complied with the law.

At least two reasons explain why you can and should consider your own interest yet act ethically for your firm. First, as the decision maker, you are impacted by the decision. Whether deserved or not, the decision maker is often credited or blamed for the success or failure of the course of action chosen. You may also be a stakeholder in other ways. For example, if you are an executive in the factory in Sacramento, you and your family may be required to move to Juarez (or El Paso, Texas, which borders Juarez) if the factory relocates. It is valid to consider a decision's impact on you and your family, although it should not be given undue weight.

A second, and more important, reason to consider your own interest is that your decision may be better for your firm and other stakeholders if you also consider your selfish interest. For example, suppose when you were charged to lead the inquiry into the firm's decision whether to move to Juarez, it was made clear that the CEO preferred to close the Sacramento factory and move operations to Juarez.

Suppose also that you would be required to move to Juarez. Your spouse has a well-paying job in Sacramento, and your teenage children are in a good school system and have very supportive friends. You have a strong relationship with your parents and siblings, who also live within 50 miles of your family in Sacramento. You believe that you and your family could find new friends and good schools in El Paso or Juarez, and the move would enhance your position in the firm and increase your chances of a promotion. Nonetheless, overall you and your spouse have determined that staying in the Sacramento area is best for your family. So you are considering quitting your job with the firm and finding another job in the Sacramento area rather than make an attempt to oppose the CEO's preference.

If you quit your job, even in protest, you will have no role in the decision and your resignation will likely have no impact on the firm's Sacramento–Juarez decision. Had you stayed with the firm, you could have led a diligent inquiry into all the facts that may have concluded that the prudent and ethical decision for the firm was to stay in Sacramento. Without your input and guidance, the firm may make a less prudent and ethical decision.

You can think of other examples where acting selfishly also results in better decisions. Suppose a top-level accounting executive, to whom you are directly responsible, has violated accounting standards and the law by pressuring the firm's auditors to book as income in the current year a contract that will not be performed for two years. You could quit your job and blow the whistle, but you may be viewed as a disgruntled employee and your story given no credibility. You could confront the executive, but you may lose your job or at least jeopardize your chances for a promotion while tipping off the executive, who will cover her tracks. As an alternative, the more effective solution may be to consider how you can keep your job and prospects for promotion while achieving your objective to blow the whistle on the executive. One alternative may be to go through appropriate channels in the firm, such as discussing the matter with the firm's audit committee or legal counsel.

Finding a way to keep your job will allow you to make an ethical decision that benefits your firm, whereas your quitting may leave the decision to someone else who would not act as prudently. The bottom line is this. While sometimes ethical conduct requires acting unselfishly, in other contexts consideration of your self-interest is not only consistent with ethical conduct, but also necessary to produce a moral result.

What Are the Ethics of Each Alternative?

Because our goal is to make a decision that not only is prudent for the firm but also ethical, we must consider the ethics of each alternative, not from one but a variety of ethical viewpoints. Our stakeholders' values comprise many ethical theories; ignoring any one theory will likely cause an incomplete consideration of the issues and may result in unforeseen consequences.

What Would a Utilitarian Do? A utilitarian would choose the alternative that promises the highest net welfare to society as a whole. If we define our society as the United States, moving to Juarez may nonetheless produce the highest net benefit, because the benefits to American citizens from a lower cost of televisions and to American shareholders from higher profits may more than offset the harm to our employees and other citizens of Sacramento. Another benefit of the move may be the reduced cost of the American government dealing with illegal immigration as Mexican workers decide to work at our plant in Juarez. Another cost may be the increased labor cost for a Texas business that would have hired Mexican workers had we not hired them.

If we define society as all countries in the North American Free Trade Agreement (NAFTA was signed by the United States, Mexico, and Canada), the benefit to workers in Juarez may completely offset the harm to workers in Sacramento. For example, the benefit to Juarez workers may be greater than the harm to Sacramento employees if many Juarez employees would otherwise be underemployed and Sacramento employees can find other work or are protected by a severance package or retirement plan.

As we discussed above in the discussion of ethical theories, finding and weighing all the benefits and costs of an alternative are difficult tasks. Even if we reject this theory as the final determinant, it is a good exercise for ensuring that we maximize the number of facts we consider when making a decision.

What Would a Profit Maximizer Do? A profit maximizer will choose the alternative that produces the most long-run profits for the company, within the limits of the law. This may mean, for example, that the firm should keep the factory in Sacramento if that will produce the most profits for the next 10 to 15 years.

This does not mean that the firm may ignore the impact of the decision on Juarez's community and workers. It may be that moving to Juarez will create a more affluent population in Juarez and consequently increase the firm's television sales in Juarez. But that impact is judged not by whether society as a whole is bettered (as with utilitarian analysis) or whether Juarez workers are more deserving of jobs (as with justice theory analysis), but is solely judged by how it impacts the firm's bottom line.

Nonetheless, profit maximization compels a decision maker to consider stakeholders other than the corporation and its shareholders. A decision to move to Juarez may mobilize American consumers to boycott our TVs, for example, or cause a public relations backlash if our Juarez employees receive wages far below our Sacramento workers. These and other impacts on corporate stakeholders may negatively impact the firm's profits.

Although projecting profits is not a precise science, tools you learned in finance classes should enhance your ability to select an alternative that maximizes your firm's profits within the limits of the law.

What Would a Rights Theorist Do? A follower of modern rights theory will determine whether anyone's rights are negatively affected by an alternative. If several rights are affected, the rights theorist will determine which right is more important or trumps the other rights, and choose the alternative that respects the most important right.

For example, if the alternative is to move to Juarez, the Sacramento employees, among others, are negatively affected. Yet if we do not move, potential employees in Juarez are harmed. Are these equal rights, a mere wash, or is it more important to retain a job one already has than to be deprived of a job one has never had?

Are other rights at work here, and how are they ranked? Is it more important to maintain manufacturing production in the firm's home country for national security and trade balance reasons than to provide cheaper televisions for the firm's customers? Does the right of all citizens to live in a global economy that spreads wealth worldwide and promotes international harmony trump all other rights?

While apparently difficult to identify and rank valid rights, this theory has value even to a utilitarian and a profit maximizer. By examining rights that are espoused by various stakeholders, we are more likely to consider all the costs and benefits of our decision and know which rights can adversely affect the firm's profitability if we fail to take them into account.

What Would a Justice Theorist Do? A justice theorist would choose the alternative that allocates society's benefits and burden most fairly. This requires the decision maker to consider whether everyone is getting what he deserves. If we follow the preaching of John Rawls, the firm should move to Juarez if the workers there are less advantaged than those in Sacramento, who may be protected by savings, severance packages, and retirement plans.

If we follow Nozick's libertarian approach, it is sufficient that the firm gives Sacramento workers an opportunity to compete for the plant by matching the offer the firm has received from Juarez workers. Under this analysis, if Sacramento workers fail to match the Juarez workers' offer of lower wages, for example, it would be fair to move the factory to Juarez, even if Sacramento workers are denied their right to jobs.

Even if the firm has difficulty determining who most deserves jobs with our firm, justice theory, like rights theory, helps the firm identify constituents who suffer from our decision and who can create problems impacting the firm's profitability if the firm ignores their claims.

What Are the Practical Constraints of Each Alternative?

As we evaluate alternatives, it is important to consider each alternative's practical problems before we implement it. For example, is it feasible for us to implement an alternative? Do we have the necessary money, labor, and other resources?

Suppose one alternative is to maintain our manufacturing plant in Sacramento as we open a new plant in Juarez, gradually shutting down the Sacramento plant as employees retire and quit. That alternative sounds like an ethical way to protect the jobs of all existing and prospective employees, but what are the costs of having two plants? Will the expense make that alternative infeasible? Will the additional expense make it difficult for the firm to compete with other TV manufacturers? Is it practicable to have a plant in Sacramento operating with only five employees who are 40 years old and will not retire for 15 years?

It is also necessary to consider potential problems with the facts that have led us to each alternative. Did we find all the facts relevant to our decision? How certain are we of some facts? For example, are we confident about our projections of labor and transportation costs if we move to Juarez? Are we sure that sales of our products will drop insubstantially due to consumer boycotts?

What Course of Action Should Be Taken and How Do We Implement It?

Ultimately, we have to stop our analysis and make a decision by choosing one alternative. Yet even then our planning is not over.

We must determine how to put the alternative into action. How do we implement it? Who announces the decision? Who is told of the decision and when? Do some people, like our employee's labor union, receive advance notice of our plans and have an opportunity to negotiate a better deal for our Sacramento employees? When do we tell shareholders, government officials, lenders, suppliers, investments analysts, and the media and in what order? Do we antagonize a friend or an enemy and risk killing a deal if we inform someone too soon or too late?

Finally, we have to prepare for the worst case scenario. What do we do if, despite careful investigation, analysis, and planning, our course of action fails? Do we have backup plans? Have we anticipated all the possible ways our plan may fail and readied responses to those failures?

Nearly two decades ago, The Coca-Cola Company decided to change the flavor of Coke in response to Coke's shrinking share of the cola market. Despite careful market research, Coca-Cola failed to anticipate Coke drinkers' negative response to the new Coke formula and was caught without a response to the outcry. Within three months, Coca-Cola realized it had to revive the old Coke formula under the brand name Coca-Cola Classic. In the meantime, Coke lost significant market share to rival Pepsi. Today, one would expect Coke executives introducing a reformulated drink to predict more consumers' reactions to the drink and to prepare a response to each reaction.

Knowing When to Use the Guidelines

You can probably see that following these factors will result in better decisions in a variety of contexts, including some that appear to have no ethical concerns. For example, in the next few years, most of you will consider what major course of study to select at college or what job to take with which firm in which industry. This framework can help you make a better analysis that should result in a better decision.

The Guidelines can be used also to decide mundane matters in your personal life, such as whether to eat a high-fat hamburger or a healthful salad for lunch, whether to spend the next hour exercising at the gym or visiting a friend in the hospital, and whether or not to brush your teeth every day after lunch . But for most of us, using the Guidelines every day for every decision would occupy so much of our time that little could be accomplished, what is sometimes called "paralysis by analysis."

Practicality, therefore, requires us to use the Guidelines only for important decisions and those that create a potential for ethical problems. We can identify decisions requiring application of the Guidelines if we carefully reflect from time to time about what we have done and are doing. This requires us to examine our past, current, and future actions.

It may not surprise you how seldom people, including business executives, carefully preview and review their actions. The pressures and pace of daily living give us little time to examine our lives critically. Most people are reluctant to look themselves in the mirror and ask themselves whether they are doing the right thing for themselves, their families, their businesses, and their communities. Few know or follow the words of Socrates, "The unexamined life is not worth living."

Ask yourself whether you believe that executives at bankrupt energy trader Enron used anything like the Guidelines for Ethical Decision Making before creating off-balance-sheet partnerships with no economic value to Enron. Do you think the employees at now defunct accounting firm Arthur Andersen carefully examined their decision to accept Enron's accounting for off-balance-sheet partnerships? Did those in charge at Andersen review their decision to order the shredding of evidence in light of the Ethical Guidelines? Did the CEO and other insiders at ImClone consider any ethical issues before trading on confidential, nonpublic information that the FDA had denied approval of a new ImClone drug?

Merely by examining our past and prospective actions, we can better know when to apply the Guidelines. In the last section of this chapter, Resisting Requests to Act Unethically, you will learn additional tools to help you identify when to apply the Guidelines.

Thinking Critically

Part of ethical decision making is being able to think critically, that is, to evaluate arguments logically, honestly, and without bias in favor of your own arguments and against those of others.

Even if someone uses the Guidelines for Ethical Decision Making, there is a risk that they have been misapplied if a person makes errors of logic or uses fallacious arguments. In this section, we want to help you identify when your arguments and thinking may be flawed and how to correct them. Equally important, we want to help you identify flaws in others' thinking. The purpose is to help you think critically and not to accept at face value everything you read or hear and to be careful before you commit your arguments to paper or voice them.

This chapter's short coverage of critical thinking covers only a few of the errors of logic and argument that are covered in a college course or book devoted to the subject. Here are 15 common fallacies.

Non Sequiturs

A *non sequitur* is a conclusion that does not follow from the facts or premises one sets out. The speaker is missing the point or coming to an irrelevant conclusion. For example, suppose a consumer uses a corporation's product and becomes ill. The consumer argues that because the corporation has lots of money, the corporation should pay for his medical expenses. Clearly, the consumer is missing the point. The issue is whether the corporation's product *caused* his injuries, not whether

money should be transferred from a wealthy corporation to a poor consumer.

You see this also used when employees attempt to justify stealing pens, staplers, and paper from their employers. The typical *non sequitur* goes like this: "I don't get paid enough, so I'll take a few supplies. My employer won't even miss them."

Business executives fall prey to this fallacy also. Our firm may consider which employees to let go during a downturn. Company policy may call for retaining the best employees in each department, yet instead we release those employees making the highest salary in each position in order to save more money. Our decision does not match the standards the company set for downsizing decisions and is a *non sequitur*, unless we admit that we have changed company policy.

Appeals to Pity

A common fallacy seen in the American press is the appeal to pity or compassion. This argument generates support for a proposition by focusing on a victim's predicament. It usually is also a *non sequitur*. Examples are antismoking advertisements that focus on the physical miseries (such as cancer and emphysema) of cigarette smokers and the impact on their families, especially children. None of those ads point out that many ill smokers knew the harms of tobacco before they started smoking.

Appeals to pity are effective because humans are compassionate. We have to be careful, however, not to be distracted from the real issues at hand. For example, in the trial against accused 9/11 co-conspirator Zacarias Moussaoui, federal prosecutors want to introduce testimony by the families of the victims. While it is terrible what the families of 9/11 suffered, the victim's families hold no evidence of Moussaoui's role in 9/11. Instead, their testimonies are appeals to pity likely to distract the jury from its main task of determining whether Moussaoui was a part of the 9/11 conspiracy.

You see many appeals to pity used against corporations. Here is a typical argument: a corporation has a chemical plant near a neighborhood; children are getting sick and dying in the neighborhood; someone should pay for this suffering; the corporation should pay. You can also see that this reasoning is a *non sequitur*.

False Analogies

An analogy essentially argues that since something is like something else in one or more ways, it is also like it in another respect. Arguers often use analogies to make a point vividly, and therefore analogies have strong appeal. Nonetheless, while some analogies are apt, we should make sure that the two situations are sufficiently similar to make the analogy valid.

Suppose an executive argues that our firm should not create any off-balance-sheet partnerships, because the company will become bankrupt just like Enron. This analogy may be invalid because our off-balance-sheet partnerships may have real economic value, we may be motivated by a desire to reduce our risk and not to misstate our financial position, and we may be committed to recognize income from the partnerships only after we receive cash from customers.

Analogies can also be used to generate support for a proposal, such as arguing that since Six Sigma worked for General Electric, it will work for our firm also. It is probable that factors other than Six Sigma contributed to GE's success during the Jack Welch era, factors our firm may or may not share with GE.

Nonetheless, analogies can identify potential opportunities, which we should evaluate prudently to determine whether the analogy is valid. Analogies can also suggest potential problems that require us to examine a decision more carefully before committing to it.

Begging the Question

An arguer begs the question when she takes for granted or assumes the thing that she is setting out to prove. For example, you might say that we should tell the truth because lying is wrong. That is **circular reasoning** and makes no sense, because telling the truth and not lying are the same things. Another example is arguing that democracy is the best form of government because the majority is always right.

Examples of begging the question are difficult to identify sometimes because they are hidden in the language of the speaker. It is best identified by looking for arguments that merely restate what the speaker or questioner has already stated, but in different words. For an example in the business context, consider this interchange between you and someone working under you.

You: Can I trust these numbers you gave to me?

Co-worker: Yes, you can trust them.

You: Why can I trust them?

Co-worker: Because I'm an honest person.

The co-worker used circular reasoning, since whether the numbers can be trusted is determined by whether he is honest, yet he provided no proof of his honesty or trustworthiness.

Argumentum ad Populum

Argumentum ad populum means argument to the people. It is an emotional appeal to popular beliefs, values, or wants. The fallacy is that merely because many or all people believe something does not mean it is true. It is common for newspapers to poll its readers about current issues, such as support for a presidential decision. For example, a newspaper poll may show that 60 percent of Americans support the president. The people may be right, but it is also possible that the president's supporters are wrong: they may be uninformed or base their support of the president on invalid reasoning.

Arguments to the people are commonly used by corporations in advertisements, such as beer company ads showing friends having a good time while drinking beer. The point of such ads is that if you want to have a good time with friends, you should drink beer. While some beer drinkers do have fun with friends, you probably can also point to other people who drink beer alone.

Bandwagon Fallacy

The bandwagon fallacy is similar to *argumentum ad populum.* A bandwagon argument states that we should or should not do something merely because one or more other people or firms do or do not do it. A June 2002 issue of *Sports Illustrated* quoted baseball player Ken Caminiti's justification for using steroids: "At first I felt like a cheater. But I looked around, and everyone was doing it." Some people justify cheating on their taxes for the same reason.

This reasoning can be fallacious because probably not everyone is doing it, and even if many or all people do something, it is not necessarily right. For example, while some baseball players do use steroids, there are serious negative side effects including impotency and acute psychosis, which make its use risky. Cheating on taxes may be common, but it is still illegal and can result in the cheater's imprisonment. Business executives often jump on the bandwagon when they adopt a management tactic used by other corporations without investigating whether the tactic is right for their firm.

Argumentum ad Baculum

Argumentum ad baculum means argument to club. The arguer uses threats or fear to bolster his position. This is a common argument in business and family settings. For example, when a parent asks a child to take out the garbage, the child may ask, "Why?" Some parents respond,

"Because if you don't, you'll spend the rest of the afternoon in your room."

In the business context, bosses explicitly and implicitly use the club, often generating support for their ideas from subordinates who fear they will not be promoted unless they support the boss's plans. An executive who values input from subordinates will ensure that they do not perceive that the executive is wielding a club over them.

Enron's CFO Andrew Fastow used this argument against investment firm Goldman Sachs when it balked at lending money to Enron. He told Goldman that he would not do anything with a presentation Goldman had prepared unless it made the loan.

By threatening to boycott a company's products, consumers and other interest groups use this argument against corporations perceived to act unethically. It is one reason that profit maximization requires decision makers to consider a decision's impact on all stakeholders.

Argumentum ad Hominem

Argumentum ad hominem means "argument against the man." This tactic attacks the speaker, not his reasoning. For example, a Republican senator criticizes a Democratic senator who opposes the use of force to oust a dictator in the Middle East by saying, "You can't trust him. He never served in the armed forces." Such an argument attacks the Democratic senator's character, not the validity of his reasons for not ousting the dictator.

When a CEO proposes a new compensation plan for corporate executives, an opponent may argue, "Of course he wants the new plan. He'll make a lot of money from it." Again, this argument doesn't address whether the plan is a good one or not; it only attacks the CEO's motives. While the obvious conflict of interest the CEO has may cause us to doubt the sincerity of the reasons he presents for the plan (such as to attract and retain better management talent), merely pointing out this conflict does not rebut his reasons.

One form of *ad hominem* argument is attacking a speaker's consistency, such as, "Last year you argued for something different." Another common form is appealing to personal circumstances. One woman may say to another, "As a woman, how can you be against corporate policies that set aside executive positions for women?" By personalizing the argument, the speaker is trying to distract the listener from the real issue. A proper response to the personal attack may be, "As a women and a human, I believe in equal opportunity for all people. I see no need for any woman or myself to have special privileges to compete with men. I can compete on my own. By having

quotas, the corporation cheapens my accomplishments by suggesting that I need the quota. Why do you, as a woman, think you need a quota?"

Guilt by association is the last *ad hominem* argument we will consider. This argument attacks the speaker by linking her to someone unpopular. For example, if you make the libertarian argument that government should not restrict or tax the consumption of marijuana, someone may attack you by saying, "Mass murderer Charles Manson also believed that." Your attacker suggests that by believing as you do, you are as evil as Charles Manson. Some corporate critics use guilt by association to paint all executives as unethical people motivated to cheat their corporations. For example, if a CEO asks for stock options as part of her compensation package, someone may say, "Enron's executives wanted stock options also." The implication is that the CEO should not be trusted because some Enron executives who were corrupt also wanted stock options.

No *ad hominem* argument is necessarily fallacious, because a person's character, motives, consistency, personal characteristics, and associations may suggest further scrutiny of a speaker's arguments is necessary. However, merely attacking the speaker does not expose flaws in her arguments.

Argument from Authority

Arguments from authority rely on the quality of an expert or person in a position of authority, not the quality of the expert's or authority's argument. For example, if someone says, "The president says we need to stop drug trafficking in the United States, and that is good enough for me," he has argued from authority. He and the president may have good reasons to stop drug trafficking, but we cannot know that from his statement.

Another example is "Studies show that humans need to drink 10 glasses of water a day." What studies? What were their methodologies? Did the sample sizes permit valid conclusions? A form of argument to authority is **argument to reverence or respect,** such as "Who are you to disagree with the CEO's decision to terminate 5,000 employees?" The arguer is trying to get you to abandon your arguments, not because they are invalid, but because they conflict with the views of an authority. Your response to this question should not attack the CEO (to call the CEO an idiot would be *ad hominem* and also damage your prospects in the firm), but state the reasons you believe the company would be better off not terminating 5,000 employees.

It is natural to rely on authorities who have expertise in the area on which they speak. But should we give credibility to authorities speaking on matters outside the scope of their competency? For example, does the fact that Julia Roberts is an Academy Award-winning actress have any relevance when she is testifying before Congress about Rett Syndrome, a neurological disorder that leaves infants unable to communicate and control body functions? Is she any more credible as a Rett Syndrome authority because she narrated a film on the Discovery Health Channel about children afflicted with the disease?

This chapter includes several examples of arguments from authority when we cite Kant, Bentham, and others who have formulated ethical theories. What makes their theories valid, however, is not whether they are recognized as experts, but whether their reasoning is sound.

False Cause

This fallacy results from observing two events and concluding that there is a causal link between them when there is no such link. Often we commit this fallacy because we do not attempt to find all the evidence proving or disproving the causal connection. For example, if as a store manager you change the opening hour for your store to 6 A.M. from 8 A.M., records for the first month of operation under the new hours may show an increase in revenue. While you may be tempted to infer that the revenue increase is due to the earlier opening hour, you should not make that conclusion until at the very least you examine store receipts showing the amount of revenue generated between 6 A.M. and 8 A.M.

The fallacy of false cause is important to businesses, which need to make valid connections between events in order to judge the effectiveness of decisions. Whether, for example, new products and an improved customer relations program increases revenues and profits should be subjected to rigorous testing, not some superficial causal analysis. Measurement tools you learn in other business classes help you eliminate false causes.

The Gambler's Fallacy

This fallacy results from the mistaken belief that independent prior outcomes affect future outcomes. Consider this example. Suppose you flip a coin five times and each time it comes up heads. What is the probability that the next coin flip will be heads? If you did not answer 50 percent, you committed the gambler's fallacy. Each coin flip is an independent event, so no number of consecutive flips producing heads will reduce the likelihood that the next flip will also be heads. That individual probability is true even though the probability

of flipping six consecutive heads is 0.5 to the sixth power, or only 1.5625 percent.

What is the relevance of the gambler's fallacy to business? We believe and are taught that business managers and professionals with higher skills and better decision-making methods are more likely to be successful than those with lesser skills and worse methods. Yet we have not discussed the importance of luck or circumstance to success. When a corporation has five years of profits rising by 30 percent, is it due to good management or because of expanding consumer demand or any number of other reasons? If a mutual fund has seven years of annual returns of at least 15 percent, is the fund's manager an investment genius or is she lucky? If it is just luck, one should not expect the luck to continue. The point is that you should not be seduced by a firm's, manager's, or even your own string of successes and immediately jump to the conclusion that the successes were the result of managerial excellence. Instead, you should use measurement tools taught in your finance, marketing, and other courses to determine the real reasons for success.

Reductio ad Absurdum

Reductio ad absurdum carries an argument to its logical end, without considering whether it is an inevitable or probable result. This is often called the **slippery slope fallacy.**

For example, if I want to convince someone not to eat fast food, I might argue, "Eating fast food will cause you to put on weight. Putting on weight will make you overweight. Soon you will weigh 400 pounds and die of heart disease. Therefore, eating fast food leads to death. Don't eat fast food." In other words, if you started eating fast food, you are on a slippery slope and will not be able to stop until you die. Although you can see that this argument makes some sense, it is absurd for most people who eat fast food.

Scientist Carl Sagan noted that the slippery slope argument is used by both sides of the abortion debate. One side says, "If we allow abortion in the first weeks of pregnancy, it will be impossible to prevent the killing of a full-term infant." The other replies, "If the state prohibits abortion even in the ninth month, it will soon be telling us what to do with our bodies around the time of conception."

Business executives face this argument frequently. Human resource managers use it to justify not making exceptions to rules, such as saying, "If we allow you time off to go to your aunt's funeral, we have to let anyone off anytime they want." Well, no, that was not what you were asking for. Executives who reason this way often are looking for administratively simple rules that do not require them to make distinctions. That is, they do not want to think hard or critically.

Pushing an argument to its limits is a useful exercise in critical thinking, often helping us to discover whether a claim has validity. The fallacy is carrying the argument to its extreme without recognizing and admitting that there are many steps along the way that are more likely consequences.

Appeals to Tradition

Appeals to tradition infer that because something has been done a certain way in the past, it should be done the same way in the future. You probably have heard people say, "I don't know why we do it, but we've always done it that way, and it's always worked, so we'll continue to do it that way." Although there is some validity to continuing to do what has stood the test of time, the reasons a business strategy has succeeded in the past may be independent of the strategy itself. The gambler's fallacy would suggest that perhaps we have just been lucky in the past. Also, changed circumstances may justify departing from previous ways of doing business.

The Lure of the New

The opposite of appeals to tradition is the lure of the new, the idea that we should do or buy something merely because it is "just released" or "improved." You see this common theme in advertising that promotes "new and improved" Tide or Windows 2005. Experience tells us that sometimes new products are better. But we can also recount examples of new car models with defects and new software with bugs that were fixed in a later version.

The lure of the new is also a common theme in management theories, as some managers have raced to embrace one new craze after another, depending on which is the hottest fad, be it Strategic Planning, Total Quality Management, Reengineering the Corporation, or Six Sigma. The point here is the same. Avoid being dazzled by claims of newness. Evaluations of ideas should be based on substance.

Sunk Cost Fallacy

The sunk cost fallacy is an attempt to recover invested time, money, and other resources, by spending still more time, money, or other resources. It is sometimes expressed as "throwing good money after bad." Stock market investors do this often. They invest $30,000 in the latest tech stock. When the investment declines to $2,000, rather than evaluate whether it is better to withdraw that $2,000 and invest it elsewhere, an investor who falls for the sunk cost fallacy might say, "I can't stop investing now, otherwise what I've invested so far will be lost." While the latter part of the statement is true, the fallacy is in the first part. Of the money already invested, $28,000 is lost whether or not the investor continues to invest. If the tech stock is not a good investment *at this time,* the rational decision is to withdraw the remaining $2,000 and not invest more money.

There are other statements that indicate business executives may fall victim to the sunk cost fallacy: "It's too late for us to change plans now." Or "If we could go back to square one, then we could make a different decision." The best way to spend the firm's remaining labor and money may be to continue a project. But that decision should be unaffected by a consideration of the labor and money already expended. The proper question is this: What project will give the firm the best return on its investment of money and other resources *from this point forward.* To continue to invest in a hopeless project is irrational, and may be a pathetic attempt to delay having to face the consequences of a poor decision.

A decision maker acts irrationally when he attempts to save face by throwing good money after bad. If you want a real world example of ego falling prey to the sunk cost fallacy, consider that President Lyndon Johnson committed American soldiers to the Vietnam Conflict after he had determined that America and South Vietnam could never defeat the Viet Cong. By falling for the sunk cost fallacy, the United States lost billions of dollars and tens of thousands of soldiers in the pursuit of a hopeless cause.

LOG ON

Go to
http://gncurtis.home.texas.net/mainpage.html
Maintained by Gary Curtis, *The Fallacy Files* cover more than 45 fallacies. Click on the link to "Taxonomy of Fallacies" to find explanations of fallacies and links to valuable resources.
Go to
www.philosophy.unimelb.edu.au/reason/critical/index.htm
Tim van Gelder's *Critical Thinking on the Web* lists some of the best websites with information about reasoning and critical thinking.

Resisting Requests to Act Unethically

Even if we follow the Guidelines for Ethical Decision Making and avoid the pitfalls of fallacious reasoning, not everyone is a CEO or his own boss and able to make decisions that everyone else follows. Sure, if you control a firm, you will do the right thing. But the reality is that for most people in the business world, other people make many decisions that you are asked to carry out. What do you do when asked to do something unethical? How can you resist a boss's request to act unethically? What could employees at WorldCom have done when its CFO instructed them to falsify the firm's books, or employees at Arthur Andersen when a partner ordered them to shred evidence?

Recognizing Unethical Requests and Bosses

A person must recognize whether he has been asked to do something unethical. While this sounds simple considering we have spent most of this chapter helping you make just that kind of decision, there are structural problems that interfere with your ability to perform an ethical analysis when a boss or colleague asks you to do something. Many of us are inclined to "do as we are told" by a superior. Therefore, it is important to recognize any tendency to accept appeals to authority and to resist the temptation to follow orders blindly. We do not want to be like the Enron accounting employee who returned to his alma mater and was asked by a student there, "What do you do at Enron?" When considering that question, apparently a question he never posed to himself, he realized that his only job was to remove liabilities from Enron's balance sheet.

For most bosses' orders, such an analysis will be unnecessary. Most of the time, a boss is herself ethical and will not ask us to do something wrong. But there are exceptions that require us to be on the lookout. Moreover, some bosses have questionable integrity, and they are more likely to give us unethical orders. Therefore, it will be helpful if we can identify bosses who have shaky ethics, for whom we should put up our ethical antennae when they come to us with a task.

Business ethicists have attempted to identify executives with questionable integrity by their actions. Ethical bosses have the ability to "tell it like it is" while those with less integrity say one thing and do another. Ethical bosses have the ability to acknowledge that they have failed, whereas those with low integrity often insist on being right all the time. Ethical bosses try to build a consensus before making an important decision; unethical bosses may generate support for their decisions with intimidation through anger and threats. Ethical bosses can think about the needs of others beside themselves. Bosses with low integrity who misuse their workers by asking them to act unethically often mistreat other people also, like secretaries and waiters.

If we pay attention to these details, we will be better able to consider the "source" when we are asked to do something by a boss and, therefore, more sensitive to the need to scrutinize the ethics of a boss's request.

Buying Time

If we think a requested action is or might be unethical, what is done next? How can we refuse to do something a boss has ordered us to do? One key is to buy some time before you have to execute the boss's order. Buying time allows you to find more facts, to understand an act's impact on the firm's stakeholders, and to evaluate the ethics of the action. It also lets you find other alternatives that achieve the boss's objectives without compromising your values. Delay also gives you time to speak with the firm's ethics officer and other confidants.

How do you buy time? If the request is in an e-mail, you might delay responding to it. Or you could answer that you have received the e-mail and will give your attention to it when you finish with the task you are working on. Similar tactics can be used with phone calls and other direct orders. Even a few hours can help your decision. Depending on the order and your ability to stack delay on top of delay, you may be able to give yourself days or weeks to find a solution to your dilemma.

The most important reason for buying time is it allows you to seek advice and assistance from other people, especially those in the firm. That brings us to the next tactic for dealing with unethical requests.

Find a Mentor and a Peer Support Group

Having a support system is one of the most important keys to survival in any organization, and it is best to put a system in place when you start working at the firm. Your support system can improve and help defend your decisions. It can also give you access to executives who hold the power to overrule your boss. Your support system should include a mentor and a network of other employees with circumstances similar to your own.

A mentor who is well established, well respected, and highly placed in the firm will help you negotiate the pitfalls that destroy employees who are ignorant of a firm's culture. A mentor can be a sounding board for your decisions; he can provide information on those who can be expected to help you and those who could hurt you; he can advise you of the procedures you should follow to avoid antagonizing potential allies. A mentor can also defend you and provide protection when you oppose a boss's decision. Many firms have a mentorship program, but if not or if your assigned mentor is deficient, you should find an appropriate mentor soon after you join the firm. Be sure to keep him updated regularly on what you are doing. By letting a mentor know that you care to keep him informed, he becomes invested in you and your career.

You should also build a community of your peers by creating a network of other workers who share your values and interests. You may want to find others who joined the firm at about the same time you did, who are about the same age, who share your passion for the firm's products and services, and who have strong ethical values. To cement the relationship, your peer support group should meet regularly, such as twice a week at work during 15-minute coffee breaks. This group can give you advice, help with difficult decisions, and unite to back up your ethical decisions.

Find Win-win Solutions

As we learned from the Guidelines for Ethical Decision Making, many times there are more than the two options of doing and not doing something. There are a number of choices in between those extremes, and the best solution may be one unconnected to them. For example, suppose your boss has ordered you to fire someone who works under you. The worker's productivity may be lagging, and perhaps he has made a few costly mistakes. Yet you think it would be wrong to fire the worker at this time. What do you do?

Find a win-win solution, that is, a compromise that works for you and your boss. First, discover your boss's wants. Probably you will find that your boss wants an employee who makes no or few mistakes and has a certain level of productivity. Next determine what is needed for the affected employee to reach that level. If you find the employee is having emotional problems that interfere with his work, are they temporary or can we help him handle them? Can we make him more productive by giving him more training? Is the employee unmotivated or is he unaware that he lags behind other workers? Should we give him a warning and place him on probationary status for a month, releasing him if there is no satisfac-

tory improvement? These alternatives may address your boss's concerns about the employee without compromising your ethical values.

In other contexts, you may need to approach your boss directly and show that her order is not right for the firm. Using the Guidelines for Ethical Decision Making and valid arguments, you may be able to persuade your boss to accept your perspective and avoid an otherwise unethical decision. Finding a win-win solution is possible only when there is room for compromise. The Ethical Guidelines and logical arguments are effective when your boss respects reason and wants to act ethically. However, when you face an intractable executive demanding you do something illegal, a different response is needed.

Work within the Firm to Stop the Unethical Act

Suppose you receive an order from an executive you know or suspect to be corrupt. For example, a CFO is motivated to increase the price of the firm's stock in order to make her stock options more valuable. She orders you to book in the current year revenue that in fact will not be received for at least two years, if ever. Booking that revenue would be fraudulent, unethical, and illegal. You are convinced the CFO knows of the illegality and will find someone else to book the revenue if you refuse. You probably will lose your job if you do not cooperate. What do you do?

This is when your mentor, peer support group, and corporate ethics officer can help you. Your mentor may have access to the CEO or audit committee, who if honest should back you and fire the CFO. Your peer support group might have similar access. The corporate ethics officer, especially if she is a lawyer in the firm's legal department, can also provide her backing and that of the legal department.

There is one large caveat however. While the situation just described should and probably will result in your support system rallying to your support, in other situations that are ethically ambiguous, you, your mentor, and your support group may find that fighting a battle against a top corporate executive ineffectively expends your and your colleagues' political capital. In other words, you need to pick your battles carefully lest you and your colleagues at the firm be labeled whiners and troublemakers who unnecessarily seek intervention from higher level corporate executives. This is why we have listed this alternative near the end of our discussion. In most situations, it is better to rely on your colleagues as advisors

CONCEPT REVIEW

Resisting Requests to Do Unethical Acts

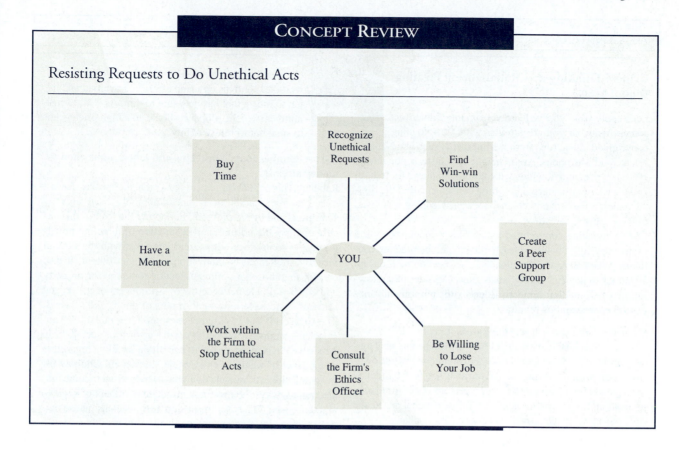

and to execute win-win solutions in cooperation with your boss.

But if neither compromise nor other intra-firm tactics protect you from unethical requests, you are left with a final tactic.

Prepare to Lose Your Job

This is the last tactic, because by quitting or losing your job you are deprived of your ability to help the firm make ethical decisions. Only as an employee can you craft win-win solutions or work within the firm to do the right thing.

But if a firm's executives and its internal governance are so corrupted that neither compromise nor reason can steer the firm away from an unethical and illegal course, you must be willing to walk away from your job or be fired for standing up for your values. Do not want your job and the status it brings so much that you are willing

to compromise more important values. It is tough losing a job when one has obligations to family, banks, and other creditors as well as aspirations for a better life. But if you prepare yourself financially from day one, putting away money for an ethical rainy day, you will protect more important values.

Problems and Problem Cases

1. You are one of three owners of a consulting company with annual revenues of $80,000,000. You are the partner in charge of human resources. One of the company's senior staff consultants, Libby Hope, has worked for your firm for seven years. Libby is the head of her household, supporting her three school-age children and disabled husband. For the last three months, Libby's work performance has declined below her usually high level. Her productivity is now in the lower quarter of the

ETHICS IN ACTION

Critical Thinking and Rationalizing Pirating Digital Music

Let's apply what you've learned from the chapter to a context many of you are familiar with: downloading copyrighted music files from the Internet at sites like Napster, Kazaa, and Morpheus. At the height of Napster's popularity, 100 users a second downloaded copyrighted music for free. In 2002, each month nearly 20 million consumers used the digital underground to download bootlegged copies of music, movies, games, and software.

Downloading copyrighted music files without permission of the copyright owner is clearly illegal, yet the practice continues. Why? Because downloaders use five common rationalizations to justify stealing music files. Consider the following excuses and their rebuttals. Identify the possible fallacies in each excuse and its rebuttal.

Excuse number one: Everybody does it.
Rebuttal: That just isn't true. Far fewer than all people steal music files. Less than 20 percent of American Internet users download music without paying for it. Even at its height, Napster had only 60,000,000 users, less than 25 percent of the American population. But even if more people did steal digital music, the folly of following the crowd in every context is clear.

Second excuse: It's the music labels' fault. They release albums with only one good track per album, yet charge 15 to 20 dollars at retail.
Rebuttal: There's some truth in that excuse, because there is evidence of market failure, of the music labels' failure to respond to some consumers' wants. And there is some evidence that labels have conspired to keep the price of CDs high. The excuse's flaw is this: taken literally it means that you can exact vigilante justice, that you are allowed to steal a seller's property if the price is too high or the seller engages in illegal conduct itself. It would excuse, for example, your stealing someone's house if you think his asking price is too high. Instead, the proper response to a high price is: don't buy.

Excuse number three: I wouldn't buy the CD anyway.
Rebuttal: This argument intends to prove that the stolen music has no value to the music thief, so he should not pay. That explanation exposes the flaw in the excuse. Of course the music has value to the thief, just as it does for any other listener. That value may not approach the price the music label

charges, but it is clear that no one, not even a thief, would expend his time and effort to download and listen to music that has no value to him. As with excuse number two, the proper response to a high price is not to steal but to refuse to buy.

Excuse number four: Musicians and labels make enough money already.
Rebuttal: This populist argument shows that the speaker doesn't trust the free market. It is one commonly used also by shoplifters and office pilferers. Following the lead of this excuse disrupts the normal market function of directing profits to those who produce output, and interferes with the flow of incentives essential to innovation and higher output. It also creates an atmosphere of disrespect or contempt for property and erects a divide between haves—producers of goods and services—and have nots—consumers of goods and services. The speaker of this excuse believes not in capitalism, but instead in socialism, and perhaps only a form of socialism in which wealth is redistributed to benefit the speaker, regardless of his level of wealth. For example, consumers who pay for music subsidize those who don't pay, yet those who pirate music aren't always the most downtrodden members of society, and those who do pay for music and the musicians whose music is stolen are often not among the wealthiest.

Excuse number five: I'm merely sampling the music to decide if I like it, just as I test drive a car before I buy it.
Rebuttal: That excuse is easy to rebut for most thieves, who in fact don't merely sample or test the music, but retain it and listen to it multiple times. But even if a digital thief is merely testing music, that doesn't justify taking control over another's property without the owner's permission. You can't test-drive a car unless you obtain the dealer's consent and agree to the dealer's conditions. You can't, for example, during a test drive take a dealer's SUV for two days on a weekend vacation in Yellowstone National Park. That's called grand theft auto.

Music labels and other owners of music should and do have the right to determine how their music will be sampled, such as allowing downloads of only partial tracks or limiting the number of times a downloaded song will play. To do otherwise removes an essential right from a property owner's bundle of rights: the power to control who possesses the property and when.

firm's staff consultants. Many of the firm's consultants with years fewer experience are outperforming her. Libby's salary is near the highest of the firm's consultants. What do the Guidelines for Ethical Decision Making suggest you do first?

2. You are a director of Dorsey Entertainment Company, a business in the family entertainment industry operating theme parks and producing motion pictures. During its 70-year history, Dorsey has produced only G-rated and PG-rated movies, which are suitable for nearly all audiences. The corporation has refused to enter the lucrative teenage- and adult-movie market of PG-13 and R-rated movies, some of which espouse questionable moral values regarding criminal conduct, drugs, language, and sex. In each of the last three years, Dorsey's motion picture revenues have decreased 5 percent and earnings from movie operations are flat. In an attempt to increase profitability, Dorsey's CEO has proposed to the board of directors that the company produce R-rated movies aimed at high school and college students. The movies will contain a mix of drug use and sexual promiscuity attractive to the teenage and young adult demographic. Projections show that if Dorsey produces R-rated movies, its motion picture profits will increase by 15 percent in each of the next five years. You are a Dorsey director. Using the Guidelines for Ethical Decision Making, what do you want to know before you decide whether you will support the proposal of the CEO?

3. You are a director of SeaGold Canning Company. SeaGold's business is canning tuna and salmon for sale to consumers. Its annual revenue is $575,000,000, 75 percent from tuna sales. SeaGold buys tuna from independent fishermen whose fishing methods do not always permit them to determine whether they are catching tuna or dolphins. The result is that many dolphins are killed. The Society to Protect All Sea Mammals (SPASM) has discovered that fishermen selling to SeaGold have been killing dolphins and has asked SeaGold to demand that the fishermen not kill dolphins and to refuse to buy tuna from fishermen who kill dolphins. If SeaGold does not comply with SPASM's request, SPASM will call a press conference to urge consumers to stop buying SeaGold tuna and salmon.

For fisherman to change their fishing methods would result in SeaGold paying an additional $3,000,000 each year for tuna. If SeaGold passes the cost on to consumers, the price of tuna will increase from $2.05 per can from the present $1.95 per can. Since SeaGold tuna now sells for the same price as other tuna brands, SeaGold expects its sales to fall by 10 percent if it increases the price of its

tuna. What would a rights theorist do? What would you do as a SeaGold director?

4. One of your employees is a widower with two preteen children. By working full time for your firm, he is able to make just enough to support his family. He has asked that you allow him to have more flexible work hours than the firm's policies allow, including permitting him to do some work at home. The flexible hours would let him help his children get ready for school and greet them at home when the school day ends. He is able to prove that he can complete all the tasks you give him despite having more flexible hours. Using justice theory, how would you justify a decision to exempt him from the firm's office-hours policies? Would a profit maximizer make the same decision?

5. Marigold Dairy Corporation sells milk products, including powdered milk formula for infants. Marigold hopes to increase sales of its powdered milk formula in Ethiopia and other African nations where mothers are often malnourished due to drought and war. Marigold's marketing department has created a marketing plan to convince mothers and expectant mothers not to breast-feed their babies and instead to use Marigold formula. Doctors generally favor breastfeeding as beneficial to mothers (it helps the uterus return to normal size), to babies (it is nutritious and strengthens the bonds between the infant and the mother), and to families (it is inexpensive). Marigold's marketing plan stresses the good nutrition of its formula and the convenience to parents of using it, including not having to breastfeed.

You are the Senior Vice President of Marketing for Marigold. Do you approve this marketing plan? What would a rights theorist do? What would a utilitarian do? What would a profit maximizer do?

6. During World War II, the insecticide DDT was used successfully to halt a typhus epidemic spread by lice and to control mosquitoes and flies. After World War II, it was used extensively to control agricultural and household pests. Today, DDT may not be used legally in the United States and most other countries. Although DDT has a rather low immediate toxicity to humans and other vertebrates, it becomes concentrated in fatty tissues of the body. In addition, it degrades slowly, remaining toxic in the soil for years after its application. But there has never been any credible evidence that this residue has caused any harm. Even so, DDT has been blamed for the near extinction of bald eagles, whose population has increased greatly since DDT was banned.

In 2002, over 3,600 people in the United States were infected by and over 210 people killed after contracting

West Nile virus, which is carried to humans by mosquitoes. CDC director Julie Geberding called West Nile virus an "emerging, infectious disease epidemic" that could be spread all the way to the Pacific Coast by birds and mosquitoes. Pesticides such as malathion, resmethrin, and sumithrin can be effective in killing mosquitoes but are significantly limited because they do not stay in the environment after spraying.

As an executive for Eartho Chemical Company, you have been asked by Eartho's CEO to study whether Eartho should resume the manufacture of DDT. What would a utilitarian decide? What would a profit maximizer do?

7. Gexxeg Company manufactures electrical capacitors. During the manufacturing process, toxic wastes are produced. Gexxeg hires Tox-Rid Corporation to dispose of the waste. Tox-Rid charges $2,000 per day, half the charge of any other toxic waste disposal company. A year after Tox-Rid began disposing Gexxeg's toxic wastes, as vice president of business operations, you discover that Tox-Rid is not disposing of the waste properly, but merely dumping it in a field. The waste has contaminated the dirt in the field and ground water beneath it.

A corporation that knowingly has another person dispose of its toxic waste illegally is subject to a fine of $50,000 per day. However, there is only a 2 percent chance that the dumping will be detected in the next 10 years. Besides, no one else at Gexxeg knows about the illegal dumping and no one knows that you know about the dumping. Hence, it would be difficult, if not impossible, to prove that Gexxeg knowingly had someone dispose of its toxic waste illegally.

What do you do if you believe that ethics requires you to maximize Gexxeg's profits?

8. You are a partner in an investment banking firm. One of your clients is a software company that has seen dramatic increases in its revenues and profits in the last three years. The firm's CEO has dominated the company for its entire five-year life. The CEO and her children own 80 percent of the company's shares, and the corporation's directors comprise only the CEO, her three children, and three of her closest friends.

As the investment banker, you recommend that the corporation go public by selling an additional 30,000,000 shares in an initial public offering (IPO). After the IPO, 40 percent of the company's shares will be held by persons outside the CEO's family. The CEO will control a majority of the shares.

You want to optimize the price of the IPO shares by making the shares more attractive to public investors. What corporate governance improvements do you recommend the client adopt to increase the IPO's price?

9. In 2002, the National Council of Women's Organizations demanded that the all-male Augusta National Golf Club, which hosts the annual Masters Tournament in April, admit women as members. When rebuffed by Augusta National, the NCWO approached IBM and The Coca-Cola Company, sponsors of the Masters Tournament, to attempt to encourage them to withdraw as sponsors of the Masters. NCWO also contacted CBS Television, the national television broadcaster, asking that CBS not broadcast the tournament. On a national sports radio show, the NCWO admitted that Augusta has the legal right to be an all-male club under the laws of Georgia and the United States. When asked to explain why August National should open its membership to women, an NCWO representative stated that discriminating against women is wrong. When asked to explain further, the representative said, "Because it's the right thing to do in our society." The radio host asked the NCWO representative why she thought the club excluded women, and she replied, "This is just men being men."

Can you identify the fallacies used by the NCWO?

10. You are hired as a staff consultant by a large national consulting firm. Your office has 50 partners and 250 staff consultants. You are one of 15 new staff consultants hired by the firm. Assigned to the information technology practice of the firm, you, three other new hires, and five other staff consultants are directed by two senior staff consultants, who answer to one of the firm's partners. Draft a plan that will help you identify and resist requests by a client or firm employee to do an unethical act.

Online Research: Josephson Institute of Ethics

Josephson Institute of Ethics is a leading source of materials for businesses and executives who want to act ethically.

- Find the Josephson website.
- List the "Five Steps to Principled Reasoning" and the "Six Pillars of Character."
- You can also participate in discussions on ethics at the Josephson chatroom.

PART TWO

CRIMES AND TORTS

5

CRIMES

Notra Trulock served as Director of the Office of Intelligence of the U.S. Department of Energy (DOE) from 1994 to 1998. During his years with the DOE, Trulock claimed to have uncovered evidence that Chinese spies had infiltrated the Los Alamos Nuclear Weapons Laboratory and other U.S. weapons facilities, and that the White House, the Federal Bureau of Investigation (FBI), and the Central Intelligence Agency (CIA) had ignored his warnings about this espionage. Trulock testified before congressional committees on this subject and, after he no longer worked for the DOE, published a related article that criticized the White House, the FBI, and the CIA. He contended that the article revealed no classified information.

Linda Conrad, a DOE employee, owned a townhouse where she and Trulock lived. After Trulock had left the department, Conrad's DOE supervisor contacted her. According to Conrad, the supervisor informed her that FBI agents wanted to talk with her about Trulock, that the FBI had a warrant to search her townhouse, and that if she did not cooperate, FBI agents would break down the townhouse's door while members of the press watched. Conrad submitted to a three-hour interview by FBI agents, who asked about Trulock's personal records and computer files. Conrad told the agents that she and Trulock shared a computer, which was located at the townhouse. She also said, however, that she and Trulock maintained separate password-protected files on the computer's hard drive, and that neither knew the other's password. Therefore, she was unable to access his private files. At the end of the interview, Conrad signed a form whose terms revealed her supposed consent to a search of the townhouse. The FBI agents said nothing to Conrad about whether they had a search warrant. In fact, they did not have one.

The FBI agents searched the townhouse pursuant to Conrad's supposed consent. They did not seek Trulock's permission. During the search, the agents found the computer Conrad had mentioned during the interview. One of the agents, aided by an FBI computer specialist, searched the computer's files for approximately 90 minutes. According to allegations made by Trulock and Conrad in an eventual legal challenge to the FBI's actions, the agent examined Trulock's password-protected files.

Think about the above scenario and these questions as you read Chapter 5:

• On which provision of the U.S. Constitution were Trulock and Conrad relying in their legal challenge to the FBI's actions?

• Assuming that a warrantless search by government agents does not violate the Constitution if there has been valid consent to the search, did Conrad provide valid consent?

• Assuming for the sake of argument that Conrad legitimately consented to the search, was her consent binding on *Trulock* with regard to the FBI agents':

    A. search of the townhouse itself?

    B. examination of computer files to which both Conrad and Trulock had access?

    C. examination of Trulock's password-protected computer files?

THE LIST FEATURES FAMILIAR names: Enron, Arthur Andersen, WorldCom, Adelphia, ImClone, Global Crossing, and Tyco, as well as others not mentioned here. These firms and their executives dominated the headlines during 2002, but not for reasons any corporation or executive would find desirable. Instead, they acquired the notoriety associated with widely publicized financial scandals, related civil litigation, and criminal prosecutions that were actually pursued by the government, seriously contemplated by prosecutors, or argued for by the public and political figures of varying stripes.

In the previous edition of this text, the first paragraph of Chapter 5 noted the importance of studying criminal law as part of a business manager's education but conceded that "[w]hen one lists legal topics relevant to business, criminal law comes to mind less readily than contracts, torts, agency, corporations, and various other subjects dealt with in this text." That statement, of course, was written prior to 2002. Given the media, public, and governmental attention devoted to corporate scandals during 2002, it might be argued that criminal law now comes to mind *more* readily than certain other subjects on the list of legal topics relevant to business. At the very least, recent events involving high-profile firms and executives have demonstrated that business managers create considerable risk for themselves and their firms if they ignore the criminal law or lack a working understanding of it.

Role of the Criminal Law

This century has witnessed society's increasing tendency to use the criminal law as a major device for controlling corporate behavior. Many regulatory statutes establish criminal and civil penalties for statutory violations. The criminal penalties often apply to individual employees as well as to their employers.

Advocates of using the criminal law in this way typically argue that doing so achieves a deterrence level superior to that produced by damage awards and other civil remedies. Corporations may be inclined to treat damage awards as simply a business cost and to violate regulatory provisions when doing so makes economic sense. Criminal prosecutions, however, threaten corporations with the stigma of a criminal conviction. In some cases, the criminal law allows society to penalize employees who would not be directly affected by a civil judgment against their employer. Moreover, by alerting private parties to a violation that could also give rise to a civil lawsuit for damages, criminal prosecutions may increase the likelihood that a corporation will bear the full costs of its actions.

Our examination of the criminal law's role in today's legal environment of business begins with consideration of the nature and essential components of the criminal law. The chapter then explores various problems encountered in applying the criminal law to the corporate setting.

Nature of Crimes

Crimes are *public wrongs*—acts prohibited by the state or federal government. Criminal prosecutions are initiated by a prosecutor (an elected or appointed government employee) in the name of the state or the United States, whichever is appropriate. Persons convicted of crimes bear the stigma of a criminal conviction and face the punitive force of the criminal sanction.

Our legal system also contemplates noncriminal consequences for violations of legal duties. The next two chapters deal with *torts,* private wrongs for which the wrongdoer must pay money damages to compensate the harmed victim. In some tort cases, the court may also assess punitive damages in order to punish the wrongdoer. Only the criminal sanction, however, combines the threat to life or liberty with the stigma of conviction.

Crimes are typically classified as felonies or misdemeanors. A **felony** is a serious crime such as murder, rape, arson, drug-dealing, or a theft or fraud offense of sufficient magnitude. Most felonies involve significant moral culpability on the offender's part. Felonies are punishable by lengthy confinement of the convicted offender to a penitentiary, as well as by a fine. A person convicted of a felony may experience other adverse consequences, such as disenfranchisement (loss of voting rights) and disqualification from the practice of certain professions (e.g., law or medicine). A **misdemeanor** is a lesser offense such as disorderly conduct or battery resulting in minor physical harm to the victim. Misdemeanor offenses usually involve less—sometimes much less—moral culpability than felony offenses. As such, misdemeanors are punishable by lesser fines and/or limited confinement in jail. Depending on their seriousness and potential for harm to the public, traffic violations are classified either as misdemeanors or as less serious **infractions.** Really only quasi-criminal, infractions usually are punishable by fines but not by confinement in jail.

Purpose of the Criminal Sanction

Disagreements about when the criminal sanction should be employed sometimes stem from a dispute over its purpose. Persons accepting the *utilitarian* view believe that prevention of socially undesirable behavior is the only proper purpose of criminal penalties. This prevention goal includes three major components: deterrence, rehabilitation, and incapacitation.

Deterrence theorists maintain that the threat or imposition of punishment deters the commission of crimes in two ways. The first, *special deterrence,* occurs when punishment of an offender deters him from committing further crimes. The second, *general deterrence,* results when punishment of a wrongdoer deters other persons from committing similar offenses. Factors influencing the probable effectiveness of deterrence include the respective likelihoods that the crime will be detected, that detection will be followed by prosecution, and that prosecution will result in a conviction. The severity of the probable punishment also serves as a key factor.

A fundamental problem attending deterrence theories is that we cannot be certain whether deterrence works, because we cannot determine reliably what the crime rate would be in the absence of punishment. Similarly, high levels of crime and recidivism (repeat offenses by previously punished offenders) may indicate only that sufficiently severe and certain criminal sanctions have not been employed, not that criminal sanctions in general cannot ef-

fectively deter. Deterrence theory's other major problem is its assumption that potential offenders are rational beings who consciously weigh the threat of punishment against the benefits derived from an offense. The threat of punishment, however, may not deter the commission of criminal offenses produced by irrational or unconscious drives.

Rehabilitation of convicted offenders—changing their attitudes or values so that they are not inclined to commit future offenses—serves as another way to prevent undesirable behavior. Critics of rehabilitation commonly point to high rates of recidivism as evidence of the general failure of rehabilitation efforts to date. Even if rehabilitation efforts fail, however, *incapacitation* of convicted offenders contributes to the goal of prevention. While incarcerated, offenders have much less ability to commit other crimes.

Prevention is not the only asserted goal of the criminal sanction. Some persons see *retribution*—the infliction of deserved suffering on violators of society's most fundamental rules—as the central focus of criminal punishment. Under this theory, punishment satisfies community and individual desires for revenge and reinforces important social values.

Figure 1   *State and Federal Approaches to Sentencing of Convicted Offenders*

Typical State Approaches

As a general rule, state laws on criminal punishments seek to further the deterrence, rehabilitation, and incapacitation purposes discussed in the text. State statutes usually set forth ranges of sentences (e.g., minimum and maximum amounts of fines and imprisonment) for each crime established by law. The court sets the convicted offender's sentence within the appropriate range unless the court places the defendant on probation.

Probation is effectively a conditional sentence that suspends the usual imprisonment and/or fine if the offender "toes the line" and meets other judicially imposed conditions for the period specified by the court. It is sometimes granted to first-time offenders and other convicted defendants deemed suitable candidates by the court. In deciding whether to order probation or an appropriate sentence within the statutory range, the court normally places considerable reliance on information contained in a presentence investigation conducted by the state probation office.

The Federal Approach

The federal approach to sentencing was essentially the same until the Federal Sentencing Guidelines set by the U.S. Sentencing Commission took effect. In the Sentencing Reform Act of 1984, Congress created the Sentencing Commission and authorized it to develop sentencing guidelines. Congress thereby sought to reduce judicial discretion in sentencing and to minimize disparities among sentences imposed by judges on similar offenders. The Sentencing Guidelines, which are binding on federal courts and have been criticized by some judges, contain a table with more than 40 levels of seriousness of offense. Where a particular offender's crime and corresponding sentence are listed on the table depends on various factors associated with the offense and on the offender's prior criminal history. The court normally must sentence the defendant to what the table shows, although departures are allowed in the event of exceptional circumstances specified by the court. A special subset of rules known as the Corporate Sentencing Guidelines (discussed later in this chapter) governs the sentencing of organizations convicted of federal crimes.

For various crimes, the Federal Sentencing Guidelines appear to have led to the imposition of more severe—sometimes much more severe—sentences than had previously been the case. Although the prospect of probation for certain offenses still exists, an increased use of incarceration of individuals convicted of serious offenses also appears to have resulted. As for what purposes incarceration should serve, the Sentencing Reform Act specifically rejected rehabilitation as one of them. Instead, the statute stated that the goals of punishment should be education, deterrence, and incapacitation.

Figure 1 explains how state and federal law approach the proper determination of a convicted offender's punishment.

Essentials of Crime

To convict a defendant of a crime, the government ordinarily must: (1) demonstrate that his alleged acts violated a criminal statute; (2) prove beyond a reasonable doubt that he committed those acts; and (3) prove that he had the capacity to form a criminal intent. Crimes are *statutory* offenses. A given behavior is not a crime unless Congress or a state legislature has criminalized it.[1] As illustrated by the *Sun-Diamond Growers* case, which follows, courts normally interpret criminal statutes narrowly.

---

[1]Infractions of a minor criminal or quasi-criminal nature (such as traffic offenses) are often established by city or county ordinances but will not be considered here. For discussion of ordinances as a type of law, see Chapter 1.

United States v. Sun-Diamond Growers of California
526 U.S. 398 (U.S. Sup. Ct. 1999)

Sun-Diamond Growers of California was a trade association engaged in marketing and lobbying activities on behalf of its member cooperatives, which were owned by 5,000 producers of raisins, figs, walnuts, prunes, and hazelnuts. A federal grand jury indicted Sun-Diamond for an alleged violation of the illegal gratuity statute, 18 USC Section 201(c)(1)(A), which criminalizes a private party's giving of "anything of value" to a public official "for or because of any official act performed or to be performed" by the public official.

According to the indictment, Sun-Diamond violated Section 201(c)(1)(A) by giving then-Secretary of Agriculture Michael Espy approximately $5,900 in gratuities (tickets to the U.S. Open Tennis Tournament, luggage, meals, a framed print, and a crystal bowl). The indictment alluded to two Department of Agriculture–related matters in which Sun-Diamond had an interest in favorable treatment at the time Sun-Diamond gave the gifts to Secretary Espy. Nevertheless, the indictment did not allege a specific connection between either of the two matters and Sun-Diamond's conferral of the gifts. A federal district court jury found Sun-Diamond guilty. Holding that the district judge erred in instructing the jury that "it is sufficient if Sun-Diamond provided Espy with unauthorized compensation simply because he held public office," the U.S. Court of Appeals for the District of Columbia Circuit reversed and remanded. The U.S. Supreme Court granted certiorari.

Scalia, Justice In this case, we consider whether conviction under the illegal gratuity statute requires any showing beyond the fact that a gratuity was given because of the recipient's official position. The district court's instructions suggested that Section 201(c)(1)(A) did not require any connection between Sun-Diamond's intent [in giving the gifts] and a specific official act. [The statute] would be satisfied, according to the instructions, merely by a showing that Sun-Diamond gave Secretary Espy a gratuity because of his official position—perhaps, for example, to build a reservoir of goodwill that might ultimately affect one or more of a multitude of unspecified acts, now and in the future. The United States contends that [this interpretation of the statute] was correct.

This interpretation does not fit comfortably with the statutory text, which prohibits only gratuities given "for or because of *any official act* performed or to be performed" (emphasis added). It seems to us that this means "for or because of some particular official act of whatever identity"— just as the question "Do you like any composer?" normally means "Do you like some particular composer?" It is lin-

guistically possible, of course, for the phrase to mean "for or because of official acts in general, without specification as to which one"—just as the question "Do you like any composer?" could mean "Do you like all composers, no matter their names or music?" But the former seems to us the more natural meaning. Why go through the trouble of requiring that the gift be made "for or because of any official act" . . . and then defining "official act" (in Section 201(a)(3)) to mean "any decision or action on any question, matter, cause, suit, proceeding or controversy, which may at any time be pending, or which may by law be brought before any public official in such official's official capacity," when, if the Government's interpretation were correct, it would have sufficed to say "for or because of such official's ability to favor the donor in executing the functions of his office"? The insistence upon an "official act," carefully defined, seems pregnant with the requirement that some particular official act be identified and proved.

Besides thinking that this is the more natural meaning of Section 201(c)(1)(A), we are inclined to believe it correct because of the peculiar results that the Government's alternative reading would produce. It would criminalize, for example, token gifts to the President based on his official position and not linked to any identifiable act—such as the replica jerseys given by championship sports teams each year during ceremonial White House visits. Similarly, it would criminalize a high school principal's gift of a school baseball cap to the Secretary of Education, by reason of his office, on the occasion of the latter's visit to the school. That these examples are not fanciful is demonstrated by the fact that counsel for the United States maintained at oral argument that a group of farmers would violate Section 201(c)(1)(A) by providing a complimentary lunch for the Secretary of Agriculture in conjunction with his speech to the farmers concerning various matters of USDA policy—so long as the Secretary had before him, or

had in prospect, matters affecting the farmers. Of course the Secretary of Agriculture *always* has before him or in prospect matters that affect farmers, just as the President always has before him or in prospect matters that affect college and professional sports, and the Secretary of Education matters that affect high schools.

A statute in this field that can linguistically be interpreted to be either a meat axe or a scalpel should reasonably be taken to be the latter. We hold that in order to establish a violation of 18 USC Section 201(c)(1)(A), the Government must prove a link between a thing of value conferred upon a public official and a specific "official act" for or because of which it was given.

Judgment of Court of Appeals affirmed.

Constitutional Limitations on Power to Criminalize Behavior

The U.S. Constitution prohibits *ex post facto* criminal laws. This means that a defendant's act must have been prohibited by statute at the time she committed it and that the penalty imposed must be the one provided for at the time of her offense.

The Constitution places other limits on legislative power to criminalize behavior. If behavior is constitutionally protected, it cannot be deemed criminal. For example, the **right of privacy** held implicit in the Constitution caused the Supreme Court, in *Griswold v. Connecticut* (1965), to strike down state statutes that prohibited the use of contraceptive devices and the counseling or assisting of others in the use of such devices. This decision provided the constitutional basis for the Court's historic *Roe v. Wade* (1973) decision, which limited the states' power to criminalize abortions.

By prohibiting laws that unreasonably restrict **freedom of speech,** the First Amendment plays a major role in limiting governmental power to enact and enforce criminal laws. As explained in Chapter 3, the First Amendment protects a broad range of noncommercial speech, including expression of a political, literary, or artistic nature as well as speech that deals with economic, scientific, or ethical issues or with other matters of public interest or concern. The First Amendment protection for noncommercial speech is so substantial that it is called "full" protection.

Commercial speech, on the other hand, receives a less substantial First Amendment shield known as "intermediate" protection. Does a speaker or writer with a profit motive (e.g., the author who hopes to make money on her book) therefore receive only intermediate First Amendment protection? No, as a general rule, because the mere presence of a profit motive does not keep expression from being fully protected noncommercial speech. Moreover, the commercial speech designation is usually reserved for what the Supreme Court has termed "speech that does no more than propose a commercial transaction." The best example of commercial speech is an advertisement for a product, service, or business.

Despite receiving less-than-full protection, commercial speech is far from a First Amendment outcast. Recent Supreme Court decisions, as noted in Chapter 3, have effectively raised commercial speech's intermediate protection to a level near that of full protection. Therefore, regardless of whether it is full or intermediate in strength, the First Amendment protection extended to expression means that governmental attempts to hold persons criminally liable for the content of their written or spoken statements are often unconstitutional.

Some speech falls outside the First Amendment umbrella, however. In a long line of cases, the Supreme Court has established that *obscene* expression receives no First Amendment protection. Purveyors of obscene books, movies, and other similar works may therefore be criminally convicted of violating an obscenity statute even though it is the works' content (i.e., the speech) that furnishes the basis for the conviction. Expression is obscene only if the government proves each element of the controlling obscenity test, which the Supreme Court established in *Miller v. California* (1973):

(a) [That] the average person, applying contemporary community standards, would find that the work, taken as a whole, appeals to the prurient interest; (b) [that] the work depicts or describes, in a patently offensive way, [explicit] sexual conduct specifically defined by the applicable state law; and (c) [that] the work, taken as a whole, lacks serious literary, artistic, political, or scientific value.

If any of the three elements is not proven, the work is not obscene; instead, it is entitled to First Amendment protection.

The *Miller* test's final element is the one most likely to derail the government's obscenity case against a defendant. Books, movies, and other materials that contain explicit sexual content are not obscene if they have serious literary, artistic, political, or scientific value—and they generally do. In view of the *Miller* test's final element, moreover, certain publications that might fairly be regarded as "pornographic" are likely to escape being classified as obscene.

Although nonobscene expression carries First Amendment protection, Supreme Court decisions have allowed the government limited latitude to regulate *indecent* speech in order to protect minors from being exposed to such material. Indecent expression contains considerable sexual content but stops short of being obscene, often because of the presence of serious literary, artistic, political, or scientific value (for adults, at least). Assume that a state statute requires magazines available for sale at a store to be located behind a store counter rather than on an unattended display rack, if the magazines feature nudity and sexual content and the store is open to minors. This statute primarily restricts indecent expression because most magazines contemplated by the law are unlikely to be obscene. If the statute is challenged on First Amendment grounds and the court concludes that it is narrowly tailored to further the protection-of-minors purpose, it will survive First Amendment scrutiny. A law that restricts too much expression suitable for adults, however, will violate the First Amendment even if the government's aim was to safeguard minors.

In a 1997 decision and two 2002 decisions, the Supreme Court considered the First Amendment fates of the Communications Decency Act, the Child Online Protection Act, and the Child Pornography Prevention Act. Each of the three statutes was designed to protect minors against indecent or pornographic expression. The cases are discussed in two nearby Cyberlaw in Action boxes.

In addition to limiting the sorts of behavior that may be made criminal, the Constitution limits the manner in which behavior may be criminalized. The **due process** clauses of the Fifth and Fourteenth Amendments (dis-

cussed in Chapter 3) require that criminal statutes define the prohibited behavior precisely enough to enable law enforcement officers and ordinary members of the public to understand which behavior violates the law. Statutes that fail to provide such fair notice may be challenged as unconstitutionally vague. The Fourteenth Amendment's **equal protection** clause (also discussed in Chapter 3) prohibits criminal statutes that discriminatorily treat certain persons of the same class or arbitrarily discriminate among different classes of persons. Legislatures usually are extended considerable latitude in making statutory classifications if the classifications have a rational basis. "Suspect" classifications, such as those based on race, are subjected to much closer judicial scrutiny, however.

Finally, the Constitution limits the type of punishment imposed on convicted offenders. The Eighth Amendment forbids **cruel and unusual punishments.** This prohibition furnishes, for example, the constitutional basis for judicial decisions establishing limits on imposition of the death penalty. Although various Supreme Court cases indicate that the Eighth Amendment may bar a sentence whose harshness is disproportionate to the seriousness of the defendant's offense, the Court has signaled that any Eighth Amendment concerns along these lines are unlikely to be triggered unless the sentence–crime disproportionality is exceedingly gross.

Proof beyond a Reasonable Doubt The serious matters at stake in a criminal case—the life and liberty of the accused—justify our legal system's placement of significant limits on the government's power to convict a person of a crime. A fundamental safeguard is the *presumption of innocence*; defendants in criminal cases are presumed innocent until proven guilty. The due process clauses require the government to overcome this presumption by proving beyond a reasonable doubt every element of the offense charged against the defendant.[2] Requiring the government to meet this stern burden of proof minimizes the risk of erroneous criminal convictions.

Defendant's Criminal Intent and Capacity Most serious crimes require *mens rea,* or criminal intent, as an element. The level of fault required for a criminal violation depends on the wording of the relevant

---

[2]The beyond a reasonable doubt standard required of the government in criminal cases contemplates a stronger and more convincing showing than that required of plaintiffs in civil cases. As explained in Chapter 2, plaintiffs in civil cases need only prove the elements of their claims by a preponderance of the evidence.

CYBERLAW IN ACTION

The Unconstitutional Communications Decency Act

With the Communications Decency Act of 1996 (CDA), Congress made its first attempt to protect minors from exposure to sexually explicit material on the Internet. The CDA criminalized the knowing transmission of obscene or indecent messages over the Internet to anyone under 18 years of age, as well as the knowing display of "patently offensive" material on the Internet in a manner that would allow persons under 18 to obtain access to it.

In *Reno v. American Civil Liberties Union,* 521 U.S. 844 (1997), the U.S. Supreme Court struck down most of the CDA on First Amendment grounds. Although its restrictions on obscene speech survived because such expression carries no First Amendment protection, the CDA's attempt to regulate the transmission and display of indecent or "patently offensive" material was a different story. The Court observed that "the breadth of the CDA's coverage [was] wholly unprecedented," covering not only commercial speech and other speech of businesses but also considerable expression of non-profit entities and individual persons. By not clearly defining "indecent" and "patently offensive," the CDA risked sweeping in "large amounts of nonpornographic material with serious educational or other value." Another fatal defect was that the CDA cut deeply into the realm of expression that adults were entitled to receive.

The Child Online Protection Act

After the CDA's demise, Congress enacted the Child Online Protection Act (COPA), which provides for civil and criminal actions against any person who "knowingly and with knowledge of the character of the material," uses the World Wide Web to "make any communication for commercial purposes that is available to any minor and that includes any material that is harmful to minors." The COPA defines "material . . . harmful to minors" as material that is obscene or that (1) contains graphic sexual content, (2) would be regarded by an average person "applying contemporary community standards" as designed to appeal to the prurient interest, and (3) "lacks serious literary, artistic, political, or scientific value for minors."

Shortly before the COPA was to take effect, various organizations challenged it on First Amendment grounds. A federal district court issued a preliminary injunction barring enforcement of the statute, and the Third Circuit Court of Appeals affirmed. The Supreme Court granted the Attorney General's petition for certiorari and issued a 2002 decision that may not mark the last time the Court will consider the case. In *Ashcroft v. American Civil Liberties Union,* 122 S. Ct. 1700 (2002), a majority of the Court agreed on only one key point: that contrary to the Third Circuit's conclusion, the COPA's use of "contemporary community standards" was not sufficient, *by itself,* to cause the statute to violate the First Amendment. On that narrow ground—the only issue on which the Court officially ruled—the Court vacated the Third Circuit's judgment and remanded the case for further proceedings. (As of the time this book went to press, no further developments had occurred.)

At least five justices hinted in separate opinions that the COPA, though narrower than the CDA in its speech restrictions, still suffered from the same First Amendment infirmities that doomed the CDA. Those hints may foreshadow what could happen if the case returns to the Court. Of the eight justices who agreed that COPA's community standards provision did not automatically cause a First Amendment violation, five offered nonbinding remarks suggesting that if an act of Congress imposed restrictions on speech in the Internet context, the statute would likely be on more solid First Amendment ground if it called for use of a *national* standard, as opposed to community standards, in assessing the relevant speech. It remains to be determined whether that suggestion will be transformed into a constitutional rule.

As previously noted, no First Amendment protection attaches to obscene expression. A 1982 Supreme Court decision, *New York v. Ferber,* 458 U.S. 747, established another category of unprotected expression: child pornography in which actual minors are depicted, regardless of whether the expression would be classified as obscene. *Ferber*'s rationale stressed the compelling government interest in protecting minors from the harm they would experience in actually taking part in the production of pornographic material.

Prior to 1996, the federal law prohibiting child pornography defined such material as containing depictions of actual minors. In the Child Pornography Prevention Act of 1996 (CPPA), however, Congress added provisions designed to criminalize sexually explicit materials that *appeared* to depict a minor even though no actual minor was depicted. The CPPA applied to so-called *virtual* child pornography because its provisions could be violated through the use of computer-generated images or youthful-looking adult actors, if the effect was a visual depiction of what appeared to be a minor engaging in sexual activity.

A First Amendment-based attack on the CPPA eventually made its way to the Supreme Court. In *Ashcroft v. Free Speech Coalition,* 122 S. Ct. 1389 (2002), the Court held the CPPA unconstitutional. A five-justice majority viewed the CPPA as "proscrib[ing] the visual depiction of an idea—that of teenagers engaging in sexual activity—that is a fact of modern society and has been a theme in art and literature throughout the ages." The CPPA's supposed coverage extended well beyond obscene expression by "prohibit[ing] speech despite [the] serious literary, artistic, political, or scientific value" of the overall work in which a scene with significant sexual content appears. Noting that a movie in which only adult actors appeared would violate the CPPA if an adult actor "appear[ed] to be" a minor engaging in actual or simulated sexual activity, the Court reasoned that such highly regarded moves as "Traffic" and "American Beauty" could be at risk of violating the CPPA because they included scenes in which adult actors playing teenage characters appeared to engage in sexual activity. In addition, the Court observed that the CPPA paid insufficient attention to the manner and purpose of certain visual depictions. "The CPPA applies," the Court observed, "to a picture in a psychology manual, as well as a movie depicting the horrors of sexual abuse."

The Court also noted that *Ferber*'s allowance of a ban on real child pornography (i.e., sexually explicit material depicting actual minors) was premised on such pornography's means of production, which involved the direct infliction of actual harm on participating minors. The government's attempt to restrict virtual child pornography, on the other hand, was clearly based on the content of the speech at issue. The Court emphasized that the government "cannot ban speech fit for adults simply because it may fall into the hands of children."

---

statute. Many criminal statutes require proof of intentional wrongdoing. Others impose liability for reckless conduct or, in rare instances, mere negligence. In the criminal context, recklessness generally means that the accused consciously disregarded a substantial risk that the harm prohibited by the statute would result from her actions. Negligence means that the accused failed to perceive a substantial risk of harm that a reasonable person would have perceived. As a general rule, negligent behavior is left to the civil justice system rather than being criminalized.

Criminal intent may be inferred from an accused's behavior, because a person is normally held to have intended the natural and probable consequences of her acts. The intent requirement furthers the criminal law's general goal of punishing conscious wrongdoers. Accordingly, proof that the defendant had the capacity to form the required intent is a traditional prerequisite of criminal responsibility. The criminal law recognizes three general types of incapacity: *intoxication, infancy,* and *insanity.*

Although it is not a complete defense to criminal liability, voluntary intoxication may sometimes diminish the degree of a defendant's responsibility. For example, many first-degree murder statutes require proof of *premeditation,* a conscious decision to kill. One who kills while highly intoxicated may be incapable of premeditation—meaning that he would not be guilty of first-degree murder. He may be convicted, however, of another homicide offense that does not require proof of premeditation.

The criminal law historically presumed that children younger than 14 years of age ("infants," for legal purposes) could not form a criminal intent. Today, most states treat juvenile offenders below a certain statutory age—usually 16 or 17—differently from adult offenders, with special juvenile court systems and separate detention facilities. Current juvenile law emphasizes rehabilitation rather than capacity issues. Repeat offenders or offenders charged with very serious offenses, however, may sometimes be treated as adults.

An accused's insanity at the time the charged act was committed may constitute a complete defense. This possible effect of insanity has generated public dissatisfaction. The controlling legal test for whether a defendant was insane varies among court systems. The details of the possible tests are beyond the scope of this text. Suffice it to say that as applied by courts, the tests make it a rare case in which the defendant succeeds with an insanity defense.

Criminal Procedure

Criminal Prosecutions: An Overview

Persons arrested for allegedly committing a crime are taken to the police station and booked. *Booking* is an administrative procedure for recording the suspect's arrest. In some states, temporary release on bail may be available at this stage. After booking, the police file an arrest report with the prosecutor, who decides whether to charge the suspect with an offense. If she decides to prosecute, the prosecutor prepares a complaint identifying the accused and detailing the charges. Most states require that arrested suspects be taken promptly before a magistrate or other judicial officer (such as a justice of the peace or judge whose court is of limited jurisdiction) for an *initial appearance*. During this appearance, the magistrate informs the accused of the charges and outlines the accused's constitutional rights. In misdemeanor cases in which the accused pleads guilty, the sentence may be (but need not be) imposed without a later hearing. If the accused pleads not guilty to a misdemeanor charge, the case is set for trial. In felony cases, as well as misdemeanor cases in which the accused pleads not guilty, the magistrate sets the amount of bail.

In many states, defendants in felony cases are protected against unjustified prosecutions by an additional procedural step, the *preliminary hearing*. The prosecutor must introduce enough evidence at this hearing to persuade a magistrate that there is *probable cause* to believe the accused committed a felony.[3] If persuaded that probable cause exists, the magistrate binds over the defendant for trial in the appropriate court.

After a bindover, the formal charge against the defendant is filed with the trial court. The formal charge consists of either an *information* filed by the prosecutor or an *indictment* returned by a grand jury. Roughly half of the states require that a grand jury approve the decision to prosecute a person for a felony. Grand juries are bodies of citizens selected in the same manner as the members of a trial (petit) jury; often, they are chosen through random drawings from a list of registered voters. Indictment of an accused prior to a preliminary hearing normally eliminates the need for a preliminary hearing because the indictment serves essentially the same function as a magistrate's probable cause determination.

The remainder of the states allow felony defendants to be charged by either indictment or information, at the prosecutor's discretion. An *information* is a formal charge signed by the prosecutor outlining the facts supporting the charges against the defendant. In states allowing felony prosecution by information, prosecutors elect the information method in the vast majority of felony cases. Misdemeanor cases are prosecuted by information in virtually all states.[4]

Once an information or indictment has been filed with a trial court, an *arraignment* occurs. The defendant is brought before the court, informed of the charges, and asked to enter a plea. The defendant may plead guilty, not guilty, or nolo contendere. Although technically not an admission of guilt, nolo contendere pleas indicate that the defendant does not contest the charges. This decision by the defendant will lead to a finding of guilt. Unlike evidence of a guilty plea, however, evidence of a defendant's nolo plea is inadmissible in later civil cases against that defendant based on the same conduct amounting to the criminal violation. Individuals and corporate defendants therefore may find nolo pleas attractive when their chances of mounting a successful defense to the criminal prosecution are poor and the prospect of later civil suits is likely.

At or shortly after the arraignment, the defendant who pleads not guilty chooses the type of trial that will take place. Persons accused of serious crimes for which incarceration for more than six months is possible have a constitutional right to be tried by a jury of their peers. The accused, however, may waive this right and opt for a bench trial (i.e., before a judge only).

Role of Constitutional Safeguards

The preceding pages referred to various procedural devices designed to protect persons accused of crime. The Bill of Rights, the first 10 amendments to the U.S. Constitution, sets forth other rights of criminal defendants. These rights guard against unjustified or erroneous criminal convictions and serve as reminders of government's proper role in the administration of justice in a democratic society. Justice Oliver Wendell Holmes aptly addressed this latter point when he said, "I think it less evil that some criminals should escape than that the government should play an ignoble part."

Although the literal language of the Bill of Rights refers only to federal government actions, the U.S.

---

[3]The state need not satisfy the beyond a reasonable doubt standard of proof at the preliminary hearing stage. The prosecutor sufficiently establishes probable cause by causing the magistrate to believe it is more likely than not that the defendant committed the felony alleged.

[4]For federal crimes, a prosecutor in the relevant U.S. Attorney's office files an information to institute the case if the offense involved carries a penalty of not more than one year of imprisonment. Federal prosecutions for more serious crimes with potentially more severe penalties are commenced by means of a grand jury indictment.

Supreme Court has applied the most important Bill of Rights guarantees to state government actions by "selectively incorporating" those guarantees into the Fourteenth Amendment's due process protection. Once a particular safeguard has been found to be "implicit in the concept of ordered liberty" or "fundamental to the American scheme of justice," it has been applied equally in state and federal criminal trials. This has occurred with the constitutional protections examined earlier in this chapter as well as with the Fourth, Fifth, and Sixth Amendment guarantees discussed in the following pages.

The Fourth Amendment

The Fourth Amendment protects persons against arbitrary and unreasonable governmental violations of their privacy rights. It states:

> The right of the people to be secure in their persons, houses, papers, and effects, against unreasonable searches and seizures, shall not be violated, and no Warrants shall issue, but upon probable cause, supported by Oath or affirmation, and particularly describing the place to be searched, and the persons or things to be seized.

Reasonable Expectation of Privacy The Fourth Amendment's language and judicial interpretations of it reflect the difficulties inherent in balancing citizens' legitimate expectations of privacy and government's legitimate interest in securing evidence of wrongdoing. Citizens are not protected against all searches and seizures—only against unreasonable ones. Because the Fourth Amendment safeguards reasonable privacy expectations, the Supreme Court has extended the amendment's protection to such places or items as private dwellings and immediately surrounding areas (often called the *curtilage*), telephone booths, sealed containers, and first-class mail. The Court has denied protection to places, items, or matters as to which it found no reasonable expectations of privacy, such as open fields, personal bank records, and voluntary conversations between criminal defendants and government informants. In *United States v. Hall,* which follows, the court considered whether a corporation and one of its executives possessed a reasonable expectation of privacy in the contents of garbage bags that had been placed in a dumpster on the corporation's property.

United States v. Hall   *47 F.3d 1091 (11th Cir. 1995)*

William T. Parks, a special agent of the U.S. Customs Service, was investigating allegations that Bet-Air, Inc. (a Miami-based seller of spare aviation parts and supplies) had supplied restricted military parts to Iran. Parks entered Bet-Air's property and removed, from a garbage dumpster, a bag of shredded documents. The dumpster was located near the Bet-Air offices in a parking area reserved for the firm's employees. To reach the dumpster, Parks had to travel 40 yards on a private paved road. No signs indicated that the road was private. In later judicial proceedings, Parks testified that at the time he traveled on the road, he did not know he was on Bet-Air's property.

When reconstructed, some of the previously shredded documents contained information seemingly relevant to the investigation. Parks used the shredded documents and the information they revealed as the basis for obtaining a warrant to search the Bet-Air premises. In executing the search warrant, Parks and other law enforcement officers seized numerous documents and Bet-Air records.

A federal grand jury later indicted Bet-Air's chairman, Terrence Hall, and other defendants on various counts related to the alleged supplying of restricted military parts to Iran. Contending that the Fourth Amendment had been violated, Hall filed a motion asking the court to suppress (i.e., exclude) all evidence derived from the warrantless search of the dumpster and all evidence seized during the search of the Bet-Air premises (the search pursuant to the warrant). The federal district court denied Hall's motion. Following a jury trial, Hall was convicted on all counts and sentenced to prison. Hall appealed to the 11th Circuit Court of Appeals.

Hatchett, Circuit Judge In *California v. Greenwood* (1988), the Supreme Court held that a warrantless search and seizure of garbage left in a plastic bag on the curb in front of, but outside the curtilage of, a private house did not violate the Fourth Amendment. The Court held that such a search would only violate the Fourth Amendment if the persons discarding the garbage manifested a subjective expectation of privacy in their garbage that society accepts as objectively reasonable. The Court concluded that Greenwood had exposed his garbage to the public sufficiently to render his subjective expectation of privacy objectively unreasonable.

Hall points to the fact that Parks obtained documents that were shredded, then placed inside a green garbage bag, which was in turn placed inside a garbage dumpster. We believe that the manner in which Bet-Air disposed of its garbage serves only to demonstrate that Bet-Air manifested a subjective expectation of privacy in its discarded garbage. Whether Parks's actions were proscribed by the Fourth Amendment, however, turns on whether society is prepared to accept Bet-Air's subjective expectation of privacy as objectively reasonable.

It is well established that the Fourth Amendment protections apply [not only to residential property but also] to commercial premises. The Supreme Court's treatment of the expectation of privacy that the owner of commercial property enjoys in such property has differed significantly from the protection accorded an individual's home, [however]. Such distinctions are inevitable given the fundamental difference in the nature and uses of a residence as opposed to commercial property. These distinctions are drawn into sharp focus when, as in this case, the government intrudes into the area immediately surrounding the structure. In order for persons to preserve Fourth Amendment protection in the area immediately surrounding the residence, they must not conduct an activity or leave an object in the plain view of those outside the area. The occupant of a commercial building, in contrast, must take the additional precaution of affirmatively barring the public from the area. The Supreme Court has consistently held that the government is required to obtain a search warrant only when it wishes to search those areas of commercial property from which the public has been excluded.

Relying on the fact that the dumpster was within the "commercial curtilage" of Bet-Air's property and that it could only be accessed by traveling 40 yards on a private road, Hall asserts that the company's subjective expectation of privacy was objectively reasonable. Hall's heavy emphasis on Parks's trespass onto Bet-Air's private property is misplaced. The law of trespass forbids intrusions onto land that the Fourth Amendment would not proscribe.

We note that although the road leading to Bet-Air's dumpster was private, the magistrate judge found that no "objective signs of restricted access such as signs, barricades, and the like" were present. Moreover, the magistrate judge also found that at the time Parks traveled the road, he believed it was a public road. [Bet-Air's] failure to exclude the public takes on increased significance when the asserted expectation of privacy is in discarded garbage. A commercial proprietor incurs a diminished expectation of privacy when garbage is placed in a dumpster which is located in a parking lot that the business shares with other businesses, and no steps are taken to limit the public's access to the dumpster. It is common knowledge that commercial dumpsters have long been a source of fruitful exploration for scavengers.

The Supreme Court used the concept of curtilage in *Hester v. United States* (1924) to distinguish between the area outside a person's house which the Fourth Amendment protects, and the open fields, which are afforded no Fourth Amendment protection. The Supreme Court has not squarely addressed the applicability of the common law concept of curtilage to commercial property. Given the Court's view of the relationship between the Fourth Amendment and commercial premises, however, we have little doubt that were the Court to embrace the so-called "business curtilage" concept, it would, at a minimum, require that the commercial proprietor take affirmative steps to exclude the public. In light of Bet-Air's failure to exclude the public from the area immediately surrounding its offices, we refuse to apply the so-called "business curtilage" concept in this case.

[W]e do not believe that Parks infringed upon any societal values the Fourth Amendment protects when he searched Bet-Air's garbage. Bet-Air did not take sufficient steps to restrict the public's access to its discarded garbage; therefore, its subjective expectation of privacy is not one that society is prepared to accept as objectively reasonable.

District court's denial of Hall's suppression motion affirmed.

Even when plainly protected areas or items are involved, not every governmental action is deemed sufficiently intrusive to constitute a search or seizure for Fourth Amendment purposes. Thus, for example, the Supreme Court held, in *United States v. Place* (1983), that exposing an airline traveler's luggage to a narcotics detection dog in a public place was not a search, considering the minimally intrusive nature of the intrusion and the narrow scope of information it revealed. Did a search occur when law enforcement officers, operating from a public street, aimed a thermal imaging device at a private home? The Supreme Court addressed that question in 2001's *Kyllo* case, which follows.

Kyllo v. United States   *533 U.S. 27 (U.S. Sup Ct. 2001)*

Suspicious that marijuana was being grown in Danny Lee Kyllo's home, federal agents used a thermal imaging device to scan his triplex to determine whether the amount of heat emanating from it was consistent with the amount emanated from high-intensity lamps typically used for indoor marijuana growth. The scan showed that Kyllo's roof and a side wall were relatively hot compared to the rest of his home and substantially warmer than the neighboring units. Based in part on the thermal imaging results, a federal magistrate judge issued a warrant to search Kyllo's home, where the agents found marijuana growing. After Kyllo was indicted on a federal drug charge, he unsuccessfully moved to suppress the evidence seized from his home and then entered a conditional guilty plea. The Ninth Circuit Court of Appeals ultimately affirmed, upholding the warrant and holding that the evidence was admissible. Kyllo appealed, and the U.S. Supreme Court granted certiorari.

Scalia, Justice The Fourth Amendment provides that "the right of the people to be secure in their persons, houses, papers, and effects, against unreasonable searches and seizures, shall not be violated." "At the very core" of the Fourth Amendment "stands the right of a man to retreat into his own home and there be free from unreasonable governmental intrusion." *Silverman v. United States,* 507 U.S. 990 (1961). With few exceptions, the question whether a warrantless search of a home is reasonable and hence constitutional must be answered no.

On the other hand, the antecedent question of whether or not a Fourth Amendment "search" has occurred is not so simple under our precedent. The lawfulness of warrantless visual surveillance [has long been accepted]. As we observed in *California v. Ciraolo,* 476 U.S. 207, 213 (1986), "the Fourth Amendment protection of the home has never been extended to require law enforcement officers to shield their eyes when passing by a home on public thoroughfares."

One might think that examining the portion of a house that is in plain public view [amounts to] a "search," [though] not an "unreasonable" one under the Fourth Amendment. But in fact we have held that visual observation is no "search" at all—perhaps in order to preserve somewhat more intact our doctrine that warrantless searches are presumptively unconstitutional. In assessing when a search is not a search, we have applied somewhat in reverse the principle first enunciated in *Katz v. United States,* 389 U.S. 347 (1967). *Katz* involved eavesdropping by means of an electronic listening device placed on the outside of a telephone booth—a location not within the catalog ("persons, houses, papers, and effects") that the Fourth Amendment protects against unreasonable searches. We held that the Fourth Amendment nonetheless protected Katz from the warrantless eavesdropping because he justifiably relied upon the privacy of the telephone booth. As Justice Harlan's oft-quoted concurrence described it, a Fourth Amendment search occurs when the government violates a subjective expectation of privacy that society recognizes as reason-

able. We have subsequently applied this principle to hold that a Fourth Amendment search does *not* occur—even when the explicitly protected location of a *house* is concerned—unless "the individual manifested a subjective expectation of privacy in the object of the challenged search," and "society [is] willing to recognize that expectation as reasonable." *Ciraolo,* 476 U.S. at 211. We have applied this test in holding that it is not a search for the police to use a pen register at the phone company to determine what numbers were dialed in a private home, and we have applied the test on two different occasions in holding that aerial surveillance of private homes and surrounding areas does not constitute a search.

The present case involves officers on a public street engaged in more than naked-eye surveillance of a home. We have previously reserved judgment as to how much technological enhancement of ordinary perception from such a vantage point, if any, is too much. While we upheld enhanced aerial photography of an industrial complex in *Dow Chemical Co. v. United States,* 476 U.S. 227 (1986), we noted that we found it "important that this is *not* an area immediately adjacent to a private home, where privacy expectations are most heightened." *Id.* at 237, n. 4. It would be foolish to contend that the degree of privacy secured to citizens by the Fourth Amendment has been entirely unaffected by the advance of technology. The question we confront today is what limits there are upon this power of technology to shrink the realm of guaranteed privacy.

The *Katz* test—whether the individual has an expectation of privacy that society is prepared to recognize as reasonable—has often been criticized as circular, and hence subjective and unpredictable. While it may be difficult to refine *Katz* when the search of areas such as telephone booths, automobiles, or even the curtilage and uncovered portions of residences are at issue, in the case of the search of the interior of homes—the prototypical and hence most commonly litigated area of protected privacy—there is a ready criterion, with roots deep in the common law, of the [minimum] expectation of privacy that *exists,* and that is acknowledged to be *reasonable.* To withdraw protection of this minimum expectation would be to permit police technology to erode the privacy guaranteed by the Fourth Amendment. We think that obtaining by sense-enhancing technology any information regarding the interior of the home that could not otherwise have been obtained without physical "intrusion into a constitutionally protected area," *Silverman,* 507 U.S. at 512, constitutes a search—at least where (as here) the technology in question is not in general public use. This assures preservation of that degree of privacy against government that existed when the Fourth Amendment was adopted. On the basis of this criterion, the information obtained by the thermal imager in this case was the product of a search.

The Government maintains, however, that the thermal imaging must be upheld because it detected "only heat radiating from the external surface of the house." [However,] just as a thermal imager captures only heat emanating from a house, so also a powerful directional microphone picks up only sound emanating from a house and a satellite capable of scanning from many miles away would pick up only visible light emanating from a house. We rejected such a mechanical interpretation of the Fourth Amendment in *Katz,* where the eavesdropping device picked up only sound waves that reached the exterior of the phone booth. Reversing that approach would leave the homeowner at the mercy of advancing technology—including imaging technology that could discern all human activity in the home. While the technology used in the present case was relatively crude, the rule we adopt must take account of more sophisticated systems that are already in use or in development.

The Government also contends that the thermal imaging was constitutional because it did not "detect private activities occurring in private areas." It points out that in *Dow Chemical* we observed that the enhanced aerial photography did not reveal any "intimate details." *Dow Chemical,* however, involved enhanced aerial photography of an industrial complex, which does not share the Fourth Amendment sanctity of the home. The Fourth Amendment's protection of the home has never been tied to measurement of the quality or quantity of information obtained. In *Silverman,* for example, we made clear that any physical invasion of the structure of the home, "by even a fraction of an inch," was too much, and there is certainly no exception to the warrant requirement for the officer who barely cracks open the front door and sees nothing but the nonintimate rug on the vestibule floor. In the home, our cases show, *all* details are intimate details, because the entire area is held safe from prying government eyes.

Limiting the prohibition of thermal imaging to "intimate details" would not only be wrong in principle; it would be impractical in application, failing to provide "a workable accommodation between the needs of law enforcement and the interests protected by the Fourth Amendment," *Oliver v. United States,* 466 U.S. 170, 181 (1984). To begin with, there is no necessary connection between the sophistication of the surveillance equipment and the "intimacy" of the details that it observes—which means that one cannot say (and the police cannot be assured) that use of the relatively crude equipment at issue here will always be lawful. The Agema Thermovision 210 might disclose, for example, at what hour each night the lady of the house takes her daily sauna and bath—a detail that many would consider "intimate"; and a much more sophisticated system might detect nothing more intimate than the fact that someone left a closet light on. We could not, in other words, develop a rule approving only that through-the-wall surveillance which identifies objects no smaller than 36 by 36 inches, but would have to develop a jurisprudence specifying which home activities are "intimate" and which are not. And even when (if ever) that jurisprudence were fully developed, no police officer would be able to know *in advance* whether his through-the-wall surveillance picks up "intimate" details—and thus would be unable to know in advance whether it is constitutional.

We have said that the Fourth Amendment draws "a firm line at the entrance to the house." *Payton v. New York,* 445 U.S. 573, 590 (1980). That line, we think, must be not only firm but also bright—which requires clear specification of those methods of surveillance that require a warrant. While it is certainly possible to conclude from the videotape of the thermal imaging that occurred in this case that no "significant" compromise of the homeowner's privacy has occurred, we must take the long view, from the original meaning of the Fourth Amendment forward. "The Fourth Amendment is to be construed in the light of what was deemed an unreasonable search and seizure when it was adopted, and in a manner which will conserve public interests as well as the interests and rights of individual citizens." *Carroll v. United States,* 267 U.S. 132, 149 (1925).

Where, as here, the Government uses a device that is not in general public use, to explore details of the home that would previously have been unknowable without physical intrusion, the surveillance is a "search" and is presumptively unreasonable without a warrant. Since we hold the Thermovision imaging to have been an unlawful search, it will remain for the District Court to determine whether, without the evidence it provided, the search warrant issued in this case was supported by probable cause.

Judgment of Ninth Circuit Court of Appeals reversed and case remanded for further proceedings.

Warrant Requirement and Exceptions In its treatment of the Fourth Amendment's warrant clause, the Supreme Court has engaged in similar balancing of individual and governmental interests. The warrant requirement further protects privacy interests by mandating that a judge or magistrate authorize and define the scope of intrusive governmental action. As a general rule, the Court has held that searches carried out without a proper warrant are unreasonable.

Nevertheless, the Court has devised a lengthy list of exceptions to this general rule. The Court has upheld warrantless searches of the area within an arrestee's immediate control, of premises police enter in hot pursuit of an armed suspect, and of automobiles and containers located therein under certain circumstances (because of cars' mobile nature). Warrantless seizures of contraband items in the plain view of officers acting lawfully have likewise been upheld. The Court has also authorized customs searches, stop-and-frisk searches for weapons, inventory searches of property in an arrestee's possession, and consensual searches, despite the absence of a warrant in each of these instances. Finally, the Court has upheld warrantless administrative inspections of closely regulated businesses.

Exclusionary Rule The exclusionary rule serves as the basic remedial device in cases of Fourth Amendment violations. Under this judicially crafted rule, evidence seized in illegal searches cannot be used in a subsequent trial against an accused whose constitutional rights were violated.[5] Because the exclusionary rule may result in suppression of convincing evidence of crime, it has generated controversy. The rule's supporters regard it as necessary to deter police from violating citizens' constitutional rights. The rule's opponents assert that it has no deterrent effect on police who believed they were acting lawfully. A loudly voiced complaint in some quarters has been that "because of a policeman's error, a criminal goes free."

In the past two decades, the Court has responded to such criticism by rendering decisions that restrict the operation of the exclusionary rule. For example, the Court has held that illegally obtained evidence may be introduced at trial if the prosecution convinces the trial judge that the evidence would inevitably have been obtained anyway by lawful means. The Court has also created a "good faith" exception to the exclusionary rule. This exception allows the use of evidence seized by police officers who acted pursuant to a search warrant later held invalid if the officers reasonably believed that the warrant was valid. Although the Court has not extended the good faith exception to the warrantless search setting, it has expanded the exception's scope to include searches made in reliance on a statute that is later declared invalid.

The USA PATRIOT Act Approximately six weeks after the September 11, 2001 terrorist attacks on the United States, Congress enacted the Uniting and Strengthening America by Providing Appropriate Tools Required to Intercept and Obstruct Terrorism Act. This statute, commonly known as the USA PATRIOT Act, contains numerous and broad-ranging provisions designed to protect the public against international and domestic terrorism.

Included in the USA PATRIOT Act are measures allowing the federal government significantly expanded ability, in terrorism-related investigations, to conduct searches of property, monitor Internet activities, and track electronic communications. Most, though not all, actions of that nature require a warrant from a special court known as the Foreign Intelligence Surveillance Court. The statute appears to contemplate, however, that such warrants may sometimes be issued upon less of a showing by the government than would ordinarily be required, and may be more sweeping than usual in terms of geographic application. Moreover, warrants issued by the special court for the search of property can be of the so-called "sneak and peek" variety, under which the FBI need not produce the warrant for the property owner or possessor to see and need not notify an absent property owner or possessor that the search took place (unlike the rules typically applicable to execution of "regular" warrants).

The USA PATRIOT Act also calls for banks to report seemingly suspicious monetary deposits, as well as any deposits exceeding $10,000, not only to the Treasury Department (as required by prior law) but also to the Central Intelligence Agency and other federal intelligence agencies. In addition, the statute enables federal law enforcement authorities to seek a Surveillance Court warrant for the obtaining of individuals' credit, medical, and student records, regardless of state or federal privacy laws that would otherwise have applied.

Commentators critical of the USA PATRIOT Act have argued that despite the importance of safeguarding the public against acts of terrorism, the statute tips the balance too heavily in favor of law enforcement. They have characterized the statute's definition of "domestic terrorism" as so broad that various suspected activities not normally regarded as terrorism (or as harboring or aiding terrorists) could be considered as such for purposes of the federal government's expanded investigatory tools. If that happens, the

---

[5]The Supreme Court initially authorized application of the exclusionary rule in federal criminal cases only. In *Mapp v. Ohio* (1961), the Court made the exclusionary rule applicable to state criminal cases as well.

critics contend, Fourth Amendment and other constitutional rights may easily be subverted. Others with reservations about the statute maintain that its allowance of expanded monitoring of Internet activities and electronic communications and its provisions for retrieval of records normally protected by privacy laws could give the government ready access to communications and private information of many wholly innocent persons.

The votes in Congress, however, demonstrated overwhelming support for the USA PATRIOT Act. In apparent recognition of the extraordinary action it was taking in a time of national crisis, Congress included provisions stating that portions of the statute would expire at the end of 2005. Congress also included provisions requiring the Attorney General to report to Congress on the use of the expanded investigatory powers. As of the time this book went to press, it was too early to assess the statute's effects or to determine whether, or to what extent, the civil liberties fears of critics had been borne out.

The Fifth Amendment

The Fifth and Fourteenth Amendments' due process clauses guarantee basic procedural and substantive fairness to criminal defendants. The due process clauses are discussed earlier in this chapter and in Chapter 3.

Privilege against Self-Incrimination In another significant provision, the Fifth Amendment protects against *compelled testimonial self-incrimination* by establishing that "[n]o person . . . shall be compelled in any criminal case to be a witness against himself." This provision prevents the government from coercing a defendant into making incriminating statements and thereby assisting in his own prosecution.

In *Miranda v. Arizona* (1966), the Supreme Court established procedural requirements—the now-familiar *Miranda* warnings—to safeguard this Fifth Amendment right and other constitutional guarantees. The Court did so by requiring police to inform criminal suspects, before commencing custodial interrogation of them, that they have the right to remain silent, that any statements they make may be used as evidence against them, and that they have the right to the presence and assistance of a retained or court-appointed attorney (with court appointment occurring when suspects lack the financial ability to retain counsel).[6] Incriminating statements that an in-custody suspect makes without first having been given the *Miranda* warn-

ings are inadmissible at trial. If the suspect invokes her right to silence, custodial interrogation must cease. If, on the other hand, the suspect knowingly and voluntarily waives her right to silence after having been given the *Miranda* warnings, her statements will be admissible.

The right to silence is limited, however, in various ways. For example, the traditional view that the Fifth Amendment applies only to *testimonial* admissions serves as the basis for allowing the police to compel an accused to furnish nontestimonial evidence such as fingerprints, samples of body fluids, and hair. Supreme Court decisions have recognized further limitations on the right to silence. For instance, the right has been held to include a corresponding implicit prohibition of prosecutorial comments at trial about the accused's failure to speak in his own defense. Although Supreme Court decisions still support this prohibition in general, the Court has sometimes allowed prosecutors to use the defendant's pretrial silence to impeach his trial testimony. For example, the Court has held that the Fifth Amendment is not violated by prosecutorial use of a defendant's silence (either prearrest or postarrest, but in advance of any *Miranda* warnings) to discredit his trial testimony that he killed the victim in self-defense.

Further inclination to narrow *Miranda*'s applicability and effect has sometimes been displayed by the Supreme Court during roughly the past two decades. In one case, for example, the Court upheld a suspect's waiver of his *Miranda* rights and approved the use of his confession at trial, despite the police's failure to notify the suspect that an attorney retained for him by a family member was seeking to contact him. Another decision established that an undercover police officer posing as a fellow inmate need not give a jailed suspect the *Miranda* warnings before asking questions that could lead to incriminating admissions.

Although the *Miranda* warnings have been a required feature of law enforcement practice since the Supreme Court handed down its landmark decision nearly four decades ago, a surprising 1999 decision of the U.S. Court of Appeals for the Fourth Circuit labeled the *Miranda* warnings as merely judicially created rules of procedure that were neither grounded in, nor required by, the Constitution. The Fourth Circuit's holding that the *Miranda* warnings were not of constitutional dimension led it to conclude that the warnings' required status could be eliminated by appropriate legislation, and that Congress, in a largely ignored 1968 statute, indeed had legislatively overruled the *Miranda* decision and the warnings it required. In *Dickerson v. United States,* the Supreme Court overturned the Fourth Circuit's decision and classified the *Miranda* warnings as a constitutional rule, which Congress could not legislatively overrule.

---

[6]The portions of the *Miranda* warnings dealing with the right to an attorney further Sixth Amendment interests. The Sixth Amendment is discussed later in this chapter.

Dickerson v. United States   *530 U.S. 428 (2000)*

Charles Dickerson was indicted for bank robbery and related federal crimes. Before trial, Dickerson moved to suppress a statement he had made at a Federal Bureau of Investigation office on the ground that he had not received the "Miranda warnings" before being interrogated. A federal district court granted his motion to suppress, but the U.S. Court of Appeals for the Fourth Circuit reversed the suppression order. The court held that 18 U.S.C. § 3501, a 1968 statute whose terms purported to make the admissibility of statements such as Dickerson's hinge on whether they were made voluntarily, was satisfied in this case. The court also held that the Miranda *warnings were a procedural and not a constitutional requirement, and could therefore rightfully be superseded by legislation such as § 3501. Dickerson appealed, and the U.S. Supreme Court granted certiorari.*

Rehnquist, Chief Justice In *Miranda v. Arizona,* 384 U.S. 436 (1966), we held that certain warnings must be given before a suspect's statement made during custodial interrogation could be admitted in evidence. In the wake of that decision, Congress enacted 18 U.S.C. § 3501, which in essence laid down a rule that the admissibility of such statements should turn only on whether or not they were voluntarily made.

Prior to *Miranda,* we evaluated the admissibility of a suspect's confession under a voluntariness test. The roots of this test developed in the common law, as the courts of England and then the United States recognized that coerced confessions are inherently untrustworthy. Over time, our cases recognized two constitutional bases for the requirement that a confession be voluntary to be admitted into evidence: the Fifth Amendment right against self-incrimination and the Due Process Clause of the Fourteenth Amendment. [F]or the middle third of the 20th century our cases based the rule against admitting coerced confessions primarily, if not exclusively, on notions of due process. We applied the due process voluntariness test in some 30 different cases decided [between 1936 and 1964]. Those cases refined the test into an inquiry that examines whether a defendant's will was overborne by the circumstances surrounding the giving of a confession. The due process test takes into consideration "the totality of all the surrounding circumstances—both the characteristics of the accused and the details of the interrogation." *Schneckcloth v. Bustamonte,* 412 U.S. 218, 226 (1972).

We have never abandoned this due process jurisprudence, and thus continue to exclude confessions that were obtained involuntarily. But our decisions in *Malloy v. Hogan,* 378 U.S. 1 (1964), and *Miranda* changed the focus of much of the inquiry in determining the admissibility of suspects' incriminating statements. In *Malloy,* we held that the Fifth Amendment's Self-Incrimination Clause is incorporated in the Due Process Clause of the Fourteenth Amendment and thus applies to the States. We decided *Miranda* on the heels of *Malloy.*

Because custodial police interrogation, by its very nature, isolates and pressures the individual, we stated [in *Miranda*] that "even without employing brutality, the 'third degree' or [other] specific stratagems, . . . custodial interrogation exacts a heavy toll on individual liberty and trades on the weakness of individuals." We concluded that the coercion inherent in custodial interrogation blurs the line between voluntary and involuntary statements, and thus heightens the risk that an individual will not be "accorded his privilege under the Fifth Amendment . . . not to be compelled to incriminate himself." Accordingly, we laid down "concrete constitutional guidelines for law enforcement agencies and courts to follow."

Those guidelines established that the admissibility in evidence of any statement given during custodial interrogation of a suspect would depend on whether the police provided the suspect with four warnings. These warnings (which have come to be known colloquially as "*Miranda* rights") are: a suspect "has the right to remain silent, that anything he says can be used against him in a court of law, that he has the right to the presence of an attorney, and that if he cannot afford an attorney one will be appointed for him prior to any questioning if he so desires."

Two years after *Miranda* was decided, Congress enacted § 3501. Given § 3501's express designation of voluntariness as the touchstone of admissibility, its omission of any warning requirement, and the instruction for trial courts to consider nonexclusive list of factors relevant to the circumstances of the confession, we agree with the Court of Appeals that Congress intended by its enactment to overrule *Miranda.* Because of the obvious conflict between our decision in *Miranda* and § 3501, we must address whether Congress has constitutional authority to thus supersede *Miranda.*

The law in this area is clear. This Court has supervisory authority over the Federal courts, and we may use that authority to prescribe rules of evidence and procedure that are binding in those tribunals. However, the power to judicially create and enforce nonconstitutional rules of procedure and evidence for the Federal courts exists only in the absence of a relevant Act of Congress. Congress retains the ultimate authority to modify or set aside any judicially created rules of evidence and procedure that are not required by the Constitution. But Congress may not legislatively supercede our decisions interpreting and applying the Constitution.

This case, therefore, turns on whether the *Miranda* court announced a constitutional rule or merely exercised its supervisory authority to regulate evidence in the absence of Congressional direction. We disagree with the Court of Appeals' conclusion, although we concede that there is language in some of our opinions that supports the view taken by that court. [F]irst and foremost of the factors on the other side—that *Miranda* is a constitutional decision—is that . . . *Miranda* . . . applied the rule to proceedings in state courts—to wit, Arizona, California, and New York. It is beyond dispute that we do not hold a supervisory power over the courts of the several States. With respect to proceedings in state courts, our authority is limited to enforcing the commands of the United States Constitution.

The *Miranda* opinion itself begins by stating that the Court granted *certiorari* "to explore some facets of the problems . . . of applying the privilege against self-incrimination to in-custody interrogation, *and to give concrete constitutional guidelines for law enforcement agencies and courts to follow.*" In fact, the majority opinion is replete with statements indicating that the majority thought it was announcing a constitutional rule. Indeed, the Court's ultimate conclusion was that the unwarned confessions obtained in the four cases before the Court in *Miranda* "were obtained from the defendant under circumstances that did not meet constitutional standards for protection of the privilege." Additional support for our conclusion that *Miranda* is constitutionally based is found in the *Miranda* Court's invitation for legislative action to protect the constitutional right against coerced self-incrimination.

The Court of Appeals also relied on the fact that we have, after our *Miranda* decision, made exceptions from its rule in certain cases. But we have broadened the application of the *Miranda* doctrine in [other] cases. These decisions illustrate the principle—not that *Miranda* is not a constitutional rule—but that no constitutional rule is immutable. No court laying down a general rule can possibly foresee the various circumstances in which counsel will seek to apply it, and the sort of modifications represented by these cases are as much a normal part of constitutional law as the original decision.

Whether or not we would agree with *Miranda*'s reasoning and its resulting rule, were we addressing the issue in the first instance, the principles of *stare decisis* weigh heavily against overruling it now. *Miranda* has become embedded in routine police practice to the point where the warnings have become part of our national culture. While we have overruled our precedents when subsequent cases have undermined their doctrinal underpinnings, we do not believe that this has happened to the *Miranda* decision. If anything, our subsequent cases have reduced the impact of the *Miranda* rule on legitimate law enforcement while reaffirming the decision's core ruling that unwarned statements may not be used as evidence in the prosecution's case in chief. The disadvantage of the *Miranda* rule is that statements which may be by no means involuntary, made by a defendant who is aware of his "rights," may nonetheless be excluded and a guilty defendant go free as a result. But experience suggests that the totality-of-the-circumstances test which §§ 3501 seeks to revive is more difficult than *Miranda* for law enforcement officers to conform to, and for courts to apply in a consistent manner.

[W]e conclude that *Miranda* announced a constitutional rule that Congress may not supersede legislatively. Following the rule of *stare decisis,* we decline to overrule *Miranda*.

Decision of Court of Appeals reversed.

Production of Records The preceding discussion of the privilege against self-incrimination applies to criminal defendants in general. The Fifth Amendment's scope, however, has long been of particular concern to businesspersons charged with crimes. Documentary evidence often is quite important to the government's case in white-collar crime prosecutions. To what extent does the Fifth Amendment protect business records? More than a century ago, the Supreme Court held, in *Boyd v. United States* (1886), that the Fifth Amendment protects individuals against compelled production of their private papers.

In more recent years, however, the Court has drastically limited the scope of the protection contemplated by *Boyd.* The Court has held various times that the private papers privilege is personal and thus cannot be asserted by a corporation, partnership, or other "collective entity." Because such entities have no Fifth Amendment rights, the Court has held that when an organization's individual officer or agent has custody of organization records, the officer or agent cannot assert any personal privilege to prevent their disclosure. This rule holds even if the contents of the records incriminate her personally. Finally, various decisions allow the government to require business proprietors to keep certain records relevant to transactions that are appropriate subjects for government regulation. These "required records" are not entitled to private papers protection. They may be subpoenaed and used against the record-keeper in prosecutions for regulatory violations.

The Court's business records decisions during the past three decades cast further doubt on the future of the private papers doctrine. Instead of focusing on whether subpoenaed records are private in nature, the Court now considers whether the *act of producing* the records would be sufficiently testimonial to trigger the privilege against self-incrimination. In *Fisher v. United States* (1976), the Court held that an individual subpoenaed to produce personal documents may assert his Fifth Amendment privilege only if the act of producing the documents would involve incriminating testimonial admissions. This is likely when the individual producing the records is in effect certifying the records' authenticity or admitting the existence of records previously unknown to the government (demonstrating that he had access to the records and, therefore, possible knowledge of any incriminating contents).

In *United States v. Doe* (1984), the Court extended the act-of-production privilege to a sole proprietor whose proprietorship records were subpoenaed. The Court, however, held that normal business records were not themselves protected by the Fifth Amendment because they were voluntarily prepared and thus not the product of compulsion. In view of *Doe*'s emphasis on the testimonial and potentially incriminating nature of the act of producing business records, some observers thought that officers of collective entities under government investigation might be able to assert their personal privileges against self-incrimination as a way to avoid producing incriminating business records.

Braswell v. United States (1988) dashed such hopes, however, as the Court refused to extend its *Doe* holding to cover a corporation's sole shareholder who acted in his capacity as custodian of corporate records. The Court held that Braswell (the sole shareholder), having chosen to operate his business under the corporate form, was bound by the rule that corporations and similar entities have no Fifth Amendment privilege. Because Braswell acted in a representative capacity in producing the requested records, the government could not make eviden-

tiary use of his act of production. The government, however, was free to use the contents of the records against Braswell and the corporation.

Double Jeopardy Another important Fifth Amendment provision is the double jeopardy clause. This provision protects defendants from multiple criminal prosecutions for the same offense. It prevents an accused from being charged with more than one count of the same statutory violation for one offense, such as being charged with two robbery violations for a one-time robbery of one individual. This clause also prevents a second criminal prosecution for the same offense after the defendant has been acquitted or convicted of that offense. Moreover, it bars the imposition of multiple punishments for the same offense.

The double jeopardy clause does not, however, preclude the possibility that a single criminal act may lead to more than one criminal prosecution. One criminal act may produce several statutory violations, all of which may give rise to prosecution. For example, a defendant who commits rape may also be prosecuted for battery, assault with a deadly weapon, and kidnapping if the facts of the case indicate that the relevant statutes were violated. In addition, the Supreme Court has long used a "same elements" test to determine what constitutes the same offense. This means that a single criminal act with multiple victims (e.g., a restaurant robbery in which several patrons are robbed) could result in several prosecutions because the identity of each victim would be an additional fact or element of proof in each case.

In addition, the double jeopardy clause does not protect against multiple prosecutions by different sovereigns. A conviction or acquittal in a state prosecution does not prevent a subsequent federal prosecution for a federal offense arising out of the same event, or vice versa. Finally, the double jeopardy clause does not bar a private plaintiff from pursuing a *civil* case (normally for one or more of the intentional torts discussed in Chapter 6) against a defendant who was criminally prosecuted by the government for the same alleged conduct. The headline-dominating criminal and civil cases against O. J. Simpson furnish perhaps the best-known example of this principle.

The Sixth Amendment

The Sixth Amendment applies to criminal cases in various ways. It entitles criminal defendants to a speedy trial by an impartial jury and guarantees them the right to confront and cross-examine the witnesses against them. The

Sixth Amendment also gives the accused in a criminal case the right "to have the assistance of counsel" in her defense. This provision has been interpreted to mean not only that the accused may employ her own attorney but also that an indigent criminal defendant is entitled to court-appointed counsel. Included in the previously discussed *Miranda* warnings is a requirement that the police inform the accused of his right to counsel before custodial interrogation begins. *Edwards v. Arizona* (1981) established that once the accused has requested the assistance of counsel, he may not as a general rule be interrogated further until counsel is made available to him. The Supreme Court later held that the *Edwards* rule against further questioning is triggered only by an *unambiguous* request for counsel.[7] In *McNeil v. Wisconsin* (1991), the Court provided further latitude for law enforcement officers by holding that if a defendant has made an in-court request for an attorney's assistance regarding a crime with which he has been formally charged, that request does not preclude police interrogation of him—in the absence of counsel—regarding another unrelated crime.

Finally, an accused is entitled to *effective* assistance of counsel. This means that the accused is entitled to representation at a point in the proceedings when an attorney may effectively assist him, and to reasonably competent representation by that attorney. Inadequate assistance of counsel is a proper basis for setting aside a conviction and ordering a new trial, but the standard applied to these cases makes ineffective assistance of counsel claims difficult ones for convicted defendants to invoke successfully.

White-Collar Crimes and the Dilemmas of Corporate Control

Introduction

White-collar crime is the term used to describe a wide variety of nonviolent criminal offenses committed by businesspersons and business organizations. Although this term often includes offenses committed by employees against their employers (e.g., embezzlement), our dis-

cussion will focus on criminal offenses committed by corporate employers and employees against society. Each year, corporate crime costs consumers billions of dollars. It takes various forms, from consumer fraud, securities fraud, mail or wire fraud, and tax evasion to price-fixing, environmental pollution, and other regulatory violations. Corporate crime presents our legal system with various problems that we have failed to resolve satisfactorily.

Corporations form the backbone of the most successful economic system in history. They dominate the international economic scene and provide us with substantial benefits in the forms of efficiently produced goods and services. Yet these same corporations may pollute the environment, swindle their customers, mislead investors, produce dangerously defective products, and conspire with others to injure or destroy competition. How are we to achieve effective control over these large organizations so important to our existence? Increasingly, we have come to rely on the criminal law as a major corporate control instrument. The criminal law, however, was developed with individual wrongdoers in mind. Corporate crime is *organizational* in nature. Any given corporate action may be the product of the combined actions of many individuals acting within the corporate hierarchy. It may be that no individual had sufficient knowledge to possess the *mens rea* necessary for criminal responsibility under usual criminal law principles. Moreover, criminally penalizing corporations raises special problems in view of the obvious inability to apply standard sanctions such as imprisonment to legal entities.

Evolution of Corporate Criminal Liability

The law initially rejected the notion that corporations could be criminally responsible for their employees' actions. Early corporations, small in size and number, had little impact on public life. Their small size made it relatively easy to pinpoint individual wrongdoers within the corporation.

As corporations grew in size and power, however, the social need to control their activities grew accordingly. Legislatures enacted statutes creating regulatory offenses that did not require proof of *mens rea*. By 1900, American courts had begun to impose criminal liability on corporations for general criminal offenses that required proof of *mens rea*. This expansion of corporate criminal liability involved imputing the criminal intent of employees to the corporation in a fashion similar to the im-

---

[7]In *Davis v. United States* (1994), the court concluded that "Maybe I should talk to a lawyer" was too ambiguous to trigger the *Edwards* rule.

ETHICS IN ACTION

The highly publicized financial scandals involving Enron, WorldCom, and other firms mentioned near the beginning of this chapter involved conduct that in some instances was alleged to be criminal. Regardless of whether criminal violations occurred, the alleged conduct was widely perceived to be questionable on ethical grounds and motivated by a desire for short-term gains notwithstanding the costs to others. Consider the broad-ranging and sometimes devastating effects of the perceived ethical lapses and the related legal proceedings (civil and/or criminal) faced by the firms and certain executives. These effects included:

- The crippling or near-crippling blow to the viability of the firms involved.
- The collapse in value of the firms' stock and the resulting loss to disillusioned and angry shareholders who felt they had been hoodwinked.

- The harm to the professional and personal reputations of the individuals involved in the business decisions that triggered legal scrutiny and raised serious ethical concerns.
- The job losses experienced by large numbers of employees who had nothing whatsoever to do with the questionable actions that effectively brought down the firm or made massive layoffs necessary.
- The effects on the families of those who lost their jobs.
- The lack of confidence on the part of would-be investors in the profit figures and projections put forth every day by corporations—including those that have done nothing irregular.
- The ripple effects of the above on the economy generally.

position of tort liability on corporations under the *respondeat superior* doctrine.[8]

Corporations now may face criminal liability for almost any offense if the statute in question indicates a legislative intent to hold corporations responsible. This legislative intent requirement is sometimes problematic. Many state criminal statutes may contain language suggesting an intent to hold only humans liable. For example, manslaughter statutes often define the offense as "the killing of one human being by the act of another." When statutes are framed, however, in more general terms—such as by referring to "persons"—courts are generally willing to apply them to corporate defendants.

Corporate Criminal Liability Today

Under the modern rule, a corporation may be held liable for criminal offenses committed by employees who *acted within the scope of their employment and for the benefit of the corporation.* A major corporate criminal liability issue centers around the classes of corporate employees whose intent can be imputed to the corporation. Some commentators argue that a corporation should be criminally responsible only for offenses committed by high corporate officials or those linked to them by authorization or acquiescence. (Nearly all, if not all, courts

impose criminal liability on a corporation under such circumstances.) This argument reflects fairness notions, for if any group of corporate employees can fairly be said to constitute a corporation's mind, that group is its top officers and directors.

The problem with imposing corporate liability only on the basis of top corporate officers' actions or knowledge is that such a policy often insulates the corporation from liability. Many corporate offenses may be directly traceable only to middle managers or more subordinate employees. It may be impossible to demonstrate that any higher-level corporate official had sufficient knowledge to constitute *mens rea.* Recognizing this problem, the federal courts have adopted a general rule that a corporation may be criminally liable for the actions of any of its agents, regardless of whether any link between the agents and higher-level corporate officials can be demonstrated.

Problems with Punishing Corporations Despite the legal theories that justify corporate criminal liability, the punishment of corporations remains problematic. Does a criminal conviction stigmatize a corporation in the same way it stigmatizes an individual? Perhaps the only stigma resulting from a corporate criminal conviction is felt by the firm's employees, many of whom are entirely innocent of wrongdoing. Is it just to punish the innocent in an attempt to punish the guilty?

What about the cash fine, the primary punishment imposed on convicted corporations? Most critics of

---

[8]Chapter 36 discusses *respondeat superior* in detail.

corporate control strategies maintain that fines imposed on convicted firms tend to be too small to provide effective deterrence. These critics urge the use of fines keyed in some fashion to the corporate defendant's wealth. Larger fines may lead to undesirable results, however, if the corporate defendant ultimately passes along the fines to its customers (through higher prices), shareholders (through lower dividends or no dividends), or employees (through lower wages). Moreover, fines large enough to threaten corporate solvency may harm employees and those economically dependent on the corporation's financial well-being. Most of those persons, however, neither had the power to prevent the violation nor derived any benefit from it. Moreover, the managers responsible for a violation may avoid the imposition of direct burdens on them when the fine is assessed against the corporation.

Still other deficiencies make fines less-than-adequate corporate control devices. Fine strategies assume that all corporations are rationally acting profit-maximizers. Fines of sufficient size, it is argued, will erode the profit drive underlying most corporate violations. Numerous studies of actual corporate behavior, however, suggest that many corporations are neither profit-maximizers nor rational actors. Mature firms with well-established market shares may embrace goals other than profit maximization, such as technological prominence, increased market share, or higher employee salaries. In addition, the interests of managers who make corporate decisions and establish corporate policies may not coincide with the long-range economic interests of their corporate employers. The prospect that their employer could have to pay a substantial fine at some future point may not trouble top managers, who tend to have relatively short terms in office and are often compensated in part by large bonuses keyed to year-end profitability.

Individual Liability for Corporate Crime

Individuals who commit crimes while acting in corporate capacities have always been subjected to personal criminal liability. Most European nations reject corporate criminal liability and rely exclusively on individual criminal responsibility. In view of the problems associated with imposing criminal liability on corporations, individual liability may seem a more attractive control device. Besides being more consistent with traditional criminal law notions about the personal nature of guilt, individual liability may provide better deterrence than corporate liability if it enables society to use the criminal

punishment threat against those who make important corporate decisions. The prospect of personal liability may cause individuals to resist corporate pressures to violate the law. If guilty individuals are identified and punished, the criminal law's purposes may be achieved without harm to innocent employees, shareholders, and consumers.

Problems with Individual Liability   Attractive as it may sound, individual liability also poses significant problems when applied to corporate acts. Identifying responsible individuals within the corporate hierarchy becomes difficult—and frequently impossible—if we follow traditional notions and require proof of criminal intent. Business decisions leading to corporate wrongs often result from the collective actions of numerous corporate employees, none of whom had complete knowledge or specific criminal intent. Other corporate crimes are structural in the sense that they result from internal bureaucratic failures rather than the conscious actions of any individual or group.

Proving culpability on the part of high-level executives may be particularly difficult. Bad news sometimes does not reach them; other times, they consciously avoid knowledge that would lead to criminal responsibility. It therefore may be possible to demonstrate culpability only on the part of middle-level managers. Juries may be unwilling to convict such individuals, however, if they seem to be scapegoats for their unindicted superiors.

The difficulties in imposing criminal penalties on individual employees have led to the creation of regulatory offenses that impose strict or vicarious liability on corporate officers. Strict liability offenses dispense with the requirement of proof of criminal intent but ordinarily require proof that the defendant committed some wrongful act. Vicarious liability offenses impose criminal liability on a defendant for the acts of third parties (normally, employees under the defendant's personal supervision), but may require proof of some form of *mens rea,* such as the defendant's negligent or reckless failure to supervise. Statutes often combine these two approaches by making corporate executives liable for the acts or omissions of corporate employees without requiring proof of criminal intent on the part of the employees. *United States v. Park,* discussed in Figure 2, is a famous example of such a prosecution.

Critics of strict liability offenses often argue that *mens rea* is a basic principle in our legal system and that it is unjust to stigmatize with a criminal conviction persons who are not morally culpable. In addition, critics doubt that strict liability statutes produce the deterrence sought by

---

Figure 2   *A Note on* United States v. Park, *421 U.S. 658 (U.S. Sup. Ct. 1975)*

Facts and Procedural History

John R. Park was CEO of Acme Markets, Inc., a national retail food chain with approximately 36,000 employees, 874 retail outlets, and 16 warehouses. Acme and Park were charged with five counts of violating the federal Food, Drug, and Cosmetic Act (the Act) by storing food shipped in interstate commerce in warehouses where it was exposed to rodent contamination. The violations were detected during Food and Drug Administration (FDA) inspections of Acme's Baltimore warehouse. Inspectors saw evidence of rodent infestation and unsanitary conditions, such as mouse droppings on the floor of the hanging meat room and alongside bales of lime Jell-O, and a hole chewed by a rodent in a bale of Jell-O. The FDA notified Park by letter of these findings.

Upon checking with Acme's vice president for legal affairs, Park learned that the Baltimore division vice president "was investigating the situation immediately and would be taking corrective action." An FDA inspection three months after the first one disclosed continued rodent contamination at the Baltimore warehouse despite improved sanitation there. The criminal charges were then filed against Acme and Park. Acme pleaded guilty; Park refused to do so. Park was convicted on each count, but the court of appeals overturned the conviction.

The Supreme Court's Decision

The Supreme Court, however, reversed. In sustaining Park's conviction, the Court noted that in view of the substantial public interest in purity of food, the Act did not require awareness of wrongdoing as an element of criminal conduct. This did not mean, however, that a person "remotely entangled in the proscribed shipment" was at risk of being criminally convicted. Instead, the defendant must be shown to have had "a responsible share" in the violation, such as by failing to exercise authority and supervisory responsibility. The Court emphasized that the Act imposes on supervisory personnel the "highest standard of foresight and vigilance." This includes a duty to seek out and remedy violations when they occur, and a duty to implement measures to prevent violations from occurring.

Although one who was "powerless" to prevent or correct the violation cannot be held criminally responsible under the Act, the Court emphasized that Park was hardly powerless. He had the authority and responsibility to prevent or correct the prohibited condition. The evidence showed that prior to the Baltimore warehouse inspections giving rise to the criminal charges, Park was advised by the FDA of unsanitary conditions in another Acme warehouse. According to the Court, Park thus acquired notice—prior to the time that the Baltimore warehouse violations were discovered—that he could not rely on his previously employed system of delegation to subordinates to prevent or correct unsanitary conditions at company warehouses. Despite evidence indicating Park's prior awareness of this system's deficiencies well before the Baltimore violations were discovered, Park had not instituted any new procedures designed to prevent violations of the Act. The Court therefore concluded that his conviction should stand.

---

their proponents. Such statutes may reduce the moral impact of the criminal sanction if they apply it to relatively trivial offenses. Moreover, they may not result in enough convictions or sufficiently severe penalties to produce deterrence because juries and judges are unwilling to convict or punish defendants who may not be morally culpable. Although statutes creating strict liability offenses are generally held constitutional, they are disfavored by courts. Most courts require a clear indication of a legislative intent to dispense with the *mens rea* element.

Strict liability offenses are also criticized on the ground that even if responsible individuals within the corporation are convicted and punished appropriately, individual liability unaccompanied by corporate liability is unlikely to achieve effective corporate control. If immune from criminal liability, corporations could benefit financially from employees' violations of the law. Individual liability, unlike a corporate fine, does not force a corporation to give up the profits flowing from a violation. Thus, the corporation would have no incentive to avoid future violations. Incarcerated offenders would merely be replaced by others who might eventually yield to the pressures that produced the violations in the first place. Corporate liability, however, may sometimes encourage corporate efforts to prevent future violations. When an offense has occurred but no identifiable individual is sufficiently culpable to justify an individual prosecution of him or her, corporate liability is uniquely appropriate.

New Directions

The preceding discussion suggests that future efforts at corporate control are likely to include both corporate and individual criminal liability. It also suggests, however, that new approaches are necessary if society is to gain more effective control over corporate activities.

Various novel criminal penalties have been suggested in the individual liability setting. For example, white-collar offenders could be sentenced to render public service in addition to, or in lieu of, being incarcerated or fined. Some have even suggested the licensing of managers, with license suspensions as a penalty for offenders. The common thread in these and other similar approaches is an attempt to create penalties that are meaningful yet not so severe that judges and juries are unwilling to impose them.

A promising suggestion regarding corporate liability involves imaginative judicial use of corporate probation for convicted corporate offenders. For example, courts could require convicted corporations to do self-studies identifying the source of a violation and proposing appropriate steps to prevent future violations. If bureaucratic failures caused the violation, the court could order a limited restructuring of the corporation's internal decisionmaking processes as a condition of obtaining probation or avoiding a penalty. Possible orders might include requiring the collection and monitoring of the data necessary to discover or prevent future violations and mandating the creation of new executive positions to monitor such data. Restructuring would minimize the previously discussed harm to innocent persons that often accompanies corporate financial penalties. In addition, restructuring could be a more effective way to achieve corporate rehabilitation than relying exclusively on a corporation's desire to avoid future fines as an incentive to police itself.

The Federal Sentencing Guidelines, discussed earlier in this chapter in Figure 1, contain good reasons for corporations to institute measures to prevent regulatory violations. Under the subset of rules known as the Corporate Sentencing Guidelines, organizations convicted of violating federal law may face greatly increased penalties for certain offenses, with some crimes carrying fines as high as $290 million. The penalty imposed on an organization depends on its "culpability score," which increases (thus calling for a more severe penalty) if, for example, high-level corporate officers were involved in the offense or the organization had a history of such offenses. Even apart from the potentially severe penalties, however, the Corporate Sentencing Guidelines provide an incentive for corporations to adopt compliance programs designed "to prevent and detect violations of the law." The presence of an effective compliance program can reduce the corporation's culpability score for sentencing purposes. Prior to the time the Corporate Sentencing Guidelines took effect, courts generally concluded that the existence of a compliance program should not operate as a mitigating factor in the sentencing of a convicted organization.

ETHICS IN ACTION

Enron employee Sherron Watkins received considerable praise from the public, governmental officials, and media commentators when she went public in 2002 with her concerns about certain accounting and other business practices of her employer. These alleged practices caused Enron and high-level executives of the firm to undergo considerable legal scrutiny. As this book went to press in 2002, an Enron executive had just agreed to plead guilty to certain criminal charges and various politicians and commentators were issuing calls for criminal prosecutions of the firm and other executives.

In deciding to become a whistleblower, Sherron Watkins no doubt was motivated by what she regarded as a moral obligation. The decision she made was more highly publicized than most decisions of that nature, but was otherwise of a type that many employees have faced and will continue to face. You may be among those persons at some point in your career. Various questions, including the ones set forth below, may therefore be worth pondering. As you do so, you may find it useful to consider the perspectives afforded by the ethical theories discussed in Chapter 4.

• When an employee learns of apparently unlawful behavior on the part of his or her employer, does the employee have an ethical duty to blow the whistle on the employer?

• Do any ethical duties or obligations of the employee come into conflict in such a situation? If so, what are they, and how does the employee balance them?

• What practical consequences may one face if he or she becomes a whistleblower? What role, if any, should those potential consequences play in the ethical analysis?

• What other consequences are likely to occur if the whistle is blown? What is likely to happen if the whistle isn't blown? Should these likely consequences affect the ethical analysis? If so, how?

Important White-Collar Crimes

Regulatory Offenses

Numerous state and federal regulatory statutes on a wide range of subjects prescribe criminal as well as civil liability for violations. The Food, Drug, and Cosmetic Act, at issue in the case discussed in Figure 2, is an example of such a statute. Other major federal regulatory offenses are discussed in later chapters. These include violations of the Sherman Antitrust Act, the Securities Act of 1933, the Securities Exchange Act of 1934, and certain environmental laws.

Fraudulent Acts

Many business crimes involve some fraudulent conduct. In most states, it is a crime to obtain money or property by fraudulent pretenses, issue fraudulent checks, make false credit statements, or give short weights or measures. Certain forms of fraud in bankruptcy proceedings, such as false claims by creditors or fraudulent concealment or transfer of a debtor's assets, are federal criminal offenses. The same is true of securities fraud. In addition, federal mail fraud and wire fraud statutes make criminal the use of the mail, telephone, or telegrams to accomplish a fraudulent scheme. Another federal law makes it a crime to travel or otherwise use facilities in interstate commerce in order to commit criminal acts.

Corporate Fraud—The 2002 Legislation In response to a series of highly publicized financial scandals and accounting controversies involving Enron, Arthur Andersen, Global Crossing, WorldCom, and other firms, Congress enacted the Sarbanes–Oxley Act of 2002 shortly before this book went to press. The Sarbanes–Oxley Act created the Public Company Accounting Oversight Board and charged it with regulatory responsibilities concerning public accounting firms' audits of corporations. The statute also established various requirements designed to ensure auditor independence, bring about higher levels of accuracy in corporate reporting of financial information, and promote responsible conduct on the part of corporate officers and directors, auditors, and securities analysts.

Additional portions of the broad-ranging Sarbanes–Oxley Act were given separate and more informative titles such as the Corporate and Criminal Fraud Accountability Act and the White-Collar Crime Penalty Enhancement Act. In those other portions of the statute, Congress:

- Established substantial fines and/or a maximum of 20 years of imprisonment as punishment for the knowing alteration or destruction of documents or records with the intent to impede a government investigation or proceeding.
- Made it a crime for an accountant to destroy corporate audit records prior to the appropriate time set forth in the statute and in regulations to be promulgated by the Securities and Exchange Commission.
- Classified debts resulting from civil judgments for securities fraud as nondischargeable in bankruptcy.
- Lengthened the statute of limitations period within which certain securities fraud cases may be filed.
- Provided legal protections for corporate employees who act as whistleblowers regarding instances of fraud on the part of their employers.
- Established substantial fines and/or imprisonment of up to 25 years as the punishment for certain securities fraud offenses.
- Increased the maximum term of imprisonment for mail fraud and wire fraud to 20 years.
- Made attempts and conspiracies to commit such offenses subject to the same penalties established for the offenses themselves.
- Enhanced the penalties for certain violations of the Securities Exchange Act of 1934 by providing for a maximum fine of $5 million or a maximum 20-year prison term for individual violators, and a maximum fine of $25 million for corporate violators.
- Instructed the U.S. Sentencing Commission to review the Federal Sentencing Guidelines' treatment of obstruction of justice offenses, white-collar crimes, and securities fraud offenses, in order to ensure that deterrence and punishment purposes were being adequately served.

Bribery and Giving of Illegal Gratuities

State and federal law has long made it a crime to offer public officials gifts, favors, or anything of value to influence official decisions for private benefit. The *Sun-Diamond Growers* case, which appears earlier in the chapter, deals with such a statute. In 1977, Congress enacted the Foreign Corrupt Practices Act (FCPA), which criminalized the offering or giving of anything of value to officials of *foreign* governments in an attempt to influence their official actions. Individuals who violate the FCPA's bribery prohibition may be fined up to $100,000 and/or imprisoned for a maximum of five years. Corporate violators of the

FCPA may be fined as much as $2 million. Chapter 45 discusses the FCPA in more depth. As explained in the nearby Global Business Environment box, the 1990s marked the emergence of international agreements as additional devices for addressing the problem of bribery of government officials.

Most states in the United States also have commercial bribery statutes. These laws prohibit offering or providing kickbacks and similar payoffs to private parties in order to secure some commercial advantage.

RICO

When Congress passed the Racketeer Influenced and Corrupt Organizations Act (RICO) as part of the Organized Crime Control Act of 1970, lawmakers were primarily concerned about organized crime's increasing entry into legitimate business enterprises. RICO's broad language, however, allows the statute to be applied in a wide variety of cases having nothing to do with organized crime. As a result, RICO has become one of the most controversial pieces of legislation affecting business. Supporters of RICO argue that it is an effective and much-needed tool for attacking unethical business practices. Its critics, however, see RICO as an overbroad statute that needlessly taints business reputations. Critics also argue that RICO has operated unduly to favor plaintiffs in civil litigation rather than serving as an aid to law enforcement.

Criminal RICO Under RICO, it is a federal crime for any person to: (1) use income derived from a "pattern of racketeering activity" to acquire an interest in, establish, or operate an enterprise; (2) acquire or maintain an interest in an enterprise through a pattern of racketeering activity; (3) conduct or participate in, through a pattern of racketeering activity the affairs of an enterprise by which he is employed or with which he is affiliated; or (4) conspire to do any of the preceding acts. The *King* case, which appears later in the chapter, deals with the third of the above ways in which RICO may be violated.

THE GLOBAL BUSINESS ENVIRONMENT

At varying times since the 1977 enactment of the Foreign Corrupt Practices Act, the United States has advocated the development of international agreements designed to combat bribery and similar forms of corruption on at least a regional, if not a global, scale. These efforts and those of other nations sharing similar views bore fruit during the past decade.

In 1996, the Organization of American States (OAS) adopted the Inter-American Convention Against Corruption (IACAC). When it ratified the IACAC in September 2000, the United States joined 20 other subscribing OAS nations. The IACAC prohibits the offering or giving of a bribe to a government official in order to influence the official's actions, the solicitation or receipt of such a bribe, and certain other forms of corruption on the part of government officials. It requires subscribing nations to make changes in their domestic laws, in order to make those laws consistent with the IACAC. The United States has taken the position that given the content of the Foreign Corrupt Practices Act and other U.S. statutes prohibiting the offering and solicitation of bribes as well as various other forms of corruption, its statutes already are consistent with the IACAC.

The Organization for Economic Cooperation and Development (OECD) is made up of 29 nations that are leading exporters. In 1997, the OECD adopted the Convention on Combating Bribery of Officials in International Business Transactions. The OECD Convention, subscribed to by the United States, 28 other OECD member nations, and five nonmember nations, prohibits the offering or giving of a bribe to a government official in order to obtain a business advantage from the official's action or inaction. It calls for subscribing nations to have domestic laws that contain such a prohibition. Unlike the IACAC, however, the OECD neither prohibits the government official's solicitation or receipt of a bribe nor contains provisions dealing with the other forms of official corruption contemplated by the IACAC.

In 1999, the Council of Europe adopted the Criminal Law Convention on Corruption, which calls upon European Union (EU) member nations to develop domestic laws prohibiting the same sorts of behaviors prohibited by the IACAC. Many European Union members have signed on to this convention, as have three nonmembers of the EU. One of those is the United States.

Because the IACAC, the OECD Convention, and the Criminal Law Convention are relatively recent developments, it is too early to determine whether they have been effective international instruments for combating bribery and similar forms of corruption. Much will depend upon whether the domestic laws contemplated by these conventions are enforced with consistency and regularity.

RICO is a compound statute because it requires proof of "predicate" criminal offenses that constitute the necessary pattern of racketeering activity. *Racketeering activity* includes the commission of any of more than 30 state or federal criminal offenses. Although most offenses that qualify (e.g., arson, gambling, extortion) have no relation to normal business transactions, such offenses as mail and wire fraud, securities fraud, and bribery are also included. Thus, many forms of business fraud may be alleged to be a racketeering activity. To show a *pattern* of such activity, the prosecution must first prove the defendant's commission of at least two acts of racketeering activity within a 10-year period. The pattern requirement also calls for proof that these acts are related and amount to, or pose the threat of, continuing racketeering activity. Most courts have interpreted the statutory term *enterprise* broadly, so that it includes partnerships and unincorporated associations as well as corporations.

Individuals found guilty of RICO violations are subject to substantial fines and imprisonment for up to 20 years. In addition, RICO violators risk the forfeiture of any interest gained in any enterprise as a result of a violation, as well as forfeiture of property derived from the prohibited racketeering activity. To prevent defendants from hiding assets that may be forfeitable upon conviction, federal prosecutors may seek pretrial orders freezing a defendant's assets. Some RICO critics argue that the harm such a freeze may work on a defendant's ability to conduct business, coupled with the threat of forfeiture of most or all of the business upon conviction, has led some defendants to make plea bargains rather than risk all by fighting prosecutions they believe to be unjustified.

Civil RICO   Under RICO, the government may also seek various civil penalties for violations. These include divestiture of a defendant's interest in an enterprise, dissolution or reorganization of the enterprise, and injunctions against future racketeering activities.

RICO's most controversial sections, however, allow private individuals to recover treble damages (three times their actual loss) and attorney's fees for injuries caused by a statutory violation. To qualify for recovery under RICO, a plaintiff must prove that the defendant violated RICO's provisions (as explained above) and that the plaintiff was "injured in his business or property" as a result. In the *King* case, which follows, the Supreme Court addressed the question whether the president/sole shareholder of a corporation was a "person" separate from the "enterprise" for purposes of the plaintiff's civil RICO claim against the president/sole shareholder.

Cedric Kushner Promotions Ltd. v. King   *533 U.S. 158 (U.S. Sup. Ct. 2001)*

Cedric Kushner Promotions Ltd. (Kushner), a corporate promoter of boxing matches, sued Don King, the president and sole shareholder of a rival corporation, alleging that King had conducted his corporation's affairs in violation of § 1962(c) of the Racketeer Influenced and Corrupt Organizations Act. The district court dismissed the complaint. In affirming, the Second Circuit expressed its view that §1962(c) applies only where a plaintiff shows the existence of two separate entities, a "person" and a distinct "enterprise," whose affairs that "person" improperly conducts. It was undisputed that King was an employee of his corporation and was acting within the scope of his authority. Under the Second Circuit's analysis, King was part of the corporation rather than a "person" distinct from the "enterprise" who allegedly improperly conducted the "enterprise's affairs." In cases presenting similar facts, other circuit courts of appeal had concluded that the sole shareholder of a corporation was a "person" distinct from the corporate "enterprise." Kushner appealed the Second Circuit's decision, and the Supreme Court granted certiorari.

Breyer, Justice   The Racketeer Influenced and Corrupt Organizations Act, 18 U.S.C. § 1961 *et seq.*, makes it "unlawful for any person employed by or associated with any enterprise . . . to conduct or participate . . . in the conduct of such enterprise's affairs" through the commission of two or more statutorily defined crimes—which RICO calls "a pattern of racketeering activity." § 1962(c). The language suggests, and lower courts have held, that this provision foresees two separate entities, a "person" and a distinct "enterprise."

This case focuses upon Don King, the president and sole shareholder of a closely held corporation. Kushner claims that the president has conducted the corporation's affairs through the forbidden "pattern," though for present purposes it is conceded that, in doing so, he acted within the scope of his authority as the corporation's employee. In these circumstances, are there two entities, a "person" and a separate "enterprise"? Assuming, as we must given the posture of this case, that the allegations in the complaint are true, we conclude that the "person" and "enterprise" here are distinct and that the RICO provision applies.

We do not quarrel with the basic principle that to establish liability under § 1962(c) one must allege and prove the existence of two distinct entities: (1) a "person"; and (2) an "enterprise" that is not simply the same "person" referred to by a different name. The statute's language . . . suggests that principle. The Act says that it applies to "persons" who are "employed by or associated with" the "enterprise." In ordinary English one speaks of employing, being employed by, or associating with others, not oneself. In addition, the Act's purposes are consistent with that principle. Whether the Act seeks to prevent a person from victimizing, say, a small business, or to prevent a person from using a corporation for criminal purposes, the person and the victim, or the person and the tool, are different entities, not the same.

While accepting the "distinctness" principle, [i.e., the requirement that the "person" and the "enterprise" be distinct,] we nonetheless disagree with the appellate court's application of that principle to the present circumstances— circumstances in which a corporate employee, acting within the scope of his authority, allegedly conducts the corporation's affairs in a RICO–forbidden way. The corporate owner/employee . . . is distinct from the corporation itself, a legally different entity with different rights and responsibilities due to its different legal status. [N]othing in the statute . . . requires more "separateness" than that.

Linguistically speaking, an employee who conducts the affairs of a corporation through illegal acts comes within the terms of a statute that forbids any "person" unlawfully to conduct an "enterprise," particularly when the statute explicitly defines "person" to include "any individual . . . capable of holding a legal or beneficial interest in property," and defines "enterprise" to include a "corporation." And, linguistically speaking, the employee and the corporation are different "persons," even where the employee is the corporation's sole owner. After all, incorporation's basic purpose is to create a distinct legal entity, with legal rights, obligations, powers, and privileges different from those of the natural individuals who created it, who own it, or whom it employs.

Further, to apply the RICO statute in present circumstances is consistent with the statute's basic purposes as this Court has defined them. The Court has held that RICO both protects a legitimate "enterprise" from those who would use unlawful acts to victimize it, and also protects the public from those who would unlawfully use an "enterprise" (whether legitimate or illegitimate) as a "vehicle" through which "unlawful . . . activity is committed." *National Organization for Women, Inc. v. Scheidler,* 510 U.S. 249 (1994). A corporate employee who conducts the corporation's affairs through an unlawful RICO "pattern . . . of activity," uses that corporation as a "vehicle" whether he is, or is not, its sole owner.

Conversely, the appellate court's critical legal distinction—between employees acting within the scope of corporate authority and those acting outside that authority—is inconsistent with a basic statutory purpose. It would immunize from RICO liability many of those at whom this Court has said RICO directly aims—*e.g.,* high-ranking individuals in an illegitimate criminal enterprise, who, seeking to further the purposes of that enterprise, act within the scope of their authority.

Finally, we have found nothing in the statute's legislative history that significantly favors an alternative interpretation. [A Senate report] not only refers frequently to the importance of undermining organized crime's influence upon legitimate businesses but also refers to the need to protect the public from those who would run "organizations in a manner detrimental to the public interest." This latter purpose, as we have said, invites the legal principle we endorse, namely, that in present circumstances the statute requires no more than the formal legal distinction between "person" and "enterprise" (namely, incorporation) that is present here.

[W]e hold . . . that the need for two distinct entities is satisfied; hence, the RICO provision before us applies when a corporate employee unlawfully conducts the affairs of the corporation of which he is the sole owner—whether he conducts those affairs within the scope, or beyond the scope, of corporate authority.

Second Circuit's decision reversed, and case remanded for further proceedings.

Aided by the Supreme Court's refusal, in *Sedima, S.P.R.L. v. Imrex Co.* (1985), to give a narrowing construction to the broadly phrased RICO, private plaintiffs have brought a large number of civil RICO cases in recent years. In *Sedima,* the Court rejected, as an erroneous statutory interpretation, some lower federal courts' approach of requiring civil RICO plaintiffs to prove that the defendant had actually been criminally convicted of a predicate offense. The Court also rejected the argument that civil RICO plaintiffs should be expected to prove a "distinct racketeering injury" as a precondition of recovery. The Court acknowledged lower courts' concern about RICO's breadth and noted the fact that most civil RICO cases are filed against legitimate businesses rather than against "the archetypal, intimidating mobster." Nevertheless, the Court observed that "[t]his defect—if defect it is— is inherent in the statute as written, and its correction must lie with Congress."

Various RICO reform proposals have been unsuccessfully introduced in Congress. A 1995 reform measure that did become law, however, established that a civil RICO case cannot be based on conduct that would have been actionable as securities fraud unless the conduct amounting to securities fraud had resulted in a criminal conviction.

Computer Crime

As computers have come to play an increasingly important role in our society, new opportunities for crime have arisen. In some instances, computers may be used to accomplish crimes such as theft, embezzlement, espionage, and fraud. In others, computers or the information stored there may be targets of crimes such as unauthorized access, vandalism, tampering, or theft of services. The law's response to computer crimes has evolved with this new technology. For example, computer hacking—once viewed by some as a mischievous but clever activity—can now lead to significant prison sentences and fines.

The technical nature of computer crime complicates its detection and prosecution. Traditional criminal statutes have often proven inadequate because they tend not to address explicitly the types of crime associated with the use of computers. Assume, for example, that a general statute on theft defines the offense in terms of stealing "property," and that the defendant is charged with violating the statute by taking and using

computer data without authorization. The court could decide to dismiss this case if categorizing data stored in a computer as "property" strikes the court as a strained interpretation of the statute. Although some courts have interpreted existing criminal laws narrowly so as to exclude instances of computer abuse, other courts have construed them more broadly. In light of the uncertainties attending statutory interpretation, legislatures on the state and federal levels have become increasingly aware of the need to revise their criminal codes to be certain that they explicitly cover computer crime.

Almost all states have now enacted criminal statutes specifically outlawing certain abuses of computers. Common provisions prohibit such acts as obtaining access to a computer system without authorization, tampering with files or causing damage to a system (e.g., by spreading a virus or deleting files), invading the privacy of others, using a computer to commit fraud or theft, and trafficking in passwords or access codes.

On the federal level, computer crime has been prosecuted with some success under existing federal statutes, primarily those forbidding mail fraud, wire fraud, transportation of stolen property, and thefts of property. As has been true at the state level, successful prosecution of these cases often depends on broad interpretation of the statutory prerequisites. Another federal law deals more directly with improper uses of computers. Among the crimes covered by this federal statute are intentionally gaining unauthorized access to a computer used by or for the U.S. government, trafficking in passwords and other access devices, and using a computer to obtain government information that is protected from disclosure. It is also a crime to gain unauthorized access to the computer system of a private financial institution that has a connection with the federal government (such as federal insurance for the deposits in the financial institution). In addition, the statute criminalizes the transmission of codes, commands, or information if the transmission was intended to damage such an institution's computers, computer system, data, or programs.

The federal Computer Fraud and Abuse Act (CFAA) allows the imposition of criminal and civil liability on one who "knowingly, and with intent to defraud, accesses a protected computer without authorization, or exceeds authorized access, and by means of such conduct furthers the intended fraud and obtains anything of value." For a case applying the CFAA, see the nearby Cyberlaw in Action box.

CYBERLAW IN ACTION

Explorica, Inc. was founded in 2000 to compete with EF Cultural Travel, which dominated the market in global tours for high school students. Setting Explorica's tour prices lower than EF's became an important Explorica objective.

EF's tour prices were accessible through the firm's website, where the user who desired information would enter various price-determining factors, such as desired date of departure and destination. The website would translate the user's preferences to a special code, decipherable only by the site's servers and human operators, and would submit the code to the server. From the code, the server would determine travel options and prices suited to the user's specifications, and then send them to the user's computer as a new page. Because this page's URL (Uniform Resource Locator) was the same regardless of the user's entries and the set of prices displayed, the code used in generating the page was not accessible to the user.

In view of the large number of possible factor combinations that a user might submit to EF, Explorica realized that manually obtaining price information on every tour that EF could offer would be nearly impossible. Explorica therefore wrote a "scraper" program, using code information provided by Explorica vice-president Philip Gormley, a former employee of EF. The scraper automatically submitted codes representing all possible factor combinations to EF's server and then recorded the results in an Excel spreadsheet. Explorica ran the scraper twice, first to obtain EF's 2000 tour prices and then to obtain its 2001 tour prices. The scraper compiled 60,000 lines—the rough equivalent of eight telephone books—of data. Explorica used the information to undercut EF's prices.

More than a year later, EF learned of Explorica's development and use of the scraper. EF then sued Explorica, alleging violations of the Computer Fraud and Abuse Act (CFAA). The CFAA is violated when an individual person or a corporation "knowingly, and with intent to defraud, accesses a protected computer without authorization, or exceeds authorized access, and by means of such conduct furthers the intended fraud and obtains anything of value." 18 U.S.C. § 1030(a)(4). Criminal liability for violating the CFAA may be established in appropriate cases brought by the federal government. Civil cases such as the one brought by EF are also allowed by the CFAA if the plaintiff has suffered "damage or loss" as a result of a violation of the statute.

EF sought a preliminary injunction that would bar all further use of the scraper and would require the return of all materials generated by the scraper. When a federal district court granted the preliminary injunction, Explorica appealed. In *EF Cultural Travel BV v. Explorica, Inc.,* 274 F.3d 577 (1st Cir. 2001), the U.S. Court of Appeals for the First Circuit reasoned that in order to show it was likely to succeed with its claim of a CFAA violation, EF would have to demonstrate that Explorica had "exceed[ed] authorized access" to EF's site by using the scraper. In the CFAA, Congress defined "exceed[ing] authorized access" as accessing a computer "with authorization and [using] such access to obtain or alter information in the computer that the accesser is not entitled so to obtain or alter." The First Circuit observed that a confidentiality agreement between EF and ex-employee Gormley (the Explorica vice-president) was evidence strongly pointing toward a conclusion that Explorica had exceeded authorized access.

The only remaining issue was whether EF was likely to be able to prove that it had suffered the "damage or loss" necessary to support a civil action for violation of the CFAA. The First Circuit noted that even though EF had not experienced "damage" of a demonstrable nature to its website, it could argue convincingly that it had suffered "loss" of business and goodwill. In addition, customary legal applications of the term "loss" would allow EF to seek recovery of the costs of diagnostic measures it took in an effort to determine whether its website had been compromised by Explorica's use of the scraper. Because EF had demonstrated a likelihood of success on the merits of its claim that Explorica had violated the CFAA, the First Circuit upheld the grant of the preliminary injunction.

Problems and Problem Cases

1. Intending to investigate drug transactions, police officers Nolan and Harvey entered a Chicago neighborhood known for heavy narcotics trafficking. Nolan observed a private citizen, Wardlow, who was standing next to a building holding an opaque bag. Wardlow looked in the direction of the police officers and fled. The officers cornered Wardlow, and Nolan detained him, conducting a protective patdown search of Wardlow's person. He then squeezed the bag Wardlow was carrying and felt a heavy, hard object similar in shape to a gun. Nolan opened the bag and discovered a loaded .38 caliber handgun. Nolan and Harvey then arrested Wardlow on a charge of unlawful use of a weapon by a felon. Were Wardlow's Fourth Amendment rights violated?

2. An informant told the Eagan, Minnesota, police that while walking past the window of a ground-floor apartment, he had observed people putting a white powder into bags. Officer Thielen went to the apartment building to investigate. He looked in the window through a gap in the closed blind and observed the bagging operation for several minutes. When two men left the building in a previously identified Cadillac, other police officers stopped the car. While one of the car's doors was open, the officers observed a black zippered pouch and a handgun on the floor of the vehicle. The officers arrested the car's occupants, Carter and Johns. A later search of the vehicle resulted in the discovery of pagers, a scale, and 47 grams of cocaine in plastic baggies. After seizing the car, the officers returned to the apartment and arrested its occupant, Thompson. A search of the apartment (conducted on the basis of a warrant) revealed cocaine residue on the kitchen table and plastic baggies similar to those found in the Cadillac. Officer Thielen identified Carter, Johns, and Thompson as the persons he had observed taking part in the bagging operation. It was later learned that Thompson was the apartment's lessee and that Carter and Johns, both of whom lived in Chicago, had come to the apartment for the sole purpose of packaging the cocaine. Carter and Johns had never been to the apartment before and were in the apartment for approximately two and one-half hours at the general time the bagging operation was conducted. In return for the use of the apartment, Carter and Johns had given some of the cocaine to Thompson. Carter and Johns were charged with controlled substance–related crimes. Prior to trial, they moved to suppress all evidence obtained from the apartment and the Cadillac. They contended that Officer Thielen's observation of them through the apartment window was an unreasonable search in violation of the Fourth Amendment and that all evidence obtained as a result was inadmissible. Were Carter and Johns entitled to claim the protection of the Fourth Amendment?

3. A federal grand jury was investigating "John Doe," president and sole shareholder of "XYZ" corporation, concerning possible violations of federal securities and money-laundering statutes. During the investigation, the government learned that XYZ had paid the bills for various telephone lines, including those used in Doe's homes and car. Grand jury subpoenas calling for the production of documents were then served on the custodian of XYZ's corporate records, on Doe, and on the law firm Paul, Weiss, Rifkind, Wharton & Garrison (Paul–Weiss), which represented Doe. These subpoenas sought production of telephone bills, records, and statements of account regarding certain telephone numbers, including

those used by Doe. The District Court determined after an evidentiary hearing that the documents sought were XYZ's, and not Doe's.

Paul–Weiss, which had received copies of these documents from its client, refused to produce them, arguing that it was exempted from doing so by Doe's privilege against self-incrimination. Was Paul–Weiss correct in its assertion?

4. Dow Chemical Company operated a 2,000-acre chemical manufacturing facility at Midland, Michigan. The facility consisted of numerous covered buildings, with manufacturing equipment and piping conduits between various buildings plainly visible from the air. Dow maintained elaborate security around the perimeter of the complex to bar ground-level public views of these areas. It also investigated any low-level flights by aircraft over the facility. Dow did not, however, attempt to conceal all manufacturing equipment within the complex from aerial views because the cost would have been prohibitive. With Dow's consent, enforcement officials of the Environmental Protection Agency (EPA) made an on-site inspection of two power plants in this complex. When Dow denied EPA's request for another inspection, EPA did not seek an administrative search warrant. Instead, EPA employed a commercial aerial photographer, who used a standard floor-mounted, precision aerial mapping camera to take photographs of the facility from altitudes of 12,000, 3,000, and 1,200 feet. At all times, the aircraft was lawfully within navigable airspace. EPA did not inform Dow of this aerial photography. Was EPA's taking of aerial photographs of the Dow complex a search prohibited by the Fourth Amendment?

5. Chicago's city council enacted the Gang Congregation Ordinance, which read, in pertinent part:

> Whenever a police officer observes a person he reasonably believes to be a criminal street gang member loitering in any public place with one or more other persons, he shall order all such persons to disperse and remove themselves from the area. Any person who does not properly obey such an order is in violation of this section.

The ordinance went on to define loitering as "remain[ing] in any one place with no apparent purpose." Violators of the fine could be subjected to a jail term and could be ordered to perform community service. Was the ordinance unconstitutionally vague?

6. Border Patrol Agent Cesar Cantu boarded a bus in Texas to check the immigration status of its passengers. As he walked off the bus, he squeezed the soft luggage that passengers had placed in the storage racks above

their seats. After squeezing a green canvas bag belonging to Steven DeWayne Bond, Cantu concluded that it contained a "brick-like" object. Bond allowed Cantu to open bag. Upon doing so, Cantu found a "brick" of methamphetamine, which had been wrapped in duct tape and then rolled in a pair of pants. Did Cantu's physical manipulation of Bond's luggage constitute an "unreasonable search and seizure" for purposes of the Fourth Amendment?

7. Wright and Panikkar owned adjoining parcels of land on which their families operated separate tree farms. The tree farms had not been profitable. Wright and Panikkar therefore entered into separate four-year contracts with Annulli, who was experienced in the tree farm business. The contracts called for Annulli to manage the tree farms. They provided that Annulli would receive the profits from tree sales after he had paid Wright or Panikkar (whichever was appropriate) a base fee for each tree sold. After Annulli had successfully managed Wright's tree farm for two years, Wright terminated the contract. Annulli contended that this was a breach of contract by Wright. In addition, Annulli contended that Wright wrongfully induced Panikkar to breach his contract with Annulli and that Wright and his son stole, from Annulli, certain proprietary information and the value of certain services Annulli had performed. Annulli filed a civil RICO action against Wright, Panikkar, and members of their families. The pattern of racketeering activity alleged by Annulli consisted of supposed breaches of contract as well as tortious interference with contract and theft by deception (a state law offense). Was Annulli correct in his assertion that such actions may constitute a pattern of racketeering activity for purposes of RICO?

8. Muniz was arrested on a charge of driving under the influence of alcohol. He was taken to a booking center, where he was asked several questions by a police officer without first being given the *Miranda* warnings. Videotape (which included an audio portion) was used to record the questions and Muniz's answers. The officer asked Muniz his name, address, height, weight, eye color, date of birth, and current age. Muniz stumbled over answers to two of these questions. The officer then asked Muniz the date of his sixth birthday, but Muniz did not give the correct date. At a later point, Muniz was read the *Miranda* warnings for the first time. He was later convicted of the charged offense, with the trial court denying his motion to exclude the videotape (both video and audio portions) from evidence. Assume that the video portion of the tape violated neither the Fifth Amendment nor *Miranda*. Should all or any part of the audio portion of

the tape (which contained Muniz's stumbling responses to two questions plus his incorrect answer to the sixth birthday date question) have been excluded as a violation of either the Fifth Amendment or *Miranda?*

9. Versaggi was employed by Kodak as a computer technician. Because he was responsible for maintaining and repairing certain telephone systems for the company, he had been given an "accelerator," a security device that allowed him to access the telephone systems operated by two SL-100 computers. On two occasions during the same month, thousands of telephone lines at Kodak's offices and a Kodak industrial complex were shut down and rendered inoperable for up to an hour and a half as a result of a cause that initially was not known. It was later determined that Versaggi had accessed the SL-100 systems and, without authorization, had issued commands that caused the phone lines to shut down. Versaggi was charged with violating New York's computer tampering statute, which read as follows: "A person is guilty of computer tampering . . . when he uses or causes to be used a computer or computer service and having no right to do so . . . intentionally alters in any manner or destroys computer data or a computer program of another person." Versaggi contended that he was not guilty of violating the statute because he did not "alter" any computer programs. Instead, Versaggi maintained, he merely activated existing instructions that commanded the computers to shut down. The trial court concluded that Versaggi violated the computer tampering statute. Was the trial court correct?

10. Concerned by a rise in the use of cocaine by prenatal patients, staff at a state hospital offered to cooperate in the city's prosecution of mothers whose children tested positive for drug use at birth. Accordingly, a task force made up of hospital staff, police, and local officials developed a policy under which prenatal patients' urine samples would be tested for drug use and the results sent to local law enforcement authorities. Patients who tested positive for drug use could participate in a rehabilitation and education program offered by the hospital; if they did not, they faced prosecution for drug offenses. Ten such patients who were arrested after being found to have been using cocaine contended that the hospital's policy constituted a series of unreasonable searches prohibited by the Constitution. Was the patients' contention correct?

11. A grand jury indicted Automated Medical Laboratories, Inc. (AML), Richmond Plasma Corporation (RPC) (a wholly owned AML subsidiary), and three former RPC managers for engaging in a conspiracy that included falsification of logbooks and records required to

be maintained by businesses producing blood plasma. The falsification was designed to conceal from the Food and Drug Administration (FDA) various violations of federal regulations governing the plasmapheresis process and facilities. The evidence introduced at trial indicated that the managers and several other members of the team charged with ensuring compliance with FDA regulations had actively participated in record falsification. AML was convicted and appealed on the ground that there was no evidence that any officer or director of AML knowingly or willfully participated in or authorized the unlawful practices at RPC. Was AML's conviction in the absence of such proof proper?

12. While under arrest for an unrelated offense, Raymond Levi Cobb confessed to a home burglary, but denied knowledge relating to the disappearance of a woman and child from the home. Cobb was indicted on charge of burglary, and an attorney was appointed to represent him. Later, while Cobb was out on bond, Cobb's father informed police that Cobb had confessed to him that he (Cobb) had murdered the woman and child. Police then took Cobb into custody. Cobb waived his *Miranda* rights, confessed to the murders, and led officers to the place where the bodies were buried. He appealed his consequent conviction and death sentence, arguing that because police had not secured the permission of his attorney from the burglary case before conducting the interrogation regarding the murders, his confession should have been suppressed. Was he correct?

Online Research: Corporate Codes of Ethics

Many corporations have adopted codes of ethics to which its executives and employees are subject. Search the World Wide Web for such a code of ethics, and read through it. Then prepare a short essay in which you (1) assess the code's strengths and weaknesses, and (2) offer suggestions for improvement of the code.

6

INTENTIONAL TORTS

Jonathan Harr's best-selling book, *A Civil Action,* is a dramatized account of real-life toxic tort litigation involving a tannery. The book discusses evidence that the protagonist, attorney Jan Schlichtmann, regarded as implicating tannery owner John Riley in the deaths of several children. Riley brought a defamation action against Harr and the book's publisher because, in Riley's view, the book had depicted him as a liar, a perjurer, a "killer," and a bully.

One passage cited by Riley described Schlichtmann's reaction upon discovering a certain incriminating document:

This document was thirty years old and it dealt only with tannery waste, which might or might not have contained TCE [a potentially harmful chemical]. But even so, Schlichtmann thought it had great value. Riley had sworn at his deposition that he had never dumped anything on the fifteen acres. Riley had lied then, and Schlichtmann—who didn't need much convincing—believed that Riley was also lying about using TCE.

Another passage described Schlichtmann's efforts to build a case against the tannery:

It seemed that everyone but Riley recognized the fifteen acres as a toxic waste dump. Riley must have known about the condition of the property. Perhaps, thought Schlichtmann, the tanner really had been running an unauthorized waste dump. Perhaps he had charged his neighbor, Whitney Barrel, a fee for the use of the land.

• Did Riley have a meritorious defamation claim against Harr and the publishing company on the basis of these and other similar statements?

A **TORT** IS A *civil wrong* that is not a breach of a contract. Tort cases and treatises identify different types of wrongfulness, culpability, or fault and define them in varying ways. In this chapter and in Chapter 7, we will refer to the four types of wrongfulness defined below.

1. *Intent.* We define intent as the desire to cause certain consequences or the substantial certainty that those consequences will result from one's behavior. For example, if D pulls the trigger of a loaded handgun while aiming it at P for the purpose of killing him or with a substantial certainty that P would be killed, D intended to kill P. This chapter discusses several *intentional torts,* most of which require, as the name of

this category of torts suggests, intent on the part of the defendant.

2. *Recklessness.* The form of intent involving substantial certainty blends by degrees into a different kind of fault—recklessness. We define recklessness as a conscious indifference to a known and substantial risk of harm created by one's behavior. Suppose that simply because he likes the muzzle flash and the sound, D fires his handgun at random in a crowded subway station. One of D's shots injures P. D acted recklessly if he had no desire to hit P or anyone else and was not substantially certain that anyone would be hit, but nonetheless knew that this could easily result from his

behavior. References to recklessness appear from time to time in this chapter and in Chapter 7.

3. *Negligence.* We define negligence as a failure to use reasonable care, with harm to another party occurring as a result. Negligent conduct falls below the level necessary to protect others against unreasonable risks of harm. Assume that without checking, D pulls the trigger on what he incorrectly and unreasonably thinks is an unloaded handgun. If the gun goes off and wounds P, D has negligently harmed P. Chapter 7 discusses negligence law in detail.

4. *Strict liability.* Strict liability is liability without fault or more precisely, liability irrespective of fault. In a strict liability case, the plaintiff need not prove intent, recklessness, negligence, or any other kind of wrongfulness on the defendant's part. However, strict liability is not automatic liability. A plaintiff must prove certain things in any strict liability case, but fault is not one of them. Chapter 7 discusses various types of strict liability, some of which are examined more fully in other chapters.

Tort law contemplates *civil* liability for those who commit torts. This distinguishes it from the criminal law, which also involves wrongful behavior. As you saw in Chapter 1, a civil case is normally a suit between private parties. In criminal cases, a prosecutor represents the government in confronting the defendant. The standard of proof that the plaintiff must satisfy in a tort case is the *preponderance of the evidence* standard, not the more stringent beyond-a-reasonable-doubt standard applied in criminal cases. This means that the greater weight of the evidence introduced at the trial must support the plaintiff's position on every element of the tort case. Finally, the remedy allowed in civil cases (most often, damages) differs from the punishment imposed in criminal cases (e.g., imprisonment or a fine). Of course, the same behavior may sometimes give rise to both civil and criminal liability. For example, one who commits a sexual assault is criminally liable and will also be liable for some or all of the torts of assault, battery, false imprisonment, and intentional infliction of emotional distress.

A plaintiff who wins a tort case usually recovers the compensatory damages for the harm she suffered as a result of the defendant's wrongful act. Depending on the facts of the case, these damages may be for direct and immediate harms such as physical injuries, medical expenses, and lost wages and benefits, or for seemingly less tangible harms such as loss of privacy, injury to reputation, and emotional distress. If the defendant's behavior was particularly bad, injured victims may also

be able to recover **punitive damages.** Punitive damages are not intended to compensate tort victims for their losses. Instead, they are designed to punish flagrant wrongdoers and to deter them, as well as others, from engaging in similar conduct in the future. Punitive damages are reserved for the worst kinds of wrongdoing and thus are not routinely assessed against the losing defendant in a tort case. Certainly, however, some behaviors giving rise to intentional tort liability are regarded as reprehensible enough to justify an assessment of punitive damages.

Interference with Personal Rights

This chapter examines two categories of intentional torts: (1) those involving interference with personal rights, and (2) those involving interference with property rights. A third category, business or competitive torts, will be discussed in Chapter 8.

Battery

Battery is the intentional and harmful or offensive touching of another without his consent. Contact is *harmful* if it produces bodily injury. However, battery also includes nonharmful contact that is *offensive*—calculated to offend a reasonable sense of personal dignity. The *intent* required for battery is either: (1) the intent to cause harmful or offensive contact, or (2) the intent to cause apprehension that such contact is imminent. Assume, for instance, that in order to scare Pine, Delano threatens to "shoot" Pine with a gun that Delano mistakenly believes is unloaded. If Delano ends up shooting Pine even though that had not been his specific intent, Delano is liable for battery. For battery to occur, moreover, the person who suffers the harmful or offensive contact need not be the person the wrongdoer intended to injure. Under a concept known as *transferred intent,* a defendant who intends to injure one person but actually injures another is liable to the person injured, despite the absence of any specific desire to injure him. So, if Dudley throws a rock at Thomas and hits Pike instead, Dudley is liable to Pike for battery.

As the previous examples suggest, the *touching* necessary for battery does not require direct contact between the defendant's body and the plaintiff's body. Dudley is therefore liable if he successfully lays a trap for Pike or poisons him. There is also a touching if the defendant causes contact with anything attached to the plaintiff's body. If the other elements of a battery are present, Dudley is thus liable to Pike if he shoots off Pike's hat. Finally, the plaintiff need not be aware of the battery at the time it occurs. This means that Dudley is liable if he sneaks up behind Pike and knocks Pike unconscious, without Pike's ever knowing what hit him.

There is no liability for battery, however, if the plaintiff *consented* to the touching. As a general rule, consent must be freely and intelligently given to be a defense to battery. Consent also may be inferred from a person's voluntary participation in an activity, but it is ordinarily limited to contacts that are a normal consequence of the activity. A professional boxer injured by his opponent's punches to the head, therefore, would not win a battery lawsuit against the opponent. However, a professional boxer whose ear is partially bitten off by his opponent should have a valid battery claim against the ear-biter. In addition, the law infers consent to many touchings that are customary or reasonably necessary in normal social life. Thus, Preston could not recover for battery if Dean tapped him on the shoulder to ask directions or brushed against him on a crowded street. Of course, many such contacts are neither harmful nor offensive anyway.

The *Wishnatsky* case, which follows, deals with battery's "offensiveness" requirement. Do you agree with the court's handling of the "reasonable sense of personal dignity" question?

Wishnatsky v. Huey   *584 N.W.2d 859 (N.D. Ct. App. 1998)*

Martin Wishnatsky worked as a paralegal for attorney Peter Crary. One day, while Crary was engaged in a conversation with North Dakota Assistant Attorney General David Huey in Crary's office, Wishnatsky attempted to enter the office. Huey then pushed the door closed in Wishnatsky's face, forcing him back into the hall. Wishnatsky suffered no physical injury from Huey's action.

Wishnatsky sued Huey for battery. After the trial court granted Huey's motion for summary judgment, Wishnatsky appealed.

Per Curiam [In his *Commentaries*], Blackstone explained: "The least touching of another's person willfully, or in anger, is a battery; for the law cannot draw the line between different degrees of violence, and therefore totally prohibits the first and lowest stage of it: every man's person being sacred, and no other having a right to meddle with it, in any the slightest manner." On the other hand, "in a crowded world, a certain amount of personal contact is inevitable, and must be accepted." *Prosser and Keeton on the Law of Torts,* section 9, at 42 (5th ed. 1984).

The American Law Institute has balanced the interest in preventing unwanted contacts and the inevitable contacts in a crowded world. In the *Restatement (Second) of Torts,* an actor is subject to liability to another for battery if: (a) he acts intending to cause a harmful or offensive contact with the person of the other or a third person, or an imminent apprehension of such a contact, and (b) an offensive [or harmful] contact with the person of the other directly or indirectly results. A bodily contact is offensive if it offends a reasonable sense of personal dignity. In order that a contact be offensive to a reasonable sense of personal dignity, it must be one which would offend the ordinary person, one not unduly sensitive as to his personal dignity. It must, therefore, be a contact which is unwarranted by the social usages prevalent at the time and place at which it is inflicted.

Huey supported [his] motion with his affidavit stating in part:

Attorney Clary and I had settled into a serious discussion about the case and had established a good rapport when the door to his office suddenly swung open without a knock. An unidentified individual carrying some papers then strode in unannounced. I had not been told that anyone would be entering Attorney Crary's office during the private meeting. I subsequently learned that the individual's name is Martin Wishnatsky.

Wishnatsky responded to Huey's motion with his own affidavit stating in part:

1. I am a born-again Christian and cultivate holiness in my life. As a result I am very sensitive to evil spirits and am greatly disturbed by the demonic.
2. As I began to enter the office Mr. Huey threw his body weight against the door and forced me out into the hall. I had not said a word to him. At the same time, he snarled: "You get out of here." This was very shocking and frightening to me. My blood pressure began to rise, my heartbeat accelerated, and I felt waves of fear

in the pit of my stomach. My hand began to shake and my body to tremble. Composing myself, I reentered the office, whereupon Mr. Huey began a half-demented tirade against me and stormed out into the hall.

The evidence demonstrates that Wishnatsky is unduly sensitive as to his personal dignity. The bodily contact was momentary, indirect, and incidental. Viewing the evidence in the light most favorable to Wishnatsky, we conclude that Huey's conduct, while rude and abrupt, would not be offensive to a reasonable sense of personal dignity. An ordinary person intruding upon a private conversation in Wishnatsky's manner would not have been offended by Huey's response to the intrusion.

Summary judgment for Huey affirmed.

Assault

Assault occurs when there is an intentional attempt or offer to cause a harmful or offensive contact with another person, if that attempt or offer causes a reasonable apprehension of imminent battery in the other person's mind. The necessary *intent* is the same as the intent required for battery. In an assault case, however, it is irrelevant whether the threatened contact actually occurs. Instead, the key thing is the plaintiff's *apprehension* of a harmful or offensive contact. Apprehension need not involve fear; it might be described as a mental state consistent with this thought: "I'm just about to be hit."

The plaintiff's apprehension must pertain to an anticipated battery that would be *imminent or immediate*. Threats of some future battery, therefore, do not create liability for assault. In addition, the plaintiff must experience apprehension *at the time the threatened battery occurs*. For instance, if Dinwiddie fires a rifle at Porter from a great distance and misses him, and only later does Porter learn of the attempt on his life, Dinwiddie is not liable to Porter for assault. The plaintiff's apprehension must also be *reasonable*. As a result, threatening words normally are not an assault unless they are accompanied by acts or circumstances indicating the defendant's intent to carry out the threat.

Intentional Infliction of Emotional Distress

For many years, courts refused to allow recovery for purely emotional injuries unless the defendant had committed some recognized tort. Victims of such torts as assault, battery, and false imprisonment could recover for the emotional injuries resulting from these torts, but courts would not recognize an independent tort of infliction of emotional distress. The reasons for this judicial reluctance included a fear of spurious or trivial claims, concerns about proving purely emotional harms, and uncertainty about the proper boundaries of an independent tort. However, increased confidence in our knowledge about emotional injuries and a greater willingness to compensate such harms have helped to overcome these judicial impediments. Most courts today allow recovery for severe emotional distress, under appropriate circumstances, regardless of whether the elements of any other tort are proven.

The courts are not, however, in complete agreement on the elements of this relatively new tort. All courts do require that a wrongdoer's conduct be *outrageous* before liability for emotional distress arises. The *Restatement (Second) of Torts* speaks of conduct "so outrageous in character, and so extreme in degree, as to go beyond all possible bounds of decency, and to be regarded as atrocious, and utterly intolerable in a civilized community." This means that many instances of boorish, insensitive behavior are not "bad enough" to give rise to liability for this tort. Courts also agree in requiring *severe* emotional distress. The *Restatement (Second)* sets forth another clear majority rule: that the defendant must *intentionally* or *recklessly* inflict the distress in order to be liable. A few courts, however, still fear fictitious claims and require proof of some bodily harm resulting from the victim's emotional distress.

In addition, some courts say that the plaintiff's distress must be distress that a reasonable person of ordinary sensibilities would suffer. The focus on whether the severely distressed person had ordinary sensibilities is sometimes minimized, however, when the defendant behaves outrageously by abusing a position or relation that gives him authority over another. Examples include employers, police officers, landlords, and school authorities.

The courts also differ in the extent to which they allow recovery for emotional distress suffered as a result of witnessing outrageous conduct directed at persons other than the plaintiff. The *Restatement (Second)* suggests that, at minimum, plaintiffs should be allowed to recover for severe emotional distress resulting from witnessing outrageous behavior toward a member of their immediate family.

The *Homan* case, which follows, addresses the outrageousness, intent, and severity-of-distress requirements of intentional infliction of emotional distress.

Homan v. Goyal   *711 A.2d 812 (D.C. App. 1998)*

At the trial in his intentional infliction of emotional distress case against Devinder Goyal, Robert Homan testified that he began receiving a series of telephone calls from a man he did not know. This man identified himself as Gabriel DaSilva. On each occasion, the man claimed his wife was with Homan and demanded to speak with her. Homan repeatedly explained that DaSilva had the wrong number and that Homan did not know DaSilva's wife. Eventually, Homan hung up on DaSilva, but DaSilva persisted, some nights calling as many as 20 times. Homan informed the police, and an officer spoke with DaSilva. Still, DaSilva continued to call for several days and became progressively more hostile.

When Homan asked DaSilva where he had obtained Homan's telephone number, DaSilva revealed that he had received the number from a man named Devinder Goyal. Homan telephoned Goyal and told him about DaSilva's calls. Goyal informed Homan that he (Goyal) had briefly employed DaSilva's wife. Goyal said that DaSilva had beaten his wife and that she had left him. During the year following Mrs. DaSilva's departure, Gabriel DaSilva had been "on the warpath" in search of her and had been harassing Goyal about her whereabouts. He had called Goyal roughly 20 times a day for a year and had come into Goyal's office approximately 100 times. Finally, Goyal had given DaSilva Homan's phone number, which Goyal had received from a friend. At Homan's request, Goyal agreed to tell DaSilva that Homan's number was the wrong one.

Nevertheless, the calls continued. Homan spoke with Goyal again and contacted the telephone company, which traced the calls to DaSilva. The telephone company sent DaSilva a letter threatening to cut off his service. As an apparent result, the calls stopped for about a week. Then, Homan received a "beep" at his apartment building from DaSilva, who was downstairs in front of Homan's building. As before, DaSilva demanded to see his wife. Homan went downstairs to "talk some sense into" DaSilva, and DaSilva asked to see the apartment personally. When Homan did not admit DaSilva into his apartment, DaSilva pursued him to the fifth floor, where the apartment was located. Homan locked DaSilva out, and DaSilva banged on the door for 20 minutes. Homan called the police, but no officer arrived until after DaSilva had left.

An hour or so later, DaSilva called twice, each time declaring his intent to kill Homan. Homan left his apartment, moved in with friends for a month, and obtained an unlisted number for his own apartment. He called Goyal a dozen times and informed Goyal's secretary of DaSilva's death threat. According to Homan, Goyal would not take his calls.

Homan later sued Goyal. A District of Columbia Superior Court jury, concluding that Goyal had committed the tort of intentional infliction of emotional distress, awarded Homan $40,000 in compensatory damages. The trial judge, however, granted Goyal's motion for judgment notwithstanding the verdict (JNOV). Homan appealed to the District of Columbia Court of Appeals.

Schwelb, Associate Judge   The concept of "outrageousness" is central to [intentional infliction of emotional distress,] the tort of which Goyal has been accused. Liability will be imposed only for conduct "so outrageous in character, and so extreme in degree, as to go beyond all possible bounds of decency, and to be regarded as atrocious, and utterly intolerable in a civilized community." *Drejza v. Vaccaro,* 650 A.2d 1308 (D.C. 1994). It is for the court to determine, in the first instance, whether the defendant's conduct may reasonably be regarded as so extreme and outrageous as to permit recovery, or whether it is necessarily so. Where reasonable persons may differ, it is for the jury . . . to determine whether . . . the conduct has been sufficiently extreme and outrageous to result in liability.

As we pointed out in *Drejza,* "the requirement of outrageousness is not an easy one to meet." Liability will not be imposed for "mere insults, indignities, threats, annoy-ances, petty oppressions, or other trivialities." *Waldon v. Covington,* 415 A.2d 1070, 1076 (D.C. 1980). "Against a large part of the frictions and irritations and clashing of temperaments incident to participation in a community life, a certain toughness of the mental hide is a better protection than the law could ever be." W. Page Keeton, Prosser & Keeton on Torts § 12, at 56 (5th ed. 1984) (quoting Magruder, *Mental and Emotional Disturbance in the Law of Torts,* 49 Harv. L. Rev. 1033, 1035 (1936)). Generally, a case of intentional infliction of emotional distress is made out only if "the recitation of the facts to an average member of the community would arouse his resentment against the actor, and lead him to exclaim, 'Outrageous!'" *Restatement,* § 46 comment d.

Outrageousness

In granting JNOV in Goyal's favor, the trial judge wrote that Goyal "gave Mr. DaSilva the plaintiff's name and his publicly listed address and phone number, and he falsely informed Mr. DaSilva that his wife could be found there." According to the judge, Goyal should have anticipated, on the basis of his own experience, that DaSilva "would call plaintiff, perhaps repeatedly, and that he would attempt to visit plaintiff." Nevertheless, the judge concluded "as a matter of law . . . that such calls and visits, even if they were persistent, were a mere annoyance which did not rise to the level of outrageous or intolerable conduct which would cause extreme emotional distress."

We disagree. The judge's impression that Goyal's conduct was annoying (but no worse than that) may well have represented a *permissible* view of the record, in the sense that a jury verdict in Goyal's favor could properly have been sustained. The judge's assessment of the evidence, however, was not the *only* permissible one. In particular, the trial judge's analysis overlooks the fact that DaSilva's conduct included death threats. There was thus evidentiary support for a conclusion by the jury that Goyal, whose life had been threatened by DaSilva before he gave DaSilva Homan's address, should have anticipated that DaSilva would likewise make death threats to Homan. In our view, the jury's conclusion that Goyal's conduct was extreme and outrageous was entirely rational and legitimate.

In some, indeed most, instances, a few unwelcome visits from an irrational, angry and jealous husband, and some harassing telephone calls, would not be cognizable in an action for a tort which requires proof of extreme or outrageous conduct. In this case, however, Goyal knew that he himself had endured perhaps a hundred visits and probably thousands of phone calls, and that Homan could expect to be subject to the same treatment, if not worse. In other words, Goyal deliberately exposed Homan to the near-certainty of repeated harassment. Repeated harassment may compound the outrageousness of incidents which, taken individually, might not be sufficiently extreme to warrant liability. Finally, as we have noted, . . . Goyal had reason to believe, when he gave DaSilva Homan's address, that Homan's life might well be threatened, just as Goyal's own life had been.

At a minimum, reasonable people might differ as to whether Goyal's conduct was sufficiently extreme and outrageous. Under these circumstances, the jury's resolution of the issue should have been allowed to stand.

Intent and recklessness

In the trial judge's opinion, the evidence did not support a finding that Goyal possessed the requisite intent to harm Homan. The judge based her disposition of this issue on her view that "the conduct itself was not extreme and outra-

geous." We conclude that the question of intent, like the question of outrageousness, should have been left to the jury.

We have held, notwithstanding the name of the tort for which Homan sued Goyal, that specific intent is not required; reckless infliction of emotional distress is sufficient. Liability extends to situations in which there is no certainty, but merely a high degree of probability, that the mental distress will follow, and the defendant goes ahead in conscious disregard of it.

The jury could reasonably conclude that Goyal deliberately disclosed Homan's telephone number and address to DaSilva while knowing full well that, in all probability, Homan would be harassed, tormented, and threatened by DaSilva. Indeed, Goyal gave out Homan's address after DaSilva had already, to Goyal's knowledge, begun his innumerable obsessive telephone calls. As Homan's counsel explained to the jury, Goyal "intentionally put Mr. Homan in harm's way. He intentionally said I'm tired of you stalking me, stalk him, he's got your wife, good riddance." The jury could rationally conclude that the record bore out counsel's words.

The severity of the emotional distress

Finally, the trial judge discerned insufficient support in the record for a finding that Homan "suffered any severe emotional distress which was proximately caused by defendant." Homan testified that as a direct and predictable consequence of Goyal's intentional acts, Homan was subjected to ceaseless harassing telephone calls and a harrowing visit from DaSilva, that DaSilva threatened to kill him, that Homan was driven from his home for a month in fear for his life, that he missed a day of work, that he found it difficult to concentrate when he was at work, and that for a significant period he had no idea when and if his ordeal was going to end. In our view, the jury could properly find that the distress resulting from these events was sufficiently severe to support Homan's claim for relief.

We recognize that it was DaSilva, and not Goyal, who harassed and threatened Homan and made his life miserable. [T]he jury [, however,] could reasonably find that it was Goyal who made this unfortunate outcome highly probable if not inevitable. Without Goyal's deliberate self-serving intervention—"stalk him, not me"—Homan would never have been tormented. On this record, questions relating to outrageousness, intent and severity of harm were for the jury, not for the judge.

Trial judge's grant of defendant's motion for JNOV reversed, and case remanded to trial court.

Most intentional infliction of emotional distress cases are based on allegedly outrageous *conduct*. What about allegedly outrageous *speech*? May it be the basis of a valid emotional distress claim? The potential First Amendment implications of allowing emotional distress liability to be based on speech—particularly when the plaintiff is a famous person who was the target or subject of the defendant's statements—occupied the attention of the U.S. Supreme Court in *Hustler Magazine, Inc. v. Falwell* (1986). On First Amendment grounds, the Court unanimously struck down a damages award received in the lower courts by the Rev. Jerry Falwell as a result of offensive statements about him in an adult magazine. In doing so, the Court severely restricted the ability of *public figures* to win speech-related intentional infliction of emotional distress cases by requiring that such plaintiffs prove the same stern First Amendment-based requirements imposed on public figure plaintiffs in defamation cases. (A later section in this chapter includes extensive discussion of defamation law, including the First Amendment–based requirements that public figures must satisfy when they sue for defamation.)

The Court had no occasion to rule in *Falwell* on whether the First Amendment would restrict the ability of a private figure (i.e., a person who is not well-known and thus is not a public figure) to base an emotional distress claim on a defendant's allegedly outrageous speech. Presumably, however, the First Amendment would have less of a role to play in such a case than in the public figure's case. Of course, when a defendant's *conduct*—as opposed to speech—is what the plaintiff complains about in an emotional distress case, the First Amendment does not even potentially furnish the defendant any protection against liability.

False Imprisonment

False imprisonment is the intentional *confinement* of another person for an *appreciable time* (a few minutes is enough) *without his consent*. The confinement element essentially involves the defendant's keeping the plaintiff within a circle that the defendant has created. It may result from physical barriers to the plaintiff's freedom of movement, such as locking a person in a room with no other doors or windows, or from the use or threat of physical force against the plaintiff. Confinement also may result from the unfounded assertion of legal authority to detain the plaintiff, or from the detention of the plaintiff's property (e.g., a purse containing a large sum of money). Likewise, a threat to harm another, such as the plaintiff's spouse or child, can also cause confinement if it prevents the plaintiff from moving.

The confinement must be *complete*. Partial confinement of another by blocking her path or by depriving her of one means of escape where several exist, such as locking one door of a building having several unlocked doors, is not false imprisonment. The fact that a means of escape exists, however, does not relieve the defendant of liability if the plaintiff cannot reasonably be expected to know of its existence. The same is true if using the escape route would present some unreasonable risk of harm to the plaintiff or would involve some affront to the plaintiff's sense of personal dignity.

Although there is some disagreement on the subject, courts usually hold that the plaintiff must have *knowledge* of his confinement in order for liability for false imprisonment to arise. In addition, there is no liability if the plaintiff has *consented* to his confinement. Such consent, however, must be freely given; consent in the face of an implied or actual threat of force or an assertion of legal authority is not freely given.

Today, many false imprisonment cases involve a store's detention of persons suspected of shoplifting. In an attempt to accommodate the legitimate interests of store owners, most states have passed statutes giving them a *conditional privilege* to stop suspected shoplifters. To obtain this defense, the owner usually must act with reasonable cause and in a reasonable manner, and must detain the suspect for no longer than a reasonable length of time. These privilege statutes typically extend to other intentional torts besides false imprisonment.

The *Banks* case, which follows, examines the elements of false imprisonment. It also discusses the damages recoverable by a plaintiff who proves that the defendant committed false imprisonment, assault, and battery.

Banks v. Fritsch   39 S.W.2d 474 (Ky. App. 2001)

Wade Banks sued John Fritsch for false imprisonment, assault, and battery on the basis of an incident that occurred at Bourbon County High School. Prior to this incident, Banks had skipped out of or left Agriculture Wood Construction class several times during the spring semester of his junior year at the school. Banks testified at the trial that one day, while he was walking to this class, another student informed him that the teacher, Fritsch, had a chain and was planning to chain Banks up to keep him from skipping class. When Banks entered the classroom, Fritsch had a large log chain over his shoulder and several key locks on his belt loop. Fritsch told Banks to put his leg up on a chair so that Fritsch could fasten the chain to Banks's ankle. When Banks refused, Fritsch repeated the instruction, and Banks consented. The entire class followed as Fritsch led Banks outside to a tree in an area where the class was painting wood troughs. Fritsch locked the chain to the tree and returned to the classroom. Banks then set to work unfastening the chain.

After several minutes, Banks freed his ankle and attempted to leave the school premises. Several classmates chased Banks down, tackled him, and carried him back to the tree. Fritsch returned and placed another chain around Banks's neck. Banks initially stood and held up the chain to keep its weight off his neck. After 15 minutes, he tired of holding the chain, sat down, and began crying. He told another student that the chain was bothering him, and the student went to tell Fritsch. Fritsch came out and unfastened the chain around Banks's neck, but tightened the chain on his ankle. The two began discussing Banks's grade in the class. During this discussion, Fritsch told Banks he could pass if he painted the three remaining wood troughs. Fritsch removed the chain when Banks agreed to do so.

Banks testified that he was deeply upset about the chaining and thought about it often. He received unwelcome attention from other students and the media about the subject. As a result, he spent his senior year in Columbia, Missouri, where his father lived. Banks testified that the move was traumatic for him, that he found it difficult to fit in at his new school, that he saw a psychologist once to discuss the incident, and that he continued to cry and have flashbacks from it. His family stated that he seemed emotionally withdrawn.

The trial judge held that the evidence was sufficient to create a jury issue as to whether assault, battery, and false imprisonment had taken place, but that there was no evidence that Banks had been damaged by Fritsch's conduct. The court therefore granted Fritsch's motion for a directed verdict. Banks appealed.

Knopf, Judge [A] trial judge cannot enter a directed verdict unless there is a complete absence of proof on a material issue or no disputed issues of fact exist upon which reasonable minds could differ. Where there is conflicting evidence, it is the responsibility of the jury to determine and resolve such conflicts.

In order to consider the propriety of the trial court's decision . . . we must first consider the nature of the claims asserted by Banks. The action for the tort of false imprisonment, sometimes called false arrest, is a lineal descendant of the old action of trespass to person. It protects the personal interest in freedom from physical restraint. The interest involved is in a sense a mental one, and false imprisonment may be maintained without proof of actual damages. The tort is complete after even a brief restraint on the plaintiff's freedom, and the plaintiff may recover nominal damages. The plaintiff is entitled to compensation for loss of time, for physical discomfort or inconvenience, and for any resulting physical illness or injury to health. Since the injury is in large part a mental one, the plaintiff is also entitled to damages for mental suffering, humiliation, and the like.

[F]alse imprisonment requires that the restraint be wrongful, improper, or without a claim of reasonable justification, authority, or privilege. Fritsch's potential liability does not arise out of his efforts to keep Banks from leaving the class, and there is no contention that Fritsch was acting within the scope of his authority as a teacher. Rather,

Fritsch's primary defense is that there was no imprisonment because Banks consented to being chained.

There are no Kentucky cases which directly discuss what evidence is necessary to prove damages from false imprisonment. However, a number of cases are instructive insofar as they address evidentiary issues relating to submission of the issue of damages to the jury. The common thread among all these cases is that a plaintiff may be entitled to at least nominal damages arising from the humiliation, emotional distress or damage to reputation caused by the false imprisonment. [T]he degree of humiliation or embarrassment actually suffered by the plaintiff is a factual matter for the jury to decide.

There was clearly a factual issue concerning whether Fritsch's conduct constituted an unlawful imprisonment of Banks. Furthermore, Banks testified that he suffered humiliation, embarrassment, emotional distress and he was held up to the ridicule of his peers by being publicly chained. There was contrary evidence that Banks did not express any distress during the chaining. Nevertheless, we are satisfied from the record that the jury could have returned a verdict for Banks for an amount greater than nominal damages. Consequently, we find that the trial court's decision to dismiss this claim was erroneous.

Banks's second claim is that Fritsch's conduct amounted to an assault and battery. Assault is a tort which merely requires the threat of unwanted touching of the victim, while battery requires an actual unwanted touching. Since intent is an essential element of assault and battery, the trial court properly left to the jury the issue of Banks's consent to the chaining. However, a plaintiff need not prove actual damages in a claim for battery because a showing of actual damages is not an element of assault or battery and, when no actual damages are shown for a battery, nominal damages may be awarded. Furthermore, a recovery for emotional distress caused by the assault or battery is allowable as an element of damages in an action based upon those torts. Consequently, we find that the trial court's dismissal of Banks's claims for assault and battery also was erroneous.

Banks [also] argues that he was entitled to an instruction on punitive damages. The trial court did not address this issue because it dismissed the action based upon lack of evidence of compensatory damages. In false imprisonment cases, punitive damages are not justified absent a showing that the acts were either willful or malicious or that they were performed in such a way as would indicate a gross neglect or disregard for the rights of the person wronged. [When Banks's false imprisonment, assault, and battery claims are tried on remand,] the trial court should consider the propriety of an instruction on punitive damages based upon the evidence presented at trial.

Judgment of the trial court reversed, and case remanded for new trial.

Defamation

The tort of defamation protects the individual's interest in his reputation. Defamation is ordinarily defined as the (1) unprivileged (2) publication of (3) false and defamatory (4) statements concerning another. Before examining each of these elements, we must consider the distinction between two forms of defamation: **libel** and **slander.**

The Libel–Slander Distinction Libel refers to written or printed defamation or to other defamation having a more or less permanent physical form, such as a defamatory picture, sign, or statue. Slander refers to all other defamatory statements—mainly oral defamation. Today, however, the great majority of courts treat defamatory statements in radio and television broadcasts as libel. The same is true of defamatory statements made on the Internet.

Why does the libel–slander distinction matter? Because of libel's more permanent nature and the seriousness we usually attach to the written word, the common law has traditionally allowed plaintiffs to recover for libel without proof of **special damages** (actual reputional injury and other actual harm). **Presumed damages** have long been allowed by the common law in libel cases. Described by the U.S. Supreme Court as an "oddity of tort law," presumed damages "compensate" for reputational harm that is presumed to have occurred but does not have to be proven by the plaintiff.

Slander, on the other hand, is generally not actionable without proof of special damages, unless the nature of the slanderous statement is so serious that it can be classified as *slander per se.* In cases of slander per se, presumed damages are allowed by the common law. Slander per se ordinarily includes false statements that the plaintiff: (1) has committed a crime involving moral turpitude or potential imprisonment, (2) has a loathsome disease, (3) is professionally incompetent or guilty of professional misconduct, or (4) is guilty of serious sexual misconduct.

False and Defamatory Statement Included among the elements of defamation are the separate requirements that the defendant's statement be both *false* and *defamatory.* Truth is a complete defense in a defamation case. A defamatory statement is one that is likely to harm the reputation of another by injuring his community's estimation of him or by deterring others from associating or dealing with him.

"Of and Concerning" the Plaintiff Because the defamation cause of action serves to protect reputation, an essential element of the tort is that the alleged defamatory statement must be "of and concerning" the plaintiff. That is, the statement must be about—and thus bear upon the reputation of—the party who brought the case. This requirement presents problems whose many complexities are beyond the scope of this text. The rules sketched below, therefore, are sometimes subject to exceptions not explained here.

What about allegedly *fictional accounts* whose characters resemble real people? Most courts say that fictional accounts may be defamatory if a reasonable reader would identify the plaintiff as the subject of the story. Similarly, *humorous or satirical accounts* ordinarily are not defamation unless a reasonable reader would believe that they purport to describe real events. Statements of pure *opinion* do not amount to defamation because they are not statements of "fact" concerning the plaintiff. However, statements that mix elements of opinion with elements of supposed "fact" may be actionable.

Do defamatory statements concerning particular *groups* of people also defame the individuals who belong to those groups? Generally, an individual member of a defamed group cannot recover for damage to her own reputation unless the group is so small that the statement can reasonably be understood as referring to individual group members.

Finally, courts have placed some limits on the persons or entities that can suffer injury to reputation. No liability attaches, for example, to defamatory statements concerning the dead. Corporations and other business entities have reputational interests and can recover for defamatory statements that harm them in their business or deter others from dealing with them. Statements about a corporation's officers, employees, or shareholders normally are not defamatory regarding the corporation, however, unless the statements also reflect on the manner in which the corporation conducts its business.[1]

Publication   Liability for defamation requires **publication** of the defamatory statement. As a general rule, no widespread communication of a defamatory statement is necessary for publication. The defendant's communication of the defamatory statement to one person other than the person defamed ordinarily suffices.

So long as no one else receives or overhears it, however, an insulting message communicated directly from the defendant to the plaintiff is not actionable. The long-standing rule is that publication does not take place when *the plaintiff herself* communicates the offensive statement to another. In recent years, some courts have made an exception to this rule in cases where a discharged employee is forced to tell a potential future employer about false and defamatory statements made to her by her prior employer.

Some courts still follow the older rule that intracorporate statements (statements by one corporate officer or employee to another officer of the same corporation) do not involve publication. Most courts, however, follow the modern trend and hold that there is publication in such situations.

The general rule is that one who repeats a false and defamatory statement is liable for defamation. This is

true even if he identifies the source of the statement or expresses his disagreement with it.

A party other than the person who initially made a defamatory statement may be liable along with the original speaker or writer if that other party served as a *publisher* of the defamatory falsehood, but not if the other party was a mere *distributor*. According to defamation law's traditional publisher vs. distributor distinction, a company that publishes a book or a newspaper may be held liable for defamation on the basis of statements that appear in the book or in the newspaper's articles. The rationale is that the publishing company possessed considerable editorial control over the content of the book or the articles, and would have had the ability to remove the defamatory falsehoods. (The writer of the statements, of course, would be liable as well.) Libraries and bookstores, however, are mere distributors because they lack the editorial control that publishers have. Therefore, libraries and bookstores are not liable for defamation even if defamatory falsehoods appear in books they lend to users or sell to customers.

The *Carafano* case, which is discussed in a Cyberlaw in Action box later in the chapter, approached the publisher vs. distributor issue from an Internet–related perspective. The case involved consideration of a statute enacted by Congress to protect "provider[s] or user[s] of an interactive computer service" from being labeled as publishers of information or statements provided by someone else.

Defenses and Privileges   Even though defamation is called an intentional tort, the common law contemplated a form of strict liability for defamation. Defenses are available, however, in certain defamation cases. Of course, the truth of the defamatory statement is a complete defense to liability. Defamatory statements may be *privileged* as well. Privileges to defamation liability recognize that in some circumstances, other social interests are more important than an individual's right to reputation. Privileges can be *absolute* or *conditional*.

An **absolute privilege** shields the author of a defamatory statement regardless of her knowledge, motive, or intent. When such a privilege applies, it operates as a complete defense to defamation liability. Absolutely privileged statements include those made by participants in judicial proceedings, by legislators or witnesses in the course of legislative proceedings, by certain executive officials in the course of their duties, and by one spouse to the other in private. In each case, the theory underlying the privilege is that complete freedom of expression is essential to the proper functioning of the relevant

---

[1] As Chapter 8 reveals, statements concerning the quality of a corporation's products or the quality of its title to land or other property may be the basis of an injurious falsehood claim.

activity, and that potential liability for defamation would inhibit free expression.

Conditional (or qualified) privileges give the defendant a defense unless the privilege is *abused*. What constitutes abuse varies with the privilege in question. In general, conditional privileges are abused when the statement is made with knowledge of its falsity or with reckless disregard for the truth, when the statement does not advance the purposes supporting the privilege, or when it is unnecessarily made to inappropriate people.

There are various conditional privileges. One important conditional privilege involves *statements made to protect or further the legitimate interests of another.* One of the most common business-related examples is the employment reference. Suppose that Parker's former employer, Dorfman, has good reason to believe—and does in fact believe—that Parker embezzled money from Dorfman's business while Parker was a Dorfman employee. Trumbull, who is deciding whether to hire Parker, contacts Dorfman to ask about Parker's work record and performance as an employee. During the conversation, Dorfman tells Trumbull that he believes Parker committed embezzlement while working for him. On these facts, Dorfman will be protected by a conditional privilege against defamation liability to Parker because Dorfman's statement was designed to further Trumbull's legitimate interest in making an intelligent hiring decision. Dorfman's good-faith and reasonably based belief in the truth of his statement about Parker is critical to his ability to rely on the conditional privilege. If Dorfman had known his statement was false or had made it with reckless disregard for the truth, Dorfman would have abused the conditional privilege and would have lost its protection against liability.

A second important type of conditional privilege concerns *statements made to promote a common interest.* Intracorporate communications are one example. Such communications normally would abuse the privilege, however, if they are also communicated to the public at large. Finally, the privilege called *fair comment* protects fair and accurate media reports of defamatory matter that appears in proceedings of official government action or originates from public meetings.

Defamation and the Constitution Until four decades ago, the First Amendment's guarantees of freedom of speech and press were not considered relevant to defamation cases. The common law's strict liability approach meant that unless one of the privileges discussed earlier applied, a speaker or writer who made a false statement believing it to be true had no more protection against defamation liability than the deliberate liar had. In a

series of cases dating back to 1964, however, the U.S. Supreme Court has concluded that the common law's approach may be too heavily weighted in favor of plaintiffs' reputational interests and not sufficiently protective of defendants' free speech and free press interests. The Court has recognized that when coupled with the potential availability of presumed damages, a strict liability regime could deter would-be speakers from contributing true statements to public debate out of fear of the costly liability that might result if the jury somehow concluded that the statements were false. Recognizing the need to guard against this "chilling effect" and the resulting restriction on the flow of information that is important to a free society, the Court determined in *New York Times Co. v. Sullivan* (1964) that the First Amendment has a role to play in certain defamation cases. The Court reasoned that judicial enforcement of the legal rules of defamation served as the government action necessary to trigger application of the First Amendment.

Public Official Plaintiff Cases In *New York Times,* the Court held that when a *public official* brings a defamation case, he or she must prove not only the usual elements of defamation but also a First Amendment–based fault requirement known as **actual malice.** The Court gave actual malice a special meaning: knowledge of falsity or reckless disregard for the truth. Thus, after *New York Times,* a defendant who makes a false and defamatory statement about a public official plaintiff will not be held liable unless the public official proves that the defendant made the statement either (1) knowing it was false, or (2) recklessly. Moreover, the Court held in *New York Times* that as a further First Amendment–based safeguard, the public official plaintiff must prove actual malice by *clear and convincing evidence*—a higher standard of proof than the preponderance of the evidence standard applicable to every other element of a defamation claim and to civil cases generally. The public official category includes many high-level government officials, whether elected or appointed.

Public Figure Plaintiff Cases Three years after *New York Times,* the Supreme Court extended the proof-of-actual-malice requirement to defamation cases in which the plaintiff is a *public figure.* The Court also mandated that such a plaintiff prove actual malice by clear and convincing evidence. Individual persons or corporations are public figures if they either (1) are well-known to large segments of society through their own voluntary efforts, or (2) have voluntarily placed themselves, in the words of the Supreme Court, at "the forefront of a particular public controversy." The first type of public figure, sometimes given the "general-purpose" designation, includes well-known corporations, political candidates who are not already holders of public office, and ex-government officials. It also includes a diverse collection of celebrities, near-celebrities, and well-known persons ranging from familiar actors, entertainers, and media figures to famous athletes or coaches and others with high public visibility in their chosen professions. The second type of public figure, sometimes assigned the "limited-purpose" label, is not well-known by large segments of society but has chosen to take a prominent leadership role regarding a matter of public debate (e.g., the abortion rights controversy, the debate over whether certain drugs should be legalized, or disputes over the extent to which environmental regulations should restrict business activity). A general-purpose public figure must prove actual malice in any defamation case in which he, she, or it is the plaintiff. A limited-purpose public figure, on the other hand, must prove actual malice when the statement giving rise to the case relates in some sense to the public controversy as to which the plaintiff is a public figure.

The proof-of-actual-malice requirement poses a very substantial hurdle for public officials and public figures to clear. That is by design, according to the Supreme Court. Defendants have especially strong First Amendment interests in regard to statements about public officials and public figures, given the high level of public interest and concern that attaches almost automatically to matters involving such persons.

Knowledge of falsity—one of the two forms of actual malice—is difficult to prove. When the defendant who made a false statement can point to an arguably credible source on which he, she, or it relied as a supposed indicator of the statement's truth, the defendant presumably

did not have knowledge of the statement's falsity. Neither did the defendant speak or write with the other form of actual malice—*reckless disregard for the truth*—in such an instance. According to the Supreme Court, reckless disregard has been demonstrated when the plaintiff proves either: (1) that the defendant "in fact entertained serious doubts" about the statement's truth but made the statement anyway; or (2) that the defendant consciously rejected overwhelming evidence of falsity and chose instead to rely on a much less significant bit of evidence that would have indicated truth only if the contrary evidence had not also been part of the picture. When the defendant relied on an arguably credible source that tended to indicate the statement was true, the defendant presumably did not entertain serious doubts and did not consciously reject overwhelming evidence of falsity. Such a defendant, therefore, did not display reckless disregard for the truth. If a reasonable person in the defendant's position would not have relied on a lone source despite its credibility and would have ascertained the statement's falsity through further investigation, the defendant who failed to investigate further has been negligent. Negligence, however, is not as severe a degree of fault as reckless disregard and does not constitute actual malice.

Most defamation cases brought by public official or public figure plaintiffs are won by the defendant—if not at trial, then on appeal. That is often the result because the plaintiff was unable to prove actual malice even though the statement was false and tended to harm reputation. Sometimes, however, the public official or public figure plaintiff accomplishes the daunting task of proving actual malice. When that occurs, the First Amendment does not bar such a plaintiff from winning the case and recovering compensatory damages (including those of the presumed variety) as well as punitive damages.

The *Tucker* case, which follows, addresses certain basic elements of defamation but focuses primarily on the actual malice requirement.

Tucker v. Fischbein   *237 F.3d 275 (3d Cir. 2001)*

C. Dolores Tucker, a former state official in Pennsylvania, was known for crusading against "gangsta rap" music because of its allegedly misogynistic and demeaning lyrics. She and her husband filed suit against the estate of deceased rapper Tupac Shakur and other defendants, alleging that lyrics in two songs from a Shakur album had attacked Mrs. Tucker. The plaintiffs sought damages for medical expenses and mental injury. The complaint alleged that Mr. Tucker had, "as a result of his wife's injuries, suffered a loss of advice, companionship, and consortium." According to a typical definition, loss of consortium may include, but is not limited to, "impairment of capacity for sexual intercourse."

Various newspaper and magazine articles reported on the filing of the case and focused on the loss of consortium claim. In an interview printed in the Philadelphia Daily News, *Richard Fischbein, attorney for the Shakur estate, was quoted as saying that "[i]t is hard for me to conceive how these lyrics could destroy their sex life . . . but we can only wait for the proof to be revealed in court." Wire and news services picked up the story and released articles quoting or paraphrasing Fischbein's remark. A* Newsweek *article by Johnnie L. Roberts entitled "Grabbing at a Dead Star" stated: "Even C. Dolores Tucker, the gangsta rap foe, wants a chunk [of Tupac Shakur's estate]. She and her husband claim that a lyrical attack by Tupac iced their sex life." The article went on to quote Fischbein regarding the loss-of-consortium claim: "I can't wait to hear testimony on that subject." The Tuckers later alleged that Roberts had interviewed Richard C. Angino, their attorney, before speaking to Fischbein, and that Angino had made clear that loss of consortium did not mean loss of sex in this case.*

After Fischbein was served with an August 27, 1997, amended complaint that included an additional claim against him for making "false and misleading statements" about the Tuckers' cause of action, Fischbein was interviewed by Belinda Luscombe, a reporter for Time *magazine.* Time *soon published an article entitled "Shakur Booty" about the Tucker case. Its author, Luscombe, admitted that the article was based on other articles, most of them derived from Fischbein's earlier comment, and on her interview with Fischbein, in which he told her that loss of sex was an issue in the case.*

The Tuckers then filed the complaint at issue here. They alleged that Time, Inc., Newsweek, Inc., Fischbein, Roberts, and Luscombe had defamed them by characterizing the earlier loss of consortium claim as a claim for impairment of sexual relations. The defendants moved for summary judgment. When a federal district court granted each defendant's motion, the Tuckers appealed to the U.S. Court of Appeals for the Third Circuit.

Alito, Circuit Judge Under Pennsylvania law, a defamation plaintiff bears the burden to show: (1) the defamatory character of the communication; (2) its publication by the defendant; (3) its application to the plaintiff; (4) the understanding by the recipient of its defamatory meaning; (5) the understanding by the recipient of it as intended to be applied to the plaintiff.

A statement is defamatory if "it tends so to harm the reputation of another as to lower him in the estimation of the community or to deter third persons from associating or dealing with him." *Corabi v. Curtis Publ'g Co.*, 441 Pa. 432 (Pa. 1971). A court must examine the meaning of the allegedly defamatory statement in context, and must evaluate "the effect [it] is fairly calculated to produce, the impression it would naturally engender, in the minds of the average persons among whom it is intended to circulate." *Id.*

The district court concluded that [the defendants' statements] could not support a cause of action for defamation. The court stated: "There is a vast difference between being annoyed and/or embarrassed on the one hand, and being disgraced and ridiculed to the extent that one's reputation is harmed and lowered in the estimation of the community, on the other." We cannot agree with the district court's analysis. Statements considerably milder than or comparable to those at issue here have been held by the Pennsylvania Supreme Court to be capable of a defamatory meaning.

Reading the statements at issue in this case in context and looking at the impression that they were likely to engender in the minds of the average reader, we conclude that each is capable of a defamatory meaning. Mrs. Tucker has led a campaign against the immorality of gangsta rap and those who profit from it. The statements made by the defendants—

to the effect that Mrs. Tucker and her husband brought a $10 million lawsuit because Shakur's lyrics damaged their sex life—carry numerous disparaging implications. Because of the inherent implausibility of the idea that lyrics alone could cause millions of dollars of damage to a couple's sexual relationship, the statements were capable of making the Tuckers look insincere, excessively litigious, avaricious, and perhaps unstable. Furthermore, the statements tended to suggest that the Tuckers are hypocritical, that after condemning the gangsta rap industry for profiting from pornography, the Tuckers were only too willing to open up their own sex life for public inspection in order to reap a pecuniary gain. Such statements were capable of lowering the Tuckers' reputation in the eyes of the community and of causing others to avoid associating with them. In short, the district court erred when it held that the defendants' statements were not capable of a defamatory meaning.

We must therefore examine whether the First Amendment poses a bar to the Tuckers' claim. [In the district court, the plaintiffs had conceded they were public figures.] When a public official or public figure sues for defamation, the First Amendment demands that the plaintiff prove both that the statement was false and that it was made with "actual malice." Under *New York Times v. Sullivan*, 376 U.S. 254 (1964), and its progeny, actual malice means "knowledge that [the statement] was false or . . . reckless disregard of whether it was false or not." *New York Times*, 376 U.S. at 279–80.

1. Fischbein

The Tuckers assert two grounds for holding that Fischbein acted with actual malice. First, the Tuckers argue that

Fischbein, as a lawyer, should have known that a claim for loss of consortium may not have anything to do with damage to sexual relations. It follows, the Tuckers contend, that Fischbein was at least reckless when he told the press that Mrs. Tucker was trying to recover for injury to her sex life.

We reject this argument. A claim for loss of consortium may concern damage to sexual relations and, with respect to the period prior to the service of the Tuckers' First Amended Complaint, there is no evidence that Fischbein was informed that Mr. Tucker's consortium claim did not refer to damage to sexual relations. Nor is there evidence from which a jury could find that Fischbein entertained serious doubts about the truthfulness of his statements at any time before the filing of the First Amended Complaint. Consequently, the record is insufficient to show by clear and convincing evidence that Fischbein was guilty during this period of anything more than negligence in jumping to the conclusion that Mr. Tucker's loss-of-consortium claim related, at least in part, to sex. The Tuckers point out that Fischbein, as the representative of Shakur's estate, had a motive for discrediting Mrs. Tucker, but circumstantial evidence of Fischbein's motive alone cannot satisfy the actual malice standard.

The Tuckers' second argument regarding Fischbein, however, does have merit. [O]n August 27, 1997, the Tuckers filed their First Amended Complaint, which added Fischbein as a defendant and sought millions of dollars in damages. The basis for adding Fischbein was set out in Paragraph 46, which averred that Fischbein had "made false and misleading statements regarding the claim herein, through published statements that C. Delores Tucker filed suit because of a 'loss of her sex life.' " It is undisputed that Fischbein was personally served with this complaint before his interview with *Time* magazine reporter Belinda Luscombe. Nevertheless, according to Luscombe's deposition, Fischbein told her during this interview that the Tuckers were attempting to recover for damage to their sexual relationship.

[W]e are convinced that a reasonable jury could find by clear and convincing evidence that, at least as of the date of the service of the First Amended Complaint, Fischbein had actual knowledge that the Tuckers were not seeking to recover for damage to their sexual relationship. Since the First Amended Complaint alleged that Fischbein had defamed the Tuckers by stating that they were attempting to recover for damage to their sexual relations, a reasonable jury could certainly conclude that an attorney who read the complaint would understand that the Tuckers were not going to attempt to recover for such damage. (Indeed, it would

be hard to interpret the First Amended Complaint any other way.) Fischbein states that he did not read the First Amended Complaint before speaking to Luscombe, but a reasonable jury could believe that a person who is added as a defendant in a multimillion dollar lawsuit is very likely to read the complaint shortly after receiving it in order to see why he or she has been sued. A reasonable jury could disbelieve Fischbein's story and find by clear and convincing evidence that Fischbein did read the First Amended Complaint before the interview. We must therefore reverse the judgment of the district court insofar as it dismissed the Tuckers' claim against Fischbein with regard to the statements to Luscombe.

2. Roberts and *Newsweek*

The Tuckers' case against Roberts and *Newsweek* includes some evidence from which a reasonable jury could infer actual malice, but not the clear and convincing evidence needed to survive summary judgment. Viewing the evidence in the light most favorable to the Tuckers, their attorney, Richard C. Angino, spoke with Roberts on August 20, 1997, six days before Roberts wrote "Grabbing at a Dead Star." According to Angino, he told Roberts in the course of this phone call that "consortium can mean, in some cases, sex. I said most of the time it doesn't and it doesn't in this case."

Other statements in Angino's deposition severely weaken the Tuckers' position, however, and make it impossible for them to satisfy the clear and convincing standard. For instance, when asked exactly what he said to put Roberts on notice that the Tuckers' claim did not involve impairment of sexual relations, Angino replied: "I said only in the rarest of cases would you have a count that actually involves sex. I'm under oath, so I cannot say to you that I said specifically this case does not involve sex." Actual malice requires a plaintiff to establish that the defendant had a subjective belief that the statement was false when made, and Angino's equivocation about the exact words he used defeats any hope the Tuckers might have of proving actual malice on the part of Roberts or *Newsweek* by clear and convincing evidence. Therefore, we affirm the district court's entry of summary judgment in favor of those parties.

3. Luscombe and *Time*

The Tuckers set forth 24 theories under which, they assert, it could be found that Belinda Luscombe and *Time* acted with actual malice in connection with the "Shakur Booty" article of September 15, 1997. Many of these theories are grounded on allegations of poor journalistic practices—e.g., that Luscombe had a preconceived story-line; that she did not follow *Time's* editorial guidelines; that she failed to conduct a thorough investigation; and that she copied from other stories but changed their language without a factual basis. As the district court found, these theories of actual malice are without support in the case law. The Supreme Court has made clear that even an extreme departure from professional standards, without more, will not support a finding of actual malice. Moreover, there is no evidence here

from which a reasonable jury would find that Luscombe was on notice that the facts related in her story were false. Accordingly, we affirm the district court's grant of summary judgment in favor of *Time* and Luscombe.

District court's grant of summary judgment affirmed as to **Time** *and* **Newsweek** *and their reporters, and reversed in part as to Fischbein.*

Private Figure Plaintiff Cases What about defamation cases brought by *private figures,* those corporations that are not public figures and those individual persons who are neither public figures nor public officials? In *Gertz v. Robert Welch, Inc.* (1974), the Supreme Court concluded that private figure plaintiffs should not be expected to prove actual malice in order to win defamation cases, despite defendants' meaningful free speech and press interests. The Court noted that such plaintiffs have neither sought, nor do they command, the higher level of attention desired and achieved by public officials and public figures. Requiring private figure plaintiffs to prove actual malice would tip the balance too heavily in favor of defendants' First Amendment interests and would do so at the expense of plaintiffs' reputational interests. The Court sought to balance the respective interests more suitably by developing, in *Gertz,* a two-rule approach under which the first rule focused on liability and the second focused on damages.

The first *Gertz* rule provided that in order to win a defamation case, the private figure plaintiff must prove some level of fault as set by state law, so long as that level of fault was at least negligence (in the sense discussed earlier). After *Gertz,* nearly every state chose negligence as the applicable fault requirement. The second *Gertz* rule addressed recoverable damages. It provided that if a private figure plaintiff proved only negligence on the defendant's part—the level of fault necessary to enable the plaintiff to win the case—the recoverable damages would be restricted to compensatory damages for proven reputational harm and other actual injury. Presumed damages and punitive damages would not be recoverable in such an instance. The second *Gertz* rule also spoke to the availability of presumed and punitive damages by providing that if the private figure plaintiff wanted to recover such damages (either instead of or in addition to damages for demonstrated harm), he,

she, or it would need to prove actual malice by clear and convincing evidence.

In a 1985 decision, *Dun & Bradstreet, Inc. v. Greenmoss Builders, Inc.,* the Court injected a *public concern vs. private concern* distinction into at least the second, if not both, of the two *Gertz* rules. The Court held in *Dun & Bradstreet* that the second *Gertz* rule (the one requiring proof of actual malice as a condition of recovering presumed and punitive damages) applies only when the private figure plaintiff's case is based on a statement that addressed a matter of public concern. If the private figure plaintiff's case pertains to a statement that addressed a matter of only private concern, the second *Gertz* rule does not apply—meaning that presumed and punitive damages are recoverable instead of or in addition to damages for proven actual injury, even though the plaintiff established nothing more than the negligence presumably necessary to win the case. "Presumably necessary" is an apt characterization because it is a matter of interpretation and debate whether, after *Dun & Bradstreet,* the basic fault requirement of negligence still applies to a private figure plaintiff case involving a statement on a matter of private concern.

Only the second *Gertz* rule was at issue in *Dun & Bradstreet,* which, according to the Court, was a private figure/private concern case. Negligence on the defendant's part was present in the facts and was not a contested issue when the case reached the Supreme Court. Even so, it is not unreasonable to assert that if the Court was injecting a public concern qualifier into the second *Gertz* rule, it logically would also have been contemplating a public concern qualifier for the first *Gertz* rule (the rule requiring proof of at least negligence to establish liability). Under this reading of *Dun & Bradstreet,* the common law's liability-without-fault approach would again govern defamation cases of the private figure/private concern variety. Those who read *Dun & Bradstreet* more narrowly, however, are inclined to restrict it to what the Supreme

Court actually held (i.e., that a public concern element is part of the second *Gertz* rule) and to assume that the basic fault requirement of negligence continues to apply to *all* private figure plaintiff cases until the Supreme Court specifically holds to the contrary. The narrower reading of *Dun & Bradstreet* may have slightly more adherents among lower courts and legal commentators, but it is a close call.

As the above discussion indicates, public concern determinations have become important in private figure plaintiff cases. (Note that the Supreme Court has not made the public concern–private concern distinction a requirement for public officials' and public figures' defamation cases—probably because the public concern character of statements about such prominent persons is essentially a "given" that may safely be assumed.) What sorts of statements, then, deal with matters of public concern? The Supreme Court provided little guidance on this issue in *Dun & Bradstreet.* Lower court decisions, however, have consistently established that statements dealing with crime address matters of public concern. The same is true of a broad range of statements dealing with public health, safety, or welfare, or with comparably important matters that capture society's attention.

The Media–Nonmedia Issue (or Non-Issue?) A final set of issues concerning defamation's First Amendment–based fault requirements is whether they apply only when the defendant is a member of the media (i.e., the press), or in all defamation cases regardless of the defendant's media or nonmedia status. In phrasing its holdings in certain defamation decisions, the Supreme Court has sometimes employed media-oriented language. That may have been done, however, because the cases involved media defendants. The Court contributed to confusion on this point in one decision with an inaccurate footnote asserting that the Court had never decided whether the First Amendment–based fault requirements apply in nonmedia defendant cases. Yet the Court clearly had made such a decision. The landmark *New York Times* case included media and nonmedia defendants. There, the Court held that the public official plaintiff needed to prove actual malice on the part of all of the defendants.

Although the Court has not officially addressed the media–nonmedia issue in recent decisions, some justices have unofficially "rejected" such a distinction by making comments along those lines in concurring and dissenting opinions. In view of those comments, the decision in *New York Times,* the equal billing the First Amendment gives to freedom of "speech" and freedom of the "press," and the disapproval of a media–nonmedia distinction by most lower courts and an overwhelming majority of legal commentators, it seems extremely likely that if the Supreme Court now faced the issue squarely, it would hold that the First Amendment–based fault requirements apply to all defamation cases without regard for whether the defendant is a member of the media.

Figure 1 summarizes the major First Amendment aspects of defamation law.

Figure 1	*Constitutional Aspects of Defamation—Fault Requirements and Rules on Damages* *		
	Public Official Plaintiff or Public Figure Plaintiff	**Private Figure Plaintiff and Subject of Public Concern**	**Private Figure Plaintiff and Subject of Private Concern**
What Plaintiff Must Prove to Win Case	Actual malice, by clear and convincing evidence	Fault, at least negligence	Perhaps (probably?) fault, at least negligence
Damages Recoverable if Plaintiff Wins Case	Damages for proven actual injury and/or presumed damages, as well as punitive damages	Damages for proven actual injury, if plaintiff proves only negligence. For presumed and punitive damages, plaintiff must prove actual malice, by clear and convincing evidence.	Damages for proven actual injury and/or presumed damages, as well as punitive damages

*These requirements and rules apply at least in defamation cases against a media defendant. Although the Supreme Court has left some uncertainty on this point, the requirements and rules set forth here probably apply in all defamation cases, regardless of the defendant's media or nonmedia status.

Invasion of Privacy

In tort law, the term **invasion of privacy** refers to four distinct torts. Each involves a different sense of the term privacy.

Intrusion on Solitude or Seclusion Any intentional intrusion on the solitude or seclusion of another constitutes an invasion of privacy if that intrusion would be highly offensive to a reasonable individual.

The intrusion in question may be physical, such as an illegal search of a person's home or body or the opening of his mail. It may also be a nonphysical intrusion such as tapping another's telephone, examining her bank account, or subjecting her to harassing telephone calls. However, the tort applies only where there is a reasonable expectation of privacy. As a general rule, therefore, there is no liability for examining public records concerning a person, or for observing or photographing him in a public place.

ETHICS IN ACTION

Jeffrey Polinski was employed by Sky Harbor Air Service, Inc., and United Airlines, Inc. For each firm, he was an employee-at-will—meaning that his employment could be terminated at any time. Polinski's jobs with Sky Harbor and United necessitated that he have access to certain nonpublic portions of the airfield at a facility managed by the Omaha Airport Authority (OAA). Only persons with an OAA–issued identification badge were given access to the airfield's nonpublic portions. Polinski had been issued such a badge by the OAA.

During his employment with Sky Harbor, Polinski had received a copy of the company's drug-free workplace policy. He had signed a copy of a Sky Harbor letter indicating that he had read it and understood its contents. The letter stated that employees could be terminated for being under the influence of drugs, that Sky Harbor reserved the right to test employees for drug use, either randomly or on the basis of reasonable cause, and that employees who refused a drug test could be fired or otherwise disciplined.

After Sky Harbor's attorneys acquired information that the OAA was preparing to bring in federal Drug Enforcement Agents to test Sky Harbor employees because OAA suspected some of them of drug use, Sky Harbor decided to drug-test nearly all of its employees. Before the test was conducted, Polinski signed a form in which he ostensibly consented to the test. The results showed Polinski as testing positive for marijuana. Sky Harbor then fired Polinski, informing him that his violation of the drug-free workplace policy was the reason. In addition, Sky Harbor returned Polinski's identification badge to the OAA and informed the OAA of Polinski's drug-test results. Without an identification badge, Polinski could not obtain access to the nonpublic portions of the airfield. United therefore suspended him and ultimately fired him when he could not regain his identification badge.

Polinski filed suit against Sky Harbor. In his first cause of action, he alleged that the defendant had violated a Nebraska invasion of privacy statute through its drug-test policy and its

accusation of illegal drug use on his part. The statute provided that "[a]ny person, firm, or corporation that trespasses or intrudes upon any natural person in his or her place of solitude or seclusion, if the intrusion would be highly offensive to a reasonable person, shall be liable for invasion of privacy." Polinski testified in his deposition that he found the accusation of illegal conduct humiliating. In a separate cause of action, Polinski contended that when it informed the OAA of the results of his drug test, Sky Harbor violated a Nebraska drug-testing statute that prohibited disclosure of employment-related drug-test results to the "public." Although Polinski based his claim on the drug-testing statute, the claim resembled an invasion of privacy cause of action of the *public disclosure of private facts* variety.

The Nebraska Court of Appeals affirmed the trial court's grant of summary judgment in favor of Sky Harbor. In *Polinski v. Sky Harbor Air Service, Inc.,* 640 N.W.2d 391 (2002), the Nebraska Supreme Court affirmed. Concerning Polinski's first cause of action, the Supreme Court observed that the drug test at issue complied with the Nebraska's drug-testing statutes. The court also concluded that an accusation of drug use at the workplace, without more, would not be highly offensive to a reasonable person and thus could not give rise to a valid claim for intrusion on solitude. Regarding Polinski's claim that Sky Harbor acted unlawfully in disclosing his drug-test results to the OAA, the court noted that the OAA was "involved in Polinski's chain of employment." This fact caused the court to conclude that Sky Harbor's disclosure to the OAA was not a disclosure to the "public" and that Polinski therefore did not have a valid claim.

The *Polinski* case raises interesting questions regarding judicial reasoning and matters of public policy. Consider these:

• Do you agree with the court that being accused of illegal drug use would not be highly offensive to a reasonable person? Does the potential for such an accusation to be highly offensive depend on whether the accused person actually had engaged in illegal drug use (i.e., would an *innocent* reasonable person be more likely to take great offense at such an accusation?)?

- In identifying reasons to reject Polinski's invasion of privacy of claim, might the court have thought it important not to allow Polinski a "back-door" way to attack Sky Harbor's drug-testing policy, its accusation that he had used illegal drugs, and its termination of his employment? The "front-door" openings, after all, probably were closed to Polinski. A direct attack by Polinski on Sky Harbor's drug-testing policy would likely have failed because such a policy was allowed by state law; a defamation claim concerning the illegal drug-use accusation would likely have failed because the accusation, even if communicated by Sky Harbor to someone other than Polinski, was either true or at least supported by credible evidence, and probably was conditionally privileged; and a claim challenging the legality of his termination would not have been successful because the employment-at-will rule permitted Sky Harbor to fire him at any time, with no reason being necessary.

Drug testing and disclosure issues of the sort present in *Polinski* may also have ethical dimensions. Private companies' policies of drug-testing employees are frequently permissible under applicable law. Consider, however, such policies from the perspectives of ethical analysis.

- What are the ethical arguments against drug testing of employees of private companies? What are the ethical arguments in favor of such drug testing? Which arguments seem stronger, and why?
- If a private employer drug-tests an employee and obtains results appearing to show illegal drug use, what ethical duties, if any, does the employer owe the employee with regard to that information? What ethical obligations, if any, does the employer owe third parties concerning that information? In the *Polinski* case, did Sky Harbor act unethically when it disclosed Polinski's test results to the OAA, or was Sky Harbor acting in accordance with an ethical obligation? What reasons or considerations support your conclusions on these questions?

Public Disclosure of Private Facts Publicizing facts concerning someone's private life can be an invasion of privacy if the publicity would be highly offensive to a reasonable person. The idea is that the public has no legitimate right to know certain aspects of a person's private life. Thus, publicity concerning someone's failure to pay his debts, humiliating illnesses he has suffered, or information about his sex life constitutes an invasion of privacy. Truth is *not* a defense to this type of invasion of privacy because the essence of the tort is giving unjustified publicity to purely private matters.

Here, in further contrast to defamation, publicity means a *widespread* communication of private details. For example, publication on the Internet would suffice.

As does defamation, this form of invasion of privacy potentially conflicts with the First Amendment. Courts have attempted to resolve this conflict in two major ways. First, no liability ordinarily attaches to publicity concerning matters of public record or legitimate public interest. Second, public figures and public officials have no right of privacy concerning information that is reasonably related to their public lives.

CYBERLAW IN ACTION

Christianne Carafano, who uses the "Chase Masterson" name professionally, is known primarily for her recurring role on the television series "Star Trek: Deep Space Nine." In *Carafano v. Metrosplash.com, Inc.,* 207 F. Supp. 2d 1055 (C.D. Cal. 2002), she alleged that Metrosplash, through its Web service known as Matchmaker.com, invaded her privacy, violated her right of publicity, and defamed her. (Metrosplash will be referred to by the Matchmaker name in the following discussion of the case.)

Matchmaker provides a "members-only" service that enables interested persons to acquire information about other members with whom they might want to develop a romantic relationship. When one becomes a Matchmaker member, he or she completes a questionnaire. His or her answers to the questionnaire, along with pictures submitted by the member, make up that member's online profile. The profile of each member is included in a database of profiles posted by other members in one of Matchmaker's various "communities," most of which are organized according to the geographic area in which the members reside. Members are provided access to this database so that they may review the profiles of other members of the same community. Matchmaker, which does not verify the information set forth in the profiles, informs members that profile information may be inaccurate.

The events giving rise to Carafano's lawsuit began when an unknown person, acting without Carafano's consent, created an account under the name "Chase529" on Matchmaker's "Los Angeles Metro" community. The profile included Carafano's home address and four photographs of her. It also contained a link to an e-mail address that prompted the following automatic response to any messages sent to it: "You think you're the one. Proof [sic] it!! [Carafano's home address and telephone number]." In addition, the profile contained statements that Carafano regarded as conveying a false and undesirable impression of her.

As a result of the profile, Carafano received obscene telephone messages and unwanted correspondence. She found it necessary to leave her home and stay with friends or in hotels. Approximately two weeks after Carafano began receiving the unwelcome messages and correspondence, the operator of Carafano's personal website learned of the profile and complained to Matchmaker's site administrator. The profile was purged from Matchmaker's servers a few days later. Carafano later sued Matchmaker on the legal theories mentioned above. Matchmaker sought summary judgment on each of Carafano's causes of action.

The CDA

Matchmaker argued that all of Carafano's causes of action were barred by § 230 of the federal Communications Decency Act of 1996 (CDA). Under § 230, no "provider or user of an interactive computer service" can be treated as a "publisher or speaker of any information provided by another information content provider." When it applies, § 230 may protect a party who might otherwise be classified as a publisher of someone else's speech from defamation or other tort liability based upon that speech. (This effect of § 230 was discussed in Chapter 1. The general rule governing defamation liability of a publisher was explained earlier in Chapter 6.)

The court concluded that Matchmaker was a "provider . . . of an interactive computer service." However, the court held that Matchmaker was not entitled to the protection of § 230 because that section insulates a defendant from speech-based liability only when the information in question was provided by "*another* information content provider" (emphasis supplied). The court noted that by requiring members to build profiles from answers to a multiple-choice questionnaire that Matchmaker had composed, Matchmaker took part in the authorship of the profiles. In so doing, the court reasoned, Matchmaker made *itself* an "information content provider." Having rejected Matchmaker's § 230 defense, the court moved on to an examination of Carafano's individual causes of action.

Public Disclosure of Private Facts Claim

According to Carafano, the private fact disclosed by Matchmaker was her home address. Matchmaker argued, however, that Carafano's home address was of legitimate public interest—and thus was not a private fact—because it was "newsworthy."

The court noted that a celebrity's home address has social value, as evidenced by the large number of tours and maps of celebrity homes throughout Los Angeles County. The court also observed that Carafano's address was a matter of public record and that disclosure of the address thus did not involve intrusion into ostensibly private matters. Finally, the court pointed out, Carafano was an entertainment celebrity who had voluntarily assumed a position of public notoriety. Members of the public have broad-ranging interests in information about celebrities. In view of these considerations, the court held that Carafano's home address was newsworthy—meaning that her public disclosure of private facts claim failed as a matter of law.

Defamation

Carafano's defamation claim rested on her contention that statements in the Matchmaker profile would give others the false impression of sexual promiscuity on her part. Carafano's notoriety as an actress, a fact that weighed against her in the analysis of her public disclosure of private facts claim, also proved significant to the resolution of her defamation claim. After detailing Carafano's many movie and television appearances in addition to the "Star Trek: Deep Space Nine" role, the court held that Carafano was a general-purpose public figure. This meant that in order to win her defamation claim, Carafano needed to prove not only that Matchmaker published false statements about her but that Matchmaker did so with *actual malice*—knowledge of falsity or reckless disregard for the truth. Holding that Carafano furnished clearly insufficient proof of actual malice, the court granted Matchmaker summary judgment on Carafano's defamation claim.

Right of Publicity

Carafano's right of publicity claim fared no better. The court concluded that the statements in the supposed profile of Carafano did not constitute an attempt by Matchmaker to use her name, likeness, or identity to help promote Matchmaker's business. Therefore, the court reasoned, the profile was neither a commercial use for purposes of the right of publicity claim nor commercial speech carrying a reduced degree of First Amendment protection. (See Chapter 3 for a discussion of the respective levels of First Amendment protection for commercial and noncommercial speech.) Because "full" First Amendment protection attached to the speech at issue and because the gist of Carafano's complaint was that false things had been said about her, the court held that the actual malice requirement applicable to her defamation claim also applied to her right of publicity claim. Carafano's inability to prove actual malice thus doomed her right of publicity cause of action to failure.

False Light Publicity Publicity that places a person in a false light in the public eye can be an invasion of privacy if that false light would be highly offensive to a reasonable person. What is required is unreasonable and highly objectionable publicity attributing to a person characteristics that she does not possess or beliefs that she does not hold. Examples include signing a person's name to a public letter that violates her deeply held beliefs or attributing authorship of an inferior scholarly or artistic work to her. As in defamation cases, truth is a defense to liability. It is not necessary, however, that a person be defamed by the false light in which he is placed. For instance, signing a pro-life person's name to a petition urging increased abortion rights would create liability for false light publicity but probably not for defamation.

In view of the overlap between false light publicity and defamation, and the obvious First Amendment issues at stake, defendants in false light cases enjoy constitutional protections matching those enjoyed by defamation defendants.

Commercial Appropriation of Name or Likeness Liability for invasion of privacy can exist when, without that person's consent, the defendant commercially uses someone's name or likeness, normally to imply his endorsement of a product or service or a nonexistent connection with the defendant's business.

This form of invasion of privacy also draws on the personal property right connected with a person's identity and his exclusive right to control it. In recent decades, recognition of this property right has given rise to a separate legal doctrine known as the *right of publicity,* under which public figures, celebrities, and entertainers have a cause of action against defendants who, without consent, use the right holders' names, likenesses, or identities for commercial purposes. Protected attributes of a celebrity's identity may include such things as a distinctive singing voice. Use of a celebrity's name or a "soundalike" of her in an advertisement for a product would be a classic example of a commercial use, as would use of an entertainer's picture as a commercially sold poster. Not all uses are commercial in nature, however, even if there is an underlying profit motive at stake. For example, though the cases are not entirely consistent on this point, a television show or movie that uses a celebrity's name, likeness, or identity is likely to be classified as noncommercial and thus not a violation of the right of publicity. Some uses, such as the one in the *Comedy III* case (which follows shortly) are close to the line and require courts to make difficult determinations regarding the use's commercial or noncommercial nature. Moreover, First Amendment issues sometimes arise in these cases, as *Comedy III* indicates.

States that recognize the right of publicity usually consider it inheritable—meaning that it may survive the death of the celebrity who held the right during his or her lifetime. There is little agreement among the states, however, on how long the right persists after the celebrity's death.

Comedy III Productions, Inc. v. Gary Saderup, Inc.
21 P.3d 747 (Cal. Sup. Ct. 2001)

At the time of the events described below, California's statute dealing with a deceased celebrity's right of publicity read as follows: "Any person who uses a deceased personality's name, voice, signature, photograph, or likeness, in any manner, on or in products, merchandise, or goods, or for purposes of advertising or selling, or soliciting purchase of, products, merchandise, goods, or services, without prior consent from [the legal owner of the deceased personality's right of publicity] shall be liable" to the right of publicity owner. The statute also set forth exemptions from the consent requirement for uses in news, public affairs, or sports broadcasts, in plays, books, magazines, newspapers, musical compositions, or film, television or radio programs, or in other works of political or news-related value. There was also an exemption for "single and original works of fine art."

Comedy III Productions, Inc. owns the rights of publicity of the deceased celebrities who, through their comedy act, had become familiar to the public as "The Three Stooges." Relying on the statute quoted above, Comedy III brought a right of publicity action against artist Gary Saderup and the corporation (Gary Saderup, Inc.) in which he was a principal. Without Comedy III's consent, the defendants (referred to here collectively as "Saderup") had produced and profited from sale of lithographs and T-shirts bearing a likeness of The Three Stooges. The likeness had been reproduced from Saderup's charcoal drawing of the Stooges. The trial court, concluding that Saderup had violated the right of publicity statute and that the First Amendment did not furnish a defense, awarded Comedy III damages of $75,000. The California Court of Appeal affirmed. Saderup appealed to the Supreme Court of California.

Mosk, Judge [The California statute] makes liable any person who, without consent, uses a deceased personality's name, voice, signature, photograph, or likeness either (1) "on or in" a product, or (2) in "advertising or selling" a product. We agree with the Court of Appeal that Saderup sold more than just the incorporeal likeness of The Three Stooges. Saderup's lithographic prints of The Three Stooges are themselves tangible personal property, . . . made as products to be sold and displayed on walls. Saderup's T-shirts are likewise tangible personal property, . . . made as products to be sold and worn on the body. Saderup thus used the likeness of The Three Stooges "on . . . products, merchandise, or goods" within the meaning of the statute. Saderup contends [, however,] that . . . the judgment against him violates his right of free speech and expression under the First Amendment.

The right of publicity is often invoked in the context of commercial speech when the appropriation of a celebrity likeness creates a false and misleading impression that the celebrity is endorsing a product. Because the First Amendment does not protect false and misleading commercial speech, and because even nonmisleading commercial speech is generally subject to somewhat lesser First Amendment protection, the right of publicity may often trump the right of advertisers to make use of celebrity figures.

But the present case does not concern commercial speech. Saderup's portraits of The Three Stooges are expressive works and not an advertisement for or endorsement of a product. Although his work was done for financial gain, "[t]he First Amendment is not limited to those who publish without charge." *Guglielmi v. Spelling-Goldberg Productions,* 603 P.2d 454 (Cal. Sup. Ct. 1979) (concurring opinion of Chief Justice Bird, whose views on First Amendment issues in case represented those of majority of court).

[T]he right of publicity has the potential of censoring significant expression by suppressing alternative versions of celebrity images that are iconoclastic or irreverent or otherwise attempt to redefine the celebrity. [As a] majority of this court recognized . . . in *Guglielmi,* the right of publicity "does not confer a shield to ward off caricature, parody, and satire. Rather, prominence invites creative comment." For similar reasons, speech about public figures is accorded heightened First Amendment protection in defamation law. Giving broad scope to the right of publicity has the potential of allowing a celebrity to accomplish through the vigorous exercise of that right the censorship of unflattering commentary that cannot be constitutionally accomplished through defamation actions.

Saderup's creations [do not] lose their constitutional protections because they are for purposes of entertaining rather than informing. As Chief Justice Bird stated in *Guglielmi,* "Our courts have often observed that entertainment is entitled to the same constitutional protection as the exposition of ideas." Nor does the fact that expression takes a form of nonverbal, visual representation remove it from the ambit of First Amendment protection. In *Bery v. City of New York,* 97 F.3d 689 (2d Cir. 1996), the court overturned an ordinance requiring visual artists—painters, printers, photographers, sculptors, etc.—to obtain licenses to sell their work in public places, but exempted the vendors of books, newspapers, or other written matter. As the court stated, "[v]isual art is as wide ranging in its depiction of ideas, concepts and emotions as any book, treatise, pamphlet or other writing, and is similarly entitled to full First Amendment protection." Nor does the fact that Saderup's art appears in large part on a less conventional avenue of communications, T-shirts, result in reduced First Amendment protection. First Amendment doctrine does not disfavor nontraditional media of expression.

But having recognized the high degree of First Amendment protection for noncommercial speech about celebrities, we need not conclude that all expression that trenches on the right of publicity receives such protection. The right of publicity, like copyright, protects a form of intellectual property that society deems to have some social utility. The present case exemplifies [the] creative labor [sometimes seen as justifying the right of publicity]. Moe and Jerome (Curly) Howard and Larry Fein fashioned personae collectively known as The Three Stooges, first in vaudeville and later in movie shorts, over a period extending from the 1920's to the 1940's. The three comic characters they created . . . possess a kind of mythic status in our culture. Through their talent and labor, they joined the relatively small group of actors who constructed identifiable, recurrent comic personalities that they brought to the many parts they were scripted to play. [S]ociety may recognize, as the legislature has done here, that a celebrity's heirs and assigns have a legitimate protectible interest in exploiting the value to be obtained from merchandising the celebrity's image, whether that interest be conceived as a kind of natural property right or as an incentive for encouraging creative work.

It is admittedly not a simple matter to develop a test that will unerringly distinguish between forms of artistic expression protected by the First Amendment and those that must give way to the right of publicity. Certainly, any such test must incorporate the principle that the right of publicity cannot . . . be a right to control the celebrity's image by censoring disagreeable portrayals. Once the celebrity thrusts himself or herself forward into the limelight, the First

Amendment dictates that the right to comment on, parody, lampoon, and make other expressive uses of the celebrity image must be given broad scope. What the right of publicity holder possesses is not a right of censorship, but a right to prevent others from misappropriating the economic value generated by the celebrity's fame through the merchandising of the "name, voice, signature, photograph, or likeness" of the celebrity.

Beyond this precept, how may courts distinguish between protected and unprotected expression? Some commentators have proposed importing the fair use defense from copyright law. We conclude that a wholesale importation of the fair use doctrine into right of publicity law would not be advisable [because some] of the factors employed in the fair use test [do not fit the right of publicity context very smoothly and would not be especially helpful] in determining whether the depiction of a celebrity likeness is protected by the First Amendment. Nonetheless, the first of [copyright law's] fair use factor[s]—the purpose and character of the use—does seem particularly pertinent to the task of reconciling the rights of free expression and publicity. As the Supreme Court has stated, the central purpose of the inquiry into this fair use factor "is to see . . . whether the new work merely 'supersedes the objects' of the original creation, or instead adds something new, with a further purpose or different character, altering the first with new expression, meaning, or message; it asks, in other words, whether and to what extent the new work is 'transformative.'" *Campbell v. Acuff-Rose Music, Inc.,* 510 U.S. 569 (1994) (citations omitted).

This inquiry into whether a work is "transformative" appears to us to be necessarily at the heart of any judicial attempt to square the right of publicity with the First Amendment. [B]oth the First Amendment and copyright law have a common goal of encouragement of free expression and creativity, the former by protecting such expression from government interference, the latter by protecting the creative fruits of intellectual and artistic labor. The right of publicity, at least theoretically, shares this goal with copyright law. When artistic expression takes the form of a literal depiction or imitation of a celebrity for commercial gain, directly trespassing on the right of publicity without adding significant expression beyond that trespass, the state law interest in protecting the fruits of artistic labor outweighs the expressive interests of the imitative artist.

On the other hand, when a work contains significant transformative elements, it is not only especially worthy of First Amendment protection, but it is also less likely to interfere with the economic interest protected by the right of publicity. As has been observed, works of parody or other

distortions of the celebrity figure are not, from the celebrity fan's viewpoint, good substitutes for conventional depictions of the celebrity and therefore do not generally threaten markets for celebrity memorabilia that the right of publicity is designed to protect. Accordingly, First Amendment protection of such works outweighs whatever interest the state may have in enforcing the right of publicity. We emphasize [, moreover,] that the transformative elements or creative contributions that require First Amendment protection are not confined to parody and can take many forms, from factual reporting to fictional protrayal, from heavy-handed lampooning to subtle social criticism. The right-of-publicity holder continues [, however,] to enforce the right to monopolize the production of conventional, more or less fungible, images of the celebrity.

We further emphasize that in determining whether the work is transformative, courts are not to be concerned with the quality of the artistic contribution—vulgar forms of expression fully qualify for First Amendment protection. On the other hand, a literal depiction of a celebrity, even if accomplished with great skill, may still be subject to a right of publicity challenge. The inquiry is in a sense more quantitative than qualitative, asking whether the literal and imitative or the creative elements predominate in the work.

Saderup argues that all portraiture involves creative decisions, that therefore no portrait portrays a mere literal likeness, and that accordingly all portraiture, including reproductions, is protected by the First Amendment. We reject any such categorical position. Without denying that all portraiture involves the making of artistic choices, we find it equally undeniable, under the test formulated above, that when an artist's skill and talent is manifestly subordinated to the overall goal of creating a conventional portrait of a celebrity so as to commercially exploit his or her fame, then the artist's right of free expression is outweighed by the right of publicity. [A]n artist depicting a celebrity must . . . create something recognizably his own [, over and above a mere depiction of the celebrity] in order to qualify for [First Amendment] protection [against a right of publicity claim].

On the other hand, we do not hold that all reproductions of celebrity portraits are unprotected by the First Amendment. The silkscreens of Andy Warhol, for example, have as their subjects the images of such celebrities as Marilyn Monroe, Elizabeth Taylor, and Elvis Presley. Through distortion and the careful manipulation of context, Warhol was able to convey a message that went beyond the commercial exploitation of celebrity images and became a form of ironic social comment on the dehumanization of celebrity itself. Such expression may well be entitled to First Amendment protection. Although the distinction between protected and unprotected expression will sometimes be subtle, it is no more so than other distinctions triers of fact are called on to make in First Amendment jurisprudence.

Turning to Saderup's work, we can discern no significant transformative or creative contribution. His undeniable skill is manifestly subordinated to the overall goal of creating literal, conventional depictions of The Three Stooges so as to exploit their fame. Indeed, were we to decide that Saderup's depictions were protected by the First Amendment, we cannot perceive how the right of publicity would remain a viable right other than in cases of falsified celebrity endorsements.

Saderup argues that it would be incongruous and unjust to protect parodies and other distortions of celebrity figures but not wholesome, reverential portraits of [them]. The test we articulate today, however, does not express a value judgment or preference for one type of depiction over another. Rather, it . . . recogni[zes] that the legislature has granted to the heirs and assigns of celebrities the property right to exploit the celebrities' images, and that certain forms of expressive activity protected by the First Amendment fall outside the boundaries of that right. [W]e are concerned not with whether conventional celebrity images should be produced but with who produces them and, more pertinently, who appropriates the value from their production. Thus, if Saderup wishes to continue to depict The Three Stooges as he has done, he may do so only with the consent of the right of publicity holder.

Judgment in favor of Comedy III affirmed.

Misuse of Legal Proceedings

Three intentional torts protect people against the harm that can result from wrongfully instituted legal proceedings. **Malicious prosecution** affords a remedy for the wrongful institution of criminal proceedings. Recovery for malicious prosecution requires proof that: (1) the defendant caused the criminal proceedings to be initiated against the plaintiff without probable cause to believe that an offense had been committed; (2) the defendant did so for an improper purpose; and (3) the criminal proceedings eventually were terminated in the plaintiff's favor. **Wrongful use of civil proceedings** is designed to protect people from wrongfully instituted civil suits. Its elements are very similar to those for malicious prosecution.

Abuse of process imposes liability on those who initiate legal proceedings, whether criminal or civil, for a primary purpose other than the one for which the proceedings were designed. Abuse of process cases often involve situations in which the legal proceedings compel the other person to take some action unrelated to the subject of the suit. For example, Rogers wishes to buy Herbert's property, but Herbert refuses to sell. To pressure him into selling, Rogers files a private nuisance suit against Herbert, contending that Herbert's activities on his land interfere with Rogers' use and enjoyment of his adjoining property. Rogers may be liable to Herbert for abuse of process even if Rogers had reason to file the case, and even if Rogers won the case.

Deceit (Fraud)

Deceit (or fraud) is the formal name for the tort claim that is available to victims of knowing misrepresentations. Liability for fraud usually requires proof of a false statement of material fact that was knowingly or recklessly made by the defendant with the intent to induce reliance by the plaintiff, along with actual, justifiable, and detrimental reliance on the plaintiff's past. Because most fraud actions arise in a contractual setting, and because a tort action is only one of the remedies available to a victim of fraud, a more complete discussion of this topic is deferred until Chapter 13.

Interference with Property Rights

Trespass to Land

Trespass to land may be defined as any unauthorized or unprivileged intentional intrusion upon another's real property. Such intrusions include: (1) physically entering the plaintiff's land; (2) causing another to do so (e.g., by chasing someone onto the land); (3) remaining on the land after one's right to remain has ceased (e.g., staying past the term of a lease); (4) failing to remove from the land anything one has a duty to remove; (5) causing an object or other thing to enter the land (although some overlap with nuisance exists here); and (6) invading the airspace above the land or the subsurface beneath it (if property law and federal, state, and local regulations give the plaintiff rights to the airspace or subsurface and do not allow the defendant to intrude).

The intent required for trespass liability is simply the intent to be on the land or to cause it to be invaded. A person therefore may be liable for trespass even though the trespass resulted from his mistaken belief that his entry was legally justified. Where the trespass was specifically intended, no actual harm to the land is required for liability, but actual harm is required for reckless or negligent trespasses.

Private Nuisance

In general, a **private nuisance** involves some interference with the plaintiff's use and enjoyment of her land.

Unlike trespass to land, nuisance usually does not involve any physical invasion of the plaintiff's property. Trespass usually requires an invasion of tangible matter, whereas nuisance involves other interferences. Examples of such other interferences include odors, noise, smoke, light, and vibration. For nuisance liability to exist, however, the interference must be *substantial* and *unreasonable*. The defendant, moreover, must intend the interference.

Despite the distinction just suggested, some courts have imposed nuisance liability in cases involving apparent invasions of tangible matter such as water, dust, and pollutants. In the following *Ahnert* case, the court treated the plaintiffs' noise claim as a nuisance action and their dust claim as a trespass action. Not all courts would agree with this court's statement of the elements of nuisance recovery.

Ahnert v. Getty 1997 Conn. Super. LEXIS 890
(Conn. Superior Court, New London 1997)

Bruno and Norma Ahnert lived across the street and approximately 500 feet from the Getty Granite Company. The Ahnerts sued Getty for nuisance and trespass to land, asserting that Getty's business produced excessive noise and dust. The noise, they further alleged, disturbed their sleep and made conversation, television watching, and radio or stereo listening difficult. The dust, the Ahnerts added, meant that they could not open their windows for ventilation, and also rendered their outdoor premises unfit for use and enjoyment. Getty moved to dismiss the Ahnerts' claims because they failed to state claims upon which relief can be granted.

Handy, Judge In order to recover under a nuisance theory, a plaintiff must prove that: (1) the action complained of had a natural tendency to create danger and inflict injury upon person or property, (2) the danger created was a continuing one, (3) the [defendant's] use of the land was unreasonable or unlawful, and (4) the existence of the nuisance was the proximate cause of the plaintiff's injuries and damage. In this case, the plaintiffs have stated facts necessary to bring a valid cause of action for private nuisance. The plaintiffs have stated that they have an ownership interest in the affected property. The plaintiffs have alleged injury to land and person in that they have been deprived of the quiet enjoyment of the property and there has been a diminution in value of the property as a result of the defendant's conduct. The plaintiffs have asserted that the injury is a continuing one in that they have cited repeated actions by the defendant dating back to 1988. The plaintiffs have arguably asserted the unreasonableness or unlawfulness of the defendant's conduct by alleging that the noise levels emanating from the defendant's land exceed those prescribed by state regulation, as well as that the plaintiffs are unable either to open windows or have a conversation in the house. The plaintiffs have also asserted that the defendant's actions were the cause in fact

of the plaintiffs' injuries. Accordingly, the court denied the defendant's motion to dismiss count one of the plaintiffs' complaint alleging nuisance.

In general, trespass is an unlawful intrusion that interferes with another's [real] property. A trespass may be committed on, or beneath, or above the surface of the earth and the phrase "surface of the earth" includes soil, water, trees, and other growths. A trespass need not be inflicted directly on another's realty, but may be committed by discharging foreign polluting matter at a point beyond the boundary of such realty.

The defendant asserts that the plaintiffs' allegation of trespass fails to allege the requisite intent for actionable trespass. However, the *Restatement* makes clear that action taken with the substantial certainty that the activity will result in entry of foreign matter on the property of another is actionable trespass. In this case, plaintiffs assert that the defendant knew or should have known that significant amounts of dust were settling outside of the defendant's premises, including on the plaintiffs' property. The plaintiffs have satisfied the intent element for trespass.

Getty's motion to dismiss denied.

Conversion

Conversion is the defendant's intentional exercise of dominion or control over the plaintiff's personal property without the plaintiff's consent. Usually, the personal property in question is the plaintiff's goods. This can happen through the defendant's: (1) *acquisition* of the plaintiff's property (e.g., theft, fraud, and even the purchase of stolen property); (2) *removal* of the plaintiff's property (e.g., taking that property to the dump or moving the plaintiff's car); (3) *transfer* of the plaintiff's property (e.g., selling stolen goods or misdelivering property); (4) *withholding possession* of the plaintiff's property (e.g., refusing to return a car one was to repair); (5) *destruction or alteration* of the plaintiff's property, or (6) *using* the plaintiff's property (e.g., driving a car left by its owner for storage purposes only).

In each case, the necessary intent is merely the intent to exercise dominion or control over the property. It is therefore possible for the defendant to be liable if she buys or sells stolen property in good faith. However, conversion is limited to *serious* interferences with the plaintiff's property rights.

If there is a serious interference and conversion, the defendant is liable for the *full value* of the property. What happens when the interference is nonserious? Although it has largely been superseded by conversion and its elements are hazy, a tort called **trespass to personal property** may come into play here. Suppose that Dalton goes to Jaffee Motors and asks to testdrive a new Ford Taurus. If Dalton either wrecks the car, causing major damage, or drives it across the United States, he is probably liable for conversion and obligated to pay Jaffee the reasonable value of the car. On the other hand, if Dalton is merely involved in a fender-bender, or keeps the car for eight hours, he is probably only liable for trespass. Therefore, he is only obligated to pay damages to compensate Jaffee for the loss in value of the car or for its loss of use of the car.

A very different application of trespass principles appears in the *Intel* case, which is discussed in the nearby Cyberlaw in Action box.

Other Examples of Intentional Tort Liability

Chapter 8 discusses three additional intentional torts that protect various economic interests and often involve unfair competition: *injurious falsehood* (a type of business "defamation"); *intentional interference with* *contractual relations;* and *interference with prospective advantage.* Chapter 51 examines an intentional tortlike recovery for wrongful discharge called the *public policy* exception to employment at will. In Chapter 27, the text discusses the recoveries some states allow for *bad faith breach of contract.*

Problems and Problem Cases

1. Betty England worked at a Dairy Queen restaurant owned by S&M Foods in Tallulah, Louisiana. One day while she was at work, her manager, Larry Garley, became upset when several incorrectly prepared hamburgers were returned by a customer. Garley expressed his dissatisfaction by throwing a hamburger that hit England on the leg. Assume that while Garley was not trying to hit England with the hamburger, he was aware that she was substantially certain to be hit as a result of his action. Also, assume that England was not harmed by the hamburger. England sued Garley for battery. Did Garley have the necessary intent for battery liability? Does England's not suffering harm defeat her battery claim?

2. High school basketball player Travis Goff filed a battery lawsuit against his coach, Craig Clarke, on the basis of an incident that occurred in the school gymnasium before a basketball practice. The incident began when Goff approached Clarke, and said teasingly, "I bet you can't take me." A playful physical confrontation ensued. According to Goff, Clarke began to twist Goff's arm behind his back. Goff contended that he asked Clarke to stop, but Clarke continued. A popping sound coming from the area of Goff's hand was then heard. Goff later found out that he had broken his wrist. Two other players witnessed the incident and heard Goff ask Clarke to stop twisting his arm. Clarke pointed out the mutual joking and playfulness that preceded the incident, and stated that he did not recall hearing Goff ask him to stop twisting his (Goff's) arm. Clarke also pointed out that the 6'1", 285-pound Goff finished the "wrestling match" on top of Clarke after performing a "wedgie" on him (meaning that Goff grabbed Clarke's shorts from behind and pulled the waistband toward Clarke's head). Immediately thereafter, Clarke contended, Goff was "high-flying" Clarke and accepting congratulations from his teammates for having beaten Clarke at wrestling. Goff sought summary judgment on his battery claim against Clarke. Was Goff entitled to summary judgment against the coach?

3. *The New Republic,* a political magazine, published an article entitled "Robespierre of the Right" about conservative political activist Paul Weyrich. The article re-

CYBERLAW IN ACTION

In *Intel Co. v. Hamidi,* 94 Cal. App. 4th 325 (2001), a California appellate court considered whether using a company's e-mail system to distribute unsolicited e-mails to employees without the company's consent constitutes trespass to personal property. After being fired from his job at Intel, Kourosh Hamidi obtained the company's e-mail address list and sent, over a period of two years, six e-mails to each of at least 8,000, and as many as 35,000, Intel employees. These e-mails discussed Hamidi's grievances against his former employer. Intel sued Hamidi, alleging that Intel owned the e-mail system, that the system was intended primarily for business use by Intel employees, that the address list was confidential, and that Hamidi had continued his mass e-mailings despite demands from Intel that he stop. Contending that Hamidi's actions amounted to trespass to chattels (i.e., trespass to personal property), Intel sought an injunction barring Hamidi from sending further e-mails to Intel employees at their Intel addresses. A California Superior Court judge later granted summary judgment in favor of Intel and issued the requested injunction

Hamidi appealed to the California Court of Appeal, which affirmed. The appellate court conceded that even though Intel was not able to demonstrate sufficient economic harm to entitle it to an award of damages, injunctive relief was appropriate in view of the disruption to Intel's business that resulted from Hamidi's intentional interference with the company's e-mail system. This interference brought the case within the ownership and possession-related interests protected by the legal theory of trespass to personal property. The appellate court regarded its application of that "somewhat arcane" theory to the modern e-mail context as an illustration of how "[t]he common law adapts to human endeavor."

The American Civil Liberties Union (ACLU), which had filed an amicus curiae (friend-of-the-court) brief, argued that any harm done to Intel flowed solely from the messages' content and that a trespass to personal property claim therefore was inappropriate. In response to the ACLU's contention that Intel was impermissibly attempting to suppress the content of messages it did not like, the court pointed out that Intel had demonstrated a loss of productivity stemming from the aggregate distraction of thousands of employees and from the hours spent by technicians in trying to block Hamidi's messages. The court accordingly concluded that Intel possessed a legitimate interest in stopping Hamidi's mass e-mailings, regardless of the content of the messages.

Another amicus curiae, the Electronic Frontier Foundation (EFF), argued that loss of productivity was a poor standard for harm. The EFF asserted that all personal e-mails received by Intel employees, not just e-mails such as Hamidi's, would distract employees momentarily and would thereby cause a loss in productivity. For the court to be consistent in applying its principle, the EFF argued, all personal e-mails sent to Intel employees would have to constitute trespass. In response to this argument, the court cited Intel's demands that Hamidi cease sending his messages—demands Hamidi had ignored. The disregarded demands distinguished Hamidi's e-mails from run-of-the-mill personal e-mails and helped support the conclusion that Hamidi's actions amounted to trespass.

Hamidi and the amici argued, finally, that the injunction violated the First Amendment and a California constitutional provision protecting free speech rights. The court rejected this argument, holding that the government action necessary to support an argument of unconstitutionality was not present. In so holding, the court declined to find government action on the basis that such action was found in *New York Times Co. v. Sullivan,* the landmark case in which the U.S. Supreme Court "constitutionalized" the law of defamation. (See this chapter's earlier discussion of *New York Times* and First Amendment issues in defamation law.) Instead, the court followed a line of Supreme Court cases indicating that First Amendment concerns are not implicated when an owner of private property excludes would-be speakers from that property and asks a court to enforce the legal rules governing trespass. In the court's view, Intel's e-mail system was private property that Intel had neither opened up, nor had an obligation to open up, to any and all speakers who would like access to it.

The California Court of Appeals' word on the matter may not be the last one heard, however. When this book went to press, the Supreme Court of California had granted Hamidi's petition for review but had not yet decided the case.

ferred to Weyrich as a "case study of the conservative mind" and presented him as an uncompromising ideologue whose stubbornness had helped to tear apart a Republican party he helped to shape. Claiming that the article contained false and defamatory statements that wrongfully portrayed him as mentally unsound and para-

noid, Weyrich sued *The New Republic* for defamation. In part, Weyrich based his case on a statement that described him as experiencing "sudden bouts of pessimism and paranoia—early symptoms of the nervous breakdown that afflicts conservatives today." Another allegedly defamatory portion of the article, according to

Weyrich, was a section that recounted certain incidents meant to illustrate Weyrich's "famous temper" and his "nutty" behavior. Assuming that Weyrich has never been professionally diagnosed as suffering from paranoia, was the statement that referred to "sudden bouts of pessimism and paranoia" a statement on which Weyrich could base a valid defamation claim? If, as Weyrich contended, some of the supposed incidents described in the article did not occur, would the article's recounting of those "incidents" give rise to a credible defamation claim?

4. Early in 1994, a K-Mart manager notified K-Mart's Birmingham, Alabama stores that Deborah Cameron and Sonja Perdue had repeatedly returned merchandise without receipts and had been given cash refunds. The manager also stated his belief that Cameron and Perdue had shoplifted the merchandise for which they had obtained supposed "refunds." Accordingly, the manager told all K-Mart loss-control managers in the area to be on the lookout for Cameron and Perdue and to monitor their activities closely. Among the recipients of this message was Doug Sharp, the loss-control manager for the Bessemer, Alabama K-Mart store. One night, after Bessemer store personnel refused to give Perdue a refund because she did not have a receipt, Sharp asked to speak with Perdue. He led Perdue to a loss-control room inside the store. Later, Sharp detained Cameron in a separate loss-control room after observing her putting a set of drapes into her purse. After Perdue accused Cameron of making her steal items and Cameron made the same accusation regarding Perdue, Cameron confessed to taking the drapes. The police arrived and arrested Perdue and Cameron for third-degree theft. Perdue and Cameron were convicted of that crime, but their convictions were reversed on appeal. Perdue and Cameron later sued Sharp and K-Mart for, among other things, false imprisonment. Were the plaintiffs entitled to win their false imprisonment claim?

5. Seattle resident Jordan Brower was active in civic affairs. At one point, he sued the city and Ackerley Communications, Inc., in an effort to have Seattle's billboard regulations enforced. Although Brower later dropped the case, his efforts prompted the city (1) to announce that Ackerley Communications had erected dozens of illegal billboards, and (2) to enact a new billboard ordinance. Over approximately a 1½-year period that began around the time he filed his lawsuit and through the time of the city's announcement regarding Ackerley Communications and the enactment of the new ordinance, Brower received a series of troubling phone calls at his home. During each of these calls, the caller was aggressive, loud,

profane, insulting, and mean-spirited. The series of calls culminated with three calls on the night the city passed the new billboard ordinance. In one of those calls, the caller referred to Brower as a "d—." In another call, the caller said that "I'm going to find out where you live and I'm going to kick your a—." The maker of the third call said, in an eerie voice, "Oooo, Jordan, oooo, you're finished; cut you in your sleep, you sack of s—." Brower complained to the police department, which traced the calls and concluded that they hade been made from the apartment of Christopher Ackerley. Ackerley and his brother, Theodore, both in their early 20s, were the sons of the founder of Ackerley Communications. Brower eventually sued Christopher and Theodore Ackerley for assault and intentional infliction of emotional distress. The trial court granted the defendants' motion for summary judgment on both claims. Was the trial court correct in doing so?

6. Irma White, a church-going woman in her late forties, was employed at a Monsanto refinery. While working in the canning department, she and three other employees were told to transfer a corrosive and hazardous chemical from a larger container into smaller containers. After they asked for rubber gloves and goggles, a supervisor sent for the equipment. In the meantime, White began cleaning up the work area and one of the other employees went to another area to do some work. The other two employees sat around waiting for the safety equipment, contrary to a work rule requiring employees to busy themselves in such situations.

After learning that the group was idle, Gary McDermott, the canning department foreman, went to the work station. Once there, he launched into a profane one-minute tirade directed at White and the other two workers present, calling them "motherf—s," accusing them of sitting on their "f—g asses," and threatening to "show them to the gate." At this, White became upset and began to experience pain in her chest, pounding in her head, and difficulty in breathing. Her family physician met her at the hospital, where he admitted her, fearing that she was having a heart attack. She was later diagnosed as having had an acute anxiety reaction.

White later sued Monsanto for intentional infliction of emotional distress. Was her distress sufficiently severe for liability? Was McDermott's behavior sufficiently outrageous for liability?

7. Jacqui Starr was general manager of a Pearle Vision retail optical store in Tulsa, Oklahoma. Three Pearle employees who were assigned to conduct an investigation met with Starr to discuss a $4,000 deficit in her store's petty cash account. Starr refused to cooperate with the investigators and was fired for that reason. The three investigating employees made certain remarks about Starr's situation to two other Pearle employees, Ballard and Ross, who were also being investigated. After Starr was fired, her successor as store manager told Winn (a friend of Starr's who was not a Pearle employee) that Starr "is no longer here" and "is in big trouble." Starr filed a defamation lawsuit against Pearle. She contended: (1) that the investigating employees' statements to Ballard and Ross met all elements of a defamation claim; (2) that she would be compelled to engage in defamatory self-publication when, in later job interviews, she would be asked about the termination of her Pearle employment; and (3) that the new manager's statements to Winn defamed her. Pearle contended that the statements by the investigating employees to Ballard and Ross did not constitute publication, that the compelled self-publication doctrine argued for by Starr should not be adopted by the court, and that the new manager's statements to Winn would not have a tendency to harm Starr's reputation and thus were not defamatory. The trial court granted Pearle's motion for summary judgment. Was the trial court correct in doing so?

8. Nineteen-year-old Elli Lake and 20-year-old Melissa Weber vacationed in Mexico with Weber's sister. During the vacation, Weber's sister took a photograph of Lake and Weber naked in the shower together. After the vacation, Lake and Weber brought five rolls of film to a Wal-Mart photo lab for processing. The negatives and all but one of the developed photographs were returned to Lake and Weber, along with a written notice stating that one of the photographs had not been printed because of its "nature." A few months later, an acquaintance of Lake and Weber alluded to the photograph of Lake and Weber in the shower and raised questions about their sexual orientation. A friend of Lake and Weber told them, a few more months later, that a Wal-Mart employee had shown her a copy of the photograph. Still later, Lake was informed that copies of the photograph were in circulation in the community. Lake and Weber sued Wal-Mart in a Minnesota trial court on four different invasion of privacy theories (intrusion on solitude, public disclosure of private facts, false light publicity, and commercial appropriation of name or likeness). Wal-Mart filed a motion to dismiss for failure to state a claim on which relief could be granted. The trial court dismissed the case, explaining that Minnesota has not recognized any of the invasion of privacy torts as valid causes of action in that state. After Minnesota's intermediate court of appeals affirmed,

Lake and Weber appealed to the Minnesota Supreme Court. How do you think that court ruled?

9. Peggy Hill purchased long distance telephone services from MCI. From then on, she paid an additional amount of money so that MCI would ensure that her number would be unlisted and that any other personal information would remain unpublished and confidential. An unidentified man ("X") began making phone calls to MCI and asking for Hill's billing information, parties Hill had called, addresses and phone numbers of parties Hill had called, and "other confidential information." MCI, over a one-week period, provided X with phone numbers and address information for 20 separate parties Hill had called. X called one such party, a close personal friend of Hill, and was later put in touch with Hill. Hill identified the voice on the line as that of her ex-husband, who had previously stalked, harassed, and threatened her. She filed suit against MCI, alleging that its actions had violated her right of privacy through public disclosure of private facts about her. Did she have a legally valid claim?

10. The Blanks purchased a lot in the Indian Fork subdivision next to a lot owned by Gary Rawson. When Rawson built his home, he located a basketball goal and dog pen immediately next to the property separating the two lots. The Blanks complained to the subdivision developer that Rawson was violating the minimum setback restrictions applicable to the subdivision and were told that Rawson had received permission from the developer to do so. They then filed a nuisance suit against Rawson. At the trial, they alleged that the sound of the basketball hitting the backboard when Rawson's son played was offensive and that when he missed, the ball could come into their yard. They also stated that the dog was a large one and that the pen was not cleaned regularly, with the result that offensive odors continued to reach their property despite the 10-foot privacy fence Rawson had erected between their properties shortly after their complaint against him was filed. Was the trial judge's order forcing Rawson to remove or relocate the goal and the dog pen proper?

11. A still photograph from the 1982 movie *Tootsie* showed Dustin Hoffman in character wearing a red long-sleeved sequined dress and high heels and standing in front of an American flag. *Los Angeles Magazine* (LAM) ran an article headed with the words "Grand Illusions" in the "Fabulous Hollywood Issue." The article used computer-imaging technology to alter famous film stills to create the appearance that the actors were wearing 1997 fashions. The final shot of the article was an altered *Tootsie* still.

Hoffman's head and the American flag remained as they were in the original, but Hoffman's body was replaced with that of a male model wearing a spaghetti-strap, cream-colored silk evening dress, and high-heeled sandals. The caption read: "Dustin Hoffman isn't a drag in a butter-colored silk gown by Richard Tyler and Ralph Lauren heels." LAM had not secured permission from Hoffman or from Columbia Pictures, the still's copyright holder. Hoffman filed suit against Capital Cities/ABC, LAM's parent company, alleging a violation of his right of publicity. Was Hoffman entitled to win the case and recover damages?

12. Peter Wallis and Kellie Rae Smith were involved in a consensual sexual relationship. According to Wallis, the two had discussed methods of contraception and had decided that Smith would take birth control pills. Wallis, who used no form of birth control himself, allegedly made clear that he did not want to father a child, and that the sexual relationship could continue only so long as Smith took birth control pills. Smith stopped taking the pills, but did not inform Wallis of her decision. She became pregnant and later gave birth. Required by New Mexico law to make child support payments for 18 years, Wallis alleged that Smith committed fraud by not informing him of her decision to cease taking birth control pills. He contended that Smith's supposed fraud had caused him significant financial harm, for which he sought compensatory damages from Smith. Wallis also asked that punitive damages be assessed against Smith. The district court, taking into account a New Mexico statute imposing strict liability on both parents for child support, dismissed Wallis's action for failure to state on claim on which relief could be granted. Was the court correct in doing so?

13. The Ammons, who lived with their children on a three-acre farm, adopted a stray dog they named "Hair Bear." Hair Bear roamed the area freely and was never licensed. A neighbor, Georgia Nuss, often complained about Hair Bear's forays onto her property. One day after she saw Hair Bear out roaming, Nuss picked up the dog and delivered him to the Trimble County Dog Warden, Robert Brewer. Before expiration of the seven-day statutory waiting period for destruction of impounded dogs, Brewer destroyed Hair Bear. He did so by shooting the dog—the method he customarily employed for destruction of impounded dogs. The Ammons filed suit against Brewer, alleging that he had wrongfully destroyed Hair Bear and that this action constituted intentional infliction of emotional distress. The trial court dismissed the Ammons' claim. Was it correct in doing so?

14. R&J Associates leased certain commercial real estate from T&C Associates, Inc. for a one-year period beginning May 1. The lease required that T&C give R&J 10 days' notice before canceling the lease. R&J operated the leased premises as a bar that featured seminude dancers but discontinued the business during the following March when it lost a necessary dance permit. In late March and early April, T&C noticed that the bar was not open and learned that R&J had lost its permit. R&J was behind on its rent at this time. Utility companies were seeking to shut off service to the premises because R&J was also behind on its utility bills. When T&C informed R&J that its monthly rent would be higher if it renewed the lease, R&J said it had no interest in renewing. For the above reasons, T&C took possession of the premises in April. T&C, however, did not give R&J the 10 days' notice referred to in the lease. T&C leased the premises to a new tenant later that month. At approximately the same time, R&J demanded the return of certain personal property items it had left on the premises. T&C told R&J to contact the new tenant, adding that there should be no problem with the return of the items of personal property. R&J contacted the new tenant, who told R&J to submit a list of its personal property because other parties were also claiming rights to what had been left on the premises. R&J did not submit this list and did not contact T&C again about the personal property items. Later, R&J sued T&C for conversion of the personal property. Did R&J have a valid conversion claim?

Online Research: The Vanna White Case

Vanna White, the familiar letter-turner on the long-running television game show *Wheel of Fortune,* was the successful plaintiff in a highly publicized right of publicity case during the 1990s. Conduct research using online sources, learn about the case, and write a brief statement setting forth what made the case both significant and controversial.

NEGLIGENCE AND STRICT LIABILITY

Universal Metrics, Inc. (UMI), sponsored an evening social gathering for its employees at a Wisconsin country club. UMI provided each attendee with two vouchers, each of which was redeemable for an alcoholic or a nonalcoholic beverage. Once the vouchers had been used, attendees could purchase additional beverages from a country club bartender.

Michael Devine and John Kreuser were among the UMI employees in attendance. They drove separately to the event. At approximately 8:30 P.M. that evening, Kreuser heard the bartender ask Devine whether he (Devine) had a ride home. Kreuser saw Devine make a motion with his head, suggesting that Kreuser would be responsible for driving Devine home. Kreuser then indicated to the bartender that he would give Devine a ride home. After this indication by Kreuser, the bartender served Devine more drinks. Kreuser saw Devine take the drinks back to a table where he had been sitting.

Between 9:00 and 9:15 P.M., Devine approached Kreuser and asked Kreuser to buy him a drink because the bartender had cut him off. Kreuser declined. He neither talked to nor saw Devine again during the evening. Kreuser and his wife left the party at approximately 10:00 P.M. As they were leaving, Kreuser decided not to give Devine a ride home. Kreuser, who had driven Devine home under similar circumstances on two other occasions, did not tell Devine or anyone else that he did not intend to drive Devine home this time.

At approximately 10:40 P.M., Devine was driving his own vehicle when he crossed the center line of the highway and struck a vehicle driven by Kathy Stephenson. Both drivers died as a result of injuries they suffered in the collision. Test results showed that Devine's blood alcohol concentration was more than three times greater than Wisconsin's legal limit.

Devine's estate, of course, was legally liable to Kathy Stephenson's estate. Ricky Stephenson, Kathy's surviving spouse and personal representative of her estate, believed that others should face liability as well. Acting on his own behalf and in his personal representative capacity, Stephenson sued UMI and Kreuser for negligence. The claim against UMI failed, however, because a Wisconsin statute insulated parties in UMI's position from liability in cases such as Stephenson's. This left Wisconsin's trial and appellate courts to decide the legal questions raised by the negligence claim against Kreuser. These questions included the following:

• When an individual indicates to a bartender that he will drive an intoxicated person home, does that individual assume a legal *duty* to drive the intoxicated person home?
• When the individual who agrees to drive subsequently does not drive the intoxicated person home, has that individual *failed to use reasonable care?* If so, may negligence liability be imposed on that individual for injury or damage experienced by parties other than the intoxicated person in a motor vehicle crash that resulted from the intoxicated person's dangerous driving?

As you read Chapter 7, consider the above questions, which relate to key components of the law of negligence. What answers do you think the Wisconsin courts gave to the questions? In addition, consider the ethical issues that may be faced by persons and entities involved in situations such as the one described above.

THE INDUSTRIAL REVOLUTION THAT changed the face of 19th-century America created serious strains on tort law. Railroads, factories, machinery, and new technologies meant increased injuries to persons and harm to their property. These injuries did not fit within the intentional torts framework because most were unintended. In response, courts created the law of **negligence.**

Negligence law initially was not kind to injured plaintiffs. One reason, some say, was the fear that if infant industries were held responsible for all the harms they caused, the country's industrial development would be seriously restricted. As a viable industrial economy emerged in the 20th century, this concern began to fade. Also fading over the same period was the 19th-century belief that there should be no tort liability without genuine fault on the defendant's part. More and more, the injuries addressed by tort law have come to be seen as the inevitable consequences of life in a highly industrialized, high-speed, technologically advanced society. Although modern negligence rules have not eliminated the fault feature, they sometimes seem consistent with a goal of imposing tort liability on the party better positioned to bear the financial costs of these consequences. That party often is the defendant. Negligence law clearly has become more proplaintiff in recent decades, though statistics indicate that defendants tend to win negligence cases as often as plaintiffs do.

Because most tort cases that do not involve intentional torts are governed by the law of negligence, the bulk of this chapter will deal with negligence principles. In a narrow range of cases, however, courts dispense with the fault requirement of negligence and impose **strict liability** on defendants. Strict liability's more limited application (as compared to that of negligence) will be addressed during the latter part of this chapter. The chapter will conclude with discussion of recent years' **tort reform** movement, whose primary aims are to (1) reduce plaintiffs' ability to prevail in tort cases, and (2) limit the amounts of damages they may receive when they win such cases.

Negligence

The previous chapter characterized negligence as conduct that falls below the level reasonably necessary to protect others against significant risks of harm. The elements of a negligence claim are: (1) that the defendant owed a **duty** of care to the plaintiff; (2) that the defendant committed a **breach** of this duty; and (3) that this breach was the **actual and proximate cause** of **injury** experienced by the plaintiff. In order to win a negligence case, the plaintiff must prove each of these three elements, which will be examined in more depth in the following pages. Later in the chapter, **defenses** to negligence liability will be considered.

Duty and Breach of Duty

Duty of Reasonable Care Negligence law rests on the premise that members of society normally should behave in ways that avoid the creation of unreasonable risks of harm to others. As a general rule, therefore, negligence law contemplates that each person must act as a *reasonable person of ordinary prudence* would have acted under the same or similar circumstances. This standard for assessing conduct is often called either the "reasonable person" test or the "reasonable care" standard. In most cases, the duty to exercise reasonable care serves as the relevant duty for purposes of a negligence claim's first element. The second element—breach of duty—requires the plaintiff to establish that the defendant failed to act as a reasonable person would have acted. Negligence law's focus on reasonableness of behavior leads to a broad range of applications in everyday personal life (e.g., a person's negligent driving of a car) and in business and professional contexts (e.g., an employer's negligent hiring of a certain employee, or an accountant's, attorney's, or physician's negligent performance of professional obligations).

Was the Duty Owed? Of course, there could not have been a breach of duty if the defendant did not owe the plaintiff a duty in the first place. It therefore becomes important, before we look further at *how* the reasonable person test is applied, to consider the ways in which courts determine *whether* the defendant even owed the plaintiff a duty of reasonable care.

Courts typically hold that the defendant owed the plaintiff a duty of reasonable care if the plaintiff was among those who would foreseeably be at risk of harm stemming from the defendant's activities or conduct, or if a special relationship logically calling for such a duty existed between the parties. Most courts today broadly define the group of foreseeable "victims" of a defendant's activities or conduct. As a result, a duty of reasonable care is held to run from the defendant to the plaintiff in a very high percentage of negligence cases—meaning that the outcome of the case will hinge on whether the defendant breached the duty or on whether the requisite causation link between the defendant's breach and the plaintiff's injury is established.

The particular circumstances present in some cases, however, cause the court to conclude that the plaintiff was not among those foreseeably at risk and that the defendant therefore did not owe the plaintiff a duty of reasonable care. When the court so holds, the plaintiff's negligence claim is dismissed for failure to prove the required initial element of such a claim.

Was the Duty Breached? Assuming that the defendant owed the plaintiff a duty of reasonable care, whether the defendant satisfied or instead breached that duty depends upon the application of the reasonable person test. This test is *objective* in two senses. First, it compares the defendant's actions with those that a hypothetical person with ordinary prudence and sensibilities would have taken (or not taken) under the circumstances. Second, the test focuses on the defendant's behavior rather than on the defendant's *subjective* mental state. The reasonable person test has another noteworthy characteristic: flexibility. In contemplating that courts consider all of the relevant facts and circumstances, the test allows courts to tailor their decisions to the facts of the particular case being decided.

When applying this objective yet flexible standard to specific cases, courts consider and balance various factors. The most important such factor is the *reasonable foreseeability* of harm. This factor does double duty, helping to determine not only whether the defendant owed the plaintiff a duty (as noted above) but also what the defendant's duty of reasonable care entailed in the case at hand. Suppose that Donald falls asleep at the wheel and causes a car accident in which another motorist, Peter, is injured. Falling asleep at the wheel involves a foreseeable risk of harm to others, so a reasonable person would remain awake while driving. Because Donald's conduct fell short of this behavioral standard, he has breached a duty to Peter. However, this probably would not be true if Donald's loss of awareness resulted from a sudden, severe, and unforeseeable blackout. On the other hand, there probably would be a breach of duty

if Donald was driving and had a blackout to which a doctor had warned him he was subject.

Negligence law does not require that we protect others against all foreseeable risks of harm. Instead, the risk created by the defendant's conduct need only be an *unreasonable* one. In determining the reasonableness of the risk, courts consider other factors besides the foreseeability of harm. One such factor is the *seriousness* or *magnitude* of the foreseeable harm. As the seriousness of the harm increases, so does the need to take action to avoid it. Another factor is the *social utility* of the defendant's conduct. The more valuable that conduct, the less likely that it will be regarded as a breach of duty. A further consideration is the *ease or difficulty of avoiding the risk.* Negligence law normally does not require that defendants make superhuman efforts to avoid harm to others.

To a limited extent, negligence law also considers the *personal characteristics* of the defendant. For example, children are generally required to act as would a reasonable person of similar age, intelligence, and experience. A physically disabled person must act as would a reasonable person with the same disability. Mental deficiencies, however, ordinarily do not relieve a person from the duty to conform to the usual reasonable person standard. The same is true of voluntary and negligent intoxication.

Finally, negligence law is sensitive to the *context* in which the defendant acted. For example, someone confronted with an emergency requiring rapid decisions and action need not employ the same level of caution and deliberation as someone in circumstances allowing for calm reflection and deliberate action.

The *Gaff* case, which follows, focuses on the duty and breach of duty elements of a negligence claim. Although the court stated that the defendant did not owe the plaintiff a duty, the real basis of the decision appears to be that the defendant did not breach the duty of reasonable care it owed to the plaintiff. The court concluded that under the circumstances, the defendant's duty of reasonable care did not include an obligation to warn the plaintiff or take the corrective action that the plaintiff asserted was necessary.

Gaff v. Johnson Oil Co.   *2002 U.S. App. LEXIS 18368 (6th Cir. 2002)*

Johnson Oil Co. operates a number of gas stations and convenience stores under the "Bigfoot Food Stores" name. On January 4, 1999, Gloria Gaff stopped at a Bigfoot store in Louisville, Kentucky, to purchase gasoline for her car and to use the store's automatic car wash. She realized that the store's parking lot was icy, and that the temperature was below freezing. In view of the parking lot's condition, Gaff walked carefully during her first two trips across the lot. The first was from her car to the store so that she could pay for the gasoline she had pumped; the second was her return from the store to the car.

Gaff then drove her car to the automatic car wash, which was located behind the store. She had difficulty engaging the car wash's automatic garage door, however. Gaff therefore crossed part of the parking lot a third time, again noticed the extent of ice on the lot, and entered the store to ask how to operate the car wash's garage door. When she left the store and proceeded toward her car, she initially walked down a fully cleared adjoining sidewalk. She then stepped onto the icy parking lot surface. Even though Gaff was proceeding cautiously, her foot slipped on the ice she encountered. She fell and sustained injuries as a result.

Gaff filed suit against Johnson Oil in a Kentucky state court. Johnson Oil exercised its right to have the case removed to the United States District Court for the Western District of Kentucky, on the basis of diversity jurisdiction principles. When the district court granted Johnson Oil's motion for summary judgment, Gaff appealed to the United States Court of Appeals for the Sixth Circuit.

Cole, Circuit Judge Gaff argues that Johnson Oil Company had a duty to remedy or warn her about the icy conditions on its parking lot prior to her accident. [Her] appeal presents one issue for our review: whether the district court properly granted Johnson Oil's motion for summary judgment on the ground that Johnson Oil owed no duty of care to [her].

Summary judgment is appropriate when there is no genuine issue of material fact and the moving party is entitled to judgment as a matter of law. Gaff [contends] that the trial court improperly granted summary judgment because whether the icy conditions in the parking lot were open and obvious, and whether Johnson Oil should have taken steps to ensure Gaff's safety, are both genuine issues of material fact that should have been submitted to a jury.

In order to recover on her negligence claim, Gaff must establish that Johnson Oil owed her a duty of care, and that its breach of that duty was responsible for her damages. An owner of commercial premises [owes] a full duty of reasonable care to a business invitee on its property. [As a customer at Johnson Oil's store, Gaff would be considered an invitee.] Despite this duty to make the property reasonably safe for the invitee, Kentucky law is not generous to business invitees who suffer an injury as a result of a risk created by an obvious, outdoor natural condition such as ice. Where the natural outdoor hazard is obvious to the invitee, then the hazard is not an unreasonable risk that the owner has a duty to remedy or about which the invitee must be warned. When an invitee knows that the weather conditions are inclement, visits during daytime hours [and is thus] able to see the condition of the parking lot, specifically notices that [the] parking lot is icy, and is forced to walk carefully to avoid falling, then the risk created by an icy parking lot is "open and obvious" and the owner has met its duty of reasonable care owed to the invitee. [In such a situation, the owner] owes no additional duty to remedy or warn. *PNC*

Bank of Kentucky, Inc. v. Green, 30 S.W.3d 185, 187 (Ky. Sup. Ct. 2000).

No exception to this rule exists where the plaintiff is forced to make multiple crossings over an icy ramp or parking lot. *See PNC Bank,* 30 S.W.3d at 186 (implicitly rejecting the [approach suggested] in *Wallingford v. Kroger Co.,* 761 S.W.2d 621, 622 (Ky. App.1988), [which appeared to contemplate] a broader duty [for] an owner of land [regarding] obvious dangers where the owner has reason to expect that the invitee will proceed to encounter the dangers). Where the owner meets this duty of reasonable care and has no additional duty to remedy or warn, there can be no breach and thus no actionable negligence.

Gaff's deposition testimony establishes that the ice in Johnson Oil's parking lot was an open and obvious outdoor natural condition of which she was aware, and that the district court properly found no genuine issue of material fact necessary for trial. Gaff's claim fails as a matter of law because she cannot establish that the full duty of reasonable care that Johnson Oil owed her required it to warn her about the naturally occurring ice or [to] remedy that condition. Gaff concedes that she knew that the parking lot was icy, that the temperature was below the freezing point, and that she walked very carefully over the lot in her three prior trips across it. As the district court concluded, Gaff "was aware of the danger of snowy and icy conditions present and, specifically, aware of the patch of ice upon which she slipped. She was also aware of the danger of these conditions and proceeded cautiously."

Since the risk created by the icy parking lot was open and obvious, Johnson Oil owed no additional duty to remedy the condition or warn Gaff. With no duty, Gaff's negligence claim fails as a matter of law.

Summary judgment in favor of Johnson Oil affirmed.

Special Duties In some situations, courts have fashioned particular negligence duties to supplement the general reasonable person standard. When performing their professional duties, for example, professionals such as doctors, lawyers, and accountants generally must exercise the knowledge, skill, and care ordinarily possessed and employed by members of the profession.[1] Also, common carriers and (sometimes) innkeepers are held to an extremely high duty of care approaching strict liability when they are sued for damaging or losing their customers' property. Many courts say that they also must exercise great caution to protect their passengers and lodgers against personal injury—especially against the foreseeable wrongful acts of third persons. This is true even though the law has long refused to recognize any general duty to aid and protect others from third-party wrongdoing unless the defendant's actions foreseeably increased the risk of such wrongdoing. Some recent decisions have imposed a duty on landlords to protect their tenants against the foreseeable criminal acts of others.

---

[1]Chapter 46 discusses professional liability in greater detail.

ETHICS IN ACTION

George Rocha, a 21-year-old college junior, drowned in a swimming accident. His parents filed a negligence-based wrongful death action against his friend, Michael Faltys, and the fraternity to which Rocha and Faltys belonged.

Several hours before Rocha's death, he and Faltys had attended a crawfish boil at their fraternity house. Rocha, who was of legal drinking age, drank beer at this event, which officially ended at 6:00 P.M. At approximately 2:45 A.M., Faltys, Rocha, and three friends went to a swimming spot at a nearby river. Faltys and Rocha climbed to the top of some cliffs hanging over the river. Faltys then dived into the river and encouraged Rocha to do the same. Rocha, who was intoxicated, jumped from a cliff but began floundering as soon as he hit the water. He did not know how to swim. Faltys and the others attempted to save Rocha, but they were unsuccessful.

In *Rocha v. Faltys,* 69 S.W.3d 315 (Tex. App. 2002), the court affirmed a lower court's grant of summary judgment in favor of Faltys and the fraternity. After noting that a person normally is not under a legal duty to control the conduct of another absent the existence of a special relationship or other special circumstances, the court held that Faltys owed Rocha no legal duty and thus could not be held liable for negligence. The court rejected the plaintiffs' argument that Faltys should be seen as having owed a duty to Rocha because he (Faltys) had created a dangerous situation by taking an intoxicated Rocha to the top of the cliffs and by encouraging him to jump into the river. According to the court, "[s]imply taking [Rocha], an adult man, to the location where [he] could choose to engage in a dangerous activity, does not constitute negligent creation of a dangerous situation. The fact that [Rocha] was intoxicated does not affect this analysis." Moreover, the court noted, the plaintiffs had not identified any Texas precedent indicating that one adult acquires a legal duty to another adult by virtue of having encouraged the other to engage in a dangerous activity.

The court observed that persons who have chosen to consume alcohol normally are obligated to control their own behavior and are held accountable for their actions while intoxicated. "[I]mpos[ing] a legal duty on Faltys because [Rocha] had consumed alcohol would be contrary to this principle," the court reasoned.

- Do you agree with the court's legal analysis? Why or why not?
- Regardless of whether Faltys owed Rocha any legal duty, did he owe and breach any *ethical* duty? Why or why not?
- Would your conclusion be any different if Rocha had been 17 years of age rather than 21? Why or why not?

The court in *Rocha v. Faltys* also concluded that the fraternity did not owe Rocha a legal duty and thus could not be held liable for negligence. Rocha's parents contended that the fraternity owed Rocha a duty of reasonable care because the trip to the river was a fraternity activity and because the fraternity had supplied beer to Rocha. The court rejected both arguments, noting the significant time lapse between the end of the crawfish boil and the trip to the river, and stressing that the swimming trip was not transformed into a fraternity activity by the simple fact that those who went to the river had been together earlier at a fraternity activity. In addition, the court noted that although Rocha had consumed alcohol at the crawfish boil, there was no evidence that the fraternity had supplied the alcohol.

- Assume now that neither state law nor university policy prohibits a fraternity or sorority from serving alcohol at official functions, so long as those served are of legal drinking age. Are any *ethical* issues raised by such serving of alcohol? If so, what are they, why do they exist, and to whom do any relevant ethical duties run? If not, why not?

Duties to Persons on Property Another important set of special duties runs from possessors of real estate (land and buildings) to those who enter that property. Negligence cases that address these duties are often called *premises liability* cases. Traditionally, the duty owed by the possessor has depended on the classification into which the entering party fits. The three classifications are:

1. *Invitees.* Invitees are of two general types, the first of which is the "business visitor" who is invited to enter the property for a purpose connected with the possessor's business. Examples include customers, patrons, and delivery persons. The second type of invitees consists of "public invitees" who are invited to enter property that is held open to the public. Examples include persons using government or municipal facilities such as parks, swimming pools, and public offices, attendees of free public lectures and church services, and people responding to advertisements that something will be given away. The entry, however, must be for the purpose for which the property is held open. Accordingly, some—though not all—courts would hold that a person who enters a public library merely to meet a friend is not an invitee.

A possessor of property must exercise reasonable care for the safety of his invitees. In particular, he must take appropriate steps to protect an invitee against dangerous on-premises conditions that he knows about, or reasonably should discover, and that the invitee is unlikely to discover.

2. *Licensees.* A licensee enters the property for her own purposes, not for a purpose connected with the possessor's business. She does, however, enter with the possessor's consent. In some states, social guests are licensees (though, as the following *Harris* case indicates, they are invitees in other states). Other examples of licensees are door-to-door salespeople, solicitors of money for charity, and sometimes persons taking a shortcut across the property. As these examples suggest, consent to enter the property is often implied. The possessor usually is obligated only to warn licensees of dangerous on-premises conditions that they are unlikely to discover.

3. *Trespassers.* A trespasser enters the land without its possessor's consent and without any other privilege. Traditionally, a possessor of land owed trespassers no duty to exercise reasonable care for their safety; instead, there was only a duty not to willfully and wantonly injure trespassers: once their presence was known.

Recent years have seen some tendency to erode these traditional distinctions. Most notably, some courts no longer distinguish between licensees and invitees and hold that the possessor owes a duty of reasonable care to persons in each of those classifications. Some courts have created additional duties that possessors owe to trespassers. For example, a higher level of care is often required as to trespassers who are known to regularly enter the land, and as to children known to be likely to trespass.

In the *Harris* case, which follows, the court discusses and applies the duty of reasonable care owed to invitees.

Harris v. Traini	759 N.E.2d 215 (Ind. App. 2001)

When Michael Traini was 15 years of age, he was arrested for possession of marijuana. His parents, Patrick and Kay Traini (the Trainis), then enrolled him in a drug treatment program. By the time Michael was 17, the Trainis owned a houseboat that was moored on Brookville Reservoir. They had given Michael permission to use the houseboat and have visitors on board with him. The Trainis, who kept alcohol in the houseboat's kitchen, did not supervise or otherwise monitor Michael's use of the houseboat on the occasion referred to below.

Michael was using the houseboat one afternoon with his parents' permission. Ron Anderson, a 21-year-old acquaintance of Michael's, arrived at the houseboat. Four minors, including Nathan Marling and 17-year-old Jessica Legear, accompanied Anderson. Anderson and the four minors had reached the houseboat by riding on a shuttle provided by the Quakertown Marina. Although Michael did not know the persons who accompanied Anderson, he invited everyone to board the houseboat, where alcohol and marijuana were already present. Anderson had visited the Trainis' houseboat as Michael's guest on previous occasions. Each time, Anderson had observed the consumption of alcohol and marijuana on board. On this occasion, Anderson left the houseboat long enough to go back to the marina, retrieve alcoholic beverages, and return with those beverages to the houseboat, again via the Quakertown shuttle.

In a deposition taken in connection with the litigation described later, Marling testified that he saw Michael, Legear, and the others consume alcohol and marijuana while on the houseboat. Michael, who denied that he smoked marijuana that day, witnessed Legear's consumption of alcohol. Later in the afternoon, Legear and Marling were sitting together at the back of the boat. Legear was talking about jumping in the water, and Marling pushed her in. Marling testified that he was "playing around" when he did this. Legear, who had not told anyone that she was unable to swim, drowned before she could be pulled out of the water. A juvenile court later entered a finding that Marling had committed reckless homicide.

Legear's mother, Naomi Harris, sued Michael, the Trainis, and Quakertown. She alleged that negligence on the part of the defendants led to her daughter's death. When the trial court granted each defendant's motion for summary judgment, Harris appealed to the Indiana Court of Appeals.

Najam, Judge Summary judgment is appropriate when the designated evidence demonstrates that there is no genuine issue of material fact and that the moving party is entitled to judgment as a matter of law.

Negligence Claim Against Michael

Harris maintains that Legear was an invitee of Michael and the Trainis and that questions of fact exist regarding whether they breached the duty of care owed to Legear. Michael and the Trainis respond that they owed no duty to protect Legear from Marling's unforeseeable criminal act. None of the defendants argues that Legear was contributorily negligent.

[Although] Michael and the Trainis . . . are not landowners with respect to the houseboat, and Legear's death did not occur on land, . . . we find that premises liability principles apply to the facts of this case. The incident occurred on a large houseboat equipped with a kitchen and bathroom. Indeed, the Trainis used the houseboat as a weekend getaway. We see no reason to distinguish the Trainis' houseboat from a residence located on land.

The tort of negligence is comprised of three elements: 1) a duty on the part of the defendant in relation to the plaintiff; 2) a failure by the defendant to conform its conduct to the requisite standard of care; and 3) an injury to the plaintiff proximately caused by the failure. The law is well-established that a person entering upon the land of another comes upon the land as an invitee, licensee, or trespasser. The person's status on the land defines the nature of the duty owed by the landowner to the visitor. Accordingly, the first step in resolving a premises liability case is to determine the plaintiff's visitor status. Our supreme court has expressly held that social guests are invitees. Legear was a social guest, [and therefore an] invitee, on the Trainis' houseboat at the time of her death.

A landowner owes the highest duty of care to an invitee; that is the duty to exercise reasonable care for his protection while he is on the landowner's property. Our supreme court has adopted the . . . definition of this duty [set forth in the *Restatement (Second) of Torts*]:

A possessor of land is subject to liability for physical harm caused to his invitees by a condition on the land if, but only if, he

(a) knows or by the exercise of reasonable care would discover the condition, and should realize that it involves an unreasonable risk of harm to such invitees, and
(b) should expect that they will not discover or realize the danger, or will fail to protect themselves against it, and
(c) fails to exercise reasonable care to protect them against the danger.

The duty of reasonable care extends not only to harm caused by a condition on the land but also to activities being conducted on the land. Where, as here, a duty of care exists, the determination of whether a breach of duty occurred is a factual question which requires an evaluation of the landowner's conduct with respect to the requisite standard of care. [I]f the facts are in dispute, or if reasonable [persons] may draw different conclusions from undisputed facts, the question of negligence is one for the jury.

"[W]hile landowners are not to be made the insurers of their invitees' safety, landowners do have a duty to take reasonable precautions to protect their invitees from foreseeable criminal attacks." *Delta Tau Delta v. Johnson,* 712 N.E.2d 968, 971 (Ind. Sup. Ct. 1999). To determine whether a criminal act was foreseeable such that a landowner owed a duty to take reasonable care to protect an invitee from the act, we implement a totality of the circumstances test. Here, Michael invited several people, including Legear, on board his parents' houseboat, and questions of fact exist regarding whether he provided alcohol and marijuana to his guests. It is undisputed, however, that Michael witnessed Legear consume alcohol on the Trainis' boat before she drowned. And Marling testified that Michael and Legear, along with the others, smoked marijuana together on the boat. Given the danger inherent in the use of alcohol and drugs aboard a boat on a reservoir, we cannot say, as a matter of law, that it was not reasonably foreseeable that one of Michael's teenaged guests would become impaired and drown. Moreover, under the circumstances, it was reasonably foreseeable that teenagers under the influence of drugs or alcohol would engage in horseplay [of the sort that] occurred when Marling gave Legear a "slight push" into the water.

Marling testified that he observed Legear consume anywhere from six to eight alcoholic beverages and smoke one or two joints on the Trainis' boat that afternoon, that everybody on board was smoking marijuana, and that he "thought" everybody was drinking alcohol. Given this evidence, we cannot say that Michael did not have a duty to ask Legear and the others to leave his parents' boat or, in the alternative, to attempt to prevent the consumption of alcohol and marijuana aboard the boat. Whether Michael exercised the requisite degree of care for Legear's safety under the circumstances is a question for a trier of fact. [T]he trial court erred when it found, as a matter of law, that Michael did not breach any duty to Legear.

Negligence Claim Against the Trainis

A determination of the Trainis' liability to Harris is, however, another matter, since they were not present at the time of Legear's death. As a general rule, the common law does not hold a parent liable for the tortious acts of her minor children. However, a child's negligence may be imputed to his parent where the parent entrusts the child with an instrumentality [that], because of the child's lack of age, judgment, or experience, may become a source of danger to others.

The Trainis gave their minor son permission to have friends aboard their houseboat. Despite Michael's history of drug abuse, and despite the known presence of alcohol on the premises, the Trainis did not supervise Michael's use of the boat [on the day in question]. Michael and his friends were using alcohol and marijuana on the Trainis' houseboat that day. Given this evidence, a jury could reasonably conclude that Michael lacked the judgment necessary to keep the houseboat from being a source of danger to invitees. Also, in light of the evidence that Anderson observed a cooler containing alcohol on deck every time he visited the

boat, a reasonable inference could be made that the Trainis knew or should have known that Michael and his friends frequently consumed alcohol on board. We conclude that questions of fact exist regarding whether Michael's negligence is imputable to the Trainis pursuant to the dangerous instrumentality exception.

Negligence Claim Against Quakertown

Harris . . . maintains that Legear was Quakertown's invitee and that questions of fact exist regarding whether Quakertown breached the duty of care owed to Legear. We cannot agree.

[Control of the relevant premises is a key consideration in negligence cases of the premises liability variety.] "Only the party who controls the land can remedy the hazardous conditions which exist upon it and only the party who controls the land has the right to prevent others from coming onto it. Thus, the party in control of the land has the exclusive ability to prevent injury from occurring." *City of Bloomington v. Kuruzovich,* 517 N.E.2d 408, 411 (Ind. App. 1987). Harris has not demonstrated that Quakertown had any control over the Trainis' houseboat at the time of Legear's death. Accordingly, the trial court did not err when it found that Quakertown did not owe Legear a duty of reasonable care once she boarded the Trainis' houseboat.

Quakertown owed [passengers on its shuttle] a duty to transport them safely to and from boats moored on Brookville Reservoir. Quakertown also had a policy prohibiting minors from transporting alcohol to boats using their shuttle service. Here, Anderson was of legal age to purchase and drink alcoholic beverages, and there is no evidence that anyone other than Anderson carried alcohol aboard the Quakertown shuttle on the date of Legear's death. [W]e conclude that, as a matter of law, Quakertown did not breach any duty of care owed to Legear.

Trial court's judgment affirmed in part and reversed in part, and case remanded for trial of claims against Michael and the Trainis.

Negligence Per Se Courts sometimes use statutes, ordinances, and administrative regulations to determine how a reasonable person would behave. Under the doctrine of **negligence per se,** the defendant's violation of such laws may create a breach of duty and may allow the plaintiff to win the case if the plaintiff (1) was within the class of persons intended to be protected by the statute or other law, and (2) suffered harm of a sort that the statute or other law was intended to protect against. In the following *Carman* case, the plaintiff lost his negligence per se claim because he was not within the class of persons to be protected by the safety regulation at issue in the case.

Carman v. Dunaway Timber Co. *949 S.W.2d 569 (Ky. Sup. Ct. 1997)*

Louis Carman, a logger, delivered some logs to the Dunaway Timber Company. The logs were secured by three chains fastened to Carman's truck by chain binders. It was Dunaway's policy for all loggers to unchain their own loads before it would accept the logs. Once the logs were unchained, Dunaway would unload them with a front-end loader. Pursuant to this policy, Carman proceeded to remove the binders and unchain the logs once he arrived at Dunaway's place of business. During this process, a log fell from the truck and injured Carman, requiring that his leg be amputated below the knee.

Carman sued Dunaway for negligence. His claim was based on a regulation promulgated pursuant to the Kentucky Occupational Safety and Health Act. The regulation said: "Binders on logs shall not be released prior to securing with unloading lines or other unloading device." Carman argued that Dunaway could have complied with this regulation by using a front-end loader to brace the load while the logs were being unchained. After a jury trial, the trial court awarded judgment to Dunaway, and an intermediate appellate court affirmed this decision. Carman appealed to the Kentucky Supreme Court.

Cooper, Justice Under proper circumstances, violations of administrative regulations constitute negligence per se. However, in order for a violation to become negligence per se, the plaintiff must be a member of the class of persons intended to be protected by the regulation, and the injury suffered must be an event which the regulation was designed to prevent. If both questions are answered in the affirmative, negligence per se is established and the applicable regulation defines the relevant standard of care. Here, although the accident was an event which the regulation was designed to prevent, Carman was not a member of the class of persons intended to be protected.

The purpose of the Kentucky Occupational Safety and Health Act is the prevention of "any detriment to the safety and health of all employees, both public and private, covered by this chapter." Each employer [must] "furnish to each of his employees employment and a place of employment which are free from recognized haz-

ards that are causing or are likely to cause death or serious physical harm to his employees." An "employee" [is] "any person employed." An "employer" [is] "any entity for whom a person is employed." Carman was not an employee, and certainly not Dunaway's employee; thus, he was not within the class of persons the regulations were designed to protect.

Since this is not a case in which the standard of care is supplied by the regulations, the duty owed to Carman by Dunaway must be defined by common law, i.e., that degree of care exercised by reasonable and prudent timber companies toward persons who sell and deliver logs to their places of business. The trial judge correctly permitted Dunaway to introduce evidence of custom within the industry to prove this standard of care. Carman was permitted to produce the regulation as evidence to the contrary.

Judgment in Dunaway's favor affirmed.

Causation of Injury

Proof that the defendant breached a duty does not guarantee that the plaintiff will win a negligence case. The plaintiff must also prove that the defendant's breach caused her to experience injury. We shall look briefly at the injury component of this *causation of injury* requirement before examining the necessary causation link in greater depth.

Types of Injury and Damages *Personal injury*—also called "physical" or "bodily" injury—is harm to the plaintiff's body. It is the type of injury present in many negligence cases. Plaintiffs who experienced personal injury and have proven all elements of a negligence claim are entitled to recover compensatory

damages. These damages may include not only amounts for losses such as medical expenses or lost wages but also sums for pain and suffering. Although the nature of the harm may make it difficult to assign a dollar value to pain and suffering, we ask judges and juries to determine the dollar value anyway. The rationale is that the plaintiff's pain and suffering is a distinct harm resulting from the defendant's failure to use reasonable care, and that merely totaling up the amounts of the plaintiff's medical bills and lost wages would not compensate the plaintiff for the full effects of the defendant's wrongful behavior.

Property damage—harm to the plaintiff's real estate or a personal property item such as a car—is another recognized type of injury for which compensatory damages are recoverable in negligence litigation. In other negligence cases, many of which arise in business or professional contexts, no personal injury or property damage is involved. Instead, the plaintiff's injury may take the form of *economic loss* such as out-of-pocket expenses, lost profits, or similar financial harms that resulted from the defendant's breach of duty but have no connection to personal injury or property damages. Compensatory damages are available, of course, for losses of this nature.

Whatever the type of injury experienced by the plaintiff, the usual rule is that only compensatory damages are recoverable in a negligence case. As noted in Chapter 6, punitive damages tend to be reserved for cases involving flagrant wrongdoing. Negligence amounts to wrongdoing, but not of the more reprehensible sort typically necessary to trigger an assessment of punitive damages.

What if the plaintiff's claimed injury is *emotional* in nature? As you learned in Chapter 6, the law has long been reluctant to afford recovery for purely emotional harms. Until fairly recently, most courts would not allow a plaintiff to recover for emotional injuries resulting from a defendant's negligence without some impact on or contact with the plaintiff's person. Many courts have now abandoned this "impact rule" and allow recovery for foreseeable emotional injuries standing alone. Many such courts, however, still require proof that physical injury or symptoms resulted from the plaintiff's emotional distress. Other courts have dispensed with the injury requirement where the plaintiff has suffered serious emotional distress as a foreseeable consequence of the defendant's negligent conduct.

Hagan v. Coca-Cola Bottling Co., a Chapter 1 case dealing with case law reasoning, addresses issues that arise in negligent infliction of emotional distress litigation.

The Causation Link Even if the defendant has breached a duty and the plaintiff has suffered actual injury, there is no liability for negligence without the necessary causation link between breach and injury. The causation question involves three issues: (1) Was the breach an *actual cause* of the injury? (2) Was the breach a *proximate cause* of the injury? and (3) What was the effect of any *intervening* cause arising after the breach and helping to cause the injury? Both actual and proximate cause are necessary for a negligence recovery. Special rules dealing with intervening causes sometimes apply, depending on the facts of the case.

Actual Cause Suppose that Dullard drove his car at an excessive speed on a crowded street and was therefore unable to stop the car in time to avoid striking and injuring Pence, who had lawfully entered the crosswalk. Dullard's conduct, being inconsistent with the behavior of a reasonable driver, was a breach of duty that served as the actual cause of Pence's injuries. To determine the existence of actual cause, courts often employ a "but for" test. This test provides that the defendant's conduct is the actual cause of the plaintiff's injury when the plaintiff would not have been hurt but for (i.e., if not for) the defendant's breach of duty. In the example employed above, Pence clearly would not have been injured if not for Dullard's duty-breaching conduct.

In some cases, however, a person's negligent conduct may combine with another person's negligent conduct to cause a plaintiff's injury. Suppose that fires negligently started by Dustin and Dibble combine to burn down Potter's house. If each fire would have destroyed Potter's house on its own, the but-for test could absolve both Dustin and Dibble. In such cases, courts apply a different test by asking whether each defendant's conduct was a *substantial factor* in bringing about the plaintiff's injury. Under this test, both Dustin and Dibble are likely to be liable for Potter's loss.

Proximate Cause The plaintiff who proves actual cause has not yet established the causation link necessary to enable her to win the case. She must also establish the existence of proximate cause—a task that sometimes, though clearly not always, is more difficult than proving actual cause.

Questions of proximate cause assume the existence of actual cause. Proximate cause concerns arise because it may sometimes seem unfair to hold a defendant liable for all the injuries actually caused by his breach—no matter how remote, bizarre, or unforeseeable they are. Thus, courts typically say that a negligent defendant is liable only for the *proximate* results of his breach. Proximate cause, then, concerns the required degree of proximity or closeness between the defendant's breach and the injury it actually caused.

Courts have not reached complete agreement on the appropriate test for resolving the proximate cause question. In reality, the question is one of social policy. When deciding which test to adopt, courts must recognize that negligent defendants may be exposed to catastrophic liability by a lenient test for proximate cause, but that a restrictive test prevents some innocent victims from recovering damages for their losses. Courts have responded in various ways to this difficult question.

A significant number of courts have adopted a test under which a defendant who has breached a duty of care is liable only for the "natural and probable consequences" of his actions. In many negligence cases, the injuries actually caused by the defendant's breach would easily qualify as natural and probable consequences because they are the sorts of harms that are both likely and logical effects of such a breach. The Dullard–Pence scenario discussed earlier would be an example. It is to be expected that a pedestrian struck by a car would sustain personal injury.

In other negligence cases, however, either the fact that the plaintiff was injured or the nature of his harms may seem unusual or in some sense remote from the defendant's breach, despite the existence of an actual causation link. The presence or absence of proximate cause becomes a more seriously contested issue in a case of that nature. A great deal will depend upon how narrowly or broadly the court defines the scope of what is natural and probable.

Other courts have limited a breaching defendant's liability for unforeseeable harms by stating that he is liable only to plaintiffs who were within the "scope of the foreseeable risk." Although this test is often characterized as

a proximate cause rule, it is actually a rule dealing with the *duty* element, because courts adopting this rule hold that a defendant owes no duty to those who are not foreseeable "victims" of his actions. The *Restatement (Second) of Torts* takes yet another approach to the proximate cause question. It suggests that a defendant's breach of duty is not the legal (i.e., proximate) cause of a plaintiff's injury if, looking back after the harm, it appears "highly extraordinary" to the court that the breach would have brought about the injury.

A further perspective on the proximate cause issue is provided by decisions such as *Interim Personnel,* a negligent hiring case in which the court held that proximate cause was lacking because the injury sustained by the plaintiff was not a foreseeable consequence of the defendant's breach. Under this approach, courts first find or assume the existence of a duty and a breach of duty, and then ask whether, given the nature of the breach, the injury was foreseeable. Read *Interim Personnel* and decide whether you agree with the court's analysis.

Interim Personnel of Central Virginia, Inc. v. Messer
559 S.E.2d 704 (Va. Sup. Ct. 2002)

Ricky Edward East, an intoxicated driver operating a stolen pickup truck, caused a motor vehicle accident near Charlottesville, Virginia, on the day after Thanksgiving 1998. The truck that East negligently operated struck the rear of a stopped vehicle, which in turn struck the rear of a stopped vehicle operated by Mildred Messer. Messer, who was injured as a result, filed the negligence lawsuit described later in this statement of facts.

The Alumni Association of the University of Virginia (Association) owned the truck that East was driving when the collision occurred. At the time, East was employed by Interim Personnel of Central Virginia, Inc. (Interim), a firm that provided temporary employees to businesses and other organizations. He was assigned to the Association as a "part-time building assistant" at the university's alumni building. The duties of this three-hours-per-day position included helping with mail processing and packaging and driving to and from the post office, which was located less than a mile away from the alumni building. According to the job description for the Association position held by East, "a valid Virginia driver's license" was required. At all times relevant to the case described below, however, East did not have a valid driver's license.

East's driver's license had been suspended since 1995, as a result of his two criminal convictions for driving under the influence of intoxicants (DUI). East neither paid the fines assessed for these convictions nor attended court-ordered alcohol counseling sessions. In January 1996, Virginia's Department of Motor Vehicles declared East to be a habitual traffic offender.

In December 1996, when East applied to work for Interim, he falsely stated that he possessed a driver's license. Interim personnel interviewed East, had him perform certain skills tests, and did some checking of his references. Interim then hired East and assigned him to various employers during the succeeding months. East later left Interim's employ but returned to work for the firm in September 1998. At that time, he completed another application form on which he falsely stated that he possessed a driver's license and wrote "child support!" as his response to this question: "Have you ever been convicted of a felony, misdemeanor or any offense other than a minor traffic violation?" During the time period referred to above, Interim did not perform criminal background checks on applicants and did not require that applicants physically produce a valid driver's license. Neither did Interim request a copy of East's driving record from the Department of Motor Vehicles.

In March 1998, an Association official contacted Interim to discuss filling the part-time building assistant position. The Association official presented Interim with the position's job description. In September 1998, the Association official asked

Interim to send an employee who met the job qualifications. Interim's sales manager informed the Association that East was qualified and stated that East "had a good driving record." Interim had found East to be a good employee who had not been involved "in any type of accidents," had never "shown up drunk on the job," and had generated no complaints "from any employer about his activities while working."

Interim sent East to be interviewed by the Association official during the latter part of September 1998. Under its arrangement with Interim, the Association had the right to accept or reject East. During the interview, the Association official handed East a copy of the job description, which required "a valid Virginia driver's license." East said that he could perform the job duties. Relying on Interim to verify that East was a licensed driver, the Association official did not ask East to produce a driver's license. No one at the Association asked East whether he possessed a valid driver's license.

The Association accepted East and found him to be an "excellent employee" during the two months preceding the November 1998 vehicle theft and resulting traffic accident. The job duties performed by East included driving to and from the post office. On the Wednesday of Thanksgiving week, East was told to keep a key to the alumni building because his supervisor was on vacation. He was instructed to lock the building before the Thanksgiving break (which consisted of Thursday and Friday) and to reopen it on the Saturday after Thanksgiving.

Because he had access to the building, East was able to procure a key to the truck he routinely operated. East took the truck without permission on the day before Thanksgiving and traveled to Richmond, Virginia. He returned to his Charlottesville home on Friday, when he began drinking beer and riding around in the truck. During the day, he consumed approximately eight quarts of beer. While intoxicated, he caused the collision in which Messer was injured.

Messer filed a negligence lawsuit against East, Interim, and the Association in an effort to collect damages for the injuries she sustained in the collision. Negligent hiring was the specific theory she employed with regard to Interim and the Association. After hearing the evidence and receiving legal instructions from the trial judge on proximate cause, foreseeability, and other negligence principles, the jury returned a verdict in favor of Messer and against all of the defendants. The defendants were held liable for $100,000 in compensatory damages. In addition, East was held liable for $25,000 in punitive damages. When the trial judge denied their motions to set aside the verdict, Interim and the Association (though not East) appealed to the Supreme Court of Virginia.

Compton, Senior Justice [T]he cause of action for negligent hiring "is based on the principle that one who conducts an activity through employees is subject to liability for harm resulting from the employer's conduct if the employer is negligent in the hiring of an improper person in work involving an unreasonable risk of harm to others." *Southeast Apartments Management v. Jackman,* 513 S.E.2d 395, 397 (Va. Sup. Ct. 1999). Liability for negligent hiring is [premised] upon an employer's failure to exercise reasonable care in placing an individual with known propensities, or propensities that should have been discovered by reasonable investigation, in an employment position in which . . . it should have been foreseeable that the hired individual posed a threat of injury to others. Mere proof of the failure to investigate a potential employee's background is not sufficient to establish an employer's liability for negligent hiring.

The tort of negligent hiring is distinct from tort liability predicated upon the doctrine of *respondeat superior.* Under the latter, an employer is vicariously liable for an employee's acts committed within the scope of employment. In contrast, the tort of negligent hiring is a doctrine of primary liability; the employer is principally liable for placing an un-

fit individual in an employment situation that involves an unreasonable risk of harm to others. Negligent hiring enables a plaintiff to recover in circumstances when *respondeat superior*'s "scope of employment" limitation protects employers from liability.

Messer contends that East had a known propensity for driving while intoxicated, or that this propensity should have been discovered by Interim and the Association had they performed a reasonable investigation. [According to Messer,] "there were facts that should have put Interim on notice that sending East to [the Association] might reasonably be a threat to the public." Messer also contends that the Association's claim of reliance on Interim "ignores the evidence of [the Association's] active negligence in giving East the job." She says the Association "failed to conduct the most basic of investigations [and failed to require] proof [that] East met the job requirement."

Additionally, Messer argues that Interim and the Association "placed East in an employment position in which, because of the circumstances of the employment, it should have been reasonably foreseeable that East posed a threat of injury to others." According to the plaintiff, it was foreseeable from Interim's standpoint that the Association would hire East, that he would drive for the Association, that he would have access to a vehicle, that he would take the vehicle, that he would drink and drive, and that he would injure someone while driving drunk. Messer also argues that from the Association's standpoint, "East was expected to drive a pickup truck as part of his job. He posed a risk to the motoring public every time he left Alumni Hall to go to the post office. He posed a special risk to the public when he was left in control of Alumni Hall over the Thanksgiving weekend, and [the Association] knew it."

We do not agree with Messer's contentions. The evidence is clear that neither Interim nor the Association had actual knowledge of East's propensities for operating a motor vehicle without a valid operator's license, for failing to obey court orders to pay fines and to attend counseling, and for driving while intoxicated. He intentionally concealed those facts from them.

The question then becomes whether those defendants should have discovered these propensities by reasonable investigation, given the fact that the position to be filled only required a three-hour daily commitment in which clerical and light labor duties were to be performed [and] incidentally requir[ed] driving only a short distance to and from a post office. For the purpose of this discussion, however, we will assume, but not decide, that both Interim and the Association should have discovered East's propensities in the exercise of reasonable care. Nevertheless, we hold that the plaintiff failed, as a matter of law, to establish that, because of the circumstances of the employment, it should have been foreseeable that East posed a threat of injury to others.

Generally, in order to warrant a finding that negligence is the proximate cause of an injury, it must appear that the injury was the natural and probable consequence of the negligent or wrongful act, and that the injury should have been foreseen in the light of the attending circumstances. Negligence carries with it liability for consequences that, in view of the circumstances, could reasonably have been anticipated by a prudent person, but not for casualties which, though possible, were wholly improbable. A party is not charged with foreseeing that which could not be expected to happen. However, the precise injury need not be foreseen by a defendant. It is sufficient that an ordinary prudent person ought, under the circumstances, to have foreseen that an injury might probably (not possibly) result from the negligent act.

[T]he mere fact that East had been convicted twice of DUI, had failed to pay fines or attend counseling, and had been declared a habitual offender, would not place a reasonable employer on notice or make it foreseeable that East would steal a truck, operate the stolen vehicle during non-business hours for his own frolic, and cause an accident on the open highway distant from the environs of his job. According to the uncontradicted evidence, East's employment history showed he had been a model employee, never had consumed alcohol at work or reported for work intoxicated, never had been in any motor vehicle accidents, never had taken any item from any employer without permission, and had no record of theft. In sum, it was not Interim's placement of East, or his subsequent acceptance for work at the Association, which was a proximate cause of the plaintiff's injuries.

Consequently, we conclude that the trial court erred in ruling that foreseeability was a jury issue, and in refusing to sustain Interim's and the Association's respective motions to set the verdict aside. Thus, that portion of the [trial court's] order entering judgment in favor of the plaintiff against Interim and the Association will be vacated, and final judgment will be entered here in favor of those defendants.

Judgment against Interim and the Association reversed.

Later Acts, Forces, or Events   In some cases, an act, force, or event occurring *after* a defendant's breach of duty may play a significant role in bringing about or worsening the plaintiff's injury. For example, suppose that after Davis sets a fire, a high wind comes up and spreads the fire to Parker's home, or that after Davis negligently runs Parker down with his car, a thief steals Parker's wallet while he lies unconscious. If the later act, force, or event was *foreseeable,* it will not relieve the defendant of liability. So, if high winds are an occurrence that may reasonably be expected from time to time in the locality, Davis is liable for the damage to Parker's home even though his fire might not have spread that far under the wind conditions that existed when he started it. In the second example, Davis is liable not only for Parker's physical injuries but also for the theft of Parker's wallet if the theft was foreseeable, given the time and location of the accident. (The thief, of course, would also be liable for the theft.)

Intervening Causes   On the other hand, if the later act, force, on event that contributes to the plaintiff's injury was *unforeseeable,* most courts hold that it is an intervening cause, which absolves the defendant of liability for harms that resulted directly from the intervening cause. For example, Dalton negligently starts a fire that causes injury to several persons. The driver of an ambulance summoned to the scene has been drinking on duty and, as a result, loses control of his ambulance and runs up onto a sidewalk, injuring several pedestrians. Given the nature of the ambulance driver's position, his drinking while on duty is likely to make the ambulance crash an unforeseeable event and thus an intervening cause. Most courts, therefore, would not hold Dalton responsible for the pedestrians' injuries. The ambulance driver, of course, would be liable to those he injured.

An important exception to the liability-absolving effect of an intervening cause deals with unforeseeable later events that produce a foreseeable harm identical to the harm risked by the defendant's breach of duty. Why should the defendant escape liability on the basis that an easily foreseeable consequence of its conduct came about through unforeseeable means? For example, if the owners of a concert hall negligently fail to install the number of emergency exits required by law, the owners will not escape liability to those burned and trampled during a fire just because the fire was caused by an insane concert-goer who set himself ablaze.

As suggested by some of the examples used above, when a defendant's breach of duty is followed by a third party's criminal or other wrongful act, the later act may be either foreseeable or unforeseeable, depending on the facts and circumstances. This state of affairs reflects the prevailing modern approach, which differs sharply from the traditional view that third parties' criminal acts were unforeseeable as a matter of law and thus were always intervening causes serving to limit or eliminate the original defendant's negligence liability. Today, courts do not hesitate to classify a third party's criminal act as foreseeable if the time and place of its commission and other relevant facts point to such a conclusion.

Assume, for instance, that XYZ, Inc. owns an apartment complex at which break-ins and prior instances of criminal activity had occurred. XYZ nevertheless fails to adopt the security-related measures that a reasonable apartment complex owner would adopt. As a result, a criminal intruder easily enters the complex. He then physically attacks a tenant. Because the intruder's act is likely to be seen as foreseeable—and thus not an intervening cause—XYZ faces negligence liability to the tenant for the injuries that the intruder directly inflicted on the tenant. (The intruder, of course, would face both criminal and civil liability for battery, but if his financial assets are limited, the injured tenant may find collecting a damages award from him either difficult or impossible.) Note that for purposes of the tenant's negligence claim, XYZ's breach of duty was a substantial factor in bringing about the plaintiff's injuries because the lack of reasonable security measures allowed the intruder to gain easy access to the premises. XYZ's

breach thus would be considered the *actual cause* of the tenant's injuries under the previously discussed substantial factor test. It would also be considered the proximate cause under the various tests described earlier.

Special Rules Whatever test for proximate cause a court adopts, most courts agree on certain basic causation rules. In case of a conflict, these rules supersede the proximate cause and intervening cause rules stated earlier. One such rule is that persons who are negligent "take their victims as they find them." This means that a negligent defendant is liable for the full extent of her victim's injuries if those injuries are aggravated by some preexisting physical susceptibility of the victim— even though this susceptibility could not have been foreseen. Similarly, negligent defendants normally are liable for diseases contracted by their victims while in a weakened state caused by their injuries. Negligent defendants typically are jointly liable—along with the attending physician—for negligent medical care that their victims receive for their injuries.

Res Ipsa Loquitur

In some cases, negligence may be difficult to prove because the defendant has superior knowledge of the circumstances surrounding the plaintiff's injury. It may not be in the defendant's best interests to disclose those circumstances if they point to liability on his part. The classic example is an 1863 case, *Byrne v. Boadle*. The plaintiff was a pedestrian who had been hit on the head by a barrel of flour that fell from a warehouse owned by the defendant. The plaintiff had no way of knowing what caused the barrel to fall; he merely knew he had been injured. The only people likely to have known the relevant facts were the owners of the warehouse and their employees, but they most likely were the ones responsible for the accident. After observing that "[a] barrel could not roll out of a warehouse without some negligence," the court required the defendant owner to show that he was not at fault.

Byrne v. Boadle eventually led to the doctrine of *res ipsa loquitur* ("the thing speaks for itself "). *Res ipsa* applies when: (1) the defendant has exclusive control of the instrumentality of harm (and therefore probable knowledge of, and responsibility for, the cause of the harm); (2) the harm that occurred would not ordinarily occur in the absence of negligence; and (3) the plaintiff was in no way responsible for his own injury. Most courts hold that when these three elements are satisfied, a presumption of breach of duty and causation arises. The defendant then runs a significant risk of losing the case if he does not produce evidence to rebut this presumption.

CYBERLAW IN ACTION

Cyberlaw in Action boxes in Chapters 1 and 6 addressed the effect of §230 of the federal Communications Decency Act (CDA) on certain defamation and injurious falsehood claims. As *Gentry v. eBay, Inc.,* 99 Cal. App. 4th 816 (2002) reveals, §230 may also apply to certain negligence claims.

Gentry was a case brought by buyers of sports memorabilia that bore autographs later determined not to be genuine. The plaintiffs contended that eBay, an online marketplace on which the items were sold, should bear legal responsibility on various legal grounds, including negligence. According to the plaintiffs, eBay had been negligent: (1) by maintaining an online forum that allowed any user, regardless of his or her purchase history, to give positive or negative feedback regarding dealers; and (2) by endorsing certain dealers on the basis of this feedback and the dealers' sales volume. The plaintiffs contended that these actions by eBay created a false sense of confidence in the collectibles' authenticity because most, if not all, of the positive feedback about a dealer would be generated either by that dealer or by another cooperating dealer.

A California appellate court held in *Gentry* that §230 of the CDA provided eBay a meritorious defense against the plaintiffs' negligence claim. Section 230 states that "[n]o provider or user of an interactive computer service shall be treated as the publisher or speaker of any information provided by another information content provider." The court reasoned that eBay was a "provider . . . of an interactive computer service" and that the plaintiffs' negligence claim amounted, in substance, to an attempt to have eBay held liable for the effects of statements made by "another *information content provider*" or providers (i.e., those who, in the online forum, posted arguably misleading "feedback"). The court therefore regarded the plaintiffs' negligence claim as an effort to have eBay treated as the "publisher" of information provided by another party. Section 230, the court held, prohibited such treatment of eBay.

Negligence Defenses

The common law traditionally recognized two defenses to negligence: **contributory negligence** and **assumption of risk.** In many states, however, one or both of these traditional defenses has been superseded by new defenses called **comparative negligence** and **comparative fault.**

Contributory Negligence Contributory negligence is the plaintiff's failure to exercise reasonable care for her own safety. Where it still applies, contributory negligence is a complete defense for the defendant if it was a substantial factor in producing the plaintiff's injury. So, if Preston steps into the path of Doyle's speeding car without first checking to see whether any cars are coming, Preston would be denied any recovery against Doyle, in view of the clear causal relationship between Preston's injury and his failure to exercise reasonable care for his own safety.

Comparative Negligence Traditionally, even a minor failure to exercise reasonable care for one's own safety—only a slight departure from the standard of reasonable self-protectiveness—gave the defendant a complete contributory negligence defense. This rule, which probably stemmed from the 19th-century desire to protect railroads and infant manufacturing interests from negligence liability, came under increasing attack in the 20th century. The main reasons were the traditional rule's harsh impact on many plaintiffs. The rule frequently prevented slightly negligent plaintiffs from recovering any compensation for their losses, even though the defendants may have been much more at fault.

In response to such complaints, all but a few states have adopted **comparative negligence** systems either by statute or by judicial decision. The details of these systems vary, but the principle underlying them is essentially the same: courts seek to determine the relative negligence of the parties and award damages in proportion to the degrees of negligence determined. The formula is:

$$\text{Plaintiff's recovery} = \text{Defendant's percentage share of the negligence causing the injury} \times \text{Plaintiff's proven damages}$$

For example, assume that Dunne negligently injures Porter and that Porter suffers $100,000 in damages. A jury determines that Dunne was 80 percent at fault and Porter 20 percent at fault. Under comparative negligence, Porter would recover $80,000 from Dunne. What if Dunne's share of the negligence is determined to be 40 percent and Porter's 60 percent? Here, the results vary depending on whether the state in question has adopted a *pure* or a *mixed* comparative negligence system. Under a pure system, courts apply the preceding formula regardless of the plaintiff's and the defendant's percentage shares of the negligence. Porter therefore would recover $40,000 in a pure comparative negligence state. Under a mixed system, the formula operates only when the defendant's share of the negligence is greater than (or, in some states, greater than or equal to) 50 percent. If the plaintiff's share of the negligence exceeds 50 percent, mixed systems provide that the defendant has a complete defense against liability. In such states, therefore, Porter would lose the case.

Assumption of Risk Assumption of risk is the plaintiff's *voluntary* consent to a *known* danger. Voluntariness means that the plaintiff accepted the risk of her own free will; knowledge means that the plaintiff was aware of the nature and extent of the risk. Often, the plaintiff's knowledge and voluntariness are inferred from the facts. This type of assumption of risk is sometimes called **implied** assumption of risk. For example, Pilson voluntarily goes for a ride in Dudley's car, even though Dudley has told Pilson that her car's brakes frequently fail. Pilson probably has assumed the risk of injury from the car's defective brakes.

A plaintiff can also **expressly** assume the risk of injury by entering into a contract that purports to relieve the

defendant of a duty of care he would otherwise owe to the plaintiff. Such contract provisions are called *exculpatory clauses*. Chapter 15 discusses exculpatory clauses and the limitations that courts have imposed on their enforceability. The most important such limitations are that the plaintiff have knowledge of the exculpatory clause (which often boils down to a question of its conspicuousness), and that the plaintiff must accept it voluntarily (which does not happen when the defendant has greatly superior bargaining power).

What happens to assumption of risk in comparative negligence states? Some of these states maintain assumption of risk as a separate and complete defense. Many other states now incorporate implied assumption of risk within the state's comparative negligence scheme. In such states, comparative negligence basically becomes **comparative fault.** Although the terms comparative negligence and comparative fault often are used interchangeably, technically the former involves only negligence and the latter involves all kinds of fault. In a comparative fault state, therefore, the factfinder determines the plaintiff's and the defendant's relative shares of the fault—including assumption of risk—that caused the plaintiff's injury.

In the *Davenport* case, which follows, the court made implied assumption of risk part of the state's mixed comparative negligence scheme (effectively making it comparative fault). Note, however, that this was not true for express assumption of risk.

Davenport v. Cotton Hope Plantation   *508 S.E.2d 565 (S.C. Sup. Ct. 1998)*

Alvin Davenport, who leased a condominium at the Cotton Hope Plantation on Hilton Head Island, South Carolina, complained to Cotton Hope that the floodlights at the bottom of the stairway to his unit were not working. Before Cotton Hope got around to fixing the floodlights, Davenport was injured when he tried to descend the stairway one night. Specifically, he fell after attempting to place his foot on what appeared to be a step but actually was a shadow caused by the inoperative floodlight.

Davenport sued Cotton Hope in negligence in a South Carolina trial court. The trial court directed a verdict against him because he had assumed the risk of his injury, and, in the alternative, because he was more than 50 percent at fault in causing the injury. After Davenport appealed, the intermediate appellate court reversed, holding that under South Carolina's comparative negligence system, assumption of risk no longer was an independent defense, that it instead was just a factor to be considered in determining the parties' relative fault, and that that issue should have gone to the jury. Cotton Hope appealed to the South Carolina Supreme Court.

Toal, Judge A threshold question is whether assumption of risk survives as a complete bar to recovery under South Carolina's comparative negligence system. In 1991, we adopted a modified version of comparative negligence. Under this system, a plaintiff in a negligence action may recover damages if his or her negligence is not greater than

that of the defendant. Not so clear was what would become of assumption of risk.

An overwhelming majority of jurisdictions that have adopted some form of comparative negligence have abolished assumption of risk as an absolute bar to recovery. In analyzing the continuing viability of assumption of risk in a comparative negligence system, many courts distinguish between express assumption of risk and implied assumption of risk. Express assumption of risk applies when the parties expressly agree in advance, either in writing or orally, that the plaintiff will relieve the defendant of his or her legal duty toward the plaintiff. Even in those comparative fault jurisdictions that have abrogated assumption of risk, the rule remains that express assumption of risk continues as an absolute defense in an action for negligence. The reason is that express assumption of risk sounds in contract, not tort, and is based upon an express manifestation of consent. Implied assumption of risk arises when the plaintiff implicitly, rather than expressly, assumes known risks.

It is contrary to the basic premise of our fault system to allow a defendant, who is at fault in causing an accident, to escape bearing any of its cost, while requiring a plaintiff, who is no more than equally at fault, to bear all of its costs. The defendant's fault is not diminished solely because the plaintiff knowingly assumes a risk. In our comparative fault system, it would be incongruous to absolve the defendant of all liability based only on whether the plaintiff assumed the risk of injury. Comparative negligence seeks to assess and compare the negligence of both the plaintiff and the defendant. This goal would clearly be thwarted by adhering to the common law defense of assumption of risk. Our conclusion that the absolute defense of assumption of risk is inconsistent with South Carolina's comparative negligence system is buttressed by our recent opinion in *Spahn v. Town of Port Royal* (1998), [where] we held that last clear chance had been subsumed by our adoption of comparative negligence. We therefore hold that a plaintiff is not barred from recovery by assumption of risk unless the degree of fault arising therefrom is greater than the negligence of the defendant.

Cotton Hope argues that we should affirm the trial court's ruling that, as a matter of law, Davenport was more than 50 percent negligent. The trial court based its ruling on the fact that Davenport knew of the danger weeks before his accident, and had a safe alternate route. However, there also was evidence suggesting that Cotton Hope was negligent in failing to properly maintain the lighting in the stairway. It could be reasonably concluded that Davenport's negligence in proceeding down the stairway did not exceed Cotton Hope's negligence. Thus, [that issue] is properly submitted for jury determination.

Court of Appeals decision returning the case to the trial court affirmed.

Strict Liability

Strict liability is liability without fault or, perhaps more precisely, irrespective of fault. This means that in strict liability cases, the defendant is liable even though he did not intend to cause the harm and did not bring it about through recklessness or negligence.

The imposition of strict liability is a social policy decision that the risk associated with an activity should be borne by those who pursue it, rather than by innocent persons who are exposed to that risk. Such liability is premised on the defendant's voluntary decision to engage in a particularly risky activity. When the defendant is a corporation that has engaged in such an activity, the assumption is that the firm can pass the costs of liability on to consumers in the form of higher prices for goods or services. Through strict liability, therefore, the economic costs created by certain harms are "socialized" by being transferred from the victims to defendants to society at large.

Strict liability, however, does not apply to the vast majority of activities. It therefore becomes important to consider which activities do trigger the liability-without-fault approach. The owners of trespassing livestock and the keepers of naturally dangerous wild animals were among the first classes of defendants on whom the courts imposed strict liability. Today, the two most important activities subject to judicially imposed strict liability are abnormally dangerous (or ultrahazardous) activities and the manufacture or sale of defective and unreasonably dangerous products. We discuss the latter in Chapter 20 and the former immediately below.

Abnormally Dangerous Activities

Abnormally dangerous (or ultrahazardous) activities are those necessarily involving a risk of harm that cannot be eliminated by the exercise of reasonable care. Among the activities treated as abnormally dangerous are blasting, crop dusting, stunt flying, and, in one case, the transportation of large quantities of gasoline by truck. (Most courts, however, would be unlikely to label the latter as abnormally dangerous.) Traditionally, contributory negligence has not been a defense in ultrahazardous activity cases, but assumption of risk has been a defense. The *Klein* case, which follows, discusses the numerous factors that courts consider before deciding whether a particular activity should be classified as abnormally dangerous.

Klein v. Pyrodyne Corporation   *810 P.2d 917 (Wash. Sup. Ct. 1991)*

Pyrodyne Corporation was hired to display the fireworks at the Western Washington State Fairgrounds in Puyallup, Washington, on July 4, 1987. During the display, one of the 5-inch mortars was knocked into a horizontal position, from which position a rocket inside ignited and flew 500 feet parallel to the earth, exploding near the crowd of onlookers. Danny and Marion Klein were injured by the explosion. They filed a strict liability suit against Pyrodyne. They also argued that Pyrodyne failed to carry out a number of the statutory and regulatory requirements for preparing and setting off fireworks. Pyrodyne argued that the accident was caused by a rocket detonating in its mortar tube without ever leaving the ground, causing another rocket to be knocked over, ignited, and set off horizontally. Pyrodyne moved for summary judgment on the ground that negligence principles should be applied to the case. When the trial court denied its motion and found it strictly liable, Pyrodyne appealed.

Guy, Justice The modern doctrine of strict liability for abnormally dangerous activities derives from *Rylands v. Fletcher* (Eng. 1866), in which the defendant's reservoir flooded mine shafts on the plaintiff's adjoining land. *Rylands v. Fletcher* has come to stand for the rule that the defendant will be liable when he damages another by a thing or activity unduly dangerous and inappropriate to the place where it is maintained, in the light of the character of that place and its surroundings.

The basic principle of *Rylands v. Fletcher* has been accepted by the *Restatement (Second) of Torts.* Section 519 of the *Restatement* provides that any party carrying on an "abnormally dangerous activity" is strictly liable for the ensuing damages. Section 520 of the *Restatement* lists six factors that are to be considered in determining whether an activity is "abnormally dangerous": (a) a high degree of risk of some harm to the person, land, or chattels of others; (b) the likelihood that the harm that results from it will be great; (c) an inability to eliminate the risk by the exercise of reasonable care; (d) the extent to which the activity is not a matter of common usage; (e) the inappropriateness of the activity to the place where it is carried on; and (f) the extent to which its value to the community is outweighed by its dangerous attributes. The comments to section 520 explain how these factors should be evaluated: "Any one of them is not necessarily sufficient of itself in a particular case, and ordinarily several of them will be required for strict liability. On the other hand, it is not necessary that each of them be present, especially if others weigh heavily."

We find that the factors stated in clauses (a), (b), and (c) are all present in the case of fireworks displays. Any time a person ignites rockets with the intention of sending them aloft to explode in the presence of large crowds of people, a high risk of serious personal injury or property damage is created. That risk arises because of the possibility that a rocket will malfunction or be misdirected. Furthermore, no matter how much care pyrotechnicians exercise, they cannot entirely eliminate the high risk inherent in setting off powerful explosives near crowds.

Pyrodyne argues that the factor stated in clause (d) is not met because fireworks are a common way to celebrate the 4th of July. Although fireworks are frequently and regularly enjoyed by the public, few persons set off special fireworks displays. Indeed, anyone wishing to do so must first obtain a license.

The Puyallup Fairgrounds is an appropriate place for the fireworks show because the audience can be seated at a reasonable distance from the display. Therefore, the clause (e) factor is not present in this case. The factor in clause (f) requires analysis of the extent to which the value of the fireworks to the community outweighs its dangerous attributes. This country has a longstanding tradition of fireworks on the 4th of July. That tradition suggests that we have decided that the value of fireworks on the day celebrating our national independence and unity outweighs the risks of injuries and damage.

In sum, we find that setting off public fireworks displays satisfies four of the six conditions under the *Restatement* test. We therefore hold that conducting public fireworks displays is an abnormally dangerous activity justifying the imposition of strict liability.

Judgment for the Kleins affirmed.

Statutory Strict Liability

Strict liability principles are also embodied in modern legislation. The most important examples are the workers' compensation acts passed by most states early in this century. Chapter 51 contains more detailed discussion of such statutes, which allow employees to recover statutorily limited amounts from their employers without any need to show fault on the employer's part and without any consideration of contributory fault on the employee's part. Employers participate in a compulsory liability insurance system and are expected to pass the costs of the system on to consumers, who then become the ultimate bearers of the human costs of industrial production. Other examples of statutory strict liability vary from state to state.

Tort Reform

The risk-spreading strategy of tort law has not been trouble-free. During roughly the past 20 years, there has been considerable talk about a supposed crisis in the liability insurance system. From time to time over that period, the insurance system has been marked by outright refusals of coverage, reductions in coverage, and escalating premiums when coverage remains available. To some, this intermittent liability insurance crisis is largely the fault of the insurance industry. Among other things, such observers argue that insurers have manufactured the crisis to obtain unjustified premium increases and to divert attention from insurer mismanagement of invested premium income.

To other observers, however, the reason for the crisis is an explosion in tort liability in recent years. Examples include the tendency toward somewhat greater imposition of strict liability, increases in the frequency and size of punitive damage awards, and similar increases in awards for noneconomic harms such as pain and suffering. The greater costs imposed on defendants, observers say, operate to increase the price and diminish the availability of liability insurance. In some cases, therefore, businesses may be required to self-insure or go without insurance coverage. In others, they may be able to obtain insurance—but only at a price that cannot be completely passed on to consumers. Where the costs can be fully passed on, the argument continues, they depress the economy by diminishing consumers' purchasing power, adding to inflation, or both. In addition, the argument concludes, the liability explosion impedes the development of new products and technologies that might result in huge awards for injured plaintiffs.

These beliefs have fueled a movement for tort reform. By the mid-1990s, most states had enacted some form of tort reform legislation. Such legislation typically follows one or both of two strategies: (1) limiting defendants' tort *liability* (plaintiffs' ability to obtain a judgment); and (2) limiting the *damages* plaintiffs can recover once they get a judgment. One example of the former is some states' legislation restricting the liability of social hosts or businesses for the damage caused by intoxicated people to whom they serve alcohol. The most common examples of the latter are statutory caps or other limits on recoveries for punitive damages and noneconomic harm.

The battle for tort reform has not ended, however. Proponents continue to seek additional reform measures. Tort reform opponents who lost the fight in the legislature have sometimes continued it in the courts. They have done so primarily by challenging tort reform measures on state constitutional grounds. Such challenges have succeeded in some states but have been rebuffed in others.

Problems and Problem Cases

1. In a rural county in Utah, a state-maintained public road known as Droubay Road intersected with railroad tracks that were still in use. Shortly before 9:00 one evening, a Union Pacific train struck an automobile at this railroad crossing. All four occupants of the car were killed. There was no indication that the train was negligently operated. Three signs on Droubay Road informed motorists that the railroad crossing would be encountered ahead. Nothing obstructed motorists' view of the tracks for several thousand feet. There were no flashing lights or other mechanical warning or safety devices at the crossing, however. The heirs of the accident victims sued Union Pacific, alleging negligent maintenance of the crossing. In view of these facts, did the heirs win the case?

2. A young man abducted R.M.V., age 10, from the sidewalk in front of her home and dragged her across the street to a vacant apartment at the Chalmette Apartments. He raped her, put her in the closet, told her not to leave, and disappeared. The apartment in question was described by the police officer called to the scene as "empty, filthy, dirty, and full of debris." Glass was broken from its windows and the front door was off its hinges. In the two years prior to the attack on R.M.V., Dallas police had investigated many serious crimes committed at the Chalmette Apartments complex. A Dallas City Ordinance established minimum standards for property owners, requiring them, among other things, to "keep the doors and windows of a vacant structure or vacant portion of a structure securely closed to prevent unauthorized entry." Gaile Nixon, R.M.V.'s mother, filed a negligence suit against Chalmette's owner and Mr. Property Management Company, Inc., the manager of the complex. Were the defendants correct in arguing that they owed no duty to R.M.V.?

3. Ludmila Hresil and her niece were shopping at a Sears retail store. There were few shoppers in the store at the time. Hresil spent about ten minutes in the store's women's department, where she observed no other shoppers. After Hresil's niece completed a purchase in another part of the store, the two women began to walk through the women's department. Hresil, who was pushing a shopping cart, suddenly lost her balance and struggled to avoid a fall. As she did so, her right leg struck the shopping cart and began to swell. Hresil observed a "gob" on the floor where she had slipped. Later, a Sears employee said that "it looked like someone spat on the floor, like it was phlegm." Under the reasonable person standard, did Sears breach a duty to Hresil by not cleaning up the gob? *Hint:* Assume that Hresil could prove that the gob was on the floor only for the ten minutes she spent in the women's department.

4. Richard Bianco, a carpet layer in training, was helping to install carpet on the second floor of an unfinished house. He had used the stairs throughout the day without carefully examining the staircase's wooden banister. Instead of carrying garbage bags full of carpet and padding scraps down the stairs, Bianco was throwing the bags over the banister to the floor below. While throwing one bag, the 155-pound Bianco leaned on the banister, which gave way. Bianco fell and, as a result, sustained serious injuries. Bianco later sued the house's builder, Frank Robino (who was not Bianco's employer), for negligence. The evidence showed that the banister was an ordinary wooden one, but that its dress cap, or handrail, had not been installed. Installation of the dress cap would have strengthened the banister, which was being held in place by two nails. An engineer testified that without the dress cap, the banister could support a force of 5 to 35 pounds. According to an expert witness for Bianco, a handrail

should normally be expected to support a minimum of 200 pounds. Robino had not yet installed the dress cap because he did not want the carpet installers to damage it. The evidence showed that leaving banisters unfinished at this stage of construction was not a common practice in the construction industry. A jury returned a verdict in favor of Bianco. Robino appealed, contending that Bianco's evidence failed to establish negligence. Was Robino correct?

5. Higgins and some friends went to a night baseball game at Comiskey Park in Chicago. Near the end of the game, Higgins went to the men's room. On his way back to his seat, he walked down a corridor that ran past a concession stand. As he passed the stand, the door to the front of the stand (a 4′ by 6′ sheet of plywood attached to the top of the stand and hooked to an eyelet in the ceiling when opened) fell from its open position and struck him on the head, causing permanent head and neck injuries. None of the eyewitnesses to the incident saw anyone touch either the door or the hook securing it, or do anything that might have caused the door to fall. There was, however, testimony that, just before the door fell, the crowd in the stadium was screaming and stamping, and that one "could feel the place tremble." Higgins sued the Chicago White Sox, owners of the stadium, arguing that *res ipsa loquitur* should be applied to the case. Was he right?

6. James and Barbara Hopper and their two-year-old granddaughter were staying at the Colonial Motel when David Wayne Clary, who was staying in the room directly above the Hoppers', accidentally fired a handgun. The bullet went through the floor of Clary's room and through the ceiling of the Hoppers' room. It then struck and wounded Barbara. When Clary and Jason Michael Bird had checked into the motel a number of days earlier, they were being sought by the police for a number of theft-related incidents. Each day during their stay, Bird had paid at the motel office in cash. Clary and Bird had kept the curtains drawn and had directed the motel staff not to perform any housekeeping services in the room. Instead, housekeepers were to deliver clean bath towels to Clary and Bird through their partially open door. The room was normally left unlit. Neither Clary nor Bird had displayed a handgun to motel personnel, and no motel employee had been informed that either of the men had engaged, or was suspected of, criminal activity. The Hoppers sued the motel for negligence. Did the Hoppers prevail?

7. A vehicle driven by Solomon Bomze collided with a vehicle driven by Tu Loi at an intersection in the parking

lot of a shopping mall leased and operated by New Plan Realty Trust. The accident occurred because Bomze failed to stop at the intersection. A stop sign previously placed at the crossing had been vandalized the day before the accident, and New Plan had not yet replaced it. However, the word "stop" was painted in yellow on the asphalt of the lane followed by Bomze. After the initial collision, Tu Loi left his car to check it for damage. In the meantime, Bomze's car continued in a circular fashion, struck a parked car, and then headed toward Tu Loi, eventually pinning him against his own car and causing him serious injury. Assume that New Plan breached a duty to Tu Loi by not immediately replacing the sign. But New Plan argues that it is not liable because the weird behavior of Bomze's car after the impact makes that car an unforeseeable intervening force. Is this a good argument?

8. While he was a freshman at Auburn University, Jason Jones became a pledge at the Kappa Alpha (KA) fraternity. Over the next year, KA brothers hazed Jones in various ways, including: (1) making him jump into a ditch filled with urine, feces, dinner leftovers, and vomit; (2) paddling his buttocks; (3) pushing and kicking him; (4) making him run a gauntlet in which he was pushed, hit, and kicked; and (5) making him attend 2:00 A.M. hazing meetings. Jones continued to participate in these and other hazing activities until he was suspended from Auburn for poor academic performance. Even though he knew that 20 to 40 percent of his pledge class had withdrawn from the pledge program, Jones kept participating because he wanted to become a full member of KA. Jones later sued the local and national KA organizations for, among other things, negligent hazing in violation of a state criminal statute that outlawed hazing. The defendants moved for summary judgment on Jones's negligence per se claim. They contended that in view of the facts, Jones had assumed the risk of hazing. Were the defendants entitled to summary judgment?

9. On April 16, 1947, the SS *Grandchamp,* a cargo ship owned by the Republic of France and operated by the French Line, was loading a cargo of fertilizer grade ammonium nitrate (FGAN) at Texas City, Texas. A fire began on board the ship, apparently as a result of a longshoreman's having carelessly discarded a cigarette or match into one of the ship's holds. Despite attempts to put out the fire, it spread quickly. Approximately an hour after the fire was discovered, the *Grandchamp* exploded with tremendous force. Fire and burning debris spread throughout the waterfront, touching off further fires and explosions in other ships, refineries, gasoline storage tanks, and chemical plants. When the conflagration was

over, 500 persons had been killed and more than 3,000 had been injured. The United States paid out considerable sums to victims of the disaster. The U.S. then sought to recoup these payments as damages in a negligence case against the Republic of France and the French Line. The evidence revealed that even though ammonium nitrate (which constituted approximately 95 percent of the FGAN) was known throughout the transportation industry as an oxidizing agent and a fire hazard, no one in charge on the *Grandchamp* had made any attempt to prohibit smoking in the ship's holds. The defendants argued that they should not be held liable because FGAN was not known to be capable of *exploding* (as opposed to simply being a fire hazard) under circumstances such as those giving rise to the disaster. Did the defendants succeed with this argument?

10. On January 9, 1979, a railroad car leased by American Cyanamid (American) and containing 20,000 gallons of acrylonitrile manufactured by American, began leaking. At the time, the car was sitting just south of Chicago in the Blue Island yard of the Indiana Harbor Belt Railroad (Indiana) awaiting switching to Conrail for delivery to its final destination. Indiana's employees stopped the leak but were uncertain about how much of the car's contents had escaped. Because acrylonitrile is flammable, highly toxic, and possibly carcinogenic, Illinois authorities ordered homes near the yard temporarily evacuated. Later, it was discovered that only about a quarter of the car's contents had leaked, but the Illinois Department of Environmental Protection, fearing that the soil and water had been contaminated, ordered Indiana to take decontamination measures costing $981,000. Indiana sued American on negligence and strict liability theories, seeking to recover its expenses. Evidence introduced at the trial included a list of 125 hazardous materials that are shipped in highest volume on the nation's railroads. Acrylonitrile was the 53rd most hazardous on the list. Was the trial court's entry of summary judgment for Indiana on the strict liability claim proper?

11. Elizabeth Culli stopped at a 24-hour self-service gas station operated by Marathon Petroleum Co. After filling her car's gas tank, she entered the station building to pay for the gas and other items she intended to purchase. After making payment, she headed toward her car. Before reaching the car, however, Culli slipped and fell on a clear or nearly clear and slippery substance that had accumulated on the parking lot pavement in a pool of approximately eight to ten inches in width and length. Culli suffered a compound fracture of her ankle. She had to use a wheelchair and a walker for the next several months. Culli sued Marathon for negligence. The evidence revealed that the Marathon station was typically staffed by one person, who primarily would stay inside and run the cash register but was also responsible for replenishing supplies of the various items sold at the station. There was also evidence that the parking lot was normally swept once per 24-hour period, during the night shift. Further evidence indicated that spills typically occurred in the parking lot area once or twice per day, and that a station employee had asked the station manager to hire more help because the station was, in the employee's view, understaffed. The manager relayed this request to his superiors, but the request went unheeded. There was no evidence, however, that any Marathon employee was actually aware of the presence of the slippery substance on the parking lot pavement at or prior to the time when Culli fell. Did Culli win her case?

Online Research: Negligent Hiring

If your college or university allows students to have access to either LEXIS or WESTLAW, use one of those on-line services to identify a *negligent hiring* case that has been decided by a court—preferably the highest court— in the state where your school is located. If you cannot locate a negligent hiring decision from one of that state's courts, identify such a decision by a court—again, preferably the highest court—in a neighboring state. (Students whose school is located in Virginia should choose to research the decisions of a neighboring state's courts, for reasons that will become apparent when you read the further instructions set forth below.)

Carefully read the case you have chosen, prepare a written case brief (see the Appendix at the end of Chapter 1), and prepare a one-page essay in which you address the following question:

> If the court that decided the case you have chosen had also decided *Interim Personnel of Central Virginia, Inc. v. Messer* (one of the text cases in Chapter 7), would that court have decided the *Messer* case as the Supreme Court of Virginia did, or would the outcome and/or analysis have been different? Explain your position, making sure to include references to appropriate aspects of the two decisions.

8

INTELLECTUAL PROPERTY
AND UNFAIR COMPETITION

Leslie Kelly is a professional photographer who specializes in photographs of the American West. Kelly has a website on which he has placed some of his photographic images. At various times, he has authorized other parties to place certain ones of the images on their websites. Ditto.com Corp. operates an Internet search engine under the Ditto.com name. Rather than displaying its results conventionally in the form of text, this search engine displays its results in thumbnail-size pictures (hereinafter, "thumbnails"). By clicking on one of the thumbnails, the Ditto.com user can then view a large version of that same picture within the context of the Ditto.com Web page.

Kelly discovered that some of his photographs had been included, without his consent, in Ditto.com's search engine database. He therefore sued Ditto.com in an effort to enforce the intellectual property rights he claimed in the photographs. Ditto.com's utilization of Kelly's photographs really consisted of two uses: (1) the thumbnails; and (2) the larger versions of the same images.

Consider this scenario and the following questions as you study Chapter 8:

• Which area of intellectual property law—patent, copyright, or trademark—provides Kelly the rights he is attempting to enforce in his case against Ditto.com?
• What specific right or rights would Kelly contend were violated by Ditto.com?
• What possible defense against liability is Ditto.com likely to raise? Which use by Ditto.com—the thumbnails or the larger versions of the photographic images—is a better candidate for the protection of this defense, or are the two uses equally strong (or weak) candidates?

THIS CHAPTER DISCUSSES LEGAL rules that limit free competition by allowing civil recoveries for abuses of that freedom. These abuses are: (1) infringement of intellectual property rights protected by patent, copyright, and trademark law; (2) the misappropriation of trade secrets; (3) the intentional torts of injurious falsehood, interference with contractual relations, and interference with prospective advantage; and (4) the various forms of unfair competition addressed by section 43(a) of the Lanham Act. Indeed, the term *unfair competition* describes the entire chapter. In general, competition is deemed unfair when: (1) it discourages creative endeavor by robbing creative people of the fruits of their innovations, or (2) it renders commercial life too uncivilized for the law to tolerate.

Protection of Intellectual Property

Patents

A patent may be viewed as an agreement between an inventor and the federal government. Under that agreement, the inventor obtains the exclusive right (for a limited time) to make, use, and sell his invention, in return for making the invention public by giving the government certain information about it. The patent holder's (or **patentee's**) monopoly encourages the creation and disclosure of inventions by stopping third parties from appropriating them once they become public. However, third parties may develop the invention in ways that do not interfere with the patentee's rights.

What Is Patentable? An inventor may patent: (1) a *process* (a mode of treatment of certain materials to produce a given result), (2) a *machine,* (3) a *manufacture* or product, (4) a *composition of matter* (a combination of elements with qualities not present in the elements taken individually, such as a new chemical compound), (5) an *improvement* of any of the above, (6) an *ornamental design* for a product, and (7) a *plant* produced by asexual reproduction. Certain business methods may also be patentable. Naturally occurring things (e.g., a new wild plant) are not patentable. In addition, abstract ideas, and scientific or mathematical concepts are not patentable, although their practical applications often are. In *Diamond v. Diehr* (1981), for instance, the Supreme Court held that a computer program may be patentable if it is part of a patentable process.[1]

Even though an invention fits within one of the above categories, it is not patentable if it lacks novelty, is obvious, or has no utility, or if the patent applicant is an inappropriate applicant.[2] One aspect of the *novelty* requirement is the rule that no patent should be issued where *before the invention's creation* it has been: (1) known or used in the United States, (2) patented in the United States or a foreign country, or (3) described in a printed publication in the United States or a foreign country. Another aspect is the requirement that no patent should be issued if more than one year before the *patent application* the invention was: (1) patented in the United States or a foreign country, (2) described in a printed publication in the United States or a foreign country, or (3) in public use or on sale in the United States. The *Pfaff* case, which follows shortly, deals with the rule just noted.

In addition, there can be no patent if the invention would have been *obvious* to a person having ordinary skill in the area. A patentable invention must also have *utility,* or usefulness. Finally, there can be no patent if the applicant did not create the invention in question, or if she abandoned the invention. *Creation* problems frequently arise where several persons allegedly contributed to the invention. *Abandonment* may be by express statement, such as publicly devoting an invention to humanity, or by implication from conduct, such as delaying for an unreasonable length of time before making a patent application.

Obtaining a Patent The United States Patent and Trademark Office handles patent applications. The application must include a *specification* describing the invention with sufficient detail and clarity to enable a person skilled in the relevant field to make and use the invention. The application must also contain a *drawing* when this is necessary for understanding the subject matter to be patented. The Patent Office then determines whether the invention meets the various tests for patentability. If the application is rejected, the applicant may resubmit it. Once any of the applicant's claims have been rejected twice, the applicant may appeal to the Office's Board of Patent Appeals and Interferences. Subsequent appeals to the federal courts are also possible.

---

[1]As discussed later in this chapter, computer programs may obtain copyright and trade secret protection.
[2]Plant and design patents are subject to requirements that are slightly different from those stated here.

Pfaff v. Wells Electronics, Inc.   *525 U.S. 55 (1998)*

Wayne Pfaff began development work on a new computer chip socket in November 1980. He prepared detailed engineering drawings that described the design and dimensions of the socket and the materials to be used in making it. Pfaff sent the drawings to a manufacturer in February or March 1981. Prior to March 17, 1981, he showed a sketch of his concept to representatives of Texas Instruments. On April 8, 1981, the Texas Instruments representatives provided Pfaff a written confirmation of a previously placed oral purchase order for 30,100 of the new sockets. The total purchase price was $91,155. In accordance with his usual business practice, Pfaff did not make and test a prototype of the socket before offering to sell it.

The manufacturer to which Pfaff sent his drawings took a few months to develop the customized tooling necessary to produce the socket. The first actual sockets were not produced until the summer of 1981. Pfaff filled the Texas Instruments order in July 1981. Other orders followed, as the socket became a commercial success. On April 19, 1982, Pfaff applied for a patent on the socket. A patent was issued to him in January 1985. Pfaff later filed an infringement action against Wells Electronics,

Inc., which produced a competing socket. Wells Electronics argued that Pfaff's patent was invalid under section 102(b) of the Patent Act of 1952, which states that a patent cannot be obtained for an invention if it has been "on sale" for more than a year before the filing of the patent application.

The federal district court rejected Wells Electronics' section 102(b) defense because Pfaff had filed the patent application less than a year after reducing the invention to practice (i.e., less than a year after the first actual sockets were produced and available for sale). The district court held Wells Electronics liable for infringement but the U.S. Court of Appeals for the Federal Circuit reversed. The Court of Appeals held that Pfaff's patent was invalid because the socket had been offered for sale on a commercial basis more than a year before the filing of the patent application. The U.S. Supreme Court granted certiorari.

Stevens, Justice   Section 102(b) of the Patent Act of 1952 provides that no person is entitled to patent an "invention" that has been "on sale" for more than one year before filing a patent application. We granted certiorari to determine whether the commercial marketing of a newly invented product may mark the beginning of the one-year period even though the invention has not yet been reduced to practice.

On April 19, 1982, Pfaff filed an application for a patent on the computer chip socket. Therefore, April 19, 1981 constitutes the critical date for purposes of the on-sale bar of section 102(b); if the one-year period began to run before that date, Pfaff lost his right to patent his invention.

The primary meaning of the word "invention" in the Patent Act unquestionably refers to the inventor's conception rather than to a physical embodiment of the idea. The statute does not contain any express requirement that an invention must be reduced to practice before it can be patented. Neither the statutory definition of the term nor the basic conditions for obtaining a patent make any mention of "reduction to practice."

It is well settled that an invention may be patented before it is reduced to practice. In 1888, this Court upheld a patent issued to Alexander Graham Bell even though he had filed his application before constructing a working telephone. [In upholding the issuance of the patent to Bell, the Court stated:]

> The law does not require that a discoverer or inventor, in order to get a patent for a process, must have succeeded in bringing his art to the highest degree of perfection. It

is enough if he describes his method with sufficient clearness and precision to enable those skilled in the matter to understand what the process is, and if he points out some practicable way of putting it into operation.

The Telephone Cases, 126 U.S. 1 (1888).

When we apply the reasoning of *The Telephone Cases* to the facts of the case before us today, it is evident that Pfaff could have obtained a patent on his novel socket when he accepted the purchase order from Texas Instruments for 30,100 units. At that time he provided the manufacturer with a description and drawings that had "sufficient clearness and precision to enable those skilled in the matter" to produce the device. The parties agree that the sockets manufactured to fill that order embody Pfaff's conception. We can find no basis in the text of section 102(b) or in the facts of this case for concluding that Pfaff's invention was not "on sale" within the meaning of the statute until after it has been reduced to practice.

When Pfaff accepted the purchase order for his new sockets prior to April 8, 1981, his invention was ready for patenting. The fact that the manufacturer was able to produce the socket using his detailed drawings and specifications demonstrates this fact. Furthermore, those sockets contained all the elements of the invention claimed in the patent. Therefore, Pfaff's patent is invalid because the invention had been on sale for more than one year in this country before he filed his patent application.

Judgment of Court of Appeals affirmed.

Ownership and Transfer of Patent Rights   Until a relatively recent change in federal law, a patent normally gave the patentee exclusive rights to make, use, and sell the patented invention for 17 years from the date the patent was granted. In order to bring the United States into compliance with the General Agreement on Tariffs and Trade (an international agreement commonly known as GATT), Congress amended the patent law to provide that the patentee's exclusive rights to make, use, and sell

the patented invention generally exist until the expiration of 20 years from the date the patent application was filed. This duration rule applies to patents that result from applications filed on or after June 8, 1995. (A design patent, however, exists for 14 years from the date it was granted.) A 1999 enactment of Congress allowed for the possible extension of a patent's duration if the Patent Office delayed an unreasonably long time in acting on and approving the patentee's application.

The patentee may transfer ownership of the patent by making a written *assignment* of it to another party. Alternatively, the patentee may retain ownership and *license* others to exercise some or all of the patent rights. International licensing and patent rights issues are discussed in a Global Business Environment box that appears later in the chapter.

Usually, the party who created the invention is the patent holder. What happens, however, when the creator of the invention is an employee and her employer seeks rights in the invention? If the invention was developed by an employee *hired to do inventive or creative work,* she must use the invention solely for the employer's benefit and must assign any patents she obtains to the employer. If the employee was hired for purposes *other than invention or creation,* however, she owns any patent she acquires. Finally, regardless of the purpose for which the employee was hired, the *shop right* doctrine gives the employer a nonexclusive, royalty-free *license* to use the employee's invention if it was created on company time and through the use of company facilities. Any patent the employee might retain is still effective against parties other than the employer.

Patent Infringement Patent infringement occurs when a defendant, without authorization from the patentee, takes action that usurps any of the patentee's rights to make, use, and sell the patented invention. Infringement may be established under principles of *literal* infringement or under a judicially developed approach known as the *doctrine of equivalents.* Infringement is literal in nature when the subject matter made, used, or sold by the defendant clearly falls within the stated terms of the claims of invention set forth in the patentee's application. Under the doctrine of equivalents, a defendant may be held liable for infringement even though the subject matter he made, used, or sold contained elements that were not identical to those described in the patentee's claim of invention, if the elements of the defendant's subject matter nonetheless may be seen as equivalent to those of the patented invention. A traditional formulation of the test posed by the doctrine of equivalents is whether the alleged infringer's subject matter performs substantially the same function as the protected invention in substantially the same way, in order to obtain the same result.

Several years ago, an alleged infringer sought to convince the Supreme Court to abolish the doctrine of equivalents on the ground that it effectively allows patentees to extend the scope of patent protection beyond the stated terms approved by the Patent Office when it issued the patent. In *Warner-Jenkinson Co. v. Hilton Davis Chemical Co.* (1997), however, the Court rejected this attack on the doctrine. The Court observed that in view of courts' longstanding use of the doctrine (use in which Congress seemingly acquiesced by not legislatively prohibiting it), arguments for abolishing the doctrine would be better addressed to Congress. The *Warner-Jenkinson* Court did acknowledge, however, that overly broad application of the doctrine of equivalents could lead to an unwarranted expansion of patent owners' rights. Therefore, the Court held that the doctrine of equivalents must be applied to the *individual elements* of the patentee's claims of invention rather than to the patentee's invention *as a whole.*

One who *actively induces* another's infringement of a patent is liable as an infringer if he knows and intends that the infringement occur. For example, if Ingram directly infringes Paxton's patent on a machine and Doyle knowingly sold Ingram an instruction manual for the machine, Doyle may be liable as an infringer. Finally, if one knowingly sells a direct patent infringer a component of a patented invention or something useful in employing a patented process, the seller may be liable for *contributory infringement.* The thing sold must be a material part of the invention and must not be a staple article of commerce with some other significant use. Suppose that Irving directly infringes Potter's patent for a radio by selling essentially identical radios. If Davis sells Irving sophisticated circuitry for the radios with knowledge of Irving's infringement, Davis may be liable for contributory infringement, assuming that the circuitry is an important component of the radios and has no other significant uses.

The basic recovery for patent infringement is damages adequate to compensate for the infringement, plus court costs and interest. The damages cannot be less than a reasonable royalty for the use made of the invention by the infringer. The court may in its discretion award damages of up to three times those actually suffered. Injunctive relief is also available, and attorney's fees may be awarded in exceptional cases.

Defenses to Patent Infringement One defense to a patent infringement suit is that the subject matter of the alleged infringement is neither within the literal scope of the patent nor substantially equivalent to the patented invention. The alleged infringer may also defend by attacking the validity of the patent. Despite having been approved by the Patent and Trademark Office, patents are sometimes declared invalid when challenged in court.

In appropriate cases, the defendant can assert that the patentee has committed *patent misuse.* This is behavior that unjustifiably exploits the patent monopoly. For example, the patentee may require the purchaser of a license on his patent to buy his unpatented goods, or may tie the obtaining of a license on one of his patented inventions to the purchase of a license on another. One who refuses the patentee's terms and later infringes the patent may attempt to escape liability by arguing that the patentee misused his monopoly position.

LOG ON

United States government websites contain a wealth of information on patent, copyright, and trademark law and procedures. For information on patents and trademarks, visit the site of the U.S. Patent and Trademark Office, at **www.uspto.gov.** Information on copyrights may be found at **www.loc.gov/copyright,** the site of the U.S. Copyright Office.

An interesting privately maintained site, **www.benedict.com,** also contains a broad range of copyright information.

Copyrights

Copyright law gives certain exclusive rights to creators of *original works of authorship.* It prevents others from using their work, gives them an incentive to innovate, and thereby benefits society. Yet copyright law also tries to balance these purposes against the equally compelling public interest in the free movement of ideas, information, and commerce. It does so mainly by limiting the intellectual products it protects and by allowing the fair use defense described later.

Coverage The federal Copyright Act protects a wide range of works of authorship, including books, periodical articles, dramatic and musical compositions, works of art, motion pictures, sound recordings, lectures, computer programs, and architectural plans. To merit copyright protection, such works must be *fixed*—set out in a tangible medium of expression from which they can be perceived, reproduced, or communicated. They also must be *original* (the author's own work) and *creative* (reflecting exercise of the creator's judgment). Unlike the inventions protected by patent law, however, copyrightable works need not be novel.

Copyright protection does not extend to ideas, facts, procedures, processes, systems, methods of operation, concepts, principles, or discoveries. Instead, it protects the *ways in which they are expressed.* The story line of a play, for instance, is protected, but the ideas, themes, or messages underlying it are not. Although there is no copyright protection over facts, the expression in nonfiction works and compilations of fact is protected.

Computer programs involve their own special problems. It is fairly well settled that copyright law protects a program's *object code* (program instructions that are machine-readable but not intelligible to humans) and *source code* (instructions intelligible to humans). There is less agreement, however, about the copyrightability of a program's nonliteral elements such as its organization, its structure, and its presentation of information on the screen. Most courts that have considered the issue hold that nonliteral elements may sometimes be protected by copyright law, but courts differ about the extent of this protection.

Creation and Notice A copyright comes into existence upon the creation and fixing of a protected work. Although a copyright owner may register the copyright with the Copyright Office of the Library of Congress, registration is not necessary for the copyright to exist. However, registration normally is a procedural prerequisite to filing a suit for copyright infringement. Even though it is not required, copyright owners often provide *notice* of the copyright. Federal law authorizes a basic form of notice for use with most copyrighted works. A book, for example, might include the term *Copyright* (or the abbreviation *Copr.* or the symbol©), the year of its first publication, and the name of the copyright owner in a location likely to give reasonable notice to readers.

Duration The U.S. Constitution's Copyright Clause (Article I, section 8) empowers Congress to "promote the progress of Science and useful arts" by enacting copyright and patent laws that "secur[e] for limited Times to Authors and Inventors the exclusive Right to their respective Writings and Discoveries." Thus, copyrights and patents cannot last forever. Even so, the history of copyright protection in the United States has featured various significant lengthenings of the "limited time" a copyright endures. When a copyright's duration ends, the underlying work enters the public domain and becomes available for any uses other parties wish to make of it. The former copyright owner, therefore, loses control over the work and forfeits what had been valuable legal rights.

With the enactment of the Sonny Bono Copyright Term Extension Act (hereinafter "CTEA") in 1998, Congress conferred a substantial benefit on copyright owners. The CTEA added 20 years to the duration of copyrights, not only for works created after the CTEA's enactment *but also for any preexisting work that was still under valid copyright protection* as of the CTEA's October 1998 effective date. Copyright owners—especially some high-profile corporations whose copyrights on older works would soon have expired if not for the enactment of the CTEA—mounted a significant lobbying effort in favor of the term extension provided by the CTEA.

The CTEA's effect cannot be understood without discussion of the copyright duration rules that existed immediately before the CTEA's enactment. One set of rules applied to works created in 1978 or thereafter; another set applied to pre-1978 works. The copyright on pre-1978 works was good for a term of 28 years from first publication of the work, plus a renewal term of 47 years. (The renewal term had been only 28 years until Congress changed the law roughly a quarter-century ago and added 19 more years to the renewal term for any work then under valid copyright protection.) As a result, 75 years of protection was available for pre-1978 works.

For works created in 1978 or thereafter, Congress scrapped the initial-term-plus-renewal-term approach, opting instead for a normally applicable rule that the copyright lasts for the life of the author/creator plus 50 years. This basic duration rule did not apply, however, if the copyrighted work, though created in 1978 or thereafter, was a work-for-hire. (The two types of work-for-hire will be explained below.) In a work-for-hire situation, the copyright would exist for 75 years from first publication of the work or 100 years from creation of it, whichever came first.

The CTEA tacked on 20 years to the durations contemplated by the rules discussed in the preceding two paragraphs. A pre-1978 work that was still under valid copyright protection as of late 1998 (when the CTEA took effect) now has a total protection period of 95 years from first publication—a 28-year initial term plus a renewal term that has been lengthened from 47 to 67 years. The copyright on Disney's "Steamboat Willie" cartoon—best-known for its introduction of the famous Mickey Mouse character—serves as an example. The protection period for the Steamboat Willie copyright began to run in the late 1920s, when the cartoon was released and distributed (i.e., published, for purposes of copyright law). Given the rule that existed immediately before the CTEA's enactment (an initial term of 28 years plus a renewal term of 47 years), the Steamboat Willie copyright would have expired within the first few years of the current century. The CTEA, however, gave Disney an additional 20 years of rights over the Steamboat Willie cartoon before it would pass into the public domain.

With the enactment of the CTEA, the basic duration rule for works created in 1978 or thereafter is now life of the author/creator plus 70 years (up from 50). The duration rule for a work-for-hire is now 95 years from first publication (up from 75) or 120 years from creation (up from 100), whichever comes first.

In late 2002, the Supreme Court heard oral arguments in *Eldred v. Ashcroft,* which presented a constitutional challenge to the CTEA. Those challenging the CTEA argued that the statute violated the purpose of the "limited times" provision in the Constitution's Copyright Clause by making copyright protection so lengthy in duration. They also contended: that the Copyright Clause's language empowering Congress to enact copyright laws to "promote the progress of science and useful arts" served as an *incentive-to-create* limitation on the exercise of that power; and that the CTEA, at least insofar as it applied to works already created as of 1998, unconstitutionally violated the incentive-to-create limitation. As of the time this book went to press, the Court had not yet decided the *Eldred* case.

Works-for-Hire A work-for-hire exists when: (1) an employee, in the course of her regular employment duties, prepares a copyrightable work; or (2) an individual or corporation and an independent contractor (i.e., nonemployee) enter into a written agreement under which the independent contractor is to prepare, for the retaining individual or corporation, one of several types of copyrightable works designated in the Copyright Act. In the first situation, the employer is legally classified as the work's author and copyright owner. In the second situation, the party who (or which) retained the independent contractor is considered the resulting work's author and copyright owner.

Ownership Rights A copyright owner has exclusive rights to reproduce the copyrighted work, prepare derivative works based on it (e.g., a movie version of a novel), and distribute copies of the work by sale or otherwise. With certain copyrighted works, the copyright owner also obtains the exclusive right to perform the work or display it publicly. Copyright ownership initially resides in the creator of the copyrighted work, but the copyright may be transferred to another party. Also, the owner may individually transfer any of the listed rights, or a portion of each, without losing ownership of the remaining rights. Most transfers of copyright ownership require a writing signed by the owner or his agent. The owner may also retain ownership while licensing the copyrighted work or a portion of it.

Infringement Those who violate any of the copyright owner's exclusive rights may be liable for copyright infringement. Infringement is fairly easily proven when direct evidence of significant copying exists; verbatim copying of protected material is an example. Usually, however, proof of infringement involves establishing that: (1) the defendant had *access* to the copyrighted work; (2) the defendant engaged in enough *copying*— either deliberately or subconsciously—that the resemblance between the allegedly infringing work and the copyrighted work does not seem coincidental; and (3) there is *substantial similarity* between the two works.

Access may be proven circumstantially, such as by showing that the copyrighted work was widely circulated. The copying and substantial similarity elements, which closely relate to each other, necessarily involve discretionary case-by-case determinations. Of course, the copying and substantial similarity must exist with regard to the copyrighted work's protected expression. Copying of general ideas, facts, themes, and the like (i.e., copying of unprotected matter) is not infringement. The defendant's having paraphrased protected expression does not constitute a defense to what otherwise appears to be infringement. Neither does the defendant's having

CYBERLAW IN ACTION

In the Digital Millennium Copyright Act of 1998 (DMCA), Congress addressed selected copyright issues as to which special rules seemed appropriate, in view of recent years' technological advances and explosion in Internet usage. One such issue was how narrowly or broadly to define the class of parties potentially liable for copyright infringement in an Internet context. If, without Osborne's consent, Jennings posts Osborne's copyrighted material on an electronic bulletin board made available by Devaney (an Internet service provider), is only Jennings liable to Osborne, or is Devaney also liable? In the DMCA, Congress enacted "safe harbor" provisions designed to protect many service providers such as Devaney from liability for the actions of direct infringers who posted or transmitted copyrighted material.

The DMCA also addressed the actions of persons who seek to circumvent technological measures (e.g., encryption, password-protection measures, and the like) that control access to or copying of a copyrighted work. With certain narrowly defined exceptions of very limited applicability, Congress outlawed both (1) the circumvention of such technological measures and (2) the activity of trafficking in programs or other devices meant to accomplish such circumvention.

In *Universal City Studios, Inc. v. Corley*, 273 F.3d 429 (2d Cir. 2001), the U.S. Court of Appeals for the Second Circuit rejected the arguments of an individual (Corley) who had been held liable to various movie studios for violating the antitrafficking provisions of the DMCA. Corley had written an article about the decryption program known as "DeCSS" and had posted the article on his website, along with a copy of the DeCSS program itself and links to other sites where DeCSS could be found. DeCSS had been developed by parties other than Corley as a means of decrypting the "CSS" encryption technology that movie studios place on copyrighted DVDs of their movies. If it is not circumvented, CSS prevents the copying of the movie that appears on the DVD. A federal district court, holding that Corley had violated the DMCA's anti-trafficking provisions, issued an injunction barring Corley from posting DeCSS on his website and from posting links to other sites where DeCSS could be found.

On appeal, Corley argued that his publication of the DeCSS program's codes was speech protected by the First Amendment and that the application of the DMCA to him was thus unconstitutional. The Second Circuit concluded that Corley was to some extent engaged in speech but that his actions also had a substantial nonspeech component. In any event, the Second Circuit reasoned, the DMCA's antitrafficking provisions served a substantial government interest in protecting the rights of intellectual property owners and were content-neutral restrictions unrelated to the suppression of free expression. The court therefore held that the antitrafficking provisions did not violate the First Amendment.

Some critics of the DMCA's anticircumvention and antitrafficking provisions have asserted that those provisions may operate to restrict users' ability to make fair use of copyrighted materials. Evidently attempting to convert this policy-based objection about what Congress enacted into a constitutional objection on which the court might be more inclined to rule, Corley argued that the fair use doctrine was required by the First Amendment and that the DMCA, insofar as it limited users' ability to rely on the fair use doctrine, was unconstitutional. The Second Circuit called it "extravagant" to assert that the fair use doctrine was constitutionally required, for there was no substantial authority to support such a contention. Moreover, the court reasoned that even if Corley's contention were not otherwise questionable, "[f]air use has never been held to be a guarantee of access to copyrighted material in order to copy it by the fair user's preferred technique or in the format of the original."

credited the copyrighted work as the source from which the defendant borrowed.

Recent years' explosion in Internet usage has led to difficult copyright questions. For instance, services such as Gnutella, KaZaA, and the now-defunct Napster have allowed easy and free-of-charge access to musical recordings in digital files. Owners of copyrights on songs and recordings have expressed concern over such services and have resorted to litigation against Napster and other providers on the theory that they materially contributed to copyright infringement by their users. The *Napster* case follows shortly.

The basic recovery for copyright infringement is the owner's actual damages plus the attributable profits received by the infringer. In lieu of the basic remedy, however, the plaintiff may usually elect to receive *statutory damages*. The statutory damages set by the trial judge or jury must fall within the range of $750 to $30,000 unless the infringement was willful, in which event the maximum rises to $150,000. These limits do not apply if the plaintiff elects the basic remedy, however. Injunctive relief and awards of costs and attorney's fees are possible in appropriate cases. Although it seldom does so, the fed-

eral government may pursue a criminal copyright infringement prosecution if the infringement was willful and for purposes of commercial advantage or private financial gain.

Fair Use The Copyright Act states that uses for such purposes as criticism or comment, news reporting, teaching, scholarship, or research may be good candidates for the protection of the fair use defense against infringement liability. However, a court's fair use determination requires the weighing of factors whose application varies from case to case. These factors are: (1) the purpose and character of the use, (2) the nature of the copyrighted work, (3) the amount and substantiality of the portion used in relation to the copyrighted work as a whole, and (4) the effect of the use on the potential markets for the copyrighted work or on its value. Even one of the supposedly good candidates may be held not to be fair use once all of the factors are weighed and balanced. In the *Napster* case, the court discusses the bases on which Napster was held liable and rejects Napster's attempt to rely on the fair use defense.

A&M Records, Inc. v. Napster, Inc.   *239 F.3d 1004 (9th Cir. 2001)*

Napster, Inc.'s MusicShare software allowed users to make MP3 music files stored on individual computer hard drives available for copying by other Napster users. It also allowed users to search for MP3 music files stored on other users' computers and to transfer exact copies of the contents of other users' MP3 files from one computer to another via the Internet. Various parties engaged in commercial recording, distribution, and sale of copyrighted musical compositions and sound recordings sued Napster, alleging that Napster users had committed copyright infringement and that Napster was liable as a contributory and vicarious infringer. The plaintiffs sought a preliminary injunction meant to prohibit allegedly infringing acts by Napster users, as well as Napster's supposed contributory and vicarious infringement. A federal district court granted the preliminary injunction, which barred Napster from "engaging in, or facilitating others in copying, downloading, uploading, transmitting, or distributing plaintiffs' copyrighted musical compositions and sound recordings, . . . without express permission of the rights owner." Napster appealed to the U.S. Court of Appeals for the Ninth Circuit, which temporarily stayed the preliminary injunction pending resolution of the appeal.

Beezer, Circuit Judge There can be no contributory infringement by a defendant without direct infringement by another [person or group of persons]. It follows that Napster does not facilitate infringement of the copyright laws in the absence of direct infringement by its users.

Plaintiffs must satisfy two requirements to present a prima facie case of direct infringement. They must: (1) show ownership of the allegedly infringed material; and (2) demonstrate that the alleged infringers violate at least one exclusive right granted [by the Copyright Act] to copyright holders. The

record supports the district court's determination that "as much as 87% of the files available on Napster may be copyrighted and more than 70% may be owned or administered by plaintiffs." We agree [with the district court] that plaintiffs have shown that Napster users infringe at least two of the copyright holders' exclusive rights: the rights of reproduction . . . and distribution. Users who upload file names to [Napster's] search index for others to copy violate plaintiffs' distribution rights. Users who download files containing copyrighted music violate plaintiffs' reproduction rights.

Napster contends [, however,] that its users do not directly infringe plaintiffs' copyrights because the users are engaged in fair use. Napster identifies [these] alleged fair uses: sampling, where users make temporary copies of a work before purchasing; and space-shifting, where users access a sound recording through the Napster system that they already own in audio CD format. The district court concluded that Napster users are not fair users. [In reviewing that conclusion, we will address the four fair use factors specified in the Copyright Act and then turn to the supposed fair uses Napster has identified.]

Purpose and Character of the Use [Factor #1]

This factor focuses on whether the [user of the copyrighted work] merely replaces the object of the original creation or instead adds a further purpose or different character. In other words, this factor asks "whether and to what extent the [use or] new work is 'transformative.' " *Campbell v. Acuff-Rose Music, Inc.,* 510 U.S. 569, 579 (1994). The district court first concluded that downloading MP3 files does not transform the copyrighted work. This conclusion is supportable. Courts have been reluctant to find fair use when an original work is merely retransmitted in a different medium.

This "purpose and character "element also requires the district court to determine whether the allegedly infringing use is commercial or noncommercial. A commercial use weighs against a finding of fair use but is not conclusive on the issue. The district court determined that Napster users engage in commercial use of the copyrighted materials largely because (1) "a host user sending a file cannot be said to engage in a personal use when distributing that file to an anonymous requester," and (2) "Napster users get for free something they would ordinarily have to buy." The district court's findings are not clearly erroneous. Direct economic benefit is not required to demonstrate a commercial use. Rather, repeated and exploitative copying of copyrighted works, even if the copies are not offered for sale, may constitute a commercial use. In the record before us, commercial use is demonstrated by a showing that repeated and exploitative unauthorized copies of copyrighted works were made to save the expense of purchasing authorized copies.

The Nature of the Use [Factor #2]

Works that are creative in nature are "closer to the core of intended copyright protection" than are more fact-based works. See *Campbell,* 510 U.S. at 586. The district court [correctly] determined that plaintiffs' "copyrighted musical compositions and sound recordings are creative in nature, which cuts against a finding of fair use under the second factor."

The Portion Used [Factor #3]

[Various cases indicate that even though copying of an entire work may be fair use in appropriate circumstances, such extensive copying often] militates against a finding of fair use. The district court determined that . . . file transfer [by Napster users] necessarily "involves copying the entirety of the copyrighted work" [and that this fair use factor therefore worked in the plaintiffs' favor]. We agree.

Effect of Use on Market [Factor #4]

Addressing this factor, the district court concluded that Napster harms the market in at least two ways: it reduces audio CD sales among college students and it "raises barriers to plaintiffs' entry into the market for the digital downloading of music." [In so concluding, the district court relied on reports submitted by the plaintiffs' three expert witnesses, who had conducted separate surveys dealing with the effect of Napster use on the market for the plaintiffs' copyrighted musical compositions and sound recordings. The court chose not to give credence to the report of Napster's expert, who had concluded that Napster benefited the music industry by stimulating more CD sales than it discouraged.]

We conclude that the district court made sound findings related to Napster's deleterious effect on the present and future digital download market. Moreover, lack of harm to an established market cannot deprive the copyright holder of the right to develop alternative markets for the works. Having digital downloads available for free on the Napster system necessarily harms the copyright holders' attempts to charge for the same downloads.

[The district court] did not abuse [its] discretion in reaching the above fair use conclusions. We next address Napster's identified uses of sampling and space-shifting, [which] Napster maintains . . . were wrongly excluded as fair uses by the district court.

Napster's First Identified Use: Sampling

Napster contends that its users download MP3 files to "sample" the music in order to decide whether to purchase the recording. Napster argues that the district court: (1) erred in concluding that sampling is a commercial use because it conflated a noncommercial use with a personal use; (2) erred in determining that sampling adversely affects the market for plaintiffs' copyrighted music . . . ; and (3) erroneously concluded that sampling is not a fair use because it determined that samplers may also engage in other infringing activity.

The district court determined that sampling remains a commercial use even if some users eventually purchase the music. Plaintiffs have established that they are likely to succeed in proving that even authorized temporary downloading of individual songs for sampling purposes is commercial in nature. The record supports a finding that free promotional downloads are highly regulated by the record company plaintiffs and that the companies collect royalties for song samples available on retail Internet sites. Evidence relied on by the district court demonstrates that the free downloads provided by the record companies consist of 30-to-60-second samples or are full songs programmed to "time out," that is, exist only for a short time on the downloader's computer. In comparison, Napster users download a full, free, and permanent copy of the recording. The determination by the district court as to the commercial purpose and character of sampling is not clearly erroneous.

The district court further found that both the market for audio CDs and market for online distribution are adversely affected by Napster's service. The record supports the court's preliminary determinations that: (1) the more music that sampling users download, the less likely they are to eventually purchase the recordings on audio CD; and (2) even if the audio CD market is not harmed, Napster has adverse effects on the developing digital download market. Napster further argues that the court erred in rejecting its evidence that the users' downloading of samples increases or tends to increase audio CD sales. The court, however, correctly noted that "any potential enhancement of plaintiffs' sales . . . would not tip the fair use analysis conclusively in favor of defendant." We agree that increased sales of copyrighted material attributable to unauthorized use should not deprive the copyright holder of the right to license the material. Nor does positive impact in one market, here the audio CD market, deprive the copyright holder of the right to develop identified alternative markets, here the digital download market. We find no error in the district court's . . . conclusion that plaintiffs will likely prevail in establishing that sampling does not constitute a fair use.

Napster's Second Identified Use: Space-Shifting

Space-shifting occurs when a Napster user downloads MP3 music files in order to listen to music he already owns on audio CD. [*Sony Corp. v. University City Studios, Inc.*, 464 U.S. 417, 423 (1984), is one of the cases on which Napster relies in arguing] that space-shifting of musical compositions and sound recordings [should be considered] fair use. [In *Sony*, the Supreme Court held] that "time-shifting," where a [VCR] owner records a television show for later viewing, is a fair use. The district court did not err when it refused to apply the "shifting" analysis of *Sony*, [a decision that is] inapposite because the . . . shifting [at issue there] did not also simultaneously involve distribution of the copyrighted material to the general public. [The time-shifting in *Sony* typically] exposed the material only to the original user. [Most VCR users] did not distribute taped television broadcasts, but merely enjoyed them at home. Conversely, it is obvious that once a user lists a copy of music he already owns on the Napster system in order to access the music from another location, the song becomes available to millions of other individuals, not just the original CD owner.

We find no error in the district court's determination that plaintiffs will likely succeed in establishing that Napster users do not have a fair use defense. Accordingly, we next address whether Napster is secondarily liable for the direct infringement under . . . contributory copyright infringement and vicarious copyright infringement.

Contributory Copyright Infringement

One who, with knowledge of the infringing activity, induces, causes, or materially contributes to the infringing conduct of another, may be held liable as a contributory infringer. It is apparent from the record that Napster has knowledge, both actual and constructive, of direct infringement. The district court found actual knowledge because: (1) a document authored by Napster co-founder Sean Parker mentioned "the need to remain ignorant of users' real names and IP addresses 'since they are exchanging pirated music'"; and (2) the Recording Industry Association of America informed Napster of more than 12,000 infringing files, some of which are still available. The district court found constructive knowledge because Napster executives have recording industry experience, . . . have enforced intellectual property rights in other instances, . . . have downloaded copyrighted songs from the system, [and] have promoted the site with "screen shots listing infringing files."

Napster claims that it is nevertheless protected from contributory liability by the teaching of *Sony*. We disagree. We observe that Napster's actual, specific knowledge of direct infringement renders *Sony*'s holding of limited assistance to Napster. The *Sony* Court refused to hold the manufacturer and retailers of [VCRs] liable for contributory infringement despite evidence that such machines could be and were used to infringe plaintiffs' copyrighted television shows. *Sony* stated that if liability "is to be imposed on [the defendants], it must rest on the fact that they have sold equipment with constructive knowledge of the fact that their customers may use that equipment to make unauthorized copies of copyrighted material." The *Sony* Court declined to impute the requisite level of knowledge where the defendants made and sold equipment capable of both infringing and "substantial noninfringing uses."

We are bound to follow *Sony,* and will not impute the requisite level of knowledge to Napster merely because peer-to-peer file sharing technology may be used to infringe plaintiffs' copyrights. We agree [with earlier court decisions holding] that if a computer system operator learns of specific infringing material available on his system and fails to purge such material from the system, the operator knows of and contributes to direct infringement. Conversely, absent any specific information which identifies infringing activity, a computer system operator cannot be liable for contributory infringement merely because the structure of the system allows for the exchange of copyrighted material. To enjoin simply because a computer network allows for infringing use would, in our opinion, violate *Sony* and potentially restrict activity unrelated to infringing use.

We nevertheless conclude that sufficient knowledge exists to impose contributory liability when linked to demonstrated infringing use of the Napster system. The record supports the district court's finding that Napster has actual knowledge that specific infringing material is available using its system, that it could block access to the system by suppliers of the infringing material, and that it failed to remove the material.

The district court [also] concluded that "without the support services defendant provides, Napster users could not find and download the music they want with the ease of which defendant boasts." [This was a proper finding] that Napster materially contributes to direct infringement. We [therefore] affirm the district court's conclusion that plaintiffs have demonstrated a likelihood of success on the merits of the contributory copyright infringement claim.

Vicarious Copyright Infringement

In the context of copyright law, vicarious liability extends . . . to cases in which a defendant has the right and ability to supervise the infringing activity and also has a direct financial interest in such activities. Ample evidence supports the district court's finding that Napster's future revenue is directly dependent upon "increases in user-base." More users register with the Napster system as the "quality and quantity of available music increases." We conclude that the district court did not err in determining that Napster financially benefits from the availability of protected works on its system.

The ability to block infringers' access to a particular environment for any reason whatsoever is evidence of the right and ability to supervise. Napster has an express reservation of rights policy, stating on its website that it expressly reserves the "right to refuse service and terminate accounts in [its] discretion, including, but not limited to, if Napster believes that user conduct violates applicable law . . . or for any reason in Napster's sole discretion, with or without cause." To escape imposition of vicarious liability, the reserved right to police must be exercised to its fullest extent. Turning a blind eye to detectable acts of infringement for the sake of profit gives rise to liability.

The district court correctly determined that Napster had the right and ability to police its system and failed to exercise that right to prevent the exchange of copyrighted material. Our review of the record requires us to accept the district court's conclusion that plaintiffs have demonstrated a likelihood of success on the merits of the vicarious copyright infringement claim. Napster's failure to police the system's "premises," combined with a showing that Napster financially benefits from the continuing availability of infringing files on its system, leads to the imposition of vicarious liability.

The district court considered ample evidence to support its determination that the balance of hardships tips in plaintiffs' favor:

> Any destruction of Napster, Inc. by a preliminary injunction is speculative compared to the statistical evidence of massive, unauthorized downloading and uploading of plaintiffs' copyrighted works—as many as 10,000 files per second by defendant's own admission. The court has every reason to believe that, without a preliminary injunction, these numbers will mushroom as Napster users, and newcomers attracted by the publicity, scramble to obtain as much free music as possible before trial.

The district court correctly recognized that a preliminary injunction against Napster's participation in copyright infringement is not only warranted but required. We believe, however, that the scope of the injunction needs modification. The preliminary injunction which we stayed is overbroad because it places on Napster the entire burden of ensuring that no "copying, downloading, uploading, transmitting, or distributing" of plaintiffs' works occur on the system. [We conclude that the plaintiffs should be expected to] provide notice to Napster of copyrighted works and files containing such works available on the Napster system before Napster has the duty to disable access to the offending content. Napster, however, also bears the burden of policing the system within the limits of the system. In crafting the injunction on remand, the district court should [make these modifications].

We . . . briefly address Napster's First Amendment argument so that it is not reasserted on remand. Napster contends that the present injunction violates the First Amendment because it is broader than necessary. The company asserts two distinct free speech rights: (1) its right to publish a "directory" (here, [Napster's] search index); and (2) its users' right to exchange information. We note that First Amendment concerns in copyright are allayed by the presence of the fair use doctrine. There was a preliminary determination here that Napster users are not fair users. Uses of copyrighted material that are not fair uses are rightfully enjoined. [Such an injunction does not] constitute a prior restraint in violation of the First Amendment.

[Finally, Napster argues] that the district court should have imposed a [compulsory] royalty payment structure in lieu of an injunction. Napster tells us that "where great public injury would be worked by an injunction, the courts might . . . award damages or a continuing royalty instead of an injunction in such special circumstances" [citations omitted]. We are at a total loss to find any "special circumstances" simply because this case requires us to apply well-established doctrines of copyright law to a new technology. Neither do we agree with Napster that an injunction would cause "great public injury." Further, we [disagree with] any suggestion that compulsory royalties are appropriate in this context. Congress has arguably limited the application of compulsory royalties to specific circumstances, none of which are present here.

The Copyright Act provides for various sanctions for infringers: [injunctions, damages, and criminal penalties in appropriate cases]. These sanctions represent a more than adequate legislative solution to the problem created by copyright infringement. Imposing a compulsory royalty payment schedule would give Napster an "easy out" of this case. If such royalties were imposed, Napster would avoid penalties for any future violation of an injunction, statutory copyright damages, and any possible criminal penalties for continuing infringement. The royalty structure would also grant Napster the luxury of either choosing to continue and pay royalties or shut down. On the other hand, the wronged parties would be forced to do business with a company that profits from the wrongful use of intellectual properties. Plaintiffs would lose the power to control their intellectual property: they could not make a business decision not to license their property to Napster, and, in the event they planned to do business with Napster, compulsory royalties would take away the copyright holders' ability to negotiate the terms of any contractual arrangement.

District court decision affirmed in part and reversed in part, and case remanded with direction that terms of preliminary injunction be modified.

Trademarks

Trademarks help purchasers identify favored products and services. For this reason, they also give sellers and manufacturers an incentive to innovate and strive for quality. However, both these ends would be defeated if competitors were free to appropriate each other's trademarks. Thus, the federal Lanham Act protects trademark owners against certain uses of their marks by third parties.[3]

Protected Marks The Lanham Act recognizes four kinds of marks. It defines a **trademark** as any word, name, symbol, device, or combination thereof used by a manufacturer or seller to identify its products and distinguish them from the products of competitors. Although trademarks consisting of single words or names are most commonly encountered, federal trademark protection has sometimes been extended to colors, pictures, label and package designs, slogans, sounds, arrangements of numbers and/or letters (e.g., "7-Eleven"), and shapes of goods or their containers (e.g., Coca-Cola bottles).

Service marks resemble trademarks but identify and distinguish services. **Certification marks** certify the origin, materials, quality, method of manufacture, and other aspects of goods and services. Here, the user of the mark and its owner are distinct parties. A retailer, for example, may sell products bearing the Good Housekeeping Seal of Approval. **Collective marks** are trademarks or service marks used by organizations to identify themselves as the source of goods or services. Trade union and trade association marks fall into this category. Although all four kinds of marks receive federal protection, this chapter focuses on trademarks and service marks, using the terms *mark* or *trademark* to refer to both.

Distinctiveness Because their purpose is to help consumers identify products and services, trademarks must

[3]In addition, the owner of a trademark may enjoy legal protection under common law trademark doctrines and state trademark statutes.

ETHICS IN ACTION

Significant ethical issues may arise as part of the clash between intellectual property rights and the claims of those who wish to make use of the protected invention, work, or item. Consider, for instance, these copyright-related questions:

- Is it ethical to use a Napster-like service to obtain free-of-charge access to copyrighted musical compositions and recordings? Does it make a difference if the user downloads music only for his or her own personal use, as opposed to sharing files with other users? Does it make a difference whether the record companies supposedly have—or have not—made significant profits already on their copyrighted recordings? Is it ethical for record companies to seek, from Internet access providers, the names of their customers who have a significant history of using

Napster-like services? (In thinking about these questions, you may find it useful to review the ethical theories discussed in Chapter 4.)

- If one has a plausible claim to the protection of the fair use doctrine, is it ethical to use portions of another party's copyrighted work even though the copyright owner has refused to grant permission for the use?
- How would profit-maximizers, utilitarians, and rights theorists, respectively, be likely to assess the lobbying efforts of copyright owners who desired the significant increase in copyright duration that Congress enacted in the Sonny Bono Copyright Term Extension Act of 1998? (Feel free to review Chapter 4's discussion of the theories referred to in this question.)

---

be *distinctive* to merit maximum Lanham Act protection. Marks fall into five general categories of distinctiveness (or nondistinctiveness):

1. *Arbitrary or fanciful marks.* These marks are the most distinctive—and the most likely to be protected—because they do not describe the qualities of the product or service they identify. The "Exxon" trademark is an example.

2. *Suggestive marks.* These marks convey the nature of a product or service only through imagination, thought, and perception. They do not actually describe the underlying product or service. The "Dietene" trademark for a dietary food supplement is an example. Although not as clearly distinctive as arbitrary or fanciful marks, suggestive marks are nonetheless classified as distinctive. Hence, they are good candidates for protection.

3. *Descriptive marks.* These marks directly describe the product or service they identify (e.g., "Realemon," for bottled lemon juice). Descriptive marks are not protected unless they acquire *secondary meaning.* This occurs when their identification with a particular source of goods or services has become firmly established in the minds of a substantial number of buyers. "Realemon," of course, now has secondary meaning. Among the factors considered in secondary-meaning determinations are the length of time the mark has been used, the volume of sales associated with that use, and the nature of the advertising employing the mark. When applied to a package delivery service, for instance, the term *overnight* is usually descriptive and thus not protectible. It may come

to deserve trademark protection, however, through long use by a single firm that advertised it extensively and made many sales while doing so. As will be seen, the same approach is taken concerning deceptively misdescriptive and geographically descriptive marks.

4. *Marks that are not inherently distinctive.* Although these marks are not distinctive in the usual senses of arbitrary nature, fanciful quality, or suggestiveness, proof of secondary meaning effectively makes these marks distinctive. They are therefore protectible if secondary meaning exists. The Supreme Court has held that under appropriate circumstances, product color is a potentially protectible trademark of this type.

5. *Generic terms.* Generic terms (e.g., "diamond" or "truck") simply refer to the general class of which the particular product or service is one example. Because any seller has the right to call a product or service by its common name, generic terms are ineligible for trademark protection.

Federal Registration   Once the seller of a product or service uses a mark in commerce or forms a bona fide intention to do so very soon, she may apply to register the mark with the U.S. Patent and Trademark Office. The office reviews applications for distinctiveness. Its decision to deny or grant the application may be contested by the applicant or by a party who feels that he would be injured by registration of the mark. Such challenges may eventually reach the federal courts.

Trademarks of sufficient distinctiveness are placed on the Principal Register of the Patent and Trademark Office. A mark's inclusion in the Principal Register: (1) is prima facie evidence of the mark's ownership, validity, and registration (which is useful in trademark infringement suits); (2) gives nationwide constructive notice of the owner's claim of ownership (thus eliminating the need to show that the defendant in an infringement suit had notice of the mark); (3) entitles the mark owner to assistance from the Bureau of Customs in stopping the importation of certain goods that, without the consent of the mark owner, bear a likeness of the mark; and (4) means that the mark will be incontestable after five years of registered status (as described later).

Even though they are not distinctive, certain other marks may merit placement on the Principal Register if they have acquired secondary meaning. These include: (1) marks that are *not inherently distinctive* (as discussed earlier); (2) *descriptive* marks (as discussed earlier); (3) *deceptively misdescriptive* marks (such as "Dura-Skin," for plastic gloves); (4) *geographically descriptive* marks (such as "Indiana-Made"); and (5) marks that are *primarily a surname* (because as a matter of general policy, persons who have a certain last name should be fairly free to use that name in connection with their businesses). Once a mark in one of these classifications achieves registered status, the mark's owner obtains the legal benefits described in the previous paragraph.

Regardless of their distinctiveness, however, some kinds of marks are denied placement on the Principal Register. These include marks that: (1) consist of the flags or other insignia of governments; (2) consist of the name, portrait, or signature of a living person who has not given consent to the trademark use; (3) are immoral, deceptive, or scandalous; or (4) are likely to cause confusion because they resemble a mark previously registered or used in the United States.

Transfer of Rights Because of the purposes underlying trademark law, transferring trademark rights is more difficult than transferring copyright or patent interests. A trademark owner may license the use of the mark, but only if the owner reserves control over the nature and quality of the goods or services as to which the licensee will use the mark. An uncontrolled "naked license" would allow the sale of goods or services bearing the mark but lacking the qualities formerly associated with it, and could confuse purchasers. Trademark rights may also be assigned or sold, but only along with the sale of the goodwill of the business originally using the mark.

Losing Federal Trademark Protection Federal registration of a trademark lasts for 10 years, with renewals for additional 10-year periods possible. However, trademark protection may be lost before the period expires. The government must cancel a registration six years after its date unless the registrant files with the Patent and Trademark Office, within the fifth and sixth years following the registration date, an affidavit detailing that the mark is in use or explaining its nonuse.

Any person who believes that he is or will be damaged by a mark's registration may petition the Patent and Trademark Office to cancel that registration. Normally, the petition must be filed within five years of the mark's registration, because the mark becomes *incontestable* as regards goods or services with which it has continuously been used for five consecutive years after the registration. A mark's incontestability means that the permissible grounds for canceling its registration are limited. Even an incontestable mark, however, may be canceled *at any time* if, among other things, it was obtained by fraud, has been abandoned, or has become the generic name for the goods or services it identifies. *Abandonment* may occur through an express statement or agreement to abandon, through the mark's losing its significance as an indication of origin, or through the owner's failure to use it. A mark acquires a *generic meaning* when it comes to refer to a class of products or services rather than a particular source's product or service. For example, this has happened to such once-protected marks as aspirin, escalator, and thermos.

Trademark Infringement A trademark is infringed when, without the owner's consent, another party uses a substantially similar mark in connection with the sale of goods or services and this is likely to cause confusion concerning their source or concerning whether there is an endorsement relationship or other affiliation between the mark's owner and the other party. The *Brookfield Communications* case, which follows shortly, deals with trademark infringement issues stemming from a World Wide Web domain name dispute. It also discusses many of the factors courts consider when determining whether the use is likely to cause confusion. A trademark owner who wins an infringement suit may obtain an injunction against uses of the mark that are likely to cause confusion. In addition, the owner may obtain money damages for provable injury resulting from the infringement, as well as attributable profits realized by the infringing defendant.

THE GLOBAL BUSINESS ENVIRONMENT

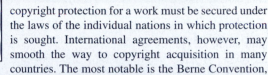

An American firm may enter the world market by licensing its product or service to a foreign manufacturer. In exchange for granting a license to the foreign licensee, the American licensor will receive royalties from the sale of the licensed product or service. Usually, the licensed product or service or the name under which it is sold will be protected by American intellectual property law, such as patent, trade secret, copyright, or trademark law. Because American intellectual property law does not protect the property outside the boundaries of the United States, a licensor needs to take steps to ensure that its intellectual property will acquire protection in the foreign nation. Otherwise, the licensor risks that a competitor may appropriate the intellectual property without penalty.

The World Trade Organization has attempted to increase the protection of intellectual property through passage of the Agreement on Trade-Related Aspects of Intellectual Property Rights **(TRIPS).** Effective in 1995, TRIPS covers patents, trade secrets, copyrights, and trademarks. It sets out minimum standards of intellectual property protection to be provided by each member nation. Some signatory nations, such as the United States, provide greater protection of intellectual property.

Patents and Trade Secrets

A patent filing must be made in each nation in which protection is desired. It is not especially difficult for a firm to acquire parallel patents in each of the major countries maintaining a patent system, because many countries (including the United States), are parties to the Paris Convention for the Protection of Industrial Property. This convention recognizes the date of the first filing in any nation as the filing date for all, but only if subsequent filings are in fact made within a year of the first filing.

When technology is not patented, either because it is not patentable or because a firm makes a business decision not to patent it, a licensor may control its use abroad under **trade secret** law. For example, an American firm can license its manufacturing know-how to a foreign manufacturer for use in a defined territory in return for promises to pay royalties and to keep the trade secret confidential.

Copyright

An American firm may license a foreign manufacturer to produce literary, artistic, or musical materials for which the firm holds an American copyright. For example, a computer software development firm may grant a license to a foreign manufacturer of software, or the American owner of copyrights protecting cartoon characters from the television program *The Simpsons* may license a Chinese firm to manufacture Homer, Marge, and Bart dolls.

There is no international copyright that automatically protects a copyrighted work everywhere in the world. Instead, copyright protection for a work must be secured under the laws of the individual nations in which protection is sought. International agreements, however, may smooth the way to copyright acquisition in many countries. The most notable is the Berne Convention, to which the United States and approximately 150 other nations subscribe. The Berne Convention guarantees that a work eligible for copyright in any signatory nation will be eligible for protection in all signatory nations. Although the Berne Convention does not completely standardize the copyright laws of the member nations, it does require each country's copyright laws to contain certain minimum guarantees of rights.

Another key aspect of the Berne Convention is its principle of *national treatment,* under which each signatory nation agrees to treat copyright owners from other subscribing countries according to the same rules it applies to copyright owners who are its own residents or citizens. Other international agreements to which the United States is a party operate in generally similar fashion. These include the Universal Copyright Convention and the World Intellectual Property Organization Copyright Treaty.

Trademarks

The holder of an American trademark may license the use of its trademark in a foreign nation. For example, McDonald's may license a French firm to use the McDonald's name and golden arches at a restaurant on the Champs-Elysees, or the holder of the Calvin Klein trademark may license a South Korean firm to manufacture Calvin Klein jeans.

An American trademark's owner, when licensing its product or services abroad, runs the risk of experiencing unwanted and largely uncontrollable uses of its trademark in a foreign market unless it has acquired trademark rights in that nation.

Trademark registrations normally must be made in each nation in which protection is desired. Parallel trademark registrations, however, may be made in compliance with the Paris Convention for the Protection of Industrial Property. Under the Paris Convention, the date of the first filing in any nation is the filing date for all nations, if the subsequent filings are made within six months of the first filing.

The European Union allows a single filing to be effective in all EU nations. An agreement known as the Madrid Protocol also permits a firm to register a trademark in all its signatory nations simultaneously by filing an application for registration in any signatory nation and with the World Intellectual Property Organization (WIPO) in Geneva. As this book went to press in late 2002, it appeared highly likely that the United States would soon join the Madrid Protocol. You can check the status of Madrid Protocol adoptions at the WIPO Web page: www.wipo.org.

Brookfield Communications, Inc. v. West Coast Entertainment Corp.
174 F.3d 1036 (9th Cir. 1999)

Brookfield Communications, Inc., produced software that provided information to entertainment industry professionals such as film studios, production companies, agents, directors, and actors. In December 1993, Brookfield introduced software that featured entertainment industry information of interest to smaller companies and individual consumers who did not want to purchase Brookfield's professional-level alternative. Brookfield used MOVIEBUFF as the name of its consumer-level software, whose searchable databases and related applications contained information such as box office receipts, film release schedules, entertainment news, and names of executives, agents, directors, and actors.

In 1996, Brookfield attempted to register the World Wide Web domain name "moviebuff.com" with Network Solutions, Inc., which was then the exclusive registrar of ".com" domain names. Brookfield learned, however, that this domain name had already been registered (in February 1996) to West Coast Entertainment Corporation, which owned a large chain of video rental stores. Brookfield therefore registered two other domain names in May and September 1996. It launched web sites bearing those domain names to sell MOVIEBUFF software and offer an online searchable database for which it also used the MOVIEBUFF name. In August 1997, Brookfield applied to the Patent & Trademark Office (PTO) for registration of MOVIEBUFF as a mark used in connection with goods and services. The PTO issued trademark and service mark registrations to Brookfield in September 1998.

Brookfield learned, in October 1998, that West Coast planned to launch a "moviebuff.com" web site that would contain a searchable entertainment database similar to Brookfield's. West Coast claimed that it had registered the "moviebuff.com" domain name nearly two years earlier because the term "movie buff" was part of its federally registered (since 1991) service mark, THE MOVIE BUFF'S MOVIE STORE. After a November 1998 press release made clear that West Coast would in fact launch the "moviebuff.com" web site featuring a searchable entertainment database, Brookfield sued West Coast for trademark infringement. Brookfield contended that West Coast's use of "moviebuff.com" would infringe Brookfield's MOVIEBUFF mark.

The district court denied Brookfield's request for a preliminary injunction that would have barred West Coast from using "moviebuff.com." The court reasoned that West Coast was effectively the senior user of MOVIEBUFF because of its long-standing service mark (THE MOVIE BUFF'S MOVIE STORE) and because it acquired rights over the "moviebuff.com" domain name before Brookfield's use of MOVIEBUFF as the name of Brookfield's Internet-based searchable database. The court also concluded that Brookfield had not established likelihood of consumer confusion. Brookfield appealed to the Ninth Circuit Court of Appeals.

O'Scannlain, Circuit Judge To resolve whether West Coast's use of "moviebuff.com" constitutes trademark infringement, we must first determine whether Brookfield has a valid, protectible trademark interest in the MOVIEBUFF mark. Brookfield's registration of the mark on the Principal Register constitutes prima facie evidence of the validity of the registered mark and of Brookfield's exclusive right to use the mark on the goods and services specified in the registration. [Although West Coast could have rebutted this presumption by showing that it used the mark in commerce first, West Coast did not make an adequate showing in this regard. Because consumers would not view "moviebuff.com" and THE MOVIE BUFF'S MOVIE STORE as virtually identical marks, the district court erred in concluding that West Coast's first use of "moviebuff.com" effectively occurred prior to or during 1991, when THE MOVIE BUFF'S MOVIE STORE became a registered mark. Moreover, even though West Coast

obtained the "moviebuff.com" domain name registration in February 1996, West Coast's first real use of "moviebuff.com," for purposes of determining trademark priority, did not occur until November 1998 (when West Coast issued a press release announcing its web site). By that time, Brookfield had made substantial use of the MOVIEBUFF mark.] [W]e must conclude that Brookfield is the senior user because it marketed MOVIEBUFF products well before West Coast began using "moviebuff.com" in commerce.

Establishing seniority, however, is only half the battle. Brookfield must also show that the public is likely to be somehow confused about the source or sponsorship of West Coast's "moviebuff.com" web site—and somehow to associate that site with Brookfield. We look to the following factors for guidance in determining [whether a] likelihood of confusion [exists]: similarity of the conflicting designations; relatedness or proximity of the two companies' products or services; strength of [the trademark owner's] mark; marketing channels used; degree of care likely to be exercised by purchasers in selecting goods; [the alleged infringer's] intent in selecting its mark; evidence of actual confusion; and likelihood of expansion in product lines. [T]his eight-factor test . . . is pliant. Some factors are much more important than others, and the relative importance of each individual factor will be case-specific. Although some factors—such as the similarity of the marks and whether the two companies are direct competitors—will always be important, it is often possible to reach a conclusion with respect to likelihood of confusion after considering only a subset of the factors.

We begin by comparing the allegedly infringing mark to the federally registered mark. [As a general rule,] the more similar the marks in terms of appearance, sound, and meaning, the greater the likelihood of confusion. [I]t is readily apparent that West Coast's allegedly infringing mark is essentially identical to Brookfield's mark MOVIEBUFF. [T]here are differences in capitalization and the addition of ".com" in West Coast's complete domain name, but these differences are inconsequential in light of the fact that web addresses are not caps-sensitive and that the ".com" top-level domain signifies the site's commercial nature.

Looks aren't everything, so we consider the similarity of sound and meaning. The two marks are pronounced the same way, except that one would say "dot.com" at the end of West Coast's mark. Because many companies use domain names comprised of ".com" as the top-level domain with their corporate name or trademark as the second-level domain, the addition of ".com" is of diminished importance in distinguishing the mark. The domain name is more than a mere address: like trademarks, second-level domain names communicate information as to source. [M]any web users are likely to associate "moviebuff.com" with the trademark MOVIEBUFF, thinking that it is operated by the company that makes MOVIEBUFF products and services.

The similarity of marks alone, [however], does not necessarily lead to consumer confusion. [W]e must . . . consider the relatedness of the products and services offered. Related goods are generally more likely than unrelated goods to confuse the public as to the producers of the goods. Here, both companies offer products and services relating to the entertainment industry generally, and their principal lines of business both relate to movies specifically. [T]he competitive proximity of their products is quite high. Just as Brookfield's MOVIEBUFF is a searchable database with detailed information on films, West Coast's web site features a similar searchable database. [T]he products are used for similar

purposes [and] the two companies compete for the patronage of an overlapping audience. The use of similar marks to offer similar products accordingly weighs heavily in favor of likelihood of confusion. [In addition,] West Coast and Brookfield both utilize the Web as a marketing and advertising facility, a factor that courts have consistently recognized as exacerbating the likelihood of confusion.

Given the virtual identity of "moviebuff.com" and MOVIEBUFF, the relatedness of the products and services accompanied by those marks, and the companies' simultaneous use of the Web as a marketing and advertising tool, many forms of consumer confusion are likely to result. People surfing the Web for information on MOVIEBUFF may confuse MOVIEBUFF with the searchable entertainment database at "moviebuff.com" and simply assume that they have reached Brookfield's web site. [E]ntering a web site takes little effort—usually one click from a linked site or a search engine's list; thus Web surfers are more likely to be confused as to the ownership of a web site than traditional patrons of a brick-and-mortar store would be of a store's ownership. Alternatively, they may incorrectly believe that West Coast licensed MOVIEBUFF from Brookfield. Other consumers may simply believe that West Coast bought out Brookfield or that they are related companies.

Yet other forms of confusion are likely to ensue. Consumers may wrongly assume that the MOVIEBUFF database they were searching for is no longer offered, having been replaced by West Coast's entertainment database, and thus simply use the services at West Coast's web site. And even where people realize, immediately upon accessing "moviebuff.com," that they have reached a site operated by West Coast and wholly unrelated to Brookfield, West Coast will still have gained a customer by appropriating the goodwill that Brookfield has developed in its MOVIEBUFF mark.

The factors that we have considered so far . . . lead us to the tentative conclusion that Brookfield has made a strong showing of likelihood of confusion. Because it is possible that the remaining factors will tip the scale back the other way . . . , we consider the remaining [ones], beginning with the strength of Brookfield's mark. The stronger a mark—meaning the more likely it is to be remembered and associated in the public's mind with the mark's owner—the greater the protection it is accorded by the trademark laws. [MOVIEBUFF is a distinctive mark because it is suggestive, making it stronger than a descriptive mark but weaker than a mark that is distinctive for reasons of fanciful nature or arbitrary assignment.] [Here, however,] the products involved are closely related and West Coast's domain name is nearly identical to Brookfield's trademark. [Therefore, in this case,] the strength of the mark is of diminished importance in the likelihood of confusion analysis.

We thus turn to intent. An inference of confusion has . . . been deemed appropriate where a mark is adopted with the intent to deceive the public. There is, however, no evidence . . . that West Coast registered "moviebuff.com" with the principal intent of confusing consumers. Brookfield correctly points out that, by the time West Coast launched its web site, it did know of Brookfield's claim to rights in the trademark MOVIEBUFF. But when it registered the domain name with Network Solutions, West Coast did not know of Brookfield's rights in MOVIEBUFF. West Coast claims that it had already invested considerable sums in developing its "moviebuff.com" web site by the time that Brookfield informed it of its rights in the trademark. Considered as a whole, this factor appears indeterminate.

The final three [likelihood of confusion] factors—evidence of actual confusion, likelihood of expansion in product lines, and purchaser care—do not affect our ultimate conclusion. Actual confusion is not relevant [in this case] because Brookfield filed suit before West Coast began actively using the "moviebuff.com" mark and thus never had the opportunity to collect information on actual confusion. The likelihood of expansion in product lines factor is relatively unimportant where two companies already compete to a significant extent.

[T]he degree of care likely to be exercised by purchasers of the products in question [deserves more comment]. Likelihood of confusion is determined on the basis of a reasonably prudent consumer. What is expected of this reasonably prudent consumer depends on the circumstances. We [sometimes] expect him to be more discerning—and less easily confused—when he is purchasing expensive items, and when the products are being marketed primarily to expert buyers. On the other hand, when dealing with inexpensive products, consumers [may be] likely to exercise less care, thus making confusion more likely. The complexity in this case arises because we must consider both entertainment professionals, who probably will take the time . . . to find the specific product they want, and movie devotees, who will be more easily confused as to the source of the database offered at West Coast's web site. Who is the reasonably prudent consumer [in this situation involving mixed buyers]? Although . . . the issue of purchaser care in mixed buyer [situations is potentially significant in some cases], [w]e need not . . . decide this question now because the purchaser confusion factor, even considered in the light most favorable to West Coast, is not sufficient to overcome the likelihood of confusion established by the other factors we have analyzed.

District court's denial of preliminary injunction reversed; case remanded for further proceedings.

Trademark Dilution In recent years, Congress granted owners of certain marks an alternative to the standard claim of trademark infringement. The Federal Trademark Dilution Act (FTDA), which took effect in 1996 and was placed in the Lanham Act as section 43(c), allows the owner of a "famous" mark to seek legal relief when another party's commercial use of a substantially similar version of the famous mark causes "dilution of [the mark's] distinctive quality." Under the FTDA, a mark need not be a registered mark in order to be "famous." Proof of likelihood of confusion—essential to a claim for trademark infringement—is not required for purposes of this claim of trademark *dilution*. The FTDA provides that if dilution is established, the owner of the famous mark will normally be entitled only to the standard remedy of an injunction against the defendant's continued use of the diluting version of the mark. Damages and the infringer's profits are recoverable by the owner of the famous mark only if the evidence reveals that the defendant willfully sought either to trade on the mark owner's reputation or to cause dilution of the mark.

For purposes of the FTDA and similar statutes that exist in roughly half the states, dilution occurs if the defendant's use of the plaintiff's trademark causes the public, which previously had associated the trademark only with the plaintiff, to associate the trademark with the defendant as well. When this takes place, the trademark's distinctiveness has been whittled away—i.e., diluted—even if the public recognizes that the plaintiff and defendant are not affiliated and that they provide different products or services. Courts interpreting the FTDA and the state dilution statutes have concluded that dilution may occur in another way: through the defendant's use of the plaintiff's trademark in an unwholesome context (normally one suggesting illicit sexual or drug-related connotations). Use of the trademark in such a context may dilute it by tarnishing its reputation.

THE GLOBAL BUSINESS ENVIRONMENT

Piracy and other unauthorized uses of American goods or technology protected by U.S. patent, copyright, and trademark law have become a major problem of American businesses. For example, foreign jeans manufacturers may without authorization place the Levi's label on their jeans, thereby damaging the business of Levi Strauss & Co. by depriving it of some of the jeans' market and damaging the value of the Levi trademark, especially if the imported jeans are of inferior quality. This is an example of **counterfeit goods**—goods that copy or otherwise purport to be those of the trademark owner whose mark has been unlawfully used on the nongenuine goods. Counterfeit goods may also unlawfully appropriate patented technology or copyrighted material. For example, a foreign musical recording company may pirate the latest Madonna album and import thousands of copies of it into the United States without copyright permission.

American firms harmed by the importation of counterfeit goods may obtain injunctions and damages under the Tariff Act of 1930, the Lanham Act, the Copyright Act, and the patent statute. In addition, the Trademark Counterfeiting Act of 1984 establishes civil and criminal penalties for counterfeiting goods. It also allows an American firm to recover from a counterfeiter three times its damages or three times the counterfeiter's profits (whichever is greater).

Patent, copyright, and trademark piracy is increasing in many parts of the world, especially in developing nations.

Some developing nations believe that technology should be transferred freely to foster their economic growth. Consequently, they either encourage piracy or choose not to oppose it.

Gray market goods are goods lawfully bearing trademarks or using patents and copyrighted material but entering the American market without authorization. For example, Parker Pen Co. may authorize a Japanese manufacturer to make and sell Parker pens only in Japan. When an American firm imports the Japanese-made Parker pens into the United States, the goods become gray market goods.

While importing gray market goods may violate the contract between the American firm and its foreign licensee, it is not clear in what contexts it violates U.S. importation, trademark, patent, or copyright law. Some courts find a Lanham Act or Tariff Act violation, but other courts do not. The Trademark Counterfeiting Act of 1984 specifically excludes gray market goods from its coverage. The Copyright Act deals with gray market goods in a provision barring the "[i]mportation into the United States, without the authority of the owner of the copyright . . . of copies or phonorecords of a work that has been acquired outside the United States." Whether the items may lawfully enter the United States depends, therefore, on whether the copyright owner has provided "authority" for this to occur.

CYBERLAW IN ACTION

As revealed earlier in the *Brookfield Communications* case, trademark infringement principles sometimes govern conflicts between one party's claim of trademark rights and another's claim of rights over a World Wide Web domain name. Such disputes sometimes raise dilution issues as well.

In a 1999 enactment, Congress paid special attention to the trademark rights–domain name rights conflict by enacting the Anticybersquatting Consumer Protection Act (hereinafter "ACPA"). The ACPA authorizes a civil action in favor of a trademark owner against any person who, having a "bad faith intent to profit" from the owner's mark, registers, sells, purchases, licenses, or otherwise uses a domain name that is identical or confusingly similar to the owner's mark (or would dilute the mark, if it is famous). Among the factors listed in the ACPA as relevant to the existence of bad faith intent to profit are a defendant's intent to divert consumers from the mark owner's online location to a site that could harm the mark's goodwill, and a defendant's offer to sell the domain name to the mark owner without having used, or intended to use, the domain name in the offering of goods or services.

If the trademark owner wins a cybersquatting action, the court may order the forfeiture or cancellation of the domain name or may order that it be transferred to the mark owner. The successful trademark owner may also recover actual damages as well as the cybersquatter's attributable profits. Borrowing the statutory damages concept from the Copyright Act, the ACPA provides that in lieu of actual damages plus profits, the trademark owner may elect to recover statutory damages falling within a range of $1,000 to $100,000 per domain name, "as the court considers just."

Many cases in which a trademark owner complains about another party's registration of a domain name have been submitted to arbitration, rather than to a court, in recent years. When a party registers an Internet address with the Internet Corporation for Assigned Names and Numbers, the registrant must agree to submit to arbitration in the event that a trademark owner claims a right to the domain name. The World Intellectual Property Organization is a leading provider of arbitrators for this process.

Trade Secrets

The law provides at least two means of protecting creative inventions. Owners of such inventions may go public and obtain monopoly patent rights. As an alternative, they may keep the invention secret and rely on trade secrets law to protect it.

The policies underlying patent protection and trade secrets protection differ. The general aim of patent law is to encourage the creation and disclosure of inventions by granting the patentee a temporary monopoly in the patented invention in exchange for his making it public. Trade secrets, however, are nonpublic by definition. Although protecting trade secrets may stimulate creative activity, it also keeps the information from becoming public knowledge. Thus, the main justification for trade secrets protection is simply to preserve certain standards of commercial morality.

Definition of a Trade Secret

A trade secret can be defined as any secret formula, pattern, process, program, device, method, technique, or compilation of information used in the owner's business, if it gives its owner an advantage over competitors who do not know it or use it.[4] Examples include chemical formulas, computer software, manufacturing processes, designs for machines, and customer lists. To be protectible, a trade secret must usually have sufficient value or originality to provide an actual or potential competitive advantage. It need not possess the novelty required for patent protection, however.

The *North Atlantic Instruments* case, which follows shortly, considers factors courts may examine when determining whether a trade secret exists. As some of the factors suggest, a trade secret must actually be *secret*. A substantial measure of secrecy is necessary, but it need not be absolute. Thus, information that becomes public knowledge or becomes generally known in the industry cannot be a trade secret. Similarly, information that is reasonably discoverable by proper means may not be protected. "Proper means" include independent invention of the secret, observation of a publicly displayed product, the owner's advertising, published literature, product analysis, and reverse engineering (starting with a legitimately acquired product and working backward to discover how it was developed).

In addition, a firm claiming a trade secret must usually show that it took *reasonable measures to ensure secrecy*. Examples include advising employees about the secret's secrecy, limiting access to the secret on a need-to-know basis, requiring those given access to sign a nondisclosure agreement, disclosing the secret only on a confidential basis, and controlling access to an office or plant. Computer software licensing agreements commonly forbid the licensee to copy the program except for backup and archival purposes, require the licensee and its employees to sign confidentiality agreements, call for those employees to use the program only in the course of their jobs, and require the licensee to use the program only in a central processing unit. Because the owner must only make *reasonable* efforts to ensure secrecy, however, she need not adopt extreme measures to block every ingenious form of industrial espionage.

Ownership and Transfer of Trade Secrets

The owner of a trade secret is usually the person who developed it or the business under whose auspices it was generated. Establishing the ownership of a trade secret can pose problems, however, when an employee develops a secret in the course of her employment. In such cases, courts often find the *employer* to be the owner if: (1) the employee was hired to do creative work related to the secret, (2) the employee agreed not to divulge or use trade secrets, or (3) other employees contributed to the development of the secret. Even when the employee owns the secret, the employer still may obtain a royalty-free license to use it through the shop right doctrine discussed in the section on patents.

The owner of a trade secret may transfer rights in the secret to third parties. This may occur by assignment (in which case the owner loses title) or by license (in which case the owner retains title but allows the transferee certain uses of the secret).

Misappropriation of Trade Secrets

Misappropriation of a trade secret can occur in various ways, most of which involve *disclosure* or *use* of the secret. For example, misappropriation liability occurs when the secret is disclosed or used by one who did one of the following:

1. Acquired it by *improper means*. Improper means include theft, trespass, wiretapping, spying, bugging, bribery, fraud, impersonation, and eavesdropping.

---

[4]This definition comes mainly from *Restatement (Third) of Unfair Competition* § 39 (1995) with some additions from *Uniform Trade Secrets Act* § 1(4) (1985). Many states have adopted the Uniform Trade Secrets Act (UTSA) in some form. The discussion in this chapter is a composite of the *Restatement*'s and the UTSA's rules.

2. Acquired it from a party who *is known or should be known* to have obtained it by improper means. For example, a free-lance industrial spy might obtain one firm's trade secrets by improper means and sell them to the firm's competitors. If those competitors know or have reason to know that the spy obtained the secrets by improper means, they are liable for misappropriation along with the spy.

3. *Breached a duty of confidentiality regarding the secret.* If an employer owns a trade secret, for example, an employee is generally bound not to use or disclose it during his employment or thereafter.[5] The *North Atlantic Instruments* case presents an application of this rule. The employee may, however, utilize general knowledge and skills acquired during her employment.

---

[5] This is an application of the agent's duty of loyalty, which is discussed in Chapter 35.

North Atlantic Instruments, Inc. v. Haber   *188 F.3d 38 (2d Cir. 1999)*

North Atlantic Instruments, Inc., manufactured electronic equipment used on ships, tanks, and aircraft. In August 1994, North Atlantic acquired Transmagnetics, Inc. (TMI), which designed, manufactured, and sold customized electronic devices to a limited number of engineers in the aerospace and high tech industries. At the time North Atlantic acquired TMI, Fred Haber was a one-third owner of TMI, as well as its president and head of sales. This position allowed Haber to develop extensive client contacts. North Atlantic conditioned its agreement to acquire TMI on Haber's continuing to work for North Atlantic in a role similar to the role he had played at TMI.

The specialized nature of TMI's business made the identity of the relatively small number of engineers who required its products especially crucial to its business success. Even in companies employing thousands of engineers, a very small number of those engineers—sometimes only two—might need the technology produced by TMI. The identity and needs of that small number of engineers (i.e., TMI's client contacts) would have been very difficult for any company to derive on its own. TMI's list of client contacts was among the intangible assets for which North Atlantic paid when it acquired TMI.

North Atlantic retained Haber as president of its new TMI division. An employment agreement between North Atlantic and Haber ran until July 31, 1997. Its terms obligated Haber not to disclose North Atlantic's customer lists, trade secrets, or other confidential information, either during his employment by North Atlantic or after that employment ceased. As president of the TMI division, Haber had access through desktop and laptop computers to information about North Atlantic's technology and customer bases, including lists of clients and information about their individual product needs and purchases. In July 1997, Haber left North Atlantic to join Apex Signal Corp., which manufactured products targeted toward the same niche market as North Atlantic's TMI division. According to North Atlantic, Apex began targeting North Atlantic's customer base, with Haber allegedly asking clients he had dealt with at North Atlantic and TMI to do business with Apex. North Atlantic also contended that Haber had taken its confidential client information with him when he joined Apex.

North Atlantic sued Haber and Apex for misappropriation of trade secrets and requested a preliminary injunction. The federal district court referred the injunction request to a magistrate, who conducted an extensive hearing and issued a report recommending issuance of the injunction. The district court adopted the magistrate's report and preliminarily enjoined Haber and Apex from using the individual client contacts Haber had developed at North Atlantic and TMI. Haber and Apex appealed.

Straub, Circuit Judge To succeed on a claim for the misappropriation of trade secrets under New York law, a party must demonstrate: (1) that it possessed a trade secret, and (2) that the defendants used the trade secret in breach of an agreement, confidential relationship, or duty, or as a result of discovery by improper means.

We first consider whether the District Court properly concluded that North Atlantic's client list, which contains the identities and preferences of its client contacts, constitutes a protectable trade secret. A trade secret is any formula, pattern, device, or compilation of information which is used in one's business, and which gives the owner an opportunity to obtain an advantage over competitors who do not know or use it. [Precedent cases indicate that a] customer list developed by a business through substantial effort and kept in confidence may be treated as a trade secret and protected at the owner's instance against disclosure to a competitor, provided the information it contains is not otherwise readily ascertainable.

The Magistrate Judge concluded that the list of *companies* to which North Atlantic's TMI division sold was not a trade secret. By contrast, [he] determined that the *identities of individual contact people* with whom Haber dealt while at North Atlantic or TMI were protectable trade secrets. The Magistrate Judge . . . determin[ed] that information on specific contact people was not readily available to others in the industry. That is, Haber generated the list of specific contact people—the people who required the customized technology produced by TMI and North Atlantic's TMI division—over the 50 years he had worked in the industry, more than half of which he spent at TMI. The Magistrate Judge relied . . . on the testimony of North Atlantic's chief executive, who described the needle-in-the-haystack character of the search for the handful of engineers in companies of 100,000 employees who might have a use for one of North Atlantic's customized products.

The Magistrate Judge [also] conclud[ed] that North Atlantic took numerous appropriate measures to prevent unauthorized disclosure of the information contained in its list of client contacts. [These measures included the use of nondisclosure provisions in employment agreements and other access restrictions.] The Magistrate Judge next assessed the value of the list of client contacts and the energy and effort necessary to create it. [H]e pointed to the testimony by North Atlantic's chief executive stating that "in the technology business, the most expensive thing to replicate is your relationships with your customers." [In addition,] the Magistrate Judge concluded that the client contact list assembled over Haber's years at TMI and North Atlantic's TMI division could probably be duplicated, but only with great difficulty.

We hold that the District Court did not err in adopting the Magistrate Judge's extensive and detailed factual determination that the identity of North Atlantic's client contacts was a protectable trade secret. Numerous cases applying New York law have held that where, as here, it would be difficult to duplicate a customer list because it reflected individual customer preferences, trade secret protection should apply.

We next consider whether the defendants' use of a trade secret—specifically the list of client contacts—was in breach of a duty. Both this Circuit and numerous New York courts have held that an agent has a duty not to use confidential knowledge acquired in his employment in competition with his principal. Such a duty exists as well after the employment is terminated as during its continuance . . . and is implied in every contract of employment. [Moreover, the employment agreement between North Atlantic and Haber] provided expressly that Haber had a comparable duty to maintain the confidentiality of TMI's and North Atlantic's trade secrets. In this way, [the employment agreement] makes explicit an employee's implied duties under New York law with respect to confidential information.

[A]t the hearing before the Magistrate Judge, North Atlantic produced a printout of confidential client information from North Atlantic's customer database, printed by Haber on September 5, 1997—over one month after he had left North Atlantic—and found in Apex's files. Haber clearly used the information on the day he printed the file. That day, he sent a fax to a contact listed on the form. Testimony at the hearing suggested that it would have been impossible for Haber to have generated th[e] information [in the file printed on September 5, 1997] unless he had taken files with him when he left North Atlantic.

Based on the facts in the record, it is clear that Haber violated the duties imposed both by the employment agreement and by New York's laws. [T]he District Court properly concluded that North Atlantic has demonstrated a likelihood of success on the merits of its misappropriation of trade secrets claim. Finally, [w]e have held [in a prior case] that the loss of trade secrets cannot be measured in money damages because a trade secret, once lost, is, of course, lost forever. We conclude that North Atlantic would be irreparably harmed in the absence of an injunction.

Decision of District Court affirmed.

Remedies for misappropriation of a trade secret include damages, which may involve both the actual loss caused by the misappropriation and the defendant's unjust enrichment. In some states, punitive damages are awarded for willful and malicious misappropriations. Also, an injunction may be issued against actual or threatened misappropriations.

Commercial Torts

In addition to the intentional torts discussed in Chapter 6, other intentional torts involve business or commercial competition. These torts may help promote innovation by protecting creative businesses against certain competitive abuses. Their main aim, however, is simply to up-hold certain minimum standards of commercial morality.

Injurious Falsehood

Injurious falsehood also goes by names such as product disparagement, slander of title, and trade libel. This tort involves the publication of false statements that disparage another's business, property, or title to property, and thus harm her economic interests. One common kind of injurious falsehood involves false statements that disparage either a person's *property rights* in land, things, or intangibles, or their *quality.* The property rights in question include virtually all legally protected property interests that can be sold; examples include leases, mineral rights, trademarks, copyrights, and corporate stock. Injurious falsehood also includes false statements that harm another's economic interests even though they do not disparage property or property rights as such.

Elements and Damages In injurious falsehood cases, the plaintiff must prove that the defendant made a false statement of the sort just described, and that the statement was communicated to a third party. The *Jefferson County School District* case, which follows shortly, deals with the sometimes difficult problem of distinguishing between false statements of "fact" and statements of opinion.

The degree of fault required for liability is unclear. Sources often say that the standard is malice, but formulations of this differ. The *Restatement* requires either knowledge that the statement is false, or reckless disregard as to its truth or falsity. There is usually no liability for false statements that are made negligently and in good faith.

The plaintiff must also prove that the false statement played a substantial part in causing him to suffer *special damages.* These may include: losses resulting from the diminished value of disparaged property; the expense of measures for counteracting the false statement (e.g., advertising or litigation expenses); losses resulting from the breach of an existing contract by a third party; and the loss of prospective business. In cases involving the loss of prospective business, the plaintiff is usually required to show that some specific person or persons refused to buy because of the disparagement. This rule is often relaxed, however, where these losses are difficult to prove.

The special damages that the plaintiff is required to prove are his usual—and virtually his only—remedy in injurious falsehood cases. Damages for personal injury or emotional distress, for instance, are generally not recoverable. However, punitive damages and injunctive relief are sometimes obtainable.

Injurious Falsehood and Defamation Injurious falsehood may or may not overlap with the tort of defamation discussed in Chapter 6. Statements impugning a businessperson's character or conduct are probably defamatory. If, on the other hand, the false statement is limited to the plaintiff's business, property, or economic interests, his normal claim is for injurious falsehood. Both claims are possible when the injurious falsehood implies something about the plaintiff's character and affects his overall reputation. An example is a defendant's false allegation that the plaintiff knowingly sells dangerous products to children.

Defamation law's absolute and conditional privileges generally apply in injurious falsehood cases.[6] Certain other privileges protect defendants who are sued for injurious falsehood. For example, a rival claimant may in good faith disparage another's property rights by asserting his own competing rights. Similarly, one may make a good faith allegation that a competitor is infringing one's patent, copyright, or trademark. Finally, a person may sometimes make unfavorable comparisons between her product and that of a competitor. This privilege is generally limited to sales talk asserting the superiority of one's own product and does not cover unfavorable statements about a competitor's product.

---

[6]Chapter 6 discusses those privileges.

The School District brought the bonds to market in late 1993. Initially, the bonds sold well. Less than two hours into the sales period, however, Moody published an article about the bonds in its "Rating News," an electronically distributed information service sent to subscribers and news services. Moody stated in the article that even though it had not been asked to rate the bonds, it intended to assign a rating to the issue subsequent to the sale. The article went on to discuss the bonds and the School District's financial condition, concluding that "the outlook on the district's general obligation debt is negative, reflecting the district's ongoing financial pressures due in part to the state's [Colorado's] past underfunding of the school finance act as well as legal uncertainties and financial constraints under Amendment 1." Amendment 1, a 1992 measure, had changed the Colorado Constitution by requiring voter approval of certain tax increases.

Within minutes after Moody released the article, Dow Jones & Company's "The Dow Jones Capital Market Reports" issued an electronic communication repeating Moody's statement about the refunding bonds' "negative outlook." According to the School District, Moody's article adversely affected the marketing of the bonds. Purchase orders ceased, several buyers canceled prior orders, and the School District found it necessary to reprice the bonds at a higher interest rate in order to complete the sale. As a result, the School District alleged, it suffered a net loss of $769,000. Contending the statement in Moody's article falsely indicated that the School District's financial condition was not creditworthy, the School District sued Moody for injurious falsehood. The federal district court dismissed the School District's complaint for failure to state a claim upon which relief could be granted. The court based its ruling on a conclusion that Moody's statement, rather than being provably false, was an expression of opinion protected by the First Amendment. The School District appealed.

Henry, Circuit Judge In *Milkovich v. Lorain Journal Co.,* 497 U.S. 1 (U.S. Sup. Ct. 1990), . . . the Supreme Court addressed [an] important limitation on the scope of defamation [and presumably injurious falsehood] laws. [T]he Court concluded [that] "a statement of opinion relating to matters of public concern which does not contain a provably false factual connotation will receive full constitutional protection." Importantly, in reaching this conclusion, the Court rejected the argument that the First Amendment creates "a wholesale defamation exception for anything that might be labeled 'opinion.'" It reasoned that expressions of opinion may often imply an assertion of objective fact:

> If a speaker says, "In my opinion, John Jones is a liar," he implies a knowledge of facts which lead to the conclusion that Jones told an untruth. Even if he states the facts upon which he bases his opinion, if those facts are either incorrect or incomplete, or if his assessment of them is erroneous, the statement may still imply a false assertion of fact. Simply couching such statements in terms of opinion does not dispel these implications; and the statement, "In my opinion Jones is a liar," can cause as much damage to reputation as the statement, "Jones is a liar."

Milkovich, 497 U.S. at 18–19.

The [*Milkovich*] Court then considered the allegedly defamatory statement in the case before it—[a statement] that anyone who had attended a wrestling meet "knows in his heart" that a coach had lied in testifying about the meet at a subsequent hearing. [Because] a reasonable factfinder could conclude that the article implied an assertion that the plaintiff had committed perjury, [and because this assertion of perjury] was sufficiently factual to be susceptible of being proved true or false, [the Court] concluded that the statement about the coach's testimony was not an expression of opinion protected by the First Amendment.

[T]he sufficiency of the School District's allegations may be assessed by considering the first line of inquiry identified in *Milkovich:* whether a reasonable factfinder could conclude that Moody's article implied a false assertion of fact about the School District's financial condition. We begin by examining the allegedly false statement that the School District maintains [was] implied by Moody's article. [This implied statement]—that the School District was not creditworthy—is no more specific than Moody's statement about the refunding bonds' "negative outlook." [A] statement regarding the creditworthiness of a bond issuer could well depend on a myriad of factors, many of them not provably true or false. [O]ne evaluator of the bonds might point to legal developments [such as] those identified by Moody in concluding that the issuer was not creditworthy. Another evaluator might point to increasing property values in making a more optimistic assessment. The difference in the evaluators' assessments of the bonds could result from differing views about the relative weight to be assigned to those factors or from other philosophical or theoretical disagreements rather than from one evaluator's reliance on inaccurate information. [I]n light of its failure to identify a more specific statement, the School District has failed to demonstrate that Moody's implied statement about its creditworthiness is provably false.

Because the alleged statement about a lack of creditworthiness is so vague, the School District's interpretation of Moody's article would be plausible only if it could establish that the article implied some other specific . . . false assertions about the School District's financial condition. [T]he article's use of the phrase "ongoing financial pressure" undermines [the School District's efforts in that regard]. The range of factors that could cause "ongoing financial pressures" is vast, ranging from constitutional and statutory changes, court decisions, property values, inflation, and labor costs to many other factors too numerous to catalogue. In order for the School District to prove that Moody's article implied an assertion about the factors causing the District's "ongoing financial pressures," it would need to identify one or [more] of these many factors, . . . demonstrate that a reasonable reader of Moody's Rating News could discern those assertions from the general references to the refunding bonds' "negative outlook" and the School District's "ongoing financial pressures," [and] prove that those specific assertions were false. The allegations of the School District's complaint do not permit such strained inferences.

We emphasize that the phrases "negative outlook" [and] "ongoing financial pressures" are not necessarily too indefinite to imply a false statement of fact. If coupled with specific factual assertions, such statements might not be immunized from [defamation or injurious falsehood] claims by the First Amendment. Moreover, the fact that Moody's article describes its evaluation as an opinion is not sufficient, standing alone, to establish that Moody's statements are protected. If such an opinion were shown to have materially false components, the issuer should not be shielded from liability by raising the word "opinion" as a shibboleth. However, in this case, the School District's failure to identify a specific false statement reasonably implied from Moody's article, combined with the vagueness of the phrases "negative outlook" and "ongoing financial pressures," indicates that Moody's article constitutes a protected expression of opinion.

District court's dismissal of complaint affirmed.

Interference with Contractual Relations

In a suit for intentional interference with contractual relations, one party to a contract claims that the defendant's interference with the other party's performance of the contract wrongly caused the plaintiff to lose the benefit of that performance. One can interfere with the performance of a contract by causing a party to repudiate it, or by wholly or partly preventing that party's performance. The means of interference can range from mere persuasion to threatened or actual violence. The agreement whose performance is impeded, however, must be an *existing* contract. This includes contracts that are voidable, unenforceable, or subject to contract defenses, but *not* void bargains, contracts that are illegal on public policy grounds, or contracts to marry. Finally, the defendant must have *intended* to cause the breach; there is usually no liability for negligent contract interferences.

Even if the plaintiff proves these threshold requirements, the defendant is liable only if his behavior was *improper.* The *RAN* case, which follows shortly, lists the factors the *Restatement* uses to decide this question. Despite the flexible, case-by-case nature of such determinations, a few generalizations about improper interference are possible.

1. If the contract's performance was blocked by such clearly improper means as threats of physical violence, misrepresentations, defamatory statements, bribery, harassment, or bad faith civil or criminal actions, the defendant usually is liable. Liability is also likely where the interference was motivated *solely* by malice, spite, or a simple desire to meddle.

2. If his means and motives are legitimate, a defendant generally escapes liability when his contract interference is in the *public interest*—for example, when he informs an airport that an air traffic controller habitually uses hallucinogenic drugs. The same is true when the defendant acts to *protect a person for whose welfare she is responsible*—for example, when a mother induces a private school to discharge a diseased student who could infect her children.

3. A contract interference resulting from the defendant's good faith effort to protect her own *existing* legal or economic interests usually does not create liability so long as appropriate means are used. For example, a landowner can probably induce his tenant to breach a sublease to a party whose business detracts from the land's value. However, business parties generally cannot interfere with existing contract rights merely to further some *prospective* competitive advantage. For example, a seller cannot entice its competitors' customers to break existing contracts with those competitors.

4. Finally, competitors are unlikely to incur liability where, as is still often true of employment contracts, the agreement interfered with is *terminable at will.* The reason is that in such cases, the plaintiff has only an expectancy that the contract will continue, and not a right to have it continued. Thus, a firm that hires away its competitors' at-will employees usually escapes liability.

The basic measure of damages for intentional interference with contractual relations is the value of the lost contract performance. Some courts also award compensatory damages reasonably linked to the interference (including emotional distress and damage to reputation). Sometimes the plaintiff may obtain an injunction prohibiting further interferences.

Interference with Prospective Advantage

The rules and remedies for intentional interference with prospective advantage parallel those for interference with contractual relations. The main difference is that the former tort involves interferences with *prospective* relations rather than existing contracts. The protected future relations are mainly potential contractual relations of a business or commercial sort. Liability for interference with such relations requires intent; negligence does not suffice.

The "improper interference" factors weighed in interference-with-contract cases generally apply to interference with prospective advantage as well. One difference, however, is that interference with prospective advantage can be justified if: (1) the plaintiff and the defendant are in competition for the prospective relation with which the defendant interferes; (2) the defendant's purpose is at least partly competitive; (3) the defendant does not use such improper means as physical threats, misrepresentations, and bad faith lawsuits; and (4) the defendant's behavior does not create an unlawful restraint of trade under the antitrust laws or other regulations. Thus, a competitor ordinarily can win customers by offering lower prices and attract suppliers by offering higher prices. Unless this is otherwise illegal, he can also refuse to deal with suppliers or buyers who also deal with his competitors.

RAN Corporation v. Hudesman   *823 P.2d 646 (Alaska Sup. Ct. 1991)*

David Hudesman leased commercial property housing the Red Dog Saloon to Don Harris, the saloon's owner and operator. The lease said that Harris could assign it to any subtenant or assignee who was financially responsible and would properly care for the premises. It also required that Hudesman consent to such an assignment, but added that this consent could not be withheld unreasonably. After Harris decided to relocate his business, he was contacted by Richard Stone, president of the RAN Corporation. Stone wanted to use the property for an artifacts gallery. Harris and Stone agreed that Harris would assign the lease for $15,000, conditional on Hudesman's approval.

About this time, a politically influential man named Jerry Reinwand contacted Hudesman about the property. In exchange for Reinwand's promise to help Hudesman secure government leases for a large building Hudesman owned, Hudesman promised Reinwand that if Harris relocated his business, Reinwand would be assigned the property. Then Hudesman told Harris that he would not consent to Harris's assignment of the lease to RAN, and that Harris would be "looking at litigation" if he tried to assign the lease to Stone. Therefore, Harris told Stone that the deal was off, returned his $15,000 deposit, and assigned the lease to Reinwand for $15,000.

RAN then sued for an injunction to invalidate Reinwand's lease and to enforce its assignment contract with Harris, and also for damages. After RAN settled with several defendants, its main remaining claims were interference with contractual relations and interference with prospective advantage claims against Hudesman. When both parties moved for summary judgment, the trial court held for Hudesman. RAN appealed.

Matthews, Justice The elements of intentional interference with contractual relations are: (1) a contract existed, (2) the defendant knew of the contract and intended to induce a breach, (3) the contract was breached, (4) the defendant's wrongful conduct engendered the breach, (5) the breach caused the plaintiff's damages, and (6) the defendant's conduct was not privileged or justified. The fourth, fifth, and sixth elements also apply to the related tort of in-

tentional interference with prospective economic advantage. As our analysis applies equally to either tort, we will refer to them collectively.

The sixth element is troublingly vague. The *Restatement (Second) of Torts* section 767 speaks not in terms of "privilege," but requires that the actor's conduct not be "improper." Other authorities used the catchword "malice." Regardless of the phrase used, the critical question is what conduct is not "privileged" or "improper" or "malicious." The *Restatement* lists seven factors for consideration: (1) the nature of the actor's conduct, (2) the actor's motive, (3) the interests of the other with which the actor's conduct interferes, (4) the interests sought to be advanced by the actor, (5) the social interests in protecting the freedom of action of the actor and the contractual interests of the other, (6) the proximity or remoteness of the actor's conduct to the interference, and (7) the relations between the parties. While these factors are relevant in some or all incarnations of the interference tort, they are hard to apply in any sort of predictive way.

Instead of relying on the *Restatement* factors, we [have] adopted a test of privilege which hold[s] that where an actor has a direct financial interest, he is privileged to interfere with a contract for economic reasons, but not where he is motivated by spite, malice, or some other improper motive. In our view, this rule applies to this case. A number of other cases have recognized that a landlord has a sufficient interest to interfere with a prospective or actual lease assignment. The right to intervene has also been recognized in the analogous setting of transfers of distributorships.

It seems beyond reasonable argument that an owner of property has a financial interest in the assignment of a lease of the property he owns. An effective lease assignment makes the assignee the tenant of the owner. The tenant has an obligation to pay rent directly to the owner, and the use, or abuse, of the property by the assignee may affect its value to the owner. Further, the owner may know of another potential assignee who will pay more rent than the prospective assignee. Moreover, the owner may wish to terminate the lease based on knowledge of a more profitable use for the property.

Since Hudesman had a direct financial interest in the proposed assignment of the lease, the essential question in determining if interference is justified is whether Hudesman's conduct is motivated by a desire to protect his economic interest, or whether it is motivated by spite, malice, or some other improper objective. As there is no evidence of spite, malice, or other improper objective—Hudesman did not even know RAN Corporation's principals—and since it is clear that Hudesman refused to approve the assignment because he believed that he would receive a greater economic benefit from a tenancy by Reinwand, the interference was justified.

Hudesman's threat of litigation does not seem relevant to RAN's claim for interference. RAN's assignment agreement with Harris was explicitly conditional on Hudesman's approval. When Hudesman disapproved of the assignment, the interference was complete. Hudesman's disapproval may have been a breach of the Hudesman/Harris lease, but it was privileged from a tort standpoint because of Hudesman's preexisting interest as a property owner-lessor. The threat of litigation may, at worst, have been another breach of the Hudesman/Harris lease. However, it too was not tortious and it was, in any case, superfluous to the interference, because RAN's prospective economic relationship was terminated by Hudesman's disapproval, not by his threat to sue.

Lower court judgment in favor of Hudesman affirmed.

Lanham Act Section 43(a)

Section 43(a) of the Lanham Act basically creates a federal law of unfair competition. Section 43(a) is not a consumer remedy; it is normally available only to commercial parties, who usually are the defendant's competitors. The section creates civil liability for a wide range of false, misleading, confusing, or deceptive representations made in connection with goods or services. Section 43(a)'s many applications include:

1. *Tort claims for "palming off" or "passing off."* This tort involves false representations that are likely to induce third parties to believe that the defendant's goods or services are those of the plaintiff. Such representations include imitations of the plaintiff's trademarks, trade names, packages, labels, containers, employee uniforms, and place of business.

2. *Trade dress infringement claims.* These claims resemble passing-off claims. A product's trade dress is its overall appearance and sales image. Section 43(a) prohibits a party from passing off its goods or services as those of a competitor by employing a substantially similar trade dress that is likely to confuse consumers as to the source of its products or services. For example, a competitor that sells antifreeze in jugs that are similar in size, shape, and color to a well-known competitor's jugs may face section 43(a) liability.

3. *Claims for infringement of both registered and unregistered trademarks.*

4. *Commercial appropriation of name or likeness claims and right of publicity claims* (discussed in Chapter 6).

5. *False advertising claims.* This important application of section 43(a) includes ads that misrepresent the nature, qualities, or characteristics of either the *advertiser's* products and services or a *competitor's* products and services. Section 43(a) applies to ads that are likely to mislead buyers even if they are not clearly false on their face, and to ads with certain deceptive *omissions*. In the *United Industries* case, the court discusses the types of statements that may violate section 43(a).

United Industries Corp. v. The Clorox Co.   *140 F.3d 1175 (8th Cir. 1998)*

The Clorox Co.'s "Combat" brand was the top-selling roach bait insecticide on the market. United Industries Corp. (hereinafter "UI") produced "Maxattrax," a relatively new roach bait insecticide. The statement that Maxattrax "kills roaches in 24 hours" appeared on the product's packaging. In a legal action filed against Clorox, UI sought a declaratory judgment that this statement did not constitute false advertising. Clorox filed an answer and counterclaim. In the counterclaim, Clorox contended that one of UI's television commercials for Maxattrax constituted false advertising in violation of Lanham Act section 43(a).

The 15-second Maxattrax commercial to which Clorox objected began with a split-screen depiction of two roach bait products on two kitchen countertops. Although the lighting was dark, the viewer could see the Maxattrax box on the left. On the right was a "Roach Box" that was generally similar to the packaging used by Clorox for its Combat brand. An announcer asked, "Can you guess which bait kills roaches in 24 hours?" As the lighting grew brighter, the camera panned beyond the boxes to reveal, on the Maxattrax side, a clean, orderly kitchen that was uninhabited by roaches. On the other side, however, the kitchen was in a chaotic state, with cupboards and drawers opening, items on the counter turning over, paper towels spinning off a dispenser, and a spice rack convulsing and losing its spices. All of this disorder was the apparent result of a major roach infestation. At the same time, the message "Based on lab tests" appeared in small print at the bottom of the screen. The two roach-bait boxes then reappeared on a split-screen, with computer-animated roaches appearing to kick over the "Roach Bait" box and dance gleefully on it. As the commercial's final visual showed the Maxattrax box, an announcer stated that "[t]o kill roaches in 24 hours, it's hot-shot Maxattrax. Maxattrax, it's the no-wait roach bait." The final phrase was also displayed in print on the screen.

Clorox filed a motion for a preliminary injunction against the commercial. When the federal district court denied the motion, Clorox appealed.

Wollman, Circuit Judge   [Lanham Act section 43(a)] prohibits commercial advertising or promotion that misrepresents the nature, characteristics, qualities, or geographic origin of the advertiser's or another person's goods, services, or commercial activities. The false statement necessary to establish a Lanham Act [section 43(a)] violation generally falls into one of two categories: (1) commercial claims that are literally false as a factual matter; and (2) claims that may be literally true or ambiguous but which implicitly convey a false impression, are misleading in context, or [are] likely to deceive consumers. Many claims will actually fall into a third category, generally known as "puffery." Puffery is exaggerated advertising, blustering, and boasting upon which no reasonable buyer would rely and is not actionable under section 43(a). Nonactionable puffery includes representations of product superiority that are vague or highly subjective. However, false descriptions of specific or absolute characteristics of a product and specific, measurable claims of product superiority based on product testing are not puffery and are actionable.

If a plaintiff proves that a challenged claim [in an advertisement] is literally false, a court may grant relief without considering whether the buying public was actually misled; actual consumer confusion need not be proved. In some circumstances, even a visual image, or a visual image combined with an audio component, may be literally false. The greater the degree to which a message relies upon the viewer or consumer to integrate its components and draw the apparent conclusion, however, the less likely it is that a finding of literal falsity will be supported. Commercial claims that are implicit, attenuated, or merely suggestive usually cannot fairly be characterized as literally false.

The district court determined that the Maxattrax commercial conveyed an explicit message that the product killed roaches in 24 hours and found that this message was literally true. Clorox argues that [in view of its combination of visual and audio elements,] the Maxattrax commercial conveyed three additional explicit messages that are literally false: (1) that Maxattrax controls roach infestations in consumers' homes within 24 hours; (2) that Combat and other roach baits are entirely ineffective in consumers' homes within 24 hours; and (3) that Maxattrax provides superior performance in consumers' homes in comparison to Combat and other roach baits.

Our review of the record satisfies us that the [district court was] clearly correct in its assessment that the audio and print components of the advertisement are literally true. The scientific evidence and expert testimony . . . satisfactorily established that Maxattrax roach bait "kills roaches in 24 hours." Clorox protests that this statement is literally true only in circumstances where a particular roach actually comes into contact with the product. This complaint rings hollow. The requirement that roaches must come into contact with the poison for it to be effective is the central premise of the roach bait line of products. We will not presume the average consumer to be incapable of comprehending the essential nature of a roach trap.

Similarly, we conclude that the district court did not err in determining that the Maxattrax commercial did not convey explicit visual messages that were literally false. The depiction of a Maxattrax box in a pristine, roach-free kitchen, coupled with the depiction of a kitchen in disarray in which animated roaches happily dance about on a generic roach trap, is not sufficient . . . to constitute literal falsity in the manner in which it was presented. [M]oreover, the audio component of the advertisement, emphasizing only the 24-hour time frame and quick roach kill with no mention of complete infestation control, fosters ambiguity regarding the intended message and renders the commercial much more susceptible to differing, plausible interpretations. Thus, . . . the district court's finding that the commercial did not explicitly convey a literally false message that Maxattrax will completely control a home roach infestation within 24 hours is not clearly erroneous.

Clorox also contends that the commercial conveys an explicit message of comparative superiority that is literally false. [When] a defendant has buttressed a claim of superiority [of the defendant's product] by attributing it to the results of scientific testing, a plaintiff must prove that the tests relied upon were not sufficiently reliable to permit one to conclude with reasonable certainty that they established the proposition for which they were cited. The Maxattrax commercial indicates in small print at the bottom of the screen that its implied answer to the posed question, "Can you guess which bait kills roaches in 24 hours?" is "[b]ased on lab tests." In order for this claim to be considered literally false, then, Clorox must establish that the tests to which the commercial referred were not sufficiently reliable to support its claims with reasonable certainty. The district court determined that the scientific research provided by UI was reliable and supported the commercial's claims. We agree. Laboratory testing indicates that the toxin in Maxattrax kills within 24 hours those roaches that come into contact with it. Some other roach bait products will not kill a roach within that interval, and in fact, are not even intended to do so.

Any additional messages in the Maxattrax commercial perceived by Clorox . . . are not sufficiently explicit or unambiguous . . . to constitute specific false claims of a literal nature. [However, statements] that are literally true or ambiguous but which nevertheless have a tendency to mislead or deceive the consumer are actionable under the Lanham Act. Where a commercial claim is not literally false but is misleading in context, proof that the advertising actually conveyed the implied message and thereby deceived a significant portion of the recipients becomes critical.

Clorox contends that when one assesses the comparative visuals and implicit messages in the commercial, a consumer might be misled to construe them as a claim that Maxattrax will completely control an infestation by killing all of the roaches in one's home within 24 hours, while its competitors will fail to do the same. In fact, Maxattrax will kill only those roaches which come into contact with the product; actual control of a roach problem may take several weeks. Whether one accepts the district court's more literal interpretation of the commercial's message or Clorox's proposed construction, however, is highly dependent upon context and inferences, and Clorox's view is unsupported at this point by expert testimony, surveys, or consumer reaction evidence of any kind. It is . . . a classic question of fact, the resolution of which we will not disturb absent a showing of clear error by the district court. Clorox has not made such a showing.

District court's denial of preliminary injunction affirmed.

Problems and Problem Cases

1. Huey J. Rivet patented an "amphibious marsh craft" for hauling loads and laying pipeline in swamps. Rivet's model could "walk" over stumps for extended periods while carrying heavy loads. Later, Robert Wilson, who had once worked for Rivet as a welder, began marketing a similar craft. The craft sold by Wilson differed from the craft described in the specification accompanying Rivet's patent application in several respects. Overall, though, the Wilson boat performed much the same functions about as effectively as the Rivet craft, and used much the same engineering techniques and concepts to do so. Has Wilson infringed Rivet's patent?

2. Lorna Nelson, half-sister of the rock star Prince, sued Prince for copyright infringement. She alleged that Prince's hit "U Got the look" infringed her copyrighted song "What's Cooking in this Book." Lorna's song, to which Prince had access, had six verses totaling 35 lines and 176 words. "U Got the look" had eight verses totaling 47 lines and 242 words. The alleged infringements concerned the following verses and words from the two songs:

a. Lorna's verse 2: "I glanced up and saw you, a smile so pretty." *Prince's verses 2 and 7:* "I woke up, I've never seen such a pretty girl."

b. Lorna's verse 3: "Makeup was rolling down my face." *Prince's verse 5:* "A whole hour just to make up your face."

c. Lorna's verse 6: "What's cooking in this book, what's cooking in . . ." *Prince's verses 4 and 6:* "U sho 'nuf do be cooking in my book."

d. Lorna's verses 1 and 6: "Take a look, Take another look." *Prince's verses 1 and 7:* "U got the look."

The main issue in the case was whether there was substantial similarity between the lyrics just quoted. Are these lyrics sufficiently similar to justify imposing liability on Prince?

3. In 1964, Roy Orbison and William Dees wrote a song titled "Oh, Pretty Woman." They assigned their rights over the song to Acuff-Rose Music, Inc., the copyright owner at all times relevant to this case. Orbison's mid-1960s' recording of "Oh, Pretty Woman" was a huge hit. In 1989, Luther Campbell, a member of the rap music group known as 2 Live Crew, wrote a song that parodied "Oh, Pretty Woman." The group sought Acuff-Rose's permission to use the parody on an album. Despite Acuff-Rose's denial of permission, 2 Live Crew used the parody on the *As Clean As They Wanna Be* album. The parody borrowed the first line of lyrics and a very recognizable bass riff from the original song. This bass riff was repeated a few times in the parody. Roughly a year after the 2 Live Crew album was released (and approximately 250,000 copies had been sold), Acuff-Rose sued 2 Live Crew and its record company for copyright infringement. What defense did the defendants raise? Did they succeed with that defense?

4. Qualitex Co. produces pads that dry-cleaning firms use on their presses. Since the 1950s, Qualitex has colored its press pads a shade of green-gold. In 1989, Jacobson Products Co. began producing press pads for sale to dry-cleaning firms. Jacobson colored its pads a green-gold resembling the shade used by Qualitex. Later in 1989, the United States Patent & Trademark Office granted Qualitex a trademark registration for the green-gold color (as used on press pads). Qualitex then added a trademark infringement claim to an unfair competition lawsuit it had previously filed against Jacobson. Qualitex won the case, but the Ninth Circuit Court of Appeals set aside the judgment on the trademark infringement claim. In the Ninth Circuit's view, the Lanham Act did not allow any party to have color alone registered as a trademark. The Supreme Court granted certiorari. How did the Supreme Court rule on the question whether color is a registrable trademark?

5. Since the 1970s, Nike, Inc., has used the word NIKE and a swoosh design as trademarks in connection with the footwear, clothing items, and related accessories it produces and sells. Both NIKE and the swoosh design are well-known, federally registered trademarks. Since 1989, Nike has used the now-familiar slogan JUST DO IT in connection with the promotion of its products. Michael Stanard began designing and selling T-shirts and sweatshirts that bore the name MIKE and a swoosh design as a takeoff on, and parody of, the Nike trademarks. Stanard, who gave the name "Just Did It" Enterprises to this business venture, chose persons named "Mike" (and their relatives) as his target market. He sought to reach these persons by mailing brochures to them. Nike sued Stanard for trademark infringement. Should Nike win the case?

6. E. I. du Pont de Nemours & Co. was building a plant to develop a highly secret unpatented process for producing methanol. During the construction, some of its trade secrets were exposed to view from the air because the plant in which they were contained did not yet have a roof. These secrets were photographed from an airplane by two photographers who were hired by persons unknown to take pictures of the new construction. Did this action amount to a misappropriation of Du Pont's trade secrets?

7. Time-Life Books published a book titled *Exercising for Fitness.* The book contained a reproduction of the famous Charles Atlas, Ltd., advertisement in which a 97-pound weakling uses Atlas's Dynamic Tension body-building program to become a real man after a bully kicks sand in his face and that of his girlfriend. The caption accompanying the reproduction told the book's readers that Atlas's program is a system of isometric exercises. On the same page, the book warned readers about the extreme dangers of isometric exercises. Atlas sued Time-Life for injurious falsehood. According to Atlas, the book's caption was false because Atlas's method was not isometric in nature. Atlas alleged that Time-Life made this false statement with knowledge of its falsity or with an intent to injure Atlas. Atlas contended that the false caption, coupled with the warning about the dangers of isometric exercises, caused it to suffer economic loss in the form of decreased sales and expenses to counteract the falsehood. Atlas's complaint did not identify any specific lost customers, however. Arguing that the allegations in Atlas's complaint were not sufficient to state a claim upon which relief could be granted, Time-Life moved to dismiss the complaint. Were Atlas's allegations sufficient to state a claim against Time-Life?

8. In 1989, Marion Merrell Dow, Inc. (MMD), developed "Cardizem CD," an improved version of a prescription diltiazem drug that MMD had introduced several years earlier. The Food and Drug Administration (FDA) approved Cardizem CD for the treatment of angina and hypertension. Cardizem CD and its predecessor versions generated huge sales figures. Approximately three years after Cardizem CD came on the market, Rhone-Poulenc Rorer Pharmaceuticals, Inc. (RPR), introduced a prescription diltiazem drug known as "Dilacor XR." It was less expensive than Cardizem CD. Dilacor XR received approval from the FDA for treatment of hypertension but not angina. Physicians may prescribe an FDA-approved drug for nonapproved uses. Federal law applicable at the time, however, prohibited the drug's manufacturer from promoting nonapproved uses. Through an advertising campaign, RPR sought to convince physicians to prescribe Dilacor XR instead of Cardizem CD. MMD responded with advertisements and promotional materials meant to dissuade physicians from prescribing Dilacor XR in place of Cardizem CD.

RPR brought a false advertising action against MMD under section 43(a) of the Lanham Act. MMD responded with a section 43(a)–based false advertising counterclaim against RPR. MMD based its counterclaim on Dilacor XR advertisements that featured images such as two similar gasoline pumps or airline tickets with dramatically different prices, accompanied by the slogan, "Which one would you choose[?]" The federal district court concluded that RPR's advertisements "contain[ed] a hidden message encouraging indiscriminate substitution" by prescribing physicians. This message, the court held, was false or misleading because it failed to disclose that Dilacor XR had not been approved by the FDA for treatment of angina. The court therefore ordered RPR to engage in corrective advertising revealing the fact that the FDA had not approved Dilacor XR for the treatment of angina. Was the court correct in concluding that RPR violated section 43(a) and that corrective advertising was an appropriate remedy?

9. The New Mexico and Arizona Land Company owned a sizable tract of land in Arizona. It leased a portion of this land, which contained water for grazing, to the Bar J Bar Cattle Company. New Mexico had the right to cancel the lease upon 30 days' notice once it sold the land. Malcolm Pace, who owned a ranch adjoining the Bar J Bar ranch and wanted its water rights, bought the land leased by Bar J Bar from New Mexico. Shortly thereafter, New Mexico gave Bar J Bar 30 days' notice of termination. Bar J Bar sued Pace for intentional interference with contractual relations. One feature of the Bar J Bar lease weakens its chances of recovery against Pace. What is that feature of the lease? *Hint:* The answer requires that you make an analogy to a subject discussed in this chapter's discussion of intentional interference with contractual relations.

10. Tony Mason created a mixed drink that he named "Lynchburg Lemonade." The drink consisted of Jack Daniel whiskey, Triple Sec, sweet and sour mix, and 7-Up. Mason, who developed the recipe one evening while seeking to ease a sore throat, served the drink at his restaurant and lounge. The drink became a very big seller for Mason. He informed only a few of his employees of the details of the recipe and instructed each of those employees not to tell anyone else. To prevent customers from learning the recipe, those in charge of mixing the beverage did so in the back of the restaurant and lounge. Winston Randle, a sales representative for Jack Daniel Distillery, drank Lynchburg Lemonade while in Mason's restaurant and lounge. Although the source of his information was unclear, Randle learned the recipe for the drink at that time. Randle informed his superiors about Lynchburg Lemonade and its recipe. Roughly one year later, Jack Daniel was developing a national promotion campaign for the drink. Mason, who never received compensation for Jack Daniel's use of the Lynchburg Lemonade recipe, sued Jack Daniel and Randle for misappropriation of a trade secret. Mason won a jury verdict. The defendants appealed. They argued, among other things, that the recipe for Lynchburg Lemonade was not a valid trade secret because it could be fairly easily duplicated and bore some resemblance to drinks classified as part of the "Collins" family of drinks. Was the recipe a valid trade secret?

11. A Quaker State Corp. television commercial asserted that "tests prove" the following claim: "At start-up Quaker State 10W-30 protects better than any other leading 10W-30 motor oil." The commercial also depicted an engine, superimposed over which were bottles of Quaker State motor oil and four competing oils, including Castrol GTX 10W-30. Nearby was a bar graph displaying the superior speed with which Quaker State oil flows to engine components once the engine is started. Castrol, Inc., sued Quaker State for false advertising under Lanham Act section 43(a). Castrol sought a preliminary injunction against Quaker State's airing the commercial. The evidence presented to the court indicated that Quaker State's oil did indeed reach engine parts faster at start-up than did its competitors' oil, but that this had no discernible effect on engine wear. The apparent reason was that the "residual oil" remaining from prior engine starts protects the engine until new oil arrives. Should an injunction be granted against the airing of the Quaker State commercial?

Online Research: The United States Copyright Office

Go to the United States Copyright Office website, at www.loc.gov/copyright. Then find the answers to these questions:

1. What is the fee for a basic registration of a claim to copyright?

2. Does the Copyright Office maintain a list of works that have fallen into the public domain (i.e., works whose copyright protection has expired)?

CONTRACTS

9

Introduction to Contracts

The 2001 catalog that Gigantic State University website sent out to prospective students described a merit-based scholarship called the "Eagle Scholarship." The catalog stated that GSU offers the Eagle Scholarship to all incoming students who are in the top 10 percent of their high school classes and have SAT scores of 1250 or above. Paul, a prospective student, read the 2001 catalog that GSU had sent to him. Money was tight for Paul, so he paid particular attention to the part of the catalog that described financial aid. He read about the Eagle Scholarship and realized that he qualified for the scholarship. Paul picked GSU over other schools in large part because of the Eagle Scholarship. He applied to GSU and GSU admitted him. Before his freshman orientation, Paul called GSU and checked to be sure that he met the requirements of the Eagle Scholarship, and the GSU representative that he talked to informed him that he did. When Paul arrived at GSU for freshman orientation, however, he received a copy of the 2002 catalog and learned that the qualifications for the Eagle Scholarship had changed and that he no longer qualified.

- *Was there a contract between GSU and Paul for the Eagle Scholarship?*
- *If so, what kind of contract was it?*
- *What body of legal rules would apply to the contract?*
- *If it wasn't a contract, is there any other basis for a legal obligation on the part of GSU?*

The Nature of Contracts

The law of contracts deals with the enforcement of promises. It is important to realize from the outset of your study of contracts that *not every promise is legally enforceable.* (If every promise were enforceable, this chapter could be one sentence long!) We have all made and broken promises without fear of being sued. If you promise to take a friend out to dinner and then fail to do so, you would be shocked to be sued for breach of contract. What separates such promises from legally enforceable contracts? The law of contracts sorts out what promises are enforceable, to what extent, and how they will be enforced.

The essence of a contract is that it is a *legally enforceable* promise or set of promises. In other words, when a set of promises has the status of *contract,* a per-

son injured by a breach of that contract is entitled to call on the government (courts) to force the breaching party to honor the contract.

The Functions of Contracts

Contracts give us the ability to enter into agreements with others with confidence that we may call on the *law*—not merely the good faith of the other party—to make sure that those agreements will be honored. Within limitations that you will study later, *contracting lets us create a type of private law*—the terms of the agreements we make—that governs our relations with others.

Contracts facilitate the planning that is necessary in a modern, industrialized society. Who would invest in a business if she could not rely on the fact that the builders and suppliers of the facilities and equipment, the suppliers of the raw materials necessary to manufacture products, and the customers who agree to purchase those products would all honor their commitments? How could we make loans, sell goods on credit, or rent property unless loan agreements, conditional sales agreements, and leases were backed by the force of the law? Contract, then, is necessary to the world as we know it. Like that world, its particulars tend to change over time, while its general characteristics remain largely stable.

The Evolution of Contract Law

The idea of contract is ancient. Thousands of years ago, Egyptians and Mesopotamians recognized devices like contracts; by the 15th century, the common law courts of England had developed a variety of theories to justify enforcing certain promises. Contract law did not, however, assume major importance in our legal system until the 19th century, when the Industrial Revolution created the necessity for greater private planning and certainty in commercial transactions.

The central principle of contract law that emerged from this period was *freedom of contract.* Freedom of contract is the idea that contracts should be enforced because they are the products of the free wills of their creators, who should, within broad limits, be free to determine the extent of their obligations. The proper role of the courts in such a system of contract was to enforce these freely made bargains but otherwise to adopt a hands-off stance. The freedom to make good deals carried with it the risk of making bad deals. As long as a person voluntarily entered a contract, it would generally be enforced against him, even if the result was grossly unfair. And since equal bargaining power tended to be assumed, the courts were usually unwilling to hear defenses based on unequal bargaining power. This judicial posture allowed the courts to create a pure contract law consisting of precise, clear, and technical rules that were capable of general, almost mechanical, application. Such a law of contract met the needs of the marketplace by affording the predictable and consistent results necessary to facilitate private planning.

The emergence of large business organizations after the Civil War produced obvious disparities of bargaining power in many contract situations, however. These large organizations found it more efficient to standardize their numerous transactions by employing standard form contracts, which also could be used to exploit their greater bargaining power by dictating the terms of their agreements.

Contract law evolved to reflect these changes in social reality. During the 20th century, there was a dramatic increase in government regulation of private contractual relationships. Think of all the statutes governing the terms of what were once purely private contractual relationships. Legislatures commonly dictate many of the basic terms of insurance contracts. Employment contracts are governed by a host of laws concerning maximum hours worked, minimum wages paid, employer liability for on-the-job injuries, unemployment compensation, and retirement benefits. In some circumstances, product liability statutes impose liability on the manufacturers and sellers of products regardless of the terms of their sales contracts. The purpose of much of this regulation has been to protect persons who lack sufficient bargaining power to protect themselves.

Courts have been increasingly concerned with creating contract rules that produce fair results. The precise, technical rules that characterized traditional common law contract have given way to permit some broader, imprecise standards such as good faith, injustice, reasonableness, and unconscionability. The reason for such standards is clear. If courts are increasingly called on to evaluate private contracts on the basis of fairness, it is necessary to fashion rules that afford the degree of judicial discretion required to reach just decisions in the increasingly complex and varied contract cases that reach the courts.

Despite the increased attention to fairness in contract law, the agreement between the parties is still the heart of every contract.

The Methods of Contracting

Many students reading about contract law for the first time may have the idea that contracts must be in writing to be enforceable. Generally speaking, that is not true. There are some situations in which the law requires certain kinds of contracts to be evidenced by a writing to be enforced. The most common examples of those situations are covered in Chapter 16. Unless the law specifically requires a certain kind of contract to be in writing, an oral contract that can be proven is as legally enforceable as a written one.

Contracts can be and are made in many ways. When most of us imagine a contract, we envision two parties bargaining for a deal, then drafting a contract on paper and signing it or shaking hands. Some contracts are negotiated and formed in that way. Far more common today, however, is the use of **standardized form contracts.** Standardized form contracts are contracts that are preprinted by one party and presented to the other party for signing. In most situations, the party who drafts and

Figure 1   *Getting to Contract*

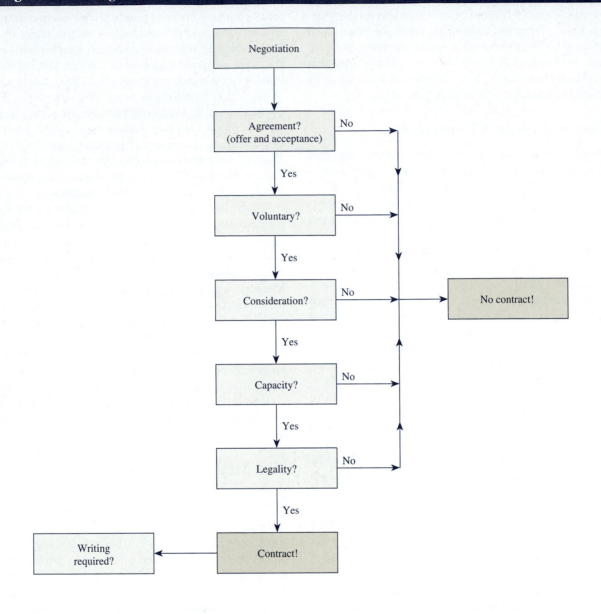

presents the standardized contract is the party who has the most bargaining power and/or sophistication in the transaction. Frequently, the terms of standardized contracts are non-negotiable. Such contracts have the advantage of providing an efficient method of standardizing common transactions. On the other hand, they present the dangers that the party who signs the contract will not know what he is agreeing to and that the party who drafts and presents the contract will take advantage of his bargaining power to include terms that are oppressive or abnormal in that kind of transaction.

Basic Elements of a Contract

Over the years, the law has developed a number of requirements that a set of promises must meet before they are treated as a contract. To qualify as a contract, a set of promises must be based on a voluntary agreement, which is made up of an **offer** and an **acceptance** of that offer. In addition, there usually must be **consideration** to support each party's promise. The contract must be between parties who have **capacity** to contract, and the objective and performance of the contract must be **legal.** (See Figure 1).

CYBERLAW IN ACTION

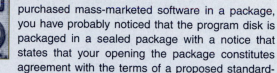

Standardized contracts are common online as well as in the physical world. You have probably entered into online standardized contracts when you downloaded software from the Internet, joined an online service, initialized an e-mail account, or purchased goods online. The terms of standardized contracts online are usually presented in a manner that requires the viewer to click on an icon indicating agreement before he can proceed in the program. Standardized online contracts presented in this way are often called **clickwrap contracts.** If you have purchased mass-marketed software in a package, you have probably noticed that the program disk is packaged in a sealed package with a notice that states that your opening the package constitutes agreement with the terms of a proposed standardized license agreement. These are called **shrinkwrap contracts** or **shrinkwrap licenses,** a name that refers to the practice of packaging software in shrinkwrapped packaging. The enforceability of clickwraps and shrinkwraps, which has been a controversial topic, will be discussed in Chapter 11.

As you study contract law, you may be surprised to learn that some transactions that you never thought of as contracts satisfy the foregoing elements and are legally treated as contracts. The following case, *Jackson v. Connecticut Lottery Corporation,* provides one example. It also provides a good introduction to a number of the issues that courts consider in determining whether and how to enforce a contract.

Each of the elements of a contract is discussed individually in subsequent chapters.

Jackson v. Connecticut Lottery Corporation   *1998 Conn. Super. LEXIS 2562 (1998)*

Clarence Jackson went to the Snack Plus convenience store in Hamden, Connecticut, and bought a Connecticut Lotto "Quick Pick" ticket for the drawing of October 13, 1995. On the back of the ticket are various provisions, including the admonition that "Prize must be claimed within one year from the drawing date. Determination of winners subject to DOSR rules and regulations." It also stated instructions for claiming the prize by presentment to any online agent or to "Lottery Claims" in Newington, Connecticut.

The drawing was held on October 13, and the winning six-number combination was announced. One of the six-number combinations on Jackson's Lotto ticket matched the six-number combination drawn in the October 13 drawing, for a prize of $5.8 million dollars. Jackson only learned of the match 15 minutes before the one-year deadline that he had won. On October 13, 1996, the Sunday anniversary of the drawing, 1,495 lottery terminals were online until midnight at sales agent locations around the state. Instead of claiming his prize online, Jackson waited till Wednesday, October 15, 1996, which was after the Columbus Day holiday, to present it in person at the Lottery Claims Center because he was under the impression that it had to be presented there.[1] The Connecticut Lottery Corporation (CLC) denied Jackson's claim because the one-year presentment period had elapsed.

Jackson sued the CLC, claiming breach of contract. The CLC moved for summary judgment because of Jackson's failure to comply with the one-year deadline.

GRAHAM, Superior Court Judge   The CLC argues that Jackson's claim must fail because Jackson did not present the Lotto ticket within one year of the drawing date as required by 12-568-5(c)(2)(B) of the Regulations of Connecticut State Agencies. It argues that the existing law becomes part of a contract when made, and therefore the one-year limitation was incorporated when Jackson's purchase of the Lotto ticket formed a contract between the parties. Jackson argues that the one-year provision

---

[1]The amount of the prize and the circumstances surrounding Jackson's failure to claim the prize in a timely manner were derived from news reports rather than from the court's statement of facts. See, e.g., Tardy Winner Loses Out on $5.8 Million, *Beloit Daily News,* June 5, 1997, http://www.beloitdailynews.com/697/4nat5.htm

was not incorporated into the contract because the provision was not "known, understood and agreed upon by the parties before the execution of the contract." Alternatively, Jackson argues that even if the term is incorporated into the contract, the one-year provision is not material to the contract.

I. Is the Lotto Ticket a Contract?

As a threshold issue, the court must first determine whether a contract exists between the parties. It has been generally held that a lottery winner's entitlement to a prize is governed by the principles of contract law. To form a binding contract, there must be an offer and acceptance based on a mutual understanding by the parties. Furthermore, a promise is generally not enforceable unless it is supported by consideration. Moreover, the contract must be definite and certain as to its terms and requirements.

In the present action, the court finds that the parties did enter into a valid, unilateral contract through the purchase of a Lotto ticket. CLC offered Jackson the chance to win prize money, and Jackson accepted that offer through the act of purchasing the Lotto ticket. The contract was supported by consideration. CLC's consideration was in the form of its promise to pay the prize money upon the fulfillment of the conditions of the contract. Jackson's act of purchasing the Lotto ticket for one dollar per drawing was sufficient consideration on his part to render the contract enforceable. There is no question that CLC made an offer and a promise to Jackson to pay the prize money upon the fulfillment of the conditions of the offer. Jackson accepted and assented through his purchase of the Lotto ticket. Consequently, there was a manifestation of mutual assent between the parties.

II. The Terms of the Contract

Jackson has claimed a material issue of fact as to whether he actually knew of the one-year presentment limitation at the time the contract was formed such that it became a mutually agreed term of the contract. But the determinative question is whether the one-year limitation provided for in Reg. 12-568-5(c)(2)(B) was incorporated into the contract as a matter of law at the time the contract was executed. If the regulation was so incorporated into the contract, Jackson's knowledge of the one-year limitation is presumed, and actual knowledge is immaterial.

Recently, the Connecticut Supreme Court stated that it was "not unmindful that when contracts are limited by statutory provisions, those provisions are generally considered to be incorporated therein as a matter of law." Jackson argues that the law only presumes the incorporation of statutes, and

not regulations into contracts. However, recent Connecticut case law, other jurisdictions' case law, and logic indicate otherwise. Such an approach is consistent with the accepted principle that validly enacted agency regulations have the same force of law as statutes. The court finds that Reg. 12-568-5(c)(2)(B) was incorporated into, and became a part of, the parties' contract when the lotto ticket was sold, regardless of whether Jackson was explicitly aware of it. The court also notes that the back of the ticket expressly indicated that the "prize must be claimed within one year from the drawing date. . . ."

IV. Materiality of Reg. 12-568-5(c)(2)(B)

The only issue remaining to be determined is whether Reg. 12-568-5(c)(2)(B) was a material term to the contract. Where a party seeking to enforce a contract is in material breach, that party will be denied enforcement of the contract. The claim that Jackson's failure to claim his prize within a year is not material ignores important consequences to the CLC of Jackson's failure. The one-year time limit is tied inflexibly under the detailed regulatory scheme to future drawing prize pools. Regulation 12-568-5(p) states "if the prize remains unclaimed at the expiration of the appropriate time period, such prize shall revert to the prize structure of future lottery games to be distributed to future winners." Jackson's position would force CLC to either ignore such provision or to pay the same prize twice. In this case, the one-year deadline expired on a Sunday and Jackson did not present a claim until the next Wednesday. It is common knowledge that the Lotto game drawings are on Tuesdays and Fridays. Jackson did not present his claim until after the prize monies had reverted to the prize structure of the drawing following the one-year deadline. CLC can reasonably expect the benefit of any winner claiming his prize within a year.

While the claim period may on rare occasion work a forfeiture on an individual winner, without it the regulatory scheme of the lottery system would be compromised. The only reasonable conclusion is that the one-year limitation provision is a material term of the lotto contract, and Jackson's failure to present the ticket for validation within one year of the drawing date is a material breach, rendering the contract unenforceable against the CLC. The one-year presentment limit is directly related to the payment of the lotto prize, the essence of every lotto contract. The one-year limit impacts the ability of a purchaser to claim a prize, the need for the CLC to pay a prize for a specific drawing, the length of time for which the CLC must reserve the funds to pay the prize, and the time at which the prize will be made available for other purchasers to win at a subsequent drawing. All these issues go to the core of a lottery ticket transaction made within the context of a regulated state lotto game.

The court finds that Section 12-568-5(c)(2)(B) of the Regulations of Connecticut State Agencies is a material term incorporated into the parties contract. Jackson's failure to present his Lotto ticket for validation within one year of the drawing relieves the CLC of any obligation to pay Jackson the prize money.

CLC's motion for summary judgment granted.

LOG ON

For helpful overviews of the law of contracts and links to many other contracts resources, see Legal Information Institute, *Law About Contracts: An Overview,*
http://www.law.cornell.edu/topics/contracts.html
and Mark Radcliffe and Diane Brinson, *Contracts Law,*
http://profs.lp.findlaw.com/contracts/index.html

Basic Contract Concepts and Types

Bilateral and Unilateral Contracts

Contracts have traditionally been classified as **bilateral** or **unilateral,** depending on whether one or both of the parties have made a promise. In unilateral contracts, only one party makes a promise. For example, Perks Café issues "frequent buyer" cards to its customers, and stamps the cards each time a customer buys a cup of coffee. Perks promises to give any customer a free cup of coffee if the customer buys 10 cups of coffee and has his "frequent buyer" card stamped 10 times. In this case, Perks has made an offer for a unilateral contract, a contract that will be created with a customer only if and when the customer buys 10 cups of coffee and has his card stamped ten times. In a bilateral contract, by contrast, *both* parties exchange promises and the contract is formed as soon as the promises are exchanged. For example, if Perks Café promises to pay Willowtown Mall $1,000 a month if Willowtown Mall will promise to lease a kiosk in the mall to Perks for the holiday season, Perks has made an offer for a bilateral contract because it is offering a promise in exchange for a promise. If Willowtown Mall makes the requested promise, a bilateral contract is formed at that point—even before the parties begin performing any of the acts that they have promised to do.

Valid, Unenforceable, Voidable, and Void Contracts

A **valid contract** is one that meets all of the legal requirements for a binding contract. Valid contracts are, therefore, enforceable in court.

An **unenforceable contract** is one that meets the basic legal requirements for a contract but may not be enforceable because of some other legal rule. You'll learn about an example of this in Chapter 16, which discusses the statute of frauds, a rule that requires certain kinds of contracts to be evidenced by a writing. If a contract is one of those for which the statute of frauds requires a writing, but no writing is made, the contract is said to be unenforceable. Another example of an unenforceable contract is an otherwise valid contract whose enforcement is barred by the applicable contract statute of limitations.

Voidable contracts are those in which one or more of the parties have the legal right to cancel their obligations under the contract. For example, a contract that is induced by fraud or duress is voidable (cancellable) at the election of the injured party. Other situations in which contracts are voidable are discussed in Chapters 13 and 14. The important feature of a voidable contract is that the injured party has the *right* to cancel the contract *if he chooses.* That right belongs only to the injured party, and if he does not cancel the contract, it can be enforced by either party.

Void contracts are agreements that create no legal obligations and for which no remedy will be given. Contracts to commit crimes, such as "hit" contracts, are classic examples of void contracts. Illegal contracts such as these are discussed in Chapter 15.

Express and Implied Contracts

In an **express contract,** the parties have directly stated the terms of their contract orally or in writing at the time the contract was formed. However, the mutual agreement necessary to create a contract may also be demonstrated by the conduct of the parties. When the surrounding facts and circumstances indicate that an agreement has in fact been reached, an **implied contract** (also called a contract implied in fact) has been created. When you go to a doctor for treatment, for example, you do not ordinarily state the terms of your agreement in advance, although it is clear that you do, in fact, have an agreement. A court would infer a promise by your doctor to use reasonable care and skill in treating you and a return promise on your part to pay a reasonable fee for her services.

Executed and Executory Contracts

A contract is **executed** when all of the parties have fully performed their contractual duties, and it is **executory** until such duties have been fully performed.

Any contract may be described using one or more of the above terms. For example, Eurocars, Inc., orders five new Mercedes-Benz 500 SLs from Mercedes. Mercedes sends Eurocars its standard acknowledgment form accepting the order. The parties have a *valid, express, bilateral* contract that will be *executory* until Mercedes delivers the cars and Eurocars pays for them.

Sources of Law Governing Contracts

Two bodies of law—Article 2 of the Uniform Commercial Code and the common law of contracts—govern contracts today. The Uniform Commercial Code, or UCC, is statutory law in every state. The common law of contracts is court-made law that, like all court-made law, is in a constant state of evolution. Determining what body of law applies to a contract problem is a very important first step in analyzing that problem.

The Uniform Commercial Code: Origin and Purposes

The UCC was created by the American Law Institute and the National Conference of Commissioners on Uniform State Laws. All of the states have adopted it except Louisiana, which has adopted only part of the Code. The drafters of the Code had several purposes in mind, the most obvious of which was to establish a uniform set of rules to govern commercial transactions, which are often conducted across state lines.[2]

In addition to promoting uniformity, the drafters of the Code sought to create a body of rules that would realistically and fairly solve the common problems occurring in everyday commercial transactions. Finally, the drafters tried to formulate rules that would promote fair dealing and higher standards in the marketplace.

The UCC contains nine articles, most of which are discussed in detail in Parts 4, 6, and 7 of this book. The most important Code article for our present purposes is Article 2, which deals with the sale of goods.

The UCC has changed and is in the process of continuing to change in response to changes in technology and business transactions. At the time of this writing, revisions to Article 2 have been proposed that may be enacted in coming years. In some instances, the creation of new bodies of uniform law have been necessary to govern transactions that are similar to but different in significant ways from the sale of goods. For example, as leasing became a more common way of executing and financing transactions in goods, a separate UCC article, Article 2A, was enacted to govern the *lease* of goods.

Application of Article 2

Article 2 expressly applies only to *contracts for the sale of goods* [2–102] (the numbers in brackets refer to specific Code sections). The essence of the definition of goods in the UCC [1–105] is that *goods are tangible, movable, personal property.* So, contracts for the sale of such items as motor vehicles, books, appliances, and clothing are covered by Article 2.

Application of the Common Law of Contracts

Article 2 of the UCC applies to contracts for the sale of goods, but it does *not* apply to contracts for the sale of real estate or intangibles such as stocks and bonds, be-

---

[2]Despite the Code's almost national adoption, however, complete uniformity has not been achieved. Many states have varied or amended the Code's language in specific instances, and some Code provisions were drafted in alternative ways, giving the states more than one version of particular Code provisions to choose from. Also, the various state courts have reached different conclusions about the meaning of particular Code sections. Work is currently under way to revise many basic sections of the Code, so uniformity will continue to be a problem as states adopt the revised sections at different rates and to different degrees.

CYBERLAW IN ACTION

Currently, many courts are using the Uniform Commercial Code in cases involving disputes over software and other information contracts. However, the UCC was designed to deal with sales of goods and may not sufficiently address the concerns that parties have when making contracts to create or distribute information. During the 1990s, contract scholars, representatives of the affected information industries, consumer groups, and others worked as a drafting committee of the National Conference of Commissioners on Uniform State Laws to draft a uniform law that would be tailored to "information contracts." Internet access contracts and software licenses are two familiar examples of information contracts. Initially, this uniform statute was conceived of as a new article of the UCC called Article 2B. Later, however, attempts to fit the uniform law within the UCC were abandoned, and it was ultimately released as a proposed statute called the Uniform Computer Information Transactions Act, or UCITA. Several UCITA positions—notably those dealing with shrinkwrap and clickwrap licenses—have been quite controversial, and at the time of this writing, only two states have adopted UCITA in full as part of their state law. For more information about UCITA, see UCITA Online, *www.ucitaonline.com.*

cause those kinds of property do not constitute goods. Article 2 also does not apply to *service* contracts. Contracts for the sale of real estate, services, and intangibles are governed by the common law of contracts.

Law Governing "Hybrid" Contracts

Many contracts involve a hybrid of both goods and services. As the following *Pittsley* case discusses, the test that the courts most frequently use to determine whether Article 2 applies to such a contract is to ask which element, goods or services, *predominates* in the contract. Is the major purpose or thrust of the agreement the rendering of a service, or is it the sale of goods, with any services involved being merely incidental to that sale? This means that contracts calling for services that involve significant elements of personal skill or judgment in addition to goods probably are not governed by Article 2. Construction contracts, remodeling contracts, and auto repair contracts are all examples of mixed goods and services contracts that may be considered outside the scope of the Code.

Pittsley v. Houser   *875 P.2d 232 (Idaho Ct. App.1994)*

In September of 1988, Jane Pittsley contracted with Hilton Contract Carpet Co. for the installation of carpet in her home for $4,402. Hilton paid the installers $700 to put the carpet in Pittsley's home. After the carpet was installed, Pittsley complained to Hilton that some seams were visible, that gaps appeared, that the carpet did not lie flat in all areas, and that it failed to reach the wall in certain locations. Although Hilton made various attempts to fix the installation, Pittsley was not satisfied with the work. Eventually, Pittsley refused any further efforts to fix the carpet. Pittsley initially paid Hilton $3,500 on the contract, but refused to pay the remaining balance of $902.

Pittsley later filed suit, seeking rescission of the contract, return of the $3,500, and other damages. Hilton counterclaimed for the balance remaining on the contract. At trial, the magistrate found that there were defects in the installation and that the carpet had been installed in an unworkmanlike manner, but that there was a lack of evidence about damages. The trial court awarded Pittsley $400 damages and awarded Hilton $902 on its counterclaim, representing the money remaining on the contract. Pittsley appealed to the district court, claiming that the transaction involved was governed by the UCC and arguing that a different result would have been reached had the UCC been applied. The district court agreed with Pittsley's argument, reversing and remanding the case to the magistrate to make additional findings of fact and to apply the UCC to the transaction. Hilton appealed.

Swanstrom, J., pro tem   Hilton argues that there were no defects in the goods that were the subject of the transaction, only in the installation, making application of the UCC inappropriate. The single question upon which this appeal depends is whether the UCC is applicable to the subject transaction. If the underlying transaction involved the sale of "goods," then the UCC would apply. If the transaction did not involve goods, but rather was for services, then application of the UCC would be erroneous. Section 2–105(1) defines "goods" as "all things which are movable at the time of identification to the contract for sale. . . ." Although there is little dispute that carpets are "goods," the transaction in this case also involved installation, a service. Such hybrid transactions, involving both goods and services, raise difficult questions about the applicability of the UCC. Two lines of authority have emerged to deal with such situations.

The first line of authority, and the majority position, utilizes the "predominant factor" test. The Ninth Circuit, applying the Idaho Uniform Commercial Code to the subject transaction, restated the predominant factor test as:

> The test for inclusion or exclusion is not whether they are mixed, but, granting that they are mixed, whether their predominant factor, their thrust, their purpose, reasonably stated, is the rendition of service, with goods incidentally involved (e.g., contract with artist for painting) or is a transaction of sale, with labor incidentally involved (e.g., installation of a water heater in a bathroom).

This test essentially involves consideration of the contract in its entirety, applying the UCC to the entire contract or not at all.

The second line of authority, which Hilton urges us to adopt, allows the contract to be severed into different parts, applying the UCC to the goods involved in the contract, but not to the non-goods involved, including services as well as other non-goods assets and property. Thus, an action focusing on defects or problems with the goods themselves would be covered by the UCC, while a suit based on the service provided or some other non-goods aspect would not be covered by the UCC. This position was advanced by the Tenth Circuit Court of Appeals in *Foster v. Colorado Radio Corp.*, which involved the sale of a radio station. The court in *Foster* held that, although there was a single contract for the purchase of a radio station, the UCC applied only to the actual goods that were covered under the contract. Thus, the court applied different analyses and remedies to two different aspects of the same contract.

We believe the predominant factor test is the more prudent rule. Severing contracts into various parts, attempting to label each as goods or non-goods and applying different law to each separate part clearly contravenes the UCC's declared purpose "to simplify, clarify and modernize the law governing commercial transactions." Section 1–102(2)(a). As the Supreme Court of Tennessee suggested in *Hudson v. Town & Country True Value Hardware, Inc.*, such a rule would, in many contexts, present "difficult and in some instances insurmountable problems of proof in segregating assets and determining their respective values at the time of the original contract and at the time of resale, in order to apply two different measures of damages."

Applying the predominant factor test to the case before us, we conclude that the UCC was applicable to the subject transaction. The record indicates that the contract between the parties called for "165 yds Masterpiece#2122—Installed" for a price of $4,319.50. There was an additional charge for removing the existing carpet. The record indicates that Hilton paid the installers $700 for the work done in laying Pittsley's carpet. It appears that Pittsley entered into this contract for the purpose of obtaining carpet of a certain quality and color. It does not appear that the installation, either who would provide it or the nature of the work, was a factor in inducing Pittsley to choose Hilton as the carpet supplier. On these facts, we conclude that the sale of the carpet was the predominant factor in the contract, with the installation being merely incidental to the purchase. Therefore, in failing to consider the UCC, the magistrate did not apply the correct legal principles to the facts as found. We must therefore vacate the judgment and remand for further findings of fact and application of the UCC to the subject transaction.

On remand, the magistrate may consider such issues as whether the carpet was properly rejected under Section 2–602 or whether the actions of Pittsley constituted acceptance under Section 2–606. If the goods were accepted, the magistrate may consider if the acceptance could have been revoked under Section 2–608. The magistrate may then consider the various remedies that are available under the UCC and any other provisions of the code that the court deems applicable.

Judgment vacated in favor of Pittsley and remanded for further proceedings.

Relationship of the UCC and the Common Law of Contracts

Two important qualifications must be made concerning the application of Code contract principles. First, the Code does not change *all* of the traditional contract rules. Where no specific Code rule exists, traditional contract law rules apply to contracts for the sale of goods. Second, and ultimately far more important, the courts have demonstrated a significant tendency to apply Code con-

Figure 2   *When the Uniform Commercial Code Applies*

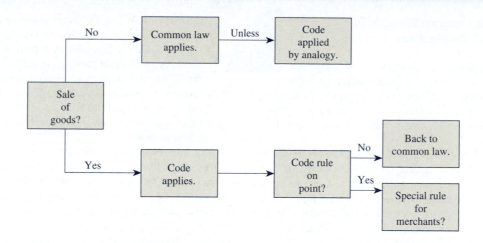

tract concepts by analogy to some contracts that are not technically covered by Article 2. For example, the Code concepts of good faith dealing and unconscionability have enjoyed wide application in cases that are technically outside the scope of Article 2. Thus, the Code is an important influence in shaping the evolution of contract law in general, and if this trend toward broader application of Code principles continues, the time may come when the dichotomy between Code principles and traditional contract rules is a thing of the past. (See Figure 2.)

Basic Differences in the Nature of Article 2 and the Common Law of Contracts

Many of the provisions of Article 2 differ from traditional common law rules in a variety of important ways. The Code is more concerned with rewarding people's legitimate expectations than with technical rules, so it is generally more flexible than the common law of contracts. A court that applies the Code is more likely to find that the parties had a contract than is a court that applies the common law of contracts [2–204]. In some cases, the Code gives less weight to technical requirements such as consideration [2–205 and 2–209].

The drafters of the Code sought to create practical rules to deal with what people actually do in today's marketplace. We live in the day of the form contract, so some of the Code's rules try to deal fairly with that fact [2–205, 2–207, 2–209(2), and 2–302]. The words *reasonable, commercially reasonable,* and *seasonably* (within a rea-

sonable time) are found throughout the Code. This reasonableness standard is different from the hypothetical reasonable person standard in tort law. A court that tries to decide what is reasonable under the Code is more likely to be concerned with what people really do in the marketplace than with what a nonexistent reasonable person would do.

The drafters of the Code wanted to promote fair dealing and higher standards in the marketplace, so they imposed a **duty of good faith** [1–203] in the performance and enforcement of every contract under the Code. Good faith means "honesty in fact," which is required of all parties to sales contracts [1–201(19)]. In addition, merchants are required to observe "reasonable commercial standards of fair dealing" [2–103(1)(b)]. The parties cannot alter this duty of good faith by agreement [1–102(3)]. Finally, the Code expressly recognizes the concept of an **unconscionable contract,** one that is grossly unfair or one-sided, and it gives the courts broad discretionary powers to deal fairly with such contracts [2–302].[3]

The Code also recognizes that buyers tend to place more reliance on professional sellers and that professionals are generally more knowledgeable and better able to protect themselves than nonprofessionals. So, the Code distinguishes between **merchants** and nonmerchants by holding merchants to a higher standard in some cases [2–201(2), 2–205, and 2–207(2)]. The Code defines the term *merchant* [2–104(1)] on a case-by-case basis. If a person regularly deals in the kind of goods being sold, or pretends to have some special knowledge about the goods, or

---

[3]Chapter 15 discusses unconscionability in detail.

THE GLOBAL BUSINESS ENVIRONMENT

Dealing with Contract Disputes in International Transactions

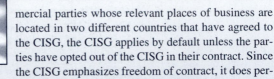

Every country has its own contract law. But what law applies when a contract is between businesses from two *different* countries? How can businesses avoid the possibility of costly litigation over international contract disputes and the added danger of being bound by an unanticipated, foreign body of law?

The **United Nations Convention on Contracts for the International Sale of Goods,** or **CISG,** is an international body of contract rules that harmonizes contract principles from many legal systems. Sixty-one countries, including the United States and Canada, have adopted the CISG to date. The CISG is intended to provide a uniform code for international commercial contracts in much the same way as the UCC provides uniformity for transactions among contracting parties in different states in the United States. Like the UCC, though, the CISG does not have provisions to cover every contract problem that might occur. It applies only to sales of goods, not services, and only to commercial parties, not consumers. When there is a contract for the sale of goods between com-

mercial parties whose relevant places of business are located in two different countries that have agreed to the CISG, the CISG applies by default unless the parties have opted out of the CISG in their contract. Since the CISG emphasizes freedom of contract, it does permit the parties to agree to exclude or vary any of the CISG rules or to opt out of the CISG completely by stating in their contract that some other body of law (such as the UCC) will apply to their contract.

Companies entering international transactions often protect themselves from disputes over what body of laws applies to their disputes by including a **choice of law clause** in their contracts. This is a provision that states the parties' agreement that a particular country or state's law will apply to their contract. (Of course, choice of law clauses are used extensively in domestic transactions as well.) In addition, it is very common for parties in international transactions to include an **arbitration clause** in their contracts, providing that future disputes between them will be resolved by arbitration.[4] Using arbitration gives the parties a relatively speedy and affordable dispute resolution process. An added benefit is that there are several international treaties that will enforce arbitration awards.

---

employed an agent in the sale who fits either of these two descriptions, that person is a merchant for the purposes of the contract in question. So, if you buy a used car from a used-car dealer, the dealer is a merchant for the purposes of your contract. But, if you buy a refrigerator from a used-car dealer, the dealer is probably not a merchant.

> **LOG ON**
>
> For links to everything you might ever want to know about the CISG, visit Pace University School of Law Database on the CISG and International Commercial Law,
> **http://www.cisg.law.pace.edu/.**
> Another good source of information is CISG Online,
> **http://www.jura.uni-freiburg.de/ipr1/cisg/.**

Influence of *Restatement (Second) of Contracts*

In 1932, the American Law Institute published the first *Restatement of Contracts,*[5] an attempt to codify and sys-

tematize the soundest principles of contract law gleaned from thousands of often conflicting judicial decisions. As the product of a private organization, the *Restatement* did not have the force of law, but as the considered judgment of some of the leading scholars of the legal profession, it was highly influential in shaping the evolution of contract law. The *Restatement (Second) of Contracts,* issued in 1979, is an attempt to reflect the significant changes that have occurred in contract law in the years following the birth of the first *Restatement.* The *Restatement (Second)* reflects the "shift from rules to standards" in modern contract law—the shift from precise, technical rules to broader, discretionary principles that produce just results.[6] In fact, many *Restatement (Second)* provisions are virtually identical to their Code analogues. For example, the *Restatement (Second)* has explicitly embraced the Code concepts of *good faith*[7] and *unconscionability.*[8]

---

[4]Arbitration is discussed in more detail in Chapter 2.

[5]See Chapter 1 for a general discussion of the *Restatement* phenomenon.

[6]Speidel, "Restatement Second: Omitted Terms and Contract Method," 67 *Cornell L. Rev.* 785, 786 (1982).

[7]*Restatement (Second) of Contracts* § 205 (1981).

[8]*Restatement (Second) of Contracts* § 208 (1981).

The *Restatement (Second)* does *not* have the force of law. Nonetheless, it can be and has been influential in shaping the evolution of contract law because courts have the option of adopting a *Restatement (Second)* approach to the contract issues presented in the cases that come before them. Particular approaches suggested by the *Restatement (Second)* will be mentioned in some of the following chapters.

"Noncontract" Obligations

Before we proceed to a discussion of the individual elements of contract law, there is one more group of introductory concepts to be considered. Although contract obligations normally require mutual agreement and an exchange of value, there are some circumstances in which the law enforces an obligation to pay for certain losses or benefits even in the absence of mutual agreement and exchange of value. We will refer to these circumstances as "noncontract" obligations because they impose the duty on a person to pay for a loss or benefit yet they do not meet the criteria for formation of a contract. These noncontract doctrines give a person who cannot establish the existence of a contract a chance to obtain compensation.

Quasi-Contract

Requiring all the elements of a binding contract before contractual obligation is imposed can cause injustice in some cases. One person may have provided goods or services to another person who benefited from them but has no contractual obligation to pay for them because no facts exist that would justify a court in implying a promise to pay for them. Such a situation can also arise in cases where the parties contemplated entering into a binding contract but some legal defense exists that prevents the enforcement of the agreement. Consider the following examples:

1. Jones paints Smith's house by mistake, thinking it belongs to Reed. Smith knows that Jones is painting his house but does not inform him of his error. There are no facts from which a court can infer that Jones and Smith have a contract because the parties have had no prior discussions or dealings.

2. Thomas Products fraudulently induces Perkins to buy a household products franchise by grossly misstating the average revenues of its franchisees. Perkins discovers the misrepresentation after he has resold some products that he has received but before he has paid Thomas for them. Perkins elects to rescind (cancel) the franchise contract on the basis of the fraud.

In the preceding examples, both Smith and Perkins have good defenses to contract liability; however, enabling Smith to get a free paint job and Perkins to avoid paying for the goods he resold would *unjustly enrich* them at the expense of Jones and Thomas. To deal with such cases and to prevent such unjust enrichment, the courts imply *as a matter of law* a promise by the benefited party to pay the *reasonable value* of the benefits he received. This idea is called **quasi-contract** (or contract implied in law) because it represents an obligation imposed by law to avoid injustice, not a contractual obligation created by voluntary consent. Quasi-contract liability has been imposed in situations too numerous and varied to detail. In general, however, quasi-contract liability is imposed when one party *confers a benefit* on another who *knowingly accepts it* and *retains it* under circumstances that make it *unjust* to do so without paying for it. So, if Jones painted Smith's house while Smith was away on vacation, Smith would probably not be liable for the reasonable value of the paint job because he did *not* knowingly accept it and because he has no way to return it to Jones. The following *Duncan* case provides another example of the application of the concept "unjust enrichment."

Duncan v. Kasim, Inc.   *810 So. 2d 968 (Fla. Ct. App. 2002)*

In October of 1997, Susan Duncan undertook the management of the beverage-lounge of a Daytona Beach, Florida, Super 8 Lodge that was owned by Kasim, Inc. Essentially, Duncan rented space in the lodge for the bar-lounge. Duncan paid fees or rent to Kasim, and she was to bear all operational expenses and the costs of renovations and remodeling. It was Duncan's sole responsibility to furnish the bar-lounge with furniture, glasses, and other equipment and stock the bar with alcohol and other items for sale. All profits of the bar-lounge were to be retained by Duncan.

Duncan made improvements to the property, placed a substantial amount of her personal property on the property, and paid for the full stocking of beverages, and managed the property until November 1998. What Duncan did not do was disclose to Kasim the fact that she was a convicted felon. Under Florida law, a person who has been convicted of a felony in the last five years cannot be employed as a bartender, manager, or person in charge of a liquor lounge licensed by the Division of Alcoholic Beverages and Tobacco. Thus, Duncan's management of the bar-lounge was illegal. A dispute arose between Duncan and Kasim, no doubt caused by Duncan's failure to disclose her conviction. In December 1998, Kasim denied Duncan access to the property and it appropriated all of her personal property, appliances, and fixtures located on the property. Duncan sued Kasim on a variety of grounds, including breach of contract and unjust enrichment. The trial court granted a summary judgment in favor of Kasim because the contract between Kasim and Duncan was illegal, and Duncan appealed.

SHARP, J.   Although some of the counts in this case were based on the illegal contract between Duncan and Kasim, we think her claims for unjust enrichment were not. For example, if a contract is entered into for the sale of illegal drugs and the buyer takes the drugs without paying for them, courts will not enforce the contract by requiring the buyer to return the drugs or pay for them. If, however, during the transaction the buyer absconds with the car used by the seller to transport the drugs and refuses to return it, an action for conversion should not be barred.

In this case, the management contract was primarily for the use of space by Duncan. She had the sole discretion to furnish and stock the premises. Her personal property and the furnishings she supplied were not sold to Kasim (or even mentioned in the contract) but, like the car in the prior example, were the means by which she hoped to earn a profit from the transaction. They were independent of the illegal contract itself.

We think the unjust enrichment claim is similar. The elements of a cause of action for unjust enrichment are: 1) the plaintiff conferred a benefit on the defendant, who has knowledge of the benefit, 2) the defendant accepts and retains the conferred benefit, and 3) under the circumstances it would be inequitable for the defendant to retain the benefit without paying for it. In this case, Duncan alleged Kasim sold her personal property, knowing the items belonged to her and accepted the benefits of the sale. The factual allegations are sufficiently distinct from the illegal contract that it should not be seen as an enforcement of the contract.

Duncan did not contract to furnish Kasim with any personal property or goods. Anything she brought onto the premises was for the purpose of selling to the public, for her sole profit, as her sole business. In addition, to the extent she improved Kasim's property with fixtures not removable from the premises, she may be entitled to an unjust enrichment claim depending on the circumstances of the case and agreements of the parties, all of which have not been defined or determined at this point in the case.

Accordingly, we reverse and remand this case to the trial court for further proceedings regarding the counts pertaining to unjust enrichment.

Summary judgment on the unjust enrichment count reversed in favor of Duncan.

Promissory Estoppel

Another very important idea that courts have developed to deal with the unfairness that would sometimes result from the strict application of traditional contract principles is the doctrine of **promissory estoppel.** In numerous situations one person may *rely* on a promise made by another even though the promise and surrounding circumstances are not sufficient to justify the conclusion that a contract has been created because one or more of the required elements is missing. To allow the person who made such a promise (the promisor) to argue that no contract was created would sometimes work an injustice on the person who relied on the promise (the promisee). For example, in *Ricketts v. Scothorn,* a grandfather's promise to pay his granddaughter interest on a demand note he gave her so that she would not have to work was enforced against him after she had quit her job in reliance on his promise.[9] The Nebraska Supreme Court acknowledged that such promises were traditionally unenforceable because they were gratuitous and not supported by any consideration, but held that the granddaughter's reliance prevented her grandfather from raising his lack of consideration defense. In the early decades of this century, many courts began to extend similar protection to relying promisees. They said that persons who made promises that produced such reliance were *estopped,* or equitably prevented, from raising any defense they had to the enforcement of their promise. Out of such cases grew the doctrine of promissory estoppel. Section 90 of the *Restatement (Second) of Contracts* states:

---

[9]57 Neb. 51, 77 N.W. 365 (1898).

Figure 3	*Contract and Noncontract Theories of Recovery*	
Theory	**Key Concept**	**Remedy**
Contract	Voluntary agreement	Enforce promise
Quasi-Contract	Unjust enrichment	Reasonable value of services
Promissory Estoppel	Foreseeable reliance	Enforce promise or recover reliance losses

A promise which the promisor should reasonably expect to induce action or forbearance on the part of the promisee or a third person and which does induce such action or forbearance is binding if injustice can be avoided only by enforcement of the promise. The remedy granted for breach may be limited as justice requires.

Thus, the elements of promissory estoppel are a *promise* that the *promisor should foresee is likely to induce reliance, reliance* on the promise by the promisee, and *injustice* as a result of that reliance. (See Figure 3.) The following *Goff-Hamel* case provides an example of promissory estoppel.

Goff-Hamel v. Obstetricians & Gynecologists, P.C.
588 N.W.2d 798 (Neb. Sup. Ct. 1999)

Julie Goff-Hamel worked for Hastings Family Planning for 11 years. Prior to leaving Hastings Family Planning, Goff-Hamel was earning $24,000 plus 6 weeks' paid maternity leave, 6 weeks' vacation, 12 paid holidays, 12 sick days, an educational reimbursement, and medical and dental insurance coverage. In June of 1993, Dr. George Adam, a part owner of Obstetricians, had approached Goff-Hamel about working for him as a patient relations and outreach coordinator at Obstetricians. Goff-Hamel initially declined the offer, explaining that she had made commitments to do some training in the fall and to hire and help train a new bookkeeper. Adam spoke to Goff-Hamel approximately one month later, asking her to reconsider and whether she was ready to "jump ship and come work for him." Goff-Hamel told Adam she would be interested in hearing some details, and an interview was set for July 27 at Adam's office.

At the meeting, Adam told Goff-Hamel the salary benefits and other conditions of the job. Obstetricians offered Goff-Hamel a job during the July 27, 1993, meeting, and she accepted the job offer at that time. She expressed concern that she be given time to finish some projects at Hastings Family Planning, and it was agreed that she would start her employment on October 4. Goff-Hamel gave notice to Hastings Family Planning in August, informing them that she would be resigning to take a job with Obstetricians.

Later, Goff-Hamel went to Obstetricians' office and was provided with uniforms for her job. She was given a copy of her schedule for the first week of work, but did not receive a copy of the employee handbook. On October 3, 1993, an Obstetricians representative told Goff-Hamel that she should not report to work the next morning as had been planned, because the wife of another part-owner of Obstetricians opposed her hiring.

Goff-Hamel brought this action against Obstetricians, seeking damages for breach of an alleged oral employment contract or, in the alternative, damages for detrimental reliance on a promise of employment. The trial court granted summary judgment in favor of Obstetricians, and Goff-Hamel appealed.

Wright, J.   It is undisputed that on July 27, 1993, Obstetricians offered Goff-Hamel employment and that she accepted. The oral agreement did not specify that the employment was for a definite period. We have consistently held that when employment is not for a definite term and there are no contractual, statutory, or constitutional restrictions upon the right of discharge, an employer may lawfully discharge an employee whenever and for whatever cause it chooses. Therefore, the trial court correctly determined as a matter of law that Goff-Hamel could not bring a claim for breach of an employment contract.

Goff-Hamel's second cause of action was based upon promissory estoppel. Promissory estoppel provides for damages as justice requires and does not attempt to provide the plaintiff damages based upon the benefit of the bargain. It requires only that reliance be reasonable and foreseeable. It does not impose the requirement that the promise giving rise to the cause of action must be so comprehensive in scope as to meet the requirements of an offer that would ripen into a contract if accepted by the promisee. We have not specifically addressed whether promissory estoppel may be asserted as the basis for a cause of action for detrimental reliance upon a promise of at-will employment. In *Merrick v. Thomas,* the employee was terminated from her job approximately 4 months after she had been hired. We determined that because the employee had worked for a time, the employer had kept his promise to employ the plaintiff and that promissory estoppel was not available. We did not consider whether a cause of action based upon promissory estoppel could be stated by a prospective at-will employee who had been induced to leave previous gainful employment based upon the promise of other employment, but who did not commence employment at the new job.

Other jurisdictions which have addressed the question of whether a cause of action for promissory estoppel can be stated in the context of a prospective at-will employee are split on the issue. Some have held that an employee can recover damages incurred as a result of resigning from the former at-will employment in reliance on a promise of other at-will employment. They have determined that when a prospective employer knows or should know that a promise of employment will induce an employee to leave his or her current job, such employer shall be liable for the reliant's damages. Recognizing that both the prospective new employer and the prior employer could have fired the employee without cause at any time, they have concluded that the employee would have continued to work in his or her prior employment if it were not for the offer by the prospective employer. Although damages have not been allowed for wages lost from the prospective at-will employment, damages have been allowed based upon wages from the prior employment and other damages incurred in reliance on the job offer.

In contrast, other jurisdictions have held as a matter of law that a prospective employee cannot recover damages incurred in reliance on an unfulfilled promise of at-will employment, concluding that reliance on a promise consisting solely of at-will employment is unreasonable as a matter of law because the employee should know that the promised employment could be terminated by the employer at any time for any reason without liability. These courts have stated that an anomalous result occurs when recovery is allowed for an employee who has not begun work, when the same employee's job could be terminated without liability 1 day after beginning work.

Having reviewed and considered decisions from other jurisdictions, we conclude under the facts of this case that promissory estoppel can be asserted in connection with the offer of at-will employment and that the trial court erred in granting Obstetricians summary judgment. Here, promissory estoppel is appropriate where Goff-Hamel acted to her detriment in order to avail herself of the promised employment.

Reversed and remanded in favor of Goff-Hamel.

When you consider these elements, it is obvious that promissory estoppel is fundamentally different from traditional contract principles. Contract is traditionally thought of as protecting *agreements* or bargains. Promissory estoppel, on the other hand, protects *reliance*. Early promissory estoppel cases applied the doctrine only to gift promises like the one made by the grandfather in the previous example. As subsequent chapters demonstrate, however, promissory estoppel is now being used by the courts to prevent offerors from revoking their offers, to enforce indefinite promises, and to enforce oral promises that would ordinarily have to be in writing.

Problems and Problem Cases

1. The Millers decided to build a house on lot 7-A in a new subdivision that was being developed by Joint Venture, Inc. (JVI). JVI had entered into agreements with

ETHICS IN ACTION

The idea that contracts should be enforced because they are voluntary agreements can obviously be justified on ethical grounds. But what about quasi-contracts and promissory estoppel? What ethical justi-fications can you give for departing from the notion of voluntary agreement in quasi-contract and promissory estoppel cases?

particular architects and contractors, who were "assigned" to the lots. JVI informed the Millers that Marks, an architect who was the principal of Architectura, an architectural firm, had been assigned to lot 7-A and the Millers would be responsible for paying Marks a fee of $25,000 for architectural services. No clear and specific agreement had been formed between JVI and Marks or between Marks and the Millers to detail what architectural services Marks would be obligated to perform for the Millers under his contract with JVI. Marks provided the Millers with two different house designs for lot 7-A. The Millers did not want either of them, however, and informed Marks that they wanted a brick Georgian-style house. They met with Marks and others in Architectura several times before closing the deal with JVI to purchase the lot. At the closing, the Millers paid a check to Marks for $25,000 that bore the notation "For: Architect Fee." The Millers thought that this $25,000 would cover all of the needed architectural services, "from soup to nuts," that would be needed to build their house. In July of 1996, Marks prepared the house plans to the Miller's specifications and delivered them to the Millers just before groundbreaking. Between July 1996 and January 1997, Marks and other Architectura personnel visited the building site to view the ongoing construction work. They did not send the Millers a bill. In March 1997, an Architectura representative noticed flaws in the house's construction and notified the Millers. The Millers requested that Marks, as part of the "architectural team," consult with Mr. Miller about these flaws, and Marks did so. Marks claimed that at this meeting, Mr. Miller orally agreed to be billed by the hour for Architectura's services, but Mr. Miller denied having any oral agreements with Marks at all. In November 1997, after Marks and others from Architectura performed corrective work on the construction of the Millers's house, Architectura sent the Millers a bill for $22,258.64. The bill listed various services performed between January and November 1997. The Millers claimed that this was the first indication they had that the $25,000 they had paid for architectural services would not cover all the architectural services to be rendered in connection with the house. The Millers declined to pay the bill and Architectura sued them and recorded a lien against their house for the amount of the bill. Must the Millers pay the additional $22,258.64?

2. Villette contracted with Sheldorado Aluminum Products for the purchase and installation of an aluminum awning on the back of her home for use as a carport. The parties signed a simple 1-page order/bill that was desig-

nated a "contract." This contract states the name of Sheldorado Aluminum Products at the top and lists the following products: awnings, windows, doors, mirrors, window treatments, storefronts, and siding. On the contract, the word "awnings" was circled. The body of the contract contains the handwritten description, "Supply and install one alum. roof" and adds dimensions, materials, design characteristics and colors. The total price was $3,000. A line for installation says "included." In June 2000, Sheldorado installed the awning on the back of Villette's house, but in January 2001, the awning collapsed on top of Villette's new Mercedes. Villette sued Sheldorado for the return of the $3,000 she paid for the awning, claiming that the UCC and its warranties applied to this transaction. Did the UCC apply to the contract between Villette and Sheldorado?

3. Advent Systems, a British company, developed an electronic document management system (EDMS), a process for transforming engineering drawings and similar documents into a computer database. Unisys Corporation decided to market Advent's EDMS in the United States. In 1987, Advent and Unisys signed contracts in which Advent agreed to provide the software and hardware making up the EDMS, as well as sales and marketing material and the technical personnel to work with Unisys employees in building and installing the document systems. The agreement was to continue for two years, subject to automatic renewal or termination on notice. Was the UCC applicable to this contract?

4. Slodov adopted a four-month-old puppy from the Animal Protective League (APL) for a fee of $45, which covered the costs of neutering or spaying, shots, collar, starter kit, and two weeks of veterinary care. She signed an adoption agreement that stipulated that the APL would treat the dog at no cost to Slodov for two weeks after the adoption. According to the agreement, the APL would not be held responsible for any treatment of the dog outside the APL clinic. The dog became ill several times and Slodov took the dog to a private veterinarian rather than to the APL clinic. She then requested that the APL pay the veterinary bills, including advertising costs of placing the dog for adoption, because her landlord would not allow dogs in the apartment, and the APL refused. Slodov brought suit against APL on a variety of theories, including breach of warranties under the UCC. She claimed that the APL was a merchant under the UCC. Was it?

5. Chow arranged through a travel agent to fly from Indianapolis to Singapore on June 27, 1986. Singapore Airlines gave him a round-trip ticket that included a TWA flight to Los Angeles. Shortly before the trip, Chow's flight was rerouted so that he had to fly to St. Louis first and then to San Francisco. During the St. Louis stopover, the flight developed engine trouble, causing a substantial delay. TWA personnel assured Chow that if he missed his connecting flight, TWA would arrange for him to take the next Singapore flight out of San Francisco. After the engine problem was fixed, TWA delayed the flight's departure an additional two hours to board additional passengers. Chow was again assured that if he missed his scheduled flight, TWA would make arrangements for him. Chow missed his Singapore flight by minutes, and was housed overnight at TWA's expense in San Francisco after once more being assured that TWA would make arrangements to get him on the next Singapore flight. When he called Singapore Airlines the next morning to see whether TWA had made him a reservation, Chow was told that no arrangements had been made. When he contacted TWA, he was told TWA would make the arrangements immediately. After waiting several hours, Chow learned TWA had still not made the arrangements and was told that TWA could no longer help him. Because Singapore Airlines no longer had economy class seats available, Chow had to buy a business class seat at an additional cost of $928. When he filed suit against TWA for that amount, TWA argued that the Conditions of Contract printed on Chow's ticket disclaimed any liability for failure to make connections. Did Chow have a valid claim against TWA?

6. Elizabeth Balano owned a building. In 1990, David Pauffhausen, a carpenter and an artist, asked Balano for permission to renovate her building because he hoped to convert the building into a fine art print shop. Balano approved Pauffhausen's request, with the understanding that he would pay her $60.00 per month after he "got the business up and running." Over the course of Pauffhausen's extensive renovations, Balano at various times signed notes to various town authorities approving his work and allowing him to procure permits. She also gave him a signed note in 1991 stating: "To Whom it may Concern—David can use my house as long as he needs it." The building was revamped sufficiently to allow Pauffhausen to host two art shows in 1994 and 1995. Balano died in October of 1995. Her personal representatives offered Pauffhausen one year of free rent, after which his rent would be $60 per month, but for no definite term. Pauffhausen rejected the offer, presumably because the tenancy after the one-year period could be terminated at will. Pauffhausen filed a claim for $12,300 against Balano's estate for the value of the work that he

had done on the building. Does Pauffhausen have any basis for his claim?

7. CCDC is the owner of a historic commercial building in Central City, Colorado. In January of 1992, CCDC entered into a five-year lease of the building with Santa Barbara Capital. The lease provided that Santa Barbara would not make alterations that would impair the historic character of the site and it gave CCDC the right to approve all plans for remodeling. Under the terms of the lease, Santa Barbara was responsible for the costs of any and all remodeling and agreed to indemnify CCDC against any liens or claims arising from the work. Santa Barbara then hired DCB Construction to perform significant remodeling work on the interior of the building, and CCDC approved the plans. Under its contract with Santa Barbara, DCB made improvements to the interior of the building. A representative of CCDC was present on the property fairly regularly during the construction, but it did not communicate with or direct DCB's work. DCB was aware of the no-lien notice and it made no attempt to place a lien on the property. DCB stopped its work in November of 1992 because of Santa Barbara's failure to pay. In all, DCB billed Santa Barbara $371,245 and Santa Barbara paid only $76,515. Santa Barbara also defaulted on its lease with CCDC and stopped paying rent. DCB claimed that CCDC, as the owner of the building, had been unjustly enriched by the improvements that DCB had made on its property, and it sued CCDC for the unpaid work that it had done on the building. Will DCB win?

8. In December 1998, Brandt had surgery at the Sarah Bush Lincoln Health Center to correct her incontinence, and a ProteGen Sling was surgically implanted in her to ameliorate her condition. Brandt experienced serious medical complications from the sling. As a result, she had it surgically removed in November 1999. Brandt sued Sarah Bush Lincoln Health Center on a number of grounds, including breach of the UCC's implied warranty of merchantability. Sarah Bush Lincoln Health Center filed a motion to dismiss Brandt's implied warranty claim, arguing that the UCC does not apply to the contract between it and Brandt. Does it?

9. Stephen Gall and his family became ill after drinking contaminated water supplied to their home by the McKeesport Municipal Water Authority. They filed suit against the utility, arguing, among other things, that the utility had breached the UCC implied warranty of merchantability when it sold them contaminated water. The utility moved to dismiss their complaint, arguing that

since water was not "goods," the UCC did not apply. Should the Galls' complaint be dismissed?

10. In 1994, Schumacher and his wife and their two daughters moved to Finland, Minnesota, to operate a bar and restaurant called the Trestle Inn, which was owned by his parents. Schumacher claims that his parents induced him to leave his previous job and to make the move by orally agreeing to provide him a job managing the Inn for life and to leave the business and a large parcel of land to him when his first parent died. Schumacher was given free reign in managing the Inn and was allowed to retain all profits of the business but was not given any salary or wage. While he was operating the Inn, Schumacher used his own funds to build a home for his family on his parents' land, install a well, buy equipment for the business, and develop various marketing tools for the business. In the fall of 1998, Schumacher suspected that his parents were about to sell the Inn and the adjoining property. He brought suit for a restraining order to prevent them from doing so, claiming breach of contract and unjust enrichment, among other claims. In October 1998, the parents notified Schumacher that his employment at the Inn and his right to possess the adjoining property were terminated. The parents moved for summary judgment. The trial court held that Schumacher's oral contract claim was invalid because the contract needed to be in writing under applicable Minnesota law. However, does Schumacher have a valid claim for unjust enrichment?

Online Research: Finding Sources of Contract Law

1. Find out what countries have signed the CISG (Contracts for International Sale of Goods). Create a hypothetical scenario in which the CISG would be applied to a contract. Use a CISG website such as Pace University School of Law's Database on the CISG and International Commercial Law, http://www.cisg.law. pace.edu/ or simply do a key word search on your favorite search engine.

2. Visit UCITA Online, www.ucitaonline.com, and find out which two states have adopted UCITA. Then use a generalized search engine to find out what major e-commerce and Internet companies are headquartered in those two states.

10

THE AGREEMENT: OFFER

Jackson read an ad in the newspaper that had been placed by the owner of a local dog track. The ad stated that the Pic-6 Jackpot for the last evening of the racing season would be $825,000. Jackson went to the track on that date, picked the winner in the six designated races, and won the jackpot. However, the owner of the track refused to pay Jackson more than $25,000, stating that it had intended the amount of the jackpot to be $25,000 and not $825,000. The reason the newspaper ad said "$825,000" was that a newspaper employee had misread the ad copy that the dog track owners had submitted to the newspaper, and had read the dollar sign in front of the 25,000 as an "8."

- *Was the ad an offer?*
- *Does the actual intent of the dog track owner determine whether the offered jackpot was $25,000 or $825,000?*
- *Did the dog track owners have the right to terminate the offer?*

THE CONCEPT OF MUTUAL agreement lies at the heart of traditional contract law. Courts faced with deciding whether two or more persons entered into a contract look first for an *agreement* between the parties. Because the formation of an agreement is normally a two-step process by which one party makes a proposal and the other responds to the proposal, it is customary to analyze the agreement in two parts: *offer* and *acceptance*. This chapter, which concerns itself with the offer, and the next chapter, which covers acceptance, focus on the tools used by courts to determine whether the parties have reached the kind of agreement that becomes the foundation of a contract.

Requirements for an Offer

An **offer** is the critically important first step in the contract formation process. An offer says, in effect, "This is it—if you agree to these terms, we have a contract." The person who makes an offer (**the offeror**) gives the person to whom she makes the offer (**the offeree**) the power to bind her to a contract simply by accepting the offer.

Not every proposal qualifies as an offer. Some proposals are vague, for example, or made in jest, or thrown out merely as a way of opening negotiations. To distinguish an offer, courts look for three requirements. First, they look for some objective indication of a *present intent to contract* on the part of the offeror. Second, they look for specificity, or *definiteness,* in the terms of the alleged offer. Third, they look to see whether the alleged offer has been *communicated to the offeree.*

The preceding chapter discussed the fact that contracts for the sale of goods are governed by Article 2 of the UCC whereas contracts for services, real estate, and intangibles are generally governed by the common law of contracts. Common law and UCC standards for contract formation have a great deal in common, but they also differ somewhat. This chapter will point out those areas in which an offer for the sale of goods would be treated somewhat differently from an offer for services, real estate, and intangibles.

Intent to Contract

For a proposal to be considered an offer, the offeror must indicate *present intent to contract.* Present intent means the intent to enter the contract upon acceptance. It signifies that the offeror is not joking, haggling, or equivocating. It makes sense that intent on the part of the offeror would be required for an offer—otherwise, an unwilling person might wrongly be bound to a contract. But what is meant by intent? Should courts look at what the offeror actually in his own mind (*subjectively*) intended? Or should intent be judged by the impression that he has given to the rest of the world through words, acts, and circumstances that *objectively* indicate that intent?

The Objective Standard of Intent Early American courts took a subjective approach to contract formation, asking whether there was truly a "meeting of the minds" between the parties. This subjective standard, however, created uncertainty in the enforcement of contracts because it left every contract vulnerable to disputes about actual intent. The desire to meet the needs of the marketplace by affording predictable and consistent results in contracts cases dictated a shift toward an *objective theory of contracts*. By the middle of the 19th century, the objective approach to contract formation, which judges agreement by looking at the parties' outward manifestations of intent, was firmly established in American law. Judge Learned Hand once described the effect of the objective contract theory as follows:

> A contract has, strictly speaking, nothing to do with the personal, or individual, intent of the parties. A contract is an obligation attached by the mere force of law to certain acts of the parties, usually words, which ordinarily accompany and represent a known intent. If however, it were proved by 20 bishops that either party when he used the words intended something else than the usual meaning which the law imposes on them, he would still be held, unless there were mutual mistake or something else of that sort.[1]

Following the objective theory of contracts, then, an offeror's intent will be judged by an objective standard—that is, what his words, acts, and the circumstances signify about his intent. If a reasonable person familiar with all the circumstances would be justified in believing that the offeror intended to contract, a court would find that the intent requirement of an offer was satisfied even if the offeror himself says that he did not intend to contract.

Definiteness of Terms

If Smith says to Ford, "I'd like to buy your house," and Ford responds, "You've got a deal," has a contract been

---

[1] *Hotchkiss v. National City Bank,* 200 F. 287, 293 (S.D.N.Y. 1911).

formed? An obvious problem here is lack of specificity. A proposal that fails to state specifically what the offeror is willing to do and what he asks in return for his performance is unlikely to be considered an offer. One reason for the requirement of definiteness is that definiteness and specificity in an offer tend to indicate an intent to contract, whereas indefiniteness and lack of specificity tend to indicate that the parties are still negotiating and have not yet reached agreement. In the conversation between Smith and Ford, Smith's statement that he'd like to buy Ford's house is merely an invitation to offer or an invitation to negotiate. It indicates a willingness to contract in the future if the parties can reach agreement on mutually acceptable terms, but not a present intent to contract. If, however, Smith sends Ford a detailed and specific written document stating all of the material terms and conditions on which he is willing to buy the house and Ford writes back agreeing to Smith's terms, the parties' intent to contract would be objectively indicated and a contract probably would be created.

A second reason definiteness is important is that courts need to know the terms on which the parties agreed in order to determine if a breach of contract has occurred and calculate a remedy if it has. Keep in mind that the offer often contains all the terms of the parties' contract. This is so because all that an offeree is allowed to do in most cases is to accept or reject the terms of the offer. If an agreement is too indefinite, a court would not have a basis for giving a remedy if one of the parties alleged that the "contract" was breached.

Definiteness Standards under the Common Law Classical contract law took the position that courts are contract enforcers, not contract makers. The prospect of enforcing an agreement in which the parties had omitted terms or left terms open for later agreement was unthinkable to courts that took a traditional, hands-off approach to contracts. Traditionally, contract law required a relatively high standard of definiteness for offers, requiring that all the essential terms of a proposed contract be stated in the offer. The traditional insistence on definiteness can serve useful ends. It can prevent a person from being held to an agreement when none was reached or from being bound by a contract term to which he never assented. Often, however, it can operate to frustrate the expectations of parties who intend to contract but, for whatever reason, fail to procure an agreement that specifies all the terms of the contract. The definiteness standard, like much of contract law, is constantly evolving. The trend of modern contract law is to tolerate a lower degree of specificity in agreements than classical contract law would have tolerated, although it is still unlikely that an agreement that leaves open important aspects of a transaction will be enforced. You can see an example of the common law's definiteness standard in the following *McCarthy* case.

McCarthy v. Kylberg   *282 F.3d 70 (1st Cir. 2002)*

Communicom Co. hired William McCarthy in February 1995 as an at-will administrative consultant at a Boston radio station that Communicom owned. Initially, McCarthy was paid $9.00 an hour, but in May 1995 he was given an annual salary of $20,000. On October 6, 1996, Richard Kylberg, the president of CCA, Communicom's general and managing partner, offered McCarthy the position of station manager, and McCarthy accepted the offer the next day. Later on that same day, McCarthy accompanied Kylberg to the airport. McCarthy claims that as they were waiting at a ticket counter, he asked Kylberg whether the station would be sold. Kylberg responded that Communicom had no present intention to sell the station but might if someone were "crazy enough to offer $7 million for it." According to McCarthy, Kylberg then added:

> "And I'll say to you guys, I have this offer. What do you think about it? Should we sell the radio station? Shouldn't we sell the radio station?" And he indicated that when push comes to shove, when it comes right down to it, it doesn't matter because he owns the radio station and he'll make the decision, but he indicated in quotes, "I don't think you'll have a problem with this if I go to Bill [McCarthy] and say Bill, here's your million dollars, Carl [DiMaria, CCA's vice president of operations], here's your million dollars, Neil [Gloude, CCA's vice president of finance], here's your million dollars. Are you going to have a problem with the fact that I sell the radio station and you get a million dollars out of it?" And I [McCarthy] said, "No, I certainly won't." He said, "Then don't worry about it."

Kylberg also told McCarthy that they would address his compensation at a later date. In December of 1996, McCarthy received a written compensation plan supplementing his annual salary of $20,000 with incentive bonuses tied to the station's advertising sales, but McCarthy never qualified for any of the bonuses.

A few months later, in early 1997, McCarthy alleges that he again discussed the $1 million bonus with Kylberg, this time over dinner at the Legal Seafoods Restaurant. According to McCarthy, Kylberg repeated the airport conversation in essence, "like a broken record." Asked in a deposition whether Kylberg ever said to him, "If I sell the station for over seven million dollars, I promise you that you will receive one million dollars," McCarthy stated that Kylberg had said, "You'll get a million dollars."

In September 1997, Communicom agreed to sell the station to One-on-One Sports for $8 million. Kylberg informed McCarthy of the deal, including the sale price. Neither mentioned the $1 million bonus. When the deal closed in December 1997, a $200,000 bonus was given to DiMaria and Gloude, and a $5,000 bonus to McCarthy and another employee. Communicom paid McCarthy an additional $50,000 severance to secure his services until the end of January 1998. In March, McCarthy sent a postcard to Communicom sending his "greetings" to the company, but once again did not mention the alleged $1 million bonus.

The next month, however, McCarthy sent a letter to Kylberg demanding the $1 million bonus. Kylberg refused and McCarthy brought suit against him, CCA, and Communicom. The trial court granted summary judgment in favor of the defendant, and McCarthy appealed.

Per Curiam   To create an enforceable contract, the parties must agree on material terms and manifest a present intention to be bound by the agreement. Summary judgment is appropriate when the evidence about the parties' intentions gleaned from their words and actions is so one-sided that no reasonable jury could find a contract.

McCarthy now concedes Kylberg's first statement is too indefinite to constitute a promise and instead focuses on the statement ("you'll get" a million dollars) allegedly made at the Legal Seafoods Restaurant. It is not clear that the "you'll get" statement was a direct quote, as opposed to McCarthy's characterization of what Kylberg said. And McCarthy said Kylberg had repeated the statement made at the airport that "[y]ou're not going to have a problem if I hand you a million dollars and give you a million dollars as a result of the sale."

In any event, the outcome is the same even if the word "get" was used somewhere in the alleged conversation (Kylberg denies that it occurred). Taking the whole body of alleged statements together, they suggest little more than a casual reassurance that McCarthy and others would gain in the unlikely event of a station sale. There were no words approximating a formal offer and none whatever of acceptance. This alone is not conclusive but two other contextual facts reinforce the inference.

First, no effort was ever made to reduce the alleged promise to writing. By contrast, other far less extraordinary promises *were* reduced to writing; the advertising sales incentive bonus plan, for instance, was detailed in the December 1996 compensation plan which made no mention of the $1 million promise. In fact, the company had a written policy stating that all employment agreements, including compensation terms, had to be in writing, although McCarthy says the policy was not strictly followed.

Second, McCarthy failed to raise the issue of a $1 million bonus when the circumstances obviously called for it, namely, when the sale occurred in December 1997. Nor did he make a claim later when he accepted his $5,000 bonus and $50,000 severance payments from Communicom. His delay in waiting till he left the company hardly suggests that he believed from the outset that he had been promised $1 million.

All of these circumstances taken together, including words used and surrounding events, persuade us that no reasonable jury could find that the parties intended to create a contract. If Kylberg made the statements attributed to him, he may have encouraged hope of a reward, but he did not create a contractual obligation to provide one.

Affirmed in favor of Kylberg.

Definiteness Standards under the UCC The UCC, with its increased emphasis on furthering people's justifiable expectations and its encouragement of a hands-on approach by the courts, often creates contractual liability in situations where no contract would have resulted at common law. Perhaps no part of the Code better illustrates this basic difference between the UCC and classical common law than does the basic Code section on contract formation [2–204]. This section says that sales contracts under Article 2 can be created "in any manner sufficient to show agreement, including conduct which recognizes the existence of a contract" [2–204(1)]. So, if the parties are acting as though they have a contract by delivering or accepting goods or payment, for example, this may be enough to create a binding contract, even if it is impossible to point to a particular moment in time when the contract was created [2–204(2)].

An important difference between Code and classical common law standards for definiteness is that under the Code, the fact that the parties left open one or more terms of their agreement does not necessarily mean that their agreement is too indefinite to enforce. A sales contract is created if the court finds that the parties intended to make a contract and that their agreement is complete enough to allow the court to reach a fair settlement of their dispute ("a reasonably certain basis for giving an appropriate remedy" [2–204(3)]). If a term is left open in a contract that meets these two standards, that open term or "gap" can be "filled" by inserting a presumption found in the Code's "gap-filling" rules. The gap-filling rules allow courts to fill contract terms left open on matters of price [2–305], quantity [2–306], delivery [2–307, 2–308, and 2–309(1)], and time for payment [2–310] when such terms have been left open by the parties.[2] Of course, if a term was left out because the parties were *unable* to reach agreement about it, this would indicate that the intent to contract was absent and no contract would result, even under the Code's more liberal rules. *Intention is still at the heart of these modern contract rules;* the difference is that courts applying Code principles seek to further the parties' *underlying* intent to contract even though the parties have failed to express their intention about specific aspects of their agreement.

---

[2]Chapter 19 discusses these Code provisions in detail.

GLOBAL BUSINESS ENVIRONMENT

Under the CISG, a proposal will be considered an offer to contract if it is addressed to one or more specific persons, is sufficiently definite, and indicates the intent of the offeror to be bound in case of acceptance. Unlike the UCC, the CISG does not consider an offer to be sufficiently definite when the price term for goods is left open. The CISG states that the offer must indicate the goods and either expressly or impliedly make a provision for determining the quantity and price.

Communication to Offeree

When an offeror communicates the terms of an offer to an offeree, he objectively indicates an intent to be bound by those terms. The fact that an offer has *not* been communicated, on the other hand, may be evidence that the offeror has not yet decided to enter into a binding agreement. For example, assume that Stevens and Meyer have been negotiating over the sale of Meyer's restaurant. Stevens confides in his friend, Reilly, that he plans to offer Meyer $150,000 for the restaurant. Reilly goes to Meyer and tells Meyer that Stevens has decided to offer him $150,000 for the restaurant and has drawn up a written offer to that effect. After learning the details of the offer from Reilly, Meyer telephones Stevens and says, "I accept your offer." Is Stevens now contractually obligated to buy the restaurant? No. Since *Stevens* did not communicate the proposal to Meyer, there was no offer for Meyer to accept.

Special Offer Problem Areas

Advertisements

Generally speaking, advertisements for the sale of goods at specified prices are *not* considered to be offers. Rather, they are treated as being invitations to offer or negotiate. The same rule is generally applied to signs, handbills, catalogs, price lists, and price quotations. This rule is based on the presumed intent of the sellers involved. It is not reasonable to conclude that a seller who has a limited number of items to sell intends to give every person who sees her ad, sign, or catalog the power to bind her to contract. Thus, if Customer sees Retailer's advertisement of Whizbang XL laptop computers for $2,000 and goes to Retailer's store indicating his intent to buy the computer, Customer is making an offer, which Retailer is free to accept or reject. This is so because *Customer* is manifesting a present intent to contract on the definite terms of the ad.

In some cases, however, particular ads have been held to amount to offers. Such ads are usually highly specific about the nature and number of items offered for sale and what is requested in return. This specificity precludes the possibility that the offeror could become contractually bound to an infinite number of offerees. In addition, many of the ads treated as offers have required some special performance by would-be buyers or have in some other way clearly indicated that immediate action by the buyer creates a binding agreement. The potential for unfairness to those who attempt to accept such ads and their fundamental difference from ordinary ads justify treating them as offers.

The issue whether a particular advertisement was an offer is explored in the following *Leonard* case.

Leonard v. Pepsico, Inc.　　　*88 F. Supp.2d 116 (U.S. Dist. Ct. S.D.N.Y. 1999)*

John Leonard saw a "Pepsi Stuff" commercial encouraging consumers to collect "Pepsi Points" from specially marked packages of Pepsi or Diet Pepsi and redeem these points for merchandise featuring the Pepsi logo. The commercial opens upon an idyllic, suburban morning and shows a paperboy on his morning route. As the newspaper hits the stoop of a house, a military drumroll introduces the subtitle, "MONDAY, 7:58 AM." Military music then introduces a teenager preparing to leave for school, dressed in a shirt emblazoned with the Pepsi logo. The drumroll sounds as the subtitle "T-SHIRT 75 PEPSI POINTS" is scrolled across the screen. The teenager strides down the hallway wearing a leather jacket, and the subtitle "LEATHER JACKET 1450 PEPSI POINTS" appears. The teenager opens the door of his house and puts on a pair of sunglasses. The drumroll then accompanies the subtitle "SHADES 175 PEPSI POINTS." A voiceover then intoned, "Introducing the new Pepsi Stuff catalog." The scene then shifts to three young boys sitting in front of a high school building. The boy in the middle is intent on his Pepsi Stuff Catalog, while the boys on either side are drinking Pepsi. The three boys gaze in awe at an object approaching overhead. The military music swells and the viewer senses the presence of a mighty plane as the extreme winds generated by its flight create a paper maelstrom in a classroom devoted to an otherwise dull physics lesson. Finally, a Harrier Jet swings into view and lands by the side of the school building, next to a bicycle rack. Several students run for cover and the velocity of the wind strips one faculty member down to his underwear. The voiceover announces, "Now the more Pepsi you drink, the more great stuff you're gonna get." The teenager opens the cockpit of the fighter and can be seen holding a Pepsi. "Sure beats the bus," he says. The military drumroll swells a final time and the following words appear: "HARRIER FIGHTER 7,000,000 PEPSI POINTS." A few seconds later, the following appears in stylized script, "Drink Pepsi—Get Stuff." With that message, the music and commercial ended with a triumphant flourish.

Inspired by the commercial, Leonard set out to get a Harrier Jet. He consulted the Pepsi Stuff catalog, which specified the number of Pepsi Points. Absent from the catalog's order form was any entry or description of the Harrier jet. The amount of Pepsi Points necessary to get the listed merchandise ranged from 15 for a "jacket tattoo" to 3300 for a mountain bike. The rear foldout pages of the Catalog contained directions for redeeming Pepsi Points for merchandise. These directions note that merchandise may be ordered "only" with the original Order Form. The Catalog notes that in the event that a consumer lacks enough Pepsi Points to obtain a desired item, additional Pepsi Points may be purchased for 10 cents each; however, at least 15 original Pepsi Points must accompany each order.

Although Leonard initially set out to collect 7,000,000 Pepsi Points by consuming Pepsi products, it soon became clear to him that he would not be able to buy or drink Pepsi fast enough. Reevaluating his strategy, he realized that buying Pepsi Points would be a more promising option. Through acquaintances, Leonard ultimately raised about $700,000. On or about March 27, 1996, Leonard submitted an Order Form, 15 original Pepsi Points, and a check for $700,008.50. At the bottom of the Order Form, Leonard wrote in "1 Harrier Jet" in the "Item" column and "7,000,000" in the "Total Points" column. In a letter accompanying his submission, he stated that the check was to purchase additional Pepsi Points for obtaining a new Harrier jet as advertised in the Pepsi Stuff commercial.

Several months later, Pepsico's fulfillment house rejected Leonard's submission and returned the check, explaining that the item he requested was not part of the Pepsi Stuff collection, and only catalog merchandise could be redeemed under this program. It also stated, "The Harrier jet in the Pepsi commercial is fanciful and is simply included to create a humorous and entertaining ad." Leonard sued Pepsico for breach of contract and Pepsico filed a declaratory judgment action. Pepsico moved for summary judgment.

Wood, U.S.D.J.   The general rule is that an advertisement does not constitute an offer. An advertisement is not transformed into an enforceable offer through completion of an order form. In *Mesaros v. United States,* for example, the plaintiffs sued the United States Mint for failure to deliver a number of Statue of Liberty commemorative coins that they had ordered. When demand for the coins proved unexpectedly robust, a number of individuals who had sent in their orders in a timely fashion were left emptyhanded. The court [held that] the spurned coin collectors could not maintain a breach of contract action because no contract would be formed until the advertiser accepted the order form and processed payment. Under these principles, Leonard's letter, with the Order Form and appropriate number of Pepsi Points, constituted the offer. There would be no enforceable contract until Pepsico accepted the Order Form and cashed the check.

The exception to the rule that advertisements do not create any power of acceptance in potential offerees is where the advertisement is clear, definite, and explicit, and leaves nothing open for negotiation. In *Lefkowitz v. Great Minneapolis Surplus Store,* defendant had published a newspaper announcement stating: "Saturday 9AM Sharp, 3 Brand New Fur Coats, Worth to $100, First Come First Served $1 Each." Mr. Morris Lefkowitz arrived at the store, dollar in hand, but was informed that under defendant's "house rules," the offer was open to ladies, but not gentlemen. The court ruled that because plaintiff had fulfilled all the terms of the advertisement and the advertisement was specific and left nothing open for negotiation, a contract had been formed. The present case is distinguishable from *Lefkowitz.* First, the commercial cannot be regarded in itself as sufficiently definite, because it specifically reserved the details of the offer to a separate writing, the Catalog. The commercial itself made no mention of the steps a potential offeree would be required to take to accept the alleged offer of a Harrier Jet. The advertisement in *Lefkowitz,* in contrast, "identified the person who could accept." *Corbin* at 119. Second, even if the Catalog had included a Harrier Jet among the items that could be obtained by redemption of Pepsi Points, the advertisement of a Harrier Jet by both the television commercial and catalog would still not constitute an offer. As the *Mesaros* court explained, the absence of any words of limitation such as "first come, first served," renders the alleged offer sufficiently indefinite that no contract could be formed. "A customer would not usually have reason to believe that the shopkeeper intended exposure to the risk of a multitude of acceptances resulting in a number of contracts exceeding the shopkeepers inventory." *Farnsworth at 242*. There was no such danger in *Lefkowitz*, owing to the limitation "first come, first served."

In opposing the present motion, Leonard largely relies on a different species of unilateral offer, involving public offers of a reward for performance of a specified act. The most venerable of these cases is the case of *Carlill v. Carbolic Smoke Ball Co*. Long a staple of law school curricula, the case arose during the London influenza epidemic of the 1890s. Among other advertisements of the time appeared solicitations for the Carbolic Smoke Ball. The specific advertisement that Mrs. Carlill saw, and relied upon, read as follows:

> £100 reward will be paid by the Carbolic Smoke Ball Company to any person who contracts the increasing epidemic influenza, colds, or any diseases caused by taking cold, after having used the ball three times daily for two weeks according to the printed directions supplied with each ball. £1000 is deposited with the Alliance Bank, Regent Street, shewing our sincerity in the matter.

On the faith of this advertisement, Mrs. Carlill purchased the smoke ball and used it as directed, but contracted influenza nevertheless. The court held that she was entitled to recover the promised reward. The advertisement was construed as offering a reward because it sought to induce performance, unlike an invitation to negotiate, which seeks a reciprocal promise. As [the judge] explained, "advertisements offering rewards . . . are offers to anybody who performs the conditions named in the advertisement, and anybody who does perform the condition accepts the offer." Like Carbolic Smoke Ball, the decisions relied upon by Leonard involve offers of reward.

Reward cases underscore the distinction between typical advertisements, in which the alleged offer is merely an invitation to negotiate for purchase of commercial goods, and promises of reward, in which the alleged offer is intended to induce a potential offeree to perform a specific action, often for noncommercial reasons. In the present case, the Harrier Jet commercial did not direct that anyone who appeared at Pepsi headquarters with 7,000,000 Pepsi Points on the Fourth of July would receive a Harrier Jet. Instead, the commercial urged consumers to accumulate Pepsi Points and to refer to the Catalog to determine how they could redeem their Pepsi Points. The commercial sought a reciprocal

promise, expressed through acceptance of, and compliance with, the terms of the Order Form. Leonard states that he noted that the Harrier Jet was not among the items described in the catalog, but this did not affect his understanding of the offer. It should have. Because the alleged offer in this case was, at most, an advertisement to receive offers rather than an offer of reward, Leonard cannot show that there was an offer made in the circumstances of this case.

Leonard's understanding of the commercial as an offer must also be rejected because the Court finds that no objective person could reasonably have concluded that the commercial actually offered consumers a Harrier Jet. In evaluating the commercial, the Court must not consider Pepsico's subjective intent in making the commercial, or Leonard's subjective view of what the commercial offered, but what an objective, reasonable person would have understood the commercial to convey. If it is clear that an offer was not serious, then no offer has been made. An obvious joke, of course, would not give rise to a contract. On the other hand, if there is no indication that the offer is evidently in jest, and that an objective, reasonable person would find that the offer was serious, then there may be a valid offer.

Leonard's insistence that the commercial appears to be a serious offer requires the Court to explain why the commercial is funny. First, the commercial suggests that use of the advertised product will transform what, for most youth, can be a fairly routine and ordinary experience. The military tattoo and stirring martial music, as well as the use of subtitles in a Courier font that scroll terse messages across the screen evoke military and espionage thrillers. The implication of the commercial is that Pepsi Stuff merchandise will inject drama and moment into hitherto unexceptional lives. The commercial in this case thus makes the exaggerated claims similar to those of many advertisements: that by consuming the featured clothing, car, beer, or potato chips, one will become attractive, stylish, desirable, and admired by all. A reasonable viewer would understand such advertisements as mere puffery, not as statements of fact. Second, the callow youth featured in the commercial is a highly improbable pilot, one who could barely be trusted with the keys to his parents' car, much less the prize aircraft of the United States Marine Corps. Finally, the teenagers's comment that flying a Harrier Jet to school "sure beats the bus" evinces an improbably insouciant attitude toward the relative difficulty and danger of piloting a fighter plane in a residential area, as opposed to taking public transportation. Third, the notion of traveling to school in a Harrier Jet is an exaggerated adolescent fantasy. In this commercial, the fantasy is underscored by how the teenager's schoolmates gape in admiration, ignoring their physics lesson. The force of the wind generated by the Harrier Jet blows off one teacher's clothes, literally defrocking an authority figure. Fourth, the primary mission of a Harrier Jet is to attack and destroy surface targets. Depiction of such a jet as a way to get to school is clearly not serious. Fifth, the number of Pepsi Points the commercial mentions as required to "purchase" the jet is 7,000,000. To amass that number of points, one would have to drink 7,000,000 Pepsis (or roughly 190 Pepsis a day for the next hundred years—an unlikely possibility), or one would have to purchase $700,000 worth of Pepsi Points. The cost of a Harrier Jet is roughly $23 million dollars, a

fact of which Leonard was aware when he set out to gather the amount he believed necessary to accept the alleged offer. Even if an objective, reasonable person were not aware of this fact, he would conclude that purchasing a fighter plane for $700,000 is a deal too good to be true.

For the reasons stated above, the Court grants Pepsico's motion for summary judgment.

Motion granted in favor of Pepsico. [Note: Leonard appealed this ruling, and the U.S. Court of Appeals for the Second Circuit affirmed the District Court's ruling in Leonard v. Pepsico, Inc., 210 F.3d 88 (2d Cir. 2000).]

Rewards

Advertisements offering rewards for lost property, for information, or for the capture of criminals are generally treated as offers for unilateral contracts. To accept the offer and be entitled to the stated reward, offerees must perform the requested act—return the lost property, supply the requested information, or capture the wanted criminal. Some courts have held that only offerees who started performance with knowledge of the offer are entitled to the reward. Other courts, however, have indicated the only requirement is that the offeree know of the reward before completing performance. In reality, the result in most such cases probably reflects the court's perception of what is fairer given the facts involved in the particular case at hand.

Auctions

Sellers at auctions are generally treated as making an invitation to offer. Those who bid on offered goods are, therefore, treated as making offers that the owner of the goods may accept or reject. Acceptance occurs only when the auctioneer strikes the goods off to the highest bidder; the auctioneer may withdraw the goods at any time before acceptance. However, when an auction is advertised as being "without reserve," the seller is treated as having made an offer to sell the goods to the highest bidder and the goods cannot be withdrawn after a call for bids has been made unless no bids are made within a reasonable time.[3]

Bids

The bidding process is a fertile source of contract disputes. Advertisements for bids are generally treated as invitations to offer. Those who submit bids are treated as offerors. According to general contract principles, bidders can withdraw their bids at any time prior to acceptance by the offeree inviting the bids and the offeree is free to accept or reject any bid. The previously announced terms of the bidding may alter these rules, however. For example, if the advertisement for bids unconditionally states that the contract will be awarded to the lowest responsible bidder, this will be treated as an offer that is accepted by the lowest bidder. Only proof by the offeror that the lowest bidder is not responsible can prevent the formation of a contract. Also, under some circumstances discussed later in this chapter, promissory estoppel may operate to prevent bidders from withdrawing their bids.

Bids for governmental contracts are generally covered by specific statutes rather than by general contract principles. Such statutes ordinarily establish the rules governing the bidding process, often require that the contract be awarded to the lowest bidder, and frequently establish special rules or penalties governing the withdrawal of bids.

Which Terms Are Included in the Offer?

After making a determination that an offer existed, a court must decide which terms were included in the offer so that it can determine the terms of the parties' contract. Put another way, which terms of the offer are binding on the offeree who accepts it? Should offerees, for example, be bound by fine-print clauses or by clauses on the back of the contract? Originally, the courts tended to hold that

[3]These rules and others concerned with the sale of goods by auction are contained in section 2–328 of the UCC.

CYBER LAW IN ACTION

One controversy regarding the terms that are included in the offer has been raised by the standardized contracting techniques that almost always accompany the transfer of computer software. For example, Stacy goes to Gigantic State University Bookstore and purchases software in a package. When Stacy opens the package, she finds that the CD containing the program is sealed in an envelope and that it bears a label stating that by opening the envelope, Stacy is accepting the terms of a license agreement that is contained somewhere in the packaging. The label states that if Stacy does not want to accept the terms of the license, she can return the software. The license contains a variety of terms that generally protect the software manufacturer. This method of contracting is often called **shrinkwrap** contracting. Stacy rips open the envelope without reading the license agreement and installs the software. If a conflict arises later concerning one of the terms of the license agreement, should the law hold that the terms of the license agreement are contractually binding? A critic of shrinkwrap contracting would argue that the terms should not be part of the contract because the contract was formed when Stacy purchased the program from Gigantic

State University Bookstore and Stacy did not know of the license or its terms at that point. Also, consumers like Stacy may not understand that by opening the sealed package they are entering a contract, the terms of which are unlikely to have read and may not understand.

The early cases dealing with shrinkwrap contracts generally decided against the enforceability of shrinkwraps. The following *ProCD, Inc. v. Zeidenberg* case, however, has been extremely influential in providing a rationale for the enforcement of shrinkwraps and turning the tide of judicial opinion toward the enforcement of shrinkwraps. The *ProCD* reasoning has been extended to the enforcement of shrinkwrap contracts accompanying the sale of computer hardware as well as software.

Other forms of standardized contracting online are familiar to us: the **click-wrap** or **click-through** agreement, which requires us to read terms presented online and click buttons indicating our agreement, and the so-called **browse-wrap** agreement, which presents purported contract terms in a separate link but does not require the reader to click to indicate agreement. These forms of contracting will be discussed in the next chapter.

---

offerees were bound by all the terms of the offer on the theory that every person had a duty to protect himself by reading agreements carefully before signing them.

In today's world of lengthy, complex form contracts, however, people often sign agreements that they have not fully read or do not fully understand. Modern courts tend to recognize this fact by saying that offerees are bound only by terms of which they had actual or reasonable notice. If the offeree actually read the term in question, or if

a reasonable person should have been aware of it, it will probably become part of the parties' contract. A fine-print provision on the back of a theater ticket would probably not be binding on a theater patron, however, because a reasonable person would not normally expect such a ticket to contain contractual terms. By contrast, the terms printed on a multipage airline ticket might well be considered binding on the purchaser if such documents would be expected to contain terms of the contract.

ProCD Inc. v. Zeidenberg   *86 F.3d 1447 (7th Cir. 1996)*

ProCD compiled information from more than 3,000 telephone directories into a computer database and sold a version of this database called SelectPhone on CD-ROM disks. The database in SelectPhone cost more than $10 million to compile and is expensive to keep current. For commercial users such as retailers and manufacturers, SelectPhone is a much cheaper alternative to the expensive mailing lists that such users otherwise would purchase from various information intermediaries. For noncommercial users, SelectPhone has less value, functioning as a substitute for calling long-distance information or other directory. ProCD decided to sell its database to the general public for personal use at a low price (approximately $150 for the set of five disks), while selling to commercial users at a higher price. If ProCD had to recover all of its cost and make a profit by charging a single price—that is, if it could not charge more to commercial users than to the general public—it would have to raise the price substantially above $150. To help ensure that no commercial users purchased the database at the lower, *noncommercial price, ProCD marketed the consumer product with a kind of contract that is popularly known as a "shrinkwrap license." A shrinkwrap license limits the ways that the person who acquires computer software can use the software. It gets its name from the fact that retail software packages are covered in plastic or cellophane "shrinkwrap." Every box containing ProCD's consumer product declares that the software comes with restrictions stated in an enclosed license. This license, which is encoded on the CD-ROM disks as well as printed in the manual, and which appears on a user's screen every time the software runs, limits use of the application program and listings to noncommercial purposes.*

Matthew Zeidenberg bought a consumer package of SelectPhone in 1994 from a retail outlet in Madison, Wisconsin, but decided to ignore the license. He formed Silken Mountain Web Services, Inc., to resell the information in the SelectPhone database. The corporation made the database available on the Internet to anyone willing to pay its price—which was less than ProCD charged its commercial customers. Zeidenberg purchased two additional SelectPhone packages, each with an updated version of the database, and made the latest information available over the World Wide Web, for a price, through his corporation. ProCD filed suit against Zeidenberg seeking an injunction against dissemination of the database that exceeds the rights specified in the licenses. The district court held the licenses ineffectual because their terms do not appear on the outside of the package. ProCD appealed.

Easterbrook, Circuit Judge   We treat the licenses as ordinary contracts accompanying the sale of products. Zeidenberg [argues] that placing the package of software on the shelf is an "offer," which the customer "accepts" by paying the asking price and leaving the store with the goods. In Wisconsin, as elsewhere, a contract includes only the terms on which the parties have agreed. One cannot agree to hidden terms. So far, so good—but one of the terms to which Zeidenberg agreed by purchasing the software is that the transaction was subject to a license.

Zeidenberg's position therefore must be that the printed terms on the outside of a box are the parties' contract—except for printed terms that refer to or incorporate other terms. But why would Wisconsin fetter the parties' choice in this way? Vendors can put the entire terms of a contract on the outside of a box only by using microscopic type, removing other information that buyers might find more useful (such as what the software does, and on which computers it works), or both. The "Read Me" included with most software, describing system requirements and potential incompatibilities, may be equivalent to 10 pages of type; warranties and license restrictions take up more space. Notice on the outside, terms on the inside, and a right to return the software for a refund if the terms are unacceptable (a right that the license expressly extends), may be a means of doing business valuable to buyers and sellers alike.

Transactions in which the exchange of money precedes the communication of terms are common. Consider the purchase of an airline ticket. The traveler calls the carrier or an agent, is quoted a price, reserves a seat, pays, and gets a ticket, in that order. The ticket contains elaborate terms, which the traveler can reject by canceling the reservation. To use the ticket is to accept the terms, even terms that in retrospect are disadvantageous. Consumer goods work the

same way. Someone who wants to buy a radio set visits a store, pays, and walks out with a box. Inside the box is a leaflet containing some terms, the most important of which usually is the warranty, read for the first time in the comfort of home. By Zeidenberg's lights, the warranty in the box is irrelevant.

Next consider the software industry itself. Only a minority of sales take place over the counter, where there are boxes to peruse. A customer may place an order by phone in response to a line item in a catalog or a review in a magazine. Much software is ordered over the Internet by purchasers who have never seen the box. Increasingly, software arrives by wire. There is no box; there is only a collection of information that includes data, an application program, instructions, many limitations, and the terms of sale. The user purchases a serial number which activates the software's features. On Zeidenberg's arguments, these unboxed sales are unfettered by terms.

A vendor, as master of the offer, may invite acceptance by conduct and may propose limitations on the kind of conduct that constitutes acceptance. A buyer may accept by performing the acts the vendor proposes to treat as acceptance. And that is what happened. ProCD proposed a contract that a buyer would accept by *using* the software after having an opportunity to read the license at leisure. This Zeidenberg did. He had no choice, because the software splashed the license on the screen and would not let him proceed without indicating acceptance. Ours is not a case in which a consumer opens a package to find an insert saying "you owe us an extra $10,000" and the seller files suit to collect. Any buyer finding such a demand can prevent formation of the contract by returning the package, as can any consumer who concludes that the terms of the license make the software worth less than the purchase price. Zeidenberg inspected the package, tried out the software, learned of the license, and did not reject the goods.

Zeidenberg has not located any case holding that the ordinary terms found in shrinkwrap licenses require any special prominence. In the end, the terms of the license are conceptually identical to the contents of the package. Just as no court would dream of saying that SelectPhone must contain 3,100 phone books rather than 3,000, or must sell for $100 rather than $150—although any of these changes would be welcomed by the customer—so, we believe, Wisconsin would not let the buyer pick and choose among terms. Terms of use are no less a part of "the product" than are the size of the database and the speed with which the software compiles listings. Competition among vendors, not judicial revision of a package's contents, is how consumers are protected in a market economy.

Reversed and remanded in favor of ProCD.

ETHICS IN ACTION

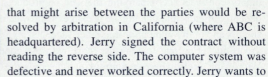

Jerry, who was in the process of opening a new small business in Connecticut, ordered an expensive new computer system from ABC Computing. As part of this transaction, ABC presented Jerry with a contract of sale. The contract was written on lightweight paper that was difficult to read. The signature line was on the bottom of the first page, but there were more contract terms on the reverse side of the page. On the reverse side, under the heading, "Warranty Service," was a provision that disclaimed all implied warranties and stated that any dispute that might arise between the parties would be resolved by arbitration in California (where ABC is headquartered). Jerry signed the contract without reading the reverse side. The computer system was defective and never worked correctly. Jerry wants to sue ABC Computing but cannot afford to go to California to do so. Is it ethical for businesses who deal with consumers and other less sophisticated parties to "hide" contract terms under misleading headings, in small print, deep in a website, or on the reverse side of the contract?

Termination of Offers

After a court has determined the existence and content of an offer, it must determine the duration of the offer. Was the offer still in existence when the offeree attempted to accept it? If not, no contract was created and the offeree is treated as having made an offer that the original offeror is free to accept or reject. This is so because, by attempting to accept an offer that has terminated, the offeree has indicated a present intent to contract on the terms of the original offer though he lacks the power to bind the offeror to a contract due to the original offer's termination.

Terms of the Offer

The offeror is often said to be "the master of the offer." This means that offerors have the power to determine the terms and conditions under which they are bound to a contract. As the following *Keller v. Bones* case indicates, an offeror may include terms in the offer that limit its effective life. These may be specific terms, such as "you must accept by December 5, 2000," or "this offer is good for five days," or more general terms such as "for immediate acceptance," "prompt wire acceptance," or "by return mail." General time limitation language in an offer can raise difficult problems of interpretation for courts trying to decide whether an offeree accepted before the offer terminated. Even more specific language, such as "this offer is good for five days," can cause problems if the offer does not specify whether the five-day period begins when the offer is sent or when the offeree receives it. Not all courts agree on such questions, so wise offerors should be as specific as possible in stating when their offers terminate.

Keller v. Bones   *8 Neb. App. 946, 2000 Neb. App. LEXIS 16 (Neb. Ct. App. 2000)*

Calvin R. Bones and Audrey J. Bones are the trustees of the Calvin R. and Audrey J. Bones Family Trust. The trust owned a ranch in Nebraska that the Boneses decided to sell. On June 11, 1997, the Boneses listed the ranch for sale with Agri Affiliates, a real estate agent. According to the listing agreement between the Boneses and Agri, if the listing sold to the current tenants, Lydic Brothers, the agent would receive only a 1 percent commission. On the other hand, if the listing sold to anyone else, the agent would receive a 6 percent commission. On July 17, 1997, Dean Keller submitted to Agri a written offer to buy the ranch for $490,000. The offer required written acceptance sent through registered mail or delivered to Keller personally. It also stated that it would be withdrawn if not accepted by July 21 at 5 P.M. Paragraph 15 of the offer states in part that "upon execution by Seller, this agreement shall become a binding contract." At 4:53 P.M. on July 21, the Boneses faxed a signed copy of the offer to Agri. In addition, at 5:12 P.M. on July 21, Loren Johnson, Agri's representative, telephoned Keller and left a voicemail message to inform him of the Boneses' acceptance. On July 22, 1997, Don Lydic, a representative of Lydic Brothers, informed the Boneses and the agent that Lydic Brothers would match Keller's offer for the ranch. The Boneses wanted to accept Don Lydic's offer and sell the ranch to Lydic Brothers. Later that same day, Agri asked Keller if he would be willing to release the Boneses from the agreement and "back out" of the deal. Keller refused and asserted that he wanted to go forward with the sale. The Boneses unequivocally informed Keller on December 5, 1997, that they would not sell the ranch to him. After the Boneses failed to close, Keller brought suit against the Boneses, seeking relief for breach of contract. The Boneses asserted that no contract existed (1) because their acceptance was not communicated to the buyer within the time specified in the offer and the attempted acceptance thus became a counteroffer and (2) because the buyer did not communicate to the sellers that he accepted their counteroffer. Both parties moved for summary judgment. The trial court found in favor of the Boneses' motion and dismissed the case. Keller appealed.

Hannon, Judge   Essentially, this case presents one question: did a contract exist between Keller and the Boneses for the sale of the ranch? Keller argues that the Boneses accepted his offer and that the contract became binding the moment the Boneses signed the offer due to the language in paragraph 15. In its most basic sense, the offer in this case was a buyer's promise to purchase real estate for a certain amount if the seller promised to sell. In this way, the Boneses' acceptance must have been communicated to Keller in order for the acceptance to be valid. This case lacks an effective communication to the offeror to create a contract. Neither the Boneses' act of signing the offer, albeit before the offer expired, nor the Boneses' act of faxing a signed copy to their agent constituted the requisite "communication" to the buyer in order to form a binding contract. Acceptance cannot become effective to create a contract until some irrevocable element occurs which places the acceptance "beyond the power or control of the sender." Neither of the Boneses' actions described above fulfills this requirement, because the acceptance never left their control. Keller argues that [his] offer included a clause which purported to make the contract binding at the moment the Boneses signed it. He also argues that parties are free to create their own terms of contracting as long as the terms do not violate public policy. Even in light of the parties' freedom to contract as they choose, acceptance

must be communicated to the offeror. Furthermore, we are considering not the terms of the parties' contract but whether the parties entered into one. With respect to the voice message left on Keller's answering machine shortly after the deadline had passed, we find that the message could not constitute an acceptance of Keller's offer. In *Kline v. Metcalfe Construction Co.,* the Nebraska Supreme Court stated:

> The offerer has a right to prescribe in his offer any conditions as to time, place, quantity, mode of acceptance, or other matters which it may please him to insert in and make a part thereof, and the acceptance, to conclude the agreement, must in every respect meet and correspond with the offer, neither falling short of nor going beyond the terms proposed, but exactly meeting them at all points and closing with them just as they stand, and, in the absence of such an acceptance, subsequent words or acts of the parties cannot create a contract.

In *Wolf v. Tastee Freez Corp.,* the court stated "[t]hat the acceptance of an offer must be made within the time specified in the offer is a general rule of law. . . . The power to create a contract by acceptance of an offer terminates at the time specified in the offer."

We believe that under a provision specifically designating the time within which notice must be given, that time is of the essence, and such provision is to be strictly construed. Keller's offer required that the Boneses accept in writing by 5 P.M. on July 21, 1997, through registered mail or delivering the acceptance to Keller personally. Additionally, paragraph 15 of the offer states in part, "Time is of the essence of this agreement and each and every provision hereof." The voice message left on Keller's answering machine was not in writing, occurred after the deadline, and was not delivered by the means specified in the offer; thus, it could not constitute an acceptance.

The Boneses' late acceptance could constitute a counteroffer. A binding contract can result from the oral accept-

ance of such a counteroffer. The Boneses' signing of the offer by Keller would constitute the written embodiment of the counteroffer, and its oral acceptance by Keller could have resulted in a contract. However, Keller does not rely upon this theory, and in any event, there was no communication from Keller to the Boneses or their agent which could be interpreted as an acceptance of any counteroffer from the Boneses. For the foregoing reasons, we affirm the district court's order granting summary judgment in favor of the Boneses because no contract existed.

Affirmed in favor of the Boneses.

Lapse of Time

Offers that fail to provide a specific time for acceptance are valid for a reasonable time. What constitutes a reasonable time depends on the circumstances surrounding the offer. How long would a reasonable person in the offeree's position believe she had to accept the offer? Offers involving things subject to rapid fluctuations in value, such as stocks, bonds, or commodities futures, have a very brief duration. The same is true for offers involving goods that may spoil, such as produce.

The context of the parties' negotiations is another factor relevant to determining the duration of an offer. For example, most courts hold that when parties bargain face-to-face or over the telephone, the normal time for acceptance does not extend past the conclusion of their conversation unless the offeror indicates a contrary intention. Where negotiations are carried out by mail or telegram, the time for acceptance would ordinarily include at least the normal time for communicating the offer and a prompt response by the offeree. Finally, in cases where the parties have dealt with each other on a regular basis in the past, the timing of their prior transactions would be highly relevant in measuring the reasonable time for acceptance.

Revocation

General Rule: Offers Are Revocable As the masters of their offers, offerors can give offerees the power to bind them to contracts by making offers. They can also terminate that power by revoking their offers. The general common law rule on revocations is that offerors may revoke their offers at any time prior to acceptance, *even if they have promised to hold the offer open for a stated period of time.*

Figure 1   When Offerors Cannot Revoke

Options	Offeror has promised to hold offer open and has received consideration for that promise
Firm Offers	Merchant offeror makes written offer to buy or sell goods, giving assurances that the offer will be held open
Unilateral Contract Offers	Offeree has started to perform requested act before offeror revokes
Promissory Estoppel	Offeree foreseeably and reasonably relies on offer being held open, and will suffer injustice if it is revoked

Exceptions to the General Rule In the following situations (summarized in Figure 1), however, offerors are *not* free to revoke their offers:

1. *Options.* An **option** is a separate contract in which an offeror agrees not to revoke her offer for a stated time in exchange for some valuable consideration. You can think of it as a contract in which an offeror sells her right to revoke her offer. For example, Jones, in exchange for $5,000, agrees to give Dewey Development Co. a six-month option to purchase her farm for $550,000. In this situation, Jones would not be free to revoke the offer during the six-month period of the option. The offeree, Dewey Development, has no obligation to accept Jones's offer. In effect, it has merely purchased the right to consider the offer for the stated time without fear that Jones will revoke it.

The following case, *Reardon v. Lautzner,* provides another example of an option contract.

Reardon v. Lautner   *1997 Mich. App. LEXIS 3294 (Mich. Ct. App. 1997)*

Timothy Reardon was a member of a partnership that entered into an agreement to purchase a parcel of real estate from Gerald and Mary Lautner. The partnership defaulted in payment on the land contract and the Lautners threatened litigation for forfeiture or foreclosure unless the partnership executed a release of the land contract. The partnership did so. On that same day, Reardon and the Lautners signed a memorandum agreement giving Reardon a six-week exclusive option to purchase the land. The memorandum provided in part:

PROPOSED OPTION AGREEMENT COMPONENTS:

1.Grant of Exclusive Option $500 for a six-week option to purchase property with amount paid credited against the purchase price in the event option is exercised; any amounts paid in option extension(s) will also be credited.

Reardon did not tender the $500 at the time the parties initialed this agreement. The Lautners later withdrew their consent to sell the property to Reardon. Reardon tendered the $500 and the Lautners refused it. Reardon sued for breach of contract. The trial court granted a motion for summary disposition in favor of the Lautners, holding that there was no legally enforceable agreement because the $500 was not tendered until after Reardon was notified that any offer was withdrawn. Reardon appealed.

Per Curiam   Options for purchasing land, if based on valid consideration, are contracts which may be specifically enforced. We note that the trial court erred in finding that until Reardon tendered the $500, the Lautners were free to revoke the "offer." The memorandum was not an offer but rather an agreement that was initialed by all parties. The memorandum agreement contains no time period for the submission of the $500 and Reardon never indicated that he did not intend to perform. Thus, if the memorandum is a valid contract, it appears that the Lautners' attorney's letter to Reardon and the subsequent refusal of the $500 constituted a repudiation of the contract.

The trial court erred in finding Reardon's execution of the release and surrender of the land contract, dated the same day as the memorandum agreement, could not constitute the consideration for the Lautners' assent to the memorandum agreement. Settlement of litigation is ordinarily sufficient to serve as consideration for a new promise, as the other party would therefore be spared the time and expense of litigating a claim of foreclosure or forfeiture. Because the parties dispute whether they intended avoidance of litigation to be consideration for the alleged agreement, the identification of the consideration for the agreement is an issue for the factfinder.

Reversed and remanded in favor of Reardon.

---

2. *Offers for unilateral contracts.* Suppose Franklin makes the following offer for a unilateral contract to Waters: "If you mow my lawn, I'll pay you $25." Given that an offeree in a unilateral contract must fully perform the requested act to accept the offer, can Franklin wait until Waters is almost finished mowing the lawn and then say "I revoke!"? Obviously, the application of the general rule that offerors can revoke at any time before acceptance creates the potential for injustice when applied to offers for unilateral contracts, because it would allow an offeror to revoke after the offeree has begun performance but before he has had a chance to complete it. To prevent injustice to offerees who rely on such offers by beginning performance, two basic approaches are available to modern courts.

Some courts have held that once the offeree has begun to perform, the offeror's power to revoke is suspended for the amount of time reasonably necessary for the offeree to complete performance. Another approach to the unilateral contract dilemma is to hold that a bilateral contract is created once the offeree begins performance.

3. *Promissory estoppel.* In some cases in which the offeree *relies* on the offer being kept open, the doctrine of promissory estoppel can operate to prevent offerors from revoking their offers prior to acceptance. Section 87(2) of the *Restatement (Second)* says:

An offer which the offeror should reasonably expect to induce action or forbearance of a substantial character on the part of the offeree before acceptance and which does induce such action or forbearance is binding as an option contract to the extent necessary to avoid injustice.

Many of the cases in which promissory estoppel has been used successfully to prevent revocation of offers involve the bidding process. For example, Gigantic General Contractor seeks to get the general contract to build a new high school gymnasium for Shadyside School District. It receives bids from subcontractors. Liny Electric submits the lowest bid to perform the electrical work on the job and Gigantic uses Liny's bid in preparing its bid for the general contract. Here, Liny has made an offer to Gigantic, but Gigantic cannot accept that offer until it knows whether it has gotten the general contract. The school district awards the general contract to Gigantic. Before Gigantic can accept Liny's offer, however, Liny attempts to revoke it. In this situation, a court could use the doctrine of promissory estoppel to hold that the offer could not be revoked.

4. *Firm offers for the sale of goods [Note: This applies to offers for the sale of goods ONLY!].* The Code makes a major change in the common law rules governing the revocability of offers by recognizing the concept of a **firm offer** [2–205]. Like an option, a firm offer is irrevocable for a period of time. In contrast to an option, however, a firm offer does not require consideration to be given in exchange for the offeror's promise to keep the offer open. Not all offers to buy or sell goods qualify as firm offers, however. To be a firm offer, an offer must:

- Be made by an offeror who is a *merchant.*
- Be contained in a signed writing.[4]
- Give assurances that the offer will be kept open.

An offer to buy or sell goods that fails to satisfy these three requirements is governed by the general common law rule and is revocable at any time prior to acceptance. If an offer *does* meet the requirements of a firm offer, however, it will be irrevocable for the time stated in the offer. If no specific time is stated in the offer, it will be irrevocable for a *reasonable* time. Regardless of the terms of the firm offer, the outer limit on a firm offer's irrevocability is *three months.* For example, if Worldwide Widget makes an offer in a signed writing in which it proposes to sell a quantity of its XL Turbo Widget to Howell Hardware and gives assurances that the offer will be kept open for a year, the offer is a firm offer, but it can be revoked after three months if Howell Hardware has not yet accepted it.

In some cases, however, offerees are the true originators of an assurance term in an offer. When offerees have effective control of the terms of the offer by providing their customers with preprinted purchase order forms or order blanks, they may be tempted to take advantage of their merchant customers by placing an assurance term in their order forms. This would allow offerees to await market developments before deciding whether to fill the order, while their merchant customers, who may have signed the order without reading all of its terms, would be powerless to revoke. To prevent such unfairness, the Code requires that assurance terms on forms provided by offerees be separately signed by the offeror to effect a firm offer. For example, if Fashionable Mfg. Co. supplies its customer, Retailer, with preprinted order forms that contain a fine-print provision giving assurances that the customer's offer to purchase goods will be held open for one month, the purported promise to keep the offer open would not be enforceable unless Retailer separately signed that provision.

Time of Effectiveness of Revocations The question of *when* a revocation is effective to terminate an offer is often a critical issue in the contract formation process. For example, Davis offers to landscape Winter's property for $1,500. Two days after making the offer, Davis changes his mind and mails Winter a letter revoking the offer. The next day, Winter, who has not received Davis's letter, telephones Davis and attempts to accept. Contract? Yes. The general rule on this point is that revocations are effective only when they are actually *received* by the offeree.

The only major exception to the general rule on effectiveness of revocations concerns offers to the general public. Because it would be impossible in most cases to reach every offeree with a revocation, it is generally held that a revocation made in the same manner as the offer is effective when published, without proof of communication to the offeree.

Rejection

An offeree may expressly reject an offer by indicating that he is unwilling to accept it. He may also impliedly reject it by making a counteroffer, an offer to contract on terms materially different from the terms of the offer. As a general rule, either form of rejection by the offeree terminates his power to accept the offer. This is so because an offeror who receives a rejection may rely on the offeree's expressed desire not to accept the offer by making another offer to a different offeree.

---

[4]Under the UCC [1–201(39)], the word *signed* includes any symbol that a person makes or adopts with the intent to authenticate a writing.

CONCEPT REVIEW

What Terminates Offers?

- Their own terms
- Lapse of time
- Revocation

- Rejection
- Death or insanity of offeror or offeree
- Destruction of subject matter

- Intervening illegality

THE GLOBAL BUSINESS ENVIRONMENT

Several of the kinds of factors that make offers irrevocable in the United States—such as consideration and, in the case of firm offers, writing—are not required to make offers irrevocable under the CISG. The CISG states that an offer cannot be revoked if it indicates that it is irrevocable or if it was reasonable for the offeree

to rely on the offer as being irrevocable and the offeree has acted in reliance on the offer. However, even when an offer is irrevocable, the CISG allows it to be revoked if the revocation reaches the offeree before or at the same time as the offer.

One exception to the general rule that rejections terminate offers concerns offers that are the subject of an option contract. Some courts hold that a rejection does not terminate an option contract and that the offeree who rejects still has the power to accept the offer later, so long as the acceptance is effective within the option period.

Time of Effectiveness of Rejections As a general rule, rejections, like revocations, are effective only when actually received by the offeror. Therefore, an offeree who has mailed a rejection could still change her mind and accept if she communicates the acceptance before the offeror receives the rejection.[5]

Death or Insanity of Either Party

The death or insanity of either party to an offer automatically terminates the offer without notice. A meeting of the minds is obviously impossible when one of the parties has died or become insane.[6]

Destruction of Subject Matter

If, prior to an acceptance of an offer, the subject matter of a proposed contract is destroyed without the knowledge or fault of either party, the offer is terminated.[7] So, if Marks offers to sell Wiggins his lakeside cottage and the cottage is destroyed by fire before Wiggins accepts, the offer was terminated on the destruction of the cottage. Subsequent acceptance by Wiggins would not create a contract.

Intervening Illegality

An offer is terminated if the performance of the contract it proposes becomes illegal before the offer is accepted. So, if a computer manufacturer offered to sell sophisticated computer equipment to another country, but two days later, before the offer was accepted, Congress placed an embargo on all sales to this country, the offer was terminated by the embargo.[8]

---

[5]Chapter 11 discusses this subject in detail.
[6]Death or insanity of a party that occurs after a contract has been formed can excuse performance in contracts that call for personal services to be performed by the person who has died or become insane. This is discussed in Chapter 18.

[7]In some circumstances, destruction of subject matter can also serve as a legal excuse for a party's failure to perform his obligations under an existing contract. Chapter 18 discusses this subject.
[8]In some circumstances, intervening illegality can also serve as a legal excuse for a party's failure to perform his obligations under an existing contract. Chapter 18 discusses this subject.

Problems and Problem Cases

1. In 1989, the New Jersey Highway Authority increased its tolls from 25 cents to 35 cents. In connection with this increase, it authorized the sale of tokens for a discounted price—$10 for a roll of 40 tokens, a savings of $4 per roll for customers—for a limited time. The authority advertised this sale through several media, including signs on the parkway itself. Shortly after the discount sale began, complaints were made that the tokens were not available. The authority explained that the shortage probably resulted from an unanticipated demand for the tokens resulting from purchasers hoarding them. The authority then began limiting the sales to certain days of the week, but even with that limitation, the demand could not be satisfied. Schlictman, a motorist who used the toll roads, sued the authority for breach of contract after trying unsuccessfully, on five different occasions within the authorized sale dates and times, to buy the discounted tokens. What should the result be?

2. Albert and Alice Vincenzi were married and divorced. After the divorce, they remained friends. Between 1987 and 1997, Albert performed household services for Alice, such as mowing the lawn, making repairs, clearing snow, taking her shopping, balancing her checkbooks, and paying her bills each month. In 1994, Alice had a stroke and Albert moved into her house for about three and a half months, during which time he kept house, made sure she got her insulin properly, and drove her to medical appointments. Albert did this because they were friends and did not expect to receive compensation for them. Periodically, Alice would give Albert money for mowing the lawn or for gas or car repairs. According to Albert, Alice said to him in 1992, "I will help you financially and make everything all right." Once she said to him, "some day I'll take care of everything, I'll take care of matters," and on another occasion she said, "Don't worry, we will get together on this matter." In 1997, Alice added Albert's name to her bank account at a savings and loan association. She did this as a convenience so that Albert could manage her finances. McKnight, Alice's nephew, was also a co-signatory on the account, but he lived out of state and Alice wanted someone geographically close to have access to her account. Alice died in May of 1997. The day after her death, Albert took her passbook to the bank and withdrew the entire $65,993.83 in the account. He deposited the entire amount in his personal bank account. He used $5,570 of the funds to pay for Alice's funeral, gave $30,000 to Alice's sister, and kept the rest. Although Albert knew that the money was not his while Alice was alive, he thought it was after she

died because his name was on the passbook and he got the passbook first. A dispute arose with McKnight, who became the executor of Alice's estate, about the money. Albert sued McKnight, claiming that he had an oral contract with Alice to perform household services in exchange for compensation, and asking for $55,000, based on $100 per week for the ten years he helped Alice, and also for reimbursement of her funeral expenses. Will he win?

3. Rodziewicz was driving a 1999 Volvo conventional tractor-trailer on I-90 in Lake County, Indiana, when he struck a concrete barrier. His truck was stuck on top of the barrier and the state police contacted Waffco Heavy Duty Towing to help in the recovery. Before Waffco began working, Rodziewicz asked how much it would cost to tow the truck. He was told that the fee would be $275, and there was no discussion of labor or other costs. Rodziewicz instructed Waffco to take his truck to a Volvo dealership. After a few minutes of work, Waffco pulled Rodziewicz's truck off the barrier and towed the truck to its towing yard a few miles away. Subsequently, Waffco notified Rodziewicz that, in addition to the $275 towing fee, he would have to pay $4,070 in labor costs. Waffco calculated its labor charges as $.11 cents per pound. Waffco would not release the truck until payment was made, so Rodziewicz paid the total amount. Was Rodziewicz contractually obligated to pay Waffco the $4,070 labor fee?

4. Schiff, a self-styled tax rebel who had made a career out of his tax protest activities, appeared live on the February 7, 1983, CBS News "Nightwatch" program. During the course of the program, which had a viewer participant format, Schiff repeated his longstanding position that "there is nothing in the Internal Revenue Code which says anyone is legally required to pay the tax." Later in the program, Schiff stated: "If anybody calls this show and cites any section of this Code that says an individual is required to file a tax return, I will pay them $100,000." Newman, an attorney, did not see Schiff live on "Nightwatch," but saw a two-minute taped segment of the original "Nightwatch" interview several hours later on the "CBS Morning News." Certain that Schiff's statements were incorrect, Newman telephoned and wrote "CBS Morning News," attempting to accept Schiff's offer by citing Internal Revenue Code provisions requiring individuals to pay federal income tax. CBS forwarded Newman's letter to Schiff, who refused to pay on the ground that Newman had not properly accepted his offer. Newman sued Schiff for breach of contract. Will Newman win?

5. Less than an hour before his estranged wife underwent emergency surgery for an ectopic pregnancy caused by another man, McAdoo was asked to sign a standard form contract prepared by St. John's Episcopal Hospital. McAdoo testified that at the time he signed the form his wife's physical appearance and declared mental state convinced him that she was near death. Further, he stated that, under such circumstances, it did not occur to him to read carefully or question the implications of the papers he was being asked to sign. The form contained a provision that read as follows:

> ASSIGNMENT OF INSURANCE BENEFITS: I hereby authorize payment directly to the above named hospital of the hospital expense benefits otherwise payable to me but not to exceed the hospital's regular charges for this period of hospitalization. I understand that I am financially responsible to the hospital for the charges not covered by my group insurance plan.

McAdoo's wife survived and was discharged from St. John's eight days later. McAdoo did not visit her after the day of the operation and had not had any further contact with her when the hospital filed suit against him to collect her hospital bill. Should St. John's be able to enforce the agreement against McAdoo?

6. Allandale Farm, Inc., employed Koch from 1988 through 1997 as the person in charge of farming. Koch was hired for "permanent employment," subject to his ability to make the farm profitable. His compensation included salary and the right to occupy a house located adjacent to the farm, and certain performance-related bonuses. On January 7, 1997, Allandale Farm terminated Koch's employment and offered him $10,000 in exchange for a general release of liability and specified services. The offer letter stated, "Assuming you have vacated 278 Allandale Road by March 7, 1997 (leaving it in broom-clean condition), have completed the Farm's pesticide reports for 1996, returned to the Farm all the Farm's tools, equipment, field reports, and other records in your possession, the Farm will pay you on March 8, 1997, the sum of $10,000 . . . in exchange for a general release. This offer, of course, will be revoked in the event you commence any legal action against the Farm or any of its officers or directors." Koch believed that he was owed more money, but he took no steps to begin legal action against the Farm at that time. On February 11, the January 7 offer was withdrawn. When Koch would not agree to the terms demanded by the Farm, the Farm sought an order for him to vacate the house. In a letter dated March 13, 1997, the Farm stated that he and his family could remain in the house for no charge until June 30, 1997. The Farm offered Koch $10,000 for his compliance with the terms of the letter, including a release of any claims relating to his ter-

mination. Koch did not accept the offer, but agreed to pay rent for his continued occupancy of the house so that he could keep his children in school. The Farm refused Koch's offer to pay rent and sued to evict him from the house. Still later, the Farm offered once more to extend Koch's occupancy if he would sign a general release, but he refused and instead vacated the house and filed a counterclaim against the Farm. In one count of this claim, Koch claimed that the Farm breached a contract to pay him $10,000. He asserts that the offer contained in the January 7 letter was wrongfully withdrawn before the expiration of time provided. Was a contract to pay the $10,000 formed between Koch and the Farm?

7. Taveras owned an approximately 95-acre parcel of land in Harvard, Massachusetts, that contained his home and several cottages. Sometime in the early 1980s, Taveras and his wife sold their home and a portion of the land, retaining approximately 41 acres of land. In the fall of 1995, O'Hagan and Papalilo, who are real estate developers, began to negotiate with Taveras to purchase a part—at least half—of the remaining 41 acres. O'Hagan and Papalilo planned to build a residential development on the land. O'Hagan and Papalilo had not, however, determined exactly how much land they would buy from Taveras. These negotiations led to the drafting of a four-page document called "the option agreement," in which Taveras granted an "irrevocable option" to O'Hagan and Papalilo to purchase "approximately 21 acres" of his land in Harvard for a period of 18 months. The option agreement continued by stating, "The consideration for the option period shall be a Three Thousand dollar nonrefundable deposit to be paid at the time of execution of this document. . . ." The parties signed the option agreement and O'Hagan and Papalilo paid the $3,000. The option agreement left the description of the portion of land to be sold—beyond the size of "approximately 21 acres"—to be determined upon the exercise of the option. It contained a clause stating that the actual subdivision line would be determined by a named engineering firm and that in the event the buyers and seller did not agree with the proposed subdivision line, the seller would refund the $3,000 to the buyers. During February and March of 1996, the engineer made three separate proposals concerning a division of the property, all of which set aside more than 21 acres for O'Hagan and Papalilo. In April, however, Taveras notified O'Hagan and Papalilo that he was declining their "offers" to purchase his land, and returned their deposit. He then entered into a contract to sell the land to a third party. Did Taveras have the right to breach the option agreement and revoke his offer to sell the land to O'Hagan and Papalilo?

8. Mariah Carey is a famous entertainer. Vian, who was Carey's stepfather before she achieved stardom, was in the business of designing, producing, and marketing gift and novelty items. Vian claimed that Carey agreed orally to give him a license to produce "Mariah dolls," which would be statuettes of the singer that would play her most popular songs. Vian asserted that this right was given in exchange for his financial and emotional support of Carey, including picking her up from late-night recording sessions, providing her with the use of a car, paying for dental care, allowing her to use his boat for business meetings and rehearsals, and giving her various items to help furnish her apartment. Vian based his claim of an oral contract on three conversations, twice in the family car and once on Vian's boat. Vian said to Carey, "Don't forget about the Mariah dolls," and "I get the Mariah dolls." According to Vian, on one occasion Carey responded, "Okay" and on other occasions, she merely smiled and nodded. Although Carey admits that Vian mentioned the dolls two or three times, she testified that she thought it was a joke. Claiming that Carey breached the contract to license dolls in her likeness, Vian brought this action for breach of contract. Was a contract formed?

9. In early 1996, the Alaska legislature was considering a teachers' retirement incentive package ("RIP") to ease the salary burdens on school districts in Alaska. The Copper River School District wanted to take advantage of this proposed legislation, and directed Kramer, the district's business manager, to study the matter. Kramer presented her analysis to the Copper River School Board at its April 2 meeting. The school board accordingly voted at its April 2 meeting in favor of the following motion:

> MOTION . . . to offer a retirement incentive equal to the employee's indebtedness for three years (8.65% of gross wages for certified [employees]. . .) to all certified and classified employees who are eligible to retire at the end of the school year and/or meet the requirements as established by the state for RIP. The employee must notify the District by April 30, 1996 if they plan to participate.

Within a few days, Kramer decided that she had erred in her analysis and she e-mailed the District's school principals, urging them to inform their eligible employees that she was waiting for a response from attorneys about the bonus offered by the school board, and stating "we may have to 're-think' the process." In early April, Goad, a teacher, called Kramer to get the specifics of the RIP offer. Kramer told her that the district's lawyer had advised the school board to rescind the incentive motion,

and that the school board would be meeting to do just that. Goad asked what would happen if the teachers accepted the incentive prior to the rescission meeting. Kramer responded, "You can't do that." On April 18, Goad and five other teachers delivered letters that communicated their acceptance of the terms of the April 2 program. On April 19, the school board met and rescinded the April 2 motion and passed a motion approving a modified retirement incentive package. The six teachers requested payment of retirement benefits under the April 2 plan, but the district refused to pay more than the April 19 plan envisioned. The six teachers sued for breach of contract. The trial court granted summary judgment in favor of the teachers. Was this appropriate?

10. Jeff visited a car dealership and test-drove a used car. After discussing the price with the salesman, Jake, and learning that he could purchase the car for $500 less than the sticker price, Jeff asked Jake to hold the car for him until 8:00 that evening so that he could bring his wife back to see the car. Jake agreed, writing out a note promising not to sell the car before 8:00 P.M. The note was written on dealership stationery, but Jake did not sign his name. The dealership broke its promise and sold the car to Jones before 8:00 P.M. Was it free to revoke its offer to Jeff? Jones, the new purchaser of the car (and a nonmerchant), later offered in a signed writing to sell the car to Jill and to hold the car for her until she returned with her husband. Could Jones revoke this offer?

Online Research: Finding Offers On the Internet

1. Browse various commercial websites, classified sections of online newspapers, pop-ups, and other online commercial solicitations. Select an example of an ad or solicitation that would be considered an invitation to negotiate rather than an offer and one that would constitute an offer. Explain why the examples you have chosen would or would not constitute offers under the standards discussed in this chapter.

2. Browse an online auction website such as Ebay (www.ebay.com) and determine under what circumstances a seller's listing of items for auction on that site constitutes an offer. That is, does the bidder form a contract by submitting the highest bid, or can the seller legally refuse to sell the item to the highest bidder? Tip: Be sure to check out the site's User Agreement and its instructions for sellers.

THE AGREEMENT: ACCEPTANCE

O n April 1, 2003, Carlos received a letter from Clear Creek School Corporation (CCSC) offering him a job as a high school mathematics teacher for the academic year 2003–04, at a salary of $32,000. Carlos considered the offer for several days and then, on April 4, he sent CCSC a letter in which he stated that he accepted its offer. In this letter, Carlos also stated, "Is CCSC willing to pay me the $2,000 signing bonus that many of my classmates are getting from other school districts?" On April 5, before CCSC had received Carlos's letter, Carlos received a letter from CCSC's superintendent stating that CCSC had decided to hire someone else and was revoking its offer to him.

- Did Carlos accept CCSC offer?
- If so, when was Carlos's acceptance effective?
- Did CCSC have the right to revoke its offer?

THE PRECEDING CHAPTER DISCUSSED the circumstances under which a proposal will constitute the first stage of an agreement: the offer. This chapter focuses on the final stage of forming an agreement: the acceptance. The acceptance is vitally important because it is with the acceptance that the contract is formed. This chapter discusses the requirements for making a valid acceptance as well as the rules concerning the time at which a contract comes into being.

What Is an Acceptance?

An **acceptance** is "a manifestation of assent to the terms [of the offer] made by the offeree in the manner invited or required by the offer."[1] In determining if an offeree accepted an offer and created a contract, a court will look for evidence of three factors: (1) the offeree intended to enter the contract, (2) the offeree accepted on the terms proposed by the offeror, and (3) the offeree communicated his acceptance to the offeror.

Intention to Accept

In determining whether an offeree accepted an offer, the court is looking for the same *present intent to contract* on the part of the offeree that it found on the part of the offeror. And, as is true of intent to make an offer, intent to accept is judged by an objective standard. The difference is that the offeree must objectively indicate a present intent to contract on the terms of the offer for a contract to result. As the master of the offer, the offeror may specify in detail what behavior is required of the offeree to bind him to a contract. If the offeror does so, the offeree must ordinarily comply with all the terms of the offer before a contract results.

The following *Specht* case analyzes how these concepts about manifestion of assent apply in the context of "browse-wrap" contracts presented online.

---

[1]*Restatement (Second) of Contracts* § 50(1)(1981).

Specht v. Netscape Communications Corp.
150 F. Supp. 2d 585 (U.S. Dist. Ct. S.D.N.Y. 2001)

Christopher Specht maintained a website from which others could download files. Four other plaintiffs in this lawsuit down-loaded Netscape's "SmartDownload" software free of charge from the Netscape website. SmartDownload is a program that makes it easier for its users to download files from the Internet without losing their interim progress when they pause to en-gage in some other task or when their Internet connection is severed. Netscape visitors wishing to obtain SmartDownload arrive at a page on which there appears a button labeled "Download." By clicking on the button, the visitor initiates the download. The only reference on this page to a License Agreement appears in text that is visible only if a visitor scrolls down through the page to the next screen. If a visitor does so, he or she sees the following invitation to review the License Agree-ment:

> Please review and agree to the terms of the Netscape SmartDownload software license agreement before download-ing and using the software.

Visitors are not required to indicate their assent to the License agreement or even to view the license agreement before proceeding with a download of the software.

If a visitor chooses to click on the underlined text in the invitation, a hypertext link takes the visitor to a web page entitled "License and Support Agreements." The first paragraph of this page instructs the visitor that the use of each Netscape soft-ware product is governed by a license agreement, and the visitor should read and agree to the terms BEFORE acquiring a product. It states, "If you do not agree to the license terms, do not download, install or use the software." One of the terms of the license agreement is an arbitration clause that provides:

> Unless otherwise agreed in writing, all disputes relating to this Agreement. . .shall be subject to final and binding ar-bitration in Santa Clara County, California, under the auspices of JAMS/EndDispute, with the losing party paying all costs of arbitration.

Specht and the other plaintiffs alleged that the usage of the software transmitted to Netscape private information about the user's file transfer activity, in violation of the Electronic Communications Privacy Act and the Computer Fraud and Abuse Act. Netscape moved to compel arbitration and stay the proceedings, arguing that the plaintiffs' disputes, like all others re-lated to the use of the software, are subject to the arbitration clause in the License Agreement.

Hellerstein, U.S. District Judge.   Promises become bind-ing when there is a meeting of the minds and consideration is exchanged. So it was at King's Bench in common law England; so it was under the common law in the American colonies; so it was through more than two centuries of ju-risprudence in this country; and so it is today. Assent may be registered by a signature, a handshake, or a click of a computer mouse transmitted across the invisible ether of the Internet. The cases before me all involve this timeless issue of assent, but in the context of free software offered on the Internet. If an offeree downloads free software, and the of-feror seeks a contractual understanding limiting its uses and applications, under what circumstances does the act of downloading create a contract? On the facts presented here, is there the requisite assent and consideration? My decision focuses on these issues.

Unless the plaintiffs agreed to the License Agreement, they cannot be bound by the arbitration clause contained therein. My inquiry focuses on whether the plaintiffs, through their acts or failures to act, manifested their assent to the terms of the License Agreement. More specifically, I must consider whether the website gave plaintiffs suffi-cient notice of the existence and terms of the License Agreement.

The sale of software, in stores, by mail, and over the In-ternet, has resulted in several specialized forms of license agreements. For example, software commonly is packaged in a container or wrapper that advises the purchaser that the use of the software is subject to the terms of a license agree-ment contained inside the package. The license agreement generally explains that, if the purchaser does not wish to enter into a contract, he or she must return the product for a refund, and that failure to return it within a certain period will constitute assent to the license terms. These so-called "shrink-wrap licenses" have been the subject of consider-able litigation. In *ProCD v. Zeidenberg*, the Seventh Circuit

Court of Appeals considered a software license agreement "encoded on the CD-ROM disks as well as printed in the manual, and which appears on a user's screen every time the software runs." The court held that the transaction, even though one "in which the exchange of money precedes the communication of detailed terms," was valid, in part because the software could not be used unless and until the offeree was shown the license and manifested his assent. Not all courts to confront the issue have enforced shrink-wrap license agreements.

For most of the products it makes available over the Internet (but not SmartDownload), Netscape uses another common type of software license, one usually identified as a "click-wrap" license. A click-wrap license presents the user with a message on his or her computer screen, requiring that the user manifest his or her assent to the terms of the license agreement by clicking on an icon. The product cannot be obtained or used unless and until the icon is clicked. The few courts that have had occasion to consider click-wrap contracts have held them to be valid and enforceable.

A third type of software license, "browse-wrap," was considered in *Pollstar v. Gigmania Ltd.* In *Pollstar,* the plaintiff's web page offered allegedly proprietary information. Notice of a license agreement appears on the plaintiff's website. Clicking on the notice links the user to a separate web page containing the full text of the license agreement, which allegedly binds any user to the information on the site. However, the user is not required to click on an icon expressing assent to this license, or even view its terms, before proceeding to use the information on the site. The court referred to this arrangement as a "browse-wrap" license.

The SmartDownload License Agreement in the case before me differs fundamentally from both click-wrap and shrink-wrap licensing, and resembles more the browse-wrap license of *Pollstar.* Where click-wrap license agreements and the shrink-wrap license agreement at issue in *ProCD* require users to perform an affirmative action unambiguously expressing assent before they may use the software, that affirmative action is equivalent to an express declaration stating, "I assent to the terms and conditions of the license agreement" or something similar. Netscape's SmartDownload, in contrast, allows a user to download and use the software without taking any action that plainly manifests assent to the terms of the associated license or indicates an understanding that a contract is being formed.

California courts carefully limit the circumstances under which a party may be bound to a contract. An offeree, regardless of apparent manifestation of his consent, is not bound by inconspicuous contractual provisions of which he was unaware, contained in a document whose contractual nature is not obvious. Netscape argues that the mere act of downloading indicates assent. However, downloading is hardly an unambiguous indication of assent. The primary purpose of downloading is to obtain a product, not to assent to an agreement. In contrast, clicking on an icon stating, "I assent" has no meaning or purpose other than to indicate such assent. Netscape's failure to require users of SmartDownload to indicate assent to its license as a precondition to downloading and using its software is fatal to its argument that a contract has been formed.

The only hint that a contract is being formed is one small box of text referring to the license agreement, text that appears below the screen used for downloading and that a user need not even see before obtaining the product: "Please review and agree to the terms of the Netscape SmartDownload software license agreement before downloading and using the software." Couched in the mild request, "Please review," this language reads as a mere invitation, not as a condition. While clearer language appears in the License Agreement itself, the language of the invitation does not require the reading of those terms or provide adequate notice either that a contract is being created or that the terms of the License Agreement will bind the user. Netscape argues that this case resembles the situation where a party has failed to read a contract and is nevertheless bound by that contract. This argument misses the point. The question before me is whether the parties have first bound themselves to the contract. If they have unequivocally agreed to be bound, the contract is enforceable whether or not they have read the terms.

The case law on software licensing has not eroded the importance of assent in contract formation. Mutual assent is the bedrock of any agreement to which the law will give force. Netscape's position, if accepted, would so expand the definition of assent as to render it meaningless. Because the user plaintiffs did not assent to the license agreement, they are not subject to the arbitration clause contained therein and cannot be compelled to arbitrate their claims against Netscape.

Motion to compel arbitration denied in favor of the plaintiffs.

Intent and Acceptance on the Offeror's Terms

Common Law: Traditional "Mirror Image" Rule

The traditional contract law rule is that an acceptance must be the *mirror image* of the offer. Attempts by offerees to change the terms of the offer or to add new terms to it are treated as counteroffers because they impliedly indicate an intent by the offeree to reject the offer instead of being bound by its terms. However, recent years have witnessed a judicial tendency to apply the mirror image rule in a more liberal fashion by holding that only *material* (important) variances between an offer and a purported acceptance result in an implied rejection of the offer.

Even under the mirror image rule, no rejection is implied if an offeree merely asks about the terms of the offer without indicating its rejection (an *inquiry regarding terms*), or accepts the offer's terms while complaining about them (a *grumbling acceptance*). Distinguishing among a counteroffer, an inquiry regarding terms, and a grumbling acceptance is often a difficult task. The fundamental issue, however, remains the same: Did the offeree objectively indicate a present intent to be bound by the terms of the offer? You will see an example of a counteroffer in the *McGurn v. Microproducts, Inc.* case, which appears later in this chapter.

UCC Standard for Acceptance on the Offeror's Terms: The "Battle of the Forms"

Strictly applying the mirror image rule to modern commercial transactions, most of which are carried out by using preprinted form contracts, would often result in frustrating the parties' true intent. Offerors use standard order forms prepared by their lawyers, and offerees use standard acceptance or acknowledgment forms drafted by their counsel. The odds that these forms will agree in every detail are slight, as are the odds that the parties will read each other's forms in their entirety. Instead, the parties to such transactions are likely to read only crucial provisions concerning the goods ordered, the price, and the delivery date called for, and if these terms are agreeable, believe that they have a contract.

If a dispute arose before the parties started to perform, a court strictly applying the mirror image rule would hold that no contract resulted because the offer and acceptance forms did not match exactly. If a dispute arose after performance had commenced, the court would probably hold that the offeror had impliedly accepted the offeree's counteroffer and was bound by its terms.

Because neither of these results is very satisfactory, the Code, in a very controversial provision often called the "Battle of the Forms" section [2–207] (see Figure 1), has changed the mirror image rule for contracts involving the sale of goods. As you will see in the following *Reilly Foam* case, UCC section 2–207 allows the formation of a contract even when there is some variance between the terms of the offer and the terms of the acceptance. It also makes it possible, under *some* circumstances, for a term contained in the acceptance form to become part of the contract. The Code provides that a *definite and timely expression of acceptance* creates a contract, even if it includes terms that are *different from those stated in the offer* or even if it states *additional terms* that the offer did not address [2–207(1)]. An attempted acceptance that *was expressly conditioned* on the offeror's agreement to the offeree's terms would *not* be a valid acceptance, however [2–207(1)].

What are the terms of a contract created by the exchange of standardized forms? The *additional* terms contained in the offeree's form are treated as "proposals for addition to the contract." If the parties are both *merchants,* the additional terms become part of the contract *unless:*

1. The offer *expressly limited acceptance* to its own terms.

2. The new terms would *materially alter* the offer, or

3. The offeror gives notice of objection to the new terms within a reasonable time after receiving the acceptance [2–207(2)].

When the offeree has made his acceptance expressly conditional on the offeror's agreement to the new terms or when the offeree's response to the offer is clearly not "an expression of acceptance" (e.g., an express rejection), no contract is created under section 2–207(1). A contract will only result in such cases if the parties engage in conduct that "recognizes the existence of a contract," such as an exchange of performance. Unlike her counterpart under traditional contract principles, however, the offeror who accepts performance in the face of an express rejection or expressly conditional acceptance is not thereby bound to all of the terms contained in the offeree's response. Instead, the Code provides that the terms of a contract created by such performance are those on which the parties' writings agree, supplemented by appropriate gap-filling provisions from the Code [2–207(3)].

As you will see in the following *Reilly Foam* case, that same approach is used by the majority of courts when there is an acceptance that contains terms that are *different* from (not merely additional to) the terms of the offer. That is, the contract will consist of those terms on which the parties' writings agree *plus* any appropriate gap-filling presumptions of the Code.

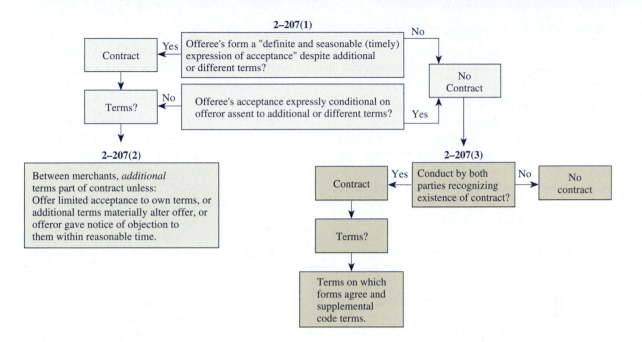

Figure 1   *The "Battle of the Forms"—A Section 2–207 Flowchart*

Reilly Foam Corp. v. Rubbermaid Corp.
2002 U.S. Dist. LEXIS 9273 (U.S. Dist. Ct. E.D. Pa. 2002)

Reilly Foam manufactures custom-order sponges and other foam products. Rubbermaid manufactures home products, including mops, nationwide. In 1997, Rubbermaid launched its "Tidal Wave Project" to introduce into the marketplace new and improved sponge mops named for a wave pattern that would be cut into the sponges. This included a "butterfly" mop that was assembled for Rubbermaid by an independent corporation, New Knight, and a roller mop that was produced "in house" by Rubbermaid. Target Stores had agreed to stock Tidal Wave sponge mop line at its stores nationwide. Initially, Rubbermaid tried to obtain sponges for the mops from Tek Pak, a competitor of Reilly Foam, but Tek Pak could not make timely deliveries of sponges to meet Target's needs, so Rubbermaid contacted Reilly Foam to see if it could fulfill its needs. Reilly Foam was able to deliver the needed products in time, and Rubbermaid began talking with Reilly Foam about a longer-term relationship. Reilly Foam needed to retool its equipment and license technology to produce the "tidal wave" sponges, and Reilly Foam was concerned that its profits on the contract would permit it to recoup its costs.

On March 26, 1999, Reilly Foam sent a letter to Rubbermaid. The letter stated that it related to the two laminates that Reilly Foam was currently working on, the roller mop and the butterfly mop, and three other products produced by New Knight. It referred to and attached a list of price quotations and quantities for these products, listing annual quantities for three products that were identified as "Other Affected Products": 340,000 for the brown sponge, 350,000 for the yellow ester with wave pattern sponge, and 300,000 for the yellow ether and white "scrubmate." The letter proposed that Rubbermaid commit to 2 million pieces of product under the subheading "Other Affected Products" over a period of two years, that the price include a surcharge of $.015 per part to amortize the cost of tooling for the wave pattern. It also proposed that Rubbermaid commit to buying all of its butterfly and roller mop laminates from Reilly Foam.

On March 30, 1999, Tony Ferrante, a Rubbermaid product manager, responded by a letter that stated in part:

This letter is to serve as Rubbermaid's commitment and authorization to procure tooling so that Reilly Foam will be in a position to make sponge products with Rubbermaid's patent pending Tidal Wave TM design. I understand that

$.015 will be added to the cost of the sponge purchase price until we have made purchases of 2 million sponges, thereby covering the tooling cost of $30,000.

Referencing the attached quotation, our commitment is as follows:

1. Any sponge mop product produced by New Knight, Inc. on behalf of Rubbermaid will source the sponge component from Reilly Foam. This includes the current product offering, as referenced in your quotation, as well as any future new products that New Knight will produce for us.

Attached to this letter was Reilly Foam's price list, marked "Approved" and signed by Ferrante.

After this exchange, Rubbermaid instructed New Knight to purchase sponges solely from Reilly Foam. New Knight complied and used Reilly Foam as its exclusive source of sponges until New Knight went bankrupt in August 2001. Rubbermaid itself made purchases of sponges listed under the "other affected products" category. At the same time, Rubbermaid continued to purchase sponges from Tek Pak for use in the Tidal Wave line of mops. Moreover, Rubbermaid did not purchase 2 million sponges within the two-year window that Reilly Foam sought.

Reilly Foam sued Rubbermaid for breach of contract. Reilly Foam moved for partial summary judgment, and Rubbermaid filed a cross-motion for summary judgment.

Schiller, Judge   Reviewing Reilly Foam's March 26 correspondence and its treatment by Rubbermaid, both parties treated the price quote as an offer and not merely as a price quote. The Court finds the March 26 correspondence contains sufficient detail and is deemed an offer as a matter of law. There can be no doubt that Rubbermaid's March 30 response accepted it. See U.C.C. § 2–207 (expression of acceptance operates to form contract even if it states additional or different terms).

If Reilly Foam's March 26 letter operates as an offer and Rubbermaid's March 30 correspondence acts as an acceptance, the Court is left with the task of determining the terms of the agreement between these merchants under U.C.C. § 2–207, commonly called the "Battle of the Forms" provision. Frequently, businessmen do not set forth all the terms of their agreements in a single, comprehensive document. Rather, deals are made on the basis of conversations and letters exchanged between the parties. Ultimately, one party reduces the terms of a proposed deal to writing which is deemed an offer. Under the common law, a document qualifying as an offer could only be accepted by a second document expressing acceptance on terms identical to the offer. This rule changed with the enactment of the Battle of the Forms provision of the U.C.C., which permits an expression of acceptance to operate as an acceptance even if it contains *additional* or *different* terms. The *additional* terms become part of the contract unless: (1) the offer expressly limits acceptance to the terms of the offer; (2) the inserted term materially alters the offer; or (3) notification of objection to the inserted terms is given within a reasonable time.

The fate of *different* terms is less clear. Section 2–207(b) does not directly address different terms in an acceptance, and the question remains: if the offer is accepted on differ-

ent terms, should the terms of the offer control or should the acceptance be followed, or should the conflicting terms cancel each other out, to be replaced by gap fillers provided by the U.C.C. The question has divided courts and scholars.

One approach considers any expression of acceptance with differing terms as actually a rejection and counteroffer. Thus, the terms outlined in the acceptance would govern. This view has been widely discredited as a revival of the common law rule, and the Court is not aware of any jurisdiction in which it is currently in force.

The minority view permits the terms of the offer to control. Professor Summers, the leading advocate of the minority rule, reasons that offerors have more reason to expect that the terms of their offer will be enforced than the recipient of an offer can hope that its inserted terms will be effective. The offeree at least had the opportunity to review the offer and object to its contents; if the recipient of an offer objected to a term, it should not have proceeded with the contract.

The final approach, held by a majority of courts, is now known as the "knockout rule." Under this approach, terms of the contract include those upon which the parties agreed and gap fillers provided by the U.C.C. provisions. This approach recognizes the fundamental tenet behind U.C.C. §2–207: to repudiate the "mirror-image" rule of the common law. One should not be able to dictate the terms of the contract merely because one sent the offer. Indeed, the knockout rule recognizes that merchants are frequently willing to proceed with a transaction even though all terms have not been assented to. It would be inequitable to lend greater force to one party's preferred terms than the other's. Advocates of the knockout rule [interpret the U.C.C.] to require the cancellation of terms in both parties' documents that conflict with one another, whether the terms are in confirmation notices or in the offer and acceptance themselves. In light of the superior policy reasons behind the knockout rule, I conclude that the Pennsylvania Supreme Court would adopt the knockout rule.

The parties have concluded a contract for the sale of sponges. Both Reilly Foam's proposal and Rubbermaid's response call for the sale of sponges of differing varieties, and they agree on the identification of particular sponges, along with dimensions and prices for each. Rubbermaid also agreed to add $.015 to the price of each sponge until Rubbermaid had made purchases of 2 million sponges. As to annual purchases of "other affected products," the price list accompanying Reilly Foam's March 26 letter set a minimum annual quantity requirement for each type of sponge. Rubbermaid's March 30 response contains no terms at odds with that requirement. To the contrary, Ferrante wrote "approved" on the page. Ferrante did consent to the $.015 surcharge on the first 2 million sponges, implying that he accepted an obligation to purchase sponges in the "other affected products" category. The letters also do not differ with respect to the time period within which Rubbermaid was to purchase 2 million sponges with a $.015 surcharge. Reilly Foam sought a two-year time frame, and Rubbermaid omitted that term in its acceptance. Rubbermaid therefore argues the two terms drop out under the knockout rule, giving Rubbermaid an infinite period of time in which to make its purchases. However, Ferrante's March 30 letter is silent as to the time period within which Rubbermaid had to make its purchases. Thus, the offer and acceptance do not differ and the two-year requirement is part of the contract.

However, as to the requirements contract clause that Reilly Foam sought respecting the butterfly and roller mop sponges, the knockout rule applies. Rubbermaid's acceptance of a requirements contract was limited to Tidal Wave project sponges produced by New Knight on behalf of Rubbermaid. Thus, Rubbermaid's commitment only related to the butterfly sponges and any new products that New Knight might produce in the future for Rubbermaid. However, Rubbermaid did not commit to purchase all of its direct requirements for sponges from Reilly Foam. Therefore, the term creating a requirements contract for all of Rubbermaid's needs for the Tidal Wave brand of sponges falls out of the contract. Rubbermaid did commit to ensuring that its purchases from New Knight are manufactured with Reilly Foam sponges. Both letters agreed on that point. All the evidence shows that Rubbermaid fulfilled its contractual duty to ensure that New Knight dealt exclusively with Reilly Foam. However, the record remains unclear as to whether Rubbermaid satisfied its obligations regarding quantity requirements of butterfly sponges.

In summary Rubbermaid has breached the contract in failing: (1) to make minimum annual purchases of "other affected products" as set forth in the March 26 price list; (2) to purchase 2 million sponges under the "other affected products" category with a $.015 surcharge within two years of the contract date. Reilly Foam may also sue for Rubbermaid's alleged failure to make good faith efforts to ensure that New Knight purchased all of its requirements of butterfly mop sponges for Rubbermaid products from Reilly Foam until New Knight went bankrupt.

Partial summary judgment granted in favor of Reilly Foam.

LOG ON

This helpful site leads a student through a §2–207 analysis: Professor Bell, *A Brief Working Guide to UCC §2–207,* **http://www.tomwbell.com/teaching/ UCC2-207.html**

Communication of Acceptance

To accept an offer for a bilateral contract, the offeree must make the promise requested by the offer. In Chapter 10, you learned that an offeror must communicate the terms of his proposal to the offeree before an offer results. This is so because communication is a necessary component of the present intent to contract required for the creation of an offer. For similar reasons, it is generally held that an offeree must communicate his intent to be bound by the offer before a contract can be created. To accept an offer for a unilateral contract, however, the offeree must perform the requested act. The traditional contract law rule on this point assumes that the offeror will learn of the offeree's performance and holds that no further notice from the offeree is necessary to create a contract unless the offeror specifically requests notice.

Manner of Communication The offeror, as the master of the offer, has the power to specify the precise time, place, and manner in which acceptance must be communicated. This is called a *stipulation*. If the offeror stipulates a particular manner of acceptance, the offeree must respond in this way to form a valid acceptance. Suppose Prompt Printing makes an offer to Jackson and the offer states that Jackson must respond by certified mail. If Jackson deviates from the offer's instructions in any significant way, no contract results unless Prompt Printing indicates a willingness to be bound by the deviating acceptance. If, however, the offer merely *suggests* a method or place of communication or is *silent* on such matters, the offeree may accept within a *reasonable time* by *any reasonable means* of communication. So, if Prompt Printing's offer did not *require* any particular manner of accepting the offer, Jackson could accept the offer by any reasonable manner of communication within a reasonable time.

When Is Acceptance Communicated?

Acceptances by Instantaneous Forms of Communication

When the parties are dealing face-to-face, by telephone, or by other means of communication that are virtually instantaneous, there are few problems determining when the acceptance was communicated. As soon as the offeree says, "I accept," or words to that effect, a contract is created, assuming that the offer is still in existence.

Acceptances by Noninstantaneous Forms of Communication

Suppose the circumstances under which the offer was made reasonably led the offeree to believe that acceptance by some noninstantaneous form of communication is acceptable, and the offeree responds by using mail, telegraph, or some other means of communication that creates a time lag between the dispatching of the acceptance and its actual receipt by the offeror. The practical problems involving the timing of acceptance multiply in such transactions. The offeror may be attempting to revoke the offer while the offeree is attempting to accept it. An acceptance may get lost and never be received by the offeror. The time limit for accepting the offer may be rapidly approaching. Was the offer accepted before a revocation was received or before the offer expired? Does a lost acceptance create a contract when it is dispatched, or is it totally ineffective?

Under the so-called *"mailbox rule,"* properly addressed and dispatched acceptances can become effective when they are *dispatched,* even if they are lost and never received by the offeror. The mailbox rule, which is discussed further in the following *Cantu v. Central Education Agency* case, protects the offeree's reasonable belief that a binding contract was created when the acceptance was dispatched. By the same token, it exposes the offeror to the risk of being bound by an acceptance that she has never received. The offeror, however, has the ability to minimize this risk by stipulating in her offer that she must actually receive the acceptance for it to be effective. Offerors who do this maximize the time that they have to revoke their offers and ensure that they will never be bound by an acceptance that they have not received.

Operation of the Mailbox Rule: Common Law of Contracts As traditionally applied by the common law of contracts, the mailbox rule would make acceptances effective upon dispatch when the offeree used a manner of communication that was expressly or impliedly **authorized** (invited) by the offeror. Any manner of communication *suggested* by the offeror (e.g., "You may respond by mail") would be expressly authorized, resulting in an acceptance sent by the suggested means being effective on dispatch. Unless circumstances indicated to the contrary, a manner of communication *used by the offeror in making the offer* would be impliedly authorized (e.g., an offer sent by mail would impliedly authorize an acceptance by mail), as would a manner of communication common in the parties' trade or business (e.g., a trade usage in the parties' business that offers are made by mail and accepted by telegram would authorize an acceptance by telegram). Conversely, an improperly dispatched acceptance or one that was sent by some means of communication that was *nonauthorized* would be effective when *received,* assuming that the offer was still open at that time. This placed on the offeree the risk of the offer being revoked or the acceptance being lost.

The mailbox rule is often applied more liberally by courts today. A modern version of the mailbox rule that is sanctioned by the *Restatement (Second)* holds that an offer that does not indicate otherwise is considered to invite acceptance by *any reasonable means* of communication, and a properly dispatched acceptance sent by a reasonable means of communication within a reasonable time is effective on dispatch. The *Cantu* case illustrates the more liberal version of the mailbox rule.

Cantu v. Central Education Agency   *884 S.W.2d 565 (Ct. App. Tex. 1994)*

Cantu was hired as a special education teacher by the San Benito Consolidated Independent School District under a one-year contract for the 1990–91 school year. On Saturday, August 18, 1990, shortly before the start of the school year, Cantu hand-delivered to her supervisor a letter of resignation, effective August 17, 1990. In this letter, Cantu requested that her final paycheck be forwarded to an address in McAllen, Texas, some fifty miles from the San Benito office where she tendered the resignation. The San Benito superintendent of schools, the only official authorized to accept resignations on behalf of the school district, received Cantu's resignation on Monday, August 20. The superintendent wrote a letter accepting Cantu's resignation the same day and deposited the letter, properly stamped and addressed, in the mail at approximately 5:15 P.M. that afternoon. At about 8:00 A.M. the next morning, August 21, Cantu hand-delivered to the superintendent's office a letter withdrawing her resignation. This letter contained a San Benito return address. In response, the superintendent hand-delivered that same day a copy of his letter mailed the previous day to inform Cantu that her resignation had been accepted and could not be withdrawn. The dispute was taken to the State Commissioner of Education, who concluded that the school district's refusal to honor Cantu's contract was lawful, because the school district's acceptance of Cantu's resignation was effective when mailed, which resulted in the formation of an agreement to rescind Cantu's employment contract. Cantu sued for judicial review of the Commissioner's final order, and the trial court affirmed the Commissioner's decision. Cantu appealed.

Smith, Justice The sole legal question presented for our review is the proper scope of the "mailbox rule" under Texas law and whether the rule was applied correctly. None of the parties to this appeal disputes that an agreement to rescind Cantu's employment contract requires the elements of an offer, acceptance, and consideration. Rather, Cantu contends in a single point of error that the trial court erred in ruling that the agreement to rescind her contract of employment became effective when the superintendent deposited his letter accepting Cantu's resignation in the mail. Cantu argues that, under Texas law, an acceptance binds the parties in contract on mailing only if the offeror has sent the offer by mail or has expressly authorized acceptance by mail. There was no express authorization for the school district to accept Cantu's offer by mail. The question presented is whether authorization to accept by mail may be implied only when the offer is delivered by mail or also when the existing circumstances make it reasonable for the offeree to so accept.

The aphorism "the offeror is the master of his offer" reflects the power of the offeror to impose conditions on acceptance of an offer, specify the manner of acceptance, or withdraw the offer before the offeree has effectively exercised the power of acceptance. However, more often than not, an offeror does not expressly authorize a particular mode, medium, or manner of acceptance. Consequently, particularly with parties communicating at a distance, a rule of law is needed to establish the point of contract formation and allocate the risk of loss and inconvenience that inevitably falls to one of the parties between the time that the offeree exercises, and the offeror receives, the accept-

ance. See 1 Arthur L. Corbin, Contracts section 78 (1963). As Professor Corbin notes, courts could adopt a rule that no acceptance is effective until received, absent express authorization by the offeror; however, the mailbox rule, which makes acceptance effective on dispatch, closes the deal and enables performance more promptly, and places the risk of inconvenience on the party who originally has power to control the manner of acceptance. Moreover, "the mailing of a letter has long been a customary and expected way of accepting [an] offer." *Id.* Therefore, "even though the offer was not made by mail and there was no [express] authorization, the existing circumstances may be such as to make it reasonable for the offeree to accept by mail and to give the offeror reason to know that the acceptance will be so made." *Id.* In short, acceptance by mail is impliedly authorized if reasonable under the circumstances.

The *Restatement* approves and adopts this approach: an acceptance by any medium reasonable under the circumstances is effective on dispatch, absent a contrary indication in the offer. *Restatement (Second) of Contracts* sections 30(2), 63(a), 65, 66 (1979). In addition, the *Restatement* specifically recognizes that acceptance by mail is ordinarily reasonable if the parties are negotiating at a distance or even if a written offer is delivered in person to an offeree in the same city.

Looking at the circumstances presented for our review, we agree with the Commissioner and the trial court that it was reasonable for the superintendent to accept Cantu's offer of resignation by mail. Cantu tendered her resignation shortly before the start of the school year—at a time when both parties could not fail to appreciate the need for immediate action by the district to locate a replacement. In fact, she delivered the letter on a Saturday, when the Superintendent could neither receive nor respond to her offer, further delaying matters by two days. Finally, Cantu's request that her final paycheck be forwarded to an address some fifty miles away indicated that she could no longer be reached in San Benito and that she did not intend to return to the school premises or school district offices. The Commissioner of Education and district court properly concluded that it was reasonable for the school district to accept Cantu's offer by mail. We affirm the trial court judgment that the Commission correctly determined that the school district accepted Cantu's resignation, rescinding her employment contract, before Cantu attempted to withdraw her offer of resignation.

Affirmed in favor of the school district.

Operation of the Mailbox Rule: UCC The UCC, like the *Restatement (Second),* provides that an offer that does not specify a particular means of acceptance is considered to invite acceptance by *any reasonable means* of communication. It also provides that a properly dispatched acceptance sent by a reasonable means of communication within a reasonable time is effective on dispatch. What is reasonable depends on the circumstances in which the offer was made. These include the speed and reliability of the means used by the offeree, the nature of the transaction (e.g., does the agreement involve goods subject to rapid price fluctuations?), the existence of any trade usage governing the transaction, and the existence of prior dealings between the parties (e.g., has the offeree previously used the mail to accept telegraphed offers from the offeror?). So, under proper circumstances, a mailed response to a telegraphed offer or a telegraphed response to a mailed offer might be considered reasonable and therefore effective on dispatch.

What if an offeree attempts to accept the offer by some means that is *unreasonable* under the circumstances or if the acceptance is not properly addressed or dispatched (e.g., misaddressed or accompanied by insufficient postage)? The UCC rejects the traditional rule that such acceptances cannot be effective until received. It provides that an acceptance sent by an unreasonable means would be effective on dispatch *if* it is received within the time that an acceptance by a reasonable means would normally have arrived.

Stipulated Means of Communication

As we discussed earlier, an offer may stipulate the means of communication that the offeree must use to accept by saying, in effect: "You must accept by mail." An acceptance by the stipulated means of communication is effective on dispatch, just like an acceptance by any other reasonable or authorized means of communication (see Figure 2). The difference is that an acceptance by other than the stipulated means does not create a contract because it is an acceptance at variance with the terms of the offer.

LOG ON

For a thorough outline of the mailbox rule complete with some helpful mnemonics and examples, see
Tom W. Bell, *The Mailbox Rule and Related Rules,*
http://www.tomwbell.com/teaching/KMailbox.html
and Richard Warner, *Warner's Tutorial on Contracts, Offer and Acceptance 1,*
http://www.kentlaw.edu/classes/rwarner/Contracts_sp2001/Offers&Acceptance/oa1/oa1_home.html

Special Acceptance Problem Areas

Acceptance in Unilateral Contracts

A unilateral contract involves the exchange of a promise for an act. To accept an offer to enter such a contract, the offeree must perform the requested act. As you learned in the last chapter, however, courts applying modern contract rules may prevent an offeror from revoking such an offer once the offeree has begun performance. This is achieved by holding either that a bilateral contract is created by the beginning of performance or that the offeror's power to revoke is suspended for the period of time reasonably necessary for the offeree to complete performance.

Figure 2   *Time of Acceptance*

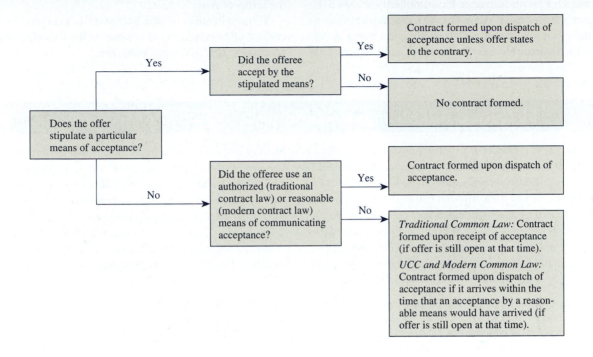

Acceptance in Bilateral Contracts

A bilateral contract involves the exchange of a promise for a promise. As a general rule, to accept an offer to enter such a contract, an offeree must *make the promise requested by the offer.* This may be done in a variety of ways. For example, Wallace sends Stevens a detailed offer for the purchase of Stevens's business. Within the time period prescribed by the offer, Stevens sends Wallace a letter that says, "I accept your offer." Stevens has *expressly* accepted Wallace's offer, creating a contract on the terms of the offer. Acceptance, however, can be *implied* as well as expressed. Offerees who take action that objectively indicates agreement risk the formation of a contract. For example, offerees who act in a manner that is inconsistent with an offeror's ownership of offered property are commonly held to have accepted the offeror's terms. So, if Arnold, a farmer, leaves 10 bushels of corn with Porter, the owner of a grocery store, saying, "Look this corn over. If you want it, it's $5 a bushel," and Porter sells the corn, he has impliedly accepted Arnold's offer. But what if Porter just let the corn sit and, when Arnold returned a week later, Porter told Arnold that he did not want it? Could Porter's failure to act ever amount to an acceptance?

Silence as Acceptance

Since contract law generally requires some objective indication that an offeree intends to contract, the general rule is that an offeree's silence, without more, is *not* an acceptance. In addition, it is generally held that an offeror cannot impose on the offeree a duty to respond to the offer. So, even if Arnold made an offer to sell corn to Porter and said, "If I don't hear from you in three days, I'll assume you're buying the corn," Porter's silence would still not amount to acceptance.

On the other hand, the circumstances of a case sometimes impose a duty on the offeree to reject the offer affirmatively or be bound by its terms. These are cases in which the offeree's silence objectively indicates an intent to accept. Customary trade practice or prior dealings between the parties may indicate that silence signals acceptance. So, if Arnold and Porter had dealt with each other on numerous occasions and Porter had always promptly returned items that he did not want, Porter's silent retention of the goods for a week would probably constitute an acceptance. Likewise, an offeree's silence can also operate as an acceptance if the offeree has indicated that it will. For example, Porter (the *offeree*) tells Arnold, "If you don't hear from me in three days, I accept."

Finally, it is generally held that offerees who accept an offeror's performance knowing what the offeror expects in return for his performance have impliedly accepted the offeror's terms. So, if Apex Paving Corporation offers to do the paving work on a new subdivision being developed by Majestic Homes Corporation, and Majestic fails to respond to Apex's offer but allows Apex to do the work, most courts would hold that Majestic is bound by the terms of Apex's offer.

The application of this exception is analyzed in the context of an employment contract in the following case, *McGurn v. Bell Microproducts, Inc.*

McGurn v. Bell Microproducts, Inc.   *284 F.3d 86 (1st Cir. 2002)*

Donald Bell, President of Bell Microproducts, met with George McGurn and discussed with him the position of Vice President for the Eastern Region. At this meeting, McGurn said that if he came to work for Bell, he would require a written contract that included a termination clause stipulating that he would receive six months salary and half his commissions in the event that he was fired. After several discussions with a Bell official, Bell extended an offer of employment to McGurn, but this initial offer had no termination clause in it, and the parties held further discussions about a termination clause. During one of these conversations, McGurn said that he would consider a termination clause that was limited to the first 24 months of his employment, and according to McGurn, Bell said that this would be acceptable. Bell issued another offer containing a termination clause, but McGurn did not agree with its termination clause. Finally, Bell sent a third offer, dated July 3, 1997. This offer contained the following termination clause:

> The Company may terminate your employment without cause. In the event that this occurs within your first twelve months of employment, you will continue to receive your base salary for a period of six (6) months following your termination of employment, [and] you will receive an additional lump-sum amount equal to $40,000 or 50 percent of annual incentive.

The letter ended with the request that McGurn "sign an acknowledgment of this offer of employment and return to me for our files." The following appeared under the signature of Bell's Director of Human Resources:

> I acknowledge my acceptance of the offer as described above and my start date will be_____.
>
> Signed_____   Date_____

McGurn signed his name and entered "7–8–97" in the other two blank spaces. In addition, he crossed out the word twelve *in the termination clause, inserted "twenty-four" directly above it, and initialed the change. The alteration was in the center of the second page of the two-page letter, five inches above McGurn's signatures. McGurn returned the letter and began work on July 8, 1997. McGurn did not tell anyone at Bell that he had modified the offer letter, and Bell officials denied having viewed the letter upon its return. Bell's Human Resources Department did receive the letter and kept it in its files.*

In April of 1998, McGurn's supervisor began to be dissatisfied with his performance, and on August 3, 1998, he fired McGurn. At some point after becoming dissatisfied with McGurn's performance but before firing him, McGurn's supervisor learned of McGurn's alteration of his offer letter. When he learned of his termination, approximately 13 months after McGurn began work at Bell, McGurn advised Bell officials that he believed his contract included a two-year termination clause. Bell refused to pay, and McGurn sued Bell for breach of contract. The district court granted summary judgment for McGurn and entered judgment for him in the amount of $120,000. Bell appealed.

Lipez, Circuit Judge.   The parties agree that McGurn's alteration of Bell's offer letter constituted a rejection of that offer and created a counteroffer. What is in dispute is whether Bell accepted McGurn's counteroffer. As a general rule, silence in response to an offer to enter into a contract does not constitute an acceptance of the offer. There is, however, an exception to the rule against acceptance by silence where an offeree takes the benefit of offered services with reasonable opportunity to reject them and reason to know that they were offered with the expectation of compensation. *Restatement (Second) of Contracts* §69.

In *Gateway C. v. Charlotte Theatres, Inc.,* a case similar to this one, the defendant had sent the plaintiff two copies of a document which reduced to writing an oral agreement for the defendant to install air conditioning in the plaintiff's movie theater, with one copy to be countersigned and returned. The plaintiff signed, but also inserted a provision that the work would be performed by a certain date. The plaintiff returned the countersigned contract with a cover letter noting its understanding that the work would be performed by that date (although the letter made no reference to the alteration of the contract itself). We stated that "in the absence of actual knowledge [of the alteration of the contract], the test is whether there was reason for [the defendant] to suppose that such addition might have been made." We held that because of the cover letter flagging the issue, defendant's silence could constitute acceptance of plaintiff's counteroffer.

Importantly, we also noted in *Gateway* that "absent the [cover] letter, the case would seem more like" *Kidder v. Greenman.* In *Kidder,* a tenant had signed and returned a lease to her landlord with the understanding that the landlord would fill in certain blank spaces pursuant to an oral agreement. The landlord then completed the lease so as to include a term contrary to the oral understanding, signed it, and returned it to the tenant, who "did not look at the lease at the time she received it." The court declined to enforce the disputed term against the tenant on the ground that she had no reason to think that the [landlord] had not completed the lease in the authorized manner and, therefore, [had] no occasion to examine it, when it was returned to her, to see if he had done so.

We distill from the *Restatement* and the *Gateway* and *Kidder* precedents the legal rule in Massachusetts that silence in response to an offer may constitute an acceptance if an offeree who takes the benefit of offered services knew or had reason to know of the existence of the offer, and had a reasonable opportunity to reject it. We turn now to the application of that rule in this case.

The relevant question is why, as a matter of law, Bell should be expected to re-read an offer it had written and signed, upon its return with McGurn's countersignature. In response to that question the district court declared that "[a] presumably sophisticated employer who receives a signed letter of engagement from a prospective employee and fails to read the letter, particularly after weeks of negotiation, does so at its own peril." Although the logic of this generalization has some appeal, its generality is an insurmountable

problem. Unless the record establishes that Bell knew or had reason to know that McGurn had modified what Bell had written—and the district court points to no facts in the record that would support such a conclusion—we cannot say that Bell's silence, as a matter of law, constituted an acceptance of McGurn's counteroffer.

We have stated that ordinarily the question of whether a contract has been made is for the jury, except where the words and actions that allegedly formed a contract are so clear themselves that reasonable people could not differ over their meaning. When, as is the case here, the facts support plausible but conflicting inferences on a pivotal issue in the case, the judge may not choose between those inferences at the summary judgment stage. In sum, we cannot say that the facts in the record compel a conclusion that Bell noticed or should have noticed McGurn's modification of Bell's offer letter, and that its silence, therefore, constituted acceptance of McGurn's offer. Instead, those issues must be resolved by the factfinder at trial.

Judgment vacated in favor of Bell and remanded for further proceedings consistent with this opinion.

SELYA, Circuit Judge (dubitante)   There is no hint here of chicanery on McGurn's part, and I doubt that ignorance induced by a party's own negligence or lassitude is a basis for escaping from contractual obligations. To the contrary, the acceptance of offered services, under circumstances in which the beneficiary of those services ought to know that the provider expected to be compensated for them in a certain way, is the functional equivalent of express assent. I believe that a party should not be able to insulate itself from contract liability by professing that it neglected to read the very document essential for the formation of the contract, especially when that document has reposed in its own files at all relevant times. Were the law otherwise and the majority's view taken to its logical extreme, an offeree could completely redefine its own responsibilities by the simple expedient of claiming that it was not aware of what its own records plainly showed. Given this doubt, I respectfully decline to join the court's opinion.

Acceptance When a Writing Is Anticipated

Frequently, the parties to a contract intend to prepare a written draft of their agreement for both parties to sign.

This is a good idea not only because the law requires written evidence of some contracts,[2] but also because it provides written evidence of the terms of the agreement

---

[2]Chapter 16 discusses this subject in detail.

ETHICS IN ACTION

Marble Publications is a publisher of various magazines and newsletters. Samanatha has a subscription to one of Marble's publications, "Parent's World." In 2003, Marble sends Samanatha a complimentary copy of another of its publications, "Gardens Unlimited," along with a letter that states that Samantha will receive Gardens Unlimited free of charge for three months, but if she does not want to receive any further copies of Gardens Unlimited,

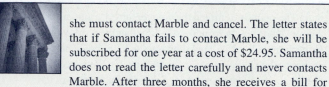

she must contact Marble and cancel. The letter states that if Samantha fails to contact Marble, she will be subscribed for one year at a cost of $24.95. Samantha does not read the letter carefully and never contacts Marble. After three months, she receives a bill for $24.95. Is this an ethical way of marketing Gardens Unlimited? What ethical problems might arise if silence were generally considered to constitute acceptance?

if a dispute arises at a later date. If a dispute arises before such a writing has been prepared or signed, however, a question may arise concerning whether the signing of the agreement was a necessary condition to the creation of a contract. A party to the agreement who now wants out of the deal may argue that the parties did not intend to be bound until both parties signed the writing. A clear expression of such an intent by the parties during the negotiation process prevents the formation of a contract until both parties have signed. However, in the absence of such a clear expression of intent, the

courts ask whether a reasonable person familiar with all the circumstances of the parties' negotiations would conclude that the parties intended to be bound only when a formal agreement was signed. If it appears that the parties had concluded their negotiations and reached agreement on all the essential aspects of the transaction, most courts would probably find a contract at the time agreement was reached, even though no formal agreement had been signed.

You will see this doctrine applied in the following *Tiburzi* case.

Tiburzi v. Department of Justice   *269 F.3d 1346 (Fed. Cir. 2001)*

Jeffrey Tiburzi was a Special Agent with the Drug Enforcement Agency of the U.S. Department of Justice. After Tiburzi allegedly became involved in a bar brawl, the agency instituted the administrative procedures to remove Tiburzi from his job based on several charges, including "Conduct Unbecoming a DEA Agent." Tiburzi appealed his removal to the Merit Systems Protection Board and an evidentiary hearing was held on July 20, 2000. During this time, Tiburzi and the agency also entered into settlement negotiations. On July 21, 2000, the administrative judge stated on the record that "the parties have entered into a settlement agreement" and invited the parties to go on the record about the specific terms of the agreement. Tiburzi's counsel then read the terms of the agreement into the record. Under the agreement, Tiburzi agreed to resign from his job effective July 21, 2000, and not to return to the DEA or make any further employment applications to the DEA and to withdraw his appeal and waive any and all claims against the agency. In return, the agency agreed to provide a neutral reference for Tiburzi and to state that he resigned from the agency "for personal reasons." All parties, including Tiburzi and his counsel, answered affirmatively when the administrative judge asked them whether they each understood the terms of the settlement agreement and whether they voluntarily entered into the settlement agreement. The parties also agreed that "this oral representation of what the settlement agreement is and the written settlement agreement will become part of the record here and enforced." The administrative judge instructed that "a copy of the written settlement agreement will be faxed to my office" on or about July 26, 2000.

On July 27, 2000, the agency sent a proposed written settlement to Tiburzi's counsel for his and Tiburzi's signature. The written proposal set forth the terms of the oral settlement agreement, except that it specified a resignation date of May 1, 2000, which was the resignation date set forth on a personnel form, as opposed to the July 21 resignation date agreed by the parties at the board meeting. Neither Tiburzi nor his counsel ever responded to this correspondence or signed the agreement.

Despite a repeated request by the agency to sign the agreement and a telephone conference between the agency and Tiburzi's counsel about a minor revision to the agreement, neither Tiburzi nor his counsel signed the written agreement.

On August 23, the administrative judge dismissed Tiburzi's appeal on the ground that the parties "lawfully and voluntarily entered into" the oral settlement agreement. Tiburzi filed a pro se *petition for review of the administrative judge's decision, requesting that the settlement agreement be vacated and a new hearing granted. The full Board denied the petition for review, and Tiburzi appealed to the U.S. Court of Appeals for the Federal Circuit.*

DYK, Circuit Judge. It is axiomatic that a settlement agreement is a contract. Tiburzi argues that the oral agreement should be set aside because he did not "sign or accept the official written agreement." In other words, Tiburzi argues that his acceptance of the oral agreement is not binding absent the parties' subsequent approval of a written memorialization of that agreement.

Parties often enter into oral contracts with the understanding that a written contract will follow that merely memorializes the oral contract. It is well-settled that if no written agreement is forthcoming, the oral agreement still governs. In *Singer Co., Librascope Div. v. United States,* for example, [a] government contractor was bound by its oral agreement with the government even though the contractor had never submitted the signed letter of acceptance that had been requested by the government. In reaching that conclusion, the trial court reasoned that the contractor had not shown that the parties intended to postpone a binding contractual commitment until the execution of a later written memorial of their agreement.

In contrast, in *Mahboob v. Department of the Navy,* we concluded that the parties had not intended an oral settlement (negotiated telephonically) to be binding until it was reduced to writing. Thus, we held that the oral agreement there was not a final settlement of plaintiff's claims that the agency had improperly removed her from her position.

In short, our cases make clear that where the parties intend to enter into an oral agreement, it is binding on the parties even if its terms are not embodied in a subsequent written instrument. Secondary sources provide further support for the proposition that an oral agreement between parties is binding even if the parties contemplate the execution of a later written agreement and no subsequent written instrument is in fact executed. The *Restatement (Second) of Contracts* makes clear that:

> Manifestations of assent that are in themselves sufficient to conclude a contract will not be prevented from so operating by the fact that the parties also manifest an intention to prepare and adopt a written memorial thereof; but the circumstances may show that the agreements are preliminary negotiations. *Id.* at § 27.

Under existing law, an oral agreement is binding absent a showing that the parties did not intend to be bound until a written contract was signed. There is no such showing here. Moreover, the hearing transcript shows that the parties intended to achieve a settlement agreement on the date of the hearing. The hearing transcript also shows that the parties and the administrative judge understood that a complete, binding agreement had been reached. Finally, all parties agreed that both the oral agreement and any subsequent written memorialization would be enforceable by the Board. In sum, substantial evidence shows that the parties intended the oral settlement agreement to be binding and enforceable even absent the execution of a subsequent written agreement.

We do note that the written agreement drafted by the agency contains one arguably material change from the oral agreement, in that the written agreement specifies an earlier resignation date for Tiburzi than did the oral agreement. But the agency's mere proposal of a different resignation date in its July 27, 2000, draft of the written agreement does not require the invalidation of the entire oral agreement. Rather, the July 21, 2000, resignation date set forth in the oral agreement continues to govern.

Affirmed in favor of the Department of Justice.

Acceptance of Ambiguous Offers

Although offerors have the power to specify the manner in which their offers can be accepted by requiring that the offeree make a return promise (a bilateral contract) or perform a specific act (a unilateral contract), often an offer is unclear about which form of acceptance is necessary to create a contract. In such a case, the offer may be accepted in any manner that is *reasonable* in light of the circumstances surrounding the offer. Thus, either a promise to perform or performance, if reasonable, creates a contract.

Acceptance by Shipment The Code specifically elaborates on the rule stated in the preceding section by stating

THE GLOBAL BUSINESS ENVIRONMENT

Under the CISG, as under U.S. law, statements or other conduct by the offeree that shows assent is an acceptance, and silence alone generally does not suffice as acceptance. And, as is true under U.S. law, a contract is concluded when an acceptance of an offer becomes effective. There are several notable differences between acceptance doctrines under U.S. law and the CISG, however. For one, the "battle of the forms," as it is formulated under the Uniform Commercial Code, does not exist under the CISG. Rather, under the CISG, a reply to an offer purports to be an acceptance but in fact contains new or different terms or limitations that are *material* is a rejection and *not* an acceptance. Examples of terms that would be considered material are terms relating to price, payment, quality, the extent of a party's liability, and settlement of disputes (such as arbitration clauses). However, a reply purporting to be an acceptance that contains *non-material* new or different terms can be an acceptance. Another major difference between U.S. law and the CISG is that, unlike the U.S. "mailbox rule," the CISG generally holds acceptances to be effective when they are received.

---

that an order requesting prompt or current shipment of goods may be accepted either by a *prompt promise to ship* or by a *prompt or current shipment* of the goods [2–206(1)(b)]. So, if Ampex Corporation orders 500 IBM personal computers from Marks Office Supply, to be shipped immediately, Marks could accept either by promptly promising to ship the goods or by promptly shipping them. If Marks accepts by shipping, any subsequent attempt by Ampex to revoke the order will be ineffective.

What if Marks did not have 500 IBMs in stock and Marks knew that Ampex desperately needed the goods? Marks might be tempted to ship another brand of computers (that is, *nonconforming goods*—goods different from what the buyer ordered), hoping that Ampex would be forced by its circumstances to accept them because by the time they arrived it would be too late to get the correct goods elsewhere. Marks would argue that by shipping the wrong goods it had made a counteroffer because it had not performed the act requested by Ampex's order. If Ampex accepts the goods, Marks could argue that Ampex has impliedly accepted the counteroffer. If Ampex rejects the goods, Marks would arguably have no liability since it did not accept the order.

The Code prevents such a result by providing that prompt shipment of either conforming goods (what the order asked for) or nonconforming goods (something else) operates as an acceptance of the order [2–206(1)(b)]. This protects buyers such as Ampex because sellers who ship the wrong goods have simultaneously accepted their offers and breached the contract by sending the wrong merchandise.[3]

But what if Marks is an honest seller merely trying to help out a customer that has placed a rush order? Must Marks expose itself to liability for breach of contract in the process? The Code prevents such a result by providing that no contract is created if the seller notifies the buyer within a reasonable time that the shipment of nonconforming goods is intended as an accommodation (an attempt to help the buyer) [2–206(1)(b)]. In this case, the shipment is merely a counteroffer that the buyer is free to accept or reject and the seller's notification gives the buyer the opportunity to seek the goods he needs elsewhere.

Who Can Accept an Offer?

As the masters of their offers, offerees have the right to determine who can bind them to a contract. So, the only person with the legal power to accept an offer and create a contract is the *original offeree*. An attempt to accept by anyone other than the offeree is treated as an offer, because the party attempting to accept is indicating a present intent to contract on the original offer's terms. For example, Price offers to sell his car to Waterhouse for $5,000. Anderson learns of the offer, calls Price, and attempts to accept. Anderson has made an offer that Price is free to accept or reject.

Problems and Problem Cases

1. In August 1993, the Panagotacoses found a house in Galaxidi, Greece, that they wanted to buy. On August 26, 1993, the Geselschaps, the owners of the house, wrote to the Panagotacoses and offered to sell it to them for $160,000. This proposal was subject to several condi-

---

[3]Chapter 19 discusses the rights and responsibilities of the buyer and seller following the shipment of nonconforming goods.

tions: first, that the money for the property be paid in Germany, and second, that delivery of the money occur no later than April 15, 1994. On January 18, 1994, the Panagotacoses wrote to the Geselschaps and enclosed a signed copy of the Geselschaps' offer letter to indicate their agreement to purchase the property. Their letter, however, included the statement that "both parties will need an attorney in Greece where papers need to be signed and the money and title exchanged." The Geselschaps wrote back on January 27, 1994, stating that the condition proposed in their offer that payment of the money occur in Germany was essential and that the Panagotacoses' remarks about payment in Greece indicated that they had failed to agree. Over the next several months, the parties continued to correspond about the property. In the meantime, the Panagotacoses set about trying to get a loan to pay for the Geselschaps' house. They intended to use some real estate that they owned in California as security for such a loan. In March of 1994, James Panagotacos applied for a loan from First Interstate Bank. He was told that it would take three or four weeks for the loan to be funded. The process of getting the loan was delayed, however, when it was discovered that Bank of America had already recorded an interest in the Panagotacoses' California property, and Interstate Bank insisted that this be cleared up before it would fund the loan. (The Panagotacoses had used the California property as security for a loan from Bank of America in 1974, and had paid it off by 1982, but Bank of America had not filed the proper documentation to clear up the title to the property.) Bank of America finally provided the correct documentation on April 12, 1994, and Interstate Bank made loan documents available to the Panagotacoses on that same date. On April 13, 1994, the Panagotacoses wrote the Geselschaps indicating a willingness to comply with the condition that payment for the property be made in Germany. They stated that they were prepared to send the money but needed an account number and, realizing that they would be unable to complete the deal prior to the April 15, 1994, deadline, they requested an extension of the agreement. They further suggested that payment of the money occur in Amsterdam or Germany in June. The Geselschaps refused to extend the agreement and sold the Greek property to another buyer on April 15, 1994. Was there a binding contract for the sale of the property between the Panagotacoses and the Geselschaps?

2. First Texas Savings Association promoted a "$5,000 Scoreboard Challenge" contest. Contestants who completed an entry form and deposited it with First Texas were eligible for a random drawing. The winner was to receive an $80 savings account with First Texas, plus four tickets to a Dallas Mavericks home basketball game chosen by First Texas. If the Mavericks held their opponent in the chosen game to 89 or fewer points, the winner was to receive an additional $5,000 money market certificate. In October 1982, Jergins deposited a completed entry form with First Texas. On November 1, 1982, First tried to amend the contest rules by posting notice at its branches that the Mavericks would have to hold their opponent to 85 or fewer points before the contest winner would receive the $5,000. In late December, Jergins was notified that she had won the $80 savings account and tickets to the January 22, 1983, game against the Utah Jazz. The notice contained the revised contest terms. The Mavericks held the Jazz to 88 points. Was Jergins entitled to the $5,000?

3. Union Carbide sold Oscar Mayer plastic casings that Oscar Mayer uses in manufacturing sausages. The parties' method of dealing was that Oscar Mayer would from time to time send large purchase orders to Union Carbide which would not be filled immediately, but instead would be filed for future reference. When Oscar Mayer actually needed casings, it would phone Union Carbide and tell it how many it need and Union Carbide would ship the casings the next day. After the casings arrived, Oscar Mayer would send Union Carbide a purchase order for the shipment on the same form used for the standing orders. At about the same time, Union Carbide would send Oscar Meyer an invoice for the shipment. The prices in Union Carbide's invoices to Oscar Mayer included two 1 percent sales taxes that are applicable to sales that originate in Chicago. In 1980, another one of Oscar Mayer's suppliers of plastic sausage casings began charging a price that was 1 percent lower than Union Carbide's. This supplier had begun accepting orders at an office outside of Chicago and had decided that therefore it did not have to pay one of the sales taxes. When Oscar Mayer informed Union Carbide of this, Union Carbide instructed its customers to send their orders to an address outside Chicago, too, and it stopped paying both sales taxes and therefore deleted them from the invoices it sent Oscar Mayer. Thus, Union Carbide had met and indeed beat the other supplier's discount by lowering its price 2 percent compared to the other supplier's reduction of 1 percent. In 1988, the Illinois tax authorities decided that the two sales taxes were due notwithstanding the change of address and assessed Union Carbide $88,000 in back taxes on sales to Oscar Mayer and $55,000 in interest on those sales. Union Carbide paid this and then attempted to recover what it had paid from Oscar Mayer. It claimed that Oscar Mayer had

agreed to indemnify it for all sales tax liability. It relied on the following provision printed on the back of its invoices to Oscar Mayer and also in a "price book" that it sent its customers:

> In addition to the purchase price, Buyer shall pay Seller the amount of all governmental taxes. . .that Seller may be required to pay with respect to the production, sale or transportation of any materials delivered hereunder.

Did this provision become part of the contract between Oscar Mayer and Union Carbide so that Oscar Mayer is obligated to pay the tax?

4. In December of 1983, Pennzoil announced an unsolicited, public tender offer for 16 million shares of Getty Oil at $100 each. Gordon Getty was a director of Getty Oil and the owner, as trustee of the Sarah C. Getty Trust, of 40.2 percent of the 79.1 million outstanding shares of Getty Oil. Shortly thereafter, Pennzoil contacted both Gordon Getty and a representative of the J. Paul Getty Museum, which held 11.8 percent of the shares of Getty Oil, to discuss the tender offer and the possible purchase of Getty Oil. The parties drafted and signed a Memorandum of Agreement providing that Pennzoil and the Trust (with Gordon Getty as trustee) were to become partners on a 3/7ths to 4/7ths basis, respectively, in owning and operating Getty Oil. The museum was to receive $110 per share for its 11.8 percent ownership, and all other outstanding public shares were to be cashed in by the company at $110 per share. The memorandum provided that it was subject to the approval of Getty Oil's board. On January 2, 1984, the board voted to reject the memorandum price as too low and made a counterproposal to Pennzoil of $110 per share plus a $10 debenture. On January 3, the board received a revised Pennzoil proposal of $110 per share plus a $3 "stub" that was to be paid after the sale of a Getty Oil subsidiary. After discussion, the board voted 15 to 1 to accept Pennzoil's proposal if the stub price was raised to $5. This counteroffer was accepted by Pennzoil later on that same day. On January 4, Getty Oil and Pennzoil issued identical press releases announcing an agreement in principle on the terms of the Memorandum of Agreement. Pennzoil's lawyers began working on a formal transaction agreement describing the deal in more detail than the outline of terms contained in the Memorandum of Agreement and press release. On January 5, the board of Texaco authorized its officers to make an offer for 100 percent of Getty Oil's stock. When the Getty Museum and Gordon Getty accepted Texaco's offer to buy their shares, the Getty Board voted to withdraw its previous counteroffer to Pennzoil and to accept Texaco's offer. Was there a binding contract between Getty Oil and Pennzoil?

5. On February 21, 1990, Barto went to Estate Motors, Ltd., to buy a new Mercedes-Benz 500SL. Barto was told that because of limited production in Germany and great demand for that model, it would be at least 18 months before a new 500SL could be delivered to him. The salesperson told Barto that Estate Motors would order the car for him if Barto would pay a $500 deposit with the order. Barto agreed and paid Estate Motors $500 with his personal check. Barto and the salesperson then executed a "Retail Buyer's Order" form. The form stated the model, body type, color, and upholstery specifications for the car. No price was specified on the form and neither the dealer nor the salesperson signed in the space provided to indicate the dealer's approval of the order. It stated at the bottom "THIS ORDER IS NOT A BINDING CONTRACT." The reverse side of the form contained 10 additional terms and conditions, including payment in cash or cashier's check upon delivery. On February 22, the day after this form was executed, Estate Motors placed an order with the manufacturer for a new 500SL with the specifications requested by Barto. On February 23, Estate Motors cashed Barto's $500 check. Nine months later, Congress amended the Internal Revenue Code to include a "luxury tax" on purchases of certain passenger vehicles, boats, and aircraft. The statute contained a "pre-existing binding contract" exception that stated that the new tax would not be imposed on sales made after December 31, 1990, if there was a binding contract for the purchase of a covered luxury item in existence as of September 30, 1990. In mid-August of 1991, nearly 18 months after Barto's payment of the $500 deposit and the execution of the order, Estate Motors notified Barto that his Mercedes would be ready for him to pick up on August 30. It also told him for the first time that he would have to pay the luxury tax on his new car ($6,995.00) when he came to pick it up. Barto believed that his car fell within the "pre-existing binding contract" exception to the luxury tax statute because his order for the car had been placed before September 30, 1990. Barto paid for the car and paid the tax, but claimed a refund from the U.S. government on the ground that he had a "binding contract" for the Mercedes-Benz in February of 1990, when the order was placed. The government, however, argued that no contract existed until August 30, 1991, when Barto paid his full purchase price and received his new car. Is Barto right?

6. On January 16, 1987, Koop, an employee of Professional Search, Inc., called Renner, the director of systems software for Northwest Airlines, to inquire about possible job openings in Renner's department. Koop explained to Renner that if Northwest Airlines hired a candidate recommended by Professional Search, Professional Search would be entitled to charge Northwest Airlines 30 percent of the candidate's starting salary. Renner told Koop that a systems analyst position was open and described the job. Renner also stated that Northwest Airlines was not currently interviewing for that position and that Koop should direct further inquiries to Northwest Airlines's human resources department. Later, Koop and Wawrzyniak discussed Wawrzyniak's desire to be placed as a systems analyst and Wawrzyniak signed a placement contract. On January 20, 1987, Koop sent Wawrzyniak's résumé to Renner. He later called Renner, who told him the résumé "looked good." On February 19, Wawrzyniak filled out an application for a systems position with Northwest Airlines, claiming he heard of the opening through a friend. On April 13, Northwest Airlines hired Wawrzyniak. Professional Search claimed that a placement contract had been formed between it and Northwest Airlines, and sought to recover its $12,000 commission. Will Professional Search prevail?

7. Gray brought a personal injury suit against the Stewarts after they were involved in a car accident. On February 28, 2001, the Stewarts made an offer to Gray to compromise her claim for $3,750. On March 6, 2001, Gray served the Stewarts with her own offer to settle the case for $5,000. This offer did not specify the manner in which an acceptance was to be communicated. On March 16, 2001, three days before the scheduled trial, the Stewarts' attorney told Gray's attorney "we accept your. . .demand of $5,000." Gray's counsel concedes that the acceptance was made, that she heard it and understood it, and that it was communicated unambiguously. The attorneys agreed that the case was settled for $5,000 and shook hands on it. The Stewarts' attorney requested the law firm's taxpayer identification number in order to expedite the settlement draft process. Gray's attorney called her office, obtained the number, and wrote it down for him. Consistent with the settlement, both attorneys also discussed and agreed on how the settlement check should be made payable. The next day, a Saturday, Gray decided to revoke her counteroffer. Over the weekend, Gray's attorney faxed a letter to the Stewarts' attorney stating that Gray was withdrawing her offer. Was it permissible for Gray to withdraw her offer?

8. Cobb owned an apartment complex. Freed, Creel, and Whirley approached Cobb about purchasing the complex. On September 5, the purchasers and Cobb entered into a sales contract stating that the purchasers would buy the complex for a sales price of $500,000—$150,000 at closing and a $350,000 purchase-money mortgage in favor of Cobb. The contract was contingent upon the purchasers obtaining a $300,000 loan from People's Bank for improvements to the property. The purchasers notified Cobb that the bank would lend them the money only on condition that Cobb subordinate his mortgage to that of the bank. On September 20, Cobb and the purchasers executed a written addendum to the contract stating that for valuable consideration, Cobb agreed that he would subordinate his mortgage to the construction loan in favor of People's Bank to be used for remodeling. Cobb then presented another addendum to the contract that changed the payment terms of the September 5 sales contract and provided for monthly payments on the amount owed to Cobb. Creel and Whirley signed the second addendum but Freed refused to. Cobb then refused to sell the complex to the purchasers. Did he have the right to do this?

9. In 1985, State Farm Mutual Insurance issued Casto an automobile insurance policy on her Jaguar. Casto also insured a second car, a Porsche, with State Farm. Some time in September or early October 1987, Casto received two renewal notices for her policy on the Jaguar, indicating that the next premium was due on October 10, 1987. State Farm sent a notice of cancellation on October 15, indicating that the policy would be canceled on October 29. Casto denied having received this notice. On October 20, Casto placed two checks, one for the Jaguar and one for the Porsche, in two preaddressed envelopes that had been supplied by State Farm. She gave these envelopes to Donald Dick, who mailed them on the same day. The envelope containing the Porsche payment was timely delivered to State Farm, but State Farm never received the Jaguar payment, and that policy was canceled. Casto was involved in an accident on November 20 while driving the Jaguar. When she made a claim with State Farm, she learned that the policy had been canceled. After the accident, the envelope containing the Jaguar payment was returned to her stamped, "Returned for postage." The envelope did not bear any postage when returned to Casto. Casto brought a declaratory judgment action seeking a declaration that her insurance policy was in effect as of the date of the accident. Was it?

10. Soldau was fired by Organon, Inc. He received a letter from Organon offering to pay him double the normal severance pay if he would sign a release giving up all claims against the company. The letter incorporated the proposed release, which Soldau signed, dated, and deposited in a mailbox outside a post office. When he returned home, Soldau found that he had received a check from Organon in the amount of the increased severance pay. He returned to the post office and persuaded a postal employee to open the mailbox and retrieve the release. Soldau cashed Organon's check and subsequently filed an age discrimination suit against Organon. Was Soldau bound by the release?

Online Research: Finding Contracts on the Internet

1. *Finding Contracts on the Internet* Surf the web and find an example of a click-wrap and an example of what the court in *Specht* calls a "browse-wrap."

2. Find a User Agreement (also called Terms of Use Agreement) on any website. How does the User Agreement that you find indicate that a user's acceptance to the terms of the agreement will be shown?

CONSIDERATION

The Valley Area Anti-Smoking Foundation (VAAF) offered to pay any Valley Area resident $500 if he or she would refrain from smoking for one year. Chad, a Valley Area resident, decided to accept this offer. He quit smoking immediately and did not smoke for a whole year. When Chad contacted VAAF to inform it of his success and collect his $500, VAAF informed him that it was only able to pay $250 because so many Valley Area residents had taken advantage of its offer. Chad reluctantly agreed to accept $250 instead of $500.

- *Was VAAF contractually obligated to pay Chad for refraining from smoking?*
- *Was there consideration to support its promise to pay $500?*
- *Are there other facts you need to know to make that determination?*
- *Is Chad entitled to receive the entire $500 or only $250?*

ONE OF THE THINGS that separates a contract from an unenforceable social promise is that a contract requires voluntary agreement by two or more parties. Not all agreements, however, are enforceable contracts. At a fairly early point in the development of classical contract law, the common law courts decided not to enforce gratuitous (free) promises. Instead, only promises supported by consideration were enforceable in a court of law. This was consistent with the notion that the purpose of contract law was to enforce freely made bargains. As one 19th-century work on contracts put it: "The common law . . . gives effect only to contracts that are founded on the mutual exigencies of men, and does not compel the performance of any merely gratuitous agreements."[1] The concept of consideration distinguishes agreements that the law will enforce from gratuitous promises, which are normally unenforceable. This chapter focuses on the concept of consideration.

Elements of Consideration

A common definition of **consideration** is *legal value, bargained for and given in exchange for an act or a promise.* Thus, a promise generally cannot be enforced against the person who made it (the *promisor*) unless the person to whom the promise was made (the *promisee*) has given up something of legal value in exchange for the promise. In effect, the requirement of consideration means that a promisee must pay the price that the promisor asked to gain the right to enforce the promisor's promise. So, if the promisor did not ask for anything in exchange for making her promise or if what the promisor asked for did not have legal value (e.g., because it was something to which she was already entitled), her promise is not enforceable against her because it is not supported by consideration.

Consider the early case of *Thorne* v. *Deas,* in which the part owner of a sailing ship named the *Sea Nymph* promised his co-owners that he would insure the ship for an upcoming voyage.[2] He failed to do so, and when the

---

[1] T. Metcalf, *Principles of the Law of Contracts* (1874), p. 161.

[2] Johns. 84 (N.Y. 1809).

ship was lost at sea, the court found that he was not liable to his co-owners for breaching his promise to insure the ship. Why? Because his promise was purely gratuitous; he had neither asked for nor received anything in exchange for making it. Therefore, it was unenforceable because it was not supported by consideration.

This early example illustrates two important aspects of the consideration requirement. First, the requirement *tended to limit the scope of a promisor's liability for his promises* by insulating him from liability for gratuitous promises and by protecting him against liability for reliance on such promises. Second, the mechanical application of the requirement *often produced unfair results.* This potential for unfairness has produced considerable dissatisfaction with the consideration concept. As the rest of this chapter indicates, the relative importance of consideration in modern contract law has been somewhat eroded by numerous exceptions to the consideration requirement and by judicial applications of consideration principles designed to produce fair results.

Legal Value

Consideration can be an act in the case of a unilateral contract or a promise in the case of a bilateral contract. An act or a promise can have legal value in one of two ways. If, in exchange for the promisor's promise, the promisee does, or agrees to do, something he had no prior legal duty to do, that provides legal value. If, in exchange for the promisor's promise, the promisee refrains from doing, or agrees not to do, something she has a legal right to do, that also provides legal value. Note that this definition does not require that an act or a promise have monetary (economic) value to amount to consideration. Thus, in a famous 19th-century case, *Hamer* v. *Sidway,*[3] an uncle's promise to pay his nephew $5,000 if he refrained from using tobacco, drinking, swearing, and playing cards or billiards for money until his 21st birthday was held to be supported by consideration. Indeed, the nephew had refrained from doing any of these acts, even though he may have benefited from so refraining. He had a legal right to indulge in such activities, yet he had refrained from doing so at his uncle's request and in exchange for his uncle's promise. This was all that was required for consideration.

Adequacy of Consideration   The point that the legal value requirement is not concerned with actual value is further borne out by the fact that the courts

generally will not concern themselves with questions regarding the adequacy of the consideration that the promisee gave. This means that as long as the promisee's act or promise satisfies the legal value test, the courts do not ask whether that act or promise was worth what the promisor gave, or promised to give, in return for it. This rule on adequacy of consideration reflects the laissez-faire assumptions underlying classical contract law. Freedom of contract includes the freedom to make bad bargains as well as good ones, so promisors' promises are enforceable if they got what they asked for in exchange for making their promises, even if what they asked for was not nearly so valuable in worldly terms as what they promised in return. Also, a court taking a hands-off stance concerning private contracts would be reluctant to step in and second-guess the parties by setting aside a transaction that both parties at one time considered satisfactory. Finally, the rule against considering the adequacy of consideration can promote certainty and predictability in commercial transactions by denying legal effect to what would otherwise be a possible basis for challenging the enforceability of a contract—the inequality of the exchange.

Several qualifications must be made concerning the general rule on adequacy of consideration. First, if the inadequacy of consideration is apparent on the face of the agreement, most courts conclude that the agreement was a disguised gift rather than an enforceable bargain. Thus, an agreement calling for an unequal exchange of money (e.g., $500 for $1,000) or identical goods (20 business law textbooks for 40 identical business law textbooks) and containing no other terms would probably be unenforceable. Gross inadequacy of consideration may also give rise to an inference of fraud, duress,[4] lack of capacity,[5] unconscionability,[6] or some other independent basis for setting aside a contract. However, inadequacy of consideration, standing alone, is never sufficient to prove lack of true consent or contractual capacity. Although gross inadequacy of consideration is not, by itself, ordinarily a sufficient reason to set aside a contract, the courts may refuse to grant specific performance or other equitable remedies to persons seeking to enforce unfair bargains.

Finally, some agreements recite "$1," or "$1 and other valuable consideration," or some other small amount as consideration for a promise. If no other consideration is

---

[3]27 N.E. 256 (N.Y.Ct. App. 1891).

[4]Fraud and duress are discussed in Chapter 13.
[5]Lack of capacity is discussed in Chapter 14.
[6]Chapter 15 discusses unconscionability in detail.

actually exchanged, this is called *nominal consideration*. Often, such agreements are attempts to make gratuitous promises look like true bargains by reciting a nonexistent consideration. Most courts refuse to enforce such agreements unless they find that the stated consideration was truly bargained for.

Bargained-For Exchange

Up to this point, we have focused on the legal value component of our consideration definition. But the fact that a promisee's act or promise provides legal value is not, in itself, a sufficient basis for finding that it amounted to consideration. In addition, the promisee's act or promise must have been bargained for and given in exchange for the promisor's promise. In effect, it must be the price that the promisor asked for in exchange for making his promise. Over a hundred years ago, Oliver Wendell Holmes, one of our most renowned jurists, expressed this idea when he said, "It is the essence of a consideration that, by the terms of the agreement, it is given and accepted as the motive or inducement of the promise."[7]

The following *Gottlieb* case illustrates the concept of bargained-for legal value.

---

[7]O. W. Holmes, *The Common Law* (1881), p. 239.

Gottlieb v. Tropicana Hotel and Casino
109 F. Supp. 2d 324 (U.S. Dist. Ct. E.D. Pa. 2000)

During the summer of 1999, Rena and Sheldon Gottlieb were vacationing in Atlantic City, New Jersey, and on July 24, they visited the Tropicana casino. Tropicana offers people membership in its "Diamond Club." To become a Diamond Club member, an individual must visit a promotional booth in the casino, obtain and fill out an application form, and show identification. There is no charge. The application form lists the person's name, address, telephone number, and e-mail address, and this information is entered into the casino's computer database. Each member receives a Diamond Club card that has a unique identification number. The member then presents or "swipes" the card in a machine each time he or she plays a game at the casino, and the casino obtains information about the member's gambling habits. The casino's marketing department then uses that information to tailor its promotions.

Rena Gottlieb was, and had been for a number of years, a member of the Diamond Club. When she entered the casino on July 24, she immediately went to the Fun House Million Dollar Wheel Promotion, which offers participants the chance to win a grand prize of $1 million. Diamond Club members were entitled to one free spin of the Million Dollar Wheel each day. She presented her Diamond Club card, a casino operator swiped it through the card reader, she pressed a button to activate the wheel, and the wheel began spinning. Gottlieb claims that the wheel landed on the $1 million grand prize, but when it did so, the casino attendant immediately swiped another card through the machine, reactivated the wheel, and the wheel landed on a prize of two show tickets. Tropicana denies that its attendant intervened and reactivated the wheel, and contends that the wheel simply landed on the lesser prize. Ms. Gottlieb sued Tropicana for breach of contract, among other theories, and Tropicana moved for summary judgment.

BARTLE, III, Judge.   According to Tropicana, participation in a promotion such as the Million Dollar Wheel cannot constitute consideration that would support the formation of an enforceable contract. We find the decision of the New Jersey Supreme Court in *Lucky Calendar Co.* v. *Cohen* to be on point. There, an advertising company brought a declaratory judgment action, seeking a determination that its promotional advertisement campaign for Acme Super Markets did not violate New Jersey's Lottery Act. The centerpiece of the campaign was a calendar that had Acme coupons bordering it, which was distributed by mass mailings. The calendar contained an explanation of the "Lucky Calendar Prize Contest." Entrants had the opportunity to win prizes in monthly drawings. All they had to do to enter was tear the entry form off the calendar, enter a name, address, and phone number, and have the form deposited in a box at any Acme store. There was no charge, and they were not required to be present for the drawing. The question in *Lucky Calendar* was whether there had been consideration for participation in the drawings. The Supreme Court of New Jersey noted that, assuming consideration was required in order for something to qualify as an illegal lottery, it need only be the minimum consideration that is necessary to form a contract. It explained:

> The consideration in a lottery, as in any form of simple contract, need not be money or the promise of money.

Nor need it be of intrinsic value; "a rose, a hawk or a peppercorn" will suffice, provided it is what is asked for by the promisor and is not illegal . . . Whether a "peppercorn" or the filling in and delivering of a coupon is sufficient consideration for a promise depends only on whether it was the requested detriment to the promisee induced by the promise.

The court determined that consideration was present "both in the form of a detriment or inconvenience to the promisee at the request of the promisor and of a benefit to the promisor. . . . Completing the coupon and arranging for the deposit of it in the box" at the store was the detriment to the promisee, and the "increase in volume of business" was the benefit to the promisor and its customer, the owner of the Acme stores. As the court pointed out, "The motives of the plaintiff and its customer [in offering the Lucky Calendar Prize Contest]. . . are in nowise altruistic."

In *Cobaugh* v. *Klick-Lewis, Inc.,* the Superior Court of Pennsylvania decided that there was adequate consideration to form a binding contract where a golfer, who was participating in a tournament, shot a hole-in-one after seeing a contest announcement offering a new car to anyone who could ace the particular hole. The court noted that the promisor benefited from the publicity of the promotional advertising, and the golfer performed an act that he was under no legal obligation to perform.

Ms. Gottlieb had to go to the casino to participate in the promotion. She had to wait in line to spin the wheel. By presenting her Diamond Club card to the casino attendant and allowing it to be swiped into the casino's machine, she was permitting the casino to gather information about her gambling habits. Additionally, by participating in the game, she was a part of the entertainment that casinos, by their very nature, are designed to offer to all of those present. All of these detriments to Ms. Gottlieb were the requested detriments to the promisee induced by the promise of Tropicana to offer her a chance to win $1 million. Tropicana's motives in offering the promotion were "in nowise altruistic." It offered the promotion in order to generate patronage of and excitement within the casino. In short, Ms. Gottlieb provided adequate consideration to form a contract with Tropicana.

Tropicana further challenges Ms. Gottlieb's breach of contract claim on the grounds that it is clear as a matter of law that she did not win the $1 million prize. Tropicana points to computer records in support of its position that Ms. Gottlieb did not win the grand prize. Ms. Gottlieb relies in part on her own testimony and the testimony of her husband, who witnessed her spin of the promotional wheel. It is for the jury, and not for the court, to resolve this factual dispute.

Motion for summary judgment on the contract claim denied in favor of Ms. Gottlieb.

Exchanges That Fail to Meet Consideration Requirements

Illusory Promises

For a promise to serve as consideration in a bilateral contract, the promisee must have promised to do, or to refrain from doing, something at the promisor's request. It seems obvious, therefore, that if the promisee's promise is illusory because it really does not bind the promisee to do or refrain from doing anything, such a promise could not serve as consideration. Such agreements are often said to lack the mutuality of obligation required for an agreement to be enforceable. So, a promisee's promise to buy "all the sugar that I want" or to "paint your house if I feel like it" would not be sufficient consideration for a

promisor's return promise to sell sugar or hire a painter. In neither case has the promisee given the promisor anything of legal value in exchange for the promisor's promise. Remember, though: So long as the promisee has given legal value, the agreement will be enforceable even though what the promisee gave is worth substantially less than what the promisor promised in return.

Effect of Cancellation or Termination Clauses

The fact that an agreement allows one or both of the parties to cancel or terminate their contractual obligations does not necessarily mean that the party (or parties) with the power to cancel has given an illusory promise. Such provisions are a common and necessary part of many business relationships. The central issue in such cases concerns whether a promise subject to cancellation or termination actually represents a binding obligation. A right to cancel or terminate at any time, for any reason, and without any notice would clearly render illusory any other promise by the party possessing such a right. However, limits on the circumstances under which cancellation may occur (such as a dealer's failure to live up to dealership obligations), or the time in which cancellation may occur (such as no cancellations for the first 90 days), or a requirement of advance notice of cancellation (such as a 30-day notice requirement) would all effectively remove a promise from the illusory category. This is so because in each case the party making such a promise has bound himself to do *something* in exchange for the other party's promise. A party's duty of good faith and fair dealing can also limit the right to terminate and prevent its promise from being considered illusory.

Effect of Output and Requirements Contracts

Contracts in which one party to the agreement agrees to buy all of the other party's production of a particular commodity (*output* contracts) or to supply all of another party's needs for a particular commodity (*requirements* contracts) are common business transactions that serve legitimate business purposes. They can reduce a seller's selling costs and provide buyers with a secure source of supply. Prior to the enactment of the UCC, however, many common law courts used to refuse to enforce such agreements on the ground that their failure to specify the quantity of goods to be produced or purchased rendered them illusory. The courts also feared that a party to such an agreement might be tempted to exploit the other party. For example, subsequent market conditions could make it profitable for the seller in an output contract or the buyer in a requirements contract to demand that the other party buy or provide more of the particular commodity than the other party had actually intended to buy or sell. The Code legitimizes requirements and output contracts. It addresses the concern about the potential for exploitation by limiting a party's demands to those quantity needs that occur in *good faith* and are not unreasonably disproportionate to any quantity estimate contained in the contract, or to any normal prior output or requirements if no estimate is stated [2–306(1)]. Chapter 19, Formation and Terms of Sales Contracts, discusses this subject in greater detail.

Effect of Exclusive Dealing Contracts

When a manufacturer of goods enters an agreement giving a distributor the exclusive right to sell the manufacturer's products in a particular territory, does such an agreement impose sufficient obligations on both parties to meet the legal value test? Put another way, does the distributor have any duty to sell the manufacturer's prod-

ucts and does the manufacturer have any duty to supply any particular number of products? Such agreements are commonly encountered in today's business world, and they can serve the legitimate interests of both parties. The Code recognizes this fact by providing that, unless the parties agree to the contrary, an exclusive dealing contract imposes a duty on the distributor to use her best efforts to sell the goods and imposes a reciprocal duty on the manufacturer to use his best efforts to supply the goods [2–306(2)].

Preexisting Duties

The legal value component of our consideration definition requires that promisees do, or promise to do, something in exchange for a promisor's promise that they had no prior legal duty to do. Thus, as a general rule, performing or agreeing to perform a preexisting duty is not consideration. This seems fair because the promisor in such a case has effectively made a gratuitous promise, since she was already entitled to the promisee's performance.

Preexisting Public Duties Every member of society has a duty to obey the law and refrain from committing crimes or torts. Therefore, a promisee's promise not to commit such an act can never be consideration. So, Thomas's promise to pay Brown $100 a year in exchange for Brown's promise not to burn Thomas's barn would not be enforceable against Thomas. Since Brown has a preexisting duty not to burn Thomas's barn, his promise lacks legal value.

Similarly, public officials, by virtue of their offices, have a preexisting legal duty to perform their public responsibilities. For example, Smith, the owner of a liquor store, promises to pay Fawcett, a police officer whose beat includes Smith's store, $50 a week to keep an eye on the store while walking her beat. Smith's promise is unenforceable because Fawcett has agreed to do something that she already has a duty to do.

Preexisting Contractual Duties and Modifications of Contracts under the Common Law The most important preexisting duty cases are those involving preexisting *contractual* duties. These cases generally occur when the parties to an existing contract agree to *modify* that contract. The general common law rule on contract modifications holds that an agreement to modify an existing contract requires *some new consideration* to be binding.

For example, Turner enters into a contract with Acme Construction Company for the construction of a new office building for $350,000. When the construction is partially completed, Acme tells Turner that due to rising labor and materials costs it will stop construction unless Turner agrees to pay an extra $50,000. Turner, having already entered into contracts to lease office space in the new building, promises to pay the extra amount. When the construction is finished, Turner refuses to pay more than $350,000. Is Turner's promise to pay the extra $50,000 enforceable against him? No. All Acme has done in exchange for Turner's promise to pay more is build the building, something that Acme had a preexisting contractual duty to do. Therefore, Acme's performance is not consideration for Turner's promise to pay more.

Although the result in the preceding example seems fair (why should Turner have to pay $400,000 for something he had a right to receive for $350,000?) and is consistent with consideration theory, the application of the preexisting duty rule to contract modifications has generated a great deal of criticism. Plainly, the rule can protect a party to a contract such as Turner from being pressured into paying more because the other party to the contract is trying to take advantage of his situation by demanding an additional amount for performance. However, mechanical application of the rule could also produce unfair results when the parties have freely agreed to a fair modification of their contract. Some critics argue that the purpose of contract modification law should be to enforce freely made modifications of existing contracts and to deny enforcement to coerced modifications. Such critics commonly suggest that general principles such as good faith and unconscionability, rather than technical consideration rules, should be used to police contract modifications.

Other observers argue that most courts in fact apply the preexisting duty rule in a manner calculated to reach fair results, because several exceptions to the rule can be used to enforce a fair modification agreement. For example, any new consideration furnished by the promisee provides sufficient consideration to support a promise to modify an existing contract. So, if Acme had promised to finish construction a week before the completion date called for in the original contract, or had promised to make some change in the original contract specifications such as to install a better grade of carpet, Acme would have done something that it had no legal duty to do in exchange for Turner's new promise. Turner's promise to pay more would then be enforceable because it would be supported by new consideration.

Many courts also enforce an agreement to modify an existing contract if the modification resulted from *unforeseen circumstances* that a party could not reasonably

be expected to have foreseen, and which made that party's performance far more difficult than the parties originally anticipated. For example, if Acme had requested the extra payment because abnormal subsurface rock formations made excavation on the construction site far more costly and time-consuming than could have been reasonably expected, many courts would enforce Turner's promise to pay more.

Courts can also enforce fair modification agreements by holding that the parties mutually agreed to terminate their original contract and then entered a new one. Because contracts are created by the will of the parties, they can be terminated in the same fashion. Each party agrees to release the other party from his contractual obligations in exchange for the other party's promise to do the same. Because such a mutual agreement terminates all duties owed under the original agreement, any subsequent agreement by the parties would not be subject to the preexisting duty rule. A court is likely to take this approach, however, only when it is convinced that the modification agreement was fair and free from coercion.

LOG ON

For a good overview of pre-existing duty concept, see Appeals on Wheels, *The Pre-Existing Duty Rule,*
http://www.appealsonwheels.com/contracts/dutyrule.htm.

Preexisting Duty and Contract Modification under the UCC The drafters of the Code sought to avoid many of the problems caused by the consideration requirement by dispensing with it in two important situations: As discussed in Chapter 10, The Agreement: Offer, the Code does not require consideration for firm offers [2–205]. The Code also provides that an agreement to modify a contract for the sale of goods needs *no consideration* to be binding [2–209(1)]. For example, Electronics World orders 200 XYZ televisions at $150 per unit from XYZ Corp. Electronics World later seeks to cancel its order, but XYZ refuses to agree to cancellation. Instead, XYZ seeks to mollify a valued customer by offering to reduce the price to $100 per unit. Electronics World agrees, but when the televisions arrive, XYZ bills Electronics World for $150 per unit. Under classical contract principles, XYZ's promise to reduce the price of the goods would not be enforceable because Electronics World has furnished no new consideration in exchange for XYZ's promise. Under the Code, no new consideration is necessary and the agreement to modify the contract is enforceable.

THE GLOBAL BUSINESS ENVIRONMENT

Like the UCC, the CISG does not require new consideration to modify a contract. The CISG states that contracts can be modified by the "mere agreement" of the parties. Another similarity between the UCC and CISG is that under the CISG, a term in a written contract stating that modifications of that contract can only be made in writing will generally preclude oral modifications.

Several things should be made clear about the operation of this Code rule. First, XYZ had no duty to agree to a modification and could have insisted on payment of $150 per unit. Second, modification agreements under the Code are still subject to scrutiny under the general Code principles of good faith and unconscionability, so unfair agreements or agreements that are the product of coercion are unlikely to be enforced. Finally, the Code contains two provisions to protect people from fictitious claims that an agreement has been modified. If the original agreement requires any modification to be in writing, an oral modification is unenforceable [2–209(2)]. Regardless of what the original agreement says, if the price of the goods in the modified contract is $500 or more, the modification is unenforceable unless the requirements of the Code's statute of frauds section [2–201] are satisfied [2–209(3)].[8]

Preexisting Duty and Agreements to Settle Debts

One special variant of the preexisting duty rule that causes considerable confusion occurs when a debtor offers to pay a creditor a sum less than the creditor is demanding in exchange for the creditor's promise to accept the part payment as full payment of the debt. If the creditor later sues for the balance of the debt, is the creditor's promise to take less enforceable? The answer depends on the nature of the debt and on the circumstances of the debtor's payment.

Liquidated Debts A **liquidated debt** is a debt that is both due and certain; that is, the parties have no good faith dispute about either the existence or the amount of the original debt. If a debtor does nothing more than pay less than an amount he clearly owes, how could this be consideration for a creditor's promise to take less? Such a debtor has actually done less than he had a preexisting legal duty to do—namely, to pay the full amount of the debt. For this reason, the creditor's promise to discharge a liquidated debt for part payment of the debt at or after its due date is _unenforceable_ for lack of consideration.

For example, Connor borrows $10,000 from Friendly Finance Company, payable in one year. On the day payment is due, Connor sends Friendly a check for $9,000 marked: "Payment in full for all claims Friendly Finance has against me." Friendly cashes Connor's check, thus impliedly promising to accept it as full payment by cashing it, and later sues Connor for $1,000. Friendly is entitled to the $1,000 because Connor has given no consideration to support Friendly's implied promise to accept $9,000 as full payment. You will see an example of this concept in the following _Schlesinger_ case.

However, had Connor done something he had no preexisting duty to do in exchange for Friendly's promise to settle for part payment, he could enforce Friendly's promise and avoid paying the $1,000. For example, if Connor had paid early, before the loan contract called for payment, or in a different medium of exchange from that called for in the loan contract (such as $4,000 in cash and a car worth $5,000), he would have given consideration for Friendly's promise to accept early or different payment as full payment.

---

[8]Chapter 16 discusses § 2–201 of the Code in detail.

Schlesinger v. Woodcock   _35 P.3d 1232 (Wyo. Sup. Ct. 2001)_

In 1997, Custom Syndicated Research, Incorporated (CSR) began experiencing financial difficulties and needed funds to make its payroll. Mary Beth Schlesinger, the sole shareholder and president, approached her friend, Ted Dixon, a financial planner and investment advisor, seeking his help in obtaining the money. Dixon made clear to Schlesinger that, to justify advising his clients to take money out of their current investments, the terms of any loans would necessarily require a high rate *of return and strong collateralization. He informed Schlesinger that, based on his experience with similar situations, the interest rate would have to be 25 percent, the loans short term, and personal liability for repayment on the part of Schlesinger in addition to CSR would be needed. Fourteen loans were entered between Dixon's clients, CSR, and Schlesinger between April 1997 and April 1998. In 1998, Dixon began experiencing serious personal problems that impaired his ability to conduct his business. Some of the loans that he arranged were documented in promissory notes, and others were not. All of the loans that were documented by promissory notes contained terms providing 25 percent interest, joint and several liability of Schlesinger and CSR, and attorney's fees.*

Dixon arranged a number of loans by Betty Jane Woodcock, a client in her seventies. Three of these loans were documented by promissory notes, one was documented by a receipt which included the notation, "Loan to CSR Inc. Standard Terms," and three were completely undocumented. No negotiations ever occurred between Schlesinger and Woodcock directly, and Woodcock relied upon Dixon to make good investments on her behalf. There was no discussion prior to the loans relating to a change of the standard terms, and Woodcock relied on those terms in making the loans.

About five months after Woodcock made the last loan to Schlesinger and CSR, Schlesinger's father presented a modified loan agreement to Woodcock and informed her that, because several of her loans were not documented by promissory notes, this modified loan agreement would provide her greater security. The modified loan agreement, which stated that it superseded all prior agreements relating to the loans, reduced the interest rate to 10 percent, eliminated the protection of joint and several liability, and extended the term of the loans. It provided no additional protection of Woodcock's legal right to repayment of the previous loans. Woodcock signed the modified loan agreement without Dixon's knowledge. Several weeks later, CSR filed for bankruptcy. Woodcock filed suit to collect on the loans. Both parties sought summary judgment on the modified loan agreement. The trial court held the modified loan agreement on the undocumented loans void for lack of consideration, and Schlesinger appealed.

KITE, Justice   The fundamental question concerning the validity of the modified loan agreement is whether the agreement is supported by any consideration. Did Woodcock receive anything of value in exchange for her supposed agreement five months after the last loan to substantially reduce the interest rate, eliminate joint and several liability, and alter other terms of the loans? Without valid consideration, the agreement is invalid.

Consideration may take a variety of forms including the performance of some act, a forbearance, or the creation, modification, or destruction of a legal relationship. The problem Schlesinger's argument faces is, the performance or promise offered as consideration cannot be for an obligation the promisor is already legally required to perform. Payment of a debt which is due and undisputed does not constitute consideration for a promise. Likewise, a mere promise to pay a debt for which the promisor is already legally bound does not constitute a consideration sufficient to support a new contract. Specifically, the promise to pay a debt already due is not sufficient consideration for a creditor's promise to forbear the time of payment.

Schlesinger has argued the modified loan agreement provided protection to assure payment of the outstanding loans over and above the protection Woodcock already had under the notes and oral agreements. However, if the terms of the oral agreement were known through the parties' course of conduct, no further protection was provided by the modified loan agreement. Certainly, the modified loan agreement provided no security or collateral which might have been adequate consideration. At bottom, the validity of the modified loan agreement and enforceability of the oral agreements are mutually exclusive. If the oral agreements are enforceable, the loan agreement offers Woodcock nothing but substantially less attractive loan terms. If the oral agreements are not enforceable, the modified loan agreement is of value to Woodcock, or at least it was prior to CSR's filing for bankruptcy.

We agree with the trial court that the terms of the oral loan agreements are knowable and certain given the parties' clear course of conduct over a year's time with fourteen different loans and four different lenders. After hearing all the evidence, the trial court made factual findings that the terms of Woodcock's agreement to loan money to Schlesinger and CSR included 25 percent interest, a term of forty days at most, joint and several liability, a 1 percent late fee, and payment by the debtor of all reasonable attorney's fees and costs of collection. Given those facts, Woodcock had an enforceable contract, and the *post hoc* modified loan agreement provided her with no greater security than that to which she was already entitled by law. To suggest, as Schlesinger does, that, because Woodcock, an elderly person not represented by counsel in the review of the loan agreement, was "thankful" to see the agreement somehow provided consideration for giving up a bargained 25 percent interest rate, joint and several liability, and costs of collection is inherently suspect. Schlesinger's contention the modified loan agreement benefitted Woodcock by the mere fact that it documented the previous loans misses the mark. It appears much more likely Schlesinger, in an attempt to avoid the admittedly onerous loan terms, took advantage of Dixon's impairment, which left Woodcock vulnerable to the suggestion the modified loan agreement was in her interest. Quite the opposite is true; the agreement removed the only protection Woodcock had for repayment of the loans—Schlesinger's personal liability.

Affirmed in favor of Woodcock.

Unliquidated Debts A good faith dispute about either the existence or the amount of a debt makes the debt an **unliquidated debt.** The settlement of an unliquidated debt is called an **accord and satisfaction.**[9] When an accord and satisfaction has occurred, the creditor cannot maintain an action to recover the remainder of the debt that he alleges is due. For example, Computer Corner, a retailer, orders 50 personal computers and associated software packages from Computech for $75,000. After receiving the goods, Computer Corner refuses to pay Computech the full $75,000, arguing that some of the computers were defective and that some of the software it received did not conform to its order. Computer Corner sends Computech a check for $60,000 marked: "Payment in full for all goods received from Computech." A creditor in Computech's position obviously faces a real dilemma. If Computech cashes Computer Corner's check, it will be held to have impliedly promised to accept $60,000 as full payment. Computech's promise to accept part payment as full payment would be enforceable because Computer Corner has given consideration to support it: Computer Corner has given up its right to have a court determine the amount it owes Computech. This is something that Computer Corner had no duty to do; by giving up this right and the $60,000 in exchange for Computech's implied promise, the consideration requirement is satisfied. The result in this case is supported not only by consideration theory but also by a strong public policy in favor of encouraging parties to settle their disputes out of court. Who would bother to settle disputed claims out of court if settlement agreements were unenforceable?

Computech could refuse to accept Computer Corner's settlement offer and sue for the full $75,000, but doing so involves several risks. A court may decide that Computer Corner's arguments are valid and award Computech less than $60,000. Even if Computech is successful, it may take years to resolve the case in the courts through the expensive and time-consuming litigation process. In addition, there is always the chance that Computer Corner may file for bankruptcy before any judgment can be collected. Faced with such risks, Computech may feel that it has no practical alternative other than to cash Computer Corner's check.[10]

Composition Agreements Composition agreements are agreements between a debtor and two or more creditors who agree to accept as full payment a stated percentage of their liquidated claims against the debtor at or after the date on which those claims are payable. Composition agreements are generally enforced by the courts despite the fact that enforcement appears to be contrary to the general rule on part payment of liquidated debts. Many courts have justified enforcing composition agreements on the ground that the creditors' mutual agreement to accept less than the amount due them provides the necessary consideration. The main reason why creditors agree to compositions is that they fear that their failure to do so may force the debtor into bankruptcy proceedings, in which case they might ultimately recover a smaller percentage of their claims than that agreed to in the composition.

Forbearance to Sue An agreement by a promisee to refrain, or forbear, from pursuing a legal claim against a promisor can be valid consideration to support a return promise—usually to pay a sum of money—by a promisor. The promisee has agreed not to file suit, something that she has a legal right to do, in exchange for the promisor's promise. The courts do not wish to sanction extortion by allowing people to threaten to file spurious claims against others in the hope that those threatened will agree to some payment to avoid the expense or embarrassment associated with defending a lawsuit. On the other hand, we have a strong public policy favoring private settlement of

---

[9]Accord and satisfaction is also discussed in Chapter 18.

[10]A provision of Article 3 of the Uniform Commercial Code, section 3–311, covers accord and satisfaction by use of an instrument such as a "full payment" check. With a few exceptions, the basic provisions of section 3–311 parallel the common law rules regarding accord and satisfaction that are described in this chapter and Chapter 18.

ETHICS IN ACTION

Rex Roofing contracted with the O'Neills to install a new roof on their house for $2,500. Rex began the work and soon realized that he had underbid the job. He informed the O'Neills that he would not do the job for $2,500 after all, but that he would complete the work for $3,200. The O'Neills promised to pay him $3,200. Assuming that there were no unforeseen conditions that affected the roof and no obvious mistakes in the bid calculations, was it ethical for Rex Roofing to refuse to do the job at the agreed-upon price? Since the O'Neills agreed to pay the higher price, are they ethically obligated to do so, even if the law does not require them to pay more than the originally agreed-upon price?

disputes. Therefore, it is generally said that the promisee must have a good faith belief in the validity of his or her claim before forbearance amounts to consideration.

Past Consideration

Past consideration—despite its name—is not consideration at all. Past consideration is an act or other benefit given in the past that was *not* given in exchange for the promise in question. Because the past act was not given in exchange for the present promise, it cannot be consideration. Consider again the facts of the famous case of *Hamer* v. *Sidway,* discussed earlier in this chapter. There, an uncle's promise to pay his nephew $5,000 for refraining from smoking, drinking, swearing, and other delightful pastimes until his 21st birthday was supported by consideration because the nephew had given legal value by refraining from participating in the prohibited activities. However, what if the uncle had said to his nephew on the eve of his 21st birthday: "Your mother tells me you've been a good lad and abstained from tobacco, hard drink, foul language, and gambling. Such goodness should be rewarded. Tomorrow, I'll give you a check for $5,000." Should the uncle's promise be enforceable against him? Clearly not, because although his nephew's behavior still passes the legal value test, in this case it was not bargained for and given in exchange for the uncle's promise.

CONCEPT REVIEW

Consideration

Consideration*	Not Consideration
Doing something you had no preexisting duty to do	Doing something you had a preexisting duty to do
Promising to do something you had no preexisting duty to do	Promising to do something you had a preexisting duty to do
Paying part of a liquidated debt prior to the date the debt is due	Nominal consideration (unless actually bargained for)
Paying a liquidated debt in a different medium of exchange than originally agreed to	Paying part of a liquidated debt at or after the date the debt is due
Agreeing to settle an unliquidated debt	Making an illusory promise
Agreeing not to file suit when you have a good faith belief in your claim's validity	Past consideration
	Preexisting moral obligation

*Assuming bargained for.

Moral Obligation As a general rule, promises made to satisfy a preexisting moral obligation are unenforceable for lack of consideration. The fact that a promisor or some member of the promisor's family, for example, has received some benefit from the promisee in the past (e.g., food and lodging, or emergency care) would not constitute consideration for a promisor's promise to pay for that benefit, due to the absence of the bargain element. Some courts find this result distressing and enforce such promises despite the absence of consideration. In addition, a few states have passed statutes making promises to pay for past benefits enforceable if such a promise is contained in a writing that clearly expresses the promisor's intent to be bound.

Exceptions to the Consideration Requirement

The consideration requirement is a classic example of a traditional contract law rule. It is precise, abstract, and capable of almost mechanical application. It can also, in some instances, result in significant injustice. Modern courts and legislatures have responded to this potential for injustice by carving out numerous exceptions to the requirement of consideration. Some of these exceptions (for example, the Code firm offer and contract modification rules) have already been discussed in this and preceding chapters. In the remaining portion of this chapter, we focus on several other important exceptions to the consideration requirement.

Promissory Estoppel

As discussed in Chapter 9, Introduction to Contracts, the doctrine of promissory estoppel first emerged from attempts by courts around the turn of this century to reach just results in donative (gift) promise cases. Classical contract consideration principles did not recognize a promisee's reliance on a donative promise as a sufficient basis for enforcing the promise against the promisor. Instead, donative promises were unenforceable because they were not supported by consideration. In fact, the essence of a donative promise is that it does not seek or require any bargained-for exchange. Yet people continued to act in reliance on donative promises, often to their considerable disadvantage.

Refer to the facts of *Thorne* v. *Deas,* discussed earlier in this chapter. The co-owners of the *Sea Nymph* clearly relied on their fellow co-owner's promise to get insurance for the ship. Some courts in the early years of this century began to protect such relying promisees by *estopping* promisors from raising the defense that their promises were not supported by consideration. In a wide variety of cases involving gratuitous agency promises (as in *Thorne* v. *Deas*), promises of bonuses or pensions made to employees, and promises of gifts of land, courts began to use a promisee's detrimental (harmful) reliance on a donative promise as, in effect, a *substitute* for consideration.

In 1932, the first *Restatement of Contracts* legitimized these cases by expressly recognizing promissory estoppel in section 90. The elements of promissory estoppel were then essentially the same as they are today: a *promise* that the promisor should reasonably expect to induce reliance, *reliance* on the promise by the promisee, and *injustice* to the promisee as a result of that reliance. Promissory estoppel is now widely used as a consideration substitute, not only in donative promise cases but also in cases involving commercial promises contemplating a bargained-for exchange. The construction contract bid cases discussed in Chapter 10 are another example of this expansion of promissory estoppel's reach. In fact, although promissory estoppel has expanded far beyond its initial role as a consideration substitute into other areas of contract law, it is probably fair to say that it is still most widely accepted in the consideration context. Promissory estoppel as a substitute for consideration is discussed in the following *Calabro* case.

Calabro v. Calabro   *1999 Tenn. App. LEXIS 732 (Ct. App. Tenn. 1999)*

Hope Calabro is the daughter of Arthur Calabro. Hope's mother and Arthur were divorced when Hope was four years old. From the time of the divorce until Hope finished high school, she lived in Oklahoma with her mother, while Arthur lived in Memphis, Tennessee. He provided financial support to Hope while she was living with her mother. While Hope was growing up, Arthur saw her during summers and on some holidays. Hope had an excellent academic record in high school. During *her senior year in high school, Arthur offered to pay for Hope's expenses to attend a distinguished, private university if she received at least $10,000 in financial aid. At the time that Hope was applying to colleges, she knew that she was eligible to attend the University of Oklahoma and receive a full scholarship, but knowing that her father would be willing to finance her college education at a private college if she received $10,000 in financial aid, Hope applied to and was accepted at Boston University, Tulane University, Pepperdine University, Stanford University, the University of California at San Diego, Southern Methodist University, and Vanderbilt University. Several of these schools offered her financial aid. In the fall of 1991, Hope enrolled in Vanderbilt University with her father paying expenses that exceeded her scholarship. During the Christmas break of 1992, Arthur informed Hope that he was no longer willing to pay for her college expenses. At that time he had prepaid her tuition for the spring of 1993 at Vanderbilt. Hope continued to attend Vanderbilt and completed her course work in the spring of 1995, earning a B.A. in psychology. Hope financed the remainder of her education by taking out student loans that became due upon her graduation.*

Hope brought a breach of contract suit against Arthur, claiming that he had breached a contract to pay for her college expenses that exceeded her scholarship. The trial granted a summary judgment in favor of Arthur, and Hope appealed.

Crawford, Judge Hope contends that there was a binding contract between the parties and that Arthur breached the contract when he refused to continue paying for her college expenses. Hope contends that she undertook to do something that she was not legally obligated to do, thereby providing the consideration needed to form a contract. She asserts that Arthur received a benefit by having his daughter close to him and away from her mother's influence, and by having a well-educated daughter. Hope further asserts that she gave up substantial scholarships and financial aid at the University of Oklahoma, Tulane, Southern Methodist University, and Pepperdine to attend Vanderbilt. Hope asserts that these foregone opportunities, along with the substantial expense she incurred to attend Vanderbilt, constitute a legal detriment to her as promisee and consideration for her father's promise to pay her education expenses. Arthur contends that the trial court properly determined that he was entitled to summary judgment as to his daughter's claim relating to expenses and debt incurred after May 1993 because there is no genuine issue of any material fact. He asserts that as a parent he has no legal obligation to pay for the educational expenses of a child that has reached the age of majority. Arthur asserts that he did not intend to enter into a contract that obligated him to pay for college expenses, but merely desired to help his daughter realize the dream she expressed to him of becoming a doctor. He further contends that even if his generosity could be construed as an obligation, it is a moral rather than a legal obligation, which is not legally enforceable. He asserts that his daughter's college attendance was not a benefit to him and that his satisfaction at having Hope attend school near his home was not an inducement, because he made no such requirement. Arthur maintains that the cause of any detriment to Hope was her failure to excel in school, and he, in fact, suffered the detriment of the expense of two years of his daughter's education. Finally Arthur asserts that in December of 1992, he made it clear to his daughter that he would pay no more after May, 1993, and it was not reasonable, necessary or justifiable for Hope to return to Vanderbilt and rely on further financial support based on his gratuitous promise.

For there to be a consideration in a contract between parties to the contract it is not necessary that something concrete and tangible move from one to the other. Any benefit to one and detriment to the other may be a sufficient consideration. The jury may draw any reasonable and natural inference from the proof and if by inference from the proof a benefit to the promisor and detriment to the promisee might be inferred this will constitute a valid consideration. In addition to the benefit, detriment paradigm, Tennessee courts have defined valid consideration in terms of the promisee's legal rights and obligations. Consideration [exists] when the promisee does something that he is under no legal obligation to do or refrains from doing [that] which he has a legal right to do. Simply stated, Hope's evidence from her deposition testimony, and the deposition of Arthur's sister, is that Arthur promised to pay her tuition and expenses over and above the $10,000 scholarship if she attended Vanderbilt. Hope had previously been entitled to various scholarship opportunities at other colleges, but she relinquished those opportunities based upon the strength of Arthur's promise. Although she preferred to go to another college, she deferred to Arthur's preference that she attend Vanderbilt. There was no condition attached to the promise to pay tuition that she maintain any sort of grade-point average or class standing, nor that she pursue any particular curriculum. Arthur's testimony by deposition indicates that he did agree to pay the tuition and other expenses, but that he did not require that his daughter attend Vanderbilt. He admits that there was no condition attached that she pursue a premed curriculum or maintain a certain grade-point average.

We believe under the proof in this case that there is sufficient evidence to create a genuine issue of material fact as to whether there was adequate consideration flowing between the parties to constitute an enforceable contract. There is a dispute as to whether a benefit was conferred on Arthur on his promise to pay the tuition and whether Hope suffered a detriment in her performance of the contract or agreement.

Hope also relies upon the doctrine of promissory estoppel. Detrimental action or forbearance by the promisee in reliance on a gratuitous promise, within limits, constitutes a substitute for consideration, or a sufficient reason for enforcement of the promise without consideration. This doctrine is known as promissory estoppel. A promisor who induces substantial change of position by the promisee in reliance on the promise is estopped to deny its enforceability as lacking consideration. The reason for the doctrine is to avoid an unjust result, and its reason defines its limits. No injustice results in refusal to enforce a gratuitous promise where the loss suffered in reliance is negligible, nor where the promisee's action in reliance was unreasonable or unjustified by the promise. The limits of promissory estoppel are: (1) the detriment suffered in reliance must be substantial in an economic sense; (2) the substantial loss to the promisee in acting in reliance must have been foreseeable by the promisor; (3) the promisee must have acted reasonably in justifiable reliance on the promise as made. 637 S.W.2d 862 at 864 (citing L. Simpson, *Law of Contracts* section 61 [2d ed. 1965]). The doctrine of promissory estoppel is also referred to as "detrimental reliance" because the plaintiff must show not only that a promise was made, but also that the plaintiff reasonably relied on the promise to his detriment. Furthermore, the promise upon which the promisee relied must be unambiguous and not unenforceably vague. However, a claim of promissory estoppel is not dependent upon the existence of an expressed contract between the parties. From our review of the record, we conclude that there are disputes of material fact as to the alleged promises of Arthur, Hope's action and response thereto, and any inferences that legitimately may be drawn therefrom. The trier of fact should first determine whether a valid contract exists between the parties. Alternatively, the trier of fact should determine whether Hope may rely upon the theory of promissory estoppel. Accordingly, the order of the trial court granting summary judgment is reversed and this case is remanded for such further proceedings as necessary.

Reversed and remanded in favor of Hope Calabro.

Promises to Pay Debts Barred by Statutes of Limitations

Statutes of limitations set an express statutory time limit on a person's ability to pursue any legal claim. A creditor who fails to file suit to collect a debt within the time prescribed by the appropriate statute of limitations loses the right to collect it. Many states, however, enforce a new promise by a debtor to pay such a debt, even though technically such promises are not supported by consideration because the creditor has given nothing in exchange for the new promise. Most states afford debtors some protection in such cases, however, by requiring that the new promise be in writing to be enforceable.

Promises to Pay Debts Barred by Bankruptcy Discharge

Once a bankrupt debtor is granted a discharge,[11] creditors no longer have the legal right to collect discharged debts. Most states enforce a new promise by the debtor to pay

---

[11]Chapter 29 discusses bankruptcy in detail.

(reaffirm) the debt regardless of whether the creditor has given any consideration to support it. To reduce creditor attempts to pressure debtors to reaffirm, the Bankruptcy Reform Act of 1978 made it much more difficult for debtors to reaffirm debts discharged in bankruptcy proceedings. The act requires that a reaffirmation promise be made prior to the date of the discharge and gives the debtor the right to revoke his promise within 30 days after it becomes enforceable. This act also requires the Bankruptcy Court to counsel individual (as opposed to corporate) debtors about the legal effects of reaffirmation and requires Bankruptcy Court approval of reaffirmations by individual debtors. In addition, a few states require reaffirmation promises to be in writing to be enforceable.

Charitable Subscriptions

Promises to make gifts for charitable or educational purposes are often enforced, despite the absence of consideration, when the institution or organization to which the promise was made has acted in reliance on the promised gift. This result is usually justified on the basis of either promissory estoppel or public policy.

Problems and Problem Cases

1. Niehaus was an employee of Delaware Valley Medical Center. The medical center distributed an employee handbook that stated that if an employee were granted an approved leave of absence, that employee, at the end of the leave, would be guaranteed the same position or one similar to the position occupied prior to the leave of absence. The handbook also stated, however, that the provisions in the handbook were not to be interpreted as a contract of employment and that either party could terminate the employment relationship at any time. Niehaus made a written request for a nine months' leave, and her request was approved. At the end of her leave, however, Delaware Valley refused to rehire Niehaus for any position. Niehaus sued the medical center, claiming breach of contract and promissory estoppel. Will she win?

2. Johnson entered into a listing agreement with Maki to sell her home in Beach Park. On December 31, 1994, Johnson entered into a real estate contract with Ganley and Phillips (the buyers) to sell her home. The buyers deposited $2,000 in earnest money, which was held by Maki in an escrow account. The real estate contract provided that Maki would not disburse the earnest money unless it was provided a written demand to do so by *both* the buyers *and* the seller. Prior to closing, Johnson and the buyers could not reach agreement over which repairs Johnson would make to the home. The buyers declared that they would not go through with the purchase and asked for the immediate return of the earnest money. Johnson at first refused, but relented after several months of litigation. In October of 1995, Johnson sent a letter to Maki directing Maki to return the earnest money to the buyers. Maki refused, demanding that Johnson sign a document entitled "Cancellation Agreement For Contract to Purchase Real Estate" before it would return the earnest money. The cancellation agreement contained a general release provision which provided as follows:

> The Buyer and Seller shall indemnify, save, and hold harmless Broker and Broker's agents from all claims, litigations, judgments, and costs arising from the cancellation of the Contract.

Johnson signed the cancellation agreement. Several months later, though, she filed suit against Maki alleging that Maki had breached its fiduciary duty to her and caused her to lose rents, incur unnecessary repair and inspection expenses, and pay attorney fees in connection with the aborted sale. Maki contended that Johnson's action was barred by the release contained in the cancellation agreement, but Johnson contended that the release

was invalid because it was not supported by consideration. Is Maki's position correct?

3. In July of 1997, Roberts was working for the Tacoma Sabercats, a professional hockey team, when Dahl, the general manager of the Yakima Sundome, contacted him and asked if he would be interested in working for Central Washington Fair Association (CWFA) in a position as senior event coordinator of the Sundome. Roberts was interested and asked for a one-year employment guarantee. He received a letter from Dahl dated July 30, 1997, offering him the job and stating that "I cannot only guarantee you will be here at least one year, but I suspect you will be in Yakima for several years to come." Roberts accepted the position and resigned his job with the Tacoma Sabercats. Roberts went to Yakima to meet with Dahl and complete some employment paperwork. Dahl gave him several papers he needed to sign, including an employee handbook. Included in the handbook was a provision that stated:

> THE CONTENTS HEREOF DO NOT FORM A CONTRACT OF EMPLOYMENT, NOR SHOULD YOU HAVE ANY EXPECTATION THAT YOUR EMPLOYMENT IS FOR ANY SPECIFIC LENGTH OF TIME.
>
> To ensure that you are aware of our local safety and Ass'n rules, and acknowledge that there is no employment guarantee or contract, we ask that you sign the bottom of this page.

Roberts cursorily reviewed the handbook and signed the acknowledgment. He did not read it first and did not realize that it had anything to do with his one-year employment guarantee. Dahl had no intent to vary the nature of Robert's employment by having him sign the acknowledgment, and he was not aware of the at-will employment policy at that time. Roberts began working for the Sundome on August 26. During his employment, he received favorable performance evaluations. In October of 1997, Dahl resigned as general manager of the Sundome. CWFA fired Roberts on November 7. Did CWFA breach a contract with Roberts when it fired him before he had worked for an entire year?

4. In November 1972, when conditions in the steel industry were highly competitive and the industry was operating at about 70 percent of its capacity, Sharon Steel Corporation agreed to sell Roth Steel Products several types of steel at prices well below Sharon's published book prices for such steel. These prices were to be effective from January 1 until December 31, 1973. In early 1973, however, an attractive export market and increased domestic demand for steel caused the entire industry to operate at full capacity, and as a consequence, nearly every domestic steel producer experienced delays in delivery. On March 23, 1973, Sharon notified Roth that it was discontinuing all price discounts. Roth protested, and Sharon agreed to continue to sell at the discount price until June 30, 1973, but refused to sell thereafter unless Roth agreed to pay a modified price that was higher than that agreed to the previous November but still lower than the book prices Sharon was charging other customers. Because Roth was unable to purchase enough steel elsewhere to meet its production requirements, it agreed to pay the increased prices. When a subsequent dispute arose between the parties over late deliveries and unfilled orders by Sharon in 1974, Roth filed a breach of contract suit against Sharon, arguing, among other things, that the 1973 modification was unenforceable. Was it?

5. Approximately four years before his death, Dr. Martin Luther King, Jr., gave Boston University possession of some of his correspondence, manuscripts, and other papers. He did this pursuant to a letter, which read as follows:

> On this 16th day of July, 1964, I name the Boston University Library the Repository of my correspondence, manuscripts, and other papers, along with a few of my awards and other material which may come to be of interest in historical and other research.
>
> In accordance with this action I have authorized the removal of most of the above-mentioned papers and other objects to Boston University, including most correspondence through 1961, at once. It is my intention that after the end of each calendar year, similar files of materials for an additional year should be sent to Boston University.
>
> All papers and other objects which thus pass into the custody of Boston University remain my legal property until otherwise indicated, according to the statements below. However, if, despite scrupulous care, any such materials are damaged or lost while in custody of Boston University, I absolve Boston University of responsibility to me for such damage or loss.
>
> I intend each year to indicate a portion of the materials deposited with Boston University to become the absolute property of Boston University as an outright gift from me, until all shall have been thus given to the University. In the event of my death, all such materials deposited with the University shall become from that date the absolute property of Boston University.
>
> Sincerely,
> Martin Luther King, Jr.

Acting in her capacity as administrator of Dr. King's estate, his widow, Coretta Scott King, sued Boston University, alleging that the King Estate, not BU, owned the papers that had been housed in the BU Library's special collection since the 1964 delivery of them. BU contended that it owned them because Dr. King had made an enforceable charitable pledge to give them to BU. Was Dr. King's promise to give ownership of his papers to BU enforceable?

6. Smith hired Jones Construction to build a detached garage on her property according to certain specifications for $15,000. The contract called for Smith to pay Jones $5,000 "up front," to disburse an additional $7,000 at various stages of the construction, and to make a final payment of $3,000 at the completion of construction. Jones built the garage but Smith complained that Jones's workmanship was substandard and that Jones had failed to build the garage to the specifications provided in the contract. Smith refused to make the final $3,000 payment. After Jones threatened to sue Smith for the $3,000, the parties came to an agreement that Smith would pay Jones $1,500 and Jones would accept the $1,500 as full payment of the contract. Smith paid Jones $1,500, making clear that it was for full payment of the contract, and Jones accepted the payment. However, Jones continued to try to collect the additional $1,500 provided for in the original contract, and when Smith refused to pay it, ultimately filed suit against Smith in small claims court. Is Smith legally obligated to pay the additional $1,500?

7. Gorham was a store manager for LensCrafters earning $38,000 when he received a phone call from Benson Optical offering him a job. After an interview, he was offered the job of area manager for half of North Carolina plus stores in Kentucky and Florida for $50,000. Terms were discussed over the phone and he was told a confirming letter and packet would follow. When he received nothing, he phoned and was told they were in the mail, and that he should quit his job with LensCrafters, which he did. He declined further negotiations with LensCrafters, flew to Chicago at his own expense, and reported for a nationwide sales meeting, which was his first day of employment. At this meeting, Gorham was "reinterviewed" and then terminated. When he sued for breach of contract, Benson defended by arguing there was no consideration because the promise of employment was unenforceable. Gorham had been promised employment at will, which gave the employer the right to fire him at any time for any reason, including on his first day of work. Can Gorham enforce the promise under the doctrine of promissory estoppel?

8. Brads became pastor of the First Baptist Church in January 1958. In June 1971, Brads had a heart attack. While he was recuperating, an officer of the church told Brads that the church had voted to pay his full salary for the remainder of his lifetime. That promise was unperformed because Brads later recovered and returned to work. In April 1980, Brads again had heart problems. On the advice of his doctor, Brads approached the deacons of the church about retirement. Brads proposed that his salary be reduced after retirement through a series of gradual step-downs to an amount approximately one-third the salary he was then receiving. Brads's proposal was accepted by the deacons. Under the terms of the agreement, the church placed Brads on disability retirement status, conferred an honorary title on him, gave him office space in the church, and allotted him retirement benefits according to the step-down schedule. Brads was required to aid, assist, and advise whomever the church called as a new pastor, to the extent Brads's health would allow. Brads and the church deacons jointly recommended to the congregation that it adopt the agreement, which the congregation did, unanimously. Brads then left his position as pastor and his benefits commenced. In 1985, the congregation was advised by a church officer that the benefits paid to Brads under the 1980 agreement should continue for Brads's lifetime. The congregation once again unanimously approved and reaffirmed the agreement. Brads received his benefits from 1980 through early July 1990, when he was notified by church officials that he had been dismissed from the membership of the church and that no more payments would be made to him. Other benefits, such as free office space, were also discontinued. Brads sued the church, contending that it breached its contract. The church contended that there was no consideration to support its promise to pay retirement benefits to Brads for life. Is the church correct?

9. In June 1999, the Cunninghams entered into a contract with Crites for the construction of their home for a total purchase price of $105,000. The Cunninghams were to pay their own closing costs and receive a $30,000 credit at closing because they owned the land on which the home was constructed. According to the contract, the construction loan was for $75,000. In separate paragraphs, the contract provided that Crites would receive a builder's fee of $12,500 and set a closing date of no later than seven days after October 30, 1999. Construction, however, was not finished until February 2000. The parties met in late January 2000 to discuss closing the sale of the home and paying the outstanding bills, and a dispute arose concerning the $12,500 builder's fee. The parties agreed that the Cunninghams would pay $10,000 worth of outstanding bills for the home and Crites would drop his claim for a $12,500 builder's fee. Was this an enforceable accord and satisfaction?

10. Tinker Construction had a contract with Scroge to build a factory addition for Scroge by a particular date. The contract contained a penalty clause exacting daily penalties for late performance, and Tinker was working hard to complete the building on time. Because prompt completion of the addition was so important to Scroge, however, Scroge offered Tinker a bonus if it completed the factory addition on time. Scroge also learned that the supplier of parts for machinery that he had contracted for had called and said that it could not deliver the parts on Scroge's schedule for the price it had agreed to. Because there was no other supplier, Scroge promised to pay the requested higher price. The factory addition was completed on time and the parts arrived on time. Scroge then refused to pay both the bonus to Tinker and the higher price for the parts. Were these promises enforceable?

Online Research: Identifying Consideration on the Web

Browse various ads in online publications or commercial websites and identify the consideration that the advertiser is proposing to give and the consideration that it requests in return.

REALITY OF CONSENT

In August of 2002, Duncan went to Smith Motors to look for a used car to buy. He test-drove a 1995 Corvette with an odometer reading of 52,000. Duncan assumed that the heater worked, but he did not turn it on to test it because it was so hot outside. The salesperson assured him that the car was in "mint condition." Duncan decided to buy the car. He later learned that the heater was broken, the radio would not work, the car would not start when the temperature dropped below 40 degrees, and that the car really had 152,000—not 52,000—miles on it.

- *Can Duncan get out of this contract and get his money back?*
- *Did Smith Motors have a duty to disclose the defects in the car?*
- *Was the statement that the car was in "mint condition" a misrepresentation?*
- *Did Duncan have the obligation to investigate the car more thoroughly?*

IN A COMPLEX ECONOMY that depends on planning for the future, it is crucial that the law can be counted on to enforce contracts. In some situations, however, there are compelling reasons for permitting people to escape or *avoid* their contracts. An agreement obtained by force, trickery, unfair persuasion, or error is not the product of mutual and voluntary consent. A person who has made an agreement under these circumstances will be able to avoid it because his consent was not *real*.

This chapter discusses five doctrines that permit people to avoid their contracts because of the absence of real consent: misrepresentation, fraud, mistake, duress, and undue influence. Doctrines that involve similar considerations will be discussed in Chapter 14, Capacity to Contract, and in Chapter 15, Illegality.

Effect of Doctrines Discussed in This Chapter

Contracts induced by misrepresentation, fraud, mistake, duress, or undue influence are generally considered to be **voidable.** This means that the person whose consent was not real has the power to **rescind** (cancel) the contract. A person who rescinds a contract is entitled to the return of anything he gave the other party. By the same token, he must offer to return anything he has received from the other party.

Necessity for Prompt and Unequivocal Rescission

Suppose Johnson, who recently bought a car from Sims Motors, learns that Sims Motors made fraudulent statements to her to induce her to buy the car. She believes the contract was induced by fraud and wants to rescind it. How does she act to protect her rights? To rescind a contract based on fraud or any of the other doctrines discussed in this chapter, she must act promptly and unequivocally. She must object promptly upon learning the facts that give her the right to rescind and must clearly express her intent to cancel the contract. She must also avoid any behavior that would suggest that she affirms or **ratifies** the contract. (Ratification of a voidable contract means that a person who had the right to rescind has elected not to do so. Ratification ends the right to rescind.) This means that she should avoid unreasonable delay in notifying the other party of her rescission, because unreasonable delay communicates that she has ratified the contract. She should also avoid any conduct that would send a "mixed message," such as continuing to accept benefits from the other party or behaving in any other way that is inconsistent with her expressed intent to rescind.

Misrepresentation and Fraud

Relationship between Misrepresentation and Fraud

A misrepresentation is an assertion that is not in accord with the truth. When a person enters a contract because of his justifiable reliance on a misrepresentation about some important fact, the contract is voidable.

It is not necessary that the misrepresentation be intentionally deceptive. Misrepresentations can be either "innocent" (not intentionally deceptive) or "fraudulent" (made with knowledge of falsity and intent to deceive). A contract may be voidable even if the person making the misrepresentation believes in good faith that what he says is true. Either innocent misrepresentation or fraud gives the complaining party the right to rescind a contract.

Fraud is the type of misrepresentation that is committed knowingly, with the intent to deceive. The legal term for this knowledge of falsity, which distinguishes fraud from innocent misrepresentation, is **scienter.** A person making a misrepresentation would be considered to do so "knowingly" if she knew that her statement was false, if she knew that she did not have a basis for making the statement, or even if she just made the statement without being confident that it was true. The intent to deceive can be inferred from the fact that the defendant knowingly made a misstatement of fact to a person who was likely to rely on it.

As is true for innocent misrepresentation, the contract remedy for fraudulent misrepresentation is rescission. The tort liability of a person who commits fraud is different from that of a person who commits innocent misrepresentation, however. A person who commits fraud may be liable for damages, possibly including punitive damages, for the tort of **deceit.**[1] As you will learn in following sections, innocent misrepresentation and fraud share a common core of elements.

Election of Remedies In some states, a person injured by fraud cannot rescind the contract *and* sue for

damages for deceit; he must elect (choose) between these remedies. In other states, however, an injured party may pursue both rescission and damage remedies and does not have to elect between them.[2]

Requirements for Rescission on the Ground of Misrepresentation

The fact that one of the parties has made an untrue assertion does not in itself make the contract voidable. Courts do not want to permit people who have exercised poor business judgment or poor common sense to avoid their contractual obligations, nor do they want to grant rescission of a contract when there have been only minor and unintentional misstatements of relatively unimportant details. A drastic remedy such as rescission should be used only when a person has been seriously misled about a fact important to the contract by someone he had the right to rely on. A person seeking to rescind a contract on the ground of innocent or fraudulent misrepresentation must be able to establish each of the following elements:

1. An untrue assertion of fact was made.

2. The fact asserted was material *or* the assertion was fraudulent.

3. The complaining party entered the contract because of his reliance on the assertion.

4. The reliance of the complaining party was reasonable.

In tort actions in which the plaintiff is seeking to recover damages for deceit, the plaintiff would have to establish a *fifth* element: injury. He would have to prove that he had suffered actual economic injury because of his reliance on the fraudulent assertion. In cases in which the injured person seeks only rescission of the contract, however, proof of economic injury usually is not required.

Untrue Assertion of Fact To have misrepresentation, one of the parties must have made an untrue assertion of fact or engaged in some conduct that is the equivalent of an untrue assertion of fact. The fact asserted must be a *past or existing fact,* as distinguished from an opinion or a promise or prediction about some future happening.

The **concealment** of a fact through some active conduct intended to prevent the other party from discovering

---

[1]The tort of deceit is discussed in Chapter 6, Intentional Torts.

[2]Under every state's law, however, a person injured by fraud in a contract for the *sale of goods* can both rescind the contract and sue for damages. This is made clear by section 2–721 of the Uniform Commercial Code, which specifically states that no election of remedies is required in contracts for the sale of goods.

the fact is considered to be the equivalent of an assertion. Like a false statement of fact, concealment can be the basis for a claim of misrepresentation or fraud. For example, if Summers is offering his house for sale and paints the ceilings to conceal the fact that the roof leaks, his active concealment constitutes an assertion of fact.

Nondisclosure can also be the equivalent of an assertion of fact. Nondisclosure differs from concealment in that concealment involves the active hiding of a fact, while nondisclosure is the failure to volunteer information. Disclosure of a fact—even a fact that will harm the speaker's bargaining position—is required in a number of situations, such as when the person has already offered *some* information but further information is needed to give the other party an accurate picture, or when there is a relationship of trust and confidence between the parties. In recent years, courts and legislatures have tended to impose a duty to disclose when a party has access to information that is not readily available to the other party. This is consistent with modern contract law's emphasis on influencing ethical standards of conduct and achieving fair results. Transactions involving the sale of real estate are among the most common situations in which this duty to disclose arises. Most states now hold that a seller who knows about a latent (hidden) defect that materially affects the value of the property he is selling has the obligation to speak up about this defect. *Stambovsky v. Ackley,* which follows, involves an interesting application of the duty to disclose in the context of a sale of real estate.

Stambovsky v. Ackley   *572 N.Y.S.2d 672 (N.Y. Sup. Ct. App. Div. 1991)*

Jeffrey Stambovsky, a resident of New York City, contracted to purchase a house in the Village of Nyack, New York, from Helen Ackley. The house was widely reputed to be possessed by poltergeists, which Ackley and members of her family had reportedly seen. Ackley did not tell Stambovsky about the poltergeists before he bought the house. When Stambovsky learned of the house's reputation, however, he promptly commenced this action for rescission. The trial court dismissed his complaint, and Stambovsky appealed.

Rubin, Justice   The unusual facts of this case clearly warrant a grant of equitable relief to the buyer who, as a resident of New York City, cannot be expected to have any familiarity with the folklore of the Village of Nyack. Not being a "local," Stambovsky could not readily learn that the home he had contracted to purchase is haunted. Whether the source of the spectral apparitions seen by Ackley are parapsychic or psychogenic, having reported their presence in both a national publication (*Reader's Digest*) and the local press (in 1977 and 1982, respectively), Ackley is estopped to deny their existence and, as a matter of law, the house is haunted. More to the point, however, no divination is required to conclude that it is Ackley's promotional efforts in publicizing her close encounters with these spirits which fostered the home's reputation in the community. In 1989, the house was included in a five-home walking tour of Nyack and described in a November 27th newspaper article as a "riverfront Victorian (with ghost)." The impact of the reputation thus created goes to the very essence of the bargain between the parties, greatly impairing both the value of the property and its potential for resale.

[*The court discussed the fact that New York law does not recognize a remedy for damages incurred as a result of the seller's mere silence, applying instead the doctrine of* caveat emptor. *The court then proceeded to discuss the availability of rescission.*]

From the perspective of a person in the position of the plaintiff, a very practical problem arises with respect to the discovery of a paranormal phenomenon: "Who you gonna call?" as the title song to the movie *Ghostbusters* asks. Applying the strict rule of *caveat emptor* to a contract involving a house possessed by poltergeists conjures up visions of a psychic or medium routinely accompanying the structural engineer and Terminix man on an inspection of every home subject to a contract of sale. The doctrine of *caveat emptor* requires that a buyer act prudently to assess the fitness and value of his purchase. It should be apparent, however, that the most meticulous inspection and the search would not reveal the presence of poltergeists at the premises or unearth the property's ghoulish reputation in the community. Therefore, there is no sound policy reason to deny Stambovsky relief for failing to discover a state of affairs which the most prudent purchaser would not be expected to even contemplate.

Where a condition which has been created by the seller materially impairs the value of the contract and is peculiarly within the knowledge of the seller or unlikely to be discovered by a prudent purchaser exercising due care, nondisclosure constitutes a basis for rescission as a matter of equity. Any other outcome places upon the buyer not merely the obligation to exercise care in his purchase but rather to be omniscient with respect to any fact which may affect the bargain. No practical purpose is served by imposing such a burden upon a purchaser. To the contrary, it encourages predatory business practice and offends the principle that equity will suffer no wrong to be without a remedy.

In the case at bar, Ackley deliberately fostered the public belief that her home was possessed. Having undertaken to inform the public at large, to whom she has no legal relationship, about the supernatural occurrences on her property, she may be said to owe no less a duty to her contract vendee. Application of the remedy of rescission is entirely appropriate to relieve the unwitting purchaser from the consequences of a most unnatural bargain.

Judgment modified in favor of Stambovsky, reinstating his action seeking rescission of the contract.

Materiality If the misrepresentation was innocent, the person seeking to rescind the contract must establish that the fact asserted was **material.** A fact will be considered to be material if it is likely to play a significant role in inducing a reasonable person to enter the contract or if the person asserting the fact knows that the other person is likely to rely on the fact. For example, Rogers, who is trying to sell his car to Ferguson and knows that Ferguson idolizes professional bowlers, tells Ferguson that a professional bowler once rode in the car. Relying on that representation, Ferguson buys the car. Although the fact Rogers asserted might not be important to most people, it would be material here because Rogers knew that his representation would be likely to induce Ferguson to enter the contract.

Even if the fact asserted was not material, the contract may be rescinded if the misrepresentation was *fraudulent.* The rationale for this rule is that a person who fraudulently misrepresents a fact, even one that is not material under the standards previously discussed, should not be able to profit from his intentionally deceptive conduct.

Actual Reliance Reliance means that a person pursues some course of action because of his faith in an assertion made to him. For misrepresentation to exist, there must have been a causal connection between the assertion and the complaining party's decision to enter the contract. If the complaining party knew that the assertion was false or was not aware that an assertion had been made, there has been no reliance.

Justifiable Reliance Courts also scrutinize the reasonableness of the behavior of the complaining party by requiring that his reliance be *justifiable.* A person does not act justifiably if he relies on an assertion that is obviously false or not to be taken seriously.

One problem involving the justifiable reliance element is determining the extent to which the relying party is responsible for investigating the accuracy of the statement on which he relies. Classical contract law held that a person who did not attempt to discover readily discoverable facts generally was not justified in relying on the other party's statements about them. For example, under traditional law, a person would not be entitled to rely on the other party's assertions about facts that are a matter of public record or that could be discovered through a reasonable inspection of available documents or records. The extent of the responsibility placed on a relying party to conduct an independent investigation has declined in modern contract law, however. Today, a court might be more likely to follow the approach of section 172 of the *Restatement,* which provides that a relying party's failure to discover facts before entering the contract does not make his reliance unjustifiable unless the degree of his fault was so extreme as to amount to a failure to act in good faith and in accordance with reasonable standards of fair dealing. Thus, today's courts tend to place a greater degree of accountability on the person who makes the assertion rather than the person who relies on the assertion.

° LOG ON

A number of useful sites provide information about the nature of Internet fraud and how to reduce the chances of being victimized. Some even provide a method of reporting Internet fraud. Here are a few examples:
The Internet Fraud Complaint Center,
http://www1.ifccfbi.gov/index.asp,
National Internet Fraud Information Center,
http://www.fraud.org/,
U.S. Securities and Exchange Commission,
Internet Fraud: How to Avoid Internet Investment Scams,
http://www.sec.gov/investor/pubs/cyberfraud. htm.

CONCEPT REVIEW

Misrepresentation and Fraud

	Innocent Misrepresentation	**Fraud**
Remedy	Rescission	Rescission *and/or* tort action for damages
Elements	1. Untrue assertion of fact (or equivalent)	1. Untrue assertion of fact (or equivalent)
	2. Assertion relates to material fact	2. Assertion made with knowledge of falsity
	3. Actual reliance	(scienter) and intent to deceive
	4. Justifiable reliance	3. Actual reliance
		4. Justifiable reliance
		5. Economic loss (in a tort action for damages)

Mistake

Nature of Mistake

Anyone who enters a contract does so on the basis of his understanding of the facts that are relevant to the contract. His decision about what he is willing to exchange with the other party is based on this understanding. If the parties are wrong about an important fact, the exchange that they make is likely to be quite different than what they contemplated when they entered the contract, and this difference is due to simple error rather than to any external events such as an increase in market price. For example, Fox contracts to sell to Ward a half-carat stone, which both believe to be a tourmaline, at a price of $65. If they are wrong and the stone is actually a diamond worth at least $2,500, Fox will have suffered an unexpected loss and Ward will have reaped an unexpected gain. The contract would not have been made at a price of $65 if the parties' belief about the nature of the stone had been in accord with the facts. In such cases, the person adversely affected by the mistake can avoid the contract under the doctrine of mistake. The purpose of the doctrine of mistake is to prevent unexpected and unbargained for losses that result when the parties are mistaken about a fact central to their contract.

What Is a Mistake? In ordinary conversation, we may use the term *mistake* to mean an error in judgment or an unfortunate act. In contract law, however, a mistake is a *belief* about a fact that is *not in accord with the*

truth.[3] The mistake must relate to facts as they exist at the time the contract is created. An erroneous belief or prediction about facts that might occur in the future would not qualify as a mistake.

As in misrepresentation cases, the complaining party in a mistake case enters a contract because of a belief that is at variance with the actual facts. Mistake is unlike misrepresentation, however, in that the erroneous belief is not the result of the other party's untrue statements.

Mistakes of Law A number of the older mistake cases state that mistake about a principle of law will not justify rescission. The rationale for this view was that everyone was presumed to know the law. More modern cases, however, have granted relief even when the mistake is an erroneous belief about some aspect of law.

Negligence and the Right to Avoid for Mistake Although courts sometimes state that relief will not be granted when a person's mistake was caused by his own negligence, they often have granted rescission even when the mistaken party was somewhat negligent. Section 157 of the *Restatement (Second) of Contracts* focuses on the *degree* of a party's negligence in making the mistake. It states that a person's fault in failing to know or discover facts before entering the contract will not bar relief unless his fault amounted to a failure to act in good faith.

---

[3]*Restatement (Second) of Contracts* § 151.

Effect of Mistake The mere fact that the contracting parties have made a mistake is not, standing alone, a sufficient ground for avoidance of the contract. The right to avoid a contract because of mistake depends on several factors that are discussed in following sections. One important factor that affects the right to avoid is whether the mistake was made by just one of the parties (**unilateral mistake**) or by both parties (**mutual mistake**).

Mutual Mistakes in Drafting Writings Sometimes, mutual mistake takes the form of erroneous *expression* of an agreement, frequently caused by a clerical error in drafting or typing a contract, deed, or other document. In such cases, the remedy is *reformation* of the writing rather than avoidance of the contract. Reformation means modification of the written instrument to express the agreement that the parties made but failed to express correctly. Suppose Arnold agrees to sell Barber a vacant lot next to Arnold's home. The vacant lot is "Lot 3, block 1"; Arnold's home is on "Lot 2, block 1." The person typing the contract strikes the wrong key, and the contract reads, "Lot 2, block 1." Neither Arnold nor Barber notices this error when they read and sign the contract, yet clearly they did not intend to have Arnold sell the lot on which his house stands. In such a case, a court will reform the contract to conform to Arnold and Baker's true agreement.

Requirements for Mutual Mistake

A mutual mistake exists when both parties to the contract have erroneous assumptions about the same fact. When *both* parties are mistaken, the resulting contract can be avoided if the three following elements are present:

1. The mistake relates to a basic assumption on which the contract was made.
2. The mistake has a material effect on the agreed-upon exchange.
3. The party adversely affected by the mistake does not bear the risk of the mistake.[4]

Mistake about a Basic Assumption Even if the mistake is mutual, the adversely affected party will not have the right to avoid the contract unless the mistake concerns a basic assumption on which the contract was based. Assumptions about the identity, existence, qual-

ity, or quantity of the subject matter of the contract are among the basic assumptions on which contracts typically are founded. It is not necessary that the parties be consciously aware of the assumption; an assumption may be so basic that they take it for granted. For example, if Peterson contracts to buy a house from Tharp, it is likely that both of them assume at the time of contracting that the house is in existence and that it is legally permissible for the house to be used as a residence.

An assumption would not be considered a basic assumption if it concerns a matter that bears an indirect or collateral relationship to the subject matter of the contract. For example, mistakes about matters such as a party's financial ability or market conditions usually would not give rise to avoidance of the contract.

Material Effect on Agreed-Upon Exchange It is not enough for a person claiming mistake to show that the exchange is something different from what he expected. He must show that the imbalance caused by the mistake is so severe that it would be unfair for the law to require him to perform the contract. He will have a better chance of establishing this element if he can show not only that the contract is *less* desirable for him because of the mistake but also that the other party has received an unbargained-for advantage.

Party Harmed by Mistake Did Not Bear the Risk of Mistake Even if the first two elements are present, the person who is harmed by the mistake cannot avoid the contract if he is considered to bear the risk of mistake.[5] Courts have the power to allocate the risk of a mistake to the adversely affected person whenever it is reasonable under the circumstances to do so.

One situation in which an adversely affected person would bear the risk of mistake is when he has expressly contracted to do so. For example, if Buyer contracted to accept property "as is," he may be considered to have accepted the risk that his assumption about the quality of the property may be erroneous.

The adversely affected party also bears the risk of mistake when he contracts with *conscious awareness* that he is ignorant or has limited information about a fact—in other words, he *knows that he does not know* the true state of affairs about a particular fact but he binds himself to perform anyway. Suppose someone gives you an old, locked safe. Without trying to open it, you sell it and "all of its contents" to one of your friends for $25.

---

[4]*Restatement (Second) of Contracts* § 152.

[5]*Restatement (Second) of Contracts* § 154.

When your friend succeeds in opening the safe, he finds $10,000 in cash. In this case, you would not be able to rescind the contract because, in essence, you gambled on your limited knowledge . . . and lost. *Estate of Nelson v. Rice,* which follows, illustrates the effect of conscious awareness and contractual assignments of risk.

Estate of Nelson v. Rice   *12 P.3d 238 (Ariz. Ct. App. 2000)*

Martha Nelson died in 1996 and Kenneth Newman and Edward Franz were appointed co-personal representatives of her estate. Newman and Franz hired Judith McKenzie-Larson to appraise the estate's personal property in preparation for an estate sale. McKenzie-Larson told them that she did not appraise fine art, and that if she saw any, they would need to hire an additional appraiser. McKenzie-Larson did not report finding any fine art, and relying on her silence and her appraisal, Newman and Franz priced the personal property and held an estate sale.

Carl Rice responded to the newspaper advertisement for the sale and attended it. At the sale he bought two oil paintings, paying the asking price of $60 for the two paintings. Rice had bought and sold some art, but he was not an educated purchaser, had never made more than $55 on any single piece, and had bought many pieces that turned out to be frauds, forgeries, or the work of lesser artists. Rice assumed that the paintings were not originals, given their price and the fact that the estate was managed by professionals. At home, he compared the signatures on the paintings to those in a book of artists' signatures, noticing that they appeared to be similar to that of Martin Johnson Heade. As they had done in the past, Rice and his wife sent pictures of the paintings to Christie's in New York, hoping that they might be Heade's work. Christie's authenticated the paintings, Magnolia Blossoms on Blue Velvet *and* Cherokee Roses, *as paintings by Heade and offered to sell them on consignment. Christie's subsequently sold the paintings at auction for $1,072,000. After subtracting the buyer's premium and the commission, the Rices realized $911,780 from the sale.*

Newman and Franz learned about the sale in February 1997 and sued McKenzie-Larson on behalf of the Estate, believing that she was responsible for the estate's loss. The following November, they settled the lawsuit because McKenzie-Larson had no assets. In January 1998, the estate sued the Rices, alleging that the sale contract should be rescinded or reformed because of mistake and unconscionability. The estate moved for summary judgment, arguing that the parties were not aware that the transaction had involved fine art, believing instead that the paintings were relatively valueless decorations. The Rices filed a cross-motion for summary judgment arguing that the estate bore the risk of the mistake. The trial court denied the estate's motion for summary judgment and granted the Rices' cross-motion. The estate's motion for a new trial was denied, and the estate appealed.

ESPINOSA, Chief Judge A contract may be rescinded on the ground of mutual mistake as to a basic assumption on which both parties made the contract. Furthermore, the parties' mutual mistake must have had such a material effect on the agreed exchange of performances as to upset the very bases of the contract. However, the mistake must not be one on which the party seeking relief bears the risk under the rules stated in § 154(b) of the Restatement. In concluding that the estate was not entitled to rescind the sale, the trial court found that, although a mistake had existed as to the value of the paintings, the estate bore the risk of that mistake under §154(b) of the Restatement. Section 154(b) states that a party bears the risk of mistake when he is aware, at the time the contract is made, that he has only limited knowledge with respect to the facts to which the mistake relates but treats his limited knowledge as sufficient. In explaining that provision, the Washington Supreme Court stated, "In such a situation there is no mistake. Instead, there is an awareness of uncertainty or conscious ignorance of the future."

The estate contends neither party bore the risk of mistake. Through its personal representatives, the estate hired two appraisers, McKenzie-Larson and an Indian art expert, to evaluate the estate's collection of Indian art and artifacts. McKenzie-Larson specifically told Newman that she did not appraise fine art. In his deposition, Newman testified that he had not been concerned that McKenzie-Larson had no expertise in fine art, believing the estate contained nothing of "significant value" except the house and the Indian art collection. Despite the knowledge that the estate contained framed art other than the Indian art, and that McKenzie-Larson was not qualified to appraise fine art, the personal representatives relied on her to notify them of any fine art or whether a fine arts appraiser was needed. Because McKenzie-Larson did not say they needed an additional appraiser, Newman and Franz did not hire anyone qualified to appraise fine art. By relying on the opinion of someone who was admittedly unqualified to appraise fine art to determine its existence, the personal representatives consciously ignored the possibility that the estate's assets might include fine art, thus assuming that risk. See *Klas v. Van Wagoner* (real estate buyers not entitled to rescind sale contract because they bore risk of mistake as to property's value; by hiring architects, decorators, and electricians to examine realty, but failing to have it appraised, purchasers executed sale contract knowing they had only limited knowledge with respect to the value of the home). Accordingly, the trial court correctly found that the estate bore the risk of mistake as to the paintings' value.

The estate asserts that the facts here are similar to those in *Renner [v. Kehl]*, in which real estate buyers sued to rescind a contract for acreage upon which they wished to commercially grow jojoba after discovering the water supply was inadequate for that purpose. The Supreme Court concluded that the buyers could rescind the contract based upon mutual mistake because both the buyers and the sellers had believed there was an adequate water supply, a basic assumption underlying formation of the contract. The parties' failure to thoroughly investigate the water supply did not preclude rescission when the risk of mistake was not allocated among the parties. The estate's reliance on *Renner* is unavailing because, as stated above, the estate bore the risk of mistake based on its own conscious ignorance.

Furthermore, under Restatement § 154(c), the court may allocate the risk of mistake to one party "on the ground that it is reasonable in the circumstances to do so." In making this determination, "the court will consider the purposes of the parties and will have recourse to its own general knowledge of human behavior in bargain transactions." Here, the estate had had ample opportunity to discover what it was selling and failed to do so; instead, it ignored the possibility that the paintings were valuable and attempted to take action only after learning of their worth as a result of the efforts of the Rices. Under these circumstances, the estate was a victim of its own folly and it was reasonable for the court to allocate to it the burden of its mistake.

Affirmed in favor of the Rices.

Requirements for Unilateral Mistake

A unilateral mistake exists when only one of the parties makes a mistake about a basic assumption on which he made the contract. For example, Plummer contracts to buy from Taylor 25 shares of Worthwright Enterprises, Inc., mistakenly believing that he is buying 25 shares of the much more valuable Worthwrite Industries. Taylor knows that the contract is for the sale of shares of Worthwright. Taylor (the "nonmistaken party") is correct in his belief about the identity of the stock he is selling; only Plummer (the "mistaken party") is mistaken in his assumption about the identity of the stock. Does Plummer's unilateral mistake give him the right to avoid the contract? Courts are more likely to allow avoidance of a contract when both parties are mistaken than when only one is mistaken. The rationale for this tendency is that in cases of unilateral mistake, at least one party's assumption about the facts was correct, and allowing avoidance disappoints the reasonable expectations of that nonmistaken party.

It is possible to avoid contracts for unilateral mistake, but to do so, proving the elements necessary for mutual mistake is just a starting point. *In addition to* proving the elements of mistake discussed earlier, a person trying to avoid on the ground of unilateral mistake must show *either* one of the following:

1. *The nonmistaken party caused or had reason to know of the mistake.* Courts permit avoidance in cases of unilateral mistake if the nonmistaken party caused the mistake, knew of the mistake, or even if the mistake was so obvious that the nonmistaken party had reason to realize that a mistake had been made.[6] For example, Ace Electrical Company makes an error when preparing a bid that it submits to Gorge General Contracting. If the mistake in Ace's bid was so obvious that Gorge knew about it when it accepted Ace's offer, Ace could avoid the contract even though Ace is the only party who was mistaken. The reasoning behind this rule is that the nonmistaken person could have prevented the loss by acting in good faith and informing the person in error that he had made a mistake. It also reflects the judgment that people should not take advantage of the mistakes of others. *Or*

2. *It would be unconscionable to enforce the contract.* A court could also permit avoidance because of unilateral mistake when the effect of the mistake was such that it would be unconscionable to enforce the contract. To show that it would be unconscionable to enforce the contract, the mistaken party would have to show that the consequences of the mistake were severe enough that it would be unreasonably harsh or oppressive to enforce

---

[6]*Restatement (Second) of Contracts* § 153.

CONCEPT REVIEW

Avoidance on the Ground of Mistake

	Mutual Mistake	Unilateral Mistake
Description	Both parties mistaken about same fact	Only one party mistaken about a fact
Needed for Avoidance of Contract	Elements of mistake: 1. Mistake about basic assumption on which contract was made 2. Material effect on agreed exchange 3. Person adversely affected by mistake does not bear the risk of the mistake	Same elements as mutual mistake *Plus* *a.* Nonmistaken party caused mistake or had reason to know of mistake *Or* *b.* Effect of mistake is to make it unconscionable to enforce contract

the contract.[7] In the example above, Ace Electrical Company made an error when preparing a bid that it submits to Gorge General Contracting. Suppose that Gorge had no reason to realize that a mistake had been made, and accepted the bid. Ace might show that it would be unconscionable to enforce the contract by showing that not only will its profit margin not be what Ace contemplated when it made its offer, but also that it would suffer a grave loss by having to perform at the mistaken price.

---

[7]The concept of unconscionability is developed more fully in Chapter 15.

CYBERLAW IN ACTION

Pricing Glitches on the Web: Legal, Ethical, and Marketing Issues

The accidental advertisement of a mistaken price for a product or service occurs sometimes in bricks-and-mortar businesses. But when e-tailers make price glitches, the impact is likely to be far greater, because news of extremely low prices travels fast on the Web through various bargain hunter websites and online bulletin boards, and by the time the company learns of and repairs the error, it may have confirmed hundreds of orders for the product or service. Amazon.com, United Air Lines, and Staples.com are a few of the e-commerce leaders that have experienced pricing glitches. In one widely reported incident, for example, United Air Lines's website accidentally listed mistaken fares to Paris and various other cities—$24.98 for a flight from San Francisco to Paris—for five hours on one day, and in that time, more than 140 people had booked trips based on the mistaken fares.[8]

Legally, the doctrine of mistake presents at least a possible avenue for avoidance of contracts that are formed based on a mistaken price, but this would depend on factors such as the size and obviousness of the discrepancy between the mistaken price and the intended price. Of equal or greater concern to the e-tailer is likely to be the issue of how to maintain good customer relations. Should it sell the product at the advertised price and absorb the loss? Refuse to honor the mistaken deal and perhaps offer the customer something else of value to preserve goodwill? Some commercial websites have a provision in their "Terms and Conditions" link that notifies customers of the possibility of pricing mistakes and purports to protect the company in cases of price glitches.

Ethical issues are also present in these situations. Is it ethical for an e-tailer to refuse to honor a contract that is based on a mistaken price? Is it ethical for a customer to insist on a contract that is based on a mistaken price?

---

[8]Frank Hayes, *A Deal's a Deal: Should Pricing Glitches Be Honored?, Computerworld* 2/26/01, http://www.itworld.com/Tech/2403/ CWSTO58053

LOG ON

For a lively discussion of some famous mistake cases in contract law, see Ron Kilgard, *Mistake in the Law of Contracts and in Translation,* http://www.dgsk.com/DOC/MISTAK~1.HTM.

Duress

Nature of Duress

Duress is wrongful coercion that induces a person to enter or modify a contract. One kind of duress is physical compulsion to enter a contract. For example, Thorp overpowers Grimes, grasps his hand, and forces him to sign a contract. This kind of duress is rare, but when it occurs, a court would find that the contract was **void.** A far more common type of duress occurs when a person is induced to enter a contract by a *threat* of physical, emotional, or economic harm. In these cases, the contract is considered *voidable* at the option of the victimized person. This is the form of duress addressed in this chapter.

The elements of duress have undergone dramatic changes. Classical contract law took a very narrow view of the type of coercion that constituted duress, limiting duress to threats of imprisonment or serious physical harm. Today, however, courts take a much broader view of the types of coercion that will constitute duress. For example, modern courts recognize that threats to a person's economic interests can be duress.

Requirements for Duress

To rescind a contract because of duress, one must be able to establish both of the following elements:

1. The contract was induced by an improper threat.
2. The victim had no reasonable alternative but to enter the contract.

Improper Threat It would not be desirable for courts to hold that every kind of threat constituted duress. If they did, the enforceability of all contracts would be in question, because every contract negotiation involves at least the implied threat that a person will not enter into the transaction unless her demands are met. What degree of wrongfulness, then, is required for a threat to constitute duress? Traditionally, a person would have to threaten to do something she was not legally entitled to do—such as threaten to commit a crime or a tort—for that threat to be duress. Some

courts still follow that rule. Other courts today follow the *Restatement* position that, to be duress, the threat need not be wrongful or illegal but must be *improper*—that is, improper to use as leverage to induce a contract.

Under some circumstances, threats to institute legal actions can be considered improper threats that will constitute duress. A threat to file either a civil or a criminal suit without a legal basis for doing so would clearly be improper. What of a threat to file a well-founded lawsuit or prosecution? Generally, if there is a good faith dispute over a matter, a person's threat to file a lawsuit to resolve that dispute is *not* considered to be improper. Otherwise, every person who settled a suit out of court could later claim duress. However, if the threat to sue is made in bad faith and for a purpose unrelated to the issues in the lawsuit, the threat can be considered improper. In one case, for example, duress was found when a husband who was in the process of divorcing his wife threatened to sue for custody of their children—something he had the right to do—unless the wife transferred to him stock that she owned in his company.[9]

Victim Had No Reasonable Alternative The person complaining of duress must be able to prove that the coercive nature of the improper threat was such that he had no reasonable alternative but to enter or modify the contract. Classical contract law applied an objective standard of coercion, which required that the degree of coercion exercised had to be sufficient to overcome the will of a person of ordinary courage. The more modern standard for coercion focuses on the alternatives open to the complaining party. For example, Barry, a traveling salesman, takes his car to Cheatum Motors for repair. Barry pays Cheatum the full amount previously agreed upon for the repair, but Cheatum refuses to return Barry's car to him unless Barry agrees to pay substantially more than the contract price for the repairs. Because of his urgent need for the return of his car, Barry agrees to do this. In this case, Barry technically had the alternative of filing a legal action to recover his car. However, this would not be a *reasonable alternative* for someone who needs the car urgently because of the time, expense, and uncertainty involved in pursuing a lawsuit. Thus, Barry could avoid his agreement to pay more money under a theory of duress.

Economic Duress

Today, the doctrine of duress is often applied in a business context. *Economic duress,* or *business compulsion,*

---

[9]*Link v. Link,* 179 S.E.2d 697 (1971).

are terms commonly used to describe situations in which one person induces the formation or modification of a contract by threatening another person's economic interests. A common coercive strategy is to threaten to breach the contract unless the other party agrees to modify its terms. For example, Moore, who has contracted to sell goods to Stephens, knows that Stephens needs timely delivery of the goods. Moore threatens to withhold delivery unless Stephens agrees to pay a higher price. Another common situation involving economic duress occurs when one of the parties offers a disproportionately small amount of money in settlement of a debt and refuses to pay more. Such a strategy exerts great economic pressure on a creditor who is in a desperate financial situation to accept the settlement because he cannot afford the time and expense of bringing a lawsuit.

Classical contract law did not recognize economic duress because this type of hard bargaining was considered neither improper nor coercive. After all, the victim of the sorts of economic pressure described above had at least the theoretical right to file a lawsuit to enforce his rights under the contract. Modern courts recognize that improper economic pressure can prevent a resulting contract or contract modification from being truly voluntary, and the concept of economic duress is well accepted today.

Undue Influence

Nature of Undue Influence

Undue influence is unfair persuasion. Like duress, undue influence involves wrongful pressure exerted on a person during the bargaining process. In undue influence, however, the pressure is exerted through *persuasion* rather than through coercion. The doctrine of undue influence was developed to give relief to persons who are unfairly persuaded to enter a contract while in a position of weakness that makes them particularly vulnerable to being preyed upon by those they trust or fear. A large proportion of undue influence cases arise after the death of the person who has been the subject of undue influence, when his relatives seek to set aside that person's contracts or wills.

Determining Undue Influence

All contracts are based on persuasion. There is no precise dividing line between permissible persuasion and impermissible persuasion. Nevertheless, several hallmarks of undue influence cases can be identified. Undue influence cases normally involve both of the following elements:

1. The relationship between the parties is either one of trust and confidence or one in which the person exercising the persuasion dominates the person being persuaded.

2. The persuasion is unfair.[10]

Relation between the Parties Undue influence cases involve people who, though they have capacity to enter a contract, are in a position of particular vulnerability in relationship to the other party to the contract. This relationship can be one of trust and confidence, in which the person being influenced justifiably believes that the other party is looking out for his interests, or at least that he would not do anything contrary to his welfare. Examples of such relationships would include parent and child, husband and wife, or lawyer and client.

The relationship also can be one in which one of the parties holds dominant psychological power that is not derived from a confidential relationship. For example, Royce, an elderly man, is dependent on his housekeeper, Smith, to care for him. Smith persuades Royce to withdraw most of his life savings from the bank and make an interest-free loan to her. If the persuasion Smith used was unfair, the transaction could be avoided because of undue influence.

Unfair Persuasion The mere existence of a close or dependent relationship between the parties that results in economic advantage to one of them is not sufficient for undue influence. It must also appear that the weaker person entered the contract because he was subjected to unfair methods of persuasion. In determining this, a court will look at all of the surrounding facts and circumstances. Was the person isolated and rushed into the contract, or did he have access to outsiders for advice and time to consider his alternatives? Was the contract discussed and consummated in the usual time and place that would be expected for such a transaction, or was it discussed or consummated at an unusual time or in an unusual place? Was the contract a reasonably fair one that a person might have entered voluntarily, or was it so lopsided and unfair that one could infer that he probably would not have entered it unless he had been unduly influenced by the other party? The answers to these and similar questions help determine whether the line between permissible and impermissible persuasion has been crossed. The following *Goldman* case provides an example of the factors that courts consider in determining undue influence.

---

[10]*Restatement (Second) of Contracts* § 177.

Goldman v. Bequai   *19 F.3d 666 (D.C. Cir. 1994)*

Florence Goldman was a woman in her 80s whose husband died after a long bout with Alzheimer's and Parkinson's diseases. For several years prior to her husband's death, Goldman had cared for him at home. During much of her husband's illness and for some time afterward, she was under the care of a psychiatrist, who treated her for depression stemming from the strain and grief she experienced because of her husband's declining health. August Bequai was an attorney and a long-time friend whom Goldman regarded as almost a member of her family. After the death of Goldman's husband, she looked to Bequai as her adviser and attorney in financial affairs.

Goldman, her son, and Bequai discussed starting a business that would employ both Goldman and her son. According to Goldman and her son, Bequai had told them that he needed to be listed as an owner of property that Goldman owned on Massachusetts Avenue in Washington, D.C., in order adequately to represent the Goldmans' interests during negotiations over the property. Bequai allegedly told Goldman's son that the transfer would be temporary and solely for the limited purpose of inflating his financial worth on paper while he looked for a business to invest in. In January 1986, three months after her husband's death, Goldman conveyed to Bequai joint tenancy with a right of survivorship (a form of joint ownership) in her condominium in Bethesda, Maryland, and a partnership interest in the Massachusetts Avenue property, for $10 consideration for the transfer of each property.

Goldman had no legal counsel or independent advice of any sort, and she alleges that Bequai did not fully explain the nature of the transactions to her. There were no witnesses to the transactions other than the notary. The Massachusetts Avenue property was sold in 1990 and the proceeds attributed to the Goldman/Bequai partnership were distributed to them. Both Bequai and Goldman were represented at the closing by an attorney hired by Bequai. After the sale of the property, Bequai accompanied Goldman to the bank, where both placed their proceeds in investment accounts that were opened that day. Bequai placed his money in an account he owned jointly with his wife, whereas Goldman placed her share in a joint account with Bequai.

Eventually, Goldman came to feel that Bequai had "deceived" her. In 1991, she brought several claims against Bequai, including fraud and breach of fiduciary duty. The trial court granted a summary judgment for Bequai on the ground that the three-year statute of limitations had run on Goldman's claim. Goldman appealed this ruling, arguing in part that the statute of limitations should be equitably tolled (that is, that time for filing suit should be extended) because Bequai had exercised undue influence on her.

Edwards, Circuit Judge Goldman argued directly and unequivocally that Bequai obtained a joint tenancy in her real estate holdings through the exercise of undue influence over her. Undue influence is a contract doctrine which serves to equitably toll the statute of limitations.

Situations amounting to undue influence may be found when "a party in whom another reposes confidence misuses that confidence to gain his own advantage while the other has been made to feel that the party in question will not act against his welfare." SAMUEL WILLISTON, 13 WILLISTON ON CONTRACTS section 1625 at 776–77.

Whether a plaintiff is subject to undue influence is a question of fact. Both Williston and the *Restatement (Second) of Contracts* agree that the alleged victim's advanced age, mental condition and poor health, as well as the consideration a defendant gave for the benefit conferred by a plaintiff, are factors to be considered in establishing undue influence. Although the District Court made much of the fact that Goldman's psychiatrist stated that she was not mentally *incompetent*, this fact is hardly dispositive of the undue influence

issue. Indeed, Williston specifically states that "[u]ndue influence in its essential elements has no real relation to mental incapacity." 13 WILLISTON section 1625 at 782.

It is a matter of basic contract law that if a plaintiff proves undue influence, the statute of limitations is equitably tolled so long as the influence continues. Goldman has alleged facts which a reasonable jury could find to constitute undue influence. She has suggested that her age, her lack of business experience, her long friendship with and reliance on Bequai, and her mental condition all made her susceptible to Bequai's manipulation. In addition, Goldman argues that Bequai was acting as her attorney, and that he accordingly had both additional influence over her and additional obligations to see to her welfare. Goldman also points to the paltry consideration she received for the enormous benefit she conferred on Bequai. These factors, if proven at trial, have the makings of a classic case of undue influence.

Reversed and remanded for further proceedings in favor of Goldman.

CONCEPT REVIEW

Wrongful Pressure in the Bargaining Process

	Duress	Undue Influence
Nature of Pressure	Coercion	Unfair persuasion of susceptible individual
Elements	1. Contract induced by improper threat	1. Relationship of trust and confidence or dominance
	2. Threat leaves party no reasonable alternative but to enter or modify contract	2. Unfair persuasion

Problems and Problem Cases

1. Mestrovic, the widow of an internationally known sculptor and artist, owned a large number of works of art created by her late husband. Mestrovic died, leaving a will in which she directed that all the works of art created by her husband were to be sold and the proceeds distributed to surviving members of the Mestrovic family. Mestrovic also owned real estate at the time of her death. 1st Source Bank, as the personal representative of the Mestrovic estate, entered into a contract to sell this real estate to the Wilkins. After taking possession of the property, the Wilkins complained to the bank that the property was left in a cluttered condition and would require substantial cleaning efforts. The trust officer of the bank offered the Wilkins two options: Either the bank would get a rubbish removal service to clean the property or the Wilkins could clean the property and keep any items of personal property they wanted. The Wilkins opted to clean the property themselves. At the time these arrangements were made, neither the bank nor the Wilkins suspected that any works of art remained on the property. During the cleanup efforts, the Wilkins found eight drawings apparently created by Mestrovic's husband. They also found a plaster sculpture of the figure of Christ with three small children. The Wilkins claimed ownership of these works of art by virtue of their agreement with the bank. The bank claimed that there was no agreement for the sale of the artwork and that there had been mutual mistake. Is the bank correct?

2. In April of 1978 and April of 1981, Wayne Carpenter entered into two separate purchases of land from an agency of the State of Alaska. The land sale contracts for both transactions contained the same disclaimer:

The Seller makes no warranty, express or implied, nor assumes any liability whatever, regarding the social, economic, or environmental aspects of the Parcel, to include, without limitation, the soil conditions, water drainage, or natural or artificial hazards.

The contracts also disclaimed any guaranty of profitability. In addition, the contracts included farm conservation or development plans, requiring the buyer to improve and develop the land as a working farm. In 1980 and 1983, Carpenter borrowed money from the Agricultural Revolving Loan Fund (ARLF), a state agency created to lend money to farmers to help them develop their land. Carpenter made repeated efforts over the years to plant, but these efforts were unsuccessful. In 1987, Carpenter abandoned efforts to farm the land. The land was reclassified as unsuitable for agriculture. Carpenter ceased making payments toward his ARLF loans. ARLF filed an action for damages, repossession, and foreclosure. Carpenter claimed he was excused from performing the contracts because of mutual mistake and misrepresentation, among other reasons. Are these good arguments in this case?

3. The Verbas sold the Rancourts a lakeshore lot in North Hero, Vermont, for $115,000. The Verbas knew that the Rancourts intended to build a residence on the lot in close proximity to the lakeshore. The Rancourts prepared the lakeshore building site by adding fill, but because this site preparation was done without permits, it violated state and federal wetland regulations. They were later ordered to remove all fill placed on the building site. On learning that they could not build near the lake, the Rancourts demanded that the Verbas rescind the transaction, refund the purchase price, and pay damages. The

Verbas refused and the Rancourts brought a rescission action based on mutual mistake. Will they win?

4. Odorizzi, an elementary school teacher, was arrested on criminal charges involving illegal sexual activity. After he was arrested, questioned by police, booked, and released on bail, and had gone 40 hours without sleep, he was visited in his home by the superintendent of the school district and the principal of his school. They told him that they were trying to help him and that they had his best interests at heart. They advised him to resign immediately, stating that there was no time to consult an attorney. They said that if he did not resign immediately, the district would dismiss him and publicize the proceedings, but that if he resigned at once, the incident would not be publicized and would not jeopardize his chances of securing employment as a teacher elsewhere. Odorizzi gave them a written letter of resignation, which they accepted. The criminal charges against Odorizzi were later dismissed, and he sought to resume his employment. When the school district refused to reinstate him, Odorizzi attempted to rescind his letter of resignation on several grounds, including undue influence. (He also alleged duress, but the facts of his case did not constitute duress under applicable state law.) Can Odorizzi avoid the contract on the ground of undue influence?

5. The Walkers owned property in Eagle River, Alaska. In 1976, they listed the property for sale with a real estate broker. They signed a multiple listing agreement, which described the property as having 580 feet of highway frontage and stated, "ENGINEER REPORT SAYS OVER 1 MILLION IN GRAVEL ON PROP." A later listing contract signed with the same broker described the property as having 580 feet of highway frontage, but listed the gravel content as "minimum 80,000 cubic yds of gravel." An appraisal prepared to determine the property's value stated that it did not take any gravel into account, but described the ground as "all good gravel base." Cousineau, a contractor who was also in the gravel extraction business, became aware of the property when he saw the multiple listing. After visiting the property with his real estate broker and discussing gravel extraction with Mr. Walker, Cousineau offered to purchase the property. He then attempted to determine the lot's road frontage but was unsuccessful because the property was covered with snow. He was also unsuccessful in obtaining the engineer's report allegedly showing "over 1 million in gravel." Walker admitted at trial that he had never seen a copy of the report, either. Nevertheless, the parties signed and consummated a contract of sale for the purchase price of $385,000. There was no reference to the amount of highway frontage in the purchase agreement. After the sale was completed, Cousineau began developing the property and removing gravel. Cousineau learned that the description of highway frontage contained in the real estate listing was incorrect when a neighbor threatened to sue him for removing gravel from the neighbor's adjacent lot. A subsequent survey revealed that the highway frontage was 410 feet—not 580 feet, as advertised. At about the same time, the gravel ran out after Cousineau had removed only 6,000 cubic yards. Cousineau stopped making payments and informed the Walkers of his intention to rescind the contract. Cousineau brought an action against the Walkers, seeking the return of his money. Does Cousineau have the right to rescind?

6. Boskett, a part-time coin dealer, paid $450 for a dime purportedly minted in 1916 at Denver and two additional coins of relatively small value. After carefully examining the dime, Beachcomber Coins, a retail coin dealer, bought the coin from Boskett for $500. Beachcomber then received an offer from a third party to purchase the dime for $700, subject to certification of its genuineness from the American Numismatic Society. That organization labeled the coin a counterfeit. Can Beachcomber rescind the contract with Boskett on the ground of mistake?

7. Retailer opened a baseball card store in vacant premises next to an existing store. The card shop was very busy on opening day, so Retailer got a clerk from the adjacent store to help out. The clerk knew nothing about baseball cards. A boy who had a large baseball card collection asked to see an Ernie Banks rookie card, which was in a plastic case with an adhesive dot attached that read "1200." The boy asked the salesclerk, "Is it really worth $12?" The salesclerk responded, "I guess so," or "I'm sure it is." The boy bought the card for $12. In fact, the true price intended by Retailer was $1,200. Can Retailer get the card back from the boy?

8. The Cablers went to Oakwood Mobile Homes lot to shop for a manufactured home. They met Patton, a salesperson, who showed them several homes. They ultimately decided upon a double-wide model home that they described as "beautiful" and "perfect." The cabinets and countertops were straight, everything matched, the trim work was correctly fitted, and every tile was in place. After talking with Patton about the features of the home and the warranties, the Cablers decided to buy the home. They wanted to buy the model home, but Patton told them they really did not want that one because it was a 1998 model. He told them the one they were ordering was a 1999 model, the newest one then available. Patton told the Cablers that their home would be exactly like the model home on the lot and promised that everything would be done to their satisfaction. He also said that Oakwood Mobile Homes were superior quality homes and that if there was ever a problem during the warranty period, it would be fixed right away. Before the Cablers's home arrived, Patton called to tell them that there was another home available. The Cablers were interested because they needed to move out of their current home by a specific date. They went to inspect the home, even though Patton discouraged them from doing so. The home was in two halves, the ceiling was "wavy," a wall was broken, the kitchen counters were crooked and "wavy looking." Patton suggested the Cablers allow him to set up the home and told them to make a list of everything that was wrong, and Oakwood Mobile Homes would fix everything to their satisfaction. The Cablers relied on Patton's promises and agreed to buy the substitute home. They then watched a video about their rights and responsibilities under the contract and were presented with a number of documents to sign. The Cablers did not read every line of these documents, but the video as well as the delivery instructions said that Oakwood Mobile Homes was not responsible for verbal promises made by employees. The manager of the Oakwood Mobile Homes lot summarized the information and showed them where to sign. The Cablers made their list of repairs, but ultimately, the only repair on the list that Oakwood Mobile Homes made was the installation of some light globes. Are the Cablers entitled to rescind the purchase of the home?

9. While reading the April 26, 1997, edition of the Costa Mesa Daily Pilot, Donovan noticed a full-page advertisement placed by RRL Corporation, an automobile dealer doing business as Lexus of Westminster. The ad promoted a "PRE-OWNED COUP-A-RAMA SALE! 2-DAY PRE-OWNED SALES EVENT" and listed, along with 15 other used automobiles, a 1995 Jaguar XJ6 Vanden Plas. The ad described the color of the automobile, included a vehicle identification number, and stated a price of $25,995. The name Lexus of Westminster was displayed prominently in three separate locations in the advertisement, which included RRL's address along with a map showing the location of the dealership. The following statements appeared in small print at the bottom of the ad: "All cars plus tax, lic., doc., smog & bank fees. On approved credit. Ad expires 4/27/97." A state statute in this state provides that it is illegal for a licensed auto

dealer to "fail to sell a vehicle to any person at the advertised total price . . . while the vehicle remains unsold, unless the advertisement states that the advertised total price is good only for a specified time and the time has elapsed." Also on April 26, Donovan visited a Jaguar dealership that offered other 1995 Jaguars for sale at $8,000 to $10,000 more than the price specified in RRL's advertisement. The following day, Donovan and his spouse drove to Lexus of Westminster and asked to test-drive the Jaguar that had been advertised. Donovan mentioned that he had seen the ad and that the price looked really good. The salesperson responded that, as a Lexus dealer, RRL might offer better prices for a Jaguar than would a Jaguar dealer, but neither party mentioned the specific advertised price. After the test drive, Donovan and his wife discussed several negative characteristics of the car, including high mileage, an apparent rust problem, and worn tires. Despite these problems, however, they still believed the advertised price was a very good price and decided to buy it. Donovan told the salesperson, "Okay. We will take it at your price, $26,000." When the salesperson did not respond, Donovan showed him the ad. The salesperson immediately stated, "That's a mistake." After some calculations, the sales manager told Donovan that he would sell the car to him for $37,016. Donovan responded, "No, I want to buy it at your advertised price, and I will write you a check right now." If the ad would be construed as an offer and Donovan's statements an acceptance, was RRL entitled to avoid the contract on the basis of mistake?

10. Reed purchased a house from King. Neither King nor his real estate agents told Reed before the sale that a woman and her four children had been murdered there 10 years earlier. Reed learned of the gruesome episode from a neighbor after the sale. She sued King and his real estate agents, seeking rescission and damages on the ground that King should have disclosed the history of the house to her. Can Reed rescind the contract?

Online Research: Reseaching Internet Fraud

Using your favorite search engine, locate an article on Internet fraud. What is the number one form of Internet fraud in recent years?

14

CAPACITY TO CONTRACT

In a state in which the age of majority for contracting purposes is 18, 17-year-old Daniel was married, employed, and living with his wife in their own apartment. Daniel and his wife went to Mattox Motors, a used car dealership, and purchased a used car for $500 cash. After driving the car for several months, Daniel was involved in a serious collision and damaged the car. He was one week over the age of 18 at this time. The next day, Daniel sent a letter to Mattox Motors stating that he was disaffirming the sales contract because he was underage at the time he entered the contract, and that he wanted his money back.

- *Does Daniel have the right to get out of his contract?*
- *Does Mattox Motors have to give him his money back?*
- *Would it make a difference if Daniel had used the car to earn a living?*
- *If, instead of being a minor at the time the contract was made, Daniel had been mentally disabled or intoxicated, would he have the right to get out of the contract?*

ONE OF THE MAJOR justifications for enforcing a contract is that the parties voluntarily consented to be bound by it. It follows, then, that a person must have the *ability* to give consent before he can be legally bound to an agreement. For truly voluntary agreements to exist, this ability to give consent must involve more than the mere physical ability to say yes or shake hands or sign one's name. Rather, the person's maturity and mental ability must be such that it is fair to presume that he is capable of representing his own interests effectively. This concept is embodied in the legal term *capacity*.

legal terms, are known as *infants*), persons suffering from mental illnesses or defects, and intoxicated persons.[1] Contract law gives them the right to *avoid* (escape) contracts that they enter during incapacity. This rule provides a means of protecting people who, because of mental impairment, intoxication, or youth and inexperience, are disadvantaged in the normal give and take of the bargaining process.

Usually, lack of capacity to contract comes up in court in one of two ways. In some cases, it is asserted by a plaintiff as the basis of a lawsuit for the money or other benefits that he gave the other party under their contract. In others, it arises as a defense to the enforcement of a

What Is Capacity?

Capacity means the ability to incur legal obligations and acquire legal rights. Today, the primary classes of people who are considered to lack capacity are minors (who, in

---

[1]In times past, married women, convicts, and aliens were also among the classes of persons who lacked capacity to contract. These limitations on capacity have been removed by statute and court rule, however.

contract when the defendant is the party who lacked capacity. The responsibility for alleging and proving incapacity is placed on the person who bases his claim or defense on his lack of capacity.

Effect of Lack of Capacity

Normally, a contract in which one or both parties lack capacity because of infancy, mental impairment, or intoxication is considered to be voidable. People whose capacity is impaired in any of these ways are able to enter a contract and enforce it if they wish, but they also have the right to avoid the contract. There are, however, some individuals whose capacity is so impaired that they do not have the ability to form even a voidable contract. A bargain is considered to be void if, at the time of formation of the bargain, a court had already **adjudicated** (adjudged or decreed) one or more of the parties to be mentally incompetent or one or more of the parties was so impaired that he could not even manifest assent (for example, he was comatose or unconscious).

Capacity of Minors

Minors' Right to Disaffirm

Courts have long recognized that minors are in a vulnerable position in their dealings with adults. Courts granted minors the right to avoid contracts as a means of protecting against their own improvidence and against overreaching by adults. The exercise of this right to avoid a contract is called **disaffirmance.** The right to disaffirm is personal to the minor. That is, only the minor or a legal representative such as a guardian may disaffirm the contract. No formal act or written statement is required to make a valid disaffirmance. Any words or acts that effectively communicate the minor's desire to cancel the contract can constitute disaffirmance.

If, on the other hand, the minor wishes to enforce the contract instead of disaffirming it, the adult party must perform. You can see that the minor's right to disaffirm puts any adult contracting with a minor in an undesirable position: He is bound on the contract unless it is to the minor's advantage to disaffirm it. The right to disaffirm has the effect of discouraging adults from dealing with minors.

Exceptions to the Minor's Right to Disaffirm

Not every contract involving a minor is voidable, however. State law often creates statutory exceptions to the minor's right to disaffirm. These statutes prevent minors from disaffirming such transactions as marriage, agreements to support their children, educational loans, life and medical insurance contracts, contracts for transportation by common carriers, and certain types of contracts approved by a court (such as contracts to employ a child actor).

LOG ON

Are you interested in the way in which concepts about capacity of minors are applied to professional child actors, athletes, and performers? In a number of states, special statutes have been enacted that create a procedure for judicial approval of such contracts. Check out this website for more information: Wallace Collins, *A Guide to Judicial Approval of Contracts for Services of Minors,* **http://wallacecollins.com/minors.html.**

Releases Signed by Parents or Guardians

Contract provisions that release a party from liability for future negligence—known as **exculpatory clauses,** releases, and liability waivers—are extremely common ways for businesses to attempt to reduce their liability. Parents are occasionally asked to sign releases that would release a party from negligence liability for harm to their minor children. For example, Happy Smiles Day Camp may ask Johnny's mother or father to sign a contract releasing Happy Smiles from liability if Johnny is injured at camp. Chapter 15 discusses the enforceability of exculpatory contracts in general, but even if an exculpatory clause would normally be valid against the person who signed it, is it enforceable when a parent signs to release rights that belong to the child? There is some disagreement among various states on that point. Several states uphold such releases on the ground that parents have the fundamental liberty to make decisions concerning their children, but the majority of courts that have considered the question agree with the outcome decided by the court in the following *Cooper* case.

Cooper v. The Aspen Skiing Company
2002 Colo. LEXIS 528 (Colo. Sup. Ct. 2002) (en banc)

In 1995, 17-year-old David Cooper had been a member of the Aspen Valley Ski Club, Inc., for about nine years and was actively involved in competitive skiing. At the beginning of the 1995–96 ski season, David and his mother signed a form titled "Aspen Valley Ski Club, Inc. Acknowledgment and Assumption of Risk and Release." The release relieved the Ski Club from:

any liability, whether known or unknown, even though that liability may arise out of negligence or carelessness on the part of the persons or entities mentioned above. The undersigned Participant and Parent or Guardian agree to accept all responsibility for the risks, conditions and hazards which may occur whether or not they are now known. . . . [T]he undersigned Participant and Parent or Guardian HEREBY AGREE TO WAIVE, RELEASE, DISCHARGE, INDEMNIFY AND HOLD HARMLESS any and all claims for damages for death, personal injury or property damage which they may have or which may hereafter accrue as a result of any participation in an Aspen Valley Ski Club, Inc. program and related activities and events. . . . By signing this Acknowledgment and Assumption of Risk and Release as the Parent or Guardian, I am consenting to the participant's participation in the Aspen Valley Ski Club, Inc. programs and related activities and acknowledge that I understand that all risk, whether known or unknown, is expressly assumed by me and all claims, whether known or unknown, are expressly waived in advance.

On December 30, 1995, David was training for a competitive, high-speed alpine race. The course had been set by his coach. During a training run, David fell and collided with a tree, sustaining severe injuries, including the loss of vision in both eyes. David brought suit against The Aspen Skiing Company, The Aspen Valley Ski Club, his coach, and the United States Ski Association. The trial court ruled that his mother's signature on the release bound David to the terms of the release, and it barred his claims against the Ski Club and the coach. The Colorado Court of Appeals affirmed, and David appealed.

RICE, Justice. We must first determine whether Colorado's public policy allows parents to contractually release their child's future claims for injury caused by negligence. While it is a well-settled principle that a minor during his minority, and acting timely on reaching his majority, may disaffirm any contract that he may have entered into during his minority, we have never specifically addressed whether a parent or guardian may release a child's cause of action on his behalf or whether Colorado's public policy allows a parent or guardian to serve as indemnitor for his minor child's claims against an indemnitee.

The General Assembly has demonstrated an ongoing commitment to afford minors significant safeguards from harm by passing numerous statutes designed to protect minor children. Most significant of these for purposes of this case are the protections accorded minors in Colorado in the post-injury claim context. Colorado laws do not allow a parent the unilateral right to foreclose a child's existing cause of action to recover for torts committed against him. Indeed, the Colorado Probate Code creates mechanisms for the appointment of a conservator to protect a minor's settlement claim rights. It also provides minors important protections by creating means by which the court may ratify the settlement of a minor's claims. Importantly, a parent may not act as a minor's conservator as a matter of right, but only when appointed by the court.

Thus, we agree with the Utah Supreme Court and the Washington Supreme Court—both of which recently analyzed the same issue presented here—that since a parent generally may not release a child's cause of action after injury, it makes little, if any, sense to conclude a parent has the authority to release a child's cause of action prior to an injury.

It may be true that parents in the pre-injury setting have less financial motivation to sign a release than a parent in the post-injury setting who needs money to care for an injured child. Nonetheless, the protections accorded minors in the post-injury setting illustrate Colorado's overarching policy to protect minors, regardless of parental motivations, against actions by parents that effectively foreclose a minor's rights of recovery. Thus, while a parent's decision to sign a pre-injury release on his child's behalf may not be in "deliberate derogation of his child's best interests," *Purdy,* 68 Wis. L. Rev. 457, 474 (1963), the effect of a release on the child in either the pre-injury or the post-injury one is the same. If the parents are unwilling or unable to care for an injured child, he may be left with no recourse against a negligent party to acquire resources needed for care and this is true regardless of when relinquishment of the child's rights might occur. In addition, while pre-injury releases might be less vulnerable to mismanagement, children still must be protected against parental actions—perhaps rash and imprudent ones—that foreclose all of the minor's potential claims for injuries caused by another's negligence.

To allow a parent or guardian to execute exculpatory provisions on his minor child's behalf would render meaningless the special protections historically accorded minors. In the tort context especially, a minor should be accorded protection not only from his own improvident decision to release his possible prospective claims for injury based on another's negligence, but also from unwise decisions made on his behalf by parents who are routinely asked to release their child's claims for liability. A minor is accorded special protection, and to allow a parent to release a child's possible future claims for injury caused by negligence may as a practical matter leave the minor in an unacceptably precarious position with no recourse, no parental support, and no method to support himself or care for his injury. Our holding comports with the vast majority of courts that have decided the issue.

Finally, we consider the validity of parental indemnity provisions. As a practical matter, release and indemnity provisions in contracts signed by parents or guardians on behalf of their minor children go hand-in-hand; having invalidated release provisions, it would be contradictory to then effectively undercut a minor's rights to sue by allowing indemnity clauses that make such suits for all realistic purposes unlikely. We agree with the reasoning of those courts invalidating parental indemnity provisions that a minor child would be unlikely to pursue claims if his parent or guardian served as the ultimate source of compensation for the negligent party's torts, and that—if the child did bring a cause of action—family discord would likely result. Moreover, the effect of a parental indemnity agreement—to assure that a negligent party will not be held financially responsible for that party's torts committed against a minor—undermines a parent's duty to protect the best interests of the child. Thus, we also agree with the Utah Supreme Court that parental indemnity provisions can only serve to undermine the parent's fundamental obligations to the child. Therefore, we also hold that parental indemnity provisions violate Colorado's public policy to protect minors and create an unacceptable conflict of interest between a minor and his parent or guardian.

Reversed in favor of David.

Period of Minority

At common law, the age of majority was 21. However, the ratification in 1971 of the 26th Amendment to the Constitution giving 18-year-olds the right to vote stimulated a trend toward reducing the age of majority. The age of majority has been lowered by 49 states. In almost all of these states, the age of majority for contracting purposes is now 18.

Emancipation

Emancipation is the termination of a parent's right to control a child and receive services and wages from him.

There are no formal requirements for emancipation. It can occur by the parent's express or implied consent or by the occurrence of some events such as the marriage of the child. In most states, the mere fact that a minor is emancipated does *not* give him capacity to contract. A person younger than the legal age of majority is generally held to lack capacity to enter a contract, even if he is married and employed full time. See the *Mitchell* case, which follows.

Mitchell v. State Farm Mutual Automobile Insurance Co.
963 S.W.2d 222 (Ky. Ct. App. 1998)

On October 14, 1995, Sherri Mitchell was injured in an automobile accident while riding in a car owned by her father and operated by her husband. On October 26, 1995, Mitchell, age seventeen, signed a release with State Farm agreeing to settle her bodily injury claim for $2,500. No conservator was appointed at the time this release was signed. Mitchell filed a motion for declaratory judgment alleging that she lacked capacity at the time the release was executed, rendering it null and void. State Farm argued that Mitchell's marriage emancipated her, removing any disability she had as a minor, including the capacity to contract. The trial court decided in favor of State Farm and Mitchell appealed.

Emberton, Judge   Ky. Rev. Stat. 387.010 defines minor as anyone under the age of eighteen. Ordinarily, a contract executed by a minor is enforceable by the minor but may be avoided by the minor if not affirmed by him after reaching adulthood. Although the minor has the legal capacity to contract, he has the privilege of avoiding the contract. Although, there are certain exceptions to this general rule, none is applicable to this case. A settlement agreement and release of a third-party tortfeasor has been held to be voidable by the infant. A repudiation of the agreement requires that the minor return the consideration paid pursuant to that agreement.

The privilege bestowed upon a minor to avoid contracts made during infancy is given for policy reasons. Infants, as with other classes of disabilities, are presumed to be insufficiently mature or experienced to effectively bargain with those who have attained legal age, and any transaction which may result in a financial loss to them or in a depletion of their estates is scrutinized with care. Marriage of the infant emancipates the minor; it does not, however, make the minor *sui juris*. In *Bensinger's CoEx'rs,* the court declined to hold that an emancipated child must be bound by his contracts and followed the general rule that:

> Although parental emancipation may free the infant from parental control, it does not remove all of the disabilities of infancy. It does

not, for example, enlarge or affect the minor's capacity or incapacity to contract.

The rule may seem antiquated in view of the arguable maturity of today's youth. It may seem ironic that a minor can drive a car yet not be bound by the contract to purchase that car or be responsible for his torts and crimes yet unable to settle a dispute against a tortfeasor. The distinction to be made is that too frequently a contract involves negotiation and thought beyond the maturity of most people under the age of eighteen. We cannot adopt a rule that marriage by the minor somehow classifies him as more mature and intelligent than his unmarried counterpart. We, as did the court in *Kiefer v. Fred Howe Motors, Inc.,* find that logic and common sense would not encourage such a result since marriage by a minor too frequently may itself be indicative of a lack of wisdom and maturity.

The legislature has provided a means through which a conservator can be appointed to protect the financial interest of a married minor. Although the lack of such appointment will not render the contract void, the minor remains free to avoid his obligation under the contract.

Reversed and remanded in favor of Mitchell.

Time of Disaffirmance

Contracts entered during minority that affect title to *real estate* cannot be disaffirmed until majority. This rule is apparently based on the special importance of real estate and on the need to protect a minor from improvidently disaffirming a transaction (such as a mortgage or conveyance) involving real estate. All other contracts entered during minority may be disaffirmed as soon as the contract is formed. The minor's power to avoid his contracts does not end on the day he reaches the age of majority. It continues for a period of time after he reaches majority.

How long after reaching majority does a person retain the right to disaffirm the contracts he made while a minor? A few states have statutes that prescribe a definite time limit on the power of avoidance. In Oklahoma, for example, a person who wishes to disaffirm a contract must do so within one year after reaching majority.[2] In

most states, however, there is no set limit on the time during which a person may disaffirm after reaching majority. In determining whether a person has the right to disaffirm, a major factor that courts consider is whether the adult has rendered performance under the contract or relied on the contract. If the adult has relied on the contract or has given something of value to the minor, the minor must disaffirm within a reasonable time after reaching majority. If he delays longer than a period of time that is considered to be reasonable under the circumstances, he will run the risk of *ratifying* (affirming) the contract. (The concept and consequences of ratification are discussed in the next section.) If the adult has neither performed nor relied on the contract, however, the former minor is likely to be accorded a longer period of time in which to disaffirm, sometimes even years after he has reached majority.

Ratification

Though a person has the right to disaffirm contracts made during minority, this right can be given up after

[2]Okla. Stat. Ann. tit. 15 sec. 18 (1983).

the person reaches the age of majority. When a person who has reached majority indicates that he intends to be bound by a contract that he made while still a minor, he surrenders his right to disaffirm. This act of affirming the contract and surrendering the right to avoid the contract is known as **ratification.** Ratification makes a contract valid from its inception. Because ratification represents the former minor's election to be bound by the contract, he cannot later disaffirm. Ratification can be done effectively only after the minor reaches majority. Otherwise, it would be as voidable as the initial contract.

There are no formal requirements for ratification. Any of the former minor's words or acts after reaching majority that indicate with reasonable clarity his intent to be bound by the contract are sufficient. Ratification can be *expressed* in an oral or written statement, or, as is more often the case, it can be *implied* by conduct on the part of the former minor. Naturally, ratification is clearest when the former minor has made some express statement of his intent to be bound. Predicting whether a court will determine that a contract has been ratified is a bit more difficult when the only evidence of the alleged ratification is the conduct of the minor. A former minor's acceptance or retention of benefits given by the other party for an unreasonable time after he has reached majority can constitute ratification. Also, a former minor's continued performance of his part of the contract after reaching majority has been held to imply his intent to ratify the contract.

Duties upon Disaffirmance

Duty to Return Consideration If neither party has performed his part of the contract, the parties' relationship will simply be canceled by the disaffirmance. Since neither party has given anything to the other party, no further adjustments are necessary. But what about the situation where, as is often the case, the minor has paid money to the adult and the adult has given property to the minor? Upon disaffirmance, each party has the duty to return to the other any consideration that the other has given. This means that the minor must return any consideration given to him by the adult that remains in his possession. However, if the minor is unable to return the consideration, most states will still permit him to disaffirm the contract.

The duty to return consideration also means that the minor has the right to recover any consideration he has given to the adult party. He even has the right to recover some property that has been transferred to third parties. One exception to the minor's right to recover property from third parties is found in section 2–403 of the Uniform Commercial Code, however. Under this section, a minor cannot recover *goods* that have been transferred to a good faith purchaser. For example, Simpson, a minor, sells a 1980 Ford to Mort's Car Lot. Mort's then sells the car to Vane, a good faith purchaser. If Simpson disaffirmed the contract with Mort's, he would *not* have the right to recover the Ford from Vane.

Must the Disaffirming Minor Make Restitution? A Split of Authority If the consideration given by the adult party has been lost, damaged, destroyed, or simply has depreciated in value, is the minor required to make restitution to the adult for the loss? The traditional rule is that the minor who cannot fully return the consideration that was given to her is *not* obligated to pay the adult for the benefits she has received or to compensate the adult for loss or depreciation of the consideration. Some states still follow this traditional rule. (As you will read in the next section, however, a minor's misrepresentation of age can, even in some of these states, make her responsible for reimbursing the other party upon disaffirmance.) The rule that restitution is not required is designed to protect minors by discouraging adults from dealing with them. After all, if an adult knew that he might be able to demand the return of anything that he transferred to a minor, he would have little incentive to refrain from entering into contracts with minors.

The traditional rule, however, can work harsh results for innocent adults who have dealt fairly with minors. It strikes many people as unprincipled that a doctrine intended to protect against unfair exploitation of one class of people can be used to unfairly exploit another class of people. As courts sometimes say, the minor's right to disaffirm was designed to be used as a "shield rather than as a sword." For these reasons, a growing number of states have rejected the traditional rule. The courts and legislatures of these states have adopted rules that require minors who disaffirm their contracts and seek refunds of purchase price to reimburse adults for the use or depreciation of their property. The *Dodson* case follows this approach.

Dodson v. Shrader   *824 W.2d 545 (Tenn. Sup.Ct. 1992)*

Joseph Dodson, age 16, bought a 1984 Chevrolet truck from Burns and Mary Shrader, owners of Shrader's Auto Sales, for $4,900 cash. At the time, Burns Shrader, believing Dodson to be 18 or 19, did not ask Dodson's age and Dodson did not volunteer it. Dodson drove the truck for about eight months, when he learned from an auto mechanic that there was a burned valve in the engine. Dodson did not have the money for the repairs, so he continued to drive the truck without repair for another month until the engine "blew up" and stopped operating. He parked the car in the front yard of his parents' house. He then contacted the Shraders, rescinding the purchase of the truck and requesting a full refund. The Shraders refused to accept the truck or to give Dodson a refund. Dodson then filed an action seeking to rescind the contract and recover the amount paid for the truck. Before the court could hear the case, a hit-and-run driver struck Dodson's parked truck, damaging its left front fender. At the time of the circuit court trial, the truck was worth only $500. The Shraders argued that Dodson should be responsible for paying the difference between the present value of the truck and the $4,900 purchase price. The trial court found in Dodson's favor, ordering the Shraders to refund the $4,900 purchase price upon delivery of the truck. The Tennessee Court of Appeals affirmed this judgment, and the Shraders appealed.

O'Brien, Justice   The law on the subject of the protection of infants' rights has been slow to evolve. The underlying purpose of the "infancy doctrine" is to protect minors from their lack of judgment and from squandering their wealth through improvident contracts with crafty adults who would take advantage of them in the marketplace.

There is, however, a modern trend among the states, either by judicial action or by statute, in the approach to the problem of balancing the rights of minors against those of innocent merchants. As a result, two minority rules have developed which allow the other party to a contract with a minor to refund less than the full consideration paid in the event of rescission. The first of these minority rules is called the "Benefit Rule." This rule holds that, upon rescission, recovery of the full purchase price is subject to a deduction for the minor's use of the merchandise. This rule recognizes that the traditional rule in regard to necessaries has been extended so far as to hold an infant bound by his contracts, where he failed to restore what he has received under them to the extent of the benefit actually derived by him from what he has received from the other party to the transaction. The other minority rule holds that the minor's recovery of the full purchase price is subject to a deduction for the minor's "use" of the consideration he or she received under the contract, or for the "depreciation" or "deterioration" of the consideration in his or her possession.

We are impressed by the statement made by the Court of Appeals of Ohio:

> At a time when we see young persons between 18 and 21 years of age demanding and assuming more responsibilities in their daily lives; when we see such persons charged with the responsibility for committing crimes; when we see such persons being sued in tort claims for acts of negligence; when we see such persons subject to military service; when we see such persons engaged in business and acting in almost all other respects as an adult, it seems timely to re-examine the case law pertaining to contractual rights and responsibilities of infants to see if the law as pronounced and applied by the courts should be redefined.

We state the rule to be followed hereafter, in reference to a contract of a minor, to be where the minor has not been overreached in any way, and there has been no undue influence, and the contract is a fair and reasonable one, and the minor has actually paid money on the purchase price, and taken and used the article purchased, that he ought not to be permitted to recover the amount actually paid, without allowing the vendor of the goods reasonable compensation for the use of, depreciation, and willful or negligent damage to the article purchased, while in his hands. If there has been any fraud or imposition on the part of the seller or if the contract is unfair, or any unfair advantage has been taken of the minor inducing him to make the purchase, then the rule does not apply. This rule will fully and fairly protect the minor against injustice or imposition, and at the same time it will be fair to a business person who has dealt with such minor in good faith.

This rule is best adapted to modern conditions under which minors are permitted to, and do in fact, transact a great deal of business for themselves, long before they have reached the age of legal majority. Many young people work and earn money and collect it and spend it oftentimes without any oversight or restriction. The law does not question their right to buy if they have the money to pay for their purchases. It seems intolerably burdensome on everyone concerned if merchants cannot deal with them safely, in a fair and reasonable way. Further, it does not appear consistent with practice of proper moral influence upon young people, tend to encourage honesty and integrity, or lead them to a good and useful business future if they are taught that they can make purchases with their own money, for their own benefit, and after paying for them, and using them until they are worn out and destroyed, go back and compel the vendor to return to them

what they have paid upon the purchase price. Such a doctrine can only lead to the corruption of principles and encourage young people in habits of trickery and dishonesty.

Reversed and remanded in favor of the Shraders.

Minors' Obligation to Pay Reasonable Value of Necessaries Though the law regarding minors' contracts is designed to discourage adults from dealing with (and possibly taking advantage of) minors, it would be undesirable for the law to discourage adults from selling minors the items that they need for basic survival. For this reason, disaffirming minors are required to pay the reasonable value of items that have been furnished to them that are classified as **necessaries.** A necessary is something that is essential for the minor's continued existence and general welfare that has not been provided by the minor's parents or guardian. Examples of necessaries include food, clothing, shelter, medical care, tools of the minor's trade, and basic educational or vocational training.

A minor's liability for necessaries supplied to him is **quasi contractual.** That is, the minor is liable for the *reasonable value* of the necessaries that she actually receives. She is not liable for the entire price agreed on if that price exceeds the actual value of the necessaries, and she is not liable for necessaries that she contracted for but did not receive. For example, Joy Jones, a minor, signs a one-year lease for an apartment in Mountain Park at a rent of $300 per month. After living in the apartment for three months, Joy breaks her lease and moves out. Because she is a minor, Joy has the right to disaffirm the lease. If shelter is a necessary in this case, however, she must pay the reasonable value of what she has actually received—three months' rent. If she can establish that the actual value of what she has received is less than $300 per month, she will be bound to pay only that lesser amount. Furthermore, she will not be obligated to pay for the remaining nine months' rent, because she has not received any benefits from the remainder of the lease.

Whether a given item is considered a necessary depends on the facts of a particular case. The minor's age, station in life, and personal circumstances are all relevant to this issue. An item sold to a minor is not considered a necessary if the minor's parent or guardian has already supplied him with similar items. For this reason, the range of items that will be considered necessaries is

broader for married minors and other emancipated minors than it is for unemancipated minors.

Effect of Misrepresentation of Age

It is not unheard of for a minor to occasionally pretend to be older than he is. The normal rules dealing with the minor's right to disaffirm and his duties upon disaffirmance can be affected by a minor's misrepresentation of his age.[3] Suppose, for example, that Jones, age 17, wants to lease a car from Acme Auto Rentals, but knows that Acme rents only to people who are at least 18. Jones induces Acme to lease a car to him by showing a false identification that represents his age to be 18. Acme relies on the misrepresentation. Jones wrecks the car, attempts to disaffirm the contract, and asks for the return of his money. What is the effect of Jones's misrepresentation? State law is not uniform on this point.

The traditional rule was that a minor's misrepresentation about his age did not affect his right to disaffirm and did not create any obligation to reimburse the adult for damages or pay for benefits received. The theory behind this rule is that one who lacks capacity cannot acquire it merely by claiming to be of legal age. As you can imagine, this traditional approach does not "sit well" with modern courts, at least in those cases in which the adult has dealt with the minor fairly and in good faith, because it creates severe hardship for innocent adults who have relied on minors' misrepresentations of age.

State law today is fairly evenly divided among those states that take the position that the minor who misrepresents his age will be *estopped* (prevented) from asserting his infancy as a defense and those that will allow a minor to disaffirm regardless of his misrepresentation of age. Among the states that allow disaffirmance despite the minor's misrepresentation, most hold the disaffirming minor responsible for the losses suffered by the adult, either by allowing the adult to counterclaim against the minor for

[3]You might want to refer back to Chapter 13 to review the elements of misrepresentation.

the tort of deceit or by requiring the minor to reimburse the adult for use or depreciation of his property.

Capacity of Mentally Impaired Persons

Theory of Incapacity

Like minors, people who suffer from a mental illness or defect are at a disadvantage in their ability to protect their own interests in the bargaining process. Contract law makes their contracts either void or voidable to protect them from the results of their own impaired perceptions and judgment and from others who might take advantage of them.

Test for Mental Incapacity

Incapacity on grounds of mental illness or defect, which is often referred to in cases and texts as "insanity," encompasses a broad range of causes of impaired mental functioning, such as mental illness, brain damage, mental retardation, or senility. The mere fact that a person suffers from some mental illness or defect does not necessarily mean that he lacks capacity to contract, however. He could still have full capacity unless the defect or illness affects the particular transaction in question.

The usual test for mental incapacity is a *cognitive* one; that is, courts ask whether the person had sufficient mental capacity to understand the nature and effect of the contract. Some courts have criticized the traditional test as unscientific because it does not take into account the fact that a person suffering from a mental illness or defect might be unable to *control* his conduct. Section 15 of the *Restatement (Second) of Contracts* provides that a person's contracts are voidable if he is unable to *act* in a reasonable manner in relation to the transaction and the other party has reason to know of his condition. Where the other party has reason to know of the condition of the mentally impaired person, the *Restatement (Second)* standard would provide protection to people who understood the transaction but, because of some mental defect or illness, were unable to exercise appropriate judgment or to control their conduct effectively.

The Effect of Incapacity Caused by Mental Impairment

The contracts of people who are suffering from a mental defect at the time of contracting are usually considered to be *voidable*. In some situations, however, severe mental or physical impairment may prevent a person from even being able to manifest consent. In such a case, no contract could be formed.

As mentioned at the beginning of this chapter, contract law makes a distinction between a contract involving a person who has been *adjudicated* (judged by a court) incompetent at the time the contract was made and a contract involving a person who was suffering from some mental impairment at the time the contract was entered but whose incompetency was not established until *after* the contract was formed. If a person is under guardianship at the time the contract is formed—that is, if a court has found a person mentally incompetent after holding a hearing on his mental competency and has appointed a guardian for him—the contract is considered *void*. On the other hand, if *after* a contract has been formed, a court finds that the person who manifested consent lacked capacity on grounds of mental illness or defect, the contract is usually considered *voidable* at the election of the party who lacked capacity (or his guardian or personal representative).

The Right to Disaffirm If a contract is found to be voidable on the ground of mental impairment, the person who lacked capacity at the time the contract was made has the right to disaffirm the contract. A person formerly incapacitated by mental impairment can ratify a contract if he regains his capacity. Thus, if he regains capacity, he must disaffirm the contract unequivocally within a reasonable time, or he will be deemed to have ratified it.

As is true of a disaffirming minor, a person disaffirming on the ground of mental impairment must return any consideration given by the other party that remains in his possession. A person under this type of mental incapacity is liable for the reasonable value of necessaries in the same manner as are minors. Must the incapacitated party reimburse the other party for loss, damage, or depreciation of non-necessaries given to him? This is generally said to depend on whether the contract was basically fair and on whether the other party had reason to be aware of his impairment. If the contract is fair, bargained for in good faith, and the other party had no reasonable cause to know of the incapacity, the contract cannot be disaffirmed unless the other party is placed in *status quo* (the position she was in before the creation of the contract). However, if the other party had reason to know of the incapacity, the incapacitated party is allowed to disaffirm without placing the other party in status quo. This distinction discourages people from attempting to take advantage of mentally impaired people, but it spares those who are dealing in good faith and have no such intent.

Contracts of Intoxicated Persons

Intoxication and Capacity

Intoxication (either from alcohol or the use of drugs) can deprive a person of capacity to contract. The mere fact that a party to a contract had been drinking when the contract was formed would *not* normally affect his/her capacity to contract, however. Intoxication is a ground for lack of capacity only when it is so extreme that the person is unable to understand the nature of the business at hand. Section 16 of the *Restatement (Second) of Contracts* further provides that intoxication is a ground for lack of capacity only if *the other party has reason to know* that the affected person is so intoxicated that he/she cannot understand or act reasonably in relation to the transaction.

The rules governing the capacity of intoxicated persons are very similar to those applied to the capacity of people who are mentally impaired. The basic right to disaffirm contracts made during incapacity, the duties upon disaffirmance, and the possibility of ratification upon regaining capacity are the same for an intoxicated person as for a person under a mental impairment. In practice, however, courts traditionally have been less sympathetic with a person who was intoxicated at the time of contracting than with minors or those suffering from a mental impairment. It is rare for a person to actually escape his contractual obligations on the ground of intoxication. A person incapacitated by intoxication at the time of contracting might nevertheless be bound to his/her contract if he/she fails to disaffirm in a timely manner.

Problems and Problem Cases

1. Webster Street owns real estate in Omaha, Nebraska. In September of 1982, Webster Street entered into a written contract to lease an apartment to Wilwerding and Sheridan for one year at a rental of $250 a month. Both Wilwerding and Sheridan were younger than the age of majority (which was 19 in their state) at the time they signed the contract, although Webster Street did not know this. Wilwerding and Sheridan could have lived at home with their parents but voluntarily left home to live on their own. They paid $150 as a security deposit and rent for the remainder of September and the month of October, for a total of $500. They failed to pay their November rent on time, however, and Webster Street notified them that they would be required to move out unless they paid immediately. Unable to pay rent, Sheridan and Wilwerding moved out of the apartment on November 12. Webster Street later demanded that they pay the expenses it incurred in attempting to rerent the property, rent for the months of November and December (apparently the two months it took to find a new tenant), and assorted damages and fees, amounting to $630.84. Sheridan and Wilwerding refused to pay any of the amount demanded on the ground of minority and demanded the return of their security deposit. Will they be able to rescind the contract?

2. Robertson, while a minor, contracted to borrow money from his father for a college education. His father mortgaged his home and took out loans against his life insurance policies to get some of the money he lent to Robertson, who ultimately graduated from dental school. Two years after Robertson's graduation, his father asked him to begin paying back the amount of $30,000 at $400 per month. Robertson agreed to pay $24,000 at $100 per month. He did this for three years before stopping the payments. His father sued for the balance of the debt. Could Robertson disaffirm the contract?

3. Green, age 16, contracted to buy a Camaro from Star Chevrolet. Green lived about six miles from school and one mile from his job, and used the Camaro to go back and forth to school and work. When he did not have the car, he used a car pool to get to school and work. Several months later, the car became inoperable with a blown head gasket, and Green gave notice of disaffirmance to Star Chevrolet. Star Chevrolet refused to refund the purchase price, claiming, in part, that the car was a necessary. Was it?

4. Farnum was 90 years old when she sold her real estate in South Yarmouth to Silvano, age 24. Farnum knew and trusted Silvano because he had done mowing and landscape work on her property. Although the fair market value of Farnum's property was $115,000 at the time of the sale, she agreed to sell it as well as the furniture and other furnishings in the house for $64,900. Silvano had reason to know of the inadequacy of the purchase price. Farnum's nephew had warned Silvano not to proceed with the sale. In addition, Silvano was able to get a mortgage for $65,000 from the bank to finance the purchase. Farnum's mental competence had begun to fail seriously three years before the sale to Silvano. She began to engage in aberrant conduct such as lamenting not hearing from her sisters, who were dead, and she would wonder where the people upstairs in her house had gone, when there was no upstairs in her house. She offered to sell her house to a neighbor for $35,000. She became abnormally forgetful, locking herself out of her house and breaking into it rather than calling on a neighbor with whom she had left a key. She hid her cat to protect it from "the cops." She would express the desire to return to Cape Cod, although she was on Cape Cod. She easily became lost. Her sister and nephew had to pay her bills and balance her checkbook. She was hospitalized several times during the three-year period preceding the sale to Silvano. Medical tests revealed organic brain disease. During the transaction in question, Farnum was represented by a lawyer that she had selected and paid for. During the closing, Farnum was cheerful and engaged in pleasantries. After the transaction, however, Farnum insisted to others that she still owned the property. Six months after the conveyance, Farnum was admitted to the hospital for dementia and seizure disorder, and was later discharged to a nursing home. Can the contract between Farnum and Silvano be voided on the ground of lack of capacity?

5. At a time when the age of majority in Ohio was 21, Lee, age 20, contracted to buy a 1964 Plymouth Fury for $1,552 from Haydocy Pontiac. Lee represented herself to be 21 when entering the contract. She paid for the car by trading in another car worth $150 and financing the balance. Immediately following delivery of the car to her, Lee permitted one John Roberts to take possession of it. Roberts delivered the car to someone else, and it was never recovered. Lee failed to make payments on the car, and Haydocy Pontiac sued her to recover the car or the amount due on the contract. Lee repudiated the contract on the ground that she was a minor at the time of purchase. Can Lee disaffirm the contract without reimbursing Haydocy Pontiac for the value of the car?

6. In March 1997, 16-year-old Schmidt was involved in a two-vehicle collision. At the time, she was driving a car owned by her grandfather and was insured with the personal injury benefits through her father's insurance company. Initially unconscious, she was transported to the Shock Trauma Unit at Prince George's Hospital, where she was given necessary treatment for brain concussion and an open scalp wound. She incurred hospital expenses of $1,756.24. Soon after release from the hospital, Schmidt filed for benefits under the coverage provided in her father's policy. During the claim process, Schmidt and her father provided the insurance company with documents about her medical expenses. Schmidt and her father signed an Assignment and Authorization of benefits instructing the insurance company to pay directly the amount owed to him. Thereafter, the insurance company issued a check in the amount of $1,756.24 to "Lewis A. Schmidt for Minor,

Michelle Schmidt" in reference to "Prince George's Hospital Center, Service Date 03-07-1997 to 03-08-1997." The check was cashed, but the funds were not paid to Prince George's Hospital. They apparently were used to purchase a replacement automobile for Schmidt. In 1999, after Schmidt had reached the age of majority, Prince George's Hospital sued her to collect the medical bills. Schmidt contended that she is not responsible for the bill because she was a minor at the time of the hospitalization. Is this correct?

7. In July 1997, 11-year-old Hawkins went to Duck Creek, Utah, for a family reunion. As part of the reunion, members of the family arranged for Navajo Trails to provide horses and guides for a trail ride. As a condition of its service, Navajo Trails required Hawkins's mother to sign a "Release Form." The form stated in part that:

> Riding and handling horses can be DANGEROUS. This form must be completed and signed before you can ride . . . . By signing this form, you agree to ASSUME THE RISK of any injury, death, or loss, or damage which you or your child . . . may suffer . . . . In consideration for the rendering of trail riding . . . service by Navajo Trails . . . [t]he undersigned on behalf of himself or for any person for whom he or she is a parent or legal guardian, does hereby indemnify (reimburse), release, and forever hold harmless, Navajo Trails . . . [for] any claims, demands, and actions or causes of action on account of death or injury or loss or damage which may occur from any cause, without regard to negligence, other than the gross negligence or willful misconduct of Navajo Trails . . . If the undersigned is a parent or guardian, he or she further agrees to indemnify (reimburse) Navajo Trails or such persons for any damages paid by or assessed against Navajo Trails. . .as a result of injury to or death of a child. . . .

Hawkins's mother signed this form. During the trail ride, Hawkins's horse was spooked and threw her, injuring her. She filed suit against Navajo Trails, alleging that it had provided an insufficient number of guides, that the guides were not adequately trained, and that the guides had failed to carry out their duties properly. One of Navajo Trails's defenses was that the Release Form relieved it of liability. Applying the general rule, was the Release Form enforceable?

8. In December 1989, 16-year-old Travis brought a 1970 Pontiac GTO into M & M Precision Body and Paint to get an estimate on repairs to the vehicle from Mizerski. After examining the vehicle, Mizerski provided Travis with an estimate for $1,550.35 in repairs and informed him that a $1,000 deposit to cover the cost of parts and materials would be required before the work was begun. Travis delivered the vehicle to Mizerski's body shop in April 1990 to have the vehicle repaired. He gave the deposit in the form of a $1,000 cashier's check. In April or May of 1990, Travis and his father went to the body shop to check on the car and to discuss and authorize additional repairs. In July, they returned to the body shop and, after an argument about the balance due, compromised on a balance of $850. This amount was paid to Mizerski in the form of a cashier's check drawn on Travis's parents' account when Travis picked up the vehicle at the end of July. Travis and his father were dissatisfied with Mizerski's workmanship, and after demanding and not receiving resolution of the problems, Travis filed suit to disaffirm the contracts that he had made for the repair work and to get his money back. In a state that follows the traditional approach to the infancy doctrine, will he succeed?

9. A boy bought an Ernie Banks rookie card for $12 from an inexperienced clerk in a baseball card store owned by Johnson. The card had been marked "1200," and Johnson, who had been away from the store at the time of the sale, had intended the card to be sold for $1,200, not $12. Can Johnson get the card back by asserting the boy's lack of capacity?

Online Research: Researching the Age of Majority

Using your favorite search engine and key word requests such as "age of majority AND states," determine what states have an age of majority older than 18.

15

ILLEGALITY

W ilson had been licensed to practice architecture in Hawaii, but his license lapsed in 1971 because he had failed to pay a required $15 renewal fee. A Hawaii statute provides that any person who practices architecture without having been registered and "without having a valid unexpired certificate of registration . . . shall be fined not more than $500 or imprisoned not more than one year, or both." In 1972, Wilson performed architectural and engineering services for Kealakekua Ranch, and billed the Ranch over $33,000 for the work.

- *Is this a legal contract?*
- *Would it matter if Wilson had never met the licensing requirements to be licensed in Hawaii?*
- *Is Kealakekua Ranch required to pay Wilson anything for his work?*

ALTHOUGH THE PUBLIC INTEREST normally favors the enforcement of contracts, there are times when the interests that usually favor the enforcement of an agreement are subordinated to conflicting social concerns. As you read in Chapter 13, Reality of Consent, and Chapter 14, Capacity to Contract, for example, people who did not truly consent to a contract or who lacked the capacity to contract have the power to cancel their contracts. In these situations, concerns about protecting disadvantaged persons and preserving the integrity of the bargaining process outweigh the usual public interest in enforcing private agreements. Similarly, when an agreement involves an act or promise that violates some legislative or court-made rule, the public interests threatened by the agreement outweigh the interests that favor its enforcement. Such an agreement will be denied enforcement on the ground of *illegality,* even if there is voluntary consent between two parties who have capacity to contract.

Meaning of Illegality

When a court says that an agreement is illegal, it does not necessarily mean that the agreement violates a criminal law, although an agreement to commit a crime is one type of illegal agreement. Rather, an agreement is illegal either because the legislature has declared that particular type of contract to be unenforceable or void or because the agreement violates a **public policy** that has been developed by courts or that has been manifested in constitutions, statutes, administrative regulations, or other sources of law.

The term *public policy* is impossible to define precisely. Generally, it is taken to mean a widely shared view about what ideas, interests, institutions, or freedoms promote public welfare. For example, in our society, there are strong public policies favoring the protection of human life and health, free competition, and private property. Judges' and legislators' perceptions of desirable public policy influence the decisions they make about the resolution of cases or the enactment of statutes. Public policy may be based on a prevailing moral code, on an economic philosophy, or on the need to protect a valued social institution such as the family or the judicial system. If the enforcement of an agreement would create a threat to a public policy, a court may determine that it is illegal.

Determining Whether an Agreement Is Illegal

If a statute states that a particular type of agreement is unenforceable or void, courts will apply the statute and refuse to enforce the agreement. Relatively few such statutes exist, however. More frequently, a legislature will forbid certain conduct but will not address the enforceability of contracts that involve the forbidden conduct. In such cases, courts must determine whether the importance of the public policy that underlies the statute in question and the degree of interference with that policy are sufficiently great to outweigh any interests that favor enforcement of the agreement.

In some cases, it is relatively easy to predict that an agreement will be held to be illegal. For example, an agreement to commit a serious crime is certain to be illegal. However, the many laws enacted by legislatures are of differing degrees of importance to the public welfare. The determination of **illegality** would not be so clear if the agreement violated a statute that was of relatively small importance to the public welfare. For example, in one Illinois case,[1] a seller of fertilizer failed to comply

---

[1]*Amoco Oil Co. v. Toppert*, 56 Ill. App. 3d 1294 (Ill. Ct. App. 1978).

with an Illinois statute requiring that a descriptive statement accompany the delivery of the fertilizer. The sellers prepared the statements and offered them to the buyers but did not give them to the buyers at the time of delivery. The court enforced the contract despite the sellers' technical violation of the law because the contract was not seriously injurious to public welfare.

Similarly, the public policies developed by courts are rarely absolute; they, too, depend on a balancing of several factors. In determining whether to hold an agreement illegal, a court will consider the importance of the public policy involved and the extent to which enforcement of the agreement would interfere with that policy. They will also consider the seriousness of any wrongdoing involved in the agreement and how directly that wrongdoing was connected with the agreement.

For purposes of our discussion, illegal agreements will be classified into three main categories: (1) agreements that violate statutes, (2) agreements that violate public policy developed by courts, and (3) unconscionable agreements and contracts of adhesion.

The *Straub* case provides an example of a contract that was held to violate public policy.

Straub v. B.M.T.   *626 N.E.2d. 848 (Ind. Ct. App. 1993)*

Edward Straub and Francine Todd began dating in 1985 when both were teachers at the same elementary school. In late 1986, Todd discussed her desire to have a child with Straub after her doctor informed her that artificial insemination would not work. Straub told Todd that he did not want the responsibility of another family on account of his age and the fact that he already had children from a previous marriage. However, when Todd threatened to end their relationship, he agreed to try to impregnate her providing she would sign a "hold harmless" agreement. Straub presented Todd with the following handwritten agreement, which Todd signed:

To Whom it may concern

I Francine Todd in sound mind & fore thought have decided not to marry, but would like to have a baby of my own. To support financially & emotionally, I have approached several men who will not be held responsible financially or emotionally who's [sic] names will be kept secret for life.

Signed Francine Todd

Dec. 15, 1986

After Todd signed the agreement, the couple began to have unprotected sex, and in March 1987, Todd became pregnant. During this period, Todd was not sexually active with any other man. Todd and Straub continued their relationship during Todd's pregnancy and for three years after the birth of their child (B.M.T.), and even after Straub's marriage to someone else, but Straub did not establish a relationship with the child. He stopped seeing Todd after she filed this action on B.M.T.'s behalf to establish paternity. The trial court found that Straub was the biological father of B.M.T. and that he had the obligation to support her. Straub appealed.

Miller, Judge   Indiana has long recognized the obligation of both parents to support their children. A parent's obligations to support his minor child is a basic tenet recognized in this state by statutes that provide civil and criminal sanctions against parents who neglect such duty. In addition, there is a well-established common-law duty and obligation of a *father* to assist in the support of his children.

It is apparent that our legislature has created a strong current public policy (and not merely maintained an ancient one) with the object of protecting the rights of children from the whims of their parents and the power of the state.

Straub first claims that "fundamental contract principles" allow him to contract around his statutory and common law duty to provide support to his daughter. He ignores other rights, such as inheritance. However, this argument fails because it amounts to the contracting away of his daughter's right to support. It is well settled that a parent cannot, by his own contract, relieve himself of the legal obligation to support his minor children. In *Ort v. Schage,* we held that an agreement to forgo court ordered child support even in exchange for a benefit (social security payments) to the child is unenforceable because a parent has no right to contract away a child's support benefits.

Although the primary goal of a paternity action is to secure support and education for illegitimate children, a legitimate subsidiary goal of the same action, however, is to protect the public interest by preventing the illegitimate child from becoming a ward of the state. Public policy considerations mandate that the state take an active interest in providing for the welfare of illegitimate children in order to avoid placing an undue burden on taxpayers.

Finally, Straub argues that the agreement signed by Todd should be enforced because he was acting merely as a "sperm donor." He argues that we should follow cases from other jurisdictions which look to the pre-conception intent of the parties involved in deciding whether to enforce their agreement. We first note, of course, arguing that Straub's and Todd's relationship was that of a sperm donor and donee ignores the facts. It is undisputed that Straub and Todd had an ongoing affair, one which began before Todd decided to become pregnant and only ended three years after B.M.T.'s birth.

Straub argues that he should be indemnified against any support claims because Todd is capable of supporting the child on her own and the "economic injury" to Straub due to her "breach of contract" would exceed $100,000. Because this argument merely seeks to circumvent public policy, it, too, must fail. First, because the agreement between the parties is void, there is no enforceable contract to breach. Second, Todd's *present* ability to care for the child on her own and the cost of the support to Straub do not change the law—Straub must provide his share of his daughter's support.

Affirmed in favor of B.M.T.

Agreements in Violation of Statute

Agreements Declared Illegal by Statute

State legislatures occasionally enact statutes that declare certain types of agreements unenforceable, void, or voidable. In a case in which a legislature has specifically stated that a particular type of contract is void, a court need only interpret and apply the statute. These statutes differ from state to state. Some are relatively uncommon. For example, an Indiana statute declares surrogate birth contracts to be void.[2] Others, such as *usury statutes* and *wagering statutes,* are common.

Usury Statutes   Federal law and the law of most states set limits on the amount of interest that can be charged for a loan or forbearance (refraining from making a demand for money that is already due). *Usury* means obtaining interest beyond the amount that is authorized by law for these transactions. The statutes that define usury and set the maximum permissible limit for interest are not uniform in their prohibitions or their penalties. When a transaction is covered by usury laws and the rate of interest charged for the use of money exceeds the statutory limit, the contract to pay that interest rate is unenforceable.

Wagering Statutes   All states either prohibit or regulate wagering, or gambling. There is a thin line separating wagering, which is illegal, from well-accepted, lawful transactions in which a person will profit from the happening of an uncertain event. The hallmark of a wager is that neither party has any financial stake or interest in the uncertain event except for the stake that

---

[2]Ind. Code 31–8–2–2 (1988).

he has created by making the bet. The person making a wager *creates* the risk that he may lose the money or property wagered upon the happening of an uncertain event. Suppose Ames bets Baker $20 that the Cubs will win the pennant this year. Ames has no financial interest in a Cubs victory other than that which he has created through his bet. Rather, he has created the risk of losing $20 for the sole purpose of bearing that risk. If, however, people make an agreement about who shall bear an *existing* risk in which one of them has an actual stake or interest, that is a legal, risk-shifting agreement. Property insurance contracts are classic examples of risk-shifting agreements. The owner of the property pays the insurance company a fee (premium) in return for the company's agreement to bear the risk of the uncertain event that the property will be damaged or destroyed. If, however, the person who takes out the policy had no legitimate economic interest in the insured property (called an **insurable interest** in insurance law), the agreement is an illegal wager.

Agreements that Violate the Public Policy of a Statute

As stated earlier, an agreement can be illegal even if no statute specifically states that that particular sort of agreement is illegal. Legislatures enact statutes in an effort to resolve some particular problem. If courts enforced agreements that involve the violation of a statute, they would frustrate the purpose for which the legislature passed the statute. They would also promote disobedience of the law and disrespect for the courts.

Agreements to Commit a Crime For the reasons stated above, contracts that require the violation of a criminal statute are illegal. If Grimes promises to pay Judge John Doe a bribe of $5,000 to dismiss a criminal case against Grimes, for example, the agreement is illegal. Sometimes the very formation of a certain type of contract is a crime, even if the acts agreed on are never carried out. An example of this is an agreement to murder another person. Naturally, such agreements are considered illegal under contract law as well as under criminal law.

Agreements that Promote Violations of Statutes Sometimes a contract of a type that is usually perfectly legal—say, a contract to sell goods—is deemed to be illegal under the circumstances of the case because it promotes or facilitates the violation of a statute. Suppose Davis sells Sims goods on credit. Sims uses the goods in some illegal manner and then refuses to pay Davis for the goods. Can Davis recover the price of the goods from Sims? The answer depends on whether Davis knew of the illegal purpose and whether he intended the sale to further that illegal purpose. Generally speaking, such agreements will be legal unless there is a direct connection between the illegal conduct and the agreement in the form of active, intentional participation in or facilitation of the illegal act. Knowledge of the other party's illegal purpose, standing alone, is generally not sufficient to render an agreement illegal. When a person is aware of the other's illegal purpose *and* actively helps to accomplish that purpose, an otherwise legal agreement—such as a sale of goods—might be labeled illegal.

Licensing Laws: Agreement to Perform an Act for Which a Party Is Not Properly Licensed Congress and the state legislatures have enacted a variety of statutes that regulate professions and businesses. A common type of regulatory statute is one that requires a person to obtain a license, permit, or registration before engaging in a certain business or profession. For example, state statutes require lawyers, physicians, dentists, teachers, and other professionals to be licensed to practice their professions. In order to obtain the required license, they must meet specified requirements such as attaining a certain educational degree and passing an examination. Real estate brokers, stockbrokers, insurance agents, sellers of liquor and tobacco, pawnbrokers, electricians, barbers, and others too numerous to mention are also often required by state statute to meet licensing requirements to perform services or sell regulated commodities to members of the public.

What is the status of an agreement in which one of the parties agrees to perform an act regulated by state law for which she is not properly licensed? This will often be determined by looking at the purpose of the legislation that the unlicensed party has violated. If the statute is **regulatory**—that is, the purpose of the legislation is to protect the public against dishonest or incompetent practitioners—an agreement by an unlicensed person is generally held to be unenforceable. For example, if Spencer, a first-year law student, agrees to draft a will for Rowen for a fee of $150, Spencer could not enforce the agreement and collect a fee from Rowen for drafting the will because she is not licensed to practice law. This result makes sense, even though it imposes a hardship on Spencer. The public interest in ensuring that people on whose legal advice others rely have an appropriate educational background and proficiency in the subject matter outweighs any interest in seeing that Spencer receives what she bargained for.

On the other hand, where the licensing statute was intended primarily as a **revenue-raising** measure—that is, as a means of collecting money rather than as a means of protecting the public—an agreement to pay a person for performing an act for which she is not licensed will generally be enforced. For example, suppose that in the example used above, Spencer is a lawyer who is licensed to practice law in her state and who met all of her state's educational, testing, and character requirements but neglected to pay her annual registration fee. In this situation, there is no compelling public interest that would justify the harsh measure of refusing enforcement and possibly inflicting forfeiture on the unlicensed person.

Whether a statute is a regulatory statute or a revenue-raising statute depends on the intent of the legislature, which may not always be expressed clearly. Generally, statutes that require proof of character and skill and impose penalties for violation are considered to be regulatory in nature. Their requirements indicate that they were intended for the protection of the public. Those that impose a significant license fee and allow anyone who pays the fee to obtain a license are usually classified as revenue raising. The fact that no requirement other than the payment of the fee is imposed indicates that the purpose of the law is to raise money rather than to protect the public. Because such a statute is not designed for the protection of the public, a violation of the statute is not as threatening to the public interest as is a violation of a regulatory statute.

It would be misleading to imply that cases involving unlicensed parties always follow such a mechanical test. In some cases, courts may grant recovery to an unlicensed party even where a regulatory statute is violated. If the public policy promoted by the statute is relatively trivial in relation to the amount that would be forfeited by the unlicensed person and the unlicensed person is neither dishonest nor incompetent, a court may conclude that the statutory penalty for violation of the regulatory statute is sufficient to protect the public interest and that enforcement of the agreement is appropriate.

The following *Bergantzel* case illustrates the effect of violating a regulatory statute.

Bergantzel v. Mlynarik   *619 N.W.2d 309 (Sup. Ct. Iowa 2000) (en banc)*

Jan Mlynarik was seriously injured in a motor vehicle accident. He entered into a written contract with Terri Bergantzel, under which Bergantzel was to "assist in the negotiation with the insurance companies and attorney, if necessary, in the settlement of [Mlynarik's] claim" resulting from the accident. Bergantzel was to receive 15 percent of the amount recovered after payment of doctors' bills. The contract stated that Bergantzel was not an attorney and that payment to her was to cover her expenses only. It stated that in the event the services of a lawyer were needed, Bergantzel would "either pay for the consultation with an attorney or, if the attorney fees exceeded the 15 percent, [would] forfeit all claims to the settlement money." Pursuant to this agreement, Bergantzel negotiated a settlement with the tortfeasor's insurance carrier for the limits of the policy—$100,000. Her work included locating witnesses, preparing affidavits, making long-distance phone calls, getting Mlynarik's medical and school records, getting a physician's opinion letter, and communicating with the insurance company. For her work, Mlynarik paid Bergantzel slightly over $12,000, which was 15 percent of the recovery after medical expenses were deducted. Bergantzel then undertook similar efforts to negotiate a settlement with Mlynarik's underinsured motorist (UIM) carrier. Bergantzel received a settlement offer from the insurance company for $35,000. She told Mlynarik that if he wanted a larger recovery, he would need to hire an attorney. Mlynarik decided to do that, and entered into a contingent fee agreement with an attorney. The attorney successfully negotiated a $65,000 settlement with the UIM carrier and received his contingent fee. Bergantzel was also paid her contingent fee, with the exception of $1,650. Bergantzel sued Mlynarik in small claims court to recover the $1,650 that remained unpaid on her contract. At trial, Mlynarik argued that Bergantzel could not recover under the contract because she engaged in the unauthorized practice of law. The trial court rejected this defense and entered judgment in favor of Bergantzel. Mlynarik appealed to the district court, and the district court affirmed. Mlynarik then appealed to the Supreme Court of Iowa.

TERNUS, Justice   This court recently reviewed the principles governing claims that a contract is unenforceable on the basis of public policy. We adopted the following rule from the *Restatement (Second) of Contracts*:

If a party is prohibited from doing an act because of his failure to comply with a licensing, registration or similar requirement, a promise in consideration of his doing that act or of his promise to do it is unenforceable on grounds of public policy if

(a) the requirement has a regulatory purpose, and

(b) the interest in the enforcement of the promise is clearly outweighed by the public policy behind the requirement.

That leaves three issues for our consideration: (1) Was Bergantzel prohibited from negotiating this settlement because she was not a licensed attorney?; (2) If so, does the attorney licensing requirement have a regulatory purpose?; and (3) Is the interest in enforcement of a contingent fee contract for the performance of legal services by a nonlawyer clearly outweighed by the public policy underlying the attorney licensing requirement? We consider each question separately.

Was Bergantzel Prohibited from Negotiating a Settlement of Mlynarik's UIM Claim Because She Was Not a Licensed Attorney?

Like many other states, Iowa has found it difficult to articulate an all-inclusive definition of the practice of law. We are not without guidance, however, in our endeavor to determine whether a particular activity is the practice of law. Such guidance is provided by Ethical Consideration 3–5 of the Iowa Code of Professional Responsibility:

The practice of law includes, but is not limited to, representing another before the courts; giving of legal advice and counsel to others relating to their rights and obligations under the law; and preparation or approval of the use of legal instruments by which legal rights of others are either obtained, secured, or transferred even if such matters never become the subject of a court proceeding. *Functionally, the practice of law relates to the rendition of services for others that call for the professional judgment of a lawyer.* The essence of the professional judgment of the lawyer is the educated ability to relate the general body and philosophy of law to a specific legal problem of a client; and thus, the public interest will be better served if only lawyers are permitted to act in matters involving professional judgment. Where this professional judgment is not involved, nonlawyers, such as court clerks, police officers, abstracters, and many governmental employees, may engage in occupations that require a special knowledge of law in certain areas. *But the services of a lawyer are essential in the public interest whenever the exercise of professional legal judgment is required.*

Based on this ethical consideration, this court in *[Comm. on Prof'l Ethics & Conduct v.] Baker* concluded that the exercise of professional judgment was at the core of the practice of law. When lawyers use their educated ability to ap-

ply an area of the law to solve a specific problem of a client, they are exercising professional judgment. In law school, lawyers learn to recognize issues first and then how to solve those issues in an ethical manner, using their knowledge of the law. This is the art of exercising professional judgment.

In reviewing Bergantzel's efforts on behalf of Mlynarik, we find her negotiations with the insurance companies of greatest concern. It appears from our review of the case law that courts considering this issues have concluded that the negotiation of a settlement on behalf of the injured party requires the exercise of professional judgment and is, therefore, the practice of law. We agree with the reasoning of these courts that the negotiation of a settlement of an injured party's claim for damages requires the exercise of professional judgment. Here, Bergantzel, in determining the amount of any settlement demand or counteroffer, was required to have an understanding of the applicable tort [and underinsured motorist] principles, a grasp of the rules of evidence, and an ability to evaluate the strengths and weaknesses of Mlynarik's case vis à vis that of the UIM carrier. By negotiating a settlement on Mlynarik's behalf, Bergantzel was indirectly advising Mlynarik on the settlement value of his claim. We hold that Bergantzel engaged in the practice of law when she represented Mlynarik in negotiation of a settlement of Mlynarik's UIM claim.

Does the Attorney Licensing Requirement Have a Regulatory Purpose?

Individuals licensed to practice law in Iowa must graduate from an accredited law school and must demonstrate proficiency in the practice of law, either by successfully passing the Iowa bar examination or by demonstrating five years of legal practice in another jurisdiction. In addition, licensed attorneys must complete 15 hours of continuing legal education each year to maintain their law license. Finally, lawyers practicing in Iowa must comply with the Iowa Code of Professional Responsibility. It is also significant that the underlying goal of the licensing and supervision of attorneys is to protect the public from the consequences of unqualified legal advisors. These facts unquestionably demonstrate that the attorney licensing requirement has a regulatory purpose.

Is the Interest in Enforcement of the Agreement Between Bergantzel and Mlynarik Clearly Outweighed by the Public Policy Behind the Attorney Licensing Requirement?

We cannot determine whether Bergantzel knew her negotiation of the settlements constituted the practice of law. It appears that Bergantzel will suffer a forfeiture in that she has already rendered her performance and will be denied compensation for those services. Although [there is] some interest in enforcement, that interest is clearly outweighed by the factors militating against enforcement. We think the public policy underlying the regulation of the practice of law is strong. The importance of the licensing requirement is further evidenced by the fact that a person who assumes to be an attorney and acts as such without authority may be held in contempt of court and fined up to one thousand dollars or imprisoned in the county jail for up to six months, or both. We think that a refusal to enforce the contract will further the public policy evidenced by the attorney licensure provisions. Taking the economic benefit out of contracts that violate public policy by holding them unenforceable very definitely would promote the public policy. Weighing all the factors, we conclude that the interest in refusing to enforce the contract must prevail. The fact that Bergantzel has already performed and Mlynarik will receive a windfall simply does not outweigh the strong public policy against the unauthorized practice of law.

Reversed and remanded in favor of Mlynarik.

Agreements That May Be in Violation of Public Policy Articulated by Courts

Courts have broad discretion to articulate public policy and to decline to lend their powers of enforcement to an agreement that would contravene what they deem to be in the best interests of society. There is no simple rule for determining when a particular agreement is contrary to public policy. Public policy may change with the times; changing social and economic conditions may make behavior that was acceptable in an earlier time unacceptable today, or vice versa. The following are examples of agreements that are frequently considered vulnerable to attack on public policy grounds.

Agreements in Restraint of Competition

The policy against restrictions on competition is one of the oldest public policies declared by the common law. This same policy is also the basis of federal and state antitrust statutes. The policy against restraints on competition is based on the economic judgment that the public interest is best served by free competition. Nevertheless, courts have long recognized that some contractual restrictions on competition serve legitimate business interests and should be enforced. Therefore, agreements that limit competition are scrutinized very closely by the courts to determine whether the restraint imposed is in violation of public policy.

If the *sole* purpose of an agreement is to restrain competition, it violates public policy and is illegal. For example, if Martin and Bloom, who own competing businesses, enter an agreement whereby each agrees not to solicit or sell to the other's customers, such an agreement would be unenforceable. Where the restriction on competition was part of (*ancillary to*) an otherwise legal contract, the result may be different because the parties may have a legitimate interest to be protected by the restriction on competition.

For example, if Martin had *purchased* Bloom's business, the goodwill of the business was part of what she paid for. She has a legitimate interest in making sure that Bloom does not open a competing business soon after the sale and attract away the very customers whose goodwill she paid for. Or suppose that Martin hired Walker to work as a salesperson in her business. She wants to assure herself that she does not disclose trade secrets, confidential information, or lists of regular customers to Walker only to have Walker quit and enter a competing business.

To protect herself, the buyer or the employer in the above examples might bargain for a contractual clause that would provide that the seller or employee agrees not to engage in a particular competing activity in a specified *geographic area* for a specified *time* after the sale of the business or the termination of employment. This type of clause is called an **ancillary covenant not to compete,** or, as it is more commonly known, a **non-competition clause** or **"non-compete."** Such clauses most frequently appear in *employment contracts, contracts for the sale of a business, partnership agreements,* and *small-business buy–sell agreements.* In an employment contract, the non-competition clause might be the only part of the contract that the parties put in writing.

Enforceability of Non-Competition Clauses Although non-competition clauses restrict competition and thereby affect the public policy favoring free competition, courts enforce them if they meet the following three criteria.

1. *Clause must serve a legitimate business purpose.* This means that the person protected by the clause must have some justifiable interest—such as an interest in protecting goodwill or trade secrets—that is to be protected by the non-competition clause. It also means that the clause must be *ancillary* to, or part of, an otherwise valid contract. For example, a non-competition clause that is one term of an existing employment contract would be ancillary to that contract. By contrast, a promise not to compete would not be enforced if the employee made the promise *after* he had already resigned his job, because the promise not to compete was not ancillary to any existing contract.

2. *The restriction on competition must be reasonable in time, geographic area, and scope.* Another way of stating this is that the restrictions must not be any greater than necessary to protect a legitimate interest. It would be unreasonable for an employer or buyer of a business to restrain the other party from engaging in some activity that is not a competing activity or from doing business in a territory in which the employer or buyer does not do business, because this would not threaten his legitimate interests.

3. *The non-competition clause should not impose an undue hardship.* A court will not enforce a non-competition clause if its restraints are unduly burdensome either on the public or on the party whose ability to compete would be restrained. In one case, for example, the court refused to enforce a non-competition clause against a gastroenterologist because of evidence that the restriction would have imposed a hardship on patients and other physicians requiring his services.[3] Non-competition clauses in employment contracts that have the practical effect of preventing the restrained person from earning a livelihood are unlikely to be enforced as well. This is discussed further in the next section.

Non-Competition Clauses in Employment Contracts In employment contracts, non-competition clauses are one form of agreement that places restric-

tions on an employee's conduct after the employment is over. Other restrictions on employees' post-employment conduct can include **confidentiality** or **nondisclosure agreements,** which constrain the employee from divulging or using certain information gained during his employment, and **non-solicitation agreements,** which forbid an employee from soliciting the employer's employees, clients, or customers. In many cases, employees sign all these forms of post-employment restrictions. In others, the post-employment restriction may reflect just one or two of these forms of restraints.

Restrictions on competition work a greater hardship on an employee than on a person who has sold a business. For this reason, courts tend to judge non-competition clauses contained in employment contracts by a stricter standard than they judge similar clauses contained in contracts for the sale of a business. In some states, statutes limit or even prohibit non-competition clauses in employment contracts. In others, there is a trend toward refusing enforcement of these clauses in employment contracts unless the employer can bring forth very good evidence that he has a protectible interest that compels enforcement of the clause. The employer can do this by showing that he has entrusted the employee with trade secrets or confidential information, or that his goodwill with "near-permanent" customers is threatened. In the absence of this kind of proof, a court might conclude that the employer is just trying to avoid competition with a more efficient competitor and refuse enforcement because there is no legitimate business interest that requires protection.

Furthermore, many courts refuse to enforce non-competition clauses if they restrict employees from engaging in a "common calling." A common calling is an occupation that does not require extensive or highly sophisticated training but instead involves relatively simple, repetitive tasks. Under this common calling restriction, various courts have refused to enforce non-competition clauses against salespersons, a barber, and an auto trim repairperson.

The following *Jay's Custom Stringing* case illustrates the way courts analyze non-competition clauses.

---

[3]*Iredell Digestive Disease Clinic, P.A. v. Petrozza,* 373 S.E.2d 449 (N.C. Ct. App. 1988).

Jay's Custom Stringing, Inc. v. Yu
2001 U.S. Dist. Lexis 9298 (U.S. Dist. Ct. S.D.N.Y. 2001)

Jay's Custom Stringing (JCS) provides specialized tennis racket customizing and stringing services to tennis professionals, including many of the top-ranked players in the world. JCS offers its clients trained personnel who provide on-site racket services at major tennis tournaments in the United States, Europe, and Australia as well as support before and after tournaments.

JCS customizes tennis rackets through a number of proprietary techniques for molding, gripping, and weighting. One of the unique features of JCS's business is the JART, a patented computerized device that enables the weight, balance point, and swing weight of a tennis racket to be duplicated automatically through a computer program that uses data supplied by the device's measuring unit and a JCS database. Rackets customized by JCS cannot be duplicated except with great difficulty through a time-consuming process of trial and error. The racket specifications recorded by JCS generally are not known to the player. In comparison to customizing, racket stringing is a relatively nontechnical process. Players typically know their preferences in terms of string type and tension and understand their other penchants such as when they like to have their racket strung (morning or evening) and whether they prefer prestretched string.

JCS records a player's customizing specifications and stringing preferences on a computer database in an individual profile. JCS's player-by-player profiles also include historical information about various tournaments attended by a player such as surface condition, weather, and ball type. This information allows JCS to provide a player with performance-related information useful at future engagements at the same tournament and may offer guidance as to how a player's racket is to be customized for a particular event. Certain of the information stored on the JCS database is posted on the company's website.

Ron Jonghwan Yu has been stringing rackets since 1987. He initially worked for JCS as an onsite stringer at the Lipton Championship in 1995 and 1998, where he was given access to the name, players' stringing preferences, and pricing information without being required to sign any confidentiality agreement. Later, JCS hired Yu as an independent contractor, and later as an employee, and trained him in the craft of customizing and stringing tennis rackets. As part of his employment, Yu was provided with a laptop computer that contained the JCS database with players' profiles, price lists, and other business information of JCS.

At the time JCS hired Yu as an independent contractor, the parties executed a Confidentiality Agreement, which obligated Yu to maintain as confidential "certain tennis racquet stringing and customizing skills, techniques, concepts, procedures, and methods and information" relating to JCS's business. With the offer of full-time employment, JCS presented Yu with an Employment Agreement, and both parties signed it. It specified that upon termination of the employment agreement, Yu was subject to a broad restrictive covenant that stated as follows:

(a) For a period of two (2) years following the termination or expiration hereof, [Yu] agrees and covenants as follows, all of which shall be applicable in the territory herein defined as being anywhere on earth ("the Territory"):

(b) [Yu] shall not directly or indirectly, as a proprietor, director, officer, shareholder, employee, partner, co-venturer, consultant or in any other capacity conduct or participate in a business which engages in tennis racquet stringing and/or customizing, and/or any other business in which JCS engages during the Term.

(c) [Yu] shall not solicit or accept any business from any competitor of JCS or from any individual or entity which is, during the Term, a client of JCS.

(d) [Yu] shall not at any time directly or indirectly request or advise any individual or entity which is, during the Term, a client or which may become a client of JCS to withdraw, curtail, or cancel its business with JCS.

(e) [Yu] agrees not to directly or indirectly induce or attempt to influence any employee of JCS to curtail or terminate her or his employment with JCS.

In January 2000, while working at the Australian Open, Yu discussed going into business with Nathan Ferguson of Priority One, a JCS competitor. In May 2000, Yu notified JCS of his intent to resign, but agreed to remain with the company through September 2000 to work the U.S. Open. In January 2001, Yu joined Priority One as a racket stringer. JCS then filed suit against Yu for breach of contract and other claims, and sought, among other remedies, a preliminary injunction prohibiting Yu from violating the terms of his employment agreements.

PAULEY, III, District Judge   A restrictive covenant will only be subject to specific enforcement to the extent that it is reasonable in time and area, necessary to protect the employer's legitimate interests, not harmful to the general public, and not unreasonably burdensome to the employee. Restrictive covenants are generally disfavored by law and are only enforced under limited circumstances. The policy underlying this strict approach rests on notions of employee mobility and free enterprise. Once the term of an employment agreement has expired, the general public policy favoring robust and uninhibited competition should not give way merely because a particular employer wishes to insulate himself from competition. Important, too, are the powerful considerations of public policy which militate against sanctioning the loss of a man's livelihood. On the other hand, the employer is entitled to protection from unfair or illegal conduct that causes economic injury.

In this case, JCS contends that the restrictive covenant is necessary to protect its proprietary business information from disclosure to third parties and to maintain its customer relationships. JCS seeks trade secret protection for four categories of its business information: players' customizing specifications, players' stringing preferences, the identity of its customers, and pricing information. Information detailing the characteristics of customer specifications and preferences may be eligible for trade secret protection. Nevertheless, trade secret protection will not attach to customer information that easily can be recalled or obtained from the customers themselves. Applying those principles here, this Court finds that the players' customizing specifications recorded on JCS's computer database are entitled to trade secret protection. The values used to customize rackets are generated by the JART, a patented device unique in the industry, and reflect precise measurements that are unknown to the players themselves. By contrast, the players' stringing preferences are not entitled to trade secret protection. The specific stringing needs and predilections of the players are readily ascertainable from the players themselves and, moreover, to large extent have been published by JCS on its website. Likewise, the identities of JCS's current or prospective customers are not confidential because they too are discoverable from JCS's website as well as from outside sources, namely any ranking of the world's top tennis professionals. Nor is JCS's pricing information to be accorded trade secret status. Yu last worked for JCS over nine months ago and whatever he can now recall about his former employer's cost and pricing margins is likely to be outdated. Significantly, Yu had access to the names of JCS's clients, players' stringing preferences, and JCS's pricing information at the Lipton Championships in 1995 and 1998 without being required to sign any confidentiality agreement. This is inconsistent with JCS's present contention that those categories of information should enjoy trade secret status.

Even assuming that all the information JCS seeks to protect could be considered a trade secret, the restrictive covenant cannot be enforced unless it is reasonably limited temporally and geographically. As stated, JCS seeks to enforce a non-competition clause that precludes Yu from working "anywhere on earth" in his chosen profession for a period of two years. This Court previously refused to uphold a restrictive covenant containing similar terms. JCS has failed to identify any New York case that supports enforcement of such a broad covenant. The extreme breadth of the covenant is exemplified further by the fact that, apart from its racket customizing and stringing business, JCS engages in the retail, travel, and concierge business. JCS's concierge business assists professional tennis players, agents, manufacturers or anybody related to a major tournament with arrangements at restaurants, nightclubs, and shows. Thus, beyond purporting to preclude Yu from working "anywhere on earth" in the tennis customizing industry, the restraint extends in similar geographic scope to the other enterprises of JCS without any apparent business justification. The restrictive covenant also aims to preclude Yu from soliciting the business of any client or prospective client of JCS. JCS's definition of a prospective client appears to include any professional tennis player. As such, the restraint on solicitation is impermissibly broad and unenforceable as a matter of law.

While tempted to exercise its discretion and "blue pencil" the restrictive covenant, this Court declines to do so. The dynamic, relationship-based nature of the tennis racket customizing industry and its lack of geographical boundaries strongly militates against a judicially-crafted agreement. The parties are best served by a modified agreement reached on mutual consent.

Motion for preliminary injunction denied in favor of Yu.

The Effect of Overly Broad Non-Competition Clauses

The courts of different states treat unreasonably broad non-competition clauses in different ways. Some courts will strike the entire restriction if they find it to be unreasonable and will refuse to grant the buyer or employer any protection. Others will refuse to enforce the restraint as written, but will adjust the clause and impose such restraints as would be reasonable. In case of breach of an enforceable non-competition clause, the person benefited by the clause may seek damages or an injunction (a court order preventing the promisor from violating the covenant).

LOG ON

Want to know more about non-competition agreements? Try these websites: Joseph Mack III and Terrence Lewis, *The ABC's of Enforcing Non-Competition Agreements, Dynamic Business Magazine* (2001), **http://www.smc.org/Fpage/0103non.htm;** Neil E. Klingshirn, *Non-Compete Agreement FAQ's,* **http://www.myemploymentlawyer.com/non-competition-faqs.htm#What%20are %20some,**

Exculpatory Clauses

An **exculpatory clause** is a provision in a contract that purports to relieve one of the parties from tort liability. Exculpatory clauses are suspect on public policy grounds for two reasons. First, courts are concerned that a party who can contract away his liability for negligence will not have the incentive to use care to avoid hurting others. Second, courts are concerned that an agreement that accords one party such a powerful advantage might have been the result of the abuse of superior bargaining power rather than truly voluntary choice. Although exculpatory agreements are often said to be "disfavored" in the law, courts do not want to prevent parties who are dealing on a fair and voluntary basis from determining how the risks of their transaction shall be borne if their agreement does not threaten public health or safety.

Courts enforce exculpatory clauses in some cases and refuse to enforce them in others, depending on the circumstances of the case, the identity and relationship of the parties, and the language of the agreement. A few ground rules can be stated. First, an exculpatory clause cannot protect a party from liability for any wrongdoing greater than negligence. One that purports to relieve a person from liability for fraud or some other willful tort will be considered to be against public policy. In some cases, in fact, exculpatory clauses have been invalidated on this ground because of broad language stating that one of the parties was relieved of "all liability." Second, exculpatory clauses will not be effective to exclude tort liability on the part of a party who owes a duty to the public (such as an airline) because this would present an obvious threat to the public health and safety.

A third possible limitation on the enforceability of exculpatory clauses arises from the increasing array of statutes and common law rules that impose certain obligations on one party to a contract for the benefit of the other party to the contract. Workers' compensation statutes and laws requiring landlords to maintain leased property in a habitable condition are examples of such laws. Sometimes the person on whom such an obligation is placed will attempt to escape it by inserting an exculpatory or waiver provision in a contract. Such clauses are often—though not always—found to be against public policy because, if enforced, they would frustrate the very purpose of imposing the duty in question. For example, an employee's agreement to relieve her employer from workers' compensation liability is likely to be held illegal as a violation of public policy.

Even if a clause is not against public policy on any of the above three grounds, a court may still refuse to enforce it if a court finds that the clause was **unconscionable,** a **contract of adhesion,** or some other product of abuse of superior bargaining power. (Unconscionability and contracts of adhesion are discussed later in this chapter.) This determination depends on all of the facts of the case. As you will see in *Leon v. Family Fitness Center,* which follows, facts that tend to show that the exculpatory clause was not the product of *knowing* consent increase the likelihood that the clause will not be enforced. A clause that is written in clear language and conspicuous print is more likely to be enforced than one written in "legalese" and presented in fine print. Facts that tend to show that the exculpatory clause was the product of *voluntary* consent increase the likelihood of enforcement of the clause. For example, a clause contained in a contract for a frivolous or unnecessary activity is more likely to be enforced than is an exculpatory clause contained in a contract for a necessary activity such as medical care.

Leon v. Family Fitness Center   71 Cal. Rptr. 2d 923 (Ct. App. Cal. 1998)

Carlos Leon joined the Family Fitness Center in June 1993, signing a contract called a "Club Membership Agreement (Retail Installment Contract)." The contract was a legal-length, single sheet of paper covered with writing front and back. The front page was divided into two columns, with the right-hand column containing blanks for insertion of financial and "Federal Truth in Lending" data plus approximately 76 lines of text of varying sizes, some highlighted with bold print. The left-hand column contained approximately 90 lines of text undifferentiated in size, with no highlighting and no paragraph headings or any other indication of its contents. The back of the agreement contained approximately 90 lines of text. The exculpatory clause was located at the bottom of the left-hand column of the front page and stated the following:

Buyer is aware that participation in a sport or physical exercise may result in accidents or injury, and Buyer assumes the risk connected with the participation in a sport or exercise and represents that Member is in good health and suffers from no physical impairment which would limit their use of FFC's facilities. Buyer acknowledges that FFC has not and will not render any medical services including medical diagnosis of Member's physical condition. Buyer specifically agrees that FFC, its officers, employees and agents shall not be liable for any claim, demand, cause of action of any kind whatsoever for, or on account of death, personal injury, property damage or loss of any kind resulting from or related to Member's use of the facilities or participation in any sport, exercise or activity within or without the club premises, and Buyer agrees to hold FFC harmless from same.

In January 1994, Leon sustained head injuries when a sauna bench on which he was lying collapsed beneath him at Family Fitness. Leon filed an action against Family Fitness for personal injuries. The trial court granted summary judgment for Family Fitness based on the release in the Club Membership Agreement, and Leon appealed.

Work, Acting P.J.   "An express release is not enforceable if it is not easily readable." *Conservatorship of Estate of Link* (1984). "Furthermore, the important operative language should be placed in a position which compels notice and must be distinguished from other sections of the document. A [layperson] should not be required to muddle through complex language to know that valuable, legal rights are being relinquished." *Id.* An exculpatory clause is unenforceable if not distinguished from other sections, if printed in the same typeface as the remainder of the document, and if not likely to attract attention because it is placed in the middle of a document. In other words, a release must not be buried in a lengthy document, hidden among other verbiage, or so encumbered with other provisions as to be difficult to find.

The trial court found the exculpatory clause was sufficiently conspicuous, citing only that it is written in 8-point type as required for retail installment contracts by Civil Code section 1803.1 and stated in plain and simple language. Although print size is an important factor, it is not the only one to be considered in assessing the adequacy of a document as a release. The court failed to address specifically other relevant characteristics of the exculpatory clause: its size, form and location within the undifferentiated paragraph in which it appears. In fact, Civil Code section 1803.2 requires warnings to protect consumers' financial interests from potential hazards in retail installment contracts by providing notice in larger, bold-face type (14-, 12-, or 10-point). Clearly, Civil Code section 1803.1's perfunctory mandate that all retail installment sales contracts be at least in 8-point type is not legislative acknowledgment that 8-point type alone is per se evidence of adequate conspicuousness so as to universally relieve a party of liability for its general negligence. Indeed, Civil Code section 1812.85 requires even a provision of lesser import, a cancellation clause in contracts for health services offered by facilities such as Family Fitness to be at least 10-point bold-face print. Here, the release clause, although a separate paragraph, is in undifferentiated type located in the middle of a document. Although some other portions are printed in bold and in enlarged print, the releasing paragraph is not prefaced by a heading to alert the reader that it is an exculpatory release, contains no bold lettering, and is in the same smaller font size as is most of the document. No physical characteristic distinguishes the exculpatory clause from the remainder of the document. The document itself is titled "Club Membership Agreement (Retail Installment Contract)" giving no notice to the reader it includes a release or waiver of liability. Of particular relevance, there is no language to alert a reader that Family Fitness intended the release to exculpate it from claims based on its own negligence. Where such exculpation is sought, the release must contain specific words "clearly and explicitly expressing that this was the intent." To be valid and enforceable, a written release purporting to exculpate a tortfeasor from damage claims based on its future negligence or misconduct must clearly, unambiguously, and explicitly express this specific intent of the subscribing parties. If a tortfeasor is to be released from such liability the language used must be clear, explicit and comprehensible in each of its essential details. Such an agreement, read as a whole, must clearly notify the prospective releasor of the effect of signing the agreement.

The membership agreement signed by Leon is prefaced with an assumption of the risk statement. The general release is unobtrusively inserted thereafter. Although some courts have treated the two interchangeably, others have separately analyzed the enforceability of either. Whether taken separately or analyzed as a whole, we conclude the general release statement is fatally ambiguous. The Restatement Second of Torts states: "In order for the agreement to assume the risk to be effective, it must also appear that its terms were intended by both parties to apply to the particular conduct of the defendant which has caused the harm. Again, where the agreement is drawn by the defendant and the plaintiff passively accepts it, its terms will ordinarily be construed strictly against the defendant." (*Rest. 2d Torts,* section 496B). In its most basic sense, assumption of risk means that one person, in advance, has given his express consent to relieve another of obligations toward himself, and to assume the chance of injury from a known risk arising from what the other is to do or leave undone. The result is the other person is relieved of a legal duty to the plaintiff;

and being under no duty, he cannot be charged with negligence solely based on the occurrence of the event anticipated. Here, an individual who understandingly entered into the membership agreement at issue can be deemed to have waived any hazard known to relate to the use of the health club facilities. These hazards typically include the risk of a sprained ankle due to improper exercise or overexertion, a broken toe from a dropped weight, injuries due to malfunctioning exercise or sports equipment, or from slipping in the locker-room shower. On the other hand, no Family Fitness patron can be charged with realistically appreciating the risk of injury from simply reclining on a sauna bench. Because the collapse of a sauna bench when properly utilized is not a "known risk," we conclude Leon cannot be deemed to have assumed the risk of this incident as a matter of law.

The Family Fitness membership agreement contained a general release or hold harmless provision as well. "[W]here a participant in an activity has expressly released the defendant from responsibility for the consequences of any act of negligence, 'the law imposes no requirement that [the participant] have had a specific knowledge of the particular risk which resulted in his death [or injury.]' . . . Not every possible specific act of negligence by the defendant must be spelled out in the agreement or discussed by the parties. . . . Where a release of all liability for any act of negligence is given, the release applies to any such negligent act, whatever it may have been. . . . 'It is only necessary that the act of negligence, which results in injury to the releasor, be reasonably related to the object or purpose for which the release is given.' " *Paralift, Inc. v. Superior Court.* Here, Family Fitness's negligence was not reasonably related to the object or purpose for which the release was given, that is, as stated, injuries resulting from participating in sports or exercise rather than from merely reclining on the facility's furniture. The objective purpose of the release Leon signed was to allow him to engage in fitness activities within the Family Fitness facilities. However, it was not this type of activity which led to his injury. Leon allegedly was lying on a fixed, nonmovable, permanent bench in the sauna room. Injuries resulting during the proper use of the bench would no more be expected to be covered by the clause than those caused by the ceiling falling on his head or from a pratfall caused by a collapsing office chair. These incidents have no relation to an individual's participation in a health club's fitness regimen. Further, the release is ineffective because, read as a whole, it does not clearly notify a customer of the effect of signing the agreement. It was not clear, unambiguous and explicit. The release begins with language that participation in a sport or physical exercise may result in accidents or injury, and buyer assumes the risk connected with the participation in such. The release is followed by a statement in large print and bold, capital letters: "Moderation Is the Key to a Successful Fitness Program and Also the Key to Preventing Injuries." Family Fitness placed the general waiver between these two statements which deal strictly with the risks inherent in an exercise or sports program without any mention that it was intended to insulate the proprietor from liability for injuries caused by its own negligence.

Reading the entire document leads to the inescapable conclusion [that] the release does not clearly, explicitly and comprehensibly set forth to an ordinary person untrained in the law, such as Leon, that the intent and effect of the document is to release claims for his own personal injuries resulting from the enterprise's own negligent acts, regardless whether related to the sports or exercise activities it marketed.

Judgment reversed in favor of Leon.

Family Relationships and Public Policy

In view of the central position of the family as a valued social institution, it is not surprising that an agreement that unreasonably tends to interfere with family relationships will be considered illegal. Examples of this type of contract include agreements whereby one of the parties agrees to divorce a spouse or agrees not to marry.

In recent years, courts have been presented with an increasing number of agreements between unmarried cohabitants that purport to agree upon the manner in which the parties' property will be shared or divided upon separation. It used to be widely held that contracts between unmarried cohabitants were against public policy because they were based on an immoral relationship. As unmarried cohabitation has become more widespread, however, the law concerning the enforceability of agreements between unmarried couples has changed. For example, in the 1976 case of *Marvin v. Marvin,* the California Supreme Court held that an agreement between an unmarried couple to pool income and share property could be enforceable.[4] To-

---

[4]134 Cal. Rptr. 815 (1976).

day, most courts hold that agreements between unmarried couples are not against public policy unless they are explicitly based on illegal sexual relations as the consideration for the contract or unless one or more of the parties is married to someone else.

Unfairness in Agreements: Contracts of Adhesion and Unconscionable Contracts

Under classical contract law, courts were reluctant to inquire into the fairness of an agreement. Because the prevailing social attitudes and economic philosophy strongly favored freedom of contract, American courts took the position that so long as there had been no fraud, duress, misrepresentation, mistake, or undue influence in the bargaining process, unfairness in an agreement entered into by competent adults did not render it unenforceable.

As the changing nature of our society produced many contract situations in which the bargaining positions of the parties were grossly unequal, the classical contract assumption that each party was capable of protecting himself was no longer persuasive. The increasing use of standardized contracts (preprinted contracts) enabled parties with superior bargaining power and business sophistication to virtually dictate contract terms to weaker and less sophisticated parties.

Legislatures responded to this problem by enacting a variety of statutory measures to protect individuals against the abuse of superior bargaining power in specific situations. Examples of such legislation include minimum wage laws and rent control ordinances. Courts became more sensitive to the fact that superior bargaining power often led to **contracts of adhesion** (contracts in which a stronger party is able to determine the terms of a contract, leaving the weaker party no practical choice but to "adhere" to the terms). Some courts responded by borrowing a doctrine that had been developed and used for a long time in courts of equity,[5] the doctrine of **unconscionability.** Under this doctrine, courts would refuse to grant the equitable remedy of specific performance for breach of a contract if they found the contract to be oppressively unfair. Courts today can use the concepts of unconscionability or adhesion to analyze contracts that are alleged to be so unfair that they should not be enforced.

---

[5]Chapter 1 discusses courts of equity.

Unconscionability

One of the most far-reaching efforts to correct abuses of superior bargaining power was the enactment of section 2–302 of the Uniform Commercial Code, which gives courts the power to refuse to enforce all or part of a contract for the sale of goods or to modify such a contract if it is found to be unconscionable. By virtue of its inclusion in Article 2 of the Uniform Commercial Code, the prohibition against unconscionable terms applies to every contract for the sale of goods. The concept of unconscionability is not confined to contracts for the sale of goods, however. Section 208 of the *Restatement (Second) of Contracts,* which closely resembles the unconscionability section of the UCC, provides that courts may decline to enforce unconscionable terms or contracts. The prohibition of unconscionability has been adopted as part of the public policy of many states by courts in cases that did not involve the sale of goods, such as banking transactions and contracts for the sale or rental of real estate. It is therefore fair to state that the concept of unconscionability has become part of the general body of contract law.

Consequences of Unconscionability The UCC and the *Restatement (Second)* sections on unconscionability give courts the power to manipulate a contract containing an unconscionable provision so as to reach a just result. If a court finds that a contract or a term in a contract is unconscionable, it can do one of three things: it can refuse to enforce the entire agreement; it can refuse to enforce the unconscionable provision but enforce the rest of the contract; or it can "limit the application of the unconscionable clause so as to avoid any unconscionable result." This last alternative has been taken by courts to mean that they can make adjustments in the terms of the contract.

Meaning of Unconscionability Neither the UCC nor the *Restatement (Second) of Contracts* attempts to define the term *unconscionability.* Though the concept is impossible to define with precision, unconscionability is generally taken to mean the *absence of meaningful choice* together with *terms unreasonably advantageous* to one of the parties.

The facts of each individual case are crucial to determining whether a contract term is unconscionable. Courts will scrutinize the process by which the contract was reached to see if the agreement was reached by fair methods and whether it can fairly be said to be the product of knowing and voluntary consent.

Procedural Unconscionability Courts and writers often refer to unfairness in the bargaining process as *procedural unconscionability.* Some facts that may point to procedural unconscionability include the use of fine print or inconspicuously placed terms, complex, legalistic language, and high-pressure sales tactics. One of the most significant facts pointing to procedural unconscionability is the lack of voluntariness as shown by a marked imbalance in the parties' bargaining positions, particularly where the weaker party is unable to negotiate more favorable terms because of economic need, lack of time, or market factors. In fact, in most contracts that have been found to be unconscionable, there has been a serious inequality of bargaining power between the parties. It is important to note, however, that the mere existence of unequal bargaining power does not make a contract unconscionable. If it did, every consumer's contract with the telephone company or the electric company would be unenforceable. Rather, in an unconscionable contract, the party with the stronger bargaining power *exploits* that power by driving a bargain containing a term or terms that are so unfair that they "shock the conscience of the court."

Substantive Unconscionability In addition to looking at facts that might indicate procedural unconscionability, courts will scrutinize the contract terms themselves to determine whether they are oppressive, unreasonably one-sided, or unjustifiably harsh. This aspect of unconscionability is often referred to as *substantive unconscionability.* Examples include situations in which a party to the contract bears a disproportionate amount of the risk or other negative aspects of the transaction and situations in which a party is deprived of a remedy for the other party's breach. In some cases, unconscionability has been found in situations in which the contract provides for a price that is greatly in excess of the usual market price.

There is no mechanical test for determining whether a clause is unconscionable. Generally, in cases in which courts have found a contract term to be unconscionable, there are elements of *both* procedural and substantive unconscionability. Though courts have broad discretion to determine what contracts will be deemed to be unconscionable, it must be remembered that the doctrine of unconscionability is designed to prevent oppression and unfair surprise—not to relieve people of the effects of bad bargains.

The cases concerning unconscionability are quite diverse. Some courts have found unconscionability in contracts involving grossly unfair sales prices. Although the doctrine of unconscionability has been raised primarily by victimized consumers, there have been cases in which

businesspeople in an inherently weak bargaining position have been successful in asserting unconscionability.

Contracts of Adhesion

A contract of adhesion is a contract, usually on a standardized form, offered by a party who is in a superior bargaining position on a "take it or leave it" basis. The person presented with such a contract has no opportunity to negotiate the terms of the contract; they are imposed on him if he wants to receive the goods or services offered by the stronger party. In addition to not having a "say" about the terms of the contract, the person who signs a standardized contract of adhesion may not even know or understand the terms of the contract that he is signing. When these factors are present, the objective theory of contracts and the normal duty to read contracts before signing them may be modified. These factors may be viewed as a form of procedural unconscionability. A court may use the word *adhesion* to describe procedural unconscionability.

All of us have probably entered contracts of adhesion at one time or another. The mere fact that a contract is a contract of adhesion does not, in and of itself, mean that the contract is unenforceable. Courts will not refuse enforcement to such a contract unless the term complained of is either substantively unconscionable or is a term that the adhering party could not reasonably expect to be included in the form that he was signing.

Unenforceable contracts of adhesion can take different forms. The first is seen when the contract of adhesion contains a term that is harsh or oppressive. In this kind of case, the party offering the contract of adhesion has used his superior bargaining power to dictate unfair terms. The second situation in which contracts of adhesion are refused enforcement occurs when a contract of adhesion contains a term that, while it may not be harsh or oppressive, is a term that the adhering party could *not* be expected to have been aware that he was agreeing to. This type of case relates to the fundamental concept of agreement in an era in which lengthy, complex, standardized contracts are common. If a consumer presented with a contract of adhesion has no opportunity to negotiate terms and signs the contract without knowing or fully understanding what he is signing, is it fair to conclude that he has consented to the terms? It is reasonable to conclude that he has consented at least to the terms that he could have expected to be in the contract, but *not* to any terms that he could not have expected to be contained in the contract. The following *Ramirez* case illustrates the concept of contract of adhesion and demonstrates the relationship between unconscionability and contracts of adhesion.

Ramirez v. Circuit City Stores, Inc.   *90 Cal. Rptr. 2d 916 (Ct. App. Cal. 1999)*

Ramirez was employed by Circuit City in Fresno, California, where he installed equipment in automobiles. At the time he applied for the job with Circuit City, Ramirez was required by Circuit City to sign an arbitration agreement under which he agreed to settle any and all claims he might have relating to his application for employment, his employment, or the termination of his employment with Circuit City, by final and binding arbitration before a neutral arbitrator and in accordance with Circuit City's "Dispute Resolution Rules and Procedures." Ramirez was given no choice but to sign the document if he wished to apply for a position with Circuit City. The arbitration agreement further provided that unless Ramirez withdrew his application within three days, he would be bound by the terms of the arbitration agreement. Circuit City's "Dispute Resolution Rules and Procedures" is a separate document, containing nine single-spaced typed pages of rules. Among other things, the rules require Circuit City's employees, termed "Associates," to arbitrate any and all employment-related disputes they have against Circuit City, including any claims arising from age discrimination, violation of civil rights, or violation of the Fair Labor Standards Act. Rule 9 deprives the arbitrator of the power to hear class actions. The rules set forth the procedures for filing and prosecuting claims and limit discovery. They require claims to be filed within one year after the date the Associate knew or should have known of the facts underlying his or her claim. They place the burden of proof on the Associate, providing that in order to prevail the Associate must prove by a preponderance of the evidence that Circuit City's conduct was a violation of applicable law. The rules describe the relief available to an Associate, providing that an Associate may obtain (1) certain forms of injunctive relief, (2) reinstatement, (3) full or partial back pay and fringe benefits for up to one year from the point that the Associate knew or should have known that a law was being violated, (4) up to 24 months of pay if reinstatement is not practical or reasonable under the circumstances, or (5) compensatory damages in accordance with applicable law. Punitive damages are limited to an amount equal to any monetary award made under (3) or (4), above, or $5,000, whichever amount is greater. The rules provide that the parties will share the costs of arbitration and that the Associate will pay his or her own attorney fees. They further provide, however, that should the Associate prevail, the arbitrator has the discretion to require Circuit City to pay the Associate's costs and award the Associate reasonable attorney fees.

On July 22, 1998, Ramirez, "on behalf of himself and all others similarly situated," filed suit against Circuit City, claiming that Circuit City had violated provisions of the Labor Code and California Code of Regulations and had committed unfair and unlawful business practices. More specifically, Ramirez alleged (1) that Circuit City failed to pay its employees at least twice the minimum wage although it required them to provide many of the tools used in the installation process; (2) that Circuit City required its employees to work overtime but did not pay them overtime at the rate of one and one-half times the minimum wage; and (3) that Circuit City was misreporting the statements of gross and net earnings of its employees. Circuit City answered Ramirez's complaint and filed a petition to compel arbitration, citing the arbitration agreement. The trial court denied Circuit City's motion, and Circuit City appealed.

Stein, Judge   The doctrine of unconscionability applies to arbitration agreements in the same manner as it applies to other contracts, and an unconscionable arbitration agreement will not be enforced. "Unconscionable agreements typically involve contractual provisions which operate in a harsh and one-sided manner without any justification. They have both a procedural and a substantive element. The procedural element focuses on two factors: oppression and surprise. Oppression arises from an inequality of bargaining power which results in no real negotiation and an absence of meaningful choice. . . . Surprise involves the extent to which the terms of the bargain are hidden in a "prolix printed form" drafted by a party in a superior bargaining position. . . . Substantive unconscionability inquires into whether the one-sidedness of an agreement is objectively justified. . . . This component is tied to procedural unconscionability and requires a balancing test, such that "the greater the unfair surprise or inequality of bargaining

power, the less unreasonable the risk reallocation which will be tolerated." *Olsen v. Breeze, Inc.* (1996).

The contract at issue here was what has been labeled an adhesion contract; i.e., a standardized contract, which, imposed and drafted by the party of superior bargaining strength, relegates to the subscribing party only the opportunity to adhere to the contract or reject it. So-called adhesion contracts are not, in and of themselves, unenforceable or even particularly objectionable, but the manner in which their terms are drafted and the language and style in which they appear are subject to an unconscionability analysis. They can satisfy the first, procedural, element of unconscionability, when the party with the weaker bargaining power has no ability to negotiate the terms, no meaningful choice other than to agree to the terms stated by the party in the stronger bargaining position, and may have no real ability to comprehend the terms to which he or she is agreeing.

Here, if Ramirez was to be considered for a position with Circuit City, he had no choice but to sign the arbitration agreement. Circuit City argues that Ramirez had a choice in that he was free to choose not to apply for a job with Circuit City. This argument, however, ignores the realities of the marketplace. Persons such as Ramirez, applying for an entry level position, presumably need a job and lack much in the way of salable skills. Circuit City was in a position to provide the needed job. In addition, although persons familiar with employment rights and employment law probably could comprehend the nature of the rights they would be giving up by agreeing to the arbitration agreement, it is unrealistic to suppose that persons such as Ramirez, seeking work and applying for positions not requiring specialized education, would have the background to understand the significance of rights they were relinquishing. A meaningful choice requires more than the choice, for applicants such as Ramirez, between forgoing the possibility of employment or applying for a job but agreeing to what, superficially, appears to be a fair means of resolving employment disputes. It follows that the procedural element of unconscionability existed here.

The lack of meaningful choice, however, would not be enough to render the agreement unenforceable if the terms of the agreement were even-handed; however, they are not. It is by now well-settled that an agreement that requires the weaker party to arbitrate any claims he or she may have, but permits the stronger party to seek redress through the courts, is presumptively unconscionable. Circuit City contends its arbitration agreement is not unilateral, but requires both parties to arbitrate their claims. In support of this contention, Circuit City cites language in Rule 2 of the Rules and Procedures:

> Arbitration shall apply to any and all such disputes, controversies or claims whether asserted against the Company and/or against any employee, officer, alleged agent, director or affiliate company.

Any suggestion that this language includes a promise by Circuit City to arbitrate claims it might have against an employee, however, is negated by the language with which Rule 2 opens, which explains just what "such disputes" are: "Except as otherwise limited herein, any and all employment-related legal disputes, controversies or claims of an Associate. . . ." Nothing is said about claims of the Company or about claims against Associates. Circuit City also cites the only language in the arbitration agreement that expressly sets forth an obligation on Circuit City's part:

> Circuit City agrees to follow this Dispute Resolution Agreement and the Dispute Resolution Rules and Procedures in connection with the Associate whose signature appears above.

This language, however, hardly can be characterized as an agreement by Circuit City to arbitrate any claims it may have against the employee; it does nothing more than bind Circuit City to follow the Rules and Procedures in connection with any claim filed by an Associate. Although it is unnecessary to look beyond the unilateral nature of Circuit City's arbitration agreement to hold it unconscionable, the agreement is suspect for other reasons. It limits or eliminates the ability of an employee to obtain relief against Circuit City by participating in a class action. Such a limitation was condemned by the Supreme Court in *Keating v. Superior Court* (1982). The court there emphasized the importance of the class action device as a means of vindicating rights asserted by large groups of persons, in that the "class suit both eliminates the possibility of repetitious litigation and provides small claimants with a method of obtaining redress for claims which would otherwise be too small to warrant individual litigation." The court found that the elimination of the device would unduly benefit the wrongdoer and unduly disadvantage the members of the affected class. It strongly suggested that where an arbitration agreement is part of an adhesion contract, a term precluding settlement of claims by means of a class action should not be enforced. "It is common knowledge that arbitration clauses frequently appear in standardized contracts of adhesion. A primary consideration which has led courts to uphold such clauses, despite the adhesive nature of the contract, is the belief that arbitration is not oppressive and does not defeat the reasonable expectations of the parties. If, however, an arbitration clause may be used to insulate the drafter of an adhesive contract from any form of class proceeding, effectively foreclosing many individual claims, it may well be oppressive and may defeat the expectations of the nondrafting party."

In addition, the arbitration agreement's limitations on punitive damages tends to subvert the accepted purpose of such awards: to punish wrongdoing and to deter future misconduct by either the defendant or other potential wrongdoers. It therefore has been suggested that such limitations violate public policy. Similarly, the arbitration agreement tends to discourage the prosecution of employee claims that are encouraged by statute. It thus makes discretionary awards of costs and attorney fees that by statute are mandatory. It also makes a complaining employee potentially liable for Circuit City's costs and attorney fees, a liability that is not authorized by statute. In short, and for all of the reasons stated above, we find that Circuit City's arbitration agreement is unconscionable and thus unenforceable.

Affirmed in favor of Ramirez.

ETHICS IN ACTION

Murphy, a welfare recipient with four minor children, saw an advertisement in the local newspaper that had been placed by McNamara, a television and stereo dealer. It stated:

> Why buy when you can rent? Color TV and stereos. *Rent to own!* Use our Rent-to-own plan and let TV Rentals deliver either of these models to your home. *We feature*—Never a repair bill—No deposit—No credit needed—No long term obligation—Weekly or monthly rates available—Order by phone—Call today—Watch color TV tonight.

As a result of the advertisement, Murphy leased a 25-inch Philco color console TV set from McNamara under the "Rent to Own" plan. The lease agreement provided that Murphy would pay a $20 delivery charge and 78 weekly payments of $16. At the end of the period, Murphy would own the set. The agreement also provided that the customer could return the set at any time and terminate the lease as long as all rental payments had been made up to the return date. Murphy entered the lease because she believed that she could acquire ownership of a TV set without first establishing credit as was stressed in McNamara's ads. At no time did McNamara inform Murphy that the terms of the lease required her to pay a total of $1,268 for the TV. The retail sales price for the same TV was $499. After making $436 in payments over a period of about six months, Murphy read a newspaper article criticizing the lease plan and realized the amount that the agreement required her to pay. She stopped making payments and McNamara sought to repossess the TV. Murphy argued that the agreement was unconscionable. Was it ethical to market the Rent to Own plan? Was McNamara ethically required to inform Murphy that the total price of the TV would be $1,268 under the Rent to Own plan?

Effect of Illegality

General Rule: No Remedy for Breach of Illegal Agreements

As a general rule, courts will refuse to give any remedy for the breach of an illegal agreement. A court will refuse to enforce an illegal agreement and will also refuse to permit a party who has fully or partially performed her part of the agreement to recover what she has parted with. The reason for this rule is to serve the public interest, not to punish the parties.

In some cases, the public interest is best served by allowing some recovery to one or both of the parties. Such cases constitute exceptions to the "hands off" rule. The following discussion concerns the most common situations in which courts will grant some remedy even though they find the agreement to be illegal.

Exceptions

Excusable Ignorance of Facts or Legislation
Though it is often said that ignorance of the law is no excuse, courts will, under certain circumstances, permit a party to an illegal agreement who was excusably ignorant of facts or legislation that rendered the agreement illegal to recover damages for breach of the agreement. This exception is used where only *one* of the parties acted in ignorance of the illegality of the agreement and the other party was aware that the agreement was illegal. For this exception to apply, the facts or legislation of which the person claiming damages was ignorant must be of a relatively minor character—that is, it must not involve an immoral act or a serious threat to the public welfare. Finally, the person who is claiming damages cannot recover damages for anything that he does after learning of the illegality. For example, Warren enters a contract to perform in a play at Craig's theater. Warren does not know that Craig does not have the license to operate a theater as required by statute. Warren can recover the wages agreed on in the parties' contract for work that he performed before learning of the illegality.

When *both* of the parties are ignorant of facts or legislation of a relatively minor character, courts will not permit them to enforce the agreement and receive what they had bargained for, but they will permit the parties to recover what they have parted with.

Rights of Parties Not Equally in the Wrong   The courts will often permit a party who is not equally in the wrong (in technical legal terms, not in pari delicto) to recover what she has parted with under an illegal agreement. One of the most common situations in which this exception is used involves the rights of "protected parties"—people who were intended to be protected by a regulatory statute—who contract with parties who are not properly licensed under that statute. Most regulatory statutes are intended to protect the pubic. As a general rule if a person guilty of violating a regulatory statute enters into an agreement with another person for whose protection the statue was adopted, the agreement will be enforceable by the party whom the legislature intended to protect,

Another common situation in which courts will grant a remedy to a party who is not equally in the wrong is one in which the less guilty party has been induced to enter the agreement by misrepresentation, fraud, duress, or undue influence.

Rescission before Performance of Illegal Act

Obviously, public policy is best served by any rule that encourages people not to commit illegal acts. People who have fully or partially performed their part of an illegal contract have little incentive to raise the question of illegality if they know that they will be unable to recover what they have given because of the courts' hands-off approach to illegal agreements. To encourage people to cancel illegal contracts, courts will allow a person who rescinds such a contract before any illegal act has been performed to recover any consideration that he has given. For example, Dixon, the owner of a restaurant, pays O'Leary, an employee of a competitor's restaurant, $1,000 to obtain some of the competitor's recipes. If Dixon has second thoughts and tells O'Leary the deal is off before receiving any recipes, he can recover the $1,000 he paid O'Leary.

Divisible Contracts

If part of an agreement is legal and part is illegal, the courts will enforce the legal part so long as it is possible to separate the two parts. A contract is said to be *divisible*—that is, the legal part can be separated from the illegal part—if the contract consists of several promises or acts by one party, each of which corresponds with an act or a promise by the other party. In other words, there must be a separate consideration for each promise or act for a contract to be considered divisible.

Where no separate consideration is exchanged for the legal and illegal parts of an agreement, the agreement is said to be *indivisible*. As a general rule, an indivisible contract that contains an illegal part will be entirely unenforceable unless it comes within one of the exceptions discussed above. However, if the major portion of a contract is legal but the contract contains an illegal provision that does not affect the primary, legal portion, courts will often enforce the legal part of the agreement and simply decline to enforce the illegal part. For example, suppose Alberts sells his barbershop to Bates. The contract of sale provides that Alberts will not engage in barbering any-

where in the world for the rest of his life. The major portion of the contract—the sale of the business—is perfectly legal. A provision of the contract—the ancillary covenant not to compete—is overly restrictive, and thus illegal. A court would enforce the sale of the business but modify or refuse to enforce the restraint provision. See Figure 1.

Problems and Problem Cases

1. In October 1998, Schlack went to work for EarthWeb in the position of Vice President, Worldwide Content. EarthWeb provides online products and services to business professionals in the information technology (IT) industry. EarthWeb and Schlack executed a written employment contract. One of the provisions of the contract was a nondisclosure agreement stating that Schlack would not disclose any confidential or proprietary information without EarthWeb's consent, either during his employment or afterward. Another provision was entitled "Limited Agreement Not To Compete." It stated that:

(c) For a period of twelve (12) months after the termination of Schlack's employment with Earth-Web, Schlack shall not, directly or indirectly:

(1) work as an employee, employer, consultant, agent, principal, partner, manager, officer, director, or in any other individual or representative capacity for any person or entity that directly competes with EarthWeb. For the purpose of this section, the term "directly competing" is defined as a person or entity or division on an entity that is

(i) an online service for Information Professionals whose primary business is to provide Information Technology Professionals with a directory of third party technology, software, and/or developer resources; and/or an online reference library, and or

(ii) an online store, the primary purpose of which is to sell or distribute third party software or products used for Internet site or software development[.]

As one of ten vice presidents at EarthWeb, Schlack was responsible for the content of all of EarthWeb's websites. In September 1999, Schlack resigned from EarthWeb because he had accepted a position with ITworld.com, a subsidiary of IDG. IDG is the world's leading provider of IT print-based information. Did Schlack breach his nondisclosure or non-competition agreement with Earth-Web by taking a job with IDG?

Figure 1   *Effect of Illegality*

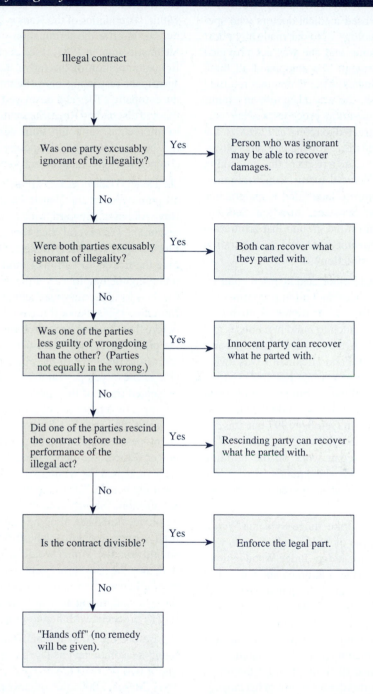

2. Broemmer, age 21, was unmarried and 16 or 17 weeks pregnant. She was a high school graduate earning less than $100 a week and had no medical benefits. Broemmer was in considerable turmoil and confusion. The father-to-be insisted that she have an abortion, but her parents advised against it. Broemmer went to Abortion Services with her mother and was escorted into an adjoining room and asked to complete three forms: a consent to treatment form, a questionnaire asking for a detailed medical history, and an agreement to arbitrate. The agreement to arbitrate stated that "any dispute arising between the Parties as a result of the fees and/or services:

would be settled by binding arbitration" and that "any arbitrators appointed by the AAA [American Arbitration Association] shall be licensed medical doctors who specialize in obstetrics/gynecology." No one made any effort to explain this to Broemmer and she was not provided with a copy of the agreement. She completed all three forms in less than five minutes. After Broemmer returned the forms to the front desk, she was taken into an examination room where preoperation procedures were performed. She was then instructed to return at 7:00 A.M. the next morning. She returned the following day and a physician performed the abortion. As a result of this procedure, Broemmer suffered a punctured uterus, which required medical treatment. Broemmer later filed a malpractice lawsuit against Abortion Services. Abortion Services moved to dismiss the suit on the ground that arbitration was required under the agreement. Should the arbitration clause be enforced in this situation?

3. Crowe, an experienced builder and licensed contractor in Mississippi, specializes in building commercial hen houses. In the fall of 1997, Crowe entered into a contract with Hickman's Egg Ranch to build hen houses and an egg processing plant in Arizona. At that time, Crowe was not licensed in Arizona, and Hickman's was aware that he was not licensed. Arizona law requires contractors to be licensed and disallows actions for compensation by unlicensed contractors. Crowe did take and pass the Arizona licensing exam in October 1997 but was not licensed or bonded until the following February, so he was unlicensed when he began work on the building project. Crowe claims that Hickman's owes him $105,709.10 on the contract. Can Crowe enforce the contract and collect this amount?

4. Strickland attempted to bribe Judge Sylvania Woods to show leniency toward one of Strickland's friends who had a case pending before the judge. Judge Woods immediately reported this to the state's attorney and was asked to play along with Strickland until the actual payment of money occurred. Strickland gave $2,500 to the judge, who promptly turned it over to the state's attorney's office. Strickland was indicted for bribery, pled guilty, and was sentenced to a four-year prison term. Three months after the criminal trial, Strickland filed a motion for the return of his $2,500. Will the court order the return of his money?

5. Steamatic of Kansas City, Inc., specialized in cleaning and restoring property damaged by fire, smoke, water, or other elements. It employed Rhea as a marketing representative. His duties included soliciting customers, preparing cost estimates, supervising restoration work, and conducting seminars. At the time of his employment, Rhea signed a non-competition agreement prohibiting him from entering into a business in competition with Steamatic within six counties of the Kansas City area for a period of two years after the termination of his employment with Steamatic. Late in 1987, Rhea decided to leave Steamatic. In contemplation of the move, he secretly extracted the agreement restricting his postemployment activity from the company's files and destroyed it. Steamatic learned of this and discharged Rhea. Steamatic filed suit against Rhea to enforce the non-competition agreement when it learned that he was entering a competing business. Will the non-competition agreement be enforced?

6. Deno, Tisdale, Adams, Fairley, and Dickerson were all employees at the Waffle House restaurant in Grand Bay, Alabama. Seward was a regular customer at the restaurant. On several occasions, Seward would travel to Florida and buy lottery tickets. On his return, he would give the tickets to various friends and family members, including the employees of the Waffle House. A drawing for the Florida lottery was scheduled for Saturday night, March 6, 1999. Seward traveled to Florida in the week before that drawing and purchased several lottery tickets. He placed each individual ticket in a separate envelope and wrote the name of the intended recipient on the outside of the envelope. On the eve of the drawing, Seward presented three of the employees with an envelope containing a ticket, but none of them won. The day after the drawing, Seward gave Dickerson and another employee envelopes containing tickets. When Dickerson opened her envelope, she determined that the numbers of her ticket matched the winning numbers drawn in the lottery the night before. The ticket won a prize of approximately $5 million. Shortly afterward, Dickerson's four co-employees sued her, alleging that they and Dickerson had orally contracted with each other that if any one of them should win, the winner would share any lottery winnings with the other ticket recipients. An Alabama statute states that "all contracts founded in whole or in part on a gambling consideration are void." Must Dickerson share the lottery proceeds with her co-employees?

7. Before the 2000 football season, The New Orleans Saints season ticket packages were for 10 games consisting of two preseason games and eight regular games. In early March 2000, the organization sent to its season ticket holders a letter setting forth the fee schedule for the upcoming season. This letter was sent before the date for payment for season tickets. It clearly informed the ticket holders that because there was to be only one home preseason game, thus reducing the number of home games to nine, each season ticket holder would receive an extra terrace seat ticket to the first home game. If there were no tickets available for that game, then the ticket holder would receive a ticket to the second home game. The invoice for a season ticket package showed only one total price rather than a per-ticket price. There were no options offered with this package; the fan either bought the package or did not buy the package. Andry purchased the season ticket package and then sued for return of the value of the extra ticket, which he asserted was about $37.00. He also alleged that the extra ticket device for the first game resulted in it being a sellout, thus generating additional TV revenues, and he sought the additional revenues to be distributed to season ticket holders as well. Andry asserted that the contract should be considered as a contract of adhesion and the extra terrace ticket clause be set aside. Does he have a good case?

8. Benjamin was a 32-year-old lawyer who had played in recreational roller and ice hockey leagues for 15 years. His team played at various rinks throughout the Phoenix metropolitan area, including the Spectrum Rink. Before playing at the Spectrum Rink, Benjamin was required to and did sign a release. The release stated in part:

> 2. [the undersigned] Acknowledge and fully understand that each participant will be engaging in activities that involve risk of serious injury, including permanent disability and death, and severe social and economic losses which might result not only from their own actions, inactions, or negligence or of any equipment used [sic]. Further, that there may be other risks not known to us, or not reasonably foreseeable, such as disability or death.

> 3. Assume all the foregoing risks and accept personal responsibility for the damages following such injury, permanent disability, or death.

> 4. Release, waive, discharge, and covenant not to sue THE CHANDLER SPORTS SPECTRUM . . . hereinafter referred to as "releases," from demands, losses, or damages on account of injury, including death or damage to property, *caused or alleged to be caused in whole or in part by the negligence of the releasee or otherwise.*

> * * *

> THE UNDERSIGNED HAVE READ THE ABOVE WAIVER AND RELEASE, UNDERSTAND THAT THEY HAVE GIVEN UP SUBSTANTIAL RIGHTS BY SIGNING IT, AND SIGN IT VOLUNTARILY.

On November 8, 1995, Benjamin was playing in a roller hockey game at the Spectrum Rink. Near the end of the game, Benjamin was racing another player for a loose puck when he fell and suffered multiple fractures to his left leg. Benjamin brought suit, contending that his left skate was stopped by a raised floor tile, resulting in his injury. Benjamin asserts the release is unenforceable. Was it?

9. Griffin, an expert skier and certified ski instructor, entered the Ironman Decathlon held at Grand Targhee ski resort, which was owned and operated by Big Valley Corporation. The decathlon was held for fun rather than profit. It consisted of several events, including swimming five pool laps, bowling one line, drinking a quart of beer, throwing darts, and skiing in both downhill and cross-country races. The downhill ski race was the first event in the decathlon. It was held early in the morning before the resort was opened to the public. Prior to the race, Griffin and all of the other downhill contestants were required to sign a document entitled "General Release of Claim." This release provided:

> In consideration of my being allowed to participate in IRONMAN DECATHLON at Targhee Resort, Alta, Wyoming, I irrevocably and forever hereby release and discharge any and all of the employees, agents, or servants and owners of Targhee Resort and the other sponsors of IRONMAN DECATHLON officially connected with this event of and from any and all legal claims or legal liability of any kind involving bodily injury or death sustained by me during my stay at Targhee Resort. I hereby personally assume all risks in connection with said event and I further release the aforementioned resort, its agents, and operators, for any harm which might befall me as a participant in this event, whether foreseen or unforeseen and further save and hold harmless said resort and persons from any claim by me or my family, estate, heirs or assigns.

/s/ Dean Griffin 4/13/84

About 10 minutes after the race began, Griffin was found unconscious approximately three-quarters of the way down the mountain. He died a few hours later. No one witnessed the incident that caused his death, but it was speculated that he lost control of his skis and hit a tree. Elizabeth Griffin, as personal representative for Griffin's estate, filed a wrongful death suit against Big Valley on behalf of Griffin's son. Will the court enforce the exculpatory agreement that Griffin signed?

10. Gianni Sport was a New York manufacturer and distributor of women's clothing. Gantos was a clothing retailer headquartered in Grand Rapids, Michigan. In 1980, Gantos's sales total was 20 times greater than Gianni Sport's, and in this industry, buyers were "in the driver's seat." In June 1980, Gantos submitted to Gianni Sport a purchase order for women's holiday clothing to be delivered on October 10, 1980. The purchase order contained the following clause:

> Buyer reserves the right to terminate by notice to Seller all or any part of this Purchase Order with respect to Goods that have not actually been shipped by Seller or as to Goods which are not timely delivered for any reason whatsoever.

Gianni Sport made the goods in question especially for Gantos. This holiday order comprised 20 to 22 percent of Gianni Sport's business. In late September 1980, before the goods were shipped, Gantos canceled the order. Was the cancellation clause unconscionable?

Online Research: Examples of Non-Competes and Exculpatory Agreements

Using your favorite search engine, find an example of a non-competition agreement and an example of a liability release (exculpatory agreement).

16

WRITING

Moore went to First National Bank and requested the president of the bank to allow his adult sons, Rocky and Mike, to open an account in the name of Texas Continental Express, Inc. Moore promised to bring his own business to the bank and orally agreed to make good any losses that the bank might incur from receiving dishonored checks from Texas Continental. The bank then furnished regular checking account and bank draft services to Texas Continental. Several years later, Texas Continental wrote checks totaling $448,942.05 that were returned for insufficient funds. Texas Continental did not cover the checks and the bank turned to Moore for payment.

- *Was Moore's **oral** promise to pay Texas Continental's dishonored checks enforceable?*
- *If not, what would have been required in the nature of a writing to make the promise enforceable?*
- *Suppose there had been a written agreement between Moore and the bank: Would the bank have been able to enforce an oral promise made by Moore that was **not** stated in the written contract?*

YOUR STUDY OF CONTRACT law so far has focused on the requirements for the formation of a valid contract. You should be aware, however, that even when all the elements of a valid contract exist, the enforceability of the contract and the nature of the parties' obligations can be greatly affected by the *form* in which the contract is set out and by the *language* that is used to express the agreement. This chapter discusses the ways in which the enforceability of a contract and the scope of contractual obligations can be affected by the manner in which people express their agreements.

The Significance of Writing in Contract Law

Purposes of Writing

Despite what many people believe, there is no general requirement that contracts be in writing. In most situations, oral contracts are legally enforceable, assuming that they can be proven. Still, oral contracts are less desirable than written contracts in many ways. They are more easily misunderstood or forgotten than written contracts. They are also more subject to the danger that a person might fabricate terms or fraudulently claim to have made an oral contract when none exists.

Writing is important in contract law and practice for a number of reasons. When people memorialize their contracts in a writing, they are enhancing their chances of proving that an obligation was undertaken and making it harder for the other party to deny making the promise. A person's signature on a written contract allows a basis for the contract to be authenticated, or proved to be genuinely the contract of the signer. In addition, signing a writing also communicates to any of us entering the contract the seriousness of the occasion. Occasionally there are problems with proving the genuineness of the writing and often there are disagreements about the interpretation of language in a contract, but the written form is still very useful in increasing the chances that you will be able to depend on the enforcement of your contracts.

LOG ON

For a discussion of some of the practical and legal problems of oral contracts, see Dummies.com's article, *Issues in Oral Contracts,* **http://www.dummies.com/Money/Small_Business/Business_Contracts/0–7645–5236–8_0002.html.**

Writing and Contract Enforcement

In contract law, there are certain situations in which a promise that is not in writing can be denied enforcement. In such situations, an otherwise valid contract can become unenforceable if it does not comply with the formalities required by state law. These situations are controlled by a type of statute called the Statute of Frauds.

Overview of the Statute of Frauds

History and Purposes

In 17th-century England, the dangers inherent in oral contracts were exacerbated by a legal rule that prohibited parties to a lawsuit from testifying in their own cases. Since the parties to an oral contract could not give testimony, the only way they could prove the existence of the contract was through the testimony of third parties. As you might expect, third parties were sometimes persuaded to offer false testimony about the existence of contracts. In an attempt to stop the widespread fraud and perjury that resulted, Parliament enacted the Statute of Frauds in 1677. It required written evidence before certain classes of contracts would be enforced. Although the possibility of fraud exists in every contract, the statute focused on contracts in which the potential for fraud was great or the consequences of fraud were especially serious. The legislatures of American states adopted very similar statutes, also known as statutes of frauds. These statutes, which require certain kinds of contracts to be evidenced by a signed writing, are exceptions to the general rule that oral contracts are enforceable.

Statutes of frauds have produced a great deal of litigation, due in part to the public's ignorance of their provisions. It is difficult to imagine an aspect of contract law that is more practical for businesspeople to know about than the circumstances under which an oral contract will not suffice.

Effect of Violation of the Statute of Frauds

The statute of frauds applies only to executory contracts. If an oral contract has been completely performed by both parties, the fact that it did not comply with the statute of frauds would not be a ground for rescission of the contract.

What happens if an executory contract is within the statute of frauds but has not been evidenced by the type of writing required by the statute? It is not treated as an illegal contract because the statute of frauds is more of a formal rule than a rule of substantive law. Rather, the contract that fails to comply with the statute of frauds is *unenforceable.* Although the contract will not be enforced, a person who has conferred some benefit on the other party pursuant to the contract can recover the reasonable value of his performance in an action based on *quasi-contract.*

Contracts Covered by the Statute of Frauds

A contract is said to be "within" (covered by) the statute of frauds if the statute requires that sort of contract to be evidenced by a writing. In almost all states, the following types of contracts are *within* the statute of frauds:

1. Collateral contracts in which a person promises to perform the obligation of another person.

2. Contracts for the sale of an interest in real estate.

THE GLOBAL BUSINESS ENVIRONMENT:

Under the CISG, there is no requirement that a contract be evidenced by a writing. A contract need not take any particular form, and can be proven by any means. The CISG does permit parties to a written contract to require that any modifications of the contract be in writing, however.

3. Bilateral contracts that cannot be performed within a year from the date of their formation.

4. Contracts for the sale of goods for a price of $500 or more.

5. Contracts in which an executor or administrator promises to be personally liable for the debt of an estate.

6. Contracts in which marriage is the consideration.

Of this list, the first four sorts of contracts have the most significance today, and our discussion will focus primarily on them.

The statutes of frauds of the various states are not uniform. Some states require written evidence of other contracts in addition to those listed above. For example, a number of states require written evidence of contracts to pay a commission for the sale of real estate. Others require written evidence of ratifications of infants' promises or promises to pay debts that have been barred by the statute of limitations or discharged by bankruptcy.

The following discussion examines in greater detail the sorts of contracts that are within most states' statute of frauds.

Collateral Contracts

A **collateral contract** is one in which one person (the *guarantor*) agrees to pay the debt or obligation that a second person (the *principal debtor*) owes to a third person (the *obligee*) if the principal debtor fails to perform. For example, Cohn, who wants to help Davis establish a business, promises First Bank that he will repay the loan that First Bank makes to Davis if Davis fails to pay it. Here, Cohn is the guarantor, Davis is the principal debtor, and First Bank is the obligee. Cohn's promise to First Bank must be in writing to be enforceable.

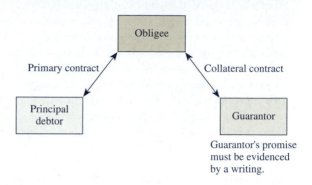

Figure 1   *Collateral Contract*

Obligee

Primary contract

Collateral contract

Principal debtor

Guarantor

Guarantor's promise must be evidenced by a writing.

Figure 1 shows that a collateral contract involves at least three parties and at least two promises to perform (a promise by the principal debtor to pay the obligee and a promise by the guarantor to pay the obligee). In a collateral contract, the guarantor promises to pay *only if the principal debtor fails to do so*. The essence of the collateral contract is that the debt or obligation is owed primarily by the principal debtor and the guarantor's debt is *secondary*. Thus, not all three-party transactions are collateral contracts.

When a person undertakes an obligation that is *not* conditioned on the default of another person, and the debt is his own rather than that of another person, his obligation is said to be *original,* not collateral. For example, when Timmons calls Johnson Florist Company and says, "Send flowers to Elrod," Timmons is undertaking an obligation to pay *her own*—not someone else's—debt.

When a contract is determined to be collateral, however, it will be unenforceable unless it is evidenced by a writing. You will see an example of this principle in the following *Gallagher* case.

Gallagher, Langlas & Gallagher, P. C. v. Burco   *587 N.W.2d 615 (Ct. App. Iowa 1998)*

Lynn Roose hired the law firm Gallagher, Langlas and Gallagher, P.C., to represent her in her divorce. Attorney Thomas Langlas signed an attorney fee contract in August 1994, and gave it to Roose to sign and return. He also requested a $2,000 retainer fee. Roose never signed or returned the contract, and did not pay the retainer fee in full. The firm represented Roose even though she did not sign the contract or pay the retainer fee in full. On April 10, 1995, the Gallagher attorneys met with Roose and her father, Gaylen Burco. The attorneys told Burco that the expense of his daughter's child custody trial would be approximately $1,000 per day. The firm would not guarantee Burco the trial would last only two or three days. The firm contends that during the meeting Burco agreed to be responsible for the remainder of Roose's account. Burco denies an agreement. At the end of the meeting Burco gave the firm a check for $1,000 to pay the outstanding balance of $ 814.92 on Roose's account and said he would pay for future services. Before trial, Mary Chicchelly, an attorney with the firm, contacted Burco *requesting an additional retainer to secure fees to be incurred and Burco told her, "My word as a gentleman should be enough. . . . I told Mr. Langlas I would pay and I will pay." Roose failed to pay her legal fees. In July 1995, the attorneys sent Burco a letter requesting $5,000 for Roose's legal fees or the signing of a promissory note. At the end of July, they sent Burco another letter asking him to sign a promissory note for $10,000. Neither Roose nor Burco paid the attorney fees or signed the notes. The firm represented Roose in the July 1995 trial. Burco took an active part in the trial by testifying and participating in conferences with counsel during recesses. After trial, Burco returned the second letter and promissory note with a notation stating he was not responsible for his daughter's attorney fees. The firm filed a motion to withdraw from Roose's case in July 1996 and the motion was granted.*

The firm filed suit against Burco and Roose for the unpaid legal fees. Among the defenses Burco raised was the statute of frauds. The trial court entered a trial judgment against Burco and a default judgment against Roose for $14,588.53. Burco appealed.

Streit, Judge   Burco contends evidence of the oral contract is barred by the statute of frauds. The statute relates to the manner of proof, but does not forbid oral contracts or render them invalid. If the statute renders evidence of the guaranty incompetent and thus inadmissible, the judgment against Burco must be reversed. The statute of frauds requires that certain contracts be evidenced by some kind of writing before they are enforceable. The statute applies to surety contracts—a promise to a creditor to answer for debt, default, or miscarriage of another. The purpose of the statute of frauds in regard to surety contracts is explained in the Restatement of Surety & Guaranty as follows:

> In the case of secondary obligations, however, the Statute also serves the cautionary function of guarding the promisor against ill-considered action. The suretyship provision of the Statute is not limited to important or complex contracts, but applies to secondary obligations created by promises made to an obligee of the underlying obligation. However, other considerations militate in favor of requiring a writing: the motivation of the secondary obligor is often essentially gratuitous; its obligation depends on a contingency that may seem remote at the time of contracting; and natural formalities that often attend an extension of credit are unlikely to provide reliable evidence of the existence and terms of the secondary obligor's undertaking. Reliance of the kinds usual in such situations—extension of credit or forbearance to pursue the principal obligor—does not render the requirement inapplicable. It should be noted that the determination of what constitutes a writing or a signature in an environment of electronic data transmission must continue to evolve. *Rest.3d Sur.* section 11 at 65 (1995).

Iowa Code section 622.32(2) codifies this doctrine:

> Except when otherwise specifically provided, no evidence of the following enumerated contracts is competent, unless it be in writing and signed by the party charged or by the party's authorized agent:

. . .

> 2. Those wherein one person promises to answer for the debt, default, or miscarriage of another, including promises by executors to pay the debt of the decedent from their own estate.

In construing Iowa Code section 622.32(2), the Iowa Supreme Court has distinguished between collateral and original promises. Original promises are made when the promise to pay the debt of another arises out of new and original consideration between the newly contracting parties. With an original promise the surety has a personal concern in the debtor's obligation and will achieve a personal benefit out of the debtor's obligation. The "leading object of his promise is to secure some benefit or business advantage for himself." Original promises are not within the statute of frauds. Collateral promises are made when a promise is made in addition to an already existing contract and the surety has no personal concern in the debtor's obligation and gains no benefit from the debtor's obligation. The "main purpose" of the promise must not be the benefit of the surety. Collateral promises fall within the statute of frauds. In addition to ascertaining whether the promisor receives a benefit, we ascertain who the credit was extended to, the promisor or the party who was rendered the services. This intention is ascertained from the promissory words used, the situation of the parties, and all surrounding circumstances when the promise was made. Whether a promise is collateral to an existing contract or creates a primary obligation on the part of the promisor is a question of fact. Thus, it is for this court to decide whether the trial court's ruling Burco's promise was original rather than collateral is supported by substantial evidence on the record. The trial court determined the promise was original rather than collateral "inasmuch as it involved his daughter and grandchild." There is nothing in the record which supports the trial court's conclusion the promise was original rather than collateral except for a vague notion his family was affected by the matter. The evidence shows the benefit to Burco was indirect in that if his daughter won custody of his granddaughter he may get to visit her more. There is no evidence this was Burco's primary motivating factor in promising to pay his daughter's debt. From this record, it cannot be found Burco gained a benefit from his promise. This being so, his promise was collateral rather than original. There is not substantial evidence supporting the court's finding Burco made an original promise which falls outside the statute of frauds. The statute of frauds renders evidence of the contract incompetent and makes it unenforceable.

Reversed in favor of Burco.

Exception: Main Purpose or Leading Object Rule There are some situations in which a contract that is technically collateral is treated like an original contract because the person promising to pay the debt of another does so for the primary purpose of securing some personal benefit. Under the **main purpose** or **leading object** rule, no writing is required where the guarantor makes a collateral promise for the main purpose of obtaining some personal economic advantage. When the consideration given in exchange for the collateral promise is something the guarantor seeks primarily for his own benefit rather than for the benefit of the primary debtor, the contract is outside the statute of frauds and does not have to be in writing. Suppose, for example, that Penn is a major creditor of Widgetmart, a retailer. To help keep Widgetmart afloat and increase the chances that Widgetmart will repay the debt it owes him, Penn orally promises Rex Industries, one of the Widgetmart's suppliers, that he will guarantee Widgetmart's payment for goods that Rex sells to Widgetmart. In this situation, Penn's oral agreement could be enforced under the main purpose rule if the court finds that Penn was acting for his own personal financial benefit.

Interest in Land

Any contract that creates or transfers an interest in land is within the statute of frauds. The inclusion of real estate contracts in the statute of frauds reflects the values of an earlier, agrarian society in which land was the primary basis of wealth. Our legal system historically has treated land as being more important than other forms of property. Courts have interpreted the land provision of the statute of frauds broadly to require written evidence of any transaction that will affect the ownership of an interest in land. Thus, a contract to sell or mortgage real estate must be evidenced by a writing, as must an option to purchase real estate or a contract to grant an easement or permit the mining and removal of minerals on land. A lease is also a transfer of an interest in land, but most states' statutes of frauds do not require leases to be in writing unless they are long-term leases, usually those for one year or more. On the other hand, a contract to erect a building or to insure a building would not be within the real estate provision of the statute of frauds because such contracts do not involve the transfer of interests in land.[1]

Exception: Full Performance by the Vendor An oral contract for the sale of land that has been completely performed by the vendor (seller) is "taken out of the statute of frauds"—that is, is enforceable without a writing. For example, Peterson and Lincoln enter into an oral contract for the sale of Peterson's farm at an agreed-on price and Peterson, the vendor, delivers a deed to the farm to Lincoln. In this situation, the vendor has completely performed and most states would treat the oral contract as being enforceable.

Exception: Part Performance (Action in Reliance) by the Vendee When the vendee (purchaser of land) does an act in clear reliance on an oral contract for the sale of land, an equitable doctrine commonly known as the "part performance doctrine" permits the vendee to enforce the contract notwithstanding the fact that it was oral. The part performance doctrine is based on both evidentiary and reliance considerations. The doctrine recognizes that a person's conduct can "speak louder than words" and can indicate the existence of a contract almost as well as a writing can. The part performance doctrine is also based on the desire to avoid the injustice that would otherwise result if the contract were repudiated after the vendee's reliance.

Under section 129 of the *Restatement (Second) of Contracts,* a contract for the transfer of an interest in land

---

[1] Note, however, that a writing might be required under state insurance statutes.

can be enforced even without a writing if the person seeking enforcement:

1. Has *reasonably relied* on the contract and on the other party's assent.

2. Has changed his position to such an extent that *enforcement of the contract is the only way to prevent injustice.*

In other words, the vendee must have done some act in reliance on the contract and the nature of the act must be such that restitution (returning his money) would not be an adequate remedy. The part performance doctrine will not permit the vendee to collect damages for breach of contract, but it will permit him to obtain the equitable remedy of **specific performance,** a remedy whereby the court orders the breaching party to perform his contract.[2]

A vendee's reliance on an oral contract could be shown in many ways. Traditionally, many states have required that the vendee pay part or all of the purchase price and either make substantial improvements on the property or take possession of it. For example, Contreras and Miller orally enter into a contract for the sale of Contreras's land. If Miller pays Contreras a substantial part of the purchase price and either takes possession of the land or begins to make improvements on it, the contract would be enforceable without a writing under the part performance doctrine. These are not the only sorts of acts in reliance that would make an oral contract enforceable, however. Under the *Restatement (Second)* approach, if the promise to transfer land is clearly proven or is admitted by the breaching party, it is not necessary that the act of reliance include making payment, taking possession, or making improvements.[3] It still is necessary, however, that the reliance be such that restitution would not be an adequate remedy. For this reason, a vendee's payment of the purchase price, standing alone, is usually *not* sufficient for the part performance doctrine.

Contracts that Cannot Be Performed within One Year

A bilateral, executory contract that cannot be performed within one year from the day on which it comes into existence is within the statute of frauds and must be evidenced by a writing. The apparent purpose of this provision is to guard against the risk of faulty or willfully inaccurate recollection of long-term contracts. Courts have tended to construe it very narrowly.

One aspect of this narrow construction is that most states hold that a contract that has been fully performed by *one* of the parties is "taken out of the statute of frauds" and is enforceable without a writing. For example, Nash enters into an oral contract to perform services for Thomas for 13 months. If Nash has already fully performed his part of the contract, Thomas will be required to pay him the contract price.

In addition, this provision of the statute has been held to apply only when the terms of the contract make it impossible for the contract to be completed within one year. If the contract is for an indefinite period of time, it is not within the statute of frauds. This is true even if, in retrospect, the contract was not completed within a year. Thus, Weinberg's agreement to work for Wolf for an indefinite period of time would not have to be evidenced by a writing, even if Weinberg eventually works for Wolf for many years. The mere fact that performance is unlikely to be completed in one year does not bring the contract within the statute of frauds. In most states, a contract "for life" is not within the statute of frauds because it is possible—since death is an uncertain event—for the contract to be performed within a year. In a few states such as New York, contracts for life are within the statute of frauds.

Computing Time In determining whether a contract is within the one-year provision, courts begin counting time on the day when the contract comes into existence. If, under the terms of the contract, it is possible to perform it within one year from this date, the contract does not fall within the statute of frauds and does not have to be in writing. If, however, the terms of the contract make it impossible to complete performance of the contract (without breaching it) within one year from the date on which the contract came into existence, the contract falls within the statute and must meet its requirements to be enforceable. Thus, if Hammer Co. and McCrea agree on August 1, 1997, that McCrea will work for Hammer Co. for one year, beginning October 1, 1997, the terms of the contract dictate that it is not possible to complete performance until October 1, 1998. Because that date is more than one year from the date on which the contract came into existence, the contract falls within the statute of frauds and must be evidenced by a writing to be enforceable.

Sale of Goods for $500 or More

The original English Statute of Frauds required a writing for contracts for the sale of goods for a price of 10 pounds sterling or more. In the United States today, the writing

---

[2]Specific performance is discussed in more detail in Chapter 18.
[3]*Restatement (Second) of Contracts* § 129, comment *d.*

CONCEPT REVIEW

Contracts within the Statute of Frauds

Provision	Description	Exceptions (Situations in Which Contract Does Not Require a Writing)
Marriage	Contracts, other than mutual promises to marry, where marriage is the consideration	—
Year	Bilateral contracts that, *by their terms,* cannot be performed within one year from the date on which the contract was formed	Full (complete) performance by one of the parties
Land	Contracts that create or transfer an ownership interest in real property	1. Full performance by vendor (vendor deeds property to vendees) or 2. "Part performance" doctrine: Vendee relies on oral contract—for example, by: a. Paying substantial part of purchase price, and b. Taking possession or making improvements
Executor's Promise	Executor promises to pay estate's debt out of his own funds	—
Sale of Goods at Price $500 or More (UCC § 2–201)	Contracts for the sale of goods for a contract price of $500 or more; also applies to modifications of contracts for goods where price as modified is $500 or more	See alternative ways of satisfying statute of frauds under UCC.
Collateral Contracts Guaranty	Contracts where promisor promises to pay the debt of another if the primary debtor fails to pay	"Main purpose" or "leading object" exception: Guarantor makes promise primarily for her own economic benefit

requirement for the sale of goods is governed by section 2–201 of the Uniform Commercial Code. This section provides that contracts for the sale of goods for the price of $500 or more are not enforceable without a writing or other specified evidence that a contract was made. There are a number of alternative ways of satisfying the requirements of section 2–201. These will be explained later in this chapter.

Modifications of Existing Sales Contracts Just as some contracts to extend the time for performance fall within the one-year provision of the statute of frauds, agreements to modify existing sales contracts can fall within the statute of frauds if the contract as modified is

for a price of $500 or more.[4] UCC section 2–209(3) provides that the requirements of the statute of frauds must be satisfied if the contract as modified is within its provisions. For example, if Carroll and Kestler enter into a contract for the sale of goods at a price of $490, the original contract does *not* fall within the statute of frauds. However, if they later modify the contract by increasing the contract price to $510, the modification falls within the statute of frauds and must meet its requirements to be enforceable.

---

[4]Modifications of sales contracts are discussed in greater detail in Chapter 12.

Promise of Executor or Administrator to Pay a Decedent's Debt Personally

When a person dies, a personal representative is appointed to administer his estate. One of the important tasks of this personal representative, who is called an executor if the person dies leaving a will or an administrator if the person dies without a will, is to pay the debts owed by the decedent. No writing is required when an executor or administrator—acting in his representative capacity—promises to pay the decedent's debts from the funds of the decedent's estate. The statute of frauds requires a writing, however, if the executor, acting in her capacity as a private individual rather than in her representative capacity, promises to pay one of the decedent's debts out of her own (the executor's) funds. For example, Thomas, who has been appointed executor of his Uncle Max's estate, is presented with a bill for $10,500 for medical services rendered to Uncle Max during his last illness by the family doctor, Dr. Barnes. Feeling bad that there are not adequate funds in the estate to compensate Dr. Barnes for his services, Thomas promises to pay Dr. Barnes from his own funds. Thomas's promise would have to be evidenced by a writing to be enforceable.

Contract in Which Marriage Is the Consideration

The statute of frauds also requires a writing when marriage is the consideration to support a contract. The marriage provision has been interpreted to be inapplicable to agreements that involve only mutual promises to marry. It can apply to any other contract in which one party's promise is given in exchange for marriage or the promise to marry on the part of the other party. This is true whether the promisor is one of the parties to the marriage or a third party. For example, if Hicks promises to deed his ranch to Everett in exchange for Everett's agreement to marry Hicks's son, Everett could not enforce Hicks's promise without written evidence of the promise.

Prenuptial (or antenuptial) agreements present a common contemporary application of the marriage provision of the statute of frauds. These are agreements between couples who contemplate marriage. They usually involve such matters as transfers of property, division of property upon divorce or death, and various lifestyle issues. Assuming that marriage or the promise to marry is the consideration supporting these agreements, they are within the statute of frauds and must be evidenced by a writing.[5]

Meeting the Requirements of the Statute of Frauds

Nature of the Writing Required

The statutes of frauds of the various states are not uniform in their formal requirements. However, most states require only a *memorandum* of the parties' agreement; they do not require that the entire contract be in writing. Essential terms of the contract must be stated in the writing. The memorandum must provide written evidence that a contract was made, but it need not have been created with the intent that the memorandum itself would be binding. In fact, in some cases, written offers that were accepted orally have been held sufficient to satisfy the writing requirement. Typical examples include letters, telegrams, receipts, or any other writing indicating that the parties had a contract. The memorandum need not be made at the same time the contract comes into being; in fact, the memorandum may be made at any time before suit is filed. If a memorandum of the parties' agreement is lost, its loss and its contents may be proven by oral testimony.

Contents of the Memorandum Although there is a general trend away from requiring complete writings to satisfy the statute of frauds, an adequate memorandum must still contain several things. The essential terms of the contract generally must be indicated in the memorandum. States differ in their requirements concerning how specifically the terms must be stated, however. The identity of the parties must be indicated in some way, and the subject matter of the contract must be identified with reasonable certainty. This last requirement causes particular problems in contracts for the sale of land, since many statutes require a detailed description of the property to be sold.

Contents of Memorandum under the UCC The standard for determining the sufficiency of the contents of a memorandum is more flexible in cases concerning

---

[5]Note, however, that "nonmarital" agreements between unmarried cohabitants who do not plan marriage are not within the marriage provision of the statute of frauds, even though the agreement may concern the same sorts of matters that are typically covered in a prenuptial agreement.

contracts for the sale of goods. This looser standard is created by the language of UCC section 2–201, which states that the writing must be sufficient to indicate that a contract for sale has been made between the parties, but a writing can be sufficient even if it omits or incorrectly states a term agreed on. However, the memorandum is not enforceable for more than the quantity of goods stated in the memorandum. Thus, a writing that does not indicate the *quantity* of goods to be sold would not satisfy the Code's writing requirement.

Signature Requirement The memorandum must be signed by the *party to be charged* or his authorized agent. (The party to be charged is the person using the statute of frauds as a defense—generally the defendant unless the statute of frauds is asserted as a defense to a counterclaim.) This means that it is not necessary for purposes of meeting the statute of frauds for both parties' signatures to appear on the document. It is, however, in the best interests of both parties for both signatures to appear on the writing; otherwise, the contract evidenced by the writing is enforceable only against the signing party. Unless the statute expressly provides that the memorandum or contract must be signed at the end, the signature may appear any place on the memorandum. Any writing, mark, initials, stamp, engraving, or other symbol placed or printed on a memorandum will suffice as a signature, as long as the party to be charged intended it to authenticate (indicate the genuineness of) the writing.

How do these standards translate to the online environment? The following *Shattuck* case discusses whether a typed signature at the end of an e-mail message meets the statute of frauds.

Shattuck v. Klotzbach   *2001 Mass. Super. LEXIS 642 (Super. Ct. Mass. 2001)*

In April 2001, Jonathon Shattuck and David and Barbara Klotzbach began discussions concerning the real estate and house located at 5 Main Street, Marion, Massachusetts. On April 9, 2001, Shattuck sent an e-mail to the Klotzbachs which contained an offer of $2,000,000 for the property. On April 10, 2001, David Klotzbach responded via e-mail by expressing his appreciation for a reasonable offer, and stated that he would be willing to accept $2,250,000. Klotzbach further stated that he and his wife Barbara "have been praying for a man such as [Shattuck] that would love the property as much as [the Klotzbachs] do." Klotzbach concluded by stating that e-mail is the "preferred" manner of communication during their negotiations. On or about April 20, 2001, Shattuck and the Klotzbachs entered into a purchase and sale agreement to sell the property for $2,200,000. That deal fell through prior to closing, however, because the Klotzbachs had been unable to procure a "wharf license" as called for in the purchase and sale agreement. The contract was thus terminated and the deposit returned to Shattuck.

Nevertheless, beginning in July 2001, the parties again began communicating via e-mail concerning the sale of the same property. In an e-mail sent July 24, 2001, Shattuck wrote to Klotzbach that he would offer $1.825 million. The e-mail also addressed various other details such as the Klotzbachs' requests for a closing to take place in less than 30 days and that there be no contingencies. Klotzbach responded later that day via e-mail stating that he would decrease the price to $2,000,000 as his counteroffer. He further stated that if Shattuck agreed to his counteroffer he would ask for "no contingencies that might tie up the property." Klotzbach specifically stated that any home inspection should take place within 5 days of the signing of the purchase and sale agreement, and there would be no financing contingency. He conceded that "other standard contingencies are fine." On August 31, 2001, Klotzbach again sent an e-mail to Shattuck which stated that the Klotzbachs "still have NOT sold" the property, and "if you are still interested in a clean deal at $1.825 mil [sic] let me know." On September 2, 2001, Shattuck sent the Klotzbachs an e-mail that stated he was still interested in doing a "clean deal" for $1,825,000. He asked if he could make a "request" that he be able to perform a "quick walk-through inspection" and if no big flaws were apparent, then he would be allowed to sign a simple purchase and sale agreement "containing only the usual boiler plate language, no financing contingency, [and] no other contingencies at all." Finally, on September 10, 2001, Shattuck sent Klotzbach an e-mail which stated that Shattuck's attorney had told him there were no complications and the attorney would draft a very standard purchase and sale agreement for $1,825,000 "with no usual contingencies." Klotzbach responded the same day by e-mail stating "once we sign the P&S we'd like to close ASAP. You may have your attorney send the P&S and deposit check for 10% of purchase price ($182,500) to my attorney." The e-mail concluded by stating that "I'm looking forward to closing and seeing you as the owner of '5 Main Street,' the prettiest spot in Marion Village." All e-mails detailed above contained a salutation at the end which consisted of the typewritten name of the respective sender.

The Klotzbachs did not sell the property to Shattuck, and he sued to enforce the contract. The Klotzbachs moved to dismiss the case on the ground that there was no signed written memorandum sufficient to satisfy the Statute of Frauds.

MURPHY, J.   G.L. c. 259, §1 provides that "no action shall be brought . . . upon a contract for the sale of lands . . . unless the promise, contract or agreement upon which such action is brought, or some memorandum or note thereof, is in writing and signed by the party to be charged. . . ." The Klotzbachs contend that the e-mails in question were not signed and thus cannot satisfy the statute of frauds.

"A memorandum is signed in accordance with the statute of frauds if it is signed by the person to be charged in his own name, or by his initials, or by his Christian name alone, or by a printed, stamped or typewritten signature, if signing in any of these methods he intended to authenticate the paper as his act." *Irving v. Goodimate Co.* Here, all e-mail correspondences between the parties contained a typewritten signature at the end. Taken as a whole, a reasonable trier of fact could conclude that the e-mails sent by Klotzbach were "signed" with the intent to authenticate the information contained therein as his act.

Moreover, courts have held that a telegram may be a signed writing sufficient to satisfy the statute of frauds. This court believes that the typed name at the end of an e-mail is more indicative of a party's intent to authenticate than that of a telegram as the sender of an e-mail types and sends the message on his own accord and types his own name as he so chooses. In the case at bar, Klotzbach sent e-mails regarding the sale of the property and intentionally and deliberately typed his name at the end of all such e-mails. A reasonable trier of fact could conclude that the e-mails sent by Klotzbach regarding the terms of the sale of the property were intended to be authenticated by Klotzbach's deliberate choice to type his name at the conclusion of all e-mails.

The Klotzbachs further contend that, even if e-mails are capable of satisfying the statute of frauds, the Klotzbachs hold title to the property jointly, and thus the signature of both the Klotzbachs would be needed. Shattuck has not alleged that Barbara Klotzbach has ever signed any written memoranda sufficient to satisfy the statute of frauds. Nevertheless, the signature of the defendant-husband may also bind the defendant-wife who impliedly gave her consent and acquiescence in the sale of jointly held property. Here, the correspondences suggest that the defendant-wife was aware of the ongoing negotiations concerning the sale of the property.

The Klotzbachs finally contend that the e-mails, even if sufficiently authenticated, do not contain the essential terms. A memorandum sufficient to satisfy the statute of frauds need not be a formal document intended to serve as a memorandum of the oral contract, but must contain the essential terms of the contract agreed upon: in the case of an interest in real estate, the parties, the locus, the nature of the transaction, and the purchase price. Multiple writings relating to the subject matter may be read together in order to satisfy the memorandum requirement so long as the writings, when considered as a single instrument, contain all the material terms of the contract and are authenticated by the signature of the party to be charged. The writings may, but need not, incorporate each other by reference.

In the case at bar, the e-mails contain terms for the sale of 5 Main Street, Marion Village, Marion, Massachusetts. The e-mails further refer to a purchase price of $1,825,000, and Klotzbach explicitly asked Shattuck to send a "deposit check for 10% of [the] purchase price ($182,500). . . ." Thus, a reasonable trier of fact could conclude that the parties had formed an agreement as to the essential terms of a land sale contract; the parties, the locus, the nature of the transaction, and the purchase price.

Motion to dismiss denied in favor of Shattuck.

Memorandum Consisting of Several Writings

In many situations, the elements required for a memorandum are divided among several documents. For example, Wayman and Allen enter into a contract for the sale of real estate, intending to memorialize their agreement in a formal written document later. While final drafts of a written contract are being prepared, Wayman repudiates the contract. Allen has a copy of an unsigned preliminary draft of the contract that identifies

LOG ON
You can learn more about e-signatures, UETA, and E-Sign at these websites: UETA Online, **http://www.uetaonline.com,** Baker & McKenzie E-Law Alert, *USA: Electronic Signatures in Global and National Commerce Act,* **http://www.bmck.com/ecommerce/E-SIGN_Act.htm,** Allston & Bird, LLP, *How the New E-Sign Act will Affect E-Commerce,* **http://www.gigalaw.com/articles/2000/alston-2000–06.html.**

CYBERLAW IN ACTION

E-Signatures and the Statute of Frauds

The necessity of being able to prove the existence of a contract is as great online as it is in offline transactions. When we communicate or transact business online, we cannot depend on the traditional means of authenticating a contract—reading a person's distinctive signature, seeing the face, or hearing the voice of the other party, for example. Practical questions flow from this state of affairs, such as how can we be sure that a transmission arrives in the same condition as it left the sender, and that it has not been altered or forged? Technologies to increase security online have been developed and new ones are emerging all the time. One method of increasing security in electronic transmissions is the use of **digital signatures.** A digital signature is an electronic identifier that tells a person receiving the document whether it is genuinely from the sender and whether it has been altered in any way. It is important to note that a digital signature is not an electronic image of a person's signature or a person's name typed out. Rather, digital signatures employ encryption technology to create a unique identifier for a sender that can be verified by the receiver.

The absence of traditional authentication methods also raises legal questions as well, such as whether a contract formed electronically, such as over e-mail or on an e-tailer's website, satisfies the statute of frauds. Few courts have dealt with this issue; the *Shattuck* case is a real rarity. However, the vast majority of states have enacted some form of legislation to accommodate formal legal requirements to the realities of e-commerce. The trouble is that this legislation has not been uniform. Some states' legislation has been tied into a particular technology, such as recognizing only digital signatures as satisfying legal requirements.

The **Uniform Electronic Transactions Act** (UETA) takes a different approach. It is a proposed uniform state law that was designed to "remove barriers to electronic commerce by validating and effectuating electronic records and signatures."[6] It is not tied to any particular technology. The UETA states that an "electronic signature" (defined as an "electronic sound, symbol, or process attached to or logically associated with an electronic record and executed or adopted by a person with the intent to sign the electronic record") satisfies any law requiring a signature. Thus, digital signatures, which are one form of electronic signature, would satisfy the UETA, but so would a more commonplace symbol or event such as a typewritten name at the end of an e-mail or a click of a mouse. The UETA has been enacted in 28 states at the time of this writing.

Against the background of lack of uniformity in state law, the federal government enacted the **Electronic Signatures in Global and National Commerce Act** (E-Sign) in 2000. E-Sign provides that in transactions that are in or affecting interstate commerce, "a signature, contract, or other record relating to such transaction may not be denied legal effect, validity, or enforceability solely because it is in electronic form," nor can "a contract relating to such a transaction be denied legal effect, validity, or enforceability solely because an electronic signature or electronic record was used in its formation." Like UETA, E-Sign broadly interprets the concept of electronic signature—using, in fact, the same statutory definition of electronic signature as that which is used in UETA. E-Sign overrides any state law that is inconsistent with UETA, thus helping to harmonize U.S. law about the interaction of formal requirements such as the statute of frauds and electronic contracts.

[6]Uniform Electronic Transactions Act, Prefatory Note (1999).

the parties and contains all of the material terms of the parties' agreement, an unsigned note written by Wayman that contains the legal description of the property, and a letter signed by Wayman that refers to the contract and to the other two documents. None of these documents, standing alone, would be sufficient to satisfy the statute of frauds. However, Allen can combine them to meet the requirements of the statute, provided that they all relate to the same agreement. This can be shown by physical attachment, as where the documents are stapled or bound together, or by references in the documents themselves that indicate that they all apply to the same transaction. In some cases, it has also been shown by the fact that the various documents were executed at the same time.

UCC: Alternative Means of Satisfying the Statute of Frauds in Sale of Goods Contracts

As you have learned, the basic requirement of the UCC statute of frauds [2–201] is that a contract for the sale of goods for the purchase price of $500 or more must be evidenced by a written memorandum that indicates the

Figure 2   *Satisfying the Statute of Frauds through a Contract for the Sale of Goods with a Price of $500 or More*

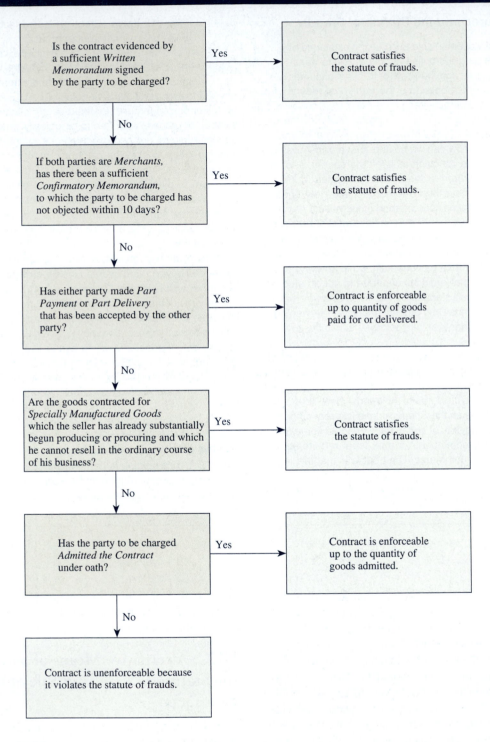

existence of the contract, states the quantity of goods to be sold, and is signed by the party to be charged. Recognizing that the underlying purpose of the statute of frauds is to provide more evidence of the existence of a contract than the mere oral testimony of one of the parties, however, the Code also permits the statute of frauds to be satisfied by any of four other types of evidence. These different methods of satisfying the UCC statute of frauds are depicted in Figure 2. Under the UCC, then, a contract for the sale of goods for a purchase price of $500 or more for which there is no written memorandum signed by the party to be charged can meet the requirements of the statute of frauds in any of the following ways:

1. *Confirmatory memorandum between merchants.* Suppose Gardner and Roth enter into a contract over the telephone for the sale of goods at a price of $5,000. Gardner then sends a memorandum to Roth confirming the deal they made orally. If Roth receives the memo and does not object to it, it would be fair to say that the parties' conduct provides some evidence that a contract exists. Under some circumstances, the UCC permits such confirmatory memoranda to satisfy the statute of frauds even though the writing is signed by the party who is seeking to enforce the contract rather than the party against whom enforcement is sought [2–201(2)]. This exception applies only when *both* of the parties to a contract are *merchants.* Furthermore, the memo must be sent within a reasonable time after the contract is made and must be sufficient to bind the person who sent it if enforcement were sought against him (that is, it must indicate that a contract was made, state a quantity, and be signed by the sender). If the party against whom enforcement is sought receives the memo, has reason to know its contents, and yet fails to give written notice of objection to the contents of the memo within 10 days after receiving it, the memo can be introduced to meet the requirements of the statute of frauds.

The following *St. Ansgar Mills* case discusses the application of the confirmatory memorandum exception.

St. Ansgar Mills, Inc. v. Streit   *613 N.W.2d 289 (Iowa Sup. Ct. 2000)*

St. Ansgar Mills, Inc. is a family-owned agricultural business. As a part of its business, St. Ansgar Mills buys corn from local grain farmers and sells corn to livestock farmers for feed. Duane Streit is a veterinarian who also raises hogs. He owns a large hog farrowing operation and a hog finishing operation. Duane purchased the Osage farm from his father, John Streit, in 1993, and John continued to help operate the Osage hog finishing facility. Both father and son were long-time customers of St. Ansgar Mills. Since 1989, Duane entered into numerous contracts with St. Ansgar Mills for the purchase of large quantities of corn and other grain products. Duane would generally initiate the purchase agreement by calling St. Ansgar Mills on the telephone to obtain a price quote. If an oral contract was made, an employee of St. Ansgar Mills would prepare a written confirmation of the sale and either mail it to Duane to sign and return, or wait for Duane or John to sign the confirmation when they would stop into the business. John would regularly stop by St. Ansgar Mills sometime during the first 10 days of each month and pay the amount of the open account Duane maintained at St. Ansgar Mills for the purchase of supplies and other materials. On those occasions when St. Ansgar Mills sent the written confirmation to Duane, it was not unusual for Duane to fail to sign the confirmation for a long period of time. He also failed to return contracts sent to him. Nevertheless, Duane had never refused delivery of grain he purchased by telephone prior to the incident which gave rise to this case.

On July 1, 1996, John telephoned St. Ansgar Mills to place two orders for the purchase of 60,000 bushels of corn for delivery in December 1996 and May 1997. This order followed an earlier conversation between Duane and St. Ansgar Mills. After the order was placed, St. Ansgar Mills completed the written confirmation but set it aside for John to sign when he was expected to stop by the business to pay the open account. The agreed price of the December corn was $3.53 per bushel. The price of the May corn was $3.73 per bushel. John failed to follow his monthly routine of stopping by the business during the month of July. St. Ansgar Mills then asked a local banker who was expected to see John to have John stop into the business, but John did not stop by St. Ansgar Mills until August 10, 1996. On that date, St. Ansgar Mills delivered the written confirmation to him. Duane later refused delivery of the corn orally purchased on July 1. The price of corn had started to decline shortly after July 1, and eventually plummeted well below the quoted price on July 1. After Duane refused delivery of the corn, he purchased corn for his hog operations on the open market at prices well below the *contract prices of July 1. St. Ansgar Mills later told Duane it should have followed up earlier with the written confirmation and had no excuse for not doing so.*

St. Ansgar Mills brought this action for breach of contract, seeking damages of $152,100, which was the difference between the contract price of the corn and the market price at the time Duane refused delivery. Duane filed a motion for summary judgment, claiming that the oral contract was unenforceable under the UCC statute of frauds. The district court granted the motion for summary judgment, and St. Ansgar Mills appealed.

CADY, Justice   Iowa's statute of frauds for the sale of goods provides:

> Except as otherwise provided in this section, a contract for the sale of goods for the price of $500 or more is not enforced by way of action or defense unless there is some writing sufficient to indicate that a contract for sale has been made between the parties and signed by the party against whom enforcement is sought.

Although the statute of frauds has been deeply engrained into our law, many of the forces which originally gave rise to the rule are no longer prevalent. This, in turn, has caused some of the rigid requirements of the rule to be modified. One statutory exception or modification to the statute of frauds which has surfaced applies to merchants. Under section [2–201(2)], the writing requirements of section [2–201(1)] are considered to be satisfied if, within a reasonable time, a writing in confirmation of the contract which is sufficient against the sender is received and the merchant receiving it has reason to know of its contents, unless written notice of objection of its contents is given within 10 days after receipt. Thus, a writing is still required, but it does not need to be signed by the party against whom the contract is sought to be enforced. The purpose of this exception was to put professional buyers and sellers on equal footing by changing the former law under which a party who received a written confirmation of an oral agreement of sale, but who had not signed anything, could hold the other party to a contract without being bound. It also encourages the common, prudent business practice of sending memoranda to confirm oral agreements. While the written confirmation exception imposes a specific 10-day requirement for a merchant to object to a written confirmation, it employs a flexible standard of reasonableness to establish the time in which the confirmation must be received.

The Uniform Commercial Code specifically defines a reasonable time for taking action in relationship to "the nature, purpose and circumstances" of the action. Additionally, the declared purpose of the Uniform Commercial Code is to permit the expansion of commercial practices through the custom and practice of the parties. Furthermore, the Uniform Commercial Code relies upon course of dealings between the parties to help interpret their conduct. Thus, all relevant circumstances, including custom and practice of the parties, must be considered in determining what constitutes a reasonable time under section [2–201(2)]. Thus, the reasonableness of time between an oral contract and a subsequent written confirmation is ordinarily a question of fact for the jury. It is only in rare cases that a determination of the reasonableness of conduct should be decided by summary adjudication. Summary judgment is appropriate only when the evidence is so one-sided that a party must prevail at trial as a matter of law. There are a host of cases from other jurisdictions which have considered the question of what constitutes a reasonable time under the written confirmation exception of the Uniform Commercial Code. Most of these cases, however, were decided after a trial on the merits and cannot be used to establish a standard or time period as a matter of law. Only a few courts have decided the question as a matter of law under the facts of the case. However, these cases do not establish a strict principle to apply in this case. The resolution of each case depends upon the particular facts and circumstances.

In this case, the district court relied upon the large amount of the sale, volatile market conditions, and lack of an explanation by St. Ansgar Mills for failing to send the written confirmation to Duane in determining St. Ansgar Mills acted unreasonably as a matter of law in delaying delivery of the written confirmation until August 10, 1996. Volatile market conditions, combined with a large sale price, would normally narrow the window of reasonable time under section [2–201(2)]. However, they are not the only factors to consider. Other relevant factors which must also be considered in this case reveal the parties had developed a custom or practice to delay delivery of the confirmation. The parties also maintained a long-time amicable business relationship and had engaged in many other similar business transactions without incident. There is also evidence to infer St. Ansgar Mills did not suspect John's failure to follow his customary practice in July of stopping by the business was a concern at the time. These factors reveal a genuine dispute over the reasonableness of the delay in delivering the written confirmation, and make the resolution of the issue appropriate for the jury. Moreover, conduct is not rendered unreasonable solely because the acting party had no particular explanation for not pursuing different conduct, or regretted not pursuing different conduct in retrospect. The reasonableness of conduct is determined by the facts and circumstances existing at the time. Considering our principles governing summary adjudication and the need to resolve the legal issue by considering the particular facts and circumstances of each case, we conclude the trial court erred by granting summary judgment.

Reversed and remanded in favor of St. Ansgar Mills.

2. *Part payment or part delivery.* Suppose Rice and Cooper enter a contract for the sale of 1,000 units of goods at $1 each. After Rice has paid $600, Cooper refuses to deliver the goods and asserts the statute of frauds as a defense to enforcement of the contract. The Code permits part payment or part delivery to satisfy the statute of frauds, but only for the quantity of goods that have been delivered or paid for [2–201(3)(c)]. Thus, Cooper would be required to deliver only 600 units rather than the 1,000 units Rice alleges that he agreed to sell.

3. *Admission in pleadings or court.* Another situation in which the UCC statute of frauds can be satisfied without a writing occurs when the party being sued admits the existence of the oral contract in his trial testimony or in any document that he files with the court. For example, Nelson refuses to perform an oral contract he made with Smith for the sale of $2,000 worth of goods, and Smith sues him. If Nelson admits the existence of the oral contract in pleadings or in court proceedings, his admission is sufficient to meet the statute of frauds. This exception is justified by the strong evidence that such an admission provides. After all, what better evidence of a contract can there be than is provided when the party being sued admits under penalty of perjury that a contract exists? When such an admission is made, the statute of frauds is satisfied as to the quantity of goods admitted [2–201(3)(b)]. For example, if Nelson admits contracting only for $1,000 worth of goods, the contract is enforceable only to that extent.

4. *Specially manufactured goods.* Finally, an oral contract within the UCC statute of frauds can be enforced without a writing in some situations involving the sale of specially manufactured goods. This exception to the writing requirement will apply only if the nature of the specially manufactured goods is such that they are not suitable for sale in the ordinary course of the seller's business. Completely executory oral contracts are not enforceable under this exception. The seller must have made a substantial beginning in manufacturing the goods for the buyer, or must have made commitments for their procurement, before receiving notice that the buyer was re-

pudiating the sale [2–201(3)(a)]. For example, Bennett Co. has an oral contract with Stevenson for the sale of $2,500 worth of calendars imprinted with Bennett Co.'s name and address. If Bennett Co. repudiates the contract before Stevenson has made a substantial beginning in manufacturing the calendars, the contract will be unenforceable under the statute of frauds. If, however, Bennett Co. repudiated the contract after Stevenson had made a substantial beginning, the oral contract would be enforceable. The specially manufactured goods provision is based both on the evidentiary value of the seller's conduct and on the need to avoid the injustice that would otherwise result from the seller's reliance.

Promissory Estoppel and the Statute of Frauds

The statute of frauds, which was created to prevent fraud and perjury, has often been criticized because it can create unjust results. One of the troubling features of the statute is that it can as easily be used to defeat a contract that was actually made as to defeat a fictitious agreement. As you have seen, courts and legislatures have created several exceptions to the statute of frauds that reduce the statute's potential for creating unfair results. In recent years, courts in some states have allowed the use of the doctrine of **promissory estoppel**[7] to enable some parties to recover under oral contracts that the statute of frauds would ordinarily render unenforceable.

Courts in these states hold that, when one of the parties would suffer serious losses because of her reliance on an oral contract, the other party is estopped from raising the statute of frauds as a defense. This position has been approved in the *Restatement (Second) of Contracts.* Section 139 of the *Restatement (Second)* provides that a promise that induces action or forbearance can be enforceable notwithstanding the statute of frauds if the reliance was foreseeable to the person making the promise

---

[7]The doctrine of promissory estoppel is discussed in Chapters 9 and 12.

and if injustice can be avoided only by enforcing the promise. The idea behind this section and the cases employing promissory estoppel is that the statute of frauds, which is designed to prevent injustice, should not be allowed to work an injustice. Section 139 and these cases also impliedly recognize the fact that the reliance required by promissory estoppel to some extent provides evidence of the existence of a contract between the parties, since it is unlikely that a person would materially rely on a nonexistent promise.

The use of promissory estoppel as a means of circumventing the statute of frauds is still controversial, however. Many courts fear that enforcing oral contracts on the basis of a party's reliance will essentially negate the statute. In cases involving the UCC statute of frauds, an additional source of concern involves the interpretation of section 2–201. Some courts have construed the provisions listing specific alternative methods of satisfying section 2–201's formal requirements to be *exclusive,* precluding the creation of any further exceptions by courts.

The Parol Evidence Rule

Explanation of the Rule

In many situations, contracting parties prefer to express their agreements in writing even when they are not required to do so by the statute of frauds. Written contracts rarely come into being without some prior discussions or negotiations between the parties, however. Various promises, proposals, or representations are usually made by one or both of the parties before the execution of a written contract. What happens when one of those prior promises, proposals, or representations is not included in the terms of the written contract? For example, suppose that Jackson wants to buy Stone's house. During the course of negotiations,

Stone states that he will pay for any major repairs that the house needs for the first year that Jackson owns it. The written contract that the parties ultimately sign, however, does not say anything about Stone paying for repairs, and, in fact, states that Jackson will take the house "as is." The furnace breaks down three months after the sale, and Stone refuses to pay for its repair. What is the status of Stone's promise to pay for repairs? The basic problem is one of defining the boundaries of the parties' agreement. Are all the promises made in the process of negotiation part of the contract, or do the terms of the written document that the parties signed supersede any preliminary agreements?

The **parol evidence rule** provides the answer to this question. The term *parol evidence* means written or spoken statements that are *not contained in the written contract.* The parol evidence rule provides that, when parties enter a *written contract* that they intend as a complete **integration** (a complete and final statement of their agreement), a court will not permit the use of evidence of *prior* or *contemporaneous* statements to add to, alter, or contradict the terms of the written contract. This rule is based on the presumption that when people enter into a written contract, the best evidence of their agreement is the written contract itself. It also reflects the idea that later expressions of intent are presumed to prevail over earlier expressions of intent. In the hypothetical case involving Stone and Jackson, assuming that they intended the written contract to be the final integration of their agreement, Jackson would not be able to introduce evidence of Stone's promise to pay for repairs. The effect of excluding preliminary promises or statements from consideration is, of course, to confine the parties' contract to the terms of the written agreement. The lesson to be learned from this example is that people who put their agreements in writing should make sure that all the terms of their agreement are included in the writing. The *Watkins & Sons* case illustrates the application of the parol evidence rule.

Watkins & Sons Pet Supplies v. the Iams Company   *254 F.3d 607 (6th Cir. 2001)*

Iams is in the business of manufacturing and selling pet foods. For many years, Watkins was a nonexclusive distributor of Iams products in Michigan. In 1986 or 1987, Iams began to require Watkins (as well as its other distributors) to sign yearly written distributorship agreements. Until 1987, Watkins was the sole distributor of Iams products in Michigan, but in 1986, Wolverton, Inc. also began selling Iams products in the state. In 1989, Iams began offering its distributors a 2 percent discount on its products in return for a commitment from the distributors to sell Iams products exclusively. The discount was significant, given the low profit margins customary in the business. Watkins alleges that in 1990, Iams promised it that if it became an exclusive Iams distributor, Iams would grant it an exclusive sales territory in Michigan when Iams changed to a distribution system of exclusive territories. Watkins claims that it became an exclusive distributor in reliance on this prom-

ise. It entered into an exclusivity agreement in July 1990 and annually thereafter through 1993. The contract of January 31, 1993 between Iams and Watkins contains the following provisions:

> Notwithstanding the appointment herein the Company [Iams] reserves the right for itself to sell Products within the Territory. In addition, the Company may appoint any other distributor to sell Products within the Territory. (§§2.1).

> This Agreement shall be effective on February 1, 1993, and shall automatically expire, without any further action by either party required, on January 31, 1994 unless earlier terminated as set forth in Section 4.2 or 4.3 or otherwise in accordance with the provisions of this Agreement. This Agreement may be renewed thereafter on terms mutually agreeable to the parties only in a writing signed by the parties hereto. . . .(§§ 4.1).

> With the exception of Schedule I, which may be unilaterally amended by the Company as provided in this Agreement . . . and except as otherwise provided in this Agreement, no change, modification or amendment of any provision of this Agreement will be binding unless made in writing and signed by the parties hereto. (§§ 11).

> THIS AGREEMENT TOGETHER WITH THE COMPANY'S STANDARD TERMS AND CONDITIONS OF SALE REPRESENT THE ENTIRE AGREEMENT BETWEEN THE PARTIES AND SUPERSEDES ALL PRIOR, EX-ISTING, AND CONTEMPORANEOUS AGREEMENTS, WHETHER WRITTEN OR ORAL, BETWEEN THE PARTIES HERETO RELATING TO THE DISTRIBUTION OR SALE OF THE COMPANY'S PRODUCTS. ALL SUCH OTHER AGREEMENTS ARE HEREBY TERMINATED, AND EACH PARTY HEREBY RELEASES THE OTHER FROM ANY AND ALL CLAIMS ARISING AS A RESULT OF OR IN ANY WAY RELATING TO THE RELATIONSHIP BETWEEN THE COMPANY AND THE DISTRIBUTOR UNDER SUCH OTHER AGREE-MENTS OR AS A RESULT OF SUCH TERMINATION, WITH THE EXCEPTION OF CLAIMS BY THE COM-PANY FOR MONEY DUE FOR GOODS AND SERVICES SOLD TO THE DISTRIBUTOR. THE UNDERSIGNED INDIVIDUALS ON BEHALF OF THE COMPANY AND THE DISTRIBUTOR, AS THE CASE MAY BE, HEREBY AFFIRM THAT THEY HAVE CAREFULLY READ THIS AGREEMENT AND FULLY UNDERSTAND THE TERMS CONTAINED IN THE AGREEMENT. (§§ 16).

Instead of making Watkins its exclusive dealer, Iams notified Watkins in September, 1993, that it would not renew its distributorship contract, and the contract expired, in accordance with its terms, on January 31, 1994. Iams subsequently entered into an exclusive distribution contract in Michigan with Wolverton.

Watkins brought suit against Iams on a number of grounds, including breach of contract, fraud, and promissory estoppel. The district court summary judgment in favor of Iams and Watkins appealed the summary judgment of its fraud and promissory estoppel claims.

ALDRICH, District Judge   Reasonable reliance is an element of both promissory estoppel and fraud. On the facts of this case, we find that Watkins's reliance on Iams's representations was unreasonable as a matter of law. In this case, the reasonableness of Watkins's reliance depends upon the effect of the integration clause. When a written contract is the final and complete statement of the parties' agreement—when, that is, it is a complete integration—the parol evidence rule prohibits the parties from introducing extrinsic evidence of the terms of their agreement. The rule is not a rule of evidence, but of substantive contract law. In other words, the parol evidence rule does not operate to prohibit proof of terms of the agreement; instead, it provides that parol terms are not terms of the agreement at all. If a written contract is completely integrated, it is unreasonable as a matter of law to rely on parol representations or promises within the scope of the contract made prior to its execution.

We find that the written agreement at issue here was a complete integration. Under Ohio law, the court determines whether a sales contract is completely integrated by considering the "four corners of the document" and evidence extrinsic to the writing. Here, §§16 of the agreement, quoted above, provides strong evidence that the parties intended their written agreement to be a complete integration. Watkins does not present extrinsic evidence to show otherwise. Instead, it merely argues that the renewal provision in the written agreement does not contain the terms of the proposed renewal, and that therefore the contract is only a partial integration—final, but not complete.

Watkins's argument is without merit. It is clear from the text of the renewal clause that the parties meant to make a final agreement and to leave the terms of a future agreement for later negotiation. This conclusion is made even clearer when one considers the integration clause. As we note in our discussion of Watkins's claim for breach of the duty of good faith, clauses such as the renewal clause in this contract may sometimes create a duty to negotiate the renewal in good faith. But a clause leaving open the possibility of a future agreement affects neither the completeness nor the finality of the present agreement.

Since the written agreement between Watkins and Iams is a complete integration, the parol evidence rule applies. There are, however, exceptions to the rule. The exception on which Watkins most heavily relies is the rule that evidence of fraud in the inducement is not barred by the parol evidence rule. But "fraud in the inducement" is a fraudulent misstatement of fact that induces a party to enter a contract, not a fraudulent promise of future performance that is within the scope of the subject matter of the written contract but that was not included in it. The parol evidence rule does apply to promissory fraud if the evidence in question is offered to show a promise which contradicts an integrated written agreement. Unless the false promise is either independent of or consistent with the written instrument, evidence thereof is inadmissible.

There is no evidence in the record sufficient to bring this case within the rule which permits claims of fraud despite the parol evidence rule when the promisor had no intention of honoring his promise and thus had actual fraudulent intent. Watkins's argument that Iams continued to make fraudulent representations after the execution of the agreement avoids the parol evidence rule, which relates only to prior representations. But because the contract is for the sale of goods that provides that modifications must be in writing, Watkins's argument runs up against Ohio Rev. Code §§1302.12(B), which provides: "A signed agreement which excludes modification or rescission except by a signed writing cannot be otherwise modified or rescinded."

Finally, Watkins's argument that Iams's representations are not within the scope of the statutory UCC parol evidence rule is without merit. The statute allows proof of course of dealing, course of performance, or usage of trade to "explain" or "supplement" the written agreement. But Watkins's evidence—evidence of parol promises of an exclusive territory and of renewal—does not explain or supplement the agreement; it contradicts the agreement. As noted above, the written contract explicitly permits Iams to "appoint any other distributor to sell Products within the Territory," and it explicitly provides for expiration of the contract on January 31, 1994, leaving renewal to future agreement of the parties.

For the foregoing reasons, we find that Watkins's reliance on Iams's representations was unreasonable as a matter of law, and therefore, that the district court properly granted summary judgment on Watkins's claims for fraud and promissory estoppel.

Affirmed in favor of Iams.

Scope of the Parol Evidence Rule

The parol evidence rule is relevant only in cases in which the parties have expressed their agreement in a written contract. Thus, it would not apply to a case involving an oral contract or to a case in which writings existed that were not intended to embody the final statement of at least part of the parties' contract. The parol evidence rule has been made a part of the law of sales in the Uniform Commercial Code [2–202], so it is applicable to contracts for the sale of goods as well as to contracts governed by the common law of contracts. Furthermore, the rule excludes only evidence of statements made *prior to* or *during* the signing of the written contract. It does not apply to statements made after the signing of the contract. Thus, evidence of subsequent statements is freely admissible.

Admissible Parol Evidence

In some situations, evidence of statements made outside the written contract is admissible notwithstanding the parol evidence rule. Parol evidence is permitted in the situations discussed below either because the writing is not the best evidence of the contract or because the evidence is offered, not to contradict the terms of the writing, but to explain the writing or to challenge the underlying contractual obligation that the writing represents.

1. *Additional terms in partially integrated contracts.* In many instances, parties will desire to introduce evidence of statements or agreements that would supplement rather than contradict the written contract. Whether they can do this depends on whether the written contract is characterized as *completely integrated* or *partially integrated*. A completely integrated contract is one that the parties intend as a *complete and exclusive statement* of their entire agreement. A partially integrated contract is one that expresses the parties' final agreement as to some but not all of the terms of their contract. When a contract is only partially integrated, the parties are permitted to use parol evidence to prove the *additional* terms of their agreement. Such evidence cannot, however, be used to

contradict the written terms of the contract. To determine whether a contract is completely or partially integrated, a court must determine the parties' intent. A court judges intent by looking at the language of the contract, the apparent completeness of the writing, and all the surrounding circumstances. It will also consider whether the contract contains a **merger clause** (also known as an **integration clause**). These clauses, which are very common in form contracts and commercial contracts, provide that the written contract is the complete integration of the parties' agreement. They are designed to prevent a party from giving testimony about prior statements or agreements and are generally effective in indicating that the writing was a complete integration. Even though a contract contains a merger clause, parol evidence could be admissible under one of the following exceptions.

2. *Explaining ambiguities.* Parol evidence can be offered to explain an ambiguity in the written contract. Suppose a written contract between Lowen and Matthews provides that Lowen will buy "Matthews's truck," but Matthews has two trucks. The parties could offer evidence of negotiations, statements, and other circumstances preceding the creation of the written contract to identify the truck to which the writing refers. Used in this way, parol evidence helps the court interpret the contract. It does not contradict the written contract.

3. *Circumstances invalidating contract.* Any circumstances that would be relevant to show that a contract is not valid can be proven by parol evidence. For example, evidence that Holden pointed a gun at Dickson and said, "Sign this contract, or I'll kill you," would be admissible to show that the contract was voidable because of duress. Likewise, parol evidence would be admissible to show that a contract was illegal or was induced by fraud, misrepresentation, undue influence, or mistake.

4. *Existence of condition.* It is also permissible to use parol evidence to show that a writing was executed with the understanding that it was *not to take effect until the occurrence of a condition* (a future, uncertain event that creates a duty to perform). Suppose Farnsworth signs a contract to purchase a car with the agreement that the contract is not to be effective unless and until Farnsworth gets a new job. If the written contract is silent about any conditions that must occur before it becomes effective, Farnsworth could introduce parol evidence to prove the existence of the condition. Such proof merely elaborates on, but does not contradict, the terms of the writing.

5. *Subsequent agreements.* As you read earlier, the parol evidence rule does not forbid parties to introduce proof of *subsequent agreements.* This is true even if the terms of the later agreement cancel, subtract from, or add to the obligations stated in the written contract. The idea here is that when a writing is followed by a later statement or agreement, the writing is no longer the best evidence of the agreement. You should be aware, however, that subsequent modifications of contracts may sometimes be unenforceable because of lack of consideration or failure to comply with the statute of frauds. In addition, contracts sometimes expressly provide that modifications must be written. In this situation, an oral modification would be unenforceable.

Interpretation of Contracts

Once a court has decided what promises are included in a contract, it is faced with *interpreting* the contract to determine the *meaning* and *legal effect* of the terms used by the parties. Courts have adopted broad, basic standards of interpretation that guide them in the interpretation process.

The court will first attempt to determine the parties' *principal objective.* Every clause will then be determined in the light of this principal objective. Ordinary words will be given their usual meaning and technical words (such as those that have a special meaning in the parties' trade or business) will be given their technical meaning, unless a different meaning was clearly intended.

Guidelines grounded in common sense are also used to determine the relationship of the various terms of the contract. Specific terms that follow general terms are presumed to qualify those general terms. Suppose that a provision that states that the subject of the contract is "guaranteed for one year" is followed by a provision describing the "one-year guarantee against defects in workmanship." Here, it is fair to conclude that the more specific term qualifies the more general term and that the guarantee described in the contract is a guarantee of workmanship only, and not of parts and materials.

Sometimes, there is internal conflict in the terms of an agreement and courts must determine which term should prevail. When the parties use a form contract or some other type of contract that is partially printed and partially handwritten, the handwritten provisions will prevail. If the contract was drafted by one of the parties, any ambiguities will be resolved against the party who drafted the contract.

If both parties to the contract are members of a trade, profession, or community in which certain words are commonly given a particular meaning (this is called a

CONCEPT REVIEW

Parol Evidence Rule

Parol Evidence Rule	Applies when:	Provides that:
	Parties create a writing intended as a final and complete integration of at least part of the parties' contract.	Evidence of statements or promises made before or during the creation of the writing cannot be used to supplement, change, or contradict the terms of the written contract.
But Parol Evidence *Can* **Be Used to**	1. Prove consistent, additional terms when the contract is *partially integrated*. 2. Explain an ambiguity in the written contract. 3. Prove that the contract is void, voidable, or unenforceable. 4. Prove that the contract was subject to a condition. 5. Prove that the parties subsequently modified the contract or made a new agreement.	

usage), the courts will presume that the parties intended the meaning that the usage gives to the terms they use. For example, if the word *dozen* in the bakery business means 13 rather than 12, a contract between two bakers for the purchase of 10 dozen loaves of bread will be presumed to mean 130 loaves of bread rather than 120. Usages can also add provisions to the parties' agreement. If the court finds that a certain practice is a matter of common usage in the parties' trade, it will assume that the parties intended to include that practice in their agreement. If contracting parties are members of the same trade, business, or community but do not intend to be bound by usage, they should specifically say so in their agreement.

Problems and Problem Cases

1. Golomb allegedly orally agreed to sell to Lee for $275,000 the Ferrari once owned by King Leopold of Belgium. Golomb ultimately refused to sell the car and Lee sued him. At trial, Golomb denied ever promising to sell the car to Lee. Can Lee enforce this alleged promise?

2. In the 1990s, Dayton's acquired the Marshall Field's department stores. The Nahigian Brothers were operating the oriental rug department in those stores at the time. During 1996 and 1997, Soomekh proposed that the Marshall Fields's rug department be consolidated with the Dayton's and Hudson's departments, and that Soomekh operate the rug departments in all three stores. At the

ETHICS IN ACTION

For those who draft and proffer standardized form contracts, the parol evidence rule can be a powerful ally because it has the effect of limiting the scope of an integrated, written contract to the terms of the writing. Although statements and promises made to a person before he signs a contract might be highly influential in persuading him to enter the contract, the parol evidence rule effectively prevents these pre-contract communications from being legally enforceable. Consider also that standardized form contracts are usually drafted for the benefit of and proffered by the more sophisticated and powerful party in a contract (e.g., the landlord rather than the tenant, the bank rather than the customer). Considering all of this, do you believe that the parol evidence rule promotes ethical behavior?

time, Nahigian Brothers still operated the Marshall Field's rug department separately. In 1997, Dayton's proposed a new one-year contract with Soomekh for operation of the Dayton's and Hudson's rug departments. Soomekh alleges that Dayton's told Soomekh that during the proposed one-year contract term, Soomekh, Nahigian Brothers, and others would have the opportunity to submit competitive proposals and bids for consolidated operation of the Dayton's, Hudson's, and Marshall Field's rug departments. Soomekh agreed to the one-year contract, which provided for an unlimited number of automatically renewable one-year terms and included a cancellation clause. The cancellation clause provided that either party could cancel the contract by providing 60 days written notice. The contract also contained an integration clause that stated: "This Agreement constitutes the entire understanding between the parties and supercedes [sic] any prior agreements between the parties hereto. . . ." It did not contain any provision for a competitive bidding process. On November 25, 1998, Dayton's gave notice of its intent to cancel the contract effective January 31, 1999, thus terminating its business relationship with Soomekh. Dayton's did not give Soomekh an opportunity to participate in a competitive bidding process. Dayton's later consolidated all of its Oriental rug departments under the operation of Nahigian Brothers in the Dayton's, Hudson's, and Marshall Field's stores. Soomekh filed suit against Dayton's. Would the parol evidence rule prevent proof of Dayton's alleged oral promise to give Soomekh the opportunity to participate in a competitive bidding?

3. On two occasions in 1980, Hodge met with Tilley, president and chief operating officer of Evans Financial Corporation, to discuss Hodge's possible employment by Evans. Hodge was 54 years old at that time and was assistant counsel and assistant secretary of Mellon National Corporation and Mellon Bank of Pittsburgh. During these discussions, Tilley asked Hodge what his conditions were for accepting employment with Evans, and Hodge replied, "Number 1, the job must be permanent. Because of my age, I have a great fear about going back into the marketplace again. I want to be here until I retire." Tilley allegedly responded, "I accept that condition." Regarding his retirement plans, Hodge later testified, "I really questioned whether I was going to go much beyond 65." Hodge later accepted Evans's offer of employment as vice president and general counsel. He moved from Pittsburgh to Washington, D.C., in September 1980 and worked for Evans from that time until he was fired by Tilley on May 7, 1981. Hodge brought a

breach of contract suit against Evans. Evans argued that the oral contract was unenforceable because of the statute of frauds. Is this correct?

4. Green owns a lot (Lot S) in the Manomet section of Plymouth, Massachusetts. In July 1980, she advertised it for sale. On July 11 and 12, the Hickeys discussed with Green purchasing Lot S and orally agreed to a sale for $15,000. On July 12, Green accepted the Hickeys' check for $500. Hickey had left the payee line of the deposit check blank because of uncertainty whether Green or her brother was to receive the check. Hickey asked Green to fill in the appropriate name. Green, however, held the check, did not fill in the payee's name, and neither cashed nor indorsed it. Hickey told Green that his intention was to sell his home and build on the lot he was buying from Green. Relying on the arrangements with Green, the Hickeys advertised their house in newspapers for three days in July. They found a purchaser quickly. Within a short time, they contracted with a purchaser for the sale of their house and accepted the purchaser's deposit check. On the back of this check, above the Hickeys' signatures indorsing the check, was noted: "Deposit on purchase of property at Sachem Rd. and First St., Manomet, Ma. Sale price, $44,000." On July 24, Green told Hickey that she no longer intended to sell her property to him and instead had decided to sell it to someone else for $16,000. Hickey offered to pay Green $16,000 for the lot, but she refused this offer. The Hickeys then filed a complaint against Green seeking specific performance. Green asserted that relief was barred by the statute of frauds. Is this correct?

5. In July 1984, Slivinsky applied for a job as a materials scientist with Watkins-Johnson Company, a large aerospace manufacturer. Directly above the signature line on the application she signed was the statement: "I understand that employment by WATKINS-JOHNSON COMPANY is conditional upon . . . execution of an Employment Agreement. I further understand that if I become employed by Watkins-Johnson Company, there will be no agreement, expressed or implied, between the company and me for any specific period of employment, nor for continuing or long-term employment." Over the next several months, Watkins-Johnson contacted Slivinsky's references, requested her transcripts, and set up a series of interviews. Slivinsky claims that at these interviews she was promised "long-term," "indefinite," and "permanent" employment, not dependent on business cycles and terminable only for cause. Finally, Watkins-Johnson made a verbal offer of employment to Slivinsky and she accepted. On January 7, 1985, which was Slivinsky's first day at work, Slivinsky signed the employee

agreement that had been referred to in her employment application. Set apart in bold type, the last paragraph of this agreement provided that there was no express or implied agreement between the parties regarding the duration of her employment and that the employment could be terminated at any time with or without cause. Watkins-Johnson terminated Slivinsky in 1986 after a down-turn in its business, and Slivinsky sued Watkins-Johnson for breach of contract. Would the parol evidence rule allow proof of the alleged promises for long-term, indefinite, and permanent employment?

6. Collins wanted to buy real estate that had formerly been used as a gas station from Marathon. He told Marathon real estate representative Jerry Jansen of his desire to purchase the Elwood property for $55,000 and use it for a used car lot. Although Jansen agreed on the price, he told Collins that Marathon preferred to lease the property before selling it so that certain work could be performed first. Accordingly, Collins signed an 18-month lease, beginning June 1, 1990. The lease required Collins to pay Marathon a security deposit and $700 per month and to repair the roof and driveway, replace the furnace, and alter the station's appearance so that it no longer resembled a Marathon station. Marathon promised to grant Collins a rent credit for the rehabilitation work he performed. Collins took possession of the property, repaired the roof and driveway, replaced the furnace, covered the building with siding, and had various other improvements done in anticipation of buying the property. Collins had spent several thousand dollars on the property when Jansen again raised the issue of Collins' buying the property. Collins approached Star Bank for a loan for the used car lot. Meanwhile, Collins received an unsigned purchase offer from Marathon. Star approved Collins for the loan, contingent upon an environmental inspection. Collins informed Jansen of this. A dispute arose regarding rent and the agreed-upon rent credit, and Collins was ultimately evicted. Can Collins enforce the contract to buy the lot?

7. Dyer purchased a used Ford from Walt Bennett Ford for $5,895. She signed a written contract, which showed that no taxes were included in the sales price. Dyer contended, however, that the salesperson who negotiated the purchase with her told her both before and after her signing of the contract that the sales tax on the automobile had been paid. The contract Dyer signed contained the following language:

> The above comprises the entire agreement pertaining to this purchase and no other agreement of any kind, verbal understanding, representation, or promise whatsoever will be recognized.

It also stated:

> This contract constitutes the entire agreement between the parties and no modification hereof shall be valid in any event and Buyer expressly waives the right to rely thereon, unless made in writing, signed by Seller.

Later, when Dyer attempted to license the automobile, she discovered that the Arkansas sales tax had not been paid on it. She paid the sales tax and sued Bennett for breach of contract. What result?

8. The Wellfleet Marine Corporation rented a slip in Wellfleet Harbor to Coady for the docking of Coady's boat. According to Coady, Wellfleet Marine orally agreed to continue to provide such storage facilities to him for the 1995 season and thereafter, for so long as he continued to require such storage and dockage facilities, and quoted him a price for the rental of slip #6 during the 1995 boating season in the amount of $1,800.00 plus excise tax. Coady further asserted that Wellfleet Marine assured him before he purchased his present boat that dockage and storage services would be available to him every year, for so long as he continued to own a boat, and required its services. Does the statute of frauds require this agreement to be evidenced by a writing?

9. Curry served as a video disc jockey (VJ) for MTV Network (MTVN). Curry also engaged in activities in the contemporary music industry that were not directly related to his MTVN employment, such as hosting radio programs and live entertainment events. In approximately June 1993, Curry met with MTVN Vice President Matthew Farber and discussed an Internet service he was developing with the Internet site address "mtv.com." Curry alleged that while Farber disclaimed any interest by MTVN in entering a joint venture, he indicated that Curry was free to continue development of the Internet site at his own expense. By approximately August 1993, Curry had announced the mtv.com address on MTVN broadcasts. On the afternoon of one August taping, Curry claimed to have had a conversation about mtv.com with Joel Stillerman, a senior MTVN executive. Curry alleged that in this conversation Stillerman "made clear that MTVN had no objection to Curry's use and development of the mtv.com address." Curry alleged that between August 1993 and April 1994 he discussed the mtv.com site with other MTVN personnel on numerous occasions, receiving encouragement in his continuing development efforts. During the period August 1993 to mid-January 1994, Curry claimed that MTVN programmers placed the graphic letters "mtv.com" on the television screen for viewers of the MTVN program, "Top Twenty Count-down." In reliance on his discussions with MTVN executives and personnel, Curry continued to develop mtv.com at his own expense. In January 1994, MTVN formally requested that Curry cease use of the mtv.com address. However Curry alleged not only that MTVN programming continued to make on-air references to the address, but that Stillerman asked him, sometime in February, to include certain materials at the mtv.com site. By the spring of 1994, Curry's mtv.com address had been accessed by millions of Internet users. Curry argued that MTVN was exploiting his development efforts to "test the waters" for their own interactive service. During the second half of 1993, MTVN and Viacom allegedly explored their options for developing online services. These efforts culminated in an agreement between MTVN and America On-Line to provide a computer link to MTVN for a fee. The AOL/MTVN service would include a performer-music professional bulletin board similar to the one Curry developed at mtv.com. Curry sued MTVN for breach of contract based on his conversations with MTVN officials in which he was allegedly promised that MTVN would not interfere with mtv.com. MTVN asserted that the statute of frauds bars enforcement of any such promise. Is this assertion correct?

10. Rosenfeld, an art dealer, claimed that Jean-Michel Basquiat, an acclaimed neo-expressionist artist, had agreed to sell to her three paintings entitled "Separation of the 'K,'" "Atlas," and "Untitled Head." She claimed that she went to Basquiat's apartment on October 25, 1982, and while she was there he agreed to sell her three paintings for $4,000 each, and that she picked out the three works. According to Rosenfeld, Basquiat asked for a cash deposit of 10 percent. She left his loft and later returned with $1,000 in cash, which she paid him. When she asked for a receipt, he insisted on drawing up a "contract," and got down on the floor and wrote it out in crayon on a large piece of paper, remarking that "some day this contract will be worth money." She identified a handwritten document listing the three paintings, bearing her signature and that of Basquiat, which stated: "$12,000 − $1,000 DEPOSIT − OCT 25 82." Is this writing sufficient to satisfy the statute of frauds?

Online Research: Coverage of the Statute of Frauds

Using your favorite search engine, find a state statute of frauds. Study the list of contracts that must be evidenced by a writing under that statute, and note whether there are any classes of contracts listed in addition to the ones discussed in this chapter.

17

RIGHTS OF THIRD PARTIES

Peterson was employed by Post-Network as a newscaster-anchorman on station WTOP-TV Channel 9 under a three-year employment contract with two additional one-year terms at the option of Post-Network. During the first year of Peterson's employment, Post-Network sold its operation license to Evening News in a sale that provided for the assignment of all contracts, including Peterson's employment contract. Peterson continued working for the station for more than a year after the change of ownership, but then found a job at a competing station and resigned. Evening News sued Peterson for breach of the employment contract.

- *Can a person who was not an original party to a contract sue to enforce it?*
- *Was the assignment of Peterson's employment contract a valid transfer, or does Peterson have a right not to have his employment transferred to another employer?*
- *Does Peterson have any right to enforce the contract between Post-Network and Evening News?*

IN PRECEDING CHAPTERS, WE have emphasized the way in which an agreement between two or more people creates legal rights and duties *on the part of the contracting parties.* Since a contract is founded on the consent of the contracting parties, it might seem to follow that they are the only ones who have rights and duties under the contract. Although this is generally true, there are two situations in which people who were not parties to a contract have legally enforceable rights under it: when a contract has been *assigned* (transferred) to a third party and when a contract is *intended to benefit a third person* (a *third-party beneficiary*). This chapter discusses the circumstances in which third parties have rights under a contract.

Assignment of Contracts

Contracts give people both rights and duties. If Murphy buys Wagner's motorcycle and promises to pay him $1,000 for it, Wagner has the *right* to receive Murphy's promised performance (the payment of the $1,000) and Murphy has the *duty* to perform the promise by paying $1,000. In most situations, contract rights can be transferred to a third person and contract duties can be delegated to a third person. The transfer of a *right* under a contract is called an **assignment.** The appointment of another person to perform a *duty* under a contract is called a **delegation.**

Nature of Assignment of Rights

A person who owes a duty to perform under a contract is called an **obligor.** The person to whom he owes the duty is called the **obligee.** For example, Samson borrows $500 from Jordan, promising to repay Jordan in six months. Samson, who owes the duty to pay the money, is the obligor, and Jordan, who has the right to receive the money, is the obligee. An assignment occurs when the obligee transfers his right to receive the obligor's performance to a third person. When there has been an assignment, the person making the assignment—the original obligee—is then called the **assignor.** The person to whom the right has been transferred is called the **assignee.** Figure 1 summarizes these key terms.

Suppose that Jordan, the obligee in the example above, assigns his right to receive Samson's payment to

Figure 1   *Assignment: Key Terms*

Obliger	Obligee	Assignment	Assignor	Assignee
Person who owes the duty to perform	Person who has the right to receive obligor's performance	Transfer of the right to receive obligor's performance	Obligee who tansfers the right to receive obligor's performance	Person to whom the right to receive obligor's performance is transferred

Figure 2   *Assignment*

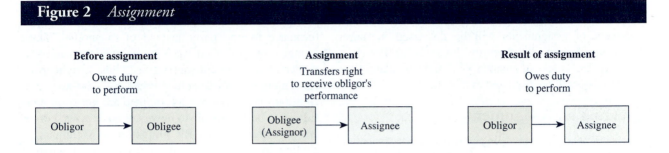

Kane. Here, Jordan is the assignor and Kane is the assignee. The relationship between the three parties is represented in Figure 2. Notice that the assignment is a separate transaction: It occurs after the formation of the original contract.

The effect of the assignment is to extinguish the assignor's right to receive performance and to transfer that right to the assignee. In the above example, Kane now owns the right to collect payment from Samson. If Samson fails to pay, Kane, as an assignee, now has the right to file suit against Samson to collect the debt.

People assign rights for a variety of reasons. A person might assign a right to a third party to satisfy a debt that he owes. For example, Jordan, the assignor in the above example, owes money to Kane, so he assigns to Kane the right to receive the $500 that Samson owes him. A person might also sell or pledge the rights owed to him to obtain financing. In the case of a business, the money owed to the business by customers and clients is called *accounts receivable*. A business's accounts receivable are an asset to the business that can be used to raise money in several ways. For example, the business may pledge its accounts receivable as collateral for a loan. Suppose Ace Tree Trimming Co. wants to borrow money from First Bank and gives First Bank a security interest (an interest in the debtor's property that secures the debtor's performance of an obligation) in its accounts re-

ceivable.[1] If Ace defaults in its payments to First Bank, First Bank will acquire Ace's rights to collect the accounts receivable. A person might also make an assignment of a contract right as a gift. For example, Lansing owes $2,000 to Father. Father assigns the right to receive Lansing's performance to Son as a graduation gift.

Evolution of the Law Regarding Assignments

Contract rights have not always been transferable. Early common law refused to permit assignment or delegation because debts were considered to be too personal to transfer. A debtor who failed to pay an honest debt was subject to severe penalties, including imprisonment, because such a failure to pay was viewed as the equivalent of theft. The identity of the creditor was of great importance to the debtor, since one creditor might be more lenient than another. Courts also feared that the assignment of debts would stir up unwanted litigation. In an economy that was primarily land-based, the extension of credit was of relatively small importance. As trade increased and became more complex, however, the practice of extending credit became more common. The needs of an increasingly commercial society demanded that people be able to trade

---

[1]Security interests in accounts and other property are discussed in Chapter 28.

freely in intangible assets such as debts. Consequently, the rules of law regarding the assignment of contracts gradually became more liberal. Today, public policy favors free assignability of contracts.

Sources of Assignment Law Today Legal principles regarding assignment are found not only in the common law of contracts but also in Articles 2 and 9 of the Uniform Commercial Code. Section 2–210 of Article 2 contains principles applicable to assignments of rights under a contract for the sale of *goods*. Article 9 governs security interests in accounts and other contract rights as well as the outright sale of accounts. Article 9's treatment of assignments will be discussed in more detail in Chapter 28, Security Interests in Personal Property, but some provisions of Article 9 relating to assignments will be discussed in this chapter.

Creating an Assignment

An assignment can be made in any way that is sufficient to show the assignor's intent to assign. No formal language is required, and a writing is not necessary unless required by a provision of the statute of frauds or some other statute. Many states do have statutes requiring certain types of assignments to be evidenced by a writing, however. Additionally, an assignment for the purposes of security must meet Article 9's formal requirements for security interests.[2]

It is not necessary that the assignee give any consideration to the assignor in exchange for the assignment. Gratuitous assignments (those for which the assignee gives no value) are generally revocable until such time as the obligor satisfies the obligation, however. They can be revoked by the assignor's death or incapacity or by notification of revocation given by the assignor to the assignee.

Assignability of Rights

Most, but not all, contract rights are assignable. Although the free assignability of contract rights performs a valuable function in our modern credit-based economy, assignment is undesirable if it would adversely affect some important public policy or if it would materially vary the bargained-for expectations of the parties. There are several basic limitations on the assignability of contract rights.

First, an assignment will not be effective if it is *contrary to public policy*. For example, most states have enacted statutes that prohibit or regulate a wage earner's assignment of future wages. These statutes are designed to protect people against unwisely impoverishing themselves by signing away their future incomes. State law may prohibit assignment of lottery prizes or certain kinds of lawsuits on grounds of public policy.

Second, an assignment will not be effective if it *adversely affects the obligor* in some significant way. An assignment is ineffective if it materially changes the obligor's duty or increases the burden or risk on the obligor. Naturally, any assignment will change an obligor's duty to some extent. The obligor will have to pay money or deliver goods or render some other performance to one party instead of to another. These changes are not considered to be sufficiently material to render an assignment ineffective. Thus, a right to receive money or goods or land is generally assignable. In addition, covenants not to compete are generally considered to be assignable to buyers of businesses. For example, Jefferson sells RX Drugstore to Waldman, including in the contract of sale a covenant whereby Jefferson promises not to operate a competing drugstore within a 30-mile radius of RX for 10 years after the sale. Waldman later sells RX to Tharp. Here, Tharp could enforce the covenant not to compete against Jefferson. The reason for permitting assignment of covenants not to compete is that the purpose of such covenants is to protect an asset of the business—goodwill—for which the buyer has paid.

An assignment could be ineffective because of its variation of the obligor's duty, however, if the contract right involved a *personal relationship* or an element of *personal skill, judgment,* or *character*. For this reason, contracts of employment in which an employee works under the direct and personal supervision of an employer cannot be assigned to a new employer. An employer could assign a contract of employment, however, if the assignee-employer could perform the contract without adversely affecting the interests of the employee, such as would be the case when an employment relationship does not involve personal supervision by an individual employer. You will see this concept discussed in the following *Managed Health Care Associates v. Kethan* case.

A purported assignment is ineffective if it significantly increases the burden of the obligor's performance. For example, if Walker contracts to sell Dwyer all of its requirements of wheat, a purported assignment of Dwyer's rights to a corporation that has much greater requirements of wheat would probably be ineffective because it would significantly increase the burden on Walker.

---

[2]These requirements are discussed in Chapter 28.

Managed Health Care Assoc. v. Kethan   *209 F.3d 923 (6th Cir. 2000)*

On December 27, 1991, Ronald Kethan signed an employment agreement with MedEcon, a group purchasing organization (GPO) for hospitals. GPOs contract for the purchase of products for use by member healthcare facilities. The contract contained a noncompetition clause preventing Kethan from competing or working for a competitor for two years within a specified geographic area, as well as some other restrictions. It also contained a provision requiring that any modifications be in writing and signed by both parties and one providing that any disputes were to be governed by Kentucky law. No clause in the contract directly addressed the issue of whether Kethan's contract could be assigned. Kethan worked as a salesman and an agreement administrator for MedEcon from 1992 through 1996. Kethan's job responsibilities included meeting with various representatives from hospitals and encouraging them to use the products covered by MedEcon's agreements. He contacted numerous representatives in Texas and Oklahoma on MedEcon's behalf. During this period, Kethan had the opportunity to develop strong business relationships with MedEcon's customers, including First Choice. Kethan eventually became the agreement administrator for the First Choice account.

In 1998, MHA, which is also a GPO, purchased most of MedEcon's assets, including Kethan's employment agreement. Neither MedEcon nor MHA obtained Kethan's written consent to the assignment. Following the transaction, Kethan continued to be an at-will employee, performing the same job, receiving the same salary and benefits, and reporting to the same supervisor. Twenty days after the sale of MedEcon's assets to MHA, Kethan gave 30-days' notice of his resignation. Two days after Kethan tendered his resignation notice, First Choice stopped using MHA/MedEcon for group purchasing services. When the 30 days had passed from Kethan's resignation notice, he went to work for First Choice. Shortly thereafter, MHA brought suit seeking to enforce Kethan's noncompetition agreement with MedEcon. MHA moved for preliminary injunction. The district court denied the request on the ground that the assignment was a modification of the contract. MHA appealed.

GILMAN, Circuit Judge The first key issue thus becomes whether MedEcon's assignment of Kethan's employment agreement was a modification of the terms of his contract. An assignment does not modify the terms of the underlying contract. It is a separate agreement between the assignor and assignee which merely transfers the assignor's contract rights, leaving them in full force and effect as to the party charged. Insofar as an assignment touches on the obligations of the other party to the underlying contract, the assignee simply moves into the shoes of the assignor. Assignments and modifications are completely different concepts, and assignability is not impacted by "boilerplate" modification provisions. Following the assignment, Kethan's contractual rights and duties as an employee did not change. The only thing that changed was the entity now entitled to enforce the terms and conditions that Kethan had previously agreed to when he entered into his employment agreement. Accordingly, we hold that the district court erred when it concluded that the assignment of Kethan's employment contract modified the terms of his agreement.

The second key issue in the present case, however, is not the general enforceability of a noncompetition clause, but whether such a clause is assignable under Kentucky law. There is only one case in Kentucky that addresses this issue. In *Choate v. Koorsen Protective Servs., Inc.,* an employee was subject to a noncompetition clause that was

silent as to whether it could be assigned. The assets of the company were later sold, and the seller assigned the noncompetition clause to the purchaser. Choate, the employee, argued that the clause was unenforceable because he did not expressly consent to the assignment. The Jefferson County Circuit Court rejected this argument and issued an injunction enforcing the noncompetition clause. This decision was affirmed by the Kentucky Court of Appeals. By the time the case reached the Kentucky Supreme Court, the one-year noncompetition clause had expired by its own terms. Because the issue was then moot, the Kentucky Supreme Court declined to address it. Consequently, the only Kentucky authority on point, as enunciated by both the trial and the appellate courts in *Choate,* recognizes that noncompetition clauses may be assigned as part of the sale of a business's assets. In addition to opinions from the lower courts of Kentucky, this court may use the rule adopted by most of the jurisdictions that have addressed the assignability issue as persuasive authority in determining how the Kentucky Supreme Court would likely decide the question. With respect to the assignability of noncompetition clauses, "[a] majority of courts permit the successor to enforce the employee's restrictive covenant as an assignee of the original covenantee (the original employer)." 6 RICHARD A. LORD, WILLISTON ON CONTRACTS §§ 13:13 (4th ed. 1995). MHA also correctly points out that if it had purchased the stock of MedEcon rather than its assets, MedEcon would have remained in existence and continued to be Kethan's employer. Because no assignment would have been necessary under such circumstances, Kethan would have had no basis to even question the enforceability of the noncompetition clause. Allowing Kethan to avoid his obligations under the circumstances of this case simply because MHA decided to structure the transaction as a purchase of assets rather than stock would exalt form over substance.

The policy behind enforcing noncompetition clauses is to protect businesses against employees resigning and taking valued clients with them. In this case, while working for MedEcon, Kethan had access to MedEcon's customer lists. He eventually became First Choice's primary advisor. Because of that, Kethan developed a special business relationship with First Choice. Shortly after First Choice decided to end its business relationship with MHA/MedEcon, Kethan ceased working for MHA and commenced working for First Choice. The reason that Kethan was able to develop his unique business relationship with First Choice, and later go to work for it, was because MedEcon employed him and placed him in charge of the First Choice account. He is thus precisely the type of employee for whom noncompetition clauses were designed. Kethan and First Choice respond by arguing that a personal services contract cannot be assigned. A personal services contract, however, requires that one of

the parties be bound to render personal services. In contrast, a noncompetition clause only requires that one of the parties abstain from certain activities. Here, Kethan was an at-will employee who was free to resign at any time. Consequently, the noncompetition clause does not require any affirmative action on the part of Kethan, and is thus assignable. Kethan and First Choice further argue that the management style and "character" changed when MHA purchased the assets of MedEcon. This, however, is irrelevant to the issue of whether the noncompetition clause is assignable because the clause was not tied to the management style or "character" of MedEcon. In fact, MedEcon could have changed its management at any time, and Kethan would have still been bound by the noncompetition clause. Similarly, management would have changed exactly as it did if MHA had purchased the stock of MedEcon rather than its assets and, as previously noted, Kethan would have had no basis to complain. Based on the opinions of the lower Kentucky courts in *Choate,* the majority rule from the other states that have addressed the issue, and the additional reasons set forth above, we believe that the Kentucky Supreme Court would conclude that noncompetition clauses are assignable. Consequently, we reverse the district court on this point.

Reversed and remanded in favor of MHA.

Contract Clauses Prohibiting Assignment A contract right may also be nonassignable because the original contract expressly forbids assignment. For example, leases often contain provisions forbidding assignment or requiring the tenant to obtain the landlord's permission for assignment.[3]

Antiassignment clauses in contracts are generally enforceable. Because of the strong public policy favoring assignability, however, such clauses are often interpreted narrowly. For example, a court might view an assignment made in violation of an antiassignment clause as a breach of contract for which damages may be recovered but not as an invalidation of the assignment. Another tactic is to interpret a contractual ban on assignment as prohibiting only the delegation of duties.

The UCC takes this latter position. Under section 2–210(2), general language prohibiting assignment of "the contract" or "all my rights under the contract" is interpreted as forbidding only the delegation of duties, un-

less the circumstances indicate to the contrary. Section 2–210 also states that a right to damages for breach of a whole sales contract or a right arising out of the assignor's performance of his entire obligation may be assigned even if a provision of the original sales contract prohibited assignment. In addition, UCC section 9–318(4) invalidates contract terms that prohibit (or require the debtor's consent to) an assignment of an account or creation of a security interest in a right to receive money that is now due or that will become due.

Nature of Assignee's Rights

When an assignment occurs, the assignee is said to "step into the shoes of his assignor." This means that the assignee acquires all of the rights that his assignor had under the contract. The assignee has the right to receive the obligor's performance, and if performance is not forthcoming, the assignee has the right to sue in his own name for breach of the obligation. By the same token, the assignee acquires no greater rights than those possessed by the assignor.

---

[3]The assignment of leases is discussed further in Chapter 25.

Because the assignee has no greater rights than did the assignor, the obligor may assert any defense or claim against the assignee that he could have asserted against the assignor, subject to certain time limitations discussed below. A contract that is void, voidable, or unenforceable as between the original parties does not become enforceable just because it has been assigned to a third party. For example, if Richards induces Dillman's consent to a contract by duress and subsequently assigns his rights under the contract to Keith, Dillman can assert the doctrine of duress against Keith as a ground for avoiding the contract.

Importance of Notifying the Obligor   An assignee should promptly notify the obligor of the assignment. Although notification of the obligor is not necessary for the assignment to be valid, such notice is of great practical importance. One reason notice is important is that an obligor who does not have reason to know of the assignment could render performance to the assignor and claim that his obligation had been discharged by performance. An obligor who renders performance to the assignor without notice of the assignment has no further liability under the contract. For example, McKay borrows $500 from Goodheart, promising to repay the debt by June 1. Goodheart assigns the debt to Rogers, but no one informs McKay of the assignment, and McKay pays the $500 to Goodheart, the assignor. In this case, McKay is not liable for any further payment. But if Rogers had immediately notified McKay of the assignment and, after receiving notice, McKay had mistakenly paid the debt to Goodheart, McKay would still have the legal obligation to pay $500 to Rogers. Having been given adequate notice of the assignment, he may remain liable to the assignee even if he later renders performance to the assignor.

An assignor who accepts performance from the obligor after the assignment holds any benefits that he receives as a trustee for the assignee. If the assignor fails to pay those benefits to the assignee, however, an obligor who has been notified of the assignment and renders performance to the wrong person may have to pay the same debt twice.

An obligor who receives notice of an assignment from the assignee will want to assure himself that the assignment has in fact occurred. He may ask for written evidence of the assignment or contact the assignee and ask for verification of the assignment. Under UCC section 9–318(3), a notification of assignment is ineffective unless it reasonably identifies the rights assigned. If requested by the account debtor (an obligor who owes money for goods sold or leased or services rendered), the assignee must furnish reasonable proof that the assignment has been made, and, unless he does so, the account debtor may disregard the notice and pay the assignor.

Defenses against the Assignee   An assignee's rights in an assignment are subject to the defenses that the obligor could have asserted against the assignor. Keep in mind that the assignee's rights are limited by the terms of the underlying contract between the assignor and the obligor. When defenses arise from the terms or performance of that contract, they can be asserted against the assignee even if they arise after the obligor receives notice of the assignment. For example, on June 1, Worldwide Widgets assigns to First Bank its rights under a contract with Widgetech, Inc. This contract obligates Worldwide Widgets to deliver a quantity of widgets to Widgetech by September 1, in return for which Widgetech is obligated to pay a stated purchase price. First Bank gives prompt notice of the assignment to Widgetech. Worldwide Widget fails to deliver the widgets and Widgetech refuses to pay. If First Bank brought an action against Widgetech to recover the purchase price of the widgets, Widgetech could assert Worldwide Widget's breach as a defense, even though the breach occurred after Widgetech received notice of the assignment.[4]

In determining what other defenses can be asserted against the assignee, the time of notification plays an important role. After notification, as we discussed earlier, payment by the obligor to the assignor will not discharge the obligor.

Subsequent Assignments

An assignee may "reassign" a right to a third party, who would be called a **subassignee.** The subassignee then acquires the rights held by the prior assignee. He should give the obligor prompt notice of the subsequent assignment, because he takes his interest subject to the same principles discussed above regarding the claims and defenses that can be asserted against him.

---

[4]Similarly, if the assignor's rights were subject to discharge because of other factors such as the nonoccurrence of a condition, impossibility, impracticability, or public policy, this can be asserted as a defense against the assignee even if the event occurs after the obligor receives notice of assignment. See *Restatement (Second) of Contracts* § 336(3). The doctrines relating to discharge from performance are explained in Chapter 18.

Successive Assignments

Notice to the obligor may be important in one other situation. If an assignor assigns the same right to two assignees in succession, both of whom pay for the assignment, a question of priority results. An assignor who assigns the same right to different people will be held liable to the assignee who acquires no rights against the obligor, but which assignee is entitled to the obligor's performance? Which assignee will have recourse only against the assignor? There are several views on this point.

In states that follow the "American rule," the first assignee has the better right. This view is based on the rule of property law that a person cannot transfer greater rights in property than he owns. In states that follow the "English rule," however, the assignee who first gives notice of the assignment to the obligor, without knowledge of the other assignee's claim, has the better right. The *Restatement (Second) of Contracts* takes a third position. Section 342 of the *Restatement (Second)* provides that the first assignee has priority unless the subsequent assignee gives value (pays for the assignment) and, without having reason to know of the other assignee's claim, does one of the following: obtains payment of the obligation, gets a judgment against the obligor, obtains a new contract with the obligor by novation, or possesses a writing of a type customarily accepted as a symbol or evidence of the right assigned (such as a passbook for a savings account).

Assignor's Warranty Liability to Assignee

Suppose that Ross, a 16-year-old boy, contracts to buy a used car for $2,000 from Donaldson. Ross pays Donaldson $500 as a down payment and agrees to pay the balance in equal monthly installments. Donaldson assigns his right to receive the balance of the purchase price to Beckman, who pays $1,000 in cash for the assignment. When Beckman later attempts to enforce the contract, however, Ross disaffirms the contract on grounds of lack of capacity. Thus, Beckman has paid $1,000 for a worthless claim. Does Beckman have any recourse against Donaldson? When an assignor is paid for making an assignment, the assignor is held to have made certain implied warranties about the claim assigned.

The assignor implicitly warrants that the claim assigned is valid. This means that the obligor has capacity to contract, the contract is not illegal, the contract is not voidable for any other reason known to the assignor (such as fraud or duress), and the contract has not been discharged prior to assignment. The assignor also warrants that he has good title to the rights assigned and that any written instrument representing the assigned claim is genuine. In addition, the assignor implicitly agrees that he will not do anything to impair the value of the assignment. These guarantees are imposed by law unless the assignment agreement clearly indicates to the contrary. One important aspect of the assigned right that the assignor does not implicitly warrant, however, is that the obligor is solvent.

Delegation of Duties

Nature of Delegation

A **delegation** of duties occurs when an obligor indicates his intent to appoint another person to perform his duties under a contract. For example, White owns a furniture store. He has numerous existing contracts to deliver furniture to customers, including a contract to deliver a sofa to Coombs. White is the *obligor* of the duty to deliver the sofa and Coombs is the *obligee*. White decides to sell his business to Rosen. As a part of the sale of the business, White assigns the rights in the existing contracts to Rosen and delegates to him the performance of those contracts, including the duty to deliver the sofa to Coombs. Here, White is the *delegator* and Rosen is the *delegatee*. White is appointing Rosen to carry out his duties to the obligee, Coombs. Figure 3 summarizes the key terms regarding delegation.

In contrast to an assignment of a right, which extinguishes the assignor's right and transfers it to the assignee, the delegation of a *duty* does *not* extinguish the duty owed by the delegator. This point is made in *Rosenberg v. Son, Inc.*, which follows this discussion. The delegator remains liable to the obligee unless the obligee agrees to substitute the delegatee's promise for that of the delegator (this is called a *novation* and will be discussed in greater detail later in this chapter). This makes sense because, if it were possible for a person to escape his duties under a contract by merely delegating them to another, any party to a contract could avoid liability by delegating duties to an insolvent acquaintance. The significance of an effective delegation is that performance by the delegatee will discharge the delegator. In addition, if the duty is a delegable one, the obligee cannot insist on performance by the delegator; he must accept the performance of the delegatee. The relationship between the parties in a delegation is shown in Figure 4.

Figure 3   *Delegation: Key Terms*

Obligor	Obligee	Delegation	Delegator	Delegatee
Person who owes the duty to perform	Person who has the right to receive obligor's performance	Appointment of another person to perform the obligor's duty to the obligee	Obligor who appoints another to perform his duty to obligee	Person who is appointed to perform the obligor's duty to the obligee

Figure 4   *Delegation*

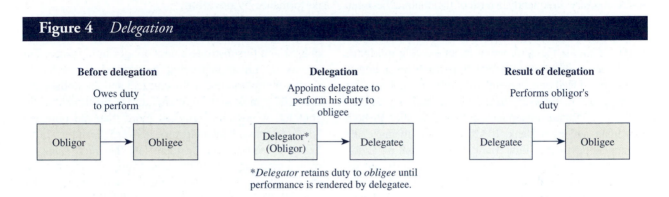

Delegable Duties

A duty that can be performed fully by a number of different persons is delegable. Not all duties are delegable, however. The grounds for finding a duty to be nondelegable resemble closely the grounds for finding a right to be nonassignable. A duty is nondelegable if delegation would violate public policy or if the original contract between the parties forbids delegation. In addition, both section 2–210(1) of the UCC and section 318(2) of the *Restatement (Second) of Contracts* take the position that a party to a contract may delegate his duty to perform to another person unless the parties have agreed to the contrary or unless the other party has a *substantial interest* in having the original obligor perform the acts required by the contract. The key factor used in determining whether the obligee has such a substantial interest is the degree to which performance is dependent on the individual traits, skill, or judgment of the person who owes the duty to perform. For example, if Jansen hires Skelton, an artist, to paint her portrait, Skelton could not effectively delegate the duty to paint the portrait to another artist. Similarly, an employee could not normally delegate her duties under an employment contract to some third person, because employment contracts are made with the understanding that the person the employer hires will perform the work. The situation in which a person hires a general

contractor to perform specific work is distinguishable, however. In that situation, the person hiring the general contractor would normally understand that at least part of the work would be delegated to subcontractors.

Language Creating a Delegation

No special, formal language is necessary to create an effective delegation of duties. In fact, since parties frequently confuse the terms *assignment* and *delegation*, one of the problems frequently presented to courts is determining whether the parties intended an assignment only or both an assignment and a delegation. Unless the agreement indicates a contrary intent, courts tend to interpret assignments as including a delegation of the assignor's duties. Both the UCC 2–210(4) and section 328 of the *Restatement (Second) of Contracts* provide that, unless the language or the circumstances indicate to the contrary, general language of assignment such as language indicating an assignment of "the contract" or of "all my rights under the contract" is to be interpreted as creating *both* an assignment and a delegation.

Assumption of Duties by Delegatee

A delegation gives the delegatee the right to perform the duties of the delegator. The mere fact that duties have been delegated does not always place legal responsibility on the delegatee to perform. The delegatee who fails to perform will not be liable to either the delegator or the obligee unless the delegatee has assumed the duty by expressly or impliedly undertaking the obligation to perform. However, both section 2–210(4) of the UCC and section 328 of the *Restatement (Second)* provide that an assignee's acceptance of an assignment is to be construed as a promise by him to perform the duties under the contract, unless the language of the assignment or the circumstances indicate to the contrary. Frequently, a term of the contract between the delegator and the delegatee provides that the delegatee assumes responsibility for performance. A common example of this is the assumption of an existing mortgage debt by a purchaser of real estate. Suppose Morgan buys a house from Friedman, agreeing to assume the outstanding mortgage on the property held by First Bank. By this assumption, Morgan undertakes personal liability to both Friedman and First Bank. If Morgan fails to make the mortgage payments, First Bank has a cause of action against Morgan personally. An assumption does *not* release the delegator from liability, however. Rather, it creates a situation in which both the delegator and the assuming delegatee owe duties to the obligee. If the assuming delegatee fails to pay, the delegator can be held liable. Thus, in the example described above, if Morgan fails to make mortgage payments and First Bank is unable to collect the debt from Morgan, Friedman would have secondary liability. Friedman, of course, would have an action against Morgan for breach of their contract.

Discharge of Delegator by Novation

As you have seen, the mere delegation of duties—even when the delegatee assumes those duties—does not release the delegator from his legal obligation to the obligee. A delegator can, however, be discharged from performance by **novation.**

A novation is a particular type of substituted contract in which the obligee agrees to discharge the original obligor and to substitute a new obligor in his place. The effects of a novation are that the original obligor has no further obligation under the contract and the obligee has the right to look to the new obligor for fulfillment of the contract. A novation requires more than the obligee's consent to having the delegatee perform the duties. In the example used above, the mere fact that First Bank accepted mortgage payments from Morgan would not create a novation. Rather, there must be some evidence that the obligee agrees to discharge the old obligor and substitute a new obligor. As you will see in the following *Rosenberg* case, this can be inferred from language of a contract or such other factors as the obligee's conduct or the surrounding circumstances.

Rosenberg v. Son, Inc.   *491 N.W.2d 71 (Sup. Ct. N.D. 1992)*

In February 1980, Mary Pratt entered into a contract to buy a Dairy Queen restaurant located in Grand Forks's City Center Mall from Harold and Gladys Rosenberg. The terms of the contract for the franchise, inventory, and equipment were a purchase price totaling $62,000, a $10,000 down payment, and $52,000 due in quarterly payments at 10 percent interest over a 15-year period. The sales contract also contained a provision denying the buyer a right of prepayment for the first five years of the contract. In October 1982, Pratt assigned her rights and delegated her duties under this contract to Son, Inc. The assignment between Pratt and Son contained a "Consent to Assignment" clause, which was signed by the Rosenbergs. It also contained a "save harmless" clause, in which Son promised to indemnify Pratt for any claims, demands, or actions that might result from Son's failure to perform the agreement. After this transaction, Pratt moved to Arizona and had no further knowledge of or involvement with the Dairy Queen business. Also following the assignment, the Dairy Queen was moved from the mall to a different location in Grand Forks.

Son assigned the contract to Merit Corporation in June 1984. This assignment did not include a consent clause, but the Rosenbergs knew of the assignment and apparently acquiesced in it. They accepted a large prepayment from Merit, reducing the principal balance to $25,000. After the assignment, Merit pledged the inventory and equipment of the Dairy Queen as collateral for a loan from Valley Bank and Trust. Payments from Merit to the Rosenbergs continued until June 1988, at which time the payments ceased, leaving an unpaid principal balance of $17,326.24 plus interest. The Rosenbergs attempted collection of the balance from Merit, but Merit filed bankruptcy. The business assets pledged as collateral for the loan from Valley Bank and Trust were repossessed. The Rosenbergs brought this action for collection of the outstanding debt against Son and Pratt. The trial court granted summary judgment in favor of Son and Pratt and against the Rosenbergs, and the Rosenbergs appealed.

Erickstad, Chief Justice   It is a well-established principle in the law of contracts that a contracting party cannot escape its liability on the contract by merely assigning its duties and rights under the contract to a third party. This rule of law applies to all categories of contracts, including contracts for the sale of goods, which is present in the facts of this case.

Thus, when Pratt entered into the "assignment agreement" with Son, a simple assignment alone was insufficient to release her from any further liability on the contract. It is not, however, a legal impossibility for a contracting party to rid itself of an obligation under a contract. It may seek the approval of the other original party for release, and substitute a new party in its place. In such an instance, the transaction is no longer called an assignment; instead, it is called a novation. If a novation occurs in this manner, it must be clear from the terms of the agreement that a novation is intended by all parties involved. Both original parties to the contract must intend and mutually assent to the discharge of the obligor from any further liability on the original contract.

It is evident from the express language of the assignment agreement between Pratt and Son that only an assignment was intended, not a novation. The agreement made no mention of discharging Pratt from any further liability on the contract. To the contrary, the latter part of the agreement contained an indemnity clause holding Pratt harmless in the event of a breach by Son. Thus, it is apparent that Pratt contemplated being held ultimately responsible for performance of the obligation. Furthermore, the agreement was between Pratt and Son; they were the parties signing the agreement, not the Rosenbergs. An agreement between Pratt and Son cannot unilaterally affect the Rosenbergs' rights under the contract. The Rosenbergs did sign a consent to the assignment at the bottom of the agreement. However, by merely consenting to the assignment the Rosenbergs did not consent to a discharge of the principal obligor—Pratt. Nothing in the language of the consent clause supports such an allegation. A creditor is free to consent to an assignment without releasing the original obligor. Thus, the express language of the agreement and intent of the parties at the time the assignment was made did not contemplate a novation by releasing Pratt and substituting Son in her stead.

The inquiry as to Pratt's liability does not end at this juncture. The trial court released Pratt from any liability on the contract due to the changes or alterations which took place following her assignment to Son. While it is true that Pratt cannot be forced to answer on the contract irrespective of events occurring subsequent to her assignment, it is also true that she cannot be exonerated for every type of alteration or change that may develop.

> The buyer can assign his right to the goods or land and can delegate performance of his duty to pay that price. But observe that he remains bound "as before"; the assignee and the seller cannot, by agreement or by waiver, make it the assignor's duty to pay a different price or on different conditions. If the seller is willing to make such a change, he must trust to the assignee alone. 4 *Corbin on Contracts* section 866 at 458–59.

The trial court decided that any alteration in the underlying obligation resulted in a release of Pratt on the contract. It appears that not every type of alteration is sufficient to warrant discharge of the assignor. As suggested by Professor Corbin in the language highlighted above, the alteration must "prejudice the position of the assignor." 4 *Corbin on Contracts* section 866 at 459.

If the changes in the obligation prejudicially affect the assignor, a new agreement has been formed between the assignee and the other original contracting party. More concisely, a novation has occurred and the assignor's original obligation has been discharged. Although we have previously determined that the terms of the assignment agreement between Pratt and Son did not contemplate a novation, there are additional methods of making a novation besides doing so in the express terms of an agreement. The question of whether or not there has been a novation is a question of fact. The trial court should not have granted summary judgment. There are questions of fact remaining as to the result of the changes in the contract. Thus, we reverse the summary judgment and remand for further proceedings.

Reversed and remanded in favor of the Rosenbergs.

Third-Party Beneficiaries

There are many situations in which the performance of a contract would constitute some benefit to a person who was not a party to the contract. Despite the fact that a nonparty may expect to derive advantage from the performance of a contract, the general rule is that no one but the parties to a contract or their assignees can enforce it. In some situations, however, parties contract for the purpose of benefiting some third person. In such cases, the benefit to the third person is an essential part of the contract, not just an incidental result of a contract that was really designed to benefit the parties. Where the parties

Figure 5   *Third-Party Beneficiaries*

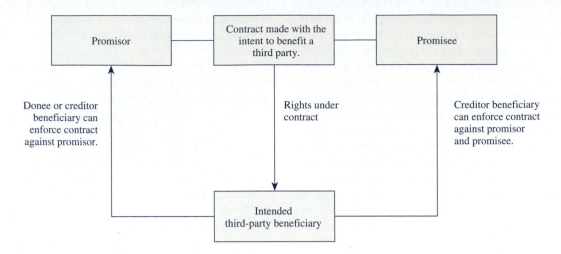

to a contract *intended* to benefit a third party, courts will give effect to their intent and permit the third party to enforce the contract. Such third parties are called **third-party beneficiaries.** Figure 5 illustrates the relationship of third-party beneficiaries to the contracting parties.

Intended Beneficiaries versus Incidental Beneficiaries

For a third person (other than an assignee) to have the right to enforce a contract, she must be able to establish that the contract was made with the intent to benefit her. A few courts have required that both parties must have intended to benefit the third party. Most courts, however, have found it to be sufficient if the person to whom the promise to perform was made (the *promisee*) intended to benefit the third party. You will see an example of this in the following *Cherry v. Crow* case. In ascertaining intent to benefit the third party, a court will look at the language used by the parties and all the surrounding circumstances. One factor that is frequently important in determining intent to benefit is whether the party making the promise to perform (the *promisor*) was to render performance directly to the third party. For example, if Allison contracts with Jones Florist to deliver flowers to Kirsch, the fact that performance was to be rendered to Kirsch would be good evidence that the parties intended to benefit Kirsch. This factor is not conclusive, however. There are some cases in which intent to benefit a third party has been found even though performance was to be

rendered to the promisee rather than to the third party. Intended beneficiaries are often classified as either *creditor* or *donee beneficiaries.* These classifications are discussed in greater detail below.

A third party who is unable to establish that the contract was made with the intent to benefit her is called an *incidental beneficiary.* A third party is classified as an incidental beneficiary when the benefit derived by that third party was merely an unintended by-product of a contract that was created for the benefit of those who were parties to it. Incidental beneficiaries acquire no rights under a contract. For example, Hutton contracts with Long Construction Company to build a valuable structure on his land. The performance of the contract would constitute a benefit to Keller, Hutton's next-door neighbor, by increasing the value of Keller's land. The contract between Hutton and Long was made for the purpose of benefiting themselves, however. Any advantage derived by Keller is purely incidental to their primary purpose. Thus, Keller could not sue and recover damages if either Hutton or Long breaches the contract.

As a general rule, members of the public are held to be incidental beneficiaries of contracts entered into by their municipalities or other governmental units in the regular course of carrying on governmental functions. A member of the public cannot recover a judgment in a suit against a promisor of such a contract, even though all taxpayers will suffer some injury from nonperformance. A different result may be reached, however, if a party contracting with a governmental unit agrees to reimburse members of the public for damages or if the party undertakes to perform some duty for individual members of the public.

Creditor Beneficiaries If the promisor's performance is intended to satisfy a legal duty that the promisee owes to a third party, the third party is a **creditor beneficiary.** The creditor beneficiary has rights against both the promisee (because of the original obligation) and the promisor. For example, Smith buys a car on credit from Jones Auto Sales. Smith later sells the car to Carmichael, who agrees to pay the balance due on the car to Jones Auto Sales. (Note that Smith is delegating his duty to pay to Carmichael, and Carmichael is assuming the personal obligation to do so.) In this case, Jones Auto Sales is a creditor beneficiary of the contract between Smith and Carmichael. It has rights against both Carmichael and Smith if Carmichael does not perform.

Donee Beneficiaries If the promisee's primary purpose in contracting is to make a gift of the agreed-on performance to a third party, that third party is classified as a *donee beneficiary.* If the contract is breached, the donee beneficiary will have a cause of action against the promisor, but not against the promisee (donor). For example, Miller contracts with Perpetual Life Insurance Company, agreeing to pay premiums in return for which Perpetual agrees to pay $100,000 to Miller's husband when Miller dies. Miller's husband is a donee beneficiary and can bring suit and recover judgment against Perpetual if Miller dies and Perpetual does not pay.

Cherry v. Crow   *845 F. Supp. 1520 (M. D. Fla. 1994)*

The Sheriff of Polk County employed Prison Health Services (PHS) to provide total health care services for inmates and detainees housed within the Polk County Jail and the Polk County Jail Annex. On December 22, 1922, Polk County Sheriff's Department (PCSD) employees booked Eddie Ronald Cherry into the jail to begin serving a 30-day sentence for driving under the influence of alcohol. At the time of his incarceration, Cherry informed the PHS medical staff that he consumed approximately one case of beer daily. Over the next two days, Cherry repeatedly requested medical attention for symptoms related to alcohol withdrawal.

Cherry's wife notified a PCSD employee by phone on December 25 that her husband had a history of delirium tremens ("DTs") during alcohol withdrawal and that he was in immediate need of a doctor's attention. About two hours later, the inmates sharing Cherry's cell asked PCSD employees to check on Cherry's condition. The employees found Cherry in his cell, hallucinating and shaking violently. The PCSD employees notified PHS Nurse Gill, who examined Cherry and reported his symptoms of DTs to PHS Nurse Smith. Nurse Smith requested that Cherry be sent to the infirmary for observation.

At the infirmary, a PCSD employee shackled Cherry, who was still hallucinating, to his bed, with the knowledge and acquiescence of Nurse Smith. The next morning, while still suffering from hallucinations associated with DTs, Cherry either walked or jumped off the end of his bed. Because the leg shackle did not allow his feet to advance beyond the top of the bed, Cherry landed head first on the concrete floor. Cherry died five days later as a result of his injuries. Cherry's wife filed suit on behalf of Cherry's estate against PHS, Nurse Smith, and the PCSD for breach of contract and other claims. The defendants moved to dismiss the suit and strike the complaint. The court's opinion follows.

Kovachevich, District Judge   Defendants assert that no cause of action exists against PHS for breach of contract, in that Cherry was not an intended third party beneficiary of the employment contract between PHS and PCSD. The Health Services Agreement between PCSD and PHS states:

> WHEREAS, the SHERIFF has the statutory and constitutional duty and responsibility to provide necessary and proper medical, psychiatric, dental and other health care services for persons remanded to his care, custody and control within the county correctional system. . . .
> WHEREAS, the SHERIFF is desirous of contracting with PHS and PHS is desirous of contracting with the SHERIFF to provide total health care services *for the inmates/detainees* . . . housed within the county correctional system facilities described above . . .

The right of a third-party beneficiary to bring suit under contract as outlined in *American Surety Co. of New York v. Smith* remains clear guidance today. The Supreme Court recognized:

Where, therefore it is manifest from the nature or terms of a contract that the formal parties thereto intended its provisions to be for the benefit of a third party, as well as for the benefit of the formal parties themselves, the benefit to such third parties being the direct and primary object of the contract, or amongst such objects, such third party may maintain an action on the contract even though he is a stranger to the consideration.

The Court finds that PCSD and PHS intended, as a result of their agreement, to benefit persons situated such as Cherry. Accordingly, defendants' motion to dismiss is denied.

Motion denied in favor of Cherry.

ETHICS IN ACTION

Westendorf bought her friend a Gateway computer, which, at her request, Gateway delivered directly to her friend. Several months later, the same friend purchased a Gateway computer, which he requested be delivered directly to Westendorf. Westendorf received and kept that computer. In the shipment, Gateway included its Standard Terms and Conditions Agreement, which contains an arbitration clause. Westendorf allegedly began experiencing numerous and serious difficulties when attempting to use the Gateway.net service. She brought a class action against Gateway. Westendorf argues that she is not bound by the arbitration clause because as a non-purchasing user of the computer she never expressly agreed to arbitration. Is it ethical to obligate a donee beneficiary such as Westendorf to the arbitration clause that was part of the contract between the friend who gave her the computer and Gateway?

Vesting of Beneficiary's Rights

Another possible threat to the interests of the third-party beneficiary is that the promisor and the promisee might modify or discharge their contract so as to extinguish or alter the beneficiary's rights. For example, Gates, who owes $500 to Sorenson, enters into a contract with Connor whereby Connor agrees to pay the $500 to Sorenson. What happens if, before Sorenson is paid, Connor pays the money to Gates and Gates accepts it or Connor and Gates otherwise modify the contract? Courts have held that there is a point at which the rights of the beneficiary vest—that is, the beneficiary's rights cannot be lost by modification or discharge. A modification or discharge that occurs after the beneficiary's rights have vested cannot be asserted as a defense to a suit brought by the beneficiary. The exact time at which the beneficiary's rights vest differs from jurisdiction to jurisdiction. Some courts have held that vesting occurs when the contract is formed, while others hold that vesting does not occur until the beneficiary learns of the contract and consents to it or does some act in reliance on the promise.

The contracting parties' ability to vary the rights of the third-party beneficiary can also be affected by the terms of their agreement. A provision of the contract between the promisor and the promisee stating that the duty to the beneficiary cannot be modified would be effective to prevent modification. Likewise, a contract provision in which the parties specifically reserved the right to change beneficiaries or modify the duty to the beneficiary would be enforced. For example, provisions reserving the right to change beneficiaries are very common in insurance contracts.

Problems and Problem Cases

1. In June 1992, Callahan settled a products liability accident case with Sentry, the tortfeasors' insurance company, for injuries he received in a rotary mower accident. Callahan and Sentry entered into a settlement agreement and release that obligated Sentry to purchase an annuity from Sentry Life Insurance Company, providing Callahan with monthly payments of $1225 starting July 1, 1992, for the remainder of his life, with a guaranteed minimum of 240 monthly payments. This guaranteed Callahan a minimum of $294,000. Several years later, Callahan and Settlement entered into a series of purchase agreements in which Settlement purchased all of Callahan's future payments in an exchange for a lump sum.

Because Callahan's original agreement with Sentry contained a non-assignability clause prohibiting him from assigning his future payments, Callahan gave Settlement a notarized instruction letter that ordered Sentry Life to send the annuity checks to Settlement's address. Callahan also represented that he would not make any changes to the instructions to Sentry Life as to where the payments should be directed. Finally, Callahan agreed that he would never interfere with Settlement's right to receive and collect the payments. Shortly thereafter, Settlement assigned its interest in Callahan's future payments from Sentry Life to Wentworth. Wentworth was aware of the non-assignability clause in the settlement agreement. This arrangement continued until August 1, 1997, when the payments to Wentworth stopped. Does Wentworth have the right to receive these payments?

2. Douglass was a highly trained servicer of hardness-testing machinery, who was employed by Page-Wilson. In August and April 1983, Douglass signed two employment agreements governing the terms and conditions of his employment with Page-Wilson. The first agreement prohibited Douglass, while he was working for Page-Wilson and for one year after the termination of his employment, from using, to Page-Wilson's detriment, any of its customer list or other intellectual property acquired from his job there. The second agreement, which applied to the same time period, prohibited Douglass from accepting employment from or serving as a consultant to any business that was in competition with Page-Wilson. In April 1987, Canrad Corporation purchased all assets and contractual rights of Page-Wilson, including Douglass's two employment contracts. Special Products Manufacturing, a wholly owned subsidiary of Canrad, assumed plant operations. Douglas worked for Special Products until his resignation in February 1988. Shortly after that time, Special Products filed suit against Douglass, alleging that Douglass had affixed his name and home telephone number to the machines he serviced, so that the ensuing maintenance calls would reach him personally. It also alleged that, following his resignation, Douglass established a competing business and actively solicited Special Products' clientele. Douglass claims that Special Products did not have the right to enforce the agreements not to compete. Is Douglass correct?

3. In May 1978, John and Judith Brooks contracted with Hayes to construct a Windsor Home (a packaged, predesigned, and precut home) on a lot that they owned. Hayes was primarily a real estate broker but also sold Windsor Homes. The construction contract required Hayes to "provide all necessary labor and materials and perform all work of every nature whatsoever to be done in the erection of a residence for" the Brookses. The Brookses and Hayes contemplated that Hayes would hire subcontractors to perform much of the home construction work and Hayes, who had no personal experience in construction, would not control the method of construction. During the construction, the Brookses requested that a "heatilator" be installed as an extra to increase the efficiency of the fireplace. Marr, the mason hired by Hayes to do the fireplace and other masonry work, installed the heatilator. The Brookses moved into the house in the winter of 1978. When they used the fireplace, they smelled smoke in areas of the house remote from the fireplace. Both the Brookses and Hayes hired several masons to inspect the fireplace system, but none of the masons was able to discover the cause of the problem. The Brookses used the fireplace with some frequency until November 1980, when a fire in the home caused structural damage around the fireplace and smoke damage to the house and the couple's personal property. It was discovered that Marr's negligence in installing the heatilator had caused the fire. The Brookses sued both Marr and Hayes. The case against Marr was dismissed because Marr went bankrupt. Is Hayes liable to the Brookses?

4. Andreson went to Monahan Beaches Jewelry Center to shop for a diamond engagement ring for his fiancée, Warren. Andreson told Monahan that the ring was to be given to Warren. Andreson and a salesperson discussed several aspects of the size, type, and style of the ring, and the salesperson made suggestions about what would be likely to be pleasing to Warren. Shortly before Christmas, Monahan sold Andreson a ring, which Monahan represented as being a diamond ring, for $3,974.25. Andreson gave the ring to Warren for Christmas as a symbol of their engagement. Warren soon noticed a small chip in the stone under the setting. She returned the ring to Monahan shortly after the Christmas holidays and Monahan agreed to replace the stone with one of equal or greater value at no charge to Warren. After making this agreement, Warren took the ring to another jeweler to have it appraised. There she learned for the first time that the alleged diamond that Monahan sold to Andreson was in fact nothing more than cut glass or cubic zirconia. Warren filed suit against Monahan on several counts, including breach of contract. Could Warren win a breach of contract suit against Monahan, even though it was her fiancé who purchased the ring?

5. Jones paid Sullivan, the chief of the Addison Police Department, $6,400 in exchange for Sullivan's cooperation in allowing Jones and others to bring marijuana by

airplane into the Addison airport without police intervention. Instead of performing the requested service, Sullivan arrested Jones. The $6,400 was turned over to the district attorney's office and was introduced into evidence in the subsequent trial in which Jones was tried for and convicted of bribery. After his conviction, Jones assigned his alleged claim to the $6,400 to Melvyn Bruder. Based on the assignment, Bruder brought suit against the state of Texas to obtain possession of the money. Will he be successful?

6. In June 1987, Barreca won a share in a prize of over two million dollars in the New Jersey Lottery. She was entitled to receive $63,500 each June for 20 years. In November of 1996 Barreca entered into an agreement with Singer Asset Finance Company in which she agreed to assign to Singer $50,000 of the payments due June 22, 1999 and June 22, 2000, in return for a present payment to her of $72,000. Singer is in the business of buying lottery prize payment streams from prizewinners in a number of states. New Jersey law holds that lottery prizes are generally unassignable, except in case of death of the lottery winner or an appropriate judicial order to assign prizes. The agreement between Barreca and Singer was conditioned upon the entry of a court order "directing the State Lottery to recognize [the agreement] and to make the Assigned Payments . . . directly to [Singer]" and a "written acknowledgement from the State Lottery . . . confirming that [Barreca] is the winner of [the assigned prize] and acknowledging the State Lottery's unqualified agreement to make all of the Assigned Payments to [Singer]." Singer assigned its right to receive the moneys to an entity entitled Lottery Receivables Trust I. Singer filed a petition in the Law Division in which it sought to proceed summarily for an order to allow the turnover of the assigned portion of Barreca's prize, an order which it characterized as an "appropriate judicial order." Should it be successful?

7. Francis brought suit against Piper and his law firm, alleging Piper committed legal malpractice when he drafted a series of wills for Heine, Francis's brother. Heine, who had never married, had no children; Francis was his sole sibling and closest living relative. In 1987, after Heine suffered a stroke, the district court appointed a conservator for him. In 1990, Heine met Resick, a waitress at a deli he frequented. In December 1991, Resick referred Heine, who did not have a will, to Piper. Piper prepared three successive wills for Heine. The first left all of Heine's estate to a church. The second left $20,000 to Resick and the remainder of Heine's estate to a church. The third left all of Heine's estate to Resick. If Heine had not executed a will, Francis would have been Heine's sole heir under the intestacy laws. After Heine's death, Resick submitted the third will to probate. Francis challenged the will, and eventually reached a settlement with Resick that provided Resick would receive $80,000 and Francis the remainder of Heine's estate. Francis then brought this action against Piper, alleging Piper was negligent because Heine was under a conservatorship, lacked testamentary capacity, and was suffering from the effects of undue influence. Piper moved for summary judgment, asserting Francis could not bring a legal malpractice action against him. Under applicable state law, an attorney is liable to a nonclient third party only if the client's sole purpose in retaining an attorney is to provide a benefit directly to the third party. Was Francis such an intended beneficiary?

8. Broadway/72nd Associates, the sponsors of the Alexandria Condominium, hired LMB to act as construction manager for the construction of the condominium. The construction management agreement between the sponsors and LMB stated in part that "[t]he sole beneficiaries of this Agreement are the parties hereto. . . . This Agreement is not intended to confer any benefit or rights upon persons other than the parties hereto . . . . " The offering plan issued by the sponsor to sell the condominium described residential units which were warranted to have been designed and constructed in a competent and workmanlike manner. However, the building developed several serious structural problems that permitted water into the interior of the building. The Board of Managers of the Alexandria Condominium claimed that LMB breached its contract with the sponsors and that it is a third party beneficiary of the contract between the sponsor and LMB. Is this correct?

9. Lewis, a dairyman, was a member of the Mountain Empire Dairymen's Association (MEDA). MEDA was the exclusive agent for marketing Lewis's dairy products. Lewis borrowed $194,850 from Mid-States Sales and secured the loan with certain of his cattle and their products. Lewis assigned his right to receive some of the proceeds from the sale of his milk each month to Mid-States, and notified MEDA of the assignment. After paying Mid-States for over a year under this agreement, MEDA received notice from Lewis that he was canceling his membership in MEDA. MEDA notified Mid-States and other assignees of Lewis that Lewis was canceling his membership, and asked them to sign a release of assignment. The other assignees signed the releases, but Mid-States did not. MEDA made the last payout on the milk it sold for Lewis directly to Lewis rather than to Mid-States. After Lewis filed for bankruptcy, Mid-States sued MEDA for the payment. Will it prevail?

Online Research: Assignment of Leases

Leases often contain clauses that specifically address the right to assign the lease. Using your favorite search engine and key words such as lease AND assignment, locate a lease that contains a provision addressing assignment. How would the concepts of this chapter apply if the lessor or the lessee of the lease you found assigns the lease?

18

PERFORMANCE AND REMEDIES

The Warrens hired Denison, a building contractor, to build a house on their property for $73,400. Denison's construction deviated somewhat from the specifications for the project. These deviations were presumably unintentional, and the cost of repairing them was $1,941.50. The finished house had a market value somewhat higher than the market value would have been without the deviations. The Warrens refused to pay the $48,400 balance due under the contract, alleging that Denison had used poor workmanship in building the house and they were under no obligation to perform further duties under the contract.

- *Do the Warrens have the right to withhold all further payment?*
- *What are the consequences of Denison's breach of contract?*
- *What are the appropriate remedies for Denison's breach of contract?*

CONTRACTS ARE GENERALLY FORMED before either of the parties renders any actual performance to the other. A person may be content to bargain for and receive the other person's promise at the formation stage of a contract because this permits him to plan for the future. Ultimately, however, all parties bargain for the *performance* of the promises that have been made to them.

In most contracts, each party carries out his promise and is *discharged* (released from all of his obligations under the contract) when his performance is complete. Sometimes, however, a party fails to perform or performs in an unsatisfactory manner. In such cases, courts are often called on to determine the respective rights and duties of the parties. This frequently involves deciding such questions as whether performance was due, whether the contract was breached, to what extent it was breached, and whether performance was excused. This task is made more difficult by the fact that contracts often fail to specify the consequences of nonperformance or defective performance. In deciding questions involving the performance of contracts and remedies for breach of contract, courts draw on a variety of legal principles that attempt to do justice, prevent forfeiture and unjust enrichment, and effectuate the parties' presumed intent.

This chapter presents an overview of the legal concepts that are used to resolve disputes arising in the performance stage of contracting. It describes how courts determine whether performance is due and what kind of performance is due, the consequences of contract breach, and the excuses for a party's failure to perform. It also includes a discussion of the remedies that are used when a court determines that a contract has been breached.

Conditions

Nature of Conditions

One issue that frequently arises in the performance stage of a contract is whether a party has the duty to perform. Some duties are *unconditional* or *absolute*—that is, the duty to perform does not depend on the occurrence of any further event other than the passage of time. For example, if Root promises to pay Downing $100, Root's duty is unconditional. When a party's duty is unconditional, he has the duty to perform unless his performance is excused. (The various excuses for nonperformance will be discussed later in this chapter.) When a duty is uncondi-

Figure 1 *Effect of Conditions*

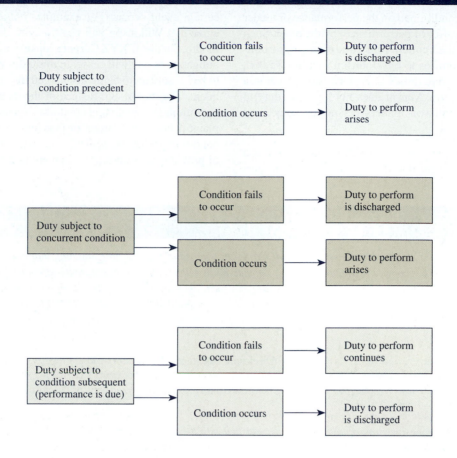

tional, the promisor's failure to perform constitutes a *breach of contract.*

In many situations, however, a promisor's duty to perform depends on the occurrence of some event that is called a **condition.** A condition is an uncertain, future event that affects a party's duty to perform. For example, if Melman contracts to buy Lance's house on condition that First Bank approve Melman's application for a mortgage loan by January 10, Melman's duty to buy Lance's house is *conditioned* on the bank's approving his loan application by January 10. When a promisor's duty is conditional, his duty to perform is affected by the occurrence of the condition. In this case, if the condition does not occur, Melman has no duty to buy the house. His failure to buy it because of the nonoccurrence of the condition will *not* constitute a breach of contract. Rather, he is discharged from further obligation under the contract.

Almost any event can be a condition. Some conditions are beyond the control of either party, such as when Morehead promises to buy Pratt's business if the prime rate drops by a specified amount. Others are within the

control of a party, such as when one party's performance of a duty under the contract is a condition of the other party's duty to perform.

Types of Conditions

There are two ways of classifying conditions. One way of classifying conditions focuses on the effect of the condition on the duty to perform. The other way focuses on the way in which the condition is created.

Classifications of Conditions Based on Their Effect on the Duty to Perform As Figure 1 illustrates, conditions vary in their effects on the duty to perform.

1. *Condition precedent.* A condition precedent is a future, uncertain event that creates the duty to perform. If the condition does not occur, performance does not become due. If the condition does occur, the duty to perform arises. In the following *Allen* case, you will see an example of a condition precedent.

2. *Concurrent condition.* When the contract calls for the parties to perform at the same time, each person's performance is conditioned on the performance or tender of performance (offer of performance) by the other. Such conditions are called **concurrent conditions.** For example, if Martin promises to buy Johnson's car for $5,000, the parties' respective duties to perform are subject to a concurrent condition. Martin does not have the duty to perform unless Johnson tenders his performance, and vice versa.

3. *Condition subsequent.* A **condition subsequent** is a future, uncertain event that **discharges** the duty to per-

form. When a duty is subject to a condition subsequent, the duty to perform arises but is discharged if the future, uncertain event occurs. For example, Wilkinson and Jones agree that Wilkinson will begin paying Jones $2,000 per month, but that if XYZ Corporation dissolves, Wilkinson's obligation to pay will cease. In this case, Wilkinson's duty to pay is subject to being discharged by a condition subsequent. The major significance of the distinction between conditions precedent and conditions subsequent is that the plaintiff bears the burden of proving the occurrence of a condition precedent, while the defendant bears the burden of proving the occurrence of a condition subsequent.

Allen v. Cedar Real Estate Group, LLP   236 F.3d 374 (7th Cir. 2001)

Cedar Real Estate Group owns a 6.2-acre parcel of real estate located in Lake County, Indiana, that had been used as a terminal for a trucking company. On June 4, 1998, Thomas Keith Allen offered to purchase the property from Cedar for $360,000. Allen made his offer on a preprinted purchase agreement that specified that the sale of the property was "as is." In addition to the preprinted purchase agreement, a typewritten page entitled "FURTHER CONDITIONS" was attached to Allen's offer. In pertinent part, this additional page provided that the offer was subject to the purchaser's approval of the following:

> 1) After purchaser's review of the Environmental Disclosure Document for Transfer of Real Property (see attached), at purchaser[']s option, a current . . .Environmental Audit with soil borings will be ordered. Cost not to exceed $5,000 and to be split on 50/50 basis between purchaser and seller. Seller shall provide completed copy of Disclosure Document. . . .

The bottom of the additional page also contained the following footnote referring to the above paragraph, "Regarding # 1— Mr. Allen will not request environmental audit if he is satisfied with the contents of the disclosure document. Mr. Allen will make the decision after it is reviewed." Although the purchase agreement specifically gave Allen the right to investigate the property to determine the existence of environmental contamination, it did not specify how such a discovery would affect the agreement to sell the property. The purchase agreement named July 15, 1998 as the closing date but also allowed a reasonable extension of time "for correcting defects in the Property noted in any inspection report."

In June of 1998, Cedar made a counteroffer that modified the first paragraph in a relatively minor way, and Allen signed and accepted the counteroffer. In accordance with the agreement, Cedar delivered the appropriate environmental disclosure documents to Allen. After reviewing these documents, Allen decided to exercise his option to order an environmental audit. He engaged the services of Enviro Solutions, Inc. (ESI) to perform an environmental assessment of the property. ESI concluded that there were adverse environmental issues on the property in the form of apparent diesel fuel contamination, but that the full extent of the contamination and the cost of cleaning it up was unknown. ESI recommended further investigatory actions. Allen submitted ESI's report to Cedar. In August 1998, Allen's real estate agent sent a memorandum to Cedar's real estate agent stating that Allen was "prepared to close the transaction within thirty (30) days after receipt of an acceptably clean environmental report for the entire property indicating it meets state standards." The memorandum said that Allen was willing to pay 50 percent of the costs of further environmental investigation up to $5,000 and 50 percent of the costs of remediation up to $10,000. It also stated, "At this time, we believe that all responsibility for future investigations, remediation, and preparation of a final environmental report is the owner's, or his agent (you)." The parties later got a tentative estimate of $30,335 for remediation costs.

During September, there were a number of communications between the parties to try to work out an arrangement for allocating the costs of remediation, each party thought the other should be responsible for remediation, and no agreement was reached. Cedar's agent finally informed Allen that Cedar had received three offers on the property and that he had instructed potential buyers to communicate their "final and best offer" to Cedar by October 2. On October 1, in response to this com-

munication, Allen's attorney advised Cedar that there was an existing contract between Cedar and Allen and "[t]he effort by Cedar Rapids Realty Group to breach this agreement by entering into agreements of sale with other parties will be resisted." Upon receipt of this letter, Cedar informed Allen's real estate agent that the agreement was terminated and directed him to return Allen's earnest money. Almost four weeks later, Allen's attorney wrote to Cedar's attorney that Allen was ready to close the transaction for the original purchase price. According to the letter, the property would be submitted to the Voluntary Remediation Program of the Indiana Department of Environmental Management, and the costs of such remediation would be forwarded to Cedar. Cedar never responded to this letter, and Allen filed suit in federal district court. The district court granted summary judgment for the defendant, finding that Allen's approval of the environmental audit was an unsatisfied condition precedent to the existence of a contract.

KANNE, Circuit Judge Allen argues that the contract to sell the Cedar property contained all essential terms and was complete and binding from the time that he signed and accepted Cedar's counteroffer. The district court, however, found that the agreement was not complete when signed because of the language that Allen inserted in the contract making Allen's "offer to purchase . . . subject to purchaser[']s approval of the following." The district court held that the insertion of this language in the purchase agreement created a condition precedent that needed to be fulfilled before the agreement became an enforceable contract. A condition precedent is either a condition which must be satisfied before an agreement becomes a binding contract or a condition which must be fulfilled before the duty to perform an already existing contract arises. Allen argues that the clause that made his offer "subject to Purchaser's approval" is not a condition precedent to contract formation but rather a condition precedent to performance of the contract. We disagree.

Contracts must be interpreted to give effect to the intentions of the parties as expressed in the four corners of the instrument. We attempt to determine the intent of the parties at the time the contract was made by examining the language that the parties used to express their rights and duties. In this case, the contract language—language inserted by Allen—shows his intent to condition his offer on an acceptable environmental report. First, the paragraph that gives Allen the right to order an environmental audit is entitled "Further Conditions." In addition, the paragraph begins by noting that, "this offer to purchase is subject to Purchaser's approval of the following." Allen's choice of the word "offer" is telling. This language makes it clear that Allen conditioned his offer on the right to order an environmental audit. The only reasonable interpretation of this language is that Allen intended to be able to opt out of the agreement if the property turned out to be contaminated.

Because the agreement contained a condition precedent to the formation of the contract, an enforceable contract only exists if the condition precedent was met. We hold that it was not. On August 7, after receiving the results of the en-

vironmental audit conducted by ESI, Allen's agent sent a memorandum to Cedar stating that Allen was willing to close on the property within 30 days of an "acceptably clean" environmental report. Although the memo stressed that Allen was still interested in the property, it also stated that "at this time we believe that all responsibility for future investigations, remediation, and preparation of a final environmental report is the owner's, or his agent (you)." By sending this memorandum, Allen made it clear that the condition precedent—an acceptable environmental report—had not been met. Allen was not willing to accept the property in an "as is" condition without changing other terms of the agreement. Allen again showed his refusal to accept the contract as written in his letter of September 21, 1998. The letter informed Cedar that Allen had obtained a legal opinion that concluded that Cedar was at least partially liable for the contamination on the property. Although Allen claims that this letter advised Cedar of its remedial obligations with respect to the property for "information purposes alone," the letter made it very clear that Allen was not willing to purchase the property "as is."

All of the subsequent communications between Allen and Cedar were simply offers and counteroffers that never resulted in a new contract. There are many reasons why a purchaser would be hesitant to buy a piece of property that was environmentally contaminated, even if another party was responsible for the remediation costs. Whether Allen had one of these reasons in mind when he inserted the condition precedent or whether he was misinformed about Indiana environmental law is immaterial. Allen specifically inserted the condition precedent requiring his approval of the environmental audit into the contract, and now he must accept the consequences of his decision.

Allen correctly points out that a condition precedent in a contract that exists solely for one party's benefit can be waived by that party. A party may waive a condition precedent expressly or by conduct. It is undisputed that Allen never expressly waived the condition, and nothing in his conduct suggested that he was willing to waive it. Allen makes much of the fact that he never threatened to walk away from the deal, but this by itself is not enough. Although Allen's conduct showed that he was still interested in the property, he never suggested that he was willing to waive the condition precedent by purchasing the property "as is." Allen's offer on October 28, 1998 to purchase the property "as is" and let Indiana environmental statutes determine who would bear remediation costs was too little, too late to constitute waiver. This offer not only came four weeks after Cedar notified Allen that the contract was terminated, but he still did not agree to purchase the property "as is."

Allen does not argue that he waived the condition precedent. Instead, he argues that because he had the option to waive the condition precedent, Cedar improperly terminated the agreement. Allen's theory is that when he received the environmental report, he had two choices: accept the property in its current environmental state or walk away from the deal. According to Allen, because he had not yet decided which of these two courses of action to pursue, the agreement was still in force. There are two problems with this argument. First, it is inaccurate. As discussed above, Allen already made clear that he was not willing to accept the contaminated property "as is." Second, even if we were to accept Allen's contention that he had not yet determined whether he was willing to waive the condition precedent, his argument still fails. If the agreement remained in force until Allen affirmatively rejected the agreement, Cedar would be required to wait indefinitely. We cannot accept this construction of the parties' agreement. By the time Allen offered to close on the property, the closing date had long since passed. Although the contract provided that a reasonable time would be allowed to correct defects in the property, no extension was made. Thus, although Allen did at one point have the right to waive the condition precedent to the formation of the contract, all indications suggest that Allen was not willing to waive it.

Affirmed in favor of Cedar.

Classifications of Conditions Based on the Way in Which They Were Created Another way of classifying conditions is to focus on the means by which the condition was created.

1. *Express condition.* An **express condition** is a condition that is specified in the language of the parties' contract. For example, if Grant promises to sell his regular season football tickets to Carson on condition that Indiana University wins the Rose Bowl, Indiana's winning the Rose Bowl is an express condition of Grant's duty to sell the tickets.

When the contract expressly provides that a party's duty is subject to a condition, courts take it very seriously. When a duty is subject to an express condition, that condition must be strictly complied with in order to give rise to the duty to perform.

2. *Implied-in-fact condition.* An **implied-in-fact condition** is one that is not specifically stated by the parties but is *implied* by the nature of the parties' promises. For example, if Summers promises to unload cargo from Knight's ship, the ship's arrival in port would be an implied-in-fact condition of Summer's duty to unload the cargo.

3. *Constructive condition.* **Constructive conditions** (also known as *implied-in-law conditions*) are conditions that are imposed by law rather than by the agreement of the parties. The law imposes constructive conditions to do justice between the parties. In contracts in which one of the parties is expected to perform before the other, the law normally infers that that performance is a constructive condition of the other party's duty to perform. For example, if Thomas promises to build a house for King, and the parties' understanding is that King will pay Thomas an agreed-on price when the house is built, King's duty to pay is subject to the constructive condition that Thomas complete the house. Without such a constructive condition, a person who did not receive the performance promised him would still have to render his own performance.

Creation of Express Conditions

Although no particular language is required to create an express condition, the conditional nature of promises is usually indicated by such words as *provided that, subject to, on condition that, if, when, while, after,* and *as soon as.* The process of determining the meaning of conditions is not a mechanical one. Courts look at the parties' overall intent as indicated in language of the entire contract.

The following discussion explores two common types of express conditions.

Example of Express Condition: Satisfaction of Third Parties It is common for building and construction contracts to provide that the property owner's duty to pay is conditioned on the builder's production of certificates to be issued by a specific architect or engineer. These certificates indicate the satisfaction of the architect or engineer with the builder's work. They are often issued at each stage of completion, after the architect or engineer has inspected the work done.

The standard usually used to determine whether the condition has occurred is a *good faith* standard. As a general rule, if the architect or engineer is acting honestly and has some good faith reason for withholding a certificate, the builder cannot recover payments due. In legal terms, the condition that will create the owner's duty to pay has not occurred.

If the builder can prove that the withholding of the certificate was fraudulent or done in bad faith (as a result of collusion with the owner, for example), the court may order that payment be made despite the absence of the certificate. In addition, production of the certificate may be excused by the death, insanity, or incapacitating illness of the named architect or engineer.

Example of Express Condition: Personal Satisfaction Contracts sometimes provide that a promisee's duty to perform is conditioned on his personal satisfaction with the promisee's performance. For example, Moore commissions Allen to paint a portrait of Moore's wife, but the contract provides that Moore's duty to pay is conditioned on his personal satisfaction with the portrait.

In determining which standard of satisfaction to apply, courts distinguish between cases in which the performance bargained for involves personal taste and comfort and cases that involve mechanical fitness or suitability for a particular purpose. If personal taste and comfort are involved, as they would be in the hypothetical case described above, a promisor who is honestly dissatisfied with the promisee's performance has the right to reject the performance without being liable to the promisee. If, however, the performance involves mechanical fitness or suitability, the court will apply a reasonable person test. If the court finds that a reasonable person would be satisfied with the performance, the condition of personal satisfaction has been met and the promisor must accept the performance and pay the contract price.

Excuse of Conditions

In most situations involving conditional duties, the promisor does not have the duty to perform unless and until the condition occurs. There are, however, a variety of situations in which the occurrence of a condition will be excused. In such a case, the person whose duty is con-

ditional will have to perform even though the condition has not occurred.

One ground for excusing a condition is that the occurrence of the condition has been *prevented* or *hindered* by the party who is benefited by the condition. For example, Connor hires Ingle to construct a garage on Connor's land, but when Ingle attempts to begin construction, Connor refuses to allow Ingle access to the land. In this case, Connor's duty to pay would normally be subject to a constructive condition that Ingle build the garage. However, since Connor prevented the occurrence of the condition, the condition will be excused, and Ingle can sue Connor for damages for breach of contract even though the condition has not occurred.

Other grounds for excuse of a condition include **waiver** and **estoppel.** When a person whose duty is conditional voluntarily gives up his right to the occurrence of the condition (waiver), the condition will be excused. Suppose that Buchman contracts to sell his car to Fox on condition that Fox pay him $2,000 by June 14. Fox fails to pay on June 14, but, when he tenders payment on June 20, Buchman accepts and cashes the check without reservation. Buchman has thereby *waived* the condition of payment by June 14.

When a person whose duty is conditional leads the other party to rely on his noninsistence on the condition, the condition will be excused because of estoppel. For example, McDonald agrees to sell his business to Brown on condition that Brown provide a credit report and personal financial statement by July 17. On July 5, McDonald tells Brown that he can have until the end of the month to provide the necessary documents. Relying on McDonald's assurances, Brown does not provide the credit report and financial statement until July 29. In this case, McDonald would be *estopped* (precluded) from claiming that the condition did not occur.

A condition may also be excused when performance of the act that constitutes the condition becomes *impossible*. For example, if a building contract provides that the owner's duty to pay is conditioned on the production of a certificate from a named architect, the condition would be excused if the named architect died or became incapacitated before issuing the certificate.

Performance of Contracts

When a promisor has performed his duties under a contract, he is discharged. Because his performance constitutes the occurrence of a constructive condition, the other party's duty to perform is also triggered, and the person who has performed has the right to receive the other party's performance. In determining whether a promisor is discharged by performance and whether the constructive condition of his performance has been fulfilled, courts must consider the standard of performance expected of him.

Level of Performance Expected of the Promisor

In some situations, no deviation from the promisor's promised performance is tolerated; in others, less-than-perfect performance will be sufficient to discharge the promisor and give him the right to recover under the contract.

Strict performance standard. A **strict performance** standard is a standard of performance that requires virtually perfect compliance with the contract terms. Remember that when a party's duty is subject to an express condition, that condition must be strictly and completely complied with in order to give rise to a duty of performance. Thus, when a promisor's performance is an express condition of the promisee's duty to perform, that performance must strictly and completely comply with the contract in order to give rise to the other promisee's duty to perform. For example, if McMillan agrees to pay Jester $500 for painting his house "on condition that" Jester finish the job no later than June 1, 1994, a standard of strict or complete performance would be applied to Jester's performance. If Jester does not finish the job by June 1, his breach will have several consequences. First, since the condition precedent to McMillan's duty to pay has not occurred, McMillan does not have a duty to pay the contract price. Second, since it

is now too late for the condition to occur, McMillan is discharged. Third, McMillan can sue Jester for breach of contract. The law's commitment to freedom of contract justifies such results in cases in which the parties have expressly bargained for strict compliance with the terms of the contract.

The strict performance standard is also applied to contractual obligations that can be performed either exactly or to a high degree of perfection. Examples of this type of obligation include promises to pay money, deliver deeds, and, generally, promises to deliver goods. A promisor who performs such promises completely and in strict compliance with the contract is entitled to receive the entire contract price. The promisor whose performance deviates from perfection is not entitled to receive the other party's performance if he does not render perfect performance within an appropriate time. He may, however, be able to recover the value of any benefits that he has conferred on the other party under a theory of quasi-contract.

Substantial performance standard. A **substantial performance** standard is a somewhat lower standard of performance that is applied to duties that are difficult to perform without some deviation from perfection *if* performance of those duties is *not* an express condition. A common example of this type of obligation is a promise to erect a building. Other examples include promises to construct roads, to cultivate crops, and to render some types of personal or professional services. Substantial performance is performance that falls short of complete performance in minor respects. It does not apply when a contracting party has been deprived of a material part of the consideration he bargained for. When a substantial performance standard is applied, the promisor who has

CONCEPT REVIEW

Substantial Performance

Definition	Application	Effects	Limitation
Performance that falls short of complete performance in some minor respect but that does not deprive the other party of a material part of the consideration for which he bargained	Applies to performance that (1) is *not* an express condition of the other party's duty to perform and (2) is difficult to do perfectly	Triggers other party's duty to perform; requires other party to pay the contract price minus any damages caused by defects in performance	Breach cannot have been willful

substantially performed is discharged. His substantial performance triggers the other party's duty to pay the contract price less any damages resulting from the defects in his performance. The obvious purpose behind the doctrine of substantial performance is to prevent forfeiture by a promisor who has given the injured party most of what he bargained for. Substantial performance is generally held to be inapplicable to a situation in which the breach of contract has been *willful*, however.

Good Faith Performance

One of the most significant trends in modern contract law is that courts and legislatures have created a duty to perform in good faith in an expanding range of contracts.[1] The Uniform Commercial Code specifically imposes a duty of good faith in every contract within the scope of any of the articles of the Code [1–203]. A growing number of courts have applied the duty to use good faith in transactions between lenders and their customers as well as insurance contracts, employment contracts, and contracts for the sale of real property.

This obligation to carry out a contract in good faith is usually called the **implied covenant of good faith and fair dealing.** It is a broad and flexible duty that is imposed by law rather than by the agreement of the parties. It is generally taken to mean that neither party to a contract will do anything to prevent the other from obtaining the benefits that he has the right to expect from the parties' agreement or their contractual relationship. The law's purpose in imposing such a term in contracts is to prevent abuses of power and encourage ethical behavior.

Breach of the implied covenant of good faith gives rise to a contract remedy. In some states, it can also constitute a tort, depending on the severity of the breach. A tort action for breach of the implied covenant of good faith is more likely to be recognized in situations in which a contract involves a special relationship of dependency and trust between the parties or where the public interest is adversely affected by a contracting party's practices. Numerous cases exist, for example, in which insurance companies' bad faith refusal to settle claims or perform duties to their insured and lenders' failure to exercise good faith in their dealings with their customers have led to large damage verdicts. Likewise, in states in which the implied duty of good faith has been held applicable to contracts of employment, employers who discharge employees in bad faith have been held liable for damages.[2]

---

[1]This trend is discussed in Chapter 9.
[2]This is discussed in Chapter 50.

Breach of Contract

When a person's performance is due, any failure to perform that is not excused is a breach of contract. Not all breaches of contract are of equal seriousness, however. Some are relatively minor deviations, whereas others are so extreme that they deprive the promisee of the essence of what he bargained for. The legal consequences of a given breach depend on the extent of the breach.

At a minimum, a party's breach of contract gives the nonbreaching party the right to sue and recover for any damages caused by that breach. When the breach is serious enough to be called a **material breach,** further legal consequences ensue.

Effect of Material Breach

A material breach occurs when the promisor's performance fails to reach the level of performance that the promisee is justified in expecting under the circumstances. In a situation in which the promisor's performance is judged by a substantial performance standard, saying that he failed to give substantial performance is the same thing as saying that he materially breached the contract.

The party who is injured by a material breach has the right to withhold his own performance. He is discharged from further obligations under the contract and may cancel it. He also has the right to sue for damages for total breach of contract.

Effect of Nonmaterial Breach By contrast, when the breach is not serious enough to be material, the nonbreaching party may sue for only those damages caused by the particular breach. In addition, he does not have the right to cancel the contract, although a nonmaterial breach can give him the right to suspend his performance until the breach is remedied. Once the breach is remedied, however, the nonbreaching party must go ahead and render his performance, minus any damages caused by the breach.

Determining the Materiality of the Breach

The standard for determining materiality is a flexible one that takes into account the facts of each individual case. The key question is whether the breach deprives the injured party of the benefits that he reasonably expected. For example, Norman, who is running for mayor, orders campaign literature from Prompt Press, to be delivered in

September. Prompt Press's failure to deliver the literature until after the election in November deprives Norman of the essence of what he bargained for and would be considered a material breach.

In determining materiality, courts take into account the extent to which the breaching party will suffer forfeiture if the breach is held to be material. They also consider the magnitude (amount) of the breach and the willfulness or good faith exercised by the breaching party. The timing of the breach can also be important. A breach that occurs early on in the parties' relationship is more likely to be viewed as material than is one that occurs after an extended period of performance. Courts also consider the extent to which the injured party can be adequately compensated by the payment of damages. The *Arnhold* case, which follows, contains an analysis of whether a breach is material.

Time for Performance A party's failure to perform on time is a breach of contract that may be serious enough to constitute a material breach, or it may be relatively trivial under the circumstances.

At the outset, it is necessary to determine when performance is due. Some contracts specifically state the time for performance, which makes it easy to determine the time for performance. In some contracts that do not specifically state the time for performance, such a time can be inferred from the circumstances surrounding the contract. In the Norman and Prompt Press campaign literature example, the circumstances surrounding the contract probably would have implied that the time for performance was some time before the election, even if the parties had not specified the time for performance. In still other contracts, no time for performance is either stated or implied. When no time for performance is stated or implied, performance must be completed within a "reasonable time," as judged by the circumstances of each case.

Consequences of Late Performance After a court determines when performance was due, it must determine the consequences of late performance. In some contracts, the parties expressly state that "time is of the essence" or that timely performance is "vital." This means that each party's timely performance by a specific date is an express condition of the other party's duty to perform. Thus, in a contract that contains a time is of the essence provision, any delay by either party normally constitutes a material breach. Sometimes, courts will imply such a term even when the language of the contract does not state that time is of the essence. A court would be likely to do this if late performance is of little or no value to the promisee. For example, Schrader contracts with the local newspaper to run an advertisement for Christmas trees from December 15, 2000, to December 24, 2000, but the newspaper does not run the ad until December 26, 2000. In this case, the time for performance is an essential part of the contract and the newspaper has committed a material breach.

When a contract does not contain language indicating that time is of the essence and a court determines that the time for performance is not a particularly important part of the contract, the promisee must accept late performance rendered within a reasonable time after performance was due. The promisee is then entitled to deduct or set off from the contract price any losses caused by the delay. Late performance is not a material breach in such cases unless it is unreasonably late.

Arnhold v. Ocean Atlantic Woodland Corp.   *284 F.3d 693 (7th Cir. 2002)*

Edith Arnhold and John Argoudelis are lifelong farmers who own 280 acres of land near Plainfield, Illinois, a far southwestern suburb of Chicago that is presently regarded as one of the fastest growing areas in the state. In exchange for $7.56 million payable over three years, Arnhold and Argoudelis agreed in August of 1997 to sell their farm to Ocean Atlantic, a sophisticated development corporation that planned to transform the land into a residential subdivision with more than 700 homes. The parties scheduled the initial closing on November 15, 1997 and agreed to cooperate and ensure that all the conditions precedent to initial closing—such as the rezoning and annexation of the land by the Plainfield Village Board—would be met in a timely manner. Despite their best efforts, however, the parties realized that they were in no position to meet the November 15, 1997 deadline, for they had neither executed the necessary documents nor obtained the Board's approval of the annexation. At this juncture, Arnhold and Argoudelis granted Ocean Atlantic's request to extend the initial closing to January 15, 1999.

Throughout the spring and summer of 1998, Ocean Atlantic met with local planning officials to discuss their proposed development involving the sellers' land. However, by the fall, Ocean Atlantic still had not presented the Board with a petition for annexation of the property. Arnhold and Argoudelis accused Ocean Atlantic of dragging its feet. Ocean Atlantic repeatedly proposed to renegotiate the purchase price of the land as well. The parties negotiated and even litigated their respective rights. They then agreed to a second extension of the contract, which pushed back the initial date of closing to November 30, 1999. The sellers thereafter notified Ocean Atlantic on numerous occasions that they would consider the contract terminated if the closing failed to occur by that date.

As the November 30 deadline loomed, Ocean Atlantic sought to delay the initial closing for a third time. After more negotiation and litigation, Arnhold and Argoudelis and Ocean Atlantic signed the settlement agreement containing the time-essence clause that is the basis of this lawsuit. The new date was scheduled for January 25, 2001. Throughout the negotiations preceding the settlement agreement, the sellers insisted upon a rigid, absolute closing date. Ocean Atlantic had the right to schedule the closing on any of the 91 days between October 26, 2000 and January 25, 2001. Nevertheless, it exercised that right by informing the sellers that it had chosen to close January 24—a mere one day prior to the "drop-dead" date. On January 18, Ocean Atlantic sent the sellers a letter demanding that they move the closing to May 1 and pay an additional $680,000 in development fees. These fees had never been the subject of any prior negotiations nor were they embodied in any prior agreement between the parties. The sellers rejected Ocean Atlantic's demand and warned that "if the closing does not occur in accordance with the terms of the settlement agreement, your clients will have no rights whatsoever to the property after January 25, 2001, as clearly spelled out in that same agreement." At this point, Ocean Atlantic withdrew its proposals and thereafter assured the sellers that it would "fully participate in the scheduled closing [January 24], pursuant to the settlement agreement." However, when the sellers arrived for the closing on the morning of January 24, they executed each and every document and were ready to close that day, but the closing failed to occur on either January 24 (the date selected by Ocean Atlantic) or January 25 (the absolute, final drop-dead date in the Settlement Agreement) because Ocean Atlantic failed to tender the purchase price of $7.267 million for deposit into the sellers' escrow account. Arnhold and Argoudelis's attorneys notified Ocean Atlantic that the contract was terminated. After receiving this notice, Ocean Atlantic pleaded with Arnhold and Argoudelis to go forward with the sale, but they refused. Ocean Atlantic sued Arnhold and Argoudelis, seeking specific performance of the contract. Arnhold and Argoudelis asked the district court to rule that the contract was null and void. The district court decided in favor of Arnhold and Argoudelis, and Ocean Atlantic appealed.

COFFEY, Circuit Judge   "What a diff'rence a day makes . . . twenty-four little hours."

The only issue before us is whether Ocean Atlantic materially breached the Settlement Agreement by failing to tender $7.267 million and close on the property by January 25, 2001.

A. The Two-Step Materiality Inquiry

Parties to a contract may make 'time is of the essence' a provision of the contract, meaning that performance by one party at the time or within the time frame specified in the contract is essential to enable him to require counterperformance by the other party. Timely performance often is an absolute requirement even if the contract does not contain the talismanic phrase "time is of the essence"; it is well-settled that the intention of the parties as expressed by the agreement controls, and courts will give effect to this provision when no peculiar circumstances have intervened to prevent or excuse strict compliance. A party that fails to perform its contractual duties is liable for breach of contract, and a material breach of the terms of the contract will serve to excuse the other party from its duty of counterperformance. In determining whether a breach is material, some

Illinois courts have stated that the question is whether performance of the disputed provision was of such a nature and such importance that the contract would not have been made without it. Other courts have stated that the question of whether a breach is material, thereby discharging the other party's duty to perform, is based on the inherent justice of the matter.

We are convinced that these cases demonstrate that the materiality inquiry focuses on two interrelated issues: (1) the intent of the parties with respect to the disputed provision; and (2) the equitable factors and circumstances surrounding the breach of the provision. When analyzing the materiality of a time-essence clause, the factfinder initially must ask whether performance by a particular date was truly of such significance that the contract would not have been made if the provision had not been included. A negative answer to this initial question means that the clause did not meet the materiality test and that the breach was minor, provided that the party has completed performance within a reasonable period of time. On the other hand, an affirmative answer to the first question does not end the materiality inquiry. Even where the parties clearly intended to regard a specific payment date as crucial, equity will refuse to enforce such a provision when to do so would be unconscionable or would give one party an unfair advantage over the other. As a result, even if the factfinder concludes that timely performance is an essential element of the contract, he or she must also decide whether to award damages and require counterperformance in spite of the breach.

The factfinder must take into account the totality of the circumstances and focus on the inherent justice of the matter. The focus should be on factors such as: whether the breach defeated the bargained-for objective of the parties, whether the nonbreaching party suffered disproportionate prejudice, and whether undue economic inefficiency and waste, or an unreasonable or unfair advantage, would inure to the nonbreaching party. We review the district court's analysis of these factors below.

1. Step one: Intent of the parties

Paragraph 15 of the settlement agreement states:

> It is intended by Sellers and Purchasers that January 25, 2001 shall be the absolute final date for closing. . . .If closing has not occurred on or before January 25, 2001, for any reason other than Sellers' default. . . .Purchaser shall have no right to purchase or otherwise encumber the Property or Homestead parcel, the Contract shall be terminated, and Purchaser shall have no rights with respect to the Property or Homestead Parcel.

The magistrate judge found that this clause was "an essential (if not 'the' essential) term of the Settlement Agreement," and we agree. In the case before us, the district court considered the language of the settlement agreement, along with the substance of the parties' negotiations and their course of performance. All three categories of evidence support a finding of materiality. The explicit and unequivocal language of the contract is an unambiguous expression of intent, referring to January 25, 2001 as an "absolute, final date for closing" that "shall" be enforced without exception. The record reflects that the initial contract contemplated closing in November 1997, and nearly three years had passed without reaching that objective. Thus, by the time the most recent settlement agreement was drafted, the sellers testified that their heart was no longer in selling their property to Ocean Atlantic, and Ocean Atlantic's president similarly testified that he was "sick and tired" of dealing with the sellers.

We are convinced that the settlement agreement reflects a compromise. The sellers agreed to continue their relationship through January 25, 2001 and give Ocean Atlantic one last, final chance to comply with the language of the contract and purchase the farmland. In exchange, Ocean Atlantic agreed that absolutely no further delays would be tolerated. We agree that the clause was a material term of the contract.

2. Step two: Totality of the circumstances

Even when the parties agree to make timely performance an essential element of the contract, the factfinder must also consider whether the breach was material as to justify the other party's subsequent refusal to perform, based upon the totality of the circumstances.

b. The relevant factors

i. Bargained-for objective

Where a contract does not set a closing date and time is not made of the essence, the law will imply that the contract is to be performed within a reasonable time. Thus, a material time-essence provision indicates that substantial but incomplete performance is not the central objective of the contract. Rather, the deal must be done on time if it may be done at all. By enforcing such provisions, courts avoid substituting their judgment for those of sophisticated parties and concomitantly extinguishing the parties' legitimate expectations in freedom of contract as well as freedom from contract.

When Ocean Atlantic failed to pay the sellers any money and failed to take title to the property by January 25, 2001, it deprived the sellers of the finality for which they had bargained. This breach went to the very heart and substance of the contract. It was material; indeed, it is difficult to imagine anything more material, given nearly three years of delays, three contract extensions, and two federal lawsuits involving the sale of this very property. The sellers displayed the patience of Job by waiting nearly 3½ years to accomplish the sale of farmland that was originally intended to be transferred within six months.

ii. Proportionality of prejudice

The proportionality-of-prejudice element of the materiality test requires the factfinder to compare the relative burdens that each side would suffer if the contract were terminated. In the case before us, the district court found that Ocean Atlantic spent $1.7 million in fees and expenses related to the annexation, rezoning, planning, preliminary engineering, and marketing of the property between 1997 and 2001. In arguing that the district court's findings are clearly erroneous, Ocean Atlantic assumes that the disparity of prejudice is calculated in terms of the absolute economic loss suffered by each party as a result of the breach, and that a $1.7 million difference is simply too much. We cannot agree. If we fully accepted Ocean Atlantic's view, then idiosyncratic parties would have the scale tipped against them and would be gravely handicapped in their efforts to obtain the full, objective, bargained-for benefits of their contract. Ocean Atlantic's million-dollar loss was, admittedly, substantial. However, a reasonable factfinder, believing that promises conditioned upon timely performance should be kept when made, could have determined that the loss was not enough to warrant granting Ocean Atlantic's motion for specific performance.

iii. Unreasonable, unfair advantage

Two important factors to consider at this juncture are: (1) whether the breaching party used reasonable efforts to perform its contractual obligations; and (2) whether the parties contemplated that the breaching party would forfeit its contractual rights if it committed the type of breach that is at issue. Neither of these factors favors Ocean Atlantic. Ocean Atlantic argues that it missed the deadline because it needed an extra day to obtain and prepare certain corporate loan guarantees requested by Yorkville National Bank on the morning of January 25, 2001. Ocean Atlantic tries to excuse its failure to complete the documents prior to the close of business that day by claiming that it could not foresee that the bank would request such materials and characterizing the bank's actions as commercially unreasonable in the context of a complex, multimillion dollar real estate transaction. The district court expressed its doubts about this testimony, however, reasoning that Ocean Atlantic is a sophisticated corporation that dealt with the bank on prior occasions, had been negotiating the loan for several weeks, should have prepared for any possible emergency, and should have been able to broker some type of deal to satisfy the bank's demands without delaying the sale. Ocean Atlantic is represented by a half dozen learned and qualified attorneys. Ocean Atlantic could have avoided forfeiture or obtained restitution for its development costs either by purchasing insurance or having the foresight to draft more favorable terms in the contract. The judge further inferred from Ocean Atlantic's historical relationship with the sellers and the language of the contract itself—a contract which was negotiated by experienced commercial attorneys—that Ocean Atlantic assumed the risk of forfeiting

title to the property if it failed to complete the necessary documents prior to the deadline. Moreover, although Ocean Atlantic blames its investment partner and its lender of choice for its failure to comply with the drop-dead clause, it appears to us that the problem more likely was caused by Ocean Atlantic waiting until the eleventh hour to execute and revise all the requisite documents. When parties wait until the last minute to comply with a deadline, they are playing with fire. Ocean Atlantic asserts that its entire legal staff needed the full six days to revamp the documents but ignores the fact that it played the waiting game for more than three years and then agreed to the very deadline it is now attacking. Furthermore, Ocean Atlantic wasted at least some time and energy contacting the sellers in a last-ditch attempt to renegotiate terms of the settlement agreement itself. If Ocean Atlantic had truly focused all of its legal resources on completing the deal, instead of trying to rewrite it, then perhaps we would not be here today. We therefore reject Ocean Atlantic's anemic attempt to find a scapegoat for its own lack of diligence. We are convinced that Ocean Atlantic failed to use reasonable efforts to complete the deal by the material date required in the contract. We agree with the district court that it would have been improper to deprive the sellers of the benefit of the drop-dead provision merely because of Ocean Atlantic's difficulties with its lender of choice. Thus, we refuse to hold that it is unfair for Ocean Atlantic to forfeit all rights to the property, while the sellers retain the same property and all improvements thereto.

Conclusion

"Never put off until tomorrow what you can do today."

Although contract law allows parties to choose the reasonable extent of their duties and obligations towards one another, neither law nor equity guarantees that a party may specifically enforce a contract if it fails to perform its material obligations thereunder. A reasonable factfinder concluded that Ocean Atlantic treated the material, bargained-for deadlines in this agreement as if they were trivial details that could be flouted with impunity. As a result, Ocean Atlantic has lost any and all rights to purchase the sellers' farmland.

Affirmed in favor of Arnhold and Argoudelis.

Time for Performance

Contract Language	Time for Performance	Consequences of Late Performance
"Time is of the essence" or similar language	The time stated in the contract	Material breach
Specific time is stated in or implied by the contract and later performance would have little or no value	The time stated in or implied by the contract	Material breach
Specific time is stated in or implied by the contract, but the time for performance is a relatively unimportant part of the contract	The time stated in or implied by the contract	Not a material breach unless performance is unreasonably late
No time for performance is stated in or implied by the contract	Within a reasonable time	Not material breach unless performance is unreasonably late

Anticipatory Repudiation

One type of breach of contract occurs when the promisor indicates before the time for his performance that he is unwilling or unable to carry out the contract. This is called **anticipatory repudiation** or **anticipatory breach.** Anticipatory breach generally constitutes a material breach of contract that discharges the promisee from all further obligation under the contract.

In determining what constitutes anticipatory repudiation, courts look for some unequivocal statement or voluntary act that clearly indicates that the promisor cannot or will not perform his duties under the contract. This may take the form of an express statement by the promisor. The promisor's intent not to perform could also be implied from actions of the promisor such as selling to a third party the property that the promisor was obligated to sell to the promisee. For example, if Ross, who is obligated to convey real estate to Davis, conveys the property to some third person instead, Ross has repudiated the contract.

When anticipatory repudiation occurs, the promisee is faced with several choices. For example, Marsh and Davis enter a contract in which Davis agrees to deliver a quantity of bricks to Marsh on September 1, 2000, and Marsh agrees to pay Davis a sum of money in two installments. The agreement specifies that Marsh will pay 50 percent of the purchase price on July 15, 2000, and 50 percent of the purchase price within 30 days after delivery. On July 1, 2000, Davis writes Marsh and unequivocally states that he will not deliver the bricks. Must Marsh go ahead and send the payment that is due on July 15? Must he wait until September 1 to bring suit for total breach of contract? The answer to both questions is no.

When anticipatory repudiation occurs, the nonbreaching party is justified in withholding his own performance and suing for damages right away, without waiting for the time for performance to arrive.[3] If he can show that he was ready, willing, and able to perform his part of the contract, he can recover damages for total breach of the contract. The nonbreaching party is not obligated to do this, however. If he chooses, he may wait until the time for performance in case the other party changes his mind and decides to perform.

Recovery by a Party Who Has Committed Material Breach

A party who has materially breached the contract (that is, has not substantially performed) does not have the right to recover the contract price. If a promisor who has

---

[3]Uniform Commercial Code rules regarding anticipatory repudiation in contracts for the sale of goods are discussed in Chapter 21.

ETHICS IN ACTION

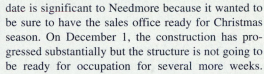

Marsh, a contractor, enters into a contract with Needmore Tree Farm to build a structure on Needmore's property that Needmore plans to use as a sales office for selling Christmas trees to the public. The contract provides that Needmore will pay Marsh $110,000 for the structure, with 50 percent of the payment in advance and 50 percent upon completion. It also provides that Marsh will complete the construction and have the structure ready for occupation by December 1. With regard to this last provision, the contract states, "time is of the essence." The December 1 date is significant to Needmore because it wanted to be sure to have the sales office ready for Christmas season. On December 1, the construction has progressed substantially but the structure is not going to be ready for occupation for several more weeks. Needmore fires Marsh and refuses to pay him the remaining 50 percent due under the contract. Assuming that Marsh has materially breached the contract, does Needmore have an ethical duty to pay Marsh for the benefit that Marsh has conferred on it?

given some performance to the promisee cannot recover under the contract, however, the promisor will face forfeiture and the promisee will have obtained an unearned gain. There are two possible avenues for a party who has committed material breach to obtain some compensation for the performance he has conferred on the nonbreaching party.

1. *Quasi-contract.* A party who has materially breached a contract might recover the reasonable value of any benefits he has conferred on the promisee by bringing an action under quasi-contract.[4] This would enable him to obtain compensation for the value of any performance he has given that has benefited the nonbreaching party. Some courts take the position that a person in material breach should not be able to recover for benefits he has conferred, however.

2. *Partial performance of a divisible contract.* Some contracts are divisible; that is, each party's performance can be divided in two or more parts and each part is exchanged for some corresponding consideration from the other party. For example, if Johnson agrees to mow Peterson's lawn for $20 and clean Peterson's gutters for $50, the contract is divisible. When a promisor performs one part of the contract but materially breaches another part, he can recover at the contract price for the part that he did perform. For example, if Johnson breached his duty to clean the gutters but fully performed his obligation to mow the lawn, he could recover at the contract price for the lawn-mowing part of the contract.

Excuses for Nonperformance

Although nonperformance of a duty that has become due will ordinarily constitute a breach of contract, there are some situations in which nonperformance is excused because of factors that arise after the formation of the contract. When this occurs, the person whose performance is made impossible or impracticable by these factors is discharged from further obligation under the contract. The following discussion concerns the most common grounds for excuse of nonperformance.

Impossibility

When performance of a contractual duty becomes impossible after the formation of the contract, the duty will be discharged on grounds of **impossibility.** This does not mean that a person can be discharged merely because he has contracted to do something that he is simply unable to do or that causes him hardship or difficulty. Impossibility in the legal sense of the word means "it cannot be done by anyone" rather than "I cannot do it." Thus, promisors who find that they have agreed to perform duties that are beyond their capabilities or that turn out to be unprofitable or burdensome are generally not excused from performance of their duties. Impossibility will provide an excuse for nonperformance, however, when some unexpected event arises after the formation of the contract and renders performance objectively impossible. The event that causes the impossibility need not have been entirely unforeseeable. Normally, however, the event will be one that the parties would not have reasonably thought of as a real possibility that would affect performance.

---

[4]Quasi-contract is discussed in Chapter 9. It involves the use of the remedy of restitution, which is discussed later in this chapter.

There are a variety of situations in which a person's duty to perform may be discharged on grounds of impossibility. The three most common situations involve illness or death of the promisor, supervening illegality, and destruction of the subject matter of the contract.

Illness or Death of Promisor Incapacitating illness or death of the promisor excuses nonperformance when the promisor has contracted to perform personal services. For example, if Pauling, a college professor who has a contract with State University to teach for an academic year, dies before the completion of the contract, her estate will not be liable for breach of contract. The promisor's death or illness does not, however, excuse the nonperformance of duties that can be delegated to another, such as the duty to deliver goods, pay money, or convey real estate. For example, if Odell had contracted to convey real estate to Ruskin and died before the closing date, Ruskin could enforce the contract against Odell's estate.

Supervening Illegality If a statute or governmental regulation enacted after the creation of a contract makes performance of a party's duties illegal, the promisor is excused from performing. Statutes or regulations that merely make performance more difficult or less profitable do not, however, excuse nonperformance.

Destruction of the Subject Matter of the Contract
If something that is essential to the promisor's performance is destroyed after the formation of the contract through no fault of the promisor, the promisor is excused from performing. For example, Woolridge contracts to sell his car to Rivkin. If an explosion destroys the car after the contract has been formed but before Woolridge has made delivery, Woolridge's nonperformance will be excused. The destruction of nonessential items that the promisor intended to use in performing does not excuse nonperformance if substitutes are available, even though securing them makes performance more difficult or less profitable. Suppose that Ace Construction Company had planned to use a particular piece of machinery in fulfilling a contract to build a building for Worldwide Widgets Company. If the piece of machinery is destroyed but substitutes are available, destruction of the machinery before the contract is performed would *not* give Ace an excuse for failing to perform.

Commercial Impracticability

Section 2–615 of the Uniform Commercial Code has extended the scope of the common law doctrine of impossibility to cases in which unforeseen developments make performance by the promisor highly impracticable, unreasonably expensive, or of little value to the promisee. Rather than using a standard of impossibility, then, the Code uses the more relaxed standard of **impracticability.** Despite the less stringent standard applied, cases actually excusing nonperformance on grounds of impracticability are relatively rare. To be successful in claiming excuse based on impracticability, a promisor must be able to establish that the event that makes performance impracticable occurred without his fault and that the contract was made with the basic assumption that this event would not occur. This basically means that the event was beyond the scope of the risks that the parties contemplated at the time of contracting and that the promisor did not expressly or impliedly assume the risk that the event would occur.

Case law and official comments to UCC section 2–615 indicate that neither increased cost nor collapse of a market for particular goods is sufficient to excuse nonperformance, because those are the types of business risks that every promisor assumes. However, drastic price increases or severe shortages of goods resulting from unforeseen circumstances such as wars and crop failures can give rise to impracticability.

If the event causing impracticability affects only a part of the seller's capacity to perform, the seller must allocate production and deliveries among customers in a "fair and reasonable" manner and must notify them of any delay or any limited allocation of the goods. You can read more about commercial impracticability in Chapter 21, Performance of Sales Contracts.

Other Grounds
for Discharge

Earlier in this chapter, you learned about several situations in which a party's duty to perform could be discharged even though that party had not himself performed. These include the nonoccurrence of a condition precedent or concurrent condition, the occurrence of a condition subsequent, material breach by the other party, and excuse from performance by impossibility, impracticability, or frustration. The following discussion deals with additional ways in which a discharge can occur.

Discharge by Mutual Agreement

Just as contracts are created by mutual agreement, they can also be discharged by *mutual agreement*. An agreement to discharge a contract must be supported by consideration to be enforceable.

Discharge by Accord and Satisfaction

An **accord** is an agreement whereby a promisee who has an existing claim agrees with the promisor that he will accept some performance different from that which was originally agreed on. When the promisor performs the accord, that is called a **satisfaction.**[5] When an accord and satisfaction occurs, the parties are discharged. For example, Root contracts with May to build a garage on May's property for $30,000. After Root has performed his part of the bargain, the parties then agree that instead of paying money, May will transfer a one-year-old Porsche to Root instead. When this is done, both parties are discharged.

Discharge by Waiver

A party to a contract may voluntarily relinquish any right he has under a contract, including the right to receive return performance. Such a relinquishment of rights is known as a **waiver.** If one party tenders an incomplete or defective performance and the other party accepts that performance without objection, knowing that the defects will not be remedied, the party to whom performance was due will have discharged the other party from his duty of performance. For example, a real estate lease requires Long, the tenant, to pay a $5 late charge for late payments of rent. Long pays his rent late each month for five months, but the landlord accepts it without objection and without assessing the late charge. In this situation, the landlord has probably waived his right to collect the late charge.

To avoid waiving rights, a person who has received defective performance should give the other party prompt notice that she expects complete performance and will seek damages if the defects are not corrected.

Discharge by Alteration

If the contract is represented by a *written* instrument, and one of the parties intentionally makes a material alteration in the instrument without the other's consent, the alteration acts as a discharge of the other party. If the other party consents to the alteration or does not object to it when he learns of it, he is not discharged. Alteration by a third party without the knowledge or consent of the contracting parties does not affect the parties' rights.

Discharge by Statute of Limitations

Courts have long refused to grant a remedy to a person who delays bringing a lawsuit for an unreasonable time.

All of the states have enacted statutes known as **statutes of limitation,** which specify the period of time in which a person can bring a lawsuit.

The time period for bringing a contract action varies from state to state, and many states prescribe time periods for cases concerning oral contracts that are different from those for cases concerning written contracts. Section 2–725 of the Uniform Commercial Code provides for a four-year statute of limitations for contracts involving the sale of goods.

The statutory period ordinarily begins to run from the date of the breach. It may be delayed if the party who has the right to sue is under some incapacity at that time (such as minority or insanity) or is beyond the jurisdiction of the state. A person who has breached a contractual duty is discharged from liability for breach if no lawsuit is brought before the statutory period elapses.

Discharge by Decree of Bankruptcy

The contractual obligations of a debtor are generally discharged by a decree of bankruptcy. Bankruptcy is discussed in Chapter 29.

Remedies for Breach of Contract

Our discussion of the performance stage of contracts so far has focused on the circumstances under which a party has the duty to perform or is excused from performing. In situations in which a person is injured by a breach of contract and is unable to obtain compensation by a settlement out of court, a further important issue remains: What remedy will a court fashion to compensate for breach of contract?

Contract law seeks to encourage people to rely on the promises made to them by others. Contract remedies focus on the economic loss caused by breach of contract, not on the moral obligation to perform a promise. The objective of granting a remedy in a case of breach of contract is simply to compensate the injured party.

Types of Contract Remedies

There are a variety of ways in which this can be done. The basic categories of contract remedies include:

1. Legal remedies (money damages).
2. Equitable remedies.
3. Restitution.

---

[5]Accord and satisfaction is also discussed in Chapter 12.

The usual remedy is an award of money damages that will compensate the injured party for his losses. This is called a **legal remedy** or **remedy at law,** because the imposition of money damages in our legal system originated in courts of law. Less frequently used but still important are **equitable remedies** such as specific performance. Equitable remedies are those remedies that had their origins in courts of equity rather than in courts of law.[6] Today, they are available at the discretion of the judge. A final possible remedy is **restitution,** which requires the defendant to pay the value of the benefits that the plaintiff has conferred on him.

LOG ON

For practical and readable summaries of the consequences of breach of contract, see What Are My Remedies in the Event There is a Breach?, **http://law.freeadvice.com/general_practice/ legal_remedies/remedies_breach.htm** and 'Lectric Law Library's *Nonperformance and Breach of Contract,* **http://www.lectlaw.com/files/bul08.htm.**

Interests Protected by Contract Remedies

Remedies for breach of contract protect one or more of the following interests that a promisee may have:[7]

1. *Expectation interest.* A promisee's **expectation interest** is his interest in obtaining the objective or opportunity for gain that he bargained for and "expected." Courts attempt to protect this interest by formulating a remedy that will place the promisee in the position he would have been in if the contract had been performed as promised.

2. *Reliance interest.* A promisee's **reliance interest** is his interest in being compensated for losses that he has suffered by changing his position in reliance on the other party's promise. In some cases, such as when a promisee is unable to prove his expectation interest with reasonable certainty, the promisee may seek a remedy to compensate for the loss suffered as a result of relying on the promisor's promise rather than for the expectation of profit.

3. *Restitution interest.* A **restitution interest** is a party's interest in recovering the amount by which he has enriched or benefited the other. Both the reliance and restitution in-

terests involve promisees who have changed their position. The difference between the two is that the reliance interest involves a loss to the promisee that does not benefit the promisor, whereas the restitution interest involves a loss to the promisee that does constitute an unjust enrichment to the promisor. A remedy based on restitution enables a party who has performed or partially performed her contract and has benefited the other party to obtain compensation for the value of the benefits that she has conferred.

Legal Remedies (Damages)

Limitations on Recovery of Damages in Contract Cases An injured party's ability to recover damages in a contract action is limited by three principles:

1. *A party can recover damages only for those losses that he can prove with reasonable certainty.* Losses that are purely speculative are not recoverable. Thus, if Jones Publishing Company breaches a contract to publish Powell's memoirs, Powell may not be able to recover damages for lost royalties (her expectation interest), since she may be unable to establish, beyond speculation, how much money she would have earned in royalties if the book had been published. (Note, however, that Powell's reliance interest might be protected here; she could be allowed to recover provable losses incurred in reliance on the contract.)

2. *A breaching party is responsible for paying only those losses that were foreseeable to him at the time of contracting.* A loss is foreseeable if it would ordinarily be expected to result from a breach or if the breaching party had reason to know of particular circumstances that would make the loss likely. For example, if Prince Manufacturing Company renders late performance in a contract to deliver parts to Cheatum Motors without knowing that Cheatum is shut down waiting for the parts, Prince will not have to pay the business losses that result from Cheatum's having to close its operation.

3. *Plaintiffs injured by a breach of contract have the duty to mitigate (avoid or minimize) damages.* A party cannot recover for losses that he could have avoided without undue risk, burden, or humiliation. For example, an employee who has been wrongfully fired would be entitled to damages equal to his wages for the remainder of the employment period. The employee, however, has the duty to minimize the damages by making reasonable efforts to seek a similar job elsewhere.

Compensatory Damages Subject to the limitations discussed above, a person who has been injured by a breach of contract is entitled to recover **compensatory**

---

[6]The nature of equitable remedies is also discussed in Chapter 1.
[7]*Restatement (Second) of Contracts* § 344.

damages. In calculating the compensatory remedy, a court will attempt to protect the expectation interest of the injured party by giving him the "benefit of his bargain" (placing him in the position he would have been in *had the contract been performed as promised*). To do this, the court must compensate the injured person for the provable losses he has suffered as well as for the provable gains that he has been prevented from realizing by the breach of contract. Normally, compensatory damages include one or more of three possible items: loss in value, any allowable consequential damages, and any allowable incidental damages.

1. *Loss in value.* The starting point in calculating compensatory damages is to determine the **loss in value** of the performance that the plaintiff had the right to expect. This is a way of measuring the expectation interest. The calculation of the loss in value experienced by an injured party differs according to the sort of contract involved and the circumstances of the breach. In contracts involving nonperformance of the sale of real estate, for example, courts normally measure loss in value by the difference between the contract price and the market price of the property. Thus, if Willis repudiates a contract with Renfrew whereby Renfrew was to purchase land worth $20,000 from Willis for $10,000, Renfrew's loss in value was $10,000. Where a seller has failed to perform a contract for the sale of goods, courts may measure loss in value by the difference between the contract price and the price that the buyer had to pay to procure substitute goods.[8] In cases in which a party breaches by rendering defective performance—say, by breaching a warranty in the sale of goods—the loss in value would be measured by the difference between the value of the goods if they had been in the condition warranted by the seller and the value of the goods in their defective condition.[9]

2. *Consequential damages.* **Consequential damages** (also called **special damages**) compensate for losses that occur as a consequence of the breach of contract. Consequential losses occur because of some special or unusual circumstances of the particular contractual relationship of the parties. For example, Apex Trucking Company buys a computer system from ABC Computers. The system fails to operate properly, and Apex is forced to pay its employees to perform the tasks manually, spending $10,000 in overtime pay. In this situation, Apex might seek to recover the $10,000 in overtime pay in addition to the loss of value that it has experienced.

Lost profits flowing from a breach of contract can be recovered as consequential damages if they are foreseeable and can be proven with reasonable certainty. It is important to remember, however, that the recovery of consequential damages is subject to the limitations on damage recovery discussed earlier.

3. *Incidental damages.* **Incidental damages** compensate for reasonable costs that the injured party incurs after the breach in an effort to avoid further loss. For example, if Smith Construction Company breaches an employment contract with Brice, Brice could recover as incidental damages those reasonable expenses he must incur in attempting to procure substitute employment, such as long-distance telephone tolls or the cost of printing new résumés.

Alternative Measures of Damages The foregoing discussion has focused on the most common formulation of damage remedies in contracts cases. The normal measure of compensatory damages is not appropriate in every case, however. When it is not appropriate, a court may use an alternative measure of damages. For example, where a party has suffered losses by performing or preparing to perform, he might seek damages based on his *reliance interest* instead of his expectation interest. In such a case, he would be compensated for the provable losses he suffered by relying on the other party's promise. This measure of damages is often used in cases in which a promise is enforceable under promissory estoppel.[10]

Nominal Damages **Nominal damages** are very small damage awards that are given when a technical breach of contract has occurred without causing any actual or provable economic loss. The sums awarded as nominal damages typically vary from 2 cents to a dollar.

Liquidated Damages The parties to a contract may expressly provide in their contract that a specific sum shall be recoverable if the contract is breached. Such provisions are called **liquidated damages** provisions. For example, Murchison rents space in a shopping mall in which she plans to operate a retail clothing store. She

---

[8]Remedies under Article 2 of the Uniform Commercial Code are discussed in detail in Chapter 22.

[9]See Chapter 20 for further discussion of the damages for breach of warranty in the sale of goods.

[10]Promissory estoppel is discussed in Chapters 9 and 12.

must make improvements in the space before opening the store, and it is very important to her to have the store opened for the Christmas shopping season. She hires Ace Construction Company to construct the improvements. The parties agree to include in the contract a liquidated damages provision stating that, if Ace is late in completing the construction, Murchison will be able to recover a specified sum for each day of delay. Such a provision is highly desirable from Murchison's point of view because, without a liquidated damages provision, she would have a difficult time in establishing the precise losses that would result from delay. Courts scrutinize these agreed-on damages carefully, however.

If the amount specified in a liquidated damages provision is reasonable and if the nature of the contract is such that actual damages would be difficult to determine, a court will enforce the provision. When liquidated damages provisions are enforced, the amount of damages agreed on will be the injured party's exclusive damage remedy. If the amount specified is unreasonably great in relation to the probable loss or injury, however, or if the amount of damages could be readily determined in the event of breach, the courts will declare the provision to be a penalty and will refuse to enforce it. The issue of reasonableness of liquidated damages is presented in the *Wojtowicz* case, which follows.

Wojtowicz v. Greeley Anesthesia Services, P.C.   *961 P.2d 520 (Ct. App. Colo. 1997)*

In 1992, Greeley Anesthesia Services (GAS), a professional corporation made up of anesthesiologists who practice at a hospital in Greeley, Colorado, hired Dr. Mark D. Wojtowicz, an anesthesiologist. GAS collects fees and distributes income for its shareholders and employees. The record indicates that GAS bills patients, collects fees, and distributes income as follows: each shareholder is paid $500 for each day worked; GAS operating expenses are paid; all remaining income is distributed to each shareholder as a bonus which is proportionate to services performed. The bonus each shareholder receives generally exceeds the sum collected as base pay. In July 1993, after Dr. Wojtowicz became a shareholder in the corporation, he and GAS entered into an employment contract. The contract contained a clause stating that if Dr. Wojtowicz terminated his employment and continued practicing anesthesiology within a 25-mile radius of Greeley, he would be required to pay GAS 50 percent of fees that he generated from practicing in competition with GAS for two years following termination. It also provided that, to compensate GAS for the harm to its goodwill, Dr. Wojtowicz would pay GAS $10,000 and would immediately forfeit any amount that might otherwise be due to him as deferred compensation

On January 12, 1995, Dr. Wojtowicz gave GAS notice of his employment termination. When GAS sought to enforce the contract, Dr. Wojtowicz sought a declaratory judgment that the noncompetition and liquidated damages provisions were invalid and unenforceable. The trial court declared valid and enforceable the liquidated damages clause requiring Dr. Wojtowicz to pay 50 percent of fees generated from practicing in competition with GAS (the noncompetition provision), but declared invalid and unenforceable the $10,000 and forfeiture clause for harm to GAS's goodwill. Both parties appealed.

Plank, Judge   The terms of the provision specifying the amount of damages are not enforceable. Section 8–2–113(3) states:

> Any covenant not to compete provision of an employment . . . between physicians which restricts the right of a physician to practice medicine . . . upon termination of such agreement, shall be void; except that all other provisions of such an agreement enforceable at law, including provisions which require the payment of damages in an amount that is reasonably related to the injury suffered by reason of termination of the agreement, shall be enforceable. Provisions which require the payment of damages upon termination of the agreement may include, but not be limited to, damages related to competition.

Here, although both parties agreed to the noncompetition provision of the contract, the statute permits enforcement of that provision only as to damages "reasonably related to the injury suffered by reason of termination of the agreement." Here, the parties agreed that, if plaintiff competes with GAS following termination of his employment, GAS will suffer harm in several ways, including lost profits.

The agreement expressly provides that Dr. Wojtowicz:

> . . .shall be free to engage in the practice of medicine in competition with the Company, except upon so competing with the Company, the Employee shall be obligated to pay the Company damages related to that competition in an amount reasonably related to the injuries suffered by the Company by reason of such competition.

The trial court found that the intended purpose of the noncompetition provision was "to discourage termination of employment without departure from the area." However, it held that such purpose was not contrary to public policy because the statute "specifically authorizes damages relating to competition," and such provisions "must necessarily discourage the setting up of rival practices." The record contains conflicting evidence, including expert testimony, as to the amount of damages GAS might suffer if plaintiff breached the agreement. Based upon the possibility that GAS and its shareholders might lose future profits if one of several hypothetical situations occurred, the trial court concluded that the noncompetition provision of the agreement provides for damages in an amount that is reasonably related to the injury. However, a damage award cannot be based on speculation or conjecture. A claim for future profits may not be sustained by evidence which is speculative, remote, imaginary, or impossible of ascertainment. Damages for lost profits are measured by the loss of net profits, meaning net earnings or the excess of returns over expenditures, but not lost gross profits or gross sales revenues. The trial court's conclusion as to the noncompetition provision is based on several theories of future lost profits which do not measure net earnings. The record indicates that net profits to GAS and its shareholders remained essentially the same as they were prior to the termination of Dr. Wojtowicz's employment contract.

Contrary to the trial court, we conclude that the noncompetition provision of the contract, which required plaintiff to pay 50 percent of his fees to GAS for two years, provides for damages that are not "reasonably related to the injury suffered" by GAS by reason of the termination of its contract with plaintiff. Hence, the language of the provision specifying the amount of damages was not enforceable under the statute.

We also conclude, as a matter of law, that the fee percentage set as liquidated damages in the noncompetition provision is disproportionate to any possible loss incurred by GAS. Thus, the noncompetition provision is also an unenforceable penalty at common law. The trial court found that there was no convincing evidence of any real harm to defendant's goodwill or its position as a service provider. The preponderance of the evidence is that no training was provided to Dr. Wojtowicz by GAS. The trial court determined that the liquidated damages portions of the goodwill provision were not enforceable because GAS suffered no harm to its goodwill and such damages were not reasonably related to its actual injury. That conclusion has support in the record, and thus, we will not disturb it on review. We conclude that the liquidated damages portions of the goodwill provision are also so disproportionate as to constitute an unenforceable penalty as a matter of law.

The portion of the judgment declaring the noncompetition provision valid and enforceable reversed in favor of Dr. Wojtowicz and the portion of the judgment declaring the goodwill provision unenforceable is affirmed in favor of Dr. Wojtowicz.

Punitive Damages **Punitive damages** are damages awarded in addition to the compensatory remedy that are designed to punish a defendant for particularly reprehensible behavior and to deter the defendant and others from committing similar behavior in the future. The traditional rule is that punitive damages are not recoverable in contracts cases unless a specific statutory provision (such as some consumer protection statutes) allows them or the defendant has committed *fraud* or some other independent tort. A few states will permit the use of punitive damages in contracts cases in which the defendant's conduct, though not technically a tort, was malicious, oppressive, or tortious in nature.

Punitive damages have also been awarded in many of the cases involving breach of the implied covenant of good faith. In such cases, courts usually circumvent the traditional rule against awarding punitive damages in contracts cases by holding that breach of the duty of good faith is an independent tort. The availability of punitive damages in such cases operates to deter a contracting party from deliberately disregarding the other party's rights. Insurance companies have been the most frequent target for punitive damages awards in bad faith cases, but employers and banks have also been subjected to punitive damages verdicts.

Equitable Remedies

In exceptional cases in which money damages alone are not adequate to fully compensate for a party's injuries, a court may grant an **equitable remedy** either alone or in combination with a legal remedy. Equitable relief is subject to several limitations, however, and will be granted only when justice is served by doing so. The primary equitable remedies for breach of contract are specific performance and injunction.[11]

Specific Performance **Specific performance** is an equitable remedy whereby the court orders the breaching party to perform his contractual duties as promised. For example, if Barnes breached a contract to sell a tract of land to Metzger and a court granted specific performance of the contract, the court would require Barnes to deed the land to Metzger. (Metzger, of course, must pay the purchase price.) This remedy can be advantageous to the injured party because he is not faced with the complexities of proving damages, he does not have to worry about whether he can actually collect the damages, and he gets exactly what he bargained for. However, the availability of this remedy is subject to the limitations discussed below.

The Availability of Specific Performance Specific performance, like other equitable remedies, is available only when the injured party has no adequate remedy at law—in other words, when money damages do not adequately compensate the injured party. This generally requires a showing that the subject of the contract is unique or at least that no substitutes are available. Even if this requirement is met, a court will withhold specific performance if the injured party has acted in bad faith, if he unreasonably delayed in asserting his rights, or if specific performance would require an excessive amount of supervision by the court.

Contracts for the sale of real estate are the most common subjects of specific performance decrees because every tract of real estate is considered to be unique. Specific performance is rarely granted for breach of a contract for the sale of goods because the injured party can usually procure substitute goods. However, there are situations involving sales of goods contracts in which specific performance is given. These cases involve goods that are unique or goods for which no substitute can be found. Examples include antiques, heirlooms, works of art, and objects of purely sentimental value.[12] Specific performance is not available for the breach of a promise to perform a personal service (such as a contract for employment, artistic performance, or consulting services). A decree requiring a person to specifically perform a

personal-services contract would probably be ineffective in giving the injured party what he bargained for. It would also require a great deal of supervision by the court. In addition, an application of specific performance in such cases would amount to a form of involuntary servitude.

Injunction Injunction is an equitable remedy that is employed in many different contexts and is sometimes used as a remedy for breach of contract. An **injunction** is a court order requiring a person to do something (**mandatory injunction**) or ordering a person to refrain from doing something (**negative injunction**). Unlike legal remedies that apply only when the breach has already occurred, the equitable remedy of injunction can be invoked when a breach has merely been *threatened*. Injunctions are available only when the breach or threatened breach is likely to cause *irreparable injury*.

In the contract context, specific performance is a form of mandatory injunction. Negative injunctions are appropriately used in several situations, such as contract cases in which a party whose duty under the contract is forbearance threatens to breach the contract. For example, Norris sells his restaurant in Gas City, Indiana, to Ford. A term of the contract of sale provides that Norris agrees not to own, operate, or be employed in any restaurant within 30 miles of Gas City for a period of two years after the sale.[13] If Norris threatens to open a new restaurant in Gas City several months after the sale is consummated, a court could *enjoin* Norris from opening the new restaurant.

Restitution

Restitution is a remedy that can be obtained either at law or in equity. Restitution applies when one party's performance or reliance has conferred a benefit on the other. A party's restitution interest is protected by compensating him for the value of benefits he has conferred on the other person.[14] This can be done through **specific restitution,** in which the defendant is required to return the exact property conferred on him by the plaintiff, or **substitutionary restitution,** in which a court awards the plaintiff a sum of money that reflects the amount by which he benefited the defendant. In an action for damages based on quasi-contract, substitutionary restitution would be the remedy.

---

[11]Another equitable remedy, *reformation,* allows a court to reform or "rewrite" a written contract when the parties have made an error in expressing their agreement. Reformation is discussed, along with the doctrine of mistake, in Chapter 13.

[12]Specific performance under § 2–716(1) of the UCC is discussed in Chapter 22.

[13]Ancillary covenants not to compete, or noncompetition agreements, are discussed in detail in Chapter 15.

[14]Quasi-contract is discussed in detail in Chapter 9.

Restitution can be used in a number of circumstances. Sometimes, parties injured by breach of contract seek restitution as an alternative remedy instead of damages that focus on their expectation interest. In other situations, a *breaching party* who has partially performed seeks restitution for the value of benefits he conferred in excess of the losses he caused. In addition, restitution often applies in cases in which a person rescinds a contract on the grounds of lack of capacity, misrepresentation, fraud, duress, undue influence, or mistake. Upon rescission, each party who has been benefited by the other's performance must compensate the other for the value of the benefit conferred. Another application of restitution occurs when a party to a contract that violates the statute of frauds confers a benefit on the other party. For example, Boyer gives Blake a $10,000 down payment on an oral contract for the sale of a farm. Although the contract is unenforceable (that is, Boyer could not get compensation for his expectation interest), the court would give Boyer restitution of his down payment.

Problems and Problem Cases

1. The Powells operate a hog farm where they "finished hogs" and provided nursery space for Swine Graphics, a hog producer. In early 1998, the Powells approached Swine Graphics about expanding to a "wean-to-finish" operation, which would entail construction of new buildings, and about extending the parties' existing contracts. Prior to the meeting, Mrs. Powell had talked to the owner of a neighboring farm, Mrs. Anderson, about the Powells' expansion project and Mrs. Anderson expressed no objection. In addition, Mr. Powell had also talked to Mr. Anderson about the project on more than one occasion. Mr. Powell had mentioned possible locations, including a location near the Andersons, the possibility of Mr. Anderson working for the Powells, and later the fact the Powells were near securing financing. Mr. Anderson expressed no objection. Before the meeting with Swine Graphics, Mrs. Powell told Weaver, a Swine Graphics manager and part owner, of potential adverse reactions to the building project by neighbors other than the Andersons, and Weaver merely shrugged his shoulders and made no mention of a need to secure the neighbors' approval. Various negotiations ensued and the Powells eventually began steps to construct a new facility near the Andersons' farm. Swine Graphics did not mention any "good neighbor" policy during the negotiations or until a substantial portion of construction had been completed. In late July 1998, the CEO of Swine Graphics told the Powells that the Andersons had recently complained about the Powells' project. On July 30, 1998, Mrs. Powell talked with Weaver prior to signing a note with Farm Credit Services in the amount of $670,000 for the project. Weaver said the project was a "go," and he made no mention of a good neighbor policy. Weaver and a Farm Credit Services employee had been discussing the Andersons' complaints prior to Weaver's conversation with Mrs. Powell. In September 1998, the Powells received a letter from Swine Graphics, stating in part that the Powells were required to get permission from their neighbors before they could build. Mrs. Powell had never heard of such a requirement before. Swine Graphics has no written good neighbor policy and has no definition of who constitutes a neighbor. Swine Graphics withdrew its endorsement of the project and the Powells sued it. Swine Graphics asserts that permission of the neighbors is a condition precedent to its duties under the contract. Is this position correct?

2. Parscale, the owner of a restaurant, entered into negotiations to acquire outdoor advertising signs for her business from Luminous Neon. At the outset of the negotiations, Luminous Neon had offered to sell the signs to Parscale for $5,600 plus tax, but Parscale ultimately leased them. Under the terms of the lease, Parscale paid a rental of $191.75 plus tax per month for a term of five years. The lease also contained a liquidated damages clause that required Parscale, in the event of breach, to pay damages equal to 80 percent of the remaining payments due. That 80 percent represented Luminous Neon's expenses incurred in manufacturing, financing, and installing the signs, as well as profit. The 20 percent of the remaining payments that were not included as liquidated damages was for maintenance and service expenses that would not be incurred due to Parscale's breach. Some time after Parscale leased the signs, the City of Topeka began construction on a street that limited access to Parscale's business. That construction had an adverse effect on Parscale's business, and it ultimately closed. Parscale stopped making payments on the signs after making a total of 19 payments. Forty-one monthly payments of $191.75 remained due and payable, resulting in liquidated damages, including tax, of $6,651.04. Luminous Neon removed the signs from Parscale's business at her request. The removal added another $300 to the damages. Luminous Neon ultimately sued Parscale to collect this money. Should Luminous Neon be able to collect these liquidated damages from Parscale?

3. Light contracted to build a house for the Mullers. After the job was completed, the Mullers refused to pay

Light the balance they owed him under the contract, claiming that he had done some of the work in an unworkmanlike manner. When Light sued for the money, the Mullers counterclaimed for $5,700 damages for delay under a liquidated damages clause in the contract. The clause provided that Light must pay $100 per day for every day of delay in completion of the construction. The evidence indicated that the rental value of the home was between $400 and $415 per month. Should the liquidated damages provision be enforced?

4. Barham entered into a contract to sell her residential building to Beverly Way Associates for $3.9 million. The contract provided for the opening of escrow (the procedure by which the sale would be consummated) and a closing within 60 days of that time. It also provided that Beverly Way's obligation to purchase the property "shall be conditioned upon" its approval of a number of specified inspections and documents and delivery of clear title. One of these items was a certified survey of the property that would show all improvements to the property and the location of all exceptions to the title. The contract gave Beverly Way 28 business days in which to inspect and approve documents after having been furnished them by Barham. On November 2, 1988, Barham furnished the material that Beverly Way required, and on December 2, Beverly Way wrote to Barham stating, "We reluctantly disapprove of the matters disclosed on the Survey and relating to the Property." This letter described in detail the reasons for its rejection. The letter expressed the hope that the parties could "keep the deal alive" and proposed two alternatives that would have changed the parties' arrangement substantially. There was no further communication between the parties until February 1989, when Beverly Way sent a second letter stating that it was prepared to waive its objections to the survey and to proceed to close the deal. Barham refused to sell the property and Beverly Way sued for specific performance. Will Beverly Way win?

5. The Bassos contracted with Dierberg to purchase her property for $1,310,000. One term of the contract stated, "[t]he sale under this contract shall be closed . . . at the office of Community Title Company . . . on May 16, 1988 at 10:00 A.M. . . . . Time is of the essence of this contract." After forming the contract, the Bassos assigned their right to purchase Dierberg's property to Miceli and Slonim Development Corp. At 10:00 A.M. on May 16, 1988, Dierberg appeared at Community Title for closing. No representative of Miceli and Slonim was there, nor did anyone from Miceli and Slonim inform Dierberg that there would be any delay in the closing. At 10:20 A.M.,

Dierberg declared the contract null and void because the closing did not take place as agreed, and she left the title company office shortly thereafter. Dierberg had intended to use the purchase money to close another contract to purchase real estate later in the day. At about 10:30 A.M., a representative of Miceli and Slonim appeared at Community Title to begin the closing, but the representative did not have the funds for payment until 1:30 P.M. Dierberg refused to return to the title company, stating that Miceli and Slonim had breached the contract by failing to tender payment on time. She had already made alternative arrangements to finance her purchase of other real estate to meet her obligation under that contract. Miceli and Slonim sued Dierberg, claiming that the contract did not require closing exactly at 10:00 A.M., but rather some time on the day of May 16. Will they prevail?

6. Winthrop Resources and Anastasi Construction entered into a Lease Agreement for computer equipment and software. The president of Anastasi Construction, Wayne Anastasi, personally guaranteed the contract. The Lease Agreement began on March 1, 1998, and provided for an initial term of 36 months. The Lease Agreement was to continue from year to year after the initial lease term until terminated by written notice at least 120 days prior to the termination date. Written notice of termination, however, would be ineffective, according to the terms of the lease, if the equipment was not returned to Winthrop. In June 1999, Winthrop, Anastasi Construction, Mr. Anastasi, and a third party, eGlobe, entered into an "Assignment and Assumption" contract under which all of Anastasi Construction's "rights and interests" in the equipment were transferred to eGlobe. Specifically, the Assignment and Assumption provided that Anastasi Construction, the assignor, would "remain principally and primarily liable for all monies, obligations, debts, liabilities, covenants and agreements associated with the Assigned Equipment and the Lease Agreement." Similarly, Anastasi agreed in the Assignment and Assumption to remain "as Guarantor under the Lease Agreement and [to] continue[] to be unconditionally bound by all of the terms and obligations of the Lease Guaranty dated January 13, 1998." Pursuant to this Assignment and Assumption, from June 1999 forward, eGlobe maintained possession and control of the equipment at issue in this case. In September 2000, Anastasi Construction sought to terminate the lease as of March 1, 2001, by written notice to Winthrop. The equipment, however, was not and has not been returned to Winthrop. On April 18, 2001, eGlobe filed bankruptcy. Winthrop sued Anastasi and Anastasi Construction alleging that because they had not returned the leased computer equipment, the Lease Agreement automatically renewed for another year. Anastasi and Anastasi Construction assert that their duty to return the computer was excused because eGlobe's bankruptcy made it impossible. Is this a good argument?

7. On December 8, 1993, Barrington Management and Paul Draper entered into a written Purchase Agreement under which Draper agreed to sell a parcel of 68 acres of commercial real estate to Barrington. Draper retained ownership of a 12-acre parcel located next to the land that was being sold. Barrington made a $1,000 earnest money deposit. The Purchase Agreement provided that "time is of the essence of this Contract." An Addendum to the Contract, which included additional terms of the Purchase Agreement also noted that "time is important." The closing of the sale was to take place within 30 days after all conditions had been satisfied or waived. The addendum also provided as follows:

4. It is a condition ("Condition # 1") of this offer that all utilities, including but not limited to sanitary sewer. . ., city water, electric, gas, storm drainage, are available to the Phase I property line and are in an adequate supply and capacity to serve the development of the entire 68 acres. . . . Purchaser shall have one hundred eighty (180) days from date of this Purchase Agreement to satisfy or waive this condition.

15. In the event any of the above listed conditions or other condition of this Purchase Agreement are not timely satisfied, Purchaser shall have the right to either waive said conditions and close or to notify Seller of the objections and terminate this Agreement. In the event Purchaser elects to terminate this Agreement, Purchaser shall be entitled to a full and immediate return of the earnest money tendered herewith, and in the event such cancellation notice is paid to the Seller, the Purchase Agreement shall terminate and be considered null and void.

Barrington experienced delays in satisfying "Condition # 1" of the Purchase Agreement; that is, in obtaining the land use and drainage approvals necessary to develop the property. Accordingly, the parties entered into a written agreement which extended the period in which Barrington could satisfy or waive this condition until December 31, 1995. However, Barrington remained unable to obtain the necessary approvals and requested an additional extension from Draper. Draper refused to grant another extension. On January 25, 1996, Barrington demanded that Draper close the transaction. Draper refused to close, however, and brought suit asking that the Pur-chase Agreement be rescinded to enable Draper to sell the real estate to another purchaser. Was Draper legally justified in refusing to go forward with the contract?

8. Shirley MacLaine Parker entered into a contract with Twentieth Century-Fox to play the female lead in Fox's contemplated production of a movie entitled *Bloomer Girl.* The contract provided that Fox would pay Parker a minimum "guaranteed compensation" of $53,571.42 per week for 14 weeks, beginning May 23, 1966, for a total of $750,000. Fox decided not to produce the movie, and in a letter dated April 4, 1966, it notified Parker that it would not "comply with our obligations to you under" the written contract. In the same letter, with the professed purpose "to avoid any damage to you," Fox instead offered to employ Parker as the leading actress in another movie, tentatively entitled *Big Country, Big Man.* The compensation offered was identical. Unlike *Bloomer Girl,* however, which was to have been a musical production, *Big Country* was to be a dramatic "western type" movie. *Bloomer Girl* was to have been filmed in California; *Big Country* was to be produced in Australia. Certain other terms of the substitute contract varied from those of the original. Parker was given one week within which to accept. She did not, and the offer lapsed. Parker then filed suit against Fox for recovery of the agreed-on guaranteed compensation. Will she prevail?

9. Ross was recruited to play basketball at Creighton University. He came from an academically disadvantaged background, and at the time he enrolled, Ross was at an academic level far below that of the average Creighton student. Creighton realized Ross's academic limitations when it admitted him, and to induce him to attend and play basketball, assured him that he would receive sufficient tutoring so that he "would receive a meaningful education while at Creighton." Ross attended Creighton from 1978 to 1982. He maintained a D average and earned 96 of the 128 credits needed to graduate. On the advice of the athletics department, he took many of these credits in courses such as marksmanship and theory of basketball, which did not count toward a university degree. He also alleged that the university hired a secretary to read his assignments and prepare and type his papers. When he left Creighton, Ross had the overall language skills of a fourth grader and the reading skills of a seventh grader. He took remedial classes for a year at a preparatory school at Creighton's expense, attending classes with grade-school children, and then enrolled at Roosevelt University. He was forced to withdraw there for lack of funds. Ross sued Creighton for breach of contract, among other theories. Can Ross win this suit?

10. In May 1991, Dalton took the SAT, which was administered by Educational Testing Service (ETS). Six months later, in November, he took the exam a second time. His combined score increased 410 points on the November exam. Because Dalton's score increased by more than 350 points, his test results fell within ETS's category of "Large Score Differences." In accordance with ETS policy, members of the ETS Test Security Office therefore reviewed his May and November answer sheets. Upon a finding of different handwriting, the answer sheets were submitted to a document examiner, who opined that they were completed by separate individuals. Dalton's case was then forwarded to the board of Review, which preliminarily decided that substantial evidence supported canceling Dalton's November score. Upon registering for the November SAT, Dalton had signed a statement agreeing to the conditions in the New York state edition of the Registration Bulletin, which reserved to ETS "the right to cancel any test score. . .if ETS believes that there is reason to question the score's validity." As specified in the Registration Bulletin, ETS informed Dalton of its preliminary decision to cancel his November score. Dalton was informed that he could supply any additional information to explain the discrepancy in the scores or proceed with one of the other options provided by ETS. Dalton opted to present additional information, including the verification that he was suffering from mononucleosis during the May exam, diagnostic test results from a preparatory course that he took between the May and November exams (he took no preparatory course prior to the May exam) that were consistent with his performance on the second exam, a statement from an ETS proctor who remembered seeing Dalton at the November exam, and a statement from two students—one previously unacquainted with Dalton—stating that he had been in the classroom during the November exam. He also provided ETS with a report from a document examiner who concluded that Dalton was the author of both sets of answer sheets. ETS submitted the tests to yet another document examiner, who concluded that different authors created the two answer sheets, and it continued to question the validity of Dalton's November scores. Dalton sued ETS, contending that ETS failed to give good faith consideration to the material that he provided. Will he be successful?

Online Research: Researching Remedies in Website Terms and Conditions

Many websites have pages called "Terms of Use" or "Terms & Conditions," and these pages often restrict the remedies that can be recovered in case of nonperformance or loss. Find a "Terms of Use" page and look for a provision that addresses remedies. What does the page you found have to say about remedies that will or will not be available in case of nonperformance?

PART FOUR

SALES

19

FORMATION AND TERMS
OF SALES CONTRACTS

Paul Reynolds used the Trek website to purchase a racing bike with a frame utilizing a newly developed high-strength but lightweight alloy. He selected the model he wanted and provided the company with the necessary information to place the $2,200 purchase price and $75.00 shipping costs on his Visa card. The bicycle was damaged during shipment when the box was punctured by a forklift truck that was loading other boxes onto the carrier's truck. Paul took the damaged bicycle to a local bicycle dealer to have it repaired. After the bicycle was repaired, but before Paul could pick it up, a clerk in the store, by mistake, sold the bicycle for $1,500 to Melissa Stevenson who bought it as a birthday gift for her boyfriend. This situation raises a number of legal issues that, among others, will be covered in this chapter, including:

- Can a legally enforceable contract for the sale of goods be formed electronically?
- Between Paul and Trek, who had the risk of loss or damage to the bicycle during the time it was under shipment to him?
- Would Paul be entitled to recover possession of the bicycle from Melissa and her boyfriend?

IN PART 3, CONTRACTS, we introduced the common law rules that govern the creation and performance of contracts generally. Throughout much of history, special rules, known as the law merchant, were developed to control mercantile transactions in goods. Because transactions in goods commonly involve buyers and sellers located in different states—and even different countries—a common body of law to control these transactions can facilitate the smooth flow of commerce. To address this need, a Uniform Sales Act was drafted in the early 1900s and adopted by about two-thirds of the states. Subsequently, the Uniform Commercial Code (UCC or Code) was prepared to simplify and modernize the rules of law governing commercial transactions.

This chapter reviews some Code rules that govern the formation of sales contracts previously discussed. It also covers some key terms in sales contracts, such as delivery terms, title, and risk of loss. Finally, it discusses the rules governing sales on trial, such as sales on approval and consignments.

Sale of Goods

The **sale of goods** is the transfer of ownership to tangible personal property in exchange for money, other goods, or the performance of services. The law of sales of goods is codified in Article 2 of the Uniform Commercial Code. While the law of sales is based on the fundamental principles of contract and personal property, it has been modified to accommodate current practices of merchants. In large measure, the Code discarded many technical requirements of earlier law that did not serve any useful purpose in the marketplace and replaced them with rules that are consistent with commercial expectations.

Article 2 of the Code applies only to *transactions in goods.* Thus, it does not cover contracts to provide services or to sell real property. However, some courts have applied the principles set out in the Code to such transactions. When a contract appears to call for the furnishing of both goods and services, a question may arise as to whether the Code

Figure 1   *Choice of Law*

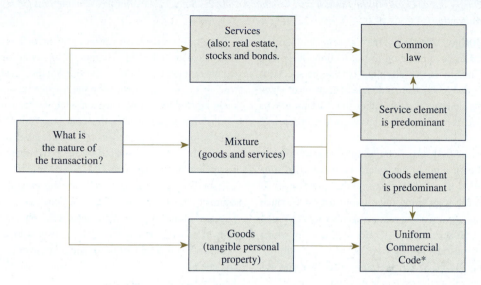

*If there is no specific Uniform Commercial Code provision governing the transaction, use the common law.

applies. For example, the operator of a hair salon may use a commercial solution intended to be used safely on humans that causes injury to a person's head. The injured person then might bring a lawsuit claiming that there was a breach of the Code's warranty of the suitability of the solution. In such cases, the courts commonly ask whether the sale of goods is the *predominant* part of the transaction or merely an *incidental* part; where the sale of goods predominates, courts normally apply Article 2. The *Baxter* case, which fol-

lows, illustrates the type of analysis courts use to determine whether a particular contract should be governed by the Code.

Thus, the first question you should ask when faced with a contracts problem is: Is this a contract for the sale of goods? If it is not, then the principles of common law that were discussed in Part 3, Contracts, apply. If the contract is one for the sale of goods, then the Code applies. This analysis is illustrated in Figure 1.

Baxter v. Maurice's Auto Repair and Towing Service, Inc.
36 UCC Rep.2d 1020 (Fla. Cty. Ct. 1994)

In December 1992, Baxter went to Maurice's Auto Repair and Towing Service for the purpose of getting his 1985 Mercedes Benz 300SD automobile fitted with a rebuilt Mercedes motor. Maurice's was in the auto repair and towing business. He sold new, used, and rebuilt parts, incidental to his repair business. Maurice's did not sell auto parts alone and did not have a parts department.

On December 16, 1992, Maurice's purchased a rebuilt motor from Rick's European Connection, and installed it in Baxter's vehicle. The repairs were completed on January 13, 1993, and Baxter picked up the vehicle from Maurice's on January 17, 1993. The express warranty for the work completed was for six months or 6,000 miles, as evidenced by the repair invoice.

In April of 1993, the motor developed an oil leak. On April 23, 1993 Baxter returned the car, from Georgia where he resided, for repairs. Repairs on a rear seal were completed by Maurice's, and on May 22, 1993, Baxter took delivery of the vehicle. During the period of the repairs, Maurice's paid for a rental car and gasoline for Baxter. In September 1993, on a trip back to Florida, the car died. It needed another new motor. At the time of its demise, the motor had 12,716 miles on it and was eight months old.

Baxter brought suit against Maurice's seeking damages for breach of contract and breach of the implied warranty of merchantability. One of the questions in the lawsuit was whether Article 2—Sales of the Uniform Commercial Code was applicable to the transaction.

Kornstein, Judge   Article 2 of the Uniform Commercial Code is limited in its application to transactions in goods. Goods are defined to mean, "all things (including specially manufactured goods) which are movable at the time of identification to the contract for sale other than the money in which the price is to be paid, investment securities and things in action." Section 2–102.

There is no doubt that the rebuilt motor in question is a good within the meaning of the statute. However, that simple determination is not dispositive of the question as to whether the entire transaction falls within the UCC, since the contract for delivery of the motor was also accompanied by the delivery of services by Maurice's. Contracts which involve both goods and services are not automatically included within the scope of Article 2 simply because the contract partially involves the exchange of goods.

One way to determine if a "mixed contract" falls within Article 2 of the UCC is the "labeling" of the arrangement. How was the contractual arrangement labeled by the parties? The first place to look would be at the invoice for this transaction. The invoice has a section identified as "DESCRIPTION OF WORK." Under that heading is the following list:

"Rebuilt Motor
"Valve Job
"Water pump
"Primer pump
"Oil Change & Filter
"Air Filter
"Fuel Filter Prim & Sec
"Antifreeze
"Thermostat & Gasket
"Fan Belt Alternator
"Upper & Lower Radiator Hoses
"Vacuum Hoses & Fuel & Shop Material."

There is also a section on the left side of the invoice for a list of parts and their costs. No parts are listed in that section. The warranty information and payment information are the only items listed on the parts section of the invoice. Below that "parts" section of the invoice is the section that either requests or waives an estimate pursuant to Florida law. The item which is marked, reads:

I do not request a written estimate as long as the repair costs do not exceed $6,024.90. The shop may not exceed this amount without my written or oral approval.

The lower right-hand corner of the invoice is the section that calculates all of the charges. It lumps all of the repair expenses together as "Total Service $5,400," and then adds towing and taxes. Nowhere on the invoice was the arrangement labeled as a "sale." By applying the facts of this case against the "labeling" test, this court must conclude that the transaction is a repair, or service, and not labeled as a sale of goods, and thus not covered by the provisions of the Uniform Commercial Code.

Another leading method used to determine if the "mixed contract" should be controlled by Article 2 is through the application of the "predominant factor test." That test for inclusion in or exclusion from sales provisions of the UCC is whether the predominant factor and purpose of the contract is for sale of goods, with labor incidentally involved, or is the predominant factor rendition of service, with goods incidentally involved. In applying the predominant factor test, this Court finds that the defendant, Maurice's Auto Repair, is predominantly selling its services, with auto parts a necessary incidental to that service.

Turning again to the invoice, Maurice's holds itself out as "Maurice's Body Repair & 24 Hour Towing Service." Maurice does not hold itself out as being in the auto parts business, but the auto repair business. Evidence produced at trial showed that Maurice's was not in the auto parts business, does not have an auto parts department, and does not sell auto parts to the general public. In fact, the evidence at the hearing clearly showed that Maurice's had to purchase the rebuilt engine from an independent dealer. It is obvious from these facts that Maurice's is primarily a service-oriented business which deals in goods as an incident to its performance of services in the auto repair business.

The preponderance of the testimony at trial clearly indicated that the transaction between the parties was for the repair of Baxter's automobile. Viewed in its entirety, this court holds that the transaction cannot be characterized in part or in its underlying nature as one for the sale of goods. The predominant factor, or purpose of the contract, can be reasonably stated as one for the delivery of ser-vices, to wit, the repair of the auto, accompanied by the acquisition of the necessary materials.

Judgment for Maurice's.

Leases

A lease of goods is a transfer of the right to possess and use goods belonging to another. Although the rights of one who leases goods (a lessee) do not constitute ownership of the goods, leasing is mentioned here because it is becoming an increasingly important way of acquiring the use of many kinds of goods, from automobiles to farm equipment. In most states, Article 2 and Article 9 of the UCC are applied to such leases by analogy. However, rules contained in these articles sometimes are inadequate to resolve special problems presented by leasing. For this reason, a new article of the UCC dealing exclusively with leases of goods, Article 2A, was written in 1987 and has been adopted by 47 states and the District of Columbia. Because of space limitations, this textbook does not cover Article 2A in detail.

Merchants

Many of the Code's provisions apply only to **merchants** or to transactions between merchants.[1] In addition, the Code sets a higher standard of conduct for merchants because persons who regularly deal in goods are expected to be familiar with the practices of that trade and with commercial law. Ordinary consumers and nonmerchants, on the other hand, frequently have little knowledge of or experience in these matters.

Code Requirements

The Code requires that parties to sales contracts act in good faith and in a commercially reasonable manner. Further, when a contract contains an unfair or unconscionable clause, or the contract as a whole is unconscionable, the courts have the right to refuse to enforce the unconscionable clause or contract [2–302].[2] The Code's treatment of unconscionability is discussed in detail in Chapter 15, Illegality.

---

[1]Under the Code, a "merchant" is defined as a "person who deals in goods of the kind or otherwise by his occupation holds himself out as having knowledge or skill peculiar to the practices or goods involved in the transaction or to whom such knowledge or skill may be attributed by his employment of an agent or broker or other intermediary who by his occupation holds himself out as having such knowledge or skill" [2–104(1)].
[2]The numbers in brackets refer to sections of the Uniform Commercial Code.

A number of the Code provisions concerning the sale of goods were discussed in the chapters on contracts. The Concept Review (page 414) lists some of the important provisions discussed earlier, together with the chapters in the text where the discussion can be found.

Terms of Sales Contracts

Gap Fillers

The Code recognizes the fact that parties to sales contracts frequently omit terms from their agreements or state terms in an indefinite or unclear manner. The Code deals with these situations by filling in the blanks with common trade practices, or by giving commonly used terms a specific meaning that is applied unless the parties' agreement clearly indicates a contrary intent.

Price Terms

A fixed price is not essential to the creation of a binding sales contract. Of course, if price has been the subject of a dispute between the parties that has never been resolved, no contract is created because a "meeting of the minds" never occurred. However, if the parties omitted a price term or left the price to be determined at a future date or by some external means, the Code supplies a price term (2–305). Under the common law, such contracts would have failed due to "indefiniteness." If a price term is simply omitted, or if the parties agreed that the price would be set by some external agency (like a particular market or trade journal) that fails to set the price, the Code says the price is a *reasonable price at the time for delivery* (2–305[1]). If the agreement gives either party the power to fix the price, that party must do so in *good faith* (2–305[2]). If the surrounding circumstances clearly indicate that the parties did not intend to be bound in the event a price was not determined in the agreed-upon manner, no contract results (2–305[4]).

Quantity Terms

In some cases, the parties may state the quantity of goods covered by their sales contract in an indefinite way. Contracts that obligate a buyer to purchase a seller's *output* of a certain item or all of the buyer's *requirements* of a certain item are commonly encountered. These contracts caused frequent problems under the common law because of the indefiniteness of the parties' obligations. If the seller decided to double its output, did the buyer have to accept the entire amount? If the market price of the

CONCEPT REVIEW

Formation of Contracts

Offer and Acceptance (Chapters 10 and 11)	1. A contract can be formed in any manner sufficient to show agreement, including conduct by both parties that recognizes the existence of a contract.
	2. The fact that the parties did not agree on all the terms of their contract does not prevent the formation of a contract.
	3. A firm written offer by a merchant that contains assurances it will be held open is irrevocable for a period of up to three months.
	4. Acceptance of an offer may be made by any reasonable manner and is effective on dispatch.
	5. A timely expression of acceptance creates a contract even if it contains terms different from the offer or states additional terms *unless* the attempted acceptance is expressly conditioned on the offer's agreement to the terms of the acceptance.
	6. An offer inviting a prompt shipment may be accepted either by a prompt promise to ship or a prompt shipment of the goods.
Consideration (Chapter 12)	1. Consideration is not required to make a firm offer in writing by a merchant irrevocable for a period of up to three months.
	2. Consideration is not required to support a modification of a contract for the sale of goods.
Statute of Frauds (Chapter 16)	
	1. Subject to several exceptions, all contracts for the sale of goods for $500 or more must be evidenced by a writing signed by the party against whom enforcement of the contract is sought. It is effective only as to the quantity of goods stated in the writing.
	2. A signed writing is not required if the party against whom enforcement is sought is a merchant, received a written memorandum from the other party, and did not object in writing within 10 days of his receipt of it.
	3. An exception to the statute of frauds is made for specially manufactured goods not suitable for sale to others on which the seller has made a substantial beginning in manufacturing or has entered into a binding contract to acquire.
	4. An exception to the statute of frauds is made for contracts that a party admits the existence of in court testimony or pleadings.
	5. If a party accepts goods or payment for goods, the statute of frauds is satisfied to the extent of the payment made or the goods accepted.
Unconscionability (Chapter 15)	If a court finds a contract for the sale of goods to be unconscionable, it can refuse to enforce it entirely, enforce it without any unconscionable clause, or enforce it in a way that avoids an unconscionable result.

CYBERLAW IN ACTION

Electronic Writings and the Statute of Frauds

The Electronic Signatures in Global and National Commerce Act (the "E-sign" act) was enacted by Congress and became effective in the United States on October 1, 2000. The E-Sign law covers many everyday transactions including sales transactions even where the law of the state involved still has a version of Article 2 that requires a "signed writing" or another means of satisfying the Article 2 statute of frauds found in Section 2–201. Federal laws "preempt", that is, displace state laws if the two sets of laws are in conflict. If state law requires a signed writing or another indicator that the purported buyer and seller actually intended to form a contract, E-Sign allows the parties to use electronic authentications instead of signed writings. E-mail messages and online orders sent by the buyer would suffice. States that have adopted the Uniform Electronic Transactions Act (UETA) also allow online communications to satisfy the Section 2–201 statute of frauds requirement.

---

item soared much higher than the contract price, could the buyer double or triple its demands?

Output and Needs Contracts

In an "output" contract, one party is bound to sell its entire output of particular goods and the other party is bound to buy that output. In a "needs" or "requirements" contract, the quantity of goods is based on the needs of the buyer. In determining the quantity of goods to be produced or taken pursuant to an output or needs contract, the rule of *good faith* applies. Thus, no quantity can be demanded or taken that is unreasonably disproportionate to any stated estimate in the contract or to "normal" prior output or requirements if no estimate is stated [2–306(2)].

For example, Farmer contracts to supply Sam's Grocery with all of the apples it requires for sale to customers. If Sam's has sold between 500 and 700 bushels of apples a year over the past 10 years, Farmer could not be required to deliver 5,000 bushels of apples to Sam's one year because Sam had an unusual demand for them. Similarly, it would not be reasonable for Sam to say he would take only 10 bushels one year.

The *Indiana-American Water Co.* case, which follows, involves an exclusive requirements contract.

Indiana-American Water Co., Inc. v. Town of Seelyville
698 N.E.2d 1255 (Ind. Ct. App. 1998)

In 1983, the Indiana-American Water Company and the Town of Seelyville entered into a contract, which provided in pertinent part as follows:

Company agrees to sell to the Town, and Town agrees to purchase from Company, at the rates hereinafter mentioned, such quantities of water as the Town may hereafter from time to time need (subject to all limitations contained in this Agreement).

The term of the contract was 25 years and was to expire in the year 2008. The contract limited the quantity of water the Town might purchase to 1 million gallons of water per day. The contract contained other limitations and provided that "in no event shall the Company be obligated to supply water in excess of the limitations on usage as provided for expressly in this Agreement. . . ."

In 1967 (many years before the contract was executed), the Town acquired land which could be used as a wellfield to supply water. In 1997 the Town announced its plan to sell bonds to finance the construction of the improvements necessary to obtain water from the wellfield.

The Water Company initiated a lawsuit seeking a declaratory judgment that the Town's plan to develop its own supply of water would constitute a breach of the contract which, Water Company contended, required the Town to purchase all the water it needed from Water Company. The trial court held that the Town had a binding agreement that permitted it to purchase its water needs from Water Company but did not require it to purchase all of its water from Water Company. The Court also held that the Town's development and utilization of its source of water diminished its need and did not violate the agreement.

Bailey, Judge

I. Indefinite Quantities or Exclusive Requirements Contract

Output and requirement contracts are governed by the Uniform Commercial Code ("UCC") as adopted in Indiana under section 2–306(1) as follows:

> A term which measures the quantity by the output of the seller or the requirements of the buyer means such actual output or requirements as may occur in good faith, except that no quantity unreasonably disproportionate to any stated estimate or in the absence of a stated estimate to any normal or otherwise comparable prior output or requirements may be tendered or demanded.

Water Company contends that the contract requires Town to purchase all its water from Water Company and, in effect, prohibits Town from developing its own water supply. Water Company asserts that any other interpretation of the contract renders it unenforceable for lack of mutuality or indefiniteness because, although Water Company is required to supply all the water Town needs (within the limitations provided in the contract), Town is not required to purchase any minimum amount of water from Water Company. Thus, Water Company raises the implied threat that, if Town does not purchase all of its water from Water Company, Water Company is not bound by the contract and is free to leave the Town "high and dry" unless the Town capitulates to its demands.

A requirements contract is one in which the purchaser agrees to buy all of its needs of a specified material exclusively from a particular supplier, and the supplier agrees, in turn, to fill all of the purchaser's needs during the period of the contract. On the other hand, an indefinite quantities contract is a contract under which the buyer agrees to purchase and the seller agrees to supply whatever quantity of goods the buyer chooses to purchase from the seller. A requirements contract differs from an indefinite quantities contract in that, under a requirements contract the buyer agrees to turn exclusively to the seller to purchase his requirements as they develop. However, in an indefinite quantities contract, even if the buyer needs the commodity in question, he is not obligated to purchase it from the seller. Thus, an indefinite quantities contract, without at least the requirement that the buyer purchase a guaranteed minimum quantity from the seller, is illusory and unenforceable. As expressed under Indiana law: "it is fundamental that a contract is unenforceable if it fails to obligate the parties to do anything."

We will strive to interpret a contract as valid rather than void. Additionally, where it is apparent that a binding exclusive requirements contract was intended, the buyer's promise to purchase from seller exclusively will be implied. Moreover, the requirements of good faith, specifically imposed under UCC section 2–306, prevent requirement contracts from being illusory or too indefinite to be enforced.

The present contract under scrutiny provides that Town will purchase "such quantities of water as the Town may hereafter from time to time need . . ." from Water Company. Moreover, the contract provides that "in no event shall the Company be obligated to supply water in excess of [1 million gallons per day]."

There has never been any contention that the contract permits Town to shop around and purchase its water needs up to 1 million gallons per day from any supplier other than Water Company. Thus, we interpret the present contract as a valid and enforceable exclusive requirements contract which requires Town to use Water Company exclusively to supply all the water it must purchase to meet its needs up to the amount of 1 million gallons of water per day.

II. Good Faith Reduction or Curtailment of Requirements

The most common problem arising out of a requirements contract is the situation where the price of the commodity is advantageous to the buyer who then demands a quantity unreasonable in excess of his needs in order to resell the excess at a profit, placing himself in competition with the seller. The provision in section 2–306(1) forbidding the "demand" by a buyer under a requirements contract to a "quantity unreasonably disproportionate to any stated estimate" applies only to this type of situation where the buyer requests more, as opposed to less, of the commodity in question.

Generally, the buyer in a requirements contract governed by UCC section 2–306(1) is required merely to exercise good faith in determining his requirements and the seller assumes the risk of all good faith variations in the buyer's requirements even to the extent of a determination to liquidate or discontinue the business. However, the buyer is not free, on any whim, to quit buying from seller. How exigent the buyer's change of circumstances must be to allow him to scale down his requirements is a difficult question. The seller assumes the risk of a change in the buyer's business that results in a substantial reduction in the buyer's needs, but the buyer assumes the risk of a less urgent change in circumstances. The essential ingredient of the buyer's good faith under such circumstances is that he not merely have had second thoughts about the terms of the contract and want to get out of it. However, if the buyer has a legitimate business reason for eliminating its requirements, as opposed to a desire to avoid its contract, the buyer acts in good faith.

It is well settled that it is not bad faith to take advantage of a technological advance which reduces the buyer's requirements. In the present case, Town had acquired a wellfield many years before the execution of the contract under scrutiny. Town's decision to develop its preexisting wellfield constitutes a legitimate, long-term business decision, and not merely a desire to avoid the terms of its contract with Water Company. Therefore, based on the above, we cannot conclude that Water Company carried its burden of overcoming the negative judgment in this case by demonstrating that the evidence leads unerringly to the conclusion that Town's development of its preexisting wellfield to reduce its need to purchase water from Water Company constitutes bad faith.

Judgment for Town affirmed.

Exclusive Dealing Contracts

The Code takes a similar approach to *exclusive dealing contracts.* Under the common law, these contracts were sources of difficulty due to the indefinite nature of the parties' duties. Did the dealer have to make any effort to sell the manufacturer's products, and did the manufacturer have any duty to supply the dealer? The Code says that unless the parties agree to the contrary, sellers have an obligation to use their best efforts to supply the goods to the buyer and the buyers are obligated to use their best efforts to promote their sale [2–306(2)].

Time for Performance

If no time for performance is stated in the sales contract, a *reasonable time* for performance is implied. If a contract requires successive performances over an indefinite period of time, the contract is valid for a reasonable time; however, either party can terminate it at any time upon the giving of reasonable notice unless the parties have agreed otherwise as to termination [2–309]. For example, Farmer Jack agrees to sell his entire output of apples each fall to a cannery at the then current market price. If the contract does not contain a provision spelling out how and when the contract can be terminated, Farmer Jack can terminate it if he gives the cannery a reasonable time to make arrangements to acquire apples from someone else.

Delivery Terms

Standardized shipping terms that through commercial practice have come to have a specific meaning are customarily used in sales contracts. The terms **FOB (free on board)** and **FAS (free alongside ship)** are basic delivery terms. If the delivery term of the contract is FOB or FAS the place at which the goods originate, the seller is obligated to deliver to the carrier goods that *conform to the contract* and *are properly prepared for shipment* to the buyer, and the seller must make a *reasonable contract for transportation of the goods* on behalf of the buyer. Under such delivery terms, the goods are at the risk of the buyer during transit and he must pay the shipping charges. If the term is *FOB destination,* the seller must deliver the goods to the designated destination and they are at the seller's risk and expense during transit. These terms will be discussed in more detail later in this chapter.

Title

Passage of Title

Title to goods cannot pass from the seller to the buyer until the goods are identified to the contract [2–401(1)]. For

CYBERLAW IN ACTION

Buying Beer on the Internet

While his parents were away from home on vacation, Hunter Butler, a minor, used a credit card in his name to order 12 bottles of beer through Beer Across America's Internet site on the World Wide Web. When his mother, Lynda Butler, returned home she found several bottles from the shipment of beer remaining in the refrigerator. Lynda Butler then filed a civil lawsuit against Beer Across America seeking damages under Section 6–5–70 of the Alabama Civil Damages Act. The Civil Damages Act provides for a civil action by the parent or guardian of a minor against anyone who knowingly sells or furnishes liquor to the minor. A threshold issue in the lawsuit was whether the sale of the beer had taken place in Alabama so that a court in Alabama would have personal jurisdiction over Beer Across America.

Beer Across America was an Illinois corporation involved in the marketing and sale of alcoholic beverages and other merchandise. The beer was brought by carrier from Illinois to Alabama. The sales invoice and shipping documents provided that the sale was F.O.B. the seller, with the carrier acting as the buyer's agent. Moreover, the invoice included a charge for sales tax but no charge for beer tax; Alabama law requires that sales tax be collected for out-of-state sale of goods which are then shipped to Alabama but requires beer tax be collected only on sales within Alabama.

The court held that the sale arranged over the Internet took place in Illinois. The court noted that under the versions of the Uniform Commercial Code in effect in both Illinois and Alabama, a sale consists in the passing of title from the seller to the buyer. Title to goods passes at the time and place of the shipment when the contract does not require the seller to make delivery at the destination. Accordingly, ownership to the beer passed to Hunter Butler upon tender of the beer to the carrier. The court then transferred the case to the U.S. District Court for the Northern District of Illinois. *Butler v. Beer Across America,* 40 UCC Rep.2d 1008 (U.S.D.C. N.D. Ala. 2000).

example, if Seller agrees to sell Buyer 50 chairs and Seller has 500 chairs in his warehouse, title to 50 chairs will not pass from Seller to Buyer until the 50 chairs that Buyer has purchased are selected and identified as the chairs sold to Buyer.

The parties may agree between themselves when title to the goods will pass from the seller to the buyer. If there is no agreement, then the general rule is that the *title to the goods passes to the buyer when the seller completes his obligations as to delivery of the goods:*

1. If the contract requires the seller to "ship" the goods to the buyer, then title passes to the buyer when the seller delivers conforming goods to the carrier.

2. If the contract requires the seller to "deliver" the goods to the buyer, title does not pass to the buyer until the goods are delivered to the buyer and tendered to him.

3. If delivery is to be made without moving the goods, then title passes at the time and place of contracting. An exception is made if title to the goods is represented by a document of title such as a warehouse receipt; then, title passes when the document of title is delivered to the buyer.

4. If the buyer rejects goods tendered to him, title reverts to the seller [2–401(4)].

Importance of Title

At common law, most of the problems relating to risks, insurable interests in goods, remedies, and similar rights and liabilities were determined on the basis of who was the technical title owner at the particular moment the right or liability arose. Under the Code, however, the rights of the seller and buyer and of third persons are determined irrespective of the technicality of who has the title, unless the provision of the Code expressly refers to title.

Determination of who has title to the goods is important in instances in which the rights of the seller's or the buyer's creditors in the goods are an issue. Another instance in which the identity of the title holder may be important is in determining whether the seller's insurance policy covers a particular loss.

The *Cardwell* case, which follows, illustrates the application of these rules.

State of Connecticut v. Cardwell   *718 A.2d 954 (Conn. Sup. Ct. 1998)*

The State of Connecticut brought suit against Roderick Cardwell, a resident of Connecticut and the owner of Ticketworld, contending that he was engaged in "ticket scalping" in violation of Connecticut law. A Connecticut statute makes it an unfair or deceptive trade practice to sell tickets to sporting and entertainment events to be held in Connecticut to purchasers located in Connecticut, for a price more than $3 in excess of the price, including tax, printed on the face of the ticket, or fixed for admission.

Cardwell was engaged in the business of selling tickets to entertainment and sporting events to be held in Connecticut. Ticketworld operated from two locations, one in Hartford and one in Springfield, Massachusetts. In order to obtain business, Ticketworld advertised in newspapers, including newspapers that circulate in Connecticut. The advertisements that appeared in Connecticut newspapers instructed prospective purchasers to telephone the Hartford office of Ticketworld for tickets to events that would take place outside of Connecticut, and to telephone the Springfield office for tickets to events that would be held in Connecticut. In the event that a prospective customer telephoned the Hartford office for tickets to a Connecticut event, the prospective customer was instructed to telephone the Springfield office in order to purchase those tickets.

On many occasions, Ticketworld sold tickets to Connecticut events from its Springfield office for which it charged a price that exceeded the fixed price of the ticket, tax included, by more than $3. The trial court found, specifically, that Ticketworld: (1) had charged Mary Lou Lupovitch $125 per ticket for tickets to an event at the Connecticut Tennis Court in New Haven, although those tickets had a fixed price of $32.50 per ticket; and (2) had charged Cyrilla Bergeron $137 per ticket for tickets to an event in Hartford, although those tickets had a fixed price of $53.50 per ticket. The court determined that Ticketworld, in selling these tickets for a price in excess of the fixed price for admission, had violated section 53–289. Consequently, it issued a permanent injunction prohibiting Cardwell from engaging in any activity within the state in connection with selling, offering for sale, attempting to sell, mailing or otherwise delivering, or advertising or promoting the sale of any ticket to an event to be held in Connecticut sold for a price more than $3 in excess of the fixed price of the ticket, including tax.

Cardwell appealed, contending that since he sold tickets to events in Connecticut only through Ticketworld's office in Springfield, Massachusetts, the "sales" did not take place in Connecticut and thus did not violate Connecticut law.

Berdon, Associate Justice   In Connecticut, the sale of goods is governed by the Connecticut Uniform Commercial Code—Sales (code). Under the code, a "sale" is defined as "the passing of title from the seller to the buyer for a price. . . ." Section 2–106(1). The code further provides that "[u]nless otherwise explicitly agreed title passes to the buyer at the time and place at which the seller completes his performance with reference to the physical delivery of the goods, despite any reservation of a security interest and even though a document of title is to be delivered at a different time or place. . . ." Section 2–401(2). In addition, the code provides that "if the contract requires or authorizes the seller to send the goods to the buyer but does not require him to deliver them at destination, title passes to the buyer at the time and place of shipment. . . ." Section 2–401(2)(a).

The latter provision reflects the distinction made by the code between "shipment" and "destination" contracts. Under the code, when a carrier is used to transport the goods sold, shipment contracts and destination contracts are the only two types of sales contracts recognized. Section 2–401(2). Furthermore, under the code, "[t]he 'shipment' contract is regarded as the [general rule]." Under a shipment contract, the seller is either required or authorized to ship

the goods to the buyer, but is not required to deliver them at a particular destination, and delivery to the carrier constitutes delivery to the buyer. Section 2–401(2)(a). Under a destination contract, the seller is required to deliver the goods to the buyer at the named destination and delivery occurs upon tender of the goods at that destination. A strong presumption against the creation of destination contracts is contained in the code such that, in the absence of specific proof of agreement by the seller to deliver the goods to a particular destination and to bear the attendant risk of loss until such delivery, a sales contract that merely provides that the goods will be shipped to a certain location will be deemed to be a shipment contract.

In this case, the contracts made by Cardwell for the sale of tickets do not contain any explicit agreement by Cardwell to deliver the goods to a particular destination or to bear the attendant risk of loss until such time as the goods are delivered. Therefore, the contracts at issue in this case are properly classified as shipment contracts. Because delivery of the goods to the carrier constitutes delivery to the buyer under a shipment contract, section 2–401(2)(a), with respect to each sale of tickets made by Cardwell, delivery is made to the post office or other commercial carrier, and hence to the buyer, within Massachusetts. As a result, the "sale" of the tickets, as defined by the code, occurs in Massachusetts. Consequently, the trial court's determination that Cardwell sells tickets within Connecticut, and thereby violates the Connecticut statute, was incorrect.

Judgment reversed in favor of Cardwell.

Title and Third Parties

Obtaining Good Title

A fundamental rule of property law is that a buyer cannot receive better title to goods than the seller had. If Thief steals a television set from Adler and sells it to Brown, Brown does not get good title to the set, because Thief had no title to it. Adler would have the right to recover the set from Brown. Similarly, if Brown sold the set to Carroll, Carroll could get no better title to it than Brown had. Adler would have the right to recover the set from Carroll.

Under the Code, however, there are several exceptions to the general rule that a buyer cannot get better title to goods than his seller had. The most important exceptions include the following: (1) a person who has a voidable title to goods can pass good title to a bona fide purchaser for value; (2) a person who buys goods in the regular course of a retailer's business usually takes free of any interests in the goods that the retailer has given to others; and (3) a person who buys goods in the ordinary course of a dealer's business takes free of any claim of a person who entrusted those goods to the dealer.

Transfers of Voidable Title

A seller who has a **voidable title** has the power to pass good title to a *good faith purchaser for value* [2–403(1)]. A seller has a voidable title to goods if he has obtained his title through fraudulent representations. For example, a person would have a voidable title if he obtained goods by impersonating another person or by paying for them with a bad check or if he obtained goods without paying the agreed purchase price when it was agreed that the transaction was to be a cash sale. Under the Code, **good faith** means "honesty in fact in the conduct or transaction concerned" [1–201(19)] and a buyer has given **value** if he has given any consideration sufficient to support a simple contract [1–201(44)].

For example, Jones goes to the ABC Appliance Store, convinces the clerk that he is really Clark, who is a good customer of ABC, and leaves with a stereo charged to Clark's account. If Jones sells the stereo to Davis, who gives Jones value for it and has no knowledge of the fraud that Jones perpetrated on ABC, Davis gets good title to the stereo. ABC cannot recover the stereo from Davis; instead, it must look for Jones, the person who deceived it. In this situation, both ABC and Davis were innocent of wrongdoing, but the law considers Davis to be the more worthy of its protection because ABC was in a better position to have prevented the wrongdoing by Jones and because Davis bought the goods in good faith and for value.

The same result would be reached if Jones had given ABC a check that later bounced and then sold the stereo to Davis, who was a good faith purchaser for value. Davis would have good title to the stereo, and ABC would have to pursue its right against Jones on the bounced check.

The *Alsafi Oriental Rugs* case, which follows, illustrates the importance of determining the identity and creditworthiness of a person to whom one sells goods. It also shows the importance of a subsequent buyer qualifying as a good faith purchaser for value so that he is able to get good title from a seller with a voidable title.

Alsafi Oriental Rugs v. American Loan Company
864.S.W.2d 41 (Tenn Ct. App. 1993)

In December 1990, Arlene Bradley entered Alsafi Oriental Rugs and advised the owner that she was an interior decorator and that she was interested in selling some of his rugs to one of her customers. Alsafi did not know Bradley and had never done business with her. However, he allowed her to take three rugs out on consignment with the understanding that she would return them if her customer was not interested. In fact, however, Bradley was not obtaining the rugs for a "customer" but was instead working for another individual, Walid Salaam, a rug dealer.

A friend of Bradley's had introduced her to Salaam earlier. Salaam had advised Bradley and her friend that he was the owner of an oriental rug store that had recently closed but he was attempting to reopen it. He offered to teach them how to become decorators and told them that when his store reopened they could operate out of the store. However, Salaam advised them that until he got his store restocked, he wanted them to "check out" rugs on approval from other rug dealers in town. As they had no experience with oriental rugs, Salaam instructed them what rugs to look for. He then instructed them to go to rug dealers in Memphis and advise them that they were interior decorators with customers that wanted to purchase oriental rugs.

After Bradley obtained possession of three rugs from Alsafi, she turned them over to Salaam, who in turn took them to a pawnshop operated by the American Loan Company. There Salaam pawned the rugs, obtaining approximately $5,000 after filling out the required paperwork. Salaam failed to redeem the rugs. Following the default, the pawnshop gave the appropriate notice that it intended to dispose of them.

In April 1991, Alsafi learned that his rugs were at the pawnshop. After visiting the pawnshop and identifying the three rugs as his, he brought suit to recover possession of them. The trial court held that the rugs had been stolen from Alsafi and awarded him possession of them. The pawnshop appealed.

Tomlin, Presiding Judge   Section 2–403(1) reads as follows:

(1) A purchaser of goods acquires all title which his transferor had or had power to transfer except that a purchaser of limited interest acquires rights only to the extent of the interest purchased. A person with voidable title has power to transfer a good title to a good faith purchaser for value. When goods have been delivered under a transaction of purchase the purchaser has such power even though:

(a) the transferor was deceived as to the identity of the purchaser, or

(b) the delivery was in exchange for a check which is later dishonored, or

(c) it was agreed that the transaction was to be a "cash sale," or

(d) the delivery was procured through fraud punishable as larcenous under the criminal law.

Section 2–403(1) empowers a purchaser with a voidable title to confer good title upon a good faith purchaser for value where the goods were procured through fraud punishable as larcenous under the criminal law. The dis-

tinction between theft and fraud in this context is found in the statutory definitions of "delivery" and "purchase." Delivery concerns a voluntary transfer of possession (1–201[14]), and purchase refers to a voluntary transaction creating an interest in property (1–201[32]). As one commentator has pointed out, "a thief who wrongfully takes goods is not a purchaser . . . but a swindler who fraudulently induces the victim to voluntarily deliver them is a purchaser."

In his sworn complaint as well as in his deposition, Alsafi characterized the transfer of possession to Bradley as a consignment—i.e., a voluntary relinquishment of possession to her. She was a purchaser as defined in sections 1–201(33) and 1–201(32). As such, she was empowered by that transaction to pass title to Salaam, who in turn passed title to American Loan Company, a good faith purchaser for value, as found by the trial court, which noted that American Loan Company had no actual knowledge or reason to believe that Salaam was not the true owner of the rugs.

Judgment reversed in favor of American Loan Company.

Buyers in the Ordinary Course of Business

A person who buys goods in the ordinary course of business from a person dealing in goods of that type takes free of any security interest in the goods given by his seller to another person [9–307(1)]. **A buyer in ordinary course** is a person who in good faith and without knowledge that the sale to him is in violation of the ownership

rights of a third party buys goods in the ordinary course of business of a person selling goods of that kind, other than a pawnbroker [1–201(9)].

For example, Brown Buick may borrow money from Bank in order to finance its inventory of new Buicks; in turn, Bank may take a security interest in the inventory to secure repayment of the loan. If Carter buys a new Buick from Brown Buick, he gets good title to the Buick free and clear of the Bank's security

CONCEPT REVIEW

Title and Third Parties

General Rule	A seller cannot pass better title to goods than he has.
Exceptions to General Rule	1. A person who has voidable title to goods can pass good title to a bona fide purchaser for value.
	2. A buyer in the ordinary course of a retailer's business usually takes free of any interests in the goods that the retailer has given to others.
	3. A person who buys goods in the ordinary course of a dealer's business takes free of any claims of a person who entrusted those goods to the dealer.

interest if he is a buyer in the ordinary course of business and without knowledge that the sale is in violation of a security interest. The basic purpose of this exception is to protect those who innocently buy from merchants and thereby to promote confidence in such commercial transactions. The exception also reflects the fact that the bank is more interested in the proceeds from the sale than in the inventory. Security interests and the rights of buyers in the ordinary course of business are discussed in more detail in Chapter 28, Security Interests in Personal Property.

Entrusting of Goods

A third exception to the general rule is that if goods are entrusted to a merchant who deals in goods of that kind, the merchant has the power to transfer all rights of the entruster to a buyer in the ordinary course of business [2–403(2)]. For example, Gail takes her watch to Jeweler, a retail jeweler, to have it repaired, and Jeweler sells the watch to Mary. Mary would acquire good title to the watch, and Gail would have to proceed against Jeweler for conversion of her watch. The purpose behind this rule is to protect commerce by giving confidence to buyers that they will get good title to the goods they buy from merchants in the ordinary course of business. However, a merchant-seller cannot pass good title to stolen goods even if the buyer is a buyer in the ordinary course of business. This is because the original owner did nothing to facilitate the transfer.

Risk of Loss

The transportation of goods from sellers to buyers can be a risky business. The carrier of the goods may lose, damage, or destroy them; floods, tornadoes, and other natural catastrophes may take their toll; thieves may steal all or part of the goods. If neither party is at fault for the loss, who should bear the risk? If the buyer has the risk when the goods are damaged or lost, the buyer is liable for the contract price. If the seller has the risk, he is liable for damages unless substitute performance can be tendered.

The common law placed the risk on the party who had technical title at the time of the loss. The Code rejects this approach and provides specific rules governing risk of loss that are designed to provide certainty and to place the risk on the party best able to protect against loss and most likely to be insured against it. Risk of loss under the Code depends on the terms of the parties' agreement, on the moment the loss occurs, and on whether one of the parties was in breach of contract when the loss occurred.

Terms of the Agreement

The contracting parties, subject to the rule of good faith, may specify who has the risk of loss in their agreement [2–509(4)]. This they may do directly or by using certain commonly accepted shipping terms in their contract. In addition, the Code has certain general rules on risk of loss that amplify specific shipping terms and control risk of loss in cases where specific terms are not used [2–509].

Shipment Contracts

If the contract requires the seller to ship the goods by carrier but does not require their delivery to a specific destination, the risk passes to the buyer when the seller delivers the goods to the carrier [2–509(1)(a)]. Shipment contracts are considered to be the normal contract where

ETHICS IN ACTION

Perils of Entrusting Goods

Suppose you are the owner of a small jewelry store that sells new and antique jewelry. A customer leaves a family heirloom—an elaborate diamond ring—with

you for cleaning and resetting. By mistake, a clerk in your store sells it to another customer. What would you do? If you were the buyer of the ring and had given it to your fiancée as a gift and then were informed of the circumstances, what would you do?

---

the seller is required to send goods to the buyer but is not required to guarantee delivery at a particular location.

The following are commonly used shipping terms that create shipment contracts:

1. *FOB (free on board) point of origin.* This term calls for the seller to deliver the goods free of expense and at the seller's risk at the place designated. For example, a contract between a seller located in Chicago and a buyer in New York calls for delivery FOB Chicago. The seller must deliver the goods at his expense and at his risk to a carrier in the place designated in the contract, namely Chicago, and arrange for their carriage. Because the shipment term in this example is FOB Chicago, the seller bears the risk and expense of delivering the goods to the carrier, but the seller is not responsible for delivering the goods to a specific destination. If the term is "FOB vessel, car, or other vehicle," the seller must load the goods on board at his own risk and expense [2–319(1)].

2. *FAS (free alongside ship).* This term is commonly used in maritime contracts and is normally accompanied by the name of a specific vessel and port—for example, "FAS Calgary [the ship], Chicago Port Authority." The seller must deliver the goods alongside the vessel *Calgary* at the Chicago Port Authority at his own risk and expense [2–319(2)].

3. *CIF (cost, insurance, and freight).* This term means that the price of the goods includes the cost of shipping and insuring them. The seller bears this expense and the risk of loading the goods [2–320].

4. *C & F.* This term is the same as CIF, except that the seller is not obligated to insure the goods [2–320].

The *Windows, Inc.* case, which follows, provides an example of the risk borne by a buyer in a shipment contract.

Windows, Inc. v. Jordan Panel Systems Corp.
38 UCC Rep.2d 267 (2nd Cir. 1999)

Windows, Inc., was a fabricator and seller of windows, based in South Dakota. Jordan Panel Systems, Inc., was a construction subcontractor, which contracted to install window wall panels at an air cargo facility at John F. Kennedy Airport in New York City. Jordan ordered custom-made windows from Windows. The purchase contract specified that the windows were to be shipped properly packaged for cross-country motor freight transit and "delivered to New York City."

Windows constructed the windows according to Jordan's specifications. It arranged to have them shipped to Jordan by a common carrier, Consolidated Freightways Corp., and delivered them to Consolidated intact and properly packaged. During the course of shipment, however, the goods sustained extensive damage. Much of the glass was broken and many of the window frames were gouged and twisted. Jordan's president signed a delivery receipt noting that approximately two-thirds of the shipment was damaged due to "load shift." Jordan, seeking to stay on its contractor's schedule, directed its employees to disassemble the window frames in an effort to salvage as much of the shipment as possible.

Jordan made a claim with Consolidated for damages it had sustained as a result of the casualty, including labor costs from its salvage efforts and other costs from Jordan's inability to perform its own contractual obligations on schedule. Jordan also ordered a new shipment from Windows, which was delivered without incident.

Jordan did not pay Windows for either the first shipment of damaged windows or the second, intact shipment. Windows filed suit to recover payment from Jordan for both shipments. Jordan counterclaimed, seeking incidental and consequential damages resulting from the damaged shipment. Windows then brought a third party claim against Consolidated. Windows settled its claims against Consolidated, and Windows later withdrew its claims against Jordan.

*   The district court granted Windows' motion for summary judgment on Jordan's counterclaim against Windows for incidental and consequential damages. Jordan appealed.*

Leval, Circuit Judge   Jordan seeks to recover incidental and consequential damages pursuant to UCC section 2–715. Under that provision, Jordan's entitlement to recover incidental and consequential damages depends on whether those damages "result[ed] from the seller's breach." A destination contract is covered by section 2–503(3); it arises where "the seller is *required to deliver* at a particular destination." Section 2–504 (emphasis added). Under a shipment contract, the seller must "put the goods in the possession of such a carrier and make such a contract for their transportation as may be reasonable having regard to the nature of the goods and other circumstances of the case." Section 2–504(a).

    Where the terms of an agreement are ambiguous, there is a strong presumption under the UCC favoring shipment contracts. Unless the parties "expressly specify" that the contract requires the seller to deliver to a particular destination, the contract is generally construed as one for shipment.

    Jordan's confirmation of its purchase order, by letter to Windows dated September 22, 1993, provided, "All windows to be shipped properly crated/packaged/boxed suitable for cross-country motor freight transit and delivered to New York City." We conclude that this was a shipment contract rather than a destination contract.

    To overcome the presumption favoring shipment contracts, the parties must have explicitly agreed to impose on Windows the obligation to effect delivery at a particular destination. The language of this contract does not do so. Nor did Jordan use any commonly recognized industry term indicating that a seller is obligated to deliver the goods to the buyer's specified destination.

    Given the strong presumption favoring shipment contracts and the absence of explicit terms satisfying both requirements for a destination contract, we conclude that the contract should be deemed a shipment contract.

    Under the terms of its contract, Windows thus satisfied its obligations to Jordan when it put the goods, properly packaged, into the possession of the carrier for shipment. Upon Windows' proper delivery to the carrier, Jordan assumed the risk of loss, and cannot recover incidental or consequential damages from the seller caused by the carrier's negligence.

    The allocation of risk is confirmed by the terms of UCC section 2–509(1)(a), entitled "Risk of Loss in the Absence of Breach." It provides that where the contract "does not require [the seller] to deliver [the goods] at a particular destination, the risk of loss passes to the buyer when the goods are duly delivered to the carrier." UCC section 2–509(1)(a). As noted earlier, Jordan does not contest the court's finding that Windows duly delivered conforming goods to the carrier. Accordingly, as Windows had already fulfilled its contractual obligations at the time the goods were damaged and Jordan had assumed the risk of loss, there was no "seller's breach" as is required for a buyer to claim incidental and consequential damages under section 2–715. Summary judgment for Windows was therefore proper.

    We are mindful of Jordan's concern that it not be left "holding the bag" for the damages it sustained through no fault of its own. The fact that Jordan had assumed the risk of loss under section 2–509(1)(a) by the time the goods were damaged does not mean it is without a remedy. Under the 1906 Carmack Amendment to the Interstate Commerce Act, a buyer or seller has long been able to recover directly from an interstate common carrier in whose care their goods are damaged. Liability attaches unless the carrier can establish one of several affirmative defenses; for example, by showing that the damage was the fault of the shipper or caused by an Act of God.

Judgment affirmed in favor of Windows.

Destination Contracts

If the contract requires the seller to deliver the goods to a specific destination, the seller bears the risk and expense of delivery to that destination [2–509(1)(b)]. The following are commonly used shipping terms that create destination contracts:

1. *FOB destination.* An FOB term coupled with the place of destination of the goods puts the expense and risk of delivering the goods to that destination on the seller [2–319(1)(b)]. For example, a contract between a seller in Chicago and a buyer in Phoenix might call for shipment FOB Phoenix. The seller must ship the goods to Phoenix at her own expense,

and she also retains the risk of delivery of the goods to Phoenix.

2. *Ex-ship.* This term does not specify a particular ship, but it places the expense and risk on the seller until the goods are unloaded from whatever ship is used [2–322].

3. *No arrival, no sale.* This term places the expense and risk during shipment on the seller. If the goods fail to arrive through no fault of the seller, the seller has no further liability to the buyer [2–324].

For example, a Chicago-based seller contracts to sell a quantity of shirts to a buyer FOB Phoenix, the buyer's place of business. The shirts are destroyed en route when the truck carrying the shirts is involved in an accident. The risk of the loss of the shirts is on the seller, and the buyer is not obligated to pay for them. The seller may have the right to recover from the trucking company, but between the seller and the buyer, the seller has the risk of loss. If the contract had called for delivery FOB the seller's manufacturing plant, then the risk of loss would have been on the buyer. The buyer would have had to pay for the shirts and then pursue any claims that he had against the trucking company.

Goods in the Possession of Third Parties

If the goods are in the possession of a bailee and are to be delivered without being moved, the risk of loss passes to the buyer upon delivery to him of a negotiable document of title for the goods; if no negotiable document of title has been used, the risk of loss passes when the bailee indicates to the buyer that the buyer has the right to the possession of the goods [2–509(2)]. For example, if Farmer sells Miller a quantity of grain currently stored at Grain Elevator, the risk of loss of the grain will shift from Farmer to Miller (1) when a negotiable warehouse receipt for the grain is delivered to Miller or (2) when Grain Elevator notifies Miller that it is holding the grain for Miller.

Risk Generally

If the transaction does not fall within the situations discussed above, the risk of loss passes to the buyer upon *receipt* of the goods if the seller is a merchant; if the seller is not a merchant, then the risk of loss passes to the buyer upon the *tender of delivery* of the goods to the buyer [2–509(3)]. If Jones bought a television set from ABC Appliance on Monday, intending to pick it up on Thursday, and the set was stolen on Wednesday, the risk of loss

remained with ABC. However, if Jones had purchased the set from his next-door neighbor and could have taken delivery of the set on Monday (i.e., delivery was tendered then), the risk of loss was Jones's.

Effect of Breach on Risk of Loss

When a seller tenders goods that do not conform to the contract and the buyer has the right to reject the goods, the risk of loss remains with the seller until any defect is cured or until the buyer accepts the goods [2–510(1)]. Where the buyer rightfully revokes his acceptance of goods, the risk of loss is with the seller to the extent that any loss is not covered by the buyer's insurance [2–510(2)]. This rule gives the seller the benefit of any insurance carried by the buyer.

For example, if Adler bought a new Buick from Brown Buick that he later returned to Brown because of serious defects in it and if through no fault of Adler the automobile was damaged while in his possession, then the risk of loss would be with Brown. However, if Adler had insurance on the automobile covering the damage to it and recovered from the insurance company, Adler would have to turn the insurance proceeds over to Brown or use them to fix the car before returning it to Brown.

When a buyer repudiates a contract for goods and those goods have already been set aside by the seller, the risk of loss stays with the buyer for a commercially reasonable time after the repudiation if the seller's insurance is not sufficient to cover any loss [2–510(3)]. Suppose Cannery contracts to buy Farmer's entire crop of peaches. Farmer picks the peaches, crates them, tenders delivery to Cannery, and stores them in his barn. Cannery then tells Farmer that it does not intend to honor the contract. Shortly thereafter, but before Farmer has a chance to find another buyer, the peaches are spoiled by a fire. If Farmer's insurance covers only part of the loss, Cannery must bear the rest of the loss.

Insurable Interest

The general practice of insuring risks is recognized and provided for under the Code. A buyer may protect his interest in goods that are the subject matter of a sales contract before he actually obtains title. The buyer obtains an insurable interest in existing goods when they are identified as the goods covered by the contract even though they are in fact nonconforming. The seller retains an insurable interest in goods so long as he has either title or a security interest in them [2–501(2)].

Risk of Loss

The point at which the risk of loss or damage to goods identified to a contract passes to the buyer is as follows:

1. If there is an agreement between the parties, the risk of loss passes to the buyer at the time they have agreed to.

2. If the contract requires the seller to ship the goods by carrier but does not require that the seller guarantee their delivery to a specific destination (shipment contract), the risk of loss passes to the buyer when the seller has delivered the goods to the carrier and made an appropriate contract for their carriage.

3. If the contract requires the seller to guarantee delivery of the goods to a specific destination (destination contract), the risk of loss passes to the buyer when the seller delivers the goods to the designated destination.

4. If the goods are in the hands of a third person and the contract calls for delivery without moving the goods, the risk of loss passes to the buyer when the buyer has the power to take possession of the goods—for example, when he receives a document of title.

5. In any situation other than those noted above where the seller is a merchant, the risk of loss passes to the buyer on his receipt of the goods.

6. In any situation other than those noted above where the seller is not a merchant, the risk of loss passes to the buyer on the tender of delivery to the buyer by the seller.

7. When a seller tenders goods that the buyer lawfully could reject because they do not conform to the contract description, the risk of loss stays on the seller until the defect is cured or the buyer accepts them.

8. When a buyer rightfully revokes acceptance of goods, the risk of loss is on the seller from the beginning to the extent it is not covered by the buyer's insurance.

9. If a buyer repudiates a contract for identified, conforming goods before risk of loss has passed to the buyer, the buyer is liable for a commercially reasonable time for any loss or damage to the goods that is not covered by the seller's insurance.

Sales on Trial

A common commercial practice is for a seller of goods to entrust possession of goods to a buyer to either give the buyer an opportunity to decide whether or not to buy them or to try to resell them to a third person. The entrusting may be known as a **sale on approval,** a **sale or return,** or a **consignment,** depending on the terms of the entrusting. Occasionally, the goods may be damaged, destroyed, or stolen, or the creditors of the buyer may try to claim them; on such occasions, the form of the entrusting will determine whether the buyer or the seller had the risk of loss and whether the buyer's creditors can successfully claim the goods.

Sale on Approval

In a sale on approval, the goods are delivered to the buyer with an understanding that he may use or test them for the purpose of determining whether he wishes to buy them [2–326(1)(a)]. In a sale on approval, neither the risk of loss nor title to the goods passes to the buyer until he accepts the goods. The buyer has the right to use the goods in any manner consistent with the purpose of the trial, but any unwarranted exercise of ownership over the goods is considered to be an acceptance of the goods. Similarly, if the buyer fails to notify the seller of his election to return the goods, he is considered to have accepted them [2–327]. For example, if Dealer agrees to let Hughes take a new automobile home to drive for a day to see whether she wants to buy it and Hughes takes the car on a two-week vacation trip, Hughes will be considered to have accepted the automobile because she used it in a manner beyond that contemplated by the trial and as if she were its owner. If Hughes had driven the automobile for a day, decided not to buy it, and parked it in her driveway for two weeks without telling Dealer of her intention to return it, Hughes would also be deemed to have accepted the automobile.

Once the buyer has notified the seller of his election to return the goods, the return of the goods is at the seller's expense and risk. Because the title and risk of

THE GLOBAL BUSINESS ENVIRONMENT

Risk of Loss in International Sales

Risk of loss is an important concept in the sale of goods—and takes on additional significance in international sales because of the substantial distances and multiple modes of transportation that may be involved. Between the time a contract is formed and the time the obligations of the parties are completed, the goods that are the subject of the contract may be lost, damaged, or stolen. Both the UCC and the Convention on Contracts for International Sale of Goods (CISG) explicitly address risk of loss in four different situations: (1) where goods are being held by the seller; (2) where goods are being held by a third person or bailee; (3) where goods are in transit; and (4) where goods are in the control of the buyer. Moreover, the CISG deals with risk of loss where goods have been sold or resold while in transit. Under both the UCC and the CISG, breach by a party may alter the basic rules regarding risk of loss.

Before discussing the CISG provisions, it is important to note that the definitions of some terms in the UCC differ from the meaning those terms may have in international trade. The International Chamber of Commerce has compiled a list of widely accepted international shipping terms in a document known as "INCOTERMS." The most recent version, INCOTERMS 2000, includes 13 different terms that are placed in four different categories, depending on the seller's responsibilities concerning the goods.

Under the first category (known as Group "E"), the seller's obligation is only to make the goods available to the buyer at the seller's place of business. This is referred to as an EXW, or EX Works, term. Risk passes from the seller to the buyer when the goods are placed at the buyer's disposal. Under the second category (known as Group "F"), the seller is required to deliver the goods to a carrier designated by the buyer. This category includes terms like "F.O.B." (Free on Board) and "F.A.S" (Free Along Side Ship). Passage of risk varies with the term.

Terms in the third category (Group "C") require the seller to contract for carriage of the goods but not to assume the risk of loss after shipment. Terms in the fourth category (Group "D") impose on the seller the costs and risks of bringing the goods to the country of destination. Under one such term, "D.A.F." (Delivered at Frontier), the seller must pay for the carriage of goods to some defined point after that where goods have been cleared for export in the country of origin but before the customs boundary of another identified, usually adjoining, country.

The CISG, like the UCC, provides a set of default rules governing risk of loss where the parties do not explicitly address risk of loss in their contract. However, it also permits parties to contract out of those rules. Parties to international agreements commonly utilize the INCOTERMS and incorporate them into contracts otherwise governed by the CISG. Thus, the INCOTERMS are used to define when risk of loss passes, and CISG, in turn, provides the legal consequences of the passage of the risk of loss in a particular case.

---

loss of goods delivered on a sale on approval remain with the seller, goods held on approval are not subject to the claims of the buyer's creditors until the buyer accepts them [2–326].

Sale or Return

In a sale or return, goods are delivered to a buyer for resale with the understanding that the buyer has the right to return them [2–326(1)(b)]. Under a sale or return, the title and risk of loss are with the buyer. While the goods are in the buyer's possession, they are subject to the claims of his creditors [2–326 and 2–327]. For example, if Publisher delivers some paperbacks to Bookstore on the understanding that Bookstore may return any of the paperbacks that remain unsold at the end of six months, the transaction is a sale or return. If Bookstore is destroyed by a fire, the risk of loss of the paperbacks was Bookstore's and it is responsible to Publisher for the purchase price. Similarly, if Bookstore becomes insolvent

and is declared a bankrupt, the paperbacks will be considered part of the bankruptcy estate. If the buyer elects to return goods held on a sale or return basis, the return is at the buyer's risk and expense.

Sale on Consignment

Sometimes, goods are delivered to a merchant on consignment. If the merchant to whom goods are consigned maintains a place of business dealing in goods of that kind under a name other than that of the person consigning the goods, then the consignor must take certain steps to protect his interest in the goods or they will be subject to the claims of the merchant's creditors. The consignor must (1) make sure that a sign indicating the consignor's interest is prominently posted at the place of business, or (2) make sure that the merchant's creditors know that he is generally in the business of selling goods owned by others, or (3) comply with the filing provisions of Article 9 of the Code—Secured Transactions.

For example, Jones operates a retail music store under the name of City Music Store. Baldwin Piano Company delivers some pianos to Jones on consignment. If no notices are posted indicating Baldwin's interest in the pianos, if Jones is not generally known to be selling from a consigned inventory, and if Baldwin does not file its interest with the recording office pursuant to Article 9 of the Code, then the goods are subject to the claims of Jones's creditors. This is crucial to Baldwin because it may have intended to retain title. However, the Code treats a consignment to a person doing business under a name other than that of the consignor as a "sale or return" [2–326(3)]. If Jones did business as the Baldwin Piano Company, Baldwin's interest would be protected from the claims of Jones's creditors without the need for Baldwin to post a sign or to file under Article 9.

The case that follows, *In Re Auclair,* illustrates the risks borne by a person who makes goods available on a sale or return or consignment basis.

In Re Auclair: Mc Gregor v. Jackson   *131 BR 185 (Bankr, MD Mass. 1991)*

Edd and Diane Auclair maintained a place of business in Covington County, Alabama, where they operated a gun shop and convenience store named Heath Grocery and Final Chapter Firearms. In November 1989, Luke Jackson delivered about 70 firearms to the Auclairs to sell on consignment. The consignment agreement provided as follows:

I Edd Auclair have received a number of guns, of which a list will be attached and I will sign. As I sell a gun I will pay James E. "Luke" Jackson or Betty King with them giving me a receipt for that particular gun. If something should happen to Luke Jackson the guns are to be returned to Betty King or at that time Betty King and Edd Auclair can enter into an agreement. If something should happen to Edd Auclair, Diane agrees to return all guns that have not been paid for to Luke Jackson or Betty King and pay for any that has [sic] been sold.

The agreement was signed by Jackson, King and the Auclairs.

On June 28, 1990, the Auclairs filed a petition in bankruptcy under Chapter 11 of the Bankruptcy Act. Shortly thereafter, Jackson removed the firearms he had consigned from the Auclairs' store. The bankruptcy trustee representing the Auclairs' creditors claimed that the firearms were the property of the bankruptcy estate.

Gordon, Bankruptcy Judge Both parties agree that section 2–326(3) regarding consignments applies to the facts of this case. Under that subsection, goods delivered on consignment are "deemed to be on sale or return." Thus, by deeming the consignee a purchaser of the goods, the consignor is precluded from asserting an ownership claim to the goods vis-a-vis the consignee's creditors.

Applying that section to the instant case, Jackson is precluded from asserting his ownership of the firearms vis-a-vis the trustee. However, the subsection is not applicable to a consignor who—

(a) Complies with an applicable law providing for a consignor's interest or the like to be evidenced by a sign, or
(b) Establishes that the person conducting the business is generally known by his creditors to be substantially engaged in selling the goods of others, or
(c) Complies with the filing provisions of the article on secured transactions (Article 9)." Section 2–326(3).

Jackson is not protected under (a) because Alabama does not have a sign law applicable to consignments. Jackson is not protected under (c) because he did not comply with the filing provisions of Article 9.

Jackson contends, but has failed to prove, that he is protected under (b). The evidence does not reflect that the debtors were "generally known by [their] creditors to be substantially engaged in selling the goods of others."

Jackson admitted that he did not notify any of the Auclairs' creditors that the firearms were placed with the Auclairs on consignment. The evidence reveals, *at best,* that only one of the Auclairs' 18 creditors had knowledge of the consignment. The court concludes that the debtors were not "generally known by [their] creditors to be substantially engaged in selling" consigned firearms.

The court holds that the firearms in question are property of this bankruptcy estate which the trustee may sell. A separate order will be entered requiring Jackson to deliver the firearms to the trustee and to account for such property or its value. Jackson will have an unsecured claim for the value of the property returned to the trustee, for which he may file a proof of claim in this case.

Judgment in favor of bankruptcy estate and against Jackson.

Problems and Problem Cases

1. Mr. and Mrs. Abelman engaged the Capitol Termite and Pest Control Company to treat their home for a termite infestation. The chemical used by Capitol was Gold Crest Termite manufactured by Velsicol Chemical Corporation. Velsicol sold the Gold Crest Termite to a distributor, which in turn sold it to Capitol in bulk—in 55-gallon drums. Capitol did not specifically buy materials for each termite job. One 55-gallon drum would service many homes. Employees of Capitol pumped the chemical from the 55-gallon drums into a 5-gallon pail at Capitol's premises. The solution was then poured from the 5-gallon pail into a 1-gallon pail, which they filled half full. Next, the half-gallon of Gold Crest Termite was poured into a fixed 50-gallon tank on the back of Capitol's trucks and then the tank was filled to capacity with water. This solution was then applied to the Abelman's residence by employees of Capitol. The Abelmans abandoned their home the day after Capitol completed treatment. Three years later they brought suit against Capitol and Velsicol contending that the termiticide had caused personal injuries and property damages. Among other things, they claimed there was a breach of express and implied warranties provided by the Uniform Commercial Code (discussed in Chapter 20). Velsicol and Capitol sought to dismiss these claims on the ground that there had not been a sale of goods and thus no warranties had arisen. Was the contract to obtain treatment for termites a sale of goods under the Uniform Commercial Code?

2. Keith Russell, a boat dealer, contracted to sell a 19-foot Kinsvater boat to Robert Clouser for $8,500. The agreement stipulated that Clouser was to make a down payment of $1,700, with the balance due when he took possession of the boat. According to the contract, Russell was to retain possession of the boat in order to install a new engine and drive train. While the boat was still in Russell's possession, it was completely destroyed when it struck a seawall. Transamerica, Russell's insurance company, refused to honor Russell's claim for the damages to the boat. The insurance policy between Transamerica and Russell covered only watercraft under 26 feet in length that were not owned by Russell. Transamerica argued that the boat was not covered by the policy since Russell still owned it at the time of the accident. Did Russell have title to the boat at the time of the accident?

3. Club Pro Golf Products was a distributor of golf products. It employed salesmen who called on customers to take orders for merchandise. The merchandise was sent by Club Pro directly to the purchaser and payment was made by the purchaser directly to Club Pro. A salesman for Club Pro, Carl Gude, transmitted orders for certain merchandise to Club Pro for delivery to several fictitious purchasers. Club Pro sent the merchandise to the fictitious purchasers at the fictitious addresses where it was picked up by Gude. Gude then sold the merchandise, worth approximately $19,000, directly to Simpson, a golf pro at a golf club. Gude then retained the proceeds of sale for himself. Club Pro discovered the fraud and brought suit against Simpson to recover the merchandise. Did Simpson get good title to the merchandise he purchased from Gude even though Gude had obtained it by fraud?

4. Shaker Valley Auto & Tire purchased a pickup truck at an auction and brought the vehicle for service to Fred Madore Chevrolet-Pontiac-Oldsmobile, an automobile dealership that sells and services vehicles. A few weeks later, Madore sold the truck to Winston Titus. Titus was unaware of Shaker Valley's ownership of the vehicle. In a subsequent court proceeding, both Titus and Shaker Valley claimed valid title to the truck. Shaker Valley argued that it never authorized the sale of the vehicle and that Madore had no title to transfer to Titus because Shaker Valley never transferred title to Madore. Does Titus have good title to the truck under the Code?

5. Legendary Homes, a home builder, purchased various appliances from Ron Mead T.V. & Appliance, a retail merchant selling home appliances. They were intended to be installed in one of Legendary Homes's houses and were to be delivered on February 1. At 5 o'clock on that day, the appliances had not been delivered. Legendary Homes's employees closed the home and left. Sometime between 5 and 6:30, Ron Mead delivered the appliances. No one was at the home so the deliveryman put the appliances in the garage. During the night, someone stole the appliances. Legendary Homes denied it was responsible for the loss and refused to pay Ron Mead for the appliances. Ron Mead then brought suit for the purchase price. Did Legendary Homes have the risk of loss of the appliances?

6. The Cedar Rapids YMCA bought a large number of cases of candy from Seaway Candy under an agreement by which any unused portion could be returned. The YMCA was to sell the candy to raise money to send boys to camp. The campaign was less than successful, and 688 cases remained unsold. They were returned to Seaway Candy by truck. When delivered to the common carrier, the candy was in good condition; when it arrived at Seaway four days later, it had melted and was completely

worthless. Seaway then brought suit against the YMCA to recover the purchase price of the candy spoiled in transit. Between Seaway and the YMCA, which had the risk of loss?

7. Richard Burnett agreed to purchase a mobile home with a shed from Betty Jean Putrell, Executrix of the Estate of Lena Holland. On Saturday, March 3, 1990, Burnett paid Putrell $6,500 and was given the certificate of title to the mobile home as well as a key to it, but no keys to the shed. At the time the certificate of title was transferred, the following items remained in the mobile home: the washer and dryer, mattress and box springs, two chairs, items in the refrigerator, and the entire contents of the shed. These items were to be retained by Putrell and removed by her. To facilitate removal she retained one key to the mobile home and the only keys to the shed. On Sunday, March 4, the mobile home was destroyed by fire through the fault of neither party. At the time of the fire, Putrell still had a key to the mobile home as well as the keys to the shed and she had not removed the contents of the mobile home or of the shed. The contents of the shed were not destroyed and were subsequently removed by Putrell. Burnett brought suit against Putrell to recover the $6,500 he had paid for the mobile home and shed. Did the seller, Putrell, have the risk of loss of the trailer?

8. Collier, a retail store operator, accepted a delivery of stereo tapes, cartridges, and equipment from B & B Sales. The invoice noted that the goods had been "sold to" Collier and stated: "Terms 30-60-90; this equipment will be picked up if not sold in 90 days." Shortly thereafter, Collier's store was burglarized and all the merchandise was stolen. B & B filed suit against Collier for the purchase price of the merchandise, claiming that the transaction was a sale and that Collier was liable to pay for the merchandise. Collier argued that the transaction was a consignment and that B & B had the risk of loss. Did Collier or B & B have the risk of loss of the merchandise?

Online Research: Using the Internet to Buy a Computer

Assume you are considering the purchase of a new computer. Use the Internet to access the website of the manufacturer of the computer you are considering. Ascertain the following: (1) the purchase price of the model you prefer; (2) the cost of having the computer shipped to you; (3) the warranties, if any, that will be provided; and (4) whether you would be able to get a full refund if you do not find the computer acceptable after it is delivered to you.

PRODUCT LIABILITY

A General Motors pickup truck driven by Paul Babcock went off the road and struck a tree. The accident rendered Mr. Babcock a paraplegic. Roughly a year later, he died as a result of complications from his injuries. The executor of his estate, Frances Babcock, sued General Motors (GM) on behalf of the estate and herself.

According to the plaintiff's version of the facts, Mr. Babcock was wearing his seat belt prior to the accident but as soon as pressure was exerted on it, the belt unbuckled and released because of a condition known as "false latching." The plaintiff claimed that the false-latching condition existed because of negligent design and/or negligent testing by GM of the seat belt mechanism, that the resulting failure of the seat belt in Mr. Babcock's pickup was a substantial factor in causing Mr. Babcock's severe—and ultimately fatal—injuries, and that a properly functioning seat belt would have protected Mr. Babcock against the injuries he sustained.

There was no direct evidence that Mr. Babcock was wearing his seat belt immediately prior to the accident. It was undisputed that when he was first seen after the accident, his seat belt was not fastened around him. The evidence showed that Mr. Babcock was covered with blood and that there was blood on the interior of the cab of the truck, but that no blood was on the seat belt straps. The plaintiff, however, offered evidence that Mr. Babcock always wore a seat belt when he drove a motor vehicle. Over GM's objection, the trial judge ruled that such "habit" evidence would be allowed and that the question of whether Mr. Babcock was wearing a seat belt at the time of the accident was for the jury. Mr. Babcock's brother, a neighbor, and a longtime friend all testified that they had ridden numerous times in a vehicle with Mr. Babcock and that he always wore his seat belt regardless of whether he was driving the vehicle or was a passenger.

Dr. Malcolm Newman testified as an expert witness for the plaintiff. He was a structural and mechanical engineering specialist with significant involvement in accident reconstruction and analysis of automobile restraint systems. Employing a method used by accident reconstruction specialists, Dr. Newman reviewed photos and other materials given to him and formed opinions as to how fast Mr. Babcock's pickup was traveling when it left the highway and when it hit the tree. He testified that in his opinion, the "impact" speed was between 20 and 25 miles per hour and that the Babcock truck had been traveling at 35 to 45 miles per hour at the time it left the highway. Dr. Newman also opined that at an impact speed of 25 miles per hour, a properly belted occupant would be fully protected by the seat belt. Therefore, Dr. Newman observed, either Mr. Babcock was not wearing his seat belt or the seat belt was defective. From examining the seat belt found in the cab of the truck, Dr. Newman concluded that it had been used just prior to impact.

Dr. Newman testified that in his opinion, Mr. Babcock's seat belt unbuckled because of false latching. With the aid of photos, the seat belt found in the cab of Mr. Babcock's truck, and a similar seat belt, Dr. Newman demonstrated how false latching can occur. When it occurs, the occupant thinks that the belt is fully latched but in reality, it is not. Moreover, according to Dr. Newman, both falsely latched and fully latched seat belts trigger the same signals in the vehicle concerning whether the seat belt is in use. Dr. Newman characterized a false-latching propensity as a design defect. He testified that in view of the design of a GM buckle, continued use of the buckle increases the danger of false latching. Using a Volvo seat belt buckle, he demonstrated that the Volvo design eliminated the risk that false latching would occur. Dr. Newman noted that the buckle on the GM truck evidently had been tested pursuant to the Federal Motor Vehicle Safety Standards. He concluded that the GM buckle could develop false latching as a result of normal wear and tear, and offered the view that any testing done by GM had not included testing for false latching.

After the jury returned a verdict holding GM liable on the plaintiff's negligence claim, GM appealed. Consider these questions as you study Chapter 20:

• May GM be held liable even though nothing it did or failed to do caused Mr. Babcock's truck to leave the highway and strike a tree?

• Did the trial judge rule appropriately in allowing the plaintiff to present "habit" evidence and opinion evidence on key issues in this product liability case?

• Did the plaintiff sufficiently prove what was necessary to establish negligent design and/or negligent testing on the part of GM?

• Were there any other legal theories on which the plaintiff might have relied in this case?

SUPPOSE YOU HOLD AN executive position in a firm that makes products for sale to the public. One of your concerns would be the company's exposure to civil liability for defects in those products. In particular, you might worry about legal developments that make such liability more likely or more expensive. In other situations, however, such developments might appeal to you—especially if *you* are harmed by defective products you purchase as a consumer. You might also appreciate certain liability-imposing legal theories if your firm wants to sue a supplier that has sold it defective products.

Each of these situations involves the law of *product liability,* the body of legal rules governing civil lawsuits for losses and harms resulting from a defendant's furnishing of defective goods. After sketching product liability law's historical evolution, this chapter discusses the most important *theories of product liability* on which plaintiffs rely. The second part of the chapter considers certain legal problems that may be resolved differently under different theories of recovery.

The Evolution of Product Liability Law
The 19th Century

A century or so ago, the rules governing suits for defective goods were very much to manufacturers' and other sellers' advantage. This was the era of *caveat emptor* (let the buyer beware). In contract cases involving defective goods, there usually was no liability unless the seller had made an express promise to the buyer and the goods did not conform to that promise. In negligence cases, the "no liability without fault" principle was widely accepted, and plaintiffs often had difficulty proving negligence because the necessary evidence was under the defendant's control. In both contract and negligence cases, finally, the doctrine of "no liability outside privity of contract"— that is, no liability without a direct contractual relationship between plaintiff and defendant—often prevented plaintiffs from recovering against parties with whom they had not directly dealt.

One reason for these prodefendant rules was the laissez-faire approach that influenced public policy and the law. One illustration of that approach was the notion that manufacturers and other sellers should be contractually bound only when they deliberately assumed such liability by making a promise to someone with whom they dealt directly. Another factor limiting manufacturers' liability for defective products was the perceived importance of promoting industrialization by preventing potentially crippling damage recoveries against infant industries. Another view of the 19th century's approach to product liability is that most plaintiffs were not especially disadvantaged by the applicable legal rules. Goods tended to be simple, so buyers often could inspect them for defects. Before the emergence of large corporations late in the 19th century, moreover, sellers and buyers often were of relatively equal size, sophistication, and bargaining power. Thus, they could deal on a relatively equal footing.

The 20th Century

Today, laissez-faire values, while still influential, do not pack the weight they once did. With the development of a viable industrial economy, there has been less perceived need to protect manufacturers from liability for defective goods. The emergence of long chains of distribution has meant that consumers often do not deal directly with the parties responsible for defects in the products they buy. Because large corporations tend to dominate the economy, consumers are less able to bargain freely with the corporate sellers with which they deal. Finally, the growing complexity of goods has made buyers' inspections of the goods more difficult.

In response to these changes, product liability law has moved from its earlier *caveat emptor* emphasis to a stance of *caveat venditor* (let the seller beware). To protect consumers, modern courts and legislatures effectively intervene in private contracts for the sale of goods and sometimes impose liability regardless of fault. As a result, sellers and manufacturers face greater liability and higher damage assessments for defects in their products. Underlying the shift toward *caveat venditor* is the belief that sellers, manufacturers, and their insurers are better able to bear the economic costs associated with product defects, and that they usually can pass on these costs through higher prices. Thus, the economic risk associated with defective products has been effectively spread throughout society, or "socialized."

The Current Debate over Product Liability Law

Modern product liability law and its socialization-of-risk rationale have come under increasing attack over the past two decades. Such attacks often focus on the difficulty sellers and manufacturers encounter in obtaining product liability insurance and the increased costs of such insurance. Some observers blame insurance industry practices for these developments, whereas others trace them to the increased liability and greater damage recoveries just discussed. Whatever their origin, these problems have sometimes put sellers and manufacturers in a difficult spot. Businesses unwilling or unable to buy expensive product liability insurance run the risk of being crippled by large damage awards unless they self-insure, which can be an expensive option today. Firms that purchase insurance, on the other hand, often must pay higher prices for it. In either case, the resulting costs may be difficult to pass on to consumers. In addition, those costs may deter the development and marketing of innovative new products.

For these reasons and others, recent years have witnessed many efforts to scale back the pro-plaintiff aspects of modern product liability law. This is one aspect of the tort reform movement discussed in Chapter 7. However, despite the introduction of various federal reform bills, Congress has yet to make significant changes in product liability law. As we note later in this chapter, however, some tort reform efforts have occurred in the states.

Theories of Product Liability Recovery

Some theories of product liability recovery are contractual and some are tort-based. The contract theories involve a product **warranty**—a promise about the nature of the product sold. In warranty cases, plaintiffs claim that the product failed to live up to the seller's promise. In tort cases, on the other hand, plaintiffs usually argue that the defendant was negligent or that strict liability should apply.

Express Warranty

Creation of an Express Warranty UCC section 2–313(1) states that an **express warranty** may be created in any of three ways.

1. *If an affirmation of fact or promise* regarding the goods becomes part of the basis of the bargain (a requirement to be discussed shortly), there is an express warranty that the goods will conform to the affirmation or promise. For instance, if a computer manufacturer's web site says that a computer has a certain amount of memory, this statement may create an express warranty to that effect.

2. Any *description* of the goods that becomes part of the basis of the bargain creates an express warranty that the goods will conform to the description. Descriptions include: (1) statements that goods are of a certain brand, type, or model (e.g., a Hewlett-Packard laser printer); (2) adjectives that characterize the product (e.g., shatterproof glass); and (3) drawings, blueprints, and technical specifications.

3. Assuming it becomes part of the basis of the bargain, a *sample* or *model* of goods to be sold creates an express warranty that the goods will conform to the sample or model. A sample is an object drawn from an actual collection of goods to be sold, whereas a model is a replica offered for the buyer's inspection when the goods themselves are unavailable.

The first two types of express warranties may often overlap; also, each may be either written or oral. "Magic" words such as *warrant* or *guarantee* are not necessary for creation of an express warranty.

Value, Opinion, and Sales Talk Statements of *value* ("This chair would bring you $2,000 at an auction") or *opinion* ("I think that this chair is an antique") do not create an express warranty. The same is true of statements that amount to *sales talk* or *puffery* ("This chair is a good buy"). No sharp line separates such statements from express warranties. In close cases, a statement is more likely to be an express warranty if it is specific rather than indefinite, if it is stated in the sales contract rather than elsewhere,[1] or if it is unequivocal rather than hedged or qualified. The relative knowledge possessed by the seller and the buyer also matters. For instance, a car salesperson's statement about a used car may be more likely to be an express warranty where the buyer knows little about

cars than where the buyer is another car dealer. The *Felley* case, which follows shortly, discusses some of the express warranty issues addressed so far, as well as the important basis-of-the-bargain requirement to which we now turn.

The Basis-of-the-Bargain Requirement Under pre-UCC law, there was no recovery for breach of an express warranty unless the buyer significantly relied on that warranty in making the purchase. The UCC, however, requires—though ambiguously—that the affirmation, promise, description, or sample or model have become *part of the basis of the bargain* in order for an express warranty to be created. Some courts read the Code's basis-of-the-bargain test as saying that significant reliance still is necessary. Others require only that the seller's warranty have been a *contributing factor* in the buyer's decision to purchase. Still others do not require any specific reliance on the buyer's part.

Advertisements Statements made in advertisements, catalogs, or brochures may be express warranties. However, such sources often are filled with sales talk. Basis-of-the-bargain problems may arise if it is unclear whether or to what degree the statement induced the buyer to make the purchase. For example, suppose that the buyer read an advertisement containing a supposed express warranty one month before actually purchasing the product.

Multiple Express Warranties What happens when a seller gives two or more express warranties and those warranties arguably conflict? UCC section 2–317 says that such warranties should be read as consistent with each other and as cumulative if this is reasonable. If not, the parties' intention controls. In determining that intention: (1) exact or technical specifications defeat a sample, a model, or general descriptive language; and (2) a sample defeats general descriptive language.

As indicated by the *Felley* case, which follows, any seller—professional or not—may make an express warranty. When such a warranty has been breached (because the goods were not as warranted), the plaintiff who demonstrates resulting losses is entitled to compensatory damages.

---

[1]Parol evidence rule problems may arise in express warranty cases. For example, a seller who used a written contract may argue that the rule excludes an alleged oral warranty. On the parol evidence rule, see Chapter 16.

Felley v. Singleton   705 N.E.2d 930 (Ill. App. 1999)

On June 8, 1997, Brian Felley went to the home of Thomas and Cheryl Singleton to look at a used car that the Singletons had offered for sale. The car, a 1991 Ford Taurus, had approximately 126,000 miles on it. Felley test-drove the car and discussed its condition with the Singletons. The Singletons told him that the car was in "good mechanical condition" and that they had experienced no brake problems. This was a primary consideration for Felley, who purchased the car from the Singletons for $5,800. Felley soon began experiencing problems with the car. On the second day after he bought it, he noticed a problem with the clutch. Over the next few days, the clutch problem worsened to the point where he was unable to shift the gears, no matter how far he pushed in the clutch pedal. He had to pay $942.76 for the removal and repair of the clutch. Within the first month that Felley owned the car, it developed serious brake problems, the repairs of which cost Felley more than $1,400.

Felley brought a small claims action against the Singletons, claiming that they had made and breached an express warranty to him. At trial, an expert witness testified that based on his examination of the car and discussion with Felley about the car and other factors, it was his opinion that the car's brake and clutch problems probably existed when Felley bought the car. The trial court ruled in Felley's favor and ordered the Singletons to pay him $2,343.03. The Singletons appealed.

Bowman, Presiding Justice On appeal, the Singletons contend that the trial court erred when it determined that the statements they made to Felley regarding the condition of the car constituted an express warranty. The Singletons argue that their statements were nothing more than expressions of opinion in the nature of puffery that could not properly be deemed an express warranty.

Section 2–313 of the Uniform Commercial Code governs the formation of express warranties by affirmation in the context of a sale of goods such as a used car. Section 2–313 provides, in relevant part:

(1) Express warranties by the seller are created as follows:

(a) Any affirmation of fact or promise made by the seller to the buyer which relates to the goods and becomes part of the basis of the bargain creates an express warranty that the goods shall conform to the affirmation or promise.

(2) It is not necessary to the creation of an express warranty that the seller use formal words such as 'warrant' or 'guarantee' or that he have a specific intention to make a warranty, but an affirmation merely of the value of the goods or a statement purporting to be merely the seller's opinion or commendation of the goods does not create a warranty.

The Singletons point to subsection (2) of section 2–313 as support for their argument that their statements to Felley did not constitute an express warranty. The Singletons also cite the official comments to subsection (2), which state:

Concerning affirmations of value or a seller's opinion or commendation under subsection (2), the basic question remains the same: What statements of the seller have in the circumstances and in objective judgment be-

come part of the basis of the bargain? As indicated above, all of the statements of the seller do so unless good reason is shown to the contrary. The provisions of subsection (2) are included, however, since common experience discloses that some statements or predictions cannot fairly be viewed as entering into the bargain.

In the Singletons' view, their statements to Felley cannot fairly be viewed as entering into the bargain. They assert that they are not automobile dealers or mechanics with specialized knowledge of the brake and clutch systems of the car and therefore their statements were merely expressions of a vendor's opinion that did not constitute an express warranty. Felley responds that the trial court correctly determined that the Singletons' statements were affirmation of fact that became a basis of the bargain and therefore constituted an express warranty. In support of his position, Felley cites *Weng v. Allison* (Ill. App. 1997).

Whether an express warranty exists is a factual issue to be determined by the trier of fact. Consequently, it is well settled that a reviewing court may not reverse a trial court judgment regarding the existence of an express or implied warranty merely because different conclusions might have been drawn. *Weng* involved the sale of a 10-year-old used car for $800. The car had 96,000 miles on it. When the buyers attempted to drive the car home, it failed to operate properly. An inspection at an automobile dealership revealed that the car was unsafe to drive and needed repairs costing about $1,500. The seller had told the buyers that the car was "mechanically sound," "in good condition," "a reliable car," "a good car," and had "no problems." The trial court ruled that such representations could not become part of the basis of the bargain unless the buyer relied on them and that no one could reasonably rely on such statements with respect to such a car. In *Weng,* the appellate court disagreed and reversed the trial court. The appellate court determined that the representations made by the sellers were affirmations of fact that created an express warranty. The court stated that affirmations of fact made during a bargaining process regarding the sale of goods are presumed to be part of the basis of the bargain unless clear affirmative proof to the contrary is shown; that a showing of reliance on the affirmations by the buyer is not necessary for the creation of an express warranty; and that the seller has the burden to establish by clear affirmative proof that the affirmations did not become part of the basis of the bargain. The court also stated that the seller may be accountable for breach of warranty where affirmations are a basis of the bargain and the goods fail to conform to the affirmations.

We believe that the principles set out in *Weng* are correct. We agree with the *Weng* court that, in the context of a used car sale, representations by the seller such as the car is "in good mechanical condition" are presumed to be affirmations of fact that become part of the basis of the bargain. Be-

cause they are presumed to be part of the basis of the bargain, such representations constitute express warranties, regardless of the buyer's reliance on them, unless seller shows by clear affirmative proof that the representations did not become part of the basis of the bargain. In this case, it is undisputed that Felley asked the Singletons about the car's mechanical condition and the Singletons responded that the car was in good mechanical condition. Under the foregoing principles, the Singletons' representations are presumed to be affirmations of fact that became a part of the basis of the bargain. Nothing in the record indicates that the Singletons made a clear and affirmative showing that their representations did not become part of the basis of the bargain. The trial court, as the fact finder in this case, could have reasonably found that the Singletons asserted a fact of which Felley was ignorant when they told Felley that the car was in good mechanical condition.

Judgment in favor of Felley affirmed.

Implied Warranty of Merchantability

An **implied warranty** is a warranty created by operation of law rather than the seller's express statements. UCC section 2–314(1) creates the Code's **implied warranty of merchantability** with this language: "[A] warranty that the goods shall be merchantable is implied in a contract for their sale if the seller is a merchant with respect to goods of that kind." This is a clear example of the modern tendency of legislatures to intervene in private contracts to protect consumers.

In an implied warranty of merchantability case, the plaintiff argues that the seller breached the warranty by selling nonmerchantable goods and that the plaintiff should therefore recover damages. Under section 2–314, such claims can succeed only where the seller is a *merchant with respect to goods of the kind sold.*[2] A housewife's sale of homemade preserves or a hardware store owner's sale of a used car, for example, do not trigger the implied warranty of merchantability.

UCC section 2–314(2) states that, to be merchantable, goods must at least: (1) pass without objection in the trade; (2) be fit for the ordinary purposes for which such goods are used; (3) be of even kind, quality, and quantity

within each unit (case, package, or carton); (4) be adequately contained, packaged, and labeled; (5) conform to any promises or statements of fact made on the container or label; and (6) in the case of fungible goods, be of fair average quality. The most important of these requirements is that the goods must be *fit for the ordinary purposes for which such goods are used.* (In the *Bako* case, which appears later in the chapter, the implied warranty of merchantability was made but was not breached, because the relevant goods were suitable for ordinary purposes.) The goods need not be perfect to be fit for their ordinary purposes. Rather, they need only meet the reasonable expectations of the average consumer.

This broad, flexible test of merchantability is almost inevitable given the wide range of products sold in the United States today and the varied defects they may present. Still, a few generalizations about merchantability determinations are possible. Goods that fail to function properly or that have harmful side effects normally are not merchantable. A computer that fails to work properly or that destroys the owner's programs, for example, is not fit for the ordinary purposes for which computers are used. In cases involving allergic reactions to drugs or other products, courts may find the defendant liable if it was reasonably foreseeable that an appreciable number of consumers would suffer the reaction. As the following revealed by the *Hong* case, which follows,

---

[2]The term *merchant* is defined in Chapter 9.

there is disagreement over the standard for food products that are alleged to be nonmerchantable because they contain harmful objects or substances. Under the *foreign–natural* test, the defendant is liable if the object or substance is "foreign" to the product, but not liable if it is "natural" to the product. Increasingly, however, courts ask whether the food product met the consumer's reasonable expectations.

Yong Cha Hong v. Marriott Corporation   3 UCC Rep. Serv. 2d 83 (D. Md. 1987)

Yong Cha Hong bought take-out fried chicken from a Roy Rogers Family Restaurant owned by the Marriott Corporation. While eating a chicken wing from her order, she bit into an object that she perceived to be a worm. Claiming permanent injuries and great physical and emotional upset from this incident, Hong sued Marriott for $500,000 in federal district court under the implied warranty of merchantability. After introducing an expert's report alleging that the object in the chicken wing was not a worm, Marriott moved for summary judgment. It claimed that the case involved no disputed issues of material fact, and that there was no breach of the implied warranty of merchantability as a matter of law.

Smalkin, District Judge It appears that the item encountered by plaintiff was probably not a worm or other parasite, although plaintiff, in her deposition, steadfastly maintains that it was a worm. If it was not a worm (i.e., if the expert analysis is correct), it was either one of the chicken's major blood vessels (the aorta) or its trachea, both of which would appear worm-like (although not meaty like a worm, but hollow). For [present] purposes, the court will assume that the item was not a worm. Precisely how the aorta or trachea wound up in this hapless chicken's wing is a fascinating, but as yet unanswered (and presently immaterial), question.

Does Maryland law provide a breach of warranty remedy for personal injury flowing from an unexpected encounter with an inedible part of the chicken's anatomy in a piece of fast food fried chicken? Marriott contends that there can be no recovery unless the offending item was a foreign object, i.e., not part of the chicken itself.

In many cases that have denied [implied] warranty recovery as a matter of law, the injurious substance was, as in this case, a natural (though inedible) part of the edible item consumed. Thus, in *Shapiro v. Hotel Statler Corp.* (1955), recovery was denied for a fish bone in "Hot Barquette of Seafood Mornay." But in all these cases the natural item was reasonably to be expected in the dish by its very nature, under the prevailing expectation of any reasonable consumer. Indeed, precisely this "reasonable expectation" test has been adopted in a number of cases. The reasonable expectation test has largely displaced the foreign–natural test adverted to by Marriott. This court is confident that Maryland would apply the reasonable expectation rule.

The court cannot conclude that the presence of a trachea or an aorta in a fast food fried chicken wing is so reasonably to be expected as to render it merchantable, as a matter of law. This is not like the situation [in a previous case] involving a one centimeter bone in a piece of fried fish. Everyone but a fool knows that tiny bones may remain in even the best filets of fish. This case is more like [another decision], where the court held that the issue was for the trier of fact, on a claim arising from a cherry pit in cherry ice cream. Thus, a question is presented that precludes the grant of summary judgment. The jury must determine whether a piece of fast food fried chicken is merchantable if it contains an inedible item of the chicken's anatomy. Of course, the jury will be instructed that the consumer's reasonable expectations form a part of the merchantability concept.

Marriott's motion for summary judgment denied.

Implied Warranty of Fitness

UCC section 2–315's **implied warranty of fitness for a particular purpose** arises where: (1) the seller has reason to know a particular purpose for which the buyer requires the goods; (2) the seller has reason to know that the buyer is relying on the seller's skill or judgment for the selection of suitable goods; and (3) the buyer actually relies on the seller's skill or judgment in purchasing the goods. If these tests are met, there is an implied warranty that the goods will be fit for the buyer's *particular* purpose. Any seller—merchant or nonmerchant—may make this implied warranty, the breach of which will give rise to liability for damages.

In many fitness warranty cases, buyers effectively put themselves in the seller's hands by making their needs known and by saying that they are relying on the seller to select goods that will satisfy those needs. This may happen, for example, when a seller sells a computer system specially manufactured or customized for a buyer's particular needs. Sellers also may be liable when the circumstances reasonably indicate that the buyer has a particular purpose and is relying on the seller to satisfy that purpose, even though the buyer fails to make either explicit. However, buyers may have trouble recovering if they are more expert than the seller, submit specifications for the goods they wish to buy, inspect the goods, actually select them, or insist on a particular brand.

As indicated in the *Bako* case, which follows shortly, the implied warranty of fitness differs from the implied warranty of merchantability. The tests for the creation of each warranty plainly are different. Under section 2–315,

moreover, sellers warrant only that the goods are fit for the buyer's *particular* purposes, not the *ordinary* purposes for which such goods are used. If a 400-pound man asks a department store for a hammock that will support his weight but is sold a hammock that can support only average-sized people, there is a breach of the implied warranty of fitness but no breach of the implied warranty of merchantability.

Bako also illustrates an important requirement applicable to all breach of warranty cases (whether express warranty or implied warranty): that the buyer must notify the seller of the breach within a reasonable time after the buyer discovers, or should have discovered, it. In *Bako,* the plaintiffs' failure to provide timely notice kept them from winning an otherwise valid claim for breach of the implied warranty of fitness for a particular purpose.

Bako v. Crystal Cabinet Works, Inc.   *2001 Ohio App. LEXIS 2120 (Ohio App. 2001)*

In 1994, David and Corrine Bako signed a contract with Don Walter Kitchen Distributors, Inc. (DW) for the purchase and installation of cabinets in their new home. DW ordered the cabinets from a manufacturer, Crystal Cabinet Works, Inc. Crystal shipped the cabinets to DW, which installed them in the Bakos' residence. Soon after the installation, Corrine Bako contacted a DW employee, Neil Mann, and asked whether DW could provide a stain to match the kitchen cabinets. She informed Mann that the stain would be applied to the wood trim primarily on the first floor of the house. Mann ordered two one-gallon cans of stain from Crystal, which shipped the stain to DW in unmarked cans. There were no labels, instructions, or warnings regarding improper use or application of the stain. The cans arrived at DW's store in unmarked cardboard boxes and were delivered to the Bakos in this manner. The stain in the cans turned out to be lacquer-based.

Shortly thereafter, Corrine Bako again contacted Mann about purchasing additional stain in a slightly different color to apply to a hardwood floor. At Mann's suggestion, she contacted Crystal's paint lab and spoke with a Crystal employee. The Crystal employee shipped the Bakos a series of samples from which Corrine ordered two gallons of stain. This stain was also a lacquer-based stain and was shipped directly from Crystal to the Bakos in unmarked cans. Once again, there were no instructions for use, no warning regarding improper use or application of the product, no label indicating that it was a lacquer-based stain, and no label indicating that a special topcoat was required because it was a lacquer-based stain. The Bakos applied the stain to their floor.

The Bakos then obtained a polyurethane topcoat sealant and applied it to the wood surfaces they had stained with the stain purchased from DW and Crystal. Following this application of the sealant, all of the stained and sealed areas suffered severe and permanent damage as a result of the nonadherence of the polyurethane sealant to the lacquer-based stain. Evidence adduced at the trial of the case referred to below established that lacquer-based stains are incompatible with the polyurethane topcoat that the Bakos applied to their home's wood surfaces.

In October 1996, the Bakos filed suit against Crystal and DW for breach of the implied warranty of merchantability and breach of the implied warranty of fitness for a particular purpose. They also claimed that the defendants had been negligent. An Ohio trial court found for the Bakos and held the defendants liable for approximately $25,000 in compensatory damages. Contending that the Bakos should not have prevailed on any of their claims, Crystal appealed to the Court of Appeals of Ohio.

Donofrio, Judge   Crystal argues that the trial court erred in determining that it . . . breached any UCC warranty. [The Ohio version of UCC § 2–314] governs the implied warranty of merchantability and provides in pertinent part:

(A) [A] warranty that goods shall be merchantable is implied in a contract for their sale if the seller is a merchant with respect to goods of that kind.

(B) Goods to be merchantable must be at least such as: . . .

(3) are fit for the ordinary purposes for which such goods are used; and

. . .

(5) are adequately contained, packaged, and labeled as the agreement may require.

An implied warranty of merchantability obligates a seller to provide goods that are fit for their ordinary purpose. The warranty is breached when the goods are not of comparable quality to that generally acceptable for goods of that kind. Therefore, in order to prove that DW and Crystal breached the implied warranty of merchantability, the Bakos needed to introduce evidence proving that the problems they experienced with the stain provided by DW and Crystal were not ordinary problems experienced or associated with stain.

A thorough review of the record shows that the defendants did not breach the implied warranty of merchantability [in regard to the] cans of stain [they sold to] the Bakos. Mrs. Bako testified that there were no problems with the application of the stain, in and of itself, to the wood trim and wood floors. [Her] testimony illustrates that the stain . . . satisfied the implied warranty of merchantability. The Bakos applied the stain and had no problems with its application. It was only when the Bakos erroneously combined the lacquer-based stain with the polyurethane sealant that the Bakos began to experience adhesion problems between the stain and the polyurethane sealant. The stain did just what stain was supposed to do: it colored the wood. As such, there was no breach of the implied warranty of merchantability.

In addition, the defendants did not breach the implied warranty of merchantability by failing to adequately package and label the stain. The Bakos failed to direct the court's attention to any agreement in the record where the stain, which DW and Crystal were to provide the Bakos, required particularized packaging or labeling instructions.

The Bakos also claim that the defendants violated the implied warranty of fitness for a particular purpose. A party must make three showings in order to show a breach of [this] implied warranty. First, the seller must have reason to know the buyer's particular purpose. Second, the seller must have reason to know that the buyer is relying on the seller's skill or judgment to furnish appropriate goods. Finally, the buyer must in fact rely upon the seller's skill or judgment

Once a party has made a successful showing of a breach of the implied warranty of fitness for a particular purpose, [Ohio law requires that] the aggrieved party notify the breaching party of its breach within a reasonable time. If the aggrieved party fails to give timely notification of breach, the party will be barred from recovering any remedy for breach. Whether a buyer gives a seller timely and reasonable notice of a breach of a contract for the sale of goods is ordinarily a question of fact to be determined from all the circumstances.

The Bakos failed to present sufficient evidence at trial to recover for breach of the implied warranty of fitness for a particular purpose. Mrs. Bako's testimony demonstrated that the Bakos did not rely upon Mann's skill and judgment when purchasing the stain from DW. As such, they may not recover against DW for breach of the implied warranty of fitness for a particular purpose.

At first glance it appears that the Bakos presented sufficient evidence showing that Crystal breached the implied warranty of fitness for a particular purpose. Crystal's catalog listed the stain in question as a lacquer-based stain. The Bakos were not provided with a copy of this catalog. Mrs. Bako testified that she notified [a Crystal paint lab employee] that the Bakos would be using a polyurethane sealant in conjunction with the stain supplied by Crystal. [The Crystal employee] failed to inform Mrs. Bako as to the incompatibility problem between the lacquer-based stain and the polyurethane sealant. The Bakos relied upon [the Crystal employee's] silence and expertise in mixing the stain with the polyurethane sealant. Therefore, the Bakos presented evidence showing that Crystal breached the implied warranty of fitness for a particular purpose.

[T]he Bakos failed[, however,] to provide Crystal with timely notice of its breach under [Ohio law], and thus the Bakos are precluded from recovering for this breach. As noted by Crystal, the Bakos presented evidence that they discovered the adhesion problems between Crystal's stain and the polyurethane topcoat sealant in approximately September 1994. The [evidence] shows that Crystal was not presented with notice of its breach until sometime around May 1995, roughly seven months after the Bakos had been alerted to the problem. While the time frame of seven months may not in and of itself be unreasonable under [Ohio law], the fact that the Bakos presented evidence showing that they notified DW of the adhesion problem in September or October 1994, yet failed to notify Crystal of the breach until roughly May 1995, shows that the Bakos failed to give timely notice of the breach to Crystal.

DW and Crystal held not to have violated implied warranty of merchantability and implied warranty of fitness for particular purpose; in portion of opinion not set forth here, however, judgment in favor of the Bakos affirmed on basis of claim that defendants were negligent.

Negligence

Product liability lawsuits brought on the **negligence** theory discussed in Chapter 7 usually allege that the seller or manufacturer breached a duty to the plaintiff by failing to eliminate a reasonably foreseeable risk of harm associated with the product. Such cases typically involve one or more of the following claims: (1) negligent *manufacture* of the goods (including improper materials and packaging), (2) negligent *inspection,* (3) negligent failure to provide *adequate warnings,* and (4) negligent *design.*

Negligent Manufacture Negligence claims alleging the manufacturer's improper assembly, materials, or packaging often encounter obstacles because the evidence needed to prove a breach of duty is under the defendant's control. However, modern discovery rules and the doctrine of *res ipsa loquitur* may help plaintiffs establish a breach in such situations.[3]

Negligent Inspection Manufacturers have a duty to inspect their products for defects that create a reasonably foreseeable risk of harm, if such an inspection would be practicable and effective. As noted above, *res ipsa loquitur* and modern discovery rules may help plaintiffs prove their case against the manufacturer.

Most courts have held that middlemen such as retailers and wholesalers have a duty to inspect the goods they sell only when they have actual knowledge or reason to know of a defect. In addition, such parties generally have no duty to inspect if inspection would be unduly difficult, burdensome, or time-consuming. Unless the product defect is obvious, for example, middlemen usually are not liable for failing to inspect goods sold in the manufacturer's original packages or containers.

On the other hand, sellers that prepare, install, or repair the goods they sell ordinarily have a duty to inspect those goods. Examples include restaurants, automobile dealers, and installers of household products. In general, the scope of the inspection need only be consistent with the preparation, installation, or repair work performed. It is unlikely, therefore, that such sellers must unearth hidden or latent defects.

If there is a duty to inspect and the inspection reveals a defect, further duties may arise. For example, a manufacturer or other seller may be required not to sell the product in its defective state, or at least to give a suitable warning.

Negligent Failure to Warn Sellers and manufacturers often have a duty to give an appropriate warning when their products pose a reasonably foreseeable risk of harm. In determining whether there was a duty to warn and whether the defendant's warning was adequate, however, courts often consider other factors besides the reasonable foreseeability of the risk. These include the *magnitude or severity* of the likely harm, the *ease or difficulty of providing an appropriate warning,* and the likely *effectiveness of a warning.* Many courts, moreover, hold there is no duty to warn if the risk is *open and obvious.*

> **LOG ON**
>
> Would you like to learn more about some of the high-profile product liability cases you have read about in the news? These sites carry news and in-depth articles about a number of major product liability cases and issues: Joe D'Addario's Cyberlaw: Product Liability, **http://www.productslaw.com/;** Lawlinks Product Liability Page, **http://resource.lawlinks.com/Content/Legal_ Subject_Index/Tort_Law_Product_Liability/ product_liability.htm;** Torts and Product Liability Law, **http://members.aol.com/ trailertot/torts.html.**

Negligent Design Manufacturers have a duty to design their products so as to avoid reasonably foreseeable risks of harm. As in failure-to-warn cases, however, design defect cases frequently involve other factors such as the *magnitude or severity* of the foreseeable harm. Three other factors are *industry practices* at the time the product was manufactured the *state of the art* (the state of existing scientific and technical knowledge) at that time, and the product's compliance or noncompliance with *government safety regulations.*

Sometimes courts employ *risk–benefit analysis* when weighing these factors. In such analyses, three other factors—the design's *social utility,* the *effectiveness of alternative designs,* and the *cost of safer designs*—may figure in the weighing process. Even when the balancing process indicates that the design was not defective, courts still may require a suitable warning.

The *Jarvis* case, which follows, illustrates various issues that arise in negligent design cases involving motor vehicles.

---

[3]Chapter 2 discusses discovery. Chapter 7 discusses *res ipsa loquitur.*

Jarvis v. Ford Motor Co.   *283 F.3d 33 (2d Cir. 2002)*

A six-day-old 1991 Ford Aerostar driven by plaintiff-appellant Kathleen Jarvis suddenly accelerated, resulting in an accident in which Jarvis sustained severe injuries. Jarvis contended that the Aerostar "took off" even though she had not depressed the accelerator and that she was unable to stop the van by pumping the brakes. She sued Ford Motor Company in a federal district court, claiming that Ford's negligence in designing the Aerostar's cruise control system led to the sudden acceleration and her accident. The injury sustained by Jarvis in the accident prevented her from returning to her previous employment.

Jarvis testified at trial that she started the Aerostar in the driveway of her home with her right foot "lightly on the brake." After she turned on the ignition, the engine suddenly revved and the vehicle "took off." As the van accelerated, Jarvis pumped the brake with both feet, looking down to make sure her feet were on the brake pedal. The van would not stop. She steered to avoid people walking in the road and then heard saplings brushing against the side of the van before she blacked out.

Jarvis's father, who was standing in the vicinity of the accident scene, testified that he saw the van starting off at an "unusually fast speed" for his daughter. As the Aerostar passed him, he saw Jarvis "holding on to the steering wheel very tight; her body was going back and forth ever so slightly." Another witness testified that she saw Jarvis's van moving quickly down the road and that she did not see any brake lights illuminated. A police officer who was called to the accident scene testified that he saw no marks on the road near the scene. Jarvis's father had been the last one to use the Aerostar before the accident. When asked at trial whether he had left the parking brake on, Jarvis's father testified that it was his "normal habit" to put it on, but that he had "no memory of it as such" in this case. When asked directly, he answered, "I'm not certain I put it in with the parking brake on."

George Pope, an accident reconstruction specialist who testified for Jarvis, stated that the van traveled approximately 330 feet and did some braking that slowed it to 15 to 20 miles per hour before it entered a ditch and turned over. Pope testified that the Aerostar had vacuum power brakes that draw their vacuum from the engine, but that the engine does not create the necessary vacuum when accelerating full throttle. Even though a check valve traps a reservoir of vacuum for use when the engine vacuum is low, this reserve can be depleted after one-and-a-half hard brake applications. Therefore, according to Pope, if Jarvis pumped the brakes in an effort to stop the Aerostar after it began accelerating at full throttle, she would have lost approximately 1000 pounds of additional force that the booster normally could have supplied to the brakes. Pope concluded that "under those circumstances . . . , it will feel to a person like they've lost their brakes, [because] they're pushing and nothing is happening."

In support of her claim that the Aerostar had suddenly accelerated even though she did not press the accelerator, Jarvis presented testimony from five Aerostar owners who recounted having had similar problems with their 1989 or 1990 Aerostars. In addition, the jury was presented with evidence that Ford had received reports of incidents of sudden acceleration in a total of 560 Aerostars.

Samuel J. Sero, an electrical engineer, testified as an expert for Jarvis. He offered a theory noting possible electrical malfunctions and mechanical reasons that could have caused the sudden acceleration to occur. This theory focused on the design and workings of Aerostar's cruise control system. Sero also testified concerning a possible alternative design of the Aerostar's cruise control system—a design that he believed would have prevented the sudden acceleration problem if the design had been implemented by Ford.

In its defense, Ford claimed principally that the acceleration was the result of a driver error by Jarvis. Ford contended that Jarvis must have been unaware that the parking brake had been set and must have mistaken the accelerator pedal for the brake pedal. Ford also presented expert testimony that the Aerostar would not have malfunctioned in the manner suggested by Jarvis's expert. In addition, Ford maintained that the existence of the Aerostar's dump valve, a spring-loaded plunger designed to open when the brake pedal is depressed, would have effectively stopped the Aerostar from accelerating when Jarvis applied the brakes, even if the cruise control had malfunctioned as Sero suggested. Jarvis's testimony regarding braking was that she tried to stop the Aerostar by pumping the brakes, as her father had taught her to do when she was first learning to drive. Jarvis offered three possible explanations at trial for why the dump valve did not permit her to stop the Aerostar from accelerating: (1) the dump valve was malfunctioning; (2) Jarvis was pumping the brakes, causing the Aerostar to reinstate an electrical malfunction in the cruise control mechanism and commence acceleration every time her foot rose from the pedal in the pumping action; or (3) Jarvis had not pressed far enough on the brakes to activate the dump valve. Although Ford's expert testified that he tested the dump valve after the accident and found that it had no leaks, there was no evidence as to whether the dump valve could have malfunctioned in a way that would not necessarily have been evident at the time Ford's expert examined the Aerostar.

The jury concluded that Ford negligently designed the Aerostar's cruise control system, that this was a substantial factor in causing the accident, and that Jarvis's negligence was also a substantial factor in causing the accident. It apportioned 65 percent of the fault to Ford and 35 percent to Jarvis, presumably because of evidence that the Aerostar owner's manual directs drivers to apply the brakes firmly with one stroke and not in a pumping action. A single application of the brakes, according to the testimony, would not have exhausted the vacuum reservoir of the power assist to the brakes and would thus have aided Jarvis's ability to stop the vehicle. The jury awarded Jarvis more than $1 million in damages for past and future medical insurance premiums, lost earnings, and pain and suffering.

Asserting that the only logical conclusion to be drawn from the evidence was that Jarvis never applied the brake pedal and mistakenly applied the accelerator instead, Ford moved for judgment as a matter of law (judgment notwithstanding the verdict). The trial judge granted Ford's motion, set aside the verdict, and entered judgment in Ford's favor. Jarvis appealed to the United States Court of Appeals for the Second Circuit.

Sotomayor, Circuit Judge Judgment as a matter of law is appropriate when "a party has been fully heard on an issue and there is no legally sufficient evidentiary basis for a reasonable jury to find for that party on that issue." Federal Rules of Civil Procedure 50(a). In ruling on a Rule 50 motion, "the trial court is required to consider the evidence in the light most favorable to the party against whom the motion was made and to give that party the benefit of all reasonable inferences that the jury might have drawn in his favor from the evidence. The court cannot assess the weight of conflicting evidence, pass on the credibility of the witnesses, or substitute its judgment for that of the jury." *Tolbert v. Queens College* (2d Cir. 2001).

The New York Court of Appeals has established that "a manufacturer is obligated to exercise that degree of care in his plan or design so as to avoid any unreasonable risk of harm to anyone who is likely to be exposed to the danger when the product is used in the manner for which the product was intended." *Micallef v. Miehle-Goss Co.* (1976). The court explained that "what constitutes reasonable care will . . . involve a balancing of the likelihood of harm, and the gravity of harm if it happens, against the burden of the precaution which would be effect to avoid the harm."

As applied to the facts of this case, the jury [instructions] on negligent design restated this standard as comprising three elements: (1) that the cruise control system in the 1991 Aerostar was defective when put on the market by Ford; (2) that the defect made it reasonably certain that the vehicle would be dangerous when put to normal use; and (3) that "Ford failed to use reasonable care in designing the cruise control system or in inspecting it or testing it for defects, or that even though Ford used reasonable care in designing, inspecting and testing the cruise control system in the 1991 Aerostar, that Ford learned of the defect before putting the product on the market and did nothing about it."

The New York Court of Appeals has held that a plaintiff's failure to prove why a product malfunctioned does not necessarily prevent a plaintiff from showing that the product was defective. [For instance, a decision of that court] rejected the contention that a plaintiff injured by an exploding can of Freon had failed to make out a *prima facie* breach of warranty claim when no particular defect in the packaged refrigerant was ever discovered. *Halloran v. Virginia Chemicals Inc.* (1977). The court stated that "if plaintiff has proven that the product has not performed as intended and excluded all causes of the accident not attributable to defendant, the fact finder may, even if the particular defect has not been proven, infer that the accident could only have occurred due to some defect in the product or its packaging." The same principles hold in product liability actions brought under a theory of negligent design. See, e.g., *Gargano v. Rosenthal* (N.Y. App. Div. 1984) (citing *Halloran* in finding that causes of action for product liability, including those under theories of negligence, breach of warranty, and strict liability, may be proven "through circumstantial evidence, by showing that the vehicle's transmission and gearshift did not perform as intended and by excluding all causes of the accident not attributable to [defendants'] conduct").

In granting Ford's motion for judgment as a matter of law, the district court relied upon the fact that Jarvis's expert had not established that the cruise control malfunctions he outlined were substantially likely to occur. The court stated that Jarvis "has offered no evidence to suggest how frequently the design defect is likely to occur," [and no] "evidence that the attenuated chain of events necessary to result in an accident is likely to occur, let alone with significant regularity."

The district court erred in requiring proof of a specific defect in the Aerostar's cruise control and in not considering Jarvis's circumstantial evidence of a defect. The malfunction in the design of the Aerostar that Jarvis has alleged is that it suddenly accelerated, opening full throttle without Jarvis depressing the accelerator pedal, and that her efforts to stop the vehicle by pumping the brakes were unavailing. If Jarvis's six-day-old Aerostar performed in this manner, a jury could reasonably conclude that it was "defective when put on the market by Ford," and that "the defect made it reasonably certain that the vehicle would be dangerous when put to normal use," as required by the first two elements of the jury [instructions] regarding negligent design. Although Ford argued that the accident was caused instead by driver error, this theory would have been rejected if the jury had believed Jarvis's testimony that she had her feet on the brake and not on the accelerator, as Ford claimed.

The final element of the [jury instructions, in] asking whether Ford breached its duty of care, required "a balancing of the likelihood of harm, and the gravity of harm if it happens, against the burden of the precaution which would be effective to avoid the harm." *Micallef v. Miehle-Goss Co.* (N.Y. 1976). Construing the evidence in Jarvis's favor and crediting her version of events, a reasonable jury could find that Ford breached its duty of care. Even accepting as true that sudden acceleration in the 1991 Aerostar would occur, at most, very infrequently when measured against all Aerostar ignition starts, the consequences of sudden acceleration could easily be catastrophic, the design of which Jarvis complains has no particular utility to balance its potential for harm, and, according to Jarvis's expert, the malfunction in the cruise control could be avoided by an inexpensive switch that would shut off power to the cruise control when not in use.

The district court also found that, apart from the issue of scientific evidence of a specific defect, "there is such an overwhelming amount of evidence in favor of the defendant that reasonable and fair minded persons could not arrive at a verdict" in favor of Jarvis. Even though the law does not require Jarvis to prove what specific defect caused the cruise control to malfunction, Ford conceivably could have offered scientific proof that the cruise control would not have malfunctioned in the manner alleged that so outweighed Jarvis's proof . . . as to warrant judgment as a matter of law for Ford. This is not such a case.

[In a hearing conducted before Jarvis's expert, Sero, was allowed to testify], the district court fully analyzed Sero's proposed testimony . . . and found the testimony admissible. The jury was entitled to consider this evidence, even if it did not conclusively demonstrate—as it need not—what specific defect caused the Aerostar's cruise control to malfunc-

tion. Jarvis also presented evidence at trial that sudden acceleration not only would open the throttle to her Aerostar but also would decrease significantly her ability to restrain the vehicle by pumping the brakes. Pope, Jarvis's expert, testified that the Aerostar had vacuum power brakes that draw their vacuum from the engine. When accelerating at full throttle, Pope testified, the engine does not create the normal vacuum that assists in braking. An additional reservoir of vacuum could be depleted by pumping the brakes, as Jarvis testified she did in this case. The expert concluded that "under those circumstances . . . , it will feel to a person like they've lost their brakes, they're pushing and nothing is happening."

The district court relied on [the testimony of Ford's expert and other evidence] as establishing that any sudden acceleration would have been prevented or terminated by the Aerostar's dump valve [if Jarvis had applied the brakes]. [T]his testimony concerning the dump valve presupposes[, however,] that it was functioning properly at the time of Jarvis's accident. If the dump valve had malfunctioned, the sudden acceleration described by Sero would have continued, despite Jarvis's depressing the brake pedal, even with both feet applying considerable force. Ford's expert testified that he tested the dump valve after the accident and found that it functioned properly at that time. Undeveloped in the record, however, is discussion of the possibility that a defect in the dump valve could cause it to malfunction in a manner that would not have been evident upon [the Ford expert's] later examination. Examining the record as a whole, and construing the evidence in the light most favorable to Jarvis, we cannot say, as a matter of law, that the fact that the Aerostar was equipped with a dump valve discredits [the evidence presented by Jarvis] in the manner found by the district court.

The district court also found that Ford had "proffered an alternative scenario that was consistent with the evidence." Ford's scenario suggests that Jarvis, unfamiliar with her new minivan, started it "unaware that her father had set the parking brake . . . , put her foot on the accelerator thinking it to be on the brake, and was startled when the engine started to race against the force of the parking brake. Continuing to believe that her foot was on the brake and not on the accelerator, plaintiff was unable to stop the car." The record as a whole, viewed in the light most favorable to Jarvis, supplies little evidence to support Ford's theory of the accident. While we agree that some evidence in the record is consistent with this theory, judgment as a matter of law demands far more. See Fed. R. Civ. P. 50(a) (requiring for judgment as a matter of law that "there is no legally sufficient evidentiary basis for a reasonable jury to find for [the nonmoving] party on that issue").

The district court [failed to give adequate consideration to] the evidence in the record that weighs heavily against Ford's theory of driver error. Ford's theory that Jarvis had the parking brake on and applied her foot to the accelerator instead of the brake is irreconcilable with Jarvis's testimony that she began with her foot "lightly" on the brake and that the Aerostar's acceleration was sudden. If her foot was placed "lightly" on the accelerator instead of the brake, and the parking brake were on, the Aerostar would have accelerated slowly, if at all. Jarvis on the other hand, testified that the Aerostar "took off." Another weakness of Ford's theory is that it assumes driver error not only as to which pedal Jarvis depressed but also as to the effect of each stroke of the pedal. Under Ford's theory, Jarvis would have felt the Aerostar *accelerate* with each application of the pedal, and slow each time she lifted her foot from the pedal. Ford's theory asks us to believe that Jarvis repeatedly applied force to the pedal without understanding the effect of her actions. Finally, Ford's theory is unable to account for Jarvis's claim that she depressed the pedal with both feet. As part of the accident reconstruction, Jarvis was asked to sit in the Aerostar and to place both feet on the accelerator. She was able to do so only by placing one foot on top of the other. When asked to do the same with the brake pedal, she found that it accommodated both feet. The jury viewed photos taken for purposes of this litigation showing Jarvis sitting in the Aerostar at the accident site. The photos also demonstrated that, when asked to put both feet on the accelerator, Jarvis had one foot placed over the other.

In sum, we find the ultimate issue of Ford's negligence to be a jury question. Ford did not present evidence that conclusively demonstrated, as a matter of law, that Jarvis's accident did not occur because of a defect in the Aerostar's cruise control mechanism. Jarvis's testimony, the testimony of other Aerostar owners who had similar experiences, and evidence of hundreds of other reported cases of sudden acceleration in Aerostars, combined with an expert's scientific explanation of how the cruise control may have malfunctioned and of an inexpensive remedy, were all found admissible by the district court. Together, this evidence provided the jury with a sufficient evidentiary basis to reasonably conclude that the cruise control mechanism had been defectively designed.

District court's judgment as matter of law for Ford vacated; case remanded to district court with instruction to reinstate jury verdict in favor of Jarvis.

Strict Liability

Strict liability for certain defective products is a relatively recent development. Only during the 1960s did courts begin to impose such liability in significant numbers. The movement toward strict liability received a critical boost when the American Law Institute promulgated section 402A of the *Restatement (Second) of Torts* in 1965. By now, the vast majority of the states have adopted some form of strict liability, either by statute or under the common law. The most important reason is the socialization-of-risk strategy discussed earlier. By not requiring plaintiffs to prove a breach of duty, strict liability makes it easier for them to recover; sellers then may pass on the costs of this liability through higher prices. Another justification for strict liability is that it stimulates manufacturers to design and build safer products.

Section 402A's Requirements Because it is the most common version of strict liability in the products context, we limit our discussion of the subject to section 402A. It provides that a "seller . . . engaged in the business of selling" a product is liable for physical harm or property damage suffered by the ultimate user or consumer of that product, if the product was "in a defective condition unreasonably dangerous to the user or consumer or to his property." This rule applies even though "the seller has exercised all possible care in the preparation and sale of his product." Thus, section 402A states a strict liability rule, which does not require plaintiffs to prove a breach of duty.

Each element required by section 402A must be present in order for strict liability to be imposed.

1. The seller must be *engaged in the business of selling the product that harmed the plaintiff.* Thus, section 402A binds only parties who resemble UCC merchants because they regularly sell the product at issue. For example, the section does not apply to a college professor's or a clothing store's sale of a used car.

2. The product must be in a *defective condition* when sold, and also must be *unreasonably dangerous* because of that condition. The usual test of a product's defective condition is whether the product meets the reasonable

THE GLOBAL BUSINESS ENVIRONMENT

By virtue of a 1985 European Union (EU) Council Directive premised on consumer protection grounds, *producers* of defective products face strict liability for the personal injuries and property damage those products cause. The 1985 Directive defined *product* as

all movables, with the exception of primary agricultural products and game, even though incorporated into another movable or into an immovable. 'Primary agricultural products' means the products of the soil, of stock-farming and of fisheries, excluding products which have undergone initial processing. 'Product' includes electricity.

A 1999 amendment, however, broadened the Directive's definition of *product* and coverage of the strict liability regime by eliminating the original version's exclusion of agricultural products. After the 1999 amendment, *product* includes "all movables even if incorporated into another movable or into an immovable." The 1999 amendment also retained the original version's inclusion of "electricity" within the definition of *product*.

The Directive states that a product is considered *defective*

when it does not provide the safety which a person is entitled to expect, taking all circumstances into account, including: (a) the presentation of the product; (b) the use to which it could reasonably be expected that the product would be put; [and] (c) the time when the product was put into circulation.

Because the Directive contemplates strict liability, the harmed consumer need not show a failure to use reasonable care on the part of the producer. The typical tendency among the states of the United States is to require, in a strict liability case, proof that the product was both defective and unreasonably dangerous. The Directive, however, takes a different approach to strict liability. Although the consumer must demonstrate personal injury or property damage resulting from use of the product, the Directive's definition of *defective* does not contemplate a separate showing that the harm-causing product was defective to the point of being unreasonably dangerous. Only limited possible defenses against liability are provided for producers in the Directive.

---

expectations of the average consumer. An unreasonably dangerous product is one that is dangerous to an extent beyond the reasonable contemplation of the average consumer. For example, good whiskey is not unreasonably dangerous even though it can cause harm, but whiskey contaminated with a poisonous substance qualifies. Some courts (such as the court in the *Hernandez* case, which follows shortly) balance the product's social utility against its danger when determining whether it is unreasonably dangerous.

Section 402A's requirement of unreasonable dangerousness means that strict liability applies to a smaller range of product defects than does the implied warranty of merchantability. A power mower that simply fails to operate is not unreasonably dangerous, although it would not be merchantable. Some courts, however, blur the requirements of defective condition and unreasonable dangerousness, and a few have done away with the latter requirement.

3. Finally, defendants may avoid section 402A liability where the product was *substantially modified* by the plaintiff or another party after the sale, and the modification contributed to the plaintiff's injury or other loss.

Applications of Section 402A Design defect and failure-to-warn claims can be brought under section 402A. Even though section 402A is a strict liability provision, the factors considered in such cases resemble those taken into account in the negligence cases discussed in the previous section.

Because it applies to sellers, section 402A covers retailers and other middlemen who market goods containing defects that they did not create and may not have been able to discover. Even though such parties often escape negligence liability, courts have held them liable under section 402A's strict liability rule. Some states, however, have given middlemen protection against 402A liability or have required the manufacturer or other responsible party to indemnity them.

What about products, such as some medications, that have great social utility but pose serious and unavoidable risks? Imposing strict liability regarding such "unavoidably unsafe" products might deter manufacturers from developing and marketing them. When products of this kind cause harm and a lawsuit follows, many courts follow comment k to section 402A. Comment k says that unavoidably unsafe products are neither defective nor unreasonably dangerous if they are properly prepared and accompanied by proper directions and a proper warning. For this rule to apply, the product must be genuinely incapable of being made safer.

The *Hernandez* case, which follows, discusses the legal requirements that govern a strict liability case involving a claim of defective design of a butane lighter.

Hernandez v. Tokai Corp.   *2 S.W.3d 251 (Tex. Sup. Ct. 1999)*

Rita Emeterio bought disposable butane lighters for use at her bar. Her daughter, Gloria Hernandez, took lighters from the bar from time to time for her personal use. Emeterio and Hernandez both knew that it was dangerous for children to play with lighters. They also knew that some lighters were made with child-resistant mechanisms, but Emeterio chose not to buy them. On April 4, 1995, Hernandez's five-year-old daughter, Daphne, took a lighter from her mother's purse on the top shelf of a closet in her grandparents' home and started a fire. Daphne's two-year-old brother, Ruben, was severely burned in the fire.

On Ruben's behalf, Hernandez sued the manufacturers and distributors of the lighter, Tokai Corporation and Scripto-Tokai Corporation (collectively, "Tokai"), in the United States District Court for the Western District of Texas. Asserting a strict liability claim, Hernandez alleged that the lighter was defectively designed and unreasonably dangerous because it did not have a child-resistant safety mechanism that would have prevented or substantially reduced the likelihood of a child's using it to start a fire. Tokai did not dispute that mechanisms for making disposable lighters child-resistant were available when the lighter Daphne used was designed and marketed, or that such mechanisms could be incorporated into lighters at nominal cost.

Tokai moved for summary judgment, contending that a disposable lighter is a simple household tool intended for adult use only, and that a manufacturer has no duty to incorporate child-resistant features into a lighter's design to protect unintended users—children—from obvious and inherent dangers. Tokai also noted that adequate warnings against access by children were provided with its lighters, even though that danger was obvious and commonly known. In response to Tokai's motion, Hernandez argued that because an alternative design in existence at the time the lighter at issue was manufactured and distributed would have made the lighter safer in the hands of children, it remained for the jury to decide whether the lighter was defective under Texas's common-law risk-utility test. The federal district court granted summary judgment for Tokai. Hernandez appealed to the United States Court of Appeals for the Fifth Circuit. The Fifth Circuit then certified the following question of state law to the Supreme Court of Texas:

Under the Texas Products Liability Act of 1993, can the legal representative of a minor child injured as a result of the misuse of a product by another minor child maintain a defective-design products liability claim against the product's manufacturer where the product was intended to be used only by adults, the risk that children might misuse the product was obvious to the product's manufacturer and to its intended users, and a safer alternative design was available?

The Supreme Court of Texas issued an opinion answering the certified question.

Hecht, Justice [T]he question . . . is whether a disposable butane lighter, intended only for adult use, can be found to be defectively designed if it does not have a child-resistant mechanism that would have prevented or substantially reduced the risk of injury from a child's foreseeable misuse of the lighter. The Fifth Circuit has disclaimed "any intention or desire that the Supreme Court of Texas confine its reply to the precise form or scope of the question certified." Thus advised, we answer . . . that:

- None of the conditions stated in the question precludes imposition of liability, but neither are they together enough to establish liability;

- Proof of an available "safer alternative design", as defined by statute, is necessary but not sufficient for liability;
- The claimant must also show that the product was unreasonably dangerous as designed, taking into consideration the utility of the product and the risk involved in its use; and
- In determining whether a product is unreasonably dangerous, the product's utility to its intended market must be balanced against foreseeable risks associated with use by its intended users.

Our answer requires the following explanation and elaboration.

The certified question references [a 1993 Texas statute, § 82.005, whose relevant portion reads] as follows:

(a) In a products liability action in which a claimant alleges a design defect, the burden is on the claimant to prove by a preponderance of the evidence that:
(1) there was a safer alternative design; and
(2) the defect was a producing cause of the personal injury, property damage, or death for which the claimant seeks recovery.
(b) In this section, "safer alternative design" means a product design other than the one actually used that in reasonable probability:
(1) would have prevented or significantly reduced the risk of the claimant's personal injury, property damage, or death without substantially impairing the product's utility; and
(2) was economically and technologically feasible at the time the product left the control of the manufacturer or seller by the application of existing or reasonably achievable scientific knowledge.

Section 82.005 does not attempt to state all the elements of a product liability action for design defect. It does not, for example, define design defect or negate the common law requirement that such a defect render the product unreasonably dangerous. Additionally, the statute was not intended to, and does not, supplant the risk-utility analysis Texas has for years employed in determining whether a defectively designed product is unreasonably dangerous. That analysis involves consideration of several factors, which we listed in *American Tobacco Co. v. Grinnell* (1997) as including:

(1) the utility of the product to the user and to the public as a whole weighed against the gravity and likelihood of injury from its use; (2) the availability of a substitute product which would meet the same need and not be unsafe or unreasonably expensive; (3) the manufacturer's ability to eliminate the unsafe character of the product without seriously impairing its usefulness or significantly increasing its costs; (4) the user's anticipated awareness of the dangers inherent in the product and their avoidability because of the general public knowledge of the obvious condition of the product, or of the existence of suitable warnings or instructions, and (5) the expectations of the ordinary consumer.

Rather, § 82.005 prescribes two elements—a safer alternative design and producing cause—that must be proved, but are not alone sufficient, to establish liability for a defectively designed product. Section 82.005 reflects the trend in our common-law jurisprudence of elevating the availability of a safer alternative design from a factor to be considered in the risk-utility analysis to a requisite element of a cause of action for defective design. Whether a defective-design action can be maintained under the circumstances posed in the certified question does not, therefore, depend entirely on § 82.005. A claimant must not only meet the proof requirements of the statute but must show, under the common law, that the product was defectively designed so as to be unreasonably dangerous, taking into consideration the utility of the product and the risk involved in its use.

The certified question inquires whether a defective-design action can be maintained under several conditions.

1. *A child was injured not by his own use of the product but by another child's use.* In [a 1969 case], we held that a bystander injured by another's use of a defective product could recover against the product manufacturer. In some situations the relationship between the product defect and the plaintiff's injury might be too attenuated to allow recovery, but that does not appear to be the case here. Thus, Ruben is not precluded from recovering against Tokai because he was burned as a result of his sister's use of the lighter and not by his own use.

2. *The injury was caused by a child's misuse of the product, the risk of which was obvious to the product manufacturer.* Implicit in the question is that it was also obvious to the manufacturer that an intended adult user would allow a child access to the product. Foreseeability of risk of harm is a requirement for liability for a defectively designed product; a product need not be designed to reduce or avoid unforeseeable risks of harm. Risk must be assessed in light of both the gravity and the likelihood of injury from a product's use. But the fact that the foreseeable risk of harm is due to a misuse of the product, rather than an intended use, is not an absolute bar to liability for that portion of an injury caused by a product's defective design. Instead, misuse of a product is a factor that must be considered in allocating responsibility for the injury. In this case, misuse of the lighter by Daphne, Hernandez, or Emeterio does not preclude Ruben from recovering damages caused by the lighter's allegedly defective design.

3. *The risk of injury from a child's misuse of the product was also obvious to the product's intended adult users.* The fact that a product user is or should be aware of the existence and avoidability of dangers inherent in a product's use that are obvious, commonly known, or warned against, is an important consideration in determining whether the product is unreasonably dangerous.

In the risk-utility analysis, that fact may even be decisive in a particular case. But in general, the obviousness of danger in and of itself is not an absolute bar—like certain affirmative defenses—to liability for a defective design. Thus, while Hernandez and Emeterio's acknowledged awareness of the dangers involved in allowing children access to lighters weighs against a finding that Tokai's lighter was unreasonably dangerous as designed, it is not, by itself, an absolute bar to recovery. Whether this factor is determinative in this case is a question that must be decided by applying the risk-utility analysis in the federal court proceeding.

4. *A safer alternative was available.* This is a prerequisite to liability under § 82.005(b), as it has come to be under the common law. The statute requires a claimant to prove that an alternative design (i) would in reasonable probability have prevented or significantly reduced the risk of the claimant's injury or damage (ii) without substantially impairing the product's utility, and (iii) was economically and technologically feasible when the product was manufactured or sold. The relevant risk of injury or damage under the statute is the risk to the claimant; in this case, the risk is that Ruben would be injured in a fire started by his minor sister with a disposable lighter obtained from their mother's purse. The relevant utility is to the intended users of the product, here all adults. To prove a safer alternative design, Hernandez must prove . . . that the child-resistant design available when the lighter was manufactured (the parties all agree that such a design was feasible then) would in reasonable probability have prevented or significantly reduced the risk of Ruben's being burned as a result of his sister's misuse of the lighter without substantially impairing the lighter's utility to the product's intended adult users. As we have already explained, however, proof of a safer alternative design under § 82.005 is necessary but not sufficient to maintain a defective-design claim. The claimant must also prove a design defect, which, under Texas common law, is a condition of the product that renders it unreasonably dangerous as designed, taking into consideration the utility of the product and the risk involved in its use.

5. *The product was intended to be used only by adults.* A product's utility and risk under the common-law test must both be measured with reference to the product's intended users. A product intended for adults need not be designed to be safe for children solely because it is possible for the product to come into a child's hands. A child may hurt himself or others with a hammer, a knife, an electrical appliance, a power tool, or a ladder; he may fall into a pool, or start a car. The manufacturers and sellers of such products need not make them childproof merely because it is possible for children to cause harm with them and certain that some children will do so. The risk that adults, for whose use the products were intended, will allow children access to them, resulting in harm, must be balanced against the products' utility to their intended users.

Even if an alternative design [exists], it still may not be sufficient for defective-design liability if it overly restricts consumer choice. Consumers are entitled to consider the risks and benefits of the different designs and choose among them. The briefs in this case suggest [these] examples: a chemistry set for teenagers that includes a Bunsen burner and chemicals that most younger children should not be allowed to use; a high-power nail gun that should be used only by experienced carpenters; and a sailboat designed for speed rather than stability that is safe only for more experienced sailors. A chemistry set designed for the ordinary teenager is not unreasonably dangerous solely because it is possible that a younger sibling could get into it and harm himself or others. Products liability law does not force experienced carpenters to use only nail guns that are safe for the garage workshop. A sailboat pilot may choose between speed and stability. To make such products safe for the least apt, and unintended, user would hold other users hostage to the lowest common denominator.

A disposable lighter without a child-resistant mechanism is safe as long as its use is restricted to adults, as its manufacturer and users intend. Tokai makes lighters with and without child-resistant devices. Adults who want to minimize the possibility that their lighter may be misused by a child may purchase the child-resistant models. Adults who prefer the other model, as Hernandez and Emeterio did, may purchase it (although we note that the federal Consumer Product Safety Commission has adopted a safety standard banning the manufacture and importation of non-child-resistant disposable lighters after July 12, 1994). Whether adult users of lighters should be deprived of this choice of product design because of the risk that some children will obtain lighters that are not child-resistant and cause harm is the proper focus of the common-law risk-utility test.

The utility of disposable lighters must be measured with reference to the intended adult users. Consumer preference . . . is one consideration. Tokai also argues that adults whose dexterity is impaired, such as by age or disease, cannot operate child-resistant lighters, but Hernandez disputes this. If Tokai were shown to be correct, then that would be an additional consideration in assessing the utility of non-child-resistant lighters.

The relevant risk includes consideration of both the likelihood that adults will allow children access to lighters and the gravity of the resulting harm. The risk is not that a child who plays with a lighter may harm himself. We assume that that risk is substantial. As Hernandez and Emeterio both acknowledged in this case, they would not allow a child to have a lighter and would discipline a child caught playing with one. Rather, the risk is that a lighter will come into a child's hands. The record before us suggests that children will almost certainly obtain access to lighters [and] that this will not happen often in comparison with the number of lighters sold, but that when it does happen the harm caused can be extreme. Each of these considerations is relevant in assessing the risk of non-child-resistant lighters.

In sum, a manufacturer's intention that its product be used only by adults does not insulate it from liability for harm caused by a child who gains access to the product, but liability standards must be applied in the context of the intended users. Tokai contends [, however,] that simple tools, like hammers and knives, whose essential utility involves intrinsic and obvious dangers to children, should not, as a matter of law, be unreasonably dangerous. A few other courts have adopted this approach, but we do not think it helpful.

The obviousness of the risk of harm and the inherent nature of the danger are, as we have explained, important factors to be considered in determining whether a product is unreasonably dangerous, and in a given case they may be conclusive of that issue. But that depends on an assessment of all the relevant considerations in the risk-utility analysis, not on whether a product can be called a simple tool. Many simple tools are not defectively designed merely because they are not child-proof, but the reason is because they are not unreasonably dangerous under the risk-utility test, not because they are simple tools.

Tokai also argues that as a simple matter of policy, parents are in a far better position to prevent children from causing harm with products like disposable lighters than manufacturers are. While we do not disagree with this, we think it should be factored into the risk-utility analysis and the determination of causation rather than used to preempt all causes of action in which it might be raised.

Certified question answered through holding of Supreme Court of Texas that claimant may maintain defective-design claim in circumstances presented by certified question if, with reference to product's intended users, design defect makes product unreasonably dangerous, "safer alternative design" as defined by state statute is available, and defect is producing cause of injury.

The *Restatement (Third)*

In 1998, the American Law Institute published its *Restatement (Third) of Torts: Product Liability.* Although many courts now discuss the new *Restatement,* it has not supplanted negligence and section 402A in most states as we write late in 2002. The *Restatement (Third),* however, may signal the likely evolution of product liability law in the coming years.

Basic Provisions The *Restatement (Third)*'s basic product liability rule states: "One engaged in the business of selling or otherwise distributing products who sells or distributes a defective product is subject to liability for harm to persons or property caused by the defect." Like section 402A, this rule covers only those who are engaged in the business of selling the kind of product that injured the plaintiff. The rule also resembles 402A in covering not only manufacturers, but other sellers down the product's chain of distribution. Unlike

402A, however, the *Restatement (Third)* does not require that the product be unreasonably dangerous.

Specific Rules The *Restatement (Third)* states special rules governing the sale of product components, prescription drugs, medical devices, food products, and used goods. More importantly, it adds substance to the general rule just stated by describing three kinds of product defects.

1. *Manufacturing defects.* A manufacturing defect occurs when the product does not conform to its intended design at the time it leaves the manufacturer's hands. This includes products that are incorrectly assembled, physically flawed, or damaged.

2. *Inadequate instructions or warnings.* Although the *Restatement (Third)* applies strict liability to manufacturing defects, liability for inadequate instructions or warnings resembles negligence more than strict liability. (The *Restatement (Third)*'s rules regarding failures to warn do not use the term *negligence,* however.) This liability exists when reasonable instructions or warnings could have reduced the product's foreseeable risk of harm, but the seller did not provide such instructions or warnings and the product thus was not reasonably safe. Manufacturers and sellers are liable only for failing to instruct or warn about *reasonably foreseeable* harms, and not about every conceivable risk their products might present. As with negligence and 402A, moreover, they need not warn about obvious and generally known risks. The other failure-to-warn factors discussed earlier probably apply under the new *Restatement* as well.

3. *Design defects.* Design defect liability under the *Restatement (Third)* is determined under principles resembling those of negligence (though the *Restatement (Third)* rule for such cases again avoids using the term *negligence*). A product is defective in design when its foreseeable risks of harm could have been reduced or avoided by a reasonable alternative design, and the omission of that design rendered the product not reasonably safe. The plaintiff must prove that a reasonable alternative design was possible at the time of the sale.

In the *Wright* case, which follows, the Iowa Supreme Court announces that in design defect cases, Iowa will follow the *Restatement (Third)*'s rule rather than the previously applied rules of strict liability and negligence.

Wright v. Brooke Group Limited *2002 Iowa Sup. LEXIS 202 (Iowa Sup. Ct. 2002)*

Robert and DeAnn Wright sued various cigarette manufacturers in federal district court in an effort to obtain damages for harms allegedly resulting from Robert's cigarette smoking. The plaintiffs made various claims, including negligence, strict liability, breach of implied warranty, breach of express warranty, fraudulent misrepresentation and nondisclosure, and civil conspiracy. The defendants' motion to dismiss was largely overruled by the federal court. Thereafter, the defendants asked the federal court to certify questions of law to the Iowa Supreme Court, in accordance with Iowa Code § 684A.1

Concluding that the case presented potentially determinative state law questions as to which there was either no controlling precedent or ambiguous precedent, the federal court certified various questions to the Iowa Supreme Court. Two of the certified questions dealt with strict liability. They read as follows: "In a design defect products liability case, what test applies under Iowa law to determine whether cigarettes are unreasonably dangerous? What requirements must be met under the applicable test?"

The Iowa Supreme Court issued an opinion answering the various questions certified by the federal court. The portions of the opinion included here dealt with the above-quoted questions regarding strict liability.

Ternus, Justice The Iowa Supreme Court first applied strict liability in tort for a product defect in 1970, adopting *Restatement (Second) of Torts* § 402A (1965). Section 402A provides:

> (1) One who sells any product in a defective condition unreasonably dangerous to the user or consumer or to his property is subject to liability for physical harm thereby caused to the ultimate user or consumer, or to his property, if
> (a) the seller is engaged in the business of selling such a product, and
> (b) it is expected to and does reach the user or consumer without substantial change in the condition in which it is sold.
> (2) The rule stated in Subsection (1) applies although
> (a) the seller has exercised all possible care in the preparation and sale of his product, and

> (b) the user or consumer has not bought the product from or entered into any contractual relation with the seller.

Our purpose in adopting this provision was to relieve injured plaintiffs of the burden of proving the elements of warranty or negligence theories, thereby insuring "that the costs of injuries resulting from defective products are borne by the manufacturers that put such products on the market." *Hawkeye-Security Insurance Co. v. Ford Motor Co.* (Iowa 1970). Consistent with this purpose, we held that a plaintiff seeking to recover under a strict liability theory need not prove the manufacturer's negligence. Moreover, we concluded that application of strict liability in tort was not exclusive and did not preclude liability based on the alternative ground of negligence, when negligence could be proved. Although *Hawkeye-Security* was a manufacturing defect case, our opinion implied that strict liability in tort was applicable to design defects as well.

In *Aller v. Rodgers Machinery Manufacturing Co.* (Iowa 1978), a design defect case, our court discussed in more detail the test to be applied in strict liability cases. In that case, the plaintiff asked the court to eliminate the "unreasonably dangerous" element of strict products liability, arguing that to require proof that the product was *unreasonably* dangerous injected considerations of negligence into strict liability, thwarting the purpose of adopting a strict liability theory. We rejected the plaintiff's request to eliminate the "unreasonably dangerous" element, concluding the theories of strict liability and negligence were distinguishable: "In strict liability the plaintiff's proof concerns the condition (dangerous) of a product which is designed or manufactured in a particular way. In negligence the proof concerns the reasonableness of the manufacturer's conduct in designing and selling the product as he did."

[This articulated distinction was], however, somewhat obscured by [*Aller*'s] explanation of the proof required in a strict liability case. Relying on comment *i* to § 402A, we held that a plaintiff seeking to prove a product was in a "defective condition unreasonably dangerous" must show that the product was "dangerous to an extent beyond that which would be contemplated by the ordinary consumer who purchases it, with the ordinary knowledge common to the community as to its characteristics." We went on, however, to discuss *how* the plaintiff is to prove the defective condition was unreasonably dangerous:

> In order to prove that a product is unreasonably dangerous, the injured plaintiff must prove the product is dangerous and that it was unreasonable for such a danger to exist. Proof of unreasonableness involves a balancing process. On one side of the scale is the utility of the product and on the other is the risk of its use. Whether the doctrine of negligence or strict liability is being used to impose liability *the same process is going on in each instance,* i.e., weighing the utility of the article against the risk of its use.

Two conclusions can be drawn from [the above] discussion in *Aller:* (1) the legal principles applied in a strict liability case include both a consumer expectation or consumer contemplation test and a risk/benefit or risk/utility analysis; and (2) the risk/benefit analysis employed in a strict liability design defect case is the same weighing process as that used in a negligence case.

Since *Aller,* this court has varied in its application of the tests set forth in that decision, sometimes applying both tests

and sometimes applying only the consumer expectation test. On the other hand, we have continued to equate the strict liability risk/benefit analysis used in a design defect case with that applied in a [negligent] design case.

One final development in product liability law in Iowa is worth mentioning before we address the precise issue in this case. In *Olson v. Prosoco* (Iowa 1994), this court rejected the distinction between negligence and strict liability claims first articulated in *Aller.* Examining a failure-to-warn case, we abandoned the analysis that differentiated strict liability from negligence on the basis that negligence focuses on the defendant's conduct while strict liability focuses on the condition of the product. We concluded that "inevitably the conduct of the defendant in a failure-to-warn case becomes the issue," and [that as a result], the product/conduct distinction had "little practical significance." Our acknowledgment that the test for negligence and strict liability were in essence the same led this court to discard the theory of strict liability in failure-to-warn cases and hold that such claims should be submitted under a theory of negligence only.

[W]e turn now to the parties' arguments on the question of the applicable test for determining whether cigarettes are unreasonably dangerous. The parties disagree as to whether the consumer contemplation test and the risk/benefit analysis are alternative tests or whether both apply in all product defect cases. The defendants assert that only the consumer contemplation test . . . should be used to determine whether cigarettes are unreasonably dangerous. Their desire for this test stems from their related argument that common knowledge of the risks of cigarette smoking precludes a finding that cigarettes are dangerous "to an extent beyond that which would be contemplated by the ordinary consumer." *Restatement (Second) of Torts* § 402A, comment *i.* The defendants argue that the risk/utility test should not be applied because it was designed for those products, unlike cigarettes, "about which the ordinary consumer would not normally have an expectation of safety or dangerousness."

The plaintiffs contend that both the consumer contemplation and risk/utility tests apply in design defect cases to determine whether a product is unreasonably dangerous. Alternatively, [the plaintiffs suggest that] this case presents an appropriate opportunity for the court to adopt the principles . . . set forth in § 2 of *Restatement (Third) of Torts: Product Liability* [hereinafter "Products Restatement].

In determining what test should be applied in assessing whether cigarettes are unreasonably dangerous, we are confronted with the anomaly of using a risk/benefit analysis for purposes of strict liability based on defective design that is identical to the test employed in proving negligence in product design. This incongruity has drawn our attention once again to the "debate over whether the distinction between strict liability and negligence theories should be maintained when applied to a design defect case." *Lovick v. Wil-Rich* (Iowa 1999). We are convinced such a distinction is illusory, just as we found[, in *Olson,*] no real difference between strict liability and negligence principles in failure-to-warn cases. Because the Products Restatement is consistent with our conclusion, we think it sets forth an intellectually sound set of legal principles for product defect cases.

Before we discuss these principles, we first explain our dissatisfaction with the consumer expectation test advocated by the defendants. As one writer has suggested, the consumer expectation test in reality does little to distinguish strict liability from ordinary negligence:

> The consumer expectations test for strict liability operates effectively when the product defect is a construction or manufacturing defect. . . . An internal standard exists against which to measure the product's condition—the manufacturer's own design standard. In essence, a product flawed in manufacture frustrates the manufacturer's own design objectives. Liability is imposed on manufacturers in these cases even if the manufacturer shows it acted reasonably in making the product. . . . When the claim of defect is based on the product's plan or design, however, the consumer expectations test is inadequate. The test seems to function as a negligence test because a consumer would likely expect the manufacturer to exercise reasonable care in designing the product and using the technology available at that time. . . . Although the consumer expectations test purports to establish [that] the manufacturer's conduct is unimportant, it does not explain what truly converts it into a standard of strict liability.

Keith Miller, *Design Defect Litigation in Iowa: The Myths of Strict Liability,* 40 Drake L. Rev. 465, 473–74 (1991). We agree that the consumer contemplation test is inadequate to differentiate a strict liability design defect claim from a negligent design case. Consequently, any attempts to distinguish the two theories in the context of a defective design are in vain. That brings us to the Products Restatement, which reflects a similar conclusion by its drafters.

The Products Restatement demonstrates a recognition that strict liability is appropriate in manufacturing defect cases, but negligence principles are more suitable for other defective product cases. Accordingly, it "establishes separate standards of liability for manufacturing defects, design defects, and defects based on inadequate instructions or warnings." Products Restatement § 2, comment *a*. Initially,

§ 1 of the Products Restatement provides: "One engaged in the business of selling or otherwise distributing products who sells or distributes a defective product is subject to liability for harm to persons or property caused by the defect." The "unreasonably dangerous" element of § 402A has been eliminated and has been replaced with a multifaceted definition of defective product. This definition is set out in § 2:

> A product is defective when, at the time of sale or distribution, it contains a manufacturing defect, is defective in design, or is defective because of inadequate instructions or warning. A product:
>
> (a) contains a manufacturing defect when the product departs from its intended design even though all possible care was exercised in the preparation and marketing of the product;
>
> (b) is defective in design when the foreseeable risks of harm posed by the product could have been reduced or avoided by the adoption of a reasonable alternative design by the seller or other distributor, or a predecessor in the commercial chain of distribution, and the omission of the alternative design renders the product not reasonably safe;
>
> (c) defective because of inadequate instructions or warnings when the foreseeable risks of harm posed by the product could have been reduced or avoided by the provision of reasonable instructions or warnings by the seller or other distributor, or a predecessor in the commercial chain of distribution, and the omission of the instructions or warnings renders the product not reasonably safe.

The commentators give the following explanation for the analytical framework adopted in the Products Restatement:

> In contrast to manufacturing defects, design defects and defects based on inadequate instructions or warnings are predicated on a different concept of responsibility. In the first place, such defects cannot be determined by reference to the manufacturer's own design or marketing standards because those standards are the very ones that the plaintiffs attack as unreasonable. Some sort of independent assessment of advantages and disadvantages, to which some attach the label "risk-utility balancing," is necessary. Products are not generically defective merely because they are dangerous. Many product-related accident costs can be eliminated only by excessively sacrificing product features that make products useful and desirable. Thus, the various trade-offs need to be considered in determining whether accident costs are more fairly and efficiently borne by accident victims, on the one hand, or, on the other hand, by consumers generally through the mechanism of higher product prices attributable to liability costs imposed by the courts on product sellers.

Products Restatement § 2, comment *a*. [T]he Products Restatement has essentially dropped the consumer expectation test traditionally used in the strict liability analysis and adopted a risk-utility analysis traditionally found in the negligence standard. The Products Restatement [, however,] does not place a conventional label, such as negligence or strict liability, on design defect cases. We question the need for or usefulness of *any* traditional doctrinal label in design defect cases because, as [a Products Restatement comment indicates], a court should not submit both a negligence claim and a strict liability claim based on the same design defect since both claims rest on an identical risk-utility evaluation. Moreover, to persist in using two names for the same claim only continues the dysfunction engendered by § 402A. Therefore, we prefer to label a claim based on a defective product design as a design defect claim without reference to strict liability or negligence.

In summary, we now adopt *Restatement (Third) of Torts: Product Liability* §§ 1 and 2 for product defect cases. Under these sections, a plaintiff seeking to recover damages on the basis of a design defect must prove "the foreseeable risks of harm posed by the product could have been reduced or avoided by the adoption of a reasonable alternative design by the seller or other distributor, or a predecessor in the commercial chain of distribution, and the omission of the alternative design renders the product not reasonably safe." Products Restatement § 2(b); *accord Hawkeye Bank v. State* (Iowa 1994) (requiring "proof of an alternative safer design that is practicable under the circumstances" in negligent design case).

Certified questions answered through Iowa Supreme Court's holding that design defect cases will be governed by the test and requirements of **Restatement (Third) of Torts: Product Liability, §§ 1 and 2.**

Other Theories of Recovery

The Magnuson-Moss Act The relevant civil-recovery provisions of the federal Magnuson-Moss Warranty Act apply to sales of *consumer products* costing more than *$10 per item*. A consumer product is tangible personal property normally used for personal, family, or household purposes. If a seller gives a *written warranty* for such a product to a *consumer,* the warranty must be designated as full or limited. A seller who gives a full warranty promises to: (1) *remedy* any defects in the product and (2) *replace* the product or *refund* its purchase price if, after a reasonable number of attempts, it cannot be repaired.[4] A seller who gives a limited warranty is bound to whatever promises it actually makes. However, neither warranty applies if the seller simply declines to give a written warranty.

Misrepresentation Product liability law has long allowed recoveries for misrepresentations made by sellers of goods. The *Restatement (Third)* does likewise. Its rule applies to merchantlike sellers engaged in the business of selling the product in question. The rule includes fraudulent, negligent, or innocent misrepresentations made by such sellers. The misrepresentation must involve a *material fact* about the product—a fact that would matter to a reasonable buyer. This means that sellers are not liable for inconsequential misstatements, sales talk, and statements of opinion. However, the product need not be defective. Unlike past law, moreover, the misrepresentation need not be made to the public, and the plaintiff need not have justifiably relied upon it. However, it must have made the plaintiff suffer personal injury or property damage.

Industrywide Liability The legal theory we call **industrywide liability** is a way for plaintiffs to bypass problems of causation that exist where several firms within an industry have manufactured a harmful standardized product, and it is impossible for the plaintiff to prove which firm produced the product that injured her. The main reasons for these proof problems are the number of firms producing the product and the time lag between exposure to the product and the appearance of the injury. Most of the cases presenting such problems have involved DES (an antimiscarriage drug that has produced various ailments in daughters of the women to whom it was administered) or diseases resulting from long-term exposure to asbestos. In such cases, each

---

[4]Also, many states have enacted so-called "lemon laws" that may apply only to motor vehicles or to various other consumer products as well. The versions applying to motor vehicles generally require the manufacturer to replace the vehicle or refund its purchase price once certain conditions are met. These conditions may include the following: a serious defect covered by warranty; a certain number of unsuccessful attempts at repair or a certain amount of downtime because of attempted repairs; and the manufacturer's failure to show that the defect is curable.

ETHICS IN ACTION

Litigation against tobacco companies has prolifer-
ated in recent years. Many cases have been brought
by cigarette smokers or the estates of deceased smokers in an effort to obtain damages for the adverse
health effects resulting from their years of smoking
cigarettes. Sometimes class-action suits brought by groups
of smokers or persons exposed to second-hand smoke have
been instituted. The federal government and many state governments have also sued tobacco companies in an effort to
recoup health care costs incurred by those governments in
regard to citizens whose health problems allegedly resulted
from smoking.

The cases against tobacco firms—particularly those
brought by private parties—have been pursued on a wide variety of legal theories that initially included breach of express
or implied warranty, negligent design, negligent failure to
warn, and strict liability. Results have been mixed, with tobacco companies frequently prevailing but plaintiffs occasionally receiving jury verdicts for very large amounts of
damages (some of which have been subject to reduction or
outright elimination by the trial judge or an appellate court).
During the past few years, plaintiffs have had greater success
in cases against tobacco companies than they once did, in
large part because plaintiffs have acquired access to old tobacco industry documents they previously did not have. Some
of these documents have helped plaintiffs augment the traditional product liability claims referred to above with claims
for fraudulent concealment of, and conspiracy to conceal, the
full extent of the health risks of smoking during a time when
tobacco firms' public pronouncements allegedly minimized
or soft-pedaled those risks. Although plaintiffs' cases against
tobacco companies remain far from sure-fire winners, there is
no doubt that plaintiffs' chances of winning such cases are
better today than they were a decade ago.

In addition to the many legal issues spawned by cases against
tobacco companies, various ethical issues come to mind. Consider, for instance, the questions set forth below. Some of them
pertain to tobacco litigation, whereas others pertain to related
issues for business and society. In considering these questions,
you may wish to employ the ethical theories outlined in Chapter 4, as well as that chapter's suggested process for making decisions that carry potential ethical implications.

• Given what is now known about the dangers of tobacco use,
  are the production and sale of tobacco products ethically

justifiable business activities? What are the arguments
each way? Does it make a difference whether the
health hazards of smoking have, or have not, been
fully disclosed by the tobacco companies?

• Would the federal government be acting ethically if it took
  the step of outlawing the production and sale of tobacco
  products? Why or why not?
• If a company that produces a product—whether tobacco or
  another product—acquires information indicating that its
  product may be or is harmful to users of it, does the company owe an ethical duty to disclose this actual or potential
  danger? If so, at what point? What considerations should be
  taken into account?
• If a manufacturer's product—whether tobacco or another
  product—is well-received by users but poses a significant
  risk of harm when used as intended by the manufacturer,
  does the manufacturer owe an ethical duty to take steps to
  redesign the product so as to lessen the risk or severity of
  the harm? Justify your conclusion, noting the considerations you have taken into account.
• When tobacco companies comply with federal law by placing the mandated health warnings on packages of their cigarettes and in their cigarette advertisements, have they simultaneously taken care of any ethical obligations they may
  have regarding disclosure of health risks? Why or why not?
• Are smokers' (or smokers' estates) lawsuits against tobacco
  companies ethically justifiable? If so, is this true of all of
  them or only some of them, and why? If only some are ethically justifiable, which ones, and why? If you believe that
  such lawsuits are not ethically justifiable, why do you hold
  that view?
• Some critics have taken the position that health care cost-
  recouping litigation brought by the federal government and
  state governments against tobacco companies reflects
  hypocrisy, because our governments extend support to tobacco farmers and collect considerable tax revenue from
  parties involved in tobacco growing, tobacco product manufacturing, and tobacco product sales. How do you weigh in
  on this issue? Are there ethical dimensions here? If our federal and state governments are "in bed" with the tobacco industry, did our governments act unethically in pursuing this
  litigation, or would our governments have been acting unethically if they had not pursued this litigation? Be prepared
  to justify your conclusions.

manufacturer of the product can argue that the plaintiff should lose because she cannot show that its product harmed her.

How do courts handle these cases? Most of the time, they continue to deny recovery under traditional causation rules because the special circumstances necessary to trigger application of industrywide liability are found not to be present. However, using various approaches whose many details are beyond the scope of this text, other courts have made it easier for plaintiffs to recover in appropriate cases. Where recovery is allowed, some of these courts have apportioned damages among the firms that might have produced the harm-causing product. Such an apportionment is typically based on market share at some chosen time.

Time Limitations

We now turn to several problems that are common to each major product liability theory but that may be resolved differently from theory to theory. One such problem is the time within which the plaintiff must sue or else lose the case. Traditionally, the main time limits on product liability suits have been the applicable contract and tort **statutes of limitations.** The usual UCC statute of limitations for express and implied warranty claims is four years after the seller offers the defective goods to the buyer (usually, four years after the sale). In tort cases, the applicable statute of limitations may be shorter, depending upon applicable state law. It begins to run, however, only when the defect was or should have been discovered—often, the time of the injury.

In part because of tort reform, some states now impose various other limitations on the time within which product liability suits must be brought. Among these additional time limitations are: (1) special statutes of limitations for product liability cases involving death, personal injury, or property damage (e.g., from one to three years after the time the death or injury occurred or should have been discovered); (2) special time limits for "delayed manifestation" injuries such as those resulting from exposure to asbestos; (3) useful safe life defenses (which prevent plaintiffs from suing once the product's "useful safe life" has passed); and (4) statutes of repose (whose aim is similar). Statutes of repose usually run for a 10- to 12-year period that begins when the product is sold to the first buyer not purchasing for resale—usually an ordinary consumer. In a state with a 10-year statute of repose, for example, such parties cannot recover for injuries that occur more than 10 years after they purchased

the product causing the harm. This is true even when the suit is begun quickly enough to satisfy the applicable statute of limitations.

Damages in Product Liability Cases

The damages obtainable under each theory of product liability recovery strongly influence a plaintiff's strategy. Here, we describe the major kinds of damages awarded in product liability cases, along with the theories under which each can be recovered. One lawsuit may involve claims for all these sorts of damages.

1. *Basis-of-the-bargain damages.* Buyers of defective goods have not received full value for the goods' purchase price. The resulting loss, usually called basis-of-the-bargain damages or **direct economic loss,** is the value of the goods as promised under the contract, minus the value of the goods as received.

Basis-of-the-bargain damages are almost never awarded in tort cases. In express and implied warranty cases, however, basis-of-the-bargain damages are recoverable where there was *privity of contract* (a direct contractual relation) between the plaintiff and the defendant. As discussed in the next section, however, only occasionally will a warranty plaintiff who lacks privity with the defendant obtain basis-of-the-bargain damages. Such recoveries most often occur where an express warranty was made to a remote plaintiff through advertising, brochures, or labels.

2. *Consequential damages.* Consequential damages include **personal injury, property damage** (damage to the plaintiff's other property), and **indirect economic loss** (e.g., lost profits or lost business reputation) resulting from a product defect. Consequential damages also include **noneconomic loss**—for example, pain and suffering, physical impairment, mental distress, loss of enjoyment of life, loss of companionship or consortium, inconvenience, and disfigurement. Noneconomic loss usually is part of the plaintiff's personal injury claim. Recently, some states have limited noneconomic loss recoveries, typically by imposing a dollar cap on them.

Plaintiffs in tort cases normally can recover for personal injury and property damage. Recoveries for foreseeable indirect economic loss sometimes are allowed.

In express and implied warranty cases where *privity exists* between the plaintiff and the defendant, the plaintiff can recover for: (1) personal injury and property damage, if either proximately resulted from the breach of warranty; and (2) indirect economic loss, if the defendant had reason to know that this was likely. As discussed in the next section, a UCC plaintiff who *lacks privity* with the defendant has a reasonably good chance of recovering for personal injury or property damage. Recovery for indirect economic loss is rare because remote sellers usually cannot foresee such losses.

3. *Punitive damages.* Unlike the compensatory damages discussed above, punitive damages are not designed to compensate the plaintiff for harms suffered (even though the plaintiff becomes entitled to collect any punitive damages assessed against the defendant). Punitive damages are intended to punish defendants who have acted in an especially outrageous fashion, and to deter them and others from so acting in the future. Of the various standards for awarding punitive damages, probably the most common is the defendant's conscious or reckless disregard for the safety of those likely to be affected by the goods. Examples include concealment of known product hazards, knowing violation of government or industry product safety standards, failure to correct known dangerous defects, and grossly inadequate product testing or quality control procedures. In view of their perceived frequency, size, and effect on business and the economy, punitive damages were targeted for some states' tort reform efforts during the 1980s and 1990s. The approaches taken by the resulting statutes vary. Some set the standards for punitive damage assessment and the plaintiff's burden of proof; some articulate factors courts should consider when ruling on punitive damage awards; and some create special procedures for punitive damage determinations. A number of states have also limited the size of punitive damage recoveries, usually by restricting them to some multiple of the plaintiff's compensatory damages or by putting a flat dollar cap on them.

Assuming that the standards just described have been met, punitive damages are recoverable in tort cases. Because of the traditional rule that punitive damages are not available in contract cases, they seldom are awarded in express and implied warranty cases.

The No-Privity Defense

Today, defective products often move through long chains of distribution before reaching the person they harm. This means that a product liability plaintiff often has not dealt directly with the party ultimately responsi-

ble for her losses. For example, in a chain of distribution involving defective component parts, the parts may move *vertically* from their manufacturer to the manufacturer of a product in which those parts are used, and then to a wholesaler and a retailer before reaching the eventual buyer. The defect's consequences may move *horizontally* as well, affecting members of the buyer's family, guests in her home, and even bystanders. If the buyer or one of these parties suffers loss because of the defect in the component parts, may she successfully sue the component parts manufacturer or any other party in the vertical chain of distribution with whom she did not directly deal?

Such cases were unlikely to succeed under 19th-century law. At that time, there was no recovery for defective goods without privity of contract between the plaintiff and the defendant. In many such cases, a buyer would have been required to sue his dealer. If the buyer was successful, the retailer might have sued the wholesaler, and so on up the chain. For various reasons, the party ultimately responsible for the defect often escaped liability.

Tort Cases

By now, the old no-liability-outside-privity rule has been severely eroded, if not eliminated, in tort cases. It has no effect in strict liability cases, where even bystanders can recover against remote manufacturers. In negligence cases, a plaintiff generally recovers against a remote defendant if the plaintiff's loss was a reasonably foreseeable consequence of the defect. Depending on the circumstances, therefore, bystanders and other distant parties may recover in a negligence case against a manufacturer. The *Restatement (Third)* suggests that tort principles should govern the privity determination. This should mean a test of reasonable foreseeability in most instances.

Warranty Cases

The no-privity defense retains some vitality in UCC cases. Unfortunately, the law on this subject is complex and confusing. Under the Code, the privity question is formally governed by section 2–318, which comes in three alternative versions. Section 2–318's language, however, is a less-than-reliable guide to the courts' actual behavior in UCC privity cases.

UCC Section 2–318 Alternative A to section 2–318 states that a seller's express or implied warranty runs to natural persons in the family or household of *his* (the seller's) buyer and to guests in his buyer's home, if they suffer personal injury and if it was reasonable to expect that they might use, consume, or be affected by the goods sold. On its face, Alternative A does little to undermine the traditional no-privity defense.

Alternatives B and C go much further. Alternative B extends the seller's express or implied warranty to any natural person who has suffered personal injury, if it was reasonable to expect that this person would use, consume, or be affected by the goods. Alternative C is much the same, but it extends the warranty to any person (not just natural persons) and to those suffering injury in general (not just personal injury). If the reasonable-to-expect test is met, these two provisions should extend the warranty to many remote parties, including bystanders.

Departures from Section 2–318 For various reasons, section 2–318's literal language sometimes has little relevance in UCC privity cases. Some states have adopted privity statutes that differ from any version of 2–318. One of the comments to section 2–318, moreover, allows courts to extend liability beyond what the section expressly permits. Finally, versions B and C are fairly open-ended as written. The plaintiff's ability to recover outside privity in warranty cases thus varies from state to state and situation to situation. The most important factors affecting resolution of this question are:

1. Whether it is *reasonably foreseeable* that a party such as the plaintiff would be harmed by the product defect in question.

2. The *status of the plaintiff.* On average, consumers and other natural persons fare better outside privity than do corporations and other business concerns.

3. The *type of damages* the plaintiff has suffered. In general, remote plaintiffs are: *(a)* most likely to recover for personal injury, *(b)* somewhat less likely to recover for property damage, *(c)* occasionally able to obtain basis-of-the-bargain damages, and *(d)* seldom able to recover for indirect economic loss. Recall from the previous section that a remote plaintiff is most likely to receive basis-of-the-bargain damages where an express warranty was made to him through advertising, brochures, or labels.

The *Minnesota Mining & Manufacturing* case, which follows, grapples with a version of Alternative C to section 2–318. How might the case be decided under the factors just listed?

Minnesota Mining & Manufacturing Co. v. Nishika, Ltd.
565 N.W.2d 16 (Minn. Sup. Ct. 1997)

James Bainbridge and Daniel Fingarette [the claimants] formulated a plan for a three-dimensional photography business through four independent companies. In January of 1988, Bainbridge met with officials of the Minnesota Mining & Manufacturing Company (3M) to seek assistance with the three-dimensional film development process. In mid-1989, 3M formulated a new emulsion that it claimed would work well with the film development process. 3M apparently understood that this emulsion would be used in combination with a backcoat sauce that 3M had also developed. In December of 1989, 3M began selling the new emulsion and backcoat sauce to two of the claimants' four companies, but not to the two others. After Bainbridge and Fingarette began using 3M's new emulsion, they encountered a problem with the film development process: the photographs faded, losing their three-dimensional effect. By early 1990, the claimants experienced a significant decline in camera sales. 3M eventually solved the problem, but the claimants' business ultimately failed.

The claimants' four companies sued 3M in a Texas trial court for, among other things, breach of express and implied warranties. They argued that the photographic fading was caused by the incompatibility of 3M's new emulsion and its old backcoat sauce. The jury concluded that 3M breached an express warranty for the emulsion and implied warranties for the emulsion and the backcoat sauce. Applying Minnesota law, the trial court awarded the four firms $29,873,599 in lost profits. An intermediate appellate court upheld this award. The Texas Supreme Court withheld final judgment and certified the following question to the Minnesota Supreme Court: "For breach of warranty under [Minnesota's version of UCC section 2–318], is a seller liable to a person who never acquired any goods from the seller, directly or indirectly, for pure economic damages (e.g., lost profits), unaccompanied by any injury to the person or the person's property?" This question arose because two of the plaintiff companies, while suffering losses due to 3M's breaches of warranty, had not dealt directly with 3M. In the following opinion, the Minnesota Supreme Court answers the Texas Supreme Court's question.

Keith, Chief Justice The certified question asks whether a seller may be held liable for breach of warranty to a plaintiff, who never used, purchased, or otherwise acquired goods from the seller, for lost profits unaccompanied by personal injury or property damage. Unlike the other two plaintiffs, two of them did not deal directly with 3M nor did they use, purchase, or otherwise acquire the 3M goods at issue. Hence, they premise their recovery of lost profits on the statutory extension of warranty protection to certain noncontracting parties ("third-party beneficiaries"). The third-party beneficiaries provision of Minnesota's Uniform Commercial Code addresses the reach of express and implied warranties to "injured" parties lacking privity of contract with the seller. Essentially, the provision broadens the reach of warranties by narrowing the lack-of-privity defense: "A seller's warranty whether express or implied extends to any person who may reasonably be expected to use, consume, or be affected by the goods and who is injured by breach of the warranty." The term "person" includes corporations and other business organizations. Minnesota's current version [of section 2–318] is somewhat broader than the broadest of three options recommended by the drafters of the model U.C.C. in 1966. We agree with 3M that the statute is not so clear and free from ambiguity that we may disregard legislative intent or the consequences of a particular construction. The term "injured" is not defined in the UCC, nor is it used elsewhere in the text of Article 2. As applied to two of the plaintiffs, the reach of the section is unclear.

Under this privity provision, this court has sanctioned the recovery of lost profits (one form of economic loss) by a third-party beneficiary whose damages arose from a remote seller's breach of warranty. We have also indicated that plaintiffs who never used, purchased, or otherwise acquired defective goods may qualify as third-party beneficiaries when they suffer property damage. But this court has never gone so far as to hold that the statute reaches a plaintiff who is seeking lost profits unaccompanied by physical injury or property damage and who never used, purchased, or otherwise acquired the goods in question. To do so would expand warranty liability well beyond the limits contemplated by the legislature.

The background and aims of this state's privity provision lead us to conclude that the scope of a seller's liability for breach of warranty should recede as the relationship between a "beneficiary" of the warranty and the seller's goods becomes more remote. Those who purchase, use, or otherwise acquire warranted goods have standing to sue for purely economic losses. Those who lack any such connection to the warranted goods must demonstrate physical injury or property damage before economic losses are recoverable. Any other result implies almost unlimited liability for sellers of warranted goods. If the section were interpreted as the plaintiffs advocate, it seems that their individual employees, or perhaps even their families, would have standing to sue 3M for causing the loss of their jobs or even a decline in their wages. The plaintiffs appear to advocate warranty recovery as a catch-all alternative for parties with no viable legal basis for suit. The risk, however, is that the fortuitous existence of a warranty—between some seller and some buyer, somewhere—would allow remote yet foreseeable parties to recover for their hampered expectations, while others in similar circumstances—but who could not identify a warranty—would not.

Confronted with liability of this magnitude, sellers would be encouraged to attempt to disclaim warranties or exclude consequential damages remedies—affecting both the immediate buyer and third-party beneficiaries alike. We therefore reject the plaintiffs' reading of the statute—an interpretation that would likely lead to a variety of unreasonable, unjust, and absurd results that we cannot imagine were intended by the legislature. In light of the statute's language and purpose, and consistent with the legislature's apparent intent, the best reading of the statute is that noncontracting parties who never used, purchased, or otherwise acquired the seller's warranted goods may not seek lost profits, unaccompanied by physical injury or property damage, for breach of warranty under the statute.

The Minnesota Supreme Court answered the Texas Supreme Court's certified question in the negative. This meant that two of the four plaintiff corporations could not recover lost profits. Later, the Texas Supreme Court applied the present case to deny these two firms recovery.

Disclaimers and Remedy Limitations

A product liability **disclaimer** is a clause in the sales contract whereby the seller attempts to eliminate *liability* it might otherwise have under the theories of recovery described earlier in the chapter. A **remedy limitation** is a clause attempting to block recovery of certain *damages*. If a disclaimer is effective, no damages of any sort are recoverable under the legal theory attacked by the disclaimer. A successful remedy limitation prevents the plaintiff from recovering certain types of damages but does not attack the plaintiff's theory of recovery. Damages not excluded still may be recovered because the theory is left intact.

The main justification for enforcing disclaimers and remedy limitations is freedom of contract. Why, however, would any rational contracting party freely accept a disclaimer or remedy limitation? Because sellers need not insure against lawsuits for defective goods accompanied by an effective disclaimer or remedy limitation, they should be able to sell those goods more cheaply. Thus, enforcing such clauses allows buyers to obtain a lower price by accepting the economic risk of a product defect. For purchases by ordinary consumers and other unsophisticated buyers, however, this argument often is illusory. Sellers normally present the disclaimer or remedy limitation in a standardized, take-it-or-leave-it fashion. It is also doubtful whether many consumers read disclaimers and remedy limitations at the time of purchase, or would comprehend them if they did read them. As a result, there is little or no genuine bargaining over disclaimers or remedy limitations in consumer situations. Instead, they are effectively dictated by a seller with superior size and organization. These observations, however, are less valid when the buyer is a business entity with the capability to engage in genuine bargaining with sellers.

Because the realities surrounding the sale differ from situation to situation, and because some theories of recovery are more hospitable to contractual limitation than others, the law on product liability disclaimers and remedy limitations is complicated. We begin by discussing implied warranty disclaimers. Then we examine disclaimers of express warranty liability, negligence liability, 402A liability, and liability under the *Restatement (Third),* before considering remedy limitations separately.

Implied Warranty Disclaimers

The Basic Tests of UCC Section 2–316(2) UCC section 2–316(2) makes it relatively easy for sellers to disclaim the implied warranties of merchantability and fitness for a particular purpose. The section states that to exclude or modify the implied warranty of merchantability, a seller must: (1) use the word *merchantability,* and (2) make the disclaimer conspicuous if it is written. To exclude or modify the implied warranty of fitness, a seller must: (1) use a writing, and (2) make the disclaimer conspicuous. A disclaimer is conspicuous if it is written so that a reasonable person ought to have noticed it. Capital letters, larger type, contrasting type, and contrasting colors usually suffice.

Unlike the fitness warranty disclaimer, a disclaimer of the implied warranty of merchantability can be oral. Although disclaimers of the latter warranty must use the word *merchantability,* no special language is needed to disclaim the implied warranty of fitness. For example, a conspicuous written statement that "THERE ARE NO WARRANTIES THAT EXTEND BEYOND THE DESCRIPTION ON THE FACE HEREOF" disclaims the implied warranty of fitness but not the implied warranty of merchantability.

Other Ways to Disclaim Implied Warranties: Section 2–316(3) According to UCC section 2–316(3)(a), sellers may also disclaim either implied warranty by using such terms as "with all faults," "as is," and "as they stand." Some courts have held that these terms must be conspicuous to be effective as disclaimers. Other courts have allowed such terms to be effective disclaimers only in sales of used goods.

UCC section 2–316(3)(b) describes two situations in which the buyer's *inspection* of the goods or her *refusal to inspect* may operate as a disclaimer. If a buyer examines the goods before the sale and fails to discover a defect that should have been reasonably apparent to her, there can be no implied warranty claim based on that defect. Also, if a seller requests that the buyer examine the goods and the buyer refuses, the buyer cannot base an implied warranty claim on a defect that would have been reasonably apparent had she made the inspection. The definition of a reasonably apparent defect varies with the buyer's expertise. Unless the defect is blatantly obvious, ordinary consumers may have little to fear from section 2–316(3)(b).

Finally, UCC section 2–316(3)(c) says that an implied warranty may be excluded or modified by *course of dealing* (the parties' previous conduct), *course of performance* (the parties' previous conduct under the same contract), or *usage of trade* (any practice regularly observed in the trade). For example, if it is accepted in the local cattle trade that buyers who inspect the seller's cattle and reject certain animals must accept all defects in the cattle actually purchased, such buyers cannot mount an implied warranty claim regarding those defects.

Unconscionable Disclaimers From the previous discussion, it seems that any seller who retains a competent attorney can escape implied warranty liability at will. In fact, however, a seller's ability to disclaim implied warranties sometimes is restricted by the doctrine of **unconscionability** established by UCC section 2–302 and discussed in Chapter 15. By now, almost all courts apply section 2–302's unconscionability standards to implied warranty disclaimers even though those disclaimers satisfy UCC section 2–316(2). Despite a growing willingness to protect smaller firms that deal with corporate giants, however, courts still tend to reject unconscionability claims where business parties have contracted in a commercial context. Implied warranty disclaimers often are declared unconscionable, however, in personal injury cases brought by ordinary consumers.

The Impact of Magnuson-Moss The Magnuson-Moss Act also limits a seller's ability to disclaim implied warranties. If a seller gives a consumer a full warranty on consumer goods whose price exceeds $10, the seller may not disclaim, modify, or limit the duration of any implied warranty. If a limited warranty is given, the seller may not disclaim or modify any implied warranty but may limit its duration to the duration of the limited warranty if this is done conspicuously and if the limitation is not unconscionable. These are significant limitations on a seller's power to disclaim implied warranties. Presumably, however, a seller still can disclaim by refusing to give a written warranty while placing the disclaimer on some other writing.

Express Warranty Disclaimers

UCC section 2–316(1) says that an express warranty and a disclaimer should be read consistently if possible, but that the disclaimer must yield if such a reading is unreasonable. Because it normally is unreasonable for a seller to exclude with one hand what he has freely and openly promised with the other, it is quite difficult to disclaim an express warranty.

Disclaimers of Tort Liability

Disclaimers of negligence liability and strict liability are usually ineffective in cases involving ordinary consumers. However, some courts enforce such disclaimers where both parties are business entities that: (1) dealt in a commercial setting, (2) had relatively equal bargaining power, (3) bargained over the product's specifications, and (4) negotiated the risk of loss from product defects (e.g., the disclaimer itself). Even though it has a provision that seems to bar all disclaimers, the same should be true under the *Restatement (Third)*.

Limitation of Remedies

In view of the expense they can create for sellers, consequential damages are the usual target of remedy limitations. When a limitation of consequential damages suc-

---

CYBERLAW IN ACTION

In Chapters 9 and 11, you read about shrinkwrap and clickwrap contracts, which are often used in sales of computer hardware and licenses of software and in establishing terms of use for access to networks and websites. It is extremely common for these shrinkwrap or clickwrap contracts to contain **warranty disclaimers** and **limitation of remedy** clauses. For some examples of how these disclaimers and limitations of remedy look, see *Warranty and Liability Disclaimer Clauses in Current Shrinkwrap and Clickwrap Contracts,* http://www.cptech.org/ecom/ucita/licenses/liability.html.

The courts that have considered the enforceability of clickwrap or shrinkwrap warranty disclaimers or limitations of remedy have upheld them. For example, in *M. A. Mortenson Company, Inc. v. Timberline Software Corp.,* 998 P.2d 305 (Wash. Sup. Ct. 2000), Mortenson, a general contractor, purchased Timberline's licensed software and used it to prepare a construction bid. Mortenson later discovered that its bid was $1.95 million too low because of a malfunction of the software. When Mortenson sued Timberline and others for breach of warranty, Timberline asserted that the limitation of remedies clause contained in the software license, which limited Mortenson's remedies to the purchase price of the software, prevented Mortenson from recovering any consequential damages caused by a defect in the software. Although Mortenson contended that it never saw or agreed to the terms of the license agreement, the Washington Supreme Court held that the terms of the license became part of the parties' contract. The terms were set forth or referenced in various places, such as the shrinkwrap packaging for the program disks, the software manuals, and the protection devices for the software. Applying the principle that limitations of remedy are generally enforceable unless they are unconscionable, the court found the limitation of remedies clause to be conscionable and enforceable.

ceeds, buyers of the product may suffer. For example, suppose that Dillman buys a computer system for $20,000 under a contract that excludes consequential damages and limits the buyer's remedies to the repair or replacement of defective parts. Suppose also that the system never works properly, causing Dillman to suffer $10,000 in lost profits. If the remedy limitation is enforceable, Dillman could only have the system replaced or repaired by the seller and could not recover his $10,000 in consequential damages.

In tort cases, the tests for the enforceability of remedy limitations resemble the previous tests for disclaimers. Under the UCC, however, the standards for remedy limitations differ from those for disclaimers. UCC section 2–719 allows the limitation of consequential damages in express and implied warranty cases unless the limitation of remedy "fails of its essential purpose" or is unconscionable. The section adds that a limitation of consequential damages is very likely to be unconscionable where the sale is for *consumer goods* and the plaintiff has suffered *personal injury*. Where the loss is "commercial," however, the limitation may or may not be unconscionable.

The *Trinity Industries* case, which follows, deals with a limitation of remedy and whether it either failed of its essential purpose or was unconscionable.

Trinity Industries, Inc. v. McKinnon Bridge Co.   *77 S.W.3d 159 (Tenn. App. 2001)*

McKinnon Bridge Company was a general contractor primarily involved in heavy construction and bridge construction. Trinity Industries, Inc., a steel fabricator, was the supplier of structural steel to McKinnon for use in building the bridge at issue in the case described below. The relationship between the parties began after the state of Tennessee awarded McKinnon a contract to build a bridge over the Tennessee River. Soon after McKinnon was awarded this contract, Trinity presented McKinnon with a bid (i.e., an offer) to supply fabricated steel for the bridge in return for payments totaling $2,535,000.00 from McKinnon. McKinnon's president, acting on behalf of the firm, accepted Trinity's offer and thereby caused the parties' contract to come into being.

During construction, McKinnon discovered that several girders and cross-frame stiffeners supplied by Trinity contained misaligned holes, which prevented proper construction and assembly of the bridge. After McKinnon notified Trinity of the problem, the parties agreed on a remedial plan that was approved by the state. Trinity's representatives went to the job site and re-drilled the holes. The re-drilled holes were approved by McKinnon. In the litigation described below, McKinnon claimed that it later encountered other problems with the steel such as incorrect length, lack of proper curvature, dimensional and fitting errors, and poor quality. None of the steel received from Trinity had been rejected by McKinnon, however, as of May 16, 1995. On that date, the partially constructed bridge collapsed.

After the collapse of the bridge, McKinnon Bridge retained experts, some of whom concluded that the steel provided by Trinity was defective and caused or contributed to the structure's collapse. McKinnon therefore ceased payment on the contract for that steel. At approximately the same time, the state informed McKinnon's president that the firm could reconstruct the bridge with Trinity-supplied steel that was in storage, as long as certain modifications were made to the steel. The state agreed to pay for these changes. McKinnon, however, ordered replacement steel from another supplier without asking Trinity to repair or replace the allegedly defective steel. When asked why his company did not use the steel from Trinity, McKinnon's president stated that it would have been necessary for the steel

to have been picked up [and] taken to Carolina . . . where it was fabricated—and all that freight and allowance, and I made a decision not to use it. . . . Cost was some consideration. It just wasn't worth it, to get in all of the trouble you could have if it didn't work. I would be responsible. They have already put the responsibility on McKinnon Bridge Company's back for that to work, and I didn't want the responsibility.

Trinity filed suit in a Tennessee state court against McKinnon, seeking the remaining $1.6 million due under the steel subcontract. McKinnon answered and counterclaimed against Trinity, alleging both negligence and breach of contract in furnishing steel that did not conform to the contract terms and specifications. (McKinnon also added third-party claims against another contractor involved in construction of the bridge, an engineering firm that worked on the project, and certain quality assurance inspectors. Those claims, however, are not addressed in the portion of the court's decision that appears below.)

Trinity moved for summary judgment on McKinnon's counterclaim. Trinity asserted two grounds: (1) that in a contract for the sale of goods, the buyer is limited to the UCC's contract remedies and cannot maintain a cause of action for negligently performing the contract of sale; and (2) that the parties' contract limited McKinnon's remedies to repair or replacement of any defective goods. The court granted Trinity summary judgment on McKinnon's counterclaim. A trial was later held on Trinity's breach of contract claim against McKinnon. After concluding that none of the nonconformities or defects in the Trinity-supplied steel caused or contributed to the collapse of the bridge, the court held in favor of Trinity for all sums still owed by McKinnon under the contract. McKinnon appealed to the Tennessee Court of Appeals.

Cantrell, Presiding Judge   Trinity's motion for summary judgment was based on two grounds: that (1) McKinnon could not sue Trinity for negligently performing the contract; and (2) that McKinnon's remedies for breach of the contract were limited to repair and/or replacement of the steel. The second [asserted ground] requires us to review the contract between the parties.

[In Paragraph 19 of the bid document setting forth the terms offered by Trinity and accepted by McKinnon, Trinity included a bold-print limited remedy clause that read as follows]:

19. GUARANTY & LIMITATION OF WARRANTY: THERE ARE NO WARRANTIES OF MERCHANTABILITY OR FITNESS OF THE MATERIALS TO BE FURNISHED PURSUANT HERETO WHICH EXTEND BEYOND A PERIOD OF ONE YEAR FROM THE DATE OF COMPLETION OF OUR WORK UNDER THIS CONTRACT. YOU SHALL GIVE US PROMPT NOTICE UPON DISCOVERY OF ANY SUCH CONDITIONS. OUR LIABILITY FOR ANY AND ALL LOSSES AND DAMAGES DIRECT AND CONSEQUENTIAL SUSTAINED BY YOU AND OTHERS ARISING OUT OF THE PERFORMANCE OF THIS CONTRACT SHALL BE LIMITED TO THE FURNISHING, FABRICATING AND DELIVERY OF MATERIAL ONLY OR REPLACEMENT OR CORRECTION OF DEFECTIVE OR NON-CONFORMITY OF MATERIALS WITHIN THE TIME ABOVE STATED.

In [an effort] to escape the [effect] of Paragraph 19, McKinnon argues that the [paragraph] is ambiguous and should be interpreted against Trinity as the party who drafted it. McKinnon [contends] that Paragraph 19 is . . . ambiguous because the first sentence of the paragraph recognizes that there are warranties of fitness and merchantability that are attached to this sale, while the last sentence disclaims these warranties. But this is not an accurate reading of the paragraph. Paragraph 19 is not a disclaimer of warranties. Rather, it limits the duration of the warranties of fitness and merchantability to one year (the first sentence) and limits the remedy for a breach of these warranties to repair or replacement of the goods (the last sentence).

The same section of the UCC that allows the parties to limit their remedies in case of a breach also provides that the limitation is unenforceable (1) if it fails of its essential purpose, Tenn. Code Ann. § 47–2–719(2), or (2) if a limitation on consequential damages is unconscionable, Tenn. Code Ann. § 47–2–719(3). When does the repair-or-replace remedy fail of its essential purpose? As a general rule, [such a] remedy fails of its essential purpose when seller is unable or unwilling to repair or replace in a reasonable time. When the seller is unable or unwilling to put conforming goods in the buyer's hands within a reasonable time, it is a repudiation of the obligations of the warranty and leaves the buyer without a remedy.

In this case the undisputed proof shows that after the bridge collapsed, McKinnon did not attempt to obtain repair or replacement from Trinity. A fair and adequate remedy not invoked by the buyer cannot be said to fail of its essential purpose. We are not prepared to say that in every case the seller must be allowed to repair or replace the goods before the buyer can assert that the limited remedy failed of its essential purpose. But the burden is on the buyer to show why he did not avail himself of the limited remedy. In this case, [McKinnon's president] stated in his discovery deposition that he decided not to demand that Trinity replace the steel because it was too much trouble.

Is the limitation on consequential damages unconscionable? This is a question of law for the court in light of the commercial setting, purpose and effect of the provision. Unconscionability may arise from a lack of a meaningful choice on the part of one party (procedural unconscionability) or from contract terms that are unreasonably harsh (substantive unconscionability). In Tennessee, we have tended to lump the two together and speak of unconscionability resulting

when the inequality of the bargain is so manifest as to shock the judgment of a person of common sense, and where the terms are so oppressive that no reasonable person would make them on one hand, and no honest and fair person would accept them on the other.

Haun v. King, 690 S.W.2d 869, 872 (Tenn. App. 1984). Where the parties possess equal bargaining power, the courts are unlikely to find that their negotiations resulted in an unconscionable bargain, and terms that are common in the industry are generally not unconscionable.

There is nothing in this record on which to base a claim that the limitation on consequential damages for any failure of the steel itself is unconscionable. Both parties were large, successful, and sophisticated businesses possessing equal bargaining power; and there is no claim that an exclusion of consequential damages is uncommon in the steel-furnishing business. Therefore, we do not think the provision of the contract providing for a limited repair or replace remedy is unconscionable.

Judgment in favor of Trinity on its breach of contract claim affirmed; judgment in favor of Trinity on McKinnon's counterclaim affirmed.

[Note: In a separate portion of the opinion not presented here, the Tennessee Court of Appeals held that McKinnon was not entitled to pursue a *negligence* counterclaim regarding matters governed by the parties' contract.]

Defenses

Various matters—for example, the absence of privity or a valid disclaimer—can be considered defenses to a product liability suit. Here, however, our concern is with product liability defenses that involve the plaintiff's behavior. Although the *Restatement (Third)* has a "comparative responsibility" provision that apportions liability among the plaintiff, the seller, and distributors, and various states have similar rules, the following discussion is limited to two-party situations.

The Traditional Defenses

Traditionally, the three main defenses in a product liability suit have been the overlapping trio of product misuse, assumption of risk, and contributory negligence. **Product misuse** (or abnormal use) occurs when the plaintiff uses the product in some unusual, unforeseeable way, and this causes the loss for which he sues. Examples include ignoring the manufacturer's instructions, mishandling the product, and using the product for purposes for which it was not intended. If, however, the defendant had reason to foresee the misuse and failed to take reasonable precautions against it, there is no defense. Product misuse traditionally has been a defense in warranty, negligence, and strict liability cases.

Assumption of risk, discussed in Chapter 7, is the plaintiff's voluntary consent to a known danger. It can occur any time the plaintiff willingly exposes herself to a known product hazard—for example, by consuming obviously adulterated food. As with product misuse, assumption of risk ordinarily has been a defense in warranty, negligence, and strict liability cases.

Contributory negligence, also discussed in Chapter 7, is the plaintiff's failure to act reasonably and prudently. In the product liability context, perhaps the most common example is the simple failure to notice a hazardous product defect. Contributory negligence is a defense in a negligence case (if state law has not replaced the contributory negligence defense with the comparative rules discussed below), but courts have disagreed about whether or when it should be a defense in warranty and strict liability cases.

Comparative Principles

Where they are allowed and proven, the three traditional product liability defenses completely absolve the defendant from liability. Dissatisfaction with this all-or-nothing situation has spurred the increasing use of comparative principles in product liability cases.[5] Rather than letting the traditional defenses completely absolve the defendant, many states now require apportionment of damages on the basis of relative fault. They do so by requiring that the fact finder establish the plaintiff's and the defendant's percentage shares of the total fault for the injury and then award the plaintiff his total provable damages times the defendant's percentage share of the fault.

Unsettled questions persist among the states that have adopted comparative principles. First, it is not always clear what kinds of fault will reduce the plaintiff's recovery. Some state comparative negligence statutes, however, have been read as embracing assumption of risk and product misuse, and state comparative fault statutes usually define fault broadly. Second, comparative principles may assume either the *pure* or the *mixed* forms described in Chapter 7. In "mixed" states, for example, the defendant has a complete defense when the

---

[5]Comparative negligence and comparative fault are discussed in Chapter 7. Although courts and commentators often use the terms comparative fault and comparative negligence interchangeably, comparative fault usually includes forms of blameworthiness other than negligence.

plaintiff was more at fault than the defendant. There is also some uncertainty about the theories of recovery and the types of damage claims to which comparative principles apply.

Problems and Problem Cases

1. Hall Farms, Inc., ordered 40 pounds of Prince Charles watermelon seed from Martin Rispens & Son, a seed dealer. Rispens had obtained the seed from Petoseed Company, Inc., a seed producer. The label on Petoseed's can stated that the seeds are "top quality seeds with high vitality, vigor and germination." Hall Farms germinated the seeds in a greenhouse, before transplanting the small watermelon plants to its fields. Although the plants had a few abnormalities, they grew rapidly. By mid-July, however, purple blotches had spread over most of the crop, and by the end of July the crop was ruined. It was later determined that the crop had been destroyed by "watermelon fruit blotch." Hall Farms' lost profits on the crop came to $180,000. Hall Farms sued Petoseed for, among other things, breach of express warranty. Petoseed moved for summary judgment, but the trial court denied the motion. Petoseed appealed. Was Petoseed entitled to summary judgment in its favor?

2. Ewers, who owned a saltwater aquarium with tropical fish, bought several seashells, a piece of coral, and a driftwood branch from the Verona Rock Shop. Just before the purchase, the salesclerk told Ewers that these items were "suitable for saltwater aquariums, if they [are] rinsed." After making the purchase, Ewers took the items home, rinsed them for 20 minutes in a saltwater solution, and put them in his aquarium. Within a week, 17 of his tropical fish died. The "rinsing" required to prevent their deaths is a week-long cleansing process that involves soaking the shells and the coral in boiling water. Suppose that you are Ewers's attorney in his express warranty case against the shop. Make an argument that the clerk's statement is an express warranty. Make an argument that this warranty was breached. Assume that Ewers did not know the correct "rinsing" procedure.

3. Steven Taterka purchased a 1972 Ford Mustang from a Ford dealer in January 1972. In October 1974, after Taterka had put 75,000 miles on the car and Ford's express warranty had expired, he discovered that the taillight assembly gaskets on his Mustang had been installed in such a way that water was permitted to enter the taillight assembly, causing rust to form. Even though the rusting problem was a recurrent one of which Ford was aware, Ford did nothing for Taterka. Was Ford liable to Taterka under the implied warranty of merchantability?

4. Peter Vamos purchased a sealed bottle of Diet Coke at a grocery store. After Vamos drank from the bottle, he discovered that it contained two AA batteries. Vamos testified that he then became ill for several days. However, there apparently was no evidence that the liquid Vamos drank was poisonous or noxious. Can the Coca-Cola Bottling Company of New York, which bottled the liquid Vamos drank, be liable to him under the implied warranty of merchantability if the liquid in fact was harmless? If so, what result under the foreign–natural test? What result under the reasonable consumer expectations test?

5. Ruby Dempsey purchased a nine-week-old pedigreed male poodle from the American Kennels Pet Stores. She named the poodle Mr. Dunphy. Dempsey later testified that before making the purchase, she told the salesperson that she wanted a dog suitable for breeding purposes. Five days after the sale, she had Mr. Dunphy examined by a veterinarian, who discovered that the poodle had one undescended testicle. This condition did not seriously affect Mr. Dunphy's fertility, but it was a genetic defect that would probably be passed on to any offspring sired. Also, a dog with this condition could not be used as a show dog. Dempsey demanded a refund from American Kennels, but her demand was denied. She then sued in small claims court, alleging that American Kennels had breached the implied warranty of fitness for a particular purpose. Was Dempsey entitled to a judgment in her favor on that claim?

6. Connie Daniell attempted to commit suicide by locking herself inside the trunk of her 1973 Ford LTD. She remained in the trunk for nine days, but survived after finally being rescued. Later, Daniell brought a negligence action against Ford in an effort to recover for her resulting physical and psychological injuries. She contended that the LTD was defectively designed because its trunk did not have an internal release or opening mechanism. She also argued that Ford was liable for negligently failing to warn her that the trunk could not be unlocked from within. Was Ford liable for negligent design and/or negligent failure to warn?

7. Gari West used Ovulen-28, a birth control medication manufactured by Searle & Company. She claimed that the Ovulen-28 caused her to develop a hepatic adenoma (a benign liver tumor), which eventually ruptured, causing a life-threatening situation. Assume that the Ovulen-28 has considerable social utility and cannot feasibly be made safer than it now is. If the Ovulen-28 actually caused West's problem, what argument can Searle make to avoid the imposition of strict liability under section 402A?

8. Curtis Hagans lost the ring finger of his left hand while operating an industrial table saw manufactured by

the Oliver Machinery Company. The saw originally was equipped with a detachable blade guard assembly that would have prevented Hagans's injury had it been attached to the saw while Hagans was working. This assembly was detachable rather than permanently affixed to the saw because many common woodworking functions could not be performed with the assembly in place. The saw exceeded industry safety practices and national and associational safety standards in effect at the time of its manufacture. In addition, few competing manufacturers included blade guards as standard equipment, and none offered a table saw with a permanently affixed blade guard.

Hagans sued Oliver for negligence and under section 402A, alleging that the saw was defectively designed because it did not include a permanent blade guard assembly. Did Hagans win? You can assume that injuries of the kind Hagans suffered were foreseeable consequences of manufacturing the saw without a permanent guard, and that Hagans was not negligent in his operation of the saw.

9. Arlyn and Rose Spindler were dairy farmers who leased a feed storage silo from Agristor Leasing. The silo was supposed to limit the oxygen reaching the feed and thus to hinder its spoilage. The Spindlers alleged that the silo was defective and that the dairy feed it contained was spoiled as a result. They further alleged that due to the spoilage of the feed, their dairy herd suffered medically and reproductively, and their milk production dropped. The Spindlers sued Agristor in negligence and under section 402A for their resulting lost income. What *type* of damages are they claiming? Under the majority rule, can they recover for such damages in negligence or under section 402A? Would your answer be different if the Spindlers had sued for the damage to the *dairy feed* itself? Assume for purposes of argument that both section 402A and negligence claims are possible under this equipment lease.

10. Even though she did not smoke cigarettes, Roxanne Ramsey-Buckingham was diagnosed with terminal lung cancer. Claiming that she contracted this disease from environmental tobacco smoke, Ramsey-Buckingham sued several prominent tobacco companies under section 402A. She asserted that the defendants' cigarettes were defective because they were unreasonably dangerous, and that they were unreasonably dangerous because (1) they were dangerous beyond the expectations of the ordinary consumer, and (2) the utility of smoking did not outweigh the risk posed by environmental smoke. She did not allege any other defect in the defendants' cigarettes.

The defendants moved to dismiss the plaintiff's claim for failure to state a claim upon which relief could be granted. The trial court granted the motion because the complaint failed to state separately that the cigarettes were defective and that the defect caused them to be unreasonably dangerous. The administrator of Ramsey-Buckingham's estate appealed after Ramsey-Buckingham's death. The administrator argued that "defective" and "unreasonably dangerous" are not separate elements of a strict liability claim, and that if cigarettes are unreasonably dangerous, they necessarily would be defective as well. Was the administrator correct, or may cigarettes be unreasonably dangerous without also being defective?

11. Duane Martin, a small farmer, placed an order for cabbage seed with the Joseph Harris Company, a large national producer and distributor of seed. Harris's order form included the following language:

> NOTICE TO BUYER: Joseph Harris Company, Inc. warrants that seeds and plants it sells conform to the label descriptions as required by Federal and State seed laws. IT MAKES NO OTHER WARRANTIES, EXPRESS OR IMPLIED, OF MERCHANTABILITY, FITNESS FOR PURPOSE, OR OTHERWISE, AND IN ANY EVENT ITS LIABILITY FOR BREACH OF ANY WARRANTY OR CONTRACT WITH RESPECT TO SUCH SEEDS OR PLANTS IS LIMITED TO THE PURCHASE PRICE OF SUCH SEEDS OR PLANTS.

All of Harris's competitors used similar clauses in their contracts.

After Martin placed his order, and unknown to Martin, Harris stopped using a cabbage seed treatment that had been effective in preventing a certain cabbage fungus. Later, Martin planted the seed he had ordered from Harris, but a large portion of the resulting crop was destroyed by fungus because the seed did not contain the treatment Harris had previously used. Martin sued Harris for his losses under the implied warranty of merchantability.

Which portion of the notice quoted above is an attempted disclaimer of implied warranty liability, and which is an attempted limitation of remedies? Will the disclaimer language disclaim the implied warranty of merchantability under UCC section 2–316(2)? If Martin had sued under the implied warranty of fitness for a particular purpose, would the disclaimer language disclaim that implied warranty as well? Assuming that the disclaimer and the remedy limitation contained the correct legal boilerplate needed to make them effective, what argument could Martin still make to block their operation? What are his chances of success with this argument?

12. Moulton purchased a 1969 Ford LTD from Hull-Dobbs, a Ford dealer. His sales contracts with Ford and

Hull-Dobbs contained valid disclaimers of the implied warranty of merchantability that satisfied UCC section 2–316(2). One year later, while Moulton was driving his car along an interstate highway, the Ford suddenly veered to the right, jumped the guardrail, and fell 26 feet to the street below. The accident was caused by a defect in the car's steering mechanism, and Moulton was seriously injured. Moulton sued Ford under the implied warranty of merchantability. Ford defended on the basis of its disclaimer. Moulton argued that the disclaimer was invalid in a personal injury case under UCC section 2–719, which makes the exclusion of consequential damages unconscionable in a case involving consumer goods and personal injury. Did Moulton's argument succeed?

13. Richard Jimenez was injured when a disc for the handheld electric disc grinder he had purchased from Sears Roebuck shattered while he used the grinder to smooth down a steel weld. When Jimenez brought a strict liability lawsuit against Sears, the defendant argued that he had misused the grinder, and that this misuse caused his injury. Assuming that Sears was right, what effect would this have in a state that has not adopted comparative negligence or comparative fault? What effect would it have in a comparative fault state?

14. On June 25, 1986, a general contractor completed the Oceanside at Pine Point Condominium. In the construction, the contractor used windows manufactured by Peachtree Doors, Inc. Peachtree delivered the windows to the contractor in December of 1985. After sale of the condominium units to the public, the condominium building suffered significant water damage around the windows. Thus, Pine Point's owners' association brought a class action product liability suit against Peachtree on December 31, 1991. The suit included claims based on Article 2 of the UCC. Have the plaintiffs satisfied Article 2's statute of limitations?

15. Roberto Martinez was injured while installing a Goodrich tire on a motor vehicle. The injury occurred after the 16-inch tire exploded while Martinez was attempting to mount it on a 16.5-inch rim. He did so despite the presence of a prominent warning label on the tire. The warning specifically stated that one should never mount a 16-inch tire on a 16.5-inch rim, and that doing so could cause severe injury or death because the tire would explode. Martinez brought a strict liability action against Goodrich in a Texas court. His theory was not that the warning was inadequate, but that the exploding tire was defective because Goodrich had failed to use a safer alternative bead design that would have kept it

from exploding. The jury found for Martinez, awarding him $5.5 million in actual damages and $11.5 million in punitive damages. After reducing the punitive damages award, the trial judge awarded Martinez $10.3 million. A Texas appeals court upheld the trial court's award of actual damages, but reversed its punitive damages award. Goodrich appealed to the Supreme Court of Texas. The question before the court was whether a manufacturer that knew of a safer alternative product design is strictly liable for injuries caused by the plaintiff's failure to follow a suitable warning. Did Goodrich's use of an adequate warning absolve Goodrich of liability for a defective design?

Online Research: SUVs and Safety

Manufacturers of sport utility vehicles (SUVs) sometimes tout the safety they provide to drivers and passengers of such vehicles when they become involved in traffic accidents. For many consumers, these safety benefits may be among the major reasons why they purchase an SUV. Some critics have asserted in recent years, however, that the added safety an SUV affords its drivers and passengers comes at a significant cost to non-SUV drivers and passengers and to society as a whole. This cost, the critics say, comes in the form of the likelihood that a traffic accident involving an SUV and a non-SUV automobile will be much worse for the non-SUV driver and passengers than an otherwise similar accident involving that same non-SUV and another non-SUV would have been. The reason, according to the critics, is the significantly greater relative size of the SUV—a size that, in certain SUV models, seems to be getting bigger in recent years. *Using at least three online sources of your choice* for supporting facts, contentions, or expressions of opinion, write an essay that sets forth and justifies your position on these questions:

> If an SUV manufacturer knows or has reason to know (a) that SUV buyers like the safety afforded by an SUV, (b) that many such consumers would be interested in purchasing even larger SUV models, and (c) that SUVs' greater size as compared to non-SUV automobiles is likely to enhance the harm to non-SUV drivers and passengers when traffic accidents between the two types of vehicles occur, does the SUV manufacturer have an ethical obligation *not* to produce the even larger SUV? Does it make a difference whether the SUV manufacturer also produces non-SUV automobiles?

21

PERFORMANCE OF SALES CONTRACTS

arah Saunders was interested in purchasing a new sport utility vehicle. Using the web page of a large volume dealer in a nearby city, she provided the dealer with the make, model color, and primary options for the vehicle she was seeking. The dealer indicated that he could obtain a vehicle meeting Sarah's specifications, quoted her a very favorable price, and offered to deliver the vehicle to her at the apartment house where she lived. Sarah accepted the offer and wired a deposit to the dealer. When the vehicle arrived, the truck driver refused to unload it from the car carrier or let Sarah inspect it until she had given him a certified check for the balance due. Then he gave her the title to the vehicle, unloaded it, and drove away. Sarah subsequently discovered a number of scratches in the paint and that some of the options she had bargained for—such as a CD player—were not on the vehicle. When she complained to the dealer, he offered her a monetary "allowance" to cover the defects. She also discovered that the vehicle had a tendency to stall and have to be restarted when she stopped at intersections. Despite repeated trips to the nearby city to have the dealer remedy the problem, those efforts have been unavailing. Sarah has indicated that she wants to return the vehicle to the dealer and get a vehicle that performs properly, but the dealer insists that she has to give him additional time to try to fix it. This situation raises a number of legal questions that, among others, will be discussed in this chapter, including:

• Did Sarah have the right to inspect the vehicle before she paid the balance of the purchase price?
• When Sarah discovered the scratches on the vehicle and that it did not conform to the contract specifications, could she have refused to accept the car and required the dealer to provide one that met the contract?
• Does Sarah have the right to return the defective vehicle to the dealer and obtain either a new vehicle or her money back, or must she give the dealer the opportunities he wants to try to remedy the defect?

IN THE TWO PREVIOUS chapters, we discussed the formation and terms of sales contracts, including those terms concerning express and implied warranties. In this chapter, the focus is on the legal rules that govern the performance of contracts. Among the topics covered are the basic obligations of the buyer and seller with respect to delivery and payment, the rights of the parties when the goods delivered do not conform to the contract,

and the circumstances that may excuse the performance of a party's contractual obligations.

General Rules

The parties to a contract for the sale of goods are obligated to perform the contract according to its terms. The

ETHICS IN ACTION

What Should You Do When the Price Rises—or Falls?

When goods that are the subject of a contract are in significantly shorter supply than when the agreement was made and the price has risen, the seller may be tempted to look for an excuse so that he can sell to someone else and realize a greater profit. This situation often arises in the sale of commodities, such as crops, fuel oil, gasoline, and natural gas. Similarly, if goods are in significantly more plentiful supply than when a contract was made, a buyer might be tempted to create an excuse to cancel so that she could buy elsewhere at a lower price. When, if ever, is a seller or buyer ethically justified in trying to find a way out of a contractual obligation because the supply or market conditions have so changed that he or she can make a much better deal elsewhere? Concomitantly, are there circumstances under which the other party, acting in an ethically responsible manner, should voluntarily release the disadvantaged party from his or her contractual commitment?

Uniform Commercial Code (UCC or Code) gives the parties great flexibility in deciding between themselves how they will perform a contract. The practices in the trade or business as well as any past dealings between the parties may supplement or explain the contract. The Code gives both the buyer and the seller certain rights, and it also sets out what is expected of them on points that they did not deal with in their contract. It should be kept in mind that the Code changes basic contract law in a number of respects.

Good Faith

The buyer and seller must act in **good faith** in the performance of a sales contract [1–203].[1] Good faith is defined to mean "honesty in fact" in performing the duties assumed in the contract or in carrying out the transaction [1–201(19)]. Thus, if the contract requires the seller to select an assortment of goods for the buyer, the selection must be made in good faith; the seller should pick out a reasonable assortment [2–311]. It would not, for example, be good faith to include only unusual sizes or colors.

Course of Dealing

The terms in the contract between the parties are the primary means for determining the obligations of the buyer and seller. The meaning of those terms may be explained by looking at any performance that has already taken place. For example, a contract may call for periodic deliveries of goods. If the seller has made a number of deliveries without objection by the buyer, the way the deliveries were made shows how the parties intended them to be made. Similarly, if there were any past contracts between the parties, the way the parties interpreted those contracts is relevant to the interpretation of the present contract. If there is a conflict between the express terms of the contract and the past course of dealing between the parties, the express terms of the contract prevail [1–205(4)].

Usage of Trade

In many kinds of businesses, there are customs and practices of the trade that are known by people in the business and that are usually assumed by parties to a contract for goods of that type. Under the Code, the parties and courts may use these trade customs and practices—known as usage of trade—in interpreting a contract [2–202; 1–205]. If there is a conflict between the express terms of the contract and trade usage, the express terms prevail [1–205(4)].

Modification

Under the Code, consideration is not required to support a modification or rescission of a contract for the sale of goods. However, the parties may specify in their agreement that modification or rescission must be in writing, in which case a signed writing is necessary for enforcement of any modification to the contract or its rescission [2–209].

Waiver

In a contract that entails a number of instances of partial performance (such as deliveries or payments) by one party, the other party must be careful to object to any late deliveries or payments. If the other party does not object, it may waive its rights to cancel the contract if other deliveries or payments are late [2–208(3), 2–209(4)]. For

---

[1]The numbers in brackets refer to sections of the Uniform Commercial Code.

CYBERLAW IN ACTION

The Internet and E-Commerce Facilitate Contract Modifications

Buyers and sellers sometimes change parts of their contracts after formation. For example, the buyer may need the goods slightly sooner or somewhat later than originally planned. Or the seller may only be able to supply yellow life jackets instead of the buyer's preferred blue and red mix of life jackets. So long as the parties agree to change the particulars of the performance contracted for, an event that Article 2 calls a "modification," they may change their contract. Modifications are quite common in deals between two merchants and are not uncommon in sales in which one lay buyer and one merchant participate.

Let's assume that the buyer decides that her customers like the first shipment of goods under a contract so much that she should order more. To change the quantity in her office, she can do several things—call the seller, send a telegram, or send a revised contract for the seller to sign and return.

E-commerce makes this easier—the buyer can send an e-mail asking the seller to send more of the same goods, preferably by specifying the number above that provided in the earlier agreement that the buyer now wishes to buy. If the buyer bought three $60 life jackets for her own use, Article 2 allows a court to enforce the seller's commitment to sell three at $60 each even without worrying about the statute of frauds in Section 2–201. However, if the buyer wanted to increase her order from three to 15 life jackets, the dollar amount of the purchase would rise above $500—and courts would not enforce the larger purchase unless the deal met the statute of frauds. How does the Internet help buyers and sellers who want to be able to enforce their agreements in court if the other party does not perform? Using either the federal E-Sign law or state-enacted versions of the Uniform Electronic Transactions Act (UETA), the party seeking to enforce the larger quantity could send an e-mail or message using a click-through form provided by a seller's website, and could use that e-mail or other electronically revised order to show the fact of the revision to the "order" and, as applicable, the existence of a reply message from the seller confirming the seller's agreement to the change.

As a further example of how e-mail and the Internet assist sales transactions, sellers now routinely send or post confirmations that shipment has occurred. These messages help buyers plan for the arrival of goods, otherwise keep track of delays in orders that they may need to act upon, and also check that their insurance is effective for a particular purchase or that their warehouse is ready to receive the goods sent.

example, a contract calls for a fish market to deliver fish to a supermarket every Thursday and for the supermarket to pay on delivery. If the fish market regularly delivers the fish on Friday and the supermarket does not object, the supermarket will be unable to cancel the contract for that reason. Similarly, if the supermarket does not pay cash but sends a check the following week, then unless the fish market objects, it will not be able to assert the late payments as grounds for later canceling the contract. A party that has waived rights to a portion of the contract not yet performed may retract the waiver by giving reasonable notice to the other party that strict performance will be required. The retraction of the waiver is effective unless it would be unjust because of a material change of position by the other party in reliance on the waiver [2–209(5)].

Assignment

Under the Code, the buyer and/or the seller may delegate their duties to someone else. If there is a strong reason for having the original party perform the duties, perhaps because the quality of the performance might differ otherwise, the parties may not delegate their duties. Also, they may not delegate their duties if the parties agree in the contract that there is to be no assignment of duties. However, they may assign rights to receive performance—for example, the right to receive goods or payment [2–210].

Delivery

Basic Obligation

The basic duty of the seller is to deliver the goods called for by the contract. The basic duty of the buyer is to accept and pay for the goods if they conform to the contract [2–301]. The buyer and seller may agree that the goods are to be delivered in several lots or installments. If there is no such agreement, then a single delivery of all the goods must be made. Where delivery is to be made in lots, the seller may demand the price of each lot upon delivery unless there has been an agreement for the extension of credit [2–307].

Place of Delivery

The buyer and seller may agree on the place where the goods will be delivered. If no such agreement is made, then the goods are to be delivered at the seller's place of business. If the seller does not have a place of business, then delivery is to be made at his home. If the goods are located elsewhere than the seller's place of business or home, the place of delivery is the place where the goods are located [2–308].

Seller's Duty of Delivery

The seller's basic obligation is to tender delivery of goods that conform to the contract with the buyer. Tender of delivery means that the seller must make the goods available to the buyer. This must be done during reasonable hours and for a reasonable period of time, so that the buyer can take possession of the goods [2–503]. The contract of sale may require the seller merely to ship the goods to the buyer but not to deliver the goods to the buyer's place of business. If this is the case, the seller must put the goods into the possession of a carrier, such as a trucking company or a railroad. The seller must also make a reasonable contract with the carrier to take the goods to the buyer. Then, the seller must notify the buyer that the goods have been shipped [2–504]. Shipment terms were discussed in Chapter 19, Formation and Terms of Sales Contracts.

If the seller does not make a reasonable contract for delivery or notify the buyer and a material delay or loss results, the buyer has the right to reject the shipment. Suppose the goods are perishable, such as fresh produce, and the seller does not ship them in a refrigerated truck or railroad car. If the produce deteriorates in transit, the buyer can reject the produce on the ground that the seller did not make a reasonable contract for shipping it.

In some situations, the goods sold may be in the possession of a bailee such as a warehouse. If the goods are covered by a negotiable warehouse receipt, the seller must indorse the receipt and give it to the buyer [2–503(4)(a)]. This enables the buyer to obtain the goods from the warehouse. Such a situation exists when grain being sold is stored at a grain elevator. The law of negotiable documents of title, including warehouse receipts, is discussed in Chapter 23, Personal Property and Bailments.

If the goods in the possession of a bailee are not covered by a negotiable warehouse receipt, then the seller must notify the bailee that it has sold the goods to the buyer and must obtain the bailee's consent to hold the goods for delivery to the buyer or release the goods to the buyer. The risk of loss as to the goods remains with the seller until the bailee agrees to hold them for the buyer [2–503(4)(b)].

Inspection and Payment

Buyer's Right of Inspection

Normally, the buyer has the right to inspect the goods before he accepts or pays for them. The buyer and seller may agree on the time, place, and manner in which the buyer will inspect the goods. If no agreement is made, then the buyer may inspect the goods at any reasonable time and place and in any reasonable manner [2–513(1)].

If the shipping terms are cash on delivery (COD), then the buyer must pay for the goods before inspecting them unless they are marked "Inspection Allowed." However, if it is obvious even without inspection that the goods do not conform to the contract, the buyer may reject them without paying for them first [2–512(1)(a)]. For example, if a farmer contracted to buy a bull and the seller delivered a cow, the farmer would not have to pay for it. The fact that a buyer may have to pay for goods before inspecting them does not deprive the buyer of remedies against the seller if the goods do not conform to the contract [2–512(2)].

If the goods conform to the contract, the buyer must pay the expenses of inspection. However, if the goods are nonconforming, he may recover his inspection expenses from the seller [2–513(2); 2–715(1)].

Payment

The buyer and seller may agree in their contract that the price of the goods is to be paid in money or in other goods, services, or real property. If all or part of the price of goods is payable in real property, then only the transfer of goods is covered by the law of sales of goods. The transfer of the real property is covered by the law of real property [2–304].

The contract may provide that the goods are sold on credit to the buyer and that the buyer has a period of time to pay for them. If there is no agreement for extending credit to the buyer, the buyer must pay for them upon delivery. The buyer usually can inspect goods before payment except where the goods are shipped COD, in which case the buyer must pay for them before inspecting them.

THE GLOBAL BUSINESS ENVIRONMENT

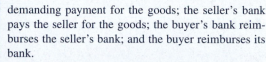

Assurance of Payment

Perhaps the most important provisions in the international sales contract cover the manner by which the buyer pays the seller. Frequently, a foreign buyer's contractual promise to pay when the goods arrive does not provide the seller with sufficient assurance of payment. The seller may not know the overseas buyer well enough to determine the buyer's financial condition or inclination to refuse payment if the buyer no longer wants the goods when they arrive. When the buyer fails to make payment, the seller will find it difficult and expensive to pursue its legal rights under the contract. Even if the seller is assured that the buyer will pay for the goods on arrival, the time required for shipping the goods often means that payment is not received until months after shipment.

To solve these problems, the seller often insists on receiving an **irrevocable letter of credit.** The buyer obtains a letter of credit from a bank in the buyer's country. The letter of credit obligates the buyer's bank to pay the amount of the sales contract to the seller. To obtain payment, the seller must produce a **negotiable bill of lading** and other documents proving that it shipped the goods required by the sales contract in conformity with the terms of the letter of credit.[1] A letter of credit is irrevocable when the buyer's bank cannot withdraw its obligation to pay without the consent of the seller and the buyer.

Letters of credit may be confirmed or advised. Under a **confirmed** letter of credit, the seller's bank agrees to assume liability on the letter of credit. Typically, under a confirmed letter of credit, the buyer's bank issues a letter of credit to the seller; the seller's bank confirms the letter of credit; the seller delivers the goods to a carrier; the carrier issues a negotiable bill of lading to the seller; the seller delivers the bill of lading to the seller's bank and presents a draft[2] drawn on the buyer

---

[1]A bill of lading is a document issued by a carrier acknowledging that the seller has delivered particular goods to it and entitling the holder of the bill of lading to receive these goods at the place of destination. Bills of lading are discussed in Chapter 23.

[2]A draft is a negotiable instrument by which the drawer (in this case, the seller) orders the drawee (the buyer) to pay the payee (the seller). Drafts are discussed in Chapter 31.

demanding payment for the goods; the seller's bank pays the seller for the goods; the buyer's bank reimburses the seller's bank; and the buyer reimburses its bank.

With an **advised** letter of credit, the seller's bank merely acts as an agent for collection of the amount owed to the seller. The seller's bank acts as agent for the seller by collecting from the buyer's bank and giving the payment to the seller. The buyer's bank is reimbursed by the buyer.

The confirmed letter of credit is the least risky payment method for sellers. The confirmation is needed because the seller, unlike the confirming bank, may not know any more about the financial integrity of the issuing bank than it knows about that of the buyer. The seller has a promise of immediate payment from an entity it knows to be financially solvent—the confirming bank. If the draft drawn pursuant to the letter of credit is not paid, the seller may sue the confirming bank, which is a bank in his home country.

Under the confirmed letter of credit, payment is made to the seller well before the goods arrive. Thus, the buyer cannot claim that the goods are defective and refuse to pay for them. When the goods are truly defective on arrival, however, the customer can commence an action for damages against the seller based on their original sales contract.

Figure 1 (page 472) summarizes the confirmed letter of credit transaction.

Conforming and Nonconforming Documents

In a letter of credit transaction, the promises made by the buyer's and seller's banks are independent of the underlying sales contract between the seller and the buyer. Therefore, when the seller presents a bill of lading and other documents that *conform* to the terms of the letter of credit, the issuing bank and the confirming bank are required to pay, even if the buyer refuses to pay its bank or even, generally, if the buyer claims to know that the goods are defective. However, if the bill of lading or other required documents do not conform to the terms of the letter of credit, a bank may properly refuse to pay. A bill of lading is *nonconforming* when, for example, it indicates the wrong goods were shipped, states the wrong person to receive the goods, or states a buyer's address differently than the letter of credit.

Unless the seller demands cash, the buyer may pay for the goods by personal check or by any other method used in the ordinary course of business. If the seller demands cash, the seller must give the buyer a reasonable amount of time to obtain it. If payment is made by check, the payment is

conditional on the check's being honored by the bank when it is presented for payment [2–511(3)]. If the bank refuses to pay the check, the buyer has not satisfied the duty to pay for the goods. In that case, the buyer does not have the right to retain the goods and must give them back to the seller.

Figure 1 *Confirmed Letter of Credit Transaction*

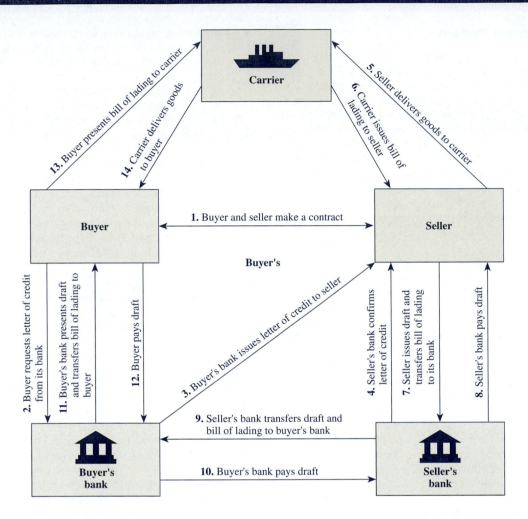

Acceptance, Revocation, and Rejection

Acceptance

Acceptance of goods occurs when a buyer, after having a reasonable opportunity to inspect them, either indicates that he will take them or fails to reject them. To **reject** goods, the buyer must notify the seller of the rejection and specify the defect or nonconformity. If a buyer treats the goods as if he owns them, the buyer is considered to have accepted them [2–606].

For example, Ace Appliance delivers a new color television set to Baldwin. Baldwin has accepted the set if, after trying it and finding it to be in working order, she says nothing to Ace or tells Ace that she will keep it. Even if the set is defective, Baldwin is considered to have accepted it if she does not give Ace timely notice that she does not want to keep it because it is not in working order. If she takes the set on a vacation trip even though she knows that it does not work properly, this is also an acceptance. In the latter case, her use of the television set would be inconsistent with its rejection and the return of ownership to the seller.

If a buyer accepts any part of a **commercial unit** of goods, he is considered to have accepted the whole unit [2–606(2)]. A commercial unit is any unit of goods that is treated by commercial usage as a single whole. It can be a single article (such as a machine), a set or quantity of articles (such as a dozen, bale, gross, or carload), or any other unit treated as a single whole [2–105(6)]. Thus, if a bushel of apples is a commercial unit, then a buyer purchasing 10 bushels of apples who accepts 8 1/2 bushels is considered to have accepted 9 bushels.

In the *Weil v. Murray* case, which follows, the buyer was considered to have accepted goods that it had handled inconsistently with a claim of rejection and return of ownership of the goods to the seller.

Weil v. Murray   *2001 WL 345222 (U.S.D.C. S.D.N.Y. 2001)*

On October 19, 1997, Mark Murray, a New York art dealer and gallery owner, traveled to Montgomery, Alabama, to view various paintings in the art collection owned by Robert Weil. Murray examined one of the paintings under ultraviolet light—a painting by Edgar Degas entitled "Aux Courses." Murray discussed the Degas with Ian Peck, another art dealer, who indicated an interest in buying it and asked Murray to arrange to have it brought to New York.

Murray and Weil executed an agreement which provided for consignment of the Degas to Murray's gallery "for a private inspection in New York for a period of a week from November 3" to be extended only with the express permission of the consignor. The director of Murray's Gallery picked up the painting, which was subsequently shown by Murray to Peck. Peck agreed to purchase the painting for $1,225,000 with Murray acting as a broker. On November 8, Murray advised Weil that he had a buyer for the Degas and they orally agreed to the sale. Subsequently, they entered into a written agreement for the sale of the painting for $1 million that indicated, among other things, that if Weil did not receive full payment by December 8, Murray would disclose the name of the undisclosed principal on whose behalf he was acting.

Neither Murray nor anyone else ever paid Weil the $1 million. Nonetheless, Murray maintained possession of the Degas from November 3, 1997, through March 25, 1998, when Weil requested its return. At some point in mid-November, Weil and Peck took the Degas to an art conservator. A condition report prepared by the conservator and dated December 3, 1997, showed that the conservator had cleaned the painting and sought to correct some deterioration. Weil brought an action to recover the price of the painting from Murray.

Mukasey, District Judge The undisputed facts establish also that Murray accepted the Degas. "Goods that a buyer has in its possession necessarily are accepted or rejected by the time a reasonable opportunity for inspecting them passes." Murray first inspected the Degas under an ultraviolet light when he viewed it at the Weils' home in late October. Murray had the opportunity to further examine the Degas at his gallery in New York pursuant to the consignment agreement and his continued possession of the painting following the expiration of the consignment agreement. It is also undisputed that Murray was present when Simon Parkes assessed the condition of the painting sometime between November 3 and November 19, 1997. Not only did Murray have a reasonable time to inspect the goods, but also it is undisputed that he actually did inspect the Degas. There is no evidence that Murray found the painting unsatisfactory or nonconforming. See *Integrated Circuits Unltd. v. E. F. Johnson Co.,* (2d Cir. 1989) (discussing acceptance as the failure to make an effective rejection after a reasonable time to inspect). Although the question of whether the buyer has had a reasonable time to inspect is generally a question for the trier of fact, no reasonable jury could find that Murray

did not accept the Degas in light of the undisputed facts that he inspected the Degas on at least two occasions, signed the written agreement, and continued to retain possession of the Degas. See *Sessa v. Riegle,* (D.C. Pa. 1977) (finding acceptance when buyer was permitted unlimited inspection of a horse and then indicated that he would buy the horse).

Moreover, it is undisputed that, without Weil's consent, Murray, at a minimum, permitted the painting to be cleaned and restored in late November or early December. Murray's participation in the alteration of the painting, regardless of whether such alteration increased its value, was an act inconsistent with Weils' ownership. See *In re Fran Char Press, Inc.,* (Bankr. E.D.N.Y. 1985) (finding that buyer had accepted posters by taking possession of them and mounting them on cardboard); *Industria De Calcados Martini Ltd. v. Maxwell Shoe Co.,* (Mass. App. Ct. 1994) (finding acceptance where buyer had shoes refinished). The Weils have established that Murray agreed to purchase the Degas, accepted it, and nonetheless failed to pay the purchase price.

Summary judgment granted in favor of the Weils.

Effect of Acceptance

Once a buyer has accepted goods, he cannot later reject them unless at the time they were accepted, the buyer had reason to believe that the nonconformity would be cured. By accepting goods, the buyer does not forfeit or waive all remedies against the seller for any nonconformities in the goods. However, if the buyer wishes to hold the seller responsible, he must give the seller timely notice that the goods are nonconforming.

The buyer is obligated to pay for goods that are accepted. If the buyer accepts all of the goods sold, she is, of course, responsible for the full purchase price. If the buyer accepts only part of the goods, she must pay for that part at the contract rate [2–607(1)].

Revocation of Acceptance

Under certain circumstances, a buyer may **revoke** or undo the acceptance. A buyer may revoke acceptance of nonconforming goods where: (1) the nonconformity substantially impairs the value of the goods and (2) the buyer accepted them without knowledge of the nonconformity because of the difficulty of discovering the nonconformity, or the buyer accepted the goods because of the seller's assurances that it would cure the defect [2–608(1)].

The buyer must exercise her right to revoke acceptance within a reasonable time after the buyer discovers or should have discovered the nonconformity. Revocation is not ef-

fective until the buyer notifies the seller of the intention to revoke acceptance. After a buyer revokes acceptance, her rights are the same as they would have been if the goods had been rejected when delivery was offered [2–608].

The right to revoke acceptance could arise, for example, where Arnold buys a new car from Dealer. While driving the car home, Arnold discovers that it has a seriously defective transmission. When she returns the car to Dealer, Dealer promises to repair it, so Arnold decides to keep the car. If the dealer does not fix the transmission after repeated efforts to fix it, Arnold could revoke her acceptance on the grounds that the nonconformity substantially impairs the value of the car, that she took delivery of the car without knowledge of the nonconformity, and that her acceptance was based on Dealer's assurances that he would fix the car. Similarly, revocation of acceptance might be involved where a serious problem with the car not discoverable by inspection shows up in the first month's use.

Revocation must occur prior to any substantial change in the goods, however, such as serious damage in an accident or wear and tear from using them for a period of time. What constitutes a "substantial impairment in value" and when there has been a "substantial change in the goods" are questions that courts frequently have to decide when an attempted revocation of acceptance results in a lawsuit. The *North River Homes* case illustrates a number of the issues that arise in situations where a buyer is seeking to revoke her acceptance.

North River Homes, Inc. v. Bosarge   *17 U.C.C Rep.2d 121 (Miss. Sup. Ct. 1992)*

On August 20, 1983, Elmer and Martha Bosarge purchased from J & J Mobile Home Sales a furnished mobile home manufactured by North River Homes. The mobile home, described by a J & J salesperson as the "Cadillac" of mobile homes, cost $23,900. Upon moving into their new home, the Bosarges immediately discovered defect after defect. The defects included a bad water leak that caused water to run all over the trailer and into the insulation, which in turn caused the trailer's underside to balloon downward, loose moldings, a warped dishwasher door, a warped bathroom door, holes in the walls, a defective heating and cooling system, cabinets with chips and holes in them, furniture that fell apart, rooms that remained moldy and mildewed, a closet that leaked rainwater, and spaces between the doors and windows and their frames that allowed the elements to come in. The Bosarges had not been able to spot the defects before taking delivery because they viewed the mobile home at night on J & J's lot and there was no light on in the mobile home.

The Bosarges immediately and repeatedly notified North River Homes of the defects, but it failed to repair the home satisfactorily. In November 1983, the Bosarges informed North River of their decision to revoke their acceptance of the defective home. On some occasions, repairmen came but did not attempt to make repairs, saying they would come back. Other times, the repairs were inadequate. For example, while looking for the water leak, a repairman cut open the bottom of the mobile home and then taped it back together with masking tape that failed to hold and resulted in the floor bowing out. Another repairman inadvertently punctured a septic line and did not properly repair the puncture, resulting in a permanent stench. Other repairmen simply left things off at the home, such as a new dishwasher door and a countertop, saying they did not have time to make the repairs.

In June 1984, the Bosarges provided North River with an extensive list of problems that had not been corrected. When they did not receive a satisfactory response, they sent a letter on October 4, 1984, saying they would make no further payments. North River made no further efforts to correct the problems. In March 1986, the Bosarges' attorney wrote to North River formally revoking acceptance of the mobile home because of its substantially impaired value, tendering the mobile home back to it, and advising North River that it could pick the home up at its earliest convenience. They then brought a lawsuit requesting return of the purchase price and seeking damages for breach of various warranties.

Prather, Justice When a consumer has accepted goods and subsequently discovers defects or a breach of implied merchantability, the consumer may invoke statutory and case law which conditions revocation of acceptance on:

(1) a nonconformity [or defect] which substantially impairs the value of the "lot or commercial unit";

(2) an acceptance
(a) (with discovery of the defect) on the reasonable assumption that the nonconformity [or defect] would be cured or
(b) (without discovery) reasonably induced by the difficulty of the discovery or by the seller's assurances;

(3) revocation within a reasonable time after the nonconformity [or defect] was discovered or should have been discovered; and

(4) revocation before a substantial change occurs in the condition of the goods not caused by their own defects.

Once the consumer has properly notified the seller of his or her intent to revoke acceptance, the seller has a right to attempt to cure the alleged defect. This right is not unlimited; that is, Mississippi law does not permit a seller to postpone revocation in perpetuity by fixing everything that goes wrong with the good. "There is a time when enough is enough"—when a consumer no longer must tolerate or endure a seller's repeated (though good faith) attempts to cure the defect. As aptly stated by a Florida Court of Appeals:

The buyer . . . is not bound to permit the seller to tinker with the article indefinitely in the hope it may ultimately be made to comply with the warranty. At some point in time, if major problems continue . . . , it must become obvious to all people that a particular [article] simply cannot be repaired or parts replaced so that the same is made free of defect.

When the "time has come," the consumer may revoke once and for all.

North River contends that the Bosarges' failure to move out of their mobile home after "rejecting it" constituted an exercise of ownership (or dominion) and waiver of their right to revoke acceptance. The Bosarges did not move out of their home in November 1983 and in October 1984—the dates when they notified North River of their intention to revoke acceptance—because they were repeatedly assured that the defects would be repaired. Their mistaken belief that North River would fulfill its assurances to repair the defects is but one reason why the Bosarges did not move out of their home. Another reason is simple and understandable:

When you tie up all your savings into purchasing a home, you cannot take it and park it somewhere. You have to live in it until you can get the people to clear your lot so you can put another one on it. It's just not like a car you can drive on the lot and hand them the keys and say, it's yours. (Testimony of Martha Bosarge.)

North River's contention that the Bosarges should have moved out reflects ignorance of case law which requires a consumer, who expresses an intention to revoke acceptance, to provide a seller with a reasonable attempt to cure the defect. The evidence unequivocally shows that the Bosarges complied with this law; indeed, one could arguably contend that they complied to an unnecessary extent. But the Bosarges' great patience is not surprising in view of their financial inability to move elsewhere.

Any excessive or unreasonable use of the home by the Bosarges may be remedied through quantum meruit recovery—*not* through ineffectuation of revocation.

North River also contends that the Bosarges "failed to prove that the mobile home in question was substantially impaired." The Bosarges counter "that the evidence showed that their North River trailer was literally falling apart." The Bosarges testimony revealed that each North River repairman who visited their home admitted to the Bosarges that their home was so defective that it "ought to be replaced." Notably, Ronnie Wilson, a HUD mobile home inspector provided testimony which is also supportive of the jury's finding; when asked if he would live in that kind of home (heating, cooling, leaking roof, mildew, ice), he answered "No, sir, my wife wouldn't let me, sir."

In sum the record is replete with evidence to support the jury's finding that the Bosarges' home was substantially impaired.

Judgment for Bosarges affirmed.

Buyer's Rights on Improper Delivery

If the goods delivered by the seller do not conform to the contract, the buyer has several options. The buyer can (1) reject all of the goods, (2) accept all of them, or (3) accept any commercial units and reject the rest [2–601]. The buyer, however, cannot accept only part of a commercial unit and reject the rest. The buyer must pay for the units accepted at the price per unit provided in the contract.

Where the contract calls for delivery of the goods in separate installments, the buyer's options are more limited. The buyer may reject an installment delivery only if the nonconformity *substantially affects the value* of that delivery and *cannot be corrected* by the seller in a timely fashion. If the nonconformity is relatively minor, the buyer must accept the installment. The seller may offer to replace the defective goods or give the buyer an allowance in the price to make up for the nonconformity [2–612].

Where the nonconformity or defect in one installment impairs the value of the whole contract, the buyer may treat it as a breach of the whole contract but must proceed carefully so as not to reinstate the remainder of the contract [2–612(3)].

Rejection

If a buyer has a basis for rejecting a delivery of goods, the buyer must act within a *reasonable time* after delivery. The buyer must also give the seller *notice* of the rejection, preferably in writing [2–602]. The buyer should be careful to state all of the defects on which he is basing the rejection, including all of the defects that a reasonable inspection would disclose. This is particularly important if these are defects that the seller might cure (remedy) and the time for delivery has not expired. In that case, the seller may notify the buyer that he intends to redeliver conforming goods.

If the buyer fails to state in connection with his rejection a particular defect that is ascertainable by reasonable inspection, he cannot use the defect to justify his rejection if the seller could have cured the defect had he been given reasonable notice of it. In a transaction taking place between merchants, the seller has, after rejection, a right to a written statement of all the defects in the goods on which the buyer bases his right to reject, and the buyer may not later assert defects not listed in justification of his rejection [2–605].

If the buyer wrongfully rejects goods, she is liable to the seller for breach of the sales contract [2–602(3)].

Right to Cure

If the seller has some reason to believe that the buyer would accept nonconforming goods, then the seller can take a reasonable time to reship conforming goods. The seller has this opportunity even if the original time for delivery has expired. For example, Ace Manufacturing contracts to sell 200 red baseball hats to Sam's Sporting Goods, with delivery to be made by April 1. On March 1, Sam's receives a package from Ace containing 200 blue baseball hats and refuses to accept them. Ace can notify Sam's that it intends to cure the improper delivery by supplying 200 red hats, and it has until April 1 to deliver the red hats to Sam's. If Ace thought that Sam's would accept the blue hats because on past shipments Sam's did not object to the substitution of blue hats for red, then Ace has a reasonable time even after April 1 to deliver the red hats [2–508]. The following *Central District Alarm* case illustrates a situation where the seller did not comply with the requirements for establishing a right to cure.

CYBERLAW IN ACTION

Providing Notice

Section 2–602 and 2–607 require that the buyer notify the seller if the buyer wishes to reject goods the seller has tendered to the buyer, or if the buyer decides to revoke acceptance of goods that the seller has promised to repair or replace and has neither repaired nor replaced the goods as promised—or where the buyer gets goods that have a latent (hard-to-find) defect. "Notice" does not have to be in writing to be effective under 2–602 or 2–607, but many buyers prefer to have a record that they gave notice to the seller and the time of the notice given.

This reduces the risk that a court will find that the buyer's failure to give notice deprives the buyer of her right to a remedy (see Section 2–607(3)(a)). Electronic commerce tools, including e-mail, allow buyers to provide speedy and reliable information to sellers in cases such as these. Buyers whose e-mail systems provide confirmation that the seller recipient actually has received the message about the buyer's concerns about the goods, or who show the time and date that the intended recipient opened the e-mail, should make providing notice easier and less expensive than using traditional means of communication.

CONCEPT REVIEW

Acceptance, Revocation, and Rejection

Acceptance	1. Occurs when buyer, having had a reasonable opportunity to inspect goods, either (a) indicates he will take them or (b) fails to reject them.
	2. If buyer accepts any part of a commercial unit, he is considered to have accepted the whole unit.
	3. If buyer accepts goods, he cannot later reject them *unless* at the time they were accepted the buyer had reason to believe that the nonconformity would be cured.
	4. Buyer is obligated to pay for goods that are accepted.
Revocation	1. Buyer may revoke acceptance of nonconforming goods where (a) the nonconformity *substantially impairs the value* of the goods and (b) buyer accepted the goods without knowledge of the nonconformity because of the difficulty of discovering the nonconformity *or* buyer accepted because of assurances by the seller.
	2. Right to revoke must be exercised within a *reasonable* time after buyer discovers *or* should have discovered the nonconformity.
	3. Revocation must be invoked before there is any *substantial* change in the goods.
	4. Revocation is not effective until buyer notifies seller of his intent to revoke acceptance.
Rejection	1. Where the goods delivered do not conform to the contract, buyer may (a) reject all of the goods, (b) accept all of the goods, or (c) accept any commercial unit and reject the rest. Buyer must pay for goods accepted.
	2. Where the goods are to be delivered in installments, an installment delivery may be rejected *only if* the nonconformity substantially affects the value of that delivery and cannot be corrected by the seller.
	3. Buyer must act within a reasonable time after delivery.

Central District Alarm, Inc. v. Hal-Tuc, Inc.   *886 S.W.2d 210 (Mo. Ct. App. 1994)*

Prior to January 1991, John Halton, president of Hal-Tuc, Inc., a company that operates retail lingerie and novelty stores, contacted Ron Weber, a security consultant for Central District Alarm (CDA), about purchasing a video surveillance system for one of its stores. Weber recommended a Javelin system and designed a system for Hal-Tuc.

On January 3, 1991, CDA and Hal-Tuc entered into a written sales agreement that provided that CDA would sell and install security equipment as described on an equipment list attached to the contract. This list included a Javelin VCR. The equipment was supposed to be new. The contract price was $7,692, of which $2,533 was paid when the contract was executed, with the balance to become due after CDA installed the equipment.

CDA ordered a new Javelin VCR but its supplier sent a new JVC VCR. CDA's supplier told CDA it would take another month to get a Javelin. When the system was installed on January 28, 1991, CDA installed a used JVC VCR instead of a new Javelin VCR. CDA did not install the new JVC VCR sent by its supplier because it would not be able to return the VCR after it had replaced it with the Javelin.

Halton called Weber the day after the installation and complained that the equipment was not Javelin and that the VCR was a used JVC VCR. Weber told Halton that the equipment was not used and that a JVC VCR was better than a Javelin. Halton telephoned other CDA personnel over a two-week period during which they denied that the equipment was used. After two weeks, when CDA's installation manager, Brian Modglin, went to the store to see the equipment, Modglin admitted for the first time that the VCR was used. No one from CDA advised Halton in advance that CDA was installing used equipment temporarily. After CDA admitted it had supplied a used JVC VCR, it offered to replace it with a new Javelin as soon as one arrived, which would take one or two months. Halton asked CDA to return Hal-Tuc's $2,533 deposit in exchange for CDA taking its equipment back. CDA refused to return the deposit. Hal-Tuc put all the equipment in boxes and stored it.

CDA brought suit against Hal-Tuc seeking damages for breach of contract. Hal-Tuc filed a counterclaim alleging fraud. The trial court found for Hal-Tuc, and CDA appealed.

Crane, Judge In this case there is no dispute that CDA supplied a VCR that did not conform. CDA argues that it has a right to cure under section 2–508(2) which provides:

(2) Where the buyer rejects a nonconforming tender which the seller had reasonable grounds to believe would be acceptable with or without money allowance the seller may if he seasonably notifies the buyer have a further reasonable time to substitute a conforming tender.

Under section 2–508(2) the seller must "seasonably" notify the buyer of the intention to cure. Seasonably means "within a reasonable time." Section 1–204(3). A "reasonable time" depends on the nature, purpose and circumstances of such action. Section 1–204(2). There was evidence from which the trial court could conclude that CDA did not seasonably notify Hal-Tuc of an intent to cure. CDA did not advise Hal-Tuc in advance that it was installing used equipment on a temporary basis. Hal-Tuc notified CDA after it discovered that CDA had installed the wrong equipment. Only after inspecting the equipment two weeks later did CDA admit the equipment was used and offer to cure with new equipment. These circumstances support a finding that CDA did not seasonably notify Hal-Tuc of its intention to cure.

Further, in order to establish a right to cure under section 2–508(2), the seller must have had reasonable grounds to believe the nonconforming tender would be acceptable. Such reasonable grounds can lie in prior course of dealing, course of performance or usage of trade as well as in the particular circumstances surrounding the making of the contract. CDA did not show any prior course of dealing, course of performance or usage of trade by which used equipment could be substituted for new equipment. CDA argues that CDA had reasonable grounds to believe the used JVC would be acceptable until the new Javelin could be obtained because Hal-Tuc wanted the security system installed as soon as possible. Although there was evidence that Hal-Tuc wanted a security system installed as soon as possible, there was no evidence that Hal-Tuc told or otherwise indicated to CDA that time was more essential than new equipment.

Under these circumstances, CDA could not have had reasonable grounds to believe that a used VCR would be acceptable when a new one had been ordered. Further, CDA could not have had reasonable grounds to believe the tender of a used VCR would be acceptable until a new one could be supplied where that tender was not accompanied by a disclosure that a used VCR was only being supplied on a temporary basis. Without such a communication, the tender was strictly a tender of a used VCR in lieu of a new VCR.

Because it did not establish seasonable notification and reasonable grounds, CDA did not establish a right to cure under section 2–508.

Judgment affirmed for Hal-Tuc on the breach of contract claim.

Buyer's Duties after Rejection

If the buyer is a merchant, then the buyer owes certain duties concerning the goods that he rejects. First, the buyer must follow any reasonable instructions that the seller gives concerning disposition of the goods. The seller, for example, might request that the rejected goods be shipped back to the seller. If the goods are perishable or may deteriorate rapidly, then the buyer must make a reasonable effort to sell the goods. The seller must reimburse the buyer for any expenses that the buyer incurs in carrying out the seller's instructions or in trying to resell perishable goods. In reselling goods, the buyer must act reasonably and in good faith [2–603(2) and (3)].

If the rejected goods are not perishable or if the seller does not give the buyer instructions, then the buyer has several options. First, the buyer can store the goods for the seller. Second, the buyer can reship them to the seller. Third, the buyer can resell them for the seller's benefit. If the buyer resells the goods, the buyer may keep his ex-penses and a reasonable commission on the sale. If the buyer stores the goods, the buyer should exercise care in handling them. The buyer also must give the seller a reasonable time to remove the goods [2–604].

If the buyer is not a merchant, then her obligation after rejection is to hold the goods with reasonable care for a sufficient time to give the seller an opportunity to remove them. The buyer is not obligated to ship the goods back to the seller [2–602].

Assurance, Repudiation, and Excuse

Assurance

The buyer or seller may become concerned that the other party may not be able to perform his contract obligations.

THE GLOBAL BUSINESS ENVIRONMENT

Insecurity in International Transactions

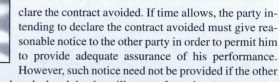

The Convention on Contracts for the International Sale of Goods (CISG) has provisions concerning insecurity, assurance, and anticipatory repudiation that parallel those in the UCC. Under Article 71 of CISG, a party may suspend performance of his obligations if after the contract is entered it "becomes apparent that the other party will not perform a substantial part of his obligations as a result of: (a) a serious deficiency in his ability to perform or his creditworthiness; or (b) his conduct in preparing to perform or in performing the contact." The party suspending performance must immediately give notice to the other party and must continue with performance if the other party provides adequate assurance of its performance.

Under Article 72 of CISG, if prior to the date of performance of a contract, it is clear that one of the parties will "commit a fundamental breach of contract," the other party may declare the contract avoided. If time allows, the party intending to declare the contract avoided must give reasonable notice to the other party in order to permit him to provide adequate assurance of his performance. However, such notice need not be provided if the other party has declared that he will not perform the contract.

In a recent case a German court[1] upheld an Italian shoe manufacturer's decision to avoid a contract and awarded damages against the German buyer. The German company had ordered 140 pairs of winter shoes from the Italian manufacturer. After the shoes were manufactured, the Italian seller demanded security for the sales price as the buyer had other accounts payable to the seller still outstanding. When the buyer neither paid nor provided security, the seller declared the contract avoided and resold the shoes to other retailers. The court allowed the seller to recover the difference between the contract price and the price it obtained in the substitute transactions.

[1]*Oberlandesgericht Dusseldorf,* 17 U 146/93, Jan. 14, 1994 (Germany), 1 UNILEX D. 1994-1 (M. J. Bonnell, ed.)

If there is a reasonable basis for that concern, the buyer or seller can demand **assurance** from the other party that the contract will be performed. If such assurances are not given within a reasonable time not exceeding 30 days, the party is considered to have repudiated the contract [2–609].

For example, a farmer contracts to sell 1,000 bushels of apples to a canner, with delivery to be made in September. In March, the canner learns that a severe frost has damaged many of the apple blossoms in the farmer's area and that 50 percent of the crop has been lost. The canner has the right to demand assurances in writing from the farmer that he will be able to fulfill his obligations in light of the frost. The farmer must provide those assurances within 30 days. Thus, he might advise the canner that his crop sustained only relatively light damage or that he had made commitments to sell only a small percentage of his total crop and expects to be able to fulfill his obligations. If the farmer does not provide such assurances in a timely manner, he is considered to have repudiated the contract. The canner then has certain remedies against the farmer for breach of contract. These remedies are discussed in the next chapter.

Anticipatory Repudiation

Sometimes, one of the parties to a contract repudiates the contract by advising the other party that he does not intend to perform his obligations. When one party repudiates the contract, the other party may suspend his performance. In addition, he may either await performance for a reasonable time or use the remedies for breach of contract that are discussed in Chapter 22 [2–610].

Suppose the party who repudiated the contract changes his mind. Repudiation can be withdrawn by clearly indicating that the person intends to perform his obligations. The repudiating party must do this before the other party has canceled the contract or has materially changed position, for example, by buying the goods elsewhere [2–611].

Excuse

Unforeseen events may make it difficult or impossible for a person to perform his contractual obligations. The Code rules for determining when a person is excused from performing are similar to the general contract rules. General contract law uses the test of **impossibility.** In most situations, however, the Code uses the test of **commercial impracticability.**

The Code attempts to differentiate events that are unforeseeable or uncontrollable from events that were part of the risk borne by a party. If the goods required for the performance of a contract are destroyed without fault of either party prior to the time that the risk of loss passed to the buyer, the contract is voided [2–613]. Suppose Jones agrees to sell and deliver an antique table to Brown. The table is damaged when Jones's antiques store is struck by lightning and catches fire. The specific table covered by the contract was damaged without fault of either party prior to the time that the risk of loss was to pass to Brown. Under the Code, Brown has the option of either canceling the contract or accepting the table with an allowance in the purchase price to compensate for the damaged condition [2–613].

If unforeseen conditions cause a delay or the inability to make delivery of the goods and thus make performance impracticable, the seller is excused from making delivery. However, if a seller's capacity to deliver is only partially affected, the seller must allocate production in any fair and reasonable manner among his customers. The seller has the option of including any regular customer not then under contract in his allocation scheme. When the seller allocates production, he must notify the buyers [2–615]. When a buyer receives this notice, the buyer may either terminate the contract or agree to accept the allocation [2–616].

For example, United Nuclear contracts to sell certain quantities of fuel rods for nuclear power plants to a number of electric utilities. If the federal government limits the amount of uranium that United has access to, so that United is unable to fill all of its contracts, United is excused from full performance on the grounds of commercial impracticability. However, United may allocate its production of fuel rods among its customers by reducing each customer's share by a certain percentage and giving the customers notice of the allocation. Then, each utility can decide whether to cancel the contract or accept the partial allocation of fuel rods.

The *Harriscom Svenska, AB,* case, which follows, illustrates a situation where government action excused a seller's nonperformance of a contract.

In the absence of compelling circumstances, courts do not readily excuse parties from their contractual obligations, particularly where it is clear that the parties anticipated a problem and sought to provide for it in the contract.

Harricom Svenska, AB v. Harris Corp.   3 F. 3d 56 (2nd Cir. 1993)

RF Systems, a division of Harris Corporation, manufactures radio communication products in Rochester, New York. In 1983, it appointed Harriscom Svenska, AB, a Sweden–based dealer, as its exclusive distributor of RF Systems' products in Iran.

On December 6, 1985, U.S. Customs Service officials detained a shipment of RF Systems' model 2301 radio spare parts ordered by Harriscom and bound for Iran. The shipment was worth $663,869. According to a 1982 determination by the United States Department of Commerce, the model 2301 radio could be exported under a general license to almost any country. But upon detaining the model 2301 radio in December 1985, the government decided to reevaluate it. State Department officials began a commodity jurisdiction proceeding, authorized by the Arms Export Control Act, to decide whether this particular radio was a military product that should be on the "Munitions List" and subject to more stringent export controls. For more than six months, RF Systems managers negotiated with officials from the Departments of Commerce, State, and Defense in an effort to speed up these administrative proceedings. The extensive negotiations revealed that the government, particularly the Defense Department, was not concerned so much with the model 2301 radio itself as with its export to Iran. RF Systems eventually negotiated a compromise in late July 1986 under which it agreed to "voluntarily withdraw from all further sales to the Iranian market." The company asserted that by so doing it would lose $5.9 million in already contracted-for orders and $10 million in potential orders to Iran. In exchange, the government ruled in September 1986 that the model 2301 radio was not subject to the stringent export controls of Munitions List products.

The State Department proceedings and resulting compromise that RF Systems and the government reached directly impacted on Harriscom's business. First, while negotiations were ongoing RF Systems could not fill any Harriscom order to Iran. Second, the government, as a result of the compromise, allowed RF Systems to fill only three of eight outstanding orders to Iran. These orders involved the disputed model 2301 radio and the model 301 radio. Harriscom's third alleged injury concerned performance bonds. In July 1986 RF Systems had performance bond guarantees of $240,000 in favor of Harriscom, but these bonds expired with shipment of the three outstanding orders. At the same time Harriscom itself had $550,000 of unconditional bond guarantees in favor of its customer, the Iranian government, and it lost $270,000 of these bonds as a result of RF Systems' failure to fill the five pending orders. Fourth, Harriscom sustained lost profits on those unfilled contracts.

Harriscom brought suit for breach of contract against RF Systems. RF Systems moved for summary judgment, citing a force majeure clause in the contract. The court granted summary judgment in favor of Harris Corporation, and Harriscom appealed.

Cardamone, Circuit Judge Before us on this appeal are two companies that contracted with one another for the sale of radios and spare parts. One is the radios' domestic manufacturer, the other is a Swedish organization, the manufacturer's distributor to the Islamic Republic of Iran. Having some doubt as to the continued viability of such trade, a force majeure clause, which is the subject of this litigation was inserted into the parties' written agreement. What began as a doubt ripened into a certainty when the United States government prohibited all sales to Iran of goods it categorized as military equipment. A shipment of the contracted-for radio spare parts enroute to Sweden, but destined for Iran, was later detained by U.S. Customs.

One of the issues before us is whether the manufacturer's refusal to ship the spare parts was a voluntary act on its part, subjecting it to liability to its distributor for damages for breach of contract. We think it a foregone conclusion that a government bureaucracy determined to prevent what it considers military goods from leaving this country and with the will to compel compliance with its directives is an irresistible force, one that cannot reasonably be controlled. The government in these circumstances may be likened to the wife of "Rumpole of the Bailey," John Mortimer's fictional barrister, who describes his wife as "she who must be obeyed."

Harriscom's first contention is that RF Systems acted voluntarily when it and the United States government reached a compromise in which RF Systems agreed not to sell its products in Iran. As support, Harriscom points to the language of RF Systems' July 24, 1986, letter to the State Department. What Harriscom ignores is the overwhelming and uncontradicted evidence that the government would not allow RF Systems to continue sales to Iran. RF Systems established the affirmative defense of commercial impracticability because it complied in good faith with the government's informal requirements. See UCC section 2–615. We reject Harriscom's assertion that good faith automatically presents an issue of fact precluding summary judgment because the record contains no evidence that RF Systems acted in bad faith. Harriscom must demonstrate more than "some metaphysical doubt as to the material facts," in order to avoid dismissal. Further, for RF Systems to have failed to comply would have been unusually foolhardy and recalcitrant, for the government had undoubted power to compel compliance.

Like commercial impracticability, a force majeure clause in a contract excuses nonperformance when circumstances beyond the control of the parties prevent performance. The contracts between these parties specifically contained force majeure clauses to excuse RF Systems' performance under the present circumstances, namely, "governmental interference."

Judgment for Harris Corporation affirmed.

Problems and Problem Cases

1. Baker was a buyer and distributor of popcorn. Ratzlaff was a farmer who grew popcorn. Baker and Ratzlaff entered into a written contract pursuant to which Ratzlaff agreed that in the current year he would raise 380 acres of popcorn and sell the popcorn to Baker. Baker agreed to furnish the seed popcorn and to pay $4.75 per hundred pounds of popcorn. The popcorn was to be delivered to Baker as he ordered it, and Baker was to pay for the popcorn as it was delivered. At Baker's request, the first delivery was made on February 2 of the following year and the second on February 4. On neither occasion did Raztlaff ask Baker to pay or Baker offer to pay. During that week, Ratzlaff and Baker had several phone conversations about further deliveries, but there was no discussion about payments. On February 11, Ratzlaff sent written notice to Baker that he was terminating the contract because Baker had not paid for the two loads of popcorn that had been delivered. In the meantime, Ratzlaff sold his remaining 1.6 million pounds of popcorn to another buyer at $8 per 100 pounds. Baker then sued Ratzlaff for breach of contract. Did Ratzlaff act in good faith in terminating the contract?

2. Harold Ledford agreed to purchase three used Mustang automobiles (a 1966 Mustang coupe, a 1965 fastback, and a 1966 convertible) from J. L. Cowan for $3,000. Ledford gave Cowan a cashier's check for $1,500 when he took possession of the coupe, with the understanding he would pay the remaining $1,500 on the delivery of the fastback and the convertible. Cowan arranged for Charles Canterberry to deliver the remaining vehicles to Ledford. Canterberry dropped the convertible off at a lot owned by Ledford and proceeded to Ledford's residence to deliver the fastback. He refused to unload it until Ledford paid him $1,500. Ledford refused to make the payment until he had an opportunity to inspect the convertible, which he suspected was not in the same condition that it had been in when he purchased it. Canterberry refused this request and returned both the fastback and the convertible to Cowan. Cowan then brought suit against Ledford to recover the balance of the purchase price. Was Ledford entitled to inspect the car before he paid the balance due on it?

3. Spada, an Oregon corporation, agreed to sell Belson, who operated a business in Chicago, two carloads of potatoes at "4.40 per sack, FOB Oregon shipping point." Spada had the potatoes put aboard railroad cars; however, it did not have floor racks placed under the potatoes, as was customary during the winter months. As a result, there was no warm air circulating and the potatoes were frozen while in transit. Spada claims that its obligations ended with the delivery to the carrier and that the risk of loss was on Belson. What argument would you make for Belson?

4. James Shelton is an experienced musician who operates the University Music Center in Seattle, Washington. On Saturday, Barbara Farkas and her 22-year-old daughter, Penny, went to Shelton's store to look at violins. Penny had been studying violin in college for approximately nine months. Mrs. Farkas and Penny advised Shelton of the price range in which they were interested, and Penny told him she was relying on his expertise. He selected a violin for $368.90, including case and sales tax. Shelton claimed that the instrument was originally priced at $465 but that he discounted it because Mrs. Farkas was willing to take it on an "as is" basis. Mrs. Farkas and Penny alleged that Shelton represented that the violin was "the best" and "a perfect violin for you" and that it was of high quality. Mrs. Farkas paid for it by check. On the following Monday, Penny took the violin to her college music teacher, who immediately told her that it had poor tone and a crack in the body and that it was not the right instrument for her. Mrs. Farkas telephoned Shelton and asked for a refund. He refused, saying that she had purchased and accepted the violin on an "as is" basis. Had Farkas "accepted" the violin so that it was too late for her to "reject" it?

5. On May 23, Deborah McCullough, a secretary, purchased a Chrysler LeBaron from Bill Swad Chrysler-Plymouth. The automobile was covered by both a limited warranty and a vehicle service contract (extended warranty). Following delivery, McCullough advised the salesperson that she had noted problems with the brakes, transmission, air conditioning, paint job, and seat panels, as well as the absence of rust proofing. The next day, the brakes failed and the car was returned to the dealer for the necessary repairs. When the car was returned, McCul-

lough discovered that the brakes had not been properly repaired and that none of the cosmetic work had been done. The car was returned several times to the dealer to correct these problems and others that developed subsequently. On June 26, the car was again returned to the dealer, who kept it for three weeks. Many of the defects were not corrected, however, and new problems with the horn and brakes arose. While McCullough was on a shopping trip, the engine abruptly shut off and the car had to be towed to the dealer. Then, while she was on her honeymoon, the brakes again failed. The car was taken back to the dealer with a list of 32 defects that needed correction. After repeated efforts to repair the car were unsuccessful, McCullough sent a letter to the dealer calling for rescission of the purchase, requesting return of the purchase price, and offering to return the car on receipt of shipping instructions. She received no answer and continued to drive it. McCullough then filed suit. In the following May, the dealer refused to do any further work on the car, claiming that it was in satisfactory condition. By the time of the trial, in June of the next year, it had been driven 35,000 miles, approximately 23,000 of which had been logged after McCullough mailed her notice of revocation. By continuing to operate the vehicle after notifying the seller of her intent to rescind the sale, did McCullough waive her right to revoke her original acceptance?

6. Walters, a grower of Christmas trees, contracted to supply Traynor with "top-quality trees." When the shipment arrived and was inspected, Traynor discovered that some of the trees were not top quality. Within 24 hours, Traynor notified Walters that he was rejecting the trees that were not top quality. Walters did not have a place of business or an agent in the town where Traynor was. Christmas was only a short time away. The trees were perishable and would decline in value to zero by Christmas Eve. Walters did not give Traynor any instructions, so Traynor sold the trees for Walters' account. Traynor then tried to recover from Walters the expenses he incurred in caring for and selling the trees. Did the buyer act properly in rejecting the trees and reselling them for the seller?

7. Creusot-Loire, a French manufacturing and engineering concern, was the project engineer to construct ammonia plants in Yugoslavia and Syria. The design process engineer for the two plants—as well as a plant being constructed in Sri Lanka—specified burners manufactured by Coppus Engineering Corporation. After the burner specifications were provided to Coppus, it sent technical and service information to Creusot-Loire.

Coppus expressly warranted that the burners were capable of continuous operation using heavy fuel oil with combustion air preheated to 260 degrees Celsius. The warranty extended for one year from the start-up of the plant but not exceeding three years from the date of shipment. In January 1989, Creusot-Loire ordered the burners for the Yugoslavia plant and paid for them; in November 1989, the burners were shipped to Yugoslavia. Due to construction delays, the plant was not to become operational until the end of 1993. In 1991, however, Creusot-Loire became aware that there had been operational difficulties with the Coppus burners at the Sri Lanka and Syria plants and that efforts to modify the burners had been futile. Creusot-Loire wrote to Coppus expressing concern that the burners purchased for the Yugoslavia plant, like those in the other plants, would prove unsatisfactory and asking for proof that the burners would meet contract specifications. When subsequent discussions failed to satisfy Creusot-Loire, it requested that Coppus take back the burners and refund the purchase price. Coppus refused. Finally, Creusot-Loire indicated that it would accept the burners only if Coppus extended its contractual guarantee to cover the delay in the start-up of the Yugoslavia plant and if Coppus posted an irrevocable letter of credit for the purchase price of the burners. When Coppus refused, Creusot-Loire brought an action for breach of contract, seeking a return of the purchase price. Coppus claimed that Creusot-Loire's request for assurance was unreasonable. How should the court rule?

8. Whelan ordered fuel oil from Griffith to be delivered to his farm home, which was located on a country road. The oil was to be delivered on a COD basis. Griffith made two attempts to deliver the oil, but each time no one was found at home. The morning after a heavy snow, the heaviest in 20 years, Griffith equipped the truck with chains and made a third attempt to deliver the oil but found on arrival that the driveway to the house was impassable due to snowdrifts approximately 6 feet high. When the driver drove past the house and attempted to turn around, the truck became stuck in the snow and had to be towed back to the main highway. Whelan ran out of oil and, as a result of having no fuel, his heating plant froze, causing substantial damage to it. Whelan sued Griffith to recover for the damage to the heating plant, claiming the breach of the contract to deliver the oil was the cause of the damage. Should Griffith be held liable?

Online Research: Using the Internet to Check Out an e-Bay Seller

Go to the e-Bay website (www.e-bay.com), select a category of goods being auctioned, and identify an item for which you might consider bidding. Assume that you would like to ascertain the experience other buyers have had dealing with that seller, including whether the seller has a reputation for (1) fairly describing the goods she puts up for auction, (2) properly preparing the goods for shipment to the winning bidder, and (3) promptly shipping the goods once payment is received. You also would like to know if other buyers have complained about this particular seller. How would you go about ascertaining this information through the e-Bay website? What information do you find concerning the seller of the item you chose?

22

REMEDIES FOR BREACH
OF SALES CONTRACTS

Kathy is engaged to be married. She contracts with the Bridal Shop for a custom-designed bridal gown in size 6 with delivery to be made by the weekend before the wedding. Kathy makes a $500 deposit against the contract price of $1,500. If the dress is completed in conformance with the specifications and on time, then Kathy is obligated to pay the balance of the agreed-on price. But what happens if either Kathy or the Bridal Shop breaches the contract? For example:

• If Kathy breaks her engagement and tells the Bridal Shop that she is no longer interested in having the dress before the shop has completed making it, what options are open to the Bridal Shop? Can it complete the dress or should it stop work on it?

• If the Bridal Shop completes the dress but Kathy does not like it and refuses to accept it, what can the Bridal Shop do? Can it collect the balance of the contract price from Kathy or must it first try to sell the dress to someone else?

• If the Bridal Shop advises Kathy that it will be unable to complete the dress in time for the wedding, what options are open to Kathy? If she has another dress made by someone else, or purchases a ready-made one, what, if any, damages can she collect from the Bridal Shop?

• If the Bridal Shop completes the dress but advises Kathy it plans to sell it to someone else who is willing to pay more money for it, does Kathy have any recourse?

These questions, and others, will be addressed in this chapter.

USUALLY, BOTH PARTIES TO a contract for the sale of goods perform the obligations that they assumed in the contract. Occasionally, however, one of the parties to a contract fails to perform his obligations. When this happens, the Uniform Commercial Code (UCC or Code) provides the injured party with a variety of remedies for breach of contract. This chapter will set forth and explain the remedies available to an injured party, as well as the Code's rules that govern buyer-seller agreements as to remedies and the Code's statute of limitations. The objective of the Code remedies is to put the injured person in the same position that he would have been in if the contract had been performed. Under the Code, an injured party may not recover consequential or punitive damages unless such damages are specifically provided for in the Code or in another statute [1–106].[1]

Agreements as to Remedies

The buyer and seller may provide their own remedies in the contract, to be applied in the event that one of the parties fails to perform. They may also limit either the remedies that the law makes available or the damages

---

[1]The numbers in brackets refer to sections of the Uniform Commercial Code.

that can be covered [2–719(1)]. If the parties agree on the amount of damages that will be paid to the injured party, this amount is known as **liquidated damages.** An agreement for liquidated damages is enforced if the amount is reasonable and if actual damages would be difficult to prove in the event of a breach of the contract. The amount is considered reasonable if it is not so large as to be a penalty or so small as to be unconscionable [2–718(1)].

For example, Carl Carpenter contracts to build and sell a display booth for $5,000 to Hank Hawker for Hawker to use at the state fair. Delivery is to be made to Hawker by September 1. If the booth is not delivered on time, Hawker will not be able to sell his wares at the fair. Carpenter and Hawker might agree that if delivery is not made by September 1, Carpenter will pay Hawker $2,750 as liquidated damages. The actual sales that

Hawker might lose without a booth would be very hard to prove, so Hawker and Carpenter can provide some certainty through the liquidated damages agreement. Carpenter then knows what he will be liable for if he does not perform his obligation. Similarly, Hawker knows what he can recover if the booth is not delivered on time. The $2,750 amount is probably reasonable. If the amount were $500,000, it likely would be void as a penalty because it is way out of line with the damages that Hawker would reasonably be expected to sustain. And if the amount were too small, say $1, it might be considered unconscionable and therefore not enforceable.

If a liquidated damages clause is not enforceable because it is a penalty or unconscionable, the injured party can recover the actual damages that he suffered. The following *Baker* case illustrates a situation where a court enforced a liquidated damages clause in a contract.

Baker v. International Record Syndicate, Inc.   *812 S.W.2d 53 (Tex. Ct. App. 1991)*

International Record Syndicate (IRS) hired Jeff Baker to take photographs of the musical group Timbuk-3. Baker mailed 37 "chromes" (negatives) to IRS via the business agent of Timbuk-3. When the chromes were returned to Baker, holes had been punched in 34 of them. Baker brought an action for breach of contract to recover for the damage done to the chromes.

A provision printed on Baker's invoice to IRS stated: "[r]eimbursement for loss or damage shall be determined by a photograph's reasonable value which shall be no less than $1,500 per transparency."

Enoch, Chief Judge   The Uniform Commercial Code provides:

Damages for breach by either party may be liquidated in the agreement but only at an amount which is reasonable in light of the anticipated harm caused by the breach, the difficulties of proof of loss, and the inconvenience or nonfeasibility of otherwise obtaining an adequate remedy. A term fixing unreasonably large liquidated damages is void as a penalty.

Under Texas law a liquidated damages provision will be enforced when the court finds (1) the harm caused by the breach is incapable of estimation, and (2) the amount of liquidated damages is a reasonable forecast of just compensation. This might be termed the "anticipated harm" test. The party asserting that a liquidated damages clause is, in fact, a penalty provision has the burden of proof. Evidence related to the difficulty of estimation and the reasonable forecast must be viewed as of the time the contract was executed.

Baker testified that he had been paid as much as $14,000 for a photo session, which resulted in 24 photographs and that several of these photographs had also been resold.

Baker further testified that he had received as little as $125 for a single photograph. Baker also testified that he once sold a photograph for $500. Subsequently, he sold reproductions of the same photograph three additional times at various prices; the total income from this one photograph was $1,500. This particular photograph was taken in 1986 and was still producing income in 1990. Baker demonstrated, therefore, that an accurate demonstration of the damages from a single photograph is virtually impossible.

Timbuk-3's potential for fame was also an important factor in the valuation of the chromes. At the time of the photo session, Timbuk-3's potential was unknown. In view of the difficulty in determining the value of a piece of art, the broad range of values and long-term earning power of photographs, and the unknown potential for fame of the subject, $1,500 is not an unreasonable estimate of Baker's actual damages.

Additionally, liquidated damages must not be disproportionate to actual damages. If the liquidated damages are shown to be disproportionate to the actual damages, then the liquidated damages can be declared a penalty and recovery limited to actual damages proven. This might be called the "actual harm" test. The burden of proving this defense is upon the party seeking to invalidate the clause. The party asserting this defense is required to prove the amount of the other party's actual damages, if any, to show that the actual loss was not an approximation of the stipulated sum.

While evidence was presented that showed the value of several of Baker's other projects, this was not evidence of the photographs in question. The evidence clearly shows that photographs are unique items with many factors bearing on their actual value. Each of the 34 chromes may have had a different value. Proof of this loss is difficult; where damages are real but difficult to prove, injustice will be done the injured party if the court substitutes the requirements of judicial proof for the parties' own informed agreement as to what is a reasonable measure of damages. The evidence offered to prove Baker's actual damages lacks probative force. IRS failed to establish Baker's actual damages as to these particular photographs.

Judgment reversed in favor of Baker.

Liability for consequential damages resulting from a breach of contract (such as lost profits or damage to property) may also be limited or excluded by agreement. The limitation or exclusion is not enforced if it would be unconscionable. Any attempt to limit consequential damages for injury caused to a person by consumer goods is considered prima facie unconscionable [2–719(3)].

Suppose an automobile manufacturer makes a warranty as to the quality of an automobile that is purchased as a consumer good. It then tries to disclaim responsibility for any person injured if the car does not conform to the warranty and to limit its liability to replacing any defective parts. The disclaimer of consequential injuries in this case would be unconscionable and therefore would not be enforced. Exclusion of or limitation on consequential damages is permitted where the loss is commercial, as long as the exclusion or limitation is not unconscionable. Where circumstances cause a limited remedy agreed to by the parties to fail in its essential purpose, the limited remedy is not enforced and the general Code remedies are available to the injured party.

The *Star-Shadow Productions* case involves the enforcement of a limitation of liability clause.

Star-Shadow Productions, Inc. v. Super 8 Sync Sound System
38 UCC Rep. 2d 1128 (R.I. Sup.Ct. 1999)

Star-Shadow Productions, Inc., and Bruce J. Haas produce and film low budget movies. One of their projects, "The Night of the Beast," was scheduled for filming from March 12 through 18, 1994, at the General Stanton Inn in Charlestown, Rhode Island. In preparation for the filming, Star-Shadow rented a Beaulieu 7008 Pro 8-millimeter camera and bought 108 rolls of Super 8 Sound high-resolution color negative film from Super 8 Sync Sound system. Unfortunately, on the first day of filming, Star-Shadow's cameraman was unable to use the Super 8 film because of loading and jamming problems. A representative of Super 8, Lisa Mattei, offered advice by phone and subsequently traveled to Charlestown with a replacement camera and Kodak Reverse film. When her troubleshooting efforts proved fruitless, she replaced the Super 8 film with Kodak Reverse film and the camera operated successfully. On March 22, 1994, Star-Shadow returned the camera and Star-Shadow's account was credited for the unused film.

Star-Shadow subsequently sued Super 8 for damages allegedly caused by the Super 8 film's inability to operate correctly. Super 8 filed a motion for summary judgment arguing that it had complied with all the terms of the contract by replacing the defective film and crediting Star-Shadow's account for the unused film. Super 8 pointed to the limitation of liability clause contained on price sheets and film boxes provided to Star-Shadow to show that Super 8 could not be subject to any additional liabilities. The limitation of liability clause's pertinent part reads: "Limitation of Liability: This product will be repaired if defective in manufacture or packing. Except for such replacement this product is sold without warranty or liability even though defect, damage, or loss is caused by negligence or other fault. . . ."

The trial court granted the motion for summary judgment. The judge found that the limitation of liability clause contained on the Super 8 film package was valid; therefore, Super 8 could not be held liable for damages beyond the value of replacement film. Star-Shadow appealed.

Per Curiam   Star-Shadow maintains that the limitation of liability clause failed its essential purpose—to adequately protect the filmmakers from damages arising from defective film. They point to the fact that the limitation of liability clause leaves them without recourse against Super 8 for the thousands of dollars of damages caused by the defective film. We have held in an analogous situation that the purchase price of goods is "not a premium for . . . insurance," and consequently, limitation of liability clauses are not unconscionable merely because buyers are not fully protected for damages that may arise from the malfunction of their purchased goods or service. In the case of defective film, the commercial film maker is not abandoned without protection [by limitation of liability clauses] but is free to purchase raw stock insurance.

The fact that Star-Shadow in this case has no protection other than their bargained-for remedy of replacement film does not make the limitation of liability clause unconscionable. "In an industry where the undertaking may vary from a multimillion dollar extravaganza to a low-budget instructional film," plaintiffs were in the better position to assess their risks and "mold the protection to the scope of [the] project" than defendant who was unaware of the breadth of plaintiffs' undertaking. Thus, Star-Shadow received what it bargained for, and the risk of equipment failure properly lay on them, not Super 8.

Judgment for Super 8 affirmed.

Statute of Limitations

The Code provides that a lawsuit for breach of a sales contract must be filed within four years after the breach occurs. The parties to a contract may shorten this period to one year, but they may not extend it for longer than four years [2–725]. Normally, a breach of warranty is considered to have occurred when the goods are delivered to the buyer. However, if the warranty covers future performance of goods (for example, a warranty on a tire for four years or 40,000 miles), then the breach occurs at the time the buyer should have discovered the defect in the product. If, for example, the buyer of the tire discovers the defect after driving 25,000 miles on the tire over a three-year period, he would have four years from that time to bring any lawsuit to remedy the breach.

Seller's Remedies

Remedies Available to an Injured Seller

A buyer may breach a contract in a number of ways. The most common are: (1) by wrongfully refusing to accept goods, (2) by wrongfully returning goods, (3) by failing to pay for goods when payment is due, and (4) by indicating an unwillingness to go ahead with the contract. When a buyer breaches a contract, the seller has a number of remedies under the Code, including the right to:

- Cancel the contract [2–703(f)].
- Withhold delivery of undelivered goods [2–703(a)].
- Complete manufacture of unfinished goods and identify them as to the contract or cease manufacture and sell for scraps [2–704].
- Resell the goods covered by the contract and recover damages from the buyer [2–706].
- Recover from the buyer the profit that the seller would have made on the sale or the damages that the seller sustained [2–708].
- Recover the purchase price of goods delivered to or accepted by the buyer [2–709].

In addition, a buyer may become insolvent and thus unable to pay the seller for goods already delivered or for goods that the seller is obligated to deliver. When a seller learns of a buyer's insolvency, the seller has a number of remedies, including the right to:

- Withhold delivery of undelivered goods [2–703(a)].
- Recover goods from a buyer upon the buyer's insolvency [2–702].
- Stop delivery of goods that are in the possession of a carrier or other bailee before they reach the buyer [2–705].

Cancellation and Withholding of Delivery

When a buyer breaches a contract, the seller has the right to cancel the contract and to hold up her own performance of the contract. The seller may then set aside any goods that were intended to fill her obligations under the contract [2–704].

If the seller is in the process of manufacturing the goods, she has two choices. She may complete manufacture of the goods, or she may stop manufacturing and sell the uncompleted goods for their scrap or salvage value. In choosing between these alternatives, the seller should select the alternative that will minimize the loss [2–704(2)]. Thus, a seller would be justified in completing the manufacture of goods that could be resold readily at the contract price. However, a seller would not be justified in completing specially manufactured goods that could not be sold to anyone other than the buyer who ordered them.

The purpose of this rule is to permit the seller to follow a reasonable course of action to mitigate (minimize) the damages. In *Madsen,* which follows, the seller, who did not complete the manufacture of goods on the buyer's repudiation, but rather dismantled and largely scrapped the existing goods, was held not to have acted in a commercially reasonable manner.

Madsen v. Murrey & Sons Co., Inc.   *743 P.2d 1212 (Utah Sup. Ct. 1987)*

Murrey & Sons Co., Inc. (Murrey), was engaged in the business of manufacturing and selling pool tables. Erik Madsen was working on an idea to develop a pool table that, through the use of electronic devices installed in the rails of the table, would produce lighting and sound effects in a fashion similar to a pinball machine. Murrey and Madsen entered into a written contract whereby Murrey agreed to manufacture 100 of its M1 4-foot by 8-foot six-pocket coin operated pool tables with customized rails capable of incorporating the electronic lighting and sound effects desired by Madsen. Under the agreement, Madsen would design the rails and provide the drawings to Murrey, who would manufacture them to Madsen's specifications. Madsen was to design, manufacture, and install the electronic components for the tables. Madsen agreed to pay $550 per table or a total of $55,000 for the 100 tables and made a $42,500 deposit on the contract.

Murrey began the manufacture of the tables while Madsen continued to work on the design of the rails and electronics. Madsen encountered significant difficulties and notified Murrey that he would be unable to take delivery of the 100 tables. Madsen then brought suit to recover the $42,500 he had paid Murrey.

Following Madsen's repudiation of the contract, Murrey dismantled the pool tables and used salvageable materials to manufacture other pool tables. A good portion of the material was simply used as firewood. Murrey made no attempt to market the 100 pool tables at a discount or at any other price in order to mitigate the damages. It claimed the salvage value of the materials it reused as $7,448. The trial court ordered Murrey to return $21,250 to Madsen and Murrey appealed.

Howe, Justice   Murrey contends that the trial court erred in concluding that it had failed to mitigate or minimize its damages in a commercially reasonable manner by not attempting to sell the 100 pool tables on the open market. It is a well-settled rule of the law of damages that "no party suffering a loss as the result of a breach of contract is entitled to any damages which could have been avoided if the aggrieved party had acted in a reasonably diligent manner in attempting to lessen his losses as a consequence of that breach." We have held:

> Where a contractual agreement has been breached by a party thereto, the aggrieved party is entitled to those damages that will put him in as good a position as he would have been had the other party performed pursuant to the agreement. A corollary to this rule is that the aggrieved party may not, either by action or inaction, aggravate the injury occasioned by the breach, but has a duty actively to mitigate his damages.

Murrey asserts that it sufficiently mitigated its damages by dismantling the pool tables and salvaging various components that could be used to manufacture other pool tables. The salvage value to Murrey was claimed to be $7,448. Murrey presented testimony that selling the tables as "seconds" would damage its reputation for quality and that the various holes, notches and routings placed in the tables to accommodate the electrical components to be installed by buyer weakened the structure of the tables so as to submit seller to potential liability if they were sold on the market.

On the other hand, Ronald Baker, who had been involved with the manufacturing and marketing of pool tables for 25 years testified on behalf of the buyer that the notches, holes and routings made in the frame to accommodate electrical wiring would not adversely affect the quality or marketability of the 100 pool tables. According to Baker, the tables could have been sold at full value or at a discounted price. In addition to this testimony, the trial court had the opportunity to view the experimental table developed by Madsen and his associates and observe the holes, notches, and routings necessary for the electrical components.

The trial court found that Murrey's action in dismantling the tables and using the materials for salvage and firewood, rather than attempting to sell or market the tables at full or discounted price, was not commercially reasonable. The court then concluded that seller had a duty to mitigate its damages and failed to do so. The finding is supported by competent evidence.

Applying the trial court's finding that the pool tables, if completed, could have been sold for at least $21,250, Murrey's damages are the difference between the market price ($21,250) and the contract price ($55,000) or $33,750. The

trial court found that Murrey was not entitled to any incidental damages. Under section 2–718(2), (3), Madsen's right to restitution of advance payments on the contract ($42,500) is subject to offset to the extent that seller establishes damages ($33,750), for a total recovery of $8,750.

Judgment for Madsen affirmed, with the recovery set at $8,750.

Resale of Goods

If the seller sets aside goods intended for the contract or completes the manufacture of such goods, he is not obligated to try to resell the goods to someone else. However, he may resell them and recover damages. The seller must make any resale in good faith and in a commercially reasonable manner. If the seller does so, he is entitled to recover from the buyer as damages the difference between the resale price and the price the buyer agreed to pay in the contract [2–706].

If the seller resells, he may also recover incidental damages, but the seller must give the buyer credit for any expenses that the seller saved because of the buyer's breach of contract. Incidental damages include storage charges and sales commissions paid when the goods were resold [2–710]. Expenses saved might be the cost of packaging the goods and/or shipping them to the buyer.

If the buyer and seller have agreed as to the manner in which the resale is to be made, the courts will enforce the agreement unless it is found to be unconscionable [2–302]. If the parties have not entered into an agreement as to the resale of the goods, they may be resold at public or private sale, but in all events the resale must be made in good faith and in a commercially reasonable manner. The seller should make it clear that the goods he is selling are those related to the broken contract.

If the goods are resold at private sale, the seller must give the buyer reasonable notification of his intention to resell [2–706(3)]. If the resale is a public sale, such as an auction, the seller must give the buyer notice of the time and place of the sale unless the goods are perishable or threaten to decline in value rapidly. The sale must be made at a usual place or market for public sales if one is reasonably available; and if the goods are not within the view of those attending the sale, the notification of the sale must state the place where the goods are located and provide for reasonable inspection by prospective bidders. The seller may bid at a public sale [2–706(4)].

The purchaser at a public sale who buys in good faith takes free from any rights of the original buyer even though the seller has failed to conduct the sale in compliance with the rules set out in the Code [2–706(5)]. The seller is not accountable to the buyer for any profit that the seller makes on a resale [2–706(6)].

Recovery of the Purchase Price

In the normal performance of a contract, the seller delivers conforming goods (goods that meet the contract specifications) to the buyer. The buyer accepts the goods and pays for them. The seller is entitled to the purchase price of all goods accepted by the buyer. She also is entitled to the purchase price of all goods that conformed to the contract and were lost or damaged after the buyer assumed the risk for their loss [2–709].

For example, a contract calls for Frank, a farmer, to ship 1,000 dozen eggs to Sutton, a grocer, with shipment "FOB Frank's Farm." If the eggs are lost or damaged while on their way to Sutton, she is responsible for paying Frank for them. Risk of loss is discussed in Chapter 19, Formation and Terms of Sales Contracts.

In one other situation, the seller may recover the purchase or contract price from the buyer. This is where the seller has made an honest effort to resell the goods and was unsuccessful or where it is apparent that any such effort to resell would be unsuccessful. This might happen where the seller manufactured goods especially for the buyer and the goods are not usable by anyone else. Assume that Sarton's Supermarket sponsors a bowling team. Sarton's orders six green-and-red bowling shirts to be embroidered with "Sarton's Supermarket" on the back and the names of the team members on the pocket. After the shirts are completed, Sarton's wrongfully refuses to accept them. The manufacturer will be able to recover the agreed purchase price if it cannot sell the shirts to someone else.

If the seller sues the buyer for the contract price of the goods, she must hold the goods for the buyer. Then, the seller must turn the goods over to the buyer if the buyer pays for them. However, if resale becomes possible before the buyer pays for the goods, the seller may resell them. Then, the seller must give the buyer credit for the proceeds of the resale [2–709(2)].

Damages for Rejection or Repudiation

When the buyer refuses to accept goods that conform to the contract or repudiates the contract, the seller does not have to resell the goods. The seller has two other ways of determining the damages that the buyer is liable for because of the breach of contract: (1) the difference between the contract price and the market price at which the goods are currently selling and (2) the "profit" that the seller lost when the buyer did not go through with the contract [2–708].

The seller may recover as damages the difference between the contract price and the market price at the time and place the goods were to be delivered to the buyer. The seller also may recover any incidental damages, but must give the buyer credit for any expenses that the seller has saved [2–708(1)]. This measure of damages most commonly is sought by a seller when the market price of the goods dropped substantially between the time the contract was made and the time the buyer repudiated the contract.

For example, on January 1, Toy Maker, Inc., contracts with the Red Balloon Toy Shop to sell the shop 100,000 trolls at $3.50 each, with delivery to be made in Boston on June 1. By June 1, the troll fad has passed and trolls are selling for $1 each in Boston. If Toy Shop repudiates the contract on June 1 and refuses to accept delivery of the 100,000 trolls, Toy Maker is entitled to the difference between the contract price of $350,000 and the June 1 market price in Boston of $100,000. Thus, Toy Maker could recover $250,000 in damages plus any incidental expenses, but less any expenses saved by it in not having to ship the trolls to Toy Shop (such as packaging and transportation costs).

If getting the difference between the contract price and the market price would not put the seller in as good a financial position as the seller would have been in if the contract had been performed, the seller may choose an alternative measure of damages based on the lost profit and overhead that the seller would have made if the sale had gone through. The seller can recover this lost profit and overhead plus any incidental expenses. However, the seller must give the buyer credit for any expenses saved as a result of the buyer's breach of contract [2–708(2)].

Using the troll example, assume that the direct labor and material cost to Toy Maker of making the trolls was

---

THE GLOBAL BUSINESS ENVIRONMENT

Seller's Remedies in International Transactions

Under the Convention on Contracts for the International Sale of Goods (CISG), an aggrieved seller has five potential remedies when the buyer breaches the contract: (1) suspension of the seller's performance; (2) "avoidance" of the contract; (3) reclamation of the goods in the buyer's possession; (4) an action for the price; and (5) an action for damages. The last two remedies can be pursued only in a judicial proceeding.

As noted in Chapter 21 (see The Global Environmental Business box entitled "Insecurity" on page 479), the seller may "suspend its performance" when it is apparent the other party to the contract will not be performing its obligations, for example, if the buyer was insolvent and unable to pay for any goods delivered to it.

Avoidance of a contract—which under the CISG essentially means canceling the contract—is a remedy most commonly utilized by buyers because the initial performance called for in contracts typically rests with the seller—for example, to deliver specified goods. When a seller has not been paid for goods, it may "avoid" the contract and seek their return from the buyer. If the buyer has possession of the goods when the contract is avoided, he must take reasonable steps to preserve them. Where the goods are perishable, the buyer might try to sell them for the seller's account but is not required to follow a seller's instructions to resell.

Where the seller has performed its obligations, the seller has the right to require the buyer to pay the contract price unless the seller has pursued an inconsistent remedy—such as reclaiming the goods. An aggrieved seller may also pursue an action for damages based on either (1) the difference between the contract price and the resale price (where the seller resold the goods) or (2) the difference between the contract price and the market price at the time the contract was avoided. The CISG also permits a measure of damages based on lost profits. Thus, in a number of respects, the UCC and CISG offer similar remedies to sellers.

75 cents each. Toy Maker could recover as damages from Toy Shop the profit Toy Maker lost when Toy Shop defaulted on the contract. Toy Maker would be entitled to the difference between the contract price of $350,000 and its direct cost of $75,000. Thus, Toy Maker could recover $275,000 plus any incidental expenses and less any expenses saved.

Seller's Remedies Where Buyer Is Insolvent

If the seller has not agreed to extend credit to the buyer for the purchase price of goods, the buyer must make payment on delivery of the goods. If the seller tenders delivery of the goods, he may withhold delivery unless the agreed payment is made. Where the seller has agreed to extend credit to the buyer for the purchase price of the goods, but discovers before delivery that the buyer is insolvent, the seller may refuse delivery unless the buyer pays cash for the goods together with the unpaid balance for all goods previously delivered under the contract [2–702(1)].

At common law, a seller had the right to rescind a sales contract induced by fraud and to recover the goods unless they had been resold to a bona fide purchaser for value. Based on this general legal principle, the Code provides that where the seller discovers that the buyer has received goods while insolvent, the seller may reclaim the goods upon demand made within 10 days after their receipt. This right granted to the seller is based on constructive deceit on the part of the buyer. Receiving goods while insolvent is equivalent to a false representation of solvency. To protect his rights, all the seller must do is to make a demand within the 10-day period; he need not actually repossess the goods.

If the buyer has misrepresented his solvency to this particular seller in writing within three months before the delivery of the goods, the 10-day limitation on the seller's right to reclaim the goods does not apply. However, the seller's right to reclaim the goods is subject to the rights of prior purchasers in the ordinary course of the buyer's business, good faith purchasers for value, creditors with a perfected lien on the buyer's inventory [2–702(2) and (3)], and of a trustee in bankruptcy. The relative rights of creditors to their debtor's collateral are discussed in Chapter 29, Security Interests in Personal Property.

CONCEPT REVIEW

Problem	Seller's Remedy
Buyer Refuses to Go Ahead with Contract and Seller Has Goods	1. Seller may cancel contract, suspend performance, and set aside goods intended to fill the contract. *a.* If seller is in the process of manufacturing, he may complete manufacture or stop and sell for scrap, picking alternative that in his judgment at the time will minimize the seller's loss. *b.* Seller can resell goods covered by contract and recover difference between contract price and proceeds of resale. *c.* Seller may recover purchase price where resale is not possible. *d.* Seller may recover damages for breach based on difference between contract price and market price, or in some cases based on lost profits.
Goods Are in Buyer's Possession	1. Seller may recover purchase price. 2. Seller may reclaim goods in possession of insolvent buyer by making a demand within 10 days after their receipt. If the buyer represented solvency to the seller in writing within three months before delivery, the 10-day limitation does not apply.
Goods Are in Transit	1. Seller may stop any size shipment if buyer is insolvent. 2. Seller may stop carload, truckload, planeload, or other large shipment for reasons other than buyer's insolvency.

Seller's Right to Stop Delivery

If the seller discovers that the buyer is insolvent, he has the right to stop the delivery of any goods that he has shipped to the buyer, regardless of the size of the shipment. If a buyer repudiates a sales contract or fails to make a payment due before delivery, the seller has the right to stop delivery of any large shipment of goods, such as a carload, a truckload, or a planeload [2–705].

To stop delivery, the seller must notify the carrier or other bailee in time for the bailee to prevent delivery of the goods. After receiving notice to stop delivery, the carrier or other bailee owes a duty to hold the goods and deliver them as directed by the seller. The seller is liable to the carrier or other bailee for expenses incurred or damages resulting from compliance with his order to stop delivery. If a nonnegotiable document of title has been issued for the goods, the carrier or other bailee does not have a duty to obey a stop-delivery order issued by any person other than the person who consigned the goods to him [2–705(3)].

Liquidated Damages

If the seller has justifiably withheld delivery of the goods because of the buyer's breach, the buyer may recover any money or goods he has delivered to the seller over and above the agreed amount of liquidated damages. If there is no such agreement, the seller may not retain an amount in excess of $500 or 20 percent of the value of the total performance for which the buyer is obligated under the contract, whichever is smaller. This right of restitution is subject to the seller's right to recover damages under other provisions of the Code and to recover the amount of value of benefits received by the buyer directly or indirectly by reason of the contract [2–718].

Buyer's Remedies

Buyer's Remedies in General

A seller may breach a contract in a number of ways. The most common are: (1) failing to make an agreed delivery, (2) delivering goods that do not conform to the contract, and (3) indicating that he does not intend to fulfill the obligations under the contract.

A buyer whose seller breaks the contract is given a number of alternative remedies. These include:

- Buying other goods (covering) and recovering damages from the seller based on any additional expense that the buyer incurs in obtaining the goods [2–712].

CYBERLAW IN ACTION

E-Commerce Aids Buyers

Electronic commerce helps solve two of the most important concerns for buyers of goods in enforcing their rights under Article 2. The first of these relates to means by which the buyer may learn—from the seller or otherwise—of a recall that affects the goods purchased. For example, sellers could notify merchant buyers that it is notifying consumer buyers that they will need to take their cars in to a dealership to have a seatbelt replaced. This early e-mail or posting on the seller's website can alert the merchant buyer to the need to train personnel how to handle recall questions from the buyers and also how to make the needed replacement. Buyers also may be able to determine in advance of their purchases whether the goods they plan to buy have been the subject of a recall and whether the recall was voluntary (a problem found by the seller) or required by the federal government, for example. Information about earlier recalls may be especially helpful to buyers of used goods, such as cars and trucks, to baby items, and anything where personal safety is critically important.

The second involves the buyer's duty to give the seller "notice" if the buyer needs a remedy from the seller. As noted in Chapter 21, Sections 2–602 and 2–607 require that the buyer notify the seller if the buyer wishes to reject goods the seller has tendered, or if the buyer decides to revoke acceptance of goods that the seller has promised to repair or replace and has neither repaired nor replaced the goods as promised—or where the buyer gets goods that have a latent defect. "Notice" does not have to be in writing to be effective, but it usually is preferable to have a record that the buyer gave notice to the seller and the time of the notice given. This reduces the risk that a court will find that the buyer's failure to give notice deprives the buyer of her right to a remedy (see Section 2–607(3)(a)). Electronic commerce tools, including e-mail, allow buyers to provide speedy and reliable information to sellers in cases such as these. Buyers whose e-mail systems provide confirmation that the seller recipient actually has received the message about the buyer's concerns about the goods, or who show the time and date that the intended recipient opened the e-mail, make providing notice easier and easier to document than using traditional methods of communication.

- Recovering damages based on the difference between the contract price and the current market price of the goods [2–713].
- Recovering damages for any nonconforming goods accepted by the buyer based on the difference in value between what the buyer got and what he should have gotten [2–714].
- Obtaining specific performance of the contract where the goods are unique and cannot be obtained elsewhere [2–716].

In addition, the buyer can in some cases recover consequential damages (such as lost profits) and incidental damages (such as expenses incurred in buying substitute goods).

Buyer's Right to Cover

If the seller fails or refuses to deliver the goods called for in the contract, the buyer can purchase substitute goods; this is known as cover. If the buyer does purchase substi-tute goods, the buyer can recover as damages from the seller the difference between the contract price and the cost of the substitute goods [2–712]. For example, Frank Farmer agrees to sell Ann's Cider Mill 1,000 bushels of apples at $10 a bushel. Farmer then refuses to deliver the apples. Cider Mill can purchase 1,000 bushels of similar apples, and if it has to pay $11 a bushel, it can recover the difference ($1 a bushel) between what it paid ($11) and the contract price ($10). Thus, Cider Mill could recover $1,000 from Farmer.

The buyer can also recover any incidental damages sustained, but must give the seller credit for any expenses saved. In addition, he may be able to obtain consequential damages. The buyer is not required to cover, however. If he does not cover, the other remedies under the Code are still available [2–712].

The case that follows, *KGM Harvesting Co.*, illustrates a situation where the aggrieved buyer chose to seek damages based on its cost of cover from the defaulting seller.

KGM Harvesting Co. v. Fresh Network	26 UCC Rep.2d 1028 (Cal. App. 1995)

KGM Harvesting Company, a California lettuce grower and distributor, and Fresh Network, an Ohio lettuce broker, began dealing with each other in 1989, and over the years the terms of the agreement were modified. As of May 1991, their agreement called for KGM to deliver 14 "loads" of lettuce a week at a price of 9 cents a pound. A load of lettuce consists of 40 bins, each of which weighs 1,000 to 1,200 pounds. At an average bin weight of 1,100 pounds, one load would equal 44,000 pounds, and the 14 loads called for in the contract would weigh 616,000 pounds. At 9 cents per pound, the cost would be approximately $55,440 per week.

Fresh Network, in turn, resold all of the lettuce to another broker (Castellani Company) who sold it to Club Chef, a company that chopped and shredded it for the fast food industry (specifically, Burger King, Taco Bell, and Pizza Hut). The transactions between Fresh Network and Castellani, and in turn between Castellani and Club Chef, were on a cost-plus basis. This meant each paid its buyer its actual cost plus a small commission.

In May and June 1991, when the price of lettuce went up dramatically, KGM refused to supply Fresh Network with lettuce at the contract price of 9 cents per pound. Instead, it sold the lettuce to others at a profit between $800,000 and $1,100,000. Fresh Network then went out on the open market and purchased lettuce to satisfy its obligations to Castellani Company. Castellani covered all of Fresh Network's extra expense except for $70,000. Fresh Network then sought to recover from KGM as damages the difference between what it was forced to spend to buy replacement lettuce and the contract price of 9 cents a pound (approximately $700,000). KGM objected on the grounds that Fresh Network had been able to pass some of the increased cost along to Castellani.

Cottle, Presiding Judge   Section 2–711 of the California Uniform Commercial Code provides a buyer with several alternative remedies for a seller's breach of contract. The buyer can " 'cover' by making in good faith and without unreasonable delay any reasonable purchase of . . . goods in substitution for those due from the seller." Section 2–712(1). In that case, the buyer "may recover from the seller as damages the difference between the cost of cover and the contract price."

Section 2–712(2). If the buyer is unable to cover or chooses not to cover, the measure of damages is the difference between the market price and the contract price. Section 2–713.

In the instant case, buyer "covered" in order to fulfill its own contractual obligations to the Castellani Company. Accordingly, it was awarded the damages called for in cover cases—the difference between the contract price and the cover price.

In appeals from judgments rendered pursuant to section 2–712, the dispute typically centers on whether the buyer acted in "good faith," whether the "goods in substitution" differed substantially from the contracted for goods, whether the buyer unreasonably delayed in purchasing substitute goods in the mistaken belief the price would go down, or whether the buyer paid too much for the substitute goods.

In this case, however, none of these typical issues is in dispute. Seller does *not* contend that buyer paid too much for the substitute lettuce or that buyer was guilty of "unreasonable delay" or lack of "good faith" in its attempt to obtain substitute lettuce. Nor does seller contend that the lettuce purchased was of a higher quality or grade and therefore not a reasonable substitute.

Instead, seller takes issue with section 2–712 itself, contending that despite the unequivocal language of section 2–712, a buyer who covers should not *necessarily* recover the difference between the cover price and the contract price. Seller points out that because of buyer's "cost plus" contract with Castellani Company, buyer was eventually able to pass on the extra expenses (except for $70,000) occasioned by seller's breach and buyer's consequent purchase of substitute lettuce on the open market. It urges this court under these circumstances not to allow buyer to obtain a "windfall."

The basic premise of contract law is to effectuate the expectations of the parties to the agreement, to give them the "benefit of the bargain" they struck when they entered into the agreement. In this case, the damage formula of section 2–712 put buyer in the identical position performance would have: it gave buyer the contracted for 14 loads of lettuce with which to carry on its business at the contracted for price of 9 cents per pound.

Despite the obvious applicability and appropriateness of section 2–712, seller argues in this appeal that the contract-cover differential of section 2–712 is inappropriate in cases, as here, where the aggrieved buyer is ultimately able to pass on its additional costs to other parties. Seller contends that section 1–106's remedial injunction to put the aggrieved party "in as good a position as if the other party had fully performed" demands that all subsequent events impacting on *buyer's* ultimate profit or loss be taken into consideration (specifically, that buyer passed on all but $70,000 of its loss to Castellani Company, which passed on all of its loss to Club Chef, which passed on most of its loss to its fast food customers).

No section 2–712 case has ever held that cover damages must be limited by section 1–106. The obvious reason is that the cover-contract differential puts a buyer who covers in the exact same position as performance would have done. This is precisely what is called for in section 1–106. In this respect, the cover/contract differential of section 2–712 is very different than the market/contract differential of section 2–713, which need bear no close relation to the buyer's actual loss.

Judgment affirmed for Fresh Network.

Incidental Damages

Incidental damages include expenses that the buyer incurs in receiving, inspecting, transporting, and storing goods shipped by the seller that do not conform to those called for in the contract. Incidental damages also include any reasonable expenses or charges that the buyer has to pay in obtaining substitute goods [2–715(1)].

Consequential Damages

In certain situations, an injured buyer is able to recover consequential damages, such as the buyer's lost profits caused by the seller's breach of contract. The buyer must be able to show that the seller knew or should have known at the time the contract was made that the buyer would suffer special damages if the seller did not perform his obligations. In case of commercial loss, the buyer must also show that he could not have prevented the damage by obtaining substitute goods [2–715(2)(a)].

Suppose Knitting Mill promises to deliver 15,000 yards of a special fabric to Dorsey by September 1. Knitting Mill knows that Dorsey wants to acquire the material to make garments suitable for the Christmas season. Knitting Mill also knows that in reliance on the contract with it, Dorsey will enter into contracts with department stores to deliver the finished garments by October 1. If Knitting Mill fails to deliver the fabric or delivers the fabric after September 1, it may be liable to Dorsey for any consequential damages that she sustains if she is unable to acquire the same material elsewhere in time to fulfill her October 1 contracts.

Consequential damages can also include an injury to a person or property caused by a breach of warranty [2–715(2)(b)]. For example, an electric saw is defective. Hanson purchases the saw, and while he is using it, the blade comes off and severely cuts his arm. The injury to Hanson is consequential damage resulting from a nonconforming or defective product.

Damages for Nondelivery

If the seller fails or refuses to deliver the goods called for by the contract, the buyer has the option of recovering damages for the nondelivery. Thus, instead of covering, the buyer can get the difference between the contract price of the goods and their market price at the time he learns of the seller's breach. In addition, the buyer may recover any incidental damages and consequential damages, but must give the seller credit for any expenses saved [2–713].

Suppose Biddle agreed on June 1 to sell and deliver 1,500 bushels of wheat to a grain elevator on September 1 for $7 per bushel and then refused to deliver on September 1 because the market price was then $10 per bushel. The grain elevator could recover $4,500 damages from Biddle, plus incidental damages that could not have been prevented by cover.

Damages for Defective Goods

If a buyer accepts defective goods and wants to hold the seller liable, the buyer must give the seller notice of the defect within a reasonable time after the buyer discovers the defect [2–607(3)]. Where goods are defective or not as warranted and the buyer gives the required notice, he can recover damages. The buyer is entitled to recover the difference between the value of the goods received and the value the goods would have had if they had been as warranted. He may also be entitled to incidental and consequential damages [2–714].

For example, Al's Auto Store sells Anders an automobile tire, warranting it to be four-ply construction. The tire goes flat when it is punctured by a nail, and Anders discovers that the tire is really only two-ply. If Anders gives the store prompt notice of the breach, she can keep the tire and recover from Al's the difference in value between a two-ply and a four-ply tire.

The *Jetpac* case, which follows, illustrates the damages available to a buyer who received defective goods.

Jetpac Group, Ltd. v. Bostek, Inc.   *942 F. Supp. 716 (D.Mass. 1996)*

Jetpac Group, Ltd., is an export/import company based in Shreveport, Louisiana. Formed in 1988, Jetpac's business generally involves selling food products, such as frozen chicken, in various countries around the world, including Russia. In 1992, it partnered with Natashquan Korotia Systems (NKS), a Canadian company headed by a former citizen of what had been the Soviet Republic of Georgia. NKS held a contract to sell 3,000 computers—in a configuration known as "Russian 286s"—to a buyer in Russia at a price of $1,050 per unit.

Jetpac contacted Bostek, Inc., a Hanover, Massachusetts, supplier of computer hardware and software that, among other things, built integrated systems to consumers' specifications, buying the components from various sources and then assembling them. On June 11, 1992, Jetpac and Bostek agreed that Bostek would build a "test shipment" of 100 units that would be shipped to the Russian customer on June 15. Bostek's price was to be $630 per unit for this smaller production run; its quote for the larger number eventually desired was $605 per unit. The parties agreed on the components to be included in the computers, including a 286/16 motherboard, a 220 volt power supply, a VGA monitor, a mouse, and a Cyrillic/English keyboard. Bostek was to ship the units directly to the customer in Russia with Jetpac paying the freight costs for shipping from Boston of $8,184. NKS and Jetpac were to split the profit on the Russian sale.

When the computers arrived in Russia, the customer notified NKS that there were significant problems. Not all the specified components were included; for example, no "mice" were shipped, although the specifications called for them. Some of the wiring in the central processing unit was either missing or disconnected. Further, the monitors did not switch automatically from 110 to 220 volts, and as a result, several of them "blew up" when initially switched on. When Jetpac's President went to Russia to meet with the very dissatisfied customer, he observed the wiring problems and when he tried to turn on five separate systems that had been in the shipment, only one booted up. In short, the "test shipment" that had been designed to impress the

Russian customer and open the way to more sales was a disaster. In an effort—unsuccessful it turned out—to regain the customer's confidence, NKS and Jetpac bought and supplied the customer with another 200 units from another supplier.

The Russian customer refused to pay fully for the first shipment and refused to buy the balance of the 3,000 computers. Thus, reasonably probable sales of 2,700 computers at $1,050 were lost. NKS charged back to Jetpac its share of the shortfall on the first shipment ($23,517). Jetpac brought suit against Bostek, claiming damages for breach of warranty, consequential damages in the form of lost profits and incidental expense, including the cost of its president's travel to Moscow to try to mollify the unhappy customer and additional shipping expenses it incurred to get components to the customer that had been omitted from the initial shipment.

O'Toole, District Judge   Jetpac and Bostek entered into a valid and binding contract for the sale of 100 computers conforming to the specifications set forth in the Bostek invoice of June 11, 1992. The contract was one for the sale of goods, and the implied warranty of merchantability imposed under the Uniform Commercial Code ("UCC") applied.

Bostek committed a breach of the contract by failing to furnish goods that conformed to the contract description. In addition, the goods furnished were defective, in breach of the warranty of merchantability.

For the breach of contract Jetpac is entitled to damages in the amount of any loss that resulted "in the ordinary course of events from the seller's breach as determined in any manner which is reasonable." [2–714(1)] For breach of the warranty, Jetpac is entitled to damages in the amount of the difference "between the value of the goods accepted and the value they would have had if they had been as warranted." [2–714(2)] In both cases, the damages can be determined by Jetpac's share of the loss incurred by NKS when the customer in Russia refused to pay the full price for the goods. Jetpac's share, as described above, was $23,517.

In addition, "[i]n a proper case any incidental and consequential damages under section 2–715 may also be recovered." Under section 2–715, recoverable consequential damages include "any loss resulting from general or particular requirements and needs of which the seller at the time of contracting had reason to know and which could not reasonably be prevented by cover or otherwise." [2–715(2)(a)]. Such damages include "prospective profits lost as the natural, primary and probable consequence of the breach."

In this case, Jetpak's president had told Bostek that the shipment of 100 computers was only the initial one in a prospective sale of 3,000 units to the buyer in Russia. Bostek thus had reason to know that a defective shipment could jeopardize that business opportunity and bring about a loss of the profits that could reasonably be earned if the full 3,000 units were to be shipped. To be sure, there was no assurance that for some other unforeseen reason the full 3,000 would not ultimately be sold. There was a firm contract for that number, however, and it is a reasonable inference that if the initial shipment had conformed to the contract specifications and the warranty of merchantability, the contract would have been fulfilled. Damages cannot be assessed upon conjecture or surmise, but by the same token the reasonable prospect of damages—such as is shown by the existence of NKS's contract with the Russian buyer—should not be defeated by conjecture or surmise, either. The plaintiff's burden is not to demonstrate its damages with mathematical certainty but only to a "fair degree of certainty." The calculation of lost profits set forth above meets the test.

Jetpac is also entitled under section 2–715(1) to incidental damages, which include the increased shipping costs and the cost of its president's trip to Moscow to try to solve the problem caused by the defective goods and thus to mitigate potential damages.

Accordingly, on its claim of breach of contract, Jetpac is entitled to damages for the direct loss in the transaction in the sum of $23,517, for consequential damages for lost prospective profits in the sum of $148,500, and for incidental damages in the sum of $6,778.33, for a total of $178,795.33.

Judgment for Jetpac affirmed.

ETHICS IN ACTION

Should the Buyer Get an Honest Answer?

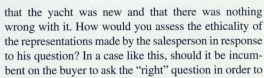

Problem case number 7 involves the sale of a yacht as new that previously had sunk in salt water. When the seller was asked by the prospective buyer why the asking price had been reduced from $102,000 to $80,000, the seller indicated it was because there had been a change in the model and they had new ones coming in. He also assured the buyer that the yacht was new and that there was nothing wrong with it. How would you assess the ethicality of the representations made by the salesperson in response to his question? In a case like this, should it be incumbent on the buyer to ask the "right" question in order to protect himself or herself, or should there be an ethical obligation on the seller to disclose voluntarily material facts that may be relevant to the buyer making an informed decision?

THE GLOBAL BUSINESS ENVIRONMENT

Buyer's Remedies in International Transactions

Under the Convention on Contracts for the International Sale of Goods (CISG), an aggrieved buyer has four potential types of remedies against a seller who has breached the contract: (1) "avoidance" of the contract; (2) an adjustment in the price; (3) specific performance; and (4) an action for damages. The first two remedies can be pursued without involving a court, and the last two require the buyer to initiate a judicial proceeding.

As noted in Chapter 21 (see The Global Business Environment box entitled "Insecurity" on page 479), a buyer has the right to suspend its performance and/or to "avoid" a contract where the seller appears unable to perform its obligations and does not provide adequate assurances that it can and will perform. A buyer may also "avoid" the contract—which under the CISG essentially means "cancel" the contract—and refuse to accept and pay for goods that are so defective or nonconforming as to constitute a "fundamental breach" of the contract.

Aggrieved buyers who receive nonconforming goods "may reduce the price" paid to the seller. The CISG provides a formula for calculating the reduction that involves comparing the value of the goods actually delivered at the time they were delivered to the value that conforming goods would have had at the time of delivery.

The CISG gives the aggrieved buyer a right to "require performance" by the seller. This follows the civil law principle that the best relief to the buyer is not damages but rather having the seller perform as promised. Thus, the CISG does not require that the goods must be "unique"—as the UCC does—in order for the buyer to be entitled to specific performance.

While the buyer has the right to seek specific performance with the assistance of a court, the buyer also has the option of seeking damages, including consequential damages. Such damages can be based either on (1) the difference between the cost of cover and the contract price or (2) on the difference between the market price and the contract price. However, unlike the UCC, the CISG requires the buyer to use the "cover" formula for calculating damages if the buyer does cover by obtaining substitute goods.

Buyer's Right to Specific Performance

Sometimes, the goods covered by a contract are unique and it is not possible for a buyer to obtain substitute goods. When this is the case, the buyer is entitled to specific performance of the contract.

Specific performance means that the buyer can require the seller to give the buyer the goods covered by the contract [2–716]. Thus, the buyer of an antique automobile such as a 1910 Ford might have a court order the seller to deliver the specified automobile to the buyer because it was one of a kind. On the other hand, the buyer of grain in a particular storage bin could not get specific performance if he could buy the same kind of grain elsewhere.

Buyer and Seller Agreements as to Remedies

As mentioned earlier in this chapter, the parties to a contract may provide remedies in addition to or as substitution for those expressly provided in the Code [2–719]. For example, the buyer's remedies may be limited by the contract to the return of the goods and the repayment of the price or to the replacement of nonconforming goods or parts. However, a court looks to see whether such a limitation was freely agreed to or whether it is unconscionable. In the latter case, the court does not enforce the limitation and the buyer has all the rights given to an injured buyer by the Code.

The *Baker* case, which follows, involves a situation where a merchant was unsuccessful in seeking to restrict an aggrieved buyer's efforts to recover the purchase price paid for defective goods.

Baker v. Burlington Coat Factory Warehouse
34 UCC Rep.2d 1052 (N.Y. City Ct. 1998)

Catherine Baker purchased a fake fur coat from the Burlington Coat Factory Warehouse store in Scarsdale, New York, paying $127.99 in cash. The coat began shedding profusely, rendering the coat unwearable. The shedding was so severe that Baker's allergies were exacerbated, necessitating a visit to her doctor and to the drugstore for a prescription.

She returned the coat to the store within two days and demanded that Burlington refund her $127.99 cash payment. Burlington refused, indicating that it would give her a store credit or a new coat of equal value, but no cash refund. Baker searched the store for a fake fur of equal value and found none. She refused the store credit, repeated her demand for a cash refund, and brought a lawsuit against Burlington when it again refused to make a cash refund.

In its store, Burlington displayed several large signs which stated, in part,

WAREHOUSE POLICY

Merchandise, in New Condition, May be Exchanged Within 7 Days of Purchase for Store Credit and Must be Accompanied by a Ticket and Receipt. No Cash Refunds or Charge Credits.

On the front of Baker's sales receipt was the following language:

Holiday Purchases May be Exchanged Through January 11th, 1998, In House Store Credit Only No Cash Refunds or Charge Card Credits.

On the back of the sales receipt was the following language:

We will be Happy to Exchange Merchandise in New Condition Within 7 Days When Accompanied By Ticket and Receipt. However, Because of Our Unusually Low Prices: No Cash Refunds or Charge Card Credits Will Be Issued. In House Store Credit Only.

At the trial, Baker claimed that she had not read the language on the receipt and was unaware of Burlington's No Cash Refunds policy.

Dickerson, Judge Under most circumstances retail stores in New York State are permitted to establish a no cash and no credit card charge refund policy and enforce it. Retail Store refund policies are governed, in part, by New York General Business Law section 218–a, Disclosure of Refund Policies, which requires conspicuous signs on the item or at the cash register or on signs visible from the cash register or at each store entrance, setting forth its refund policy including whether it is "in cash, or as credit or store credit only." If the store violates GBL section 218–a, the consumer has twenty days to return "merchandise (which) has not been used or damaged."

Baker returned the undamaged and unworn, albeit shedding, Fake Fur to Burlington Coat within two days of purchase thus coming within Burlington Coat's "7 Days of Purchase" policy and within the twenty-day claim filing period in GBL 218–a(3). Although Baker professed ignorance of Burlington Coat's refund policy, the Court finds that Burlington Coat's signs and the front and back of its sales receipt reasonably inform consumers of its no cash and no credit card charge refund policy.

Notwithstanding its visibility Burlington Coat's no cash and no credit card charge refund policy as against Baker is unenforceable. Stated simply, when a product is defective as was Baker's common and, hardly unique, shedding Fake Fur, Burlington Coat cannot refuse to return the consumer's payment whether made in cash or with a credit card.

UCC section 2–314 mandates that "a warranty that the goods shall be merchantable is implied in a contract of their sale if the seller is a merchant with respect to goods of that kind . . . (2) Goods to be merchantable must be . . . fit for the ordinary purposes for which such goods are used" [UCC section 2–314]. Should there be a breach of the implied warranty of merchantability then consumers may recover all appropriate damages including the purchase price in cash [UCC section 2–714]. The court finds that Burlington Coat sold Baker a defective and unwearable Fake Fur and breached the implied warranty of merchantability. Baker is entitled to the return of her purchase price of $127.99 in cash and all other appropriate damages. However, Baker's claim for the $15.00 co-pay for visiting her doctor and the cost of allergy medicine is denied. Baker admitted having allergies, but it is not clear that the Fake Fur exacerbated those allergies.

As between the implicit cash refund policy contained in UCC sections 2–314 and 2–714, the no cash refund policy explicitly authorized in GBL section 218–a(2), the UCC provisions are paramount and preempt any contrary provisions in GBL 218–a. To hold otherwise would allow a merchant whether in good faith or otherwise, to place in commerce a defective product and merely give credit exchange upon the product's return.

Judgment for Baker.

CONCEPT REVIEW

Buyer's Remedies (on breach by seller)

Problems	Buyer's Remedy
Seller Fails to Deliver Goods or Delivers Nonconforming Goods That Buyer Rightfully Rejects or Justifiably Revokes Acceptance Of	1. Buyer may cancel the contract and recover damages. 2. Buyer may "cover" by obtaining substitute goods and recover difference between contract price and cost of cover. 3. Buyer may recover damages for breach based on difference between contract price and market price.
Seller Delivers Nonconforming Goods That Are Accepted by Buyer	Buyer may recover damages based on difference between value of goods received and value of goods if they had been as warranted.
Seller Has the Goods but Refuses to Deliver Them and Buyer Wants Them	Buyer may seek specific performance if goods are unique and cannot be obtained elsewhere, or buyer may replevy (obtain from the seller) goods identified to contract if buyer cannot obtain cover.

Problems and Problem Cases

1. Lobianco contracted with Property Protection, Inc., for the installation of a burglar alarm system. The contract provided in part:

Alarm system equipment installed by Property Protection, Inc., is guaranteed against improper function due to manufacturing defects of workmanship for a period of 12 months. The installation of the above equipment carries a 90-day warranty. The liability of Property Protection, Inc., is limited to repair or replacement of security alarm equipment and does not include loss or damage to possessions, persons, or property.

As installed, the alarm system included a standby battery source of power in the event that the regular source of power failed. During the 90-day warranty period, burglars broke into Lobianco's house and stole $35,815 worth of jewelry. First, they destroyed the electric meter so that there was no electric source to operate the system, and then they entered the house. The batteries in the standby system were dead, and thus the standby system failed to operate. Accordingly, no outside siren was activated and a telephone call that was supposed to be triggered was not made. Lobianco brought suit, claiming damage in the amount of her stolen jewelry because of the failure of the alarm system to work properly. Did the disclaimer effectively eliminate any liability on the alarm company's part for consequential damages?

2. Parzek purchased from New England Log Homes a log home kit consisting of hand-peeled logs, window frames, and door frames. The brochure that Parzek had seen before buying the log home kit contained a statement that the logs were treated with a preservative "to protect the treated wood against decay, stain, termites, and other insects." Other statements indicated the maintenance-free nature of the logs, and there was a guarantee against any materials and engineering defects. The logs were delivered in May 1974 to the construction site, where they were stored in stacks covered with heavy tarpaulins. By fall 1976, the walls were erected and the roof was on. In 1979, Parzek discovered 15 medium-sized blue metallic beetles on the interior walls of the home. He was assured by the dealer for New England Log Homes that the problem was not serious. The following April, however, Parzek observed several hundreds of beetles and discovered larvae and "excavation channels" in the logs. When he contacted New England Log Homes, he was told that it did not guarantee that its logs were insect free. Parzek had the home treated by an exterminator and then brought suit against New England Log Homes. Relying on Section 2–725 of the Code, New England Log Homes contended that the lawsuit was filed more than four years after the date of delivery. Was the lawsuit barred by the statute of limitations because it was filed more than four years after the date of delivery?

3. Kohn ordered a custom-made suit from Meledani Tailors. A few days later, before much work had been completed, Kohn told the tailors that he did not want the suit. They, therefore, stopped its manufacture and filed suit for the entire contract price. Is Kohn liable for the full purchase price?

4. Cohn advertised a 30-foot sailboat for sale in *The New York Times*. Fisher saw the ad, inspected the sailboat, and offered Cohn $4,650 for the boat. Cohn accepted the offer. Fisher gave Cohn a check for $2,535 as a deposit on the boat. He wrote on the check, "Deposit on aux sloop, D'arc Wind, full amount $4,650." Fisher later refused to go through with the purchase and stopped payment on the deposit check. Cohn readvertised the boat and sold it for the highest offer he received, which was $3,000. Cohn then sued Fisher for breach of contract. He asked for damages of $1,679.50. This represented the $1,650 difference between the contract price and the sale price plus $29.50 in incidental expenses in reselling the boat. Is Cohn entitled to this measure of damages?

5. McCain Foods sold on credit and delivered a quantity of frozen french fries to Flagstaff Food Service Company. Several days later, when the potatoes had not yet been paid for, McCain discovered that Flagstaff was insolvent and had just filed a petition in bankruptcy. What would you advise McCain Foods to do?

6. Kneale bought two chairs from Modernage Furniture that were on sale for $97.50 apiece. The regular price of the chairs was $147.57 each, or $50.07 more than the sale price. Because the store had oversold that particular chair, it failed to deliver the items to Kneale, although she had paid the full purchase price in cash. She brought suit for breach of contract against Modernage Furniture. Modernage contended that its liability was limited to return of the purchase price. Was Modernage's liability for breach of contract limited to return of the purchase price?

7. Barr purchased from Crow's Nest Yacht Sales a 31-foot Tiara pleasure yacht manufactured by S-2 Yachts. He had gone to Crow's Nest knowing the style and type yacht he wanted. He was told that the retail price was $102,000 but that he could purchase the model they had for $80,000. When he asked about the reduction in price he was told that Crow's Nest had to move it because there was a change in the model and they had new ones coming in. He was assured that the yacht was new, that there was nothing wrong with it, and that it had only 20 hours on the engines. Barr installed a considerable amount of electronic equipment on the boat. When he began to use it, he experienced tremendous difficulties with equipment malfunctions. On examination by a marine expert it was determined that the yacht had earlier been sunk in salt water, resulting in significant rusting and deterioration in the engine, equipment, and fixtures. Other experts concluded that significant replacement and repair was required, that the engines would have only 25 percent of their normal expected life, and that following its sinking, the yacht would have only half of its original value. Barr then brought suit against Crow's Nest and S-2 Yachts for

breach of warranty. To what measure of damages is Barr entitled to recover for breach of warranty?

8. De La Hoya bought a used handgun for $140 from Slim's Gun Shop, a licensed firearms dealer. At the time, neither De La Hoya nor Slim's knew that the gun had been stolen prior to the time Slim's bought it. While De La Hoya was using the gun for target shooting, he was questioned by a police officer. The officer traced the serial number of the gun, determined that it had been stolen, and arrested De La Hoya. De La Hoya had to hire an attorney to defend himself against the criminal charges. De La Hoya then brought a lawsuit against Slim's Gun Shop for breach of warranty of title. He sought to recover the purchase price of the gun plus $8,000, the amount of his attorney's fees, as "consequential damages." Can a buyer who does not get good title to the goods he purchased recover from the seller consequential damages caused by the breach of warranty of title?

9. Certina USA is a watch manufacturer that sells its watches through traveling salespeople paid by it. Migerobe, Inc., owns and operates jewelry counters in McRae's department stores, which are located throughout the Southeast. In the summer of 1987, Migerobe contacted Gerald Murff, a Certina salesperson from whom it had previously purchased watches. It notified him that Migerobe was interested in buying Certina watches if the company decided to sell a large portion of its inventory at reduced prices. Migerobe had some reason to believe that Certina had excess inventory, and Certina in fact decided to eliminate its inventory as a result of a corporate decision to withdraw its watches from the U.S. market. Migerobe was hoping to acquire the Certina watches so that they could be used as "doorbusters" for an after-Thanksgiving sale. Doorbusters or "loss leaders" are items offered at a low price, which are designed to increase the traffic flow through a store and, thereby, increase corollary sales (the sale of nonadvertised items). On October 29, the parties agreed on the sale of over 2,000 watches at a price of $45 per watch. On November 4, the national accounts manager for Certina called Migerobe to say that Certina would not ship the watches. Migerobe brought suit against Certina to recover damages for breach of contract, including consequential damages in the form of lost profits on corollary sales. Migerobe asserted that the Certina salesperson was aware of its plan to use the watches as a loss leader by featuring them in a doorbuster Thanksgiving advertisement at a 50 percent discount. It also had data that showed it previously had increased its corollary sales by 69 to 87 percent when it had used similar doorbuster promotions. Was Migerobe entitled to recover the lost profits on corollary sales as consequential damages caused by Certina's breach of contract?

10. Schweber contracted to purchase a certain black Rolls-Royce Corniche automobile from Rallye Motors. He made a $3,500 deposit on the car. Rallye later returned his deposit to him and told him that the car was not available. However, Schweber learned that the automobile was available to the dealer and was being sold to another customer. The dealer then offered to sell Schweber a similar car, but with a different interior design. Schweber brought a lawsuit against the dealer to prevent it from selling the Rolls-Royce Corniche to anyone else and to require that it be sold to him. Rallye Motors claimed that he could get only damages and not specific performance. Approximately 100 Rolls-Royce Corniches were being sold each year in the United States, but none of the others would have the specific features and detail of this one. Is the remedy of specific performance available to Schweber?

Online Research: Use the Internet to Check for Product Recalls

Use the Internet to locate the website for the U.S. Consumer Product Safety Commission (CPSC) (www.cpsc.gov). Use it to find five products that the Commission recently has either ordered recalled or for which it has entered into voluntary settlements with manufacturers to issue recall notices. Then go to the website for one of the manufacturers and compare the information concerning the product on the manufacturer's website with the information posted on the CPSC site. What, if any, differences do you discern?

PART FIVE

PROPERTY

23

PERSONAL PROPERTY AND BAILMENTS

Claudio is a skilled craftsman employed by the Goldcasters Jewelry to make handcrafted jewelry. Working after his normal working hours and using materials he paid for himself, Claudio crafts a fine ring by skillfully weaving together strands of gold wire. He presents the ring to his fiancée, Cheryl, as an engagement ring in anticipation of their forthcoming marriage. While visiting the restroom in a steak and ribs restaurant, Cheryl removes the ring so she can wash some barbeque sauce from her hands. In her haste to get back to her table, she leaves the ring on the washstand when she exits the restroom. Sandra, a part-time janitor for the restaurant, finds the ring and slips it into her purse. When Cheryl realizes she is missing the ring and returns to the restroom to look for it, neither the ring nor Sandra are still there. Later that evening Sandra sells the ring to her cousin, Gloria, who gives her $200 for it. Several days later, Cheryl breaks her engagement to Claudio, telling him that she no longer loves him. Claudio asks Cheryl to return the ring, indicating that he only intended for her to have it if their engagement led to marriage. This situation raises a number of questions concerning rights and interests in personal property that will be discussed in this chapter. They include:

- Between Claudio and Goldcasters, who was the owner of the ring at the time Claudio created it?
- Did Claudio make an effective gift of the ring to Cheryl? Or was it a conditional gift that he could revoke when Cheryl decided to call off the marriage?
- What was Sandra's responsibility when she found the ring? Between Sandra and the restaurant, who had the better right to the ring?
- Did Gloria become the owner of the ring when she paid the $200 to Sandra? Does Cheryl have the right to recover the ring from Gloria if she finds that Gloria has it?

Nature of Property

The concept of property is crucial to the organization of society. The essential nature of a particular society is often reflected in the way it views property, including the degree to which property ownership is concentrated in the state, the extent to which it permits individual ownership of property, and the rules that govern such ownership. History is replete with wars and revolutions that arose out of conflicting claims to, or views concerning, property. Significant documents in our Anglo-American legal tradition, such as the Magna Carta and the Constitution, deal explicitly with property rights.

The word **property** is used to refer to something that is capable of being owned. It is also used to refer to a right or interest that allows a person to exercise dominion over a thing that may be owned or possessed.

When we talk about property ownership, we are speaking of a bundle of rights that the law recognizes and enforces. For example, ownership of a building includes the exclusive right to use, enjoy, sell, mortgage, or rent the building. If someone else tries to use the property without the owner's consent, the owner may use the courts and legal procedures to eject that person. Ownership of a patent includes the rights to produce, use, and sell the patented item, and to license others to do those things.

In the United States, private ownership of property is protected by the Constitution, which provides that the government shall deprive no person of "life, liberty or property without due process of law." We recognize and encourage the rights of individuals to acquire, enjoy, and use property. These rights, however, are not unlimited. For example, a person cannot use property in an unreasonable manner that injures others. Also, the state has **police power** through which it can impose reasonable regulations on the use of property, tax it, and take it for public use by paying the owner compensation for it.

Property is divided into a number of categories based on its characteristics. The same piece of property may fall into more than one class. The following discussion explores the meaning of **personal property** and the numerous ways of classifying property.

Classifications of Property

Personal Property versus Real Property

Personal property is defined by process of exclusion. The term *personal property* is used in contrast to *real property*. Real property is the earth's crust and all things firmly attached to it.[1] For example, land, office buildings, and houses are considered to be real property. All other objects and rights that may be owned are personal property. Clothing, books, and stock in a corporation are examples of personal property.

Real property may be turned into personal property if it is detached from the earth. Personal property, if attached to the earth, becomes real property. For example, marble in the ground is real property. When the marble is quarried, it becomes personal property, but if it is used in constructing a building, it becomes real property again. Perennial vegetation that does not have to be seeded every year, such as trees, shrubs, and grass, is usually treated as part of the real property on which it is growing. When trees and shrubs are severed from the land, they become personal property. Crops that must be planted each year, such as corn, oats, and potatoes, are usually treated as personal property. However, if the real property on which they are growing is sold, the new owner of the real property also becomes the owner of the crops.

When personal property is attached to, or used in conjunction with, real property in such a way as to be treated as part of the real property, it is known as a **fixture.** The law concerning fixtures is discussed in the next chapter.

Tangible versus Intangible Personal Property

Personal property may be either tangible or intangible. Tangible property has a physical existence. Cars, animals, and computers are examples. Property that has no physical existence is called intangible property. For example, rights under a patent, copyright, or trademark would be intangible property.[2]

The distinction between tangible and intangible property is important primarily for tax and estate planning purposes. Generally, tangible property is subject to tax in the state in which it is located, whereas intangible property is usually taxable in the state where its owner lives.

Public and Private Property

Property is also classified as public or private, based on the ownership of the property. If the property is owned by the government or a governmental unit, it is public property. If it is owned by an individual, a group of individuals, a corporation, or some other business organization, it is private property.

Acquiring Ownership of Personal Property

Production or Purchase

The most common ways of obtaining ownership of property are by producing it or purchasing it. A person owns the property that she makes unless the person has agreed to do the work for another party. In that case, the other party is the owner of the product of the work. For example, a person who creates a painting, knits a sweater, or develops a computer program is the owner unless she has been retained by someone to create the painting, knit the sweater, or develop the program. Another major way of acquiring property is by purchase. The law regarding the purchase of tangible personal property (that is, sale of goods) is discussed in Chapter 19.

---

[1]The law of real property is treated in Chapter 24.

[2]These important types of intangible property are discussed in Chapter 8.

Possession of Unowned Property

In very early times, the most common way of obtaining ownership of personal property was simply by taking possession of unowned property. For example, the first person to take possession of a wild animal became its owner. Today, one may still acquire ownership of personal property by possessing it if the property is unowned. The two major examples of unowned property that may be acquired by possession are wild animals and abandoned property. Abandoned property will be discussed in the next section, which focuses on the rights of finders.

The first person to take possession of a wild animal normally becomes the owner.[3] To acquire ownership of a wild animal by taking possession, a person must obtain enough control over it to deprive it of its freedom. If a person fatally wounds a wild animal, the person becomes the owner. Wild animals caught in a trap or fish caught in a net are usually considered to be the property of the person who set the trap or net. If a captured wild animal escapes and is caught by another person, that person generally becomes the owner. However, if that person knows that the animal is an escaped animal and that the prior owner is chasing it to recapture it, then he does not become the owner.

Rights of Finders of Lost, Mislaid, and Abandoned Property

The old saying "finders keepers, losers weepers" is not a reliable way of predicting the legal rights of those who find personal property that originally belonged—or still belongs—to another. The rights of the finder will be determined according to whether the property he finds is classified as abandoned, lost, or mislaid.

1. *Abandoned property.* Property is considered to be abandoned if the owner intentionally placed the property out of his possession with the intent to relinquish ownership of it. For example, Norris takes his TV set to the city dump and leaves it there. The finder who takes possession of abandoned property with intent to claim ownership becomes the owner of the property. This means he acquires better rights to the property than anyone else in the world, including the original owner. For example, if Fox finds the TV set, puts it in his car, and takes it home, Fox becomes the owner of the TV set.

2. *Lost property.* Property is considered to be lost when the owner did not intend to part with possession of the property. For example, if Barber's camera fell out of her handbag while she was walking down the street, it would be considered lost property. The person who finds lost property does not acquire ownership of it, but he acquires better rights to the lost property than anyone other than the true owner. For example, suppose Lawrence finds Barber's camera in the grass where it fell. Jones then steals the camera from Lawrence's house. Under these facts, Barber is still the owner of the camera. She has the right to have it returned to her if she discovers where it is—or if Lawrence knows that it belongs to Barber. As the finder of lost property, however, Lawrence has a better right to the camera than anyone else except Barber. This means that Lawrence has the right to require Jones to return it to him if he finds out that Jones has it.

   If the finder does not know who the true owner is or cannot easily find out, the finder must still return the property when the real owner shows up and asks for the property. If the finder of lost property knows who the owner is and refuses to return it, the finder is guilty of conversion and must pay the owner the fair value of the property.[4] A finder who sells the property that he has found can pass to the purchaser only those rights that he has; he cannot pass any better title to the property than he himself has. Thus, the true owner could recover the property from the purchaser.

3. *Mislaid property.* Property is considered to be mislaid if the owner intentionally placed the property somewhere and accidentally left it there, not intending to relinquish ownership of the property. For example, Fields places her backpack on a coatrack at Campus Bookstore while shopping for textbooks. Forgetting the backpack, Fields leaves the store and goes home. The backpack would be considered mislaid rather than lost because Fields intentionally and voluntarily placed it on the coatrack. If property is classified as mislaid, the finder acquires no rights to the property. Rather, the person in possession of the real property on which the personal property was mislaid has the right to hold the property for the true owner and has better rights to the property than anyone other than the

---

[3]As wildlife is increasingly protected by law, however, some wild animals cannot be owned because it is illegal to capture them (e.g., endangered species).

[4]The tort of conversion is discussed in Chapter 6.

true owner. For example, if Stevens found Fields's backpack in Campus Bookstore, Campus Bookstore would have the right to hold the mislaid property for Fields. Stevens would acquire neither possession nor ownership of the backpack.

The rationale for this rule is that it increases the chances that the property will be returned to its real owner. A person who knowingly placed the property somewhere but forgot to pick it up might well remember later where she left the property and return for it.

Some states have a statute that allows finders of property to clear their title to the property. The statutes generally provide that the person must give public notice of the fact that the property has been found, perhaps by putting an ad in a local newspaper. All states have statutes of limitations that require the true owner of property to claim it or bring a legal action to recover possession of it within a certain number of years. A person who keeps possession of lost or unclaimed property for longer than that period of time will become its owner.

The *Corliss* case, which follows, discusses the relative rights of a person who finds property on land owned by someone else.

Corliss v. Wenner and Anderson   *2001 Ida. App. Lexis 79 (Ct. App. Idaho 2001)*

In the fall of 1996, Jann Wenner hired Anderson Asphalt Paving to construct a driveway on his ranch. Larry Anderson, the owner of Anderson Asphalt Paving, and his employee, Gregory Corliss, were excavating soil for the driveway when they unearthed a glass jar containing paper-wrapped rolls of gold coins. Anderson and Corliss collected, cleaned, and inventoried the gold pieces dating from 1857 to 1914. The 96 coins weighed about four pounds. Initially, Anderson and Corliss agreed to split the coins among themselves, with Anderson retaining possession of all the coins. Subsequently, Anderson and Corliss argued over ownership of the coins, and Anderson fired Corliss. Anderson later gave possession of the coins to Wenner in exchange for indemnification on any claim Corliss might have against him regarding the coins.

Corliss sued Anderson and Wenner for possession of some or all of the coins. Corliss contended that the coins should be considered "treasure trove" and awarded to him pursuant to the "finders keepers" rule of treasure trove. Wenner, defending both himself and Anderson, contended that he had the better right to possession of the gold coins. The trial court held Idaho did not recognize "treasure trove" and that the coins, having been carefully concealed for safekeeping, fit within the legal classification of mislaid property, to which the right of possession goes to the landowner. Alternatively, the court ruled that the coins, like the topsoil being excavated, were a part of the property owned by Wenner and that Anderson and Corliss were merely Wenner's employees. Corliss appealed.

SCHWARTZMAN, Chief Judge At common law all found property is generally categorized in one of five ways. Those categories are:

ABANDONED PROPERTY—that which the owner has discarded or voluntarily forsaken with the intention of terminating his ownership, but without vesting ownership in any other person.

LOST PROPERTY—that property which the owner has involuntarily and unintentionally parted with through neglect, carelessness, or inadvertence and does not know the whereabouts.

MISLAID PROPERTY—that which the owner has intentionally set down in a place where he can again resort to it, and then forgets where he put it.

TREASURE TROVE—a category exclusively for gold or silver in coin, plate, bullion, and sometimes its paper money equivalents, found concealed in the earth or in a house or other private place. Treasure trove carries with it the thought of antiquity, i.e., that the treasure has been concealed for so long as to indicate that the owner is probably dead or unknown.

EMBEDDED PROPERTY—that personal property which has become a part of the natural earth, such as pottery, the sunken wreck of a steamship, or a rotted-away sack of gold-bearing quartz rock buried or partially buried in the ground.

Under these doctrines, the finder of lost or abandoned property and treasure trove acquires a right to possess the property against the entire world but the rightful owner regardless of the place of finding. The finder of mislaid property is required to turn it over to the owner of the premises who has the duty to safeguard the property for the true owner. Possession of embedded property goes to owner of the land on which the property was found.

One of the major distinctions between these various categories is that only lost property necessarily involves an element of involuntariness. The four remaining categories involve voluntary and intentional acts by the true owner in placing the property where another eventually finds it. However, treasure trove, despite not being lost or abandoned property, is treated as such in that the right to possession is recognized to be in the finder rather than the premises owner.

On appeal, Corliss argues that the district court should have interpreted the undisputed facts and circumstances surrounding of the placement of the coins in the ground to indicate that the gold coins were either lost, abandoned, or treasure trove. Wenner argues that the property was properly categorized as either embedded or mislaid property.

As with most accidentally discovered buried treasure, the history of the original ownership of the coins is shrouded in mystery and obscured by time. The coins had been wrapped in paper, like coins from a bank, and buried in a glass jar, apparently for safekeeping. Based on these circumstances, the district court determined that the coins were not abandoned because the condition in which the coins were found evidenced an intent to keep them safe, not an intent to voluntarily relinquish all possessory interest in them. The district court also implicitly rejected the notion that the coins were lost, noting that the coins were secreted with care in a specific place to protect them from the elements and from other people until such time as the original owner might return for them. There is no indication that the coins came to be buried through neglect, carelessness, or inadvertence. Accordingly, the district court properly concluded, as a matter of law, that the coins were neither lost nor abandoned.

The district court then determined that the modern trend favored characterizing the coins as property either embedded in the earth or mislaid—under which the right of possession goes to the landowner—rather than treasure trove—under which the right of possession goes to the finder. Although accepted by a number of states prior to 1950, the modern trend since then, as illustrated by decisions of the state and federal courts, is decidedly against recognizing the "finders keepers" rule of treasure trove.

We conclude that the rule of treasure trove is of dubious heritage and misunderstood application, inconsistent with our values and traditions. The danger of adopting the doctrine of treasure trove is laid out in *Morgan* v. *Wiser* (Tenn. 1985).

[We] find the rule with respect to treasure-trove to be out of harmony with modern notions of fair play. The common-law rule of treasure-trove invites trespassers to roam at large over the property of others with their metal detecting devices and to dig wherever such devices tell them property might be found. If the discovery happens to fit the definition of treasure-trove, the trespasser may claim it as his own. To paraphrase another court: The mind refuses consent to the proposition that one may go upon the lands of another and dig up and take away anything he discovers there which does not belong to the owner of the land.

The invitation to trespassers inherent in the rule with respect to treasure trove is repugnant to the common law rules dealing with trespassers in general. The common law made a trespass an actionable wrong without the necessity of showing any damage therefrom. Because a trespass often involved a breach of the peace and because the law was designed to keep the peace, the common law dealt severely with trespassers.

Recognizing the validity of the idea that the discouragement of trespassers contributes to the preservation of the peace in the community, we think this state should not follow the common law rule with respect to treasure trove. Rather, we adopt the rule suggested in the concurring opinion in *Schley* v. *Couch*. . .which we restate as follows:

> Where property is found embedded in the soil under circumstances repelling the idea that it has been lost, the finder acquires no title thereto, for the presumption is that the possession of the article found is in the owner of the locus in quo.

Landownership includes control over crops on the land, buildings and appurtenances, soils, minerals buried under those soils. The average Idaho landowner would expect to have a possessory interest in any object uncovered on his or her property. And certainly the notion that a trespassing treasure hunter, or a hired handyman or employee, could or might have greater possessory rights than a landowner in objects uncovered on his or her property runs counter to the reasonable expectations of present-day landownership.

There is no reason for a special rule for gold and silver coins, bullion, or plate as opposed to other property. Insofar as personal property (money and the like) buried or secreted on privately owned realty is concerned, the distinctions between treasure trove, lost property, and mislaid property are anachronistic and of little value. The principal point of such distinctions is the intent of the true owner which, absent some written declaration indicating such, is obscured in the mists of time and subject to a great deal of speculation.

By holding that property classed as treasure trove (gold or silver coins, bullion, plate) in other jurisdictions is classed in Idaho as personal property embedded in the soil, subject to the same limitations as mislaid property, possession will be awarded to the owner of the soil as a matter of law. Thus, we craft a simple and reasonable solution to the problem, discourage trespass, and avoid the risk of speculating about the true owner's intent when attempting to infer such from the manner and circumstances in which an object is found. Addi-

tionally, the true owner, if any, will have the opportunity to recover the property.

We hold that the owner of the land has constructive possession of all personal property secreted in, on, or under his or her land. Accordingly, we adopt the district court's reasoning and conclusion melding the law of mislaid property with that of embedded property and conclude, as a matter of law, that the landowner is entitled to possession to the exclusion of all but the true owner, absence a contract between the landowner and finder.

Judgment for Wenner affirmed.

Leasing

A lease of personal property is a transfer of the right to possess and use personal property belonging to another.[5] Although the rights of one who leases personal property (a lessee) do not constitute ownership of personal property, leasing is mentioned here because it is becoming an increasingly important way of acquiring the use of many kinds of personal property, from automobiles to farm equipment.

Articles 2 and 9 of the UCC may sometimes be applied to personal property leases by analogy. However, rules contained in these articles are sometimes inadequate to resolve special problems presented by leasing. For this reason, a new article of the UCC dealing exclusively with leases of goods, Article 2A, was written in 1987. Article 2A has been presented to state legislatures for possible adoption. Forty-seven states and the District of Columbia have adopted Article 2A.

Gifts

Title to personal property may be obtained by **gift.** A gift is a voluntary transfer of property to the **donee** (the person who receives a gift), for which the **donor** (the person who gives the gift) gets no consideration in return. To have a valid gift, all three of the following elements are necessary:

1. The donor must *intend* to make a gift.
2. The donor must make *delivery* of the gift.
3. The donee must *accept* the gift.

The most critical requirement is delivery. The donor must actually give up possession and control of the property either to the donee or to a third person who is to hold it for the donee. Delivery is important because it makes clear to the donor that he is voluntarily giving up ownership without getting something in exchange. A promise to make a gift is usually not enforceable;[6] the person must actually part with the property. In some cases, the delivery may be symbolic or constructive. For example, handing over the key to a strongbox may be symbolic delivery of the property in the strongbox. *King* v. *Trustees of Boston University,* which appears in this chapter's examination of bailments, discusses various issues concerning gifts and promises to make gifts for charitable purposes.

There are two kinds of gifts: gifts *inter vivos* and gifts *causa mortis.* A gift *inter vivos* is a gift between two living persons. For example, when Melissa's parents give her a car for her 21st birthday, that is a gift *inter vivos.* A gift *causa mortis* is a gift made in contemplation of death. For example, Uncle Earl, who is about to undergo a serious heart operation, gives his watch to his nephew, Bart, and says that he wants Bart to have it if he does not survive the operation.

A gift *causa mortis* is a conditional gift and is effective unless any of the following occurs:

1. The donor recovers from the peril or sickness under fear of which the gift was made, or
2. The donor revokes or withdraws the gift before he dies, or
3. The donee dies before the donor.

---

[5]A lease of personal property is a form of bailment, a "bailment for hire." Bailments are discussed later in this chapter.

[6]The idea is discussed in Chapter 12.

CONCEPT REVIEW

Rights of Finders of Personal Property

Character of Property	Description	Rights of Finder	Rights of Original Owner
Lost	Owner unintentionally parted with possession	Rights superior to everyone except the owner	Retains ownership; has the right to the return of the property
Mislaid	Owner intentionally put property in a place but unintentionally left it there	None; person in possession of real property on which mislaid property was found holds it for the owner, and has rights superior to everyone except owner	Retains ownership; has the right to the return of the property
Abandoned	Owner intentionally placed property out of his possession with intent to relinquish ownership of it	Finder who takes possession with intent to claim ownership acquires ownership of property	None

If one of these events takes place, ownership of the property goes back to the donor.

Conditional Gifts

Sometimes a gift is made on condition that the donee comply with certain restrictions or perform certain actions. A conditional gift is not a completed gift. It may be revoked by the donor before the donee complies with the conditions. Gifts in contemplation of marriage, such as engagement rings, are a primary example of a conditional gift. Such gifts are generally considered to have been made on an implied condition that marriage between the donor and donee will take place. The traditional rule applied in many states provides that if the donee breaks the engagement without legal justification or the engagement is broken by mutual consent, the donor will be able to recover the ring or other engagement gift. However, if the engagement is unjustifiably broken by the donor, the traditional rule generally bars the donor from recovering gifts made in contemplation of marriage. As illustrated by the *Lindh* case, which follows, a growing number of courts have rejected the traditional approach and its focus on fault. Some states have enacted legislation prescribing the rules applicable to the return of engagement presents.

Lindh v. Surman   *742 A.2d 643 (Sup. Ct. Pa. 1999)*

In August 1993, Rodger Lindh (Rodger) proposed marriage to Janis Surman (Janis). Rodger presented her with a diamond engagement ring that he had purchased for $17,400. Janis accepted the marriage proposal and the ring. Two months later, Rodger broke the engagement and asked Janis to return the ring. She did so. Rodger and Janis later reconciled, with Rodger again proposing marriage and again presenting Janis with the engagement ring. Janis accepted the proposal and the ring. In March 1994, Rodger again broke the engagement and asked Janis to return the ring. This time, however, she refused. Rodger sued her, seeking recovery of the ring or a judgment for its value. The trial court held in Rodger's favor and awarded *him damages in the amount of the ring's value. When Janis appealed, the Pennsylvania Superior Court affirmed the award of damages and held that when an engagement is broken, the engagement ring must be returned even if the donor broke the engagement. Janis appealed to the Supreme Court of Pennsylvania.*

Newman, Justice   [W]e are asked to decide whether a donee of an engagement ring must return the ring or its equivalent value when the donor breaks the engagement. We begin our analysis with the only principle on which [the] parties agree: that Pennsylvania law treats the giving of an engagement ring as a conditional gift. In *Pavlicic* v. *Vogtsberger* (Sup. Ct. Pa. 1957), the plaintiff supplied his ostensible fiancée with numerous gifts, including money for the purchase of engagement and wedding rings, with the understanding that they were given on the condition that she marry him. When the defendant left him for another man, the plaintiff sued her for recovery of these gifts. Justice Musmanno explained the conditional gift principle:

> A gift given by a man to a woman on condition that she embark on the sea of matrimony with him is no different from a gift based on the condition that the donee sail on any other sea. If, after receiving the provisional gift, the donee refuses to leave the harbor—if the anchor of contractual performance sticks in the sands of irresolution and procrastination—the gift must be restored to the donor.

[T]he parties disagree, however, [over] whether fault [on the part of the donor] is relevant to determining return of the ring.

[Janis] contends that Pennsylvania law . . . has never recognized a right of recovery in a donor who severs the engagement. [She maintains that] if the condition of the gift is performance of the marriage ceremony, [a rule allowing a recovery of the ring] would reward a donor who prevents the occurrence of the condition, which the donee was ready, willing, and eagerly waiting to perform. Janis's argument that . . . the donor [should not be allowed] to recover the ring where the donor terminates the engagement has some basis in [decisions from Pennsylvania's lower courts and in treatises]. This Court, however, has not decided the question of whether the donor is entitled to return of the ring where the donor admittedly ended the engagement.

[T]he issue we must resolve is whether we will follow the fault-based theory argued by Janis, or the no-fault rule advocated by Rodger. Under a fault-based analysis, return of the rings depends on an assessment of who broke the engagement, which necessarily entails a determination of why that person broke the engagement. A no-fault approach, however, involves no investigation into the motives or reasons for the cessation of the engagement and requires the return of the engagement ring simply upon the nonoccurrence of the marriage.

The rule concerning the return of a ring founded on fault principles has superficial appeal because, in the most outrageous instances of unfair behavior, it appeals to our sense of equity. Where one [of the formerly engaged persons] has truly "wronged" the other, justice appears to dictate that the wronged individual should be allowed to keep [the ring] or have [it] returned, depending on whether [the wronged] person was the donor . . . or the donee. However, the process of determining who is "wrong" and who is "right," when most modern relationships are complex circumstances, makes the fault-based approach less desirable. A thorough fault-based inquiry would not . . . end with the question of who terminated the engagement, but would also examine that person's reasons. In some instances the person who terminated the engagement may have been entirely justified in his or her actions. This kind of inquiry would invite the parties to stage the most bitter and unpleasant accusations against those whom they nearly made their spouse. A ring-return rule based on fault principles will inevitably invite acrimony and encourage parties to portray their ex-fiancées in the worst possible light. Furthermore, it is unlikely that trial courts would be presented with situations where fault was clear and easily ascertained.

The approach that has been described as the modern trend is to apply a no-fault rule to engagement ring cases. Courts that have applied [this rule] have borrowed from the policies of their respective legislatures that have moved away from the notion of fault in their divorce statutes. [A]ll fifty states [have] adopted some form of no-fault divorce. We agree with those jurisdictions that have looked toward the development of no-fault divorce law for a principle to decide engagement ring cases. [In addition, the] inherent weaknesses in any fault-based system lead us to adopt a no-fault approach to resolution of engagement ring disputes.

Decision of Superior Court in favor of Rodger Lindh affirmed.

Cappy, Justice, dissenting   The majority urges adoption of [the no-fault rule] to relieve trial courts from having the onerous task of sifting through the debris of the broken engagement in order to ascertain who is truly at fault. Are broken engagements truly more disturbing than cases where we ask judges and juries to discern possible abuses in nursing homes, day care centers, dependency proceedings involving abused children, and criminal cases involving horrific, irrational injuries to innocent victims? The subject matter our able trial courts address on a daily basis is certainly of equal sordidness as any fact pattern they may need to address in a simple case of who broke the engagement and why.

I can envision a scenario whereby the prospective bride and her family have expended thousands of dollars in preparation for the culminating event of matrimony and she is, through no fault of her own, left standing at the altar holding the caterer's bill. To add insult to injury, the majority would also strip her of her engagement ring. Why the majority feels compelled to modernize this relatively simple and ancient legal concept is beyond the understanding of this poor man. [A]s I see no valid reason to forego the [fault-based rule] for determining possession of the engagement ring under the simple concept of conditional gift law, I cannot endorse the modern trend advocated by the majority.

Uniform Transfers to Minors Act

The Uniform Transfers to Minors Act, which has been adopted in one form or another in every state, provides a fairly simple and flexible method for making gifts and other transfers of property to minors.[7] As defined in this act, a minor is anyone under the age of 21. Under the act, an adult may transfer money, securities, real property, insurance policies, and other property. The specific ways of doing this vary according to the type of property transferred. In general, however, the transferor (the person who gives or otherwise transfers the property) delivers, pays, or assigns the property to, or registers the property with, a custodian who acts for the benefit of the minor "under the Uniform Transfers to Minors Act." The custodian is given fairly broad discretion to use the gift for the minor's benefit and may not use it for the custodian's personal benefit. The custodian may be the transferor himself, another adult, or a trust company, depending again on the type of property transferred. If the donor or other transferor fully complies with the Uniform Transfers to Minors Act, the transfer is considered to be irrevocable.

Will or Inheritance

Ownership of personal property may also be transferred upon the death of the former owner. The property may pass under the terms of a will if the will was validly executed. If there is no valid will, the property is transferred to the heirs of the owner according to state laws. Transfer of property at the death of the owner will be discussed in Chapter 26.

Confusion

Title to personal property may be obtained by **confusion.** Confusion is the intermixing of different owners' goods in such a way that they cannot later be separated. For example, suppose wheat belonging to several different people is mixed in a grain elevator. If the mixing was by agreement or if it resulted from an accident without negligence on anyone's part, each person owns his proportionate share of the entire quantity of wheat. However, a different result would be reached if the wheat was wrongfully or negligently mixed. Suppose a thief steals a truckload of Grade #1 wheat worth $8.50 a bushel from a farmer. The thief dumps the wheat into his storage bin, which contains a lower-grade wheat worth $4.50 a bushel, with the result that the mixture is worth only $4.50 a bushel. The farmer has first claim against the entire mixture to recover the value of the higher-grade wheat that was mixed with the lower-grade wheat. The thief, or any other person whose intentional or negligent act results in confusion of goods, must bear any loss caused by the confusion.

Accession

Ownership of personal property may also be acquired by **accession.** Accession means increasing the value of property by adding materials, labor, or both. As a general rule, the owner of the original property becomes the owner of the improvements. This is particularly likely to be true if the improvement was done with the permission of the owner. For example, Hudson takes his automobile to a shop that replaces the engine with a larger engine and puts in a new four-speed transmission. Hudson is still the owner of the automobile as well as the owner of the parts added by the auto shop.

---

[7]This statute was formerly called, and is still called in some states, the Uniform Gift to Minors Act.

Problems may arise if materials are added or work is performed on personal property without the consent of the owner. If property is stolen from one person and improved by the thief, the original owner can get it back and does not have to reimburse the thief for the work done or the materials used in improving it. For example, a thief steals Rourke's used car, puts a new engine in it, replaces the tires, and repairs the muffler. Rourke is entitled to get his car back from the thief and does not have to pay him for the engine, tires, and muffler.

The result is less easy to predict, however, if property is mistakenly improved in good faith by someone who believes that he owns the property. In such a case, a court must weigh the respective interests of two innocent parties: the original owner and the improver.

For example, Johnson, a stonecarver, finds a block of limestone by the side of the road. Assuming that it has been abandoned, he takes it home and carves it into a sculpture. In fact, the block was owned by Hayes. Having fallen off a flatbed truck during transportation, the block is merely lost property, which Hayes ordinarily could recover from the finder. In a case such as this, a court could decide the case in either of two ways. The first alternative would be to give the original owner (Hayes) ownership of the improved property, but to allow the person who has improved the property in good faith (Johnson) to recover the cost of the improvements. The second alternative would be to hold that the improver, Johnson, has acquired ownership of the sculpture, but that he is required to pay the original owner the value of the property as of the time he obtained it. The greater the extent to which the improvements have increased the value of the property, the more likely it is that the court will choose the second alternative and permit the improver to acquire ownership of the improved property.

Bailments

Nature of Bailments

A **bailment** is the delivery of personal property by its owner or someone holding the right to possess it (the **bailor**) to another person (the **bailee**) who accepts it and is under an express or implied agreement to return it to the bailor or to someone designated by the bailor. Only personal property can be the subject of bailments.

Although the legal terminology used to describe bailments might be unfamiliar to most people, everyone is familiar with transactions that constitute bailments. For example, Lincoln takes his car to a parking garage where the attendant gives Lincoln a claim check and then drives the car down the ramp to park it. Charles borrows his neighbor's lawn mower to cut his grass. Tara, who lives next door to Kyle, agrees to take care of Kyle's cat while Kyle goes on a vacation. These are just a few of the everyday situations that involve bailments.

Elements of a Bailment

The essential elements of a bailment are:

1. The bailor owns the property or holds the right to possess it.
2. The bailor delivers exclusive possession of and control over the property to the bailee.
3. The bailee knowingly accepts the property with the understanding that he owes a duty to return the property as directed by the bailor.

Creation of a Bailment

A bailment is created by an express or implied contract. Whether the elements of a bailment have been fulfilled is determined by examining all the facts and circumstances of the particular situation. For example, a patron goes into a restaurant and hangs his hat and coat on an unattended rack. It is unlikely that this created a bailment, because the restaurant owner never assumed exclusive control over the hat and coat. However, if there is a checkroom and the hat and coat are checked with the attendant, a bailment will arise.

If a customer parks her car in a parking lot, keeps the keys, and may drive the car out herself whenever she wishes, a bailment has not been created. The courts treat this situation as a lease of space. Suppose, however, that she takes her car to a parking garage where an attendant, after giving her a claim check, parks the car. There is a bailment of the car because the parking garage has accepted delivery and possession of the car. However, a distinction is made between the car and packages locked in the trunk. If the parking garage was not aware of the packages, it probably would not be a bailee of them as it did not knowingly accept possession of them. The creation of a bailment is illustrated in Figure 1.

Types of Bailments

Bailments are commonly divided into three different categories:

1. Bailments for the sole benefit of the bailor.
2. Bailments for the sole benefit of the bailee.
3. Bailments for mutual benefit.

Figure 1   *Creation of a Bailment*

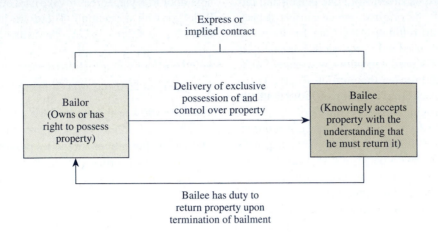

The type of bailment involved in a case can be important in determining the liability of the bailee for loss of or damage to the property. As will be discussed later, however, some courts no longer rely on these distinctions when they determine whether the bailee is liable.

Bailments for Benefit of Bailor A bailment for the sole benefit of the bailor is one in which the bailee renders some service but does not receive a benefit in return. For example, Brown allows his neighbor, Reston, to park her car in Brown's garage while she is on vacation. Brown does not ask for any compensation. Here, Reston, the bailor, has received a benefit from the bailee, Brown, but Brown has not received a benefit in return.

Bailments for Benefit of Bailee A bailment for the sole benefit of the bailee is one in which the owner of the goods allows someone else to use them free of charge. For example, Anderson lends a lawn mower to her neighbor, Moss, so he can cut his grass.

Bailments for Mutual Benefit If both the bailee and the bailor receive benefits from the bailment, it is a bailment for mutual benefit. For example, Sutton rents china for his daughter's wedding from E-Z Party Supplies for an agreed-on price. Sutton, the bailee, benefits by being able to use the china; E-Z benefits from his payment of the rental charge. On some occasions, the benefit to the bailee is less tangible. For example, a customer checks a coat at an attended coatroom at a restaurant. Even if no charge is made for the service, it is likely to be treated as a bailment for mutual benefit because the restaurant is benefiting from the customer's patronage.

Special Bailments

Certain professional bailees, such as innkeepers and common carriers, are treated somewhat differently by the law and are held to a higher level of responsibility than is the ordinary bailee. The rules applicable to common carriers and innkeepers are detailed later in this chapter.

Duties of the Bailee

The bailee has two basic duties:

1. To take care of the property that has been entrusted to her.
2. To return the property at the termination of the bailment.

The following discussion examines the scope of these duties.

Duty of Bailee to Take Care of Property

The bailee is responsible for taking steps to protect the property during the time she has possession of it. If the bailee does not exercise proper care and the property is lost or damaged, the bailee is liable for negligence. The bailee would then be required to reimburse the bailor for the amount of loss or damage. If the property is lost or damaged without the fault or negligence of the bailee, however, the bailee is not liable to the bailor. The degree of care required of the bailee traditionally has depended in large part on the type of bailment involved.

1. *Bailment for the benefit of the bailor.* If the bailment is solely for the benefit of the bailor, the bailee is expected to exercise only a minimal, or slight, degree of care for the protection of the bailed property. He would be liable, then, only if he were grossly negligent in his care of the bailed property. The rationale for this rule is that if the bailee is doing the bailor a favor, it is not reasonable to expect him to be as careful as when he is deriving some benefit from keeping the goods.

2. *Bailment for mutual benefit.* When the bailment is a bailment for mutual benefit, the bailee is expected to exercise ordinary or reasonable care. This degree of care requires the bailee to use the same care a reasonable person would use to protect his own property in the relevant situation. If the bailee is a professional that holds itself out as a professional bailee, such as a warehouse, it must use the degree of care that would be used by a person in the same profession. This is likely to be more care than the ordinary person would use. In addition, a professional bailee usually has the obligation to explain any loss of or damage to property—that is, to show it was not negligent. If it cannot do so, it will be liable to the bailor.

3. *Bailment for the benefit of the bailee.* If the bailment is solely for the benefit of the bailee, the bailee is expected to exercise a high degree of care. For instance a person who lends a sailboat to a neighbor would probably expect the neighbor to be even more careful with the sailboat than the owner might be. In such a case, the bailee would be liable for damage to the property if his action reflected a relatively small degree of negligence.

A number of courts today view the type of bailment involved in a case as just one factor to be considered in determining whether the bailee should be liable for loss of or damage to bailed goods. The modern trend appears to be moving in the direction of imposing a duty of reasonable care on bailees, regardless of the type of bailment. This flexible standard of care permits courts to take into account a variety of factors such as the nature and value of the property, the provisions of the parties' agreement, the payment of consideration for the bailment, and the experience of the bailee. In addition, the bailee is required to use the property only as was agreed between the parties. For example, Jones borrows Morrow's lawn mower to mow his lawn. If Jones uses the mower to cut the weeds on a trash-filled vacant lot and the mower is damaged, he would be liable because he was exceeding the agreed purpose of the bailment—to cut his lawn.

Bailee's Duty to Return the Property

An essential element of a bailment is the duty of the bailee to return the property at the termination of the bailment. If the bailed property is taken from the bailee by legal process, the bailee should notify the bailor and must take whatever action is necessary to protect the bailor's interest. In most instances, the bailee must return the identical property that was bailed. A person who lends a 1999 Mercury Sable to a friend expects to have that particular car returned. In some cases, the bailor does not expect the return of the identical goods. For example, a farmer who stores 1,500 bushels of Grade #1 wheat at a local grain elevator expects to get back 1,500 bushels of Grade #1 wheat when the bailment is terminated, but not the identical wheat he deposited.

The bailee must return the goods in an undamaged condition to the bailor or to someone designated by the bailor. If the goods have been damaged, destroyed, or lost, there is a rebuttable presumption of negligence on the part of the bailee. To overcome the presumption, the bailee must come forward with evidence showing that he exercised the relevant level of care.

The *Detroit Institute of Arts* case, which follows, illustrates the duty a bailee has to return the property at the termination of the bailment.

Detroit Institute of Arts v. Rose and Smith
127 F. Supp.2d 117 (U.S.D.C. D.Conn. 2001)

"The Howdy Doody Show" was a television program beloved by millions of children in what is now known as "the baby boom generation." It was produced and broadcast by the National Broadcasting Company, Inc. (NBC) from 1947 to 1960. Hosted by Robert "Buffalo Bob" Smith, the show's main character was Howdy Doody, a puppet in the image of a freckled-faced boy in cowboy clothing.

Beginning in 1952, Rufus Rose served as the puppet master, puppeteer, and caretaker for many of the puppets that appeared on the show. While the show was on the air, he created, stored, and made repairs to the puppets in his workshop in Waterford, Connecticut—and was compensated accordingly. When the show ended in 1960, Rose, pursuant to an informal agreement, kept possession of the puppets at this workshop until final arrangements were made for them. Rose acknowledged that the puppets belonged to NBC.

In 1965, Rose began a series of correspondence with NBC about payment for his maintenance and storage of the puppets, including Howdy Doody, since the end of the show in 1960. In a letter to NBC, Rose proposed that (1) NBC pay him for storage and upkeep of all the puppets since the end of the show; (2) he be allowed to keep the minor puppets but with the understanding he would not use them as Howdy Doody Show characters; and (3) the main puppets from the show, including Howdy Doody, would be turned over to a museum, the Detroit Institute of Arts (DIA), that housed the recognized museum of puppetry in America. Subsequently, he signed a release acknowledging payment for past fees and indicating his agreement to send Howdy Doody to the DIA.

In 1970, Rose, in response to a request from his friend Buffalo Bob who was making personal appearances throughout the country, sent Howdy Doody to Buffalo Bob. In an accompanying letter, Rose explained to Buffalo Bob that he had agreed with NBC that the puppet would "eventually" be placed in the DIA and that it would never be used in a commercial manner—and that the original Howdy Doody was being sent to Buffalo Bob "with this mutual understanding and responsibility." For the next 15 years, Buffalo Bob kept Howdy Doody and used him in personal appearances.

In 1992, Buffalo Bob's attorney contacted Rose's widow, NBC, and DIA, requesting that they waive the requirement that Howdy Doody be placed in the DIA. He indicated that Buffalo Bob had fallen on difficult financial times and now wished to sell the puppet and keep the proceeds. Rose's son, Christopher, replied on behalf of his mother, stating that it was his father's intention that Buffalo Bob honor the "condition" that Howdy Doody be given to the DIA. NBC refused to release Howdy Doody to him and the DIA declined to let him sell the puppet. Buffalo Bob then informed the DIA that he would transfer Howdy Doody to the museum "when he no longer wished to keep the puppet."

In 1998, Buffalo Bob and Christopher executed an agreement to sell the puppet and split the proceeds 50–50. They "certified" that Christopher had received the puppet from Buffalo Bob, and Christopher entered into a consignment agreement with an auction house to sell the "original Howdy Doody." A few days later Buffalo Bob died, and the DIA brought a lawsuit to prevent the Rose family from selling the puppet and also to gain possession of it. One of the questions in the lawsuit was whether the 1970 letter created a bailment to Buffalo Bob that obligated him to turn the puppet over to the DIA.

DRONEY, District Judge   A bailment arises when the owner or bailor "delivers personal property to another for some particular purpose with an express or implied contract to redeliver the goods when the purpose has been fulfilled, or to otherwise deal with the goods according to the bailor's directions." The bailor has a property interest in the goods bailed, while the bailee merely possesses them. The bailee's possession must be exclusive, so that he or she has sole custody and control of the property.

There are two types of bailments: those that are for the mutual benefit of the parties involved and those that are for the sole benefit of either the bailee or bailor. The latter variety, know as gratuitous bailments, typically involve no actual consideration. Instead, it is enough that the bailor suffers a detriment by giving up the present possession or custody of the property bailed on the bailee's promise that the latter will redeliver or otherwise account for it.

Bailments involve certain implied obligations, but these obligations generally are implied only in the absence of an express provision to the contrary. For example, while the law of bailment implies a general obligation to redeliver the property bailed to the owner, the parties are able to stipulate the time, place, and manner of delivery. "The general principle that the manner of a bailee's redelivery should be in accordance with the contract stipulations is too well settled to belabor." Similarly, a bailee may become liable to a third party when the bailment contract includes provisions that were incorporated for the third party's special benefit and interest.

The evidence establishes that Rufus Rose's 1970 letter to Buffalo Bob created an enforceable bailment whereby Buffalo Bob assumed a duty to turn over Howdy Doody to the DIA.

Rufus Rose delivered Howdy Doody to Buffalo Bob with an express term of the bailment that Buffalo Bob would be allowed to possess Howdy Doody "for as long as [he] personally wished to have him," but specifically conditioned Buffalo Bob's use on the same two requirements that NBC imposed upon Rufus Rose: that Howdy Doody would not be used in a commercial manner and that the puppet would "eventually be placed in the care of the Detroit Institute of Arts." These statements indicate that the bailment was express, and that Buffalo Bob, as bailee, was bound to deal with Howdy Doody according to the instructions of Rufus Rose, the bailor.

The defendants first argue that this agreement between Rufus Rose and Buffalo Bob is unenforceable as a bailment because it lacks consideration. However, actual consideration is not required for a bailment to be enforceable. As stated above, gratuitous bailments are generally not supported by actual consideration, but are still binding on the bailee. Here, it appears that the bailment was gratuitous: it was undertaken for the sole benefit of one of the parties, in this case, the bailee, Buffalo Bob. Thus, it is enough that Rufus Rose, as bailor, gave up custody of Howdy Doody based upon Buffalo Bob's promise that he would redeliver the puppet. As a result, the bailment agreement between Rufus Rose and Buffalo Bob is enforceable without actual consideration.

The defendants maintain that the 1970 agreement between Rose and Smith was satisfied by his return of Howdy Doody to the Rose family in 1998. They also argue that the 1966–1967 agreement is satisfied by "eventually" giving the puppet to the DIA. In other words, other members of the Rose or Smith family may keep the puppet so long as one day it is turned over to the DIA. However, these interpretations of Rufus Rose's words are unsupported by the language of the bailment letter itself; it states that the puppet could only be kept by Smith "personally" and does not mention that the puppet could be passed along by Buffalo Bob after the death of Rufus Rose to anyone else, other than giving it to the DIA. Also, delaying delivery of Howdy Doody through the latter interpretation would undermine the terms of the 1966–1967 agreement between Rufus Rose and NBC: it would allow Howdy Doody to be passed indefinitely, perhaps never to be sent to the DIA.

Thus, the DIA has shown that there is no genuine issue of material fact that the DIA is entitled to possession of Howdy Doody based on the agreement between NBC and Rufus Rose from 1966–1967 and the obligations of Buffalo Bob under the Rufus Rose–Buffalo Bob agreement from 1970.

Judgment in favor of Detroit Institute of Arts.

Bailee's Liability for Misdelivery

The bailee is also liable to the bailor if he misdelivers the bailed property at the termination of the bailment. The property must be returned to the bailor or to someone specified by the bailor.

The bailee is in a dilemma if a third person, claiming to have rights superior to those of the bailor, demands possession of the bailed property. If the bailee refuses to deliver the bailed property to the third-party claimant and the claimant is entitled to possession, the bailee is liable to the claimant. If the bailee delivers the bailed property to the third-party claimant and the claimant is not entitled to possession, the bailee is liable to the bailor. The circumstances may be such that the conflicting claims of the bailor and the third-party claimant can be determined only by judicial decision. In some cases, the bailee may protect himself by bringing the third-party claimant into a lawsuit along with the bailor so that all the competing claims can be adjudicated by the court before the bailee releases the property. This remedy is not always available, however.

Limits on Liability

Bailees may try to limit or relieve themselves of liability for the bailed property. Some examples include the storage receipt purporting to limit liability to $100 in the *Magee* case, signs near checkrooms such as "Not responsible for loss of or damage to checked property," and disclaimers on claim checks such as "Goods left at owner's risk." The standards used to determine whether such limitations and disclaimers are enforceable are discussed in Chapter 15.

Any attempt by the bailee to be relieved of liability for intentional wrongful acts is against public policy and will not be enforced. A bailee's ability to be relieved of liability for negligence is also limited. Courts look to see whether the disclaimer or limitation of liability was communicated to the bailor at the time of the bailment. When the customer handed her coat to the checkroom attendant, did the attendant point out the "not responsible for loss or damage" sign? Did the parking lot attendant call the car owner's attention to the disclaimer on the back of the claim check?

If not, the court may hold that the disclaimer was not communicated to the bailor and did not become part of the bailment contract. Even if the bailor was aware of the disclaimer, it still may not be enforced on the ground that it is contrary to public policy.

If the disclaimer was offered on a take-it-or-leave-it basis and was not the subject of arm's-length bargaining, it is less likely to be enforced than if it was negotiated and voluntarily agreed to by the parties. A bailee may be able to limit liability to a certain amount or to relieve himself of liability for certain perils. Ideally, the bailee will give the bailor a chance to declare a higher value and to pay an additional charge in order to be protected up to the declared value of the goods. Common carriers, such as railroads and trucking companies, often take this approach. Courts do not look with favor on efforts by a person to be relieved of liability for negligence. For this reason, terms limiting the liability of a bailee stand a better chance of being enforced than do terms completely relieving the bailee of liability.

An implied agreement as to the bailee's duties may arise from a prior course of dealing between the bailor and the bailee, or from the bailor's knowledge of the bailee's facilities or method of doing business. The bailee may, if he wishes, assume all risks incident to the bailment and contract to return the bailed property undamaged or to pay for any damage to or loss of the property.

Right to Compensation

The express or implied contract creating the bailment controls whether the bailee has the right to receive compensation for keeping the property or must pay for having the right to use it. If the bailment is made as a favor, then the bailee is not entitled to compensation even though the bailment is for the bailor's sole benefit. If the bailment involves the rental of property, the bailee must pay the agreed rental rate. If the bailment is for the storage or repair of property, the bailee is entitled to the contract price for the storage or repair services. When no specific price was agreed on but compensation was contemplated by the parties, the bailee is entitled to the reasonable value of the services provided.

In many instances, the bailee will have a lien (a charge against property to secure the payment of a debt) on the bailed property for the reasonable value of the services. For example, Silver takes a chair to Ace Upholstery to have it recovered. When the chair has been recovered, Ace has the right to keep it until the agreed price—or, if no price was set, the reasonable value of the work—is paid. This is an example of an **artisan's lien,** which is discussed in Chapter 28.

Bailor's Liability for Defects in the Bailed Property

When personal property is rented or loaned, the bailor makes an implied warranty that the property has no hidden defects that make it unsafe for use. If the bailment is for the bailee's sole benefit, the bailor is liable for injuries that result from defects in the bailed property only if the bailor knew about the defects and did not tell the bailee. For example, Price lends his car, which he knows has bad brakes, to Sloan. If Price does not tell Sloan about the bad brakes and Sloan is injured in an accident because the brakes fail, Price is liable for Sloan's injuries.

If the bailment is a bailment for mutual benefit, the bailor has a greater obligation. The bailor must use reasonable care in inspecting the property and seeing that it is safe for the purpose for which it is intended. The bailor is liable for injuries suffered by the bailee because of defects that the bailor either knew about or should have discovered through reasonable inspection. For example, Acme Rent-All, which rents trailers, does not inspect the trailers after they are returned. A wheel has come loose on a trailer that Acme rents to Hirsch. If the wheel comes off while Hirsch is using the trailer and the goods Hirsch is carrying in it are damaged, Acme is liable to Hirsch. The *Retzler* case, which follows shortly, deals with the bailor's duty of reasonable care.

In addition, product liability doctrines that apply a higher standard of legal responsibility have been applied to bailors who are commercial lessors of personal property.[8] Express or implied warranties of quality under either Article 2 or Article 2A of the UCC may apply. Liability under these warranties does not depend on whether the bailor knew about or should have discovered the defect. The only question is whether the property's condition complied with the warranty. Some courts have also imposed strict liability on the commercial lessor-bailor of defective, unreasonably dangerous goods that cause personal injury or property damage to the lessee-bailee. This liability is imposed regardless of whether the lessor was negligent.

---

[8]Product liability doctrines are discussed in Chapter 20.

Retzler v. Pratt & Whitney Co.   *1999 Ill. App. LEXIS (Ill. App. 1999)*

In August 1991, a series of financial transactions occurred with regard to a certain ATR 42-300 aircraft. First, AMR Leasing Corp. purchased the aircraft. Immediately thereafter, AMR sold the aircraft to a French company. That firm then leased the aircraft back to AMR, which subleased it to Simmons Airlines, Inc., the owner of American Eagle Airlines.

Karen Retzler was a flight attendant on a September 1991 American Eagle Airlines flight. The aircraft used for the flight was the ATR 42-300 that was the subject of the above-described transactions. Shortly after the aircraft took off from Traverse City, Michigan, for an intended destination of Chicago, the No. 4 bearing within an engine failed. The aircraft cabin and cockpit then filled with smoke. When the pilot suddenly reduced cabin pressure and began an emergency descent and landing, Retzler's body came into violent contact with the galley of the aircraft. Retzler, who sustained injuries as a result, filed suit against AMR and various other defendants. When the trial court granted AMR summary judgment, Retzler appealed.

Quinn, Justice   In her complaint, Retzler alleged that AMR is liable for the injuries she sustained in the emergency landing of the ATR 42-300. She alleged that AMR, as owner and/or lessor of the aircraft, had a duty not to place a defective aircraft into the stream of commerce. She claimed that AMR was negligent in failing to adequately test and inspect the engine to discover the defect, and [in] allowing the aircraft to be flown when AMR should have known the aircraft was not in airworthy condition. As a result of AMR's failure to detect the defect in the aircraft, Retzler alleges, the aircraft was forced into an emergency landing [and Retzler] sustained injuries. [In support of its motion for summary judgment, AMR argued that it did not owe Retzler a duty but that if any duty was owed, it was not breached.]

[T]he leasing of an aircraft is subject to the general rules regarding the bailment or lease of personal property. [When] the bailment is lucrative to the bailor-lessor, the bailor is liable to an injured third person if (1) he supplied the chattel in question; (2) the chattel was defective at the time it was supplied; (3) the defect could have been discovered by a reasonable inspection, when inspection is required (i.e., where the danger of substantial harm because of a defect is great); and (4) the defect was the proximate cause of the injury.

Retzler has clearly established three of the requirements for bailor-lessor liability. First, it is undisputed that AMR supplied the aircraft in question. In fact, not only was AMR

the lessor of the aircraft, it actually sold the aircraft to [the French firm that leased it back to AMR, which then subleased it to Simmons]. Second, the aircraft was defective at the time that it was leased to Simmons. The bearing itself was contained inside the engine since the date of the engine's assembly. Third, there is no question that the defective engine led to Retzler's injuries.

The final factor in determining whether AMR is liable under a common law bailment theory is whether the defect in the engine could have been discovered by a reasonable inspection. Such inspection may be required where the danger of substantial harm is great, as we find it is here. AMR admits that it never conducted tests or performed an inspection of the engine. AMR relies on the affidavits of Simmons employees stating that the aircraft was in a safe and airworthy condition and the engines were in good working order at the time of its transfer from AMR to Simmons. Retzler, however, submitted expert testimony that an inspection of the engine would have revealed the defect. Looking at the evidence in the light most favorable to the nonmoving party, here Retzler, we conclude that the question of whether an adequate inspection would have revealed the defect in the aircraft's engine is a genuine issue of material fact that should be resolved by a trier of fact.

Trial court's order granting summary judgment in favor of AMR reversed and case remanded.

Special Bailments

Common Carriers

Bailees that are common carriers are held to a higher level of responsibility than are bailees that are private carriers. Common carriers are licensed by governmental agencies to carry the property of anyone who requests the service. Private contract carriers carry goods only for persons selected by the carrier.

Both common carriers and private contract carriers are bailees. However, the law makes the common carrier a near-absolute insurer of the goods it carries. The common carrier is responsible for virtually any loss of or damage to the entrusted goods, unless the common

CYBERLAW IN ACTION

Online Tracking of Bailments

To lower package loss and increase consumer confidence, many large shipping companies such as UPS and FedEx provide an online tracking system. The tracking system is used by companies to identify and trace all packages as they move through the company's system to their destination. Often a package is assigned a tracking code or number that the customer can use to locate the package using an online mapping system. If a package is feared to be lost, Internet access to the tracking system allows customers immediate confirmation of its location in route, or place and time of delivery. The confidence that Internet tracking systems gives consumers increases the possibility that they will become repeat customers. Furthermore, the tracking system reveals the company's internal systems of operation to the consumer. This transparency of operation creates a forcing function that encourages companies to be certain that their shipping system is in smooth working order. Also, companies can view the tracking system to determine what shipping routes their competitors are using. Finally, the online tracking system saves a company money by lowering the cost of paying for representatives to deal with customer inquiries.

CONCEPT REVIEW

Duties of Bailees and Bailors

Type of Bailment	Duties of Bailee	Duties of Bailor
Sole Benefit of Bailee	1. Must use great care; liable for even slight negligence. 2. Must return goods to bailor or dispose of them at his direction. 3. May have duty to compensate bailor.	1. Must notify the bailee of any known defects.
Mutual Benefit	1. Must use reasonable care; liable for ordinary negligence. 2. Must return goods to bailor or dispose of them at his direction. 3. May have duty to compensate bailor.	1. Must notify bailee of all known defects and any defects that could be discovered on reasonable inspection. 2. Commercial lessors may be subject to warranties of quality and/or strict liability in tort. 3. May have duty to compensate bailee.
Sole Benefit of Bailor	1. Must use at least slight care; liable for gross negligence. 2. Must return goods to bailor or dispose of them at his direction.	1. Must notify bailee of all known defects and any hidden defects that are known or could be discovered on reasonable inspection. 2. May have duty to compensate bailee.

carrier shows that the loss or damage was caused by one of the following:

1. An act of God.
2. An act of a public enemy.
3. An act or order of the government.
4. An act of the person who shipped the goods.
5. The nature of the goods themselves.

Therefore, the common carrier is liable if goods entrusted to it are stolen by some unknown person, but not if the goods are destroyed when a tornado hits the warehouse.

THE GLOBAL BUSINESS ENVIRONMENT

Liability of Carriers of Goods

When an American firm ships goods to a foreign buyer, the goods may be shipped by ground, air, or water carrier. The duties and extent of liability of these various carriers is largely determined by domestic statutes and international law.

Ground Carriers

American trucking and railroad companies are regulated by the Interstate Commerce Act. American carriers are liable for any loss or damage to the goods with few exceptions—for example, damage caused by acts of God and acts of the shipper (usually the seller of the goods), such as poorly packaging the goods. An American carrier may limit its liability by contract, provided it allows the shipper to obtain full liability by paying a higher shipping charge.

Most European trucking companies and railroads are covered by EU rules, which place liability on carriers for damages to goods they carry with few exceptions—for example, defective packaging by the shipper and circumstances beyond the carrier's control. EU rules also limit a carrier's liability unless the shipper agrees to pay for greater liability.

Air Carriers

The Warsaw Convention governs the liability of international air carriers. Most nations have ratified the Warsaw Convention in its original or amended form. Under the Convention, an air carrier is liable to the shipper for damages to goods with few exceptions, including that it was impossible for the carrier to prevent the loss or that the damage was caused by the negligence of the shipper. The Warsaw Convention limits a carrier's liability to a stated amount per pound, unless the shipper pays for greater liability.

Water Carriers

The Hague Rules govern the liability of international water carriers. The Hague Rules were amended in Vishy, Sweden, in 1968. The United States codified the Hague Rules in the Carriage of Goods by Sea Act (COGSA), but has not ratified the Visby amendments, which do not substantially change the liability of international water carriers.

The Hague–Visby Rules and the COGSA impose on international water carriers the duties to (1) furnish a seaworthy ship and (2) stow the cargo carefully to prevent it from breaking loose during storms at sea. When these duties are met, a water carrier will not usually be liable for damages to cargo. Water carriers have no liability for damages caused by circumstances beyond their control—such as poor packaging, piracy, or acts of war. Under COGSA, liability is limited to $500 per package, unless the shipper agrees to pay a higher shipping fee. Under the Hague–Visby Rules, liability will be the value of the goods declared by the shipper. Sometimes a carrier will attempt to reduce or eliminate its liability in the shipping contract. However, COGSA does not permit a carrier to eliminate its liability for loss or damages to goods resulting from the carrier's negligence or other fault.

Under COGSA or the Hague–Visby Rules, the owner of cargo will be liable for damage his cargo does to other cargo. Also, under the ancient **maritime doctrine of general average,** when a carrier sacrifices an owner's cargo, such as throwing it overboard in order to save the ship and the other cargo, the other owners have liability to the owner whose cargo was sacrificed; liability is prorated to each owner according to the value of each owner's goods in relation to the value of the voyage (the value of the ship plus the value of the other owners' goods plus the carrier's total shipping fees).

The doctrine of general average is commonly expanded by the contract between the carrier and cargo owners in **New Jason clauses.** Typically, a New Jason clause provides that in *all* cases when goods are damaged and the carrier is not liable under COGSA, the goods owner is entitled to general average contributions from all other cargo owners. The doctrine of general average, bolstered by a New Jason clause, also requires cargo owners to pay for damages to the ship when not the result of the carrier's fault.

If goods are damaged because the shipper improperly packaged or crated them, the carrier is not liable. Similarly, if perishable goods are not in suitable condition to be shipped and therefore deteriorate in the course of shipment, the carrier is not liable so long as it used reasonable care in handling them.

Common carriers are usually permitted to limit their liability to a stated value unless the bailor declares a higher value for the property and pays an additional fee.

Hotelkeepers

Hotelkeepers are engaged in the business of offering food and/or lodging to transient persons. They hold themselves out to serve the public and are obligated to do so. As is the common carrier, the hotelkeeper is held to a higher standard of care than that of the ordinary bailee. The hotelkeeper, however, is not a bailee in the strict sense of the word. The guest does not usually surrender the exclusive possession of his property to the hotelkeeper. Even so, the hotelkeeper is treated as the virtual insurer of the guest's property. The hotelkeeper is not liable for loss of or damage to property if she shows that it was caused by one of the following:

1. An act of God.
2. An act of a public enemy.
3. An act of a governmental authority.
4. The fault of a member of the guest's party.
5. The nature of the goods.

Most states have passed laws that limit the hotelkeeper's liability, however. Commonly, the law requires the hotel owner to post a notice advising guests that any valuables should be checked into the hotel vault. The hotelkeeper's liability is then limited, usually to a fixed amount, for valuables that are not so checked.

Safe-Deposit Boxes

If a person rents a safe-deposit box at a local bank and places property in the box, the box and the property are in the physical possession of the bank. However, it takes both the renter's key and the key held by the bank to open the box. In most cases, the bank does not know the nature, amount, or value of the goods in the box. Although a few courts have held that the rental of a safe-deposit box does not create a bailment, most courts have concluded that the renter of the box is a bailor and the bank is a bailee. As such, the bank is not an insurer of the contents of the box. It is obligated, however, to use due care and to come forward and explain loss of or damage to the property entrusted to it.

Involuntary Bailments

Suppose a person owns a cottage on a beach. After a violent storm, a sailboat washed up on his beach. As the finder of lost or misplaced property, he may be considered the **involuntary bailee** or **constructive bailee** of the sailboat. This relationship may arise when a person finds himself in possession of someone else's property without having agreed to accept possession.

The duties of the involuntary bailee are not well defined. The involuntary bailee does not have the right to destroy or use the property. If the true owner shows up, the property must be returned to him. Under some circumstances, the involuntary bailee may be under an obligation to assume control of the property or to take some minimal steps to ascertain the owner's identity, or both.

Documents of Title

Storing or shipping goods, giving a warehouse receipt or bill of lading representing the goods, and transferring such a receipt or bill of lading as representing the goods are practices of ancient origin. The warehouseman or the common carrier is a bailee of the goods who contracts to store or transport the goods and to deliver them to the owner or to act otherwise in accordance with the lawful directions of the owner. The warehouse receipt or the bill of lading may be either negotiable or non-negotiable. To be negotiable, a warehouse receipt, bill of lading, or other document of title must provide that the goods are to be delivered to the bearer or to the order of a named person [7–104(1)]. The primary differences between the law of negotiable instruments and the law of negotiable documents of title are based on the differences between the obligation to pay money and the obligation to deliver specific goods.

Warehouse Receipts

A warehouse receipt, to be valid, need not be in any particular form, but if it does not embody within its written or printed form each of the following, the warehouseman is liable for damages caused by the omission to a person injured as a result of it: (1) the location of the warehouse where the goods are stored; (2) the date of issue; (3) the consecutive number of the receipt; (4) whether the goods are to be delivered to the bearer or to the order of a named person; (5) the rate of storage and handling charges; (6) a description of the goods or of the packages containing them; (7) the signature of the warehouseman or his agent; (8) whether the warehouseman is the owner of the goods, solely, jointly, or in common with others; and (9) a statement of the amount of the advances made and of the liabilities incurred for which the warehouseman claims a lien or security interest. Other terms may be inserted [7–202].

A warehouseman is liable to a purchaser for value in good faith of a warehouse receipt for nonreceipt or misdescription of goods. The receipt may conspicuously qualify the description by a statement such as "contents, condition, and quantity unknown" [7–203].

Because a warehouseman is a bailee of the goods, he owes to the holder of the warehouse receipt the duties of a mutual benefit bailee and must exercise reasonable care [7–204]. The warehouseman may terminate the relation by notification where, for example, the goods are about to deteriorate or where they constitute a threat to other goods in the warehouse [7–206]. Unless the warehouse receipt

ETHICS IN ACTION

Is It Ethical?

Suppose that you own and operate a warehouse. A local liquor store owner occasionally uses your facilities to store shipments of wine from France until he has room for the wine in his store. You are aware that from time to time your warehouse employees "borrow" a bottle from the crates of wine being stored in your warehouse. After a number of crates with a total of four bottles missing are delivered to the liquor store, the store owner queries you about the missing bottles and you tell him that they must have been broken in transit to your warehouse. Have you acted ethically?

---

provides otherwise, the warehouseman must keep separate the goods covered by each receipt; however, different lots of fungible goods such as grain may be mingled [7–207].

A warehouseman has a lien against the bailor on the goods covered by his receipt for his storage and other charges incurred in handling the goods [7–209]. The Code sets out a detailed procedure for enforcing this lien [7–210].

Bills of Lading

In many respects, the rights and liabilities of the parties to a negotiable bill of lading are the same as the rights and liabilities of the parties to a negotiable warehouse receipt. The contract of the issuer of a bill of lading is to transport goods, whereas the contract of the issuer of a warehouse receipt is to store goods. Like the issuer of a warehouse receipt, the issuer of a bill of lading is liable for nonreceipt or misdescription of the goods, but he may protect himself from liability where he does not know the contents of packages by marking the bill of lading "contents or con-

dition of packages unknown" or similar language. Such terms are ineffective when the goods are loaded by an issuer who is a common carrier unless the goods are concealed by packages [7–301].

Duty of Care

A carrier who issues a bill of lading, or a warehouse operator who issues a warehouse receipt, must exercise the same degree of care in relation to the goods as a reasonably careful person would exercise under similar circumstances. Liability for damages not caused by the negligence of the carrier may be imposed on him by a special law or rule of law. Under tariff rules, a common carrier may limit her liability to a shipper's declaration of value, provided that the rates are dependent on value [7–309]. In the case that follows, *Calvin Klein Ltd.,* a court enforced a $50 per shipment limitation that had been part of a long series of shipping contracts where the customer had the opportunity to declare a higher value and failed to do so.

Calvin Klein Ltd. v. Trylon Trucking Corp.   *892 F.2d 191 (2d. Cir. 1989)*

Trylon Trucking Corporation is a New Jersey trucking firm that engaged in the business of transporing goods from New York City's airports for delivery to its customers' facilities. For three years prior to 1986, Calvin Klein, a New York clothing company, used the services of Trylon involving hundreds of shipments. Calvin Klein, through its customs broker, would contact Trylon to pick up the shipment from the airport for delivery to Calvin Klein's facility. After completing the delivery carriage, Trylon would forward to Calvin Klein an invoice, which contained a limitation of liability provision as follows:

In consideration of the rate charged, the shipper agrees that the carrier shall not be liable for more than $50.00 on any shipment accepted for delivery to one consignee unless a greater value is declared, in writing, upon receipt at time of shipment and charge for such greater value paid, or agreed to be paid, by the shipper.

A shipment of 2,833 blouses from Hong Kong arrived at John F. Kennedy International Airport for Calvin Klein on March 27, 1986. Calvin Klein arranged for Trylon to pick up the shipment and deliver it to Calvin Klein's New Jersey warehouse. On April 2, Trylon dispatched its driver, J. Jefferson, to pick up this shipment. Jefferson signed a receipt for the shipment from Calvin Klein's broker. Later, on April 2, the parties discovered that Jefferson had stolen Trylon's truck and its shipment. The shipment was never recovered.

Calvin Klein sent a claim letter to Trylon for the full value of the lost blouses. When it did not receive a response from Trylon, Calvin Klein filed suit against Trylon, seeking to recover $150,000, the alleged value of the blouses. In the pleadings before the court, the parties agreed that Trylon was liable to Calvin Klein for the loss of the shipment and that it had been grossly negligent in the hiring and supervision of Jefferson. They also agreed that "the terms and conditions of Trylon's carriage were that liability for loss or damage to cargo is limited to $50 in accordance with the provision in Trylon's invoice forms." Calvin Klein conceded that it was aware of the limitation of liability and that it did not declare a value on the blouses at the time of shipment.

Trylon contended that its liability was limited to $50 in accordance with the provision in its invoice forms. Calvin Klein argued that the limitation clause was not enforceable for two reasons: (1) no agreement existed between it and Trylon as to the limitation of liability; and (2) even if an agreement existed, public policy would prevent its enforcement because of Trylon's gross negligence. The district court held that Calvin Klein had not assented to the limitation clause for this shipment and awarded damages to Calvin Klein of $101,542,62. Trylon appealed.

Miner, Circuit Judge   A common carrier is strictly liable for the loss of goods in its custody. Where the loss is not due to excepted causes [that is, act of God or public enemy, inherent nature of goods, or shipper's fault], it is immaterial whether the carrier was negligent or not. Even in the case of loss from theft by third parties, liability may be imposed upon a negligent common carrier. A shipper and a common carrier may contract to limit the carrier's liability in cases of loss to an amount agreed to by the parties, so long as the language of the limitation is clear, the shipper is aware of the terms of the limitation, and the shipper can change the terms by indicating the true value of the goods being shipped. Section 7-309(2). Such a limitation agreement is generally valid and enforceable despite carrier negligence. The limitation of liability provision involved here clearly provides that, at the time of delivery, the shipper may increase the limitation by written notice of the value of the goods to be delivered and by payment of a commensurately higher fee.

The parties stipulated to the fact that the $50 limitation of liability was a term and condition of carriage and that Calvin Klein was aware of that limitation. This stipulated fact removes the first issue, namely whether an agreement existed as to a liability limitation between the parties. Calvin Klein's argument that it never previously acknowledged this limitation by accepting only $50 in settlement of a larger loss does not alter this explicit stipulation. The district court erred in not accepting the limitation of liability as stipulated.

The remaining issue concerns the enforceability of the limitation clause in the light of Trylon's conceded gross negligence.

Since carriers are strictly liable for loss of shipments in their custody and are insurers of those goods, the degree of carrier negligence is immaterial. The common carrier must exercise reasonable care in relation to the shipment in its custody. Section 7-309(2). Carriers can contract with their shipping customers on the amount of liability each party will bear for the loss of a shipment, regardless of the amount of carrier negligence. Unlike a merchant acquiring a burglar alarm, the shipper can calculate the specific amount of its potential damages in advance, declare the value of the shipment based on that calculation, can pay a commensurately higher rate to carry the goods, in effect buying additional insurance from the common carrier.

In this case Calvin Klein and Trylon were business entities with an ongoing commercial relationship involving numerous carriages of Calvin Klein goods by Trylon. Where such entities deal with each other in a commercial setting, and no special relationship exists between the parties, clear limitations between them will be enforced. Here, each carriage was under the same terms and conditions as the last, including a limitation of Trylon's liability. This is not a case in which the shipper was dealing with the common carrier for the first time or contracting under new or changed conditions. Calvin Klein was aware of the terms and was free to adjust the limitation upon a written declaration of the value of a given shipment, but failed to do so with the shipment at issue here. Since Calvin Klein failed to adjust the limitation, the limitation applies here, and no public policy that dictates otherwise can be identified.

Calvin Klein also argues that the limitation is so low as to be void. The amount is immaterial because Calvin Klein had the opportunity to negotiate the amount of coverage by declaring the value of the shipment. Commercial entities can easily negotiate the degree of risk each party will bear and which party will bear the cost of insurance. Calvin Klein had the opportunity to declare a higher value and we find all of its arguments relating to the unreasonableness of the limitation to be without merit.

District court judgment reversed with instructions to enter judgment for Calvin Klein for $50.

Negotiation of Document of Title

A negotiable document of title and a negotiable instrument are negotiated in substantially the same manner. If the document of title provides for the delivery of the goods to bearer, it may be negotiated by delivery. If it provides for delivery of the goods to the order of a named person, it must be indorsed by that person and delivered. If an order document of title is indorsed in blank, it may be negotiated by delivery unless it bears a special indorsement following the blank indorsement, in which event it must be indorsed by the special indorsee and delivered [7–501].

A person taking a negotiable document of title takes as a bona fide holder if she takes in good faith and in the regular course of business. The bona fide holder of a negotiable document of title has substantially the same advantages over a holder who is not a bona fide holder or over a holder of a non-negotiable document of title as does a holder in due course of a negotiable instrument over a holder who is not a holder in due course or over a holder of a nonnegotiable instrument.

Rights Acquired by Negotiation

A person who acquires a negotiable document of title by due negotiation acquires (1) title to the document, (2) title to the goods, (3) the right to the goods delivered to the bailee after the issuance of the document, and (4) the direct obligation of the issuer to hold or deliver the goods according to the terms of the document [7–502(1)].

Under the broad general principle that a person cannot transfer title to goods he does not own, a thief—or the owner of goods subject to a perfected security interest—cannot, by warehousing or shipping the goods on a negotiable document of title and then negotiating the document of title, transfer to the purchaser of the document of title a better title than he has [7–503].

Warranties of Transferor of Document of Title

The transferor of a negotiable document of title warrants to his immediate transferee, in addition to any warranty of goods, only that the document is genuine, that he has no knowledge of any facts that would impair its validity or worth, and that his negotiation or transfer is rightful and fully effective with respect to the title to the document and the goods it represents [7–507].

Problems and Problem Cases

1. Leonard Charrier was an amateur archeologist. After researching colonial maps and records, he concluded that the Trudeau Plantation near Angola, Louisiana, was the possible site of an ancient village of the Tunica Indians. Charrier obtained the permission of the caretaker of the Trudeau Plantation to survey the property with a metal detector for possible burial locations. At the time, he mistakenly believed that the caretaker was the Plantation's owner. He located and, over the next three years, excavated approximately 150 burial sites containing beads, European ceramics, stoneware and glass bottles; iron kettles, vessels, and skillets; knives, muskets, gunflints, balls, and shots; crucifixes, rings, and bracelets; and native pottery. He began discussions with Harvard University to sell the collection to its Peabody Museum. While the University inventoried, cataloged, and displayed the items pursuant to a lease agreement, it was unwilling to go through with a sale unless Charrier could establish title to the artifacts. He then brought suit against the owners of the Trudeau Plantation seeking a declaratory judgment that he was the owner of the artifacts. The state of Louisiana intervened in the litigation to assert the rights of the lawful heirs of the artifacts. Charrier argued that the Indians abandoned the artifacts when they moved from the Trudeau Plantation in 1764. He contended that they were unowned property until he found them and reduced them to his possession. He compared them to wild game and fish, which are unowned until someone takes possession of them. Were the artifacts abandoned property of which Charrier could become the owner by taking possession?

2. Bernice Paset, a customer of the Old Orchard Bank, found $6,325 in currency on the seat of a chair in an examination booth in the bank's safety-deposit vault. The chair was partially under a table. Paset notified officers of the bank and turned the money over to them. She was told by bank officials that the bank would try to locate the owner and that she could have the money if the owner was not located within one year. The bank wrote to everyone who had been in the safety-deposit vault area either on the day of, or on the day preceding, the discovery. The bank's letter stated that some property had been found and invited the customers to describe any property they might have lost. No one reported the loss of any currency. The money remained unclaimed a year after it had been found. The bank refused to deliver the money to Paset, contending that it was mislaid, not lost, property and that it had a better right to it. Was the money mislaid property?

3. Barbara Worrell and Elizabeth Brisendine enjoyed a long-term friendship. Brisendine often spent time at the beach with Worrell's family; they saw each other at social events and occasionally traveled together. After Brisendine became terminally ill, Worrell drove her to and from the hospital and to doctors appointments. On a number of occasions Brisendine attempted to give Worrell money, but she never accepted it.

While Worrell was visiting Brisendine at her home in September 1993, Brisendine wrote a check, made an entry in her checkbook, and attempted to give the check to Worrell. Worrell refused the check, telling Brisendine that she looked after her out of friendship and did not desire payment for helping a friend. Brisendine returned the check and checkbook to her pocketbook. Worrell did not see the actual check and did not know the amount for which it was written. She was later told that the check "would be in the mail to her."

Henry Meyer, who took care of Brisendine's finances, saw an entry for $10,000 to Barbara Worrell in Brisendine's checkbook and was told by Brisendine that she was going to mail the check to Worrell. Brisendine died on October 21, 1993. Worrell did not hear anything else about the check until January 1994, when Meyer, who was then serving as one of the personal representatives of the estate, contacted her. Meyer told Worrell that a third party had endorsed her signature on the check and was trying to cash the check at NationsBank. Worrell then took an interest in the check, learned of the amount, and tried to ascertain what Brisendine had intended with the check. Worrell then filed a claim against the estate for $10,000, alleging the check was intended as a gift. The claim was denied by the personal representatives (Ray Lathan and Henry Meyer) and Worrell brought suit. Did Brisendine make a gift of the $10,000 to Worrell?

4. John Fierro and Janan Hoel became engaged to be married. At the time Fierro proposed and Hoel accepted, Fierro presented her with a diamond ring that carried a value of approximately $9,000. During the engagement, Fierro and Hoel located a condominium to purchase in New York City. Hoel, however, refused to sign mortgage documents stating that Fierro's parents had loaned them money for the purchase. Fierro later broke the engagement and asked Hoel to return the ring. When Hoel refused to return the ring, Fierro sued her. What type of gift was present in this case? Who should win the case?

5. Ochoa's Studebaker automobile was stolen. Eleven months later, the automobile somehow found its way into the hands of the U.S. government, which sold it to Rogers at a "junk" auction for $85. At the time it was purchased by Rogers, no part of the car was intact. It had no top except a part of the frame; it had no steering wheel, tires, rims, cushions, or battery; the motor, radiator, and gears were out of the car; one wheel was gone, as was one axle; the fenders were partly gone; and the frame was broken. It was no longer an automobile but a pile of broken and dismantled parts. Having purchased these parts, Rogers used them in the construction of a delivery truck at an expense of approximately $800. When the truck was completed, he put it to use in his furniture business. Several months later, Ochoa passed Rogers's place of business and recognized the vehicle from marks on the hood and the radiator. He discovered that the serial and engine numbers matched those of the car he had owned. Ochoa demanded the vehicle from Rogers, who refused to surrender it. Ochoa brought suit to recover possession of the property. In the alternative, he asked for the value of the vehicle at the time of the suit (allegedly $1,000) and for the value of the use of the car from the time Rogers purchased it from the government. Was Ochoa entitled to recover possession of his property, which Rogers had substantially improved?

6. R. B. Bewley and his family drove to Kansas City to attend a week-long church convention. When they arrived at the hotel where they had reservations, they were unable to park their car and unload their luggage because of a long line of cars. They then drove to a nearby parking lot where they took a ticket, causing the gate arm to open, and drove in 15 or 20 feet. A parking attendant told them that the lot was full, that they should leave the keys with him, and that he would park the car. They told the attendant that they had reservations at the nearby hotel and that after they checked in they would come back for their luggage. Subsequently, someone broke into the Bewley's car and stole their personal property from the car and its trunk. Was the parking lot a bailee of the property?

7. Pringle, the head of the drapery department at Wardrobe Cleaners, went to the Axelrods' home to inspect some dining room draperies for dry-cleaning purposes. He spent about 30 minutes looking at the drapes and inspecting both the drapes and the lining. He pointed out some roach spots on the lining that could not be removed by cleaning, but this was not of concern to the Axelrods. He did not indicate to them that the fabric had deteriorated from sunburn, age, dust, or air conditioning so as to make it unsuitable for dry cleaning. He took the drapes and had them dry cleaned. When the drapes were returned, they were unfit for use. The fabric had been a gold floral design on an eggshell-white background. When returned, it was a blotchy gold. Wardrobe Cleaners stated that it was difficult to predict how imported fabrics would respond to the dry-cleaning process and that the company was not equipped to pretest the fabric to see whether it was colorfast. The Axelrods sued Wardrobe Cleaners for $1,000, the replacement value of the drapes. Was Wardrobe Cleaners liable for the damage caused to the drapes during the dry-cleaning process?

8. In April, Carter brought her fur coat to Reichlin Furriers for cleaning, glazing, and storage until the next winter season. She was given a printed form of receipt, upon the front of which an employee of Reichlin had written $100 as the value of the coat. There was no discussion of the value of the coat. Carter did not realize that such a value had been written on the receipt, which she did not read at the time. A space for the customer's signature on the front of the receipt was left blank. Below this space in prominent type appeared a notice to "see reverse side for terms and conditions." The other side of the receipt stated that it was a storage contract and that by its acceptance, the customer would be deemed to have agreed to its terms unless objections were given within 10 days. Fifteen conditions were listed. One of the conditions was as follows: "Storage charges are based upon valuation herein declared by the depositor, and amount recoverable for loss or damage to the article shall not exceed its actual value or the cost of repair or replacement with materials of like kind and quality or the depositor's valuation appearing in this receipt, whichever is less." In the fall of the year, after Carter had paid the bill for storage and other services on the coat, Reichlin informed her that the coat was lost. At that time, the fair market value of the coat was $450. Carter sued Reichlin for loss of the coat and sought $450 damages. Reichlin claimed that its liability was limited to $100. Is this correct?

9. Marvin Gooden checked into a Day's Inn in Atlanta, paying in advance for two days' lodging. The next day he temporarily left his room. He left behind, in the room, a paper bag filled with approximately $9,000. Shortly after Gooden left, housekeeper Mary Carter entered his room to clean it. Carter found the bag of money. Because she saw no other personal effects, Carter assumed that Gooden had checked out. She therefore turned the bag of money over to her supervisor, Vivian Clark. Clark gave the bag to Dempsey Wilson, who was responsible for general supervision and maintenance of the grounds. During the three years he had worked for Day's Inn, Wilson had

occasionally been given items of value to turn in at the hotel's office. In the past, he had always turned in the items. This time, however, he absconded with the bag of money. There was a safe on the Day's Inn premises. Day's Inn had posted, on the door of Gooden's room, a notice concerning the safe's availability for use by guests who had valuables with them. Gooden, who had never sought the use of the safe, brought a tort action against Day's Inn, Clark, and Carter in an effort to collect $9,000 in damages. Day's Inn argued that it was protected against liability by the following Georgia statute: "The innkeeper may provide a safe or other place of deposit for valuable articles and, by posting a notice thereof, may require the guests of the innkeeper to place such valuable articles therein or the innkeeper shall be relieved from responsibility for such articles." Gooden contended, however, that the statute could not insulate an innkeeper from liability when the loss of a guest's valuables is occasioned by the negligent (or other tortious) conduct of the innkeeper's employees. Should Gooden prevail against Day's Inn, Clark, and Carter?

10. Griswold and Bateman Warehouse Company stored 337 cases of Chivas Regal Scotch Whiskey for Joseph H. Reinfeld, Inc:, in its bonded warehouse. The warehouse receipt issued to Reinfeld limited Griswold and Bateman's liability for negligence to 250 times the monthly storage rate, a total of $1,925. When Reinfeld sent its truck to pick up the whiskey, 40 cases were missing. Reinfeld then brought suit seeking the wholesale market value of the whiskey, $6,417.60. Reinfeld presented evidence of the delivery of the whiskey, the demand for its return, and the failure of Griswold and Bateman to return it. Reinfeld claimed that the burden was on Griswold and Bateman to explain the disappearance of the whiskey. Griswold and Bateman admitted that it had been negligent, but sought to limit its liability to $1,925: Is Griswold and Bateman's liability limited to $1,925?

Online Research: What Should You Do If You Find Valuable Property?

Use the Internet to determine whether your state has a law dealing with unclaimed or e-stray property. If you find a valuable item that appears to have been lost, what steps are you legally obligated to take in your state? What procedures does your state have for trying to locate the owner of such property?

24

REAL PROPERTY

Joyce and John, a married couple with two young children, are in the process of buying a house. They made an offer on a single-family house in Greenwood, a new subdivision. The house has four bedrooms, one with custom-built bunk beds in it, four bathrooms, a swimming pool, and a large basement. There is a well-equipped kitchen and a large dining room with a vintage Tiffany lamp over the dining room table. The basement is perfect for Joyce, who plans to operate a small day care center in the house. Joyce and John notice that the next-door neighbors, the Fieldings, have been dumping their garden refuse in a ravine at the back of the property that they have offered to buy, but they assume that they will be able to stop that practice once they move in.

• Are the bunk beds and Tiffany lamp considered to be part of the real property that Joyce and John have offered to buy?

• If their offer is accepted, how will Joyce and John share ownership of the property? What form of ownership will they have?

• What are the steps involved in purchasing this property?

• What rights might others, such as the Fieldings, have in the property?

• What liability might John and Joyce have to others who are injured on their property?

• What controls does the legal system place on the use of property?

LAND'S SPECIAL IMPORTANCE IN the law has long been recognized. In the agrarian society of previous eras, land served as the basic measure and source of wealth. In today's society, land functions not only as a source of food, clothing, and shelter but also as an instrument of commercial and industrial development. It is not surprising, then, that a complex body of law—the law of *real property*—exists regarding the ownership, acquisition, and use of land.

This chapter discusses the scope of real property and the various legal interests in it. In addition, the chapter examines the ways in which real property is transferred and the controls society places on an owner's use of real property.

Scope of Real Property

Real property includes not only land but also things firmly attached to or embedded in land. Buildings and other permanent structures thus are considered real property. The owner of a tract of real property also owns the air above it, the minerals below its surface, and any trees or other vegetation growing on the property.[1]

---

[1]Ownership of air above one's property is not an unlimited interest, however. Courts have held that the flight of aircraft above property does not violate the property owner's rights, so long as it does not unduly interfere with the owner's enjoyment of her land.

Unlike readily movable personal property, real property is immovable or attached to something immovable. Distinguishing between real and personal property is important because rules of law governing real property transactions such as sale, taxation, and inheritance are frequently different from those applied to personal property transactions.

Fixtures

An item of personal property may, however, be attached to or used in conjunction with real property in such a way that it ceases being personal property and instead becomes part of the real property. This type of property is called a **fixture.**

Fixtures belong to the owner of the real property. One who provides or attaches fixtures to real property without a request to that effect from the owner of the real property is normally not entitled to compensation from the owner. A conveyance (transfer of ownership) of real property also transfers the fixtures associated with that property, even if the fixtures are not specifically mentioned.

People commonly install items of personal property on the real property they own or rent. Disputes may arise regarding rights to such property. Suppose that Jacobsen buys an elaborate ceiling fan and installs it in his home. When he sells the house to Orr, may Jacobsen remove the ceiling fan, or is it part of the home Orr has bought? Suppose that Luther, a commercial tenant, installs showcases and tracklights in the store she leases from Nelson. May Luther remove the showcases and the lights when her lease expires, or do the items now belong to Nelson? If the parties' contracts are silent on these matters, courts will resolve the cases by applying the law of fixtures. As later discussion will reveal, Jacobsen probably cannot remove the ceiling fan because it is likely to be considered part of the real property purchased by Orr. Luther, on the other hand, may be entitled to remove the showcases and the lights under the special rules governing trade fixtures.

Factors Indicating Whether an Item Is a Fixture There is no mechanical formula for determining whether an item has become a fixture. Courts tend to consider these factors:

1. *Attachment.* One factor helping to indicate whether an item is a fixture is the degree to which the item is at-

tached or **annexed** to real property. If firmly attached to real property so that it cannot be removed without damaging the property, the item is likely to be considered a fixture. An item of personal property that may be removed with little or no injury to the property is less likely to be considered a fixture.

Actual physical attachment to real property is not necessary, however. A close physical connection between an item of personal property and certain real property may enable a court to conclude that the item is **constructively annexed.** For example, heavy machinery or remote control devices for automatic garage doors may be considered fixtures even though they are not physically attached to real property.

2. *Adaptation.* Another factor to be considered is **adaptation**—the degree to which the item's use is necessary or beneficial to the use of the real property. Adaptation is a particularly relevant factor when the item is not physically attached to the real property or is only slightly attached. When an item would be of little value except for use with certain real property, the item is likely to be considered a fixture even if it is unattached or could easily be removed. For example, keys and custom-sized window screens and storm windows have been held to be fixtures.

3. *Intent.* The third factor to be considered is the intent of the person who installed the item. Intent is judged not by what that person subjectively intended, but by what the circumstances indicate he intended. To a great extent, intent is indicated by the annexation and adaptation factors. An owner of real property who improves it by attaching items of personal property presumably intended those items to become part of the real estate. If the owner does not want an attached item to be considered a fixture, he must specifically reserve the right to keep the item. For instance, if a seller of a house wants to keep an antique chandelier that has been installed in the house, she should either replace the chandelier before the house is shown to prospective purchasers or specify in the contract of sale that the chandelier will be excluded from the sale.

The following *Estate of Parker* case compares the common law factors usually used to determine if an item is a fixture with a state statute determining whether mobile homes have become real property.

Estate of Parker v. Parker   *25 S.W.3d 611 (Mo. Ct. App. 2000)*

Rosa and Charles Parker were married in 1991. In that same year, they purchased an Atlanta mobile home with funds that had been Charles's prior to the marriage. They intended to affix the home to Charles's property permanently and make it their home. The mobile home was installed on property that Charles owned solely. Charles and Rosa removed the mobile home's axles and wheels and placed it on a permanent cinder block foundation. They added a screened porch to the north side of the mobile home. The roof line for the screened-in porch and the mobile home are flush.

Charles died without a will in 1997, and Rosa and his three children, Ray Parker, Susan Green, and Mary Wright, survived him. The original certificate of title to the mobile home was not available, but after Charles's death, Rosa obtained a certificate of title reflecting ownership in her name alone. She continued to live in the mobile home. As administrator of Charles's estate, Rosa filed an inventory of the personal property in the estate. She did not list the mobile home as an asset of the estate. Charles's three children filed a petition for discovery of assets, alleging that Charles's estate was entitled to the mobile home and the fair rental value of such mobile home from the date of his death to the present time. The trial court found that the mobile home did not become part of Charles's real property under a Missouri statute that details how mobile homes are converted to real property. As such, it ruled in favor of Rosa. Charles's children appealed.

HOWARD, Presiding Judge   A person converts his mobile home from personal to real property by causing the mobile home to become a fixture. A fixture is an article of the nature of personal property which has been so annexed to the realty that it is regarded as a part of the land and partakes of the legal incidents of the freehold and belongs to the person owning the land. Under the common law, the elements of a fixture are annexation to the realty, adaptation to the location, and intent of the annexor.

Section 700.111, titled "Conversion of manufactured home to real property, procedure—conversion prohibits other classification by political subdivision," states: "1. The owner of a manufactured home may convert the manufactured home to real property by: (1) Attaching the manufactured home to a permanent foundation situated on real estate owned by the manufactured home owner; and (2) The removal or modification of the transporting apparatus including but not limited to wheels, axles and hitches rendering it impractical to reconvert the real property thus created to a manufactured home." Comparing this method of statutory conversion to the common law, we see that the legislature retained the common law elements of annexation to the realty, subsection (1), and adaptation to the location, subsection (2). However, the common law element concerning the annexor's intent does not appear in the statute. In its place is the statutory element requiring the annexation to be real estate owned by the mobile home owner.

Charles's children argue that the mobile home was a fixture which had been intentionally attached or permanently annexed to the real estate according to the common law. They assert that §700.111's use of the word "may" in setting forth the method for conversion of a mobile home to real property necessarily means that it is not the sole method for doing so. Charles's children contend that the common law elements of a fixture are still a means whereby a mobile home may be converted to real property, because the legislature did not intend for §700.111 to abrogate the common law. We reject that argument. "Use of the word 'may' in a statute implies alternate possibilities and that the conferee of the power has discretion in the exercise of the power." In this case, the conferee is the mobile home owner. As used in 700.111.1, "may" is followed by the requirements for conversion of the mobile home to real property. Thus, the mobile home owner has two alternatives—he may either convert his mobile home to real property according to the statute or he may retain the mobile home as his personal property. We believe that the legislature's express direction that the common law elements cannot be used to *defeat* conversion of the mobile home to real property according to the statute necessarily implies that the common law cannot be used by a mobile home owner to *establish* conversion. Finally, in reviewing our statutes, we also consider that there is another statute that deals with the status of a mobile home being classified as personal property or real property. Section 137.115.6, relating to assessment of levy and property taxes, states in relevant part, "[a] manufactured home located in a manufactured home rental park, rental community, or *on real estate not owned by the manufactured home owner* shall be considered personal property. A manufactured home *located on real estate owned by the manufactured home owner* may be considered real property." We believe that this statute's emphasis on whether the mobile home is placed on real estate owned by the mobile home owner as determinative of how it may be treated for property tax purposes also evidences the legislature's intent to abrogate the common law conversion elements in favor of the elements set forth in §700.111. By necessary implication, §700.111's conversion elements abrogate the common law elements of conversion of a mobile home to real property.

The probate judge did not err in finding the mobile home was not an asset of Charles's estate.

Affirmed in favor of Rosa Parker.

Express Agreement If the parties to an express agreement have clearly stated their intent about whether a particular item is to be considered a fixture, a court will generally enforce that agreement. For example, the buyer and seller of a house might agree to permit the seller to remove a fence or shrubbery that would otherwise be considered a fixture.

Trade Fixtures An exception to the usual fixture rules is recognized when a tenant attaches personal property to leased premises for the purpose of carrying on her trade or business. Such fixtures, called **trade fixtures,** remain the tenant's personal property and may normally be removed at the termination of the lease. This trade fixtures exception encourages commerce and industry. It recognizes that the commercial tenant who affixed the item of personal property did not intend a permanent improvement of the leased premises.

The tenant's right to remove trade fixtures is subject to two limitations. First, the tenant cannot remove the fixtures if doing so would cause substantial damage to the landlord's realty. Second, the tenant must remove the fixtures by the end of the lease if the lease is for a definite period. If the lease is for an indefinite period, the tenant usually has a reasonable time after the expiration of the lease to remove the fixtures. Trade fixtures not removed within the appropriate time become the landlord's property.

CONCEPT REVIEW

Fixtures

Concept	A *fixture* is an item of personal property attached to or used in conjunction with real property in such a way that it is treated as being part of the real property.
Significance	A transfer of the real property will also convey the fixtures on that property.
Factors Considered in Determining Whether Property Is a Fixture	1. Attachment: Is the item physically attached or closely connected to the real property? 2. Adaptation: How necessary or beneficial is the item to the use of the real property? 3. Intent: Did the person who installed the item manifest intent for the property to become part of the real property?
Express Agreement	Express agreements clearly stating intent about whether property is a fixture are generally enforceable.
Trade Fixtures (Tenants' Fixtures)	Definition of *trade fixture:* personal property attached to leased real property by a tenant for the purpose of carrying on his trade or business. Trade fixtures can be removed and retained by the tenant at the termination of the lease except when any of the following applies: 1. Removal would cause substantial damage to the landlord's real property. 2. The tenant fails to remove the fixtures by the end of the lease (or within a reasonable time, if the lease is for an indefinite period of time). 3. An express agreement between the landlord and tenant provides otherwise.

Leases may contain terms expressly addressing the parties' rights in any fixtures. A lease might give the tenant the right to attach items or make other improvements, and to remove them later. The reverse may also be true. The lease could state that any improvements made or fixtures attached will become the landlord's property at the termination of the lease. Courts generally enforce parties' agreements on fixture ownership.

Security Interests in Fixtures Special rules apply to personal property subject to a lien or security interest at the time it is attached to real property. Assume, for example, that a person buys a dishwasher on a time-payment plan from an appliance store and has it installed in his kitchen. To protect itself, the appliance store takes a security interest in the dishwasher and perfects that interest by filing a financing statement in the appropriate real estate records office within the period of time specified by the Uniform Commercial Code. The appliance store then is able to remove the dishwasher if the buyer defaults in his payments. The store could be liable, however, to third parties such as prior real estate mortgagees for any damage removal of the dishwasher caused to the real estate. The rules governing security interests in personal property that will become fixtures are explained more fully in Chapter 29.

Rights and Interests in Real Property

When we think of real property ownership, we normally envision one person owning all of the rights in a particular piece of land. Real property, however, involves a bundle of rights subject to ownership—sometimes by different people. This discussion examines the most common forms of present *possessory interests* (rights to exclusive possession of real property): **fee simple absolute** and **life estate.** It also explores the ways in which two or more persons may share ownership of a possessory interest. Finally, it discusses the interests and rights one may have in another person's real property, such as the right to use the property or restrict the way the owner uses it.

Estates in Land

The term **estate** is used to describe the nature of a person's ownership interest in real property. Estates in land are classified as either **freehold estates** or **nonfreehold estates.** Nonfreehold (or leasehold) estates are those held by persons who lease real property. They will be discussed in the next chapter, which deals with landlord–tenant law. Freehold estates are ownership interests of uncertain duration. The most common types of freehold estates are fee simple absolute and life estates.

Fee Simple Absolute The **fee simple absolute** is what we normally think of as "full ownership" of land. One who owns real property in fee simple absolute has the right to possess and use the property for an unlimited period of time, subject only to governmental regulations or private restrictions. She also has the unconditional power to dispose of the property during her lifetime or upon her death. A person who owns land in fee simple absolute may grant many rights to others without giving up ownership. For example, she may grant a mortgage on the property to a party who has loaned her money, lease the property to a tenant, or grant rights such as those to be discussed later in this section.

Life Estate The property interest known as a **life estate** gives a person the right to possess and use property for a time measured by his or another person's lifetime. For example, if Haney has a life estate (measured by his life) in a tract of land known as Greenacre, he has the right to use Greenacre for the remainder of his life. At Haney's death, the property will revert to the person who conveyed the estate to him or will pass to some other designated person. Although a life tenant has the right to use the property, he is obligated not to commit acts that would result in permanent injury to the property.

Co-Ownership of Real Property

Co-ownership of real property exists when two or more persons share the same ownership interest in certain property. The co-owners do not have separate rights to any portion of the real property; each has a share in the whole property. Seven types of co-ownership are recognized in the United States.

Tenancy in Common Persons who own property under a **tenancy in common** have undivided interests in the property and equal rights to possess it. When property is transferred to two or more persons without specification of their co-ownership form, it is presumed that they acquire the property as tenants in common. The respective ownership interests of tenants in common may be, but need not be, equal. One tenant, for example, could have a two-thirds ownership interest in the property, with the other tenant having a one-third interest.

Each tenant in common has the right to possess and use the property. Individual tenants, however, cannot exclude the other tenants in common from also possessing and using the property. If the property is rented or otherwise produces income, each tenant is entitled to share in the income in proportion to her ownership share. Similarly, each tenant must pay her proportionate share of property taxes and necessary repair costs. If a tenant in sole possession of the property receives no rents or profits from the property, she is not required to pay rent to her cotenant unless her possession is adverse to or inconsistent with her cotenant's property interests.

A tenant in common may dispose of his interest in the property during life and at death. Similarly, his interest is subject to his creditors' claims. When a tenant dies, his interest passes to his heirs or, if he has made a will, to the person or persons specified in the will. Suppose Peterson and Sievers own Blackacre as tenants in common. Sievers dies, having executed a valid will in which he leaves his Blackacre interest to Johanns. In this situation, Peterson and Johanns become tenants in common.

Tenants in common may sever the cotenancy by agreeing to divide the property or, if they are unable to agree, by petitioning a court for *partition*. The court will physically divide the property if that is feasible, so that each tenant receives her proportionate share. If physical division is not feasible, the court will order that the property be sold and that the proceeds be appropriately divided.

Joint Tenancy   A **joint tenancy** is created when equal interests in real property are conveyed to two or more persons by means of a document clearly specifying that they are to own the property as joint tenants. The rights of use, possession, contribution, and partition are the same for a joint tenancy as for a tenancy in common. The joint tenancy's distinguishing feature is that it gives the owners the **right of survivorship,** which means that upon the death of a joint tenant, the deceased tenant's interest automatically passes to the surviving joint tenant(s). The right of survivorship makes it easy for a person to transfer property at death without the need for a will. For example, Devaney and Osborne purchase Redacre and take title as joint tenants. At Devaney's death, his Redacre interest will pass to Osborne even if Devaney did not have a will setting forth such an intent. Moreover, even if Devaney had a will that purported to leave his Redacre interest to someone other than

Osborne, the will's Redacre provision would be ineffective.

When the document of conveyance contains ambiguous language, a court may be faced with determining whether persons acquired ownership of real property as joint tenants or, instead, as tenants in common.

A joint tenant may mortgage, sell, or give away her interest in the property during her lifetime. Her interest in the property is subject to her creditors' claims. When a joint tenant transfers her interest, the joint tenancy is severed and a tenancy in common is created as to the share affected by the transaction. When a joint tenant sells her interest to a third person, the purchaser becomes a tenant in common with the remaining joint tenant(s).

Tenancy by the Entirety   Approximately half of the states permit married couples to own real property under a **tenancy by the entirety.** This tenancy is essentially a joint tenancy with the added requirement that the owners be married. As does the joint tenancy, the tenancy by the entirety features the right of survivorship. Neither spouse can transfer the property by will if the other is still living. Upon the death of the husband or wife, the property passes automatically to the surviving spouse.[2]

A tenancy by the entirety cannot be severed by the act of only one of the parties. Neither spouse can transfer the property unless the other also signs the deed. Thus, a creditor of one tenant cannot claim an interest in that person's share of property held in tenancy by the entirety. Divorce, however, severs a tenancy by the entirety and transforms it into a tenancy in common. Figure 1 compares the features of tenancy in common, joint tenancy, and tenancy by the entirety.

Community Property   A number of western and southern states recognize the **community property** system of co-ownership of property by married couples. This type of co-ownership assumes that marriage is a partnership in which each spouse contributes to the family's property base. Property acquired during the marriage through a spouse's industry or efforts is classified as *community* property. Each spouse has an equal interest in such property regardless of who produced or earned the property. Because each spouse has an equal share in community property, neither can convey community property without the other's joining in the

---

[2]In states that do not recognize the tenancy by the entirety, married couples often own real property in joint tenancy, but they are not required to elect that co-ownership form.

Figure 1   *Tenancy in Common, Joint Tenancy, and Tenancy by the Entirety*

	Tenancy in Common	Joint Tenancy	Tenancy by the Entirety
Equal Possession and Use?	Yes	Yes	Yes
Share Income?	Yes	Yes	Presumably
Contribution Requirement?	Generally	Generally	Generally
Free Conveyance of Interest?	Yes; transferee becomes tenant in common	Yes, but joint tenancy is severed on conveyance and reverts to tenancy in common	Both must agree; divorce severs tenancy
Effect of Death?	Interest transferable at death by will or inheritance	Right of survivorship; surviving joint tenant takes decedent's share	Right of survivorship; surviving spouse takes decedent's share

transaction. Various community property states permit the parties to dispose of their interests in community property at death. The details of each state's community property system vary, depending on the specific provisions of that state's statutes.

Not all property owned by a married person is community property, however. Property a spouse owned before marriage or acquired during marriage by gift or inheritance is *separate* property. Neither spouse owns a legal interest in the other's separate property. Property exchanged for separate property also remains separately owned.

Tenancy in Partnership When a partnership takes title to property in the partnership's name, the co-ownership form is called **tenancy in partnership.** This form of co-ownership is discussed in Chapter 36.

Condominium Ownership Condominiums have become very common in the United States in recent years, even in locations outside urban and resort areas. Under condominium ownership, a purchaser takes title to her individual unit and becomes a tenant in common with other unit owners in shared facilities such as hallways, elevators, swimming pools, and parking areas. The condominium owner pays property taxes on her individual unit and makes a monthly payment for the maintenance of the common areas. She may generally mortgage or sell her unit without the other unit owners' approval. For federal income tax purposes, the condominium owner is treated as if she owned a single-family

home, and is thus allowed to deduct her property taxes and mortgage interest expenses.

Cooperative Ownership In a cooperative, a building is owned by a corporation or group of persons. One who wants to buy an apartment in the building purchases stock in the corporation and holds his apartment under a long-term, renewable lease called a *proprietary lease.* Frequently, the cooperative owner must obtain the other owners' approval to sell or sublease his unit.

Interests in Real Property Owned by Others

In various situations, a person may hold a legally protected interest in someone else's real property. Such interests, to be discussed below, are not possessory because they do not give their holder the right to complete dominion over the land. Rather, they give him the right to use another person's property or to limit the way in which the owner uses the property.

Easements

An **easement** is the right to make certain uses of another person's property (*affirmative easement*) or the right to prevent another person from making certain uses of his own property (*negative easement*). The right to run a sewer line across someone else's property would be an affirmative easement. Suppose an easement prevents

Rogers from erecting, on his land, a structure that would block his neighbor McFeely's solar collector. Such an easement would be negative in nature.

If an easement qualifies as an **easement appurtenant,** it will pass with the land. This means that if the owner of the land benefited by an easement appurtenant sells or otherwise conveys the property, the new owner also acquires the right contemplated by the easement. An easement appurtenant is primarily designed to benefit a certain tract of land, rather than merely giving an individual a personal right. For example, Agnew and Nixon are next-door neighbors. They share a common driveway that runs along the borderline of their respective properties. Each has an easement in the portion of the driveway that lies on the other's property. If Agnew sells his property to Ford, Ford also obtains the easement in the driveway portion on Nixon's land. Nixon, of course, still has an easement in the driveway portion on Ford's land.

Creation of Easements

Easements may be acquired in the following ways:

1. *By grant.* When an owner of property expressly provides an easement to another while retaining ownership of the property, he is said to **grant** an easement. For example, Monroe may sell or give Madison, who owns adjoining property, the right to go across Monroe's land to reach an alley behind that land.

2. *By reservation.* When one transfers ownership of her land but retains the right to use it for some specified purpose, she is said to **reserve** an easement in the land. For example, Smythe sells land to Jones but reserves the mineral rights to the property as well as an easement to enter the land to remove the minerals.

3. *By prescription.* An **easement by prescription** is created when one person uses another's land openly, continuously, and in a manner adverse to the owner's rights for a period of time specified by state statute. The necessary period of time varies from state to state. In such a situation, the property owner presumably is on notice that someone else is acting as if she possesses rights to use the property. If the property owner does not take action during the statutory period to stop the other person from making use of his property, he may lose his right to stop that use. Suppose, for instance, that State X allows easements by prescription to be obtained through 15 years of prescriptive use. Tara, who lives in State X, uses the driveway of her next-door neighbor, Kyle. Tara does this openly, on a daily basis, and without Kyle's permission. If this use by Tara continues for the 15-year period es-

tablished by statute and Kyle takes no action to stop Tara within that time span, Tara will obtain an easement by prescription. In that event, Tara will have the right to use the driveway not only while Kyle owns the property but also when Kyle sells the property to another party. Easements by prescription resemble *adverse possession,* a concept discussed later in this chapter.

4. *By implication.* Sometimes, easements are implied by the nature of the transaction rather than created by express agreement of the parties. Such easements, called **easements by implication,** take either of two forms: easements by prior use and easements by necessity.

An *easement by prior use* may be created when land is subdivided and a path, road, or other apparent and beneficial use exists as of the time that a portion of the land is conveyed to another person. In this situation, the new owner of the conveyed portion of the land has an easement to continue using the path, road, or other prior use running across the nonconveyed portion of the land. Assume, for example, that a private road runs through Greenacre from north to south, linking the house located on Greenacre's northern portion to the public highway that lies south of Greenacre. Douglas, the owner of Greenacre, sells the northern portion to Kimball. On these facts, Kimball has an easement by implication to continue using the private road even where it runs across the portion of Greenacre retained by Douglas. To prevent such an easement from arising, Douglas and Kimball would need to have specified in their contract of sale that the easement would not exist.

An *easement by necessity* is created when real property once held in common ownership is subdivided in such a fashion that the only reasonable way a new owner can gain access to her land is through passage over another's land that was once part of the same tract. Such an easement is based on the necessity of obtaining access to property. Assume, for instance, that Tinker, the owner of Blackacre, sells Blackacre's northern 25 acres to Evers and its southern 25 acres to Chance. In order to have any reasonable access to her property, Chance must use a public road that runs alongside and just beyond the northern border of the land now owned by Evers; Chance must then go across Evers's property to reach hers. On these facts, Chance is entitled to an easement by necessity to cross Evers's land in order to go to and from her property.

Easements and the Statute of Frauds As interests in land, easements are potentially within the coverage of the statute of frauds. To be enforceable, an express agreement granting or reserving an easement must be evidenced by a suitable writing signed by the party to be charged.[3] An express grant of an easement normally must be executed with the same formalities observed in executing the grant of a fee simple interest. However, easements not granted expressly (such as easements by prior use, necessity, or prescription) are enforceable despite the lack of a writing.

Profits

A **profit** is a right to enter another person's land and remove some product or part of the land. Timber, gravel, minerals, and oil are among the products and parts frequently made the subject of profits. Generally governed by the same rules applicable to easements, profits are sometimes called *easements with a profit.*

Licenses

A **license** is a temporary right to enter another's land for a specific purpose. Ordinarily, licenses are more informal than easements. Licenses may be created orally or in any other manner indicating the landowner's permission for the licensee to enter the property. Because licenses are considered to be personal rights, they are not true interests in land. The licensor normally may revoke a license at his will. Exceptions to this general rule of revocability arise when the license is coupled with an interest (such as the licensee's ownership of personal property located on the licensor's land) or when the licensee has paid money or provided something else of value either for the license or in reliance on its existence. For example, Branch pays Leif $900 for certain trees on Leif's land. Branch is to dig up the trees and haul them to her own property for transplanting. Branch has an irrevocable license to enter Leif's land to dig up and haul away the trees.

Restrictive Covenants

Within certain limitations, real estate owners may create enforceable agreements that restrict the use of real property. These private agreements are called **restrictive covenants.** For example, Grant owns two adjacent lots. She sells one to Lee subject to the parties' agreement that Lee will not operate any liquor-selling business on the property. This use restriction appears in the deed Grant furnishes Lee. As another illustration, a subdivision developer sells lots in the subdivision and places a provision in each lot's deed regarding the minimum size of house to be built on the property.

The validity and enforceability of such private restrictions on the use of real property depend on the purpose, nature, and scope of the restrictions. A restraint that violates a statute or other expression of public policy will not be enforced. For example, the federal Fair Housing Act (discussed later in this chapter) would make unlawful an attempt by a seller or lessor of residential property to refuse to sell or rent to certain persons because of an existing restrictive covenant that purports to disqualify those prospective buyers or renters on the basis of their race, color, religion, sex, handicap, familial status, or national origin.

Public policy generally favors the unlimited use and transfer of land. A restrictive covenant therefore is unenforceable if it effectively prevents the sale or transfer of the property. Similarly, ambiguous language in a restrictive covenant is construed in favor of the less restrictive interpretation. A restraint is enforceable, however, if it is clearly expressed and neither unduly restrictive of the use and transfer of the property nor otherwise violative of public policy. Restrictions usually held enforceable include those relating to minimum lot size, building design and size, and maintenance of an area as a residential community.

An important and frequently arising question is whether subsequent owners of property are bound by a restrictive covenant even though they were not parties to the original agreement that established the covenant. Under certain circumstances, restrictive covenants are said to "run with the land" and thus bind subsequent owners of the restricted property. For a covenant to run with the land, it must have been *binding* on the original parties to it, and those parties must have *intended that the covenant bind their successors.* The covenant must also *"touch and concern"* the restricted land. This means that the covenant must involve the use, value, or character of the land, rather than being merely a personal obligation of one of the original parties. In addition, a covenant will not bind a subsequent purchaser unless she had notice of the covenant's existence when she took her interest. This notice would commonly be provided by the recording of the deed (a subject discussed later in this chapter) or other document containing the covenant.

Restrictive covenants may be enforced by the parties to them, by persons meant to benefit from them, and—if the covenants run with the land—by successors of the original parties to them. If restrictive covenants amount-

---

[3]Chapter 16 discusses the statute of frauds and compliance with the writing requirement it imposes when it is applicable.

ing to a general building scheme are contained in a subdivision plat (recorded description of a subdivision), property owners in the subdivision may be able to enforce them against noncomplying property owners.

Mains Farm Homeowners Association illustrates the difficult interpretation, enforceability, and public policy questions sometimes presented by litigation over restrictive covenants that run with the land.

Mains Farm Homeowners Association v. Worthington
854 P.2d 1072 (Wash. Sup. Ct. 1993)

A declaration of restrictive covenants for the platted Mains Farm subdivision was recorded in 1962. Worthington purchased a residential lot in Mains Farm in 1987. A house already existed on the property. Before purchasing, Worthington obtained and read a copy of the restrictive covenants, which stated, in pertinent part, that all lots in Mains Farm "shall be designated as 'Residence Lots' and shall be used for single family residential purposes only." Worthington later began occupying the residence along with four adults who paid her for 24-hour protective supervision and care. These four adults, who were not related to Worthington, were unable to do their own housekeeping, prepare their own meals, or attend to their personal hygiene. In providing this supervision and care on a for-profit basis, Worthington complied with the licensing and inspection requirements established by Washington law governing such enterprises.

The Mains Farm Homeowners Association (Association), which consisted of owners of property in the subdivision, filed suit against Worthington and asked the court to enjoin her from using her property as an adult family home business. Association asserted that Worthington's use violated the restrictive covenants quoted above. The trial court granted Association's motion for summary judgment and issued the requested injunction against Worthington's use. The Washington Court of Appeals affirmed. Worthington appealed to the Washington Supreme Court. Various organizations representing the interests of disabled adults submitted amicus curiae (friend of the court) briefs urging reversal.

Brachtenbach, Justice *Before* defendant Worthington bought the premises, she *read* the restrictive covenants. Written opposition by other property owners was made known to her immediately after her purchase. Despite that knowledge, Worthington applied for a building permit to add a fifth bedroom to the house. She was advised by the county that her intended facility did not comply with applicable zoning. Worthington later obtained the permit by stating that only her family would be living with her. In her words: "I told them what they wanted to hear." These equitable considerations must be kept in mind when we interpret the restrictive covenants at issue here. Our analysis leads to the conclusion that Worthington's commercial use is prohibited.

To reach this conclusion, we consider the meaning of "single family." The cases interpreting "family" are legion. Any of the cases must be used with caution. Some involve a state statute which bears a different relationship to zoning powers than to vested property rights embodied in a restrictive covenant. No purpose will be served by examining and comparing in detail the numerous cases which define "family." Because of the widely differing documents being interpreted, the contexts in which the word is used, and the fact-specific circumstances, it is impossible to arrive at a single, all-purpose definition of "family." The possibilities

range from the traditional notion of persons related by blood, marriage, or adoption to the broader concept of a group of people who live, sleep, cook, and eat upon the premises as a single housekeeping unit. Likewise, attempting to use one of the many dictionary classifications solves nothing. For similar reasons, the use of a phrase or two out of a dictionary to define "residential" for purposes of this covenant is not acceptable.

Some reflection leads us to attribute certain characteristics to a concept of "family," even in an extended sense. These include: (1) a sharing of responsibilities among the members and a mutual caring whether physical or emotional, (2) some commonality whether it be friendship, shared employment, mutual social or political interest, (3) some degree of existing or contemplated permanency to the relationship, and (4) a recognition of some common purpose—persons brought together by reasons other than a referral by a state agency. Here, we have four persons, all strangers before arriving at this residence. By law, they cannot be related to Worthington by birth, adoption, or marriage. By law, they cannot be below the age of 18. By regulatory definition, they must require 24-hour protective supervision and care. Worthington could not form this "family" without a license from the State, which must approve the site and is free to inspect it. Worthington meets these qualifications and provides around-the-clock care as a means of making a living.

These are not the characteristics of a single family residence. Our primary goal is to ascertain the intent of the restrictive covenants and to accord the words their ordinary and common usage. The reasonable expectations of the other lot owners who bought their family houses in reliance on the long recorded covenants would not include a State-licensed, 24-hour operating business. In this case, Worthington's main use of her property is not to provide a single family residence, but to provide 24-hour protective care and supervision in exchange for money. It must therefore be concluded that the other lot owners are entitled in equity to the injunction granted by the trial court.

As an alternative ground for reversing the trial court, Worthington argues that the restrictive covenant violates a legislative declaration of public policy and is therefore void. The public policy question should not be resolved in this case, for various reasons. First, the record made in the trial court is not adequate to identify the facts and bases upon which such a significant public policy should be considered. It is true that the Legislature has found "that adult family homes are an important part of the state's long-term care system" [citation to statute omitted]. Unfortunately, this record shows little more. We know that the Legislature has not implemented this finding beyond declaring that such homes are considered residential for *zoning* purposes. We know nothing of the number of persons qualified for adult family homes or of whether that need is being met. We know nothing of the situation along those lines in the community or county in which the Mains Farm subdivision is located. We do not know whether there exists an adequate supply of adult family homes in areas not subject to restrictive covenants. We are unaware whether efforts by individual or governmental units have been successful in locating such homes either without neighborhood opposition or by suc-

cessful negotiation with concerned owners. We have not been made aware of what coordinated efforts, if any, are being made by state or local agencies to establish adult family homes. All of these considerations would be relevant to any possible court finding that a significant public policy overrides the existing restrictive covenants at issue in this case.

In addition, the statute relied upon by Worthington as the source of a legislative declaration of public policy favoring adult family homes was not effective until after the written opinion of the trial court, and was not cited to the trial court. Moreover, the statute, in stating that an adult family home should be permitted in an area zoned for single-family dwellings, is by its very terms limited to *zoning*. When the Legislature intends to affect a *private land use restriction* (i.e., a covenant) as compared to *zoning,* it normally does so explicitly.

The cases from other jurisdictions cited by Worthington either do not reach the policy conflict presented here or are based upon entirely different statutory direction or even constitutional dictates. The various *amici curiae* raise a claimed violation of the federal Fair Housing Act. We do not consider issues raised first and only by *amicus*.

We hold that under the equities of these particular facts, the discretionary grant of an injunction was proper. We caution that the interpretation of a particular restrictive covenant is largely dependent upon the facts of the case at hand. Our holding should not be construed as an encompassing declaration concerning covenants and uses under other circumstances. Likewise, our rejection of the claimed public policy is limited to the facts herein, especially due to the record's lack of any comprehensive presentation of governmental goals, efforts, needs, and successes existing in fact.

Injunction in favor of Association and against Worthington's use of property affirmed.

Termination of Restrictive Covenants Restrictive covenants may be terminated in a variety of ways, including voluntary relinquishment or *waiver.* They may also be terminated *by their own terms* (such as when the covenant specifies that it is to exist for a certain length of time) or *by dramatically changed circumstances.* If Oldcodger's property is subject, for instance, to a

restrictive covenant allowing only residential use, the fact that all of the surrounding property has come to be used for industrial purposes may operate to terminate the covenant. When a restrictive covenant has been terminated or held invalid, the deed containing the restriction remains a valid instrument of transfer but is treated as if the restriction had been removed from the document.

Acquisition of Real Property

Title to real property may be obtained in various ways, including purchase, gift, will or inheritance, tax sale, and adverse possession. Original title to land in the United States was acquired either from the federal government or from a country that held the land prior to its acquisition by the United States. The land in the 13 original colonies had been granted by the king of England either to the colonies or to certain individuals. The states ceded the land in the Northwest Territory to the federal government, which in turn issued grants or patents of land. Original ownership of much of the land in Florida and the southwest came by grants from Spain's rulers.

Acquisition by Purchase

Selling one's real property is a basic ownership right. Unreasonable restrictions on an owner's right to sell her property are considered unenforceable because they violate public policy. Most owners of real property acquired title by purchasing the property. Each state sets the requirements for proper conveyances of real property located in that state. The various elements of selling and buying real property are discussed later in this chapter.

Acquisition by Gift

Real property ownership may be acquired by gift. For a gift of real property to be valid, the donor must deliver a properly executed deed to the donee or to some third person who is to hold it for the donee. Neither the donee nor the third person needs to take actual possession of the property. The gift's essential element is delivery of the deed. Suppose that Fields executes a deed to the family farm and leaves it in his safe-deposit box for delivery to his daughter (the intended donee) when he dies. The attempted gift will not be valid, because Fields did not deliver the gift during his lifetime.

Acquisition by Will or Inheritance

The owner of real property generally has the right to dispose of the property by will. The requirements for a valid will are discussed in Chapter 26. If the owner of real property dies without a valid will, the property passes to his heirs as determined under the laws of the state in which the property is located.

Acquisition by Tax Sale

If taxes assessed on real property are not paid when due, they become a *lien* on the property. This lien has priority over other claims to the land. If the taxes remain unpaid, the government may sell the land at a tax sale. Although the purchaser at the tax sale acquires title to the property, a number of states have statutes giving the original owner a limited time (such as a year) within which to buy the property from the tax sale purchaser for the price paid by the purchaser, plus interest.

Acquisition by Adverse Possession

Each state has a statute of limitations that gives an owner of land a specific number of years within which to bring suit to regain possession of her land from someone who is trespassing on it. This period varies from state to state, generally ranging from 5 to 20 years. If someone wrongfully possesses land and acts as if he were the owner, the actual owner must take steps to have the possessor ejected from the land. If the owner fails to do this within the statutory period, she loses her right to eject the possessor.

Assume, for example, that Titus owns a vacant lot next to Holdeman's house. Holdeman frequently uses the vacant lot for a variety of activities and appears to be the property's only user. In addition, Holdeman regularly mows and otherwise maintains the vacant lot. He has also placed a fence around it. By continuing such actions and thus staying in possession of Titus's property for the statutory period (and by meeting each other requirement about to be discussed), Holdeman may position himself to acquire title to the land by **adverse possession.**

To acquire title by adverse possession, one must possess land in a manner that puts the true owner on notice of the owner's cause of action against the possessor. The adverse possessor's acts of possession must be (1) *open,* (2) *actual,* (3) *continuous,* (4) *exclusive,* and (5) *hostile (or adverse) to the owner's rights.* The hostility element is not a matter of subjective intent. Rather, it means that the adverse possessor's acts of possession must be inconsistent with the owner's rights. If a person is in possession of another's property under a lease, as a cotenant, or with the permission of the owner, his possession is not hostile. In some states, the possessor of land must also pay the property taxes in order to gain title by adverse possession.

It is not necessary that the same person occupy the land for the statutory period. The periods of possession of several adverse possessors may be "tacked" together when calculating the period of possession if each possessor claimed rights from another possessor. The possession must, however, be continuous for the requisite time.

The following *Vezey* case applies these criteria for adverse possession.

Vezey v. Green 35 P.3d 14 (Alaska Sup. Ct. 2001)

In 1982, Angela Green's grandmother, Billie Harrild, offered Green a piece of the family's land near Shaw Creek. Billie was declining in health and wanted her granddaughter to have a home near the Harrilds' own. Green selected a parcel of land on a bluff, across Shaw Creek from her grandparents' house. The alleged gift was not recorded, and Billie and Elden Harrild, the grandparents, and John Harrild, a cousin, remained the owners of record. However, according to Green's testimony, in the 10 years following her entry onto the property, all three "absolutely" recognized the land as hers. Neighbors testified that Billie consistently referred to the land as Green's property.

Elden and Billie Harrild died in the winter of 1995–1996. Between 1982 and 1992, Green gradually built a house and cultivated grounds on the bluff. She worked on the property over the summers, and worked as a nurse and glassmaker in California for the rest of the year. In 1982, she planned the site of her house and cleared trees on the lot. In the summers of 1983 and 1984, she lived in a camper on the property, cleared more trees and stumps, and oversaw hand excavation for the foundation of the house. In the following summers, she gradually expanded the cultivated section of the property, planting lilac bushes and fruit trees and installing a coop for chickens and turkeys. She and a neighbor worked on building the house itself, and beginning in 1987 Green lived in the nearly complete house during the summers. She arranged for telephone service beginning around 1985, and dealt with fire authorities to determine how far away from the house to clear trees. In 1986, Green worked in Fairbanks the whole year and visited the property by snow machine during the winter. In 1989 she lived on the property for eight or nine months. Green lived on the bluff and with her grandmother for a month and a half in the summer of 1992, but did not come to Alaska in 1993. Green left trees standing on much of the property, but cleared undergrowth and planted native plants over an area of several acres. She also cut trees from a wide area on the southern hillside in order to clear the view from the cabin. She posted "No Trespassing" signs and built benches in some areas away from the house. She put up a chain across the road entering the property, but did not fence the entire area. In 1990, the house was considerably damaged by vandalism, and Green repaired the damage when she returned to Alaska in the spring.

Green arranged with her grandparents that, for the remainder of their lives, they could extract and sell small quantities of rock from the property but she strongly opposed use of such equipment on the property. Sometime between 1988 and 1991, the Harrilds executed a contract with an extraction company, Earthmovers, allowing them to excavate rock from the family property, including the bluff. The contract apparently included an option for Earthmovers to buy the property. According to Green, Billie's mental capacities were declining at the time of this contract, and she no longer handled her own finances or affairs. Earthmovers excavated a trench on the bluff on a day when Green was not at home. When Green returned and found the workers and equipment on the property, however, she told them that they were not allowed to excavate there. Green granted the workers permission to finish the task at hand, insisted that they arrange to repair a telephone line that they had damaged, and ordered them to leave the property.

In 1988 Allen Vezey became interested in Shaw Creek area properties. Vezey approached the Harrilds about purchasing their land. In 1994, while Vezey was still in negotiations with the Harrilds, Green called him and, according to Green, she told Vezey that the land belonged to her. In the winter of 1994–1995, Vezey purchased Elden Harrild's one-third interest in a property that included the contested bluff area. After Vezey purchased the property, Green brought suit against him and others, asserting that she owned the property. After a trial, the trial court held that Green had acquired title to the entire bluff area by adverse possession. Vezey appeals.

FABE, Chief Justice Under AS 09.10.030, Green may claim title to the bluff property by adverse possession only if she shows by clear and convincing evidence that she has possessed the property for 10 consecutive years. In order to acquire title by adverse possession, the claimant must prove, by clear and convincing evidence, that for the statutory period his use of the land was continuous, open and notorious, exclusive and hostile to the true owner. Continuity, notoriety, and exclusivity of use, we explained, are not susceptible to fixed standards, but rather depend on the character of the land in question.

1.   The Statutory Period

Judge Savell found that Green had used the bluff property from 1982 through the summer of 1993, in satisfaction of AS 09.10.030's 10-year possession requirement for adverse possession. Because Green presented the most evidence of consistent use for the period running from early summer of 1983 to early summer of 1993, we base our adverse possession analysis on those 10 years. [The] evidence supports the conclusion that Green possessed the property at least from early summer of 1983 to the same season in 1993, in fulfillment of the statutory 10-year-period requirement.

2.   Continuity

Vezey argues that because Green has spent only short periods of time on the bluff property, her occupation has not been continuous. In *Nome 2000 v. Fagerstrom,* we stated that continuity required "only that the land be used for the statutory period as an average owner of similar property would use it." This flexible standard for continuous use in adverse possession claims is appropriate to Alaska's geography and climate, and is established in our jurisprudence. We found that the *Nome 2000* claimants, a family that had made periodic subsistence use of a rural parcel of land, satisfied the continuity requirement for adverse possession. In reaching this conclusion, we cited with approval a Utah case in which pasturing sheep for three weeks each year was found sufficient to adversely possess land suitable only for grazing, and a Michigan case in which six yearly visits to a hunting cabin and some timber cutting were found sufficient to possess wild and undeveloped land. In addition, where land is best suited for seasonal use, such use may satisfy the continuity requirement. The trial court heard undisputed testimony that "it'd take a fool to live up there [on the bluff property] in the cold winter months." Given the bluff's location and unsuitability for winter use, Green used the property as an average owner of similar property would and therefore meets the requirement for continuous use.

3.   Exclusivity

Vezey argues that Earthmover's use of the bluff property demonstrates that Green's claim was not exclusive. Green also allowed her relatives to take rock from the bluff property. These facts do not preclude a finding of exclusive use. Like continuity, exclusivity requires only that the land be used for the statutory period as an average owner of similar property would use it. In *Nome 2000,* the adverse possessors

of rural property allowed others to enter the land in order to pick berries and fish, but excluded a group of campers who took and burned the family's firewood. We held that allowing berry-picking and fishing was consistent with the conduct of a hospitable landowner. We did not find, or even suggest, that exclusivity of possession had been affected by the campers' actions. Green's situation is closely analogous: She allowed moderate use of her resources, but when uninvited trespassers tried to excavate rock, she ordered them off the property. As the superior court stated, Green "acted as an owner" in directing the Earthmover crew to leave. This finding meets *Nome 2000's* requirement that an adverse possessor demonstrate exclusivity by using the land "as an average owner of similar property" would use it.

4.   Notoriety

We have stated that the function of the notoriety requirement is to afford the true owner an opportunity of notice. This requirement is fulfilled when the record owner knew or should have known of the adverse possession. In this case, we need not examine the question of constructive notice, because the record owners had actual notice. During the statutory period, the record owners of the bluff property were Billie, Elden, and John Harrild. It is undisputed that all three owners knew of Green's presence on the bluff. Therefore, the notoriety requirement has been met.

5.   Hostility

In order to meet the hostility requirement, adverse possession claimants must prove both that they acted as owners and that they did not act with the true owner's permission. The determinative question is whether or not the claimant acted toward the land as if he owned it. However, the hostility requirement is not satisfied if the adverse claimant has the record owner's permission to use the property. There is a presumption that one who possesses or uses another's property does so with the owner's permission. The adverse claimant may rebut this presumption by showing that he was not on the owner's land with permission, and that the record owner could have ejected him. Because of her extensive work on the property, Green has satisfied the first requirement of using the land as if she owned it. She has also rebutted the presumption of permissive use. The trial court found that Green held the property as an owner, not a tenant or licensee. Her occupancy was not permissive because it was not dependent on the consent or permission of the Harrilds. Therefore, it was legally hostile to the record owners. As the superior court noted, the Earthmovers incident presents particularly compelling evidence that Green's possession was hostile to the interests of all others, including the Harrilds. By excluding her grandparents' contractors from the property, Green indicated that she claimed all rights to the property as her own; she did not recognize any residual interest held by the Harrilds or any subordination of her own title to theirs. Vezey argues that because Green held the bluff property as a gift from her grandparents, her possession was permissive. Therefore, he claims, she cannot meet the hostility requirement for adverse possession. We reject this argument because possession of land based on a gift is not the same as possession by permission of the true owner. A donee who accepts a gift of land asserts a property right independent of the record owner's. The possessor's use of land in these circumstances is not permissive because the possessor's claim is not subordinate to the record owner's title; it is instead an assertion of ownership in the possessor's own right. Almost all state courts concur that land transferred by parol gift may become the donee's property through adverse possession. When a record owner gives property as a gift, the gift strengthens the possessor's claims to the property by establishing that the possessor claims full ownership, and that the record owner knows of her claim. We conclude that a parol gift of land, when proven by clear and convincing evidence, establishes two presumptions

helpful to the adverse possession claimant. First, the donee's claim to the property is presumptively hostile to the donor. As we have explained of the relationship between buyers and sellers of land, once the grantor has purported to convey property, neither he nor his grantee believe that the grantee's possession is subordinate to the grantor's title. Similarly, when a gift has been made, and both the record owner and the possessor believe that the possessor owns the property, the possessor's claim is hostile.

The more serious issue raised by Vezey is whether Green actually possessed all of the land enclosed by those boundaries. The record does not, however, offer clear evidence of where Green or the record owners believed the boundaries of the bluff property to lie. We note that an adverse possessor may claim title only to that area actually possessed for the full statutory period, from the first year to the last. It is not clear that Green has demonstrated actual possession of the entire area awarded by the superior court. Although we affirm the award as to the north, east, and south areas of the property, we remand for further findings regarding the land to the west of the house.

Affirmed in part in favor of Green but remanded in part to determine the western boundary of Green's possession.

Transfer by Sale

Steps in a Sale

The major steps normally involved in the sale of real property are:

1. Contracting with a real estate broker to locate a buyer.

2. Negotiating and signing a contract of sale.

3. Arranging for the financing of the purchase and satisfying other requirements, such as having a survey conducted or acquiring title insurance.

4. Closing the sale, which involves payment of the purchase price and transfer of the deed, as well as other matters.

5. Recording the deed.

LOG ON

For a variety of articles about practical aspects of buying, selling, or owning real estate, see Nolo.com Real Estate Law Center at **http://www.nolo.com/lawcenter/ency/index.cf m/catID/AAFB97A1-F23E-4D6F-98DBD8C64C478126.**

Contracting with a Real Estate Broker

Although engaging a real estate broker is not a legal requirement for the sale of real property, it is common for one who wishes to sell his property to "list" the property with a broker. A listing contract empowers the broker to act as the seller's agent in procuring a ready, willing, and able buyer and in managing details of the property transfer. A number of states' statutes of frauds require listing contracts to be evidenced by a writing and signed by the party to be charged.

Real estate brokers are regulated by state and federal law. They owe *fiduciary duties* (duties of trust and confidence) to their clients. Chapter 35 contains additional information regarding the duties imposed on such agents.

Types of Listing Contracts Listing contracts specify such matters as the listing period's duration, the terms on which the seller will sell, and the amount and terms of the broker's commission. There are different types of listing contracts.

1. *Open listing.* Under an open listing contract, the broker receives a *nonexclusive* right to sell the property. This means that the seller and third parties (for example, other

brokers) also are entitled to find a buyer for the property. The broker operating under an open listing is entitled to a commission only if he was the first to find a ready, willing, and able buyer.

2. *Exclusive agency listing.* Under an exclusive agency listing, the broker earns a commission if he *or any other agent* finds a ready, willing, and able buyer during the period of time specified in the contract. Thus, the broker operating under such a listing would have the right to a commission even if another broker actually procured the buyer. Under the exclusive agency listing, however, the seller has the right to sell the property himself without being obligated to pay the broker a commission.

3. *Exclusive right to sell.* An exclusive right to sell contract provides the broker the exclusive right to sell the property for a specified period of time and entitles her to a commission no matter who procured the buyer. Under this type of listing, a seller must pay the broker her commission even if it was the seller or some third party who found the buyer during the duration of the listing contract.

Contract of Sale

The contract formation, performance, assignment, and remedies principles about which you read in earlier chapters apply to real estate sales contracts. Such contracts identify the parties and subject property, and set forth the purchase price, the type of deed the purchaser will receive, the items of personal property (if any) included in the sale, and other important aspects of the parties' transaction. Real estate sales contracts often make the closing of the sale contingent on the buyer's obtaining financing at a specified rate of interest, on the seller's procurement of a survey and title insurance, and on the property's passing a termite inspection. Because they are within the statute of frauds, real estate sales contracts must be evidenced by a suitable writing signed by the party to be charged in order to be enforceable.

Financing the Purchase The various arrangements for financing the purchase of real property—such as mortgages, land contracts, and deeds of trust—are discussed in Chapter 28.

Fair Housing Act

The Fair Housing Act, enacted by Congress in 1968 and substantially revised in 1988, is designed to prevent discrimination in the housing market. Its provisions apply to real estate brokers, sellers (other than those selling their

own single-family dwellings without the use of a broker), lenders, lessors, and appraisers. Originally, the act prohibited discrimination on the basis of race, color, religion, sex, and national origin. The 1988 amendments added handicap and "familial status" to this list. The familial status category was intended to prevent discrimination in the housing market against pregnant women and families with children.[4] "Adult" or "senior citizen" communities restricting residents' age do not violate the Fair Housing Act even though they exclude families with children, so long as the housing meets the requirements of the act's "housing for older persons" exemption.[5]

The act prohibits discrimination on the above-listed bases in a wide range of matters relating to the sale or rental of housing. These matters include refusals to sell or rent, representations that housing is not available for sale or rental when in fact it is, and discriminatory actions regarding terms, conditions, or privileges of sale or rental or regarding the provision of services and facilities involved in sale or rental.[6] The act also prohibits discrimination in connection with brokerage services, appraisals, and financing of dwellings.

Prohibited discrimination on the basis of handicap includes refusals to permit a handicapped person to make (at his own expense) reasonable modifications to the property. It also includes refusals to make reasonable accommodations in property-related rules, policies, practices, or services when such modifications or accommodations are necessary to afford the handicapped person full enjoyment of the property. The act also outlaws the building of multifamily housing that is inaccessible to persons with handicaps.

A violation of the Fair Housing Act may result in a civil action brought by the government or the aggrieved individual. If the aggrieved individual sues and prevails, the court may issue injunctions, award actual and punitive damages, assess attorney's fees and costs, and grant

---

[4]"Familial status" is defined as an individual or individuals under the age of 18 who is/are domiciled with a parent, some other person who has custody over him/her/them, or the designee of the parent or custodial individual. The familial status classification also applies to one who is pregnant or in the process of attempting to secure custody of a child or children under the age of 18.
[5]The Fair Housing Act defines "housing for older persons" as housing provided under any state or federal program found by the Secretary of HUD to be specifically designed to assist elderly persons, housing intended for and solely occupied by persons 62 years old or older, or housing that meets the requirements of federal regulations and is intended for occupancy by at least one person 55 years old or older.
[6]Chapter 25 discusses the Fair Housing Act's application to rentals of residential property.

other appropriate relief. Finally, the Fair Housing Act invalidates any state or municipal law requiring or permitting an action that would be a discriminatory housing practice under federal law. *City of Edmonds v. Oxford House, Inc.*, which appears later in the chapter, illustrates the role of the Fair Housing Act when a city zoning ordinance allegedly has the effect of discriminating on the basis of handicap.

Deeds

Each state's statutes set out the formalities necessary to accomplish a valid conveyance of land. As a general rule, a valid conveyance is brought about by the execution and delivery of a **deed**, a written instrument that transfers title from one person (the grantor) to another (the grantee). Three types of deeds are in general use in the United States: *quitclaim deeds, warranty deeds,* and *deeds of bargain and sale* (also called *grant deeds*). The precise rights contemplated by a deed depend on the type of deed the parties have used.

Quitclaim Deeds A **quitclaim deed** conveys whatever title the grantor has at the time he executes the deed. It does not, however, contain warranties of title. The grantor who executes a quitclaim deed does not claim to have good title—or any title, for that matter. The grantee has no action against the grantor under a quitclaim deed if the grantee does not acquire good title. Quitclaim deeds are frequently used to cure technical defects in the chain of title to property.

Warranty Deeds A **warranty deed,** unlike a quitclaim deed, contains covenants of warranty. Besides conveying title to the property, the grantor who executes a warranty deed guarantees the title she has conveyed. There are two types of warranty deeds.

 1. *General warranty deed.* Under a general warranty deed, the grantor warrants against (and agrees to defend against) all title defects and encumbrances (such as liens and easements), including those that arose before the grantor received her title.

 2. *Special warranty deed.* Under a special warranty deed, the grantor warrants against (and agrees to defend against) title defects and encumbrances that arose after she acquired the property. If the property conveyed is subject to an encumbrance such as a mortgage, a long-term lease, or an easement, the grantor frequently provides a special warranty deed that contains a provision excepting those specific encumbrances from the warranty.

Deeds of Bargain and Sale In a **deed of bargain and sale** (also known as a **grant deed**), the grantor makes no covenants. The grantor uses language such as "I grant" or "I bargain and sell" or "I convey" property. Such a deed does contain, however, the grantor's implicit representation that he owns the land and has not previously encumbered it or conveyed it to another party.

Form and Execution of Deed

Some states' statutes suggest a form for deeds. Although the requirements for execution of deeds are not uniform, they do follow a similar pattern. As a general rule, a deed states the *name of the grantee,* contains a *recitation of consideration and a description of the property conveyed,* and is *signed by the grantor.* Most states require that the deed be notarized (acknowledged by the grantor before a notary public or other authorized officer) in order to be eligible for recording in public records.

 No technical words of conveyance are necessary for a valid deed. Any language is sufficient if it indicates with reasonable certainty the grantor's intent to transfer ownership of the property. The phrases "grant, bargain, and sell" and "convey and warrant" are commonly used. Deeds contain recitations of consideration primarily for historical reasons. The consideration recited is not necessarily the purchase price of the property. Deeds often state that the consideration for the conveyance is "one dollar and other valuable consideration."

 The property conveyed must be described in such a manner that it can be identified. This usually means that the legal description of the property must be used. Several methods of legal description are used in the United States. In urban areas, descriptions are usually by lot, block, and plat. In rural areas where the land has been surveyed by the government, property is usually described by reference to the government survey. It may also be described by a metes and bounds description that specifies the boundaries of the tract of land.

Recording Deeds

Delivery of a valid deed conveys title from a grantor to a grantee. Even so, the grantee should promptly **record** the deed in order to prevent his interest from being defeated by third parties who may claim interests in the property. The grantee must pay a fee to have the deed recorded, a process that involves depositing and indexing the deed in the files of a government office designated by state law. A recorded deed operates to provide the public at large with notice of the grantee's property interest.

Recording Statutes Each state has a **recording statute** that establishes a system for the recording of all transactions affecting real property ownership. These statutes are not uniform in their provisions. In general, however, they provide for the recording of all deeds, mortgages, land contracts, and similar documents.

Types of Recording Statutes State recording statutes also provide for priority among competing claimants to rights in real property, in case conflicting rights or interests in property should be deeded to (or otherwise claimed by) more than one person. (Obviously, a grantor has no right to issue two different grantees separate deeds to the same property, but if this should occur, recording statutes provide rules to decide which grantee has superior title.) These priority rules apply only to grantees who have given value for their deeds or other interest-creating documents (primarily purchasers and lenders), and not to donees. A given state's recording law will set up one of three basic types of priority systems: race statutes, notice statutes, and race-notice statutes. Figure 2 explains these priority systems. Although the examples used in Figure 2 deal with recorded and unrecorded deeds, recording statutes apply to other documents that create interests in real estate. Chapter 28 discusses the recording of mortgages, as well as the adverse security interest–related conse-quences a mortgagee may experience if its mortgage goes unrecorded.

Methods of Assuring Title

In purchasing real property, the buyer is really acquiring the seller's ownership interests. Because the buyer does not want to pay a large sum of money for something that proves to be of little or no value, it is important for her to obtain assurance that the seller has good title to the property. This is commonly done in one of three ways:

1. *Title opinion.* In some states, it is customary to have an attorney examine an **abstract of title.** An abstract of title is a history of what the public records show regarding the passage of title to, and other interests in, a parcel of real property. It is not a guarantee of good title. After examining the abstract, the attorney renders an opinion about whether the grantor has **marketable title,** which is title free from defects or reasonable doubt about its validity. If the grantor's title is defective, the nature of the defects will be stated in the attorney's title opinion.

2. *Torrens system.* A method of title assurance available in a few states is the **Torrens system** of title registration. Under this system, one who owns land in fee simple obtains a certificate of title. When the property is sold, the grantor delivers a deed and a certificate of title to the

Figure 2	*Three Basic Types of Priority Systems for Recording Deeds*
Race Statutes	Under a race statute—so named because the person who wins the race to the courthouse wins the property ownership "competition"—the first grantee who records a deed to a tract of land has superior title. For example, if Grantor deeds Blackacre to Kerr on March 1 and to Templin on April 1, Templin will have superior title to Blackacre if she records her deed before Kerr's is recorded. Race statutes are relatively uncommon today.
Notice Statutes	Under a notice system of priority, a later grantee of property has superior title if he acquired his interest without notice of an earlier grantee's claim to the property under an unrecorded deed. For example, Grantor deeds Greenacre to Jonson on June 1, but Jonson does not record his deed. On July 1, Marlowe purchases Greenacre without knowledge of Jonson's competing claim. Grantor executes and delivers a deed to Marlowe. In this situation, Marlowe would have superior rights to Greenacre even if Jonson ultimately records his deed before Marlowe's is recorded.
Race-Notice Statutes	The race-notice priority system combines elements of the systems just discussed. Under race-notice statutes, the grantee having priority is the one who both *takes his interest without notice* of any prior unrecorded claim and *records first.* For example, Grantor deeds Redacre to Frazier on September 1. On October 1 (at which time Frazier has not yet recorded his deed), Grantor deeds Redacre to Gill, who is then unaware of any claim by Frazier to Redacre. If Gill records his deed before Frazier's is recorded, Gill has superior rights to Redacre.

grantee. All liens and encumbrances against the title are noted on the certificate, thus assuring the purchaser that the title is good except as to the liens and encumbrances noted on the certificate. However, some claims or encumbrances, such as those arising from adverse possession, do not appear on the records and must be discovered through an inspection of the property. In some Torrens states, encumbrances such as tax liens, short-term leases, and highway rights are valid against the purchaser even though they do not appear on the certificate.

3. *Title insurance.* Purchasing a policy of **title insurance** provides the preferred and most common means of protecting title to real property. Title insurance obligates the insurer to reimburse the insured grantee for loss if the title proves to be defective. In addition, title insurance covers litigation costs if the insured grantee must go to court in a title dispute. Lenders commonly require that a separate policy of title insurance be obtained for the lender's protection. Title insurance may be obtained in combination with the other previously discussed methods of ensuring title.

Seller's Responsibilities Regarding the Quality of Residential Property

Buyers of real estate normally consider it important that any structures on the property be in good condition. This factor becomes especially significant if the buyer intends to use the property for residential purposes. The rule of *caveat emptor* (let the buyer beware) traditionally applied to the sale of real property unless the seller committed misrepresentation or fraud or made express warranties about the property's condition. In addition, sellers had no duty to disclose hidden defects in the property. In recent years, however, the legal environment for sellers—especially real estate professionals such as developers and builder-vendors of residential property—has changed substantially. This section examines two important sources of liability for sellers of real property.

Implied Warranty of Habitability

Historically, sellers of residential property were not regarded as making any **implied warranty** that the property was habitable or suitable for the buyer's use. The law's attitude toward the buyer–seller relationship in residential property sales began to shift, however, as product liability law underwent rapid change in the late 1960s.

Courts began to see that the same policies favoring the creation of implied warranties in the sale of goods applied with equal force to the sale of residential real estate.[7] Both goods and housing are frequently mass-produced. The disparity of knowledge and bargaining power often existing between a buyer of goods and a professional seller is also likely to exist between a buyer of a house and a builder-vendor (one who builds and sells houses). Moreover, many defects in houses are not readily discoverable during a buyer's inspection. This creates the possibility of serious loss, because the purchase of a home is often the largest single investment a person ever makes.

For these reasons, courts in most states now hold that builders, builder-vendors, and developers make an implied warranty of habitability when they build or sell real property for residential purposes. An ordinary owner who sells her house—in other words, a seller who was neither the builder nor the developer of the residential property—does not make an implied warranty of habitability.

The implied warranty of habitability amounts to a guarantee that the house is free of latent (hidden) defects that would render it unsafe or unsuitable for human habitation. A breach of this warranty subjects the defendant to liability for damages, measured by either the cost of repairs or the loss in value of the house.[8]

A related issue that has led to considerable litigation is whether the implied warranty of habitability extends to subsequent purchasers of the house. For example, PDQ Development Co. builds a house and sells it to Johnson, who later sells the house to McClure. May McClure successfully sue PDQ for breach of warranty if a serious defect renders the house uninhabitable? Although some courts have rejected implied warranty actions brought by subsequent purchasers, many courts today hold that an implied warranty made by a builder-vendor or developer would extend to a subsequent purchaser.

May the implied warranty of habitability be *disclaimed* or *limited* in the contract of sale? It appears at least possible to disclaim or limit the warranty through a contract provision, subject to limitations imposed by the unconscionability doctrine, public policy concerns, and contract interpretation principles.[9] Courts construe attempted disclaimers very strictly against the builder-vendor or developer, and often reject disclaimers that are not specific regarding rights supposedly waived by the purchaser.

---

[7]See Chapter 20 for a discussion of the development of similar doctrines in the law of product liability.

[8]Measures of damages are discussed in Chapter 18.

[9]The unconscionability doctrine and public policy concerns are discussed in Chapter 15. Chapter 16 addresses contract interpretation.

Duty to Disclose Hidden Defects

Traditional contract law provided that a seller had no duty to disclose to the buyer defects in the property being sold, even if the seller knew about the defects and the buyer could not reasonably find out about them on his own. The seller's failure to volunteer information, therefore, could not constitute misrepresentation or fraud. This traditional rule of nondisclosure was another expression of the prevailing *caveat emptor* notion. Although the nondisclosure rule was subject to certain exceptions,[10] the exceptions seldom applied. Thus, there was no duty to disclose in most sales of real property.

Today, courts in many jurisdictions have substantially eroded the traditional nondisclosure rule and have placed a duty on the seller to disclose any known defect that materially affects the property's value and is not reasonably observable by the buyer. The seller's failure to disclose such defects effectively amounts to an assertion that the defects do not exist—an assertion on which a judicial finding of misrepresentation or fraud may be based.[11] *Strawn v. Canuso* illustrates the trend toward expansion of the duty to disclose by holding that certain sellers of residential property may be obligated to reveal the existence of significant *off-site* physical conditions.

---

[10]These exceptions are discussed in Chapter 13.

[11]Misrepresentation and fraud are discussed in Chapter 13.

Strawn v. Canuso   657 A.2d 420 (N.J.Sup. Ct. 1995)

The Buzby Landfill was operated from 1966 to 1978. Although the landfill was not licensed to receive liquid industrial or chemical wastes, large amounts of hazardous materials and chemicals were dumped there. Toxic wastes began to escape from the landfill because it had no liner or cap. Tests performed by the New Jersey Department of Environmental Protection and Energy (DEPE) revealed ground water contamination caused by hazardous waste seepage from the landfill.

High levels of methane gas also emanated from the dump site. Various contaminants were released because there were gas leaks in a venting system that had been installed at the site to vent excessive levels of methane gas. The federal Environmental Protection Agency (EPA) investigated the situation and recommended that the Buzby Landfill site be considered for cleanup under the federal Superfund law. The cleanup did not take place, however.

During the 1980s, Canetic Corp. and Canuso Management Corp. developed a housing subdivision near the closed Buzby Landfill. Some homes in the subdivision were within half a mile of the old landfill. Twenty-six families filed a class action lawsuit against Canetic and Canuso Management on behalf of all purchasers (approximately 150 families) who bought new homes in the subdivision between 1984 and 1987. Other defendants were John B. Canuso, Sr., and John B. Canuso, Jr., who were principals in the corporations mentioned above, and Fox & Lazo, Inc., a brokerage firm that acted as selling agent for the homes in the development. Alleging fraud, negligent misrepresentation, and a violation of the New Jersey Consumer Fraud Act, the plaintiffs contended that prior to selling the plaintiffs their homes, the defendants should have disclosed that the housing development was located near an abandoned hazardous waste dump. According to the plaintiffs, the defendants had received considerable information from the EPA and the DEPE concerning the dangers of placing a housing development in the vicinity of the closed landfill. Nevertheless, the defendants followed a policy of nondisclosure to prospective purchasers.

The trial court granted summary judgment to the defendants, holding that they did not owe prospective purchasers a duty to disclose the condition "of somebody else's property." The New Jersey Appellate Division reversed, holding that Canetic, Canuso Management, and Fox & Lazo had a duty to inform potential buyers of the existence of the nearby, closed landfill. The affected defendants appealed to the Supreme Court of New Jersey.

O'Hern, Justice   [T]he doctrine of *caveat emptor* survived [as part of real property law] into the first half of the twentieth century. *[C]aveat emptor* dictates that in the absence of express agreement, a seller is not liable to the buyer or others for the condition of the land existing at the time of transfer.

In *Michaels v. Brookchester, Inc.* (1958), this Court recognized that . . . *caveat emptor* no longer applied to lease-

hold interests in property. We stated [that even though *caveat emptor* was] "suitable for the agrarian setting in which it was conceived, [it] lagged behind changes in dwelling habits and economic realities." In *Weintraub v. Krobatsch* (1974), the Court ruled that a seller of real estate had an obligation to disclose the existence of roach infestation unknown to the buyers. The Court noted that in certain circumstances, "silence may be fraudulent."

Other jurisdictions have limited the doctrine of *caveat emptor*. In California, when the seller knows of facts materially affecting the value or desirability of property and the seller also knows that such facts are not known to, or within the reach of the diligent attention and observation of the buyer, the seller is subject to a duty to disclose those facts to the buyer. [A California court decision classifies] the real estate agent or broker representing the seller [as] a party to the business transaction [and, therefore, as a party with the same duty of disclosure as the seller]. Several jurisdictions have . . . adopted mandatory disclosure laws [or] similar laws [that impose disclosure obligations on real property sellers and their brokers].

In the absence of such legislation or other regulatory requirements affecting real estate brokers, the question is whether our common-law precedent would require disclosure of off-site conditions that materially affect the value of property. By its favorable citation of California precedent, *Weintraub* establishes that a seller of real estate or a broker representing the seller would be liable for nondisclosure of on-site defective conditions if those conditions were known to them and unknown and not readily observable by the buyer. Such conditions, for example, would include radon contamination and a polluted water supply. California cases have extended this duty [of disclosure] to some off-site conditions. Whether and to what extent we should extend this duty to off-site conditions depends on an assessment of the various policies that have shaped the development of our law.

[T]he principal factors shaping the duty to disclose have been the difference in bargaining power between the professional seller of real estate and the purchaser of such housing, and the difference in access to information between the seller and the buyer. The first factor causes us to limit our holding to professional sellers of residential housing (persons engaged in the business of building or developing residential housing) and the brokers representing them. Neither the reseller of residential real estate nor the seller of commercial property has that same advantage in the bargaining process. Regarding the second factor, professional sellers of residential housing and their brokers enjoy markedly superior access to information. Hence, we believe that it is reasonable to extend to such professionals a similar duty to disclose off-site conditions that materially affect the value or desirability of the property.

[In this case, the] silence of the Fox & Lazo representative and the Canuso Management Corporation's principals and employees created a mistaken impression on the part of the purchaser. Defendants used sales-promotion brochures,

newspaper advertisements, and a fact sheet to sell the homes in the development. That material portrayed the development as located in a peaceful, bucolic setting with an abundance of fresh air and clean lake waters. Although the literature mentioned how far the property was from malls, country clubs, and train stations, neither the brochures, the newspaper advertisements, nor any sales personnel mentioned that a landfill [was] located within half a mile of some of the homes.

Is the nearby presence of a toxic-waste dump a condition that materially affects the value of property? Surely, Lois Gibbs would have wanted to know that the home she was buying in Niagara Falls, New York, was within one-quarter mile of the abandoned Love Canal site. *See* Lois M. Gibbs, *Love Canal: My Story* (1982) (recounting residents' political struggle concerning a leaking toxic-chemical dump near their homes). In the case of on-site conditions, courts have imposed affirmative obligations on sellers to disclose information materially affecting the value of property. There is no logical reason why a certain class of sellers and brokers should not disclose off-site matters that materially affect the value of property.

We know that the physical effects of abandoned dump sites are not limited to the confines of the dump. [E]ven without physical intrusion, a landfill may cause diminution in the fair market value of real property located nearby. [O]ur precedent and policy offer reliable evidence that the value of property may be materially affected by adjacent or nearby landfills. Professional sellers in southern New Jersey could not help but have been aware of the potential effects of such conditions.

In December 1983, the Real Estate Commission wrote to the Camden County Board of Realtors, stating that "[b]ecause of the potential effects on health, and because of its impact on the value of property, location of property near a hazardous waste site is a bit of information that should be supplied to potential buyers." In addition, [a New Jersey statute] requires that a broker "make reasonable effort to ascertain all pertinent information concerning every property for which he accepts an agency" [and that the broker] "shall reveal all information material to any transaction to his client or principal and when appropriate to any other party." Although not dispositive of the issues in this case, those sources certainly suggest that professionals should have been aware of some changing duty requiring them to be more forthcoming with respect to conditions affecting the value of property.

The duty that we recognize is not unlimited. We do not hold that sellers and brokers have a duty to investigate or disclose transient social conditions in the community that arguably affect the value of property. In the absence of a purchaser communicating specific needs, builders and brokers should not be held to decide whether the changing nature of a neighborhood, the presence of a group home, or the existence of a school in decline are facts material to the transaction. Rather, we root in the land the duty to disclose off-site conditions that are material to the transaction.

We hold that a builder-developer of residential real estate or a broker representing it is not only liable to a purchaser for affirmative and intentional misrepresentation, but is also liable for nondisclosure of off-site physical conditions known to it and unknown and not readily observable by the buyer, if the existence of those conditions is of sufficient materiality to affect the habitability, use, or enjoyment of the property and, therefore, render the property less desirable or valuable to the objectively reasonable buyer. Ultimately, a jury will decide whether the presence of a landfill is a factor that materially affects the value of property; whether the presence of a landfill was known by defendants and not known or readily observable by plaintiffs; and whether the presence of a landfill has indeed affected the value of plaintiffs' property.

Decision of Appellate Division affirmed.

Other Property Condition-Related Obligations of Real Property Owners and Possessors

In recent years, the law has increasingly required real property owners and possessors to take steps to further the safety of persons on the property and to make the property more accessible to disabled individuals. This section discusses two legal developments along these lines: the trend toward expansion of *premises liability* and the inclusion of property-related provisions in the *Americans with Disabilities Act.*

Expansion of Premises Liability

Premises liability is the name sometimes used for negligence cases in which property owners or possessors (such as business operators leasing commercial real estate) are held liable to persons injured while on the property. As explained in Chapter 7, property owners and possessors face liability when their *failures to exercise reasonable care* to keep their property reasonably safe result in injuries to persons lawfully on the property.[12]

The traditional premises liability case was one in which a property owner's or possessor's negligence led to the existence of a potentially hazardous condition on the property (e.g., a dangerously slick floor or similar physical condition at a business premises), and a person justifiably on the premises (e.g., a business customer) sustained personal injury upon encountering that unexpected condition (e.g., by slipping and falling).

Security Precautions against Foreseeable Criminal Acts Recent years have witnessed a judicial inclination to expand premises liability to cover other situations in addition to the traditional scenario. A key component of this expansion has been many courts' willingness to reconsider the once-customary holding that a property owner or possessor had no legal obligation to implement security measures to protect persons on the property from the wrongful acts of third parties lacking any connection with the owner or possessor. Today, courts frequently hold that a property owner's or possessor's duty to exercise reasonable care includes the obligation to take *reasonable security precautions* designed to protect persons lawfully on the premises from *foreseeable* wrongful (including criminal) acts by third parties.

This expansion has caused hotel, apartment building, and convenience store owners and operators to be among the defendants held liable—sometimes in very large damage amounts—to guests, tenants, and customers on whom third-party attackers inflicted severe physical injuries. In such cases, the property owners' or possessors' negligent failures to take security precautions restricting such wrongdoers' access to the premises served as at least a *substantial factor* leading to the

---

[12]Chapter 7 explains the law's traditional view that real property owners and possessors owe persons who come on the property certain duties that vary depending on those persons' invitee, licensee, or trespasser status. It also discusses courts' increasing tendency to merge the traditional invitee and licensee classifications and to hold that property owners and possessors owe invitees and licensees the duty to exercise reasonable care to keep the premises reasonably safe.

plaintiffs' injuries.[13] The security lapses amounting to a lack of reasonable care in a particular case may have been, for instance, failures to install deadbolt locks, provide adequate locking devices on sliding glass doors, maintain sufficient lighting, or employ security guards.

Determining Foreseeability The security precautions component of the reasonable care duty is triggered only when criminal activity on the premises is foreseeable. It therefore becomes important to determine whether the foreseeability standard has been met. In making this determination, courts look at such factors as whether previous crimes had occurred on or near the subject property (and if so, the nature and frequency of those crimes), whether the property owner or possessor knew or should have known of those prior occurrences, and whether the property was located in a high-crime area. The fact-specific nature of the foreseeability and reasonable care determinations makes the outcome of a given premises liability case difficult to predict in advance. Nevertheless, there is no doubt that the current premises liability climate gives property owners and possessors more reason than ever before to be concerned about security measures.

Americans with Disabilities Act

In 1990, Congress enacted the broad-ranging Americans with Disabilities Act (ADA). This statute was designed to eliminate longstanding patterns of discrimination against disabled persons in matters such as employment, access to public services, and access to business establishments and similar facilities open to the public. The ADA's Title III focuses on places of *public accommodation.*[14] It imposes on certain property owners and possessors the obligation to take reasonable steps to make their property accessible to disabled persons (individuals with a physical or mental impairment that substantially limits one or more major life activities).

Places of Public Accommodation Title III of the ADA classifies numerous businesses and nonbusiness enterprises as places of **public accommodation.** These include hotels, restaurants, bars, theaters, concert halls, auditoriums, stadiums, shopping centers, stores at which goods are sold or rented, service-oriented businesses (running the gamut from gas stations to law firm offices), museums, parks, schools, social services establishments (day care centers, senior citizen centers, homeless shelters, and the like), places of recreation, and various other enterprises, facilities, and establishments. Private clubs and religious organizations, however, are not treated as places of public accommodation for purposes of the statute.

Modifications of Property Under the ADA, the owner or operator of a place of public accommodation cannot exclude disabled persons from the premises or otherwise discriminate against them in terms of their ability to enjoy the public accommodation. Avoiding such exclusion or other discrimination may require alteration of the business or nonbusiness enterprise's practices, policies, and procedures. Moreover, using language contemplating the possible need for physical modifications of property serving as a place of public accommodation, the ADA includes within prohibited discrimination the property owner's or possessor's "failure to take such steps as may be necessary to ensure that no individual with a disability is excluded" or otherwise discriminated against in terms of access to what nondisabled persons are provided. The failure to take these steps does not violate the ADA, however, if the property owner or possessor demonstrates that implementing such steps would "fundamentally alter the nature" of the enterprise or would "result in an undue burden."

Prohibited discrimination may also include the "failure to remove architectural barriers and communication barriers that are structural in nature," if removal is "readily achievable." When the removal of such a barrier is not readily achievable, the property owner or possessor nonetheless engages in prohibited discrimination if he, she, or it does not adopt "alternative methods" to ensure access to the premises and what it has to offer (assuming that the alternative methods are themselves readily achievable). The ADA defines *readily achievable* as "easily accomplishable and able to be carried out without much difficulty or expense." The determination of whether an action is readily achievable involves consideration of factors such as the action's nature and cost, the nature of the enterprise conducted on the property, the financial resources of the affected property owner or possessor, and the effect the action would have on expenses and resources of the property owner or possessor.

New Construction Newly constructed buildings on property used as a place of public accommodation must

---

[13]See Chapter 7's discussion of the *causation* element of a negligence claim.

[14]42 U.S.C. §§ 12181–12189. These sections examine only Title III of the ADA. Chapter 50 discusses the employment-related provisions set forth elsewhere in the statute.

contain physical features making the buildings *readily accessible* to disabled persons. The same is true of additions built on to previous structures. The ADA is supplemented by federal regulations setting forth property accessibility guidelines designed to lend substance and specificity to the broad legal standards stated in the statute. In addition, the federal government has issued technical assistance manuals and materials in an effort to educate public accommodation owners and operators regarding their obligations under the ADA.

Remedies A person subjected to disability-based discrimination in any of the respects discussed above may bring a civil suit for injunctive relief. An injunction issued by a court must include "an order to alter facilities" to make the facilities "readily accessible to and usable by individuals with disabilities to the extent required" by the ADA. The court has discretion to award attorney's fees to the prevailing party. The U.S. Attorney General also has the legal authority to institute a civil action alleging a violation of Title III of the ADA. In such a case, the court may choose to grant injunctive and other appropriate equitable relief, award compensatory damages to aggrieved persons (when the Attorney General so requests), and assess civil penalties (up to $50,000 for a first violation and up to $100,000 for any subsequent violation) "to vindicate the public interest." When determining the amount of any such penalty, the court is to give consideration to any good faith effort by the property owner or possessor to comply with the law. The court must also consider whether the owner or possessor could reasonably have anticipated the need to accommodate disabled persons.

Land Use Control

Although a real property owner generally has the right to use his property as he desires, society has placed certain limitations on this right. This section examines the property use limitations imposed by nuisance law and by zoning and subdivision ordinances. It also discusses the ultimate land use restriction—the eminent domain power—which enables the government to deprive property owners of their land.

Nuisance Law

One's enjoyment of her land depends to a great extent on the uses her neighbors make of their land. When the uses of neighboring landowners conflict, the aggrieved party sometimes institutes litigation to resolve the conflict. A property use that unreasonably interferes with another person's ability to use or enjoy her own property may lead to an action for **nuisance** against the landowner or possessor engaging in the objectionable use.

The term *nuisance* has no set definition. It is often regarded, however, as encompassing any property-related use or activity that unreasonably interferes with the rights of others. Property uses potentially constituting nuisances include uses that are inappropriate to the neighborhood (such as using a vacant lot in a residential neighborhood as a garbage dump), bothersome to neighbors (such as keeping a pack of barking dogs in one's backyard), dangerous to others (such as storing large quantities of gasoline in 50-gallon drums in one's garage), or of questionable morality (such as operating a house of prostitution). To amount to a nuisance, a use need not be illegal. The fact that relevant zoning laws allow a given use does not mean that the use cannot be a nuisance. The use's having been in existence before complaining neighbors acquired their property does not mean that the use cannot be a nuisance, though it does lessen the likelihood that the use would be held a nuisance.

The test for determining the presence or absence of a nuisance is necessarily flexible and highly dependent on the individual case's facts. Courts balance a number of factors, such as the social importance of the parties' respective uses, the extent and duration of harm experienced by the aggrieved party, and the feasibility of abating (stopping) the nuisance.

Nuisances may be private or public. To bring a *private nuisance* action, the plaintiff must be a landowner or occupier whose enjoyment of her own land is substantially lessened by the alleged nuisance. The remedies for private nuisance include damages and injunctive relief designed to stop the offending use. A *public nuisance* occurs when a nuisance harms members of the public, who need not be injured in their use of property. For example, if a power plant creates noise and emissions posing a health hazard to pedestrians and workers in nearby buildings, a public nuisance may exist even though the nature of the harm has nothing to do with any loss of enjoyment of property. Public nuisances involve a broader class of affected parties than do private nuisances. The action to abate a public nuisance must usually be brought by the government. Remedies generally include injunctive relief and civil penalties that resemble fines. On occasion, constitutional issues may arise in public nuisance cases brought by the government. Private parties may sue for abatement of a public nuisance or for damages caused by one only when they suffered unique harm different from that experienced by the general public.

Eminent Domain

The Fifth Amendment to the Constitution provides that private property shall not be taken for public use without "just compensation." Implicit in this provision is the principle that the government has the power to take property for public use if it pays "just compensation" to the owner of the property. This power, called the power of eminent domain, makes it possible for the government to acquire private property for highways, water control projects, municipal and civic centers, public housing, urban renewal, and other public uses. Governmental units may delegate their eminent domain power to private corporations such as railroads and utility companies.

Although the eminent domain power is a useful tool of efficient government, there are problems inherent in its use. Determining when the power can be properly exercised presents an initial problem. When the governmental unit itself uses the property taken, as would be the case with property acquired for construction of a municipal building or a public highway, the exercise of the power is proper. The use of eminent domain is not so clearly justified, however, when the government acquires the property and resells it to a private developer. Although such acquisitions may be more vulnerable to challenge, recent cases have applied a very lenient standard in determining what constitutes a public use.[15]

Determining *just compensation* in a given case poses a second and frequently encountered eminent domain problem. The property owner is entitled to receive the "fair market value" of his property. Critics assert, however, that this measure of compensation falls short of adequately compensating the owner for her loss, because *fair market value* does not cover such matters as the lost goodwill of a business or one's emotional attachment to his home.

A third problem sometimes encountered is determining when there has been a "taking" that triggers the government's just compensation obligation. The answer is easy when the government institutes a formal legal action to exercise the eminent domain power (often called an action to *condemn* property). In some instances, however, the government causes or permits a serious physical invasion of a landowner's property without having instituted formal condemnation proceedings. For example, the government's dam-building project results in persistent flooding of a private party's land. Courts have recognized the right of property owners in such cases to institute litigation seeking compensation from the governmental unit whose actions effectively amounted to a physical taking of their land. In these so-called **inverse condemnation** cases, the property owner sends the message that "you have taken my land; now pay for it."

Zoning and Subdivision Laws

State legislatures commonly delegate to cities and other political subdivisions the power to impose reasonable regulations designed to promote the public health, safety, and welfare (often called the *police power*). Zoning ordinances, which regulate real property use, stem from the exercise of the police power. Normally, zoning ordinances divide a city or town into various districts and specify or limit the uses to which property in those districts may be put. They also contain requirements and restrictions regarding improvements built on the land.

Zoning ordinances frequently contain direct restrictions on land use, such as by limiting property use in a given area to single-family or high-density residential uses, or to commercial, light industry, or heavy industry uses. Other sorts of use-related provisions commonly found in zoning ordinances include restrictions on building height, limitations on the portion of a lot that can be covered by a building, and specifications of the distance buildings must be from lot lines (usually called *setback* requirements). Zoning ordinances also commonly restrict property use by establishing population density limitations. Such restrictions specify the maximum number of persons who can be housed on property in a given area and dictate the amount of living space that must be provided for each person occupying residential property. In addition, zoning ordinances often establish restrictions designed to maintain or create a certain aesthetic character in the community. Examples of this type of restriction include specifications of buildings' architectural style, limitations on billboard and sign use, and designations of special zones for historic buildings.

Many local governments also have ordinances dealing with proposed subdivisions. These ordinances often require the subdivision developer to meet certain requirements regarding lot size, street and sidewalk layout, and sanitary facilities. They also require that the city or town approve the proposed development. Such ordinances are designed to further general community interests and to protect prospective buyers of property in the

---

[15]This issue is discussed further in Chapter 3, as are other issues relating to eminent domain.

subdivision by ensuring that the developer meets minimum standards of suitability.

Nonconforming Uses A zoning ordinance has *prospective* effect. This means that the uses and buildings already existing when the ordinance is passed (**nonconforming uses**) are permitted to continue. The ordinance may provide, however, for the gradual phasing out of nonconforming uses and buildings that do not fit the general zoning plan.

Relief from Zoning Ordinances A property owner who wishes to use his property in a manner prohibited by a zoning ordinance has more than one potential avenue of relief from the ordinance. He may, for instance, seek to have the ordinance amended—in other words, attempt to get the law changed—on the ground that the proposed amendment is consistent with the essence of the overall zoning plan.

A different approach would be to seek permission from the city or political subdivision to deviate from the zoning law. This permission is called a **variance.** A person seeking a variance usually claims that the ordinance works an undue hardship on her by denying her the opportunity to make reasonable use of her land. Examples of typical variance requests include a property owner's seeking permission to make a commercial use of her property even though it is located in an area zoned for residential purposes, or permission to deviate from normal setback or building size requirements.

Attempts to obtain variances and zoning ordinance amendments frequently clash with the interests of other owners of property in the same area—owners who have a vested interest in maintaining the status quo. As a result, variance and amendment requests often produce heated battles before local zoning authorities.

Challenges to the Validity of the Zoning Ordinance A disgruntled property owner might also attack the zoning ordinance's validity on constitutional grounds. Litigation challenging zoning ordinances has become frequent in recent years, as cities and towns have used their zoning power to achieve social control. For example, assume that a city creates special zoning requirements for adult bookstores or other uses considered moral threats to the community. Such uses of the zoning power have been challenged as unconstitutional restrictions on freedom of speech. In *City of Renton v. Playtime Theatres, Inc.,* however, the Supreme Court upheld a zoning ordinance that prohibited the operation of adult bookstores within 1,000 feet of specified uses

such as residential areas and schools.[16] The Court established that the First Amendment rights of operators of adult businesses would not be violated by such an ordinance so long as the city provided them a "reasonable opportunity to open and operate" their businesses within the city. The reasonable opportunity test was satisfied in *City of Renton* even though the ordinance at issue effectively restricted adult bookstores to a small area of the community in which no property was then available to buy or rent. As lower court cases reveal, however, the fact-specific nature of the inquiry contemplated by the reasonable opportunity test means that the government is not guaranteed of passing the test in every case.[17]

Other litigation has stemmed from ordinances by which municipalities have attempted to "zone out" residential facilities such as group homes for mentally retarded adults. In a leading case, the Supreme Court held that the Constitution's Equal Protection Clause was violated by a zoning ordinance that required a special use permit for a group home for the mentally retarded.[18] (For

---

[16]475 U.S. 41 (U.S. Sup. Ct. 1986). A later case, *FW/PBS, Inc. v. City of Dallas,* 493 U.S. 215 (U.S. Sup. Ct. 1990), presented a different sort of restriction on adult businesses and resulted in a different outcome. There, the Court held that a comprehensive ordinance requiring licensing of adult cabarets and other adult entertainment establishments violated the First Amendment because the ordinance did not have appropriate procedural safeguards against arbitrary denials of licenses. The ordinance's chief defect was its failure to establish a time limit within which city authorities were required to act on license applications.

[17]See, for example, *Topanga Press, Inc. v. City of Los Angeles,* 1993 U.S. App. LEXIS 9423 (9th Cir. 1993). In that case, the Ninth Circuit Court of Appeals upheld the trial court's issuance of a preliminary injunction against the city's *City of Renton*–like zoning ordinance regarding adult businesses. The reasonable opportunity test was not passed by the city, given that much of the real estate supposedly still "available" for relocation of the adult businesses was submerged beneath the Pacific Ocean or was used as a landfill, for petroleum storage, for airport runways, or for some other purpose inconsistent with the notion that the property could somehow become available for use by adult businesses. In *Los Angeles v. Alameda Books, Inc.,* No. 00–799, (U.S. Sup. Ct. 2002), the Supreme Court upheld a city ordinance that prohibited more than one adult entertainment business in the same building. The ordinance had been enacted because of a study that indicated that crime increased in locations in which there is a concentration of adult entertainment businesses. The Court reversed a summary judgment in favor of Alameda Books, concluding that the study provided sufficient evidence to justify the city's concern about increased crime, and demonstrated that the zoning ordinance was designed to reduce crime.

[18]*City of Cleburne v. Cleburne Living Centers,* 473 U.S. 432 (U.S. Sup. Ct. 1985).

a case indicating that similar issues nonetheless may be treated differently in the *restrictive covenant*—as opposed to zoning—setting, see *Mains Farm Homeowners Association v. Worthington,* which appears earlier in this chapter.) The Fair Housing Act, which forbids discrimination on the basis of handicap and familial status, has also been used as a basis for challenging decisions that zone out group homes. Such a challenge has a chance of success when the plaintiff demonstrates that the zoning board's actions were a mere pretext for discrimination.[19] Certain applications of zoning ordinances that establish single-family residential areas may also raise Fair Housing Act–based claims of handicap discrimination. The *Oxford House* case, which follows shortly, is such a case.

Many cities and towns have attempted to restrict single-family residential zones to living units of traditional families related by blood or marriage. In enacting ordinances along those lines, municipalities have sought to prevent the presence of groups of unrelated students, commune members, or religious cult adherents by specifically defining the term *family* in a way that excludes these groups. In *Belle Terre v. Boraas,*[20] the Supreme Court upheld such an ordinance as applied to a group of unrelated students. The Court later held, however, that an ordinance defining *family* so as to prohibit a grandmother from living with her grandsons was an unconstitutional intrusion on personal freedom regarding family life.[21] Restrictive definitions of *family* have been held unconstitutional under state constitutions in some cases but narrowly construed by courts in other cases.

---

[19]See, for example, *Baxter v. City of Nashville,* 720 F. Supp. 720 (S.D. Ill. 1989), which involves a challenge by a hospice for AIDS patients to a city's denial of a special use permit.

[20]416 U.S. 1 (U.S. Sup. Ct. 1974).
[21]*Moore v. City of East Cleveland,* 431 U.S. 494 (U.S. Sup. Ct. 1977).

City of Edmonds v. Oxford House, Inc.   *514 U.S 725 (U.S. Sup. Ct. 1995)*

The zoning code of the City of Edmonds, Washington, allows only single-family dwelling units in certain designated areas of the city. One of this code's ordinances defines family as "an individual or two or more persons related by genetics, adoption, or marriage, or a group of five or fewer persons who are not related by genetics, adoption, or marriage." Oxford House, Inc., opened a group home on leased property in an area of Edmonds that was zoned for single-family residences. This group home was for 10 to 12 adults who were recovering from alcoholism and drug addiction. Upon learning that the group home was being operated, Edmonds issued criminal citations to the owner and a resident of the house. Because the Oxford House facility housed more than five unrelated persons in a single-family area, it did not conform to the Edmonds zoning code.

In an effort to keep the group home open, Oxford House relied on the federal Fair Housing Act (FHA), which bars discrimination in the sale or rental of real property on various bases, including the handicap of a buyer or renter. For purposes of the litigation described below, all parties stipulated that the residents of the Oxford House group home were recovering alcoholics or drug addicts and were therefore handicapped persons within the meaning of the FHA. Discrimination prohibited by the FHA includes the refusal to make "reasonable accommodations in rules, policies, practices, or services, when such accommodations may be necessary to afford [handicapped] persons equal opportunity to use and enjoy a dwelling." Oxford House asked Edmonds to make what Oxford House saw as a reasonable accommodation—allowing it to continue to operate the group home in the single-family residential dwelling it had leased. Edmonds denied this request.

Edmonds sued Oxford House in federal court, seeking a declaration that the FHA does not limit the operation of the city's zoning code rule defining family. The city based its case on an FHA provision that exempts from the FHA's antidiscrimination provisions "any reasonable local, State, or Federal restrictions regarding the maximum number of occupants permitted to occupy a dwelling" [FHA section 3607(b)(1)]. Oxford House counterclaimed under the FHA, alleging that in refusing to permit maintenance of the group home in a single-family zone, Edmonds had failed to make a reasonable accommodation. Holding that the Edmonds zoning code's definition of family was a reasonable maximum occupancy restriction for purposes of the FHA exemption set out in section 3607(b)(1), the federal district granted summary judgment in favor of Edmonds. The Ninth Circuit Court of Appeals reversed. It held that section 3607(b)(1)'s exemption did not apply to the Edmonds ordinance. The U.S. Supreme Court granted the city's petition for certiorari.

Ginsburg, Justice   The sole question before the Court is whether Edmonds' family composition rule qualifies as a "restrictio[n] regarding the maximum number of occupants permitted to occupy a dwelling" within the meaning of the FHA's absolute exemption [section 3607(b)(1)]. In answering this question, we are mindful of the Act's stated policy "to provide . . . for fair housing throughout the United States." We also note precedent recognizing the FHA's "broad and inclusive" compass (quoting *Trafficante v. Metropolitan Life Insurance Co.* (1972). Accordingly, we regard this case as an instance in which an exception to "a general statement of policy" is sensibly read "narrowly in order to preserve the primary operation of the [policy]" (quoting *Commissioner v. Clark* (1989)).

Congress enacted section 3607(b)(1) against the backdrop of an evident distinction between municipal land use restrictions and maximum occupancy restrictions. Land use restrictions designate "districts in which only compatible uses are allowed and incompatible uses are excluded" (quoting D. Mandelker, *Land Use Law* [3d ed. 1993]). These restrictions typically categorize uses as single-family residential, multiple-family residential, commercial, or industrial. Land use restrictions aim to prevent problems caused by the "pig in the parlor instead of the barnyard" (quoting *Village of Euclid v. Ambler Realty Co.* [1926]). [R]eserving land for single-family residences preserves the character of neighborhoods. To limit land use to single-family residences, a municipality must define the term "family"; thus, family composition rules are an essential component of single-family residential uses.

Maximum occupancy restrictions, in contradistinction, cap the number of occupants per dwelling, typically in relation to available floor space or the number and types of rooms. These restrictions ordinarily apply uniformly to *all* residents of *all* dwelling units. Their purpose is to protect health and safety by preventing dwelling overcrowding.

Section 3607 (b)(1)'s language—"restrictions regarding the maximum number of occupants permitted to occupy a dwelling"—surely encompasses maximum occupancy restrictions. But the formulation does not fit family composition rules typically tied to land use restrictions. In sum, rules that cap the total number of occupants in order to prevent overcrowding of a dwelling [clearly] fall within section 3607(b)(1)'s absolute exemption from the FHA's governance; rules designed to preserve the family character of a neighborhood, fastening on the composition of households rather than on the total number of occupants, living quarters can contain, do not.

Turning specifically to the City's [zoning code], we note that the provisions Edmonds invoked against Oxford House [the ordinance establishing single-family residential zoning for the area where the home was located and the ordinance defining *family*] are classic examples of a use restriction and complementing family composition rule. These provisions do not cap the number of people who may live in a dwelling. In plain terms, they direct that dwellings be used only to house families. A separate [Edmonds ordinance] caps the number of occupants a dwelling may house, based on the floor area. Th[e] space and occupancy standard [set forth in this separate ordinance] is a prototypical maximum occupancy restriction.

Edmonds nevertheless argues that its family composition rule falls within . . . the FHA exemption for maximum occupancy restrictions, because the rule caps at five the number of unrelated persons allowed to occupy a single-family dwelling. But Edmonds' family composition rule surely does not answer the question: "What is the maximum number of occupants permitted to occupy a house?" So long as they are related "by genetics, adoption, or marriage," any number of people can live in a house.

Family living, not living space per occupant, is what [the family composition ordinance] describes. Defining family primarily by biological and legal relationships, the provision also accommodates another group association: five or fewer unrelated people are allowed to live together as though they were family. This accommodation is the peg on which Edmonds rests its plea for section 3607(b)(1) exemption. It is curious reasoning indeed that converts a family values preserver into a maximum occupancy restriction once a town adds to a related persons prescription [a reference to a limited number of unrelated persons].

The parties have presented, and we have decided, only a threshold question: Edmonds' zoning code provision describing who may compose a "family" is not a maximum occupancy restriction exempt from the FHA under section 3607(b)(1). It remains for the lower courts to decide whether Edmonds' actions against Oxford House violate the FHA's prohibitions against discrimination.

Judgment of Ninth Circuit Court of Appeals affirmed.

Land Use Regulation and Taking

Another type of litigation seen with increasing frequency in recent years centers around zoning laws and other land use regulations that make the use of property less profitable for development.[22] Affected property owners have challenged the application of such regulations as unconstitutional takings of property without just compensation, even though these cases do not involve the actual physical invasions present in the inverse condemnation cases discussed earlier in this chapter.

States normally have broad discretion to use their police power for the public benefit, even when that means interfering to some extent with an owner's right to develop her property as she desires. Some regulations, however, may interfere with an owner's use of his property to such an extent that they constitute a taking.

For instance, in *Nollan v. California Coastal Commission,*[23] the owners of a beach-front lot (the Nollans) wished to tear down a small house on the lot and replace that structure with a larger house. The California Coastal Commission conditioned the grant of the necessary coastal development permit on the Nollans' agreeing to allow the public an easement across their property. This easement would have allowed the public to reach certain nearby public beaches more easily. The Nollans challenged the validity of the Coastal Commission's action.

Ultimately, the Supreme Court concluded that the Coastal Commission's placing the easement condition on the issuance of the permit amounted to an impermissible regulatory taking of the Nollans' property. In reaching this conclusion, the Court held that the state could not avoid paying compensation to the Nollans by choosing to do by way of the regulatory route what it would have had to pay for if it had followed the formal eminent domain route.

Regulations Denying Economically Beneficial Uses   What about a land use regulation that allows the property owner no *economically beneficial use* of his property? *Lucas v. South Carolina Coastal Commission*[24] was brought by a property owner, Lucas, who had paid nearly $1 million for two residential beach-front lots before South Carolina enacted a coastal protection statute. This statute's effect was to bar Lucas from building any permanent habitable structures on the lots. The trial court held that the statute rendered Lucas's property "valueless" and that an unconstitutional taking had occurred, but the South Carolina Supreme Court reversed. The U.S. Supreme Court, however, held that when a land use regulation denies "all economically beneficial use" of property, there normally has been a taking for which just compensation must be paid. The exception to this rule, according to the Court, would be when the economically productive use being prohibited by the land use regulation was already disallowed by nuisance law or other comparable property law principles. The Court therefore reversed and remanded the case for determination of whether there had been a taking under the rule crafted by the Court, or instead an instance in which the "nuisance" exception applied. On remand, the South Carolina Supreme Court concluded that a taking calling for compensation had occurred (and, necessarily, that the nuisance exception did not apply to Lucas's intended residential use).[25]

The mere fact that a land use regulation deprives the owner of the *highest and most profitable use* of his prop-

---

[22]This issue is also discussed in Chapter 3.
[23]483 U.S. 825 (U.S. Sup. Ct. 1987).
[24]505 U.S. 1003 (U.S. Sup. Ct. 1992).
[25]424 S.E. 2d 484 (S.C. Sup. Ct. 1992).

erty does not mean, however, that there has been a taking. If the regulation still allows a use that is economically beneficial in a meaningful sense—even though not the most profitable use—the *Lucas* analysis would seem to indicate that an unconstitutional taking probably did not occur. At the same time, *Lucas* offered hints that less-than-total takings (in terms of restrictions on economically beneficial uses) may sometimes trigger a right of compensation on the landowner's part. Thus, it appears that even as to land use regulations that restrict some but not all economically beneficial uses, property owners are likely to continue arguing (as they have in recent years) that the regulations go "too far" and amount to a taking.

There is no set formula for determining whether a regulation has gone too far. Courts look at the relevant facts and circumstances and weigh a variety of factors, such as the economic impact of the regulation, the de-

gree to which the regulation interferes with the property owner's reasonable expectations, and the character of the government's invasion. The weighing of these factors occurs against the backdrop of a general presumption that state and local governments should have reasonably broad discretion to develop land use restrictions pursuant to the police power. As a result, the outcome of a case in which *regulatory taking* allegations are made is less certain than when a *physical taking* (a physical invasion of the sort addressed in the earlier discussion of inverse condemnation cases) appears to have occurred.

You will read more about regulatory takings in the following *Palazzolo* case, including the question whether a person who acquires ownership of property after regulations are in place can bring a claim for inverse condemnation.

Palazzolo v. Rhode Island   533 U.S. 606 (U.S. Sup. Ct. 2001)

In 1959, Anthony Palazzolo decided to invest in three undeveloped, adjoining parcels along Atlantic Avenue in Westerly, Rhode Island. Most of the property is salt marsh subject to tidal flooding, and is designated as coastal wetlands under Rhode Island law. To purchase and hold the property, Palazzolo and his associates formed a corporation, Shore Gardens, Inc. (SGI). After SGI purchased the property, Palazzolo bought out his associates and became the sole shareholder of SGI. In the first decade of SGI's ownership of the property, the corporation submitted a plat to the town subdividing the property into 80 lots; and it engaged in various transactions that left it with 74 lots, which together encompassed about 20 acres. During the same period SGI also made initial attempts to develop the property and submitted intermittent applications to state agencies to fill substantial portions of the parcel. These applications were ultimately rejected.

No further attempts to develop the property were made for over a decade. In 1971, Rhode Island enacted legislation creating the Rhode Island Coastal Resources Management Council, an agency charged with the duty of protecting the State's coastal properties. Regulations promulgated by the Council designated salt marshes like those on SGI's property as protected "coastal wetlands," on which development is limited to a great extent. In 1978, SGI's corporate charter was revoked for failure to pay corporate income taxes; and title to the property passed, by operation of state law, to Palazzolo as the corporation's sole shareholder.

In 1983, Palazzolo, now the owner of the property, renewed the efforts to develop the property. He made several applications to the Council to fill the marsh land area and build a bulkhead and a private beach club on his land, and the Council rejected them. This time Palazzolo appealed the decision to the Rhode Island courts, but the Council's decision was affirmed. Palazzolo filed an inverse condemnation action in Rhode Island Superior Court, asserting that the State's wetlands regulations, as applied by the Council to his parcel, had taken the property without compensation in violation of the Fifth and Fourteenth Amendments. He sought damages in the amount of $3,150,000, a figure derived from an appraiser's estimate as to the value of a 74-lot residential subdivision. After a bench trial, the trial court ruled in favor of the Council, and the Rhode Island Supreme Court affirmed. Among the reasons for the court's ruling was that Palazzolo had no right to challenge regulations predating 1978, when he succeeded to legal ownership of the property from SGI. Palazzolo appealed.

KENNEDY, Justice The Takings Clause of the Fifth Amendment prohibits the government from taking private property for public use without just compensation. The clearest sort of taking occurs when the government en-

croaches upon or occupies private land for its own proposed use. Our cases establish that even a minimal permanent physical occupation of real property requires compensation under the Clause. In Justice Holmes's well-known, if less than self-defining, formulation, "while property may be regulated to a certain extent, if a regulation goes too far it will be recognized as a taking." We have given some, but not too specific, guidance to courts confronted with deciding whether a particular government action goes too far and effects a regulatory taking. First, we have observed, with certain qualifications, that a regulation which denies all economically beneficial or productive use of land will require compensation under the Takings Clause. Where a regulation places limitations on land that fall short of eliminating all economically beneficial use, a taking nonetheless may have occurred, depending on a complex of factors including the regulation's economic effect on the landowner, the extent to which the regulation interferes with reasonable investment-backed expectations, and the character of the government action. These inquiries are informed by the purpose of the Takings Clause, which is to prevent the government from forcing some people alone to bear public burdens which, in all fairness and justice, should be borne by the public as a whole. Palazzolo seeks compensation under these principles.

When the Council promulgated its wetlands regulations, the disputed parcel was owned not by Palazzolo but by the corporation of which he was sole shareholder. When title was transferred to Palazzolo by operation of law, the wetlands regulations were in force. The state court held the postregulation acquisition of title was fatal to the claim for deprivation of all economic use. While the first holding was couched in terms of background principles of state property law, and the second in terms of Palazzolo's reasonable investment-backed expectations, the two holdings together amount to a single, sweeping rule: A purchaser or a successive title holder like Palazzolo is deemed to have notice of an earlier-enacted restriction and is barred from claiming that it effects a taking. The theory underlying the argument that post-enactment purchasers cannot challenge a regulation under the Takings Clause seems to run on these lines: Property rights are created by the State. So, the argument goes, by prospective legislation the State can shape and define property rights and reasonable investment-backed expectations, and subsequent owners cannot claim any injury from lost value. After all, they purchased or took title with notice of the limitation.

The State may not put so potent a Hobbesian stick into the Lockean bundle. The right to improve property, of course, is subject to the reasonable exercise of state authority, including the enforcement of valid zoning and land-use restrictions. The Takings Clause, however, in certain circumstances allows a landowner to assert that a particular exercise of the State's regulatory power is so unreasonable or onerous as to compel compensation. Just as a prospective enactment, such as a new zoning ordinance, can limit the value of land without effecting a taking because it can be understood as reasonable by all concerned, other enactments are unreasonable and do not become less so through passage of time or title. Were we to accept the State's rule, the post-enactment transfer of title would absolve the State of its obligation to defend any action restricting land use, no matter how extreme or unreasonable. A State would be allowed, in effect, to put an expiration date on the Takings Clause. This ought not to be the rule. Future generations, too, have a right to challenge unreasonable limitations on the use and value of land. The State's rule would work a critical alteration to the nature of property, as the newly regulated landowner is stripped of the ability to transfer the interest which was possessed prior to the regulation. The State may not by this means secure a windfall for itself.

As the case is ripe, and as the date of transfer of title does not bar Palazzolo's takings claim, we have before us the alternative ground relied upon by the Rhode Island Supreme Court in ruling upon the merits of the takings claims. It held that all economically beneficial use was not deprived because the uplands portion of the property can still be improved. On this point, we agree with the court's decision. Palazzolo accepts the Council's contention and the state trial court's finding that his parcel retains $200,000 in development value under the State's wetlands regulations. He asserts, nonetheless, that he has suffered a total taking and contends the Council cannot [leave] "a landowner a few crumbs of value." Assuming a taking is otherwise established, a State may not evade the duty to compensate on the premise that the landowner is left with a token interest. This is not the situation of the landowner in this case, however. A regulation permitting a landowner to build a substantial residence on an 18-acre parcel does not leave the property economically idle. The case comes to us on the premise that Palazzolo's entire parcel serves as the basis for his takings claim, and, so framed, the total deprivation argument fails.

For the reasons we have discussed, the State Supreme Court erred in ruling that acquisition of title after the effective date of the regulations barred the takings claims. The court did not err in finding that Palazzolo failed to establish a deprivation of all economic value, for it is undisputed that the parcel retains significant worth for construction of a residence.

Affirmed in part in favor of Rhode Island and reversed in part in favor of Palazzolo.

Problems and Problem Cases

1. Rothermich and Toebben owned and operated St. Charles Bowl from the early 1960s, when the building housing the lanes was constructed, through 1987, when the business was ultimately sold. In January 1972, after St. Charles Bowl had been in business for several years, St. Charles Bowl entered into a lease agreement with AMF, Inc., for the installation of pinspotters in the building. The pinspotters were manufactured in three pieces and assembled inside the bowling alley. They were placed in the step-down portion of the alley lane that was re-designed to accommodate them, and screwed, bolted, and riveted to the concrete floor. The lease agreement between AMF and St. Charles Bowl provided for a lease term of 12 1/2 years and recited, in part:

> Upon any termination of this agreement, AMF shall immediately have the right to possession of the machines and AMF may enter upon the premises where the machines are located, take possession without previous demand or notice and without legal process, and remove them to the manufacturer's factory or other place of storage. . . .The machines shall at all times remain the sole and exclusive property of AMF (which reserves the right to assign or encumber the machines) and operator shall have no rights, title or interest to the machines but only the right to use them under this agreement. The machines shall remain personal property and shall not be deemed otherwise by reason of becoming attached to the premises.

In May 1987, Toebben's son, Kevin, along with several others, formed Weber's St. Charles Lanes, Inc., and purchased St. Charles Bowl. The purchase agreement between St. Charles Bowl and Weber's Lanes was made expressly contingent upon an assignment to Weber's Lanes of the lease agreement between St. Charles Bowl and AMF for the use of the pinspotters. The price paid to Rothermich and Toebben for St. Charles Bowl did not include consideration for the pinspotters, as they were considered by all parties involved to be the property of AMF. As part of the purchase agreement, Rothermich and Toebben agreed to finance part of the purchase price for St. Charles Bowl, with the remainder financed by Boatmen's Bank of O'Fallon, and Weber's Lanes executed a promissory notes in favor of all three of these parties. Each promissory note was secured by a deed of trust and recited that it conveyed to the trustee both the real property and "all buildings and appurtenances now or hereafter to the same belonging. . . ." In 1989, Weber's Lanes purchased the pinspotters from AMF through a loan from

Union Planters Bank, which was also granted a security interest in the pinspotters. Weber's Lanes defaulted on its loans. By agreement between the creditors, the pinspotters were sold at a foreclosure sale and removed from the bowling alley premises with no physical or structural damage to the property. The pinspotters were resold to another bowling alley. Rothermich and Toebben claimed that they were entitled to the proceeds from the sale of the pinspotters because the pinspotters had been fixtures subject to their deed of trust, while Union Planter's argued that it was entitled to the proceeds because the pinspotters were personal property subject to its security interest. Were the pinspotters fixtures?

2. In 1957 or 1958, the Hibbards cleared their land of overgrowth and set up a trailer park. There was no obvious boundary between their land and that of their neighbor to the east, so the Hibbards cleared the land up to a deep drainage ditch. They also built a road for use in entering and leaving the trailer park. In 1960, the Hibbards' neighbor, McMurray, discovered through a survey that the Hibbards had encroached on his land (the eastern parcel) by 20 feet. He so informed the Hibbards. The western parcel later changed hands several times until the Sanderses bought it in 1976. The use of the western parcel changed little over the years. The road remained in continuous use in connection with the trailer park. The area between the road and the drainage ditch was also used by trailer park residents for parking, storage, garbage removal, and picnicking. Trailer personnel and tenants mowed grass up to the drainage ditch and planted flowers. The Sanderses installed underground wiring and surface power poles in the area between the road and the drainage ditch. In 1978, the Chaplins bought the eastern parcel. Shortly thereafter, they had a survey conducted. This survey revealed the Sanderses' encroachments. The Chaplins then sued to quiet title to the road and its shoulder (Parcel A) and the area between the road and the drainage ditch (Parcel B). With 10 years being the relevant possession period under state law, the Sanderses asserted that they owned Parcels A and B by virtue of adverse possession. Were the Sanderses correct?

3. The Wakes owned a tract of land. They used one part of the tract as a farm and the other part as a cattle ranch. Each spring and fall, the Wakes drove cattle from the ranch over an access road on the farm to Butler Springs, which was also located on the farm. From Butler Springs, they ranged the cattle eastward to adjacent government land, where they held grazing rights. In December 1956, the Wakes sold the farm portion of the land on contract to the Hesses. The contract of sale expressly reserved an easement for the Wakes to use the Butler Springs water and the right-of-way from Butler Springs across the property to the federal land. The contract described the Butler Springs area but did not describe the access road leading to Butler Springs from the county road. In 1963, the Hesses sold the farm to the Johnsons. These parties' contract referred to the Wakes' easement. The Wakes continued to use the access road and Butler Springs until 1964, when they sold their ranch and granted the Butler Springs easement to the purchasers. The ranch later changed hands several times, but each owner continued to use the access road and Butler Springs. In 1978, shortly after the Nelsons bought the ranch, the Johnsons sent them a letter "revoking permission" to use the access road. The Johnsons later placed locks on the gates across the access road. The Nelsons alleged that they had easement rights in the Butler Springs area and the access road leading to it. Were they correct?

4. Major developed a subdivision in which he built a number of houses and offered them for sale. The Rozells bought one of the houses. Upon the first rain, water entered under the crawl space of the house. Water then accumulated to a depth of 17 inches in a room where the furnace and water heater were located. This frequently caused the water heater not to work. Major's attempts to keep the water out were unsuccessful. Water continued to accumulate in the room whenever there was a rainfall of any consequence. As a result, the house was damp and had a peculiar odor. Mildew also became a problem. Did the Rozells have a cause of action against Major? If so, what cause of action?

5. In 1968, JEP bought a fully functioning theater in the Lake of the Ozarks. The building was designed and constructed as a live theater. It contained a raked concrete floor, 1000 seats bolted to the floor, stage and backstage areas, a concession stand, and a ticket booth. In 1970, the building was converted to a movie theater. On April 1, 1973, JEP agreed to a 20-year lease with Jablonow-Komm Theatres. Shortly thereafter, and with the approval of JEP, Jablonow removed the old wooden seats and installed 733 fabric-covered plastic theater seats. Jablonow then transferred its interest in the lease and property to RKO Mid-America Theatres, Inc. In May of 1982, JEP and RKO amended the 1973 lease, giving RKO the right to remodel the theater so that it had two screens instead of one for an increase in monthly rent. Two years later, RKO transferred its interest in the lease and property to Commonwealth Theatres of Missouri. As part of this transfer, RKO gave Commonwealth a "Bill of Sale and Assignment" that purported to transfer to Commonwealth 654 theater seats, "free and clear of all liens, encumbrances, claims, clouds, charges, equities, or imperfections of any kind or nature. . . ." In May 1985, Commonwealth transferred its interest in the lease and property to Wehrenberg. In April 1993, after the lease had expired and without JEP's approval, Wehrenberg uprooted the theater seats from the floor, breaking sections of concrete and leaving behind only the inclined floor, pocked with 2,600 holes. Were these seats fixtures?

6. Manor Ridge is a development consisting of 118 one-family residential lots on a 50-acre tract. When the tract was developed in the late 1920s, the developer established various deed restrictions "to run with the land." In addition to the covenant prohibiting "outbuildings," the Manor Ridge deeds provide that (1) "no more than one house intended for not more than one family shall be built on any plot," and (2) "no house shall be erected on any property . . . costing less than Fourteen thousand ($14,000) dollars based on the cost of construction of January 1st 1926." The deeds also require any residence to be set back 40 feet from the street and any detached garage to be set back 75 feet. The evident objective of this set of deed restrictions was to establish an exclusive residential community. The Lenocis bought their home in Manor Ridge in the summer of 1994. Shortly thereafter, they contracted to do extensive renovations to the home and to construct a "pool cabana" next to an existing in-ground swimming pool. The Lenocis began construction of the cabana in late March of 1995. Sneirson, who lives two houses away, observed the construction and promptly notified the municipal building department that the structure violated the restrictive covenant prohibiting "outbuildings." The building department issued a stop work order, but later rescinded the order. The Lenocis completed construction of the cabana. It is a substantial structure that covers more than 600 square feet, and has a cathedral ceiling, bathroom, refrigerator, dryer, wet bar, and heating system. It is located only five feet from the rear boundary line between the Lenocis' property and the property of the Steigers, close to the Steigers' swimming pool. Fifteen of the 118 properties located in Manor Ridge are occupied by ancillary structures. Ten of those structures are small sheds for the storage of pool or lawn mowing equipment, one is a dollhouse, and the other four are pool cabanas. The Lenocis' cabana is the largest in Manor Ridge; the only other one nearly as large is located on a two-and-a-half-acre lot, which is five times larger than the Lenocis' half-acre lot. Should the Lenocis be compelled to remove the cabana?

7. Morton and Edna Davis entered into a contract to buy a house from Clarence and Dana Johnson for $310,000. The house was three years old. The contract required a $5,000 initial deposit payment and an additional $26,000 deposit payment within five days. After the Davises had paid the initial $5,000 deposit but before they had paid the $26,000 deposit, Mrs. Davis noticed some buckling and peeling plaster around the corner of a window frame, as well as stains on ceilings in several rooms. When Mrs. Davis inquired about this, Mr. Johnson told her that the window had had a minor problem which was corrected long ago and that the stains were wallpaper glue. The Davises then paid the remaining $26,000 deposit, and the Johnsons moved out of the house. Several days later, following a heavy rain, Mrs. Davis entered the house and discovered water gushing in from around the window frame, the ceiling of the family room, the light fixtures, the glass doors, and the stove in the kitchen. The Davises hired roofers, who reported that the roof was inherently defective and that any repairs would be temporary because the roof was "slipping." Only a new roof, at a cost of $15,000, could be watertight. The Davises then filed this action alleging, among other things, fraud on the part of the Johnsons. The Davises sought rescission of the contract and return of their deposit payments. Did the Johnsons commit fraud?

8. Voyeur Dorm operates an Internet-based website that provides a 24-hour-a-day Internet transmission portraying the lives of the residents of 2312 West Farwell Drive, Tampa, Florida. Throughout its existence, Voyeur Dorm has employed 25 to 30 different women, most of whom entered into a contract that specifies, among other things, that they are "employees," on a "stage and filming location," with "no reasonable expectation of privacy," for "entertainment purposes." Subscribers to voyeurdorm.com pay a subscription fee of $34.95 a month to watch the women employed at the premises and pay an added fee of $16.00 per month to "chat" with the women. At a zoning hearing, Voyeur Dorm's counsel conceded that five women live in the house, that there are cameras in the corners of all the rooms of the house, that for a fee a person can join a membership to a website wherein a member can view the women 24 hours a day, seven days a week, that a member, at times, can see someone disrobed, that the women receive free room and board, and that the women are paid as part of a business enterprise. From August 1998 to June 2000, Voyeur Dorm generated subscriptions and sales totaling $3,166,551.35.

Section 27–523 of Tampa's City Code defines adult entertainment establishments as:

> any premises . . . on which is offered to members of the public or any person, for a consideration, entertainment featuring or in any way including specified sexual activities . . . or entertainment featuring the displaying or depicting of specified anatomical areas. . . ; 'entertainment' as used in this definition shall include, but not be limited to, books, magazines, films, newspapers, photographs, paintings, drawings, sketches or other publications or graphic media, filmed or live plays, dances or other performances either by single individuals or groups, distinguished by their display or depiction of specified anatomical areas or specified sexual activities.

The City of Tampa argues that Voyeur Dorm is an adult use business pursuant to the express and unambiguous language of section 27–523 and, as such, cannot operate in a residential neighborhood. Is the city correct?

9. Dinsmore Farms owned land on which an asphalt processing facility was located. The processing facility, which was removable from the land, was owned by another party. That party sold the processing facility to Northern Indiana Resources (NIR) in December 1993. At essentially the same time, NIR entered into a lease agreement with Dinsmore Farms regarding use of the land. Because the processing facility had not been operated for some time, conversion and repairs were necessary in order to place it in working order. NIR's president retained Lake Electric Co. to perform electrical work at the processing facility. Over a period of about two years, Lake provided various services and materials to NIR, and NIR made partial payments. In April 1995, Lake repaired a burner control and the outside bagger system (a piece of equipment) at the processing facility. Lake again repaired the outside bagger system on May 22, 1995. That was the final work performed by Lake for NIR. NIR failed to pay Lake for most of the work it had performed from November 1993 to May 22, 1995. Lake therefore filed a notice of intention to hold a mechanic's lien on the land owned by Dinsmore Farms, as well as "all buildings, other structures, and improvements located thereon." Indiana law provided that for a mechanic's lien to be validly asserted, the lien claimant had to have filed the notice of intention to claim a lien within 60 days after the final furnishing of relevant labor or services. Lake later sued Dinsmore Farms and NIR to foreclose the mechanic's lien. Dinsmore Farms contended that the lien was not valid because the last work done by Lake was on the outside bagger system, and that is a portable piece of equipment and not part of the real property. The bagger sits on a pallet behind one of the buildings at NIR's facility. The bagger is moved up to a control center and can be detached from the control center and moved in a truck. It can be moved either by unplugging it or disconnecting the wiring. Is Dinsmore Farms's argument a good one?

10. Emma Yocum was married to James Yocum as of the time of her death in 1990. She and James had begun living together in March 1959. In July 1959, by way of a warranty deed that referred to them as "husband and wife," Emma and James took ownership of a home. She and James, however, were not yet married. Emma was still married to Joseph Perez, from whom she was divorced in April 1960. Emma and James were married in July 1960. When they acquired their home in 1959, James had provided the down payment. A mortgage executed by Emma and James at that time also referred to them as husband and wife even though they were not then married. After Emma's death in 1990, her children by her marriage to Joseph Perez filed suit in an effort to have the court determine present ownership of the home Emma and James had owned during her lifetime. Had Emma and James owned the home as *tenants in common* (meaning that Emma's interest in the property would pass to her estate, in which her children were entitled to share), or instead as either *tenants by the entirety or joint tenants* (meaning that James would then solely own the home by virtue of the right of survivorship)?

Online Research: Researching Real Property on the Web

1.   Using your favorite search engine, locate a website that lists real estate for sale. Find a property listing on one of these sites. Using the concepts discussed in this chapter, identify the property features on the listing that would be considered fixtures.

2.   Find an example online of each of the following kinds of deeds: quitclaim deed, general warranty deed, and special warranty deed.

25

LANDLORD AND TENANT

Frank Johnson and Sonia Miller, along with several other friends, were looking to rent a house near campus for the following school year. In June, they orally agreed with a landlord on a one-year lease to begin the following August 15 with a monthly rent of $1250 and provided a $1,500 security deposit. When they arrived at school in August, the current tenants were still in possession and did not move out until September 1, leaving the house a mess. The landlord told Frank and Sonia to move in and that he would clean it up later; however, he never did so despite repeated requests. They complained to the city housing department which conducted an inspection and found numerous violations of the city's housing code. The city gave the landlord 15 days to make the necessary repairs. Before any of the repairs were made, a friend who was visiting was injured when she fell through some rotten floorboards on the porch. At the end of September, Frank, Sonia and the other tenants moved out, but the landlord refused to return their security deposit.

Among the legal issues raised by this scenario are:

- Did the oral agreement create an enforceable lease?
- Were the tenants' rights violated when they were unable to take possession on August 15?
- Does the landlord have any liability to the injured friend?
- Are the tenants entitled to cancel the lease on the grounds the house is not habitable and obtain the return of their security deposit?

LANDLORD–TENANT LAW HAS undergone dramatic change during the past four decades, owing in large part to the changing nature of the relationship between landlords and tenants. In England and in early America, farms were the usual subjects of leases. The tenant sought to lease land on which to grow crops or graze cattle. Accordingly, traditional landlord–tenant law viewed the lease as primarily a conveyance of land and paid relatively little attention to its contractual aspects.

In today's society, however, the landlord–tenant relationship is typified by the lease of property for residential or commercial purposes. The tenant occupies only a small portion of the total property. He bargains primarily for the use of structures on the land rather than for the land itself. He is likely to have signed a landlord-provided form lease, the terms of which he may have had little or no opportunity to negotiate. In areas with a shortage of afford-able housing, a residential tenant's ability to bargain for favorable lease provisions is further hampered. Because the typical landlord–tenant relationship can no longer fairly be characterized as one in which the parties have equal knowledge and bargaining power, it is not always realistic to presume that tenants are capable of negotiating to protect their own interests.

Although it was initially slow to recognize the changing nature of the landlord–tenant relationship, the law now tends to place greater emphasis than it once did on the contract components of the relationship. As a result, modern contract doctrines such as unconscionability, constructive conditions, the duty to mitigate damages, and implied warranties are sometimes applied to leases. Such doctrines may operate to compensate for tenants' lack of bargaining power. In addition, state legislatures and city councils have enacted statutes and ordinances that increasingly regulate leased property and the landlord–tenant relationship.

This chapter's discussion of landlord–tenant law will focus on the nature of leasehold interests, the traditional rights and duties of landlords and tenants, and recent statutory and judicial developments affecting those rights and duties.

Leases and Tenancies

Nature of Leases

A **lease** is a contract under which an owner of property, the **landlord** (also called the *lessor*), conveys to the **tenant** (also called the *lessee*) the exclusive right to possess property for a period of time. The property interest conveyed to the tenant is called a **leasehold estate.**

Types of Tenancies

The duration of the tenant's possessory right depends upon the type of **tenancy** established by or resulting from the lease. There are four main types of tenancies.

1. *Tenancy for a term.* In a **tenancy for a term** (also called a *tenancy for years*), the landlord and tenant have agreed on a specific duration of the lease and have fixed the date on which the tenancy will terminate. For example, if Dudley, a college student, leases an apartment for the academic year ending May 25, 2004, a tenancy for a term will have been created. The tenant's right to possess the property ends on the date agreed upon without any further notice, unless the lease contains a provision permitting extension.

2. *Periodic tenancy.* A **periodic tenancy** is created when the parties agree that rent will be paid in regular successive intervals until notice to terminate is given, but do not agree on a specific lease duration. If the tenant pays rent monthly, the tenancy is from month to month; if the tenant pays yearly, as is sometimes done under agricultural leases, the tenancy is from year to year. (Periodic tenancies therefore are sometimes called *tenancies from month to month* or *tenancies from year to year.*) To terminate a periodic tenancy, either party must give advance notice to the other. The precise amount of notice required is often defined by state statutes. For example, to terminate a tenancy from month to month, most states require that the notice be given at least one month in advance.

3. *Tenancy at will.* A **tenancy at will** occurs when property is leased for an indefinite period of time and either party may choose to conclude the tenancy at any time.

CONCEPT REVIEW

Types of Tenancies

Type of Lease	Characteristics	Termination
Tenancy for a Term	Landlord and tenant agree on a specific duration of the lease and fix the date on which the tenancy will end	Ends automatically on the date agreed upon; no additional notice necessary
Periodic Tenancy	Landlord and tenant agree that tenant will pay rent at regular, successive intervals (e.g., month to month)	Either party may terminate by giving the amount of advance notice required by state law
Tenancy at Will	Landlord and tenant agree that tenant may possess property for an indefinite amount of time, with no agreement to pay rent at regular, successive intervals	May be terminated "at will" by either party, but state law requires advance notice
Tenancy at Sufferance	Tenant remains in possession after the termination of one of the leaseholds described above, until landlord brings ejectment action against tenant or collects rent from him	Landlord has choice of: 1. Treating tenant as a trespasser and bringing ejectment action against him, or 2. Accepting rent from tenant, thus creating a new leasehold

CYBERLAW IN ACTION

The Internet Facilitates Leasing Property

E-Commerce has eased the sometimes challenging and time-consuming task of finding an apartment or rental property. Now in many cities and resort-communities a person can search for a suitable rental using the Internet. There are numerous Internet portals that provide databases of available rental properties. While some are nationwide, most focus on a specific region or city. These websites allow prospective renters to list their particular requirements such as size, location, price range, and amenities. Then the site operator provides available options to the prospective renter and may periodically update the list. Some companies even provide virtual tours of apartment or house layouts that allow the prospective renter to view the property online. In some cases, a rental application may be submitted and the rental arrangements finalized via the Internet. The Internet portal sites also commonly provide links that allow customers to turn on their gas, water, telephone, and other desired utilities over the Internet.

Generally, tenancies at will involve situations in which the tenant either does not pay rent or does not pay it at regular intervals. For example, Landon allows her friend Trumbull to live in the apartment over her garage. Although this tenancy's name indicates that it is terminable "at [the] will" of either party, most states require that the landlord give reasonable advance notice to the tenant before exercising the right to terminate the tenancy.

4. *Tenancy at sufferance.* A **tenancy at sufferance** occurs when a tenant remains in possession of the property (holds over) after a lease has expired. In this situation, the landlord has two options: (1) treating the holdover tenant as a trespasser and bringing an action to eject him; and (2) continuing to treat him as a tenant and collecting rent from him. Until the landlord makes her election, the tenant is a tenant at sufferance. Suppose that Templeton has leased an apartment for one year from Larson. At the end of the year, Templeton holds over and does not move out. Templeton is a tenant at sufferance. Larson may have him ejected or may continue treating him as a tenant. If Larson elects the latter alternative, a new tenancy is created. The new tenancy will be either a tenancy for a term or a periodic tenancy, depending on the facts of the case and any presumptions established by state law. Thus, a tenant who holds over for even a few days runs the risk of creating a new tenancy he might not want.

Execution of a Lease

As transfers of interests in land, leases may be covered by the statute of frauds. In most states, a lease for a term of more than one year from the date it is made is unenforceable unless it is evidenced by a suitable writing signed by the party to be charged. A few states, however, require leases to be evidenced by a writing only when they are for a term of more than three years.

Good business practice demands that leases be carefully drafted to make clear the parties' respective rights and obligations. Care in drafting leases is especially important in cases of long-term and commercial leases. Lease provisions normally cover such essential matters as the term of the lease, the rent to be paid, the uses the tenant may make of the property, the circumstances under which the landlord may enter the property, the parties' respective obligations regarding the condition of the property, and the responsibility (as between landlord and tenant) for making repairs. In addition, leases often contain provisions allowing a possible extension of the term of the lease and purporting to limit the parties' rights to assign the lease or sublet the property. State or local law often regulates lease terms. For example, the Uniform Residential Landlord and Tenant Act (URLTA) has been enacted in a substantial minority of states. The URLTA prohibits the inclusion of certain lease provisions, such as a clause by which the tenant supposedly agrees to pay the landlord's attorney's fees in an action to enforce the lease. In states that have not enacted the URLTA, lease terms are likely to be regulated at least to a moderate degree by some combination of state statutes, common law principles, and local housing codes.

Rights, Duties, and Liabilities of the Landlord

Landlord's Rights

The landlord is entitled to receive the *agreed rent* for the term of the lease. Upon expiration of the lease, the landlord has the right to the *return of the property in as good a condition as it was when leased,* except for normal wear and tear and any destruction caused by an act of God.

Security Deposits Landlords commonly require tenants to make security deposits or advance payments of rent. Such deposits operate to protect the landlord's right to receive rent as well as her right to reversion of the property in good condition. In recent years, many cities and states have enacted statutes or ordinances designed to prevent landlord abuse of security deposits. These laws typically limit the amount a landlord may demand and require that the security deposit be refundable, except for portions withheld by the landlord because of the tenant's nonpayment of rent or tenant-caused property damage beyond ordinary wear and tear. Some statutes or ordinances also require the landlord to place the funds in interest-bearing accounts when the lease is for more than a minimal period of time. As a general rule, these laws require landlords to provide tenants a written accounting regarding their security deposits and any portions being withheld. Such an accounting normally must be provided within a specified period of time (30 days, for example) after the termination of the lease. The landlord's failure to comply with statutes and ordinances regarding security deposits may cause the landlord to experience adverse consequences that vary state by state.

Landlord's Duties

Fair Housing Act As explained in Chapter 24, the Fair Housing Act prohibits housing discrimination on the basis of race, color, sex, religion, national origin, handicap, and familial status.[1] The Fair Housing Act prohibits discriminatory practices in various transactions affecting housing, including the rental of dwellings.[2] Included within the act's prohibited instances of discrimination against a protected person are refusals to rent property to such a person, discrimination against him or her in the terms, conditions, or privileges of rental, publication of any advertisement or statement indicating any preference, limitation, or discrimination operating to the disadvantage of a protected person, and

representations that a dwelling is not available for rental to such a person when, in fact, it is available.

The act also makes it a discriminatory practice for a landlord to refuse to permit a tenant with a handicap to make—at his own expense—reasonable modifications to leased property. The landlord may, however, make this permission conditional on the tenant's agreement to restore the property to its previous condition upon termination of the lease, reasonable wear and tear excepted. In addition, landlords are prohibited from refusing to make reasonable accommodations in rules, policies, practices, or services if such accommodations are necessary to afford a handicapped tenant equal opportunity to use and enjoy the leased premises. When constructing certain types of multifamily housing for first occupancy, property owners and developers risk violating the act if they fail to make the housing accessible to persons with handicaps.

Because of a perceived increase in the frequency with which landlords refused to rent to families with children, the act prohibits landlords from excluding families with children. If, however, the dwelling falls within the act's "housing for older persons" exception, this prohibition does not apply.[3]

Implied Warranty of Possession Landlords have certain obligations that are imposed by law whenever property is leased. One of these obligations stems from the landlord's **implied warranty of possession.** This warranty guarantees the tenant's right to possess the property for the term of the lease. Suppose that Turner rents an apartment from Long for a term to begin on September 1, 2003, and to end on August 31, 2004. When Turner attempts to move in on September 1, 2003, she finds that Carlson, the previous tenant, is still in possession of the property. In this case, Long has breached the implied warranty of possession.

Implied Warranty of Quiet Enjoyment By leasing property, the landlord also makes an **implied warranty of quiet enjoyment** (or *covenant of quiet enjoyment*). This covenant guarantees that the tenant's possession will not be interfered with as a result of the landlord's act or omission. In the absence of a contrary provision in the lease or an emergency that threatens the property, the landlord may not enter the leased property during the term of the lease. If he does, he will be liable for trespass. In some cases, courts have held that the covenant of quiet enjoyment was violated when the landlord failed to stop third parties, such as trespassers or other tenants who

---

[1]Familial status is defined in Chapter 24.

[2]The act provides an exemption for certain persons who own and rent single-family houses. To qualify for this exemption, owners must not use a real estate broker or an illegal advertisement and cannot own more than three such houses at one time. It also exempts owners who rent rooms or units in dwellings in which they themselves reside, if those dwellings house no more than four families.

---

[3]The "housing for older persons" exception is described in Chapter 24.

make excessive noise, from interfering with the tenant's enjoyment of the leased premises.

Constructive Eviction The doctrine of **constructive eviction** may aid a tenant when property becomes unsuitable for the purposes for which it was leased because of the landlord's act or omission, such as the breach of a duty to repair or the covenant of quiet enjoyment. Under this doctrine, which applies both to residential and commercial property, the tenant may terminate the lease because she has effectively been evicted as a result of the poor condition or the objectionable circumstances there. Constructive eviction gives a tenant the right to vacate the property without further rent obligation if she does so *promptly* after giving the landlord reasonable notice and an opportunity to correct the problem. Because constructive eviction requires the tenant to vacate the leased premises, it is an unattractive option, however, for tenants who cannot afford to move or do not have a suitable alternative place to live.

Landlord's Responsibility for Condition of Leased Property

The common law historically held that landlords made no implied warranties regarding the *condition* or *quality* of leased premises. As an adjunct to the landlord's right to receive the leased property in good condition at the termination of the lease, the common law imposed on the *tenant* the duty to make repairs. Even when the lease contained a landlord's express warranty or express promise to make repairs, a tenant was not entitled to withhold rent if the landlord failed to carry out his obligations. This was because a fundamental contract performance principle—that a party is not obligated to perform if the other party fails to perform—was considered inapplicable to leases. In recent years, however, changing views of the landlord–tenant relationship have resulted in dramatically increased legal responsibility on the part of landlords for the condition of leased residential property.

Implied Warranty of Habitability The legal principle that landlords made no implied warranty regarding the condition of leased property arose during an era when tenants used land primarily for agricultural purposes. Buildings existing on the property were frequently of secondary importance. They also tended to be simple structures, lacking modern conveniences such as plumbing and wiring. These buildings were fairly easily inspected and repaired by the tenant, who was generally more self-sufficient than today's typical tenant. In view of the relative simplicity of the structures, landlord and tenant

were considered to have equal knowledge of the property's condition upon commencement of the lease. Thus, a rule requiring the tenant to make repairs seemed reasonable.

The position of modern residential tenants differs greatly from that of an earlier era's agricultural tenants. The modern residential tenant bargains not for the use of the ground itself but for the use of a building (or portion thereof) as a dwelling. The structures on land today are complex, frequently involving systems (such as plumbing and electrical systems) to which the tenant does not have physical access. Besides decreasing the likelihood of perceiving defects during inspection, this complexity compounds the difficulty of making repairs—something at which today's tenant already tends to be less adept than his grandparents were. Moreover, placing a duty on tenants to negotiate for express warranties and duties to repair is no longer feasible. Residential leases are now routinely executed on standard forms provided by landlords.

For these reasons, statutes or judicial decisions in most states now impose an **implied warranty of habitability** on many landlords who lease residential property. According to the vast majority of cases, this warranty is applicable only to *residential* property, and not to property leased for commercial uses. The implied warranty of habitability's content in lease settings is basically the same as in the sale of real estate: the property must be safe and suitable for human habitation. In lease settings, however, the landlord not only must deliver a habitable dwelling at the beginning of the lease but also must *maintain* the property in a habitable condition during the term of the lease. Various statutes and judicial decisions provide that the warranty includes an obligation that the leased property comply with any applicable housing codes. In the *Johnson* case, which follows shortly, the Supreme Court of Indiana takes a conservative approach to the implied warranty of habitability by holding that it may sometimes arise in the residential lease setting. Courts in other states often give this implied warranty a broader effect by ruling that it applies to all or nearly all instances of residential leasing.

Remedies for Breach of Implied Warranty of Habitability From a tenant's point of view, the implied warranty of habitability is superior to constructive eviction because a tenant does not have to vacate the leased premises in order to seek a remedy for breach of the warranty. The particular remedies for breach of the implied warranty of habitability differ from state to state. Some of the remedies a tenant may pursue include:

1. *Action for damages.* The breach of the implied warranty of habitability violates the lease and renders the landlord liable for damages. The damages generally are measured by the diminished value of the leasehold. The landlord's breach of the implied warranty of habitability may also be asserted by the tenant as a counterclaim and defense in the landlord's action for eviction and/or non-payment of rent.

2. *Termination of lease.* In extreme cases, the landlord's breach of the implied warranty of habitability may justify the tenant's termination of the lease. For this remedy to be appropriate, the landlord's breach must have been substantial enough to constitute a material breach.

3. *Rent abatement.* Some states permit rent abatement, a remedy under which the tenant withholds part of the rent for the period during which the landlord was in breach of the implied warranty of habitability. Where authorized by law, this approach allows the tenant to pay a reduced rent that reflects the *actual* value of the leasehold in its defective condition. There are different ways of computing this value. State law determines the amount by which the rent will be reduced.

4. *Repair-and-deduct.* A growing number of states have statutes permitting the tenant to have defects repaired and to deduct the repair costs from her rent. The repairs authorized in these statutes are usually limited to essential services such as electricity and plumbing. They also require that the tenant give the landlord notice of the defect and an adequate opportunity to make the repairs himself.

Housing Codes Many cities and states have enacted housing codes that impose duties on property owners with respect to the condition of leased property. Typical of these provisions is Section 2304 of the District of Columbia Housing Code, which provides: "No person shall rent or offer to rent any habitation or the furnishing thereof unless such habitation and its furnishings are in a clean, safe and sanitary condition, in repair and free from rodents or vermin." Such codes commonly call for the provision and maintenance of necessary services such as heat, water, and electricity, as well as suitable bathroom and kitchen facilities. Housing codes also tend to require that specified minimum space–per-tenant standards be met, that windows, doors, floors, and screens be kept in repair, that the property be painted and free of lead paint, that keys and locks meet certain specifications, and that the landlord issue written receipts for rent payments. A landlord's failure to comply with an applicable housing code may result in a fine or in liability for injuries resulting from the property's disrepair. The noncompliance may also result in the landlord's losing part or all of his claim to the agreed-upon rent. Some housing codes establish that tenants have the right to withhold rent until necessary repairs have been made and the right to move out in cases of particularly egregious violations of housing code requirements.

Johnson v. Scandia Associates, Inc.   *717 N.E.2d 24 (Ind. Sup. Ct. 1999)*

Scandia Associates, Inc., owned an apartment complex in Indianapolis. Terri Johnson resided in one of the apartments. While cooking in her apartment, Johnson simultaneously touched the oven and the refrigerator and received a severe electric shock. She sustained physical injuries as a result. Alleging claims for negligence and breach of the implied warranty of habitability, Johnson sued Scandia. The trial court granted Scandia's motion to dismiss the implied warranty claim but allowed the negligence claim to go to the jury. The jury returned a verdict in favor of Scandia.

Johnson appealed the dismissal of her implied warranty of habitability claim. The Indiana Court of Appeals reversed, holding that an implied warranty of habitability exists in a residential lease if the landlord is a professional in the residential apartment business. The Court of Appeals further held that the implied warranty of habitability extends to claims for personal injuries caused by a hidden or concealed dangerous condition in the leased premises. Scandia appealed to the Supreme Court of Indiana.

Shepard, Chief Justice Some Indiana [lower-court] cases have recognized that a warranty of habitability may be implied in a residential lease, giving rise to damages for breach of contract upon appropriate proof. In this appeal, we recognize for the first time that such a warranty may be implied in some leases and explore the conditions under which it may be held to exist.

This Court first imported a warranty of habitability into conveyances of real property [in a 1972 decision] holding that a warranty of fitness for habitation may be implied in a builder-vendor's sale of a new house to the first purchaser. [In a decision four years later,] we extended the protection of the implied warranty to subsequent purchasers of the house, but limited [the warranty's] scope to latent or hidden defects.

Asked whether a warranty of habitability is implied in the residential leasehold contract, the Court of Appeals held in *Breezewood Management Co. v. Maltbie* (Ind. App. 1980) that a landlord could be found liable to his tenant on a breach of implied warranty, at least where there was a housing code and city inspectors had cited the landlord with multiple violations. [The plaintiffs were awarded] damages based on the law of contract: the difference between the rents paid for the apartment as warranted and its fair rental value in the substandard condition, compensating the tenants for their economic loss.

Plainly, a warranty of habitability, whether in the sale or lease of residential dwellings, has developed in the common law of Indiana, and its roots are in the law of contract. Habitability means reasonably fit for occupation as a dwelling. Habitability is not the same as no risk of harm.

When a landlord enters a lease agreement with her tenant, she voluntarily confers certain rights upon the tenant, such as possession and quiet enjoyment for a specific term. She does this in consideration of the tenant's promise to pay rent, not to waste the property, not to use it for illegal purposes, and not to "hold over" beyond the term. The landlord agrees to this legal relationship after balancing the costs and benefits, and the same is true for the tenant.

Defining a warranty of habitability broadly as a tenant's right to be free from injury might have many effects. A broad definition might cause landlords to increase maintenance of properties, at least where doing so would still produce an economic return. It would undoubtedly prompt landlords to purchase additional insurance, spreading the risk of harm more broadly. Landlords would, of course, attempt to pass along increased insurance costs to tenants by raising rents. Increased leasing costs might also cause conversion of some properties from residential uses and outright abandonment of others. This would shrink the supply of affordable housing, which could have potentially adverse social effects and would, of course, be borne by society's poorest renters.

Potential negative outcomes also could flow from a warranty rule on injury—because high standards of upkeep could be discouraged by shifting the risk of liability, and thus economic incentive, from the landlord to the insurer. A contractual right could diminish a tenant's incentive to report or repair defects by eliminating the economic risk of contributory negligence. All of these outcomes would increase the risk of harm to tenants, residents, and guests.

In light of these considerations, we conclude that a warranty of habitability is best thought of along the lines of *Breezewood:* a landlord's promise to convey to a tenant an apartment suitable for living. Habitability is an objective factual determination which may be codified, but is not necessarily prescribed by a housing code. A community's adoption of a building or housing code is evidence of its conception of habitability standards for dwellings in that locale. These codes vary enormously in their prescriptions. Absent explicit statutory or regulatory language imposing on landlords the obligation to warrant a codified standard of habitability in a property rented as a residence, a housing code does not impose a warranty on the residential leasehold transaction.

Even though an implied warranty of habitability is not imposed by law on every residential lease contract, it may be implied in fact in the agreement between landlord and tenant. Contracts and covenants implied in fact arise from the course of dealing between the parties and may be evidenced by acts done in the course of performance or by ordinary practices in the trade. This seems the best way of viewing *Breezewood.* The warranty extended by the landlord was implied in fact from the parties' course of dealing, which included dealings related to the Bloomington Housing Code. [These dealings led to the landlord's stated but unfulfilled promise to take corrective action after the landlord was cited for housing code violations.] The Code thus provided evidence for determining that the landlord breached his promise.

Johnson does not identify any state or local law as the source of the warranty she pleads as implied in her contract. Moreover, she has not identified any facts demonstrating that a warranty of habitability was either express or implied-in-fact in the agreement.

When a landlord warrants his property to be suitable for living and then breaches that promise . . ., the tenant's remedy may take several forms, including conveyance of a suitable property, rescission and reformation of the agreement while the tenant retains possession, rescission of the contract, or damages at law. Consequential damages may be awarded in a breach of contract claim when the nonbreaching party's loss flows naturally and probably from the breach and was contemplated by the parties when the contract was made. This . . . rule . . . generally limits consequential damages to reasonably foreseeable economic losses. Accordingly, recovery for personal injury on a contract claim is allowable only when the particular injury was within the parties' contemplation during contract formation. Thus, to claim consequential damages the tenant must show the parties intended to compensate for personal injury losses caused by the apartment's unfitness. The tenant may prove the promise to compensate personal injury by showing its expression as a contract term or by pointing out evidence showing it to be implied in the agreement.

Johnson complains that her apartment was not suitable for living because its fixtures unexpectedly released an electric current, and, second, that her injuries were foreseeably caused by the breaching condition. She does not allege whether the defect was present at the time of entry or arose after [she took] possession, nor does she have any contention about giving Scandia notice of the defect. Johnson says her leasehold contract is governed by a writing, so we look within the document to see if it extended her a warranty. Because the writing does not show that Scandia expressly warranted the apartment's habitability, Johnson's assertion can mean just one thing: [in Johnson's view,] Scandia impliedly warranted the habitability of Johnson's apartment. Johnson pleads no facts which, if true, tend to show that the agreement formed with Scandia gives a warranty of habitability. Her failure to plead a factual basis showing that Scandia . . . extended the warranty as part of her agreement results in a failure to state a valid claim that the warranty was breached. Moreover, because Johnson's claim is based on an implied warranty theory, the only way she could receive the relief she requests would be through consequential damages. Inasmuch as consequential damages for physical injury are not available on a claim for breach of an implied warranty of habitability, Johnson cannot state a claim entitling her to relief.

Indiana's common law of contract governing the landlord–tenant relationship has developed a warranty of habitability. The warranty is not universally imposed by law, but derives from the agreement between the tenant and the landlord and may be express or implied. The existence of an implied warranty may be proven through evidence of the parties' course of dealing or performance and by evidence of ordinary practices in the trade. Where the warranty is express, consequential damages for injury to the person may be available as a remedy. Where the warranty is implied-in-fact, however, consequential damages may not be awarded because personal injury is outside the parties' contemplation. Johnson's complaint does not aver facts tending to show that Scandia warranted the apartment's habitability or that her injury was reasonably foreseeable within a warranty of habitability.

Decision of Court of Appeals reversed; judgment in favor of Scandia granted.

Americans with Disabilities Act Landlords leasing property constituting a *place of public accommodation* (primarily commercial property as opposed to private residential property) must pay heed to Title III of the Americans with Disabilities Act. Under Title III, owners and possessors of real property that is a place of public accommodation may be expected to make reasonable accommodations, including physical modifications of the property, in order to allow disabled persons to have access to the property. Chapter 24 contains a detailed discussion of Title III's provisions.

Landlord's Tort Liability

Traditional No-Liability Rule There were two major effects of the traditional rule that a landlord had no legal responsibility for the condition of the leased property. The first effect—that the uninhabitability of the premises traditionally did not give a tenant the right to withhold rent, assert a defense to nonpayment, or terminate a lease—has already been discussed. The second effect was that land-lords normally could not be held liable in tort for injuries suffered by tenants on leased property. This state of affairs stemmed from the notion that the tenant had the ability and responsibility to inspect the property for defects before leasing it. By leasing the property, the tenant was presumed to take it as it was, with any existing defects. As to any defects that might arise during the term of the lease, the landlord's tort immunity was seen as justified by his lack of control over the leased property once he had surrendered it to the tenant.

Traditional Exceptions to No-Liability Rule Even before the current era's protenant legal developments, however, courts created exceptions to the no-liability rule. In the following situations, landlords have traditionally owed the tenant (or an appropriate third party) a duty, the breach of which could constitute a tort:

1. *Duty to maintain common areas.* Landlords have a duty to use reasonable care to *maintain the common areas* (such as stairways, parking lots, and elevators) over which they retain control. If a tenant or a tenant's guest sustains injury as a result of the landlord's negligent maintenance of a common area, the landlord is liable.

2. *Duty to disclose hidden defects.* Landlords have the duty to disclose hidden defects about which they know, if the defects are not reasonably discoverable by the tenant. The landlord is liable if a tenant or appropriate third party suffers injury because of a hidden danger that was known to the landlord but went undisclosed.

3. *Duty to use reasonable care in performing repairs.* If a landlord repairs leased property, he must *exercise reasonable care in making the repairs.* The landlord may be liable for the consequences stemming from negligently performed repairs, even if he was not obligated to perform them.

4. *Duty to maintain property leased for admission to the public.* The landlord has a duty to suitably maintain property that is leased for *admission to the public.* A theater would be an example.

5. *Duty to maintain furnished dwellings.* The landlord who rents a *fully furnished dwelling* for a short time impliedly warrants that the premises are safe and habitable.

Except for the above circumstances, the landlord traditionally was not liable for injuries suffered by the tenant on leased property. Note that none of these exceptions would apply to one of the most common injury scenarios—when the tenant was injured by a defect in her own apartment and the defect resulted from the landlord's failure to repair, rather than from negligently performed repairs.

Current Trends in Landlord's Tort Liability

Today, there is a strong trend toward abolition of the traditional rule of landlord tort immunity. The proliferation of housing codes and the development of the implied warranty of habitability have persuaded a sizable number of courts to impose on landlords the duty to use *reasonable care* in their maintenance of the leased property. As discussed earlier, a landlord's duty to keep the property in repair may be based on an express clause in the lease, the implied warranty of habitability, or provisions of a housing code or statute. The landlord now may be liable if injury results from her negligent failure to carry out her duty to make repairs. As a general rule, a landlord will not be liable unless she had *notice* of the defect and a reasonable opportunity to make repairs.

The duty of care landlords owe tenants has been held to include the duty to take reasonable steps to protect tenants from substantial risks of harm created by other tenants. Courts have held landlords liable for tenants' injuries resulting from dangerous conditions (such as vicious animals) maintained by other tenants when the landlord knew or had reason to know of the danger.

It is not unusual for landlords to attempt to insulate themselves from negligence liability to tenants by including an *exculpatory clause* in the standard form leases they expect tenants to sign. An exculpatory clause purports to relieve the landlord from legal responsibility that the landlord could otherwise face (on negligence or other grounds) in certain instances of premises-related injuries suffered by tenants. In recent years, a number of state legislatures and courts have frowned upon exculpatory clauses when they are included in leases of residential property. There has been an increasing judicial tendency to limit the effect of exculpatory clauses or declare them unenforceable on public policy grounds when they appear in residential leases.

Landlord's Liability for Injuries Resulting from Others' Criminal Conduct Another aspect of the trend toward increasing landlords' legal accountability is that many courts have imposed on landlords the duty to take reasonable steps to protect tenants and others on their property from foreseeable criminal conduct.[4] Although landlords are not insurers of the safety of persons on their property, an increasing number of courts have found them liable for injuries sustained by individuals who were criminally attacked on the landlord's property if the attack was facilitated by the landlord's failure to comply with housing codes or maintain reasonable security. This liability has been imposed on residential and commercial landlords (such as shopping mall owners). Some courts have held that the implied warranty of habitability includes the obligation to provide reasonable security. In most states that have imposed this type of liability, however, principles of negligence or negligence per se furnish the controlling rationale.[5] The *Erichsen* case, which follows, applies negligence principles in this fashion.

---

[4]Chapter 24 contains a more extensive discussion of courts' recent inclination to impose this duty on owners and possessors of property.
[5]The law of negligence is covered in detail in Chapter 7.

Erichsen v. No-Frills Supermarkets of Omaha, Inc.
518 N.W. 2d 116 (Neb. Sup. Ct. 1994)

No-Frills Supermarkets of Omaha, Inc., operated a supermarket at a shopping center location leased from the center's owner, Harold Cooperman. Janice Erichsen had been shopping at this supermarket and was returning to her car, which was parked in the store's parking lot. Before Erichsen reached her car, she was robbed and beaten by an assailant. In the course of the attack, Erichsen, who was outside the assailant's vehicle, became entangled in the vehicle's safety belt. She was then dragged on the pavement for 1.6 miles. She sustained serious injuries as a result.

Erichsen sued No-Frills and Cooperman, alleging that they had negligently failed to warn her or take other reasonable steps to protect her against allegedly foreseeable criminal activities. Erichsen alleged that on at least 10 occasions within a 16-month period prior to the attack on her, similar crimes, including theft, purse-snatching, and robbery, had been committed in the No-Frills parking lot or in immediately surrounding areas. Erichsen also contended that No-Frills and Cooperman had a duty to foresee the type of criminal activity to which she fell victim and to take appropriate steps to guard against such harm. The district court sustained the demurrer of No-Frills and Cooperman, holding that they did not owe Erichsen a duty of reasonable care. Erichsen appealed.

Lanphier, Justice   For actionable negligence to exist, there must be a legal duty on the part of the defendant to [use reasonable care to] protect the plaintiff from injury, a failure to discharge that duty, and damage proximately resulting from such undischarged duty. A duty . . . may be defined as an obligation, to which the law will give recognition and effect, to conform to a particular standard of conduct toward another. Foreseeability is a factor in establishing a defendant's duty.

We have . . . held that a landlord is under a duty to exercise reasonable care to protect his patrons. Such care may require giving a warning or providing greater protection where there is a *likelihood* that third persons will endanger the safety of the visitors. We have applied these principles in several cases. In *Harvey v. Van Aelstyn* (1982), we held that no liability attached to the owner of a bar where [the plaintiff], a patron, was assaulted by a third party while in the bar. The assailant had not been present in the bar, but . . . entered the bar suddenly, went straight for [the plaintiff], and struck him. The assailant had been violent in the establishment on *one* prior occasion a year or more prior to the incident at issue. We stated that the possessor of the premises was not bound to anticipate the unforeseeable independent acts of third persons, nor did she have a duty to take precautionary measures to protect against such acts, because those acts could not reasonably be anticipated.

[An earlier] case, *Hughes v. Coniglio* (1946), denied recovery against a restaurant owner where a patron suffered injuries from an assault by another patron. This court noted that there was no history of any fights in the establishment and that the assault occurred suddenly and unexpectedly where no precautionary measures would have prevented the assault. In *C.S. v. Sophir* (1985), the plaintiff, a tenant

in the defendant landlord's apartment complex, was sexually assaulted. There had been one prior assault in the complex. We held that it would be unfair to impose liability upon a landlord based on a *single* prior assault at the complex.

The most recent case involving landlord liability for the acts of third persons is *K.S.R. v. Novak & Sons, Inc.* (1987). In *K.S.R.,* [the plaintiff] was sexually assaulted in the apartment complex owned by [the defendant]. The assailant had been seen by the building manager several times near the complex exhibiting inappropriate sexual behavior in public. In *K.S.R.,* we held that unlike *Sophir,* there was a history of criminal activity on the premises, and therefore the assault perpetrated against [the plaintiff] was foreseeable. [We concluded] that liability could be imposed against a landlord for reasonably foreseeable criminal acts of third parties.

This court has denied relief where the [plaintiff] based his or her allegations of negligence on a single act of violence. However, as *K.S.R.* demonstrates, a duty to undertake reasonable precautionary measures will be imposed on the landlord when there is a sufficient amount of criminal activity to make further criminal acts reasonably foreseeable. The trial court was in error in determining that the prior criminal activity must all involve the same suspect to make further criminal acts reasonably foreseeable. Under our standard of review, the allegation of many occasions of "similar" criminal activity in one fairly contiguous area in a limited timespan may make further such acts sufficiently foreseeable to create a duty to a business invitee.

[By referring in her petition to at least 10 instances of criminal activity at or near the No-Frills parking lot, Erichsen has alleged facts that] are legally sufficient to support [her] assertion that [No-Frills and Cooperman] owed her a duty of reasonable care which they breached. Although [Erichsen] concedes that not all of the criminal activities took place in the No-Frills parking lot, she did allege that at least some of the incidents of criminal activity, including a purse-snatching, actually took place on the area of the parking lot assigned to No-Frills. Criminal acts that occur near the premises in question give notice of the risk that crime may travel to the premises of the business owner. Accordingly, the district court erred in sustaining the demurrer.

District court decision reversed and case remanded for further proceedings.

ETHICS IN ACTION

Disclosing Possible Hazards to Tenants

Suppose you own an older home that in the past was painted with lead-based paint. You rent it to a family with three small children. A state law forbids using

lead-based paint on residential property after the effective date of the statute, but it does not require owners of property with residues of lead-based paint to remove it. Should you disclose the presence of the lead-based paint to your tenants?

Rights, Duties, and Liabilities of the Tenant

Rights of the Tenant

The tenant has the right to *exclusive possession* and *quiet enjoyment* of the property during the term of the lease. The landlord is not entitled to enter the leased property without the tenant's consent, unless an emergency threatens the property or the landlord is acting under an express lease provision giving her the right to enter. The tenant may use the leased premises for any lawful purpose that is reasonable and appropriate, unless the purpose for which it may be used is expressly limited in the lease. Furthermore, the tenant has both the right to receive leased residential property in a habitable condition at the beginning of the lease and the right to have the property maintained in a habitable condition for the duration of the lease.

Duty to Pay Rent

The tenant, of course, has the duty to pay rent in the agreed amount and at the agreed times. If two or more persons are cotenants, their liability under the lease is *joint and several.* This means that each cotenant has complete responsibility—not just partial responsibility—for performing the tenants' duties under the lease.

For example, Alberts and Baker rent an apartment from Caldwell, with both Alberts and Baker signing a one-year lease. If Alberts moves out after three months, Caldwell may hold Baker responsible for the entire rent, not just half of it. Naturally, Alberts remains liable on the lease— as well as to Baker under any rent-sharing agreement the two of them had—but Caldwell is free to proceed against Baker solely if Caldwell so chooses.

Duty Not to Commit Waste

The tenant also has the duty not to commit **waste** on the property. This means that the tenant is responsible for the routine care and upkeep of the property and that he has the duty not to commit any act that would harm the property. In the past, fulfillment of this duty required that the tenant perform necessary repairs. Today, the duty to make repairs has generally been shifted to the landlord by court ruling, statute, or lease provision. The tenant now has no duty to make major repairs unless the relevant damage was caused by his own negligence. When damage exists through no fault of the tenant and the tenant therefore is not obligated to make the actual repairs, the tenant nonetheless has the duty to take reasonable interim steps to prevent further damage from the elements. This duty would include, but not necessarily be limited to, informing the landlord of the problem. The duty would be triggered, for instance, when a window breaks or the roof leaks.

Assignment and Subleasing

As with rights and duties under most other types of contracts, the rights and duties under a lease may generally be assigned and delegated to third parties. **Assignment** occurs when the landlord or the tenant transfers all of her remaining rights under the lease to another person. For example, a landlord may sell an apartment building and assign the relevant leases to the buyer, who will then become the new landlord. A tenant may assign the remainder of her lease to someone else, who then acquires whatever rights the original tenant had under the lease (including, of course, the right to exclusive possession of the leased premises).

Subleasing occurs when the tenant transfers to another person some, but not all, of his remaining right to possess the property. The relationship of tenant to sublessee then becomes one of landlord and tenant. For example, Dorfman, a college student whose 18-month lease on an apartment is to terminate on December 31, 2004, sublets his apartment to Wembley for the summer months of 2004. This is a sublease rather than an assignment, because Dorfman has not transferred all of his remaining rights under the lease.

The significance of the assignment–sublease distinction is that an assignee acquires rights and duties under the lease between the landlord and the original tenant, but a sublessee does not. An assignee steps into the shoes of the original tenant and acquires any rights she had under the lease.[6] For example, if the lease contained an option to renew, the assignee would have the right to exercise this option. The assignee, of course, becomes personally liable to the landlord for the payment of rent.

Under both an assignment and a sublease, the original tenant remains liable to the landlord for the commitments made in the lease. If the assignee or sublessee fails to pay rent, for example, the tenant has the legal obligation to pay it. Figure 1 compares the characteristics of assignments and subleases.

Lease Provisions Limiting Assignment Leases commonly contain limitations on assignment and subleasing. This is especially true of commercial leases. Such provisions typically require the landlord's consent to any assignment or sublease, or purport to prohibit such a transfer of the tenant's interests. Provisions requiring the landlord's consent are upheld by the courts, although some courts hold that the landlord cannot withhold consent unreasonably. Total prohibitions

---

[6]Assignment is discussed in detail in Chapter 17.

Figure 1   Comparison of Assignment and Sublease

	Sublease	Assignment
Does the tenant transfer to the third party *all* his remaining rights under the lease?	Yes	No
Does the tenant remain liable on the lease?	Yes	Yes
Does the third party (assignee or sublessee) acquire rights and duties under the tenant's lease with the landlord?	Yes	No

against assignment may be enforced as well, but they are disfavored in the law. Courts usually construe them narrowly, resolving ambiguities against the landlord.

Tenant's Liability for Injuries to Third Persons

The tenant is normally liable to persons who suffer harm while on the portion of the property over which the tenant has control, *if the injuries resulted from the tenant's negligence.*

Termination of the Leasehold

A leasehold typically terminates because the lease term has expired. Sometimes, however, the lease is terminated early because of a party's material breach of the lease or because of mutual agreement.

Eviction

If a tenant breaches the lease (most commonly, by nonpayment of rent), the landlord may take action to **evict** the tenant. State statutes usually establish a relatively speedy eviction procedure. The landlord who desires to evict a tenant must be careful to comply with any applicable state or city regulations governing evictions. These regulations usually forbid self-help measures on the landlord's part, such as forcible entry to change locks. At common law, a landlord had a lien on the tenant's per-

Figure 2   *Termination of a Leasehold by Abandonment*

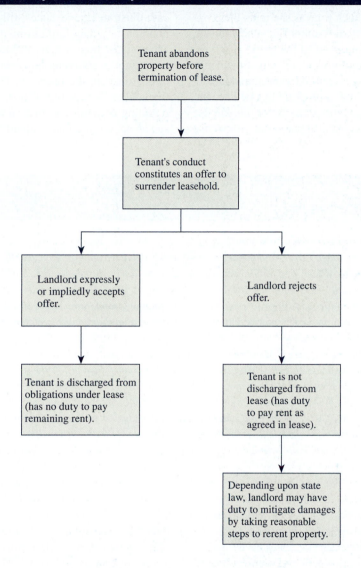

sonal property. The landlord therefore could remove and hold such property as security for the rent obligation. This lien has been abolished in many states. Where the lien still exists, it is subject to constitutional limitations requiring that the tenant be given notice of the lien, as well as an opportunity to defend and protect his belongings before they can be sold to satisfy the rent obligation.

Agreement to Surrender

A lease may terminate prematurely by mutual agreement between landlord and tenant to **surrender** the lease (i.e., return the property to the landlord prior to the end of the

lease). A valid surrender discharges the tenant from further liability under the lease.

Abandonment

Abandonment occurs when the tenant unjustifiably and permanently vacates the leased premises before the end of the lease term, and defaults in the payment of rent. If a tenant abandons the leased property, he is making an offer to surrender the leasehold. As shown in Figure 2, the landlord must make a decision at this point. If the landlord's conduct shows acceptance of the tenant's offer of surrender, the tenant is relieved of the obligation to pay rent for the remaining period of the lease. If the landlord does not accept the surrender, she may sue the tenant for the rent due until such time as she rents the property to someone else, or, if she cannot find a new tenant, for the rent due for the remainder of the term.

At common law, the landlord had no obligation to mitigate (decrease) the damages caused by the abandonment by attempting to rent the leased property to a new tenant. In fact, taking possession of the property for the purpose of trying to rent it to someone else was a risky move for the landlord—her retaking of possession might be construed as acceptance of the surrender. As the *Stonehedge* case illustrates, some states still adhere to the rule that the nonbreaching landlord has no duty to mitigate damages. Many states, however, now place the duty on the landlord to attempt to mitigate damages by making a reasonable effort to rerent the property. These states also hold that the landlord's retaking of possession for the purpose of rerenting does not constitute a waiver of her right to pursue an action to collect unpaid rent.

Stonehedge Square Limited Partnership v. Movie Merchants, Inc.
715 A.2d 1082 (Pa. Sup. Ct. 1998)

Stonehedge Square Limited Partnership owned a shopping center in Carlisle, Pennsylvania. Stonehedge leased space in the shopping center to General Video Corporation under a five-year lease that was to expire on July 6, 1995. In July 1992, General Video assigned its rights, duties, and liabilities under the lease to Movie Merchants, Inc., which operated a video rental store on the premises from July 1992 until late October 1994. In August 1994, Movie Merchants discussed with Stonehedge the possibility of terminating the lease prior to expiration of its remaining term. Stonehedge listed the premises for rent but was unable to find a tenant. Stonehedge informed Movie Merchants that until another tenant could be secured, Movie Merchants would remain liable on the lease.

Near the end of October 1994, Movie Merchants vacated the premises and failed to pay any rent thereafter. Relying on an acceleration clause in the lease (a clause triggered by Movie Merchants' having left the premises and defaulted on the rent obligation), Stonehedge then sued for the amount of the rent due from November 1, 1994 to July 5, 1995. Initially, the trial court granted judgment in favor of Stonehedge in the amount of $46,797.09, plus interest. When Movie Merchants requested a new trial, the trial court reversed itself and held that Stonehedge had a duty to mitigate damages by seeking a replacement tenant for the remainder of the lease term. Stonehedge appealed to the Superior Court of Pennsylvania, which held that Stonehedge had no duty to mitigate damages. Movie Merchants then appealed to the Supreme Court of Pennsylvania.

Flaherty, Chief Justice   The issue in this case is whether the landlord in a commercial lease is required to mitigate its damages when its tenant has breached the lease agreement by moving out before the end of the lease term.

[I]n modern landlord–tenant law, leases have a dual nature, both as conveyances of protected property interests and also as contracts. Because of . . . historical background in which leases are sometimes viewed as conveyances and sometimes as contracts, problems in leases may be resolved either by principles of property law or by principles of contract law.

At common law, the mitigation of damages in a lease was regarded as being controlled by property law. Because the lease was a conveyance of real property, the tenant owned a non-freehold estate, and the landlord had no duty to mitigate damages arising from the tenant's breach of the lease. It was of no concern to the landlord whether the tenant chose to occupy the property or not. This was so in spite of the fact that it is a general principle of contract law that the nonbreaching party to a contract has the duty to reduce his damages, if he can reasonably do so. Nonetheless, Pennsylvania has followed the common law view that a nonbreaching landlord has no duty to mitigate damages where the tenant has abandoned the property in breach of the lease.

In 1882 this court held that "if the relation of landlord and tenant was not ended by contract, [the landlord] was not bound to rent to another during the term for relief of the [tenant]." *Miller v. Becker* (Pa. Sup. Ct. 1880). Two years later, . . . this court held that "[t]he landlord may allow the property to stand idle, and hold the tenant for the entire rent; or [the landlord] may lease it and hold [the tenant] for the difference, if any." *Auer v. Penn* (Pa. Sup. Ct. 1882). And in 1928 this court [reaffirmed the rule stated in the earlier cases].

The issue becomes, then, whether we should now modify the rule of these cases. Movie Merchants argues that a lease is in the nature of a contract and is controlled by principles of contract law. Further, it argues that the common law rule leads to unfair results, encourages waste, imposes penalties, and fosters bad public policy. Movie Merchants argues that although leases traditionally have been regarded as conveyances of land, modern leases are an exchange of promises, and contract law has long recognized the duty of a nonbreaching party to mitigate damages.

Stonehedge . . . argues that the Pennsylvania rule should continue in effect because precedent requires it, because to require the landlord to mitigate damages would reward the breaching tenant for his breach, and because the requirement of mitigation would place an onerous burden on the breaching landlord, denying him the benefit of his bargain.

For the following reasons, we now hold that a nonbreaching landlord whose tenant has abandoned the property in violation of the lease has no duty to mitigate damages. First, this rule is firmly established in Pennsylvania. As the *Auer* court stated: "Nothing is better settled in Pennsylvania than that a tenant for years cannot relieve himself from his liability under his covenant to pay rent by vacating the demised premises during the term, and sending the key to his landlord." Leases have been drafted and bargained for in reliance on this rule. Business decisions and structured financial arrangements have been made with the expectation that this rule, which has been the law, will continue to be the law.

Second, the established rule has the virtue of simplicity. If the landlord is required to relet the premises, there is unlimited potential for litigation initiated by the tenant concerning the landlord's due diligence . . . and countless other questions in which the breaching tenant is permitted to mount an assault on whatever the landlord did to mitigate damages, alleging that it was somehow deficient. This potential for complexity, expense, and delay is unwelcome and would adversely affect the existing schema utilized to finance commercial development. Third, [Pennsylvania's] Landlord and Tenant Act of 1951, which is a comprehensive [statutory] scheme . . ., does not [indicate that the landlord must mitigate damages, and thus does not depart from the no-duty-to-mitigate rule] established in our cases.

Fourth, there is a fundamental unfairness in allowing the breaching tenant to require the nonbreaching landlord to mitigate the damages caused by the tenant. This unfairness takes the form of depriving the landlord of the benefit of his bargain, forcing the landlord to expend time, energy, and money to respond to the tenant's breach, and putting the landlord at risk of further expense of lawsuits and counterclaims in a matter which he justifiably assumed was closed.

Fifth, in this case, the tenant was in a position to mitigate his own damages. The lease [allowed the tenant to provide] the landlord with a sublessee and the landlord had a duty not to unreasonably withhold consent. It seems self-evident that in choosing between requiring the nonbreaching party [or] the breaching party to mitigate damages, the requirement, if any, should be placed on the breaching party, as it has been for centuries.

Superior Court decision affirmed.

Problems and Problem Cases

1. In October 1981, Cook entered into an oral lease to rent a residence to Melson. Melson agreed to pay $400 per month, in advance, as rent. In November 1987, Cook sent Melson a letter advising that the rent would be increased to $525 per month, effective January 1, 1988, and asking whether Melson was going to pay. On December 10, 1987, Melson replied that he would not pay the increased rent. On January 2, 1988, Melson sent Cook a check for $400 as rent for January. Cook returned the check and stated that the rent was now $525. Melson did not vacate the premises until February 1, 1988. Cook brought a suit against Melson for $525, allegedly the unpaid rent for the month of January. Was Melson liable for the $525?

2. A tenant rented an apartment from the landlord pursuant to a lease that required her to surrender the premises in "as good a state and condition as reasonable use and wear and tear will permit," and also required her to make a refundable security deposit. After the lease was executed, the landlord notified the tenants in the building that no tenant was to shampoo the wall-to-wall carpet on surrender of the lease because the landlord had retained a professional carpet cleaner to do it. The cost of the carpet cleaner's services was to be automatically deducted from the security deposit. When the tenant left the building, a portion of her security deposit was withheld to cover carpet cleaning and she sued for a refund of the full deposit. Is the tenant entitled to a refund?

3. Dan Maltbie and John Burke, students at Indiana University, resided in an apartment in an older house in Bloomington, Indiana. The agreed rent was $235 per month. When Maltbie and Burke moved in, they discovered numerous defects: rotting porch floorboards, broken and loose windows, an inoperable front door lock, leaks in the plumbing, a back door that would not close, a missing bathroom door, inadequate water pressure, falling plaster, exposed wiring over the bathtub, and a malfunctioning toilet. Later, they discovered more leaks in the plumbing, a leaking roof, the absence of heat and hot water, cockroach infestation, and pigeons in the attic. The City of Bloomington had a housing code in effect at that time. Code enforcement officers inspected the apartment and found over 50 violations, 11 of which were "life-safety" violations (defined as conditions that might be severely "hazardous to health of the occupant"). These conditions remained largely uncorrected after notice by the code officers and further complaints by Maltbie and Burke. Maltbie vacated the apartment before the one-year lease term expired, notified the landlord, and refused to pay any further rent. The landlord agreed to let Burke remain and pay $112.50 per month. The landlord then filed suit against Maltbie and Burke for $610.75, which was the balance due under the written rental contract plus certain charges. Maltbie and Burke filed counterclaims, seeking damages and abatement of the rent for breach of the implied warranty of habitability. Should the landlord win the case, or should Maltbie and Burke?

4. Linda Schiernbeck rented a house from Clark and Rosa Davis for the sum of $150 per month. Approximately one month after she moved in, Schiernbeck noticed a discolored circular area on one of the walls. There was a screw in the middle of this area. Schiernbeck determined that a smoke detector had been attached to the wall. No smoke detector was present, however, during the time Schiernbeck lived in the house. Schiernbeck later contended that she notified the Davises about the missing smoke detector, but the Davises denied this. Approximately one year and three months after Schiernbeck's tenancy began, a fire broke out in the house. Schiernbeck and her daughter were severely injured. Contending that the Davises should have installed a smoke detector, Schiernbeck sued them on negligence and breach of contract grounds. Did the Davises owe Schiernbeck a duty to install a smoke detector?

5. Mary Ajayi and Wemi Alakija were tenants in an apartment complex managed for the landlord by Lloyd Management, Inc. Neighboring tenants complained on various occasions to Lloyd about repeated disturbances that continued late into the night and included yelling and loud noises coming from the apartment shared by Ajayi and Alakija. The sounds of running could also be heard during these disturbances. Neighbors whose apartment walls adjoined those of the Ajayi-Alakija apartment also complained that items were knocked off their walls as a result of banging and jarring coming from the Ajayi-Alakija apartment. Do Lloyd and the landlord have any obligation to take responsive action? If so, why? What course(s) of action might they pursue?

6. Florence Trentacost, who was 61 years old, was mugged in the hallway of the apartment house where she was a tenant. The incident happened about 4 o'clock in the afternoon about 25 feet into the building at the foot of some stairs. She suffered a number of injuries, including a dislocated shoulder, a broken leg, a broken ankle, and several other fractures and cuts. She sued the landlord to recover for her personal injuries. She claimed that the landlord had been negligent by failing to maintain the safety of the common areas of the building and by failing to have a lock on the front door entrance to the building. The apartment building was located in an area where there had been civil disturbances several years earlier, and the neighborhood was considered by the police to be a high-crime area. Unauthorized persons had previously been seen in the building and reported to the landlord. Was the landlord liable to the tenant for the injuries she sustained when she was mugged in the apartment house?

7. On March 1, Sharon Fitzgerald entered into an oral lease of a house owned by Parkin. The lease was on a month-to-month basis, and the rent was set at $290 per month. Parkin also agreed to make certain repairs to the house. On July 1, Fitzgerald notified Parkin by mail of the repairs that needed to be made. These included repairs of leaky pipes, the kitchen ceiling, and the back porch. Fitzgerald also said she would withhold the rent if the repairs were not made within 30 days. On July 13, Fitzgerald had the premises inspected by a city housing inspector who found eight violations of the city code. Parkin was given notice of these violations. On July 29, Parkin served Fitzgerald with a formally correct notice to vacate the premises within 30 days. In September, he brought a lawsuit to have Fitzgerald evicted. A Minnesota statute gives a tenant a defense to an eviction action if the eviction is in retaliation for the reporting of a housing violation in good faith to city officials. Could the landlord evict the tenant from the house under these circumstances?

8. Kridel entered into a lease with Sommer, owner of the Pierre Apartments, to lease apartment 6-L for two years. Kridel, who was to be married in June, planned to move into the apartment in May. His parents and future parents-in-law had agreed to assume responsibility for the rent, because Kridel was a full-time student who had no funds of his own. Shortly before Kridel was to have moved in, his engagement was broken. He wrote Sommer a letter explaining his situation and stating that he could not take the apartment. Sommer did not answer the letter. When another party inquired about renting apartment 6-L, the person in charge told her that the apartment was already rented to Kridel.

Sommer did not enter the apartment or show it to anyone until he rented apartment 6-L to someone else when there were approximately eight months left on Kridel's lease. He sued Kridel for the full rent for the period of approximately 16 months before the new tenant's lease took effect. Kridel argued that Sommer should not be able to collect rent for the first 16 months of the lease because he did not take reasonable steps to rerent the apartment. Was Sommer entitled to collect the rent he sought?

Online Research: Check Out Your Housing Code

Use the Internet to ascertain whether the city or county in which you reside has a housing code that covers the lease of residential property. If it does not, then locate the housing code of New York City. What obligations does the code place on landlords? What rights does it give to landlords? What rights does it give to tenants? What obligations, if any, does it place on tenants?

26

ESTATES AND TRUSTS

George, an elderly widower, has no children of his own but enjoys a very close relationship with his two stepdaughters, his late wife's children by her first marriage. George's only living blood relative is his brother, from whom he has been estranged for many years. George has a substantial amount of property—his home, two cars, stocks and bonds, rental property, bank accounts, and a valuable collection of baseball cards. Though retired, George is an active volunteer for, and supporter of, several community charities and organizations. Presently, George does not have a will, but he is considering writing one.

- What will happen to George's property upon his death if he does not have a will at that time?
- What are the requirements for executing a valid will?
- What can cause a will to be invalid?
- After George's death, how would his estate be probated?
- If George decided to create a trust to benefit his stepdaughters, what is required to create a trust, and what are the duties of a trustee?

ONE OF THE BASIC features of the ownership of property is the right to dispose of the property during life and at death. You have already learned about the ways in which property is transferred during the owner's life. The owner's death is another major event for the transfer of property. Most people want to be able to choose who will get their property when they die. There are a variety of ways in which a person may control the ultimate disposition of his property. He may take title to the property in a form of joint ownership that gives his co-owner a right of survivorship. He may create a trust and transfer property to it to be used for the benefit of a spouse, child, elderly parent, or other beneficiary. He may execute a will in which he directs that his real and personal property be distributed to persons named in the will. If, however, a person makes no provision for the disposition of his property at his death, his property will be distributed to his heirs as defined by state law. This chapter focuses on the transfer of property at death and on the use of trusts for the transfer and management of property, both during life and at death.

The Law of Estates and Trusts

Each state has its own statutes and common law regulating the distribution of property upon death. Legal requirements and procedures may vary from state to state, but many general principles can be stated. The **Uniform Probate Code (UPC)** is a comprehensive, uniform law that has been enacted in 18 states. It is intended to update and unify state law concerning the disposition and administration of property at death. Several relevant UPC provisions will be discussed in this chapter.

Estate Planning

A person's **estate** is all of the property owned by that person. **Estate planning** is the popular name for the complicated process of planning for the transfer of a person's estate in later life and at death. Estate planning also concerns planning for the possibility of prolonged illness or disability. An attorney who is creating an estate plan will take an inventory of the client's assets, learn the client's objectives, and draft the instruments necessary to carry out the plan. This plan is normally guided by the desire to reduce the amount of tax liability and to provide for the orderly disposition of the estate.

Wills

Right of Disposition by Will

The right to control the disposition of property at death has not always existed. In the English feudal system, the king owned all land. The lords and knights had only the right to use land for their lifetime. A landholder's rights in land terminated upon his death, and no rights descended to his heirs. In 1215, the king granted the nobility the right to pass their interest in the land they held to their heirs. Later, that right was extended to all property owners. In the United States, each state has enacted statutes that establish the requirements for a valid will, including the formalities that must be met to pass property by will.

Nature of a Will

A **will** is a document executed with specific legal formalities by a **testator** (person making a will) that contains his instructions about the way his property will be disposed of at his death. A will can dispose only of property belonging to the testator at the time of his death. Furthermore, wills do not control property that goes to others through other planning devices (such as life insurance policies) or by operation of law (such as by right of survivorship). For example, property held in joint tenancy or tenancy by the entirety is not controlled by a will, because the property passes automatically to the surviving cotenant by right of survivorship. In addition, life insurance proceeds are controlled by the insured's designation of beneficiaries, not by any provision of a will. (Because joint tenancy and life insurance are ways of directing the disposition of property, they are sometimes referred to as "will substitutes.")

LOG ON

For discussion of why it is important to have a will, see Peter Weaver, *10 Good Reasons Why You Should Have a Will,* **http://www.thirdage.com/features/money/good will/;** Rebecca Berlin, *Wills: Why You Need One,* **http://www.alllaw.com/articles/wills_and_trusts/ article2.asp;** and Peter J. Smith, *Top Ten Reasons to Have a Will,* **http://www.soglaw.com/10will.htm.**

Common Will Terminology

Some legal terms commonly used in wills include the following:

1. *Bequest.* A **bequest** (also called **legacy**) is a gift of personal property or money. For example, a will might provide for a bequest of a family heirloom to the testator's daughter. Since a will can direct only property that is owned by the testator at the time of his death, a specific bequest of property that the testator has disposed of before his death is ineffective. This is called **ademption.** For example, Samuel's will states that Warren is to receive Samuel's collection of antique guns. If the guns are destroyed before Warren's death, however, the bequest is ineffective because of ademption.

2. *Devise.* A **devise** is a gift of real property. For example, the testator might devise his family farm to his grandson.

3. *Residuary.* The **residuary** is the balance of the estate that is left after specific devises and bequests are made by the will. After providing for the disposition of specific personal and real property, a testator might provide that the residuary of his estate is to go to his spouse or be divided among his descendants.

4. *Issue.* A person's **issue** are his lineal descendants (children, grandchildren, great-grandchildren, and so forth). This category of persons includes adopted children.

5. *Per capita.* This term and the next one, *per stirpes,* are used to describe the way in which a group of persons are to share a gift. **Per capita** means that each of that group of persons will share equally. For example, Grandfather dies, leaving a will that provides that the residuary of his estate is to go to his issue or descendants *per capita.* Grandfather had two children, Mary and Bill. Mary has two children, John and James. Bill has one child, Margaret. Mary and Bill die before Grandfather (in legal terms, *predecease* him), but all three of Grandfather's grandchildren are living at the time of his death. In this case, John, James, and Margaret would each take one-third of the residuary of Grandfather's estate.

6. *Per stirpes.* When a gift is given to the testator's issue or descendants **per stirpes** (also called **by right of representation**), each surviving descendant divides the share that his or her parent would have taken if the parent had survived. In the preceding example, if Grandfather's will had stated that the residuary of his estate was to go to his issue or descendants *per stirpes,* Margaret would take one-half and John and James would take one-quarter each (that is, they would divide the share that would have gone to their mother).

Testamentary Capacity

The capacity to make a valid will is called **testamentary capacity.** To have testamentary capacity, a person must be *of sound mind* and *of legal age,* which is 18 in most states. A person does not have to be in perfect mental health to have testamentary capacity. Because people often delay executing wills until they are weak and in ill health, the standard for mental capacity to make a will is fairly low. To be of "sound mind," a person need only be sufficiently rational to be capable of understanding the nature and character of his property, of realizing that he is making a will, and of knowing the persons who would normally be the beneficiaries of his affection. A person could move in and out of periods of lucidity and still have testamentary capacity if he executed his will during a lucid period.

Lack of testamentary capacity is a common ground upon which wills are challenged by persons who were excluded from a will. *Fraud* and *undue influence* are also common grounds for challenging the validity of a will.[1]

Execution of a Will

Unless a will is executed with the formalities required by state law, it is *void.* The courts are strict in interpreting statutes concerning the execution of wills. If a will is declared void, the property of the deceased person will be distributed according to the provisions of state laws that will be discussed later.

The formalities required for a valid will differ from state to state. For that reason, an individual should consult the laws of his state before making a will. If he should move to another state after having executed a will, he should consult a lawyer in his new state to determine whether a new will needs to be executed. All states require that a will be *in writing.* State law also requires that a formal will be *witnessed,* generally by two or three *disinterested* witnesses (persons who do not stand to inherit any property under the will), and that it be *signed* by the testator or by someone else at the testator's direction. Most states also require that the testator *publish* the will—that is, declare or indicate at the time of signing that the instrument is his will. Another formality required by most states is that the testator sign the will in the presence and the sight of the witnesses and that the witnesses sign in the presence and the sight of each other. As a general rule, an **attestation clause,** which states the formalities that have been followed in the execution of the will, is written following the testator's signature. These detailed formalities are designed to prevent fraud. Section 2–502 of the UPC requires that a will must be in writing, signed by the testator (or in the testator's name by some other individual in the testator's conscious presence and by the testator's direction), and signed by at least two individuals, each of whom signed within a reasonable time after he witnessed either the signing of the will or the testator's acknowledgment of that signature or will. Also, under the UPC, any individual who is generally competent to be a witness may witness a will, and the fact that the witness is an interested party does not invalidate the will [2–505]. When a testator has made a technical error in executing a will, however, the UPC permits the document to be treated as if it had been executed properly if it can be proven by clear and convincing evidence that the testator intended the document to constitute his will [2–503].

In some situations, a lawyer might arrange to have the execution of a will *videotaped* to provide evidence relating to the testator's capacity and the use of proper formalities. (Note that the will is executed in the normal way; the videotape merely records the execution of the will.) Some state probate codes specifically provide that videotapes of the executions of wills are admissible into evidence.

Incorporation by Reference

In some situations, a testator might want his will to refer to and incorporate an existing writing. For example, the testator may have created a list of specific gifts of personal property that he wants to incorporate in the will. A writing such as this is called an **extrinsic document**—that is, a writing apart from the will. In most states, the contents of extrinsic documents can be essentially incorporated into the will when the circumstances satisfy rules that have been designed to ensure that the document is genuine and that it was intended by the testator to be incorporated in the will. This is called **incorporation by reference.** For an extrinsic document to be incorporated by reference, it must have been *in existence at the time the will was executed.* In addition, the writing and the will must refer to each other so that the extrinsic document can be identified and so that it is clear that the testator intended the extrinsic document to be incorporated in the will. Under the UPC, incorporation by reference is allowed when the extrinsic document was in existence

---

[1]Fraud and undue influence are discussed in detail in Chapter 13.

when the will was executed, the language of the will manifests the intent to incorporate the writing, and the will describes the writing sufficiently to identify it [2–510].

Informal Wills

Some states recognize certain types of wills that are not executed with these formalities. These are:

1. *Nuncupative wills.* A **nuncupative** will is an oral will. Such wills are recognized as valid in some states, but only under limited circumstances and to a limited extent. In a number of states, for example, nuncupative wills are valid only when made by soldiers in military service and sailors at sea, and even then they will be effective only to dispose of personal property that was in the actual possession of the person at the time the oral will was made. Other states place low dollar limits on the amount of property that can be passed by a nuncupative will.

2. *Holographic wills.* **Holographic wills** are wills that are written and signed in the testator's handwriting. You will see an example of a holographic will in *Estate of Southworth v. North Shore Animal League,* which appears below. The fact that holographic wills are not properly witnessed makes them suspect. They are recognized in about half of the states and by section 2–502(b) of the UPC, even though they are not executed with the formalities usually required of valid wills. For a holographic will to be valid in the states that recognize them, it must evidence testamentary intent and must actually be *handwritten* by the testator. A typed holographic will would be invalid. Some states require that the holographic will be *entirely* handwritten—although the UPC requires only that the signature and material portions of the will be handwritten by the testator [2–502(b)]—and some also require that the will be dated.

Joint and Mutual Wills

In some circumstances, two or more people—a married couple, for example—decide together on a plan for the disposition of their property at death. To carry out this plan, they may execute a **joint will** (a single instrument that constitutes the will of both or all of the testators and is executed by both or all) or they may execute **mutual wills** (joint or separate, individual wills that reflect the common plan of distribution).

Underlying a joint or mutual will is an agreement on a common plan. This common plan often includes an express or implied contract (a contract to make a will or not to revoke the will). One issue that sometimes arises is whether a testator who has made a joint or mutual will can later change his will. Whether joint and mutual wills are revocable depends on the language of the will, on state law, and on the timing of the revocation. For example, a testator who made a joint will with his spouse may be able to revoke his will during the life of his spouse, because the spouse still has a chance to change her own will, but he may be unable to revoke or change the will after the death of his spouse. The UPC provides that the mere fact that a joint or mutual will has been executed does *not* create the presumption of a contract not to revoke the will or wills [2–514].

Construction of Wills

Even in carefully drafted wills, questions sometimes arise as to the meaning or legal effect of a term or provision. Disputes about the meaning of the will are even more likely to occur in wills drafted by the testator himself, such as holographic wills. To interpret a will, a court will examine the entire instrument in an attempt to determine the testator's intent. The following *Estate of Southworth* case provides a good example of the methods and principles courts use to interpret wills.

Estate of Southworth v. North Shore Animal League
59 Cal. Rptr. 2d 272 (Ct. App. Cal. 1996)

Dorothy Southworth never married and had no children. On March 4, 1986, in response to Southworth's request for information, North Shore Animal League (NSAL) sent a letter to her describing its lifetime pet care program and explaining how to register for it. NSAL asked that she return its enclosed pet care registration card, contact her attorney to include her bequest to NSAL in her estate, and send a copy of the bequest to NSAL. NSAL informed her that "[e]ven if you don't currently have a will, we'll accept your Registration on good faith and maintain an Active file on your pet while you're arranging the Bequest." Southworth never returned the registration card to NSAL. On September 4, 1987, Southworth requested registration with the Neptune Society for cremation of her body upon her death. On the registration form, she stated that she had never married and that Neptune should contact the Ventura County Coroner to make arrangements. On the same date, Southworth sent a letter to NSAL asking whether or not it destroyed animals. Her letter to NSAL states,

I have been terribly upset since I heard [that NSAL destroys animals] because I have always truly believed that you did not destroy animals and this was the determining factor in my selection of you as the beneficiary of my entire estate as I have no relatives and do not want the State of California, courts, or attorneys to benefit from my hard earned labor. I should appreciate greatly if you would clarify this point about the destruction of animals at your shelter and tell me honestly and truly what your policy is [and] not hedge because I have mentioned leaving my estate to your organization.

In September of 1987, NSAL wrote to assure Southworth that it would not destroy any pet. NSAL included a brochure regarding estate planning. The brochure explained that a letter or a verbal promise would not effectuate a testamentary gift; that a proper written will is required. The mailing urged members to consult an estate planning attorney to avoid the possibility that the estate might end up with "distant relatives whom you didn't even know." Southworth never prepared a formal will.

NSAL sent a donor card to Southworth. It explained that she could change her life insurance policy or provide for animals in her will by calling her attorney. It sought gifts and legacies and asked her to complete and return the donor card. On April 19, 1989, Southworth returned the donor card to NSAL. The card provided three options: naming NSAL as a beneficiary of a life insurance policy, changing one's will to leave securities or cash to NSAL, or not taking immediate action, but stating the donor's intentions. On the card, Southworth circled printed option c, which stated: "I am not taking action now, but my intention is" [in the blank space provided she wrote] "My entire estate is to be left to North Shore Animal League." The donor card also included a printed statement which read, "The total amount that the animal shelter will someday receive is" [she wrote in the blank space] "$500,000." The card then stated what she wanted the money used for. She signed and dated the donor card.

In May of 1989, NSAL sent a thank-you letter to Southworth for "letting us know that you will remember the North Shore Animal League in your will." The letter requested that Southworth have her attorney send it a copy of the will. The Neptune Society asked for additional information, and Southworth returned Neptune's supplemental form and stated that there are "[n]o living relatives" and to "[p]lease notify North Shore Animal League." She included NSAL's address, telephone numbers, and the name of the executive director of NSAL. She signed the supplemental form and dated it October 20, 1989.

On January 14, 1994, Southworth died. The Ventura County Public Administrator was appointed special administrator of her estate. The public administrator filed notice of its petition to administer her estate. NSAL filed its objection to the petition on the grounds that the donor card constituted a holographic will of Southworth. Francis See, an heir finder to whom Southworth's surviving half-siblings assigned their claims, and nephews of a deceased sister of Southworth contested the admission of the alleged holographic will. See argued that the donor card should be denied admission into probate as a holographic will because not all of its material provisions were in the handwriting of the decedent and there was no showing of testamentary intent at the time she signed the card. NSAL argued that the donor card reflected Southworth's testamentary intent and satisfied the statutory requirements for a holographic will. The trial court concluded that Southworth's handwritten statement on the donor card that "[m]y entire estate is to be left to North Shore Animal League" substantially complied with all the Probate Code requirements for a holographic will. The court viewed the preprinted parts of the donor card and the $500,000 sum written in to be immaterial. The court interpreted the preprinted words stating that "I am not taking action now, but my intention is . . ." to mean that she did not want to immediately transfer her funds to NSAL, but intended to bequeath them upon her death. The trial court admitted the donor card to probate as the last will of Southworth, and See appealed.

Gilbert, Judge A charitable donor card contains printed language showing an intent to make a future gift to the charity. In the blank space following the printed words a testator writes that her entire estate is to be left to the charity. She signs and dates the donor card. Does her handwriting on the donor card constitute a holographic will? No.

Former Civil Code section 1277 stated that "[a] [h]olographic will is one that is entirely written, dated and signed by the hand of the testator himself. It is subject to no other form, . . . and need not be witnessed." In *Estate of De Cac-*

cia (1928), our Supreme Court reversed the order of a trial court which had denied probate to an otherwise handwritten will simply because it was written under a printed letterhead stating, "Oakland, California." In 1931, the Legislature reenacted former Civil Code section 1277 as section 53 of the Probate Code and added a third sentence to codify the rule announced in the *De Caccia* case. The sentence stated, "No address, date or other matter written, printed or stamped upon the document, which is not incorporated in the provisions which are in the handwriting of the decedent, shall be considered as any part of the will." In *Estate of Black,* the decedent wrote out her will on three identical, commercially printed one-page will forms. In the blanks provided, she wrote her signature and place of domicile, and on the third page she inserted the name and gender of her executor, the date of the instrument, and the city and state where she executed it. She either struck out or ignored other printed language regarding residuary gifts, the appointment of an executor, attesting witnesses, and a testimonium clause. The trial court denied probate because the testator incorporated some of the printed language, even though it concerned perfunctory procedural matters in the form will. Our Supreme Court reversed because "none of the incorporated material is either material to the substance of the will or essential to its validity as a testamentary disposition. . . ." *Estate of Black.* The *Black* court explained that "[t]he policy of the law is toward "a construction favoring validity, in determining whether a will has been executed in conformity with statutory requirements." Moreover, we affirmed the tendency of both the courts and the Legislature . . . toward greater liberality in accepting a writing as an holographic will. Courts are to use common sense in evaluating whether a document constitutes a holographic will. The *Black* court recognized that "[i]f testators are to be encouraged by a statute like ours to draw their own wills, the courts should not adopt, upon purely technical reasoning, a construction which would result in invalidating such wills in half the cases." The law recognizes that such wills are generally made by people without legal training. The primary purpose of the statutory holographic will provisions is to prevent fraud. Because counterfeiting another's handwriting is exceedingly difficult, these statutes require the material provisions of holographic wills to be in the testator's handwriting." It was apparent to the *Black* court that the testator mistakenly believed she needed to use the printed language on the commercially printed will form regarding procedural matters. The court determined that the printed clause of the commercial will form referring to a personal representative was "patently irrelevant" to the substance—the dispositive provisions of her will. The court explained that the issue is not whether one mechanically intends to include printed material, but whether one intends to include printed material "because of its importance or materiality to the testamentary message. . . ." The inclusion of such printed procedural details does not invalidate an otherwise valid will.

Whether a document should be admitted to probate as a holographic will depends on proof of its authorship and authenticity, and whether the words establish that it was intended to be the author's last will and testament at the time she wrote

it. Our high court explained that four questions are pertinent in evaluating whether a document should be invalidated as a holographic will due to printed language in the document: "Was the particular provision relevant to the substance of the will? Was it essential to the will's validity? Did the testator intend to incorporate the provision? Would invalidation of the holograph defeat the testator's intent?" *Estate of Black.*

Accordingly, in 1983, the year after our Supreme Court decided *Black,* our Legislature replaced Probate Code section 53 with Probate Code section 6111. Section 6111 provides, in pertinent part, that "(a) A will . . . is valid as a holographic will, whether or not witnessed, if the signature and the material provisions are in the handwriting of the testator." In 1990, the Legislature added subdivision (c) which provides that "Any statement of testamentary intent contained in a holographic will may be set forth either in the testator's own handwriting or as part of a commercially printed form will."

There is no question that the handwriting on the document at issue is that of Dorothy Southworth, and that she signed and dated it. Unlike *Black,* however, the document is not a commercially printed will form. It is a donor card for a charity. It was not drafted to serve as a will. The card provides the option of informing NSAL that the donor has or intends to instruct one's attorney to change his or her will. Furthermore, the printed language Southworth incorporated from the donor card does not evince her present testamentary intent. Instead of striking the material printed words which state "I am not taking action now, but my intention is," she chose to incorporate those words with her handwritten statement," My entire estate is to be left to North Shore Animal League." The material printed language together with her handwriting evince a future intent, not present testamentary intent.

Although other evidence, such as her letter to NSAL, and the supplemental Neptune form she signed on October 20, 1989, shows that Southworth desired to leave her estate to NSAL, neither the donor card at issue nor the handwriting on it substantially complies with Probate Code requirements for holographic wills. Although courts may consider statements made before and after a holographic will is made and the surrounding circumstances, evidence of present testamentary intent provided by the instrument at issue is paramount. Here, Southworth incorporated printed language stating that she was not taking any action when she executed it. It does not establish her testamentary intent at the time she executed it. It only states her intention to make a will in the future.

The judgment is reversed in favor of See.

ETHICS IN ACTION

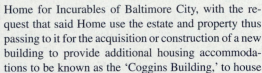

Dr. Coggins died in 1963. In his last will, Dr. Coggins gave the residue of his estate to the Mercantile-Safe Deposit & Trust Company, to be held by it as Trustee under the will. The trust provided for monthly payments to four income beneficiaries until the death of the last of them. The last of these annuitants was Dr. Coggins's widow, who died in 1998. A provision of the will stated that, upon the death of the survivor of the four annuitants, the trust would terminate and the assets and all unpaid income shall be paid over "free of trust unto the Keswick Home, formerly Home for Incurables of Baltimore City, with the request that said Home use the estate and property thus passing to it for the acquisition or construction of a new building to provide additional housing accommodations to be known as the 'Coggins Building,' to house white patients who need physical rehabilitation. If not acceptable to the Keswick Home, then this bequest shall go to the University of Maryland Hospital to be used for physical rehabilitation." What are the major ethical considerations involved in determining whether this will provision should be enforced?

Limitations on Disposition by Will

A person who takes property by will takes it subject to all outstanding claims against the property. For example, if real property is subject to a mortgage or other lien, the beneficiary who takes the property gets it subject to the mortgage or lien. In addition, the rights of the testator's creditors are superior to the rights of beneficiaries under his will. Thus, if the testator was insolvent (his debts exceeded his assets), persons named as beneficiaries do not receive any property by virtue of the will.

Under the laws of most states, the surviving spouse of the testator has statutory rights in property owned solely by the testator that cannot be defeated by a contrary will provision. This means that a husband cannot effectively disinherit his wife, and vice versa. Even if the will provides for the surviving spouse, he or she can elect to take the share of the decedent's estate that would be provided by state law rather than the amount specified in the will. In some states, personal property, such as furniture, passes automatically to the surviving spouse.

At common law, a widow had the right to a life estate in one-third of the lands owned by her husband during their marriage. This was known as a widow's **dower right.** A similar right for a widower was known as **curtesy.** A number of states have changed the right by statute to give a surviving spouse a one-third interest in fee simple in the real and personal property owned by the deceased spouse at the time of his or her death. (Naturally, a testator can leave his spouse more than this if he desires.) Under UPC 2–201, the surviving spouse's elective share varies depending on the length of the surviving spouse's marriage to the testator—the elective share increases with the length of marriage.

As a general rule, a surviving spouse is given the right to use the family home for a stated period as well as a portion of the deceased spouse's estate. In community property states, each spouse has a one-half interest in community property that cannot be defeated by a contrary will provision. (Note that the surviving spouse will obtain *full* ownership of any property owned by the testator and the surviving spouse as joint tenants or tenants by the entirety.)

Children of the testator who were born or adopted after the will was executed are called **pretermitted** children. There is a presumption that the testator intended to provide for such a child, unless there is evidence to the contrary. State law gives pretermitted children the right to a share of the testator's estate. For example, under section 2–302 of the Uniform Probate Code, a pretermitted child has the right to receive the share he would have received under the state intestacy statute unless it appears that the omission of this child was intentional, the testator gave substantially all of his estate to the child's other parent, or the testator provided for the child outside of the will.

Revocation of Wills

One important feature of a will is that it is *revocable* until the moment of the testator's death. For this reason, a will confers *no present interest* in the testator's property. A person is free to revoke a prior will and, if she wishes, to make a new will. Wills can be revoked in a variety of ways. Physical destruction and mutilation done with intent to revoke a will constitute revocation, as do other acts such as crossing out the will or creating a writing that expressly cancels the will.

In addition, a will is revoked if the testator later executes a valid will that expressly revokes the earlier will.

A later will that does not *expressly* revoke an earlier will operates to revoke only those portions of the earlier will that are inconsistent with the later will. Under the UPC, a later will that does not expressly revoke a prior will operates to revoke it by inconsistency if the testator intended the subsequent will to *replace* rather than *supplement* the prior will [2–507(b)]. Furthermore, the UPC presumes that the testator intended the subsequent will to replace rather than supplement the prior will if the subsequent one makes a complete disposition of her estate, but it presumes that the testator intended merely to supplement and not replace the prior will if the subsequent will disposes of only part of her estate [2–507(c), 2–507(d)]. In some states, a will is presumed to have been revoked if it cannot be located after the testator's death, although this presumption can be rebutted with contrary evidence.

Wills can also be revoked by operation of law without any act on the part of the testator signifying revocation. State statutes provide that certain changes in relationships operate as revocations of a will. In some states, marriage will operate to revoke a will that was made when the testator was single. Similarly, a divorce may revoke provisions in a will made during marriage that leave property to the divorced spouse. Under the laws of some states, the birth of a child after the execution of a will may operate as a partial revocation of the will.

Codicils

A **codicil** is an amendment of a will. If a person wants to change a provision of a will without making an entirely new will, she may amend the will by executing a codicil. One may *not* amend a will by merely striking out objectionable provisions and inserting new provisions. The same formalities are required for the creation of a valid codicil as for the creation of a valid will.

Advance Directives: Planning for Disability

Advances in medical technology now permit a person to be kept alive by artificial means, even in many cases in which there is no hope of the person being able to function without life support. Many people are opposed to their lives being prolonged with no chance of recovery. In response to these concerns, almost all states have enacted statutes permitting individuals to state their choices about the medical procedures that should be administered or withheld if they should become incapacitated in the future and cannot recover. Collectively, these devices are called **advance directives.** An advance directive is a written document (such as a living will or durable power of attorney) that directs others how future health care decisions should be made in the event that the individual becomes incapacitated.

Living Wills

Living wills are documents in which a person states in advance his intention to forgo or obtain certain life-prolonging medical procedures. Almost all states have enacted statutes recognizing living wills. These statutes also establish the elements and formalities required to create a valid living will and describe the legal effect of living wills. Currently, the law concerning living wills is primarily a matter of state law and differs from state to state. Living wills are typically included with a patient's medical records. Many states require physicians and other health care providers to follow the provisions of a valid living will. Because living wills are created by statute, it is important that all terms and conditions of one's state statute be followed. Figure 1 shows an example of a living will form.

Durable Power of Attorney

Another technique of planning for the eventuality that one may be unable to make decisions for oneself is to execute a document that gives another person the legal authority to act on one's behalf in the case of mental or physical incapacity. This document is called a **durable power of attorney.**

A *power of attorney* is an express statement in which one person (the **principal**) gives another person (the **attorney in fact**) the authority to do an act or series of acts on his behalf. For example, Andrews enters into a contract to sell his house to Willis, but he must be out of state on the date of the real estate closing. He gives Paulsen a power of attorney to attend the closing and execute the deed on his behalf. Ordinary powers of attorney terminate upon the principal's incapacity. By contrast, the *durable power of attorney* is not affected if the principal becomes incompetent.

A durable power of attorney permits a person to give someone else extremely broad powers to make decisions and enter transactions such as those involving real and personal property, bank accounts, and health care, and to specify that those powers will not terminate upon incapacity. The durable power of attorney is an extremely important planning device. For example, a durable power of attorney executed by an elderly parent to an adult child at

Figure 1   *Living Will*

LIVING WILL DECLARATION*

Declaration made this _____ day of _____ (month, year). I, _____, being at least eighteen (18) years of age and of sound mind, willfully and voluntarily make known my desires that my dying shall not be artificially prolonged under the circumstances set forth below, and I declare:

If at any time my attending physician certifies in writing that: (1) I have an incurable injury, disease, or illness; (2) my death will occur within a short time; and (3) the use of life prolonging procedures would serve only to artificially prolong the dying process, I direct that such procedures be withheld or withdrawn, and that I be permitted to die naturally with only the performance or provision of any medical procedure or medication necessary to provide me with comfort care or to alleviate pain, and, if I have so indicated below, the provision of artificially supplied nutrition and hydration. (Indicate your choice by initialing or making your mark before signing this declaration):

I wish to receive artificially supplied nutrition and hydration, even if the effort to sustain life is futile or excessively burdensome to me.

I do not wish to receive artificially supplied nutrition and hydration, if the effort to sustain life is futile or excessively burdensome to me.

I intentionally make no decision concerning artificially supplied nutrition and hydration, leaving the decision to my health care representative appointed under IC 16–36–1–7 or my attorney in fact with health care powers under IC 30–5–5.

In the absence of my ability to give directions regarding the use of life prolonging procedures, it is my intention that this declaration be honored by my family and physician as the final expression of my legal right to refuse medical or surgical treatment and accept the consequences of the refusal.

I understand the full import of this declaration.

Signed: _____

City, County, and State of Residence

The declarant has been personally known to me, and I believe (him/her) to be of sound mind. I did not sign the declarant's signature above for or at the direction of the declarant. I am not a parent, spouse, or child of the declarant. I am not entitled to any part of the declarant's estate or directly financially responsible for the declarant's medical care. I am competent and at least eighteen (18) years of age.

Witness _____ Date _____

Witness _____ Date _____

*From Ind. Code § 16–36 4–10 (1999).

a time in which the parent is competent would permit the child to take care of matters such as investments, property, bank accounts, and hospital admission. Without the durable power of attorney, the child would be forced to apply to a court for a guardianship, which is a more expensive and often less efficient manner in which to handle personal and business affairs.

Durable Power of Attorney for Health Care

The majority of states have enacted statutes specifically providing for **durable powers of attorney for health care** (sometimes called **health care representatives**). This is a type of durable power of attorney in which the principal specifically gives the attorney in fact the authority to make certain health care decisions for him if the principal should become incompetent. Depending on state law and the instructions given by the principal to the attorney in fact, this could include decisions such as consenting or withholding consent to surgery, admitting the principal to a nursing home, and possibly withdrawing or prolonging life support. Note that the durable power of attorney becomes relevant only in the event that the principal becomes incompetent. So long as the principal is competent, he retains the ability to make his own health care decisions. This power of attorney is also revocable at the will of the principal. The precise requirements for creation of the durable power of attorney differ from state to state, but all states require a written and signed document executed with specified formalities, such as witnessing by disinterested witnesses.

Federal Law and Advance Directives

A federal statute, The Patient Self-Determination Act,[2] requires health care providers to take active steps to educate people about the opportunity to make advance decisions about medical care and the prolonging of life and to record the choices that they make. This statute, which became effective in 1991, requires health care providers such as hospitals, nursing homes, hospices, and home health agencies, to provide written information to adults receiving medical care about their rights concerning the ability to accept or refuse medical or surgical treatment, the health care provider's policies concerning those rights, and their right to formulate advance directives. The act also requires the provider to document in the patient's medical record whether the patient has executed an advance directive, and it forbids discrimination against the patient based on the individual's choice regarding an advance directive. In addition, the provider is required to ensure compliance with the requirements of state law concerning advance directives and to educate its staff and the community on issues concerning advance directives.

Intestacy

If a person dies without making a will, or if he makes a will that is declared invalid, he is said to have died **intestate.** When that occurs, his property will be distributed to the persons designated as the intestate's heirs under the appropriate state's **intestacy** or **intestate succession** statute. The intestate's real property will be distributed according to the intestacy statute of the state in which the property is located. His personal property will be distributed according to the intestacy statute of the state in which he was **domiciled** at the time of his death. A domicile is a person's permanent home. A person can have only one domicile at a time. Determinations of a person's domicile turn on facts that tend to show that person's intent to make a specific state his permanent home.

---

[2]42 U.S.C. section 1395cc (1993).

Characteristics of Intestacy Statutes

The provisions of intestacy statutes are not uniform. Their purpose, however, is to distribute property in a way that reflects the *presumed intent* of the deceased—that is, to distribute it to the persons most closely related to him. In general, such statutes first provide for the distribution of most or all of a person's estate to his surviving spouse, children, or grandchildren. If no such survivors exist, the statutes typically provide for the distribution of the estate to parents, siblings, or nieces and nephews. If no relatives at this level are living, the property may be distributed to surviving grandparents, uncles, aunts, or cousins. Generally, persons with the same degree of relationship to the deceased person take equal shares. If the deceased had no surviving relatives, the property **escheats** (goes) to the state.

Figure 2 shows an example of a distribution scheme under an intestacy statute.

Special Rules

Under intestacy statutes, a person must have a relationship to the deceased person through blood or marriage in order to inherit any part of his property. State law includes adopted children within the definition of "children," and treats adopted children in the same way as it treats biological children. (An adopted child would inherit from his adoptive parents, not from his biological parents.) Half-brothers and half sisters are usually treated in the same way as brothers and sisters related by whole blood. An illegitimate child may inherit from his mother, but as a general rule, illegitimate children do not inherit from their fathers unless paternity has been either acknowledged or established in a legal proceeding.

A person must be alive at the time the decedent dies to claim a share of the decedent's estate. An exception may be made for pretermitted children or other descendants who are born *after* the decedent's death. If a person who is entitled to a share of the decedent's estate survives the decedent but dies before receiving his share, his share in the decedent's estate becomes part of his own estate.

Simultaneous Death

A statute known as the Uniform Simultaneous Death Act provides that where two persons who would inherit from each other (such as husband and wife) die under circumstances that make it difficult or impossible to determine who died first, each person's property is to be distributed as though he or she survived. This means, for example, that the husband's property will go to his relatives and the wife's property to her relatives.

Figure 2   *Example of a Distribution Scheme under an Intestacy Statute*

Person Dying Intestate Is Survived By	Result
1. Spouse* and child or issue of a deceased child	Spouse 1/2, Child 1/2
2. Spouse and parent(s) but no issue	Spouse 3/4, Parent 1/4
3. Spouse but no parent or issue	All of the estate to spouse
4. Issue but no spouse	Estate is divided among issue
5. Parent(s), brothers, sisters, and/or issue of deceased brothers and sisters but no spouse or issue	Estate is divided among parent(s), brothers, sisters, and issue of deceased brothers and sisters
6. Issue of brothers and sisters but no spouse, issue, parents, brothers, and sisters	Estate is divided among issue of deceased brothers and sisters
7. Grandparents, but no spouse, issue, parents, brothers, sisters, or issue of deceased brothers and sisters	All of the estate goes to grandparents
8. None of the above	Estate goes to the state

*Note, however, second and subsequent spouses who had no children by the decedent may be assigned a smaller share.

Administration of Estates

When a person dies, an orderly procedure is needed to collect his property, settle his debts, and distribute any remaining property to those who will inherit it under his will or by intestate succession. This process occurs under the supervision of a probate court and is known as the **administration process** or the **probate process.** Summary (simple) procedures are sometimes available when an estate is relatively small—for example, when it has assets of less than $7,500.

The Probate Estate

The probate process operates only on the decedent's property that is considered to be part of his **probate estate.** The probate estate is that property belonging to the decedent at the time of his death other than property held in joint ownership with right of survivorship, proceeds of insurance policies payable to a trust or a third party, property held in a revocable trust during the decedent's lifetime in which a third party is the beneficiary, or retirement benefits, such as pensions, payable to a third party. Assets that pass by operation of law and assets that are transferred by other devices such as trusts or life insurance policies do not pass through probate.

Note that the decedent's probate estate and his *taxable estate* for purposes of federal estate tax are two different concepts. The taxable estate includes all property owned or controlled by the decedent at the time of his death. For example, if a person purchased a $1 million life insurance policy made payable to his spouse or children, the policy would be included in his taxable estate, but not in his probate estate.

Determining the Existence of a Will

The first step in the probate process is to determine whether the deceased left a will. This may require a search of the deceased person's personal papers and safe-deposit box. If a will is found, it must be *proved* to be admitted to probate. This involves the testimony of the persons who witnessed the will, if they are still alive. If the witnesses are no longer alive, the signatures of the witnesses and the testator will have to be established in some other way. In many states and under UPC section 2–504, a will may be proved by an affidavit (declaration under oath) sworn to and signed by the testator and the witnesses at the time the will was executed. This is called a **self-proving affidavit.** If a will is located and proved, it will be admitted to probate and govern many of the decisions that must be made in the administration of the estate.

Selecting a Personal Representative

Another early step in the administration of an estate is the selection of a personal representative to administer the estate. If the deceased left a will, it is likely that he designated his personal representative in the will. The personal representative under a will is also known as the **ex-**

ecutor. Almost anyone could serve as an executor. The testator may have chosen, for example, his spouse, a grown child, a close friend, an attorney, or the trust department of a bank.

If the decedent died intestate, or if the personal representative named in a will is unable to serve, the probate court will name a personal representative to administer the estate. In the case of an intestate estate, the personal representative is called an **administrator.** A preference is usually accorded to a surviving spouse, child, or other close relative. If no relative is available and qualified to serve, a creditor, bank, or other person may be appointed by the court.

Most states require that the personal representative *post a bond* in an amount in excess of the estimated value of the estate to ensure that her duties will be properly and faithfully performed. A person making a will often directs that his executor may serve without posting a bond, and this exemption may be accepted by the court.

Responsibilities of the Personal Representative

The personal representative has a number of important tasks in the administration of the estate. She must see that an inventory is taken of the estate's assets and that the assets are appraised. Notice must then be given to creditors or potential claimants against the estate so that they can file and prove their claims within a specified time, normally five months. As a general rule, the surviving spouse of the deceased person is entitled to be paid an allowance during the time the estate is being settled. This allowance has priority over other debts of the estate. The personal representative must see that any properly payable funeral or burial expenses are paid and that the creditors' claims are satisfied.

Both federal and state governments impose estate or inheritance taxes on estates of a certain size. The personal representative is responsible for filing estate tax returns. The federal tax is a tax on the deceased's estate, with provisions for deducting items such as debts, expenses of administration, and charitable gifts. In addition, an amount equal to the amount left to the surviving spouse may be deducted from the gross estate before the tax is computed. State inheritance taxes are imposed on the person who receives a gift or statutory share from an estate. It is common, however, for wills to provide that the estate will pay all taxes, including inheritance taxes, so that the beneficiaries will not have to do so. The personal representative must also make provisions for filing an income tax return and for paying any income tax due for the partial year prior to the decedent's death.

When the debts, expenses, and taxes have been taken care of, the remaining assets of the estate are distributed to the decedent's heirs (if there was no will) or to the beneficiaries of the decedent's will. Special rules apply when the estate is too small to satisfy all of the bequests made in a will or when some or all of the designated beneficiaries are no longer living.

When the personal representative has completed all of these duties, the probate court will close the estate and discharge the personal representative.

Trusts

Nature of a Trust

A **trust** is a legal relationship in which a person who has legal title to property has the duty to hold it for the use or benefit of another person. The person benefited by a trust is considered to have **equitable title** to the property, because it is being maintained for his benefit. This means that he is the real owner even though the trustee has the legal title in his or her name. A trust can be created in a number of ways. An owner of property may *declare* that he is holding certain property in trust. For example, a mother might state that she is holding 100 shares of General Motors stock in trust for her daughter. A trust may also arise *by operation of law.* For example, when a lawyer representing a client injured in an automobile accident receives a settlement payment from an insurance company, the lawyer holds the settlement payment as trustee for the client. Most commonly, however, trusts are created through *express instruments* whereby an owner of property transfers title to the property to a trustee who is to hold, manage, and invest the property for the benefit of either the original owner or a third person. For example, Long transfers certain stock to First Trust Bank with instructions to pay the income to his daughter during her lifetime and to distribute the stock to her children after her death.

Trust Terminology

A person who creates a trust is known as a **settlor** or **trustor.** The person who holds the property for the benefit of another person is called the **trustee.** The person for whose benefit the property is held in trust is the **beneficiary.** Figure 3 illustrates the relationship between these parties. A single person may occupy more than one of these positions; however, if there is only one beneficiary, he cannot be the sole trustee. The property held in trust is called the **corpus** or **res.** A distinction is made between

Figure 3   Trust

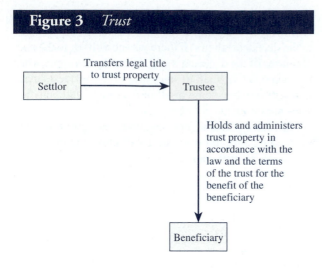

Settlor → Transfers legal title to trust property → Trustee

Trustee: Holds and administers trust property in accordance with the law and the terms of the trust for the benefit of the beneficiary

Beneficiary

the property in trust, which is the principal, and the income that is produced by the principal.

A trust that is established and effective during the settlor's lifetime is known as an **inter vivos trust.** A trust can also be established in a person's will. Such trusts take effect only at the death of the settlor. They are called **testamentary trusts.**

Why People Create Trusts

Bennett owns a portfolio of valuable stock. Her husband has predeceased her. She has two children and an elderly father for whom she would like to provide. Why might it be advantageous to Bennett to transfer the stock to a trust for the benefit of the members of her family?

First, there may be income tax or estate tax advantages in doing so, depending on the type of trust she establishes and the provisions of that trust. For example, she can establish an irrevocable trust for her children and remove the property transferred to her trust from her estate so that it is not taxable at her death. In addition, the trust property can be used for the benefit of others and may even pass to others after the settlor's death without the necessity of having a will. Many people prefer to pass their property by trust rather than by will because trusts afford more privacy: unlike a probated will, they do not become an item of public record. Trusts also afford greater opportunity for postgift management than do outright gifts and bequests. If Bennett wants her children to enjoy the income of the trust property during their young adulthood without distributing unfettered ownership of the property to them before she considers them able to manage it properly, she can ac-

complish this through a trust provision. A trust can prevent the property from being squandered or spent too quickly. Trusts can be set up so that a beneficiary's interest cannot be reached by his creditors in many situations. Such trusts, called **spendthrift trusts,** will be discussed later.

Placing property in trust can operate to increase the amount of property held for the beneficiaries if the trustee makes good investment decisions. Another important consideration is that a trust can be used to provide for the needs of disabled beneficiaries who are not capable of managing funds.

Creation of Express Trusts

There are five basic requirements for the creation of a valid express trust, although special and somewhat less restrictive rules govern the establishment of charitable trusts. The requirements for forming an express trust are:

1. *Capacity.* The settlor must have had the **legal capacity** to convey the property to the trust. This means that the settlor must have had the capacity needed to make a valid contract if the trust is an *inter vivos* trust or the capacity to make a will if the trust is a testamentary trust. For example, a trust would fail under this requirement if at the time the trust was created, the settlor had not attained the age required by state law for the creation of valid wills and contracts (age 18 in most states).

2. *Intent and formalities.* The settlor must *intend* to create a trust at the present time. To impose enforceable duties on the trustee, the settlor must meet certain formalities. Under the laws of most states, for example, the trustee must accept the trust by signing the trust instrument. In the case of a trust of land, the trust must be in writing so as to meet the statute of frauds. If the trust is a testamentary trust, it must satisfy the formal requirements for wills.

3. *Conveyance of specific property.* The settlor must convey *specific property* to the trust. The property conveyed must be property that the settlor has the *right to convey.*

4. *Proper purpose.* The trust must be created for a *proper purpose.* It cannot be created for a reason that is contrary to public policy, such as the commission of a crime.

5. *Identity of the beneficiaries.* The *beneficiaries* of the trust must be described clearly enough so that their identities can be ascertained. Sometimes, beneficiaries may be members of a specific class, such as "my children."

Charitable Trusts

A distinction is made between private trusts and trusts created for charitable purposes. In a private trust, property is devoted to the benefit of specific persons, whereas in a charitable trust, property is devoted to a charitable organization or to some other purposes beneficial to society. While some of the rules governing private and charitable trusts are the same, a number of these rules are different. For example, when a private trust is created, the beneficiary must be known at the time or ascertainable within a certain time (established by a legal rule known as the **rule against perpetuities**). However, a charitable trust is valid even though no definitely ascertainable beneficiary is named and even though it is to continue for an indefinite or unlimited period.

Doctrine of Cy Pres   A doctrine known as **cy pres** is applicable to charitable trusts when property is given in trust to be applied to a particular charitable purpose that becomes impossible, impracticable, or illegal to carry out. Under the doctrine of *cy pres,* the trust will not fail if the settlor indicated a general intention to devote the property to charitable purposes. If the settlor has not specifically provided for a substitute beneficiary, the court will direct the application of the property to some charitable purpose that falls within the settlor's general charitable intention.

Totten Trusts

A **Totten trust** is a deposit of money in a bank or other financial institution in the name of the depositor *as trustee* for a named beneficiary. For example, Bliss deposits money in First Bank in trust for his daughter, Bessie. The Totten trust creates a revocable living trust. At Bliss's death, if he has not revoked this trust, the money in the account will belong to Bessie.

Powers and Duties of the Trustee

In most express trusts, the settlor names a specific person to act as trustee. If the settlor does not name a trustee, the court will appoint one. Similarly, a court will replace a trustee who resigns, is incompetent, or refuses to act.

The trust codes of most states contain provisions giving trustees broad management powers over trust property. These provisions can be limited or expanded by express provisions in the trust instrument. The trustee must use a *reasonable degree of skill, judgment, and care* in the exercise of his duties unless he holds himself out as having a greater degree of skill, in which case he will be held to a higher standard. Section 7–302 of the UPC provides that the trustee is held to the standard of a prudent person dealing with the property of another, and if he has special skills or is named trustee based on a representation of special skills, he is required to use those special skills. He *may not commingle* the property he holds in trust with his own property or with that of another trust.

A trustee owes a *duty of loyalty* (fiduciary duty) to the beneficiaries. This means that he must administer the trust for the benefit of the beneficiaries and avoid any conflict between his personal interests and the interest of the trust. For example, a trustee cannot do business with a trust that he administers without express permission in the trust agreement. He must not prefer one beneficiary's interest to another's, and he must account to the beneficiaries for all transactions. Unless the trust agreement provides otherwise, the trustee must make the trust productive. He may not delegate the performance of discretionary duties (such as the duty to select investments) to another, but he may delegate the performance of ministerial duties (such as the preparation of statements of account).

A trust may give the trustee discretion as to the amount of principal or income paid to a beneficiary. In such a case, the beneficiary cannot require the trustee to exercise his discretion in the manner desired by the beneficiary.

Allocating between Principal and Income   One of the duties of the trustee is to distribute the principal and income of the trust in accordance with the terms of the trust instrument. Suppose Wheeler's will created a testamentary trust providing that his wife was to receive the income from the trust for life, and at her death, the trust property was to be distributed to his children. During the duration of the trust, the trust earns profits, such as interest or rents, and has expenses, such as taxes or repairs. How should the trustee allocate these items as between Wheeler's surviving spouse, who is an **income beneficiary,** and his children, who are **remaindermen?**

The terms of the trust and state law bind the trustee in making this determination. As a general rule, ordinary profits received from the investment of trust property are allocated to income. For example, interest on trust property or rents earned from leasing real property held in trust would be allocated to income. Ordinary expenses such as insurance premiums, the cost of ordinary maintenance and repairs of trust property, and property taxes, would be chargeable to income. The principal of the trust includes the trust property itself and any extraordinary receipts, such as proceeds or gains derived from the sale of trust property. Extraordinary expenses—for example, the cost of long-term permanent improvements to real property or expenses relating to the sale of property—would ordinarily be charged against principal.

Liability of Trustee

A trustee who breaches any of the duties of a trustee or whose conduct falls below the standard of care applicable to trustees may incur personal liability. For example, if the trustee invests unwisely and imprudently, the trustee may be personally liable to reimburse the trust estate for the shortfall. The language of the trust affects the trustee's liability and the level of care owed by the trustee. A settlor might, for example, include language lowering the trustee's duty of care or relieving the trustee of some liability that he might otherwise incur.

The trustee can also have liability to third persons who are injured by the operation of the trust. Because a trust is not in itself a legal entity that can be sued, a third party who has a claim (such as a tort claim or a claim for breach of contract) must file his claim against the trustee of the trust. The trustee's actual personal liability to a third party depends on the language of the trust and of any contracts he might enter on behalf of the trust as well as the extent to which the injury complained of by the third party was a result of the personal fault or omission of the trustee.

Spendthrift Trusts

Generally, the beneficiary of a trust may voluntarily assign his rights to the principal or income of the trust to another person. In addition, any distributions to the beneficiary are subject to the claims of his creditors. Sometimes, however, trusts contain provisions known as **spendthrift clauses,** which restrict the voluntary or involuntary transfer of a beneficiary's interest. Such clauses are generally enforced, and they preclude assignees or creditors from compelling a trustee to recognize their claims to the trust. The enforceability of such clauses is subject to four exceptions, however:

1. A person cannot put his own property beyond the claims of his own creditors. Thus, a spendthrift clause is not effective in a trust when the settlor makes himself a beneficiary.

2. Divorced spouses and minor children of the beneficiary can compel payment for alimony and child support.

3. Creditors of the beneficiary who have furnished necessaries can compel payment.

4. Once the trustee distributes property to a beneficiary, it can be subject to valid claims of others.

The following *Kulp* case illustrates a situation in which a court holds a spendthrift trust subject to a creditor's claims.

Kulp v. Timmons   *2002 Del. Ch. LEXIS 94 (Del. Ct. of Chancery 2002)*

Before 1985, Franklin Timmons and his wife, Kathryn, owned property adjacent to Pepper Creek in Sussex County, Delaware. The property included farmland, the Timmons's residence, and a marina called the "Boatyard," where Timmons operated the family business. The above-described land was the only real property that Timmons owned, and was the only capital asset that supported the family business. Timmons's primary income was derived from the Boatyard. At the Boatyard, Timmons rented out boat slips, assessed dry dock fees, maintained and repaired boats, and performed the day-to-day operations of the marina. According to Timmons, the business operated at a loss, but there are no records to prove that. In 1977, Timmons was sued by Charles Cannon on transactions that involved the Boatyard. Cannon was awarded a $7,700 judgment against Timmons in 1980, but Timmons never paid the judgment, claiming that he lacked sufficient funds. In 1985, Timmons and Kathryn established a Joint Irrevocable Living Trust. Timmons and Kathryn conveyed to the Trust the farm and the Boatyard, which comprised all the real property that they owned and the only significant assets that were capable of responding to a creditor judgment. Under the terms of the Trust, Timmons, Kathryn, and their son, Jimmy, were named as trustees. The Trust instrument gave trustees discretion to invade the trust principal and to sell the land for their own benefit.

Although his property was now held by the Trust, Timmons never viewed the Trust as limiting his ability to use the land for himself or to rent it to others. Timmons believed that he could continue to live on the land, operate his business on it, and use the land as his own, as he had done in the past. Two additional documents were executed in connection with the Trust instrument. The first was a partnership agreement, which created a partnership between Timmons and his son, Jimmy, for the purpose of operating the Boatyard. The Partnership Agreement identified Kathryn and Jimmy—but not Timmons—as part-

ners. The second document was a lease that called for the payment of a monthly rent for using the Boatyard, but left the specific rental amount blank. Although it was understood that the rental amount would be inserted after Timmons secured an appraisal of the Boatyard's fair market value, no rental amount was ever inserted and no rent was ever paid. Nor, insofar as the record shows, did the Trust engage in any trust activity after it was formed. Other than filing tax returns, the Trust had no financial records for any year other than 1988, or any checking or banking account; and it received no rent or other income from Timmons's use of the land. In addition, although Kathryn was the Boatyard's bookkeeper, the Trust never took any action evidenced by a formal writing.

In 1985, six months after the Trust was created, Norman Kulp, Timmons's employee, was severely injured while working at the Boatyard when Timmons instructed him to remove a gas tank from a boat docked at the Boatyard. Timmons told Kulp that he, Timmons, had personally ventilated the tank and that Jimmy would help Kulp remove it. In fact, the tank had not been emptied and Kulp was left to perform that task alone. The tank exploded and Kulp was burned over one-third of his body. Timmons did not carry workers' compensation insurance, and he did not reimburse any of Kulp's medical expenses. Kulp filed a petition for compensation due with the Industrial Accident Board (IAB) under the Delaware Workers' Compensation Act, and the IAB ordered Timmons to post a $150,000 bond and to pay Kulp's medical expenses and other benefits. Timmons did not comply with the IAB order, and several years of litigation ensued.

Timmons's son, Jimmy, died in October 1994, and Timmons's wife, Kathryn, died two years later. As a consequence, Timmons became the sole settlor, trustee, and lifetime beneficiary of the Trust. Kulp's IAB award still remained unpaid, which prompted the filing of a Superior Court proceeding to enforce payment of that award. In 1997, the Superior Court entered a money judgment in favor of Kulp, doubling the initial IAB award to $194,316.74 to compensate Kulp for the delay in payment. The Superior Court concluded, however, that it did not have the power to compel Timmons to pledge, sell, or encumber the assets held by the Trust to satisfy the judgment. In response to the Court's suggestion that Kulp's remedy would lie in equity, Kulp brought this action in this Court for a determination that the Trust was invalid and that its assets were subject to execution process. Less than one month after this action was filed, Timmons conveyed all his personal property to his daughter-in-law, Beverly, and his granddaughter, Brandi. Thereafter, Beverly and Brandi conveyed a life estate in the conveyed property to Timmons. Timmons argued that as a consequence of that conveyance, and the transfer of his (and his wife's) assets to the Trust in 1985, he has no assets from which to satisfy the judgment. Kulp moved for summary judgment.

JACOBS, Vice Chancellor As a general matter, creditors may not reach property held in a spendthrift trust to satisfy their claims against the beneficial owner. That rule, however, is not absolute. The Court first considers whether the Trust is invalid under Delaware's spendthrift trust statute. Section 3536 (a) articulates the rights of creditors to reach assets held in spendthrift trusts as follows: The creditors of a beneficiary of a trust shall have only such rights against such beneficiary's interest in the trust property or the income therefrom as shall not be denied to them by the terms of the instrument creating or defining the trust or by the laws of this State. *If such beneficiary has transferred property to the trust in defraud of the beneficiary's creditors the foregoing shall in no way limit the rights of such creditors with respect to the property so transferred.* Thus, the statute expressly permits a trust to be invalidated if it is shown that the transfer of the property to the trust operated as a fraud on the beneficiary's creditors. If a fraud is shown, the trust is void, and a creditor of the beneficiary may reach its assets to satisfy the creditor's judgment claim.

Delaware courts have held that the test of a fraudulent conveyance of property involves a two-step analysis: first, a determination of whether the transfer was made for less than fair consideration; and second, a determination of whether the transferor was rendered insolvent as a result of the transfer. Del. C. §§ 1302, as it existed when the Trust was created in 1985, stated that a person is insolvent "when the fair salable value of his assets is less than the amount that will be required to pay his probable liability on his existing debts as they become absolute and matured." In this case, the absence of financial records and other documentation precludes the Court from determining, as an evidentiary matter, whether in fact Timmons was insolvent at the time of the asset transfer. Nor does the record evidence show whether the Boatyard was transferred to the Trust for fair consideration. All the record does show is that Timmons transferred the Boatyard to a Trust controlled by himself, his wife, and his son. Where, as here, a transfer of assets occurs between relatives, collusion is difficult to prove, and therefore "a rebuttable presumption of fraud arises." That presumption requires the party asserting the validity of the transfer to show either that he was solvent after the transfer or that fair consideration was paid. Timmons has not shown either, nor has he offered any evidence on either of those issues. What evidence there is shows an intent to defraud past and future creditors. At the time the Trust was created, Cannon's judgment was outstanding and Timmons had never paid it, even though he had the resources to do so. Moreover, the Trust served no discernable economic purpose. The Trust engaged in no recorded economic activity; no rent was paid to the Trust for the use of the Boatyard; and no formal action evidenced by a writing by the Trust was ever taken. In short, Timmons has presented no evidence that rebuts the presumption that the creation and the transfer of his (and his wife's) assets to the Trust was a fraud. I conclude therefore that the Trust is invalid and has been from the outset, and must be set aside, on the basis of the fraud exception of Section 3536 (a).

In addition to, and apart from, the statute, the Trust is void because the statute does not displace the applicable principles of common law, and because under those principles the Trust is void as well. The Delaware case law has not delineated in any comprehensive "bright line" fashion the universe of common law grounds upon which a trust can be invalidated and made subject to claims of the beneficiary's creditors. The decisions do, however, clearly reflect a basic principle: our courts will not give effect to a spendthrift trust that has no economic reality and whose only function is to enable the settlor to control and enjoy the trust property without limitations or restraints, as was done before the trust was created. Apart from cases involving fraud, that principle has found expression under at least two different doctrines. Some cases express that result in terms of public policy. In such cases, our courts have denied effect to a trust agreement provision that prohibits the beneficiary's alienation of trust income or assets, where the beneficiary is also the settlor. Where, as here, the settlor or trustee is also the beneficiary, the spendthrift trust will be invalidated, because

public policy does not permit one to create a spendthrift trust with his own property for his own benefit. That is because where (as here) the trustee controls the assets and income of the trust for his own benefit, unconstrained by any fiduciary duties owed to others, the purpose of a spendthrift trust—to protect the beneficiary from his or her own improvidence—is lost. The evidence of record—undisputed by Timmons—amply supports the conclusion that at all times Timmons had—and exercised—the power to use the Trust assets as his own. The Trust instruments authorize Timmons to expend the entire corpus of the Trust at his discretion, for his own benefit and without any limitation or restriction. Timmons acknowledged that after he conveyed the property to the Trust he expected to continue to use the land as he had in the past. Timmons also admitted that he did not believe the Trust limited in any way his ability to rent the property to someone else. Further supportive of the invalidity of the Trust on public policy grounds is the fact that the Trust has no economic reality and from the outset was a sham. Most telling is the fact that the mortgage payments were made from Timmons's *personal* income (not from Trust assets), and the income from boat maintenance and repairs was reported as income to Timmons *personally,* rather than as income to the Trust. That shows that Timmons never intended for the Trust to have any economic function other than as a vehicle to avoid paying his debts. On this basis alone, the Trust is void and the Trust assets are subject to Kulp's claim as a judgment. On all of these grounds, the Trust is void under the principles of Delaware common law, and Kulp may reach the Trust's assets to satisfy his judgment claim.

Summary judgment granted in favor of Kulp.

Termination and Modification of a Trust

Normally, a settlor cannot revoke or modify a trust unless he reserves the power to do so at the time he establishes the trust. However, a trust may be modified or terminated with the consent of the settlor and all of the beneficiaries. When the settlor is dead or otherwise unable to consent, a trust can be modified or terminated by consent of all the persons with a beneficial interest, but only when this would not frustrate a material purpose of the trust. Because trusts are under the supervisory jurisdiction of a court, the court can permit a deviation from the terms of a trust when unanticipated changes in circumstances threaten accomplishment of the settlor's purpose.

Implied and Constructive Trusts

Under exceptional circumstances in which the creation of a trust is necessary to effectuate a settlor's intent or avoid unjust enrichment, the law *implies* or imposes a trust even though no express trust exists or an express trust exists but has failed. One trust of this type is a **resulting trust,** which arises when there has been an incomplete disposition of trust property. For example, if Hess transferred property to Wickes as trustee to provide for the needs of Hess's grandfather and the grandfather died before the trust funds were exhausted, Wickes will be deemed to hold the property in a resulting trust for Hess or Hess's heirs. Similarly, if Hess had transferred the property to

Wickes as trustee and the trust had failed because Hess did not meet one of the requirements of a valid trust, Wickes would not be permitted to keep the trust property as his own. A resulting trust would be implied.

A **constructive trust** is a trust created by operation of law to avoid fraud, injustice, or unjust enrichment. This type of trust imposes on the constructive trustee a duty to convey property he holds to another person on the ground that the constructive trustee would be unjustly enriched if he were allowed to retain it. For example, when a person procures the transfer of property by means of fraud or duress, he becomes a constructive trustee and is under an obligation to return the property to its original owner.

Problems and Problem Cases

1. On March 23, 1994, Evelyn Foster died, leaving a house and nearly 400 acres of land in Mercer County along with personal property. She had executed a holographic will, which was offered for probate. The will stated in part:

> I—Evelyn Foster—being of sound Mind and Body—do hereby declare—In the event of my death—I herby [sic] will the farm-house + contents to go to Judy Foster Monk—any Monies shall be divided equally—after the funeral Expenses—between Greg Foster + Judy Foster Monk—also I do herby [sic] request that the Farm *not be sold!* Any personal items shall be equally divided—
> Sincerely—
> Evelyn Foster

Foster's son claims that Foster willed only a "farm-house + contents" to his sister (Judy) and *not* the farm land. Is he correct?

2. In 1976, V.F. and Gertrude Neuhaus executed a Trust Indenture creating the Neuhaus Family Trusts, which established a number of separate individual trusts for the benefit of their children and grandchildren, Vernon and Lacey Neuhaus. The trusts were both managed by the same co-trustees, Grace Neuhaus Richards and Robert Schwarz. The initial corpus of both trusts consisted of stock in McAllen State Bank. However, in 1982, First City Bancorporation of Texas acquired all the stock of McAllen State Bank, and First City substituted its own stock for the McAllen State Bank stock in the trusts. From 1985 through 1987, the First City stock declined in value, but the trustees refused to sell until the stock in Lacey Neuhaus's trust became virtually worthless, and they delayed selling the stock in Vernon Neuhaus's trust until significant losses had been sustained. A provision of the trust states that:

> All property transferred by gift to any trust and any property acquired by the Trustees . . . shall be deemed a proper investment, and the Trustees shall be under no obligation to dispose of or convert any such property.

A second provision stated that "no Trustee shall be liable for negligence or error of judgment but shall be liable only for his willful misconduct or personal dishonesty." The Neuhauses sued both trustees alleging a breach of fiduciary duties, including a failure to exercise judgment and care, willful misconduct, and conscious disregard for the rights and welfare of the beneficiaries, among other claims. Will they win?

3. Roy and Icie Johnson established two revocable *inter vivos* trusts in 1966. The trusts provided that upon Roy and Icie's deaths, income from the trusts was to be paid in equal shares to their two sons, James and Robert, for life. Upon the death of the survivor of the sons, the trust was to be *"divided equally between all of my grandchildren, per stirpes."* James had two daughters, Barbara and Elizabeth. Robert had four children, David, Rosalyn, Catherine, and Elizabeth. James and Robert disclaimed their interest in the trust in 1979, and a dispute arose about how the trust should be distributed to the grandchildren. The trustee filed an action seeking instructions on how the trusts should be distributed. What should the court hold?

4. Kenneth Haag owned Front Royal Supply Co. Smoot had worked for Haag as the manager of the Front Royal store for a number of years. Stickley was the manager of the company's Winchester store, but had not worked for Haag as long as Smoot had. Blye was assistant manager of the Winchester store, and had worked for the company for a lesser amount of time than had Stickley. Printz was also an employee of Haag's, but was fired in 1984–85. On January 20, 1983, Haag executed a holographic will. The will contained a specific bequest of stock to his employees who were still with Front Royal at the time of his death. Read the will as shown in Figure 4.

In October 1985, Haag executed a holographic codicil. This codicil provided that "In case Chs. Smoot is deceased or any other receipitent [sic] their stare [sic] will go back in the estate." Haag died in 1986. His will was admitted to probate, and his former wife, Helen, was named executor. At the time of Haag's death, he owned 689 shares of Front Royal stock, the value of which was at least $254,000. A dispute arose between Mrs. Haag, as executor, and Stickley and Blye about whether they were entitled to any shares. Mrs. Haag maintained that the will should be interpreted to give 500 shares of stock to Smoot, and none to Stickley and Blye, with the remaining 189 shares going into the residuary

Figure 4 *Haag's Will*

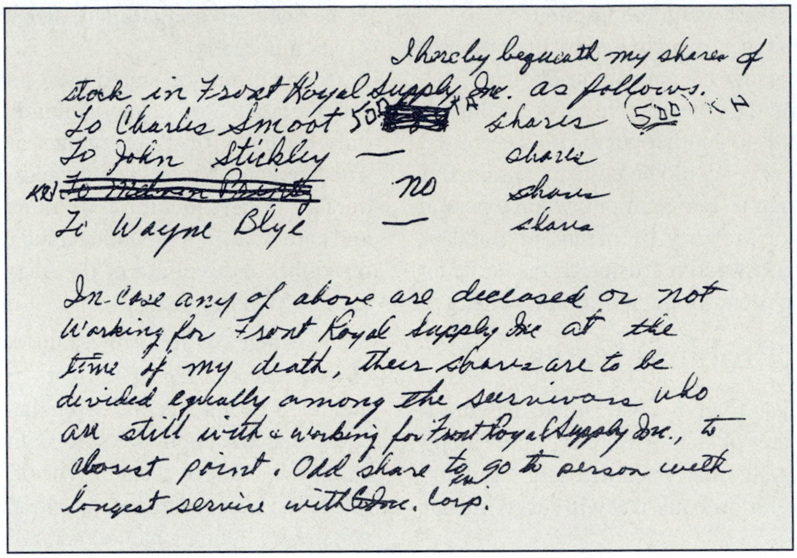
I hereby bequeath my shares of
stock in Front Royal Supply Inc. as follows.
To Charles Smoot 500 XH shares (500) XH
To John Stickley — shares
KH ~~[illegible]~~ no shares
To Wayne Blye — shares

In case any of above are deceased or not
Working for Front Royal Supply Inc at the
time of my death, their shares are to be
divided equally among the survivors who
are still with & working for Front Royal Supply Inc., to
closest point. Odd share to go to person with
longest service with Inc. Corp.

of the estate. Stickley and Blye filed this action asking the court to construe and interpret the will in order to determine their rights to the shares of stock. The court determined that Smoot should get the first 500 shares, and the remaining 189 shares should be divided equally between Stickley and Blye, with the odd share going to the person with longer service. Was this ruling correct?

5. Crawshaw bequeathed the bulk of his estate to two residuary beneficiaries, the Salvation Army and Marymount College. Crawshaw's will provided for 15 percent of the residue to go to the Salvation Army outright and 85 percent to Marymount College in trust. The stated purpose of this trust was to provide loans to nursing and other students at Marymount. Marymount ceased operation on June 30, 1989. It sought to have the trust funds directed to Marymount Memorial Educational Trust Fund. The Salvation Army challenged this, arguing that Crawshaw did not intend to benefit students attending colleges other than Marymount. It asked that the court distribute the trust funds to the Salvation Army as the remaining beneficiary of Crawshaw's residuary estate. What should the court do?

6. On September 19, 1980, Iola Wharton executed a will by signing her name in the presence of two attesting witnesses. She executed a second will on July 29, 1997. Because she had broken her right arm and lost the use of it, Iola placed her mark on the 1997 will in the presence of three attesting witnesses. One of the witnesses had typed Iola's name on the will outside the presence of the other two witnesses. All three of them witnessed Iola make her mark on the will, trust, and related documents. Iola's son, Joseph, was also present when his mother made her mark on the documents. Following Iola's death on April 1, 1998, the 1997 will was admitted to probate. Iola's daughter challenged the instruments executed by mark alleging, among other grounds, that the will and other instruments were not properly signed. Was the signature adequate?

7. Fickes, a resident of Washington, died in December 1943, leaving a will dated November 19, 1940. The will provided for the creation of a trust upon his death. The will also provided that upon the death of Fickes's last surviving child, one-half of the trust property was to be distributed to Renssalaer Polytechnic Institute and the other half of the trust property distributed "in equal portions" between Fickes's "grandchildren then living." At the time of death of Fickes's last surviving child, there were four biological grandchildren living. In addition, there were four adopted grandchildren living. Two of them, grandsons, had been adopted by Fickes's son while Fickes was still living. The other two, granddaughters, were adopted by Fickes's son in 1962 and 1965, long after Fickes's death. Were the granddaughters entitled to share in the trust distribution?

Online Research: Living Wills

Using your favorite search engine, find an example of a living will.

27

INSURANCE LAW

Prior to the September 11, 2001, attacks that destroyed the World Trade Center (WTC) towers, 22 insurance companies had issued property insurance binders covering the WTC complex. These binders were issued to Larry Silverstein, the leaseholder of the WTC complex, under an agreement with the Port Authority of New York and New Jersey. A binder is a temporary contract of insurance that is in force until a formal insurance policy is issued by the insurer. The 22 insurers intended to issue formal insurance policies to Silverstein, but very few had done so as of 9/11. Therefore, the binders established and limited their obligations to pay Silverstein after the destruction of the WTC complex.

Property insurance binders and policies often provide that the insurer's obligation to pay is triggered when a covered "occurrence" results in damage to or destruction of the relevant real estate. Binders and policies also have *policy limits,* which are both the amount of insurance coverage purchased and the maximum sum that the insurer can be obligated to pay for a covered claim. The policy limits in a property insurance binder or policy typically apply on a per-occurrence basis. For example, if the policy limits are $200,000, the insurer may become obligated to pay up to a maximum of $200,000 for losses resulting from one occurrence and up to another $200,000 on losses stemming from a separate occurrence.

Hartford Fire Insurance Company, Royal Indemnity Company, and St. Paul Fire and Marine Insurance Company—three of the 22 insurers that had issued binders regarding the WTC complex prior to 9/11—became involved in litigation with Silverstein over the amounts they were obligated to pay Silverstein after the events of 9/11. The policy limits set by the three insurers' binders totaled approximately $112 million dollars, out of a total of approximately $3.5 billion in insurance coverage contemplated by the binders and policies issued by all 22 insurers. The estimated cost of rebuilding the complex was approximately $5 billion.

In the case referred to above, a federal court agreed with an argument made by Hartford, Royal, and St. Paul: that their binders should be interpreted as containing the terms set forth in a form binder that had been circulated among the various insurers. The form binder made the insurance coverage applicable on a per-occurrence basis and contained a specific definition of *occurrence.* Silverstein argued that in all likelihood, the policies those companies ultimately would have issued would not have contained a specific definition of *occurrence* and that the definition set forth in the form binder should not necessarily guide the court's decision. The court rejected Silverstein's argument, noting that the binders were the controlling documents and that it therefore would be inappropriate to focus on the probable terms of the policies that would eventually have been issued.

Occurrence was defined this way in the form binder whose terms established the obligations of Hartford, Royal, and St. Paul:

> 'Occurrence' shall mean all losses or damages that are attributable directly or indirectly to one cause or to one series of similar causes. All such losses will be added together and the total amount of such losses will be treated as one occurrence irrespective of the period of time or area over which such losses occur.

The court then turned to the critical issue: whether, for purposes of the binders at issue, the two plane attacks that destroyed the WTC towers on 9/11 were one occurrence or, instead, two occurrences. If, as argued by Hartford, Royal, and St. Paul, the two plane attacks were one occurrence, those three insurers would be obligated to pay Silverstein a total of $112 million (the sum of their respective policy limits under the binders). If, as argued by Silverstein, the two plane attacks were two occurrences, the three insurers would be obligated to pay Silverstein a total of $224 million (twice the sum of their respective policy limits). Although the remaining insurers were not parties to the case, a determination of the extent of their liabilities to Silverstein was likely to be heavily influenced by the court's decision because it seemed reasonably likely that the other insurers would be viewed as having agreed to the same form binder terms to which Hartford, Royal, and St. Paul had agreed. Thus, although the actual amount in controversy in the case ranged from a minimum of $112 million to a maximum of $224 million, the practical economic stakes appeared to be much higher: $3.5 billion at minimum to $7 billion at maximum.

Consider the scenario described above and decide how you think the court answered this key question: whether the two plane attacks on the WTC towers on 9/11 were one occurrence or, instead, two occurrences. As you study Chapter 27, think about these related questions:

• When a court construes an insurance policy that may be subject to conflicting interpretations, what rules of interpretation should guide the court?

• What considerations should a court take into account in such a situation? In view of the risk allocations contemplated in insurance relationships, is a court justified in interpreting the policy in light of what would be "fair" or in the public interest?

• What is the nature of the relationship between insurer and insured? Should that nature affect how insurance policies are interpreted? If so, why, and how?

• What ethical obligations, if any, do insurers and insureds owe each other?

INSURANCE SERVES AS a frequent topic of discussion in various contexts in today's society. Advertisements for companies offering life, automobile, and property insurance appear daily on television and in the print media. Journalists report on issues of health insurance coverage and movements for reform. Persons engaged in business lament the excessive (from their perspective) costs of obtaining liability insurance. Insurance companies and insurance industry critics offer differing explanations for why those costs have reached their present levels.

Despite the frequency with which insurance matters receive public discussion and the perceived importance of insurance coverage, major legal aspects of insurance relationships remain unfamiliar to many persons. This chapter, therefore, examines important components of insurance law. We begin by discussing the nature of insurance relationships and exploring contract law's application to insurance policies in general. We then discuss other legal concepts and issues associated with specific types of insurance, most notably property insurance and liability insurance. The chapter concludes with an examination of an important judicial trend: allowing insurers to be held liable for compensatory and punitive damages if they refuse in bad faith to perform their policy obligations.

Nature and Benefits of Insurance Relationships

Insurance relationships arise from an agreement under which a risk of loss that one party (normally the **insured**) otherwise would have to bear is shifted to another party (the **insurer**). The ability to obtain insurance enables the insured to lessen or avoid the adverse financial effects that would be likely if certain happenings were to take place. In return for the insured's payment of necessary consideration (the **premium**), the insurer agrees to shoulder the financial consequences stemming from particular risks if those risks materialize in the form of actual events.

Each party benefits from the insurance relationship. The insured obtains a promise of coverage for losses that, if they occur, could easily exceed the amounts of the premiums paid. Along with this promise, the insured acquires the "peace of mind" that insurance companies and agents like to emphasize. By collecting premiums from many insureds over a substantial period of time, the insurer stands to profit despite its obligation to make payments covering financial losses that stem from insured-against risks. The insured-against risks, after all, are just that—risks. In some instances, events triggering the insurer's payment obligation to a particular insured may never occur (e.g., the insured's property never sustains damage from a cause contemplated by the property insurance policy). The insurer nonetheless remains entitled to the premiums collected during the policy period. Other times, events that call the insurer's payment obligation into play in a given situation may occur infrequently (e.g., a particular insured under an automobile insurance policy has an accident only every few years) or only after many years of premium collection (e.g., an insured paid premiums on his life insurance policy for 35 years prior to his death).

Insurance Policies as Contracts

Interested Parties

Regardless of the type of insurance involved, the insurance relationship is contractual. This relationship involves at least two—and frequently more than two—interested parties. As noted earlier, the insurer, in exchange for the payment of consideration (the premium), agrees to pay for losses caused by specific events (sometimes called *perils*). The insured is the person who acquires insurance on real or personal property or insurance against liability, or, in the case of life or health insurance, the person whose life or health is the focus of the policy. The person to whom the insurance proceeds are payable is the **beneficiary.** Except in the case of life insurance, the insured and the beneficiary will often be the same person. In most but not all instances, the insured will also be the policy's **owner** (the person entitled to exercise the contract rights set out in the insurance policy and in applicable law). In view of the contractual nature of the insurance relationship, insurance policies must satisfy all of the elements required for a binding contract.

Offer, Acceptance, and Consideration

The insurance industry's standard practice is to have the potential insured make an offer for an insurance contract by completing and submitting an application (provided by the insurer's agent), along with the appropriate premium, to the insurer. The insurer may then either accept or reject this offer. If the insurer accepts, the parties have an insurance contract under which the insured's initial premium payment and future premium payments furnish consideration for the insurer's promises of coverage for designated risks, and vice versa.

What constitutes acceptance of the offer set forth in the application may vary somewhat, depending on the type of insurance requested and the language of the application. As a general rule, however, acceptance occurs when the insurer (or agent, if authorized to do so) indicates to the insured an intent to accept the application. It is important to know the precise time when acceptance occurs, because the insurer's contractual obligations to the insured do not commence until acceptance has taken place. If the insured sustains losses after the submission of the application (the making of the offer) but prior to acceptance by the insurer, those losses normally must be borne by the insured rather than the insurer.

With property insurance and sometimes other types of insurance, the application may be worded so that insurance coverage begins when the insured signs the application. This arrangement provides temporary coverage until the insurer either accepts or rejects the offer contained in the application. The same result may also be achieved by the use of a *binder,* an agreement for temporary insurance pending the insurer's decision to accept or reject the risk.

Insurer's Delay in Acting on Application A common insurance law problem is the effect of the insurer's delay in acting on the application. If the applicant suffers a loss after applying but before a delaying insurer formally accepts, who must bear the loss? As a general rule, the insurer's delay does not constitute acceptance. Some states, however, have held that an insurer's retention of the premium for an unreasonable time constitutes acceptance and hence obligates the insurer to cover the insured's loss.

Other states have allowed negligence suits against insurers for delaying unreasonably in acting on an application. The theory of these cases is that insurance companies have a public duty to insure qualified applicants and that an unreasonable delay prevents applicants from obtaining insurance protection from another source. A few states have enacted statutes establishing that insurers are bound to the insurance contract unless they reject the prospective insured's application within a specified period of time.

Effect of Insured's Misrepresentation

Applicants for insurance have a duty to reveal to insurers all the material (significant) facts about the nature of the risk so that the insurer may make an intelligent decision about whether to accept the risk. When an application for property, liability, or health insurance includes an insured's false statement regarding a material matter, the insured's misrepresentation, if relied on by the insurer, has the same effect produced by misrepresentation in connection with other contracts—the contract becomes voidable at the election of the insurer. This means that the insurer may avoid its obligations under the policy. The same result is possible if the insured failed, in the application, to disclose known material facts to the insurer, which issued a policy it would not have issued if the disclosures had been made. However, special rules applicable to misrepresentations in life insurance applications may sometimes limit the life insurer's ability to use the insured's misrepresentation as a way of avoiding all obligations under the policy.

Warranty/Representation Distinction It sometimes becomes important to distinguish between **warranties** and representations that the insured makes (usually in the application) to induce the insurer to issue an insurance policy. Warranties are *express terms in the insurance policy.* They are intended to operate as conditions on which the insurer's liability is based. The insured's breach of warranty terminates the insurer's duty to perform under the policy. For example, a property insurance policy on a commercial office building specifies that the insured must install and maintain a working sprinkler system in the building, but the insured never installs the sprinkler system. The sprinkler system requirement is a warranty, which the insured breached by failing to install the system. This means that the insurer may not be obligated to perform its obligations under the policy.

Traditionally, an insured's breach of warranty has been seen as terminating the insurer's duty to perform *regardless of whether the condition set forth in the breached warranty was actually material to the insurer's risk* (unlike the treatment given to the insured's misrepresentations, which do not make the insurance policy voidable unless they pertained to a material matter). In view of the potential harshness of the traditional rule concerning the effect of a breach of warranty, some states have refused to allow insurers to escape liability on breach of warranty grounds unless the condition contemplated by the breached warranty was indeed material.

Legality

The law distinguishes between unlawful wagering contracts and valid insurance contracts. A wagering contract creates a new risk that did not previously exist. Such a contract is contrary to public policy and therefore illegal. An insurance contract, however, *transfers existing risks*—a permissible, even desirable, economic activity. A major means by which insurance law separates insurance contracts from wagering contracts is the typical requirement that the party who purchases a policy of property or life insurance must possess an **insurable interest** in the property or life being insured. Specific discussion of the insurable interest requirement appears later in the chapter.

Form and Content of Insurance Contracts

Writing State law governs whether insurance contracts are within the statute of frauds and must be evidenced by a writing. Some states require specific types of insurance contracts to be in writing. Contracts for property insurance are not usually within the statute of frauds, meaning that they may be either written or oral unless they come within some general provision of the statute of frauds— for example, the "one-year" provision.[1] Even when a writing is not legally required, however, wisdom dictates that the parties reduce their agreement to written form whenever possible.

Reformation of Written Policy As one would expect, insurance companies' customary practice is to issue written policies of insurance regardless of whether the applicable statute of frauds requires a writing. An argument sometimes raised by insureds is that the written policy issued by the insurer did not accurately reflect the content of the parties' actual agreement. For instance, after the occurrence of a loss for which the insured thought there was coverage under the insurance

contract, the insured learns that the loss-causing event was excluded from coverage by the terms expressly stated in the written policy. In such a situation, the insured may be inclined to argue that the written policy should be judicially **reformed,** so as to make it conform to the parties' supposed actual agreement.

Although reformation is available in appropriate cases, courts normally presume that the written policy of insurance should be treated as the embodiment of the parties' actual agreement. Courts consider reformation an extreme remedy. Hence, they usually refuse to grant reformation unless either of two circumstances is present. The first reformation-triggering circumstance exists when the insured and the insurer, through its agent or agents, were *mutually mistaken* about a supposedly covered event or other supposed contract term (i.e., both parties believed an event was covered by, or some other term was part of, the parties' insurance agreement but the written policy indicated otherwise). The alternative route to reformation calls for proof that the insurer committed fraud as to the terms contained in the policy or otherwise engaged in inequitable conduct. *Ridenour v. Farm Bureau Insurance Co.,* which follows, illustrates the judicial presumption that the written policy sets forth the parties' true agreement. The case also confirms that the insured's unilateral mistake—as opposed to the parties' mutual mistake—about policy terms will not warrant reformation.

---

[1]The usual provisions of the statute of frauds are discussed in detail in Chapter 16.

Ridenour v. Farm Bureau Insurance Company   *377 N.W.2d 101 (Neb. Sup. Ct. 1985)*

In August 1982, a hog confinement building owned by Charles Ridenour collapsed and was rendered a total loss. Some of Ridenour's hogs were killed as a further result of the collapse. Ridenour made a claim for these losses with his property insurer, Farm Bureau Insurance Company, whose Country Squire policy had been issued on Ridenour's property in July 1977 and had been renewed on a yearly basis after that. Farm Bureau denied the claim because the policy did not provide coverage for the collapse of farm buildings such as the hog confinement structure. Moreover, though the policy provided coverage for hog deaths resulting from certain designated causes, collapse of a building was not among the causes listed. Asserting that the parties' insurance contract was to have covered the peril of building collapse notwithstanding the terms of the written policy, Ridenour sued Farm Bureau. He asked the court to order reformation of the written policy so that it would conform to the parties' supposed agreement regarding coverage.

At trial, Ridenour testified about a February 1982 meeting in which he, his wife, and their son discussed insurance coverage with Farm Bureau agent Tim Moomey. Ridenour testified that he wanted to be certain there was insurance coverage if the hog confinement building collapsed because he had heard about the collapse of a similar structure owned by someone else. Therefore, he asked Moomey whether the Country Squire policy then in force provided such coverage. According to Ridenour, Moomey said that it did. Ridenour's wife, Thelma, testified that she asked Moomey (during the same meeting) whether there would be coverage if the floor slats of the hog confinement building collapsed and caused hogs to fall into the pit below the building. According to her testimony, Moomey responded affirmatively. The Ridenours' son, Tom, testified to the same effect. Mr. and Mrs. Ridenour both testified that they had not completely read the Country Squire policy and that because they did not understand the wording, they relied on Moomey to interpret the policy for them.

Moomey, who had ended his relationship with Farm Bureau by the time the case came to trial, testified that at no time did the Ridenours request that the hogs and the confinement building be insured so as to provide coverage for losses resulting from collapse of the building. Moomey knew that collapse coverage was not available from Farm Bureau for hog confinement buildings. In addition, Moomey testified that he met with Ridenour in April 1982 and conducted a "farm review" in which he discussed a coverage checklist and the Country Squire policy's declarations pages (which set forth the policy limits). This checklist, which Ridenour signed after Moomey reviewed it with him, made no reference to coverage for collapse losses. (Ridenour admitted in his testimony that he had signed the checklist after Moomey read off the listed items to him.) When Moomey was contacted by the Ridenours on the day the building collapsed, he had his secretary prepare a notice of loss report for submission to Farm Bureau. He also assigned an adjuster to inspect the property. Moomey and the adjuster discussed the fact that the Country Squire policy did not provide coverage for Ridenour's losses. Ridenour further testified that the day after the collapse occurred, Moomey told him he was sorry but that Farm Bureau's home office had said there was no coverage.

The trial court granted reformation, as Ridenour had requested. Farm Bureau appealed.

Caporale, Judge The principle upon which Ridenour relies is that reformation is decreed in order to effectuate the real agreement of the parties when a written instrument does not represent their true intent. In this jurisdiction reformation may be decreed where there has been a mutual mistake or where there has been a unilateral mistake caused by the fraud or inequitable conduct of the other party. To obtain reformation the evidence must be clear, convincing, and satisfactory. Such evidence is present when there has been produced in the trier of fact a firm belief or conviction that a fact to be proved exists. Moreover, there is a strong presumption that a written instrument correctly expresses the intention of the parties to it.

The record does not produce in us a firm belief or conviction that there was a mutual mistake of fact. Moomey was a trained and experienced insurance agent who, after he had no relationship with Farm Bureau, testified he knew the coverage claimed by Ridenour was not available from Farm Bureau and who denied representing that such coverage existed under the policy. Ridenour argues that Moomey's expression of sorrow over the fact that Farm Bureau's home office said there was no coverage, coupled with the facts that he caused a notice of loss report to be prepared and arranged for an adjuster to inspect the property, establishes that Moomey did think collapse coverage for the hog building existed. We conclude otherwise. Prudence dictated that Ridenour's claim be noted and investigated. Investigation of this claim to determine the facts does not imply a thought that coverage exists. Neither does an expression of regret that the home office said coverage does not exist necessarily imply an earlier belief by Moomey that there was coverage. It may as easily imply regret at the confirmation of what Moomey already knew.

Any mistake which may have existed was therefore one made only by Ridenour. Under such a circumstance he must, in order to recover, clearly, convincingly, and satisfactorily establish that the mistake was either the result of fraud on the part of Farm Bureau or due to Farm Bureau's inequitable conduct. Ridenour concedes in his brief that there was no fraud, but argues that Farm Bureau engaged in inequitable conduct by not delivering the declarations pages until after the loss. The late delivery of the declarations pages is more than adequately explained, however, by the fact that Ridenour was tardy in paying his premium. Moreover, since Ridenour admits that he did not read the policy, he cannot be heard to complain that not having the declarations pages deprived him of an opportunity to discover that he had no collapse coverage on his hog confinement building.

The nature of the conflict in the evidence in this case is not unlike that present in . . . earlier cases which resulted in a denial of reformation. [In addition,] the principal cases relied upon by Ridenour in which reformation was decreed are distinguishable from the case presently before us [because in each of the cases cited by Ridenour, the insured and the insurer's agent both testified that the agent made coverage assumptions and representations that were inconsistent with the terms of the written policy]. Indeed, in [those cases] there was no evidentiary conflict as to what the agent represented; consequently, the only conclusion which could have been reached was that there had been a mutual mistake. In the case before us, however, the evidence falls short of overcoming the presumption that the policy as written correctly expresses the intention of the parties at the time it was renewed.

Judgment and decree of reformation reversed in favor of Farm Bureau.

Interpretation of Insurance Contracts Modern courts realize that many persons who buy insurance do not have the training or background to fully understand the technical language often contained in insurance policies. As a result, courts interpret insurance policy provisions as they would be understood by an average person. In addition, courts construe ambiguities in an insurance contract against the insurer, the drafter of the contract (and hence the user of the ambiguous language). This rule of construction means that if a word or phrase used in an insurance policy is equally subject to two possible interpretations, one of which favors the insurer and the other of which favors the insured, the court will adopt the interpretation that favors the insured. The *Cope* case, which follows shortly, illustrates the application of this rule of construction to an ambiguous provision in a liability insurance policy.

A number of states purport to follow the *reasonable expectations of the insured* approach to interpretation of insurance policies. Analysis of judicial decisions reveals, however, that this approach's content and effect vary among the states ostensibly subscribing to it. Some states do little more than attach the reasonable expectations label to the familiar principles of interpretation set forth in the preceding paragraph. A few states give the reasonable expectations approach a much more significant effect by allowing courts to effectively read clauses into or out of an insurance policy, depending on whether reasonable persons in the position of the insured would have expected such clauses to be in a policy of the sort at issue. When applied in the latter manner, the reasonable expectations approach tends to resemble reformation in its effect.

Property Owners Insurance Co. v. Cope   *722 F. Supp. 1096 (N.D. Ind. 1991)*

Property Owners Insurance Co. (POI) was the insurer and Thomas Cope was the insured under a liability policy that excluded coverage except in instances of liability "with respect to the conduct of a business" owned by Cope. Cope owned a roofing business. While the policy was in force, Cope traveled to Montana with Edward Urbanski, a person with whom Cope did significant business. While on this trip, Cope snowmobiled with a group of persons that included Gregory Johnson, who died in a snowmobiling accident. Johnson's estate brought a wrongful death suit against Cope in a Montana court. POI then filed a declaratory judgment action against Cope and Johnson's estate in the U.S. District Court for the Northern District of Indiana. In this suit, POI sought a judicial determination that it had no obligations to Cope and Johnson's estate under the liability insurance policy. The parties agreed that Indiana law would control the case, which came before the court on POI's motion for summary judgment.

Moody, District Judge   POI maintains that the Montana snowmobiling trip was a recreational event rather than "the conduct of a business" owned by Cope. Thus, argues POI, the Montana trip was not covered by the insurance contract. Cope, however, maintains that he intended the Montana trip to advance both business and pleasure, thus bringing it under the policy.

The parties have not briefed, nor has the court found, any Indiana law interpreting the words "conduct of a business" in the context of an exclusion in a contract to provide liability insurance to a business owner. The closest reported case is apparently *Unigard Mutual Insurance Co. v. Martin* (1982), [an Arizona Court of Appeals case] cited by POI. The evidence before the *Martin* court showed that the object of a large annual fishing trip was both recreation and the advancement of business. The *Martin* court . . . focused on the express terms of the [liability] insurance contract. [Noting that the fishing trip was heavily recreational but only incidentally business-connected, and stressing the policy's ex-

clusion for "personal" activities that were not in "direct conduct of a business," the *Martin* court held that the policy at issue did not afford coverage.]

Applying *Martin* to this case, the court readily distinguishes the Arizona precedent on its facts. The *Martin* court relied heavily on [the] particular wording [of the policy involved there] in making its most important analytical point—namely, that the insurance contract was not ambiguous, but plainly excluded the fishing trip by its express terms. The *Martin* court focused especially on the words "direct conduct" in the exclusion before it, defining each word at length, and with particular emphasis on the word "direct." In the case at bar, the contract language is different, the limitation on coverage arising by negative implication from the words "only with respect to the conduct of a business." The word "direct" does not modify "conduct" in this case, nor does the contract expressly contrast personal and business activities. Accordingly, the *Martin* case does not present a perfect template for dealing with this action.

Whether or not the *Martin* court properly read the contract before it as unambiguous, the policy issue before this court is not resolved by the familiar Indiana rule that where an insurance contract is clear and unambiguous, the language therein must be given its plain meaning. [T]his court holds that the words "with respect to the conduct of a business" are, in this context, not sufficiently self-defining in their plain meaning. Rather, those words are ambiguous and require construction because reasonable persons might well differ on the question of whether they exclude coverage for activities furthering dual purposes of recreation and profit.

[U]nder settled principles for the interpretation of ambiguous insurance contracts . . ., this court construes the policy in favor of the insured. Thus, the court holds that the language of the contract before it does not exclude, as a matter of law, coverage for activities that serve dual purposes of recreation and profit. If insurance companies operating in Indiana desire the benefit of such an exclusion, it is a simple enough matter for them to draft their policies to unambiguously exclude coverage for recreational activities furthering business objectives.

In this case, the record on summary judgment reveals a genuine dispute over the factual nature of the Montana snowmobiling trip. This dispute is certainly material, for the factual nature of the trip will, under the express terms of the contract at issue, determine the applicability of the policy's limit on liability. It remains, however, for the court to further explore the materiality of that dispute by detailing the applicable legal standard for assessing the facts. The *Martin* court, in this regard, paints an alarming picture of insurer liability leaping up in extreme situations, perhaps even with chance meetings at Little League games. On the other hand, if hypotheticals are brought to bear, this court can readily imagine a far different situation at the other extreme, one in which a business executive who enjoys his solitude, loathes the boors to whom he must sell his product, and hopes to retire at the earliest possible moment, must nevertheless occasionally invite customers to cocktails or sporting events for the purely fictional purpose of having fun. The *Martin* court, apparently concerned with the dubious horrors of the slippery slope, seems inclined to create a bright line rule denying coverage in both situations. Given the ambiguity in the contract at issue here, however, this court is prepared to seek out a test in the law capable of discriminating among situations of mixed profit and recreation motives.

Cope advances the workmen's compensation test applied in Indiana law for many years: [whether] the activity at issue was "required by or incidental to" the insured's business. The *Martin* court rejected this type of test because the liberal coverage policy motivating workmen's compensation statutes is not at play in a private insurance contract. In this case, however, the contract is ambiguous, which brings to bear Indiana's policy of construing insurance exclusions against insurers. Thus, a significant policy of Indiana insurance law—already employed in construing the contract to cover mixed motive activities—parallels the expansive coverage policy motivating workmen's compensation, and justifies application of the same test. Accordingly, this court holds that the test for coverage under the "conduct of a business" policy at issue is whether Cope's Montana snowmobiling trip was necessary or incidental to the pursuit of profit through his business.

Of course, nothing in this opinion should be read as establishing that the Montana snowmobiling trip was sufficiently related to the insured's business to support a jury verdict of liability under the policy. Rather, this opinion merely establishes Cope's right to present evidence against exclusion at trial.

POI's motion for summary judgment denied.

Clauses Required by Law The insurance business is highly regulated by the states, which recognize the importance of the interests protected by insurance and the difference in bargaining power that often exists between insurers and their insureds. In an attempt to remedy this imbalance, many states' statutes and insurance regulations require the inclusion of certain standard clauses in insurance policies. Many states also regulate such matters as the size and style of the print used in insurance policies. Laws in a growing number of states encourage or require the use of plain, straightforward language—rather than insurance jargon and legal terms of art—whenever such language is possible to use.

Notice and Proof of Loss-Causing Event The insured (or, in the case of life insurance, the beneficiary) who seeks to obtain the benefits or protection provided by an insurance policy must notify the insurer that an event covered by the policy has occurred. In addition, the insured (or the beneficiary) must furnish reasonable proof of the loss-causing event. Property insurance policies, for instance, ordinarily require the insured to furnish a sworn statement (called a *proof of loss*) in which the covered event and the resulting damage to the insured's property are described. Under life insurance policies, the beneficiary is usually expected to provide suitable documentation of the fact that the insured person has died. Liability insurance policies call for the insured to give the insurer copies of liability claims made against the insured.

Time Limits Insurance policies commonly specify that notice and proof of loss must be given within a specified time. Policies sometimes state that compliance with these requirements is a condition of the insured's recovery and that failure to comply terminates the insurer's obligation. Other times, policies merely provide that failure to comply suspends the insurer's duty to pay until compliance occurs. Some courts

THE GLOBAL BUSINESS ENVIRONMENT

A California statute, the Holocaust Victim Insurance Relief Act of 1999 (HVIRA), requires that if an insurer presently doing business in California sold insurance policies to persons in Europe between 1920 and 1945 (Holocaust-era policies), the insurer must file certain information about those policies with the California insurance commissioner. The reporting requirement also applies to insurance companies that do business in California and are "related" to a company that sold Holocaust-era policies, even if the relationship arose after the policies were issued. A "related company" is defined as any "parent, subsidiary, reinsurer, successor in interest, managing general agent, or affiliate company of the insurer."

Insurance companies subject to HVIRA must provide this information: (1) the number of Holocaust-era insurance policies; (2) the holder, beneficiary, and current status of each such policy; and (3) the city of origin, domicile, or address for each policyholder listed in the policies. In addition, HVIRA requires the insurers to certify whichever one of the following is accurate: (1) that the proceeds of the policies were paid; (2) that the beneficiaries or heirs could not, after diligent search, be located, and the proceeds were distributed to Holocaust survivors or charities; (3) that a court of law has certified a plan for the distribution of the proceeds; or (4) that the proceeds have not been distributed. HVIRA instructs the California insurance commissioner to store the information disclosed under the statute in a Holocaust Era Insurance Registry, which is available to the public. In addition, HVIRA requires the insurance commissioner to "suspend the certificate of authority to conduct insurance business in the state of any insurer that fails to comply" with HVIRA's reporting requirements.

Various U.S.-based, German, and Italian insurance companies (referred to here as "the insurers") filed suit in a federal district court in an effort to have HVIRA invalidated on constitutional grounds. The district court held the statute unconstitutional and issued an injunction barring its enforcement. California's insurance commissioner appealed to the United States Court of Appeals for the Ninth Circuit. In *Gerling Global Reinsurance Corp. of America v. Low,* 296 F.3d 832 (9th Cir. 2002), the Ninth Circuit phrased the key question this way: "May California constitutionally require the disclosure of insurance claims-related information by an insurance company that is licensed to do business in California even though the required information may be in the hands of a related entity that is located in a foreign country?"

Answering that question "yes," the Ninth Circuit reversed the district court's decision and lifted the injunction that had barred enforcement of HVIRA. The insurers asserted that the California legislature exceeded its legislative authority and violated the U.S. Constitution's Commerce Clause (which reserves to the federal government the power to regulate commerce with other nations). More specifically, the insurers argued that HVIRA regulated extraterritorially by imposing requirements on entities located outside California's borders and by altering the substance of insurance contracts executed in foreign nations. The Ninth Circuit, however, was not persuaded. The court noted that a state legislature possesses broad-ranging power to regulate state-licensed businesses and to seek information from such entities. Rather than being a direct attempt to regulate European insurers' conduct and resulting decisions on whether to pay claims concerning Holocaust-era policies, HVIRA was merely a reporting statute designed to obtain information *about* the European-region conduct of insurers doing business in California or affiliated with insurers doing business there. The Ninth Circuit saw this as legitimate, state-related legislative activity, rather than an impermissible device for regulating foreign transactions.

The Ninth Circuit also rejected the insurers' substantive due process and equal protection arguments. With HVIRA being an economic regulation that neither involved a suspect class nor affected a fundamental right, the Ninth Circuit noted that the statute would be viewed through the lens of the lenient rational basis test. As explained in Chapter 3, a statute will be upheld under the rational basis test if the statute is reasonably related to the furtherance of a legitimate government interest. The court identified three government interests as underlying HVIRA: (1) providing California residents with information that could facilitate their resolution of legitimate Holocaust-era claims against insurance companies through an international process (or otherwise); (2) providing a means of protecting state residents from insurance companies that have not paid valid claims; and (3) providing information to California residents about the character of the family of insurance companies from which they might be contemplating buying insurance. Each of these government interests was clearly legitimate, the court held. Moreover, HVIRA was neither arbitrary nor irrational. Instead, it was reasonably related to the furtherance of the government interests at stake.

require the insurer to prove it was harmed by the insured's failure to give notice before allowing the insurer to avoid liability on the ground of tardy notice.

Cancellation and Lapse When a party with the power to terminate an insurance policy (extinguish all rights under the policy) exercises that power, **cancellation** has occurred. **Lapse** occurs at the end of the term specified in a policy written for a stated duration, unless the parties take action to renew the policy for an additional period of time. Alternatively, lapse may occur as a result of the insured's failure to pay premiums or some other significant default on the part of the insured.

Performance and Breach by Insurer

The insurer performs its obligations by paying out the sums (and taking other related actions) contemplated by the policy's terms within a reasonable time after the occurrence of an event that triggers the duty to perform. If the insurer fails or refuses to pay despite the occurrence of such an event, the insured may sue the insurer for breach of contract. By proving that the insurer's denial of the insured's claim for payment constituted a breach, the insured becomes entitled to recover compensatory damages in at least the amount that the insurer would have had to pay under the policy if the insurer had not breached.

What if the insurer's breach caused the insured to incur consequential damages that, when added to the amount due under the policy, would lead to a damages claim exceeding the dollar limits set forth in the policy? Assume that XYZ Computer Sales, Inc.'s store building is covered by a property insurance policy with Secure Insurance Co., that the building is destroyed by an accidental fire (a covered peril), and that the extent of the destruction makes the full $500,000 policy limit due from Secure to XYZ. Secure, however, denies payment because it believes—erroneously—that XYZ officials committed arson (a cause, if it had been the actual one, that would have relieved Secure from any duty to pay). Because it needs to rebuild and take other related steps to stay in business but is short on available funds as a result of Secure's denial of its claim, XYZ borrows the necessary funds from a bank. XYZ thereby incurs substantial interest costs, which are consequential damages XYZ would not have incurred if Secure had performed its obligation under the policy. Assuming that XYZ's consequential damages would have been foreseeable to Secure, most states would allow XYZ to recover the consequential damages in addition to the amount due

from Secure under the policy.[2] This is so even though the addition of the consequential damages would cause XYZ's damages recovery to exceed the dollar limit set forth in the parties' insurance policy. The breaching insurer's liability may exceed the policy limits despite the insurer's good faith (though incorrect) basis for denying the claim, because a good faith but erroneous refusal to pay is nonetheless a breach of contract. If the insurer could point to the policy limits as a maximum recovery in this type of situation, it would have an all-too-convenient means of avoiding responsibility for harms that logically flowed from its breach of contract.

Many states' laws provide that if an insured successfully sues her insurer for amounts due under the policy, the insured may recover interest on those amounts (amounts that, after all, should have been paid by the insurer much sooner and without litigation). Some states also have statutes providing that insureds who successfully sue insurers are entitled to awards of attorney's fees. Punitive damages are *not* allowed, however, when the insurer's breach of contract consisted of a *good faith (though erroneous) denial* of the insured's claim. Later in this chapter, we will explore the recent judicial trend toward allowing punitive damages when the insurer's breach was in *bad faith* and thus amounted to the tort of bad faith breach of contract.

Property Insurance

Owners of residential and commercial property always face the possibility that their property might be damaged or destroyed by causes beyond their control. These causes include, to name a few notable ones, fire, lightning, hail, and wind. Although property owners may not be able to prevent harm to their property, they can secure some protection against resulting financial loss by contracting for property insurance and thereby transferring certain risks of loss to the insurer. Persons holding prop-

---

[2]Even though the terms of the insurance policy almost certainly would state that Secure's payment obligation is limited to costs of repair or replacement or to the property's actual cash value—that is, without any coverage for consequential harms experienced by the insured—Secure cannot invoke this policy language as a defense. If Secure had performed its contract obligation, its payment obligation would have been restricted to what the policy provided in that regard. Having breached the insurance contract, however, Secure stands potentially liable for consequential damages to the full extent provided for by general contract law. For additional discussion of damages for breach of contract, see Chapter 18.

erty interests that fall short of ownership may likewise seek to benefit, as will be seen, from the risk-shifting feature of property insurance.

The Insurable Interest Requirement

As noted earlier in this chapter, in order for a property insurance contract not to be considered an illegal wagering contract, the person who purchases the policy (the policy owner) must have an **insurable interest** in the property being insured. One has an insurable interest if he, she, or it possesses a legal or equitable interest in the property and that interest translates into an economic stake in the continued existence of the property and the preservation of its condition. In other words, a person has an insurable interest if he would suffer a financial loss in the event of harm to the subject property. If no insurable interest is present, the policy is void.

Examples of Insurable Interest The legal owner of the insured property would obviously have an insurable interest. So might other parties whose legal or equitable interests in the property do not rise to the level of an ownership interest. For example, mortgagees and other lienholders would have insurable interests in the property on which they hold liens. A nonexhaustive list of other examples would also include holders of life estates in real property, buyers under as-yet unperformed contracts for the sale of real property, and lessees of real estate.[3] In the types of situations just noted, the interested party stands to lose financially if the property is damaged or destroyed.

Timing and Extent of Insurable Interest A sensible and important corollary of the insurable interest principle is that the requisite insurable interest must exist *at the time of the loss* (i.e., at the time the subject property was damaged). If an insurable interest existed when the holder thereof purchased the property insurance but the interest was no longer present when the loss occurred, the policy owner is not entitled to payment for the loss. This would mean, for example, that a property owner who purchased property insurance would not be entitled to collect from the insurer for property damage that occurred after she had transferred ownership to someone else. Similarly, a lienholder who

purchased property insurance could not collect under the policy if the loss took place after his lien had been extinguished by payment of the underlying debt or by another means.[4]

The extent of a person's insurable interest in property is limited to the value of that interest. For example, Fidelity Savings & Loan extends Williams a $95,000 loan to purchase a home and takes a mortgage on the home as security. In order to protect this investment, Fidelity obtains a $95,000 insurance policy on the property. Several years later, the house is destroyed by fire, a cause triggering the insurer's payment obligation. At the time of the fire, the balance due on the loan is $84,000. Fidelity's recovery under the insurance policy is limited to $84,000, because that amount is the full extent of its insurable interest. (An alternative way by which mortgagees protect their interest is to insist that the property owner list the mortgagee as the *loss payee* under the property owner's policy. This means that if the property is destroyed, the insurer will pay the policy proceeds to the mortgagee. Once again, however, the mortgagee's entitlement to payment under this approach would be limited to the dollar value of its insurable interest, with surplus proceeds going to the insured property owner.)

Covered and Excluded Perils

Property insurers usually do not undertake to provide coverage for losses stemming from any and all causes of harm to property. Instead, property insurers tend to either specify certain causes (**covered perils**) as to which the insured *will* receive payment for resulting losses—meaning that there is no coverage regarding a peril not specified—or set forth a seemingly broad statement of coverage but then specify certain perils concerning which there will be *no* payment for losses (**excluded perils**). Sometimes, property insurers employ a combination of these two approaches by specifying certain covered perils and certain excluded perils.

---

[3]Chapter 28 contains a detailed discussion of security interests in real property. Chapter 29 addresses security interests in personal property. Chapter 24 contains a discussion of life estates and an examination of contracts for the sale of real property. Leases of real estate are explored in Chapter 25.

[4]In the life insurance context, the requisite insurable interest *must exist at the time the policy was issued* but need not exist at the time of the insured's death. Persons who stand to suffer a financial loss in the event of the insured's death have the insurable interest necessary to support the purchase of a life insurance policy on the insured. The insured and his or her spouse, parents, children, and other dependents thus possess an insurable interest in the insured's life. In addition, the business associates of the insured may also have an insurable interest in his or her life. Such persons would include the insured's employer, business partners, or shareholders in a closely held corporation with which the insured is connected. Creditors of the insured also have an insurable interest, but only to the extent of the debt owed by the insured.

Typical Covered Perils The effects of these approaches are essentially the same, as most property insurers tend to provide coverage for the same sorts of causes of harm to property. The perils concerning which property insurance policies typically provide benefits include fire, lightning, hail, and wind. In addition, property insurance policies often cover harms to property resulting from causes such as the impact of an automobile or aircraft (e.g., an automobile or aircraft crashes into an insured building), vandalism, certain collapses of buildings, and certain accidental discharges or overflows from pipes or heating and air-conditioning systems.

Fire as a Covered Peril Historically, the importance of coverage against the peril of fire made *fire insurance* a commonly used term. Various insurance companies incorporated the term into their official firm name; the policies these companies issued came to be called *fire insurance policies* even when they covered perils in addition to fire (as policies increasingly have done in this century). As a result, judges, commentators, and persons affiliated with the insurance industry will sometimes refer to today's policies as fire insurance policies despite the usual property insurer's tendency to cover not only fire but also some combination of the other perils mentioned in the preceding paragraph. Whether the term used is *property insurance* (generally employed in this chapter) or *fire insurance,* reference is being made to the same type of policy.

Fire-related losses covered by property insurance policies are those resulting from accidental fires. An accidental fire is one other than a fire deliberately set by, or at the direction of, the insured for the purpose of damaging the property. In other words, the insured obtains no coverage for losses stemming from the insured's act of arson. This commonsense restriction on an insurer's duty to pay for losses also applies to other harms the insured deliberately caused to his property.

For purposes of fire coverage, insurance contracts often distinguish between *friendly fires,* which are those contained in a place intended for a fire (such as fires in a woodstove or fireplace), and *hostile fires,* which burn where no fire is intended to be (such as fires caused by lightning, outside sources, or electrical shorts, or those that began as friendly fires but escaped

their boundaries). Losses caused by hostile fires are covered; those stemming from friendly fires tend not to be. As a general rule, covered fire losses may extend beyond direct damage caused by the fire. Indirect damage caused by smoke and heat is usually covered, as is damage caused by firefighters in their attempts to put out the fire.

Typical Excluded Perils Although flood-related harm to property may seem similar to harm stemming from some of the weather-related causes listed earlier among the typical covered perils, it does not usually receive the same treatment. Property insurance policies frequently exclude coverage for flood damage. On this point, however, as with other questions regarding perils covered or excluded, the actual language of the policy at issue must always be consulted before a coverage issue is resolved in any given case.[5] Other typical exclusions include earthquake damage and harm to property stemming from war or nuclear reaction, radiation, or contamination. As previously indicated, property insurance policies exclude coverage for losses caused by the insured's deliberate actions that were intended to cause harm to the property.

Additional Coverages Even as to perils for which there may not be coverage in the typical property insurance policy, the property owner may sometimes be able to purchase a specialized policy (e.g., a flood insurance policy) that does afford coverage for such perils. Other times, even if coverage for a given peril is not provided by the terms of most standard property insurance policies, it may nonetheless be possible for the property owner to have coverage for that peril added to the policy by paying an additional premium. This is sometimes done, for example, by policy owners who desire earthquake coverage.

---

[5]It may be that a type of peril frequently excluded in property insurance policies is in fact a covered peril under the language of the policy at issue. Alternatively, losses that at first glance appear to have resulted from an excluded peril may sometimes be characterized as having resulted, at least in part, from a covered peril. In the latter event, there may be some coverage for the losses.

Shelter Mutual Insurance Co. v. Maples ⋅ *2002 U.S. App. LEXIS 23143 (8th Cir. 2002)*

Shelter Mutual Insurance Co. brought a declaratory judgment action against Tommy and Bessie Maples (referred to collectively as "Maples") in the United States District Court for the Western District of Arkansas. Shelter asked the court to declare that Shelter had no obligation to pay a claim made by Maples under a homeowner's insurance policy issued by Shelter. The facts set forth in the following paragraph were as stipulated (i.e., as agreed to) by the parties.

While residing in Saudi Arabia, Maples contracted for the construction of a single-family retirement home in Arkansas. Maples purchased homeowner's insurance from Shelter, whose policy, issued in November 2000, was in full effect at all times relevant to the case. The two-story residence, which had a wooden frame and a basement made of concrete, was largely complete as of November 2000. Maples, who remained in Saudi Arabia, took reasonable precautions for winter weather by leaving a key with the contractor and asking him to winterize the residence. At some unknown time, a water pipe froze and burst. As a result, between four to six inches of water stood continuously in the basement until the contractor discovered the problem in April 2001. The standing water caused only minimal structural damage to the basement, but the humidity from the standing water caused mold to form on all of the interior surfaces of the residence. As a result of the mold, the residence became uninhabitable and had to be demolished.

Maples reported the loss to Shelter, which instituted the declaratory judgment action referred to above. After the federal district court granted summary judgment in favor of Shelter, Maples appealed to the United States Court of Appeals for the Eighth Circuit.

Riley, Circuit Judge As relevant, the insurance policy provided:

PERILS WE INSURE AGAINST—SECTION I

We cover accidental direct physical loss to property covered under Dwelling and Other Structures Coverages except for losses excluded in this section.

Under Dwelling and Other Structures Coverages, we do not cover loss caused by:

1. wear and tear; marring or scratching; deterioration; inherent vice; latent defect; mechanical breakdown; rust; mold; wet or dry rot; contamination; smog, smoke from agricultural smudging or industrial operations; settling, cracking, shrinkage, bulging or expansion of pavement, patios, foundations, walls, floors, roofs, or ceilings; birds, vermin, rodents, insects or domestic animals. If, because of any of these, water escapes from a plumbing, heating, or air conditioning system or domestic appliance, we cover loss caused by the water. We also cover the cost of tearing out and replacing any part of the covered building necessary to repair the system or appliance. We do cover loss to the system or appliance from which the water escapes.

[T]he district court concluded that Shelter was entitled to summary judgment, reasoning that the policy language clearly provided that any loss due to mold was not covered.

This court reviews de novo the district court's grant of summary judgment, as well as its interpretation of Arkansas law. Under Arkansas law, insurance policies are to be construed liberally in favor of the insured, and exclusionary language that is susceptible to more than one reasonable interpretation should be construed in favor of the insured. The insurer bears the burden of proving as a matter of law that the insured's claim was excluded under the policy

Here, a covered peril, frozen pipes, caused an excluded peril, mold, which resulted in the loss. The district court concluded that the policy precluded coverage for mold damage regardless of its cause, relying on the following lead-in language from the policy:

We do not cover loss:

(a) resulting directly or indirectly from any of the following events;
   (b) which would not have occurred in the absence of any of the following events;
   (c) which occurs regardless of the cause of any of the following events; or
   (d) if loss occurs concurrently or in any sequence with any of the events.

We disagree with the court's reading of the policy, because we find this language leads into a list of ten specified items not including mold, while the mold-exclusion paragraph is separately numbered and follows the lead-in clause "Under Dwelling and Other Structures Coverages, we do not cover loss caused by." Thus, the plain language of the policy does not automatically preclude coverage. Compare *Cooper v. American Family Mutual Insurance Co.,* 184 F. Supp. 2d 960, 961–63 (D. Ariz. 2002) (no coverage for mold damage from plumbing leak where lead-in clause excluded losses regardless of any other contributing cause or event), with *West v. Umialik Insurance Co.,* 8 P.3d 1135, 1137–41 (Alaska 2000) (settling of house from broken plumbing was covered loss, where no lead-in clause precluded coverage regardless of cause).

It appears to us, then, that the determinative question is a factual one: whether the frozen pipe or the mold was the dominant and efficient cause of the loss. See 10 LEE R. RUSS & THOMAS F. SEGALLA, COUCH ON INSURANCE §§ 148:60, 148:61 (3d ed. 1998) (where covered and non-covered perils join to cause a loss, and the covered peril is the efficient and dominant cause, there is coverage under the policy); 11 COUCH ON INSURANCE § 153:96 (mold exclusions do not necessarily apply where "efficient proximate cause" of loss was a covered risk). Because the parties' factual stipulation does not answer this question, we conclude [that] a material issue of fact remains, and [that] summary judgment was improper.

District court's grant of summary judgment in favor of Shelter reversed; case remanded for consideration of causation issue.

Personal Property Insurance Although the broad term *property insurance* is what has been employed, the discussion so far in this section has centered around policies providing coverage for harm to *real* property. Items of *personal* property are, of course, insurable as well. Property insurance policies commonly known as homeowners' policies—because the real property serving as the policy's primary subject is the insured's dwelling—cover not only harm to the dwelling but also to personal property located inside the dwelling or otherwise on the subject real property. (Sometimes, depending on the policy language, there may be coverage even when the item of personal property was not located at the designated real property when the item was damaged.) Property insurance policies covering office buildings and other commercial real estate often provide some level of personal property coverage as well. When personal property coverage is included in a policy primarily concerned with real property coverage, the perils insured against in the personal property coverage tend to be largely the same as, though not necessarily identical to, those applicable to the real property coverage.

Lessees of residential or commercial real estate may obtain insurance policies to cover their items of personal property that are on the leased premises. Such policies are highly advisable, because the apartment or office building owner's insurance policy on the real property is likely to furnish little or no coverage for the tenant's personal property.

Automobile insurance policies are in part personal property insurance policies because they provide coverage (under what are usually called the *comprehensive* and *collision* sections) for car damage resulting from such causes as fire, wind, hail, vandalism, or collision with an animal or tree. As will be seen, automobile insurance policies also contain significant features of another major type of insurance policy to be discussed later—liability insurance. Other specialized types of personal property insurance are also available. For example, some farmers purchase crop insurance in order to guard against the adverse financial effects that would result if a hailstorm or other covered peril severely damaged a season's crop.

Nature and Extent of Insurer's Payment Obligation

Property insurance policies are **indemnity** contracts. This means that the insurer is obligated to reimburse the insured for his actual losses associated with a covered harm to the insured property. The insured's recovery under the policy thus cannot exceed the extent of the loss sustained. Neither may it exceed the extent of the insured's insurable interest or the amount of coverage that the insured purchased (the **policy limits**).[6]

Policy provisions other than the policy limits also help define the extent of the insurer's obligation to pay. When covered real property is damaged but not destroyed, the

---

[6]Some insurers, however, provide, in exchange for a more substantial premium than would be charged for a policy without this feature, a homeowner's policy under which the insurer could become obligated to pay *more* than the policy limits if the insured's home was destroyed and the cost to replace it would actually exceed the policy limits.

cost of repair is normally the relevant measure. Many policies provide that when covered real property is destroyed, the insurer must pay the **actual cash value** (or *fair market value*) of the property. Some policies, however, establish **cost of replacement** as the payment obligation in this situation. The policies that call for payment of the actual cash value frequently give the insurer the option to pay the cost of replacement, however, if that amount would be less than the actual cash value. As to covered personal property, the controlling standard is typically the least of the following: cost of repair, cost of replacement, or actual cash value.[7]

Many property insurance policies supplement the above provisions by obligating the insurer to pay the insured's reasonable costs of temporarily living elsewhere if the insured property was her residence and the damage to the residence made it uninhabitable pending completion of repairs or replacement. Comparable benefits may sometimes be provided in policies covering business property. Lost profits and similar consequential losses resulting from harm to or destruction of one's insured property, however, do not normally fall within the insurer's payment obligation unless a specific provision obligates the insurer along those lines.[8] Regardless of whether the damaged or destroyed property is real or personal in nature, the particular language of the policy at issue must always be consulted before a definite determination can be made concerning what is and is not within the insurer's duty to pay.

Valued and Open Policies   When insured real property is destroyed as a result of fire or another covered peril, the amount to be paid by the insurer may be further influenced by the type of policy involved. Some property insurance contracts are **valued policies.** If real property insured under a valued policy is destroyed, the insured is entitled to recover the face amount of the policy regardless of the property's fair market value. For example, in 1985, Douglas purchased a home with a fair market value of $90,000. Douglas also purchased a valued policy with a face amount of $90,000 to insure the house against various risks, including fire. The home's fair market value decreased in later years because of deterioration in the surrounding neighborhood. In 2002, when the home had a fair market value of only $75,000, it was destroyed by fire. Douglas is entitled to $90,000 (the face amount of the valued policy) despite the reduction in the home's fair market value.

Most property insurance policies, however, are open policies. Open policies allow the insured to recover the fair market value (actual cash value) of the property at the time it was destroyed, up to the limits stated in the policy. Thus, if Douglas had had an open policy in the example presented in the previous paragraph, he would have been entitled to only $75,000 when the home was destroyed by fire. Suppose instead that Douglas's home had increased in value, so that at the time of the fire its fair market value was $105,000. In that event, it would not matter what type of policy (valued or open) Douglas had. Under either type of policy, his recovery would be limited to the $90,000 face amount of the policy.

Coinsurance Clause   Some property insurance policies contain a **coinsurance clause,** which may operate as a further limit on the insurer's payment obligation and the insured's right to recovery. A coinsurance clause provides that in order for the insured to be able to recover the full cost of partial losses, the insured must obtain insurance on the property in an amount equal to a specified percentage (often 80 percent) of the property's fair market value.

For example, PDQ Corporation has a fire insurance policy on its warehouse with Cooperative Mutual Insurance Group. The policy has an 80 percent coinsurance clause. The warehouse had a fair market value of $100,000, meaning that PDQ was required to carry at least $80,000 of insurance on the building. PDQ, however, purchased a policy with a face amount of only $60,000. A fire partially destroyed the warehouse, causing $40,000 worth of damage to the structure. Because of the coinsurance clause, PDQ will recover only $30,000 from Cooperative. This figure was arrived at by taking the amount of insurance carried ($60,000) divided by the amount of insurance required ($80,000) times the loss ($40,000).

The coinsurance formula for recovery for partial losses is stated as follows:

$$\frac{\text{Amount of insurance carried}}{\text{Coinsurance percent} \times \text{Fair Market value}} \times \text{Loss} = \text{Recovery}$$

---

[7]Concerning certain designated items of personal property such as furs or jewelry, policies often set forth a maximum insurer payout (such as $1,000) that is less than the general policy limits applicable to personal property. Such a payout limitation would operate as a further restriction on the extent of the insurer's obligation.

[8]Recall, however, that if the insurer violates its payment obligation by wrongfully failing or refusing to pay what the policy contemplates, the insurer has committed a breach of contract. As noted in this chapter's earlier discussion of insurance policies as contracts, fundamental breach of contract principles dictate that the breaching insurer is potentially liable for consequential damages.

Remember that the coinsurance formula applies only to *partial* losses (i.e., damage to, but not complete destruction of, property). If PDQ's warehouse had been totally destroyed by the fire, the formula would not have been used. PDQ would have recovered $60,000—the face amount of the policy—for the total loss. If the formula had been used, it would have indicated that Cooperative owed PDQ $75,000—more than the face amount of the policy. This result would be neither logical nor in keeping with the parties' insurance contract. Whether the loss is total or partial, the insured is not entitled to recover more than the face amount of the policy.

Pro Rata Clause With the limited exception of the valued policy (discussed above), the insured cannot recover more than the amount of the actual loss. A rule allowing the insured to recover more than the actual loss could encourage unscrupulous persons to purchase policies from more than one insurer on the same property—thus substantially overinsuring it—and then intentionally to destroy the property in a way that appeared to be a covered peril (e.g., committing arson but making the fire look accidental). In order to make certain that the insured does not obtain a recovery that exceeds the actual loss, property insurance policies commonly contain a *pro rata clause,* which applies when the insured has purchased insurance policies from more than one insurer. The effect of the pro rata clause is to apportion the loss among the insurance companies. (Applicable state law sometimes contains a rule having this same effect.)

Under the pro rata clause, the amount any particular insurer must pay the insured depends on the percentage of total insurance coverage represented by that insurer's policy. For example, Mumford purchases two insurance policies to cover his home against fire and other risks. His policy from Security Mutual Insurance Corp. has a face amount of $50,000; his policy from Reliable Insurance Co. is for $100,000. Mumford's home is partially destroyed by an accidental fire, with a resulting loss of $30,000. Security Mutual must pay Mumford $10,000, with Reliable having to pay the remaining $20,000 of the loss.

The formula for determining each insurer's liability under a pro rata clause is stated as follows:

$$\frac{\text{Amount of insurer's policy}}{\text{Total coverage by all insurers}} \times \text{Loss} = \text{Liability of insurer}$$

Thus, Security Mutual's payment amount was calculated as follows:

$$\frac{\$50{,}000\ (\text{Security Mutal's policy})}{\$150{,}000\ (\text{Total of both policies})} \times \$30{,}000\ (\text{Loss}) = \$10{,}000$$

Reliable's payment amount could be similarly calculated by substituting $100,000 (Reliable's policy amount) for the $50,000 (Security Mutual's policy amount) in the numerator of the equation. This formula may be used for both partial and total losses. However, each company's payment obligation is limited by the face amount of its policy. Thus, Security Mutual could never be liable for more than $50,000. Similarly, Reliable's liability is limited to a maximum of $100,000.

Right of Subrogation

The insurer may be able in some instances to exercise a **right of subrogation** if it is required to pay for a loss under a property insurance contract. Under the right of subrogation, the insurer obtains all of the insured's rights to pursue legal remedies against anyone who negligently or intentionally caused the harm to the property. For example, Arnett purchased a property insurance policy on her home from Benevolent Insurance Company. Arnett's home was completely destroyed by a fire that spread to her property when her neighbor, Clifton, was burning leaves and negligently failed to control the fire. After Benevolent pays Arnett for her loss, Benevolent's right of subrogation entitles it to sue Clifton to recover the amount Benevolent paid Arnett. Arnett will be obligated to cooperate with Benevolent and furnish assistance to it in connection with the subrogation claim.

If the insured provides the liable third party a general release from liability, the insurer will be released from his payment obligation to the insured. Suppose that in the above scenario, Clifton persuaded Arnett to sign an agreement releasing him from liability for the fire. Because this action by Arnett would interfere with Benevolent's right of subrogation, Benevolent would not have to pay Arnett for the loss. A partial release of Clifton by Arnett would relieve Benevolent of responsibility to Arnett to the extent of her release.

Duration and Cancellation of Policy

Property insurance policies are usually effective for a designated period such as six months or a year. They are then extended for consecutive periods of like duration if the insured continues to pay the necessary premium and neither the insured nor the insurer elects to cancel the policy. The insured is normally entitled to cancel the policy at any time by providing the insurer written notice to that effect or by surrendering the policy to the insurer. Although property insurers usually have some right to cancel policies, terms of the policies themselves and/or governing law typically limit the grounds on which property insurers may do so. Permitted grounds for cancellation include the insured's nonpayment of the premium and, as a general rule, the insured's misrepresentation or fraud (see this chapter's discussion of contract law's applicability to insurance policies). Policy provisions and/or applicable law typically provide that if the property insurer intends to cancel the policy, the insured must be given meaningful advance written notice (often 30 days) of this intent before cancellation takes effect.

Another cancellation basis exists by virtue of the **increase of hazard** clauses that appear in many property insurance policies. An increase of hazard clause provides that the insurer's liability will be terminated if the insured takes any action materially increasing the insurer's risk. Some increase of hazard provisions also specify certain types of behavior that will cause termination. Common examples of such behavior include keeping highly explosive material on the property and allowing the premises to remain vacant for a lengthy period of time.

Liability Insurance

As its name suggests, liability insurance provides the insured the ability to transfer liability risks to the insurer. Under policies of liability insurance, the insurer agrees, among other things, to pay sums the insured becomes legally obligated to pay to another party. This enables the insured to minimize the troublesome or even devastating financial effects that he could experience in the event of his liability to someone else.

Types of Liability Insurance Policies

Liability insurance policies come in various types. These include, but are not limited to: **personal liability policies** designed to cover a range of liabilities an individual person could face; **business liability policies** (sometimes called *comprehensive general liability policies*) meant to apply to various liabilities that sole proprietors, partnerships, and corporations might encounter in their business operations; **professional liability policies** (sometimes called *malpractice insurance policies*) that cover physi-

cians, attorneys, accountants, and members of other professions against liabilities to clients and sometimes other persons; and **workers' compensation policies** under which insurers agree to cover employers' statutorily required obligation to pay benefits to injured workers.

Some policies combine property insurance features with liability insurance components. Automobile insurance policies, for instance, afford property insurance when they cover designated automobiles owned by the insured against perils such as vandalism, hail, and collisions with animals, telephone poles, and the like. Other sections of automobile insurance policies provide liability insurance to the insured (the policy owner), members of her household, and sometimes other authorized drivers when their use of a covered automobile leads to an accident in which they face liability to another party. Typical homeowners' policies also combine property and liability insurance features. Besides covering the insured's home and contents against perils of the types discussed earlier in this chapter, these policies normally provide the insured coverage for a range of liabilities he may face as an individual.

Liabilities Insured Against

Although the different types of liability insurance policies discussed above contain different terms setting forth the liabilities covered and not covered, liability policies commonly afford coverage against the insured's liability for negligence but not against the insured's liability stemming from deliberate wrongful acts (most intentional torts and most behavior constituting a crime). Liability policies tend to reach this common ground in the same sorts of ways property insurance policies define the scope of coverage—by listing particular liabilities that are covered and stating that an unlisted liability is not covered, by setting forth a seemingly broad statement of coverage and then specifying exclusions from coverage, or by employing a combination of the previous approaches (e.g., specifying certain covered liabilities and certain excluded liabilities).

Personal Liability and Homeowners' Policies
Personal liability policies and the liability sections of homeowners' policies often state that coverage is restricted to instances of "bodily injury" and "property damage" experienced by a third party as a result of an "occurrence" for which the insured faces liability. These sorts of policies normally define *occurrence* as an "accident" resulting in bodily injury or property damage. The provisions just noted lead to the conclusion

that intentional torts and most criminal behavior, if committed or engaged in by the insured, would fall outside the coverage of the policy at issue because they are not accidents (whereas instances of the insured's negligence would be). This conclusion is underscored by typical clauses purporting to exclude coverage for bodily injury or property damage the insured intended to cause. The occurrence, bodily injury, and property damage references in these policies also indicate that liabilities stemming from, for example, breach of contract would not be covered either (no accident, no bodily injury, no property damage). In addition, personal liability policies and liability sections of homeowners' policies also tend to specify that if bodily injury or property damage results from the insured's business or professional pursuits, it is not covered.

Business Liability Policies Business liability policies also feature coverage for bodily injury and property damage stemming from the insured's actions. The relevant range of actions, of course, is broadened to include the insured's business pursuits or "conduct of business." A major focus remains on unintentional wrongful conduct (usually negligence) of the insured, with the insured's deliberate wrongful acts normally being specifically excluded from coverage. Another typical exclusion is the pollution exclusion, which deprives the insured of coverage for actions that lead to pollution of other parties' property, unless the pollution occurs suddenly and accidentally.

Business liability policies also tend to provide the insured coverage in instances where the insured would be liable for certain torts of his employees (normally under the *respondeat superior* doctrine).[9] In addition, business liability policies sometimes afford coverage broader than instances of tortious conduct producing physical injury or property damage. Some policies, for instance, contain a clause that contemplates coverage for the insured's defamation of another person or invasion of that person's privacy (though other policies specifically exclude coverage for those same torts). Furthermore, the broad "conduct of business" language in certain poli-

cies, as well as specialized clauses (in some policies) referring to liability stemming from advertising or unfair competition, may contemplate coverage for the insured's legal wrongs that cause others to experience economic harm. In the end, the particular liabilities covered by a business liability policy cannot be determined without a close examination of the provisions in the policy at issue. It may become necessary for a court to interpret a policy provision whose meaning is unclear or scope is uncertain.

Other Liability Policies Professional liability policies also afford coverage for the insured's tortious conduct, this time in the practice of his or her profession. Negligent professional conduct producing harm to a third party (normally bodily injury in the medical malpractice setting but usually economic harm in the legal or other professional malpractice context) would be a covered liability. Wrongful professional conduct of an intentional nature typically would not be covered.

Automobile liability policies cover liability for physical injury and property damage stemming from the insured's (and certain other drivers') negligent driving. Once again, however, there is no coverage for liability arising from the insured's (or another driver's) deliberate vehicle operation acts of a wrongful nature.

Workers' compensation policies tend to approach coverage questions somewhat differently, primarily because injured employees need not prove negligence on the part of their employer in order to be entitled to benefits. Therefore, the insurer's obligation under a workers' compensation policy is phrased in terms of the liability the insured employer would face under state law.

Insurer's Obligations

Duty to Defend When another party makes a legal claim against the insured and the nature and allegations of the claim are such that the insurer would be obligated to cover the insured's liability if the claim were proven, the insurer has a **duty to defend** the insured. A commonsense precondition of this duty's being triggered is that the insured must notify the insurer that the claim has been made against her. The duty to defend means that the insurer must furnish, at its expense, an attorney to represent the insured in litigation resulting from the claim against her. If the insurer fails to perform its duty to defend in an instance where the duty arose, the insurer has breached the insurance contract. Depending on the facts, the breaching insurer would at least be liable for compensatory damages (as indicated in this chapter's

---

[9]The *respondeat superior* doctrine is discussed in Chapter 36. Although the insured's own intentional torts would not normally be covered, business liability policies sometimes provide that if the insured is liable on *respondeat superior* grounds for an employee's intentional tort such as battery, the insured will be covered unless the insured directed the employee to commit the intentional tort.

earlier discussion of insurance policies as contracts)[10] and potentially for punitive damages as well under the *bad faith* doctrine examined later in this chapter.

Sometimes it is quite clear that the insurer's duty to defend applies or does not apply, given the nature of the claim made against the insured. Other times, however, there may be uncertainty as to whether the claim alleged against the insured would fall within the scope of the liability insurance policy. Such uncertainty, of course, means that it is not clear whether the insurer has a duty to defend. Insurers tend to take one of two approaches in an effort to resolve this uncertainty. Under the first approach, the insurer files a declaratory judgment action against the insured. In this suit, the insurer asks the court to determine whether the insurer owes obligations to the insured under the policy in connection with the particular liability claim made against the insured by the injured third party. The other option insurers often pursue when it is unclear whether the liability policy applies is to retain an attorney to represent the insured in the litigation filed by the third party—thus fulfilling any duty to defend that may be owed—but to do so under a *reservation of rights* notice. By providing the reservation of rights notice to the insured, the insurer indicates that it reserves the right, upon acquisition of additional information, to conclude (or seek a later judicial determination) that it does not have the obligation to pay any damages that may be assessed against the insured as a result of the third party's claim. The insurer's reservation of rights also serves to eliminate an argument that by proceeding to defend the insured, the insurer waived the ability to argue that any actual liability would not be covered.

Duty to Pay Sums Owed by Insured If a third party's claim against the insured falls within the liabilities covered by the policy, the insurer is obligated to pay the compensatory damages held by a judge or jury to be due and owing from the insured to the third party. In addition, the insured's obligation to pay such expenses as court costs would also be covered. These payment obligations are subject, of course, to the policy limits of the insurance contract involved. For example, if the insured is held liable for compensatory damages and court costs totaling $150,000 but the policy limits of the relevant liability pol-

icy are $100,000, the insurer's contractual obligation to pay sums owed by the insured is restricted to $100,000.

Is the insurer also obligated to pay any *punitive damages* assessed against the insured as a result of a covered claim? As a general rule, the insurer will have no such obligation, either because of an insurance contract provision to that effect or because of judicial decisions holding that notions of public policy forbid arrangements by which one could transfer his punitive damages liability to an insurer. Not all courts facing this issue have so held, however, meaning that in occasional instances the insured's punitive damages liability may also be covered if the insurance policy's terms specifically contemplate such a result.

The liability insurer need not wait until litigation has been concluded to attempt to dispose of a liability claim made against the insured. Insurance policy provisions, consistent with our legal system's tendency to encourage voluntary settlements of claims, allow insurers to negotiate settlements with third parties who have made liability claims against the insured. These settlements involve payment of an agreed sum of money to the third party, in exchange for the third party's giving up her legal right to proceed with litigation against the insured. Settlements may occur regardless of whether litigation has been formally instituted by the third party or whether the claim against the insured consists of the third party's prelitigation demand for payment by the insured. If settlements are reached—and they are reached much more often than not—the substantial costs involved in taking a case all the way to trial may be avoided. The same is also true, from the insurer's perspective, of the damages that might have been assessed against the insured if the case had been tried. Note, however, that even if the defendant (the insured) wins a suit that does proceed to trial, the costs to the insurer are still substantial even though there is no award of damages to pay. Those costs include a considerable amount for attorney's fees for the insured (the insurer's obligation regardless of the outcome of the case) as well as other substantial expenses associated with protracted litigation. Accordingly, even when the insurer thinks that the insured probably would prevail if the case went to trial, the insurer may be interested in pursuing a settlement with the third party claimant if a reasonable amount—an amount less than what it would cost the insurer to defend the case—can be agreed upon.

Is There a Liability Insurance Crisis?

Since the mid-1980s, the necessary premiums for liability insurance policies of various types (particularly business and professional liability policies) have risen considerably. Sometimes, the premiums charged by liability

---

[10]The compensatory damages in such an instance would normally be the reasonable costs incurred by the insured in retaining an attorney and paying him to represent her. Of course, if the insured ended up being held liable in the third party's suit and the insurer wrongfully refused to pay the damages assessed against the insured in that case, the insured's compensatory damages claim against the breaching insurer would be increased substantially.

CYBERLAW IN ACTION

In numerous cases that were later consolidated, dissatisfied customers sued America Online Inc. Relying on a variety of legal theories, the plaintiffs contended that Version 5.0 of AOL's Internet access software ("AOL 5.0") was defective and that, as a result, they experienced harm to, and loss of use of, their computers, computer systems, and computer software and data.

AOL called upon its liability insurer, St. Paul Mercury Insurance Co., to defend it against the customers' claims. St. Paul refused, contending that the claims did not fall within the coverage obligations St. Paul had assumed. AOL retained legal counsel to defend it against the customers' claims and then sued St. Paul for an alleged breach of the contract of insurance. In *America Online, Inc. v. St. Paul Mercury Insurance Co.,* 207 F. Supp.2d 459 (E.D. Va. 2002), the court ruled on AOL's motion for summary judgment against St. Paul.

The court began its analysis by noting basic rules applicable to insurance policy interpretation and determinations of whether a liability insurer must defend its policyholder against third parties' claims: (1) that courts are "bound by the plain terms of the [insurance policy] and cannot rewrite the policy to bind the parties to obligations [to which] they did not consent;" (2) that "[i]f there is any ambiguity in the terms to be interpreted, . . . that ambiguity [is] to be construed against the insurer;" and (3) that "[an] insurer's duty to defend attaches whenever a complaint alleges claims that if proven would fall within the risk covered by the policy." Next, the court turned to the relevant provisions in the St. Paul policy, whose coverage provision stated that St. Paul would "pay amounts [AOL] is legally required to pay as damages for covered bodily injury, property damage, or premises damage that happens while this agreement is in effect and is caused by an event." The policy defined *property damage* as "physical damage to tangible property of others, including all resulting loss of use of that property; or loss of use of tangible property of others that isn't physically damaged." It defined *event* as "an accident, including continuous or repeated exposure to substantially the same generic harmful conditions.

In addition, the St. Paul policy excluded certain events or harms from coverage. Among these exclusions was a provision stating that St. Paul would not cover "property damage to impaired property, or to property which isn't physically damaged, that results from: [1] [AOL's] faulty or dangerous products or completed work; or [2] a delay or failure in fulfilling the terms of a contract or agreement." The policy defined *impaired property* as "tangible property, other than [AOL's] products or completed work, that can be restored to use by nothing more than: [1] an adjustment, repair, replacement, or removal of [AOL's] products or com-

pleted work which forms a part of it; or [2] [AOL's] fulfilling the terms of a contract or agreement."

Proceeding to interpret the St. Paul policy in light of the rules noted earlier, the court paid careful attention to the types of damages sought by the AOL customers. The court reasoned that claims seeking damages from AOL for harm to or loss of use of computer systems or computer software or data were not covered claims because systems, software, and data are not "property that can be touched" and thus "are not 'tangible' property in the common sense understanding of the word." The court also noted that computer systems, software, and data are customarily classified by courts as *intangible* property. In view of the St. Paul policy's *property damage* definition (quoted above) and its references to "tangible property," any harm to or loss of use of computer data, software, and systems would not be covered by the policy.

The claims brought against AOL, however, also alleged loss of use of the customers' computers. The court concluded that "the computer itself is tangible property because it is obviously a tactile, corporeal item" and that the claims alleging loss of use of computers therefore were "potentially covered" by the policy. The AOL customers did not allege that their computers were physically harmed. Instead, the court observed, the AOL customers really were contending that AOL 5.0 interfered with the proper operation of their computers and that loss of use of the computers resulted. The absence of a claim of physical damage to the computers meant that harm consisting of loss of use would not be covered by the portion of the *property damage* definition that referred to "physical damage to tangible property of others, including all resulting loss of use of that property."

Still potentially applicable at first glance, however, was the portion of the *property damage* definition that appeared to cover "loss of use of tangible property of others that isn't physically damaged." Yet that potential avenue to coverage was blocked, according to the court, by the St. Paul policy's "impaired property" exclusion. The plaintiffs, after all, premised their claim on the notion that AOL 5.0 was defective and that as a result, their computers were rendered inoperable. The court observed that "[t]hese claims are clearly barred by the impaired property exclusion, which states that harm to property that is not physically damaged is excluded from coverage when it is caused by a faulty or dangerous product."

Having concluded that none of the customers' claims against AOL came within the terms of the St. Paul policy, the court denied AOL's motion for summary judgment and held that St. Paul owed AOL no duty to defend it against those claims.

ETHICS IN ACTION

With the costs of medical treatment, hospitalization, and medications having increased dramatically in recent years, health insurance has become a critical means by which insured persons minimize the adverse financial consequences associated with illness and injury. The costs of serious illness or injury may be financially crippling unless insurance coverage exists. Often this coverage comes in the form of a group policy that is made available to employees of a certain company or to persons affiliated with a particular organization. Subject to certain exclusions and other contractual restrictions, group policies tend to cover a significant portion of the costs of obtaining health care services.

Although a very large percentage of the U.S. population has some form of health insurance, millions of U.S. residents do not. Public policy questions regarding health insurance availability and costs have been debated extensively in political arenas during the past decade, but sweeping legislative proposals to increase access to health coverage have not been enacted into law. Congress has opted for more limited measures, such as the Health Insurance Portability and Accountability Act of 1996, which allows most employees who had health insurance in connection with their employment to change jobs without fear of losing health coverage. This statute followed the lead of the earlier COBRA statute, under which persons who end an employment status that had entitled them to group policy coverage may continue that coverage for a limited time.

Much of the debate over whether health insurance "reform" is desirable tends to have an ethical flavor. For instance, consider the questions set forth below. In doing so, you may wish to employ the ethical theories discussed in Chapter 4.

- Is there a "right," in an ethical sense, to health insurance coverage? If so, why? If not, why not?
- Do employers have an ethical obligation to make group health insurance available to their employees? If so, why? If so, does this obligation always exist, or does it exist only under certain circumstances? If employers do not have such an obligation, why don't they?
- Would Congress be acting ethically if it enacted a law requiring the vast majority of employers in the United States to make health insurance available to their employees? Be prepared to justify your position.
- Does the U.S. government have an ethical duty to furnish health coverage to all U.S. residents? Be prepared to justify your position.

---

insurers have become so substantial that would-be insureds have concluded that they cannot afford liability insurance and therefore must go without it despite its importance. In addition, some insurers have ceased offering certain types of liability policies and/or have become much more restrictive in their decisions about which persons or firms to insure.

Insurance companies tend to blame the above state of affairs on what they see as a tort law regime under which plaintiffs win lawsuits too frequently and recover very large damage awards too often. As a result, insurers have been among the most outspoken parties calling for tort reform, a subject discussed in earlier chapters in this book. Plaintiffs' attorneys and critics of the insurance industry blame rising liability insurance premiums on, primarily, another alleged cause: questionable investment practices and other unsound business practices supposedly engaged in by insurance companies. The parties making these assertions thus oppose tort reform efforts as being unnecessary and unwise.

Liability insurance premiums in general may not be increasing as rapidly today as they once did, but they remain substantial in amount. So long as liability insurance remains unaffordable or otherwise difficult to obtain,

there is a "crisis," given the adverse financial consequences that could beset an uninsured person. This is so regardless of which of the competing explanations set forth above bears greater legitimacy.

Bad Faith Breach of Insurance Contract

Earlier in this chapter, we discussed the liability that an insurer will face if it breaches its policy obligations by means of a good faith but erroneous denial of coverage. That liability is for compensatory damages—damages designed to compensate the insured for the losses stemming from the insurer's breach—just as in breach of contract cases outside the insurance setting. Punitive damages are not available, however, when the insurer's wrongful failure or refusal to perform stemmed from a good faith (though erroneous) coverage denial. What if the insurer's failure or refusal to perform exhibited a lack of good faith? In this section, we examine the recent judicial tendency to go beyond the conventional remedy of compensatory damages and to assess punitive damages against the insurer when the insurer's refusal to perform its policy obligations amounted to the tort of **bad faith breach of contract.**

The special nature of the insurer–insured relationship tends to involve a "we'll take care of you" message that insurers communicate to insureds—at least at the outset of the relationship. Recognizing this, courts have displayed little tolerance in recent years for insurers' unjustifiable refusals to take care of insureds when taking care of them is clearly called for by the relevant policy's terms. When an insurer refuses to perform obvious policy obligations without a plausible, legitimate explanation for the refusal, the insurer risks more than being held liable for compensatory damages. If the facts and circumstances indicate that the insurer's refusal to perform stemmed not from a reasonable argument over coverage but from an intent to "stonewall," deny or unreasonably delay paying a meritorious claim, or otherwise create hardship for the insured, the insurer's breach may be of the bad faith variety. Because bad faith breach is considered an independent tort of a flagrantly wrongful nature, punitive damages—in addition to compensatory damages—have been held to be appropriate. The purposes of punitive damages in this context are the same as in other types of cases that call for punitive damages: to punish the flagrant wrongdoer and to deter the wrongdoer (as well as other potential wrongdoers) from repeating such an action.

The past two decades have witnessed bad faith cases in which many millions of dollars in punitive damages have been assessed against insurers. The types of situations in which bad faith liability has been found have included a liability insurer's unjustifiable refusal to defend its insured and/or pay damages awarded against the insured in litigation that clearly triggered the policy obligations. Various cases involving very large punitive damages assessments for bad faith liability have stemmed from property insurers' refusals to pay for the insured's destroyed property when the cause was clearly a covered peril and the insurer had no plausible rationale for denying coverage. Still other bad faith cases in which liability was held to exist have included malpractice or other liability insurers' refusals to settle certain meritorious claims against the insured within the policy limits. Bad faith liability in these cases tends to involve a situation in which the insured is held legally liable to a plaintiff for an amount well in excess of the dollar limits of the liability policy (meaning that the insured would be personally responsible for the amount of the judgment in excess of the policy limits), after the liability insurer, without reasonable justification, refused the plaintiff's offer to settle the case for an amount less than or equal to the policy limits. The *Vining* case, which follows, furnishes another example of behavior that triggers bad faith liability.

Whether bad faith liability exists in a given case depends, of course, on all of the relevant facts and circumstances. Although bad faith liability is not established in every case in which insureds allege it, cases raising a bad faith claim are of particular concern to insurers.

Vining v. Enterprise Financial Group, Inc.   *148 F.3d 1206 (10th Cir. 1998)*

Enterprise Financial Group, Inc., provided financing and credit life insurance to consumers who bought automobiles at Crown Auto World in Tulsa, Oklahoma. If purchased by a car buyer, the credit life insurance would pay off the customer's car loan in the event of his death. In March 1992, Milford Vining (Milford) purchased a jeep at Crown Auto World. Nancy Sidler, an Enterprise employee whose office was at the dealership, sold a credit life insurance policy to Milford when he purchased the jeep.

In late May 1993, Milford suffered a heart attack and died. His surviving spouse, Billie Vining (Vining), filed a claim with Enterprise for death benefits of approximately $10,000 under Milford's credit life policy. Enterprise refused to pay the claim and rescinded the policy on the supposed ground that Milford had misrepresented his health history in his application for the credit life policy. After unsuccessfully contesting the rescission, Vining sued Enterprise for breach of contract and for rescinding the policy in bad faith. In defense, Enterprise maintained that it had a legitimate basis for contesting the claim and that Milford had made material misrepresentations in his application for the credit life policy.

The evidence adduced at trial showed that in 1983, Milford suffered from coronary artery disease and underwent a triple bypass operation. After the surgery and followup tests, Milford began taking heart maintenance medication to prevent the occurrence of angina. From the time immediately following the 1983 surgery until the time of his death, Milford led an active life. He did not complain of chest pain or related symptoms.

In February 1992, Milford visited Dr. Michael Sullivan. This visit took place because Milford, who had recently moved, wanted to find a doctor closer to home. Milford's visit to Dr. Sullivan was not brought on by illness or physical symptoms. At

*the general time of this visit, Milford suffered from little, if any, angina. Dr. Sullivan continued Milford on his heart mainte-
nance medications as a preventive measure. When Milford applied for the credit life policy in March 1992, he signed an application that contained the following statement:*

> I HEREBY CERTIFY THAT I AM IN GOOD HEALTH AS OF THE EFFECTIVE DATE ABOVE. I FURTHER
> CERTIFY THAT I DO NOT PRESENTLY HAVE, NOR HAVE I EVER HAD, NOR HAVE I BEEN TOLD I HAVE,
> NOR HAVE I BEEN TREATED WITHIN THE PRECEDING 12 MONTHS FOR ANY OF THE FOLLOWING:
> ANY HEART DISEASE, OR OTHER CARDIOVASCULAR DISEASES.

*Vining presented evidence designed to show that Enterprise routinely rescinded credit life policies after insureds' deaths
and that the rescission of Milford's policy fit into this pattern. The jury returned a verdict in Vining's favor, awarding her
$400,000 in compensatory damages for financial losses, emotional distress, and related harms. In addition, the jury assessed
$400,000 in punitive damages against Enterprise, which appealed to the U.S. Court of Appeals for the Tenth Circuit.*

Ebel, Circuit Judge Both parties agree that Milford did
not intentionally attempt to mislead Enterprise [when he
signed the insurance application containing the statement
about his health], that Milford's appointment with Dr. Sullivan was his only medical visit in the 12 months preceding
the policy purchase date, and that under Oklahoma Insurance Regulations, an insurance company may consider only
the last 12 months of an applicant's medical history [when
evaluating] an insurance application.

After Milford's death, Enterprise sought all of Milford's
medical records, including Dr. Sullivan's notes. On the
same day it received Dr. Sullivan's notes, Enterprise rescinded the policy. Enterprise routinely contests all claims
on life insurance policies made within two years of a policy's effective date and investigates to find misrepresentations in the insurance application. [U]nder Oklahoma law, a
claim made more than two years after the effective date of a
life insurance policy is generally incontestable by the insurer. Debbie Cluck, Enterprise's claims examiner, denies
four out of every ten claims that she reviews. Enterprise
does not have a claims manual or any written guidelines
specifying when a claim is payable or not, and it never informed Cluck of any applicable Oklahoma law or regulation
pertaining to when a policy may be rescinded.

Cluck felt it appropriate to rescind a policy even if the
agent issued the policy with full knowledge of an applicant's medical history. Cluck's beliefs comport with Enterprise company philosophy. Cluck never paid a claim if she
had any reason to doubt whether a person's medical history
was inconsistent with the health [statement] included on the
insurance application. Cluck rescinded Milford's policy because she considered the office visit with Dr. Sullivan and
the continuation of his angina medication by Dr. Sullivan
[as] constitut[ing] treatment for triple bypass surgery. Cluck
did not investigate whether Sidler [the Enterprise employee
who dealt with Milford] was informed of Milford's medical
history, did not contact either Sidler or Vining, and did not

contact Dr. Sullivan to discuss his notes before rescinding
the policy.

Enterprise's training manual for its agents emphasizes
that applicants only need to be between the ages of 18 and
65 to purchase insurance. The manual does not discuss the
health [statement on the application] or in any way suggest
that the agent is supposed to ask the customer about his
health. [It does not suggest] that health is relevant [to a decision to issue] the policy. The manual also encourages
agents to maximize profit by overstating the actual monthly
premium that should be charged and by secretly increasing
the actual amount of monthly payments the customer agrees
to pay—for example, raising a payment from $78.22 to
$78.99 because customers look more closely at dollars than
cents. The manual informs agents that the life insurance
policies they sell are guaranteed issue policies, which means
that the coverage is in force immediately as compared to ordinary life insurance [policies, applicants for which] must
be approved by the insurer before coverage takes effect.

John Myerson was Enterprise's representative to agents
at automobile dealerships that sell Enterprise life insurance
policies. [These agents included Sidler.] Myerson testified
that he did not know what the terms used in the health [state-
ment on the application] meant and that he did not know
how Enterprise processed claims. Myerson also testified
that he does not train agents to ask about doctor visits or
medication. Sidler [was] never . . . trained . . . by Enterprise
. . . on what constituted "good health" [for purposes of the
application's health statement].

In response to numerous complaints against Enterprise
for improper rescission of life insurance policies, the Oklahoma Insurance Department conducted an investigation of
Enterprise's business practices. The Department [issued a
1992 report that] criticized Enterprise for requiring applicants to sign a disclaimer stating that they had never had any
health problems. The report sharply criticized Enterprises's
loss ratio, the ratio of benefits paid to premiums received, as

being unreasonably below accepted levels due to a large number of policy rescissions. Enterprise paid out in benefits only about 16 percent of premiums received. Oklahoma Insurance Department regulations require a 50 percent loss ratio for credit life insurance companies. Based on the report, the Oklahoma Insurance Commissioner issued an order levying a $15,000 fine against Enterprise for various violations and mandating that Enterprise lower its premiums to produce an acceptable loss ratio level. Enterprise made no changes in light of the report's criticism. In fact, loss ratios for the two years following the report continued to remain below 18 percent. Enterprise's rescission conduct and loss ratios bear some resemblance to those of the fictional insurance company portrayed in John Grisham's novel *The Rainmaker* and in the motion picture of the same name.

Numerous witnesses testified that their decedent spouses had bought life insurance from Enterprise in circumstances similar to [those of] the Vinings. Enterprise summarily rescinded those life insurance policies after the survivors made claims on the policies. In each case, Enterprise cited evidence of an insured's health problems that existed at the time the insured signed a health disclaimer statement in the insurance application as the grounds for rescission.

Finally, John Hammond testified as an expert on the handling and management of insurance claims. Hammond expressed his opinion that Enterprise's conduct was "completely inappropriate." He stated that Enterprise investigated Vining's claim by looking for a reason to rescind the policy. Hammond added that Enterprise erred by not contacting either Sidler, the agent who sold the policy, or Vining before rescinding the policy. Hammond also criticized Enterprise for not providing claims manuals detailing credit life insurance policy eligibility requirements to its claims examiners who were charged with investigating claims on those policies.

Under Oklahoma law, an insurer has a legal duty to "deal fairly and act in good faith with its insured." *Christian v. American Home Assurance Co.* (Okla. Sup. Ct. 1977). An insured may bring a cause of action in tort for bad faith if the insurer breaches this duty. The essence of a bad faith claim centers on the unreasonableness of the insurer's conduct. An insurer does not breach the duty of good faith to pay a claim "by litigating a dispute with its insured if there is a legitimate dispute as to coverage or amount of the claim, and the insurer's position is reasonable and legitimate." *Oulds v. Principal Mutual Life Insurance Co.* (10th Cir. 1993).

Enterprise argues on appeal that because it in fact had a legitimate reason for rescinding Milford's policy based on his medical history and heart condition, Enterprise is enti-

tled as a matter of law to a verdict in its favor on the claim of bad faith. An insurer does not act in bad faith if it had a "good faith belief, at the time its performance was requested, that it had justifiable reason for withholding payment under the policy." *Buzzard v. Farmers Insurance Co.* (Okla Sup. Ct. 1991). An insurer may legitimately and in good faith dispute a claim based on material misrepresentations in the insured's application for insurance.

Vining does not dispute that her husband had a heart condition and that the insurance application he signed included a disclaimer . . . certifying that he was in good health and had not been treated within the preceding 12 months for heart disease or any other cardiovascular disease. As a result, Enterprise could contest liability on the basis of a misrepresentation if it had a good faith belief that the misrepresentation was intentional. Here, Enterprise reasonably could have determined that by signing the disclaimer, Milford materially misrepresented the condition of his health. However, even a "legitimate dispute as to coverage will not act as an impenetrable shield against a valid claim of bad faith" where the insured presents "sufficient evidence reasonably tending to show bad faith" or unreasonable conduct. *Timberlake Construction Co. v. U.S. Fidelity & Guaranty Co.* (10th Cir. 1995). That is, a plaintiff may bring a bad faith cause of action even though a legitimate defense to a breach of contract claim exists if the defendant did not actually rely on that defense to deny payment under the policy.

Vining demonstrated at trial a deliberate, willful pattern of abusive conduct by Enterprise in handling claims under its life insurance policies. Vining offered evidence that as a matter of course Enterprise would rescind life insurance policies issued on a guaranteed basis as soon as claims were made. Enterprise based these rescissions on the grounds that the insured had made material misrepresentations on the insurance application regardless of whether Enterprise in fact would have declined to write the policy had it known of that information at the time the policy was written. Vining presented evidence that Enterprise engaged in a systematic, bad faith scheme of canceling policies without determining whether it had good cause to do so. Such conduct constitutes bad faith regardless of whether Enterprise legitimately might have been able to contest Vining's claim based on Milford's heart condition, because the evidence showed that Enterprise, in fact, did not dispute coverage in good faith based on Milford's heart condition.

Enterprise also raises the affirmative defense of rescission. Under [an Oklahoma statute], an insurer properly may rescind an insurance policy when the application contains a misrepresentation that (1) is fraudulent; (2) is material to the insurance company's acceptance of the risk; or (3) induced the insurer to issue the policy where it would not have done so had it known the true facts. However, Enterprise concedes that [the statute does not allow an insurer to rescind unless the insured had an intent to deceive]. Because Enterprise . . . admits that Milford did not willfully or intentionally misrepresent his health history on the application, Enterprise cannot rely on the affirmative defense of rescission.

Enterprise complains that [the district court erred in] the jury instruction [concerning what Vining needed to prove in order to establish bad faith]. Bad faith may be established by showing an unreasonable refusal to pay a claim, and the instruction set forth three alternative scenarios which are deemed to be unreasonable: (1) the insurance company "had no basis for the refusal," (2) the insurance company did not perform a proper investigation, or (3) the insurance company did not evaluate the results of the investigation properly. As we pointed out earlier, merely because there is a reasonable basis that an insurance company could invoke to deny a claim does not necessarily immunize the insurer from a bad faith claim if, in fact, it did not actually rely on that supposed reasonable basis and instead took action in bad faith. [T]he jury instruction correctly stated the applicable law.

Enterprise challenges the damages awarded to Vining as excessive and as lacking sufficient evidentiary support. Vining testified at trial regarding the distress she experienced as a result of Enterprise's conduct toward her during the three years she spent fighting the insurance company over the claim. Such evidence is sufficient in a bad faith claim to support an award for emotional distress. In addition, $400,000 for mental pain and suffering, financial losses, embarrassment, and loss of reputation in the context of bad faith insurance claims is not excessive on this record. [The award of] $400,000 in punitive damages [was also appropriate] and need not be adjusted.

Judgment in favor of Vining affirmed.

Problems and Problem Cases

1. Eighteen-year-old Arthur Smith became intoxicated at a New Year's Eve party. At 11:00 P.M., Smith left the party and began walking home. Police officer Don Czopek saw Smith walking down the center of a road and weaving from side to side. Because Smith was interfering with traffic and placing himself at risk of physical harm, Czopek pulled his patrol car alongside Smith and attempted to talk him into getting off the road. Smith refused, became argumentative, and started shouting. Czopek parked his patrol car, got out, and approached Smith in an effort to calm him down. Smith became increasingly hostile and grabbed Czopek by the lapels of his coat. Officer Herdis Petty then arrived on the scene to assist Czopek. A struggle occurred as the two officers attempted to handcuff Smith and put him into a patrol car. Smith kicked, hit, and bit the officers during this struggle, which continued for a substantial length of time. Czopek suffered frostbite on one of his hands. Petty sustained broken ribs as a result of being kicked by Smith (plus other less serious injuries). Smith was later convicted of assault and battery. He admitted that he intentionally resisted arrest but said that he did not recall hitting or kicking anyone. Officers Czopek and Petty filed a civil suit against Smith's parents, whose homeowners' policy with Group Insurance Company of Michigan (GICOM) provided liability coverage to the insureds—a status that, under the policy's terms, included Arthur Smith—for third parties' personal injury claims resulting from an "occurrence." The policy defined "occurrence" as "an accident, including injurious exposure to conditions, which results . . . in bodily injury or property damage." The policy contained an exclusion from coverage for "bodily injury or property damage which is either expected or intended from the standpoint of the insured." GICOM filed a declaratory judgment suit in which it asked the court to declare that it had no duty to defend or indemnify Arthur Smith and his parents in connection with the litigation brought by Czopek and Petty. Was GICOM entitled to such a ruling by the court?

2. Don Davis owned a lumber mill that was subject to a $248,000 mortgage held by Diversified Financial Systems, Inc. Early in 1995, Aaron Harber became interested in forming a partnership with Davis for ownership and operation of the mill. Harber and Davis orally agreed upon the terms of a partnership. Harber contended that these terms included a purchase by Harber of Diversified's interest in the mortgage on the mill. Davis later informed Harber that he (Davis) would not proceed with the partnership. Nevertheless, Harber purchased Diversified's mortgage interest in April 1995. Harber did this in reliance on the oral partnership agreement with Davis—an agreement Harber intended to enforce despite Davis's refusal to proceed.

During Harber's negotiations with Davis concerning their supposed partnership and with Diversified for purchase of its mortgage interest, Harber discovered that the mill was not covered by property insurance. Harber therefore purchased a policy from Underwriters at Lloyd's of London (Lloyd's). The policy, whose one-year term began in late May 1995, named Harber and U.S.A. Properties, Inc., a corporation set up and wholly owned by Harber, as insureds.

In mid-June 1995, one of the buildings at the mill was destroyed by fire. Approximately two weeks later, in an effort to prompt negotiations in the dispute with Davis over whether a partnership existed or would be pursued, Harber filed suit to foreclose the Diversified mortgage. The mortgage was in default at that time. Harber and Davis soon entered into a settlement agreement that provided in part for the transfer of the mill property to Harber, in exchange for Harber's giving up all of his claims against Davis. The agreement also conveyed, to Harber, whatever interest Davis had in insurance proceeds related to the building that had been destroyed by fire.

Harber and U.S.A. Properties submitted a claim to Lloyd's concerning the destroyed building. After Lloyd's denied the claim, Harber and U.S.A. Properties sued Lloyd's for payment according to the terms of the policy. A federal district court held that the plaintiffs lacked an insurable interest and that Lloyd's was therefore entitled to summary judgment. Harber and U.S.A. Properties appealed. Was the district court's holding correct?

3. In a class action suit, the plaintiffs alleged that an automobile loan program instituted by Bank of the West (BOW) violated California's Unfair Business Practices Act. No common law unfair competition claim was made in the suit. The Unfair Business Practices Act did not allow courts to award compensatory or punitive damages, but did authorize courts to order "the disgorgement of money" wrongfully obtained. BOW settled the class action suit by paying $500,000 and agreeing to make changes in the operation of the loan program. BOW contended that the $500,000 payment was covered by the terms of a liability policy issued to BOW by Industrial Indemnity Co. The policy provided coverage for "all sums which the insured shall become legally obligated to pay as damages because of advertising injury to which this insurance applies." The policy went on to define "advertising injury" as "injury arising out of . . . libel, slander, defamation, violation of right of privacy, unfair competition, or infringement of copyright, title or slogan." Industrial filed a declaratory judgment action in which it asked the court to determine that the policy did not cover the $500,000 payment made by BOW to settle the class

action suit. The trial court ruled in Industrial's favor, but the intermediate appellate court reversed. It concluded that the policy afforded coverage because the term "unfair competition" was ambiguous and thus could refer to either the common law of unfair competition or statutory claims such as those under the Unfair Business Practices Act. Was the intermediate appellate court correct?

4. In a class-action suit against Aamco Transmissions, Inc., consumers Joseph R. Tracy and Joseph P. Tracy claimed that Aamco and its network of franchisees used deceptive advertising that inaccurately described Aamco's services and lured many consumer purchasers of transmission services into paying excessively and for unnecessary repairs. The Tracys asserted that Aamco was liable under the Pennsylvania Unfair Trade Practices and Consumer Protection Law. Aamco was the insured under a comprehensive general liability insurance policy issued by Granite State Insurance Co. This policy provided liability coverage to Aamco "for personal injury or advertising injury . . . arising out of the conduct of" Aamco's business. The policy defined *advertising injury* as "injury arising . . . in the course of [Aamco's] advertising activities, if such injury arises out of libel, slander, defamation, violation of right of privacy, piracy, unfair competition, or infringement of copyright, title or slogan."

Contending that it had coverage under the "unfair competition" category of the advertising injury coverage, Aamco demanded that Granite defend and indemnify it in connection with the consumer class action case described above. When Granite declined to do so, Aamco settled the case on its own. Granite then brought a declaratory judgment action against Aamco in federal district court. Granite sought a ruling that it was not obligated to provide coverage for Aamco in the class action case brought by the Tracys. A federal district court concluded that the *unfair* competition term in the policy contemplated coverage only for common law–based claims against Aamco, not for any claims based on a state or federal statute. Because the Tracys' class action case was based on a supposed violation of a Pennsylvania statute, the district court held that Granite's policy did not furnish coverage to Aamco. In addition, the court held that the term *unfair competition* was not ambiguous and that Aamco could not have had a reasonable expectation that consumers' claims against it would be covered. Aamco appealed. Did Aamco win its appeal?

5. Sims and Dorothy Good purchased a property insurance policy on their home from Continental Insurance Co. Fire was among the covered perils. The policy contained an "increase of hazard" clause stating that Conti-

nental would not be obligated under the policy if the risk of fire was increased "by any means within the control or knowledge of the insured." After the policy took effect, a fire destroyed much of the Goods' home. While putting out the fire, firefighters discovered an illegal liquor still concealed in a false closet under the eaves of the roof. The still, encased by bricks and mortar, consisted of a 90-gallon copper vat over a butane gas burner. Firefighters also discovered 22 half-gallons of "moonshine" and many 55-gallon drums full or partially full of mash. A police detective who dismantled and examined the still's burner after the fire concluded that the still was in operation when the fire occurred. The Goods denied this, though Sims Good admitted having installed the still two years earlier, after the Continental insurance policy became effective. Continental refused to pay the Goods' claim, so the Goods sued Continental to recover proceeds under the policy. After the trial court awarded damages to the Goods, Continental appealed. Were the Goods entitled to recover damages from Continental?

6. The Plummers owned a commercial building in which they operated two businesses. The building and its contents were insured by Indiana Insurance Company (IIC). After an explosion and fire destroyed the building, the Plummers filed a claim and proof of loss with IIC. After an investigation, IIC denied the claim due to its conclusion that the Plummers had intentionally set the fire. IIC then filed a declaratory judgment action in which it asked for a determination that it had no obligation to cover losses stemming from the fire. The Plummers counterclaimed, seeking damages for breach of contract as well as punitive damages. The jury returned a verdict in favor of the Plummers on all issues. The jury awarded the Plummers approximately $700,000 in compensatory damages (an amount that exceeded the policy limits set forth in the insurance policy at issue), plus $3.5 million in punitive damages. The $700,000 compensatory damages award included not only the value of the destroyed building and its contents (what would have been due under the policy) but also $200,000 in consequential damages allegedly incurred by the Plummers as a result of IIC's lengthy investigation of the fire and ultimate denial of the Plummers' claim. For the most part, the consequential damages represented interest costs and similar expenses incurred by the Plummers—costs and expenses they would not have incurred if IIC had paid their claim. Although the evidence IIC adduced at trial included experts' testimony that the fire had been intentionally set, the jury rejected that testimony and accepted the Plummers' contrary evidence. IIC appealed, arguing that its denial of the Plummers' claim was in good faith, that it

therefore should have no liability for consequential damages and punitive damages, and that the damages awarded for breach of an insurance contract cannot exceed the policy limits set forth in the contract. Was IIC correct in these arguments?

7. In 1972, Betty DeWitt and her husband, Joseph, purchased a house. Title was taken in Betty's name. Seven years later, the DeWitts were divorced. Under the 1979 divorce decree, Joseph was given possession of the house and Betty was ordered to sign the deed over to him. Joseph died in January 1980. Soon thereafter, Betty moved into the house and purchased a fire insurance policy from American Family Mutual Insurance Company. The policy had a face value of $38,500. In August 1980, the house was completely destroyed by fire. At that time, American Family learned of her divorce and the decree ordering her to convey title to Joseph. American Family refused to pay on the policy, arguing that Betty did not have an insurable interest. Was American Family correct?

8. Robert Baer and Dareen Dahlstrom had been close friends for more than 20 years. Dahlstrom, who was in the process of separating from her husband, went to visit Baer in July 1988. On various occasions, Baer had used a recreational drug known as Ecstacy. For several years after its discovery, Ecstasy was not an illegal drug. It was, however, designated by federal law as a prohibited controlled substance beginning in March 1988. Baer believed that the use of Ecstasy had certain psychological and emotional benefits, and that using it might help Dahlstrom cope with the personal problems she was experiencing at the time of her July 1988 visit. After she and Baer discussed his beliefs regarding Ecstasy, Dahlstrom told him that she wanted to use the drug. Baer and Dahlstrom went through various rituals in preparation for use of the drug and recited a prayer that "this [may] bring harm to no one and blessing to all." Baer then removed some Ecstasy from his personal supply, which he had purchased prior to March 1988. Baer dissolved approximately one-half of his usual dose in a glass of water and gave it to Dahlstrom. She drank the mixture. Within approximately 30 minutes, she was dead. Dahlstrom's survivors filed a wrongful death suit against Baer, who asserted that the claim fell within the liability coverage provided to him by State Farm Insurance Company as part of his homeowner's policy. The policy afforded coverage for third parties' claims for physical injury resulting from an "occurrence," which was defined in terms of an "accident" that caused injury. The policy also contained an exclusion from coverage for injury that was either intended or expected by the insured. State Farm filed a declaratory judgment action in which it asked for a judicial determination that in light of the above provisions in the parties' insurance contract as well as public policy considerations, it owed Baer no coverage duties regarding the suit that stemmed from Dahlstrom's death. Was State Farm entitled to the relief it sought?

9. Jeffrey Lane was employed by Memtek, Inc., at its Arby's Restaurant. He was being trained as a cook. After 11:00 one evening, Lane finished work and clocked out. He remained in the restaurant's lobby, however, because he was waiting for the manager to complete her duties. As Lane waited, friends of other restaurant employees came to a door of the restaurant. Lane and the other employees became involved in a conversation with these persons, who included John Taylor. Lane told Taylor that he could not enter the restaurant because it was closed. Taylor did not attempt to force his way into the restaurant. Instead, he "dared" Lane to come outside. Lane left the restaurant "of [his] own will" (according to Lane's deposition) for what he assumed would be a fight with Taylor. In the fight that transpired, Lane broke Taylor's nose and knocked out three of his teeth. Lane later pleaded guilty to a criminal battery charge. Taylor filed a civil suit against Lane and Memtek in an effort to collect damages stemming from the altercation with Lane. American Family Mutual Insurance Company provided liability insurance for Memtek in connection with its restaurant. The policy stated that for purposes of American Family's duties to defend and indemnify, "the insured" included not only Memtek but also Memtek's "employees, . . . but only for acts within the scope of their employment." American Family filed a declaratory judgment action in which it asked the court to determine that it owed Lane neither a duty to defend nor a duty to indemnify in connection with the incident giving rise to Taylor's lawsuit. American Family's theory was that for purposes of that incident, Lane was not an insured within the above-quoted policy provision. Was American Family correct?

10. Earl and Vonette Crowell owned a farm in Minnesota. In 1980, they mortgaged the farm to Farm Credit Services and purchased a property insurance policy on the farm (including the farmhouse) from Delafield Farmers Mutual Insurance Co. Fire was among the perils covered by this policy, which ran from October 1985 to October 1988. When the Crowells fell behind on their mortgage payments, Farm Credit began foreclosure proceedings. Upon foreclosure, mortgagors such as the Crowells have a right of redemption for a specified time. The right of redemption allows the defaulting mortgagors to buy back their property after it has been sold to someone else in the foreclosure proceedings. In November 1987, the Crowells' right of redemption expired. Minnesota law provides, however, that farmers who lose their farms to corporate lenders are given an additional opportunity to repurchase their farms under a "right of first refusal." This right meant that Farm Credit was forbidden to sell the farm to anyone else before offering it to the Crowells at a price no higher than the highest price offered by a third party. Farm Credit allowed the Crowells to remain on the farm while they attempted to secure financing to buy the property under their right of first refusal. In November 1987, a fire substantially damaged the farmhouse. The Crowells filed a claim for the loss with Delafield. Although Delafield paid the claim concerning the Crowells' personal effects that were located inside the farmhouse and were destroyed in the fire, it denied the claim on the farmhouse itself. Delafield took the position that because the time period for the Crowells' right of redemption had expired, they no longer had an insurable interest in the farmhouse. The Crowells therefore sued Delafield. Concluding that the Crowells had an insurable interest in the farmhouse, the trial court granted summary judgment in their favor. Was the trial court correct?

Online Research: State Regulation of Insurance

Most regulation of insurance regulation is done by the individual states. Typically, a state agency named the "Department of Insurance" (or something similar) will have significant supervisory and regulatory powers with regard to insurance companies, their business practices, and the policies they issue.

Locate the website of the insurance department of a state of your choice. After reviewing information and material available on that website, prepare a brief report summarizing the insurance department's role in addressing complaints from consumers regarding insurance company practices.

CREDIT

28

INTRODUCTION TO CREDIT
AND SECURED TRANSACTIONS

Eric Richards decided to go into the commercial laundry and dry-cleaning business. He began by agreeing to buy the land, building, and equipment of a small dry cleaner. Richards agreed to pay the owner $200,000 in cash and "to assume" a $50,000 existing mortgage on the property. He next entered into a contract with a local contractor to build, within five months, a large addition to the building for $150,000 with $40,000 payable with the signing of the contract and the balance to be paid in periodic installments as the construction progressed. Because Richards had heard some horror stories from friends in the local Chamber of Commerce about contractors who walked away from jobs without completing them, he asked the contractor to post a security bond or provide a surety to assure the contract would be completed in a timely manner. Richards also had some of the existing dry-cleaning equipment picked up for repair and refurbishment. When the work was completed, the repairmen refused to redeliver it until Richards paid in full for the work, claiming he had a lien on the equipment until he was paid.

Among the questions that will be addressed in this chapter are:

- What legal rights and obligations accompany the "assumption" of a mortgage?
- Would Richards risk losing any of his rights to recover against the surety if he granted the contractor additional time to complete the construction?
- If the contractor does not pay subcontractors or companies who provide construction material for the job, would they be able to assert a lien against the property until they are paid?
- Would the person who repaired and refurbished the dry-cleaning equipment still be able to asset a lien until Richards paid for it? Would it make a difference if the repair work had been done on-site?

IN THE UNITED STATES, a substantial portion of business transactions involves the extension of credit. The term *credit* has many meanings. In this chapter, it will be used to mean transactions in which goods are sold, services are rendered, or money is loaned in exchange for a promise to repay the debt at some future date.

In some of these transactions, a creditor is willing to rely on the debtor's promise to pay at a later time; in others, the creditor wants some further assurance or security that the debtor will make good on his promise to pay. This chapter will discuss the differences between secured and unsecured credit and will detail various mechanisms that are available

to the creditor who wants to obtain security. These mechanisms include obtaining liens or security interests in personal or real property, sureties, and guarantors. Security interests in real property, sureties and guarantors, and common law liens on personal property will be covered in this chapter, and the Uniform Commercial Code (UCC or Code) rules concerning security interests in personal property will be covered in Chapter 29, Security Interests in Personal Property. The last chapter in Part 6 deals with bankruptcy law, which may come into play when a debtor is unable to fulfill his obligation to pay his debts when they are due.

Credit

Unsecured Credit

Many common transactions are based on unsecured credit. For example, a person may have a charge account at a department store or a MasterCard account. If the person buys a sweater and charges it to his charge account or MasterCard account, unsecured credit has been extended to him. He has received goods in return for his promise to pay for them later. Similarly, if a person goes to a dentist to have a tooth filled and the dentist sends her a bill payable by the end of the month, services have been rendered on the basis of unsecured credit. Consumers are not the only people who use unsecured credit. Many transactions between businesspeople utilize it. For example, a retailer buys merchandise or a manufacturer buys raw materials, promising to pay for the merchandise or materials within 30 days after receipt.

The unsecured credit transaction involves a maximum of risk to the creditor—the person who extends the credit. When goods are delivered, services are rendered, or money is loaned on unsecured credit, the creditor gives up all rights in the goods, services, or money. In return, the creditor gets a promise by the debtor to pay or to perform the promised act. If the debtor does not pay or keep the promise, the creditor's options are more limited than if he had obtained security to ensure the debtor's performance. One course of action is to bring a lawsuit against the debtor and obtain a judgment. The creditor might then have the sheriff execute the judgment on any property owned by the debtor that is subject to execution. The creditor might also try to **garnish** the wages or other moneys to which the debtor is entitled. However, the debtor might be **judgment-proof;** that is, the debtor may not have any property subject to execution or may not have a steady job. Under these circumstances, execution or garnishment would be of little aid to the creditor in collecting the judgment.

A businessperson may obtain credit insurance to stabilize the credit risk of doing business on an unsecured credit basis. However, he passes the costs of the insurance to the business, or of the unsecured credit losses that the business sustains, on to the consumer. The consumer pays a higher price for goods or services purchased, or a higher interest rate on any money borrowed, from a business that has high credit losses.

Secured Credit

To minimize his credit risk, a creditor may contract for security. The creditor may require the debtor to convey to the creditor a security interest or lien on the debtor's property. Suppose a person borrows $3,000 from a credit union. The credit union might require her to put up her car as security for the loan or might ask that some other person agree to be liable if she defaults. For example, if a student who does not have a regular job goes to a bank to borrow money, the bank might ask that the student's father or mother cosign the note for the loan.

When the creditor has security for the credit he extends and the debtor defaults, the creditor can go against the security to collect the obligation. Assume that a person borrows $18,000 from a bank to buy a new car and that the bank takes a security interest (lien) on the car. If the person fails to make his monthly payments, the bank has the right to repossess the car and have it sold so that it can recover its money. Similarly, if the borrower's father cosigned for the car loan and the borrower defaults, the bank can sue the father to collect the balance due on the loan.

Development of Security

Various types of security devices have been developed as social and economic need for them has arisen. The rights and liabilities of the parties to a secured transaction depend on the nature of the security—that is, on whether (1) the security pledged is the promise of another person to pay if the debtor does not, or (2) a security interest in goods, intangibles, or real estate is conveyed as security for the payment of a debt or obligation.

If personal credit is pledged, the other person may guarantee the payment of the debt—that is, become a guarantor—or the other person may join the debtor in the debtor's promise to pay, in which case the other person would become surety for the debt.

The oldest and simplest security device was the pledge. To have a pledge valid against third persons with an interest in the goods, such as subsequent purchasers or creditors, it was necessary that the property used as security be delivered to the pledgee or a pledge holder. Upon default by the pledger, the pledgee had the right to sell the property and apply the proceeds to the payment of the debt.

Situations arose in which it was desirable to leave the property used as security in the possession of the debtor. To accomplish this objective, the debtor would give the creditor a bill of sale to the property, thus passing title to the creditor. The bill of sale would provide that if the debtor performed his promise, the bill of sale would become null and void, thus revesting title to the property in the debtor. A secret lien on the goods was created by this device, and the early courts held that such a transaction was a fraud on third-party claimants and void as to them. An undisclosed or secret lien is unfair to creditors who might extend credit to the debtor on the strength of property that they see in the debtor's possession but that in fact is subject to the prior claim of another creditor. Statutes were enacted providing for the recording or filing of the bill of sale, which was later designated as a chattel mortgage. These statutes were not uniform in their provisions. Most of them set up formal requirements for the execution of the chattel mortgage and also stated the effect of recording or filing on the rights of third-party claimants.

To avoid the requirements for the execution and filing of the chattel mortgage, sellers of goods would sell the goods on a "conditional sales contract" under which the seller retained title to the goods until their purchase price had been paid in full. Upon default by the buyer, the seller could (a) repossess the goods or (b) pass title and recover a judgment for the unpaid balance of the purchase price. Abuses of this security device gave rise to some regulatory statutes. About one-half of the states enacted statutes providing that the conditional sales contract was void as to third parties unless it was filed or recorded.

No satisfactory device was developed whereby inventory could be used as security. The inherent difficulty is that inventory is intended to be sold and turned into cash and the creditor is interested in protecting his interest in the cash rather than in maintaining a lien on the sold goods. Field warehousing was used under the pledge, and an after-acquired property clause in a chattel mortgage on a stock of goods held for resale partially fulfilled this need. One of the devices used was the trust receipt. This short-term marketing security arrangement had its origin in the export–import trade. It was later used extensively as a means of financing retailers of consumer goods having a high unit value.

Security Interests in Personal Property

Chapter 29, Security Interests in Personal Property, will discuss how a creditor can obtain a security interest in the personal property or fixtures of a debtor. It will also explain the rights to the debtor's property of the creditor, the debtor, and other creditors of the debtor. These security interests are covered by Article 9 of the Uniform Com-

mercial Code, which sets out a comprehensive scheme for regulating security interests in personal property and fixtures. The Code abolishes the old formal distinctions between different types of security devices used to create security interests in personal property.

Security Interests in Real Property

Three types of contractual security devices have been developed by which real estate may be used as security: (1) the real estate mortgage, (2) the trust deed, and (3) the land contract. In addition to these contract security devices, all of the states have enacted statutes granting the right to mechanic's liens on real estate. Security interests in real property are covered later in this chapter.

Suretyship and Guaranty

Sureties and Guarantors

As a condition of making a loan, granting credit, or employing someone (particularly as a fiduciary), a creditor may demand that the debtor, contractor, or employee provide as security for his performance the liability of a third person as surety or guarantor. The purpose of the contract of suretyship or guaranty is to provide the creditor with additional protection against loss in the event of default by the debtor, contractor, or employee.

A **surety** is a person who is *liable for the payment of another person's debt or for the performance of another person's duty.* The surety joins with the person primarily liable in promising to make the payment or to perform the duty. For example, Kathleen Kelly, who is 17 years old, buys a used car on credit from Harry's Used Cars. She signs a promissory note, agreeing to pay $200 a month on the note until the note is paid in full. Harry's has Kathleen's father cosign the note; thus, her father is a surety. Similarly, the city of Chicago hires the B&B Construction Company to build a new sewage treatment plant. The city will probably require B&B to have a surety agree to be liable for B&B's performance of its contract. There are insurance companies that, for a fee, will agree to be a surety on the contract of a company such as B&B.

If the person who is primarily liable (the principal) defaults, the surety is liable to pay or perform. Upon default, the creditor may ask the surety to pay even if he has not asked the principal debtor to pay. If the surety makes good on his contract of suretyship, he is entitled to be reimbursed by the principal. While a contract of surety does not have to be in writing to be enforceable, it normally is.

A guaranty contract is similar to a suretyship contract in that the promisor agrees to answer for the obligation of another. However, a guarantor does not join the principal in making a promise; rather, a guarantor makes a separate promise and agrees to be liable upon the happening of a certain event. For example, a father tells a merchant, "I will guarantee payment of my daughter Rachel's debt to you if she does not pay it," or "If Rachel becomes bankrupt, I will guarantee payment of her debt to you." While a surety is *primarily liable,* a guarantor is *secondarily liable* and can be held to his guarantee only after the principal defaults and cannot be held to his promise or payment. Generally, a guarantor's promise must be made in writing to be enforceable under the statute of frauds.

The rights and liabilities of the surety and the guarantor are substantially the same. No distinction will be made between them in this chapter except where the distinction is of basic importance. Moreover, most commercial contracts and promissory notes today that are to be signed by multiple parties provide for the parties to be "jointly and severally" liable, thus making the surety relationship the predominate one.

Creation of Principal and Surety Relation

The relationship of principal and surety, or that of principal and guarantor, is created by contract. The basic rules of contract law apply in determining the existence and nature of the relationship as well as the rights and duties of the parties.

Defenses of a Surety

Suppose Jeffrey's mother agrees to be a surety for Jeffrey on his purchase of a motorcycle. If the motorcycle was defectively made and Jeffrey refuses to make further payments on it, the dealer might try to collect the balance due from Jeffrey's mother. As a surety, Jeffrey's mother can use any defenses against the dealer that Jeffrey has if they go to the merits of the primary contract. Thus, if Jeffrey has a valid defense of breach of warranty against the dealer, his mother can use it as a basis for not paying the dealer.

Other defenses that go to the merits include (1) lack or failure of consideration, (2) inducement of the contract by fraud or duress, and (3) breach of contract by the other party. Certain defenses of the principal cannot be used by the surety. These defenses include lack of capacity, such as minority or insanity, and bankruptcy. Thus, if Jeffrey is only 17 years old, the fact that he is a minor cannot be used by Jeffrey's mother to defend against the dealer.

This defense of Jeffrey's lack of capacity to contract does not go to the merits of the contract between Jeffrey and the dealer and cannot be used by Jeffrey's mother.

A surety contracts to be responsible for the performance of the principal's obligation. If the principal and the creditor change that obligation by agreement, the surety is relieved of responsibility unless the surety agrees to the change. This is because the surety's obligation cannot be changed without his consent.

For example, Fredericks cosigns a note for his friend Kato, which she has given to Credit Union to secure a loan. Suppose the note was originally for $2,500 and payable in 12 months with interest at 11 percent a year. Credit Union and Kato later agree that Kato will have 24 months to repay the note but that the interest will be 13 percent per year. Unless Fredericks consents to this change, he is discharged from his responsibility as surety. The obligation he agreed to assume was altered by the changes in the repayment period and the interest rate.

The most common kind of change affecting a surety is an extension of time to perform the contract. If the creditor merely allows the principal more time without the surety's consent, this does not relieve the surety of responsibility. The surety's consent is required only where there is an actual binding agreement between the creditor and the principal as to the extension of time.

In addition, the courts usually make a distinction between **accommodation sureties** and **compensated sureties.** An accommodation surety is a person who acts as a surety without compensation, such as a friend who cosigns a note as a favor. A compensated surety is a person, usually a professional such as a bonding company, who is paid for serving as a surety.

The courts are more protective of accommodation sureties than of compensated sureties. Accommodation sureties are relieved of liability unless they consent to an extension of time. Compensated sureties, on the other hand, must show that they will be harmed by an extension of time before they are relieved of responsibility because of a binding extension without their consent. A compensated surety must show that a change in the contract was both material and prejudicial to him if he is to be relieved of his obligation as surety.

Creditor's Duties to Surety

The creditor is required to disclose any material facts about the risk involved to the surety. If he does not do so, the surety is relieved of liability. For example, a bank (creditor) knows that an employee, Arthur, has been guilty of criminal conduct in the past. If the bank applies to a bonding company to obtain a bond on Arthur, the bank must disclose this information about Arthur. Similarly, suppose the bank has an employee, Alison, covered by a bond and discovers that Alison is embezzling money. If the bank agrees to give Alison another chance but does not report her actions to the bonding company, the bonding company is relieved of responsibility for further wrongful acts by Alison.

If the debtor posts security for the performance of an obligation, the creditor must not surrender the security without the consent of the surety. If the creditor does so, the surety is relieved of liability to the extent of the value surrendered.

In the following *New Jersey Economic Development Authority* case, the court rejected a claim by sureties that the creditors had violated their duty to the sureties.

New Jersey Economic Development Authority v. Pavonia Restaurant, Inc.
725 A.2d 1133 (N. J. Super. Ct., App. Div. 1998)

In June 1992, the New Jersey Economic Development Authority (EDA) and the Banque Nationale de Paris loaned $1,470,000 to Pavonia Restaurant, Inc. Pavonia was established to open and operate a new restaurant known as "Hudson's," to be located in a newly constructed eight-story office building in downtown Jersey City. Repayment of the loan was individually guaranteed by a number of individuals who were mostly professional and local businesspeople and, with one exception, were also stockholders in Pavonia.

To acquire the funds necessary to make the loan, the EDA issued and sold Economic Growth Bonds to investors. In order to encourage investment in the bonds, at the request of Pavonia and the guarantors, the bank issued an irrevocable letter of credit pursuant to which it agreed to repay the bondholders in the event Pavonia defaulted.

On June 1, 1992, Pavonia executed a loan agreement, a promissory note, financing statements, and a security agreement pledging its leasehold improvements and restaurant equipment as security for repayment of the loan (the loan documents). On the same date, the guarantors executed a Personal Guaranty Agreement under which they each agreed individually to guarantee repayment of the loan to EDA and the Bank.

Because of a four-month delay in the opening of the restaurant, insufficient advertising, a high-priced menu, staffing problems, and the shareholders' failure to make the necessary capital contributions, Pavonia ran into financial difficulty and the loan went into default. Consequently, as of August 19, 1994, the arrearages due from Pavonia to the EDA equaled $24,207.71, and EDA and the Bank sought payment from the guarantors in accordance with their guarantees.

Thereafter, Pavonia and the guarantors requested EDA and the Bank to forebear enforcement of their rights under the loan agreement and guarantees. EDA and the Bank agreed and, on October 17, 1994, the parties entered into a "Loan Forbearance Agreement." The agreement essentially provided that EDA and the Bank would not accelerate the loan balance for a period of time if Pavonia and the guarantors paid the delinquent amounts due and advanced monthly payments through December 1, 1994, totaling $312,970.19. In the agreement Pavonia and the guarantors acknowledged that Pavonia had defaulted on the loan, that they had not cured the default, and that they had no defenses to EDA's and the Bank's claims under the loan documents or individual guarantees.

On February 1, 1995, Pavonia again defaulted, and EDA and the Bank accelerated the loan balance. In a letter dated June 22, 1995, their counsel made a demand upon the guarantors for full payment of the loan or possession of the assets Pavonia had pledged as collateral. When the guarantors failed to respond, on July 2, 1995, EDA and the Bank filed suit against Pavonia and the guarantors seeking possession of the pledged assets and judgment in the amount of the loan balance, interest, counsel fees, and costs.

EDA and the Bank moved for summary judgment. The guarantors opposed the motion and asserted defenses grounded in fraud, bad faith, and allegations that EDA and the Bank had failed to disclose material facts at the inception of the loan that materially increased their risk under the guarantees rendering them unenforceable. Specifically, guarantors alleged that from the inception of the loan, EDA and the Bank knew and failed to disclose (1) that Pavonia's assets were insufficient to secure the loan and (2) that EDA and the Bank were relying principally, if not exclusively, upon the guarantees as the source of repayment of the loan.

Eichen, Judge   The guarantors claim that EDA and the Bank placed sole reliance on their individual guarantees for repayment of the loan. The record does not support that assertion. Rather, it reflects that both EDA and the Bank and the guarantors anticipated that the revenues from the restaurant would support repayment of the loan. The information concerning the anticipated revenues, was, in fact, derived form Pavonia's accountant, Sobel & Company. Although the guarantors maintain that the loan review document concluded that "no reliance could be placed on the 'collateral or cash flow generating ability of the restaurant,' " the record clearly belies this assertion. The record discloses that EDA and the Bank believed, based on the projections made by Pavonia's accountant, that the restaurant would generate sufficient cash flow to repay the loan. As Lloyd Cox, vice president of the Bank, indicated, the Bank never would have included the loan to Pavonia in the composite bond issue if it did not believe that Pavonia would be successful. Despite the guarantors' attempts to make it appear as though plaintiffs knew Pavonia would be unable to repay the loan and therefore insisted on the guarantees, nothing in the record supports this proposition. The guarantors have not pointed to any evidence that even suggests EDA and the Bank had information about Pavonia's ability to repay the loan which the guarantors did not have. Indeed, everyone understood that opening a restaurant in a new location was inherently risky business. EDA and the Bank hoped that the restaurant's success would comport with the financial projections of Pavonia's accountant just as the guarantors did. The obvious fact is that the external factors impeded Pavonia's success, factors which were completely unrelated to EDA and the Bank's evaluation of the loan agreements. Although Pavonia was unsuccessful in establishing a viable restaurant business, its successor, Laico's of Journal Square, has been successful.

In sum, the guarantors have utterly failed to demonstrate what facts EDA and the Bank had, but guarantors lacked, that materially increased the risk beyond that which EDA and the Bank knew the guarantors intended to assume.

Impliedly recognizing that they could not prove their case under these theories the guarantors argue that their claims are viable under the principles of law contained in the *Restatement of Security: Suretyship* section 124 (1941) (the *Restatement*). That section provides in relevant part:

> Where before [a] surety has undertaken his obligation the creditor knows facts unknown to the surety that materially increase the risk beyond that which the creditor has reason to believe the surety intends to as-

sume, and the creditor also has reason to believe that these facts are unknown to the surety and has a reasonable opportunity to communicate them to the surety, failure of the creditor to notify the surety of such facts is a defense to the surety.

The guarantors argue that EDA and the Bank violated these principles of law by failing to disclose facts to them that materially increased their risk under the guarantees, specifically, that unbeknownst to the Guarantors, EDA and the Bank were relying on their guarantees as the primary security for repayment of the loan and failed to disclose this fact to them. They maintain they would not have undertaken the risk if they had known the guarantees were the principal security for the loan.

Section 124 prescribed three conditions precedent to imposing a duty on a creditor to disclose facts it knows about the debtor to the surety: (1) the creditor must have reason to believe that those facts materially increase the risk beyond that which the surety intends to assume; (2) the creditor must have reason to believe that the facts are unknown to the surety; and (3) the creditor must have a reasonable opportunity to notify the surety of such facts.

However, the comments to section 124 of the *Restatement* explain that:

> [this rule] does not place any burden on the creditor to investigate for the surety's benefit. It does not require the creditor to take any unusual steps to assure himself that the surety is acquainted with facts which he may assume are known to both of them.

. . .

> Every surety by the nature of his obligation undertakes risks which are the inevitable concomitants of the transactions involved. Circumstances of the transactions vary the risks which will be regarded as normal and comtemplated by the surety.

For the reasons previously stated in our rejection of the guarantors' claims of fraud and bad faith, we are satisfied that the guarantors failed to raise any factual issue applying the principles derived from the *Restatement*. Suffice it to say, EDA and the Bank were not in possession of any facts that the guarantors were not aware of; both parties hoped the restaurant would generate sufficient cash flow to repay the loan. Regrettably, it did not.

Judgment affirmed for EDA and the Bank.

Subrogation, Reimbursement, and Contribution

If the surety has to perform or pay the principal's obligation, then the surety acquires all of the rights that the creditor had against the principal. This is known as the surety's **right of subrogation.** The rights acquired could include the right to any collateral in the possession of the creditor, any judgment right the creditor had against the principal on the obligation, and the rights of a creditor in bankruptcy proceedings.

If the surety performs or pays the principal's obligation, she is entitled to recover her costs from the principal; this is known as the surety's **right to reimbursement.** For example, Amado cosigns a promissory note for $2,500 at the credit union for her friend Anders. Anders defaults on the note, and the credit union collects $2,500 from Amado on her suretyship obligation. Amado then not only gets the credit union's rights against Anders under the right of subrogation, but also the right to collect $2,500 from Anders under the right of reimbursement.

Suppose several persons (Tom, Dick, and Harry) are cosureties of their friend Sam. When Sam defaults, Tom pays the whole obligation. Tom is entitled to collect one-third from both Dick and Harry since he paid more than his prorated share. This is known as the cosurety's **right to contribution.** The relative shares of cosureties, as well as any limitations on their liability, are normally set out in the contract of suretyship.

Liens on Personal Property

Common Law Liens

Under the common—or judge-made—law, artisans, innkeepers, and common carriers (such as airlines and trucking companies) were entitled to liens to secure the reasonable value of the services they performed. An arti-san such as a furniture upholsterer or an auto mechanic uses his labor or materials to improve personal property that belongs to someone else. The improvement becomes part of the property and belongs to the owner of the property. Therefore, the artisan who made the improvement is given a **lien** on the property until he is paid.

For example, the upholsterer who recovers a sofa for a customer is entitled to a lien on the sofa. The innkeeper and common carrier are in business to serve the public and are required by law to do so. Under the common law, the innkeeper, to secure payment for his reasonable charges for food and lodging, was allowed to claim a lien on the property that the guest brought to the hotel or inn. Similarly, the common carrier, such as a trucking company, was allowed to claim a lien on the goods carried for the reasonable charges for the service. The justification for such liens was that the innkeeper and common carrier were entitled to the protection of a lien because they were required by law to provide the service to anyone seeking it.

Statutory Liens

While common law liens are still generally recognized today, many states have incorporated this concept into statutes. Some of the state statutes have created additional liens, while others have modified the common law liens to some extent. The statutes commonly provide a procedure for foreclosing the lien. **Foreclosure** is the method by which the rights of the property owner are cut off so that the lienholder can realize her security interest. Typically, the statutes provide for a court to authorize the sale of the personal property subject to the lien so that the creditor can obtain the money to which she is entitled.

Carriers' liens and warehousemen's liens are provided for in Article 7, Documents of Title, of the Uniform Commercial Code. They are covered in Chapter 23, Personal Property and Bailments.

ETHICS IN ACTION

What Is the Ethical Thing to Do?

Suppose you own and operate a small loan business. A young man applies for a $1,000 loan. When you run a credit check on him, you find that he has had difficulty holding a job and has a terrible credit record. You conclude that he is a poor credit risk and inform him that you are willing to make the requested loan only if he can find someone who has a good credit rating to cosign a promissory note with him. The next day he comes by the office with a young woman who meets your criteria for a good credit rating and who indicates she is willing to cosign the note. Do you have any ethical obligation to share with the young woman the information you have about the young man's employment and credit history?

Characteristics of Liens

The common law lien and most of the statutory liens are known as **possessory liens.** They give the artisan or other lienholder the right to keep possession of the debtor's property until the reasonable charges for services have been paid. For the lien to come into play, possession of the goods must have been entrusted to the artisan. Suppose a person takes a chair to an upholsterer to have it repaired. The upholsterer can keep possession of the chair until the person pays the reasonable value of the repair work. However, if the upholsterer comes to the person's home to make the repair, the upholsterer would not have a lien on the chair as the person did not give up possession of it.

The two essential elements of the lien are: (1) possession by the improver or the provider of services and (2) a debt created by the improvement or the provision of services concerning the goods. If the artisan or other lienholder gives up the goods voluntarily, he loses the lien. For example, if a person has a new engine put in his car and the mechanic gives the car back to him before he pays for the engine, the mechanic loses the lien on the car to secure the person's payment for the work and materials. However, if the person uses a spare set of keys to regain possession, or does so by fraud or another illegal act, the lien is not lost. Once the debt has been paid, the lien is terminated and the artisan or other lienholder no longer has the right to retain the goods. If the artisan keeps the goods after the debt has been paid, or keeps the goods without the right to a lien, he is liable for conversion or unlawful detention of goods.

Another important aspect of common law liens is that the work or service must have been performed at the request of the owner of the property. If the work or service is performed without the consent of the owner, no lien is created.

The *Aircraft Repair Services* case which follows involves a situation in which the owner of property subject to a repairman's lien sought damages for breach of contract when the lien was asserted.

Aircraft Repair Services v. Stambaugh's Air Service, Inc.
175 F.3d 314 (3rd Cir. 1999)

Aircraft Repair Services (ARS) owned a Boeing 727 jet aircraft that had been kept in storage for an extended period of time, and needed to have it inspected and repaired. Pursuant to a proposal submitted by Stambaugh's Air Service, ARS retained Stambaugh's for this purpose. After Stambaugh's completed the repairs, ARS intended to lease the aircraft to Kiwi Airlines. Stambaugh's worked on the aircraft for approximately four months. After a test flight, Stambaugh's notified ARS that the aircraft would be ready by October 9, 1996, and that ARS should prepare to pay Stambaugh's repair charges and take possession of the aircraft.

On October 28, 1996, Stambaugh's submitted an invoice for $444,861.58, which it contended represented a substantial discount based on ARS's promise to give Stambaugh's additional work. ARS responded with a request for an additional credit of $151,437.56, claiming that Stambaugh's had performed unauthorized work. Because ARS refused to pay the amount Stambaugh's had billed it, Stambaugh's asserted a repairman's lien over the aircraft, refused to release the aircraft to ARS, and stated its intention to put the aircraft up for sale in satisfaction of its lien. ARS proposed to place the amount Stambaugh's claimed in escrow pending resolution of the dispute if Stambaugh's would release the aircraft. Stambaugh's rejected this suggestion.

On December 12, 1996, ARS filed in the District Court a complaint seeking replevin and damages for breach of contract. It also requested an emergency hearing to obtain a writ of replevin. In its answer, Stambaugh's asserted its repairman's lien as a defense, and counterclaimed for the amounts owed for repair charges, which it alleged to be $625,000.91. On December 18, the District Court held a hearing on the request for a writ of replevin, which it granted on the condition that ARS post a replevin bond in the amount of $1.25 million. On January 17, 1997, ARS posted the bond and took possession of the aircraft. Because of remaining problems with the aircraft and its logbooks, ARS paid additional sums for further repairs.

At trial, ARS contended that, by overstating the amount due for repairs, Stambaugh's had breached the contract between the parties. It argued that it was entitled to recover contract damages for its loss of use of the aircraft from the time Stambaugh's asserted its lien on the aircraft until ARS recovered it. Stambaugh's responded that, since it had retained possession of the aircraft lawfully under its repairman's lien, it could not be held liable for breach of contract. The District Court agreed with ARS, and instructed the jury accordingly.

The jury determined that Stambaugh's was entitled to recover $323,086.14 for its repair work, an amount which ARS at trial conceded it owed. It also found, however, that Stambaugh's had breached its duties under the contract and awarded ARS $343,017.27, apparently representing damages for both loss of use and the additional required repairs.

Stambaugh's appealed, contending that ARS was not entitled to recover damages for loss of use for the period before ARS posted a replevin bond.

Becker, Chief Judge   In Pennsylvania, a common law lien permits one who adds to the value of another person's chattel by labor, skill or material, at the other's request, to retain the chattel until he or she is paid for the value of the services rendered. As one court has explained: "A person in possession of property under a lien is owner of it against all the world and no one may disturb his possession, even the actual owner, until the claim is paid."

When a repairman asserts such a lien, the actual owner has two options: the owner may satisfy the lien and then sue for return of the alleged overcharge, or bring an action for replevin. In the latter case, the owner may recover the property by bringing an action of replevin and requesting a writ of seizure. The plaintiff may recover the property pending a final decision on its claim pursuant to a writ of seizure by posting a bond for twice the value of the chattel, or such other amount as the court deems appropriate. The repairman then loses his or her legal right to retain the chattel pending resolution of the replevin action.

The repairman's liability for damages arising out of the repair work itself is unaffected by the validity of the repairman's lien. As in this case, the actual owner is entitled to recover its costs for further repairs required as a result of inadequacies in the repairman's work. But the lienor is liable for the actual owner's loss-of-use damages for the period during which the lienor is in possession of the property before the actual owner posts a replevin bond only if the lien is found invalid. Under Pennsylvania law (and common law in general), a repairman's lien is invalid only if the lienor asserts his or her claim fraudulently or in bad faith. Accordingly, in a replevin action, ARS could not obtain damages for loss of use of the aircraft during the period prior to its payment of the replevin bond in the absence of proof of bad faith or fraud on Stambaugh's part.

ARS concedes that this is the law in a replevin case. Ordinarily, such a concession would render this case relatively straightforward. But ARS submits that this was a breach-of-contract case, not a replevin case. Accordingly, ARS contends that it should be entitled to recover those breach of contract damages not ordinarily available in a replevin ac-

tion. We disagree, believing that Pennsylvania would view this as a distinction without a difference.

The Supreme Court of Wyoming reached a similar conclusion in a case remarkably like this one. In *Rocky Mountain Turbines, Inc. v. 660 Syndicate, Inc.* (Wyo. 1981), an airplane owner brought a replevin action against a mechanic to obtain possession of its aircraft and for damages for unlawful possession of the aircraft. As in this case, the defendant raised a lien as a defense. Unlike the situation in this case, however, the mechanic refused to release the airplane even after the owner offered to post a bond for twice the value of the airplane. Such refusal was illegal, because a defendant who raises a lien as a defense to a replevin action cannot legally retain possession of the property once the plaintiff posts bond. Accordingly, the court held that the defendant had to pay the plaintiff damages for the period of time after the plaintiff offered to post bond. Significantly, however, the court did not award damages for the period prior to the plaintiff's offering to post a bond. Since the plaintiff's claim of unlawful detention for the period prior to the offer of bond in *Rocky Mountain* was identical to ARD's *Rocky Mountain* supports our conclusion.

We also find it significant that the repairman's lien itself arises out of the contractual relationship between the parties. Accordingly, we do not think that Stambaugh's can have breached the contract by asserting a valid lien which arises from that very contract.

Possessory liens are fundamentally consensual in nature, arising from an agreement, either express or implied, between the owner of the goods and the artisan who renders services for those goods. That possessory liens arise exclusively in the context of express or implied consent is long established in the jurisprudence of this commonwealth. Whenever a workman or artisan, by his labor or skill, increases the value of personal property placed in his possession to be improved he has a lien upon it for his proper charges until paid, but in order to charge a chattel with this lien, the labor for which the lien is claimed must have been done at the request of the owner or under circumstances from which his assent can be reasonably implied. It does not extend to one not in privity with the owners.

Finally, considerations of policy suggest that a plaintiff should not be able to recover damages for loss of use of a chattel retained by the defendant under a repairman's lien. ARS's argument would essentially eviscerate repairman's liens. ARS contends that a repairman need only be in beach of contract before there can be liability flowing from the assertion of the lien. We think that, if we accepted this theory, whenever a repairman attempted to enforce the lien by retaining the good pending payment, the owner of the good would sue the repairman under a contract theory for its lost use of the good while the repairman retains it. But the repairman's lien would then become almost meaningless: What repairman would attempt to enforce the lien if, in doing so, it opened itself up to potential liability much greater than the value of its lien? If, in this case, ARS had declined to post a bond until the trial nearly a year later, Stambaugh's might be liable for damages of nearly one million dollars, when its own claim was at most $625,000.91.

Judgment awarding damages to ARS reversed and remanded.

Foreclosure of Lien

The right of a lienholder to possess goods does not automatically give the lienholder the right to sell the goods or to claim ownership if his charges are not paid. Commonly, there is a procedure provided by statute for selling property once it has been held for a certain period of time. The lienholder is required to give notice to the debtor and to advertise the proposed sale by posting or publishing notices. If there is no statutory procedure, the lienholder must first bring a lawsuit against the debtor. After obtaining a judgment for his charges, the lienholder can have the sheriff seize the property and have it sold at a judicial sale.

Security Interests in Real Property

There are three basic contract devices for using real estate as security for an obligation: (1) the real estate mortgage, (2) the deed of trust, and (3) the land contract. In addition, the states have enacted statutes giving mechanics such as carpenters and plumbers, and materialmen such as lumberyards, a right to a lien on real property into which their labor or materials have been incorporated.

Historical Developments of Mortgages

A **mortgage** is a security interest in real property or a deed to real property that is given by the owner (the **mortgagor**) as security for a debt owed to the creditor (the **mortgagee**). The real estate mortgage was used as a form of security in England as early as the middle of the 12th century, but our present-day mortgage law developed from the common law mortgage of the 15th century. The common law mortgage was a deed that conveyed the land to the mortgagee, with the title to the land to return to the mortgagor upon payment of the debt secured by the mortgage. The mortgagee was given possession of the land during the term of the mortgage. If the mortgagor defaulted on the debt, the mortgagee's title to the land became absolute. The land was forfeited as a penalty, but the forfeiture did not discharge the debt. In addition to keeping the land, the mortgagee could sue on the debt, recover a judgment, and seek to collect the debt.

The early equity courts did not favor the imposition of penalties and would relieve mortgagors from such forfeitures, provided that the mortgagor's default was minor and was due to causes beyond his control. Gradually, the courts became more lenient in permitting redemptions and allowed the mortgagor to **redeem** (reclaim his property) if he tendered performance without unreasonable delay. Finally, the courts of equity recognized the mortgagor's right to redeem as an absolute right that would continue until the mortgagee asked the court of equity to decree that the mortgagor's right to redeem be foreclosed and cut off. Our present law regarding the foreclosure of mortgages developed from this practice.

Today, the mortgage is generally viewed as a lien on land rather than a conveyance of title to the land. There are still some states where the mortgagor goes through the process of giving the mortgagee some sort of legal title to the property. Even in these states, however, the mortgagee's title is minimal and the real ownership of the property remains in the mortgagor.

CYBERLAW IN ACTION

Real Estate Finance on the Internet

Recently it has become quite easy to search for financing, to compare options from multiple possible funding sources, and to apply for mortgages online when purchasing, refinancing, or remodeling a home. Many mortgage companies have developed interactive websites that allow their full array of services to be conducted over the Internet. Shopping for a mortgage on the Internet allows consumers to broaden their search to include companies outside of their city or region and to determine the best rates and options available to them. By using the Internet, consumers have the ability to search for mortgage options whenever and wherever they want without the need to visit multiple possible funding sources. Also, consumers can quickly check the status of an existing account online. Mortgage companies that offer services online significantly expand their pool of potential customers to include persons across the country, rather than just those in their immediate vicinity. Conducting transactions online can reduce their cost of doing business by reducing the number of agents they need to interact with potential customers. In addition, a customer can often fill out one online informational form that the company can make multiple uses of, thus cutting down on the need for duplicate paperwork.

Form, Execution, and Recording

Because the real estate mortgage conveys an interest in real property, it must be executed with the same formality as a deed. Unless it is executed with the required formalities, it will not be eligible for recording in the local land records. Recordation of the mortgage does not affect its validity as between the mortgagor and the mortgagee. However, if it is not recorded, it will not be effective against subsequent purchasers of the property or creditors, including other mortgagees, who have no notice of the earlier mortgage. It is important to the mortgagee that the mortgage be recorded so that the world will be on notice of the mortgagee's interest in the property.

Rights and Liabilities

The owner (mortgagor) of property subject to a mortgage can sell the interest in the property without the consent of the mortgagee. However, the sale does not affect the mortgagee's interest in the property or the mortgagee's claim against the mortgagor. In some cases, the mortgage may provide that if the property is sold, then any remaining balance becomes immediately due and payable. This is known as a "due on sale" clause.

Suppose Erica Smith owns a lot on a lake. She wants to build a cottage on the land, so she borrows $55,000 from First National Bank. She signs a note for $55,000 and gives the bank a $55,000 mortgage on the land and cottage as security for her repayment of the loan. Several years later, Smith sells her land and cottage to Melinda Mason. The mortgage she gave First National might make the unpaid balance due on the mortgage payable on sale.

If it does not, Smith can sell the property with the mortgage on it. If Mason defaults on making the mortgage payments, the bank can foreclose on the mortgage. If at the foreclosure sale the property does not bring enough money to cover the costs, interest, and balance due on the mortgage, First National is entitled to a deficiency judgment against Smith. However, some courts are reluctant to give deficiency judgments where real property is used as security for a debt. If on foreclosure the property sells for more than the debt, Mason is entitled to the surplus.

A purchaser of mortgaged property may buy it **subject to** the mortgage or may **assume** the mortgage. If she buys subject to the mortgage and there is a default and foreclosure, the purchaser is not personally liable for any deficiency. The property is liable for the mortgage debt and can be sold to satisfy it in case of default; in addition, the original mortgagor remains liable for its payment. If the buyer assumes the mortgage, then she becomes personally liable for the debt and for any deficiency on default and foreclosure.

The creditor (mortgagee) may assign his interest in the mortgaged property. To do this, the mortgagee must assign the mortgage as well as the debt for which the mortgage is security. In most jurisdictions, the negotiation of the note carries with it the right to the security and the holder of the note is entitled to the benefits of the mortgage.

Foreclosure

Foreclosure is the process by which any rights of the mortgagor or the current property owner are cut off. Foreclosure proceedings are regulated by statute in the state in which the property is located. In many states, two or more alternative methods of foreclosure are available to the mortgagee or his assignee. The methods in common use today are (1) strict foreclosure, (2) action and sale, and (3) power of sale.

A small number of states permit what is called **strict foreclosure.** The creditor keeps the property in satisfaction of the debt, and the owner's rights are cut off. This means that the creditor has no right to a deficiency and the debtor has no right to any surplus. Strict foreclosure is normally limited to situations where the amount of the debt exceeds the value of the property.

Foreclosure by **action and sale** is permitted in all states, and it is the only method of foreclosure permitted in some states. Although the state statutes are not uniform, they are alike in their basic requirements. In a foreclosure by action and sale, suit is brought in a court having jurisdiction. Any party having a property interest that would be cut off by the foreclosure must be made a defendant, and if any such party has a defense, he must enter his appearance and set up his defense. After the case is tried, a judgment is entered and a sale of the property ordered. The proceeds of the sale are applied to the payment of the mortgage debt, and any surplus is paid over to the mortgagor. If there is a deficiency, a deficiency judgment is, as a general rule, entered against the mortgagor and such other persons as are liable on the debt. Deficiency judgments are generally not permitted where the property sold is the residence of the debtor.

The right to foreclose under a **power of sale** must be expressly conferred on the mortgagee by the terms of the mortgage. If the procedure for the exercise of the power is set out in the mortgage, that procedure must be followed. Several states have enacted statutes that set out the procedure to be followed in the exercise of a power of sale. No court action is required. As a general rule, notice of the default and sale must be given to the mortgagor. After the statutory period, the sale may be held. The sale must be advertised, and it must be at auction. The sale must be conducted fairly, and an effort must be made to sell the property at the highest price obtainable. The proceeds of the sale are applied to the payment of costs, interest, and the principal of the debt. Any surplus must be paid to the mortgagor. If there is a deficiency and the mortgagee wishes to recover a judgment for the deficiency, she must bring suit on the debt.

Right of Redemption

At common law and under existing statutes, the mortgagor or an assignee of the mortgagor has what is called an **equity of redemption** in the mortgaged real estate. This means that he has the absolute right to discharge the mortgage when due and to have title to the mortgaged property restored free and clear of the mortgage debt. Under the statutes of all states, the mortgagor or any party having an interest in the mortgaged property that will be cut off by the foreclosure may redeem the property after default and before the mortgagee forecloses the mortgage. In several states, the mortgagor or any other party in interest is given by statute what is known as a redemption period (usually six months or one year, beginning either after the foreclosure proceedings are started or after a foreclosure sale of the mortgaged property has been made) in which to pay the mortgaged debt, costs, and interest and to redeem the property.

As a general rule, if a party in interest wishes to redeem, he must, if the redemption period runs after the foreclosure sale, pay to the purchaser at the foreclosure sale the amount that the purchaser has paid plus interest up to the time of redemption. If the redemption period runs before the sale, the party in interest must pay the amount of the debt plus the costs and interest. The person who wishes to redeem from a mortgage foreclosure sale must redeem the entire mortgage interest; he cannot redeem a partial interest by paying a proportionate amount of the debt or by paying a proportionate amount of the price bid at the foreclosure sale.

Deed of Trust

States typically use either the mortgage or the **deed of trust** as the primary mechanism for holding a security interest in real property. There are three parties to a deed of trust: (1) the owner of the property who borrows the money (the debtor), (2) the trustee who holds legal title to the property put up as security, and (3) the lender who is the beneficiary of the trust. The trustee serves as a fiduciary for both the creditor and the debtor. The purpose of the deed of trust is to make it easy for the security to be liquidated. However, most states treat the deed of trust like a mortgage in giving the borrower a relatively long period of time to redeem the property, thereby defeating this rationale for the arrangement.

In a deed of trust transaction, the borrower deeds to the trustee the property that is to be put up as security. The trust agreement usually gives the trustee the right to foreclose or sell the property if the debtor fails to make a required payment on the debt. Normally, the trustee does not sell the property until the lender notifies him that the borrower is in default and demands that the property be sold. The trustee must notify the debtor that

ETHICS IN ACTION

What Is the Right Thing to Do?

Suppose you have sold a farm to a young couple on a land contract that calls for them to pay off the purchase price over a 10-year period. After the couple has paid about a third of the purchase price, a serious drought damages their crop and they miss several payments, trigger- ing your right to declare a default and reclaim posses- sion of the property. Are there any ethical considerations involved in your taking such an action that you are oth- erwise legally entitled to take? If you proceed with a for- feiture action in court, what policy considerations should the court take into account in deciding whether to grant your request?

---

he is in default and that the land will be sold. The trustee advertises the property for sale. After the statutory period, the trustee will sell the property at a public or private sale. The proceeds are applied to the costs of the foreclosure, interest, and debt. If there is a surplus, it is paid to the bor- rower. If there is a deficiency, the lender has to sue the borrower on the debt and recover a judgment.

Land Contracts

The **land contract** is a device for securing the balance due the seller on the purchase price of real estate. Essen- tially, it is an installment contract for the purchase of land. The buyer agrees to pay the purchase price over a period of time. The seller agrees to convey title to the property to the buyer when the full price is paid. Usually, the buyer takes possession of the property, pays the taxes, insures the property, and assumes the other obligations of an owner. However, the seller keeps legal title and does not turn over the deed until the purchase price is paid.

If the buyer defaults, the seller usually has the right to declare a forfeiture and take over possession of the prop-

erty. The buyer's rights to the property are cut off at that point. Most states give the buyer on a land contract a lim- ited period of time to redeem his interest. Moreover, some states require the seller to go through a foreclosure proceeding. Generally, the procedure for declaring a for- feiture and recovering property sold on a land contract is simpler and less time-consuming than foreclosure of a mortgage. In most states, the procedure in case of default is set out by statute. If the buyer, after default, voluntar- ily surrenders possession to the seller, no court procedure is necessary; the seller's title will become absolute, and the buyer's equity will be cut off.

Purchases of farm property are commonly financed through the use of land contracts. As an interest in real es- tate, a land contract should be in writing and recorded in the local land records so as to protect the interests of both parties.

As can be seen in the following case, *Looney v. Farm- ers Home Administration*, some courts have invoked the equitable doctrine against forfeitures and have required that the seller on a land contract must foreclose on the property in order to avoid injustice to a defaulting buyer.

Looney v. Farmers Home Administration   *794 F.2d 310 (7th Cir. 1986)*

On October 7, 1976, Lowry and Helen McCord entered into a land contract to purchase a 260-acre farm from John and Es- ther Looney for $250,000. The contract specified that this was to be amortized over a 20-year period at an annual interest rate of 7 percent. The McCords were to make annual payments of $23,280 on November 15 of each year until the purchase price and all accrued interest was paid. They also agreed to pay real estate taxes, insurance, and maintenance costs for the property.

Four years later, the McCords received an economic emergency loan of $183,000 from the Farmers Home Administration (FmHA). They signed a promissory note for the amount of the loan with interest at 11 percent and, as security, also granted the FmHA a second mortgage on the land subject to the land sales contract.

The McCords subsequently defaulted on their obligations to the Looneys. At the time of the default, the McCords had paid $123,280 to the Looneys but still owed $249,360.12 on the contract price. At the time, the property was worth $455,000. The Looneys brought suit against the McCords and the FmHA seeking to eject the McCords from the property and forfeiture of the contract. The FmHA objected to the proposed forfeiture and argued that the court should order foreclosure proceedings.

The district court denied the FmHA's motion for foreclosure. It held that the traditional presumption under Indiana law did not apply because the McCords had made only minimal payments on the contract and had not paid their fall taxes or insurance installments. Because $249,360.12 was still owed on an initial base price of $250,000, the court found the McCords's equity to be $639.88, only .26 percent of the principal. The court therefore found forfeiture appropriate, awarded the FmHA $639.88, and extinguished the FmHA's mortgage. The FmHA appealed.

Cudahy, Circuit Judge   Under Indiana law a conditional land sales contract is considered in the nature of a secured transaction, "the provisions of which are subject to all proper and just remedies at law and in equity." *Skendzel v. Marshall.* Recognizing the common law maxim that "equity abhors forfeitures," the *Skendzel* court concluded that "judicial foreclosure of a land sales contract is in consonance with the notions of equity developed in American jurisprudence." Foreclosure generally protects the rights of all parties to a contract. Upon judicial sale the proceeds are first applied to the balance of the contract principal and interest owed the seller. Then, any junior lienholders take their share. Any surplus goes to the buyer.

Skendzel recognized, however, two instances where forfeiture was the appropriate remedy:

> In the case of an abandoning, absconding vendee, forfeiture is a logical and equitable remedy. Forfeiture would also be appropriate where the vendee has paid a minimal amount on the contract at the time of default and seeks to retain possession while the vendor is paying taxes, insurance, and other upkeep in order to preserve the premises.

The district court did not rely on the first *Skendzel* exception in finding forfeiture appropriate. No evidence in the record supports such a finding.

If forfeiture is justified, then, it is only because the second *Skendzel* exception is met. This requires that the vendee have paid only a minimum amount on the contract at the time of default. In this case, the district court concluded that "this is patently a situation contemplated by the court in *Skendzel* in which forfeiture is the logical and equitable remedy."

However, the buyers in *Skendzel* had in fact paid more than a minimum amount on the contract and the court cited no examples of what would "patently" constitute a "minimum amount." Rather, later Indiana cases have interpreted *Skendzel* as requiring a case by case analysis that examines the totality of circumstances surrounding the contract and its performance. Here, while $123,280 was paid to the Looneys, the court considered all but $639.88 to be interest rather than a part of the contract price. The court equated contract price with what was paid to reduce principal. But nothing in Indiana law compels the district court's construction of payments on the contract. On the contrary, several Indiana courts have considered and given weight to both payments to reduce principal and those to reduce interest in determining whether a buyer falls within the second *Skendzel* exception.

Even where no principal is paid, a buyer's stake in the property may be sufficient to justify foreclosure. Here, two uncontested affidavits indicate the property to be worth over $200,000 more than the McCords owe the Looneys. With the evidence of appreciation, the court was incorrect to conclusively value the McCords' equity at only $639.88.

When the second *Skendzel* exception has been invoked it frequently has been because the vendee is contributing to a decline in the value of the security. There is no allegation or evidence of waste in this case. Even the Looneys admit that the buyers "had paid substantial monies pursuant to the terms of the contracts." The Looneys received $123,280 and the McCords paid the necessary real estate taxes, insurance premiums and upkeep expenses for over six years. The Looneys make no showing that foreclosure would not satisfy their interest and the court below made no such determination. While foreclosure would appear to satisfy all parties' needs, forfeiture leaves the FmHA with a $639.88 recovery on a $183,800 loan. In view of the "totality of circumstances" this result seems inequitable.

Judgment reversed in favor of Farmers Home Administration.

Security Interests in Real Property

Type of Security Instrument	Parties	Features
Mortgage	1. Mortgagor (property owner/debtor) 2. Mortgagee (creditor)	1. Mortgagee holds a security interest (and in some states, title) in real property as security for a debt. 2. If mortgagor defaults on her obligation, mortgagee must *foreclose* on property to realize on his security interest. 3. Mortgagor has a limited time after foreclosure to *redeem* her interest.
Deed of Trust	1. Owner/debtor 2. Lender/creditor 3. Trustee	1. Trustee holds legal title to the real property put up as security. 2. If debt is satisfied, the trustee conveys property back to owner/debtor. 3. If debt is not paid as agreed, creditor notifies trustee to sell the property. 4. While intended to make foreclosure easier, most states treat it like a mortgage for purposes of foreclosure.
Land Contract	1. Buyer 2. Seller	1. Seller agrees to convey title when full price is paid. 2. Buyer usually takes possession, pays property taxes and insurance, and maintains the property. 3. If buyer defaults, seller may declare a forfeiture and retake possession (most states) after buyer has limited time to redeem; some states require foreclosure.

Mechanic's and Materialman's Liens

Each state has a statute that permits persons who contract to furnish labor or materials to improve real estate to claim a lien on the property until they are paid. There are many differences among states as to exactly who can claim such a lien and the requirements that must be met to do so.

Rights of Subcontractors and Materialmen

A general contractor is a person who has contracted with the owner to build, remodel, or improve real property. A subcontractor is a person who has contracted with the general contractor to perform a stipulated portion of the general contract. A materialman is a person who has contracted to furnish certain materials needed to perform a designated general contract.

Two distinct systems—the New York system and the Pennsylvania system—are followed by the states in allowing mechanic's liens on real estate to subcontractors and materialmen. The New York system is based on the theory of subrogation, and the subcontractors or materialmen cannot recover more than is owed to the contractor at the time they file a lien or give notice of a lien to the owner. Under the Pennsylvania system, the subcontractors or materialmen have direct liens and are entitled to liens for the value of labor and materials furnished, irrespective of the amount due from the owner to the contractor. Under the New York system, the general contractor's failure to perform his contract or his abandonment of the work has a direct effect on the lien rights of subcontractors and materialmen, whereas under the Pennsylvania system, such breach or abandonment by the general contractor does not directly affect the lien rights of subcontractors and materialmen.

Basis for Mechanic's or Materialman's Lien

Some state statutes provide that no lien shall be claimed unless the contract for the improvement is in writing and embodies a statement of the materials to be furnished and a description of the land on which the improvement is to take place and of the work to be done. Other states permit the contract to be oral, but in no state is a licensee or volunteer entitled to a lien. No lien can be claimed unless the work is done or the materials are furnished in the performance of a contract to improve specific real property. A sale of materials without reference to the improvement of specific real property does not entitle the person furnishing the materials to a lien on real property that is, in fact, improved by the use of the materials at some time after the sale.

Unless the state statute specifically includes submaterialmen, they are not entitled to a lien. For example, if a lumber dealer contracts to furnish the lumber for the erection of a specific building and orders from a sawmill a carload of lumber that is needed to fulfill the contract, the sawmill will not be entitled to a lien on the building in which the lumber is used unless the state statute expressly provides that submaterialmen are entitled to a lien.

At times, the question has arisen as to whether materials have been furnished. Some courts have held that the materialman must prove that the material furnished was actually incorporated into the structure. Under this ruling, if material delivered on the job is diverted by the general contractor or others and not incorporated into the structure, the materialman will not be entitled to a lien. Other courts have held that the materialman is entitled to a lien if he can provide proof that the material was delivered on the job under a contract to furnish the material.

Requirements for Obtaining Lien

The requirements for obtaining a mechanic's or materialman's lien must be complied with strictly. Although there is no uniformity in the statutes as to the requirements for obtaining a lien, the statutes generally require the filing of a notice of lien with a county official such as the register of deeds or the county clerk, which notice sets forth the amount claimed, the name of the owner, the names of the contractor and the claimant, and a description of the property. Frequently, the notice of lien must be verified by an affidavit of the claimant. In some states, a copy of the notice must be served on the owner or be posted on the property.

The notice of lien must be filed within a stipulated time. The time varies from 30 to 90 days, but the favored time is 60 days after the last work performed or after the last materials furnished. Some statutes distinguish between labor claims, materialmen's claims, and claims of general contractors as to time of filing. The lien, when filed, must be foreclosed within a specified time, which generally varies from six months to two years.

Priorities and Foreclosure

The provisions for priorities vary widely, but most of the statutes provide that a mechanic's lien has priority over all liens attaching after the first work is performed or after the first materials are furnished. This statutory provision creates a hidden lien on the property, in that a mechanic's lien, filed within the allotted period of time after completion of the work, attaches as of the time the first work is done or the first material is furnished, but no notice of lien need be filed during this period. And if no notice of lien is filed during this period, third persons would have no means of knowing of the existence of a lien. There are no priorities among lien claimants under the majority of the statutes.

The following case, *In Re Skyline Properties,* illustrates a number of issues that can arise when a mechanic's claim that he has a lien on certain property because of work he did concerning it is challenged by another party claiming a competing interest in the property.

In Re Skyline Properties, Inc.: Century National Bank and Trust Co. *v.* Skyline Properties, Inc.   *134 B.R. 830 (Bankr. W.D.Pa. 1992)*

In 1987, Skyline Properties commenced development of an integrated, multifaceted resort encompassing approximately 1,000 acres to be known as Hunter's Station. David Mealy was engaged to perform excavating and grading work on the project and commenced visible work on April 20, 1987. Mealy's work included bulldozing new roads, constructing parking areas, digging footers and drainage ditches, grading a basement for a new building used as a tack shop, excavation of crawl spaces for new additions to an existing building subsequently used as a sales office, grading an area for a new horse barn, and the installation of drains and fencing on the property. The sales office was substantially complete and opened for business on June 4, 1987, while work continued on construction of the tack shop.

On June 5, 1987, Century National Bank extended $150,000 credit to Skyline, took as collateral a mortgage on several of the parcels in the development, and recorded the mortgage on June 5, 1987. Mealy completed his work on August 3, 1987, and filed a notice of a mechanics' lien claim on September 23, 1987. Pennsylvania law requires that claims for such liens be filed within four months after the completion of the work.

In October 1988, the bank filed a mortgage foreclosure action against Skyline's property that it held as security for the loan. In September 1989, Mealy obtained a judgment on his claim and scheduled a Sheriff's sale of the Skyline property. The sale was halted by the filing of a involuntary petition in bankruptcy. One of the issues in the bankruptcy proceeding was the relative priority of the claims of the bank and Mealy to the Skyline property.

Bemtz, Bankruptcy Judge A mechanics' lien for services which constitute alterations and repairs takes effect and has priority as of the date the mechanics' lien claim is filed. 49 Pa. Stat. Ann. Sec. 1508(b). In the case of services constituting erection and construction, the lien of a claim takes effect and has priority "as of the date of the visible commencement upon the ground of the work of erecting or constructing the improvement." 49 Pa.Stat. Ann. Sec. 1508(a).

This matter involves the following relevant dates:

Visible commencement of construction:	April 20, 1987
Bank's mortgage:	June 5, 1987
Mealy Claim filed:	September 23, 1987

Thus, if Mealy's work is erection and construction, Mealy's claim has priority over the Bank; if the work is alteration or repair, the Bank's mortgage takes priority.

Section 1201(10) of the Mechanic's Lien Law defines "erection and construction" as follows:

"Erection and construction" means the erection and construction of a new improvement or of a substantial addition to an existing improvement or any adaption of an existing improvement rendering the same fit for a new or distinct use and effecting a material change in the interior or exterior thereof.

The Bank asserts that no buildings were erected or constructed in conjunction with Mealy's work and Mealy's lien is for alterations and repairs. Thus the Bank asserts that Mealy's lien takes priority as of the date of filing of the Claim and not the date of visible commencement of the work.

The concern in determining whether the work is "erection and construction" or "alterations or repairs" is whether a substantial change to the existing structure has occurred such that any third party, such as the Bank, would be on notice that potential liens could exist. A change in the appearance or use of a building is sufficient to give such notice.

In the present case, the evidence reveals that a farmhouse on the property, formerly used as a residential dwelling, was converted into a sales office used to sell ownership interests in the development. Skyline converted an existing farmhouse into a sales office by essentially "gutting" the structure and constructing additions to the original dwelling. The appearance of the house was transformed into a commercial building and the use was altogether different. The addition to the building made it substantially larger than it had been as a private residence. The additions are substantial enough to be considered new construction. The work was substantially completed and the sales office open for business on June 4, 1987, one day *before* the Bank recorded its mortgage. Had the Bank, which was aware of the scope of the planned construction, viewed the property at the time it recorded its mortgage, it certainly would have known that potential liens could exist.

The tack shop was built on existing concrete blocks which had served as the foundation for a building that had previously fallen down or been removed. The tack shop has both a "new use" and a "new appearance" and constitutes erection and construction.

Grading and excavation is the type of work which is properly lienable as incident to the erection or construction of an improvement. Another way of stating the test utilized by the Pennsylvania courts in determining whether a certain type of work is lienable is whether the work is incident to the construction of an improvement. Mealy graded the area for four structures—the sales office, the tack shop, the horse barn and arena, and the guardhouse. Mealy dug footers and drainage ditches for the sales office and the guardhouse and installed drains for the tack shop. The work Mealy performed was incident to the construction of these improvements and also designed to enhance their value.

Mealy's lienable work, incident to the erection and construction of four structures, as opposed to merely alteration and repair, entitles Mealy to a claim which relates back in time to the date upon which work was com-

menced and therefore, is prior to the Bank's mortgage interest.

Order upholding Mealy's lien claim.

The procedure followed in the foreclosure of a mechanic's lien on real estate follows closely the procedure followed in a court foreclosure of a real estate mortgage. The rights acquired by the filing of a lien and the extent of the property covered by the lien are set out in some of the mechanic's lien statutes. In general, the lien attaches only to the interest that the person has in the property that has been improved at the time the notice is filed. Some statutes provide that the lien attaches to the building and to the city lot on which the building stands, or if the improvement is to farm property, the lien attaches to a specified amount of land.

Waiver of Lien

The question often arises as to the effect of an express provision in a contract for the improvement of real estate that no lien shall attach to the property for the cost of the improvement. In some states, there is a statute requiring the recording or filing of the contract and making such a provision ineffective if the statute is not complied with. In some states, courts have held that such a provision is effective against everyone; in other states, courts have held that the provision is ineffective against everyone except the contractor; and in still other states, courts have held that such a provision is ineffective as to subcontractors, materialmen, and laborers. Whether the parties to the contract have notice of the waiver of lien provision plays an important part in several states in determining their right to a lien.

It is common practice that before a person who is having improvements made to his property makes final payment, he requires the contractor to sign an affidavit that all materialmen and subcontractors have been paid and to supply him with a release of lien signed by the subcontractors and materialmen.

Problems and Problem Cases

1. Rusty Jones, a used car dealer, applied to First Financial Federal Savings and Loan Association for a $50,000 line of credit to purchase an inventory of used cars. First Financial refused to make the loan to Jones alone but

agreed to do so if Worth Camp, an attorney and friend of Jones, would cosign the note. Camp agreed to cosign as an accommodation maker or surety. The expectation of the parties was that the loans cosigned by Camp would be repaid from the proceeds of the car inventory. The original note for $25,000 was signed on August 2, 1994, and renewals were executed on January 25, 1995, September 11, 1995, and March 15, 1996, and the amount was eventually increased to $50,000. In August 1995, as Camp was considering whether to sign the September renewal note, he was advised by First Financial's loan officer that the interest on the loan had been paid. In fact, interest payments were four months delinquent. In addition, unknown to Camp, as the $50,000 credit limit was approached, First Financial began making side, or personal, loans to Jones totaling about $25,000, which were also payable out of the used car inventory. Camp knew nothing of these loans and thought that Jone's used car business was making payments only on the loans he had cosigned. Jones defaulted on the $50,000 note cosigned by Camp and First Financial brought suit against Camp on his obligation as surety on the note. Was Camp relieved of his obligation as surety by First Financial's failure to disclose material facts to him?

2. Mr. and Mrs. Marshall went to Beneficial Finance to borrow money but were deemed by Beneficial's office manager, Puckett, to be bad credit risks. The Marshalls stated that their friend Garren would be willing to cosign a note for them if necessary. Puckett advised Garren not to cosign because the Marshalls were bad credit risks. This did not dissuade Garren from cosigning a note for $480 but it prompted him to ask Beneficial to take a lien or security interest in Marshall's custom-built Harley-Davidson motorcycle, then worth over $1,000. Beneficial took and perfected a security interest in the motorcycle. Marshall defaulted on the first payment. Beneficial gave notice of the default to Garren and advised him that it was looking to him for payment. Garren then discovered that Beneficial and Marshall had reached an agreement whereby Marshall would sell his motorcycle for $700; he was to receive $345 immediately, which was to be applied to the loan, and he promised to pay the balance of the loan from his pocket. Marshall paid Beneficial

$89.50 and left town without giving the proceeds of the sale to Beneficial. Because Beneficial was unable to get the proceeds from Marshall, it brought suit against Garren on his obligation as surety. When Beneficial released the security for the loan (the motorcycle) without Garren's consent, was Garren relieved of his obligation as surety for repayment of the loan?

3. Maxwell owned the timber on a certain tract of land. He hired Fitzgerald to cut the timber into logs and to put the logs in Maxwell's mill pond. Fitzgerald had the logs cut and put on the back of the mill pond, where they were levied on by a judgment creditor of Maxwell's. Fitzgerald was not paid for his work. He claimed a common law lien on the logs for his labor in cutting and hauling them. Is Fitzgerald entitled to a common law lien on the logs?

4. During May and June, John Shumate regularly parked his automobile on a vacant lot in downtown Philadelphia. At that time, no signs were posted prohibiting parking on the lot or indicating that vehicles parked there without authorization would be towed. On July 7, Shumate again left his car on the lot. When he returned two days later, the car was gone and the lot was posted with signs warning that parking was prohibited. Shumate learned that his car had been towed away by Ruffie's Towing Service and that the car was being held by Ruffie's at its place of business. Ruffie's refused to release the car until Shumate paid a towing fee of $44.50 plus storage charges of $4 per day. Shumate refused to pay the fee, and Ruffie's kept possession of the car. Did Ruffie's have a common law possessory lien on the car?

5. Philip and Edith Beh purchased some property from Alfred M. Gromer and his wife. Sometime earlier, the Gromers had borrowed money from City Mortgage. They had signed a note and had given City Mortgage a second deed of trust on the property. There was also a first deed of trust on the property at the time the Behs purchased it. In the contract of sale between the Behs and the Gromers, the Behs promised to "assume" the second deed of trust of approximately $5,000 at 6 percent interest. The Behs later defaulted on the first deed of trust. Foreclosure was held on the first deed of trust, but the proceeds of the sale left nothing for City Mortgage on its second deed of trust. City Mortgage then brought a lawsuit against the Behs to collect the balance due on the second deed of trust. When the Behs "assumed" the second deed of trust, did they become personally liable for it?

6. Pope agreed to sell certain land to Pelz and retained a mortgage on the property to secure payment of the pur-

chase price. The mortgage contained a clause providing that if Pelz defaulted, Pope had the "right to enter upon the above-described premises and sell the same at public sale" to pay the balance of the purchase price, accounting to Pelz for any surplus realized on the sale. What type of foreclosure does this provision contemplate: (1) strict foreclosure, (2) action and sale, or (3) private power of sale?

7. In October 1992, Verda Miller sold her 107-acre farm for $30,000 to Donald Kimball, who was acting on behalf of his own closely held corporation, American Wonderlands. Under the agreement, Miller retained title and Kimball was given possession pending full payment of all installments of the purchase price. The contract provided that Kimball was to pay all real estate taxes. If he did not pay them, Miller could discharge them and either add the amounts to the unpaid principal or demand immediate payment of the delinquencies plus interest. Miller also had the right to declare a forfeiture of the contract and regain possession if the terms of the agreement were not met. In 1995, Miller had to pay the real estate taxes on the property in the amount of $672.78. She demanded payment of this amount plus interest from Kimball. She also served a notice of forfeiture on him that he had 30 days to pay. Kimball paid the taxes but refused to pay interest of $10.48. Miller made continued demands on Kimball for two months, then filed notice of forfeiture with the county recorder in August 1995. She also advised Kimball of this. Was Miller justified in declaring a forfeiture and taking back possession of the land?

8. Albert Sharkey was the owner of a commercial building that was leased to Consolidated Freightways for more than 10 years before the lease was terminated by Consolidated on October 25, 1992. Consolidated's lease with Sharkey provided that Consolidated would leave the property in as good condition as received. Consolidated was responsible for damaging 10 overhead doors and contacted Dewco Building Systems to repair the damage. Dewco ordered new doors from Overhead. Overhead specially ordered the doors and paid for them on delivery from the manufacturer. On March 18, 1993, Overhead submitted its bill to Dewco. Overhead was unable to collect since Dewco had gone out of business and filed for bankruptcy. Dewco had already collected $10,397 from Consolidated and owed $6,685 to Overhead. On May 10, 1993, Overhead filed a mechanic's lien against Sharkey's property and brought a lawsuit to enforce the lien. Iowa Code Section 572.2 provides that:

> Every person who shall furnish any material or labor for, or perform any labor, upon any building or land for improvement,

alteration or repair thereof, including those engaged in the construction or repair of any work of internal or external improvement . . . by virtue of any contract with the owner, his agent, trustee, contractor, or subcontractor shall have a lien upon such building or improvement, and land belonging to the owner on which the same is situated . . ., to secure payment for material or labor furnished or labor performed.

Does Overhead have a valid claim for a mechanic's lien on Sharkey's property?

Online Research: What Protection Does Your State Give Artisans?

Use the Internet to research your state law to determine what (a) an artisan who improves personal property or (b) a contractor or supplier of materials for the improvement of real property must do to claim a lien on the property until they are paid. What steps must the lienholder do to foreclose on his lien? If your state's laws are not accessible online, then look at the law in New York or California.

SECURITY INTERESTS IN PERSONAL PROPERTY

Elaine Stanley decides that she will start a card and gift shop in leased space in a shopping mall. Her personal assets are not sufficient to finance the business so she borrows some initial working capital from a bank. She purchases some display fixtures from a local supplier, making a small down payment and agreeing to pay the balance of the purchase price over the next two years. She purchases her initial inventory from several suppliers, agreeing to either pay for the goods within 60 days or to pay interest at the rate of 15 percent per year on any unpaid balance. To attract customers, she plans to offer both a layaway plan and store charge accounts. Among the questions raised by this hypothetical are:

• How can the creditors of the business, such as the bank, the supplier of the display fixtures, and the suppliers of the inventory obtain security for the credit they have extended to Elaine?
• What steps must the creditors take to obtain maximum protection against Elaine and against her other creditors in the event she defaults on her obligations?
• What relative rights will the creditors have against each other in the event Elaine defaults on her obligations to them?
• How can Elaine protect herself when she extends credit to her customers?

IN MANY CREDIT TRANSACTIONS the creditor, in order to protect his investment, takes a security interest, or lien, in personal property belonging to the debtor. The law covering security interests in personal property is set forth in Article 9 of the Uniform Commercial Code. Article 9, entitled Secured Transactions, applies to situations that consumers and businesspeople commonly face; for example, the financing of an automobile, the purchase of a refrigerator on a time-payment plan, or the financing of business inventory.

Article 9

If a creditor wants to obtain a security interest in the personal property of the debtor, he also wants to be sure that his interest is superior to the claims of other creditors. To do so, the creditor must carefully comply with Article 9.

In Part 4 of this text, Sales, we pointed out that businesspersons sometimes leave out important terms in a contract or insert vague terms to be worked out later. Such looseness is a luxury that is not permitted in secured transactions. If a debtor gets into financial difficulties and cannot meet her obligations, even a minor noncompliance with Article 9 may cause the creditor to lose his preferred claim to the personal property of the debtor. A creditor who loses his secured interest is only a general creditor if the debtor is declared bankrupt. As a general creditor in bankruptcy proceedings, he may have little chance of recovering the money owed by the debtor because of the relatively low priority of such claims. Chapter 30, Bankruptcy, covers this in detail.

In 1998, the National Conference on Uniform State Laws adopted a "Revised Article 9" that has now been adopted by all 50 states with effective dates ranging from 2001 to 2002. Because Revised Article 9 is much more complex than the old Article 9 and because Article 9 has not been adopted in exactly the same form in every state, the law must be examined very carefully to determine the procedure in a particular state for obtaining a security interest and for ascertaining the rights of the creditors and debtors. However, the general concepts are the same in each state and will be the basis of our discussion in this chapter.

Security Interests under the Code

Security Interests

Basic to a discussion of secured consumer and commercial transactions is the term **security interest.** A security interest is an interest in personal property or fixtures obtained by a creditor to secure payment or performance of an obligation [1–201(37)].[1] For example, when a person borrows money from a bank to buy a new car, the bank takes a security interest, or puts a lien, on the car until the loan is repaid. If the person defaults on the loan, the bank can repossess the car and have it sold to cover the unpaid balance. A security interest is a property interest in the collateral.

Types of Collateral

Goods—tangible items such as automobiles and business computers—are commonly used as collateral for loans. Article 9 of the Uniform Commercial Code also covers security interests in a much broader grouping of personal property. The Code breaks down personal property into a number of different classifications, which are important in determining how a creditor obtains an enforceable security interest in a particular kind of collateral.

The Code classifications include:

1. *Instruments.* This includes checks, notes, drafts, and certificates of deposit [9–102(a)(47)].

2. *Documents of title.* This includes bills of lading, dock warrants, dock receipts, and warehouse receipts [9–102(a)(30)].

3. *Accounts.* This includes the rights to payment of a monetary obligation for goods sold or leased or for services rendered that are not evidenced by instru-

ments or chattel paper but are carried on open accounts, including lottery winnings and health care-insurance receivables. Items in the "accounts" category include such rights to payment whether or not the rights have been earned by performance [9–102(a)(2)].

4. *Chattel paper.* This includes written documents that evidence both an obligation to pay money and a security interest in specific goods [9–102(a)(11)]. A typical example of chattel paper is what is commonly known as a *conditional sales contract.* This is the type of contract that a consumer might sign when she buys a large appliance such as a refrigerator on a time-payment plan.

5. *General intangibles.* This is a catchall category that includes, among other things, patents, copyrights, software, and franchises [9–102(a)(42)].

6. *Goods.* Goods [9–102(a)(44)] are divided into several classes; the same item of collateral may fall into different classes at different times, depending on its use:

   a. *Consumer goods.* Goods used or bought primarily for personal, family, or household use, such as automobiles, furniture, and appliances [9–102(a)[23)].

   b. *Equipment.* Goods other than inventory, farm products, or consumer goods [9–102(a)(33)].

   c. *Farm products.* Crops, livestock, or supplies used or produced in farming operations as long as they are still in the possession of a debtor who is engaged in farming [9–102(a)(34)].

   d. *Inventory.* Goods held for sale or lease or to be used under contracts of service, as well as raw materials, work in process, or materials used or consumed in a business [9–102(a)(48)].

   e. *Fixtures.* Goods that will be so affixed to real property that they are considered a part of the real property [9–102(a)(41)].

7. *Investment property.* This includes securities such as stocks, bonds, and commodity contracts [9–102 (a)(49)].

8. *Deposit accounts.* This includes demand, time, savings, passbook, and similar accounts maintained with a bank [9–102(a)(29)].

It is important to note that an item such as a stove could in different situations be classified as inventory, equipment, or consumer goods. In the hands of the manufacturer or an appliance store, the stove is *inventory.* If it is being used in a restaurant, it is *equipment.* In a home, it is classified as *consumer goods.*

---

[1]The numbers in brackets refer to sections of the Uniform Commercial Code.

Obtaining a Security Interest

The goal of a creditor is to obtain a security interest in certain personal property that will be good against: (1) the debtor, (2) other creditors of the debtor, and (3) a person who might purchase the property from the debtor. In case the debtor defaults on the debt, the creditor wants to have a better right to claim the property than anyone else. Obtaining an enforceable security interest is a two-step process—attachment and perfection.

Attachment of the Security Interest

Attachment

A security interest is not legally enforceable against a debtor until it is attached to one or more particular items of the debtor's property. The **attachment** of the security interest takes place in a legal sense rather than in a physical sense. There are three basic requirements for a security interest to be attached to the goods of a debtor [9–203]. First is an *agreement* in which the debtor grants the creditor a security interest in particular property (collateral) in which the debtor has an interest. Second, the debtor must have *rights in the collateral.* Third, the creditor must give *value* to the debtor. The creditor must, for example, lend money or advance goods on credit to the debtor. Unless the debtor owes a debt to the creditor,

there can be no security interest. The purpose of obtaining a security interest is to secure a debt.

The Security Agreement

The agreement in which a debtor grants a creditor a security interest in the debtor's property must generally be authenticated by the debtor. An authenticated agreement is required in all cases except where the creditor has possession or control of the collateral [9–203]. Suppose Cole borrows $50 from Fox and gives Fox her wristwatch as a security for the loan. The agreement whereby Cole put up her watch as collateral does not have to be authenticated by Cole to be enforceable. Because the creditor (Fox) is in possession of the collateral, an oral agreement is sufficient.

The security agreement must reasonably describe the collateral so that it can readily be identified. For example, it should list the year, make, and serial number of an automobile. The security agreement usually spells out the terms of the arrangement between the creditor and the debtor. Also, it normally contains a promise by the debtor to pay certain amounts of money in a certain way. The agreement specifies which events, such as nonpayment by the buyer, constitute a default. In addition, it may contain provisions that the creditor feels are necessary to protect his security interest. For example, the debtor may be required to keep the collateral insured, not to move it without the creditor's consent, or to periodically report sales of secured inventory goods. In the case that follows, *In re Shirel,* the court found that the information contained in a credit application did not meet the requirements for a security agreement.

In Re Shirel   *251 BR 157 (Bankr., W.D. Oklahoma 2000)*

Kevin Shirel applied for a credit card from Sight'N Sound Appliance Centers, Inc. The credit application, which constituted the agreement between the parties, was a barely legible, seven-page, single-spaced, small-print document. Shirel signed it on the first page. The form contained a statement that Sight'N Sound would have a "security interest" in all "merchandise" purchased with the credit card. The statement was located approximately four pages into the application.

Shirel's credit was approved, and he purchased a new refrigerator using the credit card. Several months later, Shirel filed a bankruptcy petition listing the remaining credit card debt as unsecured and the refrigerator as exempt from the claims of creditors. Subsequently, Sight'N Sound objected to the claim of exemption. It contended that Shirel had improperly listed the debt as unsecured and asserted that it held a secured interest in the refrigerator.

BOHANON, Bankruptcy Judge The central issue here is whether the language included in the credit application is sufficient to grant a security interest under the Oklahoma Uniform Commercial Code. Neither the Oklahoma Supreme Court, nor the Court of Appeals for this Circuit, has indicated what precise language is required to create a

security interst in goods purchased with a credit card. Therefore, I will evaluate the plain language of the Uniform Commercial Code and determine whether or not this credit card application is a security agreement.

This statute defines a security interest as "an agreement which creates or provides for a security interest."

Section 9–105(h). The formal requirements are set forth in section 9–203. The relevant provision states that, "a security agreement is not enforceable against the debtor or third parties . . . unless . . . the debtor has signed a security agreement which contains a description of the collateral."

Section 9–110 of the UCC clarifies how the word "description" should be interpreted. It states that, "for the purposes of this Article any description of personal property . . . sufficient whether or not it is specific if it reasonably identifies what is described." While the UCC encourages courts to interpret "description" liberally so as to avoid requiring a precise detailed description such as a serial number, the agreement must at a minimum "do the job assigned." That job is to sufficiently describe the collateral so that a third party would reasonably identify the items which are subject to the security interest.

The credit application here states that the card issuer, "will have a purchase money security interest in all merchandise purchased on [the] account until such merchandise is paid in full." The description "all merchandise" is vague, broad, and fails to sufficiently identify a refrigerator.

It is understandable for a creditor to desire one catchall-phrase which creates a security agreement in every possible situation. However, in doing so, it may not ignore one of the primary reasons for creating a security interest which is to give notice to a third party. This can only be achieved by describing what property is subject to the security interest.

Oklahoma courts have held that the following were sufficient descriptions for section 9–110 purposes: "laundry equipment" when referring to a washing machine; "all machinery," and "paving equipment" to describe a wheel loader; and the words "pickup truck" were sufficient even though the borrower owned two pickup trucks. A reasonable party would understand those descriptions alone, with no need to inquire further. One could be reasonably certain, based on those descriptions, of what collateral is secured. This is not so with the description "all merchandise." This description could conceivably cover any type of item.

In conclusion, no reasonable party would understand that a security interest was created by merely looking to the description itself. This court can only conclude that the word "merchandise" does not sufficiently describe the collateral at issue here. Accordingly, it is determined that Sight'N Sound does not have a security interest in the refrigerator.

Judgment against Sight'N Sound.

Note: Although this case was decided under the 1972 version of Article 9, the same result would be expected under Revised Article 9, which places more emphasis on the nature of the description.

CYBERLAW IN ACTION

Revised Article 9 Is E-Commerce Friendly

The revision to Article 9 that became effective in most states on July 1, 2001, is friendlier to e-commerce than the version it replaced. It no longer requires that the debtor "sign" a "security agreement" to create an enforceable interest in the collateral that supports the loan or performance obligation. Instead, it allows an "authenticated record"—one produced by the consumer online—to substitute for the signed "writing" of the earlier versions of Article 9 and the earlier state laws that Article 9 replaced. This is very advantageous for the buyer who wants to finance, for example, the purchase of an expensive computer or camera without using a credit card to pay for the purchase. The buyer will be able to complete the purchase transaction using an Internet seller of the type of merchandise desired and also finalize the secured transaction at the same time and using the same Internet-based system provided on the seller's website. If the seller is providing financing, in a "purchase-money" transaction, the seller can obtain an enforceable sales contract, an enforceable security agreement, and get the goods heading toward the consumer from the seller's warehouse without delay. The seller in many states also will be able to file an "authenticated record" in substitution for a paper "financing statement" and can complete the filing (and perhaps even pay the filing fee) using e-commerce applications.

Like the "click-through" method of forming a contract described in Chapter 9, click-through secured transactions give the buyer and seller the time- and money-saving advantages of other online transactions. They have similar risks to those present in the pure sales portion of the transaction—of unscrupulous persons trying to take advantage of either the buyer or seller, or both. But the speed and convenience are likely to outweigh the risks for many consumers and many sellers as well.

Future Advances

A security agreement may stipulate that it covers advances of credit to be made at some time in the future [9–204(3)]. Such later extensions of credit are known as **future advances.** Future advances would be involved where, for example, a bank grants a business a line of credit for $100,000 but initially advances only $20,000. When the business draws further against its line of credit, it has received a future advance and the bank is considered to have given additional "value" at that time. The security interest that the creditor obtained earlier also covers these later advances of money.

After-Acquired Property

A security agreement may be drafted to grant a creditor a security interest in the **after-acquired property** of the debtor. After-acquired property is property that the debtor does not currently own or have rights in but that he may acquire in the future. However, the security interest does not attach until the debtor actually obtains some rights to the new property [9–203(b)(2)].[2] For example, Dan's Diner borrows $25,000 from the bank and gives it a security interest in all of its present restaurant equipment as well as all of the restaurant equipment that it may "hereafter acquire." If Dan's owns only a stove at the time, then the bank has a security interest only in the stove. However, if a month later Dan's buys a refrigerator, the bank's security interest would "attach" to the refrigerator when Dan's acquires some rights to it.

A security interest in after-acquired property may not have priority over certain other creditors if the debtor acquires his new property subject to what is known as a **purchase money security interest.** When the seller of goods retains a security interest in goods until they are paid for, or when money is loaned for the purpose of acquiring certain goods and the lender takes a security interest in those goods, the security interest is a purchase money security interest. Later in this chapter, the section entitled Priority Rules discusses the rights of the holder of a purchase money security interest versus the rights of another creditor who filed earlier on after-acquired property of the debtor.

Proceeds

The creditor is commonly interested in having his security interest cover not only the collateral described in the agreement but also the **proceeds** on the disposal of the collateral by the debtor. For example, if a bank lends money to Dealer to enable Dealer to finance its inventory of new automobiles and the bank takes a security interest in the inventory, the bank wants its interest to continue in any cash proceeds obtained by Dealer when the automobiles are sold to customers. Under the 1998 amendments to Article 9, these proceeds are automatically covered as of the time the security interest attaches to the collateral [9–203(f)].

Perfecting the Security Interest

Perfection

While attachment of a security interest to collateral owned by the debtor gives the creditor rights vis-à-vis the debtor, a creditor is also concerned about making sure that she has a better right to the collateral than any other creditor if the debtor defaults. In addition, a creditor may be concerned about protecting her interest in the collateral if the debtor sells it to someone else. The creditor gets protection against other creditors or purchasers of the collateral by perfecting her security interest. Perfection is not effective without an attachment of the security interest [9–308(a)].

Under the Code, there are three main ways of perfecting a security interest:

1. By filing a public notice of the security interest.
2. By the creditor taking possession or control of the collateral.
3. In certain transactions, by mere attachment of the security interest; this is known as automatic perfection.

Perfection by Public Filing

The most common way of perfecting a security interest is to file a **financing statement** in the appropriate public office. The financing statement serves as constructive notice to the world that the creditor claims an interest in collateral that belongs to a certain named debtor. The financing statement usually consists of a multicopy form that is available from the office of the secretary of state (see Figure 1). However, the security agreement can be

---

[2]The Code imposes an additional requirement as to security interests in after-acquired consumer goods. Security interests do not attach to consumer goods other than "accessions" unless the consumer acquires them within 10 days after the secured party gave value [9–203(b)].

Figure 1 *A Financing Statement*

UCC FINANCING STATEMENT
FOLLOW INSTRUCTIONS (front and back) CAREFULLY

A. NAME & TELEPHONE OF CONTACT AT FILER (optional)

B. SEND ACKNOWLEDGMENT TO: (Name and Address)

THE ABOVE SPACE IS FOR FILING OFFICE USE ONLY

1. DEBTOR'S EXACT FULL LEGAL NAME -insert only <u>one</u> debtor name (1a or 1b) - do not abbreviate or combine names

1a ORGANIZATION'S NAME

OR

1b INDIVIDUAL'S LAST NAME	FIRST NAME	MIDDLE NAME	SUFFIX

1c MAILING ADDRESS	CITY	STATE	POSTAL CODE	COUNTRY

1d TAX ID SSN OR EIN	ADD'L INFO RE ORGANIZATION DEBTOR	1e TYPE OF ORGANIZATION	1f JURISDICTION OF ORGANIZATION	1g ORGANIZATIONAL ID #, if any	☐ NONE

2. ADDITIONAL DEBTOR'S EXACT FULL LEGAL NAME - insert only <u>one</u> debtor name (2a or 2b) - do not abbreviate or combine names

2a ORGANIZATION'S NAME

OR

2b INDIVIDUAL'S LAST NAME	FIRST NAME	MIDDLE NAME	SUFFIX

2c MAILING ADDRESS	CITY	STATE	POSTAL CODE	COUNTRY

2d TAX ID SSN OR EIN	ADD'L INFO RE ORGANIZATION DEBTOR	2e TYPE OF ORGANIZATION	2f JURISDICTION OF ORGANIZATION	2g ORGANIZATIONAL ID #, if any	☐ NONE

3. SECURED PARTY'S NAME (or NAME of TOTAL ASSIGNEE of ASSIGNOR S/P) - insert only <u>one</u> secured party name (3a or 3b)

3a ORGANIZATION'S NAME

OR

3b INDIVIDUAL'S LAST NAME	FIRST NAME	MIDDLE NAME	SUFFIX

3c MAILING ADDRESS	CITY	STATE	POSTAL CODE	COUNTRY

4. This FINANCING STATEMENT covers the following collateral

5. ALTERNATIVE DESIGNATION (if applicable) ☐ LESEE/LESSOR ☐ CONSIGNEE/CONSIGNOR ☐ BAILEE/BAILOR ☐ SELLER/BUYER ☐ AG LIEN ☐ NON-UCC FILING

6. ☐ This FINANCING STATEMENT is to be filed (for record)(or recorded) in the REAL ESTATE RECORDS   Attach Addendum   If applicable | 7. Check to REQUEST SEARCH REPORT(S) on Debtor(s) [ADDITIONAL FEE]   (optional) ☐ ALL DEBTORS ☐ DEBTOR 1 ☐ DEBTOR 2

8. OPTIONAL FILER REFERENCE DATA

FILING OFFICE COPY—NATIONAL UCC FINANCING STATEMENT (FORM UCC1) (REV. 07/29/98)

continued

Figure 1   *A Financing Statement (continued)*

UCC FINANCING STATEMENT ADDENDUM
FOLLOW INSTRUCTIONS (front and back) CAREFULLY

9. NAME OF FIRST DEBTOR (1a or 1b) ON RELATED FINANCING STATEMENT

9a ORGANIZATION'S NAME	

OR

9b INDIVIDUAL'S LAST NAME	FIRST NAME	MIDDLE NAME SUFFIX

10. MISCELLANEOUS:

THE ABOVE SPACE IS FOR FILING OFFICE USE ONLY

11. ADDITIONAL DEBTOR'S EXACT LEGAL NAME -insert only one name (11a or 11b) - do no abbreviate or combine names

11a ORGANIZATION'S NAME

OR

11b INDIVIDUAL'S LAST NAME	FIRST NAME	MIDDLE NAME	SUFFIX

11c MAILING ADDRESS	CITY	STATE	POSTAL CODE	COUNTRY

11d TAX ID SSN OR EIN	ADD'L INFO RE ORGANIZATION DEBTOR	11e TYPE OF ORGANIZATION	11f JURISDICTION OF ORGANIZATION	11g ORGANIZATIONAL ID #, if any	☐ NONE

12. ☐ ADDITIONAL SECURED PARTY'S or ☐ ASSIGNOR S/P'S NAME -insert only one name (12a or 12b)

12a ORGANIZATION'S NAME

OR

12b INDIVIDUAL'S LAST NAME	FIRST NAME	MIDDLE NAME	SUFFIX

12c MAILING ADDRESS	CITY	STATE	POSTAL CODE	COUNTRY

13. This FINANCING STATEMENT covers ☐ timber to be cut or ☐ as extracted collateral, or is filed as a ☐ future filing.

14. Description of real estate

16. Additional collateral description

15. Name and address of a RECORD OWNER of above-described real estate (if Debtor does not have a record interest):

17. Check only if applicable and Check only one box

Debtor is a ☐ Trust or ☐ Trustee acting with respect to property held in trust or ☐ Decedent's estate

18. Check only if applicable and check only one box.
☐ Debtor is a TRANSMITTING UTILITY
☐ Filed in connection with a Manufacturing-Home Transaction—effective 30 years
☐ Filed in connection with a Public Finance Transaction—effective 30 years

FILING OFFICE COPY—NATIONAL UCC FINANCING STATEMENT ADDENDUM (FORM UCC1Ad) (REV. 07/29/98) filed as the financing statement if it contains the required information and has been signed by the debtor.

To be sufficient, the financing statement must (1) contain the names of the debtor; (2) give the name of the secured party; and (3) contain a statement indicating or describing the collateral covered by the financing statement. If the financing statement covers goods that are to become fixtures, a description of the real estate must be included.

Each state specifies by statute where the financing statement has to be filed. In all states, a financing statement that covers fixtures must be filed in the office where a mortgage on real estate would be filed [9–501]. To obtain maximum security, the secured party acquiring a security interest in property that is a fixture or is to become a fixture should double file—that is, file the security interest as a fixture and as a nonfixture.

In regard to collateral other than fixtures, most states require only central filing, usually in the office of the secretary of state. However, if you are a creditor taking a security interest, it is important to check the law in your state to determine where to file the financing statement (9–501).

A financing statement is effective for a period of five years from the date of filing, and it lapses then unless a continuation statement has been filed before that time. An exception is made for real estate mortgages that are effective as fixture filings—they are effective until the mortgage is released or terminates [9–515].

A **continuation statement** may be filed within six months before the five-year expiration date. The continuation statement must be signed by the secured party, identify the original statement by file number, and state that the original statement is still effective. Successive continuation statements may be filed [9–403(3)].

When a consumer debtor completely fulfills all debts and obligations secured by a financing statement, she is entitled to a **termination statement** signed by the secured party or an assignee of record [9–513].

Possession by Secured Party as Public Notice

Public filing of a security interest is intended to put any interested members of the public on notice of the security interest. A potential creditor of the debtor, or a potential buyer of the collateral, can check the records to see whether anyone else claims an interest in the debtor's collateral. The same objective can be reached if the debtor gives up possession of the collateral to the creditor or to a

third person who holds the collateral for the creditor. If a debtor does not have possession of collateral that he claims to own, then a potential creditor or debtor is on notice that someone else may claim an interest in it. Thus, a security interest is perfected by change of possession of collateral from the debtor to the creditor/secured party or his agent [9–313(a)]. For example, Simpson borrows $50 from a pawnbroker and leaves his guitar as collateral for the loan. The pawnbroker's security interest in the guitar is perfected by virtue of her possession of the guitar.

Change of possession is not a common or convenient way for perfecting most security interests in consumer goods. It is more practicable for perfecting security interests in commercial collateral. In fact, it is the only way to perfect a security interest in money [9–312(b)].

Possession of collateral by the creditor is often the best way to perfect a security interest in chattel paper and negotiable documents of title. Possession is also a possible way of perfecting a security interest in inventory. This is sometimes achieved through a **field warehousing arrangement.** For example, a finance company makes a large loan to a peanut warehouse to enable it to buy peanuts from local farmers. The finance company takes a security interest in the inventory of peanuts. It sets up a field warehousing arrangement under which a representative of the finance company takes physical control over the peanuts. This representative might actually fence off the peanut storage area and control access to it. When the peanut warehouse wants to sell part of the inventory to a food processor, it must make a payment to the finance company. Then the finance company's representative will allow the peanut warehouse to take some of the peanuts out of the fenced-off area and deliver them to the processor. In this way the finance company controls the collateral in which it has a security interest until the loan is repaid.

Possession by the creditor is usually not a practicable way of perfecting a security interest in equipment or farm products. In the case of equipment, the debtor needs to use it in the business. For example, if a creditor kept possession of a stove that was sold on credit to a restaurant, it would defeat the purpose for which the restaurant was buying the stove, that is, to use it in its business.

The person to whom the collateral is delivered holds it as bailee, and he owes the duties of a bailee to the parties in interest [9–207].

Perfection by possession by the secured party is illustrated in the case that follows below, *In Re 4-R Management.*

In Re 4-R Management   *208 B.R. 232 (Bankr. N.D. Ala. 1997)*

On June 10, 1994, 4-R Management, by its officers, Chris and Lucretia Ryan, executed a promissory note to the First Bank of Eva. The Ryans signed the note both personally and as officers of 4-R Management. The Ryans also executed a security agreement dated June 10, 1994, pledging one "book coin collection" and various other items, including a tractor, bush hog, farm products, and cattle, as security for the note. The promissory note was incorporated by reference in the separate security agreement. The coin collection was the property of 4-R Management, and the bank took possession of the coins on June 10. In subsequent renewal notes, 4-R Management, in its corporate capacity, expressly granted the bank a security interest in the coin collection.

On November 8, 1995, 4-R Management filed a voluntary petition for relief under the Bankruptcy Code. Subsequently, the Bankruptcy Trustee sought to recover for the bankruptcy estate the coin collection being held by the bank as security. The question of whether the bank or the Bankruptcy Trustee had the better right to the coin collection turned on whether the bank had a perfected security interest in the collection.

Caddell, Bankruptcy Judge Section 9–203(1) of the Alabama Commercial Code, which governs the attachment and enforceability of security interests, provides that a security interest attaches and becomes enforceable when:

(a) The collateral is in the possession of the secured party pursuant to agreement, or the debtor has signed a security agreement which contains a description of the collateral . . . ; and
(b) Value has been given; and
(c) The debtor has rights in the collateral.

Additionally, in order for a secured party to enforce its security interest against the trustee in bankruptcy, the secured party must have perfected its security interest prior to the commencement of the case. Sections 9–304(1) and 9–305 provide that a security interest in money shall be perfected only by the secured party's taking possession. No filing is necessary.

Initially, the court finds that the bank clearly gave "value" for the coin collection by the extension of credit to 4-R Management in satisfaction of subsection 9–203(1)(b). The court further finds that 4-R Management had sufficient rights in the coins under subsection 9–203(1)(c) to grant a security interest in same as the undisputed owner of the collateral. That leaves as the only element in question whether the collateral is in the possession of the bank pursuant to an oral agreement or whether 4-R Management executed a se-

curity agreement describing the collateral within the meaning of subsection 9–203(1)(a).

A security interest is an interest in property that secures payment or performance of an obligation. Generally, a security agreement which contains a description of the collateral and which is signed by the debtor is essential to the creation of a security interest in collateral.

On July 28, 1995, 4-R Management, by and through the Ryans, executed a renewal note to pay off the original debt and expressly granted the bank a security interest in the coin collection in its corporate capacity. On April 26, 1996, 4-R Management executed a second renewal note in satisfaction of the 1995 note and expressly pledged the coins as security for the note. The court finds that the bank has an enforceable security interest in the coins by virtue of these express grants of a security interest by the debtor. The unambiguous language in the notes clearly reflected an intent of the parties that the collateral be given as security for the debt. The court finds that bank perfected its security interest by retaining possession of the coin collection pursuant to sections 9–304(1) and 9–305 of the Alabama Code.

Judgment for First Bank of Eva.

Note: Although this case was decided under the 1972 version of Article 9, the same result would be expected under Revised Article 9. See Revised section 9–313(a).

Control

A secured party can provide a similar form of public notice by controlling the collateral [9–314]. Control is the only perfection method if the collateral is a deposit account [9–312(b)(1)]. A secured party obtains control by

one of three means: (1) the secured party is the bank with which the deposit account is maintained; (2) the debtor, secured party and the bank have agreed that the bank will comply with the secured party's instructions regarding funds in the account; or (3) the secured party becomes the bank's customer for the deposit account.

Perfection by Attachment/ Automatic Perfection

Perfection by mere attachment of the security interest, sometimes known as automatic perfection, is the only form of perfection that occurs without the giving of public notice. It occurs automatically when all the requirements of attachment are complete. This form of perfection is limited to certain classes of collateral; in addition, it may be only a temporary perfection in some situations.

A creditor who sells goods to a consumer on credit, or who lends money to enable a consumer to buy goods, can obtain limited perfection of a security interest merely by attaching the security interest to the goods. A creditor under these circumstances has what is called a **purchase money security interest in consumer goods.** For example, an appliance store sells a television set to Margaret Morse on a conditional sales contract, or time-payment plan. The store does not have to file its purchase money security interest in the set. The security interest is considered perfected just by virtue of its attachment to the set in the hands of the consumer.

Perfection by attachment is not effective if the consumer goods are motor vehicles for which the state issues certificates of title and has only limited effectiveness if the goods are fixtures [9–303]. A later section of this chapter discusses the special rules covering these kinds of collateral.

There are also major limitations to the perfection by attachment principle. As discussed later in the Priority section of this chapter, relying on attachment for perfection does not, in some instances, provide as much protection to the creditor as does public filing.

One potential concern for a creditor is that the use of the collateral will change from that anticipated when the security interest was obtained. It is important that the creditor properly perfect the security interest initially so that it will not be adversely affected by a subsequent change in use and will continue to have the benefit of its initial perfection.

Automatic perfection by attachment of the security interest is illustrated in the following case, *In re Rainer*.

In Re Rainer: Horowitz v. Green Tree Financial Corp.
40 UCC Rep.2d 1123 (Bankr. W.D. N.Y. 2000)

Rainer purchased a Sea Doo-brand personal watercraft (PWC). The purchase was financed by the Green Tree Financial Corporation, which held a purchase money security interest (PMSI) in the PWC. Green Tree Financial did not file a financing statement because it considered the PWC to be "consumer goods"—that is, not a "motor vehicle" for purposes of UCC section 9–302(1).

Rainer filed petitions under Chapter 7 of the Bankruptcy Code. The Bankruptcy Trustee took the position that he had priority over Green Tree Financial because it had filed to file a financing statement to perfect its security interests in the PWC. Green Tree contended that it should have priority over the Bankruptcy Trustee by virtue of its attachment of a purchase money security interest in consumer goods.

KAPLAN, Bankruptcy Judge The parties have framed the matter as a UCC section 9–302(1)(d) question—Is a PWC "consumer goods" but not a "motor vehicle" so that filing is not required?

Both UCC section 9–302 and New York Vehicle and Traffic Law section 2118(a) make it clear that if a vehicle must be titled in New York, then it is only by perfecting under Article 46 of the Vehicle and Traffic Law (which provides for title certificates and disclosure of lienholders on the title certificates) that one could be perfected. Section 2102 of the Vehicle and Traffic Law provides for "exclusions" from the title requirement. One finds that "any vessel under 14 feet in length" is so excluded.

"Title" is only required as to vessels that are 14 feet or longer. This is not surprising. Personal water crafts are a relatively recent development, and PWCs having such significant value as to attract the interest of bankruptcy trustees is even more recent. At the time, the 14-foot limitation was enacted by the New York Legislature (at least 15 years ago) there were few, if any, PWCs as we now know them, and consequently there were few valuable vessels of that size.

Now PWCs (most of which are under 14 feet in length) regularly cost $8,000, $10,000, or even $15,000 "new," and may be worth several thousand dollars "used." And they have become so popular that proper filing under the UCC may well be a substantial cost for volume-lenders and volume-lender/sellers. They would much prefer that the decision to file or not to file be a choice they only make in connection with whether they wish to cut-off a bona fide purchaser for personal use and without knowledge. See UCC section 9–307(2).

So we turn to the argument that the lender need not file on a PWC because of UCC section 9–302(1)(d). As adopted by the State of New York, the pertinent section reads:

1. A financing statement must be filed to perfect all security interests except the following:

(d) A purchase money security interest in consumer goods; but filing is required to perfect such a security interest in a motor vehicle required to be licensed or registered in this state.

"Motor vehicles" is currently defined in the New York State Vehicle and Traffic Law as meaning every "vehicle" that is "operated or driven upon a public highway" and which is powered by any power other than muscular power, with certain enumerated exceptions. Clearly for purposes of the Vehicle and Traffic Law, a vessel could not be a "motor vehicle."

Thus the lender argues that even though "vessels" must now be registered in this state pursuant to the Vehicle and Traffic Law, they are not "motor vehicles" required to be registered in this state. And so, they argue, vessels (at least under 14 feet in length) are not motor vehicles for purposes of the Uniform Commercial Code either.

Judgment shall now enter in favor of the lender because the PWC is too small to require "titling" and is not a "motor vehicle" in UCC terms.

Judgment for Green Tree Financial Corp.

Note: Although this case was decided under the 1972 version of Article 9, the same result would be expected under Revised Article 9.

Motor Vehicles

If state law requires a certificate of title for motor vehicles, then a creditor who takes a security interest in a motor vehicle (other than a creditor holding a security interest in inventory held for sale by a person in the business of selling goods of that kind) must have the security interest noted on the title [9-302]. Suppose a credit union lends Carlson money to buy a new car in a state that requires certificates of title for cars. The credit union cannot rely on filing or on attachment of its security interest in the car to perfect that interest; rather, it must have its security interest noted on the certificate of title.

This requirement protects the would-be buyer of the car or another creditor who might extend credit based on Carlson's ownership of the car. By checking the certificate of title to Carlson's car, a potential buyer or creditor would learn about the credit union's security interest in the car. If no security interest is noted on the certificate of title, the buyer can buy—or the creditor can extend credit—with confidence that there are no undisclosed security interests that would be effective against him.

Fixtures

The Code also provides special rules for perfecting security interests in consumer goods that become fixtures by virtue of their attachment to or use with real property. A creditor with a security interest in consumer goods (including consumer goods that will become fixtures) obtains perfection merely by attachment of her security interest to a consumer good. However, as discussed in the Priority section of this chapter, a creditor who relies on attachment for perfection will not, in some instances, prevail against other creditors who hold an interest in the real estate to which the consumer good is attached unless a special financing statement known as a fixture filing is filed with the real estate records to perfect the security interest [9–102(40); 9–334].

Priority Rules

Importance of Determining Priority

Because several creditors may claim a security interest in the same collateral of a debtor, the Code establishes a set of rules for determining which of the conflicting security interests has priority. Determining which creditor has priority or the best claim takes on particular importance in bankruptcy situations, where, unless a creditor has a perfected secured interest in collateral that fully protects the obligation owed to him, the creditor may realize nothing or only a few cents on every dollar owed to him.

General Priority Rules

The basic rule established by the Code is that when more than one security interest in the same collateral has been filed (or otherwise perfected), the first security interest to be filed (or perfected) has priority over any that is filed (or perfected) later [9–322(a)(1)]. If only one security interest has been perfected, for example, by filing, then that security interest has priority. However, if none of the conflicting security interests has been perfected, then the first security interest to be *attached* to the collateral has priority [9–322(a)(3)].

Thus, if Bank A filed a financing statement covering a retailer's inventory on February 1, 2004, and Bank B filed a financing statement on March 1, 2004, covering that same inventory, Bank A would have priority over Bank B. This is true even though Bank B might have made its loan and attached its security interest to the inventory prior to the time that Bank A did so. However, if Bank A neglected to perfect its security interest by filing and Bank B did perfect, then Bank B would prevail, as it has the only perfected security interest in the inventory.

If both creditors neglected to perfect their security interest, then the first security interest that attached would have priority [9–322(a)(3)]. For example, if Loan Company Y has a security agreement covering a dealer's equipment dated June 1, 2003, and advances money to the dealer on that date, whereas Bank Z does not obtain a security agreement covering that equipment or advance money to the dealer until July 1, 2003, then Loan Company Y has priority over Bank Z. In connection with the last situation, it is important to note that unperfected secured creditors do not enjoy a preferred position in bankruptcy proceedings, thus giving additional importance to filing or otherwise perfecting a security interest.

Purchase Money Security Interest in Inventory

There are several very important exceptions to the general priority rules. First, a **perfected purchase money security interest in inventory** has priority over a conflicting security interest in the same inventory *if* all four of these requirements are met. (1) the purchase money security interest is perfected at the time the debtor receives possession of the inventory, (2) the purchase money secured party gives notification in writing to the prior secured creditor before the debtor receives the inventory, (3) the holder of the competing security interest received notification within five years before the debtor receives the inventory, and (4) the notification states that the person expects to acquire a purchase money security interest in inventory of the debtor and describes the inventory [9–324(b)].

Assume that Bank A takes and perfects a security interest in "all present and after-acquired inventory" of a debtor. Then the debtor acquires some additional inventory from a wholesaler, which retains a security interest in the inventory until the debtor pays for it. The wholesaler perfects this security interest. The wholesaler has a *purchase money security interest* in inventory goods and will have priority over the prior secured creditor (Bank A) if the wholesaler has perfected the security interest by the time the collateral reaches the debtor and if the wholesaler sends notice of its purchase money security interest to Bank A before the wholesaler ships the goods. Thus, to protect itself, the wholesaler must check the public records to see whether any of the debtor's creditors are claiming an interest in the debtor's inventory. When it discovers that some are claiming an interest, it should file its own security interest and give notice of that security interest to the existing creditors [9–324(b) and (c)].

As the following *General Electric Capital Commercial Automotive Finance* case illustrates, the subsequent seller of inventory can obtain a priority position if it files a financing statement and notifies the prior secured party in a timely fashion.

General Electric Capital Commercial Automotive Finance, Inc. v. Spartan Motors, Inc.
675 N.Y.S. 2d 626 (New York Sup. Ct., App. Div. 1998)

On September 28, 1983, a predecessor of General Electric Capital Commercial Automotive Finance (GECC) entered into an "Inventory Security Agreement" with Spartan Motors, in connection with its "floor plan" financing of the dealership's inventory. By assignment of that agreement, GECC acquired a blanket lien (otherwise known as a "dragnet" lien) on Spartan's inventory to secure a debt in excess of $1,000,000. "Inventory" was defined in the agreement as "[a]ll inventory, of whatever kind or nature, wherever located, now owned or hereafter acquired, and all returns, repossessions, exchanges, substitutions, replacements, attachments, parts, accessories and accessions thereto and thereof, and all other goods used or intended to be used in conjunction therewith, and all proceeds thereof (whether in the form of cash, instruments, chattel paper, general intangibles, accounts or otherwise)." This security agreement was duly filed in the office of the Dutchess County Clerk and with Secretary of State for New York State.

On July 19, 1991, Spartan signed a new Wholesale Security Agreement with General Motors Acceptance Corporation (GMAC), in which the latter agreed to finance or "floor-plan" Spartan's inventory. According to its terms, Spartan agreed, inter alia, *as follows:*

In the course of our business, we acquire new and used cars, trucks and chassis ('Vehicles') from manufacturers or distributors. We desire you to finance the acquisition of such vehicles and to pay the manufacturers or distributors therefore.

We agree upon demand to pay to GMAC the amount it advances or is obligated to advance to the manufacturer or distributor for each vehicle with interest at the rate per annum designated by GMAC from time to time and then in force under the GMAC Wholesale Plan.

We also agree that to secure collectively the payment by us of the amounts of all advances and obligations to advance made by GMAC to the manufacturer, distributor or other sellers, and the interest due thereon, GMAC is hereby granted a security interest in the vehicles and the proceeds of sale thereof ("Collateral") as more fully described herein.

The collateral subject to this Wholesale Security Agreement is new vehicles held for sale or lease and used vehicles acquired from manufacturers or distributors and held for sale or lease

We understand that we may sell and lease the vehicles at retail in the ordinary course of business. We further agree that as each vehicle is sold, or leased, we will faithfully and promptly remit to you the amount you advanced or have become obligated to advance on our behalf to the manufacturer, distributor or seller.

GMAC'S Security Agreement was duly filed. In addition, by certified letter dated July 17, 1991, GMAC officially notified GECC of its competing security interest in Spartan's inventory, as follows:

This is to notify you that General Motors Acceptance Corporation holds or expects to acquire purchase money security interests in inventory collateral which will from time to time hereafter be delivered to Spartan Motors Ltd. of Poughkeepsie, New York, and in the proceeds thereof.

Such inventory collateral consists, or will consist, of the types of collateral described in a financing statement, a true copy of which is annexed hereto and made a part hereof.

On May 7, 1992, Spartan paid $121,500 of its own money to European Auto Wholesalers, Ltd. to acquire a 1992 600 SEL Mercedes-Benz. Six days later, on May 13, 1992, GMAC reimbursed Spartan and the vehicle was placed on GMAC's floor plan.

On July 7, 1992, Spartan paid $120,000 of its own money to the same seller to acquire a second 1992 600 SEL Mercedes. Two days later, on July 9, 1992, GMAC reimbursed Spartan for that amount and placed the second vehicle on its floor plan. The two vehicles remained unsold in Spartan's showroom.

A few months later, on or about October 2, 1992, GECC commenced an action against Spartan, seeking $1,180,999.98, representing money then due to GECC under its agreement with Spartan. Claims were also made against the principals of Spartan, upon their guarantees, as well as against GMAC and Mercedes-Benz of North America, Inc. (MBNA), to determine lien priority in the collateral.

After commencement of the litigation, Spartan filed a bankruptcy petition and ceased doing business. GECC, GMAC, and MBNA took possession of and liquidated their respective collateral pursuant to a prior agreement between the parties. Among the assets appropriated and sold by GMAC were two Mercedes-Benz automobiles, which were auctioned for $194,500. GECC settled its claims against all of the defendants except GMAC, which it accused of converting the two Mercedes-Benz vehicles in violation of GECC's earlier security interest.

The trial court granted GECC's motion for summary judgment, finding persuasive GECC's argument that a literal reading of GMAC's security agreement with Spartan, in conjunction with the wording of Uniform Commercial Code Section 9–107(b), required a holding that GMAC had a purchase-money secured interest only to the extent that it paid funds directly to "manufacturers, distributors and sellers" of Spartan's inventory in advance of the transfer of the merchandise to the car dealership. The court reasoned that because "[n]owhere in the contracts of adhesion signed by Spartan with GMAC is there an obligation by GMAC to reimburse Spartan for funds used to purchase automobiles," GECC's previously perfected security interest in all of Spartan's inventory should prevail. GMAC appealed.

Friedman, Judge A perfected purchase-money security interest provides an exception to the general first-in-time, first-in-right rule of conflicting security interest. Thus, a perfected purchase money security interest in inventory has priority over a conflicting prior security interest in the same inventory (see, UCC 9–312 (3)). However, the purported purchase-money security interest must fit within the Uniform Commercial Code definition to qualify for the exception.

Uniform Commercial Code Section 9–107 defines a "purchase money security interest" as a security interest:

(a) taken or retained by the seller of the collateral to secure all or part of its price; or

(b) taken by a person who by making advances or incurring an obligation gives value to enable the debtor to acquire rights in or the use of collateral if such value is in fact so used.

The issue here is therefore whether GMAC's payment as reimbursement to Spartan after it had acquired the two Mercedes-Benz vehicles on two different occasions qualifies as an "advance" or "obligation" that enabled Spartan to purchase the cars, such that GMAC acquired a purchase–money security interest in the vehicles. The arguments *against* finding a purchase-money security interest under these circumstances are basically twofold: Firstly, of the few courts to construe Uniform Commercial Code section 9–107 (b), many have been reluctant to decide that a purchase-money security interest has been created where, as here, title to and possession of the merchandise have passed to the debtor before the loan is advanced. Secondly, the literal wording of the agreement between GMAC and Spartan appears to accord GMAC purchase-money secured status only when the finance company paid Spartan's "manufacturer, distributor or other seller" directly. As the Supreme Court noted, nothing in GMAC's contract with Spartan appears to contemplate any obligation on the part of the financier to "reimburse" the auto dealership for funds that the latter had already expended to purchase merchandise. These two interrelated arguments will be discussed *seriatim*.

(1) Whether after-advanced funds may qualify for purchase-money security status under Uniform Commercial Code section 9–107(b).

Research indicates that there is no judicial authority in New York construing the application of UCC 9–107(b) to a creditor's subsequent reimbursement of a debtor for an antecedent purchase of collateral.

One factor that courts have considered is simple temporal proximity—that is, whether the value is given by the creditor "more or less contemporaneously with the debtor's acquisition of the property."

The authorities are agreed that the critical inquiry, as in all contract matters, is into the intention of the parties. In determining whether a security interest exists, the intent of the parties controls, and that intent may best be determined by examining the language used and considering the conditions and circumstances confronting the parties when the contract was made. In assessing the relationship of the transactions, the test should be whether the availability of the loan was a factor in negotiating the sale, and/or whether the lender was committed at the time of the sale to advance the amount required to pay for the items purchased.

Applying these principles to the matter before us: (1) The record establishes that GMAC's reimbursements to Spartan following its two Mercedes-Benz purchases were only six and two days apart, respectively. (2) GECC does not dispute GMAC's contention that a postpurchase reimbursement arrangement was common in the trade, as well as routine in Spartan's course of dealing with GMAC and its other financiers, depending upon the circumstances of the purchase. For example, GMAC employee Philip Canterino, who handled GMAC's account with Spartan, has averred without contradiction by GECC that although it was customary for GMAC to prepay a car manufacturer before it delivered new vehicles to Spartan's showroom, in a case of the sort at issue here—where the vehicles were difficult to obtain from the manufacturer but were readily available from a distributor—it was not uncommon for GMAC to reimburse Spartan after the cars had been delivered to Spartan's showroom, upon Spartan's presentation of proof of clear title. In the language of Uniform Commercial Code UCC 9–107(b): GMAC was committed to give value to enable the car dealership to acquire rights in the collateral. The value so extended was intended to and in fact did enable Spartan to acquire the two Mercedes-Benzes, as GECC does not seriously suggest that without GMAC's backing Spartan could have afforded to purchase the expensive vehicles. Accordingly, the literal requirements of Uniform Commercial Code section 9–107 (b) are satisfied, notwithstanding the inverted purchase-loan. Because GMAC's loans were "closely allied" with Spartan's inventory acquisitions, GMAC enjoys a purchase-money security interest in the contested merchandise.

(2) Whether GMAC's lien is circumscribed by the precise language of its agreement with Spartan.

It is well established that the terms of a written security agreement may be amplified by "other circumstances including course of dealing or usage of trade or course of performance" (UCC 1–201 (3)). Here, GECC does not deny that, although the written terms of GMAC's contract with Spartan appeared to contemplate a single method of inventory financing (i.e., GMAC's payment to Spartan's sellers in advance of the purchase transaction), in fact it was not at all unusual for the parties to pursue the same end by somewhat different means (i.e., GMAC's posttransaction reimbursement to Spartan for its inventory purchases), as GMAC employee Canterino repeatedly explained.

Generally, the express terms of an agreement and a differing course of performance, course of dealing, and/or usage of trade "shall be construed whenever reasonable as consistent with each other" (UCC 1–215 (4); 2–208 (2)). Only when a consistent construction would be "unreasonable" must express terms control over course of performance, and course of performance prevail over course of dealing and usage of trade. GMAC's election on some occasions to fund Spartan's floor planning by reimbursing the car dealership for its purchases can hardly be considered inconsistent with its decision on other occasions to accomplish the same goal by following the strict wording of the contract and prepaying the supplier directly. Rather, it is only reasonable to consider these two methods of financing to be entirely compatible with one another. Here, GMAC's security agreement and its timely notice to GECC adequately specified the precise nature of the vehicular inventory to which its lien attached, such that GECC should have been alerted to GMAC's claim to the two Mercedes-Benzes; and, as discussed above, it is clear that GMAC and Spartan intended these vehicles to be covered by their financing agreement.

Accordingly, the Supreme Court erred when it found that, having financed the two vehicles at issue here by way of reimbursements—"the very opposite of an advance"—GMAC did not acquire a purchase-money security interest pursuant to Uniform Commercial Code 9–107(b). Rather, since GMAC has established—and GECC does not deny—that GMAC was "obligated" to give value to enable Spartan to acquire rights in the two Mercedes-Benzes, and the purchase and loan transactions were only days apart, it is clear that Spartan's purchase and GMAC's subsequent reimbursement were sufficiently "closely allied" to give GMAC a purchase-money security interest in the subject vehicles. Under these circumstances, we conclude, upon searching the records, that GMAC is entitled to retain the proceeds of the sale of the two contested vehicles and to summary judgment against GECC.

Judgment in favor of GECC reversed and summary judgment granted in favor of GMAC.

Note: Although this case was decided under the 1972 version of Article 9, the same result would be expected under Revised Article 9.

Purchase Money Security Interests in Noninventory Collateral

The second exception to the general priority rule is that a purchase money security interest in collateral other than inventory has priority over a conflicting security interest in the same collateral if the purchase money security interest is perfected at the time the debtor receives the collateral or within 20 days afterward [9–324(a)].

Assume that Bank B takes and perfects a security interest in all the present and after-acquired equipment belonging to a debtor. Then, a supplier sells some equipment to the debtor, reserving a security interest in the equipment until it is paid for. If the supplier perfects the purchase money security interest by filing at the time the debtor obtains the collateral or within 20 days thereafter, it has priority over Bank B. This is because its purchase money security interest in noninventory collateral prevails over a prior perfected security interest if the purchase money security interest is perfected at the time the debtor takes possession or within 20 days afterward.

Rationale for Protecting Purchase Money Security Interests

The preference given to purchase money security interests, provided that their holders comply with the statutory procedure in a timely manner, serves several ends. First, it prevents a single creditor from closing off all other sources of credit to a particular debtor and thus possibly preventing the debtor from obtaining additional inventory or equipment needed to maintain his business. Second, the preference makes it possible for a supplier to have first claim on inventory or equipment until it is paid for, at which time it may become subject to the after-acquired property clause of another creditor's security agreement. By requiring that the first perfected creditor be given notice of a purchase money security interest at the time the new inventory comes into the debtor's inventory, the Code serves to alert the first creditor to the fact that some of the inventory on which it may be relying for security is subject to a prior secured interest until the inventory is paid for.

Buyers in the Ordinary Course of Business

A third exception to the general priority rule is that a **buyer in the ordinary course of business** (other than a person buying farm products from a person engaged in farming operations) takes free from a security interest created by his seller even though the security interest is perfected and even though the buyer knows of its existence [9–320(a)]. For example, a bank loans money to a dealership to finance that dealership's inventory of new automobiles and takes a security interest in the inventory, which it perfects by filing. Then, the dealership sells an automobile out of inventory to a customer. The customer takes the automobile free of the bank's security interest even though the dealership may be in default on its loan agreement and even if the customer knows about the bank's interest. As long as the customer is a buyer in the ordinary course of business, she is protected. The reasons for this rule are that a bank really expects to be paid from the proceeds of the dealership's automobile sales and that the rule is necessary to the smooth conduct of commerce. Customers would be very reluctant to buy goods if they could not be sure they were getting clear title to them from the merchants from whom they buy.

Artisan's and Mechanic's Liens

The Code also provides that certain liens arising by operation of law (such as an artisan's lien) have priority over a perfected security interest in the collateral [9–333]. For example, Marshall takes her automobile, on which a credit union has a perfected security interest, to Frank's Garage to have it repaired. Under common or statutory law, Frank's may have a lien on the car to secure payment for the repair work; such a lien permits Frank's to keep the car until it receives payment. If Marshall defaults on her loan to the credit union, refuses to pay Frank's for the repair work, and the car is sold to satisfy the liens, Frank's is entitled to its share of the proceeds before the credit union gets anything.

Liens on Consumer Goods Perfected by Attachment/Automatic Perfection

A retailer of consumer goods who relies on attachment of a security interest to perfect it prevails over other creditors of the debtor-buyer. However, the retailer does not prevail over someone who buys the collateral from the debtor if the buyer (1) has no knowledge of the security interest; (2) gives value for the goods; and (3) buys the goods for his personal, family, or household use [9–320(b)]. The retailer does not have priority over such a **bona fide purchaser** unless it filed its security interest.

For example, an appliance store sells a television set to Arthur for $750 on a conditional sales contract, reserving a security interest in the set until Arthur has paid for it. The store does not file a financing statement, but relies on attachment for perfection. Arthur later borrows money from a credit union and gives it a security interest in the television set. When Arthur defaults on his loans and the credit union tries to claim the set, the appliance store has a better claim to the set than does the credit union. The credit union then has the rights of an unsecured creditor against Arthur. The first to attach has priority if neither security interest is perfected [9–322(a)(2)].

Now, suppose Arthur sells the television set for $500 to his neighbor Andrews. Andrews is not aware that Arthur still owes money on the set to the appliance store. Andrews buys it to use in her home. If Arthur defaults on his obligation to the store, it cannot recover the television set from Andrews. To be protected against such a purchaser from its debtor, the appliance store must file a financing statement rather than relying on attachment for perfection [9–320(b)].

Fixtures

A separate set of problems is raised when the collateral is goods that become fixtures by being so related to particular real estate that an interest in them arises under real estate law. Determining the priorities among a secured party with an interest in the fixtures, subsequent purchasers of the real estate, and those persons who have a secured interest such as a mortgage on the real property, can involve both real estate law and the Code. The general rule is that the interest of an encumbrancer of real estate (such as a mortgagor) or the interest of the owner of real estate (other than the debtor) has priority over a security interest in fixtures [9–334(c)]. However, a perfected security interest in fixtures has priority over the conflicting interest of an encumbrancer or owner of the real property if (1) the debtor has an interest of record in the real property or is in possession of it, (2) the security interest is a purchase money security interest, (3) the interest of the encumbrancer arose before the goods became fixtures, and (4) the fixtures' security interest is perfected by a "fixtures filing" either before the goods became fixtures or within 20 days after the goods became fixtures [9–334(d)].

For example, Restaurant Supply sells Arnie's Diner a new stove on a conditional sales contract, reserving a security interest until Arnie's pays for it. The stove is to be installed in a restaurant where Arnie's is in possession under a 10-year lease. Restaurant Supply can ensure that its purchase money security interest in the stove will have priority over a conflicting claim to the stove by the owner of the restaurant and anyone holding a mortgage on the restaurant if Restaurant Supply (1) enters into a security agreement with Arnie's prior to the time the stove is delivered to him and (2) perfects its security interest by fixture filing before the stove is hooked up by a plumber or within 20 days of that time.

The Code contains several others rules concerning the relative priority of a security interest in fixtures [9–334(e)–(h)]. For example, the secured party whose interest in fixtures is perfected will have priority where (1) the fixtures are removable factory or office machines or readily removable replacements of domestic appliances that are consumer goods and (2) the security interest is perfected *prior* to the time the goods become fixtures. Suppose Harriet's dishwasher breaks and she contracts with an appliance store to buy a new one on a time-payment plan. The mortgage on Harriet's house provides that it covers the real property along with all kitchen appliances or their replacements. The appliance store's security interest will have priority on the dishwasher over the interest of the mortgage if the appliance store perfects its security interest prior to the time the new dishwasher is installed in Harriet's home [9–334(e)(2)]. Perfection in consumer goods can, of course, be obtained merely by attaching the security interest through the signing of a valid security agreement.

Note that a creditor holding a security interest in consumer goods that become fixtures who relies on attachment for perfection prevails over other creditors with an interest in the real property *only* where the consumer goods are "readily removable replacements for domestic appliances."

Suppose a hardware store takes a security interest in some storm windows. Because the storm windows are likely to become fixtures through their use with the homeowner's home, the hardware store cannot rely merely on attachment to protect its security interest. It should file a financing statement to protect that security interest against other creditors of the homeowner with an interest in his home. This rule helps protect a person interested in buying the real property or a person considering lending money based on the real property. By checking the real estate records, the potential buyer or creditor would learn of the hardware store's security interest in the storm windows.

Once a secured party has filed his security interest as a fixture filing, he has priority over purchasers or encumbrances whose interests are filed after that of the secured party [9–334(e)(1)].

Where the secured party has priority over all owners and encumbrancers of the real estate, he generally has the right on default to remove the collateral from the real estate. However, he must make reimbursement for the cost of any physical injury caused to the property by the removal.

Default and Foreclosure

Default

The Code does not define what constitutes default. Usually the creditor and debtor state in their agreement what events constitute a default by the buyer, subject to the Code requirement that the parties act in "good faith" in doing so. If the debtor defaults, the secured creditor has several options:

1. Forget the collateral, and sue the debtor on his note or promise to pay.

2. Repossess the collateral, and use strict foreclosure—in some cases—to keep the collateral in satisfaction of the remaining debt.

3. Repossess and sell the collateral, and then, depending on the circumstances, either sue for any deficiency or return the surplus to the debtor.

Right to Possession

The agreement between the creditor and the debtor may authorize the creditor to repossess the collateral in case of default. If the debtor does default, the creditor is entitled under the Code to possession of the collateral. If through self-help the creditor can obtain possession peaceably, he may do so. However, if the collateral is in the possession of the debtor and cannot be obtained without disturbing the peace, then the creditor must take court action to repossess the collateral [9–609]. See the

CONCEPT REVIEW

Outcome of Priority Contests

Parties	Outcome of Contest
Secured Party vs. Debtor	Secured party has priority [9–201(a); 9–203].

Secured Party vs. Secured Party (as to collateral other than fixtures)	1. *General rule for nonfixtures,* When more than one security interest in the collateral has been filed or otherwise perfected, the first security interest to be filed or perfected has priority over other security interests so long as there is no period after the filing or perfection when there is neither filing nor perfection [9–322(a)]. In addition,
	    a. a perfected security interest has priority over an unperfected security interest [9–322(a)].
	    b. if neither conflicting security interest is perfected, then the first security interest to attach has priority over the later-attached security interest [9–322(a)]
	2. *Purchase money security interest exceptions to the general rule.* Purchase money security interests are able to gain priority over other perfected security interests under some circumstances.
	    a. *Inventory purchase.* A perfected purchase money security interest in inventory has priority over a conflicting interest in the same inventory if the purchase money security interest is perfected when the debtor receives possession of the inventory, the purchase money secured party notifies the holder of the conflicting security interest, the holder of the conflicting security interest receives the notification within five years before the debtor receives possession of the inventory, and the notification states that the sender has or expects to acquire a purchase money security interest in inventory of the debtor and describes the inventory [9–324(b)].
	    b. *Livestock purchase money security interests.* [See 9–324(d)].
	    c. *Collateral other than inventory and livestock.* A perfected purchase money security interest in goods other than inventory or livestock has priority over a conflicting security interest in the same goods if the purchase money security interest is perfected when the debtor receives possession of the collateral or within 20 days after the debtor receives possession of the goods [9–324(a)].
	3. *Exceptions for possessory liens arising by operation of law.* Liens that arise under other state statutes—such as those that create liens in favor of artisans and mechanics—have priority over perfected security interests in the same collateral so long as the artisan has possession of the collateral unless the statute expressly provides that the lien does not have priority. To obtain priority, these liens must secure payment or performance of services or materials furnished by a person in the ordinary course of the person's business [9–333].

Secured Creditor vs. Creditor with Interest in Real Property on Which Fixture is Located	1. *General rule.* Except as expressly provided in 9–334(d)–(h), a security interest in fixtures is subordinate to a conflicting interest of an encumbrancer or owner of the related real property other than the debtor [9–334(c)].
	2. *Exceptions to the general rule*
	    a. *Purchase money security interests.* A perfected security interest in fixtures has priority over a conflicting interest of an encumbrancer or owner of the real property if the debtor has an interest of record in or is in possession of real property, the security interest of the encumbrancer or owner arises before the goods become fixtures, and the security interest is perfected by fixture filing before the goods became fixtures or within 20 days afterward.
	    b. *Interest in special classes of fixtures.* A perfected security interest in fixtures has priority over the encumbrancer or owner of record of real property if before the goods become fixtures, (1) the security interest was perfected by any of the means permitted by the Code, (2) the fixtures are readily removable, and (3) the fixtures are one of the following types: factory or office machines, equipment that is not primarily used or leased for use in the operation of the real property, or replacements of domestic appliances (such as washing machines or dishwashers that are consumer goods [9–324(e)].

CONCEPT REVIEW

Outcome of Priority Contests (concluded)

Buyers of Collateral from Debtor Versus Secured Creditor

1. *General rule.* A security interest in collateral continues despite the debtor's sale of the collateral to another person unless the secured party authorized the sale or disposition free of the security interest [9–315(a)(1)].

2. *Exceptions for buyers.* There are several exceptions to the general rule. The two most common exceptions are:

   a. *Buyers in the ordinary course of the seller's business of items in inventory.* Buyers in the ordinary course of the seller's business take free of security interests created by the seller in the favor of a secured party even if the security interest is perfected and the buyer knows of its existence. This rule applies to consumer as well as commercial buyers of inventory [9–320(a); 1–202(9)]. This rule does not cover buyers of farm products from a person engaged in farming operations.

   b. *Exceptions for buyers of consumer goods from other consumers.* Unless the secured party perfects by possession, a consumer who buys consumer goods from another consumer takes free of a security interest even if perfected if the buyer buys without knowledge of the security interest, for value, primarily for personal, family, or household purposes, and before the secured party has filed a financing statement covering the goods [9–320(b)].

Ivy v. General Motors Acceptance Corp. case, which follows shortly, for a discussion of what constitutes repossession without breach of the peace.

If the collateral is intangible, such as accounts, chattel paper, instruments, or documents, *and performance has been rendered to the debtor,* the secured party may give notice and have payments made or performance rendered to her [9–607].

Sale of the Collateral

The secured party may dispose of the collateral by sale or lease or in any manner calculated to produce the greatest benefit to all parties concerned. However, the method of disposal must be commercially reasonable [9–610; 9–627]. Notice of the time and place of a public sale must be given to the debtor, as must notice of a private sale. If the creditor decides to sell the collateral at a public sale such as an auction, then the creditor must give the debtor accurate advance notice of the time and place of the public sale. Similarly, if the creditor proposes to make a private sale of the collateral, notice must be given to the debtor. This gives the debtor a chance to object to the proposed private sale if she considers it not to be commercially reasonable or to otherwise protect her interests [9–613].

Until the collateral is actually disposed of by the creditor, the buyer has the right to *redeem* it. This means that if the buyer tenders fulfillment of all obligations secured by the collateral as well as of the expenses incurred by the secured party in retaking, holding, and preparing the collateral for disposition, she can recover the collateral from the creditor [9–623].

Consumer Goods

If the creditor has a security interest in consumer goods and the debtor has paid 60 percent or more of the purchase price or debt (and has not agreed in writing to a strict foreclosure), the creditor must sell the repossessed collateral. If less than 60 percent of the purchase price or debt related to consumer goods has been paid, and as to any other security interest, the creditor may propose to the debtor that the seller keep the collateral in satisfaction of the debt. The consumer-debtor has 20 days to object in writing. If the consumer objects, the creditor must sell the collateral. Otherwise, the creditor may keep the collateral in satisfaction of the debt [9–620].

Distribution of Proceeds

The Code sets out the order in which any proceeds are to be distributed after the sale of collateral by the creditor. First, any expenses of repossessing, storing, and selling the collateral, including reasonable attorney's fees, are paid. Second, the proceeds are used to satisfy the debt of the creditor who conducts the sale. Third, any junior interests or liens are paid. Finally, if any proceeds remain, the debtor is entitled to them. If the proceeds are not sufficient to satisfy the debt, then the creditor is usually entitled to a **deficiency judgment.** This means that the debtor remains personally liable for any debt remaining after the sale of the collateral [9–615(d)(2)].

For example, suppose a loan company lends Christy $5,000 to purchase a car and takes a security interest. After making several payments and reducing the debt to $4,800, Christy defaults. The loan company pays $50 to have the car repossessed and then has it sold at an auction, where it brings $4,500, thus incurring a sales commission of 10 percent ($450) and attorney's fees of $150. The repossession charges, sales commission, and attorney's fees, totaling $650, are paid first from the $4,500

proceeds. The remaining $3,650 is applied to the $4,800 debt, leaving a balance due of $950. Christy remains liable to the loan company for the $950 unless Chris challenges the amount of the deficiency claimed [9–626(a)].

Liability of Creditor

A creditor who holds a security interest in collateral must be careful to comply with the provisions of Article 9 of the Code. A creditor acting improperly in repossessing collateral or in its foreclosure and sale is liable to the parties injured. Thus, a creditor can be liable to a debtor if she acts improperly in repossessing or selling collateral [9–625; 9–627]. This potential liability is illustrated in the case of *Ivy v. General Motors Acceptance Corp.,* which follows.

Ivy v. General Motors Acceptance Corp.   *612 So.2d 1108 (Miss. Sup. Ct. 1992)*

Lester Ivy borrowed money from General Motors Acceptance Corp. (GMAC) to purchase a van, and GMAC acquired a security interest in the van. The security agreement contained a so-called insecurity clause that provided GMAC with the right to repossess the van immediately upon default; notice was not a prerequisite to repossession. Ivy defaulted on his obligation on the loan, and GMAC hired American Lenders Service of Jackson to repossess Ivy's van. About 6:30 A.M., Dax Freeman and Jonathan Baker of American Lenders Service drove to Ivy's home. They drove on Ivy's gravel driveway, which is about a quarter-mile long, past a chicken house and the van parked near Ivy's mobile home. They quietly attempted to start the van, but their attempt failed. They then hitched the van to their tow truck and towed it away.

When Freeman and Baker reached the end of Ivy's driveway, Freeman stopped the tow truck and checked the van. At that point he saw someone running from the chicken house toward the mobile home. Ivy testified that prior to running toward the mobile home, he ran toward the tow truck "hollering and flagging for them to stop" but Freeman and Baker apparently did not see or hear Ivy at the time Freeman jumped back into the tow truck, drove off Ivy's property, and onto an adjacent road. Ivy decided to chase after Freeman and Baker because he thought they were stealing his van. He jumped into a pickup truck, passed Freeman and Baker, and—according to them—pulled in front of the tow truck, and slammed on his brakes. Freeman claimed he was forced to slam on his brakes but was unable to avoid a slight collision with the rear bumper of Ivy's truck. Ivy claimed that he stopped well ahead of the tow truck, affording Freeman plenty of time to stop, but that he revved the engine and "rammed him." Ivy claimed that his head hit the rear window of the truck as a result of the collision and that he sustained a "severe cervical sprain." However, Ivy's medical bill totaled only $20 and he did not miss any work.

When Ivy exited his truck, Freeman showed him some "official looking documents," advised him that he worked for American Lenders, and stated that they were repossessing his truck at GMAC's request. There was a dispute as to whether Ivy sought to have the sheriff called concerning the accident. Freeman allowed Ivy to retrieve some personal belongings from the van and gave Ivy a telephone number to call to get his van back; at that point, they all departed the scene.

Seven months later, on October 20, Ivy filed a complaint against GMAC and American Lenders contending that the repossession of his van was invalid because there was a breach of the peace and he had been caused "personal injuries." Ivy sought actual and punitive damages. At the conclusion of a jury trial, the jury awarded Ivy $5,000 in actual damages and $100,000 in punitive damages. The trial court judge set aside the punitive damage award and both parties appealed.

Prather, Judge GMAC contends that its agents did not breach the peace and, therefore, it should not have been liable for actual damages. Ivy, of course, disagrees.

Mississippi law authorizes a creditor or secured party to repossess collateral without judicial process if he or she can do so without breaching the peace. Sec. 9–503. The legislature did not define "breach of peace," but this Court has provided some indication. For example, this court has held that entering a private driveway to repossess collateral without use of force does not constitute a breach of peace. This Court has also held that a creditor, who repossesses collateral despite the fact that the debtor has withheld his or her consent or has strongly objected, did not breach the peace. And, courts in other jurisdictions have generally held that the use of trickery or deceit to peaceably repossess collateral does not constitute a breach of peace.

On the other hand, a Florida Court of Appeal opined that a debtor's "physical objection"—"even from a public street"—bars repossession. A Georgia Court of Appeal found a breach of peace in a case in which: (1) the creditor repossessed the debtor's automobile by blocking it with another automobile; (2) the creditor informed the debtor that he could just "walk his a—home"; and (3) the debtor "unequivocally protested" the manner of repossession. The Ohio Supreme Court opined that the use of intimidation or acts "fraught with the likelihood of violence" constitutes a breach of peace.

In sum, much of the litigation involving self-help repossession statutes involves the issue of whether a breach of peace has occurred. Disposition of this issue is not a simple task: Since physical violence will ordinarily result in a breach of peace, the secured party's right to repossession will end if repossession evokes physical violence, either on the part of the debtor or the secured party. At the other end from physical violence, a secured party may peaceably persuade the debtor to give up the collateral so that no breach of peace occurs. Between those two extreme situations— one in which violence occurs and the other in which the debtor peaceably gives up the collateral—lies the line which divides those cases in which the secured party may exercise self-help repossession and those in which he must resort to the courts. As with most dividing lines, the line between the two extremes is sometimes hard to locate, and even if it is located, it sometimes moves.

Application of the foregoing principles to the evidence viewed in the light most favorable to the verdict leads this Court to conclude that a breach of peace did occur. This Court, therefore, affirms on this issue.

Judgment affirmed awarding actual damages and denying punitive damages.

McRae, Justice, concurring in part and dissenting in part The majority complains that Mississippi case law provides little guidance on determining whether a creditor or agent's conduct is so malicious, oppressive or fraudulent that an award of punitive damages is warranted. While it is true that this Court has not often confronted this issue, the principle is well settled throughout the jurisdictions that punitive damages are proper where creditors seize property in a manner that reflects malice, fraud, oppression, gross negligence, or reckless disregard of the rights of the chattel holder.

In *Kirkwood v. Hickman,* perhaps the only Mississippi case to directly address this question, the Court found that when a creditor commits a trespass to retrieve secured property in an "intentional and highhanded manner," punitive damages are in order even if the trespass involved no violence. What could possibly be more "highhanded" than going onto a debtor's property without permission, hooking the debtor's van to a tow truck, and hauling it away in plain view of the debtor with no explanation whatsoever? In such circumstances the debtor would naturally think his property was being stolen and would set about to recapture the property. If the conduct of GMAC and American Lenders does not qualify as "reckless disregard for the rights of the chattel holder," then I am at a loss to imagine what might fit the description.

Clearly, given Ivy's version of the events the jury was justified in concluding that the conduct of GMAC and American Lenders was oppressive, highhanded and recklessly unmindful of Ivy's rights.

This entire misadventure might have been avoided if the creditor had simply followed the replevin procedures set out in the Mississippi Code. While Mississippi still permits creditors to employ the remedy of self-help when retrieving their property from chattel holders, creditors follow that path at their peril. GMAC and American Lenders in this case took the law into their own hand, and so could be held fully responsible for the consequences. I would reverse the judgment not withstanding the verdict and reinstate the jury's award of punitive damages.

Note: This case was decided under the 1972 version of Article 9, but a similar result would be expected under Revised Article 9. See Revised Section 9–609(b).

ETHICS IN ACTION

What Is the Ethical Thing to Do?

Suppose you own an appliance business in a working-class neighborhood that makes most of its sales on credit. What considerations would you take into account in determining whether and when to foreclose or repossess items on which customers have fallen behind in making their pay-

ments? Should you be swayed by the personal circumstances of your debtors or look only to protecting your financial interests? For example, would you consider the value of the item to the debtor—such as whether it is a necessity for her life, such as a refrigerator, or a luxury? Would you consider the reason the person had fallen behind—that is whether she had been ill or recently lost her job?

Problems and Problem Cases

1. Symons, a full-time insurance salesperson, bought a set of drums and cymbals from Grinnel Brothers. A security agreement was executed between them but was never filed. Symons purchased the drums to supplement his income by playing with a band. He had done this before, and his income from his two jobs was about equal. He also played several other instruments. Symons became bankrupt, and the trustee tried to acquire the drums and cymbals as part of his bankruptcy estate. Grinnel's claimed that the drums and cymbals were consumer goods and thus it had a perfected security interest merely by attachment of the security interest. Were the drums and cymbals consumer goods?

2. On May 19, 1990, Richard Silch purchased a camcorder at Sears Roebuck by charging it to his Sears charge account. Printed on the face of the sales ticket made at that time was the following:

> This credit purchase is subject to the terms of my Sears Charge Agreement which is incorporated herein by reference and identified by the above account number. I grant Sears a security interest or lien in this merchandise, unless prohibited by law, until paid in full.

Silch's signature appeared immediately below that language on the sales ticket. The ticket also contained the brand name of the camcorder and a stock number.

Silch subsequently filed a Chapter 7 bankruptcy proceeding and was eventually discharged. Sears filed a petition to recover the camcorder from Silch, contending that it had a valid and enforceable security interest in the camcorder. Silch, in turn, contended that the sales ticket did not constitute a valid and enforceable security agreement. Does the sales ticket constitute a valid security agreement?

3. Jacob Phillips and his wife, Charlene, jointly owned the Village Variety 5 & 10 Store in Bluefield, Virginia. In addition, Mrs. Phillips was a computer science teacher at the Wytheville Community College. On December 1, 1984, Mrs. Phillips entered into a retail installment sales contract with Holdren's, Inc., for the purchase of a Leading Edge color computer and a Panasonic printer. The contract, which was also a security agreement, provided for a total payment of $3,175.68, with monthly payments of $132.32 to begin on March 5, 1985. On December 1, 1984, Holdren's assigned the contract to Creditway of America. At the time of purchase, Mrs. Phillips advised Holdren's that she was purchasing the computer for professional use in her teaching assignments as well as for use in the variety store. One of the software programs purchased was a practical accounting program for business transactions. Mrs. Phillips also received a special discount price given by Holdren's to state instructors buying for their teaching use. She used the computer in the Village Variety 5 & 10 Store until it closed in April 1985. In June, the Phillipses filed a petition under Chapter 7 of the Bankruptcy Act. At the time, they owed $2,597.79 on the computer. No financing statement was ever filed. Creditway filed a motion in the bankruptcy proceeding, claiming that it had a valid lien on the computer and seeking to be permitted to repossess it. Does Creditway have a perfected security interest in the computer?

4. Nicolosi bought a diamond ring on credit from Rike-Kumber as an engagement present for his fiancèe. He signed a purchase money security agreement giving Rike-Kumber a security interest in the ring until it was paid for. Rike-Kumber did not file a financing statement covering its security interest. Nicolosi filed for bankruptcy. The bankruptcy trustee claimed that the diamond ring was part of the bankruptcy estate because Rike-Kumber did not perfect its security interest. Rike-Kumber claimed that it had a perfected security interest in the ring. Did Rike-Kumber have to file a financing statement to perfect its security interest in the diamond ring?

5. On October 28, 1983, Steve Gresham, doing business as Midway Cycle Sales, entered into a Wholesale Financing Agreement with ITT Commercial Finance Corporation. The agreement was to finance the purchase of new motorcycles from Suzuki Motor Corporation. ITT filed a financing statement with the Indiana secretary of state on December 16, 1983. The description of the collateral in which ITT asserted a security interest included "all inventory . . . replacements and proceeds." On January 9, 1984, Union Bank filed a financing statement with the Indiana secretary of state claiming it was engaged in "floor planning of new motorcycles" for Midway Cycle Sales. In August 1984, ITT began paying Suzuki invoices for Gresham. In July 1985, ITT sent a letter to Union Bank notifying it that it expected to acquire purchase money security interests in the inventory of Stephan Gresham d/b/a Midway Cycle Sales. In early 1986, Union Bank began loaning money to Gresham under its floor planning agreement with him. Actually, Gresham was "double floor planning"—that is, he was taking invoices for motorcycles that had been paid for by ITT to the Union Bank and claiming that he had paid for the motorcycles but had decided to floor plan them. When Union Bank advanced money to him, he used the money to make payments on the loans to ITT. He made no payments to Union Bank and did not pay off all of his loan to ITT. Midway Cycle Sales went bankrupt when Union Bank repossessed 22 new Suzuki motorcycles. ITT brought suit against Union Bank, claiming it had paid for the motorcycles and had a perfected security interest in the motorcycles that had priority over Union Bank's security interest in them. Did ITT's security interest have priority over Union Bank's security interest?

6. On November 18, Firestone & Company made a loan to Edmund Carroll, doing business as Kozy Kitchen. To secure the loan, a security agreement was executed, which listed the items of property included, and concluded as follows: "together with all property and articles now, and which may hereafter be, used or mixed with, added or attached to, and/or substituted for any of the described property." A financing statement that included all the items listed in the security agreement was filed with the town clerk on November 18 and with the secretary of state on November 22. On November 25, National Cash Register Company delivered a cash register to Carroll on a conditional sales contract. National Cash Register filed a financing statement on the cash register with the town clerk on December 20 and with the secretary of state on December 21. Carroll defaulted in his payments to both Firestone and National Cash Register. Firestone repossessed all of Carroll's fixtures and equipment covered by its security agreement, including the cash register, and then sold the cash register. National Cash Register claimed that it was the title owner of the cash register and brought suit against Firestone for conversion. Did Firestone or National Cash Register have the better right to the cash register?

7. Grimes purchased a new Dodge car from Hornish, a franchised Dodge dealer. The sale was made in the ordinary course of Hornish's business. Grimes paid Hornish the purchase price of the car at the time of the sale. Hornish had borrowed money from Sterling Acceptance and had given it a perfected security interest in its inventory, including the car Grimes bought. Hornish defaulted on its loan to Sterling and Sterling then tried to recover the Dodge from Grimes. Was the car Grimes bought from Hornish still subject to Sterling Acceptance's security interest?

8. Benson purchased a new Ford Thunderbird automobile. She traded in her old automobile and financed the balance of $4,326 through the Magnavox Employees Credit Union, which took a security interest in the Thunderbird. Several months later, the Thunderbird was involved in two accidents and sustained major damage. It was taken to ACM for repairs, which took seven months and resulted in charges of $2,139.54. Benson was unable to pay the charges, and ACM claimed a garageman's lien. Does Magnavox Credit Union's lien or ACM's lien have priority?

9. In August, Norma Wade purchased a Ford Thunderbird automobile and gave Ford Motor Credit a security interest in it to secure her payment of the $7,000 balance of the purchase price. When Wade fell behind on her monthly payments, Ford engaged the Kansas Recovery Bureau to repossess the car. On the following February 10, an employee of the Recovery Bureau located the car in Wade's driveway unlocked the door, got in, and started it. He then noticed a discrepancy between the serial number of the car and the number listed in his papers. He shut off the engine, got out, and locked the car. When Wade appeared at the door to her house, he advised her that he had been sent by Ford to repossess the car but would not do so until he had straightened out the serial number. She said that she had been making payments, that he was not going to take the car, and that she had a gun, which she would use. He suggested that Wade contact Ford to straighten out the problem. She called Ford and advised its representative that if she caught anybody on her property again trying to take her car, she would use her gun to "leave him laying right where I saw him." Wade made several more payments, but Ford again contracted to have the car repossessed. At 2:00 AM on March 5, the employee of the Kansas Recovery Bureau successfully took the car from Wade's driveway. She said that she heard a car burning rubber, looked out of her window, and saw that her car was missing. There was no confrontation between Wade and the employee since he had safely left the area before she discovered that the car had been taken. Wade then brought a lawsuit against Ford claiming, that the car had been wrongfully repossessed. She sought actual and punitive damages, plus attorney's fees. Should Ford be held liable for wrongful repossession?

10. Gibson, a collector of rare old Indian jewelry, took two of his pieces to Hagberg, a pawnbroker. The two pieces, a silver belt and a silver necklace, were worth $500 each. Hagberg loaned only $45 on the belt and $50 on the necklace. Gibson defaulted on both loans, and immediately and without notice, the necklace was sold for $240. A short time later, the belt was sold for $80. At the time of their sale, Gibson owed interest on the loans of $22. Gibson sued Hagberg to recover damages for improperly disposing of the collateral. Is Gibson entitled to damages because of Hagberg's actions in disposing of the collateral?

Online Research: Using the Internet to Search for Pre-Existing Security Interests

The company you work for wants to save money by using the Internet to search for Article 9 filings against persons they may sell goods to on credit. They know that some states have all of the filings in computer databases and that some also allow searches from the Internet. Your employer asks you to search the Arizona statewide system and tell him whether you can find everything you need concerning possible Article 9 filings against a prospective customer whose business name is John J. [for Joseph] Smith.

30

BANKRUPTCY

B ob and Sue Brown are a young couple with two small children. Within the past three years they stretched themselves financially in the course of acquiring and furnishing their first home and starting their family. Recently, Bob was laid off from his job managing computer technology operations for a telecom company. Then, Sue was injured in an automobile accident and has been unable to continue substitute teaching. Bob's unemployment benefits are insufficient to provide for the ordinary family expenses, much less meet the heavy financial obligations the family has taken on. The bank has filed a notice of intent to foreclose the mortgage on their home and other creditors have sent letters threatening to repossess their car and furnishings. A friend has suggested that Bob and Sue consult with an attorney who specializes in bankruptcy matters who may be able to get them some relief from their creditors and gain a new start financially.

This situation raises a number of questions that will be addressed in this chapter. They include:

- If the Browns file a petition in bankruptcy, what assets would they be able to retain as exempt from the claims of their creditors?
- Which of their debts could be discharged in a bankruptcy proceeding?
- What advantages and disadvantages would the Browns have if they filed under Chapter 7 (liquidations) as opposed to filing under Chapter 13 (consumer debt adjustments)?

WHEN AN INDIVIDUAL, a partnership, or a corporation is unable to pay its debts to creditors, problems can arise. Some creditors may demand security for past debts or start court actions on their claims in an effort to protect themselves. Such actions may adversely affect other creditors by depriving them of their fair share of the debtor's assets. Also, quick depletion of the debtor's assets may effectively prevent the debtor who needs additional time to pay off his debts from having an opportunity to do so.

At the same time, creditors need to be protected against the actions a debtor in financial difficulty might be tempted to take to their detriment. For example, the debtor might run off with his remaining assets or might use them to pay certain favored creditors, leaving nothing for the other creditors. Finally, a means is needed by which a debtor can get a fresh start financially and not continue to be saddled with debts beyond his ability to pay. This chapter focuses on the body of law and procedure that has developed to deal with the competing interests when a debtor is unable to pay his debts in a timely manner.

The Bankruptcy Act

The Bankruptcy Act is a federal law that provides an organized procedure under the supervision of a federal court for dealing with insolvent debtors. Debtors are considered insolvent if they are unable or fail to pay their debts as they become due. The power of Congress to enact bankruptcy legislation is provided in the Constitution. Through the years, there have been many amendments to the Bankruptcy Act. Congress completely revised the act in 1978 and then passed significant amendments to it in 1984, 1986, and 1994. As this textbook went to press, legislation that would change the Bankruptcy code in a number of areas was under consideration in a House-Senate Conference Committee.

The Bankruptcy Act has several major purposes. One is to ensure that the debtor's property is fairly distributed to the creditors and that some creditors do not obtain unfair advantage over the others. At the same time, the act protects all of the creditors against actions by the debtor that would unreasonably diminish the debtor's assets to which they are entitled. The act also provides the honest debtor with a measure of protection against the demands for payment by his creditors. Under some circumstances, the debtor is given additional time to pay the creditors, freeing him of those pressures creditors might otherwise exert. If the debtor makes a full and honest accounting of his assets and liabilities and deals fairly with his creditors, the debtor may have most—if not all—of the debts discharged so as to have a fresh start.

At one time, **bankruptcy** carried a strong stigma for the debtors who became involved in it. Today, this is less true. It is still desirable that a person conduct her financial affairs in a responsible manner. However, there is a greater understanding that such events as accidents, natural disasters, illness, divorce, and severe economic dislocations are often beyond the ability of individuals to control and may lead to financial difficulty and bankruptcy.

Bankruptcy Proceedings

The Bankruptcy Act covers a number of bankruptcy proceedings. In this chapter, our focus will be on:

1. Straight bankruptcy (liquidations).
2. Reorganizations.
3. Family farms.
4. Consumer debt adjustments.

The Bankruptcy Act also contains provisions regarding municipal bankruptcies, which are not covered in this chapter.

Liquidations

A liquidation proceeding, traditionally called **straight bankruptcy,** is brought under Chapter 7 of the Bankruptcy Act. The debtor must disclose all of the property she owns and surrender this bankruptcy estate to the **bankruptcy trustee.** The trustee separates out certain property that the debtor is permitted to keep and then administers, liquidates, and distributes the remainder of the

bankrupt debtor's estate. There is a mechanism for determining the relative rights of the creditors, for recovering any preferential payments made to creditors, and for disallowing any preferential liens obtained by creditors. If the bankrupt person has been honest in her business transactions and in the bankruptcy proceedings, she is usually given a **discharge** (relieved) of her debts.

Reorganizations

Chapter 11 of the Bankruptcy Act provides a proceeding whereby a debtor can work out a plan to solve its financial problems under the supervision of a federal court. A reorganization plan is essentially a contract between a debtor and its creditors. The proceeding is intended for debtors, particularly businesses, whose financial problems may be solvable if they are given some time and guidance and if they are relieved of some pressure from creditors.

Family Farms

Historically, farmers have been accorded special attention in the Bankruptcy Code. Chapter 12 of the Bankruptcy Act provides a special proceeding whereby a debtor involved in a family farming operation can develop a plan to work out his financial difficulties. Generally, the debtor remains in possession of the farm and continues to operate it while the plan is developed and implemented.

Consumer Debt Adjustments

Under Chapter 13 of the Bankruptcy Act, individuals with regular incomes who are in financial difficulty can develop plans under court supervision to satisfy their creditors. Chapter 13 permits compositions (reductions) of debts and/or extensions of time to pay debts out of the debtor's future earnings.

The Bankruptcy Courts

Bankruptcy cases and proceedings are filed in federal district courts. The district courts have the authority to refer the cases and proceedings to bankruptcy judges, who are considered to be units of the district court. If a dispute falls within what is known as a **core proceeding,** the bankruptcy judge can hear and determine the controversy. Core proceedings include a broad list of matters related to the administration of a bankruptcy estate. However, if a dispute is not a core proceeding but rather involves a state law claim, then the bankruptcy judge can only hear the case and prepare draft findings and conclusions for review by the district court judge.

Certain proceedings affecting interstate commerce have to be heard by the district court judge if any party requests that this be done. Moreover, even the district courts are precluded from deciding certain state law claims that could not normally be brought in federal court, even if those claims are related to the bankruptcy matter. Bankruptcy judges are appointed by the president for terms of 14 years.

Chapter 7: Liquidation Proceedings

Petitions

All bankruptcy proceedings, including liquidation proceedings, are begun by the filing of a petition. The petition may be either a **voluntary petition** filed by the debtor or an **involuntary petition** filed by a creditor or creditors of the debtor. A voluntary petition in bankruptcy may be filed by an individual, a partnership, or a corporation. However, municipal, railroad, insurance, and banking corporations and savings or building and loan associations are not permitted to file for straight bankruptcy proceedings. A person filing a voluntary petition need not be insolvent—that is, her debts need not be greater than her assets. However, the person must be able to allege that she has debts. The primary purpose for filing a voluntary petition is to obtain a discharge from some or all of the debts.

Involuntary Petitions

An involuntary petition is a petition filed by creditors of a debtor. By filing it, they seek to have the debtor declared bankrupt and his assets distributed to the creditors. Involuntary petitions may be filed against many debtors. However, involuntary petitions in straight bankruptcy cannot be filed against (1) farmers; (2) ranchers; (3) nonprofit organizations; (4) municipal, railroad, insurance, and banking corporations; (5) credit unions; and (6) savings or building and loan associations.

If a debtor has 12 or more creditors, an involuntary petition to declare him bankrupt must be signed by at least 3 creditors. If there are fewer than 12 creditors, then an involuntary petition can be filed by a single creditor. The creditor or creditors must have valid claims against the debtor exceeding the value of any security they hold by $12,300 or more. To be forced into involuntary bankruptcy, the debtor must be generally not paying his debts as they become due—or have had a custodian for his property appointed within the previous 120 days.

If an involuntary petition is filed against a debtor engaged in business, the debtor may be permitted to continue to operate the business. However, the court may appoint an **interim trustee** if this is necessary to preserve the bankruptcy estate or to prevent loss of the estate. A creditor who suspects that a debtor may dismantle her business or dispose of its assets at less than fair value may apply to the court for protection.

Automatic Stay Provisions

The filing of a bankruptcy petition operates as an automatic stay, holding in abeyance various forms of creditor action against a debtor or her property. These actions include: (1) beginning or continuing judicial proceedings against the debtor; (2) actions to obtain possession of the debtor's property; (3) actions to create, perfect, or enforce a lien against the debtor's property; and (4) setoff of indebtedness owed to the debtor before commencement of the bankruptcy proceeding. A court may give a creditor relief from the stay if the creditor can show that the stay does not give her "adequate protection" and jeopardizes her interest in certain property. The relief to the creditor might take the form of periodic cash payments or the granting of a replacement lien or an additional lien on property.

Concerned that debtors were taking advantage of the automatic stay provisions to the substantial detriment of some creditors, such as creditors whose claims were secured by an interest in a single real estate asset, in 1994 Congress provided specific relief from the automatic stay for such creditors. Debtors must either file a plan of reorganization that has a reasonable chance of being confirmed within a reasonable time or must be making monthly payments to each such secured creditor that are in an amount equal to interest at a current fair market rate on the value of the creditor's interest in the real estate.

The 1994 amendments also specifically provide that the automatic stay provisions are not applicable to actions to establish paternity, to establish or modify orders for alimony, support, or maintenance, or for the collection of alimony, maintenance, or support from property that is not the property of the bankruptcy estate.

Order of Relief

Once a bankruptcy petition has been filed, the first step is a court determination that relief should be ordered. If a voluntary petition is filed by the debtor, or if the debtor does not contest an involuntary petition, this step is automatic. If the debtor contests an involuntary petition, then a trial is held on the question of whether the court should order relief. The court orders relief only (1) if the debtor is generally not paying his debts as they become due, or (2) if within 120 days of the filing of the petition a custodian was appointed or took possession of the debtor's property. The court also appoints an interim trustee pending election of a trustee by the creditors.

Meeting of Creditors and Election of Trustee

The bankrupt person is required to file a list of her assets, liabilities, and creditors and a statement of her financial affairs. Then a meeting of the creditors is called by the court. Prior to the conclusion of the meeting of creditors, the U.S. Trustee is required to examine the debtor to make sure she is aware of: (1) the potential consequences of seeking a discharge in bankruptcy, including the effects on credit history; (2) the debtor's ability to file a petition under other chapters (such as 11, 12, or 13) of the bankruptcy act; (3) the effect of receiving a discharge of debts; and (4) the effect of reaffirming a debt (discussed later in this chapter).

The creditors may elect a creditors' committee. The creditors also elect a **trustee** who, if approved by the judge, takes over administration of the bankrupt's estate. The trustee represents the creditors in handling the estate. At the meeting, the creditors have a chance to ask the debtor questions about her assets, liabilities, and financial difficulties. These questions commonly focus on whether the debtor has concealed or improperly disposed of assets. (See Figure 1.)

Duties of the Trustee

The trustee takes possession of the debtor's property and has it appraised. The debtor must also turn over her records to the trustee. For a time, the trustee may operate the debtor's business. The trustee sets aside the items of property that a debtor is permitted to keep under state exemption statutes or federal law.

The trustee examines the claims filed by various creditors and objects to those that are improper in any way. The trustee separates the unsecured property from the secured and otherwise exempt property. He also sells the bankrupt's nonexempt property as soon as possible, consistent with the best interest of the creditors.

The trustee is required to keep an accurate account of all the property and money he receives and to promptly deposit moneys into the estate's accounts. At the final meeting of the creditors, the trustee presents a detailed statement of the administration of the bankruptcy estate.

The Bankruptcy Estate

The commencement of a Chapter 7 bankruptcy case by the filing of a voluntary or involuntary petition creates a bankruptcy estate. The estate is composed of all of the debtor's legal and equitable interests in property, including certain community property. Certain property is exempted (see "Exemptions" section below.) The estate also includes:

1. Profits, royalties, rents and revenue, along with the proceeds from the debtor's estate, received during the Chapter 7 proceeding.

2. Property received by the debtor in any of the following ways within 180 days of the filing of the Chapter 7 petition: *(a)* by bequest or inheritance; *(b)* as a settlement with a divorced spouse or as a result of a divorce decree; or *(c)* as proceeds of a life insurance policy.

3. Property recovered by the bankruptcy trustee because *(a)* creditor of the debtor received a voidable preferential transfer or *(b)* the debtor made a fraudulent transfer of her assets to another person. Preferential and fraudulent transfers are discussed later in this chapter.

Exemptions

Even in a liquidation proceeding, the bankrupt is generally not required to give up all of his property; he is permitted to **exempt** certain items of property. Under the Bankruptcy Act, the debtor may choose to keep certain items or property either exempted by state law, or exempt under federal law unless state law specifically forbids use of the federal exemptions. However, any such property concealed or fraudulently transferred by the debtor may not be retained.

The debtor must elect to use *either* the set of exemptions provided by the state or the set provided by the federal bankruptcy law; she may not pick and choose between them. A husband and wife involved in bankruptcy proceedings must both elect either the federal or the state exemptions; where they cannot agree, the federal exemptions are deemed elected.

The **exemptions** permit the bankrupt person to retain a minimum amount of the assets considered necessary to life and to his ability to continue to earn a living. They are part of the fresh start philosophy that is one of the purposes of

Figure 1   *Order and Notice of Chapter 7 Bankruptcy Filing*

B16A	United States Bankruptcy Court for the District of Maryland	ORDER AND NOTICE OF CHAPTER 7 BANKRUPTCY FILING, MEETING OF CREDITORS AND FIXING OF DATES (Individual or Joint Debtor No Asset Case)

A. GENERAL INFORMATION

Name of Debtor John B. Jones D/B/A THE BATH SHOP	Address of Debtor 195 MAIN STREET ANNAPOLIS, MD. 21401

Date Filed 01/24/2003	Case Number 9060300-SD	Soc. Sec. Nos./Tax ID Nos. 050-30-4701

Addressee: WICKER PRODUCTS, INC. 2000 SMITH PIKE ALMA, MI 48030	Address of the Clerk of the Bankruptcy Court United States Bankruptcy Court 101 W. Lombard Street Baltimore, MD 21201
Name and Address of Attorney for Debtor MARC A. BURNS 215 WATER STREET BALTIMORE MD 21202	Name and Address of Trustee BRUCE A. SMITH 136 S. CHARLES STREET BALTIMORE MD 21201

B. DATE, TIME AND LOCATION OF MEETING OF CREDITORS
February 28, 2003, 09:15 A.M., U.S. Trustee, Fallon Federal Bldg., Rm. G-13, 31 Hopkins Plaza, Baltimore, MD 21201

C. DISCHARGE OF DEBTS
Deadline to File a Complaint Objecting to the Discharge of the Debtor or Dischargeability of a Debt: April 30, 2003

D. BANKRUPTCY INFORMATION

THERE APPEAR TO BE NO ASSETS AT THIS TIME FROM WHICH PAYMENT MAY BE MADE TO CREDITORS. DO NOT FILE A PROOF OF CLAIM UNTIL YOU RECEIVE NOTICE TO DO SO.

FILING OF A BANKRUPTCY CASE. A bankruptcy petition has been filed in this court for the person or persons named above as the debtor, and an order for relief has been entered. You will not receive notice of all documents filed in this case. All documents which are filed with the court, including lists for the debtor's property and debts, are available for inspection at the office of the clerk of the bankruptcy court.

CREDITORS MAY NOT TAKE CERTAIN ACTIONS. Anyone to whom the debtor owes money or property is a creditor. Under the bankruptcy law, the debtor is granted certain protection against creditors. Common examples of prohibited actions are contacting the debtor to demand re-payment, taking action against the debtor to collect money owed to creditors or to take property of the debtor, except as specifically permitted by the bankruptcy law, and starting or continuing foreclosure actions, repossessions, or wage deductions. If unauthorized actions are taken by a creditor against a debtor, the court may punish that creditor. A creditor who is considering taking action against the debtor or the property of the debtor should review 11 U.S.C. § 362 and may wish to seek legal advice. The staff of the clerk's office is not permitted to give legal advice to anyone.

MEETING OF CREDITORS. The debtor (both husband and wife in a joint case) shall appear at the meeting of creditors at the date and place set forth above in box 'B' for the purpose of being examined under oath. ATTENDANCE BY CREDITORS AT THE MEETING IS WELCOMED, BUT NOT REQUIRED. At the meeting the creditors may elect a trustee as permitted by law, elect a committee of creditors, examine the debt-or, and transact such other business as may properly come before the meeting. The meeting may be continued or adjourned from time to time without further written notice to the creditors.

LIQUIDATION OF THE DEBTOR'S PROPERTY. A trustee has been appointed in this case to collect the debtor's property, if any, and turn it into money. At this time, however, it appears from the schedules of the debtor that there are no assets from which any dividend can be paid to creditors. If at a later date it appears that there are assets from which a dividend may be paid, creditors will be notified and given an oppor-tunity to file claims.

EXEMPT PROPERTY. Under state and federal law, the debtor is permitted to keep certain money or property as exempt. If a creditor believes that an exemption of money or property is not authorized by law, the creditor may file an objection. Any objection must be filed no later than 30 days after the conclusion of the meeting of creditors.

DISCHARGE OF DEBTS. The debtor is seeking a discharge of debts. A discharge means that certain debts are made unenforceable. Credi-tors whose claims against the debtor are discharged may never take action to collect the discharged debts. If a creditor believes the debtor should not receive a discharge under 11 U.S.C. § 727 or a specific debt should not be discharged under 11 U.S.C. § 523(c) for some valid reason specified in the bankruptcy law, the creditor must take action to challenge the discharge. The deadline for challenging a discharge is set forth above in box 'C.' Creditors considering taking such action may wish to seek legal advice.

DO NOT FILE A PROOF OF CLAIM UNLESS YOU RECEIVE A COURT NOTICE TO DO SO

For the Court:	
January 31, 2003	Michael Kostishak
Date	Clerk of the Bankruptcy Court

the Bankruptcy Act. The general effect of the federal exemptions is to make a minimum exemption available to debtors in all states. States that wish to be more generous to debtors can provide more liberal exemptions.

The specific items that are exempt under state statutes vary from state to state. Some states provide fairly liberal exemptions and are considered "debtors havens." For example, in Florida none of the equity in the debtor's homestead can be used to pay off unsecured creditors, thus allowing even relatively well-off individuals to shield significant assets from creditors. Items that are commonly made exempt from sale to pay debts owed creditors include the family Bible; tools or books of the trade; life insurance policies; health aids, such as wheelchairs and hearing aids; personal and household goods; and jewelry, furniture, and motor vehicles worth up to a certain amount.

The case that follows, *In Re Kyllogen,* illustrates a claim by a debtor for an exemption under a state statute.

In Re Kyllogen   264 B.R.17 (U.S.D.C. D.Minn. 2001)

Facts

Patricia Kyllogen owns a five-acre lot with a home and pole barn located on it; the property has an estimated value of $350,000 and is subject to a $90,000 mortgage. She purchased the property from her parents in 1974 and built the home after she married in 1980. The couple has two daughters. She and her husband David also own an adjacent unimproved lot of approximately five acres located behind the lot with their home. The second lot, which is valued at $45,000, was purchased in 1988. Both lots are heavily wooded with mature oak trees and used to be part of Patricia Kyllogen's parents' family farm.

Much of the surrounding area that once had constituted the family farm has been subdivided into residential parcels of at least two-and-a-half acres or more; many of the parcels contain large, expensive and upscale homes. Three or four nearby properties are occupied by individuals who have full-time outside jobs but who also grow farm crops, primarily hay on a part-time basis.

In 1996 Kyllogen and her husband cleared one-tenth of an acre of land on the front lot and planted ginseng seeds. Ginseng is a small herbal plant harvested for its roots. The longer the root grows before it is harvested the more valuable it is and the earliest one can harvest ginseng root is about five to seven years after it is planted. The ginseng is planted under the shade of mature hardwood trees and, once an area is cleared and the ginseng planted, it requires relatively little care except for periodic weeding. Kyllogen was employed full-time at a Burlington Coat Factory; her husband did not have a regular full-time job, although he described himself as a ginseng farmer. In five years of operation (1996–2000), the ginseng "farm" had no income and approximately $28,000 in tax deductible losses.

Kyllogen filed a petition in bankruptcy. She claimed her home and the two contiguous five-acre parcels as "exempt" assets of the Bankruptcy estate. The Bankruptcy Trustee objected to the claimed exemption, asserting that Kyllogen was entitled to exempt a homestead of no more than one-half of an acre of land in area with a value of no more that $200,000.

Dreher, Bankruptcy Judge A debtor may exempt from her bankruptcy estate certain property which is exempt under applicable state law on the petition filing date.

Section 510.01 of the Minnesota Statutes specifically provides:

> The house owned and occupied by a debtor as the debtor's dwelling place, together with the land upon which it is situated to the amount hereinafter limited and defined, shall constitute the homestead of such debtor and debtor's family, and be exempt from seizure or sale under legal process on account of any debt . . . charged thereon in writing, except such as are incurred for work or materials furnished in the construction, repair, or improvement of such homestead, or for services performed by laborers or servants.

Section 510.02, in turn, defines the area limits of the homestead:

> The homestead may include any quantity of land not exceeding 160 acres, and not included in the laid out or platted portion of any city. If the homestead is within the laid out or platted portion of a city, its area must not exceed one-half of an acre. The value of the homestead exemption, whether the exemption if claimed jointly or individually, may not exceed $200,000, or, if the homestead is used primarily for agricultural purposes, $500,000, exclusive of the limitations set forth in section 510.05.

Generally speaking, exemption laws work in tandem with debt discharge to effectuate a debtor's fresh start. The intent of the homestead exemption is to secure a debtor's home against uncertainties and misfortunes of life and to preserve the home as a dwelling place for the debtor and his or her family. However, the area limitations and other requirements ensure that the debtor does not unfairly retain assets.

* * *

This case is unlike others in which the debtors are clearly family farmers who live and work on the land and use it for agricultural purposes. *Cf. In re Becker* (finding debtors who had farmed for three-plus decades a 58-acre parcel which contained a barn and several outbuildings were entitled to larger homestead exemption). While Debtor testified that she and her family always wanted to farm, nothing in this record shows that they have farmed or are farming. Debtor and, to a lesser extent, her spouse have always been principally employed off the "farm." Moreover, what little "farming" they have engaged in—a fish farm in Wisconsin, one year's worth of failed mushrooms, and upstart wood-cultivated ginseng operations—is not farming in the traditional sense, was and is small-scale, and undertaken even as they maintained outside employment. These farming operations have never provided support for Debtor and her family but instead have merely given them healthy tax write-offs year after year.

Ginseng "farming," which can be done on small plots of wooded property, can be conducted with little or no land. In five years, Debtor and her spouse have planted less than one-half of an acre of land and never expect to harvest more than one-tenth of an acre of crop per year. Debtor and her spouse do not, and never will in their lifetime, need such expansive acreage for their operations even if they stay with wood-cultivated ginseng. What they do can be termed "farming," but it is clearly not agricultural as that term is traditionally understood and is not the sort of "farm" the homestead exemption statute was designed to protect.

Debtor and her spouse fervently testified that they are ginseng farmers, but in actuality, they are a couple who own a very large house on a very large lot, which is virtually surrounded by other very large houses on very large lots, or in a few instances, some smaller houses on sizeable vacant lots, in the country. Debtor has a full-time day job and spends her evenings and weekends pulling weeds and tending small plots of ginseng, akin to a city resident who maintains a backyard vegetable garden. Her spouse likewise has historically had a full-time day job, usually as an electrical contractor, with his various "farming" operations being secondary or on the side. Debtor and her spouse are not farming their parcels in any true sense, and there is nothing inherently agricultural about what they are doing. In short, ginseng "farming" is their hobby. Therefore, given the conclusively urban use and nature of Debtor's two contiguous parcels, Debtor is only entitled to a homestead exemption of one-half of an acre up to $200,000.

Judgment Affirmed in Favor of Bankruptcy Trustee.

Eleven categories of property are exempt under the federal exemptions, which the debtor may elect in lieu of the state exemptions. The federal exemptions include:

1. The debtor's interest (not to exceed $18,450 in value) in real or personal property that the debtor or a dependent of the debtor uses as a residence.

2. The debtor's interest (not to exceed $2,950 in value) in one motor vehicle.

3. The debtor's interest (not to exceed $475 in value for any particular item) up to a total of $9,850 in household furnishings, household goods, wearing apparel, appliances, books, animals, crops, or musical instruments that are held primarily for the personal, family, or household use of the debtor or a dependent of the debtor.

4. The debtor's aggregate interest (not to exceed $1,225 in value) in jewelry held primarily for the personal, family, or household use of the debtor or a dependent of the debtor.

5. $975 in value of any other property of the debtor's choosing, plus up to $9,250 of any unused homestead exemption.

6. The debtor's aggregate interest (not to exceed $1,850 in value) in any implements, professional books, or tools of the trade.

7. Life insurance contracts.

8. Interest up to $9,850 in specified kinds of dividends or interest in certain kinds of life insurance policies.

9. Professionally prescribed health aids.

10. Social security, disability, alimony, and other benefits reasonably necessary for the support of the debtor or his dependents.

11. The debtor's right to receive certain insurance and liability payments.

The term **value** means "fair market value as of the date of the filing of the petition." In determining the debtor's interest in property, the amount of any liens against the property must be deducted.

Avoidance of Liens

The debtor is also permitted to **void** certain liens against exempt properties that impair her exemptions. Liens that can be voided on this basis are judicial liens or nonpossessionary, nonpurchase money security interests in: (1) household furnishings, household goods, wearing apparel, appliances, books, animals, crops, musical instruments, or jewelry that are held primarily for the personal, family, or household use of the debtor or a dependent of the debtor; (2) implements, professional books, or tools of the trade of the debtor or a dependent of the debtor; and (3) professionally prescribed health aids for the debtor or a dependent of the debtor. Debtors are also permitted to **redeem** exempt personal property from secured creditors by paying them the value of the collateral. Then, the creditor is an unsecured creditor as to any remaining debt owed by the debtor.

Preferential Payments

A major purpose of the Bankruptcy Act is to ensure equal treatment for the creditors of an insolvent debtor. The act also seeks to prevent an insolvent debtor from distributing her assets to a few favored creditors to the detriment of the other creditors. Thus, the trustee has the right to recover for the benefit of the bankruptcy estate all **preferential payments** in excess of $600 made by the bankrupt person.[1] A preferential payment is a payment made by an insolvent debtor within 90 days before the filing of the bankruptcy petition that enables a creditor to obtain a greater percentage of a preexisting debt than other similar creditors of the debtor. It is irrelevant whether the creditor knew that the debtor was insolvent. A debtor is presumed to have been insolvent on and during the 90 days immediately preceding the filing of a petition.

For example, Fredericks has $1,000 in cash and no other assets. He owes $650 to his friend Roberts, $1,500 to a credit union, and $2,000 to a finance company. If Fredericks pays $650 to Roberts and then files for bankruptcy, he has made a preferential payment to Roberts. Roberts has had his debt paid in full, whereas only $350 is left to satisfy the $3,500 owed to the credit union and finance company. They stand to recover only 10 cents on each dollar that Fredericks owes them. The trustee has the right to get the $650 back from Roberts.

If the favored creditor is an insider—a relative of an individual debtor or an officer, director, or related party of a company—who had reasonable cause to believe the debtor was insolvent at the time the transfer was made, then a preferential payment made to that creditor up to one year prior to the filing of the petition can be recovered by the trustee.

---

[1] In the case of an individual debtor whose debts are primarily consumer debts, the trustee is not entitled to avoid preferences unless the aggregate value of the property is $600 or more.

ETHICS IN ACTION

Should the Homestead Exemption Be Limited?

As of June 2002, six states, including Florida and Texas, provide an unlimited household exemption that allows bankrupt debtors to shield unlimited amounts of equity in a residential estate. The unlimited exemption has come under increased scrutiny in recent years as a number of public figures as well as noted wrongdoers have taken advantage of the unlimited exemption to shield significant amounts of wealth from creditors. For example, a prominent actor who was declared bankrupt in 1996 was allowed to keep a $2.5 million estate located in Hobe Sound, Florida, and a corporate executive convicted of securities fraud kept his Tampa, Florida, mansion from the claims of his creditors in bankruptcy, including federal regulators seeking to collect civil fines. When the Enron and WorldCom corporate scandals broke in 2001 and 2002, the media called attention to a $15 million mansion under construction in Boca Raton, Florida, for the former CFO of WorldCom and to a $7 million penthouse owned by the former CEO of Enron as well as to the fact that the liberal exemption laws in Florida and Texas might be utilized by them to protect a significant amount of their wealth against claims from creditors and regulators.

For some time Congress has been considering changes in the federal Bankruptcy Code to, among other things, limit the amount of equity in a residence or homestead that can be exempted in a bankruptcy proceeding. What, if anything, do you think Congress should do concerning this issue?

The 1994 amendments to the Bankruptcy Act provided that the trustee may not recover as preferential payments any bona fide payments of debts to a spouse, former spouse, or child of the debtor for alimony, maintenance, or support pursuant to a separation agreement, divorce decree, or other court order.

Preferential Liens

Preferential liens are treated in a similar manner. A creditor might try to obtain an advantage over other creditors by obtaining a lien on the debtor's property to secure an existing debt. The creditor might seek to get the debtor's consent to a lien or to obtain a lien by legal process. Such liens are considered *preferential* and are invalid if they are obtained on property of an insolvent debtor within 90 days before the filing of a bankruptcy petition and if their purpose is to secure a preexisting debt. A preferential lien obtained by an insider up to one year prior to the filing of the bankruptcy petition can be avoided.

Transactions in the Ordinary Course of Business

The Bankruptcy Act provides several exceptions to the trustee's avoiding power that are designed to allow a debtor and his creditors to engage in ordinary business transactions. The exceptions include (1) transfers that are intended by the debtor and creditor to be a contemporaneous exchange for new value or (2) the creation of a security interest in new property where new value was given by the secured party to enable the debtor to obtain the property and where the new value was in fact used by the debtor to obtain the property and perfected within 20 days after the debtor took possession of the collateral.

For example, George Grocer is insolvent. He is permitted to purchase and pay cash for new inventory, such as produce or meat, without the payment being considered preferential. His assets have not been reduced. He has simply traded money for goods to be sold in his business. Similarly, he could buy a new display counter and give the seller a security interest in the counter until he has paid for it. This would not be considered a preferential lien. The seller of the counter has not gained an unfair advantage over other creditors, and Grocer's assets have not been reduced by the transaction. The unfair advantage comes where an existing creditor tries to take a lien or obtain a payment of more than his share of the

debtor's assets. Then, the creditor has obtained a preference over other creditors, which is what the trustee is allowed to avoid.

The Bankruptcy Act also provides an exception for transfers made in payment of a debt incurred in the ordinary course of the business or financial affairs of the debtor and the transferee made in the ordinary course of business. Thus, for example, a consumer could pay her monthly utility bills in a timely fashion without the creditor/utility being vulnerable to having the transfer of funds avoided by a trustee. The purpose of this exception is to leave undisturbed normal financial relations, and it is consistent with the general policy of the preference section of the Act to discourage *unusual action* by either a debtor or her creditors when the debtor is moving toward bankruptcy.

Exceptions to the trustee's avoidance power are also made for certain statutory liens, certain other perfected security interests, and cases filed by individual debtors whose debts are primarily consumer debts and the aggregate value of all property affected by the transfer is less than $600.

Fraudulent Transfers

If a debtor transfers property or incurs an obligation with *intent to hinder, delay, or defraud creditors,* the transfer is *voidable* by the trustee. Transfers of property for less than reasonable value are similarly voidable. Suppose Kasper is in financial difficulty. She "sells" her $15,000 car to her mother for $100 so that her creditors cannot claim it. Kasper did not receive fair consideration for this transfer. The transfer could be declared void by a trustee if it was made within a year before the filing of a bankruptcy petition against Kasper. The provisions of law concerning **fraudulent transfers** are designed to prevent a debtor from concealing or disposing of his property in fraud of creditors. Such transfers may also subject the debtor to criminal penalties and prevent discharge of the debtor's unpaid liabilities.[2]

In the *Trujillo* case that follows, the Bankruptcy Court avoided the transfer of automobiles and a house as fraudulent.

---

[2]Bulk sales of a debtor's materials, supplies, merchandise, or other inventory of the business in bulk and not in the ordinary course of business have the potential to defraud creditors.

Trujillo v. Grimmett   *215 B.R. 200 (U.S. Bankr. App., 9th Cir. 1997)*

In 1991 Joseph and Toni Trujillo bought a house in Las Vegas, Nevada. Subsequently, Joseph borrowed $20,000 of his wife's savings to invest in business ventures. On November 15, 1993, the Trujillos defaulted in payment on a promissory note to Richard Hart and then into a stipulated agreement with him that was entered as a judgment on August 8, 1994.

In May of 1994, purportedly as security to his wife for the $20,000 loan, Joseph transferred the title to his Cadillac automobile to his son, Gilbert. Joseph instructed Gilbert to hold the title in trust until the loan was repaid. Later the Trujillos transferred to Gilbert the titles of two more vehicles, a Pontiac and a Volkswagen, purportedly to obtain a group insurance rate. No consideration was given for the transfer of any of the vehicles, and the Trujillos retained possession and control of all three vehicles.

On August 22, 1994, the Trujillos deeded, by a quitclaim deed, their house to their daughter, Valerie Aquino. The transfer was purportedly made to obtain a loan with Aquino's credit because Joseph's outstanding debts prevented him from obtaining credit in his own name. No consideration was given to the Trujillos for the transfer of the house, and the Trujillos retained both possession and control of the house.

On May 16, 1995, within a year of transferring the vehicles and deeding the house, the Trujillos filed a petition for relief under Chapter 7 of the Bankruptcy Code. The Bankruptcy Trustee, Tom Grimmett, filed a complaint for fraudulent conveyance, requested denial of discharge against the Trujillos, and sought recovery of the fraudulently conveyed property from Gilbert and Aquino. The Bankruptcy Court held that the transfers were avoidable fraudulent transfers. The Trujillos appealed.

Hagan, Bankruptcy Judge Section 548(a)(2) sets forth the avoidance powers of a bankruptcy trustee as they relate to fraudulent transfers of a debtor's interest in property. It provides, in relevant part:

(a) The trustee may avoid any transfer of an interest of the debtor in property, or any obligation incurred by the debtor, that was made or incurred on or within one year before the date of the filing of the petition, if the debtor voluntarily or involuntarily.

* * *

(2)(A) received less than a reasonably equivalent value in exchange for such transfer or obligation; and (B)(i) was insolvent on the date that such transfer was made or such obligation was incurred, or became insolvent as result of such transfer or obligation.

To avoid a transfer under section 548 four elements must be satisfied: (1) the debtor must have an interest in the property, (2) the debtor must have been insolvent at the time of the transfer or become insolvent as a result of the transfer, (3) the transfer must have occurred within one year of the bankruptcy filing, and (4) the debtor must have received less than a reasonably equivalent value for the transfer.

The court found the Trujillos transferred property in which they had an interest for less than equivalent value and at a time when they were insolvent. The court further held pursuant to section 522(g) that the Trujillos were not entitled to exemptions for either the value of the cars or the equity in the house because the Debtors voluntarily conveyed them.

The Trujillos argue they retained an interest in the property because transferring bare legal title is insufficient to

constitute a "transfer" under the Code. Section 101 defines "transfer" very broadly as:

[E]very mode, direct or indirect, absolute or conditional, voluntary or involuntary, of disposing of or parting with property or with an interest in property, including retention of title as a security interest and foreclosure of the debtor's equity of redemption.

11 U.S.C. section 101(54). The legislative history confirms the broadness of the term "transfer": A transfer is a disposition of an interest in property. The definition is as broad as possible. Under this definition, any transfer of an interest in property is a transfer, including a transfer of possession, custody, or control even if there is no transfer to title, because possession, custody, and control are interests in property. By the making, and recording, of the quitclaim deed to the house and the transfer of the titles to the vehicles, transfers under section 548 clearly occurred.

The four elements of a fraudulent transfer have been met. The Trujillos had an interest in both the house and the vehicles prior to the transfers. The Trujillos quitclaimed the deed to the house to Valerie and recorded it; Valerie now has marketable title in the house. Joseph transferred title to the vehicles to Gilbert; Gilbert has title to and ownership of the vehicles under state law. The Trujillos were insolvent at the time they transferred the property by their own admission. The transfers occurred within one year of the filing of their chapter 7 petition. Lastly, the Trujillos received nothing for these transfers, fulfilling the "less than reasonably equivalent value" requirement of section 548(a)(2).

Judgment affirmed in favor of Bankruptcy Trustee.

Claims

If creditors wish to participate in the estate of a bankrupt debtor, they must file a **proof of claim** in the estate within a certain time, usually six months after the first meeting of creditors. Only unsecured creditors are required to file proofs of claims. However, a secured creditor whose secured claim exceeds the value of the collateral is an unsecured creditor to the extent of the deficiency. That creditor must file a proof of claim to support the recovery of the deficiency.

Allowable Claims

The fact that a proof of claim is filed does not ensure that a creditor can participate in the distribution of the assets of the bankruptcy estate. The claim must also be allowed. If the trustee has a valid defense to the claim, he can use the defense to disallow or reduce it. For example, if the claim is based on goods sold to the debtor and the seller breached a warranty, the trustee can assert the breach as a defense. All of the defenses available to the bankrupt person are available to the trustee.

Secured Claims

The trustee must also determine whether a creditor has a lien or secured interest to secure an allowable claim. If the debtor's property is subject to a secured claim of a creditor, that creditor has first claim to it. The property is available to satisfy claims of other creditors only to the extent that its value exceeds the amount of the debt secured.

Priority Claims

The Bankruptcy Act declares certain claims to have **priority** over other claims. The nine classes of priority claims are:

1. Expenses and fees incurred in administering the bankruptcy estate.

2. Unsecured claims in involuntary cases that arise in the ordinary course of the debtor's business after the filing of the petition but before the appointment of a trustee or the order of relief.

3. Unsecured claims of up to $4,925 per individual (including vacation, severance, and sick pay) for employees' wages earned within 90 days before the petition was filed.

4. Contributions to employee benefit plans up to $4,925 per person (moreover, the claim for wages plus pension contribution is limited to $4,925 per person).

5. Unsecured claims (*a*) for grain or the proceeds of grain against a debtor who owns or operates a grain storage facility or (*b*) up to $4,925 by a U.S. fisherman against a debtor who operates a fish produce storage or processing facility and who has acquired fish or fish produce from the fisherman.

6. Claims of up to $2,225 each by individuals for deposits made in connection with the purchase, lease, or rental of property or the purchase of goods or services for personal use that were not delivered or provided.

7. Allowed for claims for debts to a spouse, former spouse, or child of the debtor for alimony to, maintenance for, or support of such spouse or child in connection with a separation agreement, divorce decree, or other court order (but not if assigned to someone else).

8. Certain taxes owed to governmental units.

9. Allowed unsecured claims based on a commitment by the debtor to a federal depository institution regulatory agency (such as the FDIC).

Distribution of the Debtor's Estate

The priority claims are paid *after* secured creditors realize on their collateral but *before* other unsecured creditors are paid. Payments are made to the nine priority classes, in order, to the extent there are funds available. Each class must be paid in full before the next class is entitled to receive anything. To the extent there are insufficient funds to satisfy all the creditors within a class, each class member receives a pro rata share of his claim.

Unsecured creditors include: (1) those creditors who had not taken any collateral to secure the debt owed to them; (2) secured creditors to the extent their debt was not satisfied by the collateral they held; and (3) priority claimholders to the extent their claims exceed the limits set for priority claims.

Unsecured creditors, to the extent any funds are available for them, share in proportion to their claims. Unsecured creditors frequently receive little or nothing on their claims. Secured claims, trustee's fees, and other priority claims often consume a large part of the bankruptcy estate.

Special rules are set out in the Bankruptcy Act for distribution of the property of a bankrupt stockbroker or commodities broker.

CONCEPT REVIEW

Distribution of Debtor's Estate

Secured Creditors

Secured creditors proceed directly against the collateral. If debt is fully satisfied, they have no further interest; if debt is only partially satisfied, they are treated as general creditors for the balance.

Debtor's Estate Is Liquidated and Distributed

↓

Priority Creditors (9 classes)

- Distribution is made to 9 classes of priority claims in order.
- Each class must be fully paid before next class receives anything.
- If funds are not sufficient to satisfy everyone in a class, then each member of the class receives the same proportion of his claim.

1. Costs and expenses of administration.

2. If involuntary proceeding, expenses incurred in the ordinary course of business after petition filed but before appointment of trustee.

3. Claims for wages, salaries, and commissions earned within 90 days of petition; limited to $4,300 per person.

4. Contributions to employee benefit plans arising out of services performed within 180 days of petition; limit of $4,300 (including claims for wages, salaries, and commissions) per person.

5. Unsecured items (*a*) for grain or the proceeds of grain against a debtor who owns or operates a grain storage facility or (*b*) up to $4,300 by a U.S. fisherman against a debtor who operates a fish produce or processing facility and who has acquired fish or fish produce from the fisherman.

6. Claims of individuals, up to $1,950 per person, for deposits made on consumer goods or services that were not received.

7. Allowed-for claims for debts to a spouse, former spouse, or child of the debtor for alimony to, maintenance for, or support of such spouse or child in connection with a separation agreement, divorce decree, or other court order (if not assigned to someone else).

8. Government claims for certain taxes.

9. Allowed unsecured claims based on a commitment by the debtor to a federal depository institution regulatory agency.

↓

General Creditors

If funds are not sufficient to satisfy all general creditors, then they each receive the same proportion of their claims.

1. General unsecured creditors.

2. Secured creditors for the portion of their debt that was not satisfied by collateral.

3. Priority creditors for amounts beyond priority limits.

Debtor

Debtor receives any remaining funds.

Discharge in Bankruptcy

Discharge

A bankrupt person who has not been guilty of certain dishonest acts and has fulfilled his duties as a bankrupt is entitled to a **discharge in bankruptcy.** A discharge relieves the bankrupt person of further responsibility for dischargeable debts and gives him a fresh start. A corporation or a partnership is not eligible for a discharge in bankruptcy. A bankrupt person may file a written waiver of his right to a discharge. An individual may not be granted a discharge if she obtained one within the previous six years.

Objections to Discharge

After the bankrupt has paid all of the required fees, the court gives creditors and others a chance to file objections to the discharge of the bankrupt. Objections may be filed by the trustee, a creditor, or the U.S. attorney. If objections are filed, the court holds a hearing to listen to them. At the hearing, the court must determine whether the bankrupt person has committed any act that is a bar to discharge. If the bankrupt has not committed such an act, the court grants the discharge. If the bankrupt has committed an act that is a bar to discharge, the discharge is denied. The discharge is also denied if the bankrupt fails to appear at the hearing on objections or if he refused earlier to submit to the questioning of the creditors.

Acts That Bar Discharge

Discharges in bankruptcy are intended for honest debtors. Therefore, the following acts bar a debtor from being discharged: (1) the unjustified falsifying, concealing, or destroying of records; (2) making false statements, presenting false claims, or withholding recorded information relating to the debtor's property or financial affairs; (3) transferring, removing, or concealing property in order to hinder, delay, or defraud creditors; (4) failing to account satisfactorily for any loss or deficiency of assets; and (5) failing to obey court orders or to answer questions approved by the court.

In the *Byrd* case, which follows, the court held that a debt owed to a bank was nondischargeable because it had been obtained on the basis of a materially false financial statement.

Byrd v. Bank of Mississippi　　　　207 B.R. 131 (S.D. Miss. 1997)

In January 1990 Dr. Anthony Byrd, a dentist, applied to the Bank of Mississippi for an unsecured loan in the amount of $20,000. Prior to this time the bank had no relationship with Dr. Byrd. The bank requested and received from Dr. Byrd a 1988 individual income tax return along with a statement of his financial condition prepared by his accountant. The bank also obtained a credit report. After considering all the information, the bank granted the loan. The promissory note was renewed on a number of occasions, beginning in July 1990. On each occasion the bank requested, and was provided, a current financial statement.

The financial statement dated June 30, 1989, showed Dr. Byrd having a net worth of approximately $649,000. Listed in the financial statements was an asset consisting of 60 acres of real property with a value of $30,000. In fact Dr. Byrd did not own the property, nor did he ever pay the property taxes on it. He later explained that he had listed it because he believed that it had passed to him on his father-in-law's death. The property was farmed by his brother-in-law. The statement also listed as an asset, a residence in Covington County, Mississippi, with an appraised value of $49,800. At the time the financial statement was submitted, the property had been sold to his brother on a conditional sale contract with a purchase price of $39,000; it also was encumbered with a deed of trust securing a $39,000 note to the Bank of Simpson County. However, neither the conditional sales contract nor the note and deed of trust was mentioned in the financial statement. Dr. Byrd later explained that this was an "oversight." The initial credit report obtained by the bank did not mention either of these elements, so the bank had no reason to disbelieve the assertion in the statement provided by Dr. Byrd.

The initial financial statement also listed as an asset a note receivable for $103,000 from Southern Outdoors, Inc., a company which the statement noted was 92 percent owned by Dr. Byrd. A subsequent statement listed the note receivable as $184,000. The last statement he submitted, omitted this loan; Dr. Byrd indicated that he had been told by his accountant that it should be considered as a capital contribution to Southern Outdoors rather than as an account receivable.

Dr. Byrd filed for bankruptcy under Chapter 7. The Bank of Mississippi commenced an adversary proceeding to have its claim arising out of the $20,000 promissory note declared nondischargeable on the grounds that it had been obtained on the basis of a materially false statement in writing concerning the debtor's financial statement which the bank had relied on in granting the loan. The Bankruptcy Court declared the debt owed by Dr. Byrd to the Bank of Mississippi to be nondischargeable on the grounds it had been obtained on the basis of a materially false financial statement. Dr. Byrd appealed.

Bramlette, District Judge Under the section of the Bankruptcy Code at issue here, an individual debtor is not discharged from any debt "for money, property, services, or an extension, renewal, or refinancing of credit, to the extent obtained by . . . use of a statement in writing (i) that is materially false; (ii) respecting the debtor's or an insider's financial condition; (iii) on which the creditor to whom the debtor is liable for such money, property, services or credit reasonably relied; and (iv) that the debtor caused to be made or published with intent to deceive . . ." 11 U.S.C. section 523(a)(2)(B).

To prevail on its claim of nondischargeability, the Bank of Mississippi was required to prove each of the following elements:

1. the existence of a statement in writing;
2. the writing must be materially false;
3. the writing must concern the debtor's financial condition;
4. the creditor must have reasonably relied on the statement; and
5. the statement must be made or published with the intent to deceive.

The bankruptcy court found that each of the financial statements provided to the bank were in writing and concerned the debtor's financial condition. While Dr. Byrd admitted that the financial statements did not accurately reflect his financial condition, he denied that they were materially false. He also contended that the bank did not reasonably rely on them, and that they were not made with the intent to deceive the bank. The bankruptcy court found against the debtor on each issue.

The debtor attempts to use a mathematical analysis to show that the financial statements were not materially false. He argues that even if the inaccuracies in his financial statements were corrected, he still would have come within the bank's net worth and income parameters, and therefore would have been granted the loan.

The Fifth Circuit Court of Appeals has stated that a materially false statement is one that 'paints a substantially untruthful picture of a financial condition by misrepresenting information of the type which would normally affect the decision to grant credit.' In determining whether a false statement is material, "a relevant although not dispositive inquiry is 'whether the lender would have made the loan had he known the debtor's true situation.'"

The bankruptcy court found that Dr. Byrd did not prove that the bank would have made the initial loan even if it had known his true financial situation. However, the court noted, even if he had proved that the bank would have loaned him the money regardless of the errors in his financial statement, that fact, while relevant, would not necessarily be dispositive of the "materially false" issue. The court concluded that the inclusion as an asset on the debtor's financial statement of 60 acres of real property valued at $30,000, which he has never owned, was a material misstatement; and that the representation that he owned a $49,000 residence free and clear, while it was subject to a deed of trust securing a debt of $39,000 and a conditional sales contract for $39,000, was a material omission.

Four financial statements were provided to the bank, one for the original loan and one for each of the three renewals. The debtor argued that the bankruptcy court should only consider whether the bank reasonably relied on the last financial statement provided. According to the debtor, by the time of the final renewal in July of 1991, the bank was aware of certain "red flags," i.e., the appearance on the July 1991 credit report of the note to the Bank of Simpson County, and the removal of the $184,000 note receivable from Southern Outdoors from the last financial statement; therefore, the bank's reliance on the last financial statement was not reasonable.

The bankruptcy court assumed for the sake of argument that the final financial statement did contain "red flags" that should have alerted the lender to possible inaccuracies in the financial statement. Nevertheless, the court concluded that where no additional money was obtained with each of the three renewals, it was the first and not the last financial statement provided to the bank that is relevant in determining the reasonableness of the bank's reliance.

The bankruptcy court below, held that since the note renewal did not represent a new debt incurred, it need consider only whether the Bank of Mississippi reasonably relied on the financial statement provided by Dr. Byrd in connection with the original note executed in January of 1990.

The bankruptcy court found that when Dr. Byrd originally approached the bank, he had no individual past loan or deposit relationship with the bank. In addition to the financial statement, Dr. Byrd provided the bank with his income tax return. The bank also obtained a credit report on Dr. Byrd prior to making the loan. The loan officer for the bank testified that neither the income tax return nor the credit report contained information that would appear to contradict Dr. Byrd's testimony.

Dr. Byrd argued that a title report on his real property would have revealed that he did not own the 60 acres in Smith County and that the Covington County residence was encumbered with a deed of trust. However, the loan officer testified that the bank does not obtain title reports when considering an unsecured loan. Dr. Byrd also argued that the existence of the $103,000 note receivable from a corporation in which he owned 92 percent of the stock was inherently suspicious and should have been considered a "red flag."

The bankruptcy court found that it was reasonable for the bank not to require a title search on property listed on a financial statement in connection with an unsecured loan. Further, the court found that the bank was not unreasonable in relying on Dr. Byrd's professionally prepared financial statement as to the amount due him from the corporation. The bankruptcy court's finding of reasonable reliance is amply supported by the record.

At trial, Dr. Byrd denied that he intended to deceive the bank, explaining that he listed the 60 acres in Smith County as an asset because he thought he owned the property as a result of a conversation with his brother-in-law. However, Dr. Byrd admitted being aware that he has never paid any taxes or received a tax bill on the property. Dr. Byrd's explanation for omitting the conditional sales contract and the deed of trust on the Covington County property was that these items were somehow mistakenly omitted from the first financial statement, and that the subsequent financial statements were simply prepared by reference to the first.

The bankruptcy court found that Dr. Byrd was a highly educated man with an extensive background in business matters. Since graduation from dental school, he had been involved in several business ventures, including a roofing business and a fishing tackle store, and was a major stockholder in a corporation named Mississippi Marine Specialties. He also owned a city block in Mount Olive, Mississippi, which he used as rental property, and owned half of the office building in which the dental practice was located. The court found that he possessed an understanding of both the incidents of real property ownership and the significance of encumbrances on real property, and thus should be held to a higher standard.

The court also found that Dr. Byrd exhibited a reckless indifference to the accuracy of his June 30, 1989, financial statement which he provided to the bank to obtain the original $20,000 unsecured loan. Therefore, the court found, Dr. Byrd had the requisite intent to deceive at the time he furnished the statement. This finding is also well supported by the record.

In conclusion, this Court finds that the financial statements of the debtor contained materially false statements; that the debtor acted with reckless indifference to, if not actual knowledge of, the materially false statements; and that the Bank of Mississippi reasonably relied on these misstatements in making the loan; therefore, a judgment of nondischargeability pursuant to section 523(a)(2)(B) was warranted.

Judgment affirmed in favor of Bank of Mississippi.

Nondischargeable Debts

Certain debts are not affected by the discharge of a bankrupt debtor. The Bankruptcy Act provides that a discharge in bankruptcy releases a debtor from all provable debts except those that:

1. Are due as a tax or fine to the United States or any state or local unit of government.
2. Result from liabilities for obtaining money by false pretenses or false representations.
3. Are due for willful or malicious injury to a person or his property.
4. Are due for alimony or child support.
5. Were created by the debtor's larceny or embezzlement or by the debtor's fraud while acting in a fiduciary capacity.
6. Are certain kinds of educational loans.
7. Were not scheduled in time for proof and allowance because the creditor holding the debt did not have notification of the proceeding even though the debtor was aware that he owed money to that creditor.
8. Secured claims in exempt assets.

The 1984 amendments established several additional grounds for nondischargeability relating to debts incurred in contemplation of bankruptcy—and the 1994 amendments made changes to them. Congress was concerned about debtors who ran up large expenditures on credit cards shortly before filing for bankruptcy relief. Cash advances in excess of $1,225 obtained by use of a credit card and a revolving line of credit at a credit union obtained within 60 days of filing a bankruptcy petition are presumed to be nondischargeable. Similarly, a debtor's purchase of more than $1,225 in *luxury goods or services* on credit from a single creditor within 60 days of filing a petition is presumed to be nondischargeable.

There are also exceptions from dischargeability for debts: (1) reflected in a judgment arising out of a debtor's operation of a motor vehicle while legally intoxicated; (2) incurred to pay a tax to the United States that would be nondischargeable; and (3) incurred by a debtor in the course of a separation agreement or divorce decree *unless* the debtor does not have the ability to pay the debt from income or property not reasonably necessary for the support of the debtor or a dependent or discharging the debt would result in a benefit to the debtor that outweighs the detrimental consequences to a spouse, former spouse, or child of the debtor.

All of these nondischargeable debts are provable debts. The creditor who owns these claims can participate in the distribution of the bankrupt's estate. However, the creditor has an additional advantage: His right to recover the unpaid balance is not cut off by the bankrupt's discharge. All other provable debts are dischargeable; that is, the right to recover them is cut off by the bankrupt's discharge.

Reaffirmation Agreements

Sometimes, creditors put pressure on debtors to reaffirm, or to agree to pay, debts that have been discharged in bankruptcy. When the 1978 amendments to the Bankruptcy Act were under consideration, some individuals urged Congress to prohibit such agreements. They argued that reaffirmation agreements were inconsistent with the fresh start philosophy of the Bankruptcy Act. Congress did not agree to a total prohibition; instead, it

set up a rather elaborate procedure for a creditor to go through to get a debt reaffirmed. Essentially, the agreement must be made *before* the discharge is granted and must contain a clear statement that advises the debtor (1) that the agreement may be rescinded at any time prior to discharge or within 60 days after filing with the court and (2) the agreement contains a clear and conspicuous statement advising the debtor that the reaffirmation is not required by the bankruptcy law and any other law or agreement. The agreement must be filed with the court accompanied by a statement from the debtor's attorney that (1) it represents a voluntary agreement by the debtor, (2) that it does not impose an undue hardship on the debtor, and (3) the attorney fully apprised the debtor of the legal affect and consequences of the agreement and of any default under such an agreement. Court approval is not required for the reaffirmation of loans secured by real property. Also, a debtor may voluntarily pay any dischargeable obligation without entering into a reaffirmation agreement.

Dismissal for Substantial Abuse

As it considered the 1984 amendments to the Bankruptcy Act, Congress was concerned that too many individuals with an ability to pay their debts over time pursuant to a Chapter 13 plan were filing petitions to obtain Chapter 7 discharges of liability. The consumer finance industry urged Congress to preclude Chapter 7 petitions where a debtor had the prospect of future disposable income to satisfy more than 50 percent of his prepetition unsecured debts. Although Congress rejected this approach, it did authorize Bankruptcy Courts to dismiss cases that they determined were a **substantial abuse** of the bankruptcy process. This provision appears to cover situations in which a debtor has acted in bad faith or has the present or future ability to pay a significant portion of her current debts. The case that follows, *In Re Huckfeldt,* illustrates a situation in which the court concluded that a petition in bankruptcy had been filed in bad faith.

In Re Huckfeldt	*39 F.3d 829 (8th Cir. 1994)*

During their 12 years of marriage, Roger and Georgianne Huckfeldt accumulated over $250,000 in debts while Roger completed college, medical school, and six years of residency in surgery and while Georgianne completed college and law school. These debts included $166,000 in student loans to Huckfeldt and $47,000 jointly borrowed from Georgianne's parents. The Huckfeldts divorced on March 26, 1992. The divorce decree ordered Roger to pay his student loans, one-half of the debt to Georgianne's parents, and other enumerated debts totaling some $241,000. The decree also ordered Roger to hold Georgianne harmless for these debts but otherwise denied Georgianne's request for maintenance.

On June 4, 1992, six months before Roger would complete his residency in surgery, he filed a voluntary Chapter 7 petition, listing assets of $1,250 and liabilities of $546,857. After filing the petition, Roger accepted a fellowship at Oregon Health Sciences University, a one- or two-year position paying $45,000 per year, substantially less than the income he could likely earn during the pendency of his Chapter 7 proceeding. Following Roger's petition, creditors of the debts assigned to him in the divorce decree began pursuing Georgianne for repayment. She filed for bankruptcy protection in March 1993.

In September 1992, Georgianne and her parents filed a motion to dismiss Roger's Chapter 7 petition on the ground that it was filed in bad faith. They alleged that Roger had threatened to file for bankruptcy during the divorce proceeding and had commenced the bankruptcy proceeding in defiance of the divorce decree for the purpose of shifting responsibility for assigned debts to Georgianne. They also alleged that Roger had deliberately taken steps to reduce his annual income to avoid payment of his debts through the Chapter 7 liquidation.

After a hearing, the bankruptcy court granted the motion to dismiss the proceeding on the grounds it was filed in bad faith, finding, among other things, that Roger could be earning $110,000 to $120,000 after expenses. The district court affirmed the decision, and Roger appealed to the court of appeals.

Loken, Circuit Judge After finding that Roger could be earning $110,000 to $120,000 per year, after all expenses except income tax, the bankruptcy court stated:

It is the purpose of the bankruptcy system to provide a fresh start for the honest but unfortunate debtor. It is not the purpose of the bankruptcy system to eliminate the obligations of a party who is capable of paying the same. The Court believes debtor filed this bankruptcy petition in bad faith and with the deliberate intention of unloading debt, particularly that to his spouse, which he could shortly begin to repay. Further this Court believes it was the intent of the debtor to leave his ex-spouse with all the debts and obligations incurred over the 12 years and force her into a bankruptcy situation also . . . Accordingly the court concludes that his case was filed in bad faith and concludes that good faith is a requirement for the filing of a bankruptcy petition no matter what the chapter.

Huckfeldt filed a Chapter 7 petition to frustrate the divorce court decree and to push his ex-wife into bankruptcy. He then manipulated his immediate earnings to ensure the Chapter 7 proceeding would achieve these noneconomic motives. That conduct meets the standard for bad faith. Indeed, such conduct has long been considered unworthy of bankruptcy protection.

The petition in this case was not filed for the purpose of a just liquidation by composition with creditors but to defeat the wife from a right of possession in and to the real estate which was to be awarded to her under the divorce proceedings. This violates the purpose and intent of the statute and, as said by the Supreme Court of the United States, under that situation, the proceedings will be halted at the outset. Huckfeldt is not an "honest but unfortunate debtor" entitled to the equitable relief of a Chapter 7 liquidation.

Judgment against Roger Huckfeldt affirmed.

Chapter 11: Reorganizations

Reorganization Proceeding

Sometimes, creditors benefit more from the continuation of a bankrupt debtor's business than from the liquidation of the debtor's property. Chapter 11 of the Bankruptcy Act provides a proceeding whereby, under the supervision of the Bankruptcy Court, the debtor's financial affairs can be reorganized rather than liquidated. Chapter 11 proceedings are available to individuals and to virtually all business enterprises, including individual proprietorships, partnerships, and corporations (except banks, savings and loan associations, insurance companies, commodities brokers, and stockbrokers).

Petitions for reorganization proceedings can be filed voluntarily by the debtor or involuntarily by its creditors. Once a petition for a reorganization proceeding is filed and relief is ordered, the court usually appoints (1) a committee of creditors holding unsecured claims, (2) a committee of equity security holders (shareholders), and (3) a trustee. The trustee may be given the responsibility for running the debtor's business. He is also usually responsible for developing a plan for handling the various claims of creditors and the various interests of persons such as shareholders.

The reorganization plan is essentially a contract between a debtor and its creditors. This contract may involve recapitalizing a debtor corporation and/or giving creditors some equity, or shares, in the corporation in exchange for part or all of the debt owed to them. The plan must (1) divide the creditors into classes; (2) set forth how each creditor will be satisfied; (3) state which claims, or classes of claims, are impaired or adversely affected by the plan; and (4) provide the same treatment to each creditor in a particular class, unless the creditors in that class consent to different treatment.

The plan is then submitted to the creditors for approval. Approval generally requires that creditors holding two-thirds in amount and one-half in number of each class of claims impaired by the plan must accept it. Once approved, the plan goes before the court for confirmation. If the plan is confirmed, the debtor is responsible for carrying it out.

However, until a plan is confirmed, the bankruptcy court has no authority to distribute any portion of the bankruptcy assets to unsecured creditors.

Use of Chapter 11

During the 1980s, attempts by a number of corporations to seek refuge in Chapter 11 as a means of escaping problems they were facing received considerable public attention. Some of the most visible cases involved efforts to obtain some protection against massive product liability claims and judgments for damages for breach of contract and to escape from collective bargaining agreements. Thus, for example, Johns-Manville Corporation filed under Chapter 11 because of the claims against it arising out of its production and sale of asbestos years earlier, while A. H. Robins Company, was concerned about a surfeit of claims arising out of its sale of the Dalkon Shield, an intrauterine birth control device. And, in 1987, Texaco, Inc., faced with a $10.3 billion judgment in favor of Pennzoil in a breach of contract action, filed a petition for reorganizational relief under Chapter 11. Companies such as LTV and Allegheny Industries sought changes in retirement and pension plans, and other companies such as Eastern Airlines sought refuge in Chapter 11 while embroiled in labor disputes.

In the 1990s, a number of companies that were the subject of highly leveraged buyouts (LBOs) financed with so-called junk bonds, including a number of re-

tailers, resorted to Chapter 11 to seek restructuring and relief from their creditors. Similarly, companies such as Pan Am and TWA that were hurt by economic slowdown and increase in fuel prices filed Chapter 11 petitions. In 2001, Enron and K-Mart filed for reorganization under Chapter 11 as did WorldCom and USAirways in 2002.

In recent years, Chapter 11 has been the subject of significant criticism and calls for its revision. Critics point out that many of the Chapter 11 cases are permitted to drag on for years, thus depleting the assets of the debtor through payments to trustees and lawyers involved in administration and diminishing the assets available to creditors.

Collective Bargaining Agreements

Collective bargaining contracts pose special problems. Prior to the 1984 amendments, there was concern that some companies would use Chapter 11 reorganizations as a vehicle to avoid executed collective bargaining agreements. The concern was heightened by the Supreme Court's 1984 decision in *NLRB v. Bildisco and Bildisco.* In that case, the Supreme Court held that a reorganizing debtor did not have to engage in collective bargaining before modifying or rejecting portions of a collective bargaining agreement and that such unilateral alterations by a debtor did not violate the National Labor Relations Act.

Congress then acted to try to prevent the misuse of bankruptcy proceedings for collective bargaining purposes. The act's 1984 amendments adopt a rigorous multistep process that must be complied with in determining whether a labor contract can be rejected or modified as part of a reorganization. Among other things that must be done before a debtor or trustee can seek to avoid a collective bargaining agreement are the submission of a proposal to the employees' representative that details the "necessary" modifications to the collective bargaining agreement and ensures that "all creditors, the debtor and all affected parties are fairly treated." Then, before the bankruptcy court can authorize a rejection of the original collective bargaining agreement, it must review the proposal and find that (1) the employees' representative refused to accept it without good cause, and (2) the balance of equities clearly favors the rejection of the original collective bargaining agreement.

The following case, *In Re Maxwell Newspapers, Inc.,* shows the scrutiny that the court gives the action of a debtor seeking to avoid a collective bargaining agreement.

In Re Maxwell Newspapers, Inc.
New York Typographical Union No. 6 v. Maxwell Newspapers, Inc.
981 F.2d 85 (2nd Cir. 1992)

In July 1974, the New York Typographical Union No. 6 agreed in a collective bargaining agreement with the Daily News, a daily newspaper in New York City, to automation of the typesetting function in return for a guarantee of lifetime employment for its members then working at the newspaper. Between 1982 and 1992, the Daily News lost approximately $100 million and its owner, Maxwell Newspapers, Inc., had filed for relief under Chapter 11. Maxwell sought a buyer for the Daily News with sufficient resources to satisfy not only its creditors and employees but also to modernize its printing plant so that it could compete in the New York metropolitan market.

In September 1992, Mortimer Zuckerman, through his affiliate New DN Company, entered negotiations with the Daily News to buy its assets. These negotiations included a so-called stand-alone plan of reorganization that was conditioned on union support. One crucial component of the plan was concessions by Local No. 6 with respect to the July 1974 collective bargaining agreement that guaranteed the printers lifetime employment.

On October 1, 1992, Maxwell, in tandem with Zuckerman, proposed to the union that the collective bargaining agreement be modified to eliminate: (1) any obligation of Maxwell to require the purchaser of the assets of the Daily News to employ any member of the union, (2) any obligation of Maxwell to continue to employ any member of the union if Maxwell ceased publication or sold the Daily News pursuant to the bankruptcy proceeding, and (3) any obligation to arbitrate any controversy regarding these matters. Maxwell also provided documentation of the impact of the union's collective bargaining agreement on the financial stability of the Daily News and asserted that it had sought in vain prospective purchasers who would honor the labor agreement.

The union made a counterproposal on October 14 in which it expressed a willingness to forgo the lifetime job guarantees. The union proposed a progressive reduction in the number of shifts worked conditioned on a cash buyout for each union member, three years' contribution to the pension and welfare funds, and an early retirement enhancement. Negotiations, including a series of counteroffers, continued until October 21, when Zuckerman, on the eve of an October 22 hearing in the bankruptcy case, made a final offer. He offered a reduced number of guaranteed shifts and jobs that fell to 15 jobs a year after a new printing plant was opened. The jobs would then be guaranteed for 13 years and he proposed to make a one-time contribution of $1 million to the pension and welfare funds.

The union rejected Zuckerman's final offer to modify the collective bargaining agreement, and negotiations broke down. Maxwell asked the bankruptcy court to reject the contract with Local No. 6 and to approve the proposed sale of the Daily News to Zuckerman. The bankruptcy court granted the motions, and the union appealed. The district court reversed the bankruptcy court concerning the rejection of the collective bargaining agreement, holding that the union had "good cause" to reject Zuckerman's final offer.

Cardamone, Circuit Judge We first analyze whether the union in fact had "good cause" to refuse Zuckerman's final offer. Section 1113 of the Bankruptcy code controls the rejection of collective bargaining agreements in Chapter 11 proceedings. The statute puts in place "safeguards designed to insure that employers did not use Chapter 11 as medicine to rid themselves of corporate indigestion." Employers may only propose those necessary modifications in the employees benefits and protections that are "necessary to permit" the effective reorganization of the debtor. A debtor may sell the assets of the business unencumbered by a collective bargaining agreement if that agreement has been rejected pursuant to section 1113. This statute requires unions to face those changed circumstances that occur when a company becomes insolvent, and it requires all affected parties to compromise in the face of financial hardship. At the same time, section 1113 also imposes requirements on the debtor to prevent it from using bankruptcy as a judicial hammer to break the union. Rejection of a collective bargaining agreement is permitted only if the debtor fulfills the requirements of section 1113(b)(1), the union fails to reject the debtor's proposal with good cause, and the balance of equities clearly favors rejection.

More importantly, the statute imposes the obligation on the parties to negotiate in good faith. This obligation is properly analyzed under section 1113(c)(2), which permits rejection of a labor agreement only when the union has rejected the debtor's proposal without good cause.

The district court reasoned that the statute covers not only the contents of an employer's proposed modification of a labor contract, but also how the offer is made. It ruled because the offer was made on October 21—on the eve of the bankruptcy hearing—and on a take-it-or-leave-it basis, the union had no meaningful opportunity to consider and make a counter-proposal.

What "good cause" means is difficult to answer in the abstract apart from the moorings of a given case. A more constructive and perhaps more answerable inquiry is why this term is in the statute. We think good cause serves as an incentive to the debtor trying to have its labor contract modified to propose in good faith only those changes necessary to its successful reorganization, while protecting it from the union's refusal to accept the changes without a good reason.

To that end, the entire thrust of section 1113 is to ensure that well-informed and good faith negotiations occur in the market place, not as part of the judicial process. Reorganization proceedings are designed to encourage such a negotiated voluntary modification. Knowing that it cannot turn down an employer's proposal without good cause gives the union an incentive to compromise on modifications of the collective bargaining agreement, so as to prevent its complete rejection. Because the employer has the burden of proving its proposals are necessary, the union is protected from an employer whose proposals may be offered in bad faith.

The bankruptcy court found that the debtor measures its workforce by calculating "full time equivalents" (FTEs) derived from dividing payroll expenses by five, which is the number of days in a week worked by a full-time employee. The bankruptcy judge further found that from September 1990 to August 1992, FTEs for debtor's employees declined as follows: for managers 58 percent, guild members 34 percent, drivers 46 percent, pressmen 47 percent, mailers 45 percent, paperhandlers 54 percent, machinists and electricians 21 percent, engravers and stereotypers 27 percent. In stark contrast, the Local 6 typographers workforce declined only 13 percent, and these employees are by far the highest hourly paid employees of the debtor. No other employees or unions suffered so small an FTE cut as Local No. 6.

Moreover, unsecured creditors, the court observed, are estimated to obtain only 13 to 18 cents on the dollar and the value of stockholders' equity is nearly worthless. Yet, the bankruptcy judge declared, the union did not offer an alternative that focused on the needs of its employer's organization, but instead adhered to its position that Local 6's excess employees had to be given an incentive to induce them to leave. Neither the debtor or purchaser could fund this demand.

We reverse the district court's ruling not only on the contents of the rejection order but also concerning the manner in which Zuckerman made his final offer to the union. First, Local No. 6 did not complain that it had too little time to respond to the employer's proposal on October 21. In addition, parties to collective bargaining agreements routinely negotiate for many hours under imperative deadlines. In that negotiating universe, 10 hours is ample time to consider and respond to a proposal. Consequently, the bankruptcy court correctly concluded that Local No. 6 rejected the employer's proposal without good cause.

Judgment reversed in favor of Maxwell Newspapers, Inc.

ETHICS IN ACTION

Using Bankruptcy to Manage Product Liability or to Change Labor Contracts

As noted above, in recent years a number of corporations have resorted to Chapter 11 to deal with their exposure to product liability claims or to see changes in labor contracts. Is it ethical for a company like A. H. Robbins Company that is faced with significant liability for birth-control devices it made and sold, or for a company like Johns-Manville that faces multimillion claims from individuals who were exposed to asbestos it made to seek the protection accorded by the bankruptcy laws? Similarly, is it ethical for a company that believes it is hampered by a labor contract under which it incurs higher costs than some of its competitors to try to use a Chapter 11 proceeding to get out of the labor contract?

THE GLOBAL BUSINESS ENVIRONMENT

Transnational Insolvency Proceedings

As the volume of international trade and the number of multinational corporations have grown, there has been a concomitant increase in transnational insolvency cases. When a company engaged in international business transactions becomes insolvent, commonly some kind of insolvency proceeding will be initiated in each country where the company does business. Different laws and different national interests can produce a challenging—if not difficult—situation for creditors of the insolvent enterprise. Where and how should the creditor go about protecting its interests? Should it seek to have its claim allowed in any one—or more—of the various proceedings? What rights will it be accorded in those proceedings, particularly the foreign forums?

Historically, two different approaches have been used to deal with transnational insolvencies. The first uses the principle of "territoriality" where each country takes control of the enterprises assets within that country and administers them according to the law of that country, giving little attention to what may be happening in other forums or to foreign interests. A second approach, often referred to as "universalism," seeks a cooperative or coordinated approach to transnational insolvency. This might be achieved through the identification of a single forum or proceeding where all assets of a company would be administered and all claims and interests addressed. Another variant of this approach is to identify a primary proceeding that has the lead in conjunction with a number of coordinated ancillary proceedings in other countries.

The U.S. Bankruptcy Code permits a foreign entity to file a case in a United States Bankruptcy court to protect assets as an ancillary case connected to a primary insolvency proceeding being conducted elsewhere in world. The bankruptcy court has considerable discretion as to whether or not to grant the requested relief and can consider factors such as whether United States creditors would be prejudiced in the foreign proceeding and what respect the foreign court would give to a United States entity if the roles were reversed.

In an effort to encourage cooperation among countries and to try to harmonize the competing and conflicting schemes, the United Nations Commission on International Trade Law has adopted a Model Law on Cross-Border Insolvency. On a regional level, the European Union has adopted a "Convention on Insolvency Proceedings" to coordinate and harmonize such proceedings in EU countries. And the American Law Institute has a Transnational Insolvency Project to develop principles of cooperation in transnational insolvency cases among the members (United States, Canada, and Mexico) of the North American Free Trade Agreement (NAFTA).

Chapter 12: Family Farms

Relief for Family Farmers

Historically, farmers have been accorded special treatment in the Bankruptcy Code. In the 1978 act, as in earlier versions, small farmers were exempted from involuntary proceedings. Thus, a small farmer who filed a voluntary Chapter 11 or 13 petition could not have the proceeding converted into a Chapter 7 liquidation over his objection so long as he complied with the act's requirements in a timely fashion. Additional protection was also accorded through the provision allowing states to opt out of the federal exemption scheme and to provide their own exemptions. A number of states used this flexibility to provide generous exemptions for farmers so they would be able to keep their tools and implements.

Despite these provisions, the serious stress on the agricultural sector in the mid-1980s led Congress in 1986 to further amend the Bankruptcy Act by adding a new Chapter 12 targeted to the financial problems of the family farm. During the 1970s and 1980s, farmland prices appreciated and many farmers borrowed heavily to expand their productive capacity, creating a large debt load in the agricultural sector. When land values subsequently dropped and excess production in the world kept farm product prices low, many farmers faced extreme financial difficulty.

Chapter 12 is modeled after Chapter 13, which is discussed next. It is available only for family farmers with regular income. To qualify, a farmer and spouse must have not less than 80 percent of their total noncontingent, liquidated debts arising out of their farming operations. The aggregate debt must be less than $1.5 million and at least 50 percent of an individual's or couple's income during the year preceding the filing of the petition must have come from the farming operation. A corporation or partnership can also qualify, provided that more than 50 percent of the stock or equity is held by one family or its relatives and they conduct the farming operation. Again, 80 percent of the debt must arise from the farming operation; the aggregate debt ceiling is $1.5 million.

The debtor is usually permitted to remain in possession to operate the farm. Although the debtor in possession has many of the rights of a Chapter 11 trustee, a trustee is appointed under Chapter 12 and the debtor is subject to his supervision. The trustee is permitted to sell unnecessary assets, including farmland and equipment, without the consent of secured creditors and before a plan is approved. However, the secured creditor's interest attaches to the proceeds of the sale.

The debtor is required to file a plan within 90 days of the filing of the Chapter 12 petition—although the bankruptcy court has the discretion to extend the time. A hearing is held on the proposed plan, and it can be confirmed over the objection of creditors. The debtor may release to any secured party the collateral that secures the claim to obtain confirmation without the acceptance by that creditor.

Unsecured creditors are required to receive at least liquidation value under the Chapter 12 plan. If an unsecured creditor or the trustee objects to the plan, the court may still confirm the plan despite the objection so long as it calls for full payment of the unsecured creditor's claim or it provides that the debtor's disposable income for the duration of the plan is applied to making payments on it. A debtor who fulfills his plan, or is excused from full performance because of subsequent hardship, is entitled to a discharge.

Chapter 13: Consumer Debt Adjustments

Relief for Individuals

Chapter 13 of the Bankruptcy Act, entitled Adjustments of Debts for Individuals, gives individuals who do not want to be declared bankrupt an opportunity to pay their debts in installments under the protection of a federal court. Under Chapter 13, the debtor has this opportunity free of such problems as garnishments and attachments of her property by creditors. Only individuals with regular incomes (including sole proprietors of businesses) who owe individually (or with their spouse) liquidated, unsecured debts of less than $307,675 and secured debts of less than $922,975 are eligible to file under Chapter 13. Under the pre-1978 Bankruptcy Act, Chapter 13 proceedings were known as "wage earner plans." The 1978 amendments expanded the coverage of these proceedings.

Procedure

Chapter 13 proceedings are initiated only by the voluntary petition of a debtor filed in the Bankruptcy Court. Creditors of the debtor may not file an involuntary petition for a Chapter 13 proceeding. The debtor in the petition states that he is insolvent or unable to pay his debts as they mature and that he desires to effect a composition or an extension, or both, out of future earnings or income. A **composition of debts** is an arrangement whereby the amount the person owes is reduced, whereas an **extension** provides the person a longer period of time in which to pay his debts. Commonly, the debtor files at the same time a list of his creditors as well as a list of his assets, liabilities, and executory contracts.

Following the filing of the petition, the court calls a meeting of creditors, at which time proofs of claims are received and allowed or disallowed. The debtor is examined, and she submits a plan of payment. The plan is submitted to the secured creditors for acceptance. If they accept the plan and if the court is satisfied that the plan is proposed in good faith, meets the legal requirements, and is in the interest of the creditors, the court approves the plan. The court then appoints a trustee to carry out the plan. The plan must provide for payments over three years or less, unless the court approves a longer period of up to five years.

No plan may be approved if the trustee or an unsecured creditor objects, unless the plan provides for the objecting creditor to be paid the present value of what he is owed or provides for the debtor to commit all of his projected disposable income for a three-year period to pay his creditors.

In the case that follows, *In the Matter of Kelly,* a proposed plan was rejected on the grounds it had not been proposed in good faith.

In the Matter of Kelly   *217 B.R. 273 (Bankr. D. Neb. 1997)*

Paul Kelly was a graduate student at the University of Nebraska, who had been working on his Ph.D. since 1991. He expected to complete it in 1999. He was also working as a clerk in a liquor store approximately 32 hours per week and earned $5.85 per hour. His monthly expenses were $743.00, and his monthly take-home pay was $761.00. Kelly borrowed money through *student loans to enable him to pay tuition, fees, books, and other school-related expenses and expected to continue to do so until he finished his Ph.D.*

On July 26, 1994, the U.S. District Court in Minnesota entered a judgment in the amount of $30,000 against Kelly and in favor of Capitol Indemnity Corporation. The judgment was based on a misappropriation of funds by Kelly from a bank insured by Capitol. The court's order provided that the judgment was not dischargeable in bankruptcy.

Kelly filed a Chapter 13 petition. In his Chapter 13 plan, Kelly proposed to pay a total of $7,080 by paying off $118 per month, $100 of which would come from student loans. In the proceeding, Kelly testified that among other things, he was currently qualified to teach at the college or university level and could earn about $20,000 but he preferred to work part-time as a clerk while he completed graduate school. Capitol objected to the proposed plan on the grounds it was not proposed in good faith. Capitol contended that Kelly should not be allowed to languish in graduate school, remain underemployed, and obtain the benefit of a Chapter 13 discharge. Capitol asserted that Kelly was attempting to discharge a debt that was nondischargeable under Chapter 7, proposed to make payments primarily from his student loans, and would be paying a dividend to unsecured creditors of only 8 1/2 percent. These factors, Capitol contended, demonstrated that the plan had not been proposed in good faith and that it should not be confirmed.

Minahan, Bankruptcy Judge Capitol objects to confirmation of the proposed Chapter 13 plan on three grounds:

1. The debtor is not an individual with regular income as required by 11 U.S.C. section 109(e);
2. The plan is not feasible; and
3. The plan was not proposed in good faith.

The Eighth Circuit Court of Appeals provided a nonexclusive list of factors to be considered in determining whether a Chapter 13 plan is filed in good faith. *United States v. Estus* (1982). The factors listed in *Estus* are: (1) the amount of the proposed payments and the amount of the debtor's surplus; (2) the debtor's employment history, ability to earn and the likelihood of future increases in income; (3) the probable or expected duration of the plan; (4) the accuracy of the plan's statements of the debts, expenses and percentage repayment of unsecured debt and whether any inaccuracies are an attempt to mislead the court; (5) the extent of preferential treatment between classes of creditors; (6) the extent to which secured claims are modified; (7) the type of debt sought to be discharged and whether any such debt is nondischargeable in Chapter 7; (8) the existence of special circumstances such as inordinate medical expenses; (9) the frequency with which the debtor has sought relief under the Bankruptcy Reform Act; (10) the motivation and sincerity of the debtor in seeking Chapter 13 relief; and (11) the burden which the plan's administration would place upon the trustee.

Section 1325(b) of the Bankruptcy Code was added in 1984, which subsumes most of the *Estus* factors; however, in determining whether a Chapter 13 plan is filed in good faith, the eighth circuit has stated that the totality of the circumstances analysis adopted in *Estus* remains in place.

Capitol's assertion that the debtor is not eligible for Chapter 13 relief because he does not receive regular income is without merit. The debtor has regular income from his employment as a clerk. This income is sufficiently stable and regular to enable the debtor to make payments under a Chapter 13 plan. The debtor has regular income and is eligible for relief under Chapter 13.

Capitol's objections regarding feasibility and good faith are addressed together. Capitol essentially asserts that the plan is not feasible because plan payments are funded from student loans. Without the student loans, it will not be feasible for the debtor to make the proposed plan payments. Capitol contends that the debtor should not be allowed to languish in graduate school, remain underemployed, and obtain the benefit of a Chapter 13 discharge. Capitol asserts that the fact the debtor is attempting to discharge a debt that is nondischargeable under Chapter 7, proposes to make payments primarily from his student loans, and is paying a dividend to unsecured creditors of only 8 1/2 percent are all factors which demonstrate that the plan has not been proposed in good faith.

I conclude that the debtor's plan has not been proposed in good faith. Total payments are $7,080 under the Chapter 13 plan. After payment of secured and priority claims, unsecured claims will be paid pro rata yielding a dividend of only 8 1/2 percent. The plan does not provide for the repayment of student loans which may become payable during the life of the plan. The debtor failed to list over $38,500 in student loans on his bankruptcy schedules until the Chapter 13 Trustee objected to confirmation of the original plan. Over half of the unsecured debt is owed to Capitol and Capitol asserts that this debt would be excepted from discharge in Chapter 7 under section 523(a)(4). The debtor stated in a deposition that he is currently qualified to teach at the college or university level and could earn about $20,000 annually. However, he has elected to work part time as a clerk while he attends graduate school. The debtor proposes to fund his plan primarily with student loans. Without these student loan funds, the debtor's disposable income is only $18.00 per month. From these facts, I conclude that the debtor's plan is not proposed in good faith.

Because the plan has not been proposed in good faith, it should not be confirmed. Although the debtor is arguably utilizing all his disposable income to make payments un-

der the proposed Chapter 13 plan, it is simply not equitable for the debtor to voluntarily remain underemployed, to obtain the benefit of an advanced college degree, and to discharge his obligations to creditors upon payment of a nominal dividend.

Objection of Capitol Indemnity Corporation to confirmation of law sustained.

Under the 1984 amendments, a Chapter 13 debtor must begin making the installment payments proposed in her plan within 30 days after the plan is filed. The interim payments must continue to be made until the plan is confirmed or denied. If the plan is denied, the money, less any administrative expenses, is returned to the debtor by the trustee. The interim payments give the trustee an opportunity to observe the debtor's performance and thus to be in a better position to make a recommendation about whether the plan should be approved.

Once approved, a plan may be subsequently modified on petition of a debtor or a creditor where there is a material change in the debtor's circumstances.

Suppose Curtis Brown has a monthly take-home pay of $1,000 and a few assets. He owes $1,500 to the credit union, borrowed for the purchase of furniture; he is supposed to repay the credit union $75 per month. He owes $1,800 to the finance company on the purchase of a used car; he is supposed to repay the company $90 a month. He has also run up charges of $1,200 on a MasterCard account, primarily for emergency repairs to his car; he must pay $60 per month to MasterCard. His rent is $350 per month, and food and other living expenses run him another $425 per month. Curtis was laid off from his job for a month and fell behind on his payments to his creditors. He then filed a Chapter 13 petition. In his plan, he might, for example, offer to repay the credit union $50 a month, the finance company $60 a month, and MasterCard $40 a month—with the payments spread over three years rather than the shorter time for which they are currently scheduled.

Discharge

When the debtor has completed her performance of the plan, the court issues an order that discharges her from the debts covered by the plan. The debtor may also be

discharged even though she did not complete her payments within the three years if the court is satisfied that the failure is due to circumstances for which the debtor cannot justly be held accountable. An active Chapter 13 proceeding stays, or holds in abeyance, any straight bankruptcy proceedings and any actions by creditors to collect consumer debts. However, if the Chapter 13 proceeding is dismissed (for example, because the debtor fails to file an acceptable plan or defaults on an accepted plan), straight bankruptcy proceedings may begin.

Advantages of Chapter 13

A debtor may choose to file under Chapter 13 to avoid the stigma of bankruptcy or to retain more of his property than is exempt from bankruptcy under state or federal law. Nonexempt property would have to be surrendered to the Trustee in a Chapter 7 liquidation proceeding. Chapter 13 can provide some financial discipline to a debtor as well as an opportunity to get his financial affairs back in good shape. It also gives him relief from the pressures of individual creditors so long as he makes the payments called for by the plan. The debtor's creditors may benefit by recovering a greater percentage of the debt owed to them than would be obtainable in straight bankruptcy.

Problems and Problem Cases

1. Tony Griffin was a debtor in a Chapter 7 bankruptcy proceeding. He claimed that his 1985 Hobie Magnum sailboat was exempt from his creditors under a Texas statute that provided an exemption for "athletic and sporting" equipment. A creditor objected to the claim of exemption. Should the sailboat be considered athletic and sporting equipment and thus exempt from the claims of the debtor's creditors?

CONCEPT REVIEW

Comparison of Major Forms of Bankruptcy Proceedings

Purpose	Chapter 7 Liquidation	Chapter 11 Reorganization	Chapter 12 Adjustments of Debts	Chapter 13 Adjustments of Debts
Eligible Debtors	Individuals, and partnerships, and corporations *except* municipal corporations, railroads, insurance companies, banks, and savings and loan associations. Farmers and ranchers are eligible only if they petition voluntarily.	Generally, same as Chapter 7 except a railroad may be a debtor, and a stockholder and commodity broker may not be a debtor under Chapter 11	Family farmer with regular income, at least 50 percent of which comes from farming, and less than $1.5 million in debts, at least 80 percent of which is farm related.	Individual with regular income with liquidated unsecured debts less than $269,250 and secured debts of less than $807,750.
Initiation of Proceeding	Petition by debtor (voluntary). Petition by creditors (involuntary).	Petition by debtor (voluntary). Petition by creditors (involuntary).	Petition by debtor.	Petition by debtor.
Basic Procedure	1. Appointment of trustee. 2. Debtor retains exempt property. 3. Nonexempt property is sold and proceeds distributed based on priority of claims. 4. Dischargeable debts are terminated.	1. Appointment of trustee and committees of creditors and equity security holders. 2. Debtor submits reorganization plan. 3. If plan is approved and implemented, debts are discharged.	1. Trustee is appointed but debtor usually remains in possession of farm. 2. Debtor submits a plan in which unsecured creditors must receive at least liquidation value. 3. If plan is approved and fulfilled, debtor is entitled to a discharge.	1. Debtor indicates in petition that he is seeking a composition of debts or an extension. 2. If plan is approved after submitted to creditors, then trustee is appointed. 3. If plan is approved and fulfilled, debts covered by plan are discharged.
Advantages	After liquidation and distribution of assets, most or all debts may be discharged and debtor gets a fresh start.	Debtor remains in business and debts are liquidated through implementation of approved reorganization plan.	Debtor generally remains in possession and has opportunity to work out of financial difficulty over period of time (usually three years) through implementation of approved plan.	Debtor has opportunity to work out of financial difficulty over period of time (usually three years) through implementation of approved plan.

2. Gary Johnson filed a Chapter 13 bankruptcy petition. Acting on the advice of his lawyer shortly before filing the petition, Johnson sold an interest in real estate and used the proceeds to buy a life insurance policy with a face value of $31,460 and a cash value of $12,118. His wife was named as the beneficiary. Johnson claimed that the policy was exempt under South Dakota law, which provides for an exemption of up to $20,000 for the proceeds of a life insurance policy payable directly to the insured, his surviving spouse, or his family. A creditor objected to the exemption but made no showing of fraudulent intent on Johnson's part. Should the exemption be allowed?

3. William Kranich, Jr., was the sole shareholder in the DuVal Financial Corporation (DFC). On November 10, 1991, Kranich filed a voluntary petition for relief under Chapter 7; on January 6, 1992, DFC also filed a voluntary petition under Chapter 7. Prior to the commencement of the Chapter 7 proceedings, Kranich conveyed his personal residence in Clearwater, Florida, to DFC. The transfer was wholly without consideration. Shortly thereafter, DFC transferred the property to William Kranich III and June Elizabeth Kranich, Kranich's son and daughter, as tenants in common. This transfer was also without consideration. The bankruptcy trustee brought suit to recover the property from the son and daughter on the grounds that the transfer was fraudulent. Could the trustee recover the property on the grounds that its transfer, without consideration, was fraudulent?

4. David Hott was a college graduate with a degree in business administration who was employed as an insurance agent. He and his wife graduated from college in 1996. At the time he graduated, Hott had outstanding student loans of $14,500 for which he was given a grace period before he had to repay them. Hott became unemployed. Bills began to accumulate and a number of his outstanding bills were near the credit limits on his accounts. About that time, he received a promotional brochure by mail from Signal Consumer Discount Company, offering the opportunity to borrow several thousand dollars. The Hotts decided it appeared to be an attractive vehicle for them to use to consolidate their debts. Hott went to the Signal office and filled out a credit application. He did not list the student loan as a current debt. He later claimed that someone in the office told him he didn't have to list it if he owned an automobile but there was significant doubt about the credibility of this claim. Had he listed it, he would not have met the debt–income ratio required by Signal and it would not have made the loan. As it was, Signal agreed to make the loan on the condition Hott pay off a car debt in order to reduce his debt–income ratio and Hott agreed to do so. On March 30, 1997, Signal loaned the Hotts $3,458.01. On June 24, 1998, the Hotts filed for bankruptcy. Signal objected to discharge of the balance remaining on its loan on the ground it had been obtained through the use of a materially false financial statement. Was discharge of the debt barred on the ground it had been obtained through the use of a materially false financial statement?

5. While attending college, Barbara Barrington obtained a student loan from the New York State Higher Education Services Corporation. Barrington had depressive illnesses all her life, as had previous generations in her family. Her grandmother was institutionalized, and her mother had been on medication for a long time. Barrington was discharged by Eastman Kodak Company because she could not face the problems and stress of her job. Since that time, she had stayed at home, slept a lot, and played with her dog. She made little or no effort to find other employment because of her depressed condition. She also filed for bankruptcy. In the bankruptcy proceeding, one of the questions was whether payment of her student loan would impose an undue hardship on Barrington, and thus whether the loan was dischargeable. Should the student loan be discharged?

6. Brian Scholz was involved in an automobile collision with a person insured by The Travelers Insurance Company. At the time, Scholz was cited for, and pled no contest to, a criminal charge of driving under the influence of alcohol arising out of the accident. The Travelers paid its insured $4,303.68 and was subrogated to the rights of its insured against Scholz. Subsequently, The Travelers filed a civil action against Scholz to recover the amount it had paid, and a default judgment was entered against Scholz. Eleven months later, Scholz sought relief from the bankruptcy court by filing a voluntary petition undue Chapter 7. One of the questions in the bankruptcy proceeding was whether the debt owing to The Travelers was nondischargeable. Is the debt dischargeable?

7. Bryant filed a Chapter 7 petition on January 7, 1984. On March 8, she filed an application to reaffirm an indebtedness owed to General Motors Acceptance Corporation (GMAC) on her 1980 Cadillac automobile. Bryant was not married, and she supported two teenage daughters. She was not currently employed, and she collected $771 a month in unemployment benefits and $150 a month in rental income from her mother. Her monthly house payments were $259. The present value of the Cadillac was $9,175; she owed $7,956.37 on it, and her monthly payments were $345.93. Bryant indicated that she wanted to keep the vehicle because it was reliable. GMAC admitted that Bryant had been, and continued to be, current in her payments. GMAC said that the car was in no danger of being repossessed but that, absent reaffirmation, it might decide to repossess it. Under the law at the time, permission of the court was required for a reaffirmation agreement. Should the court grant Bryant's petition to reaffirm her indebtedness to GMAC?

8. John and Christine Newsom were noncommissioned officers in the U.S. Air Force who each earned $1,408 net a month. In October 1986, they filed a voluntary petition in bankruptcy under Chapter 7. At the time, they had three secured debts totaling $21,956, $21,820 of which stemmed from the purchase of a 1986 Ford Bronco and a 1985 Pontiac Trans Am. They proposed to surrender the Bronco and a secured television set to the trustee, leaving only the secured debt, $10,000, owing on the Pontiac. Their unsecured debts totaled $20,911: $6,611 from bank card use, $12,764 from retail credit, and $1,350 from credit union loans. Of the unsecured debt, $11,563 was incurred in 1986. The Newsoms filed an income and expense schedule showing that their monthly expenses totaled $2,232, including $100 for recreation and $150 for cigarettes and "walking around money." This left a surplus of $276 a month. The Bankruptcy Court, on its own motion, issued an order to the Newsoms to show why their petition should not be dismissed pursuant to the substantial abuse provision of the Bankruptcy Code. Should the Chapter 7 petition be dismissed as a substantial abuse of the provisions of the Bankruptcy Act?

9. The A. H. Robbins Company is a publicly held company that filed a voluntary petition for relief under Chapter 11 of the Bankruptcy Code. Robbins sought refuge in Chapter 11 because of a multitude of civil actions filed against it by women who alleged they were injured by use of the Dalkon Shield intrauterine device that it manufactured and sold as a birth control device. Approximately 325,000 notices of claim against Robbins were received by the Bankruptcy Court.

In 1985, the court appointed the Official Committee of Security Holders to represent the interest of Robbins' public shareholders. In April 1987, Robbins filed a proposed plan of reorganization but no action was taken on the proposed plan because of a merger proposal submitted by Rorer Group, Inc. Under this plan, Dalkon Shield claimants would be compensated out of a $1.75 billion fund, all other creditors would be paid in full, and the Robbins' stockholders would receive stock of the merged corporation. However, it being a time of other critical activity in the bankruptcy proceeding, no revised plan incorporating the merger proposal had been filed or approved.

Earlier, in August 1986, the court had appointed Ralph Mabey as an examiner to evaluate and suggest proposed elements of a plan of reorganization. On Mabey's suggestion, a proposed order was put before the district court supervising the proceeding that would require Robbins to establish a $15 million emergency treatment fund "for the purpose of assisting in providing tubal reconstructive surgery or in-vitro fertilization to eligible Dalkon Shield claimants." The purpose of the emergency fund was to assist those claimants who asserted that they had become infertile as a consequence of their use of the product. A program was proposed for administering the fund and for making the medical decisions required.

On May 21, 1987, the district court ordered that the emergency treatment fund be created. This action was challenged by the committee representing the equity security holders. Was the court justified in ordering the distribution of some of the bankrupt's assets on an emergency basis before a reorganization plan was approved?

10. Winifred Doersam was the borrower on three student loans made to her by First Federal Savings and Loan and guaranteed by the state of Ohio Student Loan Commission (OSLC) totaling $10,000 to finance her graduate education at the University of Dayton. Doersam also signed as the cosigner for a $5,000 student loan for her daughter, also made by First Federal and guaranteed by OSLC. With the use of the loans, she was able to obtain a position as a systems analyst with NCR Corporation, which required her to obtain a master's degree in order to retain her position at an annual salary of $24,000. Approximately six weeks before her graduation, and before the first payment on her student loans was due, Doersam filed a petition and plan under Chapter 13. In her plan, she proposed to pay $375 a month to her unsecured creditors over a 36-month period. Doersam's total unsecured debt was $18,418, 81 percent of which was comprised of the outstanding student loans. Her schedules provided for payment of rent of $300 per month and food of $400 per month. Her listed dependents included her 23-year-old daughter and her 1-year-old granddaughter. At the time, her daughter was employed in the Ohio Work Program, a program designed to help welfare recipients, for which she was paid a small salary. The OLSC objected to the plan proposed by Doersam on the grounds that it was filed in bad faith. Should the bankruptcy court refuse to confirm the plan on the grounds it was not filed in good faith?

Online Research: Current Corporate Reorganizations

Use the Internet to locate articles from *The Wall Street Journal* and other financial publications concerning one of the recent major corporate bankruptcies and ascertain the following information concerning the bankruptcy case: (1) When was the bankruptcy petition filed? (2) Was the petition filed under Chapter 7 (liquidation) or under Chapter 11 (reorganization)? (3) Who were/are the major creditors or holders of claims against the bankrupt entity? (4) If the matter is in Chapter 11, has a reorganization plan been filed and what were/are its major elements? (5) Has the bankruptcy proceeding been completed? (6) If it has been completed, how did the major creditors appear to fare?

COMMERCIAL PAPER

31

NEGOTIABLE INSTRUMENTS

Chances are that you are using a variety of negotiable instruments in your everyday life, perhaps without realizing the special qualities that have led to their widespread use in commerce and the rules that govern them. If you have a job, your employer probably pays you by check, and you likely have a checking account that you use to make purchases and pay your bills. If you have accumulated some savings, you may have invested them in a certificate of deposit at a bank. And, if you have borrowed money, you very likely were asked to sign a promissory note acknowledging the debt and committing to repay it on specified terms. This chapter introduces the law of negotiable instruments, including:

- The special qualities and benefits of negotiable instruments.
- The basic types of commercial paper and their defining characteristics.
- The formal requirements that must be met for instruments such as checks, notes, and certificates of deposit to qualify as negotiable instruments.
- What happens if you write or receive a check in which there is a conflict between the amount set forth in figures and the amount set out in words.

AS COMMERCE AND TRADE developed, people moved beyond exclusive reliance on barter to the use of money and then to the use of substitutes for money. The term *commercial paper* encompasses substitutes in common usage today such as checks, promissory notes, and certificates of deposit.

History discloses that every civilization that engaged to an appreciable extent in commerce used some form of commercial paper. Probably the oldest commercial paper used in the carrying on of trade is the promissory note. Archaeologists found a promissory note made payable to bearer that dated from about 2100 B.C. The merchants of Europe used commercial paper—which, under the law merchant, was negotiable—in the 13th and 14th centuries. Commercial paper does not appear to have been used in England until about A.D. 1600.

This chapter and the three following chapters outline and discuss the body of law that governs commercial paper. Of particular interest are those kinds of commercial

paper having the attribute of *negotiability*—that is, they can generally be transferred from party to party and accepted as a substitute for money. This chapter discusses the nature and benefits of negotiable instruments and then outlines the requirements an instrument must meet to qualify as a negotiable instrument. Subsequent chapters discuss transfer and negotiation of instruments, the rights and liabilities of parties to negotiable instruments, and the special rules applicable to checks.

Nature of Negotiable Instruments

When a person buys a television set and gives the merchant a check drawn on his checking account, that person uses a form of negotiable commercial paper. Similarly, a person who goes to a bank or a credit union to borrow money might sign a promissory note agreeing to pay the money back in 90 days. Again, the bank and borrower use a form of negotiable commercial paper.

Commercial paper is basically a *contract for the payment of money.* It may serve as a substitute for money payable immediately, such as a check. Or, it can be used as a means of extending credit. When a television set is bought by giving the merchant a check, the check is a substitute for money. If a credit union loans a borrower money now in exchange for the borrower's promise to repay it later, the promissory note signed by the borrower is a means of extending credit.

Uniform Commercial Code

The law of commercial paper is covered in Article 3 (Negotiable Instruments) and Article 4 (Bank Deposits and Collections) of the Uniform Commercial Code. Other negotiable documents, such as investment securities and documents of title, are treated in other articles of the Code. The original Code Articles 3 and 4, adopted initially in the 1960s, generally followed the basic, centuries-old rules governing the use of commercial paper; but at the same time they adopted modern terminology and coordinated, clarified, and simplified the law. However, business practices continued to evolve and new technological developments have changed the way that banks process checks. Accordingly, in 1990, a joint effort by the American Law Institute and the National Conference of Commissioners on Uniform State Laws produced a Revised Article 3 and related amendments to Articles 1 and 4. The purpose was to clarify Articles 3 and 4, to bring them into better harmony with current business practice, and to acknowledge recent technological developments.

Because virtually all of the states (except New York) have adopted the 1990 revision to Article 3 and the related amendments to Article 4, we use them as the basis for this edition of the textbook. The reader should keep in mind that instruments may be interpreted under the version of the Code that was in effect when the instruments were issued.

For the student of negotiable instruments law, this is an interesting—but also a particularly difficult—time to study this area of the law. Revised Article 3 and the related amendments introduce new concepts, change definitions and the wording of key elements, and delete numerous provisions from the original version of Article 3. As a result, in drafting this chapter and the three chapters that follow, the authors have relied heavily on tracking the language of the revised article and on statements by the drafters as to their intent. Further complicating the picture is the fact that, in a number of respects, the revision is more complex than the original version. Moreover, while more than 30 years of case law had helped flesh out the meaning of the original Article 3, the revision has diminished some of the value of that case law. Virtually all of the cases to date arose under the original version of Article 3 and are of mixed—and sometimes very limited—value in trying to assess how courts will decide issues under the revision.

Just as these factors posed a challenge to the authors of this edition of the textbook, they will pose a challenge to you and your instructor as you work your way through the material on negotiable instruments. More questions are likely to be left up in the air than is true in other, more settled areas of the law. It will take a number of years, considerable experience, and new case law to clarify the updated law of negotiable instruments.

Negotiable Instruments

The two basic types of negotiable instruments are *promises to pay money* and *orders to pay money.* Promissory notes and certificates of deposit issued by banks are promises to pay someone money. Checks and drafts are orders to another person to pay money to a third person. A check, which is a type of draft, is an order directed to a certain kind of person, namely a bank, to pay money from a person's account to a third person.

Negotiability

Negotiable instruments are a special kind of commercial paper that can pass readily through our financial system and is accepted in place of money. This gives negotiable instruments many advantages.

For example, Searle, the owner of a clothing store in New York, contracts with Amado, a swimsuit manufacturer in Los Angeles, for $10,000 worth of swimsuits. If negotiable instruments did not exist, Searle would have to send or carry $10,000 across the country, which would be both inconvenient and risky. If someone stole the money along the way, Searle would lose the $10,000 unless he could locate the thief. By using a check in which Searle orders his bank to pay $10,000 from his account to Amado, or to someone designated by Amado, Searle makes the payment in a far more convenient manner. He sends only a single piece of paper to Amado. If the check is properly prepared and sent, sending the check is less risky than sending money. Even if someone steals the check along the way, Searle's bank may not

Figure 1   *Promissory Note*

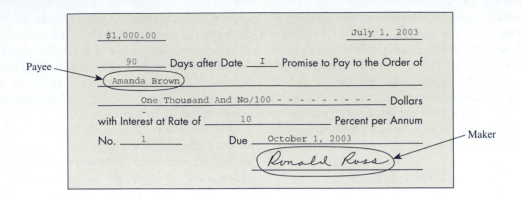

pay it to anyone but Amado or someone authorized by Amado. And, because the check gives Amado the right either to collect the $10,000 or to transfer the right to collect it to someone else, the check is a practical substitute for cash to Amado as well as to Searle.

In this chapter and in the three following chapters, we discuss the requirements necessary for a contract for the payment of money to qualify as a negotiable instrument. We also explain the features that not only distinguish a negotiable instrument from a simple contract but also led to the widespread use of negotiable instruments as a substitute for money.

Kinds of Negotiable Instruments

Promissory Notes

The promissory note is the simplest form of commercial paper; it is simply a promise to pay money. A **promissory note** is a two-party instrument in which one person (known as the **maker**) makes an unconditional promise in writing to pay another person (the **payee**), a person specified by that person, or the bearer of the instrument, a fixed amount of money, with or without interest, either on demand or at a specified, future time [3–104].[1]

The promissory note, shown in Figures 1 and 2, is a credit instrument; it is used in a wide variety of transactions in which credit is extended. For example, if a per-

son purchases an automobile using money borrowed from a bank, the bank has the person sign a promissory note for the unpaid balance of the purchase price. Similarly, if a person borrows money to purchase a house, the lender who makes the loan and takes a mortgage on the house has the person sign a promissory note for the amount due on the loan. The note probably states that it is secured by a mortgage. The terms of payment on the note should correspond with the terms of the sales contract for the purchase of the house.

Certificates of Deposit

The certificate of deposit given by a bank or a savings and loan association when a deposit of money is made is a type of note, namely a note of a bank. A **certificate of deposit** is an instrument containing (1) an acknowledgment by a bank that it has received a deposit of money and (2) a promise by the bank to repay the sum of money [3–104(j)]. Figure 3 is an example of a certificate of deposit.

Most banks no longer issue certificates of deposit (CD) in paper form. Rather, the bank maintains an electronic deposit and provides the customer with a statement indicating the amount of principal held on a CD basis and the terms of the CD, such as the maturity and interest rate. In these instances, the certificate of deposit is not in negotiable instrument form.

Drafts

A **draft** is a form of commercial paper that involves an *order* to pay money rather than a promise to pay money [3–104(e)]. The most common example of a draft is a

---

[1]The numbers in brackets refer to the sections of the 1990 Revised Article 3 (and the conforming amendments to Articles 1 and 4) of the Uniform Commercial Code.

Figure 2   *Promissory Note (Consumer Loan Note)*

The National BANK OF WASHINGTON

CONSUMER LOAN NOTE

Date ___November 21,___ , 20 _03_

#

The words I and me mean all borrowers who signed this note. The word bank means The National Bank of Washington.

Promise to Pay

___30 months from today,___ I promise to pay to the order of (The National Bank of Washington)

Seventy-Eight Hundred Seventy Five and no/100 - - - - - - - - - - -dollars ($ ___7,875.00___).

Payee

Responsibility

Although this note may be signed below by more than one person, I understand that we are each as individuals responsible for paying back the full amount.

Breakdown of Loan

This is what I will pay:

Amount of loan	1.$	6,800.00
Credit Life Insurance (optional)	2.$	100.00
Other (describe)	3.$	-0-
Amount Financed (Add 1 and 2 and 3)	4.$	6,900
FINANCE CHARGE	5.$	975.00
Total of Payments (Add 4 and 5)	$	7,875.00
ANNUAL PERCENTAGE RATE		10.5%

Repayment

This is how I will repay:
I will repay the amount of this note in ___30___ equal uninterrupted monthly installments of $ _262.50_ each on the __1st__ day of each month starting on the __1st__ day of _December_ , 20 _03_ and ending on ___May 1___ , _____ ___2007___

Prepayment

I have the right to prepay the whole outstanding amount of this note at any time. If I do, or if this loan is refinanced—that is, replaced by a new note—you will refund the unearned finance charge, figured by the rule of 78—a commonly used formula for figuring rebates on installment loans.

Late Charge

Any installment not paid within ten days of its due date shall be subject to a late charge of 5% of the payment, not to exceed $5.00 for any such late installment.

Security

To protect the National Bank of Washington, I give what is known as a security interest in my auto and/or other: (Describe) _Ford Thunderbird_

 # Serial #115117-12-

See the security agreement.

Credit Life Insurance

Credit life insurance is not required to obtain this loan. The bank need not provide it and I do not need to buy it unless I sign immediately below. The cost of credit life insurance is $___100.00___ for the term of the loan.

Signed: _A. J. Smith_

Date: ___November 21, 2003___

Default

If for any reason I fail to make any payment on time, I shall be in default. The bank can then demand immediate payment of the entire remaining unpaid balance of this loan, without giving anyone further notice. If I have not paid the full amount of the loan when the final payment is due, the bank will charge me interest on the unpaid balance at six percent (6%) per year.

Right of Offset

If this loan becomes past due, the bank will have the right to pay this loan from any deposit or security I have at this bank without telling me ahead of time. Even if the bank gives me an extension of time to pay this loan, I still must repay the entire loan.

Collection Fees

If this note is placed with an attorney for collection, then I agree to pay an attorney's fee of fifteen percent (15%) of the unpaid balance. This fee will be added to the unpaid balance of the loan.

Co-borrowers

If I am signing this note as a co-borrower, I agree to be equally responsible with the borrower for this loan. The bank does not have to notify me that this note has not been paid. The bank can change the terms of payment and release any security without notifying or releasing me from responsibility for this loan.

Copy Received

I received a completely filled in copy of this note. If I have signed for Credit Life Insurance, I received a copy of the Credit Life Insurance certificate.

Borrower: (_A. J. Smith_) ◄——— *Maker*
A. J. Smith
3412 Brookdale, S. W. Washington D.C.
Address

Co-borrower: (_Andrea H. Smith_) ◄——— *Co-maker*
Andrea H. Smith
3412 Brookdale, S. W. Washington D.C.
Address

Co-borrower: _____
Address

CONSUMER CREDIT HOTLINE: If you have any questions, please call us immediately at (202) 624-3450.

NBW 437 (Rev. 11-78)   1-Bank's copy   2-File copy   3-Customer's copy

Source: The National Bank of Washington.

check. A draft has three parties to it: one person (known as the **drawer**) orders a second person (the **drawee**) to pay a certain sum of money to a third person (the **payee**), to a person specified by that person, or to bearer.

Drafts other than checks are used in a variety of commercial transactions. If Brown owes Ames money, Ames may draw a draft for the amount of the debt, naming Brown as drawee and herself or her bank as payee, and

Figure 3 *Certificate of Deposit*

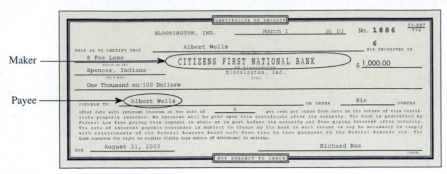

Source: Citizens First National Bank of Bloomington.

send the draft to Brown's bank for payment. Alternatively, Ames might send a draft providing for payment on a certain day in the future to Brown for "acceptance." Brown could "accept" the draft by signing his name to it, thereby obligating himself to pay the amount specified in the draft on that day in the future to Ames or to someone specified by Ames.

In freight shipments in which the terms are "cash on delivery," the seller commonly ships the goods to the buyer on an "order bill of lading" consigned to himself at the place of delivery. The seller then indorses the bill of lading and attaches a draft naming the buyer as drawee. He then sends the bill of lading and the draft through banking channels to the buyer's bank. A bank in the buyer's locale presents the draft to the buyer's bank for payment, and when the former bank receives payment, delivers the bill of lading to the buyer. Through this commercial transaction, the buyer gets the goods and the seller gets his money.

When credit is extended, the same procedure is followed, but the seller uses a time draft—a draft payable at some future time (see Figure 4). In such a transaction, the buyer "accepts" the draft (instead of paying it) and obligates herself to pay the amount of the draft when due. In these cases, the *drawee* (now called the **acceptor**) should date her signature so that the date at which payment is due is clear to all [3–409(c)].

Checks

A **check** is a *draft payable on demand* and drawn on a bank (i.e., a bank is the drawee or person to whom the order to pay is addressed). Checks are the most widely used form of commercial paper. The issuer of a check orders the bank at which she maintains an account to pay a specified person, or someone designated by that person, a fixed amount of money from the account. For example, Elizabeth Brown has a checking account at the National Bank of Washington. She goes to Sears Roebuck and agrees to buy a washing machine priced at $459.95. If she writes a check to pay for it, she is the drawer of the

---

CYBERLAW IN ACTION

E-Checks

In addition to checks, electronic funds transfers through the use of ATMs or in retail stores, and telephone-initiated checks, larger retailers such as grocers and department stores use e-commerce instead of traditional paper checks. This process, called "check conversion," starts with the buyer giving the seller a paper check. The seller uses special equipment to gather information from the paper check; this information includes the buyer's bank account number, the "routing number" that identifies the buyer's bank, and the check's serial number. Then, the seller hands the paper check back to the buyer and completes the transaction by naming itself as the payee of the transaction and by coding in the amount of the purchase. Check conversion is one of the fastest-growing means of taking payments from consumer buyers and saves the seller time and money it otherwise would spend collecting the paper check from the buyer's bank. The legal rules concerning e-checks are discussed in Chapter 34—Checks and Electronic Transfers.

Figure 4   *Draft*

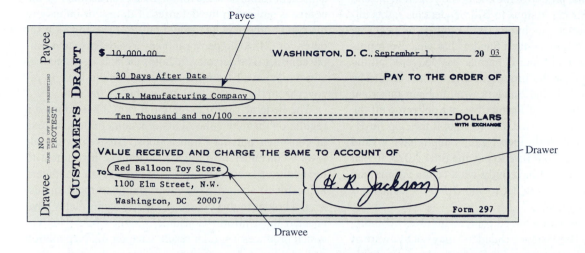

Figure 5   *Check*

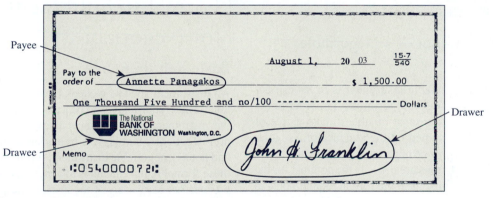

Source: The National Bank of Washington.

check, the National Bank of Washington is the drawee, and Sears is the payee. By writing the check, Elizabeth is ordering her bank to pay $459.95 from her account to Sears or to Sears's order—that is, to whomever Sears asks the bank to pay the money (see Figure 5).

An instrument may qualify as a "check" and be governed by Article 3 even though it is described on its face by another term, such as "money order." The Code definition of a "check" includes a "cashier's check" and a "teller's check." A **cashier's check** is a draft on which the drawer and drawee are the same bank (or branches of the same bank); a **teller's check** is a draft drawn by a bank (as drawer) on another bank or payable at or through a bank [3–104(g) and (h)]. For example, a check

drawn by a credit union on its account at a federally insured bank would be a teller's check.

Benefits of Negotiable Instruments

Rights of an Assignee of a Contract

As we noted in Chapter 17, Rights of Third Parties, the assignee of a contract can obtain no greater rights than the assignor had at the time of the assignment. For example, Frank Farmer and Neam's Market enter into a contract providing that Farmer will sell Neam's a dozen crates of fresh eggs a week for a year and that Neam's will pay Farmer $4,000 at the end of the year. If at the end of the year Farmer assigns to Bill Sanders his rights under the contract—including the right to collect the money from Neam's—then Sanders has whatever rights Farmer had at that time. If Farmer has delivered all the eggs to Neam's as he promised, then Farmer would be entitled to $4,000 and Sanders would obtain that right from him. However, if Farmer has not delivered all the eggs that he had promised to deliver, or if the eggs he delivered were not fresh, then Neam's might have a valid defense or reason to refuse to pay the full $4,000. In that case, Sanders would have only what rights Farmer had and also would be subject to the defense Neam's has against full payment.

Taking an assignment of a contract involves assuming certain risks. The assignee (Sanders) may not be aware of the nature and extent of any defenses that the party liable on the contract (Neam's) might have against the assignor (Farmer). An assignee who does not know what rights he is getting, or which risks he is assuming, may be reluctant to take an assignment of the contract.

Rights of a Holder of a Negotiable Instrument

The object of a negotiable instrument is to have it accepted readily as a substitute for money. In order to accept it readily, a person must be able to take it free of many of the risks assumed by the assignee of a regular contract. Under the law of negotiable instruments, this is possible if two conditions are met: (1) the contract for the payment of money must meet the formal requirements to qualify as a negotiable instrument; and (2) the person who acquires the instrument must qualify as a holder in due course. Basically, a *holder in due course* is a person who has good title to the instrument, paid value for it, acquired it in good faith, and had no notice of certain claims or defenses against payment. In addition, the instrument cannot bear facial irregularities (evidence of forgery or alteration or questions concerning its authenticity).

The next section of this chapter discusses the formal requirements for a negotiable instrument. Chapter 32, Negotiation and Holder in Due Course, outlines the requirements that a person must meet to qualify as a holder in due course.

A holder in due course of a negotiable instrument takes the instrument free of all defenses and claims to the instrument except those that concern its validity. For example, a holder in due course of a note given in payment for goods may enforce the obligation in spite of the buyer's claim that the seller breached a warranty. However, if the maker of a note wrote it under duress, such as a threat of force, or was a minor, then even a holder in due course is subject to the defenses of duress or infancy to the extent other law (1) would nullify the obligation for duress or (2) would permit infancy as a defense to a simple contract. The person who holds the note could not obtain the payment from the maker but would have to recover from the person from whom he got the note.

The Federal Trade Commission (FTC) has adopted a regulation that alters the rights of a holder in due course in consumer purchase transactions. This regulation allows a consumer who gives a negotiable instrument to use additional defenses (breach of warranty or fraudulent inducement) against payment of the instrument against even a holder in due course. Similarly, some states have enacted the Uniform Consumer Credit Code (UCCC), which produces a similar result. Chapter 32, Negotiation and Holder in Due Course, discusses the rights of a holder in due course, as well as the FTC rule.

Formal Requirements for Negotiability

Basic Requirements

An instrument such as a check or a note must meet certain formal requirements to be a negotiable instrument. If the instrument does not meet these requirements, it is non-negotiable; that is, it is treated as a simple contract and not as a negotiable instrument. A primary purpose for these formal requirements is to ensure the willingness of prospective purchasers of the instrument, particularly financial institutions such as banks, to accept it as a substitute for money.

For an instrument to be negotiable, it must:

1. Be in writing.

2. Be signed by the issuer (the *maker* in the case of a person undertaking to pay or the *drawer* in the case of a person giving an order or instruction to pay).

3. Contain an unconditional promise or order to pay a fixed amount of money, with or without interest or other charges described in the promise or order.

4. Be payable to order or to bearer at the time it is issued or first comes into possession of a holder.

5. Be payable on demand or at a definite time.

6. Not state any other undertaking or instruction by the person promising or ordering to do any act in addition to the payment of money (but it may contain

(*a*) an undertaking or promise relative to collateral to secure payment, (*b*) an authorization for confession of judgment, or (*c*) a waiver of benefit of any law intended for the advantage or protection of an obligor) [3–103; 3–104].

In addition, an instrument that otherwise qualifies as a check can be negotiable even if it is not explicitly payable to order or to bearer [3–104(c)]. As explained later, this means that a check that reads "pay John Doe" could be negotiable even though the normal form for a check is "pay to the order of _____."

A promise or order other than a check is not a negotiable instrument if at the time it is issued or first comes into the possession of a holder it contains a conspicuous statement that the promise or order is not negotiable or is not an instrument governed by Article 3 [3–104(d)]. For example, if a promissory note contained the legend "NON-NEGOTIABLE," it would not qualify as a negotiable instrument even if it otherwise met the formal requirements for one.

Importance of Form

Whether or not an instrument satisfies these formal requirements is important only for the purpose of determining whether an instrument is negotiable or non-negotiable. Negotiability should not be confused with validity or collectibility. If an instrument is negotiable, the law of negotiable instruments in the Code controls in determining the rights and liabilities of the parties to the instrument. If an instrument is non-negotiable, the general rules of contract law control. The purpose of determining negotiability is to ascertain whether a possessor of the instrument can become a holder in due course.

An instrument that meets all of the formal requirements is a negotiable instrument even though it is void, voidable, unenforceable, or uncollectible for other reasons. Negotiability is a matter of form and nothing else. Suppose a person gives an instrument in payment of a gambling debt in a state that has a statute declaring that any instrument or promise given in payment of a gambling debt is void. The instrument is a negotiable instru-

ment if it is negotiable in form even though it is absolutely void. Also, an instrument that is negotiable in form is a negotiable instrument even though it is issued by a minor. The instrument is voidable at the option of the minor if state law makes infancy a defense to a simple contract, but it is negotiable.

In Writing

To be negotiable, an instrument must be in writing. An instrument that is handwritten, typed, or printed is considered to be in writing [1–201(46)]. The writing does not have to be on any particular material; all that is required is that the instrument be in writing. A person could create a negotiable instrument in pencil on a piece of wrapping paper. It would be poor business practice to do so, but the instrument would meet the statutory requirement that it be in writing.

Signed

To qualify as a negotiable instrument, an instrument in the form of a note must be signed by the person undertaking to pay (the maker) and an instrument in the form of a draft must be signed by the person giving the instruction to pay (the drawer) [3–103]. An instrument has been signed if the maker or drawer has put a name or other symbol on it with the intention of validating it [3–401(b)]. Normally, the maker or drawer signs an instrument by writing his name on it; however, this is not required. A person or company may authorize an agent to sign instruments for it. A typed or rubber-stamped signature is sufficient if it was put on the instrument to validate it. A person who cannot write her name might make an X or some other symbol and have it witnessed by someone else.

In the *Interbank of New York* case, which follows, the court considered whether pre-authorized checks containing the notation "verbally authorized by your depositor" met the requirement that an instrument must be "signed," among other things, in order to qualify as a negotiable instrument,

---

Interbank of New York v. Fleet Bank   *45 UCC Rep.2d 167 (New York Civ. Ct. 2001)*

Interbank of New York brought an action against Fleet Bank to recover on four drafts in the total sum of $3,361.25 paid out by Interbank from the account of its customer Dimittrous Tasoulis. Two of the drafts were issued by and made payable to Sprint PCS and two were issued by and made payable to Atlantic Mobile, Inc. The drafts are known commonly in the banking industry as pre-authorized drafts or "telechecks." The drafts are created when a consumer has agreed to pay for goods *or services by allowing a vendor to prepare and issue a pre-authorized check drawn on the consumer's account at the consumer's designated financial institution. The consumer provides the vendor with the necessary account number and bank at which it is maintained, and the vendor then issues a check drawn on the consumer's account.*

In this case, Sprint and Atlantic Mobile issued drafts on the account of Tasoulis to pay for telephone services. The drafts contained the typed notation "verbally authorized by your depositor." Bell and Atlantic Mobile deposited the drafts in their respective accounts at Fleet, and the drafts were ultimately paid by Interbank.

Thereafter, Tasoulois advised Interbank that he had never authorized Atlantic Mobile or Sprint to issue the drafts and executed affidavits to that effect as to each draft. Interbank then sued Fleet Bank to recover the amount of the drafts.

Fleet took the position that the pre-authorized checks should be treated like any other check and that in accordance with the UCC a depository bank such as Fleet could not be held liable for accepting a check on which the signature of the drawer is forged, unless it knew the signature was forged (this will be discussed in Chapter 33, Liability). Interbank took the position that a pre-authorized check cannot be treated as an ordinary check and is not a negotiable instrument.

EDMEAD, Judge Section 3–104(a) of the UCC provides that for a writing to be a negotiable instrument it must be signed by the maker or drawer. Interbank argues that since the subject drafts are not signed by the maker, but merely contain the notation "verbally authorized by your depositor," the drafts do not constitute negotiable instruments.

UCC section 1–201(3) provides that "signed" includes any symbol executed or adopted by a party with a present intention to authenticate a writing. UCC section 3–401(2) provides that a signature is made by any word or mark used in lieu of a written signature.

In accordance with these sections of the UCC, if a drawer or maker intended the notation "verbally authorized by your depositor" to authenticate the checks and intended that the notation take the place of a written signature, then the check would be a negotiable instrument.

Clearly, if Tasoulis had authorized Atlantic Mobile to issue the check with the notation "verbally authorized by your depositor," in place of his written signature, the check would qualify as a negotiable instrument. The only infirmity

in the subject drafts is that Tasoulis did not authorize their issuance. Thus, the notation "verbally authorized by your depositor," which could constitute a signature under the UCC, is unauthorized.

The unauthorized use of a stamped printed signature constitutes a forgery. So too here the notation "verbally authorized by your depositor," which can constitute a signature under the UCC, when unauthorized, constitutes a forged signature. Accordingly, the pre-authorized checks should be treated as any other check that contains a forged signature. These pre-authorized checks constitute negotiable instruments.

Summary Judgment granted to Fleet.

Note: The case did not address the issue of whether Atlantic Mobile and Sprint would be liable to Interbank if they did not have the proper authorization from Tasoulis. It should also be noted that this case was decided under the pre-1990 version of Articles 3 and 4 as New York has not adopted the 1990 Revision of Articles 3 and 4. However, the same result would be expected if it had adopted the Revised Articles.

Unconditional Promise or Order

Requirement of a Promise or Order

If an instrument is promissory in nature, such as a note or a certificate of deposit, it must contain an unconditional promise to pay or it cannot be negotiable. Merely acknowledging a debt is not sufficient [3–103(9)]. For example, the statement "I owe you $100" does not constitute a promise to pay. An IOU in this form is not a negotiable instrument.

If an instrument is an order to pay, such as a check or a draft, it must contain an unconditional order. A simple request to pay as a favor is not sufficient; however, a politely phrased demand, such as "please pay," can meet the requirement. Checks commonly use the language "Pay to the order of." This satisfies the requirement that the check contain an order to pay. The order is the word "pay," not the word "order." The word "order" has another function—that of designating the instrument as payable "to order" or "to bearer" for purposes of negotiability.

CYBERLAW IN ACTION

E-Payments Compared to "Negotiable Instruments"

Article 3 has numerous requirements for the appearance and content of promises to pay (notes) and orders to pay (drafts/checks) if they are to qualify as negotiable instruments and be readily transferable. Two of these requirements contemplate paper-based transactions—the requirement that promises to pay and orders to pay be "in writing" (see 3–103) and be "signed" (see 3–104). For this reason, at present, it would be difficult to "electrify" negotiable instruments successfully.

In contrast, e-payments—more commonly substitutes for traditional "check" payments—are neither in writing or "signed" by affixing a signature in ink to a sheet of paper. Instead, the transaction is documented electronically—such as by sending an e-mail message or fax to a bank to direct them to pay a third-party seller of goods or services (such as the purchase of an online information product).

The buyer and seller using e-payments have many of the same concerns as buyers and sellers using traditional payments methods: they want to be certain that they are dealing with each other honestly, that it will not be easier for the seller to double-charge the buyer's account or to get away with taking payment but not delivering the goods or services that the buyer seeks from the transaction, and they want to guard against unscrupulous persons hacking into their records and stealing from either the buyer or seller. Because of legal uncertainty about which body of law—federal consumer protection laws designed to govern credit-card payments or "electronic funds transfers" or state-created laws such as Articles 3 and 4 of the Uniform Commercial Code—will govern the transaction, the majority of consumers have continued to use traditional, paper-based payments methods and credit cards that they understand better than newer e-payments methods of payment. For e-commerce to reach its fullest potential, more consumers will have to become comfortable with e-payments methods in addition to better-known checks and credit cards.

Promise or Order Must Be Unconditional

An instrument is not negotiable unless the promise or order is unconditional. For example, a note that provides, "I promise to pay to the order of Karl Adams $100 if he replaces the roof on my garage," is not negotiable because it is payable on a condition.

To be negotiable, an instrument must be written so that a person can tell from reading the instrument alone what the obligations of the parties are. If a note contains the statement, "Payment is subject to the terms of a mortgage dated November 20, 2003," it is not negotiable. To determine the rights of the parties on the note, one would have to examine another document—the mortgage.

However, a reference to another document for a statement of rights with respect to collateral, prepayment, or acceleration does not destroy the negotiability of a note [3–106(b)]. For example, a note could contain this statement: "This note is secured by a mortgage dated August 30, 2003" without affecting its negotiability. In this case, the mortgage does not affect rights and duties of the parties to the note. It would not be necessary to examine the mortgage document to determine the rights of the parties to the note; the parties need only examine the note.

The negotiability of an instrument is not affected by a statement of the consideration for which the instrument was given or by a statement of the transaction that gave rise to the instrument. For example, a negotiable instrument may state that it was given in payment of last month's rent or that it was given in payment of the purchase price of goods. The statement does not affect the negotiability of the instrument.

A check may reference the account to be debited without making the check non-negotiable. For example, a check could contain the notation, "payroll account" or "petty cash." Similarly, the account number that appears on personal checks does not make the instrument payable only out of a specific fund. Under original Article 3, a check (other than a governmental check) that stated that it was payable only out of a specific fund or account was treated as a conditional order and thus was not negotiable. Revised Article 3 changed this rule so that limiting payment to a particular fund or source does not make the promise or order conditional [3–106(b)].

Revised Article 3 also addresses the negotiability of traveler's checks that commonly require, as a condition to payment, a countersignature of a person whose specimen signature appears on the draft. Under the revision, the condition does not prevent the instrument from meeting the "unconditional promise or order" requirement [3–106(c)]. However, if the person whose specimen signature appears on the instrument fails to countersign it, the failure to sign becomes a defense to the obligation of the issuer to pay. This concept will be discussed in the following chapter.

A conditional *indorsement* does not destroy the negotiability of an otherwise negotiable instrument. The Code determines negotiability at *issuance,* so that indorsements do not affect the underlying negotiability of the instrument. We discuss conditional indorsements in Chapter 32, Negotiation and Holder in Due Course.

Fixed Amount of Money

Fixed Amount

The promise or order in an instrument must be to pay a fixed amount of money, with or without interest or other charges described in the promise or order. The requirement of a "fixed amount" applies only to principal; the amount of any interest payable is that described in the instrument. Interest may be stated in an instrument as a fixed or variable amount of money or it may be expressed as a fixed or variable rate or rates. If a variable rate of interest is prescribed, the amount of interest is calculated by reference to the formula or index referenced in the instrument. For example, a note might provide for interest at "three percent (3.00%) over Chase Manhattan Prime Rate to be adjusted monthly." If the description of interest in the instrument does not allow the amount of interest to be ascertained, then interest is payable at the judgment rate in effect at the place of payment at the time interest first accrues [3–112]. The judgment rate is the rate of interest courts impose on losing parties until they pay the winning parties.

Under the original version of Article 3, a promise or order had to be to pay a "sum certain." Generally, to meet this requirement, a person had to be able to compute from the information in the instrument the amount required to discharge—or pay off—the instrument at any given time. Among other things, this caused problems when applied to variable rate instruments that came into common commercial usage in the United States after the original Article 3 was drafted. Some state courts held that instruments providing for variable interest rates ascertainable through reference to indexes outside the instrument were not negotiable; other courts sought to interpret the Code to accommodate this new commercial practice. As noted above, the negotiability

of instruments that provide for variable interest rates has now been resolved in Revised Article 3.

Payable in Money

The amount specified in the instrument must be payable in money, which is a medium of exchange authorized or adopted by a domestic or foreign government and includes a monetary unit of account established by an intergovernmental organization or by agreement between two or more nations [1–201(24)]. Unless the instrument otherwise provides, an instrument that states the amount payable in foreign money may be paid in the foreign money or in an equivalent dollar amount [3–107]. If the person obligated to pay off an instrument can do something other than pay money, the instrument is not negotiable. For example, if a note reads, "I promise to pay to the order of Sarah Smith, at my option, $40 or five bushels of apples, John Jones," the note is not negotiable.

Payable on Demand or at a Definite Time

To be negotiable, the promise or order must be payable either on demand or at a specified time in the future. This is so that the time when the instrument is payable can be determined with some certainty. An instrument that is payable on the happening of some uncertain event is not negotiable. Thus, a note payable "when my son graduates from college" is not negotiable, even though the son does graduate subsequently.

Payable on Demand

A promise or order is "payable on demand" if (1) it states that it is payable on "demand" or "sight" (or otherwise at the will of the holder of the instrument) or (2) does not state any time for payment [3–108(a)]. For example, if the maker forgets to state when a note is payable, it is payable immediately at the request of the holder of the note.

An instrument may be antedated or postdated, and normally an instrument payable on demand is not payable before the date of the instrument [3–113(a)]. Revised Article 3 makes an important exception for checks: a payor bank (a bank that is the drawee of a draft) may pay a postdated check before the stated date *unless* the drawer has notified the bank of postdating pursuant to a procedure set out in the Code [3–113(a); 4–401(c)] that is similar to the process involved in stopping payment on a check.

Payable at a Definite Time

A promise or order is "payable at a definite time" if it is payable at a fixed date or dates or at a time or times readily ascertainable at the time the promise or order is issued [3–108(b)]. Thus, a note dated March 25, 2003, might be made payable at a fixed time after a stated date, such as "30 days after date."

Under the Code, an instrument that names a fixed date or time for payment—without losing its negotiable character—also may contain a clause permitting the time for payment to be accelerated at the option of the maker. Similarly, an instrument may allow an extension of time at the option of the holder or allow a maker or acceptor to extend payment to a further definite time. Or, the due date of a note might be triggered by the happening of an event, such as the filing of a petition in bankruptcy against the maker. The Code permits these clauses so long as one can determine the time for payment with certainty [3–108].

A promise or order also is "payable at a definite time" if it is payable on elapse of a definite period of time after "sight" or "acceptance." A draft payable at a specified time—such as "15 days after sight"—is, in effect, payable at a fixed time after the draft is presented to the drawee for acceptance.

If an instrument is undated, its "date" is the date it is issued by the maker or drawer [3–113(b)].

Payable to Order or Bearer

Except for checks, to be negotiable an instrument must be "payable to order or to bearer." A note that provides, "I promise to pay to the order of Sarah Smith" or "I promise to pay to Sarah Smith or bearer" is negotiable. However, one that provides "I promise to pay to Sarah Smith" is not. The words "to the order of" or "to bearer" show that the drawer of a draft, or the maker of a note, intends to issue a negotiable instrument. The drawer or maker is not restricting payment of the instrument to just Sarah Smith but is willing to pay someone else designated by Sarah Smith. This is the essence of negotiability.

In the original version of Article 3, an order in the form of a check also had to be "payable to order or bearer" to qualify as a negotiable instrument. However, the drafters of Revised Article 3 created an exception for instruments that otherwise meet the requirements for a negotiable instrument as well as the definition of a check [3–104(c)]. Under the revised article, a check that reads "Pay John Doe" could qualify as a negotiable instrument.

As a result, the Code treats checks, which are payment instruments, as negotiable instruments whether or not they contain the words "to the order of." The drafters explained that most checks are preprinted with these words but that occasionally the drawer may strike out the words before issuing the check and that a few check forms have been in use that do not contain these words. In these instances, the drafters preferred not to limit the rights of holders of such checks who may pay money or give credit for a check without being aware that it is not in the conventional form for a negotiable instrument.

A promise or order is considered to be payable "to order" if it is payable (1) to the order of an identified person or (2) to an identified person or that person's order [3–109(b)]. Examples would include: "Pay to the order of Sandy Smith" and "Pay to Sandy Smith or order." The most common forms of a promise or order being payable to bearer use the words "pay to bearer," "pay to the order of bearer," "pay to cash," or "pay to the order of cash" [3–109(a)]. A check sent with the payee line blank is payable to bearer. However, it is also considered an incomplete instrument, the rules concerning which will be discussed in the following two chapters.

The original payee of a draft or a note can transfer the right to receive payment to someone else. By making the instrument payable "to the order of " or "to bearer," the drawer or maker is giving the payee the chance to negotiate the instrument to another person and to cut off certain defenses that the drawer or maker may have against payment of the instrument.

An instrument that is payable to the order of a specific person is known as "order paper." Order paper can be negotiated or transferred only by indorsement. An instrument payable "to bearer" or "to cash" is known as "bearer paper"; it can be negotiated or transferred by delivery of possession without indorsement [3–201(b)]. The rules governing negotiation of instruments will be detailed in the next chapter.

An instrument can be made payable to two or more payees. For example, a check could be drawn payable "to the order of John Jones and Henry Smith." Then, both Jones and Smith have to be involved in negotiating it or enforcing its payment. An instrument also can be made payable to alternative persons—for example, "to the order of Susan Clark or Betsy Brown." In this case, either Clark or Brown could negotiate it or enforce its payment [3–110(d)].

A number of recent cases have addressed the use of the punctuation mark the virgule (/) to separate the names of the payees. The following *Purina Mills* case illustrates how the courts typically have applied the UCC to such situations.

Purina Mills, Inc. v. Security Bank & Trust   *547 N.W.2d 336 (Mich. Ct. App. 1996)*

From February 10, 1992, to June 17, 1992, K-R Summers & Sons Livestock drew 10 checks totaling over $21,000 on its account at Security Bank & Trust. The checks were made payable to "International Livestock/Purina Mills." International Livestock indorsed the checks and presented them to Mid America Bank in Wisconsin. Mid America honored the checks and presented them to Security Bank & Trust as the drawee bank, which also honored the checks without Purina Mills's indorsement. Purina Mills filed a lawsuit to recover the amount of the checks from Security Bank & Trust. Security Bank & Trust filed a motion for summary judgment, which the trial court granted. Purina Mills appealed.

Reilly, Judge Whether the virgule separating the names of two or more payees on an instrument indicates that the instrument is payable to all parties listed, or to the parties in the alternative, is an issue of first impression in Michigan.

Courts in other jurisdictions that have decided this issue have concluded that its use indicates that the instrument is payable in the alternative.

We agree with these authorities that a check drawn to payees whose names are separated by a virgule allows payment to the payees alternatively. A virgule is defined as "an oblique stroke (/) used between two words to show that an

appropriate one may be chosen to complete the sense of the text." The Random House Dictionary, Revised Edition (1975). Thus the virgule is used to separate alternatives. According to UCC Section 3–110(d), "[i]f an instrument is payable to two or more persons alternatively, it is payable to any of them and may be negotiated, discharged, or enforced by any of them in possession of the instrument." The banks properly honored the checks that were presented with the indorsement of one of the payees.

Judgment affirmed for Security Bank & Trust.

Special Terms

Additional Terms

Generally, if an instrument is to qualify as a negotiable instrument, the person promising or ordering payment may not state undertakings or instructions in addition to the payment of money [3–104(a)(3). However, the instrument may include clauses concerning (1) giving, maintaining, or protecting collateral to secure payment, (2) an authorization to confess judgment or to realize on or dispose of collateral, and (3) waiving the benefit of any law intended for the protection or benefit of any person obligated on the instrument.

Thus, a term authorizing the confession of judgment on an instrument when it is due does not affect the negotiability of the instrument. A confession of judgment clause authorizes the creditor to go into court if the debtor defaults and, with the debtor's acquiescence, to have a judgment entered against the debtor. However, some states prohibit confessions of judgment.

Banks and other businesses often use forms of commercial paper that meet their particular needs. These

forms may include certain other terms that do not affect the negotiability of an instrument. For example, a note may designate a place of payment without affecting the instrument's negotiability. Where the instrument does not specify a place of payment, the Code sets out rules for ascertaining where payment is to be made [3–111].

Ambiguous Terms

Occasionally, a person may write or receive a check on which the amount written in figures differs from the amount written in words. Or a note may have conflicting terms or an ambiguous term. Where a conflict or an ambiguous term exists, there are general rules of interpretation that are applied to resolve the conflict or ambiguity: Typewritten terms prevail over printed terms, handwritten terms prevail over printed and typewritten terms, and where words and numbers conflict, the words control the numbers [3–114].

The following *Galatia Community State Bank v. Kindy* case involves a check on which there was a difference between the numbers on the check placed there by a check-writing machine and those written by hand.

Galatia Community State Bank v. Kindy   *307 Ark. 467 (Ark. Sup. Ct. 1991)*

Galatia Community State Bank honored a check it took for collection for $5,550, which was the amount imprinted by a check-writing machine in the center underlined section of the check commonly used for stating the amount in words. The imprint looked like this:

Registered
No. 497345 **5550 DOL'S 00 CTS

*The impression made by the check-writing machine could be felt on the front and back of the check, and "**5550 DOL'S 00 CTS" was imprinted in red ink. In the box on the right-hand side of the check commonly used for numbers, "6,550.00" appeared in handwriting. The check was in partial payment of the purchase price of two engines that Eugene Kindy was buying from the payee on the check, Tony Hicks. Kindy postdated the check by a month and deliberately placed two different amounts on the check because he thought the bank would check with him before paying it. Kindy wanted to be sure that the engines had been delivered to Canada before he paid the $6,550 balance of the purchase price.*

After the check was deposited in the Galatia Bank and Hicks was given $5,550, an employee of the bank altered the "6" by hand to read "5." Because Kindy had stopped payment on the check, the drawee bank refused to pay it to Galatia Bank. Galatia Bank then brought suit against Kindy as the drawer of the check. One of the issues in the lawsuit was how the check should be constructed. The trial court found that the rules on construction provided in the Code were not helpful because they were contradictory. The trial court held in favor of Kindy, and Galatia Bank appealed.

Newbern, Justice The trial court reviewed Code section 3–118(b) and (c) (1987) which has since been superseded by section 3–114 (1991) but which was in effect at the time in question in this case. The statute provided in relevant part:

3–118. Ambiguous terms and rules of construction. The following rules apply to every instrument:

* * * * *

(b) Handwritten terms control typewritten and printed terms, and typewritten control printed.
(c) Words control figures except that if the words are ambiguous figures control.

The frustration expressed by the trial court with respect to section 3–118 which stated the applicable rules of construction for negotiable instruments is understandable.

The $5550.00 amount imprinted by the check writing machine upon the line customarily used for words is expressed in figures and not in words. One question is whether imprinted numbers located where words are customarily placed on a check control figures placed where figures are customarily placed. Another question is whether handwritten figures control printing.

We find both questions satisfactorily answered in *St. Paul Fire & Marine Ins. Co. v. Bank of Salem*. In that case, there was a conflict between an amount imprinted by a check imprinting machine and numbers expressed in typewritten figures. The court recognized the imprinted amount was not expressed in words but held "the purposes of the

UCC are best served by considering an amount imprinted by a check writing machine as 'words' for the purpose of resolving an ambiguity between an amount and an amount entered upon the line usually used to express the amount in figures." The court quoted from a pre-UCC case, *United States Fidelity and Guaranty Co. v. First National Bank of South Carolina* (1964), as follows:

A prime purpose, as we see it, of making a sum payable when expressed in words controlling over the sum payable expressed in figures is the very fact that words are much more difficult to alter. The perforated imprinting by a check-writing machine, while fully expressing the sum payable in figures, is even more difficult to successfully alter than a sum payable in written words.

Because a check imprinting machine's purpose is to protect against alterations, the amount shown on the imprint should control whether the number is in words or figures.

Turning to the question of whether typewriting controls printing, the court in *United States Fidelity and Guaranty Co.* stated:

As the section makes clear, in the event of an ambiguity between printed terms and typewritten terms, the latter would control. We do not consider the impression made by the check imprinter to be "printed terms" under this section.

A conflict between the two amounts on a check would be resolved by section 3–118 which states that words control figures. Arguably, the amount imprinted by the check writing machine upon the line customarily expressing the amount in words, is expressed in figures . . . We think, however, that the purposes of the UCC are best served by considering an amount imprinted by a check writing machine as "words" for the purpose of resolving an ambiguity between that amount and an amount entered upon the line usually used to express the amount in figures.

Although the court did not say specifically that it regarded the portion written by the check writing machine as the equivalent of handwriting, that is the clear effect of the decision.

In *United States v. Hibernia National Bank,* a typed numerical amount was located in the place customarily used for words. The amount conflicted with the amount located in the place customarily used for figures. The court found the typed amount controlling despite the fact it was not expressed in words.

Judgment for Kindy reversed on other grounds.

———

Note: Although, as the court notes, this case was decided under the original version of Article 3, the dilemma posed, and the conclusion reached by the court on the construction of the check, would likely be the same under Revised Article 3.

Problems and Problem Cases

1. Is the following instrument a note, a check, or a draft? Why? If it is not a check, how would you have to change it to make it a check?

> To: Arthur Adams January 1, 2004
> TEN DAYS AFTER DATE PAY TO THE ORDER OF:
> Bernie Brown
> THE SUM OF: Ten thousand and no/100 DOLLARS
> SIGNED: Carl Clark

2. Frank agrees to build a garage for Sarah for $15,000. Sarah offers either to sign a contract showing her obligation to pay Frank $15,000 or to sign a negotiable promissory note for $15,000 payable to the order of Frank. Would you advise Frank to ask for the contract or the promissory note? Explain.

3. Wiley, Tate & Irby, buyers and sellers of used cars, sold several autos to Houston Auto Sales. Houston wrote out the order for payment on the outside of several envelopes. He signed them and they were drawn on his bank, Peoples Bank & Trust Co., to be paid on the demand of Wiley, Tate & Irby. Can the envelopes qualify as negotiable instruments?

4. Is the following a negotiable instrument?

> IOU, A. Gay, the sum of seventeen and 5/100 dollars for value received.
> John R. Rooke

5. Holly Hill Acres, Ltd., executed a promissory note and mortgage and delivered them to Rogers. The note contained the following stipulation:

> this note with interest is secured by a mortgage on real estate of even herewith, made by the maker hereof in

favor of the said payee, and shall be construed and enforced according to the laws of the State of Florida. The terms of said mortgage are by this reference made a part hereof.

Is the note a negotiable instrument?

6. Strickland ordered a swimming pool from Kafko Manufacturing and gave it a check for the purchase price that included the following words in the space following the word *memo:* "for pool kit to be delivered." Is the check negotiable?

7. Olde Town Investment Corporation borrowed $18,000 from VMC Mortgage Company and signed a promissory note secured by a deed of trust on land it owned. The note provided for interest at "three percent (3.00%) over Chase Manhattan Prime to be adjusted monthly." Is a note providing for a variable amount of interest, not ascertainable from the face of the note, a negotiable instrument?

8. Darryl Young presented five photocopied checks to the Lynnwood Check-X-Change on five different days between June 13 and June 21. Lynwood cashed the first four checks presented. The fifth check, which was presented on a Saturday, was drawn on a different account from the first four checks and was payable on the following Monday. Lynnwood's practice was to cash checks on Saturday that are dated the following Monday. Young was convicted of five counts of forgery. On appeal, Young argued that the postdated check was not a legal instrument for purposes of the forgery statute. The crime of forgery requires an instrument that, if genuine, may have legal effect or be the foundation of legal liability. Young argued that the postdated check did not meet this requirement "because the time for payment had not arrived and thus the check could not have created any

CONCEPT REVIEW

Requirements for Negotiability

Requirement	Basic Rules
Must Be in Writing	1. The instrument may be handwritten, typed, or printed.
Must Be Signed by the Maker or Drawer	1. Person issuing the instrument must sign with intent of validating his or her obligation. 2. Person issuing may affix the signature in a variety of ways—for example, by word, mark, or rubber stamp. 3. Agent or authorized representative may supply the "signature."
Must Contain a Promise or Order to Pay	1. Promise must be more than acknowledgment of a debt. 2. Order requirement is met if the drawer issues an instruction to "pay."
Promise or Order Must Be Unconditional	1. Entire obligation must be found in the instrument itself and not in another document or documents. 2. Payment cannot be conditioned on the occurrence of an event.
Must Call for Payment of a Fixed Amount of Money	1. Must be able to ascertain the principal from the face of the instrument. 2. May contain a clause providing for payment of interest or other charges such as collection or attorney's fees.
Must Be Payable in Money	1. Obligation must be payable in a medium of exchange authorized or adopted by a government or by an international organization or agreement between two or more nations. 2. Maker or drawer cannot have the option to pay in something other than money.
Must Be Payable on Demand or at a Definite Time	1. Requirement is met if instrument says it is payable on demand or, if no time for payment is stated, it is payable on demand. 2. Requirement is met if it is payable on a stated date, at a fixed time after a stated date, or a fixed time "after sight." 3. Instrument may contain an acceleration clause or a clause allowing maker or holder to extend the payment date.
Generally Must Be Payable to Bearer or to Order	1. Bearer requirement is met if instrument is payable "to bearer" or "to cash." 2. Order requirement is met if instrument is payable "to the order of" a specified person or persons. 3. Exception from requirement is made for instruments meeting both the definition of a check and all the other requirements for a negotiable instrument.
May Not State Any Other Undertaking or Instruction by the Person Promising or Ordering Payment to Do Any Act in Addition to the Payment of Money	1. However, it may contain (*a*) an undertaking or power to give, maintain, or protect collateral to secure payment, (*b*) an authorization or power to the holder to confess judgment or realize on or dispose of collateral, or (*c*) a waiver of the benefit of any law intended for the advantage or protection of an obligor on the instrument.

legal liability on the part of any person at that time." If a check is postdated, can it qualify as a negotiable instrument and create legal liability?

9. Nation-Wide Check Corporation sold money orders to drugstores. The money orders contained the words, "Payable to," followed by a blank. Can the money order qualify as a negotiable instrument?

10. Emmett McDonald, acting as the personal representative of the estate of Marion Cahill, wrote a check payable to himself, individually, on the estate checking account in the Commercial Bank & Trust Company. The instrument contained an obvious variance between the numbers and the written words that indicated the amount of the check. It said: "Pay to the order of Emmett E. McDonald $10075.00 Ten hundred seventy five . . . Dollars." The bank paid the $10,075 sum stated by the numerals to McDonald, who absconded with the funds. Yates, the successor representative, sued the bank on behalf of the es-

tate to recover the $9,000 difference between that amount and the $1,075 that was written out. Did the bank pay the correct amount on the check?

Online Research: Accessing Information from Your Bank

Use the Internet to locate the website for the bank or financial institution where you maintain a checking account. From the website ascertain the following information: (1) what is the monthly fee (if any) for maintaining the type of checking account you maintain? (2) does the institution charge a fee for each check you use or if you exceed a certain number of transactions per month? (3) what rate of interest does the institution pay on a $10,000, five-year certificate of deposit (CD)? and (4) what rate of interest does the institution charge on secured personal loans such as a loan for the purchase of a new car?

32

NEGOTIATION AND HOLDER IN DUE COURSE

Rachel Allen purchases a used Honda from Friendly Fred's Used Cars, paying $1,500 down and signing a promissory note in which she promises to pay $2,000 to Fred or to his order 12 months from the date of the note with interest at 8.5 percent. Fred assures Rachel that the car is in good condition and has never been involved in an accident. Fred indorses (signs) his name on the back of the promissory note and discounts (assigns) the note to Factors, Inc. Subsequently, Rachel discovers that, contrary to Fred's assurance, the Honda had in fact been involved in an accident that caused a front-end alignment problem. When Factors notifies her of the assignment to it of the note and asks for payment on the due date, Rachel wants to assert a defense of failure of consideration or breach of contract (warranty) against full payment of the note.

Among the legal issues raised in this scenario are:

• When Fred transferred the promissory note to Factors after signing his name to the back of it, what rights did Factors obtain?
• Will Rachel be able to assert a defense of failure of consideration or breach of contract against full payment of the note to Factors?
• If the promissory note contained the clause required by the Federal Trade Commission in consumer notes or installment sales contracts, would it change Rachel's rights?

THE PRECEDING CHAPTER DISCUSSED the nature and benefits of negotiable instruments. It also outlined the requirements an instrument must meet to qualify as a negotiable instrument and thus possess the qualities that allow it to be accepted as a substitute for money.

This chapter focuses on negotiation—the process by which rights to a negotiable instrument pass from one person to another. Commonly, this involves an indorsement and transfer of the instrument. This chapter also develops the requirements that a transferee of a negotiable instrument must meet to qualify as a holder in due course and thus attain special rights under negotiable instruments law. These rights, which put a holder in due course in an enhanced position compared to an assignee of a contract, are discussed in some detail.

Negotiation

Nature of Negotiation

Under Revised Article 3, **negotiation** is the transfer of possession (whether voluntary or involuntary) of a negotiable instrument by a person (other than the issuer) to another person who becomes its *holder* [3–201]. A person is a **holder** if she is in possession of an instrument (1) that is payable to bearer or (2) made payable to an identified person and she is that identified person [1–201(20)].[1]

---

[1]The numbers in parentheses refer to sections of the Uniform Commercial Code (UCC), which is reproduced in the appendix.

For example, when an employer gives an employee, Susan Adams, a paycheck payable "to the order of Susan Adams," she is the holder of the check because she is in possession of an instrument payable to an identified person (Susan Adams) and she is that person. When she indorses (writes her name) on the back of the check and exchanges it for cash and merchandise at Ace Grocery, she has negotiated the check to the grocery store and the store is now the holder because it is in possession by transfer of a check and unless she specifies the grocery store by name, the check now is payable to bearer. Similarly, if Susan Adams indorsed the check "Pay to the Order of Ace Grocery, Susan Adams" and transferred it to the grocery store, it would be a holder through the negotiation of the order check to it. The grocery store would be in possession of an instrument payable to an identified person (Ace Grocery) and is the person identified in the check.

In certain circumstances, Revised Article 3 allows a person to become a holder by negotiation even though the transfer of possession is involuntary. For example, if a negotiable instrument is payable to bearer and is stolen by Tom Thief or found by Fred Finder, Thief or Finder becomes the holder when he obtains possession. The involuntary transfer of possession of a bearer instrument results in a negotiation to Thief or Finder.

Formal Requirements for Negotiation

The formal requirements for negotiation are very simple. If an instrument is payable to the order of a specific payee, it is called **order paper** and it can be negotiated by transfer of possession of the instrument after indorsement by the person specified [3–201(b)].

For example, if Rachel's father gives her a check payable "to the order of Rachel Stern," then Rachel can negotiate the check by indorsing her name on the back of the check and giving it to the person to whom she wants to transfer it. Note that the check is order paper, not because the word *order* appears on the check but rather because it named a specific payee, Rachel Stern.

If an instrument is payable "to bearer" or "to cash," it is called **bearer paper** and negotiating it is even simpler. An instrument payable to bearer may be negotiated by transfer of possession alone [3–201(b)]. Thus, if someone gives you a check that is made payable "to the order of cash," you can negotiate it simply by giving it to the person to whom you wish to transfer it. No indorsement is necessary to negotiate an instrument payable to bearer. However, the person who takes the instrument may ask for an indorsement for her protection. By indorsing the check, you agree to be liable for its payment to that person if it is not paid by the drawee bank when it is presented for payment. This liability will be discussed in Chapter 33, Liability of Parties.

Nature of Indorsement

An indorsement is made by adding the signature of the holder of the instrument to the instrument, usually on the back of it, either alone or with other words. **Indorsement** is defined to mean "a signature (other than that of a maker, drawer or acceptor) that alone or accompanied by other words, is made on an instrument for purpose of (i) negotiating the instrument, (ii) restricting payment of the instrument, or (iii) incurring indorser's liability on the instrument" [3–204(a)]. The negotiation and restriction of payment aspects of indorsements will be discussed below; indorser's liability will be covered in the next chapter.

The signature constituting an indorsement can be supplied or written either by the holder or by someone who is authorized to sign on behalf of the holder. For example, a check payable to "H&H Meat Market" might be indorsed "H&H Meat Market by Jane Frank, President," if Jane is authorized to do this on behalf of the market.

Wrong or Misspelled Name

When indorsing an instrument, the holder should spell his name in the same way as it appears on the instrument. If the holder's name is misspelled or wrong, then legally the indorsement can be made either in his name or in the name that is on the instrument. However, any person who pays the instrument or otherwise gives value for it may require the indorser to sign both names [3–204(d)].

Suppose Joan Ash is issued a check payable to the order of "Joanne Ashe." She may indorse the check as either "Joan Ash" or "Joanne Ashe." However, if she takes the check to a bank to cash, the bank may require her to sign both "Joanne Ashe" and "Joan Ash."

Checks Deposited without Indorsement

Occasionally, when a customer deposits a check to her account with a bank, she may forget to indorse the check. It is common practice for depository banks to receive unindorsed checks under what are known as "lock-box" arrangements with customers who receive a high volume of checks. Normally, a check payable to the order of an identified person would require the indorsement of that person in order for a negotiation to the depository bank to take place and for it to become a holder. Under the original Article 3, the depository bank, in most cases, had the right to supply the customer's indorsement. Instead of actually signing the customer's name to the check as the indorsement, the bank might just stamp on it that it was deposited by the customer or credited to her account. Banks did not have the right to put the customer's indorsement on a check that the customer has deposited if the check specifically required the payee's signature. Insurance and government checks commonly require the payee's signature.

The revision to Article 3 and the conforming amendments to Articles 1 and 4 address the situation where a check is deposited in a depositary bank without indorsement differently. The depositary bank becomes a holder of an item delivered to it for collection, whether or not it is indorsed by the customer, if the customer at the time of delivery qualified as a holder [4–205]. Concomitantly, the depositary bank warrants to other collecting banks, the payor bank (drawee), and the drawer that it paid the amount of the item to the customer or deposited the amount to the customer's account.

Transfer of Order Instrument

Except for the special provisions concerning depositary banks, if an order instrument is transferred without indorsement, the instrument has not been negotiated and the transferee cannot qualify as a holder. For example, Sue Brown gives a check payable "to the order of Susan Brown" to a drugstore in payment for some cosmetics. Until Sue indorses the check, she has not "negotiated" it and the druggist could not qualify as a "holder" of the check.

Transfer of an instrument, whether or not the transfer is a negotiation, vests in the transferee, such as the drugstore, any right of Sue, the transferor, to enforce the instrument. However, the transferee cannot obtain the rights of a holder in due course (discussed later in this chapter) if he is engaged in any fraud or illegality affecting the instrument. Unless otherwise agreed, if an instrument is transferred for value but without a required indorsement, the transferee has the right to obtain the unqualified indorsement of the transferor; however, the "negotiation" takes place only when the transferor applies her indorsement [3–203(c)].

The *Town of Freeport* case, which follows, illustrates these principles.

Town of Freeport v. Ring	*727 A.2d 901 (Maine Sup. Jud. Ct. 1999)*

Thorton Ring was the owner of real property located on Main Street in Freeport, Maine. In August 1994, the Town sent Ring a letter noting that his 1993–1994 real estate taxes were unpaid and notified him of the Town's intent to file a lien on the property if payment was not received within 30 days. The taxes remained unpaid and a tax lien was filed on the property. On January 26, 1996, because a portion of the taxes still remained unpaid, the Town sent a Notice of Impending Foreclosure of the Tax Lien Certificate to Ring by certified mail, advising him that the tax lien would be deemed to be foreclosed on February 27, 1996. Ring subsequently was in default for his 1994–1995 taxes and similar notices were sent.

In January of 1997, Ring delivered to the Town a check in the amount of $11,347.09. The check was issued by Advest, Inc., and made payable to the order of Thornton D. Ring. The back of the check was inscribed as follows:

Payable to Town of Freeport
Property Taxes
2 Main St[.]

The check was accompanied by a letter, signed by Ring and dated January 20, 1997, which reads, "I have paid $11,347.09 of real estate taxes and request the appropriate action to redeem the corresponding property." On February 3, 1997, Ring received a letter from the Town which explained that the Town was returning the check because the 1994 tax lien on the property had matured in 1996.

The Town filed suit seeking a declaratory judgment that it had good title to the Main Street property. One of the issues was whether the delivery of the check by Ring constituted payment of his outstanding taxes.

Clifford, Justice With respect to a check that is made payable to the order of a specific person, negotiation occurs, and the person receiving the check becomes a holder of a negotiable instrument, if possession of the check is transferred and the check is indorsed by the transferor. An indorsement is a signature of someone other than the maker, or some other designation identifying the indorser, that is made on an instrument for the purpose of negotiating the instrument. *Kelly v. Central Bank & Trust Co.* (writing on back of check which reads "For deposit only" to an account other than the payee's and without payee's signature is not an effective indorsement). If negotiation occurs and the holder qualifies as a holder in due course, the holder can demand payment of the instrument subject only to real defenses.

The check Ring sent to the Town was issued by Advest, Inc., payable to the order of Thornton D. Ring. Because it was payable to Ring's order, the check could only be negotiated by Ring through indorsement and transfer of possession. Ring's signature, however, does not appear on the back of the check. The words that do appear on the back of the check—"Payable to Town of Freeport[/]Property Taxes[/]2 Main St[.]"—do not identify Ring. The words only indicate to whom the instrument should have been payable had the check been properly indorsed. Thus, the writing is an incomplete attempt to create a special indorsement. A special indorsement is an indorsement that identifies a person to whom the indorser is making the check payable.

The statement included within the letter accompanying the check does not serve as a valid indorsement either. In determining whether an instrument is properly indorsed, any papers affixed to the instrument are considered part of the instrument. See section 3–204(1). This language specifically references only "affixed" documents. Courts interpreting this language have concluded that a signature on a separate, unattached piece of paper is not an indorsement of the instrument. Ring does not dispute that there is no evidence on record to suggest that the letter was physically attached to the check.

Relying on sections 3–203(3) and 3–203(2), Ring also contends that even in the absence of an indorsement, the check should have been accepted as payment of his outstanding taxes because the Town (1) had a statutory right to demand an indorsement of the check, or (2) was entitled to enforce the instrument without the indorsement. Section 3–203(3) provides that

> if an instrument is transferred for value and the transferee does not become a holder because of lack of indorsement by the transferor, the transferee has a specifically enforceable right to the unqualified indorsement of the transferor. . . ." Section 3–203(2) provides "Transfer of an instrument, whether or not the transfer is a negotiation, vests in the transferee any right of the transferor to enforce the instrument.

Even if the Town could demand an indorsement pursuant to section 3–203(3), negotiation does not occur until the indorsement is made. See section 3–203(3). Thus, at the time the check was received, the Town had a right to demand an indorsement, but could not go to the bank to demand payment of the check. Pursuant to section 3–203(2), the bank also had the right to enforce the instrument as the transferee of an instrument from a holder. That right, however, could be enforced only through a judicial proceeding. Such contingent rights to receive payment are not sufficient to redeem property subject to a municipal tax lien. Checks are meant to be the functional equivalent of cash when they are properly issued and negotiated. If the Town has to institute a judicial proceeding to receive the cash equivalent of the check, the check has not served its purpose. The unindorsed check presented to the Town is not the type of payment the redemption option of the tax lien statute contemplates.

Judgment for Town affirmed.

Indorsements

Effects of an Indorsement

There are three functions to an indorsement. First, an indorsement is necessary in order for the negotiation of an instrument that is payable to the order of a specified person. Thus, if a check is payable "to the order of James Lee," James must indorse the check before it can be negotiated. Second, the form of the indorsement that the indorser uses also affects future attempts to negotiate the instrument. For example, if James indorses it "Pay to the order of Sarah Hill," Sarah must indorse it before it can be negotiated further.

Third, an indorsement generally makes a person liable on the instrument. By indorsing an instrument, a person incurs an obligation to pay the instrument if the person primarily liable on it (for example, the maker of a note) does not pay it. We discuss the contractual liability of indorsers in Chapter 33. In this chapter, we discuss the effect of an indorsement on further negotiation of an instrument.

Kinds of Indorsements

There are three basic kinds of indorsements: (1) special, (2) blank, and (3) restrictive. In addition, an indorsement may be "qualified."

Special Indorsement A **special indorsement** contains the signature of the indorser along with words indicating to whom, or to whose order, the instrument is payable. For example, if a check is drawn "Pay to the Order of Marcia Morse" and Marcia indorses it "Pay to the Order of Sam Smith, Marcia Morse," or "Pay to Sam Smith, Marcia Morse," it has been indorsed with a special indorsement. An instrument that is indorsed with a special indorsement remains "order paper." It can be negotiated only with the indorsement of the person specified [3–205(a)]. In this example, Sam Smith must indorse the check before he can negotiate it to someone else.

Blank Indorsement If an indorser merely signs his name and does not specify to whom the instrument is payable, he has indorsed the instrument **in blank.** For example, if a check drawn "Pay to the Order of Natalie Owens" is indorsed "Natalie Owens" by Natalie, Natalie has indorsed it in blank. An instrument indorsed in blank is payable to the bearer (person in possession of it) and from that act is "bearer paper." As such, the bearer negotiates it by transfer alone and no further indorsement is necessary for negotiation [3–205(b)].

If Natalie indorsed the check in blank and gave it to Kevin Foley, Kevin would have the right to convert the blank indorsement into a special indorsement [3–205(c)]. He could do this by writing the words "Pay to the Order of Kevin Foley" above Natalie's indorsement. Then Kevin would have to indorse the check before it could be further negotiated.

If Kevin took the check indorsed in blank to a bank and presented it for payment or for collection, the bank normally would ask him to indorse the check. It asks not because it needs his indorsement for the check to be negotiated to it; the check indorsed in blank can be negotiated merely by delivering it to the bank cashier. Rather, the bank asks for his indorsement because it wants to make him liable on the check if it is not paid when the bank sends it to the drawee bank for payment. Chapter 33, Liability of Parties, discusses the liability of indorsers.

Restrictive Indorsement A **restrictive indorsement** is one that specifies the purpose of the indorse-

ment or specifies the use to be made of the instrument. Among the more common restrictive indorsements are:

1. Indorsements for deposit. For example, "For Deposit Only" or "For Deposit to My Account at First National Bank."

2. Indorsements for collection, which are commonly put on by banks involved in the collection process. For example, "Pay any bank, banker, or trust company" or "For collection only."

3. Indorsements indicating that the indorsement is for the benefit of someone other than the person to whom it is payable. For example, "Pay to Arthur Attorney in Trust for Mark Minor."

Generally, the person who takes an instrument with a restrictive indorsement must pay or apply any money or other value he gives for the instrument consistently with the indorsement. In the case of a check indorsed "for deposit" or "for collection," any person other than a bank who purchases the check is considered to have **converted** the check unless (1) the indorser received the amount paid for it or (2) the bank applied the amount of the check consistently with the indorsement (e.g., deposited it to the indorser's account). Similarly, a depositary bank (a bank that takes an item for collection) or payor bank (the drawee bank) that takes an instrument for deposit or for immediate payment over the counter that has been indorsed "for deposit" or "for collection" will be liable for conversion unless the indorser received the amount paid for the instrument or the proceeds or the bank applied the amount consistently with the indorsement [3–206(c)].[2]

By way of illustration, assume that Robert Franks has indorsed his paycheck "For Deposit to My Account No. 4068933 at Bank One." While on his way to the bank he loses the check, and Fred Finder finds it. If Finder tries to cash the check at a check-cashing service, the service must ensure that any value it gives for the check either is deposited to Franks' account at Bank One or is received by Franks. If it gives the money to Finder, it will be liable to Franks for converting his check. This principle is illustrated in *Lehigh Presbytery,* which involves a bank that failed to apply value given for checks consistently with restrictive indorsements on the checks.

---

[2]Otherwise, a payor bank as well as an intermediary bank may disregard the indorsement and is not liable if the proceeds of the instrument are not received by the indorser or applied consistently with the indorsement [3–206(c)(4)].

Lehigh Presbytery v. Merchants Bancorp. Inc.
17 UCC Rep. 2d 163 (Penn. Super. Ct. 1991)

Mary Ann Hunsberger was hired by the Lehigh Presbytery as a secretary/bookkeeper. In this capacity, she was responsible for opening the Presbytery's mail, affixing a rubber-stamp indorsement to checks received by the Presbytery, and depositing the checks into the Presbytery's account at Merchants Bancorp, Inc. Over a period of more than five years, Hunsberger deposited into her own account 153 of these checks. Each check was indorsed: "For Deposit Only To The Credit of Presbytery of Lehigh, Ernest Hutcheson, Treas." The bank credited the checks to Hunsberger's account, despite the rubber stamp restrictive indorsement, because it relied solely on the account number handwritten on the deposit slips submitted by Hunsberger with the checks at the time of deposit. Hunsberger obtained the deposit slips in the lobby of the bank, wrote the proper account title, "Lehigh Presbytery," but inserted her own account number rather than the account number of her employer.

When Lehigh Presbytery discovered the diversionary scheme, it sued the bank to recover the funds credited to Hunsberger's account. The primary issue in the case was whether the bank was bound to follow the restrictive indorsements on the 153 checks that it instead had deposited to the personal account of Hunsberger. The trial court ruled in favor of the bank and Lehigh Presbytery appealed.

McEwen, Judge   UCC Section 3–205 provides:

An indorsement is restrictive which either:

* * * * *

(3) includes the words "for collection," "for deposit," "pay any bank," or like terms signifying a purpose of deposit or collection; or

* * * * *

It is undisputed that the indorsement stamped on each check by Ms. Hunsberger is a restrictive indorsement within the meaning of section 3–205.

Section 3–206 of the UCC addresses the effect of such an indorsement and provides, in pertinent part:

(c) Conditional or specified purpose indorsement.—Except for an intermediary bank, any transferee under an indorsement which is conditional or includes the words "for collection," "for deposit," "Pay any bank," or like terms (section 3–205(1) and (3) (relating to restrictive indorsements) must pay or apply any value given by him for or on the security of the instrument consistently with

the indorsement and to the extent he does he becomes a holder for value.

Thus, the UCC mandates application of the value of the checks consistently with the indorsement, i.e., for deposit to Lehigh Presbytery's account.

Courts considering the significance of a restrictive indorsement have consistently concluded that the UCC imposes an unwaivable obligation upon the bank to follow the indorsement. New York State's highest court has held that "[t]he presence of a restriction imposes upon the depositary bank an obligation not to accept that item other than in accord with the restriction. By disregarding the restriction, it not only subjects itself to liability for any losses resulting from its actions, but it also passes up what may be the best opportunity to prevent the fraud."

Judgment reversed in favor of Lehigh Presbytery.

Note: Although this case was decided under the original version of Article 3, the same result would be expected under Revised Article 3.

Some indorsements indicate payment to the indorsee as an agent, trustee, or fiduciary. A person who takes an instrument containing such an indorsement from the indorsee may pay the proceeds to the indorsee without regard to whether the indorsee violates a fiduciary duty to the indorser *unless* he is on *notice* of any breach of fiduciary duty that the indorser may be committing [3–206(d)]. A person would have such notice if he took the instrument in any transaction that benefited the indorsee personally [3–307]. Suppose a person takes a

check indorsed to "Arthur Attorney in Trust for Mark Minor." The money given for the check should be put in Mark Minor's trust account. A person would not be justified in taking the check in exchange for a television set that he knew Attorney was acquiring for his own—rather than Minor's—use.

There are two other kinds of indorsements that the original Article 3 treated as restrictive indorsements but that the revised Article 3 no longer considers as restrictive indorsements. They are:

THE GLOBAL BUSINESS ENVIRONMENT

Convention on International Bills of Exchange and International Promissory Notes

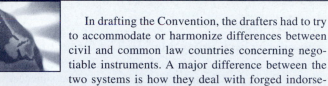

In 1988 the Convention on International Bills of Exchange and International Promissory Notes was adopted by the United Nations. The Convention is applicable to drafts and notes but not to checks. Under the Convention, a bill of exchange is an order to pay money while a promissory note is a promise to pay money. To be covered, they must have the attributes of negotiability. They also must be international in nature in that at least two of the places where their operations occur—such as the address of the drawer or promissory, the address of the payee, or the place of payment—must be in different countries. The Convention also requires that the parties must affirmatively elect to be covered by the Convention by placing a specified legend on the instrument.

In drafting the Convention, the drafters had to try to accommodate or harmonize differences between civil and common law countries concerning negotiable instruments. A major difference between the two systems is how they deal with forged indorsements. Under the common law and UCC Articles 3 and 4, a forged indorsement is not effective to negotiate an instrument to the indorsee while under the civil law it is. Under the civil law, the indorsee takes title to the instrument, acquires the rights of a holder, and payment to the indorsee discharges makers and drawers. As discussed in this and the following chapter, under the UCC, an indorsee taking an instrument with a forged indorsement does not gain these rights and a maker or drawer is not discharged by making payment to that indorsee. The resolution of these differences in the Convention is too complex to discuss in this textbook.

1. Indorsements purporting to prohibit further negotiation. For example, "Pay to Carl Clark Only."
2. Conditional indorsements, which indicate that they are effective only if the payee satisfies a certain condition. For example, "Pay to Bernard Builder Only if He Completes Construction on My House by November 1, 2003."

Under Revised Article 3, any indorsement that purports to limit payment to a particular person, or to prohibit further transfer or negotiation of the instrument, is not effective to prevent further transfer or negotiation [3–206(a)]. Thus, if a note is indorsed "Pay to Carl Clark Only" and given to Clark, he may negotiate the note to subsequent holders who may ignore the restriction on the indorsement.

Indorsements that state a condition to the right of the indorsee to receive payment do not affect the right of the indorsee to enforce the instrument. Any person who pays the instrument or takes it for value or for collection may disregard the condition. Moreover, the rights and liabilities of the person are not affected by whether the condition has been fulfilled [3–206(b)].

Qualified Indorsement   A **qualified indorsement** is one where the indorser disclaims her liability to make the instrument good if the maker or drawer defaults on it. Words such as "Without Recourse" are used to qual-

ify an indorsement. They can be used with either a blank indorsement or a special indorsement and thus make it a qualified blank indorsement or a qualified special indorsement. The use of a qualified indorsement does not change the negotiable nature of the instrument. Its effect is to eliminate the contractual liability of the particular indorser. Chapter 33, Liability of Parties, will discuss this liability in detail.

Rescission of Indorsement

Negotiation is effective to transfer an instrument even if the negotiation is (1) made by a minor, a corporation exceeding its powers, or any other person without contractual capacity; (2) obtained by fraud, duress, or mistake of any kind; (3) made in breach of duty; or (4) part of an illegal transaction. A negotiation made under the preceding circumstances is subject to **rescission** before the instrument has been negotiated to a transferee who can qualify as a holder in due course or a person paying the instrument in good faith and without knowledge of the factual basis for rescission or other remedy [3–202]. The situation in such instances is analogous to a sale of goods where the sale has been induced by fraud or misrepresentation. In such a case, the seller may rescind the sale and recover the goods, provided that the seller acts before the goods are resold to a bona fide purchaser for value.

CONCEPT REVIEW

Indorsements
(Assume a check is payable "To The Order of Mark Smith.")

Type	Example	Consequences
Blank	Mark Smith	1. Satisfies the indorsement requirement for the negotiation of order paper. 2. The instrument becomes bearer paper and can be negotiated by delivery alone. 3. The indorser becomes obligated on the instrument. (See Chapter 33, Liability of Parties.)
Special	Pay to the Order of Joan Brown, Mark Smith	1. Satisfies the indorsement requirement for the negotiation of order paper. 2. The instrument remains order paper and Joan Brown's indorsement is required for further negotiation. 3. The indorser becomes obligated on the instrument. (See Chapter 33.)
Restrictive	For deposit only to my account in First American Bank, Mark Smith	1. Satisfies the indorsement requirement for the negotiation of order paper. 2. The person who pays value for the instrument is obligated to pay it consistent with the indorsement (i.e., to pay it into Mark Smith's account at First American Bank). 3. The indorser becomes obligated on the instrument. (See Chapter 33.)
Qualified	Mark Smith (without recourse)	1. Satisfies the indorsement requirement for negotiation of order paper. 2. Eliminates the indorser's obligation. (See Chapter 33.)

Holder in Due Course

A person who qualifies as a holder in due course of a negotiable instrument gets special rights. Normally, the transferee of an instrument—like the assignee of a contract—gets only those rights in the instrument that are held by the person from whom he got the instrument. But a holder in due course can get better rights. A holder in due course takes a negotiable instrument free of all **personal defenses, claims to the instrument,** and **claims in recoupment** either of the obligor or of a third party. A holder in due course does not take free of the **real defenses,** which go to the validity of the instrument or of claims that develop after he becomes a holder. We develop the differences between "personal" and "real defenses" in more detail later in this chapter and also explain claims to the instrument and claims in recoupment. The following example illustrates the advantage that a holder in due course of a negotiable instrument may have.

Assume that Carl Carpenter contracts with Helen Hawkins to build her a garage for $18,500, payable on October 1 when he expects to complete the garage. Assume further that Carpenter assigns his right to the $18,500 to First National Bank in order to obtain money for materials. If the bank tries to collect the money from Hawkins on October 1 but Carpenter has not finished building the garage, then Hawkins may assert the fact that the garage is not complete as a defense to paying the bank. As assignee of a simple contract, the bank has only those rights that its assignor, Carpenter, has and is subject to all claims and defenses that Hawkins has against Carpenter.

Now assume that instead of simply signing a contract with Hawkins, Carpenter had Homeowner give him a negotiable promissory note in the amount of $18,500 payable to the order of Carpenter on October 1 and that Carpenter then negotiated the note to the bank. If the bank is able to qualify as a holder in due course, it may collect the $18,500 from Hawkins on October 1 even though she might have a personal defense against payment of the note because Carpenter had not completed the work on the garage. Hawkins cannot assert that personal defense against a holder in due course. She would have to pay the note to the bank and then independently seek to recover from Carpenter for breach of their agreement. The bank's improved position is due to its status as a holder in due course of a negotiable instrument. If the instrument in question was not negotiable, or if the bank could not qualify as a holder in due course, then it would be in the same position as the assignee of a simple contract and would be subject to Homeowner's personal defense.

We turn now to a discussion of the requirements that must be met for the possessor of a negotiable instrument to qualify as a holder in due course.

General Requirements

In order to become a **holder in due course,** a person who takes a negotiable instrument must be a *holder,* and take the instrument for *value,* in *good faith, without notice* that it is *overdue* or has been *dishonored* or notice that there is any uncured default with respect to payment of another instrument issued as part of the same series, *without notice* that the instrument *contains an unauthorized signature or has been altered, without notice of any claim of a property or possessory interest in it,* and *without notice* that any party has any *defense against it* or *claim in recoupment to it* [3–302].

In addition, the revision to Article 3 requires "that the instrument when issued or negotiated to the holder does not bear such *apparent evidence of forgery or alteration* or is not otherwise so *irregular* or *incomplete* as to call into question its authenticity" [3–302(a)(1)].

If a person who takes a negotiable instrument does not meet these requirements, he is not a holder in due course. Then the person is in the same position as an assignee of a contract.

Holder

To be a **holder** of a negotiable instrument, a person must have possession of an instrument that is either payable to "bearer" or that is payable to him. For example, if Teresa Gonzales is given a check by her grandmother that is made payable "to the order of Teresa Gonzales," Teresa is a holder of the check because it is made out to her. If Teresa indorses the check "Pay to the order of Ames Hardware, Teresa Gonzales" and gives it to Ames Hardware in payment for some merchandise, then Ames Hardware is the holder of the check. Ames Hardware is a holder because it is in possession of a check that is indorsed to its order. If Ames Hardware indorses the check "Ames Hardware" and deposits it in its account at First National Bank, the bank becomes the holder. The bank is in possession of an instrument that is indorsed in blank and thus is payable to bearer.

It is important that all indorsements on the instrument at the time it is payable to the order of someone are *authorized indorsements.* With limited exceptions (discussed later), a forged indorsement is not an effective indorsement and prevents a person from becoming a holder.

To be a holder, a person must have a complete chain of authorized indorsements. Suppose the Internal Revenue Service mails to Robert Washington an income tax refund check payable to him. Tom Turner steals the check from Washington's mailbox, signs (indorses) "Robert Washington" on the back of the check, and cashes it at a shoe store. The shoe store is not a holder of the check because its transferor, Turner, was not a holder and because it needs Washington's signature to have a good chain of authorized indorsements. Robert Washington has to indorse the check in order for there to be a valid chain of indorsements. Turner's signature is not effective for this purpose because Washington did not authorize him to sign Washington's name to the check [1–201(20); 3–403(a); 3–416(a)(2)].

The *Golden Years Nursing Home* case illustrates that a party in possession of a check indorsed in blank is a holder of the instrument.

Golden Years Nursing Home, Inc. v. Gabbard
682 N.E. 2d 731 (Ohio Ct. App. 1996)

From 1972 until 1991, Nancy Gabbard, the office manager for the Golden Years Nursing Home, received at the nursing home Social Security checks drawn on the United States Treasury and made payable either to individual patients or to "Golden Years Nursing Home for [an individual patient]." From 1986 until 1991, Gabbard engaged in an embezzling scheme whereby she would have certain patients indorse their own checks in blank, that is, each patient would sign his own name on the back of the check placing no restrictions on the manner in which the check could subsequently be negotiated. Gabbard would then cash the checks and either keep the cash or deposit the funds into her personal bank account.

In 1992, after Gabbard's scheme was discovered, Golden Years brought suit against Gabbard and also against the Star Bank Corporation where the checks had been cashed. The patients had in other documents assigned their interests in the checks to Golden Years, and the claim against the bank alleged that it had converted Golden Years' property by cashing checks with forged indorsements. One of the issues in the lawsuit was whether the checks had been properly negotiated to Star Bank. The trial court granted summary judgment to Golden Years, finding that the bank was not a holder in due course because the checks contained "forged indorsements." Star Bank appealed.

Per Curiam The Star Bank argues that the genuine indorsement of the individual payee designated on face of an instrument cannot constitute an unauthorized signature or a forged indorsement. Under the circumstances presented in this case, we agree.

Under the Ohio Uniform Commercial Code, the term "unauthorized signature" "includes both a forgery and a signature made by an agent exceeding his actual or apparent authority," i.e., it occurs in the context of an agency relationship. Golden Years does not argue that the patients forged their own signatures as that term is commonly understood. Rather, it contends that the signatures constitute unauthorized indorsements and, thus, were also forged indorsements because "for purposes of a [section 3–419] conversion action, a forged indorsement and an unauthorized indorsement are synonymous." In addition, Golden Years does not argue that the patients were agents of the nursing home who signed the checks without actual or apparent authority. Rather, Golden Years contends that because the patients had assigned their beneficial interest in the checks to Golden Years, any signature other than Golden Years' corporate stamp was "unauthorized."

We note that Golden Years use of the term "unauthorized signature" does not fall within the scope of the UCC definition of that term, i.e., "made without actual, implied or apparent authority." More important, assuming that the patients had assigned their interest in the checks to Golden Years, any separate agreement between the patient-payees and Golden Years would not affect the negotiability of patients' checks bearing the patients' genuine indorsements.

UCC section 3–119(2) provides that a "separate agreement does not affect the negotiability of an instrument." Negotiability "is always to be determined by what appears on the face of the instrument alone. . . ." A separate writing may affect the terms of an instrument but the Official Comment makes clear that the inquiry is controlled by what *the instrument itself* states or reflects, not, what the collateral agreement says.

If an instrument is payable to order it is negotiated by delivery with any necessary indorsement. (UCC 3–202). "However, once a payee indorses the check in blank, it becomes bearer paper which can be "negotiated by delivery alone" (UCC 3–204). "Negotiation is the transfer of an instrument in such form that the transferee becomes a holder" (UCC 3–202). Thus, in this case, Gabbard became a holder of the checks when the checks, indorsed in blank by the patient-payees, were delivered to her. When Star Bank accepted the checks that were indorsed with the genuine signatures of the payees, the checks bore no indication that they had been assigned to Golden Years. Star Bank cashed the checks in good faith without notice of any defenses and thus became a holder in due course.

This analysis does not change even if Gabbard presented the checks to the payees for their indorsement with the intent to embezzle the funds eventually:

Assuming that the stolen bearer instrument does not bear a restrictive indorsement, the thief will himself be a holder and whether or not he is a holder, he can constitute his transferee a holder simply by transfer. If his transferee then cashes the check and so gives value in good faith and without notice of any defense, that transferee will be a holder in due course under 3–302, free of all claims to the instrument on the part of any person and free of all defenses to it.

Judgment for Star Bank.

Note: Ohio's adoption of Revised Articles 3 and 4 was not effective until Aug 19, 1994, after the events that gave rise to this action. However, the same result would be expected under Revised Articles 3 and 4.

Value

To qualify as a holder in due course of a negotiable instrument, a person must give **value** for it. Value is not identical to simple consideration. Under the provisions of the Revised Article 3, a holder takes for value if: (1) the agreed-upon promise of performance has been performed—for example, if the instrument was given in exchange for a promise to deliver a refrigerator and the refrigerator has been delivered; (2) he acquires a security interest in, or a lien on, the instrument; (3) he takes the instrument in payment of, or as security for, an antecedent claim; (4) he gives a negotiable instrument for it; or (5) he makes an irrevocable commitment to a third person [3–303]. Thus, a person who gets a check as a gift or merely makes an executory promise in return for a check has not given value for it and cannot qualify as a holder in due course.

A bank or any person who discounts an instrument in the *regular course of trade* has given value for it. In this context the discount essentially is a means for increasing the return or the rate of interest on the instrument. Likewise, if a loan is made and an instrument is pledged as security for the repayment of the loan, the secured party has given value for the instrument to the amount of the loan. If Axe, who owes Bell a past-due debt, indorses and delivers to Bell, in payment of the debt or as security for its repayment, an instrument issued to Axe, Bell has given value for the instrument. If a bank allows a customer to draw against a check deposited for collection, it has given value to the extent of the credit drawn against.

If the promise of performance that is the consideration for an instrument has been partially performed, the holder may assert rights as a holder in due course of the instrument only to the fraction of the amount payable under the instrument equal to the partial performance divided by the value of the promised performance [3–302(d)]. For example, Arthur Wells agrees to purchase a note payable to the order of Helda Parks. The note is for the sum of $5,000. Wells pays Parks $1,000 on the negotiation of the note to him and agrees to pay the balance of $4,000 in 10 days. Initially, Wells is a holder in due course for one-fifth of the amount of the note. If he later pays the $4,000 due he may become a holder in due course for the full amount.

Good Faith

To qualify as a holder in due course of a negotiable instrument, a person must take it in **good faith,** which means that the person obtained it honestly and in the observance of reasonable commercial standards of fair dealing [3–103(a)(4)]. If a person obtains a check by trickery or with knowledge that it has been stolen, the person has not obtained the check in good faith and cannot be a holder in due course. A person who pays too little for an instrument, perhaps because she suspects that something may be wrong with the way it was obtained, may have trouble meeting the good faith test. Suppose a finance company works closely with a door-to-door sales

company that engages in shoddy practices. If the finance company buys the consumers' notes from the sales company, it will not be able to meet the good faith test and qualify as a holder in due course of the notes.

Overdue or Dishonored

In order to qualify as a holder in due course, a person must take a negotiable instrument before he has notice that it either is **overdue** or has been **dishonored.** The reason for this is that one should perform obligations when they are due. If a negotiable instrument is not paid when it is due, the Code considers the person taking it to be on notice that there may be defenses to the payment of it.

Overdue Instruments If a negotiable instrument is payable on demand, it is overdue: (1) the day after demand for payment has been made in a proper manner and form; (2) 90 days after its date if it is a check; and (3) if it is an instrument other than a check, when it has been outstanding for an unreasonably long period of time in light of the nature of the instrument and trade practice [3–304(a)]. Thus, a check becomes stale after 90 days. For other kinds of instruments, one must consider trade practices and the facts of the particular case. In a farming community, the normal period for loans to farmers may be six months. A demand note might be outstanding for six or seven months before it is considered overdue. On the other hand, a demand note issued in an industrial city where the normal period of such loans is 30 to 60 days would be considered overdue in a much shorter period of time.

If a negotiable instrument due on a certain date is not paid by that date, normally then it will be overdue at the beginning of the next day after the due date. For example, if a promissory note dated January 1 is payable "30 days after date," it is due on January 31. If it is not paid by January 31, it is overdue beginning on February 1.

As to instruments payable at a definite time, Revised Article 3 sets out the following rules: (1) if the principal is not payable in installments and the due date has not been accelerated, the instrument is overdue on the day after the due date; (2) if the principal is due in installments and a due date has not been accelerated, the instrument is overdue upon default for nonpayment of an installment and remains overdue until the default is cured; (3) if a due date for the principal has been accelerated, the instrument is overdue on the day after the accelerated due date; and (4) unless the due date of the principal has been accelerated, an instrument does not become overdue if there is a default in payment of interest but no default in payment of principal [3–304(b)].

Dishonored Instruments To be a holder in due course, a person not only must take a negotiable instrument before he has notice that it is overdue but also must take it before it has been dishonored. A negotiable instrument has been *dishonored* when the holder has *presented* it for payment (or acceptance) and payment (or acceptance) has been refused.

For example, Susan writes a check on her account at First National Bank that is payable "to the order of Sven Sorensen." Sven takes the check to First National Bank to cash it but the bank refuses to pay it because Susan has insufficient funds in her account to cover it. The check has been dishonored. If Sven then takes Susan's check to Harry's Hardware and uses it to pay for some paint, Harry's cannot be a holder in due course of the check if it is on notice that the check has been dishonored. Harry's would have such notice if First National had stamped the check "Payment Refused NSF" (not sufficient funds).

Similarly, suppose Carol Carson signs a 30-day note payable to Ace Appliance for $500 and gives it to Ace as payment for a stereo set. When Ace asks Carol for payment, she refuses to pay because the stereo does not work properly. If Ace negotiates the note to First National Bank, First National cannot be a holder in due course if it knows about Carol's refusal to pay.

Notice of Unauthorized Signature or Alteration

A holder who has notice that an instrument contains an unauthorized signature or has been altered cannot qualify as a holder in due course of the instrument. For example, Frank makes out a check in the amount of $5 payable to George Grocer and gives it to his daughter, Jane, to take to the grocery store to purchase some groceries. The groceries Frank wants cost $20 and Jane changes the check to read $25, giving it to Grocer in exchange for the groceries and $5 in cash. Grocer cannot qualify as a holder in due course if he sees Jane make the alteration to the check or otherwise is on notice of it. [See 3–302(a)(1).]

Notice of Claims

If a person taking a negotiable instrument is *on notice of an adverse claim* to the instrument by someone else (for example, that a third person is the rightful owner of the instrument) or that someone earlier sought to rescind a prior negotiation of the instrument, the current holder cannot qualify as a holder in due course. For example, a U.S. Treasury check is payable to Susan Samuels. Samuels loses the check and it is found by Robert Burns.

Burns takes the check to a hardware store, signs "Susan Samuels" on the back of the check in the view of a clerk, and seeks to use it in payment of merchandise. The hardware store cannot be a holder in due course because it is on notice of a potential claim to the instrument by Susan Samuels.

Notice of Breach of Fiduciary Duty One situation in which the Code considers a person to be on notice of a claim is if she is taking a negotiable instrument from a fiduciary, such as a trustee. If a negotiable instrument is payable to a person as a trustee or an attorney for someone, then any attempt by that person to negotiate it for his own behalf or for his use (or benefit) or to deposit it in an account other than that of the fiduciary puts the person on notice that the beneficiary of the trust may have a claim [3–307].

For example, a check is drawn "Pay to the order of Arthur Adams, Trustee for Mary Minor." Adams takes the check to Credit Union, indorses his name to it, and uses it to pay off the balance on a loan Adams had from Credit Union. Credit Union cannot be a holder in due course because it should know that the negotiation of the check is in violation of the fiduciary duty Adams owes to Mary Minor. Ace should know this because Adams is negotiating the check for his own benefit, not Mary's.

Notice of Defenses and Claims in Recoupment To qualify as a holder in due course, a person must also acquire a negotiable instrument without notice that any party to it has any **defenses** or **claims in recoupment.** Potential defenses include infancy, duress, fraud, and failure of consideration. Thus, if a person knows that a signature on the instrument was obtained by fraud, misrepresentation, or duress, the person cannot be a holder in due course.

A *claim in recoupment* is a claim of the obligor against the original payee of the instrument. The claim must arise from the transaction that gave rise to the instrument. An example of a claim in recoupment would be as follows: Buyer purchases a used automobile from Dealer for $8,000, giving the dealer a note for $8,000 payable in one year. Because the automobile is not as warranted, Buyer has a breach of warranty claim that could be asserted against Dealer as counterclaim or "claim in recoupment" to offset the amount owing on the note.

Irregular and Incomplete Instruments

A person cannot be a holder in due course of a negotiable instrument if, when she takes it, the instrument is irregular or some important or material term is blank. If the negotiable instrument contains a facial irregularity, such as an obvious alteration in the amount, then it is considered to be **irregular paper.** If you take an irregular instrument, you are considered to be on notice of any possible defenses to it. For example, Kevin writes a check for "one dollar" payable to Karen. Karen inserts the word "hundred" in the amount, changes the figure "$1" to "$100," and gives the check to a druggist in exchange for a purchase of goods. If the alterations in the amount should be obvious to the druggist, perhaps because there are erasures, different handwritings, or different inks, then the druggist cannot be a holder in due course. She would have taken irregular paper and would be on notice that there might be defenses to it. These defenses include Kevin's defense that he is liable for only $1 because that is the amount for which he made the check.

Similarly, if someone receives a check that has been signed but the space where the amount of the check is to be written is blank, then the person cannot be a holder in due course of that check. The fact that a material term is blank means that the instrument is **incomplete** and should put the person on notice that the drawer may have a defense to payment of it. To be material, the omitted term must be one that affects the legal obligation of the parties to the negotiable instrument. Material terms include the amount of the instrument and the name of the payee. If a negotiable instrument is unauthorizedly completed after the obligor signed it but before a person acquires it, the person can qualify as a holder in due course if she had no notice about the unauthorized completion. A person has notice if she knows or should know of the unauthorized completion.

Payee as Holder in Due Course

The original Article 3 provided explicitly that a *payee* could be a holder in due course if he complied with all the requirements for a holder in due course. Revised Article 3 drops the explicit statement; the drafters stated that they intended no change in the law but that they were concerned that the explicit provision suggested that use of holder-in-due-course status by payees was the normal situation. It is not the normal situation, because a payee usually will have notice or knowledge of any defenses to the instrument and will know whether it is overdue or has been dishonored; consequently, the payee is unlikely to qualify as a holder in due course. For example, Drew draws a check on First Bank as drawee, payable to the order of Parks, but leaves the amount blank. Drew delivers the check to Axe, his

agent, and instructs Axe to fill in $300 as the amount. Axe, however, fills in $500 as the amount, and Parks gives Axe $500 for the check. Axe then gives Drew $300 and absconds with the extra $200. In such a case, Parks, as payee, is a holder in due course of the check because he has taken it for value, in good faith, and without notice of defenses.

Similarly, assume that Jarvis owes Fields $200. Jarvis agrees to sell Kirk a used television set for $200; Jarvis assures Kirk it is in working condition. In fact, the set is broken. Jarvis asks Kirk to make her check for $200 payable to Fields and then delivers the check to Fields in payment of the debt. Fields, as the payee, can be a holder in due course of the check if he is not aware of the misrepresentation that Jarvis made to Kirk in order to obtain the check.

Shelter Rule

The transferee of an instrument—whether or not the transfer is a negotiation—obtains those rights that the transferor had, including (1) the transferor's right to enforce the instrument and (2) any right as a holder in due course [3–203(b)]. This means that any person who can trace his title to an instrument back to a holder in due course receives rights similar of a holder in due course even if he cannot meet the requirements himself. This is known as the **shelter rule** in Article 3. For example, Archer makes a note payable to Bryant. Bryant negotiates the note to Carlyle, who qualifies as a holder in due course. Carlyle then negotiates the note to Darby, who cannot qualify as a holder in due course because she knows the note is overdue. Because Darby can trace her title back to a holder in due course (Carlyle), Darby has rights like a holder in due course when she seeks payment of the note from Archer.

There is, however, a limitation on the shelter rule. A transferee who has himself been a party to any fraud or illegality affecting the instrument cannot improve his position by taking, directly or indirectly, from a later holder in due course [3–203(b)]. For example, Archer, through fraudulent representations, induced Bryant to execute a negotiable note payable to Archer and then negotiated the instrument to Carlyle, who took as a holder in due course. If Archer thereafter took the note for value from Carlyle, Archer could not acquire Carlyle's rights as a holder in due course. Archer was a party to the fraud that induced the note, and, accordingly, cannot improve his position by negotiating the instrument and then reacquiring it.

The shelter rule is illustrated in the *Triffin* case, which follows.

Triffin v. Cigna Insurance Co.   *31 UCC Rep.2d 1040 (N.J. Sup. Ct., App. Div. 1997)*

James Mills received a draft in the amount of $484.12 dated July 7, 1993, from one of Cigna Insurance Company's constituent companies. The draft had been issued for worker's compensation benefits. Mills falsely indicated to the issuer that he had not received the draft because of a change in his address and requested that payment be stopped and a new draft issued to him. The insurer complied and stopped payment on the initial draft. Mills nevertheless negotiated the draft to Sun Corp. t/a Sun's Market before the stop payment notation was placed on the draft. Sun Corp. was a holder in due course of the draft.

Sun Corp. presented the draft for payment through depositary and collecting banks. The issuer's bank dishonored the draft in accordance with its customer's direction, stamped it "Stop Payment," and returned it to Sun Corp. At that point, as a holder in due course, Sun Corp. would have been able to enforce the draft against the issuer.

Thereafter, Triffin, who is in the business of purchasing dishonored instruments, received an assignment of Sun Corp.'s interest in the draft and brought suit against the issuer. The trial court awarded summary judgment to Cigna and Triffin appealed.

DREIER, Presiding Judge Triffin does not contend that he is a holder in due course of the instrument by virtue of it being negotiated to him for value, in good faith, without notice of dishonor under the former holder in due course statute (section 3–302[1]), nor under the present statute (Revised section 3–302a[2]).

Such negotiation is, of course, only one way for a holder to claim the status of a holder in due course. There exists a second method by which one may become a holder in due course. The shelter provisions of former 3–201(1), which was in effect when Triffin obtained his assignment of this instrument, state clearly that "[t]ransfer of an instrument vests in the transferee such rights as the transferor has therein. . . ." Official Comment 3 to that section sets to rest any question of whether this section applies to the transfer by assignment of the rights of a holder in due course. The Comment reads: "A holder in due course may transfer his rights as such. . . .[The] policy is to assure the holder in due course a free market for the paper." Example (a) following this comment could have been drawn from this case, but is even stronger because it adds an element of fraud and posits a gratuitous transfer rather than a purchase, as in our case.

(a) A [Mills] induces M [Cigna] by fraud to make an instrument payable to A. A negotiates it to B [Sun Corp.], who takes it as a holder in due course. After the instrument is overdue, B gives it to C [Triffin], who has notice of the fraud. C succeeds to B's rights as a holder in due course, cutting off the defense.

If the 1995 amendments [Revised Article 3] are to be given retroactive effect, the law governing the rights of a transferee who merely has accepted the transfer of the instrument is now found in section 3–203(b). It restates the principle of the former Official Comment 3, example (a), as substantive law. This section states:

Transfer of an instrument, whether or not the transfer is a negotiation, vests in the transferee any right of the transferor to enforce the instrument, including any right as a holder in due course. . . ."

The Uniform Commercial Code Comment to this section similarly states:

Under subsection (b) a holder in due course that transfers an instrument transfers those rights as a holder in due course to the purchaser. The policy is to assure the holder in due course a free market for the instrument.

These sections could not be clearer. Triffin received by assignment the right of a holder in due course to this instrument, which apparently had been presented and then dishonored because of Cigna's stop payment order. The draft itself remained the basis of a claim upon which Triffin or its assignor had three years to sue after dishonor of the draft or ten years after the date of the draft, whichever period expired first (3–118c).

Judgment reversed in favor of Triffin.

Requirements for a Holder in Due Course

Requirement	Rule
1. Must be a *holder.*	A holder is a person in possession of an instrument payable to bearer or payable to an identified person and he is that person.
2. Must take *for value.*	A holder has given value: *a.* To the extent the agreed-on consideration has been paid or performed. *b.* To the extent a security interest or lien has been obtained in the negotiable instrument. *c.* By taking the negotiable instrument in payment of—or as security for—an antecedent claim. *d.* By giving a negotiable instrument for it. *e.* By making an irrevocable commitment to a third person.
3. Must take in *good faith.*	Good faith means honesty in fact and the observance of reasonable commercial standards of fair dealing.
4. Must take *without notice* that the instrument is *overdue.*	An instrument payable on demand is overdue the day after demand for payment has been duly made. A check is overdue 90 days after its date. If it is an instrument other than a check and payable on demand, when it has been outstanding for an unreasonably long period of time in light of nature of the instrument and trade practice. If it is an instrument due on a certain date, then it is overdue at the beginning of the next day after the due date.
5. Must take *without notice* that the instrument has been *dishonored.*	An instrument has been dishonored when the holder has presented it for payment (or acceptance) and payment (or acceptance) has been refused.
6. Must take *without notice* of any *uncured default* with respect to payment of another instrument issued as part of the same series.	If there is a series of notes, holder must take without notice that there is an uncured default as to any other notes in the series.
7. Must take *without notice* that the instrument contains an *unauthorized signature* or has been *altered.*	Notice of unauthorized signature or alteration—that is, a change in a material term—prevents holder from obtaining HDC status.
8. Must take *without notice* of any *claim of a property or possessory interest* in it.	Claims of property or possessory interest include: *a.* Claim by someone that she is the rightful owner of the instrument. *b.* Person seeking to rescind a prior negotiation of the instrument. *c.* Claim by a beneficiary that a fiduciary negotiated the instrument for his own benefit.
9. Must take *without notice* that any party has a *defense* against it.	Defenses include real defenses that go to the validity of the instrument and personal defenses that commonly are defenses to a simple contract.
10. Must take *without notice* of a *claim in recoupment* to it.	A claim in recoupment is a claim of the obligor on the instrument against the original payee that arises from the transaction that gave rise to the instrument.
11. The instrument must not bear *apparent evidence of forgery or alteration* or be *irregular* or *incomplete.*	The instrument must not contain obvious reasons to question its authenticity.

Rights of a Holder in Due Course

Claims and Defenses Generally

Revised Article 3 establishes four categories of claims and defenses. They are:

1. *Real defenses*—which go to the validity of the instrument.

2. *Personal defenses*—which generally arise out of the transaction that gave rise to the instrument.

3. *Claims to an instrument*—which generally concern property or possessory rights in an instrument or its proceeds.

4. *Claims in recoupment*—which also arise out of the transaction that gave rise to the instrument.

These defenses and claims are discussed in some detail below.

Importance of Being a Holder in Due Course

In the preceding chapter, we explained that one advantage of negotiable instruments over other kinds of contracts is that they are accepted as substitutes for money. People are willing to accept them as substitutes for money because, generally, they can take them free of claims or defenses to payment between the original parties to the instrument. On the other hand, a person who takes an assignment of a simple contract gets only the same rights as the person had who assigned the contract.

There are two qualifications to the ability of a person who acquires a negotiable instrument to be free of claims or defenses between the original parties. First, the person in possession of a negotiable instrument must be a *person entitled to enforce the instrument* as well as a *holder in due course* (or must be a holder who has the rights of a holder in due course through the shelter rule). If the person is neither, then she is subject to all claims or defenses to payment that any party to it has. Second, the only claims or defenses that the holder in due course has to worry about are so-called real defenses—those that affect the validity of the instrument—or claims that arose after she became a holder. For example, if the maker or drawer did not have legal capacity because she was a minor, the maker or drawer has a real defense. The holder in due course does not

have to worry about other defenses and claims that do not go to the validity of the instrument—the so-called personal defenses.

Real Defenses

There are some claims and defenses to payment of an instrument that go to the validity of the instrument. These claims and defenses are known as **real defenses.** They can be used as reasons against payment of a negotiable instrument to any holder, including a holder in due course (or a person who has the rights of a holder in due course). Real defenses include:

1. *Minority or infancy* that under state law makes the instrument void or voidable. For example, if Mark Miller, age 17, signs a promissory note as maker, he can use his lack of capacity to contract as a defense against paying it even to a holder in due course.

2. *Incapacity* that under state law makes the instrument void. For example, if a person has been declared mentally incompetent by a court, then the person has a real defense if state law declares all contracts entered into by the person after the adjudication of incompetency to be void.

3. *Duress* that voids or nullifies the obligation of a party liable to pay the instrument. For example, if Harold points a gun at his grandmother and forces her to execute a promissory note, the grandmother can use duress as a defense against paying it even to a holder in due course.

4. *Illegality* that under state law renders the obligation void. For example, in some states, checks and notes given in payment of gambling debts are void.

5. *Fraud in the essence (or fraud in the factum).* This occurs where a person signs a negotiable instrument without knowing or having a reasonable opportunity to know that it is a negotiable instrument or of its essential terms. For example, Amy Jones is an illiterate person who lives alone. She signs a document that is actually a promissory note but is told that it is a grant of permission for a television set to be left in her house on a trial basis. Amy has a real defense against payment of the note even to a holder in due course. Fraud in the essence is distinguished from fraud in the inducement, discussed below, which is only a personal defense.

6. *Discharge in bankruptcy.* For example, if the maker of a promissory note has had the debt discharged in a bankruptcy proceeding, she no longer is liable on it and has a real defense against payment [3–305(a)(1)].

Real defenses can be asserted even against a holder in due course of a negotiable instrument because it is more desirable to protect people who have signed negotiable instruments in these situations than it is to protect persons who have taken negotiable instruments in the ordinary course of business.

The *Kedzie & 103rd Currency Exchange* case, which follows, involves the question of whether a drawer who issued a check to an unlicensed plumber has a real defense of illegality that can be asserted against a holder in due course. It also highlights the difficult public policy issue inherent in section 3–305.

Kedzie & 103rd Currency Exchange, Inc. v. Hodge
21 UCC Rep. 2d 682 (Ill. Sup. Ct. 1993)

Pursuant to a written "work order," Fred Fentress agreed to install a "flood control system" at the home of Eric and Beulah Hodge of Chicago for $900. In partial payment for the work, Beulah Hodge drafted a personal check payable to "Fred Fentress—A-OK Plumbing" for $500 from the Hodges' joint account at Citicorp Savings.

The system's components were not delivered to the Hodges' home as scheduled. And when Fentress failed to appear on the date set for installation, Eric Hodge telephoned Fentress to advise him the contract was "canceled." Hodge also told Fentress that he would order Citicorp Savings not to pay the check Fentress had been given. Later that day Citicorp received a stop-payment order from Hodge.

Fentress presented the check at the Kedzie & 103rd Street Currency Exchange, indorsing it as "sole owner" of A-OK Plumbing and obtained payment. However, when the Currency Exchange later presented the check for payment at Citicorp Savings, payment was refused in accordance with the stop-payment order.

The Currency Exchange, alleging that it was a holder in due course, then sued Beulah Hodge as the drawer of the check, and Fentress. Hodge moved to dismiss the action against her on the grounds that under section 3–305 she had a defense against payment that could be asserted against a holder in due course, namely that the transaction was illegal because Fentress was not a licensed plumber as required by Illinois law. The circuit court granted the motion and the appeals court affirmed. Currency Exchange then appealed to the Illinois Supreme Court.

Freeman, Justice The Illinois Plumbing License Law requires that all plumbing, including "installation . . . or extension of" drains be performed by plumbers licensed under the Act. The affidavits establish that Fentress was not licensed either by the City of Chicago or the State of Illinois. That failure is a violation of the Illinois Plumbing License Law and is punishable as a misdemeanor. No counter affidavit was supplied.

No material fact remains to be resolved. The question is simply whether Hodge is entitled, as a matter of law, to a judgment of dismissal in view of the defense asserted under section 3–305. Section 3–305 provides, in relevant part:

> [A] holder in due course . . . takes the instrument free from. . .
>> (2) all defenses of any party to the instrument with whom the holder has not dealt except. . .
>>> (b) . . . illegality of the transaction, as renders the obligation of the party a nullity.

The concern is whether noncompliance by Fentress with the Illinois Plumbing License Law gives rise to "illegality of the transaction" with respect to the contract for plumbing services as to bar the claim of the Currency Exchange, a holder in due course of the check initially given to Fentress.

The issue of "illegality" arises under a variety of statutes. In view of the diverse constructions to which statutory enactments are given, "illegality" is, accordingly, a matter "left to the local law." Even so, it is only when an obligation is made "entirely null and void" under "local law" that "illegality" exists as one of the "real defenses" under section 3–305 to defeat the claim of a holder in due course. In effect, the obligation must be no obligation at all. If it is "merely voidable" at the election of the obligor, the defense is unavailable.

Historically, this court has recognized "illegality" to arise only in view of legislative declaration affecting both the underlying contract or transaction and the instrument exchanged upon it. A contract or transaction which is void must certainly negate the obligation to pay arising from it as between the contracting parties. But, unless an instrument memorializing the obligation is also made void, an innocent third party who has no knowledge of the circumstances of the initial contract or transaction may yet claim payment of it against the drawer or maker.

Thus, "illegality" has been held to defeat the claims of holders in due course in cases involving contracts of a gaming nature or for retirement of gambling debts. Owing to a deep-seated hostility toward nongovernmental sanctioned gambling, our legislature has declared that any instrument associated with such activity is void, independent of the status of who may possess it. The absence of a similar legislative declaration as for an instrument given upon a usurious contract must account, in part, for a conclusion that usury has not been held to give rise to "illegality" as a defense against a holder in due course.

Several other jurisdictions also find reason to draw a distinction between the voidness of a negotiable instrument and the underlying contract or obligation upon which it is exchanged. A plaintiff is precluded from recovering on a suit involving an illegal contract because the plaintiff is a wrongdoer. But a holder in due course is an innocent third party.

In adopting the UCC and, in particular section 3–305, our legislature chose to confer on a holder in due course of a negotiable instrument considerable protection against claims by persons to it. Our legislature also continues to declare certain obligations void because of the circumstances of the agreements from which they arise and without regard to the status of who may claim ownership. The selective negation of obligations reflects a legislative aim to declare what will and will not give rise to "illegality" in cases now governed by the UCC. As legislative direction indicates which obligations are always void, legislative silence indicates when the protection afforded a holder in due course must be honored.

We therefore reaffirm today the view this court has consistently recognized in cases predating the UCC. Unless the instrument arising from a contract or transaction is, itself, made void by statute, the "illegality" defense under section 3–305 is not available to bar the claim of a holder in due course.

Judgment for Hodge reversed.

Bilandic, Justice, dissenting I would affirm the trial court's dismissal of the Currency Exchange's complaint. The majority here incorporates into section 3–305 of the UCC an additional requirement that must be met before the defense of illegality can be met to defeat the claim of an alleged holder in due course. That additional requirement is not found anywhere in the plain language of section 3–305, however.

With respect to the defenses of duress and illegality, the comments to section 3–305 state, in pertinent part, that "[t]hey are primarily a matter of local concern and local policy. All such matters are therefore left to the local law. If under that law the effect of the duress or the illegality is such to make the *obligation* entirely null and void, the defense may be asserted against a holder in due course.

The plain language of section 3–305 and the comments to the section make it clear that where the illegality of a transaction renders the *obligation* of the maker of an instrument a nullity, the illegal transaction can be raised as a defense by the maker of the instrument, even against a holder in due course. Section 3–305 does not state that illegality is a defense only where the *instrument* arising from a contract or transaction has been expressly declared void by the legislature due to the illegality of the transaction. Had the legislature intended for illegality to be a defense only where it had expressly declared an instrument void due to the illegality of the underlying transaction, it could easily have done so.

The only inquiry necessary to resolve the issue presented in this case then is whether the contract between Hodge and Fentress is void on the grounds of illegality. An examination of the statute providing for the licensing of plumbers, the public policy behind the statute, and the Illinois case law concerning contracts made in contravention of professional licensing laws establishes that the contract between Hodge and Fentress is illegal and void.

Courts in other states have ruled that the defense of illegality of the contract may be asserted against a holder in due course without requiring that a negotiable instrument in question be expressly declared void by statute. In *Wilson v. Steele* (Cal. 1989), the court held that a contract made by an unlicensed home contractor was void and illegal and that this defense could be asserted against a holder in due course. In *Columbus Check Cashiers, Inc. v. Stiles* (Ohio 1990), the court likewise held that a check given as consideration for a contract between a homeowner and an unlicensed home contractor is illegal and void and that the defense of illegality could be asserted against the holder in due course.

In *Columbus Check Cashiers* and *Wilson,* as in the instant case, the subject matter of the contract, performance by an unlicensed individual was prohibited by law. Accordingly, the courts held the contract was illegal and void and that this defense could be asserted against a holder in due course. More importantly, the courts in these two cases did not require that a statute expressly declare the note in question void in order for the defense of illegality to be available. Such a requirement is likewise not a part of Illinois version of section 3–305. In contrast, under New Jersey law, which the majority here purports to follow, the comments to that state's version of section 3–305 expressly state that "[i]n New Jersey, a holder in due course takes free and clear of the defense of illegality, *unless the statute which declares the act illegal also indicates that payment thereunder is void.*" (Emphasis added.)

The majority asserts that to bar recovery by Currency Exchange in this case would be unfair because the Currency Exchange is an innocent third party which had no knowledge of the circumstances of the contract between Hodge and Fentress. However, section 3–305 clearly provides that the general policy favoring free negotiability is not absolute. There is a competing policy disfavoring certain transactions, such as those involving infancy, duress, illegality or misrepresentation as to the true nature of an instrument (i.e. fraud in the factum). Pursuant to section 3–305, the Currency Exchange takes a check subject to these and certain other real defenses. The Illinois legislature has provided that, by definition, a holder in due course is one who does not have notice of *any* of the real defenses listed in section 3–305. By statute, the innocence of the holder in due course cannot defeat *any* of the real defenses listed in section 3–305, including illegality. Accordingly, the argument that the Currency Exchange could not have known that the underlying transaction was illegal is simply misplaced. Such reasoning would lead to the conclusion that all of the defenses listed in section 3–305 should be unavailable to defeat the claim of a holder in due course, a conclusion obviously contrary to the provisions of section 3–305.

For the above reasons, I dissent. I would affirm the judgment of the appellate court which affirmed the circuit court's dismissal of the Currency Exchange's action against Hodge.

Note: Although this case was decided under the original version of Article 3, the same result would be anticipated under Revised Article 3.

In addition to the real defenses discussed above, there are several other reasons why a person otherwise liable to pay an instrument would have a defense against payment that would be effective even against a holder in due course. They include:

1. *Forgery.* For example, if a maker's signature has been put on the instrument without his authorization and without his negligence, the maker has a defense against payment of the note.

2. *Alteration of a completed instrument.* This is a partial defense against a holder in due course (or a person having the rights of a holder in due course) and a complete defense against a nonholder in due course. A holder in due course can enforce an altered instrument against the maker or drawer according to its original tenor (terms).

3. *Discharge.* If a person takes an instrument with knowledge that the obligation of any party obligated on the instrument has been discharged, the person takes subject to the discharge even if the person is a holder in due course.

Personal Defenses

Personal defenses are legal reasons for avoiding or reducing liability of a person who is liable on a negotiable instrument. Generally, personal defenses arise out of the transaction in which the negotiable instrument was issued and are

ETHICS IN ACTION

Asserting the Defense of Illegality against Payment of a Gambling Debt

Assume that in the course of a vacation you drop by the casino in the hotel where you were staying. You decide to play a few hands of blackjack. After winning your first few hands, you then go on a sustained losing streak. Believing your luck is about to change, you keep going until you have lost $10,000, much more than you intended or could readily afford. At the end of the evening, you write the casino a check. Later in the hotel bar, you tell your sad tale to a fellow drinker who is a local lawyer and who informs you that a state law makes gambling obligations void. Would it be ethical for you to stop payment on the check and then assert the defense of illegality against the holder of the check?

based on negotiable instruments law or contract law. A holder in due course of a negotiable instrument (or one who can claim the rights of one) is not subject to any personal defenses or claims that may exist between the original parties to the instrument. Personal defenses include:

1. *Lack or failure of consideration.* For example, a promissory note for $100 was given to someone without intent to make a gift and without receiving anything in return [3–303(b)].

2. *Breach of contract, including breach of warranty.* For example, a check was given in payment for repairs to an automobile but the repair work was defective.

3. *Fraud in the inducement of any underlying contract.* For example, an art dealer sells a lithograph to Cheryl, telling her that it is a Picasso, and takes Cheryl's check for $500 in payment. The art dealer knows that the lithograph is not a genuine Picasso but a forgery. Cheryl has been induced to make the purchase and to give her check by the art dealer's fraudulent representation. Because of this fraud, Cheryl has a personal defense against having to honor her check to the art dealer.

4. *Incapacity to the extent that state law makes the obligation voidable, as opposed to void.* For example, where state law makes the contract of a person of limited mental capacity but who has not been adjudicated incompetent voidable, the person has a personal defense to payment.

5. *Illegality that makes a contract voidable, as opposed to void.* For example, where the payee of a check given for certain professional services was required to have a license from the state but did not have one.

6. *Duress, to the extent it is not so severe as to make the obligation void but rather only voidable.* For example, if the instrument was signed under a threat to prosecute the maker's son if it was not signed, the maker might have a personal defense.

7. *Unauthorized completion or alteration of the instrument.* For example, the instrument was completed in an unauthorized manner, or was altered after it left the maker's or drawer's possession.

8. *Nonissuance of the instrument, conditional issuance, and issuance for a special purpose.* For example, the person in possession of the instrument obtained it by theft or by finding it, rather than through an intentional delivery of the instrument to him [3–105(b)].

9. *Failure to countersign a traveler's check* [3–106(c)].

10. *Modification of the obligation by a separate agreement* [3–117].

11. *Payment that violates a restrictive indorsement* [3–206(f)].

12. *Breach of warranty when a draft is accepted* (discussed in following chapter) [3–417(b)].

The following example illustrates the limited extent to which a maker or drawer can use personal defenses as a reason for not paying a negotiable instrument he signed. Suppose Trent Tucker bought a used truck from Honest Harry's and gave Harry a 60-day promissory note for $2,750 in payment for the truck. Honest Harry's "guaranteed" the truck to be in "good working condition," but in fact the truck had a cracked engine block. If Harry tries to collect the $2,750 from Trent, Trent could claim breach of warranty as a reason for not paying Harry the full $2,750 because Harry is not a holder in due course. However, if Harry negotiated the note to First National Bank and the bank was a holder in due course, the situation would be changed. If the bank tried to collect the $2,750 from Trent, Trent would have to pay the bank. Trent cannot use his defense or claim of breach of warranty as a reason for not paying the bank, which qualified as a holder in due course. It is a personal defense. Trent must pay the bank the $2,750 and then pursue his breach of warranty claim against Harry.

The rule that a holder in due course takes a negotiable instrument free of any personal defenses or claims to it has been modified to some extent, particularly in relation to instruments given by consumers. These modifications will be discussed in the next section of this chapter.

Claims to the Instrument

For purposes of Revised Article 3, the term *claims* to an instrument can include:

1. A claim to ownership of the instrument by one who asserts that he is the owner and was wrongfully deprived of possession.

2. A claim of a lien on the instrument.

3. A claim for rescission of an indorsement.

A holder in due course takes free of claims that arose before he became a holder but is subject to those arising when or after she becomes a holder in due course. For example, if a holder impairs the collateral given for an obligation, he may be creating a defense for an obligor.

Claims in Recoupment

A *claim in recoupment* is not actually a defense to an instrument but rather an *offset to liability.* For example, Ann Adams purchases a new automobile from Dealership, giving it a note for the balance of the purchase price beyond her down payment. After accepting delivery, she discovers a breach of warranty that the dealer fails to remedy. If Dealer has sold the note to a bank that subsequently seeks payment on the note from Adams, she has a claim in recoupment for breach of warranty. If the bank is a holder in due course, the claim in recoupment cannot be asserted against it. However, if the bank is not a holder in due course, then Adams can assert the claim in recoupment to reduce the amount owing on the instrument at the time the action is brought against her on the note. Her claim could serve only to reduce the amount owing and not as a basis for a net recovery from the bank. However, if Dealer was the person bringing an action to collect the note, Adams could assert the breach of warranty claim as a counterclaim and potentially might recover from Dealer any difference between the claim and the damages due for breach of warranty.

The obligor may assert a claim up to the amount of the instrument if the holder is the original payee but cannot assert claims in recoupment against a holder in due course. In addition, the obligor may assert a claim against a transferee who does not qualify as a holder in due course, but only to reduce the amount owing on the instrument at the time it brought the claim in recoupment.

Changes in the Holder in Due Course Rule

Consumer Disadvantages

The rule that a holder in due course of a negotiable instrument is not subject to personal defenses between the

---

Claims and Defenses against Payment of Negotiable Instruments

Claim or Defense	Examples
Real Defense Valid against all holders, including holders in due course and holders who have the rights of holders in due course.	1. Minority that under state law makes the contract void or voidable. 2. Other lack of capacity that makes the contract void. 3. Duress that makes the contract void. 4. Illegality that makes the contract void. 5. Fraud in the essence (fraud in the factum). 6. Discharge in bankruptcy.
Personal Defense Valid against plain holders of instruments—but not against holders in due course or holders who have the rights of in due course holders through the shelter rule.	1. Lack or failure of consideration. 2. Breach of contract (including breach of warranty). 3. Fraud in the inducement. 4. Lack of capacity that makes the contract voidable (except minority). 5. Illegality that makes the contract voidable. 6. Duress that makes the contract voidable. 7. Unauthorized completion of an incomplete instrument, or material alteration of the instrument. 8. Nonissuance of the instrument. 9. Failure to countersign a traveler's check. 10. Modification of the obligation by a separate agreement. 11. Payment that violates a restrictive indorsement. 12. Breach of warranty when a draft is accepted.
Claim to an Instrument	1. Claim of ownership by someone who claims to be the owner and that he was wrongfully deprived of possession. 2. Claim of a lien on the instrument. 3. Claim for rescission of an indorsement.
Claims in Recoupment	1. Breach of warranty in the sale of goods for which the instrument was issued.

original parties to it makes negotiable instruments a readily accepted substitute for money. This rule can also result in serious disadvantages to consumers. Consumers sometimes buy goods or services on credit and give the seller a negotiable instrument such as a promissory note. They often do this without knowing the consequences of their signing a negotiable instrument. If the goods or services are defective or not delivered, the consumer would like to withhold payment of the note until the seller corrects the problem or makes the delivery. Where the note is still held by the seller, the consumer can do this because any defenses of breach of warranty or nonperformance are good against the seller.

However, the seller may have negotiated the note at a discount to a third party such as a bank. If the bank qualifies as a holder in due course, the consumer must pay the note in full to the bank. The consumer's personal defenses are not valid against a holder in due course. The consumer must pay the holder in due course and then try to get her money back from the seller. This may be difficult if the seller cannot be found or will not accept responsibility. The consumer would be in a much stronger position if she could just withhold payment, even against the bank, until the goods or services are delivered or the performance is corrected.

State Consumer Protection Legislation

Some state legislatures and courts have limited the holder in due course rule, particularly as it affects consumers. State legislation limiting the doctrine typically amended state laws dealing with consumer credit transactions. For example, some state laws prohibit a seller from taking a negotiable instrument other than a check from a consumer in payment for consumer goods and services. Other states require promissory notes given by consumers in payment for goods and services to carry the words *consumer paper*. Holders of instruments with the legend "consumer paper" are not eligible to be holders in due course.[3] [3–106(d)]

Federal Trade Commission Regulation

The Federal Trade Commission (FTC) has promulgated a regulation designed to protect consumers against operation of the holder in due course rule. The FTC rule applies to persons who sell to consumers on credit and have the consumer sign a note or an installment sale contract or arrange third-party financing of the purchase. The seller must ensure that the note or the contract contains the following clause:

NOTICE: ANY HOLDER OF THIS CONSUMER CREDIT CONTRACT IS SUBJECT TO ALL CLAIMS AND DEFENSES WHICH THE DEBTOR COULD ASSERT AGAINST THE SELLER OF THE GOODS OR SERVICES OBTAINED PURSUANT HERETO OR WITH THE PROCEEDS HEREOF. RECOVERY HEREUNDER BY THE DEBTOR SHALL NOT EXCEED AMOUNTS PAID BY THE DEBTOR HEREUNDER.

The effect of the notice is to make a potential holder of the note or contract subject to all claims and defenses of the consumer. This is illustrated in *Music Acceptance Corp.*, which follows. If the note or contract does not include the clause required by the FTC rule, the consumer does not gain any rights that he would not otherwise have under state law, and a subsequent holder may qualify as a holder in due course. However, the FTC does have the right to seek a fine of as much as $10,000 against the seller who failed to include the clause.

---

[3]Revised Article 3 expressly deals with these state variations in section 3–106(d) and Official Comments 3 to 3–106 and Comments 3 to 3–305. Section 3–106(d) permits instruments containing legends or statements required by statutory or administrative law that preserve the obligator's right to assert claims or defenses against subsequent holders as within Article 3 except that no holder can be a holder in due course.

Music Acceptance Corp. v. Lofing   39 Cal. Rptr. 159 (Cal. Ct. App. 1995)

Dan Lofing purchased a Steinway grand piano from Sherman Clay & Co., Steinway & Sons' Sacramento dealer, and received financing through Sherman Clay's finance company, Music Acceptance Corporation (MAC). The consumer note for $19,650.94 prepared by MAC and signed by Lofing included the following in boldface type:

NOTICE

ANY HOLDER OF THIS CONSUMER CREDIT CONTRACT IS SUBJECT TO ALL CLAIMS AND DEFENSES WHICH THE DEBTOR COULD ASSERT AGAINST THE SELLER OF GOODS OR SERVICES OBTAINED

PURSUANT HEREIN OR WITH THE PROCEEDS HEREOF. RECOVERY HEREUNDER SHALL NOT EX-
CEED AMOUNTS PAID BY THE DEBTOR HEREUNDER.

Lofing received a warranty from Steinway that provided the company "will promptly repair or replace without charge any part of this piano which is found to have a defect in material or workmanship within five years" from the date of sale.

Lofing became disenchanted with the piano after experiencing a variety of problems with it. There was a significant deterioration in the action and tonal quality of the piano which the Sherman Clay piano technician was unable to remedy despite lengthy and repeated efforts. A Steinway representative who was called in to inspect the piano concluded that it was in "terrible condition" and expressed surprise that it had ever left the factory. He concluded that the piano would have to be completely rebuilt at the factory.

Because the piano was impossible to play and was ruining his technique, Lofing stopped making payments on the piano. To mitigate his damages, Lofing sold the piano for $7,000 and purchased a Kawai piano from another dealer. He brought suit against Sherman Clay, Steinway, and MAC for, among other things, breach of warranty. One of the issues in the litigation was whether the Notice in the note allowed him to assert the breach of warranty as a grounds for not continuing to pay off the note to MAC.

Sparks, Associate Justice The FTC adopted a rule which makes it an unfair or deceptive act or practice for a seller to take or receive a consumer credit application which does not contain the following provision in large boldface type:

NOTICE
ANY HOLDER OF THIS CONSUMER CREDIT CONTRACT IS SUBJECT TO ALL CLAIMS AND DEFENSES WHICH THE DEBTOR COULD ASSERT AGAINST THE SELLER OF GOODS OR SERVICES OBTAINED PURSUANT HEREIN OR WITH THE PROCEEDS HEREOF. RECOVERY HEREUNDER SHALL NOT EXCEED AMOUNTS PAID BY THE DEBTOR HEREUNDER.

This notice is identical to that included in Lofing's sales contract.

The FTC enacted this rule because it believed it was "an unfair practice for a seller to employ procedures in the course of arranging the financing of a consumer deal which separate[d] the buyer's duty to pay for goods or services from the seller's reciprocal duty to perform as promised." The FTC explained: "Our primary concern . . . has been the distribution or allocation of costs occasioned by seller misconduct in credit sale transactions. These costs arise from breaches of contract, breaches of warranty, misrepresentation, and even fraud. The current commercial system which enables sellers and creditors to divorce a consumer's obligation to pay for goods and services from the seller's obligation to perform as promised, allocates all of these costs to the consumer/buyer."

In its "Guidelines on Trade Regulation Rule Concerning Preservation of Consumers' Claims and Defenses," the FTC explained further:

[The] dramatic increase in consumer credit over the past thirty years has caused certain problems. Evolving doc-

trines and principles of contract law have not kept pace with changing social needs. One such legal doctrine which has worked to deprive consumers of the protection needed in credit sales is the so-called "holder in due course doctrine." Under this doctrine, the obligation to pay for goods or services is not conditioned upon the seller's corresponding duty to keep his promises.

Typically, the circumstances are as follows: A consumer relying in good faith on what the seller has represented to be a product's characteristics, service warranty, etc., makes a purchase on credit terms. The consumer then finds the product unsatisfactory; it fails to measure up to the claims made on its behalf by the seller, or the seller refuses to provide promised maintenance. The consumer, therefore, seeks relief from his debt obligations only to find that no relief is possible. His debt obligation, he is told, is not to the seller but to a third party whose claim to payment is legally unrelated to any promise made about the product.

The seller may, prior to the sale, have arranged to have the debt instrument held by someone other than himself; he may have sold the debt instrument at a discount after the purchase.

From the consumer's point of view, the timing and means by which the transfer was effected are irrelevant. He has been left without ready recourse. He must pay the full amount of his obligation. He has a product that yields less than its promised value. And he has been robbed of the only realistic leverage he possessed that might have forced the seller to provide satisfaction—his power to withhold payment.

As one court noted, before this rule was adopted "[t]he reciprocal duties of the buyer and seller which were mutually dependent under ordinary contract law became independent of one another. Thus, the buyer's duty to pay the creditor was not excused upon the seller's failure to perform. In abrogating the holder in due course rule in consumer credit transactions, the FTC preserved the consumer's claims and defenses against the creditor-assignee. The FTC rule was therefore designed to reallocate the cost of seller misconduct to the creditor. The commission felt the creditor was in a better position to absorb the loss or recover the cost from the guilty party—the seller."

MAC contends the FTC rule is inapplicable here. MAC cites comments in the FTC guidelines discussing possible limitations on the rule. Specifically, the FTC points out that because the regulation's definition of "Financing a Sale" expressly refers to the Truth-in-Lending Act, it "thus incorporate[s] the limitations contained in these laws. As a result, even with respect to transactions involving a sale of consumer goods or services, a purchase involving an expenditure of more than $25,000 is not affected by the Rule." MAC argues that since the cash price of the piano, including sales tax, was $25,650.94, the transaction is exempt from these requirements.

MAC's argument is unavailing as it is based on the guideline's unfortunate use of the phrase "expenditure of more than $25,000." As Lofing points out, the exemption referred to in the Truth-in-Lending Act does not speak of expenditures of more than $25,000, but of transactions in which the "total amount financed exceeds $25,000." Here, because Lofing traded in his piano, the total amount financed was $19,650.94, well below the exemption level.

More importantly, it is irrelevant whether the FTC rule applies. Even if such a notice was not required to be given, the fact remains that it was: Lofing's contract included the precise language mandated by the FTC rule. Put simply, Lofing is in the same position whether we apply the FTC rule or the language of his particular contract. The jury's finding that Sherman Clay breached its warranties mandates that the judgment in favor of MAC and against Lofing be reversed.

Judgment in favor of Lofing.

Figure 1   *The Transfer of Commercial Paper*

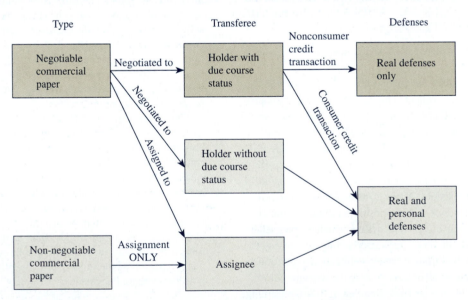

Source: "Charting the Way Through the Transfer of Commercial Paper," Janell Kurtz and Wayne Wells, *Journal of Legal Studies Education* 13 (1995), p. 191.

Problems and Problem Cases

1. Stone & Webster drew three checks in the total amount of $64,755.44 payable to the order of Westinghouse Electric Corporation. An employee of Stone & Webster obtained possession of the checks, forged Westinghouse's indorsement to them, and cashed them at the First National Bank & Trust Company and put the proceeds to his own use. The first two checks were indorsed in typewriting, "For Deposit Only: Westinghouse Electric Corporation By: Mr. O. D. Costine, Treasury Representative," followed by the ink signature "O. D. Costine." The third check was indorsed in typewriting, "Westinghouse Electric Corporation by: [Sgd.] O. D. Costine, Treasury Representative." Were the checks negotiated to the bank?

2. A bank cashed the checks of its customer, Dental Supply, Inc., presented to the bank by an employee of Dental Supply named Wilson. The checks were indorsed in blank with a rubber stamp of Dental Supply, Inc. Wilson had been stealing the checks by taking cash rather than depositing them to Dental Supply, Inc's. account. What could Dental Supply have done to avoid this situation?

3. Raye Walker was a bookkeeper for O. K. Moving & Storage Company. She opened a checking account in her name at Elgin National Bank. She then took checks that were made payable to O. K. Moving & Storage, indorsed them "For Deposit Only, O. K. Moving & Storage Co., 80 Carson Drive, N. E., Fort Walton, Florida," and deposited them in her individual account at Elgin National Bank. In a period of one year, she deposited, and Elgin Bank accepted for deposit to her account, checks totaling $19,356.01. When O. K. Moving & Storage discovered this, it sued Elgin Bank for $19,356.01 for conversion of its checks. Should Elgin Bank have permitted the checks restrictively indorsed "For Deposit Only" to a corporation's account to be deposited to an individual account?

4. Reggie Bluiett worked at the Silver Slipper Gambling Hall and Saloon. She received her weekly paycheck made out to her from the Silver Slipper. She indorsed the check in blank and left it on her dresser at home. Fred Watkins broke into Bluiett's house and stole the check. Watkins took the check to the local auto store, where he bought two tires at a cost of $71.21. He obtained the balance of the check in cash. Could the auto store qualify as a holder in due course?

5. Horton wrote a check for $20,000 to Axe, who in turn indorsed it to Halbert. In return, Halbert advanced $8,000 in cash to Axe and promised to cancel a $12,000 debt owed him by Axe. The check, when presented by Halbert to the bank, was not paid due to insufficient funds. Halbert thus never regarded the debt as canceled. To what extent can Halbert be a holder in due course of the check?

6. Charles Alcombrack was appointed guardian for his son, Chad Alcombrack, who was seven years old and the beneficiary of his grandfather's life insurance policy. The insurance company issued a check for $30,588.39 made payable to "Charles Alcombrack, Guardian of the Estate of Chad Stephen Alcombrack, a Minor." The attorney for the son's estate directed the father to take the check, along with the letters of guardianship issued to the father, to the bank and open up a guardianship savings and checking account. Instead, the father took the check, without the letters of guardianship, to the Olympic Bank and opened a personal checking and a personal savings account. Despite the fact that the check was payable to the father in his guardianship capacity, the bank allowed the father to place the entire amount in his newly opened personal accounts. The father used all but $320.60 of the trust money for his personal benefit. A new guardian, J. David Smith, was appointed for Chad. Smith brought suit against the Olympic Bank, on Chad's behalf, to recover the amount of the check. Was the bank a holder in due course of the check?

7. Two smooth-talking salesmen for Rich Plan of New Orleans called on Leona and George Henne at their home. They sold the Hennes a home food plan. One of the salesmen suggested that the Hennes sign a blank promissory note. The Hennes refused. The salesman then wrote in ink "$100" as the amount and "4" as the number of installments in which the note was to be paid, and the Hennes signed the note. Several days later, the Hennes received a payment book from Nationwide Acceptance. The payment book showed that a total of $843.38 was due, payable in 36 monthly installments. Rich Plan had erased the "$100" and "4" on the note and typed in the figures "$843.38" and "36." The erasures were cleverly done but were visible to the naked eye. Rich Plan then negotiated the Hennes' note to Nationwide Acceptance. The Hennes refused to pay the note. Nationwide claimed that it was a holder in due course and was entitled to receive payment. Was Nationwide Acceptance a holder in due course?

8. Panlick, the owner of an apartment building, entered into a written contract with Bucci, a paving contractor whereby Bucci was to install asphalt paving on the parking lot of the building. When Bucci finished the job, Panlick gave Bucci a check for $6,500 and a promissory note for $7,593 with interest at 10 percent due six months from its date. When the note came due, Panlick refused to pay it. Bucci brought suit to collect the note, and Pan-lick claimed that there had been a failure of consideration because the asphalt was defectively installed. Can Pan-lick assert this defense against Bucci?

9. Ralph Herrmann wrote a check for $10,000 payable to Ormsby House, a hotel-casino in Carson City, Nevada, and exchanged it for three counter checks he had written earlier that evening to acquire gaming chips. Ormsby House was unable to collect the proceeds from the check because Herrmann had insufficient funds in his account. The debt evidenced by the check was assigned to Sea Air Support, Inc., d/b/a Automated Accounts Associates, for collection. Sea Air was also unsuccessful in its attempts to collect and filed a lawsuit against Herrmann to recover on the dishonored check. Nevada law then provided that all instruments drawn for the purpose of reimbursing or repaying any money knowingly lent or advanced for gaming are "utterly void, frustrate, and of none effect." Is Herrmann still liable to Sea Air?

10. Arnold takes his old TV set to an appliance store for repair and purchases a new TV from the store. He signs a promissory note, which provides for installment pay-ments, for the balance due on the new set. The note contains the notice that the FTC requires be included in consumer credit instruments. Arnold discovers that the TV is defective after making the first payment on the note to the appliance store. The appliance store assigns the promissory note to Acme Finance Company, which notifies Arnold of its interest in the note and that he should make his payments on the note to it. Arnold advises Acme Finance that he will not make any further payments on the promissory note until the TV is repaired. If Arnold has a valid claim for breach of warranty of merchantability of the TV set, can he assert this as a defense against paying the note to the appliance store and/or to Acme Finance?

Online Research: Does Your State Void Instruments Given for Gambling Debts?

Use the Internet slocate the statutes for your state. Ascertain whether in your state checks and notes given in satisfaction of gambling debts are void.

33

LIABILITY OF PARTIES

When you sign a promissory note, you expect that you will be liable for paying the note on the day it is due. Similarly, when you sign a check and mail it off to pay a bill, you expect that it will be paid by your bank out of your checking account and that if there are not sufficient funds in the account to cover it, you will have to make it good out of other funds you have. The liability of the maker of a note and of the drawer of a check is commonly understood.

However, there are other ways a person can become liable on a negotiable instrument. Moreover, some of the usual liability rules are modified when a party is negligent in issuing or paying a negotiable instrument—or otherwise contributes to a potential loss.

The issues that will be discussed in this chapter include:

• Suppose you indorse a check that is payable to your order and "cash" it at a check cashing service. What liability have you assumed by indorsing and transferring the check?

• Suppose you make out a check in such a way that someone is able to raise (change) the amount of the check from $1 to $1,000 and then obtain payment of the check from the drawee bank. Will your bank be entitled to charge your account for $1,000 or can you limit the charge to $1, the original amount of the check?

• Suppose one of your employees who has responsibility for writing checks makes some of them payable to people you normally do business with and then keeps the checks, indorses the checks in the name of the named payee, and obtains payment of the checks for her own purposes. Are you entitled to have your account re-credited for the amount of the checks on the grounds they were paid over a forged indorsement?

THUS FAR IN PART 7, Commercial Paper, the focus has been on the nature of, and requirements for, negotiable instruments as well as the rights that an owner of an instrument can obtain and how to obtain them. Another important aspect to negotiable instruments concerns how a person becomes liable on a negotiable instrument and the nature of the liability incurred.

negotiable instrument or has authorized someone else to sign it. The liability depends on the capacity in which the person signs the instrument. Liability also arises from (1) transfer or presentment of an instrument, (2) negligence relating to the issuance, alteration, or indorsement of the instrument, (3) improper payment, or (4) conversion.

Liability in General

Liability on negotiable instruments flows from signatures on the instruments as well as actions taken concerning them. It can arise from the fact that a person has signed a

Contractual Liability

When a person signs a negotiable instrument, whether as maker, drawer, indorser, or in some other capacity, she generally becomes contractually liable on the instrument. As mentioned above, this contractual liability depends on the capacity in which the person signed the instrument. The terms of the contract of the parties to a negotiable instrument are not set out in the text of the instrument. Rather, Article 3 of the Uniform Commercial Code supplies the terms, which are as much a part of the instrument as if they were part of its text.

Primary and Secondary Liability

A party to a negotiable instrument may be either *primarily liable* or *secondarily liable* for payment of it. A person who is primarily liable has agreed to pay the negotiable instrument. For example, the maker of a promissory note is the person who is primarily liable on the note. A person who is secondarily liable is like a guarantor on a contract; Article 3 requires a secondary party to pay the negotiable instrument only if a person who is primarily liable defaults on that obligation. Chapter 27, Introduction to Credit and Secured Transactions, discusses guarantors.

Obligation of a Maker

The **maker** of a promissory note is primarily liable for payment of it. The maker makes an unconditional promise to pay a fixed amount of money and is responsible for making good on that promise. The obligation of the maker is to pay the negotiable instrument according to its terms at the time he issues it or, if it is not issued, then according to its terms at the time it first came into possession of a holder [3–412].[1] If the material terms of the note are not complete when the maker signs it, then the maker's obligation is to pay the note as it is completed, provided that the terms filled in are as authorized. If the instrument is incomplete when the maker signs it and it is completed in an unauthorized manner, then the maker's liability will depend on whether the person seeking to enforce the instrument can qualify as a holder in due course.

The obligation of the maker is owed to (1) a *person entitled to enforce the instrument* or (2) any indorser who paid the instrument pursuant to her indorser's liability (discussed below). A person entitled to enforce an instrument includes: (1) the holder of the instrument; (2) a nonholder in possession of the instrument who has the rights of a holder; and (3) a person not in possession of the instrument who has the right to enforce the instrument under section 3–309, which deals with lost, destroyed, or stolen instruments.

---

[1] The numbers in brackets refer to sections of the Uniform Commercial Code (UCC), which is reproduced in the appendix.

Revised Article 3 provides that the *drawer of a cashier's check* has the same obligation as the maker or issuer of a note. Thus, it treats the bank drawer of a draft drawn on a bank the same as a note for purposes of the issuer's liability rather than treating the issuer as a drawer of a draft [3–412].

Obligation of a Drawee or an Acceptor

The **acceptor** of a draft is obligated to pay the draft according to the terms at the time of its acceptance. As was discussed in Chapter 31, acceptance is the drawee's signed engagement to honor the draft as presented—and is commonly indicated by the signature of the acceptor on the instrument itself. The acceptor's obligation extends to (1) a person entitled to enforce the draft, (2) the drawer, and (3) an indorser who paid the instrument pursuant to her indorser's liability [3–413].

If the certification of a check or other acceptance of a draft states the amount certified or accepted, the obligation of the acceptor is that amount. If the certification or acceptance does not state an amount, if the amount of the instrument is subsequently raised and then the instrument is negotiated to a holder in due course, the obligation of the acceptor is the amount of the instrument at the time a holder in due course takes it [3–413(b)].

At the time a payee receives possession of a check or other draft, the payee gets the drawer's contract to pay the instrument if the drawee—bank or buyer of goods—does not pay. (This liability is discussed elsewhere in this chapter.) *Issuance* of the check or draft, however, does not obligate the *drawee* to pay it. Like other Article 3 contracts discussed in this chapter, the drawee does not have liability on the instrument until it *signs* the instrument.

The drawer or a holder of the check may ask the drawee bank to accept or certify the check. The drawee bank certifies the check by signing its name to the check and, with that act, accepts liability as acceptor. The drawee bank debits, or takes the money out of, the drawer's account and holds the money to pay the check. If the drawee bank certifies the check, it becomes primarily, or absolutely, liable for paying the check as it reads at the time of its acceptance [3–413], and its acceptance discharges the drawer and indorsers who indorsed before the acceptance. Similarly, when a trade draft is presented for acceptance or payment, and the named drawee accepts it, then the drawee accepts the obligation set forth in the instrument and the drawer and earlier indorsers are discharged.

A drawee has no liability on a check or other draft unless it certifies or accepts the check or draft—that is, agrees to be liable on it. However, a drawee bank that refuses to pay a check when it is presented for payment may be liable to the drawer for wrongfully refusing payment, assuming the drawer had sufficient funds in his checking account to cover it. The next chapter discusses this liability of a drawee bank.

The principle that a drawee has no liability on an instrument to a holder unless it has certified or accepted the instrument is illustrated in the following case, *Harrington v. MacNab*.

Harrington v. MacNab	*45 UCC Rep.2d 698 (U.S.D.C.D. Maryland 2001)*

Harrington, an experienced attorney, conducted a settlement on a piece of property in Cambridge, Maryland, being purchased by a couple named MacNab. They showed up for the settlement without certified funds, but rather with a personal check drawn on their Merrill Lynch cash management account for $150,128.70. Instead of refusing to go forward with the settlement, Harrington phoned the Merrill Lynch office in Delaware where the MacNabs had their account. He was told by a Ms. Ruark of Merrill Lynch, in response to his inquiry, that there were sufficient funds in the MacNabs' account to cover the check and that she would put a hold on the account in the amount of the check. When asked to confirm this in writing, Ms. Ruark sent a fax to Harrington that read as follows: "This letter is to verify that the funds are available in the Merrill Lynch account. There is a pend on the funds for the check that was given to you."

Harrington interpreted "pend" to mean that a hold would be placed on the MacNabs' account to cover the check in question. Merrill Lynch later claimed it meant that the funds deposited to cover that check were not themselves yet cleared. In fact, the MacNabs' account did not contain sufficient cleared funds to cover the check, which bounced. Subsequent promises by the MacNabs to make the check good came to naught. Harrington obtained a judgment against the MacNabs, but it was never satisfied in full. Harrington then brought suit against Merrill Lynch for negligent misrepresentation.

SMALKIN, District Judge There are no reported cases in Maryland in which a payee on a check has recovered against the drawee (or one, like Merrill Lynch, in the position of a drawee) for a negligent statement that there were sufficient (cleared) funds in the drawee's account to cover a check and/or that a hold would correspondingly be placed on the account. This court is of the opinion that the Court of Appeals of Maryland would not recognize a cause of action on these facts.

Here, there is no contractual privity or its equivalent between Mr. Harrington and Merrill Lynch which was in a position equivalent to that of the drawee on the MacNabs' check (a check is a species of draft, see section 3–104[f]), nor can any argument be made that Mr. Harrington was a third-party beneficiary of the MacNab cash management account agreement any more than the Baltimore Gas and Electric Company is, by virtue of the fact I draw it a check to cover my utility bill, the third party beneficiary of my checking-account contract with my bank.

To hold that such a relationship existed in this case would lead to the result that any payee on a check who makes inquiry is in the equivalent of contractual privity with the drawee, a proposition that would place substantial and potential unlimited liability on drawees for uncertified checks in contravention of the basic policies underlying the checking system in the United States as codified in the Uniform Commercial Code. For example, the UCC section 3–408 specifically provides that a drawee is not liable as an assignee of the drawer on a check. Even more to the point, a drawee has no contract liability on a check to a payee unless and until it has accepted the check, viz, certified it. See UCC sections 3–408 and 3–409. Acceptance requires the formality of the drawee's signature on the check. See UCC section 3–409(a).

To recognize a cause of action under the circumstances of this case essentially would create a tort remedy allowing suit to be brought for oral certification of checks, in clear violation of the policies of the Uniform Commercial Code and hundreds of years of commercial law.

Furthermore . . . it can hardly be claimed that reliance by an experienced real estate attorney on the statements in this case in lieu of adhering to the sound practice of requiring the buyer to pay with an accepted draft (certified check) or bank draft is justifiable. Indeed, the reason for the practice of requiring certified or bank checks is that in the eyes of the UCC, such instruments are the equivalent of cash as far as satisfying the underlying obligation goes. See UCC section 3–310(a).

Summary judgment granted for Merrill Lynch.

ETHICS IN ACTION

Would Qualifying an Indorsement Be Ethical?

Suppose you have taken a promissory note for $3,500 payable in 12 months with interest at 10 percent as payment for some carpentry work you did for a friend. You have some reason to believe the maker of the note is in finan-

cial difficulty and may not be able to pay the note when it is due. You discuss with an elderly neighbor the possibility of her buying the note from you as an investment, and she agrees to buy it from you for $3,000. Would it be ethical for you to indorse the note with a qualified indorsement ("without recourse")?

Obligation of a Drawer

The **drawer**'s obligation is that if the drawee dishonors an unaccepted check (or draft), the drawer will pay the check (or draft) according to its terms at the time he issued it or, if it was not issued, according to its terms at the time it first came into possession of a holder. If the draft was not complete when issued but was completed as authorized, then the obligation is to pay it as completed. If any completion is not authorized, then the obligation will depend on whether the person seeking to enforce the instrument can qualify as a holder in due course. A person entitled to enforce the draft or an indorser who paid the draft pursuant to his indorser's liability may enforce the drawer's obligation [3–414(b)].

For example, Janis draws a check on her account at First National Bank payable to the order of Collbert. If First National does not pay the check when Collbert presents it for payment, then Janis is liable to Collbert on the basis of her drawer's obligation.

If a draft is accepted by a bank—for example, if the drawee bank certifies a check—the drawer is discharged of her drawer's obligation. If someone other than a bank accepts a draft, then the obligation of the drawer to pay the draft, if the draft is dishonored, is the same as an indorser (discussed next) [3–414(c) and (d)].

Obligation of an Indorser

A person who indorses a negotiable instrument usually is secondarily liable. Unless the indorser qualifies or otherwise disclaims liability, the **indorser**'s obligation on dishonor of the instrument is to pay the amount due on the instrument according to its terms at the time he indorsed it or if he indorsed it when incomplete, then according to its terms when completed, provided that it is completed as authorized. The indorser owes the obligation to a person entitled to enforce the instrument or to any subsequent indorser who had to pay it [3–415].

The indorser can avoid this liability only by qualifying his indorsement, such as "without recourse," on the instrument when he indorses it [3–415(b)].

Indorsers are liable to each other in the chronological order in which they indorse, from the last indorser back to the first. For example, Mark Maker gives a promissory note to Paul Payee. Payee indorses it and negotiates it to Fred First, who indorses it and negotiates it to Shirley Second. If Maker does not pay the note when Second takes it to him for payment, then Second can require First to pay it to her. First is secondarily liable on the basis of his indorsement. First, in turn, can require Payee to pay him because Payee also became secondarily liable when he indorsed it. Then, Payee is left to try to collect the note from Maker. Second also could have skipped over First and proceeded directly against Payee on his indorsement. First has no liability to Payee, however, because First indorsed after Payee indorsed the note.

If a bank accepts a draft (for example, by certifying a check) after an indorsement is made, the acceptance discharges the liability of the indorser [3–415(d)]. If notice of dishonor is required and proper notice is not given to the indorser, she is discharged of liability [3–415(c)]. And, where no one presents a check or gives it to a depositary bank for collection within 30 days after the date of an indorsement, the indorser's liability is discharged [3–415(e)].

Obligation of an Accommodation Party

An **accommodation party** is a person who signs a negotiable instrument for the purpose of lending her credit to another party to the instrument but is not a direct beneficiary of the value given for the instrument. For example, a bank might be reluctant to lend money to—and take a note from—Payee because of his shaky financial condition. However, the bank may be willing to lend money to Payee if he signs the note and has a relative or a friend also sign the note as an accommodation maker.

The obligation of an accommodation party depends on the capacity in which the party signs the instrument [3–419]. If Maker has his brother Sam sign a note as an accommodation maker, then Sam has the same contractual liability as a maker. Sam is primarily liable on the note. The bank may ask Sam to pay the note before asking Maker to pay. However, if Sam pays the note to the bank, he has the right to recover his payment from Maker, the person on whose behalf he signed.

Similarly, if a person signs a check as an accommodation indorser, his contractual liability is that of an indorser. If the accommodation indorser has to make good on that liability, he can collect in turn from the person on whose behalf he signed.

Signing an Instrument

No person is contractually liable on a negotiable instrument unless she or her authorized agent has signed it and the signature is binding on the represented person. A signature can be any name, word, or mark used in place of a written signature [3–401]. As discussed earlier, the capacity in which a person signs an instrument determines his liability on the instrument.

Signature by an Authorized Agent

An authorized agent can sign a negotiable instrument. If Sandra Smith authorized her attorney to sign checks as her agent, then she is liable on any checks properly signed by the attorney as her agent. All negotiable instruments signed by corporations have to be signed by an agent of the corporation who is authorized to sign negotiable instruments.

If a person purporting to act as a representative signs an instrument by signing either the name of the represented person or the name of the signer, that signature binds the represented person to the same extent she would be bound if the signature were on a simple contract. If the represented person has authorized the signature of the representative, it is the "authorized signature of the represented person" and the represented person is liable on the instrument, whether or not identified in the instrument. This brings the Code in line with the general principle of agency law that binds an undisclosed principal on a simple contract. For example, if Principal authorizes Agent to borrow money on Principal's behalf and Agent signs her name to a note without disclosing that the signature was on behalf of Principal, Agent is liable on the note. In addition, if the person entitled to enforce the note can show that Principal authorized Agent to sign on his behalf, then Principal is liable on the note as well.

When a representative signs an authorized signature to an instrument, then the representative is not bound provided the signature shows "unambiguously" that the signature was made on behalf of the represented person who is named in the instrument [3–402(b)(1)]. For example, if a note is signed "XYZ, Inc. by Flanigan, Treasurer," Flanigan is not liable on the instrument in his own right but XYZ, Inc., is liable.

If an authorized representative signs his name as the representative of a drawer of a check without noting his representative status but the check is payable from an account of the represented person who is identified on the check, the signer is not liable on the check as long as his signature was authorized [3–402(c)]. The rationale for this provision is that because most checks today identify the person on whose account the check is drawn, no one is deceived into thinking that the person signing the check is meant to be liable.

Except for the check situation noted above, a representative is personally liable to a holder in due course that took the instrument without notice that the representative was not intended to be liable if (1) the form of the signature does not show unambiguously that the signature was made in a representative capacity or (2) the instrument does not identify the represented person. As to persons other than a holder in due course without notice of the representative nature of the signature, the representative is liable *unless* she can prove that the original parties did not intend her to be liable on the instrument [3–402(b)(2)].

Thus, if an agent or a representative signs a negotiable instrument on behalf of someone else, the agent should indicate clearly that he is signing as the representative of someone else. For example, Kim Darby, the president of Swimwear, Inc., is authorized to sign negotiable instruments for the company. If Swimwear borrows money from the bank and the bank asks her to sign a 90-day promissory note, Darby should sign it either "Swimwear, Inc., by Kim Darby, President" or "Kim Darby, President, for Swimwear, Inc." If Kim Darby signed the promissory note merely "Kim Darby," she could be personally liable on the note. Similarly, if Clara Carson authorizes Arthur Anderson, an attorney, to sign checks for her, Anderson should make sure either that the checks identify Clara Carson as the account involved or should sign them "Clara Carson by Arthur Anderson, Agent." Otherwise, he risks being personally liable on them.

Unauthorized Signature

If someone signs a person's name to a negotiable instrument without that person's authorization or approval, the signature does not bind the person whose name appears. However, the signature is effective as the signature of the unauthorized signer in favor of any person who in good faith pays the instrument or takes it for value [3–403(a)]. For example, if Tom Thorne steals Ben Brown's checkbook and signs Brown's name to a check, Brown is not liable on the check because Brown had not authorized Thorne to sign Brown's name. Thorne can be liable on the check, however, because he did sign it, even though he did not sign it in his own name. Thorne's forgery of Brown's signature operates as Thorne's signature. Thus, if Thorne cashed the check at the bank, Thorne would be liable to it or if he negotiated it to a store for value, he would be liable to the store to make it good.

Even though a signature is not "authorized" when it is put on an instrument initially, it can be ratified later by the person represented [3–403(a)]. It also should be noted that if more than one person must sign to constitute the authorized signature of an organization, the signature of the organization is unauthorized if one of the required signatures is lacking [3–403(b)]. Corporate and other accounts sometimes require multiple signatures as a matter of maintaining sound financial control.

Contractual Liability in Operation

To bring the contractual liability of the various parties to a negotiable instrument into play, it generally is necessary that the instrument be *presented for payment*. In addition, to hold the parties that are secondarily liable on the instrument to their contractual liability, it generally is necessary that the instrument be *presented for payment* and *dishonored*.

Presentment of a Note

The maker of a note is primarily liable to pay it when it is due. Normally, the holder takes the note to the maker at the time it is due and asks the maker to pay it. Sometimes, the note may provide for payment to be made at a bank or the maker sends the payment to the holder at the due date. The party to whom the holder presents the instrument, without dishonoring the instrument, may (1) require the exhibition of the instrument, (2) ask for reasonable identification of the person making presentment, (3) ask for evidence of his authority to make it if he is making it for another person, or (4) return the instrument for lack of any necessary indorsement, (5) ask that a receipt be signed for

any payment made, and (6) surrender the instrument if full payment is made [3–501].

Dishonor of a note occurs if the maker does not pay the amount due when: (1) it is presented in the case of (*a*) a demand note or (*b*) a note payable at or through a bank on a definite date that is presented on or after that date, or (2) if it is not paid on the date payable in the case of a note payable on a definite date but not payable at or through a bank [3–502]. If the maker or payor dishonors the note, the holder can seek payment from any persons who indorsed the note before the holder took it. The basis for going after the indorsers is that they are secondarily liable. To hold the indorsers to their contractual obligation, the holder must give them notice of the dishonor. The notice can be either written or oral [3–503].

For example, Susan Strong borrows $1,000 from Jack Jones and gives him a promissory note for $1,000 at 9 percent annual interest payable in 90 days. Jones indorses the note "Pay to the order of Ralph Smith" and negotiates the note to Ralph Smith. At the end of the 90 days, Smith takes the note to Strong and presents it for payment. If Strong pays Smith the $1,000 and accrued interest, she can have Smith mark it "paid" and give it back to her. If Strong does not pay the note to Smith when he presents it for payment, then she has dishonored the note. Smith should give notice of the dishonor to Jones and advise him that he intends to hold Jones secondarily liable on his indorsement. Smith may collect payment of the note from Jones. Jones, after making the note good to Smith, can try to collect the note from Strong on the ground that she defaulted on the contract she made as maker of the note. Of course, Smith also could sue Strong on the basis of her maker's obligation.

Presentment of a Check or a Draft

The holder should present a check or draft to the drawee. The presentment can be either for payment or for acceptance (certification) of the check or draft. Under Revised Article 3, the presentment may be made by any commercially reasonable means, including a written, oral, or electronic communication [3–501]. The drawee is not obligated on a check or draft unless it accepts (certifies) it [3–408]. An acceptance of a draft is the drawee's signed commitment to honor the draft as presented. The acceptance must be written on the draft, and it may consist of the drawee's signature alone [3–409].

A drawer who writes a check issues an order to the drawee to pay a certain amount out of the drawer's account to the payee (or to someone authorized by the payee). This order is not an assignment of the funds in the drawer's account [3–408]. The drawee bank does not have an obligation to the payee to pay the check unless it certifies the check. However, the drawee bank usually does have a separate contractual obligation (apart from Article 3) to the drawer to pay any properly payable checks for which funds are available in the drawer's account.

For example, Janet Payne has $850 in a checking account at First National Bank and writes a check for $100 drawn on First National and payable to Ralph Smith. The writing of the check is the issuance of an order by Payne to First National to pay $100 from her account to Smith or to whomever Smith requests it to be paid. First National owes no obligation to Smith to pay the $100 unless it has certified the check. However, if Smith presents the check for payment and First National refuses to pay it even though there are sufficient funds in Payne's account, then First National is liable to Payne for breaching its contractual obligation to her to pay items properly payable from existing funds in her account. Chapter 34, Checks and Electronic Transfers, discusses the liability of a bank for wrongful dishonor of checks in more detail.

If the drawee bank does not pay or certify a check when it is properly presented for payment or acceptance (certification), the drawee bank has dishonored the check [3–502]. Similarly, if a draft is not paid on the date it is due (or accepted by the drawee on the due date for acceptance), it has been dishonored. The holder of the draft or check then can proceed against either the drawer or any indorsers on their liability. To do so, the holder must give them notice of the dishonor [3–503]. Notice of dishonor, like presentment, can be by any commercially reasonable means, including oral, written, or electronic communication. Under certain circumstances, set out in section 3–504, presentment or notice of dishonor may be excused.

Suppose Matthews draws a check for $200 on her account at a bank payable to the order of Williams. Williams indorses the check "Pay to the order of Clark, Williams" and negotiates it to Clark. When Clark takes the check to the bank, it refuses to pay the check because there are insufficient funds in Matthews's account to cover the check. The check has been presented and dishonored. Clark has two options: He can proceed against Williams on Williams's secondary liability as an indorser (because by putting an unqualified indorsement on the check, Williams is obligated to make the check good if it was not honored by the drawee). Or, he can proceed against Matthews on Matthews's obligation as drawer because in drawing the check, Matthews must pay any person entitled to enforce the check if it is dishonored. Because Clark dealt with Williams, Clark is probably more likely to return the check to Williams for payment. Williams then has to go against Matthews on Matthews's liability as drawer.

Time of Presentment

If an instrument is payable at a definite time, the holder should present it for payment on the due date. In the case of a demand instrument, the nature of the instrument, trade or bank usage, and the facts of the particular case determine a reasonable time for presentment for acceptance or payment. In a farming community, for example, a reasonable time to present a promissory note that is payable on demand may be six months or within a short time after the crops are ready for sale, because the holder commonly expects payment from the proceeds of the crops.

Warranty Liability

Whether or not a person signs a negotiable instrument, a person who transfers such an instrument or presents it for payment or acceptance may incur liability on the basis of certain implied warranties. These warranties are (1) **transfer warranties,** which persons who transfer negotiable instruments make to their transferees; and (2) **presentment warranties,** which persons who present negotiable instruments for payment or acceptance (certification) make to those who pay or accept.

Transfer Warranties

A person who transfers a negotiable instrument to someone else and for consideration makes five warranties to his immediate transferee. If the transfer is by indorsement, the transferor makes these warranties to all subsequent transferees. The five transfer warranties are:

1. The warrantor is a person entitled to enforce the instrument. (In essence the transferor warrants that there are no unauthorized or missing indorsements that prevent the transferor from making the transferee a person entitled to enforce the instrument.)

2. All signatures on the instrument are authentic or authorized.

3. The instrument has not been altered.

4. The instrument is not subject to a defense or a claim in recoupment that any party can assert against the warrantor.

5. The warrantor has no knowledge of any insolvency proceedings commenced with respect to the maker or acceptor or, in the case of an unaccepted draft, the

CONCEPT REVIEW

Transfer Warranties

The five transfer warranties made by a person who transfers a negotiable instrument to someone else for consideration are:

1. The warrantor is entitled to enforce the instrument.

2. All signatures on the instrument are authentic or authorized.

3. The instrument has not been altered.

4. The instrument is not subject to a defense or a claim in recoupment that any party can assert against the warrantor.

5. The warrantor has no knowledge of any insolvency proceedings commenced with respect to the maker or acceptor or, in the case of an unaccepted draft, the drawer.

Who	What Warranties	To Whom
Nonindorsing Transferor	Makes all five transfer warranties	To his immediate transferee only
Indorsing Transferor	Makes all five transfer warranties	To his immediate transferee and all subsequent transferees

drawer [3–416(a)]. Note that this is not a warranty against difficulty in collection or insolvency—the warranty stops with the warrantor's knowledge.

Revised Article 3 provides that in the event of a breach of a transfer warranty, a beneficiary of the transfer warranties who took the instrument in good faith may recover from the warrantor an amount equal to the loss suffered as a result of the breach. However, the damages recoverable may not be more than the amount of the instrument plus expenses and loss of interest incurred as a result of the breach [3–416(b)].

Transferors of instruments other than checks may disclaim the transfer warranties. Unless the warrantor receives notice of a claim for breach of warranty within 30 days after the claimant has reason to know of the breach and the identity of the warrantor, the delay in giving notice of the claim may discharge the warrantor's liability to the extent of any loss the warrantor suffers from the delay, such as the opportunity to proceed against the transferor [3–416(c)].

Although contractual liability often furnishes a sufficient basis for suing a transferor when the party primarily obligated does not pay, warranties are still important. First, they apply even when the transferor did not indorse. Second, unlike contractual liability, they do not depend on presentment, dishonor, and notice, but may be utilized before presentment has been made or after the

time for giving notice has expired. Third, a holder may find it easier to return the instrument to a transferor on the ground of breach of warranty than to prove her status as a holder in due course against a maker or drawer.

Presentment Warranties

Persons who present negotiable instruments for payment or drafts for acceptance also make warranties, but their warranties differ from those transferors make. If an unaccepted draft (such as a check) is presented to the drawee for payment or acceptance and the drawee pays or accepts the draft, then the person obtaining payment or acceptance warrants to the drawee making payment or accepting the draft in good faith that:

1. The warrantor is, or was, at the time the warrantor transferred the draft, a person entitled to enforce the draft or authorized to obtain payment or acceptance of the draft on behalf of a person entitled to enforce the draft.

2. The draft has not been altered.

3. The warrantor has no knowledge that the signature of the drawer of the draft has not been authorized [3–417(a)].

These warranties also are made by any prior transferor of the instrument at the time the person transfers the instrument; the warranties run to the drawee who makes payment or accepts the draft in good faith. Such a drawee would include a drawee bank paying a check presented to it for payment directly or through the bank collection process.

The effect of the third presentment warranty is to leave with the drawee the risk that the drawer's signature is unauthorized, unless the person presenting the draft for payment, or a prior transferor, had knowledge of any lack of authorization.

A drawee who makes payment may recover as damages for any breach of a presentment warranty an amount equal to the amount paid by the drawee less the amount the drawee received or is entitled to receive from the drawer because of the payment. In addition, the drawee is entitled to compensation for expenses and loss of interest resulting from the breach [3–417(b)]. The drawee's right to recover damages for breach of warranty is not affected by any failure on the part of the drawee to exercise ordinary care in making payment.

If a drawee asserts a claim for breach of a presentment warranty based on an unauthorized indorsement of the draft or an alteration of the draft, the warrantor may defend by showing that the indorsement is effective under the *impostor* or *fictitious payee* rules (discussed later in this chapter) or that the drawer's negligence precludes him from asserting against the drawee the unauthorized indorsement or alteration (also discussed below) [3–417(c)].

If (1) a *dishonored draft* is presented for payment to the drawer or an indorser or (2) any other instrument (such as a note) is presented for payment to a party obligated to pay the instrument and the presenter receives payment, the presenter makes the following presentment warranty:

> The person obtaining payment is a person entitled to enforce the instrument or authorized to obtain payment on behalf of a person entitled to enforce the instrument [3–417(d)].

On breach of this warranty, the person making the payment may recover from the warrantor an amount equal to the amount paid plus expenses and loss of interest resulting from the breach.

With respect to checks, the party presenting the check for payment cannot disclaim the presentment warranties [3–417(e)]. Unless the payor or drawee provides notice of a claim for breach of a presentment warranty to the warrantor within 30 days after the claimant has reason to know of the breach and the identity of the warrantor, the warrantor is discharged to the extent of any loss caused by the delay in giving notice of the claim of breach.

Payment or Acceptance by Mistake

A longstanding general rule of negotiable instruments law is that payment or acceptance is final in favor of a holder in due course or payee who changes his position in reliance on the payment or acceptance. Revised Article 3 retains this concept by making payment final in favor of a person who took the instrument in good faith and for value. However, payment is not final—and may be

---

CONCEPT REVIEW

Presentment Warranties

If an unaccepted draft (such as a check) is presented for payment or acceptance and the drawee pays or accepts the draft, then the person obtaining payment or acceptance and prior transferors warrant to the drawee:

1. The warrantor is a person entitled to enforce payment or authorized to obtain payment or acceptance on behalf of a person entitled to enforce the draft.

2. The draft has not been altered.

3. The warrantor has no knowledge that the signature of the drawer of the draft has not been authorized.

If (a) a dishonored draft is presented for payment to the drawer or indorser or (b) any other instrument (such as a note) is presented for payment to a party obligated to pay the instrument and the presenter receives payment, the presenter (as well as a prior transferor of the instrument) makes the following warranty to the person making payment in good faith:

> The person obtaining payment is a person entitled to enforce the instrument or authorized to obtain payment on behalf of a person entitled to enforce the instrument.

recovered from—a person who does not meet these criteria where the drawee acted on the mistaken belief that (1) payment of a draft or check has not been stopped, and (2) the signature of the purported drawer of the draft was authorized [3–418(a)]. In some jurisdictions, the drawee's mistaken belief that the account held available funds also could serve as a basis for recovery of the payment [3–418(b)].

As a result, this means that if the drawee bank mistakenly paid a check over a stop-payment order, paid a check with a forged or unauthorized drawer's signature on it, or paid despite the lack of sufficient funds in the drawer's account to cover the check, the bank cannot recover if it paid the check to a presenter who had taken the instrument in good faith and for value. In that case, the drawee bank would have to pursue someone else, such as the forger or unauthorized signer, or seller whose goods proved to be defective. On the other hand, if the presenter had not taken in good faith or for value, the bank could, in these enumerated instances, recover from the presenter the payment it made by mistake.

The *Fergang v. Morgan Guaranty* case, which follows, illustrates the operation of presentment and transfer warranties.

Fergang v. Morgan Guaranty Trust Co. of New York
665 N.Y.S. 2d 785 (New York Sup. Ct. 1997)

Melvin Fergang drew a check on his account at Morgan Guaranty Trust in the amount of $101,000 and payable to Ronald Burk. Burk was selling his home to Fergang's daughter and the check apparently was intended to facilitate that transaction. The check containing a forged indorsement in Burk's name was presented to and paid by Chemical Bank. Morgan Guaranty Trust settled with Chemical Bank and charged the item against Fergang's account. The identity of the forger was unclear, but the case involved an allegation that Fergang's daughter had received the proceeds of the check.

Fergang brought suit against Morgan Guaranty Trust seeking to have his account recredited because the check had been paid based on a forged indorsement of the payee. Morgan Guaranty Trust in turn commenced a third-party action against Chemical Bank for its violation of transfer and presentment warranties.

Phelan, Justice The relationship between the bank and its depositor being that of debtor and creditor, the bank cannot charge an account of the depositor with moneys paid out without authority. There is a high standard of contractual responsibility imposed on banks in paying money chargeable against their depositors' accounts. A bank must, in paying out a deposit, comply with its agreement with the depositor; and in the absence either of prior or subsequent negligence or misleading conduct on the part of the depositor, the bank cannot charge him with any payments except such as are made in conformity with his genuine orders. Payments otherwise made cannot be charged against the depositor regardless of the care exercised and the precaution taken by the bank. Indeed, it is settled that a depositor-drawer of a check on which the payee's indorsement is forged may prevent a drawee bank which pays the check from charging the payment to his account, or may require a bank so charging the account to recredit it. However, as mentioned above, a depositor who has been negligent may lose such right of recovery. UCC section 3–406.

UCC 4–401 permits a bank to charge a customer's account only on items that are "properly payable." A check which has been cashed on the forged indorsement of the payee is *not* "properly payable" under the Code. A forged endorsement operates as an "unauthorized" signature [UCC 1–201(43)] and such is wholly inoperative as that of the person whose name is signed [UCC 3–404(1)]. A drawee bank that charged its customer's account on such a check is liable to its customer for the full amount of the check.

Chemical, joined by Morgan, claims that since the check was intended as a loan or gift to his daughter, which was achieved, Fergang suffered no loss and hence has no valid claim against Morgan. This claim lacks merit. Whether Fergang intended a gift or loan to his daughter is irrelevant. Fergang did not make the check payable to his daughter but rather to Ronald Burk. Since Burk never received the proceeds, Fergang's intentions that the check proceeds go to Burk in furtherance of his daughter's purchase of Burk's house were not met. Indeed, Fergang's daughter cannot be found to have received either a gift or loan for use as intended by Fergang.

Fergang suffered a loss. A drawer suffers a loss when the true payee never actually received the proceeds of the original certified check for the purpose intended by the drawer.

A drawee bank remains answerable to the drawer for the amount of a check paid upon a forged indorsement of the payee's name. Fergang has established his cause of action as a matter of law based upon unrefuted facts and is entitled to summary judgment. Therefore, this court hereby grants summary judgment to Fergang against Morgan for the face amount of the check. Morgan, as drawee, is liable to Fergang for the funds paid from his account based upon the fact the payee's indorsement was forged.

Under well-established principles of law, the risk of loss on a forged indorsement falls upon Chemical, the first collecting bank in the transaction and the bank best positioned to discover the forgery. Chemical breached its warranty that it had good title to the item under UCC 4–207(1)(a) when it transferred and presented the forged check to Morgan; and Chemical's liability is absolute. Since the check had a forged indorsement, Chemical neither had good title or other authorization to obtain payment or acceptance on behalf of one who has good title, because a forger does not have good title. Therefore, Chemical, the collecting bank, breached the warranty of good title when it presented the check with a forged indorsement to the payer bank. Thus, Morgan is entitled to recover against Chemical on breach of warranty which arose under UCC 4–207(1) which, in turn, includes recovery of its attorney's fees incurred as a result of said breach pursuant to UCC 4–207(3).

In so holding, the court notes that originally, Chemical denied any basis for indemnification. Thus, it is particularly fitting that such collecting bank be liable for attorney's fees where the payor bank, as here, is forced to litigate the collecting bank's obligation to indemnify despite the collecting bank's clear breach of warranty.

Judgment in favor of Fergang against Morgan Guaranty Trust and in favor of Morgan Guaranty Trust against Chemical Bank.

Operation of Warranties

Following are three scenarios that show how the transfer and presentment warranties shift the liability back to a wrongdoer or to the person who dealt immediately with a wrongdoer and thus was in the best position to avert the wrongdoing.

Scenario 1 Arthur makes a promissory note for $2000 payable to the order of Betts. Carlson steals the note from Betts, indorses her name on the back, and gives it to Davidson in exchange for a television set. Davidson negotiates the note for value to Earle, who presents the note to Arthur for payment. Assume that Arthur refuses to pay the note because Betts has advised him that it has been stolen and that he is the person entitled to enforce the instrument. Earle then can proceed to recover the face amount of the note from Davidson on the grounds that as a transferor Davidson has warranted that he is a person entitled to enforce the note and that all signatures were authentic. Davidson, in turn, can proceed against Carlson on the same basis—if he can find Carlson. If he cannot, then Davidson must bear the loss caused by Carlson's wrongdoing. Davidson was in the best position to ascertain whether Carlson was the owner of the note and whether the indorsement of Betts was genuine. Of course, even though Arthur does not have to pay the note to Earle, Arthur remains liable for his underlying obligation to Betts.

Scenario 2 Anderson draws a check for $10 on her checking account at First Bank payable to the order of Brown. Brown cleverly raises the check to $110, indorses it, and negotiates it to Carroll. Carroll then presents the check for payment to First Bank, which pays her $110 and charges Anderson's account for $110. Anderson then asks the bank to recredit her account for the altered check, and it does so. The bank can proceed against Carroll for breach of the presentment warranty that the instrument had not been altered, which she made to the bank when she presented the check for payment. Carroll in turn can proceed against Brown for breach of her transfer warranty that the check had not been altered—if she can find her. Unless she was negligent in drawing the check, Article 3 limits Anderson's liability to $10 because her obligation is to pay the amount in the instrument at the time she issued it.

Scenario 3 Bates steals Albers's checkbook and forges Albers's signature to a check for $100 payable to "cash," which he uses to buy $100 worth of groceries from a grocer. The grocer presents the check to Albers's bank. The bank pays the amount of the check to the grocer and charges Albers's account. Albers then demands that the bank recredit his account. The bank can recover against the grocer only if the grocer knew that Albers's signature had been forged. Otherwise, the bank must look for Bates. The bank had the responsibility to recognize the true signature of its drawer, Albers, and not to pay the check that contained an unauthorized signature. The bank may be able to resist recrediting Albers's account if it can show he was negligent. The next section of this chapter discusses negligence.

Other Liability Rules

Normally, a bank may not charge against (debit from) the drawer's account a check that has a forged payee's indorsement. Similarly, a maker does not have to pay a note to the person who currently possesses the note if the payee's signature has been forged. If a check or note has been altered—for example, by raising the amount—the drawer or maker usually is liable only for the instrument in the amount for which he originally issued it. However, there are a number of exceptions to these usual rules. These exceptions, as well as liability based on conversion of an instrument, are discussed below.

Negligence

A person can be so negligent in writing or signing a negotiable instrument that she in effect invites an alteration or an unauthorized signature on it. If a person has been negligent, Article 3 precludes her from using the alteration or lack of authorization as a reason for not paying a person that in good faith pays the instrument or takes it for value [3–406]. For example, Mary Maker makes out a note for $10 in such a way that someone could alter it to read $10,000. Someone alters the note and negotiates it to Katherine Smith, who can qualify as a holder in due course. Smith can collect $10,000 from Maker. Maker's negligence precludes her from claiming alteration as a defense to paying it. Maker then has to find the person who "raised" her note and try to collect the $9,990 from him.

Where the person asserting the preclusion failed to exercise ordinary care in taking or paying the instrument and that failure substantially contributed to the loss, Article 3 allocates the loss between the two parties based on their comparative negligence [3–406(b)]. Thus, if a drawer was so negligent in drafting a check that he made it possible for the check to be altered and the bank that paid the check, in the exercise of ordinary care, should have noticed the alteration, then any loss occasioned by the fact that the person who made the alteration could not be found would be split by the drawer and the bank based on their comparative fault.

Impostor Rule

Article 3 establishes special rules for negotiable instruments made payable to impostors and fictitious persons.

An impostor is a person who poses as someone else and convinces a drawer to make a check payable to the person being impersonated—or to an organization the person purports to be authorized to represent. When this happens, the Code makes any indorsement "substantially similar" to that of the named payee effective [3–404(a)]. Where the impostor has impersonated a person authorized to act for a payee, such as claiming to be Jack Jones, the president of Jones Enterprises, the impostor has the power to negotiate a check drawn payable to Jones Enterprises.

An example of a situation involving the impostor rule would be the following: Arthur steals Paulsen's automobile and finds the certificate of title in the automobile. Then, representing himself as Paulsen, he sells the automobile to Berger Used Car Company. The car dealership draws its check payable to Paulsen for the agreed purchase price of the automobile and delivers the check to Arthur. Any person can negotiate the check by indorsing it in the name of Paulsen.

The rationale for the impostor rule is to put the responsibility for determining the true identity of the payee on the drawer or maker of a negotiable instrument. The drawer is in a better position to do this than some later holder of the check who may be entirely innocent. The impostor rule allows that later holder to have good title to the check by making the payee's signature valid although it is not the signature of the person with whom the drawer or maker thought he was dealing. It forces the drawer or maker to find the wrongdoer who tricked him into signing the negotiable instrument or to bear the loss himself.

Fictitious Payee Rule

A fictitious payee commonly arises in the following situation: A dishonest employee draws a check payable to someone who does not exist—or to a real person who does business with the employer but to whom the dishonest employee does not intend to send the check. If the employee has the authority to do so, he may sign the check himself. If he does not have such authority, he gives the check to his employer for signature and represents that the employer owes money to the person named as the payee of the check. The dishonest employee then takes the check, indorses it in the name of the payee, presents it for payment, and pockets the money. The employee may be in a position to cover up the wrongdoing by intercepting the canceled checks or juggling the company's books.

The Code allows any indorsement in the name of the fictitious payee to be effective as the payee's indorsement in favor of any person that pays the instrument in good faith or takes it for value or for collection [3–404(b) and (c)]. For example, Anderson, an accountant in charge of accounts payable at Moore Corporation, prepares a false invoice naming Parks, Inc., a supplier of Moore Corporation, as having supplied Moore Corporation with goods, and draws a check payable to Parks, Inc., for the amount of the invoice. Anderson then presents the check to Temple, Treasurer of Moore Corporation, together with other checks with invoices attached. Temple signs all of these checks and returns them to Anderson for mailing. Anderson then withdraws the check payable to Parks, Inc. Anyone, including Anderson, can negotiate the check by indorsing it in the name of Parks, Inc.

The rationale for the fictitious payee rule is similar to that for the impostor rule. If someone has a dishonest employee or agent who is responsible for the forgery of some checks, the employer of the wrongdoer should bear the immediate loss of those checks rather than some other innocent party. In turn, the employer must locate the unfaithful employee or agent and try to recover from him.

The *C & N Contractors* case, which follows, illustrates the operation of the fictitious payee rule. As you read the case, determine how the contractor might have prevented the loss it suffered.

C & N Contractors v. Community Bancshares, Inc.
616 So.2d 1357 (Ala. Sup. Ct. 1994)

C & N Contractors is a construction and general contracting company in Gardendale, Alabama, that performs work at job sites throughout the southeastern United States. Mary Bivens was employed by C & N and performed general administrative duties for it.

Each Wednesday morning, the foreman at each job site telephoned Bivens and gave her the names of the employees working on the job site and the number of hours they had worked. Bivens then conveyed this information to Automatic Data Processing (ADP), whose offices are in Atlanta, Georgia. ADP prepared payroll checks based on the information given by Bivens and sent the checks to the offices of C & N in Gardendale for authorized signatures. Bivens was not an authorized signatory. After the checks were signed, Bivens sent the checks to the job site foreman for delivery to the employees.

In 1991, Bivens began conveying false information to ADP about employees and hours worked. On the basis of this false information, ADP prepared payroll checks payable to persons who were actual employees but had not worked the hours Bivens had indicated. After obtaining authorized signatures from C & N, Bivens intercepted the checks, forged the indorsement of the payees, and either cashed the checks at Community Bancshares or deposited them into her account at Community Bancshares, often presenting numerous checks at one time. Bivens continued this practice for almost a year, forging over 100 checks, until Jimmy Nation, vice president of C & N, discovered the embezzlement after noticing payroll checks payable to employees who had not recently performed services for the corporation. Bivens subsequently admitted forging the indorsements.

C & N brought suit against Community Bancshares for conversion when it cashed or accepted for deposit the numerous payroll checks containing forged payee indorsements. The trial court awarded summary judgment to Community Bancshares, and C & N Contractors appealed.

Almon, Justice With regard to the claim of conversion, the circuit court, in its summary judgment, held that under the "padded payroll" rule of section 3–405(1)(c) the forged indorsement of Bivens was effective and that, therefore, the loss caused by the forged indorsements fell on C & N. Section 3–405 provides in pertinent part:

(1) An indorsement by any person in the name of a named payee is effective if:

    (c) An agent or employee of the maker or drawer has supplied him with the name of the payee intending the latter to have no interest in the instrument.

A forged indorsement is ordinarily ineffective to pass title to an instrument to a collecting bank or, generally, to author-

ize a drawee bank to pay the instrument. Section 3–405(1) creates a limited exception to these general rules.

Although section 3–405(1) does not explicitly impose liability on the drawer for the loss caused by the payment of a forged instrument, it has the general legal effect of shifting liability to the drawer from the party who took from the forger. By making effective an otherwise ineffective indorsement in the special circumstances provided in section 3–405 (1)(a), (b) and (c), section 3–405(1) generally precludes the liability of a drawee bank to a drawer under section 4–401 and the liability of a collecting bank to a drawee/payor bank under section 4–207.

Under section 4–207, each party who obtains payment from the drawee and each prior transferor warrants to the party who pays the check that he has good title to the instrument. This warranty is breached when the check has a forged or unauthorized signature. If in good faith and in accordance with commercially reasonable standards, a depositary or collecting bank accepts a check with a forged indorsement and then presents it for payment to the drawee/payor bank and if the drawee/payor bank pays the check, the drawee/payor bank is generally liable to the drawer under section 4–401 because it did not properly pay the check to the drawer's order.

After recrediting the drawer's account, the drawee/payor bank may seek indemnification against the collecting bank that made presentment under section 4–207, alleging breach of warranty of good title. Liability on the basis of breach of warranty travels backward through the chain of collection and is ultimately placed on the party who took the check from the forger. Thus, when a depositary bank accepts a forged instrument, it is generally liable for the amount of the check paid by the payor. The rationale for this system of allocating liability is that the party who took from the forger should be liable for the loss because that party is in the best position to prevent such fraud by checking the authenticity of indorsements.

Section 3–405(1) is a narrow exception to this general system of allocating loss. Because this section makes an indorsement on a forged signature effective, the drawee/payor bank is authorized to pay the instrument and is generally not liable, therefore, to the drawer under section 4–401. Further, because this section makes an indorsement on a forged signature effective, title to the instrument passes, as though there had been no forgery, and a collecting bank is entitled to payment from parties liable on the instrument. Thus, no conversion action by the drawer against either the drawee or the depositary bank will lie where section 3–405 controls. The official comment to section 3–405 states the rationale for allocating liability to the drawer in the circumstances covered by section 3–405(1):

> The principle followed is that the loss should fall upon the employer as a risk of his business enterprise rather than upon the subsequent holder or drawee. The reasons are that the employer is normally in a better position to prevent such forgeries by reasonable care in the supervision of his employees, or, if he is not, is at least in a better position to cover the loss by fidelity insurance; and that the cost of such insurance is properly a cost of the business rather than of the holder or drawee.

The circuit court held, and Community Bancshares argues, that under section 3–405(1)(c) Community Bancshares is not liable in the circumstances of this case because Bivens, an employee of C & N, supplied her employer with the names of the payees of the payroll checks with the intent that the payees would take no interest in them. Community Bancshares argues that this is a "padded payroll" case and that by virtue of section 3–405(1)(c) the loss falls on the drawer of the checks, C & N.

We conclude that the circuit court correctly held an action for conversion will not be because there is no genuine issue of material fact regarding the application of section 3–405(1)(c) in the circumstances of this case.

Judgment affirmed for Community Bancshares.

Note: This case was decided under the original version of Article 3. Although Revised Article 3 changes the wording of the "fictitious payee rule" and sets it out in section 3–404 of Revised Article 3, the results would be the same under the revision.

Comparative Negligence Rule Concerning Impostors and Fictitious Payees

Revised Article 3 also establishes a comparative negligence rule if (1) the person, in a situation covered by the impostor or fictitious payee rule, pays the instrument or takes it for value or collection without exercising ordinary care in paying or taking the instrument, and (2) that failure substantially contributes to the loss resulting from payment of the instrument. In these instances, the person bearing the loss may recover an allocable share of the loss from the person who did not exercise ordinary care [3–404(d)].

Fraudulent Indorsements by Employees

Revised Article 3 specifically addresses employer responsibility for fraudulent indorsements by employees and adopts the principle that the risk of loss for such indorsements by employees who are entrusted with responsibilities for instruments (primarily checks) should fall on the employer rather than on the bank that takes the check or pays it [3–405]. As to any person who in good faith pays an instrument or takes it for value, a fraudulent indorsement by a responsible employee is effective as the indorsement of the payee if it is made in the name of the payee or in a substantially similar name [3–405(b)]. If the person taking or paying the instrument failed to exercise ordinary care and that failure substantially contributed to loss resulting from the fraud, the comparative negligence doctrine guides the allocation of the loss.

A fraudulent indorsement includes a forged indorsement purporting to be that of the employer on an instrument payable to the employer; it also includes a forged indorsement purporting to be that of the payee of an instrument on which the employer is drawer or maker [3–405(a)(2)]. "Responsibility" with respect to instruments means the authority to (1) sign or indorse instruments on behalf of the employer, (2) process instruments received by the employer, (3) prepare or process instruments for issue in the name of the employer, (4) control the disposition of instruments to be issued in the name of the employer, or (5) otherwise act with respect to instruments in a responsible capacity. "Responsibility" does not cover those who simply have access to instruments as they are stored, transported, or that are in incoming or outgoing mail [3–405(a)(3)].

Conversion

Conversion of an instrument is an unauthorized assumption and exercise of ownership over it. A negotiable instrument can be converted in a number of ways. For example, it might be presented for payment or acceptance, and the person to whom it is presented might refuse to pay or accept and refuse to return it. An instrument also is converted if a person pays an instrument to a person not entitled to payment—for example, if it contains a forged indorsement.

Revised Article 3 modifies and then expands the previous treatment of conversion and provides that the law applicable to conversion of personal property applies to instruments. It also specifically provides that conversion occurs if (1) an instrument lacks an indorsement necessary for negotiation and (2) it is (*a*) purchased, (*b*) taken for collection, or (*c*) paid by a drawee to a person not entitled to payment. An action for conversion may not be brought by (1) the maker, drawer, or acceptor of the instrument or (2) a payee or an indorsee who did not receive delivery of the instrument either directly or through delivery to an agent or copayee [3–420].

Thus, if a bank pays a check that contains a forged indorsement, the bank has converted the check by wrongfully paying it. The bank then becomes liable for the face amount of the check to the person whose indorsement was forged [3–420]. For example, Arthur Able draws a check for $50 on his account at First Bank, payable to the order of Bernard Barker. Carol Collins steals the check, forges Barker's indorsement on it, and cashes it at First Bank. First Bank has converted Barker's property, because it had no right to pay the check without Barker's valid indorsement. First Bank must pay Barker $50, and then it can try to locate Collins to get the $50 back from her.

As is true under the original version of Article 3, if a check contains a restrictive indorsement (such as "for deposit" or "for collection") that shows a purpose of having the check collected for the benefit of a particular account, then any person who purchases the check or any depositary bank or payor bank that takes it for immediate payment converts the check unless the indorser receives the proceeds or the bank applies them consistent with the indorsement [3–206].

Discharge of Negotiable Instruments

Discharge of Liability

The obligation of a party to pay an instrument is discharged (1) if he meets the requirements set out in Revised Article 3 or (2) by any act or agreement that would discharge an obligation to pay money on a simple contract. Discharge of an obligation is not effective against a person who has the rights of a holder in due course of the instrument and took the instrument without notice of the discharge [3–601].

The most common ways that an obligor is discharged from his liability are:

1. Payment of the instrument.

2. Cancellation of the instrument.

3. Alteration of the instrument.

4. Modification of the principal's obligation that causes loss to a surety or impairs the collateral.

5. Unexcused delay in presentment or notice of dishonor with respect to a check (discussed earlier in this chapter).

6. Acceptance of a draft [3–414(c) or (d); 3–415(d)]; as noted earlier in the chapter, a drawer is discharged of liability of a draft that is accepted by a bank (e.g., if a check is certified by a bank) because at that point the holder is looking to the bank to make the instrument good.

Discharge by Payment

Generally, payment in full discharges liability on an instrument to the extent payment is (1) by or on behalf of a party obligated to pay the instrument and (2) to a person entitled to enforce the instrument. For example, Arthur makes a note of $100 payable to the order of Bryan. Bryan indorses the note "Pay to the order of my account no. 16154 at First Bank, Bryan." Bryan then gives the note to his employee, Clark, to take to the bank. Clark takes the note to Arthur, who pays Clark the $100. Clark then runs off with the money. Arthur is not discharged of his primary liability on the note because he did not make his payment consistent with the restrictive indorsement. To be discharged, Arthur has to pay the $100 into Bryan's account at First Bank.

To the extent of payment, the obligation of a party to pay the instrument is discharged even though payment is made with knowledge of a claim to the instrument by some other person. However, the obligation is not discharged if: (1) there is a claim enforceable against the person making payment and payment is made with knowledge of the fact that payment is prohibited by an injunction or similar legal process, or (2) in the case of an instrument other than a cashier's, certified, or teller's check, the person making the payment had accepted from the person making the claim indemnity against loss for refusing to make payment to the person entitled to enforce payment. The obligation also is not discharged if he knows the instrument is a stolen instrument and pays someone he knows is in wrongful possession of the instrument [3–602].

Discharge by Cancellation

A person entitled to enforce a negotiable instrument may discharge the liability of the parties to the instrument by canceling or renouncing it. If the holder mutilates or destroys a negotiable instrument with the intent that it no longer evidences an obligation to pay money, the holder has canceled it [3–604]. For example, a grandfather lends $1,000 to his grandson for college expenses. The grandson gives his grandfather a promissory note for $1,000. If the grandfather later tears up the note with the intent that the grandson no longer owes him $1,000, the grandfather has canceled the note.

An accidental destruction or mutilation of a negotiable instrument is not a cancellation and does not discharge the parties to it. If an instrument is lost, mutilated accidentally, or destroyed, the person entitled to enforce it still can enforce the instrument. In such a case, the person must prove that the instrument existed and that she was its holder when it was lost, mutilated, or destroyed.

Altered Instruments; Discharge by Alteration

A person paying a fraudulently altered instrument, or taking it for value, in good faith and without notice of the alteration, may enforce the instrument (1) according to its original terms or (2) in the case of an incomplete instrument later completed in an unauthorized manner, according to its terms as completed [3–407(c)]. An alteration occurs if there is (1) an unauthorized change that modifies the obligation of a party to the instrument or (2) an unauthorized addition of words or numbers or other change to an incomplete instrument that changes the obligation of any party [3–407]. A change that does not affect the obligation of one of the parties, such as dotting an *i* or correcting the grammar, is not considered to be an alteration.

Two examples illustrate the situations in which Revised Article 3 allows fraudulently altered instruments to be enforced. First, assume the amount due on a note is fraudulently raised from $10 to $10,000. The contract of the maker has been changed: the maker promised to pay $10, but after the change has been made, he would be promising to pay much more. If the note is negotiated to or paid by a person who was without notice of the alteration, that person can enforce the note against the maker only according to its original terms. It would pursue the alterer or the person taking from the alterer for the balance on a presentment or transfer warranty [3–417; 3–416]. If the maker's negligence substantially contributed to the alteration, then the maker would be responsible for as much as the entire $10,000 [3–407(c); 3–406].

Second, assume Swanson draws a check payable to Frank's Nursery, leaving the amount blank. He gives it to his gardener with instructions to purchase some fertilizer at Frank's and to fill in the purchase price of the fertilizer when it is known. The gardener fills in the check for $100 and gives it to Frank's in exchange for the fertilizer ($7.25) and the difference in cash ($92.75). The gardener then leaves town with the cash. If Frank's had no knowledge of the unauthorized completion, it could enforce the check for $100 against Swanson. A similar situation is illustrated in *American Federal Bank, FSB v. Parker.*

American Federal Bank, FSB v Parker   *392 SE.2d 798 (S.C. Ct. App. 1990)*

Thomas Kirkman was involved in the horse business and was a friend of John Roundtree, a loan officer for American Federal Bank. Kirkman and Roundtree conceived a business arrangement in which Kirkman would locate buyers for horses and the buyers could seek financing from American Federal. Roundtree gave Kirkman blank promissory notes and security agreements from American Federal. Kirkman was to locate the potential purchaser, take care of the paperwork, and bring the documents to the bank for approval of the purchaser's loan.

Kirkman entered into a purchase agreement with Gene Parker, a horse dealer, to copurchase for $35,000 a horse named Wills Hightime that Kirkman represented he owned. Parker signed the American Federal promissory note in blank and also executed in blank a security agreement that authorized the bank to disburse the funds to the seller of the collateral. Kirkman told Parker he would cosign the note and fill in the details of the transaction with the bank. While Kirkman did not cosign the note, he did complete it for $85,000 as opposed to $35,000. Kirkman took the note with Parker's signature to Roundtree at American Federal and received two checks from the bank payable to him in the amounts of $35,000 and $50,000. Kirkman took the $35,000 and gave it to the real owner of the horse. Parker then received the horse.

Parker began making payments to the bank and called on Kirkman to assist in making the payments pursuant to their agreement. However, Kirkman skipped town, taking the additional $50,000 with him. Parker repaid the $35,000 but refused to pay any more. He argued that he agreed to borrow only $35,000 and the other $50,000 was unauthorized by him. American Federal Bank filed suit to recover the balance due on the note. The trial court held in favor of the bank and Parker appealed.

Cureton, Judge   Parker executed a promissory note in blank. Under the Uniform Commercial Code, the maker of a note agrees to pay the instrument according to its tenor at the time of engagement "or as completed pursuant to section 3–115 on incomplete instruments." Under section 3–115(2) if the completion of an instrument is unauthorized the rules as to material alteration apply. Under section 3–407(1)(b) the completion of an incomplete instrument otherwise than as authorized is considered an alteration. However, under section 3–407(3) a subsequent holder in due course may enforce an incomplete instrument as completed. Official comment 4 indicates that where blanks are filled or an incomplete instrument is otherwise completed, the loss is placed upon the party who left the instrument incomplete and the holder is permitted to enforce it according to its completed form.

We agree with the trial court that the bank was entitled to the directed verdicts. The responsibility for the situation rests with Parker. He and Kirkman negotiated their deal. Parker signed a blank promissory note. He relied upon Kirkman to cosign the note and fill it in for $35,000. Parker's negligence substantially contributed to the material alteration as a matter of law.

Parker argues that it was not reasonable commercial practice for American Federal to give Kirkman possession of blank promissory notes. After the fact, Parker argues the bank should have contacted him or checked to be sure everything was correct before disbursing the proceeds of the loan to Kirkman. There is no evidence in the record to establish the bank had any reason to inquire into the facial validity of the note. The note was complete when presented to the bank and there were no obvious alterations on it.

The record establishes American Federal took the note in good faith and without notice of any defense to it by Parker. American Federal gave value for the note when it disbursed the funds to Kirkman. As a holder in due course, American Federal may enforce the note against Parker as completed. Sections 3–302; 3–407(3).

Judgment for American Federal affirmed.

Note: Although this case was decided under the original version of Article 3, the same result would be reached under Revised Article 3 so long as the court found Kirkman's completion (alteration) to be fraudulent.

In any other case, a fraudulent alteration **discharges** any party whose obligation is affected by the alteration *unless* (1) the party assents or (2) is precluded from asserting the alteration (e.g. because of the party's negligence). Assume that Anderson signs a promissory note for $100 payable to Bond. Bond indorses the note "Pay to the order of Connolly, Bond" and negotiates it to Connolly. Connolly changes the $100 to read $100,000. Connolly's change is unauthorized and fraudulent. As a result, Anderson is discharged from her liability as maker of the note and Bond is discharged from her liability as indorser. Neither of them has to pay Connolly. The obligations of both Anderson and Bond were changed because the amount for which they are liable was altered.

No other alteration—that is, one that is not fraudulent—discharges any party and a holder may enforce the instrument according to its *original* terms. Thus, there would be no discharge if a blank is filled in the honest belief that it is authorized or if a change is made, without any fraudulent intent, to give the maker on a note the benefit of a lower interest rate.

Discharge of Indorsers and Accommodation Parties

If a person entitled to enforce an instrument agrees, with or without consideration, to a material modification of the obligation of a party to the instrument, including an extension of the due date, then any accommodation party or indorser who has a right of recourse against the person whose obligation is modified is discharged *to the extent the modification causes a loss to the indorser or accommodation party.* Similarly, if collateral secures the obligation of a party to an instrument and a person entitled to enforce the instrument impairs the value of the collateral, the obligation of the indorser or accommodation party having the right of recourse against the obligor is discharged to the extent of the impairment. These discharges are not effective unless the person agreeing to the modification or causing the impairment knows of the accommodation or has notice of it. Also, no discharge occurs if the obligor assented to the event or conduct, or if the obligor has waived the discharge [3–605].

For example, Frank goes to Credit Union to borrow $4,000 to purchase a used automobile. The credit union has Frank sign a promissory note and takes a security interest in the automobile (i.e., takes it as collateral for the loan). It also asks Frank's brother, Bob, to sign the note as an accommodation maker. Subsequently, Frank tells the credit union he wants to sell the automobile and it releases its security interest. Because release of the collateral adversely affects Bob's obligation as accommodation maker, he is discharged from his obligation as accommodation maker in the amount of the value of the automobile.

Problems and Problem Cases

1. Terance Fitzgerald drew a check for $4,000 payable to New Look Auto Trim and Upholstery and delivered it to Yuvonne Goss and Benii Arrazza the owners of New Look. Goss and Arrazza each indorsed the check in blank and deposited it in Goss's personal account at the Cincinnati Central Credit Union. When the the credit union presented the check to Fitzgerald's bank, the check was dishonored for insufficient funds. The credit union then demanded that Goss and Arrazza honor the check. Are Goss and Arrazza obligated to make the check good to the credit union?

2. Janota's signature appeared on a note under the name of a corporation acknowledging a $1,000 debt. No other wording appeared other than Janota's name and the corporate name. The holder of the note sues Janota on the note. What will Janota argue and what will be the result?

3. In 1997, Maryellen Peterson was a part-time employee of Textiles Specialties & Chemicals doing business as CS Industries. On April 17, 1997, Peterson signed a check in the amount of $13,789.80 on the account of CS Industries and payable to Holtrachem, Inc. The check was imprinted with name of CS Industries. However, Peterson signed only her name and did not indicate she was signing in her representative capacity on behalf of CS Industries. The drawee bank returned the check to Holtrachem due to insufficient funds in CS Industries' account. Holtrachem filed suit against Peterson, seeking to hold her liable in her personal capacity as the drawer of the check. Is an individual who signs a check drawn on a corporate account without indicating she is signing in representative capacity personally liable on the instrument?

4. Clay Haynes was the bookkeeper for Johnstown Manufacturing, Inc. He had express check signing authority, and his signature was on the signature card for the account that Johnstown maintained at BancOhio National Bank. Haynes was also the bookkeeper of another corporation, Lynn Polymers, Inc., which was operated by the same individuals that operated Johnstown. Over a period of a year, Haynes engaged in a check cashing scheme from which he pocketed approximately $70,000. Haynes wrote 35 corporate checks to the order of BancOhio National Bank, and the bank, in return, gave the cash to Haynes. Johnstown brought suit against BancOhio to recover $300 for the one check written on the Johnstown account the bank paid to Haynes. Johnstown claimed that the check was written without the express authority of the corporation, and thus it contained an "unauthorized" signature. Was Haynes's signature on the check "unauthorized" as that term is used in the Uniform Commercial Code?

5. First National Bank certified Smith's check in the amount of $29. After certification, Smith altered the check so that it read $2,900. He presented the check to a

merchant in payment for goods. The merchant then submitted the check to the bank for payment. The bank refused, saying it had certified the instrument for only $29. Can the merchant recover the $2,900 from the bank?

6. A check was drawn on First National Bank and made payable to Howard. It came into the possession of Carson, who forged Howard's indorsement and cashed it at Merchant's Bank. Merchant's Bank then indorsed it and collected payment from First National. Assuming that Carson is nowhere to be found, who bears the loss caused by Carson's forgery?

7. Mrs. Gordon Neely hired Louise Bradshaw as the bookkeeper for a Midas Muffler shop the Neelys owned and operated as a corporation, J. Gordon Neely Enterprises, Inc. (Neely). Bradshaw's duties included preparing company checks for Mrs. Neely's signature and reconciling the checking account when the company received a bank statement and canceled checks each month. Bradshaw prepared several checks payable to herself and containing a large space to the left of the amount written on the designated line. When Mrs. Neely signed the checks, she was aware of the large gaps. Subsequently, Bradshaw altered the checks by adding a digit or two to the left of the original amount and then cashed them at American National Bank, the drawee bank. Several months later, the Neelys hired a new accountant, who discovered the altered checks. Neely brought suit against American National Bank to have its account recredited for the altered checks, claiming that American was liable for paying out on altered instruments. The bank contended that Neely's negligence substantially contributed to alterations of the instruments and thus Neely was precluded from asserting the alteration against the bank. Between Neely and American National Bank, who should bear the loss caused by Bradshaw's fraud?

8. Clarice Rich was employed by the New York City Board of Education as a clerk. It was her duty to prepare requisitions for checks to be issued by the board, to prepare the checks, to have them signed by authorized personnel, and to send the checks to the recipients. In some instances, however, she retained them. Also, on a number of occasions she prepared duplicate requisitions and checks, which, when signed, she likewise retained. She then forged the indorsement of the named payees on the checks she had retained and cashed the checks at Chemical Bank, where the Board of Education maintained its account. After the board discovered the forgeries, it demanded that Chemical Bank credit its account for the amount of the forged checks. Is Chemical Bank required to credit the board's account as requested?

9. Stockton's housekeeper stole some of his checks, forged his name as drawer, and cashed them at Gristedes Supermarket where Stockton maintained check-cashing privileges. The checks were presented to Stockton's bank and honored by it. Over the course of 18 months, the scheme netted the housekeeper in excess of $147,000 on approximately 285 forged checks. Stockton brought suit against Gristedes Supermarket for conversion, seeking to recover the value of the checks it accepted and for which it obtained payment from the drawee bank. Was Gristedes Supermarket liable to Stockton for conversion for accepting and obtaining payment of the stolen and forged checks?

10. Charles Peterson, a farmer and rancher, was indebted to Crown Financial Corporation on a $4,450,000 promissory note that was due on December 29, 1992. Shortly before the note was due, Crown sent Peterson a statement of interest due on the note ($499,658.85). Petersen paid the interest and executed a new note in the amount of $4,450,000 that was to mature in December 1995. The old note was then marked "canceled" and returned to Peterson. In 1995, Crown billed Peterson for $363,800 in interest that had been due on the first note but apparently not included in the statement. Peterson claimed that the interest had been forgiven and that he was not obligated to pay it. Was Peterson still obligated to pay interest on the note that had been returned to him marked "canceled"?

Online Research: The FTC's Holder in Due Course Rule

Use the Internet to locate the site for the Federal Trade Commission. Review the FTC's presentation of the Holder in Due Course rule and note when someone taking a negotiable instrument from a consumer needs to be concerned with its implications.

34

CHECKS AND ELECTRONIC TRANSFERS

Susan Williams opened a checking account at the First National Bank. She made an initial deposit of $1,800, signed a signature card that indicated to the bank that she was the authorized signator on the account, and was given a supply of blank checks. She also received an ATM card that, when used along with an assigned PIN (personal identification number), allowed her to make deposits to her account as well as to obtain cash from it. Each month the bank sent her a statement reflecting the activity in the account during the previous month along with the canceled checks. Several months after she opened the account, the bank erroneously refused to pay a check she had written to a clothing store even though she had sufficient funds in her account. As a result, the store filed a complaint with the local prosecutor indicating she had written a "bad check." On one occasion, Susan called the bank to stop payment on a check she had written to cover repairs to her automobile because while driving the car home, she discovered the requested repair had not been made. However, the bank paid the check later that day despite the stop payment order she had given the bank. Another time, Susan's wallet fell out of her purse while she was shopping at a mall. She received a call the next morning indicating the wallet had been found and she retrieved it at that time. However, when she received her next monthly statement from the bank, she discovered that someone had apparently used her ATM card to withdraw $200 from her account on the day her wallet had been lost. Susan's experience raises a number of legal issues that will be covered in this chapter, including:

• What rights does Susan have against the bank for refusing to pay the check to the clothing store despite the fact she had sufficient funds on deposit to cover it?
• What rights does Susan have against the bank for failing to honor the stop payment order she placed on the check she had written to the repair shop?
• What rights does Susan have against the bank because of the unauthorized use of her ATM card? What must she do to preserve those rights?

FOR MOST PEOPLE, a checking account provides the majority of their contact with negotiable instruments. This chapter focuses on the relationship between the drawer with a checking account and the drawer's bank, known as the drawee bank.

The Drawer–Drawee Relationship

There are two sources that govern the relationship between the depositor and the drawee bank: the deposit agreement and Articles 3 and 4 of the Code. Article 4,

CYBERLAW IN ACTION

Account Aggregation

"Account aggregation" is a financial management tool offered by banks and by third-party, Internet-based companies. Consumers who want to use this tool will allow a bank or third-party to gather information from many accounts (checking, savings, pension funds, certificates of deposit, securities firms, and insurance companies) by giving the account aggregator key information such as the account numbers and passwords for the consumer's various accounts. The aggregator then gathers information from the websites of the different financial services firms (insurance companies, banks, investment planners, securities brokers, etc.) and makes it possible for the consumer to view all of this information on one screen, and in some cases to transfer funds between accounts.

Some consumer advocates argue that "account aggregation"—also known as "screen scraping"—is more risky for consumers than accessing each financial service provider's website separately. They worry that the possibility of hacking into such an information heavy account increases the chance that a criminal could wipe out the entire holdings of one consumer or a group of consumers. Consumers like "account aggregation" because it gives them all of their financial accounts essentially on one "page" on their computer screens. Other consumers like it because "account aggregation" allows them to move funds between their various accounts quickly from their computers without waiting to speak to each specific financial services provider to complete transactions.

---

which governs Bank Deposits and Collections, allows the depositor and drawee bank (which Article 4 calls the "payor bank") to vary Article 4's provisions with a few important exceptions. The deposit agreement cannot disclaim the bank's responsibility for its own lack of good faith or failure to exercise ordinary care or limit the measure of damages for the lack or failure; however, the parties may determine by agreement the standards by which to measure the bank's responsibility so long as the standards are not manifestly unreasonable [4–103].

The deposit agreement establishes many important relationships between the depositor and drawee/payor bank. The first of these is their relationship as creditor and debtor, respectively, so that when a person deposits money in an account at the bank, the law no longer considers him the owner of the money. Instead, he is a creditor of the bank to the extent of his deposits and the bank becomes his debtor. Also, when the depositor deposits a check to a checking account, the bank also becomes his agent for collection of the check. The bank as the person's agent owes a duty to him to follow his reasonable instructions concerning payment of checks and other items from his account and a duty of ordinary care in collecting checks and other items deposited to the account.

Bank's Duty to Pay

When a bank receives a properly drawn and payable check on a person's account and there are sufficient funds to cover the check, the bank is under a duty to pay

it. If the person has sufficient funds in the account and the bank refuses to pay, or dishonors, the check, the bank is liable for the actual damages proximately caused by its wrongful dishonor as well as consequential damages [4–402]. Actual damages may include charges imposed by retailers for returned checks as well as damages for arrest or prosecution of the customer. Consequential damages include injury to the depositor's credit rating that results from the dishonor.

For example, Donald Dodson writes a check for $1,500 to Ames Auto Sales in payment for a used car. At the time that Ames Auto presents the check for payment at Dodson's bank, First National Bank, Dodson has $1,800 in his account. However, a teller mistakenly refuses to pay the check and stamps it NSF (not sufficient funds). Ames Auto then goes to the local prosecutor and signs a complaint against Dodson for writing a bad check. As a result, Dodson is arrested. Dodson can recover from First National the damages that he sustained because the bank wrongfully dishonored his check, including the damages involved in his arrest, such as his attorney's fees.

Bank's Right to Charge to Customer's Account

The drawee bank has the right to charge any properly payable check to the account of the customer or drawer. The bank has this right even though payment of the check creates an overdraft in the account [4–401]. If an account is overdrawn, the customer owes the bank the amount of the overdraft and the bank may take that amount out of the next deposit that the customer makes or from another account that the depositor maintains with the bank. Alternatively, the bank might seek to collect the amount directly from the customer. If there is more than one customer who can draw from an account, only that customer—or those customers—who sign the item or who benefit from the proceeds of an overdraft are liable for the overdraft.

Stale Checks The bank does not owe a duty to its customer to pay any checks out of the account that are more than six months old. Such checks are called **stale checks.** However, the bank acting in good faith may pay a check that is more than six months old and charge it to the drawer-depositor's account [4–404].

Altered and Incomplete Items If the bank in good faith pays a check drawn by the drawer-depositor but subsequently altered, it may charge the customer's account with the amount of the check as originally drawn. Also, if an incomplete check of a customer gets into circulation, is completed, and is presented to the drawee bank for payment, and the bank pays the check, the bank can charge the amount as completed to the customer's account even though it knows that the check has been completed, unless it has notice that the completion was improper [4–401(d)]. The respective rights, obligations, and liabilities of drawee banks and their drawer-customers concerning forged and altered checks are discussed in more detail later in this chapter.

Limitations on Bank's Right or Duty Article 4 recognizes that the bank's right or duty to pay a check or to charge the depositor's account for the check (including exercising its right to set off an amount due to it by the depositor) may be terminated, suspended, or modified by the depositor's order to stop payment (which is discussed in the next section of this chapter). In addition, it may be stopped by events external to the relationship between the depositor and the bank. These external events include the filing of a bankruptcy petition by the depositor or by the depositor's creditors, and the garnishment of the account by a creditor of the depositor. The bank must receive the stop-payment order from its depositor or the notice of the bankruptcy filing or garnishment before the bank has certified the check, paid it in cash, settled with another bank for the amount of the item without a right to revoke the settle-

ment, or otherwise become accountable for the amount of the check under Article 4, or the cut-off hour on the banking day after the check is received if the bank established a cut-off hour [4–303]. These restrictions on the bank's right or duty to pay are discussed in later sections of this chapter.

Postdated Checks Under original Articles 3 and 4, a postdated check was not properly payable by the drawee bank until the date on the check. The recent amendments to Article 4 change this. Under the revision, an otherwise properly payable postdated check that is presented for payment before the date on the check may be paid and charged to the customer's account *unless* the customer has given notice of it to the bank. The customer must give notice of the postdating in a way that describes the check with reasonable certainty. It is effective for the same time periods as Article 4 provides for stop-payment orders (discussed below). The customer must give notice to the bank at such time and in such a manner as to give the bank an opportunity to act on it before the bank takes any action with respect to paying the check. If the bank charges the customer's account for a postdated check before the date stated in the notice given to the bank, the bank is liable for damages for any loss that results. Such damages might include those associated with the dishonor of subsequent items [3–113(a); 4–401(c)].

There are a variety of reasons why a person might want to postdate a check. For example, a person might have a mortgage payment due on the first of the month at a bank located in another state. To make sure that the check arrives on time, the customer may send the payment by mail several days before the due date. However, if the person is depending on a deposit of her next monthly paycheck on the first of the month to cover the mortgage payment, she might postdate the check to the first of the following month. Under the original version of Articles 3 and 4, the bank could not properly pay the check until the first of the month. However, under the revisions it could be properly paid by the bank before that date if presented earlier. To avoid the risk that the bank would dishonor the check for insufficient funds if presented before the first, the customer should notify the drawee bank in a manner similar to that required for stop payment of checks.

Stop-Payment Order

A stop-payment order is a request made by a customer of a drawee bank instructing it not to pay or certify a

> **Figure 1**   *Stop-Payment Order*

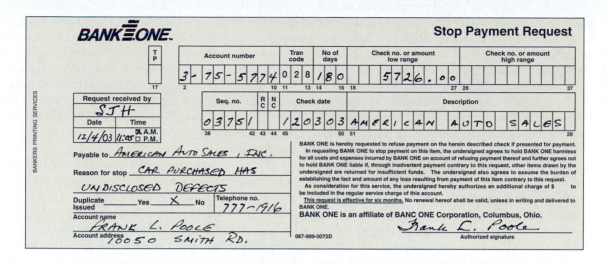

specified check. As the drawer's agent in the payment of checks, the drawee bank must follow the reasonable orders of the drawer-customer about payments made on the drawer's behalf. Any person authorized to draw a check may stop payment of it. Thus, any person authorized to sign a check on the account may stop payment even if she did not sign the check in question [4–403(a)].

To be effective, a payor bank must receive the stop-payment order in time to give the bank a reasonable opportunity to act on the order. This means that the bank must receive the stop-payment order before it has paid or certified the check. In addition, the stop-payment order must come soon enough to give the bank time to instruct its tellers and other employees that they should not pay or certify the check [4–403(a)]. The stop-payment order also must describe the check with "reasonable certainty" so as to provide the bank's employees the ability to recognize it as the check corresponding to the stop-payment order.

The customer may give a stop-payment order orally to the bank, but it is valid for only 14 days unless the customer confirms it in writing during that time. A written stop-payment order is valid for six months and the customer can extend it for an additional six months by giving the bank instructions in writing to continue the order [4–403(b)]. (See Figure 1.)

Sometimes the information given the bank by the customer concerning the check on which payment is to be stopped is incorrect. For example, there may be an error in the payee's name, the amount of the check, or the number of the check. The question then arises whether the

customer has accorded the bank a reasonable opportunity to act on his request. A common issue is whether the stop-payment order must have the dollar amount correct to the penny. Banks often take the position that the stop-payment order must be correct to the penny because they program and rely on computers to focus on the customer's account number and the amount of the check in question to avoid paying an item subject to a stop-payment order. The amendments to Article 4 do not resolve this question. In the Official Comments, the drafters indicate that "in describing an item, the customer, in the absence of a contrary agreement, must meet the standard of what information allows the bank under the technology then existing to identify the check with reasonable certainty." In the Stop-Payment Order in Figure 1, the bank takes a more lenient approach than some: it asks for the range of number or low and high dollar of the check the customer does not want the bank to pay.

Bank's Liability for Payment after Stop-Payment Order

While a stop-payment order is in effect, the drawee bank is liable to the drawer of a check that it pays for any loss that the drawer suffers by reason of such payment. However, the drawer-customer has the burden of establishing the fact and amount of the loss. To show a loss, the drawer must establish that the drawee bank paid a person against whom the drawer had a valid defense to payment. To the extent that the drawer has such a defense, he has suffered a loss due to the drawee's failure to honor the stop-payment order.

For example, Brown buys what is represented to be a new car from Foster Ford and gives Foster Ford his check for $16,280 drawn on First Bank. Brown then discovers that the car is in fact a used demonstrator model and calls First Bank, ordering it to stop payment on the check. If Foster Ford presents the check for payment the following day and First Bank pays the check despite the stop-payment order, Brown can require the bank to recredit his account. (The depositor-drawer bases her claim to recredit on the fact that the bank did not follow her final instruction—the instruction not to pay the check.) Brown had a valid defense of misrepresentation that she could have asserted against Foster Ford if it had sued her on the check. Foster Ford would have been required to sue on the check or on Brown's contractual obligation to pay for the car.

Assume, instead, that Foster Ford negotiated the check to Smith and that Smith qualified as a holder in due course. Then, if the bank paid the check to Smith over the stop-payment order, Brown would not be able to have her account recredited, because Brown would not be able to show that she sustained any loss. If the bank had refused to pay the check, so that Smith came against Brown on her drawer's liability, Brown could not use her personal defense of misrepresentation of the prior use of the car as a reason for not paying Smith. Brown's only recourse would be to pursue Foster Ford on her misrepresentation claim.

The bank may ask the customer to sign a form in which the bank tries to disclaim or limit its liability for the stop-payment order, or, as in Figure 1, for damages if it fails to obey the stop-payment order. As explained at the beginning of this chapter, the bank cannot disclaim its responsibility for its failure to act in good faith or to exercise ordinary care in paying a check over a stop-payment order [4–103].

If a bank pays a check after it has received a stop-payment order and has to reimburse its customer for the improperly paid check, it acquires all the rights of its customer against the person to whom it originally made payment, including rights arising from the transaction on which the check was based [4–407]. In the previous example involving Brown and Foster Ford, assume that Brown was able to have her account recredited because First Bank had paid the check to Foster Ford over her stop-payment order. Then, the bank would have any rights that Brown had against Foster Ford for the misrepresentation.

If a person stops payment on a check and the bank honors the stop-payment order, the person may still be liable to the holder of the check. Suppose Peters writes a check for $450 to Ace Auto Repair in payment for repairs to her automobile. While driving the car home, she concludes that the car was not repaired properly. She calls her bank and stops payment on the check. Ace Auto negotiated the check to Sam's Auto Parts, which took the check as a holder in due course. When Sam's takes the check to Peters's bank, the bank refuses to pay because of the stop-payment order. Sam's then comes after Peters on her drawer's liability. All Peters has is a personal defense against payment, which is not good against a holder in due course. So, Peters must pay Sam's the $450 and pursue her claim separately against Ace. If Ace were still the holder of the check, however, the situation would be different. Peters could use her personal defense concerning the faulty work against Ace to reduce or possibly to cancel her obligation to pay the check.

In the following case, *Seigel v. Merrill Lynch, Pierce, Fenner & Smith, Inc.*, the drawer was not entitled to have his account recredited for checks paid over a stop-payment order because he was unable to show he had suffered any loss.

Seigel v. Merrill Lynch, Pierce, Fenner & Smith, Inc.
745 A.2d 301 (D.C. Ct. App. 2000)

Walter Seigel, a Maryland resident, traveled to Atlantic City, New Jersey, to gamble. While there, Seigel wrote a number of checks to various casinos and, in exchange, received gambling chips with which to wager. The checks were drawn on Seigel's cash management account at Merrill, Lynch, Pierce, Fenner & Smith, which was established through its District of Columbia offices. There were sufficient funds in the accounts to cover all the checks.

Seigel eventually gambled away all the chips he had received for the checks. Upon returning to Maryland, Seigel discussed the outstanding checks with Merrill Lynch, informing his broker of the gambling nature of the transactions and his desire to avoid realizing the apparent losses. Merrill Lynch informed Seigel that it was possible to escape paying the checks by placing a stop-payment order and liquidating his cash management account. He took the advice and instructed Merrill

Lynch to close his account, liquidate the assets, and to not honor any checks drawn on the account. Merrill Lynch agreed and confirmed Seigel's instructions.

Many of the checks were subsequently dishonored. However, Merrill Lynch accidentally paid several of the checks totaling $143,000, despite the stop payment order and account closure. Merrill Lynch then debited Seigel's margin account to cover the payments.

Seigel brought suit in the District of Columbia against Merrill Lynch for paying the checks over his stop-payment order. He argued that the District of Columbia Code precluded enforcement of the checks as void gambling debts, or in the alternative that New Jersey law prohibited the enforcement of the check. Therefore, he contended, Merrill Lynch had no rights by way of subrogation as a defense to payment over the stop-payment order. Merrill lynch denied the applicability of the DC statute or any New Jersey law and contended that it stood in the shoes of the casinos to whom valid and enforceable checks had been given.

Steadman, Associate Judge We begin with an examination of the statutory scheme relating to stop-payment orders, because we believe these provisions are determinative of this appeal. The relevant sections are found in the Uniform Commercial Code as enacted in the District of Columbia, and in particular §§ 4–403 and 4–407.

The basic right of the depositor to stop payment on any item drawn on the depositor's account is set forth in section 4–403(a). However, liability on the bank for payment over a stop payment order is far from automatic. On the contrary, section 4–403(c) provides: "The burden of establishing the fact and amount of loss resulting from the payment of an item contrary to a stop-payment order or order to close an account is on the customer."

The provision, which places the burden on the customer to show actual loss, is reinforced by the extensive rights of subrogation given to the payor bank by section 4–407. Under that section, as to the drawer or make (that is, the depositor), the bank is subrogated both to the rights of "any holder in due course on the item" and to the rights of "the payee or any other holder of the item against the drawer or maker either on the item or under the transaction out of which the item arose." As a leading authority on the Uniform Commercial Code has noted, this section "contemplates that the bank will use its subrogation rights primarily to defend against a suit by the customer to recover payment." 2 WHITE & SUMMERS, UNIFORM COMMERCIAL CODE § 21–6, at 396 n.11 (4th ed. 1995).

As applied to the facts here, then, Seigel is required to bear the burden of establishing that he in fact suffered a loss as a result of the payment of the checks. In assessing whether any such loss was actually incurred, Merrill Lynch must be treated as the subrogee of any rights of the casino payees against Seigel. As a payee of a dishonored check, the casino would have a prima facie right to recover its amount from Seigel as drawer, § 3–414(b), and the burden would be on Seigel to establish any defense he might assert

on the instrument. § 3–308(b). Seigel asserts two such defenses: duress and illegality. We turn to an examination of those defenses.

Seigel first argues that the casinos would have no right to enforce the checks even under New Jersey law because he is a compulsive gambler. He contends that enforcement of checks by a casino against a compulsive gambler would run counter to New Jersey's Casino Control Act, or against the common law, and therefore the checks are invalid. N.J.S.A. § 5:12–1 *et seq* (1998). Nothing in the New Jersey Casino Control Act, however, specifically prohibits the cashing and redemption of checks made by "compulsive gamblers."

With regard to Seigel's common law argument, it appears to be true that intoxication, duress, and unconscionability may, in certain circumstances, be valid defenses to the enforcement of gambling contracts in New Jersey. However, compulsive gambling, in and of itself, is not a defense to a contract action in new Jersey. Rather, the facts of a particular transaction may reveal "some overreaching or imposition resulting from a bargaining disparity between the parties, or such patent unfairness in the contract that no reasonable person not acting under compulsion or out of necessity would accept its terms." The question, therefore, is whether Seigel has set forth adequate facts to raise a genuine issue regarding the enforceability of the checks in light of his alleged compulsion and duress flowing from that disorder.

The entirety of Seigel's duress argument emanates from a single sentence in his affidavit: "For years I have had [a] gambling problem." If not ambiguous, the statement is conclusory. Unlike the gambler in *Lomonaco v. Sands Hotel Casino*, Seigel fails to produce any evidence in the record, specific or otherwise, regarding his problem and its relation to any unconscionable duress in the transactions at issue. In *Lomonaco,* the gambler described an abusive and bizarre "marathon gambling session" that included unsolicited credit increases from the casino, the existence of an alleged psychological disorder, and the gambler's concomitant use of pain killers, during which he lost $285,000 in little over two days. The record—even when viewed in the light most favorable to Seigel on whom the burden of proof rests—simply does not present a genuine disputed issue of fact as to whether the contracts evidenced by the checks were made under duress, and therefore unenforceable. We therefore conclude that Seigel's assertion that the checks would be unenforceable in New Jersey fails.

Seigel also invokes the fact that these checks were given in order to obtain chips with which to gamble, and cites us in particular to D.C. Code § 16–1701(a) (1997 Repl.). Modeled after the English "Statute of Anne," 9 Anne, 14, § 1 (1710), that section provides that:

A thing in action, judgment, mortgage, or other security or conveyance made and executed by a person in which any part of the consideration is for money or other valuable things won by playing at any game whatsoever, or by betting on the sides or hands of persons who play, or for the reimbursement or payment of any money knowingly lent or advanced for the purpose, or lent or advanced at the time and place of the play or bet, to a person so playing or betting or who, during the play, so plays or bets, is void.

In substance, Seigel claims that this statute would serve as a defense if the casinos were to seek to enforce the checks in the first instance in a District of Columbia court, and therefore this same statute requires that he be entitled to affirmatively recover from Merrill Lynch the amount of the checks in a District of Columbia court, regardless of the checks' enforceability elsewhere.

We may assume for present purposes that this statute would prevent direct enforcement of the checks in the District of Columbia, a somewhat dubious proposition in itself given the validity of the checks where made. But that is not this case. Rather, the question is whether under the relevant provisions of the Uniform Commercial Code, Seigel has met his burden of proof to establish actual loss. We think he has not.

As already indicated, even if payment had been stopped, the casinos could have enforced the checks in New Jersey, where the transaction was entered into. Merrill Lynch therefore, under the Code scheme, conceptually has the same right. Furthermore, even if there were a problem in asserting jurisdiction over Seigel in New Jersey, Maryland would have provided an appropriate forum for enforcing the checks. The highest Maryland court has squarely held that because there is no longer a strong public policy against gambling per se, but only against illegal gambling, the doctrine of *lex loci contractus* prevails in full, and that therefore Maryland courts will enforce gambling debts if legally incurred in a foreign jurisdiction. Accordingly, the casinos, and hence derivatively Merrill Lynch, could enforce the checks directly against Seigel in the state of his residence—Maryland.

We conclude that Seigel failed to establish that he ultimately suffered any actual loss as a result of the payment of the checks by Merrill Lynch.

Judgment for Merrill Lynch affirmed.

ETHICS IN ACTION

What Is the Ethical Thing to Do?

Suppose you take your car to a body shop to have it repainted. When you go to pick it up, you are not happy with the quality of the work, but the body shop refuses to release the car to you unless you pay in full for the work. You give the shop a check in the amount requested, and on your way home you stop at your bank and request that the bank stop payment on the check you have just written, an action you decided to take when you were writing the check. Have you acted ethically?

Certified Check

Normally, a drawee bank is not obligated to certify a check. When a drawee bank does certify a check, it substitutes its undertaking (promise) to pay the check for the drawer's undertaking and becomes obligated to pay the check. At the time the bank certifies a check, the bank usually debits the customer's account for the amount of the certified check and shifts the money to a special account at the bank. It also adds its signature to the check

Figure 2   *Certified Check*

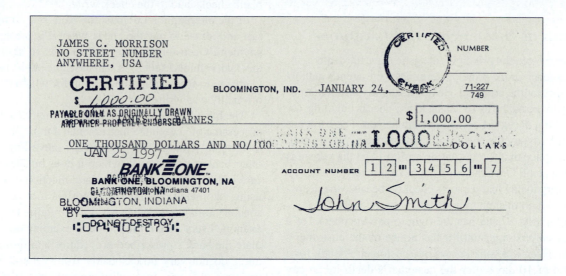

Figure 3   *Cashier's Check*

to show that it has accepted primary liability for paying it. The bank's signature is an essential part of the certification: the bank's signature must appear on the check [3–409]. If the holder of a check chooses to have it certified, rather than seeking to have it paid at that time, the holder has made a conscious decision to look to the certifying bank for payment and no longer may rely on the drawer or the indorsers to pay it. See Figure 2 for an example of a certified check.

If the drawee bank certifies a check, then the drawer and any persons who previously indorsed the check are discharged of their liability on the check [3–414(c); 3–415(d)].

Cashier's Check

A cashier's check differs from a certified check. A check on which a bank is both the drawer and the drawee is a cashier's check. The bank is primarily liable on the cashier's check. See Figure 3 for an example of a cashier's check. A teller's check is similar to a cashier's check. It is a check on which one bank is the drawer and another bank is the drawee. An example of a teller's check is a check drawn by a credit union on its account at a bank.

Death or Incompetence of Customer

Under the general principles of agency law, the death or incompetence of the principal terminates the agent's authority to act for the principal. However, slightly different rules apply to the authority of a bank to pay checks out of the account of a deceased or incompetent person. The bank has the right to pay the checks of an incompetent person until it has notice that a court has determined that the person is incompetent. Once the bank learns of this fact, it loses its authority to pay that person's checks—because the depositor is not competent to issue instructions to pay.

Similarly, a bank has the right to pay the checks of a deceased customer until it has notice of the customer's death. Even if a bank knows of a customer's death, for a period of 10 days after the customer's death it can pay checks written by the customer prior to his death. However, the deceased person's heirs or other persons claiming an interest in the account can order the bank to stop payment [4–405].

Forged and Altered Checks

Bank's Right to Charge Account

A check that bears a forged signature of the drawer or payee is generally not properly payable from the customer's account because the bank is not following the instructions of the depositor precisely as he gave them. The bank is expected to be familiar with the authorized signature of its depositor. If it pays such a check, Article 4 will treat the transaction as one in which the bank paid out its own funds, rather than the depositor's funds.

Similarly, a check that was altered after the drawer made it out—for example, by increasing the amount of the check—is generally not properly payable from the customer's account. However, as noted earlier, if the drawer is negligent and contributes to the forgery or alteration, he may be barred from claiming it as the reason that a particular check should not be charged to his account.

For example, Barton makes a check for $1 in a way that makes it possible for someone to easily alter it to read $101, and it is so altered. If the drawee bank pays the check to a holder in good faith, it can charge the $101 to Barton's account if Barton's negligence contributed to the alteration. Similarly, if a company uses a mechanical

check writer to write checks, it must use reasonable care to see that unauthorized persons do not have access to blank checks and to the check writer.

If the alteration is obvious, the bank should note that fact and refuse to pay the check when it is presented for payment. Occasionally, the alteration is so skillful that the bank cannot detect it. In that case, the bank is allowed to charge to the account the amount for which the check originally was written.

The bank has a duty to exercise "ordinary care" in the processing of negotiable instruments; it must observe the reasonable commercial standards prevailing among other banks in the area in which it does business. In the case of banks that take checks for collection or payment using automated means, it is important to note that reasonable commercial standards do not require the bank to examine every item *if* the failure to examine does not violate the bank's prescribed procedures and those procedures do not vary unreasonably from general banking practice or are not disapproved by the Code [3–107(a)(7); 4–103(c)]. For example, the bank's practice may be to examine those checks for more than $1,000 and a sample of smaller checks. Thus, if it did not examine a particular check in the amount of $250 for evidence of alteration or forgery, its action would be commercially reasonable so long as (1) it followed its own protocol, (2) that protocol was not a great variance from general banking usage, and (3) the procedure followed was not specifically disallowed in the Code.

In a case where both a bank and its customer fail to use ordinary care, a comparative negligence standard is used [4–406(e)].

Customer's Duty to Report Forgeries and Alterations

A bank must send a monthly (or quarterly) statement listing the transactions in an account, and it commonly returns the canceled checks to the customer. Revised Article 3 recognizes the modern bank practice of truncating (or retaining) checks and permits the bank to supply only a statement showing the item number, amount, and date of payment [4–406(a)]. When the bank does not return the paid items to the customer, the bank must either retain the items or maintain the capacity to furnish legible copies of the items for seven years after their receipt. The customer may request an item and the bank has a reasonable time to provide either the item or a legible copy of it [4–406(b)].

If the bank sends or makes available a statement of account or items, the customer must exercise reasonable promptness to examine the statement or items to determine whether payment was not authorized because of an alteration of any item or because a signature of the customer was not authorized. If, based on the statement or items provided, the customer should discover the unauthorized payment, the customer must notify the bank of the relevant facts promptly [4–406(c)].

These principles are illustrated in the *American Airlines Employees Federal Credit Union* case that follows.

American Airlines Employees Federal Credit Union v. Martin
29 S.W.3d 86 (Tex. Sup. Ct. 2000)

The American Airlines Employees Federal Credit Union is a federal credit union whose members are primarily employees of American Airlines and certain related entities, and their spouses and families. In 1990, Tim Martin, an American Airlines employee, opened a savings account (called a "share account") at the Credit Union. He completed and signed a Credit Union membership application, which provided that his account would be "subject to any and all rules, regulations, bylaws and policies of the Credit Union and its Board of Directors now in effect and as changed, amended or adopted hereafter." Thereafter, Martin received quarterly account statements.

In May 1994, the Credit Union adopted a Deposit Account Agreement, which contained the following paragraph:

1. Account Statements. You are responsible for promptly examining each account statement. Any objection that you may have respecting any item shown on a statement will be waived unless made in writing to us, and received on or before the sixtieth (60th) day following the date the statement is mailed, subject to applicable law. You agree that we will not be liable for any forged or altered item drawn on or deposited to your account if you fail to notify us within that sixty-day period . . . .

The Credit Union notified its members about this Deposit Agreement through its newsletter and account statements. As well, the Credit Union specifically noted on the account statements that any errors on the statement were to be reported to the Credit Union within sixty days.

On June 10, 1995, the Credit Union received a Membership Account Change Card in the mail, adding Molly Blair to Martin's account as a joint owner. Blair was Martin's girlfriend and also was a member of the Credit Union. She had recently added Martin's name to her own account. The change card contained a signature purporting to be Martin's. The Credit Union changed the ownership status of the account after verifying the personal and account information on the card and comparing Martin's purported signature on the change card to his original signature card. Martin's signature on the change card turned out to be a forgery.

Between June 12 and November 16 of 1995, Blair transferred a total of $49,800 from Martin's account to her own. She made fourteen transfers altogether—12 by telephone and two in person. To execute a telephone transfer, Blair would call the Credit Union and speak to a teller, who would verify Blair's identity by confirming certain personal and account information. The teller would complete the transaction by preparing and signing a "journal voucher" that identified the date of the transaction, the amount of the transfer, and the accounts involved. These journal vouchers were then mailed to Martin's address, on the day of the transaction or the next day. The Credit Union also prepared journal vouchers for those transfers that Blair requested in person; these vouchers were given to Blair directly.

In addition to the 12 journal vouchers, the Credit Union also mailed two quarterly statements to Martin during the period that Blair made her withdrawals. The first was mailed between July 8 and July 20, 1995, and the second was mailed between October 6 and October 18, 1995. These statements documented 10 of Blair's transfers (the other four being made after the period covered by the second statement). The first quarterly statement listed Blair as a joint owner of the account, and disclosed that she had made two withdrawals totaling $8,000. The second quarterly statement again listed Blair as a joint owner and revealed that she had made eight more withdrawals, totaling $36,500. Martin denies receiving these statements or the journal vouchers, although there is no dispute that they were mailed to the correct address. In any event, he did not contact the Credit Union to request either quarterly statement.

On December 20, 1995, Martin went to the Credit Union to make a deposit and discovered that the balance in his account was not what he expected it to be. He immediately notified the Credit Union of the discrepancy. Subsequently, Martin sued the Credit Union to recover the $49,800 transferred from his account. Among other things, he alleged breach of the Credit Union's duties to him under Articles 3 and 4 of the Uniform Commercial Code. The Credit Union defended principally on *the basis of section 4.406, which requires a bank customer to discover and report his unauthorized signature on an item within a year after the item and the account statement documenting the transaction are made available to the customer. The Credit Union further maintained that the Deposit Agreement reduced the one-year period set out in section 4–406(d) to 60 days, and that Martin had failed to notify it of the majority of Blair's unauthorized withdrawals within that time period.*

Following a bench trial, the trial court rendered judgment in Martin's favor for $49,800. The Credit Union appealed, and the court of appeals affirmed. The court of appeals agreed with the trial court that the 60-day notice provision in the Deposit Agreement was vague, ambiguous, and inconspicuous, and that Martin did not intentionally and knowingly relinquish the right to a year to give notice contained in section 4.406(d). The Credit Union appealed to the Texas Supreme Court.

ENOCH, Justice Article 4 of the UCC, of which section 4–406 is a part, establishes the rights and duties between banks and their customers regarding deposits and collections. Under Article 4's liability scheme, a bank is liable to its customer if it charges the customer's account for an item that is not properly payable from that account. An item with an unauthorized signature is not properly payable.

Section 4–406 specifies the customer's corresponding obligation concerning items with unauthorized signatures:

(a) When a bank sends to its customer a statement of account accompanied by items paid in good faith in support of the debit entries or . . . otherwise in a reasonable manner makes the statement and items available to the customer, the customer must exercise reasonable care and promptness to examine the statement and items to discover his unauthorized signature or any alteration on an item and must notify the bank promptly after discovery thereof.

Section 4–406 also provides the bank with certain defenses when the customer fails to comply with this obligation. The Credit Union here relied on two of these defenses. First, the customer cannot assert his unauthorized signature against the bank when one wrongdoer makes a series of unauthorized transactions on the same account if the customer fails to discover and report the first unauthorized transaction within 14 days. This defense is not available when the bank has failed to exercise ordinary care in paying the items.

Second, and the defense on which the Credit Union places the most emphasis, the customer is absolutely precluded from asserting his unauthorized signature on an item against the bank if the customer fails to discover and report the unauthorized signature within a year after the bank makes available the item and the account statement showing the transaction.

This statutory scheme reflects an underlying policy decision that furthers the UCC's objective of promoting certainty and predictability in commercial transactions. The UCC facilitates financial transactions, benefiting both consumers and financial institutions, by allocating responsibility among the parties according to whoever is best able to prevent a loss. Because the customer is more familiar with his own signature, and should know whether or not he authorized a particular withdrawal or check, he can prevent further unauthorized activity better than a financial institution, which may process thousands of transactions in a single day. Section 4–406 acknowledges that the customer is best situated to detect unauthorized transactions on his own account by placing the burden on the customer to exercise reasonable care to discover and report such transactions. The customer's duty to exercise this care is triggered when the bank satisfies its burden to provide sufficient information to the customer. As a result, if the bank provides sufficient information, the customer bears the loss when he fails to detect and notify the bank about unauthorized transactions.

Section 4–103(a) permits parties to vary the effect of Article 4's provisions by agreement, as long as that agreement does not "disclaim a bank's responsibility for its own lack of good faith or failure to exercise ordinary care," or "limit the measure of damages for such lack or failure." The comments to this section note that it "confers blanket power to vary all provisions of the Article by agreements of the ordinary kind. . . . In the absence of a showing that the standards manifestly are unreasonable, the agreement controls."

When he opened his account at the Credit Union, Martin signed the Credit Union membership application, which as noted above, contained the statement, "I . . . agree that this account and all agreements pertaining thereto are subject to any and all rules, regulations, bylaws and policies of the Credit Union and its Board of Directors now in effect and as changed, amended or adopted hereafter." Such signature cards establish a contract between banking institution and customer, regardless of whether the customer reads all the provisions to which he is agreeing. In May 1994, the Credit Union adopted the Deposit Agreement containing the sixty-day notice provision, notified all its members including Martin, made the agreement available, although Martin did not attempt to obtain a copy at the time, and sent account statements specifying the critical 60-day time frame. Thereafter,

Martin continued to maintain his account at the Credit Union. These actions are, as a matter of law, sufficient to demonstrate that the parties agreed to be bound by the terms of the Deposit Agreement. Consequently, the 60-day notice provision in the Deposit Agreement is enforceable.

We hold that section 4–406 of the Business and Commerce Code places a duty on bank customers to discover and report account irregularities. We further hold that the

one-year notice period of section 4–406(d) can be modified by agreement, and that the Credit Union and Martin entered into an enforceable agreement to reduce the notice period to 60 days. Martin failed to notify the bank within 60 days as to 10 of Blair's 14 withdrawals.

Judgment in part for Credit Union.

Multiple Forgeries or Alterations Revised Article 3 provides a special rule to govern the situation in which the same wrongdoer makes a series of unauthorized drawer's signatures or alterations. The customer generally cannot hold the bank responsible for paying, in good faith, any such checks after the statement of account or item that contained the first unauthorized customer's signature or an alteration was available to the customer for a reasonable period, not exceeding 30 calendar days. This rule holds (1) if the customer did not notify the bank of the unauthorized signature or alteration, and (2) the bank proves it suffered a loss because of the customer's failure to examine his statement and notify the bank [4–406(d)]. Unless the customer has notified the bank about the forgeries or alterations that he should have discovered by reviewing the statement or item, the customer generally bears responsibility for any subsequent forgeries or alterations by the same wrongdoer.

Suppose that Allen employs Farnum as an accountant and that over a period of three months, Farnum forges Allen's signature to 10 checks and cashes them. One of the forged checks is included in the checks returned to Allen at the end of the first month. Within 30 calendar days after the return of these checks, Farnum forges two more checks and cashes them. Allen does not examine the returned checks until three months after the checks that included the first forged check were returned to her. The bank would be responsible for the first forged check and for the two checks forged and cashed within the 30-day period after it sent the first statement and the canceled checks (unless the bank proves that it suffered a loss because of the customer's failure to examine the checks and notify it more promptly). It would not be liable for the seven forged checks cashed after the expiration of the 30-day period.

Regardless of which party may have been negligent, a customer must discover and report to the bank any unau-

thorized customer's signature or any alteration within one year from the time after the statement or items are made available to him. If the customer does not do so, he cannot require the bank to recredit his account for such items. [4–406(f)].

Check Collection and Funds Availability

Check Collection

As Chapter 31, Negotiable Instruments, describes, checks and other drafts collected through the banking system usually have at least three parties—the drawer, the drawee bank, and the payee. If the payee deposits the check at the same bank as the drawee bank, the latter will take a series of steps necessary to reflect the deposit as a credit to the payee's account and to decide whether to pay the check from the drawer's account. In connection with its handling of the deposit for the payee's benefit, it will make one ledger entry showing the deposit as a credit to the payee's account. In connection with its decision to pay, the bank's employees and computers will perform several steps commonly referred to as the process of posting. Original Article 4 contained special rules describing the process of posting and the legal effect. The amendments to Article 4 deleted these special rules because automated check processing limited the legal significance of particular acts in posting [4–109, 4–213(a), and 4–303(a)]. These steps need not be taken in any particular order, but they customarily include determining whether there are sufficient funds to pay, debiting the drawer's account for the amount of the check, and placing the check into a folder for later return to the drawer (to satisfy its obligations under the "bank statement" rule) [4–406]. Banks in those states that have not enacted the amendments to Article 4 will also compare the drawer's signature on the check with that on the deposit agreement as part of this process.

If the payee deposits the check at a bank other than the drawee bank, the depositary bank, acting as the agent of the payee, will make the ledger entry showing the deposit as a credit to the payee's account. The next step of the collection process depends on where the depositary bank is located. If the drawee and depositary banks are in the same town or county, the depositary bank will indorse the check and deliver (present) it to the drawee bank for payment. It may deliver it by courier or through a local association of banks known as a "clearing house" [4–104(1)(d)]. Under Article 4, the drawee-payor bank must settle for the check before midnight of the banking day of its receipt of the check, which means that it must give the depositary bank funds or a credit equal to the amount of the check. Once it settles for the check, the drawee-payor bank has until midnight of the banking day after the banking day of receipt to pay the check or to return the check or send notice of dishonor. This deadline for the drawee-payor bank's action on the check is known as the bank's "midnight deadline" [4–104(1)(h)]. The drawee-payor bank's failure to settle by midnight of the banking day of receipt, or its failure to pay or return the check, or send notice of dishonor, results in the drawee-payor bank's becoming "accountable" for the amount of the check, which means it must pay the amount of the check [4–302(a)].

If the drawee and depositary banks are located in different counties, or in different states, the depositary bank will use an additional commercial bank, and one or more of the regional Federal Reserve Banks, in the collection of the check. In these cases, the depositary bank will send the check on to the drawee-payor bank through these "collecting banks." Each bank in the sequence must use ordinary care in presenting the check or sending it for presentment, and in sending notice of dishonor or returning the check after learning that the check has not been paid [4–202(a)]. The depositary and collecting banks have until their respective midnight deadlines—or, in some cases, a further reasonable time—to take the action required of them in the sequence of collection steps.

If the drawee-payor bank dishonors the check prior to its midnight deadline or shortly after the midnight deadline under circumstances specified in "Regulation CC" of the Federal Reserve Board (described in the next section of this chapter), it will send the check back to the depositary bank. Until September 1, 1988, the drawee-payor bank customarily sent the dishonored check back

to the collecting bank from which it received the check, and the collecting bank sent it back to the bank from which it had received it, and through any other bank that handled the check in the "forward collection" process until the check again reached the depositary bank. The provisions of Article 4 still describe this sequence as the "return collection" process, although Regulation CC imposes new responsibilities on the payor bank and on any other "returning bank." Each bank in the return sequence adjusts its accounts to reflect the return and has until its midnight deadline to send the check back to the bank from which it originally had received the check. After September 1, 1988 (or in states that previously had adopted "direct return" [Original 4–212(b)], the drawee-payor bank may return the check directly to the depositary bank—skipping all of the collecting banks and the delay represented by the midnight deadlines that each bank otherwise would have had.

Direct return also increases the likelihood that the depositary bank will know whether the check has been dishonored by the day on which Regulation CC requires the depositary bank to allow the payee to write checks or otherwise make withdrawals against the deposit. The next section of this chapter discusses this aspect of Regulation CC in more detail.

On receipt of the dishonored check, the depositary bank will return the check or otherwise notify its depositor (the payee) of the dishonor and will debit or charge back her account for the check it did not collect. The depositary bank may charge back the deposit even if it previously had allowed the payee-depositor to withdraw against the credit given for the deposit.

When the depositor receives the notice of dishonor and returned check it will take one of several steps, depending on whether it received the check directly from the drawer or took it by indorsement from another person. If the depositor was not the original payee of the check, it usually will prefer to return the check—giving notice of dishonor unless already given by the drawee bank or another collecting bank—to the person who negotiated the check to her, the prior indorser. Recall that an indorser is obligated to pay the check following dishonor and notice of dishonor [3–415].

If the depositor received the check directly from the drawer, for example as payee, the depositor normally will demand payment from the drawer. Recall that the drawer is obligated to pay the check upon dishonor [3–414]; alternatively, the payee may seek to enforce the underlying obligation for which the drawer originally issued the check, such as the purchase of groceries or an automobile.

Funds Availability

When a bank takes a check for deposit to a customer's account, it typically places a hold on the funds represented by the deposited check because it runs a number of risks in allowing a customer to withdraw deposits that it has not collected from the drawee bank. The risks that the check may be returned include: (1) there may be insufficient funds in the drawer's account or the account may have been closed; (2) the check may contain a forged drawer's or indorser's signature, or there may have been a material alteration of the check; (3) the possibility that the drawer is kiting checks or playing two accounts off against each other; or (4) a stop-payment order may have been placed against the check. These are real concerns to a depositary bank, and it has a significant interest in protecting itself against these possibilities.

Until recently, the risks run by a depositary bank were complicated by a very slow process used by drawee-payor banks in returning a dishonored check or notifying the bank of the dishonor. Moreover, depositary banks did not get direct notice from drawee-payor banks when they paid checks. Accordingly, banks often restricted the depositor's use of the deposit by placing relatively long holds on checks deposited with them for collection; these sometimes ran 15 to 20 days for items drawn on other than local banks.

The extensive use of holds, and a growing public sentiment that they were excessive and often unfair, led to the passage by Congress in 1987 of the Expedited Funds Availability Act. In the act, Congress set out mandatory schedules limiting check holds and specifying when funds are to be made available to customers by depositary institutions. The act also delegated to the Federal Reserve Board the authority to speed up the check-processing system. The regulations adopted by the Board to speed up check processing supersede the provisions of Article 4 of the UCC (Bank Deposits and Collections) in a number of respects but will not be covered in this text.

The key elements of the mandatory funds availability schedules, which are set out in Federal Reserve Board Regulation CC, are:

1. Local checks (those drawn on banks in the same Federal Reserve check region as the depositary bank) must be made available for the depositor to draw against by the second business day following deposit.

2. Nonlocal checks (those drawn on banks located in the United States but outside the Federal Reserve check processing region in which the depositary bank is located) must be made available by the fifth business day following deposit.

3. Certain items must be made available by the next day after the day of deposit. These include:

    a. Cash deposits where the deposit is made in person to an employee of the depositary bank (i.e., not at an ATM).

    b. Electronic payments.

    c. Checks drawn on the U.S. Treasury.

    d. U.S. Postal Service money orders.

    e. Checks drawn on a Federal Reserve Bank or Federal Home Loan Bank.

    f. Checks drawn by a state or a unit of local government (under certain conditions).

    g. Cashier's, certified, or teller's checks.

    h. Checks drawn on the depositary bank.

    i. The lesser of $100 or the aggregate deposit on any one banking day.

4. If the next-day items are not deposited in person with an employee of the depositary institution but rather are deposited in an ATM machine or by mail, then the deposit does not have to be made available for withdrawal until the second business day after deposit.

5. Generally, the depositary bank must begin accruing interest to a depositor's interest-bearing account from the day it receives credit for cash and check deposits to an interest-bearing account.

There are six major exceptions to the mandatory availability schedules set out above that are designed to safeguard depositary banks against higher risk situations. The exceptions are:

1. *New account exception.* The depositary bank may suspend the availability rules for new accounts and can limit the next-day and second-day availability to the first $5,000 deposited.

2. *Large deposit exception.* The hold periods can be extended to the extent the aggregate deposit on any banking day exceeds $5,000.

3. *Redeposited check exception.* The hold period can be extended where a check has been returned one or more times.

4. *Repeated overdraft exception.* A longer hold period may be required for deposits to accounts that have been overdrawn repeatedly.

5. *Reasonable cause exception.* The scheduled availability may be extended where the bank has reasonable cause to believe the check is uncollectible.

6. *Emergency conditions exception.* The scheduled availability may be extended under certain emergency conditions such as a communications interruption or a computer failure.

Banks are required to disclose their funds availability policy to all of their customers; they may provide different policies to different classes or categories of customers.

Electronic Banking

With the development of computer technology, many banks are encouraging their customers to transfer funds electronically by using computers rather than paper drafts and checks. A bank customer may use a specially coded card at terminals provided by the bank to make deposits to an account, to transfer money from one checking or savings account to another, to pay bills, or to withdraw cash from an account. These new forms of transferring money have raised questions about the legal rules that apply to them, and the questions are only beginning to be resolved.

Electronic Funds Transfer Act

The consumer who used electronic funds transfer systems (EFTs), the so-called cash machines or electronic tellers, in the early years often experienced problems in identifying and resolving mechanical errors resulting from malfunctioning EFTs. In response to these problems, Congress passed the Electronic Funds Transfer Act in 1978 to provide "a basic framework, establishing the rights, liabilities, and responsibilities of participants in electronic funds transfer systems" and especially to provide "individual consumer rights."

The four basic EFT systems are: (1) automated teller machines; (2) point-of-sale terminals, which allow consumers to use their EFT cards like checks at retail establishments; (3) preauthorized payments, such as automatic paycheck deposits or mortgage or utility payments; and (4) telephone transfers between accounts or to pay specific bills by phone.

Similar to the Truth in Lending Act and the Fair Credit Billing Act (FCBA) discussed in Chapter 47, the EFT Act requires disclosure of the terms and conditions of electronic fund transfers at the time the consumer contracts for the EFT service. Among the nine disclosures required are the following: the consumer's liability for unauthorized electronic fund transfers (those resulting from loss or theft), the nature of the EFT services under the consumer's account, any pertinent dollar or frequency limitations, any charges for the right to make EFTs, the consumer's right to stop payment of a preauthorized transfer, the financial institution's liability to the consumer for failure to make or stop payments, and the consumer's right to receive documentation of transfers both at the point or time of transfer and periodically. The act also requires 21 days' notice prior to the effective date of any change in the terms or conditions of the consumer's account that pertains to the required disclosures.

The EFT Act does differ from the Fair Credit Billing Act in a number of important respects. For example, under the EFT Act, the operators of EFT systems have a maximum of 10 working days to investigate errors or provisionally recredit the consumer's account, whereas issuers of credit cards have a maximum of 60 days under the FCBA. The liability of the consumer also is different if an EFT card is lost or stolen than it is if a credit card is lost or stolen.

The *Kruser* case illustrates the application of the EFT Act's provisions that require a customer to provide timely notification of any unauthorized use of his card in order to limit his liability for the unauthorized use of the card.

Kruser v. Bank of America NT & SA   *281 Cal. Rptr. 463 (Cal. Ct. App. 1991)*

Lawrence and Georgene Kruser maintained a joint checking account with the Bank of America. The bank issued each of them a "Versatel" card and separate personal identification numbers that would allow access to funds in their account from automatic teller machines. The Krusers also received with their cards a "Disclosure Booklet" that provided to the Krusers a summary of consumer liability, the bank's business hours, and the address and telephone number by which they could notify the bank in the event they believed an unauthorized transfer had been made.

The Krusers believed Mr. Kruser's card had been destroyed in September 1986. The December 1986 account statement mailed to the Krusers by the bank reflected a $20 unauthorized withdrawal of funds by someone using Mr. Kruser's card at an automatic teller machine. The Krusers reported this unauthorized transaction to the bank when they discovered it in August or September 1987.

Mrs. Kruser underwent surgery in late 1986 or early 1987 and remained hospitalized for 11 days. She then spent a period of six or seven months recuperating at home. During this time, she reviewed the statements the Krusers received from the bank.

In September 1987, the Krusers received bank statements for July and August 1987 that reflected 47 unauthorized withdrawals totaling $9,020 made from an automatic teller machine, again by someone using Mr. Kruser's card. They notified the bank of these withdrawals within a few days of receiving the statements. The bank refused to credit the Kruser's account with the amount of the unauthorized withdrawals. The Krusers sued the bank claiming damages for the unauthorized withdrawals from their account. The trial court ruled in favor of the bank on the grounds that the Krusers had failed to comply with the note and reporting requirements of the Electronic Funds Transfer Act (EFTA). The Krusers appealed.

Stone, Associate Justice The ultimate issue we address is whether, as a matter of law, the unauthorized $20 withdrawal which appeared on the December 1986 statement barred the Krusers from recovery for the losses incurred in July and August 1987. Resolution of the issue requires the interpretation of the EFTA and section 205.6 of Regulation E, one of the regulations prescribed by the Board of Governors of the Federal Reserve System in order to carry out the EFTA.

Section 205.6 of Regulation E mirrors [the EFTA] and in particular provides:

(b) Limitations on the amount of liability. The amount of a consumer's liability for an unauthorized electronic fund transfer or a series of related unauthorized transfers shall not exceed $50 or the amount of unauthorized transfers that occur before notice to the financial institution . . . whichever is less, unless one of the following exceptions apply:

* * * * *

(2) If the consumer fails to report within 60 days of transmittal of the periodic statement any unauthorized electronic fund transfer that appears on the statement, the consumer's liability shall not exceed the sum of (i) The lesser of $50 or the amount of unauthorized electronic fund transfers that appear on the periodic statement during the 60-day period and (ii) The amount of unauthorized electronic fund transfers that occur after the close of the 60 days and before notice to the financial institution and that the financial institution establishes would not have occurred but for the failure of the consumer to notify the financial institution within that time.

* * * * *

(4) If a delay in notifying the financial statements was due to extenuating circumstances, such as extended travel or hospitalization, the time periods specified above shall be extended to a reasonable time.

The trial court concluded the Bank was entitled to judgment as a matter of law because the unauthorized withdrawals of July and August 1987 occurred more than 60 days after the Krusers received a statement which reflected an unauthorized transfer in December 1986. The court relied upon section 205.6(b)(2) of Regulation E.

The Krusers contend the December withdrawal of $20 was so isolated in time and minimal in an amount that it cannot be considered in connection with the July and August withdrawals. They assert the court's interpretation of section 205.6(b)(2) of Regulation E would have absurd results which would be inconsistent with the primary objective of the EFTA—to protect the consumer. They argue that if a consumer receives a bank statement which reflects an unauthorized minimal electronic transfer and fails to report the transaction to the bank within 60 days of transmission of the bank statement, unauthorized transfers many years later, perhaps totaling thousands of dollars, would remain the responsibility of the consumer.

The result the Krusers fear is avoided by the requirement that the bank establish the subsequent unauthorized transfers could have been prevented had the consumer notified the bank of the first unauthorized transfer. Here, although the unauthorized transfer of $20 occurred approximately seven months before the unauthorized transfers totaling $9,020, it is undisputed that all transfers were made by using Mr. Kruser's card which the Krusers believed had been destroyed prior to December 1986. According to the declaration of Yvonne Maloon, the Bank's Versatel risk manager, the Bank could have and would have canceled Mr. Kruser's card had it been timely notified of the December unauthorized transfer. In that event Mr. Kruser's card could not have been used to accomplish the unauthorized transactions in July and August.

In the alternative, the Krusers contend the facts establish that Mrs. Kruser, who was solely responsible for reconciling the bank statements, was severely ill and was also caring for a terminally ill relative when the December withdrawal occurred. Therefore they claim they were entitled to an extension of time within which to notify the bank.

The evidence the Krusers rely upon indicates in late 1986 or early 1987 Mrs. Kruser underwent surgery and remained in the hospital for 11 days. She left her house infrequently during the first six or seven months of 1987 during which she was recuperating. Mrs. Kruser admits, however, she received and reviewed bank statements during her recuperation. Therefore, we need not consider whether Mrs. Kruser's illness created circumstances which might have excused her failure to notice the unauthorized withdrawal pursuant to the applicable sections. She in fact did review the statements in question.

Judgment for Bank of America affirmed.

CYBERLAW IN ACTION

E-Checks

Chapter 31—Negotiable Instruments—notes that the process known as "check conversion" is utilized by a number of large retailers. The process begins with the buyer giving the seller a paper check. The seller uses special equipment to gather information from the paper check; this information includes the buyer's bank account number, the bank routing number, and the serial number of the check. The retailer then names itself as the payee, codes in the amount of the purchase, and forwards it for collection through an automated clearing house (ACH) transaction instead of the collection route for paper checks.

The Federal Reserve Board recently decided that the Electronic Funds Transfer Act (EFTA) and Regulation E would govern "check conversion" transactions. The EFTA will govern even if the consumer gives a blank and unsigned check to the merchant. The Act also governs if the merchant uses a paper check as a "source document" (source of critical account- and bank-related information) and then uses an electronic fund transfer rather than the ACH transfer mentioned above.

Problems and Problem Cases

1. Skov sold fish to hotels and restaurants. He acquired his fish under an agreement whereby the supplier stored the fish that Skov had purchased for future delivery and no payment was made until such delivery. Following delivery of one shipment, Skov gave his supplier a check drawn on First National Bank. The bank erroneously refused to honor the check and the supplier canceled the agreement. Can Skov recover damages from the bank for the loss of this agreement?

2. Louise Kalbe drew a check in the amount of $7,260 payable to the "order of cash" on her account at the Pulaski State Bank. The check was lost or stolen but Kalbe did not report this to the bank nor did she attempt to stop payment on it. When the check was received by the Pulaski State Bank, Kalbe had only about $700 in her checking account. However, the bank paid the check, creating an overdraft in her account of $6,542.12. The bank then sued Kalbe to recover the amount of the overdraft. Kalbe asserted that the check was not properly payable from her account. Was the bank legally entitled to pay a check that exceeded the balance in the drawer's account and to recover the overdraft from the drawer?

3. J. E. B. Stewart received a check in the amount of $185.48 in payment of a fee from a client. Stewart presented the check, properly indorsed, to the Citizen's & Southern Bank. The bank refused to cash the check even though there were sufficient funds in the drawer's account. Stewart then sued the bank for actual damages of $185.48 for its failure to cash a valid check drawn against a solvent account in the bank. Does Stewart have a good cause of action against the bank?

4. Dr. Sherrill purchased a Buick Skylark from Frank Morris Buick. He gave the auto dealer a check for $4,960.61 drawn on his account at First Alabama Bank. The check was dated "2/6/1976," was payable "to the order of Frank Morris Buick," and was not numbered. After buying the Skylark, Sherrill became concerned about whether he had gotten valid title to it. The day after he gave the dealer the check, he called in an oral stop-payment order on it. He later confirmed the stop-payment order in writing. In the stop-payment order, Sherrill stated that the check was not numbered, was payable to "Walter Morris Buick," was date "6/3/76," and was in the amount of $4,960.61. The bank paid the check when it was presented for payment. Sherrill then claimed that the bank should recredit his account for $4,960.61 because it paid the check over a valid stop-payment order. Did the stop-payment order describe the check accurately enough to constitute a valid stop-payment order?

5. Brenda Jones, who did business as Country Kitchen, purchased some cookware from an itinerant salesman, giving him a check in the amount of $200 for the purchase price. The salesman cashed the check at the First National Bank before noon on May 22 the day of the sale. Jones later became concerned about the lack of documentation from the salesman, thinking that the cookware might be stolen, and placed a stop-payment order with her bank, the State Bank of Conway Springs, at 3:30 that afternoon. State Bank refused to honor the check when it was presented for payment through banking channels. First National Bank claiming to be a holder in due course, then brought suit against Jones to recover the $200 value of the check. Is the drawer of a check on which a stop-payment order was placed and honored by the bank liable to pay the check to a holder in due course?

6. John Doe had a checking account at Highland National Bank in New York. Two days after John Doe died in Florida, but before Highland National knew of his death, John's sister appeared at the bank. She had a check signed by John Doe but with the amount and name of the payee left blank. She told the bank that her brother wanted to close his account. She asked how much was in the account, filled the check in for that amount, and made the check payable to herself. The bank checked her identification and verified the signature of John Doe. Then it paid the check to the sister. The executor of John Doe's estate sued Highland National Bank to recover the amount of money that was in John's account on the day he died. The executor claimed that the bank had no authority to pay checks from John Doe's account after his death. May a bank pay checks drawn on the account of a deceased customer?

7. In December, Whalley Company hired Nancy Cherauka as its bookkeeper. Her duties included preparing checks, taking deposits to the bank, and reconciling the monthly checking account statements. She was not authorized to sign or cash checks. Between the following January 24 and May 31, Cherauka forged 49 checks on the Whalley account at National City Bank. Each month, National City Bank sent Whalley a statement and the canceled checks (including the forgeries) it had paid the previous month. The president of Whalley looked at the statement to see the balance in the account but he did not look at the individual checks. Then he gave the statement and checks to the bookkeeper. The January 24 forged check was sent to Whalley on February 3. In June, Whalley discovered that Cherauka was forging checks and fired her. It then brought a lawsuit against National City Bank to force it to recredit Whalley's account with the total

amount of the 49 checks. Whalley claimed that the checks were not properly payable from the account. Is National City required to recredit Whalley's account?

8. On August 16, Frederick Ognibene went to the ATM area at a Citibank branch and activated one of the machines with his Citibank card, provided his personal identification code, and withdrew $20. When he approached the machine a person was using the customer service telephone located between two ATM machines and appeared to be telling customer service that one of the machines was malfunctioning. As Ognibene was making his withdrawal, the person said into the telephone, "I'll see if his card works in my machine." He then asked Ognibene if he could use his card to see if the other machine was working. Ognibene handed his card to him and saw him insert it into the adjoining machine at least two times while saying into the telephone, "Yes, it seems to be working." When Ognibene received his Citibank statement, it showed that two withdrawals of $200 each from his account were made at 5:42 P.M. and 5:43 P.M., respectively, on August 16. His own $20 withdrawal was made at 5:41 P.M. At the time, Ognibene was unaware that any withdrawals from his account were being made from the adjoining machine. Ognibene sought to have his account recredited for $400, claiming that the withdrawals had been unauthorized. Citibank had been aware for some time of a scam being perpetrated against its customers by persons who observed the customer inserting his personal identification number into an ATM and then obtaining access to the customer's ATM card in the same manner as Ognibene's card was obtained. After learning about the scam, Citibank posted signs in ATM areas containing a red circle approximately 2 1/2 inches in diameter in which was written "Do Not Let Your Citicard Be Used For Any Transaction But Your Own." Was Citibank required under the Electronic Fund Transfer Act to recredit Ognibene's account on the grounds that the withdrawal of the $400 was unauthorized?

Online Research: How Does Your Bank Handle Stop Payment Orders

Use the Internet to locate the website for the bank or other financial institution where you maintain a checking account. Ascertain from the website what the bank's policy is concerning stopping payment on checks, including (1) the means by which the bank will accept a stop-payment order, (2) the information it requires, (3) the charge it imposes for entering a stop-payment order, and (4) any qualifications or limitations it makes to its responsibility to follow your instruction to stop payment.

AGENCY LAW

35

THE AGENCY RELATIONSHIP

Upon graduating from college, Rita Morales was hired as a software consultant by IPQ Company, a large computer manufacturing and services company. Rita negotiated a high salary and even a nice signing bonus, yet after a few years of work she found that her spending often outstripped her earnings and savings. As her credit card bills piled up, Rita started her own consulting firm. Initially, Rita provided software consulting for her clients only on nights and weekends after she had finished her IPQ work for the day. As her business grew, she began seeing clients during normal weekday working hours and calling them from her office at IPQ. To find new clients, Rita downloaded IPQ's client information from IPQ's database. She contacted over 200 IPQ clients and asked them to switch from IPQ to Rita's business. Over two dozen IPQ clients switched to Rita.

- Do you see any potential problems with Rita's actions?
- What legally and practically can IPQ do to prevent Rita from taking its clients?

OFTEN, BUSINESSES ARE LEGALLY bound by the actions of their employees or other representatives. For example, corporations frequently are liable on contracts their employees make or for torts their employees commit. We take such liability for granted, but why should we? A corporation is an artificial legal person distinct from the officers, employees, and other representatives who contract on its behalf and who may commit torts while on the job. Similarly, a sole proprietor is distinct from the people he may employ. How can these and other business actors be bound on contracts they did not make or for torts they did not commit? The reason is the law of **agency.**

Agency is a two-party relationship in which one party (the **agent**) is authorized to act on behalf of, and under the control of, the other party (the **principal**). Examples include hiring a salesperson to sell goods, retaining an attorney, and engaging a real estate broker to sell a house. Agency law's most important social function has been to stimulate commercial activity. It does so by enabling businesses to increase the number of transactions they can complete within a given time. Without agency, for instance, a sole proprietor's ability to engage in trade would be limited by the need to make each of her purchase or sale contracts in person. As artificial persons, moreover, corporations can act only through their agents.

Agency law divides into two rough categories. The first involves legal relations between the principal and the agent. These include the rules governing formation of an agency, the duties the principal and the agent owe each other, and the ways an agency can be terminated. These topics are the main concern of this chapter. Chapter 36 discusses the principal's and the agent's relations with third parties. Here, our main concerns are the principal's and the agent's liability on contracts the agent makes and for torts the agent commits.

Creation of an Agency and Related Subjects

Formation

An agency is created by the manifested agreement of two parties that one party (the agent) will act for the benefit of the other (the principal) under the principal's direction. As the term *manifested* suggests, the test for an agency's existence is *objective*. If the parties' behavior and the surrounding facts and circumstances indicate an agreement that one person is to act for the benefit and under the control of another, the relationship exists. The *Euclid Plaza* case later in this chapter is an application of the agency definition.

If the facts establish an agency, neither party need know about the agency's existence or subjectively desire that it exist. In fact, an agency may be present even where the parties expressly say that they do not intend to create it, or intend to create some other legal relationship instead.

Often, parties create an agency by a written contract. But an agency contract may be oral unless state law provides otherwise. Some states, for example, require written evidence of contracts to pay an agent a commission for the sale of real estate. More important, the agency relation need not be contractual at all. Thus, consideration is not necessary to form an agency.

Capacity

A principal or agent who lacks the necessary mental capacity when the agency is formed ordinarily can release himself from the agency at his option. Examples include those who are minors or are mentally incapacitated when the agency is created. Of course, incapacity may occur at other times as well; we discuss such situations later in this chapter.

As you have seen, corporations can and must appoint agents. In a partnership, each partner normally acts as the agent of the partnership in transacting partnership business, and partnerships can appoint nonpartner agents as well. In addition, corporations, partnerships, and other business organizations themselves can act as agents.

Nondelegable Obligations

Certain duties or acts must be performed personally and cannot be delegated to an agent. Examples include making statements under oath, voting in public elections, and signing a will. The same is true for service contracts in which the principal's personal performance is crucial—for example, certain contracts by lawyers, doctors, artists, and entertainers.

Agency Concepts, Definitions, and Types

Agency law includes various concepts, definitions, and distinctions. These matters often determine the rights, duties, and liabilities of the principal, the agent, and third parties. In addition, they sometimes are important outside agency law. Because these basic topics are so cru-

cial in so many different situations, we outline them together here.

Authority

Although agency law lets people multiply their dealings by employing agents, a principal is not always liable for his agent's acts. Normally, an agent can bind his principal only when the agent has **authority** to do so. Authority is an agent's ability to affect his principal's legal relations. It comes in two main forms: **actual authority** and **apparent authority.** Each is based on the principal's manifested consent that the agent may act for and bind the principal. For actual authority this consent must be communicated to the *agent,* while for apparent authority it must be communicated to the *third party.*

Actual authority comes in two forms: **express authority** and **implied authority. Express authority** is created by the principal's *actual words* (whether written or oral). Thus, an agent has express authority to bind her principal in a certain fashion only when the principal has made a fairly precise statement to that effect.

However, it is often impractical for a principal to specify the agent's authority fully and exactly. To avoid unnecessarily restricting an agent's ability to represent her principal, agency law also gives agents **implied authority** to bind their principals. An agent generally has implied authority to do whatever it is reasonable to assume that the principal wanted him to do, given the principal's express statements and the surrounding circumstances. Relevant factors include the principal's express statements, the nature of the agency, the acts reasonably necessary to carry on the agency business, and the acts customarily done when conducting that business.

Sometimes an agent who lacks actual authority may still *appear* to have such authority, and third parties may reasonably rely on this appearance of authority. To protect third parties in such situations, agency law lets agents bind the principal on the basis of their apparent authority. **Apparent authority** arises when the principal's behavior causes a third party to believe reasonably that the agent is authorized to act in a certain way.

Apparent authority depends on what the principal communicates to the third party—either directly or through the agent. A principal might clothe an agent with apparent authority by making direct statements to the third party, telling an agent to do so, or allowing an agent to behave in a way that creates an appearance of authority. Communications to the agent are irrelevant unless they become known to the third party or affect the agent's behavior. Also, agents cannot give themselves apparent authority, and apparent authority does not exist where an agent creates an appearance of authority without the principal's consent. Finally, the third party must *reasonably* believe in the agent's authority. Trade customs and business practices can help courts determine whether such a belief was reasonable.

Authority is important in a number of agency contexts. Chapter 36 examines its most important agency application—determining a principal's liability on contracts made by his agent. The following *Euclid Plaza* case considers whether an agency exists by examining the alleged agent's actual and apparent authority to act for the purported principal.

Euclid Plaza Associates, L.L.C. v. African American Law Firm, L.L.C.
55 S.W.3d 446 (Mo. Ct. App. 2001)

Del-Mar Development Corp. failed to pay real property taxes on an office building it owned. The Collector of Revenue for the City of St. Louis sold the office building at a tax sale on July 14, 1998, to Euclid Plaza Associates, L.L.C. The sale was not effective until approved by a state court, which occurred on September 10.

Between the date of the tax sale in July and the court's approval of the sale in September, Del-Mar and African American Law Firm L.L.C. (Tenants) entered into a three-year lease to begin immediately with lease payments of $1,500 per month. During the interim between the sale and the court's confirmation of the sale, Del-Mar continued to collect rent from Tenants.

After the sale confirmation date, Euclid claimed that it was not bound on the lease made between Del-Mar and Tenants. Euclid was willing to continue leasing the building to Tenants, but only at the rate of $2,033 per month. When Tenants refused, Euclid brought an action to evict Tenants.

Tenants argued that Euclid was bound on the lease made by Del-Mar and Tenants, because Del-Mar was Euclid's agent acting within its actual and apparent authority. The trial court found no agency relationship and entered judgment for Euclid. Tenants appealed.

Russell, Judge The creation of an agency relationship requires the presence of three characteristics, and absent any one of them, no claim of agency exists. First, the agent possesses the power to alter legal relations between the principal and third persons and between the principal and himself. Second, the agent acts as a fiduciary regarding matters within the scope of the agency. Third, the principal has the right to control the agent's conduct with regard to matters entrusted to the agent. *Restatement (Second) of Agency* sections 12–14.

The nature of the agency relationship is consensual, and actual authority is created when the principal instructs the agent specifically how to act on the principal's behalf. We find no actual authority existed. There was no testimony that Euclid vested Del-Mar with any of its powers, that Euclid controlled Del-Mar's actions, or that Del-Mar acted on Euclid's behalf as a fiduciary or in any other respect. Further, there was no evidence that Euclid requested Del-Mar to act in any particular manner. Del-Mar, therefore, had no actual authority to execute the lease with Tenants on Euclid's behalf.

We also find that Del-Mar did not possess any apparent authority corollary to an agency relationship. Apparent authority is created when the principal acts in such a manner that a third party believes the agent is authorized to act on behalf of the principal. Apparent authority develops solely from acts of the alleged principal and not from acts of the purported agent. In order to claim the existence of apparent authority, the third party must act in reliance upon the belief that the agent possesses authority to act on the principal's behalf. Apparent authority cannot arise where a third party does not know the identity of the principal or where the third party is undisclosed.

There was no evidence that Tenants acted on the belief that Euclid was the principal party when signing the lease. The lease contained Del-Mar's name and the signatures of two of its representatives, and there was no mention of Euclid's name. Furthermore, Tenants' testimony indicates that they had no knowledge of Euclid's acquisition at the tax sale when they entered the lease with Del-Mar. We find the trial court was correct in finding that an agency relationship did not exist.

Judgment in favor of Euclid Plaza Associates affirmed.

General and Special Agents

Although it may be falling out of favor with courts, the blurred distinction between general agents and special agents still has some importance. A **general agent** is continuously employed to conduct a series of transactions, while a **special agent** is employed to conduct a single transaction or a small, simple group of transactions. Thus, a continuously employed general manager, construction project supervisor, or purchasing agent normally is a general agent; and a person employed to buy or sell a few objects on a one-shot basis usually is a special agent. In addition to being employed on a continuous basis, general agents often serve for longer periods, perform more acts, and deal with more parties than do special agents.

Gratuitous Agents

An agent who receives no compensation for his services is called a **gratuitous agent.** Gratuitous agents have the same power to bind their principals as do paid agents with the same authority. However, the fact that an agent is gratuitous sometimes lowers the duties principal and agent owe each other and also may increase the parties' ability to terminate the agency without incurring liability.

Subagents

A **subagent** basically is an agent of an agent. More precisely, a subagent is a person appointed by an agent to perform tasks that the agent has undertaken to perform for his principal. For example, if you retain an accounting firm as your agent, the accountant actually handling your affairs is the firm's agent and your subagent. For a subagency to exist, an agent must have the authority to make the subagent *his agent* for conducting the principal's business. Sometimes, however, a party appointed by an agent is not a subagent because the appointing agent only had authority to appoint agents *for the principal.* For instance, sales agents appointed by a corporation's sales manager probably are agents of the corporation, not agents of the sales manager.

When an agent appoints a true subagent, the agent becomes a principal with respect to the subagent, his agent. Thus, the legal relations between agent and subagent closely parallel the legal relations between principal and

agent. But a subagent is also the *original principal's agent.* Here, though, the normal rules governing principals and agents do not always apply. We occasionally refer to such situations in the pages ahead.

Employees and Independent Contractors

Many legal questions depend on whether an agent or some other party who contracts with the principal is classed as an **employee** (or servant) or as an **independent contractor.**[1] No sharp line separates employees from independent contractors; the following *Circle C* case lists some factors considered in making such determinations. The most important of these factors is the principal's *right to control the physical details of the work.* Employees typically are subject to such control. Independent contractors, on the other hand, generally contract with the principal to produce some result, and determine for themselves how that result will be accomplished.

Although many employees perform physical labor or are paid on an hourly basis, corporate officers usually are employees as well. Professionals such as brokers, accountants, and attorneys often are independent contractors, although they sometimes are employees. Consider the difference between a corporation represented by an attorney engaged in her own practice and a corporation that maintains a staff of salaried in-house counsel. Finally, franchisees usually are independent contractors.

As Chapter 36 makes clear, the employee–independent contractor distinction often is crucial in determining the principal's liability for an agent's torts. The distinction also helps define the coverage of some employment laws discussed in Chapter 51. Unemployment compensation, the Fair Labor Standards Act (the subject of *Circle C*), and workers' compensation are clear examples.

---

[1] When are employees and independent contractors agents? According to the *Restatement (Second) of Agency,* employees always are agents, while independent contractors may or may not be agents. An independent contractor is an agent when the tests for the existence of an agency—most important, sufficient control by the principal—are met.

Reich v. Circle C Investments, Inc.   *998 F.2d 324 (5th Cir. 1993)*

Circle C Investments operated two nightclubs featuring topless dancers. The secretary of labor sued to compel Circle C to observe the minimum-wage, maximum-hours, and record-keeping provisions of the Fair Labor Standards Act (FLSA). Following a bench trial, the district court concluded that because the dancers were employees, the FLSA applied to Circle C's nightclubs. Thus, the court enjoined Circle C from further violating the FLSA, and also restrained it from withholding $539,630 in back wages. Circle C appealed.

Reavley, Circuit Judge To determine employee status under the FLSA, we focus on whether the alleged employee, as a matter of economic reality, is economically dependent upon the business to which she renders her services. Our focal inquiry is whether the individual is, as a matter of economic reality, in business for herself. We consider five factors: (1) the degree of control exercised by the alleged employer, (2) the relative investments of the worker and the alleged employer, (3) the degree to which the worker's opportunity for profit and loss is determined by the alleged employer, (4) the skill and initiative required in performing the job, and (5) the permanency of the relationship. These factors are merely aids in determining the underlying question of dependency, and no single factor is determinative.

Degree of Control

The dancers are required to comply with weekly work schedules. Circle C instructs the dancers to charge at least $10 for table dances and $20 for couch dances. The dancers supply their own costumes, but the costumes must meet standards set by Circle C. The dancers can express a preference for a certain type of music, but they do not have the final say. Dancers were expected to mingle with customers when not dancing. Circle C has promulgated many other rules. Circle C enforces these rules by fining infringers. The record fully supports the district court's finding of significant control.

Relative Investment of Worker and Alleged Employer

A dancer's investment is limited to her costumes and a padlock. (One dancer testified that she spends $600 per month on costumes, while another testified that she spends approximately $40 per month.) [However,] a dancer's invest-

ment is relatively minor [compared] to the considerable investment Circle C has in operating a nightclub.

Degree to Which Employee's Profit and Loss Determined by Employer

A dancer's initiative, hustle, and costume significantly contribute to the amount of her tips. But Circle C has a significant role in drawing customers to its nightclubs. Circle C is responsible for advertising, location, business hours, maintenance, aesthetics, and beverages and food. Given its control over determinants of customer volume, Circle C exercises a high degree of control over a dancer's opportunity for "profit." The dancers are far more akin to wage earners toiling for a living, than to entrepreneurs seeking a return on their capital investments.

Skill and Initiative Required

The dancers do not need long training or highly developed skills to dance at a Circle C nightclub. The ability to develop and maintain rapport with customers is not the type of "initiative" [relevant here]. A dancer's initiative is essentially limited to decisions involving her costumes and dance routines. The dancers do not exhibit the skill or initiative indicative of persons in business for themselves.

Permanency of the Relationship

The parties agree, and the district court found, that most dancers have short-term relationships with Circle C.

On balance, the five factors favor employee status. Here, the economic reality is that the dancers are not in business for themselves but are dependent upon finding employment in the business of others.

District court decision on the FLSA's applicability affirmed; case remanded on other issues.

Duties of Agent to Principal

If an agency is created by contract, the agent must perform according to its terms. Regardless of whether the relationship is contractual, agency law also establishes certain *fiduciary duties* that the agent owes the principal. These duties supplement the duties created by an agency contract. They exist because agency is a relationship of trust and confidence. (Often, however, the parties may eliminate or modify fiduciary duties by agreement.) The principal's many remedies for an agent's breach of her fiduciary duties include termination of the agency and recovery of damages, if any, from the agent.

A gratuitous agent usually has the same fiduciary duties as a paid agent, but a gratuitous agent need not perform as promised. She normally can terminate the agency without incurring liability, and her fiduciary duties cease once the agency ends. However, a gratuitous agent *is* liable for failing to perform as promised when her promise causes the principal to rely upon her to undertake certain acts, and the principal suffers losses because he refrained from performing those acts himself.

A subagent owes the agent (his principal) all the duties agents owe their principals. A subagent who knows of the original principal's existence also owes that principal all the duties agents owe their principals, except for duties arising solely from the original principal's contract with the agent. Finally, the agent who appointed the subagent generally is liable to the original principal when the principal is harmed by the subagent's conduct.

Agent's Duty of Loyalty

Because agency is a relationship of trust and confidence, an agent has a **duty of loyalty** to his principal. Thus, an agent must subordinate his personal concerns by: (1) avoiding conflicts of interest with the principal, and (2) not disclosing confidential information received from the principal.

Conflicts of Interest   An agent whose interests conflict with the principal's interests may be unable to represent his principal effectively. When conducting the principal's business, therefore, an agent is forbidden to *deal with himself.* For example, an agent authorized to sell property cannot sell that property to himself. Many courts extend the rule to include transactions with the agent's relatives or business associates or with business organizations in which the agent has an interest. However, an agent may engage in self-dealing transactions if the principal consents. For this consent to be effective, the agent must disclose all relevant facts to the principal before dealing with the principal on his own behalf.

Unless the principal agrees otherwise, an agent also is forbidden to *compete with the principal* regarding the agency business so long as he remains an agent. Thus, an agent employed to purchase specific property may not buy it himself if the principal still desires it. Furthermore, an agent ordinarily may not solicit customers for a planned competing business while still employed by the principal.

Finally, an agent who is authorized to make a certain transaction cannot *act on behalf of the other party* to the transaction unless the principal knowingly consents. Thus, one ordinarily cannot act as agent for both parties to a transaction without first disclosing the double role to, and obtaining the consent of, both principals. Here, the agent must disclose to each principal all the factors reasonably affecting that principal's decision. Occasionally, though, an agent who acts as a middleman may serve both parties to a transaction without notifying either. For instance, an agent may simultaneously be employed as a "finder" by a firm seeking suitable businesses to acquire and a firm looking for prospective buyers, so long as neither principal expects the agent to advise it or negotiate for it.

Confidentiality   Unless otherwise agreed, an agent may not *use or disclose confidential information* acquired through the agency. Confidential information means facts that are valuable to the principal because they are not widely known or that would harm the principal's business if they became widely known. Examples include the principal's business plans, financial condition, contract bids, technological discoveries, manufacturing methods, customer files, and other trade secrets. In the absence of an agreement to the contrary, after the agency ends an agent may compete with her principal after termination of the agency. But as the following *ABKCO* case illustrates, the duty not to use or disclose confidential information continues after the agency ends. The former agent may, however, utilize general knowledge and skills acquired during the agency.

ABKCO Music Inc. v. Harrisongs Music, Ltd.   *722 F.2d 988 (2d Cir. 1983)*

In 1963, a song called "He's So Fine" was a huge hit in the United States and Great Britain. In February 1971, Bright Tunes Music Corporation, the copyright holder of "He's So Fine," sued ex-Beatle George Harrison and Harrisongs, Music, Ltd. in federal district court. Bright Tunes claimed that the Harrison composition "My Sweet Lord" infringed its copyright to "He's So Fine." At this time, Harrison's business affairs were handled by ABKCO Music, Inc., and Allen B. Klein, its president. Shortly after the suit began, Klein unsuccessfully tried to settle it by having ABKCO purchase Bright Tunes.

Shortly thereafter, Bright Tunes went into receivership, and it did not resume the suit until 1973. At this time, coincidentally, ABKCO's management contract with Harrison expired. In late 1975 and early 1976, however, Klein continued his efforts to have ABKCO purchase Bright Tunes. As part of these efforts, he gave Bright Tunes three schedules summarizing Harrison's royalty income from "My Sweet Lord," information he possessed because of his previous service to Harrison. Throughout the 1973–76 period, Harrison's attorneys had been trying to settle the copyright infringement suit with Bright Tunes. Because Klein's activities not only gave Bright Tunes information about the economic potential of its suit but also gave it an economic alternative to settling with Harrison, Klein may have impeded Harrison's efforts to settle.

When the copyright infringement suit finally came to trial in 1976, the court found that Harrison had infringed Bright Tunes' copyright. The issue of damages was scheduled for trial at a later date and this trial was delayed for some time. In 1978, ABKCO purchased the "He's So Fine" copyright and all rights to the infringement suit from Bright Tunes. This made ABKCO the plaintiff in the 1979 trial for damages on the infringement suit. At trial, Harrison counterclaimed for damages resulting from Klein's and ABKCO's alleged breaches of the duty of loyalty. Finding a breach of duty, the district judge issued a complex order reducing ABKCO's recovery. ABKCO appealed.

Pierce, Circuit Judge The relationship between Harrison and ABKCO prior to termination of the management agreement in 1973 was that of principal and agent. An agent has a duty not to use confidential knowledge acquired in his employment in competition with his principal. This duty exists as well after the employment as during its continuance. On the other hand, use of information based on general business knowledge is not covered by the rule, and the former agent is permitted to compete with his former principal in reliance on such publicly available information. The principal issue before us, then, is whether Klein (hence, ABKCO) improperly used confidential information, gained as Harrison's former agent, in negotiating for the purchase of Bright Tunes' stock in 1975–76.

One aspect of this inquiry concerns the nature of the schedules of "My Sweet Lord" earnings which Klein furnished to Bright Tunes in connection with the 1975–76 negotiations. It appears that at least some of [this] information was confidential. The evidence is not at all convincing that the information was publicly available.

Another aspect of the breach of duty issue concerns the timing and nature of Klein's entry into the negotiation picture and the manner in which he became a plaintiff in this action. We find this case analogous to those where an employee, with the use of information acquired through his former employment, completes for his own benefit a transaction originally undertaken on the former employer's behalf. Klein had commenced a purchase transaction with Bright Tunes in 1971 on behalf of Harrison, which he pursued on his own account after termination of his fiduciary relationship with Harrison. Klein pursued the later discussions armed with the intimate knowledge not only of Harrison's business affairs, but of the value of this lawsuit. Taking all of these circumstances together, we agree that Klein's conduct during the period 1975–78 did not meet the standard required of him as a former fiduciary.

Judgment in favor of Harrison affirmed.

Agent's Duty to Obey Instructions

Because an agent acts under the principal's control and for the principal's benefit, she has a duty to *obey the principal's reasonable instructions* for carrying out the agency business. However, a gratuitous agent need not obey his principal's order to continue to act as an agent. Also, agents generally have no duty to obey orders to behave illegally or unethically. Thus, a sales agent need not follow directions to misrepresent the quality of the principal's goods, and professionals such as attorneys and accountants are not obligated to obey directions that conflict with the ethical rules of their professions.

Agent's Duty to Act with Care and Skill

A paid agent must *possess and exercise the degree of care and skill* that is standard in the locality for the kind of work the agent performs. A gratuitous agent need only exercise the care and skill required of nonagents who perform similar gratuitous undertakings. Paid agents who represent that they possess a higher than customary level of skill may be held to a correspondingly higher standard of performance. Similarly, an agent's duty may change if the principal and the agent agree that the agent must possess and exercise greater than customary care and skill.

Agent's Duty to Notify the Principal

An agent must promptly communicate to the principal matters within the agent's knowledge that are reasonably relevant or material to the agency business and that he knows or should know are of concern to the principal. The basis for the duty to notify is the principal's interest in being informed of matters that are important to the agency business.

However, there is no duty to notify where the agent receives privileged or confidential information. For example, an attorney may acquire confidential information from a client and thus be obligated not to disclose it to a second client. If the attorney cannot properly represent the second client without revealing this information, he should refuse to represent that client.

The following *Olsen* case involves both the agent's duty to notify and his duty not to act on behalf of the other party.

| Olsen v. Vail Associates Real Estate, Inc. | 935 P.2d 975 (Colo. Sup. Ct. 1997) |

Following the death of J. Perry Olsen, his ranch (the estate property) was put on the market through an open listing. Initially, the listing included an adjacent parcel of land (the children's property) owned by Olsen's children. In March 1989, Vail Associates Real Estate, Inc. introduced the children to Magnus Lindholm, who was interested in buying both properties. Eventually, the Olsen children decided not to include the children's property in the sale and withdrew that parcel from the negotiations. Lindholm felt that ownership of the estate property alone was not sufficient to ensure control over the development of the area in which both properties were located. Lindholm's attorney therefore suggested that he explore the purchase of the only other parcel of land in the area, a ranch owned by Del Rickstrew (the Rickstrew property), because that property had the primary access roads to both the estate property and the children's property.

In December 1989, Lindholm asked Vail Associates to inquire whether the Rickstrew property was available for purchase. However, Rickstrew refused to negotiate through Vail Associates or any other real estate agent and demanded to negotiate personally with Lindholm. On January 5, 1990, Lindholm and Rickstrew commenced preliminary negotiations. During this time, Vail Associates performed certain tasks to facilitate the arrangement, such as introducing the parties, providing a model contract, and delivering a sealed package of unknown content to Rickstrew. However, Vail Associates did not directly participate in the discussions or negotiations between Rickstrew and Lindholm.

On January 13, 1990, Lindholm agreed to purchase the Rickstrew property, contingent upon a closing on the sale of the estate property. Although aware that negotiations were taking place, Vail Associates did not inform the Olsens that Lindholm was attempting to purchase the Rickstrew property. On January 18, 1990, Lindholm signed contracts to purchase both the estate property and the Rickstrew property. On March 20, 1990, the parties closed on the estate property, at which time the Olsen children received their asking price, and Vail Associates received its commission. The closing on the Rickstrew property occurred in June 1990; Vail Associates did not receive a commission for that sale. Lindholm paid $6,000 per acre for the Rickstrew property and $400 per acre for the estate property.

Upon learning of the sale of the Rickstrew property and the price Lindholm had paid for that property, the Olsens sued Vail Associates, alleging a breach of fiduciary duty. The trial court found for Vail Associates and against the Olsens. The court of appeals affirmed the trial court's judgment. The Olsens appealed to the Colorado Supreme Court.

Scott, Justice A real estate broker owes a fiduciary duty of good faith and loyalty to its principal, the seller. The Olsens contend that Vail Associates breached the fiduciary duty it owed to them by not revealing that Lindholm was negotiating to purchase the Rickstrew property and the ultimate sale price of that property.

A breach of fiduciary duty occurs if the broker, as agent, conceals from the seller, as principal, material information, i.e., information that bears upon the transaction in question.

An agent is required to disclose to the principal any facts which might reasonably affect the principal's decision. Thus, the question presented here is whether the information known to and withheld by Vail Associates would, if disclosed, have assumed actual significance in the deliberations of the Olsens in regard to the sale of the estate property or significantly altered the total mix of information available to them. The trial court concluded that, although Vail Associates knew that Lindholm was negotiating to purchase the Rickstrew property, it was not aware of any specific facts—e.g., that a contract had actually been entered into, its details, or the sale price—until after Lindholm and the Olsens had entered into a contract for the sale of the estate property.

It was not knowledge of Lindholm's negotiations for the Rickstrew property that would have been valuable to the Olsens, but rather the actual price offered or paid for that property. The Olsens' attorney testified that, in the past, other potential buyers' negotiations with Rickstrew had not caused the Olsens to alter their position in regard to the estate property and that only the fact of a contract for the sale of the Rickstrew property and the price to be paid under such contract would have been material to the deliberations of the Olsens in their dealings with Lindholm. Therefore, we do not consider failure to disclose the fact of preliminary negotiations between Lindholm and Rickstrew to be material to the Olsens.

The Olsens testified and the trial court recognized that the per-acre price of the Rickstrew property would have been valuable information to the Olsens in their dealings with Lindholm. However, the trial court determined that Vail Associates did not have this information prior to the signing of the sale contract for the estate property and therefore could not have disclosed it to the Olsens. Although Vail Associates did not disclose this [price] information even after it learned of it, the Olsens failed to demonstrate how knowledge of the sale price after the contract for the estate property was signed would have in any way affected their decisionmaking as it related to the transaction. We therefore conclude that the trial court's determination that any omission by Vail Associates was not material is amply supported in the record and should not be disturbed on review.

The Olsens also assert that Vail Associates breached its fiduciary duty by engaging in a dual agency. In the context of residential real estate transactions, it is a widely accepted rule of agency law that a real estate broker stands in an agency relationship with the seller. However, no such agency relationship generally exists between the selling broker and the buyer in a residential real estate transaction, nor is any such agency created solely on the basis of the selling broker's contacts with the purchaser and efforts expended to find the purchaser a home. Under Colorado law, a real estate broker or salesperson is expressly prohibited from engaging in a dual agency—i.e., representing both the seller and the buyer in the same real estate transaction—unless the parties know of and consent to the arrangement. Nothing, however, precludes a real estate broker from representing different principals in different transactions. Vail Associates did not engage in a dual agency relationship as to the sale of the estate property.

Moreover, although not directly pertinent to the question of a dual agency, we agree that Vail Associates did not act as agents for Lindholm in the sale of the Rickstrew property. First, the record reveals that, in connection with the sale of the estate property, Vail Associates only had contact with Lindholm which was necessary to facilitate the sale. Indeed, even Vail Associates' contact with Lindholm regarding the Rickstrew property was made in an effort to sell the estate property. Second, Vail Associates was not involved directly with Lindholm's attempt to purchase the Rickstrew property because Mr. Rickstrew had specifically refused to deal with real estate brokers. Vail Associates performed only certain ministerial tasks, such as contacting Rickstrew, introducing him to Lindholm, and assembling a "discussion draft contract," and had done so only because it knew that Lindholm would not purchase the estate property without simultaneously purchasing the Rickstrew property. Finally, while Vail Associates received a substantial commission for the sale of the estate property, it received no commission for the sale of the Rickstrew property.

Judgment in favor of Vail Associates affirmed.

Agent's Duties to Account

An agent's duties of loyalty and care require that she give the principal any money or property received in the course of the agency business. This includes profits resulting from the agent's breach of the duty of loyalty, or other duties. It also includes incidental benefits received through the agency business. Examples include bribes, kickbacks, and gifts from parties with whom the agent deals on the principal's behalf. However, the principal and the agent may agree that the agent can retain certain benefits received during the agency. Courts may imply such an agreement when it is customary for agents to retain tips or accept entertainment while doing the principal's business.

Another type of **duty to account** concerns agents whose business involves collections, receipts, or expenditures. Such agents must keep accurate records and ac-

ETHICS IN ACTION

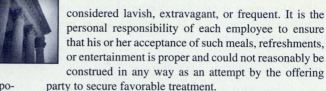

Corporations give special attention to rooting out conflicts of interests that result from kickbacks, bribes, and gifts to the corporations' employees. To ensure independence of auditors, auditing firms commonly have rules banning their audit staff from receiving anything of value from clients. In other contexts, most corporations permit their employees to receive items or services of nominal value only. Most firms have detailed rules, such as the following from Lockheed Martin's code of ethics:

> Lockheed Martin employees may accept meals, refreshments, or entertainment of nominal value in connection with business discussions. While it is difficult to define "nominal" by means of a specific dollar amount, a common sense determination should dictate what would be

considered lavish, extravagant, or frequent. It is the personal responsibility of each employee to ensure that his or her acceptance of such meals, refreshments, or entertainment is proper and could not reasonably be construed in any way as an attempt by the offering party to secure favorable treatment.

Lockheed Martin employees are not permitted to accept funds in any form or amount, or any gift that has a retail or exchange value of $20 or more from individuals, companies, or representatives of companies having or seeking business relationships with Lockheed Martin. If you have any questions about the propriety of a gift, gratuity, or item of value, contact your Ethics Officer or the Corporate Office of Ethics and Business Conduct for guidance.

THE GLOBAL BUSINESS ENVIRONMENT

While all modern nations regulate the relationship of agents and principals, associations of professional agents often reinforce or augment these legal duties with codes of ethics. For the real estate industry, you can find codes of ethics in 23 countries at the website of the International Consortium of Real Estate Associations, www.icrea.org.

Excerpts from Chapter 2 of the Code of Ethics of Korea's National Association of Real Estate Brokers are below. Note how these listed rules relate to the agent's fiduciary duties we have studied.

Article 11: Member tries to obtain current information about public policy, regulations, and circulation status in an effort to best serve clients.

Article 13: Member should not report the property status with overstatement and deceptive descriptions. The duty of Member, as an expert, is to rationally analyze a property.

Article 14: Member is expected to have a sincere attitude toward the protection of clients' rights and has the duty to help all clients.

Article 15: Member needs to have sufficient background to handle client transactions related to general intermediary contracts and to real estate transfer rights.

Article 16: If Member discovers facts that impede the consummation of a contract, remedies should be promptly proposed to clients, in which case, Member should consider the best solution to the problem.

Article 19: If there are two prospective clients for the same property, the duty of Member is to deal with each prospect equally and fairly. Member should equally report the contents to clients and consider their decisions without bias.

counts of all transactions and disclose these to the principal once the principal makes a reasonable demand for them. Also, an agent who obtains or holds property for the principal usually may not commingle that property with her own property. For example, an agent ordinarily cannot deposit the principal's funds in her own name or in her own bank account.

Duties of Principal to Agent

If an agency is formed by contract, the contract normally states the duties the principal owes the agent. In addition, the law implies certain duties from the existence of an agency relationship, however formed. The most important of these duties are the principal's obligations to **compensate** the agent, to **reimburse** the agent for money spent in the principal's service, and to **indemnify** the agent for losses suffered in conducting the principal's business. These duties generally can be eliminated or modified by agreement between the parties.

Duty to Compensate Agent

If the agency contract states the compensation the agent is to receive, it usually controls questions about the agent's pay. In other cases, the relationship of the parties and the surrounding circumstances determine whether and in what amount the agent is to be compensated. If there is no contract provision on compensation, for example, a principal generally is not required to pay for undertakings that she did not request, services to which she did not consent, and tasks that typically are undertaken without pay. Also, a principal usually need not compensate an agent who has materially breached the agency contract or has committed a serious breach of a fiduciary duty. Where compensation is due but its amount is not expressly stated, the amount is the market price or the customary price for the agent's services or, if neither is available, their reasonable value.

Sometimes an agent's compensation depends on the accomplishment of a specific result. For instance, a plaintiff's attorney may be retained on a contingent fee basis (being paid a certain percentage of the recovery if the suit succeeds or is settled), or a real estate broker may be entitled to a fee only if a suitable buyer is found. In such cases, the agent is not entitled to compensation unless he achieves the result within the time stated or, if no time is stated, within a reasonable time. This is true no matter how much effort or money the agent expends. However, the principal must cooperate with the agent in achieving the result and must not do anything to frustrate the agent's efforts. Otherwise, the agent is entitled to compensation despite the failure to perform as specified.

There is no duty to compensate a gratuitous agent. An agent's duties to a subagent are the same as a principal's duties to an agent. If there is no agreement to the contrary, however, the original principal has no contractual liability to a subagent. For example, such a principal normally is not obligated to compensate a subagent. But a principal must reimburse and indemnify subagents as he would agents.

Duties of Reimbursement and Indemnity

If an agent makes expressly or impliedly authorized expenditures while acting on the principal's behalf, the agent normally is entitled to **reimbursement** for those expenditures. Unless otherwise agreed, for example, an agent requested to make overnight trips as part of his agency duties can recover reasonable transportation and hotel expenses.

A principal's duty of reimbursement overlaps with her duty of **indemnity.** Agency law implies a promise by the principal to indemnify an agent for losses that result from the agent's authorized activities. These include authorized payments made on the principal's behalf and payments on contracts on which the agent was authorized to become liable. A principal may also have to indemnify an agent if the agent's authorized acts constitute a breach of contract or a tort for which the agent is required to pay damages to a third party.

So long as the principal did not benefit from such behavior, however, he is *not* required to indemnify an agent for losses resulting: (1) from unauthorized acts, or (2) solely from the agent's negligence or other fault. Even where the principal directed the agent to commit a tortious act, moreover, there is no duty to indemnify if the agent knew the act was tortious. But the principal must indemnify the agent for tort damages resulting from authorized conduct that the agent did not believe was tortious. For example, if a principal directs his agent to repossess goods located on another's property and the agent, believing her acts legal, becomes liable for conversion or trespass, the principal must indemnify the agent for the damages the agent pays.

Termination of an Agency

An agency can terminate in many ways. These fall under two general headings: (1) termination by act of the parties, and (2) termination by operation of law.

Termination by Act of the Parties

Termination by act of the parties occurs:

1. *At a time or upon the happening of an event stated in the agreement.* If no such time or event is stated, the agency terminates after a reasonable time.

2. *When a specified result has been accomplished, if the agency was created to accomplish a specified result.* For example, if an agency's only objective is to sell certain property, the agency terminates when the property is sold.

3. *By mutual agreement of the parties,* at any time.

4. *At the option of either party.* This is called **revocation** when done by the principal and **renunciation** when done by the agent. Revocation or renunciation occurs when either party manifests to the other that he does not wish the agency to continue. This includes conduct inconsistent with the agency's continuance. For example, an agent may learn that his principal has hired another agent to perform the same job.

A party can revoke or renounce even if this violates the agency agreement. However, although either party has the *power* to terminate in such cases, there is no *right* to do so. This means that where one party terminates in violation of the agreement, she need not perform any further, but she may be liable for damages to the other party. However, a gratuitous agency normally is terminable by either party without liability. Also, the terminating party is not liable where the revocation or renunciation is justified by the other party's serious breach of a fiduciary duty.

Termination by Operation of Law

Termination by operation of law usually involves situations where it is reasonable to believe that the principal would not wish the agent to act further, or where accomplishment of the agency objectives has become impossible or illegal. Although courts may recognize exceptions in certain cases, an agency relationship usually is terminated by:

1. *The death of the principal.* This normally is true even where the agent has no notice of the principal's death.

2. *The death of the agent.*

3. *The principal's permanent loss of capacity.* This is a *permanent* loss of capacity occurring *after* creation of the agency—most often, due to the principal's insanity. The principal's permanent incapacity ends the agency even without notice to the agent. The *Trepanier* case (page 796) presents one approach to a related problem: the principal's *temporary* incapacity.

4. *The agent's loss of capacity* to perform the agency business. The scope of this basis for termination is unclear. As Chapter 36 states, an agent who becomes insane or otherwise incapacitated after the agency is formed still can bind his principal to contracts with third parties. Thus, it probably makes little sense to treat the agency as terminated in such cases. As a result, termination under this heading may be limited to such situations as the loss of a license needed to perform agency duties.

5. *Changes in the value of the agency property or subject matter* (e.g., a significant decline in the value of land to be sold by an agent).

6. *Changes in business conditions* (e.g., a much lower supply and a much increased price for goods to be purchased by an agent).

7. *The loss or destruction of the agency property or subject matter or the termination of the principal's interest therein* (e.g., where a house to be sold by a real estate broker burns down or is taken by a mortgage holder to satisfy a debt owed by the principal).

8. *Changes in the law that make the agency business illegal* (e.g., where drugs to be sold by an agent are banned by the government).

9. *The principal's bankruptcy*—as to transactions the agent should realize the principal no longer desires. For example, consider the likely effect of the principal's bankruptcy on an agency to purchase antiques for the principal's home versus its likely effect on an agency to purchase necessities of life for the principal.

10. *The agent's bankruptcy*—where the agent's financial condition affects his ability to serve the principal. This could occur where an agent is employed to purchase goods on his own credit for the principal.

11. *Impossibility of performance by the agent.* This covers various events, some of which fall within the categories just stated. The *Restatement*'s definition of impossibility, for example, includes: (*a*) destruction of the agency subject matter, (*b*) termination of the principal's interest in the agency subject matter (as, for example, by the principal's bankruptcy), and (*c*) changes in the law or in other circumstances that make it impossible for the agent to accomplish the agency's aims.

12. *A serious breach* of the agent's duty of loyalty.

13. *The outbreak of war*—where this leads the agent to the reasonable belief that his services are no longer desired. An example might be the outbreak of war between the principal's country and the agent's country.

Termination of Agency Powers Given as Security

An agency power given as security for a duty owed by the principal, sometimes called an **agency coupled with an interest,** is an exception to some of the termination rules just discussed. Here, the agent has an interest in the subject matter of the agency that is distinct from the principal's interest and that is not exercised for the principal's benefit. This interest exists to benefit the agent or a third person by securing performance of an obligation owed by the principal. A common example is a secured loan agreement authorizing a lender (the agent) to sell property used as security if the debtor (the principal) defaults. For instance, suppose that Allen lends Peters $100,000 and Peters gives Allen a lien or security interest on Peters's land to secure the loan. The agreement might authorize Allen to act as Peters's "agent" to sell the land if Peters fails to repay the loan.

Because the power given the "agent" in such cases is not for the principal's benefit, it sometimes is said that an agency coupled with an interest is not truly an agency. In any event, courts distinguish it from genuine agency relations in which the agent is compensated from the profits or proceeds of property held for the principal's bene-

fit. For example, if an agent is promised a commission for selling the principal's property, the relationship is not an agency coupled with an interest. Here, the power exercised by the agent (selling the principal's property) benefits the principal.

Why is the agency coupled with an interest important? The main reason is that it is not terminated by: (1) the principal's revocation, (2) the principal's or the agent's loss of capacity, (3) the agent's death, and (4) (usually) the principal's death. However, unless an agency coupled with an interest is held for the benefit of a third party, the agent can voluntarily surrender it. Of course, an agency coupled with an interest terminates when the principal performs her obligation.

Trepanier v. Bankers Life & Casualty Co.   *706 A.2d 943 (Vt. Sup. Ct. 1997)*

On March 2, 1993, Bankers Life & Casualty Co. proposed in a letter addressed to Gaston Trepanier that he accept a lump sum settlement of $20,000 in exchange for release from a disability income policy that paid him a $400-a-month benefit. The letter stated that should Mr. Trepanier decide "to accept our offer," he could "jot a note at the bottom of this letter and return it." According to Mrs. Clemence Trepanier, she discussed the idea with her husband, who decided to accept the offer and directed her to write a note on the bottom of the March letter as directed. She did so on April 6, and placed the letter in an envelope, intending to send it the following day. On April 7, Mr. Trepanier was hospitalized and the letter was not mailed. Mr. Trepanier fell into a coma on April 8. On April 12, Mrs. Trepanier tried to accept the offer by mailing the letter to Bankers Life. On April 14, Mr. Trepanier died. Bankers Life subsequently revoked its offer and issued a final disability payment.

Clemence Trepanier then filed a breach-of-contract action against Bankers Life on behalf of her husband's estate, alleging that a valid contract had been formed when she accepted the $20,000 offer on her husband's behalf. Mrs. Trepanier moved for partial summary judgment on the issue of whether a binding contract had been formed. In response, Bankers Life filed a cross-motion for summary judgment, arguing that Clemence Trepanier's authority to act as agent for her husband terminated when he lapsed into a coma on April 8, four days before she mailed the acceptance. The trial court denied Clemence's motion and entered a summary judgment in favor of Bankers Life. Clemence appealed, and the case found its way to the Supreme Court of Vermont.

By the Court The sole issue on appeal is whether Mrs. Trepanier's agency terminated when Mr. Trepanier lapsed into a coma on April 8. The general rule is that an agency terminates with the death or permanent incapacity of the principal. Mrs. Trepanier argues that her power of agency was coupled with an interest, an exception to the general rule which allows the agency to survive the death or permanent incapacity of the principal. We need not decide whether Mrs. Trepanier's agency fits within this exception, however, for an individual in a comatose state is generally not considered to be permanently incapacitated under general agency principles. The rule has been stated as follows: "A comatose person is mentally incompetent while his coma continues and . . . when an agent under a power of attorney acts during the mental incapacity of a principal who has not been adjudicated incompetent and for whom no court-appointed committee or conservator has been desig-

nated, the act is at most voidable, and not void." This rule is predicated on the view that comatose individuals are only temporarily incapacitated, as they may recover, and acts by individuals temporarily incapacitated are at most voidable. With respect to such voidable contracts, the power to affirm or disaffirm rests solely with the principal or an authorized representative, which can include the estate of the principal. The contract here was not voided by Mr. Trepanier, and there is no claim or evidence that he would have done so prior to his death.

We hold, therefore, that the trial court erred in concluding as a matter of law that Mrs. Trepanier's agency terminated when Mr. Trepanier lapsed into a coma, and in entering summary judgment on this basis.

Summary judgment in favor of Bankers Trust reversed; case remanded to the trial court.

Effect of Termination on Agent's Authority

Sometimes former agents continue to act on their ex-principals' behalf even though the agency has ended. Once an agency terminates by any of the means just described, the agent's *express* and *implied* authority end as well. Such "agents" may retain apparent authority to bind their former principals.

Third parties who are unaware of the termination may reasonably believe that an ex-agent still has authority. To protect third parties who rely on such a reasonable appearance of authority, an agent's *apparent authority* often persists after termination. Thus, a former agent may be able to bind the principal under his apparent authority even though the agency has ended. But apparent authority ends where the termination was caused by: (1) the principal's death, (2) the principal's loss of capacity, or (3) impossibility. Note from the previous discussion that certain other bases for termination may also end the agent's apparent authority because they fit within the broad category of impossibility.

Notice to Third Parties Apparent authority also ends when the third party receives appropriate notice of the termination. In general, any facts known to the third party that reasonably indicate the agency's termination constitute suitable notice. Some bases for termination by operation of law (e.g., changed business conditions) may provide such notice.

To protect themselves against unwanted liability, however, prudent principals may want to notify third parties themselves. The required type of notification varies with the third party in question.

1. *For third parties who have previously dealt with the agent* or who have begun to deal with the agent, **actual notification** is necessary. This can be accomplished by: (1) a direct personal statement to the third party; or (2) a writing delivered to the third party personally, to his place of business, or to some other place reasonably believed to be appropriate.

2. *For all other parties,* **constructive notification** suffices. Usually, these other parties are aware of the agency but did no business with the agent. Constructive notification normally can be accomplished by advertising the agency's termination in a newspaper of general circulation in the place where the agency business regularly was carried on. If no suitable publication exists, notification by other means reasonably likely to inform third parties—for example, posting a notice in public places—may be enough.

Problems and Problem Cases

1. Bobby and Modell Warren took their cotton crops to cotton gins that ginned and baled the cotton. Pursuant to the Warrens' instructions, the gins obtained bids for the cotton from prospective buyers. The Warrens told the gins which bids to accept, and the gins sold the cotton to the designated buyers and collected the proceeds. At the Warrens' instruction, the gins deferred paying the proceeds of the cotton sales to the Warrens until a year after the year in which each sale was made. The Internal Revenue Service argued that the Warrens were required to report the proceeds from the sale of cotton on their tax returns for the year of the sale, not the year in which the gins paid the proceeds to the Warrens. What was the basis for the IRS's argument?

2. Paul Stieger gave his Chevy Chase Bank credit card to a Ms. Garrett during a business trip. He told her to use the card only for a car rental and for hotel lodging. After Stieger returned from the trip, he found that Garrett had used his card for 15 charges other than car rental and hotel lodging. For 13 of the charges, Garrett signed Stieger's name; for the other two, she signed her own name. Is Stieger liable for the 15 charges?

3. VIP Tours, Inc. arranged tours of central Florida's attractions. Cynthia Hoogland conducted 29 such tours for VIP between July 1980 and March 1981. Both Hoogland and VIP considered Hoogland an independent contractor. She worked for VIP only when it needed her services, and could reject particular assignments. She was also free to work for other tour services, and did so.

Once Hoogland accepted a job from VIP, she was told where to report and was given instructions about the job. She also had to use a VIP-furnished vehicle and wear a uniform with the VIP logo when conducting tours. Aside from ensuring that she departed on time, however, VIP did not tell her how long to stay or what kind of tour to conduct at each tourist attraction. Finally, Hoogland was paid on a per tour basis.

Hoogland later filed a claim for unemployment compensation benefits with the Florida Division of Labor and Employment Security. The Division concluded that she was entitled to these benefits because she was VIP Tours' employee. Was Hoogland an employee or an independent contractor?

4. Tadlock was a tenant on Lest's farm. Without any authorization from Lest, Tadlock ordered a new irrigation pump for the farm from Killinger. Tadlock told Killinger that he was Lest's tenant and that he had authority to purchase a new pump on Lest's behalf. Killinger then installed a new pump and billed Lest for $2,048. Lest denied liability on this bill, claiming that Tadlock's purchase was unauthorized. Tadlock did not have actual authority to purchase the pump, but was his statement to Killinger enough to give him *apparent* authority to make the purchase?

5. Ronald Chernow is in the business of auditing telephone bills for customers. In October of 1982, Chernow hired Angelo Reyes as an auditor. The employment lasted until July of 1983, when Reyes either quit or was fired. Prior to leaving Chernow's employment and without his knowledge, Reyes took various steps to form and operate a business that competed with Chernow's business. Most important, he obtained three auditing contracts and performed work under those contracts during that period. He also solicited a fourth account, but did no work for that firm until after ceasing to work for Chernow. None of these businesses was an existing customer of Chernow. Reyes's soliciting and auditing activities did not take place during his regular working hours, which he devoted to Chernow's business. Is Reyes liable to Chernow for breach of an agent's duty of loyalty?

6. In July of 1987, Marsha Levin bought her daughter a round-trip plane ticket from New York City to Paris from Kasmir World Travel, Inc. Upon arriving in Paris, Mrs. Levin's daughter was denied entry and was placed on the next return flight to the United States because she did not have a visa. The apparent reason for the visa requirement was the French government's effort to deal with terrorist activities directed at Americans abroad. Neither Mrs. Levin nor her daughter was aware of the requirement; indeed, a few years earlier Mrs. Levin had traveled to France without being required to present a visa. Did Kasmir breach its duty to notify the Levins about matters relevant to the agency business?

7. GMAC suggested to Gordon, Jean, Robert, and Dayonne Rose that GMAC finance the Roses' purchase of a Hyundai automobile dealership. The Roses' longtime legal counsel, Crenshaw, Dupree & Milam, L.L.P.

(CDM), advised both GMAC and the Roses during the negotiations that led to the Roses' buying the dealership with financing provided by GMAC. During the negotiations, GMAC wanted to ensure that the Roses understood that CDM had a conflict of interest and that GMAC would not be liable to the Roses for that reason. Therefore, GMAC directed CDM to obtain from the Roses a "Waiver of Conflict of Interest." Although CDM had the Roses sign such a form, it eventually was ruled unenforceable because CDM had failed to explain the form and CDM had not given the Roses an opportunity to obtain other legal counsel. As a result, when the dealership and the Roses became bankrupt, the Roses sued and obtained a settlement from GMAC. On what grounds did GMAC attempt to recover its loss from CDM?

8. Lawyers Title Insurance Company hired lawyer David Groff as Lawyer Title's settlement agent and attorney for the lender in a real estate transaction involving property in Londonderry, New Hampshire. Prior to closing the real estate sale, Groff retained a title abstractor to conduct a title search and prepare an abstractor's report. Because the title abstractor negligently failed to find and disclose a construction mortgage on the property, Groff issued title insurance policies to both the lender and the buyers without excepting the mortgage. As a result, the construction mortgage was not discharged prior to the closing of the sale. The mortgagee asserted its rights and threatened to foreclose on the property until Lawyers Title paid the mortgagee $152,000. On what grounds did Lawyers Title seek to recover a portion of its loss from Groff?

9. Wormhoudt Lumber Company employed Jon Cloyd to find construction jobs that would utilize Wormhoudt's materials. Cloyd would find property owners seeking to build, and link them up with construction contractors. Cloyd computed costs for materials and labor, including a profit for the contractor; if the contractor and the owner were satisfied with the terms, they would make a contract between themselves. If the contractor bought his materials from Wormhoudt and paid it within 30 days of the billing, it would get a 10 percent discount. Cloyd persuaded several contractors to split the 10 percent discount with him, in exchange for being recommended by him. Has Cloyd breached his duty to account?

10. Marjorie and Randall Bender owned a ranch they wished to sell, so they hired Johnson Realty as the listing agent. Johnson Realty found a buyer of the ranch, who relied on a brochure describing the ranch and its historic crop yields. The Benders authorized the production and distribution of the brochure by Johnson Realty. The buyer later sued Johnson Realty and the Benders on the grounds that the crop yields in the brochure were inflated. Although Johnson Realty and the Benders won that case, Johnson Realty suffered the expense of legal fees and other legal costs amounting to $45,000. On what grounds did Johnson Realty attempt to recover those costs from the Benders?

11. Brenda Smith was injured by a falling ceiling in a building owned by the Cynfax Corporation. She retained Floyd Goldsman as her attorney, and Goldsman sued Cynfax on her behalf. On February 4, 1992, Cynfax's insurer, the Cumberland Mutual Fire Insurance Company, made Smith a $7,000 settlement offer through Goldsman. Goldsman immediately tried to inform Smith of the offer, but learned that she had died on February 2. Later, Goldsman accepted Cumberland's offer to Smith. Did he have authority to do so? In answering this question, consider whether we have an agency coupled with an interest here, and why it would matter if we did.

Online Research: Changing Agency Law

AgencyLaw.com is dedicated to preserve the historic fiduciary duties of agency law, especially in its application to the real estate agent, buyer, and seller.

- Find the proposed law that was introduced in Connecticut House Bill No. 6981. What parts of this bill contradict the common law of agency?
- Find consumer advocate Ralph Nader's attack of this bill. What did Mr. Nader find offensive?
- Try to find whether real estate industry groups have attempted to change the law of agency in your state.

36

THIRD-PARTY RELATIONS OF THE PRINCIPAL AND THE AGENT

You are vice president of acquisitions for a medium-sized consumer food products company, Bon Vivant Foods, Inc. The company's board of directors has given you authority to negotiate acquisitions of consumer food brands on behalf of Bon Vivant. The board has told you in written and oral instructions that you have the power to acquire any consumer products brand if the acquisition price is not greater than $10,000,000, which is the authority typically held by most vice presidents of acquisitions for businesses like yours. The board's written instructions also indicate, however, that you have no authority to purchase or negotiate the purchase of a cola drink brand. Others in your position in the consumer food industry typically have authority to purchase a cola drink brand for their companies. The board also tells you that the company wants to buy the Eddie's ice cream brand from its owner, Eddie Ghahraman, at a price not greater than $9,000,000. The board is fearful, however, that if Eddie knows the company wants to buy the Eddie's ice cream brand, he will demand a higher price. The board tells you, therefore, not to disclose to Eddie that you are buying for Bon Vivant, and instead to make it appear that you are buying for your own company. They suggest you make up a name for this fictitious company. You decide to use the name Psudeau, Inc.

Assess the risks to you and Bon Vivant. Consider the following questions:

• If you make a contract in the name of Bon Vivant to buy a snack-cracker brand for $3,000,000, will Bon Vivant be bound on that contract?

• If you make a contract in the name of Bon Vivant to buy a cola brand for $7,500,000, will Bon Vivant be bound on that contract?

• If you make a contract in the name of Bon Vivant to buy a canned soup brand for $40,000,000, will Bon Vivant be bound on that contract? Will Bon Vivant be bound on that contract if you present the contract to the board, the board decides to accept the contract, and then the board later rejects the contract as too costly?

• Suppose you make a contract for Bon Vivant to purchase the Eddie's ice cream brand for $8,200,000. The contract is signed by Eddie. You sign Psudeau's name and also your own name as agent for Psudeau. Who is liable on that contract?

BY LETTING PRINCIPALS CONTRACT through their agents and thereby multiply their dealings, agency law stimulates business activity. For this process to succeed, there must be rules for determining when the principal and the agent are liable on the agent's contracts. Principals need to predict and control their liability on agreements their agents make. Also, third parties need assurance that such agreements really bind the principal. Furthermore, both agents and third parties have an interest in knowing when an agent is bound on these contracts. The first half of this chapter discusses the principal's and the agent's contract liability.

While acting on the principal's behalf, agents sometimes harm third parties. Normally, this makes the agent liable to the injured party in tort. Sometimes, moreover, a principal is liable for his agent's torts. Because tort judgments can be expensive, the rules for determining the principal's and the agent's tort liability are of great concern to principals, their agents, and third parties. Thus, we examine these subjects in this chapter's second half.

Contract Liability of the Principal

A principal normally is liable on a contract made by his agent if the agent had **express, implied, or apparent authority** to make the contract. Occasionally, however, a principal's contract liability may be affected by other factors. Even where the agent lacked authority to contract, moreover, a principal may bind herself by later **ratifying** the agent's contract.

Express Authority

Express authority is created by a principal's *words* to his agent, whether written or oral. Thus, an agent has express authority to bind her principal to a contract if the principal clearly told the agent that she could make that contract on the principal's behalf. Express authority is part of an agent's **actual authority.** For example, suppose that Payne instructs his agent Andrews to contract to sell a specific antique chair for $400 or more. If Andrews contracts to sell the chair to Tucker for $425, Payne is liable to Tucker on the basis of Andrews's express authority. However, Andrews would not have express authority to sell the chair for $375, or to sell a different chair.

Implied Authority

Often it is difficult for a principal to specify his agent's authority completely and precisely. Thus, agents can also bind their principals on the basis of the agent's **implied authority.** An agent generally has implied authority to do whatever it is reasonable to assume that his principal wanted him to do, in light of the principal's express statements and the surrounding circumstances. Relevant factors include the principal's express statements, the nature of the agency, the acts reasonably necessary to carry on the agency business, the acts customarily done when conducting that business, and the relations between principal and agent.

Implied authority usually derives from a grant of express authority by the principal and is part of an agent's actual authority. On occasion, however, implied authority may exist even though there is no relevant grant of express authority. Here, courts generally derive implied authority from the nature of the agency business, the relations between principal and agent, customs in the trade, and other facts and circumstances. For example, there may be implied authority to make a certain contract if the agent has made similar past contracts with the principal's knowledge and without his objection.

No matter what its source, an agent's implied authority cannot contradict the principal's express statements. Thus, there is no implied authority to contract where a principal has limited her agent's authority by express statement or clear implication and the contract would conflict with that limitation. But as we will see, apparent authority may still exist in such cases.

Examples of Implied Authority   Courts have created general rules or presumptions for determining the implied authority of certain agents in certain situations. For example:

1. An agent hired to *manage a business* normally has implied authority to make contracts that are reasonably necessary for conducting the business or that are customary in the business. These include contracts for obtaining equipment and supplies, making repairs, employing employees, and selling goods or services. However, a manager ordinarily has no power to borrow money or issue negotiable instruments in the principal's name unless the principal is a banking or financial concern regularly performing such activities.

2. An agent given *full control over real property* has implied authority to contract for repairs and insurance and may rent the property if this is customary. But such an agent may not sell the property or allow any third-party liens or other interests to be taken on it.

3. Agents appointed to *sell the principal's goods* may have implied authority to make customary warranties on those goods. In states that still recognize the distinction, the general agent described in Chapter 35 is more likely to have such authority than a special agent.

Apparent Authority

Apparent authority arises when the principal's behavior causes a third party to form a reasonable belief that the agent is authorized to act in a certain way. In other words, apparent authority is based on: (1) communications *by the principal* to the third party (2) that create a *reasonable appearance* of authority in the agent. Background factors such as trade customs and

THE GLOBAL BUSINESS ENVIRONMENT

Electronic Agents

In the Internet Age, evolving business practices show an increasing use of software programs known as electronic agents in e-commerce transactions. A common definition of an electronic agent is a computer program or an electronic or other automated means used to initiate an action or to respond to electronic messages without review by an individual.

In the legal context, an electronic agent can be an automated means for making or performing contracts. In automated transactions, an individual does not deal with another individual, but one or both parties are represented by electronic agents. You have probably dealt with an electronic agent if you have ordered books, CDs, airline tickets, and other goods and services from an Internet site like Amazon.com or Travelocity.com.

The legal relationship between the principal and the automated agent is not fully equivalent to common law agency, but takes into account that the electronic agent is not a human actor. Nonetheless, parties who employ or deal with electronic agents are ordinarily bound by the results of their operations.

Most modern countries have laws that indicate when a person can be bound by the action of its electronic agent. In the United States, the Uniform Computer Information Transactions Act recognizes the ability of electronic agents to bind their principals, even if no individual is aware of or reviews the agent's operation or the results of the operation. In the Philippines, a contract may not be denied legal validity solely because it was created using an electronic agent, provided the electronic agent is under the control of or its actions attributable to the person sought to be bound. India's Electronic Commerce Act states that a contract may be formed between an individual and an electronic agent if the individual has reason to know she is dealing with an electronic agent. In Canada, the Uniform Electronic Commerce Act permits contracts to be formed by electronic agents, but if an individual deals with an electronic agent and makes an error, the individual will not be bound on the contract if the electronic agent provided no opportunity to correct the error and the individual immediately notifies the other party of the error.

---

established business practices often determine whether it is reasonable for the third party to believe that the agent has authority. In other words, apparent authority exists because it *appears* that the agent may act for the principal, based on what the principal has manifested to the third party.

Principals can give their agents apparent authority through the statements they make, or tell their agents to make, *to third parties* and through the actions they knowingly allow their agents to take *with third parties*. Thus, a principal might create apparent authority by telling a third party that the agent has certain authority, or by directing the agent to do the same. A principal might also create apparent authority by appointing his agent to a position that customarily involves the authority to make certain contracts. For instance, if Penn makes Alba his sales manager, and if that position customarily involves the power to sell the firm's goods, Alba would have apparent authority to sell those products. Here, Penn's behavior in appointing Alba to the position of sales manager, as reasonably interpreted in light of business customs, gives Alba apparent authority. However, because agents cannot give themselves apparent authority, there

would be no such authority if, without Penn's knowledge or permission, Alba falsely told third parties that he had been promoted to sales manager.

Apparent authority protects third parties who reasonably rely on the principal's manifestations that the agent has authority. It assumes special importance in cases where the principal has told the agent not to make certain contracts that the agent ordinarily would have actual authority to make, but the third party knows nothing about this limitation and has no reason to know about it. Suppose that Perry employs Arthur as general sales agent for his manufacturing business. Certain warranties customarily accompany the products Perry sells, and agents like Arthur ordinarily are empowered to give these warranties. But Perry tells Arthur not to make any such warranties to buyers, thus cutting off Arthur's express and implied authority. Despite Perry's orders, however, Arthur makes the usual warranties in a sale to Thomas, who is familiar with customs in the trade. If Thomas did not know about the limitation on Arthur's authority, Perry is bound by Arthur's warranties.

The following *Opp* case discusses whether an agent has express, implied, or apparent authority.

Opp v. Wheaton Van Lines, Inc.   *231 F.3d 1060 (7th Cir. 2000)*

Shelley Opp lived in California with her husband, Richard Opp, until they sought a divorce in August 1996. In June 1997, Ms. Opp contacted Soraghan Moving and Storage, an agent of Wheaton Van Lines, to move her personal property from California to Illinois. Ms. Opp told Soraghan she wanted to insure her property for its full value of $10,000. Soraghan faxed to Ms. Opp an "Estimate/Order for Service" form which stated that Ms. Opp intended to declare that the value of the goods shipped was $10,000. Ms. Opp signed the form. According to Soraghan, it explained to Ms. Opp that she or her representative must advise the mover at the time the shipment was picked up whether Ms. Opp would like full replacement coverage of $10,000. According to Ms. Opp, she was never informed that the person releasing her property in California would have to sign anything, declare any value for her property, or do anything other than give the movers access to her belongings. The estimate form also provided a location where Ms. Opp could designate someone as her "true and lawful representative," but she made no such designation.

On the day of the move, the movers in California called Ms. Opp in Illinois to tell her they would be late arriving at the California home due to a flat tire. Ms. Opp then phoned Mr. Opp at his office and asked him to go to the house, open the door, and let the movers in. Ms. Opp also told Soraghan that "someone" would be at the California home to give the movers access to her property. Mr. Opp met the movers at the house, and he signed the bill of lading on a line that indicated that he was Ms. Opp's authorized agent, and he allegedly agreed to limit the carriers' liability for her property at 60 cents per pound. Mr. Opp also signed an inventory of the property that indicated that he was its "owner or authorized agent."

On July 8, 1997, the truck carrying Ms. Opp's belongings was struck by a train, damaging most of her property. Ms. Opp inspected her damaged property and estimated its full replacement value to be over $10,000. Soraghan claimed that its liability was limited by the bill of lading to $2,625. Ms. Opp sued Sorghan and Wheaton to recover $10,000 for property damage. The carriers moved for summary judgment, which the district court granted, finding that Mr. Opp had the actual and apparent authority to sign the bill of lading as Ms. Opp's agent. Ms. Opp appealed.

Manion, Circuit Judge An agent's authority may be either actual or apparent, and actual authority may be express or implied. Only the words or conduct of the alleged principal, not the alleged agent, establish the actual or apparent authority of an agent. We first note that Mr. Opp never received the express authority to represent Ms. Opp and to limit the carriers' liability. An agent has express authority when the principal explicitly grants the agent the authority to perform a particular act. There is no evidence that Ms. Opp explicitly granted authority to Mr. Opp to bind her to an agreement that limited the carriers' liability for her goods. Ms. Opp never requested or intended Mr. Opp to do anything other than to open the door and allow the movers to remove her property.

We next determine whether Mr. Opp had the implied authority to limit the carriers' liability. An agent has implied authority for the performance or transaction of anything reasonably necessary to effective execution of his express authority. *Restatement (Second) of Agency* § 35. Thus we must determine whether it was reasonably necessary for Mr. Opp to sign the bill of lading in order to execute his express authority to open the door to give the movers access to Ms. Opp's property.

The carriers argue that because Ms. Opp allegedly knew that the bill of lading had to be signed when her property

was picked up, but she arranged for Mr. Opp to be the only person present in California for the move, Ms. Opp's request for Mr. Opp to tender the goods to the movers also included the necessary authority for him to sign the bill of lading. But as noted above, Ms. Opp only told Mr. Opp to open the door. She made no request for him to sign anything, or to make any agreement as to the carriers' liability. Ms. Opp also testified that she was never informed that the person releasing her property in California would have to sign a bill of lading and declare a value for her property. Moreover, it is unclear whether Mr. Opp ever inferred from Ms. Opp's request that he was also authorized to limit the carriers' liability, or whether he merely thought that he was signing forms to confirm that Ms. Opp's goods were taken from the home. Thus we conclude that there is insufficient evidence to support a grant of summary judgment for the carriers on this issue.

We must then consider whether Mr. Opp had the apparent authority to sign the bill of lading and limit the carriers' liability. Under the doctrine of apparent authority, a principal will be bound not only by the authority that it actually gives to another, but also by the authority that it appears to give. Apparent authority arises when a principal creates, by its words or conduct, the reasonable impression in a third party that the agent has the authority to perform a certain act on its behalf. Thus we must determine whether the evidence demonstrates that Ms. Opp's words or conduct created a reasonable impression in the carriers that Mr. Opp had the authority to sign the bill of lading and limit their liability.

The carriers argue that they reasonably believed that Mr. Opp had the authority to sign the bill of lading because Ms. Opp allegedly knew that a bill of lading had to be signed when her goods were picked up, and she had also arranged for Mr. Opp to be the only person present at the California home to tender the goods. But material facts in the record also justify a reasonable inference that Mr. Opp did not have the apparent authority to limit the carriers' liability. It is undisputed that Ms. Opp told Soraghan that she wanted the full replacement value of $10,000 on her goods, which is reflected on the Estimate/Order for Service form. Ms. Opp never designated a "lawful representative" on the space provided on the estimate form, and thus Soraghan's own form lacked any indication that Mr. Opp was her agent. And when the movers were delayed by a flat tire on their moving truck, they called to notify Ms. Opp in Illinois, not Mr. Opp in California. Additionally, Ms. Opp testified that the carriers never informed her that the person releasing her property in California would have to sign anything, declare any value for her property, or do anything other than to give the movers access to her belongings, which indicates that the carriers could not reasonably conclude that she knew that the bill of lading had to be signed in California, and that Mr. Opp had that authority. And there is no evidence in the record that the carriers had any knowledge that Ms. Opp ever discussed the valuation of her property with Mr. Opp. We conclude, therefore, that summary judgment is precluded because the record provides sufficient evidence to enable a reasonable jury to find that Mr. Opp lacked the apparent authority to limit the carriers' liability.

Judgment reversed in favor of Ms. Opp. Remanded to the district court.

Agent's Notification and Knowledge

Sometimes the general agency rules regarding *notification and knowledge* affect a principal's contract liability. If a third party gives proper notification to an agent with actual or apparent authority to receive it, the principal is bound as if the notification had been given directly to him. Similarly, notification to a third party by an agent with the necessary authority is considered notification by the principal.

In certain circumstances, an agent's knowledge of facts is imputed to the principal. This means that the principal's rights and liabilities are what they would have been if the principal had known what the agent knew. Generally, an agent's knowledge is imputed to a principal when it is relevant to activities that the agent is authorized to undertake, or when the agent is under a duty to disclose the knowledge to the principal. Suppose that Ames contracts with Timmons on Pike's behalf, knowing that Timmons is completely mistaken about a matter material to the contract. Even though Pike knew nothing about Timmons's unilateral mistake, Timmons probably can avoid his contract with Pike.

Ratification

Ratification is a process whereby a principal binds himself to an unauthorized act done by an agent, or by a person purporting to act as an agent. Usually, the act in question is a contract. Ratification relates back to the time when the contract was made. It binds the principal as if the agent had possessed authority at that time.

Conduct Amounting to Ratification Ratification can be express or implied. An *express ratification* occurs when the principal communicates an intent to ratify by words, whether written or oral. *Implied ratification* arises when the principal's behavior evidences an intent to ratify. Examples include the principal's part performance of a contract made by an agent, or the principal's acceptance of benefits under such a contract. Sometimes even a principal's silence, acquiescence, or failure to repudiate the transaction may constitute ratification. This can occur where the principal would be expected to object if he did not consent to the contract, the principal's silence leads the third party to believe that he does consent, and the principal is aware of all relevant facts.

Additional Requirements Even if a principal's words or behavior indicate an intent to ratify, other requirements must be met before ratification occurs. These requirements have been variously stated; the following list is typical.

1. The act ratified must be one that was *valid* at the time it was performed. For example, an agent's illegal contract cannot be made binding by the principal's subsequent ratification. However, a contract that was voidable when

made due to the principal's incapacity may be ratified by a principal who has later attained or regained capacity.

2. The principal must have been *in existence* at the time the agent acted. However, as discussed in Chapter 42, corporations may bind themselves to their promoters' preincorporation contracts by adopting such contracts.

3. When the contract or other act occurred, the agent must have indicated to the third party that she was acting for a principal and not for herself. But the agent need not have disclosed the principal's identity.

4. The principal must be *legally competent* at the time of ratification. For instance, an insane principal cannot ratify.

5. As the following *Work Connection* case makes clear, the principal must have *knowledge of all material facts* regarding the prior act or contract at the time it is ratified. Here, an agent's knowledge is not imputed to the principal.

6. The principal must ratify the *entire* act or contract. He cannot ratify the beneficial parts of a contract and reject those that are detrimental.

7. In ratifying, the principal must use the *same formalities* required to give the agent authority to execute the transaction. As Chapter 35 stated, few formalities normally are needed to give an agent authority. But where the original agency contract requires a writing, ratification likewise must be written.

Note that a principal's ratification is binding even if not communicated to the third party. Also, once a principal has ratified a contract, the principal may not revoke the ratification.

Intervening Events Certain events occurring after an agent's contract but before the principal's ratification may cut off the principal's power to ratify. These include: (1) the third party's *withdrawal* from the contract; (2) the third party's *death or loss of capacity;* (3) the principal's *failure to ratify within a reasonable time* (assuming that the principal's silence did not already work a ratification); and (4) *changed circumstances* (especially where the change places a greater burden on the third party than he assumed when the contract was made).

The Work Connection, Inc. v. Universal Forest Products, Inc.
2002 Minn. App. LEXIS 659 (Minn. Ct. App. 2002)

The Work Connection, Inc. (Connection) is a temporary employment agency that provides workers to customers for a fee. In February 1995, Doyle Olson, a sales representative for Connection, contacted Universal Forest Products, Inc. (Universal). Olson spoke with Ken Von Bank, Universal's production manager and the individual with direct supervisory authority over temporary workers. Universal hired some of Connection's employees, including Wayne DeLage, to construct fence panels at its Shakopee plant.

Olson gave Universal work verification forms that were used as employee timecards. Universal filled out and signed the forms, which contained the worker's name, date, and hours worked. Submission of a completed, signed form was required for an employee to be paid, and Connection processed the forms through its payroll department. The work verification forms contained the following language:

CUSTOMER AGREES TO THE TERMS AND CONDITIONS SET FORTH ON THE REVERSE SIDE HEREOF AND CERTIFIES THAT THE LISTED EMPLOYEES HAVE SATISFACTORILY PERFORMED SERVICES FOR THE HOURS SHOWN ABOVE.

The back of the verification form stated the following:

CONDITIONS OF UNDERTAKING

* * * *

3. CUSTOMER agrees to indemnify, hold harmless and defend THE WORK CONNECTION against claims, damages, or penalties under the following circumstances:

* * * *

(b) From any claims for bodily injury (including death), or loss of, and loss of use of, or damage to, property arising out of the use of or operation of CUSTOMER'S owned, nonowned, or leased vehicles, machinery or equipment by

THE WORK CONNECTION employees.

The parties never discussed the language on the back of the work verification form. The parties' oral agreement did not include a term that required Universal to provide workers' compensation insurance for Connection's employees. Nonetheless, Von Bank signed the verification forms for Universal from March 1995 through July 1995, when the office manager, Yvonne Kohout, took over signing duties. At some point, Universal ran out of original work verification forms. Kohout simply photocopied the front side of the form and, thereafter, submitted forms that were blank on the back.

In August 1995, DeLage severed three of his fingers while operating a radial arm saw. DeLage received $75,000 in workers' compensation benefits from Connection. Connection then asked Universal to indemnify it pursuant to the language on the back of the verification form. Universal refused to pay, and Connection sued Universal for breach of contract. The trial court granted Universal's motion for a directed verdict. Connection appealed.

The Minnesota Court of Appeals held that Von Bank and Kohout had no actual or apparent authority to bind Universal to the indemnification clause. The court then considered whether Universal had ratified the indemnification clause by accepting the benefits of the employment contract for DeLage's labors.

Halbrooks, Judge Connection contends that Universal agreed to be liable for workers' compensation costs based on a theory of ratification. Ratification occurs when a principal retains the benefits of an agent's unauthorized act. Once the principal has received the benefit, it is estopped from disclaiming liability based on the fact that the act was unauthorized. Connection contends that because Universal received the benefit of the temporary worker's labor, it also accepted the associated burden of the indemnification clause on the back of the verification form.

This argument is not viable. Ratification does not occur if the principal is ignorant of material facts surrounding the transaction. Ratification by a party of another's unauthorized acts occurs where the party with full knowledge of all material facts confirms, approves, or sanctions the other's acts. Where a principal accepts and retains the benefits of an unauthorized act of an agent with full knowledge of all the facts he thereby ratifies the act.

Here Universal lacked knowledge of a material fact: that the original timecards that Kohout signed contained language committing Universal to indemnify appellant for a workers' compensation claim. Given that Universal lacked full information regarding Kohout's actions, it did not ratify her conduct.

Judgment for Universal affirmed.

Contracts Made by Subagents

The rules governing a principal's liability for her agent's contracts generally apply to contracts made by her subagents. If an agent has authorized his subagent to make a certain contract and this authorization is within the authority granted the agent by his principal, the principal is bound to the subagent's contract.

Also, a subagent contracting within the authority conferred by her principal (the agent) binds the *agent* in an appropriate case. In addition, both the principal and the agent probably can ratify the contracts of subagents.

Contract Liability of the Agent

When are *agents* liable on contracts they make on their principals' behalf? For the most part, this question depends on a different set of variables than the variables determining the principal's liability. The most important of these variables is the *nature of the principal.* Thus, this section first examines the liability of agents who contract for several different kinds of principals. Then it discusses two ways that an agent can be bound after contracting for any type of principal.

The Nature of the Principal

Disclosed Principal A principal is **disclosed** if a third party knows or has reason to know: (1) that the agent is acting for a principal, and (2) the principal's identity. Unless he agrees otherwise, an agent who represents a disclosed principal is *not liable* on authorized contracts made for such a principal. Suppose that Adkins, a sales agent for Parker, calls on Thompson and presents a business card clearly identifying her as Parker's agent. If Adkins contracts to sell Parker's goods to Thompson with authority to do so, Adkins is not bound because Parker is a disclosed principal. This rule usually is consistent with the third party's intentions; for example, Thompson probably intended to contract only with Parker.

Partially Disclosed Principal A principal is **partially disclosed** if the third party: (1) knows or has reason to know that the agent is acting for a principal, but (2) lacks knowledge or reason to know the principal's *identity*. This can occur where an agent simply neglects to disclose his principal's identity. Also, a principal may tell her agent to keep her identity secret to preserve her bargaining position.

Among the factors affecting anyone's decision to contract are the integrity, reliability, and creditworthiness of the other party to the contract. Where the principal is partially disclosed, the third party ordinarily cannot judge these matters. As a result, he usually depends on the agent's reliability to some degree. For this reason, and to give the third party additional protection, an agent is liable on contracts made for a partially disclosed principal unless the parties agree otherwise.

Undisclosed Principal A principal is **undisclosed** where the third party lacks knowledge or reason to know both the principal's existence *and* the principal's identity. This can occur where a principal judges that he will get a better deal if his existence and identity remain secret, or where the agent neglects to make adequate disclosure.

A third party who deals with an agent for an undisclosed principal obviously cannot assess the principal's reliability, integrity, and creditworthiness. Indeed, here the third party reasonably believes that the *agent* is the other party to the contract. Thus, the third party may hold an agent liable on contracts made for an undisclosed principal.

When the third party discovers that the agent has acted for an undisclosed principal and learns the identity of the principal, the third party has a choice: the third party may choose to hold either the principal or the agent liable on the contract. The third party may not usually refuse to perform the contract merely because the principal was undisclosed. This means that an undisclosed principal may enforce a contract against a third party who refuses to perform at all.

Nonexistent Principals Unless there is an agreement to the contrary, an agent who purports to act for a **legally nonexistent** principal, such as an unincorporated association, is personally liable. This is true even where the third party knows that the principal is nonexistent.

Liability of Agent by Agreement

An agent may bind herself to contracts she makes for a principal by *expressly agreeing* to be liable. This is true regardless of the principal's nature. An agent may expressly bind herself by: (1) making the contract in her own name rather than in the principal's name, (2) joining the principal as an obligor on the contract, or (3) acting as surety or guarantor for the principal.

Problems of contract interpretation can arise when it is claimed that an agent has expressly promised to be bound. The two most important factors affecting the agent's liability are the wording of the contract and the way the agent has signed it. An agent who wishes to avoid liability should make no express promises in her own name and should try to ensure that the agreement obligates only the principal. In addition, the agent should use a signature form that clearly identifies the principal and indicates the agent's representative capacity—for example, "Parker, by Adkins," or "Adkins, for Parker." Simply adding the word "agent" when signing her name ("Adkins, Agent") or signing without any indication of her status ("Adkins") could subject the agent to liability. Sometimes, the body of the agreement suggests one result and the signature form another. In such contexts, oral evidence or other extrinsic evidence of the parties' understanding may help resolve the uncertainty.

Implied Warranty of Authority

An agent also may be liable to a third party if he contracts for the principal while lacking authority to do so. Here, the principal is not bound, yet it is arguably unfair to leave the third party without any recovery. Thus, an agent normally is bound on the theory that he made an implied warranty of his authority to contract. This liability exists regardless of whether the agent is otherwise bound to the third party.

To illustrate, suppose that Allen is a salesperson for Prine, a seller of furs. Allen has actual authority to receive offers for the sale of Prine's furs but not to make sale contracts, which must be approved by Prine himself. Prine has long followed this practice, and it is customary in the markets where his agents work. Representing himself as Prine's agent but saying nothing about his authority, Allen contracts to sell Prine's furs to Thatcher on Prine's behalf. Thatcher, who should have known better, honestly believes that Allen has authority to contract to sell Prine's furs. Prine is not liable on Allen's contract because Allen lacked actual or apparent authority to bind him. But Allen is liable to Thatcher for breaching his implied warranty of authority.

However, an agent is *not* liable for making an unauthorized contract if:

1. The third party *actually knows* that the agent lacks authority. Note from the previous example, however, that the agent still is liable where the third party had *reason to know* that authority was lacking.

2. The principal subsequently *ratifies* the contract. Here, the principal is bound, and there is arguably little reason to bind the agent.

3. The agent adequately *notifies* the third party that he does not warrant his authority to contract.

Is the *Reed* case, which follows, best regarded as proceeding under the first exception just stated, or the third? In any event, do you agree with the result?

Reed v. National Foundation Life Insurance Co.
1996 Tenn. App. LEXIS 807 (Tenn. Ct. App. 1996)

On January 7, 1994, Mark Bradshaw, an agent for the National Foundation Life Insurance Company (NFLIC), tried to sell a health insurance policy to Bobby Reed. Reed was informed by Mark Bradshaw that his health insurance coverage would become effective upon the signing of certain insurance forms and the payment of the first monthly premium. Reed stated that he did not read the insurance forms because he was assured by Bradshaw that he had full coverage.

On the same day, Reed signed documents that contained these provisions:

I understand that the agent cannot change, alter or amend any NFLIC information requirement. I also understand that the agent cannot change, alter or amend the policy. I further understand that the agent has no authority to make any representations about the conditions under which NFLIC will issue a policy or make a policy effective.

I understand that the insurance applied for shall be subject to the provisions and conditions of the policy, and that the policy shall not be effective until the policy has been actually issued, with first premium paid and delivered to the insurer while the health of all persons named in this application remains as stated herein . . . I further understand that losses due to Pre-existing Conditions, diseases, or bodily injuries occurring prior to the Effective Date of the Policy are not covered . . . unless otherwise provided.

Another document signed by Reed informed him that the application process might take as long as two weeks. Reed did not read any of these documents.

The NFLIC received Reed's application on January 12, 1994. On January 19, it called Reed's telephone number and was informed that he had suffered a heart attack on January 15. The NFLIC thereupon notified Reed that it was postponing consideration of his application because his health condition had changed since the application was submitted. No policy was ever issued. Reed had paid the first monthly premium.

Reed then sued Bradshaw, arguing that Bradshaw had impliedly warranted that he possessed authority to contractually bind the NFLIC upon the happening of certain events, and that he breached that warranty. After the trial court denied Bradshaw's motion for summary judgment, he appealed.

Inman, Senior Judge Reed's theory of recovery against agent Bradshaw is apparently based on the principle that an agent purporting to make an unauthorized contract on behalf of his principal may be liable to a third party on the ground that he warrants his authority to enter into the contract. It is well settled that one who purports as agent to enter into a contract, upon which the principal is not bound because of the fact that the agent has contracted without authority or in excess of his authority, is personally liable for the damage thus occasioned by the other contracting party. However, as is here determinative, it is essential to any such third party's right of action that the third party purporting to hold the agent liable must have acted without knowledge, or imputed knowledge, of the agent's lack of authority. The *Restatement (Second) of Agency* section 329 provides: "A person who purports to make a contract, conveyance or representation on behalf of another who has full capacity but whom he has no power to bind, thereby becomes subject to liability to the other party thereto upon an implied warranty of authority, unless he has manifested that he does not make such warranty or the other party knows that the agent is not so authorized." Thus, if the agent, in ac-

cordance with the prior course of business between them, sends a notification of such lack of warranty, or if a statement of the same purport is conspicuously placed upon the memorandum of the contract, the fact that the third person does not read the notification is immaterial.

The documents signed by Reed acknowledging the lack of authority of agent Bradshaw are a complete refutation of his purported cause of action against the agent. He cannot assert a claim against the agent while acknowledging that he was aware that the agent had no authority in the premises. The motion of the agent for summary judgment is therefore well-taken.

Judgment reversed in favor of NFLIC.

Contract Suits Against Principal and Agent

Figure 1 sketches the most important situations in which the principal, the agent, or both are liable due to the agent's contracts. As it suggests, a third party usually has someone to sue if neither the principal nor the agent performs.

Without ratification, a principal is not liable on contracts made by an agent who lacks authority. Here, though, the agent usually is bound under an implied warranty of authority. In addition, the agent is bound on the

contract where the principal was partially disclosed, undisclosed, or legally nonexistent. Authorized contracts for a disclosed principal do not bind an agent unless he has agreed to be bound. But here the agent's actual or apparent authority binds the principal.

As Figure 1 further illustrates, in certain situations both principal and agent are liable on a contract made by the agent. This can occur where an agent with appropriate authority contracts on behalf of a partially disclosed or undisclosed principal. Also, an agent can bind himself by express agreement in situations where the principal also is bound.

Figure 1   *Liability of Principal and Agent: The Major Possibilities*

Principal	Agent's Authority		
	Actual	**Apparent**	**None**
Disclosed	P liable on the contract: A not liable on the contract unless agreement	P liable on the contract; A not liable on the contract unless agreement	P not liable on the contract; A usually liable for breach of the implied warranty of authority
Partially Disclosed	P liable on the contract; A liable on the contract	P liable on the contract; A liable on the contract	P not liable on the contract; A liable on the contract or for breach of the implied warranty of authority
Undisclosed	P liable on the contract; A liable on the contract	Impossible	P not liable on the contract; A liable on the contract

Tort Liability of the Principal

Besides contracting on the principal's behalf, an agent may also commit torts. A principal's liability for those torts involves four distinct subjects, which we consider in turn.

Respondeat Superior Liability

Under the doctrine of **respondeat superior** (let the master answer), a principal who is an **employer** is liable for torts committed by agents: (1) who are **employees** and (2) who commit the tort while acting within the **scope of their employment.** *Respondeat superior* makes the principal liable both for an employee's negligence and for her intentional torts. Chapter 35 outlined the main factors courts consider when determining whether an agent is an employee. The most important of these factors is a principal's right to control the physical details of an agent's work.

Respondeat superior is a rule of *imputed* or *vicarious* liability because it bases an employer's liability on his relationship with the employee rather than his own fault. This imputation of liability reflects the following beliefs: (1) that the economic burdens of employee torts can best be borne by employers, (2) that employers often can protect themselves against such burdens by self-insuring or purchasing insurance, and (3) that the resulting costs frequently can be passed on to consumers, thus "socializing" the economic risk posed by employee torts. *Respondeat superior* also motivates employers to ensure that their employees avoid tortious behavior. Because they typically control the physical details of the work, employers are fairly well positioned to do so.

Scope of Employment *Respondeat superior*'s scope-of-employment requirement has been stated in many ways and is notoriously ambiguous. In the past, for example, some courts considering this question asked whether the employee was on a "frolic" of his own, or merely made a "detour" from his assigned activity. According to the *Restatement,* an employee's conduct is within the scope of his employment if it meets *each* of the following four tests:

1. It was of the *kind* that the employee was employed to perform. To meet this test, an employee's conduct need only be of the same general nature as work expressly authorized or be incidental to its performance.

2. It occurred substantially within the authorized *time period.* This is simply the employee's assigned time of work. Beyond this, there is an extra period of time during which the employment may continue. For instance, a security guard whose regular quitting time is 5:00 probably meets the time test if he unjustifiably injures an intruder at 5:15. Doing the same thing three hours later, however, would probably put the guard outside the scope of employment.

3. It occurred substantially within the *location* authorized by the employer. This includes locations not unreasonably distant from the authorized location. For example, a salesperson told to limit her activities to New York City probably would satisfy the location requirement while pursuing the employer's business in suburbs just outside the city limits but not while pursuing the same business in Philadelphia. Generally, the smaller the authorized area of activity, the smaller the departure from that area needed to put the employee outside the scope of employment. For example, consider the different physical distance limitations that should apply to a factory worker and a traveling salesperson.

4. It was motivated *at least in part* by the *purpose* of serving the employer. This test is met where the employee's conduct was motivated *to any appreciable extent* by the desire to serve the employer. Thus, an employee's tort may be within the scope of employment even if the motives for committing it were partly personal. For example, suppose that a delivery employee is behind schedule and for that reason has an accident while speeding to make a delivery in his employer's truck. The employee would be within the scope of employment even if another reason for his speeding was to impress a friend who was riding with him.

Direct Liability

A principal's **direct liability** for an agent's torts differs considerably from *respondeat superior* liability. Here, the principal himself is at fault, and there is no need to impute liability to him. Also, no scope-of-employment requirement exists in direct liability cases, and the agent need not be an employee. Of course, a principal might incur both direct liability and *respondeat superior* liability in cases where due to the principal's fault, an employee commits a tort within the scope of her employment.

A principal is directly liable for an agent's tortious conduct if the principal directs that conduct and intends that it occur. In such cases, the *agent*'s behavior might be intentional, reckless, or negligent. For instance, if Petty tells

ETHICS IN ACTION

Principal's Liability for Agent's Torts

We have covered the reasons the law makes employers liable for the torts of employees under *respondeat superior,* including the ability of employers to bear the burden or to socialize the cost of paying for damages caused by an employee's tort.

- Do you think those are good reasons to make someone liable for the actions of another person? What kind of behavior is the rule of *respondeat superior* likely to foster? Does the rule encourage employers to train and supervise their employees better?

- Do you think *respondeat superior* makes employers liable for too many acts of their employees? Does the rule discourage some businesses from using employees? Does any discouragement affect both prospective employers and prospective employees?

- Do you think the law should make employers liable for all the torts of their employees?

- Do you think it is the right thing to do for an employer to pay for all damages caused to others by the tort of an employee? When forming your answers, consider the ethical theories we covered in Chapter 4.

---

his agent Able to beat up Tabler and Able does so, Petty is directly liable to Tabler. Petty also would be liable for harm to third parties that results from his telling Able to do construction work in a negligent, substandard fashion.

The typical direct liability case, however, involves harm caused by the principal's negligence regarding the agent. Examples of direct liability for negligence include: (1) giving the agent improper or unclear instructions; (2) failing to make and enforce appropriate regulations to govern the agent's conduct; (3) hiring an unsuitable agent; (4) failing to discharge an unsuitable agent; (5) furnishing an agent with improper tools, instruments, or materials; and (6) carelessly supervising an agent. Today, suits for negligent hiring are common.

LOG ON

www.toolkit.cch.com/text/P12_8045.asp
The CCH Business Owners Toolkit is a font of information on managing the liability of employers for the acts of employees. The URL above goes to an article, "Negligent Hiring and Supervision," that gives advice on how an employer may avoid vicarious and direct liability for the torts of employees.

The next case, *Millan,* covers both direct liability and *respondeat superior.*

Millan v. Dean Witter Reynolds, Inc.   *2001 Tex. App. LEXIS 7957 (Tex. Ct. App. 2001)*

Maria Millan opened two brokerage accounts at Dean Witter Reynolds, Inc. One was for herself and the other for her as trustee for her son James. The broker for both accounts was her other son Miguel, an employee of Dean Witter. Over the course of the next three years, Miguel systematically looted his mother's account, ultimately stealing from her more than $287,000. He managed to do this by forging her signature on an account application form and opening an additional account in her name. This account had check-writing privileges and a credit card attached to it that Miguel used liberally. Dean Witter did not verify Millan's signature, as its policy required, when the bogus account was opened.

Miguel took his mother's periodic deposits, usually consisting of several thousand dollars, deposited these checks into this fictitious account, and wrote himself checks from the account, usually made out to "cash." Miguel covered his tracks by opening a post office box, filing a false change of address form on which he forged his mother's signature, and creating false account statements purporting to be from Dean Witter. In one instance, Miguel forged a check he stole from his mother's checkbook and made it payable to "cash" in the amount of $35,000. Disregarding Dean Witter written policy, a Dean Witter supervisor did not verify the check despite the high amount, the payment to "cash," and the concerns of a Dean Witter employee who first handled the check.

Millan sued her son and Dean Witter for unauthorized transactions, negligence, and gross negligence. The trial court directed a verdict for Dean Witter on the issues of vicarious liability. The jury was given the issue regarding Dean Witter's direct liability to Millan, and it found Dean Witter negligent and liable for 15 percent of her damages. Millan was found responsible for 85 percent of her damages on the grounds that she should have discovered the fraud earlier than she did. Millan appealed the trial court's decision to a Texas court of appeals. The court of appeals upheld the jury verdict that Dean Witter was only 15 percent responsible for Millan's damages under direct liability. The court then considered the vicarious liability issue using the doctrine of respondeat superior.

Stone, Justice The crux of Dean Witter's argument is that Miguel, by acting in a criminal manner, was acting outside the scope of his authority; thus, Dean Witter contends it should not be vicariously liable for his acts. It is not a defense to liability to claim an agent was authorized only to do those acts that would be lawful. If an agent acts within the scope of his general authority, his wrongful act, although not authorized, will subject his principal to liability. In general, an agent's authority is presumed to be coextensive with the business entrusted to his care. When an agent acts for a principal, the principal is liable for the agent's fraud and misrepresentations, even though the principal has no knowledge of the fraud or misrepresentation and received no benefit from the fraud or misrepresentation. Were this not so, a firm could actually rely upon its agents to embezzle from accounts, then claim ignorance. An exception to the principle of *respondeat superior,* usually applied in cases involving serious criminal activity, is that an employer is not liable for intentional and malicious acts that are unforeseeable considering the employee's duties. Thus, we must examine Miguel's scope of authority and consider whether his acts were foreseeable.

The test to determine an employer's liability for the acts of its employees is whether on the occasion in question, the master had the right and power to direct and control the servant in the performance of the causal act or omission at the very instance of the act or neglect. To meet this test, the employee's act must 1) fall within the scope of the employee's general authority, (2) be in furtherance of the employer's business, and (3) be for the accomplishment of the object for which the employee was hired.

The key inquiry appears to center on whether the act, if performed properly, is part of an employee's general authority. For example, it is not ordinarily within the scope of a servant's authority to commit an assault on a third person. However, an employer will be held liable for its employee's assault on a third party if that assault stems directly from the employee's exercise (however inappropriate or excessive) of a delegated right or duty, such as being in charge of admissions to a club.

Here, Miguel was entrusted with the business of opening brokerage accounts for clients, receiving deposits to those accounts, making purchases of securities as directed by clients, and selling them as directed. These acts comprised the scope of his general authority; he misused his authority, but the acts were not "utterly unrelated" to his duties. Even those acts he may have undertaken outside of his place of employment—pilfering his mother's checks, renting a post office box, rifling his mother's mailbox—were merely additional acts that furthered his fraud. We conclude that Miguel acted within the course and scope of his employment, albeit improperly. We further conclude that, given a broker's customary duties, it was not unforeseeable that Miguel could have used his position to defraud a customer. Indeed, Dean Witter's policy of monitoring certain accounts more closely recognizes the potential for fraudulent acts, and the jury found that Dean Witter was 15 percent negligent.

We hold there was more than a scintilla of probative evidence regarding Dean Witter's vicarious liability for fraud to support submission of the issue to the jury.

Judgment reversed in part in favor of Millan; remanded to the trial court.

Liability for Torts of Independent Contractors

A principal ordinarily is *not* liable for torts committed by independent contractors. As compared with employees, independent contractors are more likely to have the size and resources to insure against tort liability and to pass on the resulting costs themselves. Sometimes, therefore, the risk still can be socialized if only the independent contractor is held responsible. Because the principal does not control the manner in which an independent contractor's work is performed, moreover, he has less ability to prevent a contractor's torts than an employer has to prevent an employee's torts. Thus, imposing liability on principals for the torts of independent contractors may do little to eliminate the contractor's torts.

However, the rule that principals are not liable for torts committed by independent contractors has exceptions. For example:

1. A principal can be *directly* liable for tortious behavior connected with the retention of an independent contractor. One example is the hiring of a dangerously incompetent independent contractor.

2. A principal is liable for harm resulting from the independent contractor's failure to perform a *nondelegable duty.* A nondelegable duty is a duty whose proper performance is so important that a principal cannot avoid liability by contracting it away. Examples include a carrier's duty to transport its passengers safely, a municipality's duty to keep its streets in repair, a railroad's duty to maintain safe crossings, and a landlord's duties to make repairs and to use care in doing so. Thus, a landlord who retains an independent contractor to repair the stairs in an apartment building is liable for injuries caused by the contractor's failure to repair the stairs properly.

3. A principal is liable for an independent contractor's negligent failure to take the special precautions needed to conduct certain *highly dangerous* or *inherently dangerous* activities. Examples of such activities include excavations in publicly traveled areas, the clearing of land by fire, the construction of a dam, and the demolition of a building. For example, a contractor engaged in demolishing a building presumably has duties to warn pedestrians and to keep them at a safe distance. If injury results from the independent contractor's failure to meet these duties, the principal is liable.

Liability for Agent's Misrepresentations

Special rules apply when a third party sues a principal for **misrepresentations** made by her agent. In most cases where the principal is liable under these rules, the third party can elect to recover in tort, or to rescind the transaction.

A principal is *directly* liable for misrepresentations made by her agent during authorized transactions if she *intended* that the agent make the misrepresentation. In some states, a principal also may be directly liable if she *negligently* allows the agent to make misrepresentations. Even where a principal is not directly at fault, she may be liable for an agent's misrepresentations if the agent had *actual or apparent authority to make true statements on the subject.* Suppose that an agent authorized to sell farmland falsely states that a stream on the land has never flooded the property when in fact it does so almost every year, and that this statement induces a third party to buy the land. The principal is directly liable if she intended that the agent make this false statement. Even if the principal is personally blameless, she is liable if the agent had actual or apparent authority to make true statements about the stream.

After contemplating their potential liability under the rules just discussed, both honest and dishonest principals

---

CONCEPT REVIEW

An Outline of the Principal's Tort Liability

Respondeat Superior	1. Agent must be an employee, *and* 2. Employee must act within scope of employment while committing tort
Direct Liability	1. Principal intends and directs agent's intentional tort, recklessness, or negligence, *or* 2. Principal is negligent regarding agent
Torts of Independent Contractors	1. Principal generally is *not* liable 2. Exceptions for direct liability, highly dangerous activities, and nondelegable duties
Misrepresentation	1. Direct liability 2. Vicarious liability where agent had authority to make true statements on the subject of the misrepresentation 3. An exculpatory clause may eliminate the principal's tort liability, but the third party still can rescind

may try to escape liability for an agent's misrepresentations by including an *exculpatory clause* in contracts the agent makes with third parties. Such clauses typically state that the agent only has authority to make the representations contained in the contract and that only those representations bind the principal. Exculpatory clauses do not protect a principal who intends or expects that an agent will make false statements. Otherwise, though, they insulate the principal from *tort* liability if the agent misrepresents. But the third party still may rescind the transaction, because it would be unjust to let the principal benefit from the transaction while disclaiming responsibility for it.

Tort Liability of the Agent

Agents are usually liable for their own torts. Normally, they are not absolved from liability just because they acted at the principal's command. However, there are exceptions to this generalization.

   1. An agent can escape liability if she is *exercising a privilege of the principal.* Suppose that Tingle grants Parkham a right-of-way to transport his farm products over a private road crossing Tingle's land. Parkham's agent Adams would not be liable in trespass for driving across Tingle's land to transport farm products if she did so at Parkham's command. However, an agent must not exceed the scope of the privilege and must act for the purpose for which the privilege was given. Thus, Adams would not be protected if she took her Jeep on a midnight joyride across Tingle's land. Also, the privilege given the agent must be delegable in the first place. If Tingle had given the easement to Parkham exclusively, Adams would not be privileged to drive across Tingle's land.

   2. A principal who is *privileged to take certain actions in defense of his person or property* may often authorize an agent to do the same. In such cases, the agent escapes liability if the principal could have done so. For example, a properly authorized agent may use force to protect the life or property of his principal if the principal could have done the same.

   3. An agent who makes *misrepresentations* while conducting the principal's business is not liable in tort unless he either *knew or had reason to know* their falsity. Suppose Parker authorizes Arnold to sell his house, falsely telling Arnold that the house is fully insulated. Arnold does not know that the statement is false and could not discover its falsity through a reasonable inspection. If Arnold tells Thomas that the house is fully insulated and Thomas relies on this statement in purchasing the house, Parker is directly liable to Thomas, but Arnold is not liable.

   4. An agent is not liable for injuries to third persons caused by *defective tools or instrumentalities* furnished by the principal unless the agent had actual knowledge or reason to know of the defect.

Tort Suits Against Principal and Agent

Both principal and agent sometimes are liable for an agent's torts. Here, the parties are *jointly and severally liable.* This means that a third party may join the principal and the agent in one suit and get a judgment against each, or may sue either or both individually and get a judgment against either or both. However, once a third party actually collects in full from either the principal or the agent, no further recovery is possible.

   In some cases, therefore, either the principal or the agent has to satisfy the judgment alone despite the other party's liability. Here, the other party sometimes is required to *indemnify* the party who has satisfied the judgment. As discussed in Chapter 35, for example, sometimes a principal is required to indemnify an agent for tort liability the agent incurs. On the other hand, some torts committed by agents may involve a breach of duty to their principal, and the principal may be able to recover from an agent on this basis.

Problems and Problem Cases

   1. John Schnabl was the sole proprietor of a logging business. Due to ill health, John placed his son Wade in charge of the business, telling Wade he had authority to hire and fire employees, to seek logging contracts, to assign jobs, and to pay himself whatever he wanted. John did not, however, give Wade authority to borrow money for the business. Nonetheless, Wade borrowed $20,000 for the business and signed a promissory note obligating the business to repay the lender, Neal Hausam. When the note was not repaid, Hausam sued both Wade and John. Did Wade have actual or apparent authority to bind the business, and therefore John, on the loan?

2. Rosia Adams, a warehouse employee at a school board warehouse, was injured when she slipped on a wet floor at the warehouse. The floor was wet because it had been mopped to clean up a spill from a defective Coca-Cola vending machine leased to the school district by a local Coca-Cola bottling company (Coke). The written lease for the machine required the school board to indemnify Coke for injuries like those suffered by Adams. The lease was signed by a warehouse inventory clerk. His job was simply to receive and inventory goods delivered to the school board's warehouse.

Adams sued Coke and got a judgment against it. Coke filed a third-party suit against the school board, arguing that the lease obligated the school board to compensate Coke for Adams's injuries. Based on the facts just presented, did the warehouse clerk have express, implied, or apparent authority to bind the school board to this particular term in the lease?

3. Harry Tighe opened an investment securities account with Legg Mason Wood Walker, Inc. Legg Mason could make no investments for Tighe's account without Tighe's authorization. When Tighe receive his first monthly statement from Legg Mason, he saw that his broker had made an unauthorized $220,000 purchase of limited partnership units. Tighe called the broker and objected to the purchase. Later, the broker persuaded Tighe to hold the units to see how well the investment performed. Tighe decide to hold onto the units only because the broker told him that they were not readily marketable. In fact, the units were readily marketable. For more than two years, Tighe continued to invest in his Legg Mason account through the broker. He finally complained to a Legg Mason compliance officer, but even then did not attend to revoke the purchase of the limited partnership units. Has Tighe ratified the broker's unauthorized purchase of the units?

4. Sally Leiner was the sole shareholder, director, and president of Ecco Bella, Inc., a New Jersey Corporation. On various occasions, African Bio-Botanica, Inc. sold Leiner and/or Ecco Bella merchandise. African gave little thought to the party with whom it was dealing. Ini-

tially, its records listed Sally Leiner as the customer; later, this was changed to Ecco Bella, but without any indication that Ecco Bella was a corporation. The checks with which Leiner paid for her orders and her firm's stationery bore the name Ecco Bella, but likewise did not indicate that the firm was a corporation.

Eventually, Leiner did not pay for a shipment from African, and African sued her personally for damages in a New Jersey trial court. Leiner's defense was that only the corporation, and not herself personally, was liable. Is Leiner correct?

5. A sales representative of Wired Music, Inc. sold Frank Pierson, president of the Great River Steamboat Company, a five-year Muzak Program Service for a riverboat and restaurant owned by Great River. Pierson signed a form contract drafted by Wired Music in the following manner:

By /s/ Frank C. Pierson, Pres.
Title

The Great River Steamboat Co.
~~Port of St. Louis Investments, Inc.~~
For the Corporation

In signing, Pierson crossed out "Port of St. Louis Investments, Inc.," which had been incorrectly listed as the name of the corporation, and inserted the proper name. The contract included the following clause arguably making Pierson a surety or guarantor for Great River: "The individual signing this agreement for the subscriber guarantees that all of the above provisions shall be complied with."

Great River made approximately four payments under the contract and then ceased to pay. Wired Music brought an action for contract damages against Pierson personally. Is Pierson liable?

6. Twelve people joined together to sponsor and promote a group of Little League baseball teams called the Golden Spike Little League. They arranged to purchase $3,900 in equipment for the league from a local sporting goods store. When the store sued the 12 individuals for refusing to pay the $3,900, they defended by arguing that they were agents for a disclosed principal, the league. Did this defense work?

7. James Thurn and Deryl Hines incorporated their feedlock business as Hines & Thurn Feedlot, Inc., a corporation. The corporation made three livestock purchases from Zumbrota Livestock Auction Market totaling over $540,000. Zumbrota sent invoices addressed to "Thurn-Hines Lvstk" or "Thurn Hines Livst." The corporation paid for the livestock with three checks. Printed on each check was "Thurn-Hines Livestock, Hines-Thurn Feedlot,

Inc., Box 555, Edgewood, IA 52042." The checks were signed by Jean Offerman, a corporation employee, but did not indicate the capacity in which Offerman signed. When the corporation stopped payment on the checks, Zumbrota sued Thurn and Hines individually for the amount of the livestock purchases, claiming that Thurn and Hines were agents for an undisclosed principal. Zumbrota's vice president argued that he knew the business only as "Thurn & Hines." Were Thurn and Hines liable to Zumbrota?

8. Redford had been a backhoe operator for five years. Although he had worked for other sign companies, he had spent 90 percent of his time during the past three years working for Tube Art Display, Inc. Redford generally dug holes exactly as directed by the sign company employing him. He did, however, pay his own business taxes, and he did not participate in any of the fringe benefits available to Tube Art employees.

Tube Art obtained a permit to install a sign in the parking lot of a combination commercial and apartment building. Telling Redford how to proceed, Tube Art's service manager laid out the exact location of a 4 × 4-foot square on the asphalt surface with yellow paint and directed that the hole be 6 feet deep. After Redford began the job, he negligently struck a small natural gas pipeline with the backhoe. He examined the pipe, and, finding no indication of a leak or break, concluded that the line was not in use and left the worksite. Later, an explosion and fire occurred in the building serviced by the line. As a result, a business owned by Massey was destroyed. Massey sued Tube Art for Redford's negligence under the doctrine of *respondeat superior*. Will Massey recover?

9. A. J. Gatzke, a district manager for the Walgreen Company, spent several weeks in Duluth, Minnesota, supervising the opening of a new Walgreen restaurant there. He remained at the restaurant approximately 17 hours a day, and he was on call 24 hours a day. While in Duluth, he lived at the Edgewater Motel at Walgreen's expense. After some heavy drinking late one night, Gatzke returned to his motel room and began filling out an expense account required by his employer. Shortly after Gatzke went to bed, a fire broke out in his motel room. Gatzke escaped, but fire damage to the motel totaled over $330,000. The fire was caused by Gatzke's dumping a burning cigarette or match in a wastebasket near the desk at which he worked.

Edgewater sued Walgreen for Gatzke's negligence. Did Gatzke act within the scope of his employment when he negligently started the fire?

10. The State of Indiana hired Mogul Construction Company to repair a 10-mile stretch of highway. Part of the job was to repair a bridge over a river. Mogul subcontracted this job to Wonder Construction Company. The repair of a bridge is a fairly dangerous activity that requires special precautions to keep automobile accidents from occurring. One of those precautions was to devise safe procedures for getting automobiles over the bridge while still getting the repair work done. Mogul did not tell Wonder exactly how to proceed or supervise how it did the job. Instead, the job was Wonder's to do as it saw fit.

Unfortunately, Wonder's standards of fitness evidently weren't too high. One night, 10 cars went off the bridge and into the river because the signs Wonder used to direct them around the construction work were all screwed up. Because Wonder had too few assets, the various negligence plaintiffs sued Mogul as well. Will Mogul be liable under *respondeat superior* here? Under what other theory might Mogul be liable?

11. Paula hires Albert to sell her house. She tells Albert to tell potential buyers that the house is fully insulated, which Paula knows is a lie. Albert, who has no reason to doubt Paula and cannot inspect the house, sincerely tells Tom that the house is fully insulated. As a result, Tom buys the house. The written sale contract, however, does not claim that the house is fully insulated, and it also contains an exculpatory clause saying that Paula is not bound by Albert's representations, unless they also appear in the written contract. Paula drafted this contract herself with full knowledge that Albert would be making false statements about the insulation.

After Tom discovers that the house is not fully insulated, he sues Paula for Albert's misrepresentations. Tom sues Albert too. The presence or absence of insulation was material to his decision to buy. Will either suit be successful?

Online Research: Workplace Violence Research Institute

The Workplace Violence Research Institute is a provider of workplace violence prevention programs. In part a response to employers' risk exposure due to violent employees, the Institute has resources that help an employer identify potentially dangerous employees.

- Find the Workplace Violence Research Institute website.
- Find the article by Steve Kaufer, "Corporate Liability: Sharing the Blame for Workplace Violence." Create a list of steps that an employer should take to protect its employees from violent fellow workers and thereby reduce the employer's risk of liability for the violent acts of employees.

PART NINE

PARTNERSHIPS

37

INTRODUCTION TO FORMS OF BUSINESS AND FORMATION OF PARTNERSHIPS

After working for a large company for 10 years, you decide to give expression to your entrepreneurial urges and start a business. Your business plan is to help small firms that are struggling with finding ways to make new information technologies affordable and effective for their business. You envision that your business will need a capital infusion of $500,000 for the first year, during which you project the business will have a net loss of $200,000, which reflects in part your salary of $80,000. Beginning with the second year, you believe that the business will generate enough cash flow to finance internally all its normal capital expenditures. You expect second-year losses to be $100,000. Beginning with the third year, the business will be profitable.

You have $120,000 of savings that you are willing to invest in the business. You hope to obtain the remaining $380,000 of initial capital from investors. While you are willing to give a portion of the equity of the business to the investors, you want to control the business, including day-to-day operations. It is especially important that the other investors not be able to expel you from the business or its management.

- What business forms are best for your business?
- How will you modify the default rules of some business forms to make those forms work for you?

IN THIS CHAPTER, YOU begin your study of business organizations. Early in this chapter, you will preview the basic characteristics of the most important forms of business and learn how to select an appropriate form for a business venture. Following that introduction, you will begin your in-depth study of partnerships, learning their characteristics and the formalities for their creation.

Choosing a Form of Business

One of the most important decisions made by a person beginning a business is choosing a **form of business.** This decision is important because the business owner's liability and control of the business vary greatly among the many forms of business. In addition, some business forms offer significant tax advantages to their owners.

Although other forms of business exist, usually a person starting a business will wish to organize the business as a sole proprietorship, partnership, limited liability partnership, limited partnership, limited liability limited partnership, corporation, or limited liability company.

Sole Proprietorship

A **sole proprietorship** has only one owner. The sole proprietorship is merely an extension of its only owner, the **sole proprietor.**

As the only owner, the sole proprietor has the right to make all the management decisions of the business. In addition, all the profits of the business are his. A sole proprietor assumes great liability: He is personally liable for all the obligations of the business. All the debts of the business, including debts on contracts signed only in the name of the business, are his debts. If the assets of the business are insufficient to pay the claims of its creditors, the creditors may require the sole proprietor to pay the claims using his individual, nonbusiness assets such as money from his bank account and the proceeds from the sale of his house. A sole proprietor may lose everything if his business becomes insolvent. Hence, the sole proprietorship is a risky form of business for its owner.

Despite this risk, there are two reasons why a person may organize a business as a sole proprietorship. First, the sole proprietorship is formed very easily and inexpensively. No formalities are necessary. Second, few people consider the business form decision. They merely begin their businesses. Thus, by default, a person going into business by herself automatically creates a sole proprietorship when she fails to choose another business form. These two reasons explain why the sole proprietorship is the most common form of business in the United States.

Because the sole proprietorship is merely an extension of its owner, it has no life apart from its owner. Therefore, while the business of a sole proprietorship may be freely sold to someone else, legally the sole proprietorship as a form of business cannot be transferred to another person. The buyer of the business must create his own form of business to continue the business.

A sole proprietorship is not a legal entity. It cannot sue or be sued. Instead, creditors must sue the owner. The sole proprietor—in his own name—must sue those who harm the business.

A sole proprietor may hire employees for the business, but they are employees of the sole proprietor. Under the law of agency, the sole proprietor is responsible for her employees' authorized contracts and for the torts they commit in the course of their employment. Also, a sole proprietorship is not a tax-paying entity for federal income tax purposes. All of the income of a sole proprietorship is income to its owner and must be reported on the sole proprietor's individual federal income tax return. Likewise, any business losses are deductible without limit on the sole proprietor's individual tax return. This loss-deduction advantage explains why some wealthier taxpayers use the sole proprietorship for selected business investments—when losses are expected in the early years of the business, yet the risk of liability is low. Such an investor may form a sole proprietorship and hire a professional manager to operate the business.

Many sole proprietorships have trade names. For example, Caryl Stanley may operate her bagel shop under the name Caryl's Bagel Shop. Caryl would be required to file the trade name under a state statute requiring the registration of fictitious business names. If she were sued by a creditor, the creditor would address his complaint to "Caryl Stanley, doing business as Caryl's Bagel Shop."

Partnership

A **partnership** has two or more owners, called **partners.** The partners have the right to make all the management decisions for the business. In addition, all the profits of the business are shared equally by the partners.

The partners assume personal liability for all the obligations of the business. All the debts of the business are the debts of all the partners. Likewise, partners are liable for the torts committed in the course of business by their partners or by partnership employees. If the assets of the business are insufficient to pay the claims of its creditors, the creditors may require one or more of the partners to pay the claims using their individual, nonbusiness assets. Thus, a partner may have to pay more than his share of partnership liabilities.

Like the sole proprietorship, the partnership is not a tax-paying entity for federal income tax purposes. All of the income of the partnership is income to its partners and must be reported on the individual partner's federal income tax return whether or not it is distributed to the partners. Likewise, any business losses are deductible without limit on the partner's individual tax return.

The partnership has a life apart from its owners. When a partner dies or otherwise leaves the business, the partnership usually continues. A partner's ownership interest in a partnership is not freely transferable: A purchaser of the partner's interest is not a partner of the partnership, unless the other partners agree to admit the purchaser as a partner.

Why would persons organize a business as a partnership? Formation of a partnership requires no formalities and may be formed by default. A partnership is created automatically when two or more persons own a business together without selecting another form. Also, each partner's right to manage the business and the deductibility of partnership losses on individual tax returns are attractive features.

Limited Liability Partnership

A limited liability partnership is a partnership whose partners have elected limited liability status. Reacting to the large personal liability sometimes imposed on accountants and lawyers for the professional malpractice of their partners, Texas enacted in 1991 the first statute permitting the formation of **limited liability partnerships (LLP).** An LLP is identical to a partnership except that an LLP partner has no liability for most LLP obligations; however, an LLP partner retains unlimited liability for his *own* wrongful acts, such as his malpractice liability to a client.

LLP partners may elect to have the LLP taxed like a partnership or a corporation. If an LLP is taxed like a corporation, it pays federal income tax on its income, but the partners pay federal income tax only on the compensation paid and the partnership profits distributed to the partners.

The formation of an LLP requires filing a form with the secretary of state; some states require LLPs to maintain adequate professional insurance or have a high net worth.

The LLP is an especially good form of business for professionals such as consultants and auditors, allowing them management flexibility while insulating them mostly from personal liability. The LLP is the preferred form of business for professionals who do not incorporate.

Limited Partnership

A **limited partnership** has one or more general partners and one or more limited partners. General partners have rights and liabilities similar to partners in a partnership. They manage the business of the limited partnership and have unlimited liability for the obligations of the limited partnership. Typically, however, the only general partner is a corporation, thereby protecting the human managers from unlimited liability.

Limited partners usually have no liability for the obligations of the limited partnership once they have paid their capital contributions to the limited partnership. Limited partners have no right to manage the business, but if they do manage, they nonetheless retain their limited liability.

Like an LLP, a limited partnership may elect to be taxed either as a partnership or as a corporation. If a limited partnership is taxed like a partnership, general partners report their shares of the limited partnership's income and losses on their individual federal income tax returns. For general partners, losses of the business are deductible without limit. A limited partner must pay federal income tax on his share of the profits of the business, but he may deduct his share of losses only to the extent of his investment in the business. As a passive investor, a limited partner may use the losses only to offset income from other passive investments.

If a limited partnership is taxed like a corporation, the limited partnership pays federal income tax on its net income. The partners pay federal income tax only on compensation paid and profits distributed to them.

A limited partnership may have a life apart from its owners. When a limited partner dies or otherwise leaves the business, the limited partnership is not dissolved. When a general partner dies or withdraws, however, the limited partnership may be dissolved if there is no remaining general partner. A general or limited partner's rights may not be wholly transferred to another person unless the other partners agree to admit the new person as a partner.

Unlike a sole proprietorship or partnership, a limited partnership may be created only by complying with a state statute permitting limited partnerships. Thus, no limited partnership may be created by default.

There are three main reasons why persons organize a business as a limited partnership. First, by using a corporate general partner, no human will have unlimited liability for the debts of the business. Second, if the limited partnership is taxed like a partnership, losses of the business are deductible on the owners' federal income tax returns. Third, investors may contribute capital to the business yet avoid unlimited liability and the obligation to manage the business. Thus, the limited partnership has the ability to attract large amounts of capital, much more than the sole proprietorship, which has only one owner, or the partnership, whose partners' fear of unlimited liability restricts the size of the business. Hence, for a business needing millions of dollars of capital and expecting to lose money in its early years, the limited partnership is a particularly good form of business.

Limited Liability Limited Partnership

A **limited liability limited partnership (LLLP)** is a limited partnership whose partners have elected limited liability status for all the partners. An LLLP is created by making a filing with the secretary of state. The LLLP is designed to give the same limited liability advantages to general partners in a limited partnership as have been granted to partners who manage an LLP or a limited liability company (LLC). The LLC is explained below.

The LLLP is identical to a limited partnership in its management and the rights and duties of its partners. However, by electing LLLP status, both the limited partners and the general partners in a limited partnership will have no liability for most obligations of the LLLP. Nonetheless, a general partner will have unlimited liability for any wrongs he commits while acting for the LLLP.

Corporation

A **corporation** is owned by shareholders who elect a board of directors to manage the business. The board of directors often selects officers to run the day-to-day affairs of the business. Consequently, ownership and management of a corporation may be completely separate: No shareholder has the right to manage, and no officer or director needs to be a shareholder.

Shareholders have limited liability for the obligations of the corporation, even if a shareholder is elected as a director or selected as an officer. Directors and officers have no liability for the contracts they or the corporation's employees negotiate in the name of the corporation. While managers have liability for their own misconduct, they have no liability for corporate torts committed by other corporate managers or employees. Therefore, shareholders, officers, and directors have limited liability for the obligations of the business.

The usual corporation is a tax-paying entity for federal income tax purposes. The corporation pays taxes on its profits. Shareholders do not report their shares of corporation profits on their individual federal income tax returns. Instead, only when the corporation distributes its profits to the shareholders in the form of dividends or the shareholders sell their investments at a profit do the shareholders report income on their individual returns. This creates a double-tax possibility, as profits are taxed once at the corporation level and again at the shareholder level when dividends are paid.

Also, shareholders do not deduct corporate losses on their individual returns. They may, however, deduct their investment losses after they have sold their shares of the corporation.

There is one important exception to these corporate tax rules. The shareholders may elect to have the corporation and its shareholders taxed under Subchapter S of the Internal Revenue Code. By electing **S Corporation** status, the corporation and its shareholders are taxed nearly entirely like a partnership: Income and losses of the business are reported on the shareholders' individual federal income tax returns. A corporation electing S Corporation status may have no more than 75 shareholders, have only one class of shares, and be owned only by individuals and trusts.

A corporation has a life separate from its owners and its managers. When a shareholder or manager dies or otherwise leaves the business, the corporation is not dissolved. A shareholder may sell his shares of the corporation to other persons without limitation unless there is a contrary agreement. The purchaser becomes a shareholder with all the rights of the selling shareholder.

There are several reasons why persons organize a business as a corporation. First, no human has unlimited liability for the debts of the business. As a result, businesses in the riskiest industries—such as manufacturing—incorporate. Second, because investors may contribute capital to the business, avoid unlimited liability, escape the obligation to manage the business, and easily liquidate their investments by selling their shares, the corporation has the ability to attract large amounts of capital, even more than the limited partnership, whose partner-

ship interests are not as freely transferable. Thus, the corporation has the capacity to raise the largest amount of capital.

The S Corporation has an additional advantage: Losses of the business are deductible on individual federal income tax returns. However, because the S Corporation is limited to 75 shareholders, its ability to raise capital is severely limited. Also, while legally permitted to sell their shares, S Corporation shareholders may be unable to find investors willing to buy their shares or may be restricted from selling their shares pursuant to an agreement between the shareholders.

Professional Corporation

All states permit professionals such as accountants, physicians, and dentists to incorporate their professional practices. The **professional corporation** is identical to a business corporation in most respects. It is formed only by a filing with the secretary of state, and it is managed by a board of directors, unless a statute permits it to be managed like a partnership. The rigid management structure makes the professional corporation inappropriate for some smaller professional practices.

While professional shareholders have no personal liability for the obligations of the professional corporation, such as a building lease, they retain unlimited liability to their clients for their professional malpractice. A professional will have no personal liability, however, for the malpractice of a fellow shareholder or associate.

Only professionals holding the same type of license to practice a profession may be shareholders of a professional corporation. For example, only physicians licensed to practice medicine may be shareholders of a professional corporation that practices medicine.

Professional corporation shareholders may elect for the corporation to be taxed like a corporation, or they may elect S Corporation tax treatment.

Fewer and fewer professionals incorporate each year. All of the liability and taxation advantages of the professional corporation have been assumed by the LLP. In addition, most professionals like the flexible management structure of the LLP better.

Limited Liability Company

A **limited liability company** (LLC) is a business form intended to combine the nontax advantages of corporations with the favorable tax treatment of partnerships. An LLC is owned by members, who may manage the LLC themselves or elect the manager or managers who will operate the business. Members have limited liability for the obligations of the LLC.

Some states permit professionals to organize as LLCs. Professionals in a professional LLC have unlimited liability, however, for their own malpractice. Like an LLP or LLLP, members of an LLC may elect to have the LLC taxed like a partnership or a corporation.

There is a lack of free transferability of the members' ownership interests. Transfer of a membership interest entitles the transferee to receive only the member's distributions from the LLC, unless all members or the LLC agreement permits the transferee to become a member. The death, retirement, or bankruptcy of any member usually does not dissolve or cause the liquidation of the LLC.

What are the advantages of the LLC? The LLC has the limited liability advantage and, if manager-managed, the management advantage of the corporation. The LLC and its members receive federal tax treatment similar to the S Corporation and its shareholders, yet the LLC has no limit on the number or type of owners, as does an S Corporation.

See Figure 1 for a summary of the general characteristics of business forms.

LOG ON

www.onlinewbc.gov
The Women's Business Center at the website for the Small Business Association has valuable resources for anyone starting a business. Click on the "Business Basics" link and you will find a link to "Starting Your Own Business." Listed under the "Basics of Starting a Business" is a section describing some forms of business and listing the tax forms necessary to those business forms.

THE GLOBAL BUSINESS ENVIRONMENT

Globally, businesses have a wide choice of business forms, and many of them are forms shared by many countries. For example, the partnership is recognized not only in the United States but also in Australia, Canada, Cyprus, England, India, Israel, Russia, South Africa, Turkey, and, Zimbabwe. In the Chinese province of Hong Kong, the sole proprietorship, partnership, limited partnership, and company are the typical business forms. Limited partnerships in Hong Kong are limited to 20 partners, one of whom must be a general partner with unlimited liability. Limited liability partnerships and limited liability limited partnerships do not exist in Hong Kong as yet, or the rest of the world for that matter. Limited liability companies in Hong Kong are like American corporations.

German law recognizes the public stock corporation (*AG* or *Aktiengesellschaft*). Its shares are freely transferable like those of American corporations, so it may have an unlimited number of shareholders. More common is the limited liability company (*GmbH* or *Gesellschaft mit beschrankter Haftung*), first created in 1892. It permits the owners to restrict the transfer of its shares. The majority of German subsidiaries of foreign corporations are *GmbH*s rather than *AG*s. Owners of *AG*s and *GmbH*s have liability limited to their capital contributions. The German general commercial partnership (*OHG* or *offene Handelgesellschaft*) and the limited commercial partnership (*KG* or *Kommanditgesellschaft*) are essentially the same as the general and limited partnerships in the United States.

For a large list of the world's business forms, their definitions, and the countries recognizing those forms, go to the World Trade Press website at www.worldtradepress.com/eit/wfb/ie/088eit.asp

ETHICS IN ACTION

Two people who carefully consider which American business form to use for their business can achieve nearly any combination of characteristics. For example, by choosing LLP status, they can limit their personal liability, totally control the business, and deduct business losses on their individual federal income tax returns. They can do the same with an LLC or S Corporation. They will have no liability for the contracts or the business, even though they make all business decisions and even make all contracts for the business. When the business becomes profitable, they can elect to have the business form taxed like a corporation, and if the corporate tax rate is lower than their individual tax rate, they will derive tax savings by retaining earnings in the business.

- Is it ethical for a business owner who controls the business to escape liability for the business's contracts and torts by hiding behind the veil of the business organization?
- Would you ever choose to use the partnership form when the LLP form is available?
- Is it ethical for a business owner to select a business form and elect a tax treatment that minimizes her tax liability?

Figure 1 *General Characteristics of Forms of Business*

	Sole Proprietorship	Partnership	Limited Liability Partnership	Limited Partnership	Limited Liability Limited Partnership	Corporation	S Corporation	Limited Liability Company
Formation	When one person owns a business without forming a corporation or LLC	By agreement of owners *or* by default when two or more owners conduct business together without forming a limited partnership, an LLC, or a corporation	By agreement of owners; must comply with limited liability partnership statute	By agreement of owners; must comply with limited partnership statute	By agreement of owners; must comply with limited liability limited partnership statute	By agreement of owners; must comply with corporation statute	By agreement of owners; must comply with corporation statute; must elect S Corporation status under Subchapter S of Internal Revenue Code	By agreement of owners; must comply with limited liability company statute
Duration	Terminates on death or withdrawal of sole proprietor	Usually unaffected by death or withdrawal of partner	Usually unaffected by death or withdrawal or partner	Unaffected by death or withdrawal of partner, unless sole general partner dissociates	Unaffected by death or withdrawal of partner, unless sole general partner dissociates	Unaffected by death or withdrawal of shareholder	Unaffected by death or withdrawal of shareholder	Usually unaffected by death or withdrawal of member
Management	By sole proprietor	By partners	By partners	By general partners	By general partners	By board of directors	By board of directors	By managers or members
Owner Liability	Unlimited	Unlimited	Mostly limited to capital contribution	Unlimited for general partners; limited to capital contribution for limited partners	Limited to capital contribution	Limited to capital contribution	Limited to capital contribution	Limited to capital contribution
Transferability of Owners' Interest	None	None	None	None, unless agreed otherwise	None, unless agreed otherwise	Freely transferable, although shareholders may agree otherwise	Freely transferable although shareholders usually agree otherwise	None, unless agreed otherwise
Federal Income Taxation	Only sole proprietor taxed	Only partners taxed	Usually only partners taxed; may elect to be taxed like a corporation	Usually only partners taxed; may elect to be taxed like a corporation	Usually only partners taxed; may elect to be taxed like a corporation	Corporation taxed; shareholders taxed on dividends (double tax)	Only shareholders taxed	Usually only members taxed; may elect to be taxed like a corporation

Partnerships

The basic concept of partnership is as ancient as the history of collective human activity. Partnerships were known in ancient Babylonia, ancient Greece, and the Roman Empire. Hammurabi's Code of 2300 B.C. regulated partnerships. The definition of a partnership in the 6th-century Justinian Code of the Roman Empire does not differ materially from that in our laws today. The partnership was likewise known in Asian countries, including China. During the Middle Ages, much trade between nations was carried on by partnerships.

By the close of the 17th century, the partnership was recognized in the English common law. When the United States became an independent nation and adopted the English common law in 1776, the English law of partnerships became a part of American law. In the early part of the 19th century, the partnership became the most important form of association in the United States.

Today, the American common law of partnership has been largely replaced by statutory law. Every state has a statute on partnership law. The Revised Uniform Partnership Act (RUPA) of 1994, with the 1997 amendments, is a model partnership statute that is the product of the National Conference of Commissioners on Uniform State Laws, a group of practicing lawyers, judges, and law professors. The aims of the RUPA are to codify partnership law in one document, to make that law more nearly consistent with itself, and to attain uniformity throughout the country.

In recent years, the RUPA has supplanted the Uniform Partnership Act (UPA) of 1914 as the dominant source of partnership law in the United States. As of December 2002, 32 states plus the District of Columbia, Puerto Rico, and the Virgin Islands have adopted the RUPA. The RUPA is the framework of your study of partnerships and limited liability partnerships. (See Figure 2.)

Creation of Partnership

No formalities are necessary to create a partnership. Two or more persons may become partners in accordance with a written partnership contract (articles of partnership), they may agree orally to be partners, or they may become partners merely by arranging their affairs as if they were partners. If partners conduct business under a trade name, they must file the name with the secretary of state in compliance with state statutes requiring the registration of fictitious business names.

When people decide to become partners, they should employ a lawyer to prepare a written partnership agreement. Although a partnership agreement is not required to form a partnership, it is highly desirable for the same reasons that written contracts are generally preferred. In addition, the statute of frauds requires a writing for a partnership having a term exceeding one year.

More importantly, when partners do not define their relationship as partners, the default rules of the RUPA determine the rights of the partners vis-à-vis each other. While the RUPA rules are sensible and meet the needs of many partners, they may not meet the specific interests of other partners. Thus, having a written partnership agreement will allow the partners to define their rights and duties appropriately for them.

When there is no written partnership agreement, a dispute may arise over whether persons who are associated in some enterprise are partners. For example, someone may assert that she is a partner and, therefore, claim a share of the value of a successful enterprise. More frequently, an unpaid creditor may seek to hold a person liable for a debt incurred by another person in the same enterprise. To determine whether there is a partnership in the absence of an express agreement, the courts use the definition of partnership in the RUPA.

RUPA Definition of Partnership

The RUPA defines a partnership as an "association of two or more persons to carry on as co-owners a business for profit." If the definition is satisfied, then the courts will treat those involved as partners. A relationship may meet the RUPA definition of partnership even when a person does not believe he is a partner, and occasionally, even if the parties agree that they are not partners.

Association of Two or More Persons As an association, a partnership is a *voluntary and consensual relationship*. It cannot be imposed on a person; a person must agree expressly or impliedly to have a person associate with her. For example, a partner cannot force her partners to accept her daughter into the partnership.

No person can be a partner with herself—a partnership must have *at least two partners*. A person may be a partner with her spouse.

Nearly everyone or everything may be a partner. An individual, trust, partnership, limited partnership, corporation, or other association may be a partner.

Carrying On a Business Any trade, occupation, or profession may qualify as a business. Carrying on a

---

Figure 2   *Principal Characteristics of Partnerships under the RUPA*

1. A partnership may be created with no formalities. Two or more people merely need to agree to own and conduct a business together in order to create a partnership.

2. Partners have unlimited liability for the obligations of the business.

3. Each partner, merely by being an owner of the business, has a right to manage the business of the partnership. He is an agent of the partnership and may make the partnership liable for contracts, torts, and crimes. Because partners are liable for all obligations of the partnership, in effect each partner is an agent of the other partners. Each partner may hire agents, and every partner is liable for the agents' authorized contracts and for torts that the agents commit in the course of their employments.

4. A partnership is not an employer of the partners, for most purposes. As a result, for example, a partner who leaves a partnership is not entitled to unemployment benefits.

5. Partners are fiduciaries of the partnership. They must act in the best interests of the partnership, not in their individual best interests.

6. The profits or losses of the business are shared by the partners, who report their shares of the profits or losses on their individual federal income tax returns, because the partnership does not pay federal income taxes. Nonetheless, a partnership does keep its own financial records and must file an information return with the Internal Revenue Service.*

7. A partnership may own property in its own name.

8. A partnership may sue or be sued in its own name. The partners may also be sued on a partnership obligation.

9. A partner may sue her partners during the operation of the partnership.

10. A partner's ownership interest in a partnership is not freely transferable. A purchaser of a partner's interest does not become a partner, but is entitled to receive only the partner's share of the partnership's profits.

11. Generally, a partnership has a life apart from its owners. If a partner dies, the partnership usually continues.

*The federal income tax return filed by a partnership is merely an information return in which the partnership indicates its gross income and deductions and the names and addresses of its partners (IRC Sec. 6031). The information return allows the Internal Revenue Service to determine whether the partners accurately report partnership income on their individual returns.

---

business usually requires a series of transactions conducted over a period of time. For example, a group of farmers that buys supplies in quantity to get lower prices is not carrying on a business but only part of one. If the group buys harvesting equipment with which it intends to harvest crops for others for a fee for many years, it is carrying on a business.

Co-Ownership Partners must *co-own the business* in which they associate. There is no requirement that the capital contributions or the assets of the business be co-owned. Also, by itself, co-ownership of assets does not establish a partnership. For example, two persons who own a building as joint tenants are not necessarily partners. To be partners, they must co-own a business.

The two most important factors in establishing co-ownership of the business are the sharing of profits and the sharing of management of the business. The RUPA declares that a person's **sharing the profits** of a business is presumptive evidence that she is a partner in the business. This means that persons sharing profits are partners, unless other evidence exists to disprove they are partners. The rationale for this rule is that a person ordinarily would not be sharing the profits of a business unless she were a co-owner. This rule brings under partnership law many persons who fail to realize that they are partners. For example, two college students who purchase college basketball tickets, resell them, and split the profits are partners.

Sharing the gross revenues of a business does not create a presumption of partnership. The profits, not the gross receipts, must be shared. For example, a broker who receives a commission on a sale of land is not a partner of the seller of that land.

Although sharing profits usually is presumptive proof of a partnership, the RUPA provides that no presumption of partnership is made when a share of profits is received in payment

1. of a debt.

2. of interest on a loan.

3. of wages to an employee or services to an independent contractor.

4. of rent.

5. of an annuity or other retirement or health benefit to a beneficiary or representative of a deceased partner.

6. for the sale of the goodwill of a business or other property.

These exceptions reflect the normal expectations of the parties that no partnership exists in such situations. **Sharing management** of a business is additional evidence tending to prove the existence of a partnership. However, by itself, participation in management is not conclusive proof of the existence of a partnership. For example, a creditor may be granted considerable control in a business, such as a veto power over partnership decisions and the right of consultation, without becoming a partner. Also, a sole proprietor may hire someone to manage his business, yet the manager will not be a partner of the sole proprietor.

However, when the parties claim that they share profits for one of the six reasons above, the sharing of management may overcome the presumption that they are not partners. When the parties arrange their affairs in a manner that otherwise establishes an objective intent to create a partnership, the courts find that a partnership exists. For example, when a nonmanagerial employee initially shares profits as a form of employment compensation, the employee is not a partner of his employer. But when the employer and employee modify their relationship by having the employee exercise the managerial control of a partner and fail to reaffirm that the manager is merely an employee, a partnership may exist.

Creditors occupy a privileged position. Many cases have permitted creditors to share profits and to exercise considerable control over a business without becoming partners. Creditor control is often justified on the grounds that it is merely reasonable protection for the creditor's risk.

For Profit   The owners of an enterprise must *intend to make a profit* to create a partnership. If the enterprise suffers losses, yet the owners intend to make a profit, a partnership may result. When an endeavor is carried on by several people for charitable or other nonprofit objectives, it is not a partnership. For example, Alex and Geri operate a restaurant booth at a county fair each year to raise money for a Boy Scout troop. Their relationship is not a partnership but merely an association. (Nonetheless, like partners, they may be individually liable for the debts of the enterprise.)

Intent   Frequently, courts say that there must be intent to form a partnership. This rule is more correctly stated as follows: *The parties must intend to create a relationship that the law recognizes as a partnership.* A partnership may exist even if the parties entered it inadvertently, without considering whether they had created a partnership. A written agreement to the effect that the parties do not intend to form a partnership is not conclusive if their actions provide evidence of their intent to form a relationship that meets the RUPA partnership test.

There are several important consequences of being a partner. See Figure 3 for a summary of the most important consequences.

Figure 3   *Important Consequences of Being a Partner*

1. You share ownership of the business. For example, you want to bring an employee into your business, which is worth $250,000. If you and the employee conduct your affairs like partners, your employee will become your partner and own half of your business.

2. You share the profits of the business.

3. You share management of the business. Your partner must be allowed to participate in management decisions.

4. Your partner is an agent of the partnership. You are liable for your partner's torts and contracts made in the ordinary course of business.

5. You owe fiduciary duties to your partnership and your partner, such as the duties not to compete with the business, not to self-deal, and not to disclose confidential matters.

6. You have unlimited personal liability for all the obligations of the partnership.

The *Southex* case, which follows the next section, considers whether two businesses are partners.

Creation of Joint Ventures

Courts frequently distinguish **joint ventures** from partnerships. A joint venture may be found when a court is reluctant to call an arrangement a partnership because the purpose of the arrangement is not to establish an ongoing business involving many transactions; instead, it is limited to a single project. For example, an agreement to buy, develop, and resell for profit a particular piece of real estate is likely to be viewed as a joint venture rather than a partnership. In all other respects, joint ventures are created just as partnerships are created. The joint venturers may have a formal written agreement. In its absence, a court applies the RUPA definition of partnership—modified so as not to require the carrying on of a business—to determine whether a joint venture has been created.

The legal implications of the distinction between a partnership and a joint venture are not entirely clear. Generally, partnership law applies to joint ventures. For example, all of the participants in a joint venture are personally liable for its debts, and joint venturers owe each other the fiduciary duties imposed on partners. Joint ventures are treated as partnerships for federal income tax purposes. The most significant difference between joint venturers and partners is that joint venturers are usually held to have *less implied and apparent authority* than partners, because of the limited scope of the enterprise.

Southex Exhibitions, Inc. v. Rhode Island Builders Association., Inc.
279 F. 3d 94 (1st Cir. 2002)

The Rhode Island Builder's Association, Inc. (RIBA), is an association of home construction companies. In 1974, RIBA's executive director, Ross Dagata, made an agreement with Sherman Exposition Management, Inc. (SEM), a professional show owner and producer, regarding future productions of the RIBA home shows at the Providence Civic Center. The preamble in the 1974 Agreement announced that "RIBA wishes to participate in such shows as sponsors and partners." The term of the 1974 Agreement was five years, renewable by mutual agreement.

RIBA also agreed to sponsor and endorse only shows produced by SEM, to persuade RIBA members to exhibit at those shows, and to permit SEM to use RIBA's name for promotional purposes. In turn, SEM promised to obtain all necessary leases, licenses, permits and insurance, to indemnify RIBA for show-related losses, to grant RIBA the right to accept or reject any exhibitor, to audit show income, and to advance all the capital required to finance the shows. Net show profits were to be shared: 55 percent to SEM; 45 percent to RIBA.

The 1974 Agreement provided that all show dates and admission prices, as well as the Rhode Island banking institution at which show-related business would be transacted, required agreement by both parties. If the Civic Center became unavailable for reasons beyond SEM's control, SEM was to be excused from its production duties, provided that SEM promoted no other home show in Rhode Island. RIBA retained the right to conduct a home show at another venue, after notice to SEM.

When the 1974 Agreement was being negotiated, SEM and RIBA had conversations relating to the meaning of the term "partners" in the agreement. Manual Sherman, SEM's president, informed RIBA's Ross Dagata that he "wanted no ownership of the show" because he was uncertain about the financial prospects for home shows in the Rhode Island market. Sherman advised Dagata: "After the first year, if I'm not happy, we can't produce the show properly or make any money, we'll give you back the show." Although SEM owned other home shows which it produced outside Rhode Island, Sherman consistently described himself simply as the "producer" of the RIBA shows.

In 1994, Southex Exhibitions, Inc., acquired SEM's interest under the 1974 Agreement. By 1998, Southex determined that in order to maintain its financial stake in the RIBA home shows, the 1974 Agreement either needed to be renegotiated or allowed to expire according to its terms in 1999. RIBA in turn expressed dissatisfaction with Southex's performance, and eventually entered into a management contract with another producer, Yoffee Exposition Services, Inc.

Southex sued RIBA to enjoin the RIBA 2000 home show on the grounds that the 1974 Agreement established a partnership between RIBA and Southex's predecessor, SEM. Southex argued that RIBA breached its fiduciary duties to Southex by its wrongful dissolution of their partnership and its subsequent appointment of another producer. The federal district court denied Southex's request for a preliminary injunction and found that the 1974 Agreement did not create a partnership. Southex appealed.

Cyr, Senior Circuit Judge Under Rhode Island law, a partnership is an association of two or more persons to carry on as co-owners a business for profit. The receipt by a person of a share of the profits of a business is prima facie evidence that he or she is a partner in the business.

Southex insists that the 1974 Agreement contains ample indicia that a partnership was formed, including: (1) a 55-45 percent sharing of profits; (2) mutual control over designated business operations, such as show dates, admission prices, choice of exhibitors, and "partnership" bank accounts; and (3) the respective contributions of valuable property to the partnership by the partners. In our view, the evidence indicating a nonpartner relationship cannot be dismissed as insubstantial.

First, the 1974 Agreement is simply entitled "Agreement," rather than "Partnership Agreement." Second, rather than an agreement for an indefinite duration, it prescribed a fixed (albeit renewable) term. Third, rather than undertake to share operating costs with RIBA, SEM not only agreed to advance all monies required to produce the shows, but to indemnify RIBA for all show-related losses as well. State law normally presumes that partners share equally or at least proportionately in partnership losses. Although partners may agree to override such statutory "default" provisions, there is no evidence that SEM and RIBA meant to do so, notwithstanding an intent to form a partnership.

Similarly, although RIBA involved itself in some management decisions, SEM was responsible for the lion's share. Partners normally share equal rights in management. Furthermore, Southex not only entered into contracts but conducted business with third parties, in its own name, rather than in the name of the putative partnership. As a matter of fact, their mutual association was never given a name. It is noteworthy as well that Southex never filed either a federal or state partnership tax return.

Similarly, the evidence as to whether either SEM or RIBA contributed any corporate property with the intent that it become jointly-owned partnership property is highly speculative, particularly since their mutual endeavor simply involved a periodic event, i.e., an annual home show, which neither generated, nor necessitated, ownership interests in significant tangible properties, aside from cash receipts. Unlike tangible real and personal property, whose ownership is more readily established, the intangible intellectual property involved here, such as clientele lists, goodwill, and business expertise, did not so readily lend itself to evidentiary establishment. As a consequence, in the present circumstances the requisite mutual intent to convert intangible intellectual properties into partnership assets may well depend much more importantly upon a clear contractual expression of mutual intention to form a partnership.

Finally, even assuming that the 1974 Agreement, as a whole, is ambiguous, (i) Manual Sherman testified that he regarded SEM as simply the producer of the annual RIBA shows; and (ii) Dagata testified that SEM specifically disclaimed any ownership interest in the home shows in 1974.

Southex urges that the 1974 Agreement necessitated a finding of partnership formation, in that it unambiguously describes the contracting parties as "partners." The labels the parties assign to their intended legal relationship, while probative of partnership formation, are not necessarily dispositive as a matter of law, particularly in the presence of countervailing evidence—e.g., the provision in the 1974 Agreement indemnifying RIBA for all show-related losses—which would tend to refute the partnership characterization. Although the manner in which the parties themselves characterize the relationship is probative, the question ultimately is objective intent.

Although the courts should refrain from resorting to extrinsic evidence where a contract is utterly unambiguous, the lone reference to "partners" in the 1974 Agreement's prefatory clause is so inconclusive as to carry minimal interpretive weight, especially since it arguably conflicted with other contract provisions. Had the parties intended otherwise, it would seem entirely reasonable to expect the 1974 Agreement to have been entitled "Partnership Agreement," rather than simply "Agreement."

Judgment for RIBA affirmed.

Creation of Mining Partnerships

Although similar to an ordinary partnership or a joint venture, a mining partnership is recognized as a distinct relationship in a number of states. Persons who cooperate in the working of either a mine or an oil or gas well are treated as mining partners if there is (1) joint ownership of a mineral interest, (2) joint operation of the property, and (3) sharing of profits and losses. Joint operation requires more than merely financing the development of a mineral interest, but it does not require active physical participation in operations; it may be proved by furnishing labor, supplies, services, or advice. The delegation of sole operating responsibility to one of the participants does not bar treatment as a mining partnership.

Creation of Limited Liability Partnerships

Unlike an ordinary partnership, a limited liability partnership (LLP) may not be created merely by partners conducting a business together. The partners must expressly agree to create an LLP by complying with a limited liability partnership statute. The formation of an LLP requires filing a form with the secretary of state, paying an annual fee, and adding the words "Registered Limited Liability Partnership," "Limited Liability Partnership," or the acronym "RLLP" or "LLP" to the partnership's name. Some states also require an LLP to maintain a minimum level of professional liability insurance or net worth.

Purported Partners

Two persons may not be partners, yet in the eyes of a third person they may **appear** to be partners. If the third person deals with one of the apparent partners, he may be harmed and seek to recover damages from both of the apparent partners. The question, then, is whether the third person may collect damages from both of the apparent partners, even though they are not partners in fact.

For example, Thomas thinks that Wilson, a wealthy person, is a partner of Porter, a poor person. Thomas decides to do business with Porter on the grounds that if Porter does not perform as agreed, he can recover damages from Wilson. If Thomas is wrong and Wilson is not Porter's partner, Thomas ordinarily has no recourse against Wilson. RUPA Section 308(e) states that "persons who are not partners as to each other are not liable as partners to other persons." However, if Thomas can prove that Wilson misled him to believe that Wilson and Porter were partners, he may sue Wilson for damages suffered when Porter failed to perform as agreed. This is an application of the doctrine of **purported partners.**

The liability of a purported partner is based on substantial, detrimental reliance on the appearance of partnership. A person will be a purported partner and have liability when three elements are met:

1. A person purports to be or consents to being represented as a partner of another person or partnership.
2. A third party relies on the representation.
3. The third party transacts with the actual or purported partnership.

The third party may hold liable the persons who purported to be partners or consented to being represented as the partner of the actual or purported partnership.

Purporting to Be a Partner

A person may purport to be a partner by referring to himself as another person's partner. Or he might appear frequently in the office of a purported partner and confer with him. Perhaps he and another person share office space, have one door to an office with both of their names on it, have one telephone number, and share a secretary who answers the phone giving the names of both persons.

More difficult is determining when a person *consents* to being represented as another's partner. Mere knowledge that one is being held out as a partner is not consent. But a person's silence in response to a statement that the person is another's partner is consent.

For example, suppose Chavez tells Eaton that Gold is a partner in Birt's new retail shoe business. In fact, Gold is not Birt's partner. Later, Gold learns of the conversation between Chavez and Eaton. Gold does not have to seek out Chavez and Eaton to tell them that he is not Birt's partner in order to avoid being held liable as a partner for Birt's business debts. Had Chavez made the statement to Eaton in Gold's presence, however, Gold must deny the partnership relation or he will be held liable for Eaton's subsequent reliance on Gold's silence.

Note also that if a person makes a public representation that she is a partner of another, the purported partner is liable to any third person who relies on the representation, even if the purported partner is not aware of the reliance.

Reliance Resulting in a Transaction with the Partnership

A purported partner is liable only to those persons who rely on the representation and enter into a transaction with the actual or purported partnership. This means that purported partnership is determined on a case-by-case basis. The third party must in fact rely on the appearance of partnership. For example, when Trump transacts with Doby based on Crabb's representation that Doby and Crabb are partners, Trump is able to hold both Doby and Crabb liable. If however, Trump had dealt with Doby believing Doby was in business by herself and later discovers that Crabb had purported to be Doby's partner, only Doby would be liable to Trump, because there was no reliance on Crabb's purporting to be Doby's partner when Trump transacted with Doby.

Effect of Purported Partnership

Once persons are proved to be purported partners, a person who purported to be the others' partner or who consented to being represented as the others' partner is liable as though he were a partner of those persons. He is liable on contracts entered into by third parties on their belief that he was a partner. He is liable for torts committed during the course of relationships entered by third parties who believed he was a partner. In addition, a partnership that represents that a person is a partner endows the purported partner with the apparent authority to make contracts for the partnership.

Although two persons are purported partners to a person who knows of the representation and who relies on it, the purported partners are not partners in fact and do not share the profits, management, or value of the business of the purported partnership. Purported partnership is merely a device to allow creditors to sue persons who mislead the creditors into believing that a partnership exists. It does not create an actual partnership.

In the following *Palmer* case, the court found that there was a factual dispute whether the two lawyers were purported partners under the RUPA.

Palmer v. Claydon   *1999 Conn. Super. LEXIS 2661 (Conn. Super. Ct. 1999)*

Linda Palmer sued John Claydon, an attorney, for legal malpractice in connection with legal services he provided her in several land transactions. Palmer also sued George Lawler. Lawler was not a partner of Claydon, did not provide any services to Palmer, and did not participate in Claydon's services provided to Palmer. Palmer alleged, however, that Lawler was liable for Claydon's malpractice because he was a purported partner of Claydon. Lawler asked the court to grant him summary judgment.

Hodgson, Justice Lawler asserts as a first ground that he was not a law partner of Claydon and did not hold himself out to be. He states that he and Claydon were never partners but that they shared space and expenses. He states that he and Claydon "never shared clients, nor employed each other to represent our clients" and did not commingle their funds received from the practice of law nor share profits or losses from the practice of law.

Palmer asserts that the two attorneys held themselves out to be a partnership by identifying their practice as "Claydon & Lawler" on a sign at their law office and on their stationery and in their telephone directory listing. She further avers that Claydon introduced Lawler to her as his law partner; and that Lawler, in a telephone conversation with her, identified himself as Claydon's law partner. The plaintiff further avers in her affidavit that she relied on the status of the entity as a partnership:

I relied upon Attorney Claydon's and Attorney Lawler's representations that they did business as a law partnership. I believed that I would have the benefits of working with a partnership, including adequate resources and legal coverage for the real estate transactions.

Lawler states that "the only way in which Palmer can hold Lawler liable in this action is if she can prevail that there was a partnership between Lawler and Claydon." The court does not agree with this statement. While Palmer does not allege that there was an actual partnership, she alleges that Claydon and Lawler held themselves out as partners and that she relied on that representation.

Pursuant to Conn. Gen. Stat. 34–329(a), a party who purports, by words or conduct, to be a partner or consents to being represented by another as a partner in a partnership is liable to persons who rely on the representation in entering "into a transaction with the actual or purported partnership" either to the same extent as a partner for partnership liability or "jointly and severally" with any other person consenting to the representation that a partnership existed, depending on the situation.

The affidavits submitted plainly establish that there are disputed issues of material fact concerning (a) whether defendant Lawler held himself out as a participant in a partnership or allowed that impression to be created by defendant Claydon and (b) whether Palmer relied on the representation that a partnership existed. The existence of these disputed issues of material fact precludes summary judgment on the first ground raised by Lawler.

Lawler has failed to establish entitlement to summary judgment on this ground; however, he asserts a separate and distinct ground based on Palmer's release of Claydon. Lawler claims that even if he is assumed to have held himself out as a partner of Claydon, the release and withdrawal of Palmer's claims against Claydon serves to release him from liability.

In the absence of any express provision in the Act limiting the effect of releases of purported partners, the common law principles apply. The release of Claydon, about which there is no genuine dispute of material fact, as a matter of law releases Lawler from the vicarious liability imposed on him by Conn. Gen. Stat. 34–329(a).

Motion for summary judgment granted to Lawler.

ETHICS IN ACTION

Consider the ethical basis of the doctrine of purported partnership.

- Why does Kant's categorical imperative, which we studied in Chapter 4, suggest the rule of purported partnership is the right one?

- What steps will you take to avoid being a purported partner when you carry on business with an associate who is not your partner? Are those not only legal, but also ethical acts? Is there any distinction between law and ethics in this context?

Partnership Capital

When a partnership or limited liability partnership is formed, partners contribute cash or other property to the partnership. The partners' contribution is called **partnership capital.** To supplement beginning capital, other property may be contributed to the partnership as needed, such as by the partners permitting the partnership to retain some of its profits. Partnership capital is the equity of the business.

Loans made by partners to a partnership are not partnership capital but instead are liabilities of the business. Partners who make loans to a partnership are both owners and creditors.

Partnership Property

A partnership or limited liability partnership may own all or only a part of the property it uses. For example, it may own the business and perhaps a small amount of working capital in the form of cash or a checking account, yet own no other assets. All other tangible and intangible property used by the partnership may be individually or jointly owned by one or more of the partners or rented by the partnership from third parties. A determination of what is partnership property becomes essential when the partnership is dissolved and the assets are being distributed and when third persons claim that partnership property has been sold to them.

The RUPA provides that all property actually acquired by a partnership by transfer or otherwise is partnership property and, therefore, belongs to the partnership as an entity rather than to the partners. The RUPA has several rules that help determine when property is acquired by a partnership.

Property belongs to the partnership if the property is transferred (1) to the partnership in its name, (2) to any partner acting as a partner by a transfer document that names the partnership, or (3) to any partner by a transfer document indicating the partner's status as a partner or that a partnership exists. In addition, property acquired with partnership funds is presumed to be partnership property.

The presumption is very strong that property purchased with partnership funds and used in the partnership belongs to the partnership. On the other hand, property used by the partnership is presumed to belong to an individual partner when the property is purchased by a partner with her owns funds and in her own name with no indication in the transfer document of the partner's status as a partner or the existence of a partnership. However, in both situations, other factors such as an agreement among the partners may rebut the RUPA presumption of ownership.

The intent of the partners controls whether the partnership or an individual partner owns the property. It is best to have a written record of the partners' intent as to ownership of all property used by the partnership, such as a partnership agreement and partnership accounting records.

Examples

A tax accountant discovers that a partnership is using a building to which a partner, Jacob Smith, holds title. The partnership pays rent monthly to Smith, but the partnership pays for all maintenance and repairs on the building. The accountant wants to know whether the partnership or Smith should be paying real property taxes on the building. Smith is the owner and should be paying taxes on it because his partners' intent to allow Smith to retain ownership is evidenced by the partnership's paying rent to Smith.

Changing the facts, suppose the partnership pays no rent to Smith, the partnership maintains and repairs the building, and the partnership pays real property taxes on the building, but the title is in Smith's name. Who owns the building? The property belongs to the partnership, because all the objective criteria of ownership point toward partnership ownership, especially the payment of taxes. Therefore, when the partnership is liquidated, the building will be sold along with other partnership assets, and the proceeds of its sale will be distributed to partnership creditors and to all of the partners.

In the following *Holmes* case, the court held that land held in a partner's name was partnership property.

Holmes v. Holmes   849 P.2d 1140 (Ore. Ct. App. 1993)

From 1957 to 1960, Steve Holmes and his father-in-law, Bill Foss, owned a construction business, Foss & Holmes Construction. Steve continued the business after Bill's death. In 1975, Steve's son Mike joined Foss & Holmes, which was operated as a partnership.

Steve also owned a ranch from which he generated hay sales of $30,000 to $50,000 per year. In 1984 and 1985, irrigation equipment was purchased for the ranch; for tax reasons, title to the irrigation equipment was placed in Mike's name. Beginning in 1984, Steve and Mike's joint books show that the funds of the ranch and Foss & Holmes were commingled. Money and assets were shifted from the two businesses' various bank accounts as necessary to achieve tax advantages and to protect property from Steve's creditors. Ranch activities and Foss & Holmes activities were reported to and considered together by Mike and Steve's accountant for tax purposes. Mike and Steve reported their income for tax purposes not necessarily to reflect their actual distribution of income between them but to minimize their overall tax liability.

In 1985, Mike signed loan agreements with the Bank of Eastern Oregon, the proceeds of which were used by Foss & Holmes and the ranch. In 1986, Steve obtained an FHA loan to pay off the loans by Bank of Eastern Oregon. In 1987, Steve learned of a special, low-interest FHA loan available for the purchase of property from a parent. Solely to obtain the benefits of the low-interest loan, Steve deeded the ranch to Mike. No money changed hands. Mike never paid Steve for the ranch. The transfer was not treated as a sale on Steve's and Mike's books. Mike did not claim ranch income as his own after the transfer. There were no changes in ranch operations. Steve continued to operate the ranch, and the money from hay sales was used to repay loans for both Foss & Holmes and the ranch.

Eventually, a dispute arose between Steve and Mike regarding Mike's compensation and liability arising out of ranch operations. To resolve the festering dispute, Steve brought a legal action against Mike to dissolve their partnership and distribute its assets. Steve argued that he and Mike were partners in the operation of not only Foss & Holmes but also the ranch. Steve testified that the ranch was a partnership asset that should be sold to pay claims against the partnership. Mike countered that he and Steve were not partners in the ranch; Mike testified that although they never intended to give title to the ranch to him, he nonetheless owned it as compensation for money owed him by Steve. The trial court held that the ranch was partnership property; Mike appealed.

Rossman, Presiding Judge In view of the fact that the trial court has observed the witnesses' demeanor, its findings are entitled to substantial weight, particularly when the facts are in dispute and the credibility of the witnesses is an important factor. The trial court said that it was impressed by the testimony of Steve, who outlined the affairs of the parties without embellishment and with a genuine desire to get the matter concluded. The trial court was not impressed with Mike's testimony, and expressed its belief that Mike was so motivated by greed that his entire testimony was suspect.

We find that Steve and Mike were partners in the operation of the ranch, and that Steve contributed the ranch to the partnership. The fact that Steve later transferred the ranch to Mike did not end the partnership or remove the ranch as a partnership asset, if Steve and Mike intended that it would remain a partnership asset.

> It is well established that title to the real property of a partnership may reside in one of the members rather than in the entity and that the locus of the title does not necessarily affect either the entity's rights in the property or the entity's existence. *Fenton v. State Ind. Acc. Com.* (1953).

We find that the purpose of the transfer of the ranch from Steve to Mike was to lessen the partnership's overall expenses, and that there never was an intention to remove it from the partnership. We agree with thse trial court that the ranch continued to be a partnership asset.

Judgment for Steve Holmes affirmed.

Partner's Partnership Interest

As an owner of a partnership or LLP, a partner has an ownership interest in the partnership. A partner's ownership interest is called a **partnership interest,** which embodies all a partner's rights in a partnership:

1. The partner's transferable interest.
2. The partner's management and other rights.

The first right is discussed in this section. Partners' management and other rights are discussed in Chapter 37, Operation of Partnerships and Related Forms.

Note that a partner has no individual ownership rights in partnership property. The RUPA gives ownership of partnership property to the partnership only. Partners do, however, have the right to *use* partnership property for partnership purposes.

Partner's Transferable Interest

Like a shareholder owning stock in a corporation, a partner owns his partnership interest. The only part of the partnership interest, however, that may be transferred to another person is the partner's **transferable interest:** the partner's share of profits and losses and his right to receive partnership distributions. The transferable interest may be transferred or sold to any other person. It may also be used as collateral to secure a partner's debt.

Transfer The sale or transfer of a partner's transferable interest is a voluntary act of the partner. It entitles the buyer or transferee to receive the partner's distributions from the partnership, such as a share of profits. Although the transferee is the owner of the transferable interest, the transferee does not become a partner of the partnership. The transferee has no right to inspect the partnership's books and records or to manage the partnership. The transferee's only other right is to ask a court to dissolve and wind up the partnership, but only if the partnership is at will (i.e., has no term or objective). If the partnership dissolves and is wound up, the transferee will obtain the partner's claim against the partnership's assets.

By itself a partner's transfer of his transferable interest does not dissociate the partner from the partnership or effect a dissolution; the transferring partner remains a partner and may continue to manage the partnership.

The nontransferring partners may vote to expel the transferring partner from the partnership by their unanimous agreement (unless the partner merely granted a lien in the transferable interest to the partner's creditor), even if the term or objective of the partnership has not yet been met.

Charging Order A partner's personal creditor with a judgment against the partner may ask a court to issue a charging order—that is, an order charging all or part of the partner's transferable partnership interest with payment of the unsatisfied amount of the judgment. Unlike assignment, a charging order is obtained without the partner's consent. As with assignment, however, the partner remains a partner and may manage the partnership. The charging-order creditor is a lien creditor and is entitled to receive only the partner's share of the partnership distributions. If the distributions are insufficient to pay the debt, the creditor may ask the court to order foreclosure and to sell the partner's interest to satisfy the charging order.

Neither the issuance of a charging order nor the purchase of a transferable interest at a foreclosure sale dissociates the transferring partner from the partnership. But the purchaser of a transferable interest at the foreclosure sale becomes a transferee and therefore may ask a court to dissolve and wind up a partnership at will. The other partners may eliminate this potential threat to the continuation of the partnership by **redeeming the charging order.** To redeem a charging order, the other partners must pay the creditor the amount due on the judgment against the partner. If the other partners so choose, however, they may expel the partner suffering the charging order by their unanimous agreement, even if the term or objective of the partnership has not been met.

Effect of Partnership Agreement

The partners may believe that a partner's transferring her transferable partnership interest or suffering a charging order threatens the partnership. For example, they may believe that a partner may be less motivated to work for the partnership if the partner has transferred her partnership interest to a personal creditor, because she will not receive distributions from the partnership.

Consequently, the partners may restrict the transfer of a partner's transferable interest or impose negative consequences on a partner who transfers her transferable interest or suffers a charging order. For example, the partnership agreement may require a partner to offer to sell her partnership interest to the partnership prior to transferring it any other person. Or the partnership agreement may effect a dissociation of any partner who suffers a charging order and fails to redeem the charging order within 30 days.

Note that any transfer restriction must not unreasonably limit the ability of a partner to transfer her property interest. For example, a transfer restriction that bans the transfer of a partner's interest would be unreasonable and therefore unenforceable against a partner. In addition, a transfer restriction will not be enforceable against a transferee who does not have notice of the restriction.

Joint Venturers and Mining Partners Transfers of interests in joint ventures are treated in the same way as transfers of partnership interests. However, a mining partner's interest is *freely transferable.* The transferee becomes a partner with all the rights of ownership and management, and the transferor loses all of his partnership rights. The other mining partners cannot object to the transfer, and their consent to a transfer is not required.

Problems and Problem Cases

1. You are an acquisitions manager for a venture capital firm, Pro Vista Venture Partners, LLC. Your job requires you to find new business opportunities in which Pro Vista will invest, usually as a co-owner and sometimes a co-manager. Pro Vista profits from its investment by receiving a share of a venture's profits and by eventually selling its interest, such as when the business makes an initial public offering of its equity securities. Among your duties is selecting an appropriate business form for any business in which Pro Vista invests.

You are contacted by two people who three years ago started a business that manufactures artistic rugs, blankets, and tapestries. The business has made a modest profit, and the owners want to expand their manufacturing building. No bank or other lender is willing to make a loan to the business or its owners. The owners hope that Pro Vista will finance the building construction. They are willing to give up some of their equity interest in the business, but want to maintain majority ownership control. They understand that Pro Vista may want some control of management, but the owners want to have control of all day-to-day management at least. What business form do you choose for the business venture between the current owners and Pro Vista? How do you modify the default rules to accommodate the owners' and Pro Vista's interests?

2. Rick Yurko frequently purchased lottery tickets from Phyllis Huisel at the coffee shop she operated. In February 1990, Yurko bought 100 scratch-off lottery tickets, which revealed instant winners when a film covering was scratched off. Yurko asked Phyllis, Judy Fitchie, and Frances Vincent to help him scratch off the tickets. Yurko stated that if they helped him, they would be his partners and share in any winnings. Judy uncovered a ticket that gave its owner a chance to be on television and win $100,000. The owner had to complete a form on the back of the ticket and submit it for a drawing. Six tickets would be drawn for the TV appearance. Judy and Yurko urged Phyllis to fill out the ticket, but she did not want to appear on TV, so Yurko said he would. After a discussion, Frances, Judy, Phyllis, and Yurko agreed that Yurko would represent them on TV. Yurko then printed on the back of the ticket "F.J.P. Rick Yurko." F.J.P. stood for the first initials of Frances, Judy, and Phyllis. As Yurko completed the tickets, he told Phyllis that he was going to put all their initials and his name on the ticket and that they would be partners no matter what they might win.

You can predict what happened next. The ticket was drawn for the TV show, and Yurko appeared on the show and won the $100,000 prize. He did not share the winnings with the three women. Were the three women able to share the winnings by proving they were partners with Yurko?

3. Hamel, Lamb, and Adams were partners in the operation of the Breakers Hotel. Without Hamel's knowledge, Lamb and Adams sold 10 percent of their interest in the hotel business and its profits to Tamir and agreed that Tamir would be a partner of the business. Hamel had not agreed to give Lamb and Adams authority to make such an agreement. Is Tamir a partner in the hotel business?

4. OWLP, a Hawaii limited partnership, owned the Outrigger West Hotel. OWLP and Hawaii Hotels Operating Company (HHOC) agreed that OWLP and HHOC would jointly operate the hotel and share its revenues, allocating 73 percent to OWLP and 27 percent to HHOC. The agreement provided that revenues would be collected from the hotel and allocated daily according to the percentages above. However, the allocation percentages were changed six times during a four-year period to permit each party to recover out-of-pocket expenses and to provide a return of 98 percent of the net income to OWLP and of 2 percent of the net income to HHOC. Thus, any amount recovered by each party according to the predetermined percentage in excess of its expenses would be its profit. Losses were shared pro rata like the profits. Are OWLP and HHOC partners?

5. John Williams was an assistant manager of a restaurant operated by Pizzaville, Inc. He was promoted to manager and later designated a managing partner with business cards describing him so. William's compensation was a salary of $270 per week plus 70 percent of the restaurant's gross sales less the cost of food purchases and employees' wages. Pizzaville fired Williams. Williams sued Pizzaville to receive a portion of the value of the restaurant business on the ground that he was a partner with Pizzaville. Was Williams a partner?

6. The parents of Michael Milano sought medical care from The Freed Group, including Dr. Jay Freed, Dr. Mitchell Kleinberg, and Dr. Stephanie Citerman. The three doctors were not, however, partners in fact. For several months after his birth, Michael was examined by all three doctors. His parents received a bill from the Freed group in which all three names were prominently displayed. When Dr. Freed and Dr. Kleinberg examined Michael, they misdiagnosed a serious medical condition. On behalf of Michael, his parents sued all three doctors, including Dr. Citerman, even though she had not committed malpractice herself. Was Dr. Citerman held liable to Michael?

7. Padgett Carroll and Walter Fulton operated as a partnership a trucking business under the name of C & F Trucking. Carroll contributed a semi truck, which Fulton drove for the business. Carroll used $4,600 of his personal funds to purchase a used 42-foot trailer for C & F Trucking. The seller's invoice listed C & F Trucking as the purchaser of the trailer. The trailer's certificate of title listed C & F Trucking as the owner. Fulton's personal financial problems forced him to file for bankruptcy. May Fulton claim ownership of the trailer among his assets?

8. Claude Gauldin and Joe Corn formed a partnership to raise cattle and hogs on land owned by Corn. Partnership funds were used to build two buildings on the land for use by the partnership. Gauldin and Corn did not discuss who owned the buildings. Gauldin knew when the buildings were constructed that they would be permanent improvements to the land and would become part of it. The partnership paid no rent for the land, and there was no agreement to consider the use of the land as a contribution by Corn. The taxes on the land were paid by Corn, as was the cost of upkeep. When Corn left the partnership, Gauldin claimed that the buildings were partnership assets and that he was entitled to half of their fair market value. Was Gauldin correct?

9. In 1983, Odell Rogers and two other men formed MFC Partnership. In 1984, Odell Rogers gave his 41 percent interest in the partnership to his three sons: 4-year-old Shannon, 18-year-old James, and 20-year-old Arthur. Odell made the gift for the purpose of providing income to his sons to pay for their college expenses. The sons received income from MFC, which was reported on both the partnership's and the sons' individual federal income tax returns. None of the sons did any acts denoting management or control of the partnership. They did not request information from the partnership or attend its meetings or vote. They did not speak with other partners about the firm, did not know where the partnership's offices were located, and were not employed by MFC. Nonetheless, the sons were identified as partners on MFC's balance sheet on December 31, 1985. In addition, MFC's 1986 income statement listed the sons as partners. In 1987, MFC incurred liability to an employee pension fund. Was the fund trustee correct in contending that Odell's transfer of his partnership interest to his sons made them partners and therefore liable to the fund?

Online Research: The Revised Uniform Partnership Act and Your State

The National Conference of Commissioners on Uniform State Laws is the author of uniform state laws on forms of business.

- Find the website for the National Conference of Commissioners on Uniform State Laws.
- Find the link to the listing of the uniform state acts. This link will take you to the full text of the acts including the drafters' comments, which can help you understand why the acts were written as they are. Find the text of the Revised Uniform Partnership Act and its comments. Read section 202, which has the definition of partnership.
- Find the link to the "Legislative Fact Sheet" for the RUPA. Has your state adopted the RUPA?

38

OPERATION OF PARTNERSHIPS AND RELATED FORMS

After many years working with a large consulting partnership, you and several of your business associates and friends decide to form your own consulting business as a limited liability partnership. You and five of your close friends have 20 to 25 years experience in the consulting field. Each of you plans to contribute capital of $400,000 to the business. Each of you has a strong national reputation and expects to attract most of the firm's clients, at least in the first few years. You six partners will manage only a few of the firm's consulting engagements, but you six will bring to the firm clients generating $400,000,000 of annual revenue for the firm. Each of you also has experience managing consulting businesses, including expertise in personnel, financial, and marketing matters.

In addition, 15 other partners with 10 to 15 years experience will join the new firm. Each of these 15 partners will contribute capital of $200,000. They are expected to bring few clients to the firm at this time, but they are expected to service the firm's clients and to bring in new clients as their reputations and skills expand and as the six older partners retire. Chiefly, these 15 partners will take charge of consulting engagements. They will directly supervise the firm's 50 associate consultants. The associate consultants will not be partners when the partnership is formed, but are expected to be offered partnership status within five to 10 years.

- What are the default rules regarding how the partnership will be managed?
- Why are those default rules inappropriate for this partnership?
- Write the management section of the partnership agreement. Accommodate the interests of all partners.
- What are the default rules regarding how the partners are compensated?
- Why are those default rules inappropriate for this partnership?
- Write the compensation section of the partnership agreement. Accommodate the interests of all partners.

TWO RELATIONSHIPS ARE IMPORTANT during the operation of a partnership or limited liability partnership (LLP) business: (1) the relation of the partners to each other and the partnership; and (2) the relation of the partners to third parties who are affected by the business of the partnership. Partners owe duties to each other and the partnership. Partners have the ability to make the partnership liable to third parties for contracts and torts.

Duties of Partners to the Partnership and Each Other

The relation between partners and the partnership is a fiduciary relation of the highest order. It is one of mutual trust, confidence, and honesty. Therefore, under the Revised Uniform Partnership Act (RUPA) partners owe to the partnership and each other the highest degree of *loyalty.* In addition, partners must act consistently with the obligation of *good faith and fair dealing.* The duties partners owe each other are the same in ordinary partnerships and in limited liability partnerships.

Having Interest Adverse to Partnership

Unless there is a contrary agreement, a partner's sole compensation from partnership affairs is a share of partnership profits. Therefore, a partner may not deal with the partnership when the partner has an interest adverse to the partnership or acts on behalf of another person with any adverse interest. For example, a partner may not profit personally by receiving an undisclosed kickback from a partnership supplier. In addition, a partner may not profit secretly when she makes a contract with her partnership, such as selling a building she owns to her partnership without disclosing her ownership or her profit to her partners.

When a partner receives a secret profit, she has a conflict of interests, and there is a risk that she may prefer her own interests over those of the partnership. Therefore, the law permits a partner to profit personally from partnership transactions only if she deals in good faith, makes a full disclosure of all material facts affecting the transaction, and obtains approval from her partners. The remedy for a breach of this duty not to make a secret profit is a return of the profit that she made in the transaction with the partnership.

Competing against the Partnership

A partner may not compete against his partnership unless he obtains consent from the other partners. For example, a partner of a retail clothing store may not open a clothing store nearby. However, he may open a grocery store and not breach his fiduciary duty. The partnership has the remedy of recovering the profits of the partner's competing venture.

Partnership agreements often define what conduct constitutes competing with the partnership. For example, a partnership agreement of a large auditing firm may state that no partner may provide auditing services except on behalf of the partnership. It may also state that a partner may provide other accounting services not offered by the partnership after disclosure to and approval by the partnership's managing partners.

Duty to Serve

The duty to serve requires a partner to undertake his share of responsibility for running the day-to-day operations of the partnership business. The basis of this duty is the expectation that all partners will work. Sometimes, this duty is termed the duty to devote full time to the partnership.

Partners may agree to relieve a partner of the duty to serve. So-called *silent partners* merely contribute capital to the partnership. Silent partners do not have the duty to serve, but they have the same liability for partnership debts as any other partner.

The remedies for breach of the duty to serve include assessing the partner for the cost of hiring a person to do his work and paying the other partners additional compensation.

Duty of Care

In transacting partnership business, each partner owes a **duty of care.** A partner is not liable to her partnership for losses resulting from honest errors in judgment, but a partner is liable for losses resulting from her gross negligence, reckless conduct, intentional misconduct, or knowing violation of the law. She must make an **investigation** before making a decision so that she has an adequate basis for making the decision. The decision she makes must be one she has **grounds to believe is in the best interests of the partnership.**

In the partnership agreement, the partners may reduce or increase the duty of care owed to the partnership. They may not, however, eliminate the duty of care. It is common for partnership agreements to excuse partners from liability if they act in good faith and with the honest belief that their actions are in the best interests of the partnership. Such a provision is designed to encourage honest partners to take reasonable business risks without fearing liability.

Duty to Act within Actual Authority

A partner has the duty not to exceed the authority granted him by the partnership agreement or, if there is no agreement, the authority normally held by partners in his position. He is responsible to the partnership for losses resulting from unauthorized transactions negotiated in the name of the partnership. For example, suppose partners agree that no partner shall purchase supplies from Jasper Supply Company, which is unaware of the limitation on the partners' authority. When one partner purchases supplies from Jasper and the partnership suffers a loss because the supplies are of low quality, the wrongdoing partner must bear the loss caused by her breach of the partnership agreement.

Duty to Account

Partners have a duty to account for their use or disposal of partnership funds and partnership property, as well as their receipt of any property, benefit, or profit, without the consent of the other partners. Partnership property should be used for partnership purposes, not for a partner's personal use. In addition, a partner may not misappropriate a business opportunity in which the partnership had an interest or expectancy.

For example, when a partner of a firm that leases residential property to college students allows his daughter to live in a partnership-owned apartment, the partner must collect rent for the partnership from his daughter or risk breaching the duty to account.

Each partner owes a duty to keep a reasonable record of all business transacted by him for the partnership and to make such records available to the person keeping the partnership books. The books must be kept at the partnership's chief executive office. Every partner must at all times have access to them and may inspect and copy them.

Closely related to the duty to account is the right of a partner to be indemnified for payments made from personal funds and for personal liabilities incurred during the ordinary conduct of the business. For example, a partner uses her own truck to pick up some partnership supplies, which she pays for with her personal check. The partner is entitled to be reimbursed for the cost of the supplies and for her cost of picking up the supplies, including fuel.

Other Duties

A partner must maintain the **confidentiality** of partnership information such as a trade secret or a customer list. This means a partner should not disclose to third parties confidential information of the partnership unless disclosure benefits the partnership.

On the other hand, each partner owes a duty to disclose to the other partners all information that is material to the partnership business. She also owes a duty to inform the partners of notices she has received that affect the rights of the partnership. For example, Gordon Gekko, a partner of a stock brokerage firm, learns that National Motors Corporation is projecting a loss for the current year. The projection reduces the value of National stock, which the firm has been recommending that its customers buy. Gekko has a duty to disclose the projection to his partners to allow them to advise customers of the brokerage.

In the following case, the court considered a partner's liability for failing to account and for denying his partner access to partnership property.

| Brosseau v. Ranzau | 81 S.W.3d 381 (Tex. Ct. App. 2002) |

Dennis Ranzau and William Brosseau formed a partnership to buy the Casa T, a house in Acapulco, Mexico. Their intent was to use the Casa T as a vacation home for a few weeks each year, to lease the Casa T for the remainder of each year, and to share the rental income after expenses. The Casa T was the sole asset of a Canadian corporation, 80451 Holdings, Ltd. Therefore, the partnership could control the Casa T by buying the stock of 80451 Holdings. To purchase the stock, Brosseau and Ranzau each agreed to pay $60,000 down and co-sign a promissory note for $800,000. Because Brosseau did not have time to draw up the partnership papers, Ranzau's purchase of the stock went through one of Brosseau's companies, Argos Properties, Inc. Argos, therefore, became the sole owner of 80451 stock.

Ranzau soon became concerned that Brosseau was not accounting for the expenses and income of Casa T, which rented for $1,500 a day. In spite of numerous requests from Ranzau, Brosseau failed to provide receipts for the substantial expenses he claimed were being expended on the house. In addition, on one occasion Ranzau's wife and some of her friends were locked out of the house by an agent of Brosseau. Ranzau sued Brosseau claiming breach of a partner's fiduciary duty. The trial court found that Brosseau breached his fiduciary duty and awarded to Ranzau damages of $107,196.75. Brosseau appealed to a Texas court of appeals.

Gaultney, Judge Partners have a duty to one another to make full disclosure of all matters affecting the partnership and to account for all partnership profits and property. Partners owe one another a fiduciary duty, including a strict duty of good faith and candor. Ranzau agreed that Brosseau, either individually or through Argos Properties, would take paper title to 80451 Holdings and relied on Brosseau's promise that a half interest would be transferred to Ranzau later. In addition, Ranzau allowed Brosseau to manage the maintenance and rental of Casa T. This evidence supports the conclusion that Brosseau was the managing partner. A managing partner owes his partners the highest fiduciary duty recognized in the law. In spite of their agreement to divide both expenses and income equally, Brosseau did not forward rental income to Ranzau. This evidence is sufficient to support the breach of fiduciary duty finding.

Brosseau contends there is insufficient evidence to support the trial court's award of actual damages. Brosseau claims Ranzau failed to prove Brosseau's "unfair gain" from the alleged breach of fiduciary duty. The record reveals evidence of damages or injury, apart from Ranzau's initial investment, including the following: Ranzau's payment to Brosseau on the monthly note and Brosseau's fail-

ure to then pay that amount to the bank; Brosseau's failure to account for any profits from the lease of Casa T and his letting a friend have "total run of the house" over Ranzau's objection; Ranzau's wife being locked out of and denied access to the house and having to make other accommodation arrangements for herself and her guests; Ranzau's loss of use and enjoyment of Casa T; and Ranzau's payment of expenses at Brosseau's insistence without being given an adequate accounting of those expenses.

Judgment for Ranzau affirmed.

Joint Ventures and Mining Partnerships

The fiduciary duties of partners also exist in joint ventures and mining partnerships, although there are a few special rules regarding their enforcement. For example, a joint venturer may seek an accounting to settle claims between the joint venturers, or he may sue his joint venturers to recover joint property or to be indemnified for expenditures that he has made on behalf of the joint venture. A mining partner's remedy against his partners is an accounting; however, a mining partner has a lien against his partners' shares in the mining partnership for his expenditures on behalf of the mining partnership. The lien can be enforced against purchasers of his partners' shares.

Compensation of Partners

A partner's compensation for working for a partnership or limited liability partnership is a share of the profits of the business. The RUPA continues the UPA rule that a

partner is not entitled to a salary or wages, even if he spends a disproportionate amount of time conducting the business of the partnership.

Profits and Losses

Unless there is an agreement to the contrary, partners share partnership profits equally, according to the number of partners, and not according to their capital contributions or the amount of time that each devotes to the partnership. For example, a partnership has two partners, Juarez, who contributes $85,000 of capital to the partnership and does 35 percent of the work, and Easton, who contributes $15,000 and does 65 percent of the work. If they have made no agreement how to share profits, when the partnership makes a $50,000 profit in the first year, each partner receives $25,000, half of the profits.

Losses   When the partnership agreement is silent on how to share losses, losses are shared in the same proportion that profits are shared. The basis of this rule is

---

THE GLOBAL BUSINESS ENVIRONMENT

Partner's Relations and Fiduciary Duties

All modern societies share a common set of values that are reflected not only generally in their laws but also specifically in partnership law. Thus, there is substantial agreement from nation to nation in the duties partners owe each other under partnership law. In India and the United Kingdom, for example, partner's duties are nearly identical in name and substance to those in American law. Likewise in Canada, basic values of loyalty, good faith, honesty, and avoidance of conflicts of interest are fundamental to a partner's duties.

In other societies, there are mostly similarities but also a few differences. For example, among the Inuit and other aboriginal groups in Canada, the culture requires partners to "celebrate one another." In his book, *Hunters in the Barrens: The Naskapi on the Edge of the White Man's World,* Georg Henriken notes that in a joint venture, while the Naskapi partners watch one another, examine contracts and bank statements, and even sue one another, they should respect and recognize their respective contributions.

the presumption that partners want to share benefits and detriments in the same proportions. Nonetheless, the presumption does not work in reverse. If a partnership agreement specifies how losses are shared but does not specify how profits are shared, profits are shared equally by the partners, not as losses are shared.

Examples For example, when there is no agreement regarding how profits or losses are shared, profits are shared equally, and because losses are shared like profits, losses are shared equally as well. When two partners agree to share profits 70–30 and make no agreement on losses, both profits and losses are shared 70–30.

However, when two partners make no agreement how to share profits but agree to share losses 60–40, losses are shared in that proportion but profits are shared equally.

Partners may agree to split profits on one basis and losses on another basis for many reasons, including their making different capital and personal service contributions or a partner's having higher outside income than the other partners, which better enables him to use a partnership loss as a tax deduction.

Effect of Agreement on Creditors' Rights Each partner has unlimited personal liability to partnership creditors. Loss-sharing agreements between partners do not bind partnership creditors unless the creditors agree to be bound. For example, two partners agree to share losses 60–40, the same proportion in which they contributed capital to the partnership. After the partnership assets have been distributed to the creditors, $50,000 is still owed to them. The creditors may collect the entire $50,000 from the partner who agreed to assume only 60 per-

cent of the losses. That partner may, however, collect $20,000—40 percent of the amount—from the other partner.

Compensation in Large Partnerships In a large accounting or other partnership that has thousands of partners, the partnership agreement often has a detailed section on compensation. Usually, each partner is entitled to a monthly draw or salary. The amount of each partner's draw may be established yearly by the partnership's compensation committee or be determined by a rigid formula that takes into account a partner's capital contribution to the partnership, years of service as a partner, level of partner (such as managing partner, senior partner, or junior partner), area of practice (such as consulting, auditing, or tax), and other factors. In addition, the compensation article will state how partners share profits and when profits are distributed to partners. While partners in a small partnership usually share profits according to each partner's capital contribution, in a large partnership the calculation may be very complex, including also the partner's area of practice, level of partner, revenue received from a partner's clients, and hours billed by a partner. Usually, the profits are distributed four times a year, in January, April, June, and September, coinciding with the quarterly payment dates for estimated federal and state income taxes. In addition, the compensation articles will provide for partners' expense accounts, vacations and leaves, and other fringe benefits, such as health insurance.

In the following *Warren* case, the court held that the partners' oral agreement regarding partners' compensation bound the partners.

Warren v. Warren   *784 S.W.2d 247 (Mo. App. 1989)*

In 1969, brothers Harold and Ray Warren formed a partnership to operate a funeral home in Columbia, Missouri. In 1970, they created a second partnership, The Warren Yard and Tree Service. The brothers based their partnerships solely on oral agreements, never putting them in writing. They adopted a system under which each partner drew from the partnerships' funds a reasonable compensation for his actual services rendered to the two businesses.

After a few years, Harold—a licensed embalmer and funeral director—spent an increasing amount of his time in the funeral home, performing all the lab work and specialized mortuary services. By 1978, Harold spent nearly all his time at the funeral home. Ray—licensed only as a funeral director—devoted most of his time to the tree service partnership, spending only a few hours each week assisting with funerals. Consequently, during the term of their partnership, Harold drew large sums of compensation from the funeral home partnership and only about $400 from the tree service partnership. Ray drew his primary compensation from the tree service partnership and a smaller compensation from the funeral home partnership. Because the funeral home was the more profitable business, Harold's total compensation exceeded Ray's by a considerable amount.

In 1983, Ray sued Harold, claiming that he was entitled to receive compensation equal to Harold for the entire 14-year term of the funeral home partnership. Ray asked the trial court to order Harold to pay Ray an amount that would equalize their 14-year compensation. The trial court held that Ray was not entitled to additional compensation, and Ray appealed.

Nugent, Chief Judge Ray Warren first asserts that the trial court erred in finding that an oral agreement bound each partner to draw compensation commensurate with his services. The Warren brothers adopted a compensation system abstruse as to a method of payment but clear as to intent and business customs. There was an agreement between Ray and Harold under which Ray would run the tree service, Harold the funeral home, and each would draw compensation commensurate with his input of services. For nearly 15 years, Ray knew of and did not protest the perquisites afforded his brother by the funeral home partnership, such as use of an apartment above the funeral home and of a car.

Section 18 of the Uniform Partnership Act enunciates the rules determining the rights and duties of a partner: "The rights and duties of the partners in relation to the partnership shall be determined, subject to any agreement between them, by the following rules: . . . (f) No partner is entitled to remuneration for acting in the partnership business." The oral agreement between the brothers negates the statute's proscription of compensation to partners. Missouri law recognizes the validity of oral and implied agreements between partners. Indeed, for more than a century, Missouri has recognized that, in the presence of an agreement linking compensation to a partner's efforts, partners providing services vital to the enterprise, or those devoting much of their time to the partnership's commonweal, deserve compensation often far in excess of that owed partners providing less important services or those giving only a little time to the business.

Harold provided the expert services vital to the partnership. His skills in the mortuary business far exceeded Ray's. The brothers agreed that Harold would run the funeral home and Ray, the tree service. Thus, implicitly if not expressly, they acknowledged each other's expertise, and, accordingly, each concentrated his efforts in the area of his own ability.

Moreover, Ray derived substantial financial benefit from the funeral home, to which he contributed but minimal efforts. Concomitantly, Harold succeeded in continuing to operate the business despite the effective withdrawal of Ray. Thus, Harold became entitled to suitable compensation for his efforts.

Judgment for Harold Warren affirmed.

Management Powers of Partners

Individual Authority of Partners

In a partnership or limited liability partnership, every partner is a general manager of the business. This power is expressed in the RUPA, which states that a partnership is bound by the act of every partner for apparently carrying on in the ordinary course the business of the partnership or business of the kind carried on by the partnership. Such authority derives from the nature of the business. It permits a partner to bind the partnership and his partners for acts within the ordinary course of business. The scope of this **implied authority** is determined with reference to what is usual business for partnerships of the same general type.

Implied authority of a partner may not contradict a partner's **express authority,** which is created by agreement of the partners. An agreement among the partners can expand, restrict, or even completely eliminate the implied authority of a partner. For example, the partners in a newspaper publishing business may agree that one partner shall have the authority to purchase a magazine business for the partnership and that another partner shall not have the authority to sell advertising space in the newspaper. The partners may agree also that all partners must consent to borrow money for the partnership. The partners' implied authority to be general managers is modified in accordance with these express agreements.

Express authority may be stated orally or in writing, or it may be obtained by acquiescence. Regardless of the method of agreement, all of the partners must agree to the modification of implied authority. Partners may give everyone notice of a partner's authority or limitation on a partner's authority by filing a **Statement of Partnership Authority** or **Statement of Denial** with the secretary of state or the real estate recording office. Together, a partner's express and implied authority constitute her **actual authority.**

Apparent Authority Apparent authority exists because it reasonably appears to a third party that a partner has authority to do an act. Often, the implied authority and apparent authority of a partner are coincident. However, when a partner's implied authority is restricted or eliminated, the partnership risks the possibility that **apparent authority** to do a denied act will remain. To prevent apparent authority from continuing when there is a limitation of a partner's actual authority, third persons with whom the partner deals must have knowledge of the limitation of his actual authority or have received notification of the limitation, such as receiving an e-mail or fax or otherwise having the limitation brought to their attention. Filing a Statement of Partnership Authority or Statement of Denial may help notify third parties of a partner's limited authority. Just as a principal must notify third persons of limitations of an agent's authority, so must a partnership notify its customers, suppliers, and others of express limitations of the actual authority of partners.

Suppose that Carroll, Melton, and Ramirez are partners and that they agree that Carroll will be the only purchasing agent for the partnership. This agreement must be communicated to third parties selling goods to the partnership, or Melton and Ramirez will have apparent authority to bind the partnership on purchase contracts. Melton and Ramirez do not have express authority to purchase goods, because they have agreed to such a restriction on their authority. They do not have implied authority to purchase, because implied authority may not contradict express authority.

Ratification A partnership may ratify the unauthorized acts of partners. Essentially, **ratification** occurs when the partners accept an act of a partner who had no actual or apparent authority to do the act when it was done.

For example, suppose Cabrillo and Boeglin are partners in an accounting firm. They agree that only Cabrillo has authority to make contracts to perform audits of clients, an agreement known by Mantron Company. Nonetheless, Boeglin and Mantron contract for the partnership to audit Mantron's financial statements. At this point, the partnership is not liable on the contract, because Boeglin has no express, implied, or apparent authority to make the contract. But suppose Boeglin takes the contract to Cabrillo, who reads it and says, "OK, we'll do this audit." Cabrillo, as the partner with express authority to make audit contracts, has ratified the contract and thereby bound the partnership to the contract.

Special Transactions

The validity of some partner's actions is affected by special partnership rules that reflect a concern for protecting important property and the credit standing of partners. This concern is especially evident in the rules for conveying the partnership's real property and for borrowing money in the name of the partnership.

Power to Convey Partnership Real Property To bind the partnership, an individual partner's conveyance of a partnership's real property must be expressly, impliedly, or apparently authorized or be ratified by the partnership. For example, the partners may expressly agree that a partner may sell the partnership's real property.

The more difficult determination is whether a partner has *implied* and *apparent* authority to convey real property. A partner has implied and apparent authority to sell real property if a partnership sells real property in the usual course of the partnership business. Such would be the case with the partner of a real estate investment partnership that buys and sells land as its regular business. By contrast, a partner has no implied or apparent authority to sell the building in which the partnership's retail business is conducted. Here, unanimous agreement of the partners is required, since the sale of the building may affect the ability of the firm to continue. In addition, a partner has no implied or apparent authority to sell land held for investment not in the usual course of business. A sale of such land would be authorized only if the partners concurred.

When title to partnership real property is recorded in the name of the partners and not the partnership, those partners in whose name title is recorded have apparent authority to convey title to a bona fide purchaser unaware of the partnership's interest in the real property. However, purchasers are deemed to have knowledge of a limitation on a partner's authority to convey real property that is contained in a Statement of Partnership Authority or Statement of Denial that is filed in the real estate recording office.

Borrowing Money Partnership law restricts the ability of a partner to borrow money in the name of a partnership. Essentially, a partner must possess express, implied, or apparent authority to borrow. Express authority presents few problems. Finding implied and apparent authority to borrow is more difficult.

Although the RUPA does not explicitly recognize the distinction, a number of courts have distinguished between trading and nontrading partnerships for purposes of determining whether a partner has implied or apparent authority to borrow money on behalf of the partnership. A **trading partnership** has an inventory; that is, its regular business is buying and selling merchandise, such as retailing, wholesaling, importing, or exporting. For example, a toy store and a clothing store are trading partnerships. Since there is a time lag between the date they pay for their inventory and the date they sell inventory to their customers, these firms ordinarily need to borrow to avoid cash flow problems. Therefore, a partner of a trading partnership has implied and apparent authority to borrow money for the partnership.

A **nontrading partnership** has no substantial inventory and is usually engaged in providing services—for example, accounting services or real estate brokerage. Such partnerships have no normal borrowing needs. Therefore, a partner of a nontrading partnership has no implied or apparent authority to borrow money for the partnership.

The distinction between trading and nontrading partnerships is not always clear. Businesses such as general contracting, manufacturing, and dairy farming, although not exclusively devoted to buying and selling inventory, have been held to be trading partnerships. The rationale for their inclusion in this category is that borrowing is necessary in the ordinary course of business to augment their working capital.

This suggests why the distinction between trading partnerships and nontrading partnerships is useless or misleading. There is no necessary connection between borrowing money and buying and selling. The more important inquiry should be whether a partner's borrowing is in the ordinary course of business. When borrowing is in the ordinary course of business, a partner has implied and apparent authority to borrow money. If borrowing is not in the ordinary course of business, then no individual partner has implied or apparent authority to borrow money.

If a court finds that a partner has authority to borrow money, the partnership is liable for his borrowings on behalf of the partnership. There is a limit, however, to a partner's capacity to borrow. A partner may have authority to borrow, yet borrow beyond the ordinary needs of the business. A partnership will not be liable for any loan whose amount exceeds the ordinary needs of the business, unless otherwise agreed by the partners.

The power to borrow money on the firm's credit will ordinarily carry with it the power to grant the lender a lien or security interest in firm assets to secure the repayment of the borrowed money. Security interests are a normal part of business loan transactions.

Issuing Negotiable Instruments A partner who has the authority to borrow money also has authority to issue negotiable instruments such as promissory notes for that purpose. When a partnership has a checking account and a partner's name appears on the signature card filed with the bank, the partner has express authority to draw checks. A partner whose name is not on the signature card filed with the bank has apparent authority to issue checks, but only in respect to a third person who has no knowledge or notification of the limitation on the partner's authority.

Negotiating Instruments A partnership receives many negotiable instruments during the course of its business. For example, an accounting firm's clients often pay fees by check. Even though borrowing money and issuing negotiable instruments may be beyond a partner's implied and apparent authority, a partner usually has implied and apparent authority to transfer or negotiate instruments on behalf of the partnership.

For example, when a partnership has a bank account, a partner has implied and apparent authority to indorse and deposit in the account checks drawn payable to the partnership. As a general rule, a partner also has implied and apparent authority to indorse and cash checks drawn payable to the order of the partnership. Likewise, partners have implied authority to indorse drafts and notes payable to the order of the partnership and to sell them at a discount.

Admissions and Notice A partnership is bound by admissions or representations made by a partner concerning partnership affairs that are within her express, implied, or apparent authority. Likewise, notice to a partner is considered to be received by the partnership. Also, a partner's knowledge of material information relating to partnership affairs is **imputed** to the partnership. These rules reflect the reality that a partnership speaks, sees, and hears through its partners.

Disagreement among Partners: Ordinary Course of Business

Usually, partners will discuss management decisions among themselves before taking action, even when doing so is not required by a partnership agreement and even when a partner has the implied authority to take the action by herself. When partners discuss a prospective action, they will usually vote on what action to take. Each partner has one vote, regardless of the relative sizes of their partnership interests or their shares of the profits. On matters in the ordinary course of business, the vote of a majority of the partners controls ordinary business decisions and, thereby, limits the actual authority of the partners. Nonetheless, the apparent authority of the partners to bind the partnership on contracts in the ordinary course of business is unaffected by the majority vote of partners, unless the limitation on the partners' actual authority is communicated to third parties.

Unanimous Partners' Agreement Required

Some partnership actions are so important that one partner should not be able to do them by himself. To make clear that no single partner has implied or apparent authority to do certain acts, in the absence of a contrary agreement, the UPA requires unanimity for several actions. The RUPA, however, deletes such a list. Instead, the RUPA requires that any partnership act not in the ordinary course of business be approved by all partners, absent a contrary agreement of the partners.

For example, a decision to build a new executive offices complex must be approved by all partners. Similarly, the decision of a small accounting partnership in Sacramento to open a second office in San Jose would require unanimity. When other actions, such as submitting a partnership claim to arbitration, are in the ordinary course of business, any partner has authority to do the actions.

Joint Ventures and Mining Partnerships

Most of the authority rules of partnerships apply to joint ventures and mining partnerships. These business organizations are in essence partnerships with limited purposes. Therefore, their members have less implied and apparent authority than do partners. Joint venturers have considerable apparent authority if third persons are unaware of the limited scope of the joint venture. A mining partner has no implied authority to borrow money or issue negotiable instruments. As with partners, joint venturers and mining partners may by agreement expand or restrict each other's agency powers.

Effect of Partnership Agreement

The partners may modify the rules of management by their unanimous agreement. They may agree that a partner will relinquish his management right, thus removing the partner's express and implied authority to manage the partnership. They may grant sole authority to manage the business to one or more partners. Such removals or delegations of management powers will not, however, eliminate a partner's apparent authority to bind the partnership for his acts within the usual course of business unless a third party has knowledge or notification of the limitation.

A partnership agreement may create classes of partners, some of which will have the power to veto certain actions. Some classes of partners may be given greater voting rights. Unequal voting rights are often found in very large partnerships, such as an accounting firm with hundreds or thousands of partners.

For example, in a large accounting partnership, the partnership agreement will have a management section. The management articles may give a managing partner or a managing partners' committee control over much of the firm's day-to-day management, such as the hiring, firing, and promotion of employees, investing the firm's excess cash, and drawing and indorsing partnership checks. The managing partners or a compensation committee may be given power to determine the partners' draws or salaries. Individual partners may have most of their management powers taken away but may be granted the power to hire a personal assistant or to make expenditures within limits from an expense account, such as buying a laptop computer. Other matters may require approval of all the partners (such as selling the partnership's real property and moving the partnership's place of business), a supermajority of partners (such as 75 percent approval to bind the partnership to a bank loan), a majority of partners (such as installing new carpeting), or the partners in a particular area of practice (such as requiring approval of a majority of consulting partners for a consulting engagement over $20,000,000).

In small partnerships of 10 or fewer partners, the partnership agreement often requires unanimous partners' agreement for many actions, such as hiring employees and making large contracts. In small partnerships, these and other actions have a greater impact on each partner. This impact is evident in the next case, *NBN Broadcasting,* in which a partnership agreement that was designed to prevent and resolve conflicts between the two partners eventually caused serious disagreements. It illustrates the necessity for careful drafting of partnership agreements.

NBN Broadcasting, Inc. v. Sheridan Broadcasting Networks, Inc.
105 F.3d 72 (2d Cir. 1997)

NBN Broadcasting, Inc., and Sheridan Broadcasting Networks, Inc., operated competing radio networks. In 1991, NBN and Sheridan agreed to form American Urban Radio Network (AURN), a Pennsylvania partnership that combined NBN's and Sheridan's networks. Sheridan owned 51 percent of the partnership; NBN owned 49 percent. They agreed to maintain NBN's offices in New York and Sheridan's offices in Pittsburgh to allow direct oversight and input by AURN's cochairmen and co-CEOs, Sydney Small (chairman of NBN) and Ronald R. Davenport (chairman of Sheridan). NBN and Sheridan wanted equal rights in management of the partnership. The partners' equal right to manage AURN was modified by the partnership agreement in sections 5.2 and 5.3. Section 5.2 created a five-member Management Committee comprising two members selected by NBN and two by Sheridan; a seat on the Management Committee was to be vacant and would be filled only when the Management Committee was deadlocked. Section 5.2 also provided:

The Management Committee shall be responsible for the following functions of the partnership and contractual arrangements relating thereto:

    (i) Sales and marketing;
    (ii) Promotions and public relations;
    (iii) Affiliate relations and compensation;
    (iv) Network programming;
    (v) Personnel administration; and
    (vi) Budgeting, accounting, and finance.

Section 5.3 provides:

(a) In the event that three of the four members of the Management Committee are unable to reach agreement on any issue or issues relating to items (i) through (v) above and remain so unable for a period of thirty days, then Ronald R. Davenport, Chairman of Sheridan, shall have the right to fill the vacant seat on the Management Committee for the purpose of reaching an agreement, and only until an agreement is reached, on such issue or issues.

Section 5.3 did not authorize appointment of a fifth member of the Management Committee when there was a deadlock regarding budgeting, accounting, or finance or any matter other than those listed in Section 5.2(i) through (v). As to budgeting, accounting, and finance and matters not listed in Section 5.2(i) through (v), NBN and Sheridan were equal partners, and all decisions on such matters required their agreement.

At a Management Committee meeting on September 14, 1995, Davenport proposed that AURN open an expensive new office in Washington, D.C., hire Skip Finley as chief operating officer, and employ Richard Boland. When NBN's representatives opposed opening the new office and hiring Finley and Boland, Davenport scheduled a meeting solely to appoint a fifth member to break the deadlock. On September 15, NBN asked a Pennsylvania state trial court to grant a preliminary injunction and a permanent injunction against Sheridan's opening a new AURN office in Washington and hiring Finley and Boland, on the grounds that the proposals related to budgeting, accounting, and finance and were, therefore, not subject to the deadlock voting provision. On October 13, the state trial court denied NBN's motion for a preliminary injunction. The state trial court held that Sheridan had the right to invoke the deadlock provision to "make additions to personnel" by hiring Finley and Boland. The trial court did not rule on NBN's request for a permanent injunction.

At an October 16 Management Committee meeting, Davenport appointed a fifth member of the committee. By a 3–2 vote, the Management Committee voted to hire Finley and Boland, with NBN's representatives opposing. At that meeting, Davenport also proposed to relocate AURN's New York offices from NBN's office space in New York to other office space in the New York area; to transfer to Pittsburgh from New York AURN's traffic, billing, and collection functions; and to require Finley to make cuts in AURN's New York–based marketing and research personnel. NBN's representatives opposed the proposals, and Davenport scheduled a meeting on November 28 to break the deadlock.

Sensing that the Pennsylvania state trial court would dismiss its request for a permanent injunction and hoping to litigate the issues at a later time, NBN sought to withdraw its motion for a permanent injunction. On November 28, 1995, while the state trial court judge was considering NBN's request to withdraw its lawsuit, a meeting of AURN's Management Committee was held. Davenport again invoked the deadlock provision and appointed his son as fifth member of the Management Committee. By a 3–2 vote, the Management Committee agreed to relocate AURN's New York offices from NBN's office space, to transfer AURN functions to Pittsburgh from New York, and to authorize Finley to make cuts in AURN's New York–based marketing and research personnel. Davenport also proposed to promote Finley to chief executive officer and Boland to vice president of administration. NBN Chairman Small objected, and Davenport scheduled another meeting to break the deadlock.

On November 29 and 30, the state trial court, wanting to put "a final end to this unnecessary litigation," ordered the discontinuance of NBN's lawsuit with prejudice, meaning that NBN could appeal the ruling to an appellate court but would not be permitted to have another trial court litigate the same issues. NBN chose not to appeal the decision of the Pennsylvania state trial court.

After the November 28 meeting, Sheridan located new office space for AURN in New York and entered a new lease with a minimum annual liability of $900,000, yet Sheridan never revealed the location of the space to NBN or sought NBN approval of the relocation or new lease. On January 18, 1996, at the next Management Committee meeting, Davenport again appointed his son as the fifth member. By a 3–2 vote, with NBN's representatives opposing, the Management Committee appointed Finley as CEO and Boland as vice president of administration.

On January 31, 1996, NBN filed a federal lawsuit seeking an injunction against Sheridan's alleged violations of the equal management rights of the partners by hiring Finley and Boland, interfering with AURN's personnel and customer relations, and relocating AURN's New York offices. Sheridan asked the federal district court to dismiss the suit on the grounds of res judicata; that is, Sheridan argued that NBN was raising legal issues that the Pennsylvania state trial court had already considered or that NBN should have brought to the Pennsylvania trial court. Thus, Sheridan argued, because the Pennsylvania trial court had already dismissed NBN's request for an injunction with prejudice, the federal district court should not reconsider these issues. The federal district court agreed with Sheridan and dismissed NBN's lawsuit. NBN appealed to the federal court of appeal.

Pollack, Judge A discontinuance with prejudice is deemed a final adjudication on the merits for res judicata purposes on the claims asserted or which could have been asserted in the suit. Any issue concerning the relocation of the New York Office could not have been raised in the State Court suit commenced on September 15, 1995, or until the voting deadlock thereon on November 28, 1995. The NBN claim on the relocation of the New York Office was a claim based on new conduct that could have only arisen long after the filing of NBN's State Court suit. Since a plaintiff has no obligation to expand its suit in order to add a claim that it could not have asserted at the time the suit was commenced, a later suit based on subsequent conduct is not barred by res judicata.

The res judicata effect is limited to those claims that had arisen at the time that NBN brought the State Court Action.

They did not include the relocation of the New York office, which had not yet even been brought to an initial vote. There was no submission to the State Court of NBN's equal right to decide whether the New York Office should be moved from its existing location as part of NBN's premises.

The doctrine of res judicata embraces all claims of NBN, excluding those claims relating to the relocation of the New York Office, which were passed on by the Management Committee prior to the filing of NBN's State Court action; the claims asserted therein and the dismissal thereof on the grounds of res judicata is affirmed.

Judgment for Sheridan affirmed in part; judgment in part reversed in favor of NBN. Remanded to the district court.

LOG ON

www.mhhe.com/mallor12e
Go to your textbook's website above to find a
model partnership agreement. Note that the
agreement repeats the fiduciary duties we
studied. A well-drafted partnership agreement
will expand that section to make clear what each
duty covers, such as stating what activities
constitute competition with the partnership.
In England and India, partnership agreements
are called partnership deeds. See examples at:
www.thebharat.com/legal/agreements/
partnershipdeed.html.
and
www.link2content.co.uk/uploads/Partnership
%20Deed(1).doc
There are several commercial websites that sell
model partnership agreements. One is
UrgentBusinessForms.com. See a list of
partnership agreements for sale at
www.urgentbusinessforms.com/partnership_
agreement.asp

Liability for Torts and Crimes

Torts

The standards and principles of agency law's *respondeat superior* are applied in determining the liability of the partnership and of the other partners for the torts of a partner and other partnership employees. In addition, the partnership and the other partners are liable jointly and severally for the torts of a partner committed within the ordinary course of partnership business or within the authority of that partner. Finally, when a partner commits a breach of trust, the partnership and all of the partners are liable. For example, all of the partners in a stock brokerage firm are liable for a partner's embezzlement of a customer's securities and funds.

Intentional Torts While a partnership and its partners are usually liable for a partner's negligence, they usually have no liability for a partner's intentional torts. The reason for this rule is that intentional torts are not usually within the ordinary scope of business or within the ordinary authority of a partner.

A few intentional torts impose liability on a partnership and its partners. For example, a partner who repossesses consumer goods from debtors of the partnership may trespass on consumer property or batter a consumer. Such activities have been held to be in the ordinary course of business. Also, a partner who authorizes a partner to commit an intentional tort is liable for such torts.

Partners' Remedies When a partnership and the other partners are held liable for a partner's tort, they may recover the amount of their vicarious liability from the wrongdoing partner. This rule places ultimate liability on the wrongdoing partner without affecting the ability of tort victims to obtain recovery from the partnership or the other partners.

Tort Liability and Limited Liability Partnerships

State legislatures created the limited liability partnership (LLP) as a means of reducing the personal liability of professional partners, such as accountants. Consequently, an innocent partner of an LLP has no liability for the professional malpractice of his partners. LLP statutes grant partners broad protection, eliminating an innocent partner's liability for errors, omissions, negligence, incompetence, or malfeasance of his partners or employees.

Under the RUPA, the protection afforded LLP partners is even broader. LLP partners have no liability for other debts of the business, such as a supplier's bill, lease obligations, and bank loans.

That is the limit of protection, however. The LLP itself is liable for the tort of a wrongdoing partner or employee under the doctrine of *respondeat superior*. In addition, a wrongdoing partner is liable for his own malpractice or negligence. Also, the partner supervising the work of the wrongdoing partner has unlimited liability for the wrongdoing partner's tort. Thus, the LLP's assets, the wrongdoing partner's personal assets, and the supervising partner's personal assets are at risk.

Crimes

When a partner commits a crime in the course and scope of transacting partnership business, rarely are his partners criminally liable. But when the partners have participated in the criminal act or authorized its commission, they are liable. They may also be liable when they know of a partner's criminal tendencies yet place him in a position in which he may commit a crime.

Until recent times, a partnership could not be held liable for a crime in most states because it was not viewed as a legal entity. However, modern criminal codes usually define a partnership as a "person" that may commit a crime when a partner, acting within the scope of his authority, engages in a criminal act.

ETHICS IN ACTION

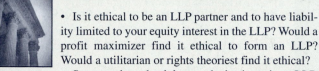

You and your friends consider forming a consulting partnership. If you form the business as a partnership, each partner has personal liability for all the contacts and torts of the partnership. If you form the business as an LLP, in general you and the other partners have no liability for partnership obligations beyond the assets of the LLP, that is, beyond each partner's equity interest in the business.

• As your form of business, will you choose the partnership or LLP?

• Is it ethical to be an LLP partner and to have liability limited to your equity interest in the LLP? Would a profit maximizer find it ethical to form an LLP? Would a utilitarian or rights theorist find it ethical?

• Suppose that a bank knows the business is an LLP, lends money to the LLP, but does not obtain the LLP partners' individual promises to repay the loan. Is it ethical that the LLP partners are not liable to the bank on the loan if the LLP's assets are insufficient to repay the loan?

Lawsuits by and against Partnerships and Partners

Under the RUPA, a partnership may sue in its own name. Since suing someone is usually an ordinary business decision, ordinarily any partner has authority to initiate a lawsuit.

The RUPA also permits a partnership to be sued in its own name. Partners may also be sued individually on partnership obligations. Partners are jointly and severally liable for partnership obligations, whether based in contract or tort. This means that in addition to suing the partnership, a creditor may sue all of the partners (jointly) or sue fewer than all the partners (severally). If a creditor sues the partnership and all of the partners, the judgment may be satisfied from the assets of the partnership and, if partnership assets are exhausted, from the assets of the partners. If the partnership and fewer than all the partners are sued severally, the judgment may be satisfied only from the assets of the partnership and the assets of the partners sued. Again, partners cannot be required to pay until partnership assets have been exhausted.

When fewer than all the partners are sued and made to pay a partnership obligation, the partners paying may seek **indemnification** and **contribution** from the other partners for their shares of the liability.

Limited Liability Partnerships

For LLP partners, only the LLP is liable on a contractual obligation, and only the LLP may be sued on such a claim. For tort obligations, the LLP is liable as well as the partner who committed the tort. LLP partners who had no role in the commission of the tort have no liability.

In the following *Ross & Hardies* case, a court held a partnership liable for the fraud of its partner.

Thomas v. Ross & Hardies   *9 F. Supp. 2d 547 (D.Ct. Md. 1998)*

Michael Clott had been convicted of violations of the federal racketeering statute, transportation of stolen securities, and bank and mail fraud. Clott was released from prison on supervised release in May 1994. A condition of Clott's supervised release was his agreement not to engage in the financial securities business in Maryland. In the fall of 1994, Clott retained the services of a law firm partnership, Ross & Hardies. Its partner, Steven Kersner, was the partner primarily assigned to Clott's account. Clott retained Kersner and Ross & Hardies to provide Clott's company, Capital Financial Group, Inc., a legal framework in which Clott could conduct business in the finance, securities, mortgage, and investment banking industries in Maryland.

In September 1994 acting through Capital, Clott created what was known as the 7.5% Program. The 7.5% Program was a mortgage loan program marketed to minority homeowners. The minority homeowners would mortgage their homes for the maximum amount possible. The homeowners would then turn the proceeds of the mortgages over to another firm controlled by Clott, Phoenix Financial Service, Inc., which would then either pay off each mortgage in full or would purchase it from the mortgage company. In exchange for doing this, the company would grant the homeowners a line of credit with a 7.5% interest rate. The rate would stay at 7.5% regardless of increases in the market rate.

Several homeowners, including Lionel and Hazel Thomas, participated in the 7.5% Program. They alleged that the Program was a fraud. While the homeowners did take out mortgages and turned proceeds over to Clott, the money was never used to pay off the mortgages and the homeowners never had access to lines of credit. Instead, the complaint alleged that Clott diverted the money and the homeowners were left with a significant mortgage on their property. The scheme fell apart sometime during the summer of 1995, and both Clott and Kersner pled guilty to felony charges brought by the United States Attorney. Both are in jail.

The homeowners sued Kersner and his partnership, Ross and Hardies, for their role in the fraud. The homeowners alleged that Kersner helped pitch the Program to legitimate mortgage lenders as early as December 1994, and allowed Clott to use the Ross & Hardies office in Washington, D.C., to conduct Capital's business. They alleged that Kersner and John Fornaciaria, another Ross & Hardies partner, prepared paperwork and affidavits for Clott that falsely represented the nature of Clott's involvement with Phoenix. Kersner allegedly wrote false letters under the Ross & Hardies letterhead concerning Clott's sentencing. These acts were done even though Kersner and Fornaciaria knew that they were misleading as to Clott's involvement in the business and that Clott's activities were fraudulent in nature.

The homeowners also alleged that Kersner played a key role in perpetuating the scheme by meeting and assuring the victim homeowners. For example, Kersner helped resolve a problem that arose when Clott "whited-out" a limited indorsement on a check from a cautious homeowner. Homeowners who were potential Program participants met with Kersner in Ross & Hardies's D.C. office and talked with him by phone, during which time Kersner assured them that the Program was legitimate and had Ross & Hardies's backing. In addition, the homeowners alleged that Kersner aided Clott in fraudulently transferring the loan proceeds to various bank accounts, opening empty accounts in the names of the participants to deceive them into believing that lines of credit had been established, preparing false documents to make it appear that the mortgages had been paid off, making monthly payments on some of the mortgages to conceal the fact that they had not been paid in full, telling lenders to contact Kersner with questions and not call the homeowners, and forging and altering certain checks.

The Thomases and the other homeowners sued Ross & Hardies, under the Racketeering Influenced Corrupt Organization Act (RICO). RICO provides a private cause of action for persons injured by a violation of RICO section 1962(c). Section 1962(c) makes it unlawful for:

> any person employed by or associated with any enterprise engaged in, or the activities of which affect, interstate or foreign commerce, to conduct or participate, directly or indirectly, in the conduct of such enterprise's affairs through a pattern of racketeering activity or collection of unlawful debt.

Ross & Hardies asked the court to dismiss the lawsuit against the partnership on the grounds that under RICO it was not liable for the fraudulent conduct of its partner.

Memorandum A difficult question facing the Court is whether there is partnership liability under RICO. The Court's primary concern is that it not allow a plaintiff to use partnership liability to reach a party that Congress did not wish to hold liable under RICO.

The general rule of partnership liability is that a partner is an agent for the partnership, and a partnership is liable for the wrongful acts of its partners committed in the ordinary course of the business of the partnership. See Revised Uniform Partnership Act sections 301, 305 (1994); Md. Code Ann. Corps. &Ass'ns. section 9–305 (Supp. 1997). With fraud claims, it is especially appropriate to hold a partnership liable when it benefited from the fraudulent acts of its partner.

Holding a partnership liable for the RICO violations of its partner under doctrines of partnership liability serves Congress's goal of deterring individuals from controlling

organizations through a pattern of racketeering activity. Imposing liability under vicarious liability (or in this case partnership liability) is consistent with RICO's compensatory goal. Holding a partnership liable when it benefits from the acts of its partners will prevent the partnership from being unjustly enriched and will help serve Congress's goal of compensating victims of racketeering activities.

The Thomases' allegation is that Kersner violated RICO while providing services to Clott and Capital. Kersner's alleged acts of transferring money, making fraudulent representations to victims, and pitching the Program to potential lenders are acts that fall within the scope of the work of a large law firm representing a corporate client. Capital was a paying client of Ross & Hardies, and the firm benefited from Kersner's representation of that client, including the alleged RICO violations. Holding Ross & Hardies liable for the RICO violations of Kersner would provide the firm, and other law firms, with a powerful incentive to take steps to prevent future violations and will assist in providing compensation to the victims of the racketeering activity.

According to the complaint, Clott and Kersner used Capital to run the 7.5% Program scheme, whereby they persuaded homeowners to mortgage their homes and turn over the proceeds to Phoenix. Kersner allegedly helped direct the recruitment of homeowners and mortgage lenders, and also helped direct the fraudulent transfers of the mortgage proceeds. These were the key acts of the scheme, and if the allegations are true then Kersner may be liable for directing an enterprise through a pattern of racketeering activity. The acts, if committed, were within the scope of Ross & Hardies's business as a large law firm serving the needs of corporate clients. As a result, Ross & Hardies may be held liable under section 1962(c) following traditional doctrines of partnership liability.

Ross & Hardies's motion to dismiss the Thomases' complaint is denied. The case proceeds to trial.

Problems and Problem Cases

1. Walter Levy and Henry Disharoon formed a partnership to purchase a jet airplane and to operate a charter airline business. Disharoon located a jet and informed Levy that the price was $963,000. After Levy approved the purchase, Disharoon contracted to buy the jet for $860,000. The partnership borrowed $975,000 to pay for the jet. Disharoon paid the seller $860,000 and deposited in Disharoon's personal bank account the $103,000 difference between the actual purchase price and the purchase price represented to Levy. Has Disharoon breached a fiduciary duty?

2. Larry Rose, Paul G. Veale, Sr., Paul G. Veale, Jr., Gary Gibson, and James Parker offered professional accounting services as partners under the firm name of Paul G. Veale and Co. Their written partnership agreement expressed the general duties of the partners, but it recognized that Veale, Sr., and Rose had outside investments and a number of other business commitments. All of the partners were allowed to pursue other business activities so long as the activities did not conflict with the partnership practice of public accounting or materially interfere with the partners' duties to the partnership. While a partner, Larry Rose performed accounting services for Right Away Foods and Ed Payne. He was paid personally by those clients. Rose was an officer and shareholder of Right Away. In addition, Rose used the partnership's employees and computers to service those clients. Has Rose breached a fiduciary duty owed to his partners?

3. Bill Lund and Don Albrecht formed Terramics Associates, a partnership in the business of acquiring, developing, and selling real property. At the same time, Lund was a partner in Wilshire Redevelopment, a real property development firm that competed with Terramics. Lund disclosed his interest in Wilshire to Albrecht. Lund and Albrecht decided to terminate the partnership. Before terminating the partnership, they negotiated the price at which Albrecht would buy Lund's interest in the partnership. During the negotiations, Albrecht and Lund valued at $8 million one of the partnership's properties, a 190-acre lot of land (Parcel D). Lund agreed to a partnership buyout price based in part on that valuation of Parcel D. Albrecht had not disclosed to Lund, however, that during the negotiations Albrecht had received four offers for Parcel D ranging from $10 million to $12 million. Have Lund and Albrecht breached any fiduciary duties?

4. Two brothers, Sydney and Ashley Altman, operated several partnerships in Pennsylvania. They shared equally in the management of the partnerships. They agreed that each would receive identical salaries and that each was permitted to charge an equal amount of personal expenses to the partnerships. After Sydney moved to Florida, Sydney commuted to Pennsylvania every week to work for two to three days. After a year passed, Sydney told Ashley that he was considering retiring and remaining in Florida permanently. They tried to reach an agreement on Ashley's purchase of Sydney's partnership interests but were unable to do so. Ashley continued to manage the businesses by himself for nearly four years. During that time, Ashley paid himself salaries in excess of what the brothers had agreed. Has Ashley received excessive compensation as a partner?

5. Nicolas Marsch and Ronald Williams formed a partnership, Horizon Properties, to develop a golf course and luxury home sites in Rancho Santa Fe, California. The partnership was a disaster. When the partnership ended, its assets were $27 million less than the claims against the partnership. Williams demanded that Marsch pay half of the $27 million loss by contributing $13,500,000 to the partnership. Marsch objected on the grounds that section 2.02 of their partnership agreement stated: "Additional capital contributions to the Partnership shall only be by prior mutual agreement of the Partners." Also Section 2.03 stated: "No Partner may make any voluntary contribution of capital to the Partnership without the prior consent of the other Partner." Is Marsch liable for half of the $27 million partnership loss?

6. Dean Wilkerson and Walter Helms formed DWA of Tennessee, Inc., a furniture manufacturer. Shortly thereafter they created H&W Partnership, a general partnership, for the purpose of purchasing DWA's furniture manufacturing facility and leasing it back to DWA. DWA failed to pay a $438,000 debt for the purchase of leather from Lackawanna Leather Co. Through Wilkerson, DWA issued to Lackawanna a promissory note to pay the debt. A few days before the note was due, Wilkerson requested an extension of time for payment. Lackawanna agreed if H&W was included on the note as a maker. Wilkerson then signed the new note on behalf of DWA and H&W. Did Wilkerson have the authority to sign the note on behalf of H&W?

7. Holland lent Dalton Waldrop $12,500 to buy well-drilling equipment that was described in the loan agreement between Holland and Dalton. A year later, Dalton formed a well-drilling partnership with his brother Thomas. They used the equipment Dalton had purchased with the money borrowed from Holland. Are the partnership and Thomas liable on the Holland loan?

8. L. G. Patel and S. L. Patel, husband and wife, owned the City Center Motel in Eureka, California. The Patels formed a partnership with their son, Raj, to own and operate the motel. The partnership agreement required Raj's approval of any sale of the motel building. Real estate records were not changed, however, and the motel building remained recorded only in the names of L. G. and S. L. Patel. L. G. and S. L. contracted to sell the motel building to P. V. and Kirit Patel, who were unaware of Raj's interest as a partner. When Raj was informed of the contract to sell the motel building, he refused to grant his approval. Is the contract enforceable against the partnership?

9. Florence and Michael Acri were married and also partners in the Acri Cafe, which they jointly managed. For the first 15 years of their marriage, Michael had been in and out of sanitaria for the treatment of mental disorders. Although he had beaten Florence when they had marital problems, he had not attacked anyone else.

Michael and Florence separated, and Michael assumed full control and management of the cafe. A few months after the Acris' separation, Stephen Vrabel and a friend went into the Acri Cafe. Without provocation, Michael shot and killed Vrabel's companion and seriously injured Vrabel while they were seated and drinking at the cafe's bar. Was Florence liable for Vrabel's injuries?

Online Research: The Saga of Arthur Andersen LLP

In October 2002, the world's fifth largest accounting firm was fined $500,000 for its criminal obstruction of the federal government's investigation of former energy trading firm Enron. Judge Melinda Harmon assessed the maximum penalty permitted by law. Andersen partner David Duncan had earlier pled guilty to obstruction of justice for his role in shredding Andersen documents that would have revealed Andersen's failure to challenge Enron's accounting practices that inflated its earnings. Andersen was convicted of the crime of obstruction of justice in part based on the actions of Duncan and Andersen legal counsel Nancy Temple, who ordered Duncan to shred incriminating documents.

The fine is only one chapter in the saga of Andersen, a firm once revered for its high professional auditing standards. Since its indictment in April 2002 and continuing through its conviction in June 2002 and announcement of the fine in October 2002, Andersen's employees have dropped from 85,000 to 3,000. Its license to conduct audits has been revoked. Many partners have left the partnership to join other public auditing firms. Actions by defrauded Enron investors against Andersen and its partners will drag on for years.

Andersen is appealing its conviction, and some partners hope to preserve the partnership. Follow what happens to Andersen's appeal, the firm, and its partners by reading current articles and archives at the websites of newspapers like *The Wall Street Journal* and *The New York Times*.

• Has the court of appeals ruled on Andersen's guilt?
• Has Arthur Andersen LLP survived? What is its likely future?
• Many Andersen partners had invested millions of dollars in Andersen. What has happened to the Andersen partners' capital investments in the firm?

39

PARTNERS' DISSOCIATION AND PARTNERSHIPS' DISSOLUTION AND WINDING UP

You are planning the formation of a 50-partner venture capital partnership. Knowing the attributes, weaknesses, and faults of humans, you expect that some partners will die, become ill, and act irresponsibly during the term of the partnership. You know that some partners will want to leave the partnership for good reasons and some for bad reasons. You know that when a partner leaves the partnership, the leaving partner will want to be paid the value of her partnership interest. You also know it is human nature for partners to disagree about the value of a partnership interest. You are also concerned about how the partnership will fund its repurchase of the leaving partner's interest without causing several liquidity problems for the firm. You know that some of the firm's clients have strong business and personal attachments to one or more firm partners; therefore, when those partners leave the partnership, the firm may lose the business of those partners' clients. Finally, you know that the firm will need to add new partners from time to time to ensure the firm's survival.

- What are the default rules that apply when partners leave and enter a partnership?
- Why may the default rules be unacceptable to you?
- Write the sections of the partnership agreement regarding partners' leaving and entering the partnership.

THIS CHAPTER IS ABOUT the death of partnerships. Four terms are important in this connection: dissociation, dissolution, winding up, and termination. Dissociation is a change in the relation of the partners, as when a partner dies. Dissolution is the commencement of the winding up process. Winding up is the orderly liquidation of the partnership assets and the distribution of the proceeds to those having claims against the partnership. Termination, the end of the partnership's existence, automatically follows winding up. A partner in a limited liability partnership dissociates from the LLP and the LLP is dissolved, wound up, and terminated in the same manner as an ordinary partnership.

Dissociation

Dissociation is defined in the Revised Uniform Partnership Act (RUPA) as a change in the relation of the partners caused by any partner ceasing to be associated in the carrying on of the business. A dissociation may be caused by a partner's retirement, death, expulsion, or bankruptcy filing, among other things. Whatever the cause of dissociation, however, it is characterized by a partner's *ceasing to take part in the carrying on of the partnership's business.*

Dissociation is the starting place for the dissolution, winding up (liquidation), and termination of a partnership. Although winding up does not always follow dissociation, it often does. Winding up usually has a severe effect on a business: It usually ends the business, because the assets of the business are sold and the proceeds of the sale are distributed to creditors and partners.

A partner has the *power* to dissociate from the partnership *at any time,* such as by withdrawing from the partnership. A partner does not, however, always have the *right* to dissociate.

When a partner's dissociation does not violate the partnership agreement and otherwise is nonwrongful, the partner has the right to dissociate from the partnership: Such a dissociation is **nonwrongful.** When a partner's dissociation violates the partnership agreement or otherwise is wrongful, the partner has the power—but not the right—to dissociate from the partnership: Such a dissociation is **wrongful.** The consequences that follow a nonwrongful dissocation may differ from those that follow a wrongful dissociation.

Nonwrongful Dissociation

A dissociation is nonwrongful when the dissociation does not violate the partnership agreement and is not otherwise wrongful. The following events are nonwrongful dissociations:

1. Death of a partner.

2. Withdrawal of a partner at any time from a partnership at will. A partnership at will is a partnership whose partnership agreement does not specify any term or undertaking to be accomplished.

3. In a partnership for a term or completion of an undertaking, withdrawal of a partner within 90 days after another partner's death, adjudicated incapacity, appointment of a custodion over his property, or wrongful dissociation. This dissociation is deemed nonwrongful to protect a partner who may think her interests are impaired by the premature departure of an important partner.

4. Withdrawal of a partner in accordance with the partnership agreement. For example, a partnership agreement allows the partners to retire at age 55. A partner who retires at age 60 has dissociated from the partnership nonwrongfully.

5. Automatic dissociation by the occurrence of an event agreed to in the partnership agreement. For example, a partnership may require a partner to retire at age 70.

6. Expulsion of a partner in accordance with the partnership agreement. For example, the removal of a partner who has been convicted of a crime causes a dissociation from the partnership if the partnership agreement allows removal on such grounds.

7. Expulsion of a partner who has transferred his transferable partnership interest or suffered a charging order against his transferable interest. Under the RUPA, such an expulsion must be approved by all the other partners, absent a contrary partnership agreement.

8. Expulsion of a partner with whom it is unlawful for the partnership to carry on its business. Under the RUPA, this expulsion must be approved by all the other partners, absent a contrary agreement.

9. A partner's assigning his assets for the benefit of creditors or consenting to the appointment of a custodian over his assets.

10. Appointment of a guardian over a partner or a judicial determination that a partner is incapable of performing as a partner. For example, a court rules that a partner who has suffered a stroke and has permanent brain damage is unable to continue as a partner of a consulting partnership.

In addition, there are a few special rules for dissociations of nonhuman partners, such as corporations.

Wrongful Dissociation

A partner wrongfully dissociates from a partnership when she dissociates in violation of the partnership agreement or in any other wrongful way. The following are wrongful dissociations:

1. Withdrawal of a partner that breaches an express provision in the partnership agreement.

2. Withdrawal of a partner before the end of the partnership's term or completion of its undertaking, unless the partner withdraws within 90 days after another partner's death, adjudicated incapacity, appointment of a custodion over his property, or wrongful dissociation.

3. A partner's filing a bankruptcy petition or being a debtor in bankruptcy.

4. Expulsion of a partner by a court at the request of the partnership or another partner. The grounds for judicial dissociation are when
   a. A partner's wrongful conduct adversely and materially affects the partnership business,
   b. A partner wilfully and persistently breaches the partnership agreement or her fiduciary duties, or
   c. A partner's conduct makes it not reasonably practicable to conduct partnership business with the partner.

For example, a partner may persistently and substantially use partnership property for his own benefit. Or three partners may refuse to allow two other partners to manage the partnership's business. The harmed partners may seek judicial dissociation. For the expelled, wrong-doing partners, the dissociation is wrongful.

In addition, there are a few wrongful dissociations that apply only to nonhuman partners, such as a corporation.

Consequences of Wrongful Dissociation A partner who wrongfully dissociates from a partnership has no right to demand that the partnership be dissolved and its business wound up. That means the remaining partners may continue the partnership and its business. If at least 50 percent of the remaining partners so choose, however, the partnership will be wound up.

Should the other partners choose to wind up the business, the wrongfully dissociated partner has no right to perform the winding up. Nonetheless, a wrongfully dissociated partner is entitled to his share of the value of his partnership interest, minus the damages he caused the partnership. Damages may include the cost of obtaining new financing and the harm to the partnership goodwill caused by the loss of a valuable partner. Moreover, the wrongfully dissociated partner is not entitled to receive the buyout price until the term of the partnership has expired.

Acts Not Causing Dissociation

Many events that you think may cause a dissociation in fact do not. For example, a partner's transfer of his transferable partnership interest, by itself, does not cause a dissociation from the partnership, and neither does a creditor's obtaining a charging order. Also, the addition of a partner to a partnership is not a dissociation, because no one ceases to be associated in the business.

Mere disagreements, even irreconcilable differences, between partners are expectable, and therefore by themselves are not grounds for dissociation. If the disagreements threaten the economic viability of the partnership, however, a court may order a dissolution, as will be discussed below.

Effect of Partnership Agreement

The dissociations listed in the RUPA are merely default rules. The partners may limit or expand the definition of dissociation and those dissociations that are wrongful, and they may change the effects of nonwrongful and wrongful dissociations. For example, the partners may require dissociation if a partner transfers his transferable partnership interest, if a partner does not redeem a charging order within 15 days of the order, or if a partner fails to make a capital contribution required by the partnership agreement. The partnership agreement may also reduce the number of partners that must approve the expulsion of a partner, such as a two-thirds vote, and expand the

grounds for expulsion. If one partner is very powerful, the partnership agreement might allow that partner to dissociate at any time without penalty.

Dissolution and Winding Up the Partnership Business

When a partner dissociates from a partnership, the next step may be dissolution and **winding up** of the partnership's business. This involves the orderly liquidation—or sale—of the assets of the business. Liquidation may be accomplished asset by asset; that is, each asset may be sold separately. It may also be accomplished by a sale of the business as a whole. Or it may be accomplished by a means somewhere between these two extremes.

Winding up does not always require the sale of the assets or the business. When a partnership has valuable assets, the partners may wish to receive the assets rather than the proceeds from their sale. Such *distributions-in-kind* are rarely permitted.

During winding up, the partners continue as fiduciaries to each other, especially in negotiating sales or making distributions of partnership assets to members of the partnership. Nonetheless, there is a termination of the fiduciary duties unrelated to winding up. For example, a partner who is not winding up the business may compete with his partnership during winding up.

Events Causing Dissolution and Winding Up

Recognizing that a partnership business is worth more as a going concern, the RUPA contemplates that the partnership business will usually continue after a partner's dissociation. Many dissociations, such as one caused by a partner's death, will not automatically result in the dissolution and winding up of a partnership.

Nonetheless, the RUPA provides that a partnership will be dissolved and wound up in the following situations:

1. When the partnership's term has expired.

2. When the partnership has completed the undertaking for which it was created.

3. When all the partners agree to wind up the business.

4. When an event occurs that the partnership agreement states will cause a winding up of the partnership.

5. For a partnership at will, when any partner expressly withdraws from the partnership, other than a partner who

is deceased, was expelled, is a debtor in bankruptcy, assigned his assets for the benefit of creditors, had a custodian appointed over his assets, or was automatically dissociated by the occurrence of an event agreed to in the partnership agreement.

6. For a partnership for a term or completion of an undertaking, when at least half the remaining partners vote to dissolve and wind up the partnership within 90 days after a partner dies, wrongfully dissociates, assigns his property for the benefit of his creditors, or consents to the appointment of a custodian over his property.

7. When the business of the partnership is unlawful.

8. Upon the request by a partner, when a court determines that the economic purpose of the partnership is likely to be unreasonably frustrated, a partner's conduct makes it not reasonably practicable to carry on the business with that partner, or it is not reasonably practicable to conform with the partnership agreement.

9. Upon the request of a transferee of a partner's transferable interest in a partnership at will or a partnership whose term or undertaking has been completed, when a court determines that it is equitable to wind up the partnership business.

Effect of Partnership Agreement The above causes of winding up are the RUPA's default rules, which except for the last three may be changed by the partnership agreement. For example, the partnership agreement may provide that at any time two-thirds of the partners may cause a winding up or that upon the death or retirement of a partner no partner has the right to force a winding up. Partners will frequently want to limit the events that cause dissolution and winding up, because they believe the business will be worth more as a going concern than by being liquidated.

In addition, if dissolution has occurred, the partners may agree to avoid winding up and to continue the business. To avoid winding up after dissolution has occurred, all the partners who have not wrongfully dissociated must consent to continuing the business. That means that any partner who has not wrongfully dissociated may force winding up if dissolution has occurred.

Joint Ventures and Mining Partnerships

The partnership rules of dissociation and dissolution apply to joint ventures. Mining partnerships are difficult to dissolve, because of the free transferability of mining partnership interests. The death of a mining partner does not effect a dissolution. In addition, a mining partner may sell his interest to another person and dissociate from the carrying on of the mining partnership business without causing a dissolution.

In the following *Horizon* case, the court considered grounds for dissolution that were contained in the RUPA and a partnership agreement, and whether a partner could be held liable for damages caused by a dissolution. The case points out the importance of careful drafting of partnership agreements.

Horizon/CMS Healthcare Corp. v. Southern Oaks Health Care, Inc.
732 So. 2d 1156 (Fla. Ct. App. 1999)

Horizon/CMS Healthcare Corporation is a large, publicly traded provider of both nursing home facilities and management for nursing home facilities. In 1993, it decided to expand into Kissimmee, Florida, by entering partnerships with Southern Oaks Health Care, Inc., which already operated the Southern Oaks Health Care Center in the area and held the rights to open another 120-bed facility. They agreed that Horizon would manage both the Southern Oaks facility and the new facility. Southern Oaks and Horizon entered into several partnership contracts having terms of 20 years.

In 1996, Southern Oaks filed suit against Horizon alleging that Horizon had breached the 20-year agreements. Horizon also sued Southern Oaks and asked the trial court to dissolve the partnerships on the grounds that the partners had irreconcilable differences regarding how profits would be calculated and divided. The trial court found largely in favor of Southern Oaks, concluding that Horizon breached its obligations under two different partnership agreements. The court ordered the dissolution of the partnerships, finding that the partners were incapable of continuing to operate in business together. The court also ruled that neither partner was entitled to damages as a result of the dissolution.

Southern Oaks appealed to the Florida Court of Appeals, asking the court to award damages because Horizon unilaterally and wrongfully sought dissolution of the partnerships. Southern Oaks asked for a damage award equal to the loss of the partnerships' 17 remaining years' future profits.

Goshorn, Justice Southern Oaks argues Horizon wrongfully caused the dissolution because the basis for dissolution cited by the court is not one of the grounds for which the parties contracted. The pertinent partnership contracts provided in section 7.3 "Causes of Dissolution":

> In addition to the causes for dissolution set forth in Section 7.2(c), the Partnership shall be dissolved in the event that: (a) the Partners mutually agree to terminate the Partnership; (b) the Partnership ceases to maintain any interest (which term shall include, but not be limited to, a security interest) in the Facility; (c) the Partnership, by its terms as set forth in this Agreement, is terminated; (d) upon thirty (30) days' prior written notice to the other Partner, either Partner elects to dissolve the Partnership on account of an Irreconcilable Difference which arises and cannot, after good faith efforts, be resolved; (e) the Partners determine, based on the opinion of Partnership counsel, that the Partnership cannot legally remain in existence or continue its business operations without material detriment; (f) the Transferring Partner sells its Partnership Interest to the Purchasing Partner; (g) pursuant to a court decree; or (h) on the date specified in Section 2.4.

The term "irreconcilable difference" used in the above quote is defined in the contracts as

> A reasonable and good faith difference of opinion between the Partners where either (i) the existence of the difference of opinion has a material and adverse impact on the conduct of the Partnerships' Business, or (ii) such difference is as to (x) the quality of services which is or should be provided at the long-term care facilities owned by the Partnership, (y) the adoption of a budget for a future fiscal year, or (z) any matter requiring unanimous approval of the Partners under the terms of this Agreement.

Southern Oaks argues that what Horizon relied on at trial as showing irreconcilable differences—the decisions of how profits were to be determined and divided—were not "good faith differences of opinion," nor did they have "a material and adverse impact on the conduct of the Partnerships' Business." Horizon's refusal to pay Southern Oaks according to the terms of the contracts was not an "irreconcilable difference" as defined by the contract, Southern Oaks asserts, pointing out that Horizon's acts were held to be breaches of the contracts. Because there was no contract basis for dissolution, Horizon's assertion of dissolution was wrongful, Southern Oaks concludes.

Southern Oaks contends further that not only were there no contractual grounds for dissolution, dissolution was also wrongful under the Florida Statutes. Southern Oaks argues that pursuant to section 620.8602, Horizon had the power to

dissociate from the partnership, but, in the absence of contract grounds for the dissociation, Horizon wrongfully dissociated. It asserts that it is entitled to lost future profits under Florida's partnership law, relying on subsection 620.8602(3), Florida Statutes.

We find Southern Oaks' argument without merit. First, the trial court's finding that the parties are incapable of continuing to operate in business together is a finding of "irreconcilable differences," a permissible reason for dissolving the partnerships under the express terms of the partnership agreements. Thus, dissolution was not "wrongful," assuming there can be "wrongful" dissolutions, and Southern Oaks was not entitled to damages for lost future profits. Additionally, the partnership contracts also permit dissolution by "judicial decree." Although neither party cites this provision, it appears that pursuant thereto, the parties agreed that dissolution would be proper if done by a trial court for whatever reason the court found sufficient to warrant dissolution.

Second, even assuming the partnership was dissolved for a reason not provided for in the partnership agreements, damages were properly denied. Under RUPA, it is clear that wrongful dissociation triggers liability for lost future profits. See section 620.8602(3) ("A partner who wrongfully dissociates is liable to the partnership and to the other partners for damages caused by the dissociation. The liability is in addition to any other obligation of the partner to the partnership or to the other partners."). However, RUPA does not contain a similar provision for dissolution; RUPA does not refer to the dissolutions as rightful or wrongful. Section 620.8801, "Events causing dissolution and winding up of partnership business," outlines the events causing dissolution without any provision for liability for damages.

Under subsection 620.8801(5), the statute recognizes judicial dissolution:

> A partnership is dissolved, and its business must be wound up, only upon the occurrence of any of the following events:
>
> (5) On application by a partner, a judicial determination that:
>
> (a) The economic purpose of the partnership is likely to be unreasonably frustrated;
>
> (b) Another partner has engaged in conduct relating to the partnership business which makes it not reasonably practicable to carry on the business in partnership with such partner; or
>
> (c) It is not otherwise reasonably practicable to carry on the partnership business in conformity with the partnership agreement; . . .

Paragraph (5)(c) provides the basis for the trial court's dissolution in this case. While "reasonably practicable" is not defined in RUPA, the term is broad enough to encompass the inability of partners to continue working together, which is what the court found.

Certainly the law predating RUPA allowed for recovery of lost profits upon the wrongful dissolution of a partnership. However, RUPA brought significant changes to partnership law, among which was the adoption of the term "dissociation." In RUPA, dissociation appears to have taken the place of "dissolution" as that word was used pre-RUPA. "Dissolution" under RUPA has a different meaning. It follows that the pre-RUPA cases providing for future damages upon wrongful dissolution are no longer applicable to a partnership dissolution. In other words a "wrongful dissolution" referred to in the pre-RUPA case law is now, under RUPA, known as " wrongful dissociation." Simply stated,

only when a partner dissociates and the dissociation is wrongful can the remaining partners sue for damages.

Southern Oaks' attempt to bring the instant dissolution under the statute applicable to dissociation is rejected. The trial court ordered dissolution of the partnership, not the dissociation of Horizon for wrongful conduct. There no longer appears to be "wrongful" dissolution—either dissolution is provided for by contract or statute or the dissolution was improper and the dissolution order should be reversed. In the instant case, because the dissolution either came within the terms of the partnership agreements or paragraph 620.8801(5)(c) (judicial dissolution where it is not reasonably practicable to carry on the partnership business), Southern Oaks' claim for lost future profits is without merit.

Judgment for Horizon affirmed.

Performing Winding Up

For the well-planned partnership, the partnership agreement will indicate who may perform the process of winding up for the partnership, what is the power of the persons performing winding up, and what their compensation is for performing the service.

In the absence of a partnership agreement, the RUPA provides that any partner who has not wrongfully dissociated from the partnership may perform the winding up. A winding up partner is entitled to reasonable compensation for her winding up services, in addition to her usual share of profits.

Partner's Authority during Winding Up

Express and Implied Authority During winding up, a partner has the express authority to act as the partners have agreed. The implied authority of a winding up partner is the power to do those acts *appropriate for winding up* the partnership business. That is, he has the power to bind the partnership in any transaction necessary to the liquidation of the assets. He may collect money due, sue to enforce partnership rights, prepare assets for sale, sell partnership assets, pay partnership creditors, and do whatever else is appropriate to wind up the business. He may maintain and preserve assets or enhance them for sale, for example, by painting a building or by paying a debt to prevent foreclosure on partnership land. A winding up partner may temporarily

continue the business when the effect is to preserve the value of the partnership.

Performing Executory Contracts The implied authority of a winding up partner includes the power to perform executory contracts (made before dissolution but not yet performed). A partner may not enter into *new* contracts unless the contracts aid the liquidation of the partnership's assets. For example, a partner may fulfill a contract to deliver coal if the contract was made before dissolution. She may not make a new contract to deliver coal unless doing so disposes of coal that the partnership owns or has contracted to purchase.

Borrowing Money Usually, the implied authority of a winding up partner includes no power to borrow money in the name of the partnership. Nonetheless, when a partner can preserve the assets of the partnership or enhance them for sale by borrowing money, he has implied authority to engage in new borrowing. For example, a partnership may have a valuable machine repossessed and sold far below its value at a foreclosure sale unless it can refinance a loan. A partner may borrow the money needed to refinance the loan, thereby preserving the asset. A partner may also borrow money to perform executory contracts.

Apparent Authority Winding up partners have apparent authority to conduct business as they did before dissolution, when notice of dissolution is not given to those persons who knew of the partnership prior to its dissolution. For example, a construction partnership dissolves and begins winding up but does not notify anyone of its dissolution. After dissolution, a partner makes a contract with a customer to remodel the customer's building. The partner would have no implied authority to make the contract, because the contract is new business and does not help liquidate assets. Nonetheless, the contract may be within the partner's apparent authority, because to persons unaware of the dissolution, it appears that a partner may continue to make contracts that have been in the ordinary course of business.

To eliminate the apparent authority of a winding up partner to conduct business in the ordinary way, the partnership must ensure that one of the following occurs:

1. A third party knows or has reason to know that the partnership has been dissolved.

2. A third party has received notification of the dissolution by delivery of a communication to the third party's place of business. For example, an e-mail message is sent to a creditor of the partnership.

3. The dissolution has come to the attention of the third party. For example, a partnership creditor was told of the dissolution by another creditor.

4. A partner has filed a Statement of Dissolution with the secretary of state, which limits the partners' authority during winding up. A third party is deemed to have notice of a limitation on a partner's authority 90 days after the filing of a Statement of Dissolution.

To be safe, a dissolved partnership should eliminate its partners' apparent authority to conduct business in the ordinary way by directly informing parties with whom it has previously conducted business, such as by e-mail, fax, or a phone call. The partnership should be able to identify such parties from its records. As for parties that may know about the partnership but with whom the partnership has not done business, the partnership should post notice of the dissolution at its place of business and in newspapers of general circulation in its area, increasing the chance that third parties will know of the dissolution. Also, the partnership should file a Statement of Dissolution: 90 days after its filing, no one should be able to rely on the apparent authority of a partner to conduct any business that is not appropriate to winding up. The partnership agreement of a well-planned partnership will require the partnership to take these steps when dissolution occurs.

Disputes among Winding Up Partners When more than one partner has the right to wind up the partnership, the partners may disagree concerning which steps should be taken during winding up. For decisions in the ordinary course of winding up, the decision of a majority of the partners controls. When the decision is an extraordinary one, such as continuing the business for an extended period of time, unanimous partner approval is required.

In the following case, *Paciaroni v. Crane,* the court found that the business of the partnership to train and race a horse should continue during winding up. The drafters of the RUPA expressly noted that this case is a model for continuing a business during winding up.

Paciaroni v. Crane   408 A.2d 946 (Del. Ct. Ch. 1979)

Black Ace, a harness racehorse of exceptional speed, was the fourth best pacer in the United States in 1979. He was owned by a partnership: Richard Paciaroni owned 50 percent; James Cassidy, 25 percent; and James Crane, 25 percent. Crane, a professional trainer, was in charge of the daily supervision of Black Ace, including training. It was understood that all of the partners would be consulted on the races in which Black Ace would be entered, the selection of drivers, and other major decisions; however, the recommendations of Crane were always followed by the other partners because of his superior knowledge of harness racing.

In 1979, Black Ace won $96,969 through mid-August. Seven other races remained in 1979, including the prestigious Little Brown Jug and the Messenger at Roosevelt Raceway. The purse for these races was $600,000.

A disagreement among the partners arose when Black Ace developed a ringbone condition and Crane followed the advice of a veterinarian not selected by Paciaroni and Cassidy. The ringbone condition disappeared, but later Black Ace became uncontrollable by his driver, and in a subsequent race he fell and failed to finish the race. Soon thereafter, Paciaroni and Cassidy sent a telegram to Crane dissolving the partnership and directing him to deliver Black Ace to another trainer they had selected. Crane refused to relinquish control of Black Ace, so Paciaroni and Cassidy sued him in August 1979, ask-

ing the court to appoint a receiver who would race Black Ace in the remaining 1979 stakes races and then sell the horse. Crane objected to allowing anyone other than himself to enter the horse in races. Before the trial court issued the following decision, Black Ace had entered three additional races and won $40,000.

Brown, Vice Chancellor It is generally accepted that once dissolution occurs, the partnership continues only to the extent necessary to close out affairs and complete transactions begun but not then finished. It is not generally contemplated that new business will be generated or that new contractual commitments will be made. This, in principle, would work against permitting Black Ace to participate in the remaining few races for which he is eligible.

However, in Delaware, there have been exceptions to this. Where, because of the nature of the partnership business, a better price upon final liquidation is likely to be obtained by the temporary continuation of the business, it is permissible, during the winding up process, to have the business continue to the degree necessary to preserve or enhance its value upon liquidation, provided that such continuation is done in good faith with the intent to bring affairs to a conclusion as soon as reasonably possible. And one way to accomplish this is through an application to the Court for a winding up, which carries with it the power of the Court to appoint a receiver for that purpose.

The business purpose of the partnership was to own and race Black Ace for profit. The horse was bred to race. He has the ability to be competitive with the top pacers in the country. He is currently "racing fit" according to the evidence. He has at best only seven more races to go over a period of the next six weeks, after which time there are established horse sales at which he can be disposed of to the highest bidder. The purse for these remaining stake races is substantial. The fact that he could possibly sustain a disabling injury during this six-week period appears to be no greater than it was when the season commenced. Admittedly, an injury could occur at any time. But this is a fact of racing life which all owners and trainers are forced to accept. And the remaining stake races are races in which all three partners originally intended that he would compete, if able.

Under these circumstances, I conclude that the winding up of the partnership affairs should include the right to race Black Ace in some or all of the remaining 1979 stakes races for which he is now eligible. The final question, then, is who shall be in charge of racing him.

On this point, I rule in favor of Paciaroni and Cassidy. They may, on behalf of the partnership, continue to race the horse through their new trainer, subject, however, to the conditions hereafter set forth. Crane does have a monetary interest in the partnership assets that must be protected if Paciaroni and Cassidy are to be permitted to test the whims of providence in the name of the partnership during the next six weeks. Accordingly, I make the following ruling:

1. Paciaroni and Cassidy shall first post security in the sum of $100,000 so as to secure to Crane his share of the value of Black Ace.

2. If Paciaroni and Cassidy are unable or unwilling to meet this condition, then they shall forgo the right to act as liquidating partners. In that event, each party, within seven days, shall submit to the Court the names of two persons who they believe to be qualified, and who they know to be willing, to act as receiver for the winding up of partnership affairs.

3. In the event that no suitable person can be found to act as receiver, or in the event that the Court should deem it unwise to appoint any person from the names so submitted, then the Court reserves the power to terminate any further racing by Black Ace and to require that he simply be maintained and cared for until such time as he can be sold as a part of the final liquidation of the partnership.

Judgment for Paciaroni and Cassidy.

Distribution of Dissolved Partnership's Assets

After the partnership's assets have been sold during winding up, the proceeds are distributed to those persons who have claims against the partnership. Not only creditors but also partners have claims against the proceeds. As you might expect, the claims of creditors must be satisfied first, yet a partner who is also a creditor of the partnership is entitled to the same priority as other creditors of the partnership. Thus a partner who has loaned money to the partnership is paid when other creditors of the partnership are paid.

After the claims of creditors have been paid, the remaining proceeds from the sale of partnership assets will be distributed to the partners according to the net amounts in their capital accounts. A partner's capital account is credited (increased) for any capital contributions the partner has made to the partnership plus the partner's share of partnership profits, including profits from the sale of partnership assets during winding up. The partner's capital account is charged (decreased) for the partner's share of partnership losses, including losses from the sale of partnership assets during winding up, and any distributions made to the partners, such as a distribution of profits or a return of capital. The net amount in the partner's account is distributed to the partner.

If the net amount in a partner's capital account is negative, the partner is obligated to contribute to the partnership an amount equal to the excess of charges over credits in the partner's account. Some partners may have a positive capital account balance and other partners may have a negative capital account balance. This means that during winding up, some partners may be required to contribute to enable the partnership to pay the claim of another partner.

In many partnerships that have been unprofitable, all the partners will have negative capital accounts. This means that the partnership assets have been exhausted and yet some of the partnership creditors have not been paid their claims. If partnership creditors cannot be paid from the partnership assets, the creditors may proceed against the partners, including a partner who may have already received a portion of partnership assets on account of her being a creditor also.

Since partners have liability for all the obligations of a partnership, if one partner fails to contribute the amount equal to her negative capital account balance, the other partners are obligated to contribute to the partnership in the proportions in which they share the losses of the partnership. The partner who fails to contribute as required is liable, however, to the partners who pay the defaulting partner's contribution.

The RUPA eliminates the old UPA's concept of marshaling of assets. While partnership creditors still have a priority over a partner's creditors with regard to partnership assets, partnership and partners' creditors share pro rata in the assets of individual partners.

Asset Distributions in a Limited Liability Partnership

The asset distribution rules are modified for a limited liability partnership, because in an LLP most partners have no liability for partnership obligations. If the LLP has been profitable, each partner will receive the net amount in her capital account. If creditors' claims exceed the LLP's assets, however, an LLP partner is not ordinarily required to contribute an amount equal to the negative balance in her account, and the creditors may not sue the partner to force the partner to pay the debt. This result is necessary to protect the limited liability of innocent partners who did not commit a wrong against the creditors.

If, however, a partner has committed malpractice or another wrong for which LLP statutes do not provide protection from liability, that wrongdoing partner must

---

THE GLOBAL ENVIRONMENT OF BUSINESS

Dissolutions around the Globe

For most nations, partnership law on dissolutions is more like the old Uniform Partnership Act than the RUPA, which was drafted to create better default rules when partners leave a partnership. In countries other than the United States, dissolution is defined much like dissociation is defined under the RUPA, a change in the partners' relation. Unlike dissociation in the United States, dissolution in those countries (and in American states that still follow the UPA) often results in the end of the partnership and its business, absent a contrary agreement of the partners. Well-planned partnerships, however, have partnership agreements that in many situations provide for continuation of the partnership and its business by the remaining partners, despite dissolution.

In India, dissolution may be caused by a court, by agreement of the partners, automatically by operation of law, upon the happening of certain contingencies, and by notice. An In-

dian court may dissolve a partnership due to a partner's insanity, permanent incapacity, conduct that prejudicially affects the carrying on of the business of the firm, willful or persistent breach of the partnership agreement, and transfer of his partnership interest, or if the partnership cannot be carried on except as a loss. Partners in an Indian partnership may dissolve the partnership by their unanimous agreement. An Indian partnership dissolves automatically if its term ends or undertaking is accomplished, if a partner dies or is insolvent, or if the partnership's business is illegal. Finally, a partnership at will in India may be dissolved by action of any partner.

In Austria, a partnership is dissolved by expiration of the period for which it was entered into, by resolution of the partners, by institution of bankruptcy proceedings against the partnership assets or the assets of a partner, by death of a partner, by notice of termination by a partner, and by judicial decision.

contribute to the partnership an amount equal to her share of the unpaid liability. Creditors may sue such a partner when the partnership fails to pay the liability. If more than one partner has liability, they must contribute to the partnership in proportion in which they share liability. If one is unable to pay, the other liable partners must contribute the shortfall. The partners who are not liable for the obligation cannot be forced to pay the debt.

Termination

After the assets of a partnership have been distributed, **termination** of the partnership occurs automatically.

When the Business Is Continued

Dissolution and winding up need not follow a partner's dissociation from a partnership. The partners may choose not to seek dissolution and winding up, or the partnership agreement may provide that the business may be continued by the remaining partners.

When there is no winding up and the business is continued, the claims of creditors against the partnership and the partners may be affected, because old partners are no longer with the business and new partners may enter the business.

Successor's Liability for Predecessor's Obligations

When the business of a partnership is continued after dissociation, creditors of the partnership are creditors of the person or partnership continuing the business. In addition, the original partners remain liable for obligations incurred prior to dissociation unless there is agreement with the creditors to the contrary. Thus, partners may not usually escape liability by forming a new partnership or a corporation to carry on the business of the partnership.

Dissociated Partner's Liability for Obligations Incurred while a Partner

Dissociated partners remain liable to partnership creditors for partnership liabilities incurred while they were partners; however, a dissociated partner's liability may be eliminated by the process of **novation**. Novation occurs when the following two conditions are met:

1. The continuing partners release a dissociated partner from liability on a partnership debt, and

2. A partnership creditor releases the dissociated partner from liability on the same obligation.

Continuing partners are required to indemnify dissociated partners from liability on partnership obligations. To complete the requirements for novation, a dissociated partner must also secure his release by the partnership's creditors. A creditor's agreement to release an outgoing partner from liability may be express, but usually it is implied. *Implied* novation may be proved by a creditor's knowledge of a partner's withdrawal and his continued extension of credit to the partnership. In addition, a *material modification* in the nature or time of payment of an obligation operates as a novation for an outgoing partner, when the creditor has knowledge of the partner's dissociation.

When former partners release a dissociated partner from liability but creditors do not, there is not a novation. As a result, creditors may enforce a partnership liability against a dissociated partner. However, the outgoing partner may recover from his former partners who have indemnified him from liability.

Dissociated Partner's Liability for Obligations Incurred after Leaving the Partnership

Ordinarily, a dissociated partner has no liability for partnership obligations incurred after he leaves the partnership. Nonetheless, a third party may believe that a dissociated partner is still a partner of the continuing partnership and transact with the partnership while holding that belief. In such a context, a dissociated partner could be liable to the third party even though the dissociated partner will not benefit from the transaction between the partnership and the third party.

The RUPA makes a dissociated partner liable as a partner to a party that entered into a transaction with the continuing partnership, unless:

1. The other party did not reasonably believe the dissociated partner was still a partner.

2. The other party knew or should have known or has received notification of the partner's dissociation.

3. The transaction was entered into more than 90 days after the filing of a Statement of Dissociation with the secretary of state, or

4. The transaction was entered into more than two years after the partner has dissociated.

Moreover, although a dissociated partner's right to manage the partnership has terminated upon his dissociation, unless one of the above can be proved the dissociated partner retains his apparent authority to bind the partnership on matters in the ordinary course of business.

This means that when dissociation occurs, a partnership should take steps similar to those it took to reduce the apparent authority of a winding up partner: that is, the partnership should directly inform parties with whom it has previously conducted business, such as by e-mail, fax, or a phone call, that the partner has dissociated. It should also post notice of the dissociation at its place of business and in newspapers of general circulation in its area. Finally, the partnership should cause the filing of a Statement of Dissociation,

limiting the authority of the dissociated partner and notifying the public that the partner is no longer a partner. Taking these steps will reduce the risk that the dissociated partner will be liable for future obligations of the partnership, and it will help eliminate the apparent authority of the dissociated partner to act on behalf of the partnership. The partnership agreement of a well-planned partnership will require that these steps be taken by the partnership immediately upon the dissociation of a partner.

In the following case, *In Re Labrum & Doak,* the court considered both the UPA and RUPA rules regarding liability of dissociated partners.

In Re Labrum & Doak, LLP   *237 B.R. 275 (Bank. Ct. E. Pa. 1999)*

Labrum & Doak, LLP, was a law partnership that began in 1904 in Pennsylvania. In 1997, its partners dissolved the partnership. The partnership entered reorganization under Chapter 11 of the federal Bankruptcy Code in January 1998. A reorganization plan was confirmed in December 1998, which authorized the reorganization administrator to bring a deficiency proceeding against the partners of Labrum & Doak, seeking to hold individual partners liable on obligations of the partnership.

John Seehousen, Jonathan Herbst, and James Hilly were former partners of Labrum & Doak. Seehousen withdrew from the partnership in 1992, Herbst resigned from the partnership in early 1996, and James Hilly resigned in late 1995. They argued that because of their dissociations from Labrum & Doak, they were not liable for partnership obligations—in particular, liability for the malpractice of other partners—that were incurred after their resignations. The bankruptcy court was asked to rule on the matter.

Scholl, Justice A very difficult issue is presented in ascertaining whether withdrawing former partners of the Debtor partnership are liable for all of the Debtor's deficiency, even those obligations which arose after their withdrawal. The determination of this issue requires interpretation of several principles of general partnership law.

We note that Pennsylvania Uniform Partnership Act (PAUPA) does not address the effect of dissociation on future liabilities. PAUPA was modeled after the Uniform Partnership Act of 1914. The UPA also does not address the effects of dissociation. At the most, the UPA, section 36, suggests that dissolution does not have any effect on the existing liability of any given partner. Accordingly, under these strictures, Seehousen, Herbst, and Hilly would be liable for the deficiencies incurred regardless of the fact that some of the deficiency claims at issue arose after their dissociation from the Debtor partnership.

The reasoning behind this conclusion is as follows. A partner may be discharged from any existing liability upon dissolution by an agreement to that effect between himself,

the partnership creditor, and the person or partnership continuing the business. UPA section 36(2). None of the partners submitted into evidence, nor testified of the existence of, any such agreement. As a result, we can only conclude that no such agreement existed, and that therefore Seehousen, Herbst, and Hilly are liable for all of the deficiencies at hand.

Conscious of these consequences, the drafters of the Revised Uniform Partnership Act (RUPA) tried to clarify the effects of dissociation of partners from a partnership. For this reason, RUPA section 703, which corresponds somewhat to the UPA, section 36, provides as follows:

SECTION 703. DISSOCIATED PARTNER'S LIABILITY TO OTHER PERSONS.

(a) A partner's dissociation does not of itself discharge the partner's liability for a partnership obligation incurred before dissociation. A dissociated partner is not liable for a partnership obligation incurred after dissociation, except as otherwise provided in subsection (b).

(b) A partner who dissociates without resulting in a dissolution and winding up of the partnership business is liable as a partner to the other party in a transaction entered into by the partnership, or a surviving partnership under Article 9, within two years after the partner's dissociation, only if at the time of entering into the transaction the other party:

(1) reasonably believed that the dissociated partner was then a partner;

(2) did not have notice of the partner's dissociation; and,

(3) is not deemed to have had knowledge under Section 303(e) or notice under Section 704 (c).

However, as of this date, RUPA has been only adopted in nineteen jurisdictions. Pennsylvania is not one of them. Moreover, assuming arguendo that RUPA did indeed apply in this jurisdiction, we would be forced to arrive at the same conclusion. Section 703(b) of RUPA simply states that a dissociated partner is not liable for partnership obligations incurred after dissociation, only if at the time the partnership enters into a given transaction with a third party, the party in question had notice of the dissociation. See RUPA, section 703(b)(2).

Although Pennsylvania case law is scarce on these issues, it is important to note that dated, but viable and therefore controlling, Pennsylvania cases arrived at similar conclusions when facing analogous problems.

In the instant factual setting the Defendant Partners presented no evidence of their having provided any notice of their dissociation from the Debtor to any of the Debtor's creditors. Moreover, no evidence was submitted to support the conclusion that any of these parties were discharged from any liability by an agreement to that effect between themselves, the partnership creditors, and/or the Debtor. Accordingly, they remain liable for all of the deficiencies at issue, even those which arose after they withdrew as partners from the Debtor.

Judgment for the bankruptcy reorganization administrator.

Buyout of Dissociated Partners

When the partnership is continued, the partnership is required to purchase the dissociated partner's partnership interest. In well-planned partnerships, the purchase price and timing of the buyout will be included in the partnership agreement. For example, the partnership agreement may require the payment of an amount equal to the current value of the partnership multiplied by the partner's proportionate share of profits or capital. The partnership agreement may specify how to value the partnership, such as average annual profits plus partners' salaries for the last three years multiplied by seven. The agreement may also permit deductions against the value of the partnership interest if the dissociated partner acted wrongly. The agreement will state when the buyout is effected; for example, it may require the payment in a lump sum 30 days after dissociation, or it may allow the partnership to pay the amount in monthly installments over the course of two years.

In the absence of a partnership agreement, the RUPA spells outs the amount and timing of the buyout of the dissociated partner's interest. The buyout price is the greater of the amount that would have been in the dissociated partner's capital account had the partnership liquidated all its assets on the dissociation date *or* the amount in the capital account had it sold the entire business as a going concern on that date. If the partner has wrongfully dissociated from the partnership, the buyout price is reduced by any damages caused by the wrongfully dissociated partner, such as the reduction in the goodwill of the business caused by the loss of a valuable partner.

When the dissociated partner has not wrongfully dissociated and there is no partnership agreement on the issue, the RUPA requires the partnership to pay the dissociated partner in cash within 120 days after he has demanded payment in writing. The buyout amount must include interest from the date of dissociation. If the dissociated partner and the partnership cannot agree on the buyout price, the partnership must, within 120 days of the written demand for payment, pay in cash to the partner the partnership's estimate of the buyout price, plus interest. The partner may challenge the sufficiency of the buyout price tendered by the partnership by asking a court to determine the buyout price.

If a partner has wrongfully dissociated, the partnership may wait to buy out the partner until the end of the partnership's term, unless the partner shows that the partnership will suffer no undue hardship by paying earlier.

In the following case, *Creel v. Lilly,* the court applied the partners' buyout agreement and noted the RUPA's bias in favor of continuing the business of the partnership.

Creel v. Lilly   729 A.2d 385 (Md. Ct. App. 1999)

In 1993, Joseph Creel began a retail business selling NASCAR racing memorabilia. His business was originally located in a section of his wife Anne's florist shop, but after about a year and a half he decided to raise capital from partners so that he could expand and move into his own space. On September 20, 1994, Mr. Creel entered into a partnership agreement—apparently prepared without the assistance of a lawyer—with Arnold Lilly and Roy Altizer to form a general partnership called "Joe's Racing." The partnership agreement covered such matters as the partnership's purpose, location, operations, and termination of the business upon a partner's death.

The three-man partnership operated a retail store in the St. Charles Towne Center Mall in Waldorf, Maryland. For their initial investment in Joe's Racing, Lilly and Altizer each paid $6,666 in capital contributions, with Mr. Creel contributing his inventory and supplies valued at $15,000. Pursuant to the partnership agreement, Lilly and Altizer each paid $3,333 to Mr. Creel "for the use and rights to the business known as Joe's Racing Collectables."

Joe's Racing had been in existence for almost nine months when Mr. Creel died on June 14, 1995. Mrs. Creel was appointed personal representative of his estate. Lilly and Altizer attempted to wind up the partnership, but were frustrated by Mrs. Creel's control of the partnership's bank checking account, the balance of which she refused to remit to Lilly and Altizer. The lease on the store premises occupied by the partnership expired on August 31, 1995, and on that date Lilly conducted an inventory of all merchandise in the store. Based on that inventory, an accountant computed the value of the partnership business. After August 1995, Lilly and Altizer ceased doing business as Joe's Racing, but continued the business together under the name Good Ole Boys Racing.

Mrs. Creel sued Lilly and Altizer asserting that, instead of winding up the affairs of Joe's Racing in accordance with her demand, Lilly and Altizer had continued the partnership business under a new name, using the assets of the partnership. Lilly and Altizer, as general partners of Joe's Racing, sued Mrs. Creel seeking to recover the $18,115.93 that was in the partnership's checking account and asking the court to determine the value of Mr. Creel's partnership interest.

The trial court refused to force Lilly and Altizer to sell all the assets of the partnership at a liquidation sale and required them to pay to Mr. Creel's estate the value of his partnership interest, $21,631. The court ordered that Mrs. Creel could withdraw the $18,115.93 in the checking account and that Lilly and Altizer should pay Mrs. Creel the difference between the amount of those funds and $21,631.00. The Court of Special Appeals affirmed the judgment of the trial court. Mrs. Creel appealed to the Maryland Court of Appeals.

Chasanow, Justice The Uniform Partnership Act (UPA), which has governed partnerships in this State for the past 80 years, has been repealed since this litigation commenced. The Act that now governs Maryland partnerships is the Revised Uniform Partnership Act (RUPA), which was adopted in July 1998 with a phase-in period. Therefore, until December 31, 2002, both UPA and RUPA will coexist.

Historically, under many courts and commentators' interpretation of UPA, when a partner died and the partnership automatically dissolved because there was no consent by the estate to continue the business nor was there a written agreement allowing for continuation, the estate had the right to compel liquidation of the partnership assets. However, while winding up has often traditionally been regarded as synonymous with liquidation, this "fire sale" of assets has been viewed by many courts and commentators as a harsh and destructive measure. Consequently, to avoid the drastic result of a forced liquidation, many courts have adopted judicial alternatives to this potentially harmful measure.

RUPA's underlying philosophy differs radically from UPA's. RUPA adopts the "entity" theory of partnership as opposed to the "aggregate" theory that the UPA espouses. RUPA's entity theory allows for the partnership to continue even with the departure of a member because it views the partnership as "an entity distinct from its partners." This adoption of the entity theory, which permits continuity of the partnership upon changes in partner identity, allows for several significant changes in RUPA. Of particular importance to the instant case is that under RUPA "a partnership no longer automatically dissolves due to a change in its membership, but rather the existing partnership may be continued if the remaining partners elect to buy out the dissociating partner." In contrast to UPA, RUPA's "buyout" option does not have to be expressly included in a written partnership agreement in order for it to be exercised; however, the surviving partners must still actively choose to exercise the option, as "continuation is not automatic as with a corporation." Critically, under RUPA the estate of the deceased partner no longer has to consent in order for the business to be continued nor does the estate have the right to compel liquidation.

In this appeal, however, we would arrive at the same holding regardless of whether UPA or RUPA governs.

Because a partnership is governed by any agreement between or among the partners, we must begin our analysis of the compelled liquidation issue by examining the Joe's Racing partnership agreement. We reiterate that both UPA and RUPA only apply when there is either no partnership agreement governing the partnership's affairs, the agreement is silent on a particular point, or the agreement contains provisions contrary to law.

The pertinent paragraph and subsections of the Joe's Racing partnership agreement are as follows:

7. TERMINATION
(a) That, at the termination of this partnership a full and accurate inventory shall be prepared, and the assets, liabilities, and income, both in gross and net, shall be ascertained: the remaining debts or profits will be distributed according to the percentages shown above in the 6(e).

* * *

(d) Upon the death or illness of a partner, his share will go to his estate. If his estate wishes to sell his interest, they must offer it to the remaining partners first.

Even though the partnership agreement uses the word "termination," paragraph 7(a) is really discussing the dissolution of the partnership and the attendant winding up process that ultimately led to termination. Paragraph 7(a) requires that the assets, liabilities, and income be "ascertained," but it in no way mandates that this must be accomplished by a forced sale of the partnership assets. Indeed, a liquidation or sale of assets is not mentioned anywhere in 7(a).

In this case, the winding up method outlined in 7(a) was followed exactly by the surviving partners: a full and accurate inventory was prepared on August 31, 1995; this information was given to an accountant, who ascertained the assets, liabilities, and income of the partnership; and finally, the remaining debt or profit was distributed according to the percentages listed in 6(e).

Paragraph 6(e) of the partnership agreement states "that the net profits or net losses be divided as follows:

Joseph Creel 28%
Arnold Lilly 24%
Joseph Cudmore 24%
Roy Altizer 24%"

As determined by the trial court, the interest of Joseph Cudmore, who never signed the partnership agreement, reverted to Joseph Creel, who was entitled to a 52 percent share.

Thus, when we look to the intention of the parties as reflected in 7(a) of the partnership agreement, the trial judge could conclude that the partners did not anticipate that a "fire sale" of the partnership assets would be necessary to ascertain the true value of Joe's Racing. Paragraph 7(a) details the preferred winding up procedure to be followed, to include an inventory, valuation, and distribution of debt or profit to the partners.

Moreover, paragraph 7(d), which discusses what happens to a partner's share of the business upon his death, also makes no mention of a sale or liquidation as being essential in order to determine the deceased partner's proportionate interest of the partnership. On the contrary, 7(d) appears to be a crude attempt to draft a "continuation clause" in the form of a buyout option by providing that the deceased partner's share of the partnership goes to his estate, and if the estate wishes to sell this interest it must first be offered to the remaining partners. In contrast to consenting to the continuation of the business, Mrs. Creel made it plain that she wanted the business dissolved and the affairs of the company wound up; however, this does not mean a liquidation was required. Particularly in light of Maryland's recent adoption of RUPA, paragraph 7(d) of the partnership agreement can be interpreted to mean that because Mrs. Creel did not wish to remain in business with Lilly and Altizer, they had the option to buy out her deceased husband's interest.

Therefore, the trial judge could have concluded that Lilly and Altizer exercised this 7(d) buyout option, and subsequently began a new partnership, when they followed the winding up procedure dictated by 7(a) and presented the Creel estate with its share of Joe's Racing.

We now explore the "true value of the partnership" issue and whether liquidation is the only way to obtain it.

In accordance with the partnership agreement, Lilly and Altizer provided Mrs. Creel with an accounting, which was based on the valuation performed by the accountant they hired. Mrs. Creel maintains that the only way to ascertain the true value of her deceased husband's interest in Joe's Racing is to liquidate all of its assets but we agree with the trial court, which held: "The surviving parties under the Code and existing case law had to account for the inventory and pay to the Estate its appropriate share, but not sell off the assets in a liquidation sale." In making his findings, the trial judge looked to paragraph 7(a) of the partnership agreement. The court held:

The partnership assets are $ 44,589.44. The Court accepts the valuation prepared by Mr. Johnson [the accountant] as the correct statement of value. The Court determines the debts to creditors to be the accounting fees due Mr. Johnson in the amount of $875.00. The debts owed to partners are: (1) $495.00 to Mrs. Creel; (2) $2,187.00 to Mr. Lilly; and (3) $900.00 to Mr. Altizer. The capital contributions are determined to be $15,000.00 to Mr. Creel and $6,666 each to Mr. Altizer and Mr. Lilly. The Estate is also due 52% of the balance of the $11,800.00 or $ 6,136.00. The total due to the Estate, therefore, is declared to be $21,631.00 ($15,000.00 + $495.00 + $6,136.00).

Finally, Mrs. Creel contends that the accountant's valuation improperly considered only the book value of the business and not its market value. "Book value" refers to the assets of the business, less its liabilities plus partner contributions or "equity." "Market value" includes the value of such intangibles as goodwill, the value of the business as an ongoing concern, and established vendor and supplier lines, among other factors. Again, we concur with the trial court's findings as to the valuation of Joe's Racing.

In making no finding of goodwill value, for example, the trial court likely considered the fact that Joe's Racing had only been operating a little over a year before the partnership was formed, and after Lilly and Altizer became partners with Mr. Creel the business was only in existence for nine months before Mr. Creel died. On these facts, it is reasonable for the trial court to conclude that a small business selling NASCAR memorabilia, which had been operating for barely two years, did not possess any goodwill value.

Judgment for Lilly and Altizer affirmed.

ETHICS IN ACTION

The default rules of the RUPA provide that any partner who leaves the partnership is entitled to the value of her partnership interest. The default valuation method uses the greater of the partnership's liquidation or going concern value. If a partner wrongfully dissociates, however, damages are deducted from the partner's interest and the partner need not be paid until the partnership ends.

- Why would partners want a partnership agreement that sets out a different valuation method than the default rule?
- What risk is taken by relying on the default rule? Among other things, under the default rule a court will value a partnership interest when partners cannot agree on the valuation. Why would partners not want a court to valuate a partnership interest?
- Using profit maximization analysis, is it ethical to delay payment to a wrongfully dissociating partner for the value of her partnership interest until the partnership terminates? Does utilitarian analysis change your answer? What are the costs and benefits of delaying payment?
- When do you propose your partnership should pay a partner who dissociates due to death, disability, retirement at an expected age, and unexpected dissociations? What ethical arguments would you make to justify the rules you propose?

Partners Joining an Existing Partnership

Frequently, a partnership will admit new partners. For example, many of you hope to be admitted to a well-established consulting or accounting partnership after you graduate and have practiced for several years. The terms under which a new partner is admitted to a partnership are usually clearly stated in the partnership agreement and in the partner's admission agreement. The terms usually include the procedure for admission as well as the new partner's capital contribution, compensation including salary and share of profits, and power to manage the business. In the absence of a partnership agreement, the RUPA sets the rules for the partner's admission and rights and duties upon admission.

Liability of New Partners

An important question is what level of liability a new partner should have for obligations of the new partnership. It makes sense for a new partner to be fully liable for all partnership obligations incurred *after* he becomes a partner, for he clearly benefits from the partnership during that time. This is the RUPA rule.

CONCEPT REVIEW

Consequences of Partner's Death or Retirement under the RUPA's Default Rules

Death of Partner

A. Is a nonwrongful dissociation
B. Does not by itself effect a dissolution
C. Rights of estate of deceased partner
   1. Receive the amount in the deceased partner's capital account at the time of death, valuing partnership or its assets at the greater of
      a. liquidation value or
      b. going concern value.
   2. Payment must be made not later than 120 days after a written demand by the estate
D. Rights of other partners
   1. In a partnership at will: any partner may dissociate at any time and effect a dissolution
   2. In a partnership for a term
      a. Any partner may dissociate within 90 days of death:
         1) that dissociation will not dissolve the partnership
         2) that dissociated partner must be paid the amount in her capital account within 120 days after a written demand by the partner
      b. By a vote of at least 50 percent of partners within 90 days of death, the partnership may be dissolved and its business wound up

Retirement (Withdrawal) of Partner

A. Is a dissociation
   1. Is a nonwrongful dissociation if the partnership is at will
   2. Is a wrongful dissociation if the partnership is for a term, the term has not expired, and the partnership agreement does not permit the partner's withdrawal
B. Automatically effects a dissolution if the partnership is at will
C. Rights of dissociated partner
   1. If nonwrongful dissociation, dissociated partner
      a. may wind up the business, if a partnership at will, or
      b. receives the amount in the dissociated partner's capital account within 120 days after a written demand
   2. If wrongful dissociation, dissociated partner
      a. may not dissolve the partnership and
      b. receives the amount in the dissociated partner's capital account, less damages, at the end of the partnership's term, unless no undue hardship to partnership by paying earlier
D. Rights of other Partners
   1. In a partnership at will, any partner may dissociate at any time and effect a dissolution
   2. In a partnership for a term if the retirement is a wrongful dissociation,
      a. any partner may dissociate within 90 days of the retirement;
      b. by a vote of at least 50 percent of partners within 90 days of the retirement, the partnership may be dissolved and its business wound up
   3. In a partnership for a term if the retirement is a nonwrongful dissociation, the remaining partners have no rights created by the retirement

What should be his liability for partnership obligations incurred *before* he became a partner? The RUPA states that a new partner has no liability for partnership obligations incurred before he became a partner. However, many partnership agreements modify this rule by requiring a partner to assume liability for all the obligations of the business as a condition of being admitted to the partnership.

Effect of LLP Statutes If a new partner enters an LLP, however, the RUPA provides that the partner has no liability for the obligations of the LLP beyond his capital contribution, whether incurred before or after his admission, unless the new partner has committed malpractice or other wrong for which he is personally responsible. LLP partnership agreements should not change this rule.

LOG ON

www.nccusl.org
At the website for the National Conference of Commissioners on Uniform State Laws, you can find the complete text and comments of the RUPA. You can find the complex default rules regarding dissociation, dissolution, and buyouts of partners in Articles 6, 7, and 8. Pay particular attention to sections 601, 701, 801, and 802. Knowing the content of these sections will help you draft the partnership agreement dealing with a partner leaving the partnership.

Problems and Problem Cases

1. James Rhue and John Dawson formed a partnership to acquire and develop a shopping center. Rhue did the day-to-day management of the business, and Dawson contributed most of the capital and promised to obtain bank financing for the project. Rhue found two adjacent shopping centers, which could be purchased and renovated for $11.8 million. To help obtain bank financing, Dawson obtained an appraisal of the projected value of the renovated shopping centers, $15.6 million, which would return a profit of $1.9 million to each partner. Seven days later, Dawson pressured Rhue into signing a partnership agreement with a buyout clause that allowed Dawson to buyout Rhue merely by paying back Rhue's capital contribution, which was a minimal amount. Rhue was unaware that the buyout clause was in the agreement, because previous drafts of the agreement did not contain the clause and Dawson did not give Rhue time to read the agreement before signing. Later, when Rhue and Dawson had a disagreement, Dawson locked Rhue out of the partnership's office and invoked the buyout clause. Has Dawson wrongfully dissolved the partnership?

2. Byron Bennett and Louis Gagliardi were partners in a law practice. Gagliardi received 60 percent of partnership profits and Bennett received 40 percent. When Gagliardi died, Bennett continued to practice law at the partnership location in Philadelphia, Pennsylvania. While winding up partnership cases, Bennett commin-

gled all of the revenue generated from partnership case files with his own personal funds. In addition, he spent all but approximately $2,000 of the partnership's revenue for personal and other nonpartnership purposes. Bennett expended 563.5 hours and incurred costs of $2,938 in winding up the partnership cases. Bennett paid $750 to a CPA for preparation of the partnership's 1993 tax return. He spent 73.5 hours and paid $618.87 to produce the accountings of the partnerships affairs. Did Bennett do anything wrong? Was Bennett entitled to compensation for his time and reimbursement of expenses for winding up the affairs of the partnership?

3. In 1968, Hal Bolinger and his son Bud Bolinger created a partnership that operated a ranch. The partnership agreement set a value of $48,000 for the partnership and stated that the value controlled in the event of a sale or dissolution of the partnership. The terms also stated that each year the partners would update the value, which will serve for the following year as the value of the partnership. In the event of Hal's or Bud's death, the agreement gave the surviving partner the right to purchase the deceased partner's interest at the value established in the agreement. Despite this agreement, Hal and Bud never updated the valuation of the partnership. In 1995, Bud died and was survived by his children. The partnership dissolved, but Hal continued the business. Bud's estate sought the value of his partnership interest. The fair value of the partnership was over $400,000, far above the 1968 valuation of $48,000 that was never updated. To determine the value of Bud's partnership interest, did the court use the 1968 valuation or did it determine the fair value of the partnership?

4. Junior Nestle and Eric Ellis owned Red Rocks Meat and Deli, a partnership, which they operated in a building that they leased from Wester & Company. Nestle left the partnership, and Wester received notice that Nestle was no longer a partner. Wester did not object to the change in partners or request that Nestle remain liable. A year later, Wester and Ellis modified the lease to include adjacent space and to increase the rent. Four months later, Ellis failed to pay the rent; Wester sued Nestle. Was Nestle liable to Wester?

5. Robert Weiss was a partner in the Hillman Group, which operated a hotel in Tampa, Florida. Weiss was the manager of the hotel and received 50 percent of its profits. The hotel became unprofitable because of Weiss's mismanagement. The partners were asked to make an additional capital contribution to the partnership, but Weiss failed to contribute as required by the partnership agreement. Pursuant to the partnership agreement, Weiss was

expelled from the partnership. The partners continuing the partnership agreed to relieve Weiss from liability on the partnership's obligations. Did the partners' agreement relieve Weiss from liability to partnership creditors on obligations incurred prior to his explusion?

6. Longview Estates, a partnership, issued a promissory note to Conklin Farms in which Longview promised to pay $9 million plus 9 percent interest. Three years later, Doris Liebowitz was admitted as a new partner of Longview. After she entered the partnership, interest continued to accrue on the promissory note. Two years after Liebowitz was admitted to the partnership, the partnership defaulted on the note. Conklin Farms sued Liebowitz. Is Liebowitz liable for the $9 million principal amount of the note? Is she liable for the interest on the loan that accrued while she was a partner?

7. As partners, Joseph Kalichman and Joseph Klein owned and managed an apartment building in the Bronx. The partnership borrowed $189,000 from National Savings Bank of Albany. Joseph Klein died; his interest in the partnership passed to his sons, Jack and Frank, who received Joseph Klein's share of the partnership income. Jack and Frank did not, however, share in the management of the partnership business. The partnership defaulted on the loan from National Savings Bank, which sued Jack and Frank. Are Jack and Frank liable to National Savings Bank?

8. NFL Associates was a partnership of three partners: Herb Friedman, Strelsa Lee Langness, and the O Street Carpet Shop, Inc. When the partnership was created, O Street Carpet contributed a contract worth $9,000, Langness contributed $14,000 in cash, and Friedman contributed his legal services, which were not valued. The partners used part of Langness's contribution to make an $8,000 payment to O Street Carpet. They used the remaining $6,000 to purchase investment property and to provide working capital for the partnership. Later, O Street Carpet contributed an additional $4,005 in capital. The partners agreed that Friedman would receive 10 percent of the profits and that each of the other two partners would receive 45 percent of the profits. They also agreed that Langness would receive payments of $116.66 each month. During the term of the partnership, Langness received monthly checks from the partnership totaling $6,300.30. Langness did not pay income tax on these monthly payments, and the partnership did not take expense deductions for the payments. When the partnership was dissolved and wound up, the partnership assets were sold for $52,001.20. Partnership creditors were owed $3,176.79. Who received what amounts from the proceeds of the sale of partnership assets?

9. Ralph Neitzert and his brother were the only partners of Jolly Jug Liquors, a retail liquor store. The partners signed a contract to lease refrigeration equipment from Colo-Tex Leasing, Inc. A month later, Ralph sold his interest in the partnership to his sister. Ralph did not notify Colo-Tex that he sold his interest to his sister. A year later, when the partnership breached the lease, Colo-Tex sued Ralph, his brother, and his sister. Is Ralph liable to Colo-Tex?

Online Research: Your State and the Revised Uniform Partnership Act

Go to the website of the National Conference of Commissioners on Uniform State Laws.

• Check the legislative update to see whether your state has adopted the RUPA and its modern rules for partner dissociations and partnership dissolutions.

• Find the law on partnership dissolutions under the old Uniform Partnership Act. Note the differences between the RUPA and the UPA.

Limited Liability Companies, Limited Partnerships, and Limited Liability Limited Partnerships

You are planning two business ventures. The first venture is a business that will own self-service businesses, such as laundromats, car washes, and warehouse storage. Due to start-up costs and accelerated write-offs of expenses and assets, you expect the business to generate losses in the first year or two, after which it should earn a yearly return on equity of over 20 percent. You prefer to own this business entirely yourself, yet you want to hire someone with experience in the business to do most of the day-to-day operations of the business. While you prefer that person not be an owner of the business, you may be willing to grant a small amount of ownership or a share of profits to her.

The other business venture will purchase and develop 320 acres of land on the outskirts of your city. You plan to construct several commercial buildings on the site and to lease the building space to several tenants. The venture will generate losses during the first four or five years of construction prior to full occupancy of the buildings. You want the business to be owned by members of your family. You want to be the only manager of the business; other family members will be passive owners only. You hope that this business will generate enough income to provide a moderate level of income to every member of your family in perpetuity.

• Why is the limited liability company an especially good business form for the first venture?
• Why should you choose the limited liability limited partnership for the family-owned commercial development?

STATE LEGISLATURES AND THE Internal Revenue Service have cooperated to permit the creation of three business forms that offer taxation advantages similar to the sole proprietorship and the partnership, yet have simple default rules that promote management of the business by fewer than all the owners and extend limited liability to some or all of the owners. These forms are the limited liability company (LLC), limited partnership, and limited liability limited partnership (LLLP).

Limited Liability Companies

The limited liability company (LLC) is the product of attempts by state legislators to create a new business organization that combines the nontax advantages of the corporation and the favorable tax status of the partnership. Wyoming, in 1977, passed the first LLC statute. Every state and the District of Columbia have adopted an

LLC statute. The National Commissioners on Uniform State Laws has adopted the **Uniform Limited Liability Company Act of 1996 (ULLCA).** The ULLCA provides default rules that govern an LLC in the absence of a contrary agreement of its owners. The ULLCA treats LLCs and their owners similar to the way the Revised Uniform Partnership Act (RUPA) treats limited liability partnerships (LLPs) and their partners.

> **LOG ON**
>
> www.nccusl.org
> You can find the Uniform Limited Liability Company Act of 1996 at the website for the National Conference of Commissioners on Uniform State Laws.

Tax Treatment of LLCs

An LLC may elect to be taxed like a partnership or a corporation for federal income tax purposes. LLC members usually elect for the LLC to be recognized as a partnership for federal income tax purposes. As a result, the LLC pays no federal income tax. Instead, all income and losses of the LLC are reported by the LLC's owners on their individual income tax returns. Typically, the LLC is a tax shelter for wealthy investors, allowing such investors to reduce their taxable income by deducting LLC losses on their federal income tax returns to the extent they are *at risk,* that is, their capital contributions to the LLC. Moreover, passive investors in an LLC, like limited partners in a limited partnership, may use their shares of LLC losses to offset only income from other *passive* investments.

Formation of LLCs

To create an LLC, one or more persons must file **articles of organization** with the secretary of state. The articles must include the name of the LLC, its duration, and the name and address of its registered agent. The name of the LLC must include the words "limited liability company," "limited company," or an abbreviation such as "LLC" or "L.L.C.," indicating that the liability of its owners is limited.

The owners of an LLC are called **members.** An individual, partnership, corporation, and even another LLC may be a member of an LLC.

The LLC articles of organization must state whether the LLC is member-managed or manager-managed. If it is manager-managed, the names of the initial managers must be listed. The articles must also indicate whether the LLC has a term. If no term is stated, the LLC is at-will, meaning a member may dissociate at any time and do so rightfully.

Although not required, an LLC will typically have an operating agreement, which is an agreement of the members. It will cover how members share profits, manage the LLC, and withdraw from the LLC, among other things. Well-planned LLCs have detailed operating agreements that cover all aspects of the LLC's operation and members' relations, often restating much of what is contained in the ULLCA but with changes to suit the members' needs.

Once formed, an LLC is an entity separate from its members. It may sue and be sued in its own name. It can buy, hold, and sell property. It can make contracts and incur liabilities.

> **LOG ON**
>
> www.medlawplus.com/legalforms/instruct/
> sample-llc.pdf
> It is easy to find model and even actual LLC operating agreements on the web. The link above is typical. You can find others by typing "LLC operating agreement" in a search engine. There are also websites that charge for downloads of LLC operating agreements. One such site is
> www.uslegalforms.com

Foreign LLCs An LLC that is created in one state but does business in another state is domestic in its creating state and foreign in the other state. While all states are required to recognize and respect the status of a foreign LLC, a foreign state may nonetheless require the foreign LLC to obtain a certificate of authority to transact business in the foreign state.

The application process for a certificate of authority is fairly simple, requiring a filing with the foreign state's secretary of state, which includes the LLC's name and address and the LLC's agent for service of process in the foreign state. The name of the LLC must be distinguishable from other business names in the foreign state. The application also must be accompanied by the payment of

---

Figure 1   *Principal Characteristics of LLCs*

1. An LLC may be created only *in accordance with a statute.*
2. An LLC is owned by *members.* Members usually have *liability limited to their capital contributions* to the business.
3. LLC members *share equally in the profits* of the business, unless members agree otherwise.
4. An LLC may be *member-managed or manager-managed.* If it is member-managed, each member has an equal right to manage the business.
5. A member who manages the LLC owes *fiduciary duties* to the LLC and its members.
6. A member's ownership interest in an LLC is *not freely transferable.* A transferee of a member's distributional interest receives only the member's share of LLC distributions.
7. The death or other withdrawal of a member *does not usually dissolve an LLC.*
8. Members of an LLC may choose to have the LLC *taxed as a partnership or as a corporation.*

---

a fee. If the LLC continues to transact business in the foreign state, it must pay a yearly fee and file an annual report with the secretary of state.

There are few penalties imposed against a foreign LLC that has failed to obtain a certificate of authority when required to do so. Contracts made in the foreign state are valid despite the failure. LLC members also retain their limited liability. However, the LLC may be required to pay back fees and fines and will be disabled from using the foreign state's courts to bring an action against someone who has breached a contract or otherwise harmed the LLC, unless it subsequently obtains a certificate of authority. The foreign LLC that has improperly failed to obtain a certificate of authority also appoints the foreign state's secretary of state as its agent for service of process in the state.

Members' Rights and Liabilities

Limited Liability   An LLC member has no individual liability on LLC contracts, unless she also signs LLC contracts in her personal capacity. Therefore, a member's liability is usually limited to her capital contributions to the LLC. She is, however, liable for torts she commits while acting for the LLC.

In addition, a member must make capital contributions to the LLC as she has agreed. This includes the initial capital she agreed to contribute and additional calls for capital that can be made on members according to the operating agreement.

Management Rights   Under the ULLCA, an LLC must choose to be member-managed or manager-managed. Each member in a **member-managed LLC** shares equal rights in the management of the business merely by being a member of the LLC. Each member is an agent of the LLC with implied authority to carry on its

ordinary business. If a member-managed LLC has limited the implied authority of one of its members, that member will retain apparent authority to transact for the LLC with a third party who did not know and had no notice that the member's authority was restricted.

The LLC operating agreement may modify the default rules of the ULLCA by granting more power to some members, such as creating a class of members whose approval is required for certain contracts. The agreement could also provide that members share power in relation to their capital contributions.

Managers in a **manager-managed LLC** are elected and removed by a vote of a majority of LLC members. The powers of a manager to act for the LLC are similar to the power of members in a member-managed LLC. Each manager in a manager-managed LLC shares equal rights in the management of the business as an agent of the LLC with implied authority to carry on the LLC's ordinary business. If a manager-managed LLC has limited the implied authority of one of its managers, that manager retains apparent authority to transact for the LLC with a third party who did not know and had no notice that the manager's authority was restricted.

Under the ULLCA, most matters in an LLC may be conducted by individual managing members or managers, or by a vote of a majority of managing members or managers. This facilitates the conduct of ordinary business. Some matters, however, required the consent of all members, including amendment of the operating agreement, admission of new members, the redemption of a member's interest, and the sale of substantially all the LLC's assets.

In addition to being contractually liable for the acts of its members or managers acting within their express, implied, or apparent authority, the LLC is also liable for the torts and other wrongful acts of managing members and other managers acting within their authority. The LLC is not ordinarily liable for the wrongful acts of members not designated as managers in a manager-managed LLC.

Duties Each member in a member-managed LLC and each manager in a manager-managed LLC is a fiduciary of the LLC and its members. The managing member or manager must account for LLC property and funds and not compete with the LLC. They owe a duty of care that imposes liability on them for harming the LLC due to their gross negligence, recklessness, intentional misconduct, or knowing violation of the law. This duty of care can be increased or it can be decreased within limits set by the ULLCA.

Nonmanaging members of a manager-managed LLC owe no fiduciary duties to the LLC. Nonetheless, whether or not they are managers, all members owe a duty of good faith and fair dealing when exercising their rights as members. This means all members must act honestly and treat each other fairly.

Member's Distributions A member's most important right in an LLC is to receive distributions (usually profits) from the LLC. The ULLCA provides that members share profits and other distributions equally, regardless of differences in their capital contributions. The LLC members will often wish to state a different method of sharing profits in the LLC operating agreement. For example, the operating agreement may simply state that managing members are entitled to salaries and that all members share profits after salaries in proportion to their capital contributions to the LLC. At the other extreme, the LLC operating agreement may have complex rules determining how profits are allocated, including factors such as hours a member works for the LLC, the revenue from clients acquired for the LLC by a member, and a member's capital contribution.

Member's Ownership Interest An LLC member's ownership interest in an LLC is the personal property of the member. However, unlike a corporation in which a shareholder may freely transfer her shares and all her rights to another person, a member has limited ability to sell or transfer her rights in the LLC. Under the ULCCA, a member may transfer her **distributional interest** in the LLC to another person; however, the transferee is not a member of the LLC. The transferee's most important right is to receive the transferring member's right to distributions from the partnership, that is, a share of profits and the value of the member's interest when the LLC is liquidated. A transferee has no right to manage the business and has only a limited right to

information about the LLC's accounts. A transferee may also obtain judicial dissolution of the LLC if it is at will or its term has expired.

The LLC operating agreement may provide that a transferee of a member's distributional interest becomes an LLC member. If so, the transferee has the rights, powers, and liabilities of the transferring member, which may include the right to manage the LLC, the right to access LLC records, and the duty to make additional capital contributions.

A personal creditor of a member may obtain from a court a charging order that charges the member's distributional interest with the payment of the debt owed to the creditor. The creditor with a charging order receives, therefore, the member's share of distributions for the life of the charging order. The creditor does not own the distribution interest, but instead only has a lien or security interest against it. To own the distributional interest and acquire all the rights of a transferee, the creditor must foreclose against the interest and purchase it at a foreclosure sale.

The ULLCA states that a member who has transferred all her distributional interest has dissociated from the LLC. This includes a member whose distributional interest has been purchased by a creditor at a foreclosure sale.

Members' Dissociations and LLC Dissolution

Under the ULLCA, members dissociate from an LLC in ways similar to those by which a partner dissociates from a partnership or LLP under the RUPA. Dissolution of an LLC is also similar to that of a partnership or LLP. Therefore, generally, when an LLC member dies or otherwise withdraws from the LLC, the LLC's business will continue, preserving its going concern value.

Member Dissociations A member's dissociation is a change in the relationship among the dissociated member, the LLC, and the other members caused by a member ceasing to be associated in the carrying on of the business. Under the ULLCA, a partner has the power to dissociate by withdrawing from the LLC at any time. Dissociations are also caused by a member's death, having a guardian appointed over her affairs, being adjudged legally incompetent by a court, being a debtor in bankruptcy, transferring all her distributional interest in the LLC, or being expelled by the other members. The other members may expel a member if it is unlawful to carry on business with her, she has suffered a charging order against her distributional interest, or she has transferred substantially all her distributional interest in the LLC. At the request of the LLC or a member, a court may also expel a member because she has harmed the LLC's business, breached the LLC operating agreement, or engaged in conduct that makes it not practicable to carry on business with her. Judicial expulsion would be appropriate when a member persistently breaches the duty of good faith or competes against the LLC. There are also other causes of dissociation for non-human members.

A member's dissociation may be wrongful or non-wrongful. Wrongful dissociations breach the LLC operating agreement. Under the ULLCA, a member has wrongfully dissociated by withdrawing before an LLC's term expires, being a debtor in bankruptcy, or being expelled by a court. When dissolution is wrongful, the dissociating member is liable to the LLC for damages caused by the dissociation, such as the loss of business due to the member's withdrawal.

When a member dissociates, his right to manage the business terminates, as do his duties to the LLC, for the most part. He may, however, have apparent authority to transact for the LLC, unless notice of his dissociation is given to third parties. This apparent authority can be eliminated by giving personal notice to LLC creditors that a member has dissociated or by filing a Statement of Dissociation with the secretary of state.

Dissociation also terminates a member's status as a member. A dissociated member is treated as a transferee of a member's distributional interest.

Payment to a Dissociated Member Under the ULLCA, the dissociated member has no right after her dissociation to force the LLC to dissolve and to liquidate its assets. Therefore, if the remaining LLC members choose to continue the business, the LLC must pay the dissociated member the value of her distributional interest.

If the LLC is at will and is not dissolved, the LLC must purchase his interest at fair value within 120 days after the member's dissociation. If the LLC has a term and is not dissolved, the LLC may continue its business and pay the dissociated member the value of his interest within 120 days after the end of the LLC's term.

LLC Dissolution When an LLC is dissolved, ordinarily it must be wound up. Since a business usually is worth more as a going concern, the ULLCA has few events that automatically cause dissolution of an LLC. For example, death and withdrawal of member do not by themselves cause dissolution of an LLC. Instead, the ULLCA mostly lets members decide the causes of dissolution.

The few grounds for dissolution in the ULLCA include an event making it unlawful for the LLC business to continue, judicial dissolution at the request of a member or transferee of a member's distributional interest, and administrative dissolution by the secretary of state. A member or dissociated member may ask for a judicial dissolution if, for example, the LLC cannot practicably carry on its business, the LLC is being managed illegally or oppressively, or the LLC failed to purchase a dissociated member's distributional interest on the date required. The ULLCA allows the members to state in the operating agreement the events that will dissolve the LLC. The operating agreement may also allow the members to dissolve the LLC by their vote, which may be any percentage of members that the members choose.

When an LLC dissolves, any member who has not wrongly dissociated may wind up the business. Winding-up members should liquidate the assets, yet they may preserve the LLC's assets or business as a going concern for a reasonable time in order to optimize the proceeds from the liquidation.

The LLC is bound by the reasonable acts of its members during winding up, and may be liable for actions that continue the business and are inconsistent with winding up, unless the LLC gives third parties notice of dissolution. Notice can be given in a reasonable manner, such as by e-mail, letter, or phone call, and by filing a Notice of Dissociation with the secretary of state, which is effective against all parties 90 days after filing.

Distribution of Dissolved LLC's Assets After all the LLC assets have been sold, the proceeds will be distributed first to LLC creditors, including members who are creditors. If there are excess proceeds, members' contributions are returned next. Any remaining proceeds are distributed in equal shares to the members.

If the LLC's assets are insufficient to pay all creditors' claims, ordinarily creditors have no recourse, because the LLC's members have liability limited to the assets of the LLC. If an LLC member has not paid in all the capital she was required to pay, however, creditors may sue the member to force the member to contribute the additional capital.

Effect of Operating Agreement The default dissociation and dissolution rules of the ULLCA may be unacceptable to members of an LLC. Therefore, a well-drafted operating agreement will cover this area completely, defining the grounds for dissociation, such as death, withdrawal, and disability of a member. The agreement should also state when a member may be expelled by the other members and a court. The ULLCA gives the members much flexibility to arrange their affairs the way they want. For example, the operating agreement may eliminate a member's power to withdraw from the LLC prior to the end of its term.

The operating agreement will state the amount and timing of payments to a dissociated member for the value of her ownership interest. For example, the operating agreement may provide for a lump sum payment within 90 days after a member dies, becomes disabled, or withdraws at age 55 or later. If a member withdraws before age 55, the agreement may provide for payment in quarterly installments over a five-year period.

The agreement will also state when dissolution and winding up occur. For example, the agreement may provide that no member has the power to seek dissolution at any time. Instead, the agreement may permit 75 percent of the members to commence winding up if any member dies or withdraws before the time permitted in the LLC operating agreement. It may require unanimous approval by the members in all other contexts. The agreement should also stipulate which members will have the right to participate in winding up.

The LLC operating agreement may also modify how proceeds are distributed to members during winding up after creditors are paid. For example, the agreement may state that all proceeds beyond creditors' claims are distributed equally to members, regardless of their capital contributions.

The following case considers both the effects of a member's dissociation and the management rights of a member in an LLC.

In Re Garrison-Ashburn, LC   *253 B.R. 700 (E. D. 2000)*

Cralle Comer and Stephen Chapman formed two manager-managed limited liability companies, Garrison-Ashburn, L.C. and Garrison-Woods, L.C. Comer and Chapman each owned a 50 percent membership interest in each LLC. While Chapman was the initial operating manager, Comer later replaced him as operating manager.

In 1999, Chapman filed a voluntary petition in bankruptcy under Chapter 11 of the United States Bankruptcy Code. In the course of the bankruptcy proceeding, Comer wished to sell a parcel of land owned by Garrison-Woods. Chapman argued that Garrison-Woods could not sell the land without his consent on the grounds that the LLC's operating agreement required all deeds and sales contracts be executed by both members. He refused to sign the contract of sale or the deed. Comer argued that as operating manager he was fully authorized to execute the contract. The bankruptcy court ruled in favor of Comer, and Chapman moved for the court to reconsider its judgment.

Mayer, Judge   The court is satisfied that Comer can bind Garrison-Woods and consummate the contract without Chapman's consent or participation.

The heart of Chapman's argument is Article IV, Section 6 of the Operating Agreement which addresses the powers of the Operating Manager. This section states in part:

Operating Manager. The Operating Manager shall be the chief executive officer of the Company and shall have the general charge of the business and affairs of the Company, subject, however, to the right of the Members to confer specified powers on officers and subject generally to the direction of Members. . . . The Operating Manager shall also have the sole and complete control of the management and operation of the affairs and business of the Company. Without limiting the foregoing, the Operating Manager shall have full and complete authority in his sole and exclusive discretion to execute on behalf of the company, any listing agreement, contract or other paper.

Article IV, Section 11 of the Operating Agreement states in part:

Signature Authority. Without limiting the foregoing, the signatures of both the Operating Manager and the Assistant\Operating Manager shall be required for, and they shall have full and complete authority in their sole and exclusive discretion to:

a. Execute on behalf of the Company, any bond or deed, execute or endorse promissory notes and renew the same from time to time;

b. Draw upon any bank or banks or any corporations, associations, or individuals for any sum or sums of money that may be to the credit of the Company, or which the Company may be entitled to receive;

c. Make all necessary deeds and conveyances thereof of Company real and/or personal property, wheresoever located, with all necessary covenants, warranties, and assurances, and to sign, seal, and acknowledge and deliver the same;

Chapman argues that pursuant to Article IV, Section 11, he along with Comer must also sign such a contract for it to be legally binding. This argument is contrary to the plain meaning of the Operating Agreement. The Operating Agreement plainly vests in the Operating Manager "the sole and complete control of the management and operation of the affairs and business of the Company" and the "full and complete authority. . . to execute on behalf of the Company" any contract. Operating Agreement, Article IV, Section 6. The Operating Manager controls the business affairs of the company pursuant to Section 6. This includes the ability to sell the principal property of the company thereby realizing the company's objective. Section 11 by its express terms does not limit this authority. Moreover, it does not require both members to execute a deed, as suggested in the Motion, but rather two officers, the Operating Manager and the Assistant Operating Manager. At best, if Chapman is the Assistant Operating Manager, Section 11 requires the deed that would be necessary to consummate the contract be signed by Comer as Operating Manager and Chapman as Assistant Operating Manager.

Chapman fails to consider the effect of the filing of his voluntary petition in bankruptcy on his rights in the limited liability company. The Code of Virginia provides that a member is "dissociated" from a limited liability company upon the occurrence of certain events, one of which is filing a petition in bankruptcy.

Dissociation of a member does not dissolve the company. The company continues in existence. The effect on a member of becoming dissociated from a limited liability company is to divest the member of all rights as a member to participate in the management or operation of the company. The only rights remaining are the dissociated member's economic rights, his membership interest. That is to say, the dissociated member is expelled from the company, but does not forfeit the value of his ownership interest.

The question presented by Chapman is whether Garrison-Woods can lawfully execute and consummate a contract for the sale of its real estate. Under present Virginia law, when Chapman filed his voluntary petition, he ceased to be a member and had no further voice or vote in the management of Garrison-Woods. Comer, as the sole remaining member, has the unilateral power to remove Chapman as Assistant Operating Manager at any time and elect a new Assistant Operating Manager. The new Assistant Operating Manager need not be a member of the company. In any event, Comer could elect himself the new Assistant Operating Manager. Article IV, Section 1 of the Operating Agreement provides that any two or more offices may be held by the same person. The restriction Chapman raises in his motion to reconsider would not prevent Garrison-Woods from executing the sales contract for its parcel or from consummating the sale. The legal authority, and the intention, to execute the contract and consummate it are both present. The contract approved by the court can be fully consummated.

Chapman's motion to reconsider is denied. Judgment for Comer.

THE GLOBAL BUSINESS ENVIRONMENT

The limited liability company is known in many countries throughout the world. However, LLCs formed under the laws of other nations are a bit different from American LLCs.

In Germany, which claims to be the first nation to permit them in 1892, LLCs are known as *Gesellschaft mit beschrankter Haftung* (GmbH). Other countries soon followed Germany's lead, including Portugal (1917), Brazil (1919), Chile (1923), Turkey (1926), Uruguay (1933), Mexico (1934), and Belgium (1935). In France, the *societes de responsabilite limitee* is more popular than the more traditional stock corporation.

In these countries, LLC law confers limited liability on the members, requires use of the word *limited* in the entity's name, permits members to control admission of new members to the entity, and allows the entity to be dissolved by death of a member, unless otherwise expressly stated in the articles of association. Most countries provide for management of LLCs by one or more managing directors. Many countries also limit the number of members in an LLC, making the LLC an entity inappropriate for a publicly held company. Some experts refer to these LLCs as private limited companies, which more accurately describes what they are: corporations with a limited number of owners.

Limited Partnerships and Limited Liability Limited Partnerships

The partnership form—with managerial control and unlimited liability for all partners—is not acceptable for all business arrangements. Often, business managers want an infusion of capital into a business yet are reluctant to surrender managerial control to those contributing capital. Investors wish to contribute capital to a business and share in its profits yet limit their liability to the amount of their investment and be relieved of the obligation to manage the business.

As you have already seen in this chapter and the other partnership chapters, an LLC may have an operating agreement and a limited liability partnership (LLP) may have a partnership agreement that accomplishes these objectives by limiting the management right to fewer than all of the LLC's members or LLP's partners. The **limited partnership,** however, has a basic, default structure that serves these needs. The limited partnership has

two classes of owners: **general partners,** who contribute capital to the business, manage it, share in its profits, and possess unlimited liability for its obligations; and **limited partners,** who contribute capital and share profits, but possess no management powers and have liability limited to their investments in the business.

A variant of the limited partnership is the **limited liability limited partnership (LLLP).** An LLLP is a limited partnership that has elected limited liability status for all its partners, including general partners. Except for the liability of general partners, limited partnerships and LLLPs are identical. For that reason, every well-planned limited partnership should also elect LLLP status, when available. Today, every state recognizes limited partnerships and many recognize LLLPs as well.

The Uniform Limited Partnership Acts

In 2001 the National Conference of Commissioners on Uniform State Laws drafted a new Uniform Limited Partnership Act (ULPA) to replace the Revised Uniform Partnership Act of 1976 and its 1985 amendments. The ULPA of 2001 is the first comprehensive statement of American limited partnership law. As shown in Figure 2,

---

Figure 2 *Principal Characteristics of Limited Partnerships and LLLPs*

1. A limited partnership or LLLP may be *created only in accordance with a statute.*
2. A limited partnership or LLLP has two types of partners: *general partners* and *limited partners.* It must have one or more of each type.
3. All partners, limited and general, *share the profits* of the business.
4. Each limited partner has liability *limited to his capital contribution* to the business. Each general partner of a limited partnership has *unlimited liability* for the obligations of the business. A general partner in an LLLP, however, has liability *limited to his capital contribution.*
5. Each general partner has a *right to manage* the business, and she is an agent of the limited partnership or LLLP. A limited partner has *no right to manage* the business or to act as its agent, but he does have the right to vote on fundamental matters. A limited partner they manage the business, yet retain limited liability for partnership obligations.
6. General partners, as agents, are *fiduciaries* of the business. Limited partners are not fiduciaries.
7. A partner's rights in a limited partnership or LLLP *are not freely transferable.* A transferee of a general or limited partnership interest is not a partner, but is entitled only to the transferring partner's share of capital and profits, absent a contrary agreement.
8. The death or other withdrawal of a partner does not usually dissolve a limited partnership or LLLP, unless there is no surviving general partner.
9. Usually, a limited partnership or LLLP is taxed like a partnership. However, a limited partnership or LLLP may elect to be taxed like a corporation.

many characteristics of a limited partnership under the ULPA are similar to those of a partnership or LLP under the Revised Uniform Partnership Act. While the ULPA copies much of the law of the RUPA, only the ULPA applies to limited partnerships.

Although most states at this time have enacted the RULPA, we will study the ULPA of 2001, which will soon be the dominant limited partnership law in the United States. The ULPA governs both limited partnerships and LLLPs. Under the ULPA, limited partnerships and LLLPs are identical except for the liability of general partners. Therefore, when this chapter addresses limited partnership law (other than the rules regarding the liability of general partners), the law applies to LLLPs as well.

LOG ON

www.nccusl.org
You can find the Uniform Limited Partnership Act of 2001 at the website for the National Conference of Commissioners on Uniform State Laws.

Use of Limited Partnerships and LLLPs

The limited partnership (or LLLP) form is used primarily in tax shelter ventures and activities such as real estate investment, oil and gas drilling, and professional sports. When the limited partnership elects to be taxed as a partnership, it operates as a tax shelter by allowing partners to reduce their personal federal income tax liability by deducting limited partnership losses on their individual income tax returns. General partners, however, receive a greater tax shelter advantage than do limited partners. Losses of the business allocated to a general partner offset his income from any other sources. Losses of the business allocated to limited partners may be used to offset only income from other *passive* investments and only to the extent limited partners are *at risk,* that is, to the extent of their capital contributions to the limited partnership. If a limited partner has sold her limited partnership interest or the limited partnership has terminated, her loss offsets any income. Limited partnerships are also used by family businesses for estate planning purposes. Regardless of the use, the ULPA presumes that its partners want a strongly centralized, strongly entrenched management (the general partners) and passive investors with little control and little right to exit the limited partnership (limited partners).

Creation of Limited Partnerships and LLLPs

A limited partnership (or LLLP) may be created only by complying with the applicable state statute. Yet the statutory requirements of the RULPA are minimal. A certificate of limited partnership must be executed and submitted to the secretary of state. The certificate must be signed by all general partners. A limited partnership begins its existence at the time the certificate is filed by the office of the secretary of state. The limited partnership may ask the secretary of state to issue a Certificate of Existence, which is conclusive proof the limited partnership exists.

The ULPA requires that the limited partnership certificate submitted by the limited partnership include its address, its registered agent for service of process, its general partners' names and addresses, and whether it is a limited partnership or an LLLP. The name of a limited partnership must include the words *limited partnership* or the letters *L.P.* or *LP*. The name of a limited liability limited partnership must contain the words *limited liability limited partnership* or the letters L.L.L.P. or LLLP. The name of a limited partnership or LLLP may include the name of any partner, general or limited.

It is expected that many limited partnerships (or LLLPs) will have unlimited duration. Therefore, the ULPA provides for the perpetual life of a limited partnership (or LLLP). The limited partnership certificate or limited partnership agreement, however, may place a limit on the limited partnership's duration.

The certificate is not required to address many other matters that are essential to the limited partnership, such as the limited partners' names, the partners' capital contributions, the partners' shares of profits and other distributions, or the acts that cause a dissolution of the limited partnership. A well-planned limited partnership will usually include those and other matters in the certificate or in a separate **limited partnership agreement.**

Any *person* may be a general or limited partner. Persons include a natural person, partnership, LLC, trust, estate, association, or corporation. Hence, as commonly occurs, a corporation may be the sole general partner of a limited partnership.

Creation of LLLPs

A well-planned limited partnership should shield all its partners from liability by electing LLLP status, when available. This election is simple, requiring no special filing. LLLP status is elected by making a statement in the limited partnership certificate submitted to the secretary of state that the business is an LLLP.

Defective Compliance with Limited Partnership Statute

The ULPA requires at least *substantial compliance* with the previously listed requirements to create a limited partnership. If the persons attempting to create a limited partnership do not substantially comply with the ULPA, a limited partnership does not exist; therefore, a limited partner may lose her limited liability and have unlimited liability for limited partnership obligations. A general partner in an LLLP may also have unlimited liability if the LLLP was formed defectively.

A lack of substantial compliance might result from failing to file a certificate of limited partnership or from filing a defective certificate. A defective certificate might, for example, misstate the name of the limited partnership or erroneously identify the business form as a limited partnership when an LLLP was intended.

Limited Partners Infrequently, a person will believe that she is a limited partner but discover later that she has been designated a general partner or that the general partners have not filed a certificate of limited partnership. In such circumstances and others, she may be liable as a general partner unless she in good faith believes she is a limited partner and upon discovering she is not a limited partner she either:

1. Causes a proper certificate of limited partnership (or an amendment thereto) to be filed with the secretary of state, or
2. Withdraws from future equity participation in the firm by filing a certificate declaring such withdrawal with the secretary of state.

However, such a person remains liable as a general partner to third parties who previously believed in good faith that the person was a general partner.

General Partners The ULPA of 2001 has no provision protecting general partners who erroneously believe an LLLP has been formed. Consequently, a general partner in a limited partnership who believes wrongly that an LLLP has been created has unlimited liability for the obligations of the limited partnership.

In the following *Briargate Condominium* case, the court considered the liability of new investors who believed they were limited partners although a limited partnership certificate had not been filed.

Briargate Condominium Assoc. v. Carpenter   *976 F.2d 868 (4th Cir. 1992)*

In 1984, Judith Carpenter invested in Briargate Homes, a business that purchased several condominium units in the Briargate Condominium complex. Although Carpenter believed that Briargate was a limited partnership and that she was a limited partner, in fact Briargate Homes was a partnership and she was a general partner. No attempt had been made to achieve actual or substantial compliance with the North Carolina limited partnership statute.

Carpenter never signed the partnership agreement or saw copies of the partnership's K-1 tax returns, which clearly identified her as a general partner. However, deductions for partnership losses that Carpenter claimed on her individual income tax returns were allowable only if she was a general partner. In early 1987, Carpenter or her attorneys had possession of documents explicitly stating that Briargate Homes was a general partnership and that her interest was one of a general partner. In June and December 1987, Carpenter received additional documents identifying Briargate Homes as a general partnership. Carpenter was an experienced businesswoman, served on the board of directors of a bank, and had ready access to legal and other professional advice.

As an owner of condominiums, the partnership was liable to the Briargate Condominium Association for assessments for maintenance, repair, and replacement of common areas in the complex. In late 1987 and early 1988, the partnership failed to pay the Association assessed fees of $85,106. The Association sued the partnership and its partners.

On February 5, 1988, Carpenter notified the other partners and the Association that she was withdrawing from any equity participation and renouncing any interest in the profits of the partnership.

At the trial, Carpenter contended that because she believed she was a limited partner, she should not be liable to the Association for the fees. The district court found that because Carpenter had not promptly withdrawn from the partnership upon discovering she was a general partner, she was liable for the full amount of the debt. Carpenter appealed.

Hamilton, Circuit Judge Carpenter's defense is grounded in the Revised Uniform Limited Partnership Act sec. 304, which provides:

(a) Except as provided in subsection (b), a person who makes a contribution to a business enterprise and erroneously but in good faith believes that he has become a limited partner in the enterprise is not a general partner in the enterprise and is not bound by its obligations, . . . if, on ascertaining the mistake, he:

(1) Causes an appropriate certificate of limited partnership to be executed and filed; or

(2) Withdraws from future equity participation in the enterprise.

(b) A person who makes a contribution of the kind described in subsection (a) is liable as a general partner to any third party who transacts business with the enterprise (i) before the person withdraws from the enterprise, or (ii) before the person gives notice to the partnership of his withdrawal from future equity participation, but only if the third party actually believed in good faith that the person was a general partner at the time of the transaction.

First, the person must have a good faith belief that he has become a limited partner. Second, the person must on ascertaining the mistake take one of two courses of action. He may file an appropriate certificate of limited partnership. Under this option, the person may continue in the business with limited liability. In the alternative, the person may give notice and withdraw completely from future equity participation in the business. If the two elements are met, then the person is liable *only* as a limited partner, effectively cutting off all personal liability of a general partner, unless subsection (b) applies.

Subsection (b) sets forth the *only* circumstances under which a person who meets the requirements of subsection (a) may incur liability like a general partner. Personal liability to third parties arises when the third party transacts business with the enterprise before the person files a proper certificate or withdraws. Imposition of liability is limited, however, by the requirement that at the time he transacts business, the third party actually believed in good faith that the person was a general partner at the time of the transaction. Reliance of the third party in the resources of the general partner is absolutely essential before liability may be imposed for transactions occurring before withdrawal.

Unlike its predecessor statute, RULPA sec. 304 does not specify how quickly a proper certificate or notice of withdrawal must be filed after a person ascertains he is not a limited partner. The current statute deletes the word "promptly" contained in the prior statute. The present statute also added the language in subsection (b) regarding reliance. This difference between the old and new statutes reflects a shift in emphasis away from the speed with which withdrawal is effected to an emphasis on protection of reliance by third parties. The key to liability is reliance by the third party on a person's apparent status as a general partner.

Given this interpretation of the statute, we believe the judgment of the district must be vacated, and the case remanded to the district court for additional findings. First, the district court must determine whether or not Carpenter held a good faith belief that she was a limited partner at the time she initially joined and contributed to the partnership. The district court did conclude that by at least mid-1987, Carpenter could not have held a good faith belief she was a limited partner, but the key date is the date of the contribution to the enterprise. Should the district court conclude that Carpenter did not have a good faith belief that she was a limited partner at the time of the initial contribution, then the statute affords her no relief.

Second, assuming Carpenter demonstrates a good faith belief at the time she invested, then her notice of withdrawal effectively cut off liability for any fees accrued after such notice. To hold Carpenter liable for fees accrued prior to the notice, the district court must determine if and when the Association actually believed in good faith that Carpenter was a general partner. Carpenter may be held liable only for those assessments made in reliance on the belief that the Association could look to assets of Carpenter as a general partner to satisfy the debt.

Carpenter points to statements indicating that agents of the Association apparently believed they were dealing with a limited partnership and were totally unaware of Carpenter's interest in the partnership until the time of her notice withdrawing from any equity participation and renouncing any interest in the profits of the partnership. We decline, however, to rule on the issue. It does not appear that this issue received much attention at trial. The district court should, on remand, review the record and may take additional evidence if necessary to aid its fact-finding on this issue.

Judgment for the Association vacated; remanded to the district court.

Foreign Limited Partnerships

A limited partnership is **domestic** in the state in which it is organized; it is **foreign** in every other state. The ULPA makes it clear that the laws of the domestic state apply to the internal affairs of the limited partnership, protecting limited partners in a limited partnership and all partners in an LLLP regardless of where business is conducted.

Nonetheless, to be privileged to transact business in a foreign state, a limited partnership must apply for *authority* to do business in that state. To obtain authority to transact business, a limited partnership must file an application for a **certificate of authority** with the secretary of state of the foreign state. The application must include the name and address of the limited partnership, the names and addresses of the general partners, the name and address of an agent for service of process, and whether or not the limited partnership is an LLLP. The secretary of state reviews the application and, if all requirements are met, issues a **certificate of authority.**

There are few penalties for failing to register as a foreign limited partnership. The ULPA does not impose fines for a failure to register. However, an unregistered foreign limited partnership may not use the foreign state's courts to sue to enforce any right or contract. Once it registers, a limited partnership may use the state's courts, even when it sues to enforce a contract that was made before it registered.

Failure to register does not invalidate any contracts made in the foreign state or prevent a limited partnership from defending itself in a suit brought in the state's courts. The failure to register does not make a limited partner liable for partnership obligations.

Rights and Liabilities of Partners in Limited Partnerships or LLLPs

The partners of a limited partnership (or LLLP) have many rights and liabilities. Some are common to both general and limited partners, while others are not shared.

Rights and Liabilities Shared by General and Limited Partners

Capital Contributions A partner may contribute any property or other benefit to the limited partnership. This includes cash, tangible or intangible property, services rendered, a promissory note, or a promise to contribute cash, property, or services. A partner is obligated to contribute as he promised. This obligation may be enforced by the limited partnership or by any of its creditors, illustrated by the *Builders Steel* case, which follows this section.

Share of Profits and Losses Under the ULPA, profits and losses are shared on the basis of the value of each partner's capital contribution unless there is a written agreement to the contrary. For example, if 2 general partners contribute $1,000 each and 20 limited partners contribute $20,000 each, and the profit is $40,200, each general partner's share of the profits is $100 and each limited partner's share is $2,000.

Because most limited partnerships are tax shelters, partnership agreements often provide for limited partners to take all the losses of the business, up to the limit of their capital contributions.

Voting Rights The ULPA of 2001 requires few actions to be approved by all the partners. Only amendment of the limited partnership agreement, amendment of the limited partnership certificate, and sale or other transfer of substantially all the limited partnership's assets outside the ordinary course of business require approval of all the partners. In a well-planned limited partnership, the limited partnership agreement may require that certain transactions be approved by general partners, by limited partners, or by all the partners. The agreement may give each general partner more votes than it grants limited partners, or vice versa.

The ULPA makes it clear that limited partners have no inherent right to vote on any matter as a class. They may receive such a right only by agreement of the partners.

Admission of New Partners Under the ULPA, the default rule is that no new partner may be admitted unless each partner has consented to the admission. The limited partnership agreement may provide for other admission procedures. For example, the general partners may be given the power to admit new limited partners without the consent of existing limited partners. Usually, this power is given to general partners to facilitate the ability of the limited partnership to raise capital, but the power should be restricted to prevent any significant dilution of the ownership interests of existing limited partners.

The limited partnership agreement may also provide for the election of new general partners, such as when a general partner dies or retires. Instead of requiring approval of all partners, the agreement may provide that a majority of the partners may elect a replacement general partner. Another option is to give to limited partners the power to replace a general partner. Another alternative is to grant such power to the partners owning a majority of the limited partnership, measured by their capital contributions.

In general, the ULPA does not grant partners much power to expel other partners from the partnership. When we discuss partners' dissociations later in the chapter, we will examine the few grounds for expulsion.

Derivative Actions A partner may sue to enforce a limited partnership right of action against a person who has harmed the limited partnership. This right of action is called a derivative action or **derivative suit.** Because usually the general partners hold the power to sue on behalf of the limited partnership, individual partners, especially limited partners, cannot ordinarily bring a derivative suit on behalf of the partnership.

However, if a partner asks the general partners to sue someone who has harmed the limited partnership and they refuse, then the partner may bring a derivative suit. The partner may also bring the suit if he shows that asking the general partners to sue would be a futile effort, such as when a limited partner wants to sue the general partners for mismanaging the business. Any recovery obtained by the partner goes to the limited partnership, because it is the party that was harmed directly.

Partner's Transferable Interest Each partner in a limited partnership owns a transferable interest in the limited partnership. It is his personal property. He may sell or transfer it to others, such as his personal creditors.

Or his personal creditor may obtain a charging order against it. Generally, a buyer or transferee—or a creditor with a charging order—is entitled to receive only the partner's share of distributions. The ULPA treats charging orders like ordinary partnership law does.

When the limited partnership agreement so provides or all the partners consent, a buyer or transferee of a partner's transferable interest may become a partner. The new partner then assumes all the rights and liabilities of a partner, except for liabilities unknown to her at the time she became a partner.

A partner's transfer of his transferable interest has no effect on his status as a partner, absent a contrary agreement. The partner has not disassociated and the limited partnership has not dissolved merely as a result of the transfer. However, the limited partnership agreement may create consequences, such as expulsion of the transferring partner.

Power and Right to Withdraw Partners have the power to withdraw from the limited partnership at any time. The expectation, however, is that a limited partnership will have perpetual duration. Consequently, the ULPA gives the partners no right to withdraw, absent a contrary provision in the limited partnership agreement.

One result, therefore, under the ULPA, is that a withdrawing partner has no right to receive the value of her partnership interest. This means that a partner who withdraws from a limited partnership will not receive a return of her investment, unless the limited partnership agreement provides for a buyout of the withdrawing partner or the limited partnership dissolves and liquidates.

Builders Steel Co. v. Hycore Inc.   877 P.2d 1168 (Okla. Ct. App. 1994)

Max A. Heidenreich, as general partner, formed a limited partnership, Brookside Realty, Ltd. (BRL), for the purpose of purchasing and developing a commercial and retail center to be known as Brookside Center. BRL's limited partners included Gilbert Grubbs, Ray Phillips, Jack Herrold, Donald Herrold, and Ron Main. The limited partnership certificate stated the limited partners' contributions as follows: Grubbs agreed to contribute $20,000 cash, assume personal liability of $225,000, render no services, and be liable for a future assessment of $145,000; Phillips agreed to contribute $5,000 cash, assume personal liability of $127,500, render no services, and be liable for a future assessment of $72,500; the Herrolds and Main each agreed to contribute $5,000 cash, assume personal liability of $63,750, render no services, and be liable for a future assessment of $36,250.

Builders Steel was one of the suppliers that sold materials on credit to BRL for the construction of the Brookside Center. When Builders Steel was not paid in full, Heidenreich, as the general partner, sought to escape personal liability under the federal bankruptcy code, but was denied discharge on the grounds that he defrauded the creditors. Nonetheless, Builders Steel sued the limited partners of BRL. Because the limited partners had not paid all the assessments required by the limited partnership certificate, Builders Steel claimed that as a creditor of BRL, Builders Steel was entitled to require the payment of those assessments to the extent of BRL's indebtedness to Builders Steel. The trial court granted the limited partners' motion for summary judgment that they were not liable to Builders Steel. Builders Steel appealed.

Brightmire, Judge   Builders Steel contends that it has a right under Oklahoma law, as a creditor of the partnership, to require payment of the assessments by the limited partners. They cite 54 O.S.1991 section 329(C):

> Unless otherwise provided in the partnership agreement, the obligation of a partner to make a contribution or return money or other property paid or distributed in violation of this act may be compromised only by consent of all the partners. Notwithstanding the compromise, a creditor of a limited partnership who extends credit or otherwise acts in reliance on that obligation after the partner signs a writing which reflects this obligation and before the amendment or cancellation thereof to reflect the compromise, may enforce the original obligation.

In this regard, Builders Steel attached to its response a copy of the certificate of limited partnership filed with the Oklahoma Secretary of State which does in fact list specific future assessments owed by each of the limited partners, and copies of correspondence from Max Heidenreich to various limited partners discussing the assessments.

The limited partners, however, argue that paragraph 5 of the first amendment to the Certificate of Limited Partnership is a disclaimer and therefore eliminates any basis for Builders Steel's reliance on the limited partners' future liability to the partnership. Paragraph 5, as amended, provides:

> Future assessments indicated above may be called only for limited purposes specifically authorized by the general partner and pursuant to the terms of the Partnership Agreement. No other creditor may rely on the above information as a representation of future assessments for the purpose of any claim.

The trouble is this argument overlooks the notice limitation of 54 O.S.1991 section 316:

> The fact that a certificate of limited partnership is on file in the Office of the Secretary of State is notice that the partnership is a limited partnership and the persons designated therein as general partners are general partners, *but it is not notice of any other fact.*

We conclude, therefore, that the trial court was not justified in basing a summary judgment on a finding that no further obligations are due to the limited partnership from the limited partners.

Judgment reversed in favor of Builders Steel.

Other Rights of General Partners

A general partner of a limited partnership or an LLLP has the same right to manage and the same agency powers as a partner in an ordinary partnership. He has the express authority to act as the partners have agreed he should and the implied authority to do what is in the ordinary course of business. In addition, he may have apparent authority to bind the partnership to contracts when his implied authority is limited yet no notice of the limitation has been given to third parties.

A general partner has no right to compensation beyond his share of the profits, absent an agreement to the contrary. Since most limited partnerships are tax shelters that are designed to lose money during their early years of operation, most limited partnership agreements provide for the payment of salaries to general partners.

Other Liabilities of General Partners

Liability   A general partner in a limited partnership has unlimited liability to the creditors of the limited partnership. In an LLLP, however, a general partner's liability is limited to his capital contribution to the business.

Even so, in an LLLP a general partner may not escape liability for torts he commits in the course of the LLLP's business. Suppose a general partner drives a car on LLLP business and negligently injures a pedestrian. Not only may the LLLP be liable, but also the general partner will have personal liability to the pedestrian. Yet the LLLP form does protect the general partner from most torts of the business. For example, the general partner in an LLLP will not have personal liability for the torts of her fellow general partners.

Fiduciary Duties   Any general partner, whether in a limited partnership or an LLLP, is in a position of trust when she manages the business and therefore owes fiduciary duties to the limited partnership and the other partners. The general partner must account for limited partnership property, not compete against the partnership, and not self-deal with the partnership.

In addition, a general partner owes a duty of care when transacting for the partnership. The ULPA provides considerable protection for general partners under the duty of care, imposing liability to the limited partnership only if she engages in grossly negligent or reckless conduct, intentional misconduct, or knowing violations of the law. The limited partnership agreement may increase the general partners' duty of care, although that is not typical. The ULPA permits the partners to reduce the general partners' duty of care, if not unreasonable, but gives no clue to what is reasonable or unreasonable.

Other Rights of Limited Partners

Limited partners have the right to be informed about partnership affairs. The ULPA obligates the general partners to provide financial information and tax returns to the limited partners on demand. In addition, a limited partner may inspect and copy a list of the partners, information concerning contributions by partners, the certificate of limited partnership, tax returns, and partnership agreements.

Other Liabilities of Limited Partners

Liability Once a limited partner has contributed all of his promised capital contribution, generally he has no further liability for partnership losses or obligations.

Under the RULPA of 1976, a limited partner who participates in the control of the business may be liable to creditors of the limited partnership. Under the RULPA, a limited partner who participates in control is liable only to those persons who transact with the limited partnership reasonably believing, based on the limited partner's conduct, that the limited partner is a general partner.

The ULPA of 2001 eliminates this liability risk. The ULPA extends to limited partners the same protection given to owners who manage LLCs and LLPs: liability limited to their capital contributions, regardless whether they manage the business.

Duties No limited partner owes fiduciary duties to the limited partnership or his partners solely by being a limited partner. That means, for example, a limited partner in an oil and gas limited partnership may also invest as a limited partner in other oil and gas limited partnerships. However, all limited partners owe a duty to act in good faith and to deal fairly with the limited partnership. For example, a limited partner who lends money to the partnership is expected to disclose his interest and to transact fairly with the limited partnership. In addition, a limited partner who is an agent of the limited partnership owes the fiduciary duties imposed by agency law. For example, a limited partner who is a leasing agent for a limited partnership that owns apartment buildings owes the duty to account for rental income and a duty of skill and care.

Partner Who Is Both a General Partner and a Limited Partner

Although unusual, a person may be both a general partner and a limited partner in a limited partnership or LLLP. A general partner may wish to be a limited partner to increase his share of limited partnership profits. A partner who is both a general and limited partner has the duties of a general partner when acting as a general partner and the duties of a limited partner when acting as a limited partner.

A general partner's liability in a limited partnership is not reduced merely because he is also a limited partner, but a limited partner who became a general partner would lose his limited liability. In an LLLP, liability is unaffected by whether a partner is both a general and limited partner, as the liability is the same for both types of partners in an LLLP.

Partners' Dissociations and Limited Partnership Dissolution

The ULPA of 2001 greatly changed the law regarding dissolutions of limited partnerships and LLLPs. The ULPA adopts much of the terminology and framework of partnership law. Reflecting the intent that limited partnerships and LLLPs are for long-term businesses, the ULPA makes it harder for limited partnership to dissolve and provides few rights for partners who dissociate from the limited partnership before the partners expect.

Partners' Dissociations

Because the roles of limited partners and general partners are different in a limited partnership or LLLP, the ULPA's default rules for dissociations by a limited partner are in part different from the default rules for dissociations by a general partner.

Limited Partner Dissociations A limited partner will dissociate upon the limited partner's death, withdrawal, or expulsion from the partnership.

A limited partner may be expelled by the other partners or by a court. The other partners may expel a limited partner if she has transferred all of her transferable interest or suffered a charging order against her partnership interest. She can also be expelled if it is illegal to conduct business with the limited partner, such as a securities investment firm limited partner who has been convicted of securities fraud. The other partners' vote to expel must be unanimous.

At the request of the limited partnership, a court may also expel a limited partner if she has engaged in wrongful conduct that negatively affects the business or if she has willfully and persistently breached the partnership agreement or the limited partner's duty of good faith and fair dealing.

The ULPA also defines dissociations for nonhuman limited partners, such as corporations, LLCs, and trusts. For example, the other partners may expel an LLC that has been dissolved and is winding up its business.

A dissociated limited partner is not a limited partner, has no rights as a limited partner, and is treated as a mere transferee of the dissociated limited partner's transferable interest. That means the dissociated limited partner has no right to vote or exercise any other partners' powers, but does have the right to receive distributions (profits) from the limited partnership and has the right to receive the liquidation value of her transferable interest at the termination of the limited partnership.

General Partner Dissociations The ULPA treats general partners' dissociations the same as the RUPA treats partners' dissociations in a partnership. A general partner's death, withdrawal, or expulsion causes dissociation, just as with limited partners. In addition, a general partner dissociates if he becomes mentally or physically unable to care for himself (such as when a court appoints a guardian over his affairs) or he is unable to perform as a general partner (as determined by a court). A general partner also dissociates if he is a debtor in bankruptcy, assigns his assets for the benefit of creditors, or has a custodian appointed over his property. In addition, a general partner may be expelled by a vote of all the other partners or by a court for the same grounds that limited partners may be expelled. The ULPA also provides for dissociation of nonhuman general partners, such as the termination of a corporation that is a general partner.

Like a dissociated limited partner, a dissociated general partner is treated as a transferee of the dissociated general partner's transferable interest. He will receive the liquidation value of the partnership interest at the termination of the partnership.

While a general partner always has the power to dissociate, his dissociation may be wrongful. A general partner wrongfully dissociates by leaving the partnership before it terminates, violating the limited partnership agreement, being a debtor in bankruptcy, or being ex-

pelled by a court. A general partner who has wrongfully dissociated is liable to the limited partnership and other partners for damages caused by his dissociation.

Authority and Liability of Dissociated General Partners Dissociation ends a general partner's right to manage the limited partnership. The dissociated general partner is released from most of his fiduciary duties. For example, the duty not to compete would no longer apply, so the dissociated general partner could set up a competing business. The duty of confidentiality, however, exists after dissociation to protect the limited partnership's trade secrets and other proprietary information.

While a general partner's express and implied authority to act for the limited partnership terminates upon his dissociation, he may retain apparent authority to transact for the limited partnership. Moreover, his liability for partnership obligations does not terminate merely due to his dissociation. Therefore, the dissociated general partner and the limited partnership must take steps to notify creditors and other parties of the dissociation to protect the limited partnership and the dissociated general partner from liability.

There are several ways to eliminate a dissociated partner's apparent authority to act for the limited partnership in the same way he did prior to the dissociation. The best way is for the limited partnership to give notice of the dissociation, such as by e-mail or phone calls. To give notice of a dissociation that is effective against everyone, the ULPA permits the filing of a Notice of Dissociation, which is effective 90 days after filing. In addition, two years after the dissociation, the apparent authority of a dissociated general partner automatically ends.

A disassociated general partner will remain liable on a limited partnership obligation incurred while he was a partner unless the creditor agrees to release him from liability. The dissociated general partner will not be liable for limited partnership obligations incurred after he dissociated, if notice has been given of his association or more than two years have passed since his dissociation.

In an LLLP, however, there is no need for the dissociated general partner to be released from liability by existing creditors or to give notice of the dissolution, because a general partner in an LLLP has liability limited to his contribution to the LLLP.

Effect of Limited Partnership Agreement The partners may agree to modify the default dissociation rules in the ULPA. For example, the partners may agree that no limited partner may withdraw from the limited partnership. While such a provision will not prevent dissociation upon a limited partner's death, it would otherwise require a limited partner to remain with the limited partnership until its term ends. The partnership agreement may also state the events that cause dissociation, such as a general partner becoming a manager of a competing business. The partners may also provide grounds to expel a partner, such as when a partner fails to contribute additional capital as required by the partnership agreement. The agreement may also reduce the percentage of partners required to expel a partner, such as requiring only 80 percent approval or giving expulsion power to general partners.

While a limited partner's power to withdraw may be eliminated, the limited partnership agreement may not restrict a general partner's right to withdraw. The grounds for this distinction is that a general partner should be able to withdraw from his duties to manage the limited partnership, while the limited partner as a passive investor has no such need to be relieved of that burden.

It may be unacceptable to the partners in a limited partnership that the dissociated partners do not receive the value of their partnership interests until the partnership terminates. Therefore, the limited partnership agreement may provide for the buyout of a partner's interest. A well written buyout agreement should state the events that trigger a buyout, the valuation method, and when and how the dissociated partner will be paid (for example, in a lump sum 120 days after dissociation or in quarterly installments for five years). To protect creditors, the ULPA prohibits any payment to a dissociated partner if the limited partnership is insolvent.

To protect the limited partnership's competitive position, the partners' agreement may also limit a dissociated general partner's ability to compete against the partnership. For example, a noncompete agreement may prohibit a dissociated general partner from competing for five years in the geographic area served by the limited partnership.

Limited Partnership Dissolutions

Recognizing that a limited partnership is usually worth more as a going concern, the ULPA provides that a limited partnership (or LLLP) is not dissolved, its business is not wound up, and it does not terminate merely because a partner has dissociated from the limited partnership. The ULPA provides that a limited partnership is dissolved and its business wound up only if all general partners and limited partners owning a majority of the claims to limited partner distributions (such as profits) vote for dissolution, if a general partner dissociates and partners owning a majority of the claims to partners' distributions vote for dissolution, if the last general or limited partner dissociates and is not replaced within 90 days, or if a court dissolves the limited partnership because it is not reasonably practicable to carry on the business of the limited partnership. Administrative dissolution by the secretary of state is also possible if the limited partnership fails to pay fees and taxes due to the secretary of state or fails to deliver an annual report to the secretary.

When a limited partnership dissolves, winding up of its business follows automatically. The general partners have the power to wind up the business. Dissociated general partners have no right to wind up.

If there is no remaining general partner, the limited partners may appoint a general partner to conduct the winding up. The limited partnership is bound by the acts of a general partner that are appropriate to winding up, such as selling assets of the business and completing contracts. No new business should be conducted by the winding up general partners.

After dissolution, a general partner has no express or implied authority to continue the business, except as necessary to liquidation. The general partners may have apparent authority to continue business in the usual way, however, and therefore bind the limited partnership. To avoid liability for the act of a general partner outside the scope of winding up, the limited partnership should give notice of its dissolution to all parties. One way to give notice is by filing a certificate of dissolution, which is effective against everyone after 90 days.

Distribution of Assets After the general partners have liquidated the assets of the limited partnership, the proceeds are distributed to those having claims against the limited partnership. First paid are creditors, which may include partners who, for example, have sold goods or made loans to the limited partnership.

If the proceeds from the sale of limited partnership assets exceed creditors' claims, the remainder is paid to the partners in the same proportions that they share distributions. This modifies the RULPA rule that repaid partners' capital contributions prior to distributing the remainder according to how partners share distributions. The ULPA rule may result in a wealth transfer from partners who have disproportionately larger contributions than their shares of distributions to partners who have disproportionately larger shares of distributions in relation to their capital contributions. If this is unacceptable, the partners may modify the ULPA rule in the limited partnership agreement, such as by requiring a return of capital con-

THE GLOBAL BUSINESS ENVIRONMENT

Limited Partnerships in Other Countries

All modern commercial countries permit the creation of limited partnerships, but almost none allow the creation of LLLPs. England and its former colonies, including the United States, Canada, Singapore, and Australia, use the term *limited partnership*. In Italy, the limited partnership form is named *Societa in accomandita semplice* (S.a.s.); in Latin American countries, the *Sociedad en comandita;* in Austria the *Kommanditgesellschaft* (Kg).

These business forms are mostly identical to American limited partnerships, having general partners who manage the business and possess unlimited liability and limited partners who may not manage and are granted limited liability. Most countries also permit the partners to restrict the transfer of a partner's interest and usually provide for the continuation of the business despite the death of a limited partner.

ETHICS IN ACTION

You now know the characteristics and default rules of LLCs, limited partnerships, and LLLPs. If you are a profit maximizer, which one of these forms would you find less desirable than the others? The answer is that the limited partnership is less desirable, because a limited partnership, LLLP, and LLC may have the same tax and management benefits, yet only the LLLP and LLC extend limited liability to all the owners. General partners in a limited partnership have unlimited liability for the limited partnership's obligations. Therefore, you reduce your risk and increase your return relative to risk by choosing the LLLP or LLC.

If you believe in utilitarianism, rights theory, or justice theory, does the distinction between limited partnerships and LLLPs and LLCs make sense to you? Why grant limited liability only to owners who know enough to create an LLLP or LLC? Is the business of an LLLP or LLC more important to society than the business of a limited partnership merely because the managers in a limited partnership have failed to acquire limited liability status? Is it fair for the law to protect someone better than others merely because she is more knowledgeable about the law?

tributions before distributing the remaining proceeds in the manner that partners share profits.

If a limited partnership's assets are insufficient to pay a creditor's claim, the persons who were general partners when the obligation was incurred must contribute cash to allow the limited partnership to pay the obligation. The general partners contribute in the same proportions that they shared distributions (considering only distributions to general partners) when the obligation was incurred.

In an LLLP, general partners are not required to contribute additional cash when the LLLP's assets are insufficient to pay creditors' claim because the liability of general partners in an LLLP is limited to their capital contributions.

Problems and Problem Cases

1. Eric Stratum and Terese Brown formed ESTB, L.L.C., a member-managed limited liability company created for the purpose of owning and leasing a residential apartment building. The term of the LLC was 25 years. Their operating agreement provided that each owned 50 percent of the LLC. Stratum contributed $120,000 cash as his contribution to the business. Brown contributed $10,000 cash at the time of the LLC's creation, with the expectation that she would contribute to the LLC with services to be performed in the future. The agreement, however, listed Brown's capital contribution as $10,000 and did not stipulate by how much it should be increased as Brown continued to manage the business. Although Brown was expected to be the primary manager of the business, nothing in the operating agreement gave more power to Brown or removed power from Stratum. For the first two years, Brown did most of the day-to-day management of the LLC. She and Stratum agreed on other actions, including replacing carpeting in apartments and reroofing the building. After two years, Brown claimed she was entitled to a larger share of the LLC's profits. Is she?

Suppose that Stratum responded by appointing his son to manage the LLC along with Brown. May Brown object to Stratum's son managing the LLC?

Suppose the relationship between Stratum and Brown has so deteriorated that she withdraws from the LLC. She demands to receive the value of her interest in the LLC. The LLC has a current value of $500,000. How much must Brown receive? When?

Suppose after she leaves the LLC, Brown purchases a residential apartment building that competes against the LLC. May Stratum prevent Brown from competing with the LLC?

2. In 1994, Steven Mossbrook, Sandra Mossbrook, and Michael Lieberman created Wyoming.com LLC. Lieberman contributed initial capital of $20,000 consisting of services rendered and to be rendered. He was given a 40 percent ownership interest in the LLC. The Mossbrooks contributed $30,000 and received a 60 percent ownership interest. In 1995, two new members were added to the LLC, each contributing $25,000 and receiving a 2.5 percent ownership interest. Lieberman's ownership interest and his stated capital contribution remained the same.

In 1998, Lieberman was terminated as vice president of Wyoming.com by the other members of Wyoming. Two weeks later, Lieberman withdrew from the LLC and demanded the immediate return of his share of the current value of the company, which he estimated at $400,000. The other members accepted Lieberman's withdrawal, chose to continue the LLC's business, and approved the return of Lieberman's $20,000 capital contribution, which Lieberman refused to accept. Is Lieberman entitled to the fair market value of his ownership interest?

3. Brookwood Fund was a limited partnership formed to trade investment securities. The original certificate of limited partnership filed in April 1987 listed Kenneth Stein as the "General Partner" and Barbara Stein as the "Original Limited Partner." Between May and August 1987, additional limited partners were added to Brookwood. The new limited partners did not participate in the management of Brookwood. However, an amended certificate of limited partnership reflecting the new limited partners was not filed. What should the new limited partners do to protect themselves from having the liability of general partners?

4. Virginia Partners, Ltd., a limited partnership organized in Florida, was in the business of drilling oil wells. When Virginia Partners injected acid into an oil well in Kentucky, a bystander, Robert Day, was injured by acid that sprayed on him from a ruptured hose. Virginia Partners had failed to register as a foreign limited partnership in Kentucky. Are the limited partners of Virginia Partners liable to Day for his injuries?

5. Horne-Long Associates was a limited partnership with one general partner and 18 limited partners. Horne-Long breached a contract with Northampton Valley Construction. The limited partnership agreement stated that the general partner could require the limited partners to make additional contributions to meet the obligations of the limited partnership. Was Northampton correct when it argued that this provision made the limited partners liable as general partners on the grounds that the general partner should have required the limited partners to contribute?

6. Seven Hills Associates, a limited partnership, owned and operated an office building. Raphael Silver was the only general partner. The building obtained its heat and utilities from equipment located in an adjacent building owned by a corporation controlled by Silver. One limited partner believed that the limited partnership's expenses were higher because of the utility arrangement. Is the limited partner permitted to bring an action in the name of Seven Hills Associates against Silver?

7. Blinder, Robinson & Co. as limited partner and Combat Promotions, Inc., as general partner created Combat Associates to promote an eight-round exhibition match between Muhammad Ali and Lyle Alzado, the pro football player. Combat Associates promised to pay Alzado $100,000 for his participation in the match.

Combat Promotions was owned entirely by Alzado, his accountant, and his professional agent. Alzado was also vice president of Combat Promotions. Blinder, Robinson used its Denver office as a ticket outlet for the match, gave two parties to promote the match, and provided a meeting room for Combat Associates' meetings. Meyer Blinder, president of Blinder, Robinson, personally appeared on a TV talk show and gave TV interviews to promote the match.

Few tickets were sold, and the match was a financial debacle. Alzado received no payments for participating in the match. Alzado sued Blinder, Robinson claiming that since it acted like a general partner it had the liability of a general partner. The case was decided under the law of the RULPA. Was Blinder, Robinson liable to Alzado? Would Blinder, Robinson be liable to Alzado under the ULPA of 2001?

Online Research: Your State and the ULLCA and the ULPA

Go to the website of the National Conference of Commissioners on Uniform State Laws.

• Check the legislative update to see whether your state has adopted the ULLCA and the ULPA.

• If your state has not adopted the ULLCA, find your state law for LLCs. Find the differences between the ULLCA and your state's LLC law.

• If your state has not adopted the ULPA, find the Revised Uniform Limited Partnership Act as amended in 1985. Note the differences between the RULPA and the ULPA of 2001.

PART TEN

CORPORATIONS

41

HISTORY AND NATURE OF CORPORATIONS

You and three friends create an online retailer, which is incorporated in California under the name Gifts&Awards.com, Inc. The website will sell awards, clocks, desk sets, and other merchandise that businesses want as gifts for their clients and as promotional items for their employees. Physically, Gifts&Awards.com, Inc. will be located exclusively in San Jose, California. All its shareholders, employees, and assets will be in California. As an online retailer, however, Gifts&Awards.com's merchandise will be available to anyone anywhere in the world. Businesses worldwide will place orders through the website, which will be filled by the Gifts&Awards.com's staff. Gifts&Awards.com will ship about 20 percent of the merchandise ordered from a warehouse it leases in California. The other 80 percent will be shipped directly from the manufacturers or importers of the items. For that 80 percent, Gifts&Awards.com will take orders from customers and direct the orders to the appropriate manufacturers or importers, some of which will be in California but most of which will be dispersed throughout the United States.

You estimate that Gifts&Awards.com will have $4,000,000 in annual sales, $60,000 of which will be sold to customers resident in Arizona. The goods will be delivered to customers by U.P.S., a third party carrier whose fee will be added to the price of the goods. Some of the goods will be shipped from Gifts&Awards.com's warehouse in California, and some from manufacturers in other states, including Arizona. Consider the following questions regarding the State of Arizona's regulation of Gifts&Awards.com, Inc., a California corporation:

• May the State of Arizona require Gifts&Awards.com, Inc. to obtain a certificate of authority to do business in Arizona and collect a fee from Gifts&Awards.com for the privilege of doing business in the state?
• May the State of Arizona impose its state income tax on a portion of Gifts&Awards.com's worldwide income?
• May the State of Arizona require Gifts&Awards.com to collect the Arizona sales tax on sales to Arizona residents?
• If Gifts&Awards.com sells defective awards to a customer in Arizona, may the customer sue Gifts&Awards.com in an Arizona trial court? Will your answer affect Gifts&Awards.com policy on customers' returns and refunds?

THE MODERN CORPORATION HAS facilitated the rapid economic development of the last 150 years by permitting businesses to attain economies of scale. Businesses organized as corporations can attain such economies because they have a greater capacity to raise capital than do other business forms. This capital-raising advantage is ensured by corporation law, which allows persons to invest their money in a corporation and become owners without imposing unlimited liability or management responsibilities on themselves. Many people are willing to invest their savings in a large, risky business if they have limited liability and no management responsibilities. Far fewer are willing to invest in a partnership or other business form in which owners have unlimited liability and management duties.

History of Corporations

Although modern corporation law emerged only in the last 150 years, ancestors of the modern corporation existed in the times of Hammurabi, ancient Greece, and the Roman Empire. As early as 1248 in France, privileges of incorporation were given to mercantile ventures to encourage investment for the benefit of society. In England, the corporate form was used extensively before the 16th century.

The famous British trading companies—such as the Massachusetts Bay Company—were the forerunners of the modern corporation. The British government gave these companies monopolies in trade and granted them powers to govern in the areas they colonized. They were permitted to operate as corporations because of the benefits they would confer on the British empire, such as the development of natural resources. Although these trading companies were among the few corporations of the time whose owners were granted limited liability, they sought corporate status primarily because the government granted them monopolies and governmental powers.

American Corporation Law

Beginning in 1776, corporation law in the United States evolved independently of English corporation law. Early American corporations received **special charters** from state legislatures. These charters were granted one at a time by special action of the legislatures; few special charters were granted.

In the late 18th century, general incorporation statutes emerged in the United States. Initially, these statutes permitted incorporation only for limited purposes beneficial to the public, such as operating toll bridges and water systems. Incorporation was still viewed as a privilege, and many restrictions were placed on corporations: incorporation was permitted for only short periods of time;

Figure 1   *Principal Characteristics of Corporations*

1. *Creation.* A corporation may be created only by *permission of a government.*

2. *Legal status.* A corporation is a legal person and a legal entity independent of its owners (*shareholders*) and its managers (officers and the *board of directors*). Its life is unaffected by the retirement or death of its shareholders, officers, and directors. A corporation is a person under the Constitution of the United States.

3. *Powers.* A corporation may *acquire, hold, and convey property* in its own name. A corporation may *sue and be sued* in its own name. Harm to a corporation is not harm to the shareholders; therefore, with few exceptions, a shareholder may not sue to enforce a claim of the corporation.

4. *Management.* Shareholders elect a board of directors, which manages the corporation. The board of directors may delegate management duties to officers. A shareholder has *no right or duty to manage* the business of a corporation, unless he is elected to the board of directors or is appointed an officer. The directors and officers need not be shareholders.

5. *Owners' liability.* The shareholders have *limited liability.* With few exceptions, they are not liable for the debts of a corporation after they have paid their promised capital contributions to the corporation.

6. *Transferability of owner's interest.* Generally, the ownership interest in a corporation is *freely transferable.* A shareholder may sell her shares to whomever she wants whenever she wants. The purchaser becomes a shareholder with the same rights that the seller had.

7. *Taxation.* Usually, a corporation pays *federal income taxes* on its income. Shareholders have personal income from the corporation only when the corporation makes a distribution of its income to them. For example, a shareholder would have personal income from the corporation when the corporation pays him a dividend. This creates a *double-taxation* possibility: The corporation pays income tax on its profits, and when the corporation distributes the after-tax profits as dividends, the shareholders pay tax on the dividends.

maximum limits on capitalization were low; and ownership of real and personal property was often restricted.

During the last 150 years, such restrictive provisions have disappeared in most states. Today, modern incorporation statutes are mostly enabling, granting the persons who control a corporation great flexibility in establishing, financing, and operating it.

See Figure 1 for a statement of the characteristics of corporations.

Classifications of Corporations

Corporations may be divided into three classes: (1) corporations **for profit,** (2) corporations **not for profit,** and (3) **government-owned** corporations. State corporation statutes establish procedures for the incorporation of each of these classes and for their operation. In addition, a large body of common law applies to all corporations.

Most business corporations are **for-profit corporations.** For-profit corporations issue stock to their shareholders, who invest in the corporation with the expectation that they will earn a profit on their investment. That profit may take the form of dividends paid by the corporation or increased market value of their shares.

Nearly all for-profit corporations are incorporated under the **general incorporation law** of a state. All of the states require professionals who wish to incorporate, such as physicians, dentists, lawyers, and accountants, to incorporate under **professional corporation acts.** In addition, for-profit corporations that especially affect the public interest, such as banks, insurance companies, and savings and loan associations, are usually required to incorporate under special statutes.

For-profit corporations range from huge international organizations such as General Motors Corporation to small, one-owner businesses. GM is an example of a **publicly held corporation** because its shares are generally available to public investors. The publicly held corporation tends to be managed by professional managers who own small percentages of the corporation. Nearly all the shareholders of the typical publicly held corporation are merely investors who are not concerned in the management of the corporation.

Corporations with very few shareholders whose shares are not available to the general public are called **close corporations.** In the typical close corporation, the controlling shareholders are the only managers of the business.

Usually, close corporations and publicly held corporations are subject to the same rules under state corporation law. Many states, however, allow close corporations greater latitude in the operation of their internal affairs than is granted to public corporations. For example, the shareholders of a close corporation may be permitted to dispense with the board of directors and manage the close corporation as if it were a partnership.

A Subchapter S corporation, or **S Corporation,** is a special type of close corporation. It is treated nearly like a partnership for federal income tax purposes. Its shareholders report the earnings or losses of the business on their individual federal income tax returns. This means that an S Corporation's profits are taxed only once—at the shareholder level, eliminating the double-taxation penalty of incorporation. All shareholders must consent to an S corporation election. The Internal Revenue Code requires an S corporation to have only one class of shares and 75 or fewer shareholders. Shareholders may be only individuals or trusts.

Not-for-profit corporations do not issue stock and do not expect to make a profit. Instead, they provide services to their members under a plan that eliminates any profit motive. These corporations have **members** rather than shareholders, and none of the surplus revenue from their operations may be distributed to their members. Since they generally pay no income tax, nonprofit corporations can reinvest a larger share of their incomes in the business than can for-profit corporations. Examples of nonprofit corporations are charities, churches, fraternal organizations, community arts councils, cooperative grocery stores, and cooperative farmers' feed and supplies stores.

Some corporations are owned by governments and perform governmental and business functions. A municipality (city) is one type of **government-owned corporation.** Other types are created to furnish more specific services—for example, school corporations and water companies. Others—such as the Tennessee Valley Authority and the Federal Deposit Insurance Corporation—operate much like for-profit corporations except that at least some of their directors are appointed by governmental officials, and some or all of their financing frequently comes from government. The TVA and the FDIC are chartered by Congress, but government-owned corporations may also be authorized by states. Government-operated businesses seek corporate status to free themselves from governmental operating procedures, which are more cumbersome than business operating procedures.

THE GLOBAL BUSINESS ENVIRONMENT

Corporations around the Globe

The corporate form of business is recognized throughout the world, and regardless of the country, the form has essentially the same characteristics: limited liability for its owners, free transferability of shares, and separation of management from ownership. In Italy, the name is *Societa per azioni*. In Zimbabwe and England, corporations are called limited companies. In Germany, the term is *Aktiengesellschaft* (AG). In Brazil, the name is *sociedade anonima*. You can learn a lot about Brazilian corporations at www.law.du.edu/elliot/sfeinle/businesslaw.htm.

Regulation of For-Profit Corporations

To become a corporation, a business must **incorporate** by complying with an incorporation statute. Incorporation is a fairly simple process usually requiring little more than paying a fee and filing a document with a designated government official—usually the secretary of state of the state of incorporation. Incorporation of for-profit businesses has been entrusted primarily to the governments of the 50 states.

State Incorporation Statutes

State incorporation statutes set out the basic rules regarding the relationship between the corporation, its shareholders, and its managers. For example, an incorporation statute sets the requirements for a business to incorporate, the procedures for shareholders' election of directors, and the duties directors and officers owe to the corporation. Although a corporation may do business in several states, usually the relationship between the corporation, its shareholders, and its managers is regulated only by the state of incorporation.

The American Bar Association's Committee on Corporate Laws has prepared a *model* statute for adoption by state legislatures. The purpose of the model statute is to improve the rationality of corporation law. It is called the **Model Business Corporation Act (MBCA).** It was last revised in 1999.

The revised MBCA is the basis of corporation law in most states. Your study of statutory corporation law in this book concentrates on the revised MBCA. Delaware and several other major commercial and industrial states such as New York and California do not follow the MBCA. Therefore, selected provisions of the Delaware and other acts will be addressed.

Several states have special provisions or statutes that are applicable only to close corporations. The ABA's Committee on Corporate Laws has adopted the *Statutory Close Corporation Supplement to the Model Business Corporation Act.* The Supplement is designed to provide a rational, statutory solution to the special problems facing close corporations.

LOG ON

Go to
www.wvu.edu/~law/wvli/bus-corp.html
You can view the MBCA, as revised in 1999, by visiting the website of the West Virginia Law Institute.

State Common Law of Corporations

Although nearly all of corporation law is statutory law, including the courts' interpretation of the statutes, there is a substantial body of common law of corporations (judge-made law). Most of this common law deals with creditor and shareholder rights. For example, the law of piercing the corporate veil, which you will study later in this chapter, is common law protecting creditors of corporations.

Regulation of Nonprofit Corporations

Nonprofit corporations are regulated primarily by the states. Nonprofit corporations may be created only by complying with a nonprofit incorporation statute. Incorporation under state law requires delivering articles of incorporation to the secretary of state. The existence of a nonprofit corporation begins when the secretary of state files the articles. Most states have statutes based on the revised **Model Nonprofit Corporation Act (MNCA).** Because of constitutional protection of freedom of religion, many states have special statutes regulating nonprofit religious organizations.

The law applied to nonprofit corporations is substantially similar to for-profit corporation law. At various points in the corporations chapters of this book, you will study the law of nonprofit corporations and examine how this form of business and its laws differ from the for-profit corporation and its laws. The Model Nonprofit Corporation Act will be the basis of your study of nonprofit corporation law.

Regulation of Foreign and Alien Corporations

A corporation may be incorporated in one state yet do business in many other states in which it is not incorporated. The corporation's contacts with other persons in those states may permit the states to regulate the corporation's transactions with their citizens, to subject the corporation to suits in their courts, or to tax the corporation. The circumstances under which states may impose their laws on a business incorporated in another state is determined by the law of foreign corporations.

A corporation is a **domestic corporation** in the state that has granted its charter; it is a **foreign corporation** in all the other states in which it does business. For example, a corporation organized in Delaware and doing business in Florida is domestic in Delaware and foreign in Florida. Note that a corporation domiciled in one country is an **alien corporation** in other countries in which it does business. Many of the rules that apply to foreign corporations apply as well to alien corporations.

Generally, a state may impose its laws on a foreign corporation if such imposition does not violate the Constitution of the United States, notably the Due Process Clause of the Fourteenth Amendment and the Commerce Clause.

Due Process Clause

The Due Process Clause requires that a foreign corporation have sufficient contacts with a state before a state may exercise jurisdiction over the corporation. The leading case in this area is the *International Shoe* case.[1] In that case, the Supreme Court ruled that a foreign corporation must have "certain minimum contacts" with the state such that asserting jurisdiction over the corporation does not offend "traditional notions of fair play and substantial justice." The Supreme Court justified its holding

with a **benefit theory:** When a foreign corporation avails itself of the protection of a state's laws, it should suffer any reasonable burden that the state imposes as a consequence of such benefit. In other words, a foreign corporation should be required to pay for the benefits that it receives from the state.

Commerce Clause

Under the commerce clause, the power to regulate interstate commerce is given to the federal government. The states have no power to exclude or to discriminate against foreign corporations that are engaged solely in *interstate* commerce. Nevertheless, a state may require a foreign corporation doing interstate business in the state to comply with its laws if the application of these laws does not unduly burden interstate commerce. When a foreign corporation enters interstate commerce to do *intrastate* business in a state, the state may regulate the corporation's activities, provided again that the regulation does not unduly burden interstate commerce.

A state law regulating the activities of a foreign corporation does not unduly burden interstate commerce if (1) the law serves a legitimate state interest, (2) the state has chosen the least burdensome means of promoting that interest, and (3) that legitimate state interest outweighs the statute's burden on interstate commerce. Because conducting intrastate business increases a corporation's contact with a state, it is easier to prove that the state has a legitimate interest and that there is no undue burden on interstate commerce when the state regulates a corporation that is conducting intrastate business.

Doing Business To aid their determination of whether a state may constitutionally impose its laws on a foreign corporation, courts have traditionally used the concept of **doing business.** Courts have generally held that a foreign corporation is subject to the laws of a state when it is doing business in the state. The activities that constitute doing business differ, however, depending on the purpose of the determination. There are four such purposes: (1) to determine whether a corporation is subject to a lawsuit in a state's courts, (2) to determine whether the corporation's activities are subject to taxation, (3) to determine whether the corporation must qualify to carry on its activities in the state, and (4) to determine whether the state may regulate the internal affairs of the corporation.

Subjecting Foreign Corporations to Suit

The Supreme Court of the United States has held that a foreign corporation may be brought into a state's court in

---

[1] *International Shoe Co. v. State of Washington,* 326 U.S. 310 (1945).

connection with its activities within the state, provided that the state does not violate the corporation's due process rights under the Fourteenth Amendment of the Constitution and its rights under the commerce clause.

The *International Shoe* minimum contacts test must be met. Subjecting the corporation to suit cannot offend "traditional notions of fair play and substantial justice." A court must weigh the corporation's contacts within the state against the inconvenience to the corporation of requiring it to defend a suit within the state. The burden on the corporation must be reasonable in relation to the benefit that it receives from conducting activities in the state.

Under the minimum contacts test, even an isolated event may be sufficient to confer jurisdiction on a state's courts. For example, driving a truck from Arizona through New Mexico toward a final destination in Florida provides sufficient contacts with New Mexico to permit a suit in New Mexico's courts against the foreign corporation for its driver's negligently causing an accident within New Mexico.

Most of the states have passed **long-arm statutes** to permit their courts to exercise jurisdiction under the decision of the *International Shoe* case. These statutes frequently specify several kinds of corporate activities that make foreign corporations subject to suit within the state, such as the commission of a tort, the making of a contract, or the ownership of property. Most of the long-arm statutes grant jurisdiction over causes of action growing out of any transaction within the state.

In the following Global Business Environment box, the court considers whether a Liechtenstein corporation may be sued in a New Hampshire court.

THE GLOBAL BUSINESS ENVIRONMENT

Jet Wine & Spirits, Inc. v. Bacardi & Co., Ltd., 298 F.3d 1 (1st Cir. 2002)

Bacardi & Co., a Liechtenstein corporation, was sued in a New Hampshire court by a New Hampshire liquor distributor, Jet Wine & Spirits, Inc. Bacardi & Co. (BACO) has its primary place of business in the Bahamas and is wholly owned by Bacardi International Limited, which is almost wholly owned by Bacardi Limited, a Bermuda corporation with its primary place of business in Bermuda. Bacardi Limited also wholly owns Bacardi U.S.A. (BUSA), a Delaware corporation with its primary place of business in Florida.

BACO owns several brands of Dewar's Scotch and Bombay Gin, which it acquired from Diageo, which had a relationship with Jet Wine & Spirits. Jet Wine had previously distributed Dewar's in several New England states, including New Hampshire, under a contract it had with subsidiaries of the companies that merged to form Diageo, including Schieffelin. BACO assumed Schieffelin's contract with Jet Wine when it acquired the Dewar's brand from Diageo.

BACO does no business directly in New Hampshire, except possibly through its website. From November 1998 to September 1999, www.bacardi.com sold some Bacardi promotional items (clothing and keychains, not alcohol), including two sales to New Hampshire addresses for a total of $30.75. This money went to National Corporate Services Unlimited, an unrelated company that buys merchandise from BUSA and sells it over the website. BACO owns one trademark, "Havana Club," that is registered in New Hampshire.

Acting under authority given it by BACO, BUSA terminated Jet Wine as distributor. Jet Wine then sued a number of members of the Bacardi corporate family, including BACO, under breach of contract and the tort of interfering with a contractual relation. BACO argued it had nothing to do with New Hampshire and moved to dismiss for lack of personal jurisdiction. The District Court granted BACO's motion, and Jet Wine appealed.

Lynch, Judge   Jet Wine bears the burden of establishing personal jurisdiction. To do that, it must show that BACO has had "certain minimum contacts" with New Hampshire "such that maintenance of the suit does not offend traditional notions of fair play and substantial justice." *Int'l Shoe Co. v. Washington,* 326 U.S. 310, 316 (1945).

The most important contact that Jet Wine alleges between BACO and New Hampshire is BACO's alleged assumption of Schieffelin's obligations under the Dewar's contract when BACO and Diageo signed the Dewar's Agreement. The primary fact produced is the provision in the Dewar's Agreement by which BACO assumed "all liabilities and obligations that arise out of or relate to the Transferred Assets (including under any Contract) [or] the Dewar's Business." Jet Wine argues that its contract with Schieffelin creates an obligation that arises out of, and relates to, the Dewar's Business, defined as "the marketing, sales and distribution of Scotch whisky" under the trade names here at issue. We agree that is a quite plausible interpretation, sufficient for a prima facie showing of jurisdiction.

The second significant contact that Jet Wine alleges between BACO and New Hampshire is BUSA's termination of Jet Wine as the distributor of Dewar's in New Hampshire and BUSA's subsequent use of another distributor for Dewar's in New Hampshire. Jet Wine claims that the district court should have imputed these actions to BACO for jurisdictional purposes because BUSA acted as BACO's agent.

Jet Wine has argued that BUSA was BACO's agent for the purpose of distributing Dewar's in New Hampshire, because [a June 16 letter from BACO to BUSA] identifies BUSA as BACO's "exclusive brand agent and distributor" and authorizes BUSA "to take all legal steps necessary to effectuate the sale of our products in the United States of America." The existence of the letter satisfies Jet Wine's burden to support its allegation that BUSA acted as BACO's agent in terminating Jet Wine as the Dewar's distributor for New Hampshire.

We must consider whether Jet Wine's claims against BACO arise out of or are related to BACO's contacts with New Hampshire. For the contract claim, the answer is a straightforward yes. Jet Wine's action against BACO for breach of contract arises out of BACO's alleged assumption of Jet Wine's contract with Schieffelin. That assumption was a contact with the state of New Hampshire that relates intimately to Jet Wine's claim.

Ordinarily, the personal jurisdiction analysis for tort claims differs from that for contract claims. When, however, the tort is intentional interference with a contractual or business relationship, the two inquiries begin to resemble each other. Intentional interference with a contractual or business relationship concerning the sale of goods in New Hampshire is a contact with New Hampshire for much the same reasons that the assumption of the contract is such a contact.

Jet Wine must also demonstrate that BACO purposefully availed itself of the privilege of doing business in New Hampshire. There must be some voluntary action that BACO has taken that should have put it fairly on notice that it might one day be called to defend itself in a New Hampshire court. If BACO assumed the various obligations of Diageo to its distributors in the Dewar's Agreement, including Schieffelin's to Jet Wine, that was a voluntary act from which BACO should have known that it was rendering itself liable to suit in many places throughout the world. From the schedules attached to the Agreement, it knew that one of those places was New Hampshire.

We acknowledge that there is some burden on BACO if it must appear in New Hampshire's courts. New Hampshire is far removed from Liechtenstein, where BACO is incorporated, and also far from the Bahamas, BACO's primary place of business. BACO is, however, an international corporation that does business in the United States, including through its purported agent, BUSA. It cannot wholly expect to escape the reach of United States courts.

We add a final note addressing an argument made by BACO. BACO says that because the agreements between Schieffelin and Jet Wine contain clauses consenting to the jurisdiction of the federal district courts within New York as the fora for resolving disputes, it is unreasonable to subject BACO to the jurisdiction of New Hampshire. Contractual language consenting to the jurisdiction of one forum, however, is not the same as language specifying one forum and excluding all others.

Judgment reversed in favor of Jet Wine. Remanded to the district court.

Taxation

A state may tax a foreign corporation if such taxation does not violate the due process clause or the commerce clause. Generally, a state's imposition of a tax must serve a legitimate state interest and be reasonable in relation to a foreign corporation's contacts with the state. For example, a North Carolina corporation's property located in Pennsylvania is subject to property tax in Pennsylvania. The corporation enjoys Pennsylvania's protection of private property. It may be required to pay its share of the cost of such protection.

Greater contacts are needed to subject a corporation to state income and sales taxation in a state than are needed to subject it to property taxation. A state tax does not violate the commerce clause when the tax (1) is applied to an activity with a substantial connection with the taxing state, (2) is fairly apportioned, (3) does not discriminate against interstate commerce, and (4) is fairly related to the services provided by the state.

For example, New Jersey has been permitted to tax a portion of the entire net income of a corporation for the privilege of doing business, employing or owning capital or property, or maintaining an office in New Jersey when the portion of entire net income taxed is determined by an average of three ratios: in-state property to total property, in-state to total receipts, and in-state to total wages, salaries, and other employee compensation.[2] However, Pennsylvania could not assess a flat tax on the operation of all trucks on Pennsylvania highways. The flat tax imposed a disproportionate burden on interstate trucks as compared with intrastate trucks because interstate trucks traveled fewer miles per year on Pennsylvania highways.[3] A state may tax an interstate sale by a foreign cor-

---

[2]*Amerada Hess Corp. v. Director of Taxation,* 490 U.S. 66 (1989).
[3]*American Trucking Assns., Inc. v. Scheiner,* 483 U.S. 266 (1987).

THE GLOBAL BUSINESS ENVIRONMENT

Offshore Tax Havens

In recent years, a few large American companies have reincorporated in Caribbean countries that offer favorable tax treatment compared to American law. For example, consulting firm Accenture incorporated in Bermuda in 2001, as did Ingersoll-Rand. Tyco in 1997 and Fruit of the Loom in 1999 also incorporated in Bermuda. Cayman Island is another popular tax haven.

Offshore reincorporation is a response to U.S. federal income tax law, which taxes all of an American corporation's income, regardless where it is earned. Bermuda, by contrast, does not tax corporate profits. Instead, a Bermuda corporation doing business in many countries—as is typical for the multinational corporations organized there—pays income tax in each country only on the amount of income earned there.

Fewer than 30 of the thousands of publicly traded American corporations have reincorporated in the Caribbean. Yet in three-fourths of the mergers between U.S. and foreign firms from 1998 to 2000, the resulting companies chose to incorporate in the foreign country. For example, Daimler Chrysler says it elected to organize in Germany because of American tax law. Proponents point to these and other examples of corporate flight as proof that American tax law must be revised to assess income taxes based on where profits are earned, not merely where the company is incorporated.

Opponents brand fleeing businesses as corporate traitors. Already, efforts are underway to restrict or prohibit offshore reincorporation or to punish firms that reincorporate offshore. One proposal would ban offshore companies from receiving lucrative federal government contracts. The 10 biggest companies that have relocated to Bermuda did over one billion dollars of federal contract business in 2001.

Some U.S. congressmen and the President are backing a moratorium on relocations, until federal tax law can be changed to make it more competitive internationally. The proposed American Competitiveness and Corporate Accountability Act of 2002 would impose a three-year moratorium on offshore reincorporation, remove the tax incentives for U.S. companies to reincorporate offshore, and change American taxation of U.S. multinationals to enable them to compete better in a global marketplace.

---

poration to an in-state consumer if the seller has a physical presence in the state, such as a retail outlet.[4]

State taxation of interstate Internet transactions has become a potential source for state revenue. However, the federal Congress placed a moratorium on new Internet taxes that is due to expire in 2003. Congress is considering new legislation that will prohibit state taxation of interstate Internet business.

Qualifying to Do Business

A state may require that foreign corporations **qualify** to conduct **intrastate business** in the state. The level of doing business that constitutes intrastate business for qualification purposes has been difficult to define. To help clarify the confusion in this area, the MBCA lists several activities that do *not* require qualification. For example, soliciting—by mail or through employees—orders that require acceptance outside the state is not doing intrastate business requiring qualification. Selling through independent contractors or owning real or personal property does not require qualification.

Also classified as not doing business for qualification purposes is conducting an **isolated transaction** that is completed within 30 days and is not one in the course of repeated transactions of a like nature. This isolated transaction safe harbor allows a tree grower to bring Christmas trees into a state in order to sell them to one retailer. However, a Christmas tree retailer who comes into a state for 29 days before Christmas and sells to consumers from a street corner is required to qualify. Although both merchants have consummated their transactions within 30 days, the grower has engaged in only one transaction, but the retailer has engaged in a series of transactions.

Maintaining an office to conduct intrastate business, selling personal property not in interstate commerce, entering into contracts relating to local business or sales, or owning or using real estate for general corporate purposes does constitute doing intrastate business. Passive ownership of real estate for investment, however, is not doing intrastate business.

Maintaining a stock of goods within a state from which to fill orders, even if the orders are taken or accepted outside the state, is doing intrastate business requiring qualification. Performing service activities such as machinery repair and construction work may be doing intrastate business.

---

[4]*Quill Corp. v. North Dakota,* 504 U.S. 298 (1992).

Qualification Requirements To qualify to do intrastate business in a state, a foreign corporation must apply for a **certificate of authority** from the secretary of state, pay an application fee, maintain a registered office and a registered agent in the state, file an annual report with the secretary of state, and pay an annual fee.

Doing intrastate business without qualifying usually subjects a foreign corporation to a fine, in some states as much as $10,000. The MBCA disables the corporation to use the state's courts to bring a lawsuit until it obtains a certificate of authority. The corporation may defend itself in the state's courts, however, even if it has no certificate of authority.

LOG ON

Go to
www.usregisteredagents.com
Several online businesses have been created to relieve corporations of the burden of qualifying to do business and maintaining a registered agent in each state in which it does business. US Registered Agents is one such business. Can you find the cost of hiring US Registered Agents to be a corporation's registered agent?

In the following *Gosch* case, the Texas court of appeals allowed a Delaware corporation to sue in a Texas court even though the corporation had not obtained a certificate of authority.

Gosch v. B & D Shrimp, Inc.   *830 S.W.2d 652 (Tex. Ct. App. 1992)*

B & D Shrimp, Inc., a Delaware corporation, entered a contract in Texas with Donald Gosch and Jesse Bach. The contract required Gosch and Bach to purchase a commercial shrimp boat from Shrimp, Inc. Gosch and Bach paid $5,000 down and received immediate possession of the boat; Gosch and Bach would get marketable title to the shrimp boat after transferring a cabin cruiser to Shrimp, Inc., and paying 15 percent of the cash proceeds generated from the shrimp boat's daily shrimp catches for the next calendar year. When Gosch and Bach defaulted on its obligation, Shrimp, Inc., sued Gosch. After the trial court found Gosch liable to Shrimp, Inc., Gosch asked the trial court to set aside its judgment on the grounds that Shrimp, Inc., had not obtained a certificate of authority to do business from the Texas secretary of state and, therefore, was not allowed to use Texas's courts to enforce the contract. The trial court denied Gosch's request, and Gosch appealed.

O'Connor, Justice The Texas Business Corporation Act prohibits a foreign corporation from maintaining any action in this State until it has obtained a certificate of authority to do business. Shrimp, Inc., argues that it was not necessary for it to obtain a certificate. A corporation is not considered to be transacting business in Texas if it conducts an isolated transaction that is completed within 30 days and the transaction is not in the course of a number of repeated transactions that are similar. Shrimp, Inc., contends that it fell within this exception to the statute requiring a certificate of authority. We disagree. Here, it is implicit in the agreement that the transaction could not be completed within 30 days. The transfer of title would not occur until, in addition to two other conditions, 15 percent of the cash proceeds generated

from the daily shrimp catches for the *next calendar year* were paid.

Shrimp, Inc., also contends it was within the trial court's discretion to disregard Gosch's plea. We agree. Here, Gosch did not raise the issue of Shrimp, Inc.'s authority until 20 days after the judgment was signed, in a motion to set aside the judgment. By waiting until after the trial, Gosch waived the issue of Shrimp, Inc.'s capacity to prosecute the suit. Even if Gosch had not waived the issue, at the hearing on the motion to set aside the judgment, Shrimp, Inc., filed a certificate of authority. The trial court did not abuse its discretion in overruling the motion to set aside the judgment.

Judgment for B & D Shrimp, Inc., affirmed.

Regulation of a Corporation's Internal Affairs

Regulation of the internal affairs of a corporation—that is, the relation between the corporation and its directors, officers, and shareholders—is usually exercised only by the state of incorporation. Nonetheless, a foreign corporation may conduct most of its business in a state other than the one in which it is incorporated. Such a corporation is called a **pseudo-foreign corporation** in the state in which it conducts most of its business.

A few states subject pseudo-foreign corporations to extensive regulation of their internal affairs, regulation similar to that imposed on their domestic corporations. California's statute requires corporations that have more than 50 percent of their business and ownership in California to elect directors by cumulative voting, to hold annual directors' elections, and to comply with California's dividend payment restrictions. Foreign corporations raise many constitutional objections to the California statute, including violations of the Commerce Clause and the Due Process Clause.

Regulation of Foreign Nonprofit Corporations

The Model Nonprofit Corporation Act and other laws impose the same requirements and penalties on nonprofit corporations as are imposed on for-profit corporations. For example, the MNCA requires a foreign nonprofit corporation to qualify to do intrastate business in a state. The failure to qualify prevents the foreign nonprofit corporation from using the state's courts to bring lawsuits and subjects it to fines for each day it transacts intrastate business without a certificate of authority.

Piercing the Corporate Veil

A corporation is a legal entity separate from its shareholders. Corporation law erects an imaginary wall between a corporation and its shareholders that protects shareholders from liability for a corporation's actions. Once shareholders have made their promised capital contributions to the corporation, they have no further financial liability. This means that contracts of a corporation are not contracts of its shareholders, and debts of a corporation are not debts of its shareholders.

Nonetheless, in order *to promote justice and to prevent inequity,* courts will sometimes ignore the separateness of a corporation and its shareholders by **piercing the corporate veil.** The primary consequence of piercing the corporate veil is that a corporation's shareholders may lose their limited liability.

Two requirements must exist for a court to pierce the corporate veil: (1) **domination** of a corporation by its shareholders; and (2) use of that domination for an **improper purpose.**

As an entity separate from its shareholders, a corporation should act for itself, not for its shareholders. If the shareholders cause the corporation to act to its detriment and to the personal benefit of shareholders, *domination*—the first requirement for piercing the corporate veil—is proved. For example, shareholders' directing a corporation to pay a shareholder's personal expenses is domination. Domination is also proved if the shareholders cause the corporation to fail to observe corporate formalities (such as failing to hold shareholder and director meetings or to maintain separate accounting records). Some courts say that shareholder domination makes the corporation the *alter ego* (other self) of the shareholders. Other courts say that domination makes the corporation an *instrumentality* of the shareholders.

To prove domination, it is not sufficient, or even necessary, to show that there is only one shareholder. Many one-shareholder corporations will never have their veils pierced. However, nearly all corporations whose veils are pierced are close corporations, since domination is more easily accomplished in a close corporation than in a publicly held one.

In addition to domination, there must be an *improper use* of the corporation. The improper use may be any of three types: defrauding creditors, circumventing a statute, or evading an existing obligation.

Defrauding Creditors Shareholders must organize a corporation with sufficient capital to meet the initial capital needs of the business. Inadequate capitalization, called **thin capitalization,** is proved when capitalization is very small in relation to the nature of the business of the corporation and the risks the business necessarily entails.

Thin capitalization defrauds creditors of a corporation. An example of thin capitalization is forming a business with a high debt-to-equity ratio, such as a $10-million-asset business with only $1,000 of equity capital, with the shareholders sometimes contributing the remainder of the needed capital as secured creditors. By doing so, the shareholders elevate a portion of their bankruptcy repayment priority to a level above that of general creditors, thereby reducing the shareholders' risk. The high debt-to-equity ratio harms nonshareholder-creditors by failing to provide an equity cushion sufficient to protect their claims. In such a situation, either the shareholders will be liable for the corporation's debts or the shareholders' loans to the corporation will be subordinated to the claims of other creditors. As a result, the nonshareholder-creditors are repaid all of their claims prior to the shareholder-creditors receiving payment from the corporation.

Transfers of corporate assets to shareholders for less than fair market value (called **looting**) also defraud creditors. For example, shareholder-managers loot a corporation by paying themselves excessively high salaries or by having the corporation pay their personal credit card bills. When such payments leave insufficient assets in the corporation to pay creditors' claims, a court will hold the shareholders liable to the creditors.

Frequently, the same shareholders may own two corporations that transact with each other. The shareholders may cause one corporation to loot the other. When such looting occurs between corporations of common ownership, courts pierce the veils of these corporations. This makes each corporation liable to the creditors of the other corporation. For example, a shareholder-manager operates two corporations from the same office. Corporation 1 transfers inventory to Corporation 2, but it receives less than fair market value for the inventory. Also, both corporations employ the same workers, but all of the wages are paid by Corporation 1. In such a situation, the veils of the corporations will be pierced, allowing the creditors of Corporation 1 to satisfy their claims against the assets of Corporation 2.

Looting may occur also when one corporation (called the **parent corporation**) owns at least a majority of the shares of another corporation (called the **subsidiary corporation**). Ordinarily, the parent is liable for its own obligations and the subsidiary is liable for its own obligations, but the parent is not liable for its subsidiary's debts and the subsidiary is not liable for the parent's debts. Nonetheless, because a parent corporation is able to elect the directors of its subsidiary and therefore can control the management of the subsidiary, the parent may cause its subsidiary to transact with the parent in a manner that benefits the parent but harms the subsidiary.

For example, a parent corporation may direct its subsidiary to sell its assets to the parent for less than fair value. Because the subsidiary has given more assets to the parent than it has received from the parent, creditors of the subsidiary have been defrauded. Consequently, a court will pierce the veil between the parent and its subsidiary and hold the parent liable to the creditors of the subsidiary.

Affiliated corporations must not commingle their assets. Each corporation must have its own books of accounts. Transactions between affiliated corporations must be recorded on the books of both corporations, and such transactions must be executed at fair value.

Circumventing a Statute A corporation should not engage in a course of conduct that is prohibited by a statute. For example, a city ordinance prohibits retail businesses from being open on consecutive Sundays. To avoid the statute, a retail corporation forms a subsidiary owned entirely by the retail corporation; on alternate weeks, it leases its building and inventory to the subsidiary. A court will pierce the veil because the purpose of creating the subsidiary corporation is to circumvent the statutory prohibition. Consequently, both the parent and the subsidiary will be liable for violating the statute.

Evading an Existing Obligation Sometimes, a corporation will attempt to escape liability on a contract by reincorporating or by forming a subsidiary corporation. The new corporation will claim that it is not bound by the contract, even though it is doing the same business as was done by the old corporation. In such a situation, courts pierce the corporate veil and hold the new corporation liable on the contract.

For example, to avoid an onerous labor union contract, a corporation creates a wholly owned subsidiary and sells its entire business to the subsidiary. The subsidiary will claim that it is not a party to the labor contract and may hire nonunion labor. A court will pierce the veil between the two corporations because the subsidiary was created only to avoid the union contract.

Nonprofit Corporations

Like a for-profit corporation, a nonprofit corporation is an entity separate and distinct from its members. A member is not personally liable for a nonprofit corporation's acts or liabilities merely by being a member. However, a court may pierce the veil of a nonprofit corporation if it is used to defraud creditors, circumvent a statute, or evade an existing obligation, the same grounds on which a for-profit corporation's veil may be pierced.

For a summary of the law of piercing the corporate veil, see Figure 2.

In the *Bingham* case, at this section's end, the court considered a full range of reasons to pierce a corporation's veil.

Figure 2   *Examples of Piercing the Corporate Veil*

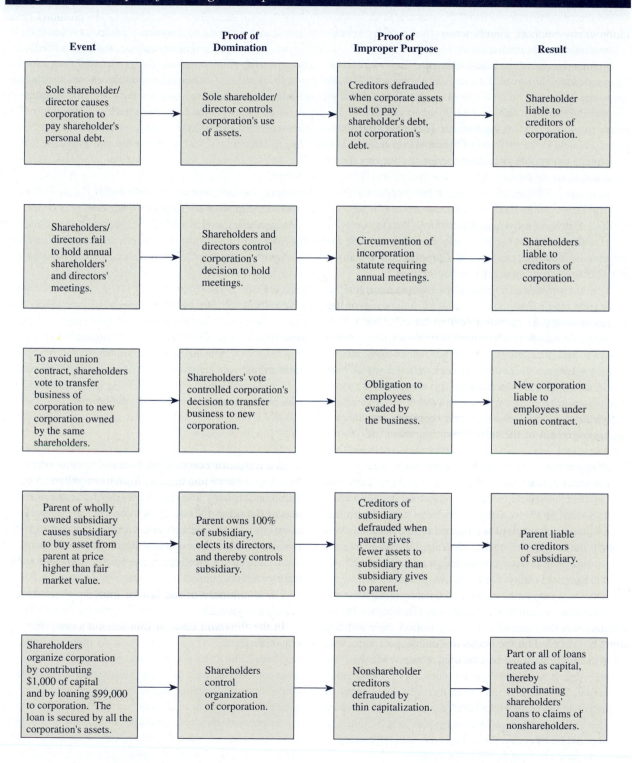

Event	Proof of Domination	Proof of Improper Purpose	Result
Sole shareholder/director causes corporation to pay shareholder's personal debt.	Sole shareholder/director controls corporation's use of assets.	Creditors defrauded when corporate assets used to pay shareholder's debt, not corporation's debt.	Shareholder liable to creditors of corporation.
Shareholders/directors fail to hold annual shareholders' and directors' meetings.	Shareholders and directors control corporation's decision to hold meetings.	Circumvention of incorporation statute requiring annual meetings.	Shareholders liable to creditors of corporation.
To avoid union contract, shareholders vote to transfer business of corporation to new corporation owned by the same shareholders.	Shareholders' vote controlled corporation's decision to transfer business to new corporation.	Obligation to employees evaded by the business.	New corporation liable to employees under union contract.
Parent of wholly owned subsidiary causes subsidiary to buy asset from parent at price higher than fair market value.	Parent owns 100% of subsidiary, elects its directors, and thereby controls subsidiary.	Creditors of subsidiary defrauded when parent gives fewer assets to subsidiary than subsidiary gives to parent.	Parent liable to creditors of subsidiary.
Shareholders organize corporation by contributing $1,000 of capital and by loaning $99,000 to corporation. The loan is secured by all the corporation's assets.	Shareholders control organization of corporation.	Nonshareholder creditors defrauded by thin capitalization.	Part or all of loans treated as capital, thereby subordinating shareholders' loans to claims of nonshareholders.

Bingham v. Goldberg, Marchesano, Kohlman, Inc.   *637 A.2d 81 (D.C. App 1994)*

In the summer 1983, Joan Bingham, Mortimer Zuckerman, and Anne Peretz formed a corporation, PFP, Inc., to explore the feasibility of publishing a weekly newspaper in Washington, D.C. The newspaper would be named The Washington Weekly. *Initially, they contributed $50,000 to the corporation. At the organization meeting, Bingham, Zuckerman, and Peretz were named initial directors, Bingham was elected president, and James Glassman was appointed vice president, treasurer, secretary, and acting publisher. In December 1983, after it was determined that such a newspaper would be feasible, further contributions were made to PFP. Bingham contributed $427,500, Anne Peretz invested $125,500, the Peretz Family Investments put in $100,000, Zuckerman contributed $100,000, and Martin Peretz added $7,000.*

In late 1983, PFP hired Goldberg, Marchesano, Kohlman, Inc. (GMK), to assist with advertising and marketing The Washington Weekly. *Glassman signed the contract for PFP. The contract provided for continuing the relationship on a month-to-month basis.*

In April 1984, in order to raise additional capital for the newspaper, a limited partnership, Washington Weekly Limited (WWL), was formed. The sole general partner of WWL was PFP. Bingham signed the limited partnership agreement as president of the general partner, PFP. When WWL was formed, PFP contributed capital of $1,022,727 to the limited partnership, including all ownership of the newspaper The Washington Weekly. *None of PFP's liabilities were transferred to WWL. PFP retained cash assets of $79,000. PFP also expected to receive management fees from WWL in exchange for its managing WWL as the general partner.*

GMK provided advertising and marketing services to The Washington Weekly *until September 1984. PFP made payments of more than $77,000 to GMK after the limited partnership was formed, but was delinquent in other payments to GMK. In late August, GMK contacted PFP about the late payments. In response, James Rice,* The Washington Weekly's *general manager, sent a letter to GMK terminating the monthly retainer agreement with GMK. The letter included Bingham's signature and listed her as publisher. In late September, Bingham wrote to Goldberg confirming the termination of the monthly retainer agreement and concluding, "We really appreciated all your good advice." Between February and September 1984, PFP paid GMK over $79,000, but still owed over $46,000.*

Subsequently, The Washington Weekly *was unprofitable and the decision was made to cease its publication. The assets of PFP were insufficient to pay the remaining $46,000 debt owed to GMK. GMK then sued Bingham, claiming that she was personally liable to GMK. The trial court found Bingham liable to GMK, and Bingham appealed.*

Wagner, Associate Judge   GMK contends that Bingham used the corporation as an alter-ego and so dominated its affairs that she should be subject to personal liability for the debt owed by PFP to GMK. The general rule has been that the corporate entity will be respected and that its obligations will not be imposed upon a particular individual unless a party seeking to disregard the corporate entity has proved that there is (1) unity of ownership and interest, and (2) use of the corporate form to perpetrate fraud or wrong. We have recognized a modification to this rule which rejects the requirement that fraud must be shown. Instead, considerations of justice and equity may justify piercing the corporate veil. Whether there is sufficient showing of a unity of ownership and interest will depend upon such factors as (1) whether corporate formalities have been disregarded, (2) whether corporate funds and assets have been extensively intermingled with personal assets, (3) inadequate initial capitalization, and (4) fraudulent use of the corporation to protect personal business from the claims of creditors.

When the evidence is viewed against these standards, there is no basis to conclude that there was a unity of ownership and interest. The record contains numerous documents evidencing the corporation's observance of corporate formalities. Among them are copies of the articles, the D.C. Certificate of Incorporation, the Resolution for Bank Accounts, minutes of meetings of the Board of Directors and of shareholders, consent to postponement of meeting, corporate by-laws, and stock certificates. Final decisionmaking authority rested with the Board of Directors of the corporation, and it was the Board's decision to terminate publication of the paper.

There is also no evidence that Bingham's personal funds were commingled with the corporation's assets or that the corporation made a preferential payment to her. What the evidence shows is that, in addition to her capital contribution to the corporation, Bingham loaned the corporation $300,000 and that she later forgave the debt. Contrary to GMK's assertion, there is no evidence that Bingham actually seized the

ETHICS IN ACTION

Large multinational corporations and smaller closely held corporations use multiple corporations to manage their tax, contract, and tort liability. As we will learn in Chapter 42, American corporations set up subsidiaries in Delaware to take advantage of its low taxes. Also, if a corporation wants to engage in a risky new venture in a country with a volatile political climate, the corporation will almost always conduct the business in a wholly owned subsidiary.

Even in the absence of an abnormal risk, many corporations create a structure like the following, in which parts of the corporation's business, such as finance, sales, and manufacturing, are placed in separate corporations, each wholly owned by the parent corporation:

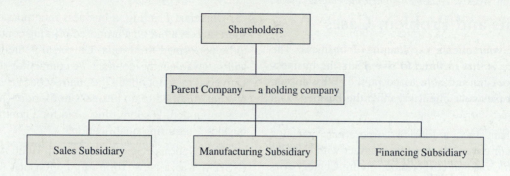

The parent company is a holding company that owns all the shares of the subsidiaries. Often, it also provides management services to the subsidiaries; in such cases, usually all employees working for the subsidiaries are assigned by the parent holding company, which receives a management fee from the subsidiaries and allocates employees to the subsidiaries as needed. The holding company will also be the capital-raising arm of the business because its cost of capital is usually lower than the individual subsidiaries' costs of capital.

As far as corporation law is concerned, this parent–subsidiary structure allows the business to isolate liability. Thus, if one subsidiary is unable to pay its obligations and its assets lost, the assets of the other subsidiaries are preserved.

- Is it ethical for a business to set up such a parent–subsidiary structure? Would a profit maximizer be likely to set up such a structure?

- If a subsidiary becomes insolvent and is unable to pay its debts, would its creditors appreciate that neither the parent nor the other subsidiaries are liable to the creditors? Is it important that a creditor chose to do business with the subsidiary and could have examined its financial position before extending credit to the subsidiary?

- Would a tort victim who was injured by a product sold by the sales subsidiary appreciate that only its assets are available to pay his tort claim? Is it important that the victim is ignorant of corporation law and is not aware that the parent and subsidiaries are separate corporations? Does a tort victim have the same ability as a contract creditor to check out the corporate structure of the business before being injured by the product? Would a believer in justice theory see a difference between a contract creditor and a tort victim?

corporation's computer equipment, although there is evidence that she had a security interest in it. Thus, we do not agree with GMK that there was either a commingling of assets or a preferential payment.

Finally, there is no basis to conclude that the corporation was undercapitalized initially or that the transfer of assets to PFP was undertaken as a fraud on creditors. On the contrary, cash in excess of $1 million was invested into the corpora-tion initially. We find no attempt to defraud creditors in the formation of WWL and PFP's purchase of a general partnership interest in the partnership. Thus, the basic elements for disregarding the corporate entity are absent here. The trial court's ruling imposing personal liability upon Bingham cannot be premised upon piercing the corporate veil.

Judgment reversed in favor of Bingham.

Problems and Problem Cases

1. One of your clients is planning a business. The client's hope is that in three to five years the business will be successful and able to go public. Why do you recommend that your client organize the business as a corporation?

2. Sculptchair, Inc., a Florida corporation, owned a patent to chair covers. It signed a contract with Century Arts, Ltd., a Canadian corporation, giving Century Arts exclusive rights under the patent to manufacture and sell chair covers. Century Arts was owned entirely by Mary Bien and Phyllis Rich. Almost immediately, Century Arts failed to make payments under the contract to Sculptchair, which terminated the contract. Century Arts went out of business. Bien and Rich formed a new Canadian corporation, Chair Décor, Inc., which carried on the business of Century Arts. Soon after, Sculptchair sued Chair Décor in a Florida court on the grounds that it was infringing Sculptchair's patent. Chair Décor argued that it could not be sued in a Florida court. Was Chair Décor right?

3. Debra Hervish, a resident of Florida, purchased 14 pieces of furniture from Growables, Inc., a furniture store incorporated and doing business in Florida. Planning to move to Louisiana, she asked Growables to ship the furniture to Louisiana. Growables hired Ryder Truck Lines to ship the furniture to Louisiana. When the furniture arrived in Louisiana, Hervish found that every piece was damaged. Hervish sued Growables in a Louisiana trial court. Does the Louisiana trial court have jurisdiction over Growables?

4. A Hawaiian statute imposed a 20 percent wholesale excise tax on liquor sold in Hawaii. To encourage the development of Hawaiian liquor, the statute exempted from taxation Okolehao, a brandy distilled from the root of the ti plant, a native Hawaiian shrub. Bacchus Imports, a liquor wholesaler, claimed that the excise tax violated the commerce clause. Was Bacchus correct?

5. Universal Printing, a business incorporated in Missouri, makes a bid on a proposed printing contract that is to be performed in Florida. Universal is the low bidder and is awarded the contract. A competitor argues that Universal may not obtain the contract because Universal had not qualified to do business in Florida when the bid was submitted. Is submitting a bid for a contract "doing business" requiring qualification?

6. The National Steeplechase and Hunt Association (NSHA) was a New York corporation that sanctioned, regulated, and supervised steeplechase races. NSHA sanctioned three steeplechase races in Kentucky. Each sanctioned event lasted no more than four days each year. NSHA promulgated steeplechase rules; approved the racecourses, race officials, and the financial responsibility of the sponsoring organization; received entries for each event by telephone or mail; assembled the information on the events; and prepared a booklet and identification badges for each meet. All these functions were performed in NSHA's New York office. The NSHA had no employees or offices in Kentucky. All communications were conducted by telephone or mail. NSHA leased fences and jumps to the sponsoring organization; the NSHA driver did not assist the local organization in setting up the equipment. Was NSHA required to qualify to do business in Kentucky?

7. Montana Merchandising, Inc. (MMI), is the sole shareholder of ECA Environmental Management Services, Inc. For over a year, ECA has held no shareholders or board of directors meetings. Every ECA director is also a director of MMI. MMI manages ECA's bank accounts. MMI regularly transfers ECA's funds into MMI's accounts without compensation. MMI has financed ECA's operations by lending $1,500,000 to ECA, a debt that is secured by all of ECA's assets. Has MMI risked being liable for ECA's liabilities?

8. Eric Dahlbeck incorporated Viking Construction, Inc. with an initial capital of $3,000. Dahlbeck also made a $7,000 loan to Viking. Viking had as assets 65 lots of land held for development, which lots cost $430,000. Viking became unable to pay its creditors, who sought to pierce the corporate veil and hold Dahlbeck liable. Were the creditors successful?

9. New York law required that every taxicab company carry $10,000 of accident liability insurance for each cab in its fleet. The purpose of the law was to ensure that passengers and pedestrians injured by cabs operated by these companies would be adequately compensated for their injuries. Carlton organized 10 corporations, each owning and operating two taxicabs in New York City. Each of these corporations carried $20,000 of liability insurance. Carlton was the principal shareholder of each corporation. The vehicles, the only freely transferable assets of these corporations, were collateral for claims of secured creditors. The 10 corporations were operated more or less as a unit with respect to supplies, repairs, and employees. Walkovszky was severely injured when he was run down by one of the taxicabs. He sued Carlton personally, alleging that the multiple corporate structure amounted to fraud upon those who might be injured by the taxicabs. Should the court pierce the corporate veil to reach Carlton individually?

10. Kommak, Inc. is a financial consulting company. It has 10 shareholders, all of whom are on the company's board of directors. Kommak is considering expanding its business by entering two new lines of business: investment banking and venture capital investment. Some of the shareholder–directors of the corporation have expressed concern that the new lines of business create new risks for the corporation and threaten to bring down the entire company if liabilities incurred by those parts of the business cannot be paid from income produced by those parts. Propose a parent–subsidiary structure that best manages Kommak's liability risks associated with the new lines of business. List the actions that should be taken and to prevent any piercing of the veils between the parent and the subsidiaries.

11. Castleberry, Branscum, and Byboth each owned one-third of the shares of a furniture-moving business, Texan Transfer, Inc. Branscum formed Elite Moving Company, a business that competed with Texan Transfer. Castleberry objected and sued to claim part ownership of Elite Moving. Branscum threatened Castleberry that he would not receive any return on his investment in Texan Transfer unless he abandoned his claim of ownership of Elite Moving. Consequently, Castleberry sold his shares back to Texan Transfer for a $42,000 promissory note. Gradually, Elite Moving took over more and more of the business of Texan Transfer. Texan Transfer allowed Elite Moving to use its employees and trucks. Elite Moving advertised for business, while Texan Transfer did not. Elite Moving prospered, while Texan Transfer's business declined. As a result, Castleberry was paid only $1,000 of the $42,000 promissory note. Did Castleberry have any grounds to hold Branscum liable for the unpaid portion of the note?

Online Research: Your State's or Country's Corporation Law

Find a website that posts the corporation law of your state or country. All state governments have online access to their statutes, and a few countries do as well. When you find the statute, determine what a foreign or alien corporation must do in your state or country to qualify to do business.

42

ORGANIZATION AND FINANCIAL STRUCTURE OF CORPORATIONS

A client has sought your assistance before incorporating a business that will buy and sell fine art. The client will enter the business with three other associates, all about 35 years old. They plan to own equal shares of the business and to manage it together. The business has not yet been incorporated.

• Your client and her associates identify five valuable paintings they want to purchase. To reduce their personal liability on the contracts to purchase the paintings, what do you recommend they do prior to signing the purchase contracts?

• Your client states that she wants to incorporate the business because a corporation's shares are freely transferable, making it easy for shareholders to liquidate their investments. You know better. Explain to your client why free transferability of the shares as a legal matter is a problem for her and her associates. Also explain to your client why free transferability of the shares as a practical matter does not exist. What should your client do to address the share transferability issues?

A PERSON DESIRING TO incorporate a business must comply with the applicable corporation law. Failing to comply can create various problems. For example, a person may make a contract on behalf of the corporation before it is incorporated. Is the corporation liable on this contract? Is the person who made the contract on behalf of the prospective corporation liable on the contract? Do the people who thought that they were shareholders of a corporation have limited liability, or do they have unlimited liability as partners of a partnership?

Promoters and Preincorporation Transactions

A **promoter** of a corporation incorporates a business, organizes its initial management, and raises its initial capital. Typically, a promoter discovers a business or an idea

to be developed, finds people who are willing to invest in the business, negotiates the contracts necessary for the initial operation of the proposed venture, incorporates the business, and helps management start the operation of the business. Consequently, a promoter may engage in many acts prior to the incorporation of the business. As a result, the promoter may have liability on the contracts he negotiates on behalf of the prospective corporation. In addition, the corporation may *not* be liable on the contracts the promoter makes on its behalf.

Corporation's Liability on Preincorporation Contracts

A nonexistent corporation has no liability on contracts made by a promoter prior to its incorporation. This is because the corporation does not exist.

Even when the corporation comes into existence, it does not automatically become liable on a preincorporation contract made by a promoter on its behalf. It cannot be held liable as a principal whose agent made the contracts because the promoter was not its agent and the corporation was not in existence when the contracts were made.

The only way a corporation may become bound on a promoter's preincorporation contracts is by the corporation's **adoption** of the promoter's contracts. Adoption is similar to the agency concept of ratification, which is covered in Chapter 36. For a corporation to adopt a promoter's contract, the corporation must accept the contract with knowledge of all its material facts.

Acceptance may be express or implied. The corporation's knowing receipt of the benefits of the contract is sufficient for acceptance. For example, a promoter makes a preincorporation contract with a genetic engineer, requiring the engineer to work for a prospective corporation for 10 years. After incorporation, the promoter presents the contract to the board of directors. Although the board takes no formal action to accept the contract, the board allows the engineer to work for the corporation for one year as the contract provides and pays him the salary required by the contract. The board's actions constitute an acceptance of the contract, binding the corporation to the contract for its 10-year term. The *Crye-Leike* case is another example of a corporation adopting a preincorporation contract.

Promoter's Liability on Preincorporation Contracts

A promoter and her copromoters are jointly and severally liable on preincorporation contracts the promoter negotiates in the name of the nonexistent corporation. This liability exists even when the promoters' names do not appear on the contract. Promoters are also jointly and severally liable for torts committed by their copromoters prior to incorporation.

A promoter retains liability on a preincorporation contract until **novation** occurs. For novation to occur, the corporation and the third party must agree to release the promoter from liability and to substitute the corporation for the promoter as the party liable on the contract. Usually, novation will occur by express or implied agreement of all the parties.

If the corporation is not formed, a promoter remains liable on a preincorporation contract unless the third party releases the promoter from liability. In addition, the mere formation of the corporation does not release a promoter from liability. A promoter remains liable on a preincorporation contract even after the corporation's adoption of the contract, since adoption does not auto-

matically release the promoter. The corporation cannot by itself relieve the promoter of liability to the third party; the third party must also agree, expressly or impliedly, to release the promoter from liability.

A few courts have held that a promoter is not liable on preincorporation contracts if the third party *knew of the nonexistence* of the corporation yet insisted that the promoter sign the contract on behalf of the nonexistent corporation. Other courts have found that the promoter is not liable if the third party clearly stated that he would *look only to the prospective corporation* for performance.

Recently, courts have held that the Model Business Corporation Act (MBCA) permits a promoter to escape liability for preincorporation contracts when the promoter has made some effort to incorporate the business and believes the corporation is in existence. The MBCA rule is discussed below in the section titled, Defective Attempts to Incorporate. The *Sivers* case, which follows that section, is an example of the application of the MBCA promoter liability rule.

Obtaining a Binding Preincorporation Contract

While it may be desirable for the promoter to escape liability on a preincorporation contract, there is one disadvantage: Only when the promoter is liable on the preincorporation contract is the other party liable on the contract. This means that when the promoter is not liable on the contract, the other party to the contract may rescind the contract at any time prior to adoption by the corporation. Once the corporation has adopted the contract, the corporation and the third party are liable on it, and the contract cannot be rescinded without the consent of both parties.

To maintain the enforceability of a preincorporation contract prior to adoption, a promoter may want to be liable on a preincorporation contract at least until the corporation comes into existence and adopts the contract. To limit his liability, however, the promoter may wish to have his liability cease automatically upon adoption. The promoter should ensure that the contract has an **automatic novation clause.** For example, a preincorporation contract may read that "the promoter's liability on this contract shall terminate upon the corporation's adoption of this contract."

Instead of using automatic novation clauses, today most well-advised promoters incorporate the business prior to making any contracts for the corporation. By doing so, only the corporation and the third party—and not the promoter—have liability on the contract.

Crye-Leike Realtors, Inc. v. WDM, Inc.
1998 Tenn. App. LEXIS 641 (Ct. App. Tenn. 1998)

On November 10, 1993, George Richert and Colman Borowsky executed a real estate brokerage agreement under which Richert appointed Borowsky, a real estate broker with Crye-Leike Realtors, Inc., as his sole and exclusive real estate broker to obtain commercial space for Richert's business. Although the term of the agreement was 12 months, it could be terminated by either party upon 30 days' written notice. Both parties understood that Richert would form a new corporation that would actually lease the property. Richert represented that he would be the chief executive officer of the new company and that he would have the authority to execute agreements on its behalf. Because the corporation was not yet in existence, however, Richert signed the agreement in his individual capacity. Borowsky signed the agreement on behalf of Crye-Leike.

In late November or early December, Borowsky first learned that Richert's new company would be named WDM, Inc. Richert formed WDM, Inc., on December 7, 1993. Initially, Richert and two other people owned all of WDM's stock. They later sold the stock to a subsidiary of Derlan Industries. Richert became WDM's president and chief executive officer.

Sometime in December 1993, Borowsky showed Richert a potential space at Interstate Industrial Park in Memphis. Borowsky prepared a written offer to lease the space and submitted it to the landlord, Belz Enterprises. The offer was made on behalf of WDM, Inc., and Richert signed the offer as WDM's president. Borowsky believed that a lease agreement with Belz was "a done deal." When the deal was not consummated as planned, however, Borowsky became concerned that Richert and WDM were "bailing out" on him. At some point, Borowsky began to suspect that Richert was instead dealing with another real estate broker, a violation of the contract signed by Richert and Borowsky.

On February 22, 1994, Richert, on behalf of WDM and with the assistance of a broker other than Borowsky, executed a lease agreement for space in the Bellbrook Business Park. Neither Borowsky nor Crye-Leike received a commission from the lease transaction. By letter dated February 23, 1994, Richert terminated his agreement with Crye-Leike and Borowsky. Richert wrote the letter on WDM stationery, and he signed the letter on behalf of WDM as its president and chief executive officer.

Crye-Leike brought an action for breach of contract against WDM. The trial court granted WDM's motion for summary judgment on the grounds that WDM was not bound on the contract with Crye-Leike because it had not adopted or ratified the contract. Crye-Leike appealed.

Farmer, Justice   A corporation may become liable on a preincorporation contract executed by its promoter if the corporation subsequently ratifies or adopts the contract. Ratification is the express or implied adoption and confirmation by the corporation of a contract entered into on the corporation's behalf by a promoter who purported to have the authority to act as the corporation's agent. In order for a ratification to occur, the corporation, having full knowledge of the facts, must accept the benefits of the promoter's contract. Moreover, the corporation, either by the circumstances or by its affirmative election, must indicate an intention to adopt the contract as its own.

After it was incorporated, WDM began to receive the benefits of Richert's contract with Crye-Leike. Borowsky continued to search for suitable property for WDM to conduct its business. These efforts included contacting various landlords and other brokers, showing different properties to WDM, and preparing an offer to lease space on behalf of WDM. The corporation also had full knowledge of the facts in this case because Richert, WDM's president and chief executive officer, had full knowledge of the contract executed by Richert and of

Borowsky's subsequent efforts to find suitable space for WDM. Finally, the corporation intended to adopt the contract. Pursuant to the contract, in January 1994 Borowsky submitted an offer to Belz Enterprises on behalf of WDM for the lease of industrial space. Richert signed the offer on behalf of WDM, Inc., as the corporation's president. This evidence supports Crye-Leike's claim that WDM ratified or adopted the contract after its incorporation and that, in actuality, Borowsky was representing WDM, and not Richert.

WDM and Richert contend that Richert's knowledge of the facts could not be imputed to WDM and that, upon becoming a corporate officer, Richert could not ratify his prior actions as a promoter. This argument is without merit. Although, as a general rule, the knowledge of a single promoter cannot be imputed to the corporation, exceptions to this rule have been found where the promoters become directors and stockholders in the corporation or are the sole or controlling stockholders. Moreover, WDM was aware of the pertinent facts in this case. During all times relevant hereto, Richert had authority to act on the corporation's behalf and to bind the corporation.

We also reject the contention that WDM could not ratify or adopt the contract with Crye-Leike because Richert signed the contract in his individual capacity and not on behalf of the corporation. WDM accepted the benefits of the contract between Richert and Crye-Leike. These benefits consisted of Borowsky's continued efforts to locate suitable space for WDM to conduct its business. WDM never sought to reject the contract or the benefits it received thereunder. When Borowsky submitted a lease proposal to Belz Enterprises, Richert signed the proposal on behalf of WDM as the corporation's president. Even when Richert sent the letter to Borowsky notifying him that the agreement was being terminated, Richert used WDM stationery and signed the letter as WDM's president and chief executive officer. We conclude that this is sufficient evidence of WDM's ratification of the contract, despite the fact that Richert signed the contract in his individual capacity rather than in his capacity as an officer of the to be formed corporation.

Judgment reversed in favor of Crye-Leike; remanded for trial.

Preincorporation Share Subscriptions

Promoters sometimes use **preincorporation share subscriptions** to ensure that the corporation will have adequate capital when it begins its business. Under the terms of a share subscription, a prospective shareholder offers to buy a specific number of the corporation's shares at a stated price. Under the Model Business Corporation Act (MBCA), a prospective shareholder may not revoke a preincorporation subscription for a six-month period, in the absence of a contrary provision in the subscription. Generally, corporate acceptance of preincorporation subscriptions occurs by action of the board of directors after incorporation.

Promoters have no liability on preincorporation share subscriptions. They have a duty, however, to make a good faith effort to bring the corporation into existence. When a corporation fails to accept a preincorporation subscription or becomes insolvent, the promoter is not liable to the disappointed subscriber, in the absence of fraud or other wrongdoing by the promoter.

Today, most promoters incorporate the business and obtain promises to buy shares from prospective shareholders. These promises, which may take the form of postincorporation subscriptions, are discussed later in this chapter.

Relation of Promoter and Prospective Corporation

A promoter of a nonexistent corporation is not an agent of the prospective corporation but nonetheless owes fiduciary duties to it. A promoter is not an agent of prospective investors in the business because they did not appoint him and they have no power to control him.

Although not an agent of the proposed corporation or its investors, a promoter owes a **fiduciary duty** to the corporation and to its prospective investors. A promoter owes such parties a duty of full disclosure and honesty. For example, a promoter breaches this duty when she diverts money received from prospective shareholders to pay her expenses, unless the shareholders agree to such payment. The fiduciary duty also prevents a promoter from diverting a business opportunity from the corporation and giving it to himself instead. In addition, the promoter may not purchase shares of the corporation at a price lower than that paid by the public shareholders.

A promoter may not profit personally by transacting secretly with the corporation in his personal capacity. The promoter's failure to disclose her interest in the transaction and the material facts permits the corporation to rescind the transaction or to recover the promoter's secret profit. On the other hand, the promoter's full disclosure of her interest and the material facts of the transaction to an independent board of directors that approves the transaction prevents the corporation from recovering the promoter's profit. Note, however, that when a promoter is a director, approval of the transaction by the board of directors is not sufficient; the transaction must be intrinsically fair to the corporation.

Liability of Corporation to Promoter

Valuable as the services of a promoter may be to a prospective corporation and to society, a corporation is generally not required to compensate a promoter for her promotional services, or even her expenses, unless the corporation has agreed expressly to compensate the promoter. The justification for this rule is that the promoter is self-appointed and acts for a corporation that is not in existence.

Nonetheless, a corporation may choose to reimburse the promoter for her reasonable expenses and to pay her the value of her services to the corporation. Corporations often compensate their promoters with shares. The MBCA permits the issuance of shares for a promoter's preincorporation services.

To ensure that she is compensated for her services, a promoter may tie herself to a person or property that the corporation needs to succeed. For example, a promoter may purchase the invention that the corporation was formed to exploit. Another way to ensure compensation is by the promoter's dominating the board of directors during the early months of its life. By doing so, the promoter may direct the corporation to compensate her.

Incorporation

Anyone seeking to incorporate a business must decide where to do so. If the business of a proposed corporation is to be primarily *intrastate,* it is usually cheaper to incorporate in the state where the corporation's business is to be conducted. For the business that is primarily *interstate,* however, the business may benefit by incorporating in a state different from the state in which it has its principal place of business.

Incorporation fees and taxes, annual fees, and other fees such as those on the transfer of shares or the dissolution of the corporation vary considerably from state to state. Delaware has been a popular state in which to incorporate because its fees and taxes tend to be low.

Promoters frequently choose to incorporate in a state whose corporation statute and court decisions grant managers broad management discretion. For example, it is easier to pay a large dividend and to effect a merger in Delaware than in many other states.

Steps in Incorporation

There are only a few requirements for incorporation. It is a fairly simple process and can be accomplished inexpensively in most cases. The steps prescribed by the incorporation statutes of the different states vary, but they generally include the following, which appear in the MBCA:

1. Preparation of articles of incorporation.
2. Signing and authenticating the articles by one or more incorporators.
3. Filing the articles with the secretary of state, accompanied by the payment of specified fees.
4. Receipt of a copy of the articles of incorporation stamped "Filed" by the secretary of state, accompanied by a fee receipt. (Some states retain the old MBCA rule requiring receipt of a certificate of incorporation issued by the secretary of state.)
5. Holding an organization meeting for the purpose of adopting bylaws, electing officers, and transacting other business.

Articles of Incorporation The basic governing document of the corporation is the **articles of incorporation** (sometimes called the charter). The articles are similar to a constitution. They state many of the rights and responsibilities of the corporation, its management, and its shareholders. Figure 1 lists the contents of the articles.

The corporation must have a name that is distinguishable from the name of any other corporation incorporated or qualified to do business in the state. The name must in-

ETHICS IN ACTION

Domestic Tax Havens

In recent years, some American companies have reincorporated all or part of their businesses in states that offer favorable tax treatment. For example, Limited Brands Inc., the owner of the Limited, Bath & Body Works, and Victoria's Secret chains, has incorporated seven subsidiaries in Delaware. The primary function of the subsidiaries is to own the chains' trademarks. The subsidiaries charge the retail chains high fees to use the trademarks. This parent–subsidiary structure allows the business to transfer hundreds of millions of dollars each year from retail outlets in high-tax states like New York into Delaware subsidiaries that

pay no state tax. Delaware is the most used domestic tax haven, but Nevada and Florida also provide favorable tax treatment for corporations.

- Is it ethical and socially responsible for an American corporation to incorporate its business wholly or in part in states that have low tax rates? Would a profit maximizer incorporate where tax rates are lowest? Would a believer in rights theory?
- If you were a state legislator in a state with high income taxes that is losing incorporations to Delaware, what legislation would you introduce? Would your answer depend on whether you were a utilitarian or a believer in justice theory?

Figure 1   *Contents of Articles of Incorporation (pursuant to MBCA)*

The following *must* be in the articles:

1. The name of the corporation.
2. The number of shares that the corporation has authority to issue.
3. The address of the initial registered office of the corporation and the name of its registered agent.
4. The name and address of each incorporator.

The following *may* be included in the articles:

1. The names and addresses of the individuals who are to serve as the initial directors.
2. The purpose of the corporation.
3. The duration of the corporation.
4. The par value of shares of the corporation.
5. Additional provisions not inconsistent with law for managing the corporation, regulating the internal affairs of the corporation, and establishing the powers of the corporation and its directors and shareholders.

clude the word *corporation, incorporated, company,* or *limited,* or the abbreviation *corp., inc., co.,* or *ltd.*

The MBCA does not require the inclusion of a statement of purpose in the articles. When a purpose is stated, it is sufficient to state, alone or together with specific purposes, that the corporation may engage in "any lawful activity."

The MBCA permits a corporation to have perpetual existence. If desired, the articles of incorporation may provide for a shorter duration.

Most of the state corporation statutes require the articles to recite the initial capitalization of the business. Usually, the statutes require that there be a minimum amount of initial capital, such as $1,000. Since such a small amount of capital is rarely enough to protect creditors adequately, the MBCA dispenses with the need to recite a minimum amount of capital.

The articles may contain additional provisions not inconsistent with law for managing the corporation, regulating the internal affairs of the corporation, and establishing the powers of the corporation and its directors and shareholders. For example, these additional provisions may contain the procedures for electing directors, the quorum requirements for shareholders' and directors' meetings, and the dividend rights of shareholders.

The MBCA specifies that one or more persons, including corporations, partnerships, and unincorporated associations, may serve as the **incorporators.** Incorporators have no function beyond lending their names and signatures to the process of bringing the corporation into existence. No special liability attaches to a person merely because she serves as an incorporator.

Filing Articles of Incorporation The articles of incorporation must be delivered to the office of the secretary of state, and a filing fee must be paid. The office of the secretary of state reviews the articles of incorporation that are delivered to it. If the articles contain everything that is required, the secretary of state stamps the articles "Filed" and returns a copy of the stamped articles to the corporation along with a receipt for payment of incorporation fees. Some states require a duplicate filing of the articles with an office—usually the county recorder's office—in the county in which the corporation has its principal place of business.

The existence of the corporation begins when the articles are filed by the secretary of state. Filing of the articles is conclusive proof of the existence of the corporation.

Because the articles of incorporation embody the basic contract between a corporation and its shareholders, shareholders must approve most changes in the articles. For example, when the articles are amended to increase the number of authorized shares, shareholder approval is required.

The Organization Meeting After the articles of incorporation have been filed by the secretary of state, an organization meeting is held. Usually, it is the first formal meeting of the directors. Frequently, only bylaws are adopted and officers elected. The function of the bylaws is to supplement the articles of incorporation by defining more precisely the powers, rights, and responsibilities of the corporation, its managers, and its shareholders and by stating other rules under which the corporation and its activities will be governed. Its common contents are listed in Figure 2.

Figure 2   *Contents of the Bylaws*

1. The authority of the officers and the directors, specifying what they may or may not do.
2. The time and place at which the annual shareholders' meetings will be held.
3. The procedure for calling special meetings of shareholders.
4. The procedures for shareholders' and directors' meetings, including whether more than a majority is required for approval of specified actions.
5. Provisions for special committees of the board, defining their membership and the scope of their activities.
6. The procedures for the maintenance of share records.
7. The machinery for the transfer of shares.
8. The procedures and standards for the declaration and payment of dividends.

The MBCA gives the incorporators or the initial directors the power to adopt the initial bylaws. The board of directors holds the power to repeal and to amend the bylaws, unless the articles reserve this power to the shareholders. Under the MBCA, the shareholders, as the ultimate owners of the corporation, always retain the power to amend the bylaws, even if the directors also have such power. To be valid, bylaws must be consistent with the law and with the articles of incorporation.

If the organization meeting is the first meeting of the board of directors, the board may adopt a corporate seal for use on corporate documents, approve the form of share certificates, accept share subscriptions, authorize the issuance of shares, adopt preincorporation contracts, authorize reimbursement for promoters' expenses, and fix the salaries of officers.

Filing Annual Report   To retain its status as a corporation in good standing, a corporation must file an annual report with the secretary of state of the state of incorporation and pay an annual franchise fee or tax. The amount of annual franchise tax varies greatly from state to state. While the annual report includes very little information and repeats information already filed in the articles of incorporation, failure to file an annual report or pay the annual fee or tax may result in a dissolution of the corporation and an imposition of monetary penalties.

Close Corporation Elections

Close corporations face problems that normally do not affect publicly held corporations. In recognition of these problems, nearly half of the states have statutes that attend to the special needs of close corporations. For example, some corporation statutes allow a close corporation to be managed by its shareholders.

To take advantage of these close corporation statutes, most statutes require that a corporation make an *election* to be treated as a close corporation. The Statutory Close Corporation Supplement to the MBCA permits a corporation with *fewer than 50 shareholders* to elect to become a close corporation. The Close Corporation Supplement requires the articles of incorporation to state that the corporation is a statutory close corporation.

There is no penalty for a corporation's failure to make a close corporation election. The only consequence of a failure to meet the requirements is that the close corporation statutory provisions are inapplicable. Instead, statutory corporation law will treat the corporation as it treats any other general corporation.

Note, however, that even when a corporation fails to meet the statutory requirements for treatment as a close corporation, a court may decide to apply special *common law* rules applicable only to close corporations.

LOG ON

www.corporate.com
The Corporation Company is one of many Internet businesses providing incorporation assistance to new businesses. While incorporation services do not facilitate the drafting of articles and bylaws meeting the special needs of a corporation and its shareholders, at least they reduce the cost and burden of incorporating.

Defective Attempts to Incorporate

When business managers attempt to incorporate a business, sometimes they fail to comply with all the conditions for incorporation. For example, the incorporators may not have filed articles of incorporation or the directors may not have held an organization meeting. These are examples of **defective attempts to incorporate.**

One possible consequence of defective incorporation is to make the managers and the purported shareholders *personally liable* for the obligations of the defectively formed corporation. For example, an employee of an insolvent corporation drives the corporation's truck over a pedestrian. If the pedestrian proves that the corporation was defectively formed, he may be able to recover damages for his injuries from the managers and the shareholders.

A second possible consequence of defective incorporation is that a party to a contract involving the purported corporation may claim nonexistence of the corporation in order to avoid a contract made in the name of the corporation. For example, a person makes an ill-advised contract with a corporation. If the person proves that the corporation was defectively formed, he may escape liability on the contract because he made a contract with a nonexistent person, the defectively formed corporation. As an alternative, the defectively formed corporation may escape liability on the contract on the grounds that its nonexistence makes it impossible for it to have liability.

The courts have tried to determine when these two consequences should arise by making a distinction between de jure corporations, de facto corporations, corporations by estoppel, and corporations so defectively formed that they are treated as being nonexistent.

De Jure Corporation

A de jure corporation is formed when the promoters substantially comply with each of the **mandatory conditions precedent** to the incorporation of the business. Mandatory provisions are distinguished from directory provisions by statutory language and the purpose of the provision. Mandatory provisions are those that the corporation statute states "shall" or "must" be done or those that are necessary to protect the public interest. Directory provisions are those that "may" be done and that are unnecessary to protect the public interest.

For example, statutes provide that the incorporators shall file the articles of incorporation with the secretary of state. This is a mandatory provision, not only because of the use of the word *shall* but also because of the importance of a filing to protect the public interest. Other mandatory provisions include conducting an organization meeting. Directory provisions include minor matters such as the inclusion of the incorporators' addresses in the articles of incorporation.

If a corporation has complied with each mandatory provision, it is a de jure corporation and is treated as a corporation for all purposes. The validity of a de jure corporation cannot be attacked, except in a few states in which the state, in a *quo warranto* proceeding, may attack the corporation for noncompliance with a condition subsequent to incorporation, such as a failure to file an annual report with the secretary of state.

De Facto Corporation

A de facto corporation exists when the incorporators fail in some material respect to comply with all of the mandatory provisions of the incorporation statute yet comply with most mandatory provisions. There are three requirements for a de facto corporation:

1. There is a valid statute under which the corporation could be organized.

2. The promoters or managers make an honest attempt to organize under the statute. This requires substantial compliance with the mandatory provisions taken as a whole.

3. The promoters or managers exercise corporate powers. That is, they act as if they were acting for a corporation.

Generally, failing to file the articles of incorporation with the secretary of state will prevent the creation of a de facto corporation. However, a de facto corporation will exist despite the lack of an organization meeting or the failure to make a duplicate filing of the articles with a county recorder.

A de facto corporation is treated as a corporation against either an attack by a third party or an attempt of the business itself to deny that it is a corporation. The state, however, may attack the claimed corporate status of the business in a *quo warranto* action.

Corporation by Estoppel

When people hold themselves out as representing a corporation or believe themselves to be dealing with a corporation, a court will estop those people from denying the existence of a corporation. This is called **corporation by estoppel.** For example, a manager states that a business has been incorporated and induces a third person to contract with the purported corporation. The manager will not be permitted to use a failure to incorporate as a defense to the contract because he has misled others to believe reasonably that a corporation exists.

Under the doctrine of estoppel, each contract must be considered individually to determine whether either party to the contract is estopped from denying the corporation's existence.

Liability for Defective Incorporation

If people attempt to organize a corporation but their efforts are so defective that not even a corporation by estoppel is found to exist, the courts have generally held such persons to be partners with unlimited liability for the contracts and torts of the business. However, most courts impose the unlimited *contractual* liability of a partner only on those who are *actively engaged in the management* of the business or who are responsible for the defects in its organization. *Tort* liability, however, is generally imposed on everyone—the managers and the purported shareholders of the defectively formed corporation.

Modern Approaches to the Defective Incorporation Problem

As you can see, the law of defective incorporation is confusing. It becomes even more confusing when you consider that many of the defective incorporation cases look like promoter liability cases, and vice versa. A court may have difficulty deciding whether to apply the law of promoter liability or the law of defective incorporation to preincorporation contracts. It is not surprising, therefore, that modern corporation statutes have attempted to eliminate this confusion by adopting simple rules for determining the existence of a corporation and the liability of its promoters, managers, and shareholders.

The MBCA states that incorporation occurs when the articles are filed by the secretary of state. The filing of the articles is conclusive proof of the existence of the corporation, except in a proceeding brought by the state. Consequently, the incorporators may omit even a mandatory provision, yet create a corporation, provided that the secretary of state has filed the articles of incorporation. Conversely, courts have held that a failure to obtain a filing of the articles is conclusive proof of the nonexistence of the corporation, on the grounds that the MBCA eliminates the concepts of de facto corporation and corporation by estoppel.

Liability for Defective Incorporation under the MBCA The MBCA imposes joint and several liability on those persons who purport to act on behalf of a corporation and know that there has been no incorporation. Thus, managers and shareholders who both (1) *participate* in the operational decisions of the business and (2) *know* that the corporation does not exist are liable for the purported corporation's contracts and torts.

The MBCA releases from liability shareholders and others who either (1) take no part in the management of the defectively formed corporation *or* (2) mistakenly believe that the corporation is in existence. Consequently, *passive* shareholders have no liability for the obligations of a defectively formed corporation even when they know that the corporation has not been formed. Likewise, managers of a defectively formed corporation have no liability when they believe that the corporation exists.

In the following case, a promoter who mistakenly thought the corporation was in existence was not liable on a preincorporation contract he made on behalf of the corporation.

Sivers v. R & F Capital Corp.   *858 P.2d 895 (Ore. Ct. App. 1995)*

Dennis Sivers owned a warehouse in Milwaukee, Oregon. On January 12, 1990, purporting to act on behalf of R & F Capital Corporation in the position of chairman, Roy Rose signed a contract to lease the warehouse from Sivers. R & F was not yet incorporated when Rose signed the lease on behalf of R & F; R & F did not come into existence until February 9, 1990. Later in 1990, R & F breached the lease, and Sivers sued Rose claiming that Rose was personally liable on the lease. Rose asked the trial court for a directed verdict, but the trial court denied Rose's motion. Rose appealed to the Oregon Court of Appeals.

Warren, Judge   Ore. Rev. Stat. 60.054 provides:

> All persons purporting to act as or on behalf of a corporation, knowing there was no corporation, are jointly and severally liable for liabilities created while so acting.

This provision was adopted in 1987 as part of SB 303 and is virtually identical to section 2.04 of the Revised Model Business Corporation Act (RMBCA). Section 2.04 is a codification of the judicial exceptions to the general rule that those who prematurely act as, or on behalf of, a corpo-ration are personally liable on all transactions entered into or liabilities incurred before incorporation.

In proposing adoption of section 2.04 of the RMBCA in Oregon, the Task Force of the Oregon State Bar Business Law Section, which authored SB 303, wrote:

> The Bill protects participants who act honestly but subject to the mistaken belief that the articles have been filed. This section is consistent with the Revised Uniform Limited Partnership Act, which provides that limited partners who contribute capital to a partnership with

a mistaken belief that a limited partnership certificate has been filed are protected from liability.

The wording of Ore. Rev. Stat. 60.054 and the drafters' comments clearly indicate that the test for imposition of personal liability is one of actual knowledge.

Sivers argues that there are facts from which the jury could find that Rose knew that R & F was not incorporated when he signed the lease. We disagree.

Rose testified that he was a businessman who created financing packages to buy companies. His highest net worth at one point was $56 million. He had been involved in setting up many corporations. However, he had no specific experience with incorporating, because his attorneys handled those aspects of his business. For example, he did not know when a corporation formally began its existence, although he understood that documents need to be filed with the state and a copy would be returned upon incorporation.

With respect to R & F, Rose had no participation in its daily operation, other than attending board meetings and signing documents as "chairman." He entrusted Flaherty, a director of R & F, with those daily duties. Rose did not read the articles of incorporation of R & F until he was sued. He recalled that the document was given to him and he signed it in December 1989.

Rose and another R & F director testified that Flaherty was entrusted to incorporate R & F in December of 1989, but failed to do that. They both believed that R & F was incorporated in December of 1989. Rose also testified that he started investing based on that belief, and that he would not have signed any document on behalf of a corporation if he had known that it was not incorporated.

Sivers does not argue that there is direct evidence that Rose knew that the corporation had not been formed when he signed the lease. To support his argument that there was circumstantial evidence, he points to Rose's vast experience as a businessman, his failure to read the articles of incorporation, and his complete lack of responsibility for filing necessary corporate documents with the Secretary of State. His reliance on those facts is misplaced. At most they show Rose should have inquired into R & F's status and should have known that the corporation was not formed. They do not rise to the level of knowledge required by Ore. Rev. Stat. 60.054. Sivers would have us require a test of constructive knowledge. However, had the legislature intended to adopt such a test, it would not have used the unmodified term "knowing."

A more fundamental argument Sivers raises is that, although Rose testified that he believed that R & F was incorporated at the time he signed the lease, the jury could disbelieve him and affirmatively find that he had the requisite actual knowledge. That argument goes too far. Although a jury may disbelieve a witness based on demeanor, bias, motives, interest, or inconsistent statements, there must be evidence, direct or circumstantial, from which the jury can *reasonably* find that a defendant possesses the requisite knowledge. In this case, Rose maintained throughout the trial that he honestly believed that R & F was incorporated when he signed the lease. Sivers produced nothing to contradict that. The trial court should have granted Rose's motion for a directed verdict.

Judgment reversed in favor of Rose.

Incorporation of Nonprofit Corporations

Nonprofit corporations are incorporated in substantially the same manner as for-profit corporations. One or more persons serve as incorporators and deliver articles of incorporation to the secretary of state for filing. A nonprofit corporation's articles must include the name and address of the corporation and state its registered agent. Unlike a for-profit corporation, a nonprofit corporation must state that it is either a public benefit corporation, a mutual benefit corporation, or a religious corporation. A public benefit corporation is incorporated primarily for the benefit of the public—for example, a community arts council that promotes the arts. A mutual benefit corporation is designed to benefit its members—for example, a golf country club. An example of a religious corporation is a church.

A nonprofit corporation's articles must also state whether it will have members. While it is typical for nonprofit corporations to have members, the Model Nonprofit Corporation Act (MNCA) does not require a nonprofit corporation to have members. An example of a nonprofit corporation having no members is a public benefit corporation established to promote business development in a city, whose directors are appointed by the city's mayor.

A nonprofit corporation's articles may include the purpose of the corporation, its initial directors, and any matter regarding the rights and duties of the corporation and its directors and members. Each incorporator and director named in the articles must sign the articles.

A nonprofit corporation's existence begins when the secretary of state files the articles. After incorporation, the initial directors or incorporators hold an organization meeting to adopt bylaws and conduct other business.

Liability for Preincorporation Transactions

Nonprofit corporation status normally protects the members and managers from personal liability. However, when a nonprofit corporation is not formed or is defectively formed, promoters and others who transact for the nonexistent nonprofit corporation have the same liability as promoters and others who transact for a nonexistent for-profit corporation. The MNCA states the same rule as the MBCA: Persons who act on behalf of a corporation knowing there is no corporation are jointly and severally liable for all liabilities created while so acting.

Similarly, promoters have no authority to make contracts for a nonexistent nonprofit corporation. The corporation becomes liable on preincorporation contracts when its board of directors adopts the contracts.

Financing For-Profit Corporations

Any business needs money to operate and to grow. One advantage of incorporation is the large number of sources of funds that are available to businesses that incorporate. One such source is the sale of corporate **securities,** including shares, debentures, bonds, and long-term notes payable.

In addition to obtaining funds from the sale of securities, a corporation may be financed by other sources. A bank may lend money to the corporation in exchange for the corporation's short-term promissory notes, called commercial paper. Earnings provide a source of funds once the corporation is operating profitably. In addition, the corporation may use normal short-term financing, such as accounts receivable financing and inventory financing.

In this section, you will study only one source of corporate funds—a corporation's sale of securities. A corporate security may be either (1) a share in the corporation or (2) an obligation of the corporation. These two kinds of securities are called equity securities and debt securities.

Equity Securities

Every business corporation issues equity securities, which are commonly called stock or **shares.** The issuance of shares creates an ownership relationship: the holders of the shares—called stockholders or **shareholders**—are the owners of the corporation.

Modern statutes permit corporations to issue several classes of shares and to determine the rights of the various classes. Subject to minimum guarantees contained in the state business corporation law, the shareholders' rights are a matter of contract and appear in the articles of incorporation, in the bylaws, in a shareholder agreement, and on the share certificates.

Common Shares Common shares (or common stock) are a type of equity security. Ordinarily, the owners of common shares—called **common shareholders**—have the exclusive right to elect the directors, who manage the corporation.

The common shareholders often occupy a position inferior to that of other investors, notably creditors and preferred shareholders. The claims of common shareholders are subordinate to the claims of creditors and other classes of shareholders when liabilities and dividends are paid and when assets are distributed upon liquidation.

In return for this subordination, however, the common shareholders have an exclusive claim to the corporate earnings and assets that exceed the claims of creditors and other shareholders. Therefore, the common shareholders bear the major risks of the corporate venture, yet stand to profit the most if it is successful.

Preferred Shares Shares that have preferences with regard to assets or dividends over other classes of shares are called preferred shares (or preferred stock). **Preferred shareholders** are customarily given liquidation and dividend preferences over common shareholders. A corporation may have several classes of preferred shares. In such a situation, one class of preferred shares may be given preferences over another class of preferred shares. Under the MBCA, the preferences of preferred shareholders must be set out in the articles of incorporation.

The **liquidation preference** of preferred shares is usually a stated dollar amount. During a liquidation, this amount must be paid to each preferred shareholder before any common shareholder or other shareholder subordinated to the preferred class may receive his share of the corporation's assets.

Dividend preferences may vary greatly. For example, the dividends may be cumulative or noncumulative. Dividends on **cumulative** preferred shares, if not paid in any year, accumulate until paid. The entire accumulation must be paid before any dividends may be paid to common shareholders. Dividends on **noncumulative** preferred shares do not accumulate if unpaid. For such shares, only the current year's dividends must be paid to preferred shareholders prior to the payment of dividends to common shareholders.

Participating preferred shares have priority up to a stated amount or percentage of the dividends to be paid by the corporation. Then, the preferred shareholders participate with the common shareholders in additional dividends paid.

Some close corporations attempt to create preferred shares with a **mandatory dividend** right. These mandatory dividend provisions have generally been held illegal as unduly restricting the powers of the board of directors. Today, a few courts and some special close corporation statutes permit mandatory dividends.

A **redemption** provision in the articles allows a corporation at its option to repurchase preferred shareholders' shares at a price stated in the articles, despite the shareholders' unwillingness to sell. Some statutes permit the articles to give the shareholders the right to force the corporation to redeem preferred shares.

Preferred shares may be **convertible** into another class of shares, usually common shares. A **conversion** right allows a preferred shareholder to exchange her preferred shares for another class of shares, usually common shares. The conversion rate or price is stated in the articles.

Preferred shares have **voting rights** unless the articles provide otherwise. Usually, most voting rights are taken from preferred shares, except for important matters such as voting for a merger or a change in preferred shareholders' dividend rights. Rarely are preferred shareholders given the right to vote for directors, except in the event of a corporation's default in the payment of dividends.

Authorized, Issued, and Outstanding Shares

Authorized shares are shares that a corporation is permitted to issue by its articles of incorporation. A corporation may not issue more shares than are authorized. **Issued** shares are shares that have been sold to shareholders. **Outstanding** shares are shares that are currently held by shareholders. The distinctions between these terms are important. For example, a corporation pays cash, property, and share dividends only on outstanding shares. Only outstanding shares may be voted at a shareholders' meeting.

Canceled Shares Sometimes, a corporation will purchase its own shares. A corporation may cancel repurchased shares. Canceled shares do not exist: they are neither authorized, issued, nor outstanding. Since canceled shares do not exist, they cannot be reissued.

Shares Restored to Unissued Status Repurchased shares may be restored to unissued status instead of being canceled. If this is done, the shares are merely authorized and they may be reissued at a later time.

Treasury Shares If repurchased shares are neither canceled nor restored to unissued status, they are called **treasury shares.** Such shares are authorized and issued, but not outstanding. They may be sold by the corporation at a later time. The corporation may not vote them at shareholders' meetings, and it may not pay a cash or property dividend on them.

The MBCA abolishes the concept of treasury shares. It provides that repurchased shares are restored to unissued status and may be reissued, unless the articles of incorporation require cancellation.

Options, Warrants, and Rights

Equity securities include options to purchase common shares and preferred shares. The MBCA expressly permits the board of directors to issue **options** for the purchase of the corporation's shares. Share options are often issued to top-level managers as an incentive to increase the profitability of the corporation. An increase in profitability should increase the market value of the corporation's shares, resulting in increased compensation to the employees who own and exercise share options.

Warrants are options evidenced by certificates. They are sometimes part of a package of securities sold as a unit. For example, they may be sold along with notes, bonds, or even shares. Underwriters may receive warrants as part of their compensation for aiding a corporation in selling its shares to the public.

Rights are short-term certificated options that are usually transferable. Rights are used to give present security holders an option to subscribe to a proportional quantity of the same or a different security of the corporation. They are most often issued in connection with a **preemptive right** requirement, which obligates a corporation to offer each existing shareholder the opportunity to buy the corporation's newly issued shares in the same proportion as the shareholder's current ownership of the corporation's shares.

Debt Securities

Corporations have inherent power to borrow money necessary for their operations by issuing debt securities. Debt securities create a debtor–creditor relationship between the corporation and the security holder. With the typical debt security, the corporation is obligated to pay interest periodically and to pay the amount of the debt (the principal) on the maturity date. Debt securities include debentures, bonds, and notes payable.

Debentures are long-term, unsecured debt securities. Typically, a debenture has a term of 10 to 30 years. Debentures usually have indentures. An indenture is a contract that states the rights of the debenture holders. For example, an indenture defines what acts constitute default by the corporation and what rights the debenture holders have upon default. It may place restrictions on the corporation's right to issue other debt securities.

Bonds are long-term, secured debt securities that usually have indentures. They are identical to debentures except that bonds are secured by collateral. The collateral for bonds may be real property such as a building, or personal property such as a commercial airplane. If the debt is not paid, the bondholders may force the sale of the collateral and take the proceeds of the sale.

Generally, **notes** have a shorter duration than debentures or bonds. They seldom have terms exceeding five years. Notes may be secured or unsecured.

It is not uncommon for notes or debentures to be **convertible** into other securities, usually preferred or common shares. The right to convert belongs to the holder of the convertible note or debenture. This conversion right permits an investor to receive interest as a debt holder and, after conversion, to share in the increased value of the corporation as a shareholder.

Consideration for Shares

The board of directors has the power to issue shares on behalf of the corporation. The board must decide at what *price* and for what *type of consideration* it will issue the shares. Corporation statutes restrict the discretion of the board in accepting specified kinds of consideration and in determining the value of the shares it issues.

Quality of Consideration for Shares

Not all kinds of consideration in contract law are acceptable as legal consideration for shares in corporation law. To protect creditors and other shareholders, the statutes require legal consideration to have *real value*. Modern statutes, however, place few limits on the type of consideration that may be received for shares. The MBCA permits shares to be issued in return for any tangible or intangible *property* or *benefit to the corporation,* including cash, promissory notes, services performed for the corporation, contracts for services *to be performed* for the corporation, and securities of the corporation or another corporation. The rationale for the MBCA rule is a recognition that future services and promises of future services have value that is as real as that of tangible property. Consequently, for example, a corporation may issue common shares to its president in exchange for the president's commitment to work for the corporation for three years or in exchange for bonds of the corporation or debentures issued by another corporation. In addition, the MBCA permits corporations to issue shares to their promoters in consideration for their promoters' preincorporation services. This rule acknowledges that a corporation benefits from a promoter's preincorporation services.

Several states' constitutions place stricter limits on permissible consideration for shares. They provide that shares may be issued only for money paid to the corporation, labor done for the corporation, or property actually received by the corporation. Such a rule prohibits a corporation from issuing its shares for a promise to pay money or a promise to provide services to the corporation in the future.

Quantity of Consideration for Shares

The board is required to issue shares for an adequate dollar amount of consideration. Whether shares have been issued for an adequate amount of consideration depends in part on the *par value* of the shares. The more important concern, however, is whether the shares have been issued for *fair value.*

Par Value Par value is an arbitrary dollar amount that may be assigned to the shares by the articles of incorporation. Par value does not reflect the fair market value of the shares, but par value is the minimum amount of consideration for which the shares may be issued.

Shares issued for less than par value are called **discount shares.** The board of directors is liable to the corporation for issuing shares for less than par value. A shareholder who purchases shares from the corporation for less than par value is liable to the corporation for the difference between the par value and the amount she paid.

Fair Value It is not always enough, however, for the board to issue shares for their par value. Many times, shares are worth more than their par value. In addition, many shares today do not have a par value. In fact, the MBCA purports to eliminate the concept of par value as it affects the issuance of shares. In all cases, the board must exercise care to ensure that the corporation receives the *fair value* of the shares it issues. If there are no par value problems, the board's judgment as to the amount of consideration that is received for the shares is *conclusive* when the board acts in good faith, exercises the care of ordinarily prudent directors, and acts in the best interests of the corporation.

Disputes may arise concerning the value of property that the corporation receives for its shares. The board's valuation of the consideration is conclusive if it acts in good faith with the care of prudent directors and in a manner it reasonably believes to be in the best interests of the corporation. When the board impermissibly overvalues the consideration for shares, the shareholder receives **watered shares.** Both the board and the shareholder are liable to the corporation when there is a watered shares problem.

When a shareholder pays less than the amount of consideration determined by the board of directors, the corporation or its creditors may sue the shareholder to recover the deficit. When a shareholder has paid the proper amount of consideration, the shares are said to be *fully paid and nonassessable.*

Accounting for Consideration Received The consideration received by a corporation for its equity securities appears in the equity or capital accounts in the shareholders' equity section of the corporation's balance sheet. The **stated capital** account records the product of the number of shares outstanding multiplied by the par value of each share. When the shares are sold for more than par value, the excess or surplus consideration received by the corporation is **capital surplus.**

Under the MBCA, the terms *stated capital* and *capital surplus* have been eliminated. All consideration received for shares is lumped under one accounting entry for that class of shares, such as common equity.

Resales of Shares The par value of shares is important *only when the shares are issued* by the corporation. Since treasury shares are issued but not outstanding, the corporation does not issue treasury shares when it resells them. Therefore, the board may sell treasury shares for less than par, provided that it sells the shares for an amount equal to their fair value.

Because par value and fair value are designed to ensure only that the corporation receives adequate consideration for its shares, a shareholder may buy shares from another

---

THE GLOBAL BUSINESS ENVIRONMENT

Corporation Law Worldwide: Proper Consideration for Shares

There is substantial similarity in corporation laws from country to country. Even in many countries where corporation law is different from American law, there are legislative attempts to modernize the law by making it more nearly consistent with U.S. law. One example is Israel, whose Knesset is likely soon to bring its corporation law in line with Western law, especially American law.

Examining the requirements to incorporate and the limits on consideration for shares, there are some differences globally, but generally not much more than one sees from state to state in the United States. For example, although the MBCA permits corporate shares to be issued for any benefit to the corporation, the laws of many countries retain the historic American rule (which is still law in many states) that certain types of benefits are improper consideration. For example, the corporate law of the Dominion of Melchizedek (which comprises a slice of Antarctica and five Pacific islands) states that consideration for the issuance of shares shall consist of money or other property, tangible or intangible, or labor or services actually received by or performed for the corporation or for its benefit or in its formation or reorganization. Its law prohibits the issuance of shares for future payments or future services. Anguilla has the same rules.

Chinese law is bit more restrictive, allowing shareholders to make their investments only in cash, in kind, in industrial property rights, in nonpatented technology, or land use rights. The Kingdom of Bhutan is more limiting, however, forbidding share issuances for consideration other than cash, unless shareholders approve.

shareholder for less than par value or fair value and incur no liability. However, if the purchasing shareholder *knows* that the selling shareholder bought the shares from the corporation for less than par value, the purchasing shareholder is liable to the corporation for the difference between the par value and the amount paid by the selling shareholder.

Share Subscriptions

Under the terms of a **share subscription,** a prospective shareholder promises to buy a specific number of shares of a corporation at a stated price. If the subscription is accepted by the corporation and the subscriber has paid for the shares, the subscriber is a shareholder of the corporation, even if the shares have not been issued. Under the MBCA, subscriptions need not be in writing to be enforceable. Usually, however, subscriptions are written.

Promoters use written share subscriptions in the course of selling shares of a proposed corporation to ensure that equity capital will be provided once the corporation comes into existence. These are called **preincorporation subscriptions,** which were covered in this chapter's discussion of promoters. Preincorporation subscriptions are not contracts binding on the corporation and the shareholders until the corporation comes into existence and its board of directors accepts the share subscriptions.

Close corporations may use share subscriptions when they seek to sell additional shares after incorporation. These are examples of **postincorporation subscriptions,** subscription agreements made *after* incorporation. A postincorporation subscription is a contract between the corporation and the subscriber at the time the subscription agreement is made.

A subscription may provide for payment of the price of the shares on a specified day, in installments, or upon the demand of the board of directors. The board may not discriminate when it demands payment: It must demand payment from all the subscribers of a class of shares or from none of them.

A share certificate may not be issued to a share subscriber until the price of the shares has been fully paid. If the subscriber fails to pay as agreed, the corporation may sue the subscriber for the amount owed.

Issuance of Shares

Uniform Commercial Code (UCC) Article 8 regulates the issuance of securities. Under Article 8, a corporation has a duty to issue only the number of shares authorized by its articles. Overissued shares are void.

When a person is entitled to overissued shares, the corporation may not issue the shares. However, the person has two remedies. The corporation must obtain identical shares and deliver them to the person entitled to issuance or the corporation must reimburse the person for the value paid for the shares plus interest.

The directors may incur liability, including criminal liability, for an overissuance of shares. To prevent overissuance through error in the issuance or transfer of their shares, corporations often employ a bank or a trust company as a registrar.

A share certificate is evidence that a person has been issued shares, owns the shares, and is a shareholder. The certificate states the corporation's name, the shareholder's name, and the number and class of shares. A person can be a shareholder without receiving a share certificate, such as a holder of a share subscription.

Under the MBCA, a corporation is not required to issue share certificates. If a corporation does not issue share certificates, it must provide each shareholder a written statement with the information required in a certificate.

Transfer of Shares

Because share certificates are evidence of the ownership of shares, their transfer is evidence of the transfer of the ownership of shares. The MBCA and UCC Article 8 cover the registration and transfer of shares, as represented by certificates.

Share certificates are issued in *registered* form; that is, they are registered with the corporation in the name of a specific person. The indorsement of a share certificate on its back by its registered owner and the delivery of the certificate to another person transfers ownership of the shares to the other person. The transfer of a share certificate without naming a transferee creates a *street certificate.* The transfer of a street certificate may be made by delivery without indorsement. Any holder of a street certificate is presumed to be the owner of the shares it represents. Therefore, a transferee should ask the corporation to reregister the shares in his name.

Under the UCC, a corporation owes a duty to register the transfer of any registered shares presented to it for registration, provided that the shares have been properly indorsed. If the corporation refuses to make the transfer, it is liable to the transferee for either conversion or specific performance.

When an owner of shares claims that his certificate has been lost, destroyed, or stolen, the corporation must issue a new certificate to the owner if the corporation has not received notice that the shares have been acquired by a bona fide purchaser, the owner files with the corporation a sufficient indemnity bond, and the owner meets any other reasonable requirements of the corporation. A bona fide purchaser is a purchaser of the shares for value in good faith with no notice of any adverse claim against the shares.

If, after the issuance of the new certificated shares, a bona fide purchaser of the original shares presents them for registration, the corporation must register the transfer, unless overissuance would result. In addition, the corporation may recover the new certificated shares from the original owner.

Restrictions on Transferability of Shares

Historically, a shareholder has been free to sell her shares to whomever she wants whenever she wants. Such free transferability is important to shareholders in a publicly held corporation. Because shares are freely transferable, in a publicly held corporation shareholders know that they can easily liquidate their investment by selling their shares, often on a stock exchange.

In close corporations, however, free transferability as a legal matter is a threat to the balance of power among shareholders. For example, if one of three shareholders owning a third of a corporation sells his shares to one of the other shareholders, the buying shareholder will own two-thirds of the corporation and may be able to dominate the third shareholder. In addition, as a practical matter, free transferability of close corporation shares is illusory, as few people other than existing shareholders are willing to purchase shares in a close corporation.

Consequently, many close corporations restrict the transfer of shares to insure those in control of a corporation will continue in control. Share transfer restrictions can also be used to guarantee a market for the shares when a shareholder dies or retires from the corporation.

The courts have been reluctant to allow restrictions on the free transferability of shares, even if the shareholder agreed to a restriction on the transfer of her shares. Gradually, the courts and the legislatures have recognized that there are good reasons to permit the use of some restrictions on the transfer of shares. Today, modern corporation statutes allow most transfer restrictions, especially for close corporations.

Types of Restrictions on Transfer   There are four categories of transfer restrictions that may be used to accomplish the objectives addressed above: (1) rights of first refusal and option agreements, (2) buy-and-sell agreements, (3) consent restraints, and (4) provisions disqualifying purchasers.

A **right of first refusal** grants to the corporation or the other shareholders the right to match the offer that a selling shareholder receives for her shares. An **option agreement** grants the corporation or the other shareholders an option to buy the selling shareholder's shares at a price determined by the agreement. An option agreement will usually state a formula used to calculate the price of the shares.

A **buy-and-sell agreement** compels a shareholder to sell his shares to the corporation or to the other shareholders at the price stated in the agreement. It also obligates the corporation or the other shareholders to buy the selling shareholder's shares at that price. The price of the shares is usually determined by a stated formula.

A **consent restraint** requires a selling shareholder to obtain the consent of the corporation or the other shareholders before she may sell her shares. A **provision disqualifying purchasers** may be used in rare situations to exclude unwanted persons from the corporation. For example, a transfer restriction may prohibit the shareholders from selling to a competitor of the business.

Uses of Transfer Restrictions   A corporation and its shareholders may use transfer restrictions to maintain the balance of shareholder power in the corporation. For example, four persons may own 25 shares each in a corporation. No single person can control such a corporation. If one of the four can buy 26 additional shares from the other shareholders, he will acquire control. The shareholders may therefore agree that each shareholder is entitled or required to buy an equal amount of any shares sold by any selling shareholder. The right of first refusal, option agreement, or buy-and-sell agreement may serve this purpose.

A buy-and-sell agreement is the preferred transfer restriction for nearly every context in well-planned close corporations, because certainty is obtained by both sides being obligated, one required to buy and the other to sell. For example, a buy-and-sell agreement may be used to guarantee a shareholder a market for his shares. In a close corporation, there may be no ready market for the shares of the corporation. To ensure that a shareholder can obtain the value of her investment upon her retirement or death, the shareholders or the corporation may be required to buy a shareholder's shares upon the occurrence of a specific event such as death or retirement.

A buy-and-sell agreement may also be used to determine who should be required to sell and who should be required to buy shares when there is a severe disagreement between shareholders that threatens the profitability of the corporation. It could also be worded to require majority shareholders to buy the shares of minority shareholders when a lucrative merger offer for the corporation is rejected by the majority but favored by the minority. The agreement could set the buyout price as the price offered in the merger.

If minority shareholders are afraid of being frozen in a close corporation that will never go public and give shareholders a chance to sell their shares on the market and get a return on investment, a buy-and-sell agreement could require the corporation to repurchase the minority's shares if the corporation has not gone public after a specified number of years.

In a close corporation, the shareholders may want only themselves or other approved persons as shareholders. A buy-and-sell agreement or right of first refusal may be used to prevent unwanted persons from becoming shareholders.

A provision disqualifying purchasers may be used in limited situations only, such as when the purchaser is a competitor of the business or has a criminal background.

A consent restraint is used to preserve a close corporation or Subchapter S taxation election. Close corporation statutes and Subchapter S of the Internal Revenue Code limit the number of shareholders that a close corporation or S Corporation may have. A transfer restriction may prohibit the shareholders from selling shares if, as a result of the sale, there would be too many shareholders to preserve a close corporation or S Corporation election. A consent restraint is also used to preserve an exemption from registration of a securities offering. Under the Securities Act of 1933 and the state securities acts, an offering of securities is exempt from registration if the offering is to a limited number of investors, usually 35. A transfer restriction may require a selling shareholder to obtain permission from the corporation's legal counsel, which permission will be granted upon proof that the shareholder's sale of the shares does not cause the corporation to lose its registration exemption.

Legality of Transfer Restrictions Corporation statutes permit the use of option agreements, rights of first refusal, and buy-and-sell agreements with virtually no restrictions. The MBCA authorizes transfer restrictions for any reasonable purpose. The reasonableness of a restraint is judged in light of the character and needs of the corporation.

Consent restraints and provisions disqualifying purchasers may be used if they are not *manifestly unreasonable.* The MBCA makes per se reasonable any consent restraint that maintains a corporation's status when that status is dependent on the number or identity of shareholders, as with close corporation or S Corporation status. The MBCA also makes per se reasonable any restriction that preserves registration exemptions under the Securities Act of 1933 and state securities laws.

Enforceability To be enforceable against a shareholder, a transfer restriction must be contained in the articles of incorporation, the bylaws, an agreement among the shareholders, or an agreement between the corporation and the shareholders. In addition, the shareholder must either agree to the restriction or purchase the shares with notice of the restriction. Under the MBCA, a purchaser of the shares has notice of a restriction if it is noted conspicuously on the face or the back of a share certificate or a written statement provided to shareholders if no certificates were issued. A purchaser also has notice if he knows of the restriction when he buys the shares.

In the following *Stufft* case, the court considered whether a right of first refusal was invoked by the corporation's decision to sell all its assets and to dissolve.

Stufft v. Stufft   *916 P.2d 104 (Mont. Sup. Ct. 1996)*

Stufft Farms, Inc., was a Montana corporation that owned and operated a family farm. Esther Stufft owned 17,077 shares of the corporation, Carmen Stufft 17,018 shares, Carol Stufft Larson 20 shares, Dorene Stufft Badgett 20 shares, and David Stufft 20 shares. To maintain control of the corporation in the hands of the Stufft family, the bylaws of the corporation included a right of first refusal share transfer restriction. Article XII, entitled Restrictions on Transfer of Shares, reads in relevant part:

No shareholder shall have the right or power to pledge, sell or otherwise dispose of, except by will, any share or shares of this company, without first offering the said share or shares for sale to the company and shareholders at the then book value.

On December 27, 1994, the board of directors of Stufft Farms adopted a resolution to dissolve and liquidate the corporation. Neil Johnson emerged as a possible purchaser of the corporation's assets, but tax considerations caused the shareholders to consider selling their shares instead of the corporation's assets. On February 24, 1995, Johnson offered to buy all of Stufft Farms's shares; the offer was contingent on all shareholders selling their shares to Johnson. All the shareholders, except David Stufft, agreed to accept Johnson's offer. On March 9, 1995, David Stufft attempted to invoke Article XII of the bylaws and to exercise his right of first refusal to buy the other shareholders' shares. David Stufft argued that the other shareholders' acceptance of Johnson's offer to buy their stock triggered Article XII, giving him a right of first refusal to purchase their stock at book value. The other shareholders refused David Stufft's demand to sell to them at book value, and instead, they offered to sell their shares to David Stufft at the same price Johnson offered. David Stufft rejected their offer, and the other shareholders elected not to sell their shares to anyone. On March 27, 1995, the board of directors approved the sale of Stufft Farms's assets to Johnson. David Stufft sued the other shareholders and Stufft Farms to void the asset sale to Johnson on the grounds that his rights under Article XII made him the equitable owner of all the shares. He argued that only he should have been entitled to vote all the shares of stock and, therefore, the agreement to sell the corporation's assets to Johnson was void. The district court dismissed David Stufft's suit, and he appealed to the Supreme Court of Montana.

Turnage, Chief Justice   David Stufft argues that his right of first refusal was triggered by the other stockholders' acceptance of Johnson's February 24, 1995, offer to purchase all of the corporation's outstanding stock, and again by the March 10, 1995 offer of the majority stockholders to sell their stock to him at the price at which the stock had been offered to Johnson, a price not shown or claimed to be book value. He maintains that the right of first refusal is triggered by a willingness, a desire, or an attempt by stockholders to dispose of their stock, citing *Weintz v. Bumgarner* (Mont. Sup. Ct. 1967).

A critical distinction between *Weintz* and the present case is that in *Weintz*, not only was there a willingness to sell on the part of the property owners, but actual agreements were reached to sell the various interests in the subject property. In the present case, no agreements were reached to sell the stock at issue.

Johnson's offer to purchase the stock in Stufft Farms, Inc., was an offer to purchase *all* of the stock in the corporation. Johnson's offer was not accepted by shareholder David Stufft. Because of the contingent nature of Johnson's offer, when Stufft elected not to sell, Johnson's offer to buy was withdrawn. Therefore, no agreement was reached. The corporation did not accept Johnson's offer.

Similarly, the other shareholders' March 10 offer to sell stock to David Stufft on the same terms as those offered by

Johnson was counteroffer to David Stufft's March 9 offer to purchase the stock at book value. David Stufft's offer was not accepted. The counteroffer was not accepted.

Stufft's right of first refusal to purchase Stufft Farms, Inc., stock was not triggered, because the other shareholders did not "pledge, sell or otherwise dispose of" their shares of stock. The other stockholders still own their stock in the corporation.

Stufft also contends that the other shareholders and Johnson are attempting to circumvent his right of first refusal. The District Court noted:

> The court is very aware of the purpose of corporate restrictive stock transfer bylaws and in particular those of a closely held family corporation. The purpose of such restrictions is to facilitate keeping the corporation closely held and to restrict the transfer of stock beyond family members. Such restrictive agreements and bylaws are specifically allowed under Montana law. However, neither the state statute nor restrictive agreements were intended to prohibit liquidation of a corporation and the sale of its assets.

We agree. The wording of Article XII does not suggest that it applies to an intended sale of the entire corporation or its assets. We conclude that David Stufft's right of first refusal was not violated.

Judgment for the other shareholders affirmed.

Statutory Solution to Close Corporation Share Transfer Problems   Although transfer restrictions are important to close corporations, many close corporation shareholders fail to address the share transferability problem. Therefore, a few states provide statutory resolution of the close corporation transferability problem. In these states, statutes offer solutions to the transferability problem that are similar to the solutions that the shareholders would have provided had they thought about the problem. Not all transferability problems are settled by the Close Corporation

Supplement, however. For example, there is no statutory buy-and-sell provision.

LOG ON

www.mhhe.com/mallor12e
Check out a model share transfer restriction at the website for this textbook. Note that the buy–sell agreement has four essential components: the events triggering a buyout, the persons obligated to buy and shareholders required to sell, the buyout price, and the timing of the payments to the selling shareholder.

Financing Nonprofit Corporations

Nonprofit corporations are financed differently from for-profit corporations. This is especially true of a public benefit corporation such as a public television station, which obtains annual financing from government sources, private foundations, members, and public contributors. A religious corporation such as a church receives weekly offerings from its congregation and may occasionally conduct capital drives to obtain additional funding from its members. A mutual benefit corporation, such as a fraternal or social organization like an Elks Club or golf country club, obtains initial funding from its original members to build facilities and assesses its members annually and monthly to pay operating expenses. In addition, nonprofit corporations have the power to obtain debt financing, such as borrowing from a bank or issuing notes and debentures.

A nonprofit corporation may admit members whether or not they pay consideration for their membership. There is no statutory limit on the number of members a nonprofit corporation may admit, although the articles may place a limit on the number of members. Social clubs typically limit the number of members. Members must be admitted in compliance with procedures stated in the articles or the bylaws.

Generally, memberships in a nonpublic corporation are not freely transferable. No member of a public benefit corporation or religious corporation may transfer her membership or any rights she possesses as a member. A member of a mutual benefit corporation may transfer her membership and rights only if the articles or bylaws permit. When transfer rights are permitted, restrictions on transfer are valid only if approved by the members, including the affected member.

Problems and Problem Cases

1. Joe Smith, Steve Smith, and Joe Bitter planned to open a bar in a college town. In the name of Gomer's, Inc., a corporation not yet formed, all three signed an offer to purchase a building in which to operate the bar. After Gomer's, Inc., was incorporated, the Smiths as corporate officers signed a contract to purchase the building in the name of Gomer's, Inc. Differences developed between the Smiths and Bitter. As shareholders and officers, the Smiths took control of the corporation, including the building. Bitter sued the Smiths arguing that the Smiths and Bitter collectively as individuals owned the building, not the corporation they formed. Was Bitter correct?

2. Garry Fox met with Coopers & Lybrand to request a tax opinion and other accounting services. Fox told Coopers that he was acting on behalf of a corporation that he was in the process of forming, to be named G. Fox and Partners, Inc. Coopers knew that the corporation was not in existence. Fox and Coopers had no agreement regarding Fox's personal liability for payment of the fee for the services. G. Fox and Partners, Inc., was incorporated, and a few weeks later Coopers completed its work. The corporation did not pay for the work, so Coopers sued Fox. Is Fox liable to Coopers?

3. Warthan and Knettel owned an insurance agency in St. Cloud, Minnesota. Koltes, McMahill, and Ketlin owned an insurance agency in Minnetonka, Minnesota. They agreed to transfer their businesses to a newly formed corporation, to be named Midwest Consolidated Insurance Agencies, Inc. (MCIA), equally owned by the St. Cloud and the Minnetonka groups. Articles of incorporation for MCIA were filed with the Minnesota secretary of state. The two groups had difficulties combining their operations. No shares of stock were issued, and no formal shareholder or directors' meetings were held. Although bylaws were drafted, they were never approved. Has MCIA's existence begun?

4. On August 30, the secretary of state filed the articles of incorporation of AC&C Wreckers, Inc. AC&C failed, however, to submit a copy of its articles for filing with the county recorder and to publish the articles of incorporation in a newspaper, as required by the state's corporation law. Nonetheless, AC&C transacted business as a corporation and had its own assets. The following February, an AC&C employee was injured on the job. He sued AC&C's majority shareholder—Collins—alleging that Collins was liable because AC&C was not properly incorporated. Is Collins liable to the employee?

5. Three friends decide to incorporate a vanity press business. They want complete control of the business, yet they need additional capital to start the business. The three friends enter negotiations with 10 business associates willing to provide capital to the corporation. The associates agree that they will not be allowed to elect directors, but they want to make sure that they will receive a return on their investments by receiving payments from the corporation quarterly or semi-annually. What securities with what rights should the corporation create to achieve the objectives of the friends and acquaintances? For each security you create, sketch the rights of the holders.

6. Eastern Oklahoma Television Corporation was incorporated to operate KTEN, a television station. To assist the station's start-up, Bill Hoover, an owner and operator of a radio station, pledged his radio station as collateral for KTEN's obligations, personally guaranteed the new corporation's obligations for the purchase of equipment, designed the television studio, planned operations, and hired and trained personnel. Hoover also became a director of the corporation. By action of the board of directors, the corporation issued some of the common shares to Hoover in consideration for his experience in broadcasting, his standing with the Federal Communications Commission, and his personal guarantee of the station's debt. Has Hoover paid a proper type of consideration for the shares?

7. Kirk's Auto Electric, Inc., issued 11 shares of common stock to Billy Bone, 10 shares to Andre Bone, and 5 shares to Joe Bone. In exchange, the Bones gave the corporation unsecured interest-bearing promissory notes payable on demand. No payments were ever made on the notes. Have the Bones paid proper consideration for the shares?

8. Robert Haft was president and CEO of Crown Books Corporation. After Haft served two years in those positions, the corporation issued 100,000 shares to Haft for a total price of $203,750. The board of directors issued the shares in recognition of Haft's past services rendered to the corporation and a promissory note in the amount of $203,750 due 15 years after the issuance. Did Crown's board issue the shares to Haft for proper consideration?

9. Bruce Bowman received 1,500 shares of Ling and Company Class A common shares. The shares were the subject of an option agreement contained in the articles of incorporation requiring Bowman to offer the shares to the corporation before selling them to any other person. On the front of Bowman's share certificate, in small print, it was stated that transfer of the shares was subject to the provisions of the articles, that a copy of the articles could be obtained from Ling or from the secretary of state, and that the back of the share certificate stated which sections of the articles contained the content of the option agreement. On the back of the share certificate, in small print, the reference to the restriction was again made, and specific reference was given to Article 4 of the articles of incorporation, in which the restriction was contained. Bowman borrowed money from Trinity Savings and Loan. When Bowman defaulted on the loan, Trinity attempted to sell the shares, but Ling objected, invoking the option agreement. Is the option agreement enforceable against Trinity?

10. Bianca Gates, Carly Jagger, and Melinda Fiorina decide to create a corporation that will manufacture blankets, quilts, and pillows. Each will contribute $160,000 initial capital to the business. They want to be equal owners and share equal management of the corporation. They do not expect the business to go public at any time, but they would not be averse to selling the business at a huge profit to a large textile company after five years. They are concerned that they will not receive a return on their investment because there will be no market for their shares. What agreement do they use to ensure that they may obtain a return on their investment through capital appreciation of their shares? Sketch the contents of that agreement.

Online Research: Pricing Incorporation

Type "incorporate" in your Internet search engine and you will obtain a list of companies that assist persons who wish to incorporate a business. Most incorporation websites quote their fees for assisting incorporation and also fees assessed by the state of incorporation. Find which website offers the most services at the best price.

Note that some websites sell corporate kits. A corporate kit is a notebook with sample bylaws, organization meeting minutes, stock certificates, and a stock transfer ledger. Corporate kits usually include a corporate seal, which is used to emboss the corporation's name on official documents. Banks and other institutions may require that all documents signed by a corporation bear the corporate seal.

43

MANAGEMENT OF CORPORATIONS

Clestra Corporation is a manufacturer of consumer products ranging from canned and packaged foods like spaghetti sauce and popcorn to over-the-counter health aids like toothpaste and mouthwash. Its annual worldwide revenues are just under $6 billion. Clestra brands are not among the top two in any of its product lines, each brand ranking from fourth to ninth in annual sales in countries in which it markets its products. Clestra's CEO has been discussing the company's future with its consultant, KRNP Consulting LLP. KRNP has suggested that Clestra consider acquiring Ballmax, Inc., a consumer products company with two billion dollars annual sales. Ballmax's brands are complementary to Clestra's brands, and while smaller than Clestra, Ballmax has a distribution system that will give Clestra access to markets in which Clestra is not currently a significant seller.

Clestra's CEO also wants to improve consumer recognition of the Clestra brand. She suggests that Clestra acquire naming rights to a stadium being built for a baseball team in northern Virginia, the Virginia Hatchets. The CEO thinks that Clestra has the inside track to acquire naming rights because the family of one of Clestra's board members owns the baseball team that will own and operate the stadium.

• What legal standard will determine whether Clestra's board of directors has acted properly when approving Clestra's acquisition of Ballmax, Inc.? What role may KRNP Consulting take in helping Clestra's board of directors meet its duties under that legal standard?
• What legal standard will judge whether Clestra's board of directors has acted properly when acquiring naming rights to the Virginia Hatchets stadium? What role may KRNP Consulting take in helping Clestra's board of directors meet its duties under that legal standard?
• Suppose Clestra's CEO is concerned that Clestra may be a target for a takeover by one of the larger consumer goods companies. If Clestra wants to remain an independent company, what should Clestra's board of directors do now to increase the chances that it may fend off a hostile takeover? What legal standard will judge whether Clestra's board has acted properly in adopting defenses against a hostile takeover? What should Clestra's board do now to increase the likelihood that the board will comply with that legal standard when it opposes a hostile takeover?

ALTHOUGH SHAREHOLDERS OWN a corporation, they traditionally have possessed no right to manage the business of the corporation. Instead, shareholders elect individuals to a *board of directors,* to which management is entrusted. Often, the board delegates much of its management responsibilities to *officers.*

This chapter explains the legal aspects of the board's and officers' management of the corporation. Their management of the corporation must be consistent with the objectives and powers of the corporation, and they owe duties to the corporation to manage it prudently and in the best interests of the corporation and the shareholders as a whole.

Corporate Objectives

The traditional objective of the business corporation has been to *enhance corporate profits and shareholder gain.* According to this objective, the managers of a corporation must seek the accomplishment of the profit objective to the exclusion of all inconsistent goals. Interests other than profit maximization may be considered, provided that they do not hinder the ultimate profit objective.

Nonetheless, some courts have permitted corporations to take *socially responsible actions* that are *beyond the profit maximization requirement.* In addition, every state recognizes corporate powers that are not economically inspired. For example, corporations may make contributions to colleges, political campaigns, child abuse prevention centers, literary associations, and employee benefit plans, regardless of economic benefit to the corporations. Also, every state expressly recognizes the right of shareholders to choose freely the extent to which profit maximization captures all of their interests and all of their sense of responsibility.

Most states have enacted **corporate constituency statutes,** which broaden the legal objectives of corporations. Such statutes permit or require directors to take into account the interests of constituencies other than shareholders, including employees, suppliers, and customers. These statutes direct the board to act in the best interests of the corporation, not just the interests of the shareholders, and to maximize corporate profits *over the long term.* The new laws promote the view that a corporation is a collection of interests working together for the purpose of producing goods and services at a profit, and that the goal of corporate profit maximization over the long term is not necessarily the same as the goal of stock price maximization over the short term.

Corporate Powers

The actions of management are limited not only by the objectives of business corporations but also by the *powers* granted to business corporations. Such limitations may appear in the state statute, the articles of incorporation, and the bylaws.

The primary source of a corporation's powers is the corporation statute of the state in which it is incorporated. Some state corporation statutes expressly specify the powers of corporations. These powers include making gifts for charitable and educational purposes, lending money to corporate officers and directors, and purchasing and disposing of the corporation's shares. Other state corporation statutes limit the powers of corporations, such as prohibiting the acquisition of agricultural land by corporations.

Modern statutes attempt to authorize corporations to engage in any activity. The Model Business Corporation Act (MBCA) states that a corporation has the power to do *anything that an individual may do.*

Purpose Clauses in Articles of Incorporation

Most corporations state their purposes in the articles of incorporation. The purpose is usually phrased in broad terms, even if the corporation has been formed with only one type of business in mind. Most corporations have purpose clauses stating that they may engage in any lawful business.

Under the MBCA, the inclusion of a purpose clause in the articles is optional. Any corporation incorporated under the MBCA has the purpose of engaging in any lawful business, unless the articles state a narrower purpose.

The *Ultra Vires* Doctrine Historically, an act of a corporation beyond its powers was a nullity, as it was *ultra vires,* which is Latin for "beyond the powers." Therefore, any act not permitted by the corporation statute or by the corporation's articles of incorporation was void due to lack of capacity.

This lack of capacity or power of the corporation was a defense to a contract assertable either by the corporation or by the other party that dealt with the corporation. Often, *ultra vires* was merely a convenient justification for reneging on an agreement that was no longer considered desirable. This misuse of the doctrine has led to its near abandonment.

ETHICS IN ACTION

Corporate Constituency Statutes

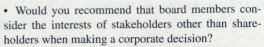

About two-thirds of the states have enacted corporate constituency stakeholder laws that permit directors to weigh the interests of constituencies other than shareholders. Only one state, Connecticut, requires the consideration of other constituencies. The other states permit, but do not require, directors to consider interests other than those of shareholders.

- Would you recommend that board members consider the interests of stakeholders other than shareholders when making a corporate decision?
- Which ethical theories that we studied in Chapter 4 permit directors to consider the interests of constituencies other than shareholders?
- Under profit maximization, what is the significance of nonshareholders' interests? Can a corporation maximize its profits without considering the interests of persons other than shareholders?

Today, the *ultra vires* doctrine is of small importance for two reasons. First, nearly all corporations have broad purpose clauses, thereby preventing any *ultra vires* problem. Second, the MBCA and most other statutes do not permit a corporation or the other party to an agreement to avoid an obligation on the ground that the corporate action is *ultra vires.*

Under the MBCA, *ultra vires* may be asserted by only three types of persons: (1) by a shareholder seeking to enjoin a corporation from executing a proposed action that is *ultra vires,* (2) by the corporation suing its management for damages caused by exceeding the corporation's powers, and (3) by the state's attorney general, who may have the power to enjoin an *ultra vires* act or to dissolve a corporation that exceeds its powers.

Powers of Nonprofit Corporations

Nonprofit corporations, like for-profit corporations, have the power to transact business granted by the incorporation statute, the articles, and the bylaws. The Model Nonprofit Corporation Act (MNCA), like the MBCA, grants nonprofit corporations the power to engage in any lawful activity and to do anything an individual may do. Thus, a nonprofit corporation may sue and be sued, purchase, hold, and sell real property, lend and borrow money, and make charitable and other donations, among its many powers.

Commonly, a nonprofit corporation's articles will limit its powers pursuant to a purpose clause. For example, a nonprofit corporation established to operate a junior baseball league may limit its powers to that business and matters reasonably connected to it. When a nonprofit

corporation limits its powers, a risk arises that the corporation may commit an *ultra vires* act. The MNCA adopts the same rules for *ultra vires* contracts as does the MBCA: Generally, neither the corporation nor the other party may use *ultra vires* as a defense to a contract.

The Board of Directors

Traditionally, the **board of directors** has had the authority and the duty to manage the corporation. Yet in a large publicly held corporation, it is impossible for the board to manage the corporation on a day-to-day basis, because many of the directors are high-level executives in other corporations and devote most of their time to their other business interests. Therefore, the MBCA permits a corporation to be managed *under the direction of* the board of directors. Consequently, the board of directors delegates major responsibility for management to committees of the board such as an executive committee, to individual board members such as the chairman of the board, and to the officers of the corporation, especially the chief executive officer (CEO). In theory, the board supervises the actions of its committees, the chairman, and the officers to ensure that the board's policies are being carried out and that the delegatees are managing the corporation prudently.

Board Authority under Corporation Statutes

A corporation's board of directors has the authority to do almost everything within the powers of the corporation. The board's authority includes not only the general power to manage or direct the corporation in the ordinary course of its business but also the power to issue shares of stock and to set the price of shares. Among its other powers, the board may repurchase shares, declare dividends, adopt and amend bylaws, elect and remove officers, and fill vacancies on the board.

Some corporate actions require *board initiative* and shareholder approval. That is, board approval is necessary to *propose such actions to the shareholders,* who then must approve the action. Board initiative is required for important changes in the corporation, such as amendment of the articles of incorporation, merger of the corporation, the sale of all or substantially all of the corporation's assets, and voluntary dissolution.

Committees of the Board

Most publicly held corporations have committees of the board of directors. These committees, which have fewer members than the board has, can more efficiently handle management decisions and exercise board powers than can a large board. Only directors may serve on board committees.

Although many board powers may be delegated to committees of the board, some decisions are so important that corporation statutes require their *approval by the board as a whole.* Under the MBCA, the powers that may not be delegated concern important corporate actions such as declaring dividends, filling vacancies on the board or its committees, adopting and amending bylaws, approving issuances of shares, and approving repurchases of the corporation's shares.

The most common board committee is the **executive committee.** It is usually given authority to act for the board on most matters when the board is not in session. Generally, it consists of the inside directors and perhaps one or two outside directors who can attend a meeting on short notice. An inside director is an officer of the corporation who devotes substantially full time to the corporation. Outside directors have no such affiliation with the corporation.

Audit committees are directly responsible for the appointment, compensation, and oversight of independent public accountants. They supervise the public accountants' audit of the corporate financial records. The Sarbanes–Oxley Act of 2002 requires that all publicly held firms have audit committees comprising independent directors. That act was a response to unethical and criminal conduct by corporate CEOs and auditors at firms like Enron, WorldCom, and Arthur Andersen in the 1990s and early 2000s.

Nominating committees choose management's slate of directors that is to be submitted to shareholders at the annual election of directors. Nominating committees also often plan generally for management succession. Nominating committees wholly or largely comprise outside directors.

Compensation committees review and approve the salaries, bonuses, stock options, and other benefits of high-level corporate executives. Although compensation committees usually comprise directors who have no affiliation with the executives or directors whose compensation is being approved, compensation committees may also set the compensation of their members. Directors of a typical corporation receive annual compensation between $30,000 to $60,000.

A **shareholder litigation committee** is given the task of determining whether a corporation should sue someone who has allegedly harmed the corporation. Usually, this committee of disinterested directors is formed when a shareholder asks the board of directors to cause the corporation to sue some or all of the directors for mismanaging the corporation.

Powers, Rights, and Liabilities of Directors as Individuals

A director is not an agent of the corporation *merely* by being a director. The directors may manage the corporation only when they act as a board, unless the board of directors grants agency powers to the directors individually.

A director has the *right to inspect* corporate books and records that contain corporate information essential to the director's performance of her duties. The director's right of inspection is denied when the director has an interest adverse to the corporation, as in the case of a director who plans to sell a corporation's trade secrets to a competitor.

Normally, a director does not have any personal liability for the contracts and torts of the corporation.

Election of Directors

Generally, any individual may serve as a director of a corporation. A director need not even be a shareholder. Nonetheless, a corporation is permitted to specify qualifications for directors in the articles of incorporation.

A corporation must have the number of directors required by the state corporation law. The MBCA and several state corporation statutes require a minimum of one director, recognizing that in close corporations with a single shareholder-manager, additional board members are superfluous. Several statutes, including the New York statute, require at least three directors, unless there are fewer than three shareholders, in which case the corporation may have no fewer directors than it has shareholders.

A corporation may have more than the minimum number of directors required by the corporation statute. The articles of incorporation or bylaws will state the number of directors of the corporation. Most large publicly held corporations have boards with more than 10 members.

Directors are elected by the shareholders at the annual shareholder meeting. Usually, each shareholder is permitted to vote for as many nominees as there are directors to be elected. The shareholder may cast as many votes for each nominee as he has shares. The top votegetters among the nominees are elected as directors. This voting process, called **straight voting,** permits a holder of more than 50 percent of the shares of a corporation to dominate the corporation by electing a board of directors that will manage the corporation as he wants it to be managed.

To avoid domination by a large shareholder, some corporations allow class voting or cumulative voting. **Class voting** may give certain classes of shareholders the right to elect a specified number of directors. **Cumulative voting** permits shareholders to multiply the number of their shares by the number of directors to be elected and to cast the resulting total of votes for one or more directors. As a result, cumulative voting may permit minority shareholders to obtain representation on the board of directors.

Directors usually hold office for only one year, but they may have longer terms. The MBCA permits **staggered terms** for directors. A corporation having a board of nine or more members may establish either two or three approximately equal classes of directors, with only one class of directors coming up for election at each annual shareholders' meeting. If there are two classes of directors, the directors serve two-year terms; if there are three classes, they serve three-year terms.

The original purpose of staggered terms was to permit continuity of management. Staggered terms also frustrate the ability of minority shareholders to use cumulative voting to elect their representatives to the board of directors.

The Proxy Solicitation Process Most individual investors purchase corporate shares in the public market to increase their wealth, not to elect or to influence the directors of corporations. Nearly all institutional investors—such as pension funds, mutual funds, and bank trust departments—have the same profit motive. Generally, they are passive investors with little interest in exercising their shareholder right to elect directors by attending shareholder meetings.

Once public ownership of the corporation's shares exceeds 50 percent, the corporation cannot conduct any business at its shareholder meetings unless some of the shares of these passive investors are voted. This is because the corporation will have a shareholder quorum requirement, which usually requires that 50 percent or more of the shares be voted for a shareholder vote to be valid. Since passive investors rarely attend shareholder meetings, the management of the corporation must solicit proxies if it wishes to have a valid shareholder vote. Shareholders who will not attend a shareholder meeting must be asked to appoint someone else to vote their shares for them. This is done by furnishing each such shareholder with a proxy form to sign. The proxy designates a person who may vote the shares for the shareholder.

Management Solicitation of Proxies To ensure its perpetuation in office and the approval of other matters submitted for a shareholder vote, the corporation's management solicits proxies from shareholders for directors' elections and other important matters on which shareholders vote, such as mergers. The management designates an officer, a director, or some other person to vote the proxies received. The person who is designated to vote for the shareholder is also called a proxy. Typically, the chief executive officer (CEO) of the corporation, the president, or the chairman of the board of directors names the person who serves as the proxy.

Usually, the proxies are merely signed and returned by the public shareholders, including the institutional shareholders. Passive investors follow the **Wall Street rule:** Either support management or sell the shares. As a result, management almost always receives enough votes from its proxy solicitation to ensure the reelection of directors and the approval of other matters submitted to the shareholders, even when other parties solicit proxies in opposition to management.

Management's solicitation of proxies may produce a result quite different from the theory of corporate management that directors serve as representatives of the shareholders. The CEO usually nominates directors of his choice, and they are almost always elected. The directors appoint officers chosen by the CEO. The CEO's nominees for director are not unduly critical of his programs or of his methods for carrying them out. This is particularly true if a large proportion of the directors are officers of the company and thus are more likely to be dominated by the CEO. In such situations, the board of directors may not function effectively as a representative of the shareholders in supervising and evaluating the CEO and the other officers of the corporation. The board members and the other officers are subordinates of the CEO, even though the CEO is not a major shareholder of the corporation.

Proposals for improving corporate governance in public-issue corporations seek to develop a board that is capable of functioning independently of the CEO by changing the composition or operation of the board of directors. Some corporate governance critics propose that a federal agency such as the Securities and Exchange Commission (SEC) appoint one or more directors to serve as watchdogs of the public interest. Other critics would require that shareholders elect at least a majority of directors without prior ties to the corporation, thus excluding shareholders, suppliers, and customers from the board. The New York Stock Exchange has proposed for its listed companies that independent directors be a majority of the board and that audit and compensation committees comprise only independent directors.

Other proposals recommend changing the method by which directors are nominated for election. One proposal would encourage shareholders to make nominations for directors. Supporters of this proposal argue that in addition to reducing the influence of the CEO, it would also broaden the range of backgrounds represented on the board. The SEC recommends that publicly held corporations establish a nominating committee composed of outside directors. Many publicly held corporations have nomination committees.

Due to pressure from the public after the corporate scandals of the 1990s and early 2000s, Congress, the SEC, the NYSE, and NASDAQ have made or proposed wide changes in corporate governance. In the next few years, we should see corporate boards that are more nearly independent of the CEO not only in structure but also in action. Boards will comprise mostly independent directors, and they will meet more frequently by themselves, independent of the CEO and other officers.

For a complete treatment of the corporate social responsibility debate, including proposals to improve corporate governance, see Chapter 4.

In the following case, *Grimes v. Donald*, the court considered whether a board of directors abdicated its duty to direct the corporation by delegating unlimited power to the CEO.

Grimes v. Donald   *673 A.2d 1207 (Del. Sup. Ct. 1996)*

James Donald was the chief executive officer of DSC Communications, a Delaware corporation headquartered in Plano, Texas. In 1990, DSC's board of directors entered an employment agreement with Donald that ran until his 75th birthday. The employment agreement provided that Donald "shall be responsible for the general management of the affairs of the company and report to the Board." Donald's employment could be terminated by death, disability, for cause, and without cause. The agreement provided, however, that Donald could declare a "Constructive Termination Without Cause" by DSC, if there was "unreasonable interference, in the good faith judgment of Donald, by the Board or a substantial stockholder of DSC, in Donald's carrying out of his duties and responsibilities." When there was termination without cause, the employment agreement provided that Donald was entitled to payment of his annual base salary ($650,000) for the remainder of the contract, his annual incentive award ($300,000), and other benefits. The total amount of payments and benefits for the term of the contract was about $20,000,000.

C. L. Grimes, a DSC shareholder, sued Donald on behalf of the corporation asking the court to invalidate the employment agreement between Donald and DSC on the grounds that the agreement illegally delegates the duties and responsibilities of DSC's board of directors to Donald. The Delaware Chancery Court dismissed the case, and Grimes appealed to the Supreme Court of Delaware.

Veasey, Chief Justice   Grimes claims that the potentially severe financial penalties which DSC would incur in the event that the Board attempts to interfere in Donald's management will inhibit and deter the Board from exercising its duties. We disagree.

Grimes has pleaded, at most, that Donald would be entitled to $20 million in the event of a Constructive Termina-tion. In light of the financial size of DSC, this amount would not constitute a *de facto* abdication.

Directors may not delegate duties which lie at the heart of the management of the corporation. A court cannot give legal sanction to agreements which have the effect of removing from directors in a very substantial way their duty to use their own best judgment on management matters. The

Donald agreement does not formally preclude the DSC board from exercising its statutory powers and fulfilling its fiduciary duty.

With certain exceptions, an informed decision to delegate a task is as much an exercise of business judgment as any other. Likewise, business decisions are not an abdication of directorial authority merely because they limit a board's freedom of future action. A board which has decided to manufacture bricks has less freedom to decide to make bottles. In a world of scarcity, a decision to do one thing will commit a board to a certain course of action and make it costly and difficult to change course and do another. This is an inevitable fact of life and is not an abdication of directorial duty.

If the market for senior management, in the business judgment of the board, demands significant severance packages, boards will inevitably limit their future range of action by entering into employment agreements. Large severance payments will deter boards, to some extent, from dismissing senior officers. If an independent and informed board, acting in good faith, determines that the services of a particular individual warrant large amounts of money, whether in the form of current salary or severance provisions, the board has made a business judgment. That judgment normally will receive the protection of the business judgment rule unless the facts show that such amounts, compared with services to be received in exchange, constitute waste or could not otherwise be the product of a valid exercise of business judgment.

The Board of DSC retains the ultimate freedom to direct the strategy and affairs of DSC. If Donald disagrees with the Board, DSC may or may not be required to pay a substantial amount of money in order to pursue its chosen course of action. So far, we have only a rather unusual contract, but not a case of abdication.

Judgment for Donald affirmed.

Vacancies on the Board The MBCA permits the directors to fill vacancies on the board. A majority vote of the remaining directors is sufficient to select persons to serve out unexpired terms, even though the remaining directors are less than a quorum.

Removal of Directors Modern corporation statutes permit shareholders to remove directors *with or without cause.* The rationale for the modern rule is that the shareholders should have the power to judge the fitness of directors at any time.

However, most corporations have provisions in their articles authorizing the shareholders to remove directors *only for cause.* Cause for removal would include mismanagement or conflicts of interest. Before removal for cause, the director must be given notice and an opportunity for a hearing.

A director elected by a class of shareholders may be removed only by that class of shareholders, thereby protecting the voting rights of the class. A director elected by cumulative voting may not be removed if the votes cast against her removal would have been sufficient to elect

THE GLOBAL BUSINESS ENVIRONMENT

Corporate Governance in Germany

Corporate governance varies somewhat from country to country. In Germany, for example, the *Aktiengesellschaft* (AG) has a **management board** and a **supervisory board.** The AG's management board represents and manages the company. Its members are not directly answerable to shareholders, but are appointed by the AG's supervisory board. All members of the management board manage the company together. However, the articles may provide that the company may be represented by two members of the management board.

The members of the AG's supervisory board are like the outside directors of an American company. They are elected by the AG's shareholders and, if German co-determination rules apply, by the employees. The supervisory board is charged with protecting the interests of the company, which may not coincide with those of the shareholders. To enable the supervisory board to carry out its oversight function, the management board is required to report regularly on the current status of the company's business and corporate planning. However, the supervisory board has no say in the day-to-day management of the company.

The Shop Constitution Act (*Betriebsverfassungsgesetz*) covers AGs with more than 500 employees. It provides that one third of supervisory board members be employee representatives. Under the Co-determination Act (*Mitbestimmungsgesetz*), the supervisory boards of AGs with more than 2,000 employees must have equal numbers of shareholder and employee representatives.

her to the board, thereby protecting the voting rights of minority shareholders.

Directors' Meetings

For the directors to act, a *quorum of the directors must be present*. The quorum requirement ensures that the decision of the board will represent the views of a substantial portion of the directors. A *quorum is usually a majority* of the number of directors.

Each director has *one vote*. If a quorum is present, a vote of a majority of the directors present is an act of the board, unless the articles or the bylaws require the vote of a greater number of directors. Such *supermajority voting provisions* are common in close corporations but not in publicly held corporations. The use of supermajority voting provisions by close corporations is covered later in this chapter.

Directors are entitled to reasonable notice of all *special meetings,* but not of regularly scheduled meetings. The MBCA does not require the notice for a special meeting to state the purpose of the meeting. A director's attendance at a meeting waives any required notice, unless at the beginning of the meeting the director objects to the lack of notice.

Traditionally, directors could act only when they were properly convened as a board. They could not vote by proxy or informally, as by telephone. This rule was based on a belief in the value of consultation and collective judgment.

Today, the corporation laws of a majority of the states and the MBCA specifically permit action by the directors without a meeting if all of the directors consent in writing to the action taken. Such authorization is useful for dealing with routine matters or for formally approving an action based on an earlier policy decision made after full discussion.

The MBCA also permits a board to meet by telephone, television, or Internet hookup. This section permits a meeting of directors who may otherwise be unable to convene. The only requirement is that the directors be able to hear one another simultaneously.

Officers of the Corporation

The board of directors has the authority to appoint the officers of the corporation. Many corporation statutes provide that the officers of a corporation shall be the *president,* one or more *vice presidents,* a *secretary,* and a *treasurer.* Usu-

ally, any two or more offices may be held by the same person, except for the offices of president and secretary.

The MBCA requires only that there be an officer performing the duties normally granted to a corporate secretary. Under the MBCA, one person may hold several offices, including the offices of president and secretary.

The officers are agents of the corporation. As agents, officers have *express authority* conferred on them by the bylaws or the board of directors. In addition, officers have *implied authority* to do the things that are reasonably necessary to accomplish their express duties. Also, officers have *apparent authority* when the corporation leads third parties to believe reasonably that the officers have authority to act for the corporation. Like any principal, the corporation may *ratify* the unauthorized acts of its officers. This may be done expressly by a resolution of the board of directors or impliedly by the board's acceptance of the benefits of the officer's acts.

The most perplexing issue with regard to the authority of officers is whether an officer has *inherent authority* merely by virtue of the title of his office. Courts have held that certain official titles confer authority on officers, but such powers are much more restricted than you might expect.

Traditionally, a *president* possesses no power to bind the corporation by virtue of the office. Instead, she serves merely as the presiding officer at shareholder meetings and directors' meetings. A president with an additional title such as *general manager* or *chief executive officer* has broad implied authority to make contracts and do other acts in the ordinary business of the corporation.

A *vice president* has no authority by virtue of that office. An executive who is vice president of a specified department, however, such as a vice president of marketing, will have the authority to transact the normal corporate business falling within the function of the department.

The *secretary* usually keeps the minutes of directors' and shareholder meetings, maintains other corporate records, retains custody of the corporate seal, and certifies corporate records as being authentic. Although the secretary has no authority to make contracts for the corporation by virtue of that office, the corporation is bound by documents certified by the secretary.

The *treasurer* has custody of the corporation's funds. He is the proper officer to receive payments to the corporation and to disburse corporate funds for authorized purposes. The treasurer binds the corporation by his receipts, checks, and indorsements, but he does not by virtue of that office alone have authority to borrow money, to issue negotiable instruments, or to make other contracts on behalf of the corporation.

Like any agent, a corporate officer ordinarily has *no liability on contracts* that he makes on behalf of his principal, the corporation, if he signs for the corporation and not in his personal capacity.

Officers serve the corporation at the pleasure of the board of directors, which may remove an officer at any time with or without cause. An officer who has been removed without cause has no recourse against the corporation, unless the removal violates an employment contract between the officer and the corporation

Managing Close Corporations

Many of the management formalities that you have studied in this chapter are appropriate for publicly held corporations yet inappropriate for close corporations. For example, each close corporation shareholder may want to be *involved in management* of the corporation. If a close corporation shareholder is not involved in management, he may want to protect his interest by placing *restrictions on the managerial discretion* of those who do manage the corporation.

Modern close corporation statutes permit close corporations to dispense with most, if not all, management formalities. The Statutory Close Corporation Supplement to the MBCA permits a close corporation to *dispense with a board of directors* and to be *managed by the shareholders.* The California General Corporation Law permits the close corporation to be managed *as if it were a partnership.*

LOG ON

www.ss.ca.gov/business/corp/corp_artsclose
info.htm
This website for California's Secretary of State
will show you how to create a close corporation
in California.

When a close corporation chooses to have a traditional board of directors, a minority shareholder may be dominated by the shareholders who control the board of directors. To protect minority shareholders, close corporations may impose **supermajority voting** requirements for board actions and **restrictions on the managerial discretion** of the board of directors.

Any corporation may require that board action be possible only with the approval of more than a majority of the directors, such as three-fourths or unanimous approval. A supermajority vote is often required to terminate the employment contract of an employee-shareholder, to reduce the level of dividends, and to change the corporation's line of business. Supermajority votes are rarely required for ordinary business matters, such as deciding with which suppliers the corporation should deal.

Traditionally, shareholders could not restrict the managerial discretion of directors. This rule recognized the traditional roles of the board as manager and of the shareholders as passive owners. Modern close corporation statutes permit shareholders to intrude into the sanctity of the boardroom. The Statutory Close Corporation Supplement grants the shareholders *unlimited* power to restrict the discretion of the board of directors. For example, the shareholders may agree that the directors may not terminate or reduce the salaries of employee-shareholders and may not lower or eliminate dividends. And, as was stated above, close corporation statutes even permit the shareholders to dispense with a board of directors altogether and to manage the close corporation as if it were a partnership.

Of course, any article or bylaw protecting the rights of minority shareholders should not be changeable, unless the minority shareholders consent.

Managing Nonprofit Corporations

A nonprofit corporation is managed under the direction of a board of directors. The board of directors must have at least three directors. All corporate powers are exercised by or under the authority of the board of directors. Any person may serve as a director; however, the Model Nonprofit Corporation Act has an optional provision stating that no more than 49 percent of directors of a public service corporation may be financially interested in the business of the public service corporation. An interested person is, for example, the musical director of a city's symphony orchestra who receives a salary from the nonprofit corporation operating the orchestra.

If a nonprofit corporation has members, typically the members elect the directors. However, the articles may provide for the directors to be appointed or elected by other persons. Directors serve for one year, unless the articles or bylaws provide otherwise. Directors who are elected may not serve terms longer than five years, but appointed directors may serve longer terms.

Directors may be elected by straight or cumulative voting and by class voting. Members may elect directors in person or by proxy. Directors may be removed at any time with or without cause by the members or other persons who elected or appointed the directors. When a director engages in fraudulent or dishonest conduct or breaches a fiduciary duty, members holding at least 10 percent of the voting power may petition a court to remove the wrongdoing director. Generally, a vacancy may be filled by the members or the board of directors; however, if a removed director was elected by a class of members or appointed by another person, only the class or person electing or appointing the director may fill the vacancy.

The board is permitted to set directors' compensation. Typically, directors of public benefit corporations and religious corporations are volunteers and receive no compensation.

Directors of a nonprofit corporation usually act at a meeting at which all directors may simultaneously hear each other, such as a meeting in person or by telephone conference call. The board may also act without a meeting if all directors consent in writing to the action. The board has the power to do most actions that are within the powers of the corporation, although some actions, such as mergers and amendments of the articles, require member action also. Ordinarily, an individual director has no authority to transact for a nonprofit corporation.

The board of directors of a nonprofit corporation may delegate some of its authority to committees of the board and to officers. A nonprofit corporation is not required to have officers, except for an officer performing the duties of corporate secretary. If a corporation chooses to have more officers, one person may hold more than one office. The board may remove an officer at any time with or without cause.

Officers have the authority granted them by the bylaws or by board resolution. However, a nonprofit corporation is bound by a contract signed by both the presiding officer of the board and the president, when the other party had no knowledge that the signing officers had no authority. The corporation is also bound to a contract signed by either the presiding officer or the president which is also signed by either a vice president, the secretary, the treasurer, or the executive director.

Directors' and Officers' Duties to the Corporation

Directors and officers are in positions of trust; they are entrusted with property belonging to the corporation and with power to act for the corporation. Therefore, directors and officers owe **fiduciary duties** to the corporation. They are the duties to act within the authority of the position and within the objectives and powers of the corporation, to act with due care in conducting the affairs of the corporation, and to act with loyalty to the corporation.

Acting within Authority

An officer or director has a duty to **act within the authority** conferred on her by the articles of incorporation, the bylaws, and the board of directors. The directors and officers must act within the scope of the powers of the corporation. An officer or a director may be liable to the corporation if it is damaged by an act exceeding that person's or the corporation's authority.

Duty of Care

Directors and officers are liable for losses to the corporation resulting from their lack of *care or diligence*. The MBCA expressly states the standard of care that must be exercised by directors and officers. MBCA section 8.30 states:

(a) Each member of the board of directors . . . shall act:
(1) in good faith, and
(2) in a manner the director reasonably believes to be in the best interests of the corporation.

(b) The members of the board of directors or a committee of the board, when becoming informed in connection with their decision-making function or devoting attention to their oversight function, shall discharge their duties with the care that a person in a like position would reasonably believe appropriate under the circumstances.

The MBCA section 8.42 imposes almost the same duty on corporate officers:

(a) An officer . . . shall act:
(1) in good faith;
(2) with the care that a person in a like position would reasonably exercise under similar circumstances; and
(3) in a manner the officer reasonably believes to be in the best interests of the corporation.

Managers need merely meet the standard of the **ordinarily prudent person in the same circumstances,** a standard focusing on the basic manager attributes of common sense, practical wisdom, and informed judgment. The duty of care does not hold directors and officers to the standard of a prudent businessperson, a person of some undefined level of business skill. A director or officer's performance is evaluated at the time of the decision, thereby preventing the application of hindsight in judging her performance.

The MBCA duty of care test requires that a director or officer make **a reasonable investigation** and **honestly believe** that her decision is in the **best interests of the corporation.** For example, the board of directors decides to purchase an existing manufacturing business for $15 million without inquiring into the value of the business or examining its past financial performance. Although the directors may believe that they made a prudent decision, they have no reasonable basis for that belief. Therefore, if the plant is worth only $5 million, the directors will be liable to the corporation for its damages—$10 million—for breaching the duty of care.

The Business Judgment Rule The directors' and officers' duty of care is sometimes expressed as the **business judgment rule:** Absent bad faith, fraud, or breach of fiduciary duty, the judgment of the board of directors is conclusive. When directors and officers have complied with the business judgment rule, they are protected from liability to the corporation for their harmful decisions. The business judgment rule precludes the courts from substituting their business judgment for that of the corporation's managers. The business judgment rule recognizes that the directors and officers—not the shareholders and the courts—are best able to make business judgments and should not ordinarily be vulnerable to second-guessing. Shareholders and the courts are ill-equipped to make better business decisions than those made by the officers and directors of a corporation, who have more business experience and are more familiar with the needs, strengths, and limitations of the corporation.

Three requirements must be met for the business judgment rule to protect managers from liability:

1. The managers must make an **informed decision.** They must take the steps necessary to become informed about the relevant facts by making a **reasonable investigation** before making a decision.

2. The managers may have **no conflicts of interest.** The managers may not benefit personally—other than as shareholders—when they transact on behalf of the corporation.

3. The managers must have a **rational basis** for believing that the decision is in the best interests of the corporation. The rational basis element requires only that the managers' decision have a *logical connection to the facts* revealed by a reasonable investigation or that the decision *not be manifestly unreasonable.* Some courts have held that the managers'

wrongdoing must amount to *gross negligence* for the directors to lose the protection of the business judgment rule.

If the business judgment rule does not apply because one or more of its elements are missing, a court may *substitute its judgment* for that of the managers.

Nonetheless, courts rarely refuse to apply the business judgment rule. As a result, the rule has been criticized frequently as providing too much protection for the managers of corporations. In one famous case, the court applied the business judgment rule to protect a 1965 decision made by the board of directors of the Chicago Cubs not to install lights and not to hold night baseball games at Wrigley Field.[1] Yet the business judgment rule is so flexible that it protected the decision of the Cubs' board of directors to install lights in 1988.

The *Trans Union* case[2] is one of the few cases that has held directors liable for failing to comply with the business judgment rule. The Supreme Court of Delaware found that the business judgment rule was not satisfied by the board's approval of an acquisition of the corporation for $55 per share. The board approved the acquisition after only two hours' consideration. The board received no documentation to support the adequacy of the $55 price. Instead, it relied entirely on a 20-minute *oral* report of the chairman of the board. No written summary of the acquisition was presented to the board. The directors failed to obtain an investment banker's report, prepared after careful consideration, that the acquisition price was fair.

In addition, the court held that the mere fact that the acquisition price exceeded the market price by $17 per share did not legitimize the board's decision. The board had frequently made statements prior to the acquisition that the market had undervalued the shares, yet the board took no steps to determine the intrinsic value of the shares. Consequently, the court found that at a minimum, the directors had been grossly negligent.

Complying with the Business Judgment Rule While the *Trans Union* case created some fear among directors that they could easily be held liable for making a decision that harms the corporation, nothing could be further from the truth. The *Trans Union* case and the business judgment rule provide a blueprint for how directors, with the assistance of investment bankers and other consultants, can avoid liability. First, to make an informed decision, the board must perform a reasonable

---

[1]*Shlensky v. Wrigley,* 237 N.E.2d 776 (Ill. Ct. App. 1968).
[2]*Smith v. Van Gorkom,* 488 A.2d 858 (Del. Sup. Ct. 1985).

investigation or reasonably rely on someone who has made a reasonable investigation, such as consultants, corporate officers, and employees. For example, few boards have the financial skills to value a product line that the corporation wants to sell, yet investment bankers are skilled at valuations. Therefore, a board will make an informed decision when an investment banker makes a reasonable investigation, informs the board of its finding in a written report delivered to the board several days prior to the board meeting, makes a presentation at the board meeting, and takes questions from the board, provided the board makes its decision after giving sufficient time and care to its deliberation of the facts.

Second, the business judgment rule will not apply unless the board has no conflicts of interest. By compiling a list of questions and quizzing the board members, consultants can help the board determine whether any member has a financial or other improper interest in the matter before the board.

Third, for the board to have a rational basis to believe that the decision is in the best interests of the corporation, the decision must fit with the firm's corporate strategy and the facts revealed by a reasonable investigation. Investment bankers and consultants can help, first by defining the corporation's strategy and second by demonstrating the fit between the course of action, the facts, and the corporate strategy.

Changes in the Duty of Care   Despite the low risk of liability, many state legislatures have changed the wording of the duty of care, typically imposing liability only for willful or wanton misconduct or for gross negligence. Some states allow corporations to reduce the duty of care in their articles of incorporation. For example, the MBCA allows corporations to reduce or eliminate directors' liability for monetary damages, unless a director has received an improper financial benefit or intended to violate the law or harm the corporation.

In the following *Omnibank* case, the court considered whether a bank loan officer complied with the business judgment rule.

Omnibank of Mantee v. United Southern Bank   *607 So.2d 76 (Miss. Sup. Ct. 1992)*

James R. Gray was president and managing officer of the Peoples Bank and Trust Company in Olive Branch, Mississippi, a branch bank owned by United Southern Bank (USB). Gray had complete charge of the day-to-day banking business of Peoples Bank. He had discretionary loan authority, subject to USB's limits for all senior loan officers: $75,000 for unsecured loans and $150,000 for secured loans.

Frank Piecara was an established customer of Peoples Bank. Piecara was president of Mirage Construction, Inc., which was obligated on a subcontract to provide earthwork and roadwork for Rogers Construction Company at the Picacho Pumping Plant in Arizona. Gray directed Peoples Bank to make loans in the amount of $536,000 to a trust managed by Piecara. The loan proceeds were used to provide working capital for Mirage. In addition, Gray directed Peoples Bank to issue a $300,000 irrevocable letter of credit to Rogers Construction for the purpose of securing Mirage's performance as Rogers's subcontractor. Gray called USB's senior vice president, Edward P. Peacock III, to request authorization of the letter of credit. Gray and Peacock each had $150,000 authority to make secured loans, which they combined to issue the letter of credit. As security for the loans and letter of credit, Gray obtained a security interest in Mirage's accounts receivable and contract rights, in particular the payments Rogers might make to Mirage under the subcontract. Gray did not perfect the security interest in the subcontract. Gray did not notify Rogers or the owner of the Picacho Pumping Plant of the security interest or require Rogers or the owner to remit subcontract payments directly to Peoples Bank.

Piecara and Mirage defaulted on the loans and letter of credit, with USB suffering a loss of almost $600,000. USB sued Gray alleging his breach of a fiduciary duty. The trial court found Gray liable to USB. Gray appealed to the Mississippi Supreme Court.

Robertson, Justice   The law devolves upon those in the upper echelons of a corporate entity certain duties owing to the entity, over and above those of an ordinary agent or employee. The question is whether Gray is one of those so burdened. We doubt a definitional line may be drawn with precision or permanence. For the moment, we are prepared to accept that

"Officer" means (a) the chief executive, operating, financial, legal and accounting officers of a corporation; (b) to the extent not encompassed by the foregoing, the chairman of the board of directors . . . , president, treasurer, and secretary, and a *vice-president or vice-chairman who is in charge of a principal business unit, division,* or function

. . . and (c) any other individual designated by the corporation as an officer.

American Law Institute, *Principles of Corporate Governance: Analysis and Recommendations,* section 1.27.

His title aside, Gray served USB as the chief operating official at Peoples Bank where he had substantial discretionary authority. We think a banking office such as the Peoples Bank branch is one of USB's principal business units. Gray was the man in charge. He presided over a branch worth over twenty million dollars, had substantial loan authority, and had considerable autonomy in directing the day-to-day operations of the branch. The trial court was correct in treating Gray as an officer of USB.

By law, officer Gray owed USB two principal duties: a duty of care and a duty of loyalty and fair dealing. These duties differ in nature and content, though they doubtless intersect and overlap. There is a bit of lore born no doubt of thought of failed banks and helpless widows that we ought demand more of bank officers than one who runs a foundry or a pest control company.

We begin with the duty of care. A director or officer has a duty to the corporation to perform the director's or officer's functions in good faith, in a manner he or she reasonably believes to be in the best interests of the corporation, and with the care that an ordinarily prudent person would reasonably be expected to exercise in a like position and under similar circumstances. The duty includes the obligation to make, or cause to make, an inquiry when, but only when, the circumstances would alert a reasonable director or officer to the need therefor. The extent of such inquiry shall be such as the director or officer reasonably believes to be necessary.

We long ago recognized this duty in a banking setting and said an officer who "very negligently" makes unreasonably risky loans may on his borrowers' default be held personally to make good the bank's loss.

The duty of care is subject to a well-settled common law, known as the business judgment rule. That rule has recently been stated with care:

A director or officer who makes a business judgment in good faith fulfills the duty . . . [of care] if the director or officer:

(1) is not interested . . . in the subject of the business judgment;

(2) is informed with respect to the subject of the business judgment to the extent the director or officer reasonably believes to be appropriate under the circumstances; and

(3) rationally believes that the business judgment is in the best interests of the corporation.

Principles of Corporate Governance, section 4.01. *See* MBCA section 8.42.

Gray's defaults in the Piecara loans are apparent. To be sure, there is nothing improper about a banker securing a credit by taking a security interest in contract rights or assignment of accounts. On the other hand, there are risks associated with the receivables form of collateral not associated with more tangible security, and a prudent loan officer must reasonably assess and control these risks. These risks are exacerbated where, as here, the subcontract is to be performed some 1,500 miles away.

Gray made no inquiry of the financial responsibility of Rogers or the owner of the Picacho Pumping Plant. A prudent loan officer taking such collateral will give notice of his bank's interest to the prime contractor and the owner and demand that all payments due under the subcontract be routed through the bank. Gray did none of this, nor did he monitor performance of the subcontract and have Piecara remit as his company was paid. Gray failed to perfect the security interest. Moreover, it appears clear the value of the collateral was far below what prudently should have been required for credit of this size. We accept the trial court's holding that Gray breached his duty of care to USB in handling the Piecara loans.

Gray's argument in reply is laced with implied references to the business judgment rule. He insists he acted in subjective good faith at all times, and of this there is little doubt. The trial court found Gray had no "interest" in any of the credits at issue. Gray insists he reasonably believed the debtors would respond to their obligations in a reasonably timely fashion. Gray insists he thought the risks reasonable and, where unsecured, backed by adequate financial statements. Reports of these loans, their terms, and periodic status were routinely available to USB, which offered nothing but praise until a state bank examiner's probe in January 1985.

These are not irrelevancies. They are evidence that Gray may have acted with reasonable business judgment. Most assuredly, the duty of care holds no truck with Monday morning quarterbacking, and the business judgment rule stands to prevent this. A loan officer is no guarantor of the success of each credit extension. The prudence of the practice is judged objectively in the circumstances then existing and reasonably knowable by the officer.

The defense ultimately founders. The trial court impliedly found unreasonable Gray's belief regarding the extent to which he should have informed himself at the time regarding these debtors. Further, the court impliedly found there was no rational basis for a belief that his handling of these matters was in USB's best interest.

Judgment for United Southern Bank affirmed.

Board Opposition to Acquisition of Control of a Corporation

In the last 35 years, many outsiders have attempted to acquire control of publicly held corporations. Typically, these outsiders (called **raiders**) will make a **tender offer** for the shares of a corporation (called the **target**). A tender offer is an offer to the shareholders to buy their shares at a price above the current market price. The raider hopes to acquire a majority of the shares, which will give it control of the target corporation.

Most tender offers are opposed by the target corporation's management. The defenses to tender offers are many and varied, and they carry colorful names, such as the Pac-Man defense, the white knight, greenmail, the poison pill, and the lock-up option. See Figure 1 for definitions of these and other defenses.

When takeover defenses are successful, shareholders of the target may lose the opportunity to sell their shares at a price up to twice the market price of the shares prior to the announcement of the hostile bid. Frequently, the loss of this opportunity upsets shareholders, who then decide to sue the directors who have opposed the tender offer. Shareholders contend that the directors have opposed the tender offer only to preserve their corporate jobs. Shareholders also argue that the target corporation's interests would have been better served if the tender offer had succeeded.

Generally, courts have refused to find directors liable for opposing a tender offer because the business judgment rule applies to a board's decision to oppose a tender offer. Nonetheless, the business judgment rule will not apply when the directors make a decision to oppose the tender offer before they have carefully studied it. In addition, if the directors' actions indicate that they opposed the tender offer in order to preserve their jobs, they will be liable to the corporation.

Court decisions have seemingly modified the business judgment rule as it is applied in the tender offer context. For example, in *Unocal Corp. v. Mesa Petroleum Co.,*[3] the Supreme Court of Delaware upheld the application of the business judgment rule to a board's decision to block a hostile tender offer by making a tender offer for its own shares that excluded the raider.[4] But in so ruling, the court held that the board may use only those defense tactics that are *reasonable* compared to the takeover threat. The board may consider a variety of concerns, including the inadequacy of the price offered, nature and timing of the offer, questions of illegality, the impact on constituencies other than shareholders

(i.e., creditors, customers, employees, and perhaps even the community generally), the risk of nonconsummation, and the quality of securities being offered in the exchange.

In *Unocal,* the threat was a two-tier, highly coercive tender offer. In the typical two-tier offer, the raider first offers cash for a majority of the shares. After acquiring a majority of the shares, the offeror initiates the second tier, in which the remaining shareholders are forced to sell their shares for a package of securities less attractive than the first tier. Because shareholders fear that they will be forced to take the less attractive second-tier securities if they fail to tender during the first tier, shareholders—including those who oppose the offer—are coerced into tendering during the first tier. *Unocal* and later cases specifically authorize the use of defenses to defeat a coercive two-tier tender offer.

Since its decision in *Unocal,* the Supreme Court of Delaware has applied this modified business judgment rule to validate a poison pill tender offer defense tactic in *Moran v. Household Int'l, Inc.*[5] and to invalidate a lock-up option tender offer defense in the *Revlon*[6] case. These cases confirmed the *Unocal* holding that the board of directors must show that:

1. It had reasonable grounds to believe that a danger to corporate policy and effectiveness was posed by the takeover attempt.

2. It acted primarily to protect the corporation and its shareholders from that danger.

3. The defense tactic was reasonable in relation to the threat posed to the corporation.

Such a standard appeared to impose a higher standard on directors than the rational basis requirement of the business judgment rule, which historically has been interpreted to require only that a decision of a board not be manifestly unreasonable. In addition, the *Revlon* case required the board to establish an auction market for the company and to sell it to the highest bidder when the directors have abandoned the long-term business objectives of the company by embracing a bust-up of the company.

In the following *Paramount v. Time* case, the Supreme Court of Delaware expanded board discretion in fighting hostile takeovers, holding that a board may oppose a hostile takeover provided the board had a *preexisting, deliberately conceived corporate plan* justifying its opposition. The existence of such a plan enabled Time's board to meet the reasonable-tactic element of the *Unocal* test.

---

[3] 493 A.2d 946 (Del. Sup. Ct. 1985).
[4] Discriminatory tender offers are now illegal pursuant to Securities Exchange Act Rule 13e-4.

[5] 500 A.2d 346 (Del. Sup. Ct. 1985).
[6] Revlon Inc. v. MacAndrews & Forbes Holdings, Inc., 506 A.2d 173 (Del. S. Ct. 1986).

Figure 1   *Tender Offer Defenses*

Greenmail

The target's repurchase of its shares from the raider at a substantial profit to the raider, upon the condition that the raider sign a standstill agreement in which it promises not to buy additional shares of the target for a stated period of time.

White Knight

A friendly tender offeror whom management prefers over the original tender offeror — called a black knight. The white knight rescues the corporation from the black knight (the raider) by offering more money for the corporation's shares.

Pac-Man

The target corporation turns the tables on the tender offeror or raider (which is often another publicly held corporation) by making a tender offer for the raider's shares. As a result, two tender offerors are trying to buy each other's shares. This is similar to the Pac-Man video game, in which Pac-Man and his enemies chase each other.

Golden Parachutes

An incentive to attract top managers, a golden parachute requires a corporation to make a large severance payment to a top-level executive such as the CEO when there is a change in control of the corporation. Payments to an individual executive may exceed $500 million. The severance agreement in *Grimes v. Donald* was a golden parachute.

Scorched Earth Tactics

Borrowed from a war tactic, scorched earth tactics attack the raider and its management directly and indiscriminately, like a tank with a flame thrower. These tactics include public relations campaigns in which the target points out the business, legal, and ethical failings of the raider and its management. The target typically warns its employees and communities that the raider will close the target's business in its current locations and move the jobs to another state or country. Finally, the target sues the raider alleging that the hostile takeover violates state corporation law, federal and state securities law, and antitrust law.

Long-Range Acquisition Strategy

A corporation should have a long-run strategy for expansion of its business, including by acquisition. That strategy may be to maintain a narrow business plan that allows the corporation and its management to focus on its core competencies. Or the strategy may be to seek new business opportunities that complement current business operations. An acquisition strategy allows the board of directors to oppose a hostile takeover that threatens the strategy, in accordance with the *Unocal* test. In the *Paramount* case, Time, Inc. was better set to oppose Paramount's bid because Time's board had a long-range acquisition strategy requiring protection of the editorial integrity of Time's magazine.

Lock-Up Option

Used in conjunction with a white knight to ensure the success of the white knight's bid. The target and the white knight agree that the white knight will buy a highly valuable asset of the target at a very attractive price for the white knight (usually a below-market price) if the raider succeeds in taking over the target. For example, a movie company may agree to sell its film library to the white knight.

Friendly Shareholders

Establishing employee stock option plans (ESOPs), by which employees of the corporation purchase the corporation's shares, and selling the corporation shares to other shareholders likely to be loyal to management, such as employee pension funds and people in the community in which the corporation conducts its business, may create a significant percentage of friendly shareholders that are not likely to tender their shares to a raider who may be perceived as hostile to the continuation of the corporation's business in the local community. Thus, building and maintaining a base of friendly shareholders make it easier to defeat a raider.

Poison Pill

Also called a shareholders' rights plan. There are many types, but the typical poison pill involves the target's issuance of a new class of preferred shares to its common shareholders. The preferred shares have rights (share options) attached to them. These rights allow the target's shareholders to purchase shares of the raider or shares of the target at less than fair market value. The poison pill deters hostile takeover attempts by threatening the raider and its shareholders with severe dilutions in the value of the shares they hold.

Stock Trading Surveillance Program

A target should watch the volume of trading in its stock, looking for unexplained spikes in volume that would indicate a future hostile bidder is acquiring a toe-hold in the target's stock prior to announcing a hostile takeover. By detecting abnormal trading in its stock, the target obtains advance knowledge of an impending hostile bid and will have additional time to implement its anti-takeover strategy.

Control Share Law

A target company may incorporate in state with a so-called Control Share Law. When a raider acquires 20 percent of the target's shares in a short period of time (say 90 days), the share control law renders the shares nonvoting, unless the target's board of directors opts out of the control share law or the target shareholders vote to allow the raider to vote the shares. The effect is to diminish the ability of a raider to acquire voting control of the target without the consent of the target. Since most raiders are unwilling to risk that shareholders will deny them voting power, hostile takeovers of companies incorporated in control share law states are mostly deterred.

Paramount Communications, Inc. v. Time, Inc.   *571 A.2d 1140 (Del. Sup. Ct. 1989)*

Since 1983, Time, Inc., had considered expanding its business beyond publishing magazines and books, owning Home Box Office and Cinemax, and operating television stations. In 1988, Time's board approved in principle a strategic plan for Time's acquisition of an entertainment company. The board gave management permission to negotiate a merger with Warner Communications, Inc. The board's consensus was that a merger of Time and Warner was feasible, but only if Time controlled the resulting corporation, preserving the editorial integrity of Time's magazines. The board concluded that Warner was the superior candidate because Warner could make movies and TV shows for HBO, Warner had an international distribution system, Warner was a giant in the music business, Time and Warner would control half of New York City's cable TV system, and the Time network could promote Warner's movies.

Negotiations with Warner broke down when Warner refused to agree to Time's dominating the combined companies. Time continued to seek expansion, but informal discussions with other companies terminated when it was suggested the other companies purchase Time or control the resulting board. In January 1989, Warner and Time resumed negotiations, and on March 4, 1989, they agreed to a combination by which Warner shareholders would own 62 percent of the resulting corporation, to be named Time-Warner. To retain the editorial integrity of Time, the merger agreement provided for a board committee dominated by Time representatives.

On June 7, 1989, Paramount Communications, Inc., announced a cash tender offer for all of Time's shares at $175 per share. (The day before, Time shares traded at $126 per share.) Time's financial advisers informed the outside directors that Time's auction value was materially higher than $175 per share. The board concluded that Paramount's $175 offer was inadequate. Also, the board viewed the Paramount offer as a threat to Time's control of its own destiny and retention of the Time editorial policy; the board found that a combination with Warner offered greater potential for Time.

In addition, concerned that shareholders would not comprehend the long-term benefits of the merger with Warner, on June 16, 1989, Time's board recast its acquisition with Warner into a two-tier acquisition, in which it would make a tender offer to buy 51 percent of Warner's shares for cash immediately and later buy the remaining 49 percent for cash and securities. The tender offer would eliminate the need for Time to obtain shareholder approval of the transaction.

On June 23, 1989, Paramount raised its offer to $200 per Time share. Three days later, Time's board rejected the offer as a threat to Time's survival and its editorial integrity; the board viewed the Warner acquisition as offering greater long-term value for the shareholders. Time shareholders and Paramount then sued Time and its board to enjoin Time's acquisition of Warner. The trial court held for Time. Paramount and Time shareholders appealed to the Supreme Court of Delaware.

Horsey, Justice   Our decision does not require us to pass on the wisdom of the board's decision. That is not a court's task. Our task is simply to determine whether there is sufficient evidence to support the initial Time-Warner agreement as the product of a proper exercise of business judgment.

We have purposely detailed the evidence of the Time board's deliberative approach, beginning in 1983–84, to expand itself. Time's decision in 1988 to combine with Warner was made only after what could be fairly characterized as an exhaustive appraisal of Time's future as a corporation. Time's board was convinced that Warner would provide the best fit for Time to achieve its strategic objectives. The record attests to the zealousness of Time's executives, fully supported by their directors, in seeing to the preservation of Time's perceived editorial integrity in journalism. The Time board's decision to expand the business of the company through its March 4 merger with Warner was entitled to the protection of the business judgment rule.

The revised June 16 agreement was defense-motivated and designed to avoid the potentially disruptive effect that Paramount's offer would have had on consummation of the proposed merger were it put to a shareholder vote. Thus, we decline to apply the traditional business judgment rule to the revised transaction and instead analyze the Time board's June 16 decision under *Unocal*.

In *Unocal*, we held that before the business judgment rule is applied to a board's adoption of a defensive measure, the burden will lie with the board to prove (a) reasonable grounds for believing that a danger to corporate policy and effectiveness existed; and (b) that the defensive measure adopted was reasonable in relation to the threat posed.

Paramount argues a hostile tender offer can pose only two types of threats: the threat of coercion that results from a two-tier offer promising unequal treatment for nontendering shareholders; and the threat of inadequate value from an all-shares, all-cash offer at a price below what a target board in good faith deems to be the present value of its shares.

Paramount would have us hold that only if the value of Paramount's offer were determined to be clearly inferior to the value created by management's plan to merge with Warner could the offer be viewed—objectively—as a threat.

Paramount's position represents a fundamental misconception of our standard of review under *Unocal* principally because it would involve the court in substituting its judgment as to what is a "better" deal for that of a corporation's board of directors. The usefulness of *Unocal* as an analytical tool is precisely its flexibility in the face of a variety of fact scenarios. Thus, directors may consider, when evaluating the threat posed by a takeover bid, the inadequacy of the price offered, nature and timing of the offer, questions of illegality, the impact on constituencies other than shareholders, the risk of nonconsummation, and the quality of securities being offered in the exchange.

The Time board reasonably determined that inadequate value was not the only threat that Paramount's all-cash, all-shares offer could present. Time's board concluded that Paramount's offer posed other threats. One concern was that Time shareholders might elect to tender into Paramount's cash offer in ignorance or a mistaken belief of the strategic benefit which a business combination with Warner might produce.

Paramount also contends that Time's board had not duly investigated Paramount's offer. We find that Time explored the available entertainment companies, including Paramount, before determining that Warner provided the best strategic "fit." In addition, Time's board rejected Paramount's offer because Paramount did not serve Time's ob-jectives or meet Time's needs. Time's board was adequately informed of the potential benefits of a transaction with Paramount. Time's failure to negotiate cannot be fairly found to have been uninformed. The evidence supporting this finding is materially enhanced by the fact that 12 of Time's 16 board members were outside independent directors.

We turn to the second part of the *Unocal* analysis. The obvious requisite to determining the reasonableness of a defensive action is a clear identification of the nature of the threat. This requires an evaluation of the importance of the corporate objective threatened; alternative methods of protecting that objective; impacts of the defensive action; and other relevant factors.

The fiduciary duty to manage a corporate enterprise includes the selection of a time frame for achievement of corporate goals. Directors are not obliged to abandon a deliberately conceived corporate plan for a short-term shareholder profit unless there is clearly no basis to sustain the corporate strategy. Time's responsive action to Paramount's tender offer was not aimed at "cramming down" on its shareholders a management-sponsored alternative, but rather had as its goal the carrying forward of a preexisting transaction in an altered form. Thus, the response was reasonably related to the threat. The revised agreement did not preclude Paramount from making an offer for the combined Time-Warner company or from changing the conditions of its offer so as not to make the offer dependent upon the nullification of the Time-Warner agreement. Thus, the response was proportionate.

Judgment for Time affirmed.

Duties of Loyalty

Directors and officers owe a duty of **utmost loyalty and fidelity** to the corporation. Judge Benjamin Cardozo stated this duty of trust. He declared that a director:

owes loyalty and allegiance to the corporation—a loyalty that is undivided and an allegiance that is influenced by no consideration other than the welfare of the corporation. Any adverse interest of a director will be subjected to a scrutiny rigid and uncompromising. He may not profit at the expense of his corporation and in conflict with its rights; he may not for personal gain divert unto himself the opportunities which in equity and fairness belong to his corporation.[7]

---

[7]*Meinhard v. Salmon,* 164 N.E.2d 545, 546 (N.Y. Ct. App. 1928).

Directors and officers owe the corporation the same duties of loyalty that agents owe their principals, though many of these duties have special names in corporation law. The most important of these duties of loyalty are the duties not to *self-deal,* not to *usurp a corporate opportunity,* not to *oppress minority shareholders,* and not to *trade on inside information.*

Conflicting Interest Transactions

A director or officer has a conflicting interest when a director or officer deals with his corporation. The director or officer with a **conflict of interest** may prefer his own interests over those of the corporation. The director's or officer's interest may be *direct,* such as his interest in selling his land to the corporation, or it may be *indirect,* such as his interest in having another business of which he or his family is an owner, director, or officer supply goods to the corporation. When a director has a conflict of interest, the director's transaction with the corporation may be voided or rescinded.

Under the MBCA, a director's conflicting interest transaction will not be voided merely on the grounds of a director's conflict of interest when *any one* of the following is true:

1. The transaction has been approved by a majority of informed, disinterested directors,

2. The transaction has been approved by a majority of the shares held by informed, disinterested shareholders, or

3. The transaction is fair to the corporation.

Nonetheless, even when disinterested directors' or shareholders' approval has been obtained, courts will void a conflict-of-interest transaction that is unfair to the corporation. Therefore, every corporate transaction in which a director has a conflict of interest must be fair to the corporation. If the transaction is fair, the interested director is excused from liability to the corporation. A transaction is fair if reasonable persons in an *arm's-length bargain* would have bound the corporation to it. This standard is often called the **intrinsic fairness standard.**

The function of disinterested director or disinterested shareholder approval of a conflict-of-interest transaction is merely to shift the burden of proving unfairness. The burden of proving fairness lies initially on the interested director. The burden of proof shifts to the corporation that is suing the interested officer or director if the transaction was approved by the board of directors or the shareholders. Nonetheless, when disinterested directors approve an interested person transaction, substantial deference is given to the decision in accordance with the business judgment rule, especially when the disinterested directors compose a majority of the board.

Generally, *unanimous* approval of an interested person transaction by informed shareholders *conclusively* releases an interested director or officer from liability even if the transaction is unfair to the corporation. The rationale for this rule is that fully informed shareholders should know what is best for themselves and their corporation.

Complying with the Intrinsic Fairness Standard

Complying with the intrinsic fairness standard is not much different than complying with the business judgment rule, despite the higher standard of conduct. The board must make a reasonable investigation to discover facts that will permit an informed decision. Almost always, the board will be aided in its investigation by officers and other employees of the corporation and by investment bankers, other consultants, and legal counsel. When relying on others' investigations, the board must receive written and oral reports in sufficient time to absorb the information, to ask questions of those who

---

ETHICS IN ACTION

Sarbanes–Oxley Act of 2002 Prohibits Loans to Management

Early corporation law prohibited loans by a corporation to its officers or directors, on the grounds that such loans may result in looting of corporate assets. Today, however, the MBCA and most other general corporation statutes allow loans to directors and officers, although they require either shareholder approval or compliance with conflicting interest transaction rules.

In 2002, Congress took steps to return to the past. After it was revealed that several executives of public companies were using their corporations as personal banks to fund extravagant lifestyles—some of which loans were never repaid and some of which corporations became bankrupt—Congress included in the Sarbanes–Oxley Act of 2002 a section generally prohibiting public companies from making loans to their

directors or executive officers. This includes the company's CEO and CFO, any vice president in charge of a principal business unit or function, and any other officer or other person who performs a policy-making function. If the corporation is not a public company or if the loan is made to a nonexecutive, the Sarbanes–Oxley Act does not prohibit the corporate loan.

- Do you think the Congress has gone too far in banning loans to directors and officers? What are the ethical justifications to ban loans? What would a rights theorist argue? What would a utilitarian argue? What would a profit maximizer argue?
- Do you think that the Sarbanes–Oxley Act should have banned all corporation loans to its employees? Would you prohibit a bank from making loans to its employees, officers, and directors?

made the investigation, and to debate and to deliberate after receiving all relevant information.

Investment bankers, other consultants, and legal counsel are especially helpful in ascertaining and disclosing any director's conflict of interest. By compiling a list of questions and quizzing the board members, consultants can help the board determine the extent of a director's conflict and ensure that the conflict is fully disclosed to the board. They should also make sure that only board members who are independent of the conflicted directors approve the conflicting interest transaction.

Finally, the board must make a decision that is fair to the corporation. Investment bankers and other consultants can help with this determination by demonstrating the decision's close fit with the firm's corporate strategy and the facts revealed by a reasonable investigation. They must ensure the decision is one that a reasonable person would make acting at arm's length.

Parent-Subsidiary Transactions Self-dealing is a concern when a parent corporation *dominates* a subsidiary corporation. Often, the subsidiary's directors will be directors or officers of the parent also. When persons with dual directorships approve transactions between the parent and the subsidiary, the opportunity for *overreaching* arises. There may be *no arm's-length bargaining* between the two corporations. Hence, such transactions must meet the *intrinsic fairness* test.

Usurpation of a Corporate Opportunity

Directors and officers may steal not only assets of their corporations (such as computer hardware and software)

but also *opportunities* that their corporations could have exploited. Both types of theft are equally wrongful. As fiduciaries, directors and officers are liable to their corporation for **usurping corporate opportunities.**

The opportunity must come to the director or officer *in her corporate capacity.* Clearly, opportunities received at the corporate offices are received by the manager in her corporate capacity. In addition, courts hold that CEOs and other high-level officers are nearly always acting in their corporate capacities, even when they are away from their corporate offices.

The opportunity must have a *relation or connection* to an *existing or prospective* corporate activity. Some courts apply the *line of business test,* considering how closely related the opportunity is to the lines of business in which the corporation is engaged. Other courts use the *interest or expectancy test,* requiring the opportunity to relate to property in which the corporation has an existing interest or in which it has an expectancy growing out of an existing right.

The corporation must be *able financially* to take advantage of the opportunity. Managers are required to make a good faith effort to obtain external financing for the corporation, but they are not required to use their personal funds to enable the corporation to take advantage of the opportunity.

A director or officer is free to exploit an opportunity that has been rejected by the corporation.

In the following case, *Guth v. Loft,* the court found that an opportunity to become the manufacturer of Pepsi-Cola syrup was usurped by the president of a corporation that manufactured beverage syrups and operated soda fountains.

Guth v. Loft, Inc.　5 A. 2d 503 (Del. Sup. Ct. 1939)

Loft, Inc., manufactured and sold candies, syrups, and beverages and operated 115 retail candy and soda fountain stores. Loft sold Coca-Cola at all of its stores, but it did not manufacture Coca-Cola syrup. Instead, it purchased its 30,000-gallon annual requirement of syrup and mixed it with carbonated water at its various soda fountains.

In May 1931, Charles Guth, the president and general manager of Loft, became dissatisfied with the price of Coca-Cola syrup and suggested to Loft's vice president that Loft buy Pepsi-Cola syrup from National Pepsi-Cola Company, the owner of the secret formula and trademark for Pepsi-Cola. The vice president said he was investigating the purchase of Pepsi syrup.

Before being employed by Loft, Guth had been asked by the controlling shareholder of National Pepsi, Megargel, to acquire the assets of National Pepsi. Guth refused at that time. However, a few months after Guth had suggested that Loft purchase Pepsi syrup, Megargel again contacted Guth about buying National Pepsi's secret formula and trademark for only $10,000. This time, Guth agreed to the purchase, and Guth and Megargel organized a new corporation, Pepsi-Cola Company, to acquire the Pepsi-Cola secret formula and trademark from National Pepsi. Eventually, Guth and his family's corporation owned a majority of the shares of Pepsi-Cola Company.

Very little of Megargel's or Guth's funds were used to develop the business of Pepsi-Cola. Instead, without the knowledge or consent of Loft's board of directors, Guth used Loft's working capital, credit, plant and equipment, and executives and employees to produce Pepsi-Cola syrup. In addition, Guth's domination of Loft's board of directors ensured that Loft would become Pepsi-Cola's chief customer.

By 1935, the value of Pepsi-Cola's business was several million dollars. Loft sued Guth, asking the court to order Guth to transfer to Loft his shares of Pepsi-Cola Company and to pay Loft the dividends he had received from Pepsi-Cola Company. The trial court found that Guth had usurped a corporate opportunity and ordered Guth to transfer the shares and to pay Loft the dividends. Guth appealed.

Layton, Chief Justice   Public policy demands of a corporate officer or director the most scrupulous observance of his duty to refrain from doing anything that would deprive the corporation of profit or advantage. The rule that requires an undivided and unselfish loyalty to the corporation demands that there shall be no conflict between duty and self-interest.

The real issue is whether the opportunity to secure a very substantial stock interest in a corporation to be formed for the purpose of exploiting a cola beverage on a wholesale scale was so closely associated with the existing business activities of Loft, and so essential thereto, as to bring the transaction within that class of cases where the acquisition of the property would throw the corporate officer purchasing it into competition with his company.

Guth suggests a doubt whether Loft would have been able to finance the project. The answer to this suggestion is two-fold. Loft's net asset position was amply sufficient to finance the enterprise, and its plant, equipment, executives, personnel and facilities were adequate. The second answer is that Loft's resources were found to be sufficient, for Guth made use of no other resources to any important extent.

Guth asserts that Loft's primary business was the manufacturing and selling of candy in its own chain of retail stores, and that it never had the idea of turning a subsidiary product into a highly advertised, nationwide specialty. It is contended that the Pepsi-Cola opportunity was not in the line of Loft's activities, which essentially were of a retail nature.

Loft, however, had many wholesale activities. Its wholesale business in 1931 amounted to over $800,000. It was a large company by any standard, with assets exceeding $9 million, excluding goodwill. It had an enormous plant. It paid enormous rentals. Guth, himself, said that Loft's success depended upon the fullest utilization of its large plant facilities. Moreover, it was a manufacturer of syrups and, with the exception of cola syrup, it supplied its own extensive needs. Guth, president of Loft, was an able and experienced man in that field. Loft, then, through its own personnel, possessed the technical knowledge, the practical business experience, and the resources necessary for the development of the Pepsi-Cola enterprise. Conceding that the essential of an opportunity is reasonably within the scope of a corporation's activities, latitude should be allowed for development and expansion. To deny this would be to deny the history of industrial development.

We cannot agree that Loft had no concern or expectancy in the opportunity. Loft had a practical and essential concern with respect to some cola syrup with an established formula and trademark. A cola beverage has come to be a business necessity for soft drink establishments; and it was essential to the success of Loft to serve at its soda fountains an acceptable five-cent cola drink in order to attract into its stores the great multitude of people who have formed the habit of drinking cola beverages.

When Guth determined to discontinue the sale of Coca-Cola in the Loft stores, it became, by his own act, a matter of urgent necessity for Loft to acquire a constant supply of some satisfactory cola syrup, secure against probable attack, as a replacement; and when the Pepsi-Cola opportunity presented itself, Guth having already considered the availability of the syrup, it became impressed with a Loft interest and expectancy arising out of the circumstances and the urgent and practical need created by him as the directing head of Loft.

The fiduciary relation demands something more than the morals of the marketplace. Guth did not offer the Pepsi-Cola opportunity to Loft, but captured it for himself. He invested little or no money of his own in the venture, but commandeered for his own benefit and advantage the money, resources, and facilities of his corporation and the services of his officials. He thrust upon Loft the hazard, while he reaped the benefit. In such a manner he acquired for himself 91 percent of the capital stock of Pepsi-Cola, now worth many millions. A genius in his line he may be, but the law makes no distinction between the wrongdoing genius and the one less endowed.

Judgment for Loft affirmed.

Oppression of Minority Shareholders

Directors and officers owe a duty to manage a corporation in the best interests of the corporation and the shareholders as a whole. When, however, a group of shareholders has been isolated for beneficial treatment to the detriment of another isolated group of shareholders, the disadvantaged group may complain of **oppression.**

For example, oppression may occur when directors of a close corporation who are also the majority shareholders pay themselves high salaries yet refuse to pay dividends or to hire minority shareholders as employees of the corporation. Since there is no market for the shares of a close corporation (apart from selling to the other shareholders), these oppressed minority shareholders have investments that provide them no return. They receive no dividends or salaries, and they can sell their shares only to the other shareholders, who are usually unwilling to pay the true value of the shares.

Generally, courts treat oppression of minority shareholders the same way courts treat director self-dealing: The transaction must be intrinsically fair to the corporation and the minority shareholders.

A special form of oppression is the **freeze-out.** A freeze-out is usually accomplished by merging a corporation with a newly formed corporation under terms by which the minority shareholders do not receive shares of the new corporation but instead receive only cash or other securities. The minority shareholders are thereby *frozen out as shareholders.*

Going private is a special term for a freeze-out of shareholders of *publicly owned corporations.* Some public corporations discover that the burdens of public ownership—such as the periodic disclosure requirements of the SEC—exceed the benefits of being public. Many of these publicly owned companies choose to freeze out their minority shareholders to avoid such burdens.

Freeze-Out Methods The two easiest ways to freeze out minority shareholders are the freeze-out merger and the reverse share split. With the freeze-out merger, the majority shareholders form a new corporation owned only by the majority shareholders. Articles of merger are drafted that will merge the old corporation into the new corporation. Under the merger terms, only shareholders of the new corporation will survive as shareholders of the surviving new corporation; the shareholders of the old corporation will receive cash only. Since the majority shareholders control both cor-

porations, the articles of merger will be approved by the directors and shareholders of both corporations. The freeze-out merger was used in the *Coggins* case, which follows at the end of this section.

Using a reverse share split to freeze out the minority shareholders is simpler. Here the articles are amended to reduce the number of outstanding shares by a multiplier, say 1/50,000, that will result in the majority shareholder having whole shares but the minority shareholders having only fractional shares. The articles amendment will be approved by directors and shareholders since the majority shareholder controls the corporation. After the reverse share split, corporation law permits the corporation to repurchase any fractional shares, even if the shareholders don't consent. The corporation buys the minority shareholders' fractional shares for cash, leaving only the majority shareholder owning the corporation.

Legal Standard Often, going private transactions appear abusive because the corporation goes public at a high price and goes private at a much lower price. Some courts have adopted a fairness test and a business purpose test for freeze-outs. Most states apply the **total fairness test** to freeze-outs. In the freeze-out context, total fairness has two basic aspects: *fair dealing* and *fair price.* Fair dealing requires disclosing material information to directors and shareholders and providing an opportunity for negotiation. A determination of fair value requires the consideration of all the factors relevant to the value of the shares, except speculative projections.

Some states apply the **business purpose test** to freeze-outs. This test requires that the freeze-out accomplish some legitimate business purpose and not serve the special interests of the majority shareholders or the managers.

Other states place no restrictions on freeze-outs provided a shareholder has a **right of appraisal,** which permits a shareholder to require the corporation to purchase his shares at a fair price.

In addition, the SEC requires a *publicly held* company to make a statement on the fairness of its proposed going private transaction and to discuss in detail the material facts on which the statement is based.

In the *Coggins* case, the court required that a freeze-out of minority shareholders of the New England Patriots football team meet both the business purpose and intrinsic fairness tests. The court held that freezing out the minority shareholders merely to allow the corporation to repay the majority shareholder's personal debts was not a proper business purpose.

Coggins v. New England Patriots Football Club, Inc.
492 N.E.2d 1112 (Mass. Sup. Jud. Ct. 1986)

In 1959, the New England Patriots Football Club, Inc. (Old Patriots), was formed with one class of voting shares and one class of nonvoting shares. Each of the original 10 voting shareholders, including William H. Sullivan, purchased 10,000 voting shares for $2.50 per share. The 120,000 nonvoting shares were sold for $5 per share to the general public in order to generate loyalty to the Patriots football team. In 1974, Sullivan was ousted as president of Old Patriots. In November 1975, Sullivan succeeded in regaining control of Old Patriots by purchasing all 100,000 voting shares for $102 per share. He again became a director and president of Old Patriots.

To finance his purchase of the voting shares, Sullivan borrowed $5,350,000 from two banks. The banks insisted that Sullivan reorganize Old Patriots so that its income could be used to repay the loans made to Sullivan and its assets used to secure the loans. To make the use of Old Patriots' income and assets legal, it was necessary to freeze out the nonvoting shareholders. In November 1976, Sullivan organized a new corporation called the New Patriots Football Club, Inc. (New Patriots). Sullivan was the sole shareholder of New Patriots. In December 1976, the shareholders of Old Patriots approved a merger of Old Patriots and New Patriots. Under the terms of the merger, Old Patriots went out of business, New Patriots assumed the business of Old Patriots, Sullivan became the only owner of New Patriots, and the nonvoting shareholders of Old Patriots received $15 for each share they owned.

David A. Coggins, a Patriots fan from the time of its formation and owner of 10 Old Patriots nonvoting shares, objected to the merger and refused to accept the $15 per share payment for his shares. Coggins sued Sullivan and Old Patriots to obtain rescission of the merger. The trial judge found the merger to be illegal and ordered the payment of damages to Coggins and all other Old Patriots shareholders who voted against the merger and had not accepted the $15 per share merger payment. Sullivan and Old Patriots appealed to the Massachusetts Supreme Judicial Court.

Liacos, Justice   When the director's duty of loyalty to the corporation is in conflict with his self-interest, the court will vigorously scrutinize the situation. The dangers of self-dealing and abuse of fiduciary duty are greatest in freeze-out situations like the Patriots merger, when a controlling shareholder and corporate director chooses to eliminate public ownership. Because the danger of abuse of fiduciary duty is especially great in a freeze-out merger, the court must be satisfied that the freeze-out was for the advancement of a legitimate corporate purpose. If satisfied that elimination of public ownership is in furtherance of a business purpose, the court should then proceed to determine if the transaction was fair by examining the totality of the circumstances. Consequently, Sullivan and Old Patriots bear the burden of

proving, first, that the merger was for a legitimate business purpose, and second, that, considering the totality of circumstances, it was fair to the minority.

Sullivan and Old Patriots have failed to demonstrate that the merger served any valid corporate objective unrelated to the personal interests of Sullivan, the majority shareholder. The sole reason for the merger was to effectuate a restructuring of Old Patriots that would enable the repayment of the personal indebtedness incurred by Sullivan. Under the approach we set forth above, there is no need to consider further the elements of fairness of a transaction that is not related to a valid corporate purpose.

Judgment for Coggins affirmed as modified.

Trading on Inside Information

Officers and directors have *confidential access* to nonpublic information about the corporation. Sometimes, directors and officers purchase their corporation's securities with knowledge of confidential information. Often, disclosure of previously nonpublic, **inside information** affects the value of the corporation's securities. Therefore, directors and officers may make a profit when the prices

of the securities increase after the inside information has been disclosed publicly. Shareholders of the corporation claim that they have been harmed by such activity, either because the directors and officers misused confidential information that should have been used only for corporate purposes or because the directors and officers had an unfair informational advantage over the shareholders.

In this century, there has been a judicial trend toward finding a duty of directors and officers to disclose information that they have received confidentially from the corporation before they buy or sell the corporation's securities. As will be discussed fully in Chapter 45, Securities Regulation, the illegality of insider trading is already federal law under the Securities Exchange Act; however, it remains only a minority rule under state corporation law.

Director's Right to Dissent

A director who assents to an action of the board of directors may be held liable for the board's exceeding its authority or its failing to meet its duty of due care or loyalty. A director who attends a board meeting is deemed to have assented to any action taken at the meeting, unless he dissents.

Under the MBCA, to register his dissent to a board action, and thereby to protect himself from liability, the director must not vote in favor of the action and must make his position clear to the other board members. His position is made clear either by requesting that his dissent appear in the minutes or by giving written notice of his dissent to the chairman of the board at the meeting or to the secretary immediately after the meeting. These procedures ensure that the dissenting director will attempt to dissuade the board from approving an imprudent action.

Generally, directors are not liable for failing to attend meetings. However, a director is liable for *continually failing* to attend meetings, with the result that the director is unable to prevent the board from harming the corporation by its self-dealing.

Duties of Directors and Officers of Nonprofit Corporations

Directors and officers of nonprofit corporations owe fiduciary duties to their corporations that are similar to the duties owed by managers of for-profit corporations. Directors and officers owe a duty of care and duties of loyalty to the nonprofit corporation. They must act in good faith, with the care of an ordinarily prudent person, and with a reasonable belief that they are acting in the best interests of the corporation. In addition, a director should not have a conflict of interest in any transaction of the nonprofit corporation. As with for-profit corporations, conflict-of-interest transactions must meet the intrinsic fairness standard. Finally, a nonprofit corporation may not lend money to a director.

Liability concerns of directors of nonprofit corporations, especially public benefit corporations in which directors typically receive no compensation, have made it difficult for some nonprofit corporations to find and retain directors. Therefore, the Model Nonprofit Corporation Act permits nonprofit corporations to limit or eliminate the liability of directors for breach of the duty of care. The articles may not limit or eliminate a director's liability for failing to act in good faith, engaging in intentional misconduct, breaching the duty of loyalty, or having a conflict of interest.

THE GLOBAL BUSINESS ENVIRONMENT

Directors' Duties around the Globe

The fiduciary duties that American directors owe to their corporations are echoed in corporate law throughout the world. In Brazil, for example, an officer must apply the same principles he would apply in his own business. A Brazilian director breaches the duty of loyalty if the director uses inside information for his own benefit or for that of third parties, acts negligently in the use or protection of the company's rights, or engages in a business opportunity to gain personal advantage. For public companies, Brazil adds a duty that does not exist under American corporation law: to supply information to the shareholders and the public. In the United States, this duty is generally imposed on the corporation, not the directors.

Under German law, the management board and supervisory board of an AG owe shareholders a duty of loyalty. Members of the management board have a statutory obligation of confidentiality, and each member of the management board must exercise the care of a diligent and prudent business executive.

ETHICS IN ACTION

Sarbanes–Oxley Act Imposes New Duties and Liabilities on Corporate Management

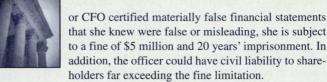

In the last few years, it has been revealed that some high-level officers of public corporations reaped millions of dollars of bonuses and profits from their sale of their corporations' stock during periods in which the corporations' profits were fraudulently inflated. In the Sarbanes–Oxley Act of 2002, Congress took a two-barreled approach, increasing top management's responsibility for the accuracy of financial statements and eliminating managements' ability to profit personally from misstated financial data.

First, the Sarbanes–Oxley Act requires the CEO and the CFO of public companies to certify that to their knowledge all financial information in annual and quarterly reports filed with the Securities and Exchange Commission fairly present the financial condition of the company and do not include untrue or misleading material statements. The purpose of the certification requirement is to protect shareholders and investors who rely on corporate financial statements. If a CEO or CFO certified materially false financial statements that she knew were false or misleading, she is subject to a fine of $5 million and 20 years' imprisonment. In addition, the officer could have civil liability to shareholders far exceeding the fine limitation.

Second, the Act requires the CEO and the CFO of a public company to disgorge any bonus, incentive-based or equity-based compensation, and the profit from the sale of corporate securities received during any period in which the corporation was required to restate a financial statement due to a wrongful material noncompliance with a financial reporting requirement. This requirement to reimburse the corporation applies to the CEO and the CFO even if the wrongdoing was by some other officer or employee. In addition, the Act expands the disgorgement remedy available against any wrongdoing officer who receives bonuses or stock profits during the period of time the stock price is inflated by false financial information. The Act permits recovery of not only improper gains but also any other relief necessary to protect and to mitigate harm to investors.

Corporate and Management Liability for Torts and Crimes

When directors, officers, and other employees of the corporation commit torts and crimes while conducting corporate affairs, the issue arises concerning who has liability. Should the individuals committing the torts and crimes be held liable, the corporation, or both?

Liability of the Corporation

For **torts,** the vicarious liability rule of *respondeat superior* applies to corporations. The only issue is whether an employee acted within the scope of her employment, which encompasses not only acts the employee is authorized to commit but may also include acts that the employee is expressly instructed to avoid. Generally, under the doctrine of *respondeat superior,* a corporation is liable for an employee's tort that is reasonably connected to the authorized conduct of the employee.

The traditional view was that a corporation could not be guilty of a **crime** because criminal guilt required intent. A corporation, not having a mind, could form no intent. Other courts held that a corporation was not a person for purposes of criminal liability.

Today, few courts have difficulty holding corporations liable for crimes. Modern criminal statutes either expressly provide that corporations may commit crimes or define the term *person* to include corporations. In addition, some criminal statutes designed to protect the public welfare do not require intent as an element of some crimes, thereby removing the grounds used by early courts to justify relieving corporations of criminal liability.

Courts are especially likely to impose criminal liability on a corporation when the criminal act is requested, authorized, or performed by:

1. The board of directors,
2. An officer,

3. Another person having responsibility for formulating company policy, or

4. A high-level administrator having supervisory responsibility over the subject matter of the offense and acting within the scope of his employment.

In addition, courts hold a corporation liable for crimes of its agent or employee committed within the scope of his authority, even if a higher corporate official has no knowledge of the act and has not ratified it.

Directors' and Officers' Liability for Torts and Crimes

A person is always *liable for his own torts and crimes,* even when committed on behalf of his principal. Every person in our society is expected to exercise independent judgment and not merely to follow orders. Therefore, directors and officers are personally liable when they commit torts or crimes during the performance of their corporate duties.

A director or officer is usually not liable for the torts of employees of the corporation, since the corporation, not the director or the officer, is the principal. He will have **tort** liability, however, if he *authorizes* the tort or *participates* in its commission. A director or officer has **criminal** liability if she *requests, authorizes, conspires,* or *aids and abets* the commission of a crime by an employee.

In the *USX* case, which follows, the court considered the liability of the sole officers and directors of a corporation that illegally dumped toxic waste.

United States v. USX Corporation — 68 F.3d 811 (3rd Cir. 1995)

Atlantic Disposal Service, Inc. (ADS), was in the business of hauling waste from commercial and industrial firms. Alvin White and Charles Carite were the sole shareholders, directors, and officers of ADS, each owning 50 percent of the shares. One of ADS's clients was a plant operated by USX Corporation in Camden, New Jersey. In 1976, the local county dump refused to accept ADS's truckload of 55-gallon drums of toxic liquid waste from USX; ADS then arranged to dispose of the drums on a one-acre wooded parcel in Tabernacle, New Jersey, owned by an ADS employee. In 1982, health department investigators discovered 193 barrels and containers at the Tabernacle site. Sampling by the Environmental Protection Agency revealed a release of hazardous substances to the soil and groundwater. After the EPA cleaned the site, it brought an action in a federal district court to recover the cost from ADS, White, and Carite under section 107(a)(4) of the Comprehensive Environmental Response, Compensation, and Liability Act (CERCLA). Section 107(a)(4) imposes liability on any person—commonly referred to as a "transporter"—who accepts hazardous substances for transport to a disposal facility selected by that person, from which there is a release of a hazardous substance. ADS was held liable as a transporter based on its employees' transportation of the drums of toxic waste to the Tabernacle site. White and Carite were held liable on the grounds they exercised control over ADS in 1976 when the drums were dumped at the Tabernacle site. ADS, White, and Carite appealed to the court of appeals.

Vanaskie, Judge Congress enacted CERCLA to facilitate cleanup of potentially dangerous hazardous waste sites, with a view to the preservation of the environment and human health. *Tippins, Inc. v. USX* (1994). One of the principal purposes of CERCLA is to force polluters to pay for costs associated with remedying their pollution.

Liability of a "transporter" is established by showing that a person accepted hazardous substances for transport and either selected the disposal facility or had substantial input into deciding where the hazardous substance should be disposed. The United States presented the testimony of the ADS mechanic who leased the Tabernacle site and who had been paid by ADS to accept the drummed liquid waste for storage. The United States also presented the testimony of the ADS mechanic's former wife, who said that she witnessed the dumping of barrels from ADS trucks on the Tabernacle site. The ADS dispatcher at the time said that he had sent drummed liquid to the Tabernacle site. At least one of the drums found at the sight had attached to it USX shipping documents, and other drums bore the name USX. Accordingly, the judgment that ADS is liable for cleanup costs is affirmed.

The appeal from the judgment against White and Carite presents an issue of first impression in this Court:

what standard of liability did Congress intend to establish under CERCLA for principal shareholders and officers of a closely-held corporation that transports hazardous substances?

In *Tippins,* we held that section 107(a)(4) imposed liability on a waste transportation corporation not only if it ultimately selects the disposal facility, but also when it actively participates in the disposal decision to the extent of having had substantial input into which facility was ultimately chosen. This "active participation" standard advances the objectives of CERCLA by recognizing the reality that transporters often play an influential role in the decision to dispose of waste at a given facility.

The express terms of section 107(a)(4) limit liability to those persons who accept hazardous substances for transport and have a substantial input into the selection of the disposal facility. Thus, section 107(a)(4) plainly imposes liability on corporate officers and shareholders if they participate in the liability-creating conduct.

The United States contends that Congress also intended to impose liability on those who control the affairs of a responsible corporation, irrespective of whether those in control actually participate in the liability-creating conduct. According to the United States, the courts have generally construed CERCLA as permitting recovery from those corporate officers who participated in the management of or exercised control over a corporate entity. Extending liability to those controlling a corporation, according to the United States, is consistent with CERCLA's goal of placing the ultimate responsibility for cleanup on those responsible for problems caused by the disposal of chemical poisons.

CERCLA, of course, is to be construed liberally to effectuate its goals. Liberal construction, however, may not be employed as a means for filling in the blanks so as to discern a congressional intent to impose liability under nearly every conceivable scenario. In light of the established principle of limited liability that protects corporate officers or employees who do not actually participate in liability-creating conduct, there must be some basis in the statute itself, beyond its general purpose, to support the conclusion that Congress intended to impose liability on those who control the corporation's day-to-day activities.

Congress could have specified that majority shareholders or officers of corporations engaged in the waste hauling business are personally responsible for releases of hazardous substances from disposal facilities selected by their companies. On the contrary, the sparse legislative history indicates that Congress anticipated that issues of liability not resolved by CERCLA shall be governed by evolving principles of common law. Under these circumstances, it is appropriate to limit liability to those persons who are clearly made liable by the language Congress used—those who actively participate in the process of accepting hazardous substances for transport and have a substantial role in the selection of the disposal site.

Contrary to the assertion of White and Carite, however, liability under section 107(a)(4) is not limited to those who personally participated in the transportation of hazardous wastes. It is not necessary that the officer personally accept the waste for transport. Nor is it necessary that the officer participate in the selection of the disposal facility. Liability may be imposed where the officer is aware of the acceptance of materials for transport and of his company's substantial participation in the selection of the disposal facility. An officer who has authority to control disposal decisions should not escape liability when she has actual knowledge that a subordinate has selected a disposal site and, effectively, acquiesces in the subordinate's actions.

Although there was indeed substantial evidence that White and Carite were actively involved in the day-to-day affairs of ADS at the time of the disposal of waste drums at the Tabernacle site, there was also countervailing evidence that White and Carite were not "hands on" managers during the relevant time period. Moreover, White disavowed knowledge of disposal of drums at the Tabernacle site. Corroboration for White's assertion may be inferred from the fact that during the relevant time frame he supervised the sales and administrative staff and did not have active involvement in the operational aspects of the business.

Tony Carite, the younger brother of Charles Carite, testified that Charles Carite had few specific responsibilities in the day-to-day business. Tony Carite was the operations manager of ADS. The ADS dispatcher and truck drivers at the time of the dumping testified that they reported directly to Tony Carite and had little, if any, involvement with Charles Carite.

Under these circumstances, the United States was not entitled to summary judgment against White and Carite.

Judgment against ADS affirmed; judgment reversed in favor of White and Carite.

Insurance and Indemnification

The extensive potential liability of directors deters many persons from becoming directors. They fear that their liability for their actions as directors may far exceed their fees as directors. To encourage persons to become directors, corporations **indemnify** them for their outlays associated with defending lawsuits brought against them and paying judgments and settlement amounts. In addition, or as an alternative, corporations purchase **insurance** that will make such payments for the directors. Indemnification and insurance are provided for officers, also.

Mandatory Indemnification of Directors

Under the MBCA, a director is entitled to *mandatory indemnification* of her reasonable litigation expenses when she is sued and *wins completely* (is *wholly successful*). The greatest part of such expenses is attorney's fees. Because indemnification is mandatory in this context, when the corporation refuses to indemnify a director who has won completely, she may ask a court to order the corporation to indemnify her.

Permissible Indemnification of Directors

Under the MBCA, a director who loses a lawsuit *may* be indemnified by the corporation. This is called *permissible indemnification,* because the corporation is permitted to indemnify the director but is not required to do so.

The corporation must establish that the director acted in *good faith* and reasonably believed that she acted in the *best interests* of the corporation. When a director seeks indemnification for a *criminal* fine, the corporation must establish a third requirement—that the director had no reasonable cause to believe that her conduct was unlawful. Finally, any permissible indemnification must be approved by someone independent of the director receiving indemnification—a disinterested board of directors, disinterested shareholders, or independent legal counsel. Permissible indemnification may cover not only the director's reasonable expenses but also fines and damages that the director has been ordered to pay.

A corporation may not elect to indemnify a director who was found to have received a *financial benefit* to which he was not entitled. Such a rule tends to prevent indemnification of directors who acted from self-interest. If a director received no financial benefit but was held liable to his corporation or paid an amount to the corporation as part of a *settlement,* the director may be indemnified only for his reasonable expenses, not for the amount that he paid to the corporation. The purpose of these rules is to avoid the circularity of having the director pay damages to the corporation and then having the corporation indemnify the director for the same amount of money.

Advances A director may not be able to afford to make payments to her lawyer prior to the end of a lawsuit. More important, a lawyer may refuse to defend a director who cannot pay legal fees. Therefore, the MBCA permits a corporation to make advances to a director to allow the director to afford a lawyer, if the director affirms that she meets the requirements for permissible indemnification and she promises to repay the advances if she is found not entitled to indemnification.

Court-Ordered Indemnification A court may order a corporation to indemnify a director if it determines that the director meets the standard for *mandatory* indemnification or if the director is *fairly and reasonably* entitled to indemnification in view of all the relevant circumstances.

ETHICS IN ACTION

Expanding Indemnification

The MBCA permits a corporation to expand the grounds on which it may indemnify a director, within limits. For example, the corporation may provide for indemnification of a director's liability (including a judgment paid to the corporation) when the director acted carelessly and in bad faith, but did not intend to harm the corporation or its shareholders and did not receive an improper financial benefit.

- Do you think it is ethical for a corporation to indemnify a director in the context above for the amount for which she was liable to the corporation? Would a rights theorist support indemnification in that context? Would a utilitarian? Would a profit maximizer?
- Would you be a shareholder in a corporation that permits indemnification in the context above?
- Would you be a director in a corporation if it did not indemnify you in that context?

Indemnification of Nondirectors Under the MBCA, officers and employees who are not directors are entitled to the same mandatory indemnification rights as directors.

Insurance

The MBCA does not limit the ability of a corporation to purchase insurance on behalf of its directors, officers, and employees. Insurance companies, however, are unwilling to insure all risks. In addition, some risks are *legally uninsurable as against public policy*. Therefore, liability for misconduct such as self-dealing, usurpation, and securities fraud is uninsurable.

Nonprofit Corporations

A nonprofit corporation may obtain insurance and indemnify its officers and directors for liabilities incurred in the course of their performance of their official duties. The MNCA requires indemnification when the director or officer wins the lawsuit completely. A corporation is permitted to indemnify an officer or director who is found liable if he acted in good faith and reasonably believed he acted in the best interests of the corporation.

Problems and Problem Cases

1. Pantry Pride, Inc., made a hostile tender offer to acquire the shares of Revlon, Inc., for $47.50 per share. Pantry Pride's plan thereafter was to sell Revlon's various lines of business individually. Recognizing that a takeover was inevitable, Revlon's board negotiated a friendly acquisition with Forstmann Little & Co. for $56 per share. Revlon's board also agreed to break up the company by selling its cosmetic division. Forstmann wanted to sell two other Revlon divisions after the purchase. Eventually, Forstmann upped its offer price to $57.25. In return, Revlon's board gave Forstmann a lock-up option, promising to sell two valuable divisions to Forstmann at nearly $200 million below their market value if Pantry Pride took over Revlon instead of Forstmann. The purpose and effect of the lock-up option was to prevent any other bidder, including Pantry Pride, from being willing to purchase Revlon. What standard or test judges whether Revlon's board acted properly in giving a lock-up option to Forstmann? Did Revlon's board comply with that test?

2. The board of directors of Pine Belt Producers Cooperative, Inc., authorized any two of its three officers to withdraw funds from its account at First National Bank of Ruston. The board also authorized its president, Claude

O'Bryan, to borrow up to $80,000 in the name of Pine Belt. O'Bryan obtained a $57,000 loan for Pine Belt from the bank in the form of a check payable to Pine Belt. O'Bryan indorsed the check in the name of Pine Belt and gave the check back to the bank for the purpose of paying a personal debt of the vice president of Pine Belt. Pine Belt later claimed that the bank acted improperly by honoring the check because it was indorsed by O'Bryan only. Pine Belt also claimed the bank acted improperly by allowing corporate funds to be used to pay a noncorporate debt. The bank defended by arguing that O'Bryan had authority to indorse checks payable to Pine Belt and to direct how Pine Belt's funds would be used. Who won?

3. Deborah Goode, Thomas Goode, Cynthia Mann, and Hodges Mann were the only shareholders and directors of Star Communications, Inc. Each owned 25 shares. The Goodes were married to each other, as were the Manns. When the Goodes had marital problems, notice was given for a directors' meeting, the stated purpose of which was to oust Mrs. Goode as a director. The Goodes and Manns attended the meeting. There was some discussion whether the meeting was a directors' or shareholders' meeting, but the issue was never clearly resolved. Nonetheless, a vote was taken to remove Mrs. Goode as a director. The Manns voted for removal, Mrs. Goode voted against, and Mr. Goode abstained. May Mrs. Goode invalidate her removal on grounds that she was removed without cause and that she was removed by action of the directors, not the shareholders?

4. Lillian Pritchard was a director of Pritchard & Baird Corporation, a business founded by her husband. After the death of her husband, her sons took control of the corporation. For two years, they looted the assets of the corporation through theft and improper payments. The corporation's financial statements revealed the improper payments to the sons, but Mrs. Pritchard did not read the financial statements. She did not know what her sons were doing to the corporation or that what they were doing was unlawful. When Mrs. Pritchard was sued for failing to protect the assets of the corporation, she argued that she was a figurehead director, a simple housewife who served as a director as an accommodation to her husband and sons. Was Mrs. Pritchard held liable?

5. The Chicago National League Ball Club, Inc. (Chicago Cubs), operated Wrigley Field, the Cubs' home park. Through the 1965 baseball season, the Cubs were the only major league baseball team that played no home games at night because Wrigley Field had no lights for nighttime baseball. Philip K. Wrigley, director and president of the corporation, refused to install lights because of

his personal opinion that baseball was a daytime sport and that installing lights and scheduling night baseball games would result in the deterioration of the surrounding neighborhood. The other directors assented to this policy. From 1961 to 1965, the Cubs suffered losses from their baseball operations. The Chicago White Sox, whose weekday games were generally played at night, drew many more fans than did the Cubs. A shareholder sued the board of directors to force them to install lights at Wrigley Field and to schedule night games. What did the court rule?

6. Paramount Communications, Inc., was the target of an unsolicited $90 per share takeover bid by QVC Network, Inc. To thwart QVC's bid, Paramount's board of directors adopted defense tactics to facilitate a friendly takeover by Viacom, Inc. at a price of $85 per share. Paramount agreed to grant Viacom a lock-up option to purchase almost 20 percent of Paramount's shares at a bargain price. In addition, Paramount promised to pay Viacom a termination fee of $100,000,000, which was about 10 percent of Paramount's assets, if Paramount terminated the merger because of a competing transaction or if its shareholders voted against the merger. Has Paramount's board of directors acted legally?

7. Micom Holding Company was owned entirely by the Edwin Walhof family. Micom Holding owned 93 percent of the shares of Micom Corporation. To freeze out the 7 percent minority shareholders of Micom Corporation, Walhof decided to merge Micom Corporation and Micom Holding Company. Under the merger terms, Micom Holding Company was the surviving corporation, the Walhof family were the only surviving shareholders, and the minority shareholders received $10 per share. What standards must the freeze-out merger meet to be legal?

8. Lindenhurst Drugs, Inc., was owned equally by Allen Becker, Burton Steinberg, and Marvin Steinberg. Each was also an officer and director. The corporation operated a drugstore in leased space in the Linden Plaza Shopping Center. Burton was the manager of the drugstore. In 1979, wanting more retail space to expand their product lines, Becker and the Steinbergs offered to purchase the Ben Franklin store franchise in the Linden Plaza Shopping Center. Their offer was rejected, but the corporation still had an interest in buying the Ben Franklin store. In 1981, the Linden Plaza Shopping Center notified the corporation that its lease would not be renewed at the end of the year. Becker did not immediately inform the Steinbergs of the termination notice. He did nothing to find a new space for the store. Instead, Becker purchased the Ben Franklin store in the name of his own corporation and leased space for the Ben Franklin store

from Linden Plaza Shopping Center. Has Becker done anything wrong?

9. Butch Stanko was an officer and shareholder of Cattle King Packing Company, Inc., which operated a meat-packing plant in Adams County, Colorado. Gary Waderich was a general sales manager primarily responsible for commercial sales of meat food products and for the daily operation of Cattle King. Stanko set company policies and practices to circumvent the Federal Meat Inspection Act (FMIA), which policies and practices he instructed Waderich and other employees to follow. When Stanko returned to his home in Scottsbluff, Nebraska, he monitored operations by phone and visits to the plant to make certain that the policies and practices that he had established were being followed. For example, spoiled meat rejected by a buyer and returned to Cattle King was in bags that were puffy with gas caused by the spoilage. On instructions by Waderich, an employee reworked the meat by poking the bags to release the gas, and the meat was reshipped to the same buyer. Were Waderich, Stanko, and Cattle King guilty of criminal violations of the FMIA?

10. On behalf of Gregg Corporation, shareholders of the corporation successfully sued Gregg's independent directors for making a $35,000,000 loan to Gregg's CEO. The directors forgave the loan because they believed it was in the best interests of Gregg not to seek repayment from the CEO, who was bankrupt. The board initially made the loan as part of the CEO's total compensation package under the belief that the CEO would leave Gregg if the loan were not made. Gregg's directors believed that the best interests of Gregg were served by retaining the CEO. May Gregg indemnify the independent directors for their litigation expenses in defending against the shareholder suit? May Gregg indemnify the independent directors for the judgment they were ordered to pay Gregg?

Online Research: Independent Directors

In 2002, the New York Stock Exchange and NASDAQ proposed corporate governance changes designed to increase the power of independent directors, especially in the membership of board committees with responsibility over executive compensation and audits. NYSE and NASDAQ rules apply to companies with stock listed on the exchanges.

• Find the websites for the NYSE and NASDAQ, determine the status of their corporate governance proposals, and list the changes and proposed changes in their corporate governance rules.

44

SHAREHOLDERS' RIGHTS AND LIABILITIES

Four business associates create a business that will develop and sell information technology software. The business will be incorporated. The four will provide 90 percent of the initial capital needs of the business, but none of them has the IT skills to develop marketable software. In addition, none of the four want to be involved in the day-to-day management of the business. The four associates have found, however, an IT engineer to develop software and another person who is willing to manage the business. The engineer and the general manager each want a 5 percent equity interest in the corporation, which the four associates are willing to grant to them. Although the engineer and the GM would each like to elect a representative to the corporation's board of directors, the four associates want to control the business absolutely, with each associate owning an equal share of the corporation and sitting on the board.

• Using classes of shares, create an equity structure for the corporation that meets the wants of the four associates, the engineer, and the GM.
• In this context, why is using classes of shares preferable to using one class of shares with cumulative voting for directors?

THE SHAREHOLDERS ARE THE ultimate owners of a corporation, but a shareholder has *no right to manage* the corporation. Instead, a corporation is managed by its board of directors and its officers for the benefit of its shareholders.

The shareholders' role in a corporation is limited to electing and removing directors, approving certain important matters, and ensuring that the actions of the corporation's managers are consistent with the applicable state corporation statute, the articles of incorporation, and the bylaws.

Shareholders also assume a few responsibilities. For example, all shareholders are required to pay the promised consideration for shares. Shareholders are liable for receiving dividends beyond the lawful amount. In addition, controlling shareholders may owe special duties to minority shareholders.

Close corporation shareholders enjoy rights and owe duties beyond the rights and duties of shareholders of publicly owned corporations. In addition, some courts have found close corporation shareholders to be fiduciaries of each other.

This chapter's study of the rights and responsibilities of shareholders begins with an examination of shareholders' meetings and voting rights.

Shareholders' Meetings

The general corporation statutes of most states and the Model Business Corporation Act (MBCA) provide that an **annual meeting of shareholders** shall be held. The purpose of an annual shareholders' meeting is to elect new directors and to conduct other necessary business. Often, the shareholders are asked to approve the corporation's independent auditors and to vote on shareholders' proposals.

Special meetings of shareholders may be held whenever a corporate matter arises that requires immediate shareholders' action, such as the approval of a merger that cannot wait until the next annual shareholders' meeting. Under the MBCA, a special shareholders' meeting may be called by the board of directors or by a person authorized to do so by the bylaws, usually the president or the chairman of the board. In addition, the holders of at least 10 percent of the shares entitled to vote at the meeting may call a special meeting.

Notice of Meetings

To permit shareholders to arrange their schedules for attendance at shareholders' meetings, the MBCA requires the corporation to give shareholders **notice** of annual and special meetings of shareholders. Notice of a *special meeting* must list the purpose of the meeting. Under the MBCA, notice of an *annual meeting* need not include the purpose of the meeting unless shareholders will be asked to approve extraordinary corporate changes—for example, amendments to the articles of incorporation and mergers.

Notice need be given only to shareholders entitled to vote who are **shareholders of record** on a date fixed by the board of directors. Shareholders of record are those whose names appear on the share-transfer book of the corporation. Usually, only shareholders of record are entitled to vote at shareholders' meetings.

Conduct of Meetings

To conduct business at a shareholders' meeting, a **quorum** of the outstanding shares must be represented at the meeting. If the approval of more than one class of shares is required, a quorum of each class of shares must be present. A quorum is a majority of shares outstanding, unless a greater percentage is established in the articles. The president or the chairman of the board usually presides at shareholders' meetings. Minutes of shareholders' meetings are usually kept by the secretary.

A majority of the votes cast at the shareholders' meeting will decide issues that are put to a vote. If the approval of more than one class of shares is required, a majority of the votes cast by each class must favor the issue. The articles may require a greater than majority vote. Ordinarily, a shareholder is entitled to cast as many votes as he has shares.

Shareholders have a right of *full participation* in shareholders' meetings. This includes the right to offer resolutions, to speak for and against proposed resolutions, and to ask questions of the officers of the corporation.

Typical shareholder resolutions are aimed at protecting or enhancing the interests of minority shareholders and promoting current social issues. Proposals have included limiting corporate charitable contributions, restricting the production of nuclear power, banning the manufacture of weapons, and requiring the protection of the environment.

Shareholder Action without a Meeting

Generally, shareholders can act only at a properly called meeting. However, the MBCA permits shareholders to act without a meeting if *all of the shareholders entitled to vote consent in writing* to the action.

Shareholders' Election of Directors

Straight Voting

The most important shareholder voting right exercised at a shareholder meeting is the right to elect the directors. Normally, directors are elected by a single class of shareholders in **straight voting,** in which each share has one vote for each new director to be elected. With straight voting, a shareholder may vote for as many nominees as there are directors to be elected; a shareholder may cast for each such nominee as many votes as she has shares. For example, in a director election in which 15 people have been nominated for 5 director positions, a shareholder with 100 shares can vote for up to 5 nominees and can cast up to 100 votes for each of those 5 nominees.

Under straight voting, the nominees with the most votes are elected. Consequently, straight voting allows a majority shareholder to elect the entire board of directors. Thus, minority shareholders are unable to elect any representatives to the board without the cooperation of the majority shareholder.

Straight voting is also a problem in close corporations in which a few shareholders own equal numbers of shares. In such corporations, no shareholder individually controls the corporation, yet if the holders of a majority of the shares act together, those holders will elect all of the directors and control the corporation. Such control may be exercised to the detriment of the other shareholders.

Two alternatives to straight voting aid minority shareholders' attempts to gain representation on the board and prevent harmful coalitions in close corporations: cumulative voting and class voting.

Cumulative Voting

With cumulative voting, a corporation allows a shareholder to cumulate her votes by multiplying the number

Figure 1 Cumulative Voting Formula

The formula for determining the minimum number of shares required to elect a desired number of directors under cumulative voting is:

$$X = \frac{S \times R}{D + 1} + 1$$

X = Number of shares needed to elect the desired number of directors

S = Total number of shares voting at the shareholders' meeting

R = Number of director representatives desired

D = Total number of directors to be elected at the meeting

Example: Sarah Smiles wants to elect two of the five directors of Oates Corporation. One thousand shares will be voted. In this case:

$S = 1,000$

$R = 2$

$D = 5$

Therefore:

$$X = 334.33$$

Fractions are ignored; thus, Sarah will need to hold at least 334 shares to be able to elect two directors.

of directors to be elected by the shareholder's number of shares. A shareholder may then allocate her votes among the nominees as she chooses. She may vote for only as many nominees as there are directors to be elected, but she may vote for fewer nominees. For example, she may choose to cast all of her votes for only one nominee.

See Figure 1 for a further explanation of the mechanics of cumulative voting.

Classes of Shares

A corporation may have several classes of shares. The two most common classes are *common shares* and *preferred shares,* but a corporation may have several classes of common shares and several classes of preferred shares. Many close corporations have two or more classes of common shares with different voting rights. Each class may be entitled to elect one or more directors, in order to balance power in a corporation.

For example, suppose a corporation has four directors and 100 shares held by four shareholders—each of whom owns 25 shares. With straight voting and no classes of shares, no shareholder owns enough shares to elect himself as a director, because 51 shares are necessary to elect a director. Suppose, however, that the corporation has four classes of shares, each with the right to elect one of the directors. Each class of shares is issued to only one shareholder. Now, as the sole owner of a class of shares entitling the class to elect one director, each shareholder can elect himself to the board.

Using classes of shares is the cleanest way to allocate among shareholders the power to elect directors, as well as allocate equity ownership of the corporation. To protect such allocations, however, the articles should require approval of every class of shares to change the rights of any class or to create a new class of shares.

Shareholder Control Devices

While cumulative voting and class voting are two useful methods by which shareholders can allocate or acquire voting control of a corporation, there are other devices that may also be used for these purposes: voting trusts; shareholder voting agreements; and proxies, especially irrevocable proxies.

Voting Trusts With a **voting trust,** shareholders transfer their shares to one or more voting trustees and receive voting trust certificates in exchange. The shareholders retain many of their rights, including the right to receive dividends, but the voting trustees vote for directors and other matters submitted to shareholders.

The purpose of a voting trust is to control the corporation through the concentration of shareholder voting power in the voting trustees, who often are participating shareholders. If several minority shareholders collectively own a majority of the shares of a corporation, they may create a voting trust and thereby control the corporation. You may ask why shareholders need a voting trust when they are in apparent agreement on how to vote their shares. The reason is that they may have disputes in the future that could prevent the shareholders from agreeing how to vote. The voting trust ensures that the shareholder group will control the corporation despite the emergence of differences.

The MBCA limits the duration of voting trusts to 10 years, though all or part of the participating shareholders may agree to extend the term for another 10 years. Also, a voting trust must be made public, with copies of the voting trust document available for inspection at the corporation's offices.

Shareholder Voting Agreements As an alternative to a voting trust, shareholders may merely agree how they will vote their shares. For example, shareholders collectively owning a majority of the shares may agree to vote for each other as directors, resulting in each being elected to the board of directors.

A shareholder voting agreement must be written; only shareholders signing the agreement are bound by it. When a shareholder refuses to vote as agreed, courts specifically enforce the agreement.

Shareholder voting agreements have two advantages over voting trusts. First, their duration may be *perpetual.* Second, they may be kept secret from the other shareholders; they usually do not have to be filed in the corporation's offices.

Proxies A shareholder may appoint a **proxy** to vote his shares. If several minority shareholders collectively own a majority of the shares of a corporation, they may appoint a proxy to vote their shares and thereby control the corporation. The ordinary proxy has only a limited duration—11 months under the MBCA—unless a longer term is specified. Also, the ordinary proxy is *revocable* at any time. As a result, there is no guarantee that control agreements accomplished through the use of revocable proxies will survive future shareholder disputes.

However, a proxy is *irrevocable* if it is coupled with an interest. A proxy is coupled with an interest when, among other things, the person holding the proxy is a party to a shareholder voting agreement or a buy-and-sell agreement. The principal use of irrevocable proxies is in conjunction with shareholder voting agreements.

In the *Eliason* case, which follows, the court considered the legality of a shareholder voting agreement and whether a proxy is irrevocable. Note that for Louise Eliason to win on the bigger issue, she had to argue that the proxy given to her by her father had been revoked.

Eliason v. Englehart   *733 A.2d 944 (Del. Sup. Ct. 1999)*

Brosius-Eliason Co. is a building and materials company whose stock is owned by three families. The Eliason family owns a majority of the 9,900 shares outstanding, with James Eliason (3,928 shares) and his sister Sarah Englehart (1,260 shares) holding the controlling block. The Brosius family owns a total of 3,690 shares, and Frank Hewlett owns the remaining 1,062 shares. On July 31, 1997, James Eliason executed a proxy giving his daughter, Louise Eliason, authority to vote his shares. Two weeks later, James and his sister Sarah entered into a voting agreement that assured Eliason family control over the company. The agreement provided, among other things, that James and Sarah would (1) grant each other irrevocable proxies to vote their shares in accordance with the agreement and (2) not sell or transfer their stock without the prior consent of the other. The second clause—requiring consent to sell or transfer the shares—made the proxies coupled with an interest. Immediately after signing the voting agreement, James (acting through Louise) and Sarah executed written consents to remove the incumbent board and elect new board members.

Over the next few months, Louise started asserting her family's control over the company by proposing a buyout of the Brosius family stock and a reorganization of the business. Sarah disagreed with Louise. On February 6, 1998, Sarah joined with the two other families, removed the incumbent directors, and replaced them with representatives from each of the three families.

Louise responded by suing to invalidate the election of the new directors. The trial court held that the rightful directors were the new directors elected in 1998. The court reasoned that the 1998 election was effective if Sarah's votes counted toward the majority, and Sarah's votes could be counted if she was not bound by her voting agreement with James. The issue was whether the 1997 proxy James gave to Louise was irrevocable. The trial court held that it was irrevocable and that Louise held James's voting power. Since the proxy predated the voting agreement by two weeks, the trial court concluded that James had no power to vote his shares by the time he contracted with Sarah. Therefore, the trial court concluded that James's voting agreement with Sarah failed for lack of consideration given by James.

Louise appealed to the Supreme Court of Delaware. To win the case, she had to argue that the proxy her father, James, gave to her was revocable. If it was revocable, then James could revoke it at any time. Louise argued that James revoked the proxy by entering the voting agreement with his sister Sarah. Thus, Louise argued that both James and Sarah gave voting rights to each other in the voting agreement, supplying the necessary consideration to make the agreement enforceable. In the following decision, the Delaware Supreme Court agreed with Louise.

Per Curiam   A proxy is evidence of an agent's authority to vote shares owned by another. To be effective as a proxy, a document must identify the shares that are to be voted by the agent and include some indication of authenticity, such as the stockholder's signature or a facsimile of the signature. Proxies are revocable unless they satisfy the requirements of 8 Delaware Code section 212(e):

> A duly executed proxy shall be irrevocable if it states that it is irrevocable and if, and only as long as, it is coupled with an interest sufficient in law to support an irrevocable power. . . .

The parties agree that the proxy James gave to Louise meets the statutory requirement that it be coupled with an interest. The question is whether it "states that it is irrevocable." The disputed proxy provides, in relevant part:

PROXY
KNOW ALL MEN BY THESE PRESENTS:
That James T. Eliason, III, as the record owner of 3,928 shares of the issued and outstanding shares of voting stock of Brosius-Eliason Co., a Delaware corporation ("BEC"), for good and valuable consideration the legal sufficiency of which is hereby acknowledged by the undersigned, do hereby constitute and appoint Louise R. Eliason as attorney and agent for him . . . to vote as his proxy (i) at all annual and special meetings of the shareholders of BEC, . . . and (ii) on all consents or dissents by shareholders of BEC . . . and any other matter, as fully as he could act, giving to said proxy, agent and attorney, full power of substitution and revocation. This proxy shall terminate on July 31, 1999.
Date: 7/31, 1997   /s/ James T. Eliason III

On this 31 day of July, 1997, before me a Notary Public in and for said County and State, personally appeared James T. Eliason, III, known to me to be the person whose name is subscribed to the within Irrevocable Proxy and acknowledged to me that he executed the same.
/s/ Notary Public

The word "irrevocable" appears only in the acknowledgment. Thus, the question becomes whether the acknowledgment may be construed to be part of the proxy for purposes of section 212(e). We conclude that section 212(e) requires that the word "irrevocable" appear somewhere in the proxy, but an acknowledgment is not part of the proxy.

Generally, proxies are revocable. If a proxy is to be irrevocable, section 212(e) requires, among other things, that it state that it is irrevocable. The purpose of this requirement is apparent—to distinguish between revocable and irrevocable proxies and to put interested parties (the stockholder, proxy holder and corporation) on notice that the proxy is irrevocable. The statutory language is simple and direct. A proxy must state that it is irrevocable, which means that the word "irrevocable," or perhaps a synonym, must appear in the proxy.

The problem is that section 212 does not specify whether an acknowledgment of the stockholder's signature is considered part of the proxy. From our review of acknowledgments, generally, we conclude that it is not. An acknowledgment is a means by which the signature on an instrument may be authenticated. There is no requirement that proxies be acknowledged, but even if there were, the acknowledgment ordinarily forms no part of the substance of the instrument. A proper acknowledgment does not validate an otherwise invalid instrument. Since an acknowledgment does not affect the substance of the instrument being acknowledged, we conclude that it cannot be used to satisfy the statutory requirement that a proxy state that it is irrevocable.

This conclusion recognizes the restricted function of an acknowledgment and also promotes the statutory goal of providing notice to interested parties. The acknowledgment normally appears after the signature line on an instrument. In this case, the acknowledgment was on the same page as the proxy, but it could have been on the following page. In either event, the location of the acknowledgment, combined with its lack of substantive impact, creates a real risk that the party signing the document will never read it.

We hold that the proxy James gave to his daughter, Louise, failed to satisfy the requirements of section 212(e), and, therefore, is revocable.

Judgment reversed in favor of Louise Eliason. Remanded to the trial court.

Fundamental Corporate Changes

Other matters besides the election of directors require shareholder action, some because they make fundamental changes in the structure or business of the corporation.

Because the articles of incorporation embody the basic contract between a corporation and its shareholders, shareholders must approve most **amendments of the articles of incorporation.** For example, when the articles are amended to increase the number of authorized shares or reduce the dividend rights of preferred shareholders, shareholder approval is needed.

ETHICS IN ACTION

By using classes of shares (or a perpetual shareholder voting agreement), shareholders that individually are minority shareholders but collectively control a majority of the corporation's shares may control the corporation absolutely. For example, suppose five shareholders create a corporation and decide at incorporation that it will have five classes of shares, one for each of the five shareholders. They decide that each of the five classes will elect his own director to the board of directors and that the consent of each class is required to amend the articles of incorporation, such as to increase the number of authorized shares of a class or to create a new class of shares. They also could agree that no shares may be issued without the consent of each class of shares. In the future, if they want to issue shares to employees of the corporation or public investors, by a vote of the five classes of shareholders they could create a class of shares that has a small (say 20 percent) equity interest in the corporation, either has no right to vote for directors or elects a nonvoting

director, has a preferential right to dividends, and has no right to veto any action the five original classes of shares approve. The creation of the new share class would permit the five original shareholders to continue their control of the corporation while receiving an infusion of capital into the company.

- Do you think it is ethical for the five original shareholders to dominate the corporation in this way? If you were one of the five original shareholders, would you set up a different equity structure? Would you give more rights to the shareholders of the class with limited rights?
- Would you buy shares of the class that has limited rights? If you did buy those shares, would it be ethical for you to argue for greater rights?
- Would your answers change if the corporation became a public company with over 2,000 shareholders?

A **merger** is a transaction in which one corporation merges into a second corporation. Usually, the first corporation dissolves; the second corporation takes all the business and assets of both corporations and becomes liable for the debts of both corporations. Usually, the shareholders of the dissolved corporation become shareholders of the surviving corporation. Ordinarily, both corporations' shareholders must approve a merger.

Corporation law allows great flexibility in the terms of a merger. For example, a merger may freeze out minority shareholders by paying them cash only while allowing majority shareholders to remain as shareholders of the surviving corporation.

A **consolidation** is similar to a merger except that both old corporations go out of existence and a new corporation takes the business, assets, and liabilities of the old corporations. Both corporations' shareholders must approve the consolidation. Modern corporate practice makes consolidations obsolete, since it is usually desirable to have one of the old corporations survive. The MBCA does not recognize consolidations. However, the effect of a consolidation can be achieved by creating a new corporation and merging the two old corporations into it.

A **share exchange** is a transaction by which one corporation becomes the owner of all of the outstanding shares of a second corporation through a *compulsory* exchange of shares: The shareholders of the second corpo-

ration are compelled to exchange their shares for shares of the first corporation. The second corporation remains in existence and becomes a wholly owned subsidiary of the first corporation. Only the selling shareholders must approve the share exchange.

A **sale of all or substantially all of the assets** of the business other than in the regular course of business must be approved by the shareholders of the selling corporation, since it drastically changes the shareholders' investment. Thus, a corporation's sale of all its real property and equipment is a sale of substantially all its assets, even though the corporation continues its business by leasing the assets back from the purchaser. However, a corporation that sells its building, but retains its machinery with the intent of continuing operations at another location, has not sold all or substantially all of its assets. Under the MBCA, a corporation that retains at least 25 percent of its business activity and either its income or revenue has not disposed of substantially all its assets.

A **dissolution** is the first step in the termination of the corporation's business. The typical dissolution requires shareholder approval. Dissolution of corporations is covered more fully at the end of this chapter.

The articles of incorporation and the bylaws may require or permit other matters to be submitted for shareholder approval. For example, loans to officers, self-dealing transactions, and indemnifications of managers for litigation expenses may be approved by shareholders.

Also, many of the states require shareholder approval of share option plans for high-level executive officers, but the MBCA does not.

Procedures Required

Similar procedures must be met to effect each of the above fundamental changes. The procedures include approval of the board of directors, notice to all of the shareholders whether or not they are entitled to vote, and majority approval of the votes held by shareholders entitled to vote under the statute, articles, or bylaws. Majority approval will be insufficient if a corporation has a supermajority shareholder voting requirement, such as one requiring two-thirds approval.

If there are two or more classes of shares, the articles may provide that matters voted on by shareholders must be approved by each class substantially affected by the proposed transaction. For example, a merger may have to be approved by a majority of the preferred shareholders and a majority of the common shareholders. As an alternative, the articles may require only the approval of the shareholders as a whole.

Under the MBCA, voting by classes is required for mergers, share exchanges, and amendments of the articles if these would substantially affect the rights of the classes. For example, the approval of preferred shareholders is required if a merger would change the dividend rights of preferred shareholders.

In many states, no approval of shareholders of the *surviving corporation* is required for a merger *if the merger does* not fundamentally alter the character of the business or substantially reduce the shareholders' voting or dividend rights.

Also, many statutes, including the MBCA, permit a merger between a parent corporation and its subsidiary without the approval of the shareholders of either corporation. Instead, the board of directors of the parent approves the merger and sends a copy of the merger plan to the subsidiary's shareholders. This simplified merger is called a **short-form merger.** It is available only if the parent owns a high percentage of the subsidiary's shares—90 percent under the MBCA and the Delaware statute.

Dissenters' Rights

Many times, shareholders approve a corporate action by less than a unanimous vote, indicating that some shareholders oppose the action. For the most part, the dissenting shareholders have little recourse. Their choice is to remain shareholders or to sell their shares. For close corporation shareholders, there is no choice—the dissenting close corporation shareholder has no ready market for her shares, so she will remain a shareholder.

Some corporate transactions, however, so materially change a shareholder's investment in the corporation or have such an adverse effect on the value of a shareholder's shares that it has been deemed unfair to require the dissenting shareholder either to remain a shareholder (because there is no fair market for the shares) or to suffer a loss in value when he sells his shares on a market that has been adversely affected by the news of the corporate action. Corporate law has therefore responded by creating **dissenters' rights** (right of appraisal) for shareholders who disagree with specified fundamental corporate transactions. Dissenters' rights require the corporation to pay dissenting shareholders the *fair value* of their shares.

Under the MBCA, the dissenters' rights cover mergers, short-form mergers, share exchanges, significant amendments of the articles of incorporation, and sales of all or substantially all the assets other than in the ordinary course of business. Some statutes cover consolidations also.

A dissenting shareholder seeking payment of the fair value of his shares must have the *right to vote* on the action to which he objects; however, a shareholder of a subsidiary in a short-form merger has dissenters' rights despite his lack of voting power. In addition, the shareholder must *not vote in favor* of the transaction. The shareholder may either vote against the action or abstain from voting.

The MBCA and many states' statutes exclude from dissenters' rights shares that are traded on a recognized securities exchange such as the New York Stock Exchange. Instead, these statutes expect a shareholder to sell his shares on the stock exchange if he dissents to the corporate action. The MBCA also excludes shares held by at least 2,000 holders or having a market value of at least $20 million.

Generally, a shareholder must notify the corporation of his intent to seek payment before the shareholders have voted on the action. Next, the corporation informs a dissenting shareholder how to demand payment. After the dissenting shareholder demands payment, the corporation and the shareholder negotiate a mutually acceptable price. If they cannot agree, a court will determine the fair value of the shares and order the corporation to pay that amount.

To determine fair value, most judges use the **Delaware Block Method,** a weighted average of several valuation techniques—such as market value, comparisons with other similar companies, capitalization of earnings, and book value. Ironically, the Supreme Court of Delaware has abandoned the Delaware Block Method, recognizing the need for courts to value shares by methods generally considered acceptable to the financial community. The MBCA values shares using "customary and current valuation concepts and techniques generally employed for similar businesses." The following *Cede & Co.* case further elaborates on the modern Delaware method of appraising shares.

Cede & Co. v. Cinerama, Inc.   684 A.2d 289 (Del. Sup. Ct. 1996)

Technicolor, Inc., was a Delaware corporation engaged in a number of businesses, including videocassette duplicating (one of the largest facilities in the world), photographic film processing for professionals, and motion picture licensing. In May 1981, Technicolor's CEO and chairman, Morton Kamerman, proposed—and its board of directors approved—an ambitious venture to develop a nationwide network of one-hour consumer film processing stores. Unfortunately, execution of the venture fell behind schedule, and Technicolor suffered severe fiscal problems, reporting an 80 percent decline in net income.

In late summer 1982, Ronald Perelman, controlling shareholder of MacAndrews & Forbes Group, Inc. (MAF), identified Technicolor as an attractive takeover target. Negotiations between Perelman and Kamerman resulted in MAF and Technicolor's agreement to MAF's two-step acquisition of Technicolor. The first step was an all-cash tender offer of $23 per share for all of Technicolor's outstanding shares; if not all Technicolor shareholders tendered their shares to MAF, the second step was a merger of MAF and Technicolor, by which all remaining Technicolor shareholders would receive $23 per share and Technicolor would merge with MAF. By December 3, 1982, MAF had acquired 82 percent of Technicolor's shares under the first step of the acquisition. Immediately, as controlling shareholder, MAF began looking for buyers of Technicolor's less profitable divisions, including the one-hour consumer film processing business. On January 24, 1983, Technicolor's shareholders approved the second step.

Several Technicolor shareholders, including Cinerama, Inc., which owned 201,200 shares, dissented from the merger and sought to have the Delaware Court of Chancery appraise their shares under their statutory dissenters' rights. Cinerama argued that the chancery court should value Technicolor with regard to the strategies that had been conceived and implemented by MAF and Perelman as of the merger date (the Perelman Plan). Technicolor argued that the court of chancery should consider Technicolor without regard to the Perelman Plan and only as Technicolor existed prior to October 29, 1982, with the strategies implemented by Kamerman (the Kamerman Plan). The dispute was whether the trial court should value Perelman's Technicolor—a company whose business plans and strategies focused on the processing and duplication of film and videotape and expected to generate $50 million in cash during 1983 from the sale of unwanted or unprofitable business; or Kamerman's Technicolor—a company that had diversified away from a concentration on film processing and videotape duplication for the professional market toward consumer-oriented businesses. The chancery court valued Technicolor as of October 29, 1982, holding that the value added by the Perelman Plan was excluded from the appraisal because it was value arising from the merger or its expectations. Cinerama appealed to the Delaware Supreme Court.

Holland, Justice The Delaware appraisal statute provides that the Court of Chancery:

> shall appraise the shares, determining their fair value exclusive of any element of value arising from the accomplishment or expectation of the merger or consolidation. In determining such fair value, the Court shall take into account all relevant factors. Del. Code section 262(h).

In *Weinberger* v. *UOP* (1983), the Delaware Supreme Court reconciled the dual mandates of section 262(h), which direct the court to determine fair value based on all relevant factors, but to exclude any element of value arising from the accomplishment or expectation of the merger. In making that reconciliation, the *Weinberger* court said:

> Only the speculative elements of value that may arise from the "accomplishment or expectation" of the merger are excluded. We take this to be a very narrow exception to the appraisal process, designed to eliminate use of pro forma data and projections of a speculative variety relating to the completion of a merger. But elements of future value, including the nature of the enterprise, which are known or susceptible of proof as of the date of the merger and not the product of speculation, may be considered. Fair value also includes any damages, resulting from the taking, which the stockholders sustain as a class. If that was not the case, then the obligation to consider "all relevant factors" in the valuation process would be eroded.

The underlying assumption in an appraisal valuation is that the dissenting shareholders would be willing to maintain their investment position had the merger not occurred. Accordingly, the Court of Chancery's task in an appraisal proceeding is to value what has been taken from the shareholder, i.e., the proportionate interest in the going concern. To that end, the corporation must be valued as an operating entity. We conclude that the Court of Chancery did not adhere to this principle.

The Court of Chancery determined that Perelman had a fixed view of how Technicolor's assets would be sold before the merger and had begun to implement it prior to January 24, 1983. Consequently, the Court of Chancery found that the Perelman Plan for Technicolor was the operative reality on the date of the merger. Nevertheless, the Court of Chancery held that Cinerama was not entitled to an appraisal of Technicolor as it was actually functioning on the date of the merger pursuant to the Perelman Plan. The Court of Chancery reasoned that valuing Technicolor as a going concern, under the Perelman Plan, on the date of the merger, would be tantamount to awarding Cinerama a proportionate share of a control premium, which the Court of Chancery deemed economically undesirable. Thus, the Court of Chancery concluded that value added by a majority acquiror is not a part of the going concern in which a dissenting shareholder has a legal right to participate.

In a two-step merger, to the extent that value has been added following a change in majority control before cashout, it is still value attributable to the going concern, i.e., the extant "nature of the enterprise," on the date of the merger.

Consequently, value added to the going concern by the majority acquiror during the transient period of a two-step merger, accrues to the benefit of all shareholders and must be included in the appraisal process on the date of the merger.

By failing to accord Cinerama the full proportionate value of its shares in the going concern on the date of the merger, the Court of Chancery imposed a penalty upon Cinerama for lack of control. Consequently, the Court of Chancery permitted MAF to reap a windfall from the appraisal process by cashing out a dissenting shareholder for less than the fair value of its interest in Technicolor as a going concern on the date of the merger.

Technicolor must be viewed and valued as an ongoing enterprise, and occupying a particular market position in the light of future prospects. All elements of future value, including the nature of the enterprise, which are known or susceptible of proof as of the date of the merger and not the product of speculation, may and should be considered.

This appraisal action will be remanded to the Court of Chancery for a recalculation of Technicolor's fair value on the date of the merger. It is within the Court of Chancery's discretion to select one of the parties' valuation models as its general framework, or fashion its own. Its choice of framework does not require it to adopt any one expert's model, methodology, or mathematical calculation in toto.

Judgment reversed in favor of Cinerama; remanded to the Court of Chancery for appraisal of the shares.

Shareholders' Inspection and Information Rights

Inspecting a corporation's books and records is sometimes essential to the exercise of a shareholder's rights. For example, a shareholder may be able to decide how to vote in a director election only after examining corporate financial records that reveal whether the present directors are managing the corporation profitably. Also, a close corporation shareholder may need to look at the books to determine the value of his shares.

Many corporate managers are resistant to shareholders' inspecting the corporation's books and records,

charging that shareholders are nuisances or that shareholders often have improper purposes for making such an inspection. Sometimes, management objects solely on the ground that it desires secrecy.

Most of the state corporation statutes specifically grant shareholders inspection rights. The purpose of these statutes is to facilitate the shareholder's inspection of the books and records of corporations whose managements resist or delay proper requests by shareholders. A shareholder's lawyer or accountant may assist the shareholder's exercise of his inspection rights.

The MBCA grants shareholders an **absolute right of inspection** of an alphabetical listing of the shareholders entitled to notice of a meeting, including the number of shares owned. Access to a shareholder list allows a shareholder to contact other shareholders about important matters such as shareholder proposals.

The MBCA also grants an absolute right of inspection of, among other things, the articles, bylaws, and minutes of shareholder meetings within the past three years.

Shareholders have a **qualified right to inspect** other records, however. To inspect accounting records, board and committee minutes, and shareholder minutes more than three years old, a shareholder must make the demand in *good faith* and have a *proper purpose*. Proper purposes include inspecting the books of account to determine the value of shares or the propriety of dividends. On the other hand, learning business secrets and aiding a competitor are clearly improper purposes.

Shareholders also have the right to receive from the corporation **information** that is important to their voting and investing decisions. The MBCA requires a corporation to furnish its shareholders *financial statements,* including a balance sheet, an income statement, and a statement of changes in shareholders' equity. The Securities Exchange Act of 1934 also requires publicly held companies to furnish such statements, as well as other information that is important to shareholders' voting and investing decisions. To protect shareholders of public companies, the Sarbanes–Oxley Act of 2002 requires the CEO and the CFO of public companies to certify that to their knowledge all financial information filed with the Securities and Exchange Commission fairly presents the financial condition of the company and does not include untrue or misleading material statements.

Preemptive Right

The market price of a shareholder's shares will be reduced if a corporation issues additional shares at a price less than the market price. In addition, a shareholder's proportionate voting, dividend, and liquidation rights may be adversely affected by the issuance of additional shares. For example, if a corporation's only four shareholders each own 100 shares worth $10 per share, then each shareholder has shares worth $1,000, a 25 percent interest in any dividends declared, 25 percent of the voting power, and a claim against 25 percent of the corporation's assets after creditors' claims have been satisfied. If the corporation subsequently issues 100 shares to another person for only $5 per share, the value of each shareholder's shares falls to $900 and his dividend, voting, and liquidation rights are reduced to 20 percent. In a

worst-case scenario, the corporation issues 201 shares to one of the existing shareholders, giving that shareholder majority control of the corporation and reducing the other shareholders' interests to less than 17 percent each. As a result, the minority shareholders will be dominated by the majority shareholder and will receive a greatly reduced share of the corporation's dividends.

Such harmful effects of an issuance could have been prevented if the corporation had been required to offer each existing shareholder a percentage of the new shares equal to her current proportionate ownership. If, for example, in the situation described above, the corporation had offered 50 shares to each shareholder, each shareholder could have remained a 25 percent owner of the corporation; her interests in the corporation would not have been reduced, and her total wealth would not have been decreased.

Corporation law recognizes the importance of giving a shareholder the option of maintaining the value of his shares and retaining his proportionate interest in the corporation. This is the shareholder's **preemptive right,** an option to subscribe to a new issuance of shares in proportion to the shareholder's current interest in the corporation.

The MBCA adopts a comprehensive scheme for determining preemptive rights. It provides that the preemptive right does not exist except to the extent provided by the articles. The MBCA permits the corporation to state expressly when the preemptive right arises.

When the preemptive right exists, the corporation must notify a shareholder of her option to buy shares, the number of shares that she is entitled to buy, the price of the shares, and when the option must be exercised. Usually, the shareholder is issued a **right,** a written option that she may exercise herself or sell to a person who wishes to buy the shares.

Distributions to Shareholders

During the life of a corporation, shareholders may receive distributions of the corporation's assets. Most people are familiar with one type of distribution—dividends—but there are other important types of distributions to shareholders, including payments to shareholders upon the corporation's repurchase of its shares.

There is one crucial similarity among all the types of distributions to shareholders: Corporate assets are transferred to shareholders. Consequently, an asset transfer to shareholders may harm the corporation's creditors and others with claims against the corporation's assets. For example, a distribution of assets may impair a corporation's ability to pay its creditors. In addition, a distribution to one class of shareholders may harm another class of shareholders that has a liquidation priority over the class of shareholders receiving the distribution. The existence of these potential harms compels corporation law to restrict the ability of corporations to make distributions to shareholders.

Dividends

One important objective of a business corporation is to make a profit. Shareholders invest in a corporation primarily to share in the expected profit either through appreciation of the value of their shares or through dividends. There are two types of dividends: *cash or property dividends* and *share dividends*. Only cash or property dividends are distributions of the corporation's assets. Share dividends are *not* distributions.

Cash or Property Dividends Dividends are usually paid in cash. However, other assets of the corporation—such as airline discount coupons or shares of another corporation—may also be distributed as dividends. Cash or property dividends are declared by the board of directors and paid by the corporation on the date stated by the directors. Once declared, dividends are *debts* of the corporation and shareholders may sue to force payment of the dividends. The board's dividend declaration, including the amount of dividend and whether to declare a dividend, is protected by the business judgment rule.

Preferred shares nearly always have a set dividend rate stated in the articles of incorporation. Even so, unless the preferred dividend is mandatory, the board has discretion to determine whether to pay a preferred dividend and what amount to pay. Most preferred shares are *cumulative preferred shares,* on which unpaid dividends cumulate. The entire accumulation must be paid before common shareholders may receive any dividend. Even when preferred shares are noncumulative, the current dividend must be paid to preferred shareholders before any dividend may be paid to common shareholders.

The following *Dodge v. Ford* case is one of the few cases in which a court ordered the payment of a dividend to common shareholders. The court found that Henry Ford had the wrong motives for causing Ford Motor Company to refuse to pay a dividend.

Dodge v. Ford Motor Co.   *170 N.W. 668 (Mich. Sup Ct. 1919)*

In 1916, brothers John and Horace Dodge owned 10 percent of the common shares of the Ford Motor Company. Henry Ford owned 58 percent of the outstanding common shares and controlled the corporation and its board of directors. Starting in 1911, the corporation paid a regular annual dividend of $1.2 million, which was 60 percent of its capital stock of $2 million but only about 1 percent of its total equity of $114 million. In addition, from 1911 to 1915, the corporation paid special dividends totaling $41 million.

The policy of the corporation was to reduce the selling price of its cars each year. In June 1915, the board and officers agreed to increase production by constructing new plants for $10 million, acquiring land for $3 million, and erecting an $11 million smelter. To finance the planned expansion, the board decided not to reduce the selling price of cars beginning in August 1915 and to accumulate a large surplus.

A year later, the board reduced the selling price of cars by $80 per car. The corporation was able to produce 600,000 cars annually, all of which, and more, could have been sold for $440 instead of the new $360 price, a forgone revenue of $48 million. At the same time, the corporation announced a new dividend policy of paying no special dividend. Instead, it would reinvest all earnings except the regular dividend of $1.2 million.

Henry Ford announced his justification for the new dividend policy in a press release: "My ambition is to employ still more men, to spread the benefits of this industrial system to the greatest possible number, to help them build up their lives and their homes." The corporation had a $112 million surplus, expected profits of $60 million, total liabilities of $18 million, $52.5 million in cash on hand, and municipal bonds worth $1.3 million.

The Dodge brothers sued the corporation and the directors to force them to declare a special dividend. The trial court ordered the board to declare a dividend of $19.3 million. Ford Motor Company appealed.

Ostrander, Chief Justice It is a well-recognized principle of law that the directors of a corporation, and they alone, have the power to declare a dividend of the earnings of the corporation, and to determine its amount. Courts will not interfere in the management of the directors unless it is clearly made to appear that they are guilty of fraud or misappropriation of the corporate funds, or they refuse to declare a dividend when the corporation has a surplus of net profits which it can, without detriment to the business, divide among its stockholders, and when a refusal to do so would amount to such an abuse of discretion as would constitute a fraud, or breach of that good faith that they are bound to exercise towards the shareholders.

The testimony of Mr. Ford convinces this court that he has to some extent the attitude towards shareholders of one who has dispensed and distributed to them large gains and that they should be content to take what he chooses to give. His testimony creates the impression that he thinks the Ford Motor Company has made too much money, has had too large profits, and that, although large profits might be still earned, a sharing of them with the public, by reducing the price of the output of the company, ought to be undertaken. We have no doubt that certain sentiments, philanthropic and altruistic, creditable to Mr. Ford, had large influence in determining the policy to be pursued by the Ford Motor Company.

There should be no confusion of the duties that Mr. Ford conceives that he and the shareholders owe to the general public and the duties that in law he and his co-directors owe to protesting, minority shareholders. A business corporation is organized and carried on primarily for the profit of the shareholders. The powers of the directors are to be employed for that end.

We are not, however, persuaded that we should interfere with the proposed expansion of the Ford Motor Company. In view of the fact that the selling price of products may be increased at any time, the ultimate results of the larger business cannot be certainly estimated. The judges are not business experts. It is recognized that plans must often be made for a long future, for expected competition, for a continuing as well as an immediately profitable venture. We are not satisfied that the alleged motives of the directors, in so far as they are reflected in the conduct of the business, menace the interests of shareholders.

Assuming the general plan and policy of expansion were for the best ultimate interest of the company and therefore of its shareholders, what does it amount to in justification of a refusal to declare and pay a special dividend? The Ford Motor Company was able to estimate with nicety its income and profit. It could sell more cars than it could make. The profit upon each car depended upon the selling price. That being fixed, the yearly income and profit was determinable, and, within slight variations, was certain.

There was appropriated for the smelter $11 million. Assuming that the plans required an expenditure sooner or later of $10 million for duplication of the plant, and for land $3 million, the total is $24 million. The company was a cash business. If the total cost of proposed expenditures had been withdrawn in cash from the cash surplus on hand August 1, 1916, there would have remained $30 million.

The directors of Ford Motor Company say, and it is true, that a considerable cash balance must be at all times carried by such a concern. But there was a large daily, weekly, monthly receipt of cash. The output was practically continuous and was continuously, and within a few days, turned into cash. Moreover, the contemplated expenditures were not to be immediately made. The large sum appropriated for the smelter plant was payable over a considerable period of time. So that, without going further, it would appear that, accepting and approving the plan of the directors, it was their duty to distribute on and near the 1st of August 1916, a very large sum of money to stockholders.

Judgment for the Dodge brothers affirmed.

To protect the claims of the corporation's creditors, all of the corporation statutes limit the extent to which dividends may be paid. The MBCA imposes two limits: (1) the *solvency test* and (2) the *balance sheet test*.

Solvency Test A dividend may not make a corporation insolvent; that is, unable to pay its debts as they come due in the usual course of business. This means that a corporation may pay a dividend to the extent it has *excess solvency*—that is, liquidity that it does not need to pay its currently maturing obligations. This requirement protects creditors, who are concerned primarily with the corporation's ability to pay debts as they mature.

Balance Sheet Test After the dividend has been paid, the corporation's assets must be sufficient to cover its liabilities and the liquidation preference of shareholders having a priority in liquidation over the shareholders receiving the dividend. This means that a corporation may pay a dividend to the extent it has *excess assets*—that is, assets it does not need to cover its liabilities and the liquidation preferences of shareholders having a priority in liquidation over the shareholders receiving the dividends. This requirement protects not only creditors but also preferred shareholders. It prevents a corporation from paying to common shareholders a dividend that will impair the liquidation rights of preferred shareholders.

Example Batt Company has $27,000 in excess liquidity that it does not need to pay its currently maturing obligations. It has assets of $200,000 and liabilities of $160,000. It has one class of common shareholders. Its one class of preferred shareholders has a liquidation preference of $15,000. Examining these facts, we find that Batt's excess solvency is $27,000, but its excess assets are only $25,000 ($200,000 − 160,000 − 15,000). Therefore, Batt's shareholders may receive a maximum cash or property dividend of $25,000, which will eliminate all of Batt's excess assets and leave Batt with $2,000 of excess solvency.

Share Dividends and Share Splits Corporations sometimes distribute additional shares of the corporation to their shareholders. Often, this is done in order to give shareholders something instead of a cash dividend so that the cash can be retained and reinvested in the business. Such an action may be called either a **share dividend** or a **share split.**

A **share dividend** of a *specified percentage of outstanding shares* is declared by the board of directors. For example, the board may declare a 10 percent share dividend. As a result, each shareholder will receive 10 percent more shares than she currently owns. A share dividend is paid on outstanding shares only. Unlike a cash or property dividend, a share dividend may be revoked by the board after it has been declared.

A **share split** results in shareholders receiving a specified number of shares in exchange for each share that they currently own. For example, shares may be split two for one. Each shareholder will now have two shares for each share that he previously owned. A holder of 50 shares will now have 100 shares instead of 50.

The MBCA recognizes that a share split or a share dividend in the same class of shares does not affect the value of the corporation or the shareholders' wealth, because no assets have been transferred from the corporation to the shareholders. The effect is like that produced by taking a pie with four pieces and dividing each piece in half. Each person may receive twice as many pieces of the pie, but each piece is worth only half as much. The total amount received by each person is unchanged.

Therefore, the MBCA permits share splits and share dividends of the same class of shares to be made merely by action of the directors. The directors merely have the corporation issue to the shareholders the number of shares needed to effect the share dividend or split. The corporation must have a sufficient number of authorized, unissued shares to effect the share split or dividend; when it does not, its articles must be amended to create the required number of additional authorized shares.

Reverse Share Split A *reverse share split* is a decrease in the number of shares of a class such that, for example, two shares become one share. Most of the state corporation statutes require shareholder action to amend the articles to effect a reverse share split because the number of authorized shares is reduced. The purpose of a reverse share split is usually to increase the market price of the shares.

A reverse share split may also be used to freeze out minority shareholders. By setting a high reverse split ratio, a majority shareholder will be left with whole shares while minority shareholders will have only fractional shares. Corporation law allows a corporation to repurchase fractional shares without the consent of the fractional shareholders. Freeze-outs are discussed in Chapter 43.

Share Repurchases

Declaring a cash or property dividend is only one of the ways in which a corporation may distribute its assets. A corporation may also distribute its assets by repurchasing its shares from its shareholders. Such a repurchase may be either a *redemption* or an *open-market repurchase.*

The right of **redemption** (or a call) is usually a right of the corporation to force an *involuntary* sale by a shareholder at a fixed price. The shareholder must sell the shares to the corporation at the corporation's request; in most states, the shareholder cannot force the corporation to redeem the shares.

Under the MBCA, the right of redemption must appear in the articles of incorporation. It is common for a corporation to issue preferred shares subject to redemption at the corporation's option. Usually, common shares are not redeemable.

In addition, a corporation may repurchase its shares **on the open market.** A corporation is empowered to purchase its shares from any shareholder who is willing to sell them. Such repurchases are usually *voluntary* on the shareholder's part, requiring the corporation to pay a current market price to entice the shareholder to sell. However, a corporation may force a shareholder with a fractional share to sell that fractional share back to the corporation.

A corporation's repurchase of its shares may harm creditors and other shareholders. The MBCA requires a corporation repurchasing shares to meet tests that are the same as its cash and property dividend rules, recognizing that financially a repurchase of shares is no different from a dividend or any other distribution of assets to shareholders.

Ensuring a Shareholder's Return on Investment

Obtaining a return on her investment in a corporation is important to every shareholder. In a publicly held corporation, a shareholder may receive a return in the form of dividends and more significantly an increase in the value of her shares, which she may sell in the public securities markets.

For a shareholder in a close corporation, obtaining a return on his investment is often a problem, especially for minority shareholders. The majority shareholders dominate the board of directors, who usually choose not to pay any dividend to shareholders. And since the close corporation has no publicly traded shares, minority shareholders have little if any ability to sell their shares. The majority shareholders in a close corporation don't suffer the same effect, because they are usually officers and employees of the corporation and receive a return on their investment in the form of salaries.

What can a minority shareholder do? Rarely will a court, as in *Dodge v. Ford,* require the payment of a dividend. The only way a minority shareholder can protect himself is to bargain well prior to becoming a shareholder. For example, a prospective minority shareholder may insist on a mandatory dividend, that he be employed by the corporation, or that the corporation or majority shareholders be required to repurchase his shares upon the occurrence of certain events, such as the failure of the corporation to go public after five years. There is a limit to what a minority shareholder may demand, however, for the majority shareholders may refuse to sell shares to a prospective shareholder who asks too much.

Shareholders' Lawsuits

Shareholders' Individual Lawsuits

A shareholder has the right to sue in his own name to prevent or redress a breach of the shareholder's contract. For example, a shareholder may sue to recover dividends declared but not paid or dividends that should have been declared, to enjoin the corporation from committing an *ultra vires* act, to enforce the shareholder's right of inspection, and to enforce preemptive rights.

Shareholder Class Action Suits

When several people have been injured similarly by the same persons in similar situations, one of the injured people may sue for the benefit of all the people injured. Likewise, if several shareholders have been similarly affected by a wrongful act of another, one of these shareholders may bring a **class action** on behalf of all the affected shareholders.

An appropriate class action under state corporation law would be an action seeking a dividend payment that has been brought by a preferred shareholder for all of the preferred shareholders. Any recovery is prorated to all members of the class.

A shareholder who successfully brings a class action is entitled to be reimbursed from the award amount for his *reasonable expenses,* including attorney's fees. If the class action suit is unsuccessful and has no reasonable foundation, the court may order the suing shareholder to pay the defendants' reasonable litigation expenses, including attorney's fees.

LOG ON

http://securities.stanford.edu
Stanford Law School maintains the Securities Class Action Clearinghouse. It provides detailed information relating to the prosecution, defense, and settlement of federal class action securities litigation.

Shareholders' Derivative Actions

When a corporation has been harmed by the actions of another person, the right to sue belongs to the corporation and any damages awarded by a court belong to the corporation. Hence, as a general rule, a shareholder has no right to sue in his own name when someone has harmed the corporation, and he may not recover for himself damages from that person. This is the rule even when the value of the shareholder's investment in the corporation has been impaired.

Nonetheless, one or more shareholders are permitted under certain circumstances to bring an action for the benefit of the corporation when the directors have failed to pursue a corporate cause of action. For example, if the corporation has a claim against its chief executive for wrongfully diverting corporate assets to her personal use, the corporation may not sue the chief executive because she controls the board of directors. Clearly, the CEO should not go unpunished. Consequently, corporation law authorizes a shareholder to bring a **derivative action** (or derivative suit) against the CEO on behalf of the corporation and for its benefit. Such a suit may also be used to bring a corporate claim against an outsider.

If the derivative action succeeds and damages are awarded, the damages ordinarily go to the corporate treasury for the benefit of the corporation. The suing shareholder is entitled only to reimbursement of his reasonable attorney's fees that he incurred in bringing the action.

Eligible Shareholders Although allowing shareholders to bring derivative suits creates a viable procedure for suing wrongdoing officers and directors, this procedure is also susceptible to abuse. **Strike suits** (lawsuits brought to gain out-of-court settlements for the complaining shareholders personally or to earn large attorney's fees, rather than to obtain a recovery for the corporation) have not been uncommon. To discourage strike suits, the person bringing the action must be a current shareholder who also held his shares at the time the alleged wrong occurred. In addition, the shareholder must fairly and adequately represent the interests of shareholders similarly situated in enforcing the right of the corporation.

One exception to these rules is the **double derivative suit,** a suit brought by a shareholder of a parent corporation on behalf of a subsidiary corporation owned by the parent. Courts regularly permit double derivative suits.

Demand on Directors Since a decision to sue someone is ordinarily made by corporate managers, a shareholder must first **demand** that the board of directors bring the suit. A demand informs the board that the corporation may have a right of action against a person that the board, in its business judgment, may decide to pursue. Therefore, if a demand is made and the board decides to bring the suit, the shareholder may not institute a derivative suit.

Ordinarily, a shareholder's failure to make a demand on the board prevents her from bringing a derivative suit. Nonetheless, the shareholder may initiate the suit if she proves that a demand on the board would have been useless or **futile.** Demand is futile, and therefore **excused,** if the board is unable to make a disinterested decision regarding whether to sue. Futility may be proved when all or a majority of the directors are interested in the challenged transaction, such as in a suit alleging that the directors issued shares to themselves at below-market prices.

If a shareholder makes a demand on the board and it **refuses** the shareholder's demand to bring a suit, ordinarily the shareholder is not permitted to continue the derivative action. The decision to bring a lawsuit is an ordinary business decision appropriate for a board of directors to make. The business judgment rule, therefore, is available to insulate from court review a board's decision not to bring a suit.

Of course, if a shareholder derivative suit accuses the board of harming the corporation, such as by misappropriating the corporation's assets, the board's refusal will not be protected by the business judgment rule because the board has a conflict of interest in its decision to sue. In such a situation, the shareholder may sue the directors despite the board's refusal.

Shareholder Litigation Committees In an attempt to ensure the application of the business judgment rule in demand refusal and demand futility situations, interested directors have tried to isolate themselves from the decision whether to sue by creating a special committee of the board, called a *shareholder litigation committee* (SLC) (or independent investigation committee) whose purpose is to decide whether to sue. The SLC should consist of directors who are not defendants in the derivative suit, who are not interested in the challenged action, are independent of the defendant directors, and if possible, were not directors at the time the wrong occurred. Usually, the SLC has independent legal counsel that assists its determination whether to sue. Because the SLC is a committee of the board, its decision may be protected by the business judgment rule. Therefore, an SLC's decision not to sue may prevent a shareholder from suing.

Shareholders have challenged the application of the business judgment rule to an SLC's decision to dismiss a shareholder derivative suit against some of the directors. The suing shareholders argue that it is improper for an SLC to dismiss a shareholder derivative suit because there is a *structural bias.* That is, the SLC members are motivated by a desire to avoid hurting their fellow directors and adversely affecting future working relationships within the board.

When demand is **not futile,** most of the courts that have been faced with this question have upheld the decisions of special litigation committees that comply with the business judgment rule. The courts require that the SLC members be *independent* of the defendant directors, be *disinterested* with regard to the subject matter of the suit, make a *reasonable investigation* into whether to dismiss the suit, and act in *good faith.*

When demand is **futile or excused,** most courts faced with the decision of an SLC have applied the rule of the *Zapata* case, which follows.

The MBCA has adopted the *Zapata* rule in all contexts, whether or not an SLC is used. When a majority of directors are not independent, the corporation has the burden of proving that the *Zapata* test has been met:

good faith and reasonable investigation by the directors making the decision to dismiss the action and a determination by those directors that the best interests of the corporation are served by dismissal. If, however, a majority of the directors are independent, the shareholders bringing the derivative action have the burden of proving that there was bad faith or no reasonable investigation or that bringing the action is in the best interest of the corporation.

Zapata Corp. v. Maldonado   430 A.2d 779 (Del. Sup. Ct. 1981)

Zapata Corporation had a share option plan that permitted its executives to purchase Zapata shares at a below-market price. Most of the directors participated in the share option plan. In 1974, the directors voted to advance the share option exercise date in order to reduce the federal income tax liability of the executives who exercised the share options, including the directors. An additional effect, however, was to increase the corporation's federal tax liability.

William Maldonado, a Zapata shareholder, believed that the board action was a breach of a fiduciary duty and that it harmed the corporation. In 1975, he instituted a derivative suit in a Delaware court on behalf of Zapata against all of the directors. He failed to make a demand on the directors to sue themselves, alleging that this would be futile since they were all defendants.

The derivative suit was still pending in 1979, when four of the defendants were no longer directors. The remaining directors then appointed two new outside directors to the board and created an Independent Investigation Committee consisting solely of the two new directors. The board authorized the committee to make a final and binding decision regarding whether the derivative suit should be brought on behalf of the corporation. Following a three-month investigation, the committee concluded that Maldonado's derivative suit should be dismissed as against Zapata's best interests.

Zapata asked the Delaware court to dismiss the derivative suit. The court refused, holding that Maldonado possessed an individual right to maintain the derivative action and that the business judgment rule did not apply. Zapata appealed to the Supreme Court of Delaware.

Quillen, Justice We find that the trial court's determination that a shareholder, once demand is made and refused, possesses an independent, individual right to continue a derivative suit for breaches of fiduciary duty over objection by the corporation, as an absolute rule, is erroneous.

Derivative suits enforce corporate rights, and any recovery obtained goes to the corporation. We see no inherent reason why a derivative suit should automatically place in the hands of the litigating shareholder sole control of the corporate right throughout the litigation. Such an inflexible rule would recognize the interest of one person or group to the exclusion of all others within the corporate entity.

When, if at all, should an authorized board committee be permitted to cause litigation, properly initiated by a derivative stockholder in his own right, to be dismissed? The problem is relatively simple. If, on the one hand, corporations can consistently wrest bona fide derivative actions away from well-meaning derivative plaintiffs through the use of the committee mechanism, the derivative suit will lose much, if not all, of its effectiveness as an intracorporate

means of policing boards of directors. If, on the other hand, corporations are unable to rid themselves of meritless or harmful litigation and strike suits, the derivative action, created to benefit the corporation, will produce the opposite, unintended result. It thus appears desirable to us to find a balancing point where bona fide shareholder power to bring corporate causes of action cannot be unfairly trampled on by the board of directors, but the corporation can rid itself of detrimental litigation.

We are not satisfied that acceptance of the business judgment rationale at this stage of derivative litigation is a proper balancing point. We must be mindful that directors are passing judgment on fellow directors in the same corporation and fellow directors, in this instance, who designated them to serve both as directors and committee members. The question naturally arises whether a "there but for the grace of God go I" empathy might not play a role. And the further question arises whether inquiry as to independence, good faith and reasonable investigation is sufficient safeguard against abuse, perhaps subconscious abuse.

We thus steer a middle course between those cases that yield to the independent business judgment of a board committee and this case as determined below, which would yield to unbridled shareholder control.

We recognize that the final substantive judgment whether a particular lawsuit should be maintained requires a balance of many factors—ethical, commercial, promotional, public relations, employee relations, fiscal, as well as legal. We recognize the danger of judicial overreaching but the alternatives seem to us to be outweighed by the fresh view of a judicial outsider.

After an objective and thorough investigation of a derivative suit, an independent committee may cause its corporation to file a motion to dismiss the derivative suit. The Court should apply a two-step test to the motion. First, the Court should inquire into the independence and good faith of the committee and the bases supporting its conclusions. The corporation should have the burden of proving independence, good faith, and reasonable investigation, rather than presuming independence, good faith, and reasonableness. If the Court determines either that the committee is not independent or has not shown reasonable bases for its conclusions, or if the Court is not satisfied for other reasons relating to the process, including but not limited to the good faith of the committee, the Court shall deny the corporation's motion to dismiss the derivative suit.

The second step provides the essential key in striking the balance between legitimate corporate claims as expressed in a derivative stockholder suit and a corporation's best interests as expressed by an independent investigating committee. The Court should determine, applying its own independent business judgment, whether the motion should be granted. The second step is intended to thwart instances where corporate actions meet the criteria of step one, but the result does not appear to satisfy its spirit, or where corporate actions would simply prematurely terminate a stockholder grievance deserving of further consideration in the corporation's interest. The Court of course must carefully consider and weigh how compelling the corporate interest in dismissal is when faced with a non-frivolous lawsuit. The Court should, when appropriate, give special consideration to matters of law and public policy in addition to the corporation's best interests.

The second step shares some of the same spirit and philosophy of the statement of the trial court: "Under our system of law, courts and not litigants should decide the merits of litigation."

Judgment reversed in favor of Zapata. Case remanded to the trial court.

Litigation Expenses If a shareholder is successful in a derivative suit, she is entitled to a reimbursement of her reasonable litigation expenses out of the corporation's damage award. On the other hand, if the suit is unsuccessful and has been brought without reasonable cause, the shareholder must pay the defendants' expenses, including attorney's fees. The purpose of this rule is to deter strike suits by punishing shareholders who litigate in bad faith.

ETHICS IN ACTION

After reading *Zapata Corp. v. Maldonado* and the MBCA rules for dismissal of shareholder derivative actions, you may predict that a court will almost always respect the recommendation of a shareholder litigation committee, even when a former or existing board member is a defendant. That is not always the case because the corporation does not have a valid right of action against a director, but often because an SLC has adopted the right process (good faith and reasonable inquiry) and easily can justify that the expense of litigation and the distraction of current management outweigh the likely recovery to the corporation from the wrongdoing director.

• Do you think is it ethical for an SLC to recommend dismissal of an action against a director who has harmed the corporation? Is that sending the right message to other directors and officers? Are there other ways to discipline a director or officer than by suing them? Are those alternatives sufficient deterrents or punishments?

• Do you think it would be justifiable for an SLC to recommend dismissal of an action against former officers who, like some top officers in WorldCom, Tyco, and Enron, either looted the corporation or caused it to overstate its earnings or understate its liabilities? Would a utilitarian or profit maximizer be more likely to recommend dismissal than a rights theorist?

Defense of Corporation by Shareholder

Occasionally, the officers or managers will refuse to defend a suit brought against a corporation. If a shareholder shows that the corporation has a valid defense to the suit and that the refusal or failure of the directors to defend is a breach of their fiduciary duty to the corporation, the courts will permit the shareholder to defend for the benefit of the corporation, its shareholders, and its creditors.

Shareholder Liability

Shareholders have many responsibilities and liabilities in addition to their many rights. You have already studied shareholder liability when a shareholder pays too little consideration for shares, when a corporation is defectively formed, and when a corporation's veil is pierced. In this section, four other grounds for shareholder liability are discussed.

Shareholder Liability for Illegal Distributions

Dividends and other distributions of a corporation's assets received by a shareholder with *knowledge of their illegality* may be recovered on behalf of the corporation. Under the MBCA, primary liability is placed on the directors who, failing to comply with the business judgment rule, authorized the unlawful distribution. However, the directors are entitled to contribution from shareholders who received an asset distribution knowing that it was illegally made. These liability rules enforce the limits on asset distributions that were discussed earlier in this chapter.

Shareholder Liability for Corporate Debts

One of the chief attributes of a shareholder is his *limited liability:* Ordinarily, he has no liability for corporate obligations beyond his capital contribution. Defective attempts to incorporate and piercing the corporate veil are grounds on which a shareholder may be held liable for corporate debts beyond his capital contribution. In addition, a few states impose personal liability on shareholders for *wages owed to corporate employees,* even if the shareholders have fully paid for their shares.

Sale of a Control Block of Shares

The per share value of the shares of a majority shareholder of a corporation is greater than the per share value of the shares of a minority shareholder. This difference in value is due to the majority shareholder's ability to control the corporation and to cause it to hire her as an employee at a high salary. Therefore, a majority shareholder can sell her shares for a *premium* over the fair market value of minority shares.

Majority ownership is not always required for control of a corporation. In a close corporation it is required, but in a publicly held corporation with a widely dispersed, hard-to-mobilize shareholder group, minority ownership of from 5 to 30 percent may be enough to obtain control. Therefore, a holder of minority control in such a corporation will also be able to receive a premium.

Current corporation law imposes no liability on any shareholder, whether or not the shareholder is a controlling shareholder, *merely* because she is able to sell her shares for a premium. Nonetheless, if the premium is accompanied by wrongdoing, controlling shareholders have been held liable either for the amount of the premium or for the damages suffered by the corporation.

For example, a seller of control shares is liable for selling to a purchaser who harms the corporation if the seller had or should have had a *reasonable suspicion* that the purchaser would mismanage or loot the corporation. A seller may be placed on notice of a purchaser's bad motives by facts indicating the purchaser's history of *mismanagement and personal use of corporate assets,* by the purchaser's *lack of interest in the physical facilities* of the corporation, or the purchaser's great *interest in the liquid assets* of the corporation. These factors tend to indicate that the purchaser has a short-term interest in the corporation.

The mere payment of a premium is not enough to put the seller on notice. If the *premium is unduly high,* however, such as a $50 offer for shares traded for $10, a seller must doubt whether the purchaser will be able to recoup his investment without looting the corporation.

When a seller has, or should have, a reasonable suspicion that a purchaser will mismanage or loot the corporation, he must not sell to the purchaser unless a *reasonable investigation* shows there is no reasonable risk of wrongdoing.

A few courts find liability when a selling shareholder takes or sells a *corporate asset.* For example, if a purchaser wants to buy the corporation's assets and the controlling shareholder proposes that the purchaser buy her shares instead, the controlling shareholder is liable for usurping a corporate opportunity.

A more unusual situation existed in *Perlman v. Feldman*.[1] In that case, Newport Steel Corporation had excess demand for its steel production, due to the Korean War. Another corporation, in order to guarantee a steady supply of steel, bought at a premium a minority yet controlling block of shares of Newport from Feldman, its chairman and president. The court ruled that Feldman was required to share the premium with the other shareholders because he had sold a corporate asset—the ability to exploit an excess demand for steel. The court reasoned that Newport could have exploited that asset to its advantage.

Shareholders as Fiduciaries

A few courts have recognized a fiduciary duty of controlling shareholders to use their ability to control the corporation in a fair, just, and equitable manner that benefits all of the shareholders proportionately. This is a duty to be **impartial**—that is, not to prefer themselves over the minority shareholders. For example, controlling shareholders have a fiduciary duty not to cause the corporation to repurchase their own shares or to pay themselves a dividend unless the same offer is made to the minority shareholder.

One of the most common examples of impartiality is the **freeze-out** of minority shareholders, which is wrongful because of its **oppression** of minority shareholders. It occurs in close corporations when controlling shareholders pay themselves high salaries while not employing or paying dividends to noncontrolling shareholders. Since there is usually no liquid market for the shares of the noncontrolling shareholders, they have an investment that provides them no return, while the controlling shareholders reap large gains. Such actions by the majority are especially wrongful when the controlling shareholders follow with an offer to buy the minority's shares at an unreasonably low price.

Some courts have held that all close corporation shareholders—whether majority or minority owners—are fiduciaries of each other and the corporation, on the grounds that the close corporation is an incorporated partnership. Thus, like partners, the shareholders owe fiduciary duties to act in the best interests of the corporation and the shareholders as a whole.

Some statutes, such as the Statutory Close Corporation Supplement to the MBCA, permit close corporation shareholders to dispense with a board of directors or to arrange corporate affairs as if the corporation were a partnership. The effect of these statutes is to impose management responsibilities, including the fiduciary duties of directors, on the shareholders. In essence, the shareholders are partners and owe each other fiduciary duties similar to those owed between partners of a partnership.

In the following case, the court found that majority shareholders owed a fiduciary duty to minority shareholders that may have been violated by removing the minority shareholders from the board of directors and stopping all corporate payments to them.

---

[1] 219 F.2d 173 (2d Cir. 1955).

Jorgensen v. Water Works, Inc.   582 N.W.2d 98 (Wis. Ct. App. 1998)

Water Works, Inc., is a closely held Wisconsin corporation that operates an automatic car wash business in Wisconsin Rapids, Wisconsin. When incorporated in 1988, its 204 shares were issued to six persons: Duane and Sharon Jorgensen; their daughter, Doreen Barber; her husband, James Barber; and two family friends, Gary Tesch and Mary Tesch. Each received 34 shares of Water Works stock and each became a director in the corporation. Duane Jorgensen was elected president; Sharon Jorgensen, Gary Tesch, and James Barber were elected vice presidents; Mary Tesch was elected treasurer; Doreen Barber was elected secretary.

The corporation's written business plan when first formed stated that Duane Jorgensen would be in charge of management and that the six shareholders would be permanent directors. There was also an oral agreement among the shareholders that Duane Jorgensen would oversee management as long as he lived. Payments were made to every shareholder once a week since 1989. Each year the shareholders sat down and decided the amount of the weekly payments based on the profits. This weekly payment was the Jorgensens' only support.

In 1995 Duane discovered that some of the officers and directors of the corporation were engaged in illegal activities on property owned by the corporation and were using the corporation's property for their own personal benefit. Duane demanded that these activities cease. In 1996, in order to stop Duane's bullying of them, the other four shareholders removed the Jorgensens from the board of directors and stopped making payments to them. From that point, the Jorgensens were not allowed to have any say in how the corporation was run or in the distribution of money.

The Jorgensens sued the other four shareholders alleging that the four shareholders owed a fiduciary duty to the corporation and its minority shareholders (the Jorgensens) and that they breached their fiduciary duty by using corporate assets for their own personal use and by paying fees to themselves that were in fact dividends. The Jorgensens' only allegation of corporate waste, however, was that payments continued to the other four shareholders, but not to Duane and Sharon. The four defendant shareholders moved for summary judgment, which the court granted on the grounds that the Jorgensens could not sue in their own right, but were required to sue derivatively in the name of the Water Works, Inc. The Jorgensens appealed to the Wisconsin Court of Appeals.

Vergeront, Judge The Jorgensens' complaint alleges waste and mismanagement of corporate assets—injuries primarily to the corporation. However, the Jorgensens argue that they have injuries that are not primarily to the corporation but are primarily injuries to themselves as individuals. The complaint alleges that the defendant majority shareholders and directors breached their fiduciary duty to the Jorgensens and caused injury to the Jorgensens by paying themselves fees and bonuses which are, in fact, dividends, to the detriment of the Jorgensens; and caused injury by removing the Jorgensens from the board of directors and controlling the corporation as if they were the sole shareholders with no obligations to the Jorgensens. We agree with the Jorgensens that this alleges an injury that is primarily to the Jorgensens, not primarily to the corporation.

A majority stockholder cannot take the position that his self-interest is superior to that of a minority stockholder; nor can directors and managing officers claim that their self-interest and self-protection are justification for denying the rights of a minority stockholder. Directors and managing officers occupy the position of quasi trustees toward stockholders with respect to their shares of stock. Since the value of their shares and all their rights are affected by the conduct of the directors, it has been said that a trust relationship exists between the stockholders and the directors and from this relationship arises the fiduciary duties of the directors toward the stockholders in dealings which may affect the stocks and the rights of the stockholders. A majority of jurisdictions hold that a director is a trustee only as to the corporation itself, but the better rule, although a minority view, is that he is also a trustee for an individual stockholder. Wisconsin has long recognized that directors are trustees for stockholders.

It is true the fiduciary duty of a director is owed to the individual stockholders as well as to the corporation. Directors in this state may not use their position of trust to further their private interest. Thus, where some individual right of a stockholder is being impaired by the improper acts of a director, the stockholder can bring a direct suit on his own behalf because it is his individual right that is being violated.

Courts in other jurisdictions that, like Wisconsin, recognize a claim for breach of fiduciary duty by directors and majority shareholders to minority shareholders have permitted such claims in circumstances factually similar to those alleged here. See, e.g., *Wilkes v. Springside Nursing Home Inc.,* 370 Mass. 842, 353 N.E.2d 657 (Mass. 1978) (breach of fiduciary duty where majority stockholders and directors of close corporation removed plaintiff as officer and director and severed him from payroll without legitimate business purpose); *McDonald v. United States Die Casting & Dev. Co.,* 541 So. 2d 1064 (Ala. 1989) (minority shareholder entitled to trial on direct action claim that a "constructive dividend" was paid to the majority shareholder without payment to him of a proportionate amount).

Duane Jorgensen's testimony provides evidence that there was a verbal agreement among all the shareholders that they would all be directors and Duane would oversee management of the company, and this was the basis for his initial contribution to the company. His testimony also provides evidence that the profits of the company had, since 1989, been divided among all six of the shareholders; the other four directors removed him and Sharon from the board of directors and they stopped all payments to them; and this was done to cut them out of the management of the company and of their share in the profits of the company, in violation of the verbal agreements, so that the four could pay themselves more. Mary Tesch's affidavit avers that the corporation's records show the payments were officers' compensation, not dividends, and in other ways her affidavit disputes Duane Jorgensen's testimony. However, this creates, not eliminates, factual disputes. It may be that at trial the defendants will submit evidence that will persuade a jury that the actions the Jorgensens complain of were not motivated by the individual defendants' desires to increase their share of the profits of the company to the detriment of the Jorgensens and were not a breach of their fiduciary duty as directors and majority shareholders. However, there are factual disputes that entitle the Jorgensens to a trial on this claim.

Judgment reversed in favor of the Jorgensens; remanded to the trial court.

Members' Rights and Duties in Nonprofit Corporations

In a for-profit corporation, the shareholders' rights to elect directors and to receive dividends are their most important rights. The shareholders' duty to contribute capital as promised is the most important responsibility. By contrast, in a nonprofit corporation, the members' rights and duties—especially in a mutual benefit corporation—are defined by the ability of the members to use the facilities of the corporation (as in a social club) or to consume its output (as in a cooperative grocery store) and by their obligations to support the enterprise periodically with their money (such as dues paid to a social club) or with their labor (such as the duty to work a specified number of hours in a cooperative grocery store).

Nonprofit corporation law grants a corporation and its members considerable flexibility in determining the rights and liabilities of its members. The Model Nonprofit Corporation Act (MNCA) provides that all members of a nonprofit corporation have equal rights and obligations with respect to voting, dissolution, redemption of membership, and transfer of membership, unless the articles or bylaws establish classes of membership with different rights and obligations. For other rights and obligations, the MNCA provides that all members have the same rights and obligations, unless the articles or bylaws provide otherwise.

For example, a mutual benefit corporation that operates a golf country club may have two classes of membership. A full membership may entitle a full member to use all the club's facilities (including the swimming pool and tennis courts), grant the full member two votes on all matters submitted to members, and require the full member to pay monthly dues of $500. A limited membership may give a limited member the right to play the golf course only, grant the limited member one vote on all matters submitted to members, and require the limited members to pay monthly dues of $300 per month.

While members are primarily concerned about their consumption rights and financial obligations—such as those addressed above—that are embodied in the articles and the bylaws, they have other rights and obligations as well, including voting, inspection, and information rights similar to those held by shareholders of for-profit corporations.

Members' Meeting and Voting Rights

A nonprofit corporation must hold an annual meeting of its members and may hold meetings at other times as well.

Members holding at least 5 percent of the voting power may call for a special meeting of members at any time.

All members of record have one vote on all matters submitted to members, unless the articles or bylaws grant lesser or greater voting power. The articles or bylaws may provide for different classes of members. Members of one class may be given greater voting rights than the members of another class. The articles or bylaws may provide that a class has no voting power.

Members may not act at a meeting unless a quorum is present. Under the MNCA, a quorum is 10 percent of the votes entitled to be cast on a matter. However, unless at least one-third of the voting power is present at the meeting, the only matters that may be voted on are matters listed in the meeting notice sent to members. The articles or bylaws may require higher percentages.

Members may elect directors by straight or cumulative voting and by class voting. The articles or bylaws may also permit members to elect directors on the basis of chapter or other organizational unit, by region or other geographical unit, or by any other reasonable method. For example, a national humanitarian fraternity such as Lions Club may divide the United States into seven regions whose members are entitled to elect one director. Members also have the right to remove directors they have elected with or without cause.

In addition to the rights to elect and to remove directors, members have the right to vote on most amendments of the articles and bylaws, merger of the corporation with another corporation, sale of substantially all the corporation's assets, and dissolution of the corporation. Ordinarily, members must approve such matters by two thirds of the votes cast or a majority of the voting power, whichever is less. This requirement is more lenient than the rule applied to for-profit corporations. Combined with the 10 percent quorum requirement, members with less than 7 percent of the voting power may approve matters submitted to members.

However, the unfairness of such voting rules is offset by the MNCA's notice requirement. A members' meeting may not consider important matters such as mergers and articles amendments unless the corporation gave members fair and reasonable notice that such matters were to be submitted to the members for a vote.

In addition, the MNCA requires approval of each class of members whose rights are substantially affected by the matter. This requirement may increase the difficulty of obtaining member approval. For example, full members of a golf country club may not change the rights of limited members without the approval of the limited members. In addition, the articles or bylaws may require third person approval as well. For example, a city industrial development board may not be permitted to amend its articles without the consent of the mayor.

Members may vote in person or by proxy. They may also have written voting agreements. However, member voting agreements may not have a term exceeding 10 years. Members may act without a meeting if the action is approved in writing by at least 80 percent of the voting power.

Member Inspection and Information Rights

A member may not be able to exercise his voting and other rights unless he is informed. Moreover, a member must be able to communicate with other members to be able to influence the way they vote on matters submitted to members. Consequently, the MNCA grants members inspection and information rights.

Members have an absolute right to inspect and copy the articles, bylaws, board resolutions, and minutes of members' meetings. Members have a qualified right to inspect and copy a list of the members. The member's demand to inspect the members' list must be in good faith and for a proper purpose—that is, a purpose related to the member's interest as a member. Improper purposes include selling the list or using the list to solicit money. Members also have a qualified right to inspect minutes of board meetings and records of actions taken by committees of the board.

A nonprofit corporation is required to maintain appropriate accounting records, and members have a qualified right to inspect them. Upon demand, the corporation must provide to a member its latest annual financial statements, including a balance sheet and statement of operations. However, the MNCA permits a religious corporation to abolish or limit the right of a member to inspect any corporate record.

Distributions of Assets

Because it is not intended to make a profit, a nonprofit corporation does not pay dividends to its members. In fact, a nonprofit corporation is generally prohibited from making any distribution of its assets to its members.

Nonetheless, a mutual benefit corporation may purchase a membership and thereby distribute its assets to the selling member, but only if the corporation is able to pay its currently maturing obligations and has assets at least equal to its liabilities. For example, when a farmer joins a farmers' purchasing cooperative, he purchases a membership interest having economic value—it entitles him to purchase supplies from the cooperative at a bar-

gain price. The mutual benefit corporation may repurchase the farmer's membership when he retires from farming. Religious and public benefit corporations may not repurchase their memberships.

Resignation and Expulsion of Members

A member may resign at any time from a nonprofit corporation. When a member resigns, generally a member may not sell or transfer her membership to any other person. A member of a mutual benefit corporation may transfer her interest to a buyer if the articles or bylaws permit.

It is fairly easy for a nonprofit corporation to expel a member or terminate her membership. The corporation must follow procedures that are fair and reasonable and carried out in good faith. The MNCA does not require the corporation to have a proper purpose to expel or terminate a member but only to follow proper procedures. The MNCA places no limits on a religious corporation's expulsion of its members.

The MNCA does not require a nonprofit corporation to purchase the membership of an expelled member, and—as explained above—permits only a mutual benefit corporation to purchase a membership. Members of mutual benefit corporations who fear expulsion should provide for repurchase rights in the articles or bylaws.

Derivative Suits

Members of a nonprofit corporation have a limited right to bring derivative actions on behalf of the corporation. A derivative action may be brought by members having at least 5 percent of the voting power or by 50 members, whichever is less. Members must first demand that the directors bring the suit or establish that demand is futile. If the action is successful, a court may require the corporation to pay the suing members' reasonable expenses. When the action is unsuccessful and has been commenced frivolously or in bad faith, a court may require the suing members to pay the other party's expenses.

THE GLOBAL BUSINESS ENVIRONMENT

Chapter 43 covered some of the corporate governance differences between the United States and other countries, specifically Germany, including the makeup of corporate boards. There are many similarities but also quite a few differences in the powers of shareholders, including matters that must be submitted for shareholder approval. In Germany, the management board must obtain the approval of the shareholders to create new shares of the corporation, to transfer major assets, and to liquidate the company. The differences include German law requiring shareholder approval to declare dividends, issue new shares, and waive shareholders' pre-emptive right. In addition, many matters that in the United States may be included by director action in the bylaws must be included in German articles of incorporation, which cannot be modified without shareholder approval.

Shareholders of German companies have limited power to force a corporate right of action against someone who has harmed the corporation. A German corporation must sue members of the management board if a shareholders' meeting decides or if shareholders holding at least 10 percent of the shares demand the action. Beyond that, German law rarely permits an *actio pro socio,* the equivalent of an American derivative action. Moreover, German corporation law does not provide for direct actions by shareholders against members of the management board for breach of duty, such as wrongfully providing false financial information to shareholders.

Dissolution and Termination of Corporations

The MBCA provides that a corporation doing business may be dissolved by action of its directors and shareholders. The directors must adopt a dissolution resolution, and a majority of the shares outstanding must be cast in favor of dissolution at a shareholders' meeting. For a **voluntary dissolution** to be effective, the corporation must file articles of dissolution with the secretary of state. The dissolution is effective when the articles are filed.

A corporation may be also dissolved **without its consent** by administrative action of the secretary of state or by judicial action of a court. The secretary of state may commence an administrative proceeding to dissolve a corporation that has not filed its annual report, paid its annual franchise tax, appointed or maintained a registered office or agent in the state, or whose period of duration has expired. **Administrative dissolution** requires that the secretary of state give written notice to the corporation of the grounds for dissolution. If, within 60 days, the corporation has not corrected the default or demonstrated that the default does not exist, the secretary dissolves the corporation by signing a certificate of dissolution.

The shareholders, secretary of state, or the creditors of a corporation may ask a court to order the involuntary dissolution of a corporation. Any **shareholder** may obtain judicial dissolution when there is a deadlock of the directors that is harmful to the corporation, when the shareholders are deadlocked and cannot elect directors for two years, or when the directors act illegally, oppressively, or fraudulently. The **secretary of state** may obtain judicial dissolution if it is proved that a corporation obtained its articles of incorporation by fraud or exceeded or abused its legal authority. **Creditors** may request dissolution if the corporation is insolvent.

Under the MBCA, a corporation that has not issued shares or commenced business may be dissolved by the vote of a majority of its incorporators or initial directors.

Many close corporations are nothing more than incorporated partnerships, in which all the shareholders are managers and friends or relatives. Recently, corporation law has reflected the special needs of those shareholders of close corporations who want to arrange their affairs to make the close corporation more like a partnership. The Close Corporation Supplement to the MBCA recognizes that a **close corporation shareholder** should have more dissolution power, like a partner. This section, like similar provisions in many states, permits the articles of incorporation to empower any shareholder to dissolve the corporation at will or upon the occurrence of a specified event such as the death of a shareholder.

Winding Up and Termination

A dissolved corporation continues its corporate existence but may not carry on any business except that appropriate to winding up its affairs. Therefore, winding up (liquidation) must follow dissolution. Winding up is the orderly

CONCEPT REVIEW

Roles of Shareholders and the Board of Directors

Corporate Action	Board's Role	Shareholders' Role
Day-to-Day Management	Selects officers; supervises management	Elect and remove directors
Issuance of Shares	Issues shares	Protected by preemptive right
Merger and Share Exchange	Adopts articles of merger or share exhange	Vote to approve merger or share exchange; protected by dissenters' rights
Amendment of Articles of Incorporation	Proposes amendment	Vote to approve amendment
Dissolution	Proposes dissolution	Vote to approve dissolution
Dividends	Declares dividends	Receive dividends
Board of Directors Harms Individual Shareholder Rights	Has harmed shareholders	Bring individual or class action against directors or the corporation
Directors Harm Corporation	Sues wrongdoing directors	Bring derivative action against wrongdoing directors

collection and disposal of the corporation's assets and the distribution of the proceeds of the sale of assets. From these proceeds, the claims of creditors will be paid first. Next, the liquidation preferences of preferred shareholders will be paid. Then, common shareholders receive any proceeds that remain.

After winding up has been completed, the corporation's existence terminates. A person who purports to act on behalf of a terminated corporation has the liability of a person acting for a corporation prior to its incorporation. Some courts impose similar liability on a person acting on behalf of a dissolved corporation, especially when dissolution is obtained by the secretary of state, such as for the failure to file an annual report or to pay annual taxes.

Dissolution of Nonprofit Corporations

A nonprofit corporation may be dissolved voluntarily, administratively, or judicially. Voluntary dissolution will usually require approval of both the directors and the members. However, a nonprofit corporation may include a provision in its articles requiring the approval of a third person also. For example, such a third person might be a state governor who appointed some of the directors to the board of a nonprofit corporation organized to encourage industrial development in the state. The dissolution is effective when the corporation delivers articles of dissolution to the secretary of state and the secretary of state files them. The dissolved corporation continues its existence, but only for the purpose of liquidating its assets and winding up its affairs.

The secretary of state may administratively dissolve a nonprofit corporation that fails to pay incorporation taxes or to deliver its annual report to the secretary of state, among other things. Minority members or directors may obtain judicial dissolution by a court if the directors are deadlocked, the directors in control are acting illegally or fraudulently, or the members are deadlocked and cannot elect directors for two successive elections, among other reasons.

Problems and Problem Cases

1. At the annual shareholders' meeting of Levisa Oil Corporation, management proposed to increase the number of directors to five from four. Quigley and one other shareholder owning together more than 50 percent of the

outstanding shares objected to the proposal. When Quigley was ruled out of order by the chairman of the board, Quigley and the other opposing shareholder stormed out of the meeting. The remaining shareholders voted to elect a five-member board. The new board then voted to issue new shares, which were issued to the minority shareholders. The effect of the issuance was to give the minority shareholders majority ownership of the corporation. Quigley later objected to the actions taken at the meeting. Were the actions taken after Quigley left invalid due to the lack of a quorum?

2. Edward and Harry Hall each owned 50 percent of the shares of a corporation and were its only directors. Edward died leaving his shares to his wife, Margaret. In compliance with the bylaws, Harry filled the vacancy on the board of directors by appointing his wife, Florence. As directors, Harry and Florence elected each other president and vice president. Subsequently, Harry and Florence refused to call an annual shareholders' meeting, and Harry failed to attend when Margaret called a shareholders' meeting. Without a quorum, no action could be taken. As a result, Harry and Florence continued as directors and officers. Will Margaret be able to obtain a court order requiring Harry to attend a shareholders' meeting?

3. Texas International Airlines, Inc. (TIA), proposed a merger that would strengthen its financial position. The merger required the approval of each of the four classes of TIA shares. Jet Capital Corporation owned all the Class C shares. Jet Capital believed the merger would benefit TIA, but it would also cause Jet Capital to suffer adverse tax consequences due to Jet Capital's ownership of warrants to purchase TIA shares. The adverse tax impact could be eliminated by Jet Capital's exercising the warrants before the merger, but it required a cash payment of $3,000,000, which Jet Capital could not afford. In exchange for Jet Capital's agreeing to vote for the merger, TIA lent Jet Capital $3,000,000 at a below-market interest rate. Since the cash lent to Jet Capital was paid back to TIA when Jet Capital exercised the warrants, the loan had virtually no impact on TIA's financial position. The loan agreement was challenged as an illegal vote-buying agreement. Was it illegal?

4. Dale Waters was minority shareholder of Double L, Inc., a business engaged in manufacturing agricultural machinery and related products. When Double L became financially distressed, the directors agreed to sell to Pioneer Astro all of Double L's real property and equipment and to issue sufficient shares to make Pioneer Astro an 80 percent shareholder of Double L. To improve

Double L's financial position, Pioneer Astro agreed to pay cash for the assets and shares and to loan money to Double L. To allow Double L to continue its business, Pioneer Astro agreed to lease the purchased assets back to Double L. At a shareholder meeting, shareholders approved the transaction with Pioneer Astro. Waters, however, abstained from voting and demanded that Double L pay him the fair value of his shares pursuant to dissenters' rights under Idaho law. Are dissenters' rights available in this context?

5. Karen Shaw, a dairy farmer in Vermont, was a member of a cooperative stock corporation, Agri-Mark, Inc., which was formed to process and market milk and other dairy products for its member farmers in New England and New York. Agri-Mark's equity consisted of contributions from its members. Its members, however, were not shareholders. The only shareholders were directors, who were elected by regional delegates, who in turn were elected by members. If Shaw had a proper purpose, did she have the right to inspect Agri-Mark's member list and the compensation of the corporation's five highest paid executives?

6. Historically, Liggett Group, Inc., had paid quarterly dividends to its shareholders in March, June, September, and December of each year. On May 14, 1980, the Liggett board of directors recommended that shareholders accept a tender offer by GM Sub Corporation at $69 per share. The tender offer provided that if GM Sub acquired more than 50 percent of the Liggett shares, GM Sub and Liggett would merge; the Liggett shareholders who did not tender during the tender offer would receive $69 per share under the merger. Subsequently, 87.4 percent of Liggett shareholders tendered their shares. The cash-out merger was effected on August 7. Because the Liggett board believed that it would have been unfair to the shareholders who accepted the tender offer, the board skipped the June 1980 dividend. The board believed that the shareholders who did not tender should not be rewarded for refusing to tender their shares to GM Sub knowing that they would receive the same price per share in the merger. Also, the board believed that $69 was a fair price for the shares. Gabelli & Co. surrendered its Liggett shares pursuant to the merger agreement but then sued Liggett to force payment of the June 1980 dividend. Did Gabelli succeed?

7. Fred and Maxine Brandon and their four children owned all the shares of Brandon Construction Co., a family corporation. Fred and Maxine owned a majority of the shares. In 1987, the shareholders agreed that Fred and Maxine each would receive a monthly salary of $12,500.

Two months later, daughter Betty Brandon alleged that the salaries were excessive, and that Fred and Maxine were dismantling the corporation and distributing its assets to themselves, without regard for the children's rights as minority shareholders. She initiated a derivative action against her parents, but her siblings responded that Betty did not represent their interests as minority shareholders and that they were content with the salaries paid to their parents. Is Betty a proper person to bring a derivative suit?

8. Three brothers—Joseph, Myer, and Samuel Sugarman—owned equal amounts of the shares of Statler Tissue Corporation. Over time, Myer's son Leonard became the majority shareholder of the corporation: Samuel gave some of his shares to his son Hyman and to Hyman's children, James, Marjorie, and Jon Sugarman; Hyman sold his shares to Leonard; Joseph Sugarman's shares were repurchased by the corporation. By 1974, Leonard owned 61 percent of the shares and was president and chairman of the board. James, Marjorie, and Jon Sugarman owned 22 percent of the shares. Marjorie had sought employment with the corporation but was not hired. Jon was employed from 1974 until his discharge in 1978. James never sought employment with the company. After 1975, Myer's value to the corporation was nearly zero because he had Alzheimer's disease; nonetheless, Myer was employed by the corporation and received a salary equal to Hyman's salary. In 1980, Leonard caused the company to double Myer's salary to $85,000 for 1980 and 1981, when Myer was 87 and 88 years of age. Hyman received no such increase. When Myer retired in 1982, Leonard caused the corporation to pay Myer a yearly pension of $75,000. When Hyman retired in 1980, he received no pension. The corporation paid no dividends. In 1980, Leonard offered to buy Jon's and Marjorie's shares for $3.33 per share. At that time, Price Waterhouse had advised Leonard that the book value of the corporation's shares was $16.30 per share. Does Leonard have liability to Jon and Marjorie?

9. H. F. Ahmanson & Co. was the controlling shareholder of United Savings and Loan Association. There was very little trading in the Association's shares, however. To create a public market for their shares, Ahmanson and a few other shareholders of the Association incorporated United Financial Corporation and exchanged each of their Association shares for United shares. United then owned more than 85 percent of the shares of the Association. The minority shareholders of the Association were not given an opportunity to exchange their shares. United made two public offerings of its shares. As a result, trading in United shares was very active, while sales of Association shares decreased to half of the formerly low level, with United as virtually the only purchaser. United offered to purchase Association shares from the minority shareholders for $1,100 per share. Some of the minority shareholders accepted this offer. At that time, the shares held by the majority shareholders were worth $3,700. United also caused the Association to decrease its dividend payments. Has Ahmanson done anything wrong?

10. Rexford Rand Corporation had three shareholders, Selwyn Ancel, who owned 50 percent of the shares, and his sons Gregory and Albert who owned 25 percent each. It sold over 200 products to 5,800 customers in many states. In 1991, Gregory was fired as vice president and treasurer, but remained a shareholder. From that point, he received no salary from the corporation, and the corporation never paid dividends. In 1993, Rexford Rand failed to file its annual report with the State of Illinois and, as a result, was administratively dissolved. The dissolution resulted in the name Rexford Rand becoming available for other businesses. Gregory learned of the dissolution but did not inform the other shareholders. Will Gregory act wrongly if he reserves the name Rexford Rand for his own corporation?

11. Jerry Yarmouth was the sole shareholder, director, and officer of J & R Interiors, Inc. The corporation's registered agent was its lawyer. Because the corporation's lawyer closed his office, when the secretary of state mailed a notice for payment of the annual fee and filing of the annual report, Yarmouth never received the notice. Consequently, the secretary of state administratively dissolved the corporation. Believing the corporation was still in existence, Yarmouth continued to transact on behalf of J & R Interiors, including making a contract to buy a $20,000 workbench from Equipto Division Aurora Equipment. Is Yarmouth personally liabile on the contract with Equipto?

12. East Side Metals, Inc., a Missouri corporation, fails to file an annual registration statement required by Missouri corporation law. Consequently, East Side forfeits its corporate charter. Harlin, Louis, and Bernice Mitauer are East Side's directors and officers at the time of the forfeiture. Do the Mitauers risk personal liability if they continue to operate East Side's business instead of winding it up?

Online Research: Corporate Governance Policies

The Council of Institutional Investors is an organization of large pension funds that addresses investment issues. As the representative of pension funds that are signifi-cant shareholders in public corporations, the Council takes a strong stance in favor of shareholder rights. Log on to the Council's website and find its "Corporate Governance Policies." List the major items in the sections on shareholder voting rights, shareholder meeting rights, and board accountability to shareholders.

45

SECURITIES REGULATION

You are the CEO of L'Malle LLC, a developer of shopping malls. L'Malle plans to raise $4,400,000 for construction of L'Malle's newest shopping center complex, Grande L'Malle Geneva. In an effort to avoid the application of the Securities Act of 1933, L'Malle's CFO has proposed that L'Malle issue 22 Profit Participation Plans (PPP) to two insurance companies, four mutual funds, and 16 individual investors. Under the PPPs, each owner will contribute $200,000 cash to finance the construction of Grande L'Malle Geneva (GLG) and receive 3 percent of the profits generated by GLG. L'Malle will be the exclusive manager of GLG, making all decisions regarding its construction and operation, for which L'Malle will receive a fee equal to 34 percent of GLG's profits.

• Are the PPPs securities under the Securities Act of 1933?

• If the PPPs are securities, may L'Malle sell them pursuant to a registration exemption from the Securities Act of 1933 under Regulation A, Rule 504, Rule 505, or 506?

L'Malle decides to sell the PPP's directly to investors by making a Regulation A offering. As CEO, you will accompany L'Malle's CFO and communications vice president when they visit prospective investors. During those visits you and the other L'Malle's executives will present copies of the offering circular to prospective investors, make oral reports about the offering, GLG, and L'Malle's business and prospects. You will also answer the investors' questions about L'Malle and GLG.

• Should you be fearful about having liability to the investors under Section 12(a)(2) of the 1933 Act and Rule 10b–5 of the Securities Exchange Act of 1934?

L'Malle decides to make a public offering of its common shares by registering the offering under the Securities Act of 1933 and complying with the requirements of Section 5 of the 1933 Act. The shares will be sold by a firm commitment underwriting.

• Under what legal conditions may L'Malle release earnings reports and make other normal communications with its shareholders and other investors?

• After L'Malle has filed its 1933 Act registration statement with the Securities and Exchange Commission and before the SEC has declared the registration statement effective, under what legal conditions may you (the CEO) and L'Malle's CFO conduct a road show where you pitch the shares to mutual fund investment managers in several cities?

• During that waiting period, may L'Malle post its preliminary prospectus and have an FAQ page for prospective investors at the offering's website?

• After the SEC has declared the registration statement effective, under what legal conditions may L'Malle confirm the sale of shares to an investor?

• During that posteffective period, under what legal conditions may L'Malle direct prospective investors from the offering's website to L'Malle's corporate website, where investors may obtain additional information about L'Malle?

MODERN SECURITIES REGULATION AROSE from the rubble of the great stock market crash of October 1929. After the crash, Congress studied its causes and discovered several common problems in securities transactions, the most important ones being:

1. Investors lacked the necessary information to make intelligent decisions whether to buy, sell, or hold securities.
2. Disreputable sellers of securities made outlandish claims about the expected performance of securities and sold securities in nonexistent companies.

Faced with these perceived problems, Congress chose to require securities sellers to disclose the information that investors need to make intelligent investment decisions. Congress found that investors are able to make intelligent investment decisions if they are given sufficient information about the company whose securities they are to buy. This **disclosure scheme** assumes that investors need assistance from government in acquiring information but that they need no help in evaluating information.

Purposes of Securities Regulation

To implement its disclosure scheme, in the early 1930s Congress passed two major statutes, which are the hub of federal securities regulation in the United States today. These two statutes, the **Securities Act of 1933** and the **Securities Exchange Act of 1934,** have three basic purposes:

1. To require the disclosure of meaningful information about a security and its issuer to allow investors to make intelligent investment decisions.
2. To impose liability on those persons who make inadequate and erroneous disclosures of information.
3. To regulate insiders, professional sellers of securities, securities exchanges, and other self-regulatory securities organizations.

The crux of the securities acts is to impose on issuers of securities, other sellers of securities, and selected buyers of securities the affirmative duty to disclose important information, even if they are not asked by investors to make the disclosures. By requiring disclosure, Congress hoped to restore investor confidence in the securities markets. Congress wanted to bolster investor confidence in the honesty of the stock market and thus encourage more investors to invest in securities. Building investor confidence would increase capital formation

and, it was hoped, help the American economy emerge from the Great Depression of the 1930s.

Congress has reaffirmed the purposes of the securities law many times since the 1930s by passing laws that expand investor protections. Most recent is the enactment of the Sarbanes–Oxley Act of 2002, a response to widespread misstatements and omissions in corporate financial statements. Many public investors lost most of their life savings in the collapses of firms like Enron, while insiders profited. As we learned in Chapters 4 and 43 and will learn in this chapter and Chapter 46, the Sarbanes–Oxley Act imposes new duties on corporations, their officers, and their auditors and provides for a Public Company Accounting Oversight Board to establish auditing standards. The hope is that the new act will restore investor confidence in both financial statements and the securities markets by ensuring that a corporation's financial statements fairly present its financial position.

LOG ON

www.law.uc.edu/CCL/sldtoc.html
The Securities Lawyer's Deskbook is maintained by the Center for Corporate Law at the University of Cincinnati College of Law. You can find the text of all the federal securities statutes and SEC regulations.

Securities and Exchange Commission

The Securities and Exchange Commission (SEC) was created by the 1934 Act. Its responsibility is to administer the 1933 Act, 1934 Act, and other securities statutes. Like other federal administrative agencies, the SEC has legislative, executive, and judicial functions. Its legislative branch promulgates rules and regulations; its executive branch brings enforcement actions against alleged violators of the securities statutes and their rules and regulations; its judicial branch decides whether a person has violated the securities laws.

SEC Actions

The SEC is empowered to investigate violations of the 1933 Act and 1934 Act and to hold hearings to determine whether the acts have been violated. Such hearings are held before an administrative law judge (ALJ), who is an employee of the SEC. The administrative law judge is a finder of both fact and law. Decisions of the ALJ are reviewed by the commissioners of the SEC. Decisions of the commissioners are appealed to the U.S. court of appeals. Most SEC actions are not litigated. Instead, the SEC issues consent orders, by which the defendant promises not to violate the securities laws in the future but does not admit to having violated them in the past.

The SEC has the power to impose civil penalties (fines) up to $500,000 and to issue **cease and desist orders.** A cease and desist order directs a defendant to stop violating the securities laws and to desist from future violations. Nonetheless, the SEC does not have the power to issue injunctions; only courts may issue injunctions. The 1933 Act and the 1934 Act empower the SEC only to ask federal district courts for injunctions against persons who have violated or are about to violate either act. The SEC may also ask the courts to grant ancillary relief, a remedy in addition to an injunction. Ancillary relief may include, for example, the disgorgement of profits that a defendant has made in a fraudulent sale or in an illegal insider trading transaction.

To reduce the risk that a securities issuer's or other person's behavior will violate the securities law and result in an SEC action, anyone may contact the SEC's staff in advance, propose a transaction or course of action, and ask the SEC to issue a **no-action letter.** In the no-action letter, the SEC's staff states it will take no legal action against the issuer or other person if the issuer or other person acts as indicated in the no-action letter. Issuers often seek no-action letters before making exempted offerings of securities and excluding shareholder proposals from their proxy statements, issues we discuss later in the chapter. Since a no-action letter is issued by the SEC's staff and not the commissioners, it is not binding on the commissioners. Nonetheless, issuers that comply with no-action letters rarely face SEC action.

LOG ON

www.sec.gov
You can read more about the SEC at the SEC website.

What Is a Security?

The first issue in securities regulation is the definition of a security. If a transaction involves no security, then the law of securities regulation does not apply. The 1933 Act defines the term **security** broadly:

Unless the context otherwise requires the term "security" means any note, stock, treasury stock, security future, bond, debenture, evidence of indebtedness, certificate of interest of participation in any profit-sharing agreement, . . . preorganization certificate or subscription, . . . investment contract, voting trust certificate, . . . fractional undivided interest in oil, gas, or mineral rights, any put, call, straddle, option, or privilege on any security, . . . or, in general, any interest or instrument commonly known as a "security."

The 1934 Act definition of security is similar, but excludes notes and drafts that mature not more than nine months from the date of issuance.

While typical securities like common shares, preferred shares, bonds, and debentures are defined as securities, the definition of a security also includes many contracts that the general public may believe are not securities. This is because the term **investment contract** is broadly defined by the courts. The Supreme Court's three-part test for an investment contract, called the *Howey* test, has been the guiding beacon in the area for more than 50 years.[1] The *Howey* test states that an investment contract is an **investment of money** in a **common enterprise** with an expectation of **profits solely from the efforts of others.**

In the *Howey* case, the sales of plots in an orange grove along with a management contract were held to be sales of securities. The purchasers had investment motives (they intended to make a profit from, not to consume, the oranges produced by the trees). There was a common enterprise, because the investors were similarly affected by the efforts of the sellers who grew and sold the oranges for all investors. The sellers, not the buyers, did all of the work needed to make the plots profitable.

In other cases, sales of limited partnership interests, Scotch whisky receipts, and restaurant franchises have been held to constitute investment contracts and, therefore, securities.

Courts define in two ways the common enterprise element of the *Howey* test. All courts permit horizontal commonality to satisfy the common enterprise requirement. Horizontal commonality requires that investors' funds be pooled and that profits of the enterprise be shared pro rata by investors. Some courts accept vertical commonality, in which the investors are similarly affected by the efforts of the person who is promoting the investment. In the following *Unique Financial* case, the court addressed both the horizontal and vertical commonality tests.

---

[1] *SEC v. W. J. Howey Co.,* 328 U.S. 293 (U.S. Sup. Ct. 1946).

Securities and Exchange Commission v. Unique Financial Concepts, Inc.
196 F.3d 1195 (11th Cir. 1999)

In October 1997, Ernest Patti and Frederick Hollander organized Unique Financial Concepts, Inc. Unique offered investors the opportunity to purchase foreign currency options; that is, the right to buy or sell foreign currencies in the future at a price set at the time the option is purchased. Unique advertised heavily on television, newspapers, and the Internet, promising large returns on small investments. Prospective investors were sent a packet containing an offering document that described the foreign exchange market, a customer agreement, and a disclosure of risk statement.

The original customer agreement explained that the investments of all the investors would be pooled together, gains and losses would be prorated among investors, and Unique had sole discretion over the investments. In August 1998, Unique modified its customer agreement by removing the language concerning the pooling of investments and Unique's sole discretion over these investments. After receiving initial investments from investors, Unique deposited the funds into its bank account at Southern Bank in Fort Lauderdale, Florida. Unique sales representatives advised the investors which currencies they should invest in and how many currency options they should buy. The investor then spoke to a Unique compliance officer, who explained the details of the investment and requested the investors' assent to the purchase.

Unique raised over $6.5 million from investors. Of this amount, $2.5 million (38 percent) was wired to the Bahamas to clearinghouses that were responsible for carrying out the investors' option trades. The remainder of the investors' money was divided as follows: about $700,000 was paid to Unique sales representatives; about $1.2 million was paid for advertising (including $761,000 paid to DRE consulting, a company co-owned by Patti from which he received a substantial salary); about $300,000 was paid to Patti, Hollander, and Nicholas DeAngelis, the lead sales representative; and about $1.6 million was paid for business and personal expenses, including checks made payable for car rentals and personal loans. In addition, about $640,000 of the investors' funds was distributed to new investors.

After the initial investment, Unique aggressively solicited the investors for additional investments. Eventually, however, Unique representatives were extremely hard to reach and often failed to return phone calls. The investors lost significant amounts of money on their investments.

The United States Securities and Exchange Commission asked the district court to issue a preliminary injunction against Unique to stop Unique's solicitation of investors. The district court found that Unique was selling securities and thus was subject to the Securities Act.

The district court found that no credible evidence existed to show that Unique's clearinghouses ever placed trades on behalf of investors. The court could find no transaction or wire verifications indicating that the clearinghouses actually executed any trades. No bank records indicated the occurrence of the alleged trades. Patti testified that he did not know how the Bahamian clearinghouses executed the trades, and that he did not know how the clearinghouses were compensated for their services. Furthermore, Unique's compliance officer testified that she did not know what the clearinghouses did and did not even know what the term clearinghouse meant. Unique's accountant, Morris Berger, stated that the "only thing we had to deal with is really the Unique data. And we don't have the Bahamian trading data. . . . Do I know that there was actual trading in the Bahamas? The answer is, no, I don't."

In essence, the district court found that Unique was operating a Ponzi scheme. That is, rather than executing currency trades, Unique was keeping over 60 percent of the money. Unique paid the rest of the money back to the investors to fool them into thinking they were making money and should therefore invest more.

The district court awarded the SEC's request for a preliminary injunction. Unique appealed to the 11th Circuit Court of Appeals on the grounds that the SEC had no authority to regulate the transaction because there was no security involved.

Black, Circuit Judge The determinative question is whether the contracts offered and sold by Unique were investment contracts, and thus securities, under federal securities law. If the contracts were investment contracts, then the SEC had jurisdiction under the federal securities laws to bring this suit.

In *S.E.C. v. W. J. Howey Co.*, 328 U.S. 293 (1946), the Supreme Court established the classic test for determining whether a transaction is an "investment contract" within the meaning of Section 2(a)(1) of the Securities Act. In *Howey,* the Court explained that for the purposes of the Securities Act, an investment contract is "a contract, transaction, or scheme whereby a person invests his money in a common enterprise and is led to expect profits solely from the efforts of the promoter or a third party. . . ." This Court has divided the *Howey* test into the three elements: (1) an investment of money, (2) a common enterprise, and (3) the expectation of profits to be derived solely from the efforts of others. Both parties agree the first prong of this test has been satisfied. There is distinct disagreement, however, as to the second and third prongs.

With respect to the second prong, we have adopted the concept of vertical commonality, holding that a common enterprise exists where the fortunes of the investor are interwoven with and dependent on the efforts and success of those seeking the investment of third parties. The fact that an investor's return is independent of that of other investors in the scheme is not decisive. Rather, the requisite commonality is evidenced by the fact that the fortunes of all investors are inextricably tied to the efficacy of the promoter. *SEC v. Koscot Interplanetary, Inc.,* 497 F.2d 473 (5th Cir. 1974). The thrust of the common enterprise test is that the investors have no desire to perform the chores necessary for a return. Unlike the more stringent concept of horizontal commonality, utilized by the Second, Third, Sixth, and Seventh Circuits, this flexible standard does not require investor funds to be pooled nor does it require profits to be shared on a pro rata basis.

At trial, the district court found that the language of the original customer agreement, in conjunction with its conclusion that Unique's operations were a sham, supported the existence of a common enterprise. The agreement, in relevant part, reads as follows:

> By executing this agreement, Client authorizes [Unique] in its sole discretion to use the total funds on deposit in the omnibus account which includes the funds of the undersigned to execute single trades or transactions and to apportion the gains, losses, commissions, and clearing expenses proportionally to each account. The results of each trade will be apportioned and applied proportionately (per unit) to all accounts open on the trade and rounded down to the nearest US dollar.

On appeal, Unique contends that, despite the language of the original agreement, in actual practice it did not operate a horizontal investment pool but rather maintained individual, independent investment accounts. As support for this contention, Unique points to cash flows between Unique and the Bahamian clearinghouses, the alleged trade reports, as well as testimony regarding the trades and trade reports. Unique claims we should rely on the actual operation of its investment contracts, rather than the language of the original agreement, to hold that Unique's investment accounts do not meet the common enterprise prong.

However, given the absence of any credible documentation of trades, the absence of any persuasive testimony concerning these trades, as well as the fact that Unique invested less than 40 percent of investors' money, we conclude the record supports the district court's finding that Unique's operations were a sham. Consequently, we look, as did the district court, to the terms of the offer to determine whether Unique's activities are covered by the Securities Act. As noted above, the terms of the offer explicitly state that investors' funds will be pooled and apportioned proportionately by Unique to each account. This language clearly presents an offer for an investment in a common enterprise and thus supports the common enterprise prong of the *Howey* test.

Unique claims that the language of the original agreement was a mistake, and that the language was changed to accurately reflect Unique's operations. The district court, however, made a factual finding that Unique switched their customer agreement in August 1998 specifically to avoid liability under the federal securities laws.

There is also distinct disagreement over whether Unique's operations meet the "expectation of profits" element of the *Howey* test. In *Howey,* the Supreme Court explained that this prong requires that investors expect their "profits to come solely from the efforts of others." The courts have suggested several interpretations of the word "solely," with the disagreement centered on whether "solely" means all or merely predominant. The view this Court adopted in *Koscot* asks "whether the efforts made by those other than the investor are the undeniably significant ones, those essential managerial efforts which affect the failure or success of the enterprise." One year after *Koscot,* the Supreme Court reaffirmed *Howey* and revisited this question in *United Housing Foundation, Inc. v. Forman,* 421 U.S. 837 (1975). In *Forman,* the Supreme Court held that "the touchstone" of an investment contract for purposes of the Securities Acts is "the presence of an investment in a common venture premised on a reasonable expectation of profits to be derived from the entrepreneurial or managerial efforts of others."

In addition, this Court has clearly stated that "the crucial inquiry for the third prong is the amount of control that the investors retain under their written agreements. While we have yet to resolve the precise level of control dictated by *Forman,* we conclude Unique's operation meets any reasonable interpretation of 'solely.'"

First, contrary to Unique's assertion, Unique did not manage nondiscretionary investment accounts in which individual investors made all key strategic decisions. Rather, Unique did not engage in any actual trading, but instead operated a fraudulent scheme which misappropriated investors' funds. Thus, the investors retained no control over their investments, since there were no investments to control. Second, the original customer agreement specifically gave Unique the sole discretion to use the total funds deposited by the investors. Consequently, both the language of the agreement and Unique's actual operations support the district court's finding that Unique's operations met the third prong of the *Howey* test.

Judgment for SEC affirmed.

Courts have used the *Howey* test to hold that some contracts with typical security names are not securities. The courts point out that some of these contracts possess few of the typical characteristics of a security. For example, in *United Housing Foundation, Inc. v. Forman,*[2] the Supreme Court held that although tenants in a cooperative apartment building purchased contracts labeled as stock, the contracts were not securities. The "stock" possessed few of the typical characteristics of stock and the economic realities of the transaction bore few similarities to those of the typical stock sale: The stock gave tenants no dividend rights or voting rights in proportion to the number of shares owned, it was not negotiable, and it could not appreciate in value. More important, tenants bought the stock not for the purpose of investment but to acquire suitable living space.

However, when investors are misled to believe that the securities laws apply because a seller sold a contract bearing both the name of a typical security and significant characteristics of that security, the securities laws do apply to the sale of the security. The application of this doctrine led to the Supreme Court's rejection of the sale-of-business doctrine, which had held that the sale of 100 percent of the shares of a corporation to a single purchaser who would manage the corporation was not a security. The rationale for the sale-of-business doctrine was that the purchaser failed to meet element 3 of the *Howey* test because he expected to make a profit from his own efforts in managing the business. Today, when a business sale is effected by the sale of stock, the transaction is covered by the securities acts if the stock possesses the characteristics of stock.

In 1990, the Supreme Court further extended this rationale in *Reves v. Ernst & Young,*[3] adopting the **family resemblance test** to determine whether promissory notes were securities. The Supreme Court held that it is inappropriate to apply the *Howey* test to notes. Instead, applying the family resemblance test, the Court held that notes are presumed to be securities unless they bear a "strong family resemblance" to a type of note that is not a security.

The five characteristics of notes that are not securities are:

1. There is no recognized market for the securities.
2. The note is not part of a series of notes.
3. The buyer of the note does not need the protection of the securities laws.
4. The buyer of the note has no investment intent.
5. The buyer has no expectation that the securities laws apply to the sale of the note.

Types of notes that are not securities include consumer notes, mortgage notes, short-term notes secured by a lien on a small business, short-term notes secured by accounts receivable, and notes evidencing loans by commercial banks for current operations.

Securities Act of 1933

The Securities Act of 1933 (1933 Act) is concerned primarily with public distributions of securities. That is, the 1933 Act regulates the sale of securities while they are passing from the hands of the issuer into the hands of public investors. An issuer selling securities publicly must make necessary disclosures at the time the issuer sells the securities to the public.

The 1933 Act has two principal regulatory components: (1) registration provisions and (2) liability provisions. The registration requirements of the 1933 Act are designed to give investors the information they need to make intelligent decisions whether to purchase securities when an issuer sells its securities to the public. The

---

[2]*United Housing Foundation Inc. v. Forman,* 421 U.S. 837 (U.S. Sup. Ct. 1975).
[3]494 U.S. 56 (U.S. Sup. Ct. 1990).

various liability provisions in the 1933 Act impose liability on sellers of securities for misstating or omitting facts of material significance to investors.

Registration of Securities under the 1933 Act

The Securities Act of 1933 is primarily concerned with protecting investors when securities are sold by an issuer to investors. That is, the 1933 Act regulates the process during which issuers offer and sell their securities to investors, primarily public investors.

Therefore, the 1933 Act requires that *every* offering of securities be registered with the SEC prior to any offer or sale of the securities, unless the offering or the securities are exempt from registration. That is, an issuer and its underwriters may not offer or sell securities unless the securities are registered with the SEC or exempt from registration. Over the next few pages, we will cover the registration process. Then the exemptions from registration will be addressed.

Mechanics of a Registered Offering

When an issuer makes a decision to raise money by a public offering of securities, the issuer needs to obtain the assistance of securities market professionals. The issuer will contact a managing underwriter, the primary person assisting the issuer in selling the securities. The managing underwriter will review the issuer's operations and financial statements and reach an agreement with the issuer regarding the type of securities to sell, the offering price, and the compensation to be paid to the underwriters. The issuer and the managing underwriter will determine what type of underwriting to use.

In a **stand-by underwriting,** the underwriters obtain subscriptions from prospective investors, but the issuer sells the securities only if there is sufficient investor interest in the securities. The underwriters receive warrants—options to purchase the issuer's securities at a bargain price—as compensation for their efforts. The stand-by underwriting is typically used only to sell common shares to existing shareholders pursuant to a preemptive rights offering.

With a **best efforts underwriting,** the underwriters are merely agents making their best efforts to sell the issuer's securities. The underwriters receive a commission for their selling efforts. The best efforts underwriting is used when an issuer is not well established and the underwriter is unwilling to risk being unable to sell the securities.

The classic underwriting arrangement is a **firm commitment underwriting.** Here the managing underwriter forms an underwriting group and a selling group. The underwriting group agrees to purchase the securities from the issuer at a discount from the public offering price—for example, 25 cents per share below the offering price. The selling group agrees to buy the securities from the underwriters also at a discount—for example, 12½ cents per share below the offering price. Consequently, the underwriters and selling group bear much of the risk with a firm commitment underwriting, but they also stand to make the most profit under such an arrangement.

Securities Offerings on the Internet Increasingly, issuers are using the Internet to make public securities offerings, especially initial public offerings (IPOs) of companies' securities. The Internet provides issuers and underwriters the advantage of making direct offerings to all investors simultaneously, that is, selling directly to investors without the need for a selling group. The first Internet securities offering that was approved by the SEC was a firm commitment underwriting. Internet offerings have increased dramatically since 1998. In the future, the Internet will become the dominant medium for marketing securities directly to investors.

Registration Statement and Prospectus

The 1933 Act requires the issuer of securities to register the securities with the SEC before the issuer or underwriters may offer or sell the securities. Registration requires filing a **registration statement** with the SEC. Historical and current data about the issuer and its business, full details about the securities to be offered, and the use of the proceeds of the issuance, among other information, must be included in the registration statement prepared by the issuer of the securities with the assistance of the managing underwriter, securities lawyers, and independent accountants. Generally, the registration statement must include audited balance sheets as of the end of each of the two most recent fiscal years, in addition to audited income statements and audited statements of changes in financial position for each of the last three fiscal years.

The registration statement becomes effective after it has been reviewed by the SEC. The 1933 Act provides that the registration statement becomes effective automatically on the 20th day after its filing, unless the SEC delays or advances the effective date.

The **prospectus** is the basic selling document of an offering registered under the 1933 Act. Most of the information in the registration statement must be included in the prospectus. It must be furnished to every purchaser of the registered security prior to or concurrently with the sale of the security to the purchaser. The prospectus enables an investor to base his investment decision on all of the relevant data concerning the issuer, not merely on the favorable information that the issuer may be inclined to disclose voluntarily.

Although most prospectuses are delivered in person or by mail, the growth of the Internet as a communication tool has resulted in many issuers transmitting their prospectuses in their Web pages.

Section 5: Timing, Manner, and Content of Offers and Sales

The 1933 Act restricts the issuer's and underwriter's ability to communicate with prospective purchasers of the securities. Section 5 of the 1933 Act states the basic rules regarding the timing, manner, and content of offers and sales. It creates three important periods of time in the life of a securities offering: (1) the pre-filing period, (2) the waiting period, and (3) the post-effective period.

The Pre-Filing Period Prior to the filing of the registration statement (the pre-filing period), the issuer and any other person may **not offer or sell** the securities to be registered. The purpose of the prefiling period is to prevent premature communications about an issuer and its securities, which may encourage an investor to make a decision to purchase the security before all the information she needs is available. The prefiling period also marks the start of what is sometimes called the **quiet period,** which continues for the full duration of the securities offering. A prospective issuer, its directors and officers, and its underwriters must avoid publicity about the issuer and the prospective issuance of securities during the pre-filing period and the rest of the quiet period. Press releases, advertisements, speeches, and press conferences may be deemed offers if their intent or effect is to condition the market to receive the securities.

SEC Rule 135 permits the issuer to publish a notice about a prospective offering during the pre-filing period. The notice may contain only the name of the issuer and a basic description of the securities and the offering. It may not name the underwriters or state the price at which the securities will be offered.

The Waiting Period The waiting period is the time between the filing date and the effective date of the registration statement, when the issuer is waiting for the

SEC to declare the registration statement effective. During the waiting period, Section 5 permits the securities to be **offered but not sold.** However, not all kinds of offers are permitted. Face-to-face oral offers (including personal phone calls) are allowed during the waiting period. However, written offers may be made only by a statutory prospectus, usually a **preliminary prospectus** that often omits the price of the securities. (A final prospectus will be available after the registration statement becomes effective. It will contain the price of the securities.) Other so-called "free writings" are not permitted during the waiting period.

The waiting period is part of the quiet period, and, therefore, general publicity during the waiting period may be construed as an illegal offer because it conditions the market to receive the securities. One type of general advertisement, called the **tombstone ad,** is permitted during the waiting period and thereafter. The tombstone ad, which appears in financial publications, is permitted by SEC Rule 134, which allows disclosure of the same information as is allowed by Rule 135 plus the general business of the issuer, the price of the securities, and the names of the underwriters who are helping the issuer to sell the securities. In addition, Rule 134 requires the tombstone ad to state that it is not an offer.

Issuers making public offerings will typically send their CEOs and other top officers on the road to talk to securities analysts and institutional investors during the waiting period. These road shows are permissible, provided investors and others who attend the meetings are able to ask unlimited questions of the issuer. Otherwise, the meetings could be construed as illegal written offers.

The Internet is an exceptional medium to communicate with investors during the waiting period. Investors may easily view a tombstone ad and download a prospectus from an offering Web page. Care must be taken, however, not to allow investors to easily link to the issuer's homepage, where additional information about the issuer is available that may violate the waiting period's free writing prohibition.

There is an issue whether an Internet chatroom may permit investors to ask questions about the offering during the waiting period, because the issuer's responses will be written, not oral, and therefore may be illegal written offers. This should not be an obstacle, if investors are able to ask unlimited questions and receive immediate answers. In that case the Internet is more akin to a conversation than a written communication. Yet there can still be a problem with a chatroom if many investors ask so many questions that the issuer is unable to respond to all of them. Nonetheless, the Internet is the best

CONCEPT REVIEW

Communications with Investors by or on Behalf of Issuer Permitted by Section 5 during a 1933 Act Registration

Type of Communication	Pre-Filing Period	Filing Date of Registration Statement / Waiting Period	Effective Date of Registration Statement / Post-Effective Period
Ordinary Business Communications, such as Annual Reports, Press Releases, and Quarterly Reports	Permitted, unless designed to assist the placement of securities or arouse interest in a prospective sale of securities	Permitted, unless designed to assist the placement of securites or arouse interest in a prospecitve sale of securities	Permitted, without restriction, if used contemporaneously with or after delivery of final prospectus
Notice of Proposed Offering (Rule 135)	Permitted	Permitted	Permitted
Tombstone Ad (Rule 134)	Not permitted	Permitted	Permitted
Offer by Preliminary Prospectus	Not permitted	Permitted	Not permitted
Offer by Final Prospectus	Not permitted	Not permitted	Permitted
Oral One-on-One Offers (including telephone calls)	Not permitted	Permitted	Permitted
Oral Offers at Road Shows	Not permitted	Permitted, if each investor has an opportunity to ask unlimited questions	Permitted, if each investor has an opportunity to ask unlimited questions, or if each investor has received a final prospectus
Written Offers Other than a Prospectus (so-called free writing)	Not permitted	Not permitted	Permitted, contemporaneously with or after delivery of final prospecus
Sales	Not permitted	Not permitted	Permitted, contemporaneously with or after delivery of final prospectus

medium to provide valuable information to all investors who are seeking information on a particular issuer. The SEC has permitted webcasts of some road shows.

The waiting period is an important part of the regulatory scheme of the 1933 Act. It provides an investor with adequate time (at least 20 days) to judge the wisdom of buying the security during a period when he cannot be pressured to buy it. Not even a contract to buy the security may be made during the waiting period.

The Post-Effective Period After the effective date (the date on which the SEC declares the registration effective), Section 5 permits the security to be offered and also to be sold, provided that the buyer has received a final prospectus (a preliminary prospectus is not acceptable for this purpose). Written offers not previously allowed are permitted during the post-effective period, but only if the offeree has received a final prospectus.

The Internet can be used extensively during the post-effective period. From the issuer's Web page, an investor may be required to download a final prospectus in order to obtain access to a chatroom or other written information about the issuer and the offering. Since the final prospectus download would be a delivery of the final prospectus to the investor, all communications thereafter would be legal even if they were written.

Liability for Violating Section 5   Section 12(a)(1) of the 1933 Act imposes liability on any person who violates the provisions of Section 5. Liability extends to any *purchaser* to whom an illegal offer or sale was made. The purchaser's remedy is *rescission* or damages.

Exemptions from the Registration Requirements of the 1933 Act

Complying with the registration requirements of the 1933 Act, including the restrictions of Section 5, is a burdensome, time-consuming, and expensive process. Planning and executing an issuer's first public offering may consume six months and cost in excess of $1 million. Consequently, some issuers prefer to avoid registration when they sell securities. There are two types of exemptions from the registration requirements of the 1933 Act: securities exemptions and transaction exemptions.

Securities Exemptions

Exempt securities never need to be registered, regardless who sells the securities, how they are sold, or to whom they are sold. The following are the most important securities exemptions.[4]

1. Securities issued or guaranteed by any government in the United States and its territories.

2. A note or draft that has a maturity date not more than nine months after its date of issuance.

3. A security issued by a nonprofit religious, charitable, educational, benevolent, or fraternal organization.

4. Securities issued by banks and by savings and loan associations.

5. Securities issued by railroads and trucking companies regulated by the Interstate Commerce Commission.

6. An insurance policy or an annuity contract.

Although the types of securities listed above are exempt from the registration provisions of the 1933 Act, they are not exempt from the general antifraud provisions of the securities acts. For example, any fraud committed in the course of selling such securities can be attacked by the SEC and by the persons who were defrauded under Section 17(a) of the 1933 Act and Section 10(b) of the 1934 Act.

Transaction Exemptions

The most important 1933 Act registration exemptions are the transaction exemptions. If a security is sold pursuant to a transaction exemption, that sale is exempt from registration. Subsequent sales, however, are not automatically exempt. Future sales must be made pursuant to a registration or another exemption.

The transaction exemptions are exemptions from the registration provisions. The general antifraud provisions of the 1933 Act and the 1934 Act apply to exempted and nonexempted transactions.

The most important transaction exemptions are those available to issuers of securities. These exemptions are the intrastate offering exemption, the private offering exemption, and the small offering exemptions.

Intrastate Offering Exemption

Under section 3(a)(11), an offering of securities solely to investors in one state by an issuer resident and doing business in that state is exempt from the 1933 Act's registration requirements. The reason for the exemption is that there is little federal government interest in an offering that occurs in only one state. Although the offering may be exempt from SEC regulation, state securities law may require a registration. The expectation is that state securities regulation will adequately protect investors.

The SEC has defined the intrastate offering exemption more precisely in Rule 147. An issuer must have at least 80 percent of its gross revenues and 80 percent of its assets in the state and use at least 80 percent of the proceeds

---

[4]Excluded from the list of securities exemptions are the intrastate offering and small offering exemptions. Although the 1933 Act denotes them (except for the section 4(6) exemption) as securities exemptions, they are in practice transaction exemptions. An exempt security is exempt from registration forever. But when securities originally sold pursuant to an intrastate or small offering exemption are resold at a later date, the subsequent sales may have to be registered. The exemption of the earlier offering does not exempt a future offering. The SEC treats these two exemptions as transaction exemptions. Consequently, this chapter also treats them as transaction exemptions.

of the offering in the state. Resale of the securities is limited to persons within the state for nine months.

Although Rule 147 is not an exclusive rule, the SEC scrutinizes closely an intrastate offering that does not comply with it.

Private Offering Exemption

Section 4(2) of the 1933 Act provides that the registration requirements of the 1933 Act "shall not apply to transactions by an issuer not involving any public offering." A private offering is an offering to a small number of purchasers who can protect themselves because they are wealthy or because they are sophisticated in investment matters and have access to the information that they need to make intelligent investment decisions.

To create greater certainty about what a private offering is, the SEC adopted Rule 506. Although an issuer may exempt a private offering under either the courts' interpretation of section 4(2) or Rule 506, the SEC tends to treat Rule 506 as the exclusive way to obtain the exemption.

Rule 506 Under Rule 506, which is part of Securities Act Regulation D, the issuer must reasonably believe that each purchaser is either (a) an accredited investor or (b) an unaccredited investor who "has such knowledge and experience in financial and business matters that he is capable of evaluating the merits and risks of the prospective investment." Accredited investors include institutional investors (such as banks and mutual funds), wealthy investors, and high-level insiders of the issuer (such as executive officers, directors, and partners).

An issuer may sell to no more than 35 unaccredited purchasers who have sufficient investment knowledge and experience; it may sell to an unlimited number of accredited purchasers, regardless of their investment sophistication.

Each purchaser must be given or have access to the information she needs to make an informed investment decision. For a public company making a nonpublic offering under Rule 506, purchasers must receive information

in a form required by the 1934 Act, such as a 10-K or annual report. The issuer must provide the following audited financial statements: two years' balance sheets, three years' income statements, and three years' statements of changes in financial position.

For a nonpublic company making a nonpublic offering under Rule 506, the issuer must provide much of the same nonfinancial information required in a registered offering. A nonpublic company may, however, obtain some relief from the burden of providing audited financial statements to investors. When the amount of the issuance is $2 million or less, only one year's balance sheet need be audited. If the amount issued exceeds $2 million but not $7.5 million, only one year's balance sheet, one year's income statement, and one year's statement of changes in financial position need be audited. When the amount issued exceeds $7.5 million, the issuer must provide two years' balance sheets, three years' income statements, and three years' statements of changes in financial position. In any offering of any amount by a nonpublic issuer, when auditing would involve unreasonable effort or expense, only an audited balance sheet is needed. When a limited partnership issuer finds that auditing involves unreasonable effort or expense, the limited partnership may use financial statements prepared by an independent accountant in conformance with the requirements of federal tax law.

Rule 506 prohibits the issuer from making any general public selling effort. This prevents the issuer from using the radio, newspapers, and television. However, offers to an individual one-on-one are permitted.

In addition, the issuer must take reasonable steps to ensure that the purchasers do not resell the securities in a manner that makes the issuance a public distribution rather than a private one. Usually, the investor must hold the security for a minimum of one year.

In the *Mark* case, the issuer failed to prove it was entitled to a private offering exemption under Rule 506.

Mark v. FSC Securities Corp.   *870 F.2d 331 (6th Cir. 1989)*

FSC Securities Corp., a securities brokerage, sold limited partnership interests in the Malaga Arabian Limited Partnership to Mr. and Mrs. Mark. A total of 28 investors purchased limited partnership interests in Malaga. All investors were asked to execute subscription documents, including a suitability letter in which the purchaser stated his income level, that he had an opportunity to obtain relevant information, and that he had sufficient knowledge and experience in business affairs to evaluate the risks of the investment.

When the value of the limited partnership interests fell, the Marks sued FSC to rescind their purchase on the grounds that FSC sold unregistered securities in violation of the Securities Act of 1933. The jury held that the offering was exempt as an offering not involving a public offering. The Marks appealed.

Simpson, Judge Section 4(2) of the Securities Act exempts from registration with the SEC "transactions by an issuer not involving any public offering." There are no hard and fast rules for determining whether a securities offering is exempt from registration under the general language of section 4(2).

However, the "safe harbor" provision of Regulation D, Rule 506, deems certain transactions to be not involving any public offering within the meaning of section 4(2). FSC had to prove that certain objective tests were met. These conditions include the general conditions not in dispute here, and the following specific conditions:

(i) Limitation on number of purchasers. The issuer shall reasonably believe that there are no more than thirty-five purchasers of securities in any offering under this Section.

(ii) Nature of purchasers. The issuer shall reasonably believe immediately prior to making any sale that each purchaser who is not an accredited investor either alone or with his purchaser representative(s) has such knowledge and experience in financial and business matters that he is capable of evaluating the merits and risks of the prospective investment.

In this case, we take the issuer to be the general partners of Malaga. FSC is required to offer evidence of the issuer's reasonable belief as to the nature of each purchaser. The only testimony at trial competent to establish the issuer's belief as to the nature of the purchasers was that of Laurence Leafer, a general partner in Malaga. By his own admission, he had no knowledge about any purchaser, much less any belief, reasonable or not, as to the purchasers' knowledge and experience in financial and business matters.

Q: What was done to determine if investors were, in fact, reasonably sophisticated?

A: Well, there were two things. Number one, we had investor suitability standards that had to be met. You had to have a certain income, be in a certain tax bracket, this kind

of thing. Then in the subscription documents themselves, they, when they sign it, supposedly represented that they had received information necessary to make an informed investment decision, and that they were sophisticated. And if they were not, they relied on an offering representative who was.

Q: Did you review the subscription documents that came in for the Malaga offering?

A: No.

Q: So do you know whether all of the investors in the Malaga offering met the suitability and sophistication requirements?

A: I don't.

FSC also offered as evidence the Marks' executed subscription documents, as well as a set of documents in blank, to establish the procedure it followed in the Malaga sales offering. Although the Marks' executed documents may have been sufficient to establish the reasonableness of any belief the issuer may have had as to the Marks' particular qualifications, that does not satisfy Rule 506. The documents offered no evidence from which a jury could conclude the issuer reasonably believed each purchaser was suitable. Instead, all that was proved was the sale of 28 limited partnership interests, and the circumstances under which those sales were intended to have been made. The blank subscriptions documents simply do not amount to probative evidence, when it is the answers and information received from purchasers that determine whether the conditions of Rule 506 have been met.

Having concluded that the Malaga limited-partnership offering did not meet the registration exemption requirement of Rule 506 of Regulation D, we conclude that the Marks are entitled to the remedy of rescission.

Judgment reversed in favor of the Marks; remanded to the trial court.

Small Offering Exemptions

Sections 3(b) and 4(6) of the 1933 Act permit the SEC to exempt from registration any offering by an issuer not exceeding $5 million. Several SEC rules and regulations permit an issuer to sell small amounts of securities and avoid registration. The rationale for these exemptions is that the dollar amount of the securities offered or the number of purchasers is too small for the federal government to be concerned with registration. State securities law may require registration, however.

Rule 504 SEC Rule 504 of Regulation D allows a nonpublic issuer to sell up to $1 million of securities in a 12-month period and avoid registration. Rule 504 sets no limits on the number of offerees or purchasers. The purchasers need not be sophisticated in investment matters, and the issuer need disclose information only as required by state securities law. Rule 504 permits general selling efforts, and purchasers are free to resell the securities at any time but only if the issuer either registers the securities under state securities law or sells only to accredited investors pursuant to a state securities law exemption.

Rule 505 Rule 505 of Regulation D allows any issuer to sell up to $5 million of securities in a 12-month period and avoid registration. No general selling efforts are allowed, and purchasers may not resell the securities for at least one year. The issuer may sell to no more than 35 unaccredited purchasers, but there is no limit on the number of accredited purchasers. The purchasers need not be sophisticated in investment matters. Rule 505 has the same disclosure requirements as Rule 506.

Regulation A Regulation A permits a nonpublic issuer to sell up to $5 million of securities in a one-year period. There is no limit on the number of purchasers, no purchaser sophistication requirement, and no purchaser resale restriction.

The Regulation A disclosure document is the offering circular, which must be filed with the SEC. The offering circular is required to contain a balance sheet dated within 90 days before the filing date of the offering circular. It must also contain two years' income statements, cash flow statements, and statements of shareholder equity. Ordinarily, the financial statements need not be audited unless the issuer is otherwise required to have audited financial statements.

There is a 20-day waiting period after the filing of the offering circular, during which offers may be made. Oral offers are permitted, as are brief advertisements and written offers by an offering circular. Sales are permitted after the waiting period.

Regulation A also permits issuers to determine investors' interest in a planned offering prior to undertaking the expense of preparing an offering circular.

Securities Offerings on the Internet

With the emergence of the Internet as a significant communication tool, small issuers have sought to make offerings to investors over the Internet. Such offerings can easily run afoul of Rules 505 and 506 of Regulation D, which prohibit public solicitations of investors. Spring Street Brewing Company, the first issuer to offer securities via the Web in 1995, avoided registration by using the Regulation A exemption. Other issuers have used Rule 504, and some have made registered offerings exclusively over the Internet.

Transaction Exemptions for Nonissuers

Although it is true that the registration provisions apply primarily to issuers and those who help issuers sell their securities publicly, the 1933 Act states that every person who sells a security is potentially subject to Section 5's restrictions on the timing of offers and sales. You must learn the most important rule of the 1933 Act: **Every transaction in securities must be registered with the SEC or be exempt from registration.**

This rule applies to every person, including the small investor who, through the New York Stock Exchange, sells securities that may have been registered by the issuer 15 years earlier. The small investor must either have the issuer register her sale of securities or find an exemption from registration that applies to the situation. Fortunately, most small investors who resell securities will have an exemption from the registration requirements of the 1933 Act. The transaction ordinarily used by these resellers is Section 4(1) of the 1933 Act. It provides an exemption for "transactions by any person other than an issuer, underwriter, or dealer."

For example, if you buy GM common shares on the New York Stock Exchange, you may freely resell them without a registration. You are not an issuer (GM is). You are not a dealer (because you are not in the business of selling securities). And you are not an underwriter (because you are not helping GM distribute the shares to the public).

Application of this exemption when an investor sells shares that are already publicly traded is easy; however, it is more difficult to determine whether an investor can use this exemption when the investor sells **restricted securities.**

Sale of Restricted Securities

Restricted securities are securities issued pursuant to Rules 505 and 506 and sometimes under Rule 504. Restricted securities are supposed to be held by the purchaser for at least one year. If they are sold earlier, the investor may be deemed an underwriter who has assisted the issuer in selling the securities to the general public. Consequently, both the issuer and the investor may have violated Section 5 of the 1933 Act by selling nonexempted securities prior to a registration of the securities with the SEC. As a result, all investors who purchased securities from the issuer in the Rule 506 offering may have the remedy of rescission under Section 12(a)(1), resulting in the issuer being required to return to investors all the proceeds of the issuance.

For example, an investor buys 10,000 common shares issued by Arcom Corporation pursuant to a Rule 506 private offering exemption. One month later, the investor sells the securities to 40 other investors. The original investor has acted as an underwriter because he has helped Arcom distribute the shares to the public. The original investor may not use the issuer's private offering exemption because it exempted only the issuer's sale to him. As a result, both the original investor and Arcom have violated Section 5. The 40 investors who purchased the securities from the original investor—and all other investors who purchased common shares from the issuer in the Rule 506 offering—may rescind their purchases under Section 12(a)(1) of the 1933 Act, receiving from their seller the return of their investment.

SEC Rule 144 allows purchasers of restricted securities to resell the securities and not be deemed underwriters. The resellers must hold the securities for at least one year. Investment information concerning the issuer of the securities must be publicly available. In any three-month period, the reseller may sell only a limited number of securities—the greater of 1 percent of the outstanding securities or the average weekly volume of trading. The reseller must file a notice (Form 144) with the SEC.

If a purchaser who is not an insider of the issuer has held the restricted securities for at least two years, Rule 144 permits her to sell unlimited amounts of the securities. In addition, investment information concerning the issuer need not be publicly available.

Consequence of Obtaining a Securities or Transaction Exemption

When an issuer has obtained an exemption from the registration provisions of the 1933 Act, the Section 5 limits on when and how offers and sales may be made do not apply. Consequently, Section 12(a)(1)'s remedy of rescission is unavailable to an investor who has purchased securities in an exempt offering.

When an issuer has attempted to comply with a registration exemption and has failed to do so, any offer or sale of securities by the issuer may violate Section 5. Because the issuer has offered or sold nonexempted securities prior to filing a registration statement with the SEC, any purchaser may sue the issuer under Section 12(a)(1) of the 1933 Act.

Although the registration provisions of the 1933 Act do not apply to an exempt offering, the antifraud provisions of the 1933 Act and 1934 Act, which are discussed later, are applicable. For example, when an issuer gives false information to a purchaser in a Rule 504 offering, the issuer may have violated the antifraud provisions of the two acts. The purchaser may obtain damages from the issuer under the antifraud rules even though the transaction is exempt from registration.

ETHICS IN ACTION

Section 5 of the 1933 Act and many of the exemptions from registration put severe limits on an issuer's ability to inform prospective investors during a registered or exempted offering. For example, during the quiet period of a registered offering, the SEC takes a dim view of an issuer's attempt to publicize itself and its business. Rules 505 and 506 prohibit general solicitations.

- Are those limitations consistent with the principles of a country that has a market-based economy and elevates freedom of speech to a constitutional right? Would a rights theorist support American securities law? How about a profit maximizer?
- Might a believer in justice theory view be more likely to support American law regulating issuances of securities? Whom would a justice theorist want to see protected?
- Who is the typical securities purchaser? Is it not someone from the wealthier classes of citizens? Is securities regulation welfare for the wealthy?

Note that section 5 of the 1933 Act does not require that investors receive a preliminary prospectus during the waiting period. In fact, an issuer can completely avoid giving investors a prospectus until a sale is confirmed during the posteffective period. That means an investor may not receive a prospectus until he has made his purchase decision. Moreover, many investors find the prospectus overwhelming to read, and if they do read it, it is often couched in legalese that is difficult to understand. Finally, the prospectus mostly comprises historical information. It is more correctly a "retrospectus," not a prospectus, and contains information that is already in the marketplace. Yet professionals like auditors and investment bankers make millions of dollars by being involved in the preparation of the prospectus, which is not received by investors at the right time, not read, not readable, and not relevant to investment decisions.

- Is it ethical for professionals to profit enormously from their role of putting together a prospectus that provides little real value to investors?

CONCEPT REVIEW

Issuer's Exemptions from the Registration Requirements of the Securities Act of 1933

	Type of Issuer	Amount of Securities Sold	Number of Purchasers	Purchaser Qualifications
Rule 504	Nonpublic issuer	$1,000,000 in a 12-month period	No limit	None
Rule 505	Any issuer	$5,000,000 in a 12-month period	• 35 unaccredited purchasers and • Unlimited accredited purchasers • High level insiders • NI ≥ $200,000 • NW ≥ $1,000,000 • Institutional investors	None
Rule 506	Any issuer	Unlimited	• 35 unaccredited purchasers and • Unlimited accredited purchasers • High level insiders • NI ≥ $200,000 • NW ≥ $1,000,000 • Institutional investors	Issuer must reasonably believe that each purchaser is either • accredited or • alone or with his purchaser representative has such knowledge and experience in financial and business matters to be capable of evaluating the merits and risks of the investment
Regulation A	Nonpublic issuer	$5,000,000 in a one-year period	No limit	None
Rule 147	• Issuer organized and doing business in the offerees' and purchasers' state • Issuer has 80% of its assets in the state • Issuer generated 80% of its gross revenues from the state • Issuer uses 80% of the offering's proceeds in the state	Unlimited	No limit	All offerees and purchasers must reside in the issuer's state

CONCEPT REVIEW

Disclosure Requirements	General Solicitations	Resale Restrictions
None	Permitted, if the issuer registered the securities under state law or sold the securities only to accredited investors pursuant to a state securities exemption	No resale restrictions, if the issuer registered the securities under state law or sold the securities only to accredited investors pursuant to a state securities exemption

If issuer sells only to accredited purchasers: the issuer must give investors only the information requested by investors. If issuer sells to any unaccredited purchasers, the issuer must give investors:
• the same nonfinancial information as required for a registered offering
• audited financial statements
  • Public issuer: 2 balance sheets, 3 income statements, 3 statements of changes in financial position
  • Nonpublic issuer: if amount of securities sold is
    • ≤$2,000,000: 1 balance sheet
    • >$2,000,000 but ≤$5,000,000: 1 balance sheet, 1 income statement, 1 statement of changes in financial position
  • Nonpublic issuer, if auditing involves unreasonable effort or expense:
    • 1 balance sheet
Any information given to one investor must be given to all investors.
	Not permitted	• Investors may not sell the securities for one year
		• After one year, investors in a public issuer may sell in any three month period the greater of
		  • 1% of the issuer's outstanding shares or
		  • the average weekly volume of the issuer's shares
		• After two years, non-insider investors may sell the securities without restriction

If issuer sells only to accredited purchasers: the issuer must give the investors only the information requested by investors. If issuer sells to any unaccredited purchasers, the issuer must give investors:
• the same nonfinancial information as required for a registered offering
• audited financial statements
  • Public issuer: 2 balance sheets, 3 income statements, 3 statements of changes in financial position
  • Nonpublic issuer: if amount of securities sold is
    • ≤$2,000,000: 1 balance sheet
    • >$2,000,000 but ≤$7,500,000: 1 balance sheet, 1 income statement, 1 statement of changes in financial position
    • >$7,500,000: 2 balance sheets, 3 income statements, 3 statements of changes in financial position
  • Nonpublic issuer, if auditing involves unreasonable effort or expense:
    • 1 balance sheet
Any information given to one investor must be given to all investors.
	Not permitted	• Investors may not sell the securities for one year
		• After one year, investors in a public issuer may sell in any three month period the greater of
		  • 1% of the issuer's outstanding shares or
		  • the average weekly volume of the issuer's shares
		• After two years, non-insider investors may sell the securities without restriction

The issuer must use an Offering Circular. Financial statements in the Offering Circular: • Need not be audited unless otherwise required • 1 balance sheet, 2 income statements, 2 cash flow statements, 2 statements of shareholder equity	Permitted	No Resale Restrictions
None	Permitted	Investors may not sell the securities outside the issuer's state for nine months

Liability Provisions of the 1933 Act

To deter fraud, deception, and manipulation and to provide remedies to the victims of such practices, Congress included a number of liability provisions in the Securities Act of 1933.

Liability for Defective Registration Statements

Section 11 of the 1933 Act provides civil liabilities for damages when a 1933 Act registration statement on its effective date misstates or omits a material fact. A purchaser of securities issued pursuant to the defective registration statement may sue certain classes of persons that are listed in Section 11—the issuer, its chief executive officer, its chief accounting officer, its chief financial officer, the directors, other signers of the registration statement, the underwriter, and experts who contributed to the registration statement (such as auditors who issued opinions regarding the financial statements or lawyers who issued an opinion concerning the tax aspects of a limited partnership). The purchaser's remedy under Section 11 is for damages caused by the misstatement or omission. Damages are presumed to be equal to the difference between the purchase price of the securities less the price of the securities at the time of the lawsuit.

Section 11 is a radical liability section for three reasons. First, reliance is usually not required; that is, the purchaser need not show that she relied on the misstatement or omission in the registration statement. In fact, the purchaser need not have read the registration statement or have seen it. Second, privity is not required; that is, the purchaser need not prove that she purchased the securities from the defendant. All she has to prove is that the defendant is in one of the classes of persons liable under Section 11. Third, the purchaser need not prove that the defendant negligently or intentionally misstated or omitted a material fact. Instead, a defendant who otherwise would be liable under Section 11 may escape liability by proving that he exercised due diligence.

Section 11 Defenses A defendant can escape liability under Section 11 by proving that the purchaser knew of the misstatement or omission when she purchased the security. In addition, a defendant may raise the **due diligence defense.** It is the more important of the two defenses.

Any defendant except the issuer may escape liability under Section 11 by proving that he acted with due diligence in determining the accuracy of the registration statement. The due diligence defense basically requires the defendant to prove that he was not negligent. The exact defense varies, however, according to the class of defendant and the portion of the registration statement that is defective. Most defendants must prove that after a **reasonable investigation** they had **reasonable grounds to believe** and **did believe** that the registration statement was true and contained no omission of material fact.

Experts need to prove due diligence only in respect to the parts that they have contributed. For example, independent auditors must prove due diligence in ascertaining the accuracy of financial statements for which they issue opinions. Due diligence requires that an auditor at least comply with generally accepted auditing standards (GAAS).

Nonexperts meet their due diligence defense for parts contributed by experts if they had no reason to believe and did not believe that the expertised parts misstated or omitted any material fact. This defense does not require the nonexpert to investigate the accuracy of expertised portions, unless something alerted the nonexpert to problems with the expertised portions.

The *BarChris* case is the most famous case construing the due diligence defense of Section 11.

Escott v. BarChris Construction Corp.   *283 F.Supp. 643 (S.D.N.Y. 1968)*

BarChris Construction Corporation was in the business of constructing bowling centers. With the introduction of automatic pinsetters in 1952, there was a rapid growth in the popularity of bowling, and BarChris's sales increased from $800,000 in 1956 to over $9 million in 1960. By 1960, it was building about 3 percent of the lanes constructed, while Brunswick Corporation and AMF were building 97 percent. BarChris contracted with its customers to construct and equip bowling alleys for them. Under the contracts, a customer was required to make a small down payment in cash. After the alleys were constructed, customers gave BarChris promissory notes for the balance of the purchase price. BarChris discounted the notes with a factor. The factor kept part of the face value of the notes as a reserve until the customer paid the notes. BarChris was obligated to repurchase the notes if the customer defaulted.

In 1960, BarChris offered its customers an alternative financing method in which BarChris sold the interior of a bowling alley to a factor, James Talcott, Inc. Talcott then leased the alley either to a BarChris customer (Type A financing) or to a BarChris subsidiary that then subleased to the customer (Type B financing). Under Type A financing, BarChris guaranteed 25 percent of the customer's obligation under the lease. With Type B financing, BarChris was liable for 100 percent of its subsidiaries' lease obligations. Under either financing method, BarChris made substantial expenditures before receiving payment from customers and, therefore, experienced a constant need of cash.

In early 1961, BarChris decided to issue debentures and to use part of the proceeds to help its cash position. In March 1961, BarChris filed with the SEC a registration statement covering the debentures. The statement became effective on May 16. The proceeds of the offering were received by BarChris on May 24, 1961. By that time, BarChris had difficulty collecting from some of its customers, and other customers were in arrears on their payments to the factors of the discounted notes. Due to overexpansion in the bowling alley industry, many BarChris customers failed. On October 29, 1962, BarChris filed a petition for bankruptcy. On November 1, it defaulted on the payment of interest on the debentures.

Escott and other purchasers of the debentures sued BarChris and its officers, directors, and auditors, among others, under Section 11 of the Securities Act of 1933. BarChris's registration statement contained material misstatements and omitted material facts. It overstated current assets by $609,689 (15.6 percent), sales by $653,900 (7.7 percent), and earnings per share by 10 cents (15.4 percent) in the 1960 balance sheet and income statement audited by Peat, Marwick, Mitchell & Co. The registration statement also understated BarChris's contingent liabilities by $618,853 (42.8 percent) as of April 30, 1961. It overstated gross profit for the first quarter of 1961 by $230,755 (92 percent) and sales for the first quarter of 1961 by $519,810 (32.1 percent). The March 31, 1961, backlog was overstated by $4,490,000 (186 percent). The 1961 figures were not audited by Peat, Marwick.

In addition, the registration statement reported that prior loans from officers had been repaid, but failed to disclose that officers had made new loans to BarChris totaling $386,615. BarChris had used $1,160,000 of the proceeds of the debentures to pay old debts, a use not disclosed in the registration statement. BarChris's potential liability of $1,350,000 to factors due to customer delinquencies on factored notes was not disclosed. The registration statement represented BarChris's contingent liability on Type B financings as 25 percent instead of 100 percent. It misrepresented the nature of BarChris's business by failing to disclose that BarChris was already engaged and was about to become more heavily engaged in the operation of bowling alleys, including one called Capitol Lanes, as a way of minimizing its losses from customer defaults.

Trilling, BarChris's controller, signed the registration statement. Auslander, a director, signed the registration statement. Peat, Marwick consented to being named as an expert in the registration statement. All three would be liable to Escott unless they could meet the due diligence defense of Section 11.

McLean, District Judge The question is whether Trilling, Auslander, and Peat, Marwick have proved their due diligence defenses. The position of each defendant will be separately considered.

Trilling

Trilling was BarChris's controller. He signed the registration statement in that capacity. Trilling entered BarChris's employ in October 1960. He was Kircher's [BarChris's treasurer] subordinate. When Kircher asked him for information, he furnished it.

Trilling was not a member of the executive committee. He was a comparatively minor figure in BarChris. The description of BarChris's management in the prospectus does not mention him. He was not considered to be an executive officer.

Trilling may well have been unaware of several of the inaccuracies in the prospectus. But he must have known of

some of them. As a financial officer, he was familiar with BarChris's finances and with its books of account. He knew that part of the cash on deposit on December 31, 1960, had been procured temporarily by Russo [BarChris's executive vice president] for window-dressing purposes. He knew that BarChris was operating Capitol Lanes in 1960. He should have known, although perhaps through carelessness he did not know at the time, that BarChris's contingent liability on Type B lease transactions was greater than the prospectus stated. In the light of these facts, I cannot find that Trilling believed the entire prospectus to be true.

But even if he did, he still did not establish his due diligence defenses. He did not prove that as to the parts of the prospectus expertised by Peat, Marwick he had no reasonable ground to believe that it was untrue. He also failed to prove, as to the parts of the prospectus not expertised by Peat, Marwick, that he made a reasonable investigation which afforded him a reasonable ground to believe that it was true. As far as appears, he made no investigation. He did what was asked of him and assumed that others would properly take care of supplying accurate data as to the other aspects of the company's business. This would have been well enough but for the fact that he signed the registration statement. As a signer, he could not avoid responsibility by leaving it up to others to make it accurate. Trilling did not sustain the burden of proving his due diligence defenses.

Auslander

Auslander was an outside director, i.e., one who was not an officer of BarChris. He was chairman of the board of Valley Stream National Bank in Valley Stream, Long Island. In February 1961, Vitolo [BarChris's president] asked him to become a director of BarChris. In February and early March 1961, before accepting Vitolo's invitation, Auslander made some investigation of BarChris. He obtained Dun & Bradstreet reports that contained sales and earnings figures for periods earlier than December 31, 1960. He caused inquiry to be made of certain of BarChris's banks and was advised that they regarded BarChris favorably. He was informed that inquiry of Talcott had also produced a favorable response.

On March 3, 1961, Auslander indicated his willingness to accept a place on the board. Shortly thereafter, on March 14, Kircher sent him a copy of BarChris's annual report for 1960. Auslander observed that BarChris's auditors were Peat, Marwick. They were also the auditors for the Valley Stream National Bank. He thought well of them.

Auslander was elected a director on April 17, 1961. The registration statement in its original form had already been filed, of course without his signature. On May 10, 1961, he signed a signature page for the first amendment to the registration statement which was filed on May 11, 1961. This was a separate sheet without any document attached. Auslander did not know that it was a signature page for a registration statement. He vaguely understood that it was something "for the SEC."

At the May 15 directors' meeting, however, Auslander did realize that what he was signing was a signature sheet to a registration statement. This was the first time that he had appreciated the fact. A copy of the registration statement in its earlier form as amended on May 11, 1961, was passed around at the meeting. Auslander glanced at it briefly. He did not read it thoroughly. At the May 15 meeting, Russo and Vitolo stated that everything was in order and that the prospectus was correct. Auslander believed this statement.

In considering Auslander's due diligence defenses, a distinction must be drawn between the expertised and nonexpertised portions of the prospectus. As to the former, Aus-

lander knew that Peat, Marwick had audited the 1960 figures. He believed them to be correct because he had confidence in Peat, Marwick. He had no reasonable ground to believe otherwise.

As to the nonexpertised portions, however, Auslander is in a different position. He seems to have been under the impression that Peat, Marwick was responsible for all the figures. This impression was not correct, as he would have realized if he had read the prospectus carefully. Auslander made no investigation of the accuracy of the prospectus. He relied on the assurance of Vitolo and Russo, and upon the information he had received in answer to his inquiries back in February and early March. These inquiries were general ones, in the nature of a credit check. The information which he received in answer to them was also general, without specific reference to the statements in the prospectus, which was not prepared until some time thereafter.

It is true that Auslander became a director on the eve of the financing. He had little opportunity to familiarize himself with the company's affairs. The question is whether, under such circumstances, Auslander did enough to establish his due diligence.

Section 11 imposes liability upon a director, no matter how new he is. He is presumed to know his responsibility when he becomes a director. He can escape liability only by using that reasonable care to investigate the facts that a prudent man would employ in the management of his own property. In my opinion, a prudent man would not act in an important matter without any knowledge of the relevant facts, in sole reliance upon general information which does not purport to cover the particular case. To say that such minimal conduct measures up to the statutory standard would, to all intents and purposes, absolve new directors from responsibility merely because they are new. This is not a sensible construction of Section 11, when one bears in mind its fundamental purpose of requiring full and truthful disclosure for the protection of investors.

Auslander has not established his due diligence defense with respect to the misstatements and omissions in those portions of the prospectus other than the audited 1960 figures.

Peat, Marwick

The part of the registration statement purporting to be made upon the authority of Peat, Marwick as an expert was the 1960 figures. But because the statute requires the court to determine Peat, Marwick's belief, and the grounds thereof, "at the time such part of the registration statement became effective," for the purposes of this affirmative defense, the matter must be viewed as of May 16, 1961, and the question is whether at that time Peat, Marwick, after reasonable investigation, had reasonable ground to believe and did believe that the 1960 figures were true and that no material fact had been omitted from the registration statement which should have been included in order to make the 1960 figures not misleading. In deciding this issue, the court must consider not only what Peat, Marwick did in its 1960 audit, but also what it did in its subsequent S–1 review. The proper scope of that review must also be determined.

The 1960 Audit

Peat, Marwick's work was in general charge of a member of the firm, Cummings, and more immediately in charge of Peat, Marwick's manager, Logan. Most of the actual work was performed by a senior accountant, Berardi, who had junior assistants, one of whom was Kennedy.

Berardi was then about 30 years old. He was not yet a CPA. He had had no previous experience with the bowling industry. This was his first job as a senior accountant. He could hardly have been given a more difficult assignment.

It is unnecessary to recount everything that Berardi did in the course of the audit. We are concerned only with the evidence relating to what Berardi did or did not do with respect to those items which I have found to have been incorrectly reported in the 1960 figures in the prospectus. More narrowly, we are directly concerned only with such of those items as I have found to be material.

First and foremost is Berardi's failure to discover that Capitol Lanes had not been sold. This error affected both the sales figure and the liability side of the balance sheet. Fundamentally, the error stemmed from the fact that Berardi never realized that Heavenly Lanes and Capitol were two different names for the same alley. Berardi assumed that Heavenly was to be treated like any other completed job.

Berardi read the minutes of the board of directors meeting of November 22, 1960, which recited that "the Chairman recommended that the Corporation operate Capitol Lanes." Berardi knew from various BarChris records that Capitol Lanes, Inc., was paying rentals to Talcott. Also, a Peat, Marwick work paper bearing Kennedy's initials recorded that Capitol Lanes, Inc., held certain insurance policies.

Berardi testified that he inquired of Russo about Capitol Lanes and that Russo told him that Capitol Lanes, Inc., was going to operate an alley someday but as yet it had no alley. Berardi testified that he understood that the alley had not been built and that he believed that the rental payments were on vacant land.

I am not satisfied with this testimony. If Berardi did hold this belief, he should not have held it. The entries as to insurance and as to "operation of alley" should have alerted him to the fact that an alley existed. He should have made further inquiry on the subject. It is apparent that Berardi did not understand this transaction.

He never identified this mysterious Capitol with the Heavenly Lanes which he had included in his sales and profit figures. The vital question is whether he failed to make a reasonable investigation which, if he had made it, would have revealed the truth.

Certain accounting records of BarChris, which Berardi testified he did not see, would have put him on inquiry. One was a job cost ledger card for job no. 6036, the job number which Berardi put on his own sheet for Heavenly Lanes. This card read "Capitol Theatre (Heavenly)." In addition, two accounts receivable cards each showed both names on the same card, Capitol and Heavenly. Berardi testified that he looked at the accounts receivable records but that he did not see these particular cards. He testified that he did not look on the job cost ledger cards because he took the costs from another record, the costs register.

The burden of proof on this issue is on Peat, Marwick. Although the question is a rather close one, I find that Peat, Marwick has not sustained that burden. Peat, Marwick has not proved that Berardi made a reasonable investigation as far as Capitol Lanes was concerned and that his ignorance of the true facts was justified.

I turn now to the errors in the current assets. As to cash, Berardi properly obtained a confirmation from the bank as to BarChris's cash balance on December 31, 1960. He did not know that part of this balance had been temporarily increased by the deposit of reserves returned by Talcott to BarChris conditionally for a limited time. I do not believe that Berardi reasonably should have known this. It would not be reasonable to require Berardi to examine all of BarChris's correspondence files [which contained correspondence indicating that BarChris was to return the cash to Talcott] when he had no reason to suspect any irregularity.

The S–1 Review   The purpose of reviewing events subsequent to the date of a certified balance sheet (referred to as an S–1 review when made with reference to a registration statement) is to ascertain whether any material change has occurred in the company's financial position which should be disclosed in order to prevent the balance sheet figures from being misleading. The scope of such a review, under generally accepted auditing standards, is limited. It does not amount to a complete audit.

Berardi made the S–1 review in May 1961. He devoted a little over two days to it, a total of 20½ hours. He did not discover any of the errors or omissions pertaining to the state of affairs in 1961, all of which were material. The question is whether, despite his failure to find out anything, his investigation was reasonable within the meaning of the statute.

What Berardi did was to look at a consolidating trial balance as of March 31, 1961, which had been prepared by BarChris, compare it with the audited December 31, 1960, figures, discuss with Trilling certain unfavorable developments which the comparison disclosed, and read certain minutes. He did not examine any important financial records other than the trial balance.

In substance, Berardi asked questions, he got answers which he considered satisfactory, and he did nothing to verify them. Since he never read the prospectus, he was not even aware that there had ever been any problem about loans from officers. He made no inquiry of factors about delinquent notes in his S–1 review. Since he knew nothing about Kircher's notes of the executive committee meetings, he did not learn that the delinquency situation had grown worse. He was content with Trilling's assurance that no liability theretofore contingent had become direct. Apparently the only BarChris officer with whom Berardi communicated was Trilling. He could not recall making any inquiries of Russo, Vitolo, or Pugliese [a BarChris vice-president].

There had been a material change for the worse in BarChris's financial position. That change was sufficiently serious so that the failure to disclose it made the 1960 figures misleading. Berardi did not discover it. As far as results were concerned, his S–1 review was useless.

Accountants should not be held to a standard higher than that recognized in their profession. I do not do so here. Berardi's review did not come up to that standard. He did not take some of the steps which Peat, Marwick's written program prescribed. He did not spend an adequate amount of time on a task of this magnitude. Most important of all, he was too easily satisfied with glib answers to his inquiries.

This is not to say that he should have made a complete audit. But there were enough danger signals in the materials which he did examine to require some further investigation on his part. Generally accepted auditing standards require such further investigation under these circumstances. It is not always sufficient merely to ask questions.

Here again, the burden of proof is on Peat, Marwick. I find that burden has not been satisfied. I conclude that Peat, Marwick has not established its due diligence defense.

Judgment for Escott and the other purchasers.

Due Diligence Meeting Officers, directors, underwriters, accountants, and other experts attempt to reduce their Section 11 liability by holding a due diligence meeting at the end of the waiting period, just prior to the effective date of a registration statement. At the due diligence meeting, the participants obtain assurances and demand proof from each other that the registration statement contains no misstatements or omissions of material fact. If it appears from the meeting that there are inadequacies in the investigation of the information in the registration statement, the issuer will delay the effective date until an appropriate investigation is undertaken.

Statute of Limitations Under Section 11, a defendant has liability for only a limited period of time, pursuant to a statute of limitations. A purchaser must sue the defendant within one year after the misstatement or omission was or should have been discovered by the purchaser. In addition, the purchaser may sue the defendant not more than three years after the securities were offered to the public. Although the word "offered" is used in the statute, the three-year period does not usu-

ally begin until after the registered securities are first delivered to a purchaser. The Sarbanes–Oxley Act of 2002 arguably extends the statute of limitations to two years after discovery of facts constituting a violation of Section 11 and five years after the violation.

Other Liability Provisions

Section 12(a)(2) of the 1933 Act prohibits misstatements or omissions of material fact in any written or oral communication in connection with the general distribution of any security by an issuer (except government-issued or government-guaranteed securities). Section 17(a) prohibits the use of any device or artifice to defraud, or the use of any untrue or misleading statement, in connection with the offer or sale of any security. Two of the subsections of Section 17(a) require that the defendant merely act negligently, while the third subsection requires proof of scienter. Scienter is the intent to deceive, manipulate, or defraud the purchaser. Some courts have held that scienter also includes recklessness.

Since these liability sections are part of federal law, there must be some connection between the illegal activity and interstate commerce for liability to exist. Section

CONCEPT REVIEW

Due Diligence Defenses under Section 11 of the 1933 Act

	For Expertised Portion of the Registration Statement	For Nonexpertised Portion of the Registration Statement
Expert Liable only for the expertised portion of the registration statement contributed by the expert. Examples: Auditor that issues an audit opinion regarding financial statements; Geologist that issues a report regarding mineral reserves; Lawyer that issues a tax opinion regarding the tax deductibility of losses	After a reasonable investigation, had reason to believe and did believe that there were no misstatements or omissions of material fact in the expertised portion of the registration statement contributed by the expert.	Not liable for this portion of the registration statement
Nonexpert Liable for the entire registration statement Examples: Directors of the issuer; CEO, CFO, and CAO of the issuer; Underwriters who assist in the sale of the securities and help prepare the registration statement	Had no reason to believe and did not believe that there were any misstatements or omissions of material fact in the expertised portions of the registration statement.	After a reasonable investigation, had reason to believe and did believe that there were no misstatements or omissions of material fact in the nonexpertised portion of the registration statement.

11 merely requires the filing of a registration statement with the SEC. Sections 12(a)(1), 12(a)(2), and 17(a) require the use of the mails or other instrumentality or means of interstate communication or transportation. Chapter 46 has more information on liability under Sections 11, 12(a)(2), and 17(a).

Criminal Liability

Section 24 of the 1933 Act provides for criminal liability for any person who willfully violates the Act or its rules and regulations. The maximum penalty is a $10,000 fine and five years' imprisonment. Criminal actions under the 1933 Act are brought by the attorney general of the United States, not by the SEC.

Securities Exchange Act of 1934

The Securities Exchange Act of 1934 is chiefly concerned with requiring the disclosure of material information to investors. Unlike the 1933 Act, which is primarily a one-time disclosure statute concerned with protecting investors when an issuer sells its shares to investors, the 1934 Act requires **periodic disclosure** by issuers with publicly held equity securities. That is, the 1934 Act is primarily concerned with protecting investors after the issuer becomes a public company. An issuer with publicly traded equity securities must report annually to its

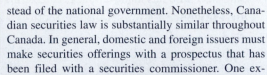

THE GLOBAL BUSINESS ENVIRONMENT

Securities Regulation of Global Issuers

All market-based economies have securities laws regulating the issuance and trading of securities. Even the Republic of China, which allows limited capitalism, has a comprehensive securities law, although not as extensive as United States law. All foreign laws regulate the issuance of securities, securities exchanges, and securities professionals.

Most countries' securities law applies equally to domestic and foreign issuers of securities. In the United States, for example, foreign issuers must register an issuance with the SEC in the same way a domestic company registers, under Regulation C.

Canadian securities law is similar to American law, although primarily enacted by the provinces and territories in-

stead of the national government. Nonetheless, Canadian securities law is substantially similar throughout Canada. In general, domestic and foreign issuers must make securities offerings with a prospectus that has been filed with a securities commissioner. One exemption from registration is the private placement offering. A typical exemption is for offerings not exceeding C$150,000. While securities qualified by a prospectus may generally be freely traded in the secondary market, securities sold through an exemption must be held by the initial purchasers for six to 18 months, depending on the exemption.

For more information on international securities law, visit the website of the International Organization of Securities Commissions at www.iosco.org.

---

shareholders and submit annual and quarterly reports to the SEC. Also, any material information about the issuer must be disclosed as the issuer obtains it, unless the issuer has a valid business purpose for withholding disclosure.

In addition, the 1934 Act regulates insiders' transactions in securities, proxy solicitations, tender offers, brokers and dealers, and securities exchanges. The 1934 Act also has several sections prohibiting fraud and manipulation in securities transactions. The ultimate purpose of the 1934 Act is to keep investors fully informed to allow them to make intelligent investment decisions at any time.

Registration of Securities under the 1934 Act

Under the 1934 Act, issuers must **register classes of securities.** This is different from the 1933 Act, which requires issuers to register issuances of securities. Under the 1933 Act, securities are registered only for the term of an issuance. Under the 1934 Act, registered classes of securities remain registered until the issuer takes steps to deregister the securities. The chief consequence of having securities registered under the 1934 Act is that the issuer is required to disclose information about itself to its owners and the SEC.

Registration Requirement Two types of issuers must register securities with the SEC under the 1934 Act.

1. An issuer whose total assets exceed $10 million must register a class of equity securities held by at least 500 holders if the securities are traded in interstate commerce.

2. An issuer must register any security traded on a national security exchange, such as common shares traded on the American Stock Exchange.

To register the securities, the issuer must file a 1934 Act **registration statement** with the SEC. The information required in the 1934 Act registration statement is similar to that required in the 1933 Act registration statement, except that offering information is omitted.

Termination of Registration An issuer may avoid the expense and burden of complying with the periodic disclosure and other requirements of the 1934 Act if the issuer terminates its registration. A 1934 Act registration of a class of securities may be terminated if the issuer has fewer than 300 shareholders of that class. In addition, a registration may be terminated if the issuer has fewer than 500 shareholders of the registered class of equity securities and assets of no more than $10 million for each of the last three years. However, an issuer with securities listed on a national securities exchange would not be able to terminate a registration of the listed securities.

Periodic Reporting Requirement To maintain a steady flow of material information to investors, the 1934 Act requires public issuers to file periodic reports with the SEC. Three types of issuers must file such reports:

1. An issuer whose total assets exceed $10 million and who has a class of equity securities held by at least 500 holders, if the securities are traded in interstate commerce.

2. An issuer whose securities are traded on a national securities exchange.

3. An issuer who has made a registered offering of securities under the 1933 Act.

The first two types of issuers—which are issuers that must also register securities under the 1934 Act—must file several periodic reports, including an annual report (Form 10-K) and a quarterly report (Form 10-Q). They must file a monthly report (Form 8-K) when material events occur. Comparable reports must also be sent to their shareholders. The third type of issuer—an issuer who must disclose under the 1934 Act only because it has made a registered offering under the 1933 Act—must file the same reports as the other issuers, except that it need not provide an annual report to its shareholders. 1934 Act disclosure required of the third type of issuer is in addition to the disclosure required by the 1933 Act.

The 10-K annual report must include audited financial statements plus current information about the conduct of the business, its management, and the status of its securities. It includes management's description and analysis of the issuer's financial condition (the so-called MDA section) and the names of directors and executive officers, including their compensation (such as salary and stock options). The 10-K auditing requirements are the same as for a 1933 Act registration statement—two years' audited balance sheets, three years' audited income statements, and three years' audited statements of changes in financial position.

The quarterly report, the 10-Q, requires only a summarized, unaudited operating statement and unaudited figures on capitalization and shareholders' equity. The 8-K monthly report must be filed within two business days of the occurrence of the event, such as a change in the amount of securities, an acquisition or disposition of assets, a change in control of the company, a revaluation of assets, or "any materially important event."

The SEC permits issuers to file reports electronically, transmitting them by telephone or by sending computer tapes or disks to the SEC. These electronic filings are made with the SEC's Electronic Data Gathering, Analysis, and Retrieval system (EDGAR).

LOG ON

www.sec.gov/edgar.shtml
The SEC's Internet homepage gives anyone access to the EDGAR database.

Issuers have historically mailed to their shareholders written copies of their annual reports and other periodic disclosure statements. Today, issuers are able to transmit such reports over the Internet. The Internet increases investors' access to information and can reduce the issuer's costs as well.

Suspension of Duty to File Reports   An issuer's duty to file periodic reports with regard to a class of securities is suspended if the issuer has fewer than 300 holders of that class. In addition, a suspension occurs if the issuer has fewer than 500 holders of that class of securities and assets of no more than $10 million. However, an issuer with securities traded on a national securities exchange would remain obligated to file periodic reports with respect to those securities.

Holdings and Trading by Insiders

Section 16 of the 1934 Act is designed to promote investor confidence in the integrity of the securities markets by limiting the ability of insiders to profit from trading in the shares of their issuers. Section 16(a) requires statutory insiders to disclose their ownership of their company's securities within 10 days of becoming owners. In addition, statutory insiders must report any subsequent transaction in such securities within two business days after the trade.

A statutory insider is a person who falls into any of the following categories:

1. An officer of a corporation having equity securities registered under the 1934 Act.

2. A director of such a corporation.

3. An owner of more than 10 percent of a class of equity securities registered under the 1934 Act.

Section 16(b) prevents an insider from profiting from short-swing trading in his company's shares. Any profit made by a statutory insider is recoverable by the issuer if the profit resulted from the purchase and sale (or the sale and purchase) of any class of the issuer's equity securities within less than a six-month period. This provision was designed to stop speculative insider trading on the basis of information that "may have been obtained by such owner, director, or officer by reason of his relationship to the issuer." The application of the provision is without regard to intent to use or actual use of inside information. However, a few cases have held that sales made by a statutory insider without actual access to inside information do not violate Section 16(b).

Proxy Solicitation Regulation

In a public corporation, shareholders rarely attend and vote at shareholder meetings. Many shareholders are able to vote at shareholder meetings only by **proxy,** a document by which shareholders direct other persons to vote their shares. Just as investors need information to be able to make intelligent investment decisions, shareholders need information to make intelligent voting and proxy decisions.

The 1934 Act regulates the solicitation of proxies. Regulation 14A requires any person soliciting proxies from holders of securities registered under the 1934 Act to furnish each holder with a **proxy statement** containing voting information. Usually, the only party soliciting proxies is the corporation's management, which is seeking proxies from common shareholders to enable it to reelect itself to the board of directors.

If the management of the corporation does not solicit proxies, it must nevertheless inform the shareholders of material information affecting matters that are to be put to a vote of the shareholders. This **information statement,** which contains about the same information as a proxy statement, must be sent to all shareholders that are entitled to vote at the meeting.

The primary purpose of the SEC rules concerning information that must be included in the proxy or information statement is to permit shareholders to make informed decisions while voting for directors and considering any resolutions proposed by the management or shareholders. Information on each director nominee must include the candidate's principal occupation, his shareholdings in the corporation, his previous service as a director of the corporation, his material transactions with the corporation (such as goods or services provided), and his directorships in other corporations. The total remuneration of the five directors or officers who are highest paid, including bonuses, grants under stock option plans, fringe benefits, and other perquisites, must also be included in the proxy statement.

SEC rules regarding the content of proxies ensure that the shareholder understands how his proxy will be voted. The proxy form must indicate in boldface type on whose behalf it is being solicited—for example, the corporation's management. Generally, the proxy must permit the shareholder to vote for or against the proposal or to abstain from voting on any resolutions on the meeting's agenda. The proxy form may ask for discretionary voting authority if the proxy indicates in bold print how the shares will be voted. For directors' elections, the share-holders must be provided with a means for withholding approval for each nominee.

Modern technology has greatly increased the ease with which shareholders may participate in shareholder votes and meetings, as well as reducing the cost of counting shareholder votes. Shareholders can vote electronically by phone and on the Internet. Some companies broadcast their shareholder meetings by satellite, and others webcast their shareholder meetings.

SEC Rule 14a–9 prohibits misstatements or omissions of material fact in the course of a proxy solicitation. If a violation is proved, a court may enjoin the holding of the shareholders' meeting, void the proxies that were illegally obtained, or rescind the action taken at the shareholders' meeting.

Proxy Contests A shareholder may decide to solicit proxies in competition with management. Such a competition is called a proxy contest, and a solicitation of this kind is also subject to SEC rules. To facilitate proxy contests, the SEC requires the corporation either to furnish a shareholder list to shareholders who desire to wage a proxy contest or to mail the competing proxy material for them.

Perhaps the most hotly contested proxy battle ever was fought in 2002 between the management of Hewlett-Packard, which wanted to merge with Compaq, and Walter Hewitt, the son of H-P's co-founder and leader of shareholders opposed to the merger. Both sides were well organized, and each deluged shareholders with proxy solicitation material. A mere 51 percent of H-P shareholders gave the merger a narrow victory. By contrast, about 90 percent of Compaq shareholders approved the merger.

Shareholder Proposals In a large public corporation, it is very expensive for a shareholder to solicit proxies in support of a proposal for corporate action that she will offer at a shareholders' meeting. Therefore, she usually asks the management to include her proposal in its proxy statement. SEC Rule 14a–8 covers proposals by shareholders.

Under SEC Rule 14a–8, the corporation must include a shareholder's proposal in its proxy statement if, among other things, the shareholder owns at least 1 percent or $2,000 of the securities to be voted at the shareholders' meeting. A shareholder may submit only one proposal per meeting. The proposal and its supporting statement may not exceed 500 words.

Under Rule 14a–8, a corporation's management may exclude many types of shareholder proposals from its proxy statement. For example, a proposal is excludable if:

1. The proposal deals with the ordinary business operations of the corporation. For example, Pacific Telesis Group was permitted on this ground to omit a proposal that the board consider adding an environmentalist director and designate a vice president for environmental matters for each subsidiary. However, TRW, Inc., was required to include in its proxy statement a proposal that it establish a shareholder advisory committee that would advise the board of directors on the interests of shareholders.

2. The proposal relates to operations that account for less than 5 percent of a corporation's total assets and is not otherwise significantly related to the company's business. For example, Harsco Corp. could not omit a proposal that it sell its 50 percent interest in a South African firm even though the investment was arguably economically insignificant—only 4.5 percent of net earnings—

because the issues raised by the proposal were significantly related to Harsco's business.

3. The proposal requires the issuer to violate a state or federal law. For example, one shareholder asked North American Bank to put a lesbian on the board of directors. The proposal was excludable because it may have required the bank to violate antidiscrimination laws.

4. The proposal relates to a personal claim or grievance. A proposal that the corporation pay the shareholder $1 million for damages that she suffered from using one of the corporation's products would be excludable.

In addition, Rule 14a–8 prevents a shareholder from submitting a proposal similar to recent proposals that have been overwhelmingly rejected by shareholders in recent years.

ETHICS IN ACTION

Sarbanes–Oxley Act of 2002

In 2001 and 2002, the discovery of financial irregularities in financial statements of nearly two dozen companies—notably Enron, Global Crossing, and World-Com—led to the bankruptcy of some companies, cost investors billions of dollars, and contributed to the bear stock market of 2001 and 2002. While many ordinary investors lost a lifetime of savings, corporate insiders received and profited from lucrative stock options, bonuses, and favorable loans that were sometimes not repaid.

Consequently, Congress passed the Sarbanes–Oxley Act of 2002, which was designed to restore integrity to corporate financial statements and revive investor confidence in the securities markets. The Sarbanes–Oxley Act attempts to accomplish these objectives by imposing a wide array of new responsibilities on public corporations and their executives and auditors. All the provisions result from the crisis of ethics, in which some corporate officers and auditors preferred their selfish interests over those of the corporation and its shareholders, creditors, and other stakeholders.

Because some public companies were manipulating their balance sheets by omitting liabilities of certain affiliate entities, the Act requires that 10-Ks and 10-Qs filed with the SEC disclose material off-balance sheet transactions. To increase the likelihood that auditors will not give in to corporate executives' pressure to account improperly for corporate transac-

tions, the Act requires greater independence between the auditor and the corporation by prohibiting the audit firm from performing most types of consulting services for the corporation. Moreover, officers and directors are prohibited from coercing auditors into creating misleading financial statements. To ensure that auditors are serving the interests of shareholders and not those of corporate managers, the Act requires auditors to be hired and overseen by an audit committee whose members are independent of the CEO and other corporate executives.

In addition, the CEO and CFO of a public company must certify that the corporation's financial reports fairly present the company's operations and financial condition. To eliminate the CEO and CFO's incentive to manipulate earnings, the CEO and CFO must disgorge bonuses, other incentive-based compensation, and profits on stock sales that were received during the 12-month period before financial statements are restated due to material misstatements or omissions. Public corporations are also generally prohibited from making loans to officers and directors. To encourage the use of ethics codes, the Act requires public companies to disclose whether they have ethics codes for senior financial officers.

Finally, the Act gives the SEC several new powers, including the authority to freeze payments to officers and directors during any lawful investigation. The SEC may also bar "unfit" persons from serving as directors and officers of public companies. The previous standard was "substantial unfitness."

Liability Provisions of the 1934 Act

To prevent fraud, deception, or manipulation and to provide remedies to the victims of such practices, Congress included provisions in the 1934 Act that impose liability on persons who engage in wrongful conduct.

Liability for False Statements in Filed Documents

Section 18 is the 1934 Act counterpart to Section 11 of the 1933 Act. Section 18 imposes liability on any person responsible for a false or misleading statement of material fact in any document filed with the SEC under the 1934 Act. (Filed documents include the 10-K report, 8-K report, and proxy statements, but not the 10-Q report.) Any person who relies on a false or misleading statement in such a filed document may sue for damages. The purchaser need not prove that the defendant was at fault. Instead, the defendant has a defense that he acted in good faith and had no knowledge that the statement was false or misleading. This defense requires only that the defendant prove that he did not act with scienter.

Section 10(b) and Rule 10b–5

The most important liability section in the 1934 Act is Section 10(b), an extremely broad provision prohibiting the use of any manipulative or deceptive device in contravention of any rules that the SEC prescribes as "necessary or appropriate in the public interest or for the protection of investors." Rule 10b–5 was adopted by the SEC under Section 10(b). The rule states:

> It shall be unlawful for any person, directly or indirectly, by use of any means or instrumentality of interstate commerce or of the mails, or of any facility of any national securities exchange,
>
>   (a) to employ any device, scheme, or artifice to defraud,
>
>   (b) to make any untrue statement of a material fact or to omit to state a material fact necessary in order to make the statements made, in the light of the circumstances under which they were made, not misleading, or
>
>   (c) to engage in any act, practice, or course of business which operates or would operate as a fraud or deceit upon any person,
>
> in connection with the purchase or sale of any security.

Rule 10b–5 applies to all transactions in all securities, whether or not registered under the 1933 Act or the 1934 Act.

Elements of a Rule 10b–5 Violation

The most important elements of a Rule 10b–5 violation are a misstatement or omission of material fact and scienter. In addition, private persons suing under the rule must be purchasers or sellers of securities who relied on the misstatement or omission.

Misstatement or Omission of Material Fact Rule 10b–5 prohibits only *misstatements or omissions of material fact.* A person **misstates** material facts, for example, when a manager of an unprofitable business induces shareholders to sell their stock to him by stating that the business will fail, although he knows that the business has become potentially profitable.

Liability for an **omission of a material fact** arises when a person fails to disclose material facts when he has a duty to disclose. For example, a securities broker is liable to his customer for not disclosing that he owns the shares that he recommends to the customer. As an agent of the customer, he owes a fiduciary duty to his customer to disclose his conflict of interest. In addition, a person is liable for omitting to tell all of the material facts after he has chosen to disclose some of them. His incomplete disclosure creates the duty to disclose all of the material facts.

Materiality Under Rule 10b–5, the misstated or omitted fact must be **material.** In essence, material information is any information that is likely to have an impact on the price of a security in the market. A fact is material if there is a substantial likelihood that a reasonable investor would consider it important to his decision, that the fact would have assumed actual significance in the deliberations of the reasonable investor, and that the disclosure of the fact would have been viewed by the reasonable investor as having significantly altered the total mix of information made available.

When there is doubt whether an important event will occur, the *Texas Gulf Sulphur* case holds that materiality of the doubtful event can be determined by "a balancing of both the indicated probability that the event will occur and the anticipated magnitude of the event in light of the totality of the company activity."

Scienter Under Rule 10b–5, the defendant is not liable unless he acted with **scienter.** Scienter is an intent to deceive, manipulate, or defraud. Scienter probably includes gross recklessness of the defendant in ascertaining the truth of his statements. Mere negligence is not scienter.

Other Elements Rule 10b–5 requires that private plaintiffs seeking damages be **actual purchasers or sellers** of securities. Persons who were deterred from purchasing securities by fraudulent statements may not recover lost profits under Rule 10b–5.

Under Rule 10b–5, private plaintiffs alleging damages caused by misstatements by the defendant must prove that they **relied** on the misstatement of material fact. The SEC as plaintiff need not prove reliance. For private plaintiffs, reliance is not usually required in omission cases; the investor need merely prove that the omitted fact was material. In addition, the misstatement or omission must **cause the investor's loss.**

The following *Carr* case considers whether an investor was entitled to rely on the misstatements of a securities salesman that contradicted a writing disclosing the risks of an investment.

Carr v. CIGNA Securities, Inc.   *95 F.3d 544 (7th Cir. 1996)*

Kenny Carr was a professional basketball player in the National Basketball Association (NBA) when in 1984 he paid CIGNA Securities, Inc., $450,000 for limited-partner interests in two commercial real estate limited partnerships that CIGNA had created. Carr said that the CIGNA salesman told him the limited partnerships were safe, conservative investments. The CIGNA salesman gave Carr documents that disclosed the riskiness of the investment, but Carr did not read or understand them. Carr also said that the salesman "knew that I didn't understand them. He said they were boilerplate kind of stuff, and breezed through them. He just explained them in his own words. He didn't say they were contrary to what he had told me. What I understood was what he told me."

When the commercial real estate market collapsed in the late 1980s, Carr lost his entire investment. Carr sued CIGNA for fraudulently selling securities in violation of Securities Exchange Act Rule 10b–5. The district court dismissed the action, and Carr appealed.

Posner, Chief Judge We are going to come directly to the merits of the fraud claim. Carr's claim is barred by a very simple, very basic, very sensible principle of the law of fraud. If a literate, competent adult is given a document that in readable and comprehensive prose says X (X might be, "this is a risky investment"), and the person who hands it to him tells him orally, not-X ("this is a safe investment"), our literate, competent adult cannot maintain an action for fraud against the issuer of the document. This principle is necessary to provide sellers of goods and services, including investments, with a safe harbor against groundless, or at least indeterminate, claims of fraud by their customers. Without such a principle, sellers would have no protection against plausible liars and gullible jurors. The sale of risky investments would be itself a very risky enterprise. Risky investments by definition often fizzle. If the documents an investor was given, warning him in capitals and bold face that it was a **RISKY** investment, do not preclude a suit, it will simply be his word against the seller's concerning the content of an unrecorded conversation.

Carr was a fully literate, fully competent adult investing $450,000, which even to an NBA player is not such chicken feed that a busy person could not realistically be expected to take the time to read a lot of fine-print legal mumbo-jumbo. Carr points out that he was not in 1984 a sophisticated investor, knowledgeable about limited partnerships or commercial real estate. He argues that CIGNA's salesman invited him to repose trust in the salesman's advice and by doing so created a fiduciary relationship. The general rule, however, is that a broker is not the fiduciary of his customer unless the customer entrusts him with discretion to select the customer's investments, which Carr did not do. But it hardly matters. A fiduciary relationship places on the fiduciary a duty of candor, and concomitantly excuses the principal from having to take the same degree of care that is expected of a participant in an arm's-length contractual relationship. But the fiduciary relationship does not excuse the principal from taking the most elementary precautions against a salesman's pitch, such as the precaution of reading a short and plain statement of what one is buying for one's $450,000.

We do not say that a written disclaimer provides a safe harbor in every fiduciary case. Not all principals of fiduciaries are competent adults; not all disclaimers are clear; and the relationship may involve such a degree of trust as to dispel any duty of self-protection by the principal. But we are dealing here with a case in which, if there is a fiduciary duty—and probably there is not—it lies at the outer limits of the fiduciary principle. In so attenuated a fiduciary relation, and with so much money at stake, the principal has a duty to read.

Carr points out that CIGNA handed him 427 pages of documents when he bought the shares of the limited partnerships.

We agree that it would be unreasonable to expect Carr to pore through 427 pages of legal and accounting mumbo-jumbo looking for nuggets of intelligible warnings. But the subscription agreements for each of the limited partnerships were only eight pages long and rich in lucid warnings, such as: "the Units are speculative investments which involve a high degree of risk of loss by the undersigned of his entire investment in the Partnership."

Professional athletes may be a common prey of financial predators. But their vulnerability does not justify a rule that would have the effect of making financial advisors the guarantors of risky investments.

Judgment for CIGNA affirmed.

Several courts have held that an investor's reliance on the availability of the securities on the market satisfies the reliance requirement of Rule 10b–5 because the securities market is defrauded as to the value of the securities. This **fraud-on-the-market theory** is based on the hypothesis that, in an open and developed securities market, the price of a company's stock is determined by the available material information regarding the company and its business. With the presence of a market, the market is interposed between seller and buyer and, ideally, transmits information to the investor in the processed form of a market price. Thus, the market is performing a substantial part of the valuation process performed by the investor in a face-to-face transaction. The market is acting as the unpaid agent of the investor, informing him that given all the information available to it, the value of the stock is the same as the market price. Misleading statements will therefore defraud purchasers of stock even if the purchasers do not directly rely on the misstatements and even if the defendants never communicated with the plaintiffs.

In *Basic, Inc. v. Levinson,* which follows this section, the Supreme Court held that the fraud-on-the-market theory permits a court to presume an investor's reliance merely from the public availability of material misrepresentations. That presumption, however, is rebuttable, such as by evidence that an investor knew the market price was incorrect.

For Rule 10b–5 to apply, the wrongful action must be accomplished *by the mails, with any means or instrumentality of interstate commerce,* or *on a national securities exchange.* This element satisfies the federal jurisdiction requirement. Use of the mails or a telephone within one state has been held to meet this element.

The scope of activities proscribed by Rule 10b–5 is not immediately obvious. While it is easy to understand that actual fraud and price manipulation are covered by the rule, two other areas are less easily mastered—the corporation's continuous disclosure obligation and insider trading.

Continuous Disclosure Obligation   The purpose of the 1934 Act is to ensure that investors have the information they need in order to make intelligent investment decisions at all times. The periodic reporting requirements of the 1934 Act are especially designed to accomplish this result. If important developments arise between the disclosure dates of reports, however, investors will not have all of the information they need to make intelligent decisions unless the corporation discloses the material information immediately. Rule 10b–5 requires a corporation to disclose material information immediately, unless the corporation has a valid business purpose for withholding disclosure. When a corporation chooses to disclose information or to comment on information that it has no duty to disclose, it must do so accurately.

Until 1988, courts had disagreed on whether Rule 10b–5 requires disclosure of merger and other acquisition negotiations prior to an agreement in principle. In *Basic, Inc. v. Levinson,* the Supreme Court of the United States held that materiality of merger negotiations is to be determined on a case-by-case basis. The Court held that materiality depends on the probability that the transaction will be consummated and on its significance to the issuer of the securities. In addition, the Court stated that a corporation that chooses to comment on acquisition negotiations must do so truthfully.

Basic Inc. v. Levinson   485 U.S. 224 (U.S. Sup. Ct. 1988)*

For over a decade, Combustion Engineering, Inc. (CEI), had been interested in acquiring Basic, Inc. When antitrust barriers to such an acquisition were eliminated in 1976, CEI's secret strategic plan listed the acquisition of Basic as an objective. Between September 1976 and October 1977, the managements of Basic and CEI privately discussed several times a possible acquisition of Basic by CEI. Throughout 1977 and 1978, despite the secrecy of merger negotiations, there were repeated instances of abnormal trading in Basic's shares on the New York Stock Exchange. On October 19 and 20, 1977, the trading volume in Basic's shares rose from an average of 7,000 shares per day to 29,000 shares. On October 21, 1977, Max Muller, the president of Basic, made a public announcement, reported in a major newspaper, that "the company knew no reason for the stock's activity and that no negotiations were under way with any company for a merger."

Secret contacts between Basic and CEI continued, however. On June 7, 1978, CEI offered $28 per share for Basic, which Basic rejected as too low. CEI stated it would make a better offer, but Muller told CEI to "hold off until we tell you," because Muller wanted to see an investment banker's valuation of Basic before evaluating any CEI offer. Muller and other Basic officials decided to ask CEI for its best offer. On July 10, 1978, Muller and CEI agreed that CEI would make an informal offer to Basic. CEI advised Muller to make no public disclosures about the negotiations.

On July 14, 1978, the price of Basic shares rose more than 12 percent to $27 per share on trading of 18,200 shares. The New York Stock Exchange called Basic and asked it to explain the trading in its shares. Basic denied that any undisclosed merger or acquisition plans or any other significant corporate development existed. On September 24, 1978, the price of Basic shares rose more than 2 points to $30 per share on volume of 31,900 shares. The next day, the price rose almost 3 points to $33 per share on volume of 28,500 shares, even though the Dow Jones Industrial Average fell more than 3 points. Again the Exchange asked Basic whether there were any undisclosed acquisition plans or any other significant corporate developments. Basic flatly denied that there were any corporate developments and issued a press release that stated:

> management is unaware of any present or pending corporate development that would result in the abnormally heavy trading activity and price fluctuation in company shares that have been experienced in the past few days.

Secret contacts between Basic and CEI continued. In early November, Basic sent a quarterly report to its shareholders in which it stated:

> With regard to the stock market activity in the Company's shares we remain unaware of any present or pending developments that would account for the high volume of trading and price fluctuations in recent months.

On November 27, 1978, CEI secretly offered to buy Basic's outstanding shares for $35 per share. Basic rejected the offer. On December 14, 1978, CEI offered $46 per share. The next day, Friday, December 15, the price of Basic's shares soared. Again Basic answered the Exchange's inquiry with a denial of corporate developments. On Monday, December 18, 1978, Basic asked the Exchange to suspend trading in Basic shares, because it had been "approached" concerning a possible merger. The next day, Basic accepted CEI's offer. On the following day, December 19, Basic announced its acceptance of CEI's offer to buy Basic's outstanding shares for $46 per share.

Max Levinson and several other Basic shareholders sold their Basic shares between October 21, 1977, and December 15, 1978, at a price lower than CEI's offer. They claimed that Basic's statements denying that any merger discussions were occurring violated Section 10(b) and Rule 10b–5 of the Securities Exchange Act of 1934. The district court held that the merger negotiations were not material. Levinson appealed to the Sixth Circuit Court of Appeals, which held that Basic possessed no general duty to disclose the merger negotiations. However, the court found that Basic released statements that were so incomplete as to be misleading. Basic appealed to the Supreme Court.

Blackmun, Justice Underlying the adoption of extensive disclosure requirements of the 1934 Act was a legislative philosophy: There cannot be honest markets without honest publicity. Manipulation and dishonest practices of the market place thrive upon mystery and secrecy.

The Court previously has explicitly defined a standard of materiality under the securities laws, concluding in the proxy-solicitation context that "[a]n omitted fact is material if there is a substantial likelihood that a reasonable shareholder would consider it important in deciding how to vote." *TSC Industries, Inc. v. Northway, Inc.* (1976). The Court was careful not to set too low a standard of materiality; it was concerned that a minimal standard might bring an overabundance of information within its reach, and lead management "simply to bury the shareholders in an avalanche of trivial information—a result that is hardly conducive to informed decisionmaking." To fulfill the materiality requirement "there must be a substantial likelihood that the disclosure of the omitted fact would have been viewed by the reasonable investor as having significantly altered the "total mix" of information made available." We now expressly adopt the *TSC Industries* standard of materiality for the Section 10(b) and Rule 10b–5 context.

The application of this materiality standard to preliminary merger discussions is not self-evident. Where the event is contingent or speculative in nature, it is difficult to ascertain whether the "reasonable investor" would have considered the omitted information significant at the time. Merger negotiations, because of the ever-present possibility that the contemplated transaction will not be effectuated, fall into this category.

Basic urges upon us the Third Circuit test for resolving this difficulty. Under this approach, preliminary merger discussions do not become material until "agreement-in-principle" as to the price and structure of the transaction has been reached between the would-be merger partners. See *Greenfield v. Heublein, Inc.* (3d Cir. 1984). By definition, then, information concerning any negotiations not yet at the agreement-in-principle stage could be withheld or even misrepresented without a violation of Rule 10b–5.

Three rationales have been offered in support of the "agreement-in-principle" test. The first derives from the concern that an investor not be overwhelmed by excessively detailed and trivial information and focuses on the substantial risk that preliminary merger discussions may collapse: because such discussions are inherently tentative, disclosure of their existence itself could mislead investors and foster false optimism. The other two justifications for the agreement-in-principle standard are based on management concerns: because the requirement of "agreement-in-principle" limits the scope of disclosure obligations, it helps preserve the confidentiality of merger discussions where

earlier disclosure might prejudice the negotiations; and the test also provides a usable, bright-line rule for determining when disclosure must be made.

None of these policy-based rationales, however, purports to explain why drawing the line at agreement-in-principle reflects the significance of the information upon the investor's decision. The first rationale "assumes that investors are nitwits, unable to appreciate—even when told—that mergers are risky propositions up until the closing." *Flamm v. Eberstadt* (7th Cir. 1987).

The second rationale, the importance of secrecy during the early stages of merger discussions, also seems irrelevant to an assessment whether their existence is significant to the trading decision of a reasonable investor. To avoid a "bidding war" over its target, an acquiring firm often will insist that negotiations remain confidential and at least one Court of Appeals has stated that "silence pending settlement of the price and structure of a deal is beneficial to most investors, most of the time." *Flamm v. Eberstadt.*

We need not ascertain, however, whether secrecy necessarily maximizes shareholder wealth—although we note that the proposition is at least disputed as a matter of theory and empirical research—for this case does not concern the timing of a disclosure; it concerns only its accuracy and completeness. We face here the narrow question whether information concerning the existence and status of preliminary merger discussions is significant to the reasonable investor's trading decision. Arguments based on the premise that some disclosure would be "premature" in a sense are more properly considered under the rubric of an issuer's duty to disclose. The "secrecy" rationale is simply inapposite to the definition of materiality.

The final justification offered in support of the agreement-in-principle test seems to be directed solely at the comfort of corporate managers. A bright-line rule indeed is easier to follow than a standard that requires the exercise of judgment in light of all the circumstances. But ease of application alone is not an excuse for ignoring the purposes of the securities acts and Congress's policy decisions.

We therefore find no valid justification for artificially excluding from the definition of materiality information concerning merger discussions, which would otherwise be considered significant to the trading decision of a reasonable investor, merely because agreement-in-principle as to price and structure has not yet been reached by the parties or their representatives.

Even before this Court's decision in *TSC Industries,* the Second Circuit had explained the role of the materiality requirement of Rule 10b–5, with respect to contingent or speculative information or events. Under such circumstances, materiality "will depend at any given time upon a balancing of both the indicated probability that the event will occur and the anticipated magnitude of the event in light of the totality of the company activity." *SEC v. Texas Gulf Sulphur Co.* (2d Cir. 1968).

The late Judge Friendly applied the *Texas Gulf Sulphur* probability/magnitude approach in the specific context of preliminary merger negotiations. He stated:

> Since a merger in which it is bought out is the most important event that can occur in a small corporation's life, to wit, its death, we think that inside information, as regards a merger of this sort, can become material at an earlier stage than would be the case as regards lesser transactions—and this even though the mortality rate of mergers in such formative stages is doubtless high. *SEC v. Geon Industries, Inc.* (2d Cir. 1976).

We agree with that analysis.

Whether merger discussions in any particular case are material therefore depends on the facts. Generally, in or-

der to assess the probability that the event will occur, a factfinder will need to look to indicia of interest in the transaction at the highest corporate levels. Board resolutions, instructions to investment bankers, and actual negotiations between principals or their intermediaries may serve as indicia of interest. To assess the magnitude of the transaction to the issuer of the securities allegedly manipulated, a factfinder will need to consider such facts as the size of the two corporate entities and of the potential premiums over market value. No particular event or factor short of closing the transaction need be either necessary or sufficient by itself to render merger discussions material.

As we clarify today, materiality depends on the significance the reasonable investor would place on the withheld or misrepresented information. Because the standard of materiality we have adopted differs from that used by both courts below, we remand the case for reconsideration.

Judgment vacated and remanded to the Court of Appeals.

In response to the *Basic* decision, in 1989 the SEC released guidelines to help public companies decide whether they must disclose merger negotiations. A company is not required to disclose merger negotiations if all three of the following requirements are met:

1. The company did not make any prior disclosures about the merger negotiations,
2. Disclosure is not compelled by other SEC rules.
3. Management determines that disclosure would jeopardize completion of the merger transaction.

Trading on Inside Information One of the greatest destroyers of public confidence in the integrity of the securities market is the belief that insiders can trade securities while possessing corporate information that is not available to the general public.

Rule 10b–5 prohibits **insider trading** on nonpublic corporate information. A person with nonpublic, confidential, inside information may not use that information when trading with a person who does not possess that information. He must either disclose the information before trading or refrain from trading. The difficult task in

the insider trading area is determining when a person is subject to this **disclose-or-refrain** rule.

In *United States v. Chiarella,*[5] the Supreme Court laid down the test for determining an insider's liability for trading on nonpublic, corporate information:

> The duty to disclose arises when one party has information that the other party is entitled to know because of a fiduciary or similar relation of trust and confidence between them. A relationship of trust and confidence exists between the shareholders of a corporation and those insiders who have obtained confidential information by reason of their position with that corporation. This relationship gives rise to a duty to disclose because of the necessity of preventing a corporate insider from taking unfair advantage of the uninformed stockholders.

Under this test, **insiders** include not only officers and directors of the corporation, but also anyone who is *entrusted with corporate information for a corporate purpose.* Insiders include outside consultants, lawyers, independent auditors, engineers, investment bankers, public

---

[5]445 U.S. 222 (U.S. Sup. Ct. 1980).

relations advisers, news reporters, and personnel of government agencies who are given confidential corporate information for a corporate purpose.

Tippees are recipients of inside information (tips) from insiders. Tippees of insiders—such as relatives and friends of insiders, stockbrokers, and security analysts—are forbidden to trade on inside information and are subject to recovery of their profits if they do.

In *SEC v. Dirks,* the Supreme Court stated the applicability of Rule 10b–5 to tippees. The Court held that a tippee has liability if (1) an insider has breached a fiduciary duty of trust and confidence to the shareholders by disclosing to the tippee and (2) the tippee knows or should know of the insider's breach. In addition, the court held that an insider has not breached her fiduciary duty to the shareholders unless she has received a personal benefit by disclosing to the tippee.

SEC v. Dirks   463 U.S. 646 (U.S. Sup. Ct. 1983)

On March 6, 1973, Raymond Dirks, a security analyst in a New York brokerage firm, received nonpublic information from Ronald Secrist, a former officer of Equity Funding of America, a seller of life insurance and mutual funds. Secrist alleged that the assets of Equity Funding were vastly overstated as the result of fraudulent corporate practices. He also stated that the SEC and state insurance departments had failed to act on similar charges of fraud made by Equity Funding employees. Secrist urged Dirks to verify the fraud and to disclose it publicly.

Dirks visited Equity Funding's headquarters in Los Angeles and interviewed several officers and employees of the corporation. The senior management denied any wrongdoing, but certain employees corroborated the charges of fraud. Dirks openly discussed the information he had obtained with a number of his clients and investors. Some of these persons sold their holdings of Equity Funding securities.

Dirks urged a Wall Street Journal *reporter to write a story on the fraud allegations. The reporter, fearing libel, declined to write the story.*

During the two-week period in which Dirks investigated the fraud and spread the word of Secrist's charges, the price of Equity Funding stock fell from $26 per share to less than $15 per share. The New York Stock Exchange halted trading in Equity Funding stock on March 27. On that date, Dirks voluntarily presented his information on the fraud to the SEC. Only then did the SEC bring an action for fraud against Equity Funding. Shortly thereafter, California insurance authorities impounded Equity Funding's records and uncovered evidence of the fraud. On April 2, The Wall Street Journal *published a front-page story based largely on information assembled by Dirks. Equity Funding immediately went into receivership.*

The SEC brought an administrative proceeding against Dirks for violating Rule 10b–5 by passing along confidential inside information to his clients. The SEC found that he had violated Rule 10b–5, but it merely censured him, since he had played an important role in bringing the fraud to light. Dirks appealed to the Court of Appeals, which affirmed the judgment. Dirks then appealed to the Supreme Court.

Powell, Justice In *U.S. v. Chiarella* (1980), we accepted the two elements set out in *In Re Cady, Roberts* (1961) for establishing a Rule 10b–5 violation: (i) the existence of a relationship affording access to inside information intended to be available only for a corporate purpose, and (ii) the unfairness of allowing a corporate insider to take advantage of that information by trading without disclosure. The Court found that a duty to disclose under Section 10(b) does not arise from the mere possession of nonpublic market information. Such a duty arises from the existence of a fiduciary relationship.

There can be no duty to disclose when the person who has traded on inside information was not the corporation's agent, was not a fiduciary, or was not a person in whom the sellers of the securities had placed their trust and confidence.

This requirement of a specific relationship between the shareholders and the individual trading on inside information has created analytical difficulties for the SEC and courts in policing tippees who trade on inside information. Unlike insiders who have independent fiduciary duties to both the corporation and its shareholders, the typical tippee has no such relationship. In view of this absence, it has been unclear how a tippee acquires the duty to refrain from trading on inside information.

Not only are insiders forbidden by their fiduciary relationship from personally using undisclosed corporate information to their advantage, but also they may not give such information to an outsider for the same improper purpose of exploiting the information for their personal gain. The transactions of those who knowingly participate with the fiduciary in such a breach are as forbidden as transactions on behalf of the trustee himself. Thus, the tippee's duty to disclose or abstain is derivative from that of the insider's duty. The tippee's obligation has been viewed as arising from his role as a participant after the fact in the insider's breach of a fiduciary duty.

A tippee assumes a fiduciary duty to the shareholders of a corporation not to trade on material nonpublic information only when the insider has breached his fiduciary duty to the shareholders by disclosing the information to the tippee and the tippee knows or should know that there has been a breach.

In determining whether a tippee is under an obligation to disclose or abstain, it thus is necessary to determine whether the insider's tip constituted a breach of the insider's fiduciary duty. Whether disclosure is a breach of duty therefore depends in large part on the purpose of the disclosure. Thus, the test is whether the insider personally will benefit, directly or indirectly, from his disclosure. Absent some personal gain, there has been no breach of duty to stockholders. And absent a breach by the insider, there is no derivative breach.

This requires courts to focus on objective criteria, i.e., whether the insider receives a direct or indirect personal benefit from the disclosure, such as a pecuniary gain or a reputational benefit that will translate into future earnings. For example, there may be a relationship between the insider and the recipient that suggests a *quid pro quo* from the latter, or an intention to benefit the particular recipient. The elements of fiduciary duty and exploitation of nonpublic information also exist when an insider makes a gift of confidential information to a relative or friend who trades. The tip and trade resemble trading by the insider himself followed by a gift of the profits to the recipient.

Under the inside-trading and tipping rules set forth above, we find that there was no violation by Dirks. Dirks was a stranger to Equity Funding, with no pre-existing fiduciary duty to its shareholders. He took no action, directly or indirectly, that induced the shareholders or officers of Equity Funding to repose trust or confidence in him. There was no expectation by Dirks's sources that he would keep their information in confidence. Nor did Dirks misappropriate or illegally obtain the information about Equity Funding. Unless the insiders breached their *Cady, Roberts* duty to shareholders in disclosing the nonpublic information to Dirks, he breached no duty when he passed it on to investors as well as to *The Wall Street Journal.*

It is clear that neither Secrist nor the other Equity Funding employees violated their *Cady, Roberts* duty to the corporation's shareholders by providing information to Dirks. Secrist intended to convey relevant information that management was unlawfully concealing, and he believed that persuading Dirks to investigate was the best way to disclose the fraud. The tippers received no monetary or personal benefit for revealing Equity Funding's secrets, nor was their purpose to make a gift of valuable information to Dirks. The tippers were motivated by a desire to expose the fraud. In the absence of a breach of duty to shareholders by the insiders, there was no derivative breach by Dirks. Dirks therefore could not have been a participant after the fact in an insider's breach of a fiduciary duty.

Judgment reversed in favor of Dirks.

In June 1997, the Supreme Court held that Rule 10b–5 liability attaches to anyone who trades in securities for personal profit using confidential information misappropriated in a breach of fiduciary duty owed to the *source of the information.* Under the **misappropriation theory,** a person violates Rule 10b–5 not only when he steals confidential information from his company and trades in its shares, but also, for example, if he steals confidential information about his firm's intent to make a tender offer for another firm and buys securities of the second firm.

Extent of Liability for Insider Trading Section 20A of the 1934 Act allows persons who traded in the securities at about the same time as the insider or tippee to recover damages from the insider or tippee. Although there may be several persons trading at about the same time, the insider or tippee's total liability cannot exceed

the profit she has made or the loss she has avoided by trading on inside information.

This limitation, which merely requires disgorgement of profits, has been assailed as not adequately deterring insider trading, because the defendant may realize an enormous profit if her trading is not discovered, but lose nothing beyond her profits if it is. In response to this issue of liability, Congress passed an amendment to the 1934 Act permitting the SEC to seek a civil penalty of three times the profit gained or the loss avoided by trading on inside information. This treble penalty is paid to the Treasury of the United States. The penalty applies only to SEC actions; it does not affect the amount of damages that may be recovered by private plaintiffs. The 1934 Act also grants the SEC power to award up to 10 percent of any triple-damage penalty as a bounty to informants who helped the SEC uncover insider trading.

CONCEPT REVIEW

Rule 10b–5 Liability for Trading on Inside Information

	For Trading by Insider	For Trading by Tippee
Insider/Tipper Liability	Liable if insider breached fiduciary duty of confidentiality by using corporate information that was disclosed to insider solely for corporate purposes.	Liable if tipper breached fiduciary duty of confidentiality, including receiving a personal benefit, by disclosing confidential information to the tippee.
Tippee Liability	Not liable	Liable if: 1. Insider/tipper breached fiduciary duty of confidentiality by disclosing confidential information to the tippee, and 2. The tippee knew or should have known of the insider/tipper's breach of the fiduciary duty.

Liability for Aiding and Abetting Persons who are not the primary actors that violate Rule 10b–5 but merely aid and abet another's violation of the rule nonetheless may be prosecuted by the SEC. To have aiding and abetting liability, there must be (1) a primary violation by another person, (2) the aider and abettor's knowledge of that violation, and (3) substantial assistance by the aider and abettor in the achievement of the primary violation. Although the SEC may prosecute aiders and abettors, investors harmed by a primary violation may recover their damages only from primary violators, not from aiders and abettors.

Securities Fraud and the Internet In recent years, the Internet has become a new source of securities fraud. In response, the SEC has included the investigation of Internet users in its antifraud arsenal. The SEC has announced that it will use search engines to conduct Internet searches of phrases such as "get high returns with low investment" to detect likely fraud. Some securities professionals have objected to the SEC tactics as an invasion of privacy.

Statute of Limitations A purchaser or seller bringing an action under Rule 10b–5 must file his suit in a timely fashion or else be precluded from litigating the issue. The Sarbanes–Oxley Act of 2002 extends the statute of limitation by requiring an action under Rule 10b–5 to be commenced within two years after discovery of the facts constituting a violation of Rule 10b–5 and within five years of the violation.

Criminal Liability

Like the 1933 Act, the 1934 Act provides for liability for criminal violations of the Act. Section 32 provides that individuals may be fined up to $5 million and imprisoned up to 20 years for willful violations of the 1934 Act or the related SEC rules. Businesses may be fined up to $25 million.

Tender Offer Regulation

Historically, the predominant procedure by which one corporation acquired another was the merger, a transaction requiring the cooperation of the acquired corporation's management. Since the early 1970s, the **tender offer** has become an often used acquisition device. A tender offer is a public offer by a **bidder** to purchase a **subject company's** equity securities directly from its shareholders at a specified price for a fixed period of time. The offering price is usually well above the market price of the shares. Such offers are often made even though there is opposition from the subject company's management. Opposed offers are called hostile tender offers. The legality of efforts opposing a tender offer is covered in Chapter 43.

The Williams Act amendments to the 1934 Act require bidders and subject companies to provide a shareholder with information on which to base his decision whether to sell his shares to a bidder. The aim of the Williams Act is to protect investors and to give the bidder and the subject company equal opportunities to present their cases to the shareholder. The intent is to encourage an auction of the shares with the highest bidder purchasing the shares. The Williams Act applies only when the subject company's equity securities are registered under the 1934 Act.

The Williams Act does not define a tender offer, but the courts have compiled a list of factors to determine whether a person has made a tender offer. The greater the number of people solicited and the lower their investment sophistication, the more likely it is that the bidder will be held to have made a tender offer. Also, the shorter the offering period, the more rigid the price, and the greater the publicity concerning the offer, the more likely it is that the purchase efforts of the bidder will be treated as a tender offer. Given these factors, a person who offers to purchase shares directly from several shareholders at a set price for only a few days risks having a court treat the offer like a tender offer. The Williams Act does not regulate a tender offer unless the bidder intends to become a holder of at least 5 percent of the subject company's shares.

A bidder making a tender offer must file a tender offer statement (Schedule TO) with the SEC when the offer commences. The information in this schedule includes the terms of the offer (for example, the price), the background of the bidder, and the purpose of the tender offer (including whether the bidder intends to control the subject company).

The SEC requires the bidder to keep the tender offer open for at least 20 business days and prohibits any purchase of shares during that time. This rule gives shareholders adequate time to make informed decisions regarding whether to tender their shares. Tendering shareholders may withdraw their tendered shares during the entire term of the offer. This rule allows the highest bidder to buy the shares, as in an auction.

All tender offers, whether made by the issuer or by a third-party bidder, must be made to all holders of the targeted class of shares. When a bidder increases the offering price during the term of the tender offer, all of the shareholders must be paid the higher price even if they tendered their shares at a lower price. If more shares are tendered than the bidder offered to buy, the bidder must prorate its purchases among all of the shares tendered. This proration rule is designed to foster careful shareholder decisions about whether to sell shares. Shareholders might rush to tender their shares if the bidder could accept shares on a first-come, first-served basis.

After an initial offering period has expired, a bidder is permitted to include a "subsequent offering period"

during which shareholders who tender will have no withdrawal rights. The SEC created the new offering period to allow shareholders a last opportunity to tender into an offer.

The management of the subject company is required to inform the shareholders of its position on the tender offer, with its reasons, within 10 days after the offer has been made. It must also provide the bidder with a list of the holders of the equity securities that the bidder seeks to acquire or mail the materials for the bidder.

SEC Rule 14e-3 prohibits persons who have knowledge of an impending tender offer from using such information prior to its public disclosure. The rule limits insider trading in the tender offer context.

Private Acquisitions of Shares

The Williams Act regulates private acquisitions of shares differently from tender offers. When the bidder privately seeks a controlling block of the subject company's shares on a stock exchange or in face-to-face negotiations with only a few shareholders, no advance notice to the SEC or disclosure to shareholders is required. However, a person making a private acquisition is required to file a Schedule 13D with the SEC and to send a copy to the subject company within 10 days after he becomes a holder of 5 percent of its shares. A Schedule 13G (which requires less disclosure than a 13D) must be filed when a 5 percent holder has purchased no more than 2 percent of the shares within the past 12 months.

State Regulation of Tender Offers

Statutes that apply to tender offers have been enacted by about two-thirds of the states. State statutes have become highly protective of subject companies. For example, the Indiana statute gives shareholders other than the bidder the right to determine whether the shares acquired by the bidder may be voted in directors' elections and other matters. The statute, which essentially gives a subject company the power to require shareholder approval of a hostile tender offer, has been copied by several states.

Other states, such as Delaware, have adopted business combination moratorium statutes. These statutes delay the effectuation of a merger of the corporation with a shareholder owning a large percentage of shares (such as 15 percent) unless the board of directors' approval is obtained. Because the typical large shareholder in a public company is a bidder who has made a tender offer, these state statutes primarily affect the ability of a bidder to effectuate a merger after a tender offer and, therefore, may have the effect of deterring hostile acquisitions.

THE GLOBAL BUSINESS ENVIRONMENT

The Foreign Corrupt Practices Act

The Foreign Corrupt Practices Act (FCPA) was passed by Congress in 1977 as an amendment to the Securities Exchange Act of 1934. Its passage followed discoveries that more than 400 American corporations had given bribes or made other improper or questionable payments in connection with business abroad and within the United States. Many of these payments were bribes to high-level officials of foreign governments for the purpose of obtaining contracts for the sale of goods or services. Officers of the companies that had made the payments argued that such payments were customary and necessary in business transactions in many countries. This argument was pressed forcefully with regard to facilitating payments. Such payments were said to be essential to get lower-level government officials in a number of countries to perform their nondiscretionary or ministerial tasks, such as preparing or approving necessary import or export documents.

In a significant number of cases, bribes had been accounted for as commission payments, as normal transactions with foreign subsidiaries, or as payments for services rendered by professionals or other firms, or had in other ways been made to appear as normal business expenses. These bribes were then illegally deducted as normal business expenses in income tax returns filed with the Internal Revenue Service.

The Payments Prohibition

The FCPA makes it a crime for any American firm—whether or not it has securities registered under the 1934 Act—to offer, promise, or make payments or gifts of anything of value to foreign officials and certain others. Payments are prohibited if the person making the payment knows or should know that some or all of it will be used for the purpose of influencing a governmental decision, even if the offer is not accepted or the promise is not carried out. The FCPA prohibits offers or payments to foreign political parties and candidates for office as well as offers and payments to government officials. Payments of kickbacks to foreign businesses and their officers are not prohibited unless it is known or should be known that these payments will be passed on to government officials or other illegal recipients.

Facilitating or grease payments are not prohibited by the FCPA. For example, suppose a corporation applies for a radio license in Italy and makes a payment to the government official who issues the licenses. If the official grants licenses to every applicant and the payment merely speeds up the processing of the application, the FCPA is not violated.

Substantial penalties for violations may be imposed. A company may be fined up to $2 million. Directors, officers, employees, or agents participating in violations are liable for fines of up to $100,000 and prison terms of up to five years.

Record-Keeping and Internal Controls Requirements

The FCPA also establishes record-keeping and internal control requirements for firms subject to the periodic disclosure provisions of the Securities Exchange Act of 1934. The purpose of such controls is to prevent unauthorized payments and transactions and unauthorized access to company assets that may result in illegal payments.

The FCPA requires the making and keeping of records and accounts "which, in reasonable detail, accurately, and fairly reflect the transactions and dispositions of the assets of the issuer" of securities. It also requires the establishment and maintenance of a system of internal accounting controls that provides "reasonable assurances" that the firm's transactions are executed in accordance with management's authorization and that the firm's assets are used or disposed of only as authorized by management.

State Securities Law

State securities laws are frequently referred to as blue-sky laws, since the early state securities statutes were designed to protect investors from promoters and security salespersons who would "sell building lots in the blue sky." The first state to enact a securities law was Kansas, in 1911. All of the states now have such legislation.

The National Conference of Commissioners on Uniform State Laws has adopted the Uniform Securities Act of 1956. The act contains antifraud provisions, requires the registration of securities, and demands broker-dealer registration. About two-thirds of the states have adopted the act, but many states have made significant changes in it.

All of the state securities statutes provide penalties for fraudulent sales and permit the issuance of injunctions to protect investors from additional or anticipated fraudulent acts. Most of the statutes grant broad power to investigate fraud to some state official—usually the attorney general or his appointee as securities administrator. All of the statutes provide criminal penalties for selling fraudulent securities and conducting fraudulent transactions.

Registration of Securities

Most of the state securities statutes adopt the philosophy of the 1933 Act that informed investors can make intelligent investment decisions. The states with such statutes have a registration scheme much like the 1933 Act, with required disclosures for public offerings and exemptions from registration for small and private offerings. Other states reject the contention that investors with full information can make intelligent investment decisions. The securities statutes in these states have a **merit registration** requirement, giving a securities administrator power to deny registration on the merits of the security and its issuer. Only securities that are not unduly risky and promise an adequate return to investors may receive administrator approval.

All state statutes have a limited number of exemptions from registration. Most statutes have private offering exemptions that are similar to Securities Act Rule 506 of Regulation D. In addition, a person may avoid the registration requirements of state securities laws by not offering or selling securities.

Registration by Coordination The Uniform Securities Act permits an issuer to register its securities by coordination. Instead of filing a registration statement under the Securities Act of 1933 and a different one as required by state law, registration by coordination allows an issuer to file the 1933 Act registration statement with the state securities administrator. Registration by coordination decreases an issuer's expense of complying with state law when making an interstate offering of its securities.

Capital Markets Efficiency Act of 1996 Congress passed the Capital Markets Efficiency Act (CMEA) to facilitate offerings of securities by small investors. The CMEA preempts state registration of offers and sales of securities to "qualified purchasers," as defined by the SEC, as well as offerings exempt under Rule 506 of Regulation D. An issuance of securities listed on the New York Stock Exchange or NASDAQ is also exempted from state registration provisions. Nonetheless, states may apply their antifraud laws despite the preemption of their registration provisions.

Problems and Problem Cases

1. A viatical settlement is a contract by which an investor purchases the life insurance policy of a terminally ill patient—typically an AIDS victim—who is in need of immediate cash to pay mounting medical expenses. Depending on the insured's life expectancy, the buyer pays 60 to 80 percent of the death benefit. When the insured dies, the investor receives the death benefit. The investor's profit is the difference between the death benefit collected from the insurer and the discounted purchase price paid to the insured, less insurance premiums paid by the investor. Life Partners, Inc. (LPI), acts as a middleman between the insured and investors. LPI assembles the purchasers of each insurance policy, selling fractional interests to investors for as little as $650. Individual investors may receive as little as 3 percent of the death benefits of a policy. The investors become owners of the insurance policy. After the purchase, LPI monitors the insured's health, makes sure the policy does not lapse, collects on the policy when the insured dies, and disburses the proceeds to the investors. Is LPI selling a security?

2. Jim Long, Jerome Atchley, and Jon and Linda Coleman invested in a cattle-feeding program offered by Shultz Cattle Company, Inc. (SCCI). They participated in SCCI's individual feeding program, under which investors would purchase and raise their own cattle. Each investor was required to sign a consulting agreement by which SCCI agreed to provide advice regarding the purchase, feeding, and sale of the investor's cattle. SCCI received only a flat-rate consulting fee of $20 per head of cattle for these services and received no share of the investors' profits. To receive tax benefits from the investment, the tax laws required investors to participate actively in farming. Therefore, SCCI required each investor to represent that "He will exert substantial and significant control over, and will, exercising independent judgment, make all principal and significant management decisions concerning his cattle feeding operations." However, investors relied solely on the advice of SCCI: they followed SCCI's recommendations regarding the purchase of cattle, the choice of feedyard, the decision when to sell, and the decision to whom to sell. Long's, Atchley's, and the Colemans' cattle were fed, along with those of many other SCCI clients, in a feedyard in which the cattle were commingled. The cattle were tagged by pen number and not by individual investor. Each investor therefore owned a percentage of the total pounds of cattle in the pen. If any cattle died, the loss was not attributed to a single investor but was distributed pro rata among the investors. Have Long, Atchley, and the Colemans purchased securities?

3. Arthur Vining Davis transferred all of his real estate holdings in coastal Florida to Arvida Corporation. A press release announcing the transfer stated that $30 million additional capital would be raised through an offering of stock to the public and that the public offering was scheduled to be made within 60 days through an investment group headed by two underwriting firms: Loeb, Rhoades and Dominick & Dominick. Arvida had not yet filed a registration statement with the SEC. Did Arvida make an illegal offer under Section 5 of the Securities Act?

4. Western-Realco Limited Partnership sold $800,000 of its limited partnership interests through the services of securities brokers. Western-Realco did not supervise the brokers and was unaware of whether the brokers solicited their clients in a newsletter or to the public in general. Will Western-Realco be able to use the private offering exemption or Rule 504 to avoid a 1933 Act registration?

5. Sonic Petroleum, Inc., was incorporated and had its corporate offices, books, and records in Utah. To obtain sufficient capital to conduct business, Sonic sold 25 million common shares to residents of Utah, raising $500,000. Seven months later, Sonic acquired an Illinois drilling corporation and transferred nearly all its assets to Illinois, having not conducted any business in Utah. At about the same time, Sonic also created a public market for its shares. As a result, Paul and Linda Busch, who were California residents, purchased Sonic shares that Sonic had issued to Utah residents seven months earlier. When Sonic's share value dropped, the Busches sued for rescission under section 12(a)(1) of the 1933 Act. Was Sonic correct that it had met the intrastate offering exemption?

6. Commonwealth Edison Co. registered 3 million common shares with the SEC and sold the shares for about $28 per share. The price of the purchasers' stock dropped to $21 when the Atomic Safety and Licensing Board denied ComEd's application to license one of its reactors. It was the first and only time the Board had denied a license application. ComEd assumed that the license would be granted; therefore, its registration statement failed to disclose the pendency of the license application. Did ComEd violate Section 11 of the Securities Act?

7. Joseph Crotty was a vice president of United Artists Communications, Inc. (UA), a corporation with equity securities registered under the Securities Exchange Act of 1934. Crotty was the head film buyer of UA's western division. He had virtually complete and autonomous control of film buying for the 351 UA theaters in the western United States, including negotiating and signing movie acquisition agreements, supervising movie distribution, and settling contracts after the movies had been shown. Crotty knew how many contracts were being negotiated at any one time and the price UA was paying for the rental of each movie. Crotty was required to consult with higher officers only if he wanted to exceed a certain limit on the amount of the cash advance paid to a distributor for a movie. This occurred no more than two or three times a year. The gross revenue from Crotty's division was about 35 percent of UA's gross revenue from movie exhibitions and around 17 percent of its total gross revenue. During a six-month period, Crotty purchased 7,500 shares of UA and sold 3,500 shares, realizing a large profit. Has Crotty violated Section 16(b) of the 1934 Act?

8. Potlatch Corporation was in the forests products industry, an industry that had experienced a wave of takeovers. The Potlatch board of directors approved a voting rights amendment to the articles of incorporation that granted four votes per share to current shareholders and other specified shareholders. New shareholders would have only one vote per share until they held the shares for four years. The effect of the amendment would be to deter and frustrate a hostile takeover of Potlatch. The board issued a proxy statement in connection with its solicitation of proxies from the shareholders. A letter issued with the proxy statement stated that the intent of the voting rights amendment was to give long-term shareholders a greater voice in the affairs of Potlatch. The voting rights amendment was approved by shareholders. Potlatch shareholders sued the company under Section 14(a) of the 1934 Act, seeking to void the shareholders' approval of the voting rights amendment. They alleged that the shareholders' votes were procured by fraud because the board failed to disclose the real purpose of the voting rights amendment—entrenchment of current management. Should the shareholders succeed?

9. J. C. Harrelson, the president and chief shareholder of Alabama Supply and Equipment Company (ASECo), and Clarence Hamilton conspired to defraud investors. They induced Frisco City, Alabama, to create the Industrial Development Board of Frisco City to issue tax-exempt bonds to investors. The Board offered and sold bonds pursuant to an offering circular, which misstated

or omitted several material facts, due to misrepresentations made by Harrelson and Hamilton. The Board used the proceeds of the bond issuance to build a manufacturing plant for ASECo. After the ASECo plant was constructed, ASECo ceased all operations and defaulted on its rental payments to the Board, causing the value of the bonds to drop precipitously. The bondholders received only $373.33 for each $1,000 bond. Clarence Bishop had purchased four of the bonds for $4,096. He never saw the offering circular or knew that one existed. He bought the bonds solely on his broker's oral representations that they were a good investment and that others in the community had purchased them. Can Bishop sue Harrelson and Hamilton under Rule 10b–5 even though he failed to read or even to seek to read the offering circular?

10. Medco Research, Inc., a pharmaceutical company that developed drugs for the treatment of heart disease, was having problems with safety and quality control problems at a manufacturing plant. As a result, Medco knew that the Food and Drug Administration was not likely to approve in the near future a new drug that was critical to Medco's prospects. Medco had even withdrawn its FDA application for the drug. Nonetheless, on April 7, 1992, Medco told shareholders and public investors that the application was on track. On the same day, Anthony LaSalle purchased Medco shares. On September 1, 1993, LaSalle sued Medco under Rule 10b–5 of the 1934 Act on the grounds that Medco had fraudulently withheld from investors information about the FDA's approval of the new drug. Medco defended on the grounds that LaSalle waited too long to sue, claiming that a dramatic drop in Medco's stock price between January and April 1992 should have alerted LaSalle to the fraud. At the time, securities law required a fraud claim to be brought within one year after discovery of facts constituting a violation of Rule 10b–5. Was Medco correct that LaSalle waited too long to sue?

11. When he was the Oklahoma Sooner football coach, Barry Switzer attended a track meet, where he spoke with friends and acquaintances, including G. Platt, a director of Phoenix Corporation and chief executive officer of Texas International Company (TIC), a business that sponsored Switzer's coach's television show. TIC owned more than 50 percent of Phoenix's shares. Switzer moved around the bleachers at the track meet in order to talk to various people. After speaking with Platt and his wife Linda for the last of five times, Switzer lay down to sunbathe on a row of bleachers behind the Platts. G. Platt, unaware that Switzer was behind him, carelessly spoke too loud while talking with his wife about his desire to sell or

liquidate Phoenix. He also talked about several companies making bids to buy Phoenix. Switzer also overheard that an announcement of a possible liquidation of Phoenix might be made within a week. Switzer used the information he obtained in deciding to purchase Phoenix shares. Did Switzer trade illegally on inside information?

12. First City Financial Corp., a Canadian company controlled by the Belzberg family, was engaged in the business of investing in publicly held American corporations. Marc Belzberg identified Ashland Oil Company as a potential target, and on February 11, 1986, he secretly purchased 61,000 shares of Ashland stock for First City. By February 26, additional secret purchases of Ashland shares pushed First City's holdings to just over 4.9 percent of Ashland's stock. These last two purchases were effected for First City by Alan "Ace" Greenberg, the chief executive officer of Bear Stearns, a large Wall Street brokerage. On March 4, Belzberg called Greenberg and told him, "It wouldn't be a bad idea if you bought Ashland Oil here." Immediately after the phone call, Greenberg purchased 20,500 Ashland shares for about $44 per share. If purchased for First City, those shares would have increased First City's Ashland holdings above 5 percent. Greenberg believed he was buying the shares for First City under a put and call agreement, under which First City had the right to buy the shares from Bear Stearns and Bear Stearns had the right to require First City to buy the shares from it. Between March 4 and 14, Greenberg purchased an additional 330,700 shares. On March 17, First City and Bear Stearns signed a formal put and call agreement covering all the shares Greenberg purchased. On March 25, First City announced publicly for the first time that it intended to make a tender offer for all of Ashland's shares. First City filed a Schedule 13D on March 26. Has First City violated the Williams Act?

13. Amenity, Inc., was incorporated with 1 million authorized shares, which were issued to Capital General Corporation (CGC) for $2,000. CGC distributed 90,000 of those shares to about 900 of its clients, business associates, and other contacts to create and maintain goodwill among its clients and contacts. CGC did not receive any monetary or other direct financial consideration from those receiving the stock. Amenity had no actual business function at this time, and its sole asset was the $2,000 CGC had paid for the 1 million shares. Through CGC's efforts, Amenity was acquired by another company, which paid CGC $25,000 for its efforts. The Utah Securities Division sought to suspend the public trading of Amenity stock on the grounds that when CGC distributed the shares it had sold them in violation of the Utah Securities Act. Was CGC's distribution a sale of securities?

Online Research: Internet Offerings of Securities

Using the term *Internet Securities Offerings,* you can find several websites that explain how an issuer may make an Internet offering of securities without violating state or federal securities law. The websites can help you answer the following questions:

- Why will an Internet offering create problems if the issuer is trying to exempt the offering under Rules 505 or 506?
- Why are Rule 504 and Regulation A good exemptions for Internet offerings?
- What are the dos and don'ts for communications during an Internet registered offering?

LEGAL AND PROFESSIONAL RESPONSIBILITIES OF AUDITORS, CONSULTANTS, AND SECURITIES PROFESSIONALS

Credit Deutsch First Chicago LLP (CDFC) is a financial consulting and investment banking firm. Angst & Yearn LLP (A&Y) is a public accounting firm. A client of both firms is Macrohard Corporation, a public issuer of securities required to file periodic reports with the Securities and Exchange Commission under the Securities Exchange Act of 1934. Because Macrohard has a short-term cash flow problem due to lower sales, CDFC advises Macrohard to issue 300 promissory notes, each with a face value of $10,000,000, interest of 6 percent, and a due date 11 months after issuance. CDFC recommends that the notes be sold to mutual funds, insurance companies, pension funds, and other institutional investors using the Rule 506 exemption from registration under the Securities Act of 1933.

The notes are offered in part by an offering circular, which includes financial statements audited by A&Y. A&Y's unqualified audit opinion is also included in the offering circular. A&Y receives a $6,500,000 fee for auditing Macrohard's financial statements and reviewing the financial statements for inclusion in the offering circular.

CDFC assists Macrohard with the offering of the notes by calling prospective investors on the phone, visiting investors in person, and sending e-mails to prospective investors urging them to buy the notes. In all three contacts, CDFC emphasizes that the notes carry an interest rate that is higher than the 30-year Treasury bond rate and, therefore, offer an excellent return on investment. As compensation for its role in the notes offering, CDFC will receive 0.5 percent of the proceeds from the sale of the notes.

- What standard of care must CDFC meet when recommending that Marcrohard issue promissory notes as a solution to its liquidity problems?
- If one of CDFC's partners during the course of the offering negligently makes false statements about Macrohard's financial position to purchasers of the notes, does CDFC have potential liability to the purchasers under Section 12(a)(2) of the Securities Act of 1933? Especially consider whether CDFC is a proper type of defendant under that section.
- Is CDFC a proper type of defendant under Rule 10b–5 of the Securities Exchange Act of 1934 due to its communications with purchasers, if one of its partners negligently made false statements?
- Should A&Y fear liability to the note purchasers under Section 12(a)(2) of the 1933 Act?
- If A&Y negligently audited Macrohard's financial statements and as a result the financial statements materially misstate Macrohard's financial position, does A&Y have potential liability to the purchasers under Rule 10b–5 of the 1934 Act? Especially consider whether A&Y is a proper type of defendant under that rule.

- Does CDFC have potential liability to any of the note purchasers under the state law of negligent misrepresentation in a state that has adopted the *Ultramares* test?
- If A&Y knows that the audited financial statements will be used in the offering circular to sell the notes, but it does not know to which institutional investors the notes will be sold, does A&Y have potential liability to any of the note purchasers under the state law of negligent misrepresentation in a state that adopted the *Ultramares* test? How about a state that has adopted the rule of the *Restatement (Second) of Torts?*

Suppose that instead of making a Rule 506 offering, Macrohard issues preferred stock in a public offering registered under the 1933 Act. CDFC is Macrohard's underwriter for the public offering, receiving a 25-cent spread for each share sold. The financial statements audited by A&Y and its audit opinion are included in the registration statement. Unknown to CDFC and A&Y, there are material misstatements of fact in the financial statements included in the registration statement, and there are also omissions of material facts in the portions of the registration statement that describe Macrohard's business and the material risks of investing in the preferred stock.

- Is CDFC a statutory defendant under section 11 of the 1933 Act? For what portions of the registration statement is CDFC liable under section 11? What is CDFC's due diligence defense for errors in the financial statements audited by A&Y? What is CDFC's due diligence defense for errors in the portions of the registration statement that describe Macrohard's business and material risks?
- Is A&Y a statutory defendant under section 11 of the 1933 Act? For what portions of the registration statement is A&Y liable under section 11? What is A&Y's due diligence defense?
- Compile a checklist that will help CDFC and A&Y meet their due diligence defenses under Section 11.

THIS CHAPTER COVERS THE legal responsibilities of accountants, auditors, consultants, and securities professionals. The chapter's primary focus is on auditors of financial statements, tax accountants, consultants who provide management and financial advice to clients, investment bankers, securities underwriters, securities analysts, and securities brokers.

This chapter will first cover the general standard of performance required of professionals. Next, we will study professionals' liability to their clients, especially under state law. The liability to third parties who are not clients comprises the largest part of this chapter. We will also examine criminal liability of professionals and end the chapter with coverage of the law protecting the integrity of communications between professionals and their clients.

General Standard of Performance

The general duty that auditors, consultants, and securities professionals owe to their clients and to other persons who are affected by their actions is to exercise the skill and care of the ordinarily prudent professional in the same circumstances. Hence, professionals must act carefully and diligently; they are *not* guarantors of the accuracy of their work or that the advice they give to clients will work out well. The professional's duty to exercise reasonable care is a subset of the negligence standard of tort law. Two elements compose the general duty of performance: skill and care.

A professional must have the **skill of the ordinarily prudent person in her profession.** This element focuses on education or knowledge, whether acquired formally at school or by self-instruction. For example, to audit financial records, an accountant must know generally accepted auditing standards (GAAS) and generally accepted accounting principles (GAAP). GAAS and GAAP are standards and principles embodied in the rules, releases, and pronouncements of the Securities and Exchange Commission, the American Institute of Certified Public Accountants (AICPA), the Financial Accounting Standards Board (FASB), and the newly created Public Company Accounting Oversight Board (PCAOB). To assist a corporate client's development of an expansion strategy, a consultant must be knowledgeable of similar businesses and the opportunities for expansion. To assist a securities issuer making an initial public offering (IPO), an investment banker must know the mechanics of a public offering and the market for securities. In recommending stocks to an investor, a broker or investment adviser must know fundamental investment analysis and portfolio theory.

The care element requires a professional to act as carefully as the ordinarily prudent person in her profession. For example, in preparing a tax return, a tax accountant must discover the income exclusions, the deductions, and the tax credits that the reasonably careful accountant would find are available to the client. When recommending a corporate acquisition to a client, an investment banker must investigate the value of the acquired firm and check the acquired firm's fit with the business and strategy of the acquiring firm. A broker recommending a security to his customer must carefully investigate the security and its fit with the customer's investment goals, securities portfolio, and financial status.

Courts and legislatures usually defer to the members of a profession in determining what the ordinarily prudent professional would do. Such deference recognizes the lawmakers' lack of understanding of the nuances of professional practice. However, a profession will not be permitted to establish a standard of conduct that is harmful to the interests of clients or other members of society.

ETHICS IN ACTION

Public Company Accounting Oversight Board

One of the main features of the Sarbanes–Oxley Act of 2002 is the creation of an independent board that will oversee the audits of public companies. Congress's perception was that auditing firms were not sufficiently independent of the public companies they audited due in part to the audit firms receiving sizable nonaudit consulting fees from their audit clients. Thus, the Sarbanes–Oxley Act creates a Public Company Accounting Oversight Board (PCAOB). Public accounting firms that audit financial statements of public companies are required to register with PCAOB and submit to its rules. The Board is charged with adopting rules establishing auditing, quality control, ethics, and independence standards. It has the power to regulate the nonaudit services that audit firms may perform for their clients. The PCAOB has the power to inspect periodically public accounting firms and to issue reports of the results of the reviews. The purpose of inspections is to assess the degree of compliance with the requirements of the Sarbanes–Oxley Act, professional auditing standards, and the rules of the PCAOB and the SEC in the performance of audits and the issuance of audit reports of public companies. In addition, the PCAOB may investigate and discipline audit firms and their partners and employees.

The PCAOB is not a federal agency, but a nonprofit corporation with broad regulatory power like the National Association of Securities Dealers, a self-regulatory organization that regulates securities brokers and dealers. It has five members, only two of which may be CPAs. No Board member may receive any share of profits or compensation from a public accounting firm.

- Do you think that the creation and work of the PCAOB will result in greater independence of auditors of public companies?
- If auditing of financial statements is required primarily for the protection of public investors, should not all PCAOB members be taken from the investment community that uses audited financial statements?

Professionals' Liability to Clients

Professionals are sometimes sued by their clients. For example, an accountant may wrongfully claim deductions on a client's tax return. When the IRS discovers the wrongful deduction, the individual will have to pay the extra tax, interest, and perhaps a penalty. The individual may sue his accountant to recover the amount of the penalty. For another example, consider a securities broker who churns the securities account of a 92-year-old investor by executing daily trades in dot-com stocks. When the value of the investor's portfolio declines from $500,000 to near zero as high commissions and capital losses mount, the investor may sue the broker for making imprudent investment decisions and for churning the account merely to earn the commissions.

When clients sue professionals, there are three principal bases of liability: contract, tort, and trust.

Contractual Liability

As a party to a contract with her client, a professional owes a duty to the client to perform as she has agreed to perform. This includes an implied duty to perform the contract as the ordinarily prudent person in the profession would perform it. If the professional fails to perform as agreed, ordinarily she is liable only for compensatory damages and those consequential damages that are contemplated by the client and the professional at the time the contract was made, such as the client's cost of hiring another consultant or auditor to complete the work. For example, an auditor agrees to provide audited financial statements for inclusion in a client's bank loan application. The loan will be used to expand the client's business. When the auditor fails to complete the audit on time, the auditor will not ordinarily be liable for the client's lost profits from the unexecuted expansion, unless the auditor had agreed to be liable for such lost profits.

A professional is not liable for breach of contract if the client obstructs the performance of the contract. For example, an investment banker is not liable for failing to make a timely public offering of a client's securities if the client delays giving the investment banker the information it needs to complete the securities offering registration statement.

A professional may not delegate his duty to perform a contract without the consent of the client. Delegation is not permitted because the performance of a contract for professional services depends on the skill, training, and character of the professional. For example, PricewaterhouseCoopers, a public accounting firm, may not delegate to Ernst & Young, another public accounting firm, the contractual duty to audit the financial statements of GM, even though both firms are nearly equally skillful and careful.

Tort Liability

Professionals' tort liability to their clients may be based on the common law concepts of negligence and fraud or on the violation of a statute, including the federal and state securities laws.

Negligence The essence of negligence is the failure of a professional to exercise the skill and care of the ordinarily prudent person in the profession. A professional is negligent when he breaches the duty to act skillfully and carefully and proximately causes damages to the client. For example, a corporate client may recover from an investment banker when the client overpays for an acquired firm due to the investment banker's careless valuation of the acquired firm.

Under the **suitability** and **know-your-customer rules** of the NASD and stock exchanges, a securities broker is required to know the financial circumstances and investment objectives of his client before recommending securities or executing securities transactions for the client. A broker who does not know his customer is negligent and may be liable for losses from securities transactions that are inappropriate for the client. A broker that warns a client of the risks and inappropriateness of an investment has met his duty and is not liable, for example, to a client that disregards the risk and authorizes trading in the risky investment. The suitability and know-your-customer rules may also justify a client's action on *contract* grounds when the customer signs an account agreement that requires a broker to handle the account in accordance with industry standards.

Audit Duties Audit engagements are a unique area of professional liability. Sometimes, an accountant will audit a company, yet fail to uncover fraud, embezzlement, or other intentional wrongdoing by an employee of the company. Ordinarily, an accountant has no specific duty to uncover employee fraud or embezzlement. Nonetheless, an accountant must uncover employee fraud or embezzlement if an ordinarily prudent accountant would have discovered it. The accountant who fails to uncover such fraud or embezzlement is negligent and liable to his client. In addition, an accountant owes a duty to investigate suspicious circumstances that tend to indicate fraud, regardless of how he became aware of those circumstances. Also, an accountant has a duty to inform a proper party of his suspicions. It is not enough to inform or confront the person suspected of fraud.

When an accountant is hired to perform a fraud audit to investigate suspected fraud or embezzlement, she has a greater duty to investigate. She must be as skillful and careful as the ordinarily prudent auditor performing a fraud audit.

When an accountant negligently fails to discover embezzlement, generally he is liable to his client only for an amount equal to the embezzlement that occurred after he should have discovered the embezzlement. The accountant is usually not liable for any part of the embezzlement that occurred prior to the time he should have uncovered the embezzlement unless his tardy discovery prevented the client from recovering embezzled funds.

In the following *Diversified Graphics* case, a consulting firm was held liable to its client for failing to meet the standard of the profession.

Diversified Graphics, Ltd. v. Groves   868 F.2d 293 (8th Cir. 1989)

Diversified Graphics, Ltd. (D.G.), hired Ernst & Whinney (E & W) to assist it in obtaining a computer system to fit its data processing needs. D.G. had a longstanding relationship with E & W during which D.G. developed great trust and reliance on E & W's services. Because D.G. lacked computer expertise, it decided to entrust E & W with the selection and implementation of an in-house computer data processing system. E & W had promised to locate a "turnkey" system, which would be fully operational without the need for extensive employee training. D.G. instead received a system that was difficult to operate and failed to meet its needs. D.G. sued E & W and its partners, including Ray Groves, for negligence. The jury found in favor of D.G.; E & W and its partners appealed.

Lay, Chief Judge   D.G.'s theory for recovery based on negligence encompasses the notion of a consultant-client relationship and therefore the existence of a professional standard of care.

The degree of skill and care that may be required of a professional is a question of fact for the jury. We find that there was substantial evidence regarding the applicable standard of a professional consultant.

E & W's Guidelines to Practice incorporates the Management Advisory Services Practice Standards which were adopted by the American Institute of Certified Public Accountants, Inc. (AICPA Standards). The AICPA Standards require that "due professional care" is to be exercised in providing management advisory services. These standards in part generally provide:

In performing management advisory services, a practitioner must act with integrity and objectivity and be independent in mental attitude.

Engagements are to be performed by practitioners having competence in the analytical approach and process, and in the technical subject matter under consideration.

Due professional care is to be exercised in the performance of a management advisory services engagement.

Before accepting an engagement, a practitioner is to notify the client of any reservations he has regarding anticipated benefits.

Before undertaking an engagement, a practitioner is to inform his client of all significant matters related to the engagement.

Engagements are to be adequately planned, supervised, and controlled.

Sufficient relevant data is to be obtained, documented, and evaluated in developing conclusions and recommendations.

All significant matters relating to the results of the engagement are to be communicated to the client.

AICPA Standards Nos. 1–8.

D.G. had determined that it required a "turnkey" computer system that would fully perform all of its data processing in-house. The term "turnkey" is intended to describe a self-sufficient system which the purchaser need only "turn the key" to commence operation. The purchaser should not have to hire programmers, and current employees should not have to undergo extensive training to be able to operate the system. To procure this type of customized and fully operational system, great care must be taken to carefully detail a business's needs and to properly develop specifications for the computer system. Potential vendors must be carefully scrutinized to discover all of the inadequacies of their data processing systems. Once a vendor is chosen, proper implementation is imperative to ensure that the purchaser truly need only "turn the key" to commence full operation of the system. A fundamental part of implementation involves testing the system through parallel data processing operation. Finally, the existence of adequate documentation regarding the operation of the system is crucial once the system is up and running. As previously stated, employees will have had only minimal training and will depend heavily on the instructions for operation. Moreover, documentation is particularly important because this type of system is highly customized and standard instruction sources will have only limited value.

Thus, the jury could conclude that E & W's conduct fell short of adhering to the applicable professional standard of care.

Judgment for Diversified Graphics affirmed.

Contributory and Comparative Negligence of Client Courts are reluctant to permit a professional to escape liability to a client merely because the client was contributorily negligent. Since the accountant or consultant has skills superior to those of the client, courts generally allow clients to rely on an accountant's duty to discover employee fraud, a consultant's duty to make reasonable recommendations, and an underwriter's advice on what type of security to issue. The client is not required to exercise reasonable care to discover these things itself.

Nonetheless, some courts allow the defense of contributory negligence or the defense of **comparative negligence,** such as when clients negligently fail to follow a consultant's advice or when clients possess information that makes their reliance on an investment banker unwarranted. The *Scioto Memorial Hospital* case considers the limits of the comparative negligence defense.

Scioto Memorial Hospital Ass'n., Inc. v. Price Waterhouse
659 N.E.2d 1268 (Ohio Sup. Ct. 1996)

Scioto Memorial Hospital Association, Inc., planned the construction of Richmond Place, a 170-unit residential retirement center in Lexington, Kentucky. Scioto hired Price Waterhouse (PW) to review the work of the architect, the financial underwriter, and the marketing consultant and to recommend whether Scioto should proceed with the Richmond Place investment. PW's engagement letter represented that PW would issue a preliminary feasibility study and review a detailed financial forecast of the project. Financial forecasts represent management's judgment of the most likely set of conditions and management's most likely course of action. Instead of reviewing a financial forecast for Richmond Place, PW reviewed only a financial projection compiled by the underwriter. As PW explained in its letter to Scioto, a projection "represents management's estimate of its possible, but not necessarily most probable, future course of action." PW's final report issued to Scioto assumed an occupancy rate of 98 percent.

During construction, presales were lagging, but PW assured Scioto's president that Richmond Place was a good project. When construction was 70 percent complete, fire destroyed most of the retirement center. Scioto used the insurance proceeds to rebuild, yet a year later, only 15 residents occupied Richmond Place.

Scioto sued PW alleging negligence and breach of contract on the grounds that PW failed adequately to assess and disclose to Scioto the risks associated with the project. Scioto claimed it would not have undertaken the project if PW's report had accurately reflected the financial forecast. PW defended on the grounds that Scioto's comparative negligence caused Scioto's damages: PW pointed to delays in construction after the fire and Scioto's lack of business-interruption insurance covering the six-month delay in construction caused by the fire. The trial court held that PW could not raise the defense of Scioto's comparative negligence, and the jury found PW liable. PW appealed to an Ohio appeals court, which affirmed, but reduced PW's liability to $8,771,000. PW appealed to the Supreme Court of Ohio.

Sweeney, Justice The main issue before this court is whether the comparative negligence defense is applicable to a professional negligence claim of a client against its accountant. We find that the comparative negligence defense is applicable in accounting negligence cases.

The audit interference rule was set forth in *National Surety Corp. v. Lybrand* (1939). At that time, New York recognized contributory negligence as a complete bar to recovery. In *National Surety,* the New York Supreme Court, Appellate Division, held that contributory negligence constituted a defense for accountants only if the client's negligence contributed to the accountant's failure to perform his contract and to report the truth. While this rule was adopted by a number of jurisdictions, a review of these cases shows that none discusses its application in a state recognizing comparative negligence, with the exception of *Fullmer v. Wohlfeiler & Beck* (1990). The audit interference rule was made to soften what was then the harsh rule of negligence law which barred recovery of damages if there was any contributory negligence on the part of the plaintiff.

However, in light of Ohio's comparative negligence statute enacted in 1980, there is no need for a special rule and, thus, we reject the application of the audit interference rule in Ohio. Hence, any negligence by a client, whether or not it directly interferes with the accountant's performance of its duties, can reduce the client's recovery. In so holding, we note that virtually all courts that have expressly considered the applicability of the audit interference rule to their comparative negligence states have agreed and rejected the rule.

As to the application of the comparative negligence defense in the present case, we note that while accountants should exercise ordinary care in conducting their accounting activities, the persons who hire accountants, usually businesspersons, should also be required to conduct their business activities in a reasonable and prudent manner. Accordingly, the trial court erred in granting the motion as to PW's comparative negligence defense and failing to give an instruction on comparative negligence to the jury.

However, despite the trial court's ruling, the record demonstrates that PW was not precluded from presenting extensive evidence tending to show that Scioto's own conduct was a cause of its losses, in addition to the negligence of PW. PW primarily argues about the trial court's exclusion of evidence regarding Scioto's business-interruption insurance. However, the $4,000,000 hole in Scioto's protective coverage was clearly and repeatedly presented to the jury. Moreover, failure to obtain such insurance constitutes comparative negligence only with regard to the damages attributable to the delays caused by the fire and not the other damages which the jury found Scioto to have sustained as a result of PW's negligence and breach of contract. The court of appeals recognized that the jury award improperly included damages that resulted from the fire and cured the error. Accordingly, we find that while the trial court should have allowed the comparative negligence defense, in this case the error was cured by the court of appeals and, therefore, did not constitute prejudicial error.

Likewise, the trial court's failure to give an instruction to the jury on comparative negligence was not prejudicial error in this case. Evidence pertaining to the negligent acts of Scioto was presented to the jury during the trial. The jury was instructed that if Scioto failed to act reasonably to avoid or reduce its losses, it could not recover any such damages. Despite these instructions, the jury still awarded Scioto all of its damages, indicating that the jury found PW the sole cause of the failure of Richmond Place. Thus, we find that even if the jury had been required to apportion the fault between the parties in this case, the outcome would have been the same. The jury found that PW was solely liable for Scioto's loss. Accordingly, since there was no prejudicial error, a new trial is not warranted.

Judgment for Scioto Memorial Hospital affirmed in part and reversed in part in favor of Price Waterhouse.

Fraud A professional is liable to his client for fraud when he misstates or omits facts in communications with his client and acts with **scienter.** A person acts with scienter when he knows of the falsity of a statement or he recklessly disregards the truth. Thus, for example, accountants are liable in fraud for their intentional or reckless disregard for accuracy in their work.

For example, an accountant chooses not to examine the current figures in a client's books of account, but relies on last year's figures because he is behind in his work for other clients. As a result, the accountant understates the client's income on an income statement that the client uses to apply for a loan. The client obtains a loan, but he has to pay a higher interest rate because his low stated income makes the loan a higher risk for the bank. Such misconduct by the accountant proves scienter and, therefore, amounts to fraud.

Scienter also includes recklessly ignoring facts, such as an auditor's finding obvious evidence of embezzlement yet failing to notify a client of the embezzlement. An investment banker defrauds its client when it withholds information concerning the value of the client's shares and causes the client to issue the shares for too little consideration, perhaps to an affiliate of the investment banker who, therefore, profits unreasonably. As you can see, fraud is extremely reprehensible conduct and deserves to be punished. Fraud actions are not designed to impose liability on honest professionals who sometimes make careless errors.

The chief advantage of establishing fraud is that the client may get a higher damage award than when the accountant is merely negligent. Usually, a client may receive only compensatory damages for a breach of contract or negligence. By proving fraud, a client may be awarded punitive damages as well.

Breach of Trust

A professional owes a duty of trust to his client. Information and assets that are entrusted to an accountant, broker, or investment banker, for example, may be used only to benefit the client. The duty of trust requires the professional to maintain the confidentiality of the client's information entrusted to the firm. Therefore, a professional may not disclose sensitive matters such as a client's income and wealth or use secret information about a client's new product to purchase the client's securities. In addition, for example, an accountant or securities broker may not use the assets of his client for his own benefit.

ETHICS IN ACTION

The Sarbanes–Oxley Act of 2002: Auditor Independence Standards

When Congress studied the causes of financial statement irregularities in 2002, it became convinced that some auditors failed to challenge their clients' financial reporting practices for fear that the audit firms would lose lucrative consulting contracts with the clients. The belief was that firms undercharged for audit services to acquire valuable consulting clients. To ensure that audit firms are free from conflict-of-interest and lack of independence charges that can undermine the quality of their audits, the Sarbanes–Oxley Act of 2002 bans most types of services by audit firms for audit clients, including:

- Bookkeeping.
- Financial information system design.
- Appraisal or valuation services.
- Actuarial services.
- Internal audit outsourcing.

- Management or human resource services.
- Broker, dealer, investment banker, and investment adviser services.
- Legal and expert services related to the audit.
- Other services as determined by the Public Company Accounting Oversight Board.

The PCAOB also has power on a case-by-case basis to exempt services performed by an audit firm for an audit client. An audit firm may provide permissible nonaudit services for an audit client, such as tax services, only if the client's audit committee approves the services in advance.

In addition, the Act requires that the audit partner-in-charge be rotated every five years at a minimum. The Act also charges the General Accounting Office to study whether all public companies should be required to rotate audit firms on a regular basis. Finally, no audit firm may audit a public company that within the past year has hired an audit firm employee as a CEO, CFO, or CAO.

THE GLOBAL BUSINESS ENVIRONMENT

International Accounting Standards Board

The International Accounting Standards Board (IASB) is an independent, privately funded accounting standard setter based in London, England. The Board's mission is to develop, in the public interest, a single set of high quality, understandable, and enforceable global accounting standards for general purpose financial statements. The IASB publishes the International Financial Reporting Standards (IFRS). It has also adopted the standards issued by the Board of the International Accounting Standards Committee: the International Accounting Standards (IAS). The Board cooperates with national accounting standard setters to achieve consistency in accounting standards. In June 2002 the European Union approved a regulation requiring all publicly traded companies in all EU states to prepare consolidated financial statements using IASB standards by no later than 2005.

Securities Law

Federal and state securities law creates several rights of action for persons harmed in connection with the purchase or sale of securities. These rights of action are based in tort. Although some securities law sections permit clients to sue professionals, they are rarely used for that purpose. Usually, only third parties (nonclients) sue under the securities law. The securities law sections that apply to professionals are discussed later in this chapter.

LOG ON

www.securitieslaw.com
The Securities Fraud & Investor Protection Resource Center provides information on the investor–broker relationship, including investors' rights of actions against brokers.

Professionals' Liability to Third Persons: Common Law

Other persons besides a professional's clients may use her work product. Banks may use financial statements reviewed by a loan applicant's accountant in deciding whether to make a loan to the applicant. Investors may use financial statements audited by a company's auditors in deciding whether to buy or sell the company's securities. These documents prepared by an accountant may prove incorrect, resulting in damages to the nonclients who relied on them. For example, banks may lend money to a corporation only because an income statement prepared by an accountant overstated the corporation's income. When the corporation fails to repay the loan, the bank may sue the accountant to recover the damages it suffered.

Nonclient actions are rarer outside the accountant context because the work product of nonaccounting professionals is infrequently used by others in an expectable way. For example, consulting advice is almost never passed from a client to a third party. A securities broker's client rarely relays the broker's investment advice to a friend; when the friend attempts to sue the broker if the advice turns out to be bad, the friend usually is not able to recover damages from the broker.

However, investment bankers often prepare documents for their clients that are created expressly to sell securities to nonclients, that is, shareholders and other holders of the client's securities. Therefore, purchasers who buy the client's securities based on false statements in a document prepared for investors by an investment banker may sue the investment banker.

Nonclients may sue professionals for common law negligence, common law fraud, and violations of the securities laws. In this section, common law negligence and fraud are discussed.

Negligence and Negligent Misrepresentation

When a professional fails to perform as the ordinarily prudent professional would perform, she risks having liability for negligence. Many courts have restricted the ability of nonclients to sue a professional for damages proximately caused by the professional's negligent conduct. These courts limit nonclient suits on the grounds that nonclient users of a professional's work product have not contracted with the professional and, therefore, are not in **privity of contract** with her. Essentially, these courts hold that a professional owes no duty to nonclients to exercise ordinary skill and care.

This judicial stance conflicts with the usual principles of negligence law under which a negligent person is liable to all persons who are reasonably foreseeably damaged by his negligence. The rationale for the restrictive judicial stance was expressed in the *Ultramares* case,[1] a decision of the highest court in New York. In that case, Judge Benjamin Cardozo refused to hold an auditor liable to third parties for mere negligence. His rationale was stated as follows:

> If liability for negligence exists, a thoughtless slip or blunder, the failure to detect a theft or forgery beneath the cover of deceptive entries, may expose accountants to a liability in an indeterminate amount for an indeterminate time to an indeterminate class.

Ultramares dominated the thinking of judges for many years, and its impact is still felt today. However, many courts understand that many nonclients use and reasonably rely on the work product of professionals, especially accountants. To varying degrees, these courts have relaxed the privity requirement and expanded the class of persons who may sue an accountant or other professional for negligent conduct. Today, most courts adopt one of the following three tests to determine whether a nonclient may sue a professional for negligence.

---

[1] *Ultramares Corp. v. Touche,* 174 N.E. 441 (N.Y.Ct.App.1931).

Primary Benefit Test The *Ultramares* court adopted a primary benefit test for imposing liability for negligence. Under this test, a professional's duty of care extends only to those persons for whose primary benefit the professional audits or prepares financial reports and other documents. The professional must actually foresee the nonclient's use and prepare the document primarily for use by a specified nonclient. That is, the nonclient must be a **foreseen user** of the professional's work product. The professional must know two things: (1) the name of the person who will use her work product and (2) the particular purpose for which that person will use the work product.

Suppose an investment banker acts as a broker for a client issuing securities to 10 mutual funds identified as prospective buyers. To assist the client's sale of the securities, the investment banker prepares an offering memorandum for the client. If due to the investment banker's negligence the offering memorandum misstates material facts, and the client gives the offering memorandum to the previously identified mutual funds, the investment banker may have liability to the mutual funds that relied on the misstated facts.

Foreseen Users and Foreseen Class of Users Test By 1965, a draft of the *Restatement (Second) of Torts* proposed that the law of professional negligence expand the class of protected persons to **foreseen users** and **users within a foreseen class of users** of reports. Under this test, the professional must know either the user of the work product or the use to be made of the work product. The protected persons are (1) those persons who a professional knows will use the work product and (2) those persons who use the work product in a way the professional knew the work product would be used.

For example, an accountant prepares an income statement that he knows his client will use to obtain a loan at Bank X. Any bank to which the client supplies the statement to obtain a loan, including Bank Y, may sue the accountant for damages caused by a negligently prepared income statement. Bank X is a foreseen user, and Bank Y is in a foreseen class of users. On the other hand, if an ac-

countant prepares an income statement for a tax return and the client, without the accountant's knowledge, uses the income statement to apply for a loan from a bank, the bank is not among the protected class of persons—the accountant did not know that the tax return would be used for that purpose.

In the securities professional context, when an underwriter prepares an offering document for a client issuing securities, the *Restatement* test extends an underwriter's liability for negligence to any purchaser of the securities whether known or not to the underwriter. This is because the underwriter knows the type of person who will use the offering document, that is, buyers of the securities.

Nonetheless, when the *Restatement* test is applied to securities brokers, liability rarely extends past the broker's client. A broker who gives investment advice to a client is rarely found liable to a nonclient who receives the advice secondhand on the grounds that investment advice is crafted specifically for the broker's client. That rationale is generally followed even in the context of a published investment newsletter, where usually only subscribers to the newsletter are permitted to sue the publisher of the newsletter.

Foreseeable Users Test A few courts have applied traditional negligence causation principles to professional negligence. They have extended liability to **foreseeable users** of an accountant's audit and other reports who suffered damages that were proximately caused by the accountant's negligence. To be liable to a nonclient under this test, an accountant need merely be reasonably able to expect or foresee the nonclient's use of the accountant's work product. It is not necessary for the nonclient to prove that the accountant actually expected or foresaw the nonclient's use.

In the following *Marcus Brothers Textiles* case, the court rejected the foreseeable users test as too broad and the *Ultramares* test as too narrow. Instead, the court applied the *Restatement*'s foreseen class of users test in the negligent misrepresentation context. Note that the dissenting opinion argues that the majority misinterpreted the *Restatement* test.

Marcus Brothers Textiles, Inc. v. Price Waterhouse, LLP
513 S.E.2d 320 (N.C. Sup. Ct. 1999)

Marcus Brothers Textiles, Inc., is a New York–based converter of textiles that buys unfinished woven material, has it finished by independent contractors, and sells it to apparel manufacturers or retailers of fabric for home sewing. Piece Goods Shops Company, L.P., a limited partnership, was a retailer of fabrics, patterns, sewing notions, needlecraft supplies, and sewing machines. Piece Goods was a frequent customer of Marcus Brothers.

Price Waterhouse, LLP, an independent public accounting firm, was hired by Piece Goods to perform audits of its year-end financial statements. Price Waterhouse audited Piece Goods's financial statements for the years 1989 through 1992. At the close of the fiscal year on July 31, 1992, Piece Goods prepared its year-end 1992 financial statements, and Price Waterhouse audited the 1992 financial statements. On September 22, 1992, following the audit, Price Waterhouse sent a letter to Piece Goods in which it stated:

> In our opinion, the accompanying balance sheet and the related statements of income and partners' equity and of cash flows present fairly, in all material respects, the financial position of Piece Goods at July 31, 1992, and the results of its operations and its cash flows for the year then ended in conformity with generally accepted accounting principles.

Piece Goods forwarded a copy of the audited 1992 financial statements to Marcus Brothers on October 29, 1992. Marcus Brothers contends that as a result of its reliance on the audited 1992 financial statements, it made several extensions of credit to Piece Goods during the period from December 1992 to April 1993.

In April 1993, Piece Goods filed a petition for reorganization under Chapter 11 of the Bankruptcy Code. At that time, Piece Goods owed Marcus Brothers nearly $290,000 as a result of the credit extensions. In August 1995, Marcus Brothers sued Price Waterhouse and five unnamed employees of Price Waterhouse, alleging gross negligence and negligent misrepresentation based on its audit of the 1992 financial statements. Marcus Brothers alleged the financial statements audited by Price Waterhouse contained several material misrepresentations and reflected numerous departures from Generally Accepted Accounting Principles (GAAP) and that Price Waterhouse's failure to alert readers of the financial statement to those departures violated Generally Accepted Auditing Standards (GAAS).

Marcus Brothers contended the audited 1992 balance sheet contained three material misrepresentations about Piece Goods's financial condition: (1) it showed a $30,332,000 receivable from a Piece Goods general partner which was uncollectible; (2) it included interest on the worthless $30,332,000 receivable; and (3) it incorrectly reflected nearly all payables for certain pattern inventories as noncurrent, long-term liabilities, but reflected the inventories for those pattern inventories as current assets. Marcus Brothers claims the result was to overstate Piece Goods's working capital and distort Piece Goods's current working capital ratio.

Price Waterhouse filed a motion for summary judgment, alleging that Marcus Brothers had failed to establish certain required elements of negligent misrepresentation, including: (1) Price Waterhouse's knowledge that Piece Goods would be supplying Marcus Brothers with the audited 1992 financial statements; and (2) Marcus Brothers' justifiable reliance upon the audited 1992 financial statements. The trial court granted Price Waterhouse's motion for summary judgment. Marcus Brothers appealed to the Court of Appeals, which reversed the trial court's decision. Price Waterhouse appealed to the North Carolina Supreme Court.

Wainwright, Justice   At the outset, we note that although a company's financial statements themselves are the representations of management, not the auditor, an audit report represents the auditor's opinion of the accuracy of the client's financial statements at a given period of time. As such, the responsibility an auditor assumes in conducting an audit and preparing a report should not be taken lightly.

The issue of the scope of an accountant's liability to persons other than the client for whom an audit report was prepared is relatively new in the annals of North Carolina jurisprudence. This Court first addressed the issue in 1988 in *Raritan River Steel Co. v. Cherry, Bekaert & Holland,* 367 S.E.2d 609 (1988). In *Raritan,* this Court stated that under certain circumstances, the tort of negligent misrepresentation set forth in section 552 of the *Restatement (Second) of Torts* could provide an appropriate remedy to plaintiffs who had been injured as a result of an accountant's negligence. Section 552 provides:

Information Negligently Supplied for the Guidance of Others

(1) One who, in the course of his business, profession or employment, or in any other transaction in which he has a pecuniary interest, supplies false information for the guidance of others in their business transactions, is subject to liability for pecuniary loss caused to them by their justifiable reliance upon the information, if he fails to exercise reasonable care or competence in obtaining or communicating the information.

(2) . . . The liability stated in Subsection (1) is limited to loss suffered

(a) by the person or one of a limited group of persons for whose benefit and guidance he intends to supply the information or knows that the recipient intends to supply it; and

(b) through reliance upon it in a transaction that he intends the information to influence or knows that the recipient so intends or in a substantially similar transaction.

Restatement (Second) of Torts section 552 (1977).

The *Restatement* approach recognizes that liability should extend not only to those with whom the accountant is in privity or near privity, but also to those persons, or classes of persons, whom he knows and intends will rely on his opinion, or whom he knows his client intends will so rely. On the other hand, as the commentary to section 552 makes clear, it prevents extension of liability in situations where the accountant "merely knows of the ever-present possibility of repetition to anyone, and the possibility of action in reliance upon [the audited financial statements], on the part of anyone to whom it may be repeated." *Restatement (Second) of Torts* section 552, comment h. As such it balances the need to hold accountants to a standard that accounts for their contemporary role in the financial world with the need to protect them from liability that unreasonably exceeds the bounds of their real undertaking.

Under this approach, in order for an auditor to be held liable to a third party, that party must demonstrate: (1) the accountant either (a) knew that the third party would rely on this information, or (b) knew that the client for whom the audit report was prepared intended to supply the information to a third party who would rely on this information; and (2) the third party justifiably relied upon this information in its decision concerning the transaction involved or one substantially similar to it. In adopting this rule, in *Raritan* this Court rejected as too expansive the position that extends liability to all persons the accountant should reasonably foresee might obtain and rely on the information generated. Further, the Court held:

> We reject the . . . "privity or near-privity" approach . . . because it provides inadequately for the central role independent accountants play in the financial world. Accountants' audit opinions are increasingly relied upon by the investing and lending public in making financial decisions. *Raritan,* 367 S.E.2d at 615.

First, we must determine whether the evidence presented is sufficient to create a genuine issue of material fact that Price Waterhouse knew either that Marcus Brothers would rely on the 1992 audited financial statements in its decision to extend credit to Piece Goods, or that Piece Goods would supply the information to Marcus Brothers intending Marcus Brothers would rely on this information in its decision to extend credit to Piece Goods.

In support of its case, Marcus Brothers cites numerous circumstances which indicate genuine issues of material fact as to the knowledge element. First, there is unrefuted testimony that Piece Goods had been a client of Price Waterhouse since 1986. In addition, there is deposition testimony from James J. Quinn, Director of Corporate Credit for Marcus Brothers, indicating that Piece Goods had been sending its audited financial statements to Marcus Brothers since 1983, and that these financial statements were regularly used in determining whether to extend credit to Piece Goods. Price Waterhouse's own internal 1989 memorandum states that "Price Waterhouse has historically reported on the financial statements of Piece Goods, and . . . vendors . . . are accustomed to receiving Piece Goods' financial statements." Further, deposition testimony from Robert Allen Smith, an audit partner for Price Waterhouse who signed off on the 1989 internal memorandum, indicates that some of Price Waterhouse's clients "typically provide" their audited financial statements to trade creditors in reference to obtaining loans or extensions of credit. There is further deposition testimony from Karen C. Frazier, an audit manager for Price Waterhouse who oversaw the audit of Piece Goods' 1992 financial statements, which indicates that audited financial statements are "used by the management of the company and possibly outsiders," and that such outsiders "could" include trade creditors such as Marcus Brothers. Marcus Brothers further cites the fact that the sixth largest check on a handwritten list of fifty "held checks" in Price Waterhouse's 1992 Piece Goods audit file is a check to Marcus Brothers in the amount of $291,337.78. Finally, Piece Goods' 1993 bankruptcy filing revealed that forty-three trade creditors had received copies of Piece Goods' audited financial statements, including Marcus Brothers.

In *Raritan,* this Court, as previously noted, adopted the *Restatement (Second) of Torts* section 552. Included in the commentary to section 552 is illustration 10 under comment h, which provides:

> A, an independent public accountant, is retained by B Company to conduct an annual audit of the customary scope for the corporation and to furnish his opinion on the corporation's financial statements. A is not informed of any intended use of the financial statements; but A knows that the financial statements, accompanied by an auditor's opinion, are customarily used in a variety of financial transactions by the corporation and that they may be relied upon by lenders, investors . . . and the like . . . In fact B Company uses the financial statements and accompanying auditor's opinion to obtain a loan from X Bank. Because of A's negligence, he issues an unqualifiedly favorable opinion upon a balance sheet that materially misstates the financial position of B Company, and through reliance upon it X Bank suffers pecuniary loss. A is not liable to X Bank.

Some confusion arises due to illustration 10 under comment h. This illustration has been read by some to mean that liability turns on whether the accountant's client specifically mentions a person or class of persons who are to receive the audited financial statements.

The *Restatement*'s text does not demand that the accountant be informed by the client himself of the audit report's intended use. The text requires only that the auditor know that his client intends to supply information to another person or limited group of persons. Whether the auditor acquires this knowledge from his client or elsewhere should make no difference. If he knows at the time he prepares his report that specific persons, or a limited group of persons, will rely on his work, and intends or knows that his client intends such reliance, his duty of care should extend to them.

The facts of the instant case are distinguishable from *Raritan* and illustration 10. In *Raritan Steel Co. v. Cherry, Bekaert & Holland,* 407 S.E.2d 178 (1991) (*Raritan II*), this Court noted that the third-party creditor did not see the audit but reviewed a summary of it published in a Dun & Bradstreet report, which apparently overstated the corporation's actual financial position. Allegedly, on the basis of the Dun & Bradstreet summary of the audit, the trade creditor extended additional open credit to the corporation, which later filed for bankruptcy. It is interesting to note that the accounting firm's engagement letter to the client provided: "If we discover that we cannot issue an unqualified opinion, we will discuss the reasons with you before submitting a different kind of report. . . . Our basic audit function is to add reliability to those financial statements." The Dun & Bradstreet report, which also contained other summarized financial information, was the only access that the third-party creditor had to the corporation financial statements. The creditor was not even aware that the audit was being performed.

As illustration 10 clearly states, A was not informed of any intended use of the financial statements. In the light most favorable to Marcus Brothers, there are genuine issues of material fact as to whether Price Waterhouse was informed of any intended use of the financial statements. Illustration 10 further states: "But A knows that the financial statements, accompanied by an auditor's opinion, are customarily used in a variety of financial transactions by the corporation and that they may be relied upon by lenders. . . ." In the instant case, the circumstances surrounding Price Waterhouse's knowledge raise issues of material fact that rise above the level of "customarily used."

At this stage of the proceedings, we conclude it can reasonably be inferred that Price Waterhouse knew Piece Goods regularly provided copies of its financial statements to a limited group of major trade creditors, of which group Marcus Brothers was a member.

Next we must determine whether the evidence presented is sufficient to create a genuine issue of material fact with regard to the second element of negligent misrepresentation, that is, Marcus Brothers' justifiable reliance upon the 1992 audited financial statements in its decision to extend credit to Piece Goods.

Marcus Brothers alleged and made a forecast of evidence that it made several extensions of credit to Piece Goods in reliance upon the audited 1992 financial statement. Whether Marcus Brothers justifiably relied on the $30,332,000 receivable from a Piece Goods general partner, the accompanying interest, and current inventory are questions of fact for a jury to determine. We conclude that Marcus Brothers presented a sufficient forecast of evidence to meet this element.

Judgment for Marcus Brothers affirmed.

Mitchell, Chief Justice, Dissenting   I do not believe that plaintiff Marcus Brothers forecast substantial evidence tending to show that defendant Price Waterhouse knew that the audited 1992 financial statements of Piece Goods would be provided to Marcus Brothers or a limited group of creditors of which Marcus Brothers was a member. Accordingly, I respectfully dissent from the decision of the majority.

The "actual knowledge" standard controlling an accountant's liability to a third party non-client for negligent misrepresentation of the financial statements of the accountant's client was established by this Court in *Raritan.* In adopting the actual knowledge standard, this Court expressly rejected the "reasonably foreseeable" standard, "because it would result in liability more expansive than an accountant should be expected to bear." Therefore, we have rejected the notion that an accountant's liability may be extended in cases such as the present case to all persons that the accountant could reasonably foresee might obtain and rely on his work. Thus, the proper standard is not what the accountant reasonably should have known, but what the accountant in fact knew.

In adopting the actual knowledge standard in *Raritan,* this Court expressly relied upon the rationale of section 552 of the *Restatement (Second) of Torts.* We explained that rationale as follows:

An accountant who audits or prepares financial information for a client owes a duty of care not only to the client but to any other person, or one of a group of persons, whom the accountant or his client intends the information to benefit; and that person reasonably relies on the information in a transaction, or one substantially similar to it, that the accountant or his client intends the information to influence. If the requisite intent is that of the client and not the accountant, then the accountant must know of his client's intent at the time the accountant audits or prepares the information.

We also explained in *Raritan* that if an accountant knows at the time he prepares his report that specific persons, or a limited group of persons, will rely on his work, and intends or knows that his client intends such reliance, his duty of care should extend to them.

Here, no evidence whatsoever was forecast tending to show that Price Waterhouse itself intended to influence plaintiff Marcus Brothers. Therefore, the issue presented by this case is whether Price Waterhouse knew of Piece Goods' intent to provide Marcus Brothers with the 1992 financial statements for the purpose of influencing Marcus Brothers, or a limited group including Marcus Brothers, in the transactions at issue in this case or in substantially similar transactions. I find nothing in the evidence to support a reasonable fact finder in finding that defendant Price Waterhouse possessed such actual knowledge at the time it performed the work in question for Piece Goods.

At most, the evidence forecast before the trial court and set forth by the majority in its opinion here might support a finding that Price Waterhouse could reasonably have foreseen that Marcus Brothers or an indeterminate group of persons including Marcus Brothers would rely on its work and that Piece Goods intended such reliance. However, the forecast of evidence relied upon by the majority does no more than raise suspicion or conjecture as to the determinative issue before this Court—whether defendant Price Waterhouse actually knew that Marcus Brothers or a limited group including Marcus Brothers would rely on its work and that its

client Piece Goods intended such reliance. Even if it is assumed arguendo that defendant Price Waterhouse had knowledge from which it could reasonably have foreseen that its work would be relied on by an unlimited group of potential trade creditors of Piece Goods, this fact would not suffice to defeat defendant Price Waterhouse's motion for summary judgment.

It is instructive that Judge Cardozo, the architect of reasonable foreseeability as the touchstone for products liability, declined to adopt the same standard for accountants' liability in *Ultramares*. Judge Cardozo distinguished accountants from manufacturers because of the potential for excessive accountants' liability. He wrote that if accountants could be held liable for negligence by those who were not in privity, or nearly in privity, accountants would face "liability in an indeterminate amount for an indeterminate time to an indeterminate class." *Ultramares Corp. v. Touche, Niven & Co.*, 174 N.E. 441, 444 (1931). Because of this potential for inordinate liability Judge Cardozo concluded, as do we, that accountants should be held liable to a narrower class of plaintiffs than the class embraced by the reasonable foreseeability test.

Although I am certain beyond all doubt that the majority has attempted in good faith to apply the actual knowledge test required by *Raritan,* its decision in this case allows a forecast of evidence to suffice which at best meets the reasonably foreseeable standard expressly rejected in *Raritan*. The result is to subject accountants such as Price Waterhouse to liability to an indeterminate class, for an indeterminate time, in an indeterminate amount, despite Judge Cardozo's warning and this Court's expressly stated desire in *Raritan* to avoid any such result. Therefore, I must respectfully dissent.

Fraud

Fraud is such reprehensible conduct that all courts have extended a professional's liability for fraud to all foreseeable users of his work product who suffered damages that were proximately caused by the fraud. Privity of contract, therefore, is not required when a person sues a professional for fraud, even in a state that has adopted the *Ultramares* test for negligence actions. To prove fraud, a nonclient must establish that a professional acted with scienter.

Some courts recognize a tort called constructive fraud that applies when a professional misstates a material fact. For a misstatement to amount to constructive fraud, the professional must have recklessly or grossly negligently failed to ascertain the truth of the statement. As with actual fraud, a professional's liability for constructive fraud extends to all persons who justifiably rely on the misstatement.

Common Law Bases of Liability of Professional to Nonclients for Use of Professional's Work Product

Privity Test Adopted by State	Basis of Liability	
	Negligence	**Fraud**
Primary Benefit Test (*Ultramares*)	Professional liable only to foreseen users (professional knew name of user and purpose of the user's use)	Regardless of test adopted, professional liable to all persons whose damages were caused by their reliance on professional's fraud
Restatement (Second) of Torts Test	Professional liable to foreseen users and users in a foreseen class of users (professional knew at least the purpose of the user's use)	
Foreseeable Users Test	Professional liable to all reasonably foreseeable users (professional can reasonably expect or foresee the purpose of the user's use)	

Professional's Liability to Third Parties: Securities Law

The slow reaction of the common law in creating a negligence remedy for third parties has led to an increased use of securities law by nonclients—that is, persons not in privity with a professional. Many liability sections in these statutes either eliminate the privity requirement or expansively define privity.

Securities Act of 1933

There are several liability sections under the Securities Act of 1933 (1933 Act). The most important liability section of the Securities Act of 1933 is Section 11, but Sections 12(a)(2) and 17(a) are also important, especially for securities professionals.

Section 11 Liability Section 11 imposes liability on underwriters and experts for misstatements or omissions of material fact in Securities Act registration statements. The 1933 Act registration statement must be filed with the Securities and Exchange Commission by an issuer making a public distribution of securities. The most common expert is an auditor who issues an opin-

ion regarding financial statements. An underwriter, although knowledgeable, skillful, and experienced in securities offerings, is not an "expert" under section 11.

An auditor or underwriter is liable to any purchaser of securities issued pursuant to a defective registration statement. The purchaser need not establish privity of contract with an underwriter or auditor. Because the underwriter is not an expert under section 11, the underwriter is liable for errors in the entire registration statement. Since an auditor is an expert, the auditor is liable only for the part of the registration statement contributed by the auditor, that is, the auditor's opinion regarding the audited financial statements and those audited financial statements. Usually, the purchaser need not prove he relied on the misstated or omitted material fact; he need not even have read or seen the defective financial statement.

For example, an auditor issues an unqualified opinion regarding a client's income statement that overstates net income by 85 percent. The defective income statement is included in the client's registration statement pursuant to which the client sells its preferred shares. Without reading the registration statement or the income statement, a person buys from the client 100 preferred shares for $105 per share. After the correct income figure is released, the price of the shares drops to $25 per share. The auditor will most likely be liable to the purchaser for $8,000, unless the auditor proves the purchaser's damages were caused by other persons or factors.

Under Section 11, auditors and underwriters may escape liability by proving that they exercised due diligence. For auditors, who are experts, this **due diligence defense** requires that an auditor issuing an opinion regarding financial statements prove that she made a reasonable investigation and that she reasonably believed that there were no misstatements or omissions of material fact in the financial statements at the time the registration statement became effective. Because the effective date is often several months after an audit has been completed, an auditor must perform an additional review of the audited statements to ensure that the statements are accurate as of the effective date. In essence, due diligence means that an auditor was not negligent, which is usually proved by showing that she complied with GAAS and GAAP.

For underwriters, who are liable for the entire registration statement, the due diligence defense varies depending on the part of the registration statement. For parts of the registration statement contributed by experts (so-called expertised portions, such as an auditor's opinion and the financial statements covered by that opinion), underwriters are entitled to rely on the expert. Therefore, the underwriter's due diligence defense for errors in audited financial statements generally requires no independent investigation by the underwriter. The underwriter will have no liability for mistakes in an expertised portion if the underwriter had no reason to believe and did not believe that there were any misstatements or omissions of material fact in the audited financial statements. If, however, the underwriter has information leading her to believe that an audited financial statement misstates or omits material facts, she has a duty to investigate until she no longer has that belief and no longer has a reason to have that belief.

For errors in parts of the registration statement not contributed by experts (the nonexpertised portion), the underwriter's defense is that after a reasonable investigation, she had a reasonable belief that there were no misstatements or omissions of material fact in those parts. The nonexpertised portion constitutes the bulk of the registration statement and includes the description of the securities, the statement of the underwriter's compensation, the use of the proceeds of the securities issuance, the description of the issuer's business, the statement of the securities' material risks, and unaudited financial statements.

Standards for complying with the due diligence defense are explained more fully in *Escott v. BarChris Construction Corp.*, which appears in Chapter 45, Securities Regulation.

Section 12(a)(2) Section 12(a)(2) imposes liability on any person who misstates or omits a material fact in connection with an offer or sale of a security that is part of a general distribution of securities by an issuer. Privity of contract between the plaintiff and the defendant apparently is required, because Section 12(a)(2) states that the defendant is liable to the person *purchasing* the security *from him.*

Under Section 12(a)(2), a defendant must have direct contact with a buyer of a security to be liable. Merely performing professional services, such as auditing financial statements, is not enough for Section 12(a)(2) liability. A person must actively solicit the sale, motivated at least by a desire to serve his own financial interest. Such a financial interest is unlikely to be met by an auditor whose compensation is a fee unconnected to the proceeds of the securities sale. In addition, the *Central Bank* case makes it fairly clear that auditors who merely *aid and abet* a client's Section 12(a)(2) violation will not have liability under Section 12(a)(2).

Securities professionals have a greater risk of liability under Section 12(a)(2), because they frequently have direct contact with purchasers. Underwriters helping clients with public offerings sell securities or at least actively solicit sales by speaking with investors and writing the prospectus or other offering document. Since underwriters receive compensation for their services in the form of a commission or a spread (the difference between the amount underwriters pay the issuer and the price they sell at), they have the requisite financial stake in the sale. Securities brokers and dealers also are sellers or actively solicit securities sales and have a financial stake in the sale when they assist issuer distributions of securities and receive a commission or spread.

In the event that a person has sufficient contact with a purchaser to incur Section 12(a)(2) liability, the defendant may escape liability by proving that she did not know and could not reasonably have known of the untruth or omission; that is, she must prove that she was not negligent.

Section 17(a) Under Section 17(a), a purchaser of a security must prove his reliance on a misstatement or omission of material fact for which an accountant or securities professional is responsible. Under two of the subsections of Section 17(a), the investor need prove only negligence by the accountant, underwriter, broker, or adviser. Under the third, the investor must prove the accountant or securities professional acted with scienter. Whether there is a private right of action for damages under Section 17(a) is unclear. The courts of appeals are in disagreement, and the Supreme Court has not ruled on the issue.

Securities Exchange Act of 1934

Two sections of the 1934 Act—Section 18 and Section 10(b)—especially affect the liability of professionals to nonclients.

Section 18   Section 18 of the 1934 Act imposes liability on persons who furnish misleading and false statements of material fact in any report or document filed with the Securities and Exchange Commission under the 1934 Act. Such reports or documents include the annual 10-K report—which includes auditors' opinions regarding financial statements—the monthly 8-K report, and proxy statements.

Under Section 18, a purchaser or seller of a security may sue an auditor if he relied on the defective statement in the filed document and it caused his damages. Usually, this means that a plaintiff must have *read and relied* on the defective statement in the filed document. The purchaser or seller may sue the auditor even if they are not in privity of contract.

An auditor may escape Section 18 liability by proving that she acted in *good faith* and had *no knowledge* that the information was misleading. That is, she must show that she acted *without scienter*. For this reason, as well as the difficulty of proving reliance, Section 18 liability for auditors is extremely rare.

Although securities professionals, such as brokers and dealers, may file reports under the 1934 Act, those documents are not the type normally used by investors making investment decisions. Section 18 liability is, therefore, not an issue for securities professionals.

Section 10(b) and Rule 10b-5   Securities Exchange Act Rule 10b-5, pursuant to Section 10(b), has been the basis for most of the recent suits investors have brought against auditors and securities professionals. Rule 10b-5 prohibits any person from making a misstatement or omission of material fact in connection with the purchase or sale of any security. Rule 10b-5 applies to misstatements or omissions in any communications with investors, including the use of audited financial statements resulting in a purchase or sale of a security. The wrongful act must have a connection with interstate commerce, the mails, or a national securities exchange.

A purchaser or seller of a security may sue an auditor, underwriter, or broker who has misstated or omitted a material fact. Privity is not required. The purchaser or seller must rely on the misstatement or omission. In omission cases, reliance may be inferred from materiality.

In addition, the defendant must act with scienter. In this context, scienter is an intent to deceive, manipulate, or defraud. Negligence is not enough.

Aiding and Abetting   Until recently, a common way investors held an auditor liable under Rule 10b-5 was to prove that the auditor aided and abetted a client's fraud. Most courts had recognized aiding and abetting liability under Rule 10b-5 by requiring (1) a primary violation by another person (such as a client fraudulently overstating its earnings), (2) the person's knowledge of the primary violation, and (3) the person's substantial assistance in the achievement of the primary violation (such as an auditor's failure to disclose a client's fraud known to the auditor.).

In 1994 in the *Central Bank* case that is mentioned in the next case (*Anixter*), the Supreme Court of the United States held that those who merely aid and abet Rule 10b–5 violations have no liability to those injured by the fraud. The court drew a distinction between those **primarily** responsible for the fraud—who retain Rule 10b–5 liability—and those **secondarily** responsible—who no longer have liability under Rule 10b–5. The distinction between primary and secondary responsibility is unclear. Issuing unqualified opinions regarding false financial statements is primary fault and would impose Rule 10b–5 liability on the auditor. However, an independent accountant's work in connection with false unaudited statements or other financial information released by a client may be only secondary and may not impose Rule 10b-5 liability on the accountant.

Although auditors are not liable to private litigants for merely secondary activities, Congress has made it clear that the SEC may prosecute accountants for aiding and abetting a client's violation of Rule 10b–5. Even so, the risk of liability is slight, because Rule 10b–5 liability is imposed only on those who act with scienter.

Securities professionals may be primarily responsible for misstatements or omissions of material facts in a variety of contexts, and therefore may have Rule 10b–5 liability to nonclients and clients. For example, an underwriter who drafts an offering memorandum for a client's Rule 506 securities offering is primarily responsible for that document, as well as oral statements the underwriter makes about the issuer and the securities to a prospective investor. Securities brokers may have Rule 10b–5 liability for churning their clients' accounts to generate high commissions for the broker. In addition, brokers may have liability under Rule 10b–5 for giving fraudulent

CONCEPT REVIEW

Liability Sections of the 1933 Act and 1934 Act

	Wrongful Conduct	Covered Communications	Who May Sue?	Must the Plaintiff Prove Reliance on the Wrongful Conduct?
Securities Act of 1933 Section 11	Misstatement or omission of material fact	1933 Act registration statement only	Any purchaser of securities issued pursuant to the registration statement	No
Securities Act of 1933 Section 12(a)(2)	Misstatement or omission of material fact	Any communication in connection with a general distribution of securities by an issuer (except government issued or guaranteed securities)	Any purchaser of the securities offered or sold	No
Securities Act of 1933 Section 17(a)	Misstatement or omission of material fact	Any communication in connection with any offer to sell or sale of any security	Any purchaser of the securities offered or sold	Yes
Securities Exchange Act of 1934 Section 10(b) and Rule 10b-5	Misstatement or omission of material fact	Any communication in connection with a purchase or sale of any security	Any purchaser or seller of the securities	Yes
Securities Exchange Act of 1934 Section 18	False or misleading statement of material fact	Any document filed with the SEC under the 1934 Act (includes the 1934 Act registration statement, 10-K, 8-K, and proxy statements)	Any purchaser or seller of a security whose price was affected by the statement	Yes

CONCEPT REVIEW

Who May Be Sued?	Must the Plaintiff and Defendant Be in Privity of Contract?	Defendant's Level of Fault	Who Has the Burden of Proving or Disproving Defendant's Level of Fault?
Issuer, underwriters, directors, signers (CEO, CFO, and CAO must sign), and experts who contribute to the registration statement (such as auditors of financial statements)	No	Negligence, except for the issuer. Issuer is liable without regard to fault.	Defendant, except issuer, may escape liability by proving due diligence. The exact defense varies, but for most defendants for most parts of the registration statement, the defense is that he made a reasonable investigation and had reason to believe and did believe there were no misstatements or omissions of material fact
Any person who sells a security or actively solicits a sale of a security	Yes (although met by a defendant who has a financial interest in a sale of securities)	Negligence	Defendant may escape liability by proving he did not know and could not reasonably have known of the misstatement or omission of material fact
Any person responsible for the misstatement or omission	No	Negligence for some parts of Section 17(a); scienter for one part	Plaintiff must prove the defendant acted negligently or with scienter, depending on the subsection
Any person primarily responsible for the misstatement or omission	No, but defendant must communicate with the plaintiff or know or should know plaintiff will receive the communication with the misstatement or omission	Scienter	Plaintiff must prove the defendant acted with scienter
Any person who made or caused the statement to be made	No	Scienter	Defendant may escape liability by proving he acted in good faith with no knowledge that the statement was false or misleading

advice to clients. Such cases are difficult to prove, as illustrated in *Carr v. CIGNA Securities, Inc.*, which appears in Chapter 45, Securities Regulation, at page 1011.

Extent of Liability The Private Securities Litigation Reform Act of 1995 limits the liability of most auditors and securities professionals to the amount of an investor's loss for which the defendant is responsible. This means that a defendant has *proportionate liability* and need no longer fear being liable for investors' entire losses when a fraudulent client is

unable to pay its share of the damages. The determination of the percentage of the loss for which a defendant is responsible is a question for the jury. Note, however, the Reform Act provides that when a person knowingly commits a violation of the securities laws, the defendant may be required to pay an investor's entire loss.

The following *Anixter* case explores the distinction between an auditor's primary violation of Section 10(b) and an auditor's merely aiding and abetting a client's violation of Section 10(b).

Anixter v. Home-Stake Production Co.   *77 F.3d 1215 (10th Cir. 1996)*

More than 30 years ago, Home-Stake Production Company began offering securities registered with the Securities and Exchange Commission in the form of interests in oil and gas drilling programs. The securities represented units of participation in annual oil production subsidiaries Home-Stake established each year between 1964 and 1972, referred to as Program Operating Corporations (Programs). These offerings purported to present investors both the promise of return on investment and attractive tax deductions of intangible drilling costs. In fact, the Home-Stake venture resembled a classic Ponzi swindle. Instead of going to oil development, investments made in later-year Programs were paid to earlier-year investors as "income" from oil production. The scheme collapsed after investors had lost tens of millions of dollars.

From 1968 to 1971, Home-Stake's independent auditor was Norman Cross. Cross prepared documents used by Home-Stake, consented to have his name appear in registration statements filed with the SEC, and issued unqualified opinions regarding Home-Stake's financial statements. Cross prepared Home-Stake's consolidated financial statements for 1968 and 1969. He also prepared the start-up balance sheets for the 1969 and 1970 Programs, which were included in the 1969 and 1970 Program registration statements and prospectuses. The registration statements and attached prospectuses were filed with the SEC. Cross consented to the use of his reports on the 1969 and 1970 Program balance sheets in the SEC filings.

Cross also provided Home-Stake with opinions on the 1969 and 1970 Programs' beginning balance sheet he prepared. These opinions were also contained in the registration statements and prospectuses filed with the SEC. Cross also provided opinion letters for Home-Stake's consolidated financial statements for 1968–70. The opinion letters for Home-Stake's financial statements, addressed to the Home-Stake board of directors, were included in Home-Stake's 1969 and 1970 annual reports but were not included in the Program prospectuses or registration statements.

In 1969 and 1970, Home-Stake also published and mailed to Program participants documents known as "Program Books" or "Black Books." These documents, which included descriptions of specific oil recovery programs and estimates of anticipated returns, were not filed with the SEC and contained information inconsistent with or contradicting the prospectuses. Home-Stake's financial statements, audited by Cross, also were included either with the Program Books or as part of Home-Stake's sales kit. The Program Books and sales kits were the primary methods of marketing Program units; the SEC-filed prospectuses were made available to investors only upon request.

Finally, Cross was also involved in the prospectus for a rescission offer made to investors in the 1970 program. In 1971, the SEC filed a complaint against Home-Stake in federal district court, alleging that its officers and directors failed to meet information requirements to investors and misstated the use of investments in the 1970 Program. As part of a consent decree entered into with the SEC, Home-Stake made a rescission offer to its 1970 Program investors. The offer documents included a Rescission Offer Prospectus. The Rescission Offer Prospectus itself failed to disclose material facts. Cross prepared an opinion on Home-Stake's 1970 consolidated financial statement and an opinion on the beginning balance sheet of the 1970 Program, included as part of the 1970 Rescission Offer Registration Statement.

In March 1973, purchasers of interests in the programs, including Ivan Anixter, filed lawsuits against Home-Stake, its officers, its outside lawyers, Cross, and brokers who sold the interests, alleging violations of Section 10(b) and Rule 10b-5 of *the Securities Exchange Act of 1934. The case went to trial in 1988, and Anixter and the other investors won jury verdicts totaling over $40 million. Cross appealed on the grounds that the court improperly instructed the jury that it could find him liable under Rule 10b-5 as an aider and abettor; he also claimed that he had not acted with scienter.*

Lucero, Circuit Judge This securities fraud case, first filed in 1973, already has been the subject of four published opinions by this court. Over the past four years it has been ordered dismissed, reinstated, remanded, and now, appealed once more.

We must resolve whether again to dismiss or remand judgments against Home-Stake's outside auditor for violating Section 10(b) of the Securities Exchange Act of 1934. The question dominating our review is whether we can let stand a general jury verdict returned on a securities fraud claim that included an instruction on aiding and abetting liability, an implied cause of action that has since been found invalid by the Supreme Court in *Central Bank of Denver* (1994). In the balance is a choice between a jury award plaintiffs won on claims filed more than 22 years ago, and maintaining judgments now totalling more than $40 million when the jury may have found liability on an invalid legal theory. We conclude the aiding and abetting instruction hopelessly taints the general verdict and that remand for a new trial is necessary.

We must first consider what acts make up a "primary" violation of Section 10(b), and how they differ from those that could be characterized only as "aiding and abetting." Unfortunately, deciding when conduct constituting aiding and abetting rises to the level of prohibited primary conduct is not well settled.

Cross argues that none of his acts constituted fraudulent misrepresentations or omissions relied on by investing plaintiffs; at most the acts only aided Home-Stake in committing the alleged fraud. Anixter points to Cross's opinion letters as evidence that Cross himself made misrepresentations or omissions sufficient to subject him to primary liability.

To establish a primary liability claim under Section 10(b), a plaintiff must prove the following facts: (1) that the defendant made an untrue statement of material fact, or failed to state a material fact; (2) that the conduct occurred in connection with the purchase or sale of a security; (3) that the defendant made the statement or omission with scienter; and (4) that plaintiff relied on the misrepresentation, and sustained damages as a proximate result of the misrepresentation. This contrasts with aider and abettor liability, which required plaintiff to prove (1) the existence of a primary violation of the securities laws by another; (2) knowledge of the primary violation by the alleged aider and abettor; and

(3) substantial assistance by the alleged aider and abettor in achieving the primary violation. The critical element separating primary from aiding and abetting violations is the existence of a representation, either by statement or omission, made by the defendant, that is relied upon by the plaintiff. Reliance only on representations made by others cannot itself form the basis of liability.

Clearly, accountants may make representations in their role as auditor to a firm selling securities. Typical representations include issuing unqualified opinions regarding financial statements and other opinion letters. An accountant's false and misleading representations in connection with the purchase or sale of any security, if made with the proper state of mind and if relied upon by those purchasing or selling a security, can constitute a primary violation. There is no requirement that the alleged violator directly communicated misrepresentations to plaintiffs for primary liability to attach. Nevertheless, for an accountant's misrepresentation to be actionable as a primary violation, there must be a showing that he knew or should have known that his representation would be communicated to investors because Section 10(b) and Rule 10b-5 focus on fraud made "in connection with the sale or purchase" of a security.

Reading the language of Section 10(b) and 10b–5 through the lens of *Central Bank of Denver,* we conclude that in order for accountants to "use or employ" a "deception" actionable under the antifraud law, they must themselves make a false or misleading statement (or omission) that they know or should know will reach potential investors. In addition to being consistent with the language of the statute, this rule, though far from a bright line, provides more guidance to litigants than a rule allowing liability to attach to an accountant or other outside professional who provided "significant" or "substantial" assistance to the representations of others.

The record in this case contains much evidence that could sustain a finding of primary liability. Most of Anixter's arguments went to representations Cross made as Home-Stake's auditor. He issued opinions on the 1969 and 1970 Program's start up balance sheets. He issued unqualified opinions regarding Home-Stake's Consolidated financial statements for those years. Cross's opinions letters were reproduced in prospectuses, annual reports, registration statements, and other Home-Stake promotional material. The jury could have concluded that any or all of these representations were false and misleading, that Cross was reckless in making the representations, and that Cross knew or should have known that his representations would reach potential investors and that they would reasonably rely on them.

Although the record supports finding Cross liable for a primary violation of Section 10(b), we still must determine whether the jury *did* find him liable as a primary violator. Cross urges us to remand for a new trial on the theory that it is not clear from the jury verdict whether his liability under Rule 10b-5 rested on finding a primary or aiding and abetting violation.

It is obvious from our discussion analyzing accountant behavior under Section 10(b) that distinctions in conduct between primary and secondary liability are elusive. The verdicts shed no light on whether the jury found Cross liable of his substantial assistance to Home-Stake's independent fraudulent acts, or whether his liability rests on actual representations he made that reached investors. The chances that the jury was confused by the aiding and abetting instructions cannot be dismissed as remote—and require us to remand.

Cross argues that remand is unnecessary, and that we should reverse the judgment because he only acted recklessly with respect to the Home-Stake fraud, and reckless-

ness does not satisfy the scienter requirement for liability in a civil action under Section 10(b). The district court correctly rejected this argument.

In *Ernst & Ernst v. Hochfelder* (1976), the Supreme Court expressly declined to address "the question whether, in some circumstances, reckless behavior is sufficient for civil liability under Section 10(b) and Rule 10b-5." The Supreme Court has still not spoken on this question. In *Hackbart v. Holmes* (1982) this court held that "recklessness" satisfies the scienter requirement for a primary violation of Section 10(b). We defined "recklessness" as "conduct that is an extreme departure from the standards of ordinary care, and which presents a danger of misleading buyers or sellers that is either known to the defendant or is so obvious that the actor must have been aware of it."

This circuit still maintains that recklessness as defined in *Hackbart* is sufficient scienter for finding civil Section 10(b) primary violations.

This is a very old case, and it is with a heavy heart that we act to prolong it. Our decision, however, is mandated by a supervening change in the law of securities fraud.

Judgment reversed in favor of Cross; remanded to the trial court.

THE GLOBAL BUSINESS ENVIRONMENT

Global Internet Offerings

In a world linked by e-mail and the Internet, local offerings of securities can become international and attract the interest of securities regulators in countries

whose citizens access a foreign securities offering website. When a foreign issuer does not register its issuance with the SEC in the United States, the issuer or a securities broker must make sure that offering materials are not sent to American investors. When offering information is sent by e-mail, there is a clear violation. When a securities offering is made on a Web page, it may be difficult to determine whether the securities offering was sent to American investors. An SEC release attempts to clarify the matter by stating that Web offerings will not come under U.S. regulation as long as the broker takes precautionary measures that are "reasonably designed to ensure that offshore Internet offers are not targeted" at the American investors. In practice, the Internet makes it difficult to discern what constitutes targeting U.S. investors. However,

the SEC provides a safe harbor for foreign brokers by allowing them to post a conspicuous disclaimer on the website either listing the countries in which the broker's services are available or stating that the services are not available to American investors.

In the United Kingdom, the Financial Services Authority (FSA) has strict provisions for the treatment of material on overseas websites that is accessible in the U.K. but not intended for U.K. investors. The law states that any Web offering will fall within the definition of restricted activities in the UK if it contains any unauthorized invitation to buy securities. Unlike U.S. law, U.K. law provides that conspicuous disclaimers by themselves are insufficient to stop an investment advertisement from being made available to U.K. investors. In Australia, the Securities and Investments Commission issued a policy statement that Australian law covers investments that target people in Australia or operate within Australia. Therefore, Australian securities law does not regulate offshore offerings that do not affect Australians.

ETHICS IN ACTION

Securities Analysts' Conflicts of Interest

For years, investors have known that stock recommendations and research reports by securities analysts in major investment banking firms are almost always overly optimistic. Few analysts have recommended that investors sell a stock. Almost all recommendations are strong buy, buy, or accumulate with a few hold recommendations sprinkled in. The reasons for such optimism vary from an unwillingness to say anything bad to a belief that a bull market will sustain rising securities prices. But the reason that caught the attention of securities regulators is that analysts may have a conflict of interest. The belief is that full-service investment firms that have securities research, brokerage, and investment banking departments discourage their securities analysts from giving poor recommendations for a public company's stock for fear that a poor recommendation will offend the company's management and cause the company to award valuable investment banking business to a more cooperative investment firm. Some investment firms even threatened to lower public companies' stock recommendations unless the companies awarded investment banking business to the firms.

The Sarbanes–Oxley Act of 2002 directed the SEC to adopt or to direct the national securities exchanges and NASD to adopt rules to address research analysts' conflicts of interest. The Act requires the rules to accomplish the following:

- Restrict prepublication approval of analysts' research reports by investment banking or other nonresearch personnel in the firm;

- Limit supervision and evaluation of securities analysts' compensation to persons not in the investment banking side of the firm;
- Prohibit investment banking personnel from retaliating against a securities analyst because of a negative research report;
- Set time periods during which firms involved in an underwriting of public issuances may not publish research reports about the issuer and its securities;
- Place information partitions to separate research analysts from review, pressure, or oversight by those whose investment banking activities might bias their judgment;
- Require securities analysts to disclose in public appearances and research reports any conflict of interest, including whether the analyst owns the issuer's securities, whether compensation has been received by the firm or analyst, and whether the issuer is currently or has been a client of the firm in the last year.

Two days after Sarbanes–Oxley was adopted, the SEC proposed Regulation AC (Analyst Certification). Although not designed to implement the requirements of the Act, Regulation AC would require an analyst's research report to include the analyst's certification that the views expressed in the report accurately reflect her personal views.

The NASD and the NYSE also passed rules on analysts' conflicts of interest prior to passage of Sarbanes–Oxley. The rules are substantially similar. They ban favorable research for pay, prohibit analyst compensation based on specific investment banking services, and limit the submission of a research report to an issuer prior to publication of the report.

State Securities Law

All states have securities statutes with liability sections. Most of the states have a liability section similar to Section 12(a)(2) of the Securities Act.

Limiting Professionals' Liability: Professional Corporations and Limited Liability Partnerships

Every state permits professionals to incorporate their business under a professional incorporation statute.

While there are significant taxation advantages to incorporation, the principal advantage of incorporation—

limited liability of the shareholders—does not isolate professionals from liability for professional misconduct. For example, an accountant who injures his client by failing to act as the ordinarily prudent accountant would act has liability to his client, despite the incorporation of the accountant's business.

When two or more professionals conduct business as co-owners, incorporation may offer them limited liability. While partners in a partnership are jointly and severally liable for each other's negligence, states permit incorporated professionals to escape liability for their associate's torts, unless the professional actually supervised the wrongdoing associate or participated in the tort.

Reacting to the large personal liability sometimes imposed on lawyers and accountants for the professional malpractice of their partners, Texas enacted in 1991 the first statute permitting the formation of limited liability partnerships (LLP). An LLP is similar to a partnership, except that a partner's liability for his partners' professional malpractice is limited to the partnership's assets, unless the partner supervised the work of the wrongdoing partner. A partner retains unlimited liability for his *own* malpractice and, in some states, for all *non*professional obligations of the partnership.

Nearly every state and the District of Columbia have passed LLP statutes. The LLP has become the preferred form of business for professionals who do not incorporate.

For more information on the limited liability partnership, see Chapters 37–39.

Qualified Opinions, Disclaimers of Opinion, Adverse Opinions, and Unaudited Statements

After performing an audit of financial statements, an independent auditor issues an opinion letter regarding the financial statements. The **opinion letter** expresses whether the audit has been performed in compliance with GAAS and whether, in the auditor's opinion, the financial statements fairly present the client's financial position and results of operations in conformity with GAAP. Usually, an auditor issues an **unqualified opinion**—that is, an opinion that there has been compliance with GAAS and GAAP. Sometimes, an auditor issues a qualified opinion, a disclaimer of opinion, or an adverse opinion. Up to this point, you have studied the liability of an auditor who has issued unqualified opinions yet has not complied with GAAS and GAAP.

What liability should be imposed on an auditor who discloses that he has not complied with GAAS and GAAP? An auditor is relieved of responsibility only to the extent that a qualification or disclaimer is specifically expressed in the opinion letter. Therefore, letters that purport to disclaim liability totally for false and misleading financial statements are too general to excuse an accountant from exercising ordinary skill and care.

For example, an auditor qualifies his opinion of the ability of financial statements to present the financial position of a company by indicating that there is uncertainty about how an antitrust suit against the company may be decided. He would not be held liable for damages resulting from an unfavorable verdict in the antitrust suit. He would remain liable, however, for failing to make an examination in compliance with GAAS that would have revealed other serious problems.

For another example, consider an auditor who, due to the limited scope of the audit, disclaims any opinion on the ability of the financial statements to present the financial position of the company. She would nonetheless be liable for the nondiscovery of problems that the limited audit should have revealed.

Likewise, an accountant who issued an adverse opinion that depreciation had not been calculated according to GAAP would not be liable for damages resulting from the wrongful accounting treatment of depreciation, but he would be liable for damages resulting from the wrongful treatment of receivables.

Merely preparing unaudited statements does not create a disclaimer as to their accuracy. The mere fact that the statements are unaudited only permits an accountant to exercise a lower level of inquiry. Even so, an accountant must act as the ordinarily prudent accountant would act under the same circumstances in preparing unaudited financial statements.

Criminal, Injunctive, and Administrative Proceedings

In addition to being held liable for damages to clients and third parties, a professional may be found criminally liable for his violations of securities, tax, and other laws. For criminal violations, he may be fined and imprisoned. His wrongful conduct may also result in the issuance of an injunction, which bars him from doing the same acts in the future. In addition, his wrongful conduct may be the subject of administrative proceedings by the Securities and Exchange Commission and state licensing boards. An administrative proceeding may result in the revocation of a professional's license to practice or the suspension from practice. Finally, disciplinary proceedings may be brought by professional societies and self regulatory organizations such as the AICPA or NASD.

Criminal Liability under the Securities Laws

Both the Securities Act of 1933 and the Securities Exchange Act of 1934 have criminal provisions that can be applied to professionals. The 1933 Act imposes criminal liability for willful violations of any section of the 1933 Act, including Sections 11, 12(a)(2), and 17(a), or any 1933 Act rule or regulation. For example, willfully making an untrue statement or omitting any material fact in a 1933 Act registration statement imposes criminal liability on a person. The maximum penalty for a criminal violation of the 1933 Act is a $10,000 fine and five years' imprisonment.

The 1934 Act imposes criminal penalties for willful violations of any section of the 1934 Act, such as Sections 10(b) and 18, and any 1934 Act rule or regulation, such as Rule 10b-5. For example, willfully making false or misleading statements in reports that are required to be filed under the 1934 Act incurs criminal liability. Such filings include 10-Ks, 8-Ks, and proxy statements. An individual may be fined up to $5 million and imprisoned for up to 20 years for a criminal violation of the 1934 Act; however, an individual who proves that he had no knowl-

edge of an SEC rule or regulation may not be imprisoned for violating that rule or regulation. A professional firm may be fined up to $25 million.

Most of the states have statutes imposing criminal penalties on professionals who willfully falsify financial statements or other reports in filings under the state securities laws and who willfully violate the state securities laws or aid and abet criminal violations of these laws by others.

In *Natelli*, accountants permitting a client to book unbilled sales after the close of the fiscal period subjected the accountants to the criminal penalties of the 1934 Act.

United States v. Natelli   *527 F.2d 311 (2d Cir. 1975)*

Anthony Natelli was the partner in charge of the Washington, D.C., office of Peat, Marwick, Mitchell & Co., a large CPA firm. In August 1968, Peat, Marwick became the independent public auditor of National Student Marketing Corporation. Natelli was the engagement partner for the audit of Student Marketing. Joseph Scansaroli was Peat, Marwick's audit supervisor on that engagement.

Student Marketing provided its corporate clients with a wide range of marketing services to help them reach the lucrative youth market. In its financial statements for the nine months ended May 31, 1968, Student Marketing had counted as income the entire amount of oral customer commitments to pay fees in Student Marketing's "fixed-fee marketing programs," even though those fees had not yet been paid. They were to be paid for services that Student Marketing would provide over a period of several years. Standard accounting practice required that part of the unpaid fees be considered income in the present year but that part be deferred as income until the years when Student Marketing actually performed the services for which the fees were paid. Therefore, in making the year-end audit, Natelli concluded that he would use a percentage-of-completion approach on these commitments, taking as income in the present year only those fees that were to be paid for services in that year.

The customer fee commitments were oral only, making it difficult to verify whether they really existed. Natelli directed Scansaroli to try to verify the fee commitments by telephoning the customers but not by seeking written verification. However, Scansaroli never called Student Marketing's clients. Instead, Scansaroli accepted a schedule prepared by Student Marketing showing estimates of the percentage of completion of services for each corporate client and the amount of the fee commitment from each client. This resulted in an adjustment of $1.7 million for "unbilled accounts receivable." The adjustment turned a loss for the year into a profit twice that of the year before.

By May 1969, a total of $1 million of the customer fee commitments had been written off as uncollectible. The effect of the write-off was to reduce 1968 income by $209,750. However, Scansaroli, with Natelli's approval, offset this by reversing a deferred tax item of approximately the same amount.

Student Marketing issued a proxy statement in September 1969 in connection with a shareholders' meeting to consider merging six companies into Student Marketing. The proxy statement was filed with the Securities and Exchange Commission. It contained several financial statements, some of which had been audited by Peat, Marwick. Others had not been audited, but Peat, Marwick had aided in their preparation. In the proxy statement, a footnote to the financial statements failed to show that the write-off of customer fee commitments had affected Student Marketing's fiscal 1968 income.

The proxy statement required an unaudited statement of nine months' earnings through May 31, 1969. This statement was prepared by Student Marketing with Peat, Marwick's assistance. Student Marketing produced a $1.2 million commitment from the Pontiac Division of General Motors Corporation two months after the end of May, but it was dated April 28, 1969. At 3 A.M. on the day the proxy statement was to be printed, Natelli informed Randall, the chief executive officer and founder of Student Marketing, that this commitment could not be included because it was not a legally binding contract. Randall responded *at once that he had "a commitment from Eastern Airlines" for a somewhat comparable amount attributable to the same period. Such a letter was produced at the printing plant a few hours later, and the Eastern commitment was substituted for the Pontiac sale in the proxy. Shortly thereafter, another Peat, Marwick accountant, Oberlander, discovered $177,547 in "bad" commitments from 1968. These were known to Scansaroli in May 1969 as being doubtful, but they had not been written off. Oberlander suggested to the company that these commitments plus others, for a total of $320,000, be written off, but Scansaroli, after consulting with Natelli, decided against the suggested write-off.*

There was no disclosure in the proxy statement that Student Marketing had written off $1 million (20 percent) of its 1968 sales and over $2 million of the $3.3 million of unbilled sales booked in 1968 and 1969. A true disclosure would have shown that Student Marketing had made no profit for the first nine months of 1969.

Subsequently, it was revealed that many of Student Marketing's fee commitments were fictitious. The attorney general of the United States brought a criminal action against Natelli and Scansaroli for violating the Securities Exchange Act of 1934 by willfully and knowingly making false and misleading statements in a proxy statement. The district court jury convicted both Natelli and Scansaroli, and they appealed.

Gurfein, Circuit Judge   The original action of Natelli in permitting the booking of unbilled sales after the close of the fiscal period in an amount sufficient to convert a loss into a profit was contrary to sound accounting practice. When the uncollectibility, and indeed, the nonexistence of these large receivables was established in 1969, the revelation stood to cause Natelli severe criticism and possible liability. He had a motive, therefore, intentionally to conceal the write-offs that had to be made.

Honesty should have impelled Natelli and Scansaroli to disclose in the footnote that annotated their own audited statement for fiscal 1968 that substantial write-offs had been taken, after year-end, to reflect a loss for the year. A simple desire to right the wrong that had been perpetrated on the stockholders and others by the false audited financial statement should have dictated that course.

The accountant owes a duty to the public not to assert a privilege of silence until the next audited annual statement comes around in due time. Since companies were being acquired by Student Marketing for its shares in this period, Natelli had to know that the 1968 audited statement was being used continuously.

Natelli contends that he had no duty to verify the Eastern commitment because the earnings statement within which it was included was unaudited. This raises the issue of the duty of the CPA in relation to an unaudited financial statement contained within a proxy statement where the figures are reviewed and to some extent supplied by the auditors. The auditors were associated with the statement and were required to object to anything they actually knew to be materially false. In the ordinary case involving an unaudited statement, the auditor would not be chargeable simply because he failed to discover the invalidity of booked accounts receivable, inasmuch as he had not undertaken an audit with verification. In this case, however, Natelli knew the history

of post-period bookings and the dismal consequences later discovered.

In terms of professional standards, the accountant may not shut his eyes in reckless disregard of his knowledge that highly suspicious figures, known to him to be suspicious, were being included in the unaudited earnings figures in the proxy statement with which he was associated.

There is some merit to Scansaroli's point that he was simply carrying out the judgments of his superior, Natelli. The defense of obedience to higher authority has always been troublesome. There is no sure yardstick to measure criminal responsibility except by measurement of the degree of awareness on the part of a defendant that he is participating in a criminal act, in the absence of physical coercion such as a soldier might face. Here the motivation to conceal undermines Scansaroli's argument that he was merely implementing Natelli's instructions, at least with respect to concealment of matters that were within his own ken. The jury could properly have found him guilty on the specification relating to the footnote.

With respect to the Eastern commitment, Scansaroli stands in a position different from that of Natelli. Natelli was his superior. He was the man to make the judgment whether or not to object to the last-minute inclusion of a new commitment in the nine-months statement. There is insufficient evidence that Scansaroli engaged in any conversations about the Eastern commitment or that he was a participant with Natelli in any check on its authenticity. Since in the hierarchy of the accounting firm it was not his responsibility to decide whether to book the Eastern contract, his mere adjustment of the figures to reflect it under orders was not a matter for his discretion.

Conviction of Natelli affirmed. Conviction of Scansaroli affirmed in part and reversed in part.

Other Criminal Law Violations

Tax Law Federal tax law imposes on professionals a wide range of penalties for a wide variety of wrongful conduct. At one end of the penalty spectrum is a $50 fine for an accountant's failing to furnish a client with a copy of his income tax return or failing to sign a client's return. At the other end is a fine of $250,000 and imprisonment of five years for tax fraud. In between is the penalty for promoting abusive tax shelters. The fine is $1,000, or 20 percent of the defendant's income from her participation in the tax shelter, whichever is greater. In addition, all of the states impose criminal penalties for specified violations of their tax laws.

Mail Fraud Several other federal statutes also impose criminal liability on professionals. The most notable of these statutes is the general mail fraud statute, which prohibits the use of the mails to commit fraud. To be held liable, a professional must know or foresee that the mails will be used to transmit materials containing fraudulent statements provided by her.

In addition, the general false-statement-to-government-personnel statute prohibits fraudulent statements to government personnel. The false-statement-to-bank statute proscribes fraudulent statements on a loan application to a bank or other financial institution.

RICO The Racketeer Influenced and Corrupt Organizations Act (RICO) makes it a federal crime to engage in a pattern of racketeering activity. Although RICO was designed to attack the activities of organized crime enterprises, it applies to professionals who conduct or participate in the affairs of an enterprise in almost any pattern of business fraud. A pattern of fraud is proved by the commission of two predicate offenses within a 10-year period. Predicate offenses include securities law violations, mail fraud, and bribery. Individuals convicted of a RICO violation may be fined up to $25,000 and imprisoned up to 20 years.

A person who is injured in his business or property by reason of a professional's conduct or participation, directly or indirectly, in an enterprise's affairs through a pattern of racketeering activity may recover treble damages (three times his actual damages) from the professional. In *Reves v. Ernst & Young*,[2] the Supreme Court held that merely by auditing financial statements that substantially overvalued a client's assets, an accounting firm was not conducting or participating in the affairs of the client's business. The Court held that the accounting firm must participate in the "operation or management" of the enterprise itself to be liable under RICO.

Injunctions

Administrative agencies such as the SEC and the Internal Revenue Service may bring injunctive actions against an auditor or securities professional in a federal district court. The purpose of such an injunction is to prevent a defendant from committing a future violation of the securities or tax laws.

After an injunction has been issued by a court, violating the injunction may result in serious sanctions. Not only may penalties be imposed for contempt, but a criminal violation may also be more easily proven.

Administrative Proceedings

The SEC has the authority to bring administrative proceedings against persons who violate the provisions of the federal securities acts. In recent years, the SEC has stepped up enforcement of SEC Rule of Practice 102(e). Rule 102(e) permits the SEC to bar temporarily or permanently from practicing before the SEC a professional who has demonstrated a lack of the qualifications required to practice before it, such as an accountant who has prepared financial statements not complying with GAAP. In the Sarbanes–Oxley Act of 2002, Congress amended the 1934 Act to include the language of Rule 102(e) almost word for word.

The SEC may discipline accountants who engage in a single instance of highly unreasonable conduct that leads to a violation of professional accounting standards. The SEC may also discipline an accountant who engages in repeated, unreasonable conduct that results in a violation of professional accounting standards. For example, an auditor's conduct in reviewing a client's financial statements is unreasonable when the auditor knew or should have known that heightened scrutiny is warranted yet failed to exercise the additional scrutiny while conducting an audit.

Rule 102(e) also permits the SEC to take action against a professional who has willfully violated or aided and abetted another's violation of the securities acts. An SEC administrative law judge hears the case and makes an initial determination. The SEC commissioners then issue a final order, which may be appealed to a federal court of appeals.

Rule 102(e) administrative proceedings can impose severe penalties on an accountant. By suspending an

---

[2]113 S. Ct. 1163 (1993).

accountant from practicing before it, the SEC may take away a substantial part of an accountant's practice. Also, the SEC may impose civil penalties up to $500,000.

In addition, state licensing boards may suspend or revoke an accountant's license to practice if she engages in illegal or unethical conduct. If such action is taken, an accountant may lose her entire ability to practice accounting.

Securities Exchange Act Audit Requirements

The Private Securities Litigation Reform Act of 1995 imposes significant public duties on independent auditors that audit the financial statements of public companies. In part added to the Securities Exchange Act as Section 10A, the Reform Act requires auditors to take specific steps if they learn during the course of an audit that a client may have committed an illegal act (that is, a violation of any law, rule, or regulation). First, the auditor is required to determine whether an illegal act has in fact occurred. If the auditor determines that the client has committed an illegal act, the auditor must calculate the prospective impact on the client's financial statements, including fines, penalties, and liability costs such as damage awards to persons harmed by the client. As soon as practical, the auditor must inform the client's management and audit committee of the auditor's determination, unless the illegal act is clearly inconsequential.

If the client's management does not take appropriate remedial action with respect to an illegal act that has a material effect on the financial statements of the client— and if the failure to take remedial action is reasonably expected to result in the auditor's issuance of a nonstandard report or resignation from the audit engagement—the auditor must make a report to the client's board of directors. The board of directors has one business day to inform the SEC of the auditor's report; if the board does not submit a report to the SEC, the auditor has one additional business day to furnish a copy of its report to the SEC, whether or not the auditor also resigns from the audit engagement.

Section 10A imposes a significant whistle-blowing duty on independent auditors, consistent with the watchdog function that Congress and the courts have continually assigned to auditors. To encourage auditors to make such reports, Section 10A also provides that an auditor

will have no liability to a private litigant for any statement in the auditor's reports given to management, the board of directors, or the SEC.

Section 10A is also the repository of many of the new securities provisions enacted under the Sarbanes–Oxley Act, including the list of services audit firms may not provide for audit clients, the audit partner rotation requirement, and the standards and duties of audit committees.

Ownership of Working Papers

The personal records that a client entrusts to a professional, such as an auditor receiving accounting records during an audit, remain the property of the client. A professional must return these records to his client. Nonetheless, material created by a professional, such as working papers produced by independent auditors, belong to the accountant, not the client.

Working papers are the records made during an audit. They include such items as work programs or plans for the audit, evidence of the testing of accounts, explanations of the handling of unusual matters, data reconciling the accountant's report with the client's records, and comments about the client's internal controls. The client has a right of access to the working papers. The accountant must obtain the client's permission before the working papers can be transferred to another accountant.

No doubt in reaction to the massive shredding of Enron-related documents by the Arthur Andersen audit firm, Congress included in the Sarbanes–Oxley Act a requirement that all audit or review working papers be retained for five years. A knowing or willful violation of the document retention rule is subject to 10 years' imprisonment, and if corruptly done, 20 years.

ETHICS IN ACTION

Rise in Audit Fees after Sarbanes–Oxley

With increased regulation of auditors a consequence of the Sarbanes–Oxley Act of 2002, it is predictable that auditor and audit firms will have two reactions: one, leave the audit field because complying with new regulations is too burdensome and the risks are too great; two, increase audit fees to compensate them for taking on greater duties and risk. Research by the *Wall Street Journal* indicates that while audit fees increased about 5 percent per year in recent years, fees could increase as much as 25 percent in 2003.

Audit firms say they face higher costs of insurance and recruiting. Auditors are logging more billable hours and using higher-priced professionals to help clients implement new accounting and reporting rules. By banning audit firms from most types of consulting for their audit clients, audits can no longer be loss leaders to attract clients with lucrative consulting work. They will need to raise rates to make up for consulting subsidies. In addition, audit committees and management have increased duties and are requesting more meetings with auditors. Finally, it appears that audit committees of large publicly held companies—having witnessed recent incidents of management greed and fraud—are willing to pay a higher audit fee to encourage auditors to make a greater effort to detect management wrongdoing.

- Is it ethical that audit firms and auditors benefit from the recent incidents of corporate fraud by having more work and charging higher fees?

Professional–Client Privilege

The attorney–client privilege is well-established as necessary to protect confidential communications between a lawyer and her client and to permit a lawyer to perform her professional duties for her client. The privilege protects communications between clients and their attorneys from the prying eyes of courts and government agencies. It also protects a lawyer's working papers from the discovery procedures available in a lawsuit.

Although other professionals owe a duty of confidentiality to their clients, in general communications between clients and nonlawyer professionals are not protected from judicial and administrative agency scrutiny when the professional's client is a party to legal or administrative action or the professional possesses evidence probative to an action. Thus, consultants, investment bankers, underwriters, brokers, and other securities professionals may be required to testify about client communications and produce documents concerning their clients, despite the objections of the client.

Accountants, however, enjoy a status somewhere between attorneys and other professionals. While the common law does not recognize an accountant–client privilege, a large number of states have granted such a privilege by statute. An accountant–client privilege of confidentiality protects communications between accountants and their clients as well as accountants' working papers. The provisions of the state statutes vary, but usually the privilege belongs to the client, and an accountant may not refuse to disclose the privileged material in a courtroom if the client consents to its disclosure.

Generally, the state-granted privileges are recognized in both state and federal courts deciding questions of state law. Nonetheless, federal courts do not recognize the privilege in matters involving federal questions, including antitrust and criminal matters.

In federal tax matters, for example, no privilege of confidentiality is recognized on the grounds that an accountant has a duty as a public watchdog to ensure that his client correctly reports his income tax liability. Consequently, an accountant can be required to bring his working papers into court and to testify as to matters involving the client's tax records and discussions with the client regarding tax matters. In addition, an accountant may be required by subpoena to make available his working papers involving a client who is being investigated by the IRS or who has been charged with tax irregularities. The same holds true for SEC investigations.

Although no accountant–client privilege exists in federal tax matters, an attorney–client privilege does exist. Moreover, the attorney–client privilege will protect communications between a client and a professional when the professional is assisting an attorney in rendering advice to the client.

Problems and Problem Cases

1. The 1136 Tenants' Corporation, a cooperative apartment house, hired Max Rothenberg & Co., a firm of certified public accountants, to perform accounting services for it. Rothenberg discovered that several invoices were missing from the financial records of the apartment house. These invoices were needed to prove that payments of $44,000 had been made to creditors of the apartment house and were not embezzled by someone with authority to make payments for the apartment house. Rothenberg noted the missing invoices on his worksheet but failed to notify the apartment house that there were missing invoices. In fact, there were no invoices. Jerome Riker, the apartment house manager, had embezzled the $44,000 from the apartment house by ordering it to make unauthorized payments to him. Riker embezzled more money after the audit was completed. Is Rothenberg liable to its client for failing to inform it of Riker's embezzlement?

2. From 1983 to 1985, Baumann-Furrie & Co. provided accounting services to Halla Nursery, Inc. During this time, Halla's bookkeeper embezzled $135,000. In 1986, Halla sued Baumann-Furrie alleging it negligently failed to detect the embezzlement. Baumann-Furrie claimed that Halla negligently failed to put in place internal financial controls to protect the company from embezzlement. The jury found Halla 80 percent at fault and Baumann-Furrie 20 percent at fault. Is Baumann-Furrie nonetheless liable to Halla?

3. Sonny Martinez opened a securities brokerage account with Edelstein & Co., depositing $680,000 in the account. Martinez was 10 years from his retirement and wanted his funds to be invested in blue chip stocks, which through capital appreciation and dividends would increase in value to $1,300,000 by the time of his retirement. Martinez's broker at Edelstein invested Martinez's funds in blue chip stocks like IBM, Proctor & Gamble, and Merck, but he traded the account almost daily, sometimes holding a stock for only a matter of days and holding no stock for longer than 13 months. The broker executed over 4,000 trades in a two-year period, generating commissions of over $200,000. As a result of the broker's trading strategy, the value of Martinez's account declined to $300,000. During the same period, the Dow Jones Industrial Average increased 22 percent. May Martinez recover from the broker under contract law, the law of negligence, and Rule 10b–5 of the 1934 Act?

4. Founded in 1980, Osborne Computer manufactured the first personal computer for the mass market. In 1983, to obtain temporary financing prior to a public securities offering, Osborne sold warrants entitling investors to buy Osborne shares at a favorable price. The investors were given and relied on an unqualified audit opinion regarding Osborne's 1982 financial statements, which indicated that Osborne had a net operating profit of $69,000 on sales of $68 million. The audit opinion, issued by Arthur Young & Company, stated that the audit had complied with GAAS, that the financial statements had been prepared in compliance with GAAP, and that the financial statements fairly presented Osborne's financial position. Arthur Young could foresee that the audited financial statements might be used by buyers of Osborne's warrants, but Arthur Young did not know that buyers of warrants would in fact use the financial statements. The buyers of the warrants lost their investments when Osborne's manufacturing problems and IBM's dominance in the PC market forced Osborne into bankruptcy. The investors sued Arthur Young on the grounds of negligent misrepresentation, because Osborne actually had a $3 million operating loss in 1982, a fact Arthur Young negligently failed to discover. Are the warrant investors permitted to sue Arthur Young for negligent misrepresentation?

5. Kibbmann & Co., an investment banking firm, acted as the underwriter for Vartarian Corporation's public issuance of common shares. Kibbmann prepared the 1933 Act registration statement that was filed with the SEC and the prospectus that investors received. Kibbmann also accompanied Vartarian's CEO and CFO to road shows where Kibbmann spoke with mutual funds and other institutional investors interested in purchasing Vartarian's stock. Kibbmann's compensation for assisting Vartarian was a 25-cent spread on each share sold. Due to its negligent investigation of Vartarian's business, Kibbmann made material misstatements of fact in the registration statement and prospectus and during the road show. Did Kibbmann have liability to purchasers of the shares who attended the road show under Section 12(a)(2) of the 1933 Act, Rule 10b–5 of the 1934 Act, and the common law of negligent misrepresentation? Did Kibbman have liability to purchasers of the shares under Section 11 of the 1933 Act?

6. Sonya Kwan, a 75-year-old retired factory worker, opened a securities account with Barton & Associates, a brokerage firm. She completed a customer account agreement form in which she disclosed her assets, liabilities, income, expenses, and investment objectives. That form indicated that it was important for her to maintain a steady income stream to augment her pension and social security income. Nonetheless, Kwan's broker advised her to purchase the stock of a high-risk company that paid no dividends to its shareholders. Kwan, who was not a sophisticated investor, followed her broker's advice and purchased the stock. Within two months, the company was dissolved and Kwan lost her entire investment. Kwan later discovered that her broker was a significant investor in the company. May Kwan recover from the analyst under Rule 10b–5 of the 1934 Act? Is Kwan able to recover under the common law of negligent misrepresentation, fraud, or breach of trust?

7. In 1986 and 1988, the Colorado Springs–Stetson Hills Public Building Authority (Authority) issued $26 million in bonds to finance public improvements at Stetson Hills, a residential and commercial development in Colorado Springs. Central Bank served as the trustee for the bondholders, undertaking a fiduciary duty to the bondholders to ensure that the Authority complied with indenture provisions protecting bondholders. The bonds were secured by liens against 522 acres of land, and the indenture required that the land be worth at least 160 percent of the bonds' outstanding principal and interest. In January 1988, AmWest Development—the developer of Stetson Hills—gave Central Bank an appraisal of the land. The appraisal showed land values almost unchanged from a 1986 appraisal, even though property values were declining in Colorado Springs. Central Bank's in-house appraiser reviewed the 1988 appraisal and decided that it was optimistic. He suggested that Central Bank use an independent outside appraiser to review the 1988 appraisal. After an exchange of letters between Central Bank and AmWest in early 1988, Central Bank agreed to delay independent review of the appraisal until the end of 1988, six months after the 1988 bonds had been issued to investors. Before the independent review was complete, the Authority defaulted on the 1988 bonds. Is Central Bank liable to the bondholders under Section 10(b) of the Securities Exchange Act of 1934?

8. Bill Thomas, a CPA, was a member of Lawhon, Thomas, Holmes & Co. (LTH), a public accounting firm. When LTH performed accounting services for Xenerex Corp., LTH received 144,000 Xenerex shares instead of cash. LTH continued to hold the Xenerex shares when the three LTH members joined the accounting firm of Oppenheim, Appel, Dixon & Co.

(OAD). LTH ceased operations and sold all its assets except the Xenerex shares to OAD. The three former LTH members, including Thomas, retained ownership of LTH. After he joined OAD, Thomas immediately solicited Xenerex as a client for OAD. Thomas, on behalf of OAD, signed a new client acceptance form for Xenerex, giving a negative response to the question, "Are there any known independence problems?" Thomas prepared and signed OAD's report on Xenerex's financial statements and annual report filed on Form 10-K with the SEC. Has Thomas violated SEC Rule of Practice 102(e)?

9. While performing a routine audit of the tax returns of Amerada Hess Corporation, the Internal Revenue Service discovered questionable payments of $7,830. The IRS issued a summons to Arthur Young & Co., the accounting firm that had prepared the tax accrual working papers that might reveal the nature of the payments. The working papers had been prepared in the process of Arthur Young's review of Amerada Hess's financial statements, as required by federal securities law. In the summons, the IRS ordered Arthur Young to make available to the IRS all of its Amerada Hess files, including its tax accrual working papers. Amerada Hess directed Arthur Young not to comply with the summons on the grounds that they were protected by an accountant–client privilege. Is Amerada Hess correct?

10. Media personality Martha Stewart is being investigated by the SEC for alleged insider trading in the stock of ImClone Systems. Stewart is a friend of Sam Waksal, founder and former chief executive of ImClone, who pleaded guilty in October 2002 to several counts of bank fraud, securities fraud, conspiracy to obstruct justice, and perjury. Stewart sold nearly 4,000 shares of ImClone stock in December 2001, just one day before the U.S. Food and Drug Administration announced it would reject ImClone's application for approval of its cancer-fighting drug Erbitux. That announcement sent the company's stock into a tailspin. The SEC believes Stewart may have been tipped off by Waksal about the looming FDA decision, but Waksal did not implicate Stewart. Stewart asserts that she told her broker, Peter Bacanovic of Merrill Lynch, to sell her shares if ImClone's stock dropped below $60 a share. The stock fell to $58 the day she sold. If the SEC wants to know all communications between Stewart and her broker Bacanovic, may Stewart invoke a professional–client privilege to prevent the SEC's discovery of her confidential communications with Bacanovic?

Online Research: Public Company Accounting Oversight Board

Keep abreast of the creation and work of the Public Company Accounting Oversight Board and the General Accounting Office's study of audit firm rotation, which are features of the Sarbanes–Oxley Act of 2002. Answer the following questions:

- Whom has the SEC appointed to the Board? Are they representatives of investors or the accounting industry?
- Has the Board adopted auditing standards?
- Has the GAO completed its study of mandatory audit firm rotation? If so, what is the GAO's recommendation?

REGULATION OF BUSINESS

47

ADMINISTRATIVE AGENCIES

During the mid-1990s, the Food and Drug Administration (FDA) adopted various regulations that restricted advertising and other marketing practices regarding tobacco products. The FDA premised these regulations on the theory that nicotine was a "drug" and cigarettes were a drug-delivery "device" for purposes of the Food, Drug & Cosmetic Act, which gives the FDA the authority to regulate such items.

Various tobacco companies and other parties challenged the regulations in federal court, arguing that Congress had not given the FDA authority to regulate tobacco products and that in any event, the advertising restrictions contemplated by the regulations violated the First Amendment. The litigation, which made its way to the ultimate forum—the United States Supreme Court—suggested fundamental questions that arise in the field of *administrative law:*

• In what subject matter area has the relevant administrative agency been granted authority to regulate by Congress or, at the state level, by the state legislature? What are the specific boundaries of that subject matter area?
• In what ways has the administrative agency been empowered by Congress or the state legislature to exercise its regulatory authority? What restrictions, if any, have been placed by Congress or the state legislature on the ways in which the agency may regulate?
• Do regulations (i.e., rules) adopted by an administrative agency have the same force of law that statutes have?
• How do constitutional provisions affect the regulatory actions that administrative agencies may take?

As you will see, the Supreme Court resolved the FDA case without having to address all of the above questions. Your understanding of administrative law, however, will be enhanced if you consider the questions as you study Chapter 47.

TODAY'S BUSINESSES OPERATE IN a highly regulated environment. The *administrative agency* serves as a primary vehicle for the creation and enforcement of modern regulation. As governmental bodies that are neither courts nor legislatures, administrative agencies have the legal power to take actions affecting the rights of private individuals and organizations. The influence of administrative agencies has become so sweeping that they are sometimes referred to as the "fourth branch" of a government that officially consists of three branches (legislative, executive, and judicial).

This chapter focuses on federal administrative agencies. It is important to remember, however, that the past century's significant growth in *federal* regulation has been accompanied by a comparable growth in *state* and *local* regulation by agencies at those levels of government.

It is difficult to think of an area of modern individual life that is not somehow touched by the actions of administrative agencies. The energy that heats and lights your home and workplace, the clothes you wear, the food you eat, the medicines you take, the design of the car you drive, the programs you watch on television, and the contents of (and label on) the pillow on which you lay your head at night are all shaped in some way by regulation. This observation is even more appropriate regarding corporations. Almost every significant aspect of contemporary corporate operations is regulated to the point that the *legal* consequences of a corporation's actions are nearly as important to its future success as the *business* consequences of its decisions.

Administrative agencies have always been objects of controversy. Are they protectors of the public or impediments to business efficiency? Are they guardians of competitive market structures or shields behind which noncompetitive firms have sought refuge from more vigorous competitors? Have they been impartial, efficient agents of the public interest or are they more often overzealous, or inept, or "captives" of the industries they supposedly regulate? At various times, and where various agencies are concerned, each of the above allegations is likely to have been true. Why, then, did we resort to such controversial entities to perform the regulatory function?

Origins of Administrative Agencies

In the 19th century's latter decades, the United States was in the midst of a dramatic transformation from an agrarian nation to a major industrial power. Improved means of transportation and communication facilitated dramatic market expansions. Large business organizations acquired unprecedented economic power, and new technologies promised additional social transformations.

The tremendous growth that resulted from these developments, however, was not attained without some cost. Large organizations sometimes abused their power at the expense of their customers, distributors, and competitors. New technologies often posed risks of harm to large numbers of citizens. Yet traditional institutions of legal control, such as courts and legislatures, were not particularly well suited to the regulatory needs of an increasingly complex, interdependent society in the throes of rapid change.

Courts, after all, are passive institutions that must await a genuine case or controversy before they can act. In addition, they are constrained by rules of procedure and evidence that make litigation a time-consuming and expensive process.

Legislatures, on the other hand, are theoretically able to anticipate social problems and to act in a comprehensive fashion to minimize social harm. In reality, however, legislatures rarely act until a problem has become severe enough to generate strong political support for a regulatory solution. Legislatures may also lack (as do courts) the expertise necessary to make rational policy regarding highly technical activities.

What was needed, therefore, was a new type of governmental entity: one that would be exclusively devoted to monitoring a particular area of activity; one that could, by its exclusive focus and specialized hiring practices, develop a reservoir of expertise concerning the relevant area; and one that could provide the continuous attention and constant policy development demanded by a rapidly changing environment. Such new entities, it was thought, could best perform their regulatory tasks if they were given considerable latitude in the approaches they utilized to achieve regulatory goals.

The modern regulatory era was born in 1887 when Congress, in response to complaints about discriminatory ratemaking practices by railroads, passed the Interstate Commerce Act. This statute created the Interstate Commerce Commission and empowered it to regulate transportation industry ratemaking practices. Since then, new administrative agencies have been added whenever *pressing social problems* (e.g., the threat to competition that led to the creation of the Federal Trade Commission) or *new technologies,* such as aviation (Federal Aviation Administration), communications (Federal Communications Commission), and nuclear power (Nuclear Regulatory Commission), have generated a political consensus in favor of regulation. More recently, developing scientific knowledge about the *dangers that modern technologies and industrial processes pose* to the environment and to industrial workers has led to the creation of new federal agencies empowered to regulate environmental pollution (Environmental Protection Agency) and promote workplace safety (Occupational Safety and Health Administration). The following sections examine the legal dimensions of the process by which such administrative agencies are created.

Agency Creation

Enabling Legislation

Administrative agencies are created when Congress passes **enabling legislation** specifying the name, composition, and powers of the agency. For example, consider the following language from Section 1 of the Federal Trade Commission Act:

> A commission is created and established, to be known as the Federal Trade Commission [FTC], which shall be composed of five commissioners, who shall be appointed by the President, by and with the advice and consent of the Senate.

Section 5 of the FTC Act prohibits "unfair methods of competition" and "unfair or deceptive acts or practices in commerce," and empowers the FTC to prevent such practices.[1] Section 5 also describes the procedures the Commission must follow to charge persons or organizations with violations of the act, and provides for judicial review of agency orders. Subsequent portions of the statute give the FTC the power "to make rules and regulations for the purpose of carrying out the provisions of the Act," to conduct investigations of business practices, to require reports from interstate corporations concerning their practices and operations, to investigate possible violations of the antitrust laws,[2] to publish reports concerning its findings and activities, and to recommend new legislation to Congress.

Thus, Congress has given the FTC powers typically associated with the three traditional branches of government. The FTC may, for instance, act in a legislative fashion by *promulgating rules* that have binding legal effect on future behavior. It may also take the executive

---

[1]Section 5 of the FTC Act is discussed in detail in Chapter 48.
[2]The antitrust laws are discussed in detail in Chapters 49 and 50.

branch–like actions of *investigating* and *prosecuting* alleged violations. Finally, the FTC may act much as courts do and *adjudicate* disputes concerning alleged violations of the law. Most other federal administrative agencies have a similarly broad mix of governmental powers, making these agencies potentially powerful agents of social control.

Great power to do good things, however, may also be great power to cause harm. Regulatory bias, zeal, insensitivity, or corruption, if left unchecked, may infringe on the basic freedoms that are the essence of our system of government. Accordingly, the fundamental problem in administrative law—a problem that will surface repeatedly in this chapter—is how to design a system of control over agency action that minimizes the potential for arbitrariness and harm yet preserves the power and flexibility that make administrative agencies uniquely valuable instruments of public policy.

Administrative Agencies and the Constitution

Because administrative agencies are governmental bodies, administrative action is *governmental action* that is subject to the basic constitutional checks discussed in Chapter 3. This "fourth branch" of government is bound by basic constitutional guarantees such as *due process, equal protection,* and *freedom of speech,* just as the three traditional branches are. The *Pearson* case, which follows, deals with First Amendment limitations on the Food and Drug Administration's regulatory authority.

Pearson v. Shalala   *164 F.3d 650 (D.C. Cir. 1999)*

A federal statute prohibits marketers of dietary supplements from including on container labels any claim characterizing the relationship of the dietary supplement to the prevention or alleviation of a disease or health-related condition, unless the claim has been submitted to the Food and Drug Administration (FDA) for preapproval. According to one of its regulations, the FDA will authorize such a "health claim" only if the FDA finds "significant scientific agreement" among experts that the claim is supported by the available evidence. Dietary supplement marketers Durk Pearson and Sandy Shaw asked the FDA to authorize four separate health claims regarding their dietary supplements' preventative effects on health conditions such as cancer or heart disease.

The FDA refused to authorize any of the four health claims, not because there was a dearth of supporting evidence but because, in the FDA's view, the evidence was inconclusive and thus failed to give rise to "significant scientific agreement." The FDA declined to consider an alternative suggested by Pearson and Shaw: permitting the making of the health claims on the appropriate labels but requiring the use of a corrective disclaimer such as "The FDA has determined that the evidence supporting this claim is inconclusive."

Pearson, Shaw, and organizations representing health care practitioners and consumers of dietary supplements sought relief in the federal district court. The court rejected their arguments and upheld the FDA's action. Pearson, Shaw, and the organizations appealed to the U.S. Court of Appeals for the District of Columbia Circuit.

Silberman, Circuit Judge Appellants raise a host of challenges to the [FDA's] action. [T]he most important are that their First Amendment rights have been impaired and that under the Administrative Procedure Act, the FDA was obliged . . . to articulate a standard a good deal more concrete than the undefined "significant scientific agreement." Normally we would discuss the non-constitutional argument first, particularly because we believe it has merit. We invert the normal order here to discuss [the argument] that the government has violated the First Amendment by declining to employ a less draconian method—the use of disclaimers—to serve the government's interests. [We do so because] even if "significant scientific agreement" were given a more concrete meaning, appellants might be entitled to make health claims that do not meet that standard—with proper disclaimers.

It is undisputed that the FDA's restrictions on appellants' health claims are [to be] evaluated under the commercial speech doctrine [and] that the FDA has unequivocally rejected the notion of requiring disclaimers to cure "misleading" health claims for dietary supplements. The government makes two alternative arguments in response to appellants' claim that it is unconstitutional for the government to refuse to entertain a disclaimer requirement for the proposed health claims: first, that health claims lacking "significant scientific agreement" are *inherently* misleading and thus entirely outside the protection of the First Amendment; and second, that even if the claims are only *potentially* misleading, . . . the government is not obliged to consider requiring disclaimers in lieu of an outright ban on all claims that lack significant scientific agreement.

If such health claims could be thought inherently misleading, that would be the end of the inquiry. [Although nonmisleading commercial speech about lawful activities receives an intermediate degree of First Amendment protection, misleading commercial speech goes wholly unprotected by the First Amendment.] [The government's] first argument runs along the following lines: that health claims lacking "significant scientific agreement" are inherently misleading because they have such an awesome impact on consumers as to make it virtually impossible for them to exercise any judgment *at the point of sale*. It would be as if the consumers were asked to buy something while hypnotized, and therefore they are bound to be misled. We think this contention is almost frivolous. We reject it. But the government's alternative argument is more substantial. It is asserted that health claims on dietary supplements should be thought at least potentially misleading because the consumer would have difficulty in independently verifying these claims. We are told, in addition, that consumers might actually assume that the government has approved these claims.

Under *Central Hudson Gas & Electric Corp. v. Public Service Commission* (U.S. Sup Ct. 1980), we are obliged to evaluate a government scheme to regulate potentially misleading commercial speech by applying a . . . test [that first asks] whether the asserted government interest is substantial. The FDA advanced two general concerns: protection of public health and prevention of consumer fraud. [In view of applicable precedent,] a substantial government interest is undeniable. The more significant questions under *Central Hudson* are the next two factors: "whether the regulation directly advances the governmental interest asserted," [quoting *Central Hudson*,] and whether the fit between the government's ends and the means chosen to accomplish those ends "is not necessarily perfect, but reasonable" [quoting *Board of Trustees v. Fox* (U.S. Sup. Ct. 1989)].

[Although any advancement of the underlying public health interest may seem more indirect than direct,] the government would appear to advance directly its interest in protecting against consumer fraud through its regulatory scheme. If it can be assumed—and we think it can—that some health claims on dietary supplements will mislead consumers, it cannot be denied that requiring FDA preapproval and setting the standard extremely, perhaps even impossibly, high will surely prevent any confusion among consumers. We also recognize that the government's interest in preventing consumer fraud/confusion may well take on added importance in the context of a product, such as dietary supplements, that can affect the public's health.

The difficulty with the government's consumer fraud justification comes at the final *Central Hudson* factor: Is there a reasonable fit between the government's goals and the means chosen to advance those goals? The government insists that it is never obliged to utilize the disclaimer approach, because the commercial speech doctrine does not embody a preference for disclosure over outright suppression. Our understanding of the doctrine is otherwise. [The Supreme Court has stated that when allegedly incomplete advertising is not inherently misleading,] "the preferred remedy is more disclosure, rather than less." *Bates v. State Bar of Arizona* (U.S. Sup. Ct. 1977). In more recent cases, the Court has reaffirmed this principle, repeatedly pointing to disclaimers as constitutionally preferable to outright suppression. [Moreover, when] government chooses a policy of suppression over disclosure—at least where there is no showing that disclosure would not suffice to [prevent or minimize] misleadingness—government disregards a far less restrictive means. [As a result, a reasonable fit between the regulatory scheme and the underlying government interest would be lacking.]

Our rejection of the government's position that there is no general First Amendment preference for disclosure over suppression . . . does not determine that any supposed weaknesses in the [health] claims at issue can be remedied by disclaimers. [We therefore examine the particular claims.] The FDA deemed the first three claims—(1) "Consumption of antioxidant vitamins may reduce the risk of certain kinds of cancers," (2) "Consumption of fiber may reduce the risk of colorectal cancer," and (3) "Consumption of omega-3 fatty acids may reduce the risk of coronary heart disease"—to lack significant scientific agreement because existing research had examined only the relationship between consumption of *foods* containing these components and the risk of these diseases. The FDA logically determined that the specific effect of the *component* of the food constituting the dietary supplement could not be determined with certainty. But certainly this concern could be accommodated, in the first claim for example, by adding a prominent disclaimer to the label along the following lines: "The evidence is inconclusive because existing studies have been performed with *foods* containing antioxidant vitamins, and the effect of those foods on reducing the risk of cancer may result from other components in those foods." A similar disclaimer would be equally effective for the latter two claims.

The FDA's concern regarding the fourth claim—".8mg of folic acid in a dietary supplement is more effective in reducing the risk of neural tube defects than a lower amount in foods in common form"—is different from its reservations regarding the first three claims: the agency simply concluded that "the scientific literature does not support the superiority of any one source over others." [W]e suspect that a clarifying disclaimer could be added to the effect that "the evidence in support of this claim is inconclusive."

The government's general concern that . . . consumers might assume that a claim on a supplement's label is approved by the government suggests an obvious answer. The agency could require the label to state that "The FDA does not approve this claim." Similarly, the government's interest in preventing the use of labels that are true but do not mention adverse effects would seem to be satisfied—at least ordinarily—by inclusion of a prominent disclaimer setting forth those adverse effects.

The government disputes that consumers would be able to comprehend appellants' proposed health claims in conjunction with the disclaimers we have suggested. [T]his mix of information would, in the government's view, create confusion among consumers. But all the government offers in support is the FDA's pronouncement that "consumers would be considerably confused by a multitude of claims with differing degrees of reliability." Although the government may have more leeway in choosing suppression over disclosure as a response to the problem of consumer confusion where the product affects health, it must still meet its burden of justifying a restriction on speech. [H]ere, the FDA's conclusory assertion falls far short.

We do not presume to draft precise disclaimers for each of appellants' four claims; we leave that task to the agency in the first instance. Nor do we rule out the possibility that where evidence in support of a claim is outweighed by evidence against the claim, the FDA could deem it incurable by a disclaimer and ban it outright. For example, if the weight of the evidence were against the hypothetical claim that "Consumption of Vitamin E reduces the risk of Alzheimer's disease," the agency might reasonably determine that adding a disclaimer such as "The FDA has determined that *no* evidence supports this claim" would not suffice to mitigate the claim's misleadingness. Finally, while we are skeptical that the government could demonstrate with empirical evidence that disclaimers similar to the ones we suggested above would bewilder consumers and fail to correct for deceptiveness, we do not rule out that possibility.

District court decision reversed; case remanded with instructions that FDA reconsider appellants' health claims.

Separation of Powers One basic constitutional principle is uniquely important when the creation of administrative agencies is at issue: the principle of *separation of powers*. A fundamental attribute of our Constitution is its allocation of governmental power among the three branches of government. Lawmaking power is given to the legislative branch, law-enforcing power to the executive branch, and law-interpreting power to the judicial branch. By limiting the powers of each branch, and by giving each branch some checks on the exercise of power by the other branches, the Constitution seeks to ensure that governmental power remains accountable to the public will.

Administrative agencies, which exercise powers resembling those of each of the three branches of government, create obvious concerns about separation of powers. In particular, the congressional delegation of legislative power to an agency in its enabling legislation may be challenged as violating the separation of powers principle if the legislation is so broadly worded as to indicate that Congress has abdicated its lawmaking responsibilities. Early judicial decisions exploring the manner in which Congress could delegate its power tended to require enabling legislation to contain fairly specific guidelines and standards limiting the exercise of agency discretion.

More recently, courts have often sustained quite broad delegations of power to administrative agencies. Section 5 of the FTC Act contains such a delegation of power. A great range of unspecified behavior falls within the statute's prohibition of "unfair methods of competition" and "unfair or deceptive acts or practices." Courts tend to approve broad delegations of power when Congress has expressed an "intelligible principle" to guide the agency's actions.[3]

The *American Trucking Associations* decision, which follows, examines the delegation of power question.

---

[3]*J. W. Hampton, Jr. & Co. v. United States* (U.S. Sup. Ct. 1928).

Whitman v. American Trucking Associations   *531 U.S. 457 (U.S. Sup. Ct. 2001)*

The federal Clean Air Act requires the Environmental Protection Agency (EPA) to promulgate and periodically revise national ambient air quality standards (NAAQS) for each air pollutant that meets certain statutory criteria. Section 109 of the statute calls for the EPA to set, for each pollutant, a standard reflecting a concentration level "requisite to protect the public health" with an "adequate margin of safety." In July 1997, the EPA issued final rules revising the NAAQS for particulate matter and ozone. Various parties, including American Trucking Associations, Inc., filed petitions for review in the United States Court of Appeals for the District of Columbia Circuit. The D.C. Circuit held, among other things, that the Clean Air Act did not permit the EPA to consider costs of implementation in setting NAAQS, and that in any event, the challenged rules had been formulated pursuant to an unconstitutional delegation of power from Congress in § 109. However, the D.C. Circuit remanded the proceedings to the EPA, in order to allow the agency to construe § 109 in a way that would cure the delegation problem.

The U.S. Supreme Court granted the EPA's petition for certiorari. In a portion of the opinion not included here, the Supreme Court agreed with the D.C. Circuit's holding that costs of implementation could not be considered by the EPA in the setting of NAAQS. The Court then turned to the delegation of power issue.

Scalia, Justice In a delegation challenge, the constitutional question is whether the statute has delegated legislative power to the agency. Article I, § 1, of the Constitution vests "all legislative Powers herein granted . . . in a Congress of the United States." This text permits no delegation of those powers, and so we repeatedly have said that when Congress confers decisionmaking authority upon agencies *Congress* must "lay down by legislative act an intelligible principle to which the person or body authorized to [act] is directed to conform." *J. W. Hampton, Jr. & Co. v. United States* (1928). We have never suggested that an agency can cure an unlawful delegation of legislative power by adopting in its discretion a limiting construction of the statute. The idea that an agency can cure an unconstitutional standardless delegation of power by declining to exercise some of that power seems to us internally contradictory. The very choice of which portion of the power to exercise—that is to say, the prescription of the standard that Congress had omitted—would *itself* be an exercise of the forbidden legislative authority. Whether the statute delegates legislative power is a question for the courts, and an agency's voluntary self-denial has no bearing upon the answer.

We agree with the Solicitor General [, who argued on behalf of the United States. According to the Solicitor General's argument,] the text of § 109 of the Clean Air Act at a minimum requires that "for a discrete set of pollutants and based on published air quality criteria that reflect the latest scientific knowledge, [the] EPA must establish uniform national standards at a level that is requisite to protect public health from the adverse effects of the pollutant in the ambient air." Requisite, in [the words of the Solicitor General], "means sufficient, but not more than necessary." These limits on the EPA's discretion are strikingly similar to the ones we approved in [a 1991 decision], which permitted the Attorney General to designate a drug as a controlled substance for purposes of criminal drug enforcement if doing so was "necessary to avoid an imminent hazard to the public safety." They also resemble the Occupational Health and

Safety Act provision requiring the agency to "set the standard which most adequately assures, to the extent feasible, on the basis of the best available evidence, that no employee will suffer any impairment of health"—which the Court upheld in [a 1980 decision].

The scope of discretion § 109 allows is in fact well within the outer limits of our nondelegation precedents. In the history of the Court we have found the requisite "intelligible principle" lacking in only two statutes, one of which provided literally no guidance for the exercise of discretion, and the other of which conferred authority to regulate the entire economy on the basis of no more precise a standard than stimulating the economy by assuring "fair competition." We have, on the other hand, upheld the validity of [a section of] the Public Utility Holding Act of 1935, which gave the Securities and Exchange Commission authority to modify the structure of holding company systems so as to ensure that they are not "unduly or unnecessarily complicated" and do not "unfairly or inequitably distribute voting power among security holders." *American Power & Light Co. v. SEC* (1946). We have approved the wartime conferral of agency power to fix the prices of commodities at a level that "will be generally fair and equitable and will effectuate the purposes of [the relevant statute]." *Yakus v. United States* (1944). And we have found an "intelligible principle" in various statutes authorizing regulation in the "public interest." See, e.g., *National Broadcasting Co. v. United States* (1943). In short, we have "almost never felt qualified to second-guess Congress regarding the permissible degree of policy judgment that can be left to those executing or applying the law." *Mistretta v. United States* (1989) (Scalia, J., dissenting).

It is true enough that the degree of agency discretion that is acceptable varies according to the scope of the power congressionally conferred. While Congress need not provide any direction to the EPA regarding the manner in which it is to define "country elevators," which are to be exempt from new stationary-source regulations governing grain elevators, it must provide substantial guidance on setting air standards that affect the entire national economy. But even in sweeping regulatory schemes we have never demanded, as the Court of Appeals did here, that statutes provide a "determinate criterion" for saying "how much [of the regulated harm] is too much." [In the controlled substance designation case referred to above,] for example, we did not require the statute to decree how "imminent" was too imminent, or how "necessary" was necessary enough, or even—most relevant here—how "hazardous" was too hazardous. Similarly, the statute at issue in [another Supreme Court decision] authorized agencies to recoup "excess profits" paid under wartime government contracts, yet we did not insist that Congress specify how much profit was too much. It is therefore not conclusive for delegation purposes that, as [American Trucking Associations and the other parties challenging the NAAQS] argue, ozone and particulate matter are "non-threshold" pollutants that inflict a continuum of adverse health effects at any airborne concentration greater than zero, and hence require the EPA to make judgments of degree. "[A] certain degree of discretion, and thus of lawmaking, inheres in most executive or judicial action. *Mistretta* (Scalia, J., dissenting).

Section 109 (b) (1) of the CAA, which we interpret as requiring the EPA to set air quality standards at the level that is "requisite"—that is, not lower or higher than is necessary—to protect the public health with an adequate margin of safety, fits comfortably within the scope of discretion permitted by our precedent.

Court of Appeals decision reversed as to delegation of power issue.

Agency Types and Organization

Agency Types

Administrative agencies may be found under a variety of labels. They may be called "administration," "agency," "authority," "board," "bureau," "commission," "department," "division," or "service." They sometimes have a governing body, which may be appointed or elected. They almost invariably have an administrative head (variously called "Chairman," "Commissioner," "Director," etc.), and a staff. Because our focus is on federal administrative agencies, it is important to distinguish between the two basic types of federal administrative agencies: executive agencies and independent agencies.

Executive Agencies Administrative agencies that reside within the Executive Office of the President or within the executive departments of the president's cabinet are called **executive agencies.** Examples of such agencies and their cabinet homes are: the Food and Drug Administration (Department of Health and Human Services); the Nuclear Regulatory Agency and the Federal Energy Regulatory Agency (Department of Energy); the Occupational Safety and Health Administration (Department of Labor); and the Internal Revenue Service (Treasury Department). In addition to their executive home, such agencies share one other important attribute. Their administrative heads serve "at the pleasure of the President," meaning that they are appointed and removable at his will.

Independent Agencies The Interstate Commerce Commission was the first independent administrative agency created by Congress. Much of the most significant regulation businesses face emanates from independent agencies such as the FTC, the National Labor Relations Board, the Consumer Product Safety Commission, the Equal Employment Opportunity Commission, the Environmental Protection Agency, and the Securities and Exchange Commission. Independent agencies are usually headed by a board or a commission (e.g., the FTC has five commissioners) whose members are appointed by the president "with the advice and consent of the Senate." Commissioners or board members are usually appointed for fixed terms (e.g., FTC commissioners serve seven-year, staggered terms) and are removable only for cause (e.g., FTC commissioners may be removed only for "inefficiency, neglect of duty, or malfeasance in office"). Enabling legislation often requires political balance in agency appointments (e.g., the FTC Act provides that "[n]ot more than three of the commissioners shall be members of the same political party").

Department of Homeland Security As this book went to press in late 2002, Congress had just enacted legislation creating the cabinet-level Department of Homeland Security. This new department, whose creation had been proposed in various versions of House and Senate bills since shortly after the September 11, 2001, attacks on the United States, will gradually absorb more than 20 different functions previously undertaken by other federal departments and agencies. The Department of Homeland Security is expected to employ roughly 170,000 workers, with the vast majority coming to that department by way of transfer from existing positions as federal government employees. With the creation of this new department and the resulting reassignments of employees and areas of responsibility, the 2002 enactment contemplates the most sweeping governmental reorganization in more than a half-century.

Agency Organization

An agency's organizational structure is largely a function of its regulatory mission. The FTC's operational side, for instance, is divided into three bureaus: the Bureau of Competition, which enforces the antitrust laws and unfair competitive practices; the Bureau of Consumer Protection, which focuses on unfair or deceptive trade practices; and the Bureau of Economics, which gathers data, compiles statistics, and furnishes technical assistance to the other bureaus. The Commission is headquartered in Washington, D.C. It maintains regional offices in Atlanta, Boston, Chicago, Cleveland, Dallas, Denver, Los Angeles, New York, San Francisco, and Seattle. This regional office system enhances the Commission's enforcement, investigative, and educational missions by locating Commission staff closer to the public it serves.

LOG ON

The Federal Web Locator, operated and maintained by the Center for Information Law and Policy at the Chicago-Kent College of Law, provides links to the websites of many departments and agencies of the United States government. The address of this useful resource is:
www.infoctr.edu.

Agency Powers and Procedures

Nature, Types, and Source of Powers

The powers administrative agencies possess may be classified in various ways. Some agencies' powers are largely *ministerial*—concerned primarily with the routine performance of duties imposed by law. The most important administrative agencies, however, have broad *discretionary* powers that necessitate the exercise of significant discretion and judgment when they are employed. The major discretionary powers agencies can possess are **investigative power, rulemaking power,** and **adjudicatory power.**

The formal powers an agency possesses are those granted by its enabling legislation. Important federal agencies such as the FTC normally enjoy significant levels of each of the discretionary powers. However, even such powerful agencies face significant limitations on the exercise of their powers. In addition to explicit limits on agency proceedings contained in enabling legislation, basic constitutional provisions restrict agency action.

A federal agency's exercise of its rulemaking and adjudicatory powers is also constrained by the *Administrative Procedure Act (APA)*. The APA was enacted by Congress in 1946 in an attempt to standardize federal agency procedures and to respond to critics who said that administrative power was out of control. The APA applies to all federal agencies, although it will not displace stricter procedural requirements contained in a particular agency's enabling legislation. Besides specifying agency procedures, the APA plays a major role in shaping the conditions under which courts will review agency actions and the standards courts will use when conducting such a review. Most states have adopted "baby APAs" to govern the activities of state administrative agencies.

Finally, as later parts of this chapter will confirm, each of the three traditional branches of government possesses substantial powers to mold and constrain the powers of the "fourth branch." That being said, one final point should be made before we turn to a detailed examination of formal agency powers and procedures. An agency's formal powers also confer on it significant *informal* power. Agency "advice," "suggestions," or "guidelines," which technically lack the legal force of formal agency regulations or rulings, may nonetheless play a major role in shaping the behavior of regulated industries because they carry with them the implicit or explicit threat of formal agency action if they are ignored. Such gentle persuasion can be a highly effective regulatory tool, and one that is subject to far fewer constraints than formal agency action.

Investigative Power

Administrative agencies need accurate information about business practices and activities not only for the detection and prosecution of regulatory violations, but also to enable the agencies to identify areas in which new rules are needed or existing rules require modification. Much of the information agencies require to do their jobs is readily available. "Public interest" groups, complaints from customers or competitors, and other regulatory agencies are all important sources of information.

However, much of the information necessary to effective agency enforcement can come only from sources that may be strongly disinclined to provide it: the individuals and business organizations subject to regulation. This reluctance may stem from the desire to avoid or de-

lay the regulatory action that disclosure would generate. It might also be the product, however, of more legitimate concerns, such as a desire to protect personal privacy, a desire to prevent competitors from acquiring trade secrets and other sensitive information from agency files, or a reluctance to incur the costs that may accompany compliance with substantial information demands. Agencies, therefore, need the means to compel unwilling possessors of information to comply with legitimate demands for information. The two most important (and most intrusive) investigative tools employed by administrative agencies are *subpoenas* and *searches and seizures*.

Subpoenas   There are two basic types of subpoena: the subpoena *ad testificandum* and the subpoena *duces tecum*. Subpoenas *ad testificandum* may be used by an agency to compel unwilling witnesses to appear and testify at agency hearings. Subpoenas *duces tecum* may be used by an agency to compel the production of most types of documentary evidence, such as accounting records and office memoranda.

Unlimited agency subpoena power risks sacrificing individual liberty and privacy in the name of regulatory efficiency. Accordingly, courts have formulated a number of limitations that seek to balance an agency's legitimate need to know against an investigatory target's legitimate privacy interests.

Agency investigations must be *authorized by law* and *conducted for a legitimate purpose*. The former requirement means that the agency's enabling legislation must have granted the agency the investigatory power it seeks to assert. The latter requirement prohibits bad faith investigations pursued for improper motives (e.g., Internal Revenue Service investigations undertaken solely to harass political opponents of an incumbent administration).

Even when the investigation is legally authorized and is undertaken for a legitimate purpose, the information sought must be *relevant to that purpose*. The Fourth Amendment to the Constitution provides this limitation on agency powers. However, an agency issuing an administrative subpoena need not possess the "probable cause" that the Fourth Amendment requires in support of regular search warrants.[4] In the words of the Supreme Court, an agency "can investigate merely on the suspicion that the law is being violated, or even just because it wants assurance that it is not."[5] This lesser standard

---

[4]The Fourth Amendment is discussed in Chapter 5.
[5]*United States v. Morton Salt* (U.S. Sup. Ct. 1950).

makes sense in the agency context, because the only evidence of many regulatory violations is documentary and "probable cause" might be demonstrable only after inspection of the target's records. In such cases, a probable cause requirement would effectively negate agency enforcement power.

Similarly, agency information demands must be *sufficiently specific* and *not unreasonably burdensome.* This requirement derives from the Fourth Amendment's prohibition against "unreasonable searches and seizures." It means that agency subpoenas must adequately describe the information the agency seeks. It also means that the cost to the target of complying with the agency's demand (e.g., the cost of assembling and reproducing the data, the disruption of business operations, or the risk that proprietary information will be indirectly disclosed to competitors) must not be unreasonably disproportionate to the agency's interest in obtaining the information.

Finally, the information sought *must not be privileged.* Various statutory and common law privileges may, at times, limit an agency's power to compel the production of information. By far the most important privilege in this respect is the Fifth Amendment *privilege against compelled testimonial self-incrimination,* or "the right to silence." As you learned in Chapter 5, however, this privilege is subject to serious limitations in the business context. The right to silence in the administrative context is further limited by the fact that it is only available in *criminal* proceedings. In some regulatory contexts, the potential sanctions for violation may be labeled "civil penalties" or "forfeitures." Only when such sanctions are essentially punitive in their intent or effect will they be considered "criminal" for the purpose of allowing the invocation of the privilege.

Public policy concerns provide another subpoena power limitation that may apply even if neither the Fifth Amendment nor another privilege bars production of the documents sought by an agency. As indicated in the *Collins* case, which follows, courts may conclude that an agency subpoena should not be enforced if its enforcement would tend to compromise important operations being conducted by another agency or arm of the government.

Commodity Futures Trading Commission v. Collins *997 F.2d 1230 (7th Cir. 1993)*

The Commodity Futures Trading Commission (CFTC) was investigating Thomas Collins for possible civil violations of the Commodity Exchange Act. Among the violations of which Collins was suspected was the trading of commodities futures contracts other than on a commodities exchange. The CFTC's staff suspected that these trades were spurious trades, which (the staff theorized) were intended to enable Collins to reallocate losses to persons who would reap the maximum tax benefits from the losses. As part of this investigation, the CFTC issued a subpoena directing Collins to produce copies of his federal income tax returns for examination by the CFTC's staff. The staff's reasoning was that the presence of tax motives would be evidence of a likely violation of rules enforced by the CFTC.

Collins resisted the subpoena on the ground that it would force him to incriminate himself. Collins argued that the tax returns contained information that could be evidence—or could lead to evidence—of felony violations of federal law. The CFTC argued that the tax returns were required records and that compelling their disclosure therefore would not violate the Fifth Amendment. [See Chapter 5's discussion of the required-records doctrine, which operates to eliminate Fifth Amendment privilege claims regarding the contents of such records.] The district court agreed with the CFTC and entered an enforcement order requiring Collins to obey the subpoena. Collins appealed.

In a portion of its opinion not set forth here, the Seventh Circuit Court of Appeals concluded that the required-records doctrine was inapplicable because the subpoena sought a taxpayer's copies of his tax returns—copies that the taxpayer was not required by law to make—rather than the actual tax returns whose preparation and filing with the Internal Revenue Service were required by law. The Seventh Circuit then (as set forth below) continued its analysis of Collins's Fifth Amendment argument and addressed other policy concerns triggered by the CFTC's subpoena.

Posner, Judge [The inapplicability of the required-records doctrine] does not end our inquiry. The [required-records] doctrine only comes into play if, were it not for the doctrine, the government would be forcing a person to incriminate himself. *Garner v. United States* (1976) holds that the taxpayer who includes incriminating information on his return is like the witness who blurts out incriminating testimony rather than invoking the Fifth Amendment and keeping mum: he has not been compelled to testify against himself, so he has no Fifth Amendment claim. *Garner* . . . is consistent with the cases which hold that there is no Fifth Amendment privilege in already created documents, because the disclosures in them were not compelled. *Garner* and [the cases dealing with already created documents] make the required-records exception to the Fifth Amendment privilege largely, perhaps entirely, superfluous, because records that are not required are by the same token not privileged. And those decisions suggest another reason for doubting that Collins has any Fifth Amendment claim: Collins created copies of his tax returns voluntarily, so any information in the copies, however incriminating, was not compelled by the government.

In light of all this it is doubtful that Collins has any constitutional leg to stand on. No matter. All constitutional concerns to one side, we think it was an abuse of discretion for the district judge to enforce this subpoena. Income tax returns are highly sensitive documents; that is why [federal law provides that agencies such as the CFTC] cannot get Collins's tax returns directly from the Internal Revenue Service. The self-reporting, self-assessing character of the income tax system would be compromised were they promiscuously disclosed to agencies enforcing regulatory programs unrelated to tax collection itself. The CFTC made no showing that it needed Collins's tax returns. All it legitimately wants to know is whether Collins traded off the exchange and if so, why. It can ask him. If it doubts his answer, it can ask for substantiation. If he refuses to furnish it on the ground that it would compel him to incriminate himself, the CFTC can draw the appropriate inference—for example, that he was trading off the exchange in order to reap tax benefits. No law forbids a regulatory agency to draw the logical inference from a regulated entity's refusing on Fifth Amendment grounds to play ball with the agency. Should the government want to prosecute Collins criminally the Fifth Amendment would be a potential bar—but a very feeble one, in light of our previous discussion.

We are not experts in the investigation of violations of the commodity laws, so we may have overlooked reasons why, despite appearances, the effectiveness of the CFTC's investigation of Collins depends on its having access to his tax returns. The CFTC has not advanced any such reasons. It asked for and obtained the enforcement of the subpoena as a matter of rote, upon its bare representation that the tax returns might contain information germane to the investigation. That is not enough, if an appropriate balance is to be struck between the privacy of income tax returns and the needs of law enforcement. [L]arger interests are at stake than those of the immediate parties—namely the interest, unrepresented by . . . the parties to this case (for the CFTC is not represented by the Department of Justice, which might be assumed to be speaking for the Internal Revenue Service as well), in the effective administration of the federal tax laws.

District court order enforcing subpoena reversed in favor of Collins.

Searches and Seizures Sometimes the evidence necessary to prove a regulatory violation can be obtained only by entering private property such as a home, an office, or a factory. When administrative agencies seek to gather information by such an entry, the Fourth Amendment's prohibition against unreasonable searches and seizures and its warrant requirement come into play. Owners of commercial property, although afforded less Fourth Amendment protection than the owners of private dwellings, do have some legitimate expectations of privacy in their business premises.

Not all agency information-gathering efforts, however, will be considered so intrusive as to amount to a prohibited search and seizure. In *Dow Chemical Co. v. United States* (U.S. Sup. Ct. 1986), for instance, the Environmental Protection Agency's warrantless aerial photography of one of Dow's plants was upheld. Furthermore, in *State of New York v. Burger* (U.S. Sup. Ct. 1987), the Supreme Court upheld the constitutionality of warrantless administrative inspections of the premises of "closely regulated" businesses so long as three criteria are satisfied: (1) there must be a substantial government interest in the regulatory scheme in question, (2) the warrantless inspections must be necessary to further the scheme, and (3) the inspection program must provide a constitutionally adequate substitute for a warrant by giving owners of commercial property adequate notice that their property is subject to inspection and by limiting the discretion of inspecting officers.

Rulemaking Power

An agency's rulemaking power derives from its enabling legislation. For example, the FTC Act gives the FTC the power "to make rules and regulations for the purpose of carrying out the provisions of this Act." The Administrative Procedure Act (APA) defines a rule as "an agency statement of general or particular applicability and future effect designed to complement, interpret or prescribe law or policy." All agency rules are compiled and published in the *Code of Federal Regulations.*

Types of Rules Administrative agencies create three types of rules: procedural, interpretive, and legislative. *Procedural rules* specify how the agency will conduct itself. For instance, agencies typically have procedural rules dealing with such matters as the manner in which advance notice of agency rulemaking proceedings will be communicated.

Interpretive rules are designed to advise regulated individuals and entities of the manner in which an agency interprets the statutes it enforces. For example, the FTC has promulgated a rule interpreting the term *consumer product,* as used in the Magnuson-Moss Warranty Act (a statute the FTC has the legal responsibility to enforce). Interpretive rules technically do not have the force of law. Therefore, they are not binding on businesses and the courts. Courts interpreting regulatory statutes often give agency interpretations substantial weight, however, in deference to the agency's familiarity with the statutes it administers and its presumed expertise in the general area being regulated. Business is also likely to pay attention to agency interpretive rules because such rules indicate the circumstances in which an agency is likely to take formal enforcement action.

If consistent with an agency's enabling legislation and the Constitution, and if created in accordance with the procedures dictated by the APA, *legislative rules* have the full force and effect of law. Legislative rules thus are binding on the courts, the public, and the agency. Federal agencies have promulgated very large numbers of legislative rules, many of which address highly specific matters. For example, an FTC legislative rule states that if a party sells a quick-freeze aerosol spray product designed for the frosting of beverage glasses and the product contains an ingredient known as Fluorocarbon 12, the seller must issue a warning (on the product label) that the product should not be inhaled in concentrated form, in view of the risk that such behavior may lead to severe harm or death.

Given the greater relative importance of legislative rules, you should not be surprised to learn that the process by which they are promulgated—unlike the process by which procedural and interpretive rules are created—is highly regulated by the APA and closely scrutinized by the courts. There are three basic types of agency rulemaking: informal, formal, and hybrid.

Informal Rulemaking *Informal rulemaking* (or "notice and comment" rulemaking) is the method most commonly employed by administrative agencies that are not forced by their enabling legislation to follow the more stringent procedures of formal rulemaking. The informal rulemaking process commences with the publication of a "Notice of Proposed Rulemaking" in the *Federal Register.* The APA requires that such notices contain: a statement of the time and place at which the proceedings will be held; a statement of the nature of the proceedings; a statement of the legal authority for the proceedings (usually the agency's enabling legislation); and either a statement of the terms of the proposed rule or a description of the matters to be addressed by the rule.

Publication of notice must then be followed by a *comment period* during which interested parties may submit written comments detailing their views about the proposed rule. After comments have been received and considered, the agency must publish the regulation in its final form in the *Federal Register.* As a general rule, the rule cannot become effective until at least 30 days after this final publication. The APA, however, recognizes a "good cause" exception to the 30-day waiting period requirement, and to the notice of rulemaking requirement as well, when notice would be impractical, unnecessary, or contrary to the public interest.

Agencies tend to favor the informal rulemaking process because it allows quick and efficient regulatory action. Such quickness and efficiency, however, are purchased at a significant cost—a minimal opportunity for interested parties to participate in the rule-formation process. Giving interested parties the opportunity to be heard may, ultimately further regulatory goals. For example, the vigorous debate about a proposed rule that a public hearing can provide may contribute to the creation of more effective rules. Also, providing interested parties an adequate opportunity to participate in the rulemaking process lends credibility to that process and the rules it produces, thereby enhancing the chances of voluntary compliance.

Formal Rulemaking *Formal rulemaking* is designed to give interested parties a far greater opportunity to make their views heard than that afforded by informal rulemaking. As does informal rulemaking, formal rulemaking begins with publication of a "Notice of Proposed Rulemaking" in the *Federal Register.* Unlike the notice employed to announce informal rulemaking procedures, however, this notice must include notice of a time and place at which a public hearing will be held. Such hearings resemble trials in that the agency must produce evidence justifying the proposed regulation, and interested parties are allowed to present evidence in opposition to it. Both sides may examine each other's exhibits and cross-examine each other's witnesses. At the conclusion of the proceedings, the agency must prepare a formal, written document detailing its findings based on the evidence presented at the hearing.

Although the formal rulemaking process affords interested parties greatly enhanced opportunities to be heard, this greater access is purchased at significant expense and at the risk that some parties will abuse their access rights in an effort to impede the regulatory process. By tireless cross-examination of government witnesses and lengthy presentations of their own, opponents seeking to derail or delay regulation may consume months, or even years, of agency time. A classic example of such behavior would be the Food and Drug Administration's hearings on a proposed rule requiring that the minimum peanut content of peanut butter be set at 90 percent. Industry forces favored an 87 percent minimum and were able to delay regulation for almost 10 years.

Hybrid Rulemaking Frustrated over the lack of access afforded by informal rulemaking and the potential for paralyzing the regulatory process that is inherent in formal rulemaking, some legislators have attempted to create a rulemaking process that combines some of the elements of informal and formal procedures. Although hybrid rulemaking procedures are insufficiently established and standardized at this point to permit a detailed discussion of them, some general tendencies are evident. Hybrid procedures bear some resemblance to those of formal rulemaking in that both involve some sort of hearing. Unlike formal rulemaking procedures, however, hybrid procedures tend to limit the right of interested parties to cross-examine agency witnesses.

Adjudicatory Power

Most major federal agencies possess substantial adjudicatory powers. Besides having the authority to investigate alleged behaviors and to produce regulations that have legal effect, agencies often have the power to conduct proceedings to determine whether regulatory or statutory violations have occurred. The administrative adjudication process is at once similar to, but substantially different from, the judicial process you studied in Chapter 2.

The administrative adjudication process normally begins with a complaint filed by the agency. The party charged in the complaint (called the *respondent*) files an answer. Respondents are normally entitled to a hearing before the agency. At this hearing, they may confront and cross-examine agency witnesses and present evidence of

their own. Respondents may be represented by legal counsel. No juries are present in administrative adjudications, however. The cases are heard by an agency employee usually called an **administrative law judge (ALJ).** Unlike criminal prosecutions, the burden of proof in administrative proceedings is normally the civil *preponderance of the evidence* standard. Constitutional procedural safeguards such as the exclusionary rule do not protect the respondent.[6]

The agency, in effect, functions as police officer, prosecutor, judge, and jury. The APA attempts to deal with the obvious potential for abuse inherent in this combination in a number of ways. First, the APA attempts to ensure that ALJs are as independent as possible by requiring internal separation between an agency's judges and its investigative and prosecutorial functions. The APA also prohibits ALJs from having private consultations with any party to an agency proceeding and shields them from agency disciplinary action other than for "good cause." Finally, insufficient separation between an agency's adjudication function and its other functions can be contrary to basic due process requirements.

After each party to the proceeding has been heard, the ALJ renders a decision stating her findings of fact and conclusions of law, and imposing whatever penalty she deems appropriate within the parameters established by the agency's enabling legislation (e.g., a fine or a cease-and-desist order). If neither party challenges the ALJ's decision, it becomes final. The losing party, however, may appeal an ALJ's decision, which will then be subjected to a **de novo review** by the governing body of the agency (e.g., appeals from FTC ALJ decisions are heard by the five FTC commissioners). *De novo review* means that the agency's governing body may treat the proceedings as if they were occurring for the first time and may ignore the ALJ's findings. Often, however, the agency's governing body will adopt the ALJ's findings. In any event, those findings will be part of the record if a disappointed respondent seeks judicial review of an agency's decision.

Finally, it is important to note that many agency proceedings are settled by a **consent order** before completion of the adjudication process. Consent orders are similar to the nolo contendere pleas discussed in Chapter 5. Respondents who sign consent orders do not admit wrongdoing, but they waive all rights to judicial review, agree to accept a specific sanction imposed by the agency, and commonly agree to discontinue the business practice that triggered the agency action.

---

[6]The exclusionary rule and the beyond a reasonable doubt standard employed in criminal cases are discussed in Chapter 5. The preponderance of the evidence standard is discussed in Chapter 6.

THE GLOBAL BUSINESS ENVIRONMENT

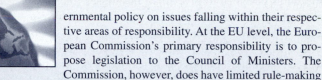

With the many administrative agencies that exist at the federal, state, and sometimes even local levels, the United States surely possesses more extensive and expansive administrative law than any other nation. (Whether this is viewed as a good or bad thing may have a great deal to do with one's philosophical and political perspectives.) Many nations that lack the vast administrative agency "infrastructure" present in the United States nevertheless tend to have some regulatory—or at least advisory—bodies charged with addressing certain types of issues that, in the United States, would fall within the regulatory authority of administrative agencies.

For instance, in the European Union (EU), individual countries typically have *ministries* that may help shape gov-

ernmental policy on issues falling within their respective areas of responsibility. At the EU level, the European Commission's primary responsibility is to propose legislation to the Council of Ministers. The Commission, however, does have limited rule-making authority that it may exercise on its own in a manner similar to—though clearly on a lesser scale than—administrative agencies' exercising of rule-making authority in the United States. In fulfilling its responsibilities, the Commission frequently relies on the research assistance, recommendations, and other input provided by subject matter-specific advisory bodies known as the Directorates General.

Controlling Administrative Agencies

By this point in our discussion, we have already encountered certain legal controls on agency action, such as the terms of an agency's enabling legislation, the procedural requirements imposed by the APA, and the basic constraints that the Constitution places on all governmental action. The following sections continue to focus on agency control by examining the various devices through which the three traditional branches of government influence and control the actions of administrative agencies.

Presidential Controls

The executive branch has at its disposal a number of tools that may be employed to shape agency action. The most obvious among them is the President's power to appoint and remove agency administrators. This presidential power is obviously more limited in the case of independent agencies than it is where executive agencies are concerned, but the President generally has the power to appoint the heads of independent agencies and demote the prior chairpersons without cause. Skillful use of the new chair's managerial powers, probably the most important of which is the power to influence agency hiring policies, can eventually effect substantial changes in agency policy. Also, significant and sustained policy differences between an independent agency and the executive branch often eventually trigger resignations by agency commissioners, thus providing the President with the opportu-

nity to appoint new members whose philosophies are more congruent with his own.

The executive branch also exercises significant control over agency action through the Office of Management and Budget (OMB). The OMB plays a major role in the creation of the annual executive budget the President presents to Congress. In the process, the OMB reviews, and sometimes modifies, the budgetary requests of executive agencies. In addition, an executive order requires executive agencies to prepare cost-benefit and least-cost analyses for all major proposed rules and to submit this information to the OMB for review prior to seeking public comments. This order and a subsequent executive order requiring agencies to give the OMB early warning of possible rule changes have made the OMB a powerful player in the rulemaking process.

Finally, the President's power to *veto* legislation concerning administrative agencies represents another point of executive influence over agency operations.

Congressional Controls

The legislative branch possesses a number of devices, both formal and informal, by which it may influence agency action. Obvious avenues of congressional control include the Senate's "advice and consent" role in agency appointments, the power to amend an agency's enabling legislation (what Congress has given, Congress can take away), and the power to pass legislation that mandates changes in agency practices or procedures. Examples of the latter include the National Environmental Policy Act (NEPA), which dictated that administrative agencies file *environmental impact statements* for every agency action that could significantly affect the quality of the environment, and the Regulatory Flexibility Act, which ordered changes in agency rulemaking procedures designed to give small businesses improved notice of agency rulemaking activities that may have a substantial impact on them. Congress can also pass *sunset legislation* providing for the automatic expiration of an agency's authority unless Congress expressly extends it by a specified date. Such legislation ensures periodic congressional review of the initial decision to delegate legislative authority to an administrative agency.

Congress enjoys several other less obvious, but no less important, points of influence over agency action. For example, Congress must authorize agency budgetary appropriations. Thus, Congress may limit or deny funding for agency programs with which it disagrees. Also, the Governmental Operations Committees of both houses of Congress exercise significant oversight over agency activities. These committees review agency programs and conduct hearings concerning proposed agency appointments and appropriations. Finally, individual members of Congress may seek to influence agency action through "casework"—informal contacts with an agency on behalf of constituents who are involved with the agency.

Judicial Review

As important as the roles of the executive and legislative branches are in controlling agency action, the courts exercise the greatest control over agency behavior, perhaps because they are the branch of government most accessible to members of the public aggrieved by agency action. The APA provides for judicial review of most agency action, which takes place either in one of the U.S. courts of appeals or a U.S. district court, depending on the nature of the agency action at issue. The Supreme Court, if it chooses to grant certiorari, is the court of last resort for review of agency action.

Not all agency actions are subject to judicial review. Moreover, only certain parties may challenge those that are reviewable. An individual or organization seeking judicial review must demonstrate that the agency action being challenged is *reviewable,* that the challenging party

has *standing to sue,* that *necessary administrative remedies have been exhausted,* and that the dispute is *ripe for judicial review.* These requirements are discussed below.

Reviewability Only reviewable agency actions may be challenged by dissatisfied individuals and organizations. Normally, it is not difficult for aggrieved parties to show that the agency action is reviewable because the APA creates a strong presumption in favor of reviewability. This presumption may be overcome only by a showing that "statutes preclude review" or that the decision in question is "committed to agency discretion by law." These limitations on reviewability come from Congress's power to dictate the jurisdiction of the federal courts and from judicial deference to the proper functions of the other branches of government (e.g., a decision relating to matters of foreign policy is likely to be seen as outside the proper province of the judiciary).

Standing to Sue Once reviewability of an agency action has been established, the challenging party must demonstrate that he, she, or it has standing to sue. This means that the individual or organization seeking judicial review is "an aggrieved party" whose interests have been substantially affected by the agency action. Initially, courts took a relatively restrictive view of this basic requirement, requiring plaintiffs to show harm to a legally protected interest. More recently, however, courts have liberalized the standing requirement somewhat, requiring plaintiffs to demonstrate that they have suffered an "injury" to an interest that lies within the "zone of interests" protected by the statute or constitutional provision that serves as the basis of their challenge. Demonstrating an economic loss remains the surest way to satisfy the "injury" requirement, but emotional, aesthetic, and environmental injuries have been found sufficient on occasion.

Lujan v. Defenders of Wildlife, which follows, demonstrates that even though the standing requirement has been liberalized over the years, an asserted injury that is overly abstract, speculative, or tenuous will be insufficient to confer standing on the plaintiff.

Lujan v. Defenders of Wildlife   504 U.S. 555 (U.S. Sup. Ct. 1992)

Section 7(a)(2) of the Endangered Species Act of 1973 divides responsibilities as to protection of endangered species between the Secretary of the Interior and the Secretary of Commerce. The statute also requires each federal agency to consult with the relevant secretary in order to ensure that any action funded by the agency would be unlikely to jeopardize the existence or habitat of an endangered or threatened species. In 1978, the secretaries referred to above promulgated a joint regulation stating that the obligations imposed by Section 7(a)(2) extend not only to actions taken in the United States but also to actions taken in foreign nations. A revised joint regulation, reinterpreting Section 7(a)(2) to require consultation only for actions taken in the United States or on the high seas, was promulgated in 1986. Defenders of Wildlife (DOW), an organization dedicated to wildlife conservation and other environmental causes, sued the Secretary of the Interior, seeking a declaratory judgment that the 1986 regulation erroneously interpreted the geographic scope of Section 7(a)(2). DOW also sought an injunction requiring the secretary to develop a new regulation restoring the interpretation set forth in the 1978 regulation. The district court denied the secretary's motion for summary judgment on the issue of whether DOW had standing to sue, granted DOW's motion for summary judgment on all issues, and ordered the secretary to develop a revised regulation. After the Eighth Circuit Court of Appeals affirmed, the Supreme Court granted certiorari.

Scalia, Justice The preliminary issue, and the only one we reach, is whether DOW has standing to seek judicial review [of the 1986 regulation]. [Article III of the U.S. Constitution] limits the jurisdiction of federal courts to "Cases" and "Controversies." Though some of its elements express merely prudential considerations that are part of judicial self-government, the core component of standing is an essential and unchanging part of the case-or-controversy requirement of Article III.

Over the years, our cases have established that the irreducible constitutional minimum of standing contains three elements: First, the plaintiff must have suffered an injury in fact—an invasion of a legally-protected interest which is (a) concrete and particularized, and (b) actual or imminent, not conjectural or hypothetical. Second, there must be a causal connection between the injury and the conduct complained of. Third, it must be likely, as opposed to merely speculative, that the injury will be redressed by a favorable decision.

The party invoking federal jurisdiction bears the burden of establishing these elements. When the suit is one challenging the legality of government action or inaction, the nature and extent of facts [necessary] to establish standing depends considerably upon whether the plaintiff is himself an object of the action (or foregone action) at issue. If he is, there is ordinarily little question that the action or inaction has caused him injury, and that a judgment preventing or requiring the action will redress it. When, however, as in this case, a plaintiff's asserted injury arises from the government's allegedly unlawful regulation (or lack of regulation) of **someone else,** . . . standing is not precluded, but it is ordinarily substantially more difficult to establish [the necessary elements outlined above].

DOW's claim to injury is that the lack of consultation with respect to certain funded activities abroad "increases the rate of extinction of endangered and threatened species." Of course, the desire to use or observe an animal species, even for purely aesthetic purposes, is undeniably a cognizable interest for purpose of standing. "But the 'injury in

fact' test requires more than an injury to a cognizable interest. It requires that the party seeking review be himself among the injured." *Sierra Club v. Morton* (1972). We shall assume for the sake of argument that [the affidavits of two DOW members, offered by DOW in opposition of the secretary's motion for summary judgment on the standing issue,] contain facts showing that certain agency-funded projects threaten listed species [a variety of crocodile in Egypt and the Asian elephant and the leopard in Sri Lanka]. [The affidavits] plainly contain no facts, however, showing how damage to the species will produce "imminent" injury to [the affiants]. That the affiants "had visited" the areas of the projects before the projects commenced proves nothing. And the affiants' profession of an "intent" to return to the places they had visited before—where they will presumably, this time, be deprived of the opportunity to observe animals of the endangered species—is simply not enough. Such "some day" intentions—without any description of concrete plans, or indeed any specification of *when* the some day will be—do not support a finding of the "actual or imminent" injury that our cases require.

[DOW also asserts theories] called, alas, the "animal nexus" approach, whereby anyone who has an interest in studying or seeing the endangered animals anywhere on the globe has standing; and the "vocational nexus" approach, under which anyone with a professional interest in such animals can sue. Under these theories, anyone who goes to see elephants in the Bronx Zoo, and anyone who is a keeper of Asian elephants in the Bronx Zoo, has standing to sue because the Director of AID did not consult with the Secretary regarding the AID-funded project in Sri Lanka. This is beyond all reason. Standing is not "an ingenious academic exercise in the conceivable." *U.S. v. Students Challenging Regulatory Agency Procedures* (1973). [Instead, standing requires] a factual showing of perceptible harm. It is clear that the person who observes or works with a particular animal threatened by a federal decision is facing perceptible harm, since the very subject of his interest will no longer exist. It is even plausible—though it goes to the outermost limit of plausibility—to think that a person who observes or works with animals of a particular species in the very area of the world where that species is threatened by a federal decision is facing such harm, since some animal that might have been the subject of his interest will no longer exist. It goes beyond the limit, however, and into pure speculation and fantasy, to say that anyone who observes or works with an endangered species, anywhere in the world, is appreciably harmed by a single project affecting some portion of that species with which he has no more specific connection.

The Court of Appeals found that DOW had standing for an additional reason: because it had suffered a "procedural injury" [by virtue of the Endangered Species Act's so-called "citizen-suit" provision stating that "any person" may bring suit to enjoin a violation of the statute]. The court held that . . . the citizen-suit provision [allows] *anyone* [to] file suit in federal court to challenge the Secretary's (or presumably any other official's) failure to follow the assertedly correct consultative procedure, notwithstanding their inability to al-

lege any discrete injury flowing from that failure. The court held that the injury-in-fact requirement [for standing purposes] had been satisfied by congressional conferral upon *all* persons of an abstract, self-contained, noninstrumental "right" to have the Executive [branch] observe the procedures required by law. We reject this view. We have consistently held that a plaintiff raising only a generally available grievance about government—claiming only harm to his and every citizen's interest in proper application of the Constitution and laws, and seeking relief that no more directly and tangibly benefits him than it does the public at large—does not state an Article III case or controversy.

[I]t is clear that in suits against the government, at least, the concrete injury requirement must remain. We hold that DOW lacks standing to bring this action.

Decision of Eighth Circuit Court of Appeals reversed in favor of Secretary of Interior.

Exhaustion and Ripeness Once standing has been established, two further obstacles—exhaustion and ripeness—confront the party challenging an agency action. Courts do not want to allow regulated parties to short-circuit the regulatory process. They also want to give agencies the chance to correct their own mistakes and to develop fully their positions in disputed matters. Accordingly, they normally insist that aggrieved parties *exhaust necessary administrative remedies* before they will grant judicial review.[7] The requirement that a dispute be *ripe* for judicial review is a general requirement emanating from the Constitution's insistence that only "cases or controversies" are judicially resolvable. In determining ripeness, the courts weigh the hardship to the parties of withholding judicial review against the degree of refinement of the issues still possible.

Legal Bases for Challenging Agency Actions Assuming that the above prerequisites to judicial review are met, there are various legal theories on which agency action may be attacked. It may be alleged that the agency's action was *ultra vires* (exceeded its authority as granted by its enabling legislation). For

example, in a 2000 case, the Supreme Court struck down the Food and Drug Administration's 1996 regulations dealing with cigarettes and smokeless tobacco. The Court held that in the Food, Drug, and Cosmetic Act, Congress neither gave, nor intended to give, the FDA authority to regulate tobacco products.[8]

Alternatively, it may be alleged that the agency *substantially deviated from procedural requirements* contained in the APA or in the agency's enabling legislation. Agency action may also be challenged as *unconstitutional* or as the product of an *erroneous interpretation of statutes*. Finally, agency action may be overturned if it is *unsubstantiated by the facts* before the agency when it acted.

Standards of Review The degree of scrutiny that courts will apply to agency action depends on the nature of issues in dispute and the type of agency proceedings that produced the challenged action. Courts are least likely to defer to agency action when *questions of law* are at issue. Although courts afford substantial consideration to an agency's interpretations of the statutes it enforces, the courts are still the ultimate arbiters of the meaning of statutes and constitutional provisions.

---

[7]Necessary administrative remedies are those a statute or regulation establishes as mandatory steps to be completed before judicial review can be sought.

[8]*Food and Drug Administration v. Brown & Williamson Tobacco Corp.* (U.S. Sup. Ct. 2000).

When *questions of fact or policy* are at issue, courts are more likely to defer to the agency because it presumably has superior expertise and because the agency fact finders who heard and viewed the evidence were better situated to judge its merit. When agency factual judgments are at stake, the APA provides for three standards of review, the most rigorous of which is *de novo* review.

When conducting a *de novo* review, courts make an independent finding of the facts after conducting a new hearing. Efficiency considerations plainly favor limited judicial review of the facts. Accordingly, *de novo* review is employed only when required by statute, when inadequate fact-finding proceedings were used in an agency adjudicatory proceeding, or when new factual issues that were not before the agency are raised in a proceeding to enforce a nonadjudicatory agency action.

When courts review formal agency adjudications or formal rulemaking, the APA calls for the application of a **substantial evidence** test. Only agency findings that are "unsupported by substantial evidence" will be overturned. In conducting substantial evidence reviews, courts look at the reasonableness of an agency's actions in relation to the facts before it rather than conducting an independent fact-finding hearing. The substantial evidence test also tends to be employed in hybrid rulemaking cases.

The judicial standard of review used in cases involving informal agency adjudications or rulemaking is the **arbitrary and capricious** test. This is the least rigorous standard of judicial review, in view of the great degree of deference it accords agency decisions. In deciding whether an agency's action was arbitrary and capricious, a reviewing court should not substitute its judgment for that of the agency. Instead, it should ask whether there was an adequate factual basis for the agency's action, and should sustain actions that do not amount to a "clear error of judgment." Although the substantial evidence and arbitrary and capricious tests are separate and distinct in theory, the distinctions often tend to blur in actual practice.

CYBERLAW IN ACTION

Since cable television's early days, cable companies have needed ways to run wires to subscribers' homes. Leasing space on telephone and electric utility poles proved to be a convenient and frequently essential way to facilitate this. Utilities, however, sometimes responded by charging monopoly rents for the use of utility pole space.

Congress addressed these utility pole transactions in 1978 by enacting the Pole Attachments Act. Section 224(b) of this statute requires the Federal Communications Commission (FCC) to "regulate the rates, terms, and conditions for pole attachments to provide that such rates, terms, and conditions are just and reasonable." In the statute's original version, § 224(a) defined *pole attachment* as "any attachment by a cable television system to a pole, duct, conduit, or right-of-way owned or controlled by a utility." A 1996 amendment expanded the definition to include, as an additional regulated category, "any attachment by a . . . provider of telecommunications service."

Pole attachments by firms providing cable television service clearly fell within the above statute and the resulting regulatory authority of the FCC. After cable companies began providing high-speed Internet service, in addition to traditional cable television service, over their wires, the FCC interpreted the statute as also covering pole attachments for these commingled services. In a 1998 order, therefore, the FCC asserted regulatory authority over pole attachments for the commingled services of cable television and high-speed Internet access. The FCC also ruled, in the same order, that the amended version of the statute was broad enough to provide the FCC regulatory authority over attachments by wireless telecommunications providers.

Several pole-owning utilities challenged the 1998 FCC order. The challenges were consolidated in the Eleventh Circuit Court of Appeals, which reversed the FCC's determination and held its order invalid. The U.S. Supreme Court granted the FCC's petition for certiorari, reversed the Eleventh Circuit's decision, and remanded the consolidated cases for further proceedings.

The Supreme Court began by addressing the commingled services question. After citing § 224(b)'s requirement that the FCC "regulate the rates, terms, and conditions for pole attachments" and § 224(a)'s inclusion of "any attachment by a cable television system" within the definition of *pole attachment,* the Court observed that "[t]hese provisions resolve the question." The Court noted the obvious—that a cable attached by a cable company in order to provide cable television service—is an "attachment by a cable television system" for purposes of the statute. It then stressed that if the cable later furnishes high-speed Internet access in addition to cable television service, "the cable does not cease, at that instant, to be an attachment 'by a cable television system.' The addition of a service does not change the character of the attaching entity—the entity the attachment is 'by.' And this is what matters under the statute."

In the Court's view, the Pole Attachments Act "unambiguous[ly]" gave the FCC regulatory authority regarding pole attachments for commingled services. The Court concluded, alternatively, that even if the statute could be regarded as ambiguous, the FCC's interpretation of it was reasonable and thus entitled to deference. According to the Court, the Eleventh Circuit had erred in holding that the two rate formulas set forth in the Pole Attachments Act operated to narrow the statutory definition of *pole attachment* and to exclude attachments for commingled services from the statute's coverage. The Eleventh Circuit's conclusion had "no foundation in the plain language" of the statute, the Court noted. Although Congress specified two rate formulas for two specific categories of pole attachments, "nothing about the text [or] structure of the [Pole Attachments] Act suggest[s] that [the two rate formulas] are the exclusive [ones] allowed." The rate formula in § 224(d) pertains to attachments "used by a cable television system solely to provide cable service." The § 224(e) rate formula applies to attachments "used by telecommunications carriers to provide telecommunications services." According to the Court, "[t]he sum of the transactions addressed by the rate formulas . . . is less than the . . . coverage of the Act as a whole," in view of § 224(a)'s statement that *pole attachment* includes "any attachment by a cable television system or provider of telecommunications service." The absence of a statutorily specified rate formula for pole attachments involving commingled services simply meant that the FCC would need to devise a rate mechanism consistent with its general obligation under the Pole Attachments Act: to see that rates are "just and reasonable."

The result reached by the Court's analysis was "more sensible" than the one reached, erroneously, by the Eleventh Circuit. The Court noted that under the Eleventh Circuit's approach, "if a cable company attempts to innovate at all and provide[s] anything other than pure television, it loses the protection of the Pole Attachments Act and subjects itself to monopoly pricing." In the Court's view, such an outcome would be inconsistent with separate statutes in which Congress instructed the FCC to "encourage the deployment" of broadband Internet capability and to "accelerate deployment of such capability by removing barriers to infrastructure investment." The Court concluded that "[t]his congressional policy underscores the reasonableness of the FCC's interpretation [under which] cable attachments providing commingled services come within the ambit of the [Pole Attachments] Act."

Next, the Court addressed the question whether pole attachments by wireless telecommunications providers were made subject to FCC regulation by the Pole Attachments Act. The Court noted that "[a]gain, the dispositive text" requires the FCC to "regulate the rates, terms, and conditions for pole attachments" (§ 224(b)) and defines *pole attachments* as including "any attachment by a . . . provider of telecommunications service" (§ 224(a)). A separate statutory section defines *telecommunications service* as the offering of telecommunications to the public for a fee, "regardless of the facilities used." Accordingly, the Court reasoned, a provider of wireless telecommunications service is a "provider of telecommunications service" for purposes of the statute—meaning that wireless service providers' attachments are pole attachments to which the statute applies.

The Court observed that the parties challenging the FCC's action had erroneously "s[ought] refuge in other parts of the statute." Although the statute defines *utility* as an entity that "owns or controls poles, ducts, conduits, or rights-of-way used, in whole or in part, for any wire communications," the Court concluded that the *utility* definition "concerns only whose poles are covered, not which attachments are covered." Therefore, contrary to the conclusion reached by the Eleventh Circuit, the *utility* definition did not serve to limit the *pole attachment* definition and thus did not place attachments by providers of wireless service outside the FCC's regulatory authority.

Because all of the pole attachments at issue in the consolidated cases fell "within the heartland" of the Pole Attachments Act, the Court held that the FCC's decision to assert regulatory authority over those attachments was "reasonable and entitled to our deference."

Information Controls

Over roughly the last four decades, Congress has enacted three major statutes aimed at controlling administrative agencies through the regulation of information. Each of these statutes represents a compromise between competing social interests of significant importance. On one hand, we have a strong democratic preference for public disclosure of governmental operations, believing that "government in the dark" is less likely to be consistent with the public interest than is "government in the sunshine." On the other hand, we recognize that some sensitive governmental activities must be shielded from the scrutiny of unfriendly parties, and that disclosure of some information may unjustifiably invade personal privacy, hinder government law enforcement efforts, or provide the competitors of a company about which information is being disclosed with proprietary information that could be used unfairly to the competitors' advantage.

Freedom of Information Act

The *Freedom of Information Act* (FOIA) has existed for nearly 35 years. Congress enacted it to enable private citizens to obtain access to documents in the government's possession. Agencies must normally respond to public requests for documents within 10 days after such a request has been received. An agency bears the burden of justifying a denial of any FOIA request. Denials are appealable to an appropriate federal district court. Successful plaintiffs may recover their costs and attorney's fees.

Not all government-held documents are obtainable under the FOIA, however. The FOIA exempts from disclosure documents that:

1. Must be kept secret in the interest of national security.

2. Concern an agency's internal personnel practices.

3. Are specifically exempted from disclosure by statute.

4. Contain trade secrets or other confidential or privileged commercial or financial information.

5. Are inter-agency or intra-agency memos or letters that would not be subject to discovery in litigation.

6. Appear in individual personnel or medical files, or in similar files if disclosure would constitute a clearly unwarranted invasion of personal privacy.

7. Would threaten the integrity of a law enforcement agency's investigations or jeopardize an individual's right to a fair trial.

8. Relate to the supervision or regulation of financial institutions.

9. Contain geological or geophysical data.

Frequent users of the FOIA include the media, industry trade associations, public interest groups, and companies seeking to obtain useful information about their competitors. The *Klamath Water Users* case, which follows shortly, deals with the fifth exemption listed above. It is important to note that although the FOIA allows agencies to refuse to disclose exempted documents, it does not impose on them the affirmative duty to do so. The Supreme Court has held that individuals cannot compel an agency to deny an FOIA request for allegedly exempt documents that contain sensitive information about them.

The FOIA has recently been the focus of considerable controversy on two points. First, budgetary cutbacks have combined with growing numbers of requests for information to produce agency delays as long as two years in responding to information requests. Courts tend to tolerate agency delays if the agency can show that it made a "due diligence" effort to respond. Second, the dramatic increase in computerized information storage that has occurred since the passage of the FOIA has created problems not specifically contemplated by the statute, which focuses on information stored in documentary form. Do interested parties have the same rights of access to data stored in agency computers that they have to government documents? May the government destroy electronic mail messages, or must it save them? Future legislative or judicial action may be necessary for definitive resolution of such questions.

Department of the Interior v. Klamath Water Users Protective Association
532 U.S. 1 (U.S. Sup. Ct. 2001)

The Department of the Interior's Bureau of Reclamation (Reclamation) administers the Klamath Irrigation Project, which uses water from the Klamath River Basin to irrigate parts of Oregon and California. After the Department began developing the Klamath Project Operation Plan (Plan) to provide water allocations among competing uses and users, the Department asked the Klamath and other Indian Tribes (Basin Tribes or Tribes) to consult with Reclamation on the matter. A memorandum of understanding between those parties called for assessment, in consultation with the Tribes, of the impacts of the Plan on tribal trust resources. During roughly same period, the Department's Bureau of Indian Affairs (Bureau) filed claims on behalf of the Klamath Tribe in an Oregon state-court proceeding intended to allocate water rights. Because the Bureau is responsible for administering land and water held in trust for Indian tribes, it consulted with the Klamath Tribe. The Bureau and the Klamath Tribe then exchanged written memos on the appropriate scope of the claims ultimately submitted by the government for the benefit of the Tribe.

The Klamath Water Users Protective Association (Water Users Association) is a nonprofit organization, most of whose members receive water from the Klamath Irrigation Project. Because of the scarcity of water, most Water Users Association members have interests adverse to the tribal interests. The Water Users Association filed a series of requests with the Bureau under the Freedom of Information Act (FOIA), seeking access to communications between the Bureau and the Basin Tribes. In response, the Bureau turned over several documents but withheld others on the basis of FOIA Exemption 5. The Water Users Association then sued the Bureau and the Department under FOIA to compel release of the documents. A federal district court granted the government summary judgment but the U.S. Court of Appeals for the Ninth Circuit reversed, holding that Exemption 5 did not apply. The U.S. Supreme Court granted the government's petition for certiorari.

Souter, Justice Upon request, FOIA mandates disclosure of records held by a federal agency, unless the documents fall within enumerated exemptions. "[T]hese limited exemptions do not obscure the basic policy that disclosure, not secrecy, is the dominant objective [of FOIA]." *Department of Air Force v. Rose* (U.S. Sup. Ct. 1976). "Consistent with [FOIA's] goal of broad disclosure, these exemptions have been consistently given a narrow compass." *Department of Justice v. Tax Analysts* (U.S. Sup. Ct. 1989).

Exemption 5 protects from disclosure "inter-agency or intra-agency memorandums or letters which would not be available by law to a party other than an agency in litigation with the agency." To qualify, a document must thus satisfy two conditions: its source must be a government agency, and it must fall within the ambit of a privilege against discovery under judicial standards that would govern litigation against the agency that holds it.

Our prior cases on Exemption 5 have addressed the second condition, incorporating civil discovery privileges. So far as they might matter here, those privileges include the privilege for attorney work product and what is sometimes called the "deliberative process" privilege. Work product protects "mental processes of the attorney" [citation omitted], while deliberative process covers "documents reflecting advisory opinions, recommendations, and deliberations comprising part of a process by which governmental decisions and policies are formulated" [citation omitted]. The deliberative process privilege rests on the obvious realization that officials will not communicate candidly among themselves if each remark is a potential item of discovery and front page news. [Its] object is to enhance the quality of agency decisions by protecting open and frank discussion among those who make them within the government.

The point is not to protect government secrecy pure and simple, however, and the first condition of Exemption 5 is no less important than the second; the communication must be "inter-agency or intra-agency." Statutory definitions underscore the apparent plainness of this text. With exceptions not relevant here, "agency" means "each authority of the Government of the United States," and "includes any executive department, military department, Government corporation, Government controlled corporation, or other estab-

lishment in the executive branch of the Government . . ., or any independent regulatory agency."

Although neither the terms of the exemption nor the statutory definitions say anything about communications with outsiders, some Courts of Appeals have held that in some circumstances a document prepared outside the government may nevertheless qualify as an "intra-agency" memorandum under Exemption 5. Typically, courts taking [this] view have held that the exemption extends to communications between government agencies and outside consultants hired by them. In such cases, the records submitted by outside consultants played essentially the same part in an agency's process of deliberation as documents prepared by agency personnel might have done. To be sure, the consultants in these cases were independent contractors and were not assumed to be subject to the degree of control that agency employment could have entailed; nor do we read the cases as necessarily assuming that an outside consultant must be devoid of a definite point of view when the agency contracts for its services. But the fact about the consultant that is constant in the typical cases is that the consultant does not represent an interest of its own, or the interest of any other client, when it advises the agency that hires it. Its only obligations are to truth and its sense of what good judgment calls for, and in those respects the consultant functions just as an employee would be expected to do.

The Department purports to rely on this consultant corollary to Exemption 5 in arguing for its application to the Klamath Tribe's communications to the Bureau in its capacity of fiduciary for the benefit of the Indian Tribes. The existence of a trust obligation is not, of course, in question. The fiduciary relationship has been described as "one of the primary cornerstones of Indian law," and has been compared to one existing under a common law trust, with the United States as trustee, the Indian tribes or individuals as beneficiaries, and the property and natural resources managed by the United States as the trust corpus. The Department is surely right in saying that confidentiality in communications with tribes is conducive to a proper discharge of its trust obligation.

From the recognition of this interest in frank communication . . ., the Department would have us infer a sufficient justification for applying Exemption 5 to communications with the Tribes, in the same fashion that Courts of Appeals have found sufficient reason to favor a consultant's advice that way. But the Department's argument skips a necessary step, for it ignores the first condition of Exemption 5, that the communication be "intra-agency or inter-agency." The Department seems to be saying that "intra-agency" is a purely conclusory term, just a label to be placed on any document the government would find it valuable to keep confidential.

There is, however, no textual justification for draining the first condition of independent vitality, and once the intra-agency condition is applied, it rules out any application of Exemption 5 to tribal communications on analogy to consultants' reports (assuming, which we do not decide, that these reports may qualify as intra-agency under Exemption 5). As mentioned already, consultants whose communications have typically been held exempt have not been communicating with the government in their own interest or on behalf of any person or group whose interests might be affected by the government action addressed by the consultant. In that regard, consultants may be enough like the agency's own personnel to justify calling their communications "intra-agency." The Tribes, on the contrary, necessarily communicate with the Bureau with their own, albeit entirely legitimate, interests in mind. While this fact alone distinguishes tribal communications from the consultants' examples recognized by several Courts of Appeals, the distinction is even sharper, in that the Tribes are self-advocates at the expense of others seeking benefits inadequate to satisfy everyone.

As to those documents bearing on the Plan, the Tribes are obviously in competition with nontribal claimants, including those irrigators represented by the Water Users Association. The record shows that documents submitted by the Tribes included, among others, "a position paper that discusses water law legal theories" and "addresses issues related to water rights of the tribes," a memorandum "containing views on policy the BIA could provide to other governmental agencies," "views concerning trust resources," and a letter "conveying the views of the Klamath Tribe concerning issues involved in the water rights adjudication." While these documents may not take the formally argumentative form of a brief, their function is quite apparently to support the tribal claims. The Tribes are thus urging a position necessarily adverse to the other claimants, the water being inadequate to satisfy the combined demand. As the Court of Appeals said, "the Tribes' demands, if satisfied, would lead to reduced water allocations to members of the [Water Users] Association and have been protested by [those] members who fear water shortages and economic injury in dry years." The position of the Klamath Tribe . . . is thus a far cry from the position of the paid consultant.

All of this boils down to requesting that we read an "Indian trust" exemption into the statute, a reading that is out of the question. There is simply no support for the exemption in the statutory text, which we have elsewhere insisted be read strictly. In FOIA, after all, a new conception of government conduct was enacted into law, "a general philosophy of full agency disclosure." *Department of Justice v. Tax Analysts* (1989) (quoting FOIA legislative history). "Congress believed that this philosophy, put into practice, would help ensure an informed citizenry, vital to the functioning of a democratic society." *Id.* Congress had to realize that not every secret under the old law would be secret under the new.

Judgment of Court of Appeals affirmed.

Privacy Act of 1974

The **Privacy Act of 1974** allows individuals to inspect files that agencies maintain on them and to request that erroneous or incomplete records be corrected. It also attempts to prevent agencies from gathering unnecessary information about individuals and forbids the disclosure of an individual's records without his written permission, except in certain specifically exempted circumstances. For example, records may be disclosed to employees of the agency that collected the information if those employees need the records to perform their duties (the "need to know" exception), to law enforcement agencies, to other agencies' personnel for "routine use" (uses for purposes compatible with the purpose for which the record was collected), and to persons filing legitimate FOIA requests. In addition, records may be disclosed if a court order requires disclosure.

Government in the Sunshine Act

The **Government in the Sunshine Act of 1976** was designed to ensure that "[e]very portion of every meeting of an agency shall be open to public observation." However, complete public access to all agency meetings could have the same negative consequences that unrestrained public access to agency records may sometimes produce. Accordingly, the Sunshine Act exempts certain agency meetings from public scrutiny under circumstances similar to those under which documents are exempt from disclosure under the FOIA.

Issues in Regulation

"Old" Regulation versus "New" Regulation

Some interested observers of regulatory developments over roughly the past 50 years have noted significant differences between the regulations that originated during the Progressive (1902 to 1914) and New Deal (1933 to 1938) eras and many regulations promulgated more recently.[9] They argue not only that the number and scope of regulatory controls have increased substantially in recent years, but also that the focus and the impact of regulation have changed significantly.

Whereas earlier regulation often focused on business practices that harmed the economic interests of specific segments of society (e.g., workers, small-business owners, investors), many modern regulations focus on the health and safety of all citizens. Furthermore, whereas earlier regulations often focused on a particular industry or group of industries (e.g., the railroads or the securities industry), many modern regulations affect large segments of industry (e.g., Title VII of the Civil Rights Act of 1964 and regulations governing environmental pollution and workplace safety). Finally, whereas earlier congressional delegations of regulatory power tended to be quite broad, many more recent regulatory statutes have been extremely detailed.

What are the consequences of these changes in the nature of regulation? Far more businesses than ever before feel the impact of federal regulation, and far more areas of internal corporate decisionmaking are affected by regulation. These changes tend to erode the historic distinction between "regulated" and other industries, and to heighten the importance of business–government relations. Detailed regulatory statutes also increase Congress's role in shaping regulatory policy at the expense of administrative discretion, making regulatory policy arguably more vulnerable to legislative lobbying efforts.

[9]See, for example, David Vogel, "The 'New' Social Regulation in Historical and Comparative Perspective." in *Regulation in Perspective.* ed. T. McGraw (Cambridge. MA: Harvard University Press, 1981). p. 155.

"Captive" Agencies and Agencies' "Shadows"

Proponents of regulation have traditionally feared that regulatory agencies would become "captives" of the industries they were charged with regulating. Through "revolving door" appointments by which key figures move back and forth between government and the private sector, and through excessive reliance on "experts" beholden to industry, the independence of administrative agencies may be compromised and their effectiveness as regulators destroyed.

More recently, commentators sympathetic to business have argued that similar dangers to agency independence exist in the form of the nonindustry "shadow" groups that public interest organizations maintain to monitor agency actions (e.g., the Center for Auto Safety, which monitors the work of the Highway Transportation Safety Administration). Agencies may develop dependency relationships with their shadows or at least make decisions based in part on their shadows' anticipated reactions. Such informal means of shaping regulatory policy, when combined with the ability to challenge agency actions in court, have made public interest organizations important players in the contemporary regulatory process.

Deregulation versus Reregulation

A useful axiom for understanding the process of social and legal evolution is that *the cost of the status quo is easier to perceive than the cost of change.* Few things are more illustrative of the operation of this axiom than the history of regulation in the United States.

In the latter years of the 19th century, the social costs of living in an unregulated environment were readily apparent. Large business organizations often abused their power at the expense of their customers, suppliers, employees, and distributors, and sought to increase their power by acquiring their competitors or driving them out of business. Market forces, standing alone, were apparently unable to protect the public from defective, and in some cases dangerous, products. As a result of these and numerous other social and historical factors, the past century witnessed a tremendous growth in government and in government regulation of business.

Regulation, too, has its costs. Regulatory bureaucracies generate their own internal momentum and have their own interests to protect. They may become insensitive to the legitimate concerns of the industries they regulate and the public they supposedly serve. They may

ETHICS IN ACTION

As noted elsewhere on these pages, a longstanding concern about administrative agencies focuses on the prospect of a "revolving door" situation in which top agency personnel leave the agency to take positions in the industry regulated by the agency, or in which agency officials' desire for an eventual position in the industry causes them to go "soft" on businesses the agency is charged with regulating. The "revolving door" prospect may take other forms, such as where an industry executive philosophically opposed to the work of a certain administrative agency ends up being appointed to a prominent position in that agency when the White House would like to see the agency become less active. Consider these potential issues regarding the revolving door situation:

- What ethical obligations does an administrative agency official owe when she leaves her agency position to accept a job in the industry regulated by the agency?
- What ethical obligations does an executive of a corporation owe when he leaves his corporate position to accept a job

with an administrative agency that regulates the industry in which the corporation does business?
- Is it ethical for an official of an administrative agency to inquire about possible employment in the very industry the agency is charged with regulating? What about the reverse of this situation?
- If the prevailing political winds lead to circumstances in which an avowed opponent of a certain administrative agency's work is appointed to a high-level position in that agency, does this new agency official have an ethical obligation to "buy in" to the work of the agency? If so, to what extent? Does this new agency official, on the other hand, have an ethical obligation to make efforts to change the agency? If so, to what extent?
- Is a revolving door between an administrative agency and its regulated industry necessarily a bad thing? May it be beneficial for the agency, the industry, and society in general? If so, in what way or ways?

---

continue to seek higher and higher levels of safety, heedless of the fact that life necessarily involves some elements of risk and that the total elimination of risk in a modern technological society may be impossible—or if possible, obtainable at a cost that we cannot afford to pay. At a time when many Americans are legitimately concerned about economic efficiency, as well as the ability of U.S. companies to compete effectively in world markets against competitors who operate in less regulated environments, these and other costs of regulation are also readily apparent.

As a result, in the last 20 to 25 years, we have witnessed substantial deregulation in a number of industries such as the airline, banking, railroad, and trucking industries. The results of these efforts are, at best, mixed. The case of airline regulation should suffice to make the point. Proponents of deregulation cite the generally lower fares that deregulation has produced. Opponents tend to point to increased airline overbooking practices, reduced or eliminated services to smaller communities, and increased safety problems, all of which, they argue, are products of deregulation. The costs of deregulation have generated predictable calls for reregulating the airline industry. The ultimate outcome of the deregulation versus reregulation debate will depend on which costs we as a society decide we would prefer to pay.

Problems and Problem Cases

1. Title X of the Public Health Service Act provides federal funding for family-planning services. Section 1008 of the statute specifies that none of the federal funds provided under Title X are to be "used in programs where abortion is a method of family planning." In 1988, the Secretary of Health and Human Services issued new regulations that, among other things, prohibited family-planning services that receive Title X funds from engaging in counseling concerning the use of abortion as a method of family planning, referrals for abortion as a method of family planning, and activities amounting to encouragement or advocacy of abortion as a method of family planning. Various Title X grantees and physicians supervising Title X funds challenged the validity of the regulations and sought an injunction against their implementation. Were the regulations a permissible interpretation of Section 1008? Did the regulations violate constitutional guarantees?

2. Section 9 of the Endangered Species Act (ESA) makes it unlawful for any person to "take" an endangered or threatened species of fish or wildlife. A definition section in the ESA states that *take* means "to harass, harm, pursue, hunt, school, wound, kill, trap, capture, or collect, or to attempt to engage in any such conduct." The

Secretary of the Department of the Interior (the Secretary) promulgated a regulation that defined the term *harm* for purposes of the statutory language just quoted. This regulation stated that *harm* "means an act which actually kills or injures wildlife" and that "[s]uch act may include significant habitat modification or degradation where it actually kills or injures wildlife by significantly impairing essential behavioral paterns, including breeding, feeding or sheltering." A declaratory judgment action attacking the validity of this regulation was brought against the Secretary by a group of landowners, logging companies, and families dependent on the forest products industries, and by organizations representing those parties' interests. The plaintiffs sought a judicial ruling that the regulation defining *harm* as including habitat modification or degradation was an unreasonable and erroneous interpretation of the ESA. The plaintiffs alleged that they had been injured economically by the government's application of the *harm* regulation to the red-cockaded woodpecker, an endangered species, and the northern spotted owl, a threatened species. Was the Department of the Interior's regulation a reasonable interpretation of the statute?

3. Small lodges in remote regions of Alaska cater to hunters and fishermen. These lodges provide food and shelter, guide services, and air transportation to and from the lodge and on side trips, all for a flat fee. Hunting and fishing guides employed by the lodges often pilot light aircraft as part of their guiding service. Beginning in 1963, the Federal Aviation Administration, through its Alaskan Region office, consistently advised guide pilots that they were not governed by FAA regulations dealing with commercial pilots. This advice stemmed from a 1963 Civil Aeronautics Board decision in a case in which the FAA had attempted to sanction a guide pilot who had not complied with FAA regulations applicable to commercial pilots. The Civil Aeronautics Board concluded that the guide pilot's flight with a hunter was merely incidental to the guiding business, that the guide pilot was not a commercial pilot, and that the FAA's commercial pilot regulations therefore did not apply. During the 1990s, officials at FAA headquarters in Washington, D.C., began expressing concern about the safety of guide pilots and their passengers. In 1998, the FAA published an announcement that was aimed at guide pilots. This announcement stated that guide pilots must abide by all FAA regulations applicable to commercial pilots. In a petition for judicial review of this FAA action, the Alaska Professional Hunters Association (APHA) attacked the validity of the announcement and the new rule it purported to adopt. APHA contended that because the FAA

sought to adopt a rule that was contrary to the longstanding interpretation of the FAA's regulations and contrary to the expectations of the guide pilots and the lodges for which they worked, the FAA at a minimum needed to follow the "notice and comment" (informal rulemaking) procedure before adopting a new rule. Simply announcing the new rule, APHA argued, was improper. Was APHA's contention correct?

4. On December 10, 1986, a federal grand jury indicted James Mallen for allegedly making false statements to the Federal Deposit Insurance Corporation (FDIC) and for allegedly making false statements to a bank for the purposes of influencing the actions of the FDIC. Mallen was the president and a director of a federally insured bank at the time he was indicted. On January 20, 1987, the FDIC issued an ex parte order stating that Mallen's continued service could "pose a threat to the interests of the bank's depositors or threaten to impair public confidence in the bank." The order suspended Mallen as president and as a director of the bank and prohibited him "from further participation in any manner in the conduct of the affairs of the bank, or any other bank insured by the FDIC." In issuing the suspension order without first holding a hearing on the matter, the FDIC acted pursuant to a section of the Financial Institutions Supervisory Act. A copy of the FDIC's order was served on Mallen on January 26, 1987. Four days later, his attorney filed a written request for an "immediate administrative hearing" to commence no later than February 9. The FDIC scheduled a hearing for February 18, but on February 6, Mallen filed suit against the FDIC. Arguing that the FDIC's action denied him due process, Mallen sought a preliminary injunction against the suspension order. Was Mallen denied due process?

5. John Doe began work at the Central Intelligence Agency (CIA) in 1973 as a clerk-typist. Periodic fitness reports consistently rated him as an excellent or outstanding employee. By 1977, he had been promoted to covert electronics technician. In January 1982, Doe voluntarily told a CIA security officer that he was a homosexual. Almost immediately, the CIA placed Doe on paid administrative leave and began an investigation of his sexual orientation and conduct. Doe submitted to an extensive polygraph examination during which he denied having sexual relations with foreign nationals and maintained that he had not disclosed classified information to any of his sexual partners. The polygraph officer told Doe that the test results indicated that his responses had been truthful. Nonetheless, a month later Doe was told that the CIA's Office of Security had determined that his

homosexuality posed a threat to security. CIA officials declined, however, to explain the nature of the danger. Doe was asked to resign. When he refused to do so he was dismissed by CIA Director William Webster, who "deemed it necessary and advisable in the interests of the United States to terminate [Doe's] employment with this Agency pursuant to section 102(c) of the National Security Act." The statutory section cited by the director allows termination of a CIA employee whenever the director "shall deem such termination necessary or advisable in the interests of the United States." Doe filed suit against the CIA, arguing that his termination was unlawful under section 102(c) and various constitutional guarantees. The CIA moved to dismiss Doe's complaint, arguing that the director's decision was a decision committed to agency discretion by law and thus was not subject to judicial review. Was the CIA's argument correct?

6. Scott Armstrong submitted a Freedom of Information Act (FOIA) request that, among other things, called for the federal government to reveal a list of names of lower-level FBI agents who attended certain meetings at the White House during the mid-1980s. When the government refused to reveal the agents' names, Armstrong filed suit under the FOIA. Upholding this refusal, the district court agreed with the government's contention that the names of FBI agents should always be exempt from disclosure under the FOIA exemption for "personnel and medical files and similar files the disclosure of which would constitute a clearly unwarranted invasion of personal privacy." On appeal, Armstrong argued that the district court erred in concluding that the FOIA's privacy exemption justifies a categorical rule that FBI agents' names are exempt from disclosure. Was Armstrong correct?

7. For many years, section 109 of the Federal Credit Union Act provided that "[f]ederal credit union membership shall be limited to groups having a common bond of occupation or association, or to groups within a well-defined neighborhood, community, or rural district." Until 1982, the National Credit Union Administration and its predecessor agencies consistently interpreted section 109 as requiring that the same common bond of occupation unite every member of an occupationally defined credit union. In 1982, however, the NCUA reversed its longstanding policy in order to permit credit unions to be composed of multiple unrelated employer groups. The NCUA thus began interpreting section 109's common bond requirement as applying only to each employer group in a multiple-group credit union, rather than to every member of that credit union.

Several banks and the American Bankers Association sought judicial review of this action by the NCUA. They alleged that the NCUA's 1982 interpretation of section 109 was improper and impermissible. Were the banks and the Bankers Association correct?

8. The federal Clean Water Act provides for two sets of water quality measures: effluent limitations, which are promulgated by the Environmental Protection Agency (EPA), and water quality standards, which are promulgated by the states. The Clean Water Act generally prohibits the discharge of effluent into a navigable body of water unless the party making such a discharge obtains a permit to do so from a state with an EPA-approved permit program or from the EPA itself. The EPA issued a Fayetteville, Arkansas, sewage treatment plant a permit to discharge effluent into an Arkansas stream that ultimately reaches the Illinois River upstream from the Oklahoma border. The permit included conditions designed to make the Fayetteville discharge comply with Oklahoma's water quality standards. Oklahoma challenged the permit's issuance and terms. Following a hearing, an EPA administrative law judge affirmed the issuance of the permit. After the EPA's chief judicial officer did the same, Oklahoma sought judicial review in federal court. What standard of review should the court follow?

9. An agent of the Pennsylvania Department of Environmental Resources saw Disposal Service's loaded trash truck backing into a building that was used to compact waste to be loaded onto tractor-trailers for transportation and final disposal. Knowing the building's purpose and that Disposal Service did not have a permit to operate it as a transfer station, as required by the state Solid Waste Management Act (SWMA), the agent entered the property, went into the building, and observed the operation. Disposal Service was later prosecuted for operating a transfer station without a permit. Disposal Service moved to suppress the agent's evidence, arguing that his warrantless entry onto the property violated the Fourth Amendment. The state argued that the SWMA's provisions allowing such warrantless inspections were constitutional. Should the evidence be suppressed?

10. Relying on the Freedom of Information Act (FOIA). Public Citizen Health Research Group asked the Food and Drug Administration (FDA) for documents relating to drug applications that had been abandoned for health or safety reasons. When the FDA denied this request, Public Citizen sued in federal court. Schering Corporation, which had submitted five investigational new drug applications (INDs) of the sort requested by Public Citizen, intervened as a defendant. The FDA and Schering contended that certain documents in the five INDs contained confidential commercial information and could therefore be withheld under Exemption 4 of the FOIA. Public Citizen argued that disclosure would prevent other drug companies "from repeating Schering's mistakes, thereby avoiding risk to human health." In addition, Public Citizen argued that under Exemption 4, the court should gauge whether the competitive harm done to the sponsor of an IND by the public disclosure of confidential information is outweighed by the strong public interest in safeguarding the health of human trial participants. Were Public Citizen's arguments regarding Exemption 4 legally correct? Were the requested documents subject to being withheld under Exemption 4?

11. Section 203(a) of the federal Communications Act required communications common carriers to file tariffs with the Federal Communications Commission (FCC). Section 203(b) of the same statute authorized the FCC to "modify any requirement made by or under" section 203. Relying on its modification authority under section 203(b), the FCC issued a series of orders during the 1980s and early 1990s. These orders made tariff filing optional for all nondominant long-distance carriers. American Telephone and Telegraph Co. (AT&T), the only long-distance carrier classified as dominant, asked the U.S. Court of Appeals for the District of Columbia Circuit to reverse these FCC orders. AT&T contended that making tariff filing optional for nondominant long-distance carriers was not a valid exercise of the FCC's modification authority under section 203(b). Was AT&T correct in this contention?

Online Research: The FCC and the FOIA

Locate the website of the Federal Communications Commission (FCC). Review it to find an explanation of how to file Freedom of Information Act (FOIA) requests. Then prepare a brief description of the filing options available to a party who wishes to submit an FOIA request to the FCC.

48

THE FEDERAL TRADE COMMISSION ACT AND CONSUMER PROTECTION LAWS

*D*oan's is a brand name used for more than 90 years for back pain medication sold on an over-the-counter basis. Shortly after its 1987 purchase of the *Doan's* trademark and the right to produce the underlying product, Ciba-Geigy Corporation (Ciba) conducted a marketing study concerning consumer perceptions of the *Doan's* medication for back pain. The study revealed that this medication had a weak image in comparison to the leading brands of analgesics, and indicated that Ciba would benefit from positioning *Doan's* as a more effective product that was strong enough for the types of pain typically experienced by persons susceptible to backaches.

In an effort to strengthen the image of *Doan's,* Ciba mounted a television and newspaper advertising campaign that lasted from 1988 to 1996. The advertisements characterized *Doan's* as an effective remedy specifically for back pain and stated that the product contained a special ingredient (magnesium salicylate) not found in other over-the-counter analgesics. Some of the advertisements displayed images of competing over-the-counter pain remedies. In 1998, the Federal Trade Commission (FTC) instituted an administrative proceeding against Ciba's successor-in-interest, Novartis Corporation, on the ground that the 1988 to 1996 advertisements for *Doan's* were deceptive, in supposed violation of § 5 of the Federal Trade Commission Act. The FTC's theory was that even though the *Doan's* advertisements were truthful in stating that the product was effective for back pain and that it contained a special ingredient not present in other over-the-counter analgesics, the combination of the two literally true statements created an implied representation for which there was no substantiation: that because of its special ingredient, *Doan's* was superior to other analgesics in relieving back pain. It was this implied representation that the FTC alleged to be deceptive. Consider the following questions as you study Chapter 48:

• In FTC administrative proceedings, what legal test controls the determination of whether an advertisement was deceptive?
• May the FTC validly base a deceptive advertising proceeding on the theory that an advertisement consisting of literally true statements may nevertheless be deceptive in what it implies?
• If the theory just noted is valid, were the *Doan's* advertisements deceptive?
• If the *Doan's* advertisements were deceptive, what potential legal consequences could follow for Novartis? In particular, may that firm be ordered to engage in corrective advertising, or would a corrective advertising order violate the firm's right to freedom of speech?

DURING THE PAST FOUR decades, *direct government regulation* of consumer matters has become a prominent feature of the legal landscape at the federal and state levels. This chapter addresses federal consumer protection regulation. It begins with a general discussion of America's main consumer watchdog, the Federal Trade Commission (FTC). After describing how the FTC operates, the chapter examines its regulation of anticompetitive, deceptive, and unfair business practices. Then we discuss various federal laws that deal with consumer credit and other consumer matters.

The Federal Trade Commission

The Federal Trade Commission was formed shortly after the 1914 enactment of the Federal Trade Commission Act (FTC Act).[1] Because the FTC is an independent federal agency, it is outside the executive branch of the federal government and is less subject to political control than agencies that are executive departments. The FTC is headed by five commissioners appointed by the President and confirmed by the Senate for staggered seven-year terms. The President designates one of the commissioners as chairman of the FTC. The FTC has a Washington headquarters and several regional offices located throughout the United States.

The FTC's Powers

The FTC's principal missions are to keep the U.S. economy both *free* and *fair.* Congress has given the Commission many tools for accomplishing these missions. By far the most important, however, is § 5 of the FTC Act, which empowers the Commission to prevent *unfair methods of competition* and *unfair or deceptive acts or practices.* We examine these bases of FTC authority later in this chapter. The Commission also enforces the consumer protection and consumer credit measures discussed in the last half of the chapter. Finally, the FTC enforces numerous other federal laws relating to specific industries or lines of commerce.

FTC Enforcement Procedures

The FTC has various legal means for ensuring compliance with the statutes it administers. The three most important FTC enforcement devices are its procedures for facilitating voluntary compliance, its issuance of trade regulation rules, and its adjudicative proceedings.

Voluntary Compliance The FTC promotes voluntary business behavior by issuing advisory opinions and industry guides. An **advisory opinion** is the Commission's response to a private party's query about the legality of proposed business conduct. The FTC is not obligated to furnish advisory opinions. The Commission may rescind a previously issued opinion when the public interest requires. When the FTC does so, however, it cannot proceed against the opinion's recipient for actions taken in good faith reliance on the opinion, unless it gives the recipient notice of the rescission and an opportunity to discontinue those actions.

Industry guides are FTC interpretations of the laws it administers. Their purpose is to encourage businesses to abandon certain unlawful practices. To further this end, industry guides are written in lay language. Although industry guides lack the force of law, behavior that violates an industry guide often violates one of the statutes or other rules the Commission enforces.

Trade Regulation Rules Unlike industry guides, FTC **trade regulation rules** are written in legalistic language and have the force of law. Thus, the FTC can proceed directly against those who engage in practices forbidden by a trade regulation rule. This may occur through the *adjudicative proceedings* discussed immediately below. The Commission may also obtain a federal district court *civil penalty* of up to $11,000 for each knowing violation of a rule. Furthermore, it may institute court proceedings to obtain various forms of *consumer redress,* including the payment of damages, the refund of money, the return of property, and the reformation or rescission of contracts.

FTC Adjudicative Proceedings Often, the FTC proceeds against violators of statutes or trade regulation rules by administrative action within the Commission itself. The FTC obtains evidence of possible violations from private parties, government bodies, and its own investigations. If the FTC decides to proceed against the alleged offender (the *respondent*), it enters a formal complaint. The case is heard in a public administrative hearing called an *adjudicative proceeding.* An FTC administrative law judge presides over this proceeding.[2]

---

[1]See Chapter 47 for further discussion of the FTC's creation, organization, powers, and status as an independent agency.

[2]Chapter 47 describes federal administrative proceedings.

The judge's decision can be appealed to the FTC's five commissioners and then to the federal courts of appeals and the U.S. Supreme Court.

The usual penalty resulting from a final decision against the respondent is an FTC **cease-and-desist order.** This is a command ordering the respondent to stop its illegal behavior. As you will see later in the chapter, however, FTC orders may go beyond the command to cease and desist. The civil penalty for noncompliance with a cease-and-desist order is up to $11,000 per violation. Where there is a continuing failure to obey a final order, each day that the violation continues is considered a separate violation.

Many alleged violations are never adjudicated by the FTC. Instead, they are settled through a **consent order.** This is an order approving a negotiated agreement in which the respondent promises to cease certain activities. Consent orders normally provide that the respondent does not admit any violation of the law. The failure to observe a consent order is punishable by civil penalties.

> **LOG ON**
>
> The Federal Trade Commission's website, **www.ftc.gov**, contains a wealth of information regarding topics addressed in this chapter.

Anticompetitive Behavior

Section 5 of the FTC Act empowers the Commission to prevent "unfair methods of competition." This language allows the FTC to regulate anticompetitive practices made unlawful by the Sherman Act. The Commission also has statutory authority to enforce the Clayton and Robinson-Patman Acts.[3]

For the most part, § 5's application to anticompetitive behavior involves the orthodox antitrust violations discussed in the following two chapters. Section 5, however, also reaches anticompetitive behavior *not covered by other antitrust statutes.* In addition, § 5 enables the FTC to proceed against *potential* or *incipient* antitrust violations.

Deception and Unfairness

Section 5 of the FTC Act also prohibits "unfair or deceptive acts or practices" in commercial settings. This language enables the FTC to regulate a wide range of activities that disadvantage consumers. In doing so, the Commission may seek to prove that the activity is *deceptive,* or that it is *unfair.* Here, we set out the general

---

[3]Chapter 49 discusses the Sherman Act. Chapter 50 discusses the Clayton and Robinson-Patman Acts.

THE GLOBAL BUSINESS ENVIRONMENT

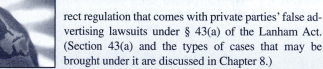

In most developed nations, the problem of misleading advertising is addressed through self-regulation and through regulatory schemes established by law. Self-regulation includes voluntary action by companies and resolution of parties' advertising-related disputes under industry codes of conduct or other agreed procedures that exist outside the formal legal system.

Since the passage of a 1984 European Union (EU) Directive on Misleading Advertising, EU nations have been obligated to have domestic laws addressing misleading advertising. The domestic laws of EU nations typically have not contemplated a significant role for direct government regulation of the sort in which the Federal Trade Commission and other government agencies engage in the United States. Instead, EU countries depend more on litigation instituted by private parties—competitors and, in some countries, consumer organizations—as the chief legal means of dealing with misleading advertising. In this sense, the approach taken by EU nations resembles a different aspect of advertising regulation in the United States: the indirect regulation that comes with private parties' false advertising lawsuits under § 43(a) of the Lanham Act. (Section 43(a) and the types of cases that may be brought under it are discussed in Chapter 8.)

Sweden and the other Scandinavian countries have established, by law, a consumer ombudsman who hears advertising complaints, resolves them when possible, and resorts to litigation if necessary. The ombudsman also has some power to promulgate advertising rules that carry legal force. In this sense, the ombudsman's role resembles that of the FTC in the United States.

Advertising laws contemplate significant regulatory roles for government agencies in New Zealand, Australia, and Japan, though industry self-regulation remains prominent in at least the latter two of those nations. In Great Britain, the traditional emphasis on self-regulation through the private Advertising Standards Authority has been supplemented during the past 15 years by government regulation through the office of the Director General of Fair Trading.

standards that the FTC uses to define each of these § 5 violations. Much of this discussion involves FTC regulation of advertising, but the standards we outline apply to many other misrepresentations, omissions, and practices. Although their details are beyond the scope of this text, the Commission also has enacted numerous trade regulation rules defining specific deceptive or unfair practices.

Deception

The FTC determines the deceptiveness of advertising and other business practices on a case-by-case basis. Courts often defer to the Commission's determinations. To be considered deceptive under the FTC's Policy Statement on Deception, an activity must: (1) involve a *material* misrepresentation, omission, or practice; (2) that is *likely to mislead* a consumer; (3) who acts *reasonably* under the circumstances.

Representation, Omission, or Practice Likely to Mislead Sometimes, sellers *expressly* make false or misleading claims in their advertisements or other representations. As revealed in the *Kraft* case, which follows shortly, an advertiser's false or misleading claims of an *implied* nature may also be challenged by the FTC. The same is true of a seller's deceptive *omissions*. Finally, certain deceptive *marketing practices* may violate section 5. In one such case, encyclopedia salespeople gained entry to the homes of potential customers by posing as surveyors engaged in advertising research.

In all of these situations, the statement, omission, or practice must be *likely to mislead* a consumer. Actual deception is not required. Determining whether an ad or practice is likely to mislead requires that the FTC evaluate the accuracy of the seller's claims. In some cases,

moreover, the Commission requires that sellers *substantiate* objective claims about their products by showing that they have a reasonable basis for making such claims.

The "Reasonable Consumer" Test To be deceptive, the representation, omission, or practice must also be likely to mislead *reasonable consumers under the circumstances*. This requirement aims to protect sellers from liability for every foolish, ignorant, or outlandish misconception that some consumer might entertain. As the Commission noted many years ago, advertising an American-made pastry as "Danish Pastry" does not violate § 5 just because "a few misguided souls believe . . . that all Danish Pastry is made in Denmark."[4] Also, § 5 normally is not violated by statements of opinion, sales talk, or "puffing," statements about matters that consumers can easily evaluate for themselves, and statements regarding subjective matters such as taste or smell. Such statements are unlikely to deceive reasonable consumers.

Materiality Finally, the representation, omission, or practice must be *material*. Material information is important to reasonable consumers and is likely to affect their choice of a product or service. Examples include statements or omissions regarding a product's cost, safety, effectiveness, performance, durability, quality, or warranty protection. In addition, the Commission presumes that express statements are material.

The *Kraft* case, which follows, illustrates the application of the FTC's deception test to an advertising claim of an implied nature. *Kraft* also reveals the Commission's broad discretion in fashioning appropriate orders once deceptive advertising has been proven.

_____
[4]*Heinz v. W. Kirchner,* 63 F.T.C. 1282, 1290 (1963).

Kraft, Inc. v. Federal Trade Commission   *970 F.2d 311 (7th Cir. 1992)*

Individually wrapped slices of cheese and cheeselike products come in two major types: process cheese food slices, *which must contain at least 51 percent natural cheese according to a federal regulation; and* imitation slices, *which contain little or no natural cheese. Kraft, Inc.'s "Kraft Singles" are* process cheese food slices. *In the early 1980s, Kraft began losing market share to other firms' less expensive* imitation slices. *Kraft responded with its "Skimp" and "Class Picture" advertisements, which were designed to inform consumers that Kraft Singles cost more because each slice is made from 5 ounces of milk. These advertisements, which ran nationally in print and broadcast media between 1985 and 1987, also stressed the calcium content of Kraft Singles.*

In the broadcast version of the Skimp advertisements, a woman stated that she bought Kraft Singles for her daughter rather than "skimping" by purchasing imitation slices. *She noted that "[i]mitation slices* use hardly any milk. But Kraft has 5 ounces per slice. Five ounces. So her little bones get calcium they need to grow." The commercial also showed milk being poured into a glass that bore the label "5 oz. milk slice." The glass was then transformed into part of the label on a package* *of Singles. In March 1987, Kraft added, as a subscript in the television commercial and as a footnote in the print media version, the disclosure that "one 3/4 ounce slice has 70% of the calcium of five ounces of milk."*

The televised version of the Class Picture advertisements cited a government study indicating that "half the school kids in America don't get all the calcium recommended for growing kids." According to the commercial, "[t]hat's why Kraft Singles are important. Kraft is made from five ounces of milk per slice. So they're concentrated with calcium. Calcium the government recommends for strong bones and healthy teeth." The commercial also included the subscript disclaimer mentioned above.

The Federal Trade Commission instituted a deceptive advertising proceeding against Kraft under § 5 of the FTC Act. According to the FTC's complaint, the Skimp and Class Picture advertisements made the false implied *claim that a Singles slice contains the same amount of calcium as 5 ounces of milk (the* milk equivalency claim*). The FTC regarded the milk equivalency claim as false even though Kraft actually uses 5 ounces of milk in making each Singles slice because roughly 30 percent of the calcium contained in the milk is lost during processing.*

The administrative law judge (ALJ) concluded that the Skimp and Class Picture advertisements made the milk equivalency claim, which was false and material. He concluded that Kraft's subscript and footnote disclosures of the calcium loss were inconspicuous and confusing and therefore insufficient to dispel the misleading impression created by the advertisements. The ALJ ordered Kraft to cease and desist making the milk equivalency claim regarding any of its individually wrapped process cheese food slices *or* imitation slices. *In addition, the ALJ ordered Kraft not to make other calcium or nutritional claims concerning its individually wrapped slices unless Kraft had reliable scientific evidence to support the claims.*

Kraft appealed to the FTC commissioners (referred to here as "the Commission"). The Commission affirmed the ALJ's decision but modified it. According to the Commission, the Skimp and Class Picture advertisements made the false and material milk equivalency claim. The Commission modified the ALJ's orders by extending their coverage from Kraft's individually wrapped slices to "any product that is a cheese, related cheese product, imitation cheese, or substitute cheese." Kraft appealed to the U.S. Court of Appeals for the Seventh Circuit. (In a portion of the opinion not set forth here, the Seventh Circuit concluded, as had the ALJ and the Commission, that some of the Kraft advertisements made a further false claim of an implied nature: that Kraft Singles slices contain more calcium than imitation slices. *The following portion of the Seventh Circuit's opinion addresses the milk equivalency claim.)*

Flaum, Circuit Judge   [A]n advertisement is deceptive under [§ 5 of the FTC Act] if it is likely to mislead consumers, acting reasonably under the circumstances, in a material respect.

In determining what claims are conveyed by a challenged advertisement, the Commission relies on two sources of information: its own viewing of the ad and extrinsic evidence. Its practice is to view the ad first and, if it is unable on its own to determine with confidence what claims are conveyed . . . , to turn to extrinsic evidence. The most convincing extrinsic evidence is a [consumer] survey . . . , but the Commission also relies on other forms of extrinsic evidence including consumer testimony, expert opinion, and copy tests of ads.

Kraft has no quarrel with this approach when it comes to determining whether an ad conveys *express* claims, but contends that the FTC should be required . . . to rely on extrinsic evidence rather than its own subjective analysis in all cases involving allegedly *implied* claims. The Commissioners, Kraft argues, are simply incapable of determining what implicit messages consumers are likely to perceive. Kraft [also] asserts that the Commissioners are predisposed to find implied claims because the claims have [already] been identified in the complaint.

Here, the Commission found implied claims based solely on its own intuitive reading of the ads (although it did reinforce that conclusion by examining the proffered extrinsic evidence). Had the Commission fully and properly relied on available extrinsic evidence, Kraft argues it would have conclusively found that consumers do not perceive the milk equivalency . . . claim in the ads. Kraft's arguments . . . are unavailing as a matter of law. Courts, including the Supreme Court, have uniformly rejected imposing such a requirement on the FTC. We hold that the Commission may rely on its own reasoned analysis to determine what claims, including implied ones, are conveyed in a challenged advertisement, so long as those claims are reasonably clear from the face of the advertisement.

[Kraft relies on] the faulty premise that implied claims are inescapably subjective and unpredictable. In fact, implied claims fall on a continuum, ranging from the obvious to the barely discernible. The Commission does not have license to go on a fishing expedition to pin liability on advertisers for barely imaginable claims. However, when [implied] claims [are] conspicuous, extrinsic evidence is unnecessary because common sense and administrative experience provide the Commission with adequate tools to make its findings. The implied claims Kraft made are reasonably clear from the face of the advertisements, and hence the Commission was not required to utilize consumer surveys in reaching its decision.

Alternatively, Kraft argues that substantial evidence does not support the FTC's finding that the Class Picture ads convey a milk equivalency claim. We find substantial [supporting] evidence in the record. Although Kraft downplays the nexus in the ads between milk and calcium, the ads emphasize visually and verbally that five ounces of milk go into a slice of Kraft Singles; this image is linked to calcium content, strongly implying that the consumer gets the calcium found in five ounces of milk. Furthermore, the Class Picture ads contained one other element reinforcing the milk equivalency claim, the phrase "5 oz. milk slice" inside the image of a glass superimposed on the Singles package.

Kraft asserts that the literal truth of the . . . ads—[Kraft Singles] *are* made from five ounces of milk and they *do* have a high concentration of calcium—makes it illogical to render a finding of consumer deception. The difficulty with this argument is that even literally true statements can have misleading implications. Here, the average consumer is not likely to know that much of the calcium in five ounces of milk (30 percent) is lost in processing, which leaves consumers with a misleading impression about calcium content.

Kraft next asserts that the milk equivalency . . . claim, even if made, [is] not material to consumers. A claim is considered material if it involves information that is important to consumers and, hence, likely to affect their choice of, or conduct regarding, a product. In determining that the milk equivalency claim was material to consumers, the FTC cited Kraft surveys showing that 71 percent of respondents rated calcium content an extremely or very important factor in their decision to buy Kraft Singles, [and that a substantial percentage of respondents] reported significant personal concerns about adequate calcium consumption. [The Commission] rationally concluded that a 30% exaggeration of calcium content was a nutritionally significant claim that would affect consumer purchasing decisions. This finding was supported by expert witnesses who agreed that consumers would prefer a slice of cheese with 100 percent of the calcium in five ounces of milk over one with only 70 percent. [T]he FTC [also] found evidence in the record that Kraft designed the ads with the intent to capitalize on consumer calcium deficiency concerns.

Significantly, the FTC found further evidence of materiality in Kraft's conduct. Before the ads even ran, ABC television raised a red flag when it asked Kraft to substantiate the milk and calcium claims in the ads. Kraft's ad agency also warned Kraft in a legal memorandum to substantiate the claims before running the ads. Moreover, in October 1985, a consumer group warned Kraft that it believed the Skimp ads were potentially deceptive. Nonetheless, a high-level Kraft executive recommended that the ad copy remain unaltered because the "Singles business is growing for the first time in four years due in large part to the copy." Finally, the FTC and the California Attorney General's Office independently notified the company in early 1986 that investigations had been initiated to determine whether the ads conveyed the milk equivalency claims. Notwithstanding these warnings, Kraft continued to run the ads and even rejected proposed alternatives that would have allayed concerns over their deceptive nature. From this, the FTC inferred—we believe, reasonably—that Kraft thought the challenged milk equivalency claim induced consumers to purchase Singles and hence that the claim was material to consumers.

The Commission's cease and desist order prohibits Kraft from running the Skimp and Class Picture ads, as well as from advertising any calcium or nutritional claims not supported by reliable scientific evidence. This order extends not only to the product contained in the deceptive advertisements (Kraft Singles), but to all Kraft cheeses and cheese-related products.

First Amendment infirmities arise, according to Kraft, from the sweep of the order: by banning commercial speech that is only *potentially* misleading, the order chills some non-deceptive advertising deserving of constitutional protection. Kraft acknowledges that sweeping bans of this variety comport with traditional FTC practice, and have been repeatedly upheld against First Amendment challenges in the past. [Kraft nevertheless argues that a First Amendment problem exists because] the order is broader than reasonably necessary to prevent deception.

We reject Kraft's argument. To begin with, the Commission determined that the ads were *actually* misleading, not *potentially* misleading, thus justifying a total ban on the ads. Moreover, even if we were to assume the order bans some potentially misleading speech, it is only constitutionally defective if it is broader than reasonably necessary to prevent the deception. Kraft mischaracterized the [Commission's order] as a categorical ban on commercial speech when in fact it identifies with particularity two nutrient claims that the Commission found actually misleading and prohibits only those claims. It further places on Kraft the minor burden of supporting future nutrient claims with reliable data. This leaves Kraft free to use any advertisement it chooses, including the Skimp and Class Picture ads, so long as it either eliminates the elements specifically identified by the FTC as contributing to consumer deception or corrects this inaccurate impression by adding prominent, unambiguous disclosures. [T]he specific prohibitions imposed on Kraft in the FTC's cease and desist order are not broader than reasonably necessary to prevent deception and hence not violative of the First Amendment.

Alternatively, Kraft argues that the scope of the order is not reasonably related to Kraft's violation of the [FTC] Act because it extends to products that were not the subject of the challenged advertisements. The FTC has discretion to issue multi-product orders, so-called "fencing-in" orders, that extend beyond violations of the Act to prevent violators from engaging in similar deceptive practices in the future.

[The Commission] concluded that Kraft's violations were serious, deliberate, and easily transferable to other Kraft products, thus warranting a broad fencing-in order. We find substantial evidence to support the scope of the order. The Commission based its finding of seriousness on the size ($15 million annually) and duration (two and one-half years) of the ad campaign and on the difficulty most con-

sumers would face in judging the truth or falsity of the calcium claims. [T]he FTC properly found that it is unreasonable to expect most consumers to perform the calculations necessary to compare the calcium content of Kraft Singles with five ounces of milk given the fact that the nutrient information given on milk cartons is not based on a five ounce serving.

As noted previously, the Commission [reasonably] found that Kraft's conduct was deliberate because it persisted in running the challenged ad copy despite repeated warnings from outside sources that the copy might be implicitly misleading. Kraft made three modifications to the ads, but two of them were implemented at the very end of the campaign, more than two years after it had begun. This dilatory response provided a sufficient basis for the Commission's conclusion. The Commission further [made the reasonable finding] that the violations were readily transferable to other Kraft cheese products given the general similarity between Singles and other Kraft cheeses.

Commission's order upheld and enforced.

Unfairness

Section 5's prohibition of *unfair* acts or practices enables the FTC to attack behavior that, while not necessarily deceptive, is objectionable for other reasons. As demonstrated by the cases discussed in a nearby Cyberlaw in Action box and an Ethics in Action box that appears later in the chapter, the FTC focuses on *consumer harm* when it attacks unfair acts or practices. To violate § 5, this harm:

1. *Must be substantial.* Monetary loss and unwarranted health and safety risks usually constitute substantial harm, but emotional distress and the perceived offensiveness of certain advertisements generally do not.

2. *Must not be outweighed by any offsetting consumer or competitive benefits produced by the challenged practice.* This element requires the Commission to balance the harm caused by the act or practice against its benefits to consumers and to competition generally. A seller's failure to give a consumer complex technical data about a product, for example, may disadvantage the consumer, but it may also reduce the product's price. Only when an act or practice is injurious in its *net effects* can it be unfair under § 5.

3. *Must be one that consumers could not reasonably have avoided.* An injury is considered reasonably unavoidable when a seller's actions significantly interfered with a consumer's ability to make informed decisions that would have prevented the injury. For example, a seller may have withheld otherwise unavailable information about important product features, or used high-pressure sales tactics on vulnerable consumers.

Remedies

Several types of orders may result from a successful FTC adjudicative proceeding attacking deceptive or unfair behavior. One possibility is an order telling the respondent to *cease* engaging in the deceptive or unfair conduct. Another is the *affirmative disclosure* of information whose absence made the advertisement deceptive or unfair. Yet another is *corrective advertising*. This requires the seller's future advertisements to correct false impressions created by its past advertisements. In certain cases, moreover, the FTC may issue an *all-products order* extending beyond the product or service whose advertisements violated § 5, and including future advertisements

CYBERLAW IN ACTION

The past decade's explosion in Internet usage has caused the FTC to exercise, in the Internet context, its general statutory authority to regulate deceptive or unfair commercial practices. For instance, in *Federal Trade Commission v. Zuccarini,* 2002 U.S. Dist. LEXIS 13324 (E.D. Pa. 2002), the FTC sought an injunction and monetary relief against a party who did business under numerous different names and engaged in a variety of practices that the FTC contended were deceptive and unfair. According to the FTC's complaint, defendant Zuccarini consistently and improperly directed consumers from their intended destinations on the World Wide Web to his websites, and then obstructed consumers from exiting his websites through a series of Web pages that displayed advertisements for goods and services. The display of these advertisements netted Zuccarini monetary gains, because affiliate marketing programs to which he was a party meant that he would be compensated for displaying those advertisements by the firms whose goods were being advertised.

The FTC alleged that Zuccarini accomplished the improper direction of consumers to his websites through using domain names that were misspellings of, or were otherwise confusingly similar to, domain names of other parties' websites. The obstruction of consumers' ability to exit his websites was accomplished, according to the FTC, by Zuc-

carini's causing multiple browser windows, pop-up windows, Web pages, or multiple copies of a consumer's browser software to launch or open when the consumer typed a domain name in her browser's address bar or used the "Close," "Exit," "X," or "Back" button. Sometimes, these windows, pages, or copies would be launched or opened when the consumer neither typed anything nor clicked on any button after reaching a Zuccarini website. The FTC contended that the above-described redirection and obstruction was unfair for purposes of § 5 of the FTC Act. The redirection was alleged to be deceptive for purposes of § 5, to the extent that it was accomplished through the use of misleading practices, including the use of domain names confusingly similar to other parties' domain names.

After hearings in which Zuccarini failed to participate, a federal district court issued an injunction barring Zuccarini from the practices described above and from participating in an affiliate marketing program of the sort in which Zuccarini had been engaged. In addition, after considering the evidence offered by the FTC, the court entered a $1.9 million judgment against Zuccarini, with the proviso that any portions of the judgment collected by the FTC would be deposited into a fund to be administered by the FTC for consumer redress.

---

for other products or services marketed by the seller. The *Kraft* case, which appeared above, illustrates such an order. Finally, the FTC may sometimes go to court to seek injunctive relief or the civil penalties or consumer redress noted earlier.

Consumer Protection Laws

The term *consumer protection* includes everything from Chapter 20's product liability law to packaging and labeling regulations. Here, we examine federal regulation of telemarketing practices, product warranties, consumer credit, and product safety.

Telemarketing and Consumer Fraud and Abuse Prevention Act

In the Telemarketing and Consumer Fraud and Abuse Prevention Act (Telemarketing Act), which was enacted in 1994, Congress required the FTC to promulgate regula-

tions defining and prohibiting *deceptive* and *abusive* telemarketing acts or practices. The FTC responded to this directive with the 1995 Telemarketing Sales Rule (TSR).

For purposes of the TSR, a *seller* is a party who (or which), in connection with a telemarketing transaction, offers or arranges to provide customers with goods or services in exchange for consideration. The TSR defines *telemarketer* as "any person who, in connection with telemarketing, initiates or receives telephone calls to or from a customer." It defines *telemarketing* as "a plan, program, or campaign which is conducted to induce the purchase of goods or services by use of one or more telephones and which involves more than one interstate telephone call." Exemptions from the telemarketing definition are provided for sellers that solicit sales through the mailing of a catalog and then receive customers' orders by telephone, and for sellers that make telephone calls of solicitation to a consumer but complete the transaction in a face-to-face meeting with the consumer.

A major feature of the TSR makes it a deceptive practice for telemarketers and sellers to fail to disclose certain information to a customer before she pays for the goods or services being telemarketed. The customer is regarded as having paid for goods or services once she provides information that may be used for billing purposes. The mandatory disclosures specified in the TSR include the total cost of the goods or services, any material restrictions or conditions on the purchase or use of the goods or services, and the terms of any refund or exchange policy mentioned in the solicitation (or, if the seller has a policy of not allowing refunds or exchanges, a disclosure of that policy). Various other disclosures are necessary if the telemarketing solicitation pertains to a prize promotion. The TSR also makes it a deceptive practice for a telemarketer or seller to misrepresent information required to be disclosed in the mandatory disclosures, or to misrepresent any other information concerning the performance, nature, or characteristics of the goods or services being offered for sale.

According to the TSR, a telemarketer or seller engages in an abusive practice if he: directs threats, intimidation, or profane or obscene language toward a customer; causes the telephone to ring, or engages a person in a telephone conversation, repeatedly and with the intent to harass, abuse, or annoy a person at the called number; or initiates a call to a person who has previously stated that she does not wish to receive a call made by or on behalf of the seller whose goods or services are being offered. What would otherwise appear to transgress the last prohibition will not be considered a violation of the TSR, however, if the seller or telemarketer has implemented procedures designed to prevent further calls to a list of persons who have said they do not want to receive calls, and the making of a further call to a listed person was merely an error.

The TSR also makes it an abusive practice for a telemarketer to call a person's residence at any time other than between 8:00 A.M. and 9:00 P.M. at the called person's location. In addition, the telemarketer engages in an abusive practice if, in a telephone call he initiated, he does not promptly and clearly disclose the identity of the seller, the sales purpose of the call, the nature of the goods or services, and the fact that no purchase or payment is necessary in order to win a prize or participate in a prize promotion (if a prize or prize promotion is being offered). Still other abusive practices are enumerated in the TSR.

The FTC and state attorneys general may bring enforcement proceedings against violators of the Telemarketing Act and the TSR. Civil penalties of up to $10,000 per violation are among the available remedies in government-initiated proceedings. Under some circumstances, private citizens may sue violators for damages and injunctive relief.

Magnuson-Moss Warranty Act

The Magnuson-Moss Warranty Act of 1975 mainly applies to *written warranties* for *consumer products*. Nothing in the act requires sellers to give a written warranty. Sellers who decline to provide such a warranty generally escape coverage. A consumer product is personal property that is ordinarily used for personal, family, or household purposes. In addition, many Magnuson-Moss provisions apply only when a written warranty is given in connection with the sale of a consumer product to a *consumer*. A consumer is a buyer or transferee who does not use the product for resale or in his own business.

Chapter 20 discusses Magnuson-Moss's provisions giving consumers minimum warranty protection. Here, we examine its rules requiring that consumer warranties contain certain information and that this information be made available to buyers before the sale. Any failure to comply with these rules violates section 5 of the FTC Act and may trigger Commission action. In addition, either the FTC or the attorney general may sue to obtain injunctive relief against such violations.

Required Warranty Information The Magnuson-Moss Act and its regulations require the simple, clear, and conspicuous presentation of certain information in written warranties to consumers for consumer products costing more than $15. That information includes: (1) the persons protected by the warranty when coverage is limited to the original purchaser or is otherwise limited; (2) the products, parts, characteristics, components, or properties covered by the warranty; (3) what the warrantor will do in case of a product defect or other failure to conform to the warranty; (4) the time the warranty begins (if different from the purchase date) and its duration; and (5) the procedure the consumer should follow to obtain the performance of warranty obligations. The act also requires that a warrantor disclose: (1) any limitations on the duration of implied warranties; and (2) any attempt to limit consequential damages or other consumer remedies.

Presale Availability of Warranty Information The regulations accompanying Magnuson-Moss also contain detailed rules requiring that warranty terms be made available to a buyer before the sale. These rules generally govern sales to consumers of consumer products costing more than $15. They set out certain duties that must be met by sellers (usually retailers) and warrantors (usually manufacturers) of such products. For example:

1. *Sellers* must make the text of the warranty available for the prospective buyer's review before the sale, either by displaying the warranty in close proximity to the product or by furnishing the warranty upon request after posting signs informing buyers of its availability.

2. *Catalog or mail-order sellers* must clearly and conspicuously disclose in their catalog or solicitation either the full text of the warranty or the address from which a free copy can be obtained.

3. *Warrantors* must give sellers the warranty materials necessary for them to comply with the duties stated above.

Truth in Lending Act

When Congress passed the Truth in Lending Act (TILA) in 1968, its main aims were to increase consumer knowledge and understanding of credit terms by compelling their *disclosure,* and to help consumers shop for credit by commanding *uniform* disclosures. Now, however, the TILA protects consumers in other ways as well.

Coverage The TILA generally applies to creditors who extend consumer credit to a debtor in an amount not exceeding $25,000.[5] A *creditor* is a party who regularly extends consumer credit. Examples include banks, credit card issuers, and savings and loan associations. Extending credit need not be a creditor's primary business. For instance, auto dealers and retail stores are creditors if they regularly extend credit. To qualify as a creditor, the party in question must also either impose a finance charge or by agreement require payment in more than four installments. *Consumer credit* is credit enabling the purchase of goods, services, or real estate used primarily for personal, family, or household purposes—not business or agricultural purposes. The TILA *debtor* must be a natural person; the act does not protect business organizations.

Disclosure Provisions The TILA's detailed disclosure provisions break down into three categories.

1. *Open-end credit.* The TILA defines an open-end credit plan as one that contemplates repeated transactions and involves a finance charge that may be computed on the unpaid balance. Examples include credit card plans and revolving charge accounts offered by retail stores. Open-end credit plans require two forms of disclosure: (1) an *initial statement* made before the first transaction under the plan; and (2) a series of *periodic statements* (usually, one for each billing cycle).

   Among the disclosures required in the initial statement are: (1) when a finance charge is imposed and how it is determined; (2) the amount of any additional charges and the method for computing them; (3) the fact that the creditor has taken or will acquire a security interest in the debtor's property; and (4) the debtor's billing rights. Periodic statements require an even lengthier set of disclosures. Much of the information contained in a monthly credit card statement, for example, is compelled by the TILA.

2. *Closed-end credit.* The TILA requires a different set of disclosures for other credit plans, which generally involve closed-end credit. Closed-end credit such as a car loan or a consumer loan from a finance company is extended for a specific time period; the total amount financed, number of payments, and due dates are all agreed on at the time of the transaction. Examples of the disclosures necessary before the completion of a closed-end credit transaction include: (1) the total finance charge; (2) the annual percentage rate (APR); (3) the amount financed; (4) the total number of payments, their due dates, and the amount of each payment; (5) the total dollar value of all payments; (6) any late charges imposed for past-due payments; and (7) any security interest taken by the creditor and the property that the security interest covers.

3. *Credit card applications and solicitations.* The TILA imposes disclosure requirements on credit card applications and solicitations. These elaborate requirements differ depending on whether the application or solicitation is made by direct mail, telephone, or other means such as catalogs and magazines. To take just one example, direct mail applications and solicitations must include information about matters such as the APR, annual fees, the grace period for paying without incurring a finance charge, and the method

---

[5]The $25,000 maximum does not apply where a creditor takes a security interest in a debtor's real property or in personal property, such as a mobile home, used as the debtor's principal dwelling. Here, the disclosure rules differ slightly from the rules for closed-end credit discussed shortly. In certain transactions of this kind, moreover, the debtor has a three-day rescission right whose details are beyond the scope of this text.

for computing the balance on which the finance charge is based.

Other TILA Provisions The TILA has provisions dealing with *consumer credit advertising.* For example, the act prevents a creditor from "baiting" customers by advertising loan or down payment amounts that it does not usually make available. To help consumers put advertised terms in perspective, if ads for open-end consumer credit plans state any of the plan's specific terms, they must state various other terms as well. For instance, an advertisement using such terms as "$100 down payment," "6 percent interest," or "$99 per month" must also state other relevant terms such as the APR.

The TILA also regulates *open-end consumer credit plans involving an extension of credit secured by a consumer's principal dwelling*—e.g., the popular home equity loans. The act controls *advertisements* for such plans, requiring certain information such as the APR if the ad states any specific terms and forbidding misleading terms such as "free money." It also imposes elaborate disclosure requirements on *applications* for such plans. These include matters such as interest rates, fees, repayment options, minimum payments, and repayment periods. The act also controls the *terms* of such a plan and the *actions* a creditor may take under it. For example: (1) if the plan involves a variable interest rate, the "index rate" to which changes in the APR are pegged must be based on some publicly available rate and must not be under the creditor's control; and (2) a creditor cannot unilaterally terminate the plan and require immediate repayment of the outstanding balance unless a consumer has made material misrepresentations, has failed to repay the balance, or has adversely affected the creditor's security.

Finally, the TILA includes rules concerning *credit cards.* The most important such rule limits a cardholder's liability for unauthorized use of the card to a maximum of $50.

Enforcement Various federal agencies enforce the TILA. Except in areas committed to a particular agency, overall enforcement authority rests in the FTC. Those who willfully and knowingly violate the act may face criminal prosecution. Civil actions by private parties, including class actions, are also possible.

Fair Credit Reporting Act

The reports credit bureaus provide may significantly affect one's ability to obtain credit, insurance, employment, and many of life's other goods. Often, affected individuals are unaware of the influence that credit reports had on such decisions. The Fair Credit Reporting Act (FCRA) was enacted in 1970 to give people protection against abuses in the process of disseminating information about their creditworthiness.

Duties of Consumer Reporting Agencies The FCRA imposes certain duties on consumer reporting agencies—agencies that regularly compile credit-related information on individuals for the purpose of furnishing consumer credit reports to users. A consumer reporting agency must adopt *reasonable procedures* to:

1. Ensure that *users employ* the information only for the following purposes: consumer credit sales, employment evaluations, the underwriting of insurance, the granting of a government license or other benefit, or any other business transaction where the user has a legitimate business need for the information. The *Scott* case, which follows shortly, addresses the legitimate business need issue.

2. Avoid including in a report *obsolete information* predating the report by more than a stated period. This period usually is 7 years; for a prior bankruptcy, it is 10 years. This duty does not apply to credit reports used in connection with certain life insurance policies, large credit transactions, and applications for employment.

3. Ensure *maximum possible accuracy* regarding the personal information in credit reports. However, the act does little to limit the *types* of data included in credit reports. In fact, all kinds of information about a person's character, reputation, personal traits, and mode of living seemingly are permitted.

Duties of Users The FCRA also imposes disclosure duties on *users* of credit reports—mainly credit sellers, lenders, employers, and insurers. One of these duties applies to users who order an *investigative consumer report*. This is a credit report that includes information on a person's character, reputation, personal traits, or mode of living and is based on interviews with neighbors, friends, associates, and the like. If a user procures such a report on a person, it must inform him that the report has been requested, that the report may contain sensitive information, and that he has a right to obtain further disclosures about the user's investigation. If the person requests such disclosures within a reasonable time, the user must reveal the nature and scope of the investigation.

Another disclosure duty arises when, because of information contained in any credit report, a user: (1) rejects an applicant for consumer credit, insurance, or employment; or (2) charges a higher rate for credit or insurance. Here, the user must maintain reasonable procedures for advising the affected individual that it relied on the credit report in making its decision and for stating the name and address of the consumer reporting agency that supplied the report.

Disclosure and Correction of Credit Report Information

After a request from a properly identified individual, a *consumer reporting agency* must normally disclose to that individual: (1) the nature and substance of all its information about the individual; (2) the sources of this information; and (3) the recipients of any credit reports that it has furnished within certain time periods. Then, a person disputing the completeness or accuracy of the agency's information can compel it to reinvestigate. The credit bureau must delete the information from the person's file if it finds the information to be inaccurate or unverifiable. An individual who is not satisfied with the agency's investigation may file a brief statement setting forth the nature of her dispute with the agency. If so, any subsequent credit report containing the disputed information must note that it is disputed and must provide either the individual's statement or a clear and accurate summary of it. An agency may also be required to notify certain prior recipients of deleted, unverifiable, or disputed information if the individual requests this. However, there is no duty to investigate or to include the consumer's version of the facts if the credit bureau has reason to believe that the individual's request is frivolous or irrelevant.

Enforcement

Violations of the FCRA are violations of FTC Act section 5; the Commission may use its normal enforcement procedures in such cases. Other federal agencies may also enforce the FCRA in certain situations. The FCRA establishes criminal penalties for persons who knowingly and willfully obtain consumer information from a credit bureau under false pretenses. The *Scott* case considers the meaning of "false pretenses." Criminal liability may also be imposed on credit bureau officers or employees who knowingly or willfully provide information to unauthorized persons. In addition, violations of the FCRA may trigger private civil suits against consumer reporting agencies and users.

Scott v. Real Estate Finance Group   *183 F.3d 97 (2d Cir. 1999)*

The owners of a certain house had listed it for rental with Gatewood Realty, Inc. Ira Simonoff, a Gatewood broker, showed the house to brothers Jonathan and Robert Scott, who offered to rent the house at a lesser monthly rate than the owners had specified. Simonoff then asked the Scotts for certain background information. Jonathan Scott responded to Simonoff's request for his social security number by telling Simonoff that he (Simonoff) was not authorized to make a credit check. Robert Scott added that he did not want his credit checked. During the discovery phase of the litigation described below, Jonathan Scott testified that Simonoff assured him no credit check would be run. Both brothers testified that they understood Simonoff would not check their credit. Simonoff, however, testified that he informed the brothers of the house owners' requirement of a credit check and that one of the brothers had simply asked Simonoff not to have a credit check done "if at all possible."

When Simonoff relayed the Scotts' offer to the owners, they insisted that credit checks be conducted. Simonoff therefore asked Peter Visconti, who was affiliated with Real Estate Finance Group (REFG), to check the Scotts' credit. According to later testimony by Visconti, Simonoff represented that he had written authorizations from the Scotts. (The Scotts denied that any such authorizations existed.) Visconti obtained credit reports on the Scotts by falsely representing to a computerized credit reporting service that he needed the reports to evaluate a mortgage application. He then supplied the credit reports to Simonoff. When a real estate broker working on behalf of the Scotts learned that Simonoff had obtained their credit reports, she so informed the Scotts.

The Scotts filed suit against REFG, Gatewood, and Simonoff for alleged violations of the Fair Credit Reporting Act (FCRA). After discovery, the Scotts moved for partial summary judgment against all defendants on the theory that they had obtained the Scotts' credit reports by means of false pretenses, in violation of the FCRA. Gatewood and Simonoff moved for summary judgment in their favor. The district court granted the Scotts' summary judgment motion as to REFG but not as to Gatewood and Simonoff. Instead, the court granted summary judgment in favor of Gatewood Realty and Simonoff and ordered dismissal of the Scotts' FRCA claim against them. REFG and the Scotts later reached a settlement. The Scotts appealed the dismissal of their FCRA claim against Gatewood and Simonoff.

Pooler, Circuit Judge [The Scotts] claim that Simonoff obtained their credit reports under false pretenses because he falsely represented to Visconti that [they] had given him written authorizations. Section 1681q of the FCRA makes criminally liable "any person who knowingly and willingly obtains information on a consumer from a consumer reporting agency under false pretenses." By virtue of [another FCRA section], a consumer may also maintain a civil action against any "user of information" who "willfully" violates § 1681q. The district court [held] that Simonoff's misrepresentation did not violate § 1681q [because] the pending lease transaction between the Scotts and Simonoff's clients constituted a permissible basis for requesting a credit report pursuant to [the FCRA]. Because Simonoff had a legitimate—albeit unstated—reason for requesting the report, the district court found that he did not obtain the report under false pretenses and thus did not violate § 1681q.

[T]he Scotts argue that the district court erred both in its legal conclusion and in its finding that the Scotts had a pending business transaction with the home owners. We agree with the district court that a requester does not violate § 1681q by giving a false reason for its request if it has an independent legitimate basis for requesting the report. Section 1681q punishes a person who "obtains information . . . under false pretenses." However, a credit reporting agency can give credit information to an entity it reasonably believes has "a legitimate business need" for the information "in connection with a business transaction involving the consumer" [quoting another FCRA section]. A person [who obtains] information to which he has a right [cannot be seen as having obtained the information] under false pretenses. Therefore, if the parties had a pending business transaction for which the credit report was a legitimate business need, Simonoff did not violate § 1681q.

However, we believe that the district court overlooked issues of fact on the legitimacy of Simonoff's business need for the report at the time he requested it. A finder of fact who credited the Scotts' testimony could find that they conditioned their offer to rent on the owners' willingness to forgo a credit check. If so, Simonoff knew that there was no longer a pending transaction between his clients and the Scotts as soon as his clients insisted on the credit report. Put in slightly different terms, we find that parties to a transaction may elect to structure their negotiations in such a way that those negotiations—no matter how apparently detailed—constitute expressions of interest that are too inchoate to give the landlord a "legitimate business need for the information in connection with a business transaction involving the consumer" within the meaning of [the FCRA]. [A]n offer to enter a lease can constitute this type of structured negotiation when it is made with the express condition that no credit check will be conducted. [T]he parties are free to contractually define whether . . . a "legitimate business need" exists "in connection with a business transaction." [W]hen a factual dispute exists as to whether the negotiations were structured in such a way, a factual dispute necessarily exists as to whether the requesting party had a legitimate need for the credit report. Because a fact finder must determine whether Simonoff had a legitimate need for the report when he requested it—and, if not, whether his noncompliance with the statute was willful—we reverse and remand.

District court's grant of summary judgment in favor of Gatewood and Simonoff reversed; case remanded for further proceedings.

Equal Credit Opportunity Act

The Equal Credit Opportunity Act (ECOA) prohibits credit discrimination on the bases of sex, marital status, age, race, color, national origin, religion, and the obtaining of income from public assistance. The ECOA covers all entities that regularly arrange, extend, renew, or continue credit. Examples include banks, savings and loan associations, credit card issuers, and many retailers, auto dealers, and realtors. The act is not limited to consumer credit; it also covers business and commercial loans.

The ECOA governs all phases of a credit transaction. As authorized by the act, the Federal Reserve Board has promulgated regulations detailing permissible and im-

permissible creditor behavior at each stage. Even when the regulations do not specifically prohibit certain creditor behavior, that behavior may still violate the act itself. Moreover, a credit practice that is neutral on its face may result in an ECOA violation if the practice has an adverse statistical impact on one of the ECOA's protected classes.[6]

The ECOA also requires that creditors notify applicants of the action taken on a credit application within

---

[6]This resembles the adverse impact or disparate impact method of proof used in employment discrimination cases under Title VII of the 1964 Civil Rights Act. See Chapter 51.

30 days of its receipt or any longer reasonable time stated in the regulations. If the action is unfavorable, an applicant is entitled to a statement of reasons from the creditor.

The ECOA is enforced by several federal agencies, with overall enforcement resting in the FTC's hands. Which agency enforces the act depends on the type of creditor or credit involved. Civil actions by aggrieved private parties, including class actions, also are possible.

Fair Credit Billing Act

The Fair Credit Billing Act is primarily aimed at credit card issuers. Although the act regulates the credit card business in other ways, its most important provisions involve billing disputes. To trigger these provisions, a cardholder must give the issuer written notice of an alleged error in a billing statement within 60 days of the time that the statement is sent to the cardholder. Then, within two complete billing cycles or 90 days (whichever is less), the issuer must either: (1) correct the cardholder's account; or (2) send the cardholder a written statement justifying the statement's accuracy. Until the issuer takes one of these steps, it may not: (1) restrict or close the cardholder's account because of her failure to pay the disputed amount; (2) try to collect the disputed amount; or (3) report or threaten to report the cardholder's failure to pay the disputed amount to a third party such as a consumer reporting agency.

Once an issuer has met the act's requirements, it must also give a cardholder at least 10 days to pay the disputed amount before making an unfavorable report to a third party. If the cardholder disputes the issuer's justification within the 10-day period allowed for payment, the issuer can make such a report only if it also tells the third party that the debt is disputed and gives the cardholder the third party's name and address. In addition, the issuer must report the final resolution of the dispute to the third party.

An issuer that fails to comply with any of these rules forfeits its right to collect $50 of the disputed amount from the cardholder. Because the issuer may still be able to collect the balance on large disputed debts, it is doubtful whether this provision does much to deter violations of the act.

Fair Debt Collection Practices Act

Concern over abusive, deceptive, and unfair practices by debt collectors led Congress to pass the Fair Debt Collection Practices Act (FDCPA) in 1977. The act applies to debts that involve money, property, insurance, or services obtained by a *consumer* for *consumer purposes*. Normally, the act covers only those who are in the business of collecting debts owed to *others*. However, creditors who collect their own debts are covered when, by using a name other than their own name, they indicate that a third party is collecting the debt. The *White* case, which follows shortly, addresses issues that arise in the latter type of case.

Communication Rules Except when necessary to locate a debtor, the FDCPA generally prevents debt collectors from contacting third parties such as the debtor's employer, relatives, or friends. The act also limits a collector's contacts with the debtor himself. Unless the debtor consents, for instance, a collector cannot contact him at unusual or inconvenient times or places, or at his place of employment if the employer forbids such contacts. A collector cannot contact a debtor if it knows that the debtor is represented by an attorney, unless the attorney consents to such contact or fails to respond to the collector's communications. In addition, a collector must cease most communications with a debtor if the debtor gives the creditor written notification that he refuses to pay the debt or that he does not desire further communications.

The FDCPA also requires a collector to give a debtor certain information about the debt within five days of the collector's first communication with the debtor. If the debtor disputes the debt in writing within 30 days after receiving this information, the collector must cease its collection efforts until it sends verification of the debt to the debtor.

Specific Forbidden Practices The FDCPA sets out categories of forbidden collector practices and lists specific examples of each category. The listed examples, however, do not exhaust the ways that debt collectors can violate the act. The categories are:

1. *Harassment, oppression, or abuse.* Examples include threats of violence, obscene or abusive language, and repeated phone calls.

2. *False or misleading misrepresentations.* Among the FDCPA's listed examples are statements that a debtor will be imprisoned for failure to pay, that a collector will take an action it is not legally entitled to take or does not intend to take, that a collector is affiliated with the government, and that misstate the amount of the debt.

3. *Unfair practices.* These include collecting from a debtor an amount not authorized by the agreement creating the debt, inducing a debtor to accept a collect call before revealing the call's true purpose, and falsely or unjustifiably threatening to take a debtor's property.

Enforcement The FTC is the main enforcement agency for the FDCPA, although other agencies enforce it in certain cases. The FDCPA also permits individual civil actions and class actions by the affected debtor or debtors.

White v. Goodman   *200 F.3d 1016 (7th Cir. 2000)*

The Fair Debt Collection Practices Act (FDCPA) prohibits a creditor from giving a debtor the false impression that a third party is involved in efforts to collect the debt owed to the creditor. North Shore Agency, Inc., is a debt-collection firm. For many years, North Shore and Book-of-the-Month Club (BOMC) had an arrangement under which BOMC would send North Shore the names and addresses of any BOMC customers from whom BOMC had been unable to collect payment. North Shore would then send these customers a letter demanding payment of the sums BOMC had reported to North Shore as due. The demand letters instructed the customers to pay BOMC directly and stated that further collection efforts would be undertaken if payment was not made.

If the demand letter to a given customer failed to elicit payment, BOMC would so notify North Shore, which would send a second demand letter. The process could be repeated a third time or even more times until either the customer paid BOMC or North Shore concluded that payment would not be forthcoming unless further collection efforts were made. BOMC paid North Shore a flat fee for every demand letter North Shore sent out. If a series of demand letters did not yield payment, it was up to North Shore whether to drop the matter—something it might often be likely to do because of the relatively small dollar amounts involved—or take other collection action. When North Shore took other collection action that resulted in payment, North Shore would keep 35 percent of the amount collected and remit the remainder to BOMC.

Patricia White, a BOMC customer who had not made payment of $18.45, received a demand letter from North Shore. Alleging that BOMC and North Shore had violated the FDCPA, White brought a class action suit on behalf of herself and other similarly situated persons. The federal district court granted summary judgment in favor of the defendants and dismissed the case. White appealed to the U.S. Court of Appeals for the Seventh Circuit.

Posner, Chief Judge One of the practices that the FDCPA . . . forbids is "flat-rating," the term popularly applied to providing a form which creates the false impression that someone (usually a collection agency) besides the actual creditor is "participating" in collecting the debt. (The provider of the form presumably charges a "flat rate" for the form; hence the popular name for the practice.) The element of deception lies less in the misrepresentation that a third-party debt collector is involved than in the signal, conveyed by turning over a debt for collection, that the creditor does not intend to drop the matter. Congress's concern was that such deception might induce debtors to abandon legitimate defenses. Whether the concern was well-founded is not for us to say.

The flat-rater is thus not the creditor, but the counterpart of a contributory infringer in the law of intellectual property; he furnishes a deceptive instrumentality to the primary violator. Another provision of [the FDCPA] brings the latter within the scope of liability by forbidding a creditor, in the collection of his debts, to use a name which suggests the involvement of a third party, unless the third party is participating in the debt collection, for then there is no deception. Conceivably this provision could be read so narrowly as to reach only the case in which the creditor is using a pseudonym; but this reading, as the cases interpreting [the statute] make clear, . . . is too narrow.

The contention that North Shore is a flat-rater is not frivolous, and if it were a flat-rater, BOMC might be liable under [the FDCPA]. But it is unconvincing. North Shore did compose, either by itself or jointly with BOMC, the dunning letter that Patricia White received; and if this were all North Shore had done to help BOMC collect the money she owed it, North Shore would indeed be a flat-rater. But it is not all that North Shore did. Because the debts that it collects on behalf of BOMC are small, North Shore's collection efforts are, we may assume, usually limited to sending a series of dunning letters. If the debtors are smart, they probably know that if they tough it out, eventually the letters will cease coming and that will be the last they hear of the matter until they discover they have earned a lousy credit rating. They are, nevertheless, in the clutches of a bona fide collection agency which, if the letters fail to collect the debt, may sue. Probably North Shore *does* sue from time to time on behalf of BOMC just so that BOMC does not get a reputation as being a particularly easy mark for people who like to get their books free. The [plaintiff seems] to think that unless the creditor assigns the debt at the start to a collection agency, the agency is a flat-rater. But there is nothing in the statute to equate participation in collection with ownership of the debt.

The plaintiffs have another claim, this one under the general provisions of the FDCPA forbidding deceptive debt collection practices. On the reverse of the dunning letters that North Shore sends appears a paragraph which begins: "The State of Colorado requires that we furnish Colorado residents with the following information. . . ." A list of the rights that Colorado residents have to limit further communications from a debt collector follows. The paragraph is not claimed to be inaccurate. The argument is, rather, that it implies that nonresidents of Colorado do not have similar rights, whereas in fact the FDCPA itself confers similar rights on debtors. In other words, the reader of the paragraph is assumed to react by saying to himself, "Since I'm not a resident of Colorado, I guess I have no right to limit further communications from this pesky debt collector." This is fantastic conjecture. Since the FDCPA does not require that a copy or summary of it be furnished with every (or any) dunning letter, it is unlikely, to say the least, that recipients of such letters, unless they happen to be class action lawyers specializing in consumer finance litigation, have any idea of what specific federal or state rights they might have, so they have no benchmark against which to compare the rights that Colorado law confers. And far from implying that Coloradans have superior rights, the paragraph by its opening sentence makes clear that Colorado merely requires that the debt collector furnish Colorado residents with the specified information. The implication is not that such residents have more rights than residents of other states, but, at most, that they are less sophisticated and therefore need more information about their rights. Realistically, the only reaction of a Colorado nonresident to the paragraph would be that it had nothing to do with him.

Any document can be misread. The FDCPA is not violated by a dunning letter that is susceptible of an ingenious misreading, for then every dunning letter would violate it. The FDCPA protects the unsophisticated debtor, but not the irrational one.

Decision of district court affirmed.

ETHICS IN ACTION

Since at least the early 1950s, the International Harvester Company's gasoline-powered tractors had been subject to "fuel geysering." This was a phenomenon in which hot liquid gasoline would shoot from the tractor's gas tank when the filler cap was opened. The hot gasoline could cause severe burns and could ignite and cause a fire. Over the years, at least 90 fuel geysering incidents involving International Harvester tractors occurred. At least 12 of these involved significant burn injuries, and at least one caused a death.

International Harvester discovered the full dimensions of the fuel geysering problem in 1963. In that year, it revised its owner's manuals to warn buyers of new gas-powered tractors not to remove the gas cap from a hot or running tractor. In 1976, it produced a new fuel tank decal with a similar warning. Because of an industrywide shift to diesel-powered tractors, however, this warning had a very limited distribution to buyers of new tractors, and it rarely reached former buyers. International Harvester never specifically warned either new or old buyers about the geysering problem until 1980, when it voluntarily made a mass mailing to 630,000 customers.

In 1980, the FTC issued a complaint against International Harvester, alleging that its failure to warn buyers of the fuel geysering problem for 17 years violated FTC Act § 5. Agreeing with the initial decision of an administrative law judge, the full Commission held that International Harvester's failure to warn was not deceptive but was unfair for purposes of § 5. *In the Matter of International Harvester,* 104 F.T.C. 949 (1984).

Applying the three-part analysis discussed earlier in this chapter, the Commission weighed the consumer injury caused by fuel geysering against the costs of providing effective warnings about it. The Commission concluded that the 12 instances of serious burns and the one death caused by fuel geysering were injuries that might have been avoided by a warning and were sufficient to outweigh the $2.8 million apparently required for an effective warning. However, the Commission's method clearly left open the possibility that in some cases, a practice's benefits to consumers or to competition might outweigh the harm it causes.

- Is it morally right to balance personal injury and human life against economic gain? Isn't each human life valuable beyond measure? Can decision-making processes such as the FTC's ever be justified?
- On the other hand, if you think that the Commission's balancing exercise *is* justifiable, how is one to strike the balance? How would you have decided *International Harvester* if ethical analysis, rather than legal standards, controlled the decision?

Product Safety Regulation

Yet another facet of consumer protection law is federal regulation of product safety. As discussed in Chapter 20, sellers and manufacturers of dangerously defective products may be held civilly liable to those injured by such products. Damage recoveries, however, are at best an after-the-fact remedy for injuries caused by such products. Thus, federal law also seeks to promote product safety through *direct regulation* of consumer products.

The Consumer Product Safety Act The most important federal product safety measure is the Consumer Product Safety Act (CPSA). The CPSA established the Consumer Product Safety Commission (CPSC), an independent regulatory agency that is the main federal body concerned with the safety of consumer products. Among the CPSC's activities are the following: (1) issuing *consumer product safety standards* (which normally pertain to the performance of consumer products or require product warnings or instructions); (2) issuing rules *banning* certain *hazardous products;* (3) bringing suit in federal district court to eliminate the dangers presented by *imminently hazardous* consumer products (products that pose an immediate and unreasonable risk of death, serious illness, or severe personal injury); and (4) *ordering private parties to address "substantial product hazards"* after receiving notice of such hazards. The CPSA's remedies and enforcement devices include injunctions, the seizure of products, civil penalties, criminal penalties, and private damage suits.

Other Federal Product Safety Regulation Other federal statutes besides the CPSA regulate various specific consumer products. Among the subjects so regulated are toys, cigarette labeling and advertising, eggs, meat, poultry, smokeless tobacco, flammable fabrics, drugs, cosmetics, pesticides, and motor vehicles. Some of these laws are enforced by the CPSC and some by other bodies.

Problems and Problem Cases

1. For many years, advertisements for Listerine Antiseptic Mouthwash had impliedly claimed that Listerine was beneficial in the treatment of colds, cold symptoms, and sore throats. An FTC adjudicative proceeding concluded that these claims were false. Thus, the Commis-

sion ordered Warner-Lambert Company, the manufacturer of Listerine, to include the following statement in future Listerine advertisements: "Contrary to prior advertising, Listerine will not help prevent colds or sore throats or lessen their severity." Warner-Lambert argued that this order was invalid because it went beyond a command to simply cease and desist from illegal behavior. Was Warner-Lambert correct?

2. Pantron I Corp. sold a shampoo and conditioner known as the Helsinki Formula. Pantron promoted the Helsinki Formula as an aid in fighting male pattern baldness. According to Pantron, polysorbate was the main ingredient that made the Helsinki Formula effective in arresting hair loss and stimulating hair growth. The Federal Trade Commission filed suit against Pantron on the theory that Pantron's advertisements made deceptive representations about the effectiveness of the Helsinki Formula, as well as deceptive representations that scientific evidence supported the effectiveness claims. The FTC sought injunctive and monetary relief. The evidence showed that the Helsinki Formula was effective for some users with male pattern baldness but that this effectiveness was probably due to the "placebo effect" (i.e., the effectiveness for some users stemmed from psychological reasons rather than from the inherent merit of the product). Because there was no scientifically valid evidence indicating that polysorbate is effective in treating hair loss or in inducing hair growth, the district court concluded that Pantron's advertisements were deceptive in representing that *scientific evidence* supported a conclusion that the Helsinki Formula was effective. The district court therefore issued an injunction that barred Pantron from representing, in its advertisements, that scientific evidence supports the alleged effectiveness of the Helsinki Formula in treating baldness or hair loss. However, because the Helsinki Formula did work for some users some of the time (whatever the reason), the district court concluded that the FTC had failed to carry its burden of proving that Pantron engaged in deceptive advertising when it represented that the Helsinki Formula was effective for persons with male pattern baldness. The court therefore refused to enjoin Pantron from making such a representation of effectiveness (i.e., a representation of effectiveness that did not go on to make the false claim of supporting scientific evidence). The court also refused to order monetary relief. In its appeal to the U.S. Court of Appeals for the Ninth Circuit, the FTC argued that when a product's effectiveness is due only to the placebo effect, an advertising claim of effectiveness is false and deceptive for purposes of the FTC Act. Was this FTC argument legally correct? Which party—the FTC or Pantron—was entitled to win the appeal?

3. Besides maintaining a private law practice, Keith Gill offered credit repair services to consumers in a business that he operated with a retired attorney, Richard Murkey. In various contexts, Gill and Murkey made representations to the effect that they could remove any accurate and non-obsolete information of a negative nature from the credit reports of consumers who used their credit repair services. The Federal Trade Commission filed suit against Gill and Murkey, alleging, among other things, that these representations violated § 5 of the Federal Trade Commission Act. Was § 5 violated?

4. Between 1966 and 1975, the Orkin Exterminating Company, the world's largest termite and pest control firm, offered its customers a "lifetime" guarantee that could be renewed each year by paying a definite amount specified in its contracts with the customers. The contracts gave no indication that the fees could be raised for any reasons other than certain narrowly specified ones. Beginning in 1980, Orkin unilaterally breached these contracts by imposing higher-than-agreed-upon annual renewal fees. Roughly 200,000 contracts were breached in this way. Orkin realized $7 million in additional revenues from customers who renewed at the higher fees. The additional fees did not purchase a higher level of service than that originally provided for in the contracts. Although some of Orkin's competitors may have been willing to assume Orkin's pre-1975 contracts at the fees stated therein, they would not have offered a fixed, locked-in "lifetime" renewal fee such as the one Orkin originally provided. Under the three-part test stated in the text, did Orkin's behavior violate FTC Act § 5's prohibition against *unfair* acts or practices?

5. Patron Aviation, Inc., an aviation company, bought an airplane engine from L&M Aircraft. The engine was assembled and shipped to L&M by Teledyne Industries, Inc. L&M installed the engine in one of Patron's airplanes. The engine turned out to be defective, so Patron sued L&M and Teledyne. One of the issues presented by the case was whether the Magnuson-Moss Act was applicable. Does the Magnuson-Moss Act apply to this transaction?

6. National Financial Services, Inc., a debt collection agency that serves magazine subscriptions clearinghouses, handled roughly 2.2 million accounts during 1986 and 1987. It sent letters to debtors whose accounts were delinquent. The average unpaid balance owed on these accounts was approximately $20. One letter sent by National Financial to a large number of debtors stated that their account "Will Be Transferred To An Attorney If It Is Unpaid After The Deadline Date!!!" Debtors who did not pay after receiving this letter received one or more letters that bore the letterhead of "N. Frank Lanocha, Attorney at Law." Lanocha prepared the text of these form letters and gave copies to National Financial's president, Smith. Smith then arranged for the letters to be prepared and mailed out. One of these letters contained the following statements: "Please Note I Am The Collection Attorney Who Represents American Family Publishers. I Have The Authority To See That Suit Is Filed Against You In This Matter." The letter also stated: "Unless This Payment Is Received In This Office Within Five Days Of The Date Of This Notice, I Will Be Compelled To Consider The Use Of The Legal Remedies That May Be Available To Effect Collection." The Federal Trade Commission sued National Financial, Smith, and Lanocha, alleging violations of the Fair Debt Collection Practices Act. How should the court rule?

7. National Credit Management Group (NCMG) offered credit monitoring and credit card services to consumers throughout the United States. NCMG used the 1-800-YES-CREDIT toll-free telephone number as the central marketing focus of its business. The company's advertisements on radio and cable television stated that persons with credit problems should call the toll-free number to receive a "confidential analysis" of their credit histories. Many of these advertisements also promised that NCMG would provide consumers with a complimentary application for a major credit card without a security deposit. In a number of the television advertisements, NCMG would flash the word "APPROVED" on the television screen or would otherwise highlight that word when the advertisement made reference to the credit card application.

NCMG received approximately 6,500 "inbound" calls per week from consumers who were responding to the radio and television advertisements. NCMG did not engage in "cold-calling" of consumers. When consumers called 1–800-YES-CREDIT, an NCMG representative offered them an initial credit analysis for an up-front fee of $95. During this phone conversation, the NCMG representative asked consumers for information—name, address, social security number, checking account number, employment information, and income information—that the representative stated was necessary to enable the credit analyst to gather information concerning the particular consumer's credit history. The NCMG representative also stated that the $95 fee was the charge associated with the accumulation and monitoring of the information contained in the credit profile of the consumer, and that the credit analyst would be telephoning the consumer in approximately two weeks to discuss the consumer's credit history. Between 5 and 9 percent of consumers who called the toll-free number purchased either the $95 initial credit analysis offered or other services (described below) that NCMG offered.

NCMG used the checking account information obtained by its representatives to set up an arrangement under which consumers' checking accounts would be debited in the amount of $95 if they accepted the initial credit analysis offer. Consumers who initially gave verbal authorization for the debiting arrangement later encountered great difficulty in attempting to cancel it. In the initial telephone conversation described above, the NCMG representatives did not tell consumers that when they used their "complimentary" application for a credit card (the application referred to in NCMG's advertisements), they could have to pay fees ranging from $50 to $100 to sponsoring banks. Neither were consumers informed that they were not guaranteed of receiving a credit card. Although sponsoring banks approved a high percentage of consumers who used the NCMG-provided application, not all applicants were approved for a credit card.

NCMG did not actually perform a credit analysis for paying consumers, nor did NCMG check those consumers' credit reports. When the supposed credit analyst made the above-described followup telephone call to a consumer, he or she did not discuss the consumer's credit history. Instead, the credit analyst attempted to sell the consumer NCMG's two-year program designed for persons who wished to establish or reestablish their credit. The two-year program, which consisted largely of NCMG's furnishing certain educational materials, ranged in cost from several hundred dollars to well over $1000, with the NCMG caller having the discretion to set the price at what seemed an appropriate level under the circumstances. The credit analyst typically did not disclose that the earlier check-debiting arrangement would be used as the payment mechanism for persons who agreed to subscribe to the two-year program.

The Federal Trade Commission (FTC) filed suit against NCMG. Among other things, the FTC alleged that NCMG violated § 5 of the FTC Act as well as the Telemarketing Sales Rule (TSR). Did NCMG violate § 5? Did NCMG violate the TSR?

8. In 1988, Vincent Mone quit his job at Sawyer of Napa, Inc., a California corporation whose president and CEO was Milton Dranow. When Mone established a competing firm, Dranow sued him for $5 million, alleg-

ing unfair competition. Three days before filing suit, Dranow had obtained a credit report on Mone from TRW, Inc., a credit reporting agency. Under the Fair Credit Reporting Act, did TRW act properly in giving Dranow the credit report on Mone?

9. When Samuel Grant sued his landlord, the landlord filed a counterclaim. Grant later was awarded a $608 judgment against the landlord, with the landlord receiving a $476.10 judgment against Grant on the counterclaim. This left Grant with a net judgment of $131.90. Approximately one year after the above case, Texaco denied Grant's application for a credit card. Texaco did so on the basis of a credit report prepared by TRW, Inc. This credit report stated that a judgment of approximately $400 had been entered against Grant in the above-described litigation between Grant and his landlord. Grant then informed TRW that the litigation involving his landlord had resulted in a net judgment in Grant's favor. TRW eventually sent Grant an "Updated Credit Profile" showing that the $400 judgment had been deleted from his file. Several months later, Grant again applied for a Texaco credit card. Texaco again denied his application because a newly issued TRW credit report indicated that a $400 judgment had been entered against him in the case involving his landlord. Grant then sued TRW on the theory that TRW had violated the Fair Credit Reporting Act (FCRA). TRW moved to dismiss the case. Should Grant's FCRA case be dismissed?

10. Sylvia Miller, a married woman, wanted to buy a pair of loveseats from a retail furniture store. The store offered to arrange financing for her through the Public Industrial Loan Company. Public later refused to extend credit to Miller unless her husband cosigned the debt obligation. The reason was a consumer reporting agency's unfavorable credit report on Miller. Was Public's action forbidden sex discrimination under the Equal Credit Opportunity Act? In any event, what other legal remedy might Miller have?

11. John E. Koerner & Co., Inc. applied for a credit card account with the American Express Company. The application was for a company account designed for business customers. Koerner asked American Express to issue cards bearing the company's name to Louis Koerner and four other officers of the corporation. Koerner was required to sign a company account form, under which he agreed that he would be jointly and severally liable with the company for all charges incurred through use of the company card. American Express issued the cards requested by the company. Thereafter, the cards were used almost totally for business purposes, although Koerner occasionally used his card for personal expenses. Later, a dispute regarding charges appearing on the company account arose. Does the Fair Credit Billing Act apply to this dispute?

12. Darlene Jenkins obtained a car loan from a bank. When she defaulted on the loan, the bank sued her to recover the balance due. The bank's attorney, George Heintz, wrote Jenkins a letter in an effort to settle the case. In the portion of the letter in which he stated the amount Jenkins allegedly owed, Heintz included $4,173 owed for insurance that the bank had purchased because Jenkins had not kept the car insured. Jenkins sued Heintz under the Fair Debt Collection Practices Act (FDCPA). She contended that Heintz's letter violated the FDCPA's prohibition against attempting to collect an amount not "authorized by the agreement creating the debt," as well as its prohibition against making a "false representation of . . . the . . . amount . . . of any debt." Jenkins conceded that the loan agreement required her to keep the car insured "against loss or damage" and permitted the bank to buy such insurance to protect the car if she failed to do so. She asserted, however, that the $4,173 policy purchased by the bank was not the kind of policy the loan agreement contemplated, because it insured the bank not only against "loss or damage" but also against her failure to repay the loan. According to Jenkins, Heintz's representation about the amount of her "debt" violated the FDCPA because the representation was false and part of an attempt to collect an amount not authorized by the loan agreement. Reasoning that the FDCPA does not apply to attorneys engaged in litigation, the federal district court dismissed Jenkins's lawsuit for failure to state a claim. The U.S. Court of Appeals for the Seventh Circuit reversed, holding that the FDCPA applies to attorneys involved in litigation. Was the Seventh Circuit correct?

Online Research: The FTC

Go to the Federal Trade Commission's website, www.ftc.gov, and review the information present there. Then briefly describe the respective responsibilities of the various offices and bureaus that exist within the FTC, and list the cities in which the FTC maintains regional offices.

49

ANTITRUST: THE SHERMAN ACT

XYZ, Inc., manufactures widgets and sells them through various wholesale dealers. Several other firms also manufacture widgets. Of course, XYZ wishes to conduct its business within the bounds of the law, including the rules of antitrust law. As you study Chapter 49, consider the following questions regarding possible courses of action and their treatment under antitrust law:

• Would XYZ violate antitrust law if XYZ deliberately causes its prices to parallel those of a competing widget manufacturer?

• If XYZ and a competing widget manufacturer agree that each will charge no more than a certain agreed amount for their widgets (i.e., a maximum price), is there an antitrust violation? What if XYZ and its competitor agree to set a minimum price in order to avoid what each sees as the potentially ruinous consequences of a price-cutting war?

• Is there an antitrust violation if XYZ and its wholesale dealers agree that the dealers will adhere to an established maximum sale price when they sell to retailers? What if the agreement between XYZ and the dealers is that the dealers will adhere to a certain minimum price when they sell to retailers?

• If XYZ and its wholesale dealers agree on exclusive sales territories within which each dealer will operate, is there an antitrust violation?

• Is there an antitrust problem if XYZ informs its dealers that it will not sell them widgets unless they also buy a certain unrelated product from XYZ, and the dealers, wanting to preserve their widget dealerships, agree to this provision?

• Would there be an antitrust violation if XYZ and some of the other widget manufacturers agree that each manufacturer will have an exclusive geographic area of business operation?

• Is there an antitrust violation if XYZ and some of the other widget manufacturers agree not to purchase, from a certain supplier, materials used in making widgets?

• If XYZ's widgets acquire a public reputation for being high in quality and this perception leads, over time, to XYZ's holding a market share so large that XYZ effectively holds monopoly status, has XYZ run afoul of antitrust law?

THE POST–CIVIL WAR EMERGENCE and growth of large industrial combines and trusts significantly altered the business environment of earlier years. A major feature of this phenomenon was the tendency of various large business entities to acquire dominant positions in their industries by buying up smaller competitors or engaging in practices aimed at driving those competitors out of business. This behavior led to public demands for legislation to preserve competitive market structures and prevent the accumulation of great economic power in the hands of a few firms.

Congress responded in 1890 with the Sherman Act. It supplemented this response by enacting the Clayton Act in 1914 and the Robinson-Patman Act in 1936.

In enacting the antitrust statutes, Congress adopted a public policy in favor of preserving and promoting free competition as the most efficient means of allocating social resources. The Supreme Court summarized, in *Times-Picayune Co. v. United States* (1953), the rationale for this faith in competition's positive effects:

> Basic to faith that a free economy best promotes the public weal is that goods must stand the cold test of competition; that the public, acting through the market's impersonal judgment, shall allocate the nation's resources and thus direct the course its economic development will take.

Congress thus presumed that competition was more likely to exist in an industrial structure characterized by a large number of competing firms than in concentrated industries dominated by a few large competitors.

Despite this longstanding policy in favor of competitive market structures, the antitrust laws have not been very successful in halting the trend toward concentration in American industry. Today's market structure in many important industries is *oligopolistic,* with the bulk of production accounted for by a few dominant firms. Traditional antitrust concepts are often difficult to apply to the behavior of firms in these highly concentrated markets. Recent years have witnessed the emergence of new ideas that challenge longstanding antitrust policy assumptions.

The Antitrust Policy Debate

Antitrust enforcement necessarily reflects fundamental public policy judgments about the economic activities to be allowed and the industrial structure best suited to foster desirable economic activity. Given the importance of such judgments to the future of the American economy, it is not surprising that antitrust policy spurs vigorous public debate.

Chicago School Theories

During the past three decades, traditional antitrust assumptions have faced an effective challenge from commentators and courts advocating the application of microeconomic theory to antitrust enforcement. These methods of antitrust analysis are commonly called **Chicago School theories** because many of their major premises were advanced by scholars affiliated with the University of Chicago.

Chicago School advocates view *economic efficiency* as the primary, if not sole, goal of antitrust enforcement. They are far less concerned with the supposed effects of industrial concentration than are traditional antitrust thinkers. Even highly concentrated industries, they argue, may engage in significant forms of nonprice competition, such as competition in advertising, styling, and warranties. They also point out that concentration in a particular industry does not necessarily preclude *interindustry competition.* For example, a concentrated glass container industry may still face significant competition from the makers of metal, plastic, and fiberboard containers. Chicago School advocates are also quick to point out that many markets today are international in scope, so that concentrated domestic industries such as automobiles, steel, and electronics may nonetheless face effective foreign competition. Moreover, they argue that the technological developments necessary for American industry to compete more effectively in international markets may require the great capital resources that result from domestic concentration.

According to the Chicago School viewpoint, the traditional antitrust focus on the structure of industry has improperly emphasized protecting *competitors* instead of protecting *competition.* Chicago School theorists argue that antitrust policy's primary thrust should feature *anticonspiracy* efforts rather than *anticoncentration* efforts. In addition, most of these theorists take a lenient view toward vertically imposed restrictions on price and distribution that have been traditionally seen as undesirable, because they believe that such restrictions can promote efficiencies in distribution. Thus, they tend to be tolerant of attempts by manufacturers to control resale prices or establish exclusive distribution systems for their products.

Traditional Antitrust Theories

Traditional antitrust thinkers, however, contend that even though economic efficiency is important, antitrust policy has historically embraced *political* as well as economic values. Concentrated economic power, they argue, is undesirable for a variety of noneconomic reasons. It may lead to antidemocratic concentrations of political power. Moreover, it may stimulate greater governmental intrusions into the economy in the same way that the post–Civil War activities of the trusts led to the passage of the antitrust laws. According to the traditional view, lessening concentration enhances individual freedom by reducing the barriers to entry that confront would-be competitors and by ensuring broader input into economic decisions having important social consequences. Judge Learned Hand summed up this perspective on antitrust policy:

> Great industrial consolidations are inherently undesirable, regardless of their economic results. Throughout the history of [the Sherman Act] it has been constantly assumed that one of [its] purposes was to perpetuate and preserve, for its own sake and in spite of possible cost, an organization of industry in small units which can effectively compete with each other.[1]

Effect of Chicago School Notions

Chicago School notions, however, have had a significant impact on the course of antitrust enforcement in recent decades. The Supreme Court and many presidential appointees to the lower federal courts, the Department of Justice, and the Federal Trade Commission have given credence to Chicago School economic arguments during the past 20 years. The presence on the federal bench of so many judges embracing Chicago School ideas means that those views are likely to continue to have an impact on the shape of antitrust law.

Jurisdiction, Types of Cases, and Standing

Jurisdiction

The Sherman Act outlaws monopolization, attempted monopolization, and agreements in restraint of trade. Because the federal government's power to regulate business originates in the commerce clause of the U.S. Constitution (discussed in Chapter 3), the federal antitrust laws apply only to behavior having some significant impact on *interstate* or *foreign* commerce. Given the interdependent nature of our national economy, it is normally fairly easy to demonstrate that a challenged activity either involves interstate commerce (the "in commerce" jurisdiction test) or has a substantial effect on interstate commerce (the "effect on commerce" jurisdiction test). Various cases indicate that a business activity may have a substantial effect on interstate commerce even if the activity occurs solely within the borders of one state. Activities that are purely *intrastate* in their effects, however, are outside the scope of federal antitrust jurisdiction and must be challenged under state law.

The federal antitrust laws have been extensively applied to activities affecting the international commerce of the United States. The conduct of American firms operating outside U.S. borders may be attacked under our antitrust laws if it has an intended effect on our foreign commerce. Likewise, foreign firms "continuously engaged" in our domestic commerce are subject to federal antitrust jurisdiction. Determining the full extent of the extraterritorial reach of our antitrust laws often involves courts in difficult questions of antitrust exemptions and immunities (to be discussed in Chapter 50). The extraterritorial reach issue also suggests the troubling political prospect that aggressive expansion of antitrust law's applicability may create tension between our antitrust policy and our foreign policy in general.

Types of Cases and the Role of Pretrial Settlements

Sherman Act violations may give rise to criminal prosecutions and civil litigation instituted by the federal government (through the Department of Justice), as well as to civil suits filed by private parties. A significant percentage of the antitrust cases brought by the Department of Justice are settled without trial through *nolo contendere* pleas in criminal cases and *consent decrees* in civil cases. Although a defendant who pleads nolo contendere technically has not admitted guilt, the sentencing court is free to impose the same penalty that would be appropriate in the case of a guilty plea or a conviction at trial. Consent decrees involve a defendant's consent to remedial measures aimed at remedying the competitive harm resulting from his actions. Because neither a nolo plea nor a consent decree is admissible as proof of a violation of the Sherman Act in a private plaintiff's later civil suit, these devices are often attractive to antitrust defendants.

LOG ON

For considerable background material dealing with antitrust law (including what is meant to be a consumer-friendly explanation of antitrust enforcement), go to the website of the United States Department of Justice, at **www.usdoj.gov.**

Criminal Prosecutions

Individuals criminally convicted of Sherman Act violations may receive a fine of up to $350,000 per violation and/or a term of imprisonment of up to three years. Corporations convicted of violating the Sherman Act may be

---

[1]*United States v. Aluminum Co. of America, Inc.* (2d Cir. 1945).

fined up to $10 million per violation. Before an individual may be found criminally responsible under the Sherman Act, however, the government must prove an *anticompetitive effect* flowing from the challenged activity, as well as *criminal intent* on the defendant's part. The level of criminal intent required for a violation is a "knowledge of [the challenged activity's] probable consequences" rather than a specific intent to violate the antitrust laws.[2] Civil violations of the antitrust laws may be proved, however, through evidence of either an unlawful purpose or an anticompetitive effect.

Civil Litigation

The federal courts have broad injunctive powers to remedy civil antitrust violations. Courts may order convicted defendants to *divest* themselves of the stock or assets of acquired companies, to *divorce* themselves from a functional level of their operations (e.g., ordering a manufacturer to sell its captive retail outlets), to refrain from particular conduct in the future, and to cancel existing contracts. In extreme cases, courts may also enter a *dissolution decree* ordering a defendant to liquidate its assets and cease business operations. Private individuals and the Department of Justice may seek such injunctive relief regarding antitrust violations.

Treble Damages for Private Plaintiffs Section 4 of the Clayton Act gives private parties a significant incentive to enforce the antitrust laws by providing that private plaintiffs injured by Sherman Act or Clayton Act violations are entitled to recover *treble damages* plus court costs and attorney's fees from the defendant. This means that once antitrust plaintiffs have demonstrated the amount of their actual losses (such as lost profits or increased costs) resulting from the challenged violation, this amount is tripled. The potential for treble damage liability plainly presents a significant deterrent threat to potential antitrust violators.

Standing

Private plaintiffs who seek to enforce the antitrust laws must first demonstrate that they have **standing** to sue. This means that they must show a *direct antitrust injury* as a result of the challenged behavior. An antitrust injury results from the unlawful aspects of the challenged behavior and is of the sort Congress sought to prevent. For example, in *Brunswick Corp. v. Pueblo Bowl-o-Mat, Inc.*

(U.S. Sup. Ct. 1977), the operator of a chain of bowling centers (Pueblo) challenged a bowling equipment manufacturer's (Brunswick's) acquisition of various competing bowling centers that had defaulted on payments owed to Brunswick for equipment purchases. In essence, Pueblo asserted that if Brunswick had not acquired them, the failing bowling centers would have gone out of business—in which event Pueblo's profits would have increased. The Supreme Court rejected Pueblo's claim because its supposed losses flowed from Brunswick's having *preserved* competition by acquiring the failing centers. Allowing recovery for such losses would be contrary to the antitrust purpose of *promoting* competition.

Importance of Direct Injury Proof that an antitrust injury is *direct* is critical because the Supreme Court has held that *indirect purchasers* lack standing to sue for antitrust violations. In *Illinois Brick Co. v. State of Illinois* (U.S. Sup. Ct. 1977), the state of Illinois and other governmental entities sought treble damages from concrete block suppliers who, they alleged, had illegally fixed the price of block used in the construction of public buildings. The plaintiffs acknowledged that the builders hired to construct the buildings had actually paid the inflated prices for the blocks, but argued that these illegal costs probably had been passed on to them in the form of higher prices for building construction. The Supreme Court refused to allow recovery, holding that granting standing to indirect purchasers would create a risk of duplicative recoveries by purchasers at various levels in a product's chain of distribution. The Court also observed that affording standing to indirect purchasers would lead to difficult problems of tracing competitive injuries through several levels of distribution and assessing the extent of an indirect purchaser's actual losses.

A number of state legislatures responded to *Illinois Brick* by enacting statutes allowing indirect purchasers to sue under *state* antitrust statutes. The Supreme Court has held that the *Illinois Brick* holding does not preempt such statutes.

Section 1–Restraints of Trade

Concerted Action

Section 1 of the Sherman Act states that "[e]very contract, combination in the form of trust or otherwise, or

---

[2]*United States v. U.S. Gypsum Co.* (U.S. Sup. Ct. 1978).

conspiracy, in restraint of trade or commerce among the several states, or with foreign nations is declared to be illegal." A **contract** is any agreement, express or implied, between *two or more* persons or business entities to restrain competition. A **combination** is a continuing *partnership* in restraint of trade. When *two or more* persons or business entities join for the purpose of restraining trade, a **conspiracy** occurs.

The above statutory language makes obvious the conclusion that § 1 of the Sherman Act is aimed at **concerted action** (i.e., *joint action*) in restraint of trade. *Purely unilateral action* by a competitor, on the other hand, cannot violate § 1. This statutory section reflects the public policy that businesspersons should make important competitive decisions on their own, rather than in conjunction with competitors. In his famous book *The Wealth of Nations* (1776), Adam Smith acknowledged both the danger to competition posed by concerted action and the tendencies of competitors to engage in such action. Smith observed that "[p]eople of the same trade seldom meet together, even for merriment and diversion, [without] the conversation end[ing] in a conspiracy against the public, or in some contrivance to raise prices."

Section 1's concerted action requirement poses two major problems. First, how separate must two business entities be before their joint activities are subject to the act's prohibitions? It has long been held that a corporation cannot conspire with itself or its employees and that a corporation's employees cannot be guilty of a conspiracy in the absence of some independent party. What about conspiracies, however, among related corporate entities? In decisions roughly 50 years ago, the Supreme Court appeared to hold that a corporation could violate the Sherman Act by conspiring with a wholly owned subsidiary. More recently, however, in *Copperweld Corp. v. Independence Tube Corp.* (U.S. Sup. Ct. 1984), the Court repudiated the "intra-enterprise conspiracy doctrine." The Court held that a parent company is legally incapable of conspiring with a wholly owned subsidiary for Sherman Act purposes, because an agreement between parent and subsidiary does not create the risk to competition that results when two independent entities act in concert. It remains to be seen whether this approach extends to corporate subsidiaries and affiliates that are not wholly owned. *Copperweld*'s logic would appear, however, to cover any subsidiary in which the parent firm has a controlling interest.

A second—and more difficult—problem frequently accompanies attempts to enforce § 1. This problem arises when courts are asked to *infer,* from the relevant circumstances, the existence of an agreement or conspiracy to restrain trade despite the lack of any *overt* agreement by the parties. Should parallel pricing behavior by several firms be enough, for instance, to justify the inference that a price-fixing conspiracy exists? Courts have consistently held that proof of pure *conscious parallelism,* standing alone, is **not** enough to establish a § 1 violation. Other evidence must be presented to show that the defendants' actions stemmed from an **agreement,** *express or implied,* rather than from independent business decisions. It therefore becomes quite difficult to attack *oligopolies* (a few large firms sharing one market) under § 1, because such firms may independently elect to follow the pricing policies of the industry "price leader" rather than risk their large market shares by engaging in vigorous price competition.

Per Se Analysis

Although § 1's language condemns "every" contract, combination, and conspiracy in restraint of trade, the Supreme Court has long held that the Sherman Act applies only to behavior that *unreasonably* restrains competition. In addition, the Court has developed two fundamentally different approaches to analyzing behavior challenged under § 1. According to the Court, some actions always have a negative effect on competition—an effect that cannot be excused or justified. Such actions are classified as **per se** unlawful. If a particular behavior falls under the per se heading, it is conclusively presumed to violate § 1. Per se rules are thought to provide reliable guidance to business. They also simplify otherwise lengthy antitrust litigation, because if per se unlawful behavior is proven, the defendant cannot assert any supposed justifications in an attempt to avoid liability.

Per se rules, however, are frequently criticized on the ground that they oversimplify complex economic realities. Recent decisions reveal that for *some* economic activities, the Supreme Court is moving away from per se rules and instead adopting **rule of reason** analysis. This trend is consistent with the Court's increased inclination to consider economic theories that seek to justify behavior previously held to be per se unlawful.

"Rule of Reason" Analysis

Behavior not classified as per se unlawful is judged under the **rule of reason.** This approach requires a detailed inquiry into the actual competitive effects of the defendant's actions. It includes consideration of any justifications that the defendant may advance. If the court concludes that the challenged activity had a significant anticompetitive effect that was not offset by any positive effect on competition or other social benefit such as enhanced economic efficiency, the activity will be held to violate § 1. On the other hand, if the court concludes that the justifications advanced by the defendant outweigh the harm to competition resulting from the defendant's activity, there is no § 1 violation.

The following subsections of this chapter examine some of the behaviors held to violate § 1. The legal treatment (per se or rule of reason) given to the respective behaviors is also considered.

Horizontal Price-Fixing

An essential attribute of a free market is that the price of goods and services is determined by the free play of the impersonal forces of the marketplace. Attempts by competitors to interfere with market forces and control prices—called **horizontal price-fixing**—have long been held per se unlawful under § 1. Price-fixing may take the form of direct agreements among competitors about the price at which they sell or buy a particular product or service. It may also be accomplished by agreements on the quantity of goods to be produced, offered for sale, or bought. In one famous case, an agreement by major oil refiners to purchase and store the excess production of small independent refiners was held to amount to price-fixing because the purpose of the agreement was to affect the market price for gasoline by artificially limiting the available supply.[3]

Some commentators have suggested that agreements among competitors to fix *maximum* prices should be treated under a rule of reason approach rather than the harsher per se standard because, in some instances, such agreements may result in savings to consumers. In addition, lower courts have occasionally sought to craft exceptions to the rule that horizontal price-fixing triggers per se treatment. It is important to note, however, that the Supreme Court continues to adhere to the longstanding rule of per se illegality for any form of horizontal price-fixing. In the *Denny's Marina* case, which follows, a federal court of appeals overturned a district court's attempt to limit the applicability of the per se rule in the horizontal price-fixing context.

---

[3] *United States v. Socony-Vacuum Oil Co.*, 310 U.S. 150 (U.S. Sup. Ct. 1940).

Denny's Marina, Inc. v. Renfro Productions, Inc.   8 F.3d 1217 (7th Cir. 1993)

Denny's Marina, Inc. filed an antitrust action, described more fully below, against various defendants: the "Renfro Defendants" (Renfro Productions, Inc., Indianapolis Boat, Sport, and Travel Show, Inc., and individuals connected with those firms); "CIMDA" (the Central Indiana Marine Dealers Association); and the "Dealer Defendants" (various boat dealers who competed with Denny's in the sale of fishing boats, motors, trailers, and marine accessories in the central Indiana market). The Renfro Defendants operate two boat shows each year, one in the spring and one in the fall, at the Indiana State Fairgrounds. The spring show has occurred annually for more than 30 years and is one of the top three boat shows in the United States. It attracts between 160,000 and 191,000 consumers each year. The fall show is a smaller operation that has occurred each year since 1987. Numerous boat dealers participate in the two shows.

Denny's participated in the fall show in 1988, 1989, and 1990. It participated in the spring show in 1989 and 1990. According to allegations made by Denny's in its antitrust complaint, Denny's was quite successful at each of these shows, apparently because it urged customers to shop the other dealers and then return to Denny's for a lower price. After the 1989 spring show, some of the Dealer Defendants began to complain (according to Denny's) to the Renfro Defendants about the sales methods used by Denny's. In addition, Denny's alleged, the Dealer Defendants spent a significant part of a CIMDA meeting venting frustration about similar sales tactics used by Denny's at the 1990 spring show. Denny's also asserted that the Dealer Defendants' complaints to the Renfro Defendants escalated, and that as a result, the Renfro Defendants informed Denny's after the 1990 fall show that Denny's could no longer participate in the boat shows.

Denny's claimed that the above-described conduct of the defendants amounted to a conspiracy, prohibited by Sherman Act § 1, to exclude Denny's from participating in the boat shows because its policy was to "meet or beat" its competitors' prices at the shows. When the district court granted the defendants' motions for summary judgment, Denny's appealed to the Seventh Circuit Court of Appeals.

Cummings, Circuit Judge   Because summary judgment was granted to the defendants, the facts alleged by Denny's and any inferences therefrom must be construed in its favor. Summary judgment will be denied if a reasonable jury could return a verdict for the plaintiff.

A successful claim under § 1 of the Sherman Act requires proof of three elements: (1) a contract, combination, or conspiracy; (2) a resultant unreasonable restraint of trade in the relevant market; and (3) an accompanying injury. The district court noted that [for purposes of a ruling on their summary judgment motions] defendants do not dispute the first and third elements of proof. Hence the parties' only argument is whether Denny's has made a sufficient showing of the second element, unreasonable restraint of trade, to withstand defendants' motions for summary judgment.

There are two standards for evaluating whether an alleged restraint of trade is unreasonable: the rule of reason and the per se rule. Because the restraint alleged by Denny's constitutes a horizontal price-fixing conspiracy, it is per se an unreasonable restraint of trade [under a long line of Supreme Court decisions]. The conspiracy in this case was horizontal because it . . . consisted of Denny's competitors and their association. That the conspiracy was joined by the operators of the . . . boat shows does not transform it into a vertical agreement.

Likewise, the conspiracy was to fix prices. Price-fixing agreements need not include "explicit agreement on prices to be charged or that one party have the right to be consulted about the other's prices." *Palmer v. BRG of Georgia, Inc.* (U.S. Sup. Ct. 1990). "Under the Sherman Act a combination formed for the purpose and with the effect of raising, depressing, fixing, pegging, or stabilizing the price of a commodity in interstate or foreign commerce is illegal per se." *United States v. Socony-Vacuum Oil Co.* (U.S. Sup. Ct. 1940). Concerted action by dealers to protect themselves from price competition by discounters constitutes horizontal price-fixing. Hence the actions of the Dealer Defendants and CIMDA, joined by the Renfro Defendants, to prevent Denny's from participating in the boat shows constitutes a horizontal price-fixing conspiracy notwithstanding the apparent lack of an explicit agreement to set prices.

So far, the position of this court is similar to that of the court below. Nevertheless, having essentially found that Denny's had adduced sufficient evidence of a horizontal price-fixing conspiracy to withstand a motion for summary judgment, the court below refused to apply the per se rule that would allow it to conclude that there had been an unreasonable restraint of trade in the relevant market. Instead, before it would apply the per se rule the court required Denny's to demonstrate a substantial potential for impact on competition in the central Indiana market as a whole. Such an exception to the per se rule against price-fixing is unwarranted by cited precedent . . . [and] would effectively require plaintiffs to make a rule of reason demonstration in order to invoke the per se rule! [In cases governed by the rule of reason], both parties are likely to present extensive economic analysis of the relevant market. It is in part to avoid such excessive costs of litigation that the per se rule is applied in cases where the anti-competitive effect of certain practices may be presumed.

As far back as 1940, it has been clear that horizontal price-fixing is illegal per se without requiring a showing of actual or likely impact on a market. *See Socony-Vacuum Oil.* This is because joint action by competitors to suppress price-cutting has the requisite "substantial potential for impact on competition" to warrant per se treatment. *Federal Trade Commission v. Superior Court Trial Lawyers Association* (U.S. Sup. Ct. 1990). The district court would require Denny's to demonstrate a particular potential for impact on the market, when one of the purposes of the per se rule is that in cases like this such a potential is so well-established as not to require individualized showings. The pernicious effects are conclusively presumed.

Since Denny's presented enough evidence for a court and jury to conclude that the defendants engaged in [per se behavior consisting of] a horizontal conspiracy to suppress price competition at boat shows, . . . the district court's grant of summary judgment to the defendants [was erroneous].

Summary judgment for defendants reversed; case remanded for trial.

Vertical Price-Fixing

Attempts by manufacturers to control the resale price of their products may also fall within the scope of § 1. This behavior, called **vertical price-fixing** or *resale price maintenance,* has long been held to be per se illegal.

Manufacturers may lawfully state a suggested retail price for their products, because such an action is purely unilateral in nature and does not involve the concerted action necessary for a violation of § 1. Per se illegality may be present, however, when there is a manufacturer-dealer *agreement* (express or implied) obligating the dealer to resell at a price dictated by the manufacturer. The latter scenario involves prohibited *concerted action*.

Unilateral Refusals to Deal   In *United States v. Colgate & Co.* (1919), the Supreme Court held that a manufacturer could *unilaterally refuse to deal* with dealers who failed to follow its suggested resale prices. The rationale underlying this holding was that a single firm may deal or not deal with whomever it chooses without violating § 1, because unilateral action is not the concerted action prohibited by the statute. Subsequent cases, however, have narrowly construed the *Colgate* doctrine. Manufacturers probably will be held to have violated § 1 if they enlist the aid of dealers who are not price-cutting to help enforce their (the manufacturers') pricing policies, or if they engage in other joint action to further those policies.

Exception to Per Se Rule   In recent years, it began to seem doubtful that per se illegality would remain the rule for all resale price maintenance agreements. Chicago School theorists argued that many of the same reasons that have been held to justify rule of reason analysis of vertically imposed *nonprice* restraints on distribution (discussed later in this chapter) were equally applicable to vertical price-fixing agreements. In particular, these critics argued that vertical restrictions limiting the maximum price at which a dealer can resell may prevent dealers with dominant market positions from exploiting consumers through price-gouging. After hinting in previous cases that it might be inclined to repudiate the rule that vertically imposed maximum price restraints trigger per se treatment, the Supreme Court overruled a longstanding precedent and held, in the 1997 *Khan* decision, that vertical maximum price-fixing should be analyzed under the rule of reason.

State Oil Co. v. Khan   *522 U.S. 3 (U.S. Sup. Ct. 1997)*

Barkat Khan operated a service station in Illinois under a contract with State Oil Co. The parties' contract called for State Oil to lease the station premises to Khan and for State Oil to supply him with gasoline and related products that he would sell at the station. According to the contract, State Oil would establish a suggested retail price for the gasoline it supplied Khan for resale under the "Union 76" brand name. State Oil would then sell the gasoline to Khan for 3.25 cents less than that price. If Khan regarded the suggested retail price as too low, he could ask State Oil to increase it. If State Oil refused to raise the suggested price and Khan increased his retail price anyway, the contract required Khan to rebate to State Oil the difference between his new price and the suggested price.

When Khan fell behind on his rent, State Oil terminated the contract. Khan then sued State Oil, alleging that the above provisions of the contract amounted to vertical maximum price-fixing in violation of § 1 of the Sherman Act. The district court held that the alleged price-fixing should be evaluated under the rule of reason approach rather than under the per se approach. When the court granted summary judgment in favor of State Oil, Khan appealed to the U.S. Court of Appeals for the Seventh Circuit. The Seventh Circuit reversed, holding that a Supreme Court precedent established the per se rule as controlling. The Supreme Court granted certiorari.

O'Connor, Justice   In *Albrecht v. Herald Co.* (U.S. Sup. Ct. 1968), this Court held that vertical maximum price-fixing is a per se violation of [§ 1 of the Sherman Act]. [W]e are asked to reconsider that decision.

The District Court found that [Khan's] allegations . . . did not establish the sort of "manifestly anticompetitive implications or pernicious effect on competition" that would justify per se prohibition of State Oil's conduct. The Court of Appeals for the Seventh Circuit reversed [the lower court's grant of summary judgment in favor of State Oil]. The [Seventh Circuit] first noted that the agreement between Khan and State Oil did indeed fix maximum gasoline prices by making it "worthless" for Khan to exceed the sug-

gested retail prices. After reviewing legal and economic aspects of price-fixing, the court concluded that State Oil's pricing scheme was a per se antitrust violation under *Albrecht*. Although the [Seventh Circuit] characterized *Albrecht* as "unsound when decided" and "inconsistent with later decisions" of this Court, it felt constrained to follow that decision.

[M]ost antitrust claims are analyzed under a "rule of reason," according to which the finder of fact must decide whether the questioned practice imposes an unreasonable restraint on competition, taking into account a variety of factors, including specific information about the relevant business, its condition before and after the restraint was imposed, and the restraint's history, nature, and effect. Some types of restraints, however, have such predictable and pernicious anticompetitive effect, and such limited potential for procompetitive benefits, that they are deemed unlawful per se.

A review of this Court's decisions leading up to and beyond *Albrecht* is relevant to our assessment of the continuing validity of the per se rule established in *Albrecht*. Beginning with [a 1911 decision], the Court recognized the illegality of agreements under which manufacturers or suppliers set the minimum resale prices to be charged by their distributors. By 1940, the Court broadly declared all business combinations "formed for the purpose and with the effect of raising, depressing, fixing, pegging, or stabilizing the price of a commodity in interstate or foreign commerce" illegal per se. *United States v. Socony-Vacuum Oil Co.* (U.S. Sup. Ct. 1940). Accordingly, the Court condemned an agreement between two affiliated liquor distillers to limit the maximum price charged by retailers in *Kiefer-Stewart Co. v. Joseph E. Seagram & Sons, Inc.* (U.S. Sup. Ct. 1951).

In subsequent cases, the Court's attention turned to arrangements through which suppliers imposed restrictions on dealers with respect to matters other than resale price. In [a 1963 decision], the Court considered the validity of a manufacturer's assignment of exclusive territories to its distributors and dealers. The Court concluded that too little was known about the competitive impact of such vertical limitations to warrant treating them as per se unlawful. Four years later, in *United States v. Arnold, Schwinn & Co.* (U.S. Sup. Ct. 1967), the Court reconsidered the status of exclusive dealer territories and held that . . . a supplier's imposition of territorial restrictions on [a] distributor was "so obviously destructive of competition" as to constitute a per se violation of the Sherman Act.

Albrecht, decided [a year after *Schwinn*], involved a newspaper publisher who had granted exclusive territories to independent carriers subject to their adherence to a maximum price on resale of the newspapers to the public. Influenced by its decisions in *Socony-Vacuum, Kiefer-Stewart*, and *Schwinn*, the Court concluded that it was per se unlawful for the publisher to fix the maximum resale price of its newspapers. The Court acknowledged that "[m]aximum and minimum price-fixing may have different consequences in many situations," but nonetheless condemned maximum price-fixing for "substituting the perhaps erroneous judgment of a seller for the forces of the competitive market."

Nine years later, in *Continental T.V., Inc. v. GTE Sylvania, Inc.* (U.S. Sup. Ct. 1977), the Court overruled *Schwinn*, thereby rejecting application of a per se rule in the context

of vertical nonprice restrictions. [The Court noted that *Schwinn*] neither explained the "sudden change in position," nor referred to the accepted requirements for per se violations set forth in [earlier cases]. The Court . . . reviewed scholarly works supporting the economic utility of vertical nonprice restraints. [It then] concluded that, because "departure from the rule-of-reason standard must be based upon demonstrable economic effect rather than—as in *Schwinn*—upon formalistic line-drawing," the appropriate course would be "to return to the rule of reason that governed vertical restrictions prior to *Schwinn*."

Subsequent decisions of the Court . . . have hinted that the analytical underpinnings of *Albrecht* were substantially weakened by *Sylvania*. We noted in [a 1982 decision] that vertical restraints are generally more defensible than horizontal restraints. [W]e explained in *324 Liquor Corp. v. Duffy* (U.S. Sup. Ct. 1987) that decisions such as *Sylvania* "recognize the possibility that a vertical restraint imposed by a single manufacturer or wholesaler may stimulate interbrand competition even as it reduces intrabrand competition."

[I]n *Atlantic Richfield Co. v. USA Petroleum Co.* (ARCO) (U.S. Sup. Ct. 1990), although *Albrecht's* continuing validity was not squarely before the Court, some disfavor with that decision was signaled by our statement that we would "assume, *arguendo,* that *Albrecht* correctly held that vertical maximum price-fixing is subject to the per se rule." More significantly, we specifically acknowledged that vertical maximum price-fixing "may have procompetitive interbrand effects," and pointed out that, in the wake of *Sylvania,* "[t]he procompetitive potential of a vertical maximum price restraint is more evident . . . than it was when *Albrecht* was decided, because exclusive territorial arrangements and other nonprice restrictions were unlawful per se in 1968."

Thus, our reconsideration of *Albrecht's* continuing validity is informed by several of our decisions, as well as a considerable body of scholarship discussing the effects of vertical restraints. Our analysis is also guided by our general view that the primary purpose of the antitrust laws is to protect interbrand competition. "Low prices," we . . . explained [in *ARCO*], "benefit consumers regardless of how those prices are set, and so long as they are above predatory levels, they do not threaten competition."

So informed, we find it difficult to maintain that vertically-imposed maximum prices could harm consumers or competition to the extent necessary to justify their per se invalidation. As Chief Judge Posner wrote for the Court of Appeals in this case:

As for maximum resale price fixing, . . . the supplier [usually] cannot squeeze his dealers' margins below a competitive level; the attempt to do so would just drive the dealers into the arms of a competing supplier. A supplier might, however, fix a maximum resale price in order to prevent his dealers from exploiting a monopoly position. . . . [S]uppose that State Oil, perhaps to encourage . . . dealer services . . . , has spaced its dealers sufficiently far apart to limit competition among them (or even given each of them an exclusive territory); and suppose further that Union 76 is a sufficiently distinctive and popular brand to give the dealers in it at least a modicum of monopoly power. Then State Oil might want to place a ceiling on the dealers' resale prices in order to prevent them from exploiting that monopoly power fully. It would do this not out of disinterested malice, but in its commercial self-interest. The higher the price at which gasoline is resold, the smaller the volume sold, and so the lower the profit to the supplier if the higher profit per gallon at the higher price is being snared by the dealer.

We recognize that the *Albrecht* decision presented a number of theoretical justifications for a per se rule against vertical maximum price-fixing. But criticism of those premises abounds. The *Albrecht* decision was grounded in the fear that maximum price-fixing by suppliers could interfere with dealer freedom. [However, as noted by Phillip Areeda in his treatise, *Antitrust Law,*] "the ban on maximum resale price limitations declared in *Albrecht* in the name of 'dealer freedom' has actually prompted many suppliers to integrate forward into distribution, thus eliminating the very independent trader for whom *Albrecht* professed solicitude."

The *Albrecht* Court also expressed the concern that maximum prices may be set too low for dealers to offer consumers essential or desired services. But such conduct, by driving away customers, would seem likely to harm manufacturers as well as dealers and consumers, making it unlikely that a supplier would set such a price as a matter of business judgment. In addition, *Albrecht* noted that vertical maximum price-fixing could effectively channel distribution through large or specially advantaged dealers. It is unclear, however, that a supplier would profit from limiting its market by excluding potential dealers. Further, although vertical maximum price-fixing might limit the viability of inefficient dealers, that consequence is not necessarily harmful to competition and consumers.

Finally, *Albrecht* reflected the Court's fear that maximum price-fixing could be used to disguise arrangements to fix minimum prices, which remains illegal per se. Although we have acknowledged the possibility that maximum pricing might mask minimum pricing, we believe that such conduct—as with the other concerns articulated in *Albrecht*—can be appropriately recognized and punished under the rule of reason. After reconsidering *Albrecht*'s rationale and the substantial criticisms the decision has received, . . . we conclude that there is insufficient economic justification for per se invalidation of vertical maximum price-fixing.

Despite what Chief Judge Posner aptly described as *Albrecht*'s "infirmities, [and] its increasingly wobbly, moth-eaten foundations," there remains the question whether *Albrecht* deserves continuing respect under the doctrine of *stare decisis*. The Court of Appeals was correct in applying that principle despite disagreement with *Albrecht,* for it is this Court's prerogative alone to overrule one of its precedents. We approach the reconsideration of decisions of this Court with the utmost caution. *Stare decisis* reflects "a policy judgment that in most matters it is more important that the applicable rule of law be settled than that it be settled right." *Agostini v. Felton* (U.S. Sup. Ct. 1997). But "[s]tare decisis is not an inexorable command." *Payne v. Tennessee* (U.S. Sup. Ct. 1991). In the area of antitrust law, there is a competing interest, well-represented in this Court's decisions, in recognizing and adapting to changed circumstances and the lessons of accumulated experience.

With the views underlying *Albrecht* eroded by this Court's precedent, there is not much of that decision to salvage. [W]e find its conceptual foundations gravely weakened. In overruling *Albrecht,* we of course do not hold that all vertical maximum price-fixing is per se lawful. Instead, vertical maximum price-fixing, like the majority of commercial arrangements subject to the antitrust laws, should be evaluated under the rule of reason.

Decision of Court of Appeals reversed; case remanded for further proceedings.

Horizontal Divisions of Markets

It has traditionally been said that **horizontal division of markets** agreements—those agreements among competing firms to divide up the available market by assigning one another certain exclusive territories or certain customers—are illegal per se. Such agreements plainly represent agreements not to compete. They result in each firm being isolated from competition in the affected market.

In *United States v. Topco Associates, Inc.* (1972), the Supreme Court reaffirmed this longstanding principle by striking down a horizontal division of markets agreement among members of a cooperative association of local and regional supermarket chains. *Topco* was widely criticized, however, on the ground that its per se approach ignored an important point: that the defendants' joint activities in promoting Topco brand products were aimed at enabling them to compete more effectively with national supermarket chains. Critics argued that when such horizontal restraints were ancillary to *procompetitive* behavior, they should be judged under the rule of reason.

Naked Restraints and Ancillary Restraints Such criticism has had an impact. Several decisions by lower federal courts have distinguished between "naked" horizontal restraints (those having no other purpose or effect except restraining competition) and "ancillary" horizontal restraints (those constituting a necessary part of a larger joint undertaking serving procompetitive ends). Although these courts continue to apply the per se rule to naked horizontal restraints, they give rule of reason treatment to ancillary restraints. In determining whether ancillary restraints are lawful under the rule of reason, courts weigh the harm to competition resulting from such restraints against the alleged offsetting benefits to competition.

Whether the Supreme Court ultimately will endorse such departures from *Topco* remains to be seen. However, the Court's post-*Topco* tendency to discard per se rules in favor of a rule of reason approach in other areas suggests that *Topco*'s critics may ultimately prevail with their arguments.

Vertical Restraints on Distribution

Vertical restraints on distribution (or *vertical nonprice restraints*) also fall within the scope of the Sherman Act. A manufacturer has always had the power to *unilaterally* assign exclusive territories to its dealers or to limit the dealerships it grants in a particular geographic area. However, manufacturers may run afoul of § 1 by causing dealers to *agree* not to sell outside their dealership territories or by placing other restrictions on their dealers' right to resell their products.

The Supreme Court once held that vertical restraints on distribution were per se illegal when applied to goods that the manufacturer had sold to its dealers. The Court changed course, however, in *Continental T.V., Inc. v. GTE Sylvania, Inc.* (1977) In *Sylvania,* the Court abandoned the per se rule in favor of a rule of reason approach to most vertical restraints on distribution. The Court accepted many Chicago School arguments concerning the potential *economic efficiencies* that could result from vertical restraints on distribution. Most notably, such restraints were alleged to offer a chance for increased *interbrand* competition among the product lines of competing manufacturers at the admitted cost of restraining *intrabrand* competition among dealers in a particular manufacturer's product. The *Orson* case, which follows shortly, illustrates this point.

Subsequent decisions on the legality of vertical restraints on distribution have emphasized the importance of the market share of the manufacturer imposing the restraints. Restraints imposed by manufacturers with large market shares are more likely to be found unlawful under the rule of reason because the resulting harm to intrabrand competition is unlikely to be offset by significant positive effects on interbrand competition.

Orson, Inc. v. Miramax Film Corp.   *79 F.3d 1358 (3d Cir. 1996)*

Orson, Inc., owned and operated the Roxy, a movie theater located in downtown Center City, Philadelphia, from January 1992 until the permanent closing of the theater in October 1994. The Roxy exhibited art films—as opposed to movies that may be characterized as mainstream—on two screens. The total seating capacity at the Roxy was 260. The Ritz theaters, which competed with the Roxy in the showing of art films in the Center City area, consisted of two five-screen facilities with a total seating capacity of approximately 1,800. The ticket prices at the Roxy and at the Ritz theaters (referred to collectively as "the Ritz") were essentially the same. In addition to the Roxy and the Ritz, there were six other Center City area theaters that showed art films at least part of the time.

Miramax Film Corp., a nationwide distributor of feature-length motion pictures (including art films), distributed movies to all of the theaters in Center City and elsewhere in the greater metropolitan Philadelphia area. Miramax licensed films for exhibition for a limited period of time. Consistent with the usual practice in the motion picture industry, these licenses normally were exclusive—meaning that during the time period established in the license, the film would not be licensed to other theaters located in a specified area. Such licenses, called clearances, *contained compensation terms entitling Miramax to a portion of the exhibiting theater's box office gross.*

In the motion picture industry, a first run *is the initial exhibition of a film in a given geographic area. A* subsequent run *is an exhibition of that film in the same geographic area after the first run has expired. Between January 1992 and February 1994 (when discovery ended in the lawsuit described below), Miramax licensed 28 films on a first-run basis, as well as one on a subsequent-run basis, to the Ritz. During the same time period, Miramax granted the Roxy one first-run license and 14 subsequent-run licenses, and issued various first-run licenses to Center City area theaters other than the Roxy and the Ritz. In addition, during the same time period, 59 distributors other than Miramax granted a total of 73 first-run licenses to the Roxy.*

All of the first-run licenses Miramax granted to the Ritz were exclusive in nature. On occasion, Orson sought a first-run, nonexclusive license on a Miramax film and indicated that Orson would offer Miramax a higher percentage of the Roxy's box office receipts than the percentage the Ritz would pay. Nevertheless, Miramax did not grant Orson the licenses it had requested for the Roxy.

Orson sued Miramax in August 1993, alleging that it had violated § 1 of the Sherman Act by conspiring with the Ritz to exclude the Roxy from the art film market. According to Orson's complaint, this conspiracy involved an agreement to (1) make the Ritz Miramax's exclusive Philadelphia exhibitor for first-run art film features, and (2) grant the Ritz exclusive first-run rights to any Miramax film the Ritz wished to exhibit. The district court concluded that rule of reason analysis was appropriate because the supposed agreement between Miramax and the Ritz was "clearly a vertical agreement" between a distributor and an exhibitor. After undertaking such an analysis, the district court granted summary judgment in favor of Miramax. Orson appealed to the U.S. Court of Appeals for the Third Circuit.

Mansmann, Circuit Judge   In rule of reason cases, the plaintiff bears the initial burden of showing that the alleged combination or agreement produced adverse, anticompetitive effects within the relevant product and geographic markets. The plaintiff may satisfy this burden by proving the existence of actual anticompetitive effects, such as reduction of output, increase in price, or deterioration in quality of goods and services. Due to the difficulty of isolating the market effects of the challenged conduct, however, such proof is often impossible to make. Accordingly, the courts allow proof of the defendant's "market power" instead. Market power [is] the ability to raise prices above those that would prevail in a competitive market. If a plaintiff meets his initial burden of adducing adequate evidence of market power or actual anticompetitive effects, the burden shifts to the defendant to show that the challenged conduct promotes a sufficiently pro-competitive objective.

Agreements between entities at different market levels are termed "vertical restraints." The Supreme Court has instructed that vertical restraints of trade, which do not present an express or implied agreement to set resale prices, are evaluated under the rule of reason. The Supreme Court has also repeatedly confirmed in vertical restraint cases that interbrand competition, as opposed to intrabrand competition, is the primary goal of the antitrust laws.

Miramax conceded for purposes of summary judgment that the relevant product market was art films and that the relevant geographic market was Center City, Philadelphia. The first issue we consider is the precise nature of the agreement between Miramax and the Ritz. Orson alleges that Miramax committed to make the Ritz its exclusive Philadelphia exhibitor for first-run art film features. [W]e disagree. The record is devoid of any proof of a promise [by Miramax] to grant first-run licenses . . . in Center City to the Ritz only. Moreover, the evidence is to the contrary; the Roxy received a first-run license from Miramax, as did [other Center City area theaters]. The record shows, instead, a series of clearances granted by Miramax to the Ritz, based on an understanding between the parties' respective principals that any time the Ritz was showing a first-run Miramax film, its license would be exclusive.

Before we consider the antitrust significance of the clearances, however, we will address the alleged conspiracy that we believe lies at the heart of Orson's . . . complaint. Orson's antitrust theory does not primarily challenge the clearances themselves; [instead, Orson] claims that the clearances were mere vehicles that Miramax and the Ritz used to further a secret conspiracy to drive the Roxy out of business by denying that theater first-run Miramax films.

[In a precedent case in which a theater owner alleged the existence of a similar conspiracy between another theater owner and a motion picture distributor, the Third Circuit required the plaintiff to prove that the defendants (1) acted in a manner contrary to their economic interests, and (2) had a motive to enter into the allegedly unlawful scheme.] Orson . . . contends that given its willingness to pay a higher percentage of the Roxy's gross for first-run Miramax films than paid by the Ritz, Miramax acted contrary to its economic well-being by choosing to grant clearances to the Ritz; [Orson] further maintains that Miramax was coerced into favoring the Ritz because the Ritz had made it clear that unless it was granted an exclusive arrangement it would use its clout and refuse to play Miramax films.

We do not find sufficient evidence in the record for either assertion. To the contrary, the evidence established that the clearances were consistent with Miramax's business interests, granted by the distributor to, as between the Roxy and the Ritz, the theater it reasonably predicted would generate greater income. The record demonstrated that the Ritz had [five times as many screens as the Roxy and nearly nine times the seating capacity of the Roxy, as well as] a solid history of box office receipts; by comparison, the Roxy was not nearly as profitable. The theaters which comprised the Ritz had been in continuous operation since their inception; the Roxy, on the other hand, had ceased operation from time to time over the years. Orson failed to show that Miramax had a motive to conspire with the Ritz to drive the Roxy out of business. Therefore, we conclude that Orson failed to sustain its burden on summary judgment regarding the essential elements of its antitrust conspiracy claim.

Our inquiry does not end here. The fact remains that clearances existed between Miramax and the Ritz, and that Orson contends that [the clearances themselves] violated § 1 of the Sherman Act. [C]learances, which involve entities at different levels of the film distribution industry, are vertical nonprice restraints of trade. As such, they are subject under § 1 to a rule of reason analysis.

[T]he reasonableness of a clearance under section 1 of the Sherman Act depends on the competitive stance of the theaters involved and the clearance's effect on competition.

[Special attention must be paid to the effect on] interbrand competition, which, as the Supreme Court has instructed, is our primary concern in an antitrust action.

[W]e begin with the fact that the parties agreed that the Roxy and the Ritz were in competition. Thus, the clearances served their accepted purpose of assuring both Miramax and the Ritz that the return from one run of a particular Miramax film would not be diminished. Turning to the touchstone of the rule of reason, the clearances' competitive effects, the uncontroverted facts . . . reveal a market in which competition thrived at both the distributor and exhibitor levels. In Center City, the Roxy, the Ritz, and [various other theaters] vied for the films of at least 59 distributors. Indeed, it is the indisputable existence of alternative sources of supply for the Roxy which negates the existence of anticompetitive effects in this case. Although the Miramax-Ritz clearances most certainly reduced intrabrand competition to some degree by disallowing the Roxy from showing on a first-run basis any Miramax film that the Ritz had selected, they undeniably promoted interbrand competition by requiring the Roxy to seek out and exhibit the films of other distributors, which it consistently accomplished. [T]he record conclusively establishes that the clearances did not produce the anticompetitive effects the Sherman Act was designed to prevent. On the contrary, competition in the relevant market was enhanced; art film consumers in Center City had more movies from which to choose. We thus conclude that Orson failed to present sufficient evidence to support its claim that the Miramax-Ritz clearances were unreasonable restraints of trade.

District court's grant of summary judgment for Miramax affirmed.

Group Boycotts and Concerted Refusals to Deal

Under the *Colgate* doctrine, a single firm may lawfully refuse to deal with certain firms. The same is not true, however, of *agreements* by two or more business entities to refuse to deal with others, to deal with others only on certain terms and conditions, or to coerce suppliers or customers not to deal with one of their competitors. Such agreements are *joint* restraints on trade. Historically, they have been per se unlawful under § 1. For example, when a trade association of garment manufacturers agreed not to sell to retailers that sold clothing or fabrics with designs pirated from legitimate manufacturers, the agreement was held to be a per se violation of the Sherman Act.[4]

Vertical Boycotts Recent antitrust developments, however, indicate that not all concerted refusals to deal will receive per se treatment. If a manufacturer terminated a distributor in response to complaints from other distributors that the terminated distributor was selling to customers outside its prescribed sales territory, the manufacturer will be held to have violated § 1 only if the termination resulted in a significant harm to competition. This result follows logically from the *Sylvania* decision.

[4]*Fashion Originators' Guild v. FTC* (U.S. Sup. Ct. 1941).

If vertical restraints on distribution are judged under the rule of reason, the same standard should apply to a vertical boycott designed to enforce such restraints.

Even distributors claiming to have been terminated as part of a per se illegal vertical price-fixing scheme have found recovery increasingly difficult to obtain in recent years. In *Monsanto v. Spray-Rite Service Corp.* (U.S. Sup. Ct. 1984), a manufacturer had terminated a discounting distributor after receiving complaints from its other distributors. The Supreme Court held that these facts would not trigger per se liability for vertical price-fixing in the absence of additional evidence tending to exclude the possibility that the manufacturer and the nonterminated distributors acted independently. In *Business Electronics Corp. v. Sharp Electronics Corp.* (U.S. Sup. Ct. 1988), the Court held that even proof of a conspiracy between a manufacturer and nonterminated distributors to terminate a price-cutter would not trigger per se liability unless it was accompanied by proof that the manufacturer and nonterminated dealers were also engaged in a vertical price-fixing conspiracy.

Horizontal Boycotts   It also appears that the Supreme Court is willing to relax the per se rule for some *horizontal* boycotts. For instance, in *Northwest Wholesale Stationers, Inc. v. Pacific Stationery & Printing Co.* (U.S. Sup. Ct. 1985), members of an office supply retailers' purchasing cooperative had expelled a member retailer that engaged in some wholesale operations in addition to retail activities. The Court held that rule of reason treatment should be extended to the alleged boycott at issue, but declined to eliminate the per se rule for all horizontal boycotts. The Court has offered only general guidance for determining which horizontal boycotts trigger rule of reason analysis and which ones amount to per se violations. The appropriate legal treatment in a given case is therefore difficult to predict.

Tying Agreements

Tying agreements occur when a seller refuses to sell a buyer a certain product (the *tying product*) unless the buyer also agrees to purchase a different product (the *tied product*) from the seller. For example, a fertilizer manufacturer refuses to sell its dealers fertilizer (the tying product) unless they also agree to buy its line of pesticides (the tied product). The potential anticompetitive effect of a tying agreement is that the seller's competitors in the sale of the tied product may be foreclosed from competing with the seller for sales to customers that have entered into tying agreements with the seller. To the extent that tying agreements are coercively imposed, they

also deprive buyers of the freedom to make independent decisions concerning their purchases of the tied product. Tying agreements may be challenged under both § 1 of the Sherman Act and § 3 of the Clayton Act.[5]

Elements of Prohibited Tying Agreements   Tying agreements are often said to be per se illegal under § 1. However, because a tying agreement must meet certain criteria before it is subjected to per se analysis, and because evidence of certain justifications is sometimes considered in tying cases, the rule against tying agreements is at best a "soft" per se rule.

Before a challenged tying agreement is held to violate § 1, these elements must be demonstrated: (1) the agreement involves *two* separate and distinct items rather than integrated components of a larger product, service, or system of doing business; (2) the tying product cannot be purchased unless the tied product is also purchased; (3) the seller has sufficient economic power in the market for the tying product (such as a patent or a large market share) to appreciably restrain competition in the tied product market; and (4) a "not insubstantial" amount of commerce in the tied product is affected by the seller's tying agreements.

Applying the above elements, a federal district court held in 2000 that Microsoft Corporation violated § 1 by tying its Internet Explorer Web browser to versions of its Windows operating system. In a 2001 decision, however, a federal court of appeals reversed that aspect of the district court's decision and remanded the tying claim for reconsideration under the rule of reason. The appellate court concluded that in the context of software used as a platform for third-party applications, tying of the sort done by Microsoft should not necessarily be presumed to have a pernicious effect on competition. The court reasoned that in order to avoid discouraging platform software-related innovation, weighing and balancing of the tying arrangement's benefits and anticompetitive effects should be undertaken. Only the rule of reason would provide the opportunity for such weighing and balancing. The court stressed, however, that it was not changing the controlling rules for tying agreements generally or for such arrangements in computer-related settings not involving platform software. (Other aspects of the appellate court's *Microsoft* decision are addressed later in this chapter.)

The *Eastman Kodak* case contains a discussion of the elements of prohibited tying arrangements, with a focus on the third element: *market power as to the tying product.*

---

[5]Section 3 of the Clayton Act applies, however, only when both the tying and the tied products are commodities. Chapter 50 discusses Clayton Act standards for tying agreement legality.

Eastman Kodak Co. v. Image Technical Services, Inc.
504 U.S. 451 (U.S. Sup. Ct. 1992)

Eastman Kodak Co. (Kodak) manufactures and sells photocopiers and micrographic equipment. In addition, Kodak provides customers with service and replacement parts for its equipment. Kodak produces some of the parts itself. The other parts are made to order for Kodak by independent original equipment manufacturers (OEMs). Rather than selling a complete system of original equipment, lifetime parts, and lifetime service for a single price, Kodak furnishes service after an initial warranty period either through annual service contracts or on a per-call basis. Kodak provides between 80 and 95 percent of the service for Kodak machines.

In the early 1980s, independent service organizations (ISOs) began repairing and servicing Kodak equipment, as well as selling parts for it. ISOs kept an inventory of parts, purchased either from Kodak or from other sources (primarily OEMs). In 1985, Kodak adopted policies designed to limit ISOs' access to parts and to make it more difficult for ISOs to compete with Kodak in servicing Kodak equipment. Kodak began selling replacement parts only to Kodak equipment buyers who used Kodak service or repaired their own machines (i.e., buyers who did not use ISOs for service). In addition, Kodak sought to limit ISO access to other sources of Kodak parts by working out agreements with OEMs that they would sell parts for Kodak equipment to no one other than Kodak, and by pressuring Kodak equipment owners and independent parts distributors not to sell Kodak parts to ISOs.

Eighteen ISOs sued Kodak, claiming that these policies amounted to (1) unlawful tying of the sale of service for Kodak machines to the sale of parts (in violation of Sherman Act § 1), and (2) monopolization or attempted monopolization of the sale of service for Kodak machines (in violation of Sherman Act § 2). A federal district court granted summary judgment in favor of Kodak on each of these claims. The Ninth Circuit Court of Appeals reversed, holding that summary judgment was inappropriate because there were genuine issues of material fact regarding the ISOs' claims. The Supreme Court granted Kodak's petition for a writ of certiorari.

Blackmun, Justice   Because this case comes to us on Kodak's motion for summary judgment, the evidence of the ISOs is to be believed, and all justifiable inferences are to be drawn in the ISOs' favor [for purposes of determining whether Kodak is entitled to summary judgment or whether a trial is instead necessary].

A tying arrangement is "an agreement by a party to sell one product but only on the condition that the buyer also purchases a different (or tied) product, or at least agrees that he will not purchase that product from any other supplier." *Northern Pacific Railway Co. v. United States* (U.S. Sup. Ct. 1958). Such an arrangement violates § 1 of the Sherman Act if the seller has "appreciable economic power" in the tying product market and if the arrangement affects a substantial volume of commerce in the tied market. *Fortner Enterprises, Inc. v. U.S. Steel Corp.* (U.S. Sup. Ct. 1969). Kodak [questions] whether its activities constituted a "tying arrangement" and whether [it] exercised "appreciable economic power" in the tying market.

For the ISOs to defeat [Kodak's] motion for summary judgment, . . . a reasonable trier of fact must be able to find, first, that service and parts are two distinct products, and second, that Kodak has tied the sale of the two products. For service and parts to be considered two distinct products, there must be sufficient consumer demand so that it is efficient for a firm to provide service separately from parts. Evidence in the record indicates that service and parts have been sold separately in the past and still are sold separately to self-service equipment owners. Kodak insists that be-

cause there is no demand for parts separate from service, there cannot be separate markets for service and parts. By that logic, we would be forced to conclude that there can never be separate markets, for example, for cameras and film, computers and software, or automobiles and tires. That is an assumption we are unwilling to make.

Kodak's assertion also appears to be incorrect as a factual matter. At least some consumers would purchase service without parts, because some service does not require parts, and some consumers, those who self-service, for example, would purchase parts without service. Enough doubt is cast on Kodak's claim of a unified market that it should be resolved by the trier of fact. [T]he ISOs have [also] presented sufficient evidence of a tie between service and parts. The record indicates that Kodak would sell parts to third parties only if they agreed not to buy service from ISOs.

[We now] consider the other necessary feature of an illegal tying arrangement: appreciable economic power in the tying market. Market power is the power "to force a purchaser to do something that he would not do in a competitive market." *Jefferson Parish Hospital Dist. No. 2 v. Hyde* (U.S. Sup. Ct. 1984). The existence of such power ordinarily is inferred from the seller's possession of a predominant share of the market.

The ISOs contend that Kodak has more than sufficient power in the parts market to force unwanted purchases of the tied market, service. The ISOs [assert or] provide evidence that certain parts are available exclusively through Kodak, . . .

that Kodak has control over the availability of parts it does not manufacture, [and that Kodak has both] prohibited independent manufacturers from selling Kodak parts to ISOs [and] pressured Kodak equipment owners and independent parts distributors to deny ISOs the purchase of Kodak parts. The ISOs also allege that Kodak's control over the parts market has excluded service competition, boosted service prices, and forced unwilling consumption of Kodak service. [They] offer evidence that consumers have switched to Kodak service even though they preferred ISO service, that Kodak service was of higher price and lower quality than the preferred ISO service, and that ISOs were driven out of business by Kodak's policies. Under our prior precedents, this evidence would be sufficient to entitle the ISOs to a trial on their claim of market power.

Kodak counters that even if it concedes monopoly *share* of the relevant parts market, it cannot actually exercise the necessary market *power* for a Sherman Act violation. This is so, according to Kodak, because competition exists in the equipment market. Kodak argues that it could not have the ability to raise prices of service and parts above the level that would be charged in a competitive market because any increase in profits from a higher price in the aftermarkets at least would be offset by a corresponding loss in profits from lower equipment sales as consumers began purchasing equipment with more attractive service costs. Kodak does not present any actual data on the equipment, service, or parts markets. Instead, it urges the adoption of a substantive legal rule that equipment competition precludes any finding of monopoly power in derivative aftermarkets. Legal presumptions that rest on formalistic distinctions rather than actual market realities are generally disfavored in antitrust law.

Even if Kodak could not raise the price of service and parts one cent without losing equipment sales, that fact would not disprove market power in the aftermarkets. Kodak's [theory] is based on the false dichotomy that there are only two prices that can be charged [for parts and service]—a competitive price or a ruinous one. But there could easily be a middle, optimum price at which the increased revenues from the higher-priced sales of service and parts would more than compensate for the lower revenues from lost equipment sales. [Contrary to the assertion in Kodak's brief], there is no immutable physical law—no "basic economic reality"—insisting that competition in the equipment market cannot coexist with market power in the aftermarkets.

[Kodak also overlooks] the existence of significant information and switching costs. These costs could create a less responsive connection between service and parts prices and equipment sales. For the service-market price to affect equipment demand, consumers must inform themselves of the total cost of the "package"—equipment, service, and parts—at the time of purchase; that is, consumers must engage in accurate lifecycle pricing. The necessary information would include data on price, quality, and availability of parts needed to operate, upgrade, or enhance the initial equipment, as well as service and repair costs, including estimates of breakdown frequency, nature of repairs, price of service and parts, length of "down-time," and losses incurred from down-time. Much of this information is difficult—some of it impossible—to acquire at the time of purchase.

Moreover, even if consumers were capable of acquiring and processing the complex body of information, they may choose not to do so. Acquiring the information is expensive. [Consumers] may not find it cost-efficient to compile the information. [It therefore] makes little sense to assume . . . that equipment-purchasing decisions are based on an accurate assessment of the total cost of equipment, service, and parts over the lifetime of the machine.

A second factor undermining Kodak's claim that supracompetitive prices in the service market lead to ruinous losses in equipment sales is the cost to current owners of switching to a different product. If the cost of switching is high, consumers who already have purchased the equipment, and are thus "locked-in," will tolerate some level of service-price increases before changing equipment brands. Under this scenario, a seller profitably could maintain supracompetitive prices in the aftermarket if the switching costs were high relative to the increase in service prices, and the number of locked-in customers were high relative to the number of new purchasers. Respondents have offered evidence that the heavy initial outlay for Kodak equipment, combined with the required support material that works only with Kodak equipment, makes switching costs very high for existing Kodak customers.

We conclude, then, that Kodak has failed to demonstrate that the ISOs' inference of market power in the service and parts markets is unreasonable. It is clearly reasonable to infer that Kodak has market power to raise prices and drive out competition in the aftermarkets, since the ISOs offer direct evidence that Kodak did so. It is also plausible . . . to infer that Kodak chose to gain immediate profits by exerting that market power where locked-in customers [and] high information costs . . . limited and perhaps eliminated any long-term loss.

In this case, . . . the balance tips against [granting Kodak's request for] summary judgment.

Denial of Kodak's motion for summary judgment affirmed; case remanded for trial.

Note: In another portion of the opinion not set forth here, the Court held that Kodak was not entitled to summary judgment on the ISOs' Sherman Act § 2 claim.

Possible Justifications for Tying Agreements

The first two elements of a prohibited tying agreement have been particularly significant in cases involving franchisors and their franchised dealers. For example, a suit by a McDonald's franchisee alleged that McDonald's violated § 1 by requiring franchisees to lease their stores from McDonald's as a condition of acquiring a McDonald's franchise. A federal court of appeals, however, rejected the franchisee's claim and held that no tying agreement was involved. Instead, the franchise and the lease were integral components of a well-thought-out system of doing business.[6]

The lower federal courts have recognized two other possible justifications for tying agreements. First, tying arrangements that are instrumental in launching a new competitor with an otherwise uncertain future may be lawful until the new business has established itself in the marketplace. The rationale for this "new business" exception is that if a tying agreement enables a fledgling firm to become a viable competitor, the agreement's net effect on competition is positive. Second, some courts have recognized that tying agreements sometimes may be necessary to protect the reputation of the seller's product line. For example, one of the seller's products functions properly only if used in conjunction with another of its products. To qualify for this exception, however, the seller must convince the court that a tying arrangement is the only viable means to protect its goodwill.

Chicago School Views on Tying Agreements

Chicago School thinkers have long criticized the traditional judicial approach to tying agreements because they do not believe that most tie-ins result in any significant economic harm. They argue that sellers who try to impose a tie-in in competitive markets gain no increased profits as a result. This is so because instead of participating in a tying agreement, buyers may turn to substitutes for the tying product or may purchase the tying product from competing sellers. The net effect of a tie-in may therefore be that any increase in the seller's sales in the tied product is offset by a loss in sales of the tying product. Only when the seller has substantial power in the tying product market is there potential that a tie-in may be used to increase the seller's power in the tied product market. However, even when the seller has such market power in the tying product, Chicago School thinkers argue that no harm to competition is likely to result if the seller faces strong competition in

the tied product market. For these and other reasons, Chicago School thinkers favor a rule of reason approach to all tying agreements. A majority of the Supreme Court has yet to accept these arguments. Some justices, however, appear willing to do so. If other members of the Court are similarly persuaded in the future, a substantial change in the legal criteria applied to tying agreements will be the result.

Reciprocal Dealing Agreements

Under a **reciprocal dealing agreement,** a buyer attempts to exploit its purchasing power by conditioning its purchases from suppliers on reciprocal purchases of some product or service offered for sale by the buyer. For example, an oil company with a chain of wholly owned gas stations refuses to purchase the tires it sells in those stations unless the tire manufacturer (the would-be supplier of the tires) agrees to purchase, from the oil company, the petrochemicals used in the tire manufacturing process. Reciprocal dealing agreements are similar in motivation and effect to tying agreements. Courts therefore tend to treat them similarly. In seeking to impose the reciprocal dealing agreement on the tire manufacturer, the oil company is attempting to gain a competitive advantage over its competitors in the petrochemical market. A court judging the legality of such an agreement would examine the oil company's economic power as a purchaser of tires and the dollar amount of petrochemical sales involved.

Exclusive Dealing Agreements

Exclusive dealing agreements require buyers of a particular product or service to purchase that product or service exclusively from a particular seller. For example, Standard Lawnmower Corporation requires its retail dealers to sell only Standard brand mowers. A common variation of an exclusive dealing agreement is the *requirements contract,* under which the buyer of a particular product agrees to purchase all of its requirements for that product from a particular supplier. For example, a candy manufacturer agrees to buy all of its sugar requirements from one sugar refiner. Exclusive dealing contracts present a threat to competition similar to that involved in tying contracts—they may reduce interbrand competition by foreclosing a seller's competitors from the opportunity to compete for sales to its customers. Unlike tying contracts, however, exclusive dealing agreements may sometimes enhance efficiencies in distribution and stimulate interbrand competition. Exclusive dealing agreements reduce a manufacturer's sales costs and provide dealers with a secure source of supply. They may also encourage dealer efforts to market the manufacturer's

---

[6] *Principe v. McDonald's Corp.,* 631 F.2d 303 (4th Cir. 1980).

products more effectively, because a dealer selling only one product line has a greater stake in the success of that line than does a dealer who sells the products of several competing manufacturers.

Because many exclusive dealing agreements involve commodities, they may also be challenged under § 3 of the Clayton Act. The legal tests applicable to exclusive dealing agreements under both acts are identical. Therefore, we defer discussing those tests until the next chapter.

Joint Ventures by Competitors

A **joint venture** is a combined effort by two or more business entities for a limited purpose such as research. Because joint ventures may yield enhanced efficiencies through integration of the resources of more than one firm, they are commonly judged under the rule of reason. Under this approach, courts tend to ask whether any competitive restraints that are incidental to the venture are necessary to accomplish its lawful objectives and, if so, whether those restraints are offset by the venture's positive effects. Joint ventures whose primary purpose is illegal per se, however, have been given per se treatment. An example of such a case would be two competing firms that form a joint sales agency and authorize it to fix the price of their products.

National Cooperative Research and Production Act

Antitrust critics have long argued that the threat of antitrust prosecution seriously inhibits the formation of joint research and development ventures, and that American firms are placed at a competitive disadvantage in world markets as a result. Such arguments have enjoyed more acceptance during roughly the past two decades. In 1984, Congress passed the National Cooperative Research Act (NCRA). This act applies to *joint research and development ventures* (JRDVs), which are broadly defined to include basic and applied research and joint activities in the licensing of technologies developed by such research. The NCRA requires the application of a reasonableness standard, rather than a per se rule, when a JRDV's legality is determined. It also requires firms contemplating a JRDV to provide the Department of Justice and the Federal Trade Commission with advance notice of their intent to do so. The NCRA provides that only actual (not treble) damages may be recovered for losses flowing from a JRDV ultimately found to be in violation of § 1. In addition, the NCRA contains a provision allowing the parties to a challenged JRDV to recover attorney's fees from an unsuccessful challenger if the suit is shown to

be "frivolous, unreasonable, without foundation, or in bad faith." Congress amended the statute in 1993 to extend its application to joint *production* ventures. In doing so, Congress renamed the statute the National Cooperative Research and Production Act.

Figure 1 summarizes the judicial treatment of potentially illegal practices under § 1 of the Sherman Act (as of early 2003, when this book went to press).

Figure 1   *Potentially Illegal Practices and Their Treatment under Sherman Act § 1*

Potentially Illegal Practice	Judicial Treatment	
	.Per Se	Rule of Reason
Horizontal price-fixing	*	
Vertical price-fixing (non-maximum)	*?	
Vertical maximum price-fixing		*
Horizontal division of markets	*?	*?
Vertical division of markets		*
Horizontal boycotts	*	*
Vertical boycotts	*	*
Tying agreements	*?	*
Reciprocal dealing agreements	*?	*
Exclusive dealing agreements		*
Joint ventures	*	*

Note: an entry with an asterisk in both columns means the facts of the individual case determine the treatment. A question mark indicates that future treatment is in question.

Section 2–Monopolization

Firms that acquire **monopoly power** in a given market have defeated the antitrust laws' objective of promoting competitive market structures. Monopolists, by definition, have the power to fix prices unilaterally because they have no effective competition. Section 2 of the Sherman Act was designed to prevent the formation of mo-

THE GLOBAL BUSINESS ENVIRONMENT

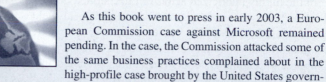

United States-based firms that engage in international business activities must remember that they may be subject to the antitrust laws of other nations. In the European Union, for instance, the European Commission serves as chief antitrust regulator through the Commission's Competition Directorate General. Articles in the Treaty of Rome contemplate bases of antitrust regulation similar, though not identical to, the legal bases in the United States under §§ 1 and 2 of the Sherman Act.

As this book went to press in early 2003, a European Commission case against Microsoft remained pending. In the case, the Commission attacked some of the same business practices complained about in the high-profile case brought by the United States government and various states against the firm. (The U.S. case receives extensive treatment at various points in this chapter.) The Commission's case also challenged other allegedly anticompetitive Microsoft practices that were not at issue in the case in the United States.

nopoly power. It provides: "Every person who shall monopolize, or attempt to monopolize, or combine or conspire with any other person to monopolize any part of trade or commerce among the several states, or with foreign nations shall be deemed guilty of a felony." Section 2 does not, however, outlaw monopolies. Instead, it outlaws the act of *monopolization*. Under § 2, a *single firm* can be guilty of monopolizing or attempting to monopolize a part of trade or commerce. The proof of joint action required for violations of § 1 is required only when two or more firms are charged with a conspiracy to monopolize under § 2.

Monopolization

Monopolization is "the willful acquisition or maintenance of monopoly power in a relevant market as opposed to growth as a consequence of superior product, business acumen, or historical accident."[7] This means that to be liable for monopolization, a defendant must have possessed not only monopoly power but also an **intent to monopolize.**

Monopoly Power   *Monopoly power* is usually defined for antitrust purposes as the power to *fix prices* or *exclude competitors* in a given market. Such power is generally inferred from the fact that a firm has captured a predominant share of the relevant market. Although the exact percentage share necessary to support an inference of monopoly power remains unclear and courts often look at other economic factors (such as the existence in the industry of barriers to the entry of new competitors), mar-

ket shares in excess of 70 percent have historically justified an inference of monopoly power.

Before a court can determine a defendant's market share, it must first define the **relevant market.** This is a crucial issue in § 2 cases because a broad definition of the relevant market normally results in a smaller market share for the defendant and a resulting reduction in the likelihood that the defendant will be found to possess monopoly power. The two components of a relevant market determination are the relevant **geographic market** and the relevant **product market.**

Economic realities prevailing in the industry determine the relevant geographic market. In which parts of the country can the defendant effectively compete with other firms in the sale of the product in question? To whom may buyers turn for alternative sources of supply? Factors such as transportation costs may also play a critical role in relevant market determinations. Thus, the relevant market for coal may be regional in nature, but the relevant market for computer chips may be national in scope.

The relevant product market is composed of those products meeting the *functional interchangeability* test, which identifies the products "reasonably interchangeable by consumers for the same purposes." This test recognizes that a firm's ability to fix the price for its products is limited by the availability of competing products that buyers view as acceptable substitutes. In a famous antitrust case, for example, Du Pont was charged with monopolizing the national market for cellophane because it had a 75 percent share. The Supreme Court concluded, however, that the relevant market was all "flexible wrapping materials," including aluminum foil, waxed paper, and polyethylene. Du Pont's 20 percent

---

[7]*United States v. Grinnell Corp.* (U.S. Sup. Ct. 1966).

share of that product market was far too small to amount to monopoly power.[8]

In the highly publicized *Microsoft* decision, a portion of which follows shortly, a federal court of appeals held that Microsoft Corporation possessed monopoly power in the worldwide market for Intel-compatible personal computer operating systems. The court concluded that Microsoft held a 95 percent share of the market.

Intent to Monopolize Proof of monopoly power standing alone, however, is never sufficient to prove a violation of § 2. The defendant's **intent to monopolize** must also be shown. Early cases required evidence that the defendant either acquired monopoly power by predatory or coercive means that violated antitrust rules (e.g., price-fixing or discriminatory pricing) or abused monopoly power in some way after acquiring it (such as by engaging in price-gouging). Contemporary courts focus on how the defendant acquired monopoly power. If the defendant *intentionally acquired it* or *attempted to maintain it* after acquiring it, the defendant possessed an intent to monopolize. Defendants are not in violation

of § 2, however, if their monopoly power resulted from the superiority of their products or business decisions, or from historical accident (e.g., the owner of a professional sports franchise in an area too small to support a competing franchise).

Purposeful acquisition or maintenance of monopoly power may be demonstrated in various ways. A famous monopolization case involved Alcoa, which had a 90 percent market share of the American market for virgin aluminum ingot. Alcoa was found liable for purposefully maintaining its monopoly power by acquiring every new opportunity relating to the production or marketing of aluminum, thereby excluding potential competitors.[9] As various cases indicate, firms that develop monopoly power by acquiring ownership or control of their competitors are likely to be held to have demonstrated an intent to monopolize.

In the following portion of the *Microsoft* decision, the court concluded that Microsoft Corporation was liable for monopolization because it possessed monopoly power in the relevant market and engaged in anticompetitive behavior in order to maintain its monopoly position.

---

[8]*United States v. E. I. du Pont de Nemours & Co.* (U.S. Sup. Ct. 1956).

[9]*United States v. Aluminum Co. of America, Inc.* (2d Cir. 1945).

United States v. Microsoft Corp.   *253 F.3d 34 (D.C. Cir. 2001)*

The United States, 19 individual states, and the District of Columbia brought civil antitrust actions against Microsoft Corporation. The cases were consolidated for trial. The plaintiffs charged, in essence, that Microsoft waged an unlawful campaign in defense of its monopoly position in the market for operating systems designed to run on Intel-compatible personal computers (PCs). More specifically, the plaintiffs claimed that Microsoft violated: (1) § 2 of the Sherman Act by engaging in monopolization through a series of exclusionary and anticompetitive acts designed to maintain its monopoly power; (2) § 2 by engaging in attempted monopolization of the Web browser market; and (3) § 1 of the Sherman Act by unlawfully tying its browser to its operating system and by entering into exclusive dealing agreements that unreasonably restrained trade. The plaintiffs other than the United States alleged that Microsoft's behavior also violated their respective antitrust laws.

The United States District Court for the District of Columbia held that Microsoft violated § 1 through unlawful tying arrangements but that Microsoft's exclusive dealing agreements did not run afoul of § 1. The court also held that Microsoft engaged in monopolization with regard to the market for Intel-compatible PC operating systems, as well as attempted monopolization of the Web browser market, in violation of § 2 and comparable state laws. In a separate decision, the district court held that the appropriate remedy was a divestiture order splitting Microsoft into two separate companies, one for the operating systems business and the other for the applications business.

Microsoft appealed to the United States Court of Appeals for the District of Columbia Circuit. In portions of the opinion not included here, the D.C. Circuit: affirmed the district court's holding that Microsoft's exclusive dealing agreements did not violate § 1; reversed the district court's holding that Microsoft violated § 1 through tying arrangements and remanded the case for reconsideration of that claim under different legal standards; and reversed the district court's holding that Microsoft violated § 2 by attempting to monopolize the Web browser market. The portions of the opinion set forth below deal with the D.C. Circuit's analysis of the claim that Microsoft violated § 2 by engaging in monopolization of the market for Intel-compatible PC operating systems. A nearby Cyberlaw in Action box examines the appellate court's treatment of the remedy issues and discusses later developments in the case.

Per Curiam   Section 2 of the Sherman Act makes it unlawful for a firm to "monopolize." The offense of monopolization has two elements: "(1) the possession of monopoly power in the relevant market, and (2) the willful acquisition or maintenance of that power as distinguished from growth or development as a consequence of a superior product, business acumen, or historic accident." *United States v. Grinnell Corp.* (U.S. Sup. Ct. 1966).

1. Monopoly Power

While merely possessing monopoly power is not itself an antitrust violation, it is a necessary element of a monopolization charge. The Supreme Court defines monopoly power as the power to control prices or exclude competition. [C]ourts . . . typically examine market structure in search of circumstantial evidence of monopoly power. [M]onopoly power may be inferred from a firm's possession of a dominant share of a relevant market that is protected by entry barriers. "Entry barriers" are factors . . . that prevent new rivals from timely responding to an increase in price above the competitive level.

Because the ability of consumers to turn to other suppliers restrains a firm from raising prices above the competitive level, the relevant market must include all products "reasonably interchangeable by consumers for the same purposes." *United States v. E. I. du Pont de Nemours Co.* (U.S. Sup. Ct. 1956). [T]he district court defined the market as "the licensing of all Intel-compatible PC operating systems worldwide," finding that there are "currently no products—and . . . there are not likely to be any in the near future—that a significant percentage of computer users worldwide could substitute for [these operating systems] without incurring substantial costs." Calling this market definition far too narrow, Microsoft argues that the court improperly excluded . . . non-Intel compatible operating systems (primarily Apple's Macintosh operating system, Mac OS) . . . and "middleware" products.

The district court found that consumers would not switch from Windows to Mac OS in response to a substantial price increase because of the costs of acquiring the new hardware needed to run Mac OS and compatible software applications, . . . because of the effort involved in learning the new system and transferring files to its format, [and because] the Apple system . . . supports fewer applications. Microsoft . . . points to [no] evidence contradicting the district court's findings. [W]e have no basis for upsetting the court's decision to exclude Mac OS from the relevant market.

This brings us to Microsoft's main challenge to the district court's market definition: the exclusion of middleware. Because of the importance of middleware to this case, we

[shall] explain what it is [and how it relates to operating systems]. Operating systems perform many functions, including allocating computer memory and . . . function[ing] as platforms for software applications. They do this by "exposing"—i.e., making available to software developers—routines or protocols that perform certain widely used functions. These are known as Application Programming Interfaces (APIs). For example, Windows contains an API that enables users to draw a box on the screen. Software developers wishing to include that function in an application need not duplicate it in their own code. Instead, they can "call"—i.e., use— the Windows API. Windows contains thousands of APIs.

"Middleware" refers to software products that expose their own APIs. Because of this, a middleware product written for Windows could take over some or all of Windows's valuable platform functions—that is, developers might begin to rely upon APIs exposed by the middleware for basic routines rather than relying upon the API set included in Windows. Ultimately, if developers could write applications relying exclusively on APIs exposed by middleware, their applications would run on any operating system on which the middleware was also present.

Microsoft argues that because middleware could usurp the operating system's platform function and might eventually take over other operating system functions . . . , the district court erred in excluding Navigator and Java from the relevant market. The court found, however, that neither Navigator, Java, nor any other middleware product could now, or would soon, expose enough APIs to serve as a platform for popular applications, much less take over all operating system functions. Whatever middleware's ultimate potential, the district court found that consumers could not now abandon their operating systems and switch to middleware in response to a sustained price for Windows above the competitive level. [B]ecause middleware is not now interchangeable with Windows, the district court had good reason for excluding middleware from the relevant market.

Having thus properly defined the relevant market, the district court found that Windows accounts for a greater than 95 percent share. The court also found that even if Mac OS were included, Microsoft's share would exceed 80 percent. [In addition], the court [properly] focused not only on Microsoft's present market share, but also on the structural barrier that protects the company's future position. That barrier—the applications barrier to entry—stems from two characteristics of the software market: (1) most consumers prefer operating systems for which a large number of applications have already been written; and (2) most developers prefer to write for operating systems that already have a substantial consumer base. This "chicken-and-egg" situation ensures that applications will continue to be written for the already dominant Windows, which in turn ensures that consumers will continue to prefer it over other operating systems.

2. Anticompetitive Conduct

[After correctly] concluding that Microsoft had monopoly power, the district court held that Microsoft had violated § 2 by engaging in a variety of exclusionary acts . . . to maintain its monopoly. Whether any particular act of a monopolist is exclusionary, rather than merely a form of vigorous competition, can be difficult to discern. [T]o be condemned as exclusionary, a monopolist's act must have an anticompetitive effect. That is, it must harm the competitive *process* and thereby harm consumers. In contrast, harm to one or more *competitors* will not suffice. [Assuming that the plaintiff] establishes a *prima facie* case under § 2 by demonstrating anticompetitive effect, the monopolist may proffer a procompetitive justification. If the monopolist asserts a procompetitive justification—a nonpretextual claim that its conduct is indeed a form of competition on the merits because it involves, for example, greater efficiency or enhanced consumer appeal—then the burden shifts back to the plaintiff to rebut that claim. [I]f the monopolist's procompetitive justification stands unrebutted, then the plaintiff must demonstrate that the anticompetitive harm of the conduct outweighs the procompetitive benefit. In cases arising under § 1 of the Sherman Act, the courts routinely apply a similar balancing approach under the rubric of the "rule of reason." With these principles in mind, we now [review] the district court's holding that Microsoft violated § 2 of the Sherman Act in a variety of ways.

a. Restrictions in Licenses Issued to Original Equipment Manufacturers (OEMs)

The district court condemned a number of provisions in Microsoft's agreements licensing Windows to OEMs, because it found that Microsoft's imposition of those provisions . . . serves to reduce usage share of Netscape's browser and, hence, protect Microsoft's operating system monopoly. Browser usage share is important because [a browser] must have a critical mass of users in order to attract software developers to write applications relying upon the APIs it exposes, and away from the APIs exposed by Windows. Applications written to a particular browser's APIs . . . would run on any computer with that browser, regardless of the underlying operating system. [The district court found that the] "overwhelming majority of consumers will only use a PC operating system for which there already exists a large and varied set of . . . applications, and for which it seems relatively certain that new types of applications and new versions of existing applications will continue to be marketed." If a consumer could have access to the applications he desired—regardless of the operating system he uses—simply by installing a particular browser on his computer, then he would no longer feel compelled to select Windows in order to have access to those applications; he could select an operating system other than Windows based solely upon its quality and price. In other words, the market for operating systems would be competitive.

The restrictions Microsoft places upon OEMs are of particular importance . . . because having an OEM pre-install a browser on a computer is one of the two most cost-effective methods by far of distributing browsing software. (The other is bundling the browser with Internet access software distributed by an Internet access provider (IAP).)

The district court concluded that [one Microsoft-imposed] license restriction—the prohibition upon the removal of desktop icons, folders, and Start menu entries—thwarts the distribution of a rival browser by preventing OEMs from removing visible means of user access to IE. The OEMs cannot practically install a second browser in addition to IE, the court found, in part because . . . a certain number of novice computer users, seeing two browser icons, will wonder which to use when and will call the OEM's support line. Support calls are extremely expensive and, in the highly competitive original equipment market, firms have a strong incentive to minimize costs. By preventing OEMs from removing visible means of user access to IE, the license restriction prevents many OEMs from pre-installing a rival browser, and therefore, protects Microsoft's monopoly from the competition that middleware might otherwise present. Therefore, we conclude that the license restriction at issue is anticompetitive.

[A] second license provision [imposed by Microsoft] prohibits OEMs from modifying the initial boot sequence—the process that occurs the first time a consumer turns on the computer. [The district court found that prior to] the imposition of that restriction, "among the programs that many OEMs inserted into the boot sequence were Internet sign-up procedures that encouraged users to choose from a list of IAPs assembled by the OEM." Microsoft's prohibition on any alteration of the boot sequence thus prevents OEMs from using that process to promote the services of IAPs, many of which—at least at the time Microsoft imposed the restriction—used Navigator rather than IE in their Internet access software. Because this prohibition has a substantial effect in protecting Microsoft's market power, and does so through a means other than competition on the merits, it is anticompetitive.

Finally, Microsoft . . . prohibits OEMs from causing any user interface other than the Windows desktop to launch automatically, from adding icons or folders different in size or shape from those supplied by Microsoft, and from using the "Active Desktop" feature to promote third-party brands. These restrictions impose significant costs upon the OEMs; prior to Microsoft's prohibiting the practice, many OEMs would change the appearance of the desktop in ways they found beneficial. The anticompetitive effect of the license restrictions is . . . that OEMs are not able to promote rival browsers, which keeps developers focused upon the APIs in Windows. This kind of promotion is not a zero-sum game; but for the restrictions in their licenses to use Windows, OEMs could promote multiple IAPs and browsers. [T]his type of license restriction . . . is anticompetitive: Microsoft reduced rival browsers' usage share not by improving its own product but, rather, by preventing OEMs from taking actions that could increase rivals' share of usage.

Microsoft argues that the license restrictions are legally justified because . . . Microsoft is simply "exercising its rights as the holder of valid copyrights." The company claims an absolute and unfettered right to use its intellectual property as it wishes: "If intellectual property rights have been lawfully acquired," it says, then, "their subsequent exercise cannot give rise to antitrust liability." That is no more correct than the proposition that use of one's personal property, such as a baseball bat, cannot give rise to tort liability. As the Federal Circuit succinctly stated: "Intellectual property rights do not confer a privilege to violate the antitrust laws." *In re Independent Service Organizations Antitrust Litigation* (Fed Cir. 2000). [Microsoft's copyright argument fails because the restrictions on OEMs are neither necessary to prevent substantial alteration of its copyrighted work nor necessary to preserve the stability of the Windows platform. Moreover,] Microsoft has not shown that the [actions OEMs otherwise would take would] reduce the value of Windows except in the sense that their promotion of rival browsers [would] undermine Microsoft's monopoly—and that is not a permissible justification for the license restrictions.

[W]e hold that . . . the OEM license restrictions represent uses of Microsoft's market power to protect its monopoly, unredeemed by any legitimate justification. The restrictions therefore violate § 2 of the Sherman Act.

b. Integration of Internet Explorer (IE) and Windows

[T]he district court found that "Microsoft's executives believed . . . its contractual restrictions placed on OEMs would not be sufficient in themselves to reverse the direction of Navigator's usage share. Consequently, . . ., Microsoft set out to bind [IE] more tightly to Windows 95." Technologically binding IE to Windows, the district court found, both prevented OEMs from pre-installing other browsers and deterred consumers from using them. [H]aving the IE software code as an irremovable part of Windows meant that pre-installing a second browser would increase an OEM's product testing costs, because an OEM must test and train its support staff to answer calls related to every software product preinstalled on the machine; moreover, pre-installing a browser in addition to IE would to many OEMs be "a questionable use of the scarce and valuable space on a PC's hard drive."

As a general rule, courts are properly very skeptical about claims that competition has been harmed by a dominant firm's product design changes. In a competitive market, firms routinely innovate in the hope of appealing to consumers, sometimes in the process making their products incompatible with those of rivals; the imposition of liability when a monopolist does the same thing will inevitably deter a certain amount of innovation. This is all the more true in a market, such as this one, in which the product itself is rapidly changing. Judicial deference to product innovation, however, does not mean that a monopolist's product design decisions are per se lawful.

The district court first condemned as anticompetitive Microsoft's decision to exclude IE from the "Add/Remove Programs" utility in Windows 98. Microsoft had included IE in the Add/Remove Programs utility in Windows 95, but when it modified Windows 95 to produce Windows 98, it took IE out of the Add/Remove Programs utility. This change reduces the usage share of rival browsers not by making Microsoft's own browser more attractive to consumers but by discouraging OEMs from distributing rival products. Because Microsoft's conduct, through something other than competition on the merits, has the effect of significantly reducing usage of rivals' products and hence protecting its own operating system monopoly, it is anticompetitive.

[T]he district court [also] condemned Microsoft's decision to bind IE to Windows 98 "by placing code specific to Web browsing in the same files as code that provided operating system functions." Putting code supplying browsing functionality into a file with code supplying operating system functionality "ensures that the deletion of any file containing browsing-specific routines would also delete vital operating system routines and thus cripple Windows." [P]reventing an OEM from removing IE deters it from installing a second browser because doing so increases the OEM's product testing and support costs; by contrast, had OEMs been able to remove IE, they might have chosen to pre-install Navigator alone.

Microsoft denies . . . that it commingled browsing and nonbrowsing code, and it maintains the district court's findings to the contrary are clearly erroneous. In view of the contradictory testimony in the record, some of which supports the district court's finding that Microsoft commingled browsing and nonbrowsing code, we cannot conclude that the finding was clearly erroneous. Microsoft proffers no [procompetitive] justification for . . . excluding IE from the Add/Remove Programs utility [or for] commingling browser and operating systems code. Accordingly, we hold that [those actions] constitute exclusionary conduct, in violation of § 2.

c. Agreements with Internet Access Providers (IAPs)

Microsoft concluded exclusive agreements with all the leading IAPs, including [America Online and other] major online services. [The] plaintiffs allege that, by closing to rivals a substantial percentage of the available opportunities for browser distribution, Microsoft managed to preserve its monopoly in the market for operating systems. The IAPs constitute one of the two major channels by which browsers can be distributed. [The district court found that] Microsoft has exclusive deals with "14 of the top 15 access providers in North America [, which] account for a large majority of all Internet access subscriptions in this part of the world." By ensuring that the majority of all IAP subscribers are offered IE either as the default browser or as the only browser, Microsoft's deals with the IAPs clearly have a significant effect in preserving its monopoly.

[With the plaintiffs] having demonstrated a harm to competition, the burden falls upon Microsoft to [justify] its exclusive dealing contracts with IAPs. Microsoft's only explanation . . . is that it wants to keep developers focused upon its APIs—which is to say [that] it wants to preserve its power in the operating system market. That is not an unlawful end, but neither is it a procompetitive justification. Accordingly, we affirm the district court's holding that Microsoft's exclusive contracts with IAPs are exclusionary devices, in violation of § 2 of the Sherman Act.

d. Dealings with Independent Software Vendors (ISVs) and Apple Computer

The district court held that Microsoft engages in exclusionary conduct in its dealings with . . . ISVs, which develop software. The court described Microsoft's deals with ISVs as [including

promises by Microsoft to provide] "preferential support, . . . technical information, and the right to use certain Microsoft seals of approval" if, in return, the ISVs agreed to "use Internet Explorer as the default browsing software for any software they develop with a hypertext-based user interface."

The court further found that the effect of these deals is to "increase the likelihood that the millions of consumers using [applications designed by ISVs subject to agreements with Microsoft] will use Internet Explorer rather than Navigator." Although the ISVs are a relatively small channel for browser distribution, they take on greater significance because [, as revealed above,] Microsoft had largely foreclosed the two primary channels to its rivals. In that light, one can tell from the record that by affecting the applications used by "millions" of consumers, Microsoft's exclusive deals with the ISVs had a substantial effect in further foreclosing rival browsers from the market. [T]he deals [thus] have an anticompetitive effect.

[In supposed justification of its ISV agreements,] Microsoft . . . states only that [the] agreements reflect an attempt "to persuade ISVs to utilize Internet-related system services in Windows rather than Navigator." [K]eeping developers focused upon Windows—that is, preserving the Windows monopoly—is a competitively neutral goal [rather than a] procompetitive justification for [Microsoft's] exclusive dealing arrangements with the ISVs. [We therefore] hold that those arrangements violate § 2.

[T]he district court [also] held that Microsoft's dealings with Apple Computer violated the Sherman Act. Apple . . . makes both software (including an operating system, Mac OS), and hardware (the Macintosh line of computers). Microsoft primarily makes software, including, in addition to its operating system, a number of popular applications. One, called "Office," is a suite of business productivity applications that Microsoft has ported to Mac OS. The district court found that "90 percent of Mac OS users running a suite of office productivity applications [use] Microsoft's Mac Office." Further, the court found that in 1997, "Apple's business was in steep decline" [and that] "many ISVs questioned the wisdom of continuing to spend time and money developing applications for the Mac OS. Had Microsoft announced in the midst of this atmosphere that it was ceasing to develop new versions of Mac Office, . . . ISVs, customers, developers, and investors would have interpreted the announcement as Apple's death notice."

Microsoft recognized the importance to Apple of its continued support of Mac Office. In June 1997 Microsoft Chairman Bill Gates [stated that] "Apple let us down on the browser by making Netscape the standard install" [and] that he had already called Apple's CEO to ask "how we should announce the cancellation of Mac Office." The district court further found that, within a month of Gates' call, Apple and Microsoft had reached an agreement pursuant to which [Microsoft promised] "to continue releasing up-to-date versions of Mac Office for at least five years" [and Apple] agreed to bundle the most current version [of IE] with Mac OS and make IE the default [browser]. The agreement also prohibit[ed] Apple from encouraging users to substitute another browser for IE, and state[d] that Apple [would] "encourage its employees to use [IE]."

This exclusive deal between Microsoft and Apple has a substantial effect upon the distribution of rival browsers. Pre-installation of a browser (which can be accomplished either by including the browser with the operating system or by the OEM installing the browser) is one of the two most important methods of browser distribution, and Apple had a not insignificant share of worldwide sales of operating systems. Because Microsoft's exclusive contract with Apple has a substantial effect in restricting distribution of rival browsers, and because [that effect] serves to protect Microsoft's monopoly, its deal with Apple must be regarded as anticompetitive. Microsoft offers no procompetitive justification for the exclusive dealing arrangement. It makes only the irrelevant claim that the IE-for-Mac Office deal is part of a multifaceted set of agreements between itself and Apple. Accordingly, we hold that the exclusive deal with Apple is exclusionary, in violation of § 2.

e. Java   Java, a set of technologies developed by Sun Microsystems, is another type of middleware posing a potential threat to Windows' position as the ubiquitous platform for software development. The Java technologies include: (1) a programming language; (2) a set of programs written in that language, called the "Java class libraries," which expose APIs; (3) a compiler, which translates code written by a developer into "bytecode"; and (4) a Java Virtual Machine ("JVM"), which translates bytecode into instructions to the operating system. Programs calling upon the Java APIs will run on any machine with a "Java runtime environment," that is, Java class libraries and a JVM.

In May 1995 Netscape agreed with Sun to distribute a copy of the Java runtime environment with every copy of Navigator. [The district court found that] "Navigator quickly became the principal vehicle by which Sun placed copies of its Java runtime environment on the PC systems of Windows users." Microsoft, too, agreed to promote the Java

technologies—or so it seemed. For at the same time, [the district court concluded,] Microsoft took steps "to maximize the difficulty with which applications written in Java could be ported from Windows to other platforms, and vice versa." The court found that Microsoft took four steps to exclude Java from developing as a viable cross-platform threat: (a) designing a JVM incompatible with the one developed by Sun; (b) entering into contracts . . . requiring major ISVs to promote Microsoft's JVM exclusively; (c) deceiving Java developers about the Windows-specific nature of the tools it distributed to them; and (d) coercing Intel to stop aiding Sun in improving the Java technologies.

The district court [erred in holding] that Microsoft engaged in exclusionary conduct by developing and promoting its own JVM, [which was incompatible with Sun's.] A monopolist does not violate the antitrust laws simply by developing a product that is incompatible with those of its rivals. In order to violate the antitrust laws, the incompatible product must have an anticompetitive effect that outweighs any procompetitive justification for the design. Microsoft's JVM is not only incompatible with Sun's, it allows Java applications to run faster on Windows than does Sun's JVM. [Microsoft's JVM thus] does not itself have . . . anticompetitive effect.

To the extent Microsoft's [agreements] with the ISVs conditioned receipt of Windows technical information upon the ISVs' agreement to promote Microsoft's JVM exclusively, they raise a different competitive concern. The district court found that . . . the deals were exclusive in practice because they required developers to make Microsoft's JVM the default in the software they developed. [T]he record indicates that Microsoft's deals with the major ISVs had a significant effect upon JVM promotion. [T]he products of [these] ISVs reached millions of consumers. Because Microsoft's agreements foreclosed a substantial portion of the field for JVM distribution and because, in so doing, they protected Microsoft's monopoly from a middleware threat, they are anticompetitive. Because . . . Microsoft has no procompetitive justification for them, we hold that the provisions in the [ISV agreements] requiring use of Microsoft's JVM as the default are exclusionary, in violation of the Sherman Act.

Microsoft's "Java implementation" included, in addition to a JVM, a set of software development tools it created to assist ISVs in designing Java applications. The district court found that, not only were these tools incompatible with Sun's cross-platform aspirations for Java—no violation, to be sure—but Microsoft deceived Java developers regarding the Windows-specific nature of the tools. Microsoft's tools included "certain 'keywords' and 'compiler directives' that could only be executed properly by Microsoft's version of the Java runtime environment for Windows." As a result, even Java "developers who were opting for portability over performance . . . unwittingly [wrote] Java applications that [ran] only on Windows." That is, developers who relied upon Microsoft's public commitment to cooperate with Sun and who used Microsoft's tools to develop what Microsoft led them to believe were cross-platform applications ended up producing applications that would run only on the Windows operating system.

Microsoft documents confirm that Microsoft intended to deceive Java developers, and predicted that the effect of its actions would be to generate Windows-dependent Java applications that their developers believed would be cross-platform; these documents also indicate that Microsoft's ultimate objective was to thwart Java's threat to Microsoft's monopoly in the market for operating systems. One Microsoft document, for example, states as a strategic goal: "Kill cross-platform Java by growing the polluted Java market." Microsoft's conduct related to its Java developer tools served to protect its monopoly of the operating system in a manner not attributable either to the superiority of the operating system or to the acumen of its makers, and therefore was anticompetitive. Unsurprisingly, Microsoft offers no procompetitive explanation for its campaign to deceive developers. [T]his conduct is exclusionary, in violation of § 2.

The district court [properly] held that Microsoft also acted unlawfully with respect to Java by using its "monopoly power to prevent firms such as Intel from aiding in the creation of cross-platform interfaces." [The record indicates that in 1995,] Intel was in the process of developing a high-performance, Windows-compatible JVM, [that] Microsoft wanted Intel to abandon [this] effort because a fast, cross-platform JVM would threaten Microsoft's monopoly in the operating system market, [and that Microsoft threatened to cease distributing] Intel technologies bundled with Windows [if Intel] did not stop aiding Sun on the multimedia front. Intel finally capitulated in 1997, after Microsoft [kept up the pressure]. Microsoft lamely characterizes its threat to Intel as "advice." The court, however, [properly concluded] that Microsoft's "advice" to Intel to stop aiding cross-platform Java was backed by the threat of retaliation. Therefore, we affirm the conclusion that Microsoft's threats to Intel were exclusionary, in violation of § 2.

District court's decision that Microsoft committed monopolization affirmed; other portions of decision affirmed in part, reversed in part, and remanded in part; remedial order of divestiture vacated and case remanded for further proceedings regarding appropriate remedies.

Attempted Monopolization

Firms that have not yet attained monopoly power may nonetheless be liable for an **attempt to monopolize** in violation of § 2 if they are dangerously close to acquiring monopoly power and are employing methods likely to result in monopoly power if left unchecked. As part of the required proof of a dangerous probability that monopoly power will be acquired, plaintiffs in attempted monopolization cases must furnish proof of the relevant market—as in monopolization cases. Attempt cases also require proof that the defendant possessed a specific intent to acquire monopoly power through anticompetitive means.

The *Microsoft* decision underscored the importance of the proof-of-relevant-market requirement in attempted monopolization cases. Although it affirmed the district court's holding that Microsoft had engaged in monopolization of the market for Intel-compatible PC operating systems, the United States Court of Appeals for the District of Columbia Circuit reversed the lower court's decision that Microsoft had attempted to monopolize the Web browser market. The D.C. Circuit stressed that the plaintiffs had failed to offer proof of—and that the district court had therefore made no appropriate finding regarding—the components and scope of any supposed browser market. Therefore, the lower court erred in basing its decision on conduct by Microsoft that, in the district court's view, seemed calculated to extend Microsoft's operating systems monopoly into another market. Whether Microsoft's conduct created a dangerous probability of monopoly power acquisition in that other market could not be determined without a definition of the latter market's boundaries—and no such definition had occurred.

A controversial issue that surfaces in many attempted monopolization cases concerns the role that *predatory pricing* may play in proving an intent to monopolize. The Supreme Court has defined predatory pricing as "pricing below an appropriate measure of cost for the purpose of eliminating competitors in the short run and reducing

CYBERLAW IN ACTION

As noted in the portion of the *Microsoft* decision included earlier, the federal district court (Thomas Penfield Jackson, District Judge) held that divestiture—in this instance, dividing Microsoft into two companies—was the appropriate remedy for Microsoft's Sherman Act violations. The D.C. Circuit Court of Appeals, however, reversed this determination and remanded the case for reconsideration of remedy-related issues.

The D.C. Circuit concluded that the district court erred in not holding a separate evidentiary hearing regarding remedies, and that because some of the bases of liability imposed by the district court had been reversed on appeal, the remedy of divestiture might no longer be the appropriate form of relief. Although the appellate court did not explicitly state that divestiture could not be ordered by the district court after it conducted further proceedings, the D.C. Circuit's opinion seemed to hint that divestiture was a more extreme remedy than was necessary. In remanding the case, the appellate court further ordered that the case be assigned to a district judge other than Judge Jackson, whose extensive participation in media interviews created the perception that he might not be impartial.

After the case was remanded, the United States, roughly half of the states that were plaintiffs, and Microsoft entered into a settlement agreement designed to resolve the case. District Judge Colleen Kollar-Kotelly held hearings on remedial and agreement-related issues, took under advisement the question whether to approve the agreement, and, shortly before this book went to press in late 2002, issued her approval. Under the settlement agreement, Microsoft became obligated to allow computer manufacturers to add icons for Microsoft competitors' software to the desktop display for the Windows operating system. Microsoft must also employ uniform licensing agreements when dealing with software manufacturers, and must furnish technical information to Internet access providers and to software and hardware vendors so that their products will work with Windows.

As of late 2002, 10 of the plaintiffs (nine states and the District of Columbia) persisted in refusing to sign on to the settlement agreement. They vowed to seek further relief in continued legal proceedings against Microsoft. Critics of the settlement agreement said it was not tough enough on Microsoft, that it would do little to benefit consumers or to curtail anticompetitive actions, and that it was, effectively, a victory for Microsoft. The U.S. Justice Department took a different view, calling the agreement a suitable and successful resolution of a case in which the plaintiffs had prevailed on their main claim of liability.

competition in the long run."[10] What constitutes "an appropriate measure of cost" in predatory pricing cases has long been a subject of debate among antitrust scholars. Although the Supreme Court has declined to resolve this debate definitively, it seems likely to take a skeptical view of predatory pricing claims in the future. The Court has described predatory pricing schemes as "rarely tried, and even more rarely successful."[11] As part of this characterization of predatory pricing schemes, the Court indicated that it agrees with economists who have argued that predatory pricing is often economically irrational because, to be successful, the predator must maintain monopoly power long enough after it has driven its competitors out of business to recoup the profits it lost through predatory pricing. The predator would be able to sustain monopoly power only if high barriers to entry prevented new competitors from being drawn into the market by the supracompetitive prices the predator would have to charge in order to recoup its losses.

Conspiracy to Monopolize

When two or more business entities **conspire to monopolize** a relevant market, § 2 may be violated. This portion of § 2 largely overlaps § 1, because it is difficult to conceive of a conspiracy to monopolize that would not also amount to a conspiracy in restraint of trade. The lower federal courts have differed on the elements necessary to prove a conspiracy to monopolize. In addition to requiring proof of the existence of a conspiracy, some courts insist on proof of the relevant market, a specific intent to acquire monopoly power, and overt action in furtherance of the conspiracy. Other courts do not require extensive proof of the relevant market. According to these courts, a violation is established through proof that the defendants conspired to exclude competitors from, or acquire control over prices in, some significant area of commerce. An approach that deemphasizes the requirement of proof of the relevant market, however, may not be consistent with Supreme Court precedent.

---

[10]*Cargill, Inc. & Excel Corp. v. Monfort of Colorado, Inc.* (U.S. Sup. Ct. 1986).

[11]*Matsushita Electric Industrial Co., Ltd. v. Zenith Radio Corp.* (U.S. Sup. Ct. 1986).

ETHICS IN ACTION

Some of the cases in this chapter recite the statement that antitrust was designed to protect competition, not competitors. How is this statement consistent with the ethical justification of markets as the most efficient form of economic organization? Consider the case of a competitor who is driven out of business by another competitor's ultimately unsuccessful predatory pricing efforts

(unsuccessful because the predator could not maintain monopoly power long enough to recoup the profits lost through predatory pricing).

• Although competition may not suffer in such a case, does the out-of-business competitor have any *ethical* or public policy-based claim to compensation?

• Should antitrust law recognize such a claim?

Problems and Problem Cases

1. Atlantic Richfield (ARCO) is an integrated oil company that sells gasoline to consumers both directly through its own stations and indirectly through ARCO-brand dealers. USA is an independent retail marketer of gasoline that buys gasoline from major petroleum companies for resale under its own brand name. USA competes directly with ARCO dealers at the retail level. Its outlets typically are low-overhead, high-volume "discount" stations that charge less than stations selling equivalent quality gasoline under major brand names. ARCO adopted a new marketing strategy in order to compete more effectively with independents such as USA. ARCO encouraged its dealers to match the retail gasoline prices offered by independents in various ways. These included making available to its dealers and distributors short-term discounts and reducing its dealers' costs by, for example, eliminating credit card sales. ARCO's strategy increased its sales and market share. When USA's sales dropped, it sued ARCO, charging that ARCO and its dealers were engaged in a per se illegal vertical price-fixing scheme. On these facts, could USA show an *antitrust injury* resulting from ARCO's actions (i.e., injury that flows from the unlawful aspects of the challenged behavior and is of a type that the antitrust laws were designed to prevent)? Does per se treatment apply to vertical price-fixing when the allegedly fixed price is of a *maximum* nature?

2. Co-Operative Theatres (Co-op), a Cleveland area movie theater booking agent, began seeking customers in southern Ohio. Shortly thereafter, Tri-State Theatre Services (Tri-State), a Cincinnati booking agent, began to solicit business in the Cleveland area. Later, however, Co-op and Tri-State allegedly entered into an agreement not to solicit each other's customers. The Justice Department prosecuted them for agreeing to restrain trade in vi-

olation of § 1 of the Sherman Act. Under a government grant of immunity, Tri-State's vice president testified that Co-op's vice president had approached him at a trade convention and threatened to start taking Tri-State's accounts if Tri-State did not stop calling on Co-op's accounts. He also testified that at a luncheon meeting he attended with officials from both firms, the presidents of both firms said that it would be in the interests of both firms to stop calling on each other's accounts. Several Co-op customers testified that Tri-State had refused to accept their business because of the agreement with Co-op. The trial court found both firms guilty of a per se violation of the Sherman Act, rejecting their argument that the rule of reason should have been applied and refusing to allow them to introduce evidence that the agreement did not have a significant anticompetitive effect. Should the rule of reason have been applied?

3. Discon, Inc., specialized in providing the service of removing obsolete telephone equipment. New York Telephone Company was a subsidiary of NYNEX Corporation. Another NYNEX subsidiary, Materiel Enterprises Company, was a purchasing entity that arranged for Discon to provide removal services for New York Telephone. After regularly doing business with Discon, Materiel switched its purchases of removal services from Discon to a Discon competitor, AT&T Technologies. According to Discon, Materiel did this as part of an attempt to defraud local telephone customers and regulatory authorities. Discon contended that Materiel would pay AT&T Technologies more than Discon would have charged for similar removal services, that Materiel would then pass those higher prices on to New York Telephone, and that New York Telephone would in turn pass those prices on to consumers in the form of higher telephone service charges that were approved by the relevant regulatory authorities. Discon further contended that at the end of the year, Materiel would receive a special rebate from AT&T Technologies, and that Materiel would share this rebate with its corporate parent, NYNEX. Discon asserted that because it refused to participate in this fraudulent scheme, Materiel would not do business with Discon, which eventually went out of business. Discon sued Materiel, New York Telephone, and NYNEX, claiming that the above facts constituted a group boycott and thus a per se violation of § 1 of the Sherman Act. If Discon's allegations are true, did a per se group boycott take place?

4. The Maricopa Foundation for Medical Care was a nonprofit organization established by the Maricopa County Medical Society to promote fee-for-service medicine. Roughly 70 percent of the physicians in Maricopa County belonged to the foundation. The foundation's trustees set maximum fees that members could charge for medical services provided to policyholders of approved medical insurance plans. To obtain the foundation's approval, insurers had to agree to pay the fees of member physicians up to the prescribed maximum. Member physicians were free to charge less than the prescribed maximum, but had to agree not to seek additional payments in excess of the maximum from insured patients. The Arizona attorney general filed suit for injunctive relief against the Maricopa County Medical Society and the foundation, arguing that the fee agreement constituted per se illegal horizontal price-fixing. The district court denied the state's motion for a partial summary judgment. The Ninth Circuit Court of Appeals affirmed on the ground that the per se rule was not applicable to the case. Was the Ninth Circuit correct?

5. In 1986, Market Force, Inc. (MFI), began operating in the Milwaukee real estate market as a buyer's broker. MFI and prospective home buyers entered into exclusive contracts providing that MFI would receive a fee equal to 40 percent of the sales commission if it located a house that the buyer ultimately purchased. This 40 percent commission was the same commission selling brokers (those who ultimately produced a buyer, but whose duty of loyalty was to the seller) earned when they sold property placed on the local multiple listing service (MLS) by other brokers. MFI's contracts anticipated that the buyer would ask the listing broker (the one who had listed the property for sale on behalf of its owners and who received 60 percent of the commission when the property was sold) to pay MFI the commission at the time of the sale. If the listing broker agreed to do so, the buyer had no further obligation to MFI. For some time after MFI began operations, other real estate firms treated it inconsistently; some paid the full 40 percent commission but others paid

nothing. In the fall of 1987, Wauwatosa Realty Co. and Coldwell Banker, the top two firms listing high-quality homes in Milwaukee, issued formal policies on splitting commissions with buyer's brokers. Wauwatosa said it would pay 20 percent of the selling agent's 40 percent commission. Coldwell Banker said it would pay 20 percent of the total sales commission. Several other real estate firms followed suit, setting their rates at 10 or 20 percent of the total sales commission, with the result that firms accounting for 31 percent of the annual listings of the MLS adopted policies and disseminated them to other MLS members. MFI filed suit against the brokers who had announced policies, arguing that they had conspired to restrain trade in violation of § 1 of the Sherman Act. At trial, the defendants introduced evidence of numerous business justifications for their policies and argued that their knowingly having adopted similar policies was not enough, standing alone, to justify a conclusion that the Sherman Act was violated. Was this argument correct?

6. When Triple-A Baseball Club Associates was in the process of building the Old Orchard Beach Ballpark, both Gemini Concerts, Inc., and Don Law Co., Inc., expressed interest in promoting concerts at the ballpark. Triple-A, however, had neither the time nor money to make the facility suitable for concerts. Gemini eventually ceased its efforts to use the facility. Law, however, persisted. After several years of discussions, Law and Triple-A signed an agreement giving Law the exclusive right to promote concerts at the ballpark for two years, with an option to renew for another five years. In return, Law paid for many of the capital improvements necessary to equip the ballpark for concerts and shared with Triple-A the cost of others. Gemini filed suit against Triple-A and Law, arguing that their exclusive dealing contract violated § 1 of the Sherman Act. Should the trial court grant the restraining order requested by Gemini?

7. Concerned that its dealers might not have sufficient spare parts to make repairs on recently purchased Subaru cars, Subaru of America (SOA) decided in 1973 to require its dealers to keep certain spare parts kits on hand. Grappone, Inc., a New Hampshire Subaru dealer, also had AMC, Pontiac, Jeep, Toyota, and Peugot franchises. Grappone acquired its cars from Subaru of New England, Inc. (SNE), a regional Subaru distributor. Grappone objected when told by SNE that it needed to purchase two "dealer's kits" containing 88 parts for 1974 cars and two "supplemental kits" containing 44 parts each (the total number of different Subaru parts being somewhere between 4,000 and 5,000). SNE refused to give Grappone its 1974 car allotment until Grappone bought the kits. Grappone went 10 months without cars; it then agreed to take the kits. Grappone later sued SNE, arguing that SNE violated § 1 of the Sherman Act by tying the sale of the parts kits to the sale of cars. The evidence introduced at trial indicated that Subaru's national market share was under 1 percent and that its share of the New Hampshire market was 3.4 percent. Was the trial court correct in granting judgment in favor of Grappone?

8. Grinnell Corporation manufactured plumbing supplies and fire sprinkler systems. It also owned 76 percent of the stock of ADT Co., 89 percent of the stock of AFA, Inc., and 100 percent of the stock of Holmes, Inc. ADT provided burglary-protection and fire-protection services. AFA provided only fire-protection services. Holmes provided only burglary-protection services. Each of the three firms offered a central station service under which hazard-detecting devices installed on the protected premises automatically transmitted an electronic signal to a central station. Other companies provided forms of protection service other than the central station variety. Subscribers to an accredited central station service (i.e., one approved by insurance underwriters) received substantially greater insurance premium reductions than the premium reductions received by users of other protection services. At the relevant time in question, ADT, AFA, and Holmes were the three largest central station service companies in terms of revenue. Together, they accounted for approximately 87 percent of the central station services provided. Contending that Grinnell, ADT, AFA, and Holmes had taken various anticompetitive actions that amounted to willful acquisition or maintenance of monopoly power, the United States government brought a monopolization action against Grinnell under § 2 of the Sherman Act. Concerning the first element of a monopolization claim (monopoly power in the relevant market), were fire-protection services and burglary-protection services too different to be part of the same market? What was the relevant market in this case? Were protection services other than those of the central station variety part of it?

9. Martindale Empowerment, a Virginia corporation, engaged in the business of providing commercial electronic-mail service to advertisers. Martindale regularly sent electronic advertising over the Internet in the form of e-mail to e-mail addresses throughout the United States. In September 1998, however, America Online, Inc., the largest commercial online service in the nation with more than 16,000,000 individual subscribers, implemented various mechanisms to block advertising

messages that Martindale had been sending to AOL subscribers for nearly two years. AOL succeeded in blocking most of those transmissions by Martindale. Contending that Martindale was using deceptive practices in an effort to mask the source and quantity of its transmissions and thereby avoid AOL's blocking and filtering technologies, AOL sued Martindale on a variety of legal theories. AOL sought an injunction against Martindale's practice of sending unsolicited bulk e-mail advertisements to AOL subscribers. Martindale responded with a counterclaim in which it alleged that AOL had engaged in monopolization, in violation of § 2 of the Sherman Act. According to Martindale, AOL had established itself as the only entity that could advertise to AOL subscribers. For purposes of the first element of a monopolization claim—monopoly power in a relevant market—Martindale contended that the relevant product or service market was e-mail advertising. Was Martindale correct in this contention?

10. In July 1977, anesthesiologist Edwin G. Hyde applied for admission to the medical staff of East Jefferson Hospital in New Orleans. The credentials committee and the medical staff executive committee recommended approval, but the hospital board denied the application because the hospital was a party to a contract providing that all anesthesiological services required by the hospital's patients would be performed by Roux & Associates, a professional medical corporation. Hyde filed suit against the board, arguing that the contract violated § 1 of the Sherman Act. The district court ruled in favor of the board, finding that the anticompetitive effects of the contract were minimal and outweighed by the benefits of improved patient care. It noted that there were at least 20 hospitals in the New Orleans metropolitan area and that roughly 70 percent of the patients residing in Jefferson Parish went to hospitals other than East Jefferson. It therefore concluded that East Jefferson lacked any significant market power and could not use the contract for anticompetitive ends. The Fifth Circuit Court of Appeals reversed, holding that the relevant market was the East Bank Jefferson Parish rather than the New Orleans metropolitan area. The court therefore concluded that because 30 percent of the parish residents used East Jefferson and "patients tend to choose hospitals by location rather than price or quality," East Jefferson possessed sufficient market power to make the contract a per se illegal tying contract. Was the Fifth Circuit correct?

11. For approximately three years, Larry and Shirley McQuillan had served as distributors of sorbothane products for a certain firm and its successor. After they lost their distributorship and their business failed, the Mc-Quillans sued both firms, as well as other affiliated companies and individuals. The McQuillans raised various legal claims, including a claim that the defendants engaged in attempted monopolization, in violation of § 2 of the Sherman Act. The evidence produced at trial revealed various instances of unfair or predatory conduct engaged in by the defendants and directed toward the McQuillans. The jury awarded the McQuillans a very substantial damages award on their attempted monopolization claim. The defendants appealed. Relying on one of its own precedents (a 1964 decision), the U.S. Court of Appeals for the Ninth Circuit held that the evidence of the defendants' unfair or predatory conduct served to satisfy the *specific intent to monopolize* and *dangerous probability of achieving monopoly power* elements of the Mc-Quillans' attempted monopolization claim, even though the McQuillans presented no proof of the relevant market or the defendants' market power therein. Was the Ninth Circuit's holding correct?

Online Research: U.S. Department of Justice, Antitrust Division

Visit the website of the United States Department of Justice, one of the major enforcers of antitrust law in the United States. Review the site's material and information regarding the Justice Department's Antitrust Division. Then prepare a brief description of the legal actions brought by the Antitrust Division against vitamin producers during the late 1990s.

50

The Clayton Act, The Robinson–Patman Act, and Antitrust Exemptions and Immunities

XYZ, Inc., the widget manufacturer referred to at the beginning of Chapter 49, may face antitrust issues that go beyond the ones addressed in that chapter. As you study Chapter 50, consider these questions regarding possible courses of action in which XYZ might engage:

• If XYZ, in selling its widgets, charges different prices to different wholesale dealers, is XYZ at risk of antitrust liability? What if XYZ charges a wholesale dealer a lower price than XYZ charges a *retailer* with which XYZ deals directly?

• If XYZ has been charging a certain price for its widgets but XYZ learns that a competing widget manufacturer is offering its widgets at a lower price, would XYZ be at risk of violating antitrust law if it lowers its price for certain customers in order to *meet* the price offered by the competitor? What if XYZ lowers its price enough to *beat* the competitor's price?

• If XYZ and a competing widget manufacturer decide to merge, what potential hurdles might antitrust law present?

• If XYZ decides to acquire a company that produces a material used in making widgets (i.e., a noncompetitor), is antitrust law a potential obstacle to XYZ's ability to carry out the acquisition?

• If, through effective lobbying efforts, XYZ helps convince a state legislature to enact a statute that may benefit XYZ at the expense of competition in the widget market, has XYZ committed an antitrust violation?

CONCENTRATION IN THE AMERICAN economy continued despite the 1890 enactment of the Sherman Act. Restrictive judicial interpretations of section 2 of the Sherman Act limited its effectiveness against many monopolists. Critics therefore sought legislation to thwart would-be monopolists before they achieved full-blown restraint of trade or monopoly power. In 1914, Congress responded by passing the Clayton Act.

Congress envisioned the Clayton Act as a vehicle for attacking practices that monopolists historically employed to acquire monopoly power. These practices included tying and exclusive dealing arrangements de-signed to squeeze competitors out of the market, mergers and acquisitions aimed at reducing competition through the elimination of competitors, interlocking corporate directorates designed to reduce competition by placing competitors under common leadership, and predatory or discriminatory pricing intended to force competitors out of business. These practices will be discussed in the following pages.

In view of the congressional intent that the Clayton Act serve as a preventive measure, only a *probability* of a significant anticompetitive effect must be shown for most Clayton Act violations. Because the Clayton Act focuses on probable harms to competition, there are no criminal penalties for violating its provisions. Private plaintiffs, however, may sue for treble damages or injunctive relief if they are injured, or threatened with injury, by another party's violation of the statute. The Justice Department and the Federal Trade Commission (FTC) share responsibility for enforcing the Clayton Act. Each has the authority to seek injunctive relief to prevent or remedy violations of the statute. In addition, the FTC has the power to enforce the Clayton Act through the use of cease and desist orders, which were discussed in Chapter 48.

Clayton Act Section 3

Section 3 of the Clayton Act makes it unlawful for any person engaged in interstate commerce to *lease or sell commodities,* or to *fix a price for commodities,* on the *condition, agreement, or understanding* that the lessee or buyer will not use or deal in the commodities of the lessor's or seller's competitors, if the effect of doing so *may be* to *substantially lessen competition* or *tend to create a monopoly* in any line of commerce. Section 3 primarily targets two potentially anticompetitive behaviors: **tying agreements** and **exclusive dealing agreements.** As you learned in the preceding chapter, these types of contracts may amount to restraints of trade in violation of Sherman Act section 1. The language of section 3, however, contains limitations on the Clayton Act's application to such agreements.

A major limitation is that section 3 applies only to tying agreements and exclusive dealing contracts involving the leasing or sale of *commodities.* Any such agreements involving services, real estate, or intangibles must therefore be attacked under the Sherman Act. Although section 3 speaks of sales and leases on the "condition, agreement, or understanding" that the buyer or lessee not deal in the commodities of the seller's or lessor's competitors, no formal agreement is required. Whenever a seller or lessor uses its economic power to prevent its customers from dealing with its competitors, potential Clayton Act concerns are triggered.

Tying Agreements

Many *tying agreements* plainly fall within at least the first portion of the section 3 language. Any agreement that requires a buyer to purchase one product (the *tied product*) from a seller as a condition of purchasing another product (the *tying product*) from the same seller necessarily prevents the buyer from purchasing the tied product from the seller's competitors.

Only tying agreements that may "*substantially lessen competition or tend to create a monopoly,*" however, violate section 3. Approximately 50 years ago, the Supreme Court appeared to indicate that a tying agreement would violate the Clayton Act if the seller either had monopoly power over the tying product or restrained a substantial volume of commerce in the tied product. Most lower federal courts today, however, require essentially the same elements for a Clayton Act violation that they require for a Sherman Act violation: the challenged agreement must involve *two separate products; sale of the tying product must be conditioned* on an accompanying sale of the tied product; the seller must have *sufficient economic power in the market for the tying product* to appreciably restrain competition in the tied product market; and the seller's tying arrangements must restrain a "*not insubstantial" amount of commerce in the tied product market.* A few courts, however, continue to apply a less demanding standard for Clayton Act tying liability by dispensing with proof of the seller's economic power in the market for the tying product as long as the seller's tying arrangements involve a "not insubstantial" amount of commerce in the tied product. The defenses to tying liability under the Sherman Act (discussed in chapter 49) are also applicable to tying claims brought under the Clayton Act.

Exclusive Dealing Agreements

In the preceding chapter, we discussed the nature of *exclusive dealing agreements.* Such contracts clearly fall under the initial portion of the section 3 language because buyers who agree to handle one seller's product exclusively, or to purchase all of their requirements for a commodity from one seller, are also agreeing not to purchase similar items from the seller's competitors. However, not all exclusive dealing agreements are unlawful. Section 3 outlaws only those agreements that may "substantially lessen competition or tend to create a monopoly."

Exclusive dealing agreements initially were treated in much the same way as tying agreements. Courts looked at the dollar amount of commerce involved and declared illegal those agreements involving a "not insubstantial" amount of commerce. This *quantitative substantiality* test was employed by the Supreme Court in *Standard Oil Co. v. United States* (1949). Standard Oil was the largest refiner and supplier of gasoline in several western states, holding approximately 14 percent of the retail market. Roughly half of these sales were made by retail outlets owned by Standard. The remaining sales were made by independent dealers who had entered into exclusive dealing contracts with Standard. Standard's six major competitors had entered into similar contracts with their own independent dealers. The Court recognized that exclusive dealing contracts, unlike tying agreements, could benefit both buyers and sellers, but declared Standard's contracts unlawful on the ground that nearly $58 million in commerce was involved.

The *Standard Oil* decision prompted considerable criticism. In *Tampa Electric Co. v. Nashville Coal Co.* (1961), however, the Supreme Court applied a broader *qualitative substantiality* test to gauge the legality of a long-term requirements contract for the sale of coal to an electric utility. In *Tampa Electric,* the Court looked at the "area of effective competition," which was the total market for coal in the geographic region from which the utility could reasonably purchase its coal needs. The Court then examined the percentage of this region's coal sales accounted for by the challenged contract. Because that percentage share was less than 1 percent of the region's coal sales, the Court upheld the agreement even though it represented more than $100 million in coal sales.

Tampa Electric, however, is distinguishable from *Standard Oil,* which the Court has not overruled. Unlike *Standard Oil, Tampa Electric* involved parties with relatively equal bargaining power and an individual agreement, rather than an industrywide practice. In addition, there were obvious reasons why an electric utility such as Tampa Electric might want to lock in its coal costs by using a long-term requirements contract. Although lower court opinions employing each test may be found, the *qualitative* approach employed in *Tampa Electric* is the one more likely to be employed by the current Court.

Clayton Act Section 7

Introduction

Section 7 of the Clayton Act was designed to attack **mergers**—a term used broadly in this chapter to refer to the acquisition of one company by another. History indicates that one way monopolists acquired monopoly power was by acquiring control of their competitors. Section 7 prohibits any party engaged in commerce or in any activity affecting commerce from *acquiring the stock or assets* of another such party if the effect, in *any line of commerce* or *any activity affecting commerce* in any section of the country, *may be to substantially lessen competition* or *tend to create a monopoly.* Rather than adopting the Sherman Act approach of waiting until a

would-be monopolist has acquired monopoly power or is dangerously close to doing so, section 7 attempts to "nip monopolies in the bud" by barring mergers that *may* have an anticompetitive effect.

Although section 7 is plainly an anticoncentration device, it has also been used (as the following text indicates) to attack mergers that have had no direct effect on concentration in a particular industry. Its future evolution, however, is uncertain, given the influence of Chicago School economic theories on contemporary antitrust law and the more tolerant stance those theories take toward mergers. During the 1980s, the Justice Department signaled a more permissive approach to merger activity than the government had previously adopted. Since then, Justice Department and FTC officials have undertaken greater scrutiny of mergers in some industries, though not necessarily on an across-the-board basis.

The Hart–Scott–Rodino Antitrust Improvement Act of 1976 requires that for planned mergers involving dollar values of stock or assets exceeding certain amounts, the parties to the merger agreement must provide advance notice to the FTC and the Justice Department. The purpose of this requirement is to provide the federal government a "heads-up" warning and to give regulators a reasonable opportunity to institute a legal challenge of the merger if a challenge seems warranted. Once the statutorily specified waiting period expires and the government has cleared the merger or at least has not taken legal action to block it, the merger may proceed. The normal waiting period is 30 days from the filing of the premerger notification form, though the waiting period is sometimes subject to extension. It should be remembered, however, that regardless of whether the government seeks to block a merger, private enforcement of section 7 is also possible.

Predictions regarding section 7's eventual judicial treatment are complicated considerably by the fact that many of the important merger cases in recent years have been settled out of court. This leaves interested observers of antitrust policy with few definitive expressions of the Supreme Court's current thinking on merger issues.

Relevant Market Determination

Regardless of the treatment section 7 ultimately receives in the courts, determining the **relevant market** affected by a merger is likely to remain a crucial component of any section 7 case. Before a court can determine whether a particular merger will have the *probable* anticompetitive effect required by the Clayton Act, it must first determine the *line of commerce* (or *relevant product mar-*

ket) and the *section of the country* (or *relevant geographic market*) that are likely to be affected by the merger. The court's adoption of a broad relevant market definition will usually enhance the government's or private plaintiff's difficulty in demonstrating the challenged merger's probable anticompetitive effect.

Relevant Product Market "Line of commerce" determinations under the Clayton Act have traditionally employed *functional interchangeability* tests similar to those employed in relevant product market determinations under the Sherman Act. Which products do the acquired and acquiring firms manufacture (assuming a

merger between competitors), and which products are reasonably interchangeable by consumers to serve the same purposes? The federal government's merger guidelines indicate that the relevant market includes those products that consumers view as good substitutes at prevailing prices. The guidelines also state that the relevant market includes any products to which a significant percentage of current customers would shift in the event of a "small, but significant and non-transitory increase" in price of the merged firms' products. The *Olin* case, which follows, discusses the making of a relevant product market determination, as does the *Staples* case, which appears later in the chapter.

Olin Corporation v. Federal Trade Commission   *986 F.2d 1295 (9th Cir. 1993)*

Sanitizing agents are used to kill algae and bacteria in swimming pools. Pool owners may use any of three sanitizing agents. One is liquid pool bleach; the other two are chemicals sold in dry form. These dry sanitizers are isocyanurates (ISOS) and calcium hypochlorite (CAL/HYPO). The chemical cyanuric acid (CA) is a precursor in the manufacturing process of ISOS. When CAL/HYPO is used as a sanitizer, CA is used along with it as a stabilizer.

Olin Corporation was the market leader in CAL/HYPO production in the United States from 1980 through 1984, with a market share of 79 to 89 percent. Olin sought to increase its ability to produce and market ISOS. After technical problems doomed Olin's attempts to produce CA and ISOS during the late 1970s and early 1980s, Olin entered into a 1984 agreement with Monsanto Co. Under this agreement, Olin provided certain ISOS precursors to Monsanto, which then produced ISOS and provided them to Olin. Olin thus became a "repackager" of ISOS.

In 1985, Olin and FMC Corporation entered into an agreement under which Olin was to purchase FMC's swimming pool chemical business. The assets of that business included FMC's sanitizers manufacturing plant at South Charleston, West Virginia. The South Charleston plant produced both CA and ISOS. The Federal Trade Commission challenged the proposed acquisition on the theory that it would likely result in a substantial lessening of competition in the relevant markets, in violation of section 7 of the Clayton Act and section 5 of the FTC Act. To avoid a possible order that would have prohibited the acquisition, Olin agreed to maintain the acquired assets in such a way that divestiture would be possible if the FTC issued a final decision holding that the acquisition violated antitrust laws. In addition, Olin agreed to a graduated withdrawal from its agreement with Monsanto. Olin and FMC were therefore allowed to consummate their transaction, pending final review by the FTC.

After a hearing, the FTC administrative law judge (ALJ) concluded that the acquisition violated the Clayton and FTC Acts because it would likely result in a substantial lessening of competition in the relevant markets. The FTC commissioners (referred to below as "the Commission") upheld the ALJ's decision as well as the ALJ's proposed remedy of divestiture. The Commission therefore ordered Olin to divest itself of the South Charleston plant it had acquired from FMC. Olin petitioned the Ninth Circuit Court of Appeals for review of the Commission's decision and order.

Tang, Circuit Judge   Normally, "a delineation of proper geographic and product markets is a necessary precondition to assessment of the probabilities of a substantial effect on competition within them." *United States v. General Dynamics Corp.* (U.S. Sup. Ct. 1974). There is no dispute in this case that the [relevant] geographic market is the entire United States. The parties have further stipulated that one relevant United States product market consists solely of

ISOS (the "ISOS-only" market). The Commission also identified over Olin's objection a second relevant United States product market, one comprised of both ISOS and CAL/HYPO (the "dry sanitizers" market). Olin contends that the finding of likely anticompetitive effect is erroneous because it is premised on . . . a relevant dry sanitizers market [whose] existence is not supported by substantial evidence. In analyzing the post-acquisition dry sanitizers market [the existence of which Olin does not concede], the Commission concluded that Olin's production capacity would be 57 percent of a market in which the four-firm concentration ratio was 95 percent.

[In *California v. American Stores Co.* (9th Cir. 1989), we] described the process of product market definition as follows:

> The outer boundaries of a product market are determined by the reasonable interchangeability of use or the cross-elasticity of demand between the product itself and substitutes for it" (quoting *Brown Shoe Co. v. United States* [U.S. Sup. Ct. 1962]). Where an increase in the price of one product leads to an increase in demand for another, both products should be included in the relevant product market.

In conducting its product market analysis for swimming pool sanitizers, the Commission discussed physical composition, usage, and technical characteristics of dry sanitizers. [T]he Commission observed that similarities in these categories "predominate over the minor [physical] differences between ISOS and CAL/HYPO. The following facts are particularly important: (1) both products are used to deliver chlorine to swimming pools; (2) each product is able to deliver chlorine with about the same efficiency—although a pool chlorinated with ISOS will remain chlorinated longer; (3) by virtue of both products' stability and other characteristics, "a pool owner can purchase a year's supply of either [product] in a single trip to the store"; and (4) both products are available to consumers in the same forms. In discussing these characteristics, the Commission apparently assumed that the relevant market is defined in terms of consumers who maintain their own pools. Although Olin challenged this assumption, we conclude there is substantial evidence in support of dealing with residential consumers as a distinct market.

Despite [the above] similarities, however, ISOS are perceived as more convenient than CAL/HYPO because, once applied, ISOS last longer than CAL/HYPO, and because CAL/HYPO requires use of a separate stabilizer (i.e., CA). Recognizing that the "convenience of [ISOS] is reflected in a price premium that [ISOS] maintain over [CAL/HYPO]," the Commission then analyzed whether this premium is sufficient to prevent inclusion of ISOS and CAL/HYPO in the same market. Ultimately, the Commission [applied a test set forth in the merger guidelines subscribed to by the Department of Justice and the FTC, and concluded that] "Olin could not profitably impose a small but significant and nontransitory increase in the price of [CAL/HYPO] because of the danger that consumers would then switch to [ISOS]."

Given this indication of cross-elasticity of demand, the Commission concluded that ISOS and CAL/HYPO together compose a relevant product market (i.e., the dry sanitizers market).

Olin argues that it is inconsistent to recognize a larger, dry sanitizers market once a relevant ISOS-only market has been identified. However, relevant submarkets are common in merger analysis. Recognizing ISOS as a submarket of the dry sanitizers market is not inherently contradictory with recognizing a dry sanitizers market.

Olin charges that the Commission had no basis on which to conclude that any significant degree of elasticity existed between ISOS and CAL/HYPO. It is evident from its opinion that the Commission relied on a narrowing of the price gap between the two products in determining cross-elasticity. The opinion [stated that] "from 1977 to 1983, . . . the price of [CAL/HYPO] increased at a faster rate than that of [ISOS]." According to the opinion, this increase in the price of CAL/HYPO came about despite direct competition from Japanese CAL/HYPO, which was later the subject of an "antidumping" order. Olin argues that the narrowing of the price gap between CAL/HYPO and ISOS was artificial—and should not be used in determining cross-elasticity—because the Japanese were "dumping" ISOS on the American market. The Commission responds convincingly that, because CAL/HYPO was subject to the same pressures as the result of Japanese CAL/HYPO dumping, the narrowing in price was not artificial. Olin ignores this explanation and shifts its focus to the Commission concession that CAL/HYPO consumers would not switch to ISOS until the price of CAL/HYPO had risen at least 10 percent.

Olin . . . attempt[s] to emphasize the 5 percent factor normally used [by the Department of Justice and the FTC when they apply the merger guidelines' test that asks whether a "small but significant and nontransitory price increase" would cause consumers to switch to another product]. [However,] research has not disclosed a case that mandates [use of the 5 percent figure in] determining relevant product markets. Indeed, [the government's merger guidelines themselves acknowledge] that a higher percent increase in price is appropriate in determining the relevant product market in certain cases. Thus, a finding of cross-elasticity between ISOS and CAL/HYPO is not precluded by the fact that a higher price increase is necessary to induce a switch; a higher increase indicates only that the relationship between the two products is somewhat inelastic—but not necessarily so inelastic as to exclude the products from the same market, particularly under the substantial evidence standard of review.

[In making its cross-elasticity finding, the Commission also reasonably relied on] a statement Olin made to the International Trade Commission [in which Olin complained about Japanese "dumping" but appeared to acknowledge that CAL/HYPO faces competition from ISOS] and a statement made by an Olin competitor indicating a competitive relationship between CAL/HYPO and ISOS. [W]e find adequate support for the Commission's finding of cross-elasticity between ISOS and CAL/HYPO.

[The Ninth Circuit went on to hold that the divestiture remedy ordered by the Commission was an appropriate exercise of the Commission's discretion.]

Olin's petition for review denied; decision and order of Commission upheld.

Relevant Geographic Market To determine a particular merger's probable anticompetitive effect on a section of the country, courts have traditionally asked where the effects of the merger will be direct and immediate. This means that the relevant geographic market may not be as broad as the markets in which the acquiring and acquired firms actually operate or, in the case of a merger between competitors, the markets in which they actually compete. The focus of the relevant market inquiry is on those sections of the country in which competition is most likely to be injured by the merger. As a result, the relevant geographic market could be drawn as narrowly as one metropolitan area or as broadly as the entire nation. All that is necessary to satisfy this aspect of section 7 is proof that the challenged merger may have a significant negative effect on competition in any economically significant geographic market.

The federal government's merger guidelines adopt a somewhat different approach to determining the relevant geographic market. They define the relevant geographic market as the geographic area in which a sole supplier of the product in question could profitably raise its price without causing outside suppliers to begin selling in the area. The guidelines contemplate beginning with the existing markets in which the parties to a merger compete, and then adding the markets of those suppliers that would enter the market in response to a "small, but significant and non-transitory increase" in price.

Horizontal Mergers

The analytical approach employed to gauge a merger's probable effect on competition varies according to the nature of the merger in question. **Horizontal mergers**— mergers among firms competing in the same product and geographic markets—have traditionally been subjected to the most rigorous scrutiny because they clearly lead to increased concentration in the relevant market.

Market Share of Resulting Firm To determine the legality of such a merger, courts look at the *market share of the resulting firm*. In *United States v. Philadelphia National Bank* (1963), the Supreme Court indicated that a horizontal merger producing a firm with an "undue percentage share" of the relevant market (33 percent in that case) and resulting in a "significant increase in concentration" of the firms in that market would be presumed illegal, absent convincing evidence that the merger would not have an anticompetitive effect.

In the past, mergers involving firms with smaller market shares than those involved in *Philadelphia National Bank* were also enjoined if other economic or historical factors pointed toward a probable anticompetitive effect. Factors that courts have traditionally considered relevant include:

1. *A trend toward concentration in the relevant market.* Has the number of competing firms decreased over time?

2. *The competitive position of the merging firms.* Are the defendants dominant firms despite their relatively small market shares?

3. *A past history of acquisitions by the acquiring firm.* Are we dealing with a would-be empire builder?

4. *The nature of the acquired firm.* Is it an aggressive, innovative competitor despite its small market share?

Recent Assessments of Merger Effects Recent developments, however, indicate that the courts and federal antitrust enforcement agencies have become increasingly less willing to presume that anticompetitive effects will result from a merger that produces a firm with a relatively large market share. Instead, a more detailed inquiry is made into the nature of the relevant market and of the merging firms in order to ascertain the likelihood of probable harm to competition as a result of a challenged merger. The federal government's merger guidelines provide that when regulators assess a horizontal merger's probable effect, the focus is on the existing concentration in the relevant market, the increase in concentration as a result of the proposed merger, and other nonmarket share factors. The more concentrated the existing market and the greater the increase in concentration that would result from the proposed merger, the more likely the merger is to be challenged by the government.

The nonmarket share factors considered by federal regulators are more traditional. They include: the existence (or absence) of barriers to the entry of new competitors into the relevant market; the prior conduct of the merging firms; and the probable future competitive strength of the acquired firm. The last factor is particularly important because courts have acknowledged that a firm's current market share may not reflect its ability to compete in the future. For example, courts have long recognized a "failing company" justification for some mergers. If the acquired firm is a failing company and no other purchasers are interested in acquiring it, its acquisition by a competitor may be lawful under section 7. Similarly,

if an acquired firm has financial problems that reflect some underlying structural weakness, or if it lacks technologies that will be necessary if it is to compete effectively in the future, its current market share may overstate its future competitive importance.

Finally, given the increased weight being assigned to economic arguments in antitrust cases, two other merger justifications may be granted greater credence in the future. Some lower federal courts have recognized the notion that a merger between two small companies may be justifiable, despite the increase in concentration stemming from the merger, if the resulting firm is able to compete more effectively with larger competitors. In a similar vein, some commentators have argued that mergers resulting in cost savings or other enhanced economic efficiencies should sometimes be allowed even though they may have some anticompetitive impact. Though courts have not been very receptive to efficiency arguments in the past, the government's merger guidelines are flexible enough to allow the Justice Department and FTC to consider efficiency claims in deciding whether to challenge a merger.

The *Staples* case, which follows, illustrates a broad range of issues that arise in horizontal merger cases.

Federal Trade Commission v. Staples, Inc.   *970 F. Supp. 1066 (D.D.C. 1997)*

Office Depot, Inc., owned the nation's largest chain of retail outlets commonly known as "office supply superstores." Staples, Inc., owned the second-largest chain of this type. Each company operated more than 500 superstores, with Office Depot's outlets existing in 38 states and the District of Columbia and Staples' superstores appearing in 28 states and the District of Columbia. The only other office supply superstore firm in the United States was OfficeMax, Inc. In 1996, Staples and Office Depot entered into a merger agreement. As required by law, they filed a Premerger Notification and Report Form with the Federal Trade Commission (FTC) and the Department of Justice.

Following a lengthy investigation, the FTC initiated an adjudicative proceeding against Staples and Office Depot on the theory that the planned merger violated section 7 of the Clayton Act. (Adjudicative proceedings are discussed in Chapters 47 and 48.) In an effort to prevent the merger from taking place while its legality was being determined in the adjudicative proceeding, the FTC filed suit against Staples and Office Depot and requested a preliminary injunction against the merger. The federal district court conducted an extensive evidentiary hearing.

Hogan, District Judge Section 7 of the Clayton Act makes it illegal for two companies to merge "where in any line of commerce or in any activity affecting commerce in any section of the country, the effect of such acquisition may be substantially to lessen competition, or to tend to create a monopoly." [The FTC Act provides that if] the Commission has reason to believe that a corporation is violating, or is about to violate, section 7 . . . , the FTC may seek a preliminary injunction to prevent a merger pending the Commission's adjudication of the merger's legality.

In order to determine whether the Commission has [made the required showing of] likelihood of success on the merits, . . . the court must consider the likely competitive effects of the merger. [This requires the court to determine the relevant product and geographic markets, as well as] the transaction's probable effect on competition in the product and geographic markets. [T]he parties . . . do not disagree . . . that [more than 40 different] metropolitan areas are the appropriate geographic markets for analyzing the competitive effects of the proposed merger. [However, the parties] sharply disagree with respect to the appropriate definition of the relevant product market. [T]o a great extent, this case hinges on the proper definition of the relevant product market.

The Commission defines the relevant product market as "the sale of consumable office supplies through office superstores," with "consumable" meaning products that consumers buy [on a recurring basis], i.e., items which "get used up" or discarded. [U]nder the Commission's definition, "consumable office supplies" would not include capital goods such as computers, fax machines, . . . or office furniture, but [would] include such products as paper, pens, file folders, post-it-notes, computer disks, and toner cartridges. The defendants . . . counter that the appropriate product market within which to assess the likely competitive consequences of a Staples–Office Depot combination is simply the overall sale of office products, of which a combined Staples–Office Depot accounted for 5.5% of total sales in North America in 1996.

The general rule when determining a relevant product market is that "the outer boundaries . . . are determined by the reasonable interchangeability of use [by consumers] or the cross-elasticity of demand between the product itself and substitutes for it." *Brown Shoe Co. v. United States* (U.S. Sup. Ct. 1962). This case . . . is an example of perfect interchangeability. The consumable office products at issue here are identical whether they are sold by Staples or Office Depot or another seller of office supplies [such as Wal-Mart or another retailer that is not an office supply superstore]. [A]s the government has argued, [however, the] functional interchangeability [of office supplies] should not end the court's analysis.

[In *United States v. E.I. Du Pont de Nemours and Co.* (U.S. Sup. Ct. 1956), the Court] did not stop after finding a high degree of functional interchangeability between cellophane and other wrapping materials. [T]he Court also found that "an element for consideration as to cross-elasticity of demand between products is the responsiveness of the sales of one product to price changes of the other." [T]he Court explained [that] "if a slight decrease in the price of cellophane causes a considerable number of customers of other flexible wrappings to switch to cellophane, it would be an indication that a high cross-elasticity of demand exists between [cellophane and other flexible wrappings, and] that the products compete in the same market." Following that reasoning . . . , the Commission has argued that a slight but significant increase in Staples–Office Depot's prices will not cause a considerable number of Staples–Office Depot's customers to purchase consumable office supplies from

other non-superstore alternatives such as Wal-Mart [or] Best Buy. . . . On the other hand, the Commission has argued that an increase in price by Staples would result in consumers' turning to another office superstore, especially Office Depot, if the consumers had that option. Therefore, the Commission [contends] that the sale of consumable office supplies by office supply superstores is the . . . relevant product market in this case, and products sold by competitors such as Wal-Mart, Best Buy, . . . and others should be excluded.

The court acknowledges that there is . . . a broad market encompassing the sale of consumable office supplies by all sellers of such supplies, and that those sellers must, at some level, compete with one another. However, the mere fact that a firm may be termed a competitor in the overall marketplace does not necessarily require that it be included in the relevant product market for antitrust purposes. The Supreme Court . . . recognized [in *Brown Shoe*] that within a broad market, "well-defined submarkets may exist which, in themselves, constitute product markets for antitrust purposes." There is a possibility, therefore, that the sale of consumable office supplies by office superstores may qualify as a submarket within a large market of retailers of office supplies in general.

[T]he FTC presented evidence comparing Staples's prices in geographic markets where Staples is the only office superstore to markets where Staples competes with Office Depot or OfficeMax, or both. [I]n markets where Staples faces no office superstore competition . . . , something which was termed a one-firm market during the hearing, prices are 13 percent higher than in three-firm markets where it competes with both Office Depot and OfficeMax. Similarly, the evidence showed that Office Depot's prices are . . . well over 5 percent higher in Depot-only markets than they are in three-firm markets.

[The FTC's evidence] suggests that office superstore prices are affected primarily by other office superstores and not by non-superstore competitors such as . . . Wal-Mart, K-Mart, or Target, wholesale clubs . . . , computer or electronic stores . . . , mail order firms . . . , and contract stationers. Though the FTC did not present the court with evidence regarding the precise amount of non-superstore competition in each of Staples's and Office Depot's one-, two-, and three-firm markets, it is clear . . . that these competitors, albeit in different combinations and concentrations, are present in every one of these markets. For example, . . . the mail order competitors compete in all of the geographic markets at issue in this case. Despite this mail order competition, . . . Staples and Office Depot are still able to charge higher prices in their one-firm markets than they do in the two-firm markets and the three-firm markets without losing a significant number of customers to the mail order firms.

The same appears to be true with respect to Wal-Mart. [A Wal-Mart executive testified] that price-checking by Wal-Mart of Staples' prices in areas where both Staples and Wal-Mart exist showed that, on average, Staples's prices were higher than where there was a Staples and a Wal-Mart but no other superstore than where there was a Staples, a Wal-Mart, and another superstore. The evidence with respect to the wholesale club stores is consistent. There is also consistent evidence with respect to computer and/or consumer electronics stores.[In addition, the] evidence shows that the defendants [lower their prices in a given geographic area] when faced with entry of another superstore [in that area], but do not do so for other retailers. There is no evidence that . . . prices fall when another non-superstore retailer enters a geographic market.

[The FTC made] a compelling showing that a small but significant increase in Staples's prices will not cause a significant number of consumers to turn to non-superstore alternatives for purchasing their consumable office supplies. Despite the high degree of functional interchangeability between consumable office supplies sold by the office superstores and other retailers of office supplies, the evidence . . . shows that even where Staples and Office Depot charge higher prices, certain consumers do not go elsewhere for their supplies.

[In addition,] both Staples and Office Depot focus primarily on competition from other superstores. [Staples's and Office Depot's own documents] show that the merging parties evaluate their "competition" as the other office superstore firms, without reference to other retailers, mail order firms, or independent stationers. When assessing key trends and making long-range plans, Staples and Office Depot focus on the plans of other superstores. [W]hen determining whether to enter a new metropolitan area, both Staples and Office Depot evaluate the extent of office superstore competition in the market and the number of office superstores the market can support. When selecting sites and markets for new store openings, the defendants repeatedly refer to markets without office superstores as "noncompetitive," even when the new store is adjacent to or near a warehouse club, consumer electronics store, or a mass-merchandiser such as Wal-Mart.

[T]he court finds that the sale of consumable office supplies through office supply superstores is the appropriate relevant product market for purposes of considering the possible anticompetitive effects of the proposed merger.

[T]he court next must consider the probable effect of a merger between Staples and Office Depot in the geographic markets previously identified. [The evidence shows] that a merged Staples–Office Depot would have a dominant market share in 42 geographic markets across the country. The combined shares of Staples and Office Depot in the office superstore market would be 100 percent in 15 metropolitan areas. In 27 other metropolitan areas, where the number of office superstore competitors would drop from three to two, the post-merger market shares would range from 45 percent to 94 percent. [T]hough the Supreme Court has established that there is no fixed threshold at which an increase in market concentration triggers the antitrust laws, this is clearly not a borderline case.

[In addition to the] market concentration evidence, [there are other] indications that a merger between Staples and Office Depot may substantially lessen competition. Much of the evidence [concerning] the relevant product market also indicates that the merger would likely have an anticompetitive effect. The evidence of the defendant's current pricing practices, for example, shows that an office superstore chain facing no competition from other superstores has the ability to profitably raise prices for consumer office supplies above competitive levels. The evidence also shows that the defendants [lower their prices] when faced with entry of another office superstore [in a particular geographic area], but do not do so for other retailers. Since prices are significantly lower in markets where Staples and Office Depot compete, eliminating this competition with one another would free the parties to charge higher prices in those markets, especially those in which the combined entity would be the sole office superstore.

In addition, allowing the defendants to merge would eliminate . . . head-to-head competition between the two . . . lowest-priced firms in the superstore market. Thus, the merger would result in the elimination of a particularly aggressive competitor in a highly concentrated market, a factor which is certainly an important consideration when analyzing possible anticompetitive effects. It is based on all of this evidence that the court finds that the Commission has shown a likelihood of success on the merits and a reasonable probability that the proposed transaction will have an anticompetitive effect.

[T]he court finds it extremely unlikely that a new office superstore will enter the market and thereby avert the anticompetitive effects from Staples's acquisition of Office Depot. [Although the defendants also argued that] expansion [by] existing companies such as U.S. Office Products and Wal-Mart [would enhance competition in the sale of office supplies, the court] finds it unlikely that expansion by U.S. Office Products and Wal-Mart would avert the anticompetitive effects which would result from the merger. The defendants' final argument with respect to entry was that existing retailers such as Sam's Club, K-Mart, and Best Buy have the capability to reallocate their shelf space to include [greater quantities and varieties] of office supplies. While [such stores may] reallocate shelf space, there is no evidence that they will in fact do this if a combined Staples–Office Depot were to raise prices . . . following a merger. In fact, the evidence indicates that [they probably] would not.

[It is not clear] whether an efficiencies defense showing that the intended merger would create significant efficiencies in the relevant market, thereby offsetting any anticompetitive effects, may be used by a defendant to rebut the government's prima facie case. The newly revised efficiencies section of the [government's] Merger Guidelines recognizes that [some mergers may achieve efficiencies and that consideration of them may sometimes be relevant to a determination of whether an acquisition would substantially lessen competition]. [H]owever, in *FTC v. Procter & Gamble Co.* (U.S. Sup. Ct. 1967), [the Supreme Court] stated that "possible economies cannot be used as a defense to illegality in section 7 merger cases." There has been great disagreement regarding the meaning of this precedent and whether an efficiencies defense is permitted. Assuming that it is a viable defense, however, the court cannot find in this case that the defendants' efficiencies evidence rebuts the [FTC's showing] that the merger may substantially lessen competition.

The defendants submitted an "Efficiencies Analysis" which predicted that the combined company would achieve savings of between $4.9 and $6.5 billion over the next five years. In addition, the defendants argued that the merger would also generate dynamic efficiencies. For example, the defendants argued that as suppliers become more efficient due to their increased sales volume to the combined Staples–Office Depot, they would be able to lower prices to their other retailers. Moreover, the defendants argued that two-thirds of the savings realized by the combined company would be passed along to consumers.

[T]he court credits the testimony and report of the Commission's expert over the testimony and efficiencies study of the defendants' witness, [a] Senior Vice President of Integration at Staples. [The testimony of the Commission's expert] was compelling, and the court finds, based primarily on [that expert's] testimony, that the defendants' cost savings estimates are unreliable [and far in excess of estimates by the defendants in proxy statements and in presentations to the defendants' boards of directors]. [T]he court also finds that the defendants' projected pass-through rate—the amount of the projected savings that the combined company expects to pass on to customers in the form of lower prices—is unrealistic. Staples and Office Depot have a proven track record of achieving cost savings through efficiencies, and then passing those savings to customers in the form of lower prices. However, in this case the defendants have projected a pass-through rate of two-thirds of the savings while the evidence shows that, historically, Staples has passed through only 15–17 percent.

[T]he court cannot find that the defendants have rebutted [the FTC's showing] that the merger will subtantially lessen competition.

FTC's motion for preliminary injunction against merger granted.

Vertical Mergers

A **vertical merger** is a merger between firms that previously had, or could have had, a supplier–customer relationship. For example, a manufacturer may seek to vertically integrate its operations by acquiring a company that controls retail outlets at which the manufacturer's products could be sold. Alternatively, the manufacturer may vertically merge by acquiring a company that makes a product the manufacturer regularly uses in its production processes. Vertical mergers, unlike horizontal mergers, do not directly result in an increase in concentration. Nonetheless, they traditionally have been thought to threaten competition in various ways.

Foreclosing Competitors in Relevant Market
First, vertical mergers may *foreclose competitors* from a share of the relevant market. If a major customer for a product acquires a captive supplier of that product, the competitors of the acquired firm are foreclosed from competing with it for sales to the acquiring firm. Similarly, if a manufacturer acquires a captive retail outlet for its products, the manufacturer's competitors are foreclosed from competing for sales to that retail outlet. A vertical merger in the latter case may also result in reduced competition at the retail level. For instance, a shoe manufacturer acquires a retail shoe store chain that carries the brands of several competing manufacturers and has a dominant share of the retail market in certain

geographic areas. If the retail chain carries only the acquiring manufacturer's brands after the merger occurs, competition among the acquiring manufacturer and its competitors is reduced in the retail market for shoes.

Creation of Increased Market Entry Barriers A second way in which vertical mergers threaten competition is that they may lead to *increased barriers to market entry* for new competitors. For example, if a major purchaser of a product acquires a captive supplier of it, the merger-related contraction of the market for the product may discourage potential producers of it from commencing production.

Elimination of Potential Competition in Acquired Firm's Market Some vertical mergers threaten competition by *eliminating potential competition* in one of two ways. First, an acquiring firm may be perceived by existing competitors in the acquired firm's market as a likely potential entrant into that market. The threat of such a potential entrant "waiting in the wings" may moderate the behavior of existing competitors because they fear that pursuing pricing policies that exploit their current market position might cause the potential entrant to react by entering the market. The acquiring firm's entry into the market by the acquisition of an existing competitor means the end of its moderating influence as a potential entrant. Second, a vertical merger may deprive the market of the potential benefits that would have resulted if the acquiring firm had entered the market in a more competitive manner, such as by creating its own entrant into the market through internal expansion or by making a toehold acquisition of a small existing competitor and then building it into a more significant competitor.

Historically, courts seeking to determine the legality of vertical mergers have tended to look at the *share of the relevant market foreclosed to competition.* If a more than insignificant market share is foreclosed to competition, courts consider other economic and historical factors. Factors viewed as aggravating the anticompetitive potential of a vertical merger include: a trend toward concentration or vertical integration in the industry; a past history of vertical integration in the industry; a past history of vertical acquisitions by the acquiring company; and significant barriers to entry resulting from the merger. This approach to determining the legality of vertical mergers has been criticized by some commentators. They argue that vertical integration may yield efficiencies of distribution and that vertical integration by merger may be more economically efficient than vertical integration by internal expansion. The Justice Department generally affords greater weight to efficiency arguments in cases involving vertical mergers than in cases

involving horizontal mergers. The department generally applies the same criteria to all nonhorizontal mergers. We discuss these criteria in the upcoming section on conglomerate mergers.

LOG ON The federal government's merger guidelines are referred to various times in this chapter. To see the actual text of the guidelines, visit the United States Department of Justice's website, at **www.usdoj.gov.** You will find the guidelines in the section dealing with the Justice Department's Antitrust Division.

Conglomerate Mergers

A **conglomerate merger** is a merger between two firms that neither compete with each other nor have a supplier–customer relationship with each other. Conglomerate mergers may be either *market extension* mergers or *product extension* mergers. In a market extension merger, the acquiring firm expands into a new geographic market by purchasing a firm already doing business in that market. For example, a conglomerate that owns an east coast grocery chain buys a west coast grocery chain. In a product extension merger, the acquiring firm diversifies its operations by purchasing a company in a new product market. For example, a conglomerate with interests in the aerospace and electronics industries purchases a department store chain.

There is considerable disagreement over the economic effects of conglomerate acquisitions. As later discussion will reveal, conglomerate mergers have been attacked with some degree of success under section 7 if they involve **potential reciprocity,** serve to **eliminate potential competition,** or give an acquired firm an **unfair advantage** over its competitors. Nevertheless, there is significant sentiment that the Clayton Act is not well-suited to dealing with conglomerate mergers. This realization has produced calls for specific legislation on the subject. Such legislation has not been enacted, however.

Potential Reciprocity Conglomerate mergers that involve *potential reciprocity* are among those sometimes held to be prohibited by section 7. A conglomerate merger may create a risk of potential reciprocity if the acquired firm produces a product regularly purchased by the acquiring firm's suppliers. Such suppliers, eager to continue their relationship with the acquiring firm, may thereafter purchase the acquired firm's products rather than those of its competitors.

Elimination of Potential Competition Some conglomerate mergers may *eliminate potential competition* in ways similar to vertical mergers, and thus may be vulnerable to attack under section 7. If existing competitors perceive the acquiring company as a potential entrant in the acquired company's market, the acquiring company's entry by means of a conglomerate acquisition may result in the loss of the moderating influence that it had while waiting in the wings. In addition, when the acquiring company actually enters the new market by acquiring a well-established competitor rather than by starting a new competitor through internal expansion or by making a toehold acquisition, the market is deprived of the potential for increased competition flowing from the reduction in concentration that would have accompanied the latter strategies.

Supreme Court decisions suggest, however, that a high degree of proof is required before either of these potential competition arguments will be accepted. Arguments that a conglomerate merger eliminated a *perceived potential entrant* must be accompanied by proof that existing competitors actually perceived the acquiring firm as a potential entrant. Arguments that a conglomerate acquisition eliminated an *actual* potential entrant (and thereby deprived the market of the benefits of reduced concentration) must be accompanied by evidence that the acquiring firm had the ability to enter the market by internal expansion or a toehold acquisition and that doing so would have ultimately yielded a substantial reduction in concentration.

Unfair Advantage to Acquired Firm Finally, conglomerate mergers may violate section 7 in certain instances when the acquired firm obtains an *unfair advantage* over its competitors. When a large firm acquires a firm that already enjoys a significant market position, the acquired firm may gain an unfair advantage over its competitors through its ability to draw on the greater resources and expertise of its new owner. This advantage may entrench the acquired firm in its market by deterring existing competitors from actively competing with it for market share and by causing other potential competitors to be reluctant to enter the market.

Nearly all of the important recent conglomerate merger cases have been settled out of court. As a result, we do not have a clear indication of the Supreme Court's current thinking on conglomerate merger issues. In recent years, the Justice Department has taken the position that the primary theories to be used by the department in attacking all *nonhorizontal* mergers are the *elimination of perceived and actual potential competition* theories. In employing these analytical tools, the department also considers other economic factors. These include: the degree of concentration in the acquired firm's market; the existence of barriers to entry into the market and the presence or absence of other firms with a comparable ability to enter; and the market share of the acquired firm (with challenges being unlikely if this is 5 percent or less and likely if it is 20 percent or more). It remains to be seen whether the Supreme Court will accept this more restrictive view of the scope of section 7.

THE GLOBAL BUSINESS ENVIRONMENT

A planned merger involving firms whose business is international in scope may face scrutiny outside the United States even if the FTC and the Justice Department decide not to challenge the merger under U.S. law. Legal regimes for controlling mergers now exist in numerous nations, with applicable rules and enforcement approaches that do not always match those of the United States. In 2001, for instance, legal objections lodged by the European Commission caused a highly publicized conglomerate merger-to-be involving the General Electric and Honeywell firms not to come about despite U.S. regulators' clearance of the deal.

The European Union's Merger Regulation, promulgated in furtherance of competition provisions in the Treaty of Rome, bars mergers that may "create or strengthen a [firm's] dominant position." As it has been applied, the Merger Regulation may focus somewhat more on protecting *competitors* than on preserving the *competitive process.* In this sense, the EU approach differs from the approach called for by the U.S. rule—

the Clayton Act provision prohibiting mergers that may "substantially lessen competition." The U.S. approach is also likely to allow greater ability to argue that a merger may produce economic efficiencies than does the EU's Merger Regulation.

In addition, the respective enforcement mechanisms in the U.S. and the EU differ. Under U.S. law, the FTC or the Justice Department normally must take legal action in court in order to block a planned merger, whereas in the EU, the Commission has considerable authority to quash a merger through its own action.

Notwithstanding the differences noted above, U.S. regulators and the European Commission fairly often reach the same conclusions regarding proposed mergers—especially those of the horizontal variety. Recent years have witnessed the development of agreements under which the EU Commission, the FTC, and the Justice Department have committed to sharing information and strategies regarding the regulation of mergers.

Clayton Act Section 8

If the same individuals control theoretically competing corporations, an obvious potential exists for anticompetitive conduct such as price-fixing or division of markets. Section 8 of the Clayton Act was designed to minimize the risks posed by such interlocks. Initially, section 8 prohibited any person from serving as a *director* of two or more corporations (other than banks or common carriers) if either had "capital, surplus, and undivided profits aggregating more than $1,000,000" and the corporations were, or had been, competitors, "so that elimination of competition by agreement between them" would violate any of the antitrust laws. The Antitrust Amendments Act of 1990 amended section 8's original language to increase the amount required to trigger the statute from $1 million to $10 million (a figure to be adjusted annually by an amount equal to the percentage increase or decrease in the gross national product).

Section 8 establishes a per se standard of liability in the sense that a violation may be demonstrated without proof that the interlock harmed competition. Until 1990, however, the statute's prohibition against interlocks was limited in scope because it barred only interlocking *directorates*. Nothing in the original language of section 8 prohibited a person from serving as an *officer* of two competing corporations, or as an officer of one firm and a director of its competitor. The Antitrust Amendments Act of 1990, however, expanded the scope of the statute by including senior "*officers*" (defined as officers elected or chosen by the board of directors) within its reach.

Although government enforcement of section 8 was historically lax, the past two decades have witnessed signs of growing government interest in the statute. Signs of renewed government interest in section 8 produced significant concern in an era of conglomerate merger activity. Given the wide diversification that characterizes many large corporations, it would be increasingly easy to demonstrate some degree of competitive overlap among a substantial number of large, diversified corporations. Critics alleged that section 8 has operated to discourage qualified persons from serving as directors when no potential for actual competitive harm exists. In response to such criticism, the Antitrust Amendments Act of 1990 specified that individuals may serve as officers or directors of competing corporations when the "competitive overlap" between them is an insignificant part of either company's total sales.

The Robinson–Patman Act

Section 2 of the Clayton Act originally prohibited *local and territorial price discrimination* by sellers, a practice monopolists frequently used to destroy smaller competitors. A large company operating in a number of geographic markets would sell at or below cost in markets where it faced local competitors, and would then make up its losses by selling at higher prices in areas where it faced no competition. Faced with such tactics, the smaller local competitors might eventually be driven out of business. Section 2 was aimed at such **primary level** (or *first line*) price discrimination.

During the 1930s, Congress was confronted with complaints that large chain stores were using their buying power to induce manufacturers to sell to them at prices lower than those offered to their smaller, independent competitors. Chain stores were also inclined to seek and obtain other payments and services their smaller competitors did not receive. Being able to purchase at lower prices and to obtain discriminatory payments and services arguably gave large firms a competitive advantage over their smaller competitors. Such price discrimination in sales to the competing customers of a particular seller is known as **secondary level** (or *second line*) price discrimination.

In addition, the customers of a manufacturer's favored customer (such as a wholesaler receiving a functional discount) may gain a competitive advantage over *their* competitors (for example, other retailers purchasing directly from the manufacturer at a higher price) if the favored customer passes on all or a portion of its discount to its customers. This form of price discrimination is known as **tertiary level** (or *third line*) price discrimination.

Congress responded to these problems by passing the Robinson-Patman Act in 1936. The Robinson–Patman Act preserved Clayton Act section 2's ban on primary level price discrimination. It also amended section 2 to outlaw secondary and tertiary level direct price discrimination, as well as indirect price discrimination in the form of discriminatory payments and services to a seller's customers. Since its enactment, the Robinson–Patman Act has been the subject of widespread dissatisfaction and criticism. Critics have long charged that the act often protects competitors at the expense of promoting competition. Government enforcement of the act has been haphazard over the years, with prominent officials in the Justice Department and the Federal Trade Commission sometimes voicing disagreement with the act's underlying policies and assumptions.

This government stance, when combined with Supreme Court decisions making private enforcement of the act difficult, raises questions about the act's future usefulness as a component of our antitrust laws.

Jurisdiction

The Robinson–Patman Act applies only to discriminatory acts that occur "in commerce." This test is narrower than the "affecting commerce" test employed under the Sherman Act. At least one of the discriminatory acts complained of must take place in interstate commerce. Thus, the act probably would not apply if a Texas manufacturer discriminated in price in sales to two Texas customers. Some lower federal courts have indicated, however, that even wholly intrastate sales may be deemed sufficiently "in commerce" if the nonfavored buyer bought the goods for resale to out-of-state customers.

Section 2(a)

Section 2(a) of the Robinson–Patman Act prohibits sellers, in certain instances, from *discriminating in price* "between different purchasers of commodities of like grade or quality." Such discrimination is prohibited when its effect may be to (1) "substantially . . . lessen competition or tend to create a monopoly in any line of commerce," or (2) "injure, destroy, or prevent competition

with any person who either grants [*primary level*] or knowingly receives [*secondary level*] the benefit of such discrimination, or with the customers of either of them [*tertiary level*]."

Price Discrimination To violate section 2(a), a seller must have made two or more sales to different purchasers at different prices. Merely quoting a discriminatory price or refusing to sell except at a discriminatory price does not violate the statute, because no actual purchase is involved. For the same reason, price discrimination in lease or consignment transactions is not covered by section 2(a). Actual sales at different prices to different purchasers will not be treated as discriminatory unless the sales were fairly close in time.

Section 2(a) does not directly address the legality of *functional discounts.* Such discounts are sometimes granted to buyers at various levels in a product's chain of distribution because of differences in the functions those buyers perform in the distribution system. As indicated in the *Texaco* case, which follows, the legality of such discounts depends on their competitive effect. If a seller charges wholesale customers lower prices than it charges retail customers, the Robinson-Patman Act is not violated unless the lower wholesale prices are somehow passed on to retailers in competition with the seller's retail customers.

Texaco Inc. v. Hasbrouck   *496 U.S. 543 (U.S. Sup. Ct. 1990)*

Ricky Hasbrouck and 11 other plaintiffs were Texaco retail service station dealers in the Spokane area. They purchased gasoline directly from Texaco and resold it at retail under the Texaco trademark. Throughout the relevant time period (1972–81), Texaco also supplied gasoline to two gasoline distributors, Dompier Oil Company and Gull Oil Company, at a price that was at various times between 2.5 cents and 5.75 cents per gallon lower than the price Hasbrouck paid.

Dompier and Gull sold the gasoline they purchased from Texaco to independent retail service stations. Dompier sold the gasoline to retailers under the Texaco trademark; Gull marketed it under private brand names. Gull's customers either sold their gasoline on consignment (in which case they set their own prices) or on commission (in which case Gull set their resale prices). Gull retained title until the gas was sold to a retail customer in either case. Some of the retail stations supplied by Dompier were owned and operated by Dompier's salaried employees. Both Dompier and Gull picked up gas at the Texaco bulk plant and delivered it to their retail customers, a service for which Dompier was compensated by Texaco at the common carrier rate.

Hasbrouck and the other dealers filed a price discrimination suit against Texaco under section 2(a) of the Robinson-Patman Act. At trial, Texaco argued that its lower prices to Gull and Dompier were lawful "functional discounts." The jury awarded the plaintiffs $1,349,700 in treble damages. When the Ninth Circuit Court of Appeals affirmed the jury award, Texaco appealed. The U.S. Supreme Court granted certiorari.

Stevens, Justice Section 2(a) contains no express reference to functional discounts. It does contain two affirmative defenses that provide protection for two categories of discounts—those that are justified by savings in the seller's

cost of manufacture, delivery, or sale, and those that represent a good faith response to the equally low prices of a competitor. In order to establish a violation of the Act, plaintiffs had the burden of proving four facts: (1) that Texaco's sales to Gull and Dompier were made in interstate commerce; (2) that the gasoline sold to them was of the same grade and quality as that sold to plaintiffs; (3) that Texaco discriminated in price as between Gull and Dompier on the one hand and plaintiffs on the other; and (4) that the discrimination had a prohibited effect on competition.

The first [three] elements of plaintiffs' case are not [at issue here]. Texaco [argues] that, at least to the extent that Gull and Dompier acted as wholesalers, the price differentials [employed by Texaco] did not injure competition.

In *FTC v. Morton Salt Co.* (1948), we held that an injury to competition may be inferred from evidence that some purchasers had to pay their supplier "substantially more for their goods than their competitors had to pay." Texaco, supported by the United States and the Federal Trade Commission as *amici curiae,* argues that this presumption should not apply to differences between prices charged to wholesalers and those charged to retailers. Moreover, they argue that it would be inconsistent with fundamental antitrust policies to construe the Act as requiring a seller to control his customers' resale prices. The seller should not be held liable for the independent pricing decisions of his customers. As the Government correctly notes, this argument endorses the position advocated 35 years ago in the Report of the Attorney General's Nation Committee to Study the Antitrust Laws (1955).

After observing that suppliers ought not to be held liable for the independent pricing decisions of their buyers, and that without functional discounts distributors might go uncompensated for the services they performed, the Committee wrote:

> On the other hand, the law should tolerate no subterfuge. For instance, where a wholesaler-retailer *buys* only part of his goods as a wholesaler, he must not claim a functional discount on all. Only to the extent that a buyer *actually* performs certain functions, assuming all the risk, investment, and costs involved, should he legally qualify for a functional discount.

We generally agree with this description of the legal status of functional discounts. A supplier need not satisfy the rigorous requirements of the cost justification defense in order to prove that a particular functional discount is reasonable and accordingly did not cause any substantial lessening of competition between a wholesaler's customers and the supplier's direct customers. The record in this case, however, adequately supports the finding that Texaco violated the Act.

The hypothetical predicate for the Committee's entire discussion of functional discounts is a price differential "that merely accords due recognition and reimbursement for actual marketing functions." Such a discount is not illegal. In this case, however, both the District Court and the Court of Appeals concluded that there was no substantial evidence indicating that the discounts to Gull and Dompier constituted a reasonable reimbursement for the value to Texaco of their actual marketing functions. Indeed, Dompier was separately compensated for its hauling function, and neither Gull nor Dompier maintained any significant storage facilities.

Both Gull and Dompier received the full discount on all their purchases even though most of their volume was resold directly to consumers. The extra margin on those sales obviously enabled them to price aggressively in both their retail and their wholesale marketing. To the extent that Dompier and Gull competed with plaintiffs in the retail market, the presumption of adverse effect on competition recognized in the *Morton Salt* case becomes all the more appropriate. The evidence indicates, moreover, that Texaco affirmatively encouraged Dompier to expand its retail business and was fully informed about the persistent and marketwide consequences of its own pricing policies. Indeed, its own executives recognized that the dramatic impact on the market was almost entirely attributable to the magnitude of the distributor discount and the hauling allowance. The special facts of this case thus make it peculiarly difficult for Texaco to claim that it is being held liable for the independent pricing decisions of Gull or Dompier.

The competitive injury component of a Robinson–Patman Act violation is not limited to the injury to competition between the favored and disfavored purchaser; it also encompasses the injury to competition between their customers. This conclusion is compelled by the statutory language, which specifically encompasses not only the adverse effect of price discrimination on persons who either grant or knowingly receive the benefit of such discrimination, but also to the "customers of either of them." Such indirect competitive effects surely may not be presumed automatically in every functional discount setting, and, indeed, one would expect that most functional discounts will be legitimate discounts that do not harm competition. At the least, a functional discount that constitutes a reasonable reimbursement for the purchasers' actual marketing functions will not violate the Act. Yet it is also true that not every functional discount is entitled to a judgment of legitimacy, and that it will sometimes be possible to produce evidence showing that a particular discount caused a price discrimination of the sort that the Act prohibits. When such anticompetitive effects are proved—as we believe they were in this case—they are covered by the Act.

Judgment for Hasbrouck affirmed.

Commodities of Like Grade and Quality Section 2(a) applies only to price discrimination in the sale of *commodities.* Price discrimination involving intangibles, real estate, or services must be challenged under the Sherman Act as a restraint of trade or an attempt to monopolize or under the FTC Act as an unfair method of competition. The essence of price discrimination is that two or more buyers are charged differing prices for the *same* commodity. Sales of commodities of varying grades or quality at varying prices, therefore, do not violate section 2(a) so long as uniform prices are charged for commodities of equal quality. Some *physical difference,* in the grade or quality of two products must be shown to justify a price differential between them. Differences solely in the brand name or label under which a product is sold—such as the seller's standard brand and a "house" brand sold to a large customer for resale under the customer's label—do not justify discriminatory pricing.

Anticompetitive Effect Only price discrimination having a *probable* anticompetitive effect is prohibited by section 2(a). Traditionally, courts have required a higher degree of proof of likely competitive injury in cases involving primary level price discrimination (which may damage the seller's competitors) than in cases involving secondary or tertiary level discrimination (which threatens competition among the seller's customers or its customers' customers). To prove a primary level violation, a market analysis must show that competitive harm has occurred as a result of the seller's engaging in significant and sustained price discrimination with the intent of punishing or disciplining a competitor. Proof of predatory pricing is often offered as evidence of a seller's anticompetitive intent. The *Brown & Williamson* case, which follows shortly, addresses predatory pricing claims under the Robinson-Patman Act and emphasizes that likely harm to competition—not merely to a competitor—remains the critical focus.

In secondary or tertiary level cases, courts tend to infer the existence of competitive injury from evidence of substantial price discrimination between competing purchasers over time. Some qualifications on this point are in order, however. Price discrimination for a short period of time ordinarily does not support an inference of competitive injury. Likewise, if the evidence indicates that nonfavored buyers could have purchased the same goods from other sellers at prices identical to those the defendant seller charged its favored customers, no competitive injury is inferred. Finally, buyers seeking treble damages for secondary or tertiary level harm must still prove that they suffered actual damages as a result of a violation of the act.

Brooke Group Ltd. v. Brown & Williamson Tobacco Corp.
509 U.S. 209 (U.S. Sup. Ct. 1993)

Brown & Williamson Tobacco Corp. (BW) and Brooke Group Ltd. (referred to here by its former corporate name, Liggett Corp.) are two of only six firms of significant consequence in the oligopolistic cigarette manufacturing industry. In 1980, BW's share of the national cigarette market was roughly 12 percent. This share placed BW a distant third behind market leaders Philip Morris and R. J. Reynolds. Liggett's share was less than half of BW's. Liggett pioneered the development of the economy segment of the national cigarette market in 1980 by introducing a popular line of "black and white" generic cigarettes (low-priced cigarettes sold in plain white packages with simple black lettering). As Liggett's sales of generic cigarettes became substantial, other cigarette manufacturers started introducing economy-priced cigarettes. In 1984, BW introduced a black and white cigarette whose net price was lower than Liggett's. BW achieved this lower price by offering volume rebates to wholesalers.

Liggett sued BW, claiming that BW's volume rebates amounted to price discrimination having a reasonable probability of injuring competition, in violation of section 2(a) of the Robinson-Patman Act. Specifically, Liggett alleged that BW's rebates were integral to a scheme of predatory pricing, under which BW reduced its net prices for generic cigarettes below average variable costs. Liggett further alleged that this pricing by BW was designed to pressure Liggett to raise its list prices on generic cigarettes, so that the percentage price difference between generic and branded cigarettes would narrow. As a result, according to Liggett, the growth of the economy segment would be restrained and BW would thereby be able to preserve its supracompetitive profits on branded cigarettes. Liggett further asserted that it could not afford to reduce its wholesale rebates without losing market share to BW. Therefore, Liggett claimed that its only choice, if it wished to avoid prolonged losses on the generic line that had become its principal product, was to raise retail prices.

After a 115-day trial, the jury returned a verdict in Liggett's favor for $49.6 million in damages. The district court trebled this amount. After reviewing the trial record, however, the district court concluded that BW was entitled to prevail as a matter of law. The court therefore set aside the jury's verdict and entered judgment in BW's favor. Liggett appealed. The Fourth Circuit Court of Appeals affirmed, holding that there cannot be liability for predatory price discrimination that allegedly takes place in the context of an oligopoly such as the cigarette industry. The Supreme Court granted certiorari.

Kennedy, Justice   Liggett contends that BW's discriminatory volume rebates to wholesalers threatened substantial competitive injury by furthering a predatory pricing scheme designed to purge competition from the economy segment of the cigarette market. This type of injury, which harms direct competitors of the discriminating seller, is known as primary-line injury. [P]rimary-line competitive injury under the Robinson–Patman Act is of the same general character as the injury inflicted by predatory pricing schemes actionable under section 2 of the Sherman Act. [T]he essence of the claim under either statute is the same.

Accordingly, whether the claim alleges predatory pricing under the Sherman Act or primary-line price discrimination under the Robinson–Patman Act, two prerequisites to recovery [exist]. First, a plaintiff seeking to establish competitive injury resulting from a rival's low prices must prove that the prices complained of are below an appropriate measure of its rival's costs. [Second, the plaintiff must demonstrate] that the competitor had a reasonable prospect [if the claim is brought under the Robinson–Patman Act], or . . . a dangerous probability [if the claim is brought under section 2 of the Sherman Act], of recouping its investment in below-cost prices. Recoupment is the ultimate object of an unlawful predatory-pricing scheme; it is the means by which a predator profits from predation. Without it, predatory pricing produces lower aggregate prices in the market, and consumer welfare is enhanced. That below-cost pricing may impose painful losses on its target is of no moment to the antitrust laws if competition is not injured.

For recoupment to occur, below-cost pricing must be capable . . . of producing the intended effects on the firm's rivals, whether driving them from the market, or, as was alleged to be the goal here, causing them to raise their prices to supracompetitive levels within a disciplined oligopoly. If circumstances indicate that below-cost pricing could likely produce its intended effect on the target, there is still the further question whether it would be likely to injure competition in the relevant market. The plaintiff must demonstrate that there is a likelihood that the predatory scheme alleged would cause a rise in prices above a competitive level that would be sufficient to compensate for the amounts expended on the predation. These prerequisites to recovery are not easy to establish, but . . . they are essential components of real market injury.

Liggett . . . allege[s] . . . that BW sought to preserve supracompetitive profits on branded cigarettes by pressuring Liggett to raise its generic cigarette prices through a process of tacit collusion with the other cigarette companies. Tacit collusion, sometimes called oligopolistic price coordination or conscious parallelism, describes the process, not in itself unlawful, by which firms in a concentrated market might in effect share monopoly power, setting their prices at a profit-maximizing, supracompetitive level by recognizing their shared economic interests and their interdependence with respect to price and output decisions.

In *Matsushita Electric Industrial Co. v. Zenith Radio Corp.* (U.S. Sup. Ct. 1986), we remarked upon the general implausibility of predatory pricing. *Matsushita* observed that such schemes are even more improbable when they require coordinated action among several firms. However unlikely predatory pricing by multiple firms may be when they conspire, it is even less likely when, as here, there is no express coordination. Firms that seek to recoup predatory losses through the conscious parallelism of oligopoly must rely on uncertain and ambiguous signals to achieve concerted action. The signals are subject to misinterpretation and are a blunt and imprecise means of ensuring smooth cooperation, especially in the context of changing or unprecedented market circumstances. This anticompetitive minuet is most difficult to compose and to perform, even for a disciplined oligopoly.

[O]n the whole, tacit cooperation among oligopolists must be considered the least likely means of recouping predatory losses. In addition to the difficulty of achieving effective tacit coordination and the high likelihood that any attempt to discipline will produce an outbreak of competition, the predator's present losses in a case like this fall on it alone, while the later supracompetitive profits must be shared with every other oligopolist in proportion to its market share, including the intended victim. In this case, for example, BW, with its 11–12 percent share of the cigarette market, would have had to generate around $9 in supracompetitive profits for each $1 invested in predation; the remaining $8 would belong to its competitors, who had taken no risk.

[However,] [t]o the extent that the Court of Appeals may have held that the interdependent pricing of an oligopoly may never provide a means for achieving recoupment and so may not form the basis of a primary-line injury claim, we disagree. A predatory pricing scheme designed to preserve or create a stable oligopoly, if successful, can injure consumers in the same way, and to the same extent, as one designed to bring about a monopoly. However unlikely that possibility may be as a general matter, when the realities of the market and the record facts indicate that it has occurred and was likely to have succeeded, theory will not stand in the way of liability. The Robinson–Patman Act . . . suggests no exclusion from coverage when primary-line injury occurs in an oligopoly setting. We decline to create a per se rule of nonliability [under the Robinson–Patman Act] for predatory price discrimination when recoupment is alleged to take place through supracompetitive oligopoly pricing.

Although Liggett's theory of liability, as an abstract matter, is within the reach of the statute, we agree with the [lower courts] that Liggett was not entitled to submit its case to the jury. Liggett . . . failed to demonstrate competitive injury as a matter of law. The evidence is inadequate to show that in pursuing [an alleged below-cost pricing] scheme, BW had a reasonable prospect of recovering its losses from below-cost pricing through slowing the growth of generics.

The only means by which BW is alleged to have established oligopoly pricing . . . is through tacit price coordination with the other cigarette firms. Yet the situation facing the cigarette companies in the 1980s would have made such tacit coordination unmanageable. Tacit coordination is facilitated by a stable market environment, fungible products, and a small number of variables upon which the firms seeking to coordinate their pricing may focus. By 1984, however, the cigarette market was in an obvious state of flux. The introduction of generic cigarettes in 1980 represented

the first serious price competition in the cigarette market since the 1930s. This development was bound to unsettle previous expectations and patterns of market conduct and to reduce the cigarette firms' ability to predict each other's behavior. The larger number of product types and pricing variables also decreased the probability of effective parallel pricing.

Even if all the cigarette companies were willing to participate in a scheme to restrain the growth of the generic segment, they would not have been able to coordinate their actions and raise prices above a competitive level unless they understood that BW's entry into the [economy] segment was not a genuine effort to compete with Liggett. If even one other firm misinterpreted BW's entry as an effort to expand share, a chain reaction of competitive responses would almost certainly have resulted, and oligopoly discipline would have broken down, perhaps irretrievably. Liggett argues that [BW's] maintaining existing list prices while offering substantial rebates to wholesalers was a signal to the other cigarette firms that BW did not intend to attract additional smokers to the generic segment by its entry. But a reasonable jury could not conclude that this pricing structure eliminated or rendered insignificant the risk that the other firms might misunderstand BW's entry as a competitive move.

We hold that the evidence cannot support a finding that BW's alleged scheme was likely to result in oligopolistic price coordination and sustained supracompetitive pricing in the generic segment of the national cigarette market. Without this, BW had no reasonable prospect of recouping its predatory losses and could not inflict the injury to competition the antitrust laws prohibit.

Judgment for BW affirmed.

Defenses to Section 2(a) Liability

There are three major statutory defenses to liability under section 2(a): *cost justification, changing conditions,* and *meeting competition in good faith.*

Cost Justification Section 2(a) legalizes price differentials that do no more than make an appropriate allowance for differences in the "cost of manufacture, sale, or delivery resulting from the differing methods or quantities" in which goods are sold or delivered to buyers. This defense recognizes the reality that it may be less costly for a seller to service some buyers than others. Sales to buyers purchasing large quantities may in some cases be more cost-effective than small-quantity

sales to their competitors. Sellers are allowed to pass on such cost savings to their customers.

Utilizing this *cost justification* defense is difficult and expensive for sellers, however, because quantity discounts must be supported by *actual evidence of cost savings.* Sellers are allowed to average their costs and classify their customers into categories based on their average sales costs. The customers included in any particular classification, however, must be sufficiently similar to justify similar treatment.

Changing Conditions Section 2(a) specifically exempts price discriminations that reflect "changing conditions in the market for or the marketability of the goods." The *changing conditions* defense has been narrowly confined to temporary situations caused by the physical nature of the goods. Examples include the deterioration of perishable goods and a declining market for seasonal goods. This defense also applies to forced judicial sales of the goods (such as during bankruptcy proceedings involving the seller) and to good faith sales by sellers that have decided to cease selling the goods in question.

Meeting Competition Section 2(b) of the Robinson–Patman Act states that price discrimination may be lawful if the discriminatory lower price was charged "in good faith to meet an equally low price of a competitor." This *meeting competition* defense is necessary to prevent the act from stifling the very competition it was designed to preserve. For example, suppose Sony Corporation has been selling a particular model of video recorder to its customers for $350 per unit. Sony then learns that Sharp Electronics is offering a comparable recorder to Acme Appliance Stores for $300 per unit. Acme, however, competes with Best Buy Video Stores, a Sony customer that has recently been charged the $350 price. Should Sony be forced to refrain from offering the lower competitive price to Acme for fear that Best Buy will charge Sony with price discrimination if it does so? If Sony cannot offer the lower competitive price to Acme, competition between Sony and Sharp will plainly suffer.

Section 2(b) avoids this undesirable result by allowing a seller to charge a lower price to certain customers if the seller has reasonable grounds for believing that the lower price is necessary to meet an equally low price offered by a competitor. Sellers may meet competition *offensively* (to gain a new customer) or *defensively* (to keep an existing customer). The meeting competition defense is subject to significant qualifications, however. First, the lower price must be necessary to meet a lower price charged by a competitor of the *seller*, not to enable a customer of the seller to compete more effectively with that customer's competitors. Second, the seller may lawfully seek only to *meet*, not *beat*, its competitor's price. A seller cannot, however, be held in violation of the act for beating a competitor's price if it did so unknowingly in a good faith attempt to meet competition. Third, the seller may reduce its price only to meet competitors' prices for products of *similar quality*.

Courts also have held that the discriminatory price must be a response to an individual competitive situation rather than the product of a seller's wholesale adoption of a competitor's discriminatory pricing system. However, a seller's competitive response need not be on a customer-by-customer basis, so long as the lower price is offered only to those customers that the seller reasonably believes are being offered a lower price by the seller's competitors.

Indirect Price Discrimination

When Congress enacted the Robinson–Patman Act, it also addressed **indirect price discrimination,** which takes the form of a seller's discriminating among competing buyers by making discriminatory payments to selected buyers or by furnishing certain buyers with services not made available to their competitors. Three sections of the act are designed to prevent such practices.

False Brokerage Section 2(c) prohibits sellers from granting, and buyers from receiving, any "commission, brokerage, or other compensation, or any allowance or discount in lieu thereof, except for services rendered in connection with the sale or purchase of goods." This provision prevents large buyers, either directly or through subsidiary brokerage agents, from receiving phony commissions or brokerage payments from their suppliers.

Section 2(c) establishes a per se standard of liability. No demonstration of probable anticompetitive effect is required for a violation. Neither the cost justification nor meeting competition defense is available in 2(c) cases. Individual plaintiffs still must prove that they have suffered some injury as a result of a 2(c) violation, however, before they are entitled to recover damages.

Discriminatory Payments and Services Sellers and their customers benefit from merchandising activities that customers employ to promote the sellers' products. Section 2(d) prohibits sellers from making *discriminatory payments* to competing customers for such customer-performed services as advertising and promotional activities or such customer-provided facilities as shelf space. Section 2(e) prohibits sellers from discriminating in the *services* they provide to competing customers, such as by providing favored customers with a display case or a demonstration kit.

A seller may lawfully make payments or provide services to customers only if the payments or services are made available to all competing customers on *proportionately equal terms*. This means that the seller must inform all customers of the availability of the payments or services and must distribute them on some rational basis, such as the quantity of goods bought by the customer. The seller must also devise a flexible plan that enables its various classes of customers to participate in the payment or services program in an appropriate way.

As does section 2(c), sections 2(d) and 2(e) create a per se liability standard. No proof of probable harm to competition is required for a violation; no cost justification defense is available. The meeting competition defense is applicable, however, to actions under sections 2(d) and 2(e).

Buyer Inducement of Discrimination

Section 2(f) of the Robinson–Patman Act makes it illegal for a buyer *knowingly to induce or receive* a discriminatory price in violation of section 2(a). The logic of the section is that buyers who are successful in demanding discriminatory prices should face liability along with the sellers charging discriminatory prices. To violate section 2(f), the buyer must know that the price the buyer received was unjustifiably discriminatory. This means that the price probably was neither cost-justified nor made in response to changing conditions. Section 2(f) does not apply to buyer inducements of discriminatory payments or services prohibited by sections 2(d) and 2(e). Such buyer actions may, however, be attacked as unfair methods of competition under section 5 of the FTC Act.

In *Great Atlantic and Pacific Tea Co. v. FTC* (1979), the Supreme Court further narrowed the effective reach of section 2(f) by holding that buyers who knowingly received a discriminatory price did not violate the act if their seller had a valid defense to the charge of violating section 2(a). The seller in *Great Atlantic* had a "meeting competition in good faith" defense. This fact was held to insulate the buyer from liability even though the buyer knew that the seller had beaten, rather than merely met, its competitor's price.

Antitrust Exceptions and Exemptions

Many economic activities occur outside the potential reach of the antitrust laws. This is so either because these activities have been specifically exempted by statute or because courts have carved out nonstatutory exceptions designed to balance our antitrust policy in favor of competition against other social policies.

Statutory Exemptions

Labor Unions and Certain Union Activities The Clayton Act and the Norris–LaGuardia Act of 1932 pro-

vide that *labor unions* are not combinations or conspiracies in restraint of trade and exempt certain union activities, including boycotts and secondary picketing, from antitrust scrutiny. This statutory exemption does not, however, exempt union combinations with nonlabor groups aimed at restraining trade or creating a monopoly. An example of such nonexempted activity would be a labor union's agreement with Employer A to call a strike at Employer B's plants. In an attempt to accommodate the strong public policy in favor of collective bargaining, courts have also created a limited nonstatutory exemption for legitimate union–employer agreements arising from the collective bargaining context.

Agricultural Cooperatives and Certain Cooperative Actions The Clayton Act and the Capper–Volstead Act exempt the formation and collective marketing activities of *agricultural cooperatives* from antitrust liability. Courts have narrowly construed this exemption, however. Cooperatives including members not engaged in the production of agricultural commodities have been denied exempt status. One such example would be a cooperative including retailers or wholesalers who do not also produce the commodity in question. The agricultural cooperatives exemption extends only to legitimate collective marketing activities. It does not legitimize coercive or predatory practices that are unnecessary to accomplish lawful cooperative goals. For example, this exemption would not prevent the antitrust laws from being applied to a boycott designed to force nonmembers of the cooperative to adopt a pricing policy established by the cooperative.

Joint Export Activities The Webb–Pomerene Act exempts the *joint export activities* of American companies, so long as those activities do not "artificially or intentionally enhance or depress prices within the United States." The purpose of the act is to encourage export activity by allowing the formation of combinations to enable domestic firms to compete more effectively with foreign cartels. Some critics assert that this exemption is no longer needed because there are fewer foreign cartels today and American firms often play a dominant role in foreign trade. Others question whether any group of American firms enjoying significant domestic market shares in the sale of a particular product could agree on an international marketing strategy, such as the amounts that they will export, without indirectly affecting domestic supplies and prices.

Business of Insurance The McCarran–Ferguson Act exempts from federal antitrust scrutiny those

aspects of the *business of insurance* that are subject to state regulation. The act provides, however, that state law cannot legitimize any agreement to boycott, coerce, or intimidate others. Because the insurance industry is extensively regulated by the states, many practices in the industry are outside the reach of the federal antitrust laws.

In recent years, however, courts have tended to decrease the scope of this exemption by narrowly construing the meaning of "business of insurance." For example, in *Union Labor Life Insurance Co. v. Pireno* (1982), the Supreme Court held that the exemption did not insulate from antitrust scrutiny a peer review system in which an insurance company used a committee established by a state chiropractic association to review the reasonableness of particular chiropractors' charges. The Court stated that to qualify for the business of insurance exemption, a challenged practice must have the effect of transferring or spreading policyholders' risk and must be an integral part of the policy relationship between the insured and the insurer. Therefore, only practices related to traditional functions of the insurance business, such as underwriting and risk-spreading, are likely to be exempt.

Other Regulated Industries Many other *regulated industries* enjoy various degrees of antitrust immunity. The airline, banking, utility, railroad, shipping, and securities industries traditionally have been regulated in the public interest. The regulatory agencies supervising such industries have frequently been given the power to approve industry practices such as rate-setting and mergers that would otherwise violate antitrust laws. In recent years, there has been a distinct tendency to deregulate many regulated industries. If this trend continues, a greater portion of the economic activity in these industries could be subjected to antitrust scrutiny.

State Action Exemption

In *Parker v. Brown* (1943), the Supreme Court held that a California state agency's regulation of the production and price of raisins was a state action exempt from the federal antitrust laws. The **state action exemption** developed in *Parker v. Brown* recognizes states' rights to regulate economic activity in the interest of their citizens. It also, however, may tempt business entities to seek "friendly" state regulation as a way of shielding anticompetitive activity from antitrust supervision. Recog-

nizing this possibility, courts have placed important limitations on the scope of the state action exemption.

First, the exemption extends only to governmental actions by a state or to actions compelled by a state acting in its sovereign capacity. Second, various decisions indicate that challenged activity cannot qualify for immunity under this exemption unless the activity is affirmatively expressed as state policy and actively supervised by the state. In other words, the price of antitrust immunity is real regulation by the state. The Supreme Court placed a further limitation on the state action exemption by holding that it does not automatically confer immunity on the actions of municipalities. Municipal conduct is immune only if it was authorized by the state legislature and its anticompetitive effects were a foreseeable result of the authorization. The Court's decision caused concern that the threat of treble damage liability might inhibit legitimate regulatory action by municipal authorities. As a result, Congress passed the Local Government Antitrust Act of 1984. This statute eliminates damage actions against municipalities and their officers, agents, and employees for antitrust violations and makes injunctive relief the sole remedy in such cases.

The *Armstrong* case, which appears shortly, discusses the state action exemption and another key exemption, the *Noerr–Pennington* doctrine.

The Noerr–Pennington Doctrine

In the *Noerr* and *Pennington* cases, the Supreme Court held that "the Sherman Act does not prohibit two or more persons from associating together in an attempt to persuade the legislature or the executive to take particular action with respect to a law that would produce a restraint or a monopoly."[1] This exemption recognizes that the right to petition government provided by the Bill of Rights takes precedence over the antitrust policy favoring competition. In a later case, the Court made the *Noerr–Pennington* exemption applicable to a party's filing of a lawsuit. The exemption does not, however, extend to sham activities that are attempts to interfere with the business activities of competitors rather than legitimate attempts to influence governmental action. The *Armstrong* case, which follows, discusses the *Noerr–Pennington* doctrine and the relationship it may sometimes have to the state action exemption.

---

[1]*Eastern R. R. President's Conference v. Noerr Motor Freight, Inc.* (U.S. Sup. Ct. 1961): *United Mine Workers v. Pennington* (U.S. Sup. Ct. 1965).

Armstrong Surgical Center, Inc. v. Armstrong County Memorial Hospital
185 F.3d 154 (3d Cir. 1999)

Armstrong Surgical Center, Inc. (the "Surgical Center"), wished to establish an ambulatory surgery center in Armstrong County, Pennsylvania. At the time, Armstrong County Memorial Hospital (the "Hospital") was the only facility with operating rooms in Armstrong County. The Hospital's 19 staff physicians performed the vast majority of surgeries in the county. The Surgical Center's proposed facility, if it had been constructed, would have provided a variety of outpatient surgical services and would have competed with the Hospital.

Pennsylvania law provides that any party wishing to establish a new health care facility must first obtain a Certificate of Need ("CON") from Pennsylvania's Department of Health. The Department reviews CON applications in an extensive proceeding consisting of an investigation, an evaluation of submitted materials, and a public hearing. Interested parties, including health care providers that supply similar services in the area, may submit information to the Department regarding any CON application.

The Surgical Center filed an application for a CON. According to the Surgical Center, the Hospital and its staff physicians then conspired to subvert establishment of the new facility. The alleged conspiracy involved an announcement by the physicians that they would not use the facility, as well as the submission of false and misleading information by the Hospital and the staff physicians to the Department of Health. The false and misleading information, according to the Surgical Center, was to the effect that the Hospital intended to open its own outpatient center. Although construction had begun on such a center, the Hospital had stopped construction at a very early stage. The Surgical Center contended that even though the Hospital had made no commitment to resume construction, the Hospital and the staff physicians falsely represented to the Department that the Hospital's center was either in use or very near completion.

The Department of Health denied the Surgical Center's CON application. The Surgical Center appealed to the Pennsylvania State Health Facility Hearing Board, which conducted its own hearing and received additional evidence. The Board affirmed the Department's denial of the CON after finding that: (1) the Surgical Center's proposed facility would result in needless duplication of existing facilities and services; and (2) the Surgical Center would not be economically viable because the Hospital's staff physicians, who performed more than 90 percent of the surgeries in Armstrong County, would not use the Surgical Center's facility. The Surgical Center appealed to a Pennsylvania court, which affirmed the Board's decision.

The Surgical Center then filed an antitrust action against the Hospital and its staff physicians (the "Hospital Defendants"). According to the Surgical Center's complaint, the Hospital Defendants' conspiracy to prevent the Surgical Center from establishing its surgery center restrained and monopolized trade, in violation of sections 1 and 2 of the Sherman Act. The federal district court dismissed the complaint after concluding that the Hospital Defendants' alleged conduct was immune from antitrust scrutiny. The Surgical Center appealed to the U.S. Court of Appeals for the Third Circuit.

Stapleton, Circuit Judge   The Hospital Defendants do not deny that [the Surgical Center's] complaint alleges a threat of a boycott that might under other circumstances constitute an antitrust violation. [T]hey contend, [however,] that their activities are insulated from antitrust scrutiny because their allegedly wrongful conduct occurred in the context of supplying information to the Pennsylvania Department of Health during the Surgical Center's CON application process and because the injuries alleged resulted solely from the Department's denial of the CON.

In *Parker v. Brown* (U.S. Sup. Ct. 1943), an agricultural producer challenged a marketing program adopted by California's Director of Agriculture as invalid under the Sherman Act. The program served to restrict competition among growers and maintain prices in commodity distribution.

"Relying on principles of federalism and state sovereignty, [the Supreme Court] held [in *Parker*] that the Sherman Act did not apply to anticompetitive restraints imposed by the States 'as an act of government.'" *City of Columbia v. Omni Outdoor Advertising, Inc.* (U.S. Sup. Ct. 1991) (quoting *Parker*).

In *Eastern R. R. Presidents Conference v. Noerr Motor Freight, Inc.* (U.S. Sup. Ct. 1961) and *United Mine Workers v. Pennington* (U.S. Sup. Ct. 1965), the Supreme Court held that antitrust liability cannot be predicated solely on petitioning to secure government action even where those efforts are intended to eliminate competition. As the Court . . . observed [in *Omni*], "*Parker and Noerr* are complementary expressions of the principle that the antitrust laws regulate business, not politics; the former decision protects the

States' acts of governing, and the latter the citizens' participation in government."

As the Surgical Center emphasizes, however, the immunity afforded to a private party under *Noerr* is not unlimited. Where the challenged private conduct is only "sham" petitioning—where it "is not genuinely aimed at procuring favorable government action as opposed to a valid effort to influence government action"—the *Noerr* immunity is not available. *Professional Real Estate Investors, Inc. v. Columbia Pictures, Inc.* (U.S. Sup. Ct. 1993). In essence, sham petitioning entails, [as noted in *Professional Real Estate Investors*], "the use of the governmental process—as opposed to the outcome of that process—as an anticompetitive weapon." Accordingly, the sham petitioning exception does not apply in a case like the one before us, where the plaintiff has not alleged that the petitioning conduct was for any purpose other than obtaining favorable government action. [In this case,] the plaintiff affirmatively alleges that [the Hospital Defendants'] purpose was to secure the outcome of the process—denial of the CON. Thus, . . .the sham exception to *Noerr* immunity [is] inapplicable here.

It is also true that a private party can be held liable even for bona fide petitioning conduct where that conduct has caused direct antitrust injury in the marketplace. *FTC v. Superior Court Trial Lawyers Association* (U.S. Sup. Ct. 1990). In *Trial Lawyers,* for example, the public defenders of the District of Columbia engaged in a concerted refusal to represent indigent defendants in order to pressure the District into raising the hourly rate paid. The Court held that the defendants could be held liable under the Sherman Act for injuries that resulted directly from the boycott, even though the boycott was intended to secure government action. The limitation on *Noerr* immunity recognized in *Trial Lawyers* is inapplicable, however, to a case where the sole antitrust injury is caused directly by the government action that the private defendant has helped to secure. Thus, even where the same petitioning conduct might give rise to antitrust liability for injury directly caused to a competitor in the marketplace, if relief is sought solely for injury as to which the state would enjoy immunity under *Parker,* the private petitioner also enjoys immunity.

Here, looking to the source of the complained-of injuries, we find that all of the Surgical Center's alleged injuries arise solely from the denial of the CON: the denial of the ability to operate the proposed facility; the losses of the CON's value, the value of the facility, and the value of the operation's proceeds; the delay in securing the CON; and other related losses. [W]here, as here, all of the plaintiff's alleged injuries result from state action, antitrust liability can-

not be imposed on a private party who induced the state action by means of concerted anticompetitive activity. It follows that the complaint fails to state a boycott claim upon which relief can be granted.

The Surgical Center's second claim is that the Hospital Defendants, as part of their conspiracy, misled the Department [and] the Board. . .into believing that the Hospital's partially constructed facility would soon open and meet the needs of the relevant market, when the Hospital Defendants knew that the facility would not be completed. The Surgical Center would have us deny antitrust immunity to the Hospital Defendants on the [ground] that they successfully opposed the issuance of a CON using information known to be false.

Although the Supreme Court suggested in *California Motor Transport Co. v. Trucking Unlimited* (U.S. Sup. Ct. 1972) that petitioning activity involving knowingly false information submitted to an adjudicative tribunal might not enjoy antitrust immunity, the Court has never so held. Moreover, since *California Motor,* the Supreme Court decided [*City of Columbia v. Omni Outdoor Advertising, Inc.* (U.S. Sup Ct. 1991), which] casts doubt on whether such an exception exists under any circumstances and dictates that . . . we honor the Hospital Defendants' claim to immunity.

In *Omni,* [a relative newcomer to the outdoor sign business alleged that a competitor and a city council] conspired to restrain competition [through the adoption of] a zoning ordinance limiting the size, spacing, and location of billboards in the city. The Supreme Court . . . concluded that [the plaintiff's] alleged injury was the result of state action, [that *Parker* immunity would therefore protect the city against liability, and that the existence of a conspiracy between city officials and a private firm did not strip the city of its immunity]. It then observed that if "conspiracy" was taken to mean "nothing more than an agreement to impose the regulation in question," the purpose of *Parker* immunity would be defeated because "it is both inevitable and desirable that public officials often agree to do what one or another group of private citizens urges upon them."

The [*Omni*] Court next considered whether *Parker* immunity is lost when it is shown that an agreement between the defendants involved governmental corruption, bribery, or other violations of state or federal law. It held that *Parker* immunity remains in such circumstances. The Court found "impractical" the contention that *Parker* immunity is forfeited by governmental corruption. Such a rule would call upon antitrust courts to speculate as to whether state action purportedly taken in the public interest was the product of an honest judgment or desire for private gain. The Court stressed that *Parker* "was not meant to shift [judgments about the public interest] from elected officials to judges and juries." With respect to the contention that *Parker* immunity should be forfeited at least where bribery or other illegal activity may have subverted the state decision making process, the Court observed that this approach had "the virtue of practicality but the vice of being unrelated to" the purposes of the Sherman Act and *Parker*. [It noted that existing statutes] other than the Sherman Act [may be utilized] to discourage such behavior.

Turning to [whether the private firm that conspired with the city council could be held liable], the *Omni* Court addressed whether *Noerr*'s immunity for private parties was subject to any of the exceptions that had been urged in the context of *Parker* immunity. It declined to restrict *Noerr* immunity in this way for the same reason it had declined to so restrict *Parker* immunity. [In so concluding, the Court noted that] "[i]n *Noerr* . . . , where the private party 'deliberately deceived the public and public officials' in its successful lobbying campaign, we said that 'deception, reprehensible as it is, can be of no consequence so far as the Sherman Act is concerned.'"

The teachings of *Omni* are pertinent here. Considerations of federalism require an interpretation of the Sherman Act that forecloses liability predicated on anticompetitive injuries that are inflicted by states acting as regulators. Liability for injuries caused by such state action is precluded even where it is alleged that a private party urging the action did so by bribery, deceit, or other wrongful conduct that may have affected the decision making process. The remedy for such conduct rests with laws addressed to it and not with courts looking behind sovereign state action at the behest of antitrust plaintiffs. Federalism requires this result both with respect to state actors and with respect to private parties who have urged the state action.

On the facts alleged in the complaint, it is . . . clear that the state decision makers were disinterested, conducted their own investigation, and afforded all interested parties an opportunity to set the record straight. The initial decision was then twice reviewed. Finally, anyone who believed that a fraud was committed on the Department or Board could have moved to reopen the proceeding and attempted to persuade them that they were materially misled.

In these circumstances, *Omni* compels us to affirm the district court. Indeed, such a result seems to follow, a fortiori, from *Omni* given the conceded presence here of disinterested decision makers, an independent investigation, an open process, and extensive opportunities for error correction. The risk that the plaintiff's injury is not the result of a bona fide execution of state policy is far less substantial here than in *Omni* and there is, accordingly, far less justification for federal court review of the state's policy judgment.

District court's dismissal of complaint affirmed.

Patent Licensing

There is a basic tension between the antitrust objective of promoting competition and the purpose of the patent law, which, as noted in Chapter 8, seeks to promote innovation by granting a limited monopoly to those who develop new products or processes. In the early case of *United States v. General Electric Company* (1926), the Supreme Court allowed General Electric to control the price at which other manufacturers sold light bulbs they had manufactured under patent licensing agreements with General Electric. The Court recognized that an important part of holding a patent was the right to license others to manufacture the patented item. This right effectively would be negated if licensees were allowed to undercut the prices that patent holders charged for their own sales of patented products.

Patent holders cannot, however, lawfully control the price at which patented items are resold by distributors purchasing them from the patent holder. Nor can patent holders use their patents to impose tying agreements on their customers by conditioning the sale of patented items on the purchase of unpatented items, unless such agreements are otherwise lawful under the Sherman and Clayton Acts. Finally, firms that seek to monopolize by acquiring most or all of the patents related to an area of commerce may face liability for violating Sherman Act section 2 or Clayton Act section 7, because a patent has been held to be an asset within the meaning of section 7.

Foreign Commerce

When foreign governments are involved in commercial activities affecting the domestic or international commerce of the United States, our antitrust policy may be at odds with our foreign policy. Congress and the courts have created a variety of antitrust exemptions aimed at reconciling this potential conflict. The Foreign Sovereign Immunities Act (FSIA) provides that the governmental actions of foreign sovereigns and their agents are

ETHICS IN ACTION

In the *Armstrong* case, which appeared earlier in this chapter, the court concluded that even if the defendants made false statements to state authorities, certain exemptions would protect them against antitrust liability. Assuming that the defendants made the false statements, how would deontologists view their behavior? How would utilitarians view their behavior? What about profit maximizers? (Refer to the discussion in Chapter 4, if necessary.)

---

exempt from antitrust liability. The commercial activities of foreign sovereigns, however, are not included within this **sovereign immunity** exemption. Significant international controversy exists concerning the proper criteria for determining whether a particular governmental act is commercial in nature. Under the FSIA, the courts employ a *nature of the act* test, holding that a commercial activity is one that an individual might customarily carry on for a profit.

The **act of state doctrine** provides that an American court cannot adjudicate a politically sensitive dispute whose resolution would require the court to judge the legality of a foreign government's sovereign act. This doctrine reflects judicial deference to the primary role of the executive and legislative branches in the adoption and execution of our foreign policy. The act of state doctrine recognizes (as does the doctrine of sovereign immunity) the importance of respecting the sovereignty of other nations. Unlike the doctrine of sovereign immunity, however, the act of state doctrine also reflects a fundamental attribute of our system of government: the principle of separation of powers.

Finally, the **sovereign compulsion doctrine** provides private parties a defense if they have been compelled by a foreign sovereign to commit, within that sovereign's territory, acts that would otherwise violate the antitrust laws because of their negative impact on our international commerce. To employ this defense successfully, a defendant must show that the challenged actions were the product of actual compulsion—as opposed to mere encouragement or approval—by a foreign sovereign.

Problems and Problem Cases

1. Mercedes-Benz of North America (MBNA), the exclusive U.S. distributor of Mercedes-Benz (Mercedes) automobiles, was a wholly owned subsidiary of Daimler-Benz Aktiengesellschaft (DBAG), the manufacturer of Mercedes automobiles. MBNA required its approximately 400 franchised Mercedes dealers to agree not to sell or use (in the repair or servicing of Mercedes automobiles) any parts other than genuine Mercedes parts. Mozart, a wholesale automotive parts distributor, filed an antitrust suit against MBNA. Mozart alleged, among other things, that MBNA had violated section 1 of the Sherman Act and section 3 of the Clayton Act by tying the sale of Mercedes parts to the sale of Mercedes automobiles. The trial court ruled in favor of MBNA. Was the trial court's ruling correct?

2. Waste Management, Inc. (WMI), a company in the solid waste disposal business, acquired the stock of EMW Ventures, Inc. EMW was a diversified holding company, one of whose subsidiaries was Waste Resources. WMI and Waste Resources each had subsidiaries operating in or near Dallas, Texas. The government challenged the merger on the theory that it violated section 7 of the Clayton Act. The trial court agreed. In finding a section 7 violation, the trial court defined the relevant market as including all forms of trash collection (except at single-family or multiple-family residences or small apartment complexes) in Dallas County plus a small fringe area. The combined WMI and Waste Resources subsidiaries had a 48.8 percent share of the relevant market. The trial court held that this market share raised a presumption of illegality and that WMI had not rebutted the presumption. WMI appealed, arguing that new firms could easily enter the trash collection business in the relevant geographic area and that the trial court should have regarded this ease of entry as a sufficient rebuttal of the presumption of illegality. Was WMI correct?

3. In 1961, Ford Motor Company acquired Autolite, a manufacturer of spark plugs, in order to enter the profitable aftermarket for spark plugs sold as replacement parts. Ford and the other major automobile manufacturers had previously purchased original equipment spark plugs (those installed in new cars when they leave the factory) from independent producers such as Autolite and Champion, either at or below the producer's cost.

The independents were willing to sell original equipment plugs so cheaply because aftermarket mechanics often replace original equipment plugs with the same brand of spark plug. GM had already moved into the spark plug market by developing its own division. Ford decided to do so by means of a vertical merger under which it acquired Autolite. Prior to the Autolite acquisition, Ford bought 10 percent of the total spark plug output. The merger left Champion as the only major independent spark plug producer. Champion's market share thereafter declined because Chrysler was the only major original equipment spark plug purchaser remaining in the market. The government filed a divestiture suit against Ford, arguing that Ford's acquisition of Autolite violated section 7 of the Clayton Act. Should Ford have been ordered to divest itself of Autolite?

4. In 1975, Tenneco, Inc., was the 15th largest industrial corporation in America. Tenneco's Walker Manufacturing Division produced and distributed a wide variety of automotive parts, the most important of which were exhaust system parts. Walker was the nation's leading seller of exhaust system parts in 1975 and 1976. Tenneco acquired control of Monroe Auto Equipment Company, a leading manufacturer of automotive shock absorbers. Monroe was the number two firm in the national market for replacement shock absorbers. Monroe and Gabriel, the industry leader, accounted for over 77 percent of replacement shock absorber sales in 1976. General Motors and Questor Corporation, the third and fourth largest firms, controlled another 15 percent of the market. The replacement shock absorber market exhibited significant barriers to the entry of new competitors. Economies of scale in the industry dictated manufacturing plants of substantial size. Furthermore, the nature of the industry required would-be entrants to acquire significant new technologies and marketing skills unique to the industry. The Federal Trade Commission (Commission) concluded that Tenneco's acquisition of Monroe violated section 7 of the Clayton Act by eliminating both perceived and actual potential competition in the replacement shock absorber market. The Commission therefore ordered Tenneco to divest itself of Monroe. Tenneco appealed. Was the Commission's decision correct?

5. The Federal Trade Commission filed an administrative complaint against six of the nation's title insurance companies. The complaint alleged that the title insurers engaged in horizontal price-fixing in their setting of uniform rates for title searches and title examinations. The challenged uniform ratesetting for title searches and title examinations occurred in various states through rating bureaus organized by the title insurers. These rating bureaus allegedly would set standard rates for search and examination services notwithstanding possible differences in efficiencies and costs as between individual title insurance companies. Though privately organized, these rating bureaus and the rates they set were potentially subject to oversight by the various states in which they operated. In Wisconsin and Montana, two of the states in which price-fixing was alleged to have occurred, the rating bureaus filed rates with state agencies that operated under the so-called negative option rule. This rule provided that the rates became effective unless they were rejected by the appropriate Wisconsin or Montana agency within a set time. At most the state agencies checked the rate filings for mathematical accuracy. Some rates were unchecked altogether. Reviewing the administrative law judge's decision in the administrative proceeding, the FTC commissioners concluded that price-fixing occurred and that the state action exemption argued for by the title insurers did not apply. On appeal, the Third Circuit Court of Appeals held that the state action exemption shielded the title insurers' from antitrust liability for the price-fixing that occurred in Wisconsin and Montana. Was the Third Circuit correct?

6. First Comics, Inc., wanted to enter the comic book publishing business. First hired World Color Press to print its comics because World used a less expensive method of printing than other comic book printers did. World allegedly promised to charge First the same price it charged its larger customers such as Marvel Comics Group and DC Comics. When First discovered it was being charged 4.3 cents per copy more than Marvel, First demanded reimbursement or a future credit. When World refused, First filed a price discrimination suit against World under the Robinson–Patman Act. Does the Robinson–Patman Act apply to this case?

7. Indian Coffee Company, a coffee roaster in Pittsburgh, Pennsylvania, sold its Breakfast Cheer coffee in the Pittsburgh area, where it had an 18 percent market share, and in Cleveland, Ohio, where it had a significant, but smaller, market share. Late in 1971, Folger Coffee Company, then the leading seller of branded coffee west of the Mississippi, entered the Pittsburgh market for the first time. In its effort to gain market share in Pittsburgh, Folger granted retailers high promotional allowances in the form of coupons. Retail customers could use these coupons to obtain price cuts. Redeeming retailers could use the coupons as credits against invoices from Folger. For a time, Indian tried to retain its market share by matching Folger's price concessions, but because Indian only operated in two areas, it could not subsidize such sales with profits from other areas. Indian, which finally was forced out of business in 1974, later filed a Robinson–Patman suit against Folger. At trial, Indian introduced evidence that Folger's Pittsburgh promotional allowances were far higher than its allowances in other geographic areas, and that Folger's Pittsburgh prices were below green (unroasted) coffee cost, below material and manufacturing costs, below total cost, and below marginal cost or average variable cost. Was the trial court's directed verdict in favor of Folger proper?

8. Bayer Corporation produced Bayferrox, a synthetic iron oxide pigment used to color paint, plastics, and building and concrete products. Hoover Color Corporation was one of several primary distributors of this pigment. Hoover therefore purchased Bayferrox from Bayer on a regular basis. For a number of years, Bayer had employed a volume-based incentive discount pricing system. Under this system, the price a distributor paid depended on the total amount of Bayferrox purchased by that distributor during the previous year. The quantities of Bayferrox purchased by Hoover were significantly smaller than those purchased by Hoover's competitors, Rockwood Industries and Landers-Segal Co. (Lansco). As a result, Hoover received smaller price discounts from Bayer than Rockwood and Lansco received. In 1992, for instance, Hoover received a 1 percent discount off Bayer's distributor market price for Bayferrox, whereas Lansco and Rockwood were given 6 percent and 10 percent discounts, respectively. Hoover sued Bayer on the theory that Bayer's volume-based incentive discount pricing system involved price discrimination, in violation of section 2(a) of the Robinson-Patman Act. Bayer contended that it set its prices in a good-faith attempt to meet competition in the marketplace, and that it was thus entitled to the protection of the affirmative defense set out in section 2(b) of the statute. Holding that Bayer was entitled to the protection of the "meeting competition" defense, the district court granted summary judgment in favor of Bayer. Was the district court's decision correct?

9. In 1982, a subsidiary of W. S. Kirkpatrick & Co. won a Nigerian Defense Ministry contract for the construction and equipment of an aeromedical center at a Nigerian Air Force base. Environmental Tectonics Corporation (Environmental), an unsuccessful bidder for the same contract, filed RICO and Robinson–Patman Act claims against Kirkpatrick. Environmental alleged that Kirkpatrick had won the contract by paying a 20 percent "commission" to bribe certain Nigerian officials. The parties agreed that the bribes, if paid, would violate Nigerian law. Was the

trial court correct in holding that the act of state doctrine barred Environmental's claim?

10. Pocahontas Coal Company filed suit against a number of other companies engaged in the mining and production of coal in West Virginia. Pocahontas alleged that the defendants were involved in a conspiracy to control the production and pricing of coal. One of Pocahontas's specific claims was that the defendants had violated section 8 of the Clayton Act by "deputizing" various persons to sit on the boards of competing subsidiaries. The defendants moved for summary judgment, noting that Pocahontas's complaint contained no factual allegations that any of the defendants were competitors, failed to name any of the alleged "deputies," and was ambiguous because it alleged that certain persons were "officers and/or directors" of competing companies. The trial court offered Pocahontas the opportunity to clarify the complaint by bringing forth additional information on these points. Did the court properly grant the defendants summary judgment when Pocahontas declined to do so?

11. Professional Real Estate Investors, Inc. (PRE), operated a resort hotel in Palm Springs, California. Having installed videodisc players in the hotel's rooms and assembled a library of more than 200 motion picture titles, PRE rented videodiscs to guests for in-room viewing. PRE also sought to develop a market for the sale of videodisc players to other hotels that wished to offer in-room viewing of prerecorded material. Columbia Pictures Industries, Inc., and seven other major motion picture studios (referred to collectively as "Columbia") owned the copyrights on the motion pictures that appeared on the videodiscs PRE had purchased. Columbia also licensed the transmission of copyrighted motion pictures to hotel rooms through a wired cable system called Spectradyne. PRE therefore competed with Columbia not only for the viewing market at PRE's hotel but also for the broader market for in-room entertainment services in hotels. Columbia sued PRE for copyright infringement on the basis of PRE's rental of videodiscs for viewing in hotel rooms. PRE counterclaimed, charging Columbia with violations of sections 1 and 2 of the Sherman Act. PRE alleged that Columbia's copyright action was a mere sham that cloaked underlying acts of monopolization and conspiracy to restrain trade. The district court granted summary judgment in favor of PRE on Columbia's copyright infringement claim. Columbia sought summary judgment on PRE's antitrust counterclaims. Columbia asserted that its copyright infringement claim had not been a sham and that the *Noerr–Pen-*

nington doctrine therefore protected Columbia against antitrust attack. PRE opposed Columbia's motion for summary judgment on PRE's antitrust counterclaims by arguing that Columbia's copyright infringement claim was a sham because Columbia did not honestly believe that the claim was meritorious. If Columbia did not subjectively believe that the claim was meritorious but there was probable cause to bring the claim, was Columbia's claim a sham for purposes of the sham exception to the *Noerr–Pennington* doctrine's protection against liability?

Online Research: The *Heinz* Case

If your college or university allows students access to LEXIS or Westlaw, use one of those services to locate *Federal Trade Commission v. H.J. Heinz Co.,* 246 F.3d 708 (D.C. Cir. 2001). In that case, a federal court of appeals ruled on the FTC's request for a preliminary injunction to stop a planned merger of two manufacturers of baby food. Read the court's decision and prepare a written case brief. (For suggested guidelines regarding case briefs, see the Appendix to Chapter 1.)

51

EMPLOYMENT LAW

Westlawn Pediatric Center advertised a job opening for a pediatric nurse practitioner. Richard and Valerie, both of whom are licensed pediatric nurse practitioners and both of whom met the published qualifications for the job, applied for the position. Westlawn hired Valerie over Richard because "women are more nurturing." No verbal agreement was made between Westlawn and Valerie about the duration of her employment. Valerie performs well at her new job and receives glowing performance reviews.

- If Valerie is injured on the job, under what circumstances must Westlawn compensate her?
- What legal regulations must Westlawn meet with regard to workplace conditions, wages, and benefits?
- What criteria are permissible for employers to use in making hiring, firing, and promotion decisions? Was it legal for Westlawn to refuse to hire Richard on the basis of a stereotype?
- Does the fact that Valerie is doing a good job mean that she cannot legally be fired?
- Under what circumstances would Westlawn have the right to monitor Valerie's communications or require a search or drug test?

YEARS AGO, IT WAS unusual to see a separate employment law chapter in a business law text. At that time, the rights, duties, and liabilities accompanying employment usually were determined by basic legal institutions such as contract, tort, and agency. Today, these common law principles still control employer–employee relations unless displaced by government regulations or by new judge-made rules applying specifically to employment. By now, however, such rules and regulations are so numerous that they touch almost every facet of employment. This chapter discusses the most important of these modern legal controls on the employer–employee relation.

Modern American employment law is so vast and complex a subject that texts designed for lawyers seldom address it in its entirety. Indeed, specialized subjects like labor law and employment discrimination often get book-length treatment in their own right. This chapter's overview of employment law emphasizes three topics that have attracted much recent attention—employment discrimination, employee privacy, and common law claims for wrongful discharge. But no discussion of employment law is complete without outlining certain basic regulations that significantly affect the conditions of employment for most Americans. Figure 1 notes these regulations and briefly states the functions they perform.

Figure 1   *The Ends and Means of Modern Employment Law*

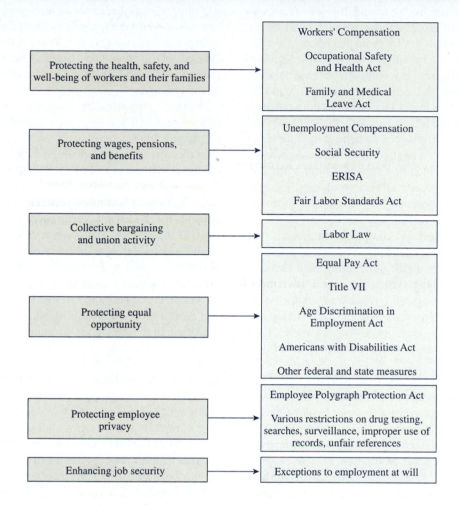

Legislation Protecting Employee Health, Safety, and Well-Being

Workers' Compensation

Nineteenth-century law made it difficult for employees to recover when they sued their employer in negligence for on-the-job injuries.[1] At that time, employers had an

---

[1]Chapter 7 discusses negligence law and most of the negligence defenses noted below.

implied assumption of risk defense under which an employee assumed all the normal and customary risks of his employment simply by taking the job. If an employee's own carelessness played some role in his injury, employers often could avoid negligence liability under the traditional rule that even a slight degree of contributory negligence is a complete defense. Another employer defense, the fellow-servant rule, said that where an employee's injury resulted from the negligence of a coemployee (or fellow servant), the employer was not liable. Finally, employees sometimes had problems proving the employer's negligence. State workers' compensation statutes, which first appeared early in the 20th century, were a response to all these problems. Today all 50 states have such systems.[2]

Basic Features Workers' compensation protects only employees, and not independent contractors.[3] However, many states exempt casual, agricultural, and domestic employees, among others. State and local government employees may be covered by workers' compensation or by some alternative state system. Also, states usually exempt certain employers—for example, firms employing fewer than a stated number of employees (often three).

Where they apply, however, all workers' compensation systems share certain basic features. They allow injured employees to recover under *strict liability*, thus removing any need to prove employer negligence. They also eliminate the employer's three traditional defenses: contributory negligence, assumption of risk, and the fellow-servant rule. In addition, they make workers' compensation an employee's *exclusive remedy* against her employer for covered injuries. There are some exceptions to the exclusivity of worker's compensation, however. In cases in which an employer *intentionally* injures an employee, the injured employee can usually sue the employer outside of worker's compensation. In some states, this intentional injury exception has expanded beyond intentional torts to situations in which the employer did something or maintained a condition in the workplace that the employer knew was substantially certain to harm the employee. An example of this approach would be holding an employer responsible outside of worker's

compensation when the employer knew that an employee was being sexually harassed but did nothing about it. In addition, in a number of states, an employee can sue outside of worker's compensation when the employer was acting in a *dual capacity* in relation to the employee. An example of this would be a case in which an employee is injured on the job by a defect in a product manufactured by the employer.

Workers' compensation basically is a social compromise. Because it involves strict liability and eliminates the three traditional employer defenses, workers' compensation greatly increases the probability that an injured employee will recover. Such recoveries usually include: (1) hospital and medical expenses (including vocational rehabilitation), (2) disability benefits, (3) specified recoveries for the loss of certain body parts, and (4) death benefits to survivors and/or dependents. But the amount recoverable under each category of damages frequently is less than would be obtained in a negligence suit. Thus, injured employees sometimes deny that they are covered by workers' compensation so that they can pursue a tort suit against their employer instead.

Although workers' compensation is usually an injured employee's sole remedy against her employer, she may be able to sue other parties whose behavior helped cause her injury. One example is a product liability suit against a manufacturer who supplies an employer with defective machinery or raw materials that cause an on-the-job injury. However, many states immunize coemployees from ordinary tort liability for injuries they inflict on other employees. Complicated questions of contribution, indemnity, and subrogation can arise where an injured employee is able to recover against both an employer and a third party.

The Work-Related Injury Requirement Another basic feature of workers' compensation is that employees recover only for *work-related* injuries. To be work-related, the injury must: (1) arise out of the employment, and (2) happen in the course of the employment. These tests have been variously interpreted.

The arising-out-of-the-employment test usually requires a sufficiently close relationship between the injury and the *nature* of the employment. Different states use different tests to define this relationship. Examples include:

1. *Increased risk.* Here, the employee recovers only if the nature of her job increases her risk of injury above the risk to which the general public is exposed. Under this test, a factory worker assaulted by a trespasser probably

---

[2]In addition, various federal statutes regulate on-the-job injuries suffered by employees of the federal government and other employees such as railroad workers, seamen, longshoremen, and harbor workers.

[3]Chapter 34 defines the terms *employee* and *independent contractor.*

would not recover, while a security guard assaulted by the same trespasser probably would.

2. *Positional risk.* Under this more liberal test, an injured employee recovers if her employment caused her to be at the place and time where her injury occurred. Here, the factory worker probably would recover The *Dulen* case on the next page seems to adopt this test.

The in-the-course-of-the-employment requirement inquires whether the injury occurred within the *time, place,* and *circumstances* of the employment. Employees injured off the employer's premises generally are outside the course of the employment. For example, injuries suffered while traveling to or from work usually are not compensable. But an employee may be covered where the off-the-premises injury occurred while she was performing employment-related duties such as going on a business trip or running an employment-related errand.

Other work-related injury problems on which courts have disagreed include mental injuries allegedly arising from the employment and injuries resulting from employee horseplay. Virtually all states, however, regard intentionally self-inflicted injuries as outside workers' compensation. Recovery for occupational diseases, on the other hand, usually is allowed today. An employee whose preexisting diseased condition is aggravated by her employment sometimes recovers as well.

Administration and Funding   Workers' compensation systems usually are administered by a state agency that adjudicates workers' claims and administers the system. Its decisions on such claims normally are appealable to the state courts. The states fund workers' compensation by compelling covered employers to: (1) purchase private insurance, (2) self-insure (e.g., by maintaining a contingency fund), or (3) make payments into a state insurance fund. Because employers generally pass on the costs of insurance to their customers, workers' compensation tends to spread the economic risk of workplace injuries throughout society.

Darco Transportation v. Dulen   *922 P.2d 591 (Okla. Sup. Ct. 1996)*

Elmer Dulen was injured and his codriver Polly Freeman was killed when a tractor-trailer rig driven by Dulen entered a railroad crossing and was struck by an oncoming train. Both Dulen and Freeman had been hired by Darco Transportation to transport goods cross-country to San Francisco. On the night of the accident, Dulen stopped his rig behind another truck when the signal arms at a railroad crossing lowered. The arms malfunctioned and came up before an oncoming train reached the intersection. The first truck proceeded across the tracks and Dulen followed. While the first truck avoided being hit, Dulen's rig was rammed by the train. The protective arms did not relower until Dulen's semi was on the tracks.

At the scene of the collision a female traffic investigator noticed that Freeman was clad only in a T-shirt. She also observed that Dulen's pants were unbuttoned, unzipped and resting at mid-hip. After Dulen was admitted to the hospital, the investigator questioned Dulen about how the accident had happened. Dulen said, "I was f—ing her and now, oh, my God, I have killed her." According to the investigator, Dulen also told her that when the accident occurred, Freeman was sitting in his lap facing him. However, in later testimony Dulen explained that by his statement at the hospital he meant that he had been living in an intimate relationship with Freeman for five months before the accident and felt responsible for her death because she was driving with him. He also denied telling the officer that Freeman was sitting in his lap and that they were having sex when the accident occurred. Other evidence revealed that there was not enough room between the steering wheel and the seat for two people of Dulen's and Freeman's size physically to fit into that space together.

Dulen sought workers' compensation benefits for what he maintained were on-the-job injuries. After various Oklahoma courts ruled in Dulen's favor, Darco appealed to the Supreme Court of Oklahoma.

Opala, Judge   When examining the compensation tribunal's factual resolutions, this court applies the any-competent-evidence standard. The trial judge's findings may not be disturbed on review if supported by competent proof.

Oklahoma's jurisprudence has long recognized that a compensable work-related injury must both: (1) occur in the course of, and (2) arise out of the worker's employment.

These two distinct elements are not to be understood as synonymous. The term "in the course of employment" relates to the time, place, or circumstances under which the injury is sustained. The term "arise out of employment" contemplates the causal connection between the injury and the risks incident to employment. We must be mindful that in this case we are applying workers' compensation law.

The concept of a worker's contributory fault, which the compensation statute discarded, must not be resurrected obliquely as a defense against the employer's liability.

The Workers' Compensation Court was faced with the task of determining if Dulen, when injured, was performing work in furtherance of his master's business—i.e., whether he was then "in the course of employment." If the trial tribunal tended to believe that Dulen and Freeman were having sex at the critical time, the question to be decided was whether the claimant's conduct is to be deemed horseplay—a complete departure from or abandonment of his employment. This issue concerns itself solely with the "course of employment" bounds—not with the risk incident to employment, i.e., the "arising out of" element.

Assuming as a fact that when the collision occurred, Dulen was having sex while also driving the rig, the trial judge could still find that this servant's acts constituted no more than a careless, negligent, or forbidden genre of performance, but did not amount to pure frolic which was tantamount to total abandonment of the master's business. On this record, such a finding would not be legally or factually incorrect. The record contains ample evidence reasonably supporting the notion that Dulen's injury was work-related, and occurred while he was en route to his assigned destination. Above all, uncontroverted is the stubborn fact that Dulen, when injured, occupied his assigned work station—the driver's seat behind the steering wheel of Darco's truck. The record offers no proof that Dulen had deviated from or abandoned his master's mission, transporting goods to San Francisco.

An injury is compensable if it arises out of the claimant's employment—i.e., was caused by a risk to which the employee was subjected by his work. Any other notion would impermissibly interject into this State's compensation regime concepts of common-law cause and foreseeability: the legal underpinnings of negligence. The only criterion for compensability is the statute's test of a connection-in-fact to the employment. The record is devoid of any proof that the protective arms were in good working order. The trial tribunal found the equipment's failure was the direct cause of the claimant's injuries. At the time of Dulen's injuries, he was employed as a Darco truck driver with an assigned task—transporting goods to the West Coast. This required his presence on the highways. A causal connection between the act in which Dulen was engaged, when injured, and his job description is clear. Because the perils of this servant's travel for his master are co-extensive with the risks of employment, Dulen's injuries undeniably arose out of his work.

Two insuperable hurdles absolutely militate against overturning the trial tribunal's findings and exonerating the employer as a matter of law. Assuming Dulen and Freeman were engaged in sexual intercourse, (1) there is undisputed proof that, when the collision occurred, Dulen remained at the steering wheel and hence cannot be deemed to have then "abandoned" his assigned work station; and (2) there is competent evidence to support the trial judge's finding which ascribes the accident's cause, not to copulation-related inattention, but to defective railroad-crossing warning equipment.

Trial court order sustained; Dulen recovers.

The Occupational Safety and Health Act

Although it may stimulate employers to remedy hazardous working conditions, workers' compensation does not directly forbid such conditions. The most important measure directly regulating workplace safety is the federal Occupational Safety and Health Act of 1970. The Occupational Safety and Health Act imposes a duty on employers to provide their employees with a workplace and jobs free from recognized hazards that may cause death or serious physical harm. Employers are required to comply with many detailed regulations promulgated by the Occupational Safety and Health Administration (OSHA). One of these regulations, for example, requires employers to inform employees who could be exposed to hazardous chemicals in the workplace about the

chemicals and to provide employees with training so that they can effectively protect themselves from harm. The Act also requires employers to report to the Secretary of Labor any on-the-job injuries that require hospitalization. Because information about workplace dangers provided by employees themselves is important to the effectiveness of the Act, employees who provide such information are protected from retaliation.

The Occupational Safety and Health Act applies to all employers engaged in a business affecting interstate commerce. Exempted, however, are the U.S. government, the states and their political subdivisions, and certain industries regulated by other federal safety legislation. The Occupational Safety and Health Act mainly is administered by the Occupational Safety and Health Administration (OSHA) of the Labor Department. It does not preempt state workplace safety regulation, but OSHA must approve any state regulatory plan.

OSHA can inspect places of employment for violations of the act and its regulations. If an employer is found to violate the act's general duty provision or any specific standard, OSHA issues a written citation.

The main sanctions for violations of the act and the regulations are various civil penalties. In addition, any employer who commits a willful violation resulting in death to an employee may suffer a fine, imprisonment, or both. Also, the secretary of labor may seek injunctive relief when an employment hazard presents an imminent danger of death or physical harm that cannot be promptly eliminated by normal citation procedures.

The Family and Medical Leave Act

After concluding that proper child-raising, family stability, and job security require that employees get reasonable work leave for family and medical reasons, Congress passed the Family and Medical Leave Act (FMLA) in 1993. In general, the act covers those employed for at least 12 months, and for 1,250 hours during those 12 months, by an employer employing 50 or more employees. Covered employers include federal, state, and local government agencies.

Under the FMLA, covered employees are entitled to a total of 12 workweeks of leave during any 12-month period for one or more of the following reasons: (1) the birth of a child and the need to care for that child; (2) the adoption of a child; (3) the need to care for a spouse, child, or parent with a serious health condition; and (4) the employee's own serious health condition. Usually, the leave is without pay. Upon the employee's return from leave, the employer ordinarily must put her in the same or an equivalent position and must not deny her any benefits accrued before the leave began.

Employers who deny any of an employee's FMLA rights are civilly liable to the affected employee for resulting lost wages or, if no wages were lost, for any other resulting monetary losses not exceeding 12 weeks' wages. Employees may also recover an additional equal amount as liquidated damages, unless the employer acted in good faith and had reasonable grounds for believing that it was not violating the act. Like the FLSA, the FMLA permits civil actions by the secretary of labor, with any sums recovered distributed to affected employees. In such actions, employees may also obtain equitable relief, including reinstatement and promotion.

Legislation Protecting Wages, Pensions, and Benefits

Social Security

Today, the law requires that employers help ensure their employees' financial security after the employment ends. One example is the federal social security system. Social security mainly is financed by the Federal Insurance Contributions Act (FICA). FICA imposes a flat percentage tax on all employee income below a certain base figure and requires employers to pay a matching amount. Self-employed people pay a different rate on a different wage base. FICA revenues finance various forms of financial assistance besides the old-age benefits that people usually call social security. These include survivors' benefits to family members of deceased workers, disability benefits, and medical and hospitalization benefits for the elderly (the medicare system).

Unemployment Compensation

Another way that the law protects employees after their employment ends is by providing unemployment compensation for discharged workers. Since 1935, federal law has authorized joint federal–state efforts in this area. Today, each state administers its own unemployment compensation system under federal guidelines. The system's costs are met by subjecting employers to federal and state unemployment compensation taxes.

Unemployment insurance plans vary from state to state but usually share certain features. States often condition the receipt of benefits on the recipient's having worked for a covered employer for a specified time period, and/or having earned a certain minimum income over such a period. Generally, those who voluntarily quit work without good cause, are fired for bad conduct, fail to actively seek suitable new work, or refuse such work are ineligible for benefits. Benefit levels vary from state to state, as do the time periods during which benefits can be received.

ERISA

Many employers voluntarily contribute to their employees' postemployment income by maintaining pension plans. For years, pension plan abuses such as arbitrary termination of participation in the plan, arbitrary benefit reduction, and mismanagement of fund assets were not uncommon. The Employee Retirement Income Security Act of 1974 (ERISA) was a response to these problems. ERISA does not require employers to establish or fund pension plans and does not set benefit levels. Instead, it tries to check abuses and to protect employees' expectations that promised pension benefits will be paid.

ERISA imposes *fiduciary duties* on pension fund managers. For example, it requires that managers diversify the plan's investments to minimize the risk of large losses, unless this is clearly imprudent. ERISA also imposes *record-keeping, reporting,* and *disclosure* requirements. For instance, it requires that covered plans provide annual reports to their participants and specifies the contents of those reports. In addition, the act has a provision *guaranteeing employee participation* in the plan. For example, certain employees who complete one year of service with an employer cannot be denied plan participation. Furthermore, ERISA contains *funding* requirements for protecting plan participants against loss of pension income. Finally, ERISA contains complex *vesting* requirements that determine when an employee's right to receive pension benefits becomes nonforfeitable. These requirements help prevent employers from using a late vesting date to avoid pension obligations to employees who change jobs or are fired before that date. ERISA's remedies include civil suits by plan participants and beneficiaries, equitable relief, and criminal penalties.

The Fair Labor Standards Act

Although federal labor law regulates several aspects of labor–management relations, it still permits many terms of employment to be determined by private bargaining. Nonetheless, sometimes the law directly regulates such key terms of employment as wages and hours worked. The most important example is the Fair Labor Standards Act (FLSA) of 1938.

The FLSA regulates *wages and hours* by entitling covered employees to: (1) a specified minimum wage whose amount changes over time, and (2) a time-and-a-half rate for work exceeding 40 hours per week. The FLSA's complicated coverage provisions basically enable its wages-and-hours standards to reach most significantly sized businesses that are engaged in interstate commerce or produce goods for such commerce. Also covered are the federal, state, and local governments. The many exemptions from the FLSA's wages-and-hours provisions include executive, administrative, and professional personnel.

The FLSA also forbids oppressive *child labor* by any employer engaged in interstate commerce or in the production of goods for such commerce, and also forbids the interstate shipment of goods produced in an establishment where oppressive child labor occurs. Oppressive child labor includes: (1) most employment of children below the age of 14; (2) employment of children aged 14–15, unless they work in an occupation specifically approved by the Department of Labor; and (3) employment of children aged 16–17 who work in occupations declared particularly hazardous by the Labor Department.

Both affected employees and the Labor Department can recover any unpaid minimum wages or overtime, plus an additional equal amount as liquidated damages, from an employer that has violated the FLSA's wages-and-hours provisions. A suit by the Labor Department terminates an employee's right to sue, but the department pays the amounts it recovers to the employee. Violations of the act's child labor provisions may result in civil penalties. Other FLSA remedies include injunctive relief and criminal liability for willful violations.

Collective Bargaining and Union Activity

Entire legal treatises are devoted to the topic of collective bargaining by unions. What follows is only a brief historical outline of the subject. Early in the 19th century, some courts treated labor unions as illegal criminal conspiracies. After this restriction disappeared around mid-century, organized labor began its lengthy—and sometimes violent—rise to power. During the late 19th and early 20th centuries, unions' growing influence and wage earners' increasing presence in the electorate spurred the passage of many laws benefiting labor. These included statutes outlawing "yellow dog" contracts (under which employees agreed not to join or remain a union member), minimum wage and maximum hours legislation, laws regulating the employment of women and children, factory safety measures, and workers' compensation. But during this period, some say, the courts tended to represent business interests. Perhaps for this reason, some pro-labor measures were struck down on constitutional grounds. Also, some courts were quick to issue temporary and permanent injunctions to restrain union picketing and boycotts and help quell strikes.

Organized labor's political power continued to grow during the first part of the 20th century. In 1926, Congress passed the Railway Labor Act, which regulates labor relations in the railroad industry, and which later included airlines. This was followed by the Norris-LaGuardia Act of 1932, which limited the circumstances in which federal courts could enjoin strikes and picketing in labor disputes, and also prohibited federal court enforcement of yellow-dog contracts.

The most important 20th-century American labor statute, however, was the National Labor Relations Act of 1935 (the NLRA or Wagner Act). The NLRA gave employees the *right to organize* by enabling them to form, join, and assist labor organizations. It also allowed them to *bargain collectively* through their own representatives. In addition, the Wagner Act prohibited certain *unfair labor practices* that were believed to discourage collective bargaining. These practices include: (1) interfering with employees' rights to form, join, and assist labor unions; (2) dominating or interfering with the formation or administration of a labor union, or giving a union financial or other support; (3) discriminating against employees in hiring, tenure, or any term of employment due to their union membership; (4) discriminating against employees because they have filed charges or given testimony under the NLRA; and (5) refusing to bargain collectively with any duly designated employee representative. The NLRA also established the National Labor Relations Board (NLRB). The NLRB's main functions are: (1) handling representation cases (which involve the process by which a union becomes the certified employee representative within a bargaining unit), and (2) deciding whether challenged employer or union activity is an unfair labor practice.

In 1947, Congress amended the NLRA by passing the Labor Management Relations Act (LMRA or Taft-Hartley Act). The act declared that certain acts by *unions* are unfair labor practices. These include: (1) restraining or coercing employees in the exercise of their guaranteed bargaining rights (e.g., their right to refrain from joining a union); (2) causing an employer to discriminate against an employee who is not a union member; (3) refusing to bargain collectively with an employer; (4) conducting a secondary strike or a secondary boycott for a specified illegal purpose;[4] (5) requiring employees covered by union-shop contracts to pay excessive or discriminatory initiation fees or dues; and (6) featherbedding (forcing an employer to pay for work not actually performed). The LMRA also established an 80-day cooling-off period for

strikes that the president finds likely to endanger national safety or health. In addition, it created a Federal Mediation and Conciliation Service to assist employers and unions in settling labor disputes.

Congressional investigations during the 1950s uncovered corruption in internal union affairs and also revealed that the internal procedures of many unions were undemocratic. In response, Congress enacted the Labor Management Reporting and Disclosure Act (or Landrum-Griffin Act) in 1959. The act established a "bill of rights" for union members and attempted to make internal union affairs more democratic. It also amended the NLRA by adding to the LMRA's list of unfair union labor practices. The proportion of U.S. workers who are members of labor unions has decreased fairly steadily over he past 40 years. Today, less than 13 percent of the workforce are members of labor unions.

Equal Opportunity Legislation

The Equal Pay Act

The Equal Pay Act (EPA), which forbids *sex* discrimination regarding *pay,* was a 1963 amendment to the FLSA. Its coverage resembles the coverage of the FLSA's minimum wage provisions. Unlike the FLSA, however, the EPA covers executive, administrative, and professional employees.

The typical EPA case involves a woman who claims that she has received lower pay than a male employee performing substantially equal work for the same employer. The substantially-equal-work requirement is met if the plaintiff's job and the higher-paid male employee's job involve *each* of the following: (1) equal effort, (2) equal skill, (3) equal responsibility, and (4) similar working conditions.

Effort basically means physical or mental exertion. *Skill* refers to the experience, training, education, and ability required for the positions being compared. Here, the question is not whether the employees being compared have equal skills but whether their jobs require or utilize substantially the same skills. *Responsibility* (or accountability) involves such factors as the degree of supervision each job requires and the importance of each job to the employer. For instance, a retail sales position in which an employee may not approve customer checks probably is not equal to a sales position in which an employee has

---

[4]These are strikes or boycotts aimed at a third party with which the union has no real dispute. Their purpose is to coerce that party not to deal with an employer with which the union does have a dispute, and thus to gain some leverage over the employer.

this authority. *Working conditions* refers to such factors as temperature, weather, fumes, ventilation, toxic conditions, and risk of injury. These need only be *similar,* not equal.

If the two jobs are substantially equal and they are paid unequally, an employer must prove one of the EPA's four defenses or it will lose the case. The employer has a defense if it shows that the pay disparity is based on: (1) seniority, (2) merit, (3) quality or quantity of production (e.g., a piecework system), or (4) any factor other than sex. The first three defenses require an employer to show some organized, systematic, structured, and communicated rating system with predetermined criteria that apply equally to employees of each sex. The any-factor-other-than-sex defense is a catchall category that includes shift differentials, bonuses paid because the job is part of a training program, and differences in the profitability of the products or services on which employees work.

The EPA's remedial scheme resembles the FLSA's scheme. Under the EPA, however, employee suits are for the amount of back pay lost because of an employer's discrimination, not for unpaid minimum wages or overtime. An employee may also recover an equal sum as liquidated damages. The EPA is enforced by the Equal Employment Opportunity Commission (EEOC) rather than the Labor Department.[5] Unlike some of the employment discrimination statutes described later, however, the EPA does not require that private plaintiffs submit their complaints to the EEOC or a state agency before mounting suit.

Title VII

Employment discrimination might be defined as employer behavior that penalizes certain individuals because of personal traits that they cannot control and that bear no relation to effective job performance. Of the many employment discrimination laws in force today, the most important is Title VII of the 1964 Civil Rights Act. Unlike the Equal Pay Act, which merely forbids sex

discrimination regarding pay, Title VII is a wide-ranging employment discrimination provision. It prohibits discrimination based on *race, color, religion, sex,* and *national origin* in hiring, firing, job assignments, pay, access to training and apprenticeship programs, and most other employment decisions.

Basic Features of Title VII

In discussing Title VII, we first examine some general rules that govern all the kinds of discrimination it forbids. Then we examine each forbidden basis of discrimination in detail.

Covered Entities Title VII covers all employers employing 15 or more employees and engaging in an industry affecting interstate commerce. Employers include individuals, partnerships, corporations, colleges and universities, labor unions and employment agencies (with respect to their own employees), and state and local governments.[6] Also, *referrals* by employment agencies are covered no matter what the size of the agency, if an employer serviced by the agency has 15 or more employees. In addition, Title VII covers certain unions—mainly those with 15 or more members—in their capacity as *employee representative.*

Procedures Although the EEOC sometimes sues to enforce Title VII, the usual Title VII suit is a private claim. The complicated procedures governing private Title VII suits are beyond the scope of this text, but a few points should be kept in mind. Private parties with a Title VII claim have no automatic right to sue. Instead, they first must file a *charge* with the EEOC, or with a state agency in states having suitable fair employment laws and enforcement schemes. This allows the EEOC or the state agency to investigate the claim, attempt conciliation if the claim has substance, or sue the employer itself. If a plaintiff files with a state agency and the state fails to act, the plaintiff still can file a charge with the EEOC. Even if the EEOC fails to act on the claim, a plaintiff still may mount her own suit. Here, the EEOC issues a "right-to-sue letter" enabling the plaintiff to sue.

Proving Discrimination The permissible methods for proving a Title VII violation are critical to its effec-

---

[5]The EEOC is an independent federal agency with a sizable staff and many regional offices. Its functions include: (1) enforcing most of the employment discrimination laws discussed in this chapter through lawsuits that it initiates or in which it intervenes, (2) conciliating employment discrimination charges (e.g., by encouraging their negotiated settlement), (3) investigating discrimination-related matters, and (4) interpreting the statutes it enforces through regulations and guidelines.

[6]Employment discrimination within the federal government is beyond the scope of this text.

tiveness against employment discrimination. Proof of discrimination is easy in cases, such as the *Johnson Controls* decision later in the chapter, where the employer had an **express policy** disfavoring one of Title VII's protected classes. **Direct evidence** of a discriminatory motive such as testimony or written evidence obviously is useful to plaintiffs as well. However, because employers can discriminate without leaving such obvious tracks, the courts have devised other methods of proving a Title VII violation. As of late 1999, two such methods predominated. Because each method's many details are beyond the scope of this text, we merely outline them here.

Title VII **disparate treatment** suits involve situations in which an employer has treated an individual differently because of the person's race, sex, color, religion, or national origin. In such suits, the plaintiff first must show a *prima facie case:* a case strong enough to create a presumption of discrimination and to require a counterargument from the defendant. The proof needed for a prima facie case varies with the nature of the challenged employment decision (e.g., hiring or promotion), but ordinarily it gives plaintiffs few difficulties. Once the plaintiff establishes a prima facie case, the employer must produce evidence that the challenged employment decision was taken for *legitimate, nondiscriminatory reasons* or it will lose the lawsuit. To establish a prima facie case in a hiring situation, for example, the plaintiff must prove that she applied for the job and was qualified for it, that she is a member of a protected class, that she was rejected, and that the employer continued to attempt to fill the job. At that point, the employer might produce evidence that it rejected the plaintiff because she did not meet its hiring criteria or was not the best qualified applicant. If the employer produces satisfactory reasons, the plaintiff then must *show that discrimination actually occurred.* She might do so by showing that the employer's alleged nondiscriminatory reasons were a *pretext* for a decision that really involved discrimination. For example, she might show that the employer's alleged hiring criteria were not applied to similarly situated male job applicants.

Title VII's **disparate impact** (or adverse impact) method is most often used when the alleged discrimination affects many employees. Here, the plaintiffs ordinarily maintain that the employer uses a particular employment practice that causes a *disparate impact* on the basis of race, color, religion, sex, or national origin. Often, the practice is an employer rule that is neutral on its face but has a disproportionate adverse effect on one of Title VII's protected groups—for example, a height, weight, or high school diploma requirement for hiring, or a written test for hiring or promotion. If the plaintiffs show a disparate impact, the employer loses unless it demonstrates that the challenged practice is *job-related for the position in question and consistent with business necessity.* For example, the employer might show that its promotion test really predicts effective job performance, and that effective performance in the relevant job is necessary for its operations. Even if the employer makes this demonstration, the plaintiffs have another option: to show that the employer's legitimate business needs can be advanced by an *alternative employment practice* that is *less discriminatory than the challenged practice.* For example, the plaintiffs might show that the employer's legitimate needs can be met by a different promotion test that has less adverse impact on the protected group. If the employer refuses to adopt this practice, the plaintiffs win.

Defenses   Even if a plaintiff proves a Title VII violation, the employer still prevails if it can establish one of Title VII's defenses. The most important such defenses are:

1. *Seniority.* Title VII is not violated if the employer treats employees differently pursuant to a *bona fide seniority system.* To be bona fide, such a system at least must treat all employees equally on its face, not have been created for discriminatory reasons, and not operate in a discriminatory fashion.

2. *The various "merit" defenses.* An employer also escapes Title VII liability if it acts pursuant to: a *bona fide merit system,* a system basing earnings on *quantity or quality of production,* or the results of a *professionally developed ability test.* Presumably, such systems and tests at least must meet the general standards for seniority systems stated above. Also, the EEOC has promulgated lengthy *Uniform Guidelines on Employee Selection Procedures* that speak to these and other matters.

3. *The BFOQ Defense.* Finally, Title VII allows employers to discriminate on the bases of sex, religion, or national origin where one of those traits is a *bona fide occupational qualification (BFOQ) that is reasonably necessary to the business in question.* The BFOQ defense is applied to cases of disparate treatment, whereas the business necessity defense, which was discussed earlier, applies in disparate impact cases. The BFOQ defense does not protect race or color discrimination. As the following *Johnson Controls* case makes clear, moreover, the defense is a narrow one even where it applies. Generally, it is available only where a certain gender, religion, or national origin is necessary for effective job performance. For example, a BFOQ probably would exist where a female is employed to model women's clothing or to fit women's undergarments. But the BFOQ defense usually is unavailable where the discrimination is based on stereotypes (e.g., that women are less aggressive than men) or on the preferences of co-workers or customers (e.g., the preference of airline travelers for female rather than male flight attendants). As *Johnson Controls* suggests, the defense also is unavailable where the employer's discriminatory practice promotes goals, such as fetal protection, that do not concern effective job performance.

Remedies   Various remedies are possible once private plaintiffs or the EEOC wins a Title VII suit. If intentional discrimination has caused lost wages, employees can obtain **back pay** accruing from a date two years before the filing of the charge. At the court's discretion, successful private plaintiffs also may recover reasonable **attorney's fees.** In addition, victims of intentional discrimination can recover **compensatory damages** for harms such as emotional distress, sickness, loss of reputation, or denial of credit. Victims of intentional discrimination also can recover **punitive damages** where the defendant discriminated with malice or with reckless indifference to the plaintiff's rights. However, the sum of the plaintiff's compensatory and punitive dam-

---

Auto Workers v. Johnson Controls, Inc.   *499 U.S. 187 (U.S. Sup. Ct. 1991)*

Johnson Controls, Inc., manufactures batteries. Lead is a primary ingredient in that manufacturing process. A female employee's occupational exposure to lead involves a risk of harm to any fetus she carries. For this reason, Johnson Controls excluded women who are pregnant or who are capable of bearing children from jobs that involve exposure to lead. Numerous plaintiffs, including a woman who had chosen to be sterilized to avoid losing her job, entered a federal district court class action alleging that Johnson Controls' policy constituted illegal sex discrimination under Title VII. The district court entered a summary judgment for Johnson Controls and the court of appeals affirmed. The plaintiffs appealed to the U.S. Supreme Court.

Blackmun, Justice   Johnson Controls' fetal-protection policy explicitly discriminates against women on the basis of their sex. The policy excludes women with childbearing capacity from lead-exposed jobs and so creates a facial classification based on gender. [But] an employer may discriminate on the basis of "religion, sex, or national origin in those certain instances where religion, sex, or national origin is a bona fide occupational qualification reasonably necessary to the normal operation of that particular business or enterprise." The BFOQ defense is written narrowly, and this Court has read it narrowly.

Johnson Controls argues that its fetal-protection policy falls within the so-called safety exception [of] the BFOQ. Discrimination on the basis of sex because of safety concerns is allowed only in narrow circumstances. In *Dothard v. Rawlinson* (1977), we allowed the employer to hire only male guards in contact areas of maximum-security male penitentiaries only because more was at stake than the individual woman's decision to weigh and accept the risks of employment. We found sex to be a BFOQ inasmuch as the employment of a female guard would create real risks of safety to others if [rape-related] violence broke out because the guard was a woman. Sex discrimination was tolerated

because sex was related to the guard's ability to do the job—maintaining prison security. Similarly, some courts have approved airlines' layoffs of pregnant flight attendants on the ground that the employer's policy was necessary to ensure the safety of passengers. In two of these cases, the courts pointedly indicated that fetal, as opposed to passenger, safety was best left to the mother.

Therefore, the safety exception is limited to instances in which sex or pregnancy actually interferes with the employee's ability to perform the job . . . [Thus,] Johnson Controls cannot establish a BFOQ. Fertile women, as far as appears in the record, manufacture batteries as efficiently as anyone else. Johnson Controls' professed moral and ethical concerns about the next generation do not suffice to establish a BFOQ of female sterility. Decisions about the welfare of future children must be left to the parents who conceive, bear, support, and raise them rather than to the employers who hire those parents.

Judgment in favor of Johnson Controls reversed; case returned to the lower courts for further proceedings consistent with the Supreme Court's opinion.

ages cannot exceed certain amounts that vary with the size of the employer. For example, they cannot total more than $300,000 for an employer with more than 500 employees.

Discrimination may also entitle successful plaintiffs to **equitable relief.** Examples include orders compelling hiring, reinstatement, or retroactive seniority. On occasion, moreover, the courts have ordered quotalike preferences in Title VII cases involving race and (occasionally) gender discrimination. For example, a court might order that whites and minorities be hired on a 50–50 basis until minority representation in the employer's work force reaches some specified percentage. Generally speaking, such orders are permissible if: (1) an employer has engaged in severe, widespread, or longstanding discrimination; (2) the order does not unduly restrict the employment interests of white people; and (3) it does not force an employer to hire unqualified workers. Minority preferences also may appear in the **consent decrees** courts issue when approving the terms on which the parties have settled a Title VII case.[7]

Race or Color Discrimination

At this point, we consider each of Title VII's prohibited bases of discrimination in more detail. *Race or color* discrimination includes discrimination against blacks, other racial minorities, Eskimos, and American Indians, among others. Title VII also prohibits racial discrimination against whites. Nonetheless, voluntary racial preferences that favor minorities who are qualified for the job in question survive a Title VII attack if they: (1) are intended to correct a racial imbalance involving underrepresentation of minorities in traditionally segregated job categories, (2) do not "unnecessarily trammel" the rights of white employees or create an absolute bar to their advancement, and (3) are only temporary.[8] Note that here our concern is not the use of minority preferences as a *remedy* for a Title VII violation, but whether such preferences *themselves* violate Title VII when voluntarily established by an employer.

National Origin Discrimination

National origin discrimination includes discrimination based on: (1) the country of one's or one's ancestors' origin; or (2) one's possession of physical, cultural, or linguistic characteristics identified with people of a particular nation. Thus, plaintiffs in national origin discrimination cases need not have been born in the country at issue. In fact, if the discrimination is based on physical, cultural, or linguistic traits identified with a particular nation, even the plaintiff's ancestors need not have been born there. Thus, a person of pure French ancestry may have a Title VII case if she suffers discrimination because she looks like, acts like, or talks like a German.

Certain formally neutral employment practices can also constitute national origin discrimination. Employers who hire only U.S. citizens may violate Title VII if their policy has the purpose or effect of discriminating against one or more national origin groups. This could happen where the employer is located in an area where aliens of a particular nationality are heavily concentrated. Also, employment criteria such as height, weight, and fluency in English may violate Title VII if they have a disparate impact on a national origin group and are not job-related.

Religious Discrimination

For Title VII purposes, the term *religion* is broadly defined. Although all courts may not agree, the EEOC says that it includes any set of moral beliefs that are sincerely held with the same strength as traditional religious views. In fact, Title VII forbids religious discrimination against atheists. It also forbids discrimination based on religious *observances or practices*—for example, grooming, clothing, or the refusal to work on the Sabbath. But such discrimination is permissible if an employer cannot reasonably accommodate the religious practice without suffering undue hardship. Undue hardship exists when the accommodation imposes more than a minimal burden on an employer.

Sex Discrimination

Title VII's ban on sex discrimination aims at *gender-based* discrimination and does not forbid discrimination on the basis of homosexuality or transsexuality.[9] Just as

---

[7]As discussed in Chapter 3, the Supreme Court has held that federal government racial discrimination against whites gets the same full strict scrutiny as racial discrimination against blacks and other racial minorities. It remains to be seen whether this change will affect the courts' ability to order remedial minority preferences or to approve such preferences when they appear in consent decrees.

[8]*United Steelworkers v. Weber,* 443 U.S. 193 (1979), a portion of which is excerpted in Chapter 1.

---

[9]However, a number of state and municipal fair employment practices laws forbid discrimination on the basis of sexual orientation. For a list of these states and municipalities, see Lambda Legal, http://www.lambdalegal.org/cgi_bin/iowa/documents/record?record= 217 (providing a summary of states and municipalities that forbid discrimination on the basis of sexual orientation).

clearly, it applies to gender discrimination against both men and women. Still, voluntary employer programs favoring women in hiring or promotion survive a Title VII attack if they meet the previous tests for voluntary racial preferences (reformulated in terms of gender). Title VII also forbids discrimination on the bases of pregnancy and childbirth, and requires employers to treat these conditions like any other condition similarly affecting working ability in their sick leave programs, medical benefit and disability plans, and so forth. Finally, sexual stereotyping violates Title VII. This is employer behavior that either: (1) denies a woman employment opportunities by assuming that she must have traditionally "female" traits (e.g., unaggressiveness), or (2) penalizes her for lacking such traits (e.g., for acting aggressively).

Sexual Harassment Unwelcome sexual advances, requests for sexual favors, and other verbal or physical conduct of a sexual nature can violate Title VII under two different theories. The first, called *quid pro quo sexual harassment*, involves some express or implied linkage between an employee's submission to sexually oriented behavior and tangible job consequences. Quid pro quo cases usually arise when, due to an employee's refusal to submit, she suffers a *tangible job detriment* of an economic nature. Quid pro quo harassment is committed only by supervisory employees, because only supervisors have the power over hiring and firing. For example, suppose that a supervisor fires a secretary because she refuses to have sexual relations with him or refuses to go out on a date with him. Such conduct would violate Title VII whether or not the supervisor expressly told the secretary that she would be fired for refusing to submit. Title VII is also violated if a supervisor denies a subordinate a deserved promotion or other job benefit for refusing to submit.

The second form of harassment, called hostile environment harassment, occurs when an employee is subjected to unwelcome, sex-related behavior that is sufficiently severe or pervasive to change the conditions of the victim's employment and create an abusive working environment. Hostile environment sexual harassment can be inflicted by both supervisors and co-workers. Because such behavior must be *unwelcome*, however, an employee may have trouble recovering if she instigated or contributed to the sex-related behavior. Also, the offending behavior must be sufficiently *severe or pervasive* to create an environment that a *reasonable victim* would find hostile or abusive.

The reach of Title VII sexual harassment law continues to expand. Courts have long held that men can recover for sexual harassment by women. The following case, *Oncale v. Sundowner*, confirms that Title VII allows recovery when the harasser(s) and the harassee are of the same gender. A few courts have granted Title VII recoveries for "sexual favoritism"—discrimination in favor of employees who submit to sexual harassment, benefit from a sexual relationship with a superior, or trade sex for personal advancement. However, some courts have refused to allow recovery for sexual favoritism. Finally, Title VII also forbids workplace harassment based on race, color, national origin, and religion.

Oncale v. Sundowner Offshore Services, Inc.   523 U.S. 75 (U.S. Sup. Ct. 1998)

Joseph Oncale was employed by Sundowner Offshore Services on a Chevron oil platform in the Gulf of Mexico. He worked as a roustabout on an eight-man crew. On several occasions, Oncale was forcibly subjected to sex-related, humiliating conduct by certain crew members in the presence of the rest of the crew. Also, two of the crew members physically assaulted Oncale in a sexual manner, and one threatened him with rape. Oncale's complaints to supervisory personnel produced no remedial action. Eventually Oncale quit his job with Sundowner, asking that his pink slip reflect that he "voluntarily left due to sexual harassment and verbal abuse." When later asked why he left Sundowner, Oncale stated, "I felt that if I didn't leave my job, that I would be raped or forced to have sex."

Oncale then sued Sundowner in federal district court, alleging sex discrimination in employment. The district court held that, as a male, Oncale had no Title VII claim for harassment by male co-workers. The Fifth Circuit Court of Appeals affirmed, and Oncale then appealed to the U.S. Supreme Court.

Scalia, Justice   This case presents the question whether workplace harassment can violate Title VII's prohibition against "discrimination . . . because of . . . sex," when the harasser and the harassed employee are of the same sex. Title VII provides that "it shall be an unlawful employment practice for an employer . . . to discriminate against any individual with respect to his compensation, terms, conditions, or privileges of employment, because of such individual's race, color, religion, sex, or national origin." We have held that this not only covers "terms" and "conditions" in the narrow contractual sense, but evinces a congressional intent to strike at the entire spectrum of disparate treatment of men and women in employment. When the workplace is permeated with discriminatory intimidation, ridicule, and insult that is sufficiently severe or pervasive to alter the conditions of the victim's employment and create an abusive working environment, Title VII is violated.

Title VII's prohibition of discrimination "because of . . . sex" protects men as well as women. . . . In *Johnson v. Transportation Agency, Santa Clara County* (1987), [furthermore], a male employee claimed that his employer discriminated against him because of his sex when it preferred a female employee for promotion. Although we ultimately rejected the claim on other grounds, we did not consider it significant that the supervisor who made that decision was also a man. We hold today that nothing in Title VII necessarily bars a claim of discrimination "because of . . . sex" merely because the plaintiff and the defendant (or the person acting on behalf of the defendant) are of the same sex.

Courts have had little trouble with that principle in cases like *Johnson,* where an employee claims to have been passed over for a job or promotion. But when the issue arises in the context of a hostile environment sexual harassment claim, the state and federal courts have taken a bewildering variety of stances. Some have held that same-sex sexual harassment claims are never cognizable under Title VII. Other decisions say that such claims are actionable only if the plaintiff can prove that the harasser is homosexual (and thus presumably motivated by sexual desire). Still others suggest that workplace harassment that is sexual in content is always actionable, regardless of the harasser's sex, sexual orientation, or motivations. We see no justification for a categorical rule excluding same-sex harassment claims from Title VII. Male-on-male sexual harassment in the workplace was assuredly not the principal evil Congress was concerned with when it enacted Title VII. But statutory prohibitions often go beyond the principal evil to cover reasonably comparable evils.

[The defendant claims] that recognizing liability for same-sex harassment will transform Title VII into a general civility code for the American workplace. But that risk is no greater for same-sex than for opposite-sex harassment, and is adequately met by careful attention to the requirements of the statute. Title VII does not prohibit all verbal or physical harassment in the workplace; it is directed only at "discrimination . . . because of . . . sex." We have never held that workplace harassment, even harassment between men and

women, is automatically discrimination because of sex merely because the words used have sexual content or connotations. The critical issue is whether members of one sex are exposed to disadvantageous terms or conditions of employment to which members of the other sex are not exposed. Courts and juries have found the inference of discrimination easy to draw in most male–female sexual harassment situations, because the challenged conduct typically involves explicit or implicit proposals of sexual activity; it is reasonable to assume those proposals would not have been made to someone of the same sex. The same chain of inference would be available to a plaintiff alleging same-sex harassment, if there were credible evidence that the harasser was homosexual. But harassing conduct need not be motivated by sexual desire to support an inference of discrimination on the basis of sex. A trier of fact might reasonably find such discrimination, for example, if a female victim is harassed in such sex-specific and derogatory terms by another woman as to make it clear that the harasser is motivated by general hostility to the presence of women in the workplace. A same-sex harassment plaintiff may also, of course, offer direct comparative evidence about how the alleged harasser treated members of both sexes in a mixed-sex workplace.

There is another requirement that prevents Title VII from expanding into a general civility code: the statute does not reach genuine but innocuous differences in the ways men and women routinely interact with members of the same sex and of the opposite sex. The prohibition of harassment on the basis of sex requires neither asexuality nor androgyny in the workplace; it forbids only behavior so objectively offensive as to alter the "conditions" of the victim's employment. Conduct that is not severe or pervasive enough to create an objectively hostile or abusive work environment—an environment that a reasonable person would find hostile or abusive—is beyond Title VII's purview. We have always regarded that requirement as crucial, and as sufficient to ensure that courts and juries do not mistake ordinary socializing in the workplace—such as male-on-male horseplay or intersexual flirtation—for discriminatory "conditions of employment."

We have emphasized, moreover, that the objective severity of harassment should be judged from the perspective of a reasonable person in the plaintiff's position, considering all the circumstances. In same-sex (as in all) harassment cases, that inquiry requires careful consideration of the social context in which particular behavior occurs and is experienced by its target. A professional football player's working environment is not severely or pervasively abusive, for example, if the coach smacks him on the buttocks as he heads onto the field—even if the same behavior would reasonably be experienced as abusive by the coach's secretary (male or female) back at the office. Common sense, and an appropriate sensitivity to social context, will enable courts and juries to distinguish between simple teasing or roughhousing among members of the same sex, and conduct which a reasonable person in the plaintiff's position would find severely hostile or abusive.

Fifth Circuit decision in favor of Sundowner reversed; case remanded for proceedings consistent with the Supreme Court's opinion.

Company Liability for Sexual Harassment Committed by Its Employees Beyond the question of what is sexual harassment is the question whether a company will be held liable for sexual harassment committed by one of its employees. Is a company liable for sexual harassment committed by one of its employees against another one even if the harassment was not reported or otherwise known? The answer to that depends on whether the harasser was a co-employee or a supervisor of the victim, whether the victim suffered a tangible job detriment, and whether the company had sexual harassment policies, training, and grievance procedures. Generally, an employer will be liable for harassment by a *co-worker* of the victim only when the employer knew or should have known about the harassment. The following case, *Burlington Industries v. Ellerth*, decides the nature of a company's liability for sexual harassment committed by a *supervisory employee*.

Burlington Industries, Inc. v. Ellerth   *524 U.S. 742 (U.S. S. Ct. 1998)*

From March 1993 until May 1994, Kimberly Ellerth worked as a salesperson in one of Burlington Industries' divisions, in a two-person office in Chicago. During her employment, she alleges, she was subjected to constant sexual harassment by her supervisor's supervisor, Ted Slowik, a mid-level manager. Slowik was a vice president in one of five business units within one of the divisions. He had authority to make hiring and promotion decisions subject to the approval of his supervisor, who signed the paperwork.

Against a background of repeated boorish and offensive remarks and gestures which Slowik allegedly made, Ellerth places particular emphasis on three alleged incidents where Slowik's comments could be construed as threats to deny her tangible job benefits. In the summer of 1993, while on a business trip, Slowik invited Ellerth to the hotel lounge, an invitation Ellerth felt compelled to accept because Slowik was her boss. When Ellerth gave no encouragement to remarks Slowik made about her breasts, he told her to "loosen up" and warned, "You know, Kim, I could make your life very hard or very easy at Burlington." In March 1994, when Ellerth was being considered for a promotion, Slowik expressed reservations during the promotion interview because she was not "loose enough." The comment was followed by his reaching over and rubbing her knee. Ellerth did receive the promotion; but when Slowik called to announce it, he told Ellerth, "You're gonna be out there with men who work in factories, and they certainly like women with pretty butts/legs."

In May 1994, Ellerth called Slowik, asking permission to insert a customer's logo into a fabric sample. Slowik responded, "I don't have time for you right now, Kim—unless you want to tell me what you're wearing." Ellerth told Slowik she had to go and ended the call. A day or two later, Ellerth called Slowik to ask permission again. This time he denied her request, but added something along the lines of, "are you wearing shorter skirts yet, Kim, because it would make your job a whole heck of a lot easier." A short time later, Ellerth's immediate supervisor cautioned her about returning telephone calls to customers in a prompt fashion. In response, Ellerth quit. She faxed a letter giving reasons unrelated to the alleged sexual harassment we have described. About three weeks later, however, she sent a letter explaining she quit because of Slowik's behavior. During her tenure at Burlington, Ellerth did not inform anyone in authority about Slowik's conduct, despite knowing Burlington had a policy against sexual harassment. In fact, she chose not to inform her immediate supervisor (not Slowik) because "it would be his duty as my supervisor to report any incidents of sexual harassment." On one occasion, she told Slowik that a comment he made was inappropriate.

In October 1994, Ellerth filed a sexual harassment suit against Burlington under Title VII. The district court granted summary judgment to Burlington. The court found Slowik's behavior, as described by Ellerth, severe and pervasive enough to create a hostile work environment, but found that Burlington neither knew nor should have known about the conduct. Ellerth appealed and the Court of Appeals initially affirmed the district court's ruling, but then on rehearing en banc, reversed in a decision which produced eight separate opinions and no consensus for a controlling rationale. Burlington appealed.

Kennedy, Justice   Cases based on threats which are carried out are referred to often as *quid pro quo* cases, as distinct from bothersome attentions or sexual remarks that are sufficiently severe or pervasive to create a hostile work environment. The terms *quid pro quo* and hostile work environment are helpful, perhaps, in making a rough demarcation between cases in which threats are carried out and those where they are not or are absent altogether. Because Ellerth's claim involves only unfulfilled threats, it should be categorized as a hostile work environment claim which requires a showing of severe or pervasive conduct. For purposes of this case, we accept the District Court's finding that the alleged conduct was severe or pervasive. The issue of real concern to the parties is whether Burlington has vicarious liability for Slowik's alleged misconduct, rather than liability limited to its own negligence.

Congress has directed federal courts to interpret Title VII based on agency principles. Section 219(1) of the *Restatement* sets out a central principle of agency law: "A master is subject to liability for the torts of his servants committed while acting in the scope of their employment." As Courts of Appeals have recognized, a supervisor acting out of gender-based animus or a desire to fulfill sexual urges may not be actuated by a purpose to serve the employer. The general rule is that sexual harassment by a supervisor is not conduct within the scope of employment. Scope of employment does not define the only basis for employer liability under agency principles. In limited circumstances, agency principles impose liability on employers even where employees commit torts outside the scope of employment. The principles are set forth in §§ 219(2) of the *Restatement:*

> (2) A master is not subject to liability for the torts of his servants acting outside the scope of their employment, unless. . . .:
> > (d) the servant purported to act or to speak on behalf of the principal . . . he was aided in accomplishing the tort by the existence of the agency relation.

Subsection 219(2)(d) concerns vicarious liability for intentional torts committed by an employee when the employee "was aided in accomplishing the tort by the existence of the agency relation" (the aided in the agency relation standard). When a party seeks to impose vicarious liability based on an agent's misuse of delegated authority, the *Restatement*'s aided in the agency relation rule appears to be the appropriate form of analysis.

We turn to the aided in the agency relation standard. In a sense, most workplace tortfeasors are aided in accomplishing their tortious objective by the existence of the agency relation: Proximity and regular contact may afford a captive pool of potential victims. Were this to satisfy the aided in the agency relation standard, an employer would be subject to vicarious liability not only for all supervisor harassment, but also for all co-worker harassment, a result enforced by neither the EEOC nor any court of appeals to have considered the issue. The aided in the agency relation standard, therefore, requires the existence of something more than the employment relation itself. At the outset, we can identify a class of cases where, beyond question, more than the mere existence of the employment relation aids in commission of the harassment: when a supervisor takes a tangible employment action against the subordinate. Every Federal Court of Appeals to have considered the question has found vicarious liability when a discriminatory act results in a tangible employment action. In the context of this case, a tangible employment action would have taken the form of a denial of a raise or a promotion. A tangible employment action constitutes a significant change in employment status, such as hiring, firing, failing to promote, reassignment with significantly different responsibilities, or a decision causing a significant change in benefits. When a supervisor makes a tangible employment decision, there is assurance the injury could not have been inflicted absent the agency relation. A tangible employment action in most cases inflicts direct economic harm. As a general proposition, only a supervisor, or other person acting with the authority of the company, can cause this sort of injury. Tangible employment actions fall within the special province of the supervisor. The supervisor has been empowered by the company as a distinct class of agent to make economic decisions affecting other employees under his or her control. For these reasons, a tangible employment action taken by the supervisor becomes for Title VII purposes the act of the employer. Whatever the exact contours of the aided in the agency relation standard, its requirements will always be met when a supervisor takes a tangible employment action against a subordinate.

In order to accommodate the agency principles of vicarious liability for harm caused by misuse of supervisory authority, as well as Title VII's equally basic policies of encouraging forethought by employers and saving action by objecting employees, we adopt the following holding in this case. An employer is subject to vicarious liability to a victimized employee for an actionable hostile environment created by a supervisor with immediate (or successively higher) authority over the employee. When no tangible employment action is taken, a defending employer may raise an affirmative defense to liability or damages, subject to proof by a preponderance of the evidence. The defense comprises two necessary elements: (a) that the employer exercised reasonable care to prevent and correct promptly any sexually harassing behavior, and (b) that the plaintiff employee unreasonably failed to take advantage of any preventive or corrective opportunities provided by the employer or to avoid harm otherwise. While proof that an employer had promulgated an antiharassment policy with complaint procedure is not necessary in every instance as a matter of law, the need for a stated policy suitable to the employment circumstances may appropriately be addressed in any case when litigating the first element of the defense. And while proof that an employee failed to fulfill the corresponding obligation of reasonable care to avoid harm is not limited to showing any unreasonable failure to use any complaint procedure provided by the employer, a demonstration of such failure will normally suffice to satisfy the employer's burden under the second element of the defense. No affirmative defense is available, however, when the supervisor's harassment culminates in a tangible employment action, such as discharge, demotion, or undesirable reassignment.

Although Ellerth has not alleged she suffered a tangible employment action at the hands of Slowik, which would deprive Burlington of the availability of the affirmative defense, this is not dispositive. In light of our decision, Burlington is still subject to vicarious liability for Slowik's activity, but Burlington should have an opportunity to assert and prove the affirmative defense to liability.

Judgment of the Court of Appeals affirmed in favor of Ellerth.

Section 1981

Where it applies, a post–Civil War civil rights statute called section 1981 sets employment discrimination standards resembling those of Title VII. Section 1981 forbids public and private employment discrimination against blacks, people of certain racially characterized national origins such as Mexicans, and ethnic groups such as gypsies and Jews. Included within such discrimination are most of the ways that an employer might disadvantage an employee.

Section 1981 is important because it gives covered plaintiffs certain advantages that Title VII does not provide. Although courts often use Title VII's methods of proof in section 1981 cases, Title VII's limitations on covered employers and its complex procedural requirements do not apply. Also, damages are apt to be greater under section 1981; in particular, Title VII's limits on compensatory and punitive damages are inapplicable. For these reasons, covered plaintiffs often include a section 1981 claim along with a Title VII claim in their complaint.

The Age Discrimination in Employment Act

The 1967 Age Discrimination in Employment Act (ADEA) prohibits age-based employment discrimination against employees who are *at least 40 years of age*. As you will see in the following *Cline* case, the favored employee may be either inside or outside the protected age group. In addition, the ADEA probably forbids age discrimination in favor of both younger and older employees.

Coverage   The ADEA covers individuals, partnerships, labor organizations and employment agencies (as to their employees), and corporations that: (1) engage in an industry affecting interstate commerce, and (2) employ at least 20 persons. The act no longer regulates state and local governments.[10] *Referrals* by an employment agency to a covered employer are within the ADEA's scope regardless of the agency's size. In addition, the ADEA reaches labor union practices affecting *union members;* usually, unions with 25 or more members are covered. The ADEA protects against age discrimination in many employment contexts, including hiring, firing, pay, job assignment, and fringe benefits.

Procedural Requirements   The complex procedural requirements for an ADEA suit are beyond the scope of this text. Before she can sue in her own right, a private plaintiff must file a charge with the EEOC or with an appropriate state agency. The EEOC also may sue to enforce the ADEA; such a suit precludes private suits

---

[10]Age discrimination in the federal government is beyond the scope of this text.

arising from the same alleged violation. For both government and private suits, the statute of limitations is three years from the date of an alleged *willful* violation and two years from the date of an alleged *nonwillful* violation.

Proof Proving age discrimination is no problem where an employer uses an express age criterion, and may be easy where there is direct evidence of discrimination such as testimony or incriminating documents. There is a split of authority among the federal Courts of Appeal whether Title VII's disparate impact theory can be used in ADEA cases. In 2002, the Supreme Court heard arguments on a case concerning this issue, but it later dismissed the case, so at the time of this writing, there is still no authoritative pronouncement from the Supreme Court about whether the disparate impact theory can be used in ADEA cases.

Defenses The ADEA allows employers to discharge or otherwise discipline an employee for *good cause,* and to use *reasonable factors other than age* in their employment decisions. It also allows employers to observe the terms of a *bona fide seniority system.* In addition, the ADEA has a *bona fide occupational qualification* (BFOQ) defense. Speaking very generally, an employer seeking to use this defense must show that its age classification is reasonably necessary to the proper performance—usually the safe performance—of the job in question. For example, an employer that refuses to hire anyone over 60 as a helicopter pilot should have a BFOQ defense if it has a reasonable basis for concluding that 60-and-over helicopter pilots pose significant safety risks, or that it is not feasible to test older pilots individually.

Remedies Remedies available after a successful ADEA suit include unpaid back wages and overtime pay resulting from the discrimination; an additional equal award of liquidated damages where the employer acted willfully; attorney's fees; and equitable relief, including hiring, reinstatement, and promotion. Most courts do not allow punitive damages and recoveries for pain, suffering, mental distress, and so forth.

Cline v. General Dynamics Land Systems, Inc.
2002 U.S. App. LEXIS 14642 (6th Cir. 2002)

Dennis Cline and 195 other employees of General Dynamics Land Systems, Inc., brought suit against their employer after their labor union, the United Auto Workers, and General Dynamics entered into a new collective bargaining agreement. The agreement took effect July 1, 1997. Before that date, the parties had been bound by a collective bargaining agreement that obligated General Dynamics to provide full health benefits to retired workers who had accumulated 30 years of seniority. With one exception, the new agreement no longer required General Dynamics to provide full health benefits to retirees. That exception held that only employees 50 years of age or older on July 1, 1997, remained eligible to receive full health benefits upon retirement. As a result, the plaintiffs sought, and obtained, a determination from the Equal Employment Opportunity Commission that the new collective bargaining agreement adversely affected General Dynamics employees who were between the ages of 40 and 49 on July 1, 1997. Cline and his fellow employees then filed suit under the ADEA, alleging that the provision of health benefits solely to those over the age of 50 constituted illegal discrimination based on age. Each of the plaintiffs was between the ages of 40 and 49 on July 1, 1997, and thus a member of the ADEA's protected class.

The district court dismissed the plaintiffs' suit, concluding that the ADEA does not recognize claims for "reverse discrimination." The court reasoned that the ADEA was drafted to aid "older workers," not those who suffer age discrimination because they are too young. Cline and the other plaintiffs appealed.

RYAN, Circuit Judge The starting point in determining how a statute is to be applied is the language of the statute itself. Legislative intent, however, is gleaned primarily from the statute's plain language, and where the statute's language is plain and unambiguous, there is no justification for resorting to legislative history to ascertain the lawmaker's intent—the words of the statute suffice.

Section 623(a)(1) of the ADEA reads:
    It shall be unlawful for an employer—
1) to fail or refuse to hire or to discharge *any individual* or otherwise discriminate against *any individual* with respect to his compensation, terms, conditions, or privileges of employment, because of such individual's age.

This language clearly and unambiguously forbids employers from defining the terms and benefits of "any individual's" employment based solely on his or her age. In §§ 631(a), Congress declared that "any individual" means those "individuals who are at least 40 years of age." Thus, by the law's plain language, an employer may not discriminate against any worker age 40 or older on the basis of age. Those younger than 40 are not protected by the ADEA. To reach the conclusion for which the defendant argues, and that was found persuasive by the district court, we would be required to hold that the plain language of §§ 623(a)(1) and §§ 631(a) does not mean what it says when it refers to "any individual," but means, instead, "older workers." Thus, only "older workers," meaning those individuals who are at least 40 years of age and, in addition, relatively older than any other group of employees with whom they are compared, are protected. This *interpretive* reading of the statute led the district court to conclude that the ADEA does not prohibit an employer from discriminating, on the basis of age, against "any individual" who is a member of the ADEA's protected class, but only prohibits discrimination against those in the protected class who are "older" than the favored employees. We think the plain meaning of the statute will not bear that reading.

Moreover, we do not share the commonly held belief that this situation is one of so-called "reverse discrimination." Insofar as we are able to determine, the expression "reverse discrimination" has no ascertainable meaning in the law. An action is either discriminatory or it is not discriminatory, and some discriminatory actions are prohibited by law. Presumably, what the district judge and others mean when they conclude that the ADEA does not prohibit "reverse discrimination" is that otherwise prohibited discrimination is permitted if the victims are literally (statutorily) within the protected class, but are a group within the class who in most cases are the beneficiaries of discrimination against others. There is no basis for this conclusion. We are not aware of any legal doctrine permitting courts to redraft antidiscrimination statutes so that they better advance the court's view of sound policy. Furthermore, even if we granted the district court its definition of "reverse discrimination," it is clear that Cline and his classmates did not suffer "reverse age discrimination." By the plain language of the ADEA they are the victims of "age discrimination." Congress has singled out the over-40 class of workers from the general workforce for protection from age discrimination by their employers. All the plaintiffs are members of the protected class created by §§ 631(a), and all properly allege that they were denied job benefits due to their age. Therefore, the protected class should be protected; to hold otherwise is discrimination, plain and simple.

If Congress wanted to limit the ADEA to protect only those workers who are *relatively* older, it clearly had the power and acuity to do so. It did not. Whatever the policy justifications for holding otherwise, we are bound by the plain language of the statute and have no occasion to look outside of the text.

Reversed in favor of Cline and the other plaintiffs.

The Americans with Disabilities Act

Before the 1990s, federal regulation of employment discrimination against people with disabilities mainly was limited to certain federal contractors and recipients of federal financial assistance. By passing Title I of the Americans with Disabilities Act of 1990 (ADA), however, Congress addressed this problem comprehensively. This portion of the ADA is primarily enforced by the EEOC, and its procedures and remedies are the same as for Title VII.

Covered Entities Title I covers employers who have 15 or more employees and who are engaged in an industry affecting interstate commerce. Employers include individuals, partnerships, corporations, colleges and universities, labor unions and employment agencies (regarding their own employees), and state and local governments. The act also covers certain labor unions in their capacity as employee representative, as well as employment agencies' discrimination against their clients.

Substantive Protections The ADA forbids covered entities from discriminating against *qualified individuals with a disability* because of that disability. It covers disability-related discrimination regarding hiring, firing, promotion, pay, and innumerable other employment decisions. The act defines a *disability* as: (1) a physical or mental impairment that substantially limits one or more of an individual's major life activities, (2) a record of such an impairment, or (3) one's being regarded as having such an impairment. (The last two categories protect those who have previously been misdiagnosed or who have recovered from earlier impairments.) Not protected, however, are those who suffer discrimination for currently engaging in the illegal use of drugs. Furthermore, homosexuality, bisexuality, transvestism, transsexualism, and various other sex-related traits or conditions are not considered disabilities. In recent years, the U.S. Supreme Court has decided several cases that narrow the concept of disability under the ADA. In *Sutton v. United Airlines,* a 1999 case, the Court decided that corrective measures must be taken into account in determining whether an impairment is a disability. There, severely near-sighted twin sisters whose vision was 20/20 with corrective lenses had been denied jobs as airline pilots because their uncorrected vision was worse than the airline's minimum vision requirement. The Court decided that their vision was not a disability within the meaning of the ADA. In the recent *Toyota* case, which follows shortly, the Court decided that for a physical impairment to constitute a disability, the life activity that it substantially limits must be one that is "central to daily life" as opposed to an activity that is used in a par-

ticular job. In a related development, the Court held in a 2002 case, *Chevron, U.S.A., Inc. v. Echazabal,* that an employer is justified in screening out an individual whose disability would constitute a "direct threat" to the individual's own health and safety in the workplace.

The ADA protects both individuals who can perform their job despite their handicap, and individuals who could perform their job if reasonable accommodation is provided. In the latter case, employers illegally discriminate if they do not provide such accommodation. *Reasonable accommodation* includes: making existing facilities readily accessible and usable, acquiring new equipment, restructuring jobs, modifying work schedules, and reassigning workers to vacant positions, among other options. Figure 2 displays the reasoning used in an ADA case.

Figure 2   *A Map through the ADA*

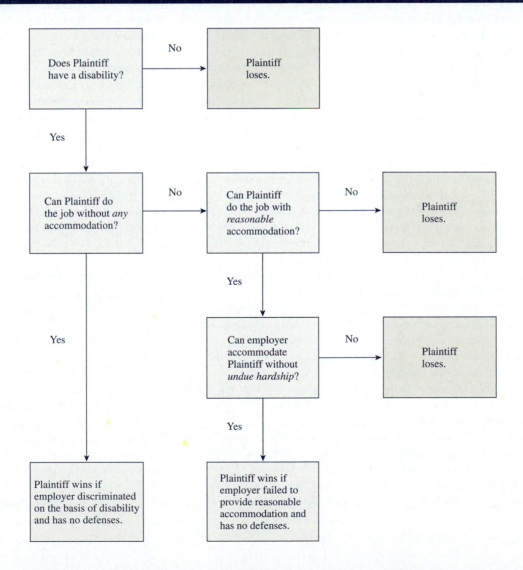

However, employers need not make reasonable accommodation where such accommodation would cause them to suffer *undue hardship*. Undue hardship is an act requiring significant difficulty or expense. Among the factors used to determine its existence are the cost of the accommodation, the covered entity's overall financial resources, and the accommodation's effect on the covered entity's activities. The ADA also protects employers whose allegedly discriminatory decisions are based on *job-related criteria and business necessity*, so long as proper job performance cannot be accomplished by reasonable accommodation.

Toyota Manufacturing Co. v. Williams   *534 U.S. 184 (U.S. Sup. Ct. 2002)*

Ella Williams began working at Toyota's automobile manufacturing plant in Georgetown, Kentucky, in August 1990. She was soon placed on an engine fabrication assembly line, where her duties included work with pneumatic tools. Use of these tools eventually caused pain in Williams's hands, wrists, and arms, and she developed bilateral carpal tunnel syndrome and bilateral tendinitis. Williams's physician placed her on permanent work restrictions. In light of these restrictions, for the next two years Toyota assigned Williams to various modified duty jobs. Nonetheless, Williams missed some work for medical leave, and eventually filed a claim under the Kentucky Workers' Compensation Act. The parties settled this claim, and Williams returned to work. She was unsatisfied by Toyota's efforts to accommodate her work restrictions, however, and responded by bringing an ADA action against Toyota, alleging that it had violated the ADA by refusing to accommodate her disability. That suit was also settled, and as part of the settlement, Williams returned to work in December 1993.

Upon her return, petitioner placed Williams on a team in Quality Control Inspection Operations (QCIO). QCIO is responsible for four tasks: (1) "assembly paint"; (2) "paint second inspection"; (3) "shell body audit"; and (4) "ED surface repair." Williams was initially placed on a team that performed only the first two of these tasks, and for a couple of years, she rotated on a weekly basis between them. In assembly paint, Williams visually inspected painted cars moving slowly down a conveyor. When Williams began working in assembly paint, inspection team members were required to open and shut the doors, trunk, and/or hood of each passing car. Sometime during Williams's tenure, however, the position was modified to include only visual inspection with few or no manual tasks. Paint second inspection required team members to use their hands to wipe each painted car with a glove as it moved along a conveyor. The parties agree that Williams was physically capable of performing both of these jobs and that her performance was satisfactory. During the fall of 1996, Toyota announced that it wanted QCIO employees to be able to rotate through all four of the QCIO processes. Williams therefore received training for the shell body audit job, in which team members apply a highlight oil to the hood, fender, doors, rear quarter panel, and trunk of passing cars at a rate of approximately one car per minute. The highlight oil has the viscosity of salad oil, and employees spread it on cars with a sponge attached to a block of wood. Wiping the cars required Williams to hold her hands and arms up around shoulder height for several hours at a time.

A short while after the shell body audit job was added to Williams's rotations, she began to experience pain in her neck and shoulders. Williams again sought care at petitioner's in-house medical service, where she was diagnosed with myotendinitis bilateral periscapular, an inflammation of the muscles and tendons around both of her shoulder blades; myotendinitis and myositis bilateral forearms with nerve compression causing median nerve irritation; and thoracic outlet compression, a condition that causes pain in the nerves that lead to the upper extremities. Williams requested that petitioner accommodate her medical conditions by allowing her to return to doing only her original two jobs in QCIO, which Williams claimed she could still perform without difficulty. According to Williams, Toyota refused her request and forced her to continue working in the shell body audit job, which caused her even greater physical injury. According to Toyota, Williams simply began missing work on a regular basis. On January 27, 1997, Williams received a letter from Toyota that terminated her employment, citing her poor attendance record.

Williams sued Toyota, claiming disability discrimination in violation of the ADA by failing to reasonably accommodate her disability and by terminating her employment. The District Court granted partial summary judgment to Toyota, finding that Williams had not been disabled, as defined by the ADA, at the time of Toyota's alleged refusal to accommodate her, and that she had therefore not been covered by the Act's protections. The Court of Appeals for the Sixth Circuit reversed the District Court's ruling on whether Williams was disabled at the time she sought an accommodation, and Toyota appealed.

O'CONNOR, Justice   The ADA requires covered entities, including private employers, to provide "reasonable accommodations to the known physical or mental limitations of an otherwise qualified individual with a disability who is an applicant or employee, unless such covered entity can demonstrate that the accommodation would impose an undue hardship." The Act defines a "qualified individual with a disability" as "an individual with a disability who, with or without reasonable accommodation, can perform the essential functions of the employment position that such individual holds or desires." In turn, a "disability" is:

(A) a physical or mental impairment that substantially limits one or more of the major life activities of such individual;

(B) a record of such an impairment; or

(C) being regarded as having such an impairment.

To qualify as disabled under subsection (A) of the ADA's definition of disability, a claimant must initially prove that he or she has a physical or mental impairment. The Rehabilitation Act regulations issued by the Department of Health, Education, and Welfare (HEW) in 1977, which appear without change in the current regulations issued by the Department of Health and Human Services, define "physical impairment," the type of impairment relevant to this case, to mean "any physiological disorder or condition, cosmetic disfigurement, or anatomical loss affecting one or more of the following body systems: neurological; musculoskeletal; special sense organs; respiratory, including speech organs; cardiovascular; reproductive, digestive, genito-urinary; hemic and lymphatic; skin; and endocrine." Merely having an impairment does not make one disabled for purposes of the ADA. Claimants also need to demonstrate that the impairment limits a major life activity. The HEW Rehabilitation Act regulations provide a list of examples of "major life activities," that includes "walking, seeing, hearing," and, as relevant here, "performing manual tasks." To qualify as disabled, a claimant must further show that the limitation on the major life activity is substantial. According to the EEOC regulations, "substantially limited" means "unable to perform a major life activity that the average person in the general population can perform"; or "significantly restricted as to the condition, manner or duration under which an individual can perform a particular major life activity as compared to the condition, manner, or duration under which the average person in the general population can perform that same major life activity." In determining whether an individual is substantially limited in a major life activity, the regulations instruct that the following factors should be con-

sidered: "the nature and severity of the impairment; the duration or expected duration of the impairment; and the permanent or long-term impact, or the expected permanent or long-term impact of or resulting from the impairment."

The question presented by this case is whether the Sixth Circuit properly determined that Williams was disabled under subsection (A) of the ADA's disability definition at the time that she sought an accommodation from Toyota. The parties do not dispute that Williams's medical conditions, which include carpal tunnel syndrome, myotendinitis, and thoracic outlet compression, amount to physical impairments. The relevant question, therefore, is whether the Sixth Circuit correctly analyzed whether these impairments substantially limited Williams in the major life activity of performing manual tasks. Answering this requires us to address an issue about which the EEOC regulations are silent: what a plaintiff must demonstrate to establish a substantial limitation in the specific major life activity of performing manual tasks.

Our consideration of this issue is guided first and foremost by the words of the disability definition itself. "Substantially" in the phrase "substantially limits" suggests "considerable" or "to a large degree." The word "substantial" thus clearly precludes impairments that interfere in only a minor way with the performance of manual tasks from qualifying as disabilities. "Major" in the phrase "major life activities" means important. "Major life activities" thus refers to those activities that are of central importance to daily life. In order for performing manual tasks to fit into this category—a category that includes such basic abilities as walking, seeing, and hearing—the manual tasks in question must be central to daily life. If each of the tasks included in the major life activity of performing manual tasks does not independently qualify as a major life activity, then together they must do so. That these terms need to be interpreted strictly to create a demanding standard for qualifying as disabled is confirmed by the first section of the ADA, which lays out the legislative findings and purposes that motivate the Act. When it enacted the ADA in 1990, Congress found that "some 43,000,000 Americans have one or more physical or mental disabilities." If Congress intended everyone with a physical impairment that precluded the performance of some isolated, unimportant, or particularly difficult manual task to qualify as disabled, the number of disabled Americans would surely have been much higher.

We therefore hold that to be substantially limited in performing manual tasks, an individual must have an impairment that prevents or severely restricts the individual from doing activities that are of central importance to most people's daily lives. The impairment's impact must also be permanent or long-term. It is insufficient for individuals attempting to prove disability status under this test to merely submit evidence of a medical diagnosis of an impairment. Instead, the ADA requires those "claiming the Act's protection . . . to prove a disability by offering evidence that the extent of the limitation [caused by their impairment] in terms of their own experience . . . is substantial." That the Act defines "disability" "with respect to an individual," makes clear that Congress intended the existence of a disability to be determined in such a case-by-case manner. An individualized assessment of the effect of an impairment is particularly necessary when the impairment is one whose symptoms vary widely from person to person. Carpal tunnel syndrome, one of Williams's impairments, is just such a condition. While cases of severe carpal tunnel syndrome are characterized by muscle atrophy and extreme sensory deficits, mild cases generally do not have either of these effects and create only intermittent symptoms of numbness and tingling. Given these large potential differences in the severity and duration of the effects of carpal tunnel syndrome, an individual's carpal tunnel syndrome diagnosis, on its own, does not indicate whether the individual has a disability within the meaning of the ADA.

When addressing the major life activity of performing manual tasks, the central inquiry must be whether the claimant is unable to perform the variety of tasks central to most people's daily lives, not whether the claimant is unable to perform the tasks associated with her specific job. There is no support in the Act, our previous opinions, or the regulations for the idea that the question of whether an impairment constitutes a disability is to be answered only by analyzing the effect of the impairment in the workplace. Even more critically, the manual tasks unique to any particular job are not necessarily important parts of most people's lives. As a result, occupation-specific tasks may have only limited relevance to the manual task inquiry. In this case, "repetitive work with hands and arms extended at or above shoulder levels for extended periods of time," the manual task on which the Court of Appeals relied, is not an important part of most people's daily lives. The court, therefore, should not have considered Williams's inability to do such manual work in her specialized assembly line job as sufficient proof that she was substantially limited in performing manual tasks.

At the same time, the Court of Appeals appears to have disregarded the very type of evidence that it should have focused upon. It treated as irrelevant "the fact that [Williams] can . . . tend to her personal hygiene [and] carry out personal or household chores." Yet household chores, bathing, and brushing one's teeth are among the types of manual tasks of central importance to people's daily lives, and should have been part of the assessment of whether Williams was substantially limited in performing manual tasks. The District Court noted that at the time Williams sought an accommodation from Toyota, she admitted that she was able to do the manual tasks required by her original two jobs in QCIO. In addition, according to Williams's deposition testimony, even after her condition worsened, she could still brush her teeth, wash her face, bathe, tend her flower garden, fix breakfast, do laundry, and pick up around the house. The record also indicates that her medical conditions caused her to avoid sweeping, to quit dancing, to occasionally seek help dressing, and to reduce how often she plays with her children, gardens, and drives long distances. But these changes in her life did not amount to such severe restrictions in the activities that are of central importance to most people's daily lives that they establish a manual-task disability as a matter of law.

Reversed and remanded in favor of Toyota.

Executive Order 11246

Executive Order 11246, issued in 1965 and later amended, forbids race, color, national origin, religion, and sex discrimination by certain federal contractors. The order is enforced by the Labor Department's Office of Federal Contract Compliance Programs (OFCCP). In the past, OFCCP enforcement has included affirmative action requirements and occasionally quotalike preferences benefiting racial minorities.

State Antidiscrimination Laws

Most states have statutes that parallel Title VII, the EPA, the ADEA, and the ADA. These statutes sometimes provide more extensive protection than their federal counterparts. In addition, some states prohibit forms of discrimination not barred by federal law. Examples include discrimination on the bases of one's marital status, physical appearance, sexual orientation, political affiliation, and off-the-job smoking.

ETHICS IN ACTION

Bookworks, Inc., requires employees to sign an agreement that they will settle any dispute or claim concerning employment through binding arbitration. Catherine, a Bookworks employee, alleged that her supervisor fired her for refusing to go on a date with him. She wants to file a sexual harassment case under Title VII against Bookworks, and Bookworks asserts that this is a claim that must be arbitrated rather than adjudicated in court. What are the ethical considerations involved in mandatory arbitration agreements that require employees to arbitrate discrimination and other employment-related claims?

Finally, some states and localities have adopted laws that adopt the employment discrimination theory called **comparable worth.** These laws, which typically apply only to public employees, often say that state governments should not discriminate in pay between female-dominated jobs and male-dominated jobs of comparable overall worth to the employer. The worth of different jobs may be determined by giving each job a point rating under factors such as skill, responsibility, effort, and working conditions; adding the ratings; and comparing the totals. It was once believed that comparable worth claims might find favor under Title VII, but that possibility has receded over the years.

Employee Privacy

The term employee privacy describes several employment issues that have assumed increasing importance recently. Uniting these issues is a concern with protecting employees' personal dignity and increasing their freedom from intrusions, surveillance, and the revelation of personal matters.

CONCEPT REVIEW

The Employment Discrimination Laws Compared

	Protected Traits	Covered Employer Decisions	Need to File Charge in Private Suit?
Equal Pay Act	Sex only	Pay only	No
Title VII	Race, color, national origin, reigion, sex	Wide range	Yes
Section 1981	Race, racially characterized national origin, perhaps alienage	Wide range	No
Age Discrimination in Employment Act	Age, if victim 40 or over	Wide range	Yes
Americans with Disabilities Act	Existence of disability, if person qualified to perform job with or without reasonable accommodation	Wide range	Yes
Executive Order 11246	Race, color, religion, national origin, sex	Wide range	Not applicable; enforced by OFCCP

Polygraph Testing

Over the years, employers have made increasing use of polygraph and other lie detector tests—most often, to screen job applicants and to investigate employee thefts. This has led to concerns about the accuracy of such tests; the personal questions examiners sometimes ask; and the tests' impact on workers' job prospects, job security, and personal privacy. Besides provoking state restrictions on polygraph testing, such worries led Congress to pass the Employee Polygraph Protection Act in 1988.

The Employee Polygraph Protection Act mainly regulates lie detector tests, which include polygraph tests and certain other devices for assessing a person's honesty. Under the act, employers may not: (1) require, suggest, request, or cause employees or prospective employees to take any lie detector test; (2) use, accept, refer to, or inquire about the results of any lie detector test administered to employees or prospective employees; and (3) discriminate or threaten to discriminate against employees or prospective employees because of the results of any lie detector test, or because such parties failed or refused to take such a test. The act also has an antiretaliation provision.

However, certain employers and tests are exempt from these provisions. They include: (1) federal, state, and local government employers; (2) certain national defense and security-related tests by the federal government; (3) certain tests by security service firms; and (4) certain tests by firms manufacturing and distributing controlled substances. The act also contains a limited exemption for private employers that use polygraph tests when investigating economic losses caused by theft, embezzlement, industrial espionage, and so forth. Finally, the act restricts the disclosure of test results by examiners and by most employers.

The Polygraph Protection Act is enforced by the Labor Department, which has issued regulations in furtherance of that mission. It does not preempt state laws that prohibit lie detector tests or that set standards stricter than those imposed by federal law. Violations of the act or its regulations can result in civil penalties, suits for equitable relief by the Labor Department, and private suits for damages and equitable relief. Workers and job applicants who succeed in a private suit can obtain employment, reinstatement, promotion, and payment of lost wages and benefits.

Drug and Alcohol Testing

Due to their impact on employees' safe and effective job performance, employers have become increasingly concerned about both on-the-job and off-the-job drug and alcohol use. Thus, employers increasingly require employees and job applicants to undergo urine tests for drugs and/or alcohol. Because those who test positive may be either disciplined or induced to undergo treatment, and because the tests themselves can raise privacy concerns, some legal checks on their use have emerged.

Drug and alcohol testing by *public* employers can be attacked under the Fourth Amendment's search-and-seizure provisions. However, such tests generally are constitutional where there is a reasonable basis for suspecting that an employee is using drugs or alcohol, or drug use in a particular job could threaten the public interest or public safety. Due to the government action requirement discussed in Chapter 3, *private-sector* employees generally have no federal constitutional protection against drug and alcohol testing. Some state constitutions, however, lack a government action requirement. In addition, several states now regulate private drug and/or alcohol testing by statute. Tort suits for invasion of privacy or infliction of emotional distress may also be possible in some cases.[11]

Despite these protections, however, federal law *requires* private-sector drug testing in certain situations. Under a Defense Department rule, for example, employers who contract with the department must agree to establish a drug-testing program requiring, for instance, that employees who work in sensitive positions sometimes be tested. Also, Transportation Department regulations require random testing of public and private employees occupying safety-sensitive or security-related positions in industries such as aviation, trucking, railroads, mass transit, and others.

Employer Searches

Employers concerned about theft, drug use, and other misbehavior by their employees sometimes conduct searches of those employees' offices, desks, lockers, files, briefcases, packages, vehicles, and even bodies to confirm their suspicions. The Supreme Court has held that public employees sometimes have a reasonable expectation of privacy in areas such as their offices, desks, or files. But it also held that searches of those areas are constitutional under the Fourth Amendment when they are reasonable under the circumstances. Determining reasonableness generally means balancing the em-

---

[11]Invasion of privacy and intentional infliction of emotional distress are discussed in Chapter 6, and negligent infliction of emotional distress is discussed in Chapter 7.

ployee's legitimate privacy expectations against the government's need for supervision and control of the workplace, with more intrusive searches demanding a higher degree of justification. Finally, the Court also said that neither probable cause nor a warrant is necessary for such searches to proceed.

As noted above, the U.S. Constitution ordinarily does not apply to private employment. Nonetheless, both private and public employees can mount common law invasion of privacy suits against employers who conduct searches. In such cases, courts usually try to weigh the intrusiveness of the search against the purposes justifying it and consider the availability of less intrusive alternatives that still would satisfy the employer's legitimate needs.

Records and References

Many states allow both public and private employees at least some access to personnel files maintained by their employers. Also, some states limit third-party access to such records. In addition, employers who transmit such data to third parties—for example, in letters of reference—may be civilly liable for defamation or invasion of privacy.[12] However, truth is a defense in defamation cases. In both defamation and invasion of privacy suits, moreover, the employer's actions may be conditionally privileged. This defense and these privileges can protect employers who are sued for truthful, accurate, relevant, good faith statements made in references concerning former employees. Finally, a few states have allowed defamation suits for so-called compelled self-disclosure by job-seeking, wrongfully discharged employees who have been required to tell potential employers their former employer's alleged reasons for firing them.

---

[12]Defamation and invasion of privacy are discussed in Chapter 6.

Employer Monitoring

Although employers have always monitored their employees' work, recent technological advances enable such monitoring to occur without those employees' knowledge. Examples include closed-circuit television, video monitoring, telephone monitoring, the monitoring of computer workstations (e.g., by counting keystrokes), and metal detectors at plant entrances. Such monitoring has encountered objections because employees often are unaware that it exists or may suffer stress when they do know or suspect its existence. Employers counter these objections by stressing that monitoring is highly useful in evaluating employee performance, improving efficiency, and reducing theft.

The amount of litigation and commentary about monitoring has grown as employers and employees are increasingly concerned about privacy. A variety of statutes exist on the federal and state levels concerning electronic privacy and security, and these may implicate some employer monitoring. Although employers have a significant amount of latitude in monitoring employees, telephone monitoring occasionally has been found illegal under federal wiretapping law. Although such claims have been uncommon, invasion of privacy suits may succeed in situations where an employer's need for surveillance is slight and it is conducted in areas, such as restrooms and lounges, in which employees have a reasonable expectation of privacy.

A growing number of companies have adopted specific policies regarding monitoring of employee communications and permissible use of company systems. Many companies have begun to inform their employees that their e-mail, voicemail, Internet usage, and other communications and transactions are subject to monitoring. Company policies may also limit the ways that employees can use company computer systems, and often subject employees who violate the policy to disciplinary penalties such as discharge. The following *TBG Insurance* case discusses the legal significance of these policies.

TBG Insurance Services Corp. v. Superior Court   *No. B153400 (Cal. Ct. App. 2002)*

For about 12 years, Robert Zieminski worked as a senior executive for TBG Insurance Services Corporation. In the course of his employment, Zieminski used two computers owned by TBG, one at the office, the other at his residence. Zieminski signed TBG's "electronic and telephone equipment policy statement" in which he agreed, among other things, that he would use the computers "for business purposes only and not for personal benefit or non-Company purposes, unless such use [was] expressly approved. Under no circumstances [could the] equipment or systems be used for improper, derogatory, defamatory, obscene or other inappropriate purposes." Zieminski consented to have his computer "use monitored by authorized company personnel" on an "as needed" basis, and agreed that communications transmitted by computer were not private. He acknowledged his understanding that his improper use of the computers could result in disciplinary action, including discharge.

In December 1998, Zieminski and TBG entered a "Shareholder Buy–Sell Agreement," pursuant to which TBG sold 4,000 shares of its stock to Zieminski at $.01 per share. One-third of the stock was to vest on December 1, 1999, one-third on December 1, 2000, and one-third on December 1, 2001, each vesting contingent upon Zieminski's continued employment. If Zieminski's employment terminated before all the shares had vested, TBG had the right to repurchase the nonvested shares at $.01 per share. One-third of Zieminski's shares vested on December 1, 1999. In March 2000, TBG's shareholders, including Zieminski, sold a portion of their TBG shares to Nationwide Insurance Company. Zieminski sold 1,230 of his 1,333 vested shares to Nationwide for $1,278,247. On November 28, 2000, three days before another 1,333 shares were to vest, TBG terminated Zieminski's employment. According to TBG, Zieminski was terminated for violating TBG's electronic policies by repeatedly accessing pornographic sites on the Internet while he was at work. According to Zieminski, the pornographic sites were not accessed intentionally but simply "popped up" on his computer.

Zieminski sued TBG, alleging that his employment had been wrongfully terminated as a pretext to prevent his substantial stock holdings in TBG from fully vesting and to allow TBG to repurchase his nonvested stock for $.01 per share. TBG asked Zieminski to return the home computer and cautioned Zieminski not to delete any information stored on the computer's hard drive. Zieminski responded that he would either return it or purchase it, but that it would be necessary for him to alter or delete some of the information on the hard drive, since "it contains personal information which is subject to a right of privacy." TBG refused to sell the computer to Zieminski and demanded its return without any deletions or alterations. TBG moved to compel production of the computer, contending it has the right to discover whether information on the hard drive proves that, as claimed by TBG, Zieminski violated his employer's policy statement. Zieminski opposed the motion and insisted that, notwithstanding the policy statement, he retained an expectation of privacy with regard to his home computer. According to Zieminski, the home computer was provided as a "perk" to all senior executives, and although it was provided so that business-related work could be done at home, it was "universally accepted and understood by all that the home computer would also be used for personal purposes as well." He said his home computer was used by his wife and children, and that it was primarily used for personal purposes and contained a significant amount of personal information and data such as details of his personal finances and income tax returns. The trial court denied TBG's motion, and TBG filed a petition for a writ of mandate, asking the appellate court to intervene.

VOGEL, Justice   A party may obtain discovery regarding any matter, not privileged, that is relevant to the subject matter involved in the pending action. In the context of discovery, evidence is relevant if it might reasonably assist a party in evaluating its case, preparing for trial, or facilitating a settlement. Here, the home computer is indisputably relevant. The issue, therefore, is whether he has a protectible privacy interest in the information to be found on the computer.

Zieminski's privacy claim is based on article I, section I, of the California Constitution, which provides: "All people are by nature free and independent and have inalienable rights. Among these are enjoying and defending life and liberty, acquiring, possessing, and protecting property, and pursuing and obtaining safety, happiness, and privacy." Assuming the existence of a legally cognizable privacy interest, the extent of that interest is not independent of the circumstances and other factors (including advance notice) may affect a person's reasonable expectation of privacy. Accordingly, our decision about the reasonableness of Zieminski's claimed expectation of privacy must take into account any accepted community norms, advance notice to

Zieminski about TBG's policy statement, and whether Zieminski had the opportunity to consent to or reject the very thing that constitutes the invasion.

We are concerned in this case with the "community norm" within 21st Century computer-dependent businesses. In 2001, the 700,000-member American Management Association reported that more than three-quarters of this country's major firms monitor, record, and review employee communications and activities on the job, including their telephone calls, e-mail, Internet connections, and computer files. Companies that engage in these practices do so for several reasons, including legal compliance, legal liability, performance review, productivity measures, and security concerns. It is hardly surprising therefore that employers are told they "should establish a policy for the use of [e-mail and the Internet], which every employee should have to read and sign. First, employers can diminish an individual employee's expectation of privacy by clearly stating in the policy that electronic communications are to be used solely for company business, and that the company reserves the right to monitor or access all employee Internet or e-mail usage." Fernandez, *Workplace Claims: Guiding Employers and Employees Safely In and Out of the Revolving Door* (1999), 614 Practicing Law Institute, Litigation and Administrative Practices Course Handbook Series, Litigation 725. For these reasons, the use of computers in the employment context carries with it social norms that effectively diminish the employee's reasonable expectation of privacy with regard to his use of his employer's computers.

TBG's advance notice to Zieminski (the company's policy statement) gave Zieminski the opportunity to consent to or reject the very thing that he now complains about, and that notice, combined with his written consent to the policy, defeats his claim that he had a reasonable expectation of privacy. Zieminski knew that TBG would monitor the files and messages stored on the computers he used at the office and at home. He had the opportunity to consent to TBG's policy or not, and had the opportunity to limit his use of his home computer to purely business matters. To state the obvious, no one compelled Zieminski or his wife or children to use the home computer for personal matters, and no one prevented him from purchasing his own computer for his personal use. With all the information he needed to make an intelligent decision, Zieminski agreed to the company's policy *and* chose to use his computer for personal matters. By any reasonable standard, Zieminski fully and voluntarily relinquished his privacy rights in the information he stored on his home computer, and he will not now be heard to say that he nevertheless had a *reasonable* expectation of privacy.

Zieminski voluntarily waived whatever right of privacy he might otherwise have had in the information he stored on the home computer. But even assuming that Zieminski has some lingering privacy interest in the information he stored on the home computer, we do not view TBG's demand for production as a serious invasion of that interest. Appropriate protective orders can define the scope of TBG's inspection and copying of information to that which is directly relevant to this litigation, and can prohibit the unnecessary copying and dissemination of Zieminski's financial and other information that has no rational bearing on this case.

Petition granted and writ issued in favor of TBG.

Job Security

The Doctrine of Employment at Will

The traditional employment-at-will rule first appeared around 1870, and by the early 20th century most state courts had adopted it. The rule says that *either party can terminate an employment contract of indefinite duration.* The termination can occur at any time; and can be for good cause, bad cause, or no cause. (However, discharged employees can recover for work actually done.) What is an employment contract of indefinite duration? The *Rooney* case addresses this question.

Rooney v. Tyson	*697 N.E.2d 571 (N.Y. Ct. App. 1998)*

In the early 1980s, Cus D'Amato, acting as agent for the young Mike Tyson, agreed with Kevin Rooney that Rooney would be Tyson's trainer "for as long as [Tyson fights] professionally." The parties also agreed that Rooney would receive 10 percent of Tyson's boxing earnings. In 1986, Tyson orally reaffirmed the agreement, stating that Rooney "will be Mike Tyson's trainer as long as Mike Tyson is a professional fighter." In 1988, apparently in connection with Rooney's alleged comments about Tyson's divorce and other business litigation, Tyson formally terminated his boxer-trainer relationship with Rooney.

In 1989, Rooney sued Tyson for breach of contract in federal district court. The jury rendered a $4,415,615 verdict for Rooney, but after that the court granted Tyson's motion for judgment notwithstanding the verdict. After Rooney appealed, the Second Circuit Court of Appeals certified a question of state law to the New York Court of Appeals, that state's highest court. The question was whether an oral personal services contract between a trainer and a boxer "for as long as the boxer fights professionally" is a definite-term agreement to which employment at will does not apply.

Bellacosa, Judge In New York, absent an agreement establishing a fixed duration, an employment relationship is presumed to be a hiring at will, terminable at any time by either party. Our previous precedents have not categorically delineated what may differentiate a "definite," "indefinite," or "fixed" employment term or duration.

This Court [has] found indefinite such temporally amorphous terms as "permanent," to "continue indefinitely and will follow [the employee] in each succeeding year," [and] to "devote [the employee's] whole time and attention" to the employer's business. This Court also adopted the at-will presumption doctrine in [a case where] a general hiring was found to result from an employment agreement that was "yearly" or "by the year." The court stated:

> In England it is held that a general hiring, or a hiring by the terms of which no time is fixed, is a hiring by the year. With us, the rule is inflexible, that a general or indefinite hiring is prima facie a hiring at will; and if the servant seeks to make it out yearly hiring, the burden is upon him to establish it by proof. A hiring at so much a day, week, month or year, no time being specified, is an indefinite hiring, and no presumption attaches that it was for a day even, but only at the rate fixed for whatever time the party may serve. . . . A contract to pay one $2,500 a year for services is not a contract for a year, but a contract to pay at the rate of $2,500 a year for services actually rendered, and is determinable at will by either party. . . . In all such cases the contract may be put an end to by either party at any time, unless the time is fixed.

New York's jurisprudence is supple and realistic, and surely not so rigid as to require that a definite duration can be found only in a determinable calendar date. Thus, although the exact end-date of Tyson's professional boxing career was not precisely calculable, the boundaries of beginning and end of the employment period are sufficiently ascertainable. That is enough to defeat a matter-of-law decision by a judge. Under the employment agreement, the durational term was understandable to the parties and reasonably determinable by the fact finders. The range of the employment relationship is established by the definable commencement and conclusion of Tyson's professional boxing career. Though the times are not precisely predictable and calculable to dates certain, they are legally and experientially limited and ascertainable by objective benchmarks.

The Court of Appeals held that a contract between a trainer and a boxer to train the boxer "for as long as the boxer fights professionally" is a contract for a definite duration and is not terminable at will.

Smith, Judge, dissenting   By its ruling, the majority heralds a new era in interpreting oral promises of potentially long-term employment. Because I believe the majority's conclusion is contrary to precedent, I dissent.

Our precedents indicate that a hiring for an "indefinite" duration includes one that may have some definable ending point, but the actual length of employment is not fixed with precision. For example, in [one case] plaintiff sought to prove that he was employed for life or at least for as long a time as the defendant remained in business based upon an oral promise of "permanent employment." We characterized the promise as "nothing more than that the employment [was] to continue indefinitely." [Also,] a contract for life is a contract for an indefinite time. Similarly, an employment contract which provides that an employee may only be terminated for "just cause" represents a hiring for an indefinite duration.

Such circumstances may be contrasted with an employment relationship where its duration is either definite or capable of being determined. In every example addressed by this Court, a "definite" duration was only determinable by reference to a precise calendar date. It would also appear that parties might specify that employment is to continue indefinitely until the happening of a particular event. However, it is only when the event precisely defines the length of employment that it will be considered of "definite" duration. Thus, a fixed duration may be precisely measured when employment lasts through summer (from the June solstice to the September equinox) or until the next election (first Tuesday in November), but not by the level of a company's stock, a lifetime, or subjective performance evaluations.

A period of time measured by an individual employer's continued professional career is indistinguishable from a [period measured by] a corporate employer's remaining in business. Similarly, career-long employment is akin to a " 'permanent' position" allegedly measured by an employee's lifetime, which we have held is employment of an indefinite duration. The majority concludes that the ending of a professional boxing career is somehow more definite than death. The distinction seen by the majority is elusive, to say the least.

The Common Law Exceptions

Because it allows employers to discharge indefinite-term employees with virtual impunity, employment at will has long been regarded as a force for economic efficiency but also as a threat to workers' job security. Although the doctrine remains important today, it has been eroded by many of the developments described in this chapter. For example, the NLRA forbids dismissal for union affiliation, and labor contracts frequently bar termination without just cause. Also, Title VII prohibits firings based on certain personal traits, the ADEA blocks discharges on the basis of age, and the ADA forbids terminations for covered disabilities.

Over the past 20 to 25 years, moreover, courts have been carving out common law exceptions to employment at will. Here we discuss the three most important such exceptions. Although a few states do not recognize any of these exceptions, most states have adopted one or more of them. In such states, a terminated employee sometimes can recover against her employer for **wrongful discharge** or **unjust dismissal.** The remedies in successful wrongful discharge suits depend heavily on whether the plaintiff's claim sounds in contract or in tort, with tort remedies being more advantageous for plaintiffs.

The Public Policy Exception The public policy exception to employment at will, which has been recognized by over four-fifths of the states, is the most common basis for a wrongful discharge suit. It usually is a tort claim. In public policy cases, the terminated employee argues that his discharge was unlawful because it violated the state's public policy. How do courts determine the content of this public policy? Although there is some disagreement on the subject, most courts limit "public policy" to the policies furthered by existing laws such as constitutional provisions, statutes, and perhaps

administrative regulations and common law rules. For this reason, employees often fail to recover where they are fired for ethical objections to job assignments or employer practices.

Successful suits under the public policy exception usually involve firings caused by an employee's: (1) refusal to commit an unlawful act (e.g., committing perjury or violating the antitrust laws), (2) performance of an important public obligation (e.g., jury duty or whistle-blowing),[13] or (3) exercise of a legal right or privilege (e.g., making a workers' compensation claim or refusing to take an illegal polygraph test). In each case, the act (or refusal to act) that caused the firing is consistent with some public policy; for this reason, the firing frustrates the policy. For example, firing an employee for filing a workers' compensation claim undermines the public policies underlying state workers' compensation statutes.

The following *Bammert* case illustrates that the mere fact that a discharge is unfounded or unfair does not mean that the public policy theory applies. Many courts, as in *Bammert,* require that the plaintiff be able to point to a clear public policy as indicated by a specific statute or other law that was violated by her discharge.

---

[13]Whistle-blowers are employees who publicly disclose dangerous, illegal, or improper behavior. Most states have passed statues protecting the employment rights of certain whistle-blowers.

Bammert v. Don's Super-Valu, Inc.   *2002 Wisc. LEXIS 483 (Sup. Ct. Wisc. 2002)*

Karen Bammert worked as the assistant manager at Don's Super-Valu in Menomonie, Wisconsin. Her husband is a Menomonie police officer. Don's is owned by Don Williams, whose wife, Nona, was arrested for drunk driving. Bammert's husband assisted in the arrest by administering a breathalyzer test. Shortly thereafter, Bammert was fired, allegedly in retaliation for her husband's participation in the arrest of her boss's wife.

Bammert sued Don's for wrongful discharge, invoking the public policy exception to the employment-at-will doctrine. Don's moved to dismiss and the trial court granted this motion. The court of appeals affirmed, and Bammert appealed.

SYKES, Justice   Bammert was an at-will employee. In general, at-will employees are terminable at will, for any reason, without cause and with no judicial remedy. Whether Bammert has an actionable claim for wrongful discharge turns on the question of whether the public policy exception to the employment-at-will doctrine can be extended to a retaliatory discharge based upon the conduct of a nonemployee spouse.

The starting point for any wrongful discharge case is *Brockmeyer.* There we adopted a public policy exception to the long-standing employment-at-will doctrine which al-

lows an at-will employee to sue for wrongful discharge when the discharge is contrary to a fundamental and well-defined public policy as evidenced by existing law. The court in *Brockmeyer* specifically declined to engraft a broad implied duty of good faith onto the at-will employment relationship. Imposing a good-faith duty would unduly restrict an employer's discretion in managing the work force and subject each discharge to judicial incursions into the amorphous conduct of bad faith. Instead, the court concluded that in the interests of employees, employers, and the public, a narrow public policy exception was justified, applicable only where the discharge clearly contravenes the public welfare and gravely violates paramount requirements of public interest.

Accordingly, to state a claim for wrongful discharge, a plaintiff must identify a constitutional, statutory, or administrative provision that clearly articulates a fundamental and well-defined public policy. Not every statutory, constitutional, or administrative provision invariably sets forth a clear public policy mandate. The determination of whether a public policy sufficient to trigger the exception is made by reference to the content of the provision. Our cases since *Brockmeyer* have cautioned against interpreting the public policy exception too broadly. The employment-at-will doctrine is a stable fixture of our common law, and has been since 1871. It is central to the free market economy and serves the interests of employees as well as employers by maximizing the freedom of both. The "antidote" to the potential for unfairness in employment-at-will is an employment contract. The prevailing general rule is that an at-will employee has no legal remedy for an employer's unjustified decision to terminate the employment relationship.

Bammert's claim must be evaluated against this backdrop. She has identified two public policies being implicated here: Wis. Stat. § 346.63, which prohibits the operation of a motor vehicle while under the influence of an intoxicant; and Wis. Stat. § 765.001(2), which describes the intent of the Family Code as including the promotion of the institution of marriage, for the preservation of the family, society, the state, morality, and indeed, all civilization. We

would be hard-pressed to say that these are not fundamental, well-established public policies. Clearly, both statutes reflect compelling public interests—one requiring the diligent pursuit and punishment of drunk drivers and the other requiring the vigorous promotion of the institution of marriage. But on the assumed facts of this case, that conclusion doesn't get us very far. Bammert was not fired for *her* participation in the enforcement of the laws against drunk driving; she was fired for *her husband's* participation in the enforcement of those laws. Discharges for conduct outside of the employment relationship by someone other than the discharged employee are not actionable under present law. The public policy generally favoring the stability of marriage, while unquestionably strong, provides an insufficient basis upon which to enlarge what was meant to be, and has always been, an extremely narrow exception to employment at will.

Bammert's claim identifies a public policy completely unrelated to her employment, being enforced by someone else, who is employed elsewhere. That the "someone else" is her husband makes her discharge obviously retaliatory, and reminds us of the sometimes harsh reality of employment-at-will, but it does not provide acceptable grounds for expansion of the public policy exception beyond its present boundaries. To expand the public policy exception to fit this case would invite future applications to retaliatory discharges based upon the conduct of any close relative, conduct which is wholly unconnected to the employment relationship.

Affirmed in favor of Don's.

The Implied Covenant of Good Faith and Fair Dealing A wrongful discharge suit based on the implied covenant of good faith and fair dealing usually is a contract claim. Here, the employee argues that her discharge was unlawful because it was not made in good faith or did not amount to fair dealing, thus breaching the implied contract term. Only about 25 percent of the states have recognized this exception to employment at will, and most of these give it a narrow scope.

Promises by Employers Using various legal theories, courts have increasingly made employers liable for breaking promises to their employees regarding termi-

nation policy. Such promises typically are express statements made by employers during hiring or employee orientation, or in their employee manuals, handbooks, personnel policies, and benefit plans. Occasionally such promises are implied from business custom and usage as well. Here, our concern is with express or implied employer promises involving matters such as discharge policies and discharge procedures. If the employer fails to follow those promises when it fires an employee, it is liable for breach of contract. At least two-thirds of the states recognize this exception to employment at will. As the following *Progress Printing* case suggests, however, employers often succeed in disclaiming liability for their own promises.

Progress Printing Co. v. Nichols   *421 S.E.2d 428 (Va. Sup. Ct. 1992)*

On January 20, 1987, William H. Nichols began work as a pressman for the Progress Printing Company. At that time, Nichols was provided with a copy of the company's Employees' Handbook. The handbook stated that Progress would not discharge or suspend an employee "without just cause" and that the company "shall give at least one warning notice in writing" before termination, except under certain circumstances not relevant here.

On February 2, 1987, however, the firm's personnel director gave Nichols a form which stated in part:

I have received a copy of the Progress Printing Employee Handbook. I recognize that an understanding of this information is important to a successful relationship between Progress Printing and myself. I agree to follow the procedures and guidelines it contains. Any questions concerning Progress Printing's policies will be directed to the Personnel Director.

The employment relationship between Progress Printing and the employee is *at will and may be terminated by either party at any time.* [Emphasis in original.]

Nichols and the personnel director both signed the form.

On March 8, 1989, Nichols became upset over Progress's failure to correct a recurring defect in a print job, and he refused to complete that job assignment as a result. Nichols was fired on the following day, without the prior written notice promised by the Employee Handbook.

Nichols then sued for wrongful discharge in a Virginia trial court. After that court ruled in his favor and awarded him $9,000 in damages, Progress appealed.

Lacy, Justice   In Virginia, as in a majority of jurisdictions, the employment relationship is presumed to be "at will," which means that the employment term extends for an indefinite period and may be terminated for any reason. This presumption may be rebutted if sufficient evidence is produced to show that the employment is for a definite, rather than an indefinite, term. Progress argues that Nichols failed to rebut the presumption because the handbook did not constitute an enforceable employment contract and, even if it did, the subsequent execution of the acknowledgment form created an at-will employment relationship.

A number of jurisdictions have held that the employer can be bound by termination-for-cause provisions contained in employee handbooks where those provisions are communicated to the employee in a sufficiently specific manner. We have held that an employment condition which allows termination only for cause sets a definite term for the duration of the employment. We nevertheless agree with Progress that the acknowledgment form specifically superseded and replaced that [just cause] provision with the agreement that the employment relationship was at will. We base this holding on a number of grounds.

The termination-for-cause language of the handbook and the employment-at-will relationship agreed to in the subsequent acknowledgment form are in direct conflict and cannot be reconciled in any reasonable way. If the documents are considered a single contract, this conflict fails to provide sufficient evidence to rebut the presumption of employment at will.

[In any event,] the acknowledgment form was not a part of the handbook and was executed 13 days after Nichols began work. Under these circumstances, the form reflects an understanding between the parties separate from that contained in the handbook. Execution of the form memorialized reciprocal commitments that satisfy the requisites of a contract—there was an offer of employment at will; the employee continued service, which constituted the consideration; and the employee accepted by performance.

We conclude that the employment relationship between Nichols and Progress was at-will employment which either party could terminate at any time. Therefore, Progress did not breach the employment contract when it terminated Nichols.

Trial court decision on Nichols's employment-at-will claim reversed in favor of Progress.

Problems and Problem Cases

1. Deborah Tolbert, a secretary employed by the Martin-Marietta Corporation, was raped by a Martin-Marietta janitor while on her way to lunch within the secured defense facility where she worked. She sued Martin-Marietta, alleging that it had negligently hired the janitor and had negligently failed to make its premises safe for employees. Martin-Marietta argued that Tolbert could not sue in negligence because workers' compensation was her sole remedy. Is the company correct under the positional-risk test? Under the increased risk test?

2. Folkerson is a professional mime who was employed by Circus Circus to perform in the guise of a life-size children's wind-up toy named "Kelbi the Living Doll." Because Folkerson was so convincing in her character, casino patrons would often wonder whether or not she was a real person. Folkerson was concerned because some patrons would try to touch her to find out if she was human. When Folkerson discussed these concerns with her supervisor, she was told that she should call security whenever she experienced problems and was provided with a sign reading "Stop, Do Not Touch," which she wore on her back. Further, Circus Circus allowed another performer, a large man dressed in a clown costume, to accompany Folkerson when she was performing. Folkerson ensured her protection further by enlisting the help of others at the casino who told her that they would call security if they saw that she was in trouble and would occasionally tell casino patrons not to touch Folkerson or other performers. Despite these precautions, Folkerson was touched by a casino patron on November 20, 1991. According to Folkerson, a casino patron approached her and said to onlookers, "I will show you how real she really is." A woman working at a nearby car rental counter warned the patron three times not to touch Folkerson. Nonetheless, the patron moved toward Folkerson with open, extended arms, as though he planned to hug her. He touched her in the shoulder area, whereupon Folkerson reached up and hit the patron in the mouth. After Folkerson's supervisor reviewed a videotape of the incident, he terminated Folkerson's employment based upon his conclusion that Folkerson did not have adequate provocation to hit the patron. Folkerson alleged that she was terminated in retaliation for her opposition to and rejection of the casino patron's sexual harassment, in violation of Title VII. Is this a good argument?

3. Dianne Rawlinson, a female applicant who was rejected for employment as a prison guard in the Alabama prison system, challenged certain state rules restricting her employment prospects under Title VII. They were: (1) requirements that all prison employees be at least 5 feet 2 inches tall and weigh at least 120 pounds, and (2) a rule expressly prohibiting women from assuming close-contact prison guard positions in maximum-security prisons (most of which were all-male). What method of proving a Title VII case should Rawlinson use in attacking the height and weight requirements? Does she need to use one of these methods to attack the second rule? What argument should the state use if Rawlinson establishes that the height and weight requirements have

an adverse impact? What Title VII defense might the state have for the second rule? With regard to the second rule, assume that at this time Alabama's maximum security prisons housed their male prisoners barracks-style rather than putting them in cells, and that they did not separate sex offenders from other prisoners.

4. Wally White, the owner of the Progressive Printing Company, had always been a civil rights pioneer. Back in the 1950s and 1960s, when such behavior was not always popular or fashionable, Wally had refused to discriminate against blacks and other racial minorities, instead hiring on a strictly color-blind basis. Now, Wally decides that the new millennium demands new, even more progressive, hiring policies for his company. Wally decides that at least 75 percent of his workforce will consist of African-Americans and other racial minorities, and these people will get first crack at all promotions. White employees and job-seekers, says Wally, will just have to wait their turn. This new plan, moreover, will be permanent. Wally's plan is challenged as race-based employment discrimination under Title VII. Will it survive a Title VII attack? Why or why not?

5. Azteca, which operates a chain of restaurants, employed Sanchez from October 1991 to July 1995. Throughout his tenure at Azteca, Sanchez was subjected to a relentless campaign of insults, name-calling, and vulgarities. Male co-workers and a supervisor repeatedly referred to Sanchez in Spanish and English as "she" and "her." Male co-workers mocked Sanchez for walking and carrying his serving tray "like a woman," and taunted him in Spanish and English as, among other things, a "faggot" and a "f--- female whore." The remarks were not stray or isolated. This conduct violated company policy. Since 1989, Azteca has expressly prohibited sexual harassment and retaliation and has directed its employees to bring complaints regarding such conduct directly to the attention of the corporate office. It also has sexual harassment training programs, in English and in Spanish. Although Sanchez attended Azteca's sexual harassment training and was familiar with the company's antiharassment policy and procedures, he never complained to the corporate EEO officer or the area manager about the harassment he experienced, as required by the corporate policy. He did, however, complain to the general manager of the Southcenter restaurant and an assistant manager as well as to Azteca's human resources director. Was this a case of sexual harassment?

6. Linda Twinkle, a receptionist for the XYZ Corporation, was stationed at the gateway to the image-conscious firm's plush offices. Linda joined a small religious cult whose members believed that it is unnatural and immoral for people to bathe. Linda followed this practice 100 percent. Soon enough, XYZ employees, potential customers, and other visitors to the firm began to be grossed out by Linda's appearance and her odor. Eventually, XYZ switched Linda to its janitorial staff. Linda sues under Title VII, alleging discrimination on the basis of her religion. Will XYZ succeed if it argues that it was not discriminating against Linda's *religion,* but rather against her appearance and her aroma? Will it succeed if it argues that Linda's small cult does not count as a "religion" under Title VII? What else can the firm argue? Will this argument work?

7. Ann Hopkins, a senior manager at the accounting firm of Price Waterhouse, was denied partnership in the firm. A persistent theme in existing partners' written comments on Hopkins's candidacy was the belief that Hopkins acted in ways inappropriate for a woman to act. Thus, one partner described her as "macho," another wrote that she "overcompensated for being a woman," yet another advised that she take "a course at charm school," and still others objected to her use of profanity. Also, a partner who tried to help Hopkins through the process told her that to improve her chances, she should walk more femininely, dress more femininely, wear makeup, have her hair styled, and wear jewelry. Assuming that these opinions were the only reason for Hopkins's failure to make partner, was that denial illegal sex discrimination under Title VII?

8. Breeden worked for Clark County School District. On October 21, 1994, Breeden's male supervisor met with Breeden and another male employee to review the psychological evaluation reports of four job applicants. The report for one of the applicants disclosed that the applicant had once commented to a co-worker, "I hear making love to you is like making love to the Grand Canyon." At the meeting Breeden's supervisor read the comment aloud, looked at Breeden and stated, "I don't know what that means." The other employee then said, "Well, I'll tell you later," and both men chuckled. Breeden later complained about the comment to the offending employee, to two assistant superintendents, and the employee's supervisor. Breeden was transferred and she claims that she was retaliated against for making these complaints. Has she stated a good claim of sexual harassment?

9. Caldwell worked for Holland's Kentucky Fried Chicken restaurant, where she had an excellent record. On Saturday, her three-year-old son awoke with a high fever, pain in his ears, and congestion. Caldwell notified her manager that she would be absent because she had to take her son to the doctor. At the emergency clinic, the son was diagnosed with an acute ear infection and put on

medication. Caldwell was also informed that he would need surgery to prevent permanent hearing loss. That night, Caldwell, a single mother, worked the night shift at another KFC owned by Holland, while her elderly mother cared for her son. When Caldwell reported to work on Monday, she was summarily fired. On a follow-up medical visit, the son had to have another course of antibiotics, and two weeks later, had surgery. Was Caldwell's leave covered by the FMLA?

10. Dey worked as a controller for the Colt Construction and Development Corporation. Her duties included maintaining Colt's payroll, payables, and receivables; making disbursements to various parties; paying office expenses; documenting project costs; and preparing various forms and reports. However, while Dey provided the data for Colt's income tax returns and its year-end financial statements, each was prepared by an outside accountant. Dey was fired from her job for reasons that are not completely clear. At that time, she was making $27,820 a year. Unlike Dey, Gagnon, her successor with Colt, was a CPA with an MBA degree. Gagnon's duties included the tasks performed by Dey plus preparation of Colt's tax returns, computerization of its financial records, and analysis of real estate investments. Gagnon was hired at a salary of $50,000. After Gagnon left Colt's employ, he was replaced by Maloney. Maloney had an MBA but had failed to pass the CPA exam. Also, he was about to be laid off by his employer. Maloney had responsibilities similar to Dey's responsibilities. Unlike Dey, however, he could execute certain documents without getting a company officer to sign them, and he supposedly continued the computerization of Colt's financial records. Colt originally offered Maloney $30,000, but upped that figure to $32,400, the amount Maloney had been making with his then-employer. Dey sued Colt, alleging that these pay discrepancies violated the Equal Pay Act. Did they?

11. The Pillsbury Company maintained an electronic mail communication system. The company repeatedly assured its employees that all e-mail communications on the system would remain confidential. Pillsbury further assured its employees that it would not intercept e-mail communications and use them as grounds for terminating or reprimanding employees. Smyth, a Pillsbury employee, received e-mails from his supervisor over Pillsbury's e-mail system on his home computer. Relying on Pillsbury's assurances, Smyth exchanged some blunt e-mails with his supervisor. One of them apparently contained a threat to "kill the back-stabbing bastards," and another seemingly referred to a firm holiday party as the "Jim Jones Kool-aid affair." Later, Pillsbury retrieved or intercepted these messages, and fired Smyth for what it deemed inappropriate and unprofessional comments over the e-mail system. Smyth sued Pillsbury for wrongful discharge under the public policy theory, alleging that public policy precludes an employer from firing an employee in violation of his privacy. Will Smyth win?

Online Research: Researching Discrimination Charges

Access the EEOC's website (http://www.eeoc.gov) and find statistics about the numbers of discrimination charges filed in particular years. What trends do you see?

52

ENVIRONMENTAL REGULATION

The B-P Paper Company is planning to build a new papermaking facility on property it owns in the Atlanta, Georgia, area that borders on the Chattahoochee River. The facility will have an industrial boiler that burns wood wastes to generate process steam for plant operation and will emit sulfur oxides, nitrogen oxides, and particulate emissions to the air. The company plans to draw water from the river to use in the papermaking process and will return it to the river after some in-house treatment to remove some of the pollutants that have been added by the process. Significant quantities of sludge from the papermaking process will have to be disposed of, as well as empty containers in which the chlorine used at the facility was delivered.

• What major requirements will the facility have to meet to control its anticipated air emissions?
• What major requirements will the facility have to meet to control its discharge of wastewater to the Chattahoochee River?
• What major requirements will the company have to meet in dealing with the waste sludge and containers?

TODAY'S BUSINESSPERSON MUST BE concerned not only with competing effectively against competitors but also with complying with a myriad of regulatory requirements. For many businesses, particularly those that manufacture goods or that generate wastes, the environmental laws and regulations loom large in terms of the requirements and costs they impose. They can have a significant effect on the way businesses have to be conducted as well as on their profitability. This area of the law has expanded dramatically over the last three decades, and environmental issues are a major concern of people and governments around the world. This chapter will briefly discuss the development of environmental law and will outline the major federal statutes that have been enacted to control pollution of air, water, and land.

Historical Perspective

Historically, people assumed that the air, water, and land around them would absorb their waste products. In recent times, however, it has become clear that nature's capacity to assimilate people's wastes is not infinite. Burgeoning population, economic growth, and the products of our industrial society can pose risks to human health and the environment. The societal challenge is to accommodate economic activity and growth and at the same time provide reasonable protection of human health and the environment.

Concern about the environment is not a recent phenomenon. In medieval England, Parliament passed smoke control acts making it illegal to burn soft coal at certain times of the year. Where the owner or operator of a piece of property is using it in such a manner as to unreasonably interfere with another owner's (or the public's) health or enjoyment of his property, the courts have long entertained suits to abate the nuisance. Nuisance actions, which are discussed in Chapter 24, Real Property, are frequently not ideal vehicles for dealing with widespread pollution problems. Rather than a hit-or-miss approach, a comprehensive across-the-board approach may be required.

Realizing this, the federal government, as well as many state and local governments, had passed laws to abate air and water pollution by the late 1950s and 1960s. As the 1970s began, concern over the quality and future of the environment produced new laws and fresh public demands for action. During the 1980s, these laws were refined and, in some cases, their coverage was extended. Environmental concerns continue to be prominent around the globe, and many countries, both individually and collectively, have programs in place to address them. Accordingly, it is increasingly important that the businessperson be cognizant of the legal requirements and the public's environmental concerns in operating a business. These requirements and concerns not only may pose challenges to businesses but can provide opportunities for them as well.

The Environmental Protection Agency

In 1970, the Environmental Protection Agency was created to consolidate the federal government's environmental responsibilities. This was an explicit recognition that the problems of air and water pollution, solid waste disposal, water supply, and pesticide and radiation control were interrelated and required a consolidated approach. Congress subsequently passed comprehensive new legislation covering, among other things, air and water pollution, pesticides, ocean dumping, and waste disposal. Among the considerations prompting these laws were protection of human health, aesthetics, economic costs of continued pollution, and protection of natural systems.

The initial efforts were aimed at problems that, by and large, could be seen, smelled, or tasted. As control requirements have been put in place and implemented by industry and government, and as significant progress has been noted in the form of cleaner air and water, attention has focused increasingly on problems that are somewhat less visible but potentially more threatening—the dangers posed by toxic substances. These dangers have come into more prominence as scientific research indicates the risks posed by some substances, as new detection technology has enabled the detection of suspect substances in ever more minute quantities in the world around us, and as increased monitoring and testing is conducted. Determination of the degree of risk posed by any particular substance or proposed action—and deciding the most appropriate control strategy—frequently triggers strong disagreements within society because of what is at stake in terms of economic costs and protection of health and the environment.

The National Environmental Policy Act

The National Environmental Policy Act (NEPA) was signed into law on January 1, 1970. The act required that an environmental impact statement be prepared for every recommendation or report on legislation and for every major federal action significantly affecting the quality of the environment. The environmental impact statement must: (1) describe the environmental impact of the proposed action, (2) discuss impacts that cannot be avoided, (3) discuss the alternatives to the proposed action, (4) indicate differences between short- and long-term impacts, and (5) detail any irreversible commitments of resources.

NEPA requires a federal agency to consider the environmental impact of a project before the project is undertaken. Other federal, state, and local agencies, as well as interested citizens, have an opportunity to comment on the environmental impact of a project before the agency can proceed. Where the process is not followed, citizens can and have gone to court to force compliance with NEPA. A number of states and local governments have passed their own environmental impact laws requiring NEPA-type statements for major public and private developments.

While the federal and state laws requiring the preparation of environmental impact statements appear directed at government actions, it is important to note that the government actions covered often include the granting of permits to private parties. Thus, businesspeople may readily find themselves involved in the preparation of an environmental impact statement—for example, in connection with a marina to be built in a navigable waterway or a resort development that will impact wetlands, both of which require permits from the U.S. Army Corps of Engineers. Similarly, a developer seeking a local zoning change so she can build a major commercial or residential development may find that she is asked to finance a study of the potential environmental impact of her proposed project.

Air Pollution

Background

Fuel combustion, industrial processes, and solid waste disposal are the major contributors to air pollution. People's initial concern with air pollution related to what they could see—visible or smoke pollution. For instance, in the 1880s, Chicago and Cincinnati enacted smoke control ordinances. As the technology became available to deal with smoke and particulate emissions, attention focused on other, less visible gases that could adversely affect human health and vegetation or that could increase the acidity of lakes, thus making them unsuitable for fish.

Clean Air Act

The comprehensive legislation enacted in 1970 and known as the **Clean Air Act** provides the basis for the present approach to air pollution control. In 1977, Congress modified the 1970 act and enacted provisions designed to prevent deterioration of the air in areas where its quality currently exceeds that required by federal law. Thirteen years then passed before Congress, in 1990, enacted a major revision to the act to deal with acid rain, toxic air pollutants, and urban smog problems that were not satisfactorily dealt with under the existing legislation.

Ambient Air Control Standards

The Clean Air Act established a comprehensive approach for dealing with air pollution. EPA is required to set **national ambient air quality standards** for the major pollutants that have an adverse impact on human health—that is, to regulate the amount of a given pollutant that may be present in the air around us. The ambient air quality standards are set at two levels: (1) **primary standards** are designed to protect the public's health from harm; and (2) **secondary standards** are designed to protect vegetation, materials, climate, visibility, and economic values. Pursuant to this statutory mandate, EPA has set national ambient air quality standards for carbon monoxide, nitrogen oxide, sulfur oxide, ozone, lead, and particulate matter.

Each state is required to develop a **state implementation plan** for meeting national ambient air quality standards. This necessitates an inventory of the various sources of air pollution and their contribution to the total air pollution in the air quality region. The major emitters of pollutants are then required to reduce their emissions to a level that ensures that overall air quality meets the national standards. For example, a factory may be required to limit its emissions of volatile organic compounds (a contributor to ozone or smog) to a certain amount per unit of production or hour of operation; similarly, a power plant might have its emissions of sulfur oxides and nitrogen oxides limited to so many pounds per Btu of energy produced. The states have the responsibility for selecting which activities must be regulated or curtailed so that overall emissions at any point in the state or area do not exceed the national standards.

Because by the late 1980s many of the nation's major urban areas were still not in compliance with the health-based standards for ozone and carbon monoxide, Congress, in its 1990 amendments, imposed an additional set of requirements on the areas that were not in compliance. Thus, citizens living in the areas and existing businesses, as well as prospective businesses seeking to locate in the designated areas, face increasingly stringent control measures designed to bring the areas into attainment with the national standards. These new requirements mean that businesses such as bakeries that are generally not thought of as major polluters of the air have to further control their emissions, and that paints and other products that contain solvents may have to be reformulated.

Acid Rain Controls

Responding to the 1970 Clean Air Act, which sought to protect the air in the area near sources of air pollution, many electric generating facilities built tall smokestacks so that the emissions were dispersed over a broader area. Unwittingly, this contributed to long-range transport of some of the pollutants, which changed chemically enroute and fell to earth many miles away in the form of acid rain, snow, fog, or dry deposition. For a number of years, a considerable debate ensued over acid rain, in particular as to whether it was a problem, what kind of damage it caused, whether anything should be done about it, and who should pay for the cost of limiting it. The 1990 amendments addressed acid deposition by among other things placing a cap on the overall emissions of the contributors to it (the oxides of sulfur and nitrogen) and requiring electric utilities to reduce their emissions to specified levels in two steps over the next decade. This required most electric generating facilities in the country to install large control devices known as scrubbers, to switch to lower sulfur coal, or to install so-called clean coal technologies. The 1990 amendments also provide an innovative system whereby companies whose emissions are cleaner than required by law can sell their rights to emit more sulfur oxide—known as *allowances*—to other companies that may be finding it more difficult to meet the standards.

Control of Toxic Air Pollutants

The 1970 Clean Air Act also required EPA to regulate the emission of toxic air pollutants. Under this authority, EPA set standards only for asbestos, beryllium, mercury, vinyl chloride, benzene, and radionuclides. Unhappy with the slow pace of regulation of toxic air pollutants, Congress in 1990 specified a list of 189 chemicals for which EPA is required to issue regulations requiring the installation of the maximum available control technology. The regulations are to be developed and the control technology installed by industry in phases. Thus, while many toxic emissions have largely gone unregulated, that situation has changed. In addition, a number of chemical companies have announced they are voluntarily reducing their

emissions of toxic chemicals to levels below those they are required to meet by law.

The case that follows, *United States v. Midwest Suspension and Brake*, involves the enforcement of an EPA regulation that controls the management and disposal of asbestos and asbestos-containing materials.

United States v. Midwest Suspension and Brake
49 F. 3d 1197 (6th Cir. 1995)

Midwest Suspension and Brake is in the business of supplying parts for heavy-duty truck suspensions, steering systems, and brakes. One of the operations it performs concerning brake systems involves the collection and rehabilitation of used brake shoes for resale. During the rehabilitation process, brake shoes are disassembled and parts that may contain asbestos are discarded. Some brake shoes are delined, a procedure performed by removing rivets that hold the brake lining to the brake table and then cleaning, sandblasting, painting, and relining the table with a new brake block. Old brake blocks and brake linings, which contain asbestos, are discarded.

During an EPA inspection of the Midwest facility, numerous emissions of asbestos were documented and the shop floor yielded detectable amounts of asbestos. As a result, EPA issued a "finding of violation" of the "no visible emission" requirement of the National Emission Standard for Hazardous Air Pollutants (NESHAP) for asbestos. To resolve the matter, Midwest agreed to the issuance of an Administrative Order (AO) that required that Midwest comply with the Clean Air Act and the asbestos NESHAP, including the no visible emission requirement.

As a preventative measure, the AO specified waste management requirements for Midwest operations including the following: (1) that delining wastes fall into a sturdy cardboard box, instead of falling to the ground; (2) that the box be securely closed and wrapped so that it would not leak when discarded; and (3) that the box bear a warning label. The AO also required that the floor of the delining area be vacuumed, not swept, and that the vacuum residue be tightly sealed before disposal. Finally, the AO required that asbestos waste be segregated and separately disposed of, without compacting, at a landfill.

Subsequent EPA inspections of the Midwest facility found numerous violations of the AO—as did inspections by the Wayne County (Michigan) Health Department. Asbestos wastes were being compacted, resulting in visible emissions. Vacuum residue was not tightly sealed, and boxes of delining wastes were improperly taped, resulting in visible emissions during landfill disposal. Asbestos-containing materials were being dropped on the shop floor, and the floor was being broom cleaned rather than vacuumed.

When efforts to have Midwest comply with the AO were unsuccessful, EPA filed suit against it in federal court. EPA sought injunctive relief as well as civil penalties of up to $25,000 per day for each violation. The federal district court found that Midwest had violated the Clean Air Act and ordered it to pay a $50,000 civil penalty. Midwest appealed, contending, among other things, that it did not fall under the Clean Air Act or the asbestos NESHAP because it did not fabricate friction products containing asbestos within the meaning of the Act.

Contie, Circuit Judge   According to the NESHAP definition of "fabrication," it includes *any* processing of a manufactured product. A plain reading of this definition is that "fabricating" is not limited to specific types of processes, such as preparing chemical substances, but entails *any* processing of a manufactured product containing asbestos. Moreover, the EPA has explained that the definition of "pro-

cessing" includes operations which "cut, shape, assemble, mix, or otherwise alter" a manufactured product that contains commercial asbestos.

The district court found that Midwest's brake refurbishing operation clearly falls within this definition of processing, and therefore Midwest is considered a business that "fabricates" friction products containing commercial asbestos within the meaning of the Act. The court found that Midwest's business involves among other things, the production and sale of rebuilt brake shoes for medium and heavy duty trucks. As described by Robert Cuipak, Midwest's general manager, Midwest's process of making rebuilt brake shoes includes the following:

> We take used brake shoes, deline them, inspect them to make sure that they are still to the manufacturer's specifications, clean them, paint them and then reline them with brake lining. And those are made available as second-hand shoes.

The district court found that Midwest "fabricated" brake shoes by "cutting" and "altering" used brake shoes by removing their linings, which contain asbestos, and by assembling refurbished brake cores with new linings, which may contain asbestos, for sale as rebuilt shoes. The court found that the entire rebuilding operation is a "process," and that Midwest's production of rebuilt brake shoes which includes a delining process, a sandblasting process, an assembly of the cores and linings, and, in some cases, the cutting, grinding, and drilling of strip stock, constitutes "fabrication" within the meaning of the Act.

We agree with the district court that these operations come within the definition of "fabrication"—the processing of friction materials containing asbestos—as contemplated by the Act. Substantial evidence in the record indicates that during Midwest's operations, particularly during the delining phase where the plow on the machines breaks and shatters the used brake linings containing asbestos, and during sandblasting, where asbestos fibers encapsulated in rust on the brake cores are pulverized into trillions of fibers, asbestos-containing material is plainly being "cut" and "otherwise altered."

Furthermore, there is evidence in the record to support the government's contention that the Asbestos NESHAP was amended specifically so that the regulations would apply to brake relining operations, such as Midwest's operation. In 1973, the EPA conducted an extensive investigation of fabricating facilities and concluded that facilities that process brake shoe linings generated significant amounts of asbestos dust. For that reason, in 1975, the EPA amended the Asbestos NESHAP to include the fabricating standard, which regulates facilities that "fabricate" friction products.

The friction product fabricating standards were promulgated in 1975 and published to provide a full opportunity for notice and comment by the public. Therefore, Midwest's allegation that the terms of the regulation were too broad to give it notice that its operations would be covered has no merit. Midwest, as a business dealing with asbestos, was under a duty to be aware of the published regulations and their interpretation.

Judgment against Midwest affirmed.

New Source Controls

The Clean Air Act requires that new stationary sources such as factories and power plants install the best available technology for reducing air pollution. EPA is required to establish the standards to be met by new stationary sources and has done so for the major stationary sources of air pollution. This means that a new facility covered by the regulations must install state of the art control technology, even if it is locating in an area where the air quality is better than that required by law. Two major policy objectives underlie this requirement: (1) to provide a level playing field for new industry irrespective of where it locates and (2) to gradually improve air quality by requiring state of the art controls whenever a new facility is built.

Permits

In the 1990 amendments to the Clean Air Act, Congress established a permit system whereby major sources of air pollution—particularly those subject to the New Source Performance Standards, air toxics, nonattainment, and acid rain provisions of the act—as well as certain other sources have to obtain permits that specify the limits on emissions from the sources. The permits also contain monitoring and reporting requirements. Once a state permitting program is approved by EPA, the permits are issued by the state in which a facility is located. A controversial issue in the permitting regulations is when a source has to seek a modification of a permit because of process or operational changes that might increase emissions. If a modification to a permit is required by an anticipated change, this can greatly complicate the timely execution of business plans.

CYBERLAW IN ACTION

Online Permitting

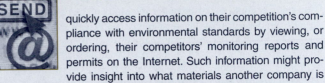

The Clean Air Act, the Clean Water Act, and the Resource Conservation and Recovery Act, as well as a number of other federal and local environmental laws, require certain businesses to obtain permits and to periodically report their discharges and/or other information to administrative agencies by filing permits or monitoring reports. Now the EPA and most, if not all, states make permit applications and motoring report forms available online. In addition, some states make specific companys' reports, or permit files, available to the public on their websites. Online permit and report transactions can streamline the process of complying with environmental law and regulations. Also, businesses can

quickly access information on their competition's compliance with environmental standards by viewing, or ordering, their competitors' monitoring reports and permits on the Internet. Such information might provide insight into what materials another company is using in its processes—or how product volume may be changing over time. Moreover, the online permitting and reporting systems make environmental regulations more transparent, which helps ensure that businesses and regulatory agencies remain accountable to the public. (See, for example, http://www.epa.gov/airmarkets/arp/permits/index.html, http://www.in.gov/idem/air/permits/Air-Permits-Online/index.html)

Enforcement

The primary responsibility for enforcing air quality standards lies with the states, but the federal government has the right to enforce the standards where the states fail to do so. The Clean Air Act also provides for suits by citizens to force industry or the government to fully comply with the act's provisions.

Automobile Pollution

The Clean Air Act provides specifically for air pollution controls on transportation sources such as automobiles. The major pollutants from automobiles are carbon monoxide, hydrocarbons, and nitrogen oxides. Carbon monoxide is a colorless, odorless gas that can dull mental performance and even cause death when inhaled in large quantities. Hydrocarbons, in the form of unburned fuel, are part of a category of air pollutants known as volatile organic compounds (VOCs). VOCs combine with nitrogen oxides under the influence of sunlight to become ozone—we know it as smog.

The 1970 Clean Air Act required a reduction of 90 percent of the carbon monoxide and hydrocarbons emitted by automobiles by 1975 and a 90 percent reduction in the nitrogen oxides emitted by 1976. At the time, these requirements were "technology forcing"; that is, the manufacturers could not rely on already existing technology to meet the standards but rather had to develop new technology. Ultimately, most manufacturers had to go beyond simply making changes in engine design and utilize pollution control devices known as catalytic converters.

Subsequently, Congress addressed the question of setting even more stringent limits on automobile emissions while at the same time requiring that the new automobiles get better gas mileage. The 1990 amendments require further limitations on emissions from tailpipes, the development of so-called clean-fueled vehicles (such as electric and natural gas fueled vehicles) for use in cities with dirty air, and the availability of oxygenated fuels (which are cleaner burning) in specified areas of the country that are having difficulty meeting the air quality limits at least part of the year. These new requirements have significant ramifications for the oil and automobile industries.

Under the Clean Air Act, no manufacturer may sell vehicles subject to emission standards without prior certification from EPA that the vehicles meet the required standards. The tests are performed on prototype vehicles and if they pass, a certificate of conformity covering that type of engine and vehicle is issued. EPA subsequently can test vehicles on the assembly line to make sure that the production vehicles covered by the certificate are meeting the standards. The manufacturers are required to warrant that the vehicle, if properly maintained, will comply with the emission standards for its useful life. If EPA discovers that vehicles in actual use exceed the emission standards, it may order the manufacturer to recall and repair the defective models; this is a power that EPA has exercised on a number of occasions.

The act also provides for the regulation and registration of fuel additives such as lead. In the 1980s, lead was largely phased out of use as an octane enhancer in gasoline. As indicated previously, the 1990 amendments provide for the availability of alternative fuels based on ethanol and methanol.

THE GLOBAL BUSINESS ENVIRONMENT

International Air Problems

During the late 1970s and 1980s, concern developed that the release of chlorine-containing substances such as chlorofluorocarbons (CFCs) used in air conditioning, refrigeration, and certain foam products was depleting the stratospheric ozone layer. This could lead to more ultraviolet radiation reaching the earth and, in turn, more skin cancer. Subsequently, a number of nations, acting under the aegis of the United Nations, signed a treaty agreeing first to limit any increases in production of chlorine-containing substances and ultimately to significantly phase out their use. The 1990 amendments to the Clean Air Act implement the obligations of the United States under the treaty and provide for the phasedown and phaseout of a number of chlorofluorocarbons; accordingly, many businesses have developed or located substitutes for those chemicals that are available only in reduced quantities, if at all.

Other air pollution issues with international dimensions that may result in multinational control efforts are acid rain and global warming/climate change resulting, in part, from increased emissions of carbon dioxide to the atmosphere.

ETHICS IN ACTION

If It's Legal, Is It Ethical?

Suppose a manufacturing facility emits into the air a chemical that it has reason to believe is inadequately regulated by EPA and that poses a significant threat to nearby residents even at levels lower than permitted by EPA. As manager of the facility, would you be satisfied to meet the EPA required level or would you install the additional controls you believe necessary to achieve a reasonably safe level?

Indoor Air Pollution

As we increased the insulation and made our buildings airtight to conserve energy, we generally reduced the air exchange and increased the concentrations of pollutants in our homes and workplaces. In recent years, attention has focused on a range of indoor air problems, sometimes known under the term *sick building syndrome,* including radon gas, asbestos, the products of combustion from fireplaces and stoves, molds and pollens, formaldehyde, cigarette smoke, pesticides, and cleaning products. Some of these problems are being dealt with on a problem-by-problem, or product-by-product, basis under various laws. Others are being addressed by providing information to consumers so that they can take appropriate actions to protect themselves. In some cases, Congress and other legislative bodies have required that steps be taken to minimize the risks, such as the federal requirement for schools to inspect for asbestos and to remove it where certain conditions are found.

Radiation Control

For many years, people have been concerned about radioactivity, particularly radioactivity from nuclear-fueled power plants. Some of these concerns were accentuated by the accident at Chernobyl in the former USSR and the one at Three Mile Island in the United States. Citizens are specifically concerned about the release of radioactivity into the environment during normal operation of the nuclear reactors, accidents through human error or mechanical failure, and disposal of the radioactive wastes generated by the reactors. They are also concerned that the discharge of heated water used to cool the reactor—thermal pollution—may cause damage to the environment. These issues are of particular concern to businesses such as utilities that operate nuclear-powered generating facilities and also to segments of the health industry—such as hospitals and other medical facilities—that may utilize low-level radioactive materials in their diagnostic and treatment activities.

Currently, the problems of reactor safety are under the jurisdiction of the Nuclear Regulatory Commission, which exercises licensing authority over nuclear power plants. EPA is responsible for setting standards for radioactivity in the overall environment and for dealing with the problem of disposal of some radioactive waste. EPA also handles the thermal pollution problem pursuant to its water pollution control authority. In addition, EPA is responsible for regulating emissions from a variety of other sources, such as uranium mill tailing piles and uranium mines.

Water Pollution

Background

History is replete with plagues and epidemics brought on by poor sanitation and polluted water. Indeed, preventing waterborne disease has always been the major reason for combating water pollution. In the early 1970s, fishing and swimming were prohibited in many bodies of water, and game fish could no longer survive in some waters where they had formerly thrived. Lake Erie was becoming choked with algae and considered to be dying. The nation recognized that water pollution could affect public health, recreation, commercial fishing, agriculture, water supplies, and aesthetics. During the 1970s, Congress enacted three major statutes to protect our water resources: the Clean Water Act; the Marine Protection, Research, and Sanctuaries Act; and the Safe Drinking Water Act.

Early Federal Legislation

Federal water pollution legislation dates back to the 19th century when Congress enacted the River and Harbor Act of 1886. In fact, this statute, recodified in the River and Harbor Act of 1899, furnished the legal basis for EPA's initial enforcement actions against polluters. The act provided that people had to obtain a discharge permit from the Army Corps of Engineers to deposit or discharge refuse into a navigable waterway. Under some contemporary court decisions, even hot water discharged from nuclear power plants was considered refuse. The permit system established pursuant to the "Refuse Act" was replaced in 1972 by a more comprehensive permit system now administered by EPA.

Congress passed the initial Federal Water Pollution Control Act (FWPCA) in 1948. Amendments to the FWPCA in 1956, 1965, 1966, and 1970 increased the federal government's role in water pollution abatement and strengthened its enforcement powers.

Clean Water Act

The 1972 amendments to the FWPCA—known as the Clean Water Act—were as comprehensive in the water pollution field as the 1970 Clean Air Act was in the air pollution field. They proclaimed two general goals for this country: (1) to achieve wherever possible by July 1, 1983, water clean enough for swimming and other recreational uses and clean enough for the protection and propagation of fish, shellfish, and wildlife; and (2) to have no discharges of pollutants into the nation's waters by 1985. These goals reflected a national frustration with the lack of progress in dealing with water pollution and a commitment to end such pollution. The new law set out a series of specific actions that federal, state, and local governments and industry were to take by certain dates and also provided strong enforcement provisions to back up the deadlines. In 1977 and again in 1987, Congress modified the 1972 act by adjusting some of the deadlines and otherwise fine-tuning the act.

State Role

Under the Clean Water Act, the states have the primary responsibility for preventing, reducing, and eliminating water pollution. The states have to do this within a national framework, and EPA is empowered to move in if the states do not fulfill their responsibilities.

Controls on Industrial Wastes

The act set a number of deadlines to control water pollution from industrial sources. It required industries discharging wastes into the nation's waterways to install the *best available water pollution control technology;* new sources of industrial pollution must use the best available demonstrated control technology. In each instance, EPA is responsible for issuing guidelines as to the best available technologies. Industries that discharge their wastes into municipal wastewater treatment systems are required to *pretreat* the wastes so that they do not interfere with the biological operation of the plant or pass through the plant without treatment.

Water Quality Standards

The act continued and expanded the previously established system of setting *water quality standards* by designating the uses of specific bodies of water for recreation, public water supply, propagation of fish and wildlife, and agricultural and industrial water supply. Then, the maximum daily loads of various pollutants are set so that the water is suitable for the designated use. The final step is to establish limits on individual dischargers of pollutants so that the water quality standards will be met.

Discharge Permits

The act requires all municipal and industrial discharges to obtain permits—known as an *NPDES permit* or National

Pollution Discharge Elimination System permit—that spell out the amounts and specific pollutants that permit holders are allowed to discharge and any steps that they must take to reduce their present or anticipated discharge. These permits are the vehicles for applying and enforcing the technology-based standards and the water quality–based limitations discussed above. Dischargers are also required to keep records, install and maintain monitoring equipment, and sample their discharges.

Enforcement

Both civil and criminal sanctions are included in the act. Criminal penalties for violating the law range from a minimum of $2,500 for a first offense up to $50,000 per day and two years in prison for subsequent violations. The act is enforced by federal and state governments. In addition, any citizen or group of citizens whose interests are adversely affected has the right to bring a court action against anyone violating an effluent standard, limitation, or order issued by EPA or a state. A significant number of cases have been brought by citizen-action groups against firms whose wastewater discharges exceeded the limits of their discharge permits. Citizens also have the right to take court action against EPA if it fails to carry out mandatory provisions of the law.

In the case that follows, *United States v. Hopkins,* a corporate officer was convicted and sentenced to prison for falsifying reports to the government concerning the discharge of pollutants.

United States v. Hopkins   53 F.3d 533 (2ND Cir. 1995)

Spirol International Corporation is a manufacturer of metal shims and fasteners located in northeastern Connecticut. Spirol's manufacturing operation involves a zinc-based plating process that generates substantial amounts of wastewater containing zinc and other toxic materials; this wastewater is discharged into the nearby Five Mile River. The U.S. Environmental Protection Agency (EPA) has delegated to the State of Connecticut's Department of Environmental Protection (DEP) the authority to administer the Clean Water Act provisions applicable to Spirol's discharges into the river. In 1987, Spirol entered into a consent order with DEP requiring Spirol to pay a $30,000 fine for past violations and to comply in the future with discharge limitations specified in the order. In February 1989, DEP issued a modified "wastewater discharge permit" imposing more restrictive limits on the quantity of zinc and other substances that Spirol was permitted to release into the river.

From 1987 through September 6, 1990, Robert Hopkins was Spirol's vice president for manufacturing. Hopkins signed the 1987 consent decree on behalf of Spirol and had the corporate responsibility for ensuring compliance with the order and the DEP permit. The DEP permit required Spirol each week to collect a sample of its wastewater and send it to an independent laboratory by Friday morning of that week. Spirol was required to report the laboratory results to DEP in a discharge monitoring report once a month. Under the DEP permit, the concentrations of zinc in Spirol's wastewater were not to exceed 2.0 milligrams per liter in any weekly sample, nor to average more than one milligram per liter in any month.

During the period March 1989 to September 1990, Spirol began its weekly sampling process on Monday. A composite sample was taken and analyzed in house. If it contained less than one milligram of zinc, it was sent to the independent laboratory with a "chain of custody" record signed by Hopkins. However, if it exceeded one milligram of zinc, it was discarded and another sample taken and tested the following day. In 54 of the 78 weeks, the samples were sent to the laboratory later than Tuesday. If the Wednesday sample also failed the in-house test, Hopkins would sometimes order that it be discarded and another taken on Thursday, but more often he instructed his subordinates doing the testing to dilute the sample with tap water or to reduce the zinc concentration using an ordinary coffee filter. Any Friday sample that failed the in-house test was always diluted or filtered so that a good sample could be sent to the laboratory by the Friday deadline. In some samples sent to the laboratory there was more tap water than wastewater.

During this period Hopkins filed with DEP monthly discharge monitoring reports consolidating the weekly tests from the independent laboratory. The reports showed no zinc concentrations above one milligram per liter. On each report, Hopkins signed the following certification.

I certify under penalty of law that this document and all attachments were prepared under my direction or supervision in accordance with a system designed to assure that qualified personnel properly gather and evaluate the information submitted. Based on my inquiry of the person or persons who administer the system, or those persons directly responsible for gathering the information, the information is, to the best of my knowledge and belief, true, accurate and complete. I am aware that there are significant penalties for submitting false information, including the possibility of fine and imprisonment for knowing violations.

Contrary to Hopkins's certifications, his subordinates testified that he had caused the samples to be tampered with about 40 percent of the time. On some 25–30 occasions when he had been told that a satisfactory sample had finally been obtained by means of dilution or filtration, Hopkins responded, "I know nothing, I hear nothing." Hopkins was told that the testing procedures were improper, yet he continued to sign the certifications and Spirol continued its discharges into the river.

In December 1993, Hopkins was charged in a three-count indictment alleging (1) that he had knowingly falsified or tampered with Spirol's discharge sampling methods, (2) that he had knowingly violated the conditions of the permit, and (3) that he had conspired to commit those offenses. Hopkins was convicted following a jury trial and sentenced to 21 months in prison, with two years probation following that, and a $7,500 fine. Hopkins appealed, arguing that the government should have been required to prove that he intended to violate the law and that he had specific knowledge of the particular statutory, regulatory or permit requirements imposed under the Clean Water Act. The government contended that it was enough to prove that he had acted voluntarily or intentionally to falsify, tamper with, or render inaccurate a monitoring method—or to violate the permit—and that he did not do so by mistake, accident or other innocent reason.

Kearse, Circuit Judge   Subsection (2) of section 1319(c), whose violation was alleged in count two of the indictment, establishes criminal penalties, including fines of up to $50,000 per day and imprisonment for up to three years, for "any person" who, inter alia, knowingly violates section 1311, 1312, 1316, 1317, 1318, 1321(b)(3), 1328, or 1345 of [Title 33], or any permit condition or limitation implementing any of such sections in a permit issued under [the Clean Water Act] by the Administrator or by a State.

Hopkins contends that the district court should have instructed the jury that it could not find him guilty of violating this section unless it found that he knew he was acting in violation of the CWA or the DEP permit. We disagree.

Section 1319(c)(2)(A) itself does not expressly state whether the adverb "knowingly" is intended to require proof that the defendant had actual knowledge that his conduct violated any of the statutory provisions that follow the phrase "knowingly violates" or had actual knowledge that his conduct violated a permit condition. As a matter of abstract logic, it would seem that a statute making it unlawful to "knowingly violate" a given statutory or permit provision would require proof that the defendant both violated and knew that he violated that provision. In defining the mental state required for conviction under a given statute, however, the courts must seek the proper "inference of the intent of Congress."

In *United States v. International Minerals & Chemical Corp.* ("International Minerals"), the Court construed a statute that authorized the Interstate Commerce Commission ("ICC") to promulgate regulations governing the transport of corrosive liquids and imposed criminal penalties on those who "knowingly violated any such regulation." The Court held that the quoted phrase required the government to prove only that the defendant knew the nature of his acts,

not that he knew his acts violated an ICC regulation. The Court stated that "where . . . dangerous or deleterious devices or products or obnoxious waste materials are involved, the probability of regulation is so great that anyone who is aware that he is in possession of them or dealing with them must be presumed to be aware of the regulation." Applying this presumption of awareness, the Court concluded that the phrase "knowingly violated any [ICC] regulation" was meant to be a "shorthand" method of referring to the acts or omissions contemplated by the statute.

Noting the general rule that ignorance of the law is no excuse, the court declined to attribute to Congress the inaccurate view that use of the word "knowingly" would require proof of knowledge of the law, as well as the facts. The mens rea presumption requires knowledge only of the facts that make the defendant's conduct illegal, lest it conflict with the related presumption, deeply rooted in the American legal system, that ordinarily ignorance of the law or a mistake of law is no defense to criminal prosecution

This court in *United States v. Laughlin* applied the *International Minerals* "presumption of awareness of regulation" in construing provisions of the Resource Conservation and Recovery Act ("RCRA") and the Comprehensive Environmental Response, Compensation and Liability Act ("CERCLA"). RCRA provides for the imposition of criminal penalties against any person who "knowingly treats, stores, or disposes of any hazardous waste identified or listed under [RCRA]" without a permit. We held that this provision did not require the government to prove that the defendant knew that the waste he dealt with was identified or listed under RCRA or that he lacked a disposal permit. Rather, we held that the government need prove only that the defendant knew the nature of the hazardous waste matter with which he dealt.

For several reasons, we view the presumption of awareness of regulation, applied to the ground-pollution offenses in *Laughlin,* to be equally applicable to the phrase "knowingly violates [the specified sections or permit]" in section 1319(c)(2)(A). Congress considered discharges of hazardous waste onto the ground, which are regulated in RCRA, as no less serious than such discharges into water. Further, the CWA sections to which section 1319(c)(2)(A) refers regulate a broad range of pollutant discharges, including "water quality related effluents," "toxic pollutants" listed in accordance with section 1317(a), "oil and hazardous substances," and "sewage sludge." The vast majority of these substances are of the type that would alert any ordinary user to the likelihood of stringent regulation. Moreover, the very fact that a governmental permit has been issued enhances the user's awareness of the existence of regulation.

Thus, we conclude that the purpose and legislative history of section 1319(c)(2)(A) indicate that Congress meant that that section would be violated if the defendant's acts were proscribed, even if the defendant was not aware of the proscription.

Judgment of conviction affirmed.

Wetlands

Another aspect of the Clean Water Act having the potential to affect businesses as well as individual property owners is the wetlands provision. Commonly, wetlands are transition zones between land and open water. Under Section 404 of the act, any *dredging or filling* activity in a wetland that is connected to the waters of the United States—as well as in any water of the United States—requires a permit before any activity begins. The permit program is administered by the Army Corps of Engineers, with the involvement of the Environmental Protection Agency.

As can be seen in the *Bersani* case, which follows, the permit requirement can significantly limit a landowner's use of his property where the fill activity is viewed as injurious to the values protected by the act.

Bersani v. U.S. Environmental Protection Agency
674 F.Supp. 405 (N.D.N.Y. 1987) aff'd 395 F.2d 36 (2d Cir. 1988)

Pyramid Companies was an association of partnerships in the business of developing, constructing, and operating shopping centers; John Bersani was a principal in one of the partnerships. In 1983, Pyramid became interested in developing a shopping mall in the Attleboro, Massachusetts, area and focused its attention on an 82-acre site known as Sweden's Swamp along an interstate highway in South Attleboro. The project contemplated altering or filling some 32 acres of the 49.6 acres of wetlands on the property. At the same time, Pyramid planned to excavate 9 acres of uplands (nonwetlands) to create new wetlands and to alter some 13 acres of existing wetlands to enhance their value for fish and wildlife.

In 1984, Pyramid applied to the U.S. Army Corps of Engineers for a permit under Section 404 of the Clean Water Act to do the dredge and fill work in the wetlands. As part of its application, it was required to submit information on practicable alternative sites for its shopping mall. One site subsequently focused on by the Corps and the Environmental Protection Agency was about three miles north in North Attleboro. Pyramid relied on several factors in claiming that the site was not a practicable alternative to its proposed site: namely, the site lacked sufficient traffic volume and access from local roads, potential department store tenants had expressed doubts about the feasibility of the site, and previous attempts to develop the site had met with strong resistance from the surrounding community. However, after Pyramid examined the site, another major developer of shopping centers had taken an option to acquire the property.

The New England Division Engineer of the Corps recommended that the permit be denied because a practicable alternative with a less adverse effect on the environment existed. The Chief of Engineers directed that the permit be issued, noting that the alternative site was not available to Pyramid because it was owned by a competitor. He also believed that even if it was considered available, Pyramid had made a convincing case that the site would not fulfill its objectives for a successful project. EPA then exercised its prerogative under the Clean Water Act to veto the permit on the grounds that filling

Sweden's Swamp to build the shopping mall would have an unacceptable adverse effect on the environment. In its view, another less environmentally damaging site had been available to Pyramid at the time it made its site selection; thus, any adverse effects on Sweden's Swamp were avoidable. Bersani and Pyramid then brought suit challenging the denial of its permit application.

McAvo, Judge   Section 404(a) authorizes the Secretary of the Army, acting through the Corps, to issue permits for the discharge of dredged or fill material at specified disposal sites. Criteria developed by the EPA in conjunction with the Corps govern these permitting decisions. Generally, the Corps must employ a "practicable alternative" analysis in determining whether to allow a proposed discharge. Section 230.10 of the regulations provides:

(a) . . . no discharge of dredged or fill material shall be permitted if there is a practicable alternative to the proposed discharge which would have less adverse impact on the aquatic ecosystem, so long as the alternative does not have other significant adverse environmental consequences. (2) An alternative is practicable if it is available and capable of being done, after taking into account cost, existing technology, and logistics in light of overall project purposes. If it is otherwise a practicable alternative, an area not presently owned by the applicant which could reasonably be obtained, utilized, expanded or managed in order to fulfill the basic purpose of the proposed activity may be considered. (3) Where the activity associated with a discharge which is proposed for a special aquatic site (including a wetland) does not require access or proximity to or siting within the special aquatic site in question to fulfill its basic purpose (i.e., is not "water dependent"), practicable alternatives that do not involve special aquatic sites are presumed to be available unless clearly demonstrated otherwise. In addition, where a discharge is proposed for a special aquatic site, all practicable alternatives to the proposed discharge which do not involve a discharge into a special aquatic site are presumed to have less adverse impact on the aquatic ecosystem, unless clearly demonstrated otherwise.

Where the proposed discharge involves a special aquatic site such as wetlands, a more stringent standard is imposed. Indeed Section 230.10(a)(3) creates a presumption that a practicable alternative exists when the discharge involves wetlands and the activity, here a shopping mall, is not "water dependent." Then the applicant must "clearly demonstrate" that no such alternative does in fact exist.

Pyramid argues that EPA's determination of feasibility was based on its erroneous conclusion that the marketplace considered the North Attleboro site suitable for a virtually identical regional shopping mall. Pyramid notes that six other shopping center developers over the past 15 years have tried and failed to develop the North Attleboro site as a shopping center. It contends that EPA has substituted its own judgment for that of the marketplace in an area in which it cannot claim expertise. The EPA, however, contends that it did not simply substitute its judgment for that of the developer. Instead, the EPA argues that the evidence on the record demonstrates that the North Attleboro site is suitable in fact for a regional shopping center mall virtually identical to that proposed by Pyramid. In this respect, the fact that a competing developer, the New England Development Company, had found the site suitable for a similar shopping mall and its own marketing analysis weighed in reaching this decision. The EPA also engaged in a review of the specific features that Pyramid found objectionable; namely, the distance from the primary trade area, lack of visibility from nearby highways, zoning, past failures of prior attempts to develop a shopping mall at the site, and various considerations. Consequently, the court finds that EPA's feasibility determination was not arbitrary.

Summary judgment granted for EPA.

Ocean Dumping

The Marine Protection, Research, and Sanctuaries Act of 1972 set up a permit system regulating the dumping of all types of materials into ocean waters. EPA has the responsibility for designating disposal sites and for establishing the rules governing ocean disposal. The Ocean Dumping Ban Act of 1987 required that all ocean dumping of municipal sewage sludge and industrial wastes be termi-

nated by December 31, 1991. Thus, the major remaining questions of ocean dumping concern the disposal of dredge spoils from dredging to keep harbors open.

Drinking Water

In 1974, Congress passed, and in 1986 and in 1996 amended, the Safe Drinking Water Act that is designed to protect and enhance the quality of our drinking water.

Under the act, EPA sets *primary drinking water standards,* minimum levels of quality for water consumed by humans. The act also establishes a program governing the injection of wastes into wells. The primary responsibility for complying with the federally established standards lies with the states. Where the states fail to enforce the drinking water standards, the federal government has the right to enforce them.

A significant number of suppliers of drinking water are privately owned—and they, as well as the publicly owned systems, have to be concerned with meeting the federal standards. In addition, factories, trailer parks, schools, and other entities that draw drinking water from wells and provide it within their facility can find that they are also subject to the drinking water regulations.

Waste Disposal

Background

Historically, concern about the environment focused on decreasing air and water pollution as well as protecting natural resources and wildlife. People paid relatively little attention to the disposal of wastes on land. Until the early 1970s, much of the solid and hazardous waste generated was disposed of in open dumps and landfills. Although some of the waste we produce can be disposed of without presenting significant health or environmental problems, some industrial, agricultural, and mining wastes—and even some household wastes—are hazardous and can present serious problems. Unless wastes are properly disposed of, they can cause air, water, and land pollution as well as contamination of the underground aquifers from which much of our drinking water is drawn. Once aquifers have been contaminated, they can take a very long time to cleanse themselves of pollutants.

In the 1970s, the discovery of abandoned dump sites such as Love Canal in New York and the Valley of the Drums in Kentucky heightened public concern about the disposal of toxic and hazardous wastes. Congress has enacted several laws regulating the generation and disposal of hazardous waste: the Resource Conservation and Recovery Act mandates proper management and disposal of wastes currently generated; and the Comprehensive Environmental Response, Compensation, and Liability Act focuses on cleaning up past disposal sites threatening public health and the environment.

The Resource Conservation and Recovery Act

Congress originally enacted the Resource Conservation and Recovery Act (RCRA) in 1976 and significantly amended it in 1984. RCRA provides the federal government and the states with the authority to regulate facilities that generate, treat, store, and dispose of hazardous waste. Most of the wastes defined as hazardous are subject to a cradle-to-the-grave tracking system and must be handled and disposed of in defined ways. RCRA requires persons who generate, treat, store, or transport specified quantities of hazardous waste to obtain permits, to meet certain standards and follow specified procedures in the handling of the wastes, and to keep records. Figure 1 illustrates the form that must accompany all shipments of hazardous waste from the point of generation until its final treatment or disposal.

In addition, operators of land waste disposal facilities must meet financial responsibility requirements and monitor groundwater quality. EPA determines whether certain wastes should be banned entirely from land disposal; a significant number of wastes must be treated before they can be disposed of in land disposal units.

Underground Storage Tanks

In 1984, Congress directed that EPA also regulate underground product storage tanks such as gasoline tanks to prevent and respond to leaks that might contaminate underground water. The regulations that EPA issued to implement these requirements impose significant costs on many businesses such as gasoline stations that utilize such storage tanks. Owners of such tanks have had to upgrade them or replace them with tanks that are corrosion resistant and can be monitored for leaks.

State Responsibilities

EPA sets minimum requirements for state RCRA programs and then delegates the responsibility for conducting programs to the states when they have the legal ability and interest to administer them. Until a state assumes partial or complete responsibility for a RCRA program, the federal government administers the program.

Enforcement

Failure to comply with the hazardous waste regulations promulgated under RCRA can subject violators to civil and criminal penalties. In the *United States v. Dean* case, which follows, an employee of a company that disposed of hazardous waste without a RCRA permit was held criminally liable.

Figure 1   *Sample "Uniform Hazardous Waste Manifest" Form*

Please Print or type   *(Form designed for use on elite (12-pitch) typewriter)*   Form Approved OMB 2000-0404 Expires 7-31-99

UNIFORM HAZARDOUS WASTE MANIFEST	1. Generator's US EPA ID No. V A D 0 0 1 2 3 4 5 6 7 0 0 0 0 7	2. Page 1 of	Information in the shaded areas is not required by federal law

3. Generator's Name and Mailing Address
GENERAL METAL PROCESSING CO.
501 MAIN ST.
SMALLTOWN, VA 23000
A. State Manifest Document Number

4. Generator's Phone No. (804) 555-0509
B. State Generator's ID

5. Transporter 1 Company Name SAFETY HAULER	6.	US EPA ID Number V A D 0 0 8 9 1 2 3 4 5	C. State Transporter's ID

D. Transporter's Phone

7. Transporter 2 Company Name	8.	US EPA ID Number	E. State Transporter's ID

F. Transporter's Phone

9. Designated Facility Name and Site Address
DISPOS-ALL, INC.
1800 NORTH AVE.
FRIENDLY TOWN, VA 2300

10. US EPA ID Number   V A D 0 0 6 7 8 9 1 2 3

G. State Facility's ID

H. Facility's Phone

11. US DOT Description *(Including Proper Shipping Name, Hazard Class, and ID Number)*	12. Containers		13. Total Quantity	13. Unit Wt/Vol	I. Waste No.
	No.	Type			
a. HAZARDOUS WASTE, LIQUID OR SOLID, NOS ORM-E NA9189	0 0 2	D M	0 0 1 1 0	GAL	
b. WASTE CYANIDE SOLUTION, NOS UN1935	0 0 1	D M	0 0 0 5 5	GAL	
c. WASTE FLAMMABLE SOLUTION, NOS UN1993	0 0 1	D M	0 0 0 5 5	GAL	
d.					

J. Additional Descriptions for Materials Listed Above	K. Handling Codes for Wastes Listed Above

15. Special Handling Instructions and Additional Information

16. Generator's Certification: I hereby declare that the contents of this consignment are fully and accurately described above by proper shipping name and classified, packed, marked, labeled, and are in all respects in proper condition for transport by highway according to applicable international and national regulations.

Unless I am a small quantity generator who has been exempted by statute or regulation from the duty to make a waste minimization certification under Section 3002(b) of RCRA. I also certify that I have a program in place to reduce the volume and toxicity of waste generated to the degree I have determined to be economically practicable and I have selected the method of treatment, storage, or disposal currently available to me which minimizes the present and future threat to human health and the environment.

Printed/ Typed Name JOSEPHINE K. DOE	Signature *Josephine K. Doe*	Month 0 8	Day 3 0	Year 0 0

17. Transporter 1 Acknowledgement of Receipt of Materials

Printed/Typed Name	Signature

18. Transporter 2 Acknowledgement of Receipt of Materials

Printed/Typed Name	Signature	Month	Day	Year

19. Discrepancy Indication Space

20. Facility Owner or Operator: Certification of receipt of hazardous materials covered by this manifest except as noted in Item 19.

Printed/Typed Name	Signature	Month	Day	Year

EPA Form 8700-22 (Rev. 4-85) Previous Edition is obsolete.

Information in the shaded areas is not required by federal law, but this or other additional information may be required by your state.

United States v. Dean   *969 F.2d 187 (6th Cir. 1992)*

General Metal Fabricators, Inc. (GMF), owned and operated a facility in Erwin, Tennessee, which was engaged in metal stamping, plating, and painting. The facility utilized hazardous chemicals and generated hazardous waste but did not have a RCRA permit nor did it maintain the required records of the treatment, storage, and disposal of hazardous substances. The hazardous waste disposal practices at GMF were discovered by chance by state waste-management authorities whose attention was caught, while driving to an appointment at another facility, by two 55-gallon drums abandoned among weeds on GMF's property.

The owners of GMF, Joseph and Jean Sanchez, as well as Clyde Griffith, the plant manager, and Gale Dean, the production manager, were indicted for conspiracy to violate RCRA, and, individually, for violations of various sections of RCRA. At his request, Dean's trial was severed from that of the other defendants.

As production manager, Dean had day-to-day supervision of GMF's production process and employees. Among his duties was the instruction of employees on hazardous waste handling and disposal. Numerous practices at GMF violated RCRA. GMF's plating operations utilized rinse baths, contaminated with hazardous chemicals, which were drained through a pipe into an earthen lagoon outside the facility. In addition, Dean instructed employees to shovel various kinds of solid wastes from the tanks into 55-gallon drums. Dean ordered the construction of a pit, concealed behind the facility, into which 38 drums of such hazardous waste were tossed. The contents spilled onto the soil from open or corroded drums. Chemical analyses of soil and solid wastes revealed that the pit and the lagoon were contaminated with chromium. In addition, the pit was contaminated with toluene and xylene solvents. All of these substances are considered hazardous under RCRA. Drums of spent chromic acid solution were also illegally stored on the premises.

Dean was familiar with the chemicals used in each of the tanks on the production line and with the manner in which the contents of the rinse tanks were deposited in the lagoon. Material Safety Data Sheets (MSDS) provided to GMF by the chemical manufacturer clearly stated that the various chemicals in use at GMF were hazardous and were subject to federal pollution control laws. Dean was familiar with the MSDS and knowledgeable about their contents. The MSDS delivered with the chromic acid made specific reference to RCRA and to related EPA regulations. Dean told investigators that he "had read this RCRA waste code but thought it was a bunch of bull—."

Dean was convicted of conspiracy to violate RCRA as well as of (1) failure to file documentation of hazardous waste generation, storage, and disposal, (2) storage of spent chromic acid without a permit, (3) disposal of chromic acid rinse water and sludges in a lagoon without a permit, and (4) disposal of paint sludge and solvent wastes in a pit without a permit, all in violation of RCRA. Dean appealed his conviction.

Joiner, Senior District Judge The first of the issues raised by Dean is that the trial court erred in denying his motion for acquittal on the permit-related counts because there was no evidence that Dean knew of RCRA's permit requirement. Dean's characterization of the evidence is inaccurate, but moreover, we see no basis on the face of the statute for concluding that knowledge of the permit requirement is an element of the crime. The statute penalizes:

Any person who— . . . (2) knowingly treats, stores or disposes of any hazardous waste identified or listed under this subchapter—(A) without a permit under this subchapter . . . ; or (B) in knowing violation of any material condition or requirement of such permit; or (C) in knowing violation of any applicable interim status or regulations. 42 U.S.C. section 6928(d)(2).

Dean was convicted of violating subsection 6928(d)(2)(A).

The question of interpretation presented by this provision is the familiar one of how far the initial "knowingly" travels. Other courts of appeals have divided on this question. We agree with the reasoning of the Court of Appeals for the Ninth Circuit in *United States v. Hoflin.* The "knowingly" which begins section 6928(d)(2) cannot be read as extending to the subsections without rendering nugatory the word "knowing" contained in subsections 6928(d)(2)(B) and (C). Subsection 6928(d)(2)(A) requires knowing treatment (or knowing storage, or knowing disposal) of hazardous waste. It also requires proof that the treatment, storage or disposal was done without a permit. It does not require that the person charged must have known that a permit was required, and that knowledge is not relevant.

Dean also contends that the district court should have granted his motion for acquittal because subsection 6928(d)(2)(A) was not intended to reach employees who are not "owners" or "operators" of facilities. By its terms, the provision applies to "any person." "Person" is a defined term meaning "an individual . . . " Dean would be hard pressed to convince the court that he is not an "individual." He argues, however, that because only owners and operators of facilities are required to obtain permits, the penalty imposed for hazardous waste handling without a permit must apply only to owners and operators.

This contention is unpersuasive for numerous reasons. Of primary importance is the fact that it is contrary to the unambiguous language of the statute.

Affirmed.

Solid Waste

Mining, commercial, and household activities generate a large volume of waste material that can present problems if not properly disposed of. As population density has increased, causing a corresponding increase in the total volume of waste, it has become more difficult to find land or incinerators where the waste material can be disposed of properly. RCRA authorizes EPA to set minimum standards for such disposkal, but states and local governments bear the primary responsibility for the siting and regulation of such activity.

As the cost and difficulty of disposing of waste increases, public attention focuses on reducing the waste to be disposed of, on looking for opportunities to recycle some of the waste material, and on changing the characteristics of the material that must ultimately be disposed of so that it poses fewer environmental problems. One of the significant challenges faced by tomorrow's businessperson will be in designing products, packaging, and production processes so as to minimize the waste products that result. A significant problem for both government and industry is the difficulty in trying to site new waste facilities. The NIMBY, or not-in-my-backyard

syndrome, is pervasive as people almost universally desire to have the wastes from their everyday lives and from the economic activity in their community disposed of in someone else's neighborhood—any place but their own. As governments try to cope with the reality of finding places to dispose of wastes in an environmentally safe manner and at the same time cope with public opposition to siting new facilities, the temptation is strong to try to bar wastes from other areas from being disposed of in local facilities.

In the landmark case *City of Philadelphia v. New Jersey,* the U.S. Supreme Court struck down an attempt by the state of New Jersey to prohibit the importation of most solid waste originating outside the state. An ironic twist is that several decades later, we find a number of other eastern and midwestern states trying to find ways to block the importation of wastes from New Jersey into their states. In recent years, the Supreme Court has had occasion to reiterate its holding in *City of Philadelphia v. New Jersey* in a series of new cases involving efforts by states to block or limit the flow of solid and hazardous waste from outside their state to disposal sites within the state. One of the cases in this series of cases, *Fort Gratiot Sanitary Landfill, Inc.,* follows.

Fort Gratiot Sanitary Landfill, Inc. v. Michigan Department of Natural Resources
112 S.Ct. 2019 (1992)

In 1978, Michigan enacted its Solid Waste Management Act (SWMA), which required every Michigan county to estimate the amount of solid waste that would be generated in the county in the next 20 years and to adopt a plan providing for its disposal at facilities that comply with state health standards. After holding public hearings, the St. Clair County Board of Commissioners adopted a solid waste plan for the St. Clair County. In 1987, the Michigan Department of Natural Resources issued a permit to Fort Gratiot Sanitary Landfill, Inc., to operate a sanitary landfill as a solid waste disposal area in the county. In December 1988, the Michigan Legislature amended the SWMA by adopting two provisions concerning the "acceptance of waste or ash generated outside the county of disposal area." The new provisions, which were effective immediately, prohibited the acceptance of out-of-county wastes unless the acceptance of such waste was explicitly authorized in the approved county solid waste management plan.

In February 1989, Fort Gratiot submitted an application to the St. Clair County Solid Waste Planning Committee for authority to accept up to 1,750 tons per day of out-of-state waste at its landfill. In the application Fort Gratiot promised to reserve sufficient capacity to dispose of all solid waste generated in the county in the next 20 years. The planning committee denied the application. Because the county's management plan did not authorize the acceptance of any out-of-county waste, Fort Gratiot was effectively prevented from receiving any solid waste that did not originate in St. Clair County.

Fort Gratiot then brought a lawsuit seeking a judgment declaring that the waste import restrictions violated the Commerce Clause of the U.S. Constitution and thus were unconstitutional and enjoining their enforcement. Fort Gratiot contended that requiring a private landfill operator to limit its business to the acceptance of local waste constituted impermissible discrimination against interstate commerce. The District Court dismissed the lawsuit. It concluded, first, that the statute did not discriminate against interstate commerce because the limitation applied equally to Michigan counties outside the county as well as to out-of-state waste. It also noted that each county had discretion to accept out-of-state waste and that any incidental burden on interstate commerce was not excessive in relation to the public health and environmental benefits derived by Michigan from the statute. The Court of Appeals affirmed the ruling, and Fort Gratiot appealed to the U.S. Supreme Court.

Stevens, Justice   In *Philadelphia v. New Jersey* (1978) we held that a New Jersey law prohibiting the importation of most "solid or liquid waste which originated or was collected outside the territorial limits of the State" violated the commerce clause of the United States Constitution. In this case petitioner challenges a Michigan law that prohibits private landfill operators from accepting solid waste that originates outside the county in which their facilities are located. Adhering to our holding in the New Jersey case we conclude that this Michigan statute is also unconstitutional.

Philadelphia v. New Jersey provides the framework for our analysis of this case. Solid waste, even if it has no value, is an article of commerce. Whether the business arrangements between out-of-state generators of waste and the Michigan operator of a waste disposal site are viewed as "sales" of garbage or "purchases" of transportation and disposal services, the commercial transactions unquestionably have an interstate character. The commerce clause thus imposes some constraints on Michigan's ability to regulate these transactions.

As we have long recognized, the "negative" or "dormant" aspect of the commerce clause prohibits States from advancing their own commercial interests by curtailing the movement of articles or commerce, either into or out of the state. A state statute that clearly discriminates against interstate commerce is therefore unconstitutional unless the discrimination is demonstrably justified by a valid factor unrelated to economic protectionism.

The Waste Import Restrictions enacted by Michigan authorize each of its 83 counties to isolate itself from the national economy. Indeed, unless a county acts affirmatively to permit other waste to enter its jurisdiction, the statute affords local waste producers complete protection from competition from out-of-state waste producers who seek to use local waste disposal areas. In view of the fact that Michigan has not identified any reason, apart from its origin, why

solid waste coming from outside the county should be treated differently from solid waste within the county, the foregoing reasoning would appear to control the disposition of this case.

Michigan and St. Clair County assert that the Waste Import Restrictions are necessary because they enable individual counties to make adequate plans for the safe disposal of future waste. Although accurate forecasts about the volume and composition of future waste flows may be an indispensable part of a comprehensive waste disposal plan, Michigan could attain that objective without discriminating between in- and out-of-state waste. Michigan could, for example, limit the amount of waste that landfill operators may accept each year. There is, however, no valid health and safety reason for limiting the amount of waste that a landfill operator may accept from outside the State, but not the amount that the operator may accept from inside the State. Of course our conclusion would be different if the imported waste raised health or other concerns not presented by Michigan waste.

For the foregoing reasons, the Waste Import Restrictions unambiguously discriminate against interstate commerce and are appropriately characterized as protectionist measures that cannot withstand scrutiny under the commerce clause.

Judgment of the Court of Appeals is reversed.

Rehnquist, Chief Justice, dissenting   When confronted with a dormant commerce clause challenge, "the crucial inquiry must be directed to determining whether the challenged statute is basically a protectionist measure, or whether it can fairly be viewed as a law directed to legitimate local concerns with effects on interstate commerce that are only incidental. Because I think the Michigan statute is at least arguably directed to legitimate local concerns, rather than improper economic protectionism, I would remand this case for further proceedings.

The substantial environmental, aesthetic, health, and safety problems flowing from this country's waste piles were already apparent at the time we decided *Philadelphia*. Those problems have only risen in the intervening years. In part, this is due to increased waste volumes, volumes that are expected to continue to rise in the foreseeable future. It is no secret why capacity is not expanding sufficiently to meet the demand—the substantial risks attendant to waste sites make them extraordinarily unattractive neighbors. The result, of course, is that while many are willing to generate waste—indeed it is a practical impossibility to solve the waste problem by banning waste production—few are willing to help dispose of it. Those locales that do provide disposal capacity to serve foreign waste effectively are affording reduced environmental and safety risks to the States that will not take charge of their own waste.

The State of Michigan has stepped into this quagmire in order to address waste problems generated by its own populace. It has done so by adopting a comprehensive approach to the disposal of solid wastes generated within its borders. The legislation challenged today is simply one part of a broad package that includes a number of features: a state-mandated statewide effort to control and plan for waste disposal; requirements that local units of government participate in the planning process; restrictions to assure safe transport; a ban on the operation of a waste disposal facility unless various design and technical requirements are satisfied and appropriate permits obtained; and commitments to promote source separation, composting, and recycling. The Michigan legislation is thus quite unlike the simple outright ban that we confronted in *Philadelphia*.

In adopting this legislation, the Michigan Legislature also appears to have concluded that, like the State, counties should reap as they have sown—hardly a novel proposition. It has accomplished this by prohibiting waste facilities from accepting waste generated from outside the county, unless special permits are obtained. In the process, of course, this facially neutral restriction (i.e. it applies equally to interstate and intrastate waste) also works to ban disposal from out-of-state sources unless appropriate permits are procured. But I cannot agree that such a requirement, when imposed as one part of a comprehensive approach to regulating in this difficult field, is the stuff of which economic protectionism is made.

Michigan has limited the ability of its own population to despoil the environment and to create health and safety risks by excessive and uncontrolled waste disposal. It does not thereby violate the commerce clause when it seeks to prevent this resource from being exported—the result if Michigan is forced to accept foreign waste in its disposal facilities.

The Court today penalizes the State of Michigan for what to all appearances is its good-faith effort, in turn encouraging each State to ignore the waste problem in the hope that another will pick up the slack. The Court's approach fails to recognize that the latter option is quite real and quite attractive for many States—and becomes even more so when the intermediate option of solving its own problems, but only its own problems, is eliminated.

Superfund

In 1980, Congress passed the Comprehensive Environmental Response, Compensation, and Liability Act (CERCLA), commonly known as Superfund, to deal with the problem of uncontrolled or abandoned hazardous waste sites. In 1986, it strengthened and expanded the law. Under the Superfund law, EPA identified and assessed the sites in the United States where hazardous wastes had been spilled, stored, or abandoned.

Eventually, EPA expects to identify 30,000 such sites. The sites are ranked on the basis of the type, quantity, and toxicity of the wastes; the number of people potentially exposed to the wastes; the different ways (e.g., in the air or drinking water) in which they might be exposed; the risks to contamination of aquifers; and other factors. The sites with the highest ranking are put on the National Priority List to receive priority federal and/or state attention for cleanup. At these sites, EPA makes careful scientific and engineering studies to determine the most appropriate cleanup plans. Once a site has been cleaned up, the state is responsible for managing it to prevent future environmental problems. EPA also has the authority to quickly initiate actions at hazardous waste sites—whether or not the site is on the priority list—to address imminent hazards such as the risk of fire, explosion, or contamination of drinking water.

The cleanup activity is financed by a tax on chemicals and feedstocks. However, EPA is authorized to require that a site be cleaned up by those persons responsible for contaminating it, either as the owner or operator of the site, a transporter of wastes to the site, or the owner of

CYBERLAW IN ACTION

The Toxic Release Inventory Is Available Online

In 1986 the Emergency Planning and Community Right-to-Know Act (EPCRA) was enacted. A primary purpose of this legislation was to ensure that communities and citizens were aware of chemical hazards in their area. Under Section 313 of the EPCRA, the EPA and the states must annually collect data on releases and transfers of certain toxic chemicals from specific facilities. In turn, the data must be made available to the general public in a Toxics Release Inventory (TRI). Now, much of the EPCRA information

and data, including data in the TRI program, is easily accessible online through the EPA website. In addition, many individual state environmental agency websites provide information on TRI for facilities within their particular state. A company's detailed toxic release data can be useful information for the company's competitors. A company could use the TRI information to determine how much of a particular chemical is being produced by their competitors, or to gain insight into what production process is being used by the competition. For more information about the TRI program, visit http://www.epa.gov/tri/.)

wastes deposited at the site. Where EPA expends money to clean up a site, it has the legal authority to recover its costs from those who were responsible for the problem. The courts have held that such persons are "jointly and severally responsible for the cost of cleanup." Chapter 7, Negligence and Strict Liability, discusses the concept of joint liability. Of concern to many businesspeople is the fact that this stringent and potentially very expensive liability can in some instances be imposed on a current owner of a site who had nothing to do with the contamination, such as a subsequent purchaser of the land.

Community Right to Know and Emergency Cleanup

As part of its 1986 amendments to Superfund, Congress enacted a series of requirements for emergency planning, notification of spills and accidents involving hazardous materials, disclosure by industry to the community of the presence of certain listed chemicals, and notification of the amounts of various chemicals being routinely released into the environment in the area of a facility. This legislation was in response to the industrial accident at Bhopal, India, in 1984 and to several similar incidents in the United States. Firms subject to the requirements have to carefully plan how they will communicate with the surrounding community what chemicals are being regularly released and what precautions the facility has taken to protect the community from regular or accidental releases. Mindful of the difficulty of explaining to a community why large emissions of hazardous substances are taking place, a significant number of companies have undertaken to reduce those emissions below levels they are currently required to meet by law.

Regulation of Chemicals

Background

More than 60,000 chemical substances are manufactured in the United States and used in a variety of products. Although these chemicals contribute much to the standard of living we enjoy, some of them are toxic or have the potential to cause cancer, birth defects, reproductive failures, and other health-related problems. These risks may be posed in the manufacturing process, during the use of a product, or as a result of the manner of disposal of the chemical or product. EPA has two statutory authorities that give it the ability to prevent or restrict the manufacture and use of new and existing chemicals to remove unreasonable risks to human health or the environment. These authorities are the Federal Insecticide, Fungicide, and Rodenticide Act and the Toxic Substances Control Act.

Regulation of Agricultural Chemicals

The vast increase in the American farmer's productivity over the past few decades has been in large measure attributable to the farmer's use of chemicals to kill the insects, pests, and weeds that have historically competed with the farmer for crops. Some of these chemicals, such as pesticides and herbicides, were a mixed blessing. They enabled people to dramatically increase productivity and to conquer disease. On the other hand, dead fish and birds provided evidence that chemicals were not only building up in the food chain but also proving fatal to some species. Unless such chemicals are carefully used and disposed of, they can present a danger to the applier and to the consumer of food and water. Gradually, people realized the need to focus on the effects of using such chemicals.

EPA enforces the Federal Insecticide, Fungicide, and Rodenticide Act (FIFRA). This act gives EPA the authority to register pesticides before they can be sold, to provide for the certification of appliers of pesticides designated for restrictive use, to set limits on the pesticide residue permitted on crops that provide food for people or animals, and to register and inspect pesticide manufacturing establishments.

When the EPA administrator has reason to believe that continued use of a particular pesticide poses an "imminent hazard," he may suspend its registration and remove the product from the market. When the administrator believes that there is a less than imminent hazard but that the environmental risks of continuing to use a pesticide outweigh its benefits, the administrator may initiate a cancellation of registration proceeding. This proceeding affords all interested persons—manufacturers, distributors, users, environmentalists, and scientists—an opportunity to present evidence on the proposed cancellation.

Cancellation of the registration occurs when the administrator finds that the product causes unreasonable adverse effects on the environment.

Companion regulations promulgated by EPA and enforced by the Food and Drug Administration control the amount of pesticide residue that can remain on raw and processed food intended for human or animal consumption. These regulations establish what are known as "tolerances."

Those involved in the food production and distribution process must keep a close watch on regulatory developments at EPA concerning the registration, cancellation, and suspension of products as well as actions it takes concerning permissible residues of pesticides on food products. During the 1980s, the agency took highly publicized actions concerning the use of ethylene dibromide (EDB), a fumigant, on citrus and grain products, sulfites on table grapes, alar on apples, and chlordane as a treatment against termite infestation. In each instance, the economic well-being of many businesses was at risk if they did not adequately anticipate and/or deal with the EPA's actions and the publicity that resulted from these actions.

CONCEPT REVIEW

Major Environmental Laws

Act	Focus
Clean Air Act	Protects quality of ambient (outdoor) air through national ambient air quality standards, state implementation plans, control of toxic air pollutants, new source performance standards, and controls on automobiles and fuels
Clean Water Act	Protects and enhances quality of surface waters by setting water quality standards and limiting discharges by industry and municipalities to those waters through permit system; also regulates dredging and filling of wetlands
Marine Protection, Research, and Sanctuaries Act	Regulates dumping of all types of material into ocean waters
Safe Drinking Water Act	Protects and enhances quality of our drinking water. Also regulates disposal of wastes in wells
Resource Conservation and Recovery Act (RCRA)	Establishes a cradle-to-the-grave regulatory system for handling and disposal of hazardous wastes; also deals with solid waste
Comprehensive Environmental Response Compensation and Liability Act (Superfund)	Provides a program to deal with hazardous waste that was inadequately disposed of in the past
Federal Insecticide, Fungicide, and Rodenticide Act (FIFRA)	Regulates the sale and use of chemicals to be used as pesticides and herbicides; companion legislation regulates residues permitted on crops intended for use as food
Toxic Substances Control Act (TSCA)	Requires preclearance of new chemicals and provides for regulation of existing chemicals that pose an unreasonable risk to health or the environment

ETHICS IN ACTION

Environmental Standards for International Operations

Suppose that a multinational chemical company with its primary manufacturing facilities in the United States plans to build a manufacturing facility in a developing country where there are few, if any, real state-imposed environmental regulations. Is it sufficient for the company to simply meet the environmental requirements of the host country? Is there any ethical obligation to do more—for example, to build the facility to meet the requirements it would have to meet in this country?

Toxic Substances Control Act

The other major statute regulating chemical use focuses on toxic substances—such as asbestos and PCBs—and on the new chemical compounds that are developed each year. The Toxic Substances Control Act, enacted in 1976, requires that chemicals be tested by manufacturers or processors to determine their effect on human health or the environment before the chemicals are introduced into commerce. The act also gives EPA the authority to regulate chemical substances or mixtures that present an unreasonable risk of injury to health or the environment and to take action against any such substances or mixtures that pose an imminent hazard.

This legislation was enacted in response to the concern that thousands of new substances were being released into the environment each year, sometimes without adequate consideration of their potential for harm, and that it was not until damage from a substance occurs that its manufacture or use was properly regulated. At the same time, a goal of the act is not to unduly impede, or create unnecessary economic barriers to, technological innovation.

Biotechnology

The development of techniques to genetically manipulate organisms—often referred to generally as biotechnology—offers considerable promise to aid our ability to provide food and health care and to generate a range of new products and production processes. At the same time, the new techniques raise concerns about their potential to adversely affect human health or the environment. Responsibility for regulating research and use of biotechnology is shared in the federal government between the Food and Drug Administration, the Department of Agriculture, the Environmental Protection Agency, and the National Institutes of Health. Generally, a review is required of such activity before it takes place. This process is of considerable import to companies that

are developing genetically engineered organisms for commercial purposes; it can affect both the speed at which they are able to get the products to market and the public's confidence that release of the organisms does not pose an unreasonable risk.

Problems and Problem Cases

1. In July 1984, Vanguard Corporation began operating a metal furniture manufacturing plant in Brooklyn, New York. The plant is located in an area that has not attained the national ambient air quality standards for ozone. The plant is a major stationary source (i.e., has the potential to emit more than 100 tons a year) of volatile organic compounds that contribute to the production of ozone in the atmosphere. The New York state implementation plan (SIP) requires that metal-coating facilities use paint that contains less than three pounds of organic solvent (minus water) per gallon at the time of coating. On August 24, 1984, EPA notified Vanguard that it was not in compliance with the SIP provision concerning coatings and issued it a notice of violation. Vanguard sought to defend against the notice of violation on the grounds that it had used its best faith efforts to comply but that full compliance was technologically and economically infeasible. It indicated that it wanted 18 more months to come into compliance. Should Vanguard be held to be in violation of the Clean Air Act?

2. In August, Tzavah Urban Renewal Corporation purchased from the city of Newark a building formerly known as the Old Military Park Hotel. While the buyer was given an opportunity to inspect the building, it was not informed by the city that the building was permeated with asbestos-containing material. At the time of the purchase, the building was in great disrepair and had been uninhabited for many years. Its proposed renovation was to be a major urban renewal project. In the following June, Tzavah contracted with Greer Industrial Corporation to "gut" the building. While the work was going on, an EPA inspector visited the site and concluded that the hotel was contaminated with asbestos. He observed Greer employees throwing asbestos-laced objects out of the windows of the building and noted an uncovered refuse pile next to the hotel that contained asbestos. The workers were not wetting the debris before heaving it out the windows and the refuse pile was also dry. As a result, asbestos dust was being released into the air. Although the hotel was located in a commercial district, there were private homes nearby. Renovation of buildings contaminated with asbestos is regulated under the Clean Air Act. The EPA regulations require building owners or operators to notify EPA before commencing renovation or demolition and prescribe various procedures for storage and removal of the asbestos. Tzavah failed to provide the required notice or to comply with procedures required. After being notified by EPA of the violation of the law, Tzavah stopped the demolition work, left the building unsecured, and left the waste piles dry and uncovered. EPA tried informally to get Tzavah to complete the work in accordance with the asbestos regulations; when Tzavah did not take action, EPA brought a lawsuit against Tzavah to do so. Should the court issue an injunction requiring Tzavah to abate the hazard posed by the dry asbestos remaining in the hotel?

3. Mall Properties, Inc., was an organization that for many years sought to develop a shopping mall in the Town of North Haven, Connecticut, a suburb of New Haven. Because the proposed development would require the filling of some wetlands, Mall Properties was required to obtain a permit from the Corps of Engineers pursuant to section 404 of the Clean Water Act. The City of New Haven opposed development of the mall—and the granting of the permit—on the grounds it would jeopardize the fragile economy of New Haven. The Corps of Engineers found the net loss of wetlands would be substantially compensated for by a proposed on-site wetland creation. Relying primarily on the socioeconomic concerns of the City of New Haven, the District Engineer rejected the proposed permit. Mall Properties then brought suit against the Corps of Engineers, claiming that the decision was arbitrary and capricious. Should the District Engineer have relied on socioeconomic factors unrelated to the project's environmental impacts in making a decision on the permit?

4. Charles Hanson owned land abutting Keith Lake, a freshwater lake that was subject to some tidal flooding as a result of its connection with tidal waters. In order to minimize the detrimental effects from the tidal activities and consequent flooding, Hanson deposited a large quantity of dirt, rock, bricks, sheet metal, and other debris along the shoreline of his property. He did so without obtaining a permit from the U.S. Army Corps of Engineers under section 404 of the Clean Water Act, which controls dumping and filling activities in navigable waters of the United States. Under the law, discharges of pollutants into navigable waters without a permit are forbidden. The term *pollutant* is defined to include "dredged spoil, solid waste, incinerator residue, sewage, garbage, sewage sludge, munitions, chemical wastes, biological materials, radioactive materials, heat, wrecked or discarded equipment, rock, sand, cellar dirt, and industrial, municipal and agricultural waste discharged into water." EPA brought an enforcement action against Hanson claiming he had violated the Clean Water Act. Should the court find that Hanson violated the act?

5. Johnson & Towers, Inc., is in the business of overhauling large motor vehicles. It uses degreasers and other industrial chemicals that contain chemicals classified as "hazardous wastes" under the Resource Conservation and Recovery Act (RCRA)—for example, methylene chloride and trichloroethylene. For some period of time, waste chemicals from cleaning operations were drained into a holding tank and, when the tank was full, pumped into a trench. The trench flowed from the plant property into Parker's Creek, a tributary of the Delaware River. Under RCRA, generators of such wastes must obtain a permit for disposal from the Environmental Protection Agency (EPA). EPA had neither issued, nor received an application for, a permit for the Johnson & Towers operations. Over a three-day period, federal agents saw workers pump waste from the tank into the trench, and on the third day toxic chemicals flowed into the creek. The company and two of its employees, Jack Hopkins, a foreman, and Peter Angel, the service manager, were indicted for unlawfully disposing of hazardous wastes. The company pled guilty. The federal district court dismissed the criminal charges against the two individuals, holding that RCRA's criminal penalty provisions imposing fines and imprisonment did not apply to employees. The government appealed. Can employees of a corporation be held criminally liable if their actions on behalf of the corporation violate the federal hazardous waste law?

6. Anne Arundel County, Maryland, enacted two related ordinances. One absolutely prohibited the disposal in and the transportation through Anne Arundel County of various hazardous wastes not originating in that county. Another ordinance required a license to dispose of hazardous waste in Anne Arundel County; it also required a license to transport hazardous wastes through

the county. Browning-Ferris, Inc. (BFI), is the owner and operator of a landfill located in Anne Arundel County that is licensed by the state of Maryland to receive hazardous wastes. BFI is also a hauler of hazardous wastes within the county. The county notified BFI that it expected BFI to comply with the new regulations, and BFI filed a lawsuit challenging the ordinances and seeking to have them enjoined. How should the court rule?

7. The Royal McBee Corporation manufactured typewriters at a factory in Springfield, Missouri. As a part of the manufacturing process, Royal McBee generated cyanide-based electroplating wastes, sludge from the bottom of electroplating tanks, and spent plating bath solution. As part of their duties, Royal McBee employees dumped the wastes onto the surface of the soil on a vacant lot adjoining the factory. This took place between 1959 and 1962. Over time, the waste materials migrated outward and downward from the original dumping site, contaminating a large area. In 1970, the manufacturing facility and lot were sold to General Electric, which operated the plant but did not engage in the dumping of wastes on the vacant lot. In the mid-1980s, General Electric was required by EPA and the state of Missouri, under the authority of the federal Superfund law, to clean up the contamination at the site. General Electric then brought a lawsuit against the successor corporation of Royal McBee's typewriter business, Litton Business Systems, to recover for the costs incurred in cleaning up the site. Under the Superfund law, "any person who at the time of disposal of any hazardous substance owned or operated any facilities at which such hazardous substances were disposed of, shall be liable for any other necessary costs of response incurred by any other person" consistent with the Superfund law and regulations. Is General Electric entitled to recover its cleanup costs from Litton?

8. Chemlawn sells pesticide products for use on residential lawns. The active ingredients in Chemlawn's products are registered with the Environmental Protection Agency pursuant to the Federal Insecticide, Fungicide, and Rodenticide Act (FIFRA). Deborah Ryan brought a lawsuit against Chemlawn seeking damages in tort for injuries she claimed that she and her son Kevin sustained from the use of Chemlawn products. Ryan claims that the products are unsafe for commercial use and that they have been inadequately tested by the EPA. Chemlawn contends that Ryan should take her complaints to EPA, which has the responsibility for determining whether the products are safe to be sold. How should the court decide?

Online Research: Online Access to Toxic Release Inventory

Locate the website for the environmental agency in your state. Does the website provide Toxics Release Inventory (TRI) data for the state? What companies are the largest contributors of toxic release to the air? What companies are the largest contributors of toxic release to the water? You may look at the EPA website (http://www.epa.gov/) as a starting point to see if your state posts information on its TRI program. If your state does not provide such information, then use the data from a neighboring state.

Appendix A

THE CONSTITUTION OF THE UNITED STATES OF AMERICA

Preamble

We the People of the United States, in Order to form a more perfect Union, establish Justice, insure domestic Tranquility, provide for the common defense, promote the general Welfare, and secure the Blessings of Liberty to ourselves and our Posterity, do ordain and establish this Constitution for the United States of America.

Article I

Section 1   All legislative Powers herein granted shall be vested in a Congress of the United States, which shall consist of a Senate and House of Representatives.

Section 2   The House of Representatives shall be composed of Members chosen every second Year by the People of the several States, and the Electors in each State shall have the Qualifications requisite for Electors of the most numerous Branch of the State Legislature.

No Person shall be a Representative who shall not have attained to the age of twenty five Years, and been seven Years a Citizen of the United States, and who shall not, when elected, be an Inhabitant of that State in which he shall be chosen.

Representatives and direct Taxes shall be apportioned among the several States which may be included within this Union, according to their respective Numbers, which shall be determined by adding to the whole Number of free Persons, including those bound to Service for a Term of Years, and excluding Indians not taxed, three fifths of all other Persons.[1] The actual Enumeration shall be made within three Years after the first Meeting of the Congress of the United States, and within every subsequent Term of ten Years, in such Manner as they shall by Law direct. The Number of Representatives shall not exceed one for every thirty Thousand, but each State shall have at Least one Representative, and until such enumeration shall be made, the State of New Hampshire shall be entitled to choose three, Massachusetts eight, Rhode-Island and Providence Plantations one, Connecticut five, New York six, New Jersey four, Pennsylvania eight, Delaware one, Maryland six, Virginia ten, North Carolina five, South Carolina five, and Georgia three.

When vacancies happen in the Representation from any State, the Executive Authority thereof shall issue Writs of Election to fill such Vacancies.

The House of Representatives shall chuse their Speaker and other Officers; and shall have the sole Power of Impeachment.

Section 3   The Senate of the United States shall be composed of two Senators from each State, chosen by the Legislature thereof,[2] for six Years; and each Senator shall have one Vote.

Immediately after they shall be assembled in Consequence of the first Election, they shall be divided as equally as may be into three Classes. The Seats of the Senators of the first Class shall be vacated at the Expiration of the second Year, of the second Class at the Expiration of the fourth Year, and of the third Class at the Expiration of the sixth Year, so that one third may be chosen every second Year; and if Vacancies happen by Resignation, or otherwise, during the Recess of the Legislature of any State, the Executive thereof may make temporary Appointments until the next Meeting of the Legislature, which shall then fill such Vacancies.[3]

No Person shall be a Senator who shall not have attained to the Age of thirty Years, and been nine Years a Citizen of the United States, and who shall not, when elected, be an Inhabitant of that State for which he shall be chosen.

The Vice President of the United States shall be President of the Senate, but shall have no Vote, unless they be equally divided.

---

[1]Changed by the Fourteenth Amendment.

[2]Changed by the Seventeenth Amendment.
[3]Changed by the Seventeenth Amendment.

The Senate shall chuse their other Officers, and also a President pro tempore, in the Absence of the Vice President, or when he shall exercise the Office of President of the United States.

The Senate shall have the sole Power to try all Impeachments. When sitting for that Purpose, they shall be on Oath or Affirmation. When the President of the United States is tried, the Chief Justice shall preside: And no Person shall be convicted without the Concurrence of two thirds of the Members present.

Judgment in Cases of Impeachment shall not extend further than to removal from Office, and disqualification to hold and enjoy any Office of honor, Trust or Profit under the United States: but the Party convicted shall nevertheless be liable and subject to Indictment, Trial, Judgment and Punishment, according to Law.

Section 4   The Times, Places and Manner of holding Elections for Senators and Representatives, shall be prescribed in each State by the Legislature thereof; but the Congress may at any time by Law make or alter such Regulations, except as to the Places of chusing Senators.

The Congress shall assemble at least once in every Year, and such Meeting shall be on the first Monday in December, unless they shall by Law appoint a different Day.[4]

Section 5   Each House shall be the Judge of the Elections, Returns and Qualifications of its own Members, and a Majority of each shall constitute a Quorum to do Business; but a smaller Number may adjourn from day to day, and may be authorized to compel the Attendance of absent Members, in such Manner, and under such Penalties as each House may provide.

Each House may determine the Rules of its Proceedings, punish its Members for disorderly Behaviour, and with the Concurrence of two thirds, expel a Member.

Each House shall keep a Journal of its Proceedings, and from time to time publish the same, excepting such Parts as may in their Judgment require Secrecy; and the Yeas and Nays of the Members of either House on any question shall, at the Desire of one fifth of those Present, be entered on the Journal.

Neither House, during the Session of Congress, shall, without the Consent of the other, adjourn for more than three days, nor to any other Place than that in which the two Houses shall be sitting.

Section 6   The Senators and Representatives shall receive a Compensation for their Services, to be ascertained by Law, and paid out of the Treasury of the United States. They shall in all Cases, except Treason, Felony and Breach of the Peace, be privileged from Arrest during their Attendance at the Session of their respective Houses, and in going to and returning from the same; and for any Speech or Debate in either House, they shall not be questioned in any other Place.

No Senator or Representative shall, during the Time for which he was elected, be appointed to any civil Office under the Authority of the United States, which shall have been created, or the Emoluments whereof shall have been encreased during such time; and no Person holding any Office under the United States, shall be a Member of either House during his Continuance in Office.

Section 7   All Bills for raising Revenue shall originate in the House of Representatives; but the Senate may propose or concur with Amendments as on other Bills.

Every Bill which shall have passed the House of Representatives and the Senate, shall, before it becomes a Law, be presented to the President of the United States; If he approves he shall sign it, but if not he shall return it, with his Objections to that House in which it shall have originated, who shall enter the Objections at large on their Journal, and proceed to reconsider it. If after such Reconsideration two thirds of that House shall agree to pass the Bill, it shall be sent, together with the Objections, to the other House, by which it shall likewise be reconsidered, and if approved by two thirds of that House, it shall become a Law. But in all such Cases the Votes of both Houses shall be determined by Yeas and Nays, and the Names of the Persons voting for and against the Bill shall be entered on the Journal of each House respectively. If any Bill shall not be returned by the President within ten Days (Sundays excepted) after it shall have been presented to him, the Same shall be a Law, in like Manner as if he had signed it, unless the Congress by their Adjournment prevent its Return, in which Case it shall not be a Law.

Every Order, Resolution, or Vote to which the Concurrence of the Senate and House of Representatives may be necessary (except on a question of Adjournment) shall be presented to the President of the United States; and before the Same shall take Effect, shall be approved by him, or being disapproved by him, shall be repassed by two thirds of the Senate and House of Representatives, according to the Rules and Limitations prescribed in the Case of a Bill.

Section 8   The Congress shall have Power To lay and collect Taxes, Duties, Imposts and Excises, to pay the Debts and provide for the common Defence and general Welfare of the United States; but all Duties, Imposts and Excises shall be uniform throughout the United States.

To borrow Money on the credit of the United States;

---

[4]Changed by the Twentieth Amendment.

To regulate Commerce with foreign Nations, and among the several States, and with the Indian Tribes;

To establish an uniform Rule of Naturalization, and uniform Laws on the subject of Bankruptcies throughout the United States;

To coin Money, regulate the Value thereof, and of foreign Coin, and fix the Standard of Weights and Measures;

To provide for the Punishment of counterfeiting the Securities and current Coin of the United States;

To establish Post Offices and post Roads;

To promote the Progress of Science and useful Arts, by securing for limited Times to Authors and Inventors the exclusive Right to their respective Writings and Discoveries;

To constitute Tribunals inferior to the supreme Court;

To define and punish Piracies and Felonies committed on the high Seas, and Offences against the Law of Nations;

To declare War, grant Letters of Marque and Reprisal, and make Rules concerning Captures on Land and Water;

To raise and support Armies, but no Appropriation of Money to that Use shall be for a longer Term than two Years;

To provide and maintain a Navy;

To make Rules for the Government and Regulation of the land and naval Forces;

To provide for calling forth the Militia to execute the Laws of the Union, suppress Insurrections and repel Invasions;

To provide for organizing, arming, and disciplining, the Militia, and for governing such Part of them as may be employed in the Service of the United States, reserving to the States respectively, the Appointment of the Officers, and the Authority of training the Militia according to the discipline prescribed by Congress;

To exercise exclusive Legislation in all Cases whatsoever, over such District (not exceeding ten Miles square) as may, by Cession of particular States, and the Acceptance of Congress, become the Seat of the Government of the United States, and to exercise like Authority over all Places purchased by the Consent of the Legislature of the State in which the Same shall be, for the Erection of Forts, Magazines, Arsenals, dock-Yards, and other needful Buildings;—And

To make all Laws which shall be necessary and proper for carrying into Execution the foregoing Powers, and all other Powers vested by this Constitution in the Government of the United States, or in any Department or Officer thereof.

Section 9   The Migration or Importation of such Persons as any of the States now existing shall think proper to admit, shall not be prohibited by the Congress prior to the Year one thousand eight hundred and eight, but a Tax or duty may be imposed on such Importation, not exceeding ten dollars for each Person.

The Privilege of the Writ of Habeas Corpus shall not be suspended, unless when in Cases of Rebellion or Invasion the public Safety may require it.

No Bill of Attainder or ex post facto Law shall be passed.

No Capitation, or other direct, Tax shall be laid, unless in Proportion to the Census of Enumeration herein before directed to be taken.[5]

No Tax or Duty shall be laid on Articles exported from any State.

No Preference shall be given by any Regulation of Commerce or Revenue to the Ports of one State over those of another: nor shall Vessels bound to, or from, one State, be obliged to enter, clear, or pay Duties in another.

No Money shall be drawn from the Treasury, but in Consequence of Appropriations made by Law; and a regular Statement and Account of the Receipts and Expenditures of all public Money shall be published from time to time.

No Title of Nobility shall be granted by the United States: And no Person holding any Office of Profit or Trust under them, shall, without the Consent of the Congress, accept of any present, Emolument, Office, or Title, of any kind whatever, from any King, Prince, or foreign State.

Section 10   No State shall enter into any Treaty, Alliance, or Confederation; grant Letters of Marque and Reprisal; coin Money; emit Bills of Credit; make any Thing but gold and silver coin a Tender in Payment of Debts; pass any Bill of Attainder, ex post facto Law, or Law impairing the Obligation of Contracts, or grant any Title of Nobility.

No State shall, without the Consent of the Congress, lay any Imposts or Duties on Imports or Exports, except what may be absolutely necessary for executing its inspection Laws: and the net Produce of all Duties and Imposts, laid by any State on Imports or Exports, shall be for the Use of the Treasury of the United States; and all such Laws shall be subject to the Revision and Controul of the Congress.

No State shall, without the consent of Congress, lay any Duty of Tonnage, keep Troops, or Ships of War in time of Peace, enter into any Agreement or Compact with another State, or with a foreign Power, or engage in War,

---

[5]Changed by the Sixteenth Amendment.

unless actually invaded, or in such imminent Danger as will not admit of delay.

Article II

Section 1 The executive Power shall be vested in a President of the United States of America. He shall hold his Office during the Term of four Years, and, together with the Vice President, chosen for the same Term, be elected, as follows

Each state shall appoint, in such Manner as the Legislature thereof may direct, a Number of Electors, equal to the whole Number of Senators and Representatives to which the State may be entitled in Congress: but no Senator or Representative, or Person holding an Office of Trust or Profit under the United States, shall be appointed an Elector.

The Electors shall meet in their respective States, and vote by Ballot for two Persons, of whom one at least shall not be an inhabitant of the same State with themselves. And they shall make a List of all the Persons voted for, and of the Number of Votes for each; which List they shall sign and certify, and transmit sealed to the Seat of the Government of the United States, directed to the President of the Senate. The President of the Senate shall, in the Presence of the Senate and House of Representatives, open all the Certificates, and the Votes shall then be counted. The Person having the greatest Number of Votes shall be the President, if such Number be a Majority of the whole Number of Electors appointed; and if there be more than one who have such Majority, and have an equal Number of Votes, then the House of Representatives shall immediately chuse by Ballot one of them for President; and if no Person have a Majority, then from the five highest on the List the said House shall in like Manner chuse the President. But in chusing the President, the Votes shall be taken by States, the Representation from each State having one Vote; A quorum for this purpose shall consist of a Member or Members from two thirds of the States, and a Majority of all the States shall be necessary to a Choice. In every Case, after the Choice of the President, the Person having the greatest Number of Votes of the Electors shall be the Vice President. But if there should remain two or more who have equal Votes, the Senate shall chuse from them by Ballot the Vice President.[6]

The Congress may determine the Time of chusing the Electors, and the Day on which they shall give their Votes; which Day shall be the same throughout the United States.

No Person except a natural born Citizen, or a Citizen of the United States, at the time of the Adoption of this Constitution, shall be eligible to the Office of President; neither shall any Person be eligible to that Office who shall not have attained to the Age of thirty five Years, and been fourteen Years a Resident within the United States.

In Case of the Removal of the President from Office, or of his Death, Resignation, or Inability to discharge the Powers and Duties of the said Office, the Same shall devolve on the Vice President, and the Congress may by Law provide for the Case of Removal, Death, Resignation or Inability, both of the President and Vice President, declaring what Officer shall then act as President, and such Officer shall act accordingly, until the Disability be removed, or a President shall be elected.[7]

The President shall, at stated Times, receive for his Services, a Compensation, which shall neither be encreased nor diminished during the Period for which he shall have been elected, and he shall not receive within that Period any other Emolument from the United States, or any of them.

Before he enter on the Execution of his Office, he shall take the following Oath or Affirmation:—"I do solemnly swear (or affirm) that I will faithfully execute the Office of President of the United States, and will to the best of my Ability, preserve, protect, and defend the Constitution of the United States."

Section 2 The President shall be Commander in Chief of the Army and Navy of the United States, and of the Militia of the several States, when called into the actual Service of the United States; he may require the Opinion, in writing, of the principal Officer in each of the executive Departments, upon any Subject relating to the Duties of their respective Offices, and he shall have Power to grant Reprieves and Pardons for Offences against the United States, except in Cases of Impeachment.

He shall have Power, by and with the Advice and Consent of the Senate, to make Treaties, provided two thirds of the Senators present concur; and he shall nominate, and by and with the Advice and Consent of the Senate, shall appoint Ambassadors, other public Ministers and Consuls, Judges of the supreme Court, and all other Officers of the United States, whose Appointments are not herein otherwise provided for, and which shall be established by Law;

---

[6]Changed by the Twelfth Amendment.

[7]Changed by the Twenty-fifth Amendment.

but the Congress may by Law vest the Appointment of such inferior Officers, as they think proper, in the President alone, in the Courts of Law, or in the Heads of Departments.

The President shall have Power to fill up all Vacancies that may happen during the Recess of the Senate, by granting Commissions which shall expire at the End of their next Session.

Section 3   He shall from time to time give to the Congress Information of the State of the Union, and recommend to their Consideration such Measures as he shall judge necessary and expedient; he may, on extraordinary Occasions, convene both Houses, or either of them, and in Case of Disagreement between them, with Respect to the Time of Adjournment, he may adjourn them to such Time as he shall think proper; he shall receive Ambassadors and other public Ministers; he shall take Care that the Laws be faithfully executed, and shall Commission all the Officers of the United States.

Section 4   The President, Vice President and all civil Officers of the United States, shall be removed from Office on Impeachment for, and Conviction of, Treason, Bribery, or other high Crimes and Misdemeanors.

Article III

Section 1   The judicial Power of the United States, shall be vested in one supreme Court, and in such inferior Courts as the Congress may from time to time ordain and establish. The Judges, both of the supreme and inferior Courts, shall hold their Offices during good Behaviour, and shall, at stated Times, receive for their Services, a Compensation, which shall not be diminished during their Continuance in Office.

Section 2   The judicial Power shall extend to all Cases, in Law and Equity, arising under this Constitution, the Laws of the United States, and Treaties made, or which shall be made, under their Authority;—to all Cases affecting Ambassadors, other public Ministers and Consuls;—to all Cases of admiralty and maritime Jurisdiction;—to Controversies to which the United States shall be a party;—to Controversies between two or more States;—between a State and Citizens of another State;[8]—between Citizens of different States;—between Citizens of the same State claiming Lands under Grants of different States, and between a State, or the Citizens thereof, and foreign States, Citizens or Subjects.

In all Cases affecting Ambassadors, other public Ministers and Consuls, and those in which a State shall be Party, the supreme Court shall have original Jurisdiction. In all the other Cases before mentioned, the supreme Court shall have appellate Jurisdiction, both as to Law and Fact, with such Exceptions, and under such Regulations as the Congress shall make.

The Trial of all Crimes, except in Cases of Impeachment, shall be by Jury: and such Trial shall be held in the State where the said Crimes shall have been committed; but when not committed within any State, the Trial shall be at such Place or Places as the Congress may by Law have directed.

Section 3   Treason against the United States, shall consist only in levying War against them, or in adhering to their Enemies, giving them Aid and Comfort. No Person shall be convicted of Treason unless on the Testimony of two Witnesses to the same overt Act, or on Confession in open Court.

The Congress shall have Power to declare the Punishment of Treason, but no Attainder of Treason shall work Corruption of Blood, or Forfeiture except during the Life of the Person attainted.

Article IV

Section 1   Full Faith and Credit shall be given in each State to the public Acts, Records, and judicial Proceedings of every other State. And the Congress may by general Laws prescribe the Manner in which such Acts, Records and Proceedings shall be proved, and the Effect thereof.

Section 2   The Citizens of each State shall be entitled to all Privileges and Immunities of Citizens in the several States.

A Person charged in any State with Treason, Felony, or other Crime, who shall flee from Justice, and be found in another State, shall on Demand of the executive Authority of the State from which he fled, be delivered up, to be removed to the State having Jurisdiction of the Crime.

No Person held to Service or Labour in one State, under the Laws thereof, escaping into another, shall, in Consequence of any Law or Regulation therein, be discharged from such Service or Labour, but shall be delivered up on Claim of the Party to whom such Service or Labour may be due.[9]

---

[8]Changed by the Eleventh Amendment.

[9]Changed by the Thirteenth Amendment.

Section 3   New States may be admitted by the Congress into this Union; but no new State shall be formed or erected within the Jurisdiction of any other State; nor any State be formed by the Junction of two or more States, or Parts of States, without the Consent of the Legislatures of the States concerned as well as of the Congress.

The Congress shall have Power to dispose of and make all needful Rules and Regulations respecting the Territory or other Property belonging to the United States; and nothing in this Constitution shall be so construed as to Prejudice any Claims of the United States, or of any particular State.

Section 4   The United States shall guarantee to every State in this Union a Republican Form of Government, and shall protect each of them against Invasion; and on Application of the Legislature, or of the Executive (when the Legislature cannot be convened) against domestic Violence.

Article V

The Congress, whenever two thirds of both Houses shall deem it necessary, shall propose Amendments to this Constitution, or, on the Application of the Legislatures of two thirds of the several States, shall call a Convention for proposing Amendments, which, in either Case, shall be valid to all Intents and Purposes, as Part of this Constitution, when ratified by the legislatures of three fourths of the several States, or by Conventions in three fourths thereof, as the one or the other Mode of Ratification may be proposed by the Congress; Provided that no Amendment which may be made prior to the Year One thousand eight hundred and eight shall in any Manner affect the first and fourth Clauses in the Ninth Section of the first Article; and that no State, without its Consent, shall be deprived of its equal Suffrage in the Senate.

Article VI

All Debts contracted and Engagements entered into, before the Adoption of this Constitution, shall be as valid against the United States under this Constitution, as under the Confederation.

The Constitution, and the Laws of the United States which shall be made in Pursuance thereof; and all Treaties made, or which shall be made, under the Authority of the United States, shall be the supreme Law of the Land; and the Judges in every State shall be bound thereby, any Thing in the Constitution or Laws of any State to the Contrary notwithstanding.

The Senators and Representatives before mentioned, and the Members of the several State Legislatures, and all executive and judicial Officers, both of the United States and of the several States, shall be bound by Oath or Affirmation, to support this Constitution; but no religious Test shall ever be required as a Qualification to any Office or public Trust under the United States.

Article VII

The Ratification of the Conventions of nine States, shall be sufficient for the Establishment of this Constitution between the States so ratifying the Same.

Done in Convention by the Unanimous Consent of the States present the Seventeenth Day of September in the Year of our Lord one thousand seven hundred and eighty seven and of the Independance of the United States of America the Twelfth. In witness whereof We have hereunto subscribed our Names.

Amendments

[The first 10 amendments are known as the "Bill of Rights."]

Amendment I (Ratified 1791)

Congress shall make no law respecting an establishment of religion, or prohibiting the free exercise thereof; or abridging the freedom of speech, or of the press; or the right of the people peaceably to assemble, and to petition the Government for a redress of grievances.

Amendment 2 (Ratified 1791)

A well regulated Militia, being necessary to the security of a free State, the right of the people to keep and bear Arms, shall not be infringed.

Amendment 3 (Ratified 1791)

No Soldier shall, in time of peace be quartered in any house, without the consent of the Owner, nor in time of war, but in a manner to be prescribed by law.

Amendment 4 (Ratified 1791)

The right of the people to be secure in their persons, houses, papers, and effects, against unreasonable searches and seizures, shall not be violated, and no Warrants shall issue, but upon probable cause, supported by Oath or affirmation, and particularly describing the place to be searched, and the persons or things to be seized.

Amendment 5 (Ratified 1791)

No person shall be held to answer for a capital, or otherwise infamous crime, unless on a presentment or indictment of a Grand Jury, except in cases arising in the land or naval forces, or in the Militia, when in actual service in time of War or public danger; nor shall any person be subject for the same offence to be twice put in jeopardy of life or limb; nor shall be compelled in any criminal case to be a witness against himself, nor be deprived of life, liberty, or property, without due process of law; nor shall private property be taken for public use, without just compensation.

Amendment 6 (Ratified 1791)

In all criminal prosecutions, the accused shall enjoy the right to a speedy and public trial, by an impartial jury of the State and district wherein the crime shall have been committed, which district shall have been previously ascertained by law, and to be informed of the nature and cause of the accusation; to be confronted with the witnesses against him; to have compulsory process for obtaining Witnesses in his favor, and to have assistance of counsel for his defence.

Amendment 7 (Ratified 1791)

In Suits at common law, where the value in controversy shall exceed twenty dollars, the right of trial by jury shall be preserved, and no fact tried by a jury, shall be otherwise re-examined in any Court of the United States, than according to the rules of the common law.

Amendment 8 (Ratified 1791)

Excessive bail shall not be required, nor excessive fines imposed, nor cruel and unusual punishments inflicted.

Amendment 9 (Ratified 1791)

The enumeration in the Constitution, of certain rights, shall not be construed to deny or disparage others retained by the people.

Amendment 10 (Ratified 1791)

The powers not delegated to the United States by the Constitution, nor prohibited by it to the States, are reserved to the States respectively, or to the people.

Amendment 11 (Ratified 1795)

The Judicial power of the United States shall not be construed to extend to any suit in law or equity, commenced or prosecuted against one of the United States by Citizens of another State, or by Citizens or Subjects of any Foreign State.

Amendment 12 (Ratified 1804)

The Electors shall meet in their respective states, and vote by ballot for President and Vice-President, one of whom, at least, shall not be an inhabitant of the same state with themselves; they shall name in their ballots the person voted for as President, and in distinct ballots the person voted for as Vice-President, and they shall make distinct lists of all persons voted for as President, and of all persons voted for as Vice-President, and of the number of votes for each, which lists they shall sign and certify, and transmit sealed to the seat of the government of the United States, directed to the President of the Senate;—The President of the Senate shall, in the presence of the Senate and House of Representatives, open all the certificates and the votes shall then be counted;—The person having the greatest number of votes for President, shall be the President, if such number be a majority of the whole number of Electors appointed; and if no person have such majority, then from the persons having the highest numbers not exceeding three on the list of those voted for as President, the House of Representatives shall choose immediately, by ballot, the President. But in choosing the President, the votes shall be taken by states, the representation from each state having one vote; a quorum for this purpose shall consist of a member or members from two-thirds of the states, and a majority of all the states shall be necessary to a choice. And if the House of Representatives shall not choose a President whenever the right of choice shall devolve upon them, before the fourth day of March next following, then the Vice-President shall act as president, as in the case of the death or other constitutional disability of the President.[10]—The person having the greatest number of votes as Vice-President, shall be the Vice-President, if such number be a majority of the whole number of Electors appointed, and if no person have a majority, then from the two highest numbers on the list, the Senate shall choose the Vice-President; a quorum for the purpose shall consist of two-thirds of the whole number of Senators, and a majority of the whole number shall be necessary to a choice. But no person constitutionally ineligible to the office of President shall be eligible to that of Vice-President of the United States.

Amendment 13 (Ratified 1865)

Section 1 Neither slavery nor involuntary servitude, except as a punishment for crime whereof the party shall

---

[10]Changed by the Twentieth Amendment.

have been duly convicted, shall exist within the United States, or any place subject to their jurisdiction.

Section 2   Congress shall have power to enforce this article by appropriate legislation.

Amendment 14 (Ratified 1868)

Section 1   All persons born or naturalized in the United States, and subject to the jurisdiction thereof, are citizens of the United States and of the State wherein they reside. No State shall make or enforce any law which shall abridge the privileges or immunities of citizens of the United States; nor shall any State deprive any person of life, liberty, or property, without due process of law; nor deny to any person within its jurisdiction the equal protection of the laws.

Section 2   Representatives shall be apportioned among the several States according to their respective numbers, counting the whole number of persons in each State, excluding Indians not taxed. But when the right to vote at any election for the choice of electors for President and Vice President of the United States, Representatives in Congress, the Executive and Judicial officers of a State, or the members of the Legislature thereof, is denied to any of the male inhabitants of such State, being twenty-one[11] years of age, and citizens of the United States, or in any way abridged except for participation in rebellion, or other crime, the basis of representation therein shall be reduced in the proportion which the number of such male citizens shall bear to the whole number of male citizens twenty-one years of age in such State.

Section 3   No person shall be a Senator or Representative in Congress, or elector of President and Vice President, or hold any office, civil or military, under the United States, or under any State, who, having previously taken an oath, as a member of Congress, or as an officer of the United States, or as a member of any State legislature, or as an executive or judicial officer of any State, to support the Constitution of the United States, shall have engaged in insurrection or rebellion against the same, or given aid or comfort to the enemies thereof. But Congress may by a vote of two-thirds of each House, remove such disability.

Section 4   The validity of the public debt of the United States, authorized by law, including debts incurred for payment of pensions and bounties for services in suppressing insurrection or rebellion, shall not be questioned. But neither the United States nor any State shall assume or pay any debt or obligation incurred in aid of insurrection or rebellion against the United States, or any claim for the loss or emancipation of any slave; but all such debts, obligations and claims shall be held illegal and void.

Section 5   The Congress shall have power to enforce, by appropriate legislation, the provisions of this article.

Amendment 15 (Ratified 1870)

Section 1   The right of citizens of the United States to vote shall not be denied or abridged by the United States or by any State on account of race, color, or previous condition of servitude.

Section 2   The Congress shall have power to enforce this article by appropriate legislation.

Amendment 16 (Ratified 1913)

The Congress shall have power to lay and collect taxes on incomes, from whatever source derived, without apportionment among the several States, and without regard to any census or enumeration.

Amendment 17 (Ratified 1913)

The Senate of the United States shall be composed of two Senators from each State, elected by the people thereof, for six years; and each Senator shall have one vote. The electors in each State shall have the qualifications requisite for electors of the most numerous branch of the State legislatures.

When vacancies happen in the representation of any State in the Senate, the executive authority of such State shall issue writs of election to fill such vacancies: *Provided,* That the legislature of any State may empower the executive thereof to make temporary appointments until the people fill the vacancies by election as the legislature may direct.

This amendment shall not be so construed as to affect the election or term of any Senator chosen before it becomes valid as part of the Constitution.

Amendment 18 (Ratified 1919; Repealed 1933)

Section 1   After one year from the ratification of this article the manufacture, sale, or transportation of intoxicating liquors within, the importation thereof into, or the exportation thereof from the United States and all territory subject to the jurisdiction thereof for beverage purposes is hereby prohibited.

Section 2   The Congress and the several States shall have concurrent power to enforce this article by appropriate legislation.

---

[11]Changed by the Twenty-sixth Amendment.

Section 3   This article shall be inoperative unless it shall have been ratified as an amendment to the Constitution by the legislatures of the several States, as provided in the Constitution, within seven years from the date of the submission hereof to the States by the Congress.[12]

Amendment 19 (Ratified 1920)

The right of citizens of the United States to vote shall not be denied or abridged by the United States or by any State on account of sex.

Congress shall have power to enforce this article by appropriate legislation.

Amendment 20 (Ratified 1933)

Section 1   The terms of the President and Vice President shall end at noon on the 20th day of January, and the terms of Senators and Representatives at noon on the 3d day of January, of the years in which such terms would have ended if this article had not been ratified; and the terms of their successors shall then begin.

Section 2   The Congress shall assemble at least once in every year, and such meeting shall begin at noon on the 3d day of January, unless they shall by law appoint a different day.

Section 3   If, at the time fixed for the beginning of the term of the President, the President elect shall have died, the Vice President elect shall become President. If a President shall not have been chosen before the time fixed for the beginning of his term, or if the President elect shall have failed to qualify, then the Vice President elect shall act as President until a President shall have qualified; and the Congress may by law provide for the case wherein neither a President elect nor a Vice President elect shall have qualified, declaring who shall then act as President, or the manner in which one who is to act shall be selected, and such person shall act accordingly until a President or Vice President shall have qualified.

Section 4   The Congress may by law provide for the case of the death of any of the persons from whom the House of Representatives may choose a President whenever the right of choice shall have devolved upon them, and for the case of the death of any of the persons from whom the Senate may choose a Vice President whenever the right of choice shall have devolved upon them.

Section 5   Sections 1 and 2 shall take effect on the 15th day of October following the ratification of this article.

Section 6   This article shall be inoperative unless it shall have been ratified as an amendment to the Constitution by the legislatures of three-fourths of the several States within seven years from the date of its submission.

Amendment 21 (Ratified 1933)

Section 1   The eighteenth article of amendment to the Constitution of the United States is hereby repealed.

Section 2   The transportation or importation into any State, Territory, or possession of the United States for delivery or use therein of intoxicating liquors, in violation of the laws thereof, is hereby prohibited.

Section 3   This article shall be inoperative unless it shall have been ratified as an amendment to the Constitution by conventions in the several States, as provided in the Constitution, within seven years from the date of the submission hereof to the States by the Congress.

Amendment 22 (Ratified 1951)

Section 1   No person shall be elected to the office of the President more than twice, and no person who has held the office of President, or acted as President, for more than two years of a term to which some other person was elected President shall be elected to the office of the President more than once. But this Article shall not apply to any person holding the office of President when this Article was proposed by the Congress, and shall not prevent any person who may be holding the office of President, or acting as President, during the term within which this Article becomes operative from holding the office of President or acting as President during the remainder of such term.

Section 2   This Article shall be inoperative unless it shall have been ratified as an amendment to the Constitution by the legislatures of three-fourths of the several States within seven years from the date of its submission to the States by the Congress.

Amendment 23 (Ratified 1961)

Section 1   The District constituting the seat of Government of the United States shall appoint in such manner as the Congress may direct:

A number of electors of President and Vice President equal to the whole number of Senators and Representatives in Congress to which the District would be entitled if it were a State, but in no event more than the least populous State; they shall be in addition to those appointed by the States, but they shall be considered, for the purposes of the election of President and Vice President, to be electors appointed by a State; and they shall meet in

---

[12]Repealed by the Twenty-first Amendment.

the District and perform such duties as provided by the twelfth article of amendment.

Section 2   The Congress shall have power to enforce this article by appropriate legislation.

Amendment 24 (Ratified 1964)

Section 1   The right of citizens of the United States to vote in any primary or other election for President or Vice President, for electors for President or Vice President, or for Senator or Representative in Congress, shall not be denied or abridged by the United States or any State by reason of failure to pay any poll tax or other tax.

Section 2   The Congress shall have power to enforce this article by appropriate legislation.

Amendment 25 (Ratified 1967)

Section 1   In case of the removal of the President from office or of his death or resignation, the Vice President shall become President.

Section 2   Whenever there is a vacancy in the office of the Vice President, the President shall nominate a Vice President who shall take office upon confirmation by a majority vote of both Houses of Congress.

Section 3   Whenever the President transmits to the President pro tempore of the Senate and the Speaker of the House of Representatives his written declaration that he is unable to discharge the powers and duties of his office, and until he transmits to them a written declaration to the contrary, such powers and duties shall be discharged by the Vice President as Acting President.

Section 4   Whenever the Vice President and a majority of either the principal officers of the executive departments or of such other body as Congress may by law provide, transmit to the President pro tempore of the Senate and the Speaker of the House of Representatives their written declaration that the President is unable to discharge the powers and duties of his office, the Vice President shall immediately assume the powers and duties of the office as Acting President.

Thereafter, when the President transmits to the President pro tempore of the Senate and the Speaker of the House of Representatives his written declaration that no inability exists, he shall resume the powers and duties of his office unless the Vice President and a majority of either the principal officers of the executive department or of such other body as Congress may by law provide, transmit within four days to the President pro tempore of the Senate and the Speaker of the House of Representatives their written declaration that the President is unable to discharge the powers and duties of his office. Thereupon Congress shall decide the issue, assembling within forty-eight hours for that purpose if not in session. If the Congress, within twenty-one days after receipt of the latter written declaration, or, if Congress is not in session, within twenty-one days after Congress is required to assemble, determines by two-thirds vote of both Houses that the President is unable to discharge the powers and duties of his office, the Vice President shall continue to discharge the same as Acting President; otherwise, the President shall resume the powers and duties of his office.

Amendment 26 (Ratified 1971)

Section 1   The right of citizens of the United States, who are eighteen years of age or older, to vote shall not be denied or abridged by the United States or by any State on account of age.

Section 2   The Congress shall have power to enforce this article by appropriate legislation.

Amendment 27 (Ratified 1992)

No law, varying the compensation for the services of the Senators and Representatives, shall take effect, until an election of Representatives shall have intervened.

INDEX